CROSSWORD LISTS AND CROSSWORD SOLVER

EDITED BY ANNE STIBBS KERR

THIRD EDITION

BLOOMSBURY INFORMATION

LONDON • NEW YORK • OXFORD • NEW DELHI • SYDNEY

BLOOMSBURY INFORMATION
Bloomsbury Publishing Plc
50 Bedford Square, London, WC1B 3DP, UK
1385 Broadway, New York, NY 10018, USA

BLOOMSBURY, BLOOMSBURY INFORMATION and the Diana logo are trademarks of
Bloomsbury Publishing Plc

First published in 1989 by Bloomsbury Publishing Plc
Second edition publishing 1997
Third edition published 2000
Fourth edition published 2004
Combined edition Crossword Lists and Solver published 2007 by
A&C Black Publishers Ltd

Crossword Solver first published 1988 by Bloomsbury Publishing Plc
Second edition published 1995
Third edition published 1997
Combined edition Crossword Lists and Solver published 2007 by
A&C Black Publishers Ltd

Crossword Lists and Crossword Solver first published 2007
Second edition published 2012
Third edition published 2019

Cover design by Jason Anscomb / rawshock design

A catalogue record for this book is available from the British Library.

A catalog record for this book is available from the Library of Congress.

ISBN:	PB:	978-1-4729-6805-0
	ePDF:	978-1-4729-6807-4
	eBook:	978-1-4729-6806-7

Typeset by Market House Books Ltd
Printed and bound in Great Britain

To find out more about our authors and books visit www.bloomsbury.com and
sign up for our newsletters.

CROSSWORD
LISTS

INTRODUCTION

This book is one of a series of reference books for lovers of crossword puzzles, including the *Bloomsbury Crossword Solver's Dictionary*, the *Bloomsbury Crossword Key*, and the *Bloomsbury Anagram Finder*. In this updated edition we have included a number of new lists. These cover such diverse topics as dams, bridges, major stock indices, sports in the Olympic Games, etc. As in previous editions we have listed words under categories – people, places, birds, animals, jewellery, canals, Greek gods, names of drinks, and so on, in the hope that the user can quickly find the required answer to a clue. We have chosen the contents for their usefulness and have tried to concentrate on words that actually appear in crosswords. We have also presented the information in the most helpful way. Usually, this means listing the words in length order – 3-letter, 4-letter, 5-letter words, etc., and then in alphabetical order within each section. In some cases we have used simple alphabetical or logical order and some information is presented in tabular form.

We have also included additional information in many of the lists; for example, the birth and death dates of people or the colours of gemstones. This is partly to help the reader to find the correct word, but we also hope that owners of the book will find it a useful reference source in its own right.

While most of the lists are collections of things, there are also lists of types of words – for example, palindromes, back words, homophones (words that sound like others), abbreviations and acronyms, common two-word phrases, anagram indicators, and split-word indicators. The book also contains a short section of familiar quotations and some well-known foreign words and phrases. To help the reader find his or her way about, there is a Contents page that lists all the tables and lists in the order in which they appear in the book. In addition, there is an index in the back of the book. This gives the tables and lists in alphabetical order, but has also been expanded to include many more cross references. For instance, a reader interested in 'jewels' will be directed to the list of gemstones, 'girl' might indicate a girl's first name, listed under first names, and so on. The index also contains hints on solving cryptic clues. There are many conventions used by setters of crosswords – 'love' often indicates the letter O, 'cardinal' might be a compass point, N, S, E, or W, 'twisted' could suggest an anagram, etc. A selection of these has been included in the index.

In using the book, the reader should also be aware of the inflection of words. The most common, for the purpose of crosswords, is the use of plurals, and it is usually apparent from the wording of the clue whether the answer is a singular or plural. When nouns have regular plurals, only the singular forms have been included. Another point is that verbs are invariably shown with -ize endings. The alternative -ise ending may have been used in the puzzle. The same principle applies to nouns with -ization.

Since the original publication of the book in 1989, a large number of useful comments and suggestions for additional lists have been received from readers. Many of these have been incorporated into the new edition. The editor would like to thank these correspondents and also thank all the people who have been involved in the production of the book. Their names are listed under Acknowledgments.

Anne Stibbs Kerr
Aylesbury, 2019

ACKNOWLEDGMENTS

Fran Alexander
Peter Blair
Beth Bonham
Eve Daintith
John Daintith
Jessica Foote
Anna Gallagher
Joan Gallagher
Amanda Garner-Hay
Robert Kerr
Jonathan Law
Sandra McQueen
David Pickering
Kathy Rooney
Mark Salad
Jessica Scholes
Gwen Shaw
Kate Smith
Brenda Tomkins
Margaret Tuthill
Sarah Walker
Linda Wells
Edmund Wright

CONTENTS

GEOGRAPHY

COUNTRIES OF THE WORLD

AFGHANISTAN
Capital: Kabul
Currency: afghani [pul, *pl.* puli (*or* puls)]
ALBANIA
Capital: Tirana (*or* Tiranë)
Currency: lek, *pl.* lekë (*or* leks) [qindar (*or* qintar *or* qindarka)]
ALGERIA
Capital: Algiers
Currency: dinar [centime (*or* santeem)]
ANDORRA
Capital: Andorra la Vella
Currency: euro [cent]
ANGOLA
Capital: Luanda
Currency: kwanza [lwei]
ANTIGUA AND BARBUDA
Capital: Saint John's
Currency: dollar [cent]
ARGENTINA
Capital: Buenos Aires
Currency: peso [austral]
ARMENIA
Capital: Yerevan
Currency: dram [louma (*or* luma)]
AUSTRALIA
Capital: Canberra
Currency: dollar [cent]
AUSTRIA
Capital: Vienna
Currency: euro [cent]
AZERBAIJAN
Capital: Baku
Currency: manat [gopik (*or* gepik)]
THE BAHAMAS
Capital: Nassau
Currency: dollar [cent]
BAHRAIN
Capital: Manama
Currency: dinar [fils]
BANGLADESH
Capital: Dhaka
Currency: taka [poisha (*or* paisa)]
BARBADOS
Capital: Bridgetown
Currency: dollar [cent]
BELARUS
Capital: Minsk
Currency: rouble [copeck (*or* kopek; *or* kapek)]

BELAU
See PALAU
BELGIUM
Capital: Brussels
Currency: euro [cent]
BELIZE
Capital: Belmopan
Currency: dollar [cent]
BENIN
Capital: Porto-Novo
Currency: CFA franc [centime]
BHUTAN
Capital: Thimphu
Currency: ngultrum, *pl.* ngultrum [chetrum]
BOLIVIA
Capital: Sucre (constitutional); La Paz (administrative)
Currency: boliviano [centavo]
BOSNIA AND HERZEGOVINA
Capital: Sarajevo
Currency: mark [fening]
BOTSWANA
Capital: Gaborone
Currency: pula [thebe]
BRAZIL
Capital: Brasília
Currency: real [centavo]
BRUNEI
Capital: Bandar Seri Begawan
Currency: dollar [sen]
BULGARIA
Capital: Sofia
Currency: lev, *pl.* leva (*or* levs) [stotinka, *pl.* stotinki]
BURKINA FASO
Capital: Ouagadougou
Currency: CFA franc [centime]
BURMA
See MYANMAR
BURUNDI
Capital: Gitega
Currency: franc [centime]
CAMBODIA
Capital: Phnom Penh
Currency: riel [sen]
CAMEROON
Capital: Yaoundé
Currency: CFA franc [centime]
CANADA
Capital: Ottawa
Currency: dollar [cent]

1

CAPE VERDE
Capital: Praia
Currency: escudo [centavo]
CENTRAL AFRICAN REPUBLIC
Capital: Bangui
Currency: CFA franc [centime]
CHAD
Capital: N'Djaména
Currency: CFA franc [centime]
CHILE
Capital: Santiago
Currency: peso [centavo]
CHINA
Capital: Beijing (or Peking)
Currency: renminbi yuan [fen]
COLOMBIA
Capital: Bogotá
Currency: peso [centavo]
COMOROS
Capital: Moroni
Currency: franc [centime]
CONGO, DEMOCRATIC REPUBLIC OF THE
Capital: Kinshasa
Currency: franc [centime]
CONGO REPUBLIC OF (or CONGO-BRAZZAVILLE)
Capital: Brazzaville
Currency: CFA franc [centime]
COSTA RICA
Capital: San José
Currency: colón, *pl.* colones (or colóns) [céntimo]
CÔTE D'IVOIRE
Capital: Yamoussoukro
Currency: CFA franc [centime]
CROATIA
Capital: Zagreb
Currency: kuna, *pl.* kune (or kuna) [lipa]
CUBA
Capital: Havana
Currency: peso [centavo]
CYPRUS
Capital: Nicosia (or Lefkosia)
Currency: euro [cent]
CZECH REPUBLIC
Capital: Prague
Currency: koruna [haler, *pl.* haleru (or haler or halura)]
DENMARK
Capital: Copenhagen
Currency: krone, *pl.* kroner (or kronen) [ø]
DJIBOUTI
Capital: Djibouti
Currency: franc [centime]
DOMINICA
Capital: Roseau
Currency: East Caribbean dollar [cent]
DOMINICAN REPUBLIC
Capital: Santo Domingo
Currency: peso [centavo]
EAST TIMOR
Capital: Dili
Currency: US dollar [cent]

ECUADOR
Capital: Quito
Currency: US dollar [cent]
EGYPT
Capital: Cairo
Currency: pound [piastre]
EL SALVADOR
Capital: San Salvador
Currency: dollar [cent]
EQUATORIAL GUINEA
Capital: Malabo
Currency: CFA franc [centime]
ERITREA
Capital: Asmara
Currency: nakfa [cent]
ESTONIA
Capital: Tallinn
Currency: euro [cent]
ETHIOPIA
Capital: Addis Adaba
Currency: birr [cent (or santim)]
FIJI
Capital: Suva
Currency: dollar [cent]
FINLAND
Capital: Helsinki
Currency: euro [cent]
FRANCE
Capital: Paris
Currency: euro [cent]
GABON
Capital: Libreville
Currency: CFA franc [centime]
THE GAMBIA
Capital: Banjul
Currency: dalasi [butut]
GEORGIA
Capital: Tbilisi
Currency: lari [tetri]
GERMANY
Capital: Berlin
Currency: euro [cent]
GHANA
Capital: Accra
Currency: cedi [pesewa]
GREECE
Capital: Athens
Currency: euro [cent]
GRENADA
Capital: St George's
Currency: East Caribbean dollar [cent]
GUATEMALA
Capital: Guatemala City
Currency: quetzal, *pl.* quetzales [centavo]
GUINEA
Capital: Conakry
Currency: franc [centime]
GUINEA-BISSAU
Capital: Bissau
Currency: CFA franc
GUYANA
Capital: Georgetown
Currency: dollar [cent]

HAITI
Capital: Port-au-Prince
Currency: gourde [centime]
HONDURAS
Capital: Tegucigalpa
Currency: lempira [centavo]
HUNGARY
Capital: Budapest
Currency: forint [fillér]
ICELAND
Capital: Reykjavik
Currency: króna, *pl.* krónur [eyrir, *pl.* aurar]
INDIA
Capital: New Delhi
Currency: rupee [paisa, *pl.* paise (or paisa)]
INDONESIA
Capital: Jakarta
Currency: rupiah [sen]
IRAN
Capital: Tehrān
Currency: rial [dinar]
IRAQ
Capital: Baghdad
Currency: dinar [fils]
IRELAND, REPUBLIC OF
Capital: Dublin
Currency: euro [cent]
ISRAEL
Capital: Jerusalem
Currency: shekel (or sheqel) [agora, *pl.* agorot]
ITALY
Capital: Rome
Currency: euro [cent]
IVORY COAST
See CÔTE D'IVOIRE
JAMAICA
Capital: Kingston
Currency: dollar [cent]
JAPAN
Capital: Tokyo
Currency: yen [sen]
JORDAN
Capital: Amman
Currency: dinar [piastre (or qirsh]
KAZAKHSTAN
Capital: Astana (or Akmola)
Currency: tenge [tiyn]
KENYA
Capital: Nairobi
Currency: shilling [cent]
KIRIBATI
Capital: Tarawa
Currency: Australian dollar [cent]
KOREA, DEMOCRATIC PEOPLE'S REPUBLIC OF
(North Korea)
Capital: P'yŏngyang
Currency: won [chon (or jun)]
KOREA, REPUBLIC OF (South Korea)
Capital: Seoul
Currency: won [chun (or jeon)]
KOSOVO
Capital: Pristina
Currency: euro [cent]

KUWAIT
Capital: Kuwait City
Currency: dinar [fils]
KYRGYZSTAN
Capital: Bishkek
Currency: som [tyin]
LAOS
Capital: Vientiane
Currency: kip [at (or att]
LATVIA
Capital: Riga
Currency: euro [cent]
LEBANON
Capital: Beirut
Currency: pound [piastre]
LESOTHO
Capital: Maseru
Currency: loti [sente, *pl.* lisente]
LIBERIA
Capital: Monrovia
Currency: dollar [cent]
LIBYA
Capital: Tripoli
Currency: dinar [dirham (or dirhem)]
LIECHTENSTEIN
Capital: Vaduz
Currency: Swiss franc [centime]
LITHUANIA
Capital: Vilnius
Currency: euro [cent]
LUXEMBOURG
Capital: Luxembourg City
Currency: euro [cent]
MACEDONIA
Capital: Skopje
Currency: denar [deni]
MADAGASCAR
Capital: Antananarivo
Currency: ariary [iraimbilanja]
MALAWI
Capital: Lilongwe
Currency: kwacha [tambala]
MALAYSIA
Capital: Kuala Lumpur
Currency: ringgit (or dollar) [sen (or cent)]
MALDIVES
Capital: Malé
Currency: rufiyaa [laari (or lari or laree)]
MALI
Capital: Bamako
Currency: CFA franc [centime]
MALTA
Capital: Valletta
Currency: euro [cent]
MARSHALL ISLANDS
Capital: Majuro
Currency: US dollar [cent]
MAURITANIA
Capital: Nouakchott
Currency: ouguiya (or ougiya) [khoum]
MAURITIUS
Capital: Port Louis
Currency: rupee [cent]

MEXICO
Capital: Mexico City
Currency: peso [centavo]
MICRONESIA, FEDERATED STATES OF
Capital: Palikir
Currency: US dollar [cent]
MOLDOVA
Capital: Kishinev (or Chişinău)
Currency: leu, *pl.* lei [ban, *pl.* bani]
MONACO
Capital: Monaco-Ville
Currency: euro [cent]
MONGOLIA
Capital: Ulaanbaatar (or Ulan Bator)
Currency: tugrik (or tögrög) [möngö]
MONTENEGRO
Capital: Podgorica
Currency: euro [cent]
MOROCCO
Capital: Rabat
Currency: dirham (or dirhem) [centime]
MOZAMBIQUE
Capital: Maputo
Currency: metical [centavo]
MYANMAR
Capital: Naypyidaw (administrative); Yangôn (or Rangoon, commercial)
Currency: kyat [pya]
NAMIBIA
Capital: Windhoek
Currency: dollar [cent]
NAURU
Capital: Yaren
Currency: Australian dollar [cent]
NEPAL
Capital: Kathmandu
Currency: rupee [paisa, *pl.* paise (or paisa)]
NETHERLANDS
Capital: Amsterdam
Currency: euro [cent]
NEW ZEALAND
Capital: Wellington
Currency: dollar [cent]
NICARAGUA
Capital: Managua
Currency: córdoba [centavo]
NIGER
Capital: Niamey
Currency: CFA franc [centime]
NIGERIA
Capital: Abuja
Currency: naira [kobo]
NORWAY
Capital: Oslo
Currency: krone, *pl.* kroner (or kronen) [ø]
OMAN
Capital: Muscat
Currency: rial [baiza]
PAKISTAN
Capital: Islamabad
Currency: rupee [paisa, *pl.* paise (or paisa)]

PALAU
Capital: Melekeok
Currency: US dollar [cent]
PANAMA
Capital: Panama City
Currency: balboa [centésimo (or cent)]
PAPUA NEW GUINEA
Capital: Port Moresby
Currency: kina [toea]
PARAGUAY
Capital: Asunción
Currency: guaraní [céntimo]
PERU
Capital: Lima
Currency: sol, *pl.* soles [céntimo]
PHILIPPINES
Capital: Manila
Currency: peso [centavo]
POLAND
Capital: Warsaw
Currency: złoty [grosz, *pl.* groszy]
PORTUGAL
Capital: Lisbon
Currency: euro [cent]
QATAR
Capital: Doha
Currency: riyal [dirham (or dirhem)]
ROMANIA
Capital: Bucharest
Currency: leu, *pl.* lei [ban, *pl.* bani]
RUSSIA
Capital: Moscow
Currency: rouble [kopeck (or copeck)]
RWANDA
Capital: Kigali
Currency: franc [centime]
SAINT KITTS (or CHRISTOPHER) AND NEVIS
Capital: Basseterre
Currency: East Caribbean dollar [cent]
SAINT LUCIA
Capital: Castries
Currency: East Caribbean dollar [cent]
SAINT VINCENT AND THE GRENADINES
Capital: Kingstown
Currency: East Caribbean dollar [cent]
SAMOA
Capital: Apia
Currency: tala [sene]
SAN MARINO
Capital: San Marino
Currency: euro [cent]
SÃO TOMÉ AND PRÍNCIPE
Capital: Sã o Tomé
Currency: dobra [cêntimo]
SAUDI ARABIA
Capital: Riyadh
Currency: riyal [halala, *pl.* halala (or halalah or halalas)]
SENEGAL
Capital: Dakar
Currency: CFA franc [centime]

SERBIA
Capital: Belgrade
Currency: dinar [para]
SEYCHELLES
Capital: Victoria
Currency: rupee [cent]
SIERRA LEONE
Capital: Freetown
Currency: leone [cent]
SINGAPORE
Capital: Singapore
Currency: dollar [cent]
SLOVAKIA
Capital: Bratislava
Currency: euro [cent]
SLOVENIA
Capital: Ljubljana
Currency: euro [cent] [stotin]
SOLOMON ISLANDS
Capital: Honiara
Currency: dollar [cent]
SOMALIA
Capital: Mogadishu
Currency: shilling [cent]
SOUTH AFRICA
Capital: Pretoria
Currency: rand [cent]
SOUTH SUDAN
Capital: Juba
Currency: pound [piastre]
SPAIN
Capital: Madrid
Currency: euro [cent]
SRI LANKA
Capital: Colombo
Currency: rupee [cent]
SUDAN
Capital: Khartoum
Currency: pound [piastre]
SURINAME
Capital: Paramaribo
Currency: dollar [cent]
SWAZILAND
Capital: Mbabane
Currency: lilangeni [cent]
SWEDEN
Capital: Stockholm
Currency: krona, *pl.* kronor [öre]
SWITZERLAND
Capital: Bern
Currency: franc [rappen or centime]
SYRIA
Capital: Damascus
Currency: pound [piastre]
TAIWAN
Capital: Taipei
Currency: dollar [cent]
TAJIKISTAN
Capital: Dushanbe
Currency: somoni [diram]
TANZANIA
Capital: Dodoma
Currency: shilling [cent]

THAILAND
Capital: Bangkok
Currency: baht [satang, *pl.* satang (or stangs or satangs)]
TOGO
Capital: Lomé
Currency: CFA franc [centime]
TONGA
Capital: Nuku'alofa
Currency: pa'anga [seniti]
TRINIDAD AND TOBAGO
Capital: Port of Spain
Currency: dollar [cent]
TUNISIA
Capital: Tunis
Currency: dinar [millime]
TURKEY
Capital: Ankara
Currency: lira, *pl.* lire [kurus]
TURKMENISTAN
Capital: Ashkhabad (or Ashgabat)
Currency: manat [tenge or tennesi]
TUVALU
Capital: Fongafale
Currency: dollar [cent]
UGANDA
Capital: Kampala
Currency: shilling [cent]
UKRAINE
Capital: Kiev
Currency: hryvnya (or hryvna) [kopiyka]
UNITED ARAB EMIRATES
Capital: Abu Dhabi
Currency: dirham [fils]
UNITED KINGDOM
Capital: London
Currency: pound [penny, *pl.* pence]
UNITED STATES OF AMERICA
Capital: Washington, DC
Currency: dollar [cent]
URUGUAY
Capital: Montevideo
Currency: peso [centésimo]
UZBEKISTAN
Capital: Tashkent
Currency: sum (or som), *pl.* sum (or sumy) [teen]
VANUATU
Capital: Vila
Currency: vatu [centime]
VATICAN CITY STATE
Capital: Vatican City
Currency: euro [cent]
VENEZUELA
Capital: Caracas
Currency: bolívar (or petro) [céntimo]
VIETNAM
Capital: Hanoi
Currency: dong [ho; xu]
YEMEN
Capital: Sana'a
Currency: riyal (or rial) [fils]

ZAMBIA
Capital: Lusaka
Currency: kwacha [ngwee]

ZIMBABWE
Capital: Harare
Currency: dollar [cent]

DEPENDENCIES

AUSTRALIA

ASHMORE AND CARTIER ISLANDS
THE AUSTRALIAN ANTARCTIC TERRITORY
CHRISTMAS ISLAND
Principal Settlement: Flying Fish Cove
COCOS (KEELING) ISLANDS
Principal Settlement: West Island
CORAL SEA ISLANDS TERRITORY
HEARD ISLAND AND MCDONALD
ISLAND
JERVIS BAY TERRITORY
NORFOLK ISLAND
Capital: Kingstown

DENMARK

FAROE ISLANDS
Capital: Torshavn
GREENLAND
Capital: Nuuk (Godtharing;b)

FRANCE

FRENCH GUIANA
Capital: Cayenne
FRENCH POLYNESIA
Capital: Papeete
GUADELOUPE
Capital: Basse-Terre
MARTINIQUE
Capital: Fort-de-France
MAYOTTE
Capital: Mamoudzou
NEW CALEDONIA
Capital: Nouméa
RÉUNION
Capital: Saint-Denis
SAINT BARTHELEMY
Capital: Gustavia
SAINT MARTIN
Capital: Marigot
SAINT PIERRE AND MIQUELON
Capital: Saint-Pierre
WALLIS AND FUTUNA
Capital: Mata-Utu

THE NETHERLANDS

ARUBA
Capital: Oranjestad
CURACAO
Capital: Willemstad
ST MARTEN
Capital: Philipsburg

NEW ZEALAND

COOK ISLANDS
Capital: Avarua
NIUE
Capital: Alofi
THE ROSS DEPENDENCY
TOKELAU

NORWAY

BOUVET ISLAND
JAN MAYEN ISLAND
PETER THE FIRST ISLAND
QUEEN MAUD LAND
SVALBARD
Principal Settlement: Longyearbyen

UNITED KINGDOM

ANGUILLA
Capital: The Valley
BERMUDA
Capital: Hamilton
BRITISH ANTARCTIC TERRITORY
BRITISH INDIAN OCEAN TERRITORY
BRITISH VIRGIN ISLANDS
Capital: Road Town
CAYMAN ISLANDS
Capital: George Town
FALKLAND ISLANDS
Capital: Stanley
GIBRALTAR
Capital: Gibraltar
GUERNSEY
Capital: St Peter Port
ISLE OF MAN
Capital: Douglas
JERSEY
Capital: St Helier
MONTSERRAT
Capital: Plymouth
PITCAIRN ISLANDS
Sole town: Adamstown
SAINT HELENA
Capital: Jamestown
SOUTH GEORGIA AND THE SOUTH SANDWICH
ISLANDS
Capital: King Edward Point
TURKS AND CAICOS ISLANDS
Capital: Cockburn Town

UNITED STATES

AMERICAN SAMOA
Capital: Pago Pago

GUAM
  Capital: Hagatna (also known as Agaña)
NORTHERN MARIANA ISLANDS
  Principal Settlement: Saipan

PUERTO RICO
  Capital: San Juan
UNITED STATES VIRGIN ISLANDS
  Capital: Charlotte Amalie

CAPITALS

CAPITAL	COUNTRY	CAPITAL	COUNTRY
ABU DHABI	UNITED ARAB EMIRATES	COPENHAGEN	DENMARK
ABUJA	NIGERIA	DAKAR	SENEGAL
ACCRA	GHANA	DAMASCUS	SYRIA
ADDIS ABABA	ETHIOPIA	DAR ES SALAAM	TANZANIA
ALGIERS	ALGERIA	DHAKA (DACCA)	BANGLADESH
AMMAN	JORDAN	DILI	EAST TIMOR
AMSTERDAM	NETHERLANDS	DJIBOUTI	DJIBOUTI
ANDORRA LA VELLA	ANDORRA	DODOMA	TANZANIA
ANKARA	TURKEY	DOHA	QATAR
ANTANANARIVO	MADAGASCAR	DUBLIN	IRELAND, REPUBLIC OF
APIA	SAMOA	DUSHANBE	TAJIKSTAN
ASHGABAT		FREETOWN	SIERRA LEONE
ASMARA	ERITREA	FUNAFUTI	TUVALU
ASTANA	KAZAKHSTAN	GABORONE	BOTSWANA
ASUNCIÓN	PARAGUAY	GEORGETOWN	GUYANA
ATHENS	GREECE	GITEGA	BURUNDI
BAGHDAD	IRAQ	GUATEMALA CITY	GUATEMALA
BAKU	AZERBAIJAN	HANOI	VIETNAM
BAMAKO	MALI	HARARE	ZIMBABWE
BANDAR SERI	BRUNEIBEGAWAN	HAVANA	CUBA
BANGKOK	THAILAND	HELSINKI	FINLAND
BANGUI	CENTRAL AFRICAN REPUBLIC	HONIARA	SOLOMON ISLANDS
		ISLAMABAD	PAKISTAN
BANJUL	THE GAMBIA	JAKARTA	INDONESIA
BASSETERRE	SAINT KITTS AND NEVIS	JERUSALEM	ISRAEL
		KABUL	AFGHANISTAN
BEIJING	CHINA	KAMPALA	UGANDA
BEIRUT	LEBANON	KATHMANDU	NEPAL
BELGRADE	SERBIA AND MONTENEGRO	KHARTOUM	SUDAN
		KIEV (*or* KYIV)	UKRAINE
BELMOPAN	BELIZE	KIGALI	RWANDA
BERLIN	GERMANY	KINGSTON	JAMAICA
BERN	SWITZERLAND	KINGSTOWN	SAINT VINCENT AND THE GRENADINES
BISHKEK	KYRGYZSTAN		
BISSAU	GUINEA-BISSAU	KINSHASA	CONGO, DEMOCRATIC REPUBLIC OF
BOGOTÁ	COLOMBIA		
BRASÍLIA	BRAZIL	KUALA LUMPUR	MALAYSIA
BRATISLAVA	SLOVAKIA	KUWAIT CITY	KUWAIT
BRAZZAVILLE	CONGO-BRAZZAVILLE	LA PAZ	BOLIVIA
BRIDGETOWN	BARBADOS	LIBREVILLE	GABON
BRUSSELS	BELGIUM	LILONGWE	MALAWI
BUCHAREST	ROMANIA	LIMA	PERU
BUDAPEST	HUNGARY	LISBON	PORTUGAL
BUENOS AIRES	ARGENTINA	LJUBLJANA	SLOVENIA
CAIRO	EGYPT	LOME	TOGO
CANBERRA	AUSTRALIA	LONDON	UNITED KINGDOM
CARACAS	VENEZUELA	LUANDA	ANGOLA
CASTRIES	SAINT LUCIA	LUSAKA	ZAMBIA
CHISNAU	MOLDOVA	LUXEMBOURG CITY	LUXEMBOURG
COLOMBO	SRI LANKA	MADRID	SPAIN
CONAKRY	GUINEA	MAJURO	MARSHALL ISLANDS

CAPITAL	COUNTRY	CAPITAL	COUNTRY
MALABO	EQUATORIAL GUINEA	ROME	ITALY
MALÉ	MALDIVES	ROSEAU	DOMINICA
MANAGUA	NICARAGUA	ST GEORGE'S	GRENADA
MANAMA	BAHRAIN	SAINT JOHN'S	ANTIGUA AND BARBUDA
MANILA	PHILIPPINES	SANA'A (administrative)	YEMEN
MAPUTO	MOZAMBIQUE	SAN JOSÉ	COSTA RICA
MASERU	LESOTHO	SAN MARINO	SAN MARINO
MBABANE	SWAZILAND	SAN SALVADOR	EL SALVADOR
MELEKEOK	PALAU	SANTIAGO	CHILE
MEXICO CITY	MEXICO	SANTO DOMINGO	DOMINICAN REPUBLIC
MINSK	BELARUS	SÃO TOMÉ	SÃO TOMÉ AND
MOGADISHU	SOMALIA		PRÍNCIPE
MONACO	MONACO	SARAJEVO	BOSNIA-HERCEGOVINA
MONROVIA	LIBERIA	SEOUL	SOUTH KOREA
MONTEVIDEO	URUGUAY	SINGAPORE	SINGAPORE
MORONI	COMOROS	SKOPJE	MACEDONIA
MOSCOW	RUSSIA	SOFIA	BULGARIA
MUSCAT	OMAN	STOCKHOLM	SWEDEN
NAIROBI	KENYA	SUCRE	BOLIVIA
NASSAU	THE BAHAMAS	SUVA	FIJI
NAYPYIDAW	MYANMAR	TAIPEI	TAIWAN
N'DJAMENA	CHAD	TALLINN	ESTONIA
NEW DELHI	INDIA	TARAWA	KIRIBATI
NIAMEY	NIGER	TASHKENT	UZBEKISTAN
NICOSIA	CYPRUS	TBILISI	GEORGIA
NOUAKCHOTT	MAURITANIA	TEGUCIGALPA	HONDURAS
NUKU'ALOFA	TONGA	TEHRAN	IRAN
OSLO	NORWAY	THIMPHU	BHUTAN
OTTAWA	CANADA	TIRANA (OR TIRANË)	ALBANIA
OUAGADOUGOU	BURKINA FASO	TOKYO	JAPAN
PALIKIR	MICRONESIA	TRIPOLI	LIBYA
PANAMA CITY	PANAMA	TUNIS	TUNISIA
PARAMARIBO	SURINAME	ULAANBAATAR	MONGOLIA (OR ULAN
PARIS	FRANCE		BATOR)
PHNOM PENH	CAMBODIA	VADUZ	LIECHTENSTEIN
PODGORICA	MONTENEGRO	VALLETTA	MALTA
PORT-AU-PRINCE	HAITI	VATICAN CITY	VATICAN CITY STATE
PORT LOUIS	MAURITIUS	VICTORIA	SEYCHELLES
PORT MORESBY	PAPUA NEW GUINEA	VIENNA	AUSTRIA
PORT OF SPAIN	TRINIDAD AND TOBAGO	VIENTIANE	LAOS
PORTO-NOVO	BENIN	VILA	VANUATU
PORT VILA	VANUATU	VILNIUS	LITHUANIA
PRAGUE	CZECH REPUBLIC	WARSAW	POLAND
PRAIA	CAPE VERDE	WASHINGTON, DC	UNITED STATES OF
PRETORIA	SOUTH AFRICA		AMERICA
PRISTINA	KOSOVO	WELLINGTON	NEW ZEALAND
P'YONGYANG	NORTH KOREA	WINDHOEK	NAMIBIA
QUITO	ECUADOR	YAMOUSSOUKRO	CÔTE D'IVOIRE
RABAT	MOROCCO	YANGÔN	MYANMAR
RANGOON	MYANMAR	YAOUNDÉ	CAMEROON
REYKJAVIK	ICELAND	YAREN	NAURU
RIGA	LATVIA	YEREVAN	ARMENIA
RIYADH	SAUDI ARABIA	ZAGREB	CROATIA

CURRENCIES

CURRENCY — COUNTRIES

AFGHANI — AFGHANISTAN
AGORA — ISRAEL
AGOROT — ISRAEL
AGOROTH — ISRAEL
ARIARY — MADAGASCAR
AT(T) — LAOS
AURAR — ICELAND
AUSTRAL — ARGENTINA
AUSTRALIAN DOLLAR — KIRIBATI, NAURU
BAHT — THAILAND
BAIZA — OMAN
BALBOA — PANAMA
BAN — MOLDOVA, ROMANIA
BANI — MOLDOVA, ROMANIA
BIRR — ETHIOPIA
BOLÍVAR — VENEZUELA
BOLIVIANO — BOLIVIA
BUTUT — THE GAMBIA
CEDI — GHANA
CENT — ANDORRA, ANTIGUA AND BARBUDA,
    ARUBA, AUSTRALIA, AUSTRIA, THE BAHAMAS,
    BARBADOS, BELGIUM, BELIZE, BERMUDA,
    BRUNEI, CANADA, THE CAYMAN ISLANDS,
    CYPRUS, DOMINICA, EAST TIMOR, ECUADOR, EL
    SALVADOR, ERITREA, ESTONIA, ETHIOPIA, FIJI,
    FINLAND, FRANCE, FRENCH GUIANA, GERMANY,
    GREECE, GRENADA, GUADELOUPE, GUAM,
    GUYANA, HONG KONG, IRELAND, JAMAICA,
    KENYA, KIRIBATI, KOSOVO, LATVIA, LIBERIA,
    LITHUANIA, LUXEMBOURG, MALAYSIA, MALTA,
    THE MARSHALL ISLANDS, MARTINIQUE,
    MAURITIUS, MAYOTTE, MICRONESIA, MONACO,
    MONTENEGRO, NAMIBIA, NAURU, THE
    NETHERLANDS, THE NETHERLANDS ANTILLES,
    NEW ZEALAND, THE NORTHERN MARIANA
    ISLANDS, PALAU, PORTUGAL, PUERTO RICO,
    RÉUNION, SAINT KITTS AND NEVIS, SAINT LUCIA,
    SAINT VINCENT AND THE GRENADINES, SAN
    MARINO, THE SEYCHELLES, SIERRA LEONE,
    SINGAPORE, SLOVAKIA, SLOVENIA, THE
    SOLOMON ISLANDS, SOMALIA, SOUTH AFRICA,
    SPAIN, SRI LANKA, SURINAM, SWAZILAND,
    TAIWAN, TANZANIA, TRINIDAD AND TOBAGO,
    TUVALU, UGANDA, THE UNITED STATES, THE
    VATICAN CITY, THE VIRGIN ISLANDS, ZIMBABWE
CÉNT — PERU
CENTAVO — BOLIVIA, BRAZIL, CAPE VERDE, CHILE,
    COLOMBIA, CUBA, DOMINICAN REPUBLIC,
    ECUADOR, EL SALVADOR, GUATEMALA,
    HONDURAS, MEXICO, MOZAMBIQUE,
    NICARAGUA, PHILIPPINES
CENTÉSIMO — PANAMA, URUGUAY
CENTIME — ALGERIA, BENIN, BURKINA FASO,
    BURUNDI, CAMEROON, CENTRAL AFRICAN
    REPUBLIC, CHAD, COMOROS, CONGO, CÔTE
    D'IVOIRE, DJIBOUTI, EQUATORIAL GUINEA,
    GABON, GUINEA, HAITI, LIECHTENSTEIN, MALI,
    MONACO, MOROCCO, NIGER, RWANDA,

SENEGAL, SWITZERLAND, TOGO, VANUATU
CÉNTIMO — COSTA RICA, PARAGUAY, PERU,
    VENEZUELA
CÊNTIMO — SÃO TOMÉ AND PRÍNCIPE
CFA FRANC — BENIN, BURKINA FASO, CAMEROON,
    CENTRAL AFRICAN REPUBLIC, CHAD, COMOROS,
    CONGO, CÔTE D'IVOIRE, EQUATORIAL GUINEA,
    GABON, GUINEA-BISSAU, MALI, NIGER, SENEGAL,
    TOGO
CHETRUM — BHUTAN
CHUN — SOUTH KOREA
COLON — COSTA RICA
COLONES — COSTA RICA
COLONS — COSTA RICA
COPECK — BELARUS, RUSSIA
COPEK — BELARUS, RUSSIA, TAJIKSTAN
CÓRDOBA — NICARAGUA
DALASI — THE GAMBIA
DENAR — MACEDONIA
DENI — MACEDONIA
DINAR — BAHRAIN, IRAN, IRAQ, JORDAN, KUWAIT,
    LIBYA, SERBIA, SUDAN, TUNISIA, YUGOSLAVIA
DIRAM — TAJIKISTAN
DIRHAM (DIRHEM) — LIBYA, MOROCCO, QATAR,
    UNITED ARAB EMIRATES
DOBRA — SÃO TOMÉ AND PRÍNCIPE
DOLLAR — ANTIGUA AND BARBUDA, AUSTRALIA,
    THE BAHAMAS, BARBADOS, BELIZE, BERMUDA,
    THE BRITISH VIRGIN ISLANDS, BRUNEI, CANADA,
    THE CAYMAN ISLANDS, DOMINICA, EAST TIMOR,
    ECUADOR, EL SALVADOR, FIJI, GRENADA,
    GUATEMALA, GUYANA, HONG KONG, JAMAICA,
    KIRIBATI, LIBERIA, MALAYSIA, THE MARSHALL
    ISLANDS, MICRONESIA, NAMIBIA, NAURU, NEW
    ZEALAND, PALAU, SAINT KITTS AND NEVIS, SAINT
    LUCIA, SAINT VINCENT AND THE GRENADINES,
    SINGAPORE, SOLOMON ISLANDS, SURINAME,
    TAIWAN, TRINIDAD AND TOBAGO, TUVALU,
    ZIMBABWE
DONG — VIETNAM
DRAM — ARMENIA
EAST CARIBBEAN DOLLAR — ANTIGUA AND
    BARBUDA, DOMINICA, GRENADA, SAINT KITTS
    AND NEVIS, SAINT LUCIA, SAINT VINCENT AND
    THE GRENADINES
ESCUDO — CAPE VERDE
EURO — ANDORRA, AUSTRIA, BELGIUM, CYPRUS,
    ESTONIA, FINLAND, FRANCE, FRENCH GUIANA,
    GERMANY, GREECE, GUADELOUPE, IRELAND,
    ITALY, KOSOVO, LATVIA, LITHUANIA,
    LUXEMBOURG, MALTA, MARTINIQUE, MAYOTTE,
    MONACO, MONTENEGRO, THE NETHERLANDS,
    PORTUGAL, RÉUNION, SAN MARINO, SLOVAKIA,
    SLOVENIA, SPAIN, VATICAN CITY
EYRIR — ICELAND
FEN — CHINA
FENING — BOSNIA AND HERZEGOVINA
FILLÉR — HUNGARY
FILS — BAHRAIN, IRAQ, KUWAIT, UNITED ARAB
    EMIRATES, YEMEN

FORINT — HUNGARY
FRANC — BURUNDI, CONGO, DJIBOUTI, GUINEA,
  RWANDA, SWITZERLAND
GITEGA — BURUNDI
GOPIK — AZERBAIJAN
GOURDE — HAITI
GROSZ — POLAND
GROSZY — POLAND
GUARANÍ — PARAGUAY
GUILDER — NETHERLANDS
HALALA — SAUDI ARABIA
HALER — CZECH REPUBLIC, SLOVAKIA
HALERU — CZECH REPUBLIC
HALURA — CZECH REPUBLIC
HO — VIETNAM
HRYVNA — UKRAINE
HRYVNYA — UKRAINE
IRAIMBILANJA — MADAGASCAR
JEON — SOUTH KOREA
JUN — NORTH KOREA
KAPEK — BELARUS
KHOUM — MAURITANIA
KINA — PAPUA NEW GUINEA
KIP — LAOS
KOBO — NIGERIA
KOPECK — BELARUS, RUSSIA, TAJIKSTAN
KOPEK — BELARUS, RUSSIA, TAJIKSTAN
KOPIYKA — UKRAINE
KORUNA — CZECH REPUBLIC
KRONA — SWEDEN
KRÓNA — ICELAND
KRONE — DENMARK, NORWAY
KRONEN — DENMARK, NORWAY
KRONER — DENMARK, NORWAY
KRONOR — SWEDEN
KRÓNUR — ICELAND
KROON — ESTONIA
KROONI — ESTONIA
KROONS — ESTONIA
KUNA — CROATIA
KUNE — CROATIA
KURUS — TURKEY
KURUSH — TURKEY
KWACHA — MALAWI, ZAMBIA
KWANZA — ANGOLA
KYAT — MYANMAR (BURMA)
LAARI — MALDIVES
LAREE — MALDIVES
LARI — GEORGIA, MALDIVES
LEI — MOLDOVA, ROMANIA
LEK — ALBANIA
LEKË — ALBANIA
LEKS — ALBANIA
LEMPIRA — HONDURAS
LEONE — SIERRA LEONE
LEU — MOLDOVA, ROMANIA
LEV — BULGARIA
LEVA — BULGARIA
LEVS — BULGARIA
LILANGENI — SWAZILAND
LIPA — CROATIA
LIRA — TURKEY

LIRE — TURKEY
LISENTE — LESOTHO
LOTI — LESOTHO
LOUMA — ARMENIA
LUMA — ARMENIA
LWEI — ANGOLA
MANAT — AZERBAIJAN, TURKMENISTAN
MARK — BOSNIA AND HERZEGOVINA
METICAL — MOZAMBIQUE
MILLIME — TUNISIA
MÖNGÖ — MONGOLIA
NAKFA — ERITREA
NAIRA — NIGERIA
NGULTRUM — BHUTAN
NGWEE — ZAMBIA
ØRE — DENMARK, NORWAY
ÖRE — SWEDEN
OUGIYA — MAURITANIA
OUGUIYA — MAURITANIA
PA'ANGA — TONGA
PAISA — BANGLADESH, INDIA, NEPAL, PAKISTAN
PAISE — INDIA, NEPAL, PAKISTAN
PARA — MACEDONIA, SERBIA
PENCE — UNITED KINGDOM
PENNIES — UNITED KINGDOM
PENNY — UNITED KINGDOM
PESEWA — GHANA
PESO — ARGENTINA, CHILE, COLOMBIA, CUBA,
  DOMINICAN REPUBLIC, MEXICO, PHILIPPINES,
  URUGUAY
PETRO — VENEZUELA
PIASTRE — EGYPT, JORDAN, LEBANON, SOUTH
  SUDAN, SUDAN, SYRIA
POISHA — BANGLADESH
POUND — EGYPT, LEBANON, SOUTH SUDAN,
  SUDAN, SYRIA, UNITED KINGDOM
PUL — AFGHANISTAN
PULA — BOTSWANA
PULI — AFGHANISTAN
PULS — AFGHANISTAN
PYA — MYANMAR (BURMA)
QAPIK — AZERBAIJAN
QINDAR — ALBANIA
QINDARKA — ALBANIA
QINTAR — ALBANIA
QUETZAL — GUATEMALA
QUETZALES — GUATEMALA
QIRSH — JORDAN
RAND — SOUTH AFRICA
RAPPEN — SWITZERLAND
REAL — BRAZIL
RENMINBI — CHINA
RIAL — IRAN, OMAN, YEMEN
RIYAL — YEMEN
RIEL — CAMBODIA
RINGGIT — MALAYSIA
RIYAL — QATAR, SAUDI ARABIA
ROUBLE — BELARUS, RUSSIA
RUFIYAA — MALDIVES
RUPEE — INDIA, MAURITIUS, NEPAL, PAKISTAN,
  SEYCHELLES, SRI LANKA
RUPIAH — INDONESIA
SANTEEM — ALGERIA

SANTIM — ETHIOPIA
SATANG — THAILAND
SATANGS — THAILAND
SEN — BRUNEI, CAMBODIA, INDONESIA, JAPAN, MALAYSIA
SENE — SAMOA
SENITI — TONGA
SENT — ESTONIA
SENTE — LESOTHO
SENTI — ESTONIA
SHEKEL — ISRAEL
SHEQEL — ISRAEL
SHILLING — KENYA, SOMALIA, TANZANIA, UGANDA
SOL — PERU
SOLES — PERU
SOM — KYRGYZSTAN, UZBEKISTAN
SOMONI — TAJIKISTAN
STANGS — THAILAND
STOTIN — SLOVENIA
STOTINKA — BULGARIA
STOTINKI — BULGARIA
SUM — UZBEKISTAN

SUMY — UZBEKISTAN
SWISS FRANC — LIECHTENSTEIN
TAKA — BANGLADESH
TALA — SAMOA
TAMBALA — MALAWI
TEEN — UZBEKISTAN
TENGE — KAZAKHSTAN, TURKMENISTAN
TENNES — TURKMENISTAN
TETRI — GEORGIA
THEBE — BOTSWANA
TIYN — KAZAKHSTAN
TOEA — PAPUA NEW GUINEA
TOG ROG — MONGOLIA
TUGRIK — MONGOLIA
US DOLLAR — BELAU, MARSHALL ISLANDS, MICRONESIA
VATU — VANUATU
WON — NORTH KOREA, SOUTH KOREA
XU — VIETNAM
YEN — JAPAN
YUAN — CHINA
ZŁ OTY — POLAND

FORMER EUROPEAN CURRENCIES

CENTAS — LITHUANIA
CENTESIMI — ITALY, SAN MARINO, VATICAN CITY
CENTESIMO — ITALY, SAN MARINO, VATICAN CITY
CENTIME — ANDORRA, BELGIUM, FRANCE, LUXEMBOURG
CÉNTIMO — ANDORRA,SPAIN
COLÓN — EL SALVADOR
DEUTSCHE MARK — GERMANY
DEUTSCHMARK — GERMANY
DRACHMA — GREECE
DRACHMAE — GREECE
DRACHMAS — GREECE
ESCUDO — PORTUGAL
FRANC — BELGIUM, FRANCE, LUXEMBOURG
GROSCHEN — AUSTRIA
HALIER(OV) — SLOVAKIA
LAT — LATVIA
LEPTA — GREECE
LEPTON — GREECE
LIRA — ITALY, SAN MARINO, VATICAN CITY

LIRE — ITALY, SAN MARINO, VATICAN CITY
LITAS — LITHUANIA
MARKA — BOSNIA-HERCEGOVINA
MARKKA — FINLAND
PENCE — IRELAND, REPUBLIC OF
PENNI — FINLAND
PENNIÄ — FINLAND
PENNIES — IRELAND, REPUBLIC OF
PENNY — IRELAND, REPUBLIC OF
PESETA — ANDORRA, SPAIN
PFENNIG — GERMANY
PFENNIGE — GERMANY
PFENNIGS — GERMANY
PUNT — IRELAND, REPUBLIC OF
ROUBLE — TAJIKISTAN
SANTIMI — LATVIA
SCHILLING — AUSTRIA
TANGA — TAJIKISTAN
TOLAR(JI) — SLOVENIA

ENGLISH COUNTIES, FORMER COUNTIES, AND SELECTED LOCAL AUTHORITIES

AUTHORITY (Administrative Centre)

AVON (Bristol)
BATH AND NORTH-EAST SOMERSET (Bath)
BEDFORDSHIRE (Bedford)
BERKSHIRE (Reading)
BRIGHTON AND HOVE
BRISTOL
BUCKINGHAMSHIRE (Aylesbury)
CAMBRIDGESHIRE (Cambridge)
CHESHIRE (Chester)
CITY OF LONDON
CLEVELAND (Middlesbrough)
CORNWALL (Truro)
COUNTY DURHAM
CUMBERLAND (Carlisle)
CUMBRIA (Carlisle)
DERBYSHIRE (Matlock)
DEVON (Exeter)
DORSET (Dorchester)
EAST RIDING (OF YORKSHIRE) (Beverley)
EAST SUSSEX (Lewes)
ESSEX (Chelmsford)
GLOUCESTERSHIRE (Gloucester)
GREATER LONDON (London)
GREATER MANCHESTER (Manchester)
HALTON (Runcorn)

HAMPSHIRE (Winchester)
HEREFORD AND WORCESTER (Worcester)
HEREFORDSHIRE (Hereford)
HERTFORDSHIRE (Hertford)
HUMBERSIDE (Beverley)
HUNTINGDONSHIRE (Huntingdon)
ISLE OF WIGHT (Newport, IOW)
KENT (Maidstone)
KIRKLEES (Huddersfield)
LANCASHIRE (Preston)
LEICESTERSHIRE (Leicester)
LINCOLNSHIRE (Lincoln)
LUTON
MEDWAY (Gillingham)
MERSEYSIDE (Liverpool)
NORFOLK (Norwich)
NORTHAMPTONSHIRE (Northampton)
NORTH-EAST LINCOLNSHIRE (Grimsby)
NORTH LINCOLNSHIRE (Scunthorpe)
NORTH SOMERSET (Weston-super-Mare)
NORTH RIDING (OF YORKSHIRE) (Middlesbrough)
NORTHUMBERLAND (Morpeth)
NORTH YORKSHIRE (Northallerton)

NOTTINGHAMSHIRE (Nottingham)
OXFORDSHIRE (Oxford)
REDCAR AND CLEVELAND (Redcar)
RUTLAND (Oakham)
SALOP (name for Shropshire between 1974 and 1980)
SHROPSHIRE (Shrewsbury)
SOMERSET (Taunton)
SOUTH GLOUCESTERSHIRE (Thornbury)
SOUTH YORKSHIRE (Barnsley)
STAFFORDSHIRE (Stafford)
SUFFOLK (Ipswich)
SURREY (Guildford)
SUSSEX (Lewes)
TELFORD AND WREKIN (Telford)
TYNE AND WEAR (Newcastle-Upon-Tyne)
WARWICKSHIRE (Warwick)
WEST BERKSHIRE (Newbury)
WEST MIDLANDS (Birmingham)
WESTMORLAND (Kendal)
WEST RIDING (OF YORKSHIRE) (Wakefield)
WEST SUSSEX (Chichester)
WEST YORKSHIRE (Wakefield)
WILTSHIRE (Trowbridge)
WIRRAL (Birkenhead)
WORCESTERSHIRE (Worcester)

WELSH COUNTIES AND SELECTED LOCAL AUTHORITIES

AUTHORITY (Administrative Centre)

ANGLESEY (Llangefni)
BLAENAU GWENT (Ebbw Vale)
*BRECONSHIRE (Brecon)
BRIDGEND
CAERPHILLY
*CAERNARFONSHIRE (Caernarfon)
CARDIFF
*CARDIGANSHIRE (Aberystwyth)
CARMARTHENSHIRE (Carmarthen)
CEREDIGION (Aberaeron)
*CLWYD (Mold)

CONWY (Bodlondeb)
DENBIGHSHIRE (Ruthin)
*DYFED (Carmarthen)
FLINTSHIRE (Mold)
*GLAMORGAN (Cardiff)
*GWENT (Cwmbran)
GWYNEDD (Caernarfon)
*MERIONETH (Dolgellan)
MERTHYR TYDFIL
*MID GLAMORGAN (Cardiff)
MONMOUTHSHIRE (Cwmbran)
*MONTGOMERYSHIRE (Welshpool)
NEATH PORT TALBOT (Port Talbot)
NEWPORT

PEMBROKESHIRE (Haverfordwest)
POWYS (Llandrindod Wells)
*RADNORSHIRE (Llandrindod Wells)
RHONDDA CYNON TAFF (Clydach Vale)
*SOUTH GLAMORGAN (Cardiff)
SWANSEA (Swansea)
TORFAEN (Pontypool)
VALE OF GLAMORGAN (Barry)
*WEST GLAMORGAN (Swansea)
WREXHAM (Wrexham)
*indicates a former county

SCOTTISH REGIONS, COUNTIES, AND SELECTED LOCAL AUTHORITIES

AUTHORITY (Administrative Centre)

ABERDEEN CITY
ABERDEENSHIRE (Aberdeen)
ANGUS (Forfar)
ARGYLL AND BUTE
  (Lochgilphead)
*ARGYLL (Lochgilphead)
*AYRSHIRE (Ayr)
*BANFF (Banff)
*BERWICK (Duns)
*BORDERS
*BUTE (Rothesay)
*CAITHNESS (Wick)
*CENTRAL (Stirling)
CLACKMANNANSHIRE (Alloa)
DUMFRIES AND GALLOWAY
  (Dumfries)
*DUMFRIES (Dumfries)
*DUNBARTONSHIRE
  (Dumbarton)
DUNDEE CITY
EAST AYRSHIRE (Kilmarnock)
EAST DUNBARTONSHIRE
  (Kirkintilloch)
EAST LOTHIAN (Haddington)

EAST RENFREWSHIRE (Giffnock)
EDINBURGH, CITY OF
EILEAN SIAR (Lewis)
FALKIRK
FIFE (Glenrothes)
GLASGOW CITY
*GRAMPIAN (Aberdeen)
HIGHLAND (Inverness)
INVERCLYDE (Greenock)
*INVERNESS (Inverness)
*KINCARDINESHIRE
  (Stonehaven)
*KINROSS (Kinross)
*KIRKCUDBRIGHT
  (Kirkcudbright)
*LANARKSHIRE (Hamilton)
*LOTHIAN (Edinburgh)
MIDLOTHIAN (Dalkeith)
MORAY (Elgin)
*NAIRN (Nairn)
NORTH AYRSHIRE (Irvine)
NORTH LANARKSHIRE
  (Motherwell)
ORKNEY (Kirkwall)
*PEEBLES (Peebles)
PERTH AND KINROSS (Perth)

*PERTHSHIRE (Perth)
RENFREWSHIRE (Paisley)
*ROSS AND CROMARTY
  (Dingwall)
*ROXBURGH (Newtown St.
  Boswells)
SCOTTISH BORDERS (Newton St.
  Boswells)
*SELKIRK (Selkirk)
SHETLAND (Lerwick)
SOUTH AYRSHIRE (Ayr)
SOUTH LANARKSHIRE (Hamilton)
STIRLING (Stirling)
*STRATHCLYDE (Glasgow)
*SUTHERLAND (Golspie)
*TAYSIDE (Dundee)
WEST DUNBARTONSHIRE
  (Dumbarton)
*WESTERN ISLES (Lewis) (now
  Eilean Siar)
WEST LOTHIAN (Livingston)
*WIGTOWNSHIRE (Stranraer)
ZETLAND (former name for
  Shetland)

*indicates a former region or
county

PROVINCES AND COUNTIES OF IRELAND

PROVINCE

COUNTY (County Town)

CONNACHT
MAYO (Castlebar)
SLIGO (Sligo)
GALWAY (Galway)
LEITRIM (Carrick-on-Shannon)
ROSCOMMON (Roscommon)

LEINSTER
LOUTH (Dundalk)
MEATH (Trim)
CARLOW (Carlow)
DUBLIN (Dublin)

OFFALY (Tullamore)
KILDARE (Naas)
WEXFORD (Wexford)
WICKLOW (Wicklow)
KILKENNY (Kilkenny)
LAOIGHIS [or LAOIS or LEIX]
  (Portlaoighise
or Portlaoise)
LONGFORD (Longford)
WESTMEATH (Mullingar)

MUNSTER
CORK (Cork)
CLARE (Ennis)
KERRY (Tralee)

LIMERICK (Limerick)
TIPPERARY (Clonmel)
WATERFORD (Waterford)

ULSTER
*DOWN (Downpatrick)
CAVAN (Cavan)
*ARMAGH (Armagh)
*ANTRIM (Belfast)
*TYRONE (Omagh)
DONEGAL (Lifford)
MONAGHAN (Monaghan)
*FERMANAGH (Enniskillen)
*LONDONDERRY (Londonderry)

*indicates counties of N Ireland

AMERICAN STATES

STATE	ABBREVIATION	NICKNAME	CAPITAL
ALABAMA	ALA	COTTON	MONTGOMERY
ALASKA	ALAS	LAST FRONTIER	JUNEAU
ARIZONA	ARIZ	GRAND CANYON	PHOENIX
ARKANSAS	ARK	LAND OF OPPORTUNITY	LITTLE ROCK
CALIFORNIA	CAL	GOLDEN	SACRAMENTO
COLORADO	COLO	CENTENNIAL	DENVER
CONNECTICUT	CONN	CONSTITUTION	HARTFORD
DELAWARE	DEL	FIRST	DOVER
FLORIDA	FLA	SUNSHINE	TALLAHASSEE
GEORGIA	GA	EMPIRE STATE OF THE SOUTH	ATLANTA
HAWAII	HA	ALOHA	HONOLULU
IDAHO	IDA	GEM	BOISE
ILLINOIS	ILL	LAND OF LINCOLN	SPRINGFIELD
INDIANA	IND	HOOSIER	INDIANAPOLIS
IOWA	IA	HAWKEYE	DES MOINES
KANSAS	KAN	SUNFLOWER	TOPEKA
KENTUCKY	KY	BLUEGRASS	FRANKFORT
LOUISIANA	LA	PELICAN	BATON ROUGE
MAINE	ME	PINE TREE	AUGUSTA
MARYLAND	MD	OLD LINE	ANNAPOLIS
MASSACHUSETTS	MASS	BAY	BOSTON
MICHIGAN	MICH	WOLVERINE	LANSING
MINNESOTA	MINN	GOPHER	ST. PAUL
MISSISSIPPI	MISS	MAGNOLIA	JACKSON
MISSOURI	MO	SHOW ME	JEFFERSON CITY
MONTANA	MONT	TREASURE	HELENA
NEBRASKA	NEBR	CORNHUSKER	LINCOLN
NEVADA	NEV	SILVER	CARSON CITY
NEW HAMPSHIRE	NH	GRANITE	CONCORD
NEW JERSEY	NJ	GARDEN	TRENTON
NEW MEXICO	N MEX	LAND OF ENCHANTMENT	SANTA FÉ
NEW YORK	NY	EMPIRE	ALBANY
NORTH CAROLINA	NC	TARHEEL	RALEIGH
NORTH DAKOTA	N DAK	FLICKERTAIL	BISMARCK
OHIO	OH	BUCKEYE	COLUMBUS
OKLAHOMA	OKLA	SOONER	OKLAHOMA CITY
OREGON	OREG	BEAVER	SALEM
PENNSYLVANIA	PA	KEYSTONE	HARRISBURG
RHODE ISLAND	RI	OCEAN	PROVIDENCE
SOUTH CAROLINA	SC	PALMETTO	COLUMBIA
SOUTH DAKOTA	S DAK	SUNSHINE	PIERRE
TENNESSEE	TENN	VOLUNTEER	NASHVILLE
TEXAS	TEX	LONE STAR	AUSTIN
UTAH	UT	BEEHIVE	SALT LAKE CITY
VERMONT	VT	GREEN MOUNTAIN	MONTPELIER
VIRGINIA	VA	OLD DOMINION	RICHMOND
WASHINGTON	WASH	EVERGREEN	OLYMPIA
WEST VIRGINIA	W VA	MOUNTAIN	CHARLESTON
WISCONSIN	WIS	BADGER	MADISON
WYOMING	WYO	EQUALITY	CHEYENNE

AUSTRALIAN STATES AND TERRITORIES

AUSTRALIAN CAPITAL TERRITORY
NEW SOUTH WALES
NORTHERN TERRITORY
QUEENSLAND

SOUTH AUSTRALIA
TASMANIA
VICTORIA
WESTERN AUSTRALIA

CANADIAN PROVINCES OR TERRITORIES

PROVINCE/TERRITORY	ABBREVIATION	PROVINCE/TERRITORY	ABBREVIATION
ALBERTA	AB	NOVA SCOTIA	NS
BRITISH COLUMBIA	BC	NUNAVUT	NU
MANITOBA	MB	ONTARIO	ON
NEW BRUNSWICK	NB	PRINCE EDWARD ISLAND	PE
NEWFOUNDLAND AND LABRADOR	NF	QUEBEC	QC
		SASKATCHEWAN	SK
NORTHWEST TERRITORIES	NT	YUKON TERRITORY	YT

NEW ZEALAND ISLANDS AND TERRITORIES

COOK ISLANDS
NIUE
NORTH ISLAND

ROSS DEPENDENCY
SOUTH ISLAND
TOKELAU

AUSTRIAN STATES

BURGENLAND
KARNTEN (CARINTHIA)
NIEDEROSTERREICH (LOWER AUSTRIA)
OBEROSTERREICH (UPPER AUSTRIA)
SALZBURG

STEIERMARK (STYRIA)
TIROL (TYROL)
VORARLBERG
WIEN (VIENNA)

FRENCH REGIONS

ALSACE
AQUITAINE
AUVERGNE
BASSE-NORMANDIE
BRITTANY (BRETAGNE)
BURGUNDY (BOURGOGNE)
CENTRE
CHAMPAGNE-ARDENNE
CORSE (CORSICA)
FRANCHE-COMTE
HAUTE-NORMANDIE

ILE-DE-FRANCE
LANGUEDOC-ROUSSILLON
LIMOUSIN
LORRAINE
MIDI-PYRENEES
NORD-PAS-DE-CALAIS
PAYS DE LA LORIE
PICARDIE
POITOU-CHARENTES
PROVENCE-ALPES-CÔTE D'AZUR
RHONE-ALPES

GERMAN STATES

BADEN-WURTTEMBERG
BAVARIA
BERLIN
BRANDENBURG
BREMEN
HAMBURG
HESSE
LOWER SAXONY

MECKLENBURG-WEST POMERANIA
NORTH RHINE-WESTPHALIA
RHINELAND-PALATINATE
SAAR
SAXONY
SAXONY-ANHALT
SCHLESWIG-HOLSTEIN
THURINGIA

SPANISH REGIONS

ANDALUSIA
ARAGON
ASTURIAS
CATALONIA
EXTREMADURA
GALICIA

MURCIA
NAVARRE
CASTILLA-LA MANCHA
CASTILLA Y LEON
VALENCIA

ITALIAN REGIONS

ABRUZZO (ABBRUZZI)
BASILICATA
BENEZIA GIULIA
CALABRIA
CAMPANIA
EMILIA ROMAGNA
FRIULI VENEZIA GIULIA
LAZIO
MARCHES (LE MARCHE)
LIGURIA
LOMBARDY (LOMBARDIA)

MOLISE
PIEMONT(E)
APULIA (PUGLIA)
SARDINIA (SARDEGNA)
SICILY (SICILIA)
TUSCANY (TOSCANA)
TRENTINO ALTO ADIGE
UMBRIA
VALLE D'AOSTA
VENETO

PORTUGUESE DISTRICTS AND AUTONOMOUS REGIONS

AVEIRO
BEJA
BRAGA
BRAGANÇA
CASTELO BRANCO
COIMBRA
EVORA
FARO
GUARDA

LEIRIA
LISBON (LISBOA)
PORTALEGRE
OPORTO (PORTO)
SANTAREM
SETUBAL
VIANA DO CASTELO
VILA REAL
VISEU

SWISS CANTONS

APPENZELL INNER-RHODES
APPENZELL OUTER-RHODES
ARGOVIA
BASLE-COUNTRY
BASLE-TOWN
BERNE
FRIBOURG
GENEVA
GLARUS
GRISONS
JURA
LUCERNE
NEUCHÂTEL

NIDWALDEN
OBWALDEN
ST GALL
SCHAFFHAU
SCHWYZ
SOLOTHURN
THURGOVIA
TICINO
URI
VALAIS
VAUD
ZUG
ZURICH

INDIAN STATES AND UNION TERRITORIES

ANDAMAN AND NICOBAR ISLANDS
ANDHRA PRADESH
ARUNCHAL PRADESH
ASSAM
BIHAR
CHANDIGARH
CHHATTISGARH
DADRA AND NAGAR HAVELI
DAMAN AND DIU
DELHI
GOA
GUJARAT
HARYANA
HIMACHAL PRADESH
JAMMU AND KASHMIR
JHARKHAND
KARNATAKA
KERALA

LAKSHADWEEP
MADHYA PRADESH
MAHARASHRA
MANIPUR
MEGHALAYA
MIZORAM
NAGALAND
ODISHA
PONDICHERRY (or PUDUCHERRY)
PUNJAB
RAJASTHAN
SIKKIM
TAMIL NADU
TRIPURA
UTTAR PRADESH
UTTARAKHAND
WEST BENGAL

PAKISTANI PROVINCES AND TERRITORIES

BALOCHISTAN (BALUCHISTAN)
ISLAMABAD CAPITAL TERRIRORY
KHYBER PAKHTUNKHWA (formerly
    NORTHWEST FRONTIER PROVINCE)

PUNJAB
SINDH
TRIBAL AREAS

NIGERIAN STATES

ABIA
ADAMAWA
AKWA IBOM
ANAMBRA
BAUCHI

BAYELSA
BERNUE
BORNO
CROSS RIVER
DELTA

EBONYI
EDO
EKITI
ENUGU
FEDERAL CAPITAL TERRITORY
GOMBE
IMO
JIGAWA
KADUNA
KANO
KATSINA
KEBBI
KOGI
KWARA

LAGOS
NASARAWA
NIGER
OGUN
ONDO
OSUN
OYO
PLATEAU
RIVERS
SOKOTO
TARABA
YOBE
ZAMFARA

CHINESE PROVINCES

ANHUI
BEIJING
CHONGQING
FUJIAN
GANSU
GUANGDONG
GUIZHOU
GUNAGXI
HAINAN
HEBEI
HEILONGJIANG
HENAN
HUBEI
HUNAN
INNER MONGOLIA (NEI MONGOL)
JIANGSU

JIANGXI
JILIN
LIAONING
NINGXIA
QINGHAI
SHAANXI
SHANDONG
SHANGHAI
SHANXI
SICHUAN
TIANJIN
TIBET (XIZANG)
XINJIANG UYGUR
YUNNAN
ZHEJIANG

BRAZILIAN REGIONS

ACRE
ALAGOAS
AMAPA
AMAZONAS
BAHIA
CEARA
DISTRITO FEDERAL
ESPIRITO SANTO
GOIAS
MARANHAO
MATO GROSSO
MATO GROSSO DO SUL
MINAS GERAIS
PARA

PARAIBA
PARANA
PERNAMBUCO
PIAUI
RIO DE JANEIRO
RIO GRANDE DO NORTE
RIO GRANDE DO SUL
RONDONIA
RORAIMA
SANTA CATARINA
SAO PAULO
SERGIPE
TOCANTINS

TOWNS AND CITIES

AFGHANISTAN

5
HERAT
KABUL

8
KANDAHAR

ALBANIA

6
TIRANA
TIRANE

ALGERIA

4
ORAN

7
ALGIERS

ANGOLA

6
HUAMBO
LOBITO
LUANDA

ARGENTINA

7
CORDOBA
LA PLATA
ROSARIO

9
LA MATANZA

11
BAHIA BLANCA
BUENOS AIRES

AUSTRALIA

5
PERTH

6
DARWIN
HOBART
SYDNEY

8
ADELAIDE
BRISBANE
CANBERRA

9
MELBOURNE
NEWCASTLE

12
ALICE
  SPRINGS

AUSTRIA

6
VIENNA

8
SALZBURG

9
INNSBRUCK

AZERBAIJAN

4
BAKU

BANGLADESH

5
DHAKA

10
CHITTAGONG

BELARUS

5
BREST
MINSK

BELGIUM

5
GHENT
LIÈGE
NAMUR
YPRES

6
BRUGES
DINANT
OSTEND

7
ANTWERP
MALINES

8
BRUSSELS

**BOSNIA-
  HERCEGOVINA**

5
TUZLA

6
MOSTAR

8
SARAJEVO

9
BANJA LUKA

BRAZIL

5
BELEM

6
MANAUS
RECIFE

8
BRASÍLIA
SALVADOR
SÃO PAULO

11
PORTO ALEGRE

12
RIO DE JANEIRO

13
BELO HORIZONTE

BULGARIA

5
SOFIA
VARNA

BURMA
SEE MYANMAR

CANADA

6
OTTAWA
QUEBEC
REGINA

7
CALGARY
HALIFAX
ST JOHN'S
TORONTO

8
EDMONTON
HAMILTON
KINGSTON
MONTREAL
VICTORIA
WINNIPEG

9
VANCOUVER
SASKATOON

10
THUNDER BAY

11
FREDERICTON

12
NIAGARA FALLS

13
CHARLOTTETOWN

CHILE

8
SANTIAGO

10
VALPARAISO

CHINA

4
LUTA
SIAN

5
WUHAN

6
ANSHAN
CANTON
DAIREN
FUSHUN
HARBIN
MUKDEN
PEKING
TSINAN

7
BEIJING
KUNMING
LANCHOW
NANKING
TAIYUAN

8
SHANGHAI
SHENYANG
TIENTSIN

9
CHANGCHUN
CHUNGKING

10
PORT ARTHUR

COLOMBIA

4
CALI

6
BOGOTÁ

8
MEDELLÍN

9
CARTAGENA

12
BARRANQUILLA

15
SANTA FÉ DE
  BOGOTÁ

**CONGO, DEMOCRATIC
  REPUBLIC OF**

6
BOKAVU

8
KINSHASA

10
LUBUMBASHI

CROATIA

5
SPLIT

6
ZAGREB

CUBA

6
HAVANA

14
SANTIAGO DE CUBA

CZECH REPUBLIC

4
BRNO

6
PRAGUE

DENMARK

5
ARHUS

6
ODENSE

10
COPENHAGEN

ECUADOR

5
QUITO

9
GUAYAQUIL

EGYPT

4
GIZA
SUEZ

5
ASWAN
CAIRO
LUXOR
TANTA

6
THEBES

7
MANSURA
MEMPHIS
ZAGAZIG

8
ISMAILIA
PORT SAID

10
ALEXANDRIA

ENGLAND

3
ELY
EYE
RYE
WEM

4
BATH
BRAY
BUDE
BURY
CLUN
DEAL
DISS
ETON
HOLT
HOVE
HULL
HYDE
INCE
LEEK
LOOE
LYDD
ROSS
RYDE
SHAP
WARE
WARK
YARM
YORK

5
ACTON
ALTON
BACUP
BLYTH
BOURN
CALNE
CHARD
CHEAM
COLNE
COWES
CREWE
DERBY
DOVER
EGHAM
EPSOM
FILEY
FOWEY
FROME
GOOLE
HAWES
HEDON
HURST
HYTHE
LEEDS
LEIGH
LEWES
LOUTH
LUTON

MARCH
OLNEY
OTLEY
POOLE
REETH
RIPON
RISCA
RUGBY
SARUM
SELBY
STOKE
STONE
TEBAY
THAME
TRING
TRURO
WELLS
WIGAN

6
ALFORD
ALSTON
ASHTON
BARNET
BARROW
BARTON
BATLEY
BATTLE
BAWTRY
BEDALE
BELPER
BODMIN
BOGNOR
BOLTON
BOOTLE
BOSTON
BRUTON
BUNGAY
BURTON
BUXTON
CASTOR
COBHAM
CROMER
DARWEN
DUDLEY
DURHAM
EALING
ECCLES
EPPING
EXETER
GORING
HANLEY
HARLOW
HARROW
HAVANT
HENLEY
HEXHAM
HOWDEN
ILFORD
ILKLEY
ILSLEY
JARROW
KENDAL
LEYTON

LONDON
LUDLOW
LYNTON
LYTHAM
MALDON
MALTON
MARLOW
MASHAM
MORLEY
NASEBY
NELSON
NESTON
NEWARK
NEWENT
NEWLYN
NEWTON
NORHAM
OAKHAM
OLDHAM
ORMSBY
OSSETT
OUNDLE
OXFORD
PENRYN
PEWSEY
PINNER
PUDSEY
PUTNEY
RAMSEY
REDCAR
RIPLEY
ROMNEY
ROMSEY
RUGELY
SEAHAM
SEATON
SELSEY
SETTLE
SNAITH
ST IVES
STROOD
STROUD
SUTTON
THIRSK
THORNE
TOTNES
WALTON
WATTON
WESTON
WHITBY
WIDNES
WIGTON
WILTON
WITHAM
WITNEY
WOOLER
YEOVIL

7
ALNWICK
ANDOVER
APPLEBY
ARUNDEL
ASHFORD

AYLSHAM	HORSHAM	TWYFORD	HELMSLEY
BAMPTON	IPSWICH	VENTNOR	HEREFORD
BANBURY	IXWORTH	WALSALL	HERNE BAY
BARKING	KESWICK	WALTHAM	HERTFORD
BECCLES	KINGTON	WANTAGE	HINCKLEY
BEDFORD	LANCING	WAREHAM	HOLBEACH
BELFORD	LANGTON	WARWICK	HUNMANBY
BERWICK	LEDBURY	WATCHET	ILKESTON
BEWDLEY	LEYBURN	WATFORD	KEIGHLEY
BEXHILL	LINCOLN	WEOBLEY	KINGSTON
BICKLEY	MALVERN	WICKWAR	LAVENHAM
BILSTON	MARGATE	WINDSOR	LECHLADE
BOURTON	MATLOCK	WINSLOW	LISKEARD
BOWFELL	MOLESEY	WINSTER	LONGTOWN
BRANDON	MORETON	WISBECK	LYNMOUTH
BRISTOL	MORPETH	WORKSOP	MARYPORT
BRIXHAM	MOSSLEY	**8**	MIDHURST
BROMLEY	NEWBURY	ABINGDON	MINEHEAD
BURNHAM	NEWPORT	ALFRETON	NANTWICH
BURNLEY	NORWICH	ALNMOUTH	NEWHAVEN
BURSLEM	OLDBURY	AMESBURY	NUNEATON
CAISTOR	OVERTON	AMPTHILL	ORMSKIRK
CATFORD	PADSTOW	AXBRIDGE	OSWESTRY
CAWSTON	PENRITH	AYCLIFFE	PENZANCE
CHARING	POULTON	BAKEWELL	PERSHORE
CHATHAM	PRESCOT	BARNSLEY	PETERLEE
CHEADLE	PRESTON	BERKELEY	PETWORTH
CHEDDAR	RAINHAM	BEVERLEY	PEVENSEY
CHESHAM	READING	BICESTER	PLAISTOW
CHESTER	REDHILL	BIDEFORD	PLYMOUTH
CHORLEY	REDRUTH	BOLSOVER	RAMSGATE
CLACTON	REIGATE	BRACKLEY	REDDITCH
CLIFTON	RETFORD	BRADFORD	RICHMOND
CRAWLEY	ROMFORD	BRAMPTON	RINGWOOD
CROYDON	ROSSALL	BRIDPORT	ROCHDALE
DARSLEY	ROYSTON	BRIGHTON	ROTHBURY
DATCHET	RUNCORN	BROMYARD	SALTBURN
DAWLISH	SALFORD	BROSELEY	SANDGATE
DEVIZES	SALTASH	CAMBORNE	SANDWICH
DORKING	SANDOWN	CARLISLE	SEDBERGH
DOUGLAS	SAXELBY	CATERHAM	SHANKLIN
DUNSTER	SEAFORD	CHERTSEY	SHELFORD
ELSTREE	SHIFNAL	CLEVEDON	SHIPSTON
ENFIELD	SHIPLEY	CLOVELLY	SIDMOUTH
EVERTON	SHIPTON	COVENTRY	SKEGNESS
EVESHAM	SILLOTH	CREDITON	SLEAFORD
EXMOUTH	SKIPTON	DAVENTRY	SOUTHEND
FAREHAM	SPILSBY	DEBENHAM	SPALDING
FARNHAM	STAINES	DEDWORTH	STAFFORD
FELTHAM	STILTON	DEPTFORD	ST ALBANS
GLOSSOP	ST NEOTS	DEWSBURY	STAMFORD
GOSPORT	SUDBURY	EGREMONT	STANHOPE
GRIMSBY	SUNBURY	EVERSLEY	STANWELL
HALIFAX	SWANAGE	FAKENHAM	ST HELENS
HAMPTON	SWINDON	FALMOUTH	STOCKTON
HARWICH	SWINTON	FOULNESS	STRATTON
HAWORTH	TAUNTON	GRANTHAM	SURBITON
HELSTON	TELFORD	GRANTOWN	SWAFFHAM
HEYWOOD	TENBURY	HADLEIGH	TAMWORTH
HITCHIN	TETBURY	HAILSHAM	THETFORD
HONITON	THAXTED	HALSTEAD	THORNABY
HORNSEA	TILBURY	HASTINGS	TIVERTON
HORNSEY	TORQUAY	HATFIELD	TUNSTALL

UCKFIELD
UXBRIDGE
WALLASEY
WALLSEND
WANSTEAD
WESTBURY
WETHERAL
WETHERBY
WEYMOUTH
WOODFORD
WOOLWICH
WORTHING
YARMOUTH

9
ALDEBURGH
ALDERSHOT
ALLENDALE
ALRESFORD
AMBLESIDE
ASHBOURNE
ASHBURTON
AVONMOUTH
AYLESBURY
BLACKBURN
BLACKPOOL
BLANDFORD
BLISWORTH
BRACKNELL
BRAINTREE
BRENTFORD
BRENTWOOD
BRIGHOUSE
BROUGHTON
CAMBRIDGE
CARNFORTH
CASTLETON
CHESILTON
CHINGFORD
CLITHEROE
CONGLETON
CRANBORNE
CRANBROOK
CREWKERNE
CRICKLADE
CUCKFIELD
DARTMOUTH
DEVONPORT
DONCASTER
DONINGTON
DROITWICH
DRONFIELD
DUNGENESS
DUNSTABLE
ELLESMERE
FAVERSHAM
FLEETWOOD
GATESHEAD
GODALMING
GRAVESEND
GREENWICH
GRINSTEAD
GUILDFORD
HARROGATE

HASLEMERE
HAVERHILL
HAWKHURST
HOLMFIRTH
ILCHESTER
IMMINGHAM
KETTERING
KING'S LYNN
KINGSWEAR
LAMBOURNE
LANCASTER
LEICESTER
LICHFIELD
LIVERPOOL
LONGRIDGE
LOWESTOFT
LYME REGIS
LYMINGTON
MAIDSTONE
MANSFIELD
MIDDLETON
NEWCASTLE
NEWMARKET
NEW ROMNEY
NORTHWICH
OTTERBURN
PEMBRIDGE
PENISTONE
PENKRIDGE
PENYGHENT
PICKERING
ROCHESTER
ROTHERHAM
SALISBURY
SALTFLEET
SEVENOAKS
SHEERNESS
SHEFFIELD
SHERBORNE
SMETHWICK
SOUTHGATE
SOUTHPORT
SOUTHWELL
SOUTHWOLD
STARCROSS
ST AUSTELL
STEVENAGE
STOCKPORT
STOKESLEY
STOURPORT
STRATFORD
TARPORLEY
TAVISTOCK
TENTERDEN
TONBRIDGE
TOWCESTER
TYNEMOUTH
ULVERSTON
UPMINSTER
UPPINGHAM
UTTOXETER
WAINFLEET
WAKEFIELD

WARKWORTH
WEYBRIDGE
WHERNSIDE
WHITHAVEN
WIMBLEDON
WINCANTON
WOKINGHAM
WOODSTOCK
WORCESTER
WYMONDHAM

10
ACCRINGTON
ALDBOROUGH
ALTRINCHAM
BARNSTAPLE
BEDLINGTON
BELLINGHAM
BILLERICAY
BIRKENHEAD
BIRMINGHAM
BRIDGNORTH
BRIDGWATER
BROMSGROVE
BROXBOURNE
BUCKINGHAM
CANTERBURY
CARSHALTON
CHELMSFORD
CHELTENHAM
CHICHESTER
CHIPPENHAM
CHULMLEIGH
COGGESHALL
COLCHESTER
CULLOMPTON
DARLINGTON
DORCHESTER
DUKINFIELD
EASTBOURNE
ECCLESHALL
FARNINGHAM
FOLKESTONE
FRESHWATER
GILLINGHAM
GLOUCESTER
HALESWORTH
HARTLEPOOL
HASLINGDON
HEATHFIELD
HORNCASTLE
HORNCHURCH
HUNGERFORD
HUNSTANTON
HUNTINGDON
ILFRACOMBE
KENILWORTH
KINGSCLERE
KIRKOSWALD
LAUNCESTON
LEAMINGTON
LEOMINSTER
LITTLEPORT
MAIDENHEAD

MALMESBURY
MANCHESTER
MEXBOROUGH
MICHELDEAN
MIDDLEWICH
MILDENHALL
NAILSWORTH
NOTTINGHAM
OKEHAMPTON
ORFORDNESS
PANGBOURNE
PATRINGTON
PEACEHAVEN
PONTEFRACT
PORTISHEAD
PORTSMOUTH
POTTER'S BAR
RAVENGLASS
ROCKINGHAM
SAXMUNDHAM
SHEPPERTON
SHERINGHAM
SHREWSBURY
STALBRIDGE
ST LEONARDS
STOWMARKET
SUNDERLAND
TEDDINGTON
TEIGNMOUTH
TEWKESBURY
THAMESMEAD
TORRINGTON
TROWBRIDGE
TWICKENHAM
WALSINGHAM
WARMINSTER
WARRINGTON
WASHINGTON
WEDNESBURY
WELLINGTON
WESTWARD HO
WHITCHURCH
WHITSTABLE
WHITTLESEY
WILLENHALL
WINCHELSEA
WINCHESTER
WINDERMERE
WINDLESHAM
WIRKSWORTH
WITHERNSEA
WOODBRIDGE
WORKINGTON

11
BASINGSTOKE
BEARMINSTER
BOGNOR REGIS
BOURNEMOUTH
BRIDLINGTON
BUNTINGFORD
CLEETHORPES
COCKERMOUTH
EAST RETFORD

GLASTONBURY
GREAT MARLOW
GUISBOROUGH
HALTWHISTLE
HAMPTON WICK
HATHERLEIGH
HIGH WYCOMBE
INGATESTONE
LEYTONSTONE
LITTLESTONE
LUDGERSHALL
LUTTERWORTH
MABLETHORPE
MANNINGTREE
MARKET RASEN
MARLBOROUGH
MUCH WENLOCK
NEW BRIGHTON
NEWTON ABBOT
NORTHAMPTON
PETERSFIELD
POCKLINGTON
RAWTENSTALL
SCARBOROUGH
SHAFTESBURY
SOUTHAMPTON
SOUTH MOLTON
STALYBRIDGE
ST MARGARET'S
STOURBRIDGE
TATTERSHALL
WALLINGFORD
WALTHAMSTOW
WESTMINSTER
WHITECHURCH
WOODHALL SPA

12
ATTLEBOROUGH
BERKHAMPSTED
BEXHILL-ON-SEA
CASTLE RISING
CHESTERFIELD
CHRISTCHURCH
GAINSBOROUGH
GREAT GRIMSBY
GREAT MALVERN
HUDDERSFIELD
INGLEBOROUGH
LONG STRATTON
LOUGHBOROUGH
MACCLESFIELD
MILTON KEYNES
MORECAMBE BAY
NORTH BERWICK
NORTH SHIELDS
NORTH WALSHAM
PETERBOROUGH
SHOEBURYNESS
SHOTTESBROOK
SOUTH SHIELDS
STOKE-ON-TRENT

13
BARNARD CASTLE

BISHOP'S CASTLE
BOROUGHBRIDGE
BRIGHTLINGSEA
BURTON-ON-TRENT
BURY ST EDMUNDS
CHIPPING ONGAR
FINCHAMPSTEAD
GODMANCHESTER
GREAT YARMOUTH
HIGHAM FERRERS
KIDDERMINSTER
KIRKBY STEPHEN
KNARESBOROUGH
LITTLEHAMPTON
LYTHAM ST ANNES
MARKET DEEPING
MARKET DRAYTON
MELCOMBE REGIS
MELTON MOWBRAY
MIDDLESBROUGH
NORTHALLERTON
SAFFRON WALDEN
SHEPTON MALLET
WOLVERHAMPTON
WOOTTON BASSET

14
BERWICK-ON-TWEED
BISHOP AUCKLAND
BISHOPS WALTHAM
CHIPPING BARNET
CHIPPING NORTON
HEMEL HEMPSTEAD
KIRKBY LONSDALE
MARKET BOSWORTH
MORTIMER'S CROSS
STOCKTON-ON-TEES
STONY STRATFORD
SUTTON COURTNEY
TUNBRIDGE WELLS
WELLINGBOROUGH
WEST HARTLEPOOL

15+
ASHTON-UNDER-LYNE
BARROW-IN-FURNESS
BISHOP'S STORTFORD
BURNHAM-ON-
  CROUCH
CASTLE DONINGTON
LEIGHTON BUZZARD
NEWCASTLE-ON-TYNE
ST LEONARDS-ON-SEA
STRATFORD-ON-AVON
SUTTON COLDFIELD
WELWYN GARDEN
  CITY
WESTON-SUPER-MARE

ERITREA

6
ASMARA
ASMERA

ESTONIA

7
TALLINN

FRANCE

3
AIX
PAU

4
ALBI
CAEN
LYON
METZ
NICE

5
ARLES
ARRAS
BREST
DIJON
EVIAN
LILLE
LYONS
MACON
NANCY
NIMES
PARIS
REIMS
ROUEN
TOURS
TULLE

6
AMIENS
BAYEUX
CALAIS
CANNES
DIEPPE
LE MANS
NANTES
RHEIMS
ST MALO
TOULON
VERDUN

7
AJACCIO
ALENÇON
AVIGNON
BAYONNE
DUNKIRK
LE HAVRE
LIMOGES
LOURDES
ORLÉANS

8
BESANÇON
BIARRITZ
BORDEAUX
BOULOGNE
CHARTRES
GRENOBLE
SOISSONS

ST TROPEZ
TOULOUSE

9
ABBEVILLE
CHERBOURG
DUNKERQUE
MARSEILLE
MONTAUBAN
PERPIGNAN
ST ETIENNE

10
MARSEILLES
MONTELIMAR
STRASBOURG
VERSAILLES

11
ARMENTIÈRES
MONTPELLIER

15
CLERMONT-FERRAND

GERMANY

4
BONN
GERA
KIEL
KÖLN
SUHL

5
ESSEN
HALLE
MAINZ
TRIER
WORMS

6
AACHEN
BERLIN
BOCHUM
BREMEN
CASSEL
ERFURT
KASSEL
LÜBECK
MUNICH
TRÈVES

7
COBLENZ
COLOGNE
COTTBUS
DRESDEN
HAMBURG
HANOVER
HOMBURG
KOBLENZ
LEIPZIG
MÜNCHEN
POTSDAM
ROSTOCK
SPANDAU

8
AUGSBURG
DORTMUND
HANNOVER
MANNHEIM
NÜRNBERG
SCHWERIN

9
BRUNSWICK
DARMSTADT
FRANKFURT
MAGDEBURG
NUREMBERG
STUTTGART
WIESBADEN
WUPPERTAL

10
BADEN BADEN
BAD HOMBURG
DÜSSELDORF
HEIDELBERG

11
BRANDENBURG
SAARBRÜCKEN

13
AIX-LA-CHAPELLE
KARL-MARX-STADT

GREECE

6
ATHENS
SPARTA
THEBES

7
CORINTH
MYCENAE
PIRAEUS

11
THESSALONIKI

HUNGARY

4
PÉCS
PUNE

8
BUDAPEST

INDIA

4
AGRA

5
AJMER
ALWAR
DELHI
KOTAH
PATNA
POONA
SIMLA
SURAT

6
BHOPAL
BOMBAY
HOWRAH
IMPHAL
INDORE
JAIPUR
JHANSI
KALYAN
KANPUR
KOHIMA
MADRAS
MEERUT
MUMBAI
MYSORE
NAGPUR
RAMPUR

7
BENARES
GWALIOR
JODHPUR
LUCKNOW

8
AGARTALA
AMRITSAR
CALCUTTA
CAWNPORE
JAMALPUR
LUDHIANA
SHILLONG
SRINAGAR
VADODARA
VARANASI

9
AHMADABAD
ALLAHABAD
BANGALORE
HYDERABAD

10
CHANDIGARH
DARJEELING
JAMSHEDPUR
TRIVANDRUM

11
BHUBANESWAR

INDONESIA

5
MEDAN

7
BANDUNG
JAKARTA

8
SEMARANG
SURABAJA

9
PALEMBANG

IRAN

6
ABADAN
SHIRAZ
TABRIZ
TEHRAN

7
ISFAHAN
MASHHAD

IRAQ

5
BASRA
MOSUL

6
KIRKUK

7
BAGHDAD
KARBALA

IRELAND, REPUBLIC OF

4
BRAY
COBH
CORK
MUFF
NAAS
TRIM
TUAM

5
BALLA
BOYLE
CAVAN
CLARE
ENNIS
KELLS
SLIGO

6
ARKLOW
BANTRY
CALLAN
CARLOW
CARNEY
CASHEL
DUBLIN
GALWAY
SHRULE
TRALEE

7
ATHLONE
BLARNEY
CARRICK
CLONMEL
DONEGAL
DUNDALK
DUNMORE
KILDARE
LIFFORD
SHANNON
WEXFORD

WICKLOW
YOUGHAL

8
BALLYBAY
BUNCRANA
CLONTARF
DROGHEDA
KILKENNY
LIMERICK
LISTOWEL
LONGFORD
MAYNOOTH
MONAGHAN
RATHDRUM

9
CASTLEBAR
CONNEMARA
KILLARNEY
MULLINGAR
ROSCOMMON
TIPPERARY
TULLAMORE
WATERFORD

10
CASTLEFINN
KILCONNELL
SHILLELAGH
SKIBBEREEN
STRANORLAR

11
LETTERKENNY

12
DUN LAOGHAIRE

13
CASTLEBLAYNEY
INNISHTRAHULL
PORTLAOIGHISE

16
CARRICK-ON-
  SHANNON

ISRAEL

4
GAZA

5
HAIFA
JAFFA

7
TEL AVIV

9
BEERSHEBA
JERUSALEM

ITALY

4
BARI
PISA
ROME

5
GENOA
MILAN
OSTIA
PADUA
PARMA
SIENA
TURIN

6
MODENA
NAPLES
REGGIO
TRENTO
VENICE
VERONA

7
BOLOGNA
BERGAMO
BRESCIA
CATANIA
FERRARA
MESSINA
PALERMO
PERUGIA
PESCARA
POMPEII
RAVENNA
SALERNO
SAN REMO
TRIESTE
VATICAN

8
CAGLIARI
FLORENCE
SYRACUSE

9
AGRIGENTO

JAPAN

4
FUGI
KOBE

5
KYOTO
OSAKA
TOKYO

6
NAGOYA
TOYOTA

7
FUKUOKA
HITACHI
SAPPORO

8
KAWASAKI
NAGASAKI
YOKOHAMA

9
HIROSHIMA

10
KITAKYUSHU

KAZAKHSTAN

6
ALMATY

9
KARAGANDA

KENYA

4
LAMU

7
MOMBASA
NAIROBI

KOREA, SOUTH

5
SEOUL

9
PANMUNJON

KYRGYZSTAN

7
BISHPEK
PISHPEK

LATVIA

4
RIGA

LEBANON

4
TYRE

5
SIDON

6
BEIRUT

7
TRIPOLI

LIBYA

4
HOMS

6
TOBRUK

7
TRIPOLI

LITHUANIA

7
VILNIUS

MACEDONIA

6
SKOPJE

MALI

6
BAMAKO

8
TIMBUKTU

MEXICO

6
JUAREZ
PUEBLA

8
ACAPULCO
VERACRUZ

9
MONTERREY

11
GUADALAJARA

MOLDOVA

8
CHIŞINA
KISHINEV

MOROCCO

3
FEZ

5
RÀ BAT

6
AGADIR
MEKNES

7
TANGIER

8
TANGIERS

9
MARRAKECH
MARRAKESH

10
CASABLANCA

MYANMAR

3
AVA

6
YANGON

7
RANGOON

8
MANDALAY

9
NAYPYIDAW

NETHERLANDS

5
BREDA
HAGUE

6
ARNHEM
LEIDEN
LEYDEN

7
UTRECHT

8
THE HAGUE

9
AMSTERDAM
DORDRECHT
EINDHOVEN
ROTTERDAM

10
MAASTRICHT

NEW ZEALAND

6
NAPIER
NELSON

7
DUNEDIN

8
AUCKLAND

10
WELLINGTON

12
CHRISTCHURCH

NIGERIA

4
KANO

5
ABUJA
ENUGU
LAGOS

6
IBADAN

NORTHERN IRELAND

5
DOAGH
GLYNN
KEADY
LARNE
NEWRY
OMAGH
TOOME

6
ANTRIM
ARMAGH
AUGHER
BANGOR

BELCOO
BERAGH
COMBER
LURGAN
RAPHOE

7
BELFAST
BELLEEK
CALEDON
CLOGHER
CRUMLIN
DERVOCK
DROMORE
FINAGHY
FINTONA
GILFORD
GLENARM
KILKEEL
LISBURN
POMEROY

8
AHOGHILL
ANNALONG
DUNGIVEN
HILLTOWN
HOLYWOOD
LIMAVADY
PORTRUSH
STRABANE
TRILLICK

9
BALLINTRA
BALLYMENA
BALLYMORE
BALLYNURE
BANBRIDGE
BUSHMILLS
CARNLOUGH
COLERAINE
COOKSTOWN
CRAIGAVON
CUSHENDUN
DUNGANNON
LISNASKEA
MONEYMORE
NEWCASTLE
PORTADOWN
RASHARKIN
ROSTREVOR
TANDRAGEE
TOVERMORE

10
ALDERGROVE
AUGHNACLOY
BALLYCLARE
BALLYGOWAN
BALLYMONEY
BALLYRONEY
CASTLEDERG
COALISLAND
CUSHENDALL
DONAGHADEE

MARKETHILL
PORTAFERRY
SAINTFIELD
STRANGFORD
TANDERAGEE

11
BALLYCASTLE
BALLYGAWLEY
CARRICKMORE
CROSSMAGLEN
DOWNPATRICK
DRAPERSTOWN
ENNISKILLEN
LONDONDERRY
MAGHERAFELT
NEWTOWNARDS
PORTGLENONE
PORTSTEWART
RANDALSTOWN
RATHFRILAND
WARRENPOINT

12
BALLYHALBERT
BALLYNAHINCH
CASTLE DAWSON
CASTLEWELLAN
FIVEMILETOWN
HILLSBOROUGH
STEWARTSTOWN

13
BROOKE-BOROUGH
CARRICKFERGUS
CRAWFORDSBURN
DERRYGONNELLY

14
NEWTOWN STEWART

NORWAY
4
OSLO
6
BERGEN
9
TRONDHEIM

PAKISTAN
6
LAHORE
MULTAN
QUETTA
7
KARACHI
8
PESHAWAR
9
HYDERABAD
ISLAMABAD
10
FAISALABAD

GUJRANWALA
RAWALPINDI

PERU
4
LIMA
5
CUZCO

PHILIPPINES
6
MANILA
10
QUEZON CITY

POLAND
4
LODZ
5
POSEN
6
DANZIG
GDANSK
KRAKOW
LUBLIN
WARSAW
7
BRESLAU
8
PRZEMYSL

PORTUGAL
6
LISBON
OPORTO

RUSSIA
3&4
UFA
OMSK
PERM
TVER
5
KAZAN
PSKOV
6
MOSCOW
SAMARA
7
IRKUTSK
YAKUTSK
8
NOVGOROD
SMOLENSK
9
ASTRAKHAN

KALINGRAD
VOLGOGRAD

11
CHELYABINSK
NOVOSIBIRSK
VLADIVOSTOK

12
EKATERINBURG
ROSTOV-NA-DONU
ST PETERSBURG

14
NIZHNY NOVGOROD

SAUDI ARABIA
5
MECCA
6
JEDDAH
MEDINA
RIYADH

SCOTLAND
3
AYR
UIG
4
ALVA
BARR
DUNS
ELIE
KIRN
LUSS
NIGG
OBAN
REAY
RONA
STOW
WICK
5
ALLOA
ANNAN
APPIN
AVOCH
AYTON
BANFF
BEITH
BRORA
BUNAW
BUSBY
CERES
CLOVA
CLUNE
CRAIL
CUPAR
DENNY
DOWNE
ELGIN
ELLON
ERROL
FYVIE

GOVAN
INSCH
ISLAY
KEISS
KEITH
KELSO
LAIRG
LARGO
LEITH
NAIRN
PERTH
SALEN
TROON

6
ABOYNE
ALFORD
BARVAS
BEAULY
BERVIE
BIGGAR
BO'NESS
BUCKIE
CARRON
CAWDOR
COMRIE
CRIEFF
CULLEN
CULTER
DOLLAR
DRYMEN
DUNBAR
DUNDEE
DUNLOP
DUNNET
DUNOON
DYSART
EDZELL
FINDON
FORFAR
FORRES
GIRVAN
GLAMIS
HAWICK
HUNTLY
IRVINE
KILLIN
KILMUN
LANARK
LAUDER
LESLIE
LINTON
LOCHEE
MEIGLE
MOFFAT
PLADDA
RESTON
RHYNIE
ROSYTH
ROTHES
SHOTTS
THURSO
TONGUE
WISHAW

YARROW

7
AIRDRIE
BALFRON
BALLOCH
BANAVIE
BOWMORE
BRAEMAR
BRECHIN
BRODICK
CANOBIE
CANTYRE
CARBOST
CARGILL
CARLUKE
CRATHIE
CULROSS
CUMNOCK
DENHOLM
DOUGLAS
DUNKELD
DUNNING
EVANTON
FAIRLIE
FALKIRK
GALSTON
GIFFORD
GLASGOW
GLENCOE
GOLSPIE
GOUROCK
GRANTON
GUTHRIE
HALKIRK
KENMORE
KESSOCK
KILMORY
KILSYTH
KINROSS
KINTORE
LAMLASH
LARBERT
LYBSTER
MACDUFF
MAYBOLE
MELDRUM
MELROSE
MELVICH
METHVEN
MILMUIR
MONIKIE
MUTHILL
NEWPORT
PAISLEY
PEEBLES
POLMONT
POOLEWE
PORTREE
PORTSOY
RENFREW
SADDELL
SARCLET
SCOURIE

SELKIRK
STANLEY
STRATHY
TARBERT
TARLAND
TAYPORT
TRANENT
TUNDRUM
TURRIFF
ULLSTER
YETHOLM

8
ABERDEEN
ABERLADY
ABINGTON
ARBROATH
ARMADALE
ARROCHAR
AULDEARN
BALLATER
BANCHORY
BARRHILL
BEATTOCK
BLANTYRE
BURGHEAD
CANISBAY
CARNWATH
CREETOWN
CROMARTY
DALKEITH
DALMALLY
DINGWALL
DIRLETON
DUFFTOWN
DUMFRIES
DUNBEATH
DUNBLANE
DUNSCORE
EARLSTON
EYEMOUTH
FINDHORN
FORTROSE
GIFFNOCK
GLENLUCE
GREENLAW
GREENOCK
HAMILTON
INVERARY
INVERURY
JEANTOWN
JEDBURGH
KILBRIDE
KILNIVER
KILRENNY
KINGHORN
KIRKWALL
LANGHOLM
LATHERON
LEUCHARS
LOANHEAD
MARKINCH
MARYKIRK
MONIAIVE

MONTROSE
MONYMUSK
MUIRKIRK
NEILSTON
NEWBURGH
NEWMILNS
PENICUIK
PITSLIGO
POOLTIEL
QUIRAING
ROTHESAY
ST FERGUS
STIRLING
STRICHEN
TALISKER
TARANSAY
TRAQUAIR
ULLAPOOL
WHITHORN
WOODSIDE

9
ABERFELDY
ABERFOYLE
ARDROSSAN
BERRIDALE
BETTYHILL
BLACKLARG
BRACADALE
BRAERIACH
BROADFORD
BROUGHTON
BUCKHAVEN
CAIRNTOUL
CALLANDER
CARSTAIRS
DUMBARTON
EDINBURGH
FERINTOSH
FOCHABERS
INCHKEITH
INVERARAY
INVERNESS
JOHNSTONE
KILDRUMMY
KINGUSSIE
KIRKCALDY
LEADHILLS
LOCHGELLY
LOCHINVAR
LOCHNAGAR
LOCKERBIE
LOGIERAIT
MAUCHLINE
MILNGAVIE
PETERHEAD
PITLOCHRY
PORT ELLEN
PRESTWICK
RICCARTON
RONALDSAY
ROTHIEMAY
SALTCOATS
SHIELDAIG

SLAMANNAN
ST ANDREWS
STEWARTON
ST FILLANS
STRANRAER
STRATHDON
STRONTIAN
THORNHILL
TOBERMORY
TOMINTOUL

10
ABBOTSFORD
ACHNASHEEN
ANSTRUTHER
APPLECROSS
ARDRISHAIG
AUCHINLECK
BALLANTRAE
BLACKADDER
CARNOUSTIE
CARSPHAIRN
CASTLETOWN
COATBRIDGE
COLDINGHAM
COLDSTREAM
DALBEATTIE
DRUMLITHIE
EAST LINTON
GLENROTHES
JOHNSHAVEN
KILCREGGAN
KILLENAULE
KILMAINHAM
KILMALCOLM
KILMARNOCK
KILWINNING
KINCARDINE
KINGSBARNS
KIRKMAIDEN
KIRKOSWALD
KIRRIEMUIR
LENNOXTOWN
LESMAHAGOW
LINLITHGOW
LIVINGSTON
MILNATHORT
MOTHERWELL
PITTENWEEM
PORTOBELLO
RUTHERGLEN
STONEHAVEN
STONEHOUSE
STONEYKIRK
STRATHAVEN
STRATHEARN
STRATHMORE
TWEEDMOUTH
WEST CALDER
WILSONTOWN

11
ABERCHIRDER
BALQUHIDDER
BANNOCKBURN

BLAIR ATHOLL
BLAIRGOWRIE
CAMPBELTOWN
CHARLESTOWN
CUMBERNAULD
DRUMMELZIER
DUNFERMLINE
ECCLEFECHAN
FETTERCAIRN
FORT WILLIAM
FRASERBURGH
HELENSBURGH
INVERGORDON
KIRKMICHAEL
LOSSIEMOUTH
LOSTWITHIEL
MAXWELLTOWN
MUSSELBURGH
PORT GLASGOW
PORT PATRICK
PRESTONPANS
PULTNEYTOWN
STRATHBLANE

12
AUCHTERARDER
BALLACHULISH
EAST KILBRIDE
FORT AUGUSTUS
GARELOCHHEAD
INNERLEITHEN
KINLOCHLEVEN
LAWRENCEKIRK
LOCHGILPHEAD
PORTMAHOMACK
STRATHPEFFER
TILLICOULTRY

13
AUCHTERMUCHTY
CASTLE DOUGLAS
COCKBURNSPATH
DALMELLINGTON
INVERKEITHING
INVERKEITHNIE
KIRKCUDBRIGHT
KIRKINTILLOCH
NEWTON
   STEWART
ROTHIEMURCHUS

**SERBIA AND
   MONTENEGRO**

3
NÍŠ

7
NOVI SAD

8
BELGRADE

9
PODGORICA

SLOVAKIA

10
BRATISLAVA

SLOVENIA

9
LJUBLJANA

SOUTH AFRICA

6
DURBAN
SOWETO

8
CAPE TOWN
MAFEKING
PRETORIA

9
KIMBERLEY
LADYSMITH

10
ALEXANDRIA
EAST LONDON
SIMONSTOWN

11
GRAHAMSTOWN
SHARPEVILLE

12
BLOEMFONTEIN
JOHANNESBURG

13
PORT ELIZABETH

16
PIETERMARITZBURG

SPAIN

4
VIGO

5
CÁDIZ

6
BILBAO
MADRID
MALAGA

7
BADAJOZ
CÓRDOBA
GRANADA
SEVILLE

8
ALICANTE
PAMPLONA
VALENCIA
ZARAGOZA

9
BARCELONA
CARTAGENA
LAS PALMAS

SANTANDER
SARAGOSSA

12
SAN SEBASTIÁN

SRI LANKA

5
GALLE
KANDY

7
COLOMBO

11
TRINCOMALEE

SUDAN

6
BERBER

7
DONGOLA

8
KHARTOUM
OMDURMAN

SWEDEN

5
MALMÖ

7
UPPSALA

8
GÖTEBORG

9
STOCKHOLM

10
GOTHENBURG

11
HELSINGBORG

SWITZERLAND

4
BÂLE
BERN

5
BASEL
BASLE

6
GENEVA
ZURICH

7
LUCERNE

8
LAUSANNE

SYRIA

4
HOMS

6
ALEPPO

7
PALMYRA

8
DAMASCUS

TAIWAN

6
TAIBEI
TAIPEI

9
KAO-HSIUNG

TAJIKSTAN

8
DUSHANBE

TANZANIA

6
DODOMA

8
ZANZIBAR

11
DAR ES SALAAM

TURKEY

5
ADANA
IZMIR

6
ANKARA
SMYRNA

7
ERZERUM

8
ISTANBUL

9
BYZANTIUM

14
CONSTANTINOPLE

TURKMENISTAN

9
ASHKHABAD

UKRAINE

4
KIEV
LVOV

5
YALTA

6
ODESSA

7
DONETSK

USA

4
GARY
LIMA
RENO
TROY
WACO
YORK

5
AKRON
BOISE
BRONX
BUTTE
FLINT
MIAMI
OMAHA
OZARK
SALEM
SELMA
TULSA
UTICA

6
ALBANY
AUSTIN
BANGOR
BILOXI
BOSTON
CAMDEN
CANTON
DALLAS
DAYTON
DENVER
DULUTH
EL PASO
EUGENE
FRESNO
LOWELL
MOBILE
NASSAU
NEWARK
OXNARD
PEORIA
ST PAUL
TACOMA
TOLEDO
TOPEKA
TUCSON
URBANA

7
ABILENE
ANAHEIM
ATLANTA
BOULDER
BUFFALO
CHICAGO
CONCORD
DETROIT
HAMPTON
HOBOKEN

HOUSTON
JACKSON
KEY WEST
LINCOLN
MADISON
MEMPHIS
MODESTO
NEW YORK
NORFOLK
OAKLAND
ORLANDO
PHOENIX
RALEIGH
READING
ROANOKE
SAGINAW
SAN JOSÉ
SEATTLE
SPOKANE
ST LOUIS
WICHITA
YONKERS

8
BERKELEY
BROOKLYN
COLUMBUS
DEARBORN
GREEN BAY
HANNIBAL
HARTFORD
HONOLULU
LAKELAND
LAS VEGAS
NEW HAVEN
OAK RIDGE
PALO ALTO
PASADENA
PORTLAND
RICHMOND
SAN DIEGO
SANTA ANA
SAVANNAH
STAMFORD
STOCKTON
SYRACUSE
WHEELING

9
ANCHORAGE
ANNAPOLIS
ARLINGTON
BALTIMORE
BETHLEHEM
CAMBRIDGE
CHAMPAIGN
CHARLOTTE
CLEVELAND
DES MOINES
FAIRBANKS
FORT WAYNE
FORT WORTH
GALVESTON
HOLLYWOOD
JOHNSTOWN

KALAMAZOO
LANCASTER
LEXINGTON
LONG BEACH
MANHATTAN
MILWAUKEE
NASHVILLE
NEW LONDON
NORTHEAST
PRINCETON
RIVERSIDE
ROCHESTER
WATERBURY
WORCESTER
YPSILANTI

10
ATOMIC CITY
BATON ROUGE
BIRMINGHAM
CHARLESTON
CINCINNATI
EVANSVILLE
GREENSBORO
GREENVILLE
HARRISBURG
HUNTSVILLE
JERSEY CITY
KANSAS CITY
LITTLE ROCK
LONG BRANCH
LOS ANGELES
LOUISVILLE
MIAMI BEACH
MONTGOMERY
NEW BEDFORD
NEW ORLEANS
PITTSBURGH
PROVIDENCE
SACRAMENTO
SAINT LOUIS
SAN ANTONIO
WASHINGTON
YOUNGSTOWN

11
ALBUQUERQUE
CEDAR RAPIDS
CHATTANOOGA
GRAND RAPIDS
MINNEAPOLIS
NEWPORT NEWS
PALM SPRINGS
SCHENECTADY
SPRINGFIELD

12
ATLANTIC CITY
BEVERLY HILLS
FAYETTEVILLE
INDEPENDENCE
INDIANAPOLIS
JACKSONVILLE
NEW BRUNSWICK
NIAGARA FALLS

OKLAHOMA CITY
PHILADELPHIA
POUGHKEEPSIE
SALT LAKE CITY
SAN FRANCISCO
SANTA BARBARA

13
CORPUS CHRISTI
ST PETERSBURGH

14
FORT LAUDERDALE

15
COLORADO SPRINGS

UZBEKISTAN

8
TASHKENT

9
SAMARKAND

VENEZUELA

7
CARACAS

9
MARACAIBO

WALES

3
USK

4
BALA
HOLT
MOLD
PYLE
RHYL

5
BARRY
CHIRK

FLINT
NEATH
NEVIN
TENBY
TOWYN

6
AMLWCH
BANGOR
BRECON
BUILTH
CONWAY
MARGAM
RUABON
RUTHIN

7
CARBURY
CARDIFF
CWMBRAN
DENBIGH
MAESTEG
NEWPORT
NEWTOWN
ST ASAPH
SWANSEA
WREXHAM

8
ABERAVON
ABERDARE
ABERGELE
BARMOUTH
BRIDGEND
CAERLEON
CARDIGAN
CHEPSTOW
DOLGELLY
EBBW VALE
HAWARDEN
HOLYHEAD
HOLYWELL

KIDWELLY
KNIGHTON
LAMPETER
LLANELLI
LLANELLY
LLANRWST
MONMOUTH
PEMBROKE
RHAYADER
SKERRIES
SKIFNESS
TALGARTH
TREDEGAR
TREGARON

9
ABERAERON
ABERDOVEY
ABERFFRAW
BEAUMARIS
BODLONDEB
CARNARVON
CRICCIETH
FESTINIOG
FISHGUARD
LLANBERIS
LLANDUDNO
NEW RADNOR
PONTYPOOL
PORTHCAWL
PORTMADOC
PWHLLHELI
WELSHPOOL

10
CADER IDRIS
CAERNARFON
CAERNARVON
CAPEL CURIG
CARMARTHEN
CRICKHOWEL
FFESTINIOG

LLANDOVERY
LLANFYLLIN
LLANGADOCK
LLANGOLLEN
LLANIDLOES
MONTGOMERY
PLINLIMMON
PONTYPRIDD
PORTH NIGEL
PORT TALBOT
PRESTEIGNE

11
ABERGAVENNY
ABERYSTWYTH
CLYDACH VALE
MACHYNLLETH
OYSTERMOUTH

12
LLANDILOFAWR
LLANTRISSANT
YSTRAD MYNACH

13
HAVERFORDWEST
MERTHYR TYDFIL

YEMEN

4
ADEN
SAN'A

5
SANA'A

ZIMBABWE

6
HARARE

8
BULAWAYO

PORTS

ALGERIA

4
ORAN

6
SKIKDA

7
ALGIERS

9
PORT ARZEW

ANGOLA

6
LOBITO
LUANDA

ARGENTINA

7
LA PLATA

11
BUENOS AIRES

AUSTRALIA

6
SYDNEY

7
DAMPIER
GEELONG

8
ADELAIDE
BRISBANE

9
MELBOURNE
NEWCASTLE

10
FREEMANTLE

11
PORT JACKSON

12
PORT ADELAIDE

BELGIUM

6
OSTEND

7
ANTWERP

9
ZEEBRUGGE

BENIN

7
COTONOU

9
PORTO NOVO

BRAZIL

4
PARA

5
BELEM

6
RECIFE
SANTOS

7
TOBARAO

10
PERNAMBUCO

12
RIO DE JANEIRO

BULGARIA

5
VARNA

BURMA
SEE MYANMAR

CAMEROON

6
DOUALA

CANADA

7
HALIFAX
KITIMAT

8
MONTREAL

9
CHURCHILL
ESQUIMALT
OWEN SOUND
VANCOUVER

11
THREE RIVERS

CHANNEL ISLANDS

8
ST HELIER

11
SAINT HELIER
ST PETER PORT
CHILE

5
ARICA

8
COQUIMBO

10
VALPARAISO

CHINA

4
AMOY

6
CHEFOO
HANKOW

SWATOW
WEIHAI

7
FOOCHOW
YINGKOW

8
SHANGHAI
TIENTSIN

10
PORT ARTHUR

COLUMBIA

9
CARTAGENA

12
BARRANQUILLA
BUENAVENTURA

**CONGO, DEMOCRATIC
 REPUBLIC OF**

6
MATADI

9
MBUJI-MAYI

CORSICA

6
BASTIA

7
AJACCIO

CUBA

6
HAVANA

14
SANTIAGO DE CUBA

CYPRUS

7
LARNACA

8
LIMASSOL

DENMARK

6
ODENSE

7
AALBORG
HORSENS

8
ELSINORE

9
HELSINGÖR

10
COPENHAGEN

13
FREDERIKSHAVN

ECUADOR

9
GUAYAQUIL

EGYPT

4
SUEZ

8
DAMIETTA
PORT SAID

10
ALEXANDRIA

ENGLAND

4
HULL

5
DOVER

6
LONDON

7
CHATHAM
GRIMSBY
HARWICH
TILBURY

8
FALMOUTH
NEWHAVEN
PENZANCE
PLYMOUTH
PORTLAND
SANDWICH
WEYMOUTH

9
AVONMOUTH
DEVONPORT
GRAVESEND
KING'S LYNN
LIVERPOOL
NEWCASTLE
SHEERNESS

10
BARNSTAPLE
COLCHESTER
FELIXSTOWE
FOLKESTONE
HARTLEPOOL
PORTSMOUTH
SUNDERLAND
TEIGNMOUTH
WHITSTABLE

11
CINQUE PORTS
SOUTHAMPTON

12
NORTH SHIELDS
PORT SUNLIGHT

13
MIDDLESBROUGH

FINLAND

8
HELSINKI

FRANCE

5
BREST

6
CALAIS
CANNES
DIEPPE
TOULON

7
DUNKIRK
LE HAVRE

8
BORDEAUX
BOULOGNE
HONFLEUR

9
CHERBOURG
FOS-SUR-MER
MARSEILLE

10
LA ROCHELLE
MARSEILLES

FRENCH GUIANA

7
CAYENNE

GERMANY

4
KIEL

5
EMDEN

6
BREMEN
WISMAR

7
HAMBURG
ROSTOCK

8
CUXHAVEN

9
FLENSBURG

10
TRAVEMÜNDE

11
BREMERHAVEN

13
WILHELMS-HAVEN

GHANA

4
TEMA

8
TAKORADI

GREECE

5
CANEA
CORFU

6
PATRAS
RHODES

7
PIRAEUS

8
NAVARINO

10
HERMOPOLIS

11
HERMOUPOLIS

HAWAII

8
HONOLULU

11
PEARL HARBOR

HUNGARY

8
BUDAPEST

INDIA

6
BOMBAY
COCHIN
HALDIA
KANDLA
MADRAS

8
CALCUTTA
COCANADA
KAKINADA

11
MASULIPATAM
PONDICHERRY

12
MASULIPATNAM

INDONESIA

6
PADANG

7
JAKARTA

8
MACASSAR
PARADEEP

IRAN

6
ABADAN

7
BUSHIRE

IRAQ

5
BASRA

IRELAND

4
COBH
CORK

7
DONEGAL
DUNDALK
YOUGHAL

12
DUN LAOGHAIRE

ISRAEL

4
ACRE
AKKO
ELAT

5
EILAT
HAIFA

6
ASHDOD

ITALY

4
BARI

5
GAETA
GENOA
OSTIA
TRANI

6
ANCONA
NAPLES
VENICE

7
LEGHORN
MARSALA
MESSINA
PALERMO
SALERNO
TRAPANI
TRIESTE

8
BRINDISI

IVORY COAST

7
ABIDJAN

JAMAICA

8
KINGSTON

9
PORT ROYAL

10
MONTEGO BAY

JAPAN

4
KOBE

5
KOCHI
OSAKA

8
HAKODATE
NAGASAKI
YOKOHAMA

9
HIROSHIMA
KAGOSHIMA

11
SHIMONOSEKI

KENYA

7
MOMBASA

KUWAIT

12
MINA AL-AHMADI

LEBANON

6
BEIRUT

LIBYA

7
TRIPOLI

8
BENGHAZI

MADAGASCAR

8
TAMATAVE

MALAYSIA

6
PENANG

9
PORT KLANG

10
GEORGE TOWN

12
KOTAKINABALU

MAURITANIA

10
NOUAKCHOTT

MAURITIUS

9
PORT LOUIS

MEXICO

7
GUAYMAS

8
VERACRUZ

MOROCCO

4
SAFI

5
CEUTA
RABAT

6
AGADIR
TETUÁN

7
MELILLA
MOGADOR
TANGIER

9
ESSAOUIRA

10
CASABLANCA

14
MINA HASSAN TANI

MOZAMBIQUE

5
BEIRA

6
MAPUTO

MYANMAR

5
AKYAB

6
SITTWE

7
RANGOON

8
MOULMEIN

NETHERLANDS

5
DELFT

8
FLUSHING

9
AMSTERDAM
EUROPOORT
ROTTERDAM

10
VLISSINGEN

NEW ZEALAND

6
NELSON

8
AUCKLAND
GISBORNE

9
LYTTELTON

NIGERIA

5
LAGOS

12
PORT HARCOURT

NORTHERN IRELAND

5
LARNE

7
BELFAST

NORWAY

4
OSLO

6
BERGEN
LARVIK
NARVIK
TROMSØ

9
STAVANGER
TRONDHEIM

10
HAMMERFEST
KRISTIANIA

12
KRISTIANSAND

PAKISTAN

6
CHALNA

7
KARACHI

PANAMA

5
COLÓN

6
BALBOA

9
CRISTOBAL

PAPUA NEW GUINEA

11
PORT MORESBY

PERU

3
ILO

6
CALLAO

8
MATARINI

10
SAN JUAN BAY

PHILIPPINES

4
CEBU

6
MANILA

POLAND

6
DANZIG
GDANSK
GDYNIA

7
STETTIN

8
SZCZECIN

9
KOLOBRZEG

PORTUGAL

6
LISBON
OPORTO

PUERTO RICO

7
SAN JUAN

ROMANIA

10
CONSTANTSA

RUSSIA

8
PECHENGA
TAGANROG

9
ARCHANGEL

11
VLADIVOSTOK

12
ST PETERSBURG

SAUDI ARABIA

6
JEDDAH

SCOTLAND

4
TAIN
WICK

5
LEITH
SCAPA

6
DUNBAR
DUNDEE

8
GREENOCK

9
ARDROSSAN
SCAPA FLOW
STORNAWAY

11
GRANGEMOUTH
PORT GLASGOW

SENEGAL

5
DAKAR

**SERBIA AND
MONTENEGRO**

3
BAR

5
KOTOR

7
CATTARO

SIERRA LEONE

8
FREETOWN

SOUTH AFRICA

6
DURBAN

8
CAPE TOWN

9
MOSSEL BAY
PORT NATAL

10
EAST LONDON
SIMONSTOWN

11
RICHARD'S BAY

13
PORT ELIZABETH

SOUTH KOREA

5
PUSAN

SPAIN

5
PALMA
PALOS

6
BILBAO
FERROL
MALAGA

7
CORUNNA
FUNCHAL

8
ALICANTE
ARRECIFE
LA CORUÑA

9
ALGECIRAS
BARCELONA
CARTAGENA
LAS PALMAS
PORT MAHON

SRI LANKA

5
GALLE

7
COLOMBO

SUDAN

6
SUAKIN

9
PORT SUDAN

SWEDEN

5
LULEA
MALMÖ
WISBY
YSTAD

6
KÄLMAR

8
GÖTEBORG
HALMSTAD
NYKÖPING

9
STOCKHOLM

10
GOTHENBURG

11
HELSINGBORG

TAIWAN
6
TAINAN

7
KEELUNG

9
KAO-HSIUNG

TANZANIA
6
MTWARA

11
DAR ES SALAAM

TRINIDAD AND TOBAGO

11
PORT-OF-SPAIN

TURKEY
5
IZMIR

6
SMYRNA

8
ISTANBUL

14
CONSTANTINOPLE

URUGUAY
10
MONTEVIDEO

USA
4
ERIE

7
DETROIT
HOUSTON

NEW YORK
NORFOLK
SEATTLE

8
NEW HAVEN

9
BALTIMORE
GALVESTON
NANTUCKET
PENSACOLA

10
BRIDGEPORT
CHARLESTON
JERSEY CITY
LOS ANGELES
NEW BEDFORD
NEW ORLEANS
PERTH AMBOY
PORTSMOUTH

11
ROCK HARBOUR

12
SAN FRANCISCO
VENEZUELA

8
LA GUIARA

12
PUERTO HIERRO

13
PUERTO CABELLO

WALES
7
CARDIFF
SWANSEA

8
HOLYHEAD
LLANELLI
PEMBROKE

9
PORTMADOC

12
MILFORD HAVEN

YEMEN
4
ADEN

5
MOCHA

6
AHMEDI

7
HODEIDA

ISLANDS

3
RUM

4
ARAN
BALI
BUTE
CEBU
CUBA
EDGE
EIGG
GUAM
IONA
JAVA
JURA
MULL
OAHU
SARK
SKYE

5
ARRAN
BANKS
CERAM
CORFU
CAPRI
CRETE

DEVON
HAITI
IBIZA
ISLAY
LEWIS
LEYTE
LUNDY
LUZON
MALTA
PANAY
SAMAR
TIMOR

6
BAFFIN
BORNEO
CYPRUS
FLORES
HAINAN
HARRIS
HAWAII
HONSHU
JERSEY
KODIAK
KYUSHU
LESBOS

MADURA
NEGROS
ORKNEY
PENANG
RHODES
SICILY
TAHITI
TAIWAN
TOBAGO

7
ANTIGUA
BAHRAIN
BARENTS
BERMUDA
CELEBES
CORSICA
CURAÇAO
GOTLAND
GRENADA
ICELAND
IRELAND
JAMAICA
MADEIRA
MAJORCA
MINDORO

OKINAWA
PALAWAN
RATHLIN
ROCKALL
ST KITTS
ST LUCIA
SHIKOKU
SUMATRA
WRANGEL

8
ALDERNEY
ANGLESEY
BARBADOS
DOMINICA
FAIR ISLE
GUERNSEY
HOKKAIDO
HONG KONG
MALAGASY
MALLORCA
MELVILLE
MINDANAO
ST HELENA
SAKHALIN
SARDINIA

SHETLAND
SOMERSET
SRI LANKA
SULAWESI
TASMANIA
TENERIFE
TRINIDAD
UNALASKA
VICTORIA
VITI LEVU
ZANZIBAR

9
ANTICOSTI
AUSTRALIA
ELLESMERE

GREENLAND
HALMAHERA
ISLE OF MAN
MANHATTAN
MAURITIUS
NANTUCKET
NEW GUINEA
ST VINCENT
SINGAPORE
VANCOUVER

10
CAPE BRETON
GUADELOUPE
HISPANIOLA
LONG ISLAND
MADAGASCAR

MARTINIQUE
NEW BRITAIN
NEW IRELAND
NEW ZEALAND
PUERTO RICO

11
AXEL HEIBERG
GUADALCANAL
ISLE OF PINES
ISLE OF WIGHT

12
BOUGAINVILLE
GREAT BRITAIN
NEW CALEDONIA

NEWFOUNDLAND
NOVAYA ZEMLYA

13
NORTH EAST LAND
PRINCE OF WALES
PRINCE PATRICK
SANTA CATALINA

14
TIERRA DEL FUEGO

15
MARTHA'S VINEYARD
WEST SPITS-BERGEN

18
PRINCE EDWARD
  ISLAND

ISLAND GROUPS

ADMIRALTY ISLANDS
AEGEAN ISLANDS
  Cyclades
  Dodecanese
  Euboea
  N. Sporades
AEOLIAN ISLANDS (also called Lipari Islands)
AHVENANMAA (Finnish name for Aland Islands)
ALAND ISLANDS (Ahvenanmaa)
ALEUTIAN ISLANDS
  Unalaska
ANDREANOF ISLANDS
  Attu
  Near Islands
AMAGER ISLANDS
ANDAMAN AND NICOBAR ISLANDS
ANTARCTIC ARCHIPELAGO (former name of Palmer
  Archipelago)
ANTIGUA AND BARBUDA
  Antigua
  Barbuda
  Redonda
ANTIPODES ISLANDS
ARAN ISLANDS
  Aranmore (or Inishmore)
  Inisheer
  Inishmaan
ARRU (or ARU) ISLANDS
ASHMORE AND CARTIER ISLANDS
AUCKLAND ISLANDS
AUSTRAL ISLANDS (also called Tubuai Islands)
BAHAMAS (or Bahama) Islands
BALEARIC ISLANDS
  Cabrera
  Formentera
  Ibiza (Spanish name: Evissa)
  Majorca (Spanish name: Mallorca)
  Minorca (Spanish name: Menorca)
BATAN ISLANDS

BELAU ISLANDS (formerly called Palau or Pelew
  Islands)
  Babelthuap
BISAYAS (Spanish name for Visayan Islands)
BISMARCK ARCHIPELAGO
  New Britain
  New Ireland
  Lavongai
  Admiralty Islands
BONIN ISLANDS (Japanese name: Ogasawara
  Gunto)
  Chichijima
BONVOULOIR ISLANDS
BRITISH VIRGIN ISLANDS
CAICOS ISLANDS
CANARY ISLANDS
  Fuerteventura
  Gomera
  Hierro
  La Palma
  Lanzarote
  Tenerife
CAROLINE ISLANDS
  Belau (formerly called Palau or Pelew Islands)
CAYMAN ISLANDS
CHANNEL ISLANDS
  Alderney
  Great Sark
  Guernsey
  Herm
  Jersey
  Jethou
  Little Sark
CHATHAM ISLANDS
CHISHIMA (Japanese name for Kuril Islands)
COCOS ISLANDS (also called Keeling Islands)
COOK ISLANDS
  Aitutaki
  Atiu
  Rarotonga

CYCLADES
  Náxos
DANISH WEST INDIES (former name of the US Virgin
  Islands)
D'ENTRECASTEAUX ISLANDS
DODECANESE ISLANDS
  Cos (or Kos)
  Rhodes
DIOMEDE ISLANDS
  Little Diomede
EAST CAROLINE ISLANDS
  Truk Islands
EAST NETHERLANDS ANTILLES
  Bonaire
EAST VIRGIN ISLANDS
  British Virgin Islands
EILEEN SIAR (another name for Outer Hebrides)
ELLICE ISLANDS (former name of Tuvalu Islands)
FAEROES (also called Faeroe Islands)
FALKLAND ISLANDS (Spanish name: Islas Malvinas)
  Palmer Islands
FARQUHAR ISLANDS
FIJI ISLANDS
  Vanua Levu
  Viti Levu
FRIENDLY ISLANDS (also called Tonga)
FRIESLAND ISLANDS
FURNEAUX ISLANDS
  Cape Barren
  Clarke
  Flinders Island
FUR SEAL ISLANDS (another name for the Pribilof
  Islands)
GALAPAGOS ISLANDS
  San Cristobal (also called Chatham Island)
GAMBIER ISLANDS (or Mangareva Islands)
  Rikitea
GILBERT ISLANDS (former name of Kiribati)
GREATER ANTILLES ISLANDS
  Cuba
  Hispaniola
  Jamaica
  Puerto Rico
GREATER SUNDA ISLANDS
  Borneo
  Java
  Nusa Tenggara
  Sulawesi
  Sumatra
GRENADINES
  Carriacou
GUADELOUPE ISLANDS
  Basse Terre
  Grande Terre
  Marie Galante
  North Saint Martin
HAWAII (formerly called Sandwich Islands)
  Kauai
  Maui
  Molokai
  Oahu

HEARD AND MCDONALD ISLANDS
INNER HEBRIDES ISLANDS
  Islay
  Jura
  Mull
  Skye
IONIAN ISLANDS
  Cephalonia
  Corfu
  Cythera
  Ithaca (Modern Greek Ithaki)
  Leukas (Spanish name: Santa Maura)
  Levkas
  Paxos
  Zante
JUAN FERNANDEZ ISLANDS
KIRIBATI (formerly Gilbert Islands)
  Banaba (Ocean Island)
  Gilbert Islands
  Phoenix Islands
KURIL ISLANDS (Japanese name: Chishima)
LACCADIVE, MINICOY and AMINDIVI ISLANDS
  (former name of the Lakshadweep Islands)
LADRONE ISLANDS (former name of the Mariana
  Islands)
LAGOON ISLANDS (former name of Tuvalu)
LAKSHADWEEP ISLANDS (formerly called Laccadive
  Minicoy and Amindivi Islands)
  Kavaratti
LEEWARD ISLANDS (French name: Isles sous le
  Vent)
  Anguilla
  Antigua
  Barbuda
  Dominica
  Guadeloupe Islands
  Montserrat
  Nevis
  Saba (Netherlands Antilles)
  St Barthelemy
  St Kitts
  St Martin North (Guadeloupe)
  St Martin South (Sint Maarten Netherlands
  Antilles)
  Sint Eustatius (Netherlands Antilles)
  Virgin Islands
LESSER ANTILLES (formerly called Caribbees)
  Barbados
  Leeward Islands
  Netherlands Antilles
  Tobago
  Trinidad
  Windward Islands
LESSER SUNDA ISLANDS (former name of Nusa
  Tenggara)
LINE ISLANDS (part of Kiribati)
  Fanning
  Jarvis
  Kiritimati (formerly called Christmas Island)
  Palmyra
  Tabuaeran
  Teraina
  Washington

LIPARI ISLANDS (also called Aeolian Islands)
   Stromboli
   Volcano
LOUISIADE ARCHIPELAGO
LOYALTY ISLANDS
MADEIRA
   Deserta
   Porto Santo
   Selvagen Islands
MALDIVE ISLANDS (or Maldives)
MALVINAS (Argentine name for the Falkland
   Islands)
MANGAREVA ISLANDS (see Gambier Islands)
MARIANA ISLANDS (former name of Ladrone
   Islands)
   Guam
   Saipan
   Tinian Islands
MARQUESAS ISLANDS (French name: Iles
   Marquises)
   Hiva Oa
   Nuku Hiva
MARSHALL ISLANDS
   Bikini
   Eniwetok
   Jaluit
   Kwajalein
   Majuro
   Ralik (Sunset)and Ratak (Sunrise) chains
MASCARENE ISLANDS (French name: Iles
   Mascareignes)
   Mauritius
   Reunion
   Rodrigues
MIDWAY ISLANDS
MOLUCCAS (or Maluku or the Molucca Islands)
   (formerly called
Spice Islands)
   Ambon
   Ceram
   Halmahera
NETHERLANDS ANTILLES
   Bonaire
   Curacao
   Saba
   Sint Maarten
   Sint Eustatius
NEW GEORGIA ISLANDS
NEW SIBERIAN ISLANDS
   Faddeyevskii
   Kotelny
   Lyakhov Islands
   New Siberia
NORTHERN MARIANA ISLANDS
   Saipan
NUSA TENGGARA (formerly called Lesser Sunda
   Islands)
   Alor
   Bali
   Flores
   Lombok
   Sumba

   Sumbawa
   Timor
ORKNEYS
   Hoy
   Mainland (or Pomona)
   Sanday
   South Ronaldsay
   Westray
OUTER HEBRIDES (Western Isles)
   Harris
   Lewis
   Saint Kilda (also known as Hirta)
   The Uists
PACIFIC ISLANDS
   Belau
   Caroline Islands
   Marianas
   Marshall Islands
PALAU ISLANDS (formerly called Belau
   Islands)
PALMER ARCHIPELAGO (formerly called Antarctic
   Archipelago)
PAPUA NEW GUINEA
   Bismark Archipelago
   D'Entrecasteaux Islands
   E New Guinea
   Louisiade Archipelago
   Trobriand Islands
   W Soloman Islands
   Woodlark Island
PELAGIAN ISLANDS
   Lampedusa
   Lampione
   Linosa
PELEW ISLANDS (formerly called Belau Islands)
PHILIPPINE ISLANDS
   Visayan Islands
PHOENIX ISLANDS
PITCAIRN ISLANDS
   Pitcairn
PRIBILOF ISLANDS (also called Fur Seal Islands)
QUEEN CHARLOTTE ISLANDS
QUEEN ELIZABETH ISLANDS
RYUKYU ISLANDS
   Okinawa
SAFETY ISLANDS (French name: Iles du Salut)
SAMOA ISLANDS (formerly called Western Samoa)
   Savai'i
   Upolu
SANDWICH ISLANDS (former name of Hawaii)
SAN JUAN ISLANDS
SCHOUTEN ISLANDS
   Biak
SCILLY ISLANDS (or Scillies)
SEA ISLANDS
SEYCHELLES
   Alderbra
   Desroches
   Farquhar
   La Digue
   Mahe
   Praslin
   Silhouette

SHETLAND OR SHETLAND ISLANDS (formerly called
  Zetland)
  Mainland
  Unst
  Yell
SOCIETY ISLANDS
  Huahine
  Leeward Islands
  Moorea
  Raiatea
  Tahiti
  Windward Islands
SOLOMON ISLANDS
  Bougainville
  Choiseul
  Guadalcanal
  Malaita
  New Georgia Islands
  San Cristobal
  Santa Isabel
SOUTH GEORGIA AND THE SOUTH SANDWICH
  ISLANDS
SOUTH NETHERLANDS ANTILLES
  Aruba
  Bonaire
  Curacao
SOUTH ORKNEY ISLANDS
SOUTH SEA ISLANDS
SOUTH SHETLAND ISLANDS
SOUTHWEST MOLUCCAS
  Aru or Arru Islands
SPICE ISLANDS (former name of the Moluccas)
SPORADES
  North Sporades
  South Sporades
SULU ISLANDS
  Basilan
  Jolo
SUNDA ISLANDS OR SOENDA ISLANDS
  Greater Sunda Islands
  Nusa Tenggara (formerly called the Lesser Sunda
  Islands)
THOUSAND ISLANDS
TOKELAU ISLANDS
  Atafu
  Fakaofo
  Nukunono
TONGA (also called Friendly Islands)
  Tongatapu
  Tres Marias Islands
TRISTAN DA CUNHA ISLANDS
  Tristan
TROBRIAND ISLANDS
  Kiriwana
TRUK ISLANDS
TUAMOTU ARCHIPELAGO
  Apataki
  Fakarava
  Rangiroa

TUBUAI ISLANDS (also called Austral Islands)
  Tubuai
  Rurutu
TURKS AND CAICOS ISLANDS
  Grand Turk
  Grand Caicos
  Salt Cay
TUVALU ISLANDS (formerly called Lagoon Islands or
  Ellice
Islands)
  Funafuti
VANUATU ISLANDS (formerly called New Hebrides)
  Espiritu Santo
VESTMANNAEYJAR ISLANDS (English name:
  Westmann Islands)
  Helgafell (volcano)
  Surtsey (emerged 1963)
VIRGIN ISLANDS (British)
  Anegada
  Jost Van Dyke
  Tortola
  Virgin Gorda
VIRGIN ISLANDS (US) (formerly called Danish West
  Indies)
  Saint Croix (or Santa Cruz)
  Saint John
  Saint Thomas
VISAYAN ISLANDS (Spanish name: Bisayas)
  Leyte
  Negros
  Panay
VOLCANO ISLANDS (Japanese name: Kazan Retto)
  Iwo Jima
WALLIS AND FUTUNA ISLANDS (or Isles de Horne
  Islands)
  Alofi
  Futuna
  Uvea
WEST CAROLINE ISLANDS
  Babelthuap
  Belau Islands
  Yap Islands
WESTERN ISLES (another name for the Outer
  Hebrides)
WEST SOCIETY ARCHIPELAGO
  Maio (Tubuai Manu)
  Mehetia
  Moorea
  Tetiaoro
WINDWARD ISLANDS (Spanish name: Islas de
  Barlovento; French
name: Iles du Vent)
  Dominica
  Martinique
  Grenada
  Northern Grenadines
  St Lucia
  St Vincent
YAP ISLANDS

OCEANS AND SEAS

3&4
ARAL (SEA)
AZOV (SEA OF)
DEAD (SEA)
JAVA (SEA)
KARA (SEA)
RED (SEA)
ROSS (SEA)
SAVA (SEA)

5
BANDA (SEA)
BLACK (SEA)
CHINA (SEA)
CORAL (SEA)
IRISH (SEA)
JAPAN (SEA OF)
NORTH (SEA)
TIMOR (SEA)
WHITE (SEA)

6
AEGEAN (SEA)
ARCTIC (OCEAN)

BALTIC (SEA)
BERING (SEA)
CELTIC (SEA)
INDIAN (OCEAN)
INLAND (SEA)
IONIAN (SEA)
LAPTEV (SEA)
NANHAI (SEA)
TASMAN (SEA)
YELLOW (SEA)

7
ANDAMAN (SEA)
ARABIAN (SEA)
ARAFURA (SEA)
BARENTS (SEA)
BEHRING (SEA)
CASPIAN (SEA)
DONG HAI (SEA)
GALILEE (SEA OF)
MARMARA (SEA OF)
OKHOTSK (SEA OF)
PACIFIC (OCEAN)

WEDDELL (SEA)

8
ADRIATIC (SEA)
AMUNDSEN (SEA)
ATLANTIC (OCEAN)
BEAUFORT (SEA)
HUANG HAI (SEA)
LIGURIAN (SEA)
SARGASSO (SEA)
TIBERIAS (SEA OF)

9
ANTARCTIC (OCEAN)
CARIBBEAN (SEA)
EAST CHINA (SEA)
GREENLAND (SEA)

10+
BELLINGSHAUSEN (SEA)
MEDITERRANEAN (SEA)
PHILIPPINE (SEA)
SETO-NAIKAI (SEA)
SOUTH CHINA (SEA)

BAYS

3
ISE (Japan)
MAL (Republic of Ireland)
TOR (England)

4
ACRE (Israel)
CLEW (Republic of Ireland)
LUCE (Scotland)
LYME (England)
PIGS (Cuba)
VIGO (Spain)
WICK (Scotland)

5
ALGOA (South Africa)
CÁDIZ (Spain)
CASCO (USA)
DVINA (Russia)
FUNDY (Canada)
HAWKE (New Zealand)
JAMES (Canada)
MILNE (New Guinea)
OMURA (Japan)
OSAKA (Japan)
SLIGO (Republic of Ireland)
TABLE (South Africa)
TAMPA (USA)
TOKYO (Japan)
URADO (Japan)
VLORË (Albania)

6
ABUKIR (Egypt)
ALASKA (USA)
ARIAKE (Japan)
BAFFIN (Baffin Island, Greenland)
BANTRY (Republic of Ireland)
BENGAL (India, Bangladesh, Myanmar)
BISCAY (France, Spain)
BOTANY (Australia)
CALLOA (Peru)
COLWYN (Wales)
DINGLE (Republic of Ireland)
DUBLIN (Republic of Ireland)
GALWAY (Republic of Ireland)
GDANSK (Poland)
HUDSON (Canada)
JERVIS (Australia)
LOBITO (Angola)
MANILA (Philippines)
MOBILE (USA)
NAPLES (Italy)
NEWARK (USA)
PLENTY (New Zealand)
RAMSEY (Isle of Man)
TASMAN (New Zealand)
TOYAMA (Japan)
TRALEE (Republic of Ireland)
UNGAVA (Canada)

VYBORG (Finland)
WALVIS (Namibia)
WIGTON (Scotland)

7
ABOUKIR (Egypt)
BRITTAS (Republic of Ireland)
CAPE COD (USA)
DELAGOA (Mozambique)
DUNDALK (Republic of Ireland)
FLORIDA (USA)
KAVÁLLA (Greece)
KILLALA (Republic of Ireland)
MONTEGO (Jamaica)
MORETON (Australia)
NEW YORK (USA)
POVERTY (New Zealand)
SETÚ BAL (Portugal)
SWANSEA (Wales)
THUNDER (Canada)
TRINITY (Canada)
WALFISH (Namibia)
WEXFORD (Republic of Ireland)
YOUGHAL (Republic of Ireland)

8
BIDEFORD (England)
BISCAYNE (USA)
BUZZARDS (USA)
CAMPECHE (Mexico)
CARDIGAN (Wales)

DELAWARE (USA)
DUNMANUS (Republic of Ireland)
FALSE BAY (South Africa)
GEORGIAN (Canada)
GWEEBARA (Republic of Ireland)
HANGZHOU (China)
JIANZHOU (China)
PLYMOUTH (USA)
QUIBERON (France)
SAN PEDRO (USA)
SANTIAGO (Cuba)
ST BRIDES (Wales)
ST MICHEL (France)
TREMADOG (Wales)

9
BOMBETOKA (Madagascar)
DISCOVERY (Australia)
ENCOUNTER (Australia)

FAMAGUSTA (Cyprus)
FROBISHER (Canada)
GIBRALTAR (Gibraltar, Spain)
GUANABARA(Brazil)
INHAMBANE (Mozambique)
LIVERPOOL (England)
MAGDALENA (Mexico)
MORECAMBE (England)
PLACENTIA(Canada)
ST AUSTELL (England)
WHITE PARK (Northern Ireland)

10
BALLYHEIGE (Republic of Ireland)
BALLYTEIGE (Republic of Ireland)
BARNSTAPLE (England)
BRIDGWATER (England)
CAERNARFON (Wales)

CAERNARVON (Wales)
CARMARTHEN (Wales)
CHESAPEAKE (USA)
CIENFUEGOS (Cuba)
GUANTÁNAMO (Cuba)

11
BRIDLINGTON (England)
LÜTZOW-HOLME (Antarctica)
PORT PHILLIP (Australia)
TRINCOMALEE (Sri Lanka)

12+
CORPUS CHRISTI (USA)
ESPÍRITO SANTO (Brazil)
MASSACHUSETTS (USA)
NARRAGANSETT (USA)
PASSAMAQUODDY (Canada, USA)
SAN FRANCISCO (USA)

STRAITS

4
BASS (Australia, Tasmania)
COOK (New Zealand)
PALK (India, Sri Lanka)

5
CANSO (Canada)
DAVIS (Canada, Greenland)
DOVER (England, France)
KERCH (Ukraine, Russia)
KOREA (South Korea, Japan)
MENAI (Wales)
SUMBA (Indonesia: Sumba, Flores)
SUNDA (Indonesia: Sumatra, Java)
TATAR (Russia)
TIRAN (Egypt, Saudi Arabia)

6
BANGKA (Indonesia: Bangka, Sumatra)
BERING (Alaska, Russia)
HAINAN (China)
HORMUZ (Iran, Oman)

HUDSON (Canada)
JOHORE (Malaysia, Singapore)
LOMBOK (Indonesia: Bali, Lombak)
SOEMBA (Indonesia: Sumba, Flores)
TAIWAN (Taiwan, China)
TORRES (Australia, New Guinea)

7
BASILAN (Philippines: Basilan, Mindanao)
DENMARK (Greenland, Iceland)
FLORIDA (USA, Cuba)
FORMOSA (Taiwan, China)
GEORGIA (Canada)
MAKASAR (Borneo, Sulawesi)
MALACCA (Peninsular Malaysia, Sumatra)
MESSINA (Sicily, Italy)
OTRANTO (Italy, Albania)

SOENDRA (Indonesia: Sumba, Java)
TSUGARU (Japan)

8
CLARENCE (Australia)
MACASSAR (Borneo, Sulawesi)
MACKINAC (Straits of; USA)
MAGELLAN (Chile, Tierra del Fuego)
MAKASSAR (Borneo, Sulawesi)
SURABAYA (Indonesia: Java, Madura)

9
BELLE ISLE (Canada)
GIBRALTAR (Gibraltar, Spain, Morocco)
LA PÉROUSE (Japan, Russia)
SOERABAJA (Indonesia: Java, Madura)

10+
GOLDEN GATE (USA)
JUAN DE FUCA (Canada, USA)
SAN BERNARDINO (Philippines: Luzon, Samar)

LAKES, LOCHS, AND LOUGHS

3&4
ARAL (Kazahkstan, Uzbekistan)
AWE (Scotland)
BALA (Wales)
CHAD (West Africa)
COMO (Italy)
ERIE (Canada, USA)
EYRE (Australia)
KIVU (Congo, Rwanda)
NEMI (Italy)
NESS (Scotland)
TANA (Ethiopia)
VAN (Turkey)

5
FOYLE (Ireland)
GARDA (Italy)
GREAT (Australia)
GREAT (USA, Canada)
HURON (USA, Canada)
KIOGA (Uganda)
KYOGA (Uganda)
LÉMAN (Switzerland, France)
LEVEN (Scotland)
LOCHY (Scotland)
MAREE (Scotland)
NEAGH (Northern Ireland)
NYASA (Malawi, Tanzania,
  Mozambique)
ONEGA (Russia)
TAUPO (New Zealand)
URMIA (Iran)

6
ALBERT (Congo, Democratic
  Republic of, Uganda)
BAIKAL (Russia)
EDWARD (Congo, Democratic
  Republic of, Uganda)
GENEVA (Switzerland, France)

KARIBA (Zambia, Zimbabwe)
LADOGA (Russia)
LOMOND (Scotland)
LOP NOR (China)
MALAWI (Malawi, Tanzania,
  Mozambique)
MOBUTU (Congo, Democratic
  Republic of, Uganda)
NASSER (Egypt)
NATRON (Tanzania)
PEIPUS (Estonia, Russia)
POYANG (China)
RUDOLF (Kenya, Ethiopia)
SAIMAA (Finland)
VÄNERN (Sweden)

7
BALATON (Hungary)
BELFAST (Northern Ireland)
DERWENT (England)
KATRINE (Scotland)
KOKO NOR (China)
LUCERNE (Switzerland)
NU JIANG (China, Burma)
ONTARIO (Canada, USA)
QINGHAI (China)
ST CLAIR (USA, Canada)
TORRENS (Australia)
TURKANA (Kenya, Ethiopia)

8
BALKHASH (Kazakhstan)
CHIEMSEE (Germany)
CONISTON (England)
DONGTING (China)
GRASMERE (England)
ISSYK KUL (Kyrgyzstan)
MAGGIORE (Italy, Switzerland)
MAZURIAN (Poland)
MENINDEE (Australia)

MICHIGAN (USA)
NEUSIEDL (Austria, Hungary)
SUPERIOR (USA, Canada)
TITICACA (Peru, Bolivia)
TONLE SAP (Cambodia)
TUNG-T'ING (China)
VICTORIA (Uganda, Tanzania,
  Kenya)
WINNIPEG (Canada)

9
ATHABASCA (Canada)
BANGWEULU (Zambia)
CHAMPLAIN (USA)
CONSTANCE (Germany)
ENNERDALE (England)
GREAT BEAR (Canada)
GREAT SALT (USA)
MARACAIBO (Venezuela)
THIRLMERE (England)
TRASIMENO (Italy)
ULLSWATER (England)
WAST WATER (England)

10+
BUTTERMERE (England)
GREAT SLAVE (Canada)
IJSSELMEER (Netherlands)
KARA-BOGAZ-GOL
  (Turkmenistan)
OKEECHOBEE (USA)
STRANGFORD (Northern
  Ireland)
TANGANYIKA (Burundi, Congo,
  Democratic Republic of,
  Tanzania, Zambia)
VIERWALDSTÄTTERSEE
  (Switzerland)
WINDERMERE (England)

RIVERS

2&3
AIN (France)
ALN (England)
BUG (Ukraine, Poland, Germany)
CAM (England)
DEE (Scotland, Wales, England)
DON (Russia, Scotland, England,
  France, Australia)
EMS (Germany, Netherlands)
ESK (Australia)
EXE (England)
FAL (England)
FLY (Papua New Guinea)
HAN (China)

KWA (Congo, Democratic
  Republic of)
LEA (England)
LEE (Republic of Ireland)
LOT (France)
OB (Russia)
PO (Italy)
RED (USA)
RUR (Germany)
RYE (England)
TAY (Scotland)
URE (England)
USK (Wales, England)
WEY (England)

WYE (Wales, England)
YEO (England)

4
ADDA (Italy)
ADUR (England)
AIRE (England, France)
AMUR (Mongolia, Russia, China)
ARNO (Italy)
ARUN (Nepal)
AUBE (France)
AVON (England)
BANN (Northern Ireland)
BEAS (India)
BURE (England)

CHER (France)
COLN (England)
DART (England)
DOON (Scotland)
DOVE (England)
EBRO (Spain)
EDEN (England, Scotland)
ELBE (Germany, Czech Republic)
EMBA (Kazakhstan)
ISIS (England)
JUBA (E. Africa)
KAMA (Russia)
KURA (Turkey, Georgia, Azerbaijan)
LAHN (Germany)
LECH (Germany, Austria)
LENA (Russia)
LUNE (England)
LÜNE (Germany)
MAAS (Netherlands)
MAIN (Germany, Northern Ireland)
MIÑO (Spain)
MOLE (England)
NILE (Sudan, Egypt)
ODER (Germany, Czech Republic, Poland)
OHIO (USA)
OISE (France)
OUSE (England)
OXUS (Turkmenistan, Uzbekistan)
PEEL (Australia,USA)
RAVI (India, Pakistan)
REDE (England)
RUHR (Germany)
SAAR (Germany, France)
SPEY (Scotland)
TAFF (Wales)
TAJO (Spain)
TARN (France)
TAWE (Wales)
TAWI (India)
TEES (England)
TEJO (Brazil)
TEST (England)
TYNE (Scotland, England)
URAL (Russia, Kazakhstan)
VAAL (South Africa)
WEAR (England)
YARE (England)

5
ADIGE (Italy)
AISNE (France)
ALLAN (Scotland, Syria)
ALLER (Spain, Germany)
ANNAN (Scotland)
BENUE (Nigeria)
BRENT (England)
CAMEL (England)
CHARI (Cameroon, Chad)
CLYDE (Scotland, Canada)
COLNE (England)

CONGO (Congo, Democratic Republic of)
DNEPR (Russia, Belarus, Ukraine)
DOUBS (France, Switzerland)
DOURO (Spain, Portugal)
DOVEY (Wales)
DRAVA (Italy, Austria, Yugoslavia, Hungary)
DUERO (Spain)
DVINA (Russia)
FORTH (Scotland)
FOYLE (Northern Ireland)
FROME (Australia)
INDUS (India, Pakistan, China)
JAMES (USA, Australia)
JUMNA (India)
JURUÁ (Brazil)
KAFUE (Zambia)
KASAI (Angola, Congo, Democratic Republic of)
KUBAN (Russia)
LAGAN (Northern Ireland)
LIPPE (Germany)
LOIRE (France)
MARNE (France)
MAROS (Indonesia)
MEUSE (France, Belgium)
MINHO (Spain, Portugal)
MUREŞ (Romania, Hungary)
NEGRO (Spain, Brazil, Argentina, Bolivia, Paraguay, Uruguay, Venezuela)
NEMAN (Belarus, Lithuania)
NIGER (Nigeria, Mali, Guinea)
OTTER (England)
PEACE (Canada, USA)
PEARL (USA, China)
PECOS (USA)
PIAVE (Italy)
PURUS (Brazil)
RANCE (France)
RHINE (Switzerland, Germany, Netherlands)
SAALE (Germany)
SAÔNE (France)
SEINE (France)
SLAVE (Canada)
SNAKE (USA)
SOMME (France)
STOUR (England)
SWALE (England)
TAGUS (Portugal, Spain)
TAMAR (England)
TIBER (Italy)
TRENT (England)
TWEED (England, Scotland)
VOLGA (Russia, USA)
VOLTA (Ghana)
WESER (Germany)
XINGU (Brazil)
ZAÏRE (Congo, Democratic Republic of)

6
ALLIER (France)
AMAZON (Peru, Brazil)
ANGARA (Russia)
BÍO-BÍO (Chile)
CHENAB (Pakistan)
CLUTHA (New Zealand)
COOPER (Australia)
COQUET (England)
CROUCH (England)
DANUBE (Germany, Austria, Romania, Hungary, Slovakia, Bulgaria)
DNESTR (Ukraine, Moldova)
ESCAUT (Belgium, France)
FRASER (Canada)
GAMBIA (The Gambia, Senegal)
GANGES (India)
GLOMMA (Norway)
HUDSON (USA)
HUNTER (Australia)
IRTYSH (China, Kazakhstan, Russia)
ITCHEN (England)
JAPURÁ (Brazil)
JORDAN (Israel, Jordan)
KOLYMA (Russia)
LIFFEY (Republic of Ireland)
LODDON (Australia, England)
MAMORÉ (Brazil, Bolivia)
MEDINA (USA)
MEDWAY (England)
MEKONG (Laos, China)
MERSEY (England)
MONNOW (England, Wales)
MURRAY (Australia, Canada)
NECKAR (Germany)
NEISSE (Poland, Germany)
OGOOUÉ (Gabon)
ORANGE (South Africa)
ORWELL (England)
PARANÁ (Brazil)
PLATTE (USA)
RIBBLE (England)
ST JOHN (Liberia, USA)
SALADO (Argentina, Cuba, Mexico)
SEVERN (England)
SUTLEJ (Pakistan, India, China)
THAMES (England)
TICINO (Italy, Switzerland)
TIGRIS (Iraq, Turkey)
TUGELA (South Africa)
USSURI (China, USSR)
VIENNE (France)
VLTAVA (Czech Republic)
WABASH (USA)
WEAVER (England)
YELLOW (China, USA, Papua New Guinea)

7
BERMEJO (Argentina)
CAUVERY (India)

DAMODAR (India)
DARLING (Australia)
DERWENT (England)
DURANCE (France)
GARONNE (France)
GIRONDE (France)
HELMAND (Afghanistan)
HOOGHLY (India)
HUANG HO (China)
LACHLAN (Australia)
LIMPOPO (South Africa, Zimbabwe, Mozambique)
LUALABA (Congo, Democratic Republic of)
MADEIRA (Brazil)
MARAÑÓN (Brazil, Peru)
MARITSA (Bulgaria)
MOSELLE (Germany)
ORONTES (Syria)
PECHORA (Russia)
POTOMAC (USA)
SALWEEN (Myanmar, China)
SCHELDT (Belgium)
SENEGAL (Senegal)
SHANNON (Republic of Ireland)
SONGHUA (Vietnam, China)
SUNGARI (China)
SUWANNEE (USA)
URUGUAY (Uruguay, Brazil)
VISTULA (Poland)
WAIKATO (New Zealand)

XI JIANG (China)
YANGTZE (China)
YENISEI (Russia)
ZAMBEZI (Zambia, Angola, Zimbabwe, Mozambique)

8

AMU DARYA (Turkmenistan, Uzbekistan)
ARAGUAIA (Brazil)
ARKANSAS (USA)
CANADIAN (USA)
CHARENTE (France)
COLORADO (USA)
COLUMBIA (USA)
DEMERARA (Guyana)
DORDOGNE (France)
GODAVARI (India)
MANAWATU (New Zealand)
MENDERES (Turkey)
MISSOURI (USA)
PARAGUAY (Paraguay)
PUTUMAYO (Ecuador)
RÍO BRAVO (Mexico)
SAGUENAY (Canada)
SYR DARYA (Uzbekistan, Kazakhstan)
TORRIDGE (England)
TUNGUSKA (Russia)
VOLTURNO (Italy)
WANSBECK (England)
WINDRUSH (England)

9

ATHABASCA (Canada)
CHURCHILL (Canada)
ESSEQUIBO (Guyana)
EUPHRATES (Iraq)
GREAT OUSE (England)
HSI CHIANG (China)
IRRAWADDY (Burma)
MACKENZIE (Australia)
MAGDALENA (Colombia)
RIO GRANDE (Jamaica)
TENNESSEE (USA)

10

CHANG JIANG (China)
CHAO PHRAYA (Thailand)
COPPERMINE (Canada)
HAWKESBURY (Australia)
SHENANDOAH (USA)
ST LAWRENCE (USA)

11

ASSINIBOINE (Canada)
BRAHMAPUTRA (China, India)
MISSISSIPPI (USA)
SUSQUEHANNA (USA)
YELLOWSTONE (USA)

12

GUADALQUIVIR (Spain)
MURRUMBIDGEE (Australia)
RÍO DE LA PLATA (Argentina, Uruguay)
SASKATCHEWAN (Canada)

MOUNTAINS AND HILLS

3

ASO (MT) (Japan)
IDA (MT) (Turkey)

4

ALPS (France, Switzerland, Italy, Austria)
BLUE (MTS) (Australia)
COOK (MT) (New Zealand)
ETNA (MT) (Sicily)
HARZ (MTS) (Germany)
JAYA (MT) (Indonesia)
JURA (MTS) (France, Switzerland)
OSSA (MT) (Australia)
RIGI (Switzerland)
URAL (MTS) (Russia)

5

ALTAI (MTS) (Russia, China, Mongolia)
ANDES (South America)
ATHOS (MT) (Greece)
ATLAS (MTS) (Morocco, Algeria)
BLACK (MTS) (Wales)

COAST (MTS) (Canada)
EIGER (Switzerland)
ELGON (MT) (Uganda, Kenya)
GHATS (India)
KAMET (MT) (India)
KENYA (MT) (Kenya)
LENIN (PEAK) (Russia)
LOGAN (MT) (Canada)
PELÉE (MT) (Martinique)
ROCKY (MTS) (USA, Canada)
SAYAN (MTS) (Russia)
SNOWY (MTS) (Australia)
TATRA (MTS) (Poland, Slovakia)
WEALD (THE) (England)

6

ANTRIM (HILLS) (Northern Ireland)
ARARAT (MT) (Turkey)
BALKAN (MTS) (Bulgaria)
CARMEL (MT) (Israel)
EGMONT (MT) (New Zealand)
ELBERT (MT) (USA)
ELBRUS (MT) (Russia, Georgia)
ELBURZ (MTS) (Iran)

EREBUS (MT) (Antartica)
HERMON (MT) (Syria, Lebanon)
HOGGAR (MTS) (Algeria)
KUNLUN (MTS) (China)
LADAKH (RANGE) (India)
MATOPO (HILLS) (Zimbabwe)
MENDIP (HILLS) (England)
MOURNE (MTS) (Northern Ireland)
OLIVES (MT OF) (Israel)
PAMIRS (Tajikistan, China, Afghanistan)
PINDUS (MTS) (Greece, Albania)
TAURUS (MTS) (Turkey)
VOSGES (France)
ZAGROS (MTS) (Iran)

7

AHAGGAR (MTS) (Algeria)
BERNINA (Switzerland)
BROCKEN (Germany)
CHEVIOT (HILLS) (United Kingdom)
CHIANTI (Italy)
EVEREST (MT) (Nepal, China)

43

OLYMPUS (MT) (Greece)
PALOMAR (MT) (USA)
RAINIER (MT) (USA)
RORAIMA (MT) (Brazil, Guyana, Venezuela)
RUAPEHU (MT) (New Zealand)
SKIDDAW (England)
SLEMISH (Northern Ireland)
SNOWDON (Wales)
SPERRIN (MTS) (Northern Ireland)
ST ELIAS (MTS) (Alaska, Yukon)
TIBESTI (MTS) (Chad, Libya)
WICKLOW (MTS) (Republic of Ireland)

8

ARDENNES (Luxembourg, Belgium, France)
BEN NEVIS (Scotland)
CAMBRIAN (MTS) (Wales)
CAUCASUS (MTS) (Georgia, Azerbaijan, Armenia)
CÉVENNES (France)
CHILTERN (HILLS) (England)
COTOPAXI (Ecuador)
COTSWOLD (HILLS) (England)
FLINDERS (RANGE) (Australia)
FUJIYAMA (Japan)
HYMETTUS (MT) (Greece)
JUNGFRAU (Switzerland)
KAIKOURA (RANGES) (New Zealand)
MUSGRAVE (RANGES) (Australia)
PENNINES (England)
PYRENEES (France, Spain)
STANOVOI (RANGE) (Russia)
TIAN SHAN (Tajikistan, China, Mongolia)
VESUVIUS (Italy)

9

ACONCAGUA (MT) (Argentina)
ALLEGHENY (MTS) (USA)
ANNAPURNA (MT) (Nepal)
APENNINES (Italy)
CAIRNGORM (MTS) (Scotland)

DOLOMITES (Italy)
DUNSINANE (Scotland)
GRAMPIANS (Scotland)
HAMERSLEY (RANGE) (Australia)
HELVELLYN (England)
HIMALAYAS (S. Asia)
HINDU KUSH (Central Asia)
HUASCARÁN (Peru)
KARAKORAM (RANGE) (China, Pakistan, India)
KOSCIUSKO (MT) (Australia)
MONT BLANC (France, Italy)
NANDA DEVI (MT) (India)
PACARAIMA (MTS) (Brazil, Venezuela, Guyana)
PARNASSUS (MT) (Greece)
RUWENZORI (MTS) (Congo, Democratic Republic of, Uganda)
TIRICH MIR (MT) (Pakistan)
ZUGSPITZE (Germany)

10

ADIRONDACK (MTS) (USA)
CADER IDRIS (Wales)
CANTABRIAN (MTS) (Spain)
CARPATHIAN (MTS) (Slovakia, Poland, Romania, Hungary, Ukraine, Moldova)
CHIMBORAZO (MT) (India)
DHAULAGIRI (MT) (Nepal)
ERZGEBIRGE (Czech Republic, Germany)
KEBNEKAISE (Sweden)
LAMMERMUIR (HILLS) (Scotland)
MACDONNELL (RANGES) (Australia)
MAJUBA HILL (South Africa)
MATTERHORN (Switzerland, Italy)
MIDDLEBACK (RANGE) (Australia)
MONTSERRAT (Spain)
MOUNT LOFTY (RANGES) (Australia)

11

ANTI-LEBANON (MTS) (Lebanon, Syria)
APPALACHIAN (MTS) (USA)
DRAKENSBERG (MTS) (South Africa)
JOTUNHEIMEN (Norway)
KILIMANJARO (MT) (Tanzania)
MONADHLIATH (MTS) (Scotland)
NANGA PARBAT (MT) (Pakistan)
SCAFELL PIKE (England)
SIERRA MADRE (Mexico)

12

CITLALTÉPETL (Mexico)
GODWIN AUSTEN (MT) (Pakistan)
GOLAN HEIGHTS (Syria)
GRAN PARADISO (Italy)
INGLEBOROUGH (England)
KANCHENJUNGA (MT) (Nepal)
PEAK DISTRICT (England)
POPOCATÉPETL (MT) (Mexico)
SIDING SPRING (MT) (Australia)
SIERRA MORENA (Spain)
SIERRA NEVADA (Spain, USA)
SLIEVE DONARD (Northern Ireland)
WARRUMBUNGLE (RANGE) (Australia)

13

CARRANTUOHILL (Republic of Ireland)
COMMUNISM PEAK (Tajikistan)
GROSSGLOCKNER (Austria)
KANGCHENJUNGA (MT) (Nepal)
KOMMUNIZMA PIK (Tajikistan)
OJOS DEL SALADO (Argentina, Chile)
SIERRA MAESTRA (Cuba)

14+

BERNESE OBERLAND (Switzerland)
FICHTELGEBIRGE (Germany)
FINSTERAARHORN (Switzerland)
MACGILLICUDDY'S REEKS (Republic of Ireland)
SHIRÉ HIGHLANDS (Malawi)

VOLCANOES

3
ASO (Japan)
AWU (Indonesia)

4
ETNA (Sicily)
FOGO (Cape Verde Islands)
GEDE (Indonesia)
KABA (Indonesia)
LAKI (Iceland)
NILA (Indonesia)
POAS (Costa Rica)
SIAU (Indonesia)
TAAL (Philippines)

5
AGUNG (Indonesia)
ASAMA (Japan)
ASKJA (Iceland)
DEMPO (Indonesia)
FUEGO (Guatemala)
HEKLA (Iceland)
KATLA (Iceland)
MANAM (Papua New Guinea)
MAYON (Philippines)
NOYOE (Iceland)
OKMOK (USA)
PALOE (Indonesia)
PELÉE (Martinique)
SPURR (USA)

6
ALCEDO (Galapagos Islands)
AMBRIM (Vanuatu)
BIG BEN (Heard Island)
BULENG (Indonesia)
COLIMA (Mexico)
DUKONO (Indonesia)
IZALCO (El Salvador)
KATMAI (USA)
LASCAR (Chile)
LASSEN (USA)
LLAIMA (Chile)
LOPEVI (Vanuatu)
MARAPI (Indonesia)
MARTIN (USA)
MEAKAN (Japan)
MERAPI (Indonesia)
MIHARA (Japan)

O'SHIMA (Japan)
OSORNO (Chile)
PACAYA (Guatemala)
PAVLOF (USA)
PURACÉ (Colombia)
SANGAY (Ecuador)
SEMERU (Indonesia)
SLAMAT (Indonesia)
TACANA (Guatemala)
UNAUNA (Indonesia)

7
ATITLAN (Guatemala)
BÁRCENA (Mexico)
BULUSAN (Philippines)
DIDICAS (Philippines)
EL MISTI (Peru)
GALERAS (Colombia)
JORULLO (Mexico)
KILAUEA (USA)
OMETEPE (Nicaragua)
PUYEHUE (Chile)
RUAPEHU (New Zealand)
SABRINA (Azores)
SOPUTAN (Indonesia)
SURTSEY (Iceland)
TERNATE (Indonesia)
TJAREME (Indonesia)
TOKACHI (Japan)
TORBERT (USA)
TRIDENT (USA)
VULCANO (Italy)

8
BOGOSLOF (USA)
CAMEROON (Cameroon)
COTOPAXI (Ecuador)
DEMAVEND (Iran)
FONUALEI (Tonga Islands)
FUJIYAMA (Japan)
HUALALAI (USA)
KERINTJI (Indonesia)
KRAKATAU (Indonesia)
KRAKATOA (Indonesia)
MAUNA LOA (USA)
NIUAFO'OU (Tonga)
RINDJANI (Indonesia)
SANGEANG (Indonesia)

TARAWERA (New Zealand)
VESUVIUS (Italy)
YAKEDAKE (Japan)

9
AMBUROMBU (Indonesia)
BANDAI-SAN (Japan)
CLEVELAND (USA)
COSEGUINA (Nicaragua)
COTACACHI (Ecuador)
GAMKONORA (Indonesia)
GRIMSVÖTN (Iceland)
MOMOTOMBO (Nicaragua)
MYOZIN-SYO (Japan)
NGAURUHOE (New Zealand)
PARICUTIN (Mexico)
RININAHUE (Chile)
SANTORINI (Greece)
STROMBOLI (Italy)
TONGARIRO (New Zealand)

10
ACATENANGO (Guatemala)
CAPELINHOS (Azores)
CERRO NEGRO (Nicaragua)
GUALLATIRI (Chile)
HIBOK HIBOK (Philippines)
LONG ISLAND (Papua New Guinea)
MIYAKEJIMA (Japan)
NYAMIAGIRA (Congo, Democratic Republic of)
NYIRAGONGO (Congo, Democratic Republic of)
SANTA MARIA (Guatemala)
SHISHALDIN (USA)
TUNGURAHUA (Ecuador)
VILLARRICA (Chile)

11
GREAT SITKIN (USA)
KILIMANJARO (Tanzania)
LA SOUFRIÈRE (Saint Vincent and the Grenadines)
TUPUNGATITO (Chile)
WHITE ISLAND (New Zealand)

12
HUAINAPUTINA (Peru)
POPOCATÉPETL (Mexico)

DAMS

4
OAHE (USA)
GURI (Venezuela)
SAND (Kenya)
ZEYA (Russia)

5
ASWAN (Egypt)
NUREK (Tajikistan)
TETON (USA)

6
BHAKRA (India)
BRATSK (Russia)
CHIXOY (Guatemala)
CONTRA (Switzerland)
GORDON (Australia)
HOOVER (USA)
IDUKKI (India)
INGURI (Georgia)
ITAIPU (Brazil/Paraguay)
KARIBA (Zambia/Zimbabwe)
KARUN-3 (Iran)
MANGLA (Pakistan)
MEROWE (Sudan)
PARKER (USA)
SAMARA (Russia)
SHASTA (USA)
VAJONT (Italy)

7
ALMANSA (Spain)
ATATURK (Turkey)
COCHITI (USA)

FONTANA (USA)
HIRAKUD (India)
LOCARNO (Switzerland)
LONGTAN (China)
MANOIKE (Japan)
SAN LUIS (USA)
TUCURUI (Brazil)
XILUODU (China)

8
AKOSOMBO (Ghana)
CORNALVO (Spain)
DWORSHAK (USA)
FORT PECK (USA)
GARDINER (Canada)
GARRISON (USA)
JINPING-I (China)
KALLANAI (India)
LAKE HOMS (Syria)
MRATINJE (Montenegro)
OROVILLE (USA)
SAN ROQUE (Philippines)
VERZASCA (Switzerland)
YACYRETA (Argentina)

9
KOLNBREIN (Austria)
SAYAMAIKE (Japan)
ST.FRANCIS (USA)

10
GLEN CANYON (USA)
HAWES WATER (England)
LAKE VYRNWY (Wales)

PROSERPINA (Spain)
SADD-E KOBAR (Iran)
TONNUR KERE (India)
W.A.C. BENNETT (Canada)
XIANGJIABA (China)

11
AFSLUITDIJK (Netherlands)
FORT RANDALL (USA)
GRAND COULEE (USA)
HOUTRIBDIJK (Netherlands)
KRASNOYARSK (Russia)
SYLVENSTEIN (Germany)
THREE GORGES (China)

12
KAERUMATAIKE (Japan)
KIELDER WATER (England)
RUTLAND WATER (England)

13
DANIEL JOHNSON (Canada)

14
NAGARJUNA SAGAR (India)
ROBERT-BOURASSA (Canada)

15
QUATINAH BARRAGE (Syria)

18
KALESHWARAM PROJECT (India)

22
ASHFORK-BAINBRIDGE STEEL
  (USA)

BRIDGES

4
CITY (Wales)
DUGE (China)
IRON (England)
LUPU (China)
SKYE (Scotland)

5
ESSEX (England)
FORTH (Scotland)
HELIX (Singapore)
KHAJU (Iran)
NANPU (China)
TAMAR (England)
TOWER (England)
TRIFT (Switzerland)
U BEIN (Burma)

6
ALBERT (Northern Ireland)
CHAPEL (Switzerland)
GOLDEN (Vietnam)

HOWRAH (India)
HUMBER (England)
KINTAI (Japan)
LONDON (England)
MONNOW (Wales)
PUTNEY (England)
RIALTO (Italy)
RUSSKY (Russia)
SEVERN (Wales)

7
CARAVAN (Turkey)
CHARLES (Czech Republic)
CLACHAN (Scotland)
DA VINCI (Norway)
DONGHAI (China)
GEORGE V (Scotland)
HA'PENNY (Ireland)
KYLESKU (Scotland)
NEWPORT (Wales)
ORESUND (Sweden/Denmark)

TAY ROAD (Scotland)
TSING MA (China)

8
ARKADIKO (Greece)
BROOKLYN (USA)
CAERLEON (Wales)
CLYDE ARC (Scotland)
CORONADO (USA)
INFINITY (England)
MACKINAC (USA)
PORT MANN (Australia)
PONT-NEUF (France)
PULTENEY (England)
SI-O-SE-POL (Iran)
SOMERSET (Bermuda)
WATERLOO (England)

9
ALCANTARA (Spain)
BOSPHORUS (Turkey)
BRIG O'DOON (Scotland)

BRITANNIA (Scotland)
CHENGYANG (China)
FORTH ROAD (Scotland)
LOSCHWITZ (Germany)
SIDU RIVER (China)
SOUTHWARK (England)
ST. JULIAN'S (Wales)
STARI MOST (Bosnia and
 Herzegovina)
SUNNIBERG (Switzerland)
TARR STEPS (England)

10
GOLDEN GATE (USA)
MILLENNIUM (England)
OAKLAND BAY (USA)
PONT DU GARD (France)
RIVER MELES (Turkey)
ROYAL GORGE (USA)
SLAUERHOFF (Netherlands)

11
CEFN VIADUCT (Wales)
HAMMERSMITH (England)
HANGZHOU BAY (China)
JIAOZHOU BAY (China)
LANGKAWI SKY (Malaysia)
PONTE VECCHIO (Italy)
SERI WAWASAN (Malaysia)
STIRLING OLD (Scotland)
VASCO DA GAMA (Portugal)
WIND AND RAIN (China)

12
AKASHI KAILYO (Japan)
CARRICK-A-REDE (Northern
 Ireland)
ESHIMA OHASHI (Japan)
GEORGE STREET (Wales)
KAPELLBRUCKE (Switzerland)

13
BRIDGE OF SIGHS (Italy)

CHESAPEAKE BAY (USA)
CONFEDERATION (Canada)
CRAIGELLACHIE (Scotland)
MILLAU VIADUCT (France)
SYDNEY HARBOUR (Australia)

14
HENDERSON WAVES (Singapore)
HONG KONG-ZHUHAI (China)
MAGDEBURG WATER (Germany)
PONTE 25 DE ABRIL (Portugal)
SZECHENYI CHAIN (Hungary)

15
BARMOUTH VIADUCT (Wales)
CONWY SUSPENSION (Wales)
HUSSAINI HANGING (Pakistan)
MENAI SUSPENSION (Wales)
TILIKUM CROSSING (USA)

16
GEORGE WASHINGTON (USA)
HALF-BRIDGE OF HOPE (Russia)
PONT ALEXANDRE III (France)
QUEEN ELIZABETH II (England)
ZHANGJIAJIE GLASS (China)

17
CAPILANO CLIFFWALK (Canada)
CLIFTON SUSPENSION (England)
FAITH SULTAN MEHMET (Turkey)
GLENFINNAN VIADUCT
 (Scotland)
LEADERFOOT VIADUCT
 (Scotland)
RIBBLEHEAD VIADUCT (England)
VERRAZZANO-NARROWS (USA)

18
GRAND CANYON SKYWALK
 (USA)

19
DANYANG KUNSHAN

GRAND (China)
GATESHEAD MILLENNIUM
 (England)
SCALE LANE FOOTBRIDGE
 (England)
QUEENSFERRY CROSSING
 (Scotland)
RUNYANG YANGTZE RIVER
 (China)

20
NEW BRUNSWICK HARTLAND
 (Canada)
NORTH BRIDGE EDINBURGH
 (Scotland)
PONTCYSYLLTE AQUEDUCT
 (Wales)
SECOND SEVERN CROSSING
 (Wales)
SOUTH BRIDGE EDINBURGH
 (Scotland)

21
CORNISH WINDSOR COVERED
 (USA)
STATE ROUTE 520 FLOATING
 (USA)

22
GREAT WESTERN RAILWAY USK
 (Wales)
OCTAVIO FRIAS DE OLIVEIRA
 (Brazil)

23
PONT JACQUES CHABAN-
 DELMAS (France)

25
LAKE PONTCHARTRAIN
 CAUSEWAY (USA)

WATERFALLS

5
PILAO, SALTO (Brazil)

6
GIETRO, CASCADE DU
 (Switzerland)
YUTAJE, SALTO (Venezuela)

7
AA FALLS (USA)
RORAIMA, SALTO (Venezuela)
SELFOSS (Iceland)

8
ITUTINGA, CACHOEIRA (Brazil)
JOG FALLS (India)
KUKENAAM, SALTO (Venezuela)

LANGFOSS (Norway)

9
BRUFOSSEN (Norway)
DETTIFOSS (Iceland)
SIPI FALLS (Uganda)
TROU DE FER, CASCADES DE
 (Réunion)

10
AIMOO FALLS (USA)
ANGEL FALLS (Venezuela)
BLUFF FALLS (New Zealand)
GREAT FALLS (USA)
KJELFOSSEN (Norway)
LEVO SAVICE, SLAPOVI (Slovenia)

RHEINFALLE (Switzerland)
WAPTA FALLS (Canada)

11
BALAIFOSSEN (Norway)
BOYOMA FALLS (Congo)
BROWNE FALLS (New Zealand)
COHOES FALLS (USA)
DONTEFOSSEN (Norway)
HALOKU FALLS (USA)
IGUACU FALLS (Brazil, Argentina,
 Paraguay)
KAHIWA FALLS (USA)
KRUNEFOSSEN (Norway)
MADDEN FALLS (Canada)
MONGEFOSSEN (Norway)

MONGEFOSSEN (Norway)
OLMAAFOSSEN (Norway)
PAPALA FALLS (USA)
SPIREFOSSEN (Norway)
SUNDIFOSSEN (Norway)
TJOTAFOSSEN (Norway)
TUGELA FALLS (South Africa)
TYSSEFOSSEN (Norway)

12

IGUASSU FALLS (Brazil,
  Argentina, Paraguay)
LAEGDAFOSSEN (Norway)
LUNGAFOSSEN (Norway)
MARENGO FALLS (Australia)
MTARAZI FALLS (Zimbabwe)
NIAGARA FALLS (USA, Canada)
ORMELIFOSSEN (Norway)
RUACANA FALLS (Namibia,
  Angola)
SPOKANE FALLS (USA)
STANLEY FALLS (former name for
  Boyoma Falls)
TRES HERMANAS, CATARATAS
  LAS (Peru)
WAIMANU FALLS (USA)
WAILELE FALLS (USA)

13

DIYALUMA FALLS (Sri Lanka)
HAFRAGILSFOSS (Iceland)
KAIETEUR FALLS (Guyana)
KAKAAUKI FALLS (USA)
KEANA'AWI FALLS (USA)
KOOTENAI FALLS (USA)
LAHOMENE FALLS (USA)
MARDALSFOSSEN (Norway)
MONUMENT FALLS (USA)
OLO'UPENA FALLS (USA)
PU'UKA'OKU FALLS (USA)
RAVINE BLANCHE, LA CASCADE
  DE (Réunion)
SENTINEL FALLS (USA)
SHOSHONE FALLS (USA)
STRUPENFOSSEN (Norway)
VICTORIA FALLS (Zimbabwe)
WAIHILAU FALLS (USA)
YOSEMITE FALLS (USA)

14

AUGRABIES FALLS (South Africa)
CHURCHILL FALLS (Canada)
DUDHSAGAR FALLS (India)
GOLD CREEK FALLS (Canada)
MURCHISON FALLS (Uganda)
PITCHFORK FALLS (USA)
SNOW CREEK FALLS (USA)
TYSSESTRENGENE (Norway)

15

BRIDAL VEIL FALLS (USA)
MANA'WAI'NUI FALLS (USA)
SILVER LAKE FALLS (USA)
SUTHERLAND FALLS (New
  Zealand)

16

ALFRED CREEK FALLS (Canada)
BASESEACHIC FALLS (Mexico)
PISSING MARE FALLS (Canada)
WILLIAMETTE FALLS (USA)
YELLOWSTONE FALLS (USA)

17

RAMNEFJELLSFOSSEN (Norway)
WHITE GLACIER FALLS (USA)

18+

AVALANCHE BASIN FALLS (USA)
COLONIAL CREEK FALLS (USA)
DESERTED RIVER FALLS (Canada)
KINGCOME VALLEY FALLS
  (Canada)
OSTRE TINJEFJELLFOSSEN
  (Norway)
SULPHIDE CREEK FALLS (USA)
YTSTE TINJEFJELLFOSSEN
  (Norway)

DESERTS

4
GILA
GOBI
THAR

5
NAMIB
NEFUD
NEGEV
OLMOS
ORDOS
SINAI
STURT

6
ARUNTA
GIBSON
MOJAVE
NUBIAN
SAHARA
SYRIAN

UST'-URT

7
ALASHAN
ARABIAN
ATACAMA
KARA KUM
MORROPE
PAINTED
SECHURA
SIMPSON

8
COLORADO
KALAHARI
KYZYL KUM
MUYUNKUM
VIZCAINO

9
BLACK ROCK
DASHT-I-LUT

DZUNGARIA

10
AUSTRALIAN
BET-PAK-DALA
GREAT SANDY
PATAGONIAN
RUB'AL KHALI

11
DASHT-I-KAVIR
DASHT-I-MARGO
DEATH VALLEY

13
GREAT SALT LAKE
GREAT VICTORIA

14
BOLSON DE MAPIMI

16
TURFAN DEPRESSION

NATIONAL PARKS

PARK	LOCATION	SPECIAL FEATURE
Abisko	Sweden	
Abruzzo	Italy	
Altos de Campana	Panama	
Amazônia	Brazil	
Angkor	Kampuchea	Khmer civilization remains
Arusha	Tanzania	
Atitlán	Guatemala	
Awāsh	Ethiopia	
Babiogórski	Poland	
Banff	Alberta, Canada	hot springs at Sulphur Mountain
Bayarischer Wald	Bavaria, Germany	
Belovezhskaya	Belorussia	
Białowieski	Poland	
Bison	Tripura, India	
Brecon Beacons	Wales	
Broads	England	
Cabo de Hornos	Chile	automatically operated lighthouse
Cairngorms	Scotland	
Canaima	Venezuela	Salto Angel
Cañon del Rio Blanco	Mexico	
Canyonlands	Utah, United States	landforms carved in the red sandstone
Carlsbad Caverns	New Mexico	largest area of caverns in the world
Carnarvon	Queensland	
Chobe	Botswana	
Corbett	Uttar Pradesh, India	
Cradle Mountain–Lake	Tasmania, Australia	Saint Clair
Daisetsuzan	Japan	
Dartmoor	England	
Denali	Alaska, United States	Mt. McKinley
Djung-kulon	Indonesia	
Etosha	Namibia	
Everglades	Florida, United States	
Exmoor	England	
Fiordland	New Zealand	
Franklin D. Roosevelt	Uruguay	
Fray Jorge	Chile	
Fuji-Hakone-Izu	Japan	
Fundy	New Brunswick, Canada	
Galápagos	Ecuador	giant iguanas and giant tortoises
Gateway Arch	Missouri, United States	
Gemsbok	Botswana	
Gir Lion	Gujarāt, India	
Glacier	Montana, United States	
Gorongosa	Mozambique	
Grand Canyon	Arizona, United States	
Gran Paradiso	Italy	
Great Smoky Mountains	North Carolina & Tennessee, United States	
Hawaii Volcanoes	Hawaii, United States	
Henri Pittier	Venezuela	

Hohe Tauern	Austria	Krimmler Waterfall
Hortobágyi	Hungary	
Huascarán	Peru	Nevado Huascarán
Iguaçu	Brazil	Iguaçu Falls
Iguazú	Argentina	Iguazú River cliffs; Iguazú Falls
Isle Royale	Michigan, United States	
Ixtacihuatl-Popocatépetl	Mexico	
Jaldapara	West Bengal, India	
Jasper	Alberta, Canada	Columbia Icefield
Kabalega	Uganda	Kabalega Falls
Kafue	Zambia	
Kaieteur	Guyana	Kaieteur Falls
Kalahari Gemsbok	Cape of Good Hope, South Africa	
Karatepe-Asiantaş	Turkey	Hittite, Roman, and Phoenician civilizations ruins
Katmai	Alaska, United States	
Kaziranga	Assam, India	
Khao Yai	Thailand	
Kilimanjaro	Tanzania	
Komoé	Ivory Coast	
Kosciusko	New South Wales, Australia	Mt. Kosciusko
Kruger	Transvaal, South Africa	
Kuno	Madhya Pradesh, India	
Lake District	England	Lake Windermere
Loch Lomond and the Trossachs	Scotland	
Los Glaciares	Argentina	glacial landforms
Machu Picchu Historic Sanctuary	Peru	
Manovo-Gounda	Central African Republic	Saint Floris
Manu	Peru	
Mayon Volcano	Phillippines	Mayon Volcano
Mesa Verde	Colorado, United States	remains of cliff dwellings of pre-Columbian Indians
Moçãmedes Reserva	Angola	
Mount Apo	Phillippines	
Mount Aspiring	New Zealand	Mt. Aspiring
Mount Carmel	Israel	
Mount Cook	New Zealand	Mt. Cook; Tasman Glacier
Nahuel Huapi	Argentina	Mt. Tronador
Nairobi	Kenya	
Namib Desert	Namibia	
New Forest	England	
Northumberland	England	
North York Moors	England	
Odzala	Congo	
Olympic	Washington, USA	
Olympus	Greece	
Peak District	England	
Pellas-Ounastunturi	Finland	
Pembrokeshire Coast	Wales	
Petrified Forest	Arizona, United States	forests of petrified trees

Pfälzerwald	Rheinland-Pfalz, Germany	
Pico de Orizaba	Mexico	Citlaltépetl volcano
Plitvič ka, Jezera	Croatia	
Puracé	Columbia	
Pyrénée Occidentales	France	
Rapa Nui	Chile	sites of an ancient civilization
Redwood	California, United States	
Retezat	Romania	
Rocky Mountain	Colorado, United States	
Rondane	Norway	
Rouge	Ontario, Canada	
Ruwenzori	Uganda	
Sarek	Sweden	
Schweizerische	Switzerland	
Serengeti	Tanzania	
Setto-Naikai	Japan	
Sierra Nevada	Venezuela	de Mérida
Skaftafell Thingvellir	Iceland	
Snowdonia	Wales	Snowdon Peak
South Downs	England	
Stirling Range	Western Australia,	Australia
Stolby Zapovednik	Russia	
Tatransky Národni	Slovakia	
Tatrzański	Poland	
Teberdinsky	Russia	Zapovednik
Tikal	Guatemala	ruins of Mayan city
Tortuguero	Costa Rica	green sea turtles
Toubkal	Morocco	
Triglavski Narodni	Slovenia	Kanjavec Peak; Savica Waterfalls
Tsavo	Kenya	
Uluru	Northern Territory, Australia	Mt. Olga; Ayers Rock
Valle de Ordesa	Spain	
Vanoise	France	
Veluwezoom, Het	Netherlands	
Victoria Falls	Zimbabwe & Zambia	Victoria Falls
Virunga	Zaire	
Volcanoes	Rwanda	
Wankie	Zimbabwe	
Waterton Lakes	Alberta, Canada	
Waza	Cameroon	
Wood Buffalo	Alberta & Northwest Territories, Canada	reserve for bison herds
W. Parc	Benin, Niger, & Burkina Faso	
Yellowstone	Wyoming, Montana, & Idaho, United States	Old Faithful
Yoho	British Columbia, Canada	Takakkaw Falls
Yorkshire Dales	England	
Yosemite	California, United States	Yosemite Falls
Zion	Utah, United States	

ANIMALS AND PLANTS

ANIMALS

2&3
AI
APE
ASS
BAT
CAT
DOG
ELK
FOX
GNU
KOB
PIG
RAT
YAK

4
ANOA
BEAR
CAVY
CONY
DEER
GAUR
GOAT
HARE
IBEX
KUDU
LION
LYNX
MINK
MOLE
MULE
ORYX
PACA
PIKA
PUMA
SAKI
SEAL
SIKA
TAHR
TITI
URUS
VOLE
WOLF
ZEBU

5
ADDAX
BISON
BONGO
CAMEL
CHIRU
CIVET

COATI
COYPU
DHOLE
DINGO
DRILL
ELAND
FOSSA
GAYAL
GENET
GORAL
HINNY
HORSE
HUTIA
HYENA
HYRAX
INDRI
KIANG
KOALA
LEMUR
LIGER
LLAMA
LORIS
MOOSE
MOUSE
NYALA
OKAPI
ORIBI
OTTER
OUNCE
PANDA
POTTO
RATEL
SABLE
SAIGA
SEROW
SHEEP
SHREW
SKUNK
SLOTH
STOAT
TAPIR
TIGER
TIGON
WHALE
ZEBRA

6
AGOUTI
ALPACA
AOUDAD
ARGALI
AUROCH

AYE-AYE
BABOON
BADGER
BEAVER
BOBCAT
CATTLE
CHITAL
COLUGO
COUGAR
COYOTE
CUSCUS
DESMAN
DIK-DIK
DONKEY
DUGONG
DUIKER
ERMINE
FENNEC
FERRET
FISHER
GALAGO
GELADA
GERBIL
GIBBON
GOPHER
GRISON
GUENON
HYAENA
IMPALA
JACKAL
JAGUAR
JERBOA
LANGUR
MARGAY
MARMOT
MARTEN
MONKEY
MUSK OX
NILGAI
NUMBAT
NUTRIA
OCELOT
OLINGO
ONAGER
POSSUM
RABBIT
RED FOX
RODENT
SEA COW
SERVAL
SIFAKA

TENREC
VERVET
VICUNA
WALRUS
WAPITI
WEASEL
WISENT
WOMBAT

7
ACOUCHI
ANT BEAR
BANTENG
BIGHORN
BLESBOK
BLUE FOX
BUFFALO
CANE RAT
CARACAL
CARIBOU
CHAMOIS
CHEETAH
COLOBUS
DASYURE
DOLPHIN
ECHIDNA
FELIDAE
GAZELLE
GEMSBOK
GERENUK
GIRAFFE
GLUTTON
GORILLA
GRAMPUS
GUANACO
GYMNURE
HAMSTER
LEMMING
LEOPARD
LINSANG
MACAQUE
MAMMOTH
MANATEE
MARKHOR
MEERKAT
MOLE RAT
MOON RAT
MOUFLON
MUSKRAT
NARWHAL
NOCTULE
OPOSSUM

PACK RAT
PANTHER
PECCARY
POLECAT
PRIMATE
RACCOON
RED DEER
ROE DEER
RORQUAL
SEALION
SIAMANG
SOUSLIK
SUN BEAR
TAMARIN
TAMAROU
TARSIER
WALLABY
WARTHOG
WILDCAT
ZORILLA

8
AARDVARK
AARDWOLF
ANTEATER
ANTELOPE
AXIS DEER
BABIRUSA
BONTEBOK
BUSHBABY
BUSHBUCK
CACHALOT
CAPYBARA
CHIPMUNK
DORMOUSE
ELEPHANT
ENTELLUS
FRUIT BAT
HEDGEHOG
IRISH ELK
KANGAROO
KINKAJOU
MANDRILL
MANGABEY
MARMOSET
MONGOOSE
MUSK DEER
MUSQUASH
PANGOLIN
PLATYPUS
PORPOISE
REEDBUCK
REINDEER

RUMINANT
SEA OTTER
SEI WHALE
SQUIRREL
STEINBOK
TALAPOIN
TAMANDUA
VISCACHA
WALLAROO
WATER RAT
WILD BOAR

9
ARCTIC FOX
ARMADILLO
BANDICOOT
BINTURONG
BLACK BEAR
BLACKBUCK
BLUE WHALE
BROWN BEAR
DEER MOUSE
DESERT RAT
DROMEDARY
FLYING FOX
GOLDEN CAT
GROUNDHOG
GUINEA PIG
HAMADRYAS
MONOTREME
MOUSE DEER
ORANG-UTAN
PACHYDERM
PALM CIVET
PAMPAS CAT
PHALANGER
POLAR BEAR
PORCUPINE
PRONGHORN
PROSIMIAN
SILVER FOX
SITATUNGA
SLOTH BEAR
SOLENODON
SPRINGBOK
THYLACINE
TREE SHREW
WATERBUCK
WATER VOLE
WOLVERINE
WOODCHUCK

10
ANGWANTIBO

BARBARY APE
BOTTLENOSE
CACOMISTLE
CHEVROTAIN
CHIMPANZEE
CHINCHILLA
CHIROPTERA
FALLOW DEER
FIELDMOUSE
GOLDEN MOLE
HARTEBEEST
HONEY MOUSE
HOODED SEAL
JAGUARUNDI
KODIAK BEAR
MONA MONKEY
OTTER SHREW
PALLAS'S CAT
PILOT WHALE
PINE MARTEN
POUCHED RAT
PRAIRIE DOG
RACCOON DOG
RHINOCEROS
RIGHT WHALE
SPERM WHALE
SPRINGHAAS
TIMBER WOLF
VAMPIRE BAT
WATER SHREW
WHITE WHALE
WILDEBEEST

11
BARBASTELLE
BARKING DEER
DOUROUCOULI
FLYING LEMUR
GRASS MONKEY
GRIZZLY BEAR
HARBOUR SEAL
HONEY BADGER
KANGAROO RAT
KILLER WHALE
LEOPARD SEAL
PATAS MONKEY
PIPISTRELLE
PRAIRIE WOLF
RAT KANGAROO
RED SQUIRREL
SEROTINE BAT
SNOW LEOPARD

12
ELEPHANT SEAL
HARVEST MOUSE
HIPPOPOTAMUS
HORSESHOE BAT
HOWLER MONKEY
JUMPING MOUSE
KLIPSPRINGER
MOUNTAIN LION
POCKET GOPHER
RHESUS MONKEY
ROAN ANTELOPE
SNOWSHOE HARE
SPIDER MONKEY
TREE KANGAROO
WATER BUFFALO
WOOLLY MONKEY

13
ANTHROPOID APE
CRABEATER SEAL
DORCAS GAZELLE
HUMPBACK WHALE
MARSUPIAL MOLE
ROYAL ANTELOPE
SABLE ANTELOPE
TASMANIAN WOLF

14
CAPUCHIN MONKEY
CLOUDED LEOPARD
FLYING SQUIRREL
GROUND SQUIRREL
MOUNTAIN BEAVER
NEW WORLD MONKEY
OLD WORLD MONKEY
PÈRE DAVID'S DEER
SPECTACLED BEAR
SQUIRREL MONKEY
TASMANIAN DEVIL

15+
CHINESE WATER DEER
DUCK-BILLED PLATYPUS
FLYING PHALANGER
PROBOSCIS MONKEY
PYGMY
   HIPPOPOTAMUS
SCALY-TAILED
   SQUIRREL
WHITE RHINOCEROS
WOOLLY RHINOCEROS
WOOLLY SPIDER
   MONKEY

ANIMALS AND THEIR GENDER

ANIMAL	MALE	FEMALE	ANIMAL	MALE	FEMALE
ANTELOPE	BUCK	DOE	HARE	BUCK	DOE
ASS	JACKASS	JENNYASS	HARTEBEAST	BULL	COW
BADGER	BOAR	SOW	HORSE	STALLION	MARE
BEAR	BOAR	SOW	IMPALA	RAM	EWE
BOBCAT	TOM	LIONESS	JACKRABBIT	BUCK	DOE
BUFFALO	BULL	COW	KANGAROO	BUCK	DOE
CAMEL	BULL	COW	LEOPARD	LEOPARD	LEOPARDESS
CARIBOU	STAG	DOE	LION	LION	LIONESS
CAT	TOM	QUEEN	MOOSE	BULL	COW
CATTLE	BULL	COW	OX	BULLOCK	COW
CHICKEN	COCK	HEN	PEACOCK	PEACOCK	PEAHEN
COUGAR	TOM	LIONESS	PHEASANT	COCK	HEN
COYOTE	DOG	BITCH	PIG	BOAR	SOW
DEER	STAG	DOE	RHINOCEROS	BULL	COW
DOG	DOG	BITCH	ROEDEER	ROEBUCK	DOEDEER
DONKEY	JACKASS	JENNYASS	SEAL	BULL	COW
DUCK	DRAKE	DUCK	SHEEP	RAM	EWE
ELAND	BULL	COW	SWAN	COB	PEN
ELEPHANT	BULL	COW	TIGER	TIGER	TIGRESS
FERRET	JACK	JILL	WALRUS	BULL	COW
FISH	COCK	HEN	WEASEL	BOAR	COW
FOX	FOX or DOG	VIXEN	WHALE	BULL	COW
GIRAFFE	BULL	COW	WOLF	DOG	BITCH
GOAT	BILLYGOAT	NANNYGOAT	ZEBRA	STALLION	MARE
GOOSE	GANDER	GOOSE			

ADJECTIVES

CREATURE	ADJECTIVE	CREATURE	ADJECTIVE
BEAR	URSINE	LOBSTER	CRUSTACEAN or CRUSTACEOUS
BEE	APIAN	MONGOOSE	VIVERRINE
BULL	TAURINE	MONKEY	SIMIAN
CAT	FELINE	MOUSE	MURINE
CHIPMUNK	SCIURINE	PIG	PORCINE
CIVET	VIVERRINE	PORPOISE	CETACEAN or CETACEOUS
COW	BOVINE	RAT	MURINE
CRAB	CRUSTACEAN or CRUSTACEOUS	SEAL	OTARID; PHOCINE
		SEA LION	OTARID
DEER	CERVID or CERVINE	SHEEP	OVINE
DOG	CANINE	SHRIMP	CRUSTACEAN or CRUSTACEOUS
DOLPHIN	CETACEAN or CETACEOUS		
DONKEY	ASININE	SKUNK	MUSTELINE
EEL	ANGUILLIFORM	SNAKE	ANGUINE; COLUBRINE; OPHIDIAN; SERPENTINE
ELEPHANT	ELEPHANTINE		
FERRET	MUSTELINE	SPIDER	ARACHNOID
FISH	PISCINE	SQUIRREL	SCIURINE
FOWL	GALLINACEOUS	TERRAPIN	CHELONIAN
FOX	VULPINE	TOAD	BATRACHIAN
FROG	BATRACHIAN	TORTOISE	CHELONIAN
GOAT	CAPRINE; HIRCINE	TURTLE	CHELONIAN
GOOSE	ANSERINE	VIPER	VIPERINE or VIPEROUS
HARE	LEPORINE	WEASEL	MUSTELINE
HORSE	EQUINE	WHALE	CETACEAN or CETACEOUS
LION	LEONINE	WOLF	LUPINE
LIZARD	SAURIAN	WORM	VERMIFORM

ANIMALS AND THEIR YOUNG

ANIMAL	YOUNG	ANIMAL	YOUNG
ANTELOPE	KID	HARE	LEVERET
BADGER	CUB	HARTEBEAST	CALF
BEAR	CUB	HAWK	CHICK
BEAVER	KITTEN	HORSE	FOAL
BOBCAT	KITTEN	JACKRABBIT	KITTEN
BUFFALO	CALF	KANGAROO	JOEY
CAMEL	CALF	LEOPARD	CUB
CARIBOU	FAWN	LION	CUB
CAT	KITTEN	MONKEY	INFANT
CATTLE	CALF	OX	STOT
CHICKEN	CHICK	PHEASANT	CHICK
COUGAR	KITTEN	PIG	PIGLET
COYOTE	PUPPY	RHINOCEROS	CALF
DEER	FAWN	ROEDEER	KID
DOG	PUPPY	SEAL	CALF
DUCK	DUCKLING	SHEEP	LAMB
ELAND	CALF	SKUNK	KITTEN
ELEPHANT	CALF	SWAN	CYGNET
ELK	CALF	TIGER	CUB
FISH	FRY	TOAD	TADPOLE
FROG	TADPOLE	WALRUS	CUB
FOX	CUB	WEASEL	KIT
GIRAFFE	CALF	WHALE	CALF
GOAT	KID	WOLF	CUB
GOOSE	GOSLING	ZEBRA	FOAL

ANIMAL SOUNDS

ANIMAL	SOUND	ANIMAL	SOUND
ASS	BRAY		SNARL
	HEE-HAW		HOWL
BEAR	GROWL		WHINE
BEE	BUZZ	DOLPHIN	CLICK
	HUM	DONKEY	BRAY
BEETLE	DRONE	DOVE	COO
BIRD	CALL	DUCK	QUACK
	SING	EAGLE	SQUAWK
	CHIRP		SCREAM
	TWEET	ELEPHANT	TRUMPET
	WARBLE	FALCON	CHANT
BULL	BELLOW	FLY	BUZZ
CAT	MEOW	FOX	BARK
	PURR		YAP
CHICKEN	CLUCK		YELP
COCK	CROW	FROG	CROAK
COW	MOO	GIRAFFE	BLEAT
	LOW		GRUNT
CROW	CAW	GOAT	BLEAT
CUCKOO	CUCKOO	GOOSE	HISS
DEER	BELL		CACKLE
DOG	BARK		HONK
	YELP	GRASSHOPPER	CHIRP
	BAY		PITTER
	YAP	GROUSE	DRUM
	GROWL	GUINEA PIG	SQUEAK

ANIMAL	SOUND	ANIMAL	SOUND
HIPPOPOTAMUS	BRAY	PEACOCK	SCREAM
HORSE	NEIGH		WAIL
	WHINNY	PIG	GRUNT
HYENA	LAUGH		OINK
KITTEN	MEW		SQUEAL
LION	ROAR	PIGEON	COO
MAGPIE	CHATTER	RAVEN	CROAK
MONKEY	CHATTER	RHINOCEROS	SNORT
	GIBBER	SEA GULL	SQUAWK
MOUSE	SQUEAK		CRY
MULE	BRAY	SEAL	BARK
NIGHTINGALE	WARBLE	SHEEP	BLEAT
	PIPE		BAA
	JUG-JUG	SNAKE	HISS
OWL	HOOT	SWAN	HISS
	SCREECH	TIGER	GROWL
OX	LOW	TURKEY	GOBBLE
	BELLOW	WOLF	BAY
PARROT	SQUAWK		HOWL

ANIMAL HOMES

ANIMAL	HOME	ANIMAL	HOME
ANT	HILL	MOUSE	MOUSEHOLE
	FORMICARY		MOUSERY
ARMADILLO	DUGOUT		NEST
BADGER	SETT	OTTER	HOLT
	HOLE		COUCH
BAT	ROOST	OWL	OWLERY
	CAVE	OX	CORRAL
BEAR	DEN		CRIB
BEAVER	LODGE	OYSTER	HIVE
BEE	HIVE	PENGUIN	PENGUINERY
BIRD	AVIARY	PHEASANT	NIDE
	NEST	PIG	PEN
CAT	CATTERY		STY
	LAIR	PIGEON	PIGEONCOTE
	DEN		LOFT
CHICKEN	COOP	RABBIT	WARREN
	BATTERY		HUTCH
	HENHOUSE		BURROW
COW	BYRE	RAT	NEST
	BARN		HOLE
DOG	KENNEL	RAVEN	RAVENRY
DOVE	DOVECOTE	SEAL	ROOKERY
EAGLE	EYRIE	SHEEP	FOLD
FOX	DEN		PEN
	LAIR	SNAIL	SNAILERY
	EARTH	SNAKE	NEST
HARE	FORM	SPIDER	WEB
HERON	HERONRY	SQUIRREL	DREY
HORNET	NEST	SWAN	SWANNERY
HORSE	STABLE	TERMITE	MOUND
	PADDOCK	TIGER	LAIR
LION	DEN	WASP	NEST
MOLE	FORTRESS		VESPIARY
	HILL	WOLF	LAIR
	BURROW		DEN

COLLECTIVE TERMS

ANIMAL	COLLECTIVE TERM	ANIMAL	COLLECTIVE TERM
ANTELOPE	HERD	GOAT	FLOCK
APE	SHREWDNESS	GOOSE	GAGGLE
ASS	DROVE	HARE	HUSKE
BADGER	CETE	HARTEBEAST	HERD
BEAR	SLEUTH	HAWK	CAST
BEAVER	COLONY	HORSE	HERD
BLOODHOUND	SUTE	IMPALA	COUPLE
BOAR	SOUNDER	JACKRABBIT	HUSK
BUFFALO	HERD	KANGAROO	TROOP or MOB
CAMEL	TRAIN	KINE	DROVE
CARIBOU	HERD	LEOPARD	LEAP
CAT	CLUSTER	LION	PRIDE
CATTLE	HERD	MOLE	LABOUR
CHAMOIS	HERD	MONKEY	TROOP
CHICKEN	FLOCK	MOOSE	HERD
CHOUGH	CHATTERING	MOUSE	NEST
COLT	RAG	OX	TEAM
COOT	FLEET	PEACOCK	PRIDE
COYOTE	PACK	PHEASANT	BROOD
DEER	HERD	PIG	TRIP
DOG	PACK	RHINOCEROS	CRASH
DOLPHIN	POD	ROEDEER	BEVY
DONKEY	DROVE	ROOK	BUILDING
DUCK	PADDLING	SEAL	POD
ELAND	HERD	SHEEP	FLOCK
ELEPHANT	HERD	SNAKE	KNOT
ELK	GANG	TOAD	NEST
FERRET	BUSINESS	WALRUS	POD
FISH	SCHOOL	WEASEL	PACK
FOX	TROOP	WHALE	SCHOOL
GELDING	BRACE	WOLF	PACK
GIRAFFE	HERD	ZEBRA	HERD

ANIMAL DISEASES AND INFECTIONS

3
EHV
EIA
GID
ORF
ROT

4
ROUP
SCUR

5
FARCY

6
APHTHA
CANKER
CAT FLU
CRUELS
EPULIS
GRAPES

GREASE
SPAVIN
STURDY
SWEENY
TEASER
WARBLE

7
BIGHEAD
FOOT ROT
FOUNDER
GOLDEYE
MOONEYE
ONYCHIA
QUITTOR
REDFOOT
YELLOWS

8
FOG FEVER
JAUNDICE

LUMPY JAW
RINGWOMB
STAGGERS
SWAY-BACK
TOE CRACK
TREMBLES
WINDGALL

9
CLOACITIS
ECLAMPSIA
HOOFBOUND
MILK FEVER
RUBBER JAW
SAND COLIC
SAND CRACK
VENT GLEET
WHISTLING

10
BABESIOSIS

BLUETONGUE
BUMBLE-FOOT
HEART-WATER
KNEE SPAVIN
NYCTALOPIA
SADDLE GALL
SALLENDERS
SEBORRHOEA
SHOVEL BEAK
SOD DISEASE
TEXAS FEVER
WATERBRAIN

11
FOWL CHOLERA
WOODY TONGUE

12
BLACK DISEASE
BORNA DISEASE
HIP DYSPLASIA

MILK LAMENESS
MILK SICKNESS
QUARTER CRACK
WOODEN TONGUE

13
ACTINOMYCOSIS

BLIND STAGGERS
BORDER DISEASE
MOON BLINDNESS

14
BABY PIG DISEASE
CALF DIPHTHERIA

15
BLACKWATER FEVER
EQUINE INFLUENZA
HYPOMAGNESAEMIA
LACTATION TETANY
MILLER'S DISEASE
PARTURIENT FEVER

16+
ACTINO BACILLOSIS
AFRICAN SWINE FEVER
ALTITUDE SICKNESS
CANINE PARVOVIRUS
MOUNTAIN SICKNESS
NEW FOREST DISEASE

BREEDS OF CATS

3
REX

4
MANX

5
CREAM
SMOKE
TABBY

6
BIRMAN
HAVANA

7
BURMESE
PERSIAN

RED SELF
SIAMESE
SPOTTED
TURKISH

8
DEVON REX
RED TABBY

9
BLUE CREAM

10
ABYSSINIAN
BROWN TABBY
CHINCHILLA
CORNISH REX

11
BLUE BURMESE
BRITISH BLUE
COLOURPOINT
RUSSIAN BLUE
SILVER TABBY

12
BROWN BURMESE

13
CHESTNUT BROWN
RED ABYSSINIAN
TORTOISESHELL

14
LONG HAIRED BLUE
TORTIE AND WHITE

15
RED-POINT SIAMESE

18
BLUE-POINTED
    SIAMESE
SEAL-POINTED SIAMESE
TORTIE-POINT SIAMESE

19
LILAC-POINTED
    SIAMESE
TABBY-POINTED
    SIAMESE

20+
CHOCOLATE-POINTED
    SIAMESE

BREEDS OF DOGS

3
PUG

4
PULI

5
BOXER
CORGI
HUSKY
SPITZ

6
BEAGLE
BORZOI
BRIARD
COLLIE
KELPIE
POODLE
SALUKI
SETTER

7
BASENJI
BULLDOG
CAVAPOO
GRIFFON
HARRIER

LOWCHEN
LURCHER
MALTESE
MASTIFF
POINTER
SAMOYED
SHELTIE
SHIH TZU
SPANIEL
SPOODLE
TERRIER
WHIPPET

8
ALSATIAN
CHOW CHOW
COCKAPOO
ELKHOUND
FOXHOUND
KEESHOND
MALEMUTE
PAPILLON
SHEEPDOG

9
CHIHUAHUA
DACHSHUND

DALMATIAN
DEERHOUND
GREAT DANE
GREYHOUND
LHASA APSO
PEKINGESE
RETRIEVER
SCHNAUZER
STAGHOUND
ST BERNARD

10
BLOODHOUND
FOX TERRIER
OTTERHOUND
POMERANIAN
ROTTWEILER
SCHIPPERKE
WEIMARANER
WELSH CORGI

11
AFGHAN HOUND
BASSET HOUND
BULL MASTIFF
BULL TERRIER
IBIZAN HOUND

IRISH SETTER
LABRADOODLE
SKYE TERRIER

12
CAIRN TERRIER
FINNISH SPITZ
IRISH TERRIER
JAPANESE CHIN
NEWFOUNDLAND
PHARAOH HOUND
SILKY TERRIER
WELSH TERRIER

13
AFFENPINSCHER
BORDER TERRIER
BOSTON TERRIER
COCKER SPANIEL
ENGLISH SETTER
HUNGARIAN PULI

14
GERMAN SHEPHERD
IRISH WOLFHOUND

15
AIREDALE TERRIER

ALASKAN MALAMUTE
GOLDEN RETRIEVER
HUNGARIAN VIZSLA
LAKELAND TERRIER
SCOTTISH TERRIER
SEALYHAM TERRIER
SPRINGER SPANIEL

16
KERRY BLUE TERRIER

PYRENEAN MOUNTAIN
SHETLAND SHEEPDOG
YORKSHIRE TERRIER

17
BEDLINGTON TERRIER
DOBERMANN
 PINSCHER
LABRADOR RETRIEVER

18
JACK RUSSELL TERRIER
KING CHARLES SPANIEL
LARGE
 MUNSTERLANDER
OLD ENGLISH
 SHEEPDOG
RHODESIAN
 RIDGEBACK

20+
DANDIE DINMONT
 TERRIER
STAFFORDSHIRE BULL
 TERRIER
WEST HIGHLAND WHITE
 TERRIER
WIREHAIRED POINTING
 GRIFFON

BREEDS OF HORSES AND PONIES

3
COB
DON

4
ARAB
BARB
FELL
POLO
RUSS

5
DALES
FJORD
HUCUL
KONIK
LOKAI
ORLOV
PINTO
SHIRE
TERSK
TIMOR
WELSH

6
ALBINO
BASUTO
EXMOOR
MERENS
MORGAN
TARPAN ·
VIATKA

7
CASPIAN
COMTOIS
CRIOLLO
FURIOSA
HACKNEY
JUTLAND
LLANERO
MUSTANG
NORIKER
QUARTER
SORRAIA

8
BUDEONNY

CAMARGUE
DARTMOOR
GALICEÑO
HIGHLAND
HOLSTEIN
KABARDIN
KARABAIR
KARABAKH
LUSITANO
PALOMINO
SHETLAND

9
AKHAL-TEKE
ALTER-REAL
APPALOOSA
CONNEMARA
FALABELLA
HAFLINGER
KNABSTRUP
NEW FOREST
OLDENBURG
PERCHERON

SCHLESWIG

10
ANDALUSIAN
AVELIGNESE
CLYDESDALE
GELDERLAND
HANOVERIAN
IRISH DRAFT
LIPIZZANER

11
NOVOKIRGHIZ

12
CLEVELAND BAY
SUFFOLK PUNCH
THOROUGHBRED

13
WELSH
 MOUNTAIN

16
TENNESSEE
 WALKING

BREEDS OF CATTLE

3
GIR

5
DEVON
KERRY
LUING

6
DEXTER
JERSEY
SUSSEX

7
BEEFALO
BRANGUS

8
AYRSHIRE
FRIESIAN
GALLOWAY
GUERNSEY
HEREFORD
HIGHLAND

LIMOUSIN

9
CHAROLAIS
SHORTHORN
SIMMENTAL

10
BROWN SWISS
LINCOLN RED
MURRAY GREY
WELSH BLACK

11
JAMAICA HOPE
MARCHIGIANA

13
ABERDEEN ANGUS
DROUGHTMASTER
TEXAS LONGHORN

BREEDS OF PIGS

5
DUROC
WELSH

8
PIETRAIN

TAMWORTH

9
BERKSHIRE
HAMPSHIRE

10
LARGE WHITE

15
SWEDISH LANDRACE

17
BRITISH SADDLEBACK
GLOUCESTER OLD
SPOT

BREEDS OF SHEEP

4
LONK
MULE
SOAY

5
CARDY
CHIOS
JACOB
LLEYN
MORFE
TEXEL

6
AWASSI
MASHAM

MERINO
ROMNEY

7
CHEVIOT
GOTLAND
KARAKUL
LACAUNE
SUFFOLK

8
HERDWICK
LONGMYND
POLWARTH
PORTLAND
SHETLAND

9
HEBRIDEAN
LONGWOOLS
OLDENBERG
ROUGH FELL
SWALEDALE
TEESWATER

10
CORRIEDALE
DORSET HORN
EXMOOR HORN
POLL DORSET

11
MANX LOGHTAN

WENSLEYDALE

13
WELSH MOUNTAIN
WILTSHIRE HORN

15
FRIES MELKSCHAAP

17
SCOTTISH BLACKFACE

18
WHITEFACED
WOODLAND

BREEDS OF POULTRY

4
BUFF (goose)

5
MARAN (chicken)
PEARL (guinea fowl)
PEKIN (duck)
ROMAN (goose)
ROUEN (duck)
WHITE (guinea fowl)

6
ANCONA (chicken)
CAYUGA (duck)
EMBDEN (goose)
SILKIE (chicken)

7
AFRICAN (goose)
CHINESE (goose)
CRESTED (duck)

DORKING (chicken)
LEGHORN (chicken)
MUSCOVY (duck)
PILGRIM (goose)

8
LAVENDER (guinea
fowl)
TOULOUSE (goose)

9
AYLESBURY (duck)
WELSUMMER (chicken)

10
BARNVELDER (chicken)
BELTSVILLE (turkey)
BOURBON RED (turkey)
INDIAN GAME (chicken)
ROSS RANGER (chicken)
SEBASTOPOL (goose)

11
CUCKOO MARAN
(chicken)
LIGHT SUSSEX
(chicken)

12
BLACK NORFOLK
(turkey)
INDIAN RUNNER (duck)
NARRAGANSETT
(turkey)
PLYMOUTH ROCK
(chicken)
WHITE HOLLAND
(turkey)

13
BUFF ORPINGTON
(duck)

KHAKI CAMPBELL
(duck)
MAMMOTH BRONZE
(turkey)
WHITE AUSTRIAN
(turkey)

14
BLACK EAST INDIE
(duck)
RHODE ISLAND RED
(chicken)
WELSH HARLEQUIN
(duck)
WHITE WYANDOTTE
(chicken)

15
CAMBRIDGE BRONZE
(turkey)

POINTS OF A HORSE

CANNON BONE	ERGOT	HIND QUARTERS	POLL
CHEEK	FEATHERS	HOCK	RIBS
CHEST	FETLOCK	HOOF	SHANK
CHESTNUT	FETLOCK JOINT	KNEE	SHEATH
CHIN GROOVE	FLANK	LOIN	SHOULDER
COFFIN BONE	FOREARM	MANE	SPLINT BONE
CORONET	FORELOCK	NAVICULAR BONE	STIFLE
CREST	FROG	PASTERN	TAIL
CROUP	GASKIN	PEDAL BONE	TENDON
DOCK	GULLET	POINT OF HIP	WINDPIPE
ELBOW	HEEL	POINT OF SHOULDER	WITHERS

BIRDS

3
AUK
EMU
JAY
MOA
OWL
TIT
TUI

4
CHAT
COLY
COOT
CROW
DODO
DOVE
DUCK
GULL
HAWK
HUIA
IBIS
KAGU
KITE
KIWI
KNOT
LARK
LORY
RAIL
RHEA
ROOK
RUFF
SHAG
SKUA
SMEW
SWAN
TEAL
TERN
WREN

5
BOOBY
CRAKE
CRANE

DIVER
EAGLE
EGRET
EIDER
FINCH
GOOSE
GREBE
HERON
HOBBY
MACAW
MYNAH
NODDY
OUZEL
PIPIT
PRION
QUAIL
RAVEN
ROBIN
SCAUP
SERIN
SNIPE
STILT
STORK

6
AVOCET
BARBET
BULBUL
CANARY
CHOUGH
CONDOR
CUCKOO
CURLEW
DARTER
DIPPER
DRONGO
DUNLIN
FALCON
FULMAR
GANNET
GODWIT
HOOPOE
JABIRU

JACANA
KAKAPO
LINNET
MAGPIE
MARTIN
MERLIN
MOTMOT
ORIOLE
OSPREY
PARROT
PEEWIT
PETREL
PIGEON
PLOVER
PUFFIN
QUELEA
RATITE
ROLLER
SHRIKE
SISKIN
TAKAHE
THRUSH
TOUCAN
TROGON
TURACO
TURKEY
WHIDAH
WHYDAH
WIGEON

7
ANTBIRD
BABBLER
BARN OWL
BITTERN
BLUETIT
BUNTING
BUSTARD
BUZZARD
COAL TIT
COURSER
DUNNOCK
EMU WREN

FANTAIL
FINFOOT
FISH OWL
GADWALL
GOSHAWK
GRACKLE
HARRIER
HAWK OWL
HOATZIN
JACAMAR
JACKDAW
KESTREL
LAPWING
MALLARD
MANAKIN
MARABOU
MINIVET
MOORHEN
OILBIRD
ORTOLAN
OSTRICH
PEACOCK
PEAFOWL
PELICAN
PENGUIN
PINTAIL
POCHARD
QUETZAL
REDPOLL
REDWING
ROSELLA
SEAGULL
SERIEMA
SKIMMER
SKYLARK
SPARROW
SUNBIRD
SWALLOW
TANAGER
TINAMOU
TOURACO
VULTURE

WAGTAIL
WARBLER
WAXBILL
WAXWING
WRYBILL
WRYNECK

8
ACCENTOR
AVADAVAT
BATELEUR
BEE-EATER
BLACKCAP
BLUEBIRD
BOATBILL
BOBOLINK
CARACARA
CARDINAL
COCKATOO
CURASSOW
DABCHICK
DOTTEREL
EAGLE OWL
FISH HAWK
FLAMINGO
GAMEBIRD
GARGANEY
GREAT TIT
GROSBEAK
HAWFINCH
HORNBILL
LOVEBIRD
LYREBIRD
MANNIKIN
MEGAPODE
MUTE SWAN
NIGHTJAR
NUTHATCH
OVENBIRD
OXPECKER
PARAKEET
PHEASANT
PYGMY OWL
REDSHANK
REDSTART
REEDLING
RIFLEMAN
ROCK DOVE
SCOPS OWL
SCREAMER
SEA EAGLE
SHELDUCK
SHOEBILL
SNOWY OWL
SONGBIRD
STARLING
SWIFTLET
TAWNY OWL
TITMOUSE
TRAGOPAN
WHEATEAR
WHIMBREL
WHINCHAT

WHIPBIRD
WHITE-EYE
WILDFOWL
WOODCHAT
WOODCOCK

9
ALBATROSS
BALD EAGLE
BLACKBIRD
BLACK SWAN
BOWERBIRD
BRAMBLING
BROADBILL
BULLFINCH
CASSOWARY
CHAFFINCH
COCKATIEL
CORMORANT
CORNCRAKE
CROSSBILL
CURRAWONG
FIELDFARE
FIRECREST
FRANCOLIN
FRIARBIRD
FROGMOUTH
GALLINULE
GOLDCREST
GOLDENEYE
GOLDFINCH
GUILLEMOT
GYRFALCON
HILL MYNAH
KITTIWAKE
LITTLE OWL
MERGANSER
MOUSEBIRD
PARTRIDGE
PHALAROPE
PTARMIGAN
RAZORBILL
RED GROUSE
RIFLEBIRD
RING OUZEL
SANDPIPER
SCRUB BIRD
SNAKEBIRD
SNOW GOOSE
SPOONBILL
STONECHAT
THICKHEAD
THORNBILL
TRUMPETER
TURNSTONE

10
ARCTIC TERN
BEARDED TIT
BRENT GOOSE
BUDGERIGAR
CHIFFCHAFF
CRESTED TIT

DEMOISELLE
DIVING DUCK
FLYCATCHER
GRASSFINCH
GREENFINCH
GREENSHANK
GUINEA FOWL
HAMMERHEAD
HARPY EAGLE
HONEYEATER
HONEY GUIDE
HOODED CROW
JUNGLE FOWL
KINGFISHER
KOOKABURRA
MALLEE FOWL
MUTTONBIRD
NIGHT HERON
NUTCRACKER
PRATINCOLE
SACRED IBIS
SADDLEBACK
SAGE GROUSE
SANDERLING
SANDGROUSE
SCREECH OWL
SHEARWATER
SHEATHBILL
SONG THRUSH
SUN BITTERN
TAILORBIRD
TROPIC BIRD
TURTLE DOVE
WEAVERBIRD
WOODPECKER
WOOD PIGEON
ZEBRA FINCH

11
BLACK GROUSE
BRUSH TURKEY
BUTCHERBIRD
BUTTON QUAIL
CANADA GOOSE
CARRION CROW
DIAMONDBIRD
FRIGATE BIRD
GNATCATCHER
GOLDEN EAGLE
HERRING GULL
HUMMINGBIRD
LAMMERGEIER
LAUGHING OWL
MOCKINGBIRD
MUSCOVY DUCK
NIGHTINGALE
REED WARBLER
SNOW BUNTING
SPARROWHAWK
STONE CURLEW
STORM PETREL
TREECREEPER
WALLCREEPER

WEAVERFINCH
WHITETHROAT
WOODCREEPER
WREN BABBLER

12
BURROWING OWL
CAPERCAILLIE
CUCKOO-SHRIKE
DABBLING DUCK
FAIRY PENGUIN
FLOWERPECKER
GREYLAG GOOSE
HEDGE SPARROW
HONEYCREEPER
HOUSE SPARROW
LANNER FALCON
MANDARIN DUCK
MARSH HARRIER
MISTLE THRUSH
MOURNING DOVE
PERCHING DUCK
SHOVELER DUCK
STANDARDWING
UMBRELLA BIRD
WHIPPOORWILL
YELLOWHAMMER

13
ADJUTANT STORK
AMERICAN EAGLE
BARNACLE GOOSE
CROCODILE BIRD
ELEPHANT BIRDS
FAIRY BLUEBIRD
HARLEQUIN DUCK
HAWAIIAN GOOSE
LONG-TAILED TIT
OYSTERCATCHER
PASSERINE BIRD
SECRETARY BIRD
WHISTLING DUCK
WHOOPING CRANE

14
BEARDED VULTURE
BIRD OF PARADISE
DARWIN'S FINCHES
EMPEROR PENGUIN
GOLDEN PHEASANT
GRIFFON VULTURE
OWLET FROGMOUTH
PLAINS-WANDERER

15+
BALTIMORE ORIOLE
GREAT CRESTED GREBE
IVORY-BILLED
 WOODPECKER
LAUGHING JACKASS
PASSENGER PIGEON
PEREGRINE FALCON
PHILIPPINE EAGLE
TYRANT FLYCATCHER

ADJECTIVES

BIRD	ADJECTIVE	BIRD	ADJECTIVE
BIRD	AVIAN	PARROT	PSITTACINE
CROW	CORVINE	SONGBIRD	OSCINE
DOVE	COLUMBINE	SPARROW	PASSERINE
EAGLE	AQUILINE	SWALLOW	HIRUNDINE
FOWL	GALLINACEOUS	THRUSH	TURDINE

FISH

3	TUNNY	PIRANHA	STINGRAY
COD		POLLACK	STURGEON
DAB	**6**	POMPANO	SWAMP EEL
EEL	BARBEL	RATFISH	TOADFISH
GAR	BELUGA	SARDINE	WOLF FISH
IDE	BLENNY	SAWFISH	
RAY	BONITO	SCULPIN	**9**
	BOWFIN	SEA BASS	ANGELFISH
4	BURBOT	SNAPPER	BARRACUDA
BASS	GUNNEL	SUNFISH	BLUE SHARK
CARP	KIPPER	TELEOST	CLINGFISH
CHAR	MARLIN	TORPEDO	CONGER EEL
CHUB	MINNOW	WHITING	GLASSFISH
DACE	MULLET		GLOBEFISH
DORY	PLAICE	**8**	GOOSEFISH
FISH	PUFFER	ALBACORE	GRENADIER
GOBY	REMORA	BLUEFISH	KILLIFISH
HAKE	SAITHE	BRISLING	LATIMERIA
LING	SALMON	BROTULID	LEMON SOLE
OPAH	TARPON	BULLHEAD	MURRAY COD
ORFE	TURBOT	CAVE FISH	PEARLFISH
PIKE	WEEVER	CHARACIN	PIKEPERCH
RUDD	WRASSE	CHIMAERA	PILOT FISH
SHAD		DEVIL RAY	PLACODERM
SOLE	**7**	DRAGONET	PORBEAGLE
TOPE	ALEWIFE	DRUMFISH	RED MULLET
TUNA	ANCHOVY	FILEFISH	RED SALMON
	BATFISH	FLATFISH	STARGAZER
5	CATFISH	FLATHEAD	STONE BASS
BLEAK	CICHLID	FLOUNDER	STONEFISH
BREAM	CROAKER	FROGFISH	SWORDFISH
BRILL	DOGFISH	GOLDFISH	SWORDTAIL
DANIO	EELPOUT	GRAYLING	THREADFIN
GRUNT	GARFISH	JOHN DORY	TIGERFISH
GUPPY	GARPIKE	LUNGFISH	TOP MINNOW
LOACH	GOURAMI	MACKEREL	TRUNKFISH
MOLLY	GROUPER	MANTA RAY	WHITEBAIT
PERCH	GUDGEON	MONKFISH	WHITEFISH
PORGY	GURNARD	MOONFISH	WRECKFISH
ROACH	HADDOCK	MORAY EEL	ZEBRA FISH
SAURY	HAGFISH	PILCHARD	
SHARK	HALIBUT	PIPEFISH	**10**
SKATE	HERRING	SAILFISH	ANGLERFISH
SMELT	HOGFISH	SEA BREAM	ARCHER FISH
SPRAT	ICEFISH	SEA HORSE	BOMBAY DUCK
TENCH	LAMPREY	SEA PERCH	COELACANTH
TETRA	MUDFISH	SEA ROBIN	CORNETFISH
TROUT	OARFISH	SKIPJACK	CYCLOSTOME

DAMSELFISH
DRAGONFISH
FLYING FISH
GHOST SHARK
GUITAR FISH
LUMPSUCKER
MIDSHIPMAN
MUDSKIPPER
NEEDLEFISH
NURSE SHARK
PADDLEFISH
PARROT FISH

PINK SALMON
PLACODERMI
RIBBONFISH
SHIELD FERN
SILVERSIDE
TIGER SHARK
WHALE SHARK
WHITE SHARK

11
ELECTRIC EEL
ELECTRIC RAY
GOBLIN SHARK

HATCHETFISH
LANTERN FISH
MOORISH IDOL
STICKLEBACK
SURGEONFISH
TRIGGERFISH

12+
BASKING SHARK
CLIMBING PERCH
FIGHTING FISH
FOUR-EYED FISH
GREENLAND SHARK

HAMMERHEAD SHARK
LABYRINTH FISH
MACKEREL SHARK
MILLER'S THUMB
MOUTHBROODER
PORCUPINE FISH
REQUIEM SHARK
SCORPION FISH
SOCKEYE SALMON
THRESHER SHARK
YELLOWFIN TUNA

SEASHELLS

3
SUN

4
HARP

5
TULIP

6
NUTMEG

7
JUNONIA
SUNDIAL

8
DYE MUREX
LION'S PAW
NOBLE PEN
PHEASANT
TURK'S CUP

9
ANGEL WING
BAT VOLUTE
BURSA FROG
GIANT CLAM
PINK CONCH
ROTA MUREX
SPINY VASE
TELESCOPE
TENT OLIVE
WEDGE CLAM

10
BLUE MUSSEL
CAMEO HELMT
COAT-OF-MAIL
CROWN CONCH
DELPHINULA
DRUPE SNAIL
EYED COWRIE
PAPERY RAPA
QUAHOG CLAM
SCALED WORM
WINGED FROG

11
BEAR PAW CLAM
CLIONE SNAIL
FRONS OYSTER
GREEN TURBAN
HEART COCKLE
MUSIC VOLUTE
ONYX SLIPPER
OSTRICH FOOT
PAPER BUBBLE
PEARL OYSTER
SACRED CHANK
TEXTILE CONE
TIGER COWRIE

12
AMORIA VOLUTE
ATLANTIC CONE
FLORIDA MITER
GAUDY ASAPHIS
GOLDEN COWRIE
GOLDEN TELLIN
LIMA FILE CLAM
MONEY COWRIES
PACIFIC AUGER
PARTRIDGE TUN
PELICAN'S FOOT
SCOTCH BONNET
SPIKED LIMPET
SPINDLE TIBIA

13
ANGULAR VOLUTE
BABLYON TURRID
BLEEDING TOOTH
CARDINAL MITER
COMMERCIAL TOP
COSTATE COCKLE
FIGHTING CONCH
GEOGRAPHY CONE
JACKKNIFE CLAM
JAPANESE CONES
PAPER NAUTILUS
PRICKLY HELMET

RIDGED ABALONE
SPIRAL BABYLON
SUNRISE TELLIN
TURKEY WING ARK
VENUS COMB CLAM

14
CHANNELED WHELK
DISTAFF SPINDLE
ELEGANT FIMBRIA
EPISCOPAL MITER
IMPERIAL VOLUTE
INDONESIAN CLAM
LEUCODON COWRIE
LEWIS' MOON SNAIL
LIGHTNING WHELK
PANAMANIAN CONE
PHILIPPINE CONE
POLYNESIAN CONE
TAPESTRY TURBAN
TRITON'S TRUMPET
VENUS COMB MUREX

15
BITTERSWEET CLAM
BULL-MOUTH HELMET
JAPANESE CARRIER
NEW ENGLAND WHELK
PANAMANIAN AUGER
PILGRIM'S SCALLOP
SUNBURST CARRIER
TURRITELLA SNAIL
WATERING POT CLAM
WEST INDIAN CHANK
WEST AFRICAN CONE

16
ASIAN MOON SCALLOP
ATLANTIC SURF CLAM
DONKEY EAR ABALONE
EDIBLE BAY SCALLOP
FRILLED DOGWINKLE
GLORY-OF-INDIA CONE
ORANGE-MOUTH OLIVE
PAGODA PERIWINKLE

PERPLICATE VOLUTE
PINK-MOUTHED MUREX
ROOSTERTAIL CONCH
WEDDING CAKE VENUS

17
AUSTRALIAN TRUMPET
CHAMBERED NAUTILUS
FLORIDA HORSE CONCH
PACIFIC WING OYSTER
SANTA CRUZ LATIAXIS
VIOLET SPIDER CONCH

18
ATLANTIC DEER
  COWRIE
GIANT KNOBBED
  CERITH
GLORY-OF-THE-SEAS
  CONE
GREAT KEYHOLE
  LIMPET
PACIFIC GRINNING TUN
PRECIOUS
  WENTLETRAP
WHITE-SPOTTED
  MARGIN

19
TANKERVILLE'S
  ANCILLA

20+
ARTHRITIC SPIDER
  CONCH
ATLANTIC THORNY
  OYSTER
COLOURFUL ATLANTIC
  MOON
ELEPHANT'S SNOUT
  VOLUTE
IMBRICATE CUP-AND-
  SAUCER
MIRACULOUS
  THATCHERIA

MARSUPIALS

5
BILBY
KOALA

6
CUSCUS
NUMBAT
WOMBAT

7
DASYURE
DUNNART

OPOSSUM
WALLABY

8
KANGAROO

9
BANDICOOT
KOALA BEAR
NATIVE CAT
PHALANGER
SPRINGBOK

THYLACINE

10
HONEY MOUSE
SPRINGBUCK

11
DIPROTODONT
NOTOTHERIUM
PYGMY GLIDER
RAT KANGAROO

13
MARSUPIAL MOLE
POLYPROTODONT

14
MARSUPIAL MOUSE
TASMANIAN DEVIL

15
FLYING PHALANGER

REPTILES AND AMPHIBIANS

3
ASP
BOA
OLM

4
FROG
NEWT
TOAD

5
ADDER
AGAMA
COBRA
GECKO
KRAIT
MAMBA
SIREN
SKINK
SNAKE
TOKAY
VIPER

6
CAYMAN
GAVIAL
IGUANA
LIZARD
MOLOCH
MUGGER
PYTHON
TAIPAN

TURTLE
ZALTYS

7
AXOLOTL
GHARIAL
REPTILE
TUATARA

8
ANACONDA
BASILISK
BULLFROG
CONGO EEL
MATAMATA
MOCCASIN
MUDPUPPY
PIT VIPER
RINGHALS
SEA SNAKE
SLOWWORM
TERRAPIN
TORTOISE
TREE FROG

9
ALLIGATOR
BLINDWORM
BOOMSLANG
BOX TURTLE
CAECILIAN
CHAMELEON

CROCODILE
HAIRY FROG
PUFF ADDER
TREE SNAKE
VINE SNAKE
WART SNAKE
WHIP SNAKE

10
BLACK SNAKE
BUSHMASTER
CHUCKWALLA
CLAWED FROG
COPPERHEAD
CORAL SNAKE
FER-DE-LANCE
GLASS SNAKE
GRASS SNAKE
HELLBENDER
HORNED TOAD
NATTERJACK
POND TURTLE
SALAMANDER
SAND LIZARD
SIDEWINDER
WATER SNAKE
WORM LIZARD

11
AMPHISBAENA
CONSTRICTOR
COTTONMOUTH

DIAMONDBACK
FLYING SNAKE
GABOON VIPER
GILA MONSTER
GOLIATH FROG
GREEN TURTLE
HORNED VIPER
MIDWIFE TOAD
RATTLESNAKE
SMOOTH SNAKE

12
FLYING LIZARD
HORNED LIZARD
KOMODO DRAGON

13
BEARDED LIZARD
FRILLED LIZARD
GIANT TORTOISE
MANGROVE SNAKE
MONITOR LIZARD
RUSSELL'S VIPER
SPADEFOOT TOAD
WATER MOCCASIN

14+
FIRE SALAMANDER
HAWKSBILL TURTLE
LEATHERBACK TURTLE
SNAKE-NECKED TURTLE
SOFT-SHELLED TURTLE

INSECTS

3
ANT
BEE
BUG
FLY

4
FLEA
GNAT
WASP

5
APHID
DRONE
LOUSE
MIDGE

6
BEDBUG
BEETLE
BOT FLY
CAPSID
CHAFER
CHIGOE
CICADA
EARWIG
GAD FLY
HORNET
LOCUST
LOOPER
MAGGOT
MANTIS
MAYFLY
SAWFL
THRIPS
WEEVIL

7
ANTLION
ARMY ANT
BLOWFLY
CRICKET
CUTWORM
DIPTERA
FIRE ANT
FIREFLY
KATYDID
PROTURA
SANDFLY
STYLOPS
TERMITE

8
ALDERFLY
ARMY WORM
BLACKFLY
BOOKWORM
CRANEFLY
FIREBRAT
FRUIT FLY
GALL WASP
GLOWWORM
GREENFLY
HONEY ANT
HONEYBEE
HORNTAIL
HORSE FLY
HOUSEFLY
HOVERFLY
LACEWING
LADYBIRD
MASON BEE
MEALWORM
MEALYBUG
MOSQUITO
PHASMIDA
PLANT BUG
SHEEP KED
SILKWORM
SNAKEFLY
STINK BUG
STONEFLY
WATER BUG
WHITE FLY
WIREWORM
WOODWASP
WOODWORM

9
AMAZON ANT
ANOPHELES
BLOODWORM
BOOKLOUSE
BUMBLEBEE
CADDIS FLY
CHINCH BUG
COCKROACH
CORN BORER
DAMSELFLY
DOBSONFLY
DOR BEETLE

DRAGONFLY
DRIVER ANT
GALL MIDGE
GROUND BUG
ICHNEUMON
LAC INSECT
OIL BEETLE
ROBBER FLY
SCREWWORM
SHIELD BUG
TSETSE FLY
WARBLE FLY
WHIRLIGIG

10
BARK BEETLE
BLUEBOTTLE
BOLL WEEVIL
COCKCHAFER
COLEOPTERA
DIGGER WASP
DROSOPHILA
DUNG BEETLE
FROGHOPPER
JUNE BEETLE
LEAF BEETLE
LEAF HOPPER
LEAF INSECT
PHYLLOXERA
POND SKATER
POTTER WASP
ROVE BEETLE
SILVERFISH
SPANISH FLY
SPIDER WASP
SPITTLEBUG
SPRINGTAIL
STAG BEETLE
TREEHOPPER
WEBSPINNER
WOOLLY BEAR

11
ASSASSIN BUG
BACKSWIMMER
BLACK BEETLE
BRISTLETAIL
BUFFALO GNAT
BUSH CRICKET

CANTHARIDIN
CATERPILLAR
CLICK BEETLE
GRASSHOPPER
MOLE CRICKET
PLANT HOPPER
SCALE INSECT
SCORPION FLY
STICK INSECT
TIGER BEETLE
WATER BEETLE

12
CACTOBLASTIS
CARPENTER BEE
CARPET BEETLE
DIVING BEETLE
GROUND BEETLE
HERCULES MOTH
SCARAB BEETLE
SEXTON BEETLE
WATER BOATMAN
WATER STRIDER

13
BLISTER BEETLE
BURYING BEETLE
COTTON STAINER
DADDY LONGLEGS
ELM BARK BEETLE
GIANT WATER BUG
GOLIATH BEETLE
LEAFCUTTER ANT
LEAFCUTTER BEE
SOLDIER BEETLE
WATER SCORPION

14+
AMBROSIA BEETLE
BOMBARDIER BEETLE
CABBAGE ROOT FLY
COLORADO BEETLE
CUCKOO-SPIT INSECT
DARKLING BEETLE
DEATHWATCH BEETLE
DEVIL'S COACH HORSE
HERCULES BEETLE
SLAVE-MAKING ANT
TORTOISE BEETLE

BUTTERFLIES

3&4
OWL
BLUE
LEAF
MONK

5
ARGUS
BROWN
DRYAD
FRIAR
HEATH
JOKER
NYMPH
SATYR
SNOUT
WHITE
ZEBRA

6
ACRAEA
APOLLO
COPPER
DIADEM
GLIDER
HERMIT
MORPHO

7
ADMIRAL

FESTOON
LEOPARD
MONARCH
RINGLET
SKIPPER
SULPHUR

8
BIRDWING
BLACK EYE
BLACK-TIP
CARDINAL
CHARAXES
CYMOTHOE
GRAYLING
MILKWEED

9
ATLAS BLUE
BATH WHITE
BRIMSTONE
CLEOPATRA
COMMODORE
GOLDEN TIP
HACKBERRY
METALMARK
ORANGE TIP
SWORDTAIL
WALL BROWN

WOOD WHITE

10
ADONIS BLUE
ARCTIC BLUE
ARRAN BROWN
BLACK SATYR
BUSH BEAUTY
CRIMSON TIP
FRITILLARY
GATEKEEPER
GRASS JEWEL
HAIRSTREAK
LARGE WHITE
PLAIN TIGER
RED ADMIRAL
SILVER-LINE
SMALL WHITE

11
AMANDA'S BLUE
FOREST QUEEN
GRASS YELLOW
MEADOW BROWN
PAINTED LADY
PARNASSIANS
SWALLOWTAIL

12
DOTTED BORDER

MAP BUTTERFLY
MARBLED WHITE
SPECKLED WOOD
WHITE ADMIRAL

13
CLOUDED YELLOW
CHALK-HILL BLUE
PEARL CRESCENT
PURPLE EMPEROR
TORTOISESHELL
WOODLAND BROWN

14
AFRICAN MIGRANT
COMMA BUTTERFLY
LEMON TRAVELLER
MOUNTAIN BEAUTY
PAINTED EMPRESS

15+
CAMBERWELL BEAUTY
GREAT SOOTY SATYR
MOTHER-OF-PEARL
   BLUE
NETTLE-TREE
   BUTTERFLY
PEACOCK BUTTERFLY
TWO-TAILED PASHA

MOTHS

2&3
IO
OWL

4
GOAT
HAWK
PUSS

5
ATLAS
EGGAR
FAIRY
GHOST
GYPSY
OWLET
REGAL

SWIFT
TIGER
YUCCA

6
BURNET
CALICO
ERMINE
LAPPET

7
BAGWORM
CLOTHES
EMPEROR
FLANNEL
PYRALID
TUSSOCK

URANIAS

8
CINNABAR
FORESTER
SILKWORM

9
AILANTHUS
BRAHMAEID
CARPENTER
CLEARWING
GEOMETRID
SALT MARSH
SATURNIID
UNDERWING

10
BLACK WITCH
LEAF ROLLER

11
HUMMINGBIRD
OLETHREUTID
PYROMORPHID

13
BLINDED SPHINX
GIANT SILKWORM

14
DEATH'S HEAD HAWK
PANDORA'S SPHINX

PLANTS AND FLOWERS

3
ABE
HOP
IVY
RYE

4
DOCK
FERN
FLAG (*Iris*)
FLAX
HEMP
IRIS (flag, sweet flag, gladdon)
JUTE
LILY
PINK (carnation)
RAPE
REED
RICE
ROSE
RUSH
TARE
UPAS
WOAD

5
AGAVE
ASTER (Michaelmas daisy)
AVENS
BRIAR
CANNA
CYCAD
DAISY
HENNA
JALAP
KUDZU
LOTUS
LUPIN
OXLIP (*Primula*)
PANSY (*Viola*)
PEONY
PHLOX
POPPY
SEDGE
SENNA
SISAL
TULIP
VIOLA (pansy, violet)

6
ALLIUM
ALSIKE (clover)
BALSAM
BLUETS
BRYONY
CACTUS
CLOVER (trefoil)
COLEUS
COTTON
COWPEA
CROCUS
DAHLIA

DARNEL
FESCUE
HYSSOP
MADDER
MEDICK
MILLET
NETTLE (*Urtica*)
ORCHID
PETREA
PEYOTE (cactus)
RATTAN
SALVIA
SPURGE
SQUILL (*Scilla*)
SUNDEW
TEASEL
THRIFT
TWITCH (couch grass)
VIOLET (*Viola*)
YARROW
ZINNIA

7
ACONITE (monkshood)
ALFALFA
ALKANET
ANEMONE
ASTILBE
BEGONIA
BISTORT (snakeroot)
BRACKEN (fern)
BUGLOSS
BULRUSH (reed mace)
BURDOCK
CAMPION
CATMINT
CLARKIA
COWSLIP (*Primula*)
DAY LILY
DOGBANE
DOG ROSE
FIGWORT
FREESIA
FROG-BIT
GENTIAN
GLADDON (*Iris*)
GUARANA
HEMLOCK
HENBANE
HONESTY (*Lunaria*)
JONQUIL (*Narcissus*)
KINGCUP (marsh marigold)
LOBELIA
MILFOIL (yarrow)
MULLEIN (Aaron's rod)
OPUNTIA (prickly pear)
PAPYRUS
PETUNIA
PIGWEED
PRIMULA (cowslip, primrose)
RAGWORT

ROSELLE
SAGUARO
SANICLE
SPURREY
THISTLE
TIMOTHY
TOBACCO
TREFOIL (clover)
VERBENA (vervain)
VERVAIN (*Verbena*)

8
ACANTHUS
AGRIMONY
ARUM LILY (cuckoopint, lords-
and-ladies)
ASPHODEL
AURICULA
BEDSTRAW
BERGENIA
BINDWEED (*Convolvulus*)
BLUEBELL
CATBRIER
CAT'S TAIL (reedmace)
CHARLOCK
CLEAVERS (goosegrass)
CLEMATIS (old man's beard,
traveller's joy)
CROWFOOT
CYLCAMEN
DAFFODIL
DIANTHUS
EELGRASS
EUCHARIS (amazon lily)
FLEABANE
FLEAWORT
FOXGLOVE (*Digitalis*)
FUMITORY
GERANIUM (*Pelargonium*)
GLOXINIA
GOUTWEED (ground elder)
HAREBELL
HAWKWEED
HENEQUEN
HIBISCUS (rose of China, rose of
Sharon)
HORNWORT
HYACINTH
ICE PLANT
KNAPWEED
LADY FERN
LARKSPUR
LUNGWORT
MARIGOLD
MILKWEED
MILKWORT
MOSS PINK (*Phlox*)
PLANTAIN
PLUMBAGO
POLYPODY
PRIMROSE (*Primula*)

REEDMACE (bulrush, cat's-tail)
ROCK ROSE
SAINFOIN
SALTWORT
SAMPHIRE
SCABIOUS
SEED FERN
SELF HEAL
SHAMROCK (clover, medick, wood sorrel)
SNOWDROP
SOAPWORT
SWEET PEA
TOAD LILY (fritillary)
TUBEROSE
VALERIAN
VERONICA (speedwell)
WAXPLANT
WOODBINE (virginia creeper)
WOODRUSH
WORMWOOD

9
AARON'S ROD (mullein)
AMARYLLIS (belladonna lily)
ANTHURIUM
AQUILEGIA (columbine)
ARROWROOT
BLUEGRASS
BROOMRAPE
BRYOPHYTE
BUCKWHEAT
BUTTERCUP
CAMPANULA (Canterbury bell)
CANDYTUFT
CARNATION (pink)
CELANDINE
CHICKWEED
CINERARIA
COCKLEBUR
COCKSFOOT (orchard grass)
COLTSFOOT
COLUMBINE (*Aquilegia*)
CORDGRASS
CORN POPPY
CORYDALIS
CYMBIDIUM (orchid)
DANDELION
DEVIL'S FIG (prickly poppy)
DOG VIOLET
EDELWEISS
EGLANTINE (sweet briar)
EYEBRIGHT
GERMANDER
GLADIOLUS
GLASSWORT
GOLDENROD (*Solidago*)
GOOSEFOOT (pigweed)
GRASS TREE
GROUND IVY
GROUNDSEL
HELLEBORE (Christmas rose)
HERB PARIS
HOLLYHOCK

HORSETAIL
HOUSELEEK
IMPATIENS (touch-me-not, busy Lizzie)
JABORANDI
MARE'S TAIL
MONEYWORT (creeping jenny)
MONKSHOOD (aconite)
MOSCHATEL (townhall clock)
NARCISSUS (jonquil)
PATCHOULI
PIMPERNEL
PYRETHRUM
QUILLWORT
ROYAL FERN
SAFFLOWER
SAXIFRAGE (London pride)
SNAKEROOT (bistort)
SPEEDWELL (*Veronica*)
SPIKENARD
STONECROP
SUNFLOWER
SWEET FLAG (*Iris*)
TORMENTIL
WATER LILY
WITCHWEED
WOUNDWORT

10
AGAPANTHUS
AMARANTHUS (love-lies-bleeding)
AMAZON LILY
ASPIDISTRA
BELLADONNA (deadly nightshade)
BUSY LIZZIE
BUTTERWORT
CHARMOMILE
CINQUEFOIL
CITRONELLA
CLIFFBREAK (fern)
CORNCOCKLE
CORNFLOWER
COUCH GRASS (twitch, quack grass)
COW PARSLEY
CRANESBILL
CUCKOOPINT (arum lily)
DAMASK ROSE
DRAGONROOT
DYER'S BROOM
FRITILLARY (snake's head, leopard lily, toad lily)
GAILLARDIA (blanket flowers)
GOATSBEARD
GOOSEGRASS (cleavers)
GRANADILLA (passionflower)
GREENBRIER (catbrier)
HELIOTROPE
HERB ROBERT
JIMSONWEED (thorn apple)
LADY'S SMOCK
MARGUERITE (oxeye daisy)

MIGNONETTE
MONTBRETIA
MOONFLOWER (morning glory)
NASTURTIUM
OPIUM POPPY
OXEYE DAISY (marguerite)
PENNYROYAL
PERIWINKLE
POLYANTHUS (*Primula*)
QUACK GRASS (couch grass)
SHIELD FERN
SNAKE'S HEAD
SNAPDRAGON (*Antirrhinum*)
SOW THISTLE
SPIDERWORT
SPLEENWORT
STITCHWORT
SWEET BRIAR (eglantine)
THORN APPLE (jimsonweed)
TOUCH-ME-NOT
WALLFLOWER
WATERCRESS
WELSH POPPY
WILLOWHERB
WOOD SORREL

11
ANTIRRHINUM (snapdragon)
BISHOP'S WEED (ground elder)
BITTERSWEET (woody nightshade)
BLADDERWORT
CALCEOLARIA
CANARY GRASS
CONVOLVULUS (bindweed)
FIG MARIGOLD
FORGET-ME-NOT
GILLYFLOWER (gilliflower, pink, carnation)
GLOBE FLOWER
GROUND ELDER (goutweed, bishop's weed)
HELLEBORINE (orchid)
HONEYSUCKLE
IPECACUANHA
KANGAROO PAW
LEOPARD LILY (fritillary, blackberry lily)
LONDON PRIDE (saxifrage)
LOVE-IN-A-MIST
MARRAM GRASS
MARSH MALLOW
MEADOWSWEET
PAMPAS GRASS
PONTENTILLA (cinquefoil)
PRICKLY PEAR (cactus)
RAGGED ROBIN
RED-HOT POKER
ROSE OF CHINA (*Hibiscus*)
RUBBER PLANT
SEA LAVENDER
SHRIMP PLANT
SPIDER PLANT
ST JOHN'S WORT

STRAWFLOWER
WELWITSCHIA
WINTERGREEN

12
AUTUMN CROCUS (meadow saffron)
CENTURY PLANT
COMPASS PLANT (turpentine plant)
GLOBE THISTLE
LADY'S SLIPPER
MONKEYFLOWER
MORNING GLORY (moonflower)
OLD MAN CACTUS
OLD MAN'S BEARD (*Clematis*)
ORCHARD GRASS (cocksfoot)
PITCHER PLANT
PRICKLY POPPY (devil's fig)
QUAKING GRASS
ROSE OF SHARON (*Hibiscus*)
SOLOMON'S SEAL
SWEET WILLIAM
VENUS FLYTRAP

13
AFRICAN VIOLET
BIRD'S NEST FERN

BLEEDING HEART
CALYPSO ORCHID
CARRION FLOWER
CHRISTMAS ROSE (hellebore)
CHRYSANTHEMUM
CREEPING JENNY (moneywort)
ELEPHANT GRASS
GARLIC MUSTARD (jack-by-the-hedge)
GRAPE HYACINTH
MARSH MARIGOLD (kingcup)
MEADOW SAFFRON (autumn crocus)
PASSIONFLOWER (granadilla)
RANUNCULACEAE
ROSE OF JERICHO
SLIPPER ORCHID
TOWNHALL CLOCK (moschatel)
TRAVELLER'S JOY (*Clematis*)
WINTER ACONITE

14
BELLADONNA LILY (*Amaryllis*)
BLACKBERRY LILY (leopard lily)
BLANKET FLOWERS
CANTERBURY BELL (*Campanula*)
CASTOR-OIL PLANT
HEDGEHOG CACTUS

JACK-BY-THE-HEDGE (garlic mustard)
LORDS-AND-LADIES (arum lily)
MAIDENHAIR FERN
TRUMPET CREEPER

15+
BIRD-OF-PARADISE FLOWER
BIRD'S NEST ORCHID
BLACK NIGHTSHADE
DEADLY NIGHTSHADE (belladonna)
DOG'S TOOTH VIOLET
ENCHANTER'S NIGHTSHADE
GRASS OF PARNASSUS
LILY-OF-THE-VALLEY
LOVE-LIES-BLEEDING (*Amaranthus*)
MICHAELMAS DAISY (*Aster*)
ORGAN-PIPE CACTUS
SNOW-ON-THE-MOUNTAIN
SQUIRTING CUCUMBER
STAR OF BETHLEHEM
TURPENTINE PLANT (compass plant)
WOODY NIGHTSHADE (bittersweet)

PARTS OF A FLOWER

3
LIP

4
CYME
SPUR

5
BRACT
CALYX
GLUME
LEMMA
OVARY
OVULE
PALEA
PETAL
SEPAL
SPIKE
STYLE
TEPAL
UMBEL

6
ANTHER
CARPEL
CATKIN
CORYMB
FLORET
POLLEN
RACEME
SPADIX
SPATHE
STAMEN
STIGMA

7
COROLLA
NECTARY
PANICLE
PEDICEL
RHACHIS

8
BRACTEDE
CYATHIUM

FILAMENT
LADICULE
NUCELLUS
PEDUNCLE
PLACENTA
SPIKELET

9
CAPITULUM
GYNOECIUM
INVOLUCEL
INVOLUCRE
POLLINIUM

10
ANDROECIUM
CARPOPHORE
HYPANTHIUM
RECEPTACLE

11
MONOCHASIUM
POLLEN GRAIN

PLANT PEOPLE

PLANT – named after

AUBRIETIA – Claude Aubriet 18th-century French painter of flowers and animals
BANKSIA – Sir Joseph Banks (1743–1820) British botanist and explorer
BARTSIA – Johann Bartsch (d. 1738) German botanist
BAUERA – Franz (1758–1840) and Ferdinand (1760–1826) Bauer, Australian botanical artists
BAUHINIA – Jean and Gaspard Bauhin 16th-century French herbalists
BEGONIA – Michel Bégon (1638–1710) French patron of science
BETONY – the Vettones an ancient Iberian tribe
BIGNONIA – the Abbé Jean-Paul Bignon (1662–1743)
BOLTONIA – James Bolton 18th-century English botanist
BOUGAINVILLEA – Louis Antoine de Bougainville (1729–1811) French navigator
BOYSENBERRY – Rudolph Boysen, US botanist who developed it
BRUCINE – James Bruce (1730–94) Scottish explorer of Africa
BUDDLEIA – A. Buddle (d. 1715) British botanist
CAMELLIA – Georg Josef Kamel (1661–1706) Moravian Jesuit missionary, who introduced it to Europe
CATTLEYA – William Cattley (d. 1832) English botanist
CLARKIA – William Clark (1770–1838) US explorer and frontiersman, who discovered it
CLAYTONIA – John Clayton (1693–1773) US botanist
CLINTONIA – De Witt Clinton (1769–1828) US politician and naturalist
COLLINSIA – Zaccheus Collins (1764–1831) US botanist
DAHLIA – Anders Dahl 18th-century Swedish botanist
DEUTZIA – Jean Deutz 18th-century Dutch patron of botany
DIEFFENBACHIA – Ernst Dieffenbach (d. 1855) German horticulturist
DOUGLAS FIR – David Douglas (1798–1834) Scottish botanist
ESCHSCHOLTZIA – J. F. von Eschscholtz (1743–1831) German naturalist
FORSYTHIA – William Forsyth (1737–1804) English botanist
FREESIA – F. H. T. Freese (d. 1876) German physician
FUCHSIA – Leonhard Fuchs (1501–66) German botanist
GAILLARDIA – Gaillard de Marentonneau 18th-century French amateur botanist
GALTONIA – Sir Francis Galton (1822–1911) English explorer and scientist
GARDENIA – Dr Alexander Garden (1730–91) US botanist
GAZANIA – Theodore of Gaza 1398–1478 translator of the botanical treatises of Theophrastus
GENTIAN – Gentius, a 2nd-century BC Ilyrian king, reputedly the first to use it medicinally
GERBERA – Traugott Gerber (d. 1743) German naturalist
GLOXINIA – Benjamin P. Gloxin 18th-century German physician and botanist who first described it
GODETIA – C. H. Godet (d. 1879) Swiss botanist
GREVILLEA – C. F. Greville (1749–1809) a founder of the Royal Horticultural Society
GRINDELIA – David Hieronymus Grindel (1777–1836) Russian botanist
GUNNERA – J. E. Gunnerus (1718–73) Norwegian bishop and botanist
HAKEA – C. L. von Hake (d. 1818) German botanist
HEUCHERA – J. H. Heucher (1677–1747) German doctor and botanist
HOSTA – N. T. Host (1761–1834) Austrian physician
HOUSTONIA – Dr. William Houston (d. 1733) Scottish botanist
INCARVILLEA – Pierre d'Incarville (1706–57) French missionary
KALMIA – Peter Kalm (1715–79) Swedish botanist and pupil of Linnaeus
KNIPHOFIA – J. H. Kniphof (1704–63) German doctor and botanist
KOCHIA – W. D. J. Koch (1771–1849) German botanist
LAVATERA – the two brothers Lavater 18th-century Swiss doctors and naturalists
LEYLAND CYPRESS – C. J. Leyland (1849–1926) British horticulturalist
LOBELIA – Matthias de Lobel (1538–1616) Flemish botanist
LOGANBERRY – James H. Logan (1841–1928) US judge and horticulturist who first grew it (1881)
MACADAMIA – John Macadam (1827–65) Australian chemist
MAGNOLIA – Pierre Magnol (1638–1715) French botanist
MAHONIA – Bernard McMahon (d. 1816) US botanist
MONTBRETIA – A. F. E. Coquebert de Montbret (1780–1801) French botanist
PAULOWNIA – Anna Paulovna, daughter of Paul I of Russia
POINCIANA – M. de Poinci 17th-century governor of the French Antilles
RAUWOLFIA – Leonhard Rauwolf (d. 1596) German botanist
RUDBECKIA – Olaus Rudbeck (1630–1702) Swedish botanist
SAINTPAULIA – Baron W. von Saint Paul (d. 1910) German soldier who discovered it

SEQUOIA – Sequoya known also as George Guess (?1770–1843) US Indian scholar and leader
STRELITZIA – Charlotte of Mecklenburg-Strelitz (1744–1818) queen of Great Britain and Ireland
THUNBERGIA – K. P. Thunberg (1743–1822) Swedish traveller and botanist
TILLANDSIA – Elias Tillands (d. 1693) Finno-Swedish botanist
TIMOTHY GRASS – a Timothy Hanson, who brought it to colonial Carolina
TRADESCANTIA – John Tradescant (1570–1638) English botanist and gardener
WEIGELA – C. E. Weigel (1748–1831) German physician
WELLINGTONIA – the 1st Duke of Wellington
WELWITSCHIA – F. M. J. Welwitsch (1807–72) Portuguese botanist, born in Austria
WISTERIA – Caspar Wistar (1761–1818) US anatomist
YOUNGBERRY – B. M. Young, US fruit-grower who was first to cultivate it (circa 1900)
ZINNIA – J. G. Zinn (d. 1759) German botanist
ZOYSIA – Karl von Zois (d. 1800) German botanist

TREES AND SHRUBS

3
ASH
BOX
ELM
FIG
FIR
MAY (hawthorn)
OAK
TEA
YEW

4
ANIL
COCA
DATE (palm)
KAVA
KOLA (cola)
NIPA (palm)
PALM
PINE
TEAK

5
ALDER
ASPEN
BALSA
BEECH (*Fagus*)
BIRCH
BROOM
CACAO
CAPER
CEDAR
EBONY
ELDER
ERICA (heath, heather)
FURZE (gorse)
GORSE (furze)
HAZEL
HEATH (*Erica*)
HOLLY
KARRI
LARCH
LILAC
MAPLE
OSIER (willow)
PECAN (hickory)

ROWAN (mountain ash)
SAVIN (juniper)
YUCCA

6
ACACIA
AZALEA
BAMBOO
BANYAN
BAOBAB
BONSAI
BO TREE
CASSIA
DAPHNE
DATURA
DEODAR (cedar)
DERRIS
DURIAN
GINKGO (maidenhair
  tree)
GOMUTI (sugar palm)
JARRAH
JINBUL (coolabar)
JUJUBE
LAUREL
LOCUST (carob tree, St
  John's bread)
MIMOSA
MOOLAR (coolabar)
MYRTLE
NUTMEG
ORACHE
POPLAR
PRIVET
PROTEA
REDBUD (judas tree)
RED GUM (*Eucalyptus*)
SALLOW (willow)
SALVIA
SAPPAN
SPRUCE
WILLOW

7
AMBOYNA
ARBUTUS

BEBEERU (greenheart)
BLUE GUM (*Eucalyptus*)
CORK OAK
CYPRESS
DOGWOOD
DURMAST (oak)
FUCHSIA
GUM TREE (*Eucalyptus*)
HEATHER (*Erica*, ling)
HEMLOCK
HICKORY (pecan)
HOLM OAK (holly oak)
JASMINE
JUNIPER
MUGWORT
  (wormwood)
OIL PALM
PALMYRA
REDWOOD
ROSEBAY (oleander)
SEQUOIA (redwood,
  wellingtonia, big tree)
SOURSOP
SPIRAEA
SYRINGA (lilac, mock
  orange)

8
BARBERRY (*Berberis*)
BASSWOOD
BAYBERRY
BERBERIS (barberry)
BERGAMOT
BLACKBOX (coolabar)
BOX ELDER (maple)
CALABASH
CAMELLIA
CINCHONA
COOLABAR (jinbul,
  moolar, blackbox,
  dwarf box)
CORKWOOD (balsa)
DWARF BOX (coolabar)
EUONYMUS (spindle
  tree)
GARDENIA

GUAIACUM
HAWTHORN (may)
HORNBEAM
IRONWOOD
JAPONICA
LABURNUM (golden
  chain, golden rain)
LAVENDER
MAGNOLIA (umbrella
  tree)
OLEANDER (rosebay)
QUANDONG
RAMBUTAN
ROSEWOOD
SAGO PALM
SALTBUSH
SILKY OAK
SWEET GUM
SWEETSOP
SYCAMORE (maple)
TAMARISK
TOLU TREE
VIBURNUM (snowball
  tree)
WISTERIA
WOODBINE (virginia
  creeper)
WORMWOOD
  (mugwort)

9
ARAUCARIA (monkey
  puzzle tree)
BEARBERRY
BUCKTHORN
CAROB TREE (locust)
CORAL TREE
EUPHORBIA (crown of
  thorns, poinsettia,
  snow-on-the-
  mountain)
FIRETHORN
  (pyracantha)
FLAME TREE
  (flamboyant)
FORSYTHIA

(golden bell)
JACARANDA
JUDAS TREE (redbud)
KALANCHOE
KAURI PINE
MANGROVES
MISTLETOE
PLANE TREE
POINCIANA
POISON IVY
SASSAFRAS
SATINWOOD
SCREW PINE
STINKWOOD
STONE PINE
SWEETWOOD
(greenheart)
TULIP TREE
WHITEBEAM

10
ARBOR VITAE
BIRD CHERRY
BRAZILWOOD
COFFEE TREE
COTTONWOOD
DOUGLAS FIR
DRAGON TREE
EUCALYPTUS (blue

gum, red gum)
FRANGIPANI (pagoda
tree, temple flower)
GOLDEN BELL
(forsythia)
GOLDEN RAIN
(laburnum)
GREENHEART
(sweetwood,
bebeeru)
JOSHUA TREE
MANGOSTEEN
MOCK ORANGE
PAGODA TREE
(frangipani)
POINSETTIA
PYRACANTHA
RAFFIA PALM
RUBBER TREE
WITCH HAZEL
YELLOWWOOD

11
BOTTLEBRUSH
CABBAGE PALM
CAMPHOR TREE
CHAULMOOGRA
COTONEASTER
CYPRESS PINE

DAWN REDWOOD
GOLDEN CHAIN
(laburnum)
GUELDER ROSE
HONEY LOCUST
JUMPING BEAN
MOUNTAIN ASH
(rowan)
PENCIL CEDAR (juniper)
PHYLLANTHUS
SERVICE TREE
SLIPPERY ELM
SPINDLE TREE
STEPHANOTIS
TALIPOT PALM

12
CHERRY LAUREL
CREOSOTE BUSH
CUCUMBER TREE
CUSTARD APPLE
(soursop, sweetsop)
INCENSE CEDAR
MONKEY PUZZLE
SNOWBALL TREE
ST JOHN'S BREAD
(locust)
SWAMP CYPRESS
TEMPLE FLOWER

(frangipani)
TREE OF HEAVEN
UMBRELLA TREE
(*Magnolia*)

13
BOUGAINVILLEA
BUTCHER'S BROOM
CROWN OF THORNS
HORSE CHESTNUT
JAPANESE CEDAR
JAPANESE MAPLE
PAPER MULBERRY
PEACOCK FLOWER
(flamboyant)
WAYFARING TREE

14+
FLAMBOYANT TREE
(flame tree, peacock
flower)
FLOWERING CURRANT
JERUSALEM CHERRY
MAIDENHAIR TREE
(ginkgo)
STRAWBERRY TREE
TRAVELLER'S TREE
TURPENTINE TREE
VIRGINIA CREEPER
(woodbine)

FRUIT, VEGETABLES, AND PULSES

3
FIG
PEA
YAM

4
BEET
EDDO (taro)
KALE
KIWI
LEEK
LIME (linden)
OKRA (lady's fingers,
gumbo)
PEAR
PLUM
SLOE
TARO (eddo, dasheen,
elephant's ear)

5
APPLE
CAROB
CHARD (swiss chard)
CRESS
GRAPE
GUAVA
GUMBO (okra)
LEMON

MANGO
MAIZE
MELON (musk,
honeydew,
canteloupe, water)
OLIVE
ONION (spring onion,
scallion)
PEACH
SWEDE

6
ALMOND
BANANA
CARROT
CASHEW
CELERY
CHERRY
CITRON
COB NUT
DAMSON
ENDIVE
GARLIC
LENTIL
LICHEE
LINDEN (lime)
LITCHI
LOQUAT

LYCHEE (litchi, lichee)
MANIOC (cassava)
MARROW
MEDLAR
ORANGE
PAWPAW
PEANUT (groundnut)
POTATO
PRUNUS (plum, almond,
apricot, cherry)
QUINCE
RADISH
SORREL
SQUASH
TOMATO
TURNIP
WALNUT

7
ALFALFA
APRICOT
AVOCADO
BRAMBLE (blackberry)
BULLACE (plum)
CABBAGE
CASSAVA (manioc)
CHICORY
CURRANT

DASHEEN (taro)
FILBERT
GENIPAP
GHERKIN
KUMQUAT
LETTUCE
PARSNIP
PUMPKIN
RHUBARB
SALSIFY
SATSUMA (tangerine)
SHALLOT
SPINACH

8
BEETROOT
BILBERRY (blaeberry,
huckleberry,
whortleberry)
BRASSICA (broccoli,
cabbage)
BROCCOLI
CAPSICUM (sweet
pepper, chilli, paprika)
CELERIAC (knob celery)
CHESTNUT
CHICK PEA
CUCUMBER

DEWBERRY
EARTHNUT (groundnut)
EGGPLANT (aubergine)
KOHLRABI (cabbage)
MANDARIN (tangerine)
MULBERRY
MUNG BEAN (green gram)
MUSHROOM
OLEASTER (Russian olive, trebizond date)
SCALLION
SUGAR PEA
SOYA BEAN
TAMARIND
ZUCCHINI (courgette)

9
ARTICHOKE
ASPARAGUS
AUBERGINE (eggplant)
BLAEBERRY (bilberry)
BROAD BEAN

CALABRESE
COCODEMER
COURGETTE (marrow, zucchini)
CRAB APPLE
CRANBERRY
CROWBERRY
DWARF BEAN
GREENGAGE
GROUNDNUT (peanut, earthnut)
MANGETOUT
NECTARINE
PERSIMMON
PETIT POIS
PINEAPPLE
PISTACHIO
RADICCHIO
RASPBERRY
SAPODILLA
STAR APPLE
SWEET CORN
TANGERINE

10
ADZUKI BEAN
BEAN SPROUT
BLACKBERRY (bramble)
BUTTER BEAN
CLEMENTINE
ELDERBERRY
FRENCH BEAN (kidney bean)
GOOSEBERRY
GRAPEFRUIT (*Citrus Paradisi*)
KIDNEY BEAN
LOGANBERRY
RED CABBAGE
REDCURRANT
RUNNER BEAN
SALAD ONION
SNAKE GOURD
STRAWBERRY
STRING BEAN
SWISS CHARD

11
CAULIFLOWER
COCONUT PALM
HORSERADISH
HUCKLEBERRY (bilberry)
POMEGRANATE
SPRING ONION
SWEET POTATO

12+
BLACKCURRANT
BRUSSELS SPROUT
ELEPHANT'S EAR (taro)
JERUSALEM ARTICHOKE
LADY'S FINGERS (okra)
MANGEL-WURZEL (beet)
SAVOY CABBAGE
WATER CHESTNUT
WHORTLEBERRY (bilberry)

FUNGI

4
CÈPE

5
MOREL
YEAST

6
AGARIC
INK CAP

7
AMANITA

BLEWITS
BOLETUS
CANDIDA
TRUFFLE

8
DEATH CAP
MUSHROOM
PUFFBALL

9
CUP FUNGUS
EARTHSTAR

FLY AGARIC
PSILOCYBE
RUST FUNGI
STINKHORN
TOADSTOOL

10
BREAD MOULD
CHAMPIGNON

11
ASCOMYCETES
ASPERGILLUS

CHANTERELLE
HONEY FUNGUS
PENICILLIUM
SLIME MOULDS

13
BRACKET FUNGUS

14
BASIDIOMYCETES

15
PARASOL MUSHROOM

FERNS

4
TREE

5
ROYAL

7
BRACKEN
OSMUNDA

8
LADY FERN
POLYPODY

STAGHORN

9
BIRD'S NEST

10
CLIFFBRAKE

DRYOPTERIS
MAIDENHAIR
SPLEENWORT

11
HART'S TONGUE

GRASSES, SEDGES, AND RUSHES

3
FOG
OAT
RYE
TEF

4
BENT
CORN
REED
RICE
RUSH

5
BROME
DURRA
MAIZE
PADDY
PANIC
SEDGE
SPELT
WHEAT

6
BAMBOO
BARLEY
DARNEL
FESCUE

FIORIN
MELICK
MILLET
QUITCH
REDTOP
ZOYSIA

7
BULRUSH
ESPARTO
FOXTAIL
PAPYRUS
SORGHUM
WILD OAT

8
CUTGRASS
DOG'S-TAIL
OAT-GRASS
REED MACE
RYEGRASS
SPARTINA
SPINIFEX
TEOSINTE
WILD RICE
WOODRUSH

9
BLUEGRASS
BROOMCORN
COCKSFOOT
CORDGRASS
CRABGRASS
GAMA GRASS
HAIR-GRASS
LYME GRASS
REED GRASS
STAR GRASS
SUGAR CANE
WIRE GRASS

10
BEACH GRASS
BEARD GRASS
BUNCH GRASS
CHINA GRASS
COUCH GRASS
HERD'S-GRASS
INDIAN CORN
INDIAN RICE
LEMON GRASS
QUACK GRASS
SPEAR GRASS

SWORD GRASS

11
CANARY GRASS
COTTON GRASS
FINGER GRASS
MARRAM GRASS
MEADOW GRASS
PAMPAS GRASS
SWITCH GRASS
TWITCH GRASS
VERNAL GRASS

12
BERMUDA GRASS
BRISTLE GRASS
BUFFALO GRASS
FEATHER GRASS
ORCHARD GRASS
QUAKING GRASS
TIMOTHY GRASS
TUSSOCK GRASS
YORKSHIRE FOG

13+
ELEPHANT GRASS
KENTUCKY BLUEGRASS
SQUIRREL-TAIL GRASS

PEOPLE

WORLD LEADERS

3

FOX, Charles James (1749–1806; British Whig politician)

FOX, Vincente (1942– ; Mexican politician)

LIE, Trygve (Halvdan) (1896–1968; Norwegian Labour politician)

MAY, Theresa Mary (1956– ; British Conservative politician)

4

BENN, Anthony Neil Wedgwood (1925–2014; British Labour politician)

BLUM, Léon (1872–1950; French socialist)

BOSE, Subhas Chandra (c. 1897–c. 1945; Indian nationalist leader)

COOK, Joseph (1860–1947; Australian statesman)

DÍAZ, Porfirio (1830–1915; Mexican soldier)

FOOT, Michael (Mackintosh) (1913–2010; British Labour politician)

GORE, Al(bert) H., Jr (1948– ; US politician)

HOLT, Harold Edward (1908–67; Australian statesman)

HOWE, Richard Edward Geoffrey, Baron (1926–2015; British Conservative politician)

HULL, Cordell (1871–1955; US Democratic politician)

KING, Jr, Martin Luther (1929–68; US Black civil-rights leader)

KING, William Lyon Mackenzie (1874–1950; Canadian statesman)

KIRK, Norman Eric (1923–74; New Zealand statesman)

KOHL, Helmut (1930–2017; German statesman)

MEIR, Golda (1898–1978; Israeli stateswoman)

NAGY, Imre (1896–1958; Hungarian statesman)

OWEN, Dr David, Baron (1938– ; British politician)

RHEE, Syngman (1875–1965; Korean statesman)

RUSK, David Dean (1909–94; US statesman)

TOJO (Hideki) (1884–1948; Japanese general)

TONE, Theobald Wolfe (1763–98; Irish nationalist)

TUTU, Desmond (1931– ; South African clergyman)

WARD, Joseph George (1856–1930; New Zealand statesman)

5

AGNEW, Spiro Theodore (1918–96; US Republican politician)

AHERN, Bertie (1951– ; Irish statesman)

ASTOR, Nancy Witcher, Viscountess (1879–1964; British politician)

BANDA, Hastings Kamuzu (1905–97; Malawi statesman)

BARAK, Ehud (1942–; Israeli politician)

BEGIN, Menachem (1913–92; Israeli statesman)

BERIA, Lavrenti Pavlovich (1899–1953; Soviet politician)

BEVAN, Aneurin (1897–1960; British Labour politician)

BEVIN, Ernest (1881–1951; British politician)

BLAIR, Tony (1953– ; British politician)

BOTHA, Louis (1862–1919; South African statesman)

BOTHA, Pieter Willem (1916–2006; South African statesman)

BROWN, Gordon (1951– ; British Labour politician)

CLARK, Charles Joseph (1939– ; Canadian statesman)

CLARK, Helen (1950– ; New Zealand politician)

CLEGG, Nick (1967– ; British Liberal Democrat politician)

DAYAN, Moshe (1915–81; Israeli general)

DEBRÉ, Michel (1912–96; French statesman)

DESAI, Shri Morarji Ranchhodji (1896–95; Indian statesman)

DE WET, Christian Rudolf (1854–1922; Afrikaner politician and soldier)

EBERT, Friedrich (1871–1925; German statesman)

EMMET, Robert (1778–1803; Irish nationalist)

FLOOD, Henry (1732–91; Irish politician)

LAVAL, Pierre (1883–1945; French statesman)

LENIN, Vladimir Ilich (V I Ulyanov, 1870–1924; Russian revolutionary)

LODGE, Henry Cabot (1850–1924; US Republican politician)

LYNCH, Jack (1917–99; Irish statesman)

LYONS, Joseph Aloysius (1879–1939; Australian statesman)

MAJOR, John, Sir (1943– ; British politician)

MANIN, Daniele (1804–57; Italian patriot)

MBEKI, Thabo (1942– ; South African politician)

MBOYA, Tom (1930–69; Kenyan politician)

MENON, Krishna (Vengalil Krishnan Krishna Menon, 1896–1974; Indian diplomat)

NEHRU, Jawaharlal (1889–1964; Indian statesman)

NKOMO, Joshua (1917–99; Zimbabwean politician)

OBAMA, Barack (1961– ; US Democrat politician)

OBOTE, Apollo Milton (1925–2005; Ugandan statesman)

PERÓN, Juan Domingo (1895–1974; Argentine statesman)

PUTIN, Vladimir (1952– ; Russian politician)

RABIN, Yitshak (1922–95; Israeli statesman)

SADAT, Anwar (1918–81; Egyptian statesman)

SMITH, Ian Douglas (1919–2007; Rhodesian politician)

SMUTS, Jan Christiaan (1870–1950; South African

statesman and general)

SPAAK, Paul Henri (1899– 1972; Belgian statesman)

STEEL, David Martin Scott, Baron Steel of Aikwood (1938– ; British politician)

TRUMP, Donald John (1946– ; US Republican politician)

VANCE, Cyrus (1917–2002; US statesman)

VILLA, Pancho (Francesco V, (1878–1923; Mexican revolutionary)

6

ARAFAT, Yassir (1929–2004; Palestinian leader)

ARROYO, Gloria Macapagal (1947– ; Filipino stateswoman)

BARTON, Edmund (1849–1920; Australian statesman)

BHUTTO, Benazir (1953–2007; Pakistani politician)

BHUTTO, Zulfikar Ali (1928–79; Pakistani statesman)

BORDEN, Robert Laird (1854–1937; Canadian statesman)

BRANDT, Willy (1913–92; West German statesman)

BRIGHT, John (1811–89; British radical politician)

BRUTON, John Gerard (1947– ; Irish statesman)

BUTLER, Richard Austen, Baron (1902–82; British Conservative politician)

CHENEY, Richard Bruce (1941– ; US politician)

CHIRAC, Jacques (1932– ; French statesman)

COATES, Joseph Gordon (1878–1943; New Zealand statesman)

COBDEN, Richard (1804–65; British politician and economist)

CRIPPS, Richard Stafford (1889–1952; British Labour politician)

CURTIN, John Joseph (1885–1945; Australian statesman)

CURZON, George Nathaniel, 1st Marquess (1859–1925 British politician)

DAVITT, Michael (1846–1906; Irish nationalist)

DEAKIN, Alfred (1856–1919; Australian statesman)

DJILAS, Milovan (1911–95; Yugoslav politician)

DUBČEK, Alexander (1921–92; Czechoslovak statesman)

DULLES, John Foster (1888–1959; US Republican politician and diplomat)

ERHARD, Ludwig (1897–1977; German statesman)

FADDEN, Arthur William (1895–1973; Australian statesman)

FISHER, Andrew (1862–1928; Australian statesman)

FLEURY, André Hercule de, Cardinal (1653–1743; French statesman)

FORBES, George William (1869–1947; New Zealand statesman)

FRANCO, Francisco (1892–1975; Spanish general and statesman)

FRASER, John Malcolm (1930–2015; Australian statesman)

FRASER, Peter (1884–1950; New Zealand statesman)

GANDHI, Indira (1917–84; Indian stateswoman)

GANDHI, Mohandas Karamchand (1869–1948; Indian nationalist leader)

GÖRING, Hermann Wilhelm (1893–1946; German Nazi politician)

GORTON, John Grey (1911–2002; Australian statesman)

GRIVAS, Georgios (1898–1974; Greek general)

HEALEY, Denis Winston, Baron (1917–2015; British politician)

HOWARD, John (1939– ; Australian politician)

HUGHES, William Morris (1864–1952; Australian statesman)

JUÁREZ, Benito Pablo (1806–72; Mexican statesman)

KAUNDA, Kenneth David (1924– ; Zambian statesman)

KRUGER, Stephanus Johannes Paulus (1825– 1904; Afrikaner statesman)

MARCOS, Ferdinand Edralin (1917–89; Philippine statesman)

MASSEY, William Ferguson (1856–1925; New Zealand statesman)

MERKEL, Angela (1954– ; German politician)

MOBUTU, Sese Seko (Joseph Désiré M, (1930–97; Zaïrese statesman)

MOSLEY, Oswald Ernald (1896–1980; British fascist)

NASSER, Gamal Abdel (1918– 70; Egyptian statesman)

O'BRIEN, Conor Cruise (1917–2008; Irish diplomat)

O'NEILL, Terence, Baron (1914–90; Northern Irish statesman)

PÉTAIN, Henri Philippe (1856–1951; French general and statesman)

POWELL, John Enoch (1912–98; British politician)

QUAYLE, Dan (1947– ; US politician)

REVERE, Paul (1735–1818; American revolutionary)

RHODES, Cecil John (1853–1902; South African financier and statesman)

SAVAGE, Michael Joseph (1872–1940; New Zealand statesman)

SEDDON, Richard John (1845–1906; New Zealand statesman)

SHARON, Ariel (1928–2014; Israeli politician)

STALIN, Joseph (1879–1953; Soviet statesman)

SUÁREZ, Adolfo, Duke of (1932–2014; Spanish statesman)

THORPE, (John) Jeremy (1929–2014; British Liberal politician)

WATSON, John Christian (1867–1941; Australian statesman)

WILKES, John (1725–97; British journalist and politician)

ZAPATA, Emiliano (?1877–1919; Mexican revolutionary)

7

ACHESON, Dean Gooderham (1893–1971; US lawyer and statesman)

ASHDOWN, Paddy (1941–2018; Social and Liberal Democrat politician)

ATATÜRK, Kemal (Mustafa Kemal, 1881–1938; Turkish statesman)

BATISTA (y Zaldívar), Fulgencio (1901–73 ; Cuban statesman)

BENNETT, Richard Bedford, Viscount (1870–1947; Canadian statesman)

BOLÍVAR, Simón (1783–1830; South American statesman)

BORMANN, Martin (1900–45; German Nazi leader)

CAMERON, David (1966– ; British Conservative politician)

CARDOSO, Fernando Henrique (1931– ; Brazilian statesman)

CLINTON, Bill (1946– ; US statesman)

CLINTON, de Witt (1769–1828; US statesman)

COLLINS, Michael (1890–1922; Irish nationalist)

GADDAFI, Moammar Al- (or Qaddafi, 1942–2011; Libyan colonel and statesman)

GILLARD, Julia (1961– ; Australian politician)

GRATTAN, Henry (1746–1820; Irish politician)

GRIMOND, Joseph (1913–93; British politician)

GROMYKO, Andrei (1909–89; Soviet statesman)

HIMMLER, Heinrich (1900–45; German Nazi politician)

HOLLAND, Sidney George (1893–1961; New Zealand statesman)

HUSSEIN (ibn Talal (1935–99; King of Jordan)

HUSSEIN, Saddam (1937–2006; Iraqi politician)

KEATING, Paul John (1944– ; Australian statesman)

JENKINS, Roy Harris (1920–2003; British politician and historian)

KINNOCK, Neil, Baron (1942– ; Labour politician)

KOSYGIN, Aleksei Nikolaevich (1904–80; Soviet statesman)

LUMUMBA, Patrice Hemery (1925–61; Congolese statesman)

MACLEOD, Iain Norman (1913–70; British Conservative politician)

MANDELA, Nelson (Rolihlahla) (1918–2013; South African lawyer and politician)

MAZZINI, Giuseppe (1805–72; Italian patriot)

MCMAHON, William (1908–80; Australian statesman)

MENZIES, Robert Gordon (1894–1978; Australian statesman)

MINTOFF, Dominic (1916–2012; Maltese statesman)

MOLOTOV, Vyacheslav Mikhailovich (1890–1986; Soviet statesman)

NYERERE, Julius Kambarage (1922–99; Tanzanian statesman)

PAISLEY, Ian, Baron (1926–2014; Northern Irish politician)

PARNELL, Charles Stewart (1846–91; Irish politician)

PEARSON, Lester Bowles (1897–1972; Canadian statesman)

RAFFLES, Thomas Stamford (1781–1826; British colonial administrator)

SALAZAR, António de Oliveira (1889–1970; Portuguese dictator)

SARKOZY, Nicolas (1955– ; French politician)

SCHMIDT, Helmut (1918–2015; German statesman)

SCULLIN, James Henry (1876–1953; Australian statesman)

SHASTRI, Shri Lal Bahadur (1904–66; Indian statesman)

SUHARTO (1921–2008; Indonesian statesman and general)

TROTSKY, Leon (1879–1940; Russian revolutionary)

TRUDEAU, Pierre Elliott (1919–2000; Canadian statesman)

VORSTER, Balthazar Johannes (1915–83; South African statesman)

WHITLAM, Edward Gough (1916–2014; Australian statesman)

YELTSIN, Boris (1931–2007; Russian statesman)

8

ADENAUER, Konrad (1876–1967; German statesman)

AMIN DADA, Idi (c. 1925–2003; Ugandan politician and president)

ARISTIDE, Jean-Bertrand (1953– ; Haitian statesman)

AYUB KHAN, Mohammad (1907–74; Pakistani statesman)

BEN BELLA, Ahmed (1918?–2012; Algerian statesman)

BIN LADEN, Osama (1957–2011; leader of al-Qaida terrorists)

BISMARCK, Otto Eduard Leopold, Prince Von (1815–98; Prussian statesman)

BOUCHARD, Lucien (1938– ; Canadian politician)

BREZHNEV, Leonid Ilich (1906–82; Soviet statesman)

BUKHARIN, Nikolai Ivanovich (1888–1938; Soviet politician)

BULGANIN, Nikolai Aleksandrovich (1895–1975; Soviet statesman)

CHRÉTIEN, Jean (1934– ; Canadian statesman)

COSGRAVE, William Thomas (1880–1965; Irish statesman)

CROSSMAN, Richard Howard Stafford (1907–74; British Labour politician)

DALADIER, Édouard (1884– 1970; French statesman)

DE GAULLE, Charles André Joseph Marie (1890–1970; French general and statesman)

DE VALERA, Eamon (1882–1975; Irish statesman)

DOLLFUSS, Engelbert (1892–1934; Austrian statesman)

DUVALIER, François (1907–71; Haitian politician)

EICHMANN, Adolf (1906–62; German Nazi politician)

FRANKLIN, Benjamin (1706–90; US diplomat)

GOEBBELS, Paul Joseph (1897–1945; German Nazi politician)

GRIFFITH, Arthur (1872–1922; Irish journalist and nationalist)

HARRIMAN, William Averell (1891–1986; US diplomat)

HASTINGS, Warren (1732–1818; British colonial administrator)

HIROHITO (1901–89; Emperor of Japan)

HOLLANDE, François (1954– ; French politician)

HOLYOAKE, Keith Jacka (1904–83; New Zealand statesman)

HONECKER, Erich (1912–94; East German statesman)

HUMPHREY, Hubert Horatio (1911–1978; US Democratic politician)

IBARRURI, Dolores (1895– 1989; Spanish politician)

KENYATTA, Jomo (c. 1891– 1978; Kenyan statesman)

KHOMEINI, Ayatollah Ruholla (1900–89; Iranian Shiite Muslim leader)

MALENKOV, Georgi Maksimilianovich (1902–88; Soviet statesman)

MCALEESE, Mary (1951– ; Irish politician)

MCCARTHY, Joseph Raymond (1908–57; US Republican senator)

MILIBAND, Ed(ward) Samuel (1969– ; Labour politician)

MORRISON, Herbert Stanley, Baron (1888–1965; British Labour politician)

MUZOREWA, Bishop Abel Tendekayi (1925–2010; Zimbabwean statesman)

O'CONNELL, Daniel (1775–1847; Irish politician)

O'HIGGINS, Bernardo (?1778–1842; Chilean national hero)

PINOCHET, Augusto (1915–2006; Chilean general)

PODGORNY, Nikolai (1903–83; Soviet statesman)

POINCARÉ, Raymond (1860–1934; French statesman)

POMPIDOU, Georges Jean Raymond (1911–74; French statesman)

QUISLING, Vidkun Abraham Lauritz Jonsson (1887–1945;

Norwegian army officer and Nazi collaborator)

RASPUTIN, Grigori Yefimovich (c. 1872–1916;Russian mystic)

SCHRÖDER, Gerhard (1944– ; German politician)

SIHANOUK, Norodim, Prince (1923–2012; King of Cambodia)

SIKORSKI, Władysław (1881–1943; Polish general and statesman)

THATCHER, Margaret, Baroness (1925–2013; British stateswoman)

ULBRICHT, Walter (1893–1973; East German statesman)

VERWOERD, Hendrik Frensch (1901–66; South African statesman)

WALDHEIM, Kurt (1918–2007; Austrian diplomat and statesman)

WEIZMANN, Chaim Azriel (1874–1952; Israeli statesman)

WELENSKY, Roy (1907–92; Rhodesian statesman)

WILLIAMS, Shirley Vivien Teresa Brittain, Baroness Williams of Crosby (1930– ; British politician)

9

AGA KHAN IV (1936– ; Imam of the Ismaili sect of Muslims)

ANDREOTTI, Giulio (1919–2013; Italian politician)

BEN-GURION, David (1886– 1973; Israeli statesman)

CASTRO RUZ, Fidel (1926–2016; Cuban statesman)

CHOU EN-LAI (or Zhou En Lai, 1898–1976; Chinese communist statesman)

CHURCHILL, Lord Randolph Henry Spencer (1849–95; British Conservative politician)

GAITSKELL, Hugh (1906–63; British politician)

GARIBALDI, Giuseppe (1807–82; Italian soldier)

GORBACHOV, Mikhail Sergeevich (1931– ; Soviet statesman)

HENDERSON, Arthur (1863–1935; British Labour politician)

HO CHI MINH (Nguyen That Thanh, 1890–1969; Vietnamese statesman)

KIM YONG UN (1984– ; North Korean politician)

KISSINGER, Henry Alfred

(1923– ; US diplomat and political scientist)

LA GUARDIA, Fiorello Henry (1882–1947; US politician)

LUXEMBURG, Rosa (1871–1919; German revolutionary)

MACDONALD, James Ramsay (1866–1937; British statesman)

MACDONALD, John Alexander (1815–91; Canadian statesman)

MILOŠEVIĆ, Slobodan (1941–2006; Serbian politician)

MUSSOLINI, Benito Amilcare Andrea (1883–1945; Italian fascist dictator)

NETANYAHU, Benjamin (1949– ; Israeli politician)

PANKHURST, Emmeline (1858–1928; British suffragette)

STEVENSON, Adlai Ewing (1900–65; US Democratic politician)

XI JINPING (1953– ; Chinese politician)

10

ABDULLAH II (1962– ; King of Jordan)

BERNADOTTE, Jean Baptiste Jules (c. 1763–1844; French marshal)

BERLUSCONI, Silvio (1936– ; Italian politician)

CARRINGTON, Peter Alexander Rupert, 6th Baron (1919–2018; British Conservative politician)

CLEMENCEAU, Georges (1841–1929; French statesman)

KHRUSHCHEV, Nikita Sergeevich (1894–1971; Soviet statesman)

LEE KUAN YEW (1923–2015; Singaporean statesman)

MAO TSE-TUNG (or Mao Ze Dong, 1893–1976; Chinese communist statesman)

MITTERRAND, François Maurice (1916–96; French statesman)

RIBBENTROP, Joachim von (1893–1946; German Nazi politician)

VOROSHILOV, Kliment Yefremovich (1881–1969; Soviet marshal and statesman)

11

ABDUL RAHMAN, Tunku (1903–73; Malaysian statesman)

CASTLEREAGH, Robert Stewart, Viscount (1769– 1822; British statesman)

DIEFENBAKER, John George

(1895–1979; Canadian statesman)

HORE-BELISHA, Isaac Leslie, 1st Baron (1893–1957;British politician)

IZETBEGOVIĆ, Alija (1925–2003; Bosnian politician)

MAKARIOS III, Mikhail Khristodolou Mouskos (1913–77; Cypriot churchman and statesman)

MOUNTBATTEN (of Burma), Louis, 1st Earl (1900–79; British admiral and colonial administrator)

SELWYN LLOYD, John, Baron (1904–78; British Conservative politician)

WILBERFORCE, William (1759–1833; British philanthropist)

12

BANDARANAIKE, Solomon (1899–1959; Sri Lankan statesman)

FREI MONTALVA, Eduardo (1911–82; Chilean statesman)

HAMMARSKJÖLD, Dag (1905–61; Swedish international civil servant)

MENDÈS-FRANCE, Pierre (1907–82; French statesman)

PAPADOPOULOS, George (1919–99; Greek colonel)

SHEVARDNADZE, Eduard Amvrosiyevich (1928–2014; Georgian statesman)

13

CHIANG KAI-SHEK (or Jiang Jie Shi, 1887–1975; Nationalist Chinese soldier and statesman)

14

ALLENDE GOSSENS, Salvador (1908–73; Chilean statesman)

CLIVE OF PLASSEY, Robert, Baron (1725–74; British soldier and colonial administrator)

15

GISCARD D'ESTAING, Valéry (1926– ; French statesman)

20+

AYATOLLAH RUHOLLA KHOMEINI. See KHOMEINI, Ayatollah Ruholla.

HAILSHAM OF ST MARYLEBONE, Baron (Quintin McGarel Hogg; 1907–)

MILITARY LEADERS

3

LEE, Robert E (1807–70; US Confederate commander)

NEY, Michel, Prince of Moscow (1769–1815; French marshal)

4

ALBA, Fernando Alvarez de Toledo, Duke of (1507–83; Spanish general)

BART, Jean (1650–1702; French admiral)

BYNG, George, Viscount Torrington (1663–1733; English admiral)

DIAZ, Porfirio (1830–1915; Mexican soldier)

FOCH, Ferdinand (1851–1929; French marshal)

HAIG, Douglas, 1st Earl (1861–1928; British field marshal)

HOOD, Samuel, 1st Viscount (1724–1816; British admiral)

HOWE, Richard, Earl (1726–99; British admiral)

JODL, Alfred (1890–1946; German general)

RAIS, Gilles de (or G de Retz 1404–40; French marshal)

RÖHM, Ernst (1887–1934; German soldier)

ROON, Albrecht, Graf von (1803–79; Prussian general)

SAXE, Maurice, Comte de (1696–1750; Marshal of France)

SLIM, William Joseph, 1st Viscount (1891–1970; British field marshal)

TOGO (Heihachiro) (1847–1934; Japanese admiral)

5

ANDRÉ, John (1751–80; British soldier)

ANSON, George Anson, Baron (1697–1762; British admiral)

BLAKE, Robert (1599–1657; English admiral)

BLIGH, William (1754–1817; British admiral)

CIMON (d. c. 450 BC; Athenian general and politician)

DEWEY, George (1837–1917; US admiral)

DRAKE, Francis (1540–96; English navigator andadmiral)

EL CID (Rodrigo Díaz de Vivar, c. 1040–99; Spanish warrior)

GATES, Horatio (?1728–1806; American general)

HAWKE, Edward, 1st Baron (1705–81; British admiral)

JONES, John Paul (1747–92; American naval commander)

LALLY, Thomas, Comte de (1702–66; French general)

LEVEN, Alexander Leslie, 1st Earl of (1580–1661; Scottish general)

MOORE, John (1761–1809; British general)

MURAT, Joachim (1767–1815; French marshal)

PERRY, Matthew C (1794–1858; US naval officer)

PRIDE, Thomas (d. 1658; English parliamentary soldier)

SULLA, Lucius Cornelius (c. 138–78 BC; Roman dictator)

TILLY, Johan Tserclaes, Graf von (1559–1632; Bavarian general)

TROMP, Maarten (1598–1653; Dutch admiral)

WOLFE, James (1727–59; British soldier)

6

AETIUS, Flavius (d. 454 AD; Roman general)

ARNOLD, Benedict (1741–1801; American general)

BAYARD, Pierre Terrail, Seigneur de (c. 1473–1524; French soldier)

BEATTY, David, 1st Earl (1871–1936; British admiral)

BENBOW, John (1653–1702; English naval officer)

CRONJE, Piet Arnoldus (c. 1840–1911; South African general)

CUSTER, George Armstrong (1839–76; US cavalry general)

DARLAN, Jean (Louis Xavier) François (1881–1942; French admiral)

DÖNITZ, Karl (1891–1981; German admiral)

DUNDEE, John Graham of Claverhouse, 1st Viscount (c. 649–89; Scottish soldier)

DUNOIS, Jean d'Orléans, Comte de (1403–68; French general)

FISHER, John Arbuthnot, 1st Baron (1841–1920; British admiral)

FRENCH, John, 1st Earl of Ypres (1852–1925; British field marshal)

FULLER, J F C (1878–1966; British soldier)

GINKEL, Godert de, 1st Earl of Athlone (1644–1703; Dutch general)

GORDON, Charles George (1833–85; British general)

GRANBY, John Manners, Marquess of (1721–70; British soldier)

GREENE, Nathaneal (1742–86; American general)

HALSEY, William F (1882–1959; US admiral)

JOFFRE, Joseph Jacques Césaire (1852–1931; French marshal)

KEITEL, Wilhelm (1882–1946; German field marshal)

KLÉBER, Jean Baptiste (1753–1800; French general)

KONIEV, Ivan Stepanovich (1897–1973; Soviet marshal)

MARIUS, Gaius (c. 157–86 BC; Roman general)

MOLTKE, Helmuth, Graf von (1800–91; Prussian field marshal)

MOREAU, Jean Victor (1763–1813; French general)

NAPIER (of Magdala), Robert Cornelis, 1st Baron (1810–90; British field marshal)

NAPIER, Charles James (1782–1853; British general)

NARSES (c. 480–574 AD; Byzantine general)

NELSON, Horatio, Viscount (1758–1805; British admiral)

NIMITZ, Chester W (1885–1966; US admiral)

OUTRAM, James (1803–63; British soldier)

PATTON, George S (1885–1945; US general)

PAULUS, Friedrich (1890–1957; German field marshal)

PÉTAIN, (Henri) Philippe (1856–1951; French general and statesman)

RAEDER, Erich (1876–1960; German admiral)

RAGLAN, Fitzroy James Henry Somerset, 1st Baron (1788–1855; British field marshal)

RODNEY, George Brydges, 1st Baron (1719–92; British admiral)

ROMMEL, Erwin (1891–1944; German general)

RUPERT, Prince (1619–82; Cavalry officer)

RUYTER, Michiel Adriaanszoon de (1607–76; Dutch admiral)

TEDDER, Arthur William, 1st Baron (1890–1967; British air marshal)

VERNON, Edward (1684–1757; British admiral)

WAVELL, Archibald Percival, 1st Earl (1883–1950; British field marshal)

WILSON, Henry Maitland, 1st Baron (1881–1964; British field marshal)

WILSON, Henry Hughes (1864–1922; British field marshal)

ZHUKOV, Georgi Konstantinovich (1896–1974; Soviet marshal)

7

AGRIPPA, Marcus Vipsanius (?63–12 BC; Roman general)

ALLENBY, Edmund Henry Hynman, 1st Viscount (1861–1936; British field marshal)

ARTIGAS, José Gervasio (1764–1850; national hero of Uruguay)

ATHLONE, Alexander Cambridge, 1st Earl of (1874–1957; British soldier)

BAZAINE, Achille François (1811–88; French marshal)

BERWICK, James Fitzjames, Duke of (1670–1734; Marshal of France)

BLÜCHER, Gebhard Leberecht von, Prince of Wahlstatt (1742–1819; Prussian general)

BRADLEY, Omar Nelson (1893–1981; US general)

DECATUR, Stephen (1779–1820; US naval officer)

DENIKIN, Anton Ivanovich (1872–1947; Russian general)

DOWDING, Hugh Caswall Tremenheere, 1st Baron (1882–1970; British air chief marshal)

FAIRFAX, Thomas, 3rd Baron (1612–71; English general)

JACKSON, Andrew (1767–1845; US statesman and general)

JACKSON, Stonewall (Thomas Jonathan J, 1824–63; US Confederate general)

KOLCHAK, Alexander Vasilievich (1874–1920; Russian admiral)

LAMBERT, John (1619–83; English parliamentary general)

LYAUTEY, Louis Hubert Gonzalve (1854–1934; French marshal)

MASSÉNA, André (?1756– 1817; French marshal)

METAXAS, Ioannis (1871–1941; Greek general)

MORTIER, Édouard Adolphe Casimir Joseph, Duc de Trévise (1768–1835; French marshal)

PHILLIP, Arthur (1738–1814; British admiral)

REGULUS, Marcus Attilus (d. c. 251 BC; Roman general)

ROBERTS, Frederick Sleigh, 1st Earl (1832–1914; British field marshal)

SHERMAN, William Tecumseh (1820–91; US Federal general)

SHOVELL, Cloudesley (1650–1707; English admiral)

SUVOROV, Aleksandr Vasilievich, Count (1729– 1800; Russian field marshal)

TANCRED (c. 1078–1112; Norman Crusader)

TIRPITZ, Alfred von (1849– 1930; German admiral)

TURENNE, Henri de la Tour d'Auvergne, Vicomte de (1611–75; French marshal)

VENDÔME, Louis Joseph, Duc de (1654–1712; French marshal)

VILLARS, Claude Louis Hector, Duc de (1653–1734; French marshal)

WALLACE, Lew (1827–1905; US soldier)

WINGATE, Orde Charles (1903–44; British soldier)

WRANGEL, Peter Nikolaievich, Baron (1878–1928; Russian general)

8

AGRICOLA, Gnaeus Julius (40–93 AD; Roman governor)

ANGLESEY, Henry William Paget, 1st Marquess of (1768–1854; British field marshal)

AUGEREAU, Pierre François Charles, Duc de Castiglione (1757–1816; French marshal)

BADOGLIO, Pietro (1871–1956; Italian general)

BERTRAND, Henri Gratien, Comte (1773–1844; French marshal)

BOURMONT, Louis Auguste Victor de Ghaisnes, Comte de (1773–1846; French marshal)

BURGOYNE, John (1722–92; British general)

CAMPBELL, Colin, Baron Clyde (1792–1863; British field marshal)

CARDIGAN, James Thomas Brudenell, 7th Earl of (1797–1868; British cavalry officer)

CARRANZA, Venustiano (1859–1920; Mexican statesman and soldier)

COCHRANE, Thomas, 10th Earl of Dundonald (1775–1860; British admiral)

CROMWELL, Oliver (1599–1658; English soldier and statesman)

GUESCLIN, Bertrand du (c. 1320–80; French commander)

HANNIBAL (247–c. 183 BC; Carthaginian general)

IRONSIDE, William Edmund, 1st Baron (1880–1959; British field marshal)

JELLICOE, John Rushworth, 1st Earl (1859–1935; British admiral)

KHAMENEI, Ayatollah Seyed Ali (1939– ; Iranian political and religious leader)

KORNILOV, Lavrentia Georgievich (1870–1918; Russian general)

LUCULLUS, Lucius Licinius (d. c. 57 BC; Roman general)

LYSANDER (d. 395 BC; Spartan general)

MARSHALL, George C (1880–1959; US general)

MONTCALM, Louis Joseph de Montcalm-Grozon, Marquis de (1712–59; French general)

O'HIGGINS, Bernardo (?1778–1842; Chilean national hero)

PERSHING, John J (1860–1948; US general)

SANDWICH, John Montagu, 4th Earl of (1718–92; first lord of the admiralty)

SHERIDAN, Philip H (1831–88; US Federal general)

STILICHO, Flavius (d. 408 AD; Roman general)

STILWELL, Joseph W (1883–1946; US general)

WOLSELEY, Garnet Joseph, 1st Viscount (1833–1913; British field marshal)

9

ANGOULÊME, Charles de Valois, Duc d' (1573–1650; French soldier)

ANTIPATER (397–319 BC; Macedonian general)

ANTONESCU, Ion (1882–1946; Romanian general)

ARISTIDES (the Just) (c. 520–c. 468 BC; Athenian statesman)

BONAPARTE, Napoleon (1769–1821; French emperor)

DUMOURIEZ, Charles François Du Périer (1739–1823; French general)

GNEISENAU, August, Graf Neithardt von (1760–1831; Prussian field marshal)

GRENVILLE, Richard (?1541–91; British sailor)

HASDRUBAL (d. 207 BC; Carthaginian general)

KITCHENER (of Khartoum), Horatio Herbert, 1st Earl (1850–1916; British field marshal)

LAFAYETTE, Marie Joseph Gilbert Motier, Marquis de (1757–1834; French general and politician)

MACARTHUR, Douglas (1880–1964; US general)

MARCELLUS, Marcus Claudius (d. 208 BC; Roman general)

MCCLELLAN, George B (1826–85; Federal general)

MILTIADES (c. 550–489 BC; Athenian general)

NEWCASTLE, William Cavendish, Duke of (1592–1676; English soldier)

OLDCASTLE, John (c. 1378–1417; English soldier)

PRETORIUS, Andries (1799–1853; Afrikaner leader)

RUNDSTEDT, Gerd von (1875–1953; German field marshal)

SANTA ANNA, Antonio López de (1794–1876; Mexican soldier)

TRENCHARD, Hugh Montague, 1st Viscount (1873–1956; The first British air marshal)

10

ABERCROMBY, Ralph (1734–1801; British general)

ALANBROOKE, Alan Francis Brooke, 1st Viscount (1883–1963; British field marshal)

ALCIBIADES (c. 450–404 BC; Athenian general and politician)

ANTIGONUS I (c. 382–301 BC; Macedonian general)

AUCHINLECK, Claude (1884–1981; British field marshal)

BELISARIUS (c. 505–65 AD; Byzantine general)

BERNADOTTE, Jean Baptiste Jules (1763–1844)

CORNWALLIS, Charles, 1st Marquess (1738–1805; British general)

CUMBERLAND, William Augustus, Duke of (1721–65; British general)

ENVER PASHA (1881–1922; Turkish soldier)

FLAMININUS, Titus Quinctius (c. 230–c. 174 BC; Roman general)

HINDENBURG, Paul von Beneckendorff und von (1847–1934; German general)

KESSELRING, Albert (1885–1960; German general)

KUBLAI KHAN (1215–94; Mongol conqueror of China)

MANNERHEIM, Carl Gustaf Emil, Baron von (1867–1951; Finnish general)

MONTGOMERY (of Alamein), Bernard Law, 1st Viscount (1887–1976; British field marshal)

OGLETHORPE, James Edward (1696–1785; English general)

RICHTHOFEN, Manfred, Freiherr von (1892–1918; German air ace)

SCHLIEFFEN, Alfred, Graf von (1833–1913; German general)

TIMOSHENKO, Semyon Konstantinovich (1895–1970; Soviet marshal)

VILLENEUVE, Pierre (1763–1806; French admiral)

WELLINGTON, Arthur Wellesley, Duke of (1769–1852; British general)

11

ALBUQUERQUE, Alfonso de (1453–1515; Portuguese governor in India)

BADEN-POWELL, Robert Stephenson Smyth, 1st Baron (1857–1941; British general)

BEAUHARNAIS, Alexandre, Vicomte de (1760–94; French general)

BRAUCHITSCH, Walther von (1881–1948; German general)

COLLINGWOOD, Cuthbert, 1st Baron (1750–1810; British admiral)

EPAMINONDAS (c. 418–362 BC; Theban general)

LIDDELL HART, Basil Henry (1895–1970; British soldier)

MARLBOROUGH, John Churchill, 1st Duke of (1650–1722; British general)

MÜNCHHAUSEN, Karl Friedrich, Freiherr von (1720–97; German soldier)

PONIATOWSKI, Józef (1763–1813; Marshal of France)

WALLENSTEIN, Albrecht Wenzel von (1583–1634; Bohemian-born general)

12

IBRAHIM PASHA (1789–1848; Ottoman general)

13

EUGÈNE OF SAVOY, Prince (1663–1736; Austrian general)

FABIUS MAXIMUS, Quintus (d. 203 BC; Roman general)

HAMILCAR BARCA (d. c. 229 BC; Carthaginian general)

14

BARCLAY DE TOLLY, Mikhail Bogdanovich, Prince (1761–1818; Russian field marshal)

CLIVE OF PLASSEY, Robert, Baron (1725–74; British soldier and colonial administrator)

15

CASSIUS LONGINUS, Gaius (d. 42 BC; Roman general)

SCIPIO AFRICANUS (236–183 BC; Roman general)

16

ALEXANDER OF TUNIS, Harold, 1st Earl (1891–1969; British field marshal)

17

HOWARD OF EFFINGHAM, Charles, 2nd Baron (1536–1624; English Lord High Admiral)

20+

BERNHARD OF SAXE-WEIMAR, Duke (1604–39; German general)

SCIPIO AEMILIANUS AFRICANUS (c. 185–129 BC; Roman general)

PRIME MINISTERS OF GREAT BRITAIN (FROM 1721)

NAME	(TERM)	NAME	(TERM)
ROBERT WALPOLE	(1721–42)	GEORGE HAMILTON GORDON,	
SPENCER COMPTON, EARL OF		EARL OF ABERDEEN	(1852–55)
WILMINGTON	(1742–43)	HENRY JOHN TEMPLE,	
HENRY PELHAM	(1743–54)	VISCOUNT PALMERSTON	(1855–58)
THOMAS PELHAM-HOLLES,		EDWARD STANLEY, EARL OF DERBY	(1858–59)
DUKE OF NEWCASTLE	(1754–56)	HENRY TEMPLE,	
WILLIAM CAVENDISH, DUKE		VISCOUNT PALMERSTON	(1859–65)
OF DEVONSHIRE	(1756–57)	JOHN RUSSELL, EARL RUSSELL	(1865–66)
THOMAS PELHAM-HOLLES,		EDWARD STANLEY, EARL OF DERBY	(1866–68)
DUKE OF NEWCASTLE	(1757–62)	BENJAMIN DISRAELI	(1868)
JOHN STUART, EARL OF BUTE	(1762–63)	WILLIAM EWART GLADSTONE	(1868–74)
GEORGE GRENVILLE	(1763–65)	BENJAMIN DISRAELI, EARL	
CHARLES WATSON-WENTWORTH,		OF BEACONSFIELD	(1874–80)
MARQUIS OF ROCKINGHAM	(1765–66)	WILLIAM EWART GLADSTONE	(1880–85)
WILLIAM PITT, EARL OF CHATHAM	(1766–68)	ROBERT GASCOYNE-CECIL,	
AUGUSTUS HENRY FITZROY,		MARQUIS OF SALISBURY	(1885–86)
DUKE OF GRAFTON	(1768–70)	WILLIAM EWART GLADSTONE	(1886)
FREDERICK NORTH	(1770–82)	ROBERT GASCOYNE-CECIL,	
CHARLES WATSON-WENTWORTH,		MARQUIS OF SALISBURY	(1886–92)
MARQUIS OF ROCKINGHAM	(1782)	WILLIAM EWART GLADSTONE	(1892–94)
WILLIAM PETTY, EARL OF SHELBURNE	(1782–83)	ARCHIBALD PHILIP PRIMROSE,	
WILLIAM HENRY CAVENDISH		EARL OF ROSEBERY	(1894–95)
BENTINCK, DUKE OF PORTLAND	(1783)	ROBERT GASCOYNE-CECIL,	
WILLIAM PITT (SON OF EARL		MARQUIS OF SALISBURY	(1895–1902)
OF CHATHAM)	(1783–1801)	ARTHUR JAMES BALFOUR	(1902–05)
HENRY ADDINGTON	(1801–04)	HENRY CAMPBELL-BANNERMAN	(1905–08)
WILLIAM PITT	(1804–06)	HERBERT HENRY ASQUITH	(1908–16)
WILLIAM WYNDHAM GRENVILLE,		DAVID LLOYD GEORGE	(1916–22)
BARON GRENVILLE	(1806–07)	ANDREW BONAR LAW	(1922–23)
WILLIAM BENTINCK, DUKE		STANLEY BALDWIN	(1923–24)
OF PORTLAND	(1807–09)	JAMES RAMSAY MACDONALD	(1924)
SPENCER PERCEVAL	(1809–12)	STANLEY BALDWIN	(1924–29)
ROBERT BANKS JENKINSON, EARL		JAMES RAMSAY MACDONALD	(1929–35)
OF LIVERPOOL	(1812–27)	STANLEY BALDWIN	(1935–37)
GEORGE CANNING	(1827)	NEVILLE CHAMBERLAIN	(1937–40)
FREDERICK JOHN ROBINSON,		WINSTON CHURCHILL	(1940–45)
VISCOUNT GODERICH	(1827–28)	CLEMENT RICHARD ATTLEE	(1945–51)
ARTHUR WELLESLEY, DUKE OF		WINSTON CHURCHILL	(1951–55)
WELLINGTON	(1828–30)	ANTHONY EDEN	(1955–57)
CHARLES GREY, EARL GREY	(1830–34)	HAROLD MACMILLAN	(1957–63)
WILLIAM LAMB, VISCOUNT		ALEC DOUGLAS-HOME	(1963–64)
MELBOURNE	(1834)	HAROLD WILSON	(1964–70)
ROBERT PEEL	(1834–35)	EDWARD HEATH	(1970–74)
WILLIAM LAMB, VISCOUNT		HAROLD WILSON	(1974–76)
MELBOURNE	(1835–41)	JAMES CALLAGHAN	(1976–79)
ROBERT PEEL	(1841–46)	MARGARET THATCHER	(1979–90)
JOHN RUSSELL	(1846–52)	JOHN MAJOR	(1990–97)
EDWARD GEORGE GEOFFREY		TONY BLAIR	(1997–2007)
SMITH STANLEY, EARL OF DERBY	(1852)	GORDON BROWN	(2007–10)
		DAVID CAMERON	(2010–16)
		THERESA MAY	(2016–)

THE PRESIDENTS OF THE UNITED STATES OF AMERICA

NAME	(TERM)	NAME	(TERM)
GEORGE WASHINGTON	(1789–97)	GROVER CLEVELAND	(1893–97)
JOHN ADAMS	(1797–1801)	WILLIAM MCKINLEY	(1897–1901)
THOMAS JEFFERSON	(1801–09)	THEODORE ROOSEVELT	(1901–09)
JAMES MADISON	(1809–17)	WILLIAM HOWARD TAFT	(1909–13)
JAMES MONROE	(1817–25)	WOODROW WILSON	(1913–21)
JOHN QUINCY ADAMS	(1825–29)	WARREN GAMALIEL HARDING	(1921–23)
ANDREW JACKSON	(1829–37)	CALVIN COOLIDGE	(1923–29)
MARTIN VAN BUREN	(1837–41)	HERBERT CLARK HOOVER	(1929–33)
WILLIAM HENRY HARRISON	(1841)	FRANKLIN DELANO ROOSEVELT	(1933–45)
JOHN TYLER	(1841–45)	HARRY S. TRUMAN	(1945–53)
JAMES KNOX POLK	(1845–49)	DWIGHT DAVID EISENHOWER	(1953–61)
ZACHARY TAYLOR	(1849–50)	JOHN FITZGERALD KENNEDY	(1961–63)
MILLARD FILLMORE	(1850–53)	LYNDON BAINES JOHNSON	(1963–69)
FRANKLIN PIERCE	(1853–57)	RICHARD MILHOUS NIXON	(1969–74)
JAMES BUCHANAN	(1857–61)	GERALD RUDOLPH FORD	(1974–77)
ABRAHAM LINCOLN	(1861–65)	JAMES EARL CARTER	(1977–81)
ANDREW JOHNSON	(1865–69)	RONALD WILSON REAGAN	(1981–89)
ULYSSES SIMPSON GRANT	(1869–77)	GEORGE HERBERT WALKER BUSH	(1989–93)
RUTHERFORD BIRCHARD HAYES	(1877–81)	WILLIAM JEFFERSON CLINTON	(1993–2001)
JAMES ABRAM GARFIELD	(1881)	GEORGE WALKER BUSH	(2001–09)
CHESTER ALAN ARTHUR	(1881–85)	BARACK OBAMA	(2009–17)
GROVER CLEVELAND	(1885–89)	DONALD TRUMP	(2017–)
BENJAMIN HARRISON	(1889–93)		

RULERS OF ENGLAND

KINGS OF KENT		EDWIN	(?590–592)
HENGEST	(c. 455–488)	ETHELFRITH	(592–616)
GERIC surnamed OISC	(488–?512)	EDWIN	(616–632)
OCTA	(?512–?)	OSRIC	(632–633)
EORMENRIC	(?–560)	OSWALD (ST.)	(633–641)
ETHELBERT I	(560–616)	OSWINE	(644–651)
EADBALD	(616–640)	ETHELWALD	(651–654)
EARCONBERT	(640–664)		
EGBERT I	(664–673)	**KINGS OF NORTHUMBRIA**	
HLOTHERE*	(673–685)	ETHELFRITH	(592–616)
EADRIC*	(685–686)	EDWIN	(616–632)
SUAEBHARD*	(676–692)	OSWALD (ST.)	(633–641)
OSWINI*	(?688–?690)	OSWIU	(654–670)
WIHTRED*	(690–725)	EGFRITH	(670–685)
ETHELBERT II*	(725–762)	ALDFRITH	(685–704)
EADBERT*	(?725–?762)	OSRED I	(704–716)
ALRIC*	(c. 750s)	COENRED	(716–718)
EARDWULF*	(747–762)	OSRIC	(718–729)
SIGERED*	(?762)	CEOLWULF	(729–737)
EANMUND*	(c. 759–765)	EADBERT	(737–758)
HEABERHT*	(764–765)	OSWULF	(c. 758)
EGBERT II	(c. 765–780)	ETHELWALD MOLL	(758–765)
EALHMUND	(784–786)	ALCHRED	(765–774)
EADBERT (PRAEN)	(796–798)	ETHELRED I	(774–778)
EADWALD	(?798 or 807)	ELFWALD I	(778–788)
CUTHRED	(798–807)	OSRED II	(788–790)
BALDRED	(?825)	ETHELRED I	(790–796)
		OSBALD	(796)
KINGS OF DEIRA		EARDWULF	(796–806)
AELLI	(c. 560–590)	ELFWALD II	(806–808)

EARDWULF	(?808)
EANRED	(808–840)
ETHELRED II	(840–844)
REDWULF	(844)
ETHELRED II	(844–849)
OSBERT	(849–862)
AELLE	(862–867)
EGBERT I	(867–873)
RICSIG	(873–876)
EGBERT II	(876–?878)

KINGS OF MERCIA

CEARL	(c. 600)
PENDA	(632–654)
WULFHERE	(657–674)
ETHELRED	(674–704)
COENRED	(704–709)
CEOLRED	(709–716)
ETHELBALD	(716–?757)
BEORNRED	(757)
OFFA	(757–796)
EGFRITH	(796)
COENWULF	(796–?821)
CEOLWULF I	(821–823)
BEORNWULF	(823–825)
LUDECAN	(825–827)
WIGLAF	(827–840)
BEORHTWULF	(840–852)
BURGRED	(852–874)
CEOLWULF II	(874–?883)

KINGS OF THE WEST SAXONS

CERDIC	(519–534)
CYNRIC	(534–560)
CEAWLIN	(560–591)
CEOL	(591–597)
CEOLWULF	(597–611)
CYNEGILS	(611–643)
CENWALH	(643–672)
SEAXBURH (Queen)	(?672–?674)
AESCWINE	(674–676)
CENTWINE	(676–685)
CAEDWALLA	(685–688)
INI	(688–726)
AETHELHEARD	(726–?740)
CUTHRED	(740–756)
SIGEBERHT	(756–757)
CYNEWULF	(757–786)
BEORHTRIC	(786–802)
EGBERT	(802–839)
ETHELWULF	(839–855)
ETHELBALD	(855–860)
ETHELBERT	(860–866)
ETHELRED	(866–871)
ALFRED	(871–899)
EDWARD THE ELDER	(899–925)
ATHELSTAN	(925–939)
EDMUND	(939–946)
EDRED	(946–955)

RULERS OF ENGLAND

EDWY	(955–959)

EDGAR	(959–975)
EDWARD THE MARTYR	(975–979)
ETHELRED	(979–1013)
SWEGN FORKBEARD	(1013–14)
ETHELRED	(1014–16)
EDMUND IRONSIDE	(1016)
CANUTE	(1016–35)
HAROLD HAREFOOT	(1035–40)
HARTACNUT	(1040–42)
EDWARD THE CONFESSOR	(1042–66)
HAROLD GODWINSON	(1066)
EDGAR ETHELING	(1066)
WILLIAM I (THE CONQUEROR)	(1066–87)
WILLIAM II (RUFUS)	(1087–1100)
HENRY I	(1100–35)
STEPHEN	(1135–54)
HENRY II	(1154–89)
RICHARD I	(1189–99)
JOHN	(1199–1216)
HENRY III	(1216–72)
EDWARD I	(1272–1307)
EDWARD II	(1307–27)
EDWARD III	(1327–77)
RICHARD II	(1377–99)
HENRY IV	(1399–1413)
HENRY V	(1413–22)
HENRY VI	(1422–61; 1470–71)
EDWARD IV	(1461–83)
EDWARD V	(1483)
RICHARD III	(1483–85)
HENRY VII	(1485–1509)
HENRY VIII	(1509–47)
EDWARD VI	(1547–53)
JANE (LADY JANE GREY)	(1553)
MARY	(1553–58)
PHILIP*	(1554–58)
ELIZABETH I	(1558–1603)
JAMES I	(1603–25)
CHARLES I	(1625–49)
THE COMMONWEALTH	(1649–60)
[OLIVER CROMWELL	(1653–58) RICHARD
CROMWELL	(1658–59)]
CHARLES II	(1660–85)
JAMES II	(1685–88)
WILLIAM AND MARY	(1689–1694)
WILLIAM III	(1694–1702)
ANNE	(1702–14)
GEORGE I	(1714–27)
GEORGE II	(1727–60)
GEORGE III	(1760–1820)
GEORGE IV	(1820–30)
WILLIAM IV	(1830–37)
VICTORIA	(1837–1901)
EDWARD VII	(1901–10)
GEORGE V	(1910–36)
EDWARD VIII (DUKE OF WINDSOR)	(1936)
GEORGE VI	(1936–52)
ELIZABETH II	(1952–)

* Joint rulers

SCOTTISH RULERS

KENNETH I (MACALPIN)	(843–58)	EDGAR	(1097–1107)
DONALD I	(858–62)	ALEXANDER I	(1107–24)
CONSTANTINE I	(862–77)	DAVID I	(1124–53)
AEDH	(877–78)	MALCOLM IV	(1153–65)
GIRAC	(878–89)	WILLIAM THE LION	(1165–1214)
EOCHA	(878–89)	ALEXANDER II	(1214–49)
DONALD II	(889–900)	ALEXANDER III	(1249–86)
CONSTANTINE II	(900–43)	MARGARET, MAID OF NORWAY	(1286–90)
MALCOLM I	(943–54)	JOHN BALLIOL	(1292–96)
INDULPHUS	(954–62)	ROBERT I (BRUCE)	(1306–29)
DUFF	(962–66)	DAVID II	(1329–71)
COLIN	(966–71)	ROBERT II	(1371–90)
KENNETH II	(971–95)	ROBERT III	(1390–1406)
CONSTANTINE III	(995–97)	JAMES I	(1406–37)
KENNETH III	(997–1005)	JAMES II	(1437–60)
MALCOLM II	(1005–34)	JAMES III	(1460–88)
DUNCAN I	(1034–40)	JAMES IV	(1488–1513)
MACBETH	(1040–57)	JAMES V	(1513–42)
MALCOLM III	(1058–93)	MARY STUART, QUEEN OF SCOTS	(1542–67)
DONALD III (BANE)	(1093–94, 1094–97)	JAMES VI OF SCOTLAND	(1567–1625)
DUNCAN II	(1094)		

ROMAN RULERS

Name (Usurpers in italics)	(Date of office)		
		MAXIMUS	(238)
		GORDIAN III	(238–244)
AUGUSTUS	(27 BC– AD 14)	PHILIP	(244–249)
TIBERIUS	(14–37)	DECIUS	(249–251)
CALIGULA	(37–41)	HOSTILIAN	(251)
CLAUDIUS	(41–54)	GALLUS	(251–253)
NERO	(54–68)	AEMILIAN	(253)
GALBA	(68–69)	VALERIAN	(253–260)
OTHO	(69)	GALLIENUS	(253–268)
VITELLIUS	(69)	CLAUDIUS II	(268–269)
VESPASIAN	(69–79)	QUINTILLUS	(269–270)
TITUS	(79–81)	AURELIAN	(270–275)
DOMITIAN	(81–96)	TACITUS	(275–276)
NERVA	(96–98)	FLORIAN	(276)
TRAJAN	(98–117)	PROBUS	(276–282)
HADRIAN	(117–138)	CARUS	(282–283)
ANTONINUS PIUS	(138–161)	CARINUS	(283–285)
MARCUS AURELIUS	(161–180)	NUMERIAN	(283–284)
LUCIUS VERUS	(161–169)	†DIOCLETIAN	(284–305; abdicated)
COMMODUS	(180–192)	*MAXIMIAN	(286–305; 306–308)
PERTINAX	(193)	*CONSTANTIUS I	(305–306)
DIDUS JULIANUS	(193)	†GALERIUS	(305–311)
NIGER	(193)	*SEVERUS	(306–307)
SEPTIMUS SEVERUS	(193–211)	†LICINIUS	(308–324)
CARACALLA	(211–217)	MAXIMIN	(310–313)
GETA	(209–212)	*MAXENTIUS	(306–312)
MACRINUS	(217–218)	CONSTANTINE I (THE GREAT)	(312–337)
ELAGABALUS	(218–222)	CONSTANTINE II	(337–340)
ALEXANDER SEVERUS	(222–235)	CONSTANS	(337–350)
MAXIMIN I	(235–238)	CONSTANTIUS II	(337–361)
GORDIAN I	(238)	MAGNENTIUS	(350–351)
GORDIAN II	(238)	JULIAN	(360–363)
BALBINUS	(238)		

JOVIAN	(363–364)
*VALENTINIAN I	(364–375)
†VALENS	(364–378)
†PROCOPIUS	(365–366)
*GRATIAN	(375–383)
*VALENTINIAN II	(375–392)
THEODOSIUS I	(379–395)
†ARCADIUS	(395–408)
*HONORIUS	(395–423)
CONSTANTINE III	(407–411)
†THEODOSIUS II	(408–450)
*CONSTANTIUS III	(421–423)
VALENTINIAN III	(423–455)
†MARCIAN	(450–457)
*PETRONIUS MAXIMUS	(455)
*AVITUS	(455–456)

†LEO I	(457–474)
*MAJORIAN	(457–461)
*LIBIUS SEVERUS	(461–467)
*ANTHEMIUS	(467–472)
*OLYBRIUS	(472–473)
GLYCERIUS	(473)
*JULIUS NEPOS	(474–475)
†LEO II	(474)
†ZENO	(474–491)
*ROMULUS AUGUSTULUS	(475–476)

*Emperors of the Western Roman Empire only

†Emperors of the Eastern Roman Empire (at Constantinople) before the fall of Rome (476). (For Eastern emperors after 476, see BYZANTINE RULERS.)

BYZANTINE RULERS

Name	(Date of office)
(Usurpers in italics)	
ZENO	(474–491)
BASILICUS	(475–76)
ANASTASIUS I	(491–518)
JUSTIN I	(518–527)
JUSTINIAN I	(527–565)
JUSTIN II	(565–578)
TIBERIUS II CONSTANTINE	(578–582)
MAURICE TIBERIUS	(582–602)
PHOCAS	(602–610)
HERACLIUS	(610–641)
HERACLIUS CONSTANTINE	(641)
HERACLONAS	(641)
CONSTANS II	(641–668)
CONSTANTINE IV	(668–685)
JUSTINIAN II RHINOTMETUS	(685–695, 705–711)
LEONTIUS	(695–698)
TIBERIUS III	(698–705?)
PHILIPPICUS	(711–713)
ANASTASIUS II	(713–716)
THEODOSIUS III	(716–717)
LEO III	(717–741)
CONSTANTINE V COPRONYMUS	(741–775)
LEO IV	(775–780)
CONSTANTINE VI	(780–797)
IRENE	(797–802)
NICEPHORUS I	(802–811)
STAURACIUS	(811)
MICHAEL I RHANGABE	(811–813)
LEO V	(813–820)
MICHAEL II BALBUS	(820–829)
THEOPHILUS	(829–842)
MICHAEL III	(842–867)
BASIL I	(867–886)
LEO VI	(886–912)
ALEXANDER	(912–913)
CONSTANTINE VII PORPHYROGENITUS	(913–959)
ROMANUS I LECAPENUS	(920–944)

ROMANUS II	(959–963)
NICEPHOROUS II PHOCAS	(963–969)
JOHN I TZIMISCES	(969–976)
BASIL II BULGAROCTONUS	(976–1025)
CONSTANTINE VIII	(1025–28)
ROMANUS III ARGYRUS	(1028–34)
MICHAEL IV	(1034–41)
MICHAEL V CALAPHATES	(1041–42)
ZOE	(1042–56)
CONSTANTINE IX MONOMACHUS	(1042–55)
THEODORA	(1055–56)
MICHAEL VI STRATIOTICUS	(1056–57)
ISAAC I COMNENUS	(1057–59)
CONSTANTINE X DUCAS	(1059–67)
ROMANUS IV DIOGENES	(1067–71)
MICHAEL VII DUCAS	(1071–78)
NICEPHORUS III BOTANIATES	(1078–81)
ALEXIUS I COMNENUS	(1081–1118)
JOHN II COMNENUS	(1118–43)
MANUEL I COMNENUS	(1143–80)
ALEXIUS II COMNENUS	(1180–83)
ANDRONICUS I COMNENUS	(1183–85)
ISAAC II ANGELUS	(1185–95, 1203–04)
ALEXIUS III ANGELUS	(1195–1203)
ALEXIUS V DUCAS MURTZUPHLUS	(1204)
*BALDWIN I	(1204–06)
*HENRY	(1206–16)
*PETER	(1217)
*YOLANDE	(1217–19)
*ROBERT	(1219–28)
*BALDWIN II	(1228–61)
*JOHN	(1231–37)
†CONSTANTINE (XI) LASCARIS	(1204–05?)
†THEODORE I LASCARIS	(1205–22)
†JOHN III DUCAS VATATZES	(1222–54)
†THEODORE II LASCARIS	(1254–58)
†JOHN IV LASCARIS	(1258–61)
MICHAEL VIII PALAEOLOGUS	(1261–82)
ANDRONICUS II PALAEOLOGUS	(1282–1328)

ANDRONICUS III PALAEOLOGUS	(1328–41)
JOHN V PALAEOLOGUS	(1341–76,
1379–90,	
1390–91)	
JOHN VI CANTACUZENUS	(1347–54)
ANDRONICUS IV PALAEOLOGUS	(1376–77)

JOHN VII PALAEOLOGUS	(1390)
MANUEL II PALAEOLOGUS	(1391–1425)
JOHN VIII PALAEOLOGUS	(1421–48)
CONSTANTINE XI PALAEOLOGUS	(1448–53)

*Latin emperors
†Nicaean emperors

ANCIENT EGYPTIAN RULERS

DYNASTIES (all dates are BC):

Earliest dynasties
I 3200–3000
II 3000–2780

Old Kingdom
III 2780–2720
IV 2720–2560
V 2560–2420
VI 2420–2270

First Intermediate Period
VII–VIII	2270–2240
IX–X	2240–2100

Middle Kingdom
XI 2100–2000	
XII	2000–1788

Second Intermediate Period
XIII–XVI	1788–1600
XVII	1600–1555

The Empire
XVIII	1555–1350
XIX	1350–1200
XX	1200–1090
XXI	1090–945
XXII	945–c.745
XXIII	c. 745–718
XXIV	718–712

Late Period
XXV	712–663
XXVI	663–525
XXVII	525–332
XXVIII	405–399
XXIX	399–379
XXX	379–341
Ptolemaic	323–30

RULERS

NARMER
MENES
AHA
DEN
HETEPSEKHEMWY
RENEB
NYNETJER
PERIBSEN
KHASEKHEM
KHASEKHEMWY
SANAKHTE
DJOSER
NETJERYKHET
SEKHEMKHET
KHABA
HUNI
SNEFRU
KHUFU
CHEOPS
REDJEDEF
SHEPSESKAF
KHAFRE
USERKAF
SAHURE
NEFERIAKARE
RENEFEREF
NUSERRE
MENKAUHOR
DJEDKARE IZEZI
UNAS
TETI
PEPI I
MERENRE
PEPI II
IBI
NEFERKARE
KHETY
MERIKARE

INYOTEF I	(2081–2065 BC)
INYOTEF II	(2065–2016 BC)
INYOTEF III	(2016–2008 BC)
MENTUHOTEP I	(2008–1957 BC)
MENTUHOTEP II	(1957–1945 BC)
MENTUHOTEP III	(1945–1938 BC)
AMENEMHET I	(1938–1908 BC)
SESOSTRIS I	(1918–1875 BC)
AMENEMHET II	(1876–1842 BC)
SESOSTRIS II	(1844–1837 BC)
SESOSTRIS III	(1836–1818 BC)
AMENEMHET III	(1818–1770 BC)
AMENEMHET IV	(1770–1760 BC)
SEBEKNEFRU	(1760–1756 BC)
APOPIS	
KAMOSE	
AHMOSE	(c. 1539–1514 BC)
AMENHOTEP I	(c. 1514–1493 BC)
THUTMOSE I	(1493–c. 1482 BC)
THUTMOSE II	(c. 1482–1479 BC)

THUTMOSE III	(1479–1426 BC)
HATSHEPSUT	(c. 1481–c.1458 BC)
AMENHOTEP II	(c. 1426–1400BC)
THUTMOSE IV	(1400–1390 BC)
AMENHOTEP III	(1390–1353 BC)
AMENHOTEP IV	(1353–1336 BC)
AKHENATON	(1353–1336 BC)
SMENKHKARE	(1335–1332 BC)
TUTANKHATEN	(1352–c. 1323 BC)
TUTANKHAMEN	(1352–c. 1323 BC)
AY	(1323–1319 BC)
HOREMHEB	(1319–c. 1292 BC)
RAMSES I	(1292–1290 BC)
SETI I	(1290–1279 BC)
RAMSES II	(1279–1213BC)
MARNEPTAH	(1213–1204 BC)
SETI II	(1204–1198 BC)
SIPTAH	(1198–1193 BC)
TAUSERT	(1193–1190 BC)
SETNAKHT	(1190–1187 BC)
RAMSES III	(1187–1156 BC)
RAMSES IV	(1156–1150 BC)
RAMSES V	(1150–1145 BC)
RAMSES VI	(1145–1137 BC)
RAMSES VII	(1137–c. 1132 BC)
RAMSES VIII	(c. 1132–1126 BC)
RAMSES IX	(1126–1108 BC)
RAMSES X	(1108–1104 BC)
RAMSES XI	(1104–c. 1075 BC)
SMENDES	(c. 1075 BC)
PINUDJEM I	
PSUSENNES I	(c. 1045–c. 997 BC)
AMENEMOPE	(c. 998–c. 989 BC)
OSORKON I	(c. 979–c. 973 BC)
PSUSENNES II	(c. 964–c. 950 BC)
SHESHONK	(c. 950–929 BC)
OSORKON II	(c. 929–c. 914 BC)
OSORKON III	(c. 888–c. 860 BC)
OSORKON IV	(c. 777–c. 750 BC)

KASHTA	
SHEPENWEPE I	
AMONIRDIS I	
BOCCHORIS	(c. 722–c. 715 BC)
SHABAKA	(c. 719–703 BC)
SHEBITKU	(703–690 BC)
TAHARQA	(690–664 BC)
TANUTAMON	(664 BC)
PSAMTIK I	(664–610 BC)
PSAMMETICHUS I	(664–610 BC)
NECHO II	(610–595 BC)
PSAMTIK II	(595–589 BC)
APRIES	(589–570 BC)
AMASIS II	(570–526 BC)
AHMOSE II	(570–526 BC)
CAMBYSES II	(526–522 BC)
DARIUS I	(522–486 BC)
ARTAXERXES I	(465–424 BC)
DARIUS II	(424–404 BC)
AMYRTAEUS	(404–399 BC)
ACHORIS	(393–380 BC)
NEPHERITES II	(380 BC)
NECTANEBO I	(380–362 BC)
TACHOS	(c. 365–360 BC)
NECTANEBO II	(360–343 BC)
PTOLEMY I SOTER	(305–282 BC)
PTOLEMY II PHILADELPHUS	(285–246 BC)
PTOLEMY III EVERGETES	(246–222 BC)
PTOLEMY IV PHILOPATOR	(222–205 BC)
PTOLEMY V EPIPHANES	(205–180 BC)
PTOLEMY VI PHILOMETOR	(180–145 BC)
PTOLEMY VIII	(145–116 BC)
EURGETES II	
PHYSCON	
PTOLEMY XII AULETES	(80–51 BC)
PTOLEMY XIII	(51–47 BC)
CLEOPATRA VII	(51–30 BC)

ARTISTS, SCULPTORS, AND ARCHITECTS

3

ARP, Jean (1887–1966; French sculptor and poet)

DOU, Gerrit (1613–75; Dutch painter)

FRY, Roger (1866–1934; British painter and art critic)

LIN, Maya (1959– ; US sculptor and architect)

LOW, David (1871–1963; New Zealand-born cartoonist)

4

ADAM, Robert (1728–92; British architect and interior designer)

CAPP, Al (Alfred Caplin, 1909–79; US cartoonist)

CUYP, Aelbert Jacobsz (1620– 91; Dutch landscape painter)

DADD, Richard (1817–86; British painter)

DALI, Salvador (1904–89; Spanish surrealist painter)

DORÉ, Gustave (1832–83; French illustrator, painter, and sculptor)

DUFY, Raoul (1877–1953; French painter)

EMIN, Tracey (1963– ; British artist)

ERTÉ (Romain de Tirtoff, 1892–1990; French fashion illustrator and designer, born in Russia)

ETTY, William (1787–1849; British painter)

GABO, Naum (Naum Neemia Pevsner, 1890–1977; Russian sculptor)

GOES, Hugo van der (c. 1440–82; Flemish painter)

GOYA, Francesco de (1746–1828; Spanish painter)

GRIS, Juan (José Victoriano González, 1887–1927; Spanish-born cubist painter)

GROS, Antoine Jean, Baron (1771–1835; French painter)

HALS, Frans (c. 1581–1666; Dutch painter)

HILL, David Octavius (1802–70; Scottish painter and photographer)

HUNT, William Holman (1827–1910; British painter)

JOHN, Augustus (1878–1961; British painter)

KAHN, Louis Isadore (1901–74; US architect)

KENT, William (1685–1748; English architect, landscape gardener, and interior designer)

KLEE, Paul (1879–1940; Swiss painter and etcher)

LAMB, Henry (1885–1960; Australian-born British painter)

LELY, Peter (Pieter van der Faes, 1618–80; English portrait painter of Dutch descent)

LOOS, Adolph (1870–1933; Austrian architect)

MAES, Nicolas (or N Maas, 1634–93; Dutch painter)

MARC, Franz (1880–1916; German expressionist painter)

MIRÓ, Joan (1893–1983; Spanish painter)

NASH, John (1752–1835; British architect)

NASH, Paul (1889–1946; British painter)

NEER, Aert van der (c. 1603–77; Dutch landscape painter)

OPIE, John (1761–1807; British portrait and history painter)

RENI, Guido (1575–1642; Italian painter)

ROSA, Salvator (1615–73; Italian painter and etcher)

SHAW, Norman (1831–1912; British architect)

WARD, Leslie (1851–1922; British caricaturist)

WEST, Benjamin (1738–1820; British painter of American birth)

WOOD, Christopher (1901–30; English painter)

WOOD, Grant (1892–1942; US painter)

WOOD, John, of Bath (1704–54; English architect)

WREN, Christopher (1632–1723; English architect and scientist)

ZORN, Anders (1860–1920; Swedish artist)

5

AALTO, Alvar (1898–1976; Finnish architect)

ATGET, Eugène (1856–1927; French photographer)

BACON, Francis (1909–92; British painter, born in Dublin)

BACON, John (1740–99; British neoclassical sculptor)

BAKST, Léon (Lev Samoilovich Rosenberg, 1866–1924; Russian artist)

BALLA, Giacomo (1871–1958; Italian futurist painter)

BARRY, Charles (1795–1860; British architect)

BLAKE, Peter, Sir (1932– ; British artist)

BLAKE, Quentin, Sir (1932– ; British artist)

BOSCH, Hieronymus (Jerome van Aeken, c. 1450–c. 1516; Dutch painter)

BOUTS, Dierick (c. 1400–75; Netherlandish painter)

BROWN, Capability (Lancelot B, 1716–83; British landscape gardener)

BROWN, Ford Madox (1821–93; British painter, born in Calais)

BURRA, Edward (1905–76; British painter)

CAMPI, Giulio (1502–72; Italian Renaissance architect)

COROT, Jean Baptiste Camille (1796–1875; French landscape painter)

CRANE, Walter (1845–1915; British illustrator, painter, and designer of textiles and wallpaper)

CROME, John (1768–1821; British landscape painter and etcher)

DAGLY, Gerhard (c. 1653–?1714; Belgian artist)

DANBY, Francis (1793–1861; Irish painter)

DANCE, George (c. 1700–68; British architect)

DAVID, Gerard (c. 1460–1523; Netherlandish painter)

DAVID, Jacques Louis (1748–1825; French painter)

DEGAS, Edgar (1834–1917; French painter and sculptor)

DENIS, Maurice (1870–1943; French painter, designer, and art theorist)

DÜRER, Albrecht (1471–1528; German painter)

ENSOR, James Sydney, Baron (1860–1949; Belgian painter)

ERNST, Max (1891–1976; German artist)

FOLEY, John Henry (1818–74; British sculptor)

FREUD, Lucian (1922–2011; German-born British painter)

GADDI, Taddeo (c. 1300– ?1366; Florentine painter)

GEHRY, Frank Owen (1929– ; US architect)

GIBBS, James (1682–1754; British architect)

GILES, Carl Ronald (1916–95; British cartoonist)

GORKY, Arshile (Vosdanig Adoian, 1905–48; US painter, born in Armenia)

GOYEN, Jan Josephszoon van (1596–1656; Dutch landscape painter and etcher)

GRANT, Duncan James Corrowr (1885–1978; British painter and designer)

GROSZ, George (1893–1959; German painter and draughtsman)

HIMID, Lubaina (1954– ; British artist)

HIRST, Damien (1965– ; British artist and sculptor)

HOMER, Winslow (1836–1910; US painter)

HOOCH, Pieter de (1629–c. 1684; Dutch painter)

HORTA, Victor (1861–1947; Belgian architect)

JOHNS, Jasper (1930– ; US artist)

JONES, Inigo (1573–1652; English classical architect)

KEENE, Charles Samuel (1823–91; British artist and illustrator)

KLIMT, Gustav (1862–1918; Viennese Art Nouveau artist)

KLINT, Kaare (1888–1954; Danish furniture designer)

LEACH, Bernard (1887–1979; British potter, born in Hong Kong)

LEECH, John (1817–64; British caricaturist)

LÉGER, Fernand (1881–1955; French painter)

LE VAU, Louis (1612–70; French baroque architect)

LIPPI, Fra Filippo (c. 1406–69; Florentine painter)

LOTTO, Lorenzo (c. 1480–1556; Venetian painter)

LOWRY, L S (1887–1976; British painter)

MACKE, August (1887–1914; German painter)

MANET, Edouard (1832–83; French painter)

MENGS, Anton Raphael (1728–79; German painter)

METSU, Gabriel (1629–67; Dutch painter)

MONET, Claude (1840–1926; French impressionist painter)

MOORE, Henry (1898–1986; British sculptor)

MOSES, Grandma (Anna Mary Robertson M, 1860–1961; US primitive painter)

MUNCH, Edvard (1863–1944; Norwegian painter and printmaker)

MYRON (5th century BC; Athenian sculptor)

NADAR (Gaspard Felix Tournachon, 1820–1910; French photographer and caricaturist)

NERVI, Pier Luigi (1891–1979; Italian architect)

NOLAN, Sidney (1917–92; Australian painter)

NOLDE, Emil (E Hansen, 1867–1956; German expressionist painter and printmaker)

OUDRY, Jean-Baptiste (1686–1755; French rococo painter and tapestry designer)

PHYFE, Duncan (or Fife, 1768–1854; US cabinetmaker and furniture designer, born in Scotland)

PIPER, John (1903–92; British painter and writer)

PUGIN, Augustus Welby Northmore (1812–52; British architect and theorist)

REDON, Odilon (1840–1916; French symbolist painter and lithographer)

RICCI, Sebastiano (1659–1734; Venetian painter)

RILEY, Bridget Louise (1931– ; British painter)

RODIN, Auguste (1840–1917; French sculptor)

SCOTT, George Gilbert (1811–78; British architect)

SHAHN, Ben (1898–1969; Lithuanian-born US artist)

SOANE, John (1753–1837; British architect)

STEEN, Jan (c. 1626–79; Dutch painter)

STOSS, Veit (c. 1445–1533; German gothic sculptor and woodcarver)

TOBEY, Mark (1890–1976; US painter)

UTZON, Jørn (1918–2008; Danish architect)

VICKY (Victor Weisz, 1913–66; British cartoonist, born in Berlin)

WATTS, George Frederick (1817–1904; British artist)

WYATT, James (1747–1813; British architect)

6

ALBERS, Josef (1888–1976; German abstract painter)

ARCHER, Thomas (1668–1743; English baroque architect)

BEATON, Cecil (1904–80; British photographer)

BEHZAD (c. 1455–c. 1536; Persian painter)

BENTON, Thomas Hart (1889–1975; US painter)

BEWICK, Thomas (1753–1828; British wood engraver)

BOUDIN, Eugène (1824–98; French painter)

BOULLE, André Charles (or Buhl, 1642–1732; French cabinetmaker)

BRANDT, Bill (1905–83; British photographer)

BRAQUE, Georges (1882–1963; French painter)

BRATBY, John (1928–92; British painter and writer)

BREUER, Marcel Lajos (1902–81; US architect, born in Hungary)

BUFFET, Bernard (1928–99; French painter)

BUTLER, Reg Cotterell (1913–81; British sculptor)

CALDER, Alexander (1898–1976; US sculptor)

CALLOT, Jacques (c. 1592–1635; French graphic artist)

CANOVA, Antonio (1757–1822; Italian sculptor)

CASSON, Hugh (1910–99; British architect)

CLOUET, Jean (c. 1485–1540; French portrait painter)

COOPER, Samuel (1609–72; British miniaturist)

COSWAY, Richard (1742–1821; British portrait miniaturist)

COTMAN, John Sell (1782–1842; British landscape watercolourist and etcher)

DELLER, Jeremy (1966– ; British artist)

DERAIN, André (1880–1954; French postimpressionist painter)

DE WINT, Peter (1784–1849; British landscape painter)

EAKINS, Thomas (1844–1916; US painter)

FLORIS, Cornelis (1514–75; Flemish artist)

FLORIS, Frans (c. 1516–70; Flemish artist)

FOSTER, Norman, Baron Foster of Thames Bank (1935– ; British architect)

FULLER, Richard Buckminster (1895–1983; US inventor and architect)

FUSELI, Henry (Johann Heinrich Füssli, 1741–1825; British painter of Swiss birth)

GÉRARD, François, Baron (1770–1837; French painter)

GIOTTO (Giotto di Bondone, c. 1266–1337; Italian painter and architect)

GIRTIN, Thomas (1775–1802; British landscape painter)

GORDON, Douglas (1966– ; British artist)

GOUJON, Jean (c. 1510–68; French Renaissance sculptor)

GREUZE, Jean-Baptiste (1725–1805; French painter)

GUARDI, Francesco (1712–93; Venetian painter)

HOLLAR, Wenceslaus (1607–77; Bohemian etcher)

HOUDON, Jean Antoine (1741–1828; French sculptor)

INGRES, Jean-Auguste-Dominique (1780–1867; French painter)

ISABEY, Jean Baptiste (1767–1855; French portrait painter and miniaturist)

JOCHHO (d. 1057; Japanese sculptor)

KAPOOR, Anish, Sir (1954– ; Indian-born British sculptor)

KNIGHT, Laura (1877–1970; British painter)

LASDUN, Denys (1914–2001; British architect)

LA TOUR, Georges de (1593–1652; French painter)

LA TOUR, Maurice-Quentin de (1704–88; French portrait pastellist)

LE BRUN, Charles (1619–90; French history and portrait painter and designer)

LE NAIN, Antoine (c. 1588–1648; French painter)

LE NAIN, Louis (c. 1593–1648; French painter)

LE NAIN, Mathieu (c. 1607–77; French painter)

LESCOT, Pierre (c. 1510–78; French architect)

LONGHI, Pietro (Pietro Falca, 1702–85; Venetian painter)

LURÇAT, Jean (1892–1966; French painter)

MARINI, Marino (1901–80; Italian sculptor and painter)

MARTEN, Helen (1985– ; British sculptor)

MARTIN, John (1789–1854; British painter)

MASSYS, Quentin (or Matsys, Messys, Metsys, c. 1466– 1530; Flemish painter)

MILLET, Jean François (1814–75; French painter)

MOREAU, Gustave (1826–98; French symbolist painter)

MORONI, Giovanni Battista (c. 1525–78; Italian painter)

MORRIS, William (1834–96; British designer and artist)

NOUVEL, Jean (1945– ; French artist)

OLIVER, Isaac (?1556–1617; English portrait miniaturist, born in France)

OROZCO, José (1883–1949; Mexican mural painter)

OSTADE, Adrian van (1610–85; Dutch painter and etcher)

PALMER, Samuel (1805–81; British landscape painter and etcher)

PAXTON, Joseph (1801–65; British architect)

PISANO, Andrea (Andrea de Pontedera, c. 1290–1348; Italian sculptor)

PISANO, Nicola (c. 1220–c. 1278; Italian sculptor)

RENOIR, Pierre Auguste (1841–1919; French impressionist painter)

RIBERA, José de (or Jusepe R, 1591– 1652; Spanish-born painter and etcher)

RIVERA, Diego (1886–1957; Mexican mural painter)

ROGERS, Richard, Baron Rogers of Riverside (1933– ; British architect)

ROMNEY, George (1734–1802; British portrait painter)

ROTHKO, Mark (Marcus Rothkovitch, 1903–70; Russian-born US painter)

RUBENS, Peter Paul (1577–1640; Flemish painter)

SCARFE, Gerald (1936– ; British cartoonist)

SEARLE, Ronald William Fordham (1920–2011; British cartoonist)

SESSHU (Sesshu Toyo, 1420–1506; Japanese landscape painter)

SEURAT, Georges (1859–91; French painter)

SIGNAC, Paul (1863–1935; French painter and art theorist)

SISLEY, Alfred (1839–99; Impressionist painter)

SLUTER, Claus (c. 1345–1406; Dutch sculptor)

SPENCE, Basil (1907–76; British architect)

STUBBS, George (1724–1806; British animal painter)

TANGUY, Yves (1900–55; French surrealist painter)

TISSOT, James Joseph Jacques (1836–1902; French painter and etcher)

TITIAN (Tiziano Vecellio, c. 1488–1576; Venetian painter)

TURNER, Joseph Mallord William (1775–1851; British landscape and marine painter)

VASARI, Giorgio (1511–74; Italian painter, architect, and writer)

VOYSEY, Charles Francis Annesley (1857–1941; British architect and designer)

WARHOL, Andy (Andrew Warhola, 1926–87; US pop artist)

WEYDEN, Rogier van der (c. 1400–64; Flemish painter)

WILKIE, David (1785–1841; Scottish painter)

WILSON, Richard (1714–82; British landscape painter)

WRIGHT, Frank Lloyd (1869–1959; US architect)

XIA GUI (or Hsia Knei, c. 1180–c. 1230, Chinese landscape painter)

ZEUXIS (late 5th century BC; Greek painter)

7

ALBERTI, Leon Battista (1404–72; Italian Renaissance architect)

ALLSTON, Washington (1779–1843; US Romantic painter)

ANTENOR (late 6th century BC; Athenian sculptor)

APELLES (4th century BC; Greek painter)

ASTBURY, John (1688–1743; English potter)

BARLACH, Ernst (1870–1938; German expressionist sculptor and playwright)

BASSANO, Jacopo (Jacopo or Giacomo da Ponte, c. 1517–92; Italian painter)

BEHRENS, Peter (1868–1940; German architect)

BELLINI, Jacopo (c. 1400–c. 1470; Venetian painter)

BERNINI, Gian Lorenzo (1598–1680; Italian sculptor and architect)

BONNARD, Pierre (1867–1947; French painter)

BORGLUM, Gutzon (1867–1941; US sculptor)

BOUCHER, François (1703–70; French rococo painter)

BROUWER, Adriaen (c. 1605–38; Flemish painter)

CAMERON, Julia Margaret (1815–79; British photographer, born in Calcutta)

CASSATT, Mary (1844–1926; US painter)

CELLINI, Benvenuto (1500–71; Florentine goldsmith and sculptor)

CENNINI, Cennino (c. 1370–c. 1440; Florentine painter)

CÉZANNE, Paul (1839–1906; French postimpressionist painter)

CHAGALL, Marc (1887–1985; Russian-born painter and printmaker)

CHARDIN, Jean-Baptiste-Siméon (1699–1779; French painter)

CHIRICO, Giorgio de (1888–1978; Italian painter)

CHRISTO (1935–2009; Bulgarian-born artist)

CIMABUE, Giovanni (Cenni de Peppi, c. 1240–c. 1302; Florentine painter)

CLODION (Claude Michel, 1738–1814; French rococo sculptor)

COURBET, Gustave (1819–77; French painter)

DAUMIER, Honoré (1808–79; French caricaturist, painter, and sculptor)

DELORME, Philibert (?1510–70; French Renaissance architect)

DELVAUX, Paul (1897–94; Belgian painter)

DUCHAMP, Marcel (1887–1968; French artist)

EL GRECO (Domenikos Theotokopoulos, 1541–1614; Painter of Greek parentage, born in Crete)

EPSTEIN, Jacob (1880– 1959; British sculptor)

EXEKIAS (6th century BC; Athenian potter and vase painter)

FABERGÉ, Peter Carl (1846–1920; Russian goldsmith and jeweller)

FLAXMAN, John Henry (1755–1826; British sculptor and book illustrator)

FONTANA, Domenico (1543–1607; Italian architect)

FOUQUET, Jean (c. 1420–81; French painter and manuscript illuminator)

GAUGUIN, Paul (1848–1903; French postimpressionist painter)

GIBBONS, Grinling (1648–1721; English wood carver and sculptor)

GILLRAY, James (1756–1815; British caricaturist)

GOZZOLI, Benozzo (Benozzo di Lese, 1420–97; Florentine painter)

GROPIUS, Walter (1883–1969; German architect)

GUARINI, Guarino (1624–83; Italian baroque architect)

HASSALL, John (1868–1948; British artist)

HERRERA, Juan de (1530–97; Spanish architect)

HOBBEMA, Meindert (1638–1709; Dutch landscape painter)

HOCKNEY, David (1937– ; British painter, draughtsman, and printmaker)

HOGARTH, William (1697–1764; British painter and engraver)

HOKUSAI (Katsushika H, 1760–1849; Japanese painter and book illustrator)

HOLLAND, Henry (1745–1806; British architect)

HOLSTAD, Christian (1972– ; US conceptual artist)

HOPPNER, John (1758–1810; British portrait painter)

ICTINUS (5th century BC; Greek architect)

JOHNSON, Cornelius (Janssen van Ceulen, 1593–1661; English portrait painter)

KNELLER, Godfrey (1646– 1723; English portrait painter)

LALIQUE, René (1860–1945; French Art Nouveau jeweller and glassmaker)

LAMERIE, Paul de (1688– 1751; English silversmith)

L'ENFANT, Pierre-Charles (1754–1825; US architect and town planner of French birth)

LE NÔTRE, André (1613–1700; French landscape gardener)

LIMBURG, Pol de (active c. 1400–c. 1416; French manuscript illuminator)

LIMOSIN, Léonard (or Limousin, c. 1505–c. 1577; French artist)

LOCHNER, Stefan (c. 1400–51; German painter)

LUTYENS, Edwin Landseer (1869–1944; British architect)

MACLISE, Daniel (1806–70; Irish portrait and history painter)

MADERNA, Carlo (1556–1629; Roman architect)

MAILLOL, Aristide (1861–1944; French sculptor)

MANSART, François (or Mansard, 1596–1666; French classical architect)

MARTINI, Simone (c. 1284–1344; Italian painter)

MATISSE, Henri (1869–1954; French painter and sculptor)

MEMLING, Hans (or Memlinc, c. 1430–1494; German painter)

MILLAIS, John Everett (1829–96; British painter)

MORANDI, Giorgio (1890–1964; Italian still-life painter and etcher)

MORISOT, Berthe (1841–95; French painter)

MORLAND, George (1763–1804; British painter)

MURILLO, Bartolomé Esteban (1617–82; Spanish painter)

NEUMANN, Balthasar (1687–1753; German architect)

O'KEEFFE, Georgia (1887–1986; US painter)

ORCAGNA, Andrea (Andrea di Cione, c. 1308–c. 1368; Florentine artist)

PALISSY, Bernard (1510–89; French potter)

PASMORE, Victor (1908–98; British artist)

PATINIR, Joachim (or Patenier, c. 1485–1524; Flemish painter)

PEVSNER, Antoine (1886–1962; Russian sculptor and painter)

PHIDIAS (c. 490–c. 417 BC; Athenian sculptor)

PICABIA, Francis (1879–1953; French painter and writer)

PICASSO, Pablo (1881–1973; Spanish artist)

POLLOCK, Jackson (1912–56; US painter)

POUSSIN, Nicolas (1594–1665; French painter)

PRUD'HON, Pierre Paul (1758–1823; French painter and draughtsman)

RACKHAM, Arthur (1867–1939; British watercolourist and book illustrator)

RAEBURN, Henry (1756–1823; Scottish portrait painter)

RAPHAEL (Raffaello Sanzio, 1483–1520; Italian Renaissance painter and architect)

REDOUTÉ, Pierre Joseph (1759–1841; French flower painter)

RICHTER, Gerhard (1932– ; German artist)

ROBERTS, Tom (1856–1931;

Australian painter, born in Britain)

ROUAULT, Georges (1871–1958; French artist)

RUBLYOV, Andrey (or A Rublev, c. 1370–1430; Russian icon painter)

SARGENT, John Singer (1856–1925; US portrait painter, born in Florence)

SCHIELE, Egon (1890–1918; Austrian expressionist painter)

SEGHERS, Hercules Pieterzoon (c. 1589–c. 1638; Dutch landscape painter and etcher)

SHEPARD, Ernest Howard (1879–1976; British artist)

SICKERT, Walter Richard (1860–1942; British impressionist, born in Munich)

SNOWDON, Antony Armstrong-Jones, Earl of (1930–2017; British photographer)

SNYDERS, Frans (1579–1657; Flemish animal painter)

SOUTINE, Chaim (1893–1943; Lithuanian-born painter, who emigrated to Paris)

SPENCER, Stanley (1891–1959; British painter)

TENNIEL, John (1820–1914; British cartoonist and book illustrator)

TIBALDI, Pellegrino (1527–96; Italian architect and painter)

TIEPOLO, Giovanni Battista (1696–1770; Venetian rococo painter)

UCCELLO, Paolo (P di Dono, 1397–1475; Florentine painter and craftsman)

UTRILLO, Maurice (1883–1955; French painter)

VAN DYCK, Anthony (or Vandyke, 1599–1641; Flemish baroque painter)

VAN EYCK, Jan (c. 1390–1441; Flemish painter)

VAN GOGH, Vincent (1853–90; Dutch postimpressionist painter)

VERMEER, Jan (1632–75; Dutch painter)

VIGNOLA, Giacomo da (1507–73; Roman mannerist architect)

WATTEAU, Antoine (1684– 1721; French rococo painter)

ZADKINE, Ossip (1890–1967; French sculptor of Russian birth)

ZOFFANY, Johann (c. 1733–1810; German-born English painter)

ZUCCARO, Federico (1543–1609; Italian painter)

ZUCCARO, Taddeo (1529–66; Italian painter)

8

AALTONEN, Wäinö (1894–1966; Finnish sculptor)

AMMANATI, Bartolommeo (1511–92; Florentine architect and sculptor)

ANGELICO, Fra (Guido di Pietro, c. 1400–55; Italian painter)

ANNIGONI, Pietro (1910–88; Italian painter)

ANTELAMI, Benedetto (active 1177–1233; Italian sculptor)

BECKMANN, Max (1884–1950; German expressionist painter)

BOCCIONI, Umberto (1882–1916; Italian futurist painter and sculptor)

BRAMANTE, Donato (1444–1514; Italian Renaissance painter)

BRANCUSI, Constantin (1876–1957; Romanian sculptor)

BRONZINO, Il (Agnolo di Cosimo, 1503–72; Florentine mannerist painter)

CAMPBELL, Duncan (1972– ; Irish video artist)

CARNEGIE, Gillian (1971– ; British painter)

CARRACCI, Annibale (1560–1609; Italian painter)

CASTAGNO, Andrea del (Andrea di Bartolo de Simone, c. 1421–57; Italian painter)

CHAMBERS, William (1723–96; British architect and interior designer)

CRESSENT, Charles (1685–1768; French cabinetmaker)

CRIVELLI, Carlo (c. 1430–95; Venetian painter)

DAUBIGNY, Charles-François (1817–78; French landscape painter)

DELAUNAY, Robert (1885–1941; French painter)

DRYSDALE, Russell (1912–81; Australian painter, born in England)

DUBUFFET, Jean (1901–85; French painter and sculptor)

FILARETE (Antonio Averlino, c. 1400–c. 1469; Italian Renaissance architect)

FRAMPTON, George James (1860–1928; British sculptor)

GHIBERTI, Lorenzo (c. 1378–1455; Florentine Renaissance sculptor)

GIORDANO, Luca (1632–1705; Neapolitan painter, nicknamed LUCA FA PRESTO)

GOSSAERT, Jan (c. 1478–c. 1532; Flemish painter)

GUERCINO (Giovanni Francesco Barbieri, 1591–1666; Italian painter)

HEPWORTH, Barbara (1903–75; British sculptor)

HILLIARD, Nicholas (1547–1619; English portrait miniaturist)

JACOBSEN, Arne (1902–71; Danish architect and designer of furniture and wallpaper)

JONGKIND, Johan Barthold (1819–91; Dutch landscape painter and etcher)

JORDAENS, Jakob (1593–1678; Flemish painter)

KIRCHNER, Ernst Ludwig (1880–1938; German expressionist painter and printmaker)

LANDSEER, Edwin Henry (1802–73; British artist)

LAWRENCE, Thomas (1769–1830; British painter)

LIPCHITZ, Jacques (1891–1973; Lithuanian cubist sculptor)

LOMBARDO, Pietro (c. 1438–1515; Italian sculptor and architect)

LYSIPPUS (4th century BC; Court sculptor of Alexander the Great)

MAGRITTE, René (1898–1967; Belgian surrealist painter)

MALEVICH, Kazimir (1878–1935; Russian painter and art theorist)

MANTEGNA, Andrea (c. 1431–1506; Italian Renaissance painter and engraver)

MASACCIO (Tommaso di Giovanni di Simone Guidi, 1401–28; Florentine painter)

MASOLINO (Tommaso di Cristoforo Fini, 1383–?1447; Italian painter)

MEEGEREN, Hans van (1889–1947; Dutch painter)

MONDRIAN, Piet (Pieter Cornelis Mondriaan, 1872–1944; Dutch painter)

MULREADY, William (1786–1863; British painter)

MUNNINGS, Alfred (1878–1959; British painter)

NIEMEYER, Oscar (1907–2012; Brazilian architect)

PALLADIO, Andrea (1508–80; Italian architect)

PIRANESI, Giambattista (1720–78; Italian etcher)

PISSARRO, Camille (1830–1903; French impressionist painter)

PONTORMO, Jacopo da (J

Carrucci, 1494–1557; Italian mannerist painter)

REYNOLDS, Joshua (1723–92; British portrait painter)

ROBINSON, William Heath (1872–1944; British cartoonist and book illustrator)

ROUSSEAU, Henri (1844–1910; French painter)

ROUSSEAU, Théodore (1812– 67; French Romantic painter)

RUISDAEL, Jacob van (?1628–82; Dutch landscape painter)

SAARINEN, Eero (1910–61; US architect, born in Finland)

SASSETTA (Stefano di Giovanni, c. 1392–c. 1450; Italian painter)

SEVERINI, Gino (1883–1966; Italian painter)

SHERATON, Thomas (1751–1806; British furniture designer)

SOUFFLOT, Jacques Germain (1713–80; French architect)

SULLIVAN, Louis Henry (1856–1924; US architect)

TERBORCH, Gerard (1617–81; Dutch painter)

VANBRUGH, John (1664–1726; English architect)

VASARELY, Victor (1908–97; Hungarian-born painter)

VERONESE, Paolo (P Caliari, 1528–88; Italian painter)

VLAMINCK, Maurice de (1876-1958; French painter)

VUILLARD, Édouard (1868–1940; French artist)

WEDGWOOD, Josiah (1730–95; British potter, industrialist, and writer)

WHISTLER, James McNeill (1834–1903; US painter)

WHISTLER, Rex (1905–44; British artist)

WOOLLETT, William (1735–85; British engraver)

ZURBARÁN, Francisco de (1598–1664; Spanish painter)

9

ALTDORFER, Albrecht (c. 1480–1538; German artist)

BARTHOLDI, Frédéric August (1834–1904; French sculptor)

BEARDSLEY, Aubrey Vincent (1872–98; British illustrator)

BONINGTON, Richard Parkes (1801–28; British painter)

BORROMINI, Francesco (1599–1667; Italian baroque architect)

BOURDELLE, Émile (1861–1929; French sculptor)

CANALETTO (Antonio Canal, 1697–1768; Venetian painter)

CARPACCIO, Vittore (c. 1460–c. 1525; Venetian painter)

CAVALLINI, Pietro (c. 1250–c. 1330; Italian painter)

COCKERELL, Charles Robert (1788–1863; British architect)

CONSTABLE, John (1776–1837; British landscape painter)

CORNELIUS, Peter von (1783–1867; German painter)

CORREGGIO (Antonio Allegri, c. 1494–1534; Italian Renaissance painter)

DE KOONING, Willem (1904–89; US painter of Dutch birth)

DELACROIX, Eugène (1798–1863; French Romantic painter)

DELAROCHE, Paul (1797–1859; French history and portrait painter)

DONATELLO (Donato de Nicolo di Betti Bardi, c. 1386–1466; Florentine sculptor)

FABRITIUS, Carel (1622–54; Dutch painter)

FEININGER, Lyonel (1871–1956; US painter and illustrator)

FRAGONARD, Jean Honoré (1732–1806; French rococo painter)

FRIEDRICH, Caspar David (1774–1840; German Romantic landscape painter)

GÉRICAULT, Théodore (1791–1824; French painter)

GIORGIONE (c. 1477–1510; Italian painter)

GREENAWAY, Kate (1846–1901; British artist and book illustrator)

GREENOUGH, Horatio (1805– 52; US neoclassical sculptor)

GRÜNEWALD, Matthias (Mathis Gothardt, d. 1528; German painter)

HAWKSMOOR, Nicholas (1661–1736; English baroque architect)

HIROSHIGE (Ando Tokitaro, 1797–1858; Japanese colour-print artist)

HONTHORST, Gerrit von (1590–1656; Dutch painter)

JAWLENSKY, Alexey von (1864–1941; Russian expressionist painter)

KANDINSKY, Wassily (1866–1944; Russian expressionist painter and art theorist)

KAUFFMANN, Angelica (1741–1807; Swiss painter)

KOKOSCHKA, Oskar (1886–1980; Austrian expressionist painter and writer)

LISSITZKY, El (Eliezer L, 1890–1941; Russian painter and architect)

MEŠTROVIĆ, Ivan (1883–1962; US sculptor, born in Yugoslavia)

MUYBRIDGE, Eadweard (Edward James Muggeridge, 1830–1904; US photographer, born in Britain)

NICHOLSON, Ben (1894–1982; British artist)

NOLLEKENS, Joseph (1737–1823; British neoclassical sculptor)

OLDENBURG, Claes; (1929– ; US sculptor, born in Sweden)

PISANELLO (Antonio Pisano, c. 1395–c. 1455; Italian international gothic painter, draughtsman, and medallist)

ROUBILLAC, Louis François (or L F Roubiliac, 1695–1762; French sculptor)

SIQUEIROS, David Alfaro (1896–1974; Mexican painter)

STIEGLITZ, Alfred (1864–1946; US photographer)

THORNHILL, James (1675–1734; English baroque decorative painter)

VELÁZQUEZ, Diego Rodriguez de Silva (1599–1660; Spanish painter)

VITRUVIUS (Marcus Vitruvius Pollio, 1st century BC; Roman architect)

WALLINGER, Mark (1959– ; British sculptor)

WOUWERMAN, Philips (1619–68; Dutch painter)

10

ALMA-TADEMA, Lawrence (1836–1912; Dutch painter)

ALTICHIERO (c. 1330–c. 1390; Italian painter)

ARCHIPENKO, Alexander (1887–1964; Russian-born sculptor and painter)

ARCIMBOLDO, Giuseppe (1527–93; Mannerist painter)

BERRUGUETE, Alonso (c. 1488–1561; Castillian painter)

BERRUGUETE, Pedro (c. 1450–c. 1504; Castillian painter)

BOTTICELLI, Sandro (Alessandro di Mariano Filipepi, c. 1445–1510; Florentine Renaissance painter)

BURLINGTON, Richard Boyle, 3rd Earl of (1694–1753; English architect)

BURNE-JONES, Edward Coley (1833–98; Pre-Raphaelite painter)

CARAVAGGIO (Michelangelo Merisi, 1573–1610; Italian painter)

CHAMPAIGNE, Philippe de (1602–74; French portrait painter)

CRUIKSHANK, George (1792–1872; British caricaturist, painter, and illustrator)

EUPHRONIOS (late 6th–early 5th centuries BC; Athenian potter and vase painter)

GIACOMETTI, Alberto (1901–66; Swiss sculptor and painter)

LORENZETTI, Ambrogio (c. 1290–?1348; Italian painter)

MACKINTOSH, Charles Rennie (1868–1928; Scottish architect and designer)

MEISSONIER, Jean-Louis-Ernest (1815–91; French painter)

MODIGLIANI, Amedeo (1884–1920; Italian painter and sculptor)

MOHOLY-NAGY, László (1895–1946; Hungarian artist)

MOTHERWELL, Robert (1915–91; US abstract painter)

POLLAIUOLO, Antonio (c. 1432–98; Florentine Renaissance artist)

POLYCLITUS (5th century BC; Greek sculptor)

PRAXITELES (mid-4th century BC; Athenian sculptor)

RICHARDSON, Henry Hobson (1838–86; US architect)

ROWLANDSON, Thomas (1756–1827; British caricaturist)

SCHWITTERS, Kurt (1887–1958; German artist and poet)

SENEFELDER, Aloys (1771–1834; German playwright and engraver)

SIGNORELLI, Luca (c. 1441–1523; Italian Renaissance painter)

SUTHERLAND, Graham Vivian (1903–80; British artist)

TANGE KENZO (1913–2005; Japanese architect)

TINTORETTO (Jacopo Robusti, 1518–94; Venetian painter)

VAN DE VELDE, Henry (1863–1957; Belgian Art Nouveau architect, interior designer, and painter)

VERROCCHIO, Andrea del (Andrea del Cione, c. 1435–88; Italian sculptor, painter, and goldsmith)

WATERHOUSE, Alfred (1830–1905; British architect)

ZUCCARELLI, Francesco (1702–88; Italian painter)

11

ABERCROMBIE, Patrick (1879–1957; British architect)

BARTOLOMMEO, Fra (Baccio della Porta, c. 1472–1517; Florentine Renaissance painter)

BUTTERFIELD, William (1814–1900; British architect)

CALLICRATES (5th century BC; Athenian architect)

CALLIMACHUS (late 5th century BC; Greek sculptor)

CHIPPENDALE, Thomas (1718–79; British cabinetmaker)

CHODOWIECKI, Daniel Nikolaus (1726–1801; German painter and engraver)

DELLA ROBBIA, Luca (1400–82; Florentine Renaissance sculptor)

DOMENICHINO (Domenico Zampieri, 1581–1641; Italian painter)

GHIRLANDAIO, Domenico (Domenico di Tommaso Bigordi, 1449–94; Florentine painter)

GIAMBOLOGNA (Giovanni da Bologna or Jean de Boulogne, 1529–1608; Italian mannerist sculptor)

GISLEBERTUS (early 12th century; French romanesque sculptor)

HEPPLEWHITE, George (d. 1786; British furniture designer and cabinetmaker)

LE CORBUSIER (Charles-Édouard Jeanneret, 1887–1965; French architect, born in Switzerland)

TERBRUGGHEN, Hendrik (1588–1629; Dutch painter)

THORVALDSEN, Bertel (or B Thorwaldsen, 1768–1844; Danish sculptor)

12

BRUNELLESCHI, Filippo (1377–1446; Italian architect)

FANTIN-LATOUR, Henri (1836–1904; French painter)

GAINSBOROUGH, Thomas (1727–88; British portrait and landscape painter)

GAUDÍ Y CORNET, Antonio (1852–1926; Spanish architect)

GIULIO ROMANO (Giulio Pippi, c. 1499–1546; Italian mannerist painter and architect)

LICHTENSTEIN, Roy (1923–97; US painter)

LUCA FA PRESTO (Nickname of Luca Giordano)

PALMA VECCHIO, Jacopo (J Negretti, c. 1480–1528;

Italian painter)

PARMIGIANINO (Girolamo Francesco Maria Mazzola, 1503–40; Italian painter)

PINTURICCHIO (Bernardino di Betto, c. 1454–1513; Italian Renaissance painter)

RAUSCHENBERG, Robert (1925–2008; US artist)

VIOLLET-LE-DUC, Eugène Emmanuel (1814–79; French architect and author)

WINTERHALTER, Franz Xavier (1806–73; German painter and lithographer)

13

LORENZO MONACO (Piero di Giovanni, c. 1370–1425; Italian painter)

PIERO DI COSIMO (P di Lorenzo, 1462–1521; Florentine Renaissance painter)

WILLIAMS-ELLIS, Clough (1883–1978; Welsh architect)

14

ANDREA DEL SARTO (Andrea d'Agnolo, 1486–1530; Italian painter)

BÉRAIN THE ELDER, Jean (1637–1711; French designer, engraver, and painter)

CARTIER-BRESSON, Henri (1908–2004; French photographer)

CLAUDE LORRAINE (Claude Gellée, 1600–82; French landscape painter)

COUSIN THE ELDER, Jean (1490–1560; French artist and craftsman)

GAUDIER-BRZESKA, Henri (1891–1915; French sculptor)

LUCAS VAN LEYDEN (Lucas Hugensz or Jacobsz, c. 1494–1533; Dutch artist)

MIES VAN DER ROHE, Ludwig (1886–1969; German architect)

15

CRANACH THE ELDER, Lucas (Lucas Müller, 1472–1553; German artist)

HARDOUIN-MANSART, Jules (1646–1708; French baroque architect)

KITAGAWA UTAMARO (1753–1806; Japanese artist)

LEONARDO DA VINCI (1452–1519; Italian artistic and scientific genius of the Renaissance)

TOULOUSE-LAUTREC, Henri de (1864–1901; French artist)

16

BRUEGHEL THE ELDER, Pieter (or

Bruegel, 1525–69; Flemish painter)

FISCHER VON ERLACH, Johann Bernhard (1656–1723; Austrian architect)

PUVIS DE CHAVANNES, Pierre (1824–98; French painter)

REMBRANDT VAN RIJN (1606–69; Dutch painter and etcher)

UTAGAWA KUNIYOSHI (Igusa Magosaburo, 1797–1861; Japanese painter and printmaker)

17

DOMENICO VENEZIANO (active c. 1438–1461; Italian painter)

GENTILE DA FABRIANO (Niccolo di Giovanni di Massio,

c. 1370–1427; Florentine painter)

HERRERA THE YOUNGER, Francisco de (1622–85; Spanish baroque painter and architect)

HOLBEIN THE YOUNGER, Hans (c. 1497–1543; German painter)

TENIERS THE YOUNGER, David (1610–90; Flemish painter)

18

ANTONELLO DA MESSINA (c. 1430–c. 1479; Italian painter)

JACOPO DELLA QUERCIA (c. 1374–1438; Italian Renaissance sculptor)

LEIGHTON OF STRETTON, Frederic, Baron (1830–96; British painter and sculptor)

19

DUCCIO DI BUONINSEGNA (c. 1255–c. 1318; Italian painter)

PIERO DELLA FRANCESCA (c. 1420–92; Italian Renaissance painter)

20

DESIDERIO DA SETTIGNANO (c. 1430–64; Italian Renaissance sculptor)

MICHELANGELO BUONARROTI (1475–1564; Italian sculptor, painter, and architect)

MICHELOZZO DI BARTOLOMMEO (1396–1472; Florentine Renaissance sculptor and architect)

WRITERS, PLAYWRIGHTS, AND POETS

2

FO, Dario (1926–2016; Italian playwright)

3

ECO, Umberto (1932–2016; Italian writer)

FRY, Christopher (C Harris, 1907–2005; British dramatist)

GAY, John (1685–1732; British poet and dramatist)

KYD, Thomas (1558–94; English dramatist)

PAZ, Octavio (1914–98; Mexican poet)

SUE, Eugène (Joseph Marie S, 1804–57; French novelist)

4

AGEE, James (1909–55; US poet and novelist)

AMIS, Kingsley (1922–95; British novelist and poet)

AMIS, Martin (1949– ; British novelist)

ASCH, Sholem (1880–1957; Jewish novelist)

BANA (7th century AD; Sanskrit writer)

BAUM, L Frank (1856–1919; US novelist)

BENN, Gottfried (1886–1956; German poet)

BLOK, Aleksandr Aleksandrovich (1880–1921; Russian symbolist poet)

BÖLL, Heinrich (1917–85; German novelist)

BOLT, Robert Oxton (1924–95; British dramatist)

BOND, Edward (1934– ; British dramatist)

BUCK, Pearl S (1892–1973; US novelist)

CARY, Joyce (1888–1957; British novelist)

CRUZ, Sor Juana Inéz de la (1651–95; Mexican poet)

DAHL, Roald (1916–90; British author)

DEUS, Joã o de (1830–96; Portuguese poet)

DU FU (or Tu Fu; 712–70 AD; Chinese poet)

FORD, Ford Madox (Ford Hermann Hueffer, 1873–1939; British novelist)

FORD, John (1586–c. 1640; English dramatist)

FOXE, John (1516–87; English religious writer)

GALT, John (1779–1839; Scottish novelist)

GIDE, André (1869–1951; French novelist and critic)

GRAY, Thomas (1716–71; British poet)

GUNN, Thomson W (1929–2004; British poet)

HARE, David, Sir (1947– ; British playwright)

HART, Moss (1904–61; US dramatist)

HILL, Geoffrey, Sir (1932–2016; British poet)

HOGG, James (1770–1835;

Scottish poet and writer)

HOOD, Thomas (1799–1845; British poet)

HOPE, Anthony (Sir Anthony Hope Hawkins; 1863–1933; British novelist)

HUGO, Victor (1802–85; French poet, dramatist, and novelist)

HUNT, Leigh (1784–1859; British poet and journalist)

KING, Stephen Edwin (1947– ; US novelist)

KIVI, Alexis (A Stenvall, 1834–72; Finnish poet, dramatist, and novelist)

LAMB, Charles (1775–1834; British essayist and critic)

LEAR, Edward (1812–88; British artist and poet)

LEVY, ANDREA (1956–62; British novelist)

LIVY (Titus Livius, 59 BC–17 AD; Roman writer)

LOTI, Pierre (Julien Viaud; 1850–1923; French novelist)

LYLY, John (c. 1554–1606; English dramatist and writer)

MANN, Thomas (1875–1955; German novelist)

MUIR, Edwin (1887–1959; Scottish poet)

NASH, Ogden (1902–71; US humorous writer)

NEXØ, Martin Andersen (1869–1954; Danish novelist)

OVID (Publius Ovidius Naso 43 BC–17 AD; Roman poet)

OWEN, Wilfred (1893–1918; British poet)

POPE, Alexander (1688–1744; British poet)

READ, Herbert (1893–1968; British poet)

RHYS, Jean (1894–1979; British novelist)

RICH, Adrienne (1929–2012; US poet)

ROTH, Philip (1933–2018; US novelist)

ROWE, Nicholas (1674–1718; British dramatist)

RUIZ, Juan (c. 1283–c. 1350; Spanish poet)

SADE, Donatien Alphonse François, Marquis de (1740–1814; French novelist)

SA'DI (Mosleh al-Din S, c. 1215–92; Persian poet)

SAKI (H H Munro, 1870–1916; British humorous short-story writer)

SAND, George (Aurore Dupin, Baronne Dudevant, 1804–76; French novelist)

SETH, Vikram (1952– ; Indian-born novelist)

SHAW, George Bernard (1856–1950; Irish dramatist)

SNOW, C P, Baron (1905–80; British novelist)

TATE, Allen (1899–1979; US poet and critic)

TATE, Nahum (1652–1715; British poet)

URFÉ, Honoré d' (1568–1625; French novelist)

VEGA, Lope Félix de (1562–1635; Spanish poet and dramatist)

WAIN, John (1925–94; British novelist and poet)

WARD, Artemus (Charles Farrar Browne, 1834–67; US humorous writer)

WARD, Mrs Humphry (1851–1920; British novelist)

WEBB, Mary (1881–1927; British novelist)

WEST, Rebecca (Cicely Isabel Fairfield, 1892–1983; British novelist and journalist)

WEST, Nathanael (Nathan Weinstein, 1903–40; US novelist)

WOOD, Mrs Henry (1814–87; British novelist)

WREN, P C (1885–1941; British novelist)

WYSS, Johann Rudolph (1782–1830; Swiss writer)

ZOLA, Émile (1840–1902; French novelist)

5

ADAMS, Douglas (1952–2001; British writer and playwright)

ADAMS, Henry (1838–1918; US historian)

ADAMS, Richard (1920–2016; British novelist)

AGNON, Shmuel Yosef (Samuel Josef Czaczkes, 1888–1970; Jewish novelist)

ALBEE, Edward (1928–2016; US dramatist)

ARANY, János (1817–82; Hungarian poet)

AUDEN, W H (1907–73; British poet)

BABEL, Isaac Emmanuilovich (1894–1941; Russian short-story writer)

BANKS, Iain Menzies (1954–2013; Scottish novelist)

BARTH, John (1930– ; US novelist)

BATES, H E (1905–74; British writer)

BEHAN, Brendan (1923–64; Irish playwright)

BELLO, Andrés (1781–1865; Venezuelan scholar and poet)

BELYI, Andrei (Boris Nikolaevich Bugaev, 1880–1934; Russian poet)

BEMBO, Pietro (1470–1547; Italian scholar)

BENDA, Julien (1867–1956; French novelist and philosopher)

BENÉT, Stephen Vincent (1898–1943; US poet and novelist)

BETTI, Ugo (1892–1953; Italian dramatist)

BLUME, Judy (1938– ; US children's writer)

BOWEN, Elizabeth (1899–1973; British novelist, born in Dublin)

BRANT, Sebastian (?1458–1521; German poet)

BROCH, Hermann (1886–1951; Austrian novelist)

BROWN, Dan (1964– ; US novelist)

BUNIN, Ivan Alekseevich (1879–1953; Russian poet and novelist)

BURNS, Robert (1759–96; Scottish poet)

BUTOR, Michel (1926–2016; French experimental novelist and critic)

BYATT, A S, Dame (1936– ; British writer)

BYRON, George Gordon, Lord (1788–1824; British poet)

CAMUS, Albert (1913–60; French novelist)

CAREW, Thomas (c. 1595–1640; British poet)

CLARE, John (1793–1864; British poet)

COLUM, Padraic (Patrick Colm; 1881–1972; Irish poet)

CRAIK, Dinah Maria Mulock (1826–87; British novelist)

CRANE, Hart (1899–1932; US poet)

CRANE, Stephen (1871–1900; US novelist)

DARÍO, Rubén (Félix García Sarmiento; 1867–1916; Nicaraguan poet)

DEFOE, Daniel (1660–1731; British novelist)

DONNE, John (1572–1631; English poet)

DOYLE, Arthur Conan (1859–1930; British author)

DOYLE, Roddy (1958– ; Irish novelist)

DUFFY, Carol Ann, Dame (1955– ; British poet)

DUMAS, Alexandre (1802–70; French novelist and dramatist)

DURAS, Marguerite (1914–; French novelist)

ELIOT, George (Mary Ann Evans, 1819–80; British novelist)

ELIOT, T S (1888–1965; Anglo-American poet, critic, and dramatist)

ELYOT, Thomas (c. 1490–1546; English scholar)

EWALD, Johannes (1743–81; Danish poet and playwright)

FRIEL, Brian (1929–2015; Irish playwright)

FROST, Robert Lee (1874–1963; US poet)

GENET, Jean (1910–86; French novelist and dramatist)

GOGOL, Nikolai Vasilievich (1809–52; Russian novelist and dramatist)

GORKI, Maksim (Aleksei Maksimovich Peshkov; 1868–1936; Russian novelist)

GOSSE, Edmund (1849–1928; British critic)

GOWER, John (c. 1330–1408; English poet)

GRASS, Günter (1927– ; German novelist and poet)

GREEN, Henry (Henry Vincent Yorke; 1905–73; British novelist)

HAFIZ, Shams al-Din Muhammad

(?1326–90; Persian lyric poet)

HALLE, Adam de la (c. 1240–90; French poet and musician)

HARDY, Thomas (1840–1928; British novelist and poet)

HARTE, Brett (1836–1902; US short-story writer)

HAŠEK, Jaroslav (1883–1923; Czech novelist)

HEINE, Heinrich (1797–1856; German Jewish poet and writer)

HENRY, O (William Sidney Porter, 1862–1910; US short-story writer)

HESSE, Hermann (1877–1962; German novelist and poet)

HOMER (8th century BC; Greek epic poet)

HOOFT, Pieter Corneliszoon (1581–1647; Dutch poet)

IBSEN, Henrik (1828–1906; Norwegian playwright and poet)

JAMES, Henry (1843–1916; US novelist and critic)

JAMES, P D, Baroness James of Holland Park (1920–2014; British novelist)

JARRY, Alfred (1873–1907; French dramatist)

JONES, David (1895–1974; Anglo-Welsh writer)

JOYCE, James (1882–1941; Irish novelist and poet)

KAFKA, Franz (1883–1924; Czech writer)

KEATS, John (1795–1821; British poet)

KEMAL, Namik (1840–88; Turkish poet, novelist, and dramatist)

KESEY, Ken (1935–2001; US novelist)

LEWIS, C S (1898–1963; British writer)

LEWIS, Matthew Gregory (1775–1818; British novelist)

LEWIS, Sinclair (1885–1951; US novelist)

LEWIS, Wyndham (1882–1957; British novelist)

LODGE, David (1935– ; British novelist)

LODGE, Thomas (1558–1625; English poet, dramatist, and writer)

LOWRY, Malcolm (1909–57; British novelist)

LUCAN (Marcus Annaeus Lucanus, 39–65 AD; Roman poet)

MAMET, David (1947– ; US playwright)

MAROT, Clément (1496–1544; French poet)

MARSH, Ngaio (1899–1981; New Zealand detective-story writer)

MARTÍ, José Julián (1853–95; Cuban poet)

MASON, A E W (1865–1948; British novelist)

MEYER, Stephanie (1973– ; US novelist)

MILNE, A A (1882–1956; British novelist and dramatist)

MOORE, Marianne (1887–1972; US poet)

MOORE, Thomas (1779–1852; Irish poet)

MOYES, Jojo (1969– ; British novelist)

MUNRO, Alice (1931– ; Canadian short story writer)

MURRY, John Middleton (1889–1957; British literary critic)

MUSIL, Robert (1880–1942; Austrian novelist)

MYERS, F W H (1843–1901; British essayist and poet)

NASHE, Thomas (1567–c. 1601; British dramatist)

NOYES, Alfred (1880–1958; British poet)

ODETS, Clifford (1906–63; US dramatist)

O'HARA, John (1905–70; US novelist)

OPITZ, Martin (1597–1639; German poet)

ORCZY, Baroness Emmusca (1865–1947; British novelist)

OTWAY, Thomas (1652–85; British dramatist)

OUIDA (Marie Louise de la Ramée, 1839–1908; British novelist)

PAN GU (or P'an Ku; 32–92 AD; Chinese historian)

PATON, Alan (1903–88; South African novelist)

PEAKE, Mervyn (1911–68; British novelist)

PEELE, George (1556–96; English dramatist)

PÉGUY, Charles (1873–1914; French poet and essayist)

PERSE, Saint-John (Alexis Saint-Léger, 1887–1975; French poet)

PLATH, Sylvia (1932–63; US poet and writer)

POUND, Ezra (1885–1972; US poet and critic)

POWYS, John Cowper (1872–1963; British novelist)

PRIOR, Matthew (1664–1721; British poet)

PULCI, Luigi (1432–84; Italian poet)

RAINE, Kathleen (1908–2003; British poet)

READE, Charles (1814–84; British novelist)

RILKE, Rainer Maria (1875–1926; Austrian poet)

ROLFE, Frederick William (1860–1913; British novelist)

SACHS, Hans (1494–1576; German poet and folk dramatist)

SACHS, Nelly (1891–1970; German Jewish poet and dramatist)

SAGAN, Françoise (Françoise Quoirez, 1935–2004; French writer)

SCOTT, Walter (1771–1832; Scottish novelist)

SETON, Ernest Thompson (1860–1946; US writer)

SHUTE, Nevil (Nevil Shute Norway, 1899–1960; British novelist)

SIMMS, William Gilmore (1806–70; US novelist)

SMART, Christopher (1722–71; British poet)

SMITH, Stevie (Florence Margaret S, 1902–71; British poet)

SPARK, Muriel (1918–2006; British novelist)

STAËL, Anne Louise Germaine Necker, Madame de (1766–1817; French writer)

STEIN, Gertrude (1874–1946; US writer)

STORM, Theodor Woldsen (1817–1888; German writer)

STOWE, Harriet Beecher (1811–96; US novelist)

SVEVO, Italo (Ettore Schmitz, 1861–1928; Italian novelist)

SWIFT, Graham (1946– ; British novelist)

SWIFT, Jonathan (1667–1745; Anglo-Irish poet and satirist)

SYNGE, John Millington (1871–1909; Anglo-Irish dramatist)

TARTT, Donna (1963– ; US novelist)

TASSO, Torquato (1544–95; Italian poet)

TIECK, Ludwig (1773–1853; German writer)

TWAIN, Mark (Samuel Langhorne Clemens, 1835–1910; US novelist)

UDALL, Nicholas (1505–56; English dramatist)

VARRO, Marcus Terentius (116–27 BC; Roman poet)

VERNE, Jules (1828–1905; French writer)

VIDAL, Gore (1925–2012; US novelist and essayist)

VIGNY, Alfred de (1797–1863; French poet, novelist, and dramatist)

WALEY, Arthur (1889–1966; British translator and poet)

WAUGH, Evelyn (1903–66; British novelist)

WEISS, Peter (1916–82; German dramatist and novelist)

WELLS, H G (1866–1946; British novelist)

WELSH, Irvine (1958– ; British novelist)

WHITE, Patrick (1912–90; Australian novelist)

WHITE, T H (1906–64; British novelist)

WILDE, Oscar (O Fingal O'Flahertie Wills W, 1854–1900; British dramatist and poet)

WOLFE, Charles (1791–1823; Irish poet)

WOLFE, Thomas (1900–38; US novelist)

WOOLF, Virginia (1882–1941; British novelist)

WYATT, Thomas (1503–42; English poet)

YEATS, William Butler (1865–1939; Irish poet and dramatist)

YONGE, Charlotte (1823–1901; British novelist)

ZWEIG, Arnold (1887–1968; East German-Jewish novelist)

ZWEIG, Stefan (1881–1942; Austrian Jewish writer)

6

ACCIUS, Lucius (170–c. 85 BC; Roman tragic dramatist)

ADAMOV, Arthur (1908–70; French dramatist)

ALCOTT, Louisa May (1832–88; US novelist)

ALDISS, Brian W (1925–2017; British novelist)

ALEMÁN, Mateo (1547–?1614; Spanish writer)

ALGREN, Nelson (1909–81; US novelist)

AMBLER, Eric (1909–98; British novelist)

ANDRIĆ, Ivo (1892–1975; Serbian writer)

ARAGON, Louis (1897–1982; French poet, novelist, and journalist)

ARNOLD, Matthew (1822–88; British poet)

ASCHAM, Roger (1515–68; English scholar and writer)

ASIMOV, Isaac (1920–92; US science fiction writer, born in Russia)

ATWOOD, Margaret (1939– ; Canadian novelist)

AUBREY, John (1626–97; English antiquary)

AUSTEN, Jane (1775–1817; British novelist)

AZORÍN (José Martinéz Ruíz, 1874–1967; Spanish novelist, essayist, and critic)

AZUELA, Mariano (1873–1952; Mexican novelist)

BALZAC, Honoré de (1799–1850; French novelist)

BARAKA, Amiri (1934–2014; US dramatist and poet; formerly known as Everett LeRoi Jones)

BARHAM, Richard Harris (1788–1845; British humorous writer)

BARKER, George (1913–91; British poet)

BARNES, William (1801–86; British poet)

BAROJA, Pío (1872–1956; Spanish novelist)

BARRÈS, Maurice (1862–1923; French writer)

BARRIE, James (1860–1937; British dramatist and novelist)

BELLAY, Joachim de (1522–60; French poet)

BELLOC, Hilaire (1870–1953; British poet and essayist)

BELLOW, Saul (1915–2005; Canadian-born US novelist)

BESANT, Walter (1836–1901; British novelist)

BIALIK, Chaim Nachman (1873–1934; Jewish poet and translator)

BIERCE, Ambrose Gwinnett (1842–?1914; US writer)

BINCHY, Maeve (1940–2012; Irish novelist)

BINYON, Laurence (1869–1943; British poet)

BLYTON, Enid (1897–1968; British writer of children's books)

BORGES, Jorge Luis (1899–1986; Argentinian novelist)

BORROW, George Henry (1803–81; British writer)

BRECHT, Bertolt (1898–1956; German dramatist and poet)

BRETON, André (1896–1966; French poet)

BRIDIE, James (Osborne Henry Mavor; 1888–1951; British dramatist)

BRONTË, Anne (1820–49; British novelist)

BRONTË, Charlotte (1816–55; British novelist)

BRONTË, Emily (1818–48; British novelist)

BROOKE, Rupert (1887–1915; British poet)

BROWNE, Thomas (1605–82; English writer)

BRYANT, William Cullen (1794–1878; US poet, journalist, and critic)

BUCHAN, John, 1st Baron Tweedsmuir (1875–1940; British novelist)

BUNYAN, John (1628–88; English writer)

BÜRGER, Gottfried (1747–94; German poet)

BURNEY, Fanny (Mrs Frances Burney D'Arblay; 1752–1840; British novelist)

BUTLER, Samuel (1612–80; British satirical poet)

BUTLER, Samuel (1835–1902; British novelist)

CAMÕES, Luís de (c. 1524–80; Portuguese poet)

CAPOTE, Truman (1924–84; US novelist)

CARSON, Rachel Louise (1907–64; US science writer)

CAVAFY, Constantine (C Kavafis, 1863–1933; Greek poet)

CÉLINE, Louis Ferdinand (L F Destouches, 1884–1961; French novelist)

CIBBER, Colley (1671–1757; British dramatist)

CLANCY, Tom (1947–2013; US novelist)

CLARKE, Marcus (1846–81; Australian novelist, born in London)

COLMAN, George (1732–94; British dramatist)

CONRAD, Joseph (Teodor Josef Konrad Watę cz Korzeniowski, 1857–1924; Polish-born British novelist)

COOPER, James Fenimore (1789–1851; US novelist)

COWLEY, Abraham (1618–67; English poet)

COWPER, William (1731–1800; British poet)

CRABBE, George (1754–1832; British poet)

CRONIN, A J (1896–1981; British novelist)

DANIEL, Samuel (?1562–1619; English poet, dramatist, and critic)

DAUDET, Alphonse (1840–97; French novelist)

DAVIES, W H (1871–1940; British poet)

DEKKER, Thomas (c. 1572–1632; British dramatist and pamphleteer)

DOWSON, Ernest (1867–1900; British poet)

DRYDEN, John (1631–1700; British poet)

DUNBAR, William (c. 1460–c. 1530; Scots poet)

ÉLUARD, Paul (Eugène Grindel, 1895–1952; French poet)

EMPSON, William (1906–84; British poet and critic)

ENNIUS, Quintus (238–169 BC; Roman poet)

EVELYN, John (1620–1706; English diarist)

FOUQUÉ, Friedrich Heinrich Karl, Baron de la Motte (1777–1843; German novelist and dramatist)

FOWLES, John (1926–2005; British novelist)

FRANCE, Anatole (Jacques Anatole François Thibault 1844–1924; French novelist)

FRISCH, Max (1911–91; Swiss dramatist and novelist)

FUGARD, Athol (1932– ; South African dramatist)

FULLER, Roy (1912–91; British poet and novelist)

FULLER, Thomas (1608–61; British historian)

GEORGE, Stefan (1868–1933; German poet)

GIBBON, Edward (1737–94; British historian)

GIBRAN, Khalil (1883–1931; Lebanese mystic and poet)

GOETHE, Johann Wolfgang von (1749–1832; German poet)

GRAVES, Robert (1895–1985; British poet, critic, and novelist)

GREENE, Graham (1904–91; British novelist)

GREENE, Robert (c. 1558–92; English dramatist)

HAMSUN, Knut (1859–1952; Norwegian novelist)

HARRIS, Joel Chandler (1848–1908; US novelist and short-story writer)

HEANEY, Seamus (1939–2013; Irish poet)

HEBBEL, Friedrich (1813–63; German dramatist)

HELLER, Joseph (1923–99; US novelist)

HESIOD (8th century BC; Greek poet)

HILTON, James (1900–54; British novelist)

HISLOP, Victoria (1959– ; British novelist)

HOLMES, Oliver Wendell (1809–94; US essayist and poet)

HORACE (Quintus Horatius Flaccus; 65–8 BC; Roman poet)

HUDSON, W H (1841–1922; British naturalist and writer)

HUGHES, Richard (1900–76; British novelist)

HUGHES, Ted (1930–98; British poet)

HUGHES, Thomas (1822–96; British writer)

HUXLEY, Aldous (1894–1963; British writer)

IRVING, Washington (1783–1859; US short-story writer)

ISAACS, Jorge (1837–95; Colombian novelist)

JENSEN, Johannes (1873–1950; Danish novelist and poet)

JONSON, Ben (1572–1637; English dramatist and poet)

KAISER, Georg (1878–1945; German dramatist)

KELLER, Gottfried (1819–90; German-Swiss poet and novelist)

KLEIST, Heinrich von (1777–1811; German dramatist)

LACLOS, Pierre Choderlos de (1741–1803; French novelist)

LANDOR, Walter Savage (1775–1864; British poet and prose writer)

LANIER, Sidney (1842–81; US poet)

LARKIN, Philip (1922–85; British poet)

LAWLER, Ray (1921– ; Australian dramatist)

LE FANU, Sheridan (1814–73; Irish novelist)

LEONOV, Leonid (1899–1994; Soviet novelist and playwright)

LESAGE, Alain-René (1668–1747; French novelist)

LIVELY, Penelope, Dame (1933– ; British novelist)

LONDON, Jack (1876–1916; US novelist)

LOWELL, Amy (1874–1925; US poet)

LOWELL, James Russell (1819–91; US poet)

LOWELL, Robert (1917–77; US poet)

LU HSÜN (or Chou Shu-jen 1881–1936; Chinese writer)

MACHEN, Arthur (1863–1947; Welsh novelist)

MAILER, Norman (1923–2007; US novelist and journalist)

MALORY, Thomas (?1400–71; English writer)

MANTEL, Hilary, Dame (1952– ; British novelist)

MARTIN, George R. R. (1948– ; US novelist)

MCEWAN, Ian (1948– ; British novelist)

MERCER, David (1928–80; British dramatist)

MILLAY, Edna St Vincent (1892–1950; US poet)

MILLER, Arthur (1915–2005; US dramatist)

MILLER, Henry (1891–1980; US novelist)

MILTON, John (1608–74; English poet)

MOLNÁR, Ferenc (1878–1952; Hungarian dramatist)

MORGAN, Charles (1894–1958; British novelist and dramatist)

MÖRIKE, Eduard Friedrich (1804–75; German poet and novelist)

MOTION, Andrew, Sir (1952– ; British poet and writer)

MUNTHE, Axel (1857–1949; Swedish author)

MUSSET, Alfred de (1810–57; French poet and dramatist)

NERUDA, Pablo (Neftalí Ricardo Reyes 1904–73; Chilean poet)

NERVAL, Gérard de (Gérard Labrunie 1808–55; French poet)

NESBIT, Edith (1858–1924; British children's writer)

O'BRIEN, Flann (Brian O'Nolan 1911–66; Irish novelist and journalist)

O'CASEY, Sean (1880–1964; Irish dramatist)

O'NEILL, Eugene (1888–1953; US dramatist)

ORWELL, George (Eric Blair; 1903–50; British novelist, born in India)

PARKER, Dorothy Rothschild (1893–1967; US humorous writer)

PAVESE, Cesare (1908–50; Italian novelist and poet)

PETÖFI, Sándor (1823–49; Hungarian poet)

PINDAR (518–438 BC; Greek poet)

PINERO, Arthur Wing (1855–1934; British dramatist)

PINTER, Harold (1930–2008; British dramatist)

PIOZZI, Hester Lynch (1741–1821; British writer)

PLOMER, William (1903–73; South African poet and novelist)

PORTER, Katherine Anne (1890–1980; US short-story writer and novelist)

PORTER, Peter (1929–2010; British poet)

POTTER, Beatrix (1866–1943; British children's writer)

POTTER, Stephen (1900–70; British writer)

POWELL, Anthony (1905–2000; British novelist)

PROUST, Marcel (1871–1922; French novelist)

RACINE, Jean (1639–99; French dramatist)

RAMSAY, Allan (?1685–1758; Scottish poet)

RANSOM, John Crowe (1888–1974; US poet)

RUNYON, Damon (1884–1946; US humorous writer)

SAPPER (H C McNeile, 1888–1937; British novelist)

SAPPHO (c. 612–c. 580 BC; Greek poet)

SARDOU, Victorien (1831–1908; French dramatist)

SARTRE, Jean-Paul (1905–80; French philosopher, novelist, dramatist, and critic)

SAVAGE, Richard (c. 1696–1743; British poet)

SAYERS, Dorothy L (1893–1957; British writer)

SIDNEY, Philip (1554–86; English poet)

SILONE, Ignazio (Secondo Tranquilli, 1900–78; Italian novelist)

SINGER, Isaac Bashevis (1904–91; US novelist and short-story writer)

SMILES, Samuel (1812–1904; British writer)

STEELE, Richard (1672–1729; British essayist and dramatist)

STERNE, Laurence (1713–68; British novelist)

STOKER, Bram (Abraham S, 1847–1912; Irish novelist)

STOREY, David (1933–2017; British novelist and dramatist)

SURREY, Henry Howard, Earl of (1517–47; English poet)

SYMONS, Arthur (1865–1945; British poet and critic)

TAGORE, Rabindranath (1861–1941; Indian poet)

THOMAS, Dylan (1914–53; Welsh poet)

THOMAS, Edward (1878–1917; British poet)

TOLLER, Ernst (1893–1939; German playwright and poet)

TRAVEN, B (Berick Traven Torsvan, 1890–1969; US novelist)

UHLAND, Ludwig (1787–1862; German poet)

UNDSET, Sigrid (1882–1949; Norwegian novelist)

UPDIKE, John (1932–2009; US novelist and short-story writer)

VALÉRY, Paul (1871–1945; French poet, essayist, and critic)

VILLON, François (1431–?1463; French poet)

VIRGIL (Publius Vergilius Maro, 70–19 BC; Roman poet)

VONDEL, Joost van den (1587–1679; Dutch dramatist and poet)

WALLER, Edmund (1606–87; British poet)

WALTON, Izaak (1593–1683; English writer)

WARTON, Joseph (1722–1800; British poet and critic)

WELDON, Fay (1931–   ; British writer)

WERFEL, Franz (1890–1945; Austrian Jewish poet, dramatist, and novelist)

WESKER, Arnold, Sir (1932–2016; British dramatist)

WILDER, Thornton (1897–1975; US novelist and dramatist)

WILSON, Angus (1913–91; British novelist)

WILSON, Colin (1931–2013; British critic and novelist)

WILSON, Edmund (1895–1972; US critic and essayist)

WILSON, Jacqueline, Dame (1945–   ; British children's writer)

WOTTON, Henry (1568–1639; English poet)

WRIGHT, Judith (1915–2000; Australian poet)

WRIGHT, Richard (1908–60; US novelist and critic)

7

ADDISON, Joseph (1672–1719; British essayist and poet)

AELFRIC (c. 955–c. 1020; Anglo-Saxon prose writer)

ALARCÓN, Pedro Antonio de (1833–91; Spanish novelist)

ALBERTI, Raphael (1902–99; Spanish poet)

ALCAEUS (6th century BC; Greek lyric poet)

ALDANOV, Mark (M Aleksandrovich Landau, 1886–1957; Russian novelist)

ALDRICH, Thomas Bailey (1836–1907; US short-story writer and poet)

ALEGRÍA, Ciro (1909–61; Peruvian novelist)

ALFIERI, Vittorio, Count (1749–1803; Italian poet and dramatist)

ALLENDE, Isabel (1942–   ; Peruvian novelist)

ANEIRIN (6th century AD; Welsh poet)

ANGELOU, Maya (1928–2014; US poet and novelist)

ARETINO, Pietro (1492–1556; Italian satirist)

ARIOSTO, Ludovico (1474–1533; Italian poet)

ARRABAL, Fernando (1932–   ; Spanish playwright and novelist)

BALCHIN, Nigel (1908–70; British novelist)

BALDWIN, James Arthur (1924–87; US novelist, essayist, and dramatist)

BARBOUR, John (1316–95; Scottish poet)

BECKETT, Samuel (1906–89; Irish novelist, dramatist, and poet)

BEDDOES, Thomas Lovell (1803–49; British poet)

BENNETT, Alan (1934–   ; British playwright and writer)

BENNETT, Arnold (1837–1931; British novelist)

BENTLEY, Edmund Clerihew (1875–1956; British writer)

BERGMAN, Hjalmar (1883–1931; Swedish novelist and dramatist)

BLUNDEN, Edmund Charles (1896–1974; British poet and critic)

BOIARDO, Matteo Maria, Conte di Scandiano (1441–94; Italian poet)

BOILEAU(-Despréaux), Nicolas (1636–1711; French poet and critic)

BOSWELL, James (1740–95; Scottish writer)

BO ZHU YI (or Po Chü-i; 772–846; Chinese poet)

BRADLEY, Andrew Cecil (1851–1935; British literary critic)

BRIDGES, Robert Seymour (1844–1930; British poet)

BÜCHNER, Georg (1813–37; German dramatist)

BURGESS, Anthony (John Burgess Wilson; 1917–93; British novelist and critic)

BURNETT, Frances Eliza Hodgson (1849–1924; British novelist)

CAEDMON (d. c. 680 AD; English poet)

CAO CHAN (or Zao Zhan; ?1715–63; Chinese novelist)

CAROSSA, Hans (1878–1956; German novelist)

CARROLL, Lewis (Charles Lutwidge Dodgson; 1832–98; British writer)

CHAPMAN, George (c. 1560–1634; British poet and dramatist)

CHAUCER, Geoffrey (c. 1342–1400; English poet)

CHEKHOV, Anton Pavlovich (1860–1904; Russian dramatist and short-story writer)

CHÉNIER, André de (1762–94; French poet, born in Istanbul)

CHU YUAN (c. 343 BC–c. 289 BC; Chinese poet)

CLAUDEL, Paul (1868–1955; French dramatist and poet)

CLELAND, John (1709–89; English novelist)

COCTEAU, Jean (1889–1963; French poet and artist)

COETZEE, J M (1940– ; South African novelist)

COLETTE (Sidonie-Gabrielle C, 1873–1954; French novelist)

COLLINS, William (1721–59; British poet)

COLLINS, William Wilkie (1824–89; British novelist)

CORELLI, Marie (1854–1924; British novelist)

CRASHAW, Richard (c. 1613–49; British poet)

CREELEY, Robert (1926–2005; US poet)

DA PONTE, Lorenzo (1749–1838; Italian author)

DELEDDA, Grazia (1871–1936; Italian novelist)

DICKENS, Charles (1812–70; British novelist)

DINESEN, Isak (Karen Blixen, Baroness Blixen-Finecke, 1885–1962; Danish author)

DOUGLAS, Gavin (?1474–1522; Scottish poet)

DOUGLAS, Norman (1868–1952; British novelist)

DRABBLE, Margaret, Dame (1939– ; British novelist)

DRAYTON, Michael (1563–1631; English poet)

DREISER, Theodore (1871–1945; US novelist)

DUHAMEL, Georges (1884–1966; French novelist)

DUNSANY, Edward John Moreton Drax Plunkett, 18th Baron (1878–1957; Irish author)

DURRELL, Lawrence George (1912–90; British novelist and poet, born in India)

EMERSON, Ralph Waldo (1803–82; US essayist and poet)

ENRIGHT, Anne (1962– ; Irish novelist)

ERCILLA, Alonso de (1533–94; Spanish poet)

EUPOLIS (late 5th century BC; Greek dramatist)

FERRIER, Susan Edmonstone (1782–1854; Scottish novelist)

FEYDEAU, Georges (1862–1921; French playwright)

FIRBANK, Ronald (1886–1926; British novelist)

FLECKER, James Elroy (1884–1915; British poet)

FLEMING, Ian (1908–64; British author)

FLEMING, Paul (1609–40; German poet)

FOLLETT, Ken (1949– ; British novelist)

FONTANE, Theodor (1819–98; German novelist)

FORSTER, E M (1879–1970; British novelist)

FOSCOLO, Ugo (1778–1827; Italian poet)

FRENEAU, Philip (1752–1832; US poet)

FRÖDING, Gustaf (1860–1911; Swedish lyric poet)

GAARDER, Jostein (1952– ; Norwegian novelist)

GASKELL, Elizabeth Cleghorn (1810–65; British novelist)

GAUTIER, Théophile (1811–72; French poet)

GILBERT, William Schwenk (1836–1911; British comic dramatist)

GISSING, George Robert (1857–1903; British novelist)

GOLDING, William (1911–93; British novelist)

GOLDONI, Carlo (1707–93; Italian comic playwright)

GRAHAME, Kenneth (1859–1932; British children's writer)

GRISHAM, John (1955– ; US novelist)

GUARINI, Giovanni Battista (1538–1612; Italian poet)

HAGGARD, H Rider (1856–1925; British novelist)

HAMMETT, Dashiell (1894–1961; US novelist)

HARTLEY, L P (1895–1972; British novelist)

HELLMAN, Lillian (1905–84; US dramatist)

HERBERT, George (1593–1633; English poet)

HERRICK, Robert (1591–1674; English poet)

HEYWOOD, Thomas (c. 1574–1641; English dramatist)

HOLBERG, Ludvig, Baron (1684–1754; Danish playwright and poet)

HOPKINS, Gerard Manley (1844–89; British poet)

HOUSMAN, A E (1859–1936; British poet and scholar)

IBN EZRA, Abraham Ben Meir (1093–1167; Hebrew poet and scholar)

IONESCO, Eugène (1912–94; French dramatist)

JEFFERS, Robinson (1887–1962; US poet)

JIMÉNEZ, Juan Ramón (1881–1958; Spanish poet)

JUVENAL (Decimus Junius Juvenalis, c. 60–c. 130 AD; Roman satirist)

KÄSTNER, Erich (1899–1974; German novelist and poet)

KAUFMAN, George S (1889–1961; US dramatist)

KENDALL, Henry (1841–82; Australian poet)

KEROUAC, Jack (1922–69; US novelist)

KIPLING, Rudyard (1865–1936; British writer and poet)

KLINGER, Friedrich Maximilian von (1752–1831; German dramatist)

LABICHE, Eugène (1815–88; French dramatist)

LARDNER, Ring (1885–1933; US short-story writer)

LAXNESS, Halldór (1902–98; Icelandic novelist and essayist)

LAYAMON (early 13th century; English poet)

LEACOCK, Stephen (1869–1944; English-born Canadian humorist)

LE CARRÉ, John (David Cornwell, 1931– ; British novelist)

LESSING, Doris (1919–2013; British novelist)

LESSING, Gotthold Ephraim (1729–81; German dramatist and writer)

LINDSAY, Vachel (1879–1931; US poet)

LYDGATE, John (c. 1370–c. 1450; English poet)

MACHAUT, Guillaume de (c. 1300–77; French poet)

MALAMUD, Bernard (1914–86; US novelist)

MALRAUX, André (1901–76; French novelist and essayist)

MANZONI, Alessandro (1785–1873; Italian poet and novelist)

MARLOWE, Christopher (1564–93; English dramatist and poet)

MARRYAT, Captain Frederick (1792–1848; British novelist)

MARSTON, John (1576–1634; English dramatist)

MARTIAL (Marcus Valerius Martialis, c. 40–c. 104 AD; Roman poet)

MARVELL, Andrew (1621–78; English poet)

MASTERS, Edgar Lee (1868–1950; US poet)

MAUGHAM, W Somerset (1874–1965; British novelist and dramatist)

MAURIAC, François (1885–1970; French novelist)

MAUROIS, André (Émile Herzog; 1885–1967; French biographer, novelist, and critic)

MCGOUGH, Roger (1937– ; British poet)

MÉRIMÉE, Prosper (1803–70; French novelist)

MISHIMA, Yukio (Kimitake Hiraoka; 1925–70; Japanese novelist and playwright)

MISTRAL, Frédéric (1830–1914; French poet)

MISTRAL, Gabriela (Lucila Godoy Alcayaga, 1889–1957; Chilean poet)

MOLIÈRE (Jean-Baptiste Poquelin, 1622–73; French dramatist)

MONTAGU, Lady Mary Wortley (1689–1762; English writer)

MONTALE, Eugenio (1896–1981; Italian poet)

MORAVIA, Alberto (Alberto Pincherle, 1907–90; Italian novelist)

MURDOCH, Iris (1919–99; British novelist)

NABOKOV, Vladimir (1899–1977; US novelist)

NAEVIUS, Gnaeus (c. 270–c. 200 BC; Roman poet)

NAIPAUL, V S (1932–2018; West Indian novelist)

NOVALIS (Friedrich Leopold, Freiherr von Hardenberg; 1772–1801; German poet and writer)

O'CONNOR, Frank (Michael O'Donovan; 1903–66; Irish short-story writer)

OSBORNE, John (1929–94; British dramatist)

PATMORE, Coventry (1823–96; British poet)

PEACOCK, Thomas Love (1785–1866; British satirical novelist)

PLAUTUS, Titus Maccius (c. 254–184 BC; Roman dramatist)

PRÉVERT, Jacques (1900–77; French poet)

PULLMAN, Philip (1946– ; British novelist)

PUSHKIN, Aleksandr (1799–1837; Russian poet, novelist, and dramatist)

PYNCHON, Thomas (1937– ; US novelist)

QUENEAU, Raymond (1903–79; French novelist and poet)

RANSOME, Arthur Mitchell (1884–1967; British journalist and children's writer)

REGNIER, Henri François Joseph de (1864–1936; French poet)

RICHLER, Mordecai (1931–2001; Canadian novelist)

RIMBAUD, Arthur (1854–91; French poet)

ROLLAND, Romain (1866–1944; French novelist, dramatist, and essayist)

ROMAINS, Jules (Louis Farigoule; 1885–1972; French poet, novelist, and dramatist)

RONSARD, Pierre de (1524–85; French poet)

ROSTAND, Edmond (1868–1918; French dramatist)

ROUSSEL, Raymond (1877–1933; French writer and dramatist)

ROWLING, J(oanne) K(athleen) (1965– ; British children's writer)

RUSHDIE, Salman, Sir (1947– ; British novelist)

SAROYAN, William (1908–81; US dramatist and fiction writer)

SASSOON, Siegfried (1886–1967; British poet and writer)

SCARRON, Paul (1610–60; French poet, dramatist, and satirist)

SEFERIS, George (Georgios Seferiadis, 1900–71; Greek poet)

SHAFFER, Peter, Sir (1926–2016; British dramatist)

SHELLEY, Percy Bysshe (1792–1822; British poet)

SIMENON, Georges (1903–89; Belgian novelist)

SIMONOV, Konstantin (1915–79; Soviet novelist, playwright, poet, and journalist)

SITWELL, Edith (1887–1964; British poet and writer)

SKELTON, John (c. 1460–1529; English poet)

SOUTHEY, Robert (1774– 1843; British poet and writer)

SOYINKA, Wole (1934– ; Nigerian dramatist and poet)

SPENDER, Stephen (1909– 95; British poet and critic)

SPENSER, Edmund (c. 1552–99; English poet)

STEVENS, Wallace (1879–1955; US poet)

SURTEES, Robert Smith (1803–64; British novelist)

TERENCE (Publius Terentius Afer, c. 185–c. 159 BC; Roman dramatist)

THESPIS (6th century BC; Greek poet)

THOMSON, James (1700–48; British poet)

THURBER, James (1894–1961; US humorous writer and cartoonist)

TOLKIEN, J R R (1892–1973; British scholar and writer)

TOLSTOY, Leo, Count (1828–1910; Russian writer)

TRAVERS, Ben (1886–1980; British dramatist)

TREMAIN, Rose (1943– ; British novelist)

TUTUOLA, Amos (1920–97; Nigerian writer)

VAN DUYN, Mona (1921–2004; US poet)

VAUGHAN, Henry (c. 1622–95; English poet)

VICENTE, Gil (c. 1465–1536; Portuguese dramatist)

WALLACE, Edgar (1875–1932; British novelist)

WALPOLE, Hugh (1884–1941; British novelist)

WEBSTER, John (c. 1580–c. 1625; English dramatist)

WHARTON, Edith (1862–1937; US novelist)

WHITMAN, Walt (1819–92; US poet)

WIELAND, Christoph Martin (1733–1813; German novelist and poet)

YESENIN, Sergei Aleksandrovich (1895–1925; Russian poet)

8

ABU NUWAS (c. 762–c. 813 AD; Arab poet)

ANACREON (6th century BC; Greek lyric poet)

ANCHIETA, José de (1534–97; Portuguese poet)

ANDERSEN, Hans Christian (1805–75; Danish author)

ANDERSON, Sherwood (1876–1941; US author)

APULEIUS, Lucius (2nd century AD; Roman writer and rhetorician)

ARMITAGE, Simon Robert (1963– ; British poet and writer)

ASTURIAS, Miguel Ángel (1899–1974; Guatemalan novelist and poet)

BANDEIRA, Manuel Carneiró de Sousa (1886–1968; Brazilian poet)

BANVILLE, Théodore Faullain de (1823–89; French poet)

BARBUSSE, Henri (1873–1935; French novelist)

BEAUMONT, Francis (1584–1616; British dramatist)

BEAUVOIR, Simone de (1908–86; French novelist and essayist)

BECKFORD, William (?1760–1844; British writer)

BEERBOHM, Max (1872–1956; British caricaturist and writer)

BELINSKY, Vissarion (1811–48; Russian literary critic)

BENCHLEY, Robert Charles (1889–1945; US humorist)

BERANGER, Pierre Jean de (1780–1857; French poet and songwriter)

BERNANOS, Georges (1888–1948; French novelist)

BETJEMAN, John (1906–84; British poet)

BJØRNSON, Bjørnstjerne (1832–1910; Norwegian novelist, poet, and playwright)

BRADBURY, Ray (1920–2012; US science-fiction writer)

BRENTANO, Clemens (1778–1842; German writer)

BROOKNER, Anita (1928–2016;

British writer and art historian)

BROWNING, Robert (1812–89; British poet)

CAMPBELL, Roy (1901–57; South African poet)

CAMPBELL, Thomas (1777–1844; British poet)

CARDUCCI, Giosuè (1835–1907; Italian poet and critic)

CASTILHO, Antonio Feliciano de (1800–75; Portuguese poet)

CATULLUS, Valerius (c. 84–c. 54 BC; Roman poet)

CHANDLER, Raymond (1888–1959; US novelist)

CHARTIER, Alain (c. 1385–c. 1440; French poet and prose writer)

CHRISTIE, Agatha (1891–1976; British author of detective fiction and playwright)

CLAUDIAN (c. 370–404 AD; Roman poet)

CONGREVE, William (1670–1729; British dramatist)

CONSTANT, Benjamin (1767–1830; French novelist)

CORNWELL, Patricia (1956– ; US novelist)

CROMPTON, Richmal (Richmal Crompton Lamburn, 1890–1969; British children's author)

CUMMINGS, e e (1894–1962; US poet)

CYNEWULF (early 9th century AD; Anglo-Saxon religious poet)

DAVENANT, William (1606–68; English dramatist and poet)

DAY LEWIS, C (1904–72; British poet and critic)

DE LA MARE, Walter (1873–1956; British poet, novelist, and anthologist)

DONLEAVY, J P (1926–2017; Irish-American novelist)

ETHEREGE, George (c. 1635–c. 1692; English dramatist)

FARQUHAR, George (1678–1707; Irish dramatist)

FAULKNER, William (1897–1962; US novelist)

FIELDING, Henry (1707–54; British novelist and dramatist)

FIRDAUSI (Abul Qasim Mansur; c. 935–c. 1020; Persian poet)

FLAUBERT, Gustave (1821–80; French novelist)

FLETCHER, John (1579–1625; English dramatist)

FORESTER, C S (1899–1966; British novelist)

GINSBERG, Allen (1926–97; US poet)

GONCOURT, Edmond de (1822–96; French writer)

HENRYSON, Robert (15th century; Scottish poet)

HOCHHUTH, Rolf (1931– ; Swiss-German dramatist)

HUYSMANS, Joris Karl (1848–1907; French novelist)

JEAN PAUL (Johann Paul Friedrich Richter, 1763–1825; German novelist)

KALIDASA (5th century AD; Indian poet)

KENEALLY, Thomas (1935– ; Australian writer)

KINGSLEY, Charles (1819–79; British writer)

KOESTLER, Arthur (1905–83; British writer)

KOTZEBUE, August von (1761–1819; German dramatist and novelist)

LAFORGUE, Jules (1860–87; French poet)

LAGERLÖF, Selma Ottiliana Lovisa (1858–1940; Swedish novelist)

LANGLAND, William (c. 1330–c. 1400; English poet)

LAS CASES, Emmanuel, Comte de (1776–1842; French writer)

LAWRENCE, D H (1885–1930; British novelist, poet, and painter)

LEOPARDI, Giacomo (1798–1837; Italian poet)

LOCKHART, John Gibson (1794–1854; Scottish biographer and journalist)

LONGINUS (1st century AD; Greek rhetorician)

LOVELACE, Richard (1618–57; English Cavalier poet)

MACAULAY, Rose (1881–1958; British novelist)

MACLEISH, Archibald (1892–1982; US poet)

MACNEICE, Louis (1907–63; Irish-born British poet)

MALHERBE, François de (1555–1628; French poet and critic)

MALLARMÉ, Stéphane (1842–98; French poet)

MARIVAUX, Pierre Carlet de Chamblain de (1688–1763; French dramatist)

MARQUAND, J P (1893–1960; US novelist)

MCCARTHY, Mary (1912–89; US novelist)

MELVILLE, Herman (1819–91; US novelist)

MENANDER (c. 341–c. 290 BC; Greek dramatist)

MEREDITH, George (1828–1909; British poet and novelist)

MICHELET, Jules (1798–1874; French historian)

MITCHELL, Margaret (1909–49; US novelist)

MORRISON, Toni (1931– ; US writer)

NEKRASOV, Nikolai Alekseevich (1821–78; Russian poet)

NICOLSON, Harold (1886–1968; British literary critic)

ONDAATJE, Michael (1943– ; Canadian writer)

PALGRAVE, Francis Turner (1824–97; British poet and anthologist)

PERELMAN, S J (1904–79; US humorous writer)

PERRAULT, Charles (1628–1703; French poet and fairytale writer)

PETRARCH (Francesco Petrarca, 1304–74; Italian poet)

PHAEDRUS (1st century AD; Roman writer)

PHILEMON (c. 368–c. 264 BC; Greek dramatist)

PLUTARCH (c. 46–c. 120 AD; Greek biographer and essayist)

RABELAIS, François (1483–1553; French satirist)

RADIGUET, Raymond (1903–23; French novelist)

RATTIGAN, Terence (1911–77; British dramatist)

REMARQUE, Erich Maria (1898–1970; German novelist)

RICHARDS, Frank (Charles Hamilton, 1876–1961; British children's writer)

RUNEBERG, Johan Ludvig (1804–77; Finnish poet)

SALINGER, J D (1919–2010; US novelist)

SANDBURG, Carl (1878–1967; US poet)

SARAMAGO, José (1922–2010; Portuguese writer)

SARRAUTE, Nathalie (1900–99; French novelist, born in Russia)

SCALIGER, Julius Caesar (1484–1558; Italian humanist scholar)

SCHILLER, Friedrich (1759–1805; German dramatist, poet, and writer)

SHADWELL, Thomas (c. 1642–92; British dramatist)

SHERIDAN, Richard Brinsley (1751–1816; Anglo-Irish dramatist)

SILLITOE, Alan (1928–2010; British novelist)

SINCLAIR, Upton (1878–1968; US novelist)

SMOLLETT, Tobias (1721–71; British novelist)

SPILLANE, Mickey (Frank Morrison S, 1918–2006; US detective-story writer)

STENDHAL (Henri Beyle, 1783–1842; French novelist)

STOPPARD, Tom, Sir (1937– ; British dramatist)

SUCKLING, John (1609–42; English poet and dramatist)

SU DONG PO (or Su Tung-p'o, 1036–1101; Chinese poet)

TALIESIN (6th century AD; Welsh poet)

TENNYSON, Alfred, Lord (1809–92; British poet)

THOMPSON, Francis (1859–1907; British poet and critic)

TIBULLUS, Albius (c. 55–c. 19 BC; Roman poet)

TOURNEUR, Cyril (c. 1575–1626; English dramatist)

TRAHERNE, Thomas (c. 1637–74; English poet)

TRILLING, Lionel (1905–75; US literary critic)

TROLLOPE, Anthony (1815–82; British novelist)

TULSIDAS (c. 1532–1623; Indian poet)

TURGENEV, Ivan (1818–83; Russian novelist)

VERLAINE, Paul (1844–96; French poet)

VOLTAIRE (François-Marie Arouet, 1694–1778; French writer)

VONNEGUT, Kurt (1922–2007; US novelist)

WEDEKIND, Frank (1864–1918; German dramatist)

WHITTIER, John Greenleaf (1807–92; US poet)

WILLIAMS, Tennessee (1911–83; US dramatist)

WILLIAMS, William Carlos (1883–1963; US poet)

ZAMYATIN, Yevgenii Ivanovich (1884–1937; Russian novelist)

9

AESCHYLUS (c. 525–456 BC; Greek tragic dramatist)

AINSWORTH, W Harrison (1805–82; British historical novelist)

AKHMATOVA, Anna (Anna Andreevna Gorenko, 1889–1966; Russian poet)

ALDINGTON, Richard (1892–1962; British poet, novelist, and biographer)

ALLINGHAM, Margery (1904–66; British detective-story writer)

ARBUTHNOT, John (1667–1735; Scottish writer)

AYCKBOURN, Alan, Sir (1939– ; British dramatist)

BLACKMORE, R D (1825–1900; British historical novelist)

BLACKWOOD, Algernon Henry (1869–1951; British novelist and short-story writer)

BLEASDALE, Alan (1946– ; British playwright)

BOCCACCIO, Giovanni (1313–75; Italian writer and poet)

BURROUGHS, Edgar Rice (1875–1950; US novelist)

BURROUGHS, William (1914–97; US novelist)

CERVANTES, Miguel de (1547–1616; Spanish novelist)

CHARTERIS, Leslie (L Charles Bowyer Yin, 1907–93; British novelist)

CHURCHILL, Charles (1731–64; British poet)

COLERIDGE, Samuel Taylor (1772–1834; British poet)

CORNEILLE, Pierre (1606–84; French dramatist)

D'ANNUNZIO, Gabriele (1863–1938; Italian poet, novelist, and dramatist)

DE LA ROCHE, Mazo (1885–1961; Canadian novelist)

DE QUINCEY, Thomas (1785–1859; British essayist and critic)

DICKINSON, Emily (1830–86; US poet)

DOOLITTLE, Hilda (1886–1961; US poet)

DOS PASSOS, John (1896–1970; US novelist)

DU MAURIER, George (1834–96; British caricaturist and novelist)

ECKERMANN, Johann Peter (1792–1854; German writer)

EDGEWORTH, Maria (1767–1849; Anglo-Irish writer)

EHRENBERG, Iliya Grigorievich (1891–1967; Soviet author)

EURIPIDES (c. 480–406 BC; Greek dramatist)

FROISSART, Jean (1337–c. 1400; French chronicler and poet)

GIRAUDOUX, Jean (1882–1944; French dramatist and novelist)

GOLDSMITH, Oliver (1730–74; Anglo-Irish writer)

GONCHAROV, Ivan Aleksandrovich (1812–91; Russian novelist)

PROPERTIUS, Sextus (c. 50–c. 16 BC; Roman poet)

RICHARDSON, Henry Handel (Ethel Florence R, 1870–1946; Australian novelist)

RICHARDSON, Samuel (1689–1761; British novelist)

RUTHERFORD, Mark (William Hale White, 1831–1913; British novelist)

SCHNITZLER, Arthur (1862–1931; Austrian Jewish dramatist and novelist)

STRINDBERG, August (1849–1912; Swedish dramatist and writer)

TANNHÄUSER (c. 1200–c. 1270; German poet)

THEOCRITUS (c. 310–250 BC; Greek poet)

VAN DER POST, Laurens (1906–96; South African novelist)

WILLIAMSON, Henry (1895–1977; British novelist)

WORDSWORTH, William (1770–1850; British poet)

XENOPHANES (6th century BC; Greek poet)

11

ANZENGRUBER, Ludwig (1839–89; Austrian dramatist and novelist)

APOLLINAIRE, Guillaume (Wilhelm de Kostrowitzky, 1880–1918; French poet)

ARCHILOCHUS (c. 680–c. 640 BC; Greek poet)

BACCHYLIDES (c. 516–c. 450 BC; Greek lyric poet)

BLESSINGTON, Marguerite, Countess of (1789–1849; Irish author)

CALLIMACHUS (c. 305–c. 240 BC; Greek poet)

CASTIGLIONE, Baldassare (1478–1529; Italian writer)

DOSTOIEVSKI, Fedor Mikhailovich (1821–81; Russian novelist)

EICHENDORFF, Josef, Freiherr von (1788–1857; German writer)

GARCÍA LORCA, Federico (1898–1936; Spanish poet and dramatist)

GRILLPARZER, Franz (1791–1872; Austrian dramatist)

KAZANTZAKIS, Nikos (1885–1957; Greek novelist and poet)

LAUTRÉAMONT, Comte de (Isidore Ducasse, 1846–70; French writer)

MAETERLINCK, Maurice (1862–1949; Belgian poet and dramatist)

MATSUO BASHO (Matsuo Munefusa, 1644–94; Japanese poet)

MAYAKOVSKII, Vladimir (1893–1930; Russian poet)

MONTHERLANT, Henry de (1896–1972; French novelist and dramatist)

'OMAR KHAYYAM (?1048–?1122; Persian poet)

PÉREZ GALDÓS, Benito (1843–1920; Spanish novelist)

SHAKESPEARE, William (1564–1616; English dramatist)

SIENKIEWICZ, Henryk (1846–1916; Polish novelist)

STIERNHIELM, Georg Olofson (1598–1672; Swedish poet)

YEVTUSHENKO, Yevgenii (1933–2017; Soviet poet)

12

ARISTOPHANES (c. 450–c. 385 BC; Greek comic dramatist)

BEAUMARCHAIS, Pierre-Augustin Caron de (1732–99; French dramatist)

BLASCO IBÁÑEZ, Vicente (1867–1928; Spanish novelist)

FERLINGHETTI, Lawrence (1919–   ; US poet)

FEUCHTWANGER, Lion (1884–1958; German novelist and dramatist)

HOFMANNSTHAL, Hugo von (1874–1929; Austrian poet and dramatist)

LÓPEZ DE AYALA, Pero (c. 1332–c. 1407; Spanish poet and chronicler)

MARTIN DU GARD, Roger (1881–1958; French novelist)

MATTHEW PARIS (c. 1200–59; English chronicler)

ROBBE-GRILLET, Alain (1922–2008; French novelist)

SAINT-EXUPÉRY, Antoine de (1900–44; French novelist)

SOLZHENITSYN, Aleksandr (1918–2008; Russian novelist)

VOZNESENSKII, Andrei (1933–2010; Soviet poet)

13

BERTRAN DE BORN (?1140–?1215; French troubadour poet)

CASTELO BRANCO, Camilo (1825–95; Portuguese novelist)

CHATEAUBRIAND, Vicomte de (1768–1848; French writer)

CSOKONAI VITÉZ, Mihaly (1773–1805; Hungarian poet)

GARCÍA MÁRQUEZ, Gabriel (1927–2014; Colombian novelist)

HARISHCHANDRA (1850–85; Hindi poet, dramatist, and essayist, also known as Bharatendu)

MARIE DE FRANCE (12th century AD; French poet)

TIRSO DE MOLINA (Gabriel Téllez, c. 1584–1648; Spanish dramatist)

ZEAMI MOTOKIYO (1363–c. 1443; Japanese playwright)

14

BRILLAT-SAVARIN, Anthelme (1755–1826; French writer)

COMPTON-BURNETT, Ivy (1892–1969; British novelist)

DAFYDD AP GWILYM (c. 1320–c. 1380; Welsh poet)

DANTE ALIGHIERI (1265–1321; Italian poet)

DROSTE-HÜLSHOFF, Annette von (1797–1848; German poet and novelist)

GÓNGORA Y ARGOTE, Luis de (1561–1627; Spanish poet)

GRIMMELSHAUSEN, Hans Jacob Christoph von (c. 1625–76; German novelist)

JACOPONE DA TODI (c. 1236–1306; Italian religious poet)

LECONTE DE LISLE, Charles Marie René (1818–94; French poet)

OEHLENSCHLÄGER, Adam (1779–1850; Danish poet and playwright)

PRÉVOST D'EXILES, Antoine François, Abbé (1697–1763; French novelist)

SULLY-PRUDHOMME, René François Armand (1839–1907; French poet)

WOLLSTONECRAFT, Mary (1759–97; British writer)

ZORRILLA Y MORAL, José (1817–93; Spanish poet and dramatist)

15

ALARCÓN Y MENDOZA, Juan Ruiz de (1581–1639; Spanish dramatist)

DIODORUS SICULUS (1st century BC; Greek historian)

PLINY THE YOUNGER (Gaius Plinius Caecilius Secundus, c. 61–c. 113 AD; Roman writer)

16

CHRÉTIEN DE TROYES (12th century AD; French poet)

CYRANO DE BERGERAC, Savinien (1619–55; French writer and dramatist)

KAWABATA YASUNARI (1899–
1972; Japanese novelist)
PETRONIUS ARBITER (1st century
AD; Roman satirist)

17
CALDERÓN DE LA BARCA, Pedro
(1600–81; Spanish dramatist)
GUILLAUME DE LORRIS (13th
century; French poet and
author)
TANIZAKI JUN-ICHIRO (1886–
1965; Japanese novelist)

18
APOLLONIUS OF RHODES (3rd
century BC; Greek epic poet)
KAKINOMOTO HITOMARO (c.

680–710; Japanese poet)
THOMAS OF ERCELDOUNE (13th
century; English poet and
prophet)

19
BENOIT DE SAINTE-MAURE (12th
century AD; French poet)
CHIKAMATSU MONZAEMON
(Sugimori Nobumori; 1653–
1724; Japanese dramatist)
VILLIERS DE L'ISLE-ADAM,
Philippe Auguste, Comte de
(1838–89; French poet,
novelist, and dramatist)

20+
BERNARDIN DE SAINT-PIERRE,

Jacques Henri (1737–1814;
French naturalist and writer)
DIONYSIUS OF HALICARNASSUS
(1st century BC; Greek historian)
DRUMMOND OF
HAWTHORNDEN, William
(1585–1649; Scots poet)
ECHEGARAY Y EIZAGUIRRE, José
(1832–1916; Spanish dramatist)
GOTTFRIED VON STRASSBURG
(13th century; German poet)
WALTHER VON DER VOGELWEIDE
(c. 1170–c. 1230; German poet)
WOLFRAM VON ESCHENBACH (c.
1170–c. 1220; German poet)

PHILOSOPHERS

4
AYER, Alfred (Jules) (1910–89;
British philosopher)
HUME, David (1711–76; Scottish
philosopher and historian)
KANT, Immanuel (1724–1804;
German philosopher)
MACH, Ernst (1838–1916; Austrian
physicist and philosopher)
MARX, Karl (Heinrich) (1818– 83;
German philosopher)
MILL, James (1773–1836; Scottish
writer and philosopher)
MORE, Henry (1614–87; English
philosopher)
MOZI (or Motzu; ?470–?391 BC;
Chinese philosopher)
RAZI, ar (or Rhazes; c. 865–c. 928
AD; Persian physician and
philosopher)
REID, Thomas (1710–96; Scottish
philosopher)
RYLE, Gilbert (1900–76; British
philosopher)
VICO, Giambattista (or Giovanni
Battista Vico; 1668– 1744;
Italian historical
philosopher)
WEIL, Simone (1909–43; French
mystic and philosopher)

5
AMIEL, Henri Frédéric (1821–81;
Swiss philosopher and writer)
BACON, Francis, 1st Baron
Verulam, Viscount St Albans
(1561–1626; English lawyer and
philosopher)
BENDA, Julien (1867–1956; French
novelist and philosopher)

BODIN, Jean (1530–96; French
philosopher and jurist)
BRUNO, Giordano (1548–1600;
Italian philosopher)
BUBER, Martin (1878–1965;
Austrian-born Jewish religious
philosopher)
BURKE, Edmund (1729–97; British
political philosopher and
politician)
CHU XI (or Chu Hsi; 1130–1200;
Chinese philosopher)
COMTE, Auguste (1798–1857;
French philosopher)
CROCE, Benedetto (1866–1952;
Italian philosopher)
DEWEY, John (1859–1952; US
philosopher and educationalist)
FLUDD, Robert (1574–1637;
English physician and
philosopher)
FROMM, Erich (1900–80; US
psychologist and philosopher)
HEGEL, Georg Wilhelm Friedrich
(1770–1831; German
philosopher)
IQBAL, Mohammed (?1875–1938;
Indian Muslim poet and
philosopher)
LACAN, Jacques (Marie Emile)
(1901–81; French psychoanalyst
and philosopher)
LOCKE, John (1632–1704; English
philosopher)
MOORE, G(eorge) E(dward)
(1873–1958; British
philosopher)
PLATO (429–347 BC; Greek
philosopher)

QUINE, Willard van Orman (1908–
2000; US philosopher)
RAMUS, Petrus (Pierre de la
Ramée; 1515–72; French
humanist philosopher and
logician)
RENAN, (Joseph; Ernest (1823–92;
French philosopher and
theologian)
SMITH, Adam (1723–90; Scottish
moral philosopher and political
economist)
SOREL, Georges (1847–1922;
French social philosopher)

6
ADORNO, Theodor
(Wiesengrund) (1903–64;
German philosopher)
AGNESI, Maria Gaetana (1718–99;
Italian mathematician and
philosopher)
ARENDT, Hannah (1906–75;
German-born US political
philosopher)
AUSTIN, John Langshaw (1911–
60; British philosopher)
BERLIN, Isaiah (1909–97; Latvian-
born British philosopher and
historian)
CARNAP, Rudolf (1891–1970;
German-born logical positivist
philosopher)
COUSIN, Victor (1792–1867;
French philosopher)
FICHTE, Johann Gottlieb (1762–
1814; German philosopher)
GODWIN, William (1756–1836;
British political philosopher and
novelist)

HERDER, Johann Gottfried (1744–1803; German philosopher and poet)

HERZEN, Aleksandr (Ivanovich) (1812–70; Russian political philosopher)

HOBBES, Thomas (1588–1679; English political philosopher)

KRIPKE, Saul (1940– ; US philosopher)

LUKACS, Giorgi (1885–1971; Hungarian Marxist philosopher)

ORESME, Nicole d' (c. 1320–82; French philosopher and churchman)

PEIRCE, Charles Sanders (1839–1914; US philosopher and logician)

POPPER, Karl Raimund (1902–94; Austrian-born philosopher)

SARTRE, Jean-Paul (1905–80; French philosopher, novelist, dramatist, and critic)

SUPPES, Patrick (1922–2014; US philosopher)

TAGORE, Rabindranath (1861–1941; Indian poet, philosopher, and teacher)

TAYLOR, Charles (1931– ; Canadian philosopher)

7

ABELARD, Peter (1079–1142; French philosopher)

ALKINDI, Abu Yusuf Ya'qub ibn Ishaq (died c. 870; Muslim Arab philosopher)

AQUINAS, St Thomas (c. 1225–74; Italian Dominican theologian, scholastic philosopher, and Doctor of the Church)

ARNAULD, Antoine (1612–94; French theologian, philosopher, and logician)

BENTHAM, Jeremy (1748–1832; British philosopher)

BERGSON, Henri (1859–1941; French philosopher and psychologist)

BLONDEL, Maurice (1861–1949; French philosopher)

BRADLEY, Francis Herbert (1846–1924; British philosopher)

BURIDAN, Jean (c. 1297–c. 1358; French scholastic philosopher)

CHARRON, Pierre (1541–1603; French theologian and philosopher)

DERRIDA, Jacques (1930–2004; French philosopher)

DESTUTT, Antoine Louis Claude, Comte de Tracy (1754–1836;

French philosopher and politician)

DIDEROT, Denis (1713–84; French philosopher and writer)

DREYFUS, Hubert (1929–2017; US philosopher)

EDWARDS, Jonathan (1703–58; American theologian and philosopher)

ERIGENA, John Scotus (c. 800–c. 877; Irish-born medieval philosopher)

GENTILE, Giovanni (1875–1944; Italian philosopher)

GUARINI, Guarino (1624–83; Italian baroque architect, philosopher, and mathematician)

HUSSERL, Edmund (1859–1938; German philosopher)

HYPATIA (d. 415 AD; Neoplatonist philosopher and mathematician)

JASPERS, Karl (Theodor) (1883–1969; German philosopher)

LEIBNIZ, Gottfried Wilhelm (1646–1716; German philosopher and mathematician)

MENCIUS (Mengzi or Mengtzu; 371–289 BC; Chinese moral philosopher)

MUMFORD, Lewis (1895–1990; US social philosopher)

MURDOCH, Iris (1919–99; British novelist and philosopher)

PROCLUS (410–85 AD; Neoplatonist philosopher)

PYRRHON (or Pyrrho; c. 360–c. 270 BC; Greek philosopher)

RUSSELL, Bertrand Arthur William, 3rd Earl (1872–1970; British philosopher)

SANKARA (or Shankara; 8th century AD; Hindu philosopher)

SCHLICK, Moritz (1882–1936; German philosopher)

SCRUTON, Roger (Vernon) (1944–; British philosopher and cultural historian)

SPENCER, Herbert (1820–1903; British philosopher)

SPINOZA, Benedict (or Baruch de S.; 1632–77; Dutch philosopher, theologian, and scientist)

8

ALFARABI, Mohammed ibn Tarkhan (d. 950; Muslim philosopher, physician, mathematician, and musician)

AVERROES (Ibn Rushd; 1126–98; Muslim philosopher)

AVICENNA (980–1037; Persian philosopher and physician)

BERDYAEV, Nikolai (1874–1948; Russian mystical philosopher)

BERKELEY, George (1685–1753; Irish bishop and idealist philosopher)

BOETHIUS, Anicius Manlius Severinus (c. 480–524 AD; Roman statesman and philosopher)

BRENTANO, Franz (1838–1916; German psychologist and philosopher)

CASSIRER, Ernst (1874–1945; German philosopher and historian)

EPICURUS (341–270 BC; Greek philosopher)

FOUCAULT, Michel (1926–84; French philosopher)

GASSENDI, Pierre (1592–1655; French physicist and philosopher)

GEULINCX, Arnold (1624–69; Belgian-born philosopher)

HAN FEI ZI (d. 233 BC; Chinese diplomat and philosopher of law)

HARTMANN, Eduard von (1842–1906; German philosopher)

HARTMANN, Nicolai (1882–1950; Russian-born German philosopher)

KROCHMAL, Nachman (1785–1840; Jewish philosopher)

PLOTINUS (205–70 AD; Greek philosopher)

PORPHYRY (232–305 AD; Syrian-born philosopher)

RAMANUJA (11th century AD; Indian-born Hindu philosopher and theologian)

ROSCELIN (died c. 1125; French scholastic philosopher)

ROUSSEAU, Jean Jacques (1712–78; French philosopher and writer)

SIDGWICK, Henry (1838–1900; British moral philosopher)

SOCRATES (c. 469–399 BC; Athenian philosopher)

SOLOVIOV, Vladimir Sergevich (1853–1900; Russian philosopher and poet)

SPENGLER, Oswald (1880–1936; German philosopher)

STRAWSON, Peter Frederick (1919–; British philosopher)

VOLTAIRE (François-Marie Arouet; 1694–1778; French philosopher)

ZHUANGZI (or Chuangtzu;

c. 369–286 BC; Chinese philosopher)

9

ALTHUSSER, Louis (1918–90; Algerian-born French philosopher)

ARISTOTLE (384–322 BC; Greek philosopher and scientist)

BOSANQUET, Bernard (1848–1923; British philosopher)

CLEANTHES (c. 310–230 BC; Greek philosopher)

CONDILLAC, Étienne Bonnot de (1715–80; French philosopher and psychologist)

CONDORCET, Marie Jean Antoine de Caritat, Marquis de (1743–94; French philosopher and politician)

CONFUCIUS (Kong Zi or K'ungfutzu; c. 551–479 BC; Chinese philosopher)

DESCARTES, René (1596–1650; French philosopher)

EPICTETUS (c. 60–110 AD; Stoic philosopher)

FEUERBACH, Ludwig Andreas (1804–72; German philosopher)

HEIDEGGER, Martin (1889–1976; German philosopher)

HELVÉTIUS, Claude Adrien (1715–71; French philosopher)

HUTCHESON, Francis (1694–1746; Scottish philosopher)

LEUCIPPUS (5th century BC; Greek philosopher)

LUCRETIUS (Titus Lucretius Carus; c. 95–c. 55 BC; Roman philosopher and poet)

NAGARJUNA (c. 150–c. 250 AD; Indian Buddhist monk and philosopher)

NIETZSCHE, Friedrich (1844–1900; German philosopher)

PLEKHANOV, Georgi Valentinovich (1857–1918; Russian revolutionary and Marxist philosopher)

PUFENDORF, Samuel von (1632–94; German philosopher)

SANTAYANA, George (1863–1952; Spanish-born US philosopher and poet)

SCHELLING, Friedrich (1775–1854; German philosopher)

WHITEHEAD, A(lfred); N(orth) (1861–1947; British philosopher and mathematician)

10

ANAXAGORAS (c. 500–428 BC; Greek philosopher)

ANAXIMENES (died c. 528 BC; Greek philosopher)

ARISTIPPUS (c. 435–c. 356 BC; Greek philosopher)

BAUMGARTEN, Alexander Gottlieb (1714–62; German philosopher)

CAMPANELLA, Tommaso (1568–1639; Italian philosopher and Dominican friar)

CUMBERLAND, Richard (1631–1718; English moral philosopher)

DEMOCRITUS (c. 460–370 BC; Greek philosopher and scientist)

DUNS SCOTUS, John (c. 1260–1308; Scottish-born Franciscan philosopher)

EMPEDOCLES (c. 490–430 BC; Sicilian Greek philosopher)

FONTENELLE, Bernard le Bovier de (1657–1757; French philosopher)

HERACLITUS (c. 535–c. 475 BC; Greek philosopher)

IBN GABIROL, Solomon (c. 1021–c. 1058; Spanish-born Jewish philosopher and poet)

IBN KHALDUN (1332–1406; Arab historian and philosopher)

MAIMONIDES, Moses (1135–1204; Jewish philosopher and physician)

PARMENIDES (c. 510–c. 450 BC; Greek philosopher)

PYTHAGORAS (6th century BC; Greek philosopher and religious leader)

SWEDENBORG, Emanuel (1688–1772; Swedish scientist, mystic, and philosopher)

WILLIAMSON, Timothy (1955– ; British philosopher)

ZENO OF ELEA (born c. 490 BC; Greek philosopher)

11

BOLINGBROKE, Henry St John, 1st Viscount (1678–1751; English statesman and philosopher)

COLLINGWOOD, R(obin); G(eorge) (1889–1943; British philosopher)

JUDAH HALEVI (or Halevy; c. 1075–1141; Jewish poet and philosopher)

KIERKEGAARD, Søren (1813–55; Danish philosopher)

MALEBRANCHE, Nicolas (1638–1715; French philosopher and theologian)

MENDELSSOHN, Moses (1729–86; German Jewish philosopher)

MONTESQUIEU, Charles Louis de Secondat, Baron de (1689–1755; French historical philosopher and writer)

VIVEKANANDA, Swami (1862–1902; Hindu philosopher)

ANAXIMANDER (c. 610–c. 546 BC; Greek philosopher)

ANTISTHENES (c. 445–c. 360 BC; Greek philosopher)

12

MERLEAUPONTY, Maurice (1908–61; French philosopher)

PHILO JUDAEUS (c. 30 BC–45 AD; Jewish philosopher)

SCHOPENHAUER, Arthur (1788–1860; German philosopher)

THEOPHRASTUS (c. 370–286 BC; Greek philosopher and scientist)

UNAMUNO Y JUGO, Miguel de (1864–1936; Spanish writer and philosopher)

WITTGENSTEIN, Ludwig (1889–1951; Austrian philosopher)

ZENO OF CITIUM (c. 335–262 BC; Greek philosopher)

13

DIO CHRYSOSTOM (2nd century AD; Greek philosopher and orator)

ORTEGA Y GASSET, José (1883–1955; Spanish philosopher and writer)

14

ALBERTUS MAGNUS, St (c. 1200–80; German bishop, philosopher, and Doctor of the Church)

WOLLSTONECRAFT, Mary (1759–97; British writer)

15

JOHN OF SALISBURY (c. 1115–80; English philosopher)

WILLIAM OF OCKHAM (c. 1285–1349; English scholastic philosopher)

16

ALEXANDER OF HALES (c. 1170–1245; English scholastic philosopher)

17

APOLLONIUS OF TYANA (1st century AD; Pythagorean philosopher)

BERNARD OF CHARTRES (died c. 1130; French scholastic philosopher)

18

PICO DELLA MIRANDOLA, Giovanni, Conte (1463–94; Italian Renaissance philosopher)

MUSICIANS AND COMPOSERS

3

BAX, Arnold Edward Trevor (1883–1953; British composer)

4

ADAM, Adolphe-Charles (1803–56; French composer)

ADÈS, Thomas (1971– ; British composer)

ARNE, Thomas Augustine (1710–78; British composer)

BACH, Johann Sebastian (1685–1750; German composer and keyboard player)

BERG, Alban (1885–1935; Austrian composer)

BING, Rudolf (1902–97; British opera administrator)

BLOW, John (1649–1708; English composer)

BÖHM, Karl (1894–1981; Austrian conductor)

BULL, John (c. 1562–1628; English composer and organist)

BUSH, Alan Dudley (1900–95; British composer)

BUTT, Clara (1873–1936; British contralto singer)

BYRD, William (?1543–1623; English composer)

CAGE, John (1912–92; US composer)

HESS, Myra (1890–1965; British pianist)

IVES, Charles (1874–1954; US composer)

LALO, Édouard (1823–92; French composer)

LILL, John (1944– ; British pianist)

LIND, Jenny (1820–87; Swedish soprano)

NONO, Luigi (1924–90; Italian composer)

ORFF, Carl (1895–1982; German composer and conductor)

PÄRT, Arvo (1935– ; Estonian composer)

WOLF, Hugo (1860–1903; Austrian composer)

WOOD, Henry (1869–1944; British conductor)

5

ADAMS, John Coolidge (1947– ; US composer)

ALKAN, Charles Henri Valentin (C H V Morhange, 1813–88; French pianist and composer)

ALLEN, Thomas, Sir (1944– ; British operatic baritone)

ARRAU, Claudio (1903–91; Chilean pianist)

AUBER, Daniel François Esprit (1782–1871; French composer)

AURIC, Georges (1899–1983; French composer)

BAKER, Janet, Dame (1933– ; British mezzo-soprano)

BERIO, Luciano (1925–2003; Italian composer)

BIZET, Georges (Alexandre César Léopold B, 1838–75; French composer)

BLISS, Arthur Edward Drummond (1891–1975; British composer)

BLOCH, Ernest (1880–1959; Swiss-born composer)

BOEHM, Theobald (1794–1881; German flautist)

BOULT, Adrian (1889–1983; British conductor)

BOYCE, William (c. 1710–79; British composer)

BREAM, Julian Alexander (1933– ; British guitarist and lutenist)

BRIAN, Havergal (1876–1972; British composer)

BRUCH, Max (1838–1920; German composer)

BÜLOW, Hans Guido, Freiherr von (1830–94; German pianist and conductor)

DAVIS, Andrew, Sir (1944– ; British conductor)

DAVIS, Colin, Sir (1927–2013; British conductor)

D'INDY, Vincent (1851–1931; French composer)

DUFAY, Guillaume (c. 1400–74; Burgundian composer)

DUKAS, Paul (1865–1935; French composer)

DUPRÉ, Jacqueline (1945–87; British cellist)

DUPRÉ, Marcel (1886–1971; French composer)

ELDER, Mark, Sir (1947– ; British conductor)

ELGAR, Edward (1857– 1934; British composer)

EVANS, Geraint (1922–92; Welsh baritone)

FALLA, Manuel de (1876–1946; Spanish composer)

FAURÉ, Gabriel (1845–1924; French composer and organist)

FIELD, John (1782–1837; Irish pianist and composer)

FRIML, Rudolph (1879–1972;

Czech-born composer and pianist)

GIGLI, Beniamino (1890–1957; Italian tenor)

GLASS, Philip (1937– ; US composer)

GLUCK, Christoph Willibald (1714–87; German composer)

GOBBI, Tito (1915–84; Italian baritone)

GOEHR, Alexander (1932– ; British composer)

GRIEG, Edvard Hagerup (1843–1907; Norwegian composer)

GROVE, George (1820– 1900; British musicologist)

HALLÉ, Charles (Karl Hallé, 1819–1895; German conductor and pianist)

HAYDN, Franz Joseph (1732–1809; Austrian composer)

HENZE, Hans Werner (1926–2012; German composer)

HOLST, Gustav (1874–1934; British composer and teacher)

IBERT, Jacques (1890–1962; French composer)

LEHÁR, Franz (Ferencz L, 1870–1948; Hungarian composer)

LISZT, Franz (Ferencz L, 1811–86; Hungarian pianist and composer)

LOCKE, Matthew (c. 1622–77; English composer)

LULLY, Jean Baptiste (Giovanni Battista Lulli, 1632–87; French composer)

MELBA, Nellie (Helen Porter Armstrong, 1861– 1931; Australian soprano)

MOORE, Gerald (1899–1987; British pianist)

MUNCH, Charles (1892–1968; French conductor)

OGDON, John (1937–89; British pianist)

PARRY, Hubert (1848–1918; British composer)

PATTI, Adelina (Adela Juana Maria, 1843–1919; Italian-born operatic soprano)

PEARS, Peter (1910–86; British tenor)

RAVEL, Maurice (1875–1937; French composer)

REGER, Max (1873–1916; German composer, organist, and teacher)

REICH, Stephen Michael (1936– ; US composer)

SATIE, Erik (1866–1925; French composer)

SHARP, Cecil (1859–1924; British musician)

SOLTI, Georg (1912–97; Hungarian-born British conductor)

SOUSA, John Philip (1854–1933; US composer and bandmaster)

SPOHR, Louis (Ludwig S, 1784–1859; German violinist and composer)

STERN, Isaac (1920–2001; Russian-born US violinist)

SZELL, George (1897–1970; Hungarian conductor)

TEYTE, Maggie (1888–1976; British soprano)

VERDI, Giuseppe (1813–1901; Italian composer)

WEBER, Carl Maria von (1786–1826; German composer)

WEILL, Kurt (1900–50; German composer)

WIDOR, Charles Marie (1844–1937; French organist and composer)

6

ARNOLD, Malcolm (1921–2006; British composer)

BARBER, Samuel (1910–81; US composer)

BARTÓK, Béla (1881–1945; Hungarian composer)

BATTLE, Kathleen (1948– ; US soprano)

BISHOP, Henry Rowley (1786–1855; British composer and conductor)

BOULEZ, Pierre (1925–2016; French composer and conductor)

BRAHMS, Johannes (1833–97; German composer)

BRIDGE, Frank (1879–1941; British composer)

BURNEY, Charles (1726–1814; British musicologist, organist, and composer)

BUSONI, Ferruccio (1866–1924; Italian virtuoso pianist and composer)

CALLAS, Maria (Maria Anna Kalageropoulos, 1923–77; US-born soprano)

CARTER, Elliott (1908–2012; US composer)

CARUSO, Enrico (1873–1921; Italian tenor)

CASALS, Pablo (Pau C, 1876–1973; Spanish cellist, conductor, and composer)

CHOPIN, Frédéric (François, 1810–49; Polish composer)

CLARKE, Jeremiah (?1673–1707; English composer and organist)

CORTOT, Alfred (1877–1962; French pianist and conductor)

COWELL, Henry (1897–1965; US composer)

CURWEN, John (1816–80; British teacher who perfected the Tonic Sol-fa system)

CURZON, Clifford (1907–82; British pianist)

DAVIES, Peter Maxwell, Sir (1934–2016; British composer)

DELIUS, Frederick (1862–1934; British composer)

DIBDIN, Charles (1745–1814; British composer, actor, and singer)

DUPARC, Henri (Marie Eugène Henri Foucques D, 1848–1933; French composer)

DVŎŘÁK, Antonín (1841–1904; Czech composer)

ENESCO, Georges (G Enescu, 1881–1955; Romanian violinist and composer)

FLOTOW, Friedrich von (1812–83; German composer)

FRANCK, César Auguste (1822–90; Belgian composer, organist, and teacher)

GALWAY, James (1939– ; Irish flautist)

GLINKA, Mikhail Ivanovich (1804–57; Russian composer)

GLOVER, Jane Alison (1949– ; British conductor)

GOUNOD, Charles François (1818–93; French composer)

GRÉTRY, André Ernest Modeste (1741–1813; Belgian composer)

GROVES, Charles (1915–92; British conductor)

HALÉVY, Jacques François (Fromental Elias Levy, 1799–1862; French composer)

HANDEL, George Frederick (1685–1759; German composer)

HARRIS, Roy (1898–1979; US composer)

HOTTER, Hans (1909–2003; German baritone)

HUMMEL, Johann Nepomuk (1778–1837; Hungarian pianist and composer)

JOCHUM, Eugen (1902–87; German conductor)

JOPLIN, Scott (1867–1917; US composer and pianist)

KODÁLY, Zoltan (1882–1967; Hungarian composer)

KRENEK, Ernst (1900–91; Austrian composer)

LASSUS, Roland de (c. 1532–94; Flemish composer)

LIGETI, György (1923–2006; Hungarian composer)

MAAZEL, Lorin (1930–2014; US conductor)

MAHLER, Gustav (1860–1911; Austrian composer and conductor)

MORLEY, Thomas (1557– 1603; English composer, music printer and organist)

MOZART, Wolfgang Amadeus (1756–91; Austrian composer)

PREVIN, André (Andreas Ludwig Priwin, 1929–2019; German-born conductor, pianist, and composer)

RAMEAU, Jean Philippe (1683–1764; French composer)

RATTLE, Simon, Sir (1955– ; British conductor)

RUBBRA, Edmund (1901–86; British composer)

SCHÜTZ, Heinrich (1585–1672; German composer)

TALLIS, Thomas (c. 1505–85; English composer)

TERFEL, Bryn, Sir (1965– ; British bass-baritone)

VARÈSE, Edgard (1883–1965; French composer)

WAGNER, Richard (1813–83; German composer)

WALTER, Bruno (B W Schlesinger, 1876–1962; German conductor)

WALTON, William (1902–83; British composer)

WATSON, Russell (1966– ; British tenor)

WEBERN, Anton von (1883–1945; Austrian composer)

7

ALBÉNIZ, Isaac Manuel Francisco (1860–1909; Spanish composer and pianist)

ALLEGRI, Gregorio (1582–1652; Italian composer)

ANTHEIL, George (1900–59; US composer)

BABBITT, Milton (1916–2011; US composer)

BEECHAM, Thomas (1879– 1961; British conductor)

BELLINI, Vincenzo (1801–35; Italian opera composer)

BENNETT, Richard Rodney, Sir (1936–2012; British composer)

BENNETT, William Sterndale (1816–75; British pianist)

BERLIOZ, Hector (1803–69;

French composer and
conductor)

BORODIN, Aleksandr Porfirevich
(1833–87; Russian composer)

BRENDEL, Alfred (1931– ;
Austrian pianist)

BRAXTON, Anthony (1945– ; US
composer)

BRITTEN, Benjamin, Baron (1913–
76; British composer and
pianist)

BRUBECK, David Warren (1920–
2012; US pianist and composer)

CABALLÉ, Montserrat (1933–2018;
Spanish soprano)

CACCINI, Giulio (c. 1545–c. 1618;
Italian singer and composer)

CAMPION, Thomas (or Campian,
1567–1620; English composer)

CAVALLI, Francesco (1602–76;
Italian composer)

COPLAND, Aaron (1900–90; US
composer)

CORELLI, Arcangelo (1653–1713;
Italian violinist and composer)

DEBUSSY, Claude (1862– 1918;
French composer)

DELIBES, Leo (1836–91; French
composer)

DOMINGO, Placido (1941– ;
Spanish tenor)

DOWLAND, John (1563–1626;
English composer and lutenist)

FARNABY, Giles (c. 1565– 1640;
English composer)

FERRIER, Kathleen (1912–53;
British contralto)

GALUPPI, Baldassare (1706– 85;
Venetian composer)

GARRETT, Lesley (1955– ; British
soprano)

GIBBONS, Orlando (1583– 1625;
English composer, organist,
and virginalist)

GIULINI, Carlo Maria (1914–2005;
Italian conductor)

GORECKI, Henryk (1933–2010;
Polish composer)

HAMMOND, Joan (1912–96;
British soprano)

HOFMANN, Joseph Casimir
(1876–1957; Polish-born pianist)

IRELAND, John Nicholson (1879–
1962; British composer)

JANÁČEK, Leoš (1854–1928;
Czech composer)

JENKINS, Katherine (1980– ;
British mezzo-soprano)

JOACHIM, Joseph (1831–1907;
Hungarian violinist and
composer)

KARAJAN, Herbert von (1908–89;
Austrian conductor)

KUBELIK, Rafael (1914–96; Czech
conductor)

LAMBERT, Constant (1905–51;
British composer and
conductor)

LEHMANN, Lilli (1848–1929;
German soprano)

LEHMANN, Lotte (1885–1976;
German soprano)

MALCOLM, George John (1917–
97; British harpsichordist)

MARTINŮ , Bohuslav (1890–1959;
Czech composer)

MENOTTI, Gian Carlo (1911–2007;
Italian-born US composer)

MENUHIN, Yehudi (1916–99;
British violinist)

MILHAUD, Darius (1892–1974;
French composer)

MONTEUX, Pierre (1875–1964;
French conductor)

NICOLAI, Otto Ehrenfried (1810–
49; German conductor and
composer)

NIELSEN, Carl (1865–1931; Danish
composer and conductor)

NIKISCH, Arthur (1855–1922;
Hungarian conductor)

NILSSON, Birgit Marta (1918–
2005; Swedish soprano)

OKEGHEM, Jean d' (c. 1425–c.
1495; Flemish composer)

ORMANDY, Eugene (E Blau,
1899–1985; Hungarian-born US
conductor)

PÉROTIN (Latin name: Perotinus
Magnus, c. 1155–c. 1202; French
composer)

POULENC, Francis (1899– 1963;
French composer)

PUCCINI, Giacomo (1858– 1924;
Italian opera composer)

PURCELL, Henry (1659–95;
English composer and organist)

RICHTER, Hans (1843–1916;
Hungarian conductor)

RICHTER, Sviatoslav (1915–97;
Ukrainian pianist)

RODRIGO, Joaquín (1902–99;
Spanish composer)

ROSSINI, Gioacchino Antonio
(1792–1868; Italian composer)

ROUSSEL, Albert (1869–1937;
French composer)

RUGGLES, Carl (1876–1971; US
composer)

SALIERI, Antonio (1750–1825;
Italian composer and
conductor)

SARGENT, Malcolm (1895–1967;
British conductor)

SCHUMAN, William (1910–91; US
composer)

SLATKIN, Leonard (1944– ; US
conductor)

SMETANA, Bedřich (1824–84;
Bohemian composer)

SOLOMON (S Cutner, 1902–88;
British pianist)

STAINER, John (1840–1901; British
composer and organist)

STAMITZ, Johann (Jan Stamic,
1717–57; Bohemian composer)

STRAUSS, Richard (1864–1949;
German composer and
conductor)

TAVENER, John, Sir (1944–2013;
British composer)

THIBAUD, Jacques (1880–1953;
French violinist)

THOMSON, Virgil (1896–1989; US
composer and conductor)

TIPPETT, Michael (1905–98;
British composer)

VIVALDI, Antonio (1678–1741;
Italian composer and violinist)

WARLOCK, Peter (Philip
Heseltine, 1894–1930; British
composer and music scholar)

WEELKES, Thomas (c. 1575–1623;
English composer and organist)

WELLESZ, Egon (1885–1974;
Austrian composer)

XENAKIS, Yannis (1922–2001;
Greek composer)

8

ALBINONI, Tomaso (1671–1750;
Italian composer)

ANSERMET, Ernest (1883–1969;
Swiss conductor)

BERKELEY, Lennox Randal
Francis (1903–89; British
composer)

BRUCKNER, Anton (1824–96;
Austrian composer and
organist)

CARRERAS, José (1946– ;
Spanish tenor)

CHABRIER, Emmanuel (1841–94;
French composer)

CHAUSSON, Ernest (1855–99;
French composer)

CIMAROSA, Domenico (1749–
1801; Italian composer)

CLEMENTI, Muzio (1752–1832;
Italian pianist and composer)

COUPERIN, François (1668– 1733;
French composer)

DOHNÁNYI, Ernö (Ernst von D,
1877–1960; Hungarian
composer and pianist)

FLAGSTAD, Kirsten Malfrid (1895–
1962; Norwegian soprano)

GARDINER, John Eliot, Sir
(1943– ; British conductor)

GERSHWIN, George (Jacob

Gershvin, 1898– 1937; US composer)

GESUALDO, Carlo, Prince of Venosa (c. 1560–1631; Italian composer)

GLAZUNOV, Aleksandr Konstantinovich (1865–1936; Russian composer)

GOOSSENS, Eugene (1893–1962; British conductor and composer)

GRAINGER, Percy Aldridge (1882–1961; Australian composer and pianist)

GRANADOS, Enrique (1867–1916; Spanish composer and pianist)

HONEGGER, Arthur (1892–1955; French composer)

HOROWITZ, Vladimir (1904–89; Russian pianist)

KREISLER, Fritz (1875–1962; Austrian violinist)

MACONCHY, Elizabeth (1907–94; British composer)

MARENZIO, Luca (1553–99; Italian composer)

MASCAGNI, Pietro (1863–1945; Italian composer)

MASSENET, Jules (1842– 1912; French composer)

MELCHIOR, Lauritz (1890–1973; Danish tenor)

MESSAGER, André (1853–1929; French composer and conductor)

MESSIAEN, Olivier (1908–92; French composer, organist, and teacher)

MILSTEIN, Nathan (1904–92; US violinist)

MUSGRAVE, Thea (1928–   ; Scottish composer)

OISTRAKH, David (1908–75; Russian violinist)

PAGANINI, Niccolò (1782–1840; Italian violinist)

PHILIDOR, André Danican (d. 1730; French musician)

RESPIGHI, Ottorino (1879–1936; Italian composer)

SCHNABEL, Artur (1882–1951; Austrian pianist)

SCHUBERT, Franz (1797–1828; Austrian composer)

SCHULLER, Gunther (1925–2015; US composer)

SCHUMANN, Elisabeth (1885–1952; German-born soprano)

SCHUMANN, Robert (1810– 56; German composer)

SCRIABIN, Alexander (1872–1915; Russian composer and pianist)

SESSIONS, Roger (1896–1985; US composer)

SIBELIUS, Jean (Johan Julius Christian S, 1865–1957; Finnish composer)

STANFORD, Charles (1852–1924; Irish composer)

SULLIVAN, Arthur (1842– 1900; British composer)

TAVERNER, John (c. 1495– 1545; English composer)

TE KANAWA, Kiri, Dame (1944–   ; New Zealand soprano)

TELEMANN, Georg Philipp (1681–1767; German composer)

VICTORIA, Tomás Luis de (c. 1548–1611; Spanish composer)

WILLIAMS, John (1941–   ; Australian guitarist)

WILLIAMS, John Towner (1932–   ; US composer)

ZABALETA, Nicanor (1907–93; Spanish harpist)

9

ADDINSELL, Richard (1904–77; British composer)

ASHKENAZY, Vladimir (1937–   ; Russian pianist and conductor)

BALAKIREV, Mili Alekseevich (1837–1910; Russian composer)

BARENBOIM, Daniel (1942–   ; Israeli pianist and composer)

BEETHOVEN, Ludwig van (1770–1827; German composer)

BERNSTEIN, Leonard (1918–90; US conductor, composer, and pianist)

BOULANGER, Nadia (1887– 1979; French composer, teacher, and conductor)

BUXTEHUDE, Dietrich (1637–1707; Danish organist and composer)

CHALIAPIN, Feodor Ivanovich (1873–1938; Russian bass)

CHERUBINI, Maria Luigi (1760–1842; Italian composer)

CHRISTOFF, Boris (1919–93; Bulgarian singer)

DOLMETSCH, Arnold (1858–1940; British musician and instrument maker)

DONIZETTI, Gaetano (1797–1848; Italian composer)

DUNSTABLE, John (d. 1453; English composer)

HINDEMITH, Paul (1895–1963; German composer and viola player)

HODDINOTT, Alun (1929–2008; Welsh composer)

KLEMPERER, Otto (1885–1973; German conductor)

LANDOWSKA, Wanda (1877–

1959; Polish-born harpsichordist)

MACKERRAS, Charles (1925–2010; US-born Australian conductor)

MALIPIERO, Gian Francesco (1882–1973; Italian composer and teacher)

MCCARTNEY, Paul, Sir (1942–   ; British singer and composer)

MEYERBEER, Giacomo (Jacob Liebmann Beer, 1791–1864; German composer and pianist)

OFFENBACH, Jacques (J Eberst, 1819–80; French composer)

PAVAROTTI, Luciano (1935–2007; Italian tenor)

PERGOLESI, Giovanni (1710–36; Italian composer)

SCARLATTI, Domenico (1685–1757; Italian composer, harpsichordist, and organist)

STOKOWSKI, Leopold (1882–1977; British-born conductor)

TORTELIER, Paul (1914–90; French cellist)

TOSCANINI, Arturo (1867– 1957; Italian conductor)

10

BARBIROLLI, John (1899–1970; British conductor)

BIRTWISTLE, Harrison, Sir (1934–   ; British composer)

BOCCHERINI, Luigi (1743–1805; Italian violoncellist and composer)

GALLI-CURCI, Amelita (1882–1963; Italian soprano)

LOS ANGELES, Victoria de (1923–2005; Spanish soprano)

MENGELBERG, William (1871–1951; Dutch conductor)

MONTEVERDI, Claudio (1567–1643; Italian composer)

MUSSORGSKI, Modest Petrovich (1839–81; Russian composer)

PADEREWSKI, Ignacy (1860–1941; Polish pianist and composer)

PALESTRINA, Giovanni Pierluigi da (?1525–94; Italian composer)

PENDERECKI, Krzysztof (1933–   ; Polish composer)

PRAETORIUS, Michael (M Schultheiss, 1571–1621; German composer)

RAWSTHORNE, Alan (1905–71; British composer)

RUBINSTEIN, Anton (1829–94; Russian pianist and composer)

RUBINSTEIN, Artur (1888–1982; Polish-born pianist)

SAINT-SAËNS, Camille (1835–1921; French composer, conductor, pianist, and organist)

SCHOENBERG, Arnold (1874–1951; Austrian-born composer)

SKALKOTTAS, Nikos (1904–49; Greek composer)

STRADIVARI, Antonio (?1644–1737; Italian violin maker)

STRAVINSKY, Igor (1882–1971; Russian-born composer)

SUTHERLAND, Joan (1926–2010; Australian soprano)

TETRAZZINI, Luisa (1871–1940; Italian soprano)

VILLA-LOBOS, Heitor (1887–1959; Brazilian composer)

11

CHARPENTIER, Gustave (1860–1956; French composer)

FURTWÄNGLER, Wilhelm (1886–1954; German conductor)

HUMPERDINCK, Engelbert (1854–1921; German composer)

LEONCAVALLO, Ruggiero (1858–1919; Italian composer)

LESCHETIZKY, Theodor (1830–1915; Polish pianist and piano teacher)

LLOYD WEBBER, Andrew, Baron (1948– ; British composer)

LLOYD WEBBER, Julian (1951– ; British cellist)

LUTOSLAWSKI, Witold (1913–94; Polish composer)

MENDELSSOHN, Felix (Jacob Ludwig Felix Mendelssohn-Bartholdy, 1809–47; German composer)

RACHMANINOV, Sergei (1873–1943; Russian composer, pianist, and conductor)

SCHWARZKOPF, Elisabeth (1915–2006; German soprano)

STOCKHAUSEN, Karlheinz (1928–2007; German composer)

SZYMANOWSKI, Karol (1882–1937; Polish composer)

TCHAIKOVSKY, Peter Ilich (1840–93; Russian composer)

WOLF-FERRARI, Ermanno (1876–1948; Italian composer)

12

DALLAPICCOLA, Luigi (1904–1975; Italian composer and pianist)

GUIDO D'AREZZO (c. 990–c. 1050; Italian monk and musical theorist)

KHACHATURIAN, Aram Ilich (1903–78; Soviet composer, born in Armenia)

KOUSSEVITSKY, Sergei (1874–1951; Russian composer)

13

ROUGET DE L'ISLE, Claude Joseph (1760–1836; French composer)

14

FISCHER-DIESKAU, Dietrich (1925–2012; German baritone)

JAQUES-DALCROZE, Émile (1865–1950; Swiss composer)

JOSQUIN DES PREZ (c. 1450–1521; Flemish composer)

RIMSKY-KORSAKOV, Nikolai (1844–1908; Russian composer)

15

COLERIDGE-TAYLOR, Samuel (1875–1912; British composer)

VAUGHAN WILLIAMS, Ralph (1872–1958; British composer)

17

STRAUSS THE YOUNGER, Johann (1825–99; Austrian violinist, conductor, and composer)

STAGE AND SCREEN PERSONALITIES

3

BOW, Clara (US film actress)

COX, Robert (English comic actor)

FOY, Eddie (US actor)

HAY, Will (British comedian)

LAW, Jude (British actor)

LEE, Gypsy Rose (US entertainer)

RAY, Satyajit (Indian film director)

RIX, Brian (British actor)

SIM, Alastair (Scottish actor)

4

ARNE, Susanna Maria (British actress)

BALE, Christian (British-US actor)

BIRD, Theophilus (English actor)

BOND, Edward (British dramatist)

CANE, Andrew (English actor)

CHAN, Jackie (Hong Kong actor-director)

COBB, Lee J (US actor)

COOK, Peter (British comedy actor)

DALY, Augustin (US theatre manager)

DEAN, James (US film actor)

DEPP, Johnny (US actor)

DIAZ, Cameron (US film actress)

DUFF, Mrs (US actress)

DUSE, Eleonora (Italian actress)

FORD, John (US film director)

FORD, Harrison (US film actor)

GISH, Lillian (US actress)

GOLD, Jimmy (British comedian)

GRAY, Dulcie (British actress)

GRAY, 'Monsewer' Eddie (British comedian)

HALL, Peter (British theatre director)

HOPE, Bob (US comedian, born in Britain)

KEAN, Edmund (British actor)

KNOX, Teddy (British comedian)

LAHR, Bert (US actor)

LANG, Fritz (German film director)

LEAN, David (British film director)

LUNT, Alfred (US actor)

NUNN, Trevor (British theatre director)

OWEN, Alun Davies (British dramatist)

PAGE, Geraldine (US actress)

PIAF, Edith (French cabaret and music-hall performer)

PITT, Brad (US actor)

RANK, J Arthur (British industrialist and film executive)

REED, Carol (British film director)

REID, Beryl (British actress)

RIGG, Diana (British actress)

SHER, Anthony (British actor)

TATE, Harry (British music-hall comedian)

TREE, Herbert Beerbohm (British actor and theatre manager)

WEST, Mae (US actress)

5

ALLEN, Chesney (British comedian)

ALLEN, Woody (US film actor and director)

ARMIN, Robert (British actor)

ASTON, Anthony (Irish actor)

BADEL, Alan (British actor)

BARON, André (French actor)

BARON, Michel (French actor)

BARRY, Elizabeth (English actress)

BARRY, Spranger (Irish actor)

BATES, Alan (British actor)

BETTY, William Henry West (British boy actor)
BLOOM, Claire (British actress)
BOOTH, Barton (British actor)
BOOTH, Edwin Thomas (US actor)
BOOTH, Junius Brutus (US actor)
BOYER, Charles (French film actor)
BRICE, Fanny (US actress)
BROOK, Peter (British theatre director)
BROWN, Pamela (British actor)
BRYAN, Dora (British actress)
CAINE, Michael (British film actor)
CAPRA, Frank (US film director, born in Italy)
CAREY, Joyce (British actress)
CARNÉ, Marcel (French film director)
CLAIR, René (French film director)
CLIVE, Kitty (British actress)
CLOSE, Glenn (US actress)
CONTI, Italia (British actress)
CROWE, Russell (Australian actor)
DAMON, Matt (US actor)
DAVIS, Bette (US film actress)
DENCH, Judi (British actress)
EDWIN, John (British actor)
EKHOF, Konrad (German actor and director)
EVANS, Edith (British actress)
FIRTH, Colin (British actor)
FLYNN, Errol (Australian actor, born in Tasmania)
FONDA, Henry (US film actor and director)
GABIN, Jean (French film actor)
GABLE, Clark (US film actor)
GARBO, Greta (Swedish actress)
GOZZI, Carlo (Italian dramatist)
GRANT, Cary (US film actor, born in England)
GRANT, Hugh (British actor)
GWYNN, Nell (English actress)
HAIGH, Kenneth (British actor)
HANDL, Irene (British actress)
HANKS, Tom (US actor)
HAWKS, Howard (US film director)
HICKS, Seymour (British actor-manager)
IRONS, Jeremy (British actor)
KAZAN, Elia (US stage and film director and novelist)
KELLY, Grace (US film actress)
KORDA, Alexander (British film producer and director)
LA RUE, Danny (British female impersonator)
LEIGH, Vivien (British actress)

LENYA, Lotte (German actress and singer)
LIFAR, Serge (Russian ballet dancer and choreographer)
LLOYD, Harold (US film comedian)
LLOYD, Marie (British music-hall entertainer)
LOPEZ, Jennifer (J-Lo; Puerto Rican film actress and singer)
LOREN, Sophia (Italian film actress)
LOSEY, Joseph (US film director)
LUCAS, George (US film director)
MALEK, Rami (US actor)
MAYER, Louis B (US film producer, born in Russia)
MILES, Bernard (British theatre director and actor)
MILLS, John (British actor)
MOORE, Dudley (British actor and songwriter)
MOORE, Julianne (US actress)
NERVO, Jimmy (British comedian)
NIVEN, David (British film actor)
PAIGE, Elaine (British actress and singer)
PASCO, Richard (British actor)
PETIT, Roland (French ballet dancer and choreographer)
POLUS (Greek tragic actor)
POPOV, Oleg Konstantinovich (Russian clown)
POWER, Tyrone (US actor)
PRYCE, Jonathan (British actor)
ROBEY, George Edward (British music-hall comedian)
RONAN, Saoirse (Irish actress)
SMITH, Maggie Natalie (British actress)
SMITH, Will (US actor)
TERRY, Ellen Alice (British actress)
TOPOL, Chaim (Israeli actor)
TRACY, Spencer (US film actor)
TUTIN, Dorothy (British actress)
WAJDA, Andrzej (Polish film director)
WAYNE, John (US film actor)

6

ADRIAN, Max (British actor)
AINLEY, Henry (British actor)
AITKEN, Maria (British actress)
ALIZON (French actor)
ALLEYN, Edward (English actor)
ALTMAN, Robert (US film director)
ARNAUD, Yvonne Germaine (French actress)
ARTAUD, Antonin (French actor, poet, producer, and theoretician of the theatre)
ASHTON, Frederick (British ballet dancer and choreographer, born in Ecuador)
ATKINS, Eileen (British actress)
BACALL, Lauren (US film actress)
BALCON, Michael (British film producer)
BARDOT, Brigitte (French film actress)
BARNUM, Phineas Taylor (US showman)
BAYLIS, Lilian (British theatre manager)
BEATTY, Warren (US film actor)
BÉJART, Joseph (French actor)
BÉJART, Maurice (French ballet dancer and choreographer)
BENSON, Frank (British actor-manager)
BLASIS, Carlo (Italian dance teacher)
BOCAGE (French actor)
BOGART, Humphrey (US film actor)
BRANDO, Marlon (US actor)
BRIERS, Richard (British actor)
BROOKE, Gustavus Vaughan (British actor)
BROUGH, Lionel (British actor)
BROWNE, Robert (English actor)
BRYANT, Michael (British actor)
BUÑUEL, Luis (Spanish film director)
BURTON, Richard Walter (British actor, born in Wales)
CAGNEY, James (US actor)
CALLOW, Simon (British actor)
CANTOR, Eddie (US singer and actor)
CASSON, Lewis (British actor and director)
CIBBER, Colley (British actor-manager)
COLMAN, Ronald (British actor)
CONWAY, William Augustus (British actor)
COOGAN, Steve (British actor and producer)
COOPER, Bradley (US actor)
COOPER, Gladys (British actress)
COOPER, Gary (US film actor)
COWARD, Noël (British dramatist, composer, and actor)
COWELL, Joe Leathley (British actor)
CRANKO, John (British choreographer, born in South Africa)
CROSBY, Bing (US popular singer and film actor)
CRUISE, Tom (US actor)
CURTIS, Tony (US film actor)
DE NIRO, Robert (US film actor)

DE SICA, Vittorio (Italian film director)

DEVINE, George Alexander Cassady (British theatre manager, director, and actor)

DIGGES, Dudley (British actor)

DISNEY, Walt (US film producer and animator)

DRAPER, Ruth (US actress)

DREYER, Carl Theodor (Danish film director)

DUNCAN, Isadora (US dancer)

FIELDS, Gracie (British popular entertainer)

FIELDS, W C (US actor)

FINLAY, Frank (British actor)

FINNEY, Albert (British actor)

FLEURY (French actor)

FOKINE, Michel (Russian ballet dancer and choreographer)

FORMAN, Miloš (Czech film director)

FORMBY, George (British music hall singer)

FOSTER, Jodie (US actress)

GIBSON, Mel (Australian film actor and director)

GODARD, Jean-Luc (French film director)

GONG LI (Chinese actress)

GORING, Marius (British actor)

GRAHAM, Martha (US ballet dancer and choreographer)

GUITRY, Sacha (French actor and dramatist)

HARLOW, Jean (US film actress)

HERZOG, Werner (German film director)

HILLER, Wendy (British actress)

HOWARD, Leslie (British actor of Hungarian descent)

HUSTON, John (US film director)

IRVING, Henry (British actor and manager)

JACOBI, Derek (British actor)

JOLSON, Al (US actor and singer)

JORDAN, Dorothy (British actress)

JOUVET, Louis (French actor and theatre director)

KEATON, Buster (US comedian of silent films)

KEATON, Michael (US actor)

KEMBLE, John Philip (British actor and manager)

KENDAL, Felicity (British actress)

KIDMAN, Nicole (Australian film actress)

LANDEN, Dinsdale (British actor)

LAUDER, Harry (Scottish singer and music-hall comedian)

LAURIE, Hugh (British actor)

LEMMON, Jack (US actor)

LESSER, Anton (British actor)

LILLIE, Beatrice Gladys (British actress, born in Canada)

LIPMAN, Maureen (British actress)

MARTIN, Mary (US actress)

MARTIN, Steve (US actor)

MASSEY, Daniel (British actor)

MASSEY, Raymond Hart (Canadian actor)

MCEWAN, Geraldine (British actress)

MCKERN, Leo (Australian actor)

MERMAN, Ethel (US actress)

MIRREN, Helen (British actress)

MONROE, Marilyn (US film actress)

MORLEY, Robert (British actor)

MURPHY, Eddie (US film actor)

NEWMAN, Paul (US film actor)

O'TOOLE, Peter (British actor)

PACINO, Al (US actor)

PETIPA, Marius (French dancer and choreographer)

PORTER, Eric (British actor)

QUAYLE, Anthony (British actor)

RACHEL (French actress)

RÉJANE (French actress)

ROBSON, Flora (British actress)

ROGERS, Ginger (US actress and singer)

ROWLEY, Thomas (English dramatist and actor)

SHUTER, Ned (British actor)

SINDEN, Donald (British actor)

SNIPES, Wesley (US actor)

SPACEY, Kevin (US actor)

STEELE, Tommy (British singer and actor)

STREEP, Meryl (US actress)

SUZMAN, Janet (British actress)

TAYLOR, Elizabeth (US film actress, born in England)

TEARLE, Godfrey Seymour (British actor)

TEMPLE, Shirley (US film actress)

TILLEY, Vesta (British music-hall entertainer)

WARREN, William (US actor, born in Britain)

WELLES, Orson (US film actor and director)

WILDER, Billy (US film director, born in Austria)

WILLIS, Bruce (US actor)

WOLFIT, Donald (British actor and manager)

7

ACHURCH, Janet (British actress)

ACKLAND, Joss (British actor)

AESOPUS, Claudius (Roman tragic actor)

AFFLECK, Ben (US actor)

ALLGOOD, Sara (Irish actress)

ANTOINE, André (French actor, director, and theatre manager)

BEAUVAL (French actor)

BELLAMY, George Anne (British actress)

BENNETT, Hywel (British actor, born in Wales)

BENNETT, Jill (British actress)

BERGMAN, Ingmar (Swedish film and stage director)

BERGMAN, Ingrid (Swedish actress)

BERGNER, Elisabeth (Austrian actress)

BLAKELY, Colin (British actor)

BOGARDE, Dirk (British film actor of Dutch descent)

BRANAGH, Kenneth (British actor)

BRESSON, Robert (French film director)

BROSNAN, Pierce (Irish actor)

BURBAGE, Richard (English actor)

BULLOCK, Sandra (US actress)

BUSSELL, Darcey (British ballet dancer)

CALVERT, Louis (British actor)

CAMERON, James (Canadian film director)

CAMPION, Jane (New Zealand film director)

CASARÉS, Maria (French actress)

CELESTE, Céline (French actress)

CHABROL, Claude (French film director)

CHAPLIN, Charlie (US film actor, born in Britain)

CLOONEY, George (US film actor)

COLBERT, Claudette (US film actress, born in France)

COLEMAN, Olivia (British actress)

COLLIER, Constance (British actress)

COMPTON, Fay (British actress)

CONDELL, Henry (English actor)

CONNERY, Sean (Scottish film actor)

COPPOLA, Francis Ford (US film director)

CORALLI, Jean (Italian ballet dancer and choreographer)

CORNELL, Katharine (US actress)

COSTNER, Kevin (US film actor and director)

DEBURAU, Jean-Gaspard (French pantomimist, born in Bohemia)

DÉJAZET, Pauline-Virginie (French actress)

DELYSIA, Alice (French actress and singer)

DE MILLE, Cecil B (US film producer and director)

DENEUVE, Catherine (French film actress)
DENISON, Michael (British actor)
DOGGETT, Thomas (British actor)
DOTRICE, Roy (British actor)
DOUGLAS, Kirk (US film actor)
DOUGLAS, Michael (US film actor)
DURANTE, Jimmy (US actor and singer, known as 'Schnozzle')
ELLIOTT, Denholm (British actor)
EJIOFOR, Chiwetel (British actor)
FELLINI, Federico (Italian film director)
FIENNES, Ralph (British actor)
FONTEYN, Margot (British ballet dancer)
FREEMAN, Morgan (US actor)
GARLAND, Judy (US singer and film actress)
GARRICK, David (English actor)
GIELGUD, John (British actor)
GINGOLD, Hermione (British actress)
GOLDWYN, Samuel (US film producer)
GOSLING, Ryan (Canadian actor and musician)
GREGORY, Lady Augusta (Irish theatre patron and dramatist)
GUTHRIE, Tyrone (British theatre director)
HANCOCK, Sheila (British actress)
HANCOCK, Tony (British comedian)
HAWTREY, Charles (British actor-manager)
HEPBURN, Audrey (British actress)
HEPBURN, Katharine (US actress)
HOFFMAN, Dustin (US film actor)
HOPKINS, Anthony (British actor)
HORDERN, Michael (British actor)
HOUDINI, Harry (US magician)
IFFLAND, August Wilhelm (German actor)
JACKMAN, Hugh (Australian actor, singer, and producer)
JACKSON, Glenda (British actress)
JACKSON, Peter (New Zealand film producer)
JOHNSON, Celia (British actress)
KARLOFF, Boris (British character actor)
KUBRICK, Stanley (US film writer, director, and producer)
LACKAYE, Wilton (US actor)
LANGTRY, Lillie (British actress, known as the 'Jersey Lily')
LAROQUE (French actor)
LÉOTARD, Jules (French acrobat and music-hall performer)

MADONNA (US pop singer and film actress)
MARCEAU, Marcel (French mime)
MARKOVA, Alicia (British ballet dancer)
MASSINE, Léonide (Russian ballet dancer and choreographer)
MCKENNA, Siobhán (Irish actress)
MCQUEEN, Steve (US film actor)
MICHELL, Keith (Australian actor)
NUREYEV, Rudolf (Russian ballet dancer)
OLIVIER, Laurence Kerr, Lord (British actor)
OXBERRY, William (British actor)
PAVLOVA, Anna (Russian ballet dancer)
PAXINOU, Katina (Greek actress)
PLUMMER, Christopher (Canadian actor)
PORTMAN, Eric (British actor)
PORTMAN, Natalie (Israeli-US actress, producer, and director)
QUILLEY, Denis (British actor)
RAMBERT, Marie (British ballet dancer and choreographer)
REDFORD, Robert (US film actor)
RISTORI, Adelaide (Italian actress)
ROBARDS, Jason (US actor)
ROBBINS, Jerome (US ballet dancer and choreographer)
ROBERTS, Julia (US film actress)
ROBESON, Paul Bustil (US Black actor)
RUSSELL, Ken (British film director)
SALVINI, Tommaso (Italian actor)
SELLERS, Peter (British comic actor)
SIDDONS, Sarah (English actress)
STEWART, James (US film actor)
STRITCH, Elaine (US actress)
TEMPEST, Marie (British actress)
ULANOVA, Galina (Russian ballet dancer)
USTINOV, Peter Alexander (British actor, director, and dramatist)
VESTRIS, Madame (British actress)
WALTERS, Julie (British actress)
WINSLET, Kate (British film actress)
WITHERS, Googie (British actress)

8

ABINGTON, Frances (British actress)
ALDRIDGE, Ira Frederick (US actor)
ANDERSON, Judith (Australian actress)

ANDREINI, Francesco (Italian actor-manager and playwright)
ANDREINI, Giovann Battista (Italian actor)
ANDREINI, Isabella (Italian actress)
ASHCROFT, Peggy (British actress)
BADDELEY, Hermione (British actress)
BANCROFT, Anne (US actress)
BANKHEAD, Tallulah (US actress)
BARRAULT, Jean-Louis (French actor and director)
BERKELEY, Busby (US dance director)
BRASSEUR, Pierre (French actor)
BUCHANAN, Jack (Scottish actor-manager)
CALDWELL, Zoë (Australian actress)
CAMPBELL, Mrs Patrick (British actress)
CHANNING, Carol (US actress and singer)
CLEMENTS, John (British actor-manager)
CRAWFORD, Joan (US film actress)
CRAWFORD, Michael (British actor)
DANCOURT, Florent (French actor and playwright)
DAY-LEWIS, Daniel (British actor)
DE LA TOUR, Frances (British actress)
DE VALOIS, Ninette (British ballet dancer and choreographer, born in Ireland)
DEVRIENT, Ludwig (German actor)
DICAPRIO, Leonardo (US film actor)
DIETRICH, Marlene (German film actress and singer)
DUFRESNE (French actor)
EASTWOOD, Clint (US film actor and director)
ESTCOURT, Richard (English actor)
FLAHERTY, Robert (US film director)
FLANAGAN, Bud (British comedian)
FLORENCE, William Jermyn (US actor)
FLORIDOR (French actor)
GRENFELL, Joyce (British actress)
GRIERSON, John (British film director)
GRIMALDI, Joseph (British clown)
GUINNESS, Alec (British actor)
HARRISON, Rex (British actor)

HELPMANN, Robert Murray (Australian ballet dancer, choreographer, and actor)
KUROSAWA, Akira (Japanese film director)
KYNASTON, Ned (English actor)
LANSBURY, Angela (US actress)
LAUGHTON, Charles (British actor)
LAWRENCE, Gertrude (British actress)
LAWRENCE, Jennifer (US actress)
LEIGHTON, Margaret (British actress)
MACLAINE, Shirley (US actress)
MACREADY, William Charles (British actor and theatre manager)
MATTHEWS, Jessie (British actress)
MCKELLEN, Ian (British actor)
MERCOURI, Melina (Greek actress and politician)
NAUGHTON, Charlie (British comedian)
NAZIMOVA, Alla (Russian actress)
NIJINSKY, Vaslav (Russian ballet dancer)
PALTROW, Gwyneth (US film actress)
PFEIFFER, Michelle (US actress)
PICKFORD, Mary (Canadian-born US film actress)
POLANSKI, Roman (Polish film director, born in Paris)
REDGRAVE, Corin (British actor)
REDGRAVE, Lynn (British actress)
REDGRAVE, Michael (British actor)
REDGRAVE, Vanessa (British actress)
REDMAYNE, Eddie (British actor)
ROBINSON, Edward G (US film actor, born in Romania)
SCOFIELD, Paul (British actor)
SCORSESE, Martin (US film director)
SELZNICK, David O (US film producer)
STROHEIM, Erich von (US film director and actor)
THOMPSON, Emma (British actress)
VISCONTI, Luchino (Italian film director)
WHITELAW, Billie (British actress)
WILLIAMS, Kenneth (British comic actor)
WILLIAMS, Michael (British actor)
WILLIAMS, Robin (US film actor)
ZIEGFELD, Florenz (US theatrical producer)

9

ALMODÓVAR, Pedro (Spanish film director)
ANTONIONI, Michelangelo (Italian film maker)
BARKWORTH, Peter (British actor)
BARRYMORE, Ethel (US actress)
BARRYMORE, John (US actor)
BARRYMORE, Lionel (US actor)
BARRYMORE, Maurice (British actor)
BELLECOUR (French actor)
BELLEROSE (French actor-manager)
BERIOSOVA, Svetlana (Russian ballet dancer)
BERNHARDT, Sarah (French actress)
BETTERTON, Thomas (English actor)
BLANCHETT, Cate (Australian actress)
CHEN KAIGE (Chinese film director)
CHEVALIER, Maurice (French singer and actor)
COURTENAY, Tom (British actor)
DEPARDIEU, Gérard (French film actor)
DIAGHILEV, Sergei (Russian ballet impresario)
DU MAURIER, Gerald (British actor-manager)
FAIRBANKS, Douglas (US film actor)
FAVERSHAM, William (US actor)
FERNANDEL (French comedian)
FEUILLÈRE, Edwige (French actress)
FISHBURNE, Larry (US actor)
GRAMATICA, Irma (Italian actress)
GROSSMITH, George (British actor)
GRÜNDGENS, Gustav (German actor)
KNIGHTLEY, Keira (British actress)
LAPOTAIRE, Jane (British actress)
MACMILLAN, Kenneth (British ballet dancer and choreographer)
MONCRIEFF, Gladys (Australian actress)
NICHOLSON, Jack (US film actor)
PECKINPAH, Sam (US film director)
PLEASENCE, Donald (British actor)
PLOWRIGHT, Joan Anne (British actress)

PREMINGER, Otto (US film director, born in Austria)
REINHARDT, Max (Austrian theatre director)
RADCLIFFE, Daniel (British actor)
SPIELBERG, Steven (US film director)
STERNBERG, Josef von (US film director, born in Austria)
STREISAND, Barbra (US singer and actress)
THORNDIKE, Sybil (British actress)
VALENTINO, Rudolf (US film actor, born in Italy)

10

BALANCHINE, George (US ballet dancer and choreographer, born in Russia)
BASSERMANN, Albert (German actor)
BELLEROCHE (French actor)
BERTOLUCCI, Bernardo (Italian film director)
BOUCICAULT, 'Dot' (British actor-manager)
BOUCICAULT, Nina (British actress)
CARTWRIGHT, William (English actor)
CUNNINGHAM, Merce (US dancer and choreographer)
D'OYLY CARTE, Richard (British theatre impresario and manager)
EISENSTEIN, Sergei (Russian film director)
FASSBINDER, Rainer Werner (German film director)
LITTLE TICH (British music-hall comedian)
LITTLEWOOD, Joan (British theatre director)
MONTFLEURY (French actor)
RICHARDSON, Ian (British actor)
RICHARDSON, Ralph (British actor)
ROSSELLINI, Roberto (Italian film director)
RUTHERFORD, Margaret (British actress)
WASHINGTON, Denzil (US film actor)
WOFFINGTON, Peg (Irish actress)
ZEFFIRELLI, G Franco (Italian director and stage designer)

11

BEAUCHÂTEAU (French actor)
BIANCOLELLI, Giuseppe Domenico (French actor)
BRACEGIRDLE, Anne (English actress)

BRAITHWAITE, Lilian (British actress)

COURTNEIDGE, Cicely (British actress)

CUMBERBATCH, Benedict (British actor)

DAUVILLIERS (French actor)

MACLIAMMÓIR, Micheál (Irish actor and dramatist)

MASTROIANNI, Marcello (Italian actor)

MISTINGUETT (French singer and comedienne)

SCHLESINGER, John (British film and theatre director)

WITHERSPOON, Reese (US actress)

12

BONHAM CARTER, Helena (British actress)

BRUSCAMBILLE (French actor)

MARX BROTHERS (US family of comic film actors)

STANISLAVSKY, Konstantin (Russian actor and theatre director)

13

ROSCIUS GALLUS, Quintus (Roman comic actor)

14

MIZOGUCHI KENJI (Japanese film director)

15

FFRANGCON-DAVIES, Gwen (British actress)

FORBES-ROBERTSON, Johnston (British actor-manager)

GRANVILLE-BARKER, Harley (British theatre director)

KOBAYASHI MASAKI (Japanese film director)

SCIENTISTS

3

CHU, Steven (1948– ; American physicist)

DAM, Carl Peter Henrik (1895–1976; Danish biochemist)

IVE, Sir Jonathan (Jony) Paul (1967– ; British computer designer)

KAY, John (1704–c. 1764; British inventor)

LEE, Tsung-Dao (1926– ; US physicist)

OHM, Georg Simon (1787–1854; German physicist)

RAY, John (1627–1705; English naturalist)

4

ABEL, Niels Henrik (1802–29; Norwegian mathematician)

ABEL, Frederick Augustus (1827–1902; British chemist)

ADER, Clément (1841–1926; French engineer and inventor)

AIRY, George Biddell (1801–92; British astronomer)

BAER, Karl Ernest von (1792–1876; Russian embryologist)

BENZ, Karl (1844–1929; German engineer)

BIRÓ, Laszlo (1900–85; Hungarian inventor)

BOHR, Niels Henrik David (1885–1962; Danish physicist)

BORN, Max (1882–1970; British physicist)

BOSE, Jagadis Chandra (1858–1937; Indian plant physiologist and physicist)

COHN, Ferdinand Julius (1839–1884; German botanist)

COKE, Thomas William, of Holkham, Earl of Leicester (1752–1842; British agriculturalist)

EADS, John Buchanan (1820–87; US civil engineer)

FUST, Johann (1400–66; German printer)

GEIM, Andre Konstantinovich (1958– ; Russian-born physicist)

GOLD, Thomas (1920–2004; Austrian-born astronomer)

GRAY, Asa (1810–88; US botanist)

HAHN, Otto (1879–1968; German chemist and physicist)

HALL, Jeffrey Connor (1945– ; US geneticist)

HECK, Richard Fred (1931–2015; American organic chemist)

HELL, Stefan (1962– ; Romanian-born German physicist)

HESS, Victor Francis (1883–1964; US physicist)

KOCH, Robert (1843–1910; German bacteriologist)

LAUE, Max Theodor Felix Von (1879–1960; German physicist)

LOEB, Jacques (1859–1924; US zoologist)

MACH, Ernst (1838–1916; Austrian physicist)

MAYO (family of US medical researchers)

OTIS, Elisha Graves (1811–61; US inventor)

OTTO, Nikolaus August (1832–91; German engineer)

RABI, Isidor Isaac (1898–88; US physicist)

RYLE, Martin (1918–84; British astronomer)

SWAN, Joseph Wilson (1828–1914; British physicist)

TODD, Alexander Robertus, Baron (1907–97; British biochemist)

UREY, Harold Clayton (1893–1981; US physicist)

YANG, Chen Ning (1922– ; US physicist)

5

ADAMS, John Couch (1819–92; English astronomer)

AIKEN, Howard Hathaway (1900–73; US mathematician)

AMANO, Hiroshi (1960– ; Japanese physicist)

AMICI, Giovanni Battista (1786–1863; Italian astronomer, microscopist, and optical instrument maker)

ASTON, Francis William (1877–1945; British chemist)

AVERY, Oswald Theodore (1877–1955; Canadian bacteriologist)

BACON, Roger (c. 1214–c. 1292; English scientist)

BAILY, Francis (1774–1844; British amateur astronomer)

BAKER, Benjamin (1840–1907; British civil engineer)

BANKS, Joseph (1743–1820; British botanist and explorer)

BATES, Henry Walter (1825–92; British naturalist and explorer)

BEEBE, Charles William (1877–1962; US explorer and naturalist)

BETHE, Hans Albrecht (1906–2005; US physicist)

BLACK, Joseph (1728–99; Scottish physician and chemist)

BLOCH, Felix (1905–83; US physicist)

BONDI, Hermann (1919–2005; British cosmologist and mathematician)

BOOLE, George (1815–64; British mathematician)

BOSCH, Carl (1874–1940; German chemist)

BOTHE, Walther Wilhelm Georg Franz (1891–1957; German experimental physicist)

BOVET, Daniel (1907–92; Swiss pharmacologist)

BOWEN, Norman Levi (1887–1956; Canadian experimental petrologist)

BOWER, Frederick Orpen (1855–1948; British botanist)

BOYLE, Robert (1627–91; British physicist and chemist)

BRAGG, William Henry (1862–1942; British physicist)

BRAHE, Tycho (1546–1601; Danish astronomer)

BROUT, Robert (1928–2011; US-Belgian theoretical physicist)

BROWN, Robert (1773–1858; Scottish botanist)

BÜRGE, Joost (1552–1632; Swiss mathematician)

CHAIN, Ernst Boris (1906–79; British biochemist)

CRICK, Francis Harry Compton (1916–2004; British biophysicist)

CURIE, Marie (1867–1934; Polish chemist)

CURIE, Pierre (1859–1906; French physicist)

DEBYE, Peter Joseph Wilhelm (1884–1966; Dutch physicist and chemist)

DIELS, Otto Paul Hermann (1876–1954; German chemist)

DIRAC, Paul Adrien Maurice (1902–84; British physicist)

ELTON, Charles (1900–91; British zoologist)

EULER, Leonhard (1707–83; Swiss mathematician)

EVANS, Oliver (1755–1819; American engineer)

FABRE, Jean Henri (1823– 1915; French entomologist)

FABRY, Charles (1867–1945; French physicist)

FERMI, Enrico (1901–54; US physicist)

FRANK, Joachim (1940– ; German-born US biophysicist)

FREGE, Gottlob (1848–1925; German mathematician and logician)

GABOR, Dennis (1900–79; British electrical engineer)

GALLE, Johann Gottfried (1812–1910; German astronomer)

GAUSS, Karl Friedrich (1777–1855; German mathematician)

GEBER (14th century; Spanish alchemist)

GIBBS, Josiah Willard (1839–1903; US physicist)

GÖDEL, Kurt (1906–78; US mathematician)

HABER, Fritz (1868–1934; German chemist and inventor)

HALES, Thomas (1958– ; US mathematician)

HARDY, Godfrey Harold (1877–1947; British mathematician)

HENRY, Joseph (1797–1878; US physicist)

HERTZ, Heinrich Rudolf (1857–94; German physicist)

HONJO, Tasuko (1942– ; Japanese immunologist)

HOOKE, Robert (1635–1703; British physicist)

HOYLE, Fred (1915–2001; British astronomer)

JEANS, James Hopwood (1877–1946; British mathematician and astronomer)

JOULE, James Prescott (1818–89; British physicist)

KOLBE, Hermann (1818–84; German chemist)

KREBS, Hans Adolf (1900–81; British biochemist)

KROTO, Harold, Sir (1939–2016; British chemist)

LAWES, John Bennet (1814–1900; British agriculturalist)

LIBBY, Willard Frank (1908–80; US chemist)

LODGE, Oliver Joseph (1851–1940; British physicist)

LYELL, Charles (1797–1875; British geologist)

MARCY, Geoffrey William (1954– ; US astronomer)

MAYER, Julius Robert Von (1814–78; German physicist)

MONGE, Gaspard (1746–1818; French mathematician)

MONOD, Jacques-Lucien (1910–76; French biochemist)

MOORE, Patrick Alfred Caldwell, Sir (1923–2012; British astronomer and broadcaster)

MOSER, Edvard (1962– ; Norwegian neuroscientist and psychologist)

MOSER, May-Britt (1963– ; Norwegian neuroscientist and psychologist)

NOBEL, Alfred Bernhard (1833–96; Swedish chemist)

NOBLE, Andrew (1831–1915; British physicist)

OMURA, Satoshi (1935– ; Japanese biologist)

PÄÄBO, Svante (1955– ; Swedish biologist)

PAULI, Wolfgang (1900–58; US physicist)

POPOV, Aleksandr Stepanovich (1859–1905; Russian physicist)

PROUT, William (1785–1850; British chemist and physiologist)

RAMAN, Chandrasekhara Venkata (1888–1970; Indian physicist)

REBER, Grote (1911–2002; US astronomer)

RHINE, Joseph Banks (1895–1980; US psychologist)

RIESS, Adam Guy (1969– ; American astrophysicist)

ROSSE, William Parsons, 3rd Earl Of (1800–67; Irish astronomer)

SEGRÈ, Emilio (1905–89; US physicist)

SINAI, Yakov Grigorevich (1935– ; Russian mathematician theoretical physicist)

SMITH, George Pearson (1941– ; US biochemist/molecular biologist)

SMITH, Keith Macpherson (1890–1955; Australian aviator)

SODDY, Frederick (1877–1956; British chemist)

STAHL, Georg Ernst (1660–1734; German physician and chemist)

TATUM, Edward Lawrie (1909–75; US geneticist)

VOLTA, Alessandro Giuseppe Antonio Anastasio, Count (1745–1827; Italian physicist)

WEBER, Ernst Heinrich (1795–1878; German physiologist)

WEISS, Rainer (1932– ; German-born US physicist)

WHITE, Gilbert (1720–93; English naturalist)

YOUNG, Michael Warren (1949– ; US geneticist)

YOUNG, Thomas (1773–1829; British physician and physicist)

ZADEH, Lotfi Aliasker (1921–2017; Azerbaijan-born US

mathematician and computer scientist)

ZHANG, Feng (1981– ; Chinese-born US neuroscientist and bioengineer)

6

ACHARD, Franz Karl (1753–1821; German chemist)

ADRIAN, Edgar Douglas, 1st Baron (1889–1977; British physiologist)

AGNESI, Maria Gaetana (1718–99; Italian mathematician)

ALFVÉN, Hannes Olof Gösta (1908–95; Swedish astrophysicist)

AMPÈRE, André Marie (1775–1836; French physicist)

APPERT, Nicolas (1750–1841; French inventor)

ARCHER, Frederick Scott (1813–57; British inventor and sculptor)

ARNOLD, Frances Hamilton (1956– ; US chemical engineer)

ARNOLD, Vladimir Igorevich (1937–2010; Russian mathematician)

ASHKIN, Arthur (1922– ; US physicist)

BAEYER, Adolf Von (1835–1917; German chemist)

BARISH, Barry Clark (1936– ; US physicist)

BEADLE, George Wells (1903–89; US geneticist)

BETZIG, Eric (1960– ; US physicist)

BODONI, Giambattista (1740–1813; Italian printer)

BOLYAI, János (1802–60; Hungarian mathematician)

BONNET, Charles (1720–93; Swiss naturalist)

BORDET, Jules Jean Baptiste Vincent (1870–1961; Belgian bacteriologist)

BOVERI, Theodor Heinrich (1862–1915; German cell biologist)

BRAMAH, Joseph (1748–1814; British engineer and inventor)

BRIGGS, Henry (1561–1630; English mathematician)

BRUNEL, Isambard Kingdom (1806–59; British engineer)

BUFFON, Georges Louis Leclerc, Comte de (1707–88; French naturalist)

BUNSEN, Robert Wilhelm (1811–99; German chemist)

CALVIN, Melvin (1911–97; US biochemist)

CANTOR, Georg (1845–1918; Russian mathematician)

CARNOT, Sadi (1796–1832; French scientist and soldier)

CARREL, Alexis (1873–1944; French surgeon)

CARVER, George Washington (1864–1943; US agriculturalist)

CAUCHY, Augustin Louis, Baron (1789–1857; French mathematician)

CAXTON, William (c. 1422–91; The first English printer)

CAYLEY, Arthur (1821–95; British mathematician)

CAYLEY, George (1773–1857; British engineer and pioneer designer of flying machines)

COTTON, Frank Albert (1930–2007; US chemist)

CUVIER, Georges, Baron (1769–1832; French zoologist)

DALTON, John (1766–1844; British chemist)

DARWIN, Charles Robert (1809–82; British naturalist)

DE BARY, Heinrich Anton (1831–88; German botanist)

DE DUVE, Christian (1917–2013; Belgian biochemist)

DOBSON, Christopher Martin, Sir (1949– ; British chemist)

DOUDNA, Jennifer Anne (1963– ; US biochemist and molecular biologist)

DREVER, Ronald William Prest (1931–2017; British physicist)

DREYER, Johan Ludvig Emil (1852–1926; Danish astronomer)

ECKERT, John Presper (1919–95; US electronics engineer)

ENDERS, John Franklin (1897–1985; US microbiologist)

ENGLER, Gustav Heinrich Adolf (1844–1930; German botanist)

EUCLID (c. 300 BC; Greek mathematician)

FERMAT, Pierre de (1601–65; French mathematician)

FINSEN, Niels Ryberg (1860–1904; Danish physician)

FOKKER, Anthony Hermann Gerard (1890–1939; Dutch aircraft manufacturer)

FRANCK, James (1882–1964; US physicist)

FRIEND, Richard Henry, Sir (1953– ; British physicist and technologist)

FRISCH, Karl Von (1886–1982; Austrian zoologist)

FRISCH, Otto Robert (1904–79; Austrian-born physicist)

FULTON, Robert (1765–1815; American inventor)

GALOIS, Évariste (1811–32; French mathematician)

GALTON, Francis (1822–1911; British scientist)

GEIGER, Hans (1882–1945; German physicist)

GESNER, Conrad (1516–65; Swiss physician)

GRAHAM, Thomas (1805–69; British physicist)

HALLEY, Edmund (1656–1742; British astronomer)

HEVESY, George Charles Von (1885–1966; Hungarian-born chemist)

HOOKER, William Jackson (1785–1865; British botanist)

HUBBLE, Edwin Powell (1889–1953; US astronomer)

HUTTON, James (1726–97; Scottish physician)

HUXLEY, Thomas Henry (1825–95; British biologist)

JANSKY, Karl Guthe (1905–50; US radio engineer)

JEMMIS, Eluvathingal Devassy (1951– ; Indian theoretical chemist)

JENSON, Nicolas (c. 1420–80; French printer)

JOLIOT, Frédéric (1900–59; French physicist)

KELVIN, William Thomson, 1st Baron (1824–1907; Scottish physicist)

KEPLER, Johannes (1571–1630; German astronomer)

KIBBLE, Thomas Walter Bannerman (1932–2016; British theoretical physicist)

KINSEY, Alfred (1894–1956; US zoologist and sociologist)

LANDAU, Lev Davidovich (1908–68; Soviet physicist)

LARTET, Édouard Armand Isidore Hippolyte (1801–71; French archaeologist)

LEVITT, Michael (1947– ; South African-born US-British-Israeli molecular biologist)

LIEBIG, Justus, Baron Von (1803–73; German chemist)

LORENZ, Konrad (1903–89; Austrian zoologist)

LOVELL, Bernard, Sir (1913–2012; British astronomer)

LOWELL, Percival (1855–1916; US astronomer)

MARKOV, Andrei Andreevich

(1856–1922; Russian mathematician)

MARTIN, Archer John Porter (1910–2002; British biochemist)

MARTIN, Pierre-Émile (1824–1915; French engineer)

MCADAM, John Loudon (1756–1836; British inventor)

MENDEL, Gregor Johann (1822–84; Austrian botanist)

MORGAN, Thomas Hunt (1866–1945; US geneticist)

MORGAN, William Jason (1935– ; US geophysicist)

MORLEY, Edward Williams (1838–1923; US chemist)

MORRIS, Desmond John (1928– ; British zoologist)

MOUROU, Gérard Albert (1944– ; French physicist and electrical engineer)

MULLER, Hermann Joseph (1890–1967; US geneticist)

MÜLLER, Paul Hermann (1899–1965; Swiss chemist)

NAPIER, John (1550–1617; Scottish mathematician)

NERNST, Walther Hermann (1864–1941; German physical chemist)

NEWTON, Isaac (1642–1727; British physicist and mathematician)

OHSUMI, Yoshinori (1945– ; Japanese cell biologist)

O'KEEFE, John (1939– ; US-born British neuroscientist)

OLBERS, Heinrich Wilhelm Matthäus (1758–1840; German astronomer)

PASCAL, Blaise (1623–62; French mathematician and physicist)

PENDRY, John Brian, Sir (1943– ; English theoretical physicist)

PENNEY, William George, Baron (1909–91; British mathematician)

PERKIN, William Henry (1838–1907; British chemist)

PERRIN, Jean-Baptiste (1870–1942; French physicist)

PLANCK, Max Karl Ernst Ludwig (1858–1947; German physicist)

POWELL, Cecil Frank (1903–69; British physicist)

PROUST, Joseph-Louis (1754–1826; French chemist)

RAMSAY, William (1852–1916; Scottish chemist)

RENNIE, John (1761–1821; British civil engineer)

SANGER, Frederick (1918–2013; British biochemist)

SAVERY, Thomas (c. 1650–1715; English engineer)

SLOANE, Hans (1660–1753; British physician and naturalist)

STOKES, George Gabriel (1819–1903; British physicist and mathematician)

STRUVE, Otto (1897–1963; US astronomer)

SÜDHOF, Thomas Christian (1955– ; German-US biochemist)

SUTTON, Walter Stanborough (1877–1916; US geneticist)

SUZUKI, Akira (1930– ; Japanese organic chemist)

TALBOT, William Henry Fox (1800–77; British botanist and physicist)

TAYLOR, Brook (1685–1737; English mathematician)

TAYLOR, Frederick Winslow (1856–1915; US engineer)

TELLER, Edward (1908–2003; US physicist)

TOWNES, Charles Hard (1915–2015; US physicist)

VAUBAN, Sébastian Le Prestre de (1633–1707; French military engineer)

VENTER, John Craig (1946– ; US biologist and businessman)

WALLIS, Barnes (1887–1979; British aeronautical engineer)

WALTON, Ernest Thomas Sinton (1903–95; Irish physicist)

WATSON, James Dewey (1928– ; US geneticist)

WIENER, Norbert (1894–1964; US mathematician)

WIGNER, Eugene Paul (1902–95; US physicist)

WILSON, Alan Herries, Sir (1906–95; British theoretical physicist and industrialist)

WILSON, Charles Thomson Rees (1869–1959; British physicist)

WILSON, Edmund Beecher (1856–1939; US biologist)

WINTER, Gregory (Greg) Paul, Sir (1951– ; British biochemist/molecular biologist)

WÖHLER, Friedrich (1800–82; German chemist)

WRIGHT, Orville (1871–1948; US aviator)

YUKAWA, Hideki (1907–81; Japanese physicist)

ZEEMAN, Pieter (1865–1943; Dutch physicist)

7

AGASSIZ, Jean Louis Rodolphe

(1807–73; Swiss natural historian)

AKASAKI, Isamu (1929– ; Japanese physicist)

ALLISON, James Patrick (1948– ; US immunologist)

ALVAREZ, Luis Walter (1911–88; US physicist)

AUDUBON, John James (1785–1851; US naturalist)

BABBAGE, Charles (1792–1871; British mathematician)

BARDEEN, John (1908–91; US physicist)

BARNARD, Edward Emerson (1857–1923; US astronomer)

BATESON, William (1861–1926; British biologist)

BATTANI, Al- (c. 858–929; Islamic astronomer)

BENNETT, Charles Henry (1943– ; US computer scientist and physicist)

BERGIUS, Friedrich (1884–1949; German chemist)

BEUTLER, Bruce (1957– ; American biologist and immunologist)

BORLAUG, Norman (1914–2009; US plant breeder)

BROUWER, Luitzen Egbertus Jan (1881–1966; Dutch mathematician)

BURBANK, Luther (1849–1926; US plant breeder)

CANDELA, Felix (1910–97; Spanish-Mexican engineer and architect)

CARDANO, Girolamo (1501–76; Italian mathematician)

CHAITIN, Gregory (1947– ; US mathematician and computer scientist)

COMPTON, Arthur Holly (1892–1962; US physicist)

CORRENS, Carl Erich (1864–1933; German botanist and geneticist)

COULOMB, Charles Augustin de (1736–1806; French physicist)

CROOKES, William (1832–1919; British physicist)

CURTISS, Glenn (1878–1930; US aviator and aeronautical engineer)

DAIMLER, Gottlieb (1834–1900; German inventor)

DANIELL, John Frederic (1790–1845; British chemist)

DAWKINS, Richard (1941– ; British evolutionary biologist)

DE LA RUE, Warren (1815–89; British astronomer)

DE VRIES, Hugo Marie (1848–1935; Dutch botanist)

DOPPLER, Christian Johann (1803–53; Austrian physicist)

DRIESCH, Hans Adolf Eduard (1867–1941; German zoologist)

EDWARDS, Robert Geoffrey, Sir (1925–2013; British biologist and medical researcher)

EICHLER, August Wilhelm (1839–87; German botanist)

ENGLERT, François (1932– ; Belgian theoretical physicist)

FARADAY, Michael (1791– 1867; British chemist and physicist)

FERINGA, Bernard Lucas (Ben) (1951– ; Dutch organic chemist)

FEYNMAN, Richard Phillips (1918–88; US physicist)

FISCHER, Emil Hermann (1852–1919; German chemist)

FLEMING, John Ambrose (1849–1945; British electrical engineer)

FOURIER, Jean Baptiste Joseph, Baron (1768–1830; French mathematician and physicist)

FRESNEL, Augustin Jean (1788–1827; French physicist)

GAGARIN, Yuri Alekseevich (1934–68; Soviet cosmonaut)

GALVANI, Luigi (1737–98; Italian physician)

GILBERT, William (1544–1603; English physicist)

GODDARD, Robert Hutchings (1882–1945; US physicist)

GREGORY, James (1638–75; Scottish mathematician and astronomer)

HAECKEL, Ernst Heinrich (1834–1919; German zoologist)

HALDANE, Frederick Duncan Michael (1951– ; British-born US theoretical physicist)

HAWKING, Stephen (1942–2018; British theoretical physicist and cosmologist)

HAWORTH, Walter Norman (1883–1950; British biochemist)

HELMONT, Jan Baptist van (1580–1644; Belgian alchemist and physician)

HENSLOW, John Stevens (1796–1861; English botanist and geologist)

HERMITE, Charles (1822–1901; French mathematician)

HILBERT, David (1862–1943; German mathematician)

HODGKIN, Alan Lloyd (1914–98; British physiologist)

HODGKIN, Dorothy Mary Crowfoot (1910–95; British biochemist)

HOPKINS, Frederick Gowland (1861–1947; British biochemist)

HUGGINS, William (1824–1910; British astronomer)

HUYGENS, Christiaan (1629–95; Dutch astronomer and physicist)

JUSSIEU (French family of botanists)

KAPITZA, Peter Leonidovich (1894–1984; Soviet physicist)

KARPLUS, Martin (1930– ; Austrian-born US theoretical chemist)

KENDALL, Edward Calvin (1886–1972; US biochemist)

KENDREW, John Cowdery (1917–97; British biochemist)

KHORANA, Har Gobind (1922–2011; US biochemist)

KIDINNU (4th century BC; Babylonian mathematician and astronomer)

KOZIREV, Nikolai Aleksandrovich (1908–83; Russian astronomer)

LALANDE, Joseph-Jérôme le Français de (1732–1807; French astronomer)

LAMARCK, Jean-Baptiste de Monet, Chevalier de (1744–1829; French naturalist)

LAMBERT, Johann Heinrich (1728–77; German mathematician and astronomer)

LANGLEY, Samuel Pierpont (1834–1906; US astronomer)

LAPLACE, Pierre Simon, Marquis de (1749–1827; French mathematician and astronomer)

LESSEPS, Ferdinand de (1805–94; French diplomat)

LOCKYER, Joseph Norman (1836–1920; British astronomer)

LORENTZ, Hendrick Antoon (1853–1928; Dutch physicist)

LUMIÈRE, Auguste (1862–1954; French photographer and inventor)

LYSENKO, Trofim Denisovich (1898–1976; Soviet biologist)

MARCONI, Guglielmo (1874–1937; Italian electrical engineer)

MAXWELL, James Clerk (1831–79; Scottish physicist)

MEITNER, Lise (1878–1968; Austrian physicist)

MESSIER, Charles (1730– 1817; French astronomer)

MOERNER, William (1953– ; US chemist/physicist)

MOSELEY, Henry Gwyn Jeffries (1887–1915; British physicist)

NEGISHI, Ei-ichi (1935– ; Japanese organic chemist)

NEUMANN, John Von (1903–57; US mathematician)

OERSTED, Hans Christian (1777–1851; Danish physicist)

ONSAGER, Lars (1903–76; US chemist)

OSTWALD, Wilhelm (1853– 1932; German chemist)

PARSONS, Charles Algernon (1854–1931; British engineer)

PASTEUR, Louis (1822–95; French chemist and microbiologist)

PAULING, Linus Carl (1901–94; US chemist)

PICCARD (family of Swiss scientists)

POISSON, Siméon Dénis (1781–1840; French mathematician)

PRANDTL, Ludwig (1875–1953; German physicist)

PTOLEMY (or Claudius Ptolemaeus, 2nd century AD; Egyptian mathematician, astronomer, and geographer)

PURCELL, Edward Mills (1912–97; US physicist)

RÉAUMUR, René-Antoine Ferchault de (1683–1757; French physicist)

RIEMANN, Georg Friedrich Bernhard (1826–66; German mathematician)

ROSBASH, Michael Morris (1944– ; US geneticist)

ROTHMAN, James Edward (1950– ; US cell biologist)

RUMFORD, Benjamin Thompson, Count (1753–1814; American-born scientist)

SANDAGE, Allan Rex (1926–2010; US astronomer)

SAUVAGE, Jean-Pierre (1944– ; French chemist)

SCHEELE, Carl Wilhelm (1742–86; Swedish chemist)

SCHMIDT, Brian P. (1967– ; American-born astrophysicist)

SCHWANN, Theodor (1810– 82; German physiologist)

SEABORG, Glenn Theodore (1912–99; US physicist)

SHEPARD, Jr, Allan Bartlett (1923–98; US astronaut)

SIEMENS, Ernst Werner von (1816–92; German electrical engineer)

SIMPSON, George Gaylord

(1902–84; US palaeontologist)

STEPTOE, Patrick Christopher (1913–1988; British physician and medical researcher)

SZILARD, Leo (1898–1964; US physicist)

TELFORD, Thomas (1757–1834; British civil engineer)

THENARD, Louis-Jacques (1777–1857; French chemist)

THOMSON, Joseph John (1856–1940; British physicist)

TUPOLEV, Andrei Niklaievich (1888–1972; Soviet designer)

TYNDALL, John (1820–93; Irish physicist)

VAVILOV, Nikolai Ivanovich (1887–1943; Soviet plant geneticist)

VILLANI, Cédric (1973– ; French mathematician)

WAKSMAN, Selman Abraham (1888–1973; US microbiologist)

WALLACE, Alfred Russel (1823–1913; British naturalist)

WARSHEL, Arieh (1940– ; Israeli-US chemist, biochemist, and molecular biologist)

WEGENER, Alfred Lothar (1880–1930; German geologist)

WILKINS, Maurice Hugh Frederick (1916–2004; New Zealand physicist)

WINSTON, Robert, Baron (1940– ; British obstetrician and gynaecologist)

ZIEGLER, Karl (1898–1973; German chemist)

8

AGRICOLA, Georgius (1494–1555; German physician and mineralogist)

ANDERSON, Carl David (1905–91; US physicist)

ÅNGSTRÖM, Anders Jonas (1814–74; Swedish physicist and astronomer)

AVOGADRO, Amedeo, Conte di Quaregna e Ceretto (1776–1856; Italian physicist)

BAKEWELL, Robert (1725–95; British agriculturalist)

BESSEMER, Henry (1813–98; British engineer and inventor)

BIRKHOFF, George David (1864–1944; US mathematician)

BJERKNES, Vilhelm Friman Koren (1862–1951; Norwegian meteorologist and physicist)

BLACKETT, Patrick Maynard Stuart, Baron (1897–1974; British physicist)

BRATTAIN, Walter Houser (1902–87; US physicist)

BREWSTER, David (1781–1868; Scottish physicist)

BRIDGMAN, Percy Williams (1882–1961; US physicist)

BRINDLEY, James (1716–72; British canal builder)

BUSHNELL, David (1742–1824; US inventor; built the first submarine)

CALMETTE, Albert Léon Charles (1863–1933; French bacteriologist)

CAMPBELL, William Cecil (1930– ; Irish-born US biologist)

CHADWICK, James (1891–1974; British physicist)

CLAUSIUS, Rudolf Julius Emanuel (1822–88; German physicist)

CULPEPER, Nicholas (1616–54; English physician)

DEDEKIND, Richard (1831–1916; German mathematician)

DE MORGAN, Augustus (1806–71; British mathematician and logician)

DUBOCHET, Jacques (1942– ; Swiss biophysicist)

EINSTEIN, Albert (1879–1955; German physicist)

ERICSSON, John (1803–89; US naval engineer and inventor)

FOUCAULT, Jean Bernard Léon (1819–68; French physicist)

GASSENDI, Pierre (1592–1655; French physicist)

GELL-MANN, Murray (1929– ; US physicist)

GUERICKE, Otto Von (1602–86; German physicist)

HAMILTON, William Rowan (1805–65; Irish mathematician)

HERSCHEL, William (1738–1822; British astronomer)

HOFFMANN, Jules A. (1941– ; Luxembourg-born French biologist)

ILYUSHIN, Sergei Vladimirovich (1894–1977; Soviet aircraft designer)

IPATIEFF, Vladimir Nikolaievich (1867–1952; US physicist)

JACQUARD, Joseph-Marie (1752–1834; French inventor)

KENNELLY, Arthur Edwin (1861–1939; US electrical engineer)

KLAPROTH, Martin Heinrich (1743–1817; German chemist)

KOROLIOV, Sergei Pavlovich (1906–66; Soviet aeronautical engineer)

LAGRANGE, Joseph Louis, Comte de (1736–1813; French mathematician and astronomer)

LANGMUIR, Irving (1881–1957; US chemist)

LAWRENCE, Ernest Orlando (1901–58; US physicist)

LEGENDRE, Adrien Marie (1752–1833; French mathematician)

LEMAÎTRE, Georges Édouard, Abbé (1894–1966; Belgian priest and astronomer)

LEUCKART, Karl Georg Friedrich Rudolph (1822–98; German zoologist)

LINNAEUS, Carolus (Carl Linné; 1707–78; Swedish botanist)

LIPSCOMB, William Nunn (1919–2011; US chemist)

LONSDALE, Kathleen (1903–71; Irish physicist)

MAUDSLAY, Henry (1771–1831; British engineer)

MCKENZIE, Dan, (1942– ; British geophysicist)

MCMILLAN, Edwin Mattison (1907–91; US physicist)

MERCATOR, Gerardus (1512–94; Flemish geographer)

MEYERHOF, Otto Fritz (1884–1951; US biochemist)

MILLIKAN, Robert Andrews (1868–1953; US physicist)

MILSTEIN, César (1927–2002; British molecular biologist)

MITCHELL, Reginald Joseph (1895–1937; British aeronautical engineer)

MOROWITZ, Harold Joseph (1927–2016; US biophysicist)

MULLIKEN, Robert Sanderson (1896–1986; US chemist and physicist)

NAKAMURA, Shuji (1954– ; Japanese-born US physicist)

NEWCOMEN, Thomas (1663–1729; English blacksmith and inventor of steam engine)

OLIPHANT, Mark Laurence Elwin (1901–2000; Australian physicist)

POINCARÉ, Jules Henri (1854–1912; French mathematician)

RAYLEIGH, John William Strutt, 3rd Baron (1842–1919; British physicist)

RHETICUS (1514–76; German mathematician)

ROBINSON, Carol Vivien, Dame (1956– ; British chemist)

ROBINSON, Robert (1886–1975; British chemist)

ROEBLING, John Augustus (1806–69; US engineer)

ROENTGEN, Wilhelm Konrad (1845–1923; German physicist)

SABATIER, Paul (1854–1941; French chemist)

SAKHAROV, Andrei Dimitrievich (1921–89; Soviet physicist)

SCHEKMAN, Randy Wayne (1948– ; US cell biologist)

SHOCKLEY, William Bradfield (1910–89; US physicist)

SHRAPNEL, Henry (1761–1842; British army officer, who invented the shrapnel shell)

SIKORSKY, Igor Ivan (1889–1972; US aeronautical engineer)

STEINMAN, Ralph Marvin (1943–2011; Canadian biologist)

STIRLING, James (1692–1770; Scottish mathematician)

STODDART, James Fraser, Sir (1942– ; British-born US chemist)

SUSSKIND, Leonard (1940– ; US theoretical physicist)

THORNTON, Janet Maureen, Dame (1949– ; British molecular biologist)

THOULESS, David James (1934– ; British theoretical physicist)

TU YOUYOU, (1930– ; Chinese medical scientist and pharmaceutical chemist)

VAN ALLEN, James Alfred (1914–2006; US physicist)

VAN'T HOFF, Jacobus Henricus (1852–1911; Dutch chemist)

WEISMANN, August Friedrich Leopold (1834–1914; German biologist)

WOODWARD, Robert Burns (1917–79; US chemist)

ZERNICKE, Frits (1888–1966; Dutch physicist)

ZWORYKIN, Vladimir Kosma (1889–1982; US physicist)

9

ABU AL-WAFA (940–98 AD; Persian mathematician and astronomer)

ARMSTRONG, Edwin Howard (1890–1954; US electrical engineer)

ARMSTRONG, William George, Baron (1810–1900; British engineer)

ARRHENIUS, Svante August (1859–1927; Swedish physicist and chemist)

BECQUEREL, Henri (1852–1908; French physicist)

BERNOULLI (family of Swiss mathematicians and physicists)

BERTHELOT, Marcelin (1827–1907; French chemist)

BERZELIUS, Jöns Jakob, Baron (1779–1848; Swedish chemist)

BOLTZMANN, Ludwig Eduard (1844–1906; Austrian physicist)

BORCHERDS, Richard Ewen (1959– ; South African-born British mathematician)

BRILLOUIN, Léon (1889–1969; French physicist)

BRONOWSKI, Jacob (1908–74; British mathematician)

CAVENDISH, Henry (1731–1810; British physicist)

CHEBISHEV, Pafnuti Lvovich (1821–94; Russian mathematician)

CHERENKOV, Pavel Alekseievich (1904–90; Russian physicist)

COCKCROFT, John Douglas (1897–1967; British physicist)

CORNFORTH, John Warcup, Sir (1917–2013; Australian chemist)

D'ALEMBERT, Jean Le Rond (1717–83; French mathematician)

DAUBENTON, Louis Jean Marie (1716–1800; French naturalist)

DAVENPORT, Charles Benedict (1866–1944; US zoologist)

EDDINGTON, Arthur Stanley (1882–1944; British theoretical astronomer)

ENDLICHER, Stephan Ladislaus (1804–49; Hungarian botanist)

FIBONACCI, Leonardo (c. 1170–c. 1230; Italian mathematician)

FLAMSTEED, John (1646–1719; English astronomer)

GAY-LUSSAC, Joseph Louis (1778–1850; French chemist and physicist)

HEAVISIDE, Oliver (1850–1925; British physicist)

HELMHOLTZ, Hermann Ludwig Ferdinand Von (1821–94; German physicist and physiologist)

HENDERSON, Richard (1945– ; British molecular biologist)

HOPKINSON, John (1849–98; British physicist and electrical engineer)

JOHANNSEN, Wilhelm Ludvig (1857–1927; Danish geneticist)

JOSEPHSON, Brian David (1940– ; British physicist)

KIRCHHOFF, Gustav Robert (1824–87; German physicist)

KURCHATOV, Igor Vasilievich (1903–60; Soviet physicist)

LANKESTER, Edwin Ray (1847–1929; British zoologist)

LAVOISIER, Antoine Laurent (1743–94; French chemist)

LEDERBERG, Joshua (1925–2008; US geneticist)

LEVERRIER, Urbain Jean Joseph (1811–77; French astronomer)

LIOUVILLE, Joseph (1809–82; French mathematician)

MACINTOSH, Charles (1766–1843; Scottish chemist)

MACMILLAN, Kirkpatrick (d. 1878; Scottish inventor)

MICHELSON, Albert Abraham (1852–1931; US physicist)

NICHOLSON, William (1753–1815; British chemist)

NIRENBERG, Marshall Warren (1927–2010; US biochemist)

NOVOSELOV, Konstantin Sergeevich (1974– ; Russian–British physicist)

PELLETIER, Pierre Joseph (1788–1842; French chemist)

PRIESTLEY, Joseph (1733–1804; British chemist)

REMINGTON, Eliphalet (1793–1863; US inventor)

SCHLEIDEN, Matthias Jakob (1804–81; German botanist)

SHECHTMAN, Dan (1941– ; Israeli material scientist)

STEINMETZ, Charles Proteus (1865–1923; US electrical engineer)

TINBERGEN, Nikolaas (1907–94; Dutch zoologist and pioneer ethologist)

VERNADSKY, Vladimir Ivanovich (1863–1945; Russian geologist and biologist)

ZSIGMONDY, Richard Adolph (1865–1929; Austrian chemist)

ZUCKERMAN, Solly, Baron (1904–93; British anatomist)

10

ARCHIMEDES (c. 287–c. 212 BC; Greek mathematician and inventor)

ARROWSMITH, Aaron (1750–1823; British cartographer)

BARKHAUSEN, Heinrich (1881–1956; German physicist)

BERTHOLLET, Claude Louis, Comte (1748–1822; French chemist and physician)

BLENKINSOP, John (1783–1831; British engineer)

CANNIZZARO, Stanislao (1826–1910; Italian chemist)

COPERNICUS, Nicolaus (1473–1543; Polish astronomer)

DOBZHANSKY, Theodosius (1900–75; US geneticist)

FEIGENBAUM, Mitchell Jay (1944– ; American mathematical physicist)

FITZGERALD, George Francis (1851–1901; Irish physicist)

FOURNEYRON, Benoît (1802–67; French engineer)

FRAUNHOFER, Joseph Von (1787–1826; German physicist)

HEISENBERG, Werner Karl (1901–76; German physicist)

HIPPARCHUS (c. 190–c. 120 BC; Greek astronomer)

HOFMEISTER, Wilhelm Friedrich Benedict (1824–77; German botanist)

INGENHOUSZ, Jan (1730–99; Dutch physician and plant physiologist)

KOLMOGOROV, Andrei Nikolaevich (1903–87; Soviet mathematician)

KOSTERLITZ, John Michael (Mike) (1943– ; British-born US theoretical physicist)

LILIENTHAL, Otto (1848–96; German aeronautical engineer)

LIPPERSHEY, Hans (d. c. 1619; Dutch lens grinder)

MAUPERTUIS, Pierre Louis Moreau de (1698–1759; French mathematician)

MENDELEYEV, Dimitrii Ivanovich (1834–1907; Russian chemist)

METCHNIKOV, Ilya Ilich (1845–1916; Russian zoologist)

MIRZAKHANI, Maryam (1977– ; Iranian mathematician)

PERLMUTTER, Saul (1959– ; American astrophysicist)

POLCHINSKI, Joseph Gerard (1954–2018; US theoretical physicist)

PONTECORVO, Bruno (1913–1993; Italian-born Russian physicist)

RUTHERFORD, Ernest, 1st Baron (1871–1937; English physicist)

SOMMERFELD, Arnold Johannes Wilhelm (1868–1951; German physicist)

STAUDINGER, Hermann (1881–1965; German chemist)

STEPHENSON, George (1781–1848; British engineer)

STRICKLAND, Donna Theo (1959– ; Canadian physicist)

SWAMMERDAM, Jan (1637–80; Dutch naturalist and microscopist)

TORRICELLI, Evangelista (1608–47; Italian physicist)

TOURNEFORT, Joseph Pitton de (1656–1708; French botanist)

TREVITHICK, Richard (1771–1833; British engineer)

WATSON-WATT, Robert Alexander (1892–1973; Scottish physicist)

WHEATSTONE, Charles (1802–75; British physicist)

11

AL-KHWARIZMI, Muhammed Ibn Musa (c. 780–c. 850 AD; Arabic mathematician)

BASKERVILLE, John (1706–75; British printer)

BEREZINSKII, Vadim L'vovich (1935–80; Soviet theoretical physicist)

BHOSKHARA II (1114–c. 1185; Indian mathematician)

CHAMBERLAIN, Owen (1920–2006; US physicist)

CHARPENTIER, Emmanuelle (1968– ; French biochemist)

GOLDSCHMIDT, Richard Benedict (1878–1958; US geneticist)

HENDRICKSON, Wayne A. (1941– ; US biophysicist)

HINSHELWOOD, Cyril Norman (1897–1967; British chemist)

JOLIOT-CURIE, Irène (1896–1956; French physicist)

LE CHÂTELIER, Henri-Louis (1850–1936; French chemist)

LEEUWENHOEK, Antonie van (1632–1723; Dutch scientist)

LOBACHEVSKI, Nikolai Ivanovich (1793–1856; Russian mathematician)

NOSTRADAMUS (1503–66; French physician and astrologer)

OPPENHEIMER, J Robert (1904–67; US physicist)

SCHRÖDINGER, Erwin (1887–1961; Austrian physicist)

SHERRINGTON, Charles Scott (1857–1952; British physiologist)

SPALLANZANI, Lazzaro (1729–99; Italian physiologist)

TSIOLKOVSKI, Konstantin Eduardovich (1857–1935; Russian aeronautical engineer)

VAN DER WAALS, Johannes Diderik (1837–1923; Dutch physicist)

12

AMBARTSUMIAN, Viktor Amazaspovich (1908–96 Armenian astrophysicist)

ATTENBOROUGH, David, Sir (1926– ; British naturalist and broadcaster)

GROTHENDIECK, Alexander (1928–2014; German-born stateless mathematician)

RAMACHANDRAN, Gopalasamudram Narayan (1922–2001; Indian physicist)

SZENT-GYÖRGYI, Albert (1893–1986; US biochemist)

13

ARAGO FRANÇOIS (1786–1853; French astronomer and physicist)

CHANDRASEKHAR, Subrahmanyan (1910–95; US astronomer)

REGIOMONTANUS (1436-76; German astronomer and mathematician)

VAN DER WAERDEN, Bartel Leendert (1903–1996; Dutch mathematician and historian of mathematics and science)

14

GALILEO GALILEI (1564–1642; Italian mathematician, physicist, and astronomer)

15

BALASUBRAMANIAN, Shankar (1966– ; Indian-born British chemist)

EUDOXUS OF CNIDUS (c. 408–c. 355 BC; Greek astronomer and mathematician)

16

HERO OF ALEXANDRIA (mid-1st century AD; Greek engineer and mathematician)

17

APOLLONIUS OF PERGA (c. 261–c. 190 BC; Greek mathematician)

18

ARISTARCHUS OF SAMOS (c. 310–230 BC; Greek astronomer)

LECOQ DE BOISBAUDRAN, Paul-Émile (1838–1912; French chemist)

PAPPUS OF ALEXANDRIA (3rd century BC; Greek mathematician)

19

DIOSCORIDES PEDANIUS (c. 40–c. 90 AD; Greek physician)

KEKULÉ VON STRADONITZ, Friedrich August (1829–96; German chemist)

20+
IOPHANTUS OF ALEXANDRIA (mid-3rd century AD; Greek mathematician)

ERATOSTHENES OF CYRENE (c. 276–c. 194 BC; Greek astronomer)
GEOFFROY SAINT-HILAIRE,

Étienne (1772–1844; French naturalist)
SOSIGENES OF ALEXANDRIA (1st century BC; Greek astronomer)

COMPUTER SCIENTISTS

4
BINA, Eric US computer scientist
BRIN, Sergey (1973–) Russian-born US computer scientist
CERF, Vinton G US computer scientist
CODD, Edgar Frank (1923–2003) British computer scientist
HOFF, Marcian Edward (1937–) US computer engineer
JOBS, Steven Paul (1955–2011) US computer engineer and entrepreneur
KAHN, Robert (1938–) US computer scientist
ZUSE, Konrad (1910–95) German computer engineer

5
AIKEN, Howard Hathaway (1900–73) US computer pioneer
BYRON, Augusta Ada, Countess of Lovelace (1815–52) British computer pioneer
KAPOR, Mitch(ell David) (1950–) US computer scientist
KNUTH, Donald Ervin (1938–) US computer programmer
LENAT, Douglas (1950–) US computer scientist
OLSEN, Kenneth Harry (1926–2011) US computer engineer and entrepreneur

6
AMDAHL, Gene Myron (1922–

2015) US computer engineer
BACKUS, John (1924–2007) US computer scientist
ECKERT, John Presper, Jr (1919–1995) US computer scientist
HOPPER, Grace (1906–92) US mathematician and computer scientist
MINSKY, Marvin Lee (1927–2016) US computer scientist
NELSON, Ted (1937–) US computer scientist
NEWELL, Allan (1927–92) US computer scientist
POSTEL, Jonathan (1943–98) US computer scientist
SALTON, Gerard (1927–95) German-born US scientist
SCHANK, Roger Carl (1946–) US computer scientist
TURING, Alan (1912–54) British computer scientist
WILKES, Maurice Vincent (1913–2010) British computer scientist

7
DENNING, Peter (1942–) US computer scientist
ELLISON, Larry (1944–) US software developer
KILDALL, Gary (1942–95) US computer scientist
MAUCHLY, John William (1907–80) US computer engineer
STIBITZ, George Robert (1904–95) US computer pioneer

8
BRICKLIN, Daniel (1951–) US computer engineer
DIJKSTRA, Edsger (1930–2002) Dutch computer scientist
MCCARTHY, John (1927–2011) US computer scientist
STRACHEY, Christopher (1916–75) British computer scientist
WINOGRAD, Terry Allen (1946–) US computer scientist

9
ATANASOFF, John Vincent (1904–95) US physicist and computer pioneer
ENGELBART, Douglas (1925–2013) US computer scientist
FORRESTER, Jay (1918–2016) US computer engineer
KASPERSKY, Eugene (1965–) Russian computer scientist

10
ANDREESSEN, Marc (1971–) US computer scientist
BERNERS-LEE, Tim, Sir (1955–) British computer scientist
FEIGENBAUM, Edward Albert (1936–) US computer scientist
HOFSTADTER, Douglas Richard (1945–) US computer scientist
SUTHERLAND, Ivan (1938–) US computer scientist

ENGINEERS AND INVENTORS

4
BELL, Alexander Graham (1847–1922) Scottish-born US inventor of the telephone
DAVY, Humphry (1778–1829) English inventor of the Davy lamp
HOWE, Elias (1819–67) US inventor of the sewing machine

IVES, Frederick Eugene (1856–1937) US inventor of halftone photography
LAND, Edwin Herbert (1909–91) US inventor of the Polaroid Land camera
MOON, William (1818–94) British inventor of the Moon writing system

TULL, Jethro (1674–1741) English inventor of the seed drill
WATT, James (1736–1819) Scottish engineer and inventor who developed the steam engine

5
BAIRD, John Logie (1888–1946) Scottish inventor of television

CREED, Frederick (1871–1957) Canadian inventor of the teleprinter

CYRIL, Saint (?827–869) Greek Christian theologian, inventor of the Cyrillic alphabet

DALEN, Nils Gustaf (1869– 1937) Swedish inventor of an automatic light-controlled valve

DYSON, James, Sir (1947–   ) British industrial designer

HOOKE, Robert (1635–1703) English physicist, chemist, and inventor of the Gregorian telescope and a balance spring for watches

MAXIM, Hiram Stevens (1840–1916) British inventor of the first automatic machine gun

MORSE, Samuel (1791–1872) US inventor of electric telegraph and Morse code

NOBEL, Alfred (1833–96) Swedish inventor of dynamite

TESLA, Nikola (1857–1943) US inventor of transformers, generators, and dynamos

6

ARCHER, Frederick Scott (1813–57) British inventor of wet collodion photographic process

BAYLIS, Trevor (1937–2018) British inventor of clockwork radio

DU MONT, Allen Balcom (1901–65) US inventor and developer of cathode-ray tube

DUNLOP, John (1840–1921) Scottish inventor of pneumatic tyre

EDISON, Thomas Alva (1847–1931) US inventor of phonograph, electric lamp, microphone, etc.

NAPIER, John (1550–1617) Scottish inventor of logarithms

NIEPCE, Joseph-Nicéphore (1765–1833) French inventor who produced first photographic image and first permanent camera photograph

PITMAN, Isaac (1813–97) British inventor of a system of shorthand

SHOLES, Christopher Latham (1819–90) US inventor of the typewriter

SINGER, Isaac Merrit (1811–75) US inventor of chain-stitch sewing machine

WILSON, Charles (1869–1959) Scottish inventor of the cloud chamber

7

BABBAGE, Charles (1792–1871) English inventor of a calculating machine (forerunner of modern electronic computers)

BRAILLE, Louis (1809–52) French inventor of the Braille system of raised writing

LAENNEC, René (1781–1826) French inventor of the stethoscope

NASMYTH, James (1808–90) British inventor of the steam hammer

SIEMENS, Ernst Werner von (1816–92) German inventor and pioneer in telegraphy

WHITNEY, Eli (1765–1825) US inventor of a mechanical cotton gin

WHITTLE, Frank (1907–96) British inventor of the jet engine

8

CROMPTON, Samuel (1753–1827) British inventor of the spinning mule

DAGUERRE, Louise (1789–1851) French inventor of photographic processes

DE FOREST, Lee (1873–1961) US inventor of radio equipment

GOODYEAR, Charles (1800–60) US inventor of vulcanized rubber

LAWRENCE, Ernest (1901–58) US inventor of the cyclotron

LIPPMANN, Gabriel (1845–1921) French inventor of a process of colour photography

ZAMENHOF, Lazarus (1859–1917) Polish inventor of Esperanto

9

ARKWRIGHT, Richard (1732–92) English inventor of the spinning wheel

COCKERELL, Christopher (1910–99) British inventor of the hovercraft

FOX TALBOT, William (1800–77) British pioneer of photography

GUTENBERG, Johann (?1398–1468) German inventor of printing by movable type

MCCORMICK, Cyrus Hall (1809–84) US inventor of the reaping machine

10

CARTWRIGHT, Edmund (1743–1823) British inventor of the power loom

FAHRENHEIT, Gabriel (1686–1736) German inventor of the mercury thermometer

HARGREAVES, James (d. 1778) English inventor of the spinning jenny

MONTGOLFIER, Jacques (1745–99) and Joseph (1740–1810) French inventors who built the first practical hot-air balloon

STEPHENSON, George (1781-1848) British inventor of the first successful steam locomotive

ENTREPRENEURS AND INDUSTRIALISTS

3

LAW, John (1671–1729) Scottish financier

4

FORD, Henry (1863–1947) US manufacturer

OWEN, Robert (1771–1858) Welsh industrialist

RANK, J Arthur, 1st Baron (1888–1972) British industrialist

TATE, Henry (1819–99) British manufacturer

5

DAWES, Charles Gates (1865–1951) US financier

FARGO, William (1818–81) US businessman

GATES, Bill (1955–   ) US businessman

GETTY, J(ean) Paul (1892–1976) US oil executive

SUGAR, Alan, Baron (1947–   ) British entrepreneur

TRUMP, Donald (1946–   ) US businessman, 45th President of the United States of America

WELLS, Henry (1805–78) US businessman

6

GEORGE, Edward (1938–2009) British banker

HAMLYN, Paul, Baron (1926–2001) British businessman

HUGHES, Howard (1905–76) US industrialist

MORGAN, John Pierpont (1837–1913) US financier

NECKER, Jacques (1732–1804) French financier

RHODES, Cecil John (1853–1902) British financier

TURNER, Robert Edward, III (1938–   ) US businessman

7

BOULTON, Matthew (1728–1809) British manufacturer

BRANSON, Richard, Sir (1950–   ) British entrepreneur

BUGATTI, Ettore (1881–1947) Italian manufacturer

CADBURY, George (1839–1922) British industrialist

DAIMLER, Gottlieb (1834–1900) German manufacturer

EASTMAN, George (1854–1932) US manufacturer

GRESHAM, Thomas (?1519–79) English financier

ONASSIS, Aristotle (1906–1975) Turkish-born Argentinian shipowner

PEABODY, George (1795–1869) US merchant

RODDICK, Anita (1942–2007) British entrepreneur

WHITNEY, Eli (1765–1825) US manufacturer

8

CARNEGIE, Andrew (1835–1919) US manufacturer

MICHELIN, André (1853–1931) French industrialist

NUFFIELD, William Richard Morris (1877–1963) English manufacturer

PATERSON, William (1658–1719) Scottish merchant

RATHENAU, Walther (1867–1922) German industrialist

SINCLAIR, Clive, Sir (1940–   ) British entrepreneur

9

ARKWRIGHT, Richard (1732–92) English manufacturer

MACARTHUR, John (1767–1834) Australian entrepreneur

WEDGEWOOD, Josiah (1730–95) British industrialist

WOOLWORTH, Frank Winfield (1852–1919) US merchant

10

CHARDONNET, (Louis Marie) Hilaire Bernigaud (1839–1924) French industrialist

GULBENKIAN, Calouste Sarkis (1869–1955) British industrialist

LEVERHULME, 1st Viscount (1851–1925) English industrialist

ROTHSCHILD, Lionel Nathan, Baron de Rothschild (1809–1879) British banker

VANDERBILT, Cornelius (1794–1877) US shipowner

11

ROCKEFELLER, John D (1839–1937) US industrialist

FASHION DESIGNERS

3

SUI, Anna (1955–) US fashion designer

4

BOSS, Hugo (1885–1948) German fashion designer

DIOR, Christian (1905–57) French fashion designer

FORD, Tom (1961–) US fashion designer

HEAD, Edith (1907–81) US fashion designer

KANE, Christopher (1982–) British fashion designer

KORS, Michael (1959–) US fashion designer

LANG, Helmut (1956–) Austrian fashion designer

WANG, Vera (1949–) US fashion designer

5

DOLCE, Domenico (1958–) Italian fashion designer

FARHI, Nicole (1946–) French fashion designer

FERRE, Gianfranco (1944–2007) Italian fashion designer

FREUD, Bella (1961–) British fashion designer

GUCCI, Guccio (1881–1953) Italian fashion designer

KARAN, Donna (1948–) US fashion designer

KLEIN, Calvin (1942– –) US fashion designer

PRADA, Miuccia (1949–) Italian fashion designer

QUANT, Mary, Dame (1934–) British fashion designer

RICCI, Nina (1883–1970) Italian fashion designer

SMITH, Paul, Sir (1946–) British fashion designer

WORTH, Charles Frederick (1825–95) British fashion designer

6

ARMANI, Giorgio (1936–) Italian fashion designer

ASHLEY, Laura (1925–85) British fashion designer

CARDIN, Pierre (1922–) French fashion designer

CHANEL, Gabrielle (Coco) (1883–1971) French fashion designer

CONRAN, Jasper (1959–) British fashion designer

JACOBS, Marc (1963–) US fashion designer

LAUREN, Ralph (1939–) US fashion designer

MIYAKE, Issey (1938–) Japanese fashion designer

MUGLER, Thierry (1948–) French fashion designer

SANDER, Jil (1943–) German fashion designer

SIMONS, Raf (1968–) Belgian fashion designer

UNGARO, Emanuel (1935–) French fashion designer

7

BALMAIN, Pierre Alexandre (1914–82) French fashion designer

BECKHAM, Victoria (1974–) British fashion designer

BLAHNIK, Manolo (1942–) Spanish Czech fashion designer

CERRUTI, Nino (1930–) Italian fashion designer

GABBANA, Stefano (1962–) Italian fashion designer

HAMNETT, Katharine (1947–) British fashion designer

HERRERA, Carolina (1939–) US fashion designer

LACROIX, Christian (1951–) French fashion designer

LACOSTE, René (1906–96) French fashion designer

MCQUEEN, Alexander (1969–2010) British fashion designer

VERSACE, Donatella (1955–) Italian fashion designer

VERSACE, Gianni (1946–97) Italian fashion designer

VUITTON, Louis (1821–92) Swiss fashion designer

8

BURBERRY, Thomas (1835–1926) British fashion designer

FERRETTI, Alberta (1950–) Italian fashion designer

GALLIANO, John (1960–) British fashion designer

GAULTIER, Jean-Paul (1952–) French fashion designer

GIVENCHY, Hubert de (1927–2018) French fashion designer

HARTNELL, Norman (1901–79) British fashion designer

HILFIGER, Tommy (1951–) US fashion designer

OLDFIELD, Bruce (1950–) British fashion designer

WESTWOOD, Vivienne (1941–) British fashion designer

9

COURRÈGES, André (1923–2016) French fashion designer

DE LA RENTA, Oscar (1932–2014) Dominican fashion designer

FERRAGAMO, Salvatore (1898–1960) Italian fashion designer

LAGERFELD, Karl (1938–2019) German fashion designer

LOUBOUTIN, Christian (1964–) French fashion designer

MACDONALD, Julien (1972–) British fashion designer

MCCARTNEY, Stella (1971–) British fashion designer

VALENTINO (Garavani) (1932–) Italian fashion designer

10+

BALENCIAGA, Cristobal (1895–1972) Spanish fashion designer

SAINT-LAURENT, Yves (1936–2008) French fashion designer

SCHIAPARELLI, Elsa (1896–1973) Italian fashion designer

VON FURSTENBERG, Diane (1946–) Belgian fashion designer

ECONOMISTS

4

LIST, Friedrich (1789–1846; German economist)

MARX, Karl (Heinrich; (1818– 83; German philosopher, economist, and revolutionary)

WARD, Barbara, Baroness Jackson (1914–81; British economist and conservationist)

WEBB, Sidney (James), Baron Passfield (1859–1947; British economist and socialist)

5

DEFOE, Daniel (1660–1731; British novelist, economist, and journalist)

FOGEL, Robert William (1926– 2013; US historian and economist)

HAYEK, Friedrich August von (1899–1992; British economist)

KLEIN, Lawrence Robert (1920– 2013; US economist)

MEADE, James Edward (1907–95; British economist)

PASSY, Frédéric (1822–1912; French economist and politician)

PIGOU, Arthur Cecil (1877– 1954; British economist)

SMITH, Adam (1723–90; Scottish moral philosopher and political economist)

TOBIN, James (1918–2002; US economist)

6

ANGELL, Norman (1874– 1967; British author, economist, and Labour politician)

BARUCH, Bernard (1870–1965; US economist)

COBDEN, Richard (1804–65; British politician and economist)

DELORS, Jacques (Lucien Jean; (1925– ; French politician and economist)

ERHARD, Ludwig (1897–1977; German statesman and economist)

FRISCH, Ragnar (1895–1973; Norwegian economist)

JEVONS, William Stanley (1835–1882; British economist, logician, and statistician)

KEYNES, John Maynard, 1st Baron (1883–1946; British economist)

MONNET, Jean (1888–1979; French economist)

MYRDAL, Gunnar (1898–1987; Swedish sociologist and economist)

PARETO, Vilfredo (1848–1932; Italian economist and sociologist)

SHARPE, William Forsyth (1934– ; US economist)

TURGOT, Anne Robert Jacques, Baron de l'Aulne (1727–81; French economist)

7

BAGEHOT, Walter (1826–77; British economist, political theorist, literary critic, and journalist)

DIAMOND, Peter (1940– ; US economist)

KRUGMAN, Paul (1953– ; US economist)

KUZNETS, Simon (1901–85; US economist)

MALTHUS, Thomas Robert (1766–1834; British clergyman and economist)

QUESNAY, François (1694–1774; French economist)

RICARDO, David (1772–1823; British political economist)

TOYNBEE, Arnold (1852–83; British economist and philanthropist)

WOOTTON, Barbara, Baroness (1897–1988; British educationalist and economist

8

BECCARIA, Cesare Bonesana, Marchese de (1738–94; Italian legal theorist and political economist)

FRIEDMAN, Milton (1912–2006; US economist)

KAHNEMAN, Daniel (1934– ; Israeli economist)

MANSHOLT, Sicco (1908–95; Dutch politician and economist)

PHILLIPS, A W (1914–75; British economist)

STIGLITZ, Joseph (1943– ; US economist)

9

BEVERIDGE, William Henry Beveridge, 1st Baron (1879– 1963; British economist, writer, and academic)

GALBRAITH, John Kenneth (1908–2006; US economist)

GREENSPAN, Alan (1926– ; US economist)

MORTENSEN, Dale (1939–2014; US economist)

TINBERGEN, Jan (1903–94; Dutch economist)

10

SCHUMPETER, Joseph (1883–1950; Austrian-US economist)

NOBEL PRIZE WINNERS

PHYSICS

1901	W RÖNTGEN (GER)
1902	H ANTOON LORENTZ (NETH)
	P ZEEMAN (NETH)
1903	A BECQUEREL (FR)
	P CURIE (FR)
	M CURIE (FR)
1904	LORD RAYLEIGH (GB)
1905	P LENARD (GER)
1906	J J THOMSON (GB)
1907	A A MICHELSON (US)
1908	G LIPPMANN (FR)
1909	G MARCONI (ITALY)
	K BRAUN (GER)
1910	J VAN DER WAALS (NETH)
1911	W WIEN (GER)
1912	N G DALÉN (SWED)
1913	H KAMERLINGH ONNES (NETH)
1914	M VON LAUE (GER)
1915	W BRAGG (GB)
	L BRAGG (GB)
1916	(NO AWARD)
1917	C BARKLA (GB)
1918	M PLANCK (GER)
1919	J STARK (GER)
1920	C GUILLAUME (SWITZ)
1921	A EINSTEIN (SWITZ)
1922	N BOHR (DEN)
1923	R MILLIKAN (US)
1924	K SIEGBAHN (SWED)
1925	J FRANCK (GER)
	G HERTZ (GER)
1926	J PERRIN (FR)
1927	A H COMPTON (US)
	C WILSON (GB)
1928	O RICHARDSON (GB)
1929	PRINCE L DE BROGLIE (FR)
1930	C RAMAN (INDIA)
1931	(NO AWARD)
1932	W HEISENBERG (GER)
1933	P A M DIRAC (GB)
	E SCHRÖDINGER (AUSTRIA)
1934	(NO AWARD)
1935	J CHADWICK (GB)
1936	V HESS (AUSTRIA)
	C ANDERSON (US)
1937	C DAVISSON (US)
	G P THOMSON (GB)
1938	E FERMI (ITALY)
1939	E LAWRENCE (US)
1943	O STERN (US)
1944	I RABI (US)
1945	W PAULI (AUSTRIA)
1946	P BRIDGMAN (US)
1947	E APPLETON (GB)
1948	P BLACKETT (GB)
1949	H YUKAWA (JAPAN)
1950	C POWELL (GB)
1951	J COCKCROFT (GB)
	E WALTON (IRE)
1952	F BLOCH (US)
	E PURCELL (US)
1953	F ZERNIKE (NETH)
1954	M BORN (GB)
	W BOTHE (GER)
1955	W LAMB, JR (US)
	P KUSCH (US)
1956	W SHOCKLEY (US)
	J BARDEEN (US)
	W BRATTAIN (US)
1957	TSUNG-DAO LEE (CHINA)
	C N YANG (CHINA)
1958	P A CHERENKOV (USSR)
	I M FRANK (USSR)
	I Y TAMM (USSR)
1959	E SEGRÈ (US)
	O CHAMBERLAIN (US)
1960	D GLASER (US)
1961	R HOFSTADTER (US)
	R MÖSSBAUER (GER)
1962	L D LANDAU (USSR)
1963	J H D JENSEN (GER)
	M G MAYER (US)
	E P WIGNER (US)
1964	C H TOWNES (US)
	N G BASOV (USSR)
	A M PROKHOROV (USSR)
1965	J S SCHWINGER (US)
	R P FEYNMAN (US)
	S TOMONAGA (JAPAN)
1966	A KASTLER (FR)
1967	H A BETHE (US)
1968	L W ALVAREZ (US)
1969	M GELL-MANN (US)
1970	H ALVÉN (SWED)
	L NÉEL (FR)
1971	D GABOR (GB)
1972	J BARDEEN (US)
	L N COOPER (US)
	J R SCHRIEFFER (US)
1973	L ESAKI (JAPAN)
	I GIAEVER (US)
	B JOSEPHSON (GB)
1974	M RYLE (GB)
	A HEWISH (GB)
1975	J RAINWATER (US)
	A BOHR (DEN)
	B MOTTELSON (DEN)
1976	B RICHTER (US)
	S TING (US)
1977	P W ANDERSON (US)
	N F MOTT (GB)
	J H VAN VLECK (US)
1978	P L KAPITSA (USSR)
	A A PENZIAS (US)
	R W WILSON (US)
1979	S L GLASHOW (US)
	A SALAM (PAK)
	S WEINBERG (US)
1980	J CRONIN (US)

	V FITCH (US)
1981	K SIEGBAHN (SWED)
	N BLOEMBERGEN (US)
	A SCHAWLOW (US)
1982	K G WILSON (US)
1983	S CHANDRASEKHAR (US)
	W FOWLER (US)
1984	C RUBBIA (ITALY)
	S VAN DER MEER (NETH)
1985	K VON KLITZING (GER)
1986	E RUSKA (GER)
	G BINNIG (GER)
	H ROHRER (SWITZ)
1987	A MÜLLER (SWITZ)
	G BEDNORZ (GER)
1988	L M LEDERMAN (US)
	M SCHWARTZ (US)
	J STEINBERGER (GER)
1989	H DEHMELT (US)
	W PAULM (GER)
	N RAMSEY (US)
1990	J FRIEDMAN (US)
	H KENDALL (US)
	R TAYLOR (CAN)
1991	P De GENNES (FR)
1992	G CHARPAK (FR)
1993	R HULSE (US)
	J TAYLOR (US)
1994	B BROCKHOUE (CAN)
	C SHULL (US)
1995	M PERL (US)
	F REINES (US)
1996	D M LEE (US)
	D D OSCHEROF (US)
	R C RICHARDSON (US)
1997	S CHU (US)
1998	R B LAUGHLIN (US)
	H L STÖRMER (GER)
	D C TSUI (US)
1999	G 't HOOFT (NETH)
	M J G VELTMAN (NETH)
2000	Z I ALFEROV (RUS)
	H KOEMER (GER)
	J S KILBY (US)
2001	E A CORNELL (US)
	W KETTERLE (GER)
	C E WIEMAN (US)
2002	R DAVIS JR (US)
	M KOSHIBA (JAPAN)
	R GIACCONI (US)
2004	A A ABRIKOSOV (US)
	V L GINZBURG (RUS)
	A J LEGGETT (US)
2005	R J GLAUBER (US)
	J L HALL (US)
	T W HÄNSCH (GER)
2006	J C MATHER (US)
	G F SMOOT (US)
2007	A FERT (FR)
	P GRÜNBERG (GER)
2008	Y NAMBU (JAPAN)
	M KOBAYASHI (JAPAN)
	T MASKAWA (JAPAN)

2009	C K KAO (CHINA)
	W S BOYLE (CAN)
	G E SMITH (US)
2010	A GEIM (USSR)
	K NOVOSELOV (USSR)
2011	S PERLMUTTER (US)
	A G REISS (US)
	B P SCHMIDT (US)
2012	S HAROCHE (FR)
	D WINELAND (US)
2013	F ENGLERT (BELG)
	P HIGGS (GB)
2014	I AKASAKI (JAPAN)
	H AMANO (JAPAN)
	S NAKAMURA (JAPAN)
2015	T KAJITA (JAPAN)
	A MCDONALD (CAN)
2016	D THOULESS (GB)
	D HALDANE (GB)
	J KOSTERLITZ (US)
2017	R WEISS (US)
	B BARISH (US)
	K THORNE (US)
2018	A ASHKIN (US)
	G MOUROU (FR)
	D STRICKLAND (CAN)

CHEMISTRY

1901	J V HOFF (NETH)
1902	E FISCHER (GER)
1903	S ARRHENIUS (SWED)
1904	W RAMSAY (GB)
1905	A VON BAEYER (GER)
1906	H MOISSAN (FR)
1907	E BUCHNER (GER)
1908	LORD RUTHERFORD (GB)
1909	W OSTWALD (GER)
1910	O WALLACH (GER)
1911	M CURIE (FR)
1912	V GRIGNARD (FR)
	P SABATIER (FR)
1913	A WERNER (SWITZ)
1914	T RICHARDS (US)
1915	R WILLSTÄTTER (GER)
1916	(NO AWARD)
1917	(NO AWARD)
1918	F HABER (GER)
1919	(NO AWARD)
1920	W NERNST (GER)
1921	F SODDY (GB)
1922	F ASTON (GB)
1923	F PREGL (AUSTRIA)
1924	(NO AWARD)
1925	R ZSIGMONDY (AUSTRIA)
1926	T SVEDBERG (SWED)
1927	H WIELAND (GER)
1928	A WINDAUS (GER)
1929	A HARDEN (GB)
	H VON EULER-CHELPIN (SWED)
1930	H FISCHER (GER)
1931	K BOSCH (GER)
	F BERGIUS (GER)
1932	I LANGMUIR (US)

1933	(NO AWARD)	1980	P BERG (US)
1934	H UREY (US)		W GILBERT (US)
1935	F JOLIOT-CURIE (FR)		F SANGER (GB)
	I JOLIOT-CURIE (FR)	1981	K FUKUI (JAPAN)
1936	P DEBYE (NETH)		R HOFFMANN (POL)
1937	W HAWORTH (GB)	1982	A KLUG (GB)
	P KARRER (SWITZ)	1983	H TAUBE (US)
1938	R KUHN (GER)	1984	R B MERRIFIELD (US)
1939	A BUTENANDT (GER)	1985	H HAUPTMAN (US)
	L RUZICKA (SWITZ)		J KARLE (US)
1943	G DE HEVESY (HUNG)	1986	D HERSCHBACH (US)
1944	O HAHN (GER)		Y TSEH LEE (US)
1945	A VIRTANEN (FIN)		J POLANYI (CAN)
1946	J SUMNER (US)	1987	D CRAM (US)
	J NORTHROP (US)		J LEHN (FR)
	W STANLEY (US)		C PEDERSEN (US)
1947	R ROBINSON (GB)	1988	J DIESENHOFER (GER)
1948	A TISELIUS (SWED)		R HUBER (GER)
1949	W GIAUQUE (US)		H MICHEL (GER)
1950	O DIELS (GER)	1989	S ALTMAN (US)
	K ALDER (GER)		T CECH (US)
1951	E MCMILLAN (US)	1990	E CORY (US)
	G SEABORG (US)	1991	R ERNST (SWITZ)
1952	A MARTIN (GB)	1992	R MARCUS (CAN)
	R SYNGE (GB)	1993	K MULLIS (US)
1953	H STAUDINGER (GER)		M SMITH (US)
1954	L C PAULING (US)	1994	G OLAH (US)
1955	V DU VIGNEAUD (US)	1995	P CRUTZEN (NETH)
1956	N SEMYONOV (USSR)		M MOLINA (MEX)
	C HINSHELWOOD (GB)		F ROWLAND (US)
1957	A TODD (GB)	1996	H KROTO (GB)
1958	F SANGER (GB)		R CURL (US)
1959	J HEYROVSKY (CZECH)		R SMALLEY (US)
1960	W LIBBY (US)	1997	P D BOYER (US)
1961	M CALVIN (US)		J C SKOU (DEN)
1962	J C KENDREW (GB)		J E WALKER (GB)
	M F PERUTZ (GB)	1998	W KOHN (US)
1963	G NATTA (ITALY)		J A POPE (GB)
	K ZIEGLER (GER)	1999	A H ZEWAIL (EGYPT & US)
1964	D M C HODGKIN (GB)	2000	A J HEEGER (US)
1965	R B WOODWARD (US)		A G MACDIARMID (US)
1966	R S MULLIKEN (US)		H SHIRAKAWA (JAPAN)
1967	M EIGEN (GER)	2001	W S KNOWLES (US)
	R G W NORRISH (GB)		R NOYORI (JAPAN)
	G PORTER (GB)		K B SHARPLESS (US)
1968	L ONSAGER (US)	2002	J B FENN (US)
1969	D H R BARTON (GB)		K TANAKA (JAPAN)
	O HASSEL (NOR)		K WUTHRICH (SWITZ)
1970	L F LELOIR (ARG)	2003	P AGRE (US)
1971	G HERZBERG (CAN)		R MACKINNON (US)
1972	C B ANFINSEN (US)	2004	A CIECHANOVER (ISRAEL)
	S MOORE (US)		A HERSHKO (ISRAEL)
	W H STEIN (US)		I ROSE (US)
1973	E FISCHER (GER)	2005	Y CHAUVIN (FR)
	G WILKINSON (GB)		R H GRUBBS (US)
1974	P J FLORY (US)		R R SCHROCK (US)
1975	J W CORNFORT (AUSTR)	2006	R D KORNBERG (US)
	V PRELOG (SWITZ)	2007	G ERTL (GER)
1976	W M LIPSCOMB (US)	2008	O SHIMOMURA (JAPAN)
1977	I PRIGOGINE (BELGIUM)		M CHALFIE (US)
1978	P MITCHELL (GB)		R Y TSIEN (US)
1979	H C BROWN (US)	2009	V RAMAKRISHNAN (US)
	G WITTIG (GER)		T A STEITZ (US)

2010	A E YONATH (ISRAEL)
	R HECK (US)
	E NEGISHI (JAPAN)
	A SUZUKI (JAPAN)
2011	D SHECHTMAN (ISRAEL)
2012	B KOBILKA (US)
	R LEFKOWITZ (US)
2013	M KARPLUS (US)
	M LEVITT (ISRAEL)
	A WARSHEL (US)
2014	E BETZIG (US)
	S HELL (ROM)
	W MOERNER (US)
2015	T LINDAHI (SWED)
	P MODRICH (US)
	A SANCAR (TUR)
2016	J SAUVAGE (FR)
	F STODDART (GB)
	B FERINGA (NETH)
2017	J DUBOCHET (SWITZ)
	J FRANK (GER)
	R HENDERSON (GB)

PHYSIOLOGY OR MEDICINE

1901	E VON BEHRING (GER)
1902	R ROSS (GB)
1903	N R FINSEN (DEN)
1904	I PAVLOV (RUSS)
1905	R KOCH (GER)
1906	C GOLGI (ITALY)
	S RAMÓN Y CAJAL (SPAIN)
1907	A LAVERAN (FR)
1908	P EHRLICH (GER)
	I MECHNIKOV (RUSS)
1909	E KOCHER (SWITZ)
1910	A KOSSEL (GER)
1911	A GULLSTRAND (SWED)
1912	A CARREL (FR)
1913	C RICHET (FR)
1914	R BÁRÁNY (AUSTRIA)
1915	(NO AWARD)
1916	(NO AWARD)
1917	(NO AWARD)
1919	J BORDET (BELG)
1920	A KROGH (DEN)
1921	(NO AWARD)
1922	A V HILL (GB)
	O MEYERHOF (GER)
1923	F G BANTING (CAN)
	J J R MACLEOD (GB)
1924	W EINTHOVEN (NETH)
1925	(NO AWARD)
1926	J FIBIGER (DEN)
1927	J W VON JAUREGG (AUSTRIA)
1928	C NICOLLE (FR)
1929	C EIJKMAN (NETH)
	F HOPKINS (GB)
1930	K LANDSTEINER (US)
1931	O WARBURG (GER)
1932	E D ADRIAN (GB)
	C SHERRINGTON (GB)
1933	T H MORGAN (US)
1934	G R MINOT (US)

	W P MURPHY (US)
	G H WHIPPLE (US)
1935	H SPEMANN (GER)
1936	H H DALE (GB)
	O LOEWI (GER)
1937	A SZENT-GYÖRGYI (HUNG)
1938	C HEYMANS (BELG)
1939	G DOMAGK (GER)
1943	H DAM (DEN)
	E A DOISY (US)
1944	J ERLANGER (US)
	H S GASSER (US)
1945	A FLEMING (GB)
	E B CHAIN (GB)
	LORD FLOREY (AUSTR)
1946	H J MULLER (US)
1947	C F CORI (US)
	G T CORI (US)
	B HOUSSAY (ARG)
1948	P MÜLLER (SWITZ)
1949	W R HESS (SWITZ)
	A E MONIZ (PORT)
1950	P S HENCH (US)
	E C KENDALL (US)
	T REICHSTEIN (SWITZ)
1951	M THEILER (S AF)
1952	S A WAKSMAN (US)
1953	F A LIPMANN (US)
	H A KREBS (GB)
1954	J F ENDERS (US)
	T H WELLER (US)
	F ROBBINS (US)
1955	A H THEORELL (SWED)
1956	W FORSSMANN (GER)
	D RICHARDS (US)
	A F COURNAND (US)
1957	D BOVET (ITALY)
1958	G W BEADLE (US)
	E L TATUM (US)
	J LEDERBERG (US)
1959	S OCHOA (US)
	A KORNBERG (US)
1960	F MACFARLANE BURNET (AUSTR)
	P B MEDAWAR (GB)
1961	G VON BÉKÉSY (US)
1962	F H C CRICK (GB)
	J D WATSON (US)
	M WILKINS (GB)
1963	J C ECCLES (AUSTR)
	A L HODGKIN (GB)
	A F HUXLEY (GB)
1964	K BLOCH (US)
	F LYNEN (GER)
1965	F JACOB (FR)
	A LWOFF (FR)
	J MONOD (FR)
1966	C B HUGGINS (US)
	F P ROUS (US)
1967	H K HARTLINE (US)
	G WALD (US)
	R A GRANIT (SWED)
1968	R W HOLLEY (US)
	H G KHORANA (US)

1969	M W NIRENBERG (US)
	M DELBRÜCK (US)
	A D HERSHEY (US)
	S E LURIA (US)
1970	J AXELROD (US)
	B KATZ (GB)
	U VON EULER (SWED)
1971	E W SUTHERLAND, JR (US)
1972	G M EDELMAN (US)
	R R PORTER (GB)
1973	K VON FRISCH (GER)
	K LORENZ (GER)
	N TINBERGEN (NETH)
1974	A CLAUDE (US)
	C DE DUVE (BELG)
	G E PALADE (BELG)
1975	D BALTIMORE (US)
	R DULBECCO (US)
	H M TEMIN (US)
1976	B S BLUMBERG (US)
	D G GAJDUSEK (US)
1977	R S YALOW (US)
	R GUILLEMIN (US)
	A V SCHALLY (US)
1978	W ARBER (SWITZ)
	D NATHANS (US)
	H SMITH (US)
1979	A M CORMACK (US)
	G N HOUNSFIELD (GB)
1980	G SNELL (US)
	J DAUSSET (FR)
	B BENACERRAF (US)
1981	R SPERRY (US)
	D HUBEL (US)
	T WIESEL (SWED)
1982	S K BERGSTROM (SWED)
	B I SAMUELSON (SWED)
	J R VANE (GB)
1983	B MCCLINTOCK (US)
1984	N K JERNE (DEN)
	G J F KÖHLER (GER)
	C MILSTEIN (GB)
1985	J GOLDSTEIN (US)
	M BROWN (US)
1986	S COHEN (US)
	R LEVI-MONTALCINI (ITALY)
1987	S TONEGAWA (JAPAN)
1988	J W BLACK (GB)
	G B ELION (US)
	G H HITCHINGS (US)
1989	M BISHOP (US)
	H VARMUS (US)
1990	J MURRAY (US)
	E THOMAS (US)
1991	E NEHER (GER)
	B SAKMANN (GER)
1992	E FISCHER (US)
	E KREBS (US)
1993	R ROBERTS (US)
	P SHARP (US)
1994	A GILMAN (US)
	M RODBELL (US)
1995	E LEWIS (US)

	C NÜESSLEIN-VOLHARD (GER)
	E WIESCHAUS (US)
1996	P DOHERTY (AUSTR)
	R ZINKERNAGEL (SWITZ)
1997	S B PRUSINER (US)
1998	R F FURCHGOTT (US)
	L J IGNARRO (US)
	F MURAD (US)
1999	G BLOBEL (US)
2000	A CARLSSON (SWED)
	P GREENGARD (US)
	E R KANDEL (US)
2001	L H HARTWELL (US)
	R T HUNT (GB)
	P M NURSE (GB)
2002	S BRENNER (GB)
	H R HORVITZ (GB)
	J E SULSTON (GB)
2003	P C LAUTERUR (US)
	P MANSFIELD (GB)
2004	R AXEL (US)
	L B BUCK (US)
2005	B MARSHALL (AUSTRALIA)
	R WARREN (AUSTRALIA)
2006	A FIRE (US)
	C MELLO (US)
2007	M CAPECCHI (US)
	M EVANS (GB)
	O SMITHIES (GB)
2008	H Z HAUSEN (GER)
	F BARRÈ-SINOUSSI (FR)
	L MONTAGNIER (FR)
2009	E BLACKBURN (AUSTRALIA)
	C W GREIDER (US)
	J W SZOSTAK (US)
2010	R G EDWARDS (GB)
2011	B BEUTLER (US)
	J A HOFFMANN (FR)
	R M STEINMAN (CAN)
2012	J GURDON (GB)
	S YAMANAKA (JAPAN)
2013	J ROTHMAN (US)
	R SCHEKMAN (US)
	T SUDHOF (GER)
2014	J O'KEEFE (US)
	M MOSER (NOR)
	E MOSER (NOR)
2015	W CAMPBELL (IRE)
	S OMURA (JAPAN)
	T YOUYOU (CHINA)
2016	Y ONSUMI (JAPAN)
2017	J HALL (US)
	M ROSBASH (US)
	M YOUNG (US)

LITERATURE

1901	S PRUDHOMME (FR)
1902	T MOMMSEN (GER)
1903	B BJØRNSON (NOR)
1904	F MISTRAL (FR)
	J ECHEGARAY Y EIZAGUIRRE (SPAIN)
1905	H SIENKIEWICZ (POL)
1906	G CARDUCCI (ITALY)

1907	R KIPLING (GB)
1908	R EUCKEN (GER)
1909	S LAGERLÖF (SWED)
1910	P VON HEYSE (GER)
1911	M MAETERLINCK (BELG)
1912	G HAUPTMANN (GER)
1913	R TAGORE (INDIA)
1914	(NO AWARD)
1915	R ROLLAND (FR)
1916	V VON HEIDENSTAM (SWED)
1917	K GJELLERUP (DEN)
	H PONTOPPIDAN (DEN)
1919	C SPITTELER (SWITZ)
1920	K HAMSUN (NOR)
1921	A FRANCE (FR)
1922	J BENAVENTE Y MARTINEZ
	(SPAIN)
1923	W B YEATS (IRE)
1924	W S REYMONT (POL)
1925	G B SHAW (IRE)
1926	G DELEDDA (ITALY)
1927	H BERGSON (FR)
1928	S UNDSET (NOR)
1929	T MANN (GER)
1930	S LEWIS (US)
1931	E A KARLFELDT (SWED)
1932	J GALSWORTHY (GB)
1933	I BUNIN (USSR)
1934	L PIRANDELLO (ITALY)
1935	(NO AWARD)
1936	E O'NEILL (US)
1937	R M DU GARD (FR)
1938	P BUCK (US)
1939	F E SILLANPÄÄ (FIN)
1940	(NO AWARD)
1941	(NO AWARD)
1942	(NO AWARD)
1943	(NO AWARD)
1944	J V JENSEN (DEN)
1945	G MISTRAL (CHILE)
1946	H HESSE (SWITZ)
1947	A GIDE (FR)
1948	T S ELIOT (GB)
1949	W FAULKNER (US)
1950	B RUSSELL (GB)
1951	P F LAGERKVIST (SWED)
1952	F MAURIAC (FR)
1953	W CHURCHILL (GB)
1954	E HEMINGWAY (US)
1955	H K LAXNESS (ICE)
1956	J R JIMÉNEZ (SPAIN)
1957	A CAMUS (FR)
1958	B L PASTERNAK (DECLINED
	AWARD) (USSR)
1959	S QUASIMODO (ITALY)
1960	S J PERSE (FR)
1961	I ANDRIĆ (YUGOS)
1962	J STEINBECK (US)
1963	G SEFERIS (GR)
1964	J-P SARTRE (DECLINED AWARD) (FR)
1965	M SHOLOKHOV (USSR)
1966	S Y AGNON (ISR)
	N SACHS (SWED)

1967	M A ASTURIAS (GUAT)
1968	K YASUNARI (JAPAN)
1969	S BECKETT (IRE)
1970	A I SOLZHENITSYN (USSR)
1971	P NERUDA (CHILE)
1972	H BÖLL (GER)
1973	P WHITE (AUSTR)
1974	E JOHNSON (SWED)
	H MARTINSON (SWED)
1975	E MONTALE (ITALY)
1976	S BELLOW (US)
1977	S ALEIXANDRE (SPAIN)
1978	I B SINGER (US)
1979	O ELYTIS (GREECE)
1980	C MILOSZ (US)
1981	E CANETTI (BULG)
1982	G GARCIA MARQUEZ (COLOMBIA)
1983	W GOLDING (GB)
1984	J SEIFERT (CZECH)
1985	C SIMON (FR)
1986	W SOYINKA (NIGERIA)
1987	J BRODSKY (US)
1988	N MAHFOUZ (EGYPT)
1989	C J CELA (SPAIN)
1990	O PAZ (MEX)
1991	N GORDIMER (S AF)
1992	D WALCOTT (ST LUCIA)
1993	T MORRISON (US)
1994	KENSABURO OË (JAPAN)
1995	S HEANEY (IRE)
1996	W SZYMBORSKA (POL)
1997	D FO (ITALY)
1998	J SARAMAGO (PORT)
1999	G GRASS (GER)
2000	G XINGJIAN (FRANCE)
2001	V S NAIPAUL (GB)
2002	I KERTESZ (HUNGARY)
2003	J M COETZEE (SA)
2004	E JELINEK (AUS)
2005	H PINTER (GB)
2006	O PARNUK (TURK)
2007	D LESSING (GB)
2008	J GUSTAVE LE CLÈZIO (FR)
2009	H MÜLLER (GER)
2010	M VARGAS LLOSA (SPAIN)
2011	T TRANSTÖMER (SWE)
2012	M YAN (CHINA)
2013	A MUNRO (CAN)
2014	P MODIANO (FR)
2015	S ALEXIEVICH (RUS)
2016	B DYLAN (US)
2017	K ISHIGURO (GB)

PEACE

1901	J H DUNANT (SWITZ)
	F PASSY (FR)
1902	E DUCOMMUN (SWITZ)
	C A GOBAT (SWITZ)
1903	W CREMER (GB)
1904	INSTITUTE OF INTERNATIONAL
	LAW (FOUNDED, 1873)
1905	BARONESS VON SUTTNER
	(AUSTRIA)
1906	T ROOSEVELT (US)

1907	E TEODORO MONETA (ITALY)
	L RENAULT (FR)
1908	K P ARNOLDSON (SWED)
1909	BARON D'ESTOURNELLES DE
	CONSTANT (FR)
	A BEERNAERT (BELG)
1910	INTERNATIONAL PEACE BUREAU
	(FOUNDED, 1891)
1911	T ASSER (NETH)
	A FRIED (AUSTRIA)
1912	E ROOT (US)
1913	H LAFONTAINE (BELG)
1914	(NO AWARD)
1915	(NO AWARD)
1916	(NO AWARD)
1917	INTERNATIONAL RED CROSS
	COMMITTEE (FOUNDED, 1863)
1918	(NO AWARD)
1919	W WILSON (US)
1920	L BOURGEOIS (FR)
1921	K BRANTING (SWED)
	C L LANGE (NOR)
1922	F NANSEN (NOR)
1923	(NO AWARD)
1924	(NO AWARD)
1925	A CHAMBERLAIN (GB)
	C G DAWES (US)
1926	A BRIAND (FR)
	G STRESEMANN (GER)
1927	F BUISSON (FR)
	L QUIDDE (GER)
1928	(NO AWARD)
1929	F B KELLOGG (US)
1930	N SÖDERBLOM (SWED)
1931	J ADDAMS (US)
	N M BUTLER (US)
1932	(NO AWARD)
1933	N ANGELL (GB)
1934	A HENDERSON (GB)
1935	C VON OSSIETZKY (GER)
1936	C S LAMAS (ARG)
1937	VISCOUNT CECIL OF CHELWOOD
(GB)	
1938	NANSEN INTERNATIONAL OFFICE
	FOR REFUGEES (FOUNDED, 1931)
1939	(NO AWARD)
1940	(NO AWARD)
1941	(NO AWARD)
1942	(NO AWARD)
1943	(NO AWARD)
1944	INTERNATIONAL RED CROSS
	COMMITTEE (FOUNDED, 1863)
1945	C HULL (US)
1946	E G BALCH (US)
	J R MOTT (US)
1947	AMERICAN FRIENDS' SERVICE
	COMMITTEE (US)
	FRIENDS' SERVICE COUNCIL
	(LONDON)
1948	(NO AWARD)
1949	LORD BOYD-ORR (GB)
1950	R BUNCHE (US)
1951	L JOUHAUX (FR)

1952	A SCHWEITZER (FR)
1953	G C MARSHALL (US)
1954	OFFICE OF THE UNITED NATIONS
	HIGH COMMISSIONER FOR
	REFUGEES (FOUNDED, 1951)
1955	(NO AWARD)
1956	(NO AWARD)
1957	L B PEARSON (CAN)
1958	D G PIRE (BELG)
1959	P J NOEL-BAKER (GB)
1960	A J LUTHULI (S AF)
1961	D HAMMARSKJÖLD (SWED)
1962	L C PAULING (US)
1963	INTERNATIONAL RED CROSS
	COMMITTEE (FOUNDED, 1863)
	LEAGUE OF RED CROSS SOCIETIES
	(GENEVA)
1964	M LUTHER KING, JR (US)
1965	UNITED NATIONS CHILDREN'S
	FUND (FOUNDED, 1946)
1966	(NO AWARD)
1967	(NO AWARD)
1968	R CASSIN (FR)
1969	INTERNATIONAL LABOUR
	ORGANISATION (FOUNDED, 1919)
1970	N E BORLAUG (US)
1971	W BRANDT (GER)
1972	(NO AWARD)
1973	H KISSINGER (US)
	LE DUC THO (DECLINED AWARD)
	(N VIET)
1974	S MACBRIDE (IRE)
	E SATO (JAPAN)
1975	A S SAKHAROV (USSR)
1976	MRS B WILLIAMS (N IRE)
	MISS M CORRIGAN (N IRE)
1977	AMNESTY INTERNATIONAL
	(FOUNDED IN UK, 1961)
1978	A SADAT (EGYPT)
	M BEGIN (ISR)
1979	MOTHER TERESA (YUGOS)
1980	A P ESQUIVEL (ARG)
1981	OFFICE OF THE U N HIGH
	COMMISSION FOR REFUGEES
	(FOUNDED, 1951)
1982	A GARCIA ROBLES (MEX)
	MRS A MYRDAL (SWED)
1983	L WALESA (POL)
1984	BISHOP D TUTU (S AF)
1985	INTERNATIONAL PHYSICIANS FOR
	THE PREVENTION OF NUCLEAR
	WAR (FOUNDED, 1980)
1986	E WIESEL (US)
1987	OSCAR ARIAS SÁNCHEZ (COSTA
	RICA)
1988	THE UNITED NATIONS PEACE-
	KEEPING FORCES
1989	DALAI LAMA (TIBET)
1990	M GORBACHOV (RUSS)
1991	A SAN SUU KYI (BURMESE)
1992	R MENCHU
1993	F W DE KLERK (S AF)
	N MANDELA (S AF)

1994	Y ARAFAT (PALESTINE)	1982	G J STIGLER (US)
	S PERES (ISR)	1983	G DEBREU (US)
	Y RABIN (ISR)	1984	R STONE (GB)
1995	J ROTBLAT (GB)	1985	F MODIGLIANI (US)
1996	J RAMOS-HORTA (E TIMOR)	1986	J M BUCHANAN, JR (US)
	C BELO (E TIMOR)	1987	R M SOLOW (US)
1997	THE INTERNATIONAL CAMPAIGN	1988	M ALLAIS (FR)
	TO BAN LANDMINES	1989	T HAAVELMO (NOR)
1998	J HUME (N IRE)	1990	H MARKOWITZ (US)
	D TRIMBLE (N IRE)		W F SHARPE (US)
1999	MÉDICINS SANS FRONTIÈRES		M MILLER (US)
2000	K DAE-JUNG (SOUTH KOREA)	1991	R H COASE (GB)
2001	UNITED NATIONS	1992	G S BECKER (US)
	K ANNAN (GHANA)	1993	R FOGEL (US)
2002	J CARTER (US)		D NORTH (US)
2003	S EBADI (IRAN)	1994	J HARSANYI (US)
2004	W MAATHAI (AFRICA)		J NASH (US)
2005	INTERNATIONAL ATOMIC ENERGY		R SELTON (GER)
	AGENCY	1995	R LUCAS (US)
	MUHAMED EL BARADEI (EGYPT)	1996	J MIRRLEES (GB)
2006	M YUNUS (BANGLADESHI)		W VICKREY (CAN)
	GRAMEEN BANK	1997	R C MERTON (US)
2007	INTERGOVERNMENTAL PANEL ON		M S SCHOLES (US)
	CLIMATE CHANGE	1998	A SEN (INDIA)
	A GORE (US)	1999	R A MUNDELL (CAN)
2008	M AHTISAARI (FIN)	2000	J J HECKMAN (US)
2009	B OBAMA (US)		D L MCFADDEN (US)
2010	L XIABO (CHINA)	2001	G A AKERLOF (US)
2011	E J SIRLEAF (AFRICA)		A M SPENCE (US)
	L GBOWEE (ARFICA)		J E STIGLITZ (US)
	T KARMAN (YEMENI)	2002	D KAHNEMAN (US)
2012	EUROPEAN UNION		V L SMITH
2013	ORGANISATION FOR THE	2003	R F ENGLE (US)
	PROHIBITION OF CHEMICAL		C W J GRANGER (GB)
	WEAPONS	2004	F E KYDLAND (NORWAY)
2014	K SATYARTHI (INDIA)		E C PRESCOTT (US)
	M YOUSAFZAI (PAK)	2005	R AUMANN (US)
2015	NATIONAL DIALOGUE QUARTET (TUN)		T SCHELLING (US)
2016	J SANTOS (COLOMBIA)	2006	E PHELPS (US)
2017	INTERNATIONAL CAMPAIGN TO	2007	L HURKICZ (USSR)
	ABOLISH NUCLEAR WEAPONS		E MASKIN (US)
2018	D MUKWEGE (DRC)		R MYERSON (US)
	N MURAD (IRAQ)	2008	P KRUGMAN (US)
		2009	E OSTROM (US)

ECONOMICS

			O E WILLIAMSON (US)
1969	R FRISCH (NOR)	2010	P A DIAMOND (US)
	J TINBERGEN (NETH)		D T MORTENSEN (US)
1970	P A SAMUELSON (US)		C A PISSARIDES (GREEK)
1971	S KUZNETS (US)	2011	T J SARGENT (US)
1972	R HICKS (GB)		C A SIMS (US)
	K J ARROW (US)	2012	A ROTH (US)
1973	W LEONTIEF (US)		L SHAPLEY (US)
1974	G MYRDAL (SWED)	2013	E FAMA (US)
	F A VON HAYEK (GB)		L HANSEN (US)
1975	L KANTOROVICH (USSR)		R SHILLER (US)
	T C KOOPMANS (US)	2014	J TIROLE (FR)
1976	M FRIEDMAN (US)	2015	A DEATON (GB)
1977	B OHLIN (SWED)	2016	O HART (GB)
	J E MEADE (GB)		B HOLSTROM (FIN)
1978	H A SIMON (US)	2017	R THALER (US)
1979	T W SCHULTZ (US)	2018	W NORDHAUS (US)
	A LEWIS (GB)		P ROMER (US)
1980	L R KLEIN (US)		
1981	J TOBIN (US)		

EXPLORERS, PIONEERS, AND ADVENTURERS

4

AEBI, Tania (1966–   ; US sailor)

BYRD, Richard E (1888–1957; US explorer)

CANO, Juan Sebastián del (c. 1460–1526; Spanish navigator)

COOK, Captain James (1728–79; British navigator)

DIAS, Bartolomeu (c. 1450–c. 1500; Portuguese navigator)

EYRE, Edward John (1815–1901; British explorer)

GAMA, Vasco da (c. 1469– 1524; Portuguese navigator)

HUME, Hamilton (1797–1873; Australian explorer)

HUNT, John, Baron (1910–98; British mountaineer)

KIDD, William (c. 1645–1701; Scottish sailor)

PARK, Mungo (1771–c. 1806; Scottish explorer)

POLO, Marco (c. 1254–1324; Venetian traveller)

ROSS, James Clark (1800–62; British explorer)

SOTO, Hernando de (?1496– 1542; Spanish explorer)

5

BAKER, Samuel White (1821–93; British explorer)

BARTH, Heinrich (1821–65; German explorer and geographer)

BOONE, Daniel (1734–1820; American pioneer)

BRUCE, James (1730–94; British explorer)

BURKE, Robert O'Hara (1820–61; Irish explorer)

CABOT, John (Giovanni Caboto, c. 1450–c. 1499; Italian explorer)

DAVIS, John (or J Davys c. 1550–1605; English navigator)

DICKS, David (1978–   ; Australian sailor)

FOGLE, Ben (1973–   ; British adventurer)

FUCHS, Vivian (1908–99; British explorer)

LAIRD, Macgregor (1808–61; Scottish explorer)

OATES, Lawrence Edward Grace (1880–1912; British explorer)

OÑATE, Juan de (d. 1630; Spanish conquistador)

PARRY, William Edward (1790–1855; British navigator)

PEARY, Robert Edwin (1856–1920; US explorer)

SCOTT, Robert Falcon (1868–1912; British explorer)

SMITH, Dick (1944–   ; Australian adventurer)

SPEKE, John Hanning (1827–64; British explorer)

STURT, Charles (1795–1869; British explorer)

TEACH, Edward (d. 1718; British pirate)

6

ALCOCK, John (1892–1919; British aviator)

BAFFIN, William (c. 1584– 1622; English navigator)

BALBOA, Vasco Núñez de (c. 1475–1517; Spanish explorer)

BERING, Vitus Jonassen (1681–1741; Danish navigator)

BRAZZA, Pierre Paul François Camille Savorgnan de (1852–1905; French explorer)

BROOKE, James (1803–68; British explorer)

BURTON, Richard (1821–90; British explorer)

CABRAL, Pedro Álvares (?1467–1520; Portuguese navigator)

CARSON, Kit (Christopher C, 1809–68; US frontiersman)

CORTÉS, Hernán (1485–1547; Spanish conquistador)

EDGLEY, Ross (1985–   ; British adventurer)

GRYLLS, Bear (1974–   ; British adventurer)

HUDSON, Henry (d. 1611; English navigator)

MORGAN, Henry (c. 1635–88; Welsh buccaneer)

NANSEN, Fridtjof (1861–1930; Norwegian explorer)

NOBILE, Umberto (1885–1978; Italian aviator)

STUART, John McDouall (1815–66; Scottish explorer)

TASMAN, Abel Janszoon (c. 1603–c. 1659; Dutch navigator)

7

BARENTS, Willem (c. 1550–97; Dutch navigator)

BLÉRIOT, Louis (1872–1936; French aviator)

BRANSON, Richard, Sir (1950–   ; British entrepreneur and adventurer)

CARPINI, Giovanni da Pian del (c. 1180–c. 1252; Italian traveller)

CARTIER, Jacques (1491– 1557; French navigator)

CÓRDOBA, Francisco Fernández de (d. 1518; Spanish explorer)

COVILHÃ, Pêro da (c. 1460–c. 1526; Portuguese explorer)

DAMPIER, William (c. 1652–1715; English explorer)

EARHART, Amelia (1898–1937; US aviator)

FIENNES, Ranulph, Sir (1944–   ; British explorer)

FRÉMONT, John C (1813–90; US explorer)

GILBERT, Humphrey (c. 1539–83; English navigator)

HAWKINS, John (1532–95; English navigator)

HILLARY, Edmund (1919–2008; New Zealand mountaineer and explorer)

HINKLER, Herbert John Lewis (1892–1933; Australian aviator)

LA SALLE, Robert Cavelier, Sieur de (1643–87; French explorer)

MCCLURE, Robert John Le Mesurier (1807–73; Irish explorer)

PIZARRO, Francisco (c. 1475–1541; Spanish conquistador)

PYTHEAS (4th century BC; Greek navigator)

RALEIGH, Walter (1554–1618; British explorer)

SELKIRK, Alexander (1676–1721; Scottish sailor)

STANLEY, Henry Morton (1841–1904; British explorer)

WILKINS, George Hubert (1888–1958; British explorer)

WRANGEL, Ferdinand Petrovich, Baron von (1794–1870; Russian explorer)

8

AMUNDSEN, Roald (1872– 1928; Norwegian explorer)

COLUMBUS, Christopher (1451–1506; Italian navigator)

COUSTEAU, Jacques Yves (1910–97; French underwater explorer)

FLINDERS, Matthew (1774– 1814; British navigator and hydrographer)

FRANKLIN, John (1786–1847; British explorer)

MAGELLAN, Ferdinand (c. 1480–1521; Portuguese explorer)

MARCHAND, Jean Baptiste (1863–1934; French explorer)

STAFFORD, Ed (1975–   ; British explorer)

VESPUCCI, Amerigo (1454–1512; Italian navigator)

9

BLANCHARD, Jean Pierre François (1753–1809; French balloonist)

CHAMPLAIN, Samuel de (1567–1635; French explorer)

FROBISHER, Martin (c. 1535–94; English navigator)

HEYERDAHL, Thor (1914–2002; Norwegian ethnologist)

IBERVILLE, Pierre Le Moyne, Sieur d' (1661–1706; French-Canadian explorer)

LEICHARDT, Ludwig (1813–48; German explorer)

LINDBERGH, Charles A (1902–74; US aviator)

MACARTHUR, Ellen, Dame (1976–   ; British sailor)

MARQUETTE, Jacques (1637–75; French explorer)

PAUSANIAS (2nd century AD; Greek traveller)

RASMUSSEN, Knud Johan Victor (1879–1933; Danish explorer)

VANCOUVER, George (c. 1758–98; British navigator)

VELÁSQUEZ, Diego (?1465–1522; Spanish explorer)

10

BARBAROSSA (Khayr ad-Din, d. 1546; Turkish pirate)

ERIC THE RED (late 10th century; Norwegian explorer)

SHACKLETON, Ernest Henry (1874–1922; British explorer)

11

IBN BATTUTAH (1304–?1368; Arab traveller)

LA CONDAMINE, Charles Marie de (1701–74; French geographer)

LIVINGSTONE, David (1813–73;

Scottish missionary and explorer)

PONCE DE LEON, Juan (1460–1521; Spanish explorer)

12

BOUGAINVILLE, Louis Antoine de (1729–1811; French navigator)

LEIF ERIKSSON (11th century; Icelandic explorer)

NORDENSKJÖLD, Nils Adolf Erik, Baron (1832–1901; Swedish navigator)

14

BELLINGSHAUSEN, Fabian Gottlieb, Baron von (1778–1852; Russian explorer)

DUMONT D'URVILLE, Jules Sébastien César (1790–1842; French navigator)

17

HENRY THE NAVIGATOR (1394–1460; Portuguese navigator and patron of explorers)

SPORTSMEN AND WOMEN

3

ALI, Muhammad (Cassius Marcellus Clay, 1942–   ; US boxer)

COE, Sebastian, Baron (1956–   ; British middle-distance runner)

LEE, Bruce (1940–73; US kung fu expert)

4

ASHE, Arthur (1943–93; US tennis player)

BOLT, Usain (1986–   ; Jamaican sprinter)

BORG, Bjorn (1956–   ; Swedish tennis player)

CLAY, Cassius. See Ali, Muhammed

CRAM, Steve (1960–   ; British middle-distance runner)

DUKE, Geoffrey E (1923–2015; British racing motorcyclist)

GRAF, Steffi (1969–   ; German tennis player)

HILL, Damon (1960–   ; British motor-racing driver)

HILL, Graham (1929–75; British motor-racing driver)

HOAD, Lewis Alan (1934–94; Australian tennis player)

HUNT, James (1947–93; British motor-racing driver)

JOHN, Barry (1945–   ; Welsh Rugby Union footballer)

KHAN, Amir (1986–   ; British boxer)

KHAN, Imran (1952–   ; Pakistani cricketer, 22nd Prime Minister of Pakistan)

KING, Billie Jean (born Moffitt, 1943–   ; US tennis player)

LARA, Brian (1969–   ; West Indian cricketer)

LOMU, Jonah (1975–2015; New Zealand Rugby Union footballer)

MILO (late 6th century BC; Greek wrestler)

MOSS, Stirling, Sir (1929–   ; British motor-racing driver)

OWEN, Michael (1979–   ; British Association footballer)

PELÉ (1940–   ; Brazilian Association footballer)

RICE, Jerry (1962–   ; US football player)

ROOT, Joe (1990–   ; British cricketer)

ROSE, Justin (1980–   ; British golfer)

RYAN, Matt (1985–   ; US football player)

WADE, Virginia (1945–   ; British tennis player)

5

BLAKE, Peter (1948–2001; New Zealand yachtsman)

BLYTH, Chay, Sir (1940–   ; British yachtsman)

BRUNO, Frank (1961–   ; British heavyweight boxer)

BUDGE, Don (1916–2000; US tennis player)

BUENO, Maria (1939–2018; Brazilian tennis player)

BUSBY, Matt (1909–94; British Association footballer)

CLARK, Jim (1937–68; British motor-racing driver)

COURT, Margaret (born Smith, 1942–   ; Australian tennis player)

CURRY, John Anthony (1949–94; British ice skater)

DALEY, Tom (1994–   ; British diver)

EVERT, Christine (1954–   ; US tennis player)

FALDO, Nick, Sir (1957–   ; British golfer)

FARAH, Mo (1983– ; British athlete)

GRACE, William Gilbert (1848–1915; British cricketer)

GREIG, Tony (1946–2012; Rhodesian-born cricketer)

HAGEN, Walter Charles (1892–1969; US professional golfer)

HOBBS, Jack (1882–1963; British cricketer)

HOGAN, Ben (1912–97; US professional golfer)

HOYLE, Edmond (1672–1769; British authority on card games)

JAMES, LeBron (1984– ; US basketball player)

JEEPS, Dickie (1931–2016; British Rugby Union footballer)

JONES, Bobby (1902–71; US amateur golfer)

KOHLI, Virat (1988– ; Indian cricketer)

LAUDA, Niki (1949–2019; Austrian motor-racing driver)

LAVER, Rod (1938– ; Australian tennis player)

LEWIS, Carl (1961– ; US athlete)

LEWIS, Lennox (1965– ; British boxer)

LLOYD, Clive (1944– ; West Indian cricketer)

LOUIS, Joe (1914–81; US boxer)

MCCOY, Tony, Sir (1974– ; Northern Irish horse-racing jockey)

MEADE, Richard (1938–2015; British three-day-event horse rider)

MEADS, Colin Earl, Sir (1935–2017; New Zealand Rugby Union footballer)

MOORE, Bobby (1941–93; British Association footballer)

NURMI, Paavo Johannes (1897–1973; Finnish middle-distance and long-distance runner)

OVETT, Steve (1955– ; British middle-distance runner)

OWENS, Jesse (1913–80; US sprinter, long jumper, and hurdler)

PERRY, Fred (1909–95; British tennis and table-tennis player)

ROSSI, Valentino (1979– ; Italian motorcycle racer)

SELES, Monica (1973– ; US tennis player)

SENNA, Ayrton (1960–94; Brazilian motor-racing driver)

SMITH, Harvey (1938– ; British showjumper and equestrian)

SPITZ, Mark Andrew (1950– ; US swimmer)

TYSON, Mike (1966– ; US boxer)

VIREN, Lasse Artturi (1949–; Finnish middle-distance and long-distance runner)

WALSH, Courtney (1962– ; Jamaican cricketer)

WARNE, Shane (1969– ; Australian cricketer)

WAUGH, Mark (1965– ; Australian cricketer)

WAUGH, Stephen (1965– ; Australian cricketer)

WOODS, Tiger (1975– ; US golfer)

6

AGASSI, Andre (1970– ; US tennis player)

ALONSO, Fernando (1981– ; Spanish motor-racing driver)

BLANCO, Serge (1958– ; French Rugby Union footballer)

BORDER, Allan (1955– ; Australian cricketer)

BOTHAM, Ian, Sir (1955– ; British cricketer)

BROOME, David (1940– ; British showjumper)

BROUGH, Louise (1923–2014; US tennis player)

BUTTON, Jenson (1980– ; British motor-racing driver)

CAWLEY, Evonne (born Goolagong, 1951– ; Australian tennis player)

CRUYFF, Johann (1947–2016; Dutch Association footballer)

D'INZEO, Colonel Piero (1923–2014; Italian show jumper and equestrian)

EDBERG, Stefan (1966– ; Swedish tennis player)

FANGIO, Juan Manuel (1911–95; Argentinian motor-racing driver)

GARCIA, Sergio (1980– ; Spanish golfer)

HADLEE, Richard, Sir (1951– ; New Zealand cricketer)

HATTON, Ricky (1978– ; British boxer)

HENDRY, Stephen (1969– ; British snooker player)

HENMAN, Tim (1974– ; British tennis player)

HESTER, Carl (1967– ; British equestrian)

HINGIS, Martina (1980– ; Swiss tennis player)

HOLMES, Kelly, Dame (1970– ; British middle-distance athlete)

HUTTON, Len (1916–90; British cricketer)

KARPOV, Anatoly (1951– ; Russian chess player)

KEEGAN, Kevin (1951– ; British footballer)

KERBER, Angelique (1988 – ; German tennis player)

LASKER, Emanuel (1868–1941; German chess player)

MORPHY, Paul Charles (1837–84; US chess player)

MURRAY, Andy, Sir (1987– ; British tennis player)

PALMER, Arnold (1929–2016; US golfer)

RAMSEY, Alf (1922–99; British Association footballer)

RHODES, Wilfred (1877–1973; British cricketer)

ROBSON, Robert (1933–2009; British footballer and manager)

SHEENE, Barry (1950–2003; British racing motorcyclist)

SMYTHE, Pat (1928–96; British showjumper and equestrian)

SOBERS, Gary, Sir (1936– ; West Indian cricketer)

THOMAS, Geraint (1986– ; British cyclist)

TUNNEY, Gene (1897–1978; US boxer)

VETTEL, Sebastian (1987– ; German racing driver)

WEBBER, Mark (1976– ; Australian racing driver)

WENGER, Arsène (1949– ; French football manager)

7

AMBROSE, Curtly, Sir (1963– ; West Indian cricketer)

BECKHAM, David (1975– ; British footballer)

BRABHAM, Jack, Sir (1926–2014; Australian motor-racing driver)

BRADMAN, Donald George (1908–2001; Australian cricketer)

CANTONA, Eric (1966– ; French footballer)

CAPELLO, Fabio (1946– ; Italian football manager)

CARLING, William (1965– ; British Rugby Union footballer)

CARNERA, Primo (1906–67; Italian boxer)

COMPTON, Denis (1918–97; British cricketer)

CONNORS, Jimmy (1952– ; US tennis player)

COWDREY, Colin (1932–2000; British cricketer)

DEMPSEY, Jack (1895–1983; US boxer)

DETTORI, Frankie (1970– ; Italian horse-racing jockey)

EDWARDS, Johnathan (1966– ; British athlete)

FEDERER, Roger (1981– ; Swiss tennis player)

FISCHER, Bobby (1943–2008; US chess player)

FRAZIER, Joe (1944–2011; US boxer)

GUNNELL, Sally (1966– ; British athlete)

HAMMOND, Wally (1903–65; British cricketer)

HUSSAIN, Nasser (1968– ; British cricketer)

JOHNSON, Michael (1967– ; US sprinter)

LENGLEN, Suzanne (1899–1938; French tennis player)

LINEKER, Gary (1960– ; British footballer)

MCBRIDE, Willie John (1940– ; Irish Rugby Union footballer)

MCENROE, John (1959– ; US tennis player)

MANSELL, Nigel (1953– ; British motor-racing driver)

PINSENT, Matthew, Sir (1970– ; British oarsman)

RONALDO, Christiano (1985– ; Portuguese football player)

SAMPRAS, Pete (1971– ; US tennis player)

SPASSKY, Boris (1937– ; Russian chess player)

STEWART, Jackie, Sir (1939– ; British motor-racing driver)

SURTEES, John (1934–2017; British racing motorcyclist and motor-racing driver)

TREVINO, Lee (1939– ; US golfer)

TRUEMAN, Fred (1931–2006; British cricketer)

WHYMPER, Edward (1840– 1911; British mountaineer)

WIGGINS, Bradley (1980– ; British cyclist)

WINKLER, Hans Günter (1926–2018; German showjumper)

ZÁTOPEK, Emil (1922–2002; Czech long-distance runner)

8

AGOSTINI, Giacomo (1942– ; Italian racing motorcyclist)

ALEKHINE, Alexander (1892–1946; French chess player)

ATHERTON, Michael (1968– ; British cricketer)

CAMPBELL, Malcolm (1885–1949;

British land- and water-speed racing driver)

CHARLTON, Bobby, Sir (1937– ; British Association footballer)

CHRISTIE, Linford (1960– ; British sprinter)

COMANECI, Nadia (1961– ; Romanian gymnast)

DJOKOVIC, Novak (1987– ; Serbian tennis player)

ERIKSSON, Sven Goran (1948– ; Swedish football manager)

FERGUSON, Alex, Sir (1941– ; Scottish football manager)

FLINTOFF, Andrew (1977– ; British cricketer)

HAILWOOD, Mike (1940–81; British racing motorcyclist)

HAKKINEN, Mika (1968– ; Finnish motor-racing driver)

HAMILTON, Lewis (1985– ; British motor-racing driver)

HAWTHORN, Mike (1929–58; British motor-racing driver)

JOSELITO (1895–1920; Spanish matador)

KAPIL DEV, (1959– ; Indian cricketer)

KORCHNOI, Victor (1931–2016; Soviet-born chess player)

LINDWALL, Raymond Russell (1921–96; Australian cricketer)

MATTHEWS, Stanley (1915–2000; British Association footballer)

MCGREGOR, Conor (1988– ; Irish martial arts fighter)

NEWCOMBE, John (1944– ; Australian tennis player)

NICKLAUS, Jack William (1940– ; US golfer)

PHILLIPS, Zara (1981– ; eventing world champion)

REDGRAVE, Steven, Sir (1962– ; British oarsman)

RICHARDS, Gordon (1904–86; British jockey)

RICHARDS, Viv, Sir (1952– ; West Indian cricketer)

ROBINSON, Sugar Ray (1920–89; US boxer)

ROSEWALL, Ken (1934– ; Australian tennis player)

RUSEDSKI, Greg (1973– ; Canadian-born British tennis player)

SULLIVAN, John Lawrence (1858–1918; US boxer)

THOMPSON, Daley (1958– ; British decathlete)

WILLIAMS, J P R (1949– ; Welsh Rugby Union footballer)

WILLIAMS, SERENA (1981– ; US tennis player)

WILLIAMS, VENUS (1980– ; US tennis player)

9

BANNISTER, Roger, Sir (1929–2018; British middle-distance runner)

BONINGTON, Chris, Sir (1934– ; British mountaineer)

BOTVINNIK, Mikhail Moiseivich (1911–95; Russian chess player)

COULTHARD, David (1971– ; British motor-racing driver)

DAVENPORT, Lindsay (1976– ; US tennis player)

D'OLIVIERA, Basil Lewis (1931–2011; South African-born cricketer)

GASCOIGNE, Paul (1967– ; British footballer)

GOOLAGONG, Evonne. See Cawley, Evonne

LLEWELLYN, Harry (1911–99; British showjumper and equestrian)

MACARTHER, Ellen, Dame (1976– ; British sailor)

PETROSIAN, Tigran Vartanovich (1929–84; Soviet chess player)

RADCLIFFE, Paula (1973– ; British long-distance runner)

RAIKKONEN, Kimi (1979– ; Finnish racing driver)

SCHMELING, Max (1905–2005; German boxer)

SHARAPOVA, Maria (1987– ; Russian tennis player)

SUTCLIFFE, Herbert (1894–1978; British cricketer)

SZEWINSKA, Irena (1946–2018; Polish athlete)

TENDULKAR, Sachin (1973– ; Indian cricketer)

UNDERWOOD, Rory (1963– ; British Rugby Union football player)

WILKINSON, Jonny (1979– ; British Rugby Union football player)

10

CARPENTIER, Georges (1894–1975; French boxer)

CULBERTSON, Ely (1891–1955; US bridge authority)

IMRAN KHAN (1952– ; Pakistani cricketer, 22nd Prime Minister of Pakistan)

JUANTORENA, Alberto (1951– ; Cuban middle-distance runner)

SCHUMACHER, Michael (1969– ; German motor-racing driver)

WILLS MOODY, Helen (1905–98; US tennis player)

11

BALLESTEROS, Severiano (1957–2011; Spanish golfer)

CONSTANTINE, Learie Nicholas, Baron (1902–71; West Indian cricketer)

FITZSIMMONS, Bob (1862–1917; New Zealand boxer)

MONTGOMERIE, Colin (1963– ; Scottish professional golfer)

NAVRATILOVA, Martina (1956– ; Czech-born US tennis player)

WEISSMULLER, Johnny (1904–84; US swimmer)

12

GREY-THOMPSON, Tanni, Dame (1969– ; British wheelchair athlete)

KNOX-JOHNSTON, Robin

(1939– ; British yachtsman)

19

CAPABLANCA Y GRAUPERA, José Raúl (1888–1942; Cuban chess player)

RANJITSINHJI VIBHAJI, Kumar Shri, Maharajah Jam Sahib of Nawanagar (1872–1933; Indian cricketer)

MURDERERS AND ASSASSINS

Murderer/Assassin	Year	Details
ALLEN, Peter and WELBY, John	1964	Murdered John West. Last two men to be hanged in Britain.
BELLINGHAM, John	1812	Assassinated UK Prime Minister, Spencer Perceval. Only UK PM to have been assassinated.
BENTLEY, Derek and CRAIG, Christoper	1952	Both men were convicted of the murder of PC Miles. Bentley was hanged, although he did not fire a shot, on the grounds that he had incited his younger partner to murder. Craig, who was too young for the death sentence, was imprisoned until 1963. This case caused considerable public disquiet and was used in the abolition-of-hanging debate.
BOOTH, John Wilkes	1865	Assassinated US president Abraham Lincoln. He was shot watching the play Our American Cousin.

BORDEN, Lizzie	1892	Accused of the murder of her father and stepmother in Fall River, Massachusetts, but was acquitted. Public opinion was that she was guilty.
		
		    Lizzie Borden took an axe
		    And gave her mother forty whacks.
		    When she saw what she had done,
		    She gave her father forty-one.

BRADY, Ian and HINDLEY, Myra	1966	Sentenced to life imprisonment for the brutal murder of five children. They were known as the Moors murders as at least three children were killed and buried on the Lancashire moors; some of the bodies were never recovered.
BURKE, William and HARE, William	1827–28	Burke was sentenced to death for the murder of Mary Patterson, James Wilson, and Margaret Docherty; Hare was granted immunity from prosecution by offering to turn King's Evidence. Burke and Hare, with the help of their partners, lured victims to their lodging house, murdered them and sold their bodies to an Edinburgh anatomist, Dr Knox. They are known to have murdered 16 people over a period of nine months, although the exact total is unknown.
BUSH, Edwin	1961	Hanged for the murder of Mrs Elsie Batten. He was identified from an indentikit portrait – the first use of the system in Britain.
CHAPMAN, George	1897–1902	Hanged for the murders of Mary Spink, Bessie Taylor, and Maud Marsh. The three women (all of whom were apparently married to Chapman) were poisoned with antimony. The police who arrested

		him believed that Chapman may have been 'Jack the Ripper'.
CHAPMAN, Mark David	1980	Shot John Lennon in the entrance of his apartment building, The Dakota.
CHRISTIE, John	1943–53	Hanged for the murder of his wife, Ethel Christie, whose body was found under the floorboards of 10 Rillington Place, London. The bodies of five other women were found behind the kitchen wall and buried in the garden.
CORDER, William	1827	Sentenced to death for the murder of Maria Marten. Although her family had been led to believe that she was happily married and living on the Isle of Wight, her mother had a dream that she had been murdered and buried in the Red Barn on Corder's father's farm. Her body was found there.
COTTON, Mary Ann	1872	Hanged for the murder of her stepson Charles Cotton. She was estimated to have killed 14 victims who were diagnosed as having died of gastric fever. She was arrested following the discovery of arsenic in the body of her stepson and the bodies of her husband, baby, and two stepchildren were exhumed. They were also found to have died of arsenical poisoning.
CRIPPEN, Dr Hawley Harvey	1910	US doctor who poisoned his actress wife Cora (called Belle Elmore) in London. He attempted to escape to America with his mistress Ethel LeNeve on the SS Montrose, but was arrested on board following one of the first uses of ship-to-shore radio.
CZOLGOSZ, Leon	1901	Shot and killed US president William McKinley.
ELLIS, Ruth	1955	Convicted of the murder of her boyfriend David Blakely. Last woman to be hanged in Britain.
GODSE, Nathuram	1948	Shot Mahatma Gandhi.
GUITEAU, Charles J	1881	Shot and killed US president James Garfield.
HAIGH, John	1949	Hanged for the murder of Olivia Durand-Deacon. Haigh thought he could not be tried for murder as he had destroyed the body in an acid bath. However, the discovery of gallstones, bone fragments, and false teeth meant that the remains could be identified.
HALLIWELL, Kenneth	1967	Murdered his lover, the British dramatist Joe Orton (1933–67).
HANRATTY, James	1961	Hanged for the murder of Michael Gregsten, after a trial lasting 21 days. Controversy surrounded the verdict. Much of the evidence was based on the identification of Hanratty by Valerie Storie (Gregsten's lover, who was present at the murder). Hanratty's alibi that he had been in Rhyl when the murder was committed was disbelieved. The uncertainty relating to the verdict added fuel to the campaign against hanging. In 2001 Hanratty's remains were exhumed to enable DNA comparison of the body with samples found at the crime scene. These matched and in 2002 the Court of Criminal Appeal ruled that Hanratty's conviction was not unsound and that there were no grounds for a posthumous pardon.
JACK THE RIPPER	1888	Brutally murdered at least five prostitutes in the Whitechapel area. There has been great controversy about the identity of the murderer.
KENT, Constance	1860	Sentenced to death, commuted to life imprisonment, for the murder of her half-brother,

		Francis. In 1885 she was released and went to Australia, where she trained as a nurse under the name of Ruth Kaye. She successfully rebuilt her life and died in 1944, at the age of 100.
LUCHENI, Luigi	1898	Assassinated Empress Elizabeth of Austria she collapsed and died two hours later, not realising she had been stabbed.
MCMAHON, Thomas	1979	Killed Louis Mountbatten 1st Earl Mountbatten of Burma, by blowing up the boat in which he was fishing.
MIJAILOVIĆ, Mijailo	2003	Stabbed Swedish Foreign minister Anna Lindh.
NEILSON, Donald	1974–75	Sentenced to life imprisonment for the murder of four men. He was know as 'The Black Panther'.
NILSEN, Denis	1979–83	Convicted of the murder of six men after the discovery of human remains in a manhole at the side of the flats where he lived. He boasted of killing over 15 men in total.
OSWALD, Lee Harvey	1963	Believed to have shot US president John F. Kennedy.
PEACE, Charles	1876	Hanged for the murder of Arthur Dyson. Peace was a burglar who carried the 'tools of his trade' in a violin case. His activities were spread over a 25 year period, during which he became notorious.
PRINCIP, Gavrilo	1914	Yugoslav nationalist who killed Archduke Franz Ferdinand of Austria precipitating WW1.
ROBINSON, John	1927	Suffocated Minnie Alice Bonati. He dismembered her body and hid it in a trunk which he handed to the left-luggage office at Charing Cross station.
SCHRANK, John	1912	Shot former US president Theodore Roosevelt.
SHIPMAN, Harold	?1974–98	A GP, Shipman was jailed in 2000 for the murder of 15 of his patients, although the total number of his victims is believed to be at least 215. He was found dead, hanging from the window bars of his prison cell, in 2004.
SINGH, Satwant and SINGH, Beant	1984	Assassinated Indira Gandhi.
SIRHAN, Sirhan	1968	Shot US Senator Robert F. Kennedy.
SMITH, George (alias Oliver Love, George Rose, Henry Williams, Oliver James, John Lloyd)	1912	Hanged for the murder of Bessie Mundy. The story became known as 'The Brides in the Bath' when it was revealed that Smith bigamously married his victims and, in three instances, killed them in their baths. In each inquest a verdict of accidental drowning was brought in, and Smith claimed the possessions or life insurance of his 'wife'.
STRATTON, Alfred and Albert	1905	Convicted of the murders of Mr and Mrs Farrow. The case made legal history because the jury was convinced of the guilt of the two brothers after a fingerprint found at the scene of the crime was found to match that of Alfred Stratton.
SUTCLIFFE, Peter	1975–80	Sentenced to life imprisonment following the murder of 13 women. Known as the 'Yorkshire Ripper', Sutcliffe claimed he had a mission from God to kill prostitutes (although several of his victims were not prostitutes).
TURPIN, Dick	1735	Hanged at York for the murder of Thomas Morris. Notorious for highway robberies, a reward of £200 was placed on his head.
WEST, Frederick and Rosemary	?1970–94	Frederick West committed suicide before his trial for the murder of 12 young women. Rosemary West was sentenced to life imprisonment for the murder of 10 young women.

THE ARTS

ART TERMS

2
OP

3
FEC
INC
OIL
POP

4
BODY
BUST
CAST
DADA
HERM
KORE
SIZE
SWAG
TERM
WASH

5
BRUSH
BURIN
CHALK
EASEL
FECIT
GESSO
GLAZE
MODEL
NAIVE
PIETÀ
PUTTO
SALON
SCULP
SECCO
SEPIA
STYLE
TONDO

6
ASHCAN
BISTRE
CANVAS
CUBISM
FRESCO
GOTHIC
GROUND
KIT-CAT
KITSCH
KOUROS

LIMNER
MAESTÀ
MEDIUM
MOBILE
MOSAIC
PASTEL
PATINA
PENCIL
PURISM
RELIEF
ROCOCO
SCHOOL
SKETCH
STUCCO
STYLUS
TUSCAN
VEDUTA
VERISM

7
ACADEMY
ARCHAIC
ATELIER
BAROQUE
BAUHAUS
BITUMEN
BODEGÓN
CABINET
CAMAÏEU
CARTOON
COLLAGE
COSMATI
DIPTYCH
DRAWING
ECORCHÉ
ETCHING
GOUACHE
IMPASTO
INCIDIT
LINOCUT
LOST WAX
MODELLO
MONTAGE
PALETTE
PIGMENT
POCHADE
REALISM
SCUMBLE
SFUMATO
SINOPIA
TEMPERA

VANITAS
VARNISH
WOODCUT

8
ABSTRACT
AIR-BRUSH
ALLEGORY
ANCIENTS
AQUATINT
ARMATURE
ARRICCIO
BARBIZON
BOZZETTO
CARYATID
CHARCOAL
DRÔLERIE
DRYPOINT
EMULSION
FIXATIVE
FROTTAGE
FUTURISM
GRAFFITI
HATCHING
INTAGLIO
INTONACO
MANDORLA
MAQUETTE
PASTICHE
PLEURANT
POUNCING
PREDELLA
REPOUSSÉ
SCULPSIT
STAFFAGE
TACHISME
TESSERAE
TRECENTO
TRIPTYCH
VENETIAN

9
ALLA PRIMA
ANTI-CERNE
AQUARELLE
AUTOGRAPH
BRUSHWORK
BYZANTINE
CAPRICCIO
COLOURIST
DISTEMPER

ENGRAVING
GRISAILLE
GROTESQUE
INTIMISME
LANDSCAPE
MAHLSTICK
MAULSTICK
MEZZOTINT
MINIATURE
POLYPTYCH
PRIMITIVE
SCULPTURE
STILL LIFE
STIPPLING
SYMBOLISM
TENEBRISM
VORTICISM

10
ARRICCIATO
ART NOUVEAU
ASSEMBLAGE
AUTOMATISM
AVANTGARDE
BIOMORPHIC
CARICATURE
CIRE-PERDUE
CRAQUELURE
FLORENTINE
METALPOINT
MONOCHROME
MORBIDEZZA
NATURALISM
PENTIMENTO
PROVENANCE
QUADRATURA
REPOUSSOIR
ROMANESQUE
SURREALISM
SYNTHETISM
TURPENTINE
XYLOGRAPHY

11
BAMBOCCANTI
BIEDERMEIER
CAROLINGIAN
CHIAROSCURO
CONTÉ CRAYON
DIVISIONISM
ECLECTICISM

ILLUSIONISM
IMPRIMATURA
LITHOGRAPHY
MASTERPIECE
PERSPECTIVE
PICTURESQUE
POINTILLISM
PORTRAITURE

RENAISSANCE
RETROUSSAGE
STYLIZATION
SUPREMATISM
TROMPE L'OEIL
WATERCOLOUR

12
ACRYLIC PAINT

ANAMORPHOSIS
CLOISONNISME
CONTRAPPOSTO
COUNTERPROOF
ILLUMINATION
PRECISIONISM
QUATTROCENTO
SUPERREALISM

13
ARCHITECTONIC
EXPRESSIONISM
FÊTE CHAMPÊTRE
IMPRESSIONISM
PAPIERS COLLÉS

14
CONSTRUCTIVISM

ART SCHOOLS AND STYLES

4
DADA

5
OP ART

6
CUBISM
KITSCH
POP ART
PURISM
ROCOCO
VERISM

7
ART BRUT
ART DECO
BAROQUE
DE STIJL
FAUVISM
FOLK ART
JUNK ART
LAND ART
ORPHISM
REALISM
TACHISM

8
FUTURISM
MOGUL ART
NAIVE ART

RAYONISM

9
INTIMISME
MANNERISM
MINOAN ART
SYMBOLISM
VORTICISM

10
ARTE POVERA
ART NOUVEAU
CLASSICISM
ISLAMIC ART
JUGENDSTIL
KINETIC ART
MINIMALISM
NATURALISM
OTTOMAN ART
SURREALISM
SYNTHETISM

11
ABSTRACT ART
ART INFORMEL
AVANT-GARDE
BLAUE REITER
CLOISONNISM
CONCRETE ART
DIVISIONISM

GRAND MANNER
POINTILLISM
REGIONALISM
ROMANTICISM
SUPREMATISM
SYNCHRONISM

12
BYZANTINE ART
CAMDEN SCHOOL
MAGIC REALISM
MOZARABIC ART
PHOTOREALISM
PRECISIONISM
PRIMITIVE ART

13
CONCEPTUAL ART
EXPRESSIONISM
FIGURATIVE ART
IMPRESSIONISM
NEOCLASSICISM
POSTMODERNISM
SIENESE SCHOOL
SOCIAL REALISM

14
ACTION PAINTING
CONSTRUCTIVISM
NEOROMANTICISM

PERFORMANCE ART
RENAISSANCE ART
VENETIAN SCHOOL

16
ENVIRONMENTAL ART
FLORENTINE SCHOOL
NEOEXPRESSIONISM
NEOIMPRESSIONISM
NEUE SACHLICHKEIT
PRE-RAPHAELITISM
SOCIALIST REALISM
TRANSAVANT-GARDE

18+
ABSTRACT
  EXPRESSIONISM
AESTHETIC MOVEMENT
ARTS AND CRAFTS
  MOVEMENT
HIGH RENAISSANCE
  ART
INTERNATIONAL
  GOTHIC
METAPHYSICAL
  PAINTING
PLEIN-AIR PAINTING
POSTIMPRESSIONISM
REPRESENTATIONAL
  ART

ARCHITECTURAL TERMS

3
BAY
CAP
DIE
EYE
KEY

4
AMBO
ANTA
APSE
ARCH
BAND
BEAD

BELL
BOSS
DADO
DAIS
DOME
FRET
FROG

FUST
NAVE
PELE
STOA

5
AISLE

AMBRY
ARRIS
ATTIC
CONGÉ
CROWN
CRYPT
DORIC
FOILS
GABLE
GLYPH
HELIX
INLAY
IONIC
LOBBY
NEWEL
ROMAN
SCAPE
SHAFT
SHANK
TALON
TENIA
TUDOR
VERGE

6
ABACUS
ACCESS
ALCOVE
ARCADE
ATRIUM
ATTICK
AUMBRY
BELFRY
BONNET
BROACH
CANOPY
CHEVET
COLUMN
CORONA
CRENEL
CUPOLA
DAGGER
DENTIL
DIAPER
FAÇADE
FILLET
FINIAL
FLÈCHE
FRESCO
FRIEZE
GABLET
GAZEBO
GOTHIC
GUTTAE
HEROIC
LESENE
LINTEL
LINTOL
LOGGIA
LOUVRE
MANTEL
MERLON
METOPE
MUTULE

NORMAN
OCULUS
PAGODA
PATERA
PLINTH
PULPIT
QUADRA
REGULA
ROCOCO
SCAPUS
SCROLL
SEDILE
SOFFIT
TROPHY
URELLA
VESTRY
VOLUTE
WREATH
XYSTUS
ZIG-ZAG

7
ANNULET
ARCH RIB
ASTYLAR
BALCONY
BAROQUE
BASTION
BOULTIN
BUTMENT
CAPITAL
CAVETTO
CHANCEL
CHEVRON
CORNICE
CROCHET
CROCKET
DISTYLE
ECHINUS
ENCARPA
ENTASIS
EUSTYLE
FESTOON
FLEURON
FLUTING
GADROON
GALILEE
GALLERY
LACUNAR
LANTERN
LATTICE
LEQUEAR
LUNETTE
NARTHEX
NULLING
OBELISK
ORATORY
PARVISE
PORTAIL
PORTICO
POSTERN
PTEROMA
REEDING
REGENCY

REREDOS
ROSETTE
ROTUNDA
ROUNDEL
SCALLOP
SPANISH
SYSTYLE
TESSARA
TONDINO
TRACERY
TRUMEAU

8
ABUTMENT
ACANTHUS
AEDICULA
APOPHYGE
ASTRAGAL
ATLANTES
BALUSTER
BARTIZAN
BASILICA
BEAK HEAD
CARYATID
CIMBORIO
CINCTURE
CRENELLE
CRESTING
CYMATIUM
DIASTYLE
DIPTERAL
DOG-TOOTH
EDGE ROLL
EXTRADOS
FORMERET
GARGOYLE
INTRADOS
KEEL ARCH
KEYSTONE
LICH GATE
LYCH GATE
MISERERE
PAVILION
PEDESTAL
PEDIMENT
PILASTER
PREDELLA
PULPITUM
ROCAILLE
SPANDREL
SPANDRIL
TORCHING
TRANSEPT
TRIGLYPH
TYMPANUM
VERANDAH
VIGNETTE
WAINSCOT

9
ACROPOLIS
ANTEFIXAE
ANTHEMION
APEX STONE

ARABESQUE
ARCH BRICK
ARCHIVOLT
ATTIC BASE
BIRD'S BEAK
BYZANTINE
CAMPANILE
CANEPHORA
CARTOUCHÈ
CAULICOLI
CLOISTERS
COLONNADE
COMPOSITE
DRIPSTONE
FOLIATION
GROTESQUE
HEXASTYLE
HYPOCAUST
HYPOSTYLE
INGLE NOOK
LABEL STOP
LACUNARIA
LINENFOLD
MEZZANINE
MOULDINGS
OCTASTYLE
PALLADIAN
REFECTORY
SGRAFFITO
STRAPWORK
STYLOBATE
TRABEATED
TRIFORIUM
TRILITHON
VESTIBULE
ZOOPHORUS

10
ACROTERION
AMBULATORY
ARAEOSTYLE
ARCHITRAVE
BALDACHINO
BALL FLOWER
BALUSTRADE
BATTLEMENT
CINQUEFOIL
COLONNETTE
CORINTHIAN
EGG AND DART
ENRICHMENT
HAGIOSCOPE
LADY CHAPEL
LANCET ARCH
MISERICORD
MODILLIONS
PIETRA DURA
PRESBYTERY
PYCNOSTYLE
QUATREFOIL
ROMANESQUE
ROOD SCREEN
ROSE WINDOW
SEXPARTITE

TETRASTYLE
TRACHELION

11
CASTELLATED
ENTABLATURE
FAN VAULTING

HARELIP ARCH
LEADED LIGHT
MANTELPIECE
MANTELSHELF
ORIEL WINDOW
RENAISSANCE
RETICULATED

12
AMPHITHEATRE
BLIND TRACERY
COCKLE STAIRS
EGG AND TONGUE
LANCET WINDOW
PORTE-COCHÈRE

13
AMPHI-PROSTYLE

14
ANGULAR CAPITAL
FLYING BUTTRESS
HYPOTRACHELION

ANTIQUE-TRADE TERMS

3
WAF

4
COST
KITE
LUMP
RING

5
AGGRO
FOLKY
FRESH
LYLE'S
MOODY
REPRO
RIGHT
ROUGH

RUN UP
TOUCH
TRADE
VICKY

6
LOOKER
MADE-UP
PERIOD
PUNTER
RUNNER
SMALLS
TOTTER

7
BREAKER
CALL-OUT
CUT DOWN

KNOCKER
MILLER'S

8
AS BOUGHT
BENT GEAR
BOUGHT IN
CHAIRMAN
DOWN TO ME
ESTIMATE
FOLLOWER
MARRIAGE
SCLENTER

9
CLEARANCE
INNER RING

SIX AND TWO

10
COMMERCIAL
FOUR AND TWO
OFF THE WALL
OLD FRIENDS

11
EIGHT AND TWO
HAMMER PRICE
OUT OF THE AIR
SIGHT UNSEEN

12+
COLLECTOR'S ITEM
KNOCKING DOWN

TYPES OF GLASS

4
AMEN
COIN
DAUM
KNOP
LAVA
RUBY
SLAG

5
AGATE
CAMEO
FLUTE
GALLE
GRAAL
WEALD

6
CLICHY
CLUTHA
GOBLET

HUMPEN
MURANO
NEVERS
RUMMER

7
AMPULLA
BACCHUS
BRISTOL
BURMESE
FAVRILE
HYALITH
LALIQUE
LOBMEYR
NAILSEA
OPALINE
POTSDAM
RATAFIA
STAINED
TIFFANY

8
AIRTWIST
BACCARAT
BOHEMIAN
CUT GLASS
FACET CUT
FRIGGERS
INTAGLIO
JACOBITE
VAUXHALL
VENETIAN
WALDGLAS

9
CHALCEDON
HARRACHOV
LITHYALIN
MOSS AGATE
NEWCASTLE
PEACH BLOW

PEACH SKIN
PILLAR CUT

10
AVENTURINE
FLUGELGLAS
MILLEFIORI
PILKINGTON

11
HOCHSCHNITT
OPAQUE TWIST
PATE-DE-VERRE
RAVENSCROFT
STANGENGLAS
STOURBRIDGE
WHITEFRIARS

16
ZWISCHENGOLDGLAS

TYPES OF WOOD

3
ASH
BOX
ELM
OAK
YEW

4
DEAL
LIME
PINE
TEAK

5
CEDAR

EBONY
HOLLY
IROKO
LARCH
MAPLE
THUJA
THUYA

6
CHERRY
PADAUK
PADOUK
WALNUT
WILLOW

7
AMBOYNA
CYPRESS
LOGWOOD

8
CHESTNUT
FUMED OAK
HARDWOOD
HAREWOOD
KINGWOOD
MAHOGANY
MULBERRY
PEARWOOD
ROSEWOOD

9
MARQUETRY
STAINWOOD

11
LIGNUM VITAE

13
ITALIAN WALNUT
MACASSAR EBONY
PARTRIDGE-WOOD

14
COROMANDEL WOOD
INDIAN ROSEWOOD

FURNITURE

3
COT

4
CRIB
DESK
SOFA

5
BENCH
BERTH
CHEST
COUCH
DIVAN
FUTON
STALL
STOOL
Z-BED

6
BUREAU
CRADLE
DAY BED
LOWBOY
SETTEE
SETTLE

7
BUNK BED
CABINET
CAMP BED
CASSONE
COMMODE
DRESSER
HAMMOCK
HIGHBOY
LECTERN

SHELVES
SOFA BED
TALLBOY
TWIN BED
WHATNOT

8
ARMCHAIR
BAR STOOL
BOOKCASE
BOX CHAIR
END TABLE
LOVE SEAT
RECLINER
TEA TABLE
WARDROBE
WATER BED

9
BOOKSHELF
CAMP CHAIR
CANE CHAIR
CARD TABLE
CLUB CHAIR
DAVENPORT
DECK CHAIR
DOUBLE BED
EASY CHAIR
EMPIRE BED
HIGH CHAIR
HOPE CHEST
PIER TABLE
SIDEBOARD
SIDE CHAIR
SIDE TABLE
SINGLE BED

WING CHAIR
WORK TABLE

10
BUCKET SEAT
CANTERBURY
CHOIR STALL
ESCRITOIRE
FEATHER BED
SECRETAIRE
TRUCKLE BED

11
BARREL CHAIR
CANOPIED BED
CARVER CHAIR
COFFEE TABLE
COLONIAL BED
DINING CHAIR
DINING TABLE
FOLDAWAY BED
GAMING TABLE
KING-SIZE BED
LOUNGE CHAIR
MORRIS CHAIR
PANELLED BED
READING DESK
ROLL-TOP DESK
SHAKER CHAIR
STUDIO COUCH
SWIVEL CHAIR
WOODEN CHAIR
WRITING DESK

12
BEDSIDE TABLE
BOSTON ROCKER

BOTTOM DRAWER
CHAISE LONGUE
CHESTERFIELD
CHINA CABINET
CONSOLE TABLE
FOLDING CHAIR
GATE-LEG TABLE
GRECIAN COUCH
KITCHEN TABLE
KNEE-HOLE DESK
LEATHER CHAIR
LIBRARY TABLE
MILKING STOOL
NURSING CHAIR
QUEEN-SIZE BED
ROCKING CHAIR
SLANT-TOP DESK
SLOPE-TOP DESK
WELSH DRESSER
WINDSOR CHAIR
WRITING TABLE

13
BENTWOOD CHAIR
CAPTAIN'S CHAIR
DOUBLE DRESSER
DRESSING TABLE
DRINKS CABINET
DROP-LEAF TABLE
FOUR-POSTER BED
LIQUOR CABINET
MIRROR CABINET
PEDESTAL TABLE
PEMBROKE TABLE
SHERATON CHAIR
STRAIGHT CHAIR

14
CHEST OF DRAWERS
CORNER CUPBOARD
PANEL-BACK CHAIR

QUEEN-ANNE CHAIR
RECLINING CHAIR
WHEEL-BACK CHAIR

15+
COCKTAIL CABINET
CONVERTIBLE SOFA

LADDER-BACK CHAIR
UPHOLSTERED CHAIR

FURNITURE TERMS

3
EAR

4
BAIL
BULB
HUSK
OGEE
SWAG

5
APRON
BEVEL
BOMBÉ
CLEAT
DOWEL
FRETS
GESSO
INLAY
LOPER
OVOLO
SHELL
SKIRT
SPLAT
SQUAB
STILE

6
DIAPER
FIGURE
FILLET
FINIAL
FLY-LEG
FRIEZE
LINING
MUNTIN
ORMOLU
PATERA
PATINA

PLINTH
REBATE
RUNNER
SCROLL
VENEER
VOLUTE

7
AMORINI
BANDING
BEADING
BLISTER
BUN FOOT
CARCASE
CASTORS
CHAMFER
CORNICE
EN SUITE
FLUTING
GALLERY
HIPPING
LOZENGE
LUNETTE
PAD FOOT
PAW FOOT
REEDING
ROUNDEL
SALTIRE
TAMBOUR
TURNING

8
ACANTHUS
ARCADING
ASTRAGAL
BALUSTER
BOW FRONT
CABOCHON

DOVETAIL
HOOP BACK
LION MASK
MOULDING
PEDIMENT
PIE CRUST
PILASTER
RAM'S HEAD
SABRE LEG
SUNBURST
SWAN-NECK
TERMINAL
WAINSCOT

9
ANTHEMION
ARABESQUE
BLIND FRET
CAMEO BACK
CARTOUCHE
DROP FRONT
FALL FRONT
GUILLOCHE
LINENFOLD
MARQUETRY
MEDALLION
PARQUETRY
RULE JOINT
SHOE-PIECE
SPADE FOOT
SPOON BACK
STRAPWORK
STRETCHER
STRIATION
STRINGING

10
BOULLE WORK

BREAK-FRONT
EGG-AND-DART
ESCUTCHEON
GADROONING
KEY PATTERN
LADDER BACK
MITRE JOINT
MONOPODIUM
QUARTERING
SERPENTINE
SHIELD-BACK
UNDER-BRACE

11
BALL-AND-CLAW
BALLOON BACK
BRACKET FOOT
CABRIOLE LEG
CHIP-CARVING
COCKBEADING
COUNTERSINK
CUP-AND-COVER
LATTICEWORK
SPIRAL TWIST

12
CRESTING RAIL
DISHED CORNER
FIELDED PANEL
OYSTER VENEER

13+
BARLEY-SUGAR TWIST
BOBBIN TURNING
BROKEN PEDIMENT
CHANNEL MOULDING
COLUMN TURNING
MORTISE-AND-TENON

POTTERY AND PORCELAIN

3&4
AULT
BOW
MING
TANG

5
DELFT
DERBY
IMARI
SPODE

6
BISQUE
BRETBY
CANTON
MINTON

PARIAN
RUSKIN
SEVRES

7
BELLEEK

BISCUIT
BRISTOL
CHELSEA
DOULTON
FAIENCE
ITALIAN
MEISSEN
MOULDED
NEW HALL
REDWARE
SATSUMA
TOBY JUG

8
CANEWARE
CAUGHLEY
CHAFFERS
COALPORT
FAIRINGS

MAIOLICA
MAJOLICA
NANTGARW
PLYMOUTH
SALOPIAN
SLIPWARE
WEDGWOOD

9
AGATE WARE
CHINA CLAY
CRACKLING
CREAMWARE
DAVENPORT
HARD PASTE
LINTHORPE
LIVERPOOL
LOWESTOFT
MOORCROFT

PEARLWARE
PRATTWARE
SOFT
  PASTE
STONEWARE
WORCESTER

10
CANTON WARE
CHINA STONE
LUSTREWARE
MARTINWARE
PILKINGTON
POLYCHROME
ROCKINGHAM
SALT-GLAZED
STONE CHINA
TERRACOTTA

11
BLACK BASALT
CAPODIMONTE
EARTHENWARE
FAMILLE ROSE
FAMILLE VERT
LONGTON HALL
PATE-SUR-PATE

12+
ASIATIC PHEASANT
BLUE AND WHITE
CAMBRIAN POTTERY
MASON'S IRONSTONE
  CHINA
NAGASAKI WARE
STAFFORDSHIRE
WILLOW PATTERN

LITERARY TERMS

3
ODE
WIT

4
EPIC
FOOT
IAMB
MYTH

5
ELEGY
FABLE
GENRE
ICTUS
IRONY
LYRIC
METRE
NOVEL
OCTET
PROSE
RHYME
STYLE
THEME
VERSE

6
BALLAD
BATHOS
CESURA
CLICHÉ
DACTYL
HUBRIS
LAMENT
MONODY
OCTAVE

PARODY
PATHOS
SATIRE
SCHOOL
SEPTET
SESTET
SIMILE
SONNET
STANZA
STRESS
SYMBOL

7
CAESURA
CONCEIT
COUPLET
DICTION
ELISION
EPIGRAM
EPISTLE
EPITAPH
EUPHONY
FABLIAU
HUMOURS
IMAGERY
NEMESIS
PARADOX
PROSODY
PYRRHIC
REALISM
SPONDEE
SUBPLOT
TRAGEDY
TROCHEE

8
ALLEGORY

ANAPAEST
AUGUSTAN
DIDACTIC
ELEMENTS
EXEMPLUM
EYE RHYME
METAPHOR
OXYMORON
PASTORAL
QUATRAIN
RHETORIC
SCANSION
SYLLABLE
TRIMETER

9
AMBIGUITY
ASSONANCE
BURLESQUE
CATHARSIS
CLASSICAL
EUPHEMISM
FREE VERSE
HALF RHYME
HEXAMETER
HYPERBOLE
MONOMETER
OCTAMETER
PARARHYME

10
BLANK VERSE
CARICATURE
DENOUEMENT
EPIC SIMILE
HEPTAMETER

MOCK HEROIC
NATURALISM
PENTAMETER
PICARESQUE
SPOONERISM
SUBJECTIVE
TETRAMETER

11
ANACHRONISM
COURTLY LOVE
END STOPPING
ENJAMBEMENT
GOTHIC NOVEL
HORATIAN ODE
MALAPROPISM
NOBLE SAVAGE
OBJECTIVITY
TRAGICOMEDY

12
ALLITERATION
ONOMATOPOEIA

13
ANTHROPOMORPH
HEROIC COUPLET
INTERNAL RHYME

14
EXISTENTIALISM
FEMININE ENDING
MILTONIC SONNET
ROMANTIC POETRY
SENTIMENTALITY

15
MASCULINE ENDING

PATHETIC FALLACY	**18**	**20+**
PERSONIFICATION	METAPHYSICAL POETRY	STREAM OF
	NEGATIVE CAPABILITY	CONSCIOUSNESS
16	OMNISCIENT NARRATOR	
PETRARCHAN SONNET		

FIGURES OF SPEECH

ALLITERATION	APOSIOPESIS	HYPERBATON	METONYMY
ANACOLUTHON	APOSTROPHE	HYPERBOLE	PERIPHRASIS
ANADIPLOSIS	ASSONANCE	IRONY	PERSONIFICATION
ANAPHORA	ASYNDETON	LITOTES	SIMILE
ANTISTROPHE	CHIASMUS	METAPHOR	SYNECDOCHE
ANTITHESIS	CONSONANCE		

PRINTING AND PUBLISHING TERMS

2&3	LINE	REPRO	GLOSSY
CCR	MATT	RESET	GUTTER
CPU	PAGE	ROMAN	HEADER
CRT	PICA	ROUGH	INDENT
CSS	PULP	RUN-ON	JACKET
DTP	REAM	SERIF	KINDLE
FIT	SEWN	SHEET	LAYOUT
KEY	SGML	SPACE	LEADED
LAY	SKID	SPINE	LEGEND
LC	TEXT	VERSO	MAKE-UP
OCR	TRIM	WIDOW	MANILA
PDF	TYPE	XHTML	MARK-UP
PE	TYPO		MARGIN
RGB	WOVE	**6**	MASKING
SC		AUTHOR	MOCK-UP
UC	**5**	BLOW UP	OCTAVO
XML	AGENT	CENTRE	OFFSET
	ALIGN	CHEMAC	ORPHAN
4	BLOCK	CICERO	OZALID
BLOG	BLURB	COLUMN	QUARTO
BOLD	COVER	CREASE	RASTER
BOOK	DRAFT	CREDIT	READER
CAPS	DUMMY	CUT-OFF	REVIEW
CASE	EBOOK	DAGGER	SIZING
CMYK	ERROR	DAMPER	SPREAD
COPY	FIBRE	DECKLE	UNSEWN
CROP	FLUSH	DELETE	WEIGHT
DATA	FOLIO	DESIGN	
EDIT	FOUNT	DRYING	**7**
EPUB	GLOSS	EDITOR	ACETATE
FILM	GRAIN	EM-DASH	ACRYLIC
FLAP	IMAGE	EN-DASH	ADVANCE
FOIL	INDEX	ERRATA	ARTWORK
FOLD	INSET	FIGURE	BINDING
FONT	LITHO	FILTER	BROMIDE
FOOT	POINT	FIXING	BUCKRAM
HEAD	PROOF	FOOTER	CALIPER
LEAF	RECTO	FORMAT	CAPTION

CHAPTER
COLLATE
DENSITY
DIAGRAM
DUOTONE
EDITION
FEATURE
FIGURES
FLYLEAF
FOLD-OUT
HEADING
IMPRINT
JUSTIFY
KEYLINE
KNOCK UP
LEADING
MASKING
OUTWORK
PASTE-UP
PICKING
PODCAST
PREFACE
PRELIMS
PRINTER
REISSUE
REPRINT
ROYALTY
TYPESET
UPRIGHT
WYSIWYG

8
ABRIDGED
ADDENDUM
APPENDIX
ASCENDER
BACKLIST
BAD BREAK
BASE LINE
BODY TEXT
BUNDLING
CONTENTS
CONTRACT
CONTRAST
DATABASE
DELETION
DIGITISE
DROP CAPS
EMBOSSED
EMULSION
EPIGRAPH
EPILOGUE
FOOTNOTE
FORE-EDGE
FOREWORD
GATEFOLD
GILT EDGE
GLOSSARY
GRAMMAGE
GRAPHICS
HALFTONE
HARDBACK
HARD COPY
HEADLINE

KEYBOARD
LAMINATE
LANGUAGE
LIGATURE
OFFPRINT
PACKAGER
PHOTOSET
PORTRAIT
PRE-PRESS
PRINT RUN
SIDE HEAD
SLIP CASE
STILLAGE
SUBTITLE
SUPERIOR
TAILBAND
TEXT AREA
TYPEFACE
TYPESIZE

9
BLANK PAGE
BLUEPRINT
BOOK PROOF
CASE BOARD
CHARACTER
CO-EDITION
COLLOTYPE
COPYRIGHT
CROP MARKS
DANDY ROLL
DESCENDER
DRY OFFSET
ENDMATTER
ENDPAPERS
EVEN PAGES
FREELANCE
HALF-SHEET
HALF TITLE
HARDBOUND
HARDCOVER
HIGHLIGHT
KEYSTROKE
LANDSCAPE
LIMPBOUND
LOOSE LEAF
LOWER CASE
MARKETING
MICROFILM
MILLBOARD
OVERPRINT
OXIDATION
PAGE PROOF
PAPER TAPE
PERFECTOR
REMAINDER
SANS SERIF
SIGNATURE
SMALL CAPS
SUB-EDITOR
SUBSCRIPT
TITLE PAGE
TRANSPOSE
TWO-COLOUR

UNDERLINE
UPPER CASE
WATERMARK
WORDSPACE

10
BACKLINING
BACK MARGIN
BACKMATTER
BIBLE PAPER
BOOK BINDER
BOOK JACKET
CORRECTION
DEDICATION
DIAZO PRINT
DIDOT POINT
HOUSE STYLE
IMPOSITION
IMPRESSION
IN REGISTER
LAMINATION
MANUSCRIPT
METAL PLATE
MICROFICHE
MONOCHROME
OVERMATTER
PAGINATION
PAPER PLATE
PERFORATED
PRODUCTION
RANGED LEFT
REVERSE OUT
SEPARATION
SUBHEADING
SUPPLEMENT
TAIL MARGIN
THUMB INDEX
TITLE VERSO
TYPE HEIGHT
TYPESCRIPT
TYPOGRAPHY

11
ADVANCE COPY
ADVERTISING
ANTIQUE WOVE
CASE BINDING
CHAPTER HEAD
CONTRIBUTOR
COPY EDITING
COPYFITTING
DIRECT LITHO
DROPPED HEAD
ENLARGEMENT
EPUBLISHING
FACING PAGES
FILMSETTING
FLAT ARTWORK
FRONT MATTER
GALLEY PROOF
HYPHENATION
KEYBOARDING
KNIFE FOLDER
LETTERSPACE

LINE ARTWORK
LINE DRAWING
LINE SPACING
MIDDLE TONES
MULTICOLOUR
OFFSET LITHO
ORIGINATION
OVEREXPOSED
POSTER PAPER
PROCESS INKS
PROOFREADER
RAGGED RIGHT
RANGED RIGHT
RUBBER PLATE
RUNNING HEAD
SPECIAL SORT
STRIPPING IN
SUPERSCRIPT
UNJUSTIFIED

12
BIBLIOGRAPHY
BIMETAL PLATE
BLADE-COATING
CENTRESPREAD
CHARACTER SET
CHEMICAL PULP
CLOTH BINDING
CODING SYSTEM
DOUBLE-COLUMN
FILM NEGATIVE
FILM POSITIVE
FRONTISPIECE
ILLUSTRATION
INTRODUCTION
LEATHERBOUND
MARBLED PAPER
MILL FINISHED
PARALLEL FOLD
PASS FOR PRESS
PERFECT BOUND
POSITIVE FILM
QUARTER-BOUND
RANGED CENTER
REPRODUCTION
SADDLE STITCH
SIDE-STITCHED
SINGLE-COLOUR
SINGLE-COLUMN
SOFTWOOD PULP
THERMOGRAPHY
TRANSPARENCY
UNDEREXPOSED

13
BASE ALIGNMENT
BLACK AND WHITE
BLACK HALFTONE
BLIND BLOCKING
CONDENSED TYPE
CYLINDER PRESS
FILM PROCESSOR
FOREIGN RIGHTS
GRAPHIC DESIGN

157

JUSTIFICATION
LINING FIGURES
LITHO PRINTING
PROCESS COLOUR
REGISTER MARKS
RIGHT-HAND PAGE
SPECIFICATION
SPIRAL BINDING
STRIKE-THROUGH
TRIMETAL PLATE
UNTRIMMED SIZE

14
CATHODE RAY TUBE
CODE CONVERSION
CONCERTINA FOLD
CROSS REFERENCE
CUT-OUT HALFTONE
DIGITAL READ-OUT
FRONT-END SYSTEM
LEATHER BINDING
PERFECT BINDING
PRINTER'S ERROR

SCREEN PRINTING

15
ANTI SET-OFF SPRAY
CALENDERED PAPER
CAST COATED PAPER
COFFEE-TABLE BOOK
DIRECT SCREENING
FLATBED PRINTING
GRAVURE PRINTING
OLD-STYLE FIGURES
PICTURE RESEARCH

16
ACKNOWLEDGEMENTS
AUTOPOSITIVE FILM
AUTOREVERSAL FILM
COLD MELT ADHESIVE
CYRILLIC ALPHABET
DOUBLE-PAGE SPREAD
INTERLINE SPACING
LINE ILLUSTRATION
PROCESS ENGRAVING
PROOFREADER'S MARK

ROUNDED AND BACKED
VANITY PUBLISHING

17
ALL RIGHTS RESERVED
DIFFUSION TRANSFER
FOLDED AND
  GATHERED
INCLUSIVE TYPE AREA

18+
ACADEMIC PUBLISHING
ACHROMATIC
  SEPARATION
CENTRAL PROCESSING
  UNIT
COLD-SET WEB
  PRINTING
COMPLEMENTARY
  COLOUR REMOVAL
DESK-TOP PUBLISHING

DISCRETIONARY
  HYPHEN

DRY-TRANSFER
  LETTERING
ELECTRONIC
  PUBLISHING
FOUR-COLOUR
  PRINTING
FOUR-COLOUR
  SEPARATION
HOT METAL
  COMPOSITION
HYPHENATION AND
  JUSTIFICATION
LINE AND TONE
  COMBINATION
OPTICAL CHARACTER
  RECOGNITION
PROOF CORRECTION
  MARKS
SILK-SCREEN PRINTING
VERTICAL
  JUSTIFICATION

BOOK AND PAPER SIZES

4
DEMY
POST
POTT

5
CROWN
FOLIO
ROYAL

6
MEDIUM
OCTAVO
QUARTO

8
FOOLSCAP
IMPERIAL

9
DUODECIMO
LARGE POST
SMALL DEMY

10
ATLAS FOLIO
CROWN FOLIO
DOUBLE DEMY
DOUBLE POST
LARGE CROWN
OCTODECIMO
ROYAL FOLIO
SMALL ROYAL
SUPER ROYAL

11
CROWN OCTAVO
CROWN QUARTO

DOUBLE CROWN
DOUBLE ROYAL
MEDIUM FOLIO
ROYAL OCTAVO
ROYAL QUARTO
SEXTODECIMO

12
MEDIUM OCTAVO
MEDIUM QUARTO

13
ELEPHANT FOLIO

14
CROWN SIXTEENMO
DOUBLE FOOLSCAP
IMPERIAL OCTAVO
ROYAL SIXTEENMO

15+
CROWN SIXTY-FOURMO
CROWN THIRTY-
  TWOMO
DOUBLE ELEPHANT
  FOLIO
MEDIUM SIXTEENMO
MEDIUM SIXTY-
  FOURMO
MEDIUM THIRTY-
  TWOMO
QUADRASEGISIMO-
  OCTAVO
ROYAL SIXTY-FOURMO
ROYAL THIRTY-TWOMO
SEXAGESIMO-QUARTO
TRIGESIMO-SEGUNDO

ARCHAEOLOGY TERMS

2&3
AMS
AXE
CRM
DIG
DNA
EDM
GIS
GPR
TL

4
ALUM
CIST
CLAY
COIN
MAYA
SILT
SITE
SLIP
SOIL
TANG
TELL
TROY
WOOD

5
BLADE
BONES
CAIRN
CHERT
DECAY
FLINT
GENUS
HENGE
HOARD
MOUND
PALEO-
QUERN
ROMAN
STONE
TOMBS
TOOLS

6
AEGEAN
BARROW
BEAKER
BURIAL
DEBRIS
GENDER
GOTHIC
GRAVES
ICE AGE
INSULA
METALS
MIDDEN
PALAEO-
TUMULI
VARVES

VILLAS

7
AEOLIAN
AZILIAN
CAPSIAN
CONTEXT
ECOLOGY
FEATURE
HOMINID
ICE CORE
IRON AGE
ISOTOPE
LAKE BED
OLDOWAN
POMPEII
POTTERY
SCRAPER

8
AMPHORAE
ARTEFACT
CHELLEAN
CROP MARK
CULTURES
EVIDENCE
GLACIALS
HALF-LIFE
HERITAGE
HILLFORT
KNAPPING
MEGALITH
METAL ORE
MUD-BRICK
OBSIDIAN
PEAT BOGS
SAVAGERY
SECTIONS
STONE AGE
TYPOLOGY

9
ACHEULIAN
BARBARISM
BIOSPHERE
BRONZE AGE
COMPONENT
ETHNICITY
EVOLUTION
FIELDWORK
FIRED CLAY
HUT CIRCLE
JEWELLERY
MICROLITH
NEOLITHIC
PRIMITIVE
SEDIMENTS
SERIATION
SOLUTREAN
SYMBOLISM

TAPHONOMY
THREE AGES
TREE RINGS

10
ANGLO-SAXON
ASSEMBLAGE
CHRONOLOGY
CLACTONIAN
COPROLITES
DERIVATIVE
EARTHWORKS
EGYPTOLOGY
EXCAVATION
GRAVE GOODS
GRAVETTIAN
HAMBURGIAN
LOWER PHASE
MESOLITHIC
METALLURGY
MOUSTERIAN
PALAEODIET
PALAEOSOLS
PALYNOLOGY
POSITIVISM
PREHISTORY
RIFT VALLEY
SETTLEMENT
STONEHENGE
STONE TOOLS
UPPER PHASE
WEATHERING

11
ABBEVILLIAN
ANTIQUARIES
ASSOCIATION
AURIGNACIAN
BURIAL MOUND
CALIBRATION
CRESWELLIAN
CROSS-DATING
ETHNOGRAPHY
FIELD SURVEY
FIELD SYSTEM
FOUNDATIONS
INSCRIPTION
MAGDALENIAN
MESOPOTAMIA
MIDDLE PHASE
NEANDERTHAL
NEW STONE AGE
OLD STONE AGE
PERIGORDIAN
PHOTOGRAPHY
PREHISTORIC
RADIOCARBON
RENAISSANCE
RITUAL SITES
ROMANTICISM

SEABED CORES

12
ANTHROPOLOGY
ARCHITECTURE
CALENDAR YEAR
CARBON DATING
CAVE DWELLERS
CHALCOLITHIC
CIVILIZATION
CONSERVATION
CRO-MAGNON MAN
DIFFUSIONISM
ETHNOGRAPHIC
FIELDWALKING
INTERGLACIAL
LAKE DWELLERS
LEVALLOISIAN
LUMINESCENCE
MAGNETOMETER
OLDUVAI GORGE
PALAEOBOTANY
PALAEOLITHIC
POLLEN GRAINS
RELATIVE AGES
ROSETTA STONE
SHELL MIDDENS
STONE CIRCLES
STRATIGRAPHY

13
ARCHAEOLOGIST
CLIFF DWELLERS
DOMESTICATION
ENLIGHTENMENT
FOLSOM CULTURE
GEOCHRONOLOGY
HUNTER-GATHERER
MAGNETIC FIELD
PARADIGM SHIFT
PROCESSUALISM
REMOTE SENSING
SAMIAN POTTERY
SITE FORMATION
VOLCANIC GLASS
WATTLE AND DAUB

14
ABSOLUTE DATING
ANTHROPOLOGIST
ANTIQUARIANISM
CHATELPERRONIAN
GEOLOGICAL TIME
MAGNETIC DATING
NEW ARCHAEOLOGY
RELATIVE DATING
STRATIFICATION
THREE AGE SYSTEM
TREE-RING DATING
ZOOARCHAEOLOGY

15
BOX TRENCH SYSTEM
CLIMATIC FACTORS
CUP AND RING MARKS
GEOLOGICAL ROCKS
ISOTOPE ANALYSIS
MATERIAL CULTURE
NOBLE SAVAGE MYTH
PALAEOMAGNETISM
PRESSURE-FLAKING
RELATIVE SYSTEMS
SOCIAL EVOLUTION

16
ARCHAEOASTRONOMY
ARCHAEOMAGNETISM
BULB OF PERCUSSION
CALIBRATION CURVE
CHARACTERIZATION
DENDROCHRONOLOGY
ETHNOARCHAEOLOGY
FIELD ARCHAEOLOGY
GEOLOGICAL STRATA
ORGANIC MATERIALS
PALAEODEMOGRAPHY
RADIOACTIVE DECAY
TERMINUS ANTE QUEM
TERMINUS POST QUEM
VOLCANIC DEPOSITS

17
ABSOLUTE TECHNIQUE
AERIAL ARCHAEOLOGY
AERIAL PHOTOGRAPHY
EXCAVATION METHODS

GEOMAGNETIC SURVEY
GEOPHYSICAL SURVEY
LANDSCAPE FEATURES
MAGNETIC SURVEYING
MIDDLE RANGE THEORY
OBSIDIAN HYDRATION
PALAEOENVIRONMENT
POSTGLACIAL PERIOD
RADIOCARBON DATING
RESCUE ARCHAEOLOGY
RESISTIVITY METERS
SELECTIVE BREEDING

18
CHRONOMETRIC DATING
DOMESTICATED PLANTS
FORMATION PROCESSES
MAGNETOMETER SURVEY
NORTH-SOUTH REVERSAL
OPEN-AREA EXCAVATION
SALVAGE ARCHAEOLOGY

19
BIBLICAL ARCHAEOLOGY
CLIMATOSTRATIGRAPHY
DOMESTICATED ANIMALS
ETHNOARCHAEOLOGICAL
MEDIEVAL ARCHAEOLOGY
NEOLITHIC REVOLUTION
RADIOACTIVE ISOTOPES

20
CLASSICAL ARCHAEOLOGY
GEOPHYSICAL TECHNIQUE
LANDSCAPE ARCHAEOLOGY
POTASSIUM-ARGON DATING

RADIOMETRIC TECHNIQUE
RESISTIVITY SURVEYING

21
ABSOLUTE DATING SYSTEMS
ARCHAEOMAGNETIC DATING
HISTORICAL ARCHAEOLOGY
INDUSTRIAL ARCHAEOLOGY
METALLURGICAL ANALYSIS
STRATIGRAPHIC SEQUENCE
UNDERWATER ARCHAEOLOGY

22+
ACCELERATOR MASS
  SPECTROMETRY
ANATOMICALLY MODERN
  HUMANS
ELECTRONIC DISTANCE
  MEASUREMENT
ENVIRONMENTAL
  ARCHAEOLOGY
EXPERIMENTAL ARCHAEOLOGY
GEOGRAPHICAL INFORMATION
  SYSTEM
GEOPHYSICAL INSTRUMENTS
GROUND PENETRATING RADAR
INTERPRETIVE ARCHAEOLOGY
MAGNETIC SUSCEPTIBILITY
  SURVEY
OBSIDIAN HYDRATION DATING
  TECHNIQUE
POSTPROCESSUAL
  ARCHAEOLOGY
SATELLITE RECONNAISSANCE
THERMOLUMINESCENCE DATING

MUSEUMS AND GALLERIES

AMERICAN MUSEUM (Bath)
ART GALLERY (Aberdeen)
ART GALLERY AND MUSEUM
  (Glasgow)
ASHMOLEAN (Oxford)
BALTIC CENTRE FOR
  CONTEMPORARY ART, THE
  (Gateshead)
BARBARA HEPWORTH MUSEUM
  (St Ives)
BEAMISH OPEN AIR MUSEUM
  (County Durham)
BEATLES STORY (Liverpool)
BIG PIT MINING MUSEUM
  (Blaenafon)
BLISTS HILL MUSEUM
  (Ironbridge Gorge)
BRIGHTON MUSEUM AND ART
  GALLERY (Brighton)
BRISTOL INDUSTRIAL MUSEUM
  (Bristol)

BRITISH MUSEUM (London)
BUCKLER'S HARD (Beaulieu)
BUILDING OF BATH MUSEUM
  (Bath)
BURRELL COLLECTION (Glasgow)
CADBURY WORLD (Bournville)
CASTLE MUSEUM (Norwich)
CENTRE FOR ALTERNATIVE
  TECHNOLOGY (Machynlleth)
CHELTENHAM ART GALLERY AND
  MUSEUM (Cheltenham)
CITY ART GALLERY (Leeds)
CITY MUSEUM AND ART
  GALLERY (Birmingham)
CITY MUSEUM AND ART
  GALLERY (Bristol)
COALPORT CHINA MUSEUM
  (Ironbridge Gorge)
CRICH NATIONAL TRAMWAY
  MUSEUM (Crich)
D-DAY MUSEUM (Portsmouth)

DESIGN MUSEUM (London)
DULWICH PICTURE GALLERY
  (London)
FITZWILLIAM MUSEUM
  (Cambridge)
FOTOGRAFISKA (London)
GOONHILLY EARTH STATION
  (Lizard Peninsular)
HAYWARD GALLERY (London)
HUNTERIAN ART GALLERY
  (Glasgow)
IMPERIAL WAR MUSEUM
  (Duxford)
IMPERIAL WAR MUSEUM
  (London)
IRONBRIDGE GORGE MUSEUM
  (Telford)
KELVINGROVE ART GALLERY
  AND MUSEUM (Glasgow)
LIVERPOOL MUSEUM
  (Liverpool)

LLECHWEDD SLATE CAVERNS (Blaenau)
LONDON DUNGEON (London)
LONDON TRANSPORT MUSEUM (London)
LOWRY GALLERY (Manchester)
MADAME TUSSAUD'S (London)
MANCHESTER ART GALLERY (Manchester)
MARITIME AND INDUSTRIAL MUSEUM (Swansea)
MARITIME MUSEUM (Southampton)
MILLENNIUM GALLERIES (Sheffield)
MUSEUM OF IRON (Ironbridge Gorge)
MUSEUM OF ISLAY LIFE (Islay)
MUSEUM OF LONDON (London)
MUSEUM OF LIVERPOOL (Liverpool)
MUSEUM OF NORTH DEVON (Barnstaple)
MUSEUM OF OXFORD (Oxford)
MUSEUM OF SCIENCE AND INDUSTRY
   (Manchester)
MUSEUM OF SCOTLAND (Edinburgh)
MUSEUM OF TRANSPORT (Glasgow)
MUSEUM OF VICTORIAN SCIENCE (Whitby)
NATIONAL COAL MINING MUSEUM (Wakefield)
NATIONAL FISHING HERITAGE CENTRE (Grimsby)
NATIONAL GALLERY (London)
NATIONAL GALLERY OF MODERN ART & DEAN
   GALLERY (Edinburgh)
NATIONAL GALLERY OF SCOTLAND (Edinburgh)
NATIONAL HORESRACING MUSEUM (Newmarket)
NATIONAL MARITIME MUSEUM (Greenwich)
NATIONAL MOTOR MUSEUM (Beaulieu)
NATIONAL MUSEUM OF PHOTOGRAPHY, FILM AND
   TELEVISION (Bradford)
NATIONAL MUSEUM OF WALES (Cardiff)
NATIONAL PORTRAIT GALLERY (London)
NATIONAL RAILWAY MUSEUM (York)
NATURAL HISTORY MUSEUM (London)
NEW WALK MUSEUM (Leicester)
NORTH CORNWALL MUSEUM AND GALLERY
   (Camelford)
NORTH DEVON MARITIME MUSEUM (Appledore)

OXFORD STORY, THE (Oxford)
PITT RIVERS MUSEUM (Oxford)
PLANETARIUM (London)
POLDARK MINE (Lizard Peninsular)
QUEEN'S GALLERY, Buckingham Palace (London)
RAF ROYAL AIR FORCE MUSEUM (Hendon)
ROMAN BATHS MUSEUM (Bath)
ROYAL ALBERT MEMORAIL MUSEUM AND ART
   GALLERY (Exeter)
ROYAL ARMOURIES MUSEUM (Leeds)
ROYAL CORNWALL (Truro)
ROYAL NAVAL MUSEUM (Portsmouth)
ROYAL OBSERVATORY GREENWICH (Greenwich)
ROYAL PUMP ROOM MUSEUM (Harrogate)
SAATCHI GALLERY (London)
SAINSBURY CENTRE FOR VISUAL ARTS (Norwich)
SCIENCE MUSEUM (London)
SCOTTISH FISHERIES MUSEUM (Anstruther)
SCOTTISH NATIONAL PORTRAIT GALLERY
   (Edinburgh)
SHERLOCK HOLMES MUSEUM (London)
ST MUNGO'S MUSEUM OF RELIGIOUS LIFE AND
   ART (Glasgow)
TATE LIVERPOOL (Liverpool)
TATE MODERN (London)
TATE ST IVES (St Ives)
THACKERY MEDICAL MUSEUM (Leeds)
UNIVERSITY MUSEUM (Oxford)
VERULAMIUM MUSEUM (St Albans)
V&A DUNDEE (Dundee)
VICTORIA AND ALBERT MUSEUM (London)
WALKER ART GALLERY (Liverpool)
WALLACE COLLECTION (London)
WHEAL MAWRTYN CHINA CLAY MUSEUM
   (Carthew)
YORK CASTLE MUSEUM (York)
YORK CITY ART GALLERY (York)
YORKSHIRE SCULPTURE PARK (Wakefield)
YORVIK VIKING CENTRE (York)

STATELY HOMES

A LA RONDE (Devonshire)
ABBOTSFORD HOUSE (Scottish borders)
ALTHORP HOUSE (Northamptonshire)
ARLINGTON COURT (Devon)
AUDLEY END (Essex)
BLENHEIM PALACE (Oxfordshire)
BLICKLING HALL (Norfolk)
BOWOOD HOUSE (Wiltshire)
BROADLANDS (Hampshire)
BURGHLEY HOUSE (Lincolnshire)
BURTON AGNES (East Yorkshire)
BURTON CONSTABLE (East Yorkshire)
CASTLE HOWARD (Yorkshire)
CHARLECOTE PARK (Warwickshire)
CHATSWORTH HOUSE (Derbyshire)
CHISWICK HOUSE (London)
CLANDON PARK (Surrey)

CLAYDON HOUSE (Buckinghamshire)
CLIVEDEN (Buckinghamshire)
CORSHAM COURT (Wiltshire)
DALEMAIN (Cumbria)
FAIRFAX HOUSE (York)
FOUNTAINS HALL (North Yorkshire)
GLYNDE PLACE (East Sussex)
GOODWOOD HOUSE (West Sussex)
GREAT DIXTER (East Sussex)
HADDON HALL (Derbyshire)
HAMPTON COURT (Surrey)
HARDWICK HALL (Derbyshire)
HAREWOOD HOUSE (West Yorkshire)
HATFIELD HOUSE (Hertfordshire)
HOLKER HALL (Cumbria)
HOLKHAM HALL (Norfolk)
HOPETOUN HOUSE (West Lothian)

HUGHENDEN MANOR (Buckinghamshire)
HUTTON-IN-THE-FOREST (Cumbria)
ICKWORTH HOUSE (Suffolk)
KEDLESTON HALL (Derbyshire)
KELMSCOTT MANOR (Oxfordshire)
KINGSTON LACY (Dorset)
KNEBWORTH HOUSE (Hertfordshire)
KNOLE (Kent)
LANHYDROCK (Cornwall)
LEIGHTON HALL (Lancashire)
LEVENS HALL (Cumbria)
LITTLE MORETON HALL (Cheshire)
LONGLEAT (Wiltshire)
MELLERSTAIN HOUSE (Scottish Borders)
MONTACUTE HOUSE (Dorset)
MOSELEY OLD HALL (Staffordshire)
NEWBY HALL (North Yorkshire)
NUNNINGTON HALL (York)
OSBOURNE HOUSE (Isle of Wight)
OXBURGH HALL (Norfolk)
PACKWOOD HOUSE (Warwickshire)

PENSHURST PLACE (Kent)
PETWORTH HOUSE (West Sussex)
PLAS NEWYDD (Denbighshire)
PLAS-YN-RHIW (Gwynedd)
QUENBY HALL (Leicestershire)
ROYAL PAVILION (Brighton)
SALTRAM HOUSE (Devon)
SANDRINGHAM (Norfolk)
SCONE PALACE (Perthshire)
SNOWSHILL MANOR (Gloucestershire)
SOMERLEYTON HALL (Suffolk)
SPEKE HALL (Merseyside)
STOURHEAD (Wiltshire)
STRATFIELD SAYE (Hampshire/Berkshire border)
SYON HOUSE (London)
TRAQUAIR HOUSE (Scottish Borders)
WADDESDON MANOR (Buckinghamshire)
WIGHTWICK MANOR (West Midlands)
WILTON HOUSE (Wiltshire)
WOBURN ABBEY (Bedfordshire)

ABBEYS AND PRIORIES

ABBEY DORE (Herefordshire)
ANGLESEY ABBEY (Cambridgeshire)
BATH ABBEY (Bath)
BATTLE ABBEY (East Sussex)
BEAULIEU ABBEY (Hampshire)
BOLTON PRIORY (North Yorkshire)
BUCKFAST ABBEY (Devon)
BUCKLAND ABBEY (Devon)
BYLAND ABBEY (North Yorkshire)
CARTMEL PRIORY (Cumbria)
CASTLE ACRE PRIORY (Norfolk)
CHRISTCHURCH PRIORY (Dorset)
DRYBURGH ABBEY (Scottish Borders)
EASBY ABBEY (North Yorkshire)
FOUNTAINS ABBEY (North Yorkshire)
FURNESS ABBEY (Cumbria)
GLASTONBURY (Somerset)
HEXHAM ABBEY (Northumberland)
INCHMAHOME PRIORY (Stirling)
JEDBURGH ABBEY (Scottish Borders)

KELSO ABBEY (Scottish Borders)
KIRKHAM PRIORY (North Yorkshire)
KIRKSTALL ABBEY (West Yorkshire)
LACOCK ABBEY (Wiltshire)
LANERCOST PRIORY (Cumbria)
LINDISFARNE PRIORY (Northumberland)
LLANTHONY PRIORY (Gwent)
MELROSE ABBEY (Scottish Borders)
MOUNT GRACE PRIORY (North Yorkshire)
RIEVAULX ABBEY (North Yorkshire)
SELBY ABBEY (West Yorkshire)
SHERBORNE ABBEY (Dorset)
ST MARY'S ABBEY (York)
ST NICHOLAS PRIORY (Devon)
TINTERN ABBEY (Gwent)
TORRE ABBEY (Devon)
WHALLEY ABBEY (Lancashire)
WHITBY ABBEY (North Yorkshire)
WOBURN ABBEY (Bedfordshire)

BRITISH CASTLES

3&4

DEAL (England)
DRUM (Scotland)
ETAL (England)
RABY (England)
ROSS (Ireland)
RYE (England)

5

AYDON (England)
BLACK (Ireland)
BOWES (England)
CABRA (Ireland)
CAREW (Wales)
CONWY (Wales)
CORFE (England)
DOUNE (Scotland)
DOVER (England)
EWLOE (Wales)
FLINT (Wales)
FYVIE (Scotland)
HEVER (England)
LEEDS (England)
LEWES (England)
UPNOR (England)
WHITE (Wales)

6

BODIAM (England)
BOLTON (England)
BROUGH (England)
CAMBER (England)
DUBLIN (Ireland)
DUFFUS (Scotland)
EDZELL (Scotland)
FRASER (Scotland)
GLAMIS (Scotland)
HAILES (Scotland)
HUNTLY (Scotland)
KELLIE (Scotland)
MORTON (Scotland)
NEWARK (England)
NORHAM (England)
NUNNEY (England)
ODIHAM (England)
ORFORD (England)
PENHOW (Wales)
RAGLAN (Wales)
ROTHES (Scotland)
TIORAM (Scotland)
TOTNES (England)
WALDEN (England)
WALMER (England)

7

ALNWICK (England)
APPLEBY (England)
ARUNDEL (England)
BARNARD (England)
BEESTON (England)

BERWICK (England)
BLARNEY (Ireland)
CARDIFF (Wales)
CARRICK (Ireland)
CRATHES (Scotland)
DENBIGH (Wales)
DINEFWR (Wales)
DONEGAL (Ireland)
DUNSTER (England)
FARNHAM (England)
HARLECH (Wales)
LINCOLN (England)
LYDFORD (England)
OLD WICK, Castle of (Scotland)
PENRITH (England)
PRUDHOE (England)
ST MAWES (England)
SKIPSEA (England)
SKIPTON (England)
STALKER (Scotland)
THREAVE (Scotland)
TUTBURY (England)
WARWICK (England)
WEOBLEY (Wales)
WICKLOW (Ireland)
WINDSOR (England)

8

ABERDOUR (Scotland)
ARDVRECK (Scotland)
BALVENIE (Scotland)
BAMBURGH (England)
BROUGHAM (England)
BUNRATTY (Ireland)
CARLISLE (England)
CHEPSTOW (Wales)
CORGARFF (Scotland)
CRICHTON (Scotland)
DELGATIE (Scotland)
DIRLETON (Scotland)
DRISHANE (Ireland)
DRYSLWYN (Wales)
DUNGIVEN (Ireland)
EYNSFORD (England)
GOODRICH (England)
GROSMONT (Wales)
HADLEIGH (England)
HELMSLEY (England)
KIDWELLY (Wales)
KILCHURN (Scotland)
LONGTOWN (England)
PEMBROKE (Wales)
PEVENSEY (England)
PORTLAND (England)
RICHMOND (England)
STIRLING (Scotland)
TAMWORTH (England)
TINTAGEL (England)
TOLQUHON (Scotland)
URQUHART (Scotland)

YARMOUTH (England)

9

BEAUMARIS (Wales)
CARDONESS (Scotland)
CASTLE ROS (Ireland)
CLAYPOTTS (Scotland)
CRICCIETH (Wales)
DARTMOUTH (England)
DROMOLAND (Ireland)
DUNNOTTAR (Scotland)
EDINBURGH (Scotland)
EDLINGHAM (England)
FINDLATER (Scotland)
GUILDFORD (England)
HEDINGHAM (England)
KILDRUMMY (Scotland)
KINGSWEAR (England)
LAUGHARNE (Wales)
LLANTILIO (Wales)
LLAWHADEN (Wales)
MANORBIER (Wales)
MIDDLEHAM (England)
PENDENNIS (England)
PENDRAGON (England)
PICKERING (England)
RESTORMEL (England)
ROCHESTER (England)
SHANKHILL (Ireland)
SKENFRITH (Wales)
SPOFFORTH (England)
TANTALLON (Scotland)
WARKWORTH (England)

10

AUCHINDOUN (Scotland)
BALLYMALOO (Ireland)
CAERNARFON (Wales)
CAERPHILLY (Wales)
CASTLE ACRE (England)
CASTLE SHAN (Ireland)
COLCHESTER (England)
CRAIGIEVAR (Scotland)
DONNINGTON (England)
GLENBUCHAT (Scotland)
KENILWORTH (England)
KILLYLEAGH (Ireland)
LAUNCESTON (England)
LINLITHGOW (Scotland)
OKEHAMPTON (England)
OLD WARDOUR (England)

11

BALLYCASTLE (Ireland)
BARDEN TOWER (England)
BAYARD'S COVE (England)
BERKHAMSTED (England)
CARISBROOKE (England)
CARRIGONNON (Ireland)
CASTELL COCH (Wales)

CASTLE KELLY (Ireland)
CASTLE SHANE (Ireland)
CHILLINGHAM (England)
CONISBROUGH (England)
CRAIGMILLAR (Scotland)
DOLWYDDELAN (Wales)
EILEAN DONAN (Scotland)
FRAMLINGHAM (England)
LINDISFARNE (England)
LLANSTEFFAN (Wales)
MACLELLAN'S (Scotland)
PORTCHESTER (England)
RAVENSCRAIG (Scotland)
SCARBOROUGH (England)
TATTERSHALL (England)
TILBURY FORT (England)

12
BERRY POMEROY (England)
CAERLAVEROCK (Scotland)
CARREG CENNEN (Wales)
CASTELL Y BERE (Wales)
CASTLE FRASER (Scotland)
CASTLE RISING (England)
DUNSTANBURGH (England)
HERSTMONCEUX (England)
HUNTINGTOWER (Scotland)
SHERBORNE OLD (England)
SPYNIE PALACE (Scotland)

13
BALLINDALLOCH (Scotland)
CASTLE DONOVAN (Ireland)
CASTLE STALKER (Scotland)

KNARESBOROUGH (England)
ST CATHERINE'S (England)
TOWER OF LONDON (England)

14
CASTLE CAMPBELL (Scotland)
FALKLAND PALACE (Scotland)

15+
CLIFFORD'S TOWER (England)
CLOUGH BALLYMORE (Ireland)
FARLEIGH HUNGERFORD
  (England)
ORCHARDTON TOWER (Scotland)
SINCLAIR GIRNIGOE (Scotland)
ST MICHAEL'S MOUNT (England)
WINCHESTER GREAT HALL
  (England)

FAMOUS BUILDINGS AND STRUCTURES

ACROPOLIS
ALHAMBRA
ARC DE TRIOMPHE
BRITISH MUSEUM
BUCKINGHAM PALACE
BURJ KHALIFA
CHICHEN ITZA
CHRYSLER BUILDING
COLOSSEUM
COLOSSUS OF RHODES
DOME OF THE ROCK
DUOMO
EDINBURGH CASTLE
EIFFEL TOWER
EMPIRE STATE BUILDING
GHERKIN
GOLDEN GATE BRIDGE
GREAT SPHINX
GREAT WALL OF CHINA
GUGGENHEIM BILBAO MUSEUM
GUGGENHEIM MUSEUM
HOOVER DAM
HOUSES OF PARLIAMENT (or PALACE OF
  WESTMINSTER)
KREMLIN
LEANING TOWER OF PISA
LIBRARY OF ALEXANDRIA

LOUVRE MUSEUM
MACAU TOWER
MACHU PICCHU
MOUNT RUSHMORE
NOTRE-DAME DE PARIS
PALACE OF VERSAILLES
PANTHEON
PARTHENON
PETRONAS TWIN TOWERS
PYRAMIDS OF GIZA
SACRÉ COEUR
SHARD
SPACE NEEDLE, SEATTLE
ST BASIL'S CATHEDRAL
ST MARK'S CATHEDRAL
ST PAUL'S CATHEDRAL
ST PETER'S BASILICA
STATUE OF LIBERTY
STONEHENGE
SYDNEY OPERA HOUSE
TAJ MAHAL
TOWER OF LONDON
WESTMINSTER ABBEY
WHITE HOUSE
WILLIS TOWER (or SEARS TOWER)
WORLD TRADE CENTER

MUSICAL TERMS

TERM – definition

1&2

F – loud
FF - very loud
MF – half loud
P – soft
PP – very soft
SF – strongly accented

3

BIS – repeat
DIM – becoming softer
PED – abbr. for pedal
PIÙ – more
PIZ – plucked
RFZ – accentuated
RIT – slowing down, holding back
SFZ – strongly accented
TEN – held
VIF – lively (Fr.)

4

CODA – final part of a movement
MOTO – motion
RALL – slowing down
SINO – up to; until
TIEF – deep; low (Ger.)

5

AD LIB – at will
ASSAI – very
BUFFO – comic
DOLCE – sweet
FORTE – loud
LARGO – very slow
LENTO – slowly
MESTO – sad, mournful
MEZZO – half
MOLTO – very much
MOSSO – moving, fast
PIANO – soft
QUASI – almost, as if
SEGNO – sign
SENZA – without
SOAVE – sweet; gentle
STARK – strong, loud (Ger.)
TACET – instrument is silent
TANTO – so much
TEMPO – the speed of a composition
TUTTI – all
ZOPPA – in syncopated rhythm

6

ADAGIO – slow
AL FINE – to the end
CHIUSO – stopped (of a note); closed
DA CAPO – from the beginning
DEHORS – outside; prominent

DIVISI – divided
DOPPIO – double
FACILE – easy, fluent
LEGATO – bound, tied (of notes), smoothly
MARCIA – march
NIENTE – nothing
NOBILE – noble
RETENU – held back
SEMPRE – always, still
SUBITO – immediately
TENUTO – held

7

AGITATO – agitated; rapid tempo
ALLEGRO – lively, brisk
AL SEGNO – as far as the sign
AMOROSO – loving, emotional
ANIMATO – spirited
ATTACCA – attack; continue without a pause
CALANDO – ebbing; lessening of tempo
CODETTA – small coda; to conclude a passage
CON BRIO – with vigour
DOLENTE – sorrowful
ESTINTO – extremely softly, almost without tone
GIOCOSO – merry; playful
MARCATO – accented
MORBIDO – soft, delicate
PESANTE – heavily, firmly
SCHNELL – fast (Ger.)
SFOGATO – effortless; in a free manner
SORDINO – mute
STRETTO – accelerating or intensifying; overlapping of entries of fugue

8

A BATTUTA – return to strict time
A PIACERE – as you please
BRILLANT – brilliant
COL CANTO – accompaniment to follow solo line
COL LEGNO – to strike strings with stick of the bow
CON FUOCO – fiery; vigorous
DAL SEGNO – from the sign
IN MODO DI – in the manner of
MAESTOSO – majestic
MODERATO – moderately
PORTANDO – carrying one note into the next
RITENUTO – slowing down, holding back
SOURDINE – mute (Fr.)
STACCATO – detached
VIVEMENT – lively (Fr.)

9

ADAGIETTO – quite slow
CANTABILE – in a singing fashion
CANTILENA – lyrical, flowing
CRESCENDO – becoming louder
FIORITURA – decoration of a melody
GLISSANDO – sliding scale played on instrument
MENO MOSSO – slower pace
MEZZA VOCE – at half power
OBBLIGATO – not to be omitted
PIUTTOSTO – somewhat
PIZZICATO – plucked
SCHNELLER – faster (Ger.)
SFORZANDO – strongly accented
SIN'AL FINE – up to the end
SLENTANDO – slowing down
SOSTENUTO – sustained
SOTTO VOCE – quiet subdued tone

10

AFFETTUOSO – tender
ALLA CACCIA – in hunting style
ALLARGANDO – broadening; more dignified
ALLEGRETTO – quite lively, brisk
DIMINUENDO – becoming softer
FORTISSIMO – very loud
MEZZOFORTE – half loud
NOBILMENTE – nobly
PERDENDOSI – dying away gradually
PIANISSIMO – very soft
PORTAMENTO – carrying one note into the next
RAVVIVANDO – quickening
RITARDANDO – slowing down, holding back
SCHERZANDO – joking; playing
SCHLEPPEND – dragging; deviating from correct speed (Ger.)
SCORREVOLE – gliding; fluent
STRINGENDO – tightening; intensification

11

ACCELERANDO – accelerating
AFFRETTANDO – hurrying
MINACCIANDO – menacing
RALLENTANDO – slowing down
RINFORZANDO – accentuated

12

ALLA CAPPELLA – in church style
LEGGERAMENTE – lightly

13

LEGGIERAMENTE – lightly

TONIC SOL-FA

DOH	RAY	ME	FAH	SOH	LAH	TE

MUSICAL INSTRUMENTS

2
UD (lute)
YÜ (scraper)

3
BIN (vina)
KIT (fiddle)
LUR (horn)
OUD (ud)
SAZ (lute)
SHÔ (mouth organ)
TAR (drum; lute)
UTI (lute)

4
BATA (drum)
BIWA (lute)
CH'IN (zither)
DRUM
FIFE
FUYE (flute)
GONG
HARP
HORN
KENA (quena)
KHEN (mouth organ)
KOTO (zither)
LIRA (fiddle)
LUTE
LYRA (lyre)
LYRE
MU YÜ (drum)
MVET (zither)
OBOE
OUTI (lute)
P'I P'A (lute)
PIPE
ROTE (lyre)
RUAN (lute)
SONA (shawm)
TRO-U (fiddle)
URUA (clarinet)
VINA (stringed
   instrument related to
   sitar)
VIOL
WHIP (percussion)
ZOBO (mirliton)

5
AULOI (shawm)

BANJO
BELLS
BHAYA (kettledrum)
BUGLE
BUMPA (clarinet)
CELLO
CHANG (dulcimer)
CHIME
CLAVE
COBZA (lute)
CORNU (trumpet)
CRWTH (lyre)
DAULI (drum)
DHOLA (drum)
DOBRO (guitar)
ERH-HU (fiddle)
FIDEL (fiddle)
FIDLA (zither)
FLUTE
GAITA (bagpipe)
GAJDY (bagpipe)
GUSLE (fiddle)
HURUK (drum)
KAKKO (drum)
KANUN (qanun)
KAZOO (mirliton)
KERAR (lyre)
KO-KIU (fiddle)
MBILA (xylophone)
NGOMA (drum)
NGURU (flute)
OKEDO (drum)
ORGAN
PIANO
PI NAI (shawm)
PU-ILU (clappers)
QANUN (zither)
QUENA (flute)
RASPA (scraper)
REBAB (fiddle)
REBEC (fiddle)
SARON (metallophone)
SHAWM
SHENG (mouth organ)
SITAR (lute)
TABLA (drum)
TABOR (drum)
TAIKO (drum)
TIBIA (shawm)
TIPLE (shawm)

TI-TZU (flute)
TUDUM (drum)
TUMYR (drum)
TUPAN (drum)
VIOLA
YUN LO (gong)
ZURLA (shawm)
ZURNA (shawm)

6
ALBOKA (hornpipe)
ARGHUL (clarinet)
BAGANA (lyre)
BINIOU (bagpipe)
CARNYX (trumpet)
CHAKAY (zither)
CHA PEI (lute)
CORNET
CURTAL (double reed)
DARBUK (drum)
FANDUR (fiddle)
FIDDLE
FUJARA (flute)
GEKKIN (lute)
GENDER (metallophone)
GONGUE (percussion)
GUITAR
HU CH'IN (fiddle)
HUMMEL (zither)
KENONG (gong)
KISSAR (lyre)
KOBORO (drum)
LIRICA (fiddle)
LIRONE (fiddle)
LITUUS (trumpet)
LONTAR (clappers)
MAYURI (lute)
MOROPI (drum)
NAKERS (drums)
NAQARA (drums)
NTENGA (drum)
O-DAIKO (drum)
OMBGWE (flute)
P'AI PAN (clappers)
POMMER (shawm)
RACKET (double reed)
RAMKIE (lute)
RATTLE
REBECK (fiddle)
SANTIR (dulcimer)
SHAING (horn)

SHAKER
SHANAI (shawm)
SHIELD (percussion)
SHOFAR (horn)
SOPILE (shawm)
SPINET
SPOONS (clappers)
SRALAY (shawm)
SURNAJ (shawm)
SWITCH (percussion)
SYRINX (panpipe)
TAM-TAM (gong)
TOM-TOM (drum)
TXISTU (flute)
VALIHA (zither)
VIELLE (fiddle)
VIOLIN
YANGUM (dulcimer)
ZITHER

7
ADENKUM (stamping
   tube)
ALPHORN (trumpet)
ANKLUNG (rattle)
ATUMPAN (kettledrum)
BAGPIPE
BARYTON (viol)
BASSOON
BODHRAN (drum)
BONNANG (gong)
BOW HARP
BOX LYRE
BUCCINA (trumpet)
BUISINE (trumpet)
BUMBASS
CELESTE
CHANGKO (drum)
CITTERN
CORNETT
COWBELL
CROTALS (percussion)
CYMBALS
DA-DAIKO (drum)
DIPLICE (clarinet)
DUGDUGI (drum)
ENZENZE (zither)
FITHELE (fiddle)
GADULKA (fiddle)
GITTERN
GLING-BU (flute)

HULA IPU (percussion)
INGUNGU (drum)
ISIGUBU (drum)
KACHAPI (zither)
KALUNGU (talking
  drum)
KAMANJE (fiddle)
KANTELE (zither)
KEMANAK (clappers)
KITHARA (lyre)
KOMUNGO (zither)
MACHETE (lute)
MANDOLA (lute)
MARACAS (percussion)
MASENQO (fiddle)
MIGYAUN (zither)
MOKUGYO (drum)
MURUMBU (drum)
MUSETTE (bagpipe)
MUSETTE (shawm)
OBUKANO (lyre)
OCARINA (flute)
OCTAVIN (wind)
ORPHICA (piano)
PANDORA (cittern)
PANPIPE
PIANINO
PIBCORN (hornpipe)
PICCOLO
PIFFARO (shawm)
QUINTON (viol)
RESHOTO (drum)
RINCHIK (cymbals)
SACKBUT (trombone)
SALPINX (trumpet)
SAMISEN (lute)
SANTOOR (dulcimer)
SARANGI (fiddle)
SARINDA (fiddle)
SAW-THAI (fiddle)
SAXHORN
SAXTUBA
SERPENT
SHIWAYA (flute)
SISTRUM (rattle)
SORDINE (kit)
SORDONE (double reed)
SPAGANE (clappers)
TAMÂM LA (gong)
TAMBURA (lute)
TERBANG (drum)
THEORBO (lute)
TIKTIRI (clarinet)
TIMPANI
TRUMPET
TSUZUMI (drum)
UJUSINI (flute)
UKULELE
VIHUELA (guitar)
VIOLONE (viol)
WHISTLE
YUN NGAO (gong)
ZUMMARA (clarinet)

8
ALGHAITA (shawm)
ALTOHORN
AUTOHARP
BANDOURA (lute)
BASS DRUM
BASS HORN
BOMBARDE (shawm)
BOUZOUKI (lute)
BOWL LYRE
BUZZ DISK
CALLIOPE (mechanical
  organ)
CARILLON
CHIME BAR
CIMBALOM (dulcimer)
CIPACTLI (flute)
CLAPPERS
CLARINET
CLAVICOR (brass family)
CLAW BELL
COURTAUT (double
  reed)
CRECELLE (cog rattle)
CRUMHORN (double
  reed)
DULCIMER
DVOYNICE (flute)
GONG DRUM
HANDBELL
HAND HORN
HAWKBELL
JEW'S HARP
KAYAKEUM (zither)
KHUMBGWE (flute)
LANGLEIK (zither)
LANGSPIL (zither)
LAP ORGAN (melodeon)
MANDOLIN (lute)
MELODEON
MELODICA
MIRLITON (kazoo)
MRIDANGA (drum)
OLIPHANT (horn)
O-TSUZUMI (drum)
OTTAVINO (virginal)
P'AI HSIAO (panpipe)
PENORCON (cittern)
POCHETTE (kit)
PSALTERY (zither)
PUTORINO (trumpet)
RECORDER
RKAN-DUNG (trumpet)
RKAN-LING (horn)
RONÉAT-EK (xylophone)
SAN HSIEN (lute)
SIDE DRUM
SLIT DRUM
SONAJERO (rattle)
SRINGARA (fiddle)
SURBAHAR (lute)
TALAMBAS (drum)
TARABUKA (drum)

TAROGATO (clarinet;
  shawm)
TIMBALES (drum)
TRIANGLE
TRO-KHMER (fiddle)
TROMBONE
VIOLETTA (viol)
VIRGINAL
YANGCHIN (dulcimer)
YUEH CH'IN (lute)
ZAMPOGNA (bagpipe)

9
ACCORDION
ANGLE HARP
ARPANETTA (zither)
BALALAIKA (lute)
BANDURRIA (lute)
BANJOLELE
BASSONORE (bassoon)
BOMBARDON (tuba)
CASTANETS
CHALUMEAU (clarinet)
COG RATTLE
COMPONIUM
  (mechanical organ)
CORNEMUSE (bagpipe)
CORNOPEAN (brass
  family)
CROOK HORN
DAIBYOSHI (drum)
DARABUKKE (drum)
DJUNADJAN (zither)
DUDELSACK (bagpipes)
DVOJACHKA (flute)
EUPHONIUM (brass
  family)
FLAGEOLET (flute)
FLEXATONE
  (percussion)
GONG AGENG
HACKBRETT (dulcimer)
HARMONICA
HARMONIUM
HYDRAULIS (organ)
KELONTONG (drum)
KÖNIGHORN (brass
  family)
LAUNEDDAS (clarinet)
MANDOBASS (lute)
MANDOLONE (lute)
MORIN-CHUR (fiddle)
ORPHARION (cittern)
PICCO PIPE (flute)
PIEN CH'ING
  (lithophone)
ROMMELPOT (drum)
SAXOPHONE
TALLHARPA (lyre)
TOTOMBITO (zither)
TUBA-DUPRÉ
WOOD BLOCK
WURLITZER
XYLOPHONE

XYLORIMBA
  (xylophone)

10
BANANA DRUM
BARREL DRUM
BASSANELLO (double
  reed)
BASSET HORN
BIBLE REGAL (organ)
BICITRABIN (vina)
BIRD SCARER
BONGO DRUMS
BULL-ROARER
CHENGCHENG (cymbals)
CHITARRONE (lute)
CLAVICHORD
CLAVIORGAN
COLASCIONE (lute)
CONTRABASS (double
  bass)
COR ANGLAIS
DIDGERIDOO (trumpet)
DOUBLE BASS
FLUGELHORN
FRENCH HORN
GEIGENWERK
  (mechanical
  harpsichord)
GONG CHIMES
GRAND PIANO
HANDLE DRUM
HURDY GURDY
KETTLEDRUM
LITHOPHONE
  (percussion)
MANDOCELLO (lute)
MELLOPHONE (horn)
MOSHUPIANE (drum)
MOUTH ORGAN
OPHICLEIDE (brass
  family)
RANASRINGA (horn)
SAXOTROMBA
SHAKUHACHI (flute)
SOUSAPHONE
SPITZHARFE (zither)
SYMPHONIUM (mouth
  organ)
TAMBOURINE (drum)
TEPONAZTLI (drum)
THUMB PIANO (jew's
  harp)
TIN WHISTLE
TLAPIZTALI (flute)
TSURI DAIKO (drum)

11
AEOLIAN HARP
ANGEL CHIMES
BARREL ORGAN
BELL CITTERN
BIVALVE BELL
BLADDER PIPE

167

BOARD ZITHER
CLAPPER BELL
FIPPLE FLUTE
GAMBANG KAYA (xylophone)
GUITAR-BANJO
HAND TRUMPET
HARPSICHORD
HECKELPHONE (oboe)
NYCKELHARPA
PAIMENSARVI (horn)
PANHUÉHUETL (drum)
SARON DEMONG (metallophone)
SLEIGH BELLS
SPIKE FIDDLE
THEORBO-LUTE
UCHIWA DAIKO (drum)
VIOLA D'AMORE (viol)
VIOLONCELLO

12
DIPLO-KITHARA (zither)
GANSA GAMBANG
 (metallophone)
GANSA JONGKOK

(metallophone)
GLOCKENSPIEL (metallophone)
GUITAR-VIOLIN
HI-HAT CYMBALS
KANTELEHARPE (lyre)
MANDOLINETTO (ukulele)
PEACOCK SITAR (lute)
RAUSCHPFEIFE (double reed)
SARRUSOPHONE (brass)
SHOULDER HARP
STOCK-AND-HORN (hornpipe)
TIPPOO'S TIGER (organ)
TUBULAR BELLS
VIOLA DA GAMBA (viol)
WHISTLE FLUTE

13
COCKTAIL DRUMS
CONTRABASSOON
DOUBLE BASSOON
 (contrabassoon)
HARDANGERFELE (fiddle)
HECKELCLARINA (clarinet)
SAVERNAKE HORN

SCHRILLPFEIFE (flute)
SLIDE TROMBONE
VIOLA BASTARDA (viol)

14
CLARINET D'AMORE
CLAVICYTHERIUM (harpsichord)
CYTHARA ANGLICA (harp)
JINGLING JOHNNY
TLAPANHUÉHUETL (drum)
TRICCABALLACCA (clappers)

15
CLASSICAL GUITAR
MOOG SYNTHESIZER
TURKISH CRESCENT (jingling
 johnny)

16
CHINESE WOOD BLOCK
CHITARRA BATTENTE (guitar)
CYLINDRICAL DRUMS
DEUTSCHE SCHALMEI (double
 reed)
STRUMENTO DI PORCO (zither)

BALLET TERMS

4
BRAS
DEMI
JETÉ
PLIÉ
POSÉ
SAUT
TUTU
VOLÉ

5
ARQUÉ
BARRE
BATTU
BEATS
BRISÉ
COLLÉ
COUPÉ
DÉCOR
ÉLÈVE
FONDU
LIGNE
PASSÉ
PIQUÉ
PIVOT
PORTÉ
ROSIN
SAUTÉ
SERRÉ
TOMBÉ

6
APLOMB
À TERRE
ATTACK
BAISSÉ
BALLON
CAMBRÉ
CHAINÉ
CHANGÉ
CHASSÉ
CROISÉ
DÉGAGÉ
DÉTIRÉ
DEVANT
ÉCARTÉ
ÉFFACÉ
ÉLANCÉ
ENTRÉE
ÉPAULÉ
ÉTENDU
ÉTOILE
FAILLI
JARRET
MONTER
PENCHÉ
POINTE
RELEVÉ
RETIRÉ
VOYAGÉ

7
ALLONGÉ
ARRONDI
ATTAQUE
BALANCÉ
DANSEUR
DÉBOITÉ
ÉCHAPPÉ
EMBOITÉ
ÉTENDRE
FOUETTÉ
JARRETÉ
LEOTARD
MAILLOT
MARQUER
POISSON
RAMASSÉ
RETOMBÉ
SISSONE
SOUTENU
TAQUETÉ

8
ASSEMBLÉ
ATTITUDE
BACK BEND
BALLONNÉ
BALLOTTÉ
BATTERIE
CABRIOLE
CAGNEAUX

CORYPHÉE
DANSEUSE
DÉBOULÉS
DERRIÈRE
DÉTOURNÉ
GLISSADE
PISTOLET
RENVERSÉ
SERPETTE
SPOTTING
STULCHIK
TONNELET

9
ARABESQUE
BALLABILE
COU DE PIED
DÉVELOPPÉ
ÉLÉVATION
ENTRECHAT

ENVELOPPÉ
ÉQUILIBRE
HORTENSIA
JUPONNAGE
LIMBERING
MARCHEUSE
PAS DE DEUX
PIROUETTE
RACCOURCI
RÉVÉRENCE
REVOLTADE

10
BATTEMENTS
ENLÈVEMENT
ÉPAULEMENT
SOUBRESAUT
TAQUETERIE

11
CONTRETEMPS

PAS DE BASQUE

12
CHOREOGRAPHY
ENCHAÎNEMENT
GARGOUILLADE

13
CHOREOGRAPHER
CORPS DE BALLET

14
CLOSED POSITION
DIVERTISSEMENT
PRIMA BALLERINA

15
AUTOUR DE LA SALLE

17
RÉGISSEUR-GÉNÉRALE

NOVEL TITLES

NOVEL (Author)

3
SHE (H Rider Haggard)

4
DR NO (Ian Fleming)
EMMA (Jane Austen)
GIGI (Colette)
NANA (Émile Zola)

5
CHÉRI (Colette)
KIPPS (H G Wells)
SCOOP (Evelyn Waugh)
SYBIL (Benjamin Disraeli)
ZADIG (Voltaire)

6
AMELIA (Henry Fielding)
BEN HUR (Lew Wallace)
CHOCKY (John Wyndham)
LOLITA (Vladimir Nabokov)
PAMELA (Samuel Richardson)
ROB ROY (Walter Scott)

7
CAMILLA (Fanny Burney)
CANDIDE (Voltaire)
CECILIA (Fanny Burney)
DRACULA (Bram Stoker)
EREWHON (Samuel Butler)
EVELINA (Fanny Burney)
IVANHOE (Walter Scott)
ORLANDO (Virginia Woolf)
REBECCA (Daphne Du Maurier)
SHIRLEY (Charlotte Brontë)

THE FALL (Albert Camus)
THE ROAD (Cormac McCarthy)
ULYSSES (James Joyce)

8
ADAM BEDE (George Eliot)
CRANFORD (Mrs Gaskell)
JANE EYRE (Charlotte Brontë)
LUCKY JIM (Kingsley Amis)
SWAN SONG (John Galsworthy)
THE IDIOT (Fyodor Mikhailovich
    Dostoevsky)
THE MAGUS (John Fowles)
THE REBEL (Albert Camus)
TOM JONES (Henry Fielding)
VILLETTE (Charlotte Brontë)
WAVERLEY (Walter Scott)
WOLF HALL (Hilary Mantel)

9
AGNES GREY (Anne Brontë)
BILLY LIAR (Keith Waterhouse)
CONINGSBY (Benjamin Disraeli)
DUBLINERS (James Joyce)
GLENARVON (Lady Caroline Lamb)
HARD TIMES (Charles Dickens)
I CLAUDIUS (Robert Graves)
KIDNAPPED (R L Stevenson)
LOVE STORY (Erich Segal)
ROGUE MALE (Geoffrey
    Household)
THE CHIMES (Charles Dickens)
THE DEVILS (Fyodor Mikhailovich
    Dostoevsky)
THE HEROES (Charles Kingsley)
THE HOBBIT (J R R Tolkien)

THE PLAGUE (Albert Camus)
VICE VERSA (F Anstey)
WIGAN PIER (George Orwell)

10
ANIMAL FARM (George Orwell)
BLEAK HOUSE (Charles Dickens)
CANCER WARD (Alexander
    Solzhenitsyn)
CLAYHANGER (Arnold Bennett)
DON QUIXOTE (Cervantes)
GOLDFINGER (Ian Fleming)
IN CHANCERY (John Galsworthy)
KENILWORTH (Walter Scott)
LORNA DOONE (R D Blackmore)
PERSUASION (Jane Austen)
THE RAINBOW (D H Lawrence)
TITUS ALONE (Mervyn Peake)
TITUS GROAN (Mervyn Peake)
VANITY FAIR (William Makepeace
    Thackeray)

11
BLACK BEAUTY (Anna Sewell)
BURMESE DAYS (George Orwell)
CAKES AND ALE (W Somerset
    Maugham)
COUSIN BETTE (Honoré de Balzac)
DAISY MILLER (Henry James)
GORMENGHAST (Mervyn Peake)
LITTLE WOMEN (Louisa M Alcott)
LOST HORIZON (James Hilton)
MIDDLEMARCH (George Eliot)
MRS DALLOWAY (Virginia Woolf)
OLIVER TWIST (Charles Dickens)
SILAS MARNER (George Eliot)

THE BIG SLEEP (Raymond Chandler)
THE OUTSIDER (Albert Camus)
WAR AND PEACE (Leo Tolstoy)
WOMEN IN LOVE (D H Lawrence)

12

ANNA KARENINA (Leo Tolstoy)
A SEVERED HEAD (Iris Murdoch)
BARNABY RUDGE (Charles Dickens)
BRIGHTON ROCK (Graham Greene)
CASINO ROYALE (Ian Fleming)
DOMBEY AND SON (Charles Dickens)
FRANKENSTEIN (Mary Shelley)
GUY MANNERING (Walter Scott)
HEADLONG HALL (Thomas Love Peacock)
LITTLE DORRIT (Charles Dickens)
MADAME BOVARY (Gustave Flaubert)
MOLL FLANDERS (Daniel Defoe)
OF MICE AND MEN (John Steinbeck)
ROGUE JUSTICE (Geoffrey Household)
ROOM AT THE TOP (John Braine)
THE DECAMERON (Boccaccio)
THE GHOST ROAD (Pat Barker)
THE GO-BETWEEN (L P Hartley)
THE LOST WORLD (Arthur Conan Doyle)
THE MOONSTONE (Wilkie Collins)
THE PROFESSOR (Charlotte Brontë)

13

A KIND OF LOVING (Stan Barstow)
A MODERN COMEDY (John Galsworthy)
BRAVE NEW WORLD (Aldous Huxley)
DANIEL DERONDA (George Eliot)
DOCTOR ZHIVAGO (Boris Pasternak)
JACOB FAITHFUL (Captain Marryat)
JUST-SO STORIES (Rudyard Kipling)
LES MISÉRABLES (Victor Hugo)
LIVE AND LET DIE (Ian Fleming)
LIZA OF LAMBETH (W Somerset Maugham)
MANSFIELD PARK (Jane Austen)
NORTH AND SOUTH (Mrs Gaskell)
PINCHER MARTIN (William Golding)
SKETCHES BY BOZ (Charles Dickens)
SMILEY'S PEOPLE (John Le Carré)
SONS AND LOVERS (D H Lawrence)
TARKA THE OTTER (Henry Williamson)
THE BLUE LAGOON (H de Vere Stacpoole)
THE CHRYSALIDS (John Wyndham)
THE GOLDEN BOWL (Henry James)
THE HISTORY MAN (Malcolm Bradbury)
THE KITE RUNNER (Khaled Hosseini)
THE LAST TYCOON (F Scott Fitzgerald)
THÉRÈSE RAQUIN (Émile Zola)
ZULEIKA DOBSON (Max Beerbohm)

14

A MAN OF PROPERTY (John Galsworthy)
A ROOM OF ONE'S OWN (Virginia Woolf)
A ROOM WITH A VIEW (E M Forster)
A TOWN LIKE ALICE (Neville Shute)
CHANGING PLACES (David Lodge)
CIDER WITH ROSIE (Laurie Lee)
CROTCHET CASTLE (Thomas Love Peacock)
DEATH ON THE NILE (Agatha Christie)

DECLINE AND FALL (Evelyn Waugh)
FRANNY AND ZOOEY (J D Salinger)
GOODBYE, MR CHIPS (James Hilton)
GO SET A WATCHMAN (Harper Lee)
JUDE THE OBSCURE (Thomas Hardy)
LORD OF THE FLIES (William Golding)
NIGHTMARE ABBEY (Thomas Love Peacock)
OUR MAN IN HAVANA (Graham Greene)
PICKWICK PAPERS (Charles Dickens)
RITES OF PASSAGE (William Golding)
ROBINSON CRUSOE (Daniel Defoe)
THE AMBASSADORS (Henry James)
THE CORAL ISLAND (R M Ballantyne)
THE FIRST CIRCLE (Alexander Solzhenitsyn)
THE FORSYTE SAGA (John Galsworthy)
THE GREAT GATSBY (F Scott Fitzgerald)
THE KRAKEN WAKES (John Wyndham)
THE LONG GOODBYE (Raymond Chandler)
THE SECRET AGENT (Joseph Conrad)
THE SILVER SPOON (John Galsworthy)
THE TIME MACHINE (H G Wells)
THE WATER-BABIES (Charles Kingsley)
THE WHITE MONKEY (John Galsworthy)
THE WOODLANDERS (Thomas Hardy)
TREASURE ISLAND (R L Stevenson)
TRISTRAM SHANDY (Laurence Sterne)
WHAT MAISIE KNEW (Henry James)

15

A CHRISTMAS CAROL (Charles Dickens)
A FAREWELL TO ARMS (Ernest Hemingway)
A PASSAGE TO INDIA (E M Forster)
COLD COMFORT FARM (Stella Gibbons)
EUSTACE AND HILDA (L P Hartley)
GONE WITH THE WIND (Margaret Mitchell)
GOODBYE TO BERLIN (Christopher Isherwood)
HEART OF DARKNESS (Joseph Conrad)
NORTHANGER ABBEY (Jane Austen)
OUR MUTUAL FRIEND (Charles Dickens)
PORTRAIT OF A LADY (Henry James)
PORTRAIT OF CLARE (Francis Brett Young)
STRAIT IS THE GATE (André Gide)
THE COUNTRY GIRLS (Edna O'Brien)
THE INVISIBLE MAN (H G Wells)
THE SECRET GARDEN (Frances Hodgson Burnett)
THE SILMARILLION (J R R Tolkien)
THE TRUMPET MAJOR (Thomas Hardy)
THE WHITE COMPANY (Arthur Conan Doyle)
THE WOMAN IN WHITE (Wilkie Collins)
THREE MEN IN A BOAT (Jerome K Jerome)

16

A CLOCKWORK ORANGE (Anthony Burgess)
A TALE OF TWO CITIES (Charles Dickens)
DAVID COPPERFIELD (Charles Dickens)
GULLIVER'S TRAVELS (Jonathan Swift)
MARTIN CHUZZLEWIT (Charles Dickens)
MR MIDSHIPMAN EASY (Captain Marryat)
NICHOLAS NICKLEBY (Charles Dickens)
TENDER IS THE NIGHT (F Scott Fitzgerald)
TEN LITTLE NIGGERS (Agatha Christie)
THE GRAPES OF WRATH (John Steinbeck)
THE PLUMED SERPENT (D H Lawrence)
THE SCARLET LETTER (Nathaniel Hawthorne)

WUTHERING HEIGHTS (Emily Brontë)

17

ALICE IN WONDERLAND (Lewis Carroll)
DR JEKYLL AND MR HYDE (R L Stevenson)
GREAT EXPECTATIONS (Charles Dickens)
KING SOLOMON'S MINES (H Rider Haggard)
MY BROTHER JONATHAN (Francis Brett Young)
POINT COUNTER POINT (Aldous Huxley)
PRIDE AND PREJUDICE (Jane Austen)
THE DEVILS OF LOUDUN (Aldous Huxley)
THE DIARY OF A NOBODY (G and W Grossmith)
THE LORD OF THE RINGS (J R R Tolkien)
THE MIDWICH CUCKOOS (John Wyndham)
THE MILL ON THE FLOSS (George Eliot)
THE WAR OF THE WORLDS (H G Wells)
THE WINGS OF THE DOVE (Henry James)
WIVES AND DAUGHTERS (Mrs Gaskell)

18

A HIGH WIND IN JAMAICA (Richard Hughes)
ANNA OF THE FIVE TOWNS (Arnold Bennett)
CRIME AND PUNISHMENT (Fyodor Dostoevsky)
NINETEEN EIGHTY-FOUR (George Orwell)
SWALLOWS AND AMAZONS (Arthur Ransome)
THE CATCHER IN THE RYE (J D Salinger)
THE MOON AND SIXPENCE (W Somerset Maugham)
THE OLD MAN AND THE SEA (Ernest Hemingway)
THE PRISONER OF ZENDA (Anthony Hope)
THE THIRTY-NINE STEPS (John Buchan)
THE THREE MUSKETEERS (Alexandre Dumas)
TO KILL A MOCKINGBIRD (Harper Lee)

19

BRIDESHEAD REVISITED (Evelyn Waugh)
FOR WHOM THE BELL TOLLS (Ernest Hemingway)
SENSE AND SENSIBILITY (Jane Austen)
THE DAY OF THE TRIFFIDS (John Wyndham)
THE GULAG ARCHIPELAGO (Alexander
  Solzhenitsyn)
THE HISTORY OF MR POLLY (H G Wells)
THE MAN IN THE IRON MASK (Alexandre Dumas)
THE OLD CURIOSITY SHOP (Charles Dickens)
THE PILGRIM'S PROGRESS (John Bunyan)
THE RIDDLE OF THE SANDS (Erskine Childers)
THE SCARLET PIMPERNEL (Baroness Orczy)
THE SCREWTAPE LETTERS (C S Lewis)
THE VICAR OF WAKEFIELD (Oliver Goldsmith)
THE WIND IN THE WILLOWS (Kenneth Grahame)
TOM BROWN'S SCHOOLDAYS (Thomas Hughes)

20+

A CONNECTICUT YANKEE IN KING ARTHUR'S
  COURT (Mark Twain)

A DANCE TO THE MUSIC OF TIME (Anthony Powell)
AS I WALKED OUT ONE MIDSUMMER MORNING
  (Laurie Lee)
CHILDREN OF THE NEW FOREST (Captain Marryat)
FAR FROM THE MADDING CROWD (Thomas Hardy)
JOHN HALIFAX, GENTLEMAN (Mrs Craik)
KEEP THE ASPIDISTRA FLYING (George Orwell)
LADY CHATTERLEY'S LOVER (D H Lawrence)
LARK RISE TO CANDLEFORD (Flora Thompson)
LITTLE LORD FAUNTLEROY (Frances Hodgson
  Burnett)
MURDER ON THE ORIENT EXPRESS (Agatha
  Christie)
OUT OF THE SILENT PLANET (C S Lewis)
AROUND THE WORLD IN EIGHTY DAYS (Jules
  Verne)
TESS OF THE D'URBERVILLES (Thomas Hardy)
THE ADVENTURES OF HUCKLEBERRY FINN (Mark
  Twain)
THE ADVENTURES OF TOM SAWYER (Mark Twain)
THE BEAUTIFUL AND DAMNED (F Scott Fitzgerald)
THE BRIDE OF LAMMERMOOR (Walter Scott)
THE BROTHERS KARAMAZOV (Fyodor Mikhailovich
  Dostoevsky)
THE CRICKET ON THE HEARTH (Charles Dickens)
THE FRENCH LIEUTENANT'S WOMAN (John Fowles)
THE HEART OF MIDLOTHIAN (Walter Scott)
THE HISTORY OF HENRY ESMOND (William
  Makepeace Thackeray)
THE HONOURABLE SCHOOLBOY (John Le Carré)
THE INNOCENCE OF FATHER BROWN (G K
  Chesterton)
THE ISLAND OF DOCTOR MOREAU (H G Wells)
THE LAST OF THE MOHICANS (James Fenimore
  Cooper)
THE MEMOIRS OF SHERLOCK HOLMES (Arthur
  Conan Doyle)
THE MYSTERIES OF UDOLPHO (Mrs Radcliffe)
THE MYSTERIOUS AFFAIR AT STYLES (Agatha
  Christie)
THE MYSTERY OF EDWIN DROOD (Charles Dickens)
THE PICTURE OF DORIAN GRAY (Oscar Wilde)
THE PRIME OF MISS JEAN BRODIE (Muriel Spark)
THE RED BADGE OF COURAGE (Stephen Crane)
THE RETURN OF THE NATIVE (Thomas Hardy)
THE TENANT OF WILDFELL HALL (Anne Brontë)
TINKER, TAILOR, SOLDIER, SPY (John Le Carré)
TWENTY THOUSAND LEAGUES UNDER THE SEA
  (Jules Verne)
TWO YEARS BEFORE THE MAST (Richard Henry
  Dana)
UNDER THE GREENWOOD TREE (Thomas Hardy)

PLAY TITLES

TITLE (Playwright)

3
ART (Yasmina Rieza)

4
LOOT (Joe Orton)
ROSS (Terence Rattigan)

5
CASTE (T W Robertson)
ENRON (Lucy Prebble)
FAUST (Goethe)
MEDEA (Euripides)
ROOTS (Arnold Wesker)

6
GHOSTS (Henrik Ibsen)
HAMLET (William Shakespeare)
HENRY V (William Shakespeare)
PHÈDRE (Jean Racine)
PLENTY (David Hare)
STRIFE (John Galsworthy)

7
AMADEUS (Peter Shaffer)
ATHALIE (Jean Racine)
BLASTED (Sarah Kane)
CANDIDA (G B Shaw)
ELECTRA (Sophocles)
GALILEO (Bertolt Brecht)
HENRY IV (William Shakespeare)
HENRY VI (William Shakespeare)
JUMPERS (Tom Stoppard)
MACBETH (William Shakespeare)
OTHELLO (William Shakespeare)
THE LARK (Jean Anouilh)
THE ROOM (Harold Pinter)
THE WEIR (Conor McPherson)
VOLPONE (Ben Jonson)

8
ANTIGONE (Sophocles)
HAY FEVER (Noël Coward)
KING JOHN (William Shakespeare)
KING LEAR (William Shakespeare)
PERICLES (William Shakespeare)
PETER PAN (J M Barrie)
TARTUFFE (Molière)
THE BIRDS (Aristophanes)
THE FROGS (Aristophanes)
THE MISER (Molière)

9
ALL MY SONS (Arthur Miller)
BILLY LIAR (Willis Hall and Keith Waterhouse)
CAVALCADE (Noël Coward)
CYMBELINE (William Shakespeare)
DR FAUSTUS (Christopher Marlowe)
FLARE PATH (Terence Rattigan)
GOLDEN BOY (Clifford Odets)

HAPPY DAYS (Samuel Beckett)
HENRY VIII (William Shakespeare)
JERUSALEM (Jez Butterworth)
PYGMALION (G B Shaw)
RICHARD II (William Shakespeare)
SAINT JOAN (G B Shaw)
THE CIRCLE (W Somerset Maugham)
THE CRITIC (Sheridan)
THE DEVILS (John Whiting)
THE RIVALS (Sheridan)

10
ALL FOR LOVE (John Dryden)
ANDROMAQUE (Jean Racine)
AURENG-ZEBE (John Dryden)
COPENHAGEN (Michael Frayn)
CORIOLANUS (William Shakespeare)
I AM A CAMERA (John Van Druten)
OEDIPUS REX (Sophocles)
RICHARD III (William Shakespeare)
THE BACCHAE (Euripides)
THE BALCONY (Jean Genet)
THE HOSTAGE (Brendan Behan)
THE SEAGULL (Anton Chekhov)
THE TEMPEST (William Shakespeare)
UNCLE VANYA (Anton Chekhov)

11
A DOLL'S HOUSE (Henrik Ibsen)
AS YOU LIKE IT (William Shakespeare)
JOURNEY'S END (R C Sherriff)
LOVE FOR LOVE (William Congreve)
PANDORA'S BOX (Frank Wedekind)
ROOKERY NOOK (Ben Travers)
THE BANKRUPT (Alexander Ostrovsky)
THE CONTRAST (Royall Tyler)
THE CRUCIBLE (Arthur Miller)
THE WILD DUCK (Henrik Ibsen)

12
AFTER THE FALL (Arthur Miller)
ANNA CHRISTIE (Eugene O'Neill)
BEDROOM FARCE (Alan Ayckbourn)
BLITHE SPIRIT (Noël Coward)
BLOOD WEDDING (García Lorca)
CHARLEY'S AUNT (Brandon Thomas)
DUEL OF ANGELS (Jean Giraudoux)
JULIUS CAESAR (William Shakespeare)
MAJOR BARBARA (G B Shaw)
PRIVATE LIVES (Noël Coward)
THE ALCHEMIST (Ben Jonson)
THE ANATOMIST (James Bridie) '
THE APPLE CART (G B Shaw)
THE BROKEN JUG (Heinrich von Kleist)
THE CARETAKER (Harold Pinter)
THE MOUSETRAP (Agatha Christie)
THREE SISTERS (Anton Chekhov)
TWELFTH NIGHT (William Shakespeare)

13
ARMS AND THE MAN (G B Shaw)

A TASTE OF HONEY (Shelagh Delaney)
HOBSON'S CHOICE (Harold Brighouse)
LE MISANTHROPE (Molière)
QUALITY STREET (J M Barrie)
THE ACHARNIANS (Aristophanes)
THE DUMB WAITER (Harold Pinter)
THE JEW OF MALTA (Christopher Marlowe)
THE LINDEN TREE (J B Priestley)
THE MAGISTRATE (Pinero)
THE MATCHMAKER (Thornton Wilder)
THE WHITE DEVIL (John Webster)
THE WINSLOW BOY (Terence Rattigan)
TIMON OF ATHENS (William Shakespeare)
UNDER MILK WOOD (Dylan Thomas)

14

AN IDEAL HUSBAND (Oscar Wilde)
MAN AND SUPERMAN (G B Shaw)
ROMEO AND JULIET (William Shakespeare)
SEPARATE TABLES (Terence Rattigan)
THE CORN IS GREEN (Emlyn Williams)
THE COUNTRY GIRL (Clifford Odets)
THE DEEP BLUE SEA (Terence Rattigan)
THE FIRE-RAISERS (Max Frisch)
THE GHOST SONATA (August Strindberg)
THE HISTORY BOYS (Alan Bennet)
THE OLD BACHELOR (William Congreve)
THE PHILANDERER (G B Shaw)
THE TROJAN WOMEN (Euripides)
THE WINTER'S TALE (William Shakespeare)
THIS HAPPY BREED (Noël Coward)

15

ANGELS IN AMERICA (Tony Kushner)
BARTHOLOMEW FAIR (Ben Jonson)
DANGEROUS CORNER (J B Priestley)
DESIGN FOR LIVING (Noël Coward)
HEARTBREAK HOUSE (G B Shaw)
LOOK BACK IN ANGER (John Osborne)
MARRIAGE À LA MODE (John Dryden)
PRESENT LAUGHTER (Noël Coward)
THE CONSTANT WIFE (W Somerset Maugham)
THE ICEMAN COMETH (Eugene O'Neill)
TITUS ANDRONICUS (William Shakespeare)
TWO NOBLE KINSMEN (William Shakespeare)
VENICE PRESERVED (Thomas Otway)
WAITING FOR GODOT (Samuel Beckett)

16

A CUCKOO IN THE NEST (Ben Travers)
AN INSPECTOR CALLS (J B Priestley)
CAT ON A HOT TIN ROOF (Tennessee Williams)
DEATH OF A SALESMAN (Arthur Miller)
LOVE'S LABOUR'S LOST (William Shakespeare)
PILLARS OF SOCIETY (Henrik Ibsen)
RING ROUND THE MOON (Jean Anouilh)
THE ADDING MACHINE (Elmer Rice)
THE AMERICAN DREAM (Edward Albee)
THE BIRTHDAY PARTY (Harold Pinter)
THE CHERRY ORCHARD (Anton Chekhov)
THE COCKTAIL PARTY (T S Eliot)
THE FAMILY REUNION (T S Eliot)
THE MASTER BUILDER (Henrik Ibsen)
WHAT THE BUTLER SAW (Joe Orton)

17

A MAN FOR ALL SEASONS (Robert Bolt)
AN ITALIAN STRAW HAT (Eugène Labiche)
ARSENIC AND OLD LACE (Joseph Kesselring)
BAREFOOT IN THE PARK (Neil Simon)
JUNO AND THE PAYCOCK (Sean O'Casey)
MEASURE FOR MEASURE (William Shakespeare)
ROMANOFF AND JULIET (Peter Ustinov)
THE BEAUX' STRATAGEM (George Farquhar)
THE COMEDY OF ERRORS (William Shakespeare)
THE DEVIL'S DISCIPLE (G B Shaw)
THE DOCTOR'S DILEMMA (G B Shaw)
THE DUCHESS OF MALFI (John Webster)
THE GLASS MENAGERIE (Tennessee Williams)
THE GOOD-NATURED MAN (Oliver Goldsmith)
THE SCHOOL FOR WIVES (Molière)
THE SUPPLIANT WOMEN (Aeschylus)
'TIS PITY SHE'S A WHORE (John Ford)

18

AN ENEMY OF THE PEOPLE (Henrik Ibsen)
ANTONY AND CLEOPATRA (William Shakespeare)
CAESAR AND CLEOPATRA (G B Shaw)
FIVE FINGER EXERCISE (Peter Shaffer)
FRENCH WITHOUT TEARS (Terence Rattigan)
LADY WINDERMERE'S FAN (Oscar Wilde)
SHE STOOPS TO CONQUER (Oliver Goldsmith)
SUDDENLY LAST SUMMER (Tennessee Williams)
THE BROWNING VERSION (Terence Rattigan)
THE ROMANS IN BRITAIN (Howard Brenton)
TROILUS AND CRESSIDA (William Shakespeare)

19

ANDROCLES AND THE LION (G B Shaw)
CHIPS WITH EVERYTHING (Arnold Wesker)
MUCH ADO ABOUT NOTHING (William
  Shakespeare)
TAMBURLAINE THE GREAT (Christopher Marlowe)
THE MERCHANT OF VENICE (William Shakespeare)
THE SCHOOL FOR SCANDAL (Sheridan)
THE TAMING OF THE SHREW (William Shakespeare)
WHAT EVERY WOMAN KNOWS (J M Barrie)

20+

ACCIDENTAL DEATH OF AN ANARCHIST (Dario Fo)
ALL GOD'S CHILLUN GOT WINGS (Eugene O'Neill)
ALL'S WELL THAT ENDS WELL (William
  Shakespeare)
A MIDSUMMER NIGHT'S DREAM (William
  Shakespeare)
A STREETCAR NAMED DESIRE (Tennessee Williams)
A WOMAN OF NO IMPORTANCE (Oscar Wilde)
CAPTAIN BRASSBOUND'S CONVERSION (G B Shaw)
ENTERTAINING MR SLOANE (Joe Orton)
INADMISSIBLE EVIDENCE (John Osborne)
MOURNING BECOMES ELECTRA (Eugene O'Neill)
MURDER IN THE CATHEDRAL (T S Eliot)
ROSENCRANTZ AND GUILDENSTERN ARE DEAD
  (Tom Stoppard)
THE ADMIRABLE CRICHTON (J M Barrie)
THE BARRETTS OF WIMPOLE STREET (Rudolf
  Besier)
THE CAUCASIAN CHALK CIRCLE (Bertolt Brecht)
THE GOVERNMENT INSPECTOR (Nikolai Gogol)

THE IMPORTANCE OF BEING EARNEST (Oscar Wilde)
THE LADY'S NOT FOR BURNING (Christopher Fry)
THE MERRY WIVES OF WINDSOR (William Shakespeare)

THE SECOND MRS TANQUERAY (Pinero)
THE TWO GENTLEMEN OF VERONA (William Shakespeare)
WHO'S AFRAID OF VIRGINIA WOOLF? (Edward Albee)

FICTIONAL CHARACTERS

CHARACTER (*Title*, Author)

3

FOX, Brer (*Uncle Remus*, J C Harris)
GOG (*The Tower of London*, W H Ainsworth)
HUR, Judah (*Ben Hur*, L Wallace)
JIM, 'Lord' (*Lord Jim*, J Conrad)
KIM (*Kim*, Rudyard Kipling)
LEE, General Robert E (*Abraham Lincoln*, J Drinkwater)
LEE, Lorelei (*Gentlemen Prefer Blondes*, Anita Loos)
OWL (*Winnie the Pooh*, A A Milne)
ROO (*Winnie the Pooh*, A A Milne)
TOM (*The Water Babies*, C Kingsley)
TOM, 'Uncle' (*Uncle Tom's Cabin*, Harriet B Stowe)

4

ABEL (*Middlemarch*, George Eliot)
CASS, Eppie (*Silas Marner*, George Eliot)
CASY, Rev Jim (*The Grapes of Wrath*, J Steinbeck)
CUFF, Sergeant (*The Moonstone*, W Collins)
DEAN, Ellen (*Wuthering Heights*, Emily Brontë)
EAST (*Tom Brown's Schooldays*, T Hughes)
EASY, John (*Mr Midshipman Easy*, Captain Marryat)
EYRE, Jane (*Jane Eyre*, Charlotte Brontë)
FAWN, Lord Frederic (*Phineas Finn*, A Trollope)
FELL, Dr Gideon (*The Black Spectacles*, J Dickson Carr)
FINN, Huckleberry (*Huckleberry Finn, Tom Sawyer*, M Twain)
FINN, Phineas (*Phineas Finn*, A Trollope)
GRAY, Dorian (*The Picture of Dorian Gray*, Oscar Wilde)
GRAY, Nelly (*Faithless Nelly Gray*, T Hood)
GUNN, Ben (*Treasure Island*, R L Stevenson)
HOOK, Captain James (*Peter Pan*, J M Barrie)
HYDE, Edward (*Dr Jekyll and Mr Hyde*, R L Stevenson)
JUDY (*Wee Willie Winkie*, R Kipling)
LAMB, Leonard (*Middlemarch*, George Eliot)
LYRA, (*His Dark Materials*, Philip Pullman)
MOLE, Mr (*The Wind in the Willows*, K Grahame)
NANA (*Peter Pan*, J M Barrie)
NASH, Richard (Beau) (*Monsieur Beaucaire*, Booth Tarkington)
PUCK (Robin Goodfellow) (*Puck of Pook's Hill*, R Kipling)
RAMA (Tiger Tiger) (*The Jungle Book*, R Kipling)
REED, Mrs (*Jane Eyre*, Charlotte Brontë)
RIDD, John (*Lorna Doone*, R D Blackmore)
SEAL, Basil (*Put Out More Flags*, E Waugh)
SMEE (*Peter Pan*, J M Barrie)
TOAD, Mr (*The Wind in the Willows*, K Grahame)
TROY, Sergeant Francis (*Far from the Madding Crowd*, T Hardy)

VANE, Harriet (*Strong Poison*, Dorothy L Sayers)
VANE, Lady Isabel (*East Lynne*, Mrs Henry Wood)
WOLF, 'Brer' (*Uncle Remus*, J C Harris)

5

ADLER, Irene (*The Adventures of Sherlock Holmes*, A Conan Doyle)
AKELA (*The Jungle Book*, R Kipling)
ALIBI, Tom (*Waverley*, W Scott)
ATHOS (*The Three Musketeers*, Alexandre Dumas)
BALOO (*The Jungle Book*, R Kipling)
BLAKE, Franklin (*The Moonstone*, W Collins)
BONES, Captain Billy (*Treasure Island*, R L Stevenson)
BOOBY, Sir Thomas (*Joseph Andrews*, H Fielding)
BRUFF (*The Moonstone*, W Collins)
BULBO, Prince (*The Rose and the Ring*, W M Thackeray)
CHANT, Mercy (*Tess of the D'Urbervilles*, T Hardy)
CLACK, Drusilla (*The Moonstone*, W Collins)
CLARE, Angel (*Tess of the D'Urbervilles*, T Hardy)
DARCY, Fitzwilliam (*Pride and Prejudice*, Jane Austen)
DEANS, Effie/Jeanie (*The Heart of Midlothian*, W Scott)
DIXON, James (*Lucky Jim*, K Amis)
DOONE, Lorna (*Lorna Doone*, R D Blackmore)
EAGER, Rev Cuthbert (*Room with a View*, E M Forster)
FANNY (*Fanny's First Play*, G B Shaw)
FLYNN, Father James (*The Dubliners*, J Joyce)
GESTE, Beau (*Beau Geste*, P C Wren)
GWYNN, Nell (*Simon Dale*, A Hope)
HANDS, Israel (*Treasure Island*, R L Stevenson)
HATCH, Bennet (*The Black Arrow*, R L Stevenson)
JONES, Tom (*Tom Jones*, H Fielding)
KANGA (*Winnie the Pooh*, A A Milne)
KIPPS, Arthur (*Kipps*, H G Wells)
LEIGH, Captain Sir Amyas (*Westward Ho!*, C Kingsley)
MAGOG (*The Tower of London*, W H Ainsworth)
MARCH, Amy/Beth/Josephine (Jo)/Meg (*Little Women*, etc, Louisa M Alcott)
MERCY (*Pilgrim's Progress*, J Bunyan)
MITTY, Walter (*The Secret Life of Walter Mitty*, J Thurber)
MOORE, Mrs (*A Passage to India*, E M Forster)
O'HARA, Kimball (*Kim*, Rudyard Kipling)
O'HARA, Scarlett (*Gone with the Wind*, Margaret Mitchell)
OTTER, Mr (*The Wind in the Willows*, K Grahame)
PAGET, Jean (*A Town like Alice*, N Shute)
POLLY, Alfred (*The History of Mr Polly*, H G Wells)
POOLE, Grace (*Jane Eyre*, Charlotte Brontë)
PORGY (*Porgy*, Du Bose Heywood)
PRISM, Miss Laetitia (*The Importance of Being Earnest*, Oscar Wilde)

PUNCH (*Wee Willie Winkie*, R Kipling)
READY, Masterman (*Masterman Ready*, F Marryat)
REMUS, Uncle (*Uncle Remus* series, J C Harris)
RYDER, Charles (*Brideshead Revisited*, E Waugh)
SALLY (*Sally in Our Alley*, H Carey)
SAMBO (*Just So Stories*, R Kipling)
SHARP, Rebecca (Becky) (*Vanity Fair*, W M Thackeray)
SLOPE, Rev Obadiah (*Barchester Towers*, A Trollope)
SLOTH (*Pilgrim's Progress*, J Bunyan)
SMITH, Winston (*1984*, G Orwell)
SNOWE, Lucy (*Villette*, Charlotte Brontë)
TARKA (*Tarka the Otter*, H Williamson)
THUMB, Tom (*The Tale of Two Bad Mice*, Beatrix Potter)
TOPSY (*Uncle Tom's Cabin*, Harriet B Stowe)
UNCAS (*The Last of the Mohicans*, J Fennimore Cooper)

6

AITKEN (*Prester John*, J Buchan)
ARAMIS (*The Three Musketeers*, Alexandre Dumas)
ASRIEL, Lord (*His Dark Materials*, Philip Pullman)
AYESHA (*She*, H Rider Haggard)
BENNET, Catherine/Elizabeth/Jane/Lydia/Mary (*Pride and Prejudice*, Jane Austen)
BESSIE (*Jane Eyre*, Charlotte Brontë)
BINKIE, Lady Grizzel (*Vanity Fair*, W M Thackeray)
BOVARY, Emma (*Madame Bovary*, G Flaubert)
BUTLER, Rhett (*Gone with the Wind*, Margaret Mitchell)
CACKLE (*Vanity Fair*, W M Thackeray)
CARDEW, Cecily (*The Importance of Being Earnest*, Oscar Wilde)
CRUSOE, Robinson (*Robinson Crusoe*, D Defoe)
DANGLE (*The Critic*, R B Sheridan)
EEYORE (*Winnie the Pooh*, A A Milne)
ELAINE (*Idylls of the King*, Lord Tennyson)
'FRIDAY' (*Robinson Crusoe*, D Defoe)
FRITHA (*The Snow Goose*, P Gallico)
GARTER, Polly (*Under Milk Wood*, D Thomas)
GATSBY, Major Jay (*The Great Gatsby*, F Scott Fitzgerald)
GEORGE (*Three Men in a Boat*, J K Jerome)
GERARD, Etienne (*The Exploits of Brigadier Gerard*, A Conan Doyle)
GILPIN, John (*John Gilpin*, W Cowper)
GLOVER, Catherine (*The Fair Maid of Perth*, W Scott)
GORDON, Squire (*Black Beauty*, A Sewell)
GRIMES (*The Water Babies*, C Kingsley)
HANNAY, Richard (*The Thirty-Nine Steps*, J Buchan)
HARKER, Jonathan/Minna (*Dracula*, Bram Stoker)
HARMAN, Joe (*A Town like Alice*, N Shute)
HAROLD, Childe (*Childe Harold's Pilgrimage*, Lord Byron)
HEARTS, King of/Knave of/Queen of (*Alice in Wonderland*, L Carroll)
HESTER, (*His Dark Materials*, Philip Pullman)
HOLMES, Mycroft (*The Return of Sherlock Holmes*, A Conan Doyle)
HOLMES, Sherlock (*A Study in Scarlet, The Sign of Four, The Hound of the Baskervilles*, etc, A Conan Doyle)
HOOPER, Fanny (*Fanny by Gaslight*, M Sadleir)
JEEVES (*Thank you, Jeeves*, P G Wodehouse)

JEKYLL, Henry (*Dr Jekyll and Mr Hyde*, R L Stevenson)
LAURIE (*Little Women*, Louisa M Alcott)
LAURIE, Annie (*Annie Laurie*, Douglass)
LEGREE, Simon (*Uncle Tom's Cabin*, Harriet B Stowe)
LINTON, Edgar (*Wuthering Heights*, Emily Brontë)
MANGAN, Boss (*Heartbreak House*, G B Shaw)
MANSON, Dr Andrew (*The Citadel*, A J Cronin)
MARPLE, Jane (*A Pocket Full of Rye*, Agatha Christie)
MERLIN (*Idylls of the King*, Lord Tennyson)
MODRED, Sir (*Idylls of the King*, Lord Tennyson)
MOREAU, André-Louis (*Scaramouche*, R Sabatini)
MOREAU, Dr (*The Island of Dr Moreau*, H G Wells)
MORGAN, Angharad/Huw (*How Green Was My Valley*, R Llewellyn)
MORGAN, Organ (*Under Milk Wood*, D Thomas)
MOWGLI (*The Jungle Book*, R Kipling)
NUTKIN, Squirrel, (*The Tale of Squirrel Nutkin*, Beatrix Potter)
OMNIUM, Duke of (Family name Palliser) (*The Barsetshire series*, Angela Thirkell)
PICKLE, Peregrine (*Peregrine Pickle*, T Smollett)
PIGLET, Henry Pootel (*Winnie the Pooh*, A A Milne)
POIROT, Hercule (*The Mysterious Affair at Styles*, Agatha Christie)
RABBIT (*Winnie the Pooh*, A A Milne)
RABBIT, 'Brer' (*Uncle Remus*, J C Harris)
RABBIT, The White (*Alice in Wonderland*, L Carroll)
RIVERS, St John (*Jane Eyre*, Charlotte Brontë)
RUSTUM (*Sohrab and Rustum*, M Arnold)
SAWYER, Tom (*The Adventures of Tom Sawyer*, M Twain)
SHANDY, Tristram (*Tristram Shandy*, L Sterne)
SILVER, Long John (*Treasure Island*, R L Stevenson)
SIMNEL, Lambert (*Perkin Warbeck*, John Ford)
SOHRAB (*Sohrab and Rustum*, M Arnold)
TEMPLE, Miss (*Jane Eyre*, Charlotte Brontë)
THORNE, Dr Thomas (*Doctor Thorne*, A Trollope)
THORPE, Isabella (*Northanger Abbey*, Jane Austen)
TILNEY, Henry (*Northanger Abbey*, Jane Austen)
TURNER, Jim (Captain Flint) (*Swallows and Amazons*, A Ransome)
UMPOPA (*King Solomon's Mines*, H Rider Haggard)
WALKER, John/Roger/Susan/Titty/Vicky (*Swallows and Amazons*, A Ransome)
WESTON, Mrs (*Emma*, Jane Austen)
WILKES, Ashley/India (*Gone with the Wind*, Margaret Mitchell)
WIMSEY, Lord Peter Death Bredon (*Whose Body?*, Dorothy L Sayers)

7

AISGILL, Alice (*Room at the Top*, J Braine)
BAGSTER (*Middlemarch*, George Eliot)
BEESLEY (*Lucky Jim*, Kingsley Amis)
BINGLEY, Charles (*Pride and Prejudice*, Jane Austen)
BRANDON, Colonel (*Sense and Sensibility*, Jane Austen)
CANDOUR, Mrs (*The School for Scandal*, R B Sheridan)
CHESNEY, Jack (*Charley's Aunt*, Brandon Thomas)
COLLINS, Rev William (*Pride and Prejudice*, Jane Austen)
CYPRESS, Mr (*Nightmare Abbey*, T L Peacock)
DANVERS, Mrs (*Rebecca*, Daphne du Maurier)
DESPAIR, Giant (*Pilgrim's Progress*, J Bunyan)

DRACULA, Count (*Dracula*, Bram Stoker)
EPICENE (*Epicene*, B Jonson)
FAIRFAX, Gwendolen (*The Importance of Being Earnest*, Oscar Wilde)
FAIRFAX, Jane (*Emma*, J Austen)
FAIRFAX, Mrs (*Jane Eyre*, Charlotte Brontë)
FAIRLIE, Frederick (*Woman in White*, W Collins)
FAUSTUS (*The History of Dr Faustus*, C Marlowe)
FORSYTE, Fleur/Irene/Jolyon/Jon/Soames (*The Forsyte Saga*, J Galsworthy)
GALAHAD (*Idylls of the King*, Lord Tennyson)
GERAINT (*Idylls of the King*, Lord Tennyson)
GRANTLY, Bishop of Barchester (*The Warden, Barchester Towers*, A Trollope)
HAWKINS, Jim (*Treasure Island*, R L Stevenson)
HENTZAU, Rupert of (*The Prisoner of Zenda*, A Hope)
HERRIES, Francis (*Rogue Herries*, H Walpole)
HIGGINS, Henry (*Pygmalion*, G B Shaw)
IVANHOE, Wilfred, Knight of (*Ivanhoe*, W Scott)
JENKINS, Rev Eli (*Under Milk Wood*, D Thomas)
KEELDAR, Shirley (*Shirley*, Charlotte Brontë)
LAMPTON, Joe (*Room at the Top*, J Braine)
LANGDON, Robert (*The DaVinci Code*, Dan Brown)
LATIMER, Darsie (*Redgauntlet*, W Scott)
LAWLESS (*The Black Arrow*, R L Stevenson)
LINCOLN, Abraham (*Abraham Lincoln*, J Drinkwater)
LUCIFER (*Faustus*, C Marlowe)
MARKHAM, Gilbert (*The Tenant of Wildfell Hall*, Anne Brontë)
MESSALA (*Ben Hur*, L Wallace)
MICHAEL, Duke of Strelsau (*The Prisoner of Zenda*, A Hope)
MINIVER, Mrs Caroline (*Mrs Miniver*, Jan Struther)
MORLAND, Catherine (*Northanger Abbey*, Jane Austen)
NOKOMIS (*Song of Hiawatha*, H W Longfellow)
PORTHOS (*The Three Musketeers*, Alexandre Dumas)
PROUDIE, Dr/Mrs (*Framley Parsonage*, A Trollope)
RAFFLES, A J (*Raffles* series, E W Hornung)
RANDALL, Rebecca (*Rebecca of Sunnybrook Farm*, Kate D Wiggin)
RATTLER, Martin (*Martin Rattler*, R M Ballantyne)
REBECCA (*Rebecca*, Daphne du Maurier)
REBECCA (*Rebecca of Sunnybrook Farm*, Kate D Wiggin)
RED KING (*Alice Through the Looking Glass*, L Carroll)
ROBSART, Amy (*Kenilworth*, W Scott)
SANDERS (Sandi) (*Sanders of the River*, E Wallace)
SHELTON, Richard (*The Black Arrow*, R L Stevenson)
SHIPTON, Mother (*The Luck of Roaring Camp*, Bret Harte)
SMOLLET, Captain (*Treasure Island*, R L Stevenson)
SORRELL, Christopher (Kit) (*Sorrell and Son*, W Deeping)
ST CLARE, Evangeline (Little Eva) (*Uncle Tom's Cabin*, Harriet B Stowe)
TIDDLER, Tom (*Adam's Opera*, Clemence Dane)
WARBECK, Perkin (*Perkin Warbeck*, John Ford)
WESTERN, Mrs/Sophia/Squire, (*Tom Jones*, H Fielding)
WILLIAM (*Just William*, Richmal Crompton)
WINSLOW, Ronnie (*The Winslow Boy*, T Rattigan)

WOOSTER, Bertie (*Thank You, Jeeves*, P G Wodehouse)

8

ABSOLUTE, Sir Anthony (*The Rivals*, R B Sheridan)
ANGELICA (*The Rose and the Ring*, W M Thackeray)
APOLLYON (*Pilgrim's Progress*, J Bunyan)
ARMITAGE, Jacob (*The Children of the New Forest*, Captain Marryat)
BACKBITE, Sir Benjamin (*The School for Scandal*, R B Sheridan)
BAGHEERA (*The Jungle Book*, R Kipling)
BLACK DOG (*Treasure Island*, R L Stevenson)
CARRAWAY, Nick (*The Great Gatsby*, F Scott Fitzgerald)
CASAUBON, Rev Edward, (*Middlemarch*, George Eliot)
CRAWFURD, David (*Prester John*, J Buchan)
CRICHTON, Bill (*The Admirable Crichton*, J M Barrie)
DASHWOOD, Henry (*Sense and Sensibility*, Jane Austen)
DE BOURGH, Lady Catherine (*Pride and Prejudice*, Jane Austen)
DE WINTER, Maximilian (*Rebecca*, Daphne du Maurier)
EARNSHAW, Catherine (*Wuthering Heights*, Emily Brontë)
EVERDENE, Bathsheba (*Far from the Madding Crowd*, T Hardy)
FFOULKES, Sir Andrew (*The Scarlet Pimpernel*, Baroness Orczy)
FLANDERS, Moll (*Moll Flanders*, D Defoe)
FLASHMAN (*Tom Brown's Schooldays*, T Hughes)
GLORIANA (*The Faërie Queen*, E Spenser)
GOLLANTZ, Emmanuel (*Young Emmanuel*, N Jacob)
GULLIVER, Lemuel (*Gulliver's Travels*, J Swift)
GUNGA DIN (*Barrack-room Ballads*, R Kipling)
HIAWATHA (*The Song of Hiawatha*, H W Longfellow)
KNIGHTLY, George (*Emma*, J Austen)
LANCELOT, Sir (*Idylls of the King*, Lord Tennyson)
LANGUISH, Lydia (*The Rivals*, R B Sheridan)
LAURENCE, Theodore (*Little Women*, Louisa M Alcott)
LESSWAYS, Hilda (*The Clayhanger Trilogy*, Arnold Bennett)
LESTRADE, of Scotland Yard (*A Study in Scarlet*, A Conan Doyle)
LOCKWOOD (*Wuthering Heights*, Emily Brontë)
MACAVITY (*Old Possum's Book of Practical Cats*, T S Eliot)
MALAPROP, Mrs (*The Rivals*, R B Sheridan)
MARY JANE (*When We Were Very Young*, A A Milne)
MORIARTY, Professor James (*Memoirs of Sherlock Holmes*, A Conan Doyle)
O'FERRALL, Trilby (*Trilby*, George du Maurier)
OLIFAUNT, Nigel (*The Fortunes of Nigel*, W Scott)
O'TRIGGER, Sir Lucius (*The Rivals*, R B Sheridan)
PALLISER, Lady Glencora/Plantagenet (*Phineas Finn*, A Trollope)
PRIMROSE, Dr Charles (*The Vicar of Wakefield*, O Goldsmith)
QUANTOCK, Mrs Daisy (*Queen Lucia*, E F Benson)
RED QUEEN (*Alice Through the Looking Glass*, L Carroll)
SHOTOVER, Captain (*Heartbreak House*, G B Shaw)

ST BUNGAY, Duke of (*Phineas Finn*, A Trollope)
SVENGALI (*Trilby*, George du Maurier)
THATCHER, Becky (*The Adventures of Tom Sawyer*, M Twain)
TRISTRAM (*Idylls of the King*, Lord Tennyson)
TULLIVER, Maggie/Tom (*The Mill on the Floss*, George Eliot)
VERINDER, Lady Julia (*The Moonstone*, W Collins)
WATER RAT (Ratty) (*The Wind in the Willows*, K Grahame)
WAVERLEY, Edward (*Waverley*, W Scott)
WHITEOAK (family) (*The Whiteoak Chronicles*, Mazo de la Roche)
WHITE-TIP (*Tarka the Otter*, Henry Williamson)
WHITTIER, Pollyanna (*Pollyanna*, Eleanor H Porter)
WILLIAMS, Percival William (*Wee Willie Winkie*, R Kipling)
WORTHING, John (*The Importance of Being Earnest*, Oscar Wilde)

9

ABBEVILLE, Horace (*Cannery Row*, J Steinbeck)
ABLEWHITE, Godfrey (*The Moonstone*, W Collins)
ALLWORTHY, Squire (*Tom Jones*, H Fielding)
BABBERLEY, Lord Fancourt (*Charley's Aunt*, Brandon Thomas)
BARRYMORE (*The Hound of the Baskervilles*, A Conan Doyle)
BRACKNELL, Lady (*The Importance of Being Earnest*, Oscar Wilde)
BULSTRODE, Nicholas (*Middlemarch*, George Eliot)
CHAINMAIL (*Crotchet Castle*, T L Peacock)
CHRISTIAN (*Pilgrim's Progress*, J Bunyan)
CHURCHILL, Frank (*Emma*, Jane Austen)
D'ARTAGNAN (*The Three Musketeers*, Alexandre Dumas)
DOOLITTLE, Eliza (*Pygmalion*, G B Shaw)
GREYSTOKE, Lord (*Tarzan* series, E R Burroughs)
GUINEVERE (*Idylls of the King*, Lord Tennyson)
INDIAN JOE (*The Adventures of Tom Sawyer*, M Twain)
LEICESTER, Earl of (*Kenilworth*, W Scott)
MACGREGOR, Robin (*Rob Roy*, W Scott)
MARCH HARE, The (*Alice in Wonderland*, L Carroll)
MARCHMAIN, Lady Cordelia/Lady Julia/Lord Sebastian/ Marquis of/Teresa/The Earl of Brideshead (*Brideshead Revisited*, E Waugh)
MEHITABEL, the cat (*Archy and Mehitabel*, D Marquis)
MERRILIES, Meg (*Guy Mannering*, W Scott)
MINNEHAHA (*The Song of Hiawatha*, H W Longfellow)
MONCRIEFF, Algernon (*The Importance of Being Earnest*, Oscar Wilde)
PENDENNIS, Arthur (Pen) (*Pendennis*, W M Thackeray)
PERCIVALE (*Idylls of the King*, Lord Tennyson)
RED KNIGHT (*Alice Through the Looking Glass*, L Carroll)
ROCHESTER, Bertha/Edward Fairfax (*Jane Eyre*, Charlotte Brontë)
SHERE KHAN (Lungri) (*The Jungle Book*, R Kipling)
SOUTHDOWN, Earl of (*Vanity Fair*, W M Thackeray)
TAMERLANE (*Tamerlane*, N Rowe)
TANQUERAY, Aubrey (*The Second Mrs Tanqueray*, A W Pinero)
TIGER LILY (*Peter Pan*, J M Barrie)

TRELAWNEY, Rose (*Trelawney of the Wells*, A W Pinero)
TRELAWNEY, Squire (*Treasure Island*, R L Stevenson)
TWITCHETT, Mrs Tabitha (*The Tale of Tom Kitten*, Beatrix Potter)
VIRGINIAN, The (*The Virginian*, O Wister)
WAYNFLETE, Lady Cicely (*Captain Brassbound's Conversion*, G B Shaw)
WOODHOUSE, Emma/Isabella (*Emma*, Jane Austen)

10

ABRAMS MOSS (*Pendennis*, W M Thackeray)
ALLAN-A-DALE (*Ivanhoe*, W Scott)
ARROWPOINT (*Daniel Deronda*, George Eliot)
BELLADONNA (*Vanity Fair*, W M Thackeray)
CHALLENGER, Professor (*The Lost World*, A Conan Doyle)
CRIMSWORTH, William (*The Professor*, Charlotte Brontë)
EVANGELINE (*Evangeline*, H W Longfellow)
FAUNTLEROY, Lord Cedric Errol (*Little Lord Fauntleroy*, F H Burnett)
GOODFELLOW, Robin (*St Ronan's Well*, W Scott)
HEATHCLIFF (*Wuthering Heights*, Emily Brontë)
HORNBLOWER, Horatio (The *Hornblower* series, C S Forester)
HUNCA MUNCA (*The Tale of Two Bad Mice*, Beatrix Potter)
HUNTER-DUNN, Joan (*A Subaltern's Love Song*, J Betjeman)
JACKANAPES (*Jackanapes*, Juliana H Ewing)
LETHBRIDGE, Daphne (*The Dark Tide*, Vera Brittain)
MAN IN BLACK (*A Citizen of the World*, O Goldsmith)
MAULEVERER, Lord (*Cranford*, Mrs Gaskell)
MOCK TURTLE, THE (*Alice in Wonderland*, L Carroll)
PUDDLEDUCK, Jemima (*The Tale of Jemima Puddleduck*, Beatrix Potter)
QUATERMAIN, Allan (*King Solomon's Mines*, H Rider Haggard)
STARKADDER, Judith/Old Mrs (*Cold Comfort Farm*, Stella Gibbons)
TINKER BELL (*Peter Pan*, J M Barrie)
TWEEDLEDEE (*Alice Through the Looking-Glass*, L Carroll)
TWEEDLEDUM (*Alice Through the Looking-Glass*, L Carroll)
UNDERSHAFT, Barbara (*Major Barbara*, G B Shaw)
WILLOUGHBY, John (*Sense and Sensibility*, Jane Austen)
WINDERMERE, Lord Arthur/Margaret (*Lady Windermere's Fan*, Oscar Wilde)

11

ADDENBROOKE, Bennett (*Raffles*, E W Hornung)
DURBEYFIELD, Tess (*Tess of the D'Urbervilles*, T Hardy)
JABBERWOCKY (*Alice Through the Looking-Glass*, L Carroll)
LEE SCORESBY, (*His Dark Materials*, Philip Pullman)
MONTMORENCY, the dog (*Three Men in a Boat*, J K Jerome)
PANTALAIMON, (*His Dark Materials*, Philip Pullman)
REDGAUNTLET, Sir Arthur Darsie (*Redgauntlet*, W Scott)
TAMBURLAINE (*Tamburlaine*, C Marlowe)

TAM O'SHANTER (*Tam O'Shanter*, R Burns)

TIGGY-WINKLE, Mrs (*The Tale of Mrs Tiggy-Winkle*, Beatrix Potter)

TITTLEMOUSE, Mrs Thomasina (*The Tale of Mrs Tittlemouse*, Beatrix Potter)

12
BROCKLEHURST (*Jane Eyre*, Charlotte Brontë)
CAPTAIN FLINT (*Swallows and Amazons*, A Ransome)
FRANKENSTEIN, Victor (*Frankenstein*, M W Shelley)
HUMPTY-DUMPTY (*Alice Through the Looking-Glass*, L Carroll)
PENNYFEATHER, Paul (*Decline and Fall*, E Waugh)

13
WINNIE-THE-POOH (Edward Bear) (*Winnie-the-Pooh*, A A Milne)

14
MEPHISTOPHELES (*Doctor Faustus*, C Marlowe)
RIKKI-TIKKI-TAVI (*The Jungle Book*, R Kipling)
SAMUEL WHISKERS (*The Tale of Samuel Whiskers*, Beatrix Potter)
WORLDLY-WISEMAN (*Pilgrim's Progress*, J Bunyan)

15
OGMORE-PRITCHARD, Mrs (*Under Milk Wood*, D Thomas)
VALIANT-FOR-TRUTH (*Pilgrim's Progress*, J Bunyan)
VIOLET ELIZABETH (*Just William*, Richmal Crompton)

DICKENSIAN CHARACTERS

CHARACTER (*Novel*)

2
JO (*Bleak House*)

3
AMY (*Oliver Twist*)
BET, Betsy (*Oliver Twist*)
BUD, Rosa (*Edwin Drood*)
CLY (*A Tale of Two Cities*)
GAY, Walter (*Dombey and Son*)
JOE (*Pickwick Papers*)
TOX, Miss (*Dombey and Son*)

4
ANNE (*Dombey and Son*)
BAPS (*Dombey and Son*)
BEGS, Mrs Ridger (*David Copperfield*)
BRAY, Madeline (*Nicholas Nickleby*)
BRAY, Walter (*Nicholas Nickleby*)
DICK, Mr (*Oliver Twist*)
DUFF (*Oliver Twist*)
FIPS, Mr (*Martin Chuzzlewit*)
FOGG (*Pickwick Papers*)
GAMP, Mrs Sarah (*Martin Chuzzlewit*)
GRIP (*Barnaby Rudge*)
HAWK, Sir Mulberry (*Nicholas Nickleby*)
HEEP, Uriah (*David Copperfield*)
HUGH (*Barnaby Rudge*)
JOWL, Mat (*The Old Curiosity Shop*)
JUPE, Cecilia (*Hard Times*)
KAGS (*Oliver Twist*)
KNAG, Miss (*Nicholas Nickleby*)
LIST, Isaac (*The Old Curiosity Shop*)
MANN, Mrs (*Oliver Twist*)
MARY (*Pickwick Papers*)
MELL, Charles (*David Copperfield*)
MIFF, Mrs (*Dombey and Son*)
OMER (*David Copperfield*)
PEAK (*Barnaby Rudge*)
PELL, Solomon (*Pickwick Papers*)
PEPS, Dr Parker (*Dombey and Son*)

POTT, Minverva (*Pickwick Papers*)
'RIAH (*Our Mutual Friend*)
RUGG, Anastasia (*Little Dorrit*)
TIGG, Montague (*Martin Chuzzlewit*)
WADE, Miss (*Little Dorrit*)
WEGG, Silas (*Our Mutual Friend*)

5
ADAMS, Jack (*Dombey and Son*)
ALLEN, Arabella/Benjamin (*Pickwick Papers*)
BATES, Charley (*Oliver Twist*)
BETSY (*Pickwick Papers*)
BRASS, Sally/Sampson (*The Old Curiosity Shop*)
BRICK, Jefferson (*Martin Chuzzlewit*)
BROWN, Alice/Mrs (*Dombey and Son*)
CASBY, Christopher (*Little Dorrit*)
CHICK, John/Louisa (*Dombey and Son*)
CLARE, Ada (*Bleak House*)
CLARK (*Dombey and Son*)
CLIVE (*Little Dorrit*)
CROWL (*Nicholas Nickleby*)
CRUPP, Mrs (*David Copperfield*)
DAISY, Solomon (*Barnaby Rudge*)
DAVID (*Nicholas Nickleby*)
DAWES, Mary (*Dombey and Son*)
DINGO, Professor (*Bleak House*)
DIVER, Colonel (*Martin Chuzzlewit*)
DONNY, Mrs (*Bleak House*)
DOYCE, Daniel (*Little Dorrit*)
DROOD, Edwin (*Edwin Drood*)
DUMPS, Nicodemus (*Pickwick Papers*)
FAGIN (*Oliver Twist*)
FLITE, Miss (*Bleak House*)
GILES (*Oliver Twist*)
GILLS, Solomon (*Dombey and Son*)
GOWAN, Harry (*Little Dorrit*)
GREEN, Tom (*Barnaby Rudge*)
GRIDE, Arthur (*Nicholas Nickleby*)
GUPPY, William (*Bleak House*)
HEXAM, Charlie/Jesse/Lizzie (*Our Mutual Friend*)
JANET (*David Copperfield*)
JONES, Mary (*Barnaby Rudge*)

KROOK (*Bleak House*)
LOBBS, Maria/'Old' (*Pickwick Papers*)
LORRY, Jarvis (*A Tale of Two Cities*)
LUCAS, Solomon (*Pickwick Papers*)
LUPIN, Mrs (*Martin Chuzzlewit*)
MEALY (*David Copperfield*)
'MELIA (*Dombey and Son*)
MIGGS, Miss (*Barnaby Rudge*)
MILLS, Julia (*David Copperfield*)
MOLLY (*Great Expectations*)
MOULD (*Martin Chuzzlewit*)
NANCY (*Oliver Twist*)
NANDY, John Edward (*Little Dorrit*)
NOGGS, Newman (*Nicholas Nickleby*)
PERCH (*Dombey and Son*)
PINCH, Ruth/Tom (*Martin Chuzzlewit*)
PRICE, 'Tilda (*Nicholas Nickleby*)
PROSS, Miss/Solomon (*A Tale of Two Cities*)
QUALE (*Bleak House*)
QUILP, Daniel (*The Old Curiosity Shop*)
RUDGE, Barnaby/Mary (*Barnaby Rudge*)
SALLY, Old (*Oliver Twist*)
SCOTT, Tom (*The Old Curiosity Shop*)
SHARP (*David Copperfield*)
SIKES, Bill (*Oliver Twist*)
SLURK (*Pickwick Papers*)
SLYME, Chevy (*Martin Chuzzlewit*)
SMIKE (*Nicholas Nickleby*)
SNOBB, The Hon (*Nicholas Nickleby*)
SQUOD, Phil (*Bleak House*)
STAGG (*Barnaby Rudge*)
TOOTS, Mr P (*Dombey and Son*)
TRABB (*Great Expectations*)
TRENT, Frederick/Nellie (*The Old Curiosity Shop*)
TWIST, Oliver (*Oliver Twist*)
VENUS, Mr (*Our Mutual Friend*)
WATTY (*Pickwick Papers*)

6

BADGER, Dr Bayham/Laura/Malta/Matthew/Quebec/
   Woolwich (*Bleak House*)
BAILEY, Benjamin (*Martin Chuzzlewit*)
BAILEY, Captain (*David Copperfield*)
BAMBER, Jack (*Pickwick Papers*)
BANTAM, Angelo Cyrus (*Pickwick Papers*)
BARKER, Phil (*Oliver Twist*)
BARKIS (*David Copperfield*)
BARLEY, Clara (*Great Expectations*)
BARNEY (*Oliver Twist*)
BEDWIN, Mrs (*Oliver Twist*)
BETSEY, Jane (*Dombey and Son*)
BITZER (*Hard Times*)
BOFFIN, Henrietta/Nicodemus (*Our Mutual Friend*)
BONNEY (*Nicholas Nickleby*)
BRIGGS (*Dombey and Son*)
BUMBLE (*Oliver Twist*)
BUNSBY, Captain (*Dombey and Son*)
BUZFUZ, Sergeant (*Pickwick Papers*)
CARKER, Harriet/James/John (*Dombey and Son*)
CARTON, Sydney (*A Tale of Two Cities*)
CHEGGS, Alick (*The Old Curiosity Shop*)
CLARKE (*Pickwick Papers*)
CODGER, Mrs (*Martin Chuzzlewit*)
CODLIN, Thomas (*The Old Curiosity Shop*)

CONWAY, General (*Barnaby Rudge*)
CORNEY, Mrs (*Oliver Twist*)
CURDLE (*Nicholas Nickleby*)
CUTLER, Mr/Mrs (*Nicholas Nickleby*)
CUTTLE, Captain Ned (*Dombey and Son*)
DARNAY, Charles (*A Tale of Two Cities*)
DARTLE, Rosa (*David Copperfield*)
DENNIS, Ned (*Barnaby Rudge*)
DIBABS, Mrs (*Nicholas Nickleby*)
DODSON (*Pickwick Papers*)
DOMBEY, Fanny/Florence/Louisa/Paul (*Dombey and Son*)
DORKER (*Nicholas Nickleby*)
DORRIT, Amy/Edward/Fanny/Frederick/William
   (*Little Dorrit*)
DOWLER, Captain (*Pickwick Papers*)
FEEDER (*Dombey and Son*)
FEENIX (*Dombey and Son*)
FIZKIN, Horatio (*Pickwick Papers*)
FOLIAR (*Nicholas Nickleby*)
GEORGE (*The Old Curiosity Shop*)
GEORGE (*Pickwick Papers*)
GEORGE, Mr (*Bleak House*)
GORDON, Lord George (*Barnaby Rudge*)
GRAHAM, Mary (*Martin Chuzzlewit*)
GROVES, 'Honest' James (*The Old Curiosity Shop*)
GUNTER (*Pickwick Papers*)
HARMON, John (*Our Mutual Friend*)
HARRIS, Mrs (*Martin Chuzzlewit*)
HAWDON, Captain (*Bleak House*)
HIGDEN, Betty (*Our Mutual Friend*)
HOMINY, Major (*Martin Chuzzlewit*)
HOWLER, Rev M (*Dombey and Son*)
JARLEY, Mrs (*The Old Curiosity Shop*)
JASPER, Jack (*Edwin Drood*)
JINGLE, Alfred (*Pickwick Papers*)
KETTLE, La Fayette (*Martin Chuzzlewit*)
LAMMLE, Alfred (*Our Mutual Friend*)
LOBLEY (*Edwin Drood*)
LUMLEY, Dr (*Nicholas Nickleby*)
MAGNUS, Peter (*Pickwick Papers*)
MALDEN, Jack (*David Copperfield*)
MARLEY, Jacob (*A Christmas Carol*)
MARTON (*The Old Curiosity Shop*)
MAYLIE, Harrie/Mrs/Rose (*Oliver Twist*)
MERDLE, Mr (*Little Dorrit*)
MILVEY, Rev Frank (*Our Mutual Friend*)
MIVINS (*Pickwick Papers*)
MODDLE, Augustus (*Martin Chuzzlewit*)
MORFIN (*Dombey and Son*)
MULLET, Professor (*Martin Chuzzlewit*)
NIPPER, Susan (*Dombey and Son*)
PANCKS (*Little Dorrit*)
PERKER (*Pickwick Papers*)
PHUNKY (*Pickwick Papers*)
PIPKIN, Nathaniel (*Pickwick Papers*)
PIRRIP, Philip (*Great Expectations*)
POCKET, Herbert/Matthew/Sarah (*Great Expectations*)
POGRAM, Elijah (*Martin Chuzzlewit*)
RADDLE, Mr and Mrs (*Pickwick Papers*)
RIGAUD, Monsieur (*Little Dorrit*)
SAPSEA, Thomas (*Edwin Drood*)

SAWYER, Bob (*Pickwick Papers*)
SCALEY (*Nicholas Nickleby*)
SLEARY, Josephine (*Hard Times*)
'SLOPPY' (*Our Mutual Friend*)
SOWNDS (*Dombey and Son*)
STRONG, Dr (*David Copperfield*)
TACKER (*Martin Chuzzlewit*)
TAPLEY, Mark (*Martin Chuzzlewit*)
TARTAR (*Edwin Drood*)
TIPPIN, Lady (*Our Mutual Friend*)
TISHER, Mrs (*Edwin Drood*)
TOODLE (*Dombey and Son*)
TUPMAN, Tracy (*Pickwick Papers*)
VARDEN, Dolly/Gabriel (*Barnaby Rudge*)
VHOLES (*Bleak House*)
VUFFIN (*The Old Curiosity Shop*)
WALKER, Mick (*David Copperfield*)
WARDLE, Emily/Isabella/Mr/Rachel (*Pickwick Papers*)
WELLER, Sam/Tony (*Pickwick Papers*)
WILFER, Bella/Lavinia/Reginald (*Our Mutual Friend*)
WILLET, Joe/John (*Barnaby Rudge*)
WINKLE, Nathaniel (*Pickwick Papers*)
WOPSLE (*Great Expectations*)

7

BAILLIE, Gabriel (*Pickwick Papers*)
BANGHAM, Mrs (*Little Dorrit*)
BARBARA (*The Old Curiosity Shop*)
BARBARY, Miss (*Bleak House*)
BARDELL, Mrs Martha/Tommy (*Pickwick Papers*)
BAZZARD (*Edwin Drood*)
BELLING, Master (*Nicholas Nickleby*)
BLIMBER, Dr (*Dombey and Son*)
BLOTTON (*Pickwick Papers*)
BOBSTER, Cecilia/Mr (*Nicholas Nickleby*)
BOLDWIG, Captain (*Pickwick Papers*)
BROGLEY (*Dombey and Son*)
BROOKER (*Nicholas Nickleby*)
BROWDIE, John (*Nicholas Nickleby*)
BULLAMY (*Martin Chuzzlewit*)
CHARLEY (*David Copperfield*)
CHESTER, Edward/Sir John (*Barnaby Rudge*)
CHILLIP, Dr (*David Copperfield*)
CHIVERY, John (*Little Dorrit*)
CHOLLOP, Hannibal (*Martin Chuzzlewit*)
CHUFFEY (*Martin Chuzzlewit*)
CLEAVER, Fanny (*Our Mutual Friend*)
CLENNAM, Arthur (*Little Dorrit*)
CLUBBER, Sir Thomas (*Pickwick Papers*)
CRACKIT, Toby (*Oliver Twist*)
CRAWLEY, Young Mr (*Pickwick Papers*)
CREAKLE (*David Copperfield*)
CREWLER, Mrs/Rev Horace/Sophy (*David Copperfield*)
CRIMPLE, David (*Martin Chuzzlewit*)
CROOKEY (*Pickwick Papers*)
DAWKINS, Jack (*Oliver Twist*)
DEDLOCK, Sir Leicester/Volumnia (*Bleak House*)
DEFARGE, Madame (*A Tale of Two Cities*)
DOLLOBY (*David Copperfield*)
DRUMMLE, Bentley (*Great Expectations*)
DUBBLEY (*Pickwick Papers*)
DURDLES (*Edwin Drood*)
EDMUNDS, John (*Pickwick Papers*)
ESTELLA (*Great Expectations*)

FLEMING, Agnes (*Oliver Twist*)
GABELLE, Theophile (*A Tale of Two Cities*)
GARGERY, Biddy/Joe/Pip (*Great Expectations*)
GARLAND, Abel/Mrs/Mr (*The Old Curiosity Shop*)
GASPARD (*A Tale of Two Cities*)
GAZINGI, Miss (*Nicholas Nickleby*)
GENERAL, Mrs (*Little Dorrit*)
GILBERT, Mark (*Barnaby Rudge*)
GRANGER, Edith (*Dombey and Son*)
GRIDLEY (*Bleak House*)
GRIMWIG (*Oliver Twist*)
GRUDDEN, Mrs (*Nicholas Nickleby*)
HAGGAGE, Dr (*Little Dorrit*)
HEYLING, George (*Pickwick Papers*)
JAGGERS (*Great Expectations*)
JELLYBY, Caddy/Mrs/Peepy (*Bleak House*)
JINKINS (*Martin Chuzzlewit*)
JOBLING, Dr John (*Martin Chuzzlewit*)
JOBLING, Tony (*Bleak House*)
JOHNSON, Mr (*Nicholas Nickleby*)
JORKINS (*David Copperfield*)
KEDGICK, Captain (*Martin Chuzzlewit*)
KENWIGS, Morleena (*Nicholas Nickleby*)
LARKINS, Mr (*David Copperfield*)
LEEFORD, Edward (*Oliver Twist*)
LEWSOME (*Martin Chuzzlewit*)
MALLARD (*Pickwick Papers*)
MANETTE, Dr/Lucie (*A Tale of Two Cities*)
MEAGLES (*Little Dorrit*)
MINERVA (*Pickwick Papers*)
MOWCHER, Miss (*David Copperfield*)
NADGETT (*Martin Chuzzlewit*)
NECKETT, Charlotte/Emma/Tom (*Bleak House*)
NUBBLES, Christopher (*The Old Curiosity Shop*)
NUPKINS, George (*Pickwick Papers*)
PAWKINS, Major (*Martin Chuzzlewit*)
PILKINS, Dr (*Dombey and Son*)
PIPCHIN, Mrs (*Dombey and Son*)
PODSNAP, Georgiana/Mr (*Our Mutual Friend*)
QUINION (*David Copperfield*)
SAMPSON, George (*Our Mutual Friend*)
SCADDER, Zephaniah (*Martin Chuzzlewit*)
SCROOGE, Ebenezer (*A Christmas Carol*)
SIMMONS, William (*Martin Chuzzlewit*)
SKEWTON, Hon Mrs (*Dombey and Son*)
SKYLARK, Mr (*David Copperfield*)
SLAMMER, Dr (*Pickwick Papers*)
SLUMKEY, Hon Samuel (*Pickwick Papers*)
SNAGSBY (*Bleak House*)
SNAWLEY (*Nicholas Nickleby*)
SNUBBIN, Sergeant (*Pickwick Papers*)
SPARSIT, Mrs (*Hard Times*)
SPENLOW, Dora (*David Copperfield*)
SQUEERS, Fanny/Wackford (*Nicholas Nickleby*)
STARTOP (*Great Expectations*)
STRYVER, C J (*A Tale of Two Cities*)
TAMAROO, Miss (*Martin Chuzzlewit*)
TODGERS, Mrs (*Martin Chuzzlewit*)
TROTTER, Job (*Pickwick Papers*)
TRUNDLE (*Pickwick Papers*)
WACKLES, Jane/Melissa/Sophie (*The Old Curiosity Shop*)
WATKINS (*Nicholas Nickleby*)

WEMMICK (*Great Expectations*)
WICKHAM, Mrs (*Dombey and Son*)
WITHERS (*Dombey and Son*)

8

AKERSHEM, Sophronia (*Our Mutual Friend*)
BAGSTOCK, Major (*Dombey and Son*)
BARNWELL, B B (*Martin Chuzzlewit*)
BILLIKIN, Mrs (*Edwin Drood*)
BLATHERS (*Oliver Twist*)
BOYTHORN, Lawrence (*Bleak House*)
BRAVASSA, Miss (*Nicholas Nickleby*)
BROWNLOW, Mr (*Oliver Twist*)
CLAYPOLE, Noah (*Oliver Twist*)
CLUPPINS (*Pickwick Papers*)
CRADDOCK, Mrs (*Pickwick Papers*)
CRATCHIT, Belinda/Bob/Tiny Tim (*A Christmas Carol*)
CRIPPLES, Mr (*Little Dorrit*)
CRUMMLES, Ninetta/Vincent (*Nicholas Nickleby*)
CRUNCHER, Jeremiah/Jerry (*A Tale of Two Cities*)
CRUSHTON, Hon Mr (*Pickwick Papers*)
DATCHERY, Dick (*Edwin Drood*)
D'AULNAIS (*A Tale of Two Cities*)
FINCHING, Mrs Flora (*Little Dorrit*)
FLEDGEBY, Old/Young (*Our Mutual Friend*)
GASHFORD (*Barnaby Rudge*)
HAREDALE, Emma/Geoffrey/Reuben (*Barnaby Rudge*)
HAVISHAM, Miss (*Great Expectations*)
HORTENSE (*Bleak House*)
JARNDYCE, John (*Bleak House*)
LA CREEVY, Miss (*Nicholas Nickleby*)
LANDLESS, Helena/Neville (*Edwin Drood*)
LANGDALE (*Barnaby Rudge*)
LENVILLE (*Nicholas Nickleby*)
LITTIMER (*David Copperfield*)
LOSBERNE (*Oliver Twist*)
MAGWITCH, Abel (*Great Expectations*)
MARY ANNE (*David Copperfield*)
MATTHEWS (*Nicholas Nickleby*)
MICAWBER, Wilkins (*David Copperfield*)
MUTANHED, Lord (*Pickwick Papers*)
NICKLEBY, Godfrey/Kate/Nicholas/Ralph (*Nicholas Nickleby*)
PEGGOTTY, Clara/Daniel/Ham/Little Em'ly (*David Copperfield*)
PICKWICK, Samuel (*Pickwick Papers*)
PLORNISH, Thomas (*Little Dorrit*)
POTATOES (*David Copperfield*)
SCADGERS, Lady (*Hard Times*)
SKIFFINS, Miss (*Great Expectations*)
SKIMPOLE, Arethusa/Harold/Kitty/Laura (*Bleak House*)
SKITTLES, Sir Barnet (*Dombey and Son*)
SMIGGERS, Joseph (*Pickwick Papers*)
SPARKLER, Edmund (*Little Dorrit*)
STIGGINS (*Pickwick Papers*)
TRADDLES, Tom (*David Copperfield*)
TROTWOOD, Betsey (*David Copperfield*)
WESTLOCK, John (*Martin Chuzzlewit*)
WRAYBURN, Eugene (*Our Mutual Friend*)

9

BELVAWNEY, Miss (*Nicholas Nickleby*)
BERINTHIA (*Dombey and Son*)

BLACKPOOL, Stephen (*Hard Times*)
BOUNDERBY, Josiah (*Hard Times*)
CHARLOTTE (*Oliver Twist*)
CHEERYBLE, Charles/Frank/Ned (*Nicholas Nickleby*)
CHICKWEED, Conkey (*Oliver Twist*)
CHUCKSTER (*The Old Curiosity Shop*)
COMPEYSON (*Great Expectations*)
FIBBITSON, Mrs (*David Copperfield*)
GRADGRIND, Louisa/Thomas (*Hard Times*)
GREGSBURY (*Nicholas Nickleby*)
GREWGIOUS (*Edwin Drood*)
HARTHOUSE, James (*Hard Times*)
HEADSTONE, Bradley (*Our Mutual Friend*)
LIGHTWOOD, Mortimer (*Our Mutual Friend*)
LILLYVICK (*Nicholas Nickleby*)
MANTALINI, Mr (*Nicholas Nickleby*)
MURDSTONE, Edward/Jane (*David Copperfield*)
OLD BARLEY (*Great Expectations*)
PARDIGGLE, Francis/O A (*Bleak House*)
PECKSNIFF, Charity/Mercy/Seth (*Martin Chuzzlewit*)
PRISCILLA (*Bleak House*)
RIDERHOOD, Pleasant/Roger (*Our Mutual Friend*)
SMALLWEED, Bartholomew/Joshua/Judy (*Bleak House*)
SMORLTORK, Count (*Pickwick Papers*)
SNODGRASS, Augustus (*Pickwick Papers*)
SUMMERSON, Esther (*Bleak House*)
SWIVELLER, Richard (*The Old Curiosity Shop*)
TAPPERTIT, Simon (*Barnaby Rudge*)
VENEERING, Anastasia/Hamilton (*Our Mutual Friend*)
VERISOPHT, Lord Frederick (*Nicholas Nickleby*)
WICKFIELD, Agnes/Mr (*David Copperfield*)
WITHERDEN, Mr (*The Old Curiosity Shop*)
WOODCOURT, Allan (*Bleak House*)

10

AYRESLEIGH, Mr (*Pickwick Papers*)
CHUZZLEWIT, Anthony/Diggory/George/Jonas/Martin/Mrs Ned/Toby (*Martin Chuzzlewit*)
CRISPARKLE, Rev Septimus (*Edwin Drood*)
FLINTWINCH, Affery/Ephraim/Jeremiah (*Little Dorrit*)
MACSTINGER, Mrs (*Dombey and Son*)
ROUNCEWELL, Mrs (*Bleak House*)
SNEVELLICI, Miss (*Nicholas Nickleby*)
SOWERBERRY (*Oliver Twist*)
STARELEIGH, Justice (*Pickwick Papers*)
STEERFORTH, James (*David Copperfield*)
TATTYCORAM (*Little Dorrit*)
TURVEYDROP, Prince (*Bleak House*)
TWINKLETON, Miss (*Edwin Drood*)
WATERBROOK (*David Copperfield*)
WITITTERLY, Julia (*Nicholas Nickleby*)

11

COPPERFIELD, Clara/David (*David Copperfield*)
'DISMAL JIMMY' (*Pickwick Papers*)
'GAME CHICKEN', The (*Dombey and Son*)
MARCHIONESS, The (*The Old Curiosity Shop*)
PUMBLECHOOK (*Great Expectations*)
SPOTTLETOES, Mrs (*Martin Chuzzlewit*)
ST EVREMONDE, Marquis de/Marquise de (*A Tale of Two Cities*)
SWEEDLEPIPE, Paul (*Martin Chuzzlewit*)
TULKINGHORN (*Bleak House*)

12
HONEYTHUNDER, Luke (*Edwin Drood*)
'SHINY WILLIAM' (*Pickwick Papers*)
SWEET WILLIAM (*The Old Curiosity Shop*)

TITE-BARNACLE, Clarence/Ferdinand/Junior/ Lord Decimus/Mr (*Little Dorrit*)

15
VON KOELDWETHOUT (*Nicholas Nickleby*)

SHAKESPEAREAN CHARACTERS

CHARACTER (*Play*)

3
HAL (*1 Henry IV*)
NYM (*Henry V, The Merry Wives of Windsor*)

4
ADAM (*As You Like It*)
AJAX (*Troilus and Cressida*)
EROS (*Antony and Cleopatra*)
FORD, Mistress (*The Merry Wives of Windsor*)
GREY (*Henry V*)
HERO (*Much Ado About Nothing*)
IAGO (*Othello*)
IRAS (*Antony and Cleopatra*)
LEAR (*King Lear*)
PAGE, Mistress (*The Merry Wives of Windsor*)
PETO (*2 Henry IV*)
PUCK (*A Midsummer Night's Dream*)
SNUG (*A Midsummer Night's Dream*)

5
AARON (*Titus Andronicus*)
ARIEL (*The Tempest*)
BELCH, Sir Toby (*Twelfth Night*)
BLUNT (*2 Henry IV*)
CAIUS, Doctor (*The Merry Wives of Windsor*)
CELIA (*As You Like It*)
CLEON (*Pericles*)
CORIN (*As You Like It*)
DIANA (*All's Well that Ends Well*)
EDGAR (*King Lear*)
ELBOW (*Measure for Measure*)
FESTE (*Twelfth Night*)
FLUTE (*A Midsummer Night's Dream*)
FROTH (*Measure for Measure*)
GOBBO, Launcelot (*The Merchant of Venice*)
JULIA (*The Two Gentlemen of Verona*)
LAFEW (*All's Well That Ends Well*)
MARIA (*Love's Labour's Lost, Twelfth Night*)
PARIS (*Troilus and Cressida*)
PERCY (*1 Henry IV*)
PHEBE (*As You Like It*)
PINCH (*The Comedy of Errors*)
POINS (*1 Henry IV, 2 Henry IV*)
PRIAM (*Troilus and Cressida*)
REGAN (*King Lear*)
ROMEO (*Romeo and Juliet*)
SNOUT (*A Midsummer Night's Dream*)
TIMON (*Timon of Athens*)
TITUS (*Titus Andronicus*)
VIOLA (*Twelfth Night*)

6
AEGEON (*The Comedy of Errors*)
ALONSO (*The Tempest*)
ANGELO (*Measure for Measure*)
ANTONY (*Antony and Cleopatra*)
ARCITE (*The Two Noble Kinsmen*)
ARMADO (*Love's Labour's Lost*)
AUDREY (*As You Like It*)
BANQUO (*Macbeth*)
BIANCA (*The Taming of the Shrew, Othello*)
BOTTOM (*A Midsummer Night's Dream*)
BRUTUS (*Coriolanus, Julius Caesar*)
CASSIO (*Othello*)
CHIRON (*Titus Andronicus*)
CLOTEN (*Cymbeline*)
DENNIS (*As You Like It*)
DROMIO (*The Comedy of Errors*)
DUMAIN (*Love's Labour's Lost*)
DUNCAN (*Macbeth*)
EDMUND (*King Lear*)
EMILIA (*Othello, The Two Noble Kinsmen*)
FABIAN (*Twelfth Night*)
FENTON (*The Merry Wives of Windsor*)
FULVIA (*Antony and Cleopatra*)
HAMLET (*Hamlet*)
HECATE (*Macbeth*)
HECTOR (*Troilus and Cressida*)
HELENA (*A Midsummer Night's Dream, All's Well That Ends Well*)
HERMIA (*A Midsummer Night's Dream*)
IMOGEN (*Cymbeline*)
JULIET (*Romeo and Juliet, Measure for Measure*)
LUCIUS (*Titus Andronicus*)
MARINA (*Pericles*)
MUTIUS (*Titus Andronicus*)
OBERON (*A Midsummer Night's Dream*)
OLIVER (*As You Like It*)
OLIVIA (*Twelfth Night*)
ORSINO (*Twelfth Night*)
OSWALD (*King Lear*)
PISTOL (*2 Henry IV, Henry V, The Merry Wives of Windsor*)
POMPEY (*Measure for Measure, Antony and Cleopatra*)
PORTIA (*The Merchant of Venice*)
QUINCE (*A Midsummer Night's Dream*)
RUMOUR (*2 Henry IV*)
SCROOP (*Henry IV*)
SILVIA (*The Two Gentlemen of Verona*)
TAMORA (*Titus Andronicus*)
THASIA (*Pericles*)
THURIO (*The Two Gentlemen of Verona*)
TYBALT (*Romeo and Juliet*)

VERGES (*Much Ado About Nothing*)

7
ADRIANA (*The Comedy of Errors*)
AEMILIA (*The Comedy of Errors*)
AGRIPPA (*Antony and Cleopatra*)
ALARBUS (*Titus Andronicus*)
ANTONIO (*The Merchant of Venice, The Tempest*)
BEROWNE (*Love's Labour's Lost*)
BERTRAM (*All's Well That Ends Well*)
CALCHAS (*Troilus and Cressida*)
CALIBAN (*The Tempest*)
CAPULET (*Romeo and Juliet*)
CESARIO (*Twelfth Night*)
CLAUDIO (*Much Ado About Nothing, Measure for Measure*)
COSTARD (*Love's Labour's Lost*)
DIONYZA (*Pericles*)
DOUGLAS (*1 Henry IV*)
ESCALUS (*Measure for Measure*)
FLAVIUS (*Timon of Athens*)
FLEANCE (*Macbeth*)
GONERIL (*King Lear*)
GONZALO (*The Tempest*)
HORATIO (*Hamlet*)
HOTSPUR (*1 Henry IV*)
IACHIMO (*Cymbeline*)
JACQUES (*As You Like It*)
JESSICA (*The Merchant of Venice*)
LAERTES (*Hamlet*)
LAVINIA (*Titus Andronicus*)
LEONTES (*The Winter's Tale*)
LORENZO (*The Merchant of Venice*)
LUCIANA (*The Comedy of Errors*)
MACBETH (*Macbeth*)
MACDUFF (*Macbeth*)
MALCOLM (*Macbeth*)
MARIANA (*Measure for Measure, All's Well That Ends Well*)
MARTIUS (*Titus Andronicus*)
MIRANDA (*The Tempest*)
NERISSA (*The Merchant of Venice*)
OCTAVIA (*Antony and Cleopatra*)
OPHELIA (*Hamlet*)
ORLANDO (*As You Like It*)
OTHELLO (*Othello*)
PALAMON (*The Two Noble Kinsmen*)
PAULINA (*The Winter's Tale*)
PERDITA (*The Winter's Tale*)
PISANIO (*Cymbeline*)
PROTEUS (*The Two Gentlemen of Verona*)
QUICKLY, Mistress (*1 Henry IV, 2 Henry IV, The Merry Wives of Windsor*)
QUINTUS (*Titus Andronicus*)
SHALLOW, Justice (*2 Henry IV, The Merry Wives of Windsor*)
SHYLOCK (*The Merchant of Venice*)
SILENCE (*2 Henry IV*)
SILVIUS (*As You Like It*)
SLENDER (*The Merry Wives of Windsor*)
SOLINUS (*The Comedy of Errors*)
THESEUS (*A Midsummer Night's Dream, The Two Noble Kinsmen*)
TITANIA (*A Midsummer Night's Dream*)

TROILUS (*Troilus and Cressida*)
ULYSSES (*Troilus and Cressida*)
WILLIAM (*As You Like It*)

8
ACHILLES (*Troilus and Cressida*)
AUFIDIUS (*Coriolanus*)
BAPTISTA (*The Taming of the Shrew*)
BARDOLPH (*Henry IV, Henry V, The Merry Wives of Windsor*)
BASSANIO (*The Merchant of Venice*)
BEATRICE (*Much Ado About Nothing*)
BELARIUS (*Cymbeline*)
BENEDICK (*Much Ado About Nothing*)
BENVOLIO (*Romeo and Juliet*)
CHARMIAN (*Antony and Cleopatra*)
CLAUDIUS (*Hamlet*)
COMINIUS (*Coriolanus*)
CORDELIA (*King Lear*)
CRESSIDA (*Troilus and Cressida*)
DIOMEDES (*Antony and Cleopatra, Troilus and Cressida*)
DOGBERRY (*Much Ado About Nothing*)
DON PEDRO (*Much Ado About Nothing*)
FALSTAFF (*The Merry Wives of Windsor, Henry IV*)
FLORIZEL (*The Winter's Tale*)
GERTRUDE (*Hamlet*)
GRATIANO (*The Merchant of Venice*)
HERMIONE (*The Winter's Tale*)
ISABELLA (*Measure for Measure*)
LUCENTIO (*The Taming of the Shrew*)
LYSANDER (*A Midsummer Night's Dream*)
MALVOLIO (*Twelfth Night*)
MENENIUS (*Coriolanus*)
MERCUTIO (*Romeo and Juliet*)
MONTAGUE (*Romeo and Juliet*)
MORTIMER (*1 Henry IV*)
OCTAVIUS (*Antony and Cleopatra*)
PANDARUS (*Troilus and Cressida*)
PAROLLES (*All's Well That Ends Well*)
PERICLES (*Pericles*)
PHILOTEN (*Pericles*)
POLONIUS (*Hamlet*)
PROSPERO (*The Tempest*)
RODERIGO (*Othello*)
ROSALIND (*As You Like It*)
ROSALINE (*Love's Labour's Lost*)
SICINIUS (*Coriolanus*)
STEPHANO (*The Tempest*)
TRINCULO (*The Tempest*)
VIOLENTA (*All's Well That Ends Well*)
VOLUMNIA (*Coriolanus*)

9
AGUECHEEK, Sir Andrew (*Twelfth Night*)
ANTIOCHUS (*Pericles*)
ARVIRAGUS (*Cymbeline*)
BASSIANUS (*Titus Andronicus*)
BRABANTIO (*Othello*)
CAMBRIDGE (*Henry V*)
CLEOPATRA (*Antony and Cleopatra*)
CYMBELINE (*Cymbeline*)
DEMETRIUS (*A Midsummer Night's Dream, Antony and Cleopatra, Titus Andronicus*)
DESDEMONA (*Othello*)

ENOBARBUS (*Antony and Cleopatra*)
FERDINAND (*Loves Labours Lost, The Tempest*)
FREDERICK (*As You Like It*)
GLENDOWER, Owen (*1 Henry IV*)
GUIDERIUS (*Cymbeline*)
HELICANUS (*Pericles*)
HIPPOLYTA (*A Midsummer Night's Dream, The Two Noble Kinsmen*)
HORTENSIO (*The Taming of the Shrew*)
KATHERINA (*The Taming of the Shrew*)
KATHERINE (*Henry V, Love's Labour's Lost*)
MAMILLIUS (*The Winter's Tale*)
PATROCLUS (*Troilus and Cressida*)
PETRUCHIO (*The Taming of the Shrew*)
POLIXENES (*The Winter's Tale*)
SEBASTIAN (*The Tempest, Twelfth Night*)
TEARSHEET, Doll (*2 Henry IV*)
VALENTINE (*The Two Gentlemen of Verona*)
VINCENTIO (*Measure for Measure, The Taming of the Shrew*)

10

ALCIBIADES (*Timon of Athens*)
ANTIPHOLUS (*The Comedy of Errors*)
CORIOLANUS (*Coriolanus*)
FORTINBRAS (*Hamlet*)
JAQUENETTA (*Love's Labour's Lost*)
LONGAVILLE (*Love's Labour's Lost*)
LYSIMACHUS (*Pericles*)
POSTHUMOUS (*Cymbeline*)
SATURNINUS (*Titus Andronicus*)
TOUCHSTONE (*As You Like It*)

11

ROSENCRANTZ (*Hamlet*)

12

GUILDENSTERN (*Hamlet*)

14

CHRISTOPHER SLY (*The Taming of the Shrew*)

CHARACTERS FROM JANE AUSTEN

CHARACTER (*Novel*)

ALLEN, Mr/Mrs (*Northanger Abbey*)
BATES, Mrs (*Emma*)
BENNET, Jane/Elizabeth/Catherine/Mary/Lydia (*Pride and Prejudice*)
BENWICK, Captain (*Persuasion*)
BERTRAM, Lady Maria/Sir Thomas/ Rev Edmund/ Maria/Julia (*Mansfield Park*)
BINGLEY, Charles/Caroline/Louisa (*Pride and Prejudice*)
BRANDON, Colonel (*Sense and Sensibility*)
CAMPBELL, Colonel/Jane (*Emma*)
CHURCHILL, Frank (*Emma*)
CLAY, Mrs (*Persuasion*)
COLLINS, Rev William (*Pride and Prejudice*)
CRAWFORD, Henry/Mary/Admiral (*Mansfield Park*)
CROFT, Admiral (*Persuasion*)
DARCY, Fitzwilliam/Lady Anne/Georgiana (*Pride and Prejudice*)
DASHWOOD, Henry/John/Fanny/Elinor/ Marianne/ Margaret (*Sense and Sensibility*)
DE BOURGH, Lady Catherine (*Pride and Prejudice*)
DIXON, Mr (*Emma*)
ELTON (*Emma*)
FAIRFAX, Jane (*Emma*)
FERRARS, Edward/Robert (*Sense and Sensibility*)
FITZWILLIAM, Colonel (*Pride and Prejudice*)
FORSTER, Colonel/Harriet (*Pride and Prejudice*)
GARDINER, Edward (*Pride and Prejudice*)
GODDARD, Mrs (*Emma*)
GRANT, Rev Dr (*Mansfield Park*)
HARVILLE, Captain (*Persuasion*)
HAYTER, Mrs (*Persuasion*)
HURST, Louisa (*Pride and Prejudice*)

JENNINGS, Mrs (*Sense and Sensibility*)
KNIGHTLEY, George/John/Isabella (*Emma*)
LUCAS, Sir William/Charlotte/Marie (*Pride and Prejudice*)
MARTIN, Robert (*Emma*)
MIDDLETON, Sir John (*Sense and Sensibility*)
MORLAND, Catherine/James/Sarah/George/Harriet (*Northanger Abbey*)
MUSGROVE, Mary/Richard/Charles/Henrietta/ Laura(*Persuasion*)
NORRIS, Mrs/Rev Mr (*Mansfield Park*)
PALMER, Mrs Charlotte (*Sense and Sensibility*)
PERRY (*Emma*)
PHILLIPS, Mrs (*Pride and Prejudice*)
PRICE, Mrs Frances/Lieutenant/Fanny/ William/Susan (*Mansfield Park*)
RUSHWORTH, Maria/James (*Mansfield Park*)
RUSSELL, Lady (*Persuasion*)
SHEPHERD, John (*Persuasion*)
SMITH, Harriet (*Emma*)
SMITH, Mrs (*Persuasion*)
SMITH, Mrs (*Sense and Sensibility*)
STEELE, Anne/Lucy (*Sense and Sensibility*)
THORPE, Mrs/Isabella/John/Edward/William (*Northanger Abbey*)
TILNEY, Henry/Eleanor/General/Captain Fred (*Northanger Abbey*)
WENTWORTH, Captain Frederick (*Persuasion*)
WESTON, Mrs (*Emma*)
WICKHAM, George (*Pride and Prejudice*)
WILLIAMS, Eliza (*Sense and Sensibility*)
WILLOUGHBY, John (*Sense and Sensibility*)
WOODHOUSE, Emma/Isabella (*Emma*)
YATES, Hon John (*Mansfield Park*)

CHARACTERS FROM LEWIS CARROLL'S 'ALICE' BOOKS

4
DODO
LION
LORY

5
ALICE
DINAH
HATTA
KITTY
MOUSE

6
EAGLET
HAIGHA

PIGEON
WALRUS

7
DUCHESS
GRYPHON
OYSTERS
PIG-BABY
UNICORN

8
DORMOUSE
FLAMINGO
RED QUEEN

9
CARPENTER
MAD HATTER
MARCH HARE
RED KNIGHT
WHITE KING

10
MOCK TURTLE
TWEEDLEDEE
TWEEDLEDUM
WHITE QUEEN

11
CATERPILLAR

CHESHIRE CAT
FISH FOOTMAN
FROG FOOTMAN
WHITE KNIGHT
WHITE RABBIT

12
HUMPTY DUMPTY
KING OF HEARTS

13
BILL THE LIZARD
FATHER WILLIAM
KNAVE OF HEARTS
QUEEN OF HEARTS

CHARACTERS FROM TROLLOPE

'BARSETSHIRE' NOVELS:
The Warden
Barchester
Towers
Doctor Thorne
Framley Parsonage
The Small House at Allington
The Last Chronicle of Barset

'PALLISER' NOVELS:
Can You Forgive Her?
Phineas Finn
The Eustace Diamonds
Phineas Redux
The Prime Minister
The Duke's Children

3
FAY, Marion (*Marion Fay*)
RAY, Rachel (*Rachel Ray*)

4
BOLD, John (*The Warden*)
DALE, Lily (*The Small House at Allington; The Last Chronicle of Barset*)
DALE, Squire (*The Small House at Allington; The Last Chronicle of Barset*)
DUNN, Onesiphorus (*The Last Chronicle of Barset*)
FAWN, Lord (*The Eustace Diamonds*)
FINN, Phineas (*Phineas Finn; Phineas Redux*)
GREX, Lady Mabel (*The Duke's Children*)
GREY, Dolly (*Mr Scarborough's Family*)
GREY, John (*Can You Forgive Her?*)
MONK, Joshua (*Phineas Finn*)
ORME, Sir Peregrine (*Orley Farm*)
ROBY, Thomas (*The Prime Minister*)
VOSS, Michel (*The Golden Lion of Granpere*)

5
CRUMP, Mrs (*The Small House at Allington*)
EAMES, Johnny (*The Small House at Allington; The Last Chronicle of Barset*)
GREEN, Archibald (*The Conors of Castle Conor*)
JONES, Henry (*Cousin Henry*)
JONES, Indefer (*Cousin Henry*)
JONES, Mrs Montacute (*Is He Popenjoy?*)

KELLY, Martin (*The Kellys and the O'Kellys*)
LOPEZ, Ferdinand (*The Prime Minister*)
LOVEL, Earl (*Frederick*) (*Lady Anna*)
LOVEL, Lady Anna (*Lady Anna*)
LYNCH, Simeon (*The Kellys and the O'Kellys*)
MASON, Lady (*Orley Farm*)
MASON, Mrs (*Orley Farm*)
MAULE, Gerard (*Phineas Redux*)
MOGGS, Ontario (*Ralph the Heir*)
ONGAR, Lady Julia (*The Claverings*)
ONGAR, Lord (*The Claverings*)
ORIEL, Rev. Caleb (*Doctor Thorne*)
PENGE, Caroline (*The US Senator*)
PRIME, Dorothea (*Rachel Ray*)
PRONG, Rev. Samuel (*Rachel Ray*)
RODEN, George (*Marion Fay*)
ROWAN, Luke (*Rachel Ray*)
SCOTT, Clementina (*The Three Clerks*)
SCOTT, Mrs Val (*The Three Clerks*)
SLOPE, Rev. Obadiah (*Barchester Towers*)
TIFTO, Major (*The Duke's Children*)
TUDOR, Alaric (*The Three Clerks*)
TUDOR, Charley (*The Three Clerks*)

6
ARABIN, Rev. Francis (*Barchester Towers*)
AYLMER, Lady (*The Belton Estate*)

BELTON, Will (*The Belton Estate*)
BODKIN, Sir Borcas (*Marion Fay*)
BOODLE, Captain ('Doodles') (*The Claverings*)
BURTON, Florence (*The Claverings*)
BURTON, Theodore (*The Claverings*)
CASHEL, Lord and Lady (*The Kellys and the O'Kellys*)
DORMER, Ayala (*Ayala's Angel*)
DORMER, Lucy (*Ayala's Angel*)
FRENCH, Arabella (*He Knew He Was Right*)
FRENCH, Camilla (*He Knew He Was Right*)
GIBSON, Rev. Mr (*He Knew He Was Right*)
GLOMAX, Captain (*The US Senator*)
GRAHAM, Felix (*Orley Farm*)
HURTLE, Winifred (*The Way We Live Now*)
LUFTON, Lord (*Framley Parsonage*)
MCKEON, Tony (*The Macdermots of Ballycloran*)
MORRIS, Lucy (*The Eustace Diamonds*)
MORTON, Reginald (*The US Senator*)
M'RUEN, Jabez (*The Three Clerks*)
NEEFIT, Mr (*Ralph the Heir*)
NEEFIT, Polly (*Ralph the Heir*)
NERONI, Signora Vesey (*Barchester Towers*)
NEWTON, Ralph (*Ralph the Heir*)
NORMAN, Harry (*The Three Clerks*)
O'GRADY, Sam (*Castle Richmond*)
O'KELLY, Frank (*The Kellys and the O'Kellys*)
O'KELLY, Guss (*The Kellys and the O'Kellys*)
O'KELLY, Sophy (*The Kellys and the O'Kellys*)
OMNIUM, Duke of ('Palliser' novels)
PETRIE, Wallachia (*He Knew He Was Right*)
PUFFLE, Mrs ('Barsetshire' novels)
ROWLEY, Nora (*He Knew He Was Right*)
STUBBS, Colonel Jonathan (*Ayala's Angel*)
THOMAS, John (*The Small House at Allington*)
THORNE, Doctor (*Doctor Thorne*)
THORNE, Mary (*Doctor Thorne*)
TOWERS, Tom (*The Warden*)
USHANT, Lady (*The US Senator*)
USSHER, Myles (*The Macdermots*)
WORTLE, Dr and Mrs (*Dr Wortle's School*)

7

AMEDROZ, Clara (*The Belton Estate*)
BANMANN, Baroness (*Is He Popenjoy?*)
BERTRAM, George (*The Bertrams*)
BONTEEN, Mr (*Phineas Redux*)
BRATTLE, Carry (*The Vicar of Bullhampton*)
CARBURY, Felix (*The Way We Live Now*)
CARBURY, Henrietta (*The Way We Live Now*)
CARBURY, Lady (*The Way We Live Now*)
COMFORT, Rev. Charles (*Rachel Ray*)
CRAWLEY, Grace ('Barsetshire' novels)
CRAWLEY, Rev. Josiah (*Framley Parsonage*; The Last Chronicle of Barset)
CROSBIE, Adolphus (*The Small House at Allington*)
DE BARON, Jack (*Is He Popenjoy?*)
DE GUEST, Earl (*The Small House at Allington*)
DESMOND, Lady (*Castle Richmond*)
DOSSETT, Aunt and Uncle (*Ayala's Angel*)
EMILIUS, Rev. Joseph ('Palliser' novels)
EUSTACE, John (*The Eustace Diamonds*)
EUSTACE, Lizzie (*The Eustace Diamonds*)
EUSTACE, Sir Florian (*The Eustace Diamonds*)
FENWICK, Rev. Frank (*The Vicar of Bullhampton*)

GERMAIN, Lord and Lady George (*Is He Popenjoy?*)
GILMORE, Harry (*The Vicar of Bullhampton*)
GOESLER, Madame Max (*Phineas Finn*)
GOTOBED, Elias (*The US Senator*)
GRANTLY, Archdeacon ('Barsetshire' novels)
GRESHAM, Fanny (*Framley Parsonage*)
GRESHAM, Frank (*Doctor Thorne*)
GRESLEY, Lord Alfred (*Sir Harry Hotspur of Humblethwaite*)
HARDING, Rev. Septimus (*The Warden*)
HOTSPUR, Emily (*Sir Harry Hotspur of Humblethwaite*)
HOTSPUR, George (*Sir Harry Hotspur of Humblethwaite*)
KENNEDY, Lady Laura (*Phineas Finn*; *Phineas Redux*)
LOWTHER, Mary (*The Vicar of Bullhampton*)
MASTERS, Gregory (*The US Senator*)
MASTERS, Mary (*The US Senator*)
MILDMAY, Aunt Ju (*Is He Popenjoy?*)
NEVILLE, Fred (*An Eye for an Eye*)
O'MAHONY, Gerald (*The Hard Leaguers*)
O'MAHONY, Rachel (*The Hard Leaguers*)
PEACOCK, Mr and Mrs (*Dr Wortle's School*)
PROSPER, Peter (*Mr Scarborough's Family*)
PROTEST, Lady Selina (*Is He Popenjoy?*)
PROUDIE, Augusta ('Barsetshire' novels)
PROUDIE, Bishop ('Barsetshire' novels)
PROUDIE, Mrs ('Barsetshire' novels)
PROUDIE, Netta ('Barsetshire' novels)
ROBARTS, Fanny (*Framley Parsonage*)
ROBARTS, Lucy (*Framley Parsonage*)
ROBARTS, Mrs Mark (*Framley Parsonage*)
ROBARTS, Rev. Mark (*Framley Parsonage*)
RUFFORD, Lord (*The US Senator*)
SOWERBY, Nathaniel (*Framley Parsonage*)
THWAITE, Daniel (*Lady Anna*)
TOOGOOD, Mr (*The Last Chronicle of Barset*)
TREFOIL, Arabella (*The US Senator*)
TREGEAR, Frank (*The Duke's Children*)
TRINGLE, Sir Thomas (*Ayala's Angel*)
TRINGLE, Tom (*Ayala's Angel*)
VAVASOR, Alice (*Can You Forgive Her?*)
VAVASOR, George (*Can You Forgive Her?*)
VAVASOR, John (*Can You Forgive Her?*)
VAVASOR, Kate (*Can You Forgive Her?*)
WESTEND, Sir Warwick (*The Three Clerks*)
WESTERN, Cecilia (*Kept in the Dark*)
WESTERN, George (*Kept in the Dark*)
WHARTON, Abel (*The Prime Minister*)
WHARTON, Emily (*The Prime Minister*)
WYNDHAM, Fanny (*The Kellys and the O'Kellys*)

8

ANNESLEY, Florence (*Mr Scarborough's Family*)
ANNESLEY, Harry (*Mr Scarborough's Family*)
ANTICANT, Dr Pessimist (*The Warden*)
BRODRICK, Isabel (*Cousin Henry*)
COLLIGAN, Dr (*The Kellys and the O'Kellys*)
DE COURCY, Lady Alexandria (*The Small House at Allington*)
DE COURCY, Lady Amelia (*Doctor Thorne*)
DUMBELLO, Lady (*The Small House at Allington*)
FLEABODY, Dr Olivia Q. (*Is He Popenjoy?*)
FURNIVAL, Mrs (*Orley Farm*)
GAUNTLET, Adela (*The Bertrams*)

GERAGHTY, Norah (*The Three Clerks*)
GLASCOCK, Hon. Charles (*He Knew He Was Right*)
GLENCORA, Lady ('Palliser' novels)
GRASCOUR, M. (*Mr Scarborough's Family*)
HARCOURT, Sir Henry (*The Bertrams*)
HOUGHTON, Mrs Adelaide (*Is He Popenjoy?*)
LOVELACE, Dean (*Is He Popenjoy?*)
MARRABLE, Sir Gregory (*The Vicar of Bullhampton*)
MARRABLE, Walter (*The Vicar of Bullhampton*)
MELMOTTE, Augustus (*The Way We Live Now*)
MELMOTTE, Madame (*The Way We Live Now*)
MELMOTTE, Marie (*The Way We Live Now*)
MONTAGUE, Paul (*The Way We Live Now*)
MOUNTJOY, Florence (*Mr Scarborough's Family*)
MULREADY, Widow (*The Macdermots*)
PALLISER, Adelaide (*Phineas Redux*)
PALLISER, Lady Glencora ('Palliser' novels)
PALLISER, Plantagenet ('Palliser' novels)
PATEROFF, Count (*The Claverings*)
SPALDING, Caroline (*He Knew He Was Right*)
ST BUNGAY, Duke of (*The Prime Minister*)
STANBURY, Aunt Jemima (*He Knew He Was Right*)
STANBURY, Dorothy (*He Knew He Was Right*)
STANBURY, Hugh (*He Knew He Was Right*)
STANDISH, Lady Laura (*Phineas Finn; Phineas Redux*)
STANHOPE, Dr and Mrs (*Barchester Towers*)
TURNBULL, Mr (*Phineas Finn*)
WOODWARD, Katie (*The Three Clerks*)

9

ALTIFIORA, Francesca (*Kept in the Dark*)
BLUESTONE, Mrs (*Lady Anna*)
BONCASSEN, Isabel (*The Duke's Children*)
BROUGHTON, Dobbs (*The Last Chronicle of Barset*)
CALDIGATE, John (*John Caldigate*)
CARBUNCLE, Mrs (*The Eustace Diamonds*)
CARSTAIRS, Lord (*Dr Wortle's School*)
CHEESACRE, Mr (*Can You Forgive Her?*)
CLAVERING, Archie (*The Claverings*)
CLAVERING, Harry (*The Claverings*)
CLAVERING, Lady (*The Claverings*)
CURLYDOWN, Mr (*John Caldigate*)
DEMOLINES, Madalina (*The Last Chronicle of Barset*)
DOCKWRATH, Mr (*Orley Farm*)
DUNSTABLE, Miss (*Doctor Thorne; Framley Parsonage*)
EFFINGHAM, Violet (*Phineas Finn*)
GERALDINE, Sir Francis (*Kept in the Dark*)
GOLIGHTLY, Clementina (*The Three Clerks*)
GORDELOUP, Madame Sophie (*The Claverings*)

GREYSTOCK, Frank (*The Eustace Diamonds*)
HAMPSTEAD, Lord (*Marion Fay*)
HARDLINES, Sir Gregory (*The Three Clerks*)
KINGSBURY, Marquess of (*Marion Fay*)
MACDERMOT, Feemy (*The Macdermots*)
MACDERMOT, Thady (*The Macdermots*)
MACKENZIE, Margaret (*Miss Mackenzie*)
MONGROBER, Lord (*The Prime Minister*)
NEVERBEND, Fidus (*The Three Clerks*)
NEVERBEND, John (*The Fixed Period*)
QUIVERFUL, Mr (*Barchester Towers*)
SCATCHERD, Roger (*Doctor Thorne*)
SENTIMENT, Mr Popular (*The Warden*)
TREVELYAN, Emily (*He Knew He Was Right*)
TREVELYAN, Louis (*He Knew He Was Right*)
TWENTYMAN, Lawrence (*The US Senator*)
UNDERWOOD, Sir Thomas (*Ralph the Heir*)
VAN SIEVER, Clara (*The Last Chronicle of Barset*)
WILKINSON, Arthur (*The Bertrams*)

10

BIRMINGHAM, Lord (*The Macdermots*)
CARRUTHERS, Lord George de Bruce (*The Eustace Diamonds*)
FITZGERALD, Burgo (*Can You Forgive Her?*)
FITZGERALD, Herbert (*Castle Richmond*)
FITZGERALD, Owen (*Castle Richmond*)
FITZGERALD, Sir Thomas (*Castle Richmond*)
FITZGIBBON, Hon. Laurence (*Phineas Finn*)
FLOOD JONES, Mary (*Phineas Finn*)
HAUTEVILLE, Lady Amaldina (*Marion Fay*)
LINLITHGOW, Lady (*The Eustace Diamonds*)
LLWDDYTHLW, Marquis of (*Marion Fay*)
MILBOROUGH, Lady (*He Knew He Was Right*)
MUSSELBORO, Mr (*The Last Chronicle of Barset*)
WADDINGTON, Caroline (*The Bertrams*)

11

GOLDSHEINER, Miss (*The Way We Live Now*)
GREENMANTLE, Mr (*The Two Heroines of Plumplington*)
SCARBOROUGH, Mountjoy (*Mr Scarborough's Family*)

12

CHAFFANBRASS, Mr (*The Three Clerks; Orley Farm; Phineas Redux*)
SILVERBRIDGE, Lord (*The Prime Minister; The Duke's Children*)
THOROUGHBUNG, Matilda (*Mr Scarborough's Family*)
WHITTLESTAFF, William (*An Old Man's Love*)

CHARACTERS FROM WALTER SCOTT

3

LEE, Alice (*Woodstock*)
LEE, Colonel Albert (*Woodstock*)
LEE, Sir Henry (*Woodstock*)

4

DODS, Meg (*St Ronan's Well*)
GRAY, Gideon (*The Surgeon's Daughter*)
GRAY, Menie (*The Surgeon's Daughter*)
LYLE, Annot (*A Legend of Montrose*)
VERE, Isabella (*The Black Dwarf*)

5

BINKS, Sir Bingo (*St Ronan's Well*)
BUNCE, Jack (*The Pirate*)
EWART, Nanty (*Redgauntlet*)
DEANS, Davie (*The Heart of Midlothian*)
DEANS, Effie (*The Heart of Midlothian*)
DEANS, Jeanie (*The Heart of Midlothian*)
GURTH (*Ivanhoe*)
ISAAC (the Jew) (*Ivanhoe*)
SMITH, Henry (*The Fair Maid of Perth*)
SMITH, Wayland (*Kenilworth*)
TROIL, Brenda (*The Pirate*)
TROIL, Magnus (*The Pirate*)
TROIL, Minna (*The Pirate*)
TROIL, Ulla (*The Pirate*)
WAMBA (*Ivanhoe*)

6

ALBANY, Duke of (*The Fair Maid of Perth*)
ASHTON, Lucy (*The Bride of Lammermoor*)
ASHTON, Sir William (*The Bride of Lammermoor*)
AVENEL, Mary (*The Monastery*)
AVENEL, Roland (*The Abbot*)
BERTHA (*Count Robert of Paris*)
BUTLER, Reuben (*The Heart of Midlothian*)
CEDRIC (*Ivanhoe*)
DE LACY, Damian (*The Betrothed*)
DE LACY, Hugo (*The Betrothed*)
DE LACY, Randel (*The Betrothed*)
DE VERE, Arthur (*Anne of Geierstein*)
ELLIOT, Hobbie (*The Black Dwarf*)
GEDDES, Joshua (*Redgauntlet*)
GLOVER, Catharine (*The Fair Maid of Perth*)
GLOVER, Simon (*The Fair Maid of Perth*)
GRAEME, Magdalen (*The Abbot*)
GRAEME, Roland (*The Abbot*)
HALCRO, Claud (*The Pirate*)
JAMES I (*The Fortunes of Nigel*)
JARVIE, Bailie Nicol (*Rob Roy*)
LE DAIN, Oliver (*Quentin Durward*)
MANLEY, Sir Edward (*The Black Dwarf*)
MORTON, Henry (*Old Mortality*)
OXFORD, Earl of (*Anne of Geierstein*)
PHILIP (of France) (*The Talisman*)
RAMSEY, Margaret (*The Fortunes of Nigel*)
ROWENA (*Ivanhoe*)
SEYTON, Catherine (*The Abbot*)
SLUDGE, Dickie (*Kenilworth*)

TALBOT, Colonel (*Waverley*)
TYRREL, Francis (*St Ronan's Well*)
VARNEY, Richard (*Kenilworth*)
VERNON, Diana (*Rob Roy*)
WARDEN, Henry (*The Monastery*)

7

BALFOUR, John (*Old Mortality*)
BERTRAM (*Castle Dangerous*)
BERTRAM, Harry (*Guy Mannering*)
BUCKLAW, Laird of (*The Bride of Lammermoor*)
DINMONT, Dandie (*Guy Mannering*)
DOUGLAS, Sir James (*Castle Dangerous*)
DURWARD, Quentin (*Quentin Durward*)
EVERARD, Colonel Markham (*Woodstock*)
FENELLA (*Peveril of the Peak*)
GLOSSIN (*Guy Mannering*)
GWENWYN (*The Betrothed*)
HARTLEY, Adam (*The Surgeon's Daughter*)
KENNETH, Sir (*The Talisman*)
LANGLEY, Sir Frederick (*The Black Dwarf*)
LATIMER, Darsie (*Redgauntlet*)
MACTURK, Captain (*St Ronan's Well*)
M'AULAY, Allan (*A Legend of Montrose*)
MERTOUN, Basil (*The Pirate*)
MERTOUN, Mordaunt (*The Pirate*)
MOWBRAY, Clara (*St Ronan's Well*)
NEVILLE, Major (*The Antiquary*)
OLDBUCK, Jonathan (*The Antiquary*)
PEEBLES, Peter (*Redgauntlet*)
PEVERIL, Julian (*Peveril of the Peak*)
PEVERIL, Sir Geoffrey (*Peveril of the Peak*)
REBECCA (*Ivanhoe*)
ROBSART, Amy (*Kenilworth*)
ROBSART, Sir Hugh (*Kenilworth*)
ROTHSAY, Duke of (*The Fair Maid of Perth*)
SALADIN (*The Talisman*)
SAMPSON, Dominie (*Guy Mannering*)
SHAFTON, Sir Piercie (*The Monastery*)
TOMKINS, Joseph (*Woodstock*)
WARDOUR, Isabella (*The Antiquary*)
WARDOUR, Sir Arthur (*The Antiquary*)

8

BEAN LEAN, Donald (*Waverley*)
BERENGER, Eveline (*The Betrothed*)
BONIFACE, Abbot (*The Monastery*)
BURGUNDY, Duke of (*Anne of Geierstein*)
CAMPBELL, Sir Duncan (*A Legend of Montrose*)
CONACHAR (*The Fair Maid of Perth*)
CROMWELL, Oliver (*Woodstock*)
DALGARNO, Lord (*The Fortunes of Nigel*)
DALGETTY, Captain Dugald (*A Legend of Montrose*)
DE WALTON, Sir John (*Castle Dangerous*)
EVANDALE, Lord (*Old Mortality*)
FAIRFORD, Alan (*Redgauntlet*)
GALEOTTI, Martius (*Quentin Durward*)
GARDINER, Colonel James (*Waverley*)
HEREWARD (*Count Robert of Paris*)
HYDER ALI (*The Surgeon's Daughter*)

L'HERMITE, Tristan (*Quentin Durward*)
MENTEITH, Earl of (*A Legend of Montrose*)
M'INTYRE, Hector (*The Antiquary*)
OLIFAUNT, Nigel (*The Fortunes of Nigel*)
RAMORNEY, Sir John (*The Fair Maid of Perth*)
STAUNTON, George (*The Heart of Midlothian*)
TRAPBOIS (*The Fortunes of Nigel*)
TRUMBULL, Thomas (*Redgauntlet*)
WAVERLEY, Edward (*Waverley*)
WAVERLEY, Sir Everard (*Waverley*)
WILDRAKE, Roger (*Woodstock*)

9

ARMSTRONG, Grace (*The Black Dwarf*)
BELLENDEN, Edith (*Old Mortality*)
BELLENDEN, Lady Margaret (*Old Mortality*)
BIEDERMAN, Arnold (*Anne of Geierstein*)
BRENHILDA (*Count Robert of Paris*)
BRIENNIUS, Nicephorus (*Count Robert of Paris*)
CHIFFINCH (*Peveril of the Peak*)
CHRISTIAN, Edward (*Peveril of the Peak*)
CLEVELAND, Clement (*The Pirate*)
DE BERKELY, Lady Augusta (*Castle Dangerous*)
DE LA MARCK, William (*Quentin Durward*)
DE VALENCE, Aymer (*Castle Dangerous*)
ELIZABETH, Queen (*Kenilworth*)
FRIAR TUCK (*Ivanhoe*)
GELLATLEY, Davie (*Waverley*)
HAGENBACH, Archibald of (*Anne of Geierstein*)
MACGREGOR, Rob Roy (*Rob Roy*)
MANNERING, Colonel Guy (*Guy Mannering*)
MANNERING, Julia (*Guy Mannering*)
MERRILIES, Meg (*Guy Mannering*)
MIDDLEMAS, Richard (*The Surgeon's Daughter*)
MONIPLIES, Richard (*The Fortunes of Nigel*)
OCHILTREE, Edie (*The Antiquary*)
PHILIPSON (*Anne of Geierstein*)
ROBIN HOOD (*Ivanhoe*)
TOUCHWOOD, Mr (*St Ronan's Well*)
YELLOWLEY, Barbara (*The Pirate*)
YELLOWLEY, Triptolemus (*The Pirate*)

10

ATHELSTANE (of Coningsburgh) (*Ivanhoe*)
BERENGARIA, Queen (*The Talisman*)
BUCKINGHAM (*Peveril of the Peak*)
HATTERAICK, Dirk (*Guy Mannering*)
HOLDENOUGH, Rev. Nehemiah (*Woodstock*)
LOWESTOFFE, Templar (*The Fortunes of Nigel*)
MACWHEEBLE, Duncan (*Waverley*)
MONTFERRAT, (Conrade of) (*The Talisman*)
MURDOCKSON, Meg (*The Heart of Midlothian*)
PENFEATHER, Lady Penelope (*St Ronan's Well*)
RAVENSWOOD, Lord (*The Bride of Lammermoor*)
RAVENSWOOD, Master of (*The Bride of Lammermoor*)
SADDLETREE, Bartoline (*The Heart of Midlothian*)
SNAILSFOOT, Bryce (*The Pirate*)

SUDDLECHOP, Dame Ursula (*The Fortunes of Nigel*)
TRESSILIAN, Edmund (*Kenilworth*)

11

ANNA COMNENA (*Count Robert of Paris*)
BALDERSTONE, Caleb (*The Bride of Lammermoor*)
BRADWARDINE, Baron of (*Waverley*)
BRADWARDINE, Rose (*Waverley*)
BRIDGENORTH, Alic (*Peveril of the Peak*)
BRIDGENORTH, Major (*Peveril of the Peak*)
DUMBIEDIKES, Laird of (*The Heart of Midlothian*)
ETHERINGTON, Earl of (*St Ronan's Well*)
FAIRSERVICE, Andrew (*Rob Roy*)
GLENDINNING, Edward (*The Monastery*)
GLENDINNING, Halbert (*The Monastery*)
GLENDINNING, Simon (*The Monastery*)
MONTREVILLE, Madame (*The Surgeon's Daughter*)
PLANTAGENET, Edith (*The Talisman*)
REDGAUNTLET, Sir Arthur Darsie (*Redgauntlet*)
TIPPOO SAHIB (*The Surgeon's Daughter*)

12

BOIS-GUILBERT, Sir Brian de (*Ivanhoe*)
FRONT-DE-BOEUF, Sir Reginald (*Ivanhoe*)
MALAGROWTHER, Sir Mungo (*The Fortunes of Nigel*)
OSBALDISTONE, Francis (*Rob Roy*)
OSBALDISTONE, Rashleigh (*Rob Roy*)
OSBALDISTONE, Sir Hildebrand (*Rob Roy*)

13

DOUSTERSWIVEL (*The Antiquary*)
FATHER EUSTACE (*The Monastery*)
MADGE WILDFIRE (*The Heart of Midlothian*)

14

CHARLES THE BOLD (*Anne of Geierstein; Quentin Durward*)
ROBERT THE BRUCE (*Castle Dangerous*)

15+

ELSHENDER THE RECLUSE (*The Black Dwarf*)
ELSHIE OF THE MUCKLESTANES (*The Black Dwarf*)
FLIBBERTIGIBBET (*Kenilworth*)
HERRIES OF BIRRENSWORK (*Redgauntlet*)
ISABELLE DE CROYE (*Quentin Durward*)
KNIGHT OF THE LEOPARD (*The Talisman*)
MAC-IVOR VICH IAN VOHR OF GLENNAQUOICH, Fergus (*Waverley*)
MAC-IVOR VICH IAN VOHR OF GLENNAQUOICH, Flora (*Waverley*)
NORNA OF THE FITFUL-HEAD (*The Pirate*)
TORQUIL OF THE OAK (*The Fair Maid of Perth*)
WANDERING WILLIE (*Redgauntlet*)
WILFRED OF IVANHOE (*Ivanhoe*)

CHARACTERS FROM MARTIN'S 'GAME OF THRONES'

4

FREY, Walder – (male) Lord of the Twins – a vassal to the House Tully

OSHA – (female) wildling who sneaked south – helped Bran and Rickon Stark escape from Theon Greyjoy

REED, Jojen – (male) helped Bran and Rickon Stark escape from Theon Greyjoy

REED, Meera – (female) helped Bran and Rickon Stark escape from Theon Greyjoy

SAND, Ellaria – (female) paramour of Oberyn Martell and mother of the four youngest "Sand Snakes"

SNOW, Jon – (male) raised as Eddard Stark's illegitimate son – House: Stark, Targaryen

WAIF, The – (female) a priestess of the Many-Faced God

WORM, Grey – (male) commander of Daenerys Targaryen's Unsullied and one of her trusted advisors

5

ARRYN, Jon – (male) Lord of the Eyrie and a father figure to both Eddard Stark and Robert Baratheon – House: Arryn

ARRYN, Lysa – (female) younger sister of Catelyn Stark – enamoured of Petyr Baelish – House: Arryn, Tully

ARRYN, Robert – (male) only child of Jon and Lysa Arryn – House: Arryn

BRONN – (male) mercenary of low birth

DROGO, Khal – (male) a warlord of the Dothraki people

FOREL, Syrio – (male) first sword of Braavos

GILLY – (female) wildling girl, daughter and wife of Craster

HODOR – (male) giant of a man, employed to carry around Bran Stark

HOTAH, Areo – (male) captain of Doran Martell's guards

MARSH, Bowen – (male) first steward of the Night's Watch

PAYNE, Ilyn – (male) the King's Justice, the royal executioner

PAYNE, Podrick – (male) a squire to Tyrion Lannister

POOLE, Jeyne – (female) best friend of Sansa Stark

ROYCE, Nestor – (male) cousin of Yohn Royce – House: Royce

ROYCE, Yohn – (male) Lord of Runestone – House: Royce

SELMY, Barristan – (male) called Barristan the Bold – Lord Commander of the kingsguard

SLYNT, Janos – (male) Commander of the City Watch – a brother in the Night's Watch

STARK, Arya – (female) third child of Eddard and Catelyn Stark – House: Stark

STARK, Benjen – (male) younger brother of Eddard Stark – House: Stark

STARK, Brandon – (male) known as Bran – fourth child of Eddard and Catelyn Stark – House: Stark

STARK, Catelyn – (female) wife of Eddard – House: Stark, Tully

STARK, Eddard – (male) known as Ned – Lord of Winterfell – House: Stark

STARK, Lyanna – (female) younger sister of Eddard Stark – House: Stark

STARK, Rickon – (male) fifth child of Eddard and Catelyn Stark – House: Stark

STARK, Robb – (male) oldest child of Eddard and Catelyn Stark – House: Stark

STARK, Sansa – (female) second child of Eddard and Catelyn Stark – House: Stark, Lannister

STORM, Edric – (male) Robert Baratheon's only acknowledged bastard

SWANN, Balon – (male) member of the kingsguard

TARLY, Randyll – (male) bannerman of House Tyrell

TARLY, Samwell – (male) known as Sam

TRANT, Meryn – (male) member of the kingsguard

TULLY, Brynden – (male) yonger brother of Hoster Tully, known as Blackfish – House: Tully

TULLY, Hoster – (male) Lord of Riverrun – father of Catelyn Stark, Lysa Arryn and Edmure Tully – House: Tully

TULLY, Edmure – (male) third child of Hoster Tully – House: Tully

VARYS – (male) a eunuch – Master of the Whispers, the spymaster for the King of the Seven Kingdoms

YOREN – (male) recruiter of the Night's Watch

6

BOLTON, Roose – (male) vassal of Eddard Stark – House: Bolton

BOLTON, Ramsay – (male) previously known as Ramsay Snow, bastard son of Roose Bolton – House: Bolton

DROGON – (dragon) Daenerys dragon named after Khal Drogo

DUNCAN – (male) the Tall – legendary knight

GENDRY – (male) one of Robert Baratheon's many bastard children

HARLAW, Rodrik – (male) Lord of Harlaw – known as the reader

H'GHAR, Jagen – (male) a member of the Faceless Men a society of assassins

QYBURN – (male) former Maester – rumoured to dabble in necromancy

RAYDER, Mance – (male) a member of the Night's Watch that deserted and became known as the King-beyond-the-Wall

RIVERS, Brynden – (male) known as Lord Bloodraven and The Three Eyed Raven – House: Targaryen

SNAKES, The Sand – (females) eight illegitimate daughters of Oberyn Martell

THORNE, Alliser – (male) Master of Arms at Castle Black

THOROS – (male) of Myr – Red priest of R'hllor

TYRELL, Mace – (male) Lord of Highgarden – House: Tyrell

TYRELL, Garlan – (male) second child of Mace Tyrell – House: Tyrell

TYRELL, Loras – (male) third child of Mace Tyrell – House: Tyrell

TYRELL, Margaery – (female) youngest child of Mace Tyrell – House: Tyrell

TYRELL, Olenna – (female) mother of Mace Tyrell – known as the Queen of Thorns – House: Tyrell

TYRELL, Willas – (male) first child of Mace Tyrell – House: Tyrell

UNELLA, Septa – (female) a member of the Most Devout

7

BAELISH, Petyr – (male) known as Littlefinger – the Treasurer of the Seven Kingdoms

BRIENNE – (female) known as Brienne of Tarth

CRASTER – (male) wildling who lives north of the Wall – incestuously fathering children with his daughters

CLEGANE, Gregor – (male) known as the Mountain – vassal to Tywin Lannister

CLEGANE, Sandor – (male) known as the Hound – a retainer to House Lannister

FLORENT, Selyse – (female) wife of Stannis Baratheon

GREYJOY, Aeron – (male) brother of Balon Greyjoy – House: Greyjoy

GREYJOY, Asha – (female) oldest child of Balon Greyjoy – House: Greyjoy

GREYJOY, Balon – (male) Lord of the Iron Islands – House: Greyjoy

GREYJOY, Euron – (male) brother of Balon Greyjoy – nicknamed Crow's Eye – House: Greyjoy

GREYJOY, Theon – (male) youngest child of Balon Greyjoy – House: Greyjoy

GREYJOY, Victarion – (male) brother of Balon Greyjoy – House: Greyjoy

MARTELL, Arianne – (female) oldest child of Doran Martell – House: Martell

MARTELL, Doran – (male) Prince of Dorne and the Lord of Sunspear – House: Martell

MARTELL, Elia – (female) younger sister of Doran Martell – wife of Rhaegar Targaryen – House: Martell, Targaryen

MARTELL, Oberyn – (male) younger brother of Doran Martell – known as the Red Viper – House: Martell

MARTELL, Quentyn – (male) second child of Doran Martell – House: Martell

MARTELL, Trystane – (male) youngest child of Doran Martell – House: Martell

MOPATIS, Illyrio – (male) a wealthy and powerful Magister

MORMONT, Jorah – (male) exiled Lord of Bear Island – House: Mormont

NAHARIS, Daario – (male) leader of the Stormcrows mercenary company

PYCELLE – (male) a Maester, served many Kings as Grand Maester

RHAEGAL – (dragon) Daenerys dragon named after Rhaegar Targaryen

SPARROW, The High – (male) prominent member of the sparrows

TOLLETT, Eddison – (male) squire from House Tollett – steward of the Night's Watch

YGRITTE – (female) a warrior wildling woman

ZO LORAQ, Hizdahr – (male) a Ghiscari noble of the city of Meereen

8

GREY WORM – (male) commander of Daenerys Targaryen's Unsullied and one of her trusted advisors

KARSTARK, Rickard – (male) Lord of Karhold – a main Stark vassal – House: Karstark

KARSTARK, Alys – (female) only daughter of Rickard Karstark – House: Karstark

MANDERLY, Wyman – (male) wealthiest of the Stark vassals

MERIBALD – (male) a septon of the Riverlands

NESTORIS, Tycho – (male) representative of the Iron Bank of Braavos

OAKHEART, Arys – (male) knight of House Baratheon's kingsguard

ZO QAGGAZ, Yezzan – (male) slave-trader from Yunkai

SEAWORTH, Davos – (male) called the Onion Knight – House: Seaworth

SIXSKINS, Varamyr – (male) a wildling skinchanger

VISERION – (dragon) Daenerys dragon named after Viserys Targaryen

WAYNWOOD, Anya – (female) Lady of Ironoaks – the head of House Waynwood – a powerful vassal to House Arryn – House: Waynwood

9

BARATHEON, Joffrey – (male) first child of Cersei and Jaime Lannister. He believed he was Robert Baratheon's son – House: Baratheon, Lannister

BARATHEON, Myrcella – (female) second child of Cersei and Jaime Lannister. She believed she was Robert Baratheon's daughter – House: Baratheon, Lannister

BARATHEON, Renly – (male) younger brother of Robert and Stannis Baratheon – House: Baratheon

BARATHEON, Robert – (male) married to Cersei Lannister – House: Baratheon

BARATHEON, Shireen – (female) only daughter of Stannis Baratheon – House: Baratheon

BARATHEON, Stannis – (male) younger brother of Robert and older brother of Renly Baratheon – House: Baratheon

BARATHEON, Tommen – (male) third child of Cersei and Jaime Lannister. He believed he was Robert Baratheon's son – House: Baratheon, Lannister

LANNISTER, Cersei – (female) only daughter of Tywin Lannister and twin with Jaime Lannister – she had an incestuous relationship with Jaime, they had three children – she married Robert Baratheon – House: Lannister, Baratheon

LANNISTER, Jaime – (male) first son of Tywin Lannister and twin with Cersei Lannister – House: Lannister

LANNISTER, Kevan – (male) Tywin Lannister's younger brother – House: Lannister

LANNISTER, Lancel – (male) Kevan Lannister's

eldest son – House: Lannister

LANNISTER, Tyrion – (male) second son of Tywin Lannister – House: Lannister

LANNISTER, Tywin – (male) Lord of Casterly Rock – House: Lannister

MISSANDEI – (female) handmaiden to Daenerys Targaryen

NIGHT KING – White Walker, supreme leader of the Army of the Dead

TARGARYEN, Aegon V – (male) House: Targaryen

TARGARYEN, Aemon – (male) became a Maester of an order of scholars and healers House: Targaryen

TARGARYEN, Aerys II – (male) The Mad King – married to his sister Rhaella – House: Targaryen

TARGARYEN, Maekar I – (male) House: Targaryen

TARGARYEN, Rhaella – (female) House: Targaryen

TARGARYEN, Rhaegar – (male) first child of Aerys II and Rhaella Targaryen – married Elia Martell –

House: Targaryen

TARGARYEN, Viserys – (male) second child of Aerys II and Rhaella Targaryen – House: Targaryen

TARGARYEN, Daenerys – (female) third child of Aerys II and Rhaella Targaryen – known as the Mother of Dragons – House: Targaryen

TARGARYEN, Aegon – (male) child of Rhaegar Targaryen and Ella Martell – House: Targaryen

10

CONNINGTON, Jon – (male) exiled Lord of Griffin's Roost – close friend of Rhaegar Targaryen

DONDARRION, Beric – (male) nicknamed the Lightening Lord – a gallant knight with great fighting skills

GIANTSBANE, Tormund – (male) wildling raider

MELISANDRE – (female) priestess of R'hllor – in service to Stannis Baratheon

CHARACTERS FROM TOLKIEN'S 'LORD OF THE RINGS'

3&4

ENT – one of the tree-people

ORC – nasty goblin-like creature – many served Saruman and Sauron

SAM – see Gamgee, Sam

TOOK, Peregrin – (hobbit) member of the Fellowship, known as Pippin

5

ARWEN – (elf) daughter of Elrond – she married Aragorn and became Queen when he was crowned King – also known as the Evenstar

DROGO – see Baggins, Drogo

EOMER – (man) Marshal of the Riders of Rohan – became King of Rohan after his uncle Théoden's death

EOWYN – (woman) Lady of Rohan, she was Théoden's niece and Éomer's sister

FRODO – see Baggins, Frodo

GIMLI – dwarf and member of the Fellowship

GLOIN – (dwarf) Gimli's father

MERRY – see Brandybuck, Meriadoc

NARYA – one of the Rings of Power – belonged to Gandalf

NENYA – one of the Rings of Power – belonged to Galadriel

STING – sword belonging to Bilbo Baggins, which he gave to Frodo Baggins – glows blue when Orcs are near

UGLUK – an Uruk-hai

VILYA – one of the Rings of Power, belonged to Elrond

6

BALROG – a creature of fire in the mines of Moria

COTTON, Rosie – (hobbit) who marries Sam Gamgee

DEAGOL – (hobbit) cousin of Sméagol – found the Ring in a river and was killed by Sméagol

ELROND – (elf) Lord of Rivendell and father of Arwen

GAMGEE, Samwise – (hobbit) best friend of Frodo Baggins and member of the Fellowship – known as Sam

GOLLUM – pitiful creature obsessed by the Ring, named for his gurgling cough. He was once a hobbit called Sméagol

HALDIR – (elf) escorted the Fellowship into Lothlórien

HOBBIT – little people, also known as 'halflings'

NARSIL – the broken sword with which Isildur cut the Ring from Sauron's hand – repaired in Rivendell for Aragorn's use – rechristened Anduril

NAZGUL – another name for a Ringwraith

PIPPIN – see Took, Peregrin

SAURON – The Dark Lord and Master of the Ring

SHELOB – huge carnivorous spider who lives in the mountains on the edge of Mordor – killed by Sam Gamgee

THEODEN – (man) King of Rohan – died in battle and was succeeded by his nephew, Éomer

7

ANDURIL – name given to the sword Narsil, after being reforged

ARAGORN – (man and ranger) sometimes known as Strider – heir of Isildur and Member of the Fellowship – named Elessar (meaning Elfstone) when he is crowned King

BAGGINS, Bilbo – (hobbit) Frodo's uncle

BAGGINS, Drogo – (hobbit) Frodo's father

BAGGINS, Frodo – (hobbit) ring-bearer and member of the Fellowship – Bilbo's nephew

BOROMIR – (man) member of the Fellowship, brother of Faramir and son of Denethor

ELENDIL – (man) Isildur's father and ancestor of Aragorn. He was once King of Gondor

ELESSAR – see Aragorn

FARAMIR – (man) Captain of Gondor – brother of Boromir and son of Denethor

GANDALF – wizard and member of the Fellowship – his Elvish name is Mithrandir

GWAIHIR – great eagle who rescued Gandalf from Isengard and Frodo and Sam from Mount Doom

ISILDUR – (man) son of Elendil and ancestor of Aragorn – he cut the Ring from Sauron's finger

LEGOLAS – see Greenleaf, Legolas

MITHRIL – dwarf-made chainmail originally belonging to Bilbo Baggins – he gave it to Frodo for the journey to Mordor

SARUMAN – a wizard

SMÉAGOL – Gollum's name when he was a hobbit

STRIDER – a name by which Aragorn is sometimes known

URUK-HAI – a particularly large and violent breed of Orc

8

ARATHORN – (man) Aragorn's father

BOMBADIL, Tom – master of wood, water, and hill – gives shelter to the four hobbits on their journey to Rivendell

CELEBORN – (elf) Lord of Lórien

DENETHOR – (man) ruling Steward of Gondor in the absence of a King – also the father of Boromir and Faramir

EVENSTAR – see Arwen

9

BUTTERBUR, Barliman – (man) Landlord of the Prancing Pony

CELEBRIAN – (elf) Wife of Elrond and mother of Arwen (daughter of Galadriel and Celeborn)

GALADRIEL – (elf) Lady of Lórien and Arwen's grandmother

GLAMDRING – sword belonging to Gandalf

GREENLEAF, Legolas – (elf) member of the Fellowship – son of Thranduil, the Elven-king of Mirkwood

SHADOWFAX – horse originally belonging to King Théoden, ridden by Gandalf

THRANDUIL – (elf) Legolas's father and Elven-king of Mirkwood

TREEBEARD – an Ent in the forest of Fangorn – oldest living thing in Middle-earth

UNDERHILL, Mr – alias used by Frodo on the journey to Mordor

10+

BLACK RIDER – another name for a Ringwraith

BRANDYBUCK, Meriadoc – (hobbit) member of the Fellowship, known as Merry

GLORFINDEL – (elf) escorted Aragorn and the hobbits to Rivendell

MITHRANDIR – see Gandalf

RINGWRAITHS – nine shadows of men who are the servants of Sauron – also known as the Nazgul or the Black Riders

SACKVILLE-BAGGINS – (hobbits) cousins of Bilbo Baggins

WITCH-KING – the Lord of the Nazgul, sometimes fully known as the Witch-king of Angmar

WORMTONGUE, Gríma – (man) servant of Théoden but secretly in league with Saruman

CHARACTERS FROM ROWLING'S 'HARRY POTTER'

3

OGG – gamekeeper at Hogwarts when Arthur and Molly Weasley were students

PYE, Augustus – trainee Healer at St Mungo's Hospital for Magical Maladies

TOM – landlord of the Leaky Cauldron, the London pub that provides the entrance to Diagon Alley

4

BANE – centaur who lives in the Forbidden Forest

BELL, Katie – student at Hogwarts and Chaser for the Gryffindor Quidditch team

BOTT, Bertie – maker of the Every Flavour Beans

DOGE, Elphias – member of the Order of the Phoenix

GRIM, the – spectral black dog that is an omen of death

FANG – large boarhound belonging to Hagrid

FIGG, Arabella – a fellow resident of Privet Drive, where the Dursley family and Harry live

NOTT, Theodore – student at Hogwarts and friend of Draco Malfoy

WOOD, Oliver – student at Hogwarts – one-time captain and Keeper for the Gryffindor Quidditch team

5

AUROR – catcher of dark wizards – works for the Ministry of Magic

AVERY – a Death Eater

BASIL – keeper of the Portkeys for the Quidditch World Cup

BINNS, Professor – History of Magic teacher at Hogwarts

BLACK, Alphard – Sirius Black's uncle

BLACK, Elladora – Sirius Black's aunt

BLACK, Mrs – Sirius Black's mother – a firm believer in pure-blood wizardry

BLACK, Regulus – Sirius Black's brother and a Death Eater

BLACK, Sirius – Harry's godfather and a member of the Order of the Phoenix – school friend of Peter Pettigrew, James Potter, and Remus Lupin – escaped from the wizard prison Azkaban, where he was falsely held for multiple murders

BONES, Amelia – head of the Department of Magical Law Enforcement at the Ministry of Magic

BONES, Edgar – brother of Amelia Bones and an original member of the Order of the Phoenix

BONES, Susan – niece of Amelia Bones, student at Hogwarts

BROWN, Lavender – student at Hogwarts, usually to be found with Parvati Patil

CHANG, Cho – student at Hogwarts and Seeker for the Ravenclaw Quidditch team

CRAGG, Elfrida – former headmistress of Hogwarts, whose portrait hangs in St Mungo's Hospital for Magical Maladies

DOBBY – A male house-elf

ERROL – ancient owl belonging to the Weasley family

FILCH, Argus – caretaker at Hogwarts

FLINT, Marcus – student at Hogwarts and captain of the Slytherin Quidditch team

FUDGE, Cornelius – Minister for Magic

GOYLE, Gregory – student at Hogwarts and one of Draco Malfoy's cronies

GRAWP – Hagrid's giant half-brother

HOOCH, Madam – teacher of Flying lessons and Quidditch at Hogwarts

JONES, Hestia – member of the Order of the Phoenix

LUPIN, Remus – Harry's third Defence Against the Dark Arts teacher – a werewolf and school friend of Peter Pettigrew, James Potter, and Sirius Black – member of the Order of the Phoenix

MOODY, Alastor 'Mad-Eye' – ex-Auror and a member of the Order of the Phoenix

MOONY – school nickname for Remus Lupin when he was in his animagus form (a werewolf)

MUNCH, Eric – Security watchwizard at the Ministry of Magic

OGDEN, Tiberius – an Elder at the Wizengamot (wizard court)

PATIL, Padma and Parvati – twin sisters and students at Hogwart's

PINCE, Madam – librarian at Hogwarts

PRANG, Ernie – driver of the Knight Bus, a bus that magically transports wizard folk up and down the UK

PUCEY, Adrian – student at Hogwarts and player for the Slytherin Quidditch team

RONAN – centaur who lives in the Forbidden Forest

SMITH, Zacharias – student at Hogwarts

SNAPE, Professor Severus – Potions teacher at Hogwarts, head of Slytherin house, and a member of the Order of the Phoenix

SQUIB – name for somebody born into a wizarding family who has no magical powers

TONKS, Andromeda – Nymphadora Tonks's mother and a cousin of Sirius Black

TONKS, Nymphadora – an Auror and member of the Order of the Phoenix – a metamorphmagus (can change her appearance at will)

TONKS, Ted – Nymphadora Tonks's father

VANCE, Emmeline – member of the Order

of the Phoenix

VEELA – beautiful women who enchant men, especially by dancing, but become physically ugly when unhappy – Bulgaria's mascots at the Quidditch World Cup

WINKY – female house-elf

6

ABBOTT, Hannah – student at Hogwarts

ARAGOG – huge spider brought up by Hagrid – lives in the Forbidden Forest

BAGMAN, Ludo – Head of the Department of Magical Games and Sports at the Ministry of Magic

CRABBE, Mr – Vincent Crabbe's father and a Death Eater

CRABBE, Vincent – student at Hogwarts and one of Draco Malfoy's cronies

CROUCH, Barty, Jr – a Death Eater who impersonated 'Mad-Eye' Moody for the whole of Harry's fourth year of school

CROUCH, Barty, Sr – one-time head of the Department of International Magical Cooperation at the Ministry of Magic

DAVIES, Roger – student at Hogwarts and captain of the Ravenclaw Quidditch team

DIGGLE, Dedalus – member of the Order of the Phoenix

DIPPET, Professor Armando Albus Dumbledore's predecessor as Headmaster of Hogwarts

FAWKES – Phoenix belonging to Albus Dumbledore – provided the feather that lies inside the wands of Harry and Voldemort

FLAMEL, Nicholas – responsible for making the Philosopher's Stone – worked on alchemy with Albus Dumbledore

FLUFFY – huge, three-headed dog that guarded the trapdoor through which the Philosopher's Stone was hidden

HAGRID, Rubeus – gamekeeper and teacher of the Care of Magical Creatures at Hogwarts

HEDWIG – snowy white owl belonging to Harry Potter

HERMES – screech owl belonging to Percy Weasley

JORDAN, Lee – student at Hogwarts and best friend of Fred and George Weasley

JUGSON – a Death Eater

KARKUS – a giant

MALFOY, Draco – student at Hogwarts and enemy of Harry Potter – became Seeker for the Slytherin Quidditch team in Harry's second year of school

MALFOY, Lucius – Draco Malfoy's father – a Death Eater and supporter of Voldemort

MALFOY, Narcissa – Draco Malfoy's mother and a cousin of Sirius Black

MALKIN, Madam – owns and runs the robe shop in Diagon Alley

MAXIME, Madame Olympe – headmistress of Beauxbatons Academy – a giantess

MUGGLE – name for a non-magic person

MURCUS – head of the merpeople who live in the lake at Hogwarts

NAGINI – snake-like creature whose venom helped restore Voldemort to human form

NORRIS, Mrs – cat with lamp-like eyes belonging to Argus Filch

PEEVES – resident poltergeist at Hogwarts

POTTER, Harry – boy wizard and central character – famously survived a murder attempt by Lord Voldemort, which left a lightning-shaped scar on his forehead – one of the champions of the Triwizard Tournament and Seeker for the Gryffindor Quidditch team – can speak Parseltongue (snake language)

POTTER, James – Harry's father who was Head Boy while at Hogwarts and school friend of Sirius Black, Remus Lupin, and Peter Pettigrew

POTTER, Lily – Harry's mother and Petunia Dursley's sister – was Head Girl at Hogwarts and an original member of the Order of the Phoenix

PRONGS – school nickname for James Potter when he was in his animagus form (a stag)

RAGNOK – a goblin

RIDDLE, Tom – Voldemort's original name

RIPPER – Marge Dursley's pet dog

ROSIER – a Death Eater

SPROUT, Professor – Herbology teacher at Hogwarts and head of Hufflepuff house

STROUT, Miriam – healer at St Mungo's Hospital for Magical Maladies, in charge of the ward where Broderick Bode died

THOMAS, Dean – student at Hogwarts and friend of Harry and Ron Weasley

TREVOR – pet toad belonging to Neville Longbottom

VECTOR, Professor – Arithmancy teacher at Hogwarts

VIOLET – portrait painting of a witch who is good friends with the Fat Lady

WILKES – a Death Eater

7

BAGNOLD, Millicent – Cornelius Fudge's predecessor as Minister for Magic

CADOGAN, Sir – portrait painting at Hogwarts

CREEVEY, Colin – student at Hogwarts

CREEVEY, Dennis – Colin Creevey's younger brother, student at Hogwarts

DERWENT, Dilys – former headmistress of Hogwarts, now present in a portrait painting in Albus Dumbledore's office – was a Healer at St Mungo's Hospital for Magical Maladies

DIGGORY, Cedric – student and Prefect at Hogwarts – one of the champions in the Triwizard Tournament – killed by Peter Pettigrew on Voldemort's orders

DURSLEY, Dudley – Harry's bullying, overweight cousin

DURSLEY, Petunia – Harry's aunt – sister of Lily Potter

DURSLEY, Vernon – Harry's uncle

EVERARD – former headmaster of Hogwarts, now present in a portrait painting in Albus Dumbledore's office

FAT LADY – portrait painting at Hogwarts through which the Gryffindor students enter their Tower

FENWICK, Benjy – an original member of the Order of the Phoenix, killed by Death Eaters

FIRENZE – centaur who lives in the Forbidden Forest next to Hogwarts

GOSHAWK, Miranda – author of the Standard Book of Spells (in various grades)

GRANGER, Hermione – best friend of Harry and Ron Weasley

HOPKIRK, Mafalda – employee of the Improper Use of Magic Office at the Ministry of Magic

JOHNSON, Angelina – student at Hogwarts and Chaser for the Gryffindor Quidditch team

JORKINS, Bertha – employee of the Ministry of Magic who was killed by Voldemort

MACNAIR, Walden – executioner at Buckbeak's trial – a Death Eater

NORBERT – dragon of the Norwegian Ridgeback variety – later taken to Romania by Charlie Weasley

PADFOOT – school nickname for Sirius Black when he was in his animagus form (a large black dog)

PERKINS – elderly colleague of Arthur Weasley's at the Ministry of Magic

PODMORE, Sturgis – member of the Order of the Phoenix

POMFREY, Madam Poppy – school nurse at Hogwarts

PREWETT, Fabian and Gideon – original members of the Order of the Phoenix

PRINGLE, Apollyon – caretaker at Hogwarts when Arthur and Molly Weasley were students

SKEETER, Rita – reporter for the Daily Prophet – can transform into a beetle

SPINNET, Alicia – student at Hogwarts and Chaser for the Gryffindor Quidditch team

TRAVERS – a Death Eater

WEASLEY, Arthur – Ron Weasley's father and a member of the Order of the Phoenix – works at the Ministry of Magic and is fascinated by anything to do with Muggles

WEASLEY, Bill – older brother of Ron – worked in Egypt breaking curses for Gringotts Wizarding Bank before moving back to England to join the Order of the Phoenix

WEASLEY, Charlie – older brother of Ron Weasley – former Hogwarts Quidditch captain, now studying dragons in Romania – member of the Order of the Phoenix

WEASLEY, Fred and George – identical twins and older brothers of Ron Weasley – fond of practical jokes – were beaters for the Gryffindor Quidditch team

WEASLEY, Ginny – younger sister of Ron Weasley – replaced Harry as Seeker for the Gryffindor Quidditch team for part of Harry's fifth year

WEASLEY, Molly – Ron Weasley's mother and a member of the Order of the Phoenix

WEASLEY, Percy – older brother of Ron Weasley – prefect and Head Boy at Hogwarts – left to work at the Ministry of Magic

WEASLEY, Ron – best friend of Harry and Hermione Granger – became both a Prefect and Keeper for the Gryffindor Quidditch team in Harry's fifth year of school

8

BASILISK – large serpent-like creature that petrified those who looked it in the eye

BUCKBEAK – a hippogriff (a cross between a horse and an eagle) belonging to Hagrid and later Sirius Black

DEARBORN, Caradoc – an original member of the Order of the Phoenix

DELACOUR, Fleur – one of the champions of the Triwizard Tournament (representing Beauxbatons Academy of Magic) – became an employee at Gringott's Wizarding Bank – partly a Veela

DELACOUR, Gabrielle – Fleur Delacour's younger sister, used as a hostage for a challenge in the Triwizard Tournament

DIMITROV – player for the Bulgarian Quidditch World Cup team

FAT FRIAR – One of the resident ghosts at Hogwarts

FINNIGAN, Seamus – student at Hogwarts and friend of Harry

FLETCHER, Mundungus – member of the Order of the Phoenix

FLITWICK, Professor – teacher of Charms at Hogwarts

GRIPHOOK – a goblin at Gringotts Wizarding Bank

KREACHER – house-elf belonging to both the Black and the Malfoy families

LOCKHART, Gilderoy – Harry's second teacher of Defence Against the Dark Arts

LOVEGOOD, Luna – student at Hogwarts

MAGORIAN – a centaur who lives in the Forbidden Forest

MCKINNON, Marlene – an original member of the Order of the Phoenix, killed by Death Eaters

MEADOWES, Dorcas – an original member of the Order of the Phoenix, killed by Voldemort

MELIFLUA, Araminta – distant relative of Sirius Black

MUDBLOOD – vulgar name for somebody with non-magic parents

MULCIBER – a Death Eater

NIGELLUS, Phineas – Sirius Black's great-great-grandfather

QUIRRELL, Professor – Harry's first Defence Against the Dark Arts teacher

ROOKWOOD, Algernon – a Death Eater

ROSMERTA, Madam – landlady of the Three Broomsticks Inn at Hogsmeade

SCABBERS – seemingly useless rat belonging Ron Weasley – turned out to be Peter Pettigrew in his animagus form

SHUNPIKE, Stan – conductor on the Knight Bus, a bus that magically transports wizard folk up and down the UK

SINISTRA, Professor – Astronomy teacher at Hogwarts

TENEBRUS – a Thestral (winged horse creatures that pull carriages) – first of its kind born in the Hogwarts forest

UMBRIDGE, Professor Dolores – Harry's fifth Defence Against the Dark Arts teacher who replaced Albus Dumbledore as headteacher for a time in Harry's fifth year of school

WORMTAIL – school nickname for Peter Pettigrew when he was in his animagus form (a rat)

9

BLETCHLEY, Miles – student at Hogwarts and Keeper for the Slytherin Quidditch team

BULSTRODE, Millicent – student at Hogwarts and one of Draco Malfoy's cronies

DEMENTORS – menacing guards of the Azkaban prison

EDGECOMBE, Marietta – student at Hogwarts and friend of Cho Chang

FORTESCUE – previous headmaster of Hogwarts, now resident in a portrait painting in Albus Dumbledore's office

FORTESCUE, Florean – owns and runs the ice cream parlour in Diagon Alley

FRIDWULFA – Hagrid's giantess mother

GOLDSTEIN, Anthony – student at Hogwarts

KARKAROFF, Professor Igor – headmaster of Durmstrang school, former Death Eater

LESTRANGE, Bellatrix – wife of Rodolphus Lestrange – a Death Eater and cousin of Sirius Black

LESTRANGE, Rabastan – brother of Rodolphus Lestrange – a Death Eater

LESTRANGE, Rodolphus – husband of Bellatrix Lestrange – Death Eater

MACMILLAN, Ernie – student at Hogwarts

PARKINSON, Pansy – student at Hogwarts and friend of Draco Malfoy

PETTIGREW, Peter – school friend of Sirius Black, James Potter, and Remus Lupin – betrayed James and Lily Potter and then hid out in the form of Scabbers the rat

PUDDIFOOT, Madam – owner of the tea shop in Hogsmeade

RAVENCLAW, Rowena – one of the four founders of Hogwarts – creator of Ravenclaw house

SLINKHARD, Wilbert – author of 'Defensive Magical Theory'

SLYTHERIN, Salazar – one of the four founders of Hogwarts and creator of Slytherin house – known for being a parselmouth

SMETHWYCK, Hippocrates – Healer-in-Charge at St Mungo's Hospital for Magical Maladies

TRELAWNEY, Cassandra – great-great-grandmother of Sybill Trelawney – a celebrated seer

TRELAWNEY, Professor Sybill – Divination teacher at Hogwarts

VOLDEMORT, Lord – dark wizard

10

DUMBLEDORE, Aberforth – Albus Dumbledore's brother and an original member of the Order of the Phoenix

DUMBLEDORE, Albus – headmaster of Hogwarts

GRYFFINDOR, Godric – one of the four founders of Hogwarts – creator of Gryffindor house

HUFFLEPUFF, Helga – one of the founders of Hogwarts – creator of Hufflepuff house

LONGBOTTOM, Algie – Neville Longbottom's great uncle

LONGBOTTOM, Alice – Neville Longbottom's

mother and an original member of the Order of the Phoenix

LONGBOTTOM, Frank – Neville Longbottom's father and an original member of the Order of the Phoenix

LONGBOTTOM, Neville – friend of Harry, Ron Weasley, and Hermione Granger

MARCHBANKS, Griselda – an Elder at the Wizengamot and head of the Wizarding Examinations Authority

MCGONAGALL, Professor Minerva – transfiguration teacher, deputy headmistress, and head of Gryffindor house – a member of the Order of the Phoenix

OLLIVANDER, Mr – owns and runs the wand shop in Diagon Alley

RACKHARROW, Urquhart – portrait painting at St Mungo's Hospital for Magical Maladies

SCRIMGEOUR – employee at the Ministry of Magic

SORTING HAT – talking wizard's hat (originally belonging to Godric Gryffindor) that famously sorts students into houses on their arrival at the Hogwarts

WARRINGTON – student at Hogwarts and player for the Slytherin Quidditch team

11

BLOODY BARON – one of the resident ghosts at Hogwarts

CROOKSHANKS – large ginger cat belonging to Hermione Granger

DEATH EATERS – supporters of Voldemort

SHACKLEBOLT, Kingsley – an Auror and member of the Order of the Phoenix

UNSPEAKABLE – name for employees who work in the Department of Mysteries at the Ministry of Magic (so-called because their work is top secret)

12+

DE MIMSY-PORPINGTON, Sir Nicholas – one of the resident ghosts at Hogwarts, more commonly known as 'Nearly Headless Nick'

FINCH-FLETCHLEY, Justin – student at Hogwarts who was petrified by the Basilisk

GOLGOMATH – a giant

GRUBBLY-PLANK, Professor Wilhelmina – teacher who temporarily took over Hagrid's Care of Magical Creatures classes

MOANING MYRTLE – ghost of a student that haunts one of the girl's bathrooms – killed by the Basilisk when Tom Riddle was at Hogwarts

NEARLY HEADLESS NICK – one of the resident ghosts at Hogwarts (full name Sir Nicholas de Mimsy-Porpington)

PIGWIDGEON 'Pig' – tiny, hyperactive owl given to Ron Weasley by Sirius Black to replace Scabbers the rat

WEIRD SISTERS, the – famous wizarding music group who play at the Yule Ball

LOVERS OF FACT AND FICTION

ANNA KARENINA AND LEON VRONSKI
ANTONY AND CLEOPATRA
AUCASSIN AND NICOLETTE
BEATRICE AND BENEDICK
BONNIE AND CLYDE
BYRON AND LADY CAROLINE LAMB
CHARLES II AND NELL GWYN
CHARLES PARNELL AND KITTY O'SHEA
CHOPIN AND GEORGE SAND
DANTE AND BEATRICE
DAPHNIS AND CHLOE
DARBY AND JOAN
DAVID AND BATHSHEBA
DIDO AND AENEAS
EDWARD VII AND LILLIE LANGTRY
EDWARD VIII AND WALLIS SIMPSON
ELIZABETH BARRETT AND ROBERT BROWNING
ELIZABETH BENNETT AND FITZWILLIAM DARCY
EROS AND PSYCHE
GEORGE IV AND MARIA FITZHERBERT
GERTRUDE STEIN AND ALICE B TOKLAS
HARLEQUIN AND COLUMBINE
HEATHCLIFF AND CATHY
HELOISE AND ABELARD
HERO AND LEANDER
HORATIO NELSON AND LADY EMMA HAMILTON

HUMPHREY BOGART AND LAUREN BACALL
JANE EYRE AND EDWARD ROCHESTER
JOHN OF GAUNT AND KATHERINE SWYNFORD
LADY CHATTERLEY AND MELLORS
LANCELOT AND GUINEVERE
NAPOLEON AND JOSEPHINE
ODYSSEUS AND PENELOPE
OSCAR WILDE AND LORD ALFRED DOUGLAS
PAOLO AND FRANCESCA
PARIS AND HELEN
PETRARCH AND LAURA
PORGY AND BESS
PYGMALION AND GALATEA
PYRAMUS AND THISBE
RICHARD BURTON AND ELIZABETH TAYLOR
RIMBAUD AND VERLAINE
ROBIN HOOD AND MAID MARIAN
ROMEO AND JULIET
ROSALIND AND ORLANDO
SAMSON AND DELILAH
SCARLETT O'HARA AND RHETT BUTLER
SPENCER TRACEY AND KATHARINE HEPBURN
TRISTAN AND ISOLDE
TROILUS AND CRESSIDA
VIRGINIA WOOLF AND VITA SACKVILLE-WEST
W B YEATS AND MAUD GONNE

FICTIONAL DETECTIVES

CHARACTER	(Creator)
MARTIN AINSWORTH	(Michael Underwood)
SUPERINTENDENT RODERICK ALLEYN	(Ngaio Marsh)
INSPECTOR ENRIQUE ALVAREZ	(Roderic Jeffries)
SIR JOHN APPLEBY	(Michael Innes)
SERGEANT NICK ATTWELL	(Michael Underwood)
INSPECTOR BILL AVEYARD	(James Fraser)
PROFESSOR ANDREW BASNETT	(E X Ferrars)
SUPERINTENDENT BATTLE	(Agatha Christie)
SERGEANT WILLIAM BEEF	(Leo Bruce)
TOMMY AND TUPPENCE BERESFORD	(Agatha Christie)
COLONEL PETER BLAIR	(J R L Anderson)
INSPECTOR BLAND	(Julian Symons)
DR WILLIAM BLOW	(Kenneth Hopkins)
INSPECTOR SALVADOR BORGES	(John and Emery Bonett)
DAME BEATRICE BRADLEY	(Gladys Mitchell)
CONSTABLE JOHN BRAGG	(Henry Wade)
MILES BREDON	(Ronald A Knox)
ERNST BRENDEL	(J C Masterman)
INSPECTOR JOHN BRENTFORD	(S B Hough)
RONALD BRIERCLIFFE	(Francis Beeding)
INSPECTOR DAVID BROCK	(R J White)
SUPERINTENDENT JOHN BROCK	(John Bingham)
FATHER BROWN	(G K Chesterton)
JANE AND DAGOBERT BROWN	(Delano Ames)
INSPECTOR THOMAS BRUNT	(John Buxton Hilton)
INSPECTOR BURNIVEL	(Edward Candy)
BROTHER CADFAEL	(Ellis Peters)
INSPECTOR THOMAS CADOVER	(Michael Innes)
RONALD CAMBERWELL	(J S Fletcher)
ALBERT CAMPION	(Margery Allingham)
	(Youngman Carter)
JOHN CARLYLE	(Henry Calvin)
SUPERINTENDENT CHARLESWORTH	(Christianna Brand)
AMBROSE CHITTERWICK	(Anthony Berkeley)
JOSHUA CLUNK	(H C Bailey)
INSPECTOR COCKRILL	(Christianna Brand)
MRS CRAGGS	(H R F Keating)
INSPECTOR CRAMBO	(Julian Symons)
PROFESSOR THEA CRAWFORD	(Jessica Mann)
SERGEANT CRIBB	(Peter Lovesey)
TESSA CRICHTON	(Anne Morice)
SERGEANT CUFF	Wilkie Collins
SUPERINTENDENT ADAM DALGLIESH	(P D James)
PROFESSOR DALY	(Eilís Dillon)
SUPERINTENDENT ANDREW DALZIEL	(Reginald Hill)
CHARMIAN DANIELS	(Jennie Melville)
DR R V DAVIE	(V C Clinton-Baddeley)
CAROLUS DEENE	(Leo Bruce)
INSPECTOR PIET DEVENTER	(J R L Anderson)
SUPERINTENDENT DITTERIDGE	(E X Ferrars)
KENNETH DUCANE (VANDOREN)	(John Bingham)
SUPERINTENDENT DUFFY	(Nigel FitzGerald)
TOBY DYKE	(E X Ferrars)
ROSA EPTON	(Michael Underwood)
MAJOR FAIDE	(Henry Wade)
KATE FANSLER	(Amanda Cross)
GIDEON FELL	(John Dickson Carr)
JACK FROST	(R D Wingfield)

SUPERINTENDENT GEORGE, DOMINIC, AND BUNTY FELSE	(Ellis Peters)
GERVASE FEN	(Edmund Crispin)
INSPECTOR FINCH (RUDD)	(June Thomson)
INSPECTOR SEPTIMUS FINCH	(Margaret Erskine)
REGGIE FORTUNE	(H C Bailey)
SUPERINTENDENT FRANCIS FOY	(Lionel Black)
VIRGINIA FREER	(E X Ferrars)
INSPECTOR JOSEPH FRENCH	(Freeman Wills Crofts)
DR HENRY FROST	(Josephine Bell)
INSPECTOR MATTHEW FURNIVAL	(Stella Phillips)
INSPECTOR ROBERT FUSIL	(Michael Alding)
SUPERINTENDENT GEORGE GENTLY	(Alan Hunter)
COLONEL ANTHONY GETHRYN	(Philip MacDonald)
INSPECTOR GANESH GHOTE	(H R F Keating)
LINDSAY GORDON	(Val McDermid)
COLONEL ALISTER GRANBY	(Francis Beeding)
INSPECTOR ALAN GRANT	(Gordon Daviot)
	(Josephine Tey)
CELIA GRANT	(John Sherwood)
DR PATRICK GRANT	(Margaret Yorke)
CORDELIA GRAY	(P D James)
EMMA GREAVES	(Lionel Black)
SID HALLEY	(Dick Francis)
SUPERINTENDENT HANNASYDE	(Georgette Heyer)
PAUL HARRIS	(Gavin Black)
JIMMIE HASWELL	(Herbert Adams)
INSPECTOR HAZLERIGG	(Michael Gilbert)
INSPECTOR HEMINGWAY	(Georgette Heyer)
SHERLOCK HOLMES	(Arthur Conan Doyle)
CHARLES HONEYBATH	(Michael Innes)
TAMARA HOYLAND	(Jessica Mann)
INSPECTOR HARRY JAMES	(Kenneth Giles)
INSPECTOR BENJAMIN JURNET	(S T Haymon)
SUPERINTENDENT RICHARD JURY	(Martha Grimes)
INSPECTOR KELSEY	(Emma Page)
INSPECTOR MIKE KENNY	(Eilís Dillon)
SUPERINTENDENT SIMON KENWORTHY	(John Buxton Hilton)
INSPECTOR DON KERRY	(Jeffrey Ashford)
INSPECTOR KYLE	(Roy Vickers)
GERALD LEE	(Kenneth Hopkins)
CORPORAL JUAN LLORCA	(Delano Ames)
INSPECTOR HENRY LOTT	(Henry Wade)
LOVEJOY	(Jonathan Gash)
ADAM LUDLOW	(Simon Nash)
SUPERINTENDENT MACDONALD	(E C R Lorac)
MAIGRET	(Georges Simenon)
ANTONY MAITLAND	(Sara Woods)
DAN MALLETT	(Frank Parrish)
INSPECTOR MALLETT	(Cyril Hare)
PROFESSOR GIDEON MANCIPLE	(Kenneth Hopkins)
PROFESSOR MANDRAKE	(John and Emery Bonett)
SUPERINTENDENT SIMON MANTON	(Michael Underwood)
PHILIP MARLOWE	(Raymond Chandler)
MISS JANE MARPLE	(Agatha Christie)
INSPECTOR GEORGE MARTIN	(Francis Beeding)
PERRY MASON	(Erle Stanley Gardner)
SUPERINTENDENT GEORGE MASTERS	(Douglas Clark)
KINSEY MILLHONE	(Sue Grafton)
SUPERINTENDENT STEVEN MITCHELL	(Josephine Bell)
INSPECTOR MONTERO	(Simon Nash)
INSPECTOR MORSE	(Colin Dexter)
ARIADNE OLIVER	(Agatha Christie)

DAI OWEN	(Henry Calvin)
CHARLES PARIS	(Simon Brett)
INSPECTOR PETER PASCOE	(Reginald Hill)
AMELIA PEABODY	(Elizabeth Peters)
JIMMY PEREZ	(Ann Cleeves)
DOUGLAS PERKINS	(Marian Babson)
SERGEANT PATRICK PETRELLA	(Michael Gilbert)
MIKAEL PETROS	(James Anderson)
FRANCIS PETTIGREW	(Cyril Hare)
SUPERINTENDENT JAMES PIBBLE	(Peter Dickinson)
SUPERINTENDENT ARNOLD PIKE	(Philip MacDonald)
MISS MELINDA PINK	(Gwen Moffat)
INSPECTOR THOMAS AND CHARLOTTE E PITT	(Anne Perry)
INSPECTOR POINTER	(A Fielding)
HERCULE POIROT	(Agatha Christie)
SUPERINTENDENT TOM POLLARD	(Elizabeth Lemarchand)
INSPECTOR JOHN POOL	(Henry Wade)
THOMAS PRESTON	(Francis Beeding)
DR LANCELOT PRIESTLEY	(John Rhode)
INSPECTOR WALTER PURBRIGHT	(Colin Watson)
DR HENRY PYM	(W J Burley)
INSPECTOR DOUGLAS QUANTRILL	(Sheila Radley)
ELLERY QUEEN	(Ellery Queen)
COLONEL RACE	(Agatha Christie)
PRECIOUS RAMOTSWE	(Alexander McCall Smith)
JOHN REBUS	(Ian Rankin)
SUPERINTENDENT GEORGE ROGERS	(Jonathan Ross)
INSPECTOR RUDD (FINCH)	(June Thomson)
ALAN RUSSELL	(Nigel FitzGerald)
DR KAY SCARPETTA	(Patricia Cornwell)
ROGER SHERINGHAM	(Anthony Berkeley)
JEMIMA SHORE	(Antonia Fraser)
MAUD SILVER	(Patricia Wentworth)
INSPECTOR C D SLOAN	(Catherine Aird)
SUPERINTENDENT BEN SPENCE	(Michael Allen)
VERA STANHOPE	(Ann Cleeves)
MATTHEW STOCK	(Leonard Tourney)
NIGEL STRANGEWAYS	(Nicholas Blake)
JEREMY STURROCK	(Jeremy Sturrock)
PROFESSOR HILARY TAMAR	(Sarah Caudwell)
INSPECTOR LUKE THANET	(Dorothy Simpson)
KATE THEOBALD	(Lionel Black)
LIZZIE THOMAS	(Anthony Oliver)
DR JOHN THORNDYKE	(R Austin Freeman)
SUPERINTENDENT GEORGE THORNE	(John Penn)
SUPERINTENDENT HENRY AND EMILY TIBBETT	(Patricia Moyes)
MARK TREASURE	(David Williams)
PHILIP TRENT	(E C Bentley)
SUPERINTENDENT PERRY TRETHOWAN	(Robert Barnard)
MISS AMY TUPPER	(Josephine Bell)
KURT WALLANDER	(Henning Mankell)
V I WARSHAWSKI	(Sara Paretsky)
MALCOLM WARREN	(C H B Kitchin)
CLAUD WARRINGTON-REEVE	(Josephine Bell)
JOHN WEBBER	(Anthony Oliver)
INSPECTOR REGINALD WEXFORD	(Ruth Rendell)
INSPECTOR WILKINS	(James Anderson)
INSPECTOR WILKINS	(Francis Beeding)
LORD PETER WIMSEY	(Dorothy L Sayers)
DR DAVID WINTRINGHAM	(Josephine Bell)
NERO WOLFE	(Rex Stout)
SUPERINTENDENT CHARLES WYCLIFFE	(W J Burley)

GILBERT AND SULLIVAN

OPERAS **Alternative title**

THESPIS (The Gods Grown Old)
TRIAL BY JURY
THE SORCERER
HMS PINAFORE (The Lass that Loved a Sailor)
THE PIRATES OF PENZANCE (The Slave of Duty)
PATIENCE (Bunthorne's Bride)
IOLANTHE (The Peer and the Peri)
PRINCESS IDA (Castle Adamant)
THE MIKADO (The Town of Titipu)
RUDDIGORE (The Witch's Curse)
THE YEOMEN OF THE GUARD (The Merryman and his Maid)
THE GONDOLIERS (The King of Barataria)
UTOPIA, LIMITED (The Flowers of Progress)
THE GRAND DUKE (The Statutory Duel)

CHARACTERS (*Operas*)

4
ADAM (*Ruddigore*)
ELLA (*Patience*)
GAMA (*Princess Ida*)
INEZ (*The Gondoliers*)
JANE (*Patience*)
KATE (*The Pirates of Penzance*)
KO-KO (*The Mikado*)
LUIZ (*The Gondoliers*)
RUTH (*The Pirates of Penzance*)

5
ALINE (*The Sorcerer*)
CELIA (*Iolanthe*)
CYRIL (*Princess Ida*)
EDITH (*The Pirates of Penzance*)
EDWIN (*Trial by Jury*)
FLETA (*Iolanthe*)
LEILA (*Iolanthe*)
MABEL (*The Pirates of Penzance*)
TESSA (*The Gondoliers*)

6
ALEXIS (*The Sorcerer*)
ANGELA (*Patience*)
ISABEL (*The Pirates of Penzance*)
PEEP-BO (*The Mikado*)
SAPHIR (*Patience*)
YUM-YUM (*The Mikado*)

7
CASILDA (*The Gondoliers*)
FLORIAN (*Princess Ida*)
KATISHA (*The Mikado*)
LEONARD (*The Yeomen of the Guard*)
MELISSA (*Princess Ida*)
PHYLLIS (*Iolanthe*)
POOH-BAH (*The Mikado*)

8
ANGELINA (*Trial by Jury*)
FREDERIC (*The Pirates of Penzance*)
GIANETTA (*The Gondoliers*)
HILARION (*Princess Ida*)
IOLANTHE (*Iolanthe*)
NANKI-POO (*The Mikado*)
PATIENCE (*Patience*)
PISH-TUSH (*The Mikado*)
SERGEANT (*The Pirates of Penzance*)
STREPHON (*Iolanthe*)

9
BUNTHORNE (*Patience*)
JACK POINT (*The Yeomen of the Guard*)
JOSEPHINE (*HMS Pinafore*)
PITTI-SING (*The Mikado*)

10
DAME HANNAH (*Ruddigore*)
HILDEBRAND (*Princess Ida*)
LADY PSYCHE (*Princess Ida*)
PIRATE KING (*The Pirates of Penzance*)
ROSE MAYBUD (*Ruddigore*)
SIR RODERIC (*Ruddigore*)

11
DICK DEADEYE (*HMS Pinafore*)
LADY BLANCHE (*Princess Ida*)
MAD MARGARET (*Ruddigore*)
MOUNTARARAT (*Iolanthe*)
PRINCESS IDA (*Princess Ida*)

12
ELSIE MAYNARD (*The Yeomen of the Guard*)
PHOEBE MERYLL (*The Yeomen of the Guard*)

SIR MARMADUKE (*The Sorcerer*)

13
LADY SANGAZURE (*The Sorcerer*)
MARCO PALMIERI (*The Gondoliers*)
ROBIN OAKAPPLE (*Ruddigore*)

14
COLONEL FAIRFAX (*The Yeomen of the Guard*)
DAME CARRUTHERS (*The Yeomen of the Guard*)
RALPH RACKSTRAW (*HMS Pinafore*)

15
CAPTAIN CORCORAN (*HMS Pinafore*)
DUKE OF DUNSTABLE (*Patience*)
DUKE OF PLAZA TORO (*The Gondoliers*)
EARL OF TOLLOLLER (*Iolanthe*)
LITTLE BUTTERCUP (*HMS Pinafore*)
SIR JOSEPH PORTER (*HMS Pinafore*)
WILFRED SHADBOLT (*The Yeomen of the Guard*)

16
COLONEL CALVERLEY (*Patience*)
GIUSEPPE PALMIERI (*The Gondoliers*)
RICHARD DAUNTLESS (*Ruddigore*)

18
ARCHIBALD GROSVENOR (*Patience*)

201

19
JOHN WELLINGTON WELLS (*The Sorcerer*)
MAJOR-GENERAL STANLEY (*The Pirates of Penzance*)

20
SIR DESPARD MURGATROYD (*Ruddigore*)
SIR RICHARD CHOLMONDELEY (*The Yeomen of the Guard*)

CHARACTERS FROM OPERA

CHARACTER (*Opera*, Composer)

3
LIU (*Turandot*, Puccini)

4
AIDA (*Aida*, Verdi)
ELSA (*Lohengrin*, Wagner)
ERDA (*Das Rheingold, Götterdämmerung, Siegfried*, Wagner)
ERIK (*The Flying Dutchman*, Wagner)
FROH (*Das Rheingold*, Wagner)
GORO (*Madame Butterfly*, Puccini)
KATE (*Madame Butterfly*, Puccini)
LOGE (*Das Rheingold*, Wagner)
LUNA, THE COUNT OF (*Il Trovatore*, Verdi)
MARY (*The Flying Dutchman*, Wagner)
MIME (*Das Rheingold, Götterdämmerung, Siegfried*, Wagner)
MIMI (*La Bohème*, Puccini)
OCHS, BARON (*Der Rosenkavalier*, Strauss)
PANG (*Turandot*, Puccini)
PING (*Turandot*, Puccini)
PONG (*Turandot*, Puccini)

5
BERTA (*The Barber of Seville*, Rossini)
BONZE, THE (*Madame Butterfly*, Puccini)
CALAF (*Turandot*, Puccini)
EDGAR; EDGARDO (*Lucy of Lammermoor*, Donizetti)
FREIA (*Das Rheingold*, Wagner)
GILDA (*Rigoletto*, Verdi)
HAGEN (*Götterdämmerung*, Wagner)
LUCIA *See* LUCY ASHTON
PETER (*Hansel and Gretel*, Humperdinck)
SENTA (*The Flying Dutchman*, Wagner)
TIMUR (*Turandot*, Puccini)
WITCH (*Hansel and Gretel*, Humperdinck)
WOTAN, THE WANDERER (*Das Rheingold, Die Walküre, Götterdämmerung, Siegfried*, Wagner)

6
AILSIE; ALISA (*Lucy of Lammermoor*, Donizetti)
ALTOUM, THE EMPEROR (*Turandot*, Puccini)
ANNINA (*Der Rosenkavalier*, Strauss; (*La Traviata*, Verdi)
ARTURO *See* ARTHUR BUCKLAW
BENOIT (*La Bohème*, Puccini)
CARMEN (*Carmen*, Bizet)
DALAN D (*The Flying Dutchman*, Wagner)
DONNER (*Das Rheingold*, Wagner)
FAFNER (*Das Rheingold, Götterdämmerung, Siegfried*, Wagner)
FASOLT (*Das Rheingold*, Wagner)
FIGARO (*The Barber of Seville*, Rossini; The

Marriage of Figaro, Mozart)
FRICKA (*Das Rheingold, Die Walküre, Götterdämmerung*, Wagner)
GRETEL (*Hansel and Gretel*, Humperdinck)
HANSEL (*Hansel and Gretel*, Humperdinck)
MANTUA, THE DUKE OF (*Rigoletto*, Verdi)
NORINA (*Don Pasquale*, Donizetti)
NORMAN; NORMANNO (*Lucy of Lammermoor*, Donizetti)
ORTRUD (*Lohengrin*, Wagner)
PAMINA (*The Magic Flute*, Mozart)
RAMFIS; RAMPHIS (*Aida*, Verdi)
ROSINA (*The Barber of Seville*, Rossini)
SOPHIE (*Der Rosenkavalier*, Strauss)
SUZUKI (*Madame Butterfly*, Puccini)
TAMINO (*The Magic Flute*, Mozart)
ZUNIGA (*Carmen*, Bizet)

7
AMNERIS (*Aida*, Verdi)
ANTONIO (*The Marriage of Figaro*, Mozart)
AZUCENA (*Il Trovatore*, Verdi)
BARTOLA, DR (*The Marriage of Figaro*, Mozart)
BARTOLO, DR (*The Barber of Seville*, Rossini)
COLLINE (*La Bohème*, Puccini)
DESPINA (*Cosi Fan Tutte*, Mozart)
DON JOSÉ (*Carmen*, Bizet)
EDGARDO *See* EDGAR
ERNESTO (*Don Pasquale*, Donizetti)
FANINAL (*Der Rosenkavalier*, Strauss)
GERTRUD (*Hansel and Gretel*, Humperdinck)
GETRUNE (*Götterdämmerung*, Wagner)
GRENVIL, DR (*La Traviata*, Verdi)
GUNTHER (*Götterdämmerung*, Wagner)
HUNDING (*Die Walküre*, Wagner)
LEONORA (*Il Trovatore*, Verdi)
MANRICO (*Il Trovatore*, Verdi)
MASETTO (*Don Giovanni*, Mozart)
MICAELA (*Carmen*, Bizet)
MUSETTA (*La Bohème*, Puccini)
RADAMES (*Aida*, Verdi)
RAMPHIS *See* RAMFIS
RODOLFO (*La Bohème*, Puccini)
SANDMAN (*Hansel and Gretel*, Humperdinck)
SCARPIA, BARON (*Tosca*, Puccini)
SUSANNA (*The Marriage of Figaro*, Mozart)
ZERLINA (*Don Giovanni*, Mozart)

8
ALBERICH (*Das Rheingold, Götterdämmerung, Siegfried*, Wagner)
ALMAVIVA, COUNTESS (*The Marriage of Figaro*, Mozart)
ALMAVIVA, COUNT (*The Barber of Seville*, Rossini; The Marriage of Figaro, Mozart)

AMONASRO (*Aida*, Verdi)
DEW FAIRY (*Hansel and Gretel*, Humperdinck)
FERRANDO (*Cosi Fan Tutte*, Mozart; *Il Trovatore*, Verdi)
FIORELLO (*The Barber of Seville*, Rossini)
GERHILDE (*Die Walküre*, Wagner)
HELMWIGE (*Die Walküre*, Wagner)
MARCELLO (*La Bohème*, Puccini)
MARIANNE (*Der Rosenkavalier*, Strauss)
NORMANNO See NORMAN
OCTAVIAN (*Der Rosenkavalier*, Strauss)
ORTLINDE (*Die Walküre*, Wagner)
PAPAGENA (*The Magic Flute*, Mozart)
PAPAGENO (*The Magic Flute*, Mozart)
RAIMONDO See BIDE-THE-BENT
SARASTRO (*The Magic Flute*, Mozart)
SIEGMUND (*Die Walküre*, Wagner)
SIEGRUNE (*Die Walküre*, Wagner)
SPOLETTA (*Tosca*, Puccini)
TURANDOT, PRINCESS (*Turandot*, Puccini)
WOGLINDE (*Das Rheingold, Götterdämmerung*, Wagner)
YAMADORI, PRINCE (*Madame Butterfly*, Puccini)

9
ANGELOTTI (*Tosca*, Puccini)
BARBARINA (*The Marriage of Figaro*, Mozart)
CHERUBINO (*The Marriage of Figaro*, Mozart)
DON CURZIO (*The Marriage of Figaro*, Mozart)
DONNA ANNA (*Don Giovanni*, Mozart)
DORABELLA (*Cosi Fan Tutte*, Mozart)
ESCAMILLO (*Carmen*, Bizet)
GRIMGERDE (*Die Walküre*, Wagner)
GUGLIELMO (*Cosi Fan Tutte*, Mozart)
LEPORELLO (*Don Giovanni*, Mozart)
LOHENGRIN (*Lohengrin*, Wagner)
MADDALENA (*Rigoletto*, Verdi)
MALATESTA, DR (*Don Pasquale*, Donizetti)
PINKERTON, LIEUTENANT B F (*Madame Butterfly*, Puccini)
ROSSWEISS (*Die Walküre*, Wagner)
SCHAUNARD (*La Bohème*, Puccini)
SHARPLESS (*Madame Butterfly*, Puccini)
SIEGFRIED (*Götterdämmerung, Siegfried*, Wagner)
SIEGLINDE (*Die Walküre*, Wagner)
VALZACCHI (*Der Rosenkavalier*, Strauss)
WALTRAUTE (*Die Walküre, Götterdämmerung*, Wagner)
WELLGUNDE (*Das Rheingold, Götterdämmerung*, Wagner)

10
BRÜNNHILDE (*Die Walküre, Götterdämmerung, Siegfried*, Wagner)
DON ALFONSO (*Cosi Fan Tutte*, Mozart)
DON BASILIO (*The Barber of Seville*, Rossini; *The Marriage of Figaro*, Mozart)
DON OTTAVIO (*Don Giovanni*, Mozart)
FIORDILIGI (*Cosi Fan Tutte*, Mozart)
FLOSSHILDE (*Das Rheingold, Götterdämmerung*, Wagner)
LUCY ASHTON; LUCIA (*Lucy of Lammermoor*, Donizetti)
MARCELLINA (*The Marriage of Figaro*, Mozart)
MONOSTATOS (*The Magic Flute*, Mozart)

11
BIDE-THE-BENT; RAIMONDO (*Lucy of Lammermoor*, Donizetti)
DON GIOVANNI (*Don Giovanni*, Mozart)
DONNA ELVIRA (*Don Giovanni*, Mozart)
DON PASQUALE (*Don Pasquale*, Donizetti)
FLORIO TOSCA (*Tosca*, Puccini)
HENRY ASHTON; ENRICO (*Lucy of Lammermoor*, Donizetti)
MARSCHALLIN (*Der Rosenkavalier*, Strauss)
SPARAFUCILE (*Rigoletto*, Verdi)

12
COMMENDATORE, THE (*Don Giovanni*, Mozart)
FLORA BERVOIX (*La Traviata*, Verdi)
SCHWERTLEITE (*Die Walküre*, Wagner)

13
ARTHUR BUCKLAW; ARTURO (*Lucy of Lammermoor*, Donizetti)

14+
ALFREDO GERMONT (*La Traviata*, Verdi)
FRIEDRICH VON TELRAMUND (*Lohengrin*, Wagner)
GIORGIO GERMONT (*La Traviata*, Verdi)
HENRY I OF GERMANY (*Lohengrin*, Wagner)
MADAME BUTTERFLY (*Madame Butterfly*, Puccini)
MARIO CAVARADOSSI (*Tosca*, Puccini)
VIOLETTA VALERY (*La Traviata*, Verdi)

CHARACTERS FROM NURSERY RHYMES

3	JUDY	SPOON	**8**	JACK SPRAT
CAT	MARY	SUKEY	BILLY BOY	JENNY WREN
COW	PAUL	TAFFY	DAME TROT	JOHN SMITH
NAN			LADYBIRD	LITTLE DOG
TOM	**5**	**6**	PUSSY CAT	WILLY WOOD
	BAKER, THE	FIDDLE	THUMBKIN	
4	PETER	JOHNNY		**10**
DISH	POLLY		**9**	BLACK SHEEP
JACK	PUNCH	**7**	AIKEN DRUM	DAPPLE GREY
JILL	ROBIN	BUTCHER, THE	COCK ROBIN	KING ARTHUR
JOHN	SANDY	RICHARD	GREEDY NAN	LUCY LOCKET

MARGERY DAW
PETER PIPER
SLEEPY-HEAD
TOMMY STOUT
TWEEDLEDEE
TWEEDLEDUM

11
BESSY BROOKS
ELSIE MARLEY
FARMER GILES
JACK AND JILL
JEMMY DAWSON
JOHNNY GREEN
JUMPING JOAN
KITTY FISHER
OLD KING COLE
SIMPLE SIMON
TOMMY O'LINN
TOMMY SNOOKS
BETTY PRINGLE
BOBBY SHAFTOE
DARBY AND JOAN
DISH AND SPOON
DOCTOR FOSTER
FARMER'S WIFE
HUMPTY DUMPTY
KING OF HEARTS
LITTLE BO-PEEP
NOTHING-AT-ALL

PETER AND PAUL
PUNCH AND JUDY
ROBERT BARNES
ROBERT ROWLEY
YANKEE DOODLE

13
ANTHONY ROWLEY
CHARLEY BARLEY
DOCTOR FAUSTUS
FATHER FRANCIS
GEORGIE PORGIE
GREGORY GRIGGS
JOHNNY PRINGLE
KNAVE OF HEARTS
LITTLE BOY BLUE
MRS SHECKLETON
QUEEN OF HEARTS
SOLOMON GRUNDY

14
DAFFY DOWN DILLY
OLD MOTHER GOOSE
ROBIN REDBREAST
THREE BLIND MICE

15
HECTOR PROTECTOR
LITTLE BETTY BLUE
LITTLE TOM TINKER
ROBIN AND RICHARD

WEE WILLIE WINKIE

16
CANDLESTICK MAKER, THE
LITTLE JACK HORNER
LITTLE MISS MUFFET
OLD MOTHER HUBBARD
OLD MOTHER SHUTTLE

17
INCEY WINCEY SPIDER
LITTLE TOMMY TUCKER

18+
ELSPETH, BETSY, AND BESS
GOOSEY GOOSEY GANDER
LITTLE NANCY ETTICOAT
LITTLE POLLY FLINDERS
LITTLE TOMMY TITTLEMOUSE
MATTHEW MARK LUKE AND JOHN
OLD MOTHER TWITCHETT
OLD WOMAN WHO LIVED IN A SHOE
THE CAT AND THE FIDDLE
THE GRAND OLD DUKE OF YORK
THEOPHILUS THISTLEDOWN
THREE LITTLE KITTENS
WILLIAM MCTRIMBLETOE

ANIMALS IN FICTION

NAME	ANIMAL	NAME	ANIMAL
ARTAX	HORSE	FLIPPER	DOLPHIN
ASLAN	LION	GREYFRIARS BOBBY	DOG
BABAR	ELEPHANT	GREYMALKIN	CAT
BABE	PIG	GWAIHIR	EAGLE
BAGHEERA	PANTHER	HATHI	ELEPHANT
BALOO	BEAR	HAZEL	RABBIT
BAMBI	DEER	HEDWIG	OWL
BILLINA	CHICKEN	LARK	HORSE
BLACK BEAUTY	HORSE	MOBY-DICK	WHALE
BLACKMALKIN	CAT	MONTMORENCY	DOG
BOXER	HORSE	NANA	DOG
BREE	HORSE	NAPOLEON	PIG
BUCK	DOG	NARA	HORSE
BULLSEYE	DOG	NIBBINS	CAT
CAPTAIN FLINT	PARROT	OLD MAJOR	PIG
CHARLOTTE	SPIDER	PADDINGTON	BEAR
CROOKSHANKS	CAT	PETER COTTONTAIL	RABBIT
DINAH	CAT	RAKSHA	WOLF
DIRIUS	DOG	RIKKI-TIKKI-TAVI	MONGOOSE
DUMBO	ELEPHANT	ROCINANTE	HORSE
EEYORE	DONKEY	ROWF	DOG
EMPRESS OF BLANDINGS	PIG	RUDOLPH	REINDEER
FIVER	RABBIT	SHADOWFAX	HORSE
FLAG	FAWN	SHARDIK	BEAR
FLICKA	HORSE	SHELOB	SPIDER

NAME	ANIMAL	NAME	ANIMAL
SHERE KHAN	TIGER	TIMMY	DOG
SILVER BLAZE	HORSE	TOBERMORY	CAT
SIPKIN	CAT	TOTO	DOG
SKIPPY	KANGAROO	TUG	CAT
SNITTER	DOG	WHITE FANG	DOG
SNOWBALL	PIG	WILBUR	PIG
SQUEALER	PIG	WINNIE THE POOH	BEAR
TIGGER	TIGER		

HISTORY, POLITICS, GOVERNMENT, AND LAW

OLD NAMES OF COUNTRIES

CURRENT NAME	OLD NAME(S) (MOST RECENT FIRST)
BANGLADESH	EAST PAKISTAN
BELAU	PALAU (or PELEW)
BELIZE	BRITISH HONDURAS
BENIN	DAHOMEY
BOLIVIA	UPPER PERU
BOTSWANA	BECHUANALAND
BURKINA FASO	UPPER VOLTA
CAYMAN ISLANDS	LAS TORTUGAS
CONGO, DEMOCRATIC REPUBLIC OF	ZAÏRE; CONGO; BELGIAN CONGO; CONGO FREE STATE
ETHIOPIA	ABYSSINIA
GHANA	GOLD COAST
GUINEA	FRENCH GUINEA; RIVIÈ RES DU SUD
GUINEA-BISSAU	PORTUGUESE GUINEA
GUYANA	BRITISH GUIANA
HAITI	SAINT-DOMINIQUE
INDONESIA	DUTCH EAST INDIES
IRAN	PERSIA
IRAQ	MESOPOTAMIA
IRELAND, REPUBLIC OF	EIRE; IRISH FREE STATE
JORDAN	TRANSJORDAN
KENYA	EAST AFRICA PROTECTORATE
KIRIBATI	GILBERT ISLANDS
LESOTHO	BASUTOLAND
MADAGASCAR	MALAGASY REPUBLIC
MALAWI	NYASALAND
MALDIVES	MALDIVE ISLANDS
MALI	FRENCH SUDAN
MONGOLIA	MONGOLIAN PEOPLE'S REPUBLIC; OUTER MONGOLIA
MYANMAR	BURMA
NAMIBIA	SOUTH WEST AFRICA
NAURU	PLEASANT ISLAND
NEW ZEALAND	STATEN LAND
NIGERIA	BIAFRA
NIUE	SAVAGE ISLAND
OMAN	MUSCAT AND OMAN
PUERTO RICO	PORTO RICO
SERBIA AND MONTENEGRO	YUGOSLAVIA
SINGAPORE	TUMASIK (or TEMASEK)
SOMALIA	BENADIR
SRI LANKA	CEYLON
SURINAME	DUTCH GUIANA
TAIWAN	FORMOSA
TANZANIA	TANGANYIKA; ZANZIBAR
THAILAND	SIAM
TOGO	FRENCH TOGOLAND
TONGA	FRIENDLY ISLANDS
TUNISIA	CARTHAGE
TURKEY	OTTOMAN EMPIRE
TUVALU	ELLICE ISLANDS
UNITED ARAB EMIRATES	TRUCIAL STATES
VANUATU	NEW HEBRIDES
ZAMBIA	NORTHERN RHODESIA
ZIMBABWE	RHODESIA; SOUTHERN RHODESIA

OLD NAMES OF CAPITAL AND MAJOR CITIES

CURRENT NAME	OLD NAME(S) (MOST RECENT FIRST)
ALMATY	ALMA-ATA; VERNY
ANTANANARIVO	TANANARIVE
ASTANA	AKMOLA
BANDAR SERI BEGAWAN	BRUNEI TOWN
BANJUL	BATHURST
BEIJING (or PEKING)	PEI-P'ING (or BEIBING); TA-TU
BISHKEK (or PISHPEK)	FRUNZE
BOGOTÁ	BACATÁ
BUJUMBURA	USUMBURA
CAIRO	EL QAHIRA; EL FUSTAT
CARACAS	SANTIAGO DE LEÓN DE CARACAS
CHARLOTTE AMALIE	SAINT THOMAS
CONSTANTINE	CIRTA
DHAKA	DACCA
DNEPROPETROVSK	EKATERINOSLAV
DONETSK	STALINO; YUZOVKA
DÚ N LAOGHAIRE	KINGSTOWN; DUNLEARY
DUSHANBE	STALINABAD; DYUSHAMBE
EKATERINBURG	SVERDLOVSK
EAST LONDON	PORT REX

FAISALABAD	LYALLPUR	N'DJAMENA	FORT LAMY
FORT-DE-FRANCE	FORT ROYAL	NIZHNY NOVGOROD	GORKY (or GORKI)
GABERONE	GABERONES	NOUMÉA	PORT-DE-FRANCE
HARARE	SALISBURY	NUUK	GODTHAÅB
HO CHI MINH CITY	SAIGON	OTTAWA	BYTOWN
ISTANBUL	CONSTANTINOPLE; BYZANTIUM	OSLO	KRISTIANIA
		PAGO PAGO	PANGO PANGO
IZMIR	SMYRNA	PALIKIR	KOLONIA
JAKARTA	BATAVIA	PERM	MOLOTOV
KANPUR	CAWNPORE	SAMARA	KUYBYSHEV
KINSHASA	LÉOPOLDVILLE	SANTO DOMINGO	CIUDAD TRUJILLO
KIROV	VYATKA	SOFIA	SERDICA
KOLKATA	CALCUTTA	ST PETERSBURG	LENINGRAD; PETROGRAD
KOROR	CORRORA	T'BILISI	TIFLIS
LUANDA	SÃO PAULO DE LOANDA	THESSALONÍKI	SALONIKA; THESSALONICA
MALABO	SANTA ISABEL		
MAPUTO	LOURENÇO MARQUES	TOKYO	EDO
MEXICO CITY	TENOCHTITLÁN	TRIPOLI	OEA
MONTREAL	VILLE-MARIE	UJANG PANDANG	MACASSAR (or MAKASAR)
MUMBAI	BOMBAY	ULAANBAATAR	URGA
NABEREZHNYE	BREZHNEV; CHELNYCHELNY	VADODARA	BARODA
NAPLES	NEAPOLIS	VOLGOGRAD	STALINGRAD; TSARITSYN

ROMAN NAMES OF CITIES

ROMAN NAME – BRITISH NAME

ANDERITUM – PEVENSEY
AQUA SULIS – BATH
CALLEVA – SILCHESTER
CAMULODUNUM – COLCHESTER
CORINIUM – CIRENCESTER
DANUM – DONCASTER
DEVA – CHESTER
DURNOVARIA – DORCHESTER
DUROLIPONTE – GRANTCHESTER
DUROVERNUM – CANTERBURY
EBORACUM – YORK
GLEVUM – GLOUCESTER
ISARIUM – ALDEBOROUGH
ISCA – CAERLEON
ISCA – EXETER
LETOCETUM – WALL
LINDINIS – ILCHESTER

ROMAN NAME – BRITISH NAME

LINDUM – LINCOLN
LONDINIUM – LONDON
LUGUVALIUM – CARLISLE
MAMUCIUM – MANCHESTER
MORIDUNUM – CARMARTHEN
NOVIOMAGUS – CHICHESTER
PETURIA – BROUGH
POTUS ADURNI – PORTCHESTER
RATAE – LEICESTER
SARUM – SALISBURY
SEGONTIUM – CAERNARFON
TAMIUM – CARDIFF
VENTA – CAERWENT
VENTA – WINCHESTER
VERTIS – WORCESTER
VERULAMIUM – ST ALBANS
VIROCONIUM – WROXETER

CELTIC TRIBES OF BRITAIN

ATREBATES
BRIGANTES
CALEDONII
CANTIUM
CATUVELLAUNI
CORIELTAUVI
CORNOVII
DECEANGELI
DEMETAE
DOBUNNI
DRUIDS
DUROTRIGES

ICENI
NOVANTAE
ORDOVICES
PARISI
SELGOVAE
SILURES
TAXALI
TRINOVANTES
VACOMAGI
VENICONES
VOTADINI

HORSES IN HISTORY

HORSE	RIDER	HORSE	RIDER
BABIECA	EL CID	LEXINGTON	WILLIAM T SHERMAN
BLACK BESS	DICK TURPIN	LITTLE SORREL	GENERAL STONEWALL JACKSON
BROWN BEAUTY or BETTY	PAUL REVERE	MARENGO	NAPOLEON
BUCEPHALA	ALEXANDER THE GREAT	MAROCCO	WILLIAM BANKS
		NELSON	GEORGE WASHINGTON
BUTTERMILK	DALE EVANS	RONALD	EARL OF CARDIGAN
CINCINNATI	LT GENERAL US GRANT	TRAVELLER	ROBERT E LEE
COMANCHE	GENERAL CUSTER	TRIGGER	ROY ROGERS
COPENHAGEN	DUKE OF WELLINGTON	WHITE SURREY	RICHARD III
INCITATUS	CALIGULA	WINCHESTER	GENERAL SHERIDAN

FAMOUS SHIPS

ARK ROYAL	English flagship against Armada	LUSITANIA	torpedoed by German U-boat, 1915
BEAGLE	carried Charles Darwin	MARY CELESTE	ship discovered with no crew or passengers, 1872
BISMARK	sank HMS Hood, 1941		
BOUNTY	mutiny aboard ship, 1789	MARY ROSE	wreck discovered in 1971; sank off Portsmouth, 1545
CARPATHIA	rescued passengers on Titanic, 1912	MAYFLOWER	carried English Pilgrims to Plymouth, Massachusetts, 1620
CUTTY SARK	clipper ship built 1869		
DISCOVERY	carried Scott and Shackleton to Antarctic		
DREADNOUGHT	revolutionary battleship, 1906	NINA	sailed by Columbus
ENDEAVOUR	research vessel commanded by James Cook	PINTA	sailed by Columbus
		QUEEN ANNE'S REVENGE	flagship of pirate Blackbeard
ENDURANCE	used by Shackleton, 1914		
GOLDEN HIND	Sir Francis Drake, 1577–1580	REVENGE	fought Spanish Armada
HOOD	sunk by Bismark 1941	SANTA MARIA	sailed by Columbus
KON TIKI	Thor Heyerdahl used to cross Pacific, 1947	TITANIC	unsinkable ship that sank after hitting an iceberg, 1912
LA AMISTAD	slave ship on which African captives revolted, 1839	VICTORY	Nelson's flagship, Battle of Trafalgar, 1805

THE EUROPEAN UNION

STATE	ACCESSION YEAR	STATE	ACCESSION YEAR
AUSTRIA	1995	ITALY	1958
BELGIUM	1958	LATVIA	2004
BULGARIA	2007	LITHUNIA	2004
CROATIA	2013	LUXEMBOURG	1958
CYPRUS	2004	MALTA	2004
CZECHIA	2004	NETHERLANDS	1958
DENMARK	1973	POLAND	2004
ESTONIA	2004	PORTUGAL	1986
FINLAND	1995	ROMANIA	2007
FRANCE	1958	SLOVAKIA	2004
GERMANY	1958	SLOVENIA	2004
GREECE	1981	SPAIN	1986
HUNGARY	2004	SWEDEN	1995
IRELAND	1973	UK	1973

MEMBERS OF THE COMMONWEALTH

ANTIGUA AND BARBUDA
AUSTRALIA
THE BAHAMAS
BANGLADESH
BARBADOS
BELIZE
BOTSWANA
BRUNEI DARUSSALAM
CAMEROON
CANADA
CYPRUS
DOMINICA
FIJI ISLANDS
THE GAMBIA
GHANA
GRENADA
GUYANA
INDIA
JAMAICA
KENYA
KINGDOM OF ESWATINI (or SWAZILAND)
KIRIBATI
LESOTHO
MALAWI
MALAYSIA
MALTA
MAURITIUS

MOZAMBIQUE
NAMIBIA
NAURU
NEW ZEALAND
NIGERIA
PAKISTAN
PAPUA NEW GUINEA
RWANDA
ST KITTS AND NEVIS
ST LUCIA
ST VINCENT AND THE GRENADINES
SAMOA
SEYCHELLES
SIERRA LEONE
SINGAPORE
SOLOMON ISLANDS
SOUTH AFRICA
SRI LANKA
TONGA
TRINIDAD AND TOBAGO
TUVALU
UGANDA
UNITED KINGDOM
UNITED REPUBLIC OF TANZANIA
VANUATU
ZAMBIA

MEMBERS OF NATO

ALBANIA
BELGIUM
BULGARIA
CANADA
CROATIA
CZECH REPUBLIC
DENMARK
ESTONIA
FRANCE
GERMANY

GREECE
HUNGARY
ICELAND
ITALY
LATVIA
LITHUANIA
LUXEMBOURG
MONTENEGRO
NETHERLANDS
NORWAY

POLAND
PORTUGAL
ROMANIA
SLOVAKIA
SLOVENIA
SPAIN
TURKEY
UNITED KINGDOM
UNITED STATES

LEGAL TERMS

2&3
BAN
BAR
CAV
DOE
FEE
JUS
NP
ROE
RUN
USE

4
ABLE
AVER
AVOW
BAIL
BANC
BILL
BOND
COST
DEED
FACT
FEME
FIND
FLAW
FREE
GIST
HEAR
LAND
LIEN
MISE
MUTE
NISI
NUDE
OATH
OPEN
PLEA
REST
ROUT
RULE
SOLE
TERM

TORT
UDAL
USER
VIEW
WAIF
WARD

5
ABATE
ADOPT
ADULT
AGIST
ALIBI
ARRAY
AVOID
AWARD
BRIEF
BRING
CHEAT
CHOSE
CLAIM
CLOSE
COUNT
COURT
COVIN
DEMUR
DEVIL
DONEE
DONOR
ENTER
ESTOP
FOLIO
IN REM
ISSUE
JOINT
JURAT
LAPSE
LIBEL
LIMIT
MESNE
MORAL
NAKED
OVERT

PANEL
PAROL
PETTY
PLEAD
POSSE
PRIVY
PROOF
PROVE
REMIT
REPLY
SHORE
SOUND
SQUAT
STALE
TALES
TENOR
THING
TITLE
TRIAL
VENUE
WASTE
WRONG

6
ABATOR
ACCRUE
ACTION
AFFIRM
AFFRAY
AMERCE
ANSWER
APPEAL
ARREST
ASSETS
ASSIGN
ATTACH
ATTORN
CAMERA
CAPIAS
CAVEAT
CESSER
CHARGE
COMMON

CONVEY
COVERT
CY PRES
DEFEAT
DELICT
DEMAND
DEPONE
DEPOSE
DEVISE
DICTUM
DISBAR
DOCKET
DOMAIN
DURESS
ENJOIN
EQUITY
ESCROW
ESTRAY
EXTENT
FOREST
GUILTY
HOLDER
INFANT
INFIRM
INJURY
INTENT
JUNIOR
LACHES
MALICE
MATTER
MAYHEM
MERGER
MOTION
NONAGE
OWELTY
PLAINT
PRAYER
PREFER
RECOUP
REJOIN
RELIEF
REMAND
REMISE
REPORT
RESCUE
RETAIN
RETURN
REVIEW
SAVING
SCRIPT
SPECIE
SUITOR
TENDER
TROVER
VACANT
VACATE
VENTER
VERIFY
VIEWER

7
ACCUSED
AFFIANT
ALIENEE

ALIENOR
ALIMONY
AMNESTY
ANCIENT
APPROVE
ASSAULT
BEQUEST
CAPITAL
CAUTION
CODICIL
COMMUTE
CONDONE
CONNIVE
CONVERT
CRUELTY
CULPRIT
CURATOR
DAMAGES
DAMNIFY
DEFAULT
DEFENCE
DERAIGN
DETINUE
DEVOLVE
DIES NON
DOWABLE
EMPANEL
ENGROSS
ESCHEAT
ESTREAT
EXAMINE
EXECUTE
EXHIBIT
EX PARTE
FICTION
FILIATE
FINDING
FOREIGN
FOREMAN
FORFEIT
GARNISH
GRANTEE
GRANTOR
IMPLEAD
JOINDER
JUS SOLI
JUSTIFY
LARCENY
MANAGER
MENS REA
MISUSER
MOVABLE
NONSUIT
OBSCENE
ONEROUS
OPENING
PORTION
PRECEPT
PRESUME
PURVIEW
RECITAL
RECOVER
REFEREE

RELATOR
RELEASE
REPLEVY
RESIDUE
REVERSE
SCANDAL
SETTLOR
SEVERAL
SLANDER
TESTIFY
VESTURE
WARRANT

8
ABEYANCE
ABSOLUTE
ACT OF GOD
ALIENATE
APPELLEE
ASSIGNEE
ASSIGNOR
AVULSION
BAILABLE
BEQUEATH
BONDSMAN
CAVEATOR
CHANCERY
CITATION
COMPOUND
CONTINUE
COPYHOLD
COVENANT
DEAD HAND
DECEDENT
DEED POLL
DEMURRER
DEPONENT
DETAINER
DISCLAIM
DISTRAIN
DISTRESS
DIVIDEND
DOMINION
DOTATION
ESTOPPEL
ESTOVERS
EVIDENCE
EXECUTOR
FELO DE SE
FEME SOLE
FIDUCIAL
FORJUDGE
FUNGIBLE
GRAVAMEN
GUARDIAN
HAND DOWN
HANDLING
HEIRSHIP
HERITAGE
IN CAMERA
INNUENDO
INSANITY
INSTRUCT
JEOPARDY

JOINTURE
JURATORY
MANDAMUS
MATERIAL
MITTIMUS
MONOPOLY
MORTMAIN
NON PROS
NOVATION
NUISANCE
OBLIVION
OCCUPANT
PERSONAL
PETITION
PLEADING
PREMISES
PRESENTS
PROPERTY
QUESTION
REBUTTER
RECOVERY
RELATION
REPLEVIN
SCHEDULE
SCIENTER
SOLATIUM
SOLUTION
SPINSTER
STRANGER
SUI JURIS
TORTIOUS
TRANSFER
TRAVERSE
TRESPASS
VOIR DIRE

9
ABANDONEE
ACCESSARY
ACCRETION
ADMINICLE
AFFIDAVIT
ALIENABLE
APPELLANT
APPELLATE
APPENDANT
ARBITRARY
ASSUMPSIT
AUTHORITY
AVOIDANCE
BAILIWICK
BLASPHEMY
BONA FIDES
CARTULARY
CHALLENGE
CHAMPERTY
COMPETENT
CONDITION
COVERTURE
CUSTOMARY
DEBATABLE
DEFALCATE
DEMANDANT
DESERTION

DEVISABLE
DILIGENCE
DISAFFIRM
DISCHARGE
DISCOMMON
DISCOVERT
DISCOVERY
DISTRAINT
EQUITABLE
EXCEPTION
EXECUTRIX
EXEMPLIFY
FIDUCIARY
FILIATION
FORECLOSE
FOREJUDGE
GARNISHEE
GRAND JURY
GUARANTEE
IMMOVABLE
IMPERFECT
INSTANTER
INTENTION
INTERVENE
JOINTRESS
LITIGABLE
MORTGAGEE
MUNIMENTS
OCCUPANCY
ONOMASTIC
PECUNIARY
PLEADINGS
PRECEDENT
PREJUDICE
PRESCRIBE
PRINCIPAL
PROPONENT
QUITCLAIM
RECAPTION
RE-EXAMINE
REJOINDER
RES GESTAE
RESIDUARY
SEQUESTER
SERVITUDE
SEVERABLE
SEVERANCE
SOLEMNITY
SPECIALTY
STATEMENT
SUBROGATE
SURCHARGE
SURRENDER
TESTAMENT
TESTIMONY
TRADITION
VEXATIOUS
VOLUNTARY
VOLUNTEER

10
ABSENTE REO
ACTIONABLE
ADMISSIBLE

AGGRAVATED
ALIENATION
AMBULATORY
APOTHECARY
APPEARANCE
ASSIGNMENT
ATTACHMENT
AUTOMATISM
BENEFICIAL
BILL OF SALE
CASE STATED
CERTIORARI
CESSIONARY
CIVIL DEATH
COEXECUTOR
COGNIZABLE
COGNIZANCE
COMMITMENT
COMMUTABLE
COMPETENCY
CONCLUSION
CONNIVANCE
CONSENSUAL
CONSORTIUM
CONSTITUTE
CONTRACTOR
CONVERSION
CONVEYANCE
COPARCENER
COPYHOLDER
DEFAMATION
DEFEASIBLE
DEPOSITION
DISINHERIT
DISORDERLY
DISTRAINEE
DISTRINGAS
EMBLEMENTS
FEME COVERT
GRATUITOUS
GROUND RENT
HEREDITARY
HOMOLOGATE
IMPARTIBLE
IMPEDIMENT
INCAPACITY
INDUCEMENT
INJUNCTION
IN PERSONAM
INTERPLEAD
LIMITATION
MEMORANDUM
MISJOINDER
NEGLIGENCE
NEXT FRIEND
NONJOINDER
OBLIGATION
PERCEPTION
PEREMPTORY
PERSONALTY
POSSESSORY
PRE-EMPTION
PREFERENCE

PRIVILEGED
PRIZE COURT
PROPOSITUS
RECOGNIZEE
RECOGNIZOR
RESCISSION
RESOLUTIVE
RESPONDENT
SECULARIZE
SETTLEMENT
SIGN MANUAL
SMART MONEY
SPOLIATION
STILLICIDE
SUBMISSION
SURPLUSAGE
SUSPENSION
TORT-FEASOR
TRIAL COURT
ULTRA VIRES
UNILATERAL

11

AFFIRMATION
ARBITRATION
ASSIGNATION
BED AND BOARD
BENEFICIARY
CLASS ACTION
COMPLAINANT
CONTENTIOUS
COPARCENARY
DECLARATION
DECLARATORY
DESCENDIBLE
DISCONTINUE
DISTRIBUTEE
DISTURBANCE
ENCUMBRANCE
EXAMINATION
FIERI FACIAS
FORBEARANCE
FORNICATION
GARNISHMENT
HYPOTHECATE
INCOMPETENT
INCORPOREAL
INHERITANCE
LOCUS STANDI
MAINTENANCE
MALFEASANCE
MARE CLAUSUM
MARE LIBERUM
MATTER OF LAW
MINISTERIAL
MISFEASANCE
MISPLEADING
NECESSARIES
NONFEASANCE
NUDUM PACTUM
PORT OF ENTRY
PRESENTMENT
PRESUMPTION
PROCURATION

PROCURATORY
PROHIBITION
QUO WARRANTO
REPLICATION
RESERVATION
RES JUDICATA
RESTITUTION
SCIRE FACIAS
SEARCH ORDER
SELF-DEFENCE
SEQUESTRATE
SPECIAL CASE
SUBROGATION
SURREBUTTAL
SURREBUTTER
UNAVOIDABLE

12

ACCUSATORIAL
AMICUS CURIAE
BONA VACANTIA
CODIFICATION
COMPURGATION
CONSTRUCTIVE
CONVENTIONAL
CO-RESPONDENT
CROSS-EXAMINE
DENUNCIATION
DETERMINABLE
DISTRIBUTION
ENCUMBRANCER
FORCE MAJEURE
HABEAS CORPUS
INDEFEASIBLE
INSTRUCTIONS
INTERPLEADER
JUS SANGUINIS
MANSLAUGHTER
MATTER OF FACT
MISADVENTURE
OBITER DICTUM
ONUS PROBANDI
PENDENTE LITE
PRESCRIPTION
RECEIVERSHIP
RECOGNIZANCE
SURREJOINDER
TRAFFIC COURT
UNAPPEALABLE
UNCOVENANTED
VENIRE FACIAS
VERIFICATION

13

A MENSA ET THORO
ATTORNEY-AT-LAW
BODY CORPORATE
BREACH OF TRUST
BURDEN OF PROOF
CERTIFICATION
CIVIL MARRIAGE
CONSIDERATION
CONSOLIDATION
CORPUS DELICTI

CRIMEN INJURIA
DETERMINATION
EMINENT DOMAIN
INQUISITORIAL
INTERLOCUTORY
IRREPLEVIABLE
JURIDICAL DAYS
NOLLE PROSEQUI
PARAPHERNALIA
PATERNITY SUIT
PREMEDITATION
PRIMOGENITURE
PROBABLE CAUSE
RECRIMINATION
SEQUESTRATION
TREASURE-TROVE

14

DIRECT EVIDENCE
FAMILY DIVISION
GRANT OF PROBATE
MENTAL DISORDER
NOLO CONTENDERE
NON PROSEQUITUR
PUBLIC NUISANCE
TIME IMMEMORIAL
ULTIMOGENITURE
UNINCORPORATED
UTTER BARRISTER

15

BREACH OF PROMISE
DISORDERLY HOUSE
HEARSAY EVIDENCE
IMPRESCRIPTIBLE
INTERROGATORIES
OFFICIAL REFEREE
RES IPSA LOQUITUR
SPECIAL PLEADING
WRIT OF EXECUTION

16

AFFILIATION ORDER
ANTON PILLER ORDER
ARREST OF JUDGMENT
BREACH OF THE PEACE
DEFERRED SENTENCE
EXEMPLARY DAMAGES
LITIGATION FRIEND
MAREVA INJUNCTION
MENTAL IMPAIRMENT
PERSONAL PROPERTY
PUBLIC PROSECUTOR
STATEMENT OF CLAIM
STATEMENTS OF CASE
TRANSITORY ACTION
UNLAWFUL ASSEMBLY

17

DISORDERLY CONDUCT
FALSE IMPRISONMENT
INSURABLE INTEREST
PERSISTENT CRUELTY

18
AGGRAVATED TRESPASS
CORPUS JURIS CIVILIS
COURT OF COMMON PLEAS
CUMULATIVE EVIDENCE
FACULTY OF ADVOCATES
PARTICULARS OF CLAIM
PECUNIARY ADVANTAGE
PLACE OF SAFETY ORDER

PRIMA-FACIE EVIDENCE

19
ADMINISTRATION ORDER
PROSECUTING ATTORNEY
RESTRICTIVE COVENANT
SPECIFIC PERFORMANCE

20+
CONTRIBUTORY NEGLIGENCE

DIMINISHED RESPONSIBILITY
INDETERMINATE SENTENCE
LETTERS OF ADMINISTRATION
OBTAINING BY DECEPTION
PSYCHOPATHIC DISORDER
STATUTORY DECLARATION
UNREASONABLE BEHAVIOUR

ECONOMIC TERMS AND THEORIES

3
GDP
GNP

4
FIFO

5
SLUMP

7
DUOPOLY
MARXISM
NEW DEAL
SLAVERY
STATICS
SURPLUS

8
FUNGIBLE
LENINISM
MONOPOLY
PROPERTY

9
BOOM CYCLE
BUST CYCLE
FREE TRADE
INELASTIC
LIQUIDITY
OLIGOPOLY
PUT OPTION
RECESSION

10
ADDED VALUE
BEAR MARKET
BROAD MONEY
BULL MARKET
CAPITALISM
DEPRESSION
FISCAL DRAG
FREE MARKET
INVESTMENT
MONETARISM

PROTECTION
TRADE CYCLE
TROTSKYISM
VALUE ADDED

11
COLONIALISM
COMPETITION
CONSUMERISM
DEMAND CURVE
IMPERIALISM
MARGINALISM
MATERIALISM
NARROW MONEY
PHYSIOCRACY
REVISIONISM
STAGFLATION
SYNDICALISM

12
ECONOMETRICS
ECONOMIC RENT
FISCAL POLICY
FIVE-YEAR PLAN
GOLD STANDARD
KEYNESIANISM
MARKET FORCES
MERCANTILISM
MIXED ECONOMY
NEW ECONOMICS
PRODUCTIVITY
PUBLIC SECTOR
SURPLUS VALUE
TRADE BARRIER

13
DEMAND ECONOMY
EXCHANGE VALUE
FUTURES MARKET
NEO-CLASSICISM
OPTIONS MARKET
PRIVATE SECTOR

14
BALANCED BUDGET

COMMAND ECONOMY
CORPORATE STATE
ECONOMIC GROWTH
ECONOMIC POLICY
MACROECONOMICS
MICROECONOMICS
MONETARY POLICY
NATIONAL INCOME
WINDFALL PROFIT

15
AGGREGATE DEMAND
INFLATIONARY GAP
POSITIONAL GOODS
SUPPLY AND DEMAND
TOTALITARIANISM
VELOCITY OF MONEY
WAGE-PRICE SPIRAL

16
COST OF PRODUCTION
DEFICIT FINANCING
DIVISION OF LABOUR
ECONOMIES OF SCALE
INSTITUTIONALISM
RETAIL PRICE INDEX
WELFARE ECONOMICS

17
MEANS OF PRODUCTION

18
DIMINISHING RETURNS
ECONOMIC CLASSICISM
ELASTICITY OF DEMAND
PERFECT COMPETITION

19+
DIALECTICAL MATERIALISM
ECONOMIC EQUILIBRIUM
GROSS DOMESTIC PRODUCT
GROSS NATIONAL PRODUCT
LAISSEZ-FAIRE ECONOMICS
PRICES AND INCOMES POLICY
SUPPLY-SIDE ECONOMICS

MAJOR STOCK INDICES

AEX
AIM
ATX
BEL
BIST
BOVESPA
BSE
CAC
CSE
DAX
DOW

DOW JONES
FTSE
HANG SENG
HNX
IBEX
IDX
KOSPI
MOEX
NASDAQ
NIFTY
NIKKEI

OMX
PSI
RTSI
S&P
SET
SHANGHAI
SMI
STANDARD & POOR
TA
WIG

SCIENCE AND TECHNOLOGY

BRANCHES OF SCIENCE

6
BOTANY
OPTICS

7
ALGEBRA
ANATOMY
BIOLOGY
ECOLOGY
GEOLOGY
OTOLOGY
PHYSICS
ZOOLOGY

8
ANALYSIS
APIOLOGY
BRYOLOGY
CALCULUS
CYTOLOGY
ETHOLOGY
GEOMETRY
MEDICINE
MYCOLOGY
ONCOLOGY
TOPOLOGY
VIROLOGY

9
ACAROLOGY
ACOUSTICS
ASTRONOMY
CHEMISTRY
COSMOGONY
COSMOLOGY
DENTISTRY
HISTOLOGY
LITHOLOGY
MECHANICS
NEUROLOGY
OSTEOLOGY
PATHOLOGY
PETROLOGY
PHYTOLOGY
RADIOLOGY
RHINOLOGY
SELENLOGY

10
ARITHMETIC
CARDIOLOGY

EMBRYOLOGY
ENTOMOLOGY
IMMUNOLOGY
METALLURGY
MINERALOGY
OCEANOLOGY
ODONTOLOGY
PALYNOLOGY
PHYSIOLOGY
POTAMOLOGY
SEISMOLOGY
SPELEOLOGY
TOXICOLOGY
TRICHOLOGY

11
AERONAUTICS
CLIMATOLOGY
DERMATOLOGY
ELECTRONICS
GERONTOLOGY
GROUP THEORY
HAEMATOLOGY
HERPETOLOGY
ICHTHYOLOGY
INFORMATICS
LIFE SCIENCE
MATHEMATICS
METEOROLOGY
ORNITHOLOGY
PAEDIATRICS
STOMATOLOGY
VOLCANOLOGY
VULCANOLOGY

12
ANTHROPOLOGY
ASTROBIOLOGY
ASTRONAUTICS
ASTROPHYSICS
BACTERIOLOGY
BIOCHEMISTRY
EARTH SCIENCE
EPIDEMIOLOGY
ETHNOBIOLOGY
GEOCHEMISTRY
MICROBIOLOGY
NUMBER THEORY
OCEANOGRAPHY
ORTHODONTICS
PARASITOLOGY

PHARMACOLOGY
SPECTROSCOPY

13
ENDOCRINOLOGY
GEOMORPHOLOGY
HEALTH PHYSICS
HELMINTHOLOGY
OPHTHALMOLOGY
PALAEONTOLOGY

14
ASTROCHEMISTRY
BIOINFORMATICS
COLEOPTEROLOGY
PHYTOCHEMISTRY
THERMODYNAMICS

15
CHEMICAL PHYSICS
COMPUTER SCIENCE
CRYSTALLOGRAPHY
PHYSICAL SCIENCE
PHYSIOCHEMISTRY
PURE MATHEMATICS

16
CIVIL ENGINEERING
GASTROENTER-OLOGY
INTEGRAL CALCULUS
ORGANIC CHEMISTRY

17
EUCLIDEAN GEOMETRY
PHYSICAL CHEMISTRY

18
APPLIED MATHEMATICS
CELESTIAL MECHANICS
INORGANIC CHEMISTRY
PALAEOANTHROPOLOGY

19
CHEMICAL ENGINEERING

20+
AERONAUTICAL ENGINEERING
DIFFERENTIAL CALCULUS
ELECTRICAL ENGINEERING
INFORMATION TECHNOLOGY
MECHANICAL ENGINEERING
NONEUCLIDEAN GEOMETRY

WEIGHTS AND MEASURES

2

CM
DR
FT
GR
HL
IN
KG
KM
LB
MG
ML
MM
OZ
YD

3

AMP
ARE
BAR
BEL
BIT
CWT
DWT
ELL
ERG
LUX
MHO
MIL
MIM
NIT
OHM
RAD
REM
ROD
TON
TUN

4

ACRE
BALE
BARN
BOLT
BYTE
CASK
CORD
CRAN
DRAM
DYNE
FOOT
GILL
GRAM
HAND
HIDE
HOUR
INCH
KILO
KNOT
LINE
LINK

MILE
MOLE
NAIL
PECK
PHON
PHOT
PICA
PINT
PIPE
POLE
REAM
ROOD
SLUG
SPAN
TORR
TROY
VOLT
WATT
YARD

5

CABLE
CARAT
CHAIN
CRITH
CUBIT
CURIE
CUSEC
CYCLE
DEBYE
FARAD
FERMI
GAUGE
GAUSS
GRAIN
HENRY
HERTZ
JOULE
LITRE
LUMEN
METRE
MINIM
NEPER
OUNCE
PERCH
POINT
POISE
POUND
QUART
QUIRE
STADE
STERE
STILB
STOKE
STONE
TESLA
THERM
TOISE
TONNE
WEBER

6

AMPERE
BARREL
BUSHEL
CANDLE
CENTAL
DEGREE
DENIER
DRACHM
FATHOM
FIRKIN
GALLON
GRAMME
KELVIN
LEAGUE
MEGOHM
MICRON
MINUTE
NEWTON
PARSEC
PASCAL
RADIAN
RÉAMUR
SECOND
STOKES

7

CALORIE
CANDELA
CENTNER
COULOMB
DECIBEL
DIOPTER
FARADAY
FURLONG
GILBERT
HECTARE
KILOBAR
KILOTON
LAMBERT
MAXWELL
MEGATON
OERSTED
POUNDAL
QUARTER
QUINTAL
RÖNTGEN
SCRUPLE
SIEMENS

8

ÅNGSTROM
CHALDRON
HOGSHEAD
KILOGRAM
KILOWATT
QUADRANT
MEGAWATT
MICROOHM
WATT-HOUR

9
BOARD-FOOT
CENTIGRAM
CUBIC FOOT
CUBIC INCH
CUBIC YARD
DECALITRE
DECAMETRE
DECILITRE
DECIMETRE
FOOT-POUND
HECTOGRAM
KILOCYCLE
KILOHERTZ
KILOLITRE
KILOMETRE
LIGHT-YEAR

MEGACYCLE
MEGAFARAD
MEGAHERTZ
METRIC TON
MICROGRAM
MICROWATT
MILLIGRAM
NANOMETRE
SCANTLING
STERADIAN

10+
BARLEYCORN
CENTILITRE
CENTIMETRE
CUBIC METRE
DECAGRAMME

DECIGRAMME
FLUID OUNCE
HECTOLITRE
HORSEPOWER
HUNDREDWEIGHT
KILOGRAMME
MICROFARAD
MILLILITRE
MILLIMETRE
NANOSECOND
PENNYWEIGHT
RUTHERFORD
SQUARE CENTIMETRE
SQUARE INCH
SQUARE KILOMETRE
SQUARE MILE
SQUARE YARD

PAPER MEASURES

4
BALE
COPY
DEMY
POST
POTT
REAM

5
ATLAS
BRIEF
CROWN
DRAFT
QUIRE
ROYAL

6
BAG CAP

BUNDLE
CASING
MEDIUM

7
EMPEROR
KENT CAP

8
ELEPHANT
FOOLSCAP
HAVEN CAP
IMPERIAL

9
CARTRIDGE
COLOMBIER
LARGE POST
MUSIC DEMY

10
DOUBLE DEMY
DOUBLE POST
GRAND EAGLE
SUPER ROYAL

11
ANTIQUARIAN
IMPERIAL CAP
PINCHED POST

14
DOUBLE ELEPHANT

15
DOUBLE LARGE POST

ELEMENTARY PARTICLES

2
XI

3
ETA
PHI
PSI

4
KAON
MUON
PION

5
BOSON
GLUON
MESON
OMEGA
QUARK
SIGMA

6
BARYON
HADRON
LAMBDA
LEPTON

PHOTON
PROTON

7
FERMION
HYPERON
NEUTRON
TACHYON

8
DEUTERON
ELECTRON
GRAVITON

NEUTRINO
POSITRON

12
ANTIPARTICLE
BETA PARTICLE

13
ALPHA PARTICLE

9
NEUTRETTO

THE CHEMICAL ELEMENTS

NAME	(SYMBOL)				
ACTINIUM	(AC)	GERMANIUM	(GE)	POTASSIUM	(K)
ALUMINIUM	(AL)	GOLD	(AU)	PRASEODYMIUM	(PR)
AMERICIUM	(AM)	HAFNIUM	(HF)	PROMETHIUM	(PM)
ANTIMONY	(SB)	HASSIUM	(HS)	PROTACTINIUM	(PA)
ARGON	(AR)	HELIUM	(HE)	RADIUM	(RA)
ARSENIC	(AS)	HOLMIUM	(HO)	RADON	(RN)
ASTATINE	(AT)	HYDROGEN	(H)	RHENIUM	(RE)
BARIUM	(BA)	INDIUM	(IN)	RHODIUM	(RH)
BERKELIUM	(BK)	IODINE	(I)	ROENTGENIUM	(RG)
BERYLLIUM	(BE)	IRIDIUM	(IR)	RUBIDIUM	(RB)
BISMUTH	(BI)	IRON	(FE)	RUTHENIUM	(RU)
BOHRIUM	(BH)	KRYPTON	(KR)	RUTHERFORDIUM	(RF)
BORON	(B)	LANTHANUM	(LA)	SAMARIUM	(SM)
BROMINE	(BR)	LAWRENCIUM	(LR)	SCANDIUM	(SC)
CADMIUM	(CD)	LEAD	(PB)	SEABORGIUM	(SG)
CAESIUM	(CS)	LITHIUM	(LI)	SELENIUM	(SE)
CALCIUM	(CA)	LIVERMORIUM	(LV)	SILICON	(SI)
CALIFORNIUM	(CF)	LUTETIUM	(LU)	SILVER	(AG)
CARBON	(C)	MAGNESIUM	(MG)	SODIUM	(NA)
CERIUM	(CE)	MANGANESE	(MN)	STRONTIUM	(SR)
CHLORINE	(CL)	MEITNERIUM	(MT)	SULPHUR	(S)
CHROMIUM	(CR)	MENDELEVIUM	(MD)	TANTALUM	(TA)
COBALT	(CO)	MERCURY	(HG)	TECHNETIUM	(TC)
COPERNICUM	(CN)	MOLYBDENUM	(MO)	TELLURIUM	(TE)
COLUMBIUM	(CB)	MOSCOVIUM	(MC)	TENNESSINE	(TS)
COPPER	(CU)	NEODYMIUM	(ND)	TERBIUM	(TB)
CURIUM	(CM)	NEON	(NE)	THALLIUM	(TL)
DARMSTADTIUM	(DS)	NEPTUNIUM	(NP)	THORIUM	(TH)
DUBNIUM	(DB)	NICKEL	(NI)	THULIUM	(TM)
DYSPROSIUM	(DY)	NIHONIUM	(NH)	TIN	(SN)
EINSTEINIUM	(ES)	NIOBIUM	(NB)	TITANIUM	(TI)
ERBIUM	(ER)	NITROGEN	(N)	TUNGSTEN	(W)
EUROPIUM	(EU)	NOBELIUM	(NO)	URANIUM	(U)
FERMIUM	(FM)	OGANESSON	(OG)	VANADIUM	(V)
FLEROVIUM	(FL)	OSMIUM	(OS)	WOLFRAM	(W)
FLUORINE	(F)	OXYGEN	(O)	XENON	(XE)
FRANCIUM	(FR)	PALLADIUM	(PD)	YTTERBIUM	(YB)
GADOLINIUM	(GD)	PHOSPHORUS	(P)	YTTRIUM	(Y)
GALLIUM	(GA)	PLATINUM	(PT)	ZINC	(ZN)
		PLUTONIUM	(PU)	ZIRCONIUM	(ZR)
		POLONIUM	(PO)		

COMMON CHEMICALS

4
ALUM
LIME
UREA

5
BORAX
ETHER
FREON
FURAN
HALON

6
BARYTA
CETANE
CRESOL
DIOXAN
ETHANE
HEXANE
IODIDE
LITHIA
LITMUS
PHENOL
POTASH
QUINOL
SILICA
XYLENE

7
ACETATE
ALUMINA
AMMONIA
ANILINE
BENZENE
BORAZON
BROMIDE
CALOMEL
CAMPHOR
CHLORAL
CYANIDE
ETHANOL
HEPTANE
PENTANE
QUINONE
REALGAR
RED LEAD
SODA ASH
STYRENE
TOLUENE

8
BERYLLIA
CATECHOL
CHLORIDE
CINNABAR
CORUNDUM
CYANOGEN
FLUORIDE
FLUORITE
FORMALIN

MAGNESIA
MELAMINE
METHANOL
NEOPRENE
PEROXIDE
PHOSGENE
PLUMBAGO
PROPANOL
SODA LIME
SODAMIDE
STRONTIA

9
ACETYLENE
AQUA REGIA
BLANC FIXE
BORIC ACID
BROMOFORM
FERROCENE
IODIC ACID
LIMEWATER
PHOSPHINE
PROPYLENE
QUICKLIME
SALTPETRE

10
CAPRIC ACID
CYANIC ACID
FORMIC ACID
LACTIC ACID
LAURIC ACID
MUSTARD GAS
NITRIC ACID
OXALIC ACID
PICRIC ACID
SLAKED LIME
TANNIC ACID
WATER GLASS
ZINC BLENDE

11
ACRYLIC ACID
BENZOIC ACID
BUTYRIC ACID
CAPROIC ACID
CAUSTIC SODA
DIPHOSPHINE
FUMARIC ACID
IODOMETHANE
LAUGHING GAS
MALONIC ACID
NITRIC OXIDE
NITROUS ACID
PRUSSIC ACID
SAL AMMONIAC
STEARIC ACID
SUGAR OF LEAD
WASHING SODA

12
ACETALDEHYDE
BENZALDEHYDE
BENZOQUINONE
CAPRYLIC ACID
CARBOLIC ACID
CARBONIC ACID
DECANOIC ACID
ETHYL ALCOHOL
FLUOROCARBON
FORMALDEHYDE
FULMINIC ACID
GREEN VITRIOL
HYDROQUINONE
NITROBENZENE
NITROUS OXIDE
OIL OF VITRIOL
PERMANGANATE
PHTHALIC ACID
TARTARIC ACID

13
ISOCYANIC ACID
METHANOIC ACID
METHYL ALCOHOL
PROPANOIC ACID
SILVER NITRATE
SODIUM CYANIDE
SULPHURIC ACID
VINYL CHLORIDE

14
CALCIUM CARBIDE
CARBON MONOXIDE
CHLORAL HYDRATE
COPPER SULPHATE
HYDROIODIC ACID
METHYL CHLORIDE
NITROCELLULOSE
PHOSPHORIC ACID
SODIUM CHLORIDE
SODIUM SULPHATE
SULPHUR DIOXIDE
TETRAETHYL LEAD

15
ABSOLUTE ALCOHOL
BLEACHING POWDER
HYDROBROMIC ACID
HYDROCYANIC ACID
HYDROGEN CYANIDE
NITROGEN DIOXIDE
PHOSPHOROUS ACID
SODIUM HYDROXIDE
SULPHUR TRIOXIDE
TETRAHYDROFURAN

16
CALCIUM CARBONATE
CALCIUM HYDROXIDE

HYDROCHLORIC ACID
HYDROFLUORIC ACID
HYDROGEN FLUORIDE
HYDROGEN PEROXIDE
HYPOCHLOROUS ACID
NITROGEN MONOXIDE

17
BICARBONATE OF SODA

MAGNESIUM CHLORIDE
POTASSIUM CHLORIDE
SODIUM BICARBONATE
VANADIUM PENTOXIDE

18
CHLOROFLUOROCARBON
DIMETHYL SULPHOXIDE
MAGNESIUM CARBONATE

19+
BUCKMINSTERFULLERENE
CARBON TETRACHLORIDE
POTASSIUM BICARBONATE
POTASSIUM PERMANGANATE

ALLOYS

ALLOY – main components

4
ALNI – iron, nickel, aluminium, copper
BETA – titanium, aluminium, vanadium, chromium

5
ALPHA – titanium, aluminium, tin, copper,
  zirconium, niobium, molybdenum
BRASS – copper, zinc
INVAR – iron, nickel
MAZAC – zinc, aluminium, magnesium, copper
MONEL – nickel, cobalt, iron
STEEL – iron, carbon

6
ALNICO – aluminium, nickel, cobalt
BABBIT – tin, lead, antimony, copper
BRONZE – copper, tin
CUNICO – iron, cobalt, copper, nickel
CUNIFE – iron, cobalt, nickel
FEROBA – iron, barium oxide, iron oxide
PEWTER – tin, lead
SOLDER – lead, tin (soft), copper, zinc (brazing)

7
ALCOMAX – aluminium, cobalt, nickel, copper, lead,
  niobium
ALUMNEL – aluminium, chromium
AMALGAM – mercury, various
CHROMEL – nickel, chromium
COLUMAN – iron, chromium, nickel, aluminium,
  nobium, copper
ELINVAR – iron, nickel, chromium, tungsten
INCONEL – nickel, chromium, iron
KANTHAL – chromium, aluminium, iron
MUMETAL – iron, nickel, copper, chromium
NIMONIC – nickel, chromium, iron, titanium,
  aluminium, manganese, silicon

8
CAST IRON – carbon, iron
DOWMETAL – magnesium, aluminium, zinc,
  manganese
GUNMETAL – copper, tin, zinc
HIPERNIK – nickel, iron

ALLOY – main components

KIRKSITE – zinc, aluminium, copper
MANGANIN – copper, manganese, nickel
NICHROME – nickel, iron, chromium
VICALLOY – iron, cobalt, vanadium
ZIRCALOY – zirconium, tin, iron, nickel, chromium

9
DURALUMIN – aluminium, copper, silicon,
  magnesium, manganese, zinc
HASTELLOY – nickel, molybdenum, iron, chromium,
  cobalt, tungsten
PERMALLOY – nickel, iron
PERMINVAR – nickel, iron, cobalt
TYPE METAL – lead, tin, antimony

10
CONSTANTAN – copper, nickel
MISCH METAL – cerium, various
MUNTZ METAL – copper, zinc
ROSE'S METAL – bismuth, lead, tin
SUPERALLOY – type of stainless steel
WOOD'S METAL – lead, tin, bismuth, cadmium

11
CUPRONICKEL – copper, nickel
ELECTROTYPE – lead, tin, antimony
SUPERMALLOY – iron, nickel
SUPERMENDUR – iron, cobalt

12
FERROSILICON – iron, silicon
GERMAN SILVER – copper, nickel, zinc, lead, tin
SILVER SOLDER – copper, silver, zinc

13
FERROCHROMIUM – iron, chromium
FERROTUNGSTEN – iron, tungsten
FERROVANADIUM – iron, vanadium

14
ADMIRALTY METAL – copper, zinc
BRITANNIA METAL – tin, antimony, copper
FERROMANGANESE – iron, manganese
PHOSPHOR BRONZE – copper, tin, phosphorus
STAINLESS STEEL – iron, chromium, vanadium

TYPES OF CHEMICAL COMPOUNDS

4
ACID
BASE

5
ALDOL
AMIDE
AMINE
ARENE
ARYNE
AZINE
ESTER
ETHER
KETAL
OXIDE
OXIME
SUGAR
YLIDE

6
ACETAL
ALKALI
ALKANE
ALKENE
ALKYNE
BORANE
CRESOL
HALIDE
IODIDE
KETENE
KETONE
LACTAM
LACTIM
LACTOL
OLEFIN
PHENOL
PURINE

7
ALCOHOL

BENZYNE
CARBIDE
CHELATE
COMPLEX
EPOXIDE
LACTONE
OZONIDE
QUINONE

8
ALDEHYDE
ALKOXIDE
ANNULENE
AROMATIC
CARBINOL
CARBONYL
CHLORIDE
CORONAND
CRYPTAND
CRYPTATE
CUMULENE
FLUORIDE
HELICENE
PEROXIDE

9
ACETYLENE
AMINO ACID
ANHYDRIDE
FATTY ACID
FULLERENE
HEMIKETAL
IMINO ACID
NAPHTHENE

10
ACYL HALIDE
CALIXARENE
CROWN ETHER
CYCLOPHANE

HEMIACETAL
PIANO STOOL
PYRIMIDINE
SACCHARIDE

11
ALKYL HALIDE
CYCLOALKANE
CYCLOALKENE
CYCLOALKYNE
HETEROARENE
HETEROARYNE
HYDROCARBON
METALLOCENE

12
CARBOHYDRATE
HALF SANDWICH
HETEROCYCLIC
INTERHALOGEN

13
ACID ANHYDRIDE
SPIRO COMPOUND

14
CARBOXILIC ACID
PSEUDOAROMATIC

15+
CHARGE TRANSFER COMPOUND
COORDINATION COMPOUND
DOUBLE DECKER SANDWICH
NITROGENOUS BASE
SANDWICH COMPOUND

BIOCHEMICAL COMPOUNDS

3
ADP
AMP
ATP
COA
DNA
FAD
FMN
NAD
RNA

4
HAEM
HEME
NADP
UREA

5
ACTIN
AUXIN
DNASE
EOSIN
HEMIN
KININ
LYASE
MUCIN
OPSIN
PRION
RENIN

6
BIOTIN
CASEIN
CHITIN
FIBRIN
FLAVIN
GLUCAN
GLUTEN
GLYCAN
INULIN
KINASE
LIGASE
LIGNIN
LIPASE
LUTEIN
MYOSIN
NIACIN
PECTIN
PEPSIN
PURINE
RENNIN
S PHASE
STARCH
STEROL
TANNIN
URACIL

7
ADENINE
ALBUMEN

ALBUMIN
AMYLASE
AMYLOSE
CHOLINE
COCAINE
CODEINE
CYSTINE
DEXTRIN
ELASTIN
ESTRIOL
ESTRONE
FLAVONE
FRUCTAN
GASTRIN
GUANINE
HEPARIN
HORMONE
INHIBIN
INSULIN
KERATIN
MELANIN
OPSONIN
PEPTIDE
PROTEIN
PTYALIN
QUININE
RELAXIN
RETINAL
STEROID
TERPENE
THYMINE
TRYPSIN
URIDINE

8
ANAPHASE
ATROPINE
CAFFEINE
CAROTENE
CATALASE
COLLAGEN
CORTISOL
CREATINE
CYTIDINE
CYTOKINE
CYTOSINE
ESTROGEN
EXOTOXIN
FLAVONOL
GLOBULIN
GLUCAGON
GLYCEROL
GLYCOGEN
INOSITOL
KILOBASE
LECITHIN
LYSOSOME
LYSOZYME
MANNITOL
MEGABASE

MORPHINE
NEOTONIN
NUCLEASE
OXYTOCIN
PROPHASE
PROTEASE
PYRUVATE
RETINENE
RIBOZYME
SECRETIN
THIAMINE
THROMBIN
TROPONIN
URIC ACID

9
ACETYL COA
ADENOSINE
AFLATOXIN
BILIRUBIN
CELLULASE
CORTISONE
CYTOKININ
DEAMINASE
ENDORPHIN
ENDOTOXIN
ESTRADIOL
FLAVONOID
FOLIC ACID
GLYCERIDE
GLYCOSIDE
GUANOSINE
HISTAMINE
HYDROLASE
KAIROMONE
LUCIFERIN
MELATONIN
METAPHASE
MYOGLOBIN
NINHYDRIN
PEPTIDASE
PORPHYRIN
PROLACTIN
PROTAMINE
RHODOPSIN
SEROTONIN
TELOPHASE
THYMIDINE
THYROXINE
UBIQUITIN

10
ACTOMYOSIN
ADRENALINE
BILIVERDIN
BRADYKININ
CADAVERINE
CALCIFEROL
CALCITONIN
CAROTENOID

CITRULLINE
COLCHICINE
CREATININE
CYTOCHROME
ENCEPHALIN
ENKEPHALIN
ERGOSTEROL
FERREDOXIN
GLYCOLIPID
HOMOGLYCAN
INTERFERON
INTERPHASE
LIPOIC ACID
LIPOTROPIN
LYMPHOKINE
NUCLEOSIDE
NUCLEOTIDE
PENICILLIN
PHYCOBILIN
POLYMERASE
PROHORMONE
PROTEINASE
PUTRESCINE
PYRIDOXINE
PYRIMIDINE
RIBOFLAVIN
STRYCHNINE
TOCOPHEROL
UBIQUINONE

11
ACTINOMYCIN
ALDOSTERONE
AMYLOPECTIN
ANGIOTENSIN
ANTHOCYANIN
CARBOXYLASE
CHLOROPHYLL
CHOLESTEROL
CYTOKERATIN
ECDYSTERONE
EPINEPHRINE
EUCHROMATIN
EXONUCLEASE
FUCOXANTHIN
FUMARIC ACID
GIBBERELLIN
GLUTATHIONE
HAEMOCYANIN
HAEMOGLOBIN
INTERLEUKIN
MENAQUINONE
MUCOPROTEIN
MYCOPROTEIN

NUCLEIC ACID
PHAEOPHYTIN
POLYPEPTIDE
PROGESTOGEN
PROTHROMBIN
THEOBROMINE
THYROTROPIN
TRANSFERASE
TRYPSINOGEN
VASOPRESSIN
XANTHOPHYLL

12
ABSCISIC ACID
ANDROSTERONE
ASCORBIC ACID
ENDONUCLEASE
ENTEROKINASE
FLAVOPROTEIN
GLYCOPROTEIN
GONADOTROPIN
HAEMATOXYLIN
HAEMERYTHRIN
NEUROHORMONE
PHOSPHOLIPID
PHYTOHORMONE
PROGESTERONE
PROTEOGLYCAN
RIBONUCLEASE
SOMATOSTATIN
SOMATOTROPIN
TESTOSTERONE
TETRAPYRROLE
THEOPHYLLINE
TRANSAMINASE
VIOLAXANTHIN
VISUAL PURPLE

13
ACETYLCHOLINE
CATECHOLAMINE
CORTICOTROPIN
DECARBOXYLASE
DEHYDROGENASE
HEMICELLULOSE
NICOTINIC ACID
NORADRENALINE
NUCLEOPROTEIN
OXYHEMOGLOBIN
PHYCOERYTHRIN
PHYLLOQUINONE
PROSTAGLANDIN
PROTEIN KINASE
SCLEROPROTEIN

14
CORTICOSTEROID
CORTICOSTERONE
CYANOCOBALAMIN
GLUCOCORTICOID
HYALURONIC ACID
HYDROCORTISONE
IMMUNOGLOBULIN
NOREPINEPHRINE
PHOSPHOPROTEIN

15
CHOLECALCIFEROL
CHOLECYSTOKININ
ENTEROPEPTIDASE
EXORIBONUCLEASE
GIBBERELLIC ACID
HETEROCHROMATIN
OXALOACETIC ACID
PANTOTHENIC ACID
PHOSPHOCREATINE
RIBONUCLEIC ACID

16
ENDORIBONUCLEASE
METALLOPORPHYRIN
TRIIODOTHYRONINE

17
AUTOIMMUNE DISEASE
DEOXYRIBONUCLEASE
GLYCOSAMINOGLYCAN
MINERALOCORTICOID

18
LIPOPOLYSACCHARIDE
MUCOPOLYSACCHARIDE

19
DEOXYCORTICOSTERONE
PTEROYLGLUTAMIC ACID

20+
ACETYLCHOLINESTERASE
ADENOSINE DIPHOSPHATE
ADENOSINE MONOPHOSPHATE
ADENOSINE TRIPHOSPHATE
DEOXYRIBONUCLEIC ACID
FLAVIN ADENINE DINUCLEOTIDE
FLAVIN MONONUCLEOTIDE
NICOTINAMIDE ADENINE
   DINUCLEOTIDE
RESTRICTION ENDONUCLEASE
REVERSE TRANSCRIPTASE
RIBULOSE BISPHOSPHATE

ORGANIC ACIDS

5
MALIC (hydroxybutanedioic)
OLEIC (octadec-9-enoic)

6
ACETIC (ethanoic)
ADIPIC (hexanedioic)
CAPRIC (decanoic)
CITRIC (2-hydroxy-propane-
1,2,3-tricarboxylic)
FORMIC (methanoic)
LACTIC (2-hydroxypropanoic)
LAURIC (dodecanoic)
MALEIC (cis-butenedioic)
OXALIC (ethanedioic)

7
BEHENIC (docosanoic)
BUTYRIC (butanoic)
CAPROIC (hexanoic)
CEROTIC (hexacosanoic)
ENATHIC (heptanoic)
FUMARIC (trans-butenedioic)
MALONIC (propanedioic)
STEARIC (octadecanoic)
VALERIC (pentanoic)

8
CAPRYLIC (octanoic)
GLUTARIC (pentanedioic)
GLYCOLIC (hydroxyethanoic)

LINOLEIC (octadeca-
9,12-dienoic)
MYRISTIC (tetradecanoic)
PALMITIC (hexadecanoic)
SUCCINIC (butanedioic)

9
ARACHIDIC (eicosanoic)
LINOLENIC (octadeca-
9,12,15-trienoic)

10
LIGNOCERIC (tetracosanoic)
PELARGONIC (nonanoic)
PROPRIONIC (propanoic)

AMINO ACIDS

6
LYSINE
SERINE
VALINE

7
ALANINE
GLYCINE
LEUCINE
PROLINE

8
ARGININE

CYSTEINE
TYROSINE

9
ASPARTINE
GLUTAMINE
HISTIDINE
ORNITHINE
THREONINE

10
ASPARAGINE
CITRULLINE

ISOLEUCINE
METHIONINE
TRYPTOPHAN

12
ASPARTIC ACID
GLUTAMIC ACID

13
PHENYLALANINE

SUGARS

6
ALDOSE
HEXOSE
KETOSE
RIBOSE

7
AMYLOSE
GLUCOSE
LACTOSE
MALTOSE
MANNOSE
PENTOSE
SUCROSE

8
DEXTROSE
FRUCTOSE
FURANOSE
MANNITOL
PYRANOSE

9
CANE SUGAR
GALACTOSE
MILK SUGAR

10
ALDOHEXOSE

GRAPE SUGAR
KETOHEXOSE
SACCHARIDE

11
ALDOPENTOSE
KETOPENTOSE

12
DISACCHARIDE

14
MONOSACCHARIDE

MATHEMATICAL TERMS

3
SET
SUM

4
BASE
CUBE
MEAN
NODE
RING
ROOT
SINE
SURD

5
ARRAY
DIGIT
FIELD
GROUP
LIMIT
LOCUS
POWER
PROOF
RATIO
UNITY

6
COSINE
FACTOR
GOOGOL
MATRIX
MEDIAN
ORIGIN
SCALAR
SECANT
SERIES
SQUARE
SUBSET
TENSOR
VECTOR

7
ALGEBRA
DIVISOR
FORMULA
FRACTAL
INTEGER
INVERSE
MODULUS
PRODUCT
TANGENT
UNKNOWN

8
ABSCISSA
ADDITION
ANALYSIS
BINOMIAL
CALCULUS
COSECANT
CUBE ROOT

DIVISION
EQUATION
EXPONENT
FRACTION
FUNCTION
FUZZY SET
GRADIENT
IDENTITY
JULIA SET
LIE GROUP
MULTIPLE
OPERATOR
QUOTIENT
SOLUTION
VARIABLE

9
ALGORITHM
ASYMPTOTE
CANTOR SET
CONJUGATE
COTANGENT
EXPANSION
FACTORIAL
INTEGRAND
INTERCEPT
ITERATION
LOGARITHM
NUMERATOR
PARAMETER
RECURSION
REMAINDER
SET THEORY
SUB-GROUP
TRANSFORM

10
DERIVATIVE
DIFFERENCE
EIGENVALUE
FRACTAL SET
GAME THEORY
GOOGOLPLEX
INEQUALITY
MULTIPLIER
PERCENTILE
POLYNOMIAL
QUATERNION
REAL NUMBER
RECIPROCAL
SQUARE ROOT

11
ALIQUOT PART
BANACH SPACE
CHAOS THEORY
COEFFICIENT
DENOMINATOR
DETERMINANT
EIGENVECTOR

GALOIS GROUP
GROUP THEORY
INTEGRATION
KLEIN BOTTLE
MAGIC SQUARE
MARKOV CHAIN
MÖBIUS STRIP
PERMUTATION
POWER SERIES
PRIME NUMBER
SUBTRACTION
VENN DIAGRAM
WHOLE NUMBER

12
BAYES' THEOREM
DECIMAL POINT
GÖDEL NUMBERS
HILBERT SPACE
LONG DIVISION
MULTIPLICAND
NEWTON METHOD
NUMBER THEORY
SIMPSON'S RULE
SQUARE NUMBER
SUBSTITUTION
TAYLOR SERIES

13
ANTILOGARITHM
ARGAND DIAGRAM
COMPLEX NUMBER
EIGENFUNCTION
EUCLID'S AXIOMS
EULER'S FORMULA
EXTRAPOLATION
FOURIER SERIES
GAUSS'S THEOREM
GEOMETRIC MEAN
GREEN'S THEOREM
INTERPOLATION
L'HÔPITAL'S RULE
MANDELBROT SET
ORDINAL NUMBER
PERFECT NUMBER
PERFECT SQUARE
QUEUING THEORY
STOKES' THEOREM

14
ARITHMETIC MEAN
ASSOCIATIVE LAW
BOOLEAN ALGEBRA
CARDINAL NUMBER
CAUCHY SEQUENCE
COMMUTATIVE LAW
EULER'S CONSTANT
HYPERBOLIC SINE
LINEAR EQUATION
MULTIPLICATION

NATURAL NUMBERS
NULL HYPOTHESIS
PROPER FRACTION
RATIONAL NUMBER
ROOT-MEAN-SQUARE
VULGAR FRACTION

15
BESSEL FUNCTIONS
BINOMIAL THEOREM
DIFFERENTIATION
DIRICHLET SERIES
DISTRIBUTIVE LAW
FOURIER ANALYSIS
HERMITIAN MATRIX
IMAGINARY NUMBER
LAPLACE OPERATOR
LEIBNIZ'S THEOREM
MACLAURIN SERIES
MERSENNE NUMBERS
MIDPOINT THEOREM
PASCAL'S TRIANGLE
RUSSELL'S PARADOX
STATIONARY POINT

16
BERNOULLI NUMBERS
DEFINITE INTEGRAL
DE MOIVRE'S FORMULA
FIBONACCI NUMBERS

HILBERT'S PROBLEMS
HYPERBOLIC COSINE
IMPROPER FRACTION
INTEGRAL CALCULUS
IRRATIONAL NUMBER
LAGRANGE'S THEOREM
MONTE CARLO METHOD
NATURAL LOGARITHM
POLAR COORDINATES
RECURRING DECIMAL
REMAINDER THEOREM
REPEATING DECIMAL

17
APOLLONIUS' THEOREM
CATASTROPHE THEORY
COMMON DENOMINATOR
EUCLIDEAN GEOMETRY
HYPERBOLIC TANGENT
PARTIAL DERIVATIVE
POINT OF INFLECTION
SIGNIFICANT FIGURE
TRANSFINITE NUMBER

18
COORDINATE GEOMETRY
FERMAT'S LAST THEOREM
FOUR-COLOUR THEOREM
INDEFINITE INTEGRAL
LEAST SQUARES METHOD

NAPIERIAN LOGARITHM
PYTHAGORAS' THEOREM
RIEMANNIAN GEOMETRY

19
BRIGGSIAN LOGARITHMS
DIOPHANTINE EQUATION
EXPONENTIAL FUNCTION
HARMONIC PROGRESSION
HIGHEST COMMON FACTOR
LEGENDRE POLYNOMIALS
POISSON DISTRIBUTION

20+
ARITHMETIC PROGRESSION
CARTESIAN COORDINATES
CHINESE REMAINDER THEOREM
DIFFERENTIAL CALCULUS
DIFFERENTIAL EQUATION
GAUSSIAN DISTRIBUTION
GEOMETRIC PROGRESSION
INFINITESIMAL CALCULUS
LOBACHEVSKIAN GEOMETRY
LOWEST COMMON
  DENOMINATOR
LOWEST COMMON MULTIPLE
SIMULTANEOUS EQUATIONS
STIRLING'S APPROXIMATION
TRIGONOMETRIC FUNCTION
TRANSCENDENTAL FUNCTION

GEOMETRIC FIGURES AND CURVES

3
ARC

4
CONE
CUBE
KITE
LINE
LOOP
LUNE
OVAL
ROSE
ZONE

5
CHORD
CONIC
HELIX
LOCUS
NAPPE
OGIVE
PLANE
PRISM
RHOMB
SHEET
SOLID

TORUS
WEDGE
WITCH

6
CIRCLE
CONOID
FOLIUM
LAMINA
NORMAL
OCTANT
PENCIL
RADIUS
SECTOR
SPHERE
SPIRAL
SPLINE
SQUARE

7
ANNULUS
CISSOID
CYCLOID
DECAGON
ELLIPSE
EVOLUTE

FRACTAL
HEXAGON
LIMAÇON
OCTAGON
PERIGON
POLYGON
PYRAMID
RHOMBUS
SEGMENT
SURFACE
TANGENT
TREFOIL
TRIDENT

8
CARDIOID
CATENARY
CATENOID
CONCHOID
CONICOID
CYLINDER
ENVELOPE
EPICYCLE
EXCIRCLE
FRUSTRUM
GEODESIC

HEPTAGON
INCIRCLE
INVOLUTE
PARABOLA
PENTAGON
PRISMOID
QUADRANT
RHOMBOID
ROULETTE
SPHEROID
TRACTRIX
TRIANGLE
TROCHOID

9
ANTIPRISM
CRUCIFORM
DIRECTRIX
DODECAGON
ELLIPSOID
HYPERBOLA
ISOCHRONE
KOCH CURVE
LOXODROME
MULTIFOIL
PENTAGRAM
PENTANGLE
RHUMB LINE
SINE CURVE
STROPHOID
TRAPEZIUM
TRAPEZOID

10
ACUTE ANGLE
ANCHOR RING
CYLINDROID
EPICYCLOID
HEMISPHERE
HEXAHEDRON
KAPPA CURVE
LEMNISCATE
OCTAHEDRON
PARABOLOID
PEANO CURVE
POLYHEDRON
PRISMATOID
QUADRANGLE
QUADREFOIL
RIGHT ANGLE
SEMICIRCLE
SERPENTINE
TRISECTRIX

11
CORNU SPIRAL
EPITROCHOID
HEPTAHEDRON
HYPERBOLOID
HYPOCYCLOID
ICOSAHEDRON
KLEIN BOTTLE
LATUS RECTUM
MÖBIUS STRIP
OBTUSE ANGLE
PENTAHEDRON

REFLEX ANGLE
TAUTOCHRONE
TETRAHEDRON

12
HYPOTROCHOID
PSEUDOSPHERE
RHOMBOHEDRON
SIGMOID CURVE

13
CIRCUMFERENCE
CUBOCTAHEDRON
PARALLELOGRAM
PARALLELOTOPE
PEDAL TRIANGLE
PERPENDICULAR
QUADRILATERAL

14
SNOWFLAKE CURVE

15
BRACHISTOCHRONE
SCALENE TRIANGLE

17
ICOSIDODECAHEDRON
ISOSCELES TRIANGLE

19
EQUILATERAL TRIANGLE

ELECTRONIC COMPONENTS

3
FET
LED
RCD

4
CHIP
FUSE
GATE

5
CHOKE
DIODE
IGFET
RELAY
SHUNT
VALVE

6
BRIDGE
DYNAMO
FILTER
JUGFET

MOSFET
SWITCH
TRIODE

7
AMMETER
BATTERY
COUNTER
MAGNETO
PENTODE
SPEAKER
TETRODE

8
ARMATURE
BISTABLE
FLIP-FLOP
INDUCTOR
RESISTOR
RHEOSTAT
SOLENOID
VARACTOR
WINDINGS

9
AMPLIFIER
CAPACITOR
GUNN DIODE
MICROCHIP
RECTIFIER
THYRISTOR
VOLTMETER
WAVEGUIDE

10
ALTERNATOR
ATTENUATOR
MICROPHONE
OSCILLATOR
TRANSDUCER
TRANSISTOR
ZENER DIODE

11
ELECTRON GUN
LOUDSPEAKER
SILICON CHIP

TRANSFORMER

12
ELECTRON LENS
ELECTRON TUBE
GALVANOMETER
LOGIC CIRCUIT
OSCILLOSCOPE
PHOTOCATHODE

13
SEMICONDUCTOR

14
CIRCUIT BREAKER
PRINTED CIRCUIT

15+
ELECTRON MULTIPLIER

FIELD-EFFECT TRANSISTOR
INTEGRATED CIRCUIT
LIGHT-EMITTING DIODE
N-TYPE SEMICONDUCTOR
PHOTOMULTIPLIER
P-TYPE SEMICONDUCTOR
THERMIONIC CATHODE
WHEATSTONE BRIDGE

COMPUTER TERMS

1&2	FAQ	BAUD	MIDI
K	FYI	BEEP	MPEG
AI	GIF	BIOS	MTBF
BS	GIG	BLOG	NERD
CD	GIT	BOOT	NODE
CR	GUI	BURN	PACK
DP	IAP	BYTE	PATH
GB	ICR	CELL	PORT
IC	IDE	CHAT	POST
IE	IOS	CHIP	PROM
IP	IRQ	CMYK	RAID
IT	ISP	COPY	SAVE
KB	JOB	CORE	SCAN
LF	KEY	COTS	SCSI
MB	LAN	CROP	SGML
NL	LCD	DATA	SLOT
OS	MEG	DIFF	SOHO
PC	NET	DISK	SPAM
UI	NIC	DRAG	SRAM
WP	NLQ	DRAM	UNDO
	OCR	DUMP	VOIP
3	OEM	ECHO	WAND
AGP	PDA	EDIT	WIFI
ASP	PDF	EPOS	WORD
BBS	PIN	EXIT	WORM
AGP	POS	FILE	ZOOM
BIT	RAM	FIND	
BOT	RGB	FLAG	**5**
BUG	RIP	FLOP	ABORT
BUS	ROM	FONT	ALIAS
CAD	RTF	GEEK	ARRAY
CAL	RUN	GIGO	ASCII
CAM	UPS	GOTO	BASIC
CBL	URL	HOST	BATCH
CGI	USB	HTML	BLINK
COM	VDA	HTTP	BLOCK
CPU	VDU	HUNG	BOARD
CRT	VPN	ICON	CACHE
CSV	WAN	IMAP	CD-ROM
CUT	WEB	IPAD	CLICK
DAT	WWW	IPOD	CLONE
DNS	XML	ISDN	CLOUD
DSL	ZIP	JAVA	CODEC
DTP		JPEG	CRASH
DVD	**4**	KILL	CYBER
EGA	ADSL	LOOP	CYCLE
EOL	ANSI	MENU	DEBUG
EPS	BASE		EMAIL

EPROM
ERASE
ERROR
FIELD
FLAME
FLOOD
FORUM
GUSET
IMAGE
INDEX
INPUT
KIOSK
LOCAL
LOGIN
LOGON
MACRO
MEDIA
MERGE
MODEM
MOUSE
OCTAL
PAINT
PASTE
PATCH
PIXEL
POP-UP
PURGE
QUEUE
SLAVE
SLEEP
SPOOL
TABLE
TWAIN
VIRUS
WHOIS
WRITE

6
ACCESS
ADWARE
ALT KEY
APACHE
APPLET
ATTACK
AVATAR
BACKUP
BANNER
BINARY
BITMAP
BITNET
BLU-RAY
BOOT UP
BRANCH
BRIDGE
BROWSE
BUFFER
BULLET
BUTTON
CHROME
CLIENT
COOKIE
CURSOR
DAEMON
DECODE

DELETE
DIAL-UP
DOMAIN
DRIVER
ESCAPE
FILTER
FORMAT
GOPHER
HACKER
HANDLE
HEADER
HOT FIX
IMPORT
IPHONE
JUMPER
KERMIT
KEYPAD
LAPTOP
LAYOUT
LOGOFF
LOGOUT
MEMORY
NEWBIE
NYBBLE
ON-LINE
OUTPUT
PACKET
PARITY
PARSER
PIRACY
PORTAL
QWERTY
RASTER
RECORD
REMOTE
ROUTER
SAFARI
SCREEN
SCRIPT
SCROLL
SECTOR
SERVER
SMILEY
SPIDER
SPRITE
STRING
TABLET
THREAD
TROJAN
UNPACK
UPLOAD
USENET
VECTOR
WIZARD

7
ADDRESS
ANDROID
ARCHIVE
ARPANET
BARCODE
BROWSER
CHANNEL
CHIPSET

CLIP ART
COMMAND
COMPILE
COUNTER
CRACKER
CRAWLER
DECIMAL
DEFAULT
DENSITY
DESKTOP
DINGBAT
DISPLAY
DYNAMIC
END USER
EURONET
FIDONET
FIREFOX
FRACTAL
GAME PAD
GARBAGE
● GATEWAY
HASHING
HISTORY
HOT SPOT
INSTALL
JOURNAL
MAILBOX
MALWARE
MESSAGE
MONITOR
NESTING
NETWORK
NEWLINE
OFF-LINE
PALMTOP
PARSING
PLOTTER
PODCAST
PRINTER
PRIVACY
PROGRAM
RESTORE
SCANNER
SORTING
SPOTIFY
SPYWARE
STORAGE
TASK BAR
TIMEOUT
TOOL BAR
TOOLBOX
TWITTER
UPGRADE
WINDOWS
WYSIWYG

8
ALIASING
ANALYZER
BETA TEST
BOOKMARK
CALL BACK
CHAT ROOM
CHECK BOX

COMPILER
COMPRESS
COMPUTER
DESELECT
DIGITIZE
DINGBATS
DISKETTE
DOT PITCH
DOWNLOAD
DOWNTIME
EMOTICON
ETHERNET
EXTRANET
FACEBOOK
FEED BACK
FILENAME
FIREWALL
FIRMWARE
FREEWARE
GIGABYTE
GRAPHICS
GREEKING
HALFWORD
HARD DISK
HARDWIRE
HELP DESK
HOME PAGE
INTERNET
INTRANET
JOYSTICK
KEYBOARD
KILOBYTE
LANGUAGE
LIGHT PEN
LINEFEED
LINKEDIN
MEGABYTE
NAVIGATE
NOTEBOOK
OPERATOR
PASSWORD
PLATFORM
PRINTOUT
PROTOCOL
QUADWORD
REAL TIME
RECOVERY
REGISTER
REPEATER
RETRIEVE
ROBOTICS
SECURITY
SNAPCHAT
SOFTWARE
TEMPLATE
TERMINAL
TYPEFACE
UNDELETE
WHATSAPP
WILD CARD

9
ALGORITHM
ASSEMBLER

BACKSPACE
BANDWIDTH
BENCHMARK
BOOTSTRAP
BROADBAND
BROADCAST
CARTRIDGE
CHARACTER
CLIPBOARD
CLOCK RATE
CONFIGURE
CYBERCAFE
DATA ENTRY
DECOMPILE
DIGITIZER
DIRECTORY
DOWNGRADE
EASTER EGG
E-COMMERCE
EXTENSION
FIXED DISK
FLOWCHART
FRAMEWORK
GREY SCALE
HANDSHAKE
HASH TABLE
HEARTBEAT
HEURISTIC
HIBERNATE
HIGHLIGHT
HYPERLINK
HYPERTEXT
INFECTION
INTERFACE
INTERRUPT
INSTAGRAM
IP ADDRESS
MAGIC WAND
MAINFRAME
MICROCHIP
NEWSGROUP
OVERWRITE
PHREAKING
POP-UP-MENU
PRIME TIME
PROCESSOR
RENDERING
SHAREWARE
SMART CARD
SOUND CARD
STREAMING
THESAURUS
TRACKBALL
UNINSTALL
USER GROUP
VOICE MAIL
WALLPAPER
WEBMASTER
WRAP-AROUND

10
ANNOTATION
ATTACHMENT
BIOMETRICS

BLACKBERRY
BOTTLENECK
CLOCK CYCLE
CLOCK SPEED
CYBERCRIME
CYBERSPACE
DATA TABLET
DIAGNOSTIC
DOWNSIZING
ENCRYPTION
FILE SERVER
FLOPPY DISK
MULTIMEDIA
NAVIGATION
NETIQUETTE
NEWSLETTER
OPEN SOURCE
PEER-TO-PEER
PERIPHERAL
PREPROCESS
PROGRAMMER
REWRITABLE
SERIAL PORT
SMARTPHONE
SOURCE CODE
TEXT EDITOR
TRANSISTOR
VACUUM TUBE
WEB ADDRESS
WELL-FORMED
WHITEBOARD

11
ACCUMULATOR
ADDRESS BOOK
APPLICATION
BAND PRINTER
BELT PRINTER
BETA TESTING
BLOGOSPHERE
BOILER PLATE
CLICKSTREAM
COMPACT DISK
COMPILATION
COMPRESSION
COPROCESSOR
CUT AND PASTE
CYBERNETICS
DOTS PER INCH
DRUM PRINTER
INTELLIGENT
INTERACTIVE
INTERPRETER
LINE PRINTER
MOTHERBOARD
MULTIPLEXER
OPTICAL DISK
PLUG AND PLAY
POINT OF SALE
PRINT SERVER
PROGRAMMING
SCREEN SAVER
SEMANTIC NET
SPREADSHEET

STAR NETWORK
SYNCHRONOUS
TIME SHARING
TRANSCEIVER
TROJAN HORSE
VIRTUAL DISK
WORKSTATION

12
ALPHANUMERIC
ASSEMBLY CODE
ASYNCHRONOUS
BROADCASTING
BUBBLE MEMORY
CHAIN PRINTER
CHARACTER SET
CLICK AND DRAG
COLOR PRINTER
CONTROL PANEL
DEVICE DRIVER
DIRECT ACCESS
ENCRYPTION
EXPERT SYSTEM
GRAPHICS CARD
HOUSEKEEPING
INTERNET CAFE
LASER PRINTER
MEMORY STICK
MINICOMPUTER
MULTITASKING
OPTICAL MOUSE
PARALLEL PORT
PERSONAL DATA
PROGRAM SUITE
PULL-DOWN MENU
SEARCH ENGINE
SPELL CHECKER
USER-FRIENDLY
WORLDWIDE WEB

13
ADMINISTRATOR
AUTHORING TOOL
BAR-CODE READER
BARREL PRINTER
BULLETIN BOARD
COMPATIBILITY
CYBERCOMMERCE
DATA STRUCTURE
DOT COM COMPANY
DYNAMIC MEMORY
FLOPTICAL DISK
GRID COMPUTING
HYPERTEXT LINK
IMPACT PRINTER
INK-JET PRINTER
LETTER QUALITY
MICROCOMPUTER
NEURAL NETWORK
PRIMARY MEMORY
SUPERCOMPUTER
TELECOMMUTING
USER INTERFACE
WINDOW MANAGER

231

WORD PROCESSOR

14
CARRIAGE RETURN
CATHODE-RAY TUBE
DATA CONTROLLER
DATA PROCESSING
ELECTRONIC MAIL
FLAT-BED PLOTTER
FRAGMENTATTION
MULTITHREADING
PAPER-TAPE PUNCH
READ-ONLY MEMORY
RICH TEXT FORMAT
SYSTEMS ANALYST
SYSTEM SOFTWARE
THEOREM PROVING
UTILITY PROGRAM
VIRTUAL REALITY
VOICE ACTIVATED
VOLATILE MEMORY
WORD PROCESSING

15
ACOUSTIC COUPLER
BATCH PROCESSING
BUNDLED SOFTWARE
CHARACTER STRING
CONTROL SEQUENCE
CRYOGENIC MEMORY
DATABASE PROGRAM
ELECTRONIC BRAIN
MULTIPROCESSING
OPERATING SYSTEM
PAPER-TAPE READER
RULE-BASED SYSTEM
SPELLING CHECKER
TERMINAL DISPLAY
WIDE AREA NETWORK
WIRELESS NETWORK

16
BUBBLE-JET PRINTER
COMPILED LANGUAGE
DIAL-IP NETWORKING
DIGITAL AUDIO TAPE
DOMAIN NAME SYSTEM
DOT-MATRIX PRINTER
INSTANT MESSAGING

INTERNET PROTOCOL
LOCAL AREA NETWORK
PERSONAL COMPUTER
SOLID-STATE MEMORY
TELECONFERENCING
TOKEN RING NETWORK
TURNKEY OPERATION
VIDEO DISPLAY UNIT

17
DAISYWHEEL PRINTER
DESKTOP PUBLISHING
HIGH-LEVEL LANGUAGE
INTEGRATED CIRCUIT
NEAR LETTER QUALITY
OPTICAL RESOLUTION
PARALLEL PROCESSOR
PERSONAL ORGANIZER

18
FOR YOUR INFORMATION
IONOGRAPHIC PRINTER
MULTI-CORE PROCESSOR
PRINTABLE CHARACTER
RANDOM-ACCESS MEMORY
RELATIONAL DATABASE
SPREADSHEET PROGRAM
UNIVERSAL SERIAL BUS

19
BULLETIN BOARD SYSTEM
COMPUTER-AIDED DESIGN
GARBAGE IN GARBAGE OUT
PERCEPTUAL COMPUTING
PROGRAMMING LANGUAGE
SEMICONDUCTOR MEMORY
TOUCHSCREEN SOFTWARE
UNIVERSL POWER SUPPLY

20
APPLICATIONS SOFTWARE
HEXADECIMAL CHARACTER
HIERARCHICAL DATABASE
LIQUID CRYSTAL DISPLAY
MODULATOR-DEMODULATOR

21
CENTRAL PROCESSING UNIT
COMPUTER-BASED LEARNING

DIGITAL SUBSCRIBER LINE
INFORMATION TECHNOLOGY
VIRTUAL PRIVATE NETWORK

22
ARTIFICIAL INTELLIGENCE
COMMON GATEWAY INTERFACE
GRAPHICAL USER INTERFACE
INTERNET ACCESS PROVIDER
MEAN TIME BETWEEN FAILURE
WHAT YOU SEE IS WHAT YOU
  GET

23+
ACCELERATED GRAPHICS PORT
COMPUTER-AIDED
  MANUFACTURE
COMPUTER-ASSISTED LEARNING
ENHANCED GRAPHICS ADAPTER
FLOATING-POINT OPERATION
FREQUENTLY ASKED QUESTIONS
INTEGRATED DRIVE
  ELECTRONICS
INTERNET SERVICE PROVIDER
NATURAL-LANGUAGE
  PROCESSING
PERSONAL DIGITAL ASSISTANT
TOUCHSCREEN HARDCOPY
  DEVICE
UNINTERRUPTIBLE POWER
  SUPPLY
OPTICAL CHARACTER
  RECOGNITION
PROGRAMMABLE READ-ONLY
  MEMORY
INDUSTRY STANDARD
  ARCHITECTURE
SMALL COMPUTER SYSTEMS
  INTERFACE
INTELLIGENT CHARACTER
  RECOGNITION
INTEGRATED SERVICES DIGITAL
  NETWORK
ERASABLE PROGRAMMABLE
  READ-ONLY MEMORY

COMPUTER LANGUAGES

4GL	FORTRAN	POSTSCRIPT
ADA	GO	PROLOG
ALGOL	HASKELL	PYTHON
APL	IPL	QUICKBASIC
ASSEMBLER	JAVA	RPG
ASSEMBLY LANGUAGE	JAVASCRIPT	RUBY
AUTOCODE	JOVIAL	SCALA
BASH	LISP	SGML
C	LOGO	SNOBOL
C++	LUA	SQL
CLOJURE	MACLISP	SWIFT
COBOL	PASCAL	TCL
COMAL	PERL	UCSD PASCAL
COMMON LISP	PHP	VBA
CORAL	PILOT	VISUAL BASIC
CPL	PL/1	VISUAL BASIC FOR
CSL	PL/360	APPLICATIONS
EULISP	POP-11	VISUAL C++
FORTH	POP-2	WORD BASIC

PLANETS AND SATELLITES

MAIN PLANETS (NAMED SATELLITES)

MERCURY

VENUS

EARTH (MOON)

MARS (PHOBOS, DEIMOS)

JUPITER (METIS, ADRASTEA, AMALTHEA, THEBE, IO, EUROPA, GANYMEDE, CALLISTO, LEDA, HIMALIA, LYSITHEA, ELARA, IOCASTE, PRAXIDIKE, HARPALYKE, ANANKE, ISONOE, ERINOME, TAYGETE, CHALDENE, CARME, PASIPHAE, KALYKE, MAGACLITE, SINOPE, CALLIRRHOE)

SATURN (PAN, ATLAS, PROMETHEUS, PANDORA, EPIMETHEUS, JANUS, MIMAS, ENCELADUS, TETHYS, TELESTO, CALYPSO, DIONE, HELENE, RHEA, TITAN, HYPERION, IAPETUS, PHOEBE)

URANUS (MIRANDA, ARIEL, UMBRIEL, TITANIA, OBERON, CALIBAN, STEPHANO, SYCORAX, PROSPERO, SETEBOS, CORDELIA, OPHELIA, BIANCA, CRESSIDA, DESDEMONA, JOLIET, PORTIA, ROSALIND, BELINDA, PUCK, CALIBAN, SYCORAX)

NEPTUNE (TRITON, NEREID, NAIAD, THALASSA, DESPINA, LARISSA, GALATEA, PROTEUS, LARISSA)

MINOR PLANETS AND PLANETOIDS

ACHILLES	HAUMEA
ADONIS	HEBE
AGAMEMNON	HEPHAISTOS
AMOR	HERMES
APOLLO	HIDALGO
ASTRAEA	HYGIEA
ATEN	ICARUS
CASTALIA	IDA
CERES	IRIS
CHIRON	JUNO
DACTYL	MAKEMAKE
DAVIDA	MATHILDE
ERIS	PALLAS
EROS	PLUTO
EUNOMIA	QUAOAR
EUPHROSYNE	SEDNA
EUROPA	THE GOBLIN
GASPRA	TOUTATIS
GEOGRAPHOS	VESTA

COMETS

4
FAYE

5
BIELA
ENCKE
KOPFF

6
HALLEY
OLBERS
TUTTLE

7
BENNETT
D'ARREST
VÄISÄLÄ
WHIPPLE

8
BORRELLY
DAYLIGHT
HALE-BOPP
KOHOUTEK
WESTPHAL

9
COMAS SOLÀ
CROMMELIN
HYAKUTAKE

10
PONS-BROOKS
SCHAUMASSE

11
AREND-ROLAND

SWIFT-TUTTLE

12
PONS-WINNECKE

13
SHOEMAKER-LEVY
STEPHAN-OTERMA

14
BRONSEN-METCALF

15
GIACOBINI-ZINNER
GRIGG-SKIELLERUP

NAMED NEAREST AND BRIGHTEST STARS

4
ROSS
VEGA
WOLF

5
CYGNI
DENEB
RIGEL
SIRUS
SPICA

6
ADHARA
ALTAIR
CASTOR
CRUCIS
KRUGER
LUYTEN
POLLUX
SHAULA
SIRIUS

7
ANTARES

CANOPUS
CAPELLA
LALANDE
PROCYON
REGULUS
TAU CETI

8
ACHERNAR
ARCTURUS
BARNARD'S
CENTAURI
KAPTEYN'S

9
ALDEBARAN
BELLATRIX
FOMALHAUT

10+
BETELGEUSE
EPSILON INDI
ALPHA CENTAURI
EPSILON ERIDANI
PROXIMA CENTAURI

THE CONSTELLATIONS

3
ARA
LEO

4
APUS
CRUX
GRUS
LYNX
LYRA
PAVO
VELA

5
ARIES
CETUS
DRACO
HYDRA
INDUS
LEPUS
LIBRA
LUPUS
MENSA
MUSCA
NORMA
ORION

PYXIS
VIRGO

6
ANTLIA
AQUILA
AURIGA
BOÖTES
CAELUM
CANCER
CARINA
CORVUS
CRATER

CYGNUS
DORADO
FORNAX
GEMINI
HYDRUS
OCTANS
PICTOR
PISCES
PUPPIS
SCUTUM
TAURUS
TUCANA
VOLANS

7
CEPHEUS
COLUMBA
LACERTA
PEGASUS
PERSEUS
PHOENIX
SAGITTA
SERPENS
SEXTANS

8
AQUARIUS
CIRCINUS
EQUULEUS
ERIDANUS
HERCULES
LEO MINOR

SCORPIUS
SCULPTOR

9
ANDROMEDA
CENTAURUS
CHAMELEON
DELPHINUS
MONOCEROS
OPHIUCHUS
RETICULUM
URSA MAJOR
URSA MINOR
VULPECULA

10
CANIS MAJOR
CANIS MINOR

CASSIOPEIA
HOROLOGIUM
TRIANGULUM

11
CAPRICORNUS
SAGITTARIUS
TELESCOPIUM

12+
CAMELOPARDALIS
CANES VENATICI
COMA BERENICES
CORONA AUSTRALIS
CORONA BOREALIS
MICROSCOPIUM
PISCIS AUSTRINUS
TRIANGULUM AUSTRALE

METEOR SHOWERS

6
LYRIDS
URSIDS

7
CYGNIDS
LEONIDS
TAURIDS

8
CEPHEIDS
GEMINIDS
ORIONIDS
PERSEIDS

10
AUSTRALIDS

OPHIUCHIDS
PHOENICIDS

11
QUADRANTIDS

12
CAPRICORNIDS

ASTRONOMERS ROYAL

JOHN FLAMSTEED (1675–1719)
EDMUND HALLEY (1720–42)
JAMES BRADLEY (1742–62)
NATHANIEL BLISS (1762–64)
NEVIL MASKELYNE (1765–1811)
JOHN POND (1811–35)
SIR GEORGE BIDDELL AIRY (1835–81)
SIR WILLIAM H M CHRISTIE (1881–1910)

SIR FRANK WATSON DYSON (1910–33)
SIR HAROLD SPENCER JONES (1933–55)
SIR RICHARD WOOLLEY (1955–71)
SIR MARTIN RYLE (1972–82)
SIR FRANCIS GRAHAM-SMITH (1982–91)
SIR ARNOLD WOLFENDALE (1991–95)
SIR MARTIN REES, BARON REES OF LUDLOW
   (1995–   )

MANNED SPACE PROGRAMS

VOSTOK (Russian; 1961–63)
MERCURY (US; 1961–63)
VOSKHOD (Russian; 1964–65)
GEMINI (US; 1965–66)
APOLLO (US; 1967–72)
SOYUZ (Russian; 1967–   )
SALYUT (Russian; 1971–86)

SKYLAB (US; 1973–79)
SPACE SHUTTLE (US; 1981–   )
SPACELAB (US; 1983–92)
MIR (Russian; 1986–99)
INTERNATIONAL SPACE STATION (1998–   )
SHENZHOU (2003)
TIANGONG (2012)

GEOLOGICAL TIME SCALE

ERA	PERIOD	EPOCH
CENOZOIC	QUATERNARY	HOLOCENE
		PLEISTOCENE
	TERTIARY	PIOCENE
		IOCENE
		OLIGOCENE
		EOCENE
		PALAEOCENE
MESOZOIC	CRETACEOUS	
	JURASSIC	
	TRIASSIC	
PALAEOZOIC	PERMIAN	
	CARBONIFEROUS	
	DEVONIAN	
	SILURIAN	
	ORDOVICIAN	
	CAMBRIAN	
PRECAMBRIAN	PRECAMBRIAN	

PREHISTORIC ANIMALS

8
EOHIPPUS
RUTIODON
SMILODON

9
IGUANODON
TRACHODON

10
ALLOSAURUS
ALTISPINAX
BAROSAURUS
DIPLODOCUS
DRYOSAURUS
EUPARKERIA
MESOHIPPUS
ORTHOMERUS
PLIOHIPPUS
PTERANODON
STEGOCERAS

11
ANATOSAURUS
ANCHISAURUS
APATOSAURUS
APHANERAMMA
COELOPHYSIS
DEINONYCHUS
KRITOSAURUS
MANDASUCHUS
MERYCHIPPUS
MONOCLONIUS
POLACANTHUS

PTERODACTYL
RIOJASAURUS
SAUROLOPHUS
SCOLOSAURUS
SPINOSAURUS
STEGOSAURUS
TARBOSAURUS
TRICERATOPS

12
ANKYLOSAURUS
BRONTOSAURUS
CAMPTOSAURUS
CERATOSAURUS
CHASMOSAURUS
DEINOCHEIRUS
HYLAEOSAURUS
KENTROSAURUS
LAMBEOSAURUS
MEGALOSAURUS
ORNITHOMIMUS
OURANOSAURUS
PLATEOSAURUS
TICINOSUCHUS

13
BRACHIOSAURUS
COMPSOGNATHUS
CORYTHOSAURUS
DESMATOSUCHUS
DILOPHOSAURUS
EDMONTOSAURUS
ERYTHROSUCHUS
HYPSELOSAURUS

HYPSILOPHODON
LESOTHOSAURUS
PANOPLOSAURUS
PENTACERATOPS
PROTOCERATOPS
PTERODACTYLUS
SCELIDOSAURUS
SCLEROMOCHLUS
STYRACOSAURUS
TENONTOSAURUS
TYRANNOSAURUS

14
BALUCHITHERIUM
CETIOSAURISCUS
CHASMATOSAURUS
EUOPLOCEPHALUS
MASSOSPONDYLUS
PSITTACOSAURUS
THESCELOSAURUS

15
PARASAUROLOPHUS
PROCHENEOSAURUS

16
PACHYRHINOSAURUS
PROCOMPSOGNATHUS

17
HETERODONTOSAURUS

18
PACHYCEPHALOSAURUS

EARLY HOMINIDS

AFRICAN EVE (*Australopithecus afarensis*)
BODO SKULL (*Homo heidelbergensis*)
BOXGROVE MAN (*Homo heidelbergensis*)
CRO-MAGNON MAN (*Homo sapiens*)
FLAT-FACED KENYA MAN (*Kenyanthropus platyops*)
HANDY MAN (*Homo habilis*)
HEIDELBERG MAN (*Homo heidelbergensis*)
HERTO MAN (*Homo sapiens idaltu*)
JAVA MAN (*Homo erectus*)
KABWE SKULL (*Homo heidelbergensis*)
KENYA MAN (*Kenyanthropus platyops*)
LUCY (*Australopithecus afarensis*)
MAUER MANDIBLE (*Homo heidelbergensis*)
MILLENNIUM MAN (*Orrorin turgensis*)
MITOCHONDRIAL EVE
MUNGO MAN (*Homo sapiens*)
NANJING MAN (*Homo erectus*)
NEBRASKA MAN (*fake*)
PEKING MAN (*Homo erectus*)
PILTDOWN MAN (*fake*)
QATZEH SKULL (*Homo heidelbergensis*)
RHODESIAN MAN (*Homo heidelbergensis*)
SOUTHERN APE (*Australopithecus*)
TAUNG CHILD (*Australopithecus afarensis*)
TURKANA BOY (*Homo erectus*)
UPRIGHT MAN (*Homo erectus*)

ROCKS AND MINERALS

4
GOLD
MICA
OPAL
RUBY
TALC

5
AGATE
BERYL
BORAX
EMERY
FLINT
SHALE
SHARD
SKARN
TOPAZ
TRONA

6
ACMITE
ALBITE
ARKOSE
AUGITE
BARITE
BASALT
COPPER
DACITE

DUNITE
GABBRO
GALENA
GARNET
GNEISS
GYPSUM
HALITE
HAÜYNE
HUMITE
ILLITE
LEVYNE
MINIUM
NORITE
NOSEAN
PELITE
PYRITE
PYROPE
QUARTZ
RUTILE
SALITE
SCHIST
SCHORL
SILICA
SILVER
SPHENE
SPINEL
URTITE
ZIRCON

7
ALNOITE
ALTAITE
ALUNITE
ANATASE
APATITE
ARSENIC
AXINITE
AZURITE
BARYTES
BAUXITE
BIOTITE
BISMUTH
BORNITE
BRECCIA
BRUCITE
CALCITE
CALOMEL
CELSIAN
CITRINE
COESITE
CUPRITE
DIAMOND
DIORITE
EMERALD
EPIDOTE
FELSITE
FOYAITE

GAHNITE
GEDRITE
GRANITE
GUMMITE
HELVITE
HESSITE
HOPEITE
HUNTITE
IJOLITE
JADEITE
KAINITE
KERNITE
KYANITE
LEUCITE
LIGNITE
MELLITE
MULLITE
OLIVINE
ORTHITE
RASPITE
REALGAR
SPARITE
SYENITE
SYLVITE
THORITE
THULITE
ZEOLITE
ZINCITE
ZOISITE

8
AEGIRINE
ALLANITE
ALUNOGEN
ANALCIME
ANALCITE
ANDESINE
ANDORITE
ANKERITE
ANTIMONY
ARCANITE
AUGELITE
AUTUNITE
BASANITE
BIXBYITE
BLOEDITE
BLUE JOHN
BOEHMITE
BORACITE
BRAGGITE
BRAUNITE
BRAVOITE
BRONZITE
BROOKITE
CALAMINE
CHIOLITE
CHLORITE
CHROMITE
CINNABAR
CORUNDUM
CROCOITE
CRYOLITE
CUBANITE
DATOLITE

DIALLAGE
DIASPORE
DIGENITE
DIOPSIDE
DIOPTASE
DOLERITE
DOLOMITE
ECLOGITE
ENARGITE
EPSOMITE
ESSEXITE
EULYTITE
EUXENITE
FAYALITE
FELDSPAR
FLUORITE
GIBBSITE
GOETHITE
GRAPHITE
HANKSITE
HAWAIITE
HEMATITE
HYACINTH
IDOCRASE
ILMENITE
IODYRITE
JAROSITE
LAZURITE
LIMONITE
LITHARGE
MARSHITE
MEIONITE
MELANITE
MELILITE
MESOLITE
MIERSITE
MIMETITE
MONAZITE
MONETITE
MYLONITE
NEPHRITE
ORPIMENT
PARISITE
PERIDOTE
PERTHITE
PETALITE
PLATINUM
PORPHYRY
PREHNITE
PSAMMITE
PYRIBOLE
PYROXENE
RHYOLITE
ROCKSALT
SANIDINE
SAPPHIRE
SELLAITE
SIDERITE
SMECTITE
SODALITE
STANNITE
STEATITE
STIBNITE

STILBITE
STOLSITE
STRUVITE
TITANITE
TONALITE
TRACHYTE
VARISITE
VATERITE
WEHRLITE
WURTZITE
XENOTIME

9
ACANTHITE
ALMANDINE
ALUMINITE
AMPHIBOLE
ANDRADITE
ANGLESITE
ANHYDRITE
ANORTHITE
ARAGONITE
ARGENTITE
ATACAMITE
BENITOITE
BRIMSTONE
BROMYRITE
BUNSENITE
BYTOWNITE
CARNALITE
CARNOTITE
CELESTITE
CERUSSITE
CHABAZITE
CHINACLAY
COBALTITE
COLUMBITE
COPIAPITE
COTUNNITE
COVELLITE
DANBURITE
DERBYLITE
DIATOMITE
ENSTATITE
ERYTHRITE
EUCAIRITE
EUCLASITE
EUDIALITE
FERBERITE
FIBROLITE
FLUORSPAR
GEHLENITE
GMELINITE
GOSLARITE
GRANULITE
GREYWACKE
GROSSULAR
GRUNERITE
HARMOTOME
HERCYNITE
HERDERITE
HORNSTONE
KAOLINITE
KIESERITE

LANARKITE
LAWSONITE
LEUCITITE
LIMESTONE
LODESTONE
MAGNESITE
MAGNETITE
MALACHITE
MALIGNITE
MANGANITE
MARCASITE
MARGARITE
MARIALITE
MENDIPITE
MICROLITE
MIGMATITE
MILLERITE
MISPICKEL
MONZONITE
MORDENITE
MUGEARITE
MUSCOVITE
NANTOKITE
NATROLITE
NEPHELINE
NICCOLITE
OLDHAMITE
OLIVENITE
PECTOLITE
PENNINITE
PERCYLITE
PERICLASE
PHENAKITE
PHONOLITE
PIGEONITE
PISTACITE
POLLUCITE
POWELLITE
PROUSTITE
PULASKITE
QUARTZITE
RHODONITE
SANDSTONE
SCAPOLITE
SCHEELITE
SCOLECITE
SCORODITE
SMALLTITE
SOAPSTONE
SPODUMENE
STRENGITE
SYLVANITE
TACHYLITE
TANTALITE
TAPIOLITE
THERALITE
THOLEIITE
TREMOLITE
TRIDYMITE
TURQUOISE
URANINITE
VIVIANITE
WAGNERITE

WAVELLITE
WILLEMITE
WITHERITE
WULFENITE
ZEUNERITE

10
ACTINOLITE
ÅKERMANITE
ALABANDITE
ANDALUSITE
ANKARAMITE
ARSENOLITE
BOROLONITE
BOURNONITE
BRONZITITE
CACOXENITE
CALEDONITE
CANCRINITE
CERVANTITE
CHALCEDONY
CHALCOCITE
CHLORITOID
CHRYSOLITE
CLAUDETITE
CLINTONITE
COLEMANITE
CONNELLITE
COQUIMBITE
CORDIERITE
DOUGLASITE
DYSCRASITE
EMPLECTITE
EMPRESSITE
EPIDIORITE
FORSTERITE
GANOMALITE
GARNIERITE
GAYLUSSITE
GEIKIELITE
GLAUBERITE
GLAUCONITE
GREENSTONE
HAMBERGITE
HEULANDITE
HORNBLENDE
HUEBNERITE
IGNIMBRITE
JAMESONITE
KIMBERLITE
LANTHANITE
LAUMONTITE
LAURIONITE
LEPIDOLITE
LHERZOLITE
LIMBURGITE
MASCAGNITE
MATLOCKITE
MEERSCHAUM
MELILITITE
MELTEIGITE
MICROCLINE
MIRABILITE
MOISSANITE

NEWBERYITE
OLIGOCLASE
ORTHOCLASE
PARAGONITE
PEKOVSKITE
PERIDOTITE
PERTHOSITE
PHLOGOPITE
PHOSGENITE
PIEMONTITE
POLYBASITE
PYRALSPITE
PYROCHLORE
PYROLUSITE
PYRRHOTITE
RHYODACITE
RICHTERITE
RIEBECKITE
SAFFLORITE
SAMARSKITE
SAPPHIRINE
SERPENTINE
SHONKINITE
SPERRYLITE
SPHALERITE
STAUROLITE
STERCORITE
STISHOVITE
TESCHENITE
THENARDITE
THOMSONITE
THORIANITE
TORBERNITE
TOURMALINE
TRAVERTINE
TROEGERITE
ULLMANNITE
ULVÓSPINEL
VANADINITE
VITROPHYRE
WEBSTERITE
WHEWELLITE
WOLFRAMITE
ZINCBLENDE

11
ALLEMONTITE
AMBLYGONITE
ANORTHOSITE
APOPHYLLITE
BADDELEYITE
BERTRANDITE
BERYLLONITE
BROCHANTITE
CALCARENITE
CALCILUTITE
CALCIRUDITE
CARBONATITE
CARBORUNDUM
CASSITERITE
CERARGYRITE
CHARNOCKITE
CHIASTOLITE
CHLOANTHITE

CHONDRODITE
CHRYSOBERYL
CHRYSOCOLLA
CLINOCHLORE
COBALTBLOOM
DAUBREELITE
EGLESTONITE
FERROAUGITE
FRANKLINITE
GLAUBER SALT
GLAUCOPHANE
GREENOCKITE
HARZBURGITE
HASTINGSITE
HAUSMANNITE
HYPERSTHENE
ICELAND SPAR
KATOPHORITE
LAPIS LAZULI
LEADHILLITE
LOELLINGITE
MANGANOSITE
MELANTERITE
MOLYBDENITE
MONTROYDITE
NEPHELINITE
NORDMARKITE
PENFIELDITE
PENTLANDITE
PHILLIPSITE
PITCHBLENDE
PLAGIOCLASE
PSILOMELANE
PUMPELLYITE
PYRARGYRITE
PYROCHROITE
RADIOLARITE
ROCK CRYSTAL
SILLIMANITE
SMITHSONITE
SPESSARTITE

TITANAUGITE
TRIPHYLLITE
VALENTINITE
VERMICULITE
VESUVIANITE
VILLIAUMITE
ZINNWALDITE

12
ANORTHOCLASE
ARSENOPYRITE
BISMUTHINITE
BOULANGERITE
CALCISILTITE
CHALCANTHITE
CHALCOPYRITE
CLAY MINERALS
CLINOPTOLITE
CLINOZOISITE
CRISTOBALITE
EDDINGTONITE
FELDSPATHOID
FERGUSSONITE
FLUORAPATITE
GROSSULARITE
HEDENBERGITE
HEMIMORPHITE
LUXULLIANITE
METACINNABAR
MONTICELLITE
PYROMORPHITE
PYROPHYLLITE
RHODOCROSITE
SENARMONTITE
SKUTTERUDITE
STRONTIANITE
SYENODIORITE
TERLINGUAITE
TETRAHEDRITE
THOMSENOLITE
TRACHYBASALT

WOLLASTONITE

13
ANTHOPHYLLITE
BREITHAUPTITE
CLINOPYROXENE
CUMMINGTONITE
JACUPIRANGITE
KALIOPHYLLITE
LEPIDOCROCITE
LITCHFIELDITE
ORTHOPYROXENE
QUARTZARENITE
RHODOCHROSITE
STILPNOMELANE
THERMONATRITE
UNCOMPAHGRITE

14
CRYOLITHIONITE
HYDROMAGNESITE
LECHATELIERITE
LITHIOPHYLLITE
ORTHOQUARTZITE
PSEUDOBROOKITE
RAMMELSBERGITE
TRACHYANDESITE
XANTHOPHYLLITE

15
MONTMORILLONITE
PSEUDOTACHYLITE
STIBIOTANTALITE

16
GALENABISMUTHITE
ORTHOFERROSILITE
PHARMACOSIDERITE

17
HYDROGROSSULARITE
TELLUROBISMUTHITE

ORES

ELEMENT – ore(s)

3
TIN – cassiterite

4
IRON – haematite, magnetite
LEAD – galena
ZINC – sphalerite, smithsonite, calamine

5
BORON – kernite

6
BARIUM – barite, witherite
CERIUM – monazite, bastnaesite
COBALT – cobaltite, smaltite, erythrite

COPPER – malachite, azurite, chalcopyrite, bornite, cuprite
ERBIUM – monazite, bastnaesite
INDIUM – sphalerite, smithsonite, calamine
NICKEL – pentlandite, pyrrhotite
OSMIUM – iridosime
RADIUM – pitchblende, carnotite
SILVER – argentite, horn silver
SODIUM – salt

7
ARSENIC – realgar, orpiment, arsenopyrite
CADMIUM – greenockite
CAESIUM – lepidolite, pollucite
CALCIUM – limestone, gypsum, fluorite
HAFNIUM – zircon

HOLMIUM – monazite
LITHIUM – lepidolite, spodumene
MERCURY – cinnabar
NIOBIUM – columbite-tantalite, pyrochlore, euxenite
RHENIUM – molybdenite
SILICON – silica
THORIUM – monazite
THULIUM – monazite
URANIUM – pitchblende, uraninite, carnotite
YTTRIUM – monazite

8
ANTIMONY – stibnite
CHROMIUM – chromite
LUTETIUM – monazite
PLATINUM – sperrylite
RUBIDIUM – lepidolite
SAMARIUM – monazite, bastnaesite
SCANDIUM – thortveitite, davidite
SELENIUM – pyrites
TANTALUM – columbite-tantalite
THALLIUM – pyrites
TITANIUM – rutile, ilmenite, sphere
TUNGSTEN – wolframite, scheelite

VANADIUM – carnotite, roscoelite, vanadinite

9
ALUMINIUM – bauxite
BERYLLIUM – beryl
GERMANIUM – germanite, argyrodite
LANTHANUM – monazite, bastnaesite
MAGNESIUM – magnesite, dolomite
MANGANESE – pyrolusite, rhodochrosite
NEODYMIUM – monazite, bastnaesite
POTASSIUM – sylvite, carnallite, polyhalite
RUTHENIUM – pentlandite, pyroxinite
STRONTIUM – celestite, strontianite
YTTERBIUM – monazite

10
DYSPROSIUM – monazite, bastnaesite
GADOLINIUM – monazite, bastnaesite
MOLYBDENUM – molybdenite, wulfenite
PHOSPHORUS – apatite

12
PRASEODYMIUM – monazite, bastnaesite
PROTACTINIUM – pitchblende

GEMSTONES

STONE (colour)

4
JADE (green, mauve, brown)
ONYX (various colours, banded)
OPAL (white, milky blue, or black with rainbow-coloured reflections)
RUBY (red)

5
AGATE (brown, red, blue, green, yellow)
BERYL (green, blue, pink)
TOPAZ (usually yellow or colourless)

6
GARNET (red)
ZIRCON (all colours)

7
CITRINE (yellow)
DIAMOND (colourless)

EMERALD (green)

8
AMETHYST (purple)
SAPPHIRE (blue and other colours except red)
SUNSTONE (whitish-red-brown flecked with gold)

9
MALACHITE (dark green banded)
MOONSTONE (white with bluish tinge)
SOAPSTONE (white or greenish)
TURQUOISE (greenish-blue)

10
AQUAMARINE (turquoise, greenish-blue)
BLOODSTONE (green with red spots)
CHALCEDONY (red, brown, grey, or black)
SERPENTINE (usually green or white)
TOURMALINE (all colours)

11
LAPIS LAZULI (deep blue)

CLOUD CLASSIFICATION

ALTOCUMULUS	CIRRUS	NIMBOSTRATUS
ALTOSTRATUS	CUMULONIMBUS	STRATOCUMULUS
CIRROCUMULUS	CUMULUS	STRATUS
CIRROSTRATUS		

NOTABLE WINDS

4
BERG
BISE
BORA
FÖHN

5
BURAN
FOEHN
GIBLI
ZONDA

6
AUSTRU
GHIBLI
HABOOB
KAMSIN
SANIEL
SIMOOM

SOLANO

7
CHINOOK
ETESIAN
GREGALE
KHAMSIN
MELTEMI
MISTRAL
MONSOON
PAMPERO
SIROCCO

8
LEVANTER
LIBECCIO
PAPAGAYO
SANTA ANA
WILLIWAW

9
HARMATTAN
LIBECCHIO
SNOW EATER

10
CAPE DOCTOR
EUROCLYDON
TRAMONTANA
TRAMONTANE
WET CHINOOK
WILLY-WILLY

11
TEHUANTEPEC

12+
BRICKFIELDER
SOUTHERLY BUSTER

MEDICINE AND HEALTH

MEDICAL FIELDS AND SPECIALITIES

7
ANATOMY
MYOLOGY
OTOLOGY
UROLOGY

8
CYTOLOGY
EUGENICS
NOSOLOGY
ONCOLOGY
SEROLOGY

9
AETIOLOGY
ANDROLOGY
AUDIOLOGY
HISTOLOGY
NECROLOGY
NEUROLOGY
ORTHOTICS
OSTEOLOGY
PATHOLOGY
PLEOPTICS
RADIOLOGY
RHINOLOGY

10
CARDIOLOGY
EMBRYOLOGY

GERIATRICS
IMMUNOLOGY
MORPHOLOGY
NEPHROLOGY
OBSTETRICS
ORTHOPTICS
PROCTOLOGY
PSYCHOLOGY
SEMEIOLOGY
TERATOLOGY

11
DERMATOLOGY
GERONTOLOGY
GYNAECOLOGY
HAEMATOLOGY
LARYNGOLOGY
LOGOPAEDICS
PAEDIATRICS
RADIOGRAPHY
STOMATOLOGY

12
CYTOGENETICS
EPHEBIATRICS
EPIDEMIOLOGY
ORTHOPAEDICS
PHARMACOLOGY
RADIOBIOLOGY
RHEUMATOLOGY

SYNDESMOLOGY
THERAPEUTICS
TRAUMATOLOGY

13
ENDOCRINOLOGY
OPHTHALMOLOGY
PSYCHOMETRICS

14
OTOLARYNGOLOGY
SYMPTOMATOLOGY

15
DERMATOGLYPHICS
NEUROPHYSIOLOGY
PSYCHOPATHOLOGY

16
GASTROENTEROLOGY
PSYCHOGERIATRICS
PSYCHOPHYSIOLOGY

17+
COGNITIVE PSYCHOLOGY
INTERVENTIONAL RADIOLOGY
NUCLEAR CARDIOLOGY
OTORHINO-LARYNGOLOGY
PSYCHOLINGUISTICS
PSYCHO-PHARMACOLOGY

MAJOR ARTERIES

AORTA
BRACHIAL
CAROTID
FEMORAL
HEPATIC

ILIAC
INNOMINATE
MESENTERIC
PULMONARY
RADIAL

RENAL
SUBCLAVIAN
THORACIC
TIBIAL
ULNAR

MAJOR VEINS

BASILIC
BRACHIAL
CEPHALIC
FEMORAL
HEPATIC
HEPATIC PORTAL

ILIAC
INFERIOR VENA CAVA
JUGULAR
PULMONARY
RENAL

SAPHENOUS
SUBCLAVIAN
SUPERIOR VENA CAVA
SUPRARENAL
TIBIAL

ALTERNATIVE THERAPIES

4
YOGA

5
REIKI

6
T'AI CHI

7
CHI KUNG
CUPPING
FASTING
HEALING
MASSAGE
ROLFING
SHIATSU

8
AYURVEDA
FENG SHUI

9
BREATHING
DREAMWORK
RADIONICS
SHAMANISM

10
ART THERAPY
BIORHYTHMS
HELLERWORK
HOMEOPATHY
MEDITATION
MYOTHERAPY
OSTEOPATHY
RELAXATION

11
ACUPRESSURE
ACUPUNCTURE
BATES METHOD
BIOFEEDBACK

COUNSELLING
FELDENKRAIS
MINDFULNESS
MOXIBUSTION
NATUROPATHY
PSYCHODRAMA
REFLEXOLOGY

12
AROMATHERAPY
CHIROPRACTIC
HYDROTHERAPY
HYPNOTHERAPY
LIGHT THERAPY
SOUND THERAPY
TREE REMEDIES

13
BIOENERGETICS
COLOUR THERAPY
FOOD COMBINING
PSYCHOTHERAPY
VISUALIZATION

14
BOWEN TECHNIQUE
CRYSTAL HEALING
DIETARY THERAPY
FLOWER REMEDIES
GESTALT THERAPY
HERBAL MEDICINE
ROSEN TECHNIQUE
TRAGER APPROACH

15
CELLOID MINERALS
ENCOUNTER GROUPS
ENERGY THERAPIES
GEOPATHIC ENERGY
MACROBIOTIC DIET
MAGNETIC THERAPY
POLARITY THERAPY

PSIONIC MEDICINE
PSYCHOSYNTHESIS
SCHUESSLER SALTS
THALASSOTHERAPY

16
COGNITIVE THERAPY
FLOTATION THERAPY
SPIRITUAL HEALING
THERAPEUTIC TOUCH

17
AUTOGENIC TRAINING
COLONIC IRRIGATION
CRANIAL OSTEOPATHY

18
ALEXANDER TECHNIQUE
APPLIED KINESIOLOGY
BACH FLOWER REMEDIES
MEGAVITAMINTHERAPY
NUTRITIONAL THERAPY

19
CRANIOSACRAL THERAPY
EXPRESSION THERAPIES

20+
BIOCHEMIC TISSUE SALTS
CHINESE HERBAL MEDICINE
ELECTROCRYSTAL THERAPY
ELECTROMAGNETIC THERAPY
ENVIRONMENTAL THERAPIES
EXTERNAL VISUALIZATION
GEM AND MINERAL ESSENCES
INTERNAL VISUALIZATION
METAMORPHIC TECHNIQUE
ORIENTAL HERBAL MEDICINE
TRADITIONAL CHINESE
    MEDICINE
TRANSACTIONAL ANALYSIS
TRANSCENDENTAL MEDITATION

THE EAR

ANVIL
AUDITORY NERVE
BASILAR MEMBRANE
COCHLEA
EARDRUM
EUSTACHIAN TUBE
FENESTRA OVALIS
FENESTRA ROTUNDA
HAMMER
INCUS
INNER EAR

LABYRINTH
MALLEUS
MEMBRANE OF REISSNER
MIDDLE EAR
ORGAN OF CORTI
OSSICLES
OVAL WINDOW
PINNA
RECEPTOR CELLS
ROUND WINDOW
SACCULE

SCALA MEDIA
SCALA TYMPANI
SCALA VESTIBULI
SEMICIRCULAR CANAL
STAPES
STIRRUP
TECTORIAL MEMBRANE
TUNNEL OF CORTI
TYMPANIC MEMBRANE
UTRICLE
VESTIBULAR NERVE

THE EYE

AQUEOUS HUMOUR
BLIND SPOT
CHOROID
CILIARY BODY
CONE
CONJUNCTIVA
CORNEA

EYELASH
FOVEA
HYALOID CANAL
IRIS
LACRIMAL GLAND
LENS
MEIBOMIAN GLAND

OPTIC NERVE
PUPIL
RETINA
ROD
SCLERA
VITREOUS HUMOUR
YELLOW SPOT

MUSCLES

4
PSOAS

5
TERES

6
BICEPS
RECTUS
SOLEUS
VASTUS

7
DELTOID
GLUTEUS
ILIACUS
TRICEPS

8
ANCONEUS
MASSETER
OPPONENS

PECTORAL
PERONEUS
PLATYSMA
POSTURAL
RHOMBOID
SCALENUS
SERRATUS
SKELETAL
TIBIALIS

9
DEPRESSOR
ILIOPSOAS
MYLOHYOID
OBTURATOR
POPLITEUS
QUADRATUS
SARTORIUS
SPHINCTER
SUPINATOR
TRAPEZIUS

VOLUNTARY

10
BRACHIALIS
BUCCINATOR
EPICRANIUS
HYOGLOSSUS
QUADRICEPS
STYLOHYOID
TEMPORALIS

11
ORBICULARIS
STERNOHYOID

12
STYLOGLOSSUS

13+
GASTROCNEMIUS
STERNOMASTOID
STERNOCLEIDOMASTOID

BONES

3
RIB

4
ULNA

5
ANVIL
COSTA
FEMUR
ILIUM
INCUS
PUBIS
SKULL
SPINE
TALUS
TIBIA
VOMER

6
CARPAL
CARPUS
COCCYX
CUBOID
FIBULA
HALLUX

HAMMER
PELVIS
RACHIS
RADIUS
SACRUM
STAPES
TARSAL
TARSUS

7
CRANIUM
HIPBONE
HUMERUS
ISCHIUM
JAWBONE
KNEECAP
KNEEPAN
MALLEUS
MASTOID
MAXILLA
PATELLA
PHALANX
SCAPULA
STERNUM
STIRRUP

8
BACKBONE
CLAVICLE
HEEL BONE
MANDIBLE
SCAPHOID
SHINBONE
SPHENOID
VERTEBRA

9
ANKLEBONE
CALCANCUS
CHEEKBONE
FUNNY BONE
HYOID BONE
MAXILLARY
NASAL BONE
PHALANGES
THIGHBONE
WRISTBONE

10
ASTRAGALUS
BREASTBONE
CANNON BONE

COLLARBONE
HAUNCH BONE
METACARPAL
METACARPUS
METATARSAL
METATARSUS

11
ETHMOID BONE
FLOATING RIB
FRONTAL BONE

12
PARIETAL BONE
SPINAL COLUMN
TEMPORAL BONE

13
OCCIPITAL BONE
SESAMOID BONES
SHOULDER BLADE
ZYGOMATIC BONE

14+
INNOMINATE BONE
VERTEBRAL COLUMN

GLANDS

5
LIVER
SWEAT

6
BUCCAL
PINEAL
TARSAL
THYMUS

7
ADRENAL

COWPER'S
GASTRIC
MAMMARY
PAROTID
THYROID

8
BRUNNER'S
DUCTLESS
EXOCRINE
PANCREAS
PROSTATE

SALIVARY

9
ENDOCRINE
MEIBOMIAN
PITUITARY
PREPUTIAL
SEBACEOUS

10
BARTHOLIN'S
SUBLINGUAL

SUPRARENAL
VESTIBULAR

11
LIEBERKÜHN'S
PARATHYROID

12
SUBMAXILLARY

13
BULBOURETHRAL
SUBMANDIBULAR

SURGICAL OPERATIONS

7
MYOTOMY – MUSCLE
LOBOTOMY – NERVE FIBRES FROM FRONTAL LOBE
OF BRAIN

8
MYECTOMY – MUSCLE
TENOTOMY – TENDON
VAGOTOMY – VAGUS NERVE
VASOTOMY – SPERM DUCT

9
AMNIOTOMY – AMNIOTIC MEMBRANES
COLECTOMY – COLON
COLOSTOMY – COLON
COLPOTOMY – VAGINA
CORDOTOMY – PART OF SPINAL CORD
CYSTOTOMY – BLADDER
GONIOTOMY – DUCT IN EYE
ILEECTOMY – ILEUM
ILEOSTOMY – ILEUM
IRIDOTOMY – IRIS
LEUCOTOMY – NERVE FIBRES IN BRAIN
LITHOTOMY – KIDNEY STONE
LOBECTOMY – LOBE OF AN ORGAN
MYOPLASTY – MUSCLE
NEUROTOMY – NERVE
OSTECTOMY – BONE
OSTEOTOMY – BONE
OTOPLASTY – EAR
PUBIOTOMY – PUBIC BONE
PYELOTOMY – PELVIS OF KIDNEY
RHIZOTOMY – NERVE ROOTS
THYROTOMY – THYROID GLAND
TOPECTOMY – PART OF BRAIN
VALVOTOMY – HEART VALVE
VASECTOMY – SPERM DUCT

10
ANTRECTOMY – PART OF STOMACH
ANTROSTOMY – BONE CAVITY
APICECTOMY – ROOT OF TOOTH
ARTHROTOMY – JOINT CAPSULE
CAECOSTOMY – CAECUM
CORDECTOMY – VOCAL CORD
CRANIOTOMY – SKULL
CYSTECTOMY – BLADDER
CYSTOSTOMY – BLADDER
EMBRYOTOMY – FETUS
ENTEROTOMY – INTESTINE
EPISIOTOMY – VAGINAL OPENING
GASTROTOMY – STOMACH
HYMENOTOMY – HYMEN
IRIDECTOMY – IRIS
JEJUNOTOMY – JEJUNUM
KERATOTOMY – CORNEA
LAPAROTOMY – ABDOMEN
LUMPECTOMY – BREAST TUMOUR
MASTECTOMY – BREAST
MYOMECTOMY – FIBROIDS

NEPHROTOMY – KIDNEY
NEURECTOMY – NERVE
ORBITOTOMY – BONE AROUND EYE
OVARIOTOMY – OVARY
PHLEBOTOMY – VEIN
PLEUROTOMY – PLEURAL MEMBRANE
PROCTOTOMY – RECTUM OR ANUS
RACHIOTOMY – BACKBONE
SCLEROTOMY – WHITE OF EYE
SCROTOTOMY – SCROTUM
STERNOTOMY – BREASTBONE
TARSECTOMY – ANKLE BONES OR EYELID TISSUE
TENOPLASTY – TENDON
THYMECTOMY – THYMUS GLAND
UVULECTOMY – UVULA
VARICOTOMY – VARICOSE VEIN
VITRECTOMY – VITREUS HUMOUR
VULVECTOMY – VULVA

11
ANGIOPLASTY – BLOOD VESSEL
ARTERIOTOMY – ARTERY
ARTHRECTOMY – JOINT
CAPSULOTOMY – LENS CAPSULE OF EYE
COLPOPLASTY – VAGINA
CYSTOPLASTY – BLADDER
EMBOLECTOMY – EMBOLUS, BLOOD CLOT
ENTERECTOMY – INTESTINE
ENTEROSTOMY – SMALL INTESTINE
FRAENECTOMY – TISSUE BENEATH TONGUE
GASTRECTOMY – STOMACH
GASTROSTOMY – STOMACH
GENIOPLASTY – CHIN
GLOSSECTOMY – TONGUE
HELCOPLASTY – SKIN ULCERS
HEPATECTOMY – LIVER
HYSTEROTOMY – WOMB
INCUDECTOMY – MIDDLE EAR OSSIDE
JEJUNECTOMY – JEJUNUM
JEJUNOSTOMY – JEJUNUM
KERATECTOMY – CORNEA
LABIOPLASTY – LIPS
LARYNGOTOMY – LARYNX
MAMMOPLASTY – BREAST
MYRINGOTOMY – EARDRUM
NEPHRECTOMY – KIDNEY
NEPHROSTOMY – KIDNEY
OMENTECTOMY – PERITONEUM OF STOMACH
ORCHIDOTOMY – TESTIS
OVARIECTOMY – OVARY
PAPILLOTOMY – PART OF BILE DUCT
PHLEBECTOMY – VEIN
PLEURECTOMY – PLEURAL MEMBRANE
POLYPECTOMY – POLYP
PROCTECTOMY – RECTUM
PYELOPLASTY – PELVIS OF KIDNEY
PYLORECTOMY – PART OF STOMACH
RHINOPLASTY – NOSE
SCLERECTOMY – WHITE OF EYE
SPLENECTOMY – SPLEEN

SYNOVECTOMY – MEMBRANE AROUND JOINT
TARSOPLASTY – EYELID
THALAMOTOMY – PART OF BRAIN
THORACOTOMY – CHEST CAVITY
TRACHEOTOMY – WINDPIPE
TYMPANOTOMY – EARDRUM
URETEROTOMY – URETER
URETHROTOMY – URETHRA
VALVULOTOMY – HEART VALVE
VARICECTOMY – VARICOSE VEINS
VESICOSTOMY – BLADDER

12
ARTERIECTOMY – ARTERY
ARTHROPLASTY – JOINT
CHEILOPLASTY – LIPS
CINGULECTOMY – PART OF BRAIN
DUODENOSTOMY – DUODENUM
GASTROPLASTY – STOMACH
GINGIVECTOMY – GUM TISSUE
HERNIOPLASTY – HERNIA
HYSTERECTOMY – WOMB
KERATOPLASTY – CORNEA
LARYNGECTOMY – LARYNX
MASTOIDOTOMY – MASTOID BONE
MENISCECTOMY – KNEE CARTILAGE
OOPHORECTOMY – OVARY
ORCHIDECTOMY – TESTIS
PALATOPLASTY – CLEFT PALATE
PALLIDECTOMY – PART OF BRAIN
PHALLOPLASTY – PENIS
PYLOROPLASTY – STOMACH OUTLET
STAPEDECTOMY – THIRD EAR OSSICLE
THORACECTOMY – RIB
THROMBECTOMY – BLOOD CLOT
TONSILLOTOMY – TONSIL
TRACHEOSTOMY – WIND PIPE
TURBINECTOMY – BONE IN NOSE
URETERECTOMY – URETER
URETEROSTOMY – URETER
URETHROSTOMY – URETHRA
VAGINOPLASTY – VAGINA

13
ADENOIDECTOMY – ADENOIDS
ARTERIOPLASTY – ARTERY
CARDIOMYOTOMY – STOMACH OPENING
DERMATOPLASTY – SKIN
HEMICOLECTOMY – PART OF COLON
HEPATICOSTOMY – LIVER
ILEOCOLOSTOMY – ILEUM AND COLON
MASTOIDECTOMY – MASTOID
MYRINGOPLASTY – EARDRUM
NEURONOPLASTY – NERVES
OESOPHAGOTOMY – GULLET
OPHTHALMOTOMY – EYE
PANCREATOTOMY – PANCREAS
PERINEOPLASTY – VAGINAL OPENING
PHALANGECTOMY – FINGER OR TOE BONES
PHARYNGECTOMY – PHARYNX
PHRENICECTOMY – PHRENIC NERVE
PNEUMONECTOMY – LUNG
PROSTATECTOMY – PROSTATE GLAND
PYLOROMYOTOMY – STOMACH OUTLET

SALPINGECTOMY – FALLOPIAN TUBE
SALPINGOSTOMY – FALLOPIAN TUBE
SIGMOIDECTOMY – PART OF COLON
STAPHYLECTOMY – UVULA
SYMPATHECTOMY – SYMPATHETIC NERVE
SYMPHYSIOTOMY – FRONT OF PELVIS
THORACOPLASTY – CHEST CAVITY
THYROIDECTOMY – THYROID GLAND
TONSILLECTOMY – TONSILS
TRABECULOTOMY – DUCT IN EYE
MYRINGOTOMY, TYMPANOTOMY – EARDRUM
TYMPANOPLASTY – EARDRUM
URETEROPLASTY – URETER
URETHROPLASTY – URETHRA
VASOVASOSTOMY – REJOINING OF SEVERED
   SPERM DUCT
VESICULECTOMY – SEMINAL VESICLE

14
APPENDICOSTOMY – APPENDIX
BLEPHAROPLASTY – EYELID
CHOLECYSTOTOMY – GALL BLADDER
CHOLEDOCHOTOMY – BILE DUCT
CLITORIDECTOMY – CLITORIS
ENDARTERECTOMY – INNER WALL OF ARTERY
EPIDIDYMECTOMY – SPERM DUCT
HYPOPHYSECTOMY – PITUITARY GLAND
OESOPHAGOSTOMY – GULLET
OPHTHALMECTOMY – EYE
PANCREATECTOMY – PANCREAS
SEQUESTRECTOMY – DEAD BONE
SPHINCTEROTOMY – SPHINCTER MUSCLE
TRABECULECTOMY – PART OF EYE

15
CHOLECYSTECTOMY – GALL BLADDER
ILEOPROCTOSTOMY – ILEUM AND RECTUM
JEJUNOILEOSTOMY – JEJUNUM AND ILEUM
LITHONEPHROTOMY – KIDNEY STONE
LYMPHADENECTOMY – LYMPH NODE
NEPHROLITHOTOMY – KIDNEY STONE
PYELOLITHOTOMY – KIDNEY STONE

16
PERICARDIOSTOMY – MEMBRANE AROUND HEART
PROCTOCOLECTOMY – RECTUM AND COLON
SPHINCTERECTOMY – SPHINCTER MUSCLE
STRICTUROPLASTY – STRICTURE
VENTRICULOSTOMY – CAVITY OF BRAIN

17
GASTROENTEROSTOMY – STOMACH AND SMALL
   INTESTINE
GASTROJEJUNOSTOMY – STOMACH AND JEJUNUM
HAEMORRHOIDECTOMY – HAEMORRHOIDS
PARATHYROIDECTOMY – PARATHYROID GLAND

18
COLPOPERINEOPLASTY – VAGINAL OPENING
EPIDIDYMOVASOSTOMY – SPERM DUCTS
GASTRODUODENOSTOMY – STOMACH AND
   DUODENUM
URETEROENTEROSTOMY – URETER AND BOWEL
VASO-EPIDIDYMOSTOMY – SPERM DUCTS

19
CHOLECYSTENTEROSTOMY – GALL BLADDER AND SMALL INTESTINE
URETERONEOCYSTOSTOMY – URETER AND BLADDER
URETEROSIGMOIDOSTOMY – URETER AND PART OF BOWEL

20+
CHOLECYSTODUODENOSTOMY –

GALL BLADDER AND DUODENUM
CHOLECYSTOGASTROSTOMY – GALL BLADDER AND STOMACH
DACRYOCYSTORHINOSTOMY – TEAR SAC AND NOSE
GASTRO-OESOPHAGOSTOMY – STOMACH AND GULLET
TRANSURETERO-URETEROSTOMY – ONE URETER TO THE OTHER

PSYCHOLOGICAL TERMS

2&3
ID
IQ
ADD
DSM
ECT
EGO
PVS
REM

4
AMOK
FEAR
KORO
MIND
PICA
PTSD
SADS
SANE
SKEW

5
ANIMA
BINGE
FUGUE
FUROR
HABIT
IMAGO
LATAH
MANIA

6
ABULIA
AFFECT
ANIMUS
ANOMIA
AUTISM
CENSOR
DÉJÀ VU
ENGRAM
EONISM
FADING
LIBIDO
MENCAP
MUTISM
PHOBIA
PSYCHE
SADISM

SCHISM
SODOMY
STRESS
TRANCE

7
AMENTIA
AMNESIA
ANXIETY
AROUSAL
BONDING
BULIMIA
COMPLEX
COUVADE
DEREISM
ECSTASY
EIDETIC
ELATION
EMOTION
EMPATHY
FANTASY
IMAGERY
INSIGHT
LERESIS
OPERANT
PARADOX
PSYCHIC
SHAPING
T-GROUP
WINDIGO
ZOOPSIA

8
ANALYSIS
ANOREXIA
APHRENIA
ASTHENIC
ATARAXIA
AVOIDANT
BISEXUAL
BLOCKING
CHAINING
CONATION
CONFLICT
DELUSION
DEMENTIA
DOPAMINE
DYSBULIA

DYSLOGIA
EUPHORIA
EXPOSURE
FREUDIAN
FROTTAGE
GENOGRAM
HEBETUDE
HYSTERIA
IDEATION
ILLUSION
INSANITY
INSTINCT
LOBOTOMY
NEUROSIS
ONEIRISM
PARANOIA
PARANOID
PSELLISM
REACTIVE
SUPEREGO

9
ADDICTION
AEROPHAGY
AGROMANIA
AKATHISIA
ANALYSAND
ANHEDONIA
ARCHETYPE
ASYNDESIS
AUTOSCOPY
BABY BLUES
CATALEPSY
CATATONIA
COCAINISM
COGNITION
DYSPHEMIA
DYSSOCIAL
ECHOLALIA
EROTICISM
EXTROVERT
FETISHISM
FLASHBACK
FRIGIDITY
GEOPHAGIA
HYPOBULIA
HYPOMANIA
IDEOMOTOR

IMITATION
IMPLOSION
INTROVERT
LALLATION
LEUCOTOMY
MASOCHISM
MENTAL AGE
MODELLING
MONOMANIA
NEOLOGISM
OBSESSION
OBSESSIVE
PALILALIA
PRECOCITY
PROMPTING
PSYCHOSIS
PYROMANIA
SCULPTING
SPLITTING
SURROGATE
SYMBOLISM
VOYEURISM
ZOOPHOBIA

10
ABREACTION
ALIENATION
ANANKASTIC
APOTREPTIC
ATTACHMENT
BELL AND PAD
BORDERLINE
CHILD ABUSE
CITALOPRAM
CLUTTERING
COMPULSION
CONVERSION
COPROLALIA
DEPENDENCE
DEPRESSION
DIPSOMANIA
DIVAGATION
DROMOMANIA
ECHOPRAXIA
EROTOMANIA
EXALTATION
EXTINCTION
FOLIE À DEUX

GESTALTISM
HANDEDNESS
HYPNAGOGIC
HYPOTHYMIA
HYSTERICAL
IMPRINTING
LESBIANISM
LOGORRHOEA
MONOPHOBIA
NARCISSISM
NECROMANIA
NEGATIVISM
OLANZAPINE
PAEDERASTY
PARAMNESIA
PAREIDOLIA
PAROXETINE
PERCEPTION
PITHIATISM
POLYPHAGIA
PROJECTION
PSYCHIATRY
PSYCHOLOGY
PSYCHOPATH
REGRESSION
REPRESSION
RUMINATION
SAMARITANS
SATYRIASIS
SERTINDOLE
SERTRALINE
STAMMERING
STEREOTYPY
STUTTERING
SUGGESTION
WITHDRAWAL
XENOPHOBIA
ZOOPHILISM

11
AGORAPHOBIA
ALEXITHYMIA
AMBIVALENCE
BIOFEEDBACK
COUNSELLING
CYCLOTHYMIA
DOUBLE-BIND
DYSPAREUNIA
ECHOKINESIS
GANSER STATE
GLOSSOLALIA
HEBEPHRENIA
HYPERPRAXIA
HYPNOPOMPIC
IDIOT SAVANT
KLEPTOMANIA
LYCANTHROPY
MEGALOMANIA
MELANCHOLIA
NEUROTICISM
NYCTOPHILIA
NYCTOPHOBIA

NYCTOPHONIA
NYMPHOMANIA
ORIENTATION
PAEDOPHILIA
PALIPHRASIA
PARAGRAPHIA
PARAPHRENIA
PARASUICIDE
PERSONALITY
PSYCHODRAMA
PSYCHOGENIC
RETARDATION
RETROGRAPHY
RISPERIDONE
ROLE PLAYING
SAD SYNDROME
SCHIZOTYPAL
SEXUAL ABUSE
SUBLIMATION
THALAMOTOMY
UNCONSCIOUS

12
BEHAVIOURISM
CANCER PHOBIA
CINGULECTOMY
CONDITIONING
DISPLACEMENT
DISSOCIATION
EXTRAVERSION
EXTROVERSION
FEINGOLD DIET
FLAGELLATION
GROUP THERAPY
HALFWAY HOUSE
HYPERGRAPHIA
HYPERKINESIA
HYPOCHONDRIA
INTRAVERSION
INTROJECTION
INTROVERSION
NECROPHILISM
NEURASTHENIA
ONOMATOMANIA
PALINGRAPHIA
PHANEROMANIA
PREPAREDNESS
PSEUDOPLEGIA
PSYCHIATRIST
PSYCHOLOGIST
PSYCHOTICISM
SOMNAMBULISM
SUBCONSCIOUS
SUBSTITUTION
TIME SAMPLING
TRANSFERENCE
TRANSVESTISM

13
ANTIPSYCHOTIC
CONFABULATION
CROSS-DRESSING

DEREALIZATION
EVENT SAMPLING
EXHIBITIONISM
FAMILY THERAPY
HALLUCINATION
HOMOSEXUALITY
MENTAL ILLNESS
NORMALIZATION
PANIC DISORDER
PERSEVERATION
PHARMACOMANIA
PSYCHOKINESIS
PSYCHOMETRICS
PSYCHOSOMATIC
PSYCHOSURGERY
PSYCHOTHERAPY
REINFORCEMENT
RORSCHACH TEST
SCHIZOPHRENIA
SLEEP-WALKING
SOMNILOQUENCE
TWILIGHT STATE
VERBIGERATION

14
AUTOSUGGESTION
CLAUSTROPHOBIA
DISORIENTATION
DRUG DEPENDENCE
EFFORT SYNDROME
ENCOUNTER GROUP
IDENTIFICATION
MENTAL HANDICAP
NOCTAMBULATION
OEDIPUS COMPLEX
ONOMATOPOIESIS
PARAPSYCHOLOGY
PROJECTIVE TEST
PSYCHOANALYSIS
PSYCHONEUROSIS
RETT'S SYNDROME
SECURITY OBJECT
SENILE DEMENTIA
TRANSSEXUALISM
WECHSLER SCALES

15
ANOREXIA NERVOSA
AVERSION THERAPY
BIPOLAR DISORDER
CAPGRAS' SYNDROME
CONDUCT DISORDER
DYSMORPHOPHOBIA
ELECTRONARCOSIS
FREE ASSOCIATION
HELLER'S SYNDROME
HETEROSEXUALITY
NEUROPSYCHIATRY
PSEUDOMUTUALITY
PSYCHOPATHOLOGY
RATIONALIZATION
RETENTION DEFECT

SEXUAL DEVIATION
THOUGHT STOPPING

16
BEHAVIOUR THERAPY
BRIQUET'S SYNDROME
COGNITIVE THERAPY
CORE-AND-CLUSTER
DEFENCE MECHANISM
EXPRESSED EMOTION
FRAGILE-X SYNDROME
GLOBUS HYSTERICUS
INTELLIGENCE TEST
LOCKED-IN SYNDROME
MENTAL DEFICIENCY
MENTAL HEALTH ACTS
MENTALIMPAIRMENT
NERVOUS BREAKDOWN
OVERCOMPENSATION
PSYCHOGERIATRICS
PSYCHOPHYSIOLOGY
SPECIAL HOSPITALS
TRICHOTILLOMANIA

17
AFFECTIVE DISORDER
ASPERGER'S
  SYNDROME
BELLE INDIFFERENCE
CIRCUMSTANTIALITY
DEPERSONALIZATION
DYSMNESIC SYNDROME
DYSTHYMIC DISORDER
FLEXIBILITAS CEREA
MENTAL RETARDATION
PSYCHOLINGUISTICS
REACTION FORMATION
RELAXATION THERAPY
SEPARATION ANXIETY
TOURETTE'S
  SYNDROME

18
ASSOCIATION OF IDEAS
ATTACHMENT
  DISORDER
CONVERSION
  DISORDER
DOPAMINE
  HYPOTHESIS
GRADED SELF-
  EXPOSURE
INFERIORITY COMPLEX
KNIGHT'S-MOVE
  THOUGHT
KORSAKOFF'S
  SYNDROME
LEARNING DISABILITY
RESPONSE PREVENTION
SENSORY DEPRIVATION

PHOBIAS BY NAME

ACAROPHOBIA – ITCHING, MITES
ACERBOPHOBIA – SOURNESS
ACEROPHOBIA – SOURNESS
ACHLUOPHOBIA – DARKNESS
ACOUSTICOPHOBIA – SOUND
ACROPHOBIA – HIGH PLACES, SHARPNESS
AEROPHOBIA – DRAUGHTS
AGORAPHOBIA – CROWDS, OPEN PLACES
AGYROPHOBIA – STREETS (CROSSING)
AILUROPHOBIA – CATS
ALGOPHOBIA – PAIN
ALTOPHOBIA – HIGH PLACES
AMATHOPHOBIA – DUST
ANAEMOPHOBIA – ANAEMIA
ANCRAOPHOBIA – WIND
ANDROPHOBIA – MEN
ANGINOPHOBIA – NARROWNESS
ANGLOPHOBIA – ENGLISH
ANTHOPHOBIA – FLOWERS
ANTHROPOPHOBIA – PEOPLE
ANTLOPHOBIA – FLOODS
APEIROPHOBIA – INFINITY
APIPHOBIA – BEES
ARACHNOPHOBIA – SPIDERS
ASTHENOPHOBIA – WEAKNESS
ASTRAPHOBIA – LIGHTNING
ASTRAPOPHOBIA – LIGHTNING
ATELOPHOBIA – IMPERFECTION
ATEPHOBIA – RUIN
AULOPHOBIA – FLUTES
AUROPHOBIA – GOLD
AUTOPHOBIA – LONELINESS
BACILLOPHOBIA – MICROBES
BACTERIOPHOBIA – BACTERIA
BALLISTOPHOBIA – BULLETS
BAROPHOBIA – GRAVITY
BATHOPHOBIA – DEPTH
BATOPHOBIA – HIGH BUILDINGS, HIGH PLACES
BATRACHOPHOBIA – REPTILES
BELONEPHOBIA – NEEDLES
BLENNOPHOBIA – SLIME
BROMIDROSIPHOBIA – BODY ODOUR
BRONTOPHOBIA – THUNDER
CARDIOPHOBIA – HEART DISEASE
CHAETOPHOBIA – HAIR
CHEIMAPHOBIA – COLD
CHEIMATOPHOBIA – COLD
CHIONOPHOBIA – SNOW
CHLOEROPHOBIA – CHOLERA
CHROMETOPHOBIA – MONEY
CHROMOPHOBIA – COLOUR
CHRONOPHOBIA – TIME (DURATION)
CIBOPHOBIA – FOOD
CLAUSTROPHOBIA – ENCLOSED PLACES
CLINOPHOBIA – BED (GOING TO BED)
CNIDOPHOBIA – INSECT STINGS
COITOPHOBIA – COITUS
COMETOPHOBIA – COMETS
COPROPHOBIA – FAECES

COPROSTASOPHOBIA – CONSTIPATION
CREMNOPHOBIA – PRECIPICES
CRYOPHOBIA – ICE, FROST
CRYSTALLOPHOBIA – CRYSTALS
CYMOPHOBIA – WAVES
CYNOPHOBIA – DOGS
DEMONOPHOBIA – DEMONS
DEMOPHOBIA – CROWDS
DERMATOPATHOPHOBIA – SKIN DISEASE
DERMATOSIOPHOBIA – SKIN
DIABETOPHOBIA – DIABETES
DIKEPHOBIA – JUSTICE
DORAPHOBIA – FUR
DROMOPHOBIA – MOTION
ECCLESIOPHOBIA – CHURCH
ECOPHOBIA – HOME
EISOPTROPHOBIA – MIRRORS
ELECTROPHOBIA – ELECTRICITY
ELEUTHEROPHOBIA – FREEDOM
EMETOPHOBIA – VOMITING
ENETOPHOBIA – PINS
ENTOMOPHOBIA – INSECTS
EOSOPHOBIA – DAWN
ERGOPHOBIA – WORK
ERMITOPHOBIA – LONELINESS
EROTOPHOBIA – SEX
ERYTHROPHOBIA – BLUSHING
FEBRIPHOBIA – FEVER
FRANCOPHOBIA – FRENCH
GALLOPHOBIA – FRENCH
GAMETOPHOBIA – MARRIAGE
GENOPHOBIA – SEX
GEPHYROPHOBIA – BRIDGES (CROSSING)
GERMANOPHOBIA – GERMANS
GEUMATOPHOBIA – TASTE
GLOSSOPHOBIA – SPEECH
GRAPHOPHOBIA – WRITING
GYNEPHOBIA – WOMEN
HADEPHOBIA – HELL
HAGIOPHOBIA – SAINTS
HAMARTOPHOBIA – SIN
HAPHOPHOBIA – TOUCH
HAPTOPHOBIA – TOUCH
HARPAXOPHOBIA – ROBBERS
HEDONOPHOBIA – PLEASURE
HELIOPHOBIA – SUN
HELMINTHOPHOBIA – WORMS
HAEMAPHOBIA – BLOOD
HAEMATOPHOBIA – BLOOD
HAEMOPHOBIA – BLOOD
HERPETOPHOBIA – REPTILES
HIEROPHOBIA – PRIESTS
HIPPOPHOBIA – HORSES
HODOPHOBIA – TRAVEL
HOMICHLOPHOBIA – FOG
HORMEPHOBIA – SHOCK
HYDROPHOBIA – WATER
HYDROPHOBOPHOBIA – RABIES
HYGROPHOBIA – DAMPNESS

HYPEGIAPHOBIA – RESPONSIBILITY
HYPNOPHOBIA – SLEEP
HYPSOPHOBIA – HIGH PLACES
ICHTHYOPHOBIA – FISH
IDEOPHOBIA – IDEAS
JAPANOPHOBIA – JAPANESE
JUDEOPHOBIA – JEWS
KAKORRAPHIAPHOBIA – FAILURE
KATAGELOPHOBIA – RIDICULE
KENOPHOBIA – VOID
KERAUNOPHOBIA – THUNDER
KINETOPHOBIA – MOTION
KLEPTOPHOBIA – STEALING
KONIOPHOBIA – DUST
KOPOPHOBIA – FATIGUE
LALIOPHOBIA – SPEECH
LALOPHOBIA – SPEECH
LIMNOPHOBIA – LAKES
LINONOPHOBIA – STRING
LOGOPHOBIA – WORDS
LYSSOPHOBIA – INSANITY
MANIPHOBIA – INSANITY
MASTIGOPHOBIA – BEATING
MECHANOPHOBIA – MACHINERY
MENINGITOPHOBIA – MENINGITIS
METALLOPHOBIA – METAL
MICROBIOPHOBIA – MICROBES
MICROPHOBIA – SMALL THINGS
MONOPHOBIA – LONELINESS
MUSICOPHOBIA – MUSIC
MUSOPHOBIA – MICE
MYSOPHOBIA – DIRT
MYXOPHOBIA – SLIME
NECROPHOBIA – CORPSES
NEGROPHOBIA – NEGROES
NEOPHOBIA – NEW THINGS
NEPHOPHOBIA – CLOUDS, DISEASE
NYCTOPHOBIA – NIGHT
OCHLOPHOBIA – MOBS
OCHOPHOBIA – VEHICLES
ODONTOPHOBIA – TEETH
OECOPHOBIA – HOME
OIKOPHOBIA – HOME
OLFACTOPHOBIA – SMELL
OMMETAPHOBIA – EYES
ONOMATOPHOBIA – NAMES
OPHICIOPHOBIA – SNAKES
OPHIOPHOBIA – SNAKES
OPHRESIOPHOBIA – SMELL
ORNITHOPHOBIA – BIRDS
OSMOPHOBIA – SMELL
OURANOPHOBIA – HEAVEN
PAEDOPHOBIA – CHILDREN
PANPHOBIA – EVERYTHING
PANTOPHOBIA – EVERYTHING
PAPAPHOBIA – POPE
PARASITOPHOBIA – PARASITES
PARTHENOPHOBIA – YOUNG GIRLS
PATHOPHOBIA – DISEASE
PATROIOPHOBIA – HEREDITY
PECCATIPHOBIA – SIN
PEDICULOPHOBIA – LICE

PENIAPHOBIA – POVERTY
PHAGOPHOBIA – SWALLOWING
PHARMACOPHOBIA – DRUGS
PHASMOPHOBIA – GHOSTS
PHILOSOPHOBIA – PHILOSOPHY
PHOBOPHOBIA – FEAR, SPEECH
PHOTOPHOBIA – LIGHT
PHRONEMOPHOBIA – THINKING
PHTHISIOPHOBIA – TUBERCULOSIS
PNEUMATOPHOBIA – SPIRITS
PNIGEROPHOBIA – SMOTHERING
PNIGOPHOBIA – SMOTHERING
POGONOPHOBIA – BEARDS
POINEPHOBIA – PUNISHMENT
POLITICOPHOBIA – POLITICS
POTAMOPHOBIA – RIVERS
POTOPHOBIA – DRINK
PTERONOPHOBIA – FEATHERS
PYROPHOBIA – FIRE
RECTOPHOBIA – RECTUM
RHABDOPHOBIA – MAGIC
RUSSOPHOBIA – RUSSIANS
RYPOPHOBIA – SOILING
SATANOPHOBIA – SATAN
SCABIOPHOBIA – SCABIES
SCIOPHOBIA – SHADOWS
SCOTOPHOBIA – DARKNESS
SIDEROPHOBIA – STARS
SINOPHOBIA – CHINESE
SITOPHOBIA – FOOD
SNAKEPHOBIA – SNAKES
SPERMATOPHOBIA – GERMS
SPERMOPHOBIA – GERMS
STASOPHOBIA – STANDING
STYGIOPHOBIA – HELL
SYMMETROPHOBIA – SYMMETRY
SYPHILOPHOBIA – SYPHILIS
TACHOPHOBIA – SPEED
TELEPHONOPHOBIA – TELEPHONE
TERATROPHOBIA – MONSTERS
TEUTONOPHOBIA – GERMANS
THAASOPHOBIA – IDLENESS
THALASSOPHOBIA – SEA
THANATOPHOBIA – DEATH
THEOPHOBIA – GOD
THERMOPHOBIA – HEAT
THIXOPHOBIA – TOUCH
TOCOPHOBIA – CHILDBIRTH
TONITROPHOBIA – THUNDER
TOPOPHOBIA – PLACES
TOXICOPHOBIA – POISON
TOXIPHOBIA – POISON
TOXOPHOBIA – POISON
TRAUMATOPHOBIA – INJURY
TREMOPHOBIA – TREMBLING
TRICHOPATHOPHOBIA – HAIR DISEASE
TRICHOPHOBIA – HAIR
TRICINOPHOBIA – TRICHINOSIS
TRISKAIDEKAPHOBIA – THIRTEEN
TRYPANOPHOBIA – INOCULATION
TUBERCULOPHOBIA – TUBERCULOSIS
TYRANNOPHOBIA – TYRANTS

URANOPHOBIA – HEAVEN
UROPHOBIA – URINE
VACCINOPHOBIA – INOCULATION
VENEROPHOBIA – VENEREAL DISEASE

VERMIPHOBIA – WORMS
XENOPHOBIA – FOREIGNERS
ZELOPHOBIA – JEALOUSY

PHOBIAS BY FEAR

ANAEMIA – ANAEMOPHOBIA
BACTERIA – BACTERIOPHOBIA
BEARDS – POGONOPHOBIA
BEATING – MASTIGOPHOBIA
BED (GOING TO BED) – CLINOPHOBIA
BEES – APIPHOBIA
BIRDS – ORNITHOPHOBIA
BLOOD – HAEMAPHOBIA, HAEMATOPHOBIA,
  HAEMOPHOBIA
BLUSHING – ERYTHROPHOBIA
BODY ODOUR – BROMIDROSIPHOBIA
BRIDGES (CROSSING) – GEPHYROPHOBIA
BULLETS – BALLISTOPHOBIA
CATS – AILUROPHOBIA
CHILDBIRTH – TOCOPHOBIA
CHILDREN – PAEDOPHOBIA
CHINESE – SINOPHOBIA
CHOLERA – CHLOEROPHOBIA
CHURCH – ECCLESIOPHOBIA
CLOUDS – NEPHOPHOBIA
COITUS – COITOPHOBIA
COLD – CHEIMAPHOBIA, CHEIMATOPHOBIA
COLOUR – CHROMOPHOBIA
COMETS – COMETOPHOBIA
CONSTIPATION – COPROSTASOPHOBIA
CORPSES – NECROPHOBIA
CROWDS – AGORAPHOBIA, DEMOPHOBIA
CRYSTALS – CRYSTALLOPHOBIA
DAMPNESS – HYGROPHOBIA
DARKNESS – ACHLUOPHOBIA, SCOTOPHOBIA
DAWN – EOSOPHOBIA
DEATH – THANATOPHOBIA
DEMONS – DEMONOPHOBIA
DEPTH – BATHOPHOBIA
DIABETES – DIABETOPHOBIA
DIRT – MYSOPHOBIA
DISEASE – NEPHOPHOBIA, PATHOPHOBIA
DOGS – CYNOPHOBIA
DRAUGHTS – AEROPHOBIA
DRINK – POTOPHOBIA
DRUGS – PHARMACOPHOBIA
DUST – AMATHOPHOBIA
ELECTRICITY – ELECTROPHOBIA
ENCLOSED PLACES – CLAUSTROPHOBIA
ENGLISH – ANGLOPHOBIA
EVERYTHING – PANPHOBIA, PANTOPHOBIA
EYES – OMMETAPHOBIA
FAECES – COPROPHOBIA
FAILURE – KAKORRAPHIAPHOBIA
FATIGUE – KOPOPHOBIA
FEAR – PHOBOPHOBIA
FEATHERS – PTERONOPHOBIA

FEVER – FEBRIPHOBIA
FIRE – PYROPHOBIA
FISH – ICHTHYOPHOBIA
FLOODS – ANTLOPHOBIA
FLOWERS – ANTHOPHOBIA
FLUTES – AULOPHOBIA
FOG – HOMICHLOPHOBIA
FOOD – CIBOPHOBIA, SITOPHOBIA
FOREIGNERS – XENOPHOBIA
FREEDOM – ELEUTHEROPHOBIA
FRENCH – FRANCOPHOBIA, GALLOPHOBIA
FROST – CRYOPHOBIA
FUR – DORAPHOBIA
GERMANS – GERMANOPHOBIA
GERMANS – TEUTONOPHOBIA
GERMS – SPERMATOPHOBIA, SPERMOPHOBIA
GHOSTS – PHASMOPHOBIA
GOD – THEOPHOBIA
GOLD – AUROPHOBIA
GRAVITY – BAROPHOBIA
HAIR – CHAETOPHOBIA, TRICHOPHOBIA
HAIR DISEASE – TRICHOPATHOPHOBIA
HEART DISEASE – CARDIOPHOBIA
HEAT – THERMOPHOBIA
HEAVEN – OURANOPHOBIA, URANOPHOBIA
HELL – HADEPHOBIA, STYGIOPHOBIA
HEREDITY – PATROIOPHOBIA
HIGH BUILDINGS – BATOPHOBIA
HIGH PLACES – ACROPHOBIA, ALTOPHOBIA,
  BATOPHOBIA, HYPSOPHOBIA
HOME – ECOPHOBIA, OECOPHOBIA, OIKOPHOBIA
HORSES – HIPPOPHOBIA
ICE – CRYOPHOBIA
IDEAS – IDEOPHOBIA
IDLENESS – THAASOPHOBIA
IMPERFECTION – ATELOPHOBIA
INFINITY – APEIROPHOBIA
INJURY – TRAUMATOPHOBIA
INOCULATION – TRYPANOPHOBIA,
  VACCINOPHOBIA
INSANITY – LYSSOPHOBIA, MANIPHOBIA
INSECTS – ENTOMOPHOBIA
INSECT STINGS – CNIDOPHOBIA
ITCHING – ACAROPHOBIA
JAPANESE – JAPANOPHOBIA
JEALOUSY – ZELOPHOBIA
JEWS – JUDEOPHOBIA
JUSTICE – DIKEPHOBIA
LAKES – LIMNOPHOBIA
LICE – PEDICULOPHOBIA
LIGHTNING – ASTRAPHOBIA, ASTRAPOPHOBIA
LIGHT – PHOTOPHOBIA

LONELINESS – AUTOPHOBIA, ERMITOPHOBIA, MONOPHOBIA
MACHINERY – MECHANOPHOBIA
MAGIC – RHABDOPHOBIA
MARRIAGE – GAMETOPHOBIA
MEN – ANDROPHOBIA
MENINGITIS – MENINGITOPHOBIA
METAL – METALLOPHOBIA
MICE – MUSOPHOBIA
MICROBES – BACILLOPHOBIA, MICROBIOPHOBIA
MIRRORS – EISOPTROPHOBIA
MITES – ACAROPHOBIA
MOBS – OCHLOPHOBIA
MONEY – CHROMETOPHOBIA
MONSTERS – TERATROPHOBIA
MOTION – DROMOPHOBIA
MOTION – KINETOPHOBIA
MUSIC – MUSICOPHOBIA
NAMES – ONOMATOPHOBIA
NARROWNESS – ANGINOPHOBIA
NEEDLES – BELONEPHOBIA
NEGROES – NEGROPHOBIA
NEW THINGS – NEOPHOBIA
NIGHT – NYCTOPHOBIA
OPEN PLACES – AGORAPHOBIA
PAIN – ALGOPHOBIA
PARASITES – PARASITOPHOBIA
PEOPLE – ANTHROPOPHOBIA
PHILOSOPHY – PHILOSOPHOBIA
PINS – ENETOPHOBIA
PLACES – TOPOPHOBIA
PLEASURE – HEDONOPHOBIA
POISON – TOXICOPHOBIA, TOXOPHOBIA
POLITICS – POLITICOPHOBIA
POPE – PAPAPHOBIA
POVERTY – PENIAPHOBIA
PRECIPICES – CREMNOPHOBIA
PRIESTS – HIEROPHOBIA
PUNISHMENT – POINEPHOBIA
RABIES – HYDROPHOBOPHOBIA
RECTUM – RECTOPHOBIA
REPTILES – BATRACHOPHOBIA, HERPETOPHOBIA
RESPONSIBILITY – HYPEGIAPHOBIA
RIDICULE – KATAGELOPHOBIA
RIVERS – POTAMOPHOBIA
ROBBERS – HARPAXOPHOBIA
RUIN – ATEPHOBIA
RUSSIANS – RUSSOPHOBIA
SAINTS – HAGIOPHOBIA
SATAN – SATANOPHOBIA
SCABIES – SCABIOPHOBIA
SEA – THALASSOPHOBIA
SEX – EROTOPHOBIA, GENOPHOBIA
SHADOWS – SCIOPHOBIA
SHARPNESS – ACROPHOBIA
SHOCK – HORMEPHOBIA
SIN – HAMARTOPHOBIA, PECCATIPHOBIA

SKIN – DERMATOSIOPHOBIA
SKIN DISEASE – DERMATOPATHOPHOBIA
SLEEP – HYPNOPHOBIA
SLIME – BLENNOPHOBIA, MYXOPHOBIA
SMALL THINGS – MICROPHOBIA
SMELL – OLFACTOPHOBIA, OPHRESIOPHOBIA, OSMOPHOBIA
SMOTHERING – PNIGEROPHOBIA
SNAKES – OPHICIOPHOBIA, SNAKEPHOBIA
SNOW – CHIONOPHOBIA
SOILING – RYPOPHOBIA
SOUND – ACOUSTICOPHOBIA
SOURNESS – ACERBOPHOBIA
SPEECH – GLOSSOPHOBIA, LALIOPHOBIA, PHONOPHOBIA
SPEED – TACHOPHOBIA
SPIDERS – ARACHNOPHOBIA
SPIRITS – PNEUMATOPHOBIA
STANDING – STASOPHOBIA
STARS – SIDEROPHOBIA
STEALING – KLEPTOPHOBIA
STREETS (CROSSING) – AGYROPHOBIA
STRING – LINONOPHOBIA
SUN – HELIOPHOBIA
SWALLOWING – PHAGOPHOBIA
SYMMETRY – SYMMETROPHOBIA
SYPHILIS – SYPHILOPHOBIA
TASTE – GEUMATOPHOBIA
TEETH – ODONTOPHOBIA
TELEPHONE – TELEPHONOPHOBIA
THINKING – PHRONEMOPHOBIA
THIRTEEN – TRISKAIDEKAPHOBIA
THUNDER – BRONTOPHOBIA, THUNDER, KERAUNOPHOBIA, TONITROPHOBIA
TIME (DURATION) – CHRONOPHOBIA
TOUCH – HAPTOPHOBIA, THIXOPHOBIA
TRAVEL – HODOPHOBIA
TREMBLING – TREMOPHOBIA
TRICHINOSIS – TRICINOPHOBIA
TUBERCULOSIS – PHTHISIOPHOBIA, TUBERCULOPHOBIA
TYRANTS – TYRANNOPHOBIA
URINE – UROPHOBIA
VEHICLES – OCHOPHOBIA
VENEREAL DISEASE – VENEROPHOBIA
VOID – KENOPHOBIA
VOMITING – EMETOPHOBIA
WATER – HYDROPHOBIA
WAVES – CYMOPHOBIA
WEAKNESS – ASTHENOPHOBIA
WIND – ANCRAOPHOBIA
WOMEN – GYNEPHOBIA
WORDS – LOGOPHOBIA
WORK – ERGOPHOBIA
WORMS – HELMINTHOPHOBIA, VERMIPHOBIA
WRITING – GRAPHOPHOBIA
YOUNG GIRLS – PARTHENOPHOBIA

RELIGION AND MYTHOLOGY

BOOKS OF THE BIBLE

OLD TESTAMENT

GENESIS
EXODUS
LEVITICUS
NUMBERS
DEUTERONOMY
JOSHUA
JUDGES
RUTH
1 SAMUEL
2 SAMUEL
1 KINGS
2 KINGS
1 CHRONICLES
2 CHRONICLES
EZRA
NEHEMIAH
ESTHER
JOB
PSALMS
PROVERBS
ECCLESIASTES
SONG OF SOLOMON
ISAIAH
JEREMIAH
LAMENTATIONS
EZEKIEL
DANIEL

HOSEA
JOEL
AMOS
OBADIAH
JONAH
MICAH
NAHUM
HABAKKUK
ZEPHANIAH
HAGGAI
ZECHARIAH
MALACHI

NEW TESTAMENT

MATTHEW
MARK
LUKE
JOHN
THE ACTS
ROMANS
1 CORINTHIANS
2 CORINTHIANS
GALATIANS
EPHESIANS
PHILIPPIANS
COLOSSIANS
1 THESSALONIANS
2 THESSALONIANS
1 TIMOTHY

2 TIMOTHY
TITUS
PHILEMON
HEBREWS
JAMES
1 PETER
2 PETER
1 JOHN
2 JOHN
3 JOHN
JUDE
REVELATION

APOCRYPHA

I ESDRAS
II ESDRAS
TOBIT
JUDITH
THE REST OF ESTHER
WISDOM
ECCLESIASTICUS
BARUCH, WITH EPISTLE OF
    JEREMIAH
SONG OF THE THREE CHILDREN
SUSANNA
BEL AND THE DRAGON
PRAYER OF MANASSES
I MACCABEES
II MACCABEES

BIBLICAL CHARACTERS

OLD TESTAMENT

AARON – elder brother of Moses; 1st high priest of
    Hebrews
ABEL – second son of Adam and Eve; murdered by
    brother Cain
ABRAHAM – father of Hebrew nation
ABSALOM – David's spoilt third son; killed after
    plotting against his father
ADAM – the first man created; husband of Eve
BAAL – fertility god of Canaanites and Phoenicians
BATHSHEBA – mother of Solomon
BELSHAZZAR – last king of Babylon, son of
    Nebuchadnezzar; Daniel interpreted his vision of
    writing on the wall as foretelling the downfall of
    his kingdom

BENJAMIN – youngest son of Jacob and Rachel. His
    descendants formed one of the 12 tribes of Israel
CAIN – first son of Adam and Eve; murdered his
    brother Abel
DANIEL – prophet at the court of Nebuchadnezzar
    with a gift for interpreting dreams
DAVID – slayed the giant Goliath
DELILAH – a Philistine seducer and betrayer of
    Samson
ELIJAH – Hebrew prophet, taken into heaven in a
    fiery chariot
ELISHA – prophet and disciple of Elijah
ENOCH – father of Methuselah
EPHRAIM – son of Joseph; founded one of the 12
    tribes of Israel
ESAU – elder of Isaac's twin sons; tricked out of his

birthright by his younger brother Jacob

ESTHER – beautiful Israelite woman; heroically protected her people

EVE – first woman; created as companion for Adam in Garden of Eden

EZEKIEL – prophet of Israel captured by Babylonians

GIDEON – Israelite hero and judge

GOLIATH – Philistine giant killed by David

HEZEKIAH – king of Judah (c 715–686BC)

ISAAC – son of Abraham and Sarah, conceived in their old age; father of Jacob and Esau

ISAIAH – the greatest old testament prophet

ISHMAEL – Abraham's son by Hagar, hand-maiden to his wife, Sarah; rival of Isaac

ISRAEL – new name given to Jacob after his reconciliation with Esau

JACOB – second son of Isaac and Rebekah, younger twin of Esau whom he tricked out of his inheritance. The 12 tribes of Israel were named after his sons and grandsons

JEREMIAH – one of the great prophets; foretold destruction of Jerusalem

JEZEBEL – cruel and lustful wife of Ahab, king of Israel

JOB – long-suffering and pious inhabitant of Uz

JONAH – after ignoring God's commands he was swallowed by a whale

JONATHAN – eldest son of Saul and close friend of David

JOSEPH – favourite son of Jacob and Rachel with his "coat of many colours"; sold into slavery by his jealous brothers

JOSHUA – succeeded Moses and led Israelites against Canaan. He defeated Jericho where the walls fell down

JUDAH – son of Jacob and Leah; founded tribe of Judah

LOT – nephew of Abraham; he escaped the destruction of Sodom, but his wife was turned into a pillar of salt for looking back

METHUSELAH – son of Enoch, the oldest person ever (969 years)

MIRIAM – sister of Aaron and Moses whom she looked after as a baby; prophetess and leader of Israelites

MOSES – Israel's great leader and lawgiver, he led the Israelites out of captivity in Egypt to the promised land of Canaan. Received ten commandments from Jehovah on Mt Sinai

NATHAN – Hebrew prophet at courts of David and Solomon

NEBUCHADNEZZAR – king of Babylon

NOAH – grandson of Methuselah, father of Shem, Ham, and Japheth; built ark to save his family and all animal species from the great flood

REBEKAH – wife of Isaac, mother of Jacob and Esau

RUTH – Moabite who accompanied her mother-in-law Naomi to Bethlehem. Remembered for her loyalty

SAMSON – Israelite judge of great physical strength; seduced and betrayed by Delilah

SAMUEL – prophet and judge of Israel

SARAH – wife of Abraham, mother of Isaac

SAUL – first king of Israel

SOLOMON – son of David and Bathsheba; remembered for his great wisdom and wealth

NEW TESTAMENT

ANDREW – fisherman and brother of Peter; one of 12 Apostles

BARABAS – Cypriot missionary; introduced Paul to the Church

BARABBAS – robber and murderer; in prison with Jesus and released instead of him

BARTHOLOMEW – possibly same person as Nathaniel, one of the 12 Apostles

CAIAPHAS – high priest of the Jews; Jesus brought to him after arrest

GABRIEL – angel who announced birth of Jesus to Mary; and of John the Baptist to Zechariah

HEROD – 1. the Great, ruled when Jesus was born 2. Antipas, son of Herod the Great, ruled when John the Baptist was murdered 3. Agrippa, killed James (brother of John) 4. Agrippa II, before whom Paul was tried

JAMES – 1. the Greater, one of 12 Apostles, brother of John 2. the Less, one of 12 Apostles 3. leader of the Church in Jerusalem and author of the New Testament epistle

JESUS – founder of Christianity

JOHN – youngest of 12 Apostles

JOHN THE BAPTIST – announced coming of Jesus, and baptized him

JOSEPH – 1. husband of Mary the mother of Jesus 2. of Arimathea, a secret disciple of Jesus

JUDAS ISCARIOT – the disciple who betrayed Jesus

LAZARUS – brother of Mary and Martha, raised from the dead by Jesus

LUKE – companion of Paul, author of Luke and Acts

MARK – author of the gospel; companion of Paul, Barnabas, and Peter

MARTHA – sister of Mary and Lazarus, friend of Jesus

MARY – 1. mother of Jesus 2. sister of Martha and Lazarus 3. Magdalene, cured by Jesus and the first to see him after the resurrection

MATTHEW – one of 12 Apostles, author of the gospel

MATTHIAS – chosen to replace the apostle Judas

MICHAEL – a chief archangel

NATHANIEL – see Bartholomew

NICODEMUS – a Pharisee who had a secret meeting with Jesus

PAUL – formerly Saul of Tarsus, persecutor of Christians; renamed after his conversion. Apostle to the Gentiles and author of epistles

PETER – Simon, one of 12 Apostles; denied Jesus before the crucifixion but later became leader of the Church

PHILIP – one of 12 Apostles

PILATE – Roman procurator of Judea; allowed Jesus to be crucified

SALOME – 1. wife of Zebedee, mother of James and John 2. daughter of Herodias; danced before Herod for the head of John the Baptist

SAUL – see Paul

SIMON – **1.** Simon Peter see Peter **2.** the Canaanite, one of 12 Apostles **3.** one of Jesus' four brothers **4.** the leper, in whose house Jesus was anointed **5.** of Cyrene, carried the cross of Jesus **6.** the tanner, in whose house Peter had his vision

STEPHEN – Christian martyr, stoned to death

THOMAS – one of 12 Apostles, named 'Doubting' because he doubted the resurrection

TIMOTHY – Paul's fellow missionary; two of Paul's epistles are to him

TITUS – convert and companion of Paul, who wrote him one epistle

PATRON SAINTS

NAME (Patron of)

AGATHA (bell-founders)
ALBERT THE GREAT (students of natural sciences)
ANDREW (Scotland)
BARBARA (gunners and miners)
BERNARD OF MONTJOUX (mountaineers)
CAMILLUS (nurses)
CASIMIR (Poland)
CECILIA (musicians)
CHRISTOPHER (wayfarers)
CRISPIN (shoemakers)
DAVID (Wales)
DIONYSIUS (DENIS) OF PARIS (France)
DUNSTAN (goldsmiths, jewellers, and locksmiths)
DYMPNA (insanity)
ELIGIUS or ELOI (metalworkers)
ERASMUS (sailors)
FIACRE (gardeners)
FRANCES CABRINI (emigrants)
FRANCES OF ROME (motorists)
FRANCIS DE SALES (writers)
FRANCIS XAVIER (foreign missions)

FRIDESWIDE (Oxford)
GEORGE (England)
GILES (cripples)
HUBERT (huntsmen)
JEROME EMILIANI (orphans and abandoned children)
JOHN OF GOD (hospitals and booksellers)
JUDE (hopeless causes)
JULIAN (innkeepers, boatmen, and travellers)
KATHERINE OF ALEXANDRIA (students, philosophers, and craftsmen)
LUKE (physicians and surgeons)
MARTHA (housewives)
NICHOLAS (children, sailors, unmarried girls, merchants, pawnbrokers, apothecaries, and perfumeries)
PATRICK (Ireland)
PETER NOLASCO (midwives)
SAVA (Serbian people)
VALENTINE (lovers)
VITUS (epilepsy and nervous diseases)
WENCESLAS (Czechoslovakia)
ZITA (domestic servants)

RELIGIOUS ORDERS

AUGUSTINIAN
BARNABITE
BENEDICTINE
BRIGITTINE
CAMALDOLESE
CAPUCHINS
CARMELITE
CARTHUSIAN
CISTERCIAN
DOMINICAN
FRANCISCAN
HOSPITALLERS
JERONYMITE

MINIMS
POOR CLARES
PREMONSTRATENSIAN
SALESIAN
SERVITE
SYLVESTRINE
TEMPLARS
THEATINE
TRAPPIST
TRINITARIAN
URSULINE
VISITANDINE, VISITATION

RELIGIOUS MOVEMENTS

3
BON
I AM
ZEN

4
AINU

5
AMISH
BOSCI
ISLAM
KEGON
THAGS
THUGS

6
BABISM
PARSIS
SHINTO
TAOISM
VOODOO

7
AJIVIKA
BAHAISM
GIDEONS
JAINISM
JUDAISM
JUMPERS

LAMAISM
MORMONS
PARSEES
QUAKERS
SHAKERS
SIKHISM
WAHABIS
ZIONISM

8
ABELIANS
ABELITES
ACOEMETI
ADAMITES
ADMADIYA
AHMADIYA
AMARITES
BAPTISTS
BUDDHISM
HINDUISM
HUMANISM
MAR THOMA
NICHIREN
NOSAIRIS
STUDITES

9
CALVINISM
CHUNTOKYO

FRANKISTS
HICKSITES
HUGUENOTS
JANSENISM
METHODIST
PANTHEISM

10
ABSTINENTS
ADVENTISTS
AGONIZANTS
AMBROSIANS
BUCHANITES
CALIXTINES
PURATINISM

11
ABODE OF LOVE
ABRAHAMITES
ANABAPTISTS
ANGLICANISM
ARMINIANISM
BASILIDEANS
BERNARDINES
CATHOLICISM
COVENANTERS

12
ABECEDARIANS

BENEDICTINES
CHRISTIANITY
SPIRITUALISM
UNITARIANISM

13
MOHAMMEDANISM
PROTESTANTISM
REDEMPTORISTS
SALVATION ARMY

14
CONGREGATIONAL
FUNDAMENTALISM

15
PRESBYTERIANISM

16
CHRISTIAN SCIENCE
PLYMOUTH
  BRETHREN
ROMAN
  CATHOLICISM

17
ANTIPAEDOBAPTISTS
CONGREGATIONALISM
JEHOVAH'S
  WITNESSES

CLERGY

ARCHBISHOP
ARCHDEACON
BISHOP
CANON
CARDINAL

CHAPLAIN
CURATE
DEACON
DEAN
ELDER

MINISTER
PADRE
PARSON
POPE

PRIEST
RECTOR
VICAR
VICAR-FORANE

POPES

POPE (DATE OF ACCESSION)

ST PETER (42)
ST LINUS (67)
ST ANACLETUS (Cletus) (76)
ST CLEMENT I (88)
ST EVARISTUS (97)
ST ALEXANDER I (105)
ST SIXTUS I (115)
ST TELESPHORUS (125)

ST HYGINUS (136)
ST PIUS I (140)
ST ANICETUS (155)
ST SOTERUS (166)
ST ELEUTHERIUS (175)
ST VICTOR I (189)
ST ZEPHYRINUS (199)
ST CALLISTUS I (217)
ST URBAN I (222)
ST PONTIAN (230)
ST ANTERUS (235)

ST FABIAN (236)
ST CORNELIUS (251)
ST LUCIUS I (253)
ST STEPHEN I (254)
ST SIXTUS II (257)
ST DIONYSIUS (259)
ST FELIX I (269)
ST EUTYCHIAN (275)
ST CAIUS (283)
ST MARCELLINUS (296)
ST MARCELLUS I (308)

ST EUSEBIUS (309)
ST MELCHIADES (311)
ST SYLVESTER I (314)
ST MARCUS (336)
ST JULIUS I (337)
LIBERIUS (352)
ST DAMASUS I (366)
ST SIRICIUS (384)
ST ANASTASIUS I (399)
ST INNOCENT I (401)
ST ZOSIMUS (417)

ST BONIFACE I (418)
ST CELESTINE I (422)
ST SIXTUS III (432)
ST LEO I (the Great) (440)
ST HILARY (461)
ST SIMPLICIUS (468)
ST FELIX III (483)
ST GELASIUS I (492)
ANASTASIUS II (496)
ST SYMMACHUS (498)
ST HORMISDAS (514)
ST JOHN I (523)
ST FELIX IV (526)
BONIFACE II (530)
JOHN II (533)
ST AGAPETUS I (535)
ST SILVERIUS (536)
VIGILIUS (537)
PELAGIUS I (556)
JOHN III (561)
BENEDICT I (575)
PELAGIUS II (579)
ST GREGORY I (the Great) (590)
SABINIANUS (604)
BONIFACE III (607)
ST BONIFACE IV (608)
ST DEUSDEDIT (Adeodatus I) (615)
BONIFACE V (619)
HONORIUS I (625)
SEVERINUS (640)
JOHN IV (640)
THEODORE I (642)
ST MARTIN I (649)
ST EUGENE I (654)
ST VITALIAN (657)
ADEODATUS II (672)
DONUS (676)
ST AGATHO (678)
ST LEO II (682)
ST BENEDICT II (684)
JOHN V (685)
CONON (686)
ST SERGIUS I (687)
JOHN VI (701)
JOHN VII (705)
SISINNIUS (708)
CONSTANTINE (708)
ST GREGORY II (715)
ST GREGORY III (731)
ST ZACHARY (741)
STEPHEN II (III)* (752)
ST PAUL I (757)
STEPHEN III (IV) (768)
ADRIAN I (772)
ST LEO III (795)

STEPHEN IV (V) (816)
ST PASCHAL I (817)
EUGENE II (824)
VALENTINE (827)
GREGORY IV (827)
SERGIUS II (844)
ST LEO IV (847)
BENEDICT III (855)
ST NICHOLAS I (858)
ADRIAN II (867)
JOHN VIII (872)
MARINUS I (882)
ST ADRIAN III (884)
STEPHEN V (VI) (885)
FORMOSUS (891)
BONIFACE VI (896)
STEPHEN VI (VII) (896)
ROMANUS (897)
THEODORE II (897)
JOHN IX (898)
BENEDICT IV (900)
LEO V (903)
SERGIUS III (904)
ANASTASIUS III (911)
LANDUS (913)
JOHN X (914)
LEO VI (928)
STEPHEN VII (VIII) (928)
JOHN XI (931)
LEO VII (936)
STEPHEN VIII (IX) (939)
MARINUS II (942)
AGAPETUS II (946)
JOHN XII (955)
LEO VIII (963)
BENEDICT V (964)
JOHN XIII (965)
BENEDICT VI (973)
BENEDICT VII (974)
JOHN XIV (983)
JOHN XV (985)
GREGORY V (996)
SYLVESTER II (999)
JOHN XVII (1003)
JOHN XVIII (1004)
SERGIUS IV (1009)
BENEDICT VIII (1012)
JOHN XIX (1024)
BENEDICT IX (1032)
GREGORY VI (1045)
CLEMENT II (1046)
BENEDICT X (1047)
DAMASUS II (1048)
ST LEO IX (1049)
VICTOR II (1055)
STEPHEN IX (X) (1057)
NICHOLAS II (1059)
ALEXANDER II (1061)

ST GREGORY VII (1073)
VICTOR III (1086)
URBAN II (1088)
PASCHAL II (1099)
GELASIUS II (1118)
CALLISTUS II (1119)
HONORIUS II (1124)
INNOCENT II (1130)
CELESTINE II (1143)
LUCIUS II (1144)
EUGENE III (1145)
ANASTASIUS IV (1153)
ADRIAN IV (1154)
ALEXANDER III (1159)
LUCIUS III (1181)
URBAN III (1185)
GREGORY VIII (1187)
CLEMENT III (1187)
CELESTINE III (1191)
INNOCENT III (1198)
HONORIUS III (1216)
GREGORY IX (1227)
CELESTINE IV (1241)
INNOCENT IV (1243)
ALEXANDER IV (1254)
URBAN IV (1261)
CLEMENT IV (1265)
GREGORY X (1271)
INNOCENT V (1276)
ADRIAN V (1276)
JOHN XXI (1276)
NICHOLAS III (1277)
MARTIN IV (1281)
HONORIUS IV (1285)
NICHOLAS IV (1288)
ST CELESTINE V (1294)
BONIFACE VIII (1294)
BENEDICT XI (1303)
CLEMENT V (1305)
JOHN XXII (1316)
BENEDICT XII (1334)
CLEMENT VI (1342)
INNOCENT VI (1352)
URBAN V (1362)
GREGORY XI (1370)
URBAN VI (1378)
BONIFACE IX (1389)
INNOCENT VII (1404)
GREGORY XII (1406)
MARTIN V (1417)
EUGENE IV (1431)
NICHOLAS V (1447)
CALLISTUS III (1455)
PIUS II (1458)
PAUL II (1464)
SIXTUS IV (1471)
INNOCENT VIII (1484)
ALEXANDER VI (1492)

PIUS III (1503)
JULIUS II (1503)
LEO X (1513)
ADRIAN VI (1522)
CLEMENT VII (1523)
PAUL III (1534)
JULIUS III (1550)
MARCELLUS II (1555)
PAUL IV (1555)
PIUS IV (1559)
ST PIUS V (1566)
GREGORY XIII (1572)
SIXTUS V (1585)
URBAN VII (1590)
GREGORY XIV (1590)
INNOCENT IX (1591)
CLEMENT VIII (1592)
LEO XI (1605)
PAUL V (1605)
GREGORY XV (1621)
URBAN VIII (1623)
INNOCENT X (1644)
ALEXANDER VII (1655)
CLEMENT IX (1667)
CLEMENT X (1670)
INNOCENT XI (1676)
ALEXANDER VIII (1689)
INNOCENT XII (1691)
CLEMENT XI (1700)
INNOCENT XIII (1721)
BENEDICT XIII (1724)
CLEMENT XII (1730)
BENEDICT XIV (1740)
CLEMENT XIII (1758)
CLEMENT XIV (1769)
PIUS VI (1775)
PIUS VII (1800)
LEO XII (1823)
PIUS VIII (1829)
GREGORY XVI (1831)
PIUS IX (1846)
LEO XIII (1878)
ST PIUS X (1903)
BENEDICT XV (1914)
PIUS XI (1922)
PIUS XII (1939)
JOHN XXIII (1958)
PAUL VI (1963)
JOHN PAUL I (1978)
JOHN PAUL II (1978)
BENEDICT XVI (2005)
FRANCIS (2013)
*Stephen II died before consecration and was dropped from the list of popes in 1961; Stephen III became Stephen II

ARCHBISHOPS OF CANTERBURY

ARCHBISHOP (DATE OF ACCESSION)

AUGUSTINE (597)
LAURENTIUS (604)
MELLITUS (619)
JUSTUS (624)
HONORIUS (627)
DEUSDEDIT (655)
THEODORUS (668)
BEORHTWEALD (693)
TATWINE (731)
NOTHELM (735)
CUTHBEORHT (740)
BREGUWINE (761)
JAENBEORHT (765)
⊡THELHEARD (793)
WULFRED (805)
FEOLOGILD (832)
CEOLNOTH (833)
⊡THELRED (870)
PLEGMUND (890)
⊡THELHELM (914)
WULFHELM (923)
ODA (942)
⊡LFSIGE (959)
BEORHTHELM (959)
DUNSTAN (960)
⊡THELGAR (988)
SIGERIC SERIO (990)
⊡LFRIC (995)
⊡LFHEAH (1005)
LYFING (1013)
⊡THELNOTH (1020)
EADSIGE (1038)
ROBERT OF JUMIÈGES (1051)
STIGAND (1052)
LANFRANC (1070)
ANSELM (1093)
RALPH D'ESCURES (1114)
WILLIAM OF CORBEIL (1123)
THEOBALD OF BEC (1139)
THOMAS BECKET (1162)

RICHARD OF DOVER (1174)
BALDWIN (1184)
REGINALD FITZJOCELIN (1191)
HUBERT WALTER (1193)
REGINALD (1205)
JOHN DE GRAY (1205)
STEPHEN LANGTON (1213)
WALTER OF EVESHAM (1128)
RICHARD GRANT (Wethershed) (1229)
RALPH NEVILL (1231)
JOHN OF SITTINGBOURNE (1232)
JOHN BLUND (1232)
EDMUND RICH (1234)
BONIFACE OF SAVOY (1245)
ADAM OF CHILLENDEN (1270)
ROBERT KILWARDBY (1273)
ROBERT BURNELL (1278)
JOHN PECHAM (1279)
ROBERT WINCHELSEY (1295)
THOMAS COBHAM (1313)
WALTER REYNOLDS (1314)
SIMON MEPHAM (1328)
JOHN STRATFORD (1334)
JOHN OFFORD (1348)
THOMAS BRADWARDINE (1349)
SIMON ISLIP (1349)
SIMON LANGHAM (1366)
WILLIAM WHITTLESEY (1369)
SIMON SUDBURY (1375)
WILLIAM COURTENAY (1381)
THOMAS ARUNDEL (1397)
ROGER WALDEN (1398)
THOMAS ARUNDEL (1399)
HENRY CHICHELE (1414)
JOHN STAFFORD (1443)
JOHN KEMPE (1452)
THOMAS BOURGCHIER (1454)
JOHN MORTON (1486)
HENRY DEANE (1501)
WILLIAM WARHAM (1504)
THOMAS CRANMER (1533)
REGINALD POLE (1556)

MATTHEW PARKER (1559)
EDMUND GRINDAL (1576)
JOHN WHITGIFT (1583)
RICHARD BANCROFT (1604)
GEORGE ABBOT (1611)
WILLIAM LAUD (1633)
WILLIAM JUXON (1660)
GILBERT SHELDON (1663)
WILLIAM SANCROFT (1678)
JOHN TILLOTSON (1691)
THOMAS TENISON (1695)
WILLIAM WAKE (1716)
JOHN POTTER (1737)
THOMAS HERRING (1747)
MATTHEW HUTTON (1757)
THOMAS SECKER (1758)
FREDERICK CORNWALLIS (1768)
JOHN MOORE (1783)
CHARLES MANNERS SUTTON (1805)
WILLIAM HOWLEY (1828)
JOHN BIRD SUMNER (1848)
CHARLES THOMAS LONGLEY (1862)
ARCHIBALD CAMPBELL TAIT (1868)
EDWARD WHITE BENSON (1883)
FREDERICK TEMPLE (1896)
RANDALL THOMAS DAVIDSON (1903)
COSMO GORDON LANG (1928)
GEOFFREY FRANCIS FISHER (1945)
ARTHUR MICHAEL RAMSEY (1961)
FREDERICK DONALD COGGAN (1974)
ROBERT ALEXANDER KENNEDY RUNCIE (1980)
GEORGE LEONARD CAREY (1991)
ROWAN DOUGLAS WILLIAMS (2003)
JUSTIN PORTAL WELBY (2013)

RELIGIOUS TERMS

2
BA
HO
OM

3
ALB
ARA
AUM
HAJ
PEW
PIX
PYX
YAD

4
AMBO
APSE
AZAN
BEMA
BUJI
BULL
COPE
COWL
FONT
HADJ
HAJJ
HALO
HELL
HOOD
HOST
HYMN
JUBE
KAMA
KNOP
LENT
MACE
MASS
NAOS
NAVE
OLAH
RAMA
SOMA
TIEN
VOID
WAKE
YOGA

5
ABBOT
ABYSS
AGATI
AISLE
ALLEY
ALTAR
AMBRY
AMICE
ANGEL
APRON
ARMOR

BANNS
BASON
BEADS
BIBLE
BIMAH
BODHI
BRIEF
BUGIA
BURSE
COTTA
CREED
CROSS
CRUET
DIKKA
EMETH
EPHOD
FALDA
GOHEI
HYLIC
IHRAM
KALPA
KARMA
LAVER
LIMBO
MOTZI
NICHE
PASCH
PESAH
PESHA
PSALM
ROSHI
SHIVA
STOUP
SYNOD
TOTEM
USHER
VEDAS
WAFER

6
ABBACY
ABODAH
ADVENT
AGUNAH
AHIMSA
AKASHA
AKEDAH
AL CHET
ANOINT
ANTHEM
AUMBRY
AVODAH
BARSOM
BAT KOL
BEADLE
BELFRY
CANTOR
CHOHAN
CHOVAH
CHRISM

CLERGY
DHARMA
DHYANA
DITTHI
DOSSAL
DUCHAN
EASTER
FLECHE
FRATER
GLORIA
HEAVEN
HEKHAL
HESPED
KAIROS
KIBLAH
KISMET
KITTEL
LITANY
MANTRA
MATINS
MISSAL
NIGGUN
NIMBUS
ORATIO
ORISON
PARVIS
PESACH
PRAYER
PULPIT
ROCHET
ROSARY
SANGHA
SERMON
SERVER
SHARI'A
SHRIVE
SPIRIT
SUTRAS
TAUHID
TIPPET
VERGER
VESTRY

7
ACCIDIA
ACCIDIE
ACOLYTE
AGRAPHA
AMPULLA
ANGELUS
APOSTIL
APOSTLE
APPAREL
ASHAMNU
ATHEISM
AUREOLE
BADCHAN
BANKERS
BAPTISM
BATHING

BELL COT
BERAKAH
BIRETTA
CASSOCK
CHALICE
CHAMETZ
CHANCEL
CHANTRY
CHAPTER
CHAZZAN
CHRISOM
COLLECT
COMPLIN
CORNICE
CROSIER
CROZIER
DHARANI
DIOCESE
DIPTYCH
EILETON
FISTULA
GAYATRI
GELILAH
GEULLAH
GRADINE
GREMIAL
HASSOCK
HEATHEN
HEKDESH
INTROIT
KHEREBU
LECTERN
LOCULUS
MANIPLE
MINARET
MOZETTA
NARTHEX
NIRVANA
NOCTURN
PALLIUM
PENANCE
PILGRIM
PURUSHA
REQUIEM
REREDOS
SAMSARA
STHIBEL
TALLITH
TONSURE
TRINITY
TZADDIK
VESPERS
WORSHIP

8
ABLUTION
ABSTEMII
A CAPELLA
AFFLATUS
AFFUSION

AFIKOMEN
AGNUS DEI
ANTIPHON
ARMORIUM
AUTO DA FE
AVE MARIA
BEADROLL
BELL COTE
BEMIDBAR
BENEFICE
BREVIARY
BUTSUDEN
CANCELLI
CANTICLE
CIBORIUM
CINCTURE
COMPLINE
CONCLAVE
CORPORAL
CRUCIFIX
DALMATIC
DIKERION
DISCIPLE
DOXOLOGY
EPIPHANY
EVENSONG
FRONTLET
HABDALAH
MANIPULE
NATIVITY
NER TAMID
NIVARANA

OBLATION
PAROKHET
PASSOVER
PREDELLA
RESPONSE
SACRISTY
SURPLICE
TASHLICH
TRIPTYCH
VESTMENT

9
ADIAPHORA
ANAMNESIS
APOCRYPHA
ARBA KOSOT
ARCHANGEL
ASPERSION
CANDLEMAS
CARTOUCHE
CATACOMBS
CATECHISM
CERECLOTH
CHALITZAH
CHRISTMAS
COLLATION
COMMUNION
EPHPHETHA
EUCHARIST
FALDSTOOL
FLABELLUM
FORMULARY

MUNDATORY
OFFERTORY
PACE-AISLE
PURGATORY
SANCTUARY
YOM KIPPUR

10
ABSOLUTION
AGATHOLOGY
ALLOCUTION
AMBULATORY
ANTECHAPEL
APOCALYPSE
BALDACHINO
BAR MITZVAH
BAS MITZVAH
BAT MITZVAH
BENEDICTUS
CATAFALQUE
CLERESTORY
CUTTY STOOL
HAGIOSCOPE
INDULGENCE
INTINCTION
INVOCATION
LADY CHAPEL
PRESBYTERY
SEXAGESIMA

11
ABBREVIATOR

ABOMINATION
AGNOSTICISM
ALITURGICAL
ANTEPENDIUM
ANTIMINSION
ASPERGILLUM
BENEDICTION
CHRISTENING
HUMERAL VEIL
INQUISITION
INVESTITURE
SCRIPTORIUM

12
ANTILEGOMENA
ARON HA-KODESH
ASH WEDNESDAY
CONFIRMATION
CONGREGATION
SEPTUAGESIMA

13
BEATIFICATION
BIRKAT HA-MAZON
EPITRACHELION

14
FOLDED CHASUBLE
MAUNDY THURSDAY

17
CONSUBSTANTIATION

RELIGIOUS BUILDINGS

3
WAT

4
CELL
KIRK

5
ABBEY
BET AM
CELLA
DUOMO
HONDO

JINGU
JINJA

6
CHAPEL
CHURCH
MOSQUE
PAGODA
PRIORY

7
CHANTRY
CONVENT

DEANERY
MINSTER

8
BASILICA
CLOISTER
HOUNFORT
LAMASERY

9
BADRINATH
CATHEDRAL
MONASTERY

SYNAGOGUE

12
BET HA-KNESSET

BET HA-MIDRASH

CHAPTER HOUSE

MEETINGHOUSE

13
ANGELUS TEMPLE

RELIGIOUS FESTIVALS

Date	Festival	Religion	Date	Festival	Religion
Jan	Epiphany	Christian	June	Dragon Boat Festival	Chinese
Jan	Imbolc	Pagan	June	Summer Solstice	Pagan
Jan, Feb	New Year	Chinese	July	Dhammacakka	Buddhist
Feb, Mar	Shrove Tuesday	Christian	July	Eid ul-Adha	Islamic
Feb, Mar	Ash Wednesday	Christian	Aug	Raksha Bandhan	Hindu
Feb, Mar	Purim	Jewish	Aug	Lammas	Pagan
Feb, Mar	Mahashivaratri	Hindu	Aug, Sept	Janmashtami	Hindu
Feb, Mar	Holi	Hindu	Sept	Moon Festival	Chinese
Mar, Apr	Easter	Christian	Sept, Oct	Rosh Hashana	Jewish
Mar, Apr	Passover	Jewish	Sept, Oct	Yom Kippur	Jewish
Mar, Apr	Holi Mohalla	Sikh	Sept, Oct	Succoth	Jewish
Mar, Apr	Rama Naumi	Hindu	Oct	Dusshera	Hindu
Mar, Apr	Ching Ming	Chinese	Oct	Samhain	Pagan
Apr	Baisakhi	Sikh	Oct, Nov	Diwali	Hindu, Sikh
Apr	Beltane	Pagan	Nov	Birthday of Guru	SikhNanak
Apr, May	Lailat ul-Isra wal Mi'raj	islamic	Nov	Bodhi Day	Buddhist
			Dec	Christmas	Christian
Apr, May	Lailat ul-Bara'h	Islamic	Dec	Hanukkah	Jewish
Apr, May	Vesak	Buddhist	Dec	Winter Festival	Chinese
May, June	Shavuoth	Jewish	Dec	Winter Solstice	Pagan
May, June	Lailat ul-Qadr	Islamic	Dec, Jan	Birthday of Guru Gobind Singh	Sikh
May, June	Eid ul-Fitr	Islamic			
May, June	Martyrdom of Guru Arjan	Sikh	Dec, Jan	Martyrdom of Guru Tegh Bahadur	Sikh

HINDU DEITIES

ADITI - goddess of heaven; mother of the gods
AGNI - god of fire
AHI or IHI - the Sistrum Player
AMARAVATI - city of the gods
AMRITA - water of life
BALI - demon who became king of heaven and earth
BRAHMA - the Creator
DEVI - a mother goddess
DITI - mother of the demons
GANDHARVAS - celestial musicians
GANESHA - god of literature, wisdom, and prosperity
GARUDA - the devourer, identified with fire and the sun
HANUMAN - a monkey chief
INDRA - king of the gods; god of war and storm
JYESTHA - goddess of misfortune
KAMA - god of desire

KARTTIKEYA - war-god; god of bravery
KUBERA - god of wealth; guardian of the north
LAKSHMI - goddess of fortune
MANASA - sacred mountain and lake
PRITHIVI - earth-goddess; goddess of fertility
SARANYU - goddess of the clouds
SARASVATI - goddess of speech
SHITALA - goddess of smallpox
SHIVA - the Destroyer
SOMA - ambrosial offering to the gods
SUGRIVA - monkey king
SURYA - the sun-god
VAYU - god of the wind
VISVAKARMA - architect for the gods
VISHNU - the Preserver
YAMA - king of the dead
VARUNA - god of water

GREEK AND ROMAN MYTHOLOGY

MYTHOLOGICAL CHARACTERS

ACHILLES – Greek hero; invulnerable except for his heel

ADONIS – renowned for his beauty

AGAMEMNON – king of Mycenae

AJAX – Greek warrior

ATLAS – bore heaven on his shoulders

BELLEROPHON – Corinthian hero who rode winged horse Pegasus

BOREAS – the north wind

CERBERUS – three-headed dog, guarded Hades

CHARON – boatman who rowed dead across river Styx

CHARYBDIS – violent whirlpool

CIRCE – sorceress who had the power to turn men into beasts

CYCLOPS – one of a race of one-eyed giants (cyclopes)

DAEDALUS – craftsman; designed and built the labyrinth in Crete

GORGONS – three sisters (Stheno, Euryale, and Medusa) who had snakes for hair and whose appearance turned people to stone

HADES – the Underworld

HELEN OF TROY – famed for her beauty; cause of Trojan war

HERACLES – famed for his courage and strength; performed the twelve labours

HERCULES – Roman name for HERACLES

HYDRA – many-headed snake

JASON – led the Argonauts in search of the Golden Fleece

LETHE – river in Hades whose water caused forgetfulness

MIDAS – King of Phrygia whose touch turned everything to gold

MINOTAUR – monster with the head of a bull and the body of a man. It was kept in the Cretan labyrinth and fed with human flesh

NARCISSUS – beautiful youth who fell in love with his own reflection

ODYSSEUS – Greek hero of the Trojan war

OEDIPUS – king of Thebes; married his mother

OLYMPUS – a mountain; the home of the gods

ORPHEUS – skilled musician

PANDORA – the first woman; opened the box that released all varieties of evil

PERSEUS – Greek hero who killed the Gorgon Medusa

POLYPHEMUS – leader of the Cyclopes

ROMULUS – founder of Rome

SATYRS – hoofed spirits of forests, fields, and streams

SCYLLA – six-headed sea monster

SIBYL – a prophetess

SIRENS – creatures depicted as half women, half birds, who lured sailors to their deaths

STYX – main river of Hades, across which Charon ferried the souls of the dead

THESEUS – Greek hero who killed the Cretan Minotaur

ULYSSES – Roman name for ODYSSEUS

GREEK GODS (ROMAN EQUIVALENT)

APHRODITE – goddess of beauty and love (VENUS)

APOLLO – god of poetry, music, and prophecy (APOLLO)

ARES – god of war (MARS)

ARTEMIS – goddess of the moon (DIANA)

ASCLEPIUS – god of medical art (AESCULAPIUS)

ATHENE – goddess of wisdom (MINERVA)

CHARITES – 3 daughters of Zeus: Euphrosyne, Aglaia, and Thalia; personified grace, beauty, and charm (GRACES)

CRONOS – god of agriculture (SATURN)

DEMETER – goddess of agriculture (CERES)

DIONYSUS – god of wine and fertility (BACCHUS)

EOS – goddess of dawn (AURORA)

EROS – god of love (CUPID)

FATES – 3 goddesses who determine man's destiny: Clotho, Lachesis, and Atropos

HEBE – goddess of youth (JUVENTAS)

HECATE – goddess of witchcraft (HECATE)

HELIOS – god of the sun (SOL)

HEPHAESTUS – god of destructive fire (VULCAN)

HERA – queen of heaven, goddess of women and marriage (JUNO)

HERMES – messenger of gods (MERCURY)

HESTIA – goddess of the hearth (VESTA)

HYPNOS – god of sleep (SOMNUS)

NEMESIS – goddess of retribution

PAN – god of woods and fields (FAUNUS)

PERSEPHONE – goddess of the Underworld (PROSERPINE)

PLUTO – god of the Underworld (PLUTO)

PLUTUS – god of wealth

POSEIDON – god of the sea (NEPTUNE)

RHEA – goddess of nature (CYBELE)

SELENE – goddess of the moon (LUNA)

THANATOS – god of death (MORS)

ZEUS – supreme god; god of sky and weather (JUPITER)

ROMAN GODS (GREEK EQUIVALENT)

AESCULAPIUS (ASCLEPIUS)

APOLLO (APOLLO)

AURORA (EOS)

BACCHUS (DIONYSUS)

CERES (DEMETER)

CUPID (EROS)

CYBELE (RHEA)

DIANA (ARTEMIS)

FAUNUS (PAN)

GRACES (CHARITES)

HECATE (HECATE)

JUNO (HERA)

JUPITER (ZEUS)

JUVENTAS (HEBE)

LUNA (SELENE)
MARS (ARES)
MERCURY (HERMES)
MINERVA (ATHENE)
MORS (THANATOS)
NEPTUNE (POSEIDON)
PLUTO (PLUTO)
PROSERPINE (PERSEPHONE)
SATURN (CRONOS)
SOL (HELIOS)
SOMNUS (HYPNOS)
VENUS (APHRODITE)
VESTA (HESTIA)
VULCAN (HEPHAESTUS)

THE TWELVE LABOURS OF HERCULES

THE NEMEAN LION
THE LERNAEAN HYDRA
THE WILD BOAR OF ERYMANTHUS
THE STYMPHALIAN BIRDS

THE CERYNEIAN HIND
THE AUGEAN STABLES
THE CRETAN BULL
THE MARES OF DIOMEDES
THE GIRDLE OF HIPPOLYTE
THE CATTLE OF GERYON
THE GOLDEN APPLES OF THE HESPERIDES
THE CAPTURE OF CERBERUS

THE NINE MUSES

CALLIOPE (EPIC POETRY)
CLIO (HISTORY)
ERATO (LOVE POETRY)
EUTERPE (LYRIC POETRY)
MELPOMENE (TRAGEDY)
POLYHYMNIA (SACRED SONG)
TERPSICHORE (DANCING)
THALIA (COMEDY)
URANIA (ASTRONOMY)

NORSE MYTHOLOGY

AEGIR – god of the sea
ALFHEIM – part of Asgard inhabited by the light
   elves
ASGARD – the home of the gods
ASK – name of the first man, created from a fallen
   tree
BALDER – god of the summer sun
BRAGI – god of poetry
EIR – goddess of healing
EMBLA – name of first woman, created from a fallen
   tree
FORSETI – god of justice
FREY – god of fertility and crops
FREYJA – goddess of love and night
FRIGG – Odin's wife; supreme goddess
GUNGNIR – Odin's magic spear
HEIMDAL – guardian of Asgard
HEL – goddess of the dead
HÖDUR – god of night
IDUN – wife of Bragi; guardian of the golden apples
   of youth

LOKI – god of evil
MIDGARD – the world of men
NORNS – three goddesses of destiny: Urd (Fate),
   Skuld (Being), and Verdandi (Necessity)
ODIN – supreme god; god of battle, inspiration, and
   death
RAGNAROK – final battle between gods and giants,
   in which virtually all life is destroyed
SIF – wife of Thor; her golden hair was cut off by
   Loki
SLEIPNIR – Odin's eight-legged horse
THOR – god of thunder
TYR – god of war
VALHALLA – hall in Asgard where Odin welcomed
   the souls of heroes killed in battle
VALKYRIES – nine handmaidens of Odin who chose
   men doomed to die in battle
YGGDRASILL – the World Tree, an ash linking all the
   worlds
YMIR – giant from whose body the world was
   formed

EGYPTIAN MYTHOLOGY

AMON-RA – supreme god
ANUBIS – jackel-headed son of Osiris; god of the
   dead
BES – god of marriage
GEB – earth-god
HATHOR – cow-headed goddess of love
HORUS – hawk-headed god of light
ISIS – goddess of fertility

MAAT – goddess of law, truth, and
   justice
MIN – god of virility
MONT – god of war
MUT – wife of Amon-Ra
NEHEH – god of eternity
NUN or NU – the primordial Ocean
NUT – goddess of the sky

OSIRIS – ruler of the afterlife
PTAH – god of the arts
RA – the sun god
RENPET – goddess of youth
SEKHMET – goddess of war

SET or SETH – god of evil
SHU – god of air
TEFNUT – goddess of dew and rain
THOTH – god of wisdom
UPUAUT – warrior-god; god of the dead

NORTH AMERICAN MYTHOLOGY

ADLIVUN – Eskimo land of the unhappy dead
AGLOOKIK – Eskimo spirit of hunters
AHSONNUTLI – chief god of the Navaho Indians
AKYCHA – the Sun
ANGAKOO – Eskimo shaman
ANGUTA – Eskimo ruler of the underworld
ANINGAN – the Moon
BIG OWL – cannibalistic monster of the Apache
   Indians
COYOTE – trickster god
DZOAVITS – Shoshone ogre
GLOOSKAP – agent of good; made the sky, earth,
   creatures, and mankind
HIAWATHA – legendary sage of the Iroquois Indians
   who founded the League of Five Nations
HINO – Iroquois god of thunder
HINUN – thunder spirit of the Iroquois Indians
ICTINIKE – trickster god of the Sioux Indians
MALSUM – agent of evil; made the mountains,
   valleys, and snakes
NANA BOZHO (MANA BOZHO) – trickster god of

the Algonquins
NANOOK – the Bear (the Pleiades)
NAPI – chief god of the Blackfoot
NATOS – sun god of the Blackfoot Indians
NAYENEZGANI – hero of Navaho legend; name
   means 'slayer of evil gods'
NEGAFOK – cold weather spirit
SEDNA – the great Sea Mother; Eskimo goddess of
   the underworld and sea
SPIDER WOMAN – benevolent creature who helped
   Nayenezgani defeat the powers of evil
TIRAWA – chief god of the Pawnee, who created
   the world and set the course of the sun, moon,
   and stars
TORNAQ – familiar of a shaman
TSOHANOAI – Navaho sun god, who carries the sun
   on his back across the sky
WAKONDA – great god of the Sioux Indians whose
   name means 'great power above'
WONOMI – sky god of the Maidu Indians who was
   abandoned in favour of Coyote

CENTRAL AND SOUTH AMERICAN MYTHOLOGY

AH PUCH – Maya god of death
BACHUE – mother goddess and protector of crops
BOCHICA – Colombian founder hero; appears as an
   old bearded man
CHAC – Maya rain god
CINTEOTL – Aztec god of maize
COATLICUE – Aztec earth goddess; a devouring
   goddess who was only satisfied by human flesh
   and blood
CUPAY (SUPAY) – Inca god of death
EHECATL – Aztec god of the winds who introduced
   sexual love to mankind
GUINECHEN – chief deity of Araucanian Indians,
   associated with fertility
HUITZILOPOCHTLI – chief god of the Aztecs
INTI – sun god from whom Inca dynasty traced its
   descent
ITZAMNA – chief god of the Maya
IXCHEL – Maya moon goddess
IXTAB – Maya goddess of suicide

IXTLILTON – Aztec god of medicine
KUAT – sun god of the Mamaiurans
MIXCOATL – Aztec god of the chase
MONTEZUMA – Aztec god whose name was taken
   from the last emperor
PACHAMAMA – Earth goddess of the Incas
PILLAN – thunder god of Araucanian Indians
QUETZALCOATL – a priest-king of Central America;
   the snake-bird god or plumed serpent
TEZCATLIPOCA – Aztec god of summer sun; bringer
   of harvests as well as drought
TLALOC – rain god of Central America, worshipped
   by the Toltecs and Aztecs
TUPAN – thunder god of the Guarani Indians
VAICA – magician and medicine-man of the Jurunas
VIRACOCHA – creator god of the Incas
XIPETOTEC – Aztec god of agriculture and self-
   torture; his name means 'flayed lord'
XOCHIQUETZAL – Aztec goddess of flowers and
   fruits

AUSTRALIAN MYTHOLOGY

AKURRA – serpent god

ALCHERA – 'Dreamtime', primeval time when the ancestors sang the world into existence

ARUNKULTA – Aranda spirit of evil

BAGADJIMBIRI – ancestral creator of gods

BIAME – god of creation

BIRRAHGNOOLOO – chief wife of Biame

BOLUNG – serpent god; giver of life

BOOMERANG – symbolizes the rainbow and the connection of opposites (e.g. heaven and earth)

BRALGU – island of the dead

BUNJIL – god of creation

BUNYIP – monster and giver of mystic healing rites

DILGA – earth goddess

DJANBUN – man who turned into a platypus after blowing too hard on a fire-stick

KAPOO – ancestral kangaroo who gave cats their spots

MANGAR-KUNGER-KUNJA – great lizard ancestor of the Aranda

MARINDI – ancestral dog whose blood turned the rocks red

PUNDJEL – creator god who made the first human being

WATI-KUTJARA – two lizard men of Central Australia

YURLUNYUR – ancestor of the Murngin of the northern Australia, known as the great copper python or the rainbow serpent

AFRICAN MYTHOLOGY

ABASSI – sky god of the Efik

ADROA – creator god of the Lugbara

ADU OGYINAE – first man of the Ashanti

ALA – mother goddess of the Ibo, eastern Nigeria

AMMA – an egg; seed of the cosmos; god of creation

ANANSI – W African trickster god

ASA – supreme god of the Akamba

BUMBA – creator god of the Bushongo of the Democratic Republic of Congo

CHINAWEJI – serpent; founder of the universe

CHUKU – supreme god of the Ibo, eastern Nigeria

DXUI – first god of creation

ESHU – messenger between High God and humans

ESHU – trickster god of the Yoruba who carried messages from the gods to mankind

EVENING STAR – wife of MWETSI, bearer of animals and people

FARO – maker of the sky

GU – heavenly blacksmith

IFA – god of medicine and prophecy

IMANA – supreme god of the Banyarwanda, Rwanda

JOK – creator god of the Alur

KAANG – creator god of the southwest African Bushmen

LEZA – supreme god of the Bantu

MAWU-LISA – twin creator gods

MBOOM – god of creation

MINIA – serpent; founder of the universe

MORNING STAR – wife of MWETSI, bearer of grass, shrubs, etc.

MOYNA – hero who invented the bull-roarer

MULUNGU – all-knowing sky god of the Nyamwezi

MWARI – High God

MWETSI – the first man

NANA – earth goddess of the Yoruba

NGAAN – god of creation

NGEWO – sky god of the Miende

NOMMO – a creator god

NTORO – the soul, in the beliefs of the Ashanti

NYAME – mother goddess

OGUN – war god of the Yoruba

PEMBA – maker of the earth

RUHANGA – high god of the Bangoro

UNKULUNKULU – supreme god of the Zulus

WELE – chief god of the Abaluyia of Kenya

WOOD – name of all the nine children of MBOOM

ARTHURIAN LEGEND

AGRAVAIN – younger brother of Gawain, helped expose Lancelot's and Guinevere's adultery to Arthur

AMFORTAS – Fisher King who looked after the Grail

ARTHUR – legendary British leader of the Knights of the Round Table

AVALON – wonderful island where Arthur was taken to be healed of his wounds

BORS – only knight to achieve the quest of the Holy

Grail, and to survive and return to Arthur's court

CAMELOT – capital of Arthur's kingdom

ECTOR – foster father of Arthur, father of Kay

EXCALIBUR – Arthur's magic sword

GALAHAD – son of Lancelot; purest of the Knights of the Round Table; succeeded in the quest of the Grail

GAWAIN – nephew of Arthur, son of Morgan Le Fay; searched for the Grail

GRAIL (SANGREAL, THE HOLY GRAIL) – said to be the vessel of the Last Supper; in the custody of the Fisher King

GUINEVERE – wife of Arthur, lover of Lancelot

IGRAINE – wife of Uther Pendragon; mother of Arthur and Morgan le Fay

KAY – foster brother of Arthur

LADY OF THE LAKE – enchantress who raised Lancelot and gave Arthur Excalibur

LANCELOT or LAUNCELOT – knight and lover of Queen Guinevere

LUCAN – most trusted of Arthur's friends

MERLIN – magician and bard who prepared Arthur for kingship

MORDRED or MODRED – son of Arthur and his half-sister Morgause

MORGAN LE FAY – sorceress and healer; half-sister of Arthur

MORGAUSE – half-sister of Arthur; mother of Mordred, Gawain, Gareth, and Agravain

NIMUE – enchantress with whom Merlin fell in love

PERCIVAL or PERCEVAL – knight who vowed to seek the Grail

UTHER PENDRAGON – father of Arthur

VIVIANE – the Lady of the Lake

CELTIC MYTHOLOGY

ANGUS – Irish god of love

ANNWN – the Underworld in Welsh mythology

ANU – earth goddess, mother of the gods of Ireland

ARAWN – Welsh king of the Underworld (Annwn)

BALOR – Irish one-eyed god of death

BANSHEE – English name for Bean Sidhe, the Irish fairy, whose wailing foretells the approach of death

BECUMA – Irish goddess, who was banished to earth

BELINUS – god of the sun

BELTAIN – first day of summer – 1st May

BRANWEN – daughter of Llyr

BRIGIT, BRIGHID – bringer of the spring – became St Bride

CERNUNNOS – god of wild beasts

CIAN – Irish father of the sun god Lugh

COCIDIUS – god of hunting

CONN – high king of Ireland

COVENTINA – goddess of water

CU CHULAINN – Irish hero, foster-son of King Conchobhar

DAGHDHA, THE – The Good God (of Ireland)

DANA – Irish mother goddess

DIAN-CECHT – Irish god of medicine

DIERDRE – daughter of the Ulster lord Felim Mac Dall who was forced to marry Conchobhar, and never smiled again

DONN – Irish god of the dead

EPONA – goddess of horsemen and animals

FINN MAC COOL (FINGAL) – legendary Irish hero who obtained wisdom from the salmon of knowledge (Fintan)

FLIDHAIS – goddess of the moon and hunting

GREEN MAN – fertility god

GWYDION – Welsh priest-king and magician

GWYNN – Welsh god of the Underworld

HERNE – the hunter

LUGH – Irish sun god

MABON – god of youth

MANANNAN – Irish sea god

MEDB – legendary Queen of Connacht – possibly prototype of Mab, British Queen of the fairies

MORRIGAN – Irish goddess of war

NUADA – high king of Ireland

OENGHUS – god of love

OSSIAN – Irish hero

PRYDERI – son of Pwyll and Rhiannon, who eventually succeeded his father as lord of Dyfed

PWYLL – Chief of Annwn (Prince of Dyfed)

RHIANNON – wife of Pwyll who was falsely accused of killing her son

SAMHAIN – first day of winter – 1st November

SHEELA-NA-GIG – goddess of fertility

SIDHE – Irish fairies of the Otherworld

TALIESIN – Welsh wizard who knew the secrets of the past, present, and future

TARANIS – the thunderer

MYTHOLOGICAL AND IMAGINARY BEINGS

3
ELF
NIX
ORC
ROC

4
FAUN
JINN
OGRE
PUCK
YETI

5
DEMON
DWARF
FAIRY
FIEND
GENIE
GHOST
GHOUL
GIANT
GNOME
GOLEM
HARPY
JOTUN
LAMIA
NYMPH
PIXIE
PRETA
SATYR
SYLPH
TROLL

6
AFREET

AZAZEL
BUNYIP
DAEMON
DRAGON
DYBBUK
FAFNIR
FURIES
GOBLIN
HOBBIT
KELPIE
KOBOLD
KRAKEN
RAVANA
SINBAD
SPHINX
SPRITE
UNDINE
ZOMBIE

7
AMAZONS
BANSHEE
BROWNIE
CENTAUR
CHIMERA
GREMLIN
GRENDEL
GRIFFIN
INCUBUS
LORELEI
MERMAID
PHOENIX
SILENUS
UNICORN
VAMPIRE

8
BABA YAGA
BARGHEST
BASILISK
BEHEMOTH
QUEEN MAB
SUCCUBUS
WEREWOLF

9
GILGAMESH
HOBGOBLIN
MANTICORE
NIBELUNGS
PIED PIPER
ROBIN HOOD

10
HIPPOGRIFF
LEPRECHAUN
SALAMANDER
SANTA CLAUS

11
AMPHISBAENA
HIPPOCAMPUS
POLTERGEIST
RIP VAN WINKLE
SCHEHEREZADE

12+
ABOMINABLE SNOWMAN
FATHER CHRISTMAS
LOCH NESS MONSTER
ROBIN GOODFELLOW

CHARACTERS FROM THE TALES OF ROBIN HOOD

ALAN A DALE
FRIAR TUCK
GUY OF GISBORNE
KING RICHARD THE LIONHEART

LITTLE JOHN
MAID MARIAN
MERRY MEN
MUCH THE MILLER

PRINCE JOHN
SHERIFF OF NOTTINGHAM
WILL SCARLET

WORK

PROFESSIONS, TRADES, AND OCCUPATIONS

2
GP
MD
MO
PM

3
DOC
DON
GYP
PRO
REP
SPY
VET

4
AMAH
AYAH
BABU
BARD
BOSS
CHAR
CHEF
COOK
CREW
DIVA
DYER
GANG
GRIP
HACK
HAND
HEAD
HERD
HIND
MAGI
MAID
MATE
MIME
PAGE
PEON
POET
SEER
SERF
SYCE
TOUT
WARD
WHIP

5
ACTOR
AD-MAN

AGENT
BAKER
BONZE
BOOTS
BOSUN
CADDY
CLERK
CLOWN
COACH
COMIC
CRIER
CRIMP
CURER
DAILY
ENVOY
EXTRA
FAKIR
FENCE
FIFER
FILER
FINER
FLIER
GIPSY
GLUER
GROOM
GUARD
GUIDE
GUILD
HAKIM
HARPY
HELOT
HIRER
HIVER
HOPPO
LEECH
LUTER
MASON
MEDIC
MINER
NAVVY
NURSE
OILER
OWLER
PILOT
PIPER
PLYER
PUPIL
QUACK
QUILL
RABBI

RATER
REEVE
RUNER
SCOUT
SEWER
SHOER
SLAVE
SMITH
SOWER
STAFF
SWEEP
TAMER
TAWER
TAXER
TILER
TUNER
TUTOR
TYLER
USHER
VALET
VINER

6
AIRMAN
ARCHER
ARTIST
AURIST
AUTHOR
BAGMAN
BAILER
BAILOR
BALKER
BANKER
BARBER
BARGEE
BARKER
BARMAN
BATMAN
BEARER
BINDER
BOFFIN
BOOKIE
BOWMAN
BREWER
BROKER
BUGLER
BURLER
BURSAR
BUSKER
BUTLER
CABBIE

CABMAN
CALKER
CANNER
CARTER
CARVER
CASUAL
CENSOR
CLERGY
CLERIC
CODIST
COINER
COMBER
CONDER
COOLIE
COOPER
COPPER
CO-STAR
COSTER
COWBOY
COWMAN
CRITIC
CUTLER
CUTTER
DANCER
DEALER
DIGGER
DOCKER
DOCTOR
DOWSER
DRAPER
DRAWER
DRIVER
DROVER
EDITOR
FABLER
FACTOR
FARMER
FELLER
FICTOR
FISHER
FITTER
FLAYER
FORGER
FOWLER
FRAMER
FULLER
GAFFER
GANGER
GAOLER
GAUCHO

GAUGER
GIGOLO
GILDER
GILLIE
GLAZER
GLOVER
GRAVER
GROCER
GUIDER
GUIDON
GUNMAN
GUNNER
HARPER
HATTER
HAWKER
HEALER
HEAVER
HODMAN
HOOPER
HORNER
HOSIER
HUNTER
INTERN
ISSUER
JAILER
JAILOR
JOBBER
JOCKEY
JOINER
JOWTER
JURIST
KEELER
KEEPER
KILLER
LACKEY
LANDER
LASCAR
LAWYER
LECTOR
LENDER
LOADER
LOGMAN
LUMPER
MARKER
MATRON
MEDICO
MENDER
MENIAL
MENTOR
MERCER
MILKER
MILLER
MINTER
MONGER
MORISK
MUMMER
MUMPER
MYSTIC
NAILER
NOTARY
NURSER
OBOIST
OILMAN

ORATOR
OSTLER
PACKER
PARSON
PASTOR
PAVIER
PAVIOR
PEDANT
PEDLAR
PENMAN
PICKER
PIEMAN
PIRATE
PITMAN
PLATER
PLAYER
PORTER
POTBOY
POTTER
PRIEST
PRUNER
PURSER
QUERRY
RABBIN
RAGMAN
RANGER
RATTER
READER
REAPER
REAVER
RECTOR
REGENT
RELIEF
RENTER
RIGGER
RINGER
ROBBER
ROOFER
ROOTER
SACKER
SAILOR
SALTER
SALVOR
SAPPER
SARTOR
SAWYER
SCRIBE
SEA-DOG
SEALER
SEAMAN
SEINER
SEIZOR
SELLER
SERVER
SETTER
SEXTON
SHROFF
SINGER
SIRCAR
SKIVVY
SLATER
SLAVER
SLAVEY

SLEUTH
SNARER
SOCMAN
SORTER
SOUTER
SPICER
SQUIRE
STAGER
STOKER
STORER
SUTLER
TABLER
TAILOR
TAMPER
TANNER
TASKER
TASTER
TELLER
TERMER
TESTER
TILLER
TINKER
TINMAN
TINNER
TOLLER
TOUTER
TRACER
TRADER
TUBMAN
TURNER
TYCOON
TYPIST
USURER
VACHER
VALUER
VAMPER
VANMAN
VASSAL
VENDER
VENDOR
VERGER
VERSER
VIEWER
WAITER
WALLER
WARDEN
WARDER
WARPER
WASHER
WEAVER
WEEDER
WELDER
WHALER
WORKER
WRIGHT
WRITER

7

ABACIST
ABIGAIL
ACOLYTE
ACOLYTH
ACROBAT
ACTRESS

ACTUARY
ALEWIFE
ALMONER
ANALYST
APPOSER
ARABIST
ARBITER
ARTISAN
ARTISTE
ASSAYER
ASSIZER
ASSURED
ASSURER
AUDITOR
AVIATOR
AWARDER
BAILIFF
BANDMAN
BARMAID
BELLBOY
BELLHOP
BEST BOY
BIRDMAN
BLASTER
BLENDER
BOATMAN
BONDMAN
BOOKMAN
BOTTLER
BRIGAND
BUILDER
BURGLAR
BUTCHER
BUTTONS
CALLBOY
CAMBIST
CARRIER
CASEMAN
CASHIER
CATERER
CAULKER
CELLIST
CHANTER
CHAPMAN
CHEMIST
CHORIST
CLEANER
CLICKER
CLIPPIE
COALMAN
COBBLER
COCKLER
COLLIER
CO-PILOT
COPYIST
CORONER
CORSAIR
COUNSEL
COURIER
COWHERD
COWPOKE
CROFTER
CROPPER

271

CURATOR	IRONIST	SADDLER	**8**
CURRIER	JANITOR	SAMPLER	ADSCRIPT
CUSTODE	JUGGLER	SAMURAI	AERONAUT
DANSEUR	JUNKMAN	SCOURER	ALGERINE
DENTIST	JURYMAN	SCRAPER	ANALYSER
DIALIST	KEELMAN	SERVANT	APHORIST
DIETIST	KNACKER	SETTLER	APIARIST
DITCHER	KNITTER	SHARPER	APRON-MAN
DOMINIE	LACEMAN	SHEARER	ARBORIST
DOORMAN	LINKBOY	SHIPPER	ARMORIST
DRAGMAN	LINKMAN	SHOPBOY	ARMOURER
DRAPIER	LOCKMAN	SHOWMAN	ARRESTOR
DRAWBOY	LOMBARD	SHUNTER	ASSESSOR
DRAYMAN	MALTMAN	SILKMAN	ATTORNEY
DREDGER	MANAGER	SIMPLER	BAGMAKER
DRESSER	MANGLER	SKINNER	BAGPIPER
DROGMAN	MARBLER	SKIPPER	BANDSMAN
DRUMMER	MARCHER	SLIPPER	BARGEMAN
DUSTMAN	MARINER	SMELTER	BEARHERD
FARRIER	MARSHAL	SNIPPER	BEDESMAN
FASCIST	MATADOR	SOCAGER	BEDMAKER
FIDDLER	MATELOT	SOLDIER	BIT-MAKER
FIREMAN	MEALMAN	SOLOIST	BLEACHER
FLESHER	MEATMAN	SPENCER	BOATSMAN
FLORIST	MIDWIFE	SPINNER	BONDMAID
FLUNKEY	MILKMAN	SPOTTER	BONDSMAN
FLUTIST	MODISTE	STAINER	BOTANIST
FOOTBOY	MONEYER	STAMPER	BOWMAKER
FOOTMAN	MONITOR	STAPLER	BOXMAKER
FOOTPAD	MOOTMAN	STATIST	BREWSTER
FOREMAN	MOULDER	STEERER	BROACHER
FOUNDER	NEWSBOY	STEWARD	CABIN BOY
FRISEUR	OCULIST	SURGEON	CELLARER
FROGMAN	OFFICER	SWABBER	CERAMIST
FUELLER	ORDERER	SWEEPER	CHANDLER
FURRIER	ORDERLY	TABORER	CHOIRBOY
GATEMAN	PACKMAN	TALLIER	CIDERIST
GIRDLER	PAGEBOY	TAPSTER	CLAQUEUR
GLAZIER	PAINTER	TAXI-MAN	CLOTHIER
GLEANER	PALMIST	TEACHER	COACHMAN
GLEEMAN	PANTLER	TIPSTER	CO-AUTHOR
GLOSSER	PEDDLER	TRACKER	CODIFIER
GRAFFER	PIANIST	TRAINER	COISTRIL
GRAFTER	PICADOR	TRAPPER	COLLATOR
GRAINER	PLANNER	TRAWLER	COMEDIAN
GRANGER	PLANTER	TRIMMER	COMPILER
GRANTEE	PLEADER	TRUCKER	COMPOSER
GRANTOR	PLUMBER	TRUSTEE	CONJURER
GRAZIER	POACHER	TUMBLER	CONVEYOR
GRINDER	POSTBOY	TURNKEY	COURTIER
GYMNAST	POSTMAN	VINTNER	COW-LEECH
HACKLER	PRESSER	VIOLIST	COXSWAIN
HARPIST	PRESTOR	WAGONER	CROUPIER
HAULIER	PRINTER	WARRIOR	CUTPURSE
HELOTRY	PUDDLER	WEBSTER	DAIRYMAN
HERBIST	RANCHER	WEIGHER	DANSEUSE
HERDMAN	REALTOR	WHEELER	DECKHAND
HERITOR	REFINER	WHETTER	DEFENDER
HIGGLER	RIVETER	WIREMAN	DESIGNER
HOGHERD	ROADMAN	WOODMAN	DIRECTOR
HOSTLER	ROASTER	WOOLMAN	DOG-LEECH
INDEXER	RUSTLER	WORKMAN	DOMESTIC
INLAYER	SACRIST	WRAPPER	DOUGHBOY

DRAGOMAN
DRUGGIST
EDUCATOR
EMBALMER
EMISSARY
ENGINEER
ENGRAVER
ENROLLER
EPIC POET
ESSAYIST
ESSOINER
EXORCIST
EXPLORER
EXPORTER
FABULIST
FACTOTUM
FALCONER
FAMULIST
FARMHAND
FERRYMAN
FIGURANT
FILMSTAR
FINISHER
FISHWIFE
FLATFOOT
FLAUTIST
FLETCHER
FODDERER
FORESTER
FORGEMAN
FUGLEMAN
GANGSTER
GARDENER
GAVELMAN
GENDARME
GLASSMAN
GOATHERD
GOVERNOR
GUARDIAN
GUNSMITH
HAMMERER
HANDMAID
HANDYMAN
HATMAKER
HAYMAKER
HEAD COOK
HEADSMAN
HELMSMAN
HENCHMAN
HERDSMAN
HIRELING
HISTRION
HOME HELP
HOTELIER
HOUSEBOY
HUCKSTER
HUNTSMAN
IMPORTER
IMPROVER
INKMAKER
INVENTOR
JAPANNER
JET PILOT

JEWELLER
JONGLEUR
KIPPERER
LABOURER
LANDGIRL
LANDLADY
LANDLORD
LAPIDARY
LARCENER
LARDERER
LEADSMAN
LECTURER
LINESMAN
LUMBERER
MAGICIAN
MAGISTER
MALTSTER
MASSEUSE
MEASURER
MECHANIC
MEDALIST
MELODIST
MERCATOR
MERCHANT
METAL-MAN
MILKMAID
MILLHAND
MILLINER
MINISTER
MINSTREL
MODELLER
MULETEER
MURALIST
MUSICIAN
NEWSHAWK
NOVELIST
ONION-MAN
OPERATOR
OPTICIAN
ORDAINER
ORDINAND
ORGANIST
OUTRIDER
OVERSEER
PARGETER
PARODIST
PENMAKER
PERFUMER
PETERMAN
PEWTERER
PICAROON
PLOUGHER
POLISHER
PORTRESS
POSTILER
POTMAKER
PREACHER
PREFACER
PRELUDER
PRESSMAN
PROBATOR
PROCURER
PROMOTER

PROMPTER
PROSAIST
PROVIDER
PSALMIST
PUBLICAN
PUGILIST
PURVEYOR
QUARRIER
RAFTSMAN
RANCHERO
RAPPEREE
RECEIVER
REGRATER
RELESSEE
RELESSOR
REPAIRER
REPORTER
RESETTER
RESTORER
RETAILER
RETAINER
REVIEWER
REWRITER
RIVETTER
ROMANCER
RUGMAKER
RUMOURER
SALESMAN
SATIRIST
SAWBONES
SCULLION
SCULPTOR
SEAMSTER
SEA-ROVER
SEASONER
SEEDSMAN
SEMPSTER
SERVITOR
SHEARMAN
SHEPHERD
SHIPMATE
SHIP'S BOY
SHOPGIRL
SHOWGIRL
SIDESMAN
SIMPLIST
SKETCHER
SMUGGLER
SPACEMAN
SPEARMAN
SPEEDCOP
SPURRIER
STARCHER
STITCHER
STOCKMAN
STOREMAN
STRIPPER
STRUMMER
STUNTMAN
SUPPLIER
SURVEYOR
SWINDLER
TABOURER

TALLYMAN
TAVERNER
TEAMSTER
THATCHER
THESPIAN
THRESHER
TIN MINER
TINSMITH
TORTURER
TOYMAKER
TRIPEMAN
TRUCKMAN
TURNCOCK
TURNSPIT
TUTORESS
UNIONIST
VALUATOR
VINTAGER
VIRTUOSO
VOCALIST
VOLUMIST
WAITRESS
WALKER-ON
WARDRESS
WARRENER
WATCHMAN
WATERMAN
WET NURSE
WHALEMAN
WHITENER
WHITSTER
WIGMAKER
WINNOWER
WOOL-DYER
WRESTLER

9
ALCHEMIST
ALLUMINOR
ANATOMIST
ANNOTATOR
ANNOUNCER
ARBORATOR
ARCHERESS
ARCHITECT
ARCHIVIST
ART CRITIC
ART DEALER
ARTIFICER
ASTRONAUT
ATTENDANT
AUTHORESS
BALLADIST
BALLERINA
BANK AGENT
BARRISTER
BARROW BOY
BEEFEATER
BEEKEEPER
BIOLOGIST
BOATSWAIN
BODYGUARD
BOILERMAN
BONDSLAVE

BONDWOMAN	DRUM-MAKER	HERB-WOMAN	MYOLOGIST
BOOKMAKER	DRYSALTER	HIRED HAND	NAVIGATOR
BOOTBLACK	ECOLOGIST	HIRED HELP	NEGOTIANT
BOOTMAKER	EMBEZZLER	HISTORIAN	NEOLOGIAN
BUCCANEER	ENAMELLER	HOG-RINGER	NEOLOGIST
BURNISHER	ENGINEMAN	HOMEOPATH	NEWSAGENT
BUS DRIVER	ENGROSSER	HOP-PICKER	NURSEMAID
CAB DRIVER	EPITOMIST	HOSTELLER	ODD JOB MAN
CAFÉ OWNER	ERRAND BOY	HOUSEMAID	OFFICE BOY
CAMERAMAN	ESTIMATOR	HOUSEWIFE	OPERATIVE
CAR DRIVER	EXAMINANT	HYGIENIST	ORDINATOR
CARETAKER	EXCAVATOR	HYPNOTIST	OSTEOPATH
CARPENTER	EXCERPTOR	INCUMBENT	OTOLOGIST
CARVANEER	EXCHANGER	INGRAFTER	OUTFITTER
CASEMAKER	EXCISEMAN	INNHOLDER	PASQUILER
CATECHIST	EXECUTIVE	INNKEEPER	PAYMASTER
CELLARMAN	EXERCITOR	INSCRIBER	PEDAGOGUE
CHARWOMAN	EXORCISER	INSPECTOR	PERFORMER
CHAUFFEUR	FABRICANT	INTENDANT	PHYSICIAN
CHEAPJACK	FASHIONER	IRONSMITH	PHYSICIST
CHORISTER	FELT-MAKER	ITINERANT	PINKMAKER
CLARIFIER	FIGURANTE	JACK-SMITH	PITSAWYER
CLERGYMAN	FILM ACTOR	JOB-MASTER	PLANISHER
CLINICIAN	FILM EXTRA	KENNEL-MAN	PLASTERER
CLOGMAKER	FILM-MAKER	LACEMAKER	PLOUGHBOY
COALMINER	FINANCIER	LACQUERER	PLOUGHMAN
COALOWNER	FIRE-EATER	LADY'S MAID	PLURALIST
COLLECTOR	FISH-CURER	LAND AGENT	POETASTER
COLOURIST	FISHERMAN	LANDREEVE	POINTSMAN
COLUMNIST	FISH-WOMAN	LARCENIST	POLICEMAN
COMPRADOR	FLAG-MAKER	LAUNDERER	POP ARTIST
CONCIERGE	FLAX-WENCH	LAUNDRESS	PORTERESS
CONDUCTOR	FLYFISHER	LEGIONARY	PORTRAYER
CONSERVER	FREELANCE	LIBRARIAN	PORTREEVE
COSMONAUT	FREIGHTER	LINOTYPER	POSTILION
COST CLERK	FRIPPERER	LIONTAMER	POSTWOMAN
COSTUMIER	FRUITERER	LIVERYMAN	POULTERER
COURTESAN	FURBISHER	LOAN AGENT	PRACTISER
COUTURIER	FURNISHER	LOCKMAKER	PRECENTOR
COWFEEDER	GALVANIST	LOCKSMITH	PRECEPTOR
COWKEEPER	GASFITTER	LOG-ROLLER	PREDICANT
CRACKSMAN	GAZETTEER	LUMBERMAN	PRELECTOR
CRAFTSMAN	GEM-CUTTER	MACHINIST	PRIESTESS
CRAYONIST	GEOLOGIST	MAGNETIST	PRIVATEER
CYMBALIST	GLADIATOR	MAJORDOMO	PROFESSOR
DAILY HELP	GLUEMAKER	MALE MODEL	PROFILIST
DAIRYMAID	GOLDSMITH	MALE NURSE	PROVEDORE
DECORATOR	GONDOLIER	MAN-AT-ARMS	PUBLICIST
DECRETIST	GOSPELLER	MANNEQUIN	PUBLISHER
DESK CLERK	GOVERNESS	MECHANIST	PULPITEER
DETECTIVE	GROUNDMAN	MEDALLIST	PUPPETEER
DICE-MAKER	GUARDSMAN	MEMOIRIST	PYTHONESS
DIE-SINKER	GUERRILLA	MERCENARY	QUALIFIER
DIETETIST	GUITARIST	MESMERIST	QUARRYMAN
DIETITIAN	GUN-RUNNER	MESSENGER	RACKETEER
DIRECTRIX	HARLEQUIN	METALLIST	RAILMAKER
DISPENSER	HARMONIST	METRICIAN	RECRUITER
DISSECTOR	HARPOONER	MILL-OWNER	REFORMIST
DISTILLER	HARVESTER	MODELGIRL	REHEARSER
DOCTORESS	HELLENIST	MORTICIAN	RIBBONMAN
DRAFTSMAN	HERBALIST	MUFFIN-MAN	ROADMAKER
DRAMATIST	HERBARIAN	MUSKETEER	ROPEMAKER
DRAWLATCH	HERBORIST	MUSKETOON	ROUNDSMAN

RUM-RUNNER
SACRISTAN
SAFEMAKER
SAILMAKER
SCARIFIER
SCAVENGER
SCENARIST
SCHOLIAST
SCHOOLMAN
SCIENTIST
SCRIVENER
SCYTHEMAN
SEA-ROBBER
SECRETARY
SHIPOWNER
SHIP'S MATE
SHOEBLACK
SHOEMAKER
SIGHTSMAN
SIGNALMAN
SINOLOGUE
SOAPMAKER
SOLICITOR
SONNETEER
SORCERESS
STABLEBOY
STABLEMAN
STAGEHAND
STATIONER
STAY-MAKER
STEERSMAN
STEVEDORE
SUBEDITOR
SUCCENTOR
SUR-MASTER
SWAN-UPPER
SWINEHERD
SWITCHMAN
SWORDSMAN
SYNDICATE
SYNOPTIST
TABLEMAID
TACTICIAN
TAILORESS
TEATASTER
TENTMAKER
TEST PILOT
THERAPIST
THEURGIST
THROWSTER
TIMBERMAN
TIREWOMAN
TOOLSMITH
TOWN CLERK
TOWNCRIER
TRADESMAN
TRAGEDIAN
TRAVELLER
TREASURER
TREPANNER
TRIBUTARY
TRUMPETER
TYMPANIST

USHERETTE
VARNISHER
VERSIFIER
VETTURINO
VEXILLARY
VIOLINIST
VOLCANIST
VOLTIGEUR
WADSETTER
WARRANTEE
WARRANTER
WASHERMAN
WAXWORKER
WHITESTER
WINEMAKER
WOOD-REEVE
WORKWOMAN
ZOOKEEPER
ZOOLOGIST
ZOOTOMIST

10
ABLE SEAMAN
ACCOMPTANT
ACCOUCHEUR
ACCOUNTANT
ACOLOTHIST
ADVERTISER
AEROLOGIST
AGROLOGIST
AGRONOMIST
AIR HOSTESS
AIR STEWARD
ALGEBRAIST
AMANUENSIS
APOTHECARY
APPRENTICE
ARBALISTER
ARBITRATOR
ASTROLOGER
ASTRONOMER
ATMOLOGIST
AUCTIONEER
AUDIT CLERK
BALLOONIST
BALLPLAYER
BANDMASTER
BASEBALLER
BASSOONIST
BEADSWOMAN
BEAUTICIAN
BELL-HANGER
BELL-RINGER
BIOCHEMIST
BIOGRAPHER
BLACKSMITH
BLADESMITH
BLOCKMAKER
BLUEJACKET
BOMBARDIER
BONDSWOMAN
BONESETTER
BOOKBINDER
BOOKHOLDER

BOOKKEEPER
BOOKSELLER
BOOTLEGGER
BRICKLAYER
BRICKMAKER
BRUSHMAKER
BUREAUCRAT
BUTTERWIFE
CARTOONIST
CARTWRIGHT
CASH-KEEPER
CAT BREEDER
CAT BURGLAR
CERAMICIST
CHAIR-MAKER
CHARGEHAND
CHARIOTEER
CHIRURGEON
CHORUS GIRL
CHRONICLER
CIRCUITEER
CLAIM AGENT
CLAPPER BOY
CLOCKMAKER
CLOG DANCER
CLOTH MAKER
COACHMAKER
COAL-BACKER
COAL-FITTER
COALHEAVER
COAL-MASTER
CO-ASSESSOR
COASTGUARD
COLLOCUTOR
COLLOQUIST
COLPORTEUR
COMEDIENNE
COMPOSITOR
COMPOUNDER
CONCORDIST
CONTRACTOR
CONTROLLER
COPYHOLDER
COPYWRITER
CORDWAINER
COUNSELLOR
CULTIVATOR
CUSTOMS MAN
CYTOLOGIST
DELINEATOR
DIRECTRESS
DISC JOCKEY
DISCOUNTER
DISCOVERER
DISHWASHER
DISPATCHER
DISTRAINER
DISTRAINOR
DOCKMASTER
DOG BREEDER
DOG-FANCIER
DOORKEEPER
DRAMATURGE

DRESSMAKER
DRUMMER-BOY
DRY CLEANER
EMBLAZONER
EMBOWELLER
ENAMELLIST
EPHEMERIST
EPITAPHIST
EPITOMIZER
EVANGELIST
EXAMINATOR
EXPLORATOR
EYE-SERVANT
FELL-MONGER
FILE-CUTTER
FILIBUSTER
FILM EDITOR
FIREMASTER
FIRE-WORKER
FISHMONGER
FLIGHT CREW
FLOWERGIRL
FLUVIALIST
FOLK-DANCER
FOLK-SINGER
FORECASTER
FRAME-MAKER
FREEBOOTER
FUND RAISER
GAMEKEEPER
GAME WARDEN
GEAR-CUTTER
GEISHA GIRL
GENETICIST
GEOGRAPHER
GLEE-SINGER
GLOSSARIST
GLUE-BOILER
GOLD-BEATER
GOLD-DIGGER
GOLD-WASHER
GOVERNANTE
GRAMMARIAN
GUNSLINGER
HACKNEY-MAN
HALL PORTER
HANDMAIDEN
HARVESTMAN
HATCHELLER
HEAD PORTER
HEAD WAITER
HIEROPHANT
HIGHWAYMAN
HORN PLAYER
HOROLOGIST
HORSECOPER
HORSE-LEECH
HOUSE AGENT
HUCKSTRESS
HUSBANDMAN
INOCULATOR
INSTITUTOR
INSTRUCTOR

INTERAGENT
IRONMONGER
IRONWORKER
JOURNALIST
JOURNEYMAN
KENNELMAID
KEYBOARDER
LAUNDRYMAN
LAW OFFICER
LEGISLATOR
LIBRETTIST
LIGHTERMAN
LIME-BURNER
LINOTYPIST
LIQUIDATOR
LOBSTERMAN
LOCK-KEEPER
LUMBERJACK
MAGISTRATE
MANAGERESS
MANICURIST
MANSERVANT
MATCHMAKER
MEAT-HAWKER
MEDICAL MAN
MILITIAMAN
MILLWRIGHT
MINERALIST
MINISTRESS
MINTMASTER
MISSIONARY
MOONSHINER
NATURALIST
NAUTCH GIRL
NEGOTIATOR
NEWSCASTER
NEWS EDITOR
NEWSVENDOR
NEWSWRITER
NIGHT NURSE
NOSOLOGIST
NURSERYMAN
OBITUARIST
OIL PAINTER
ORCHARDIST
OSTEOLOGER
OVERLOOKER
PANEGYRIST
PANTRYMAID
PARK-KEEPER
PARK-RANGER
PASQUILANT
PASTRY-COOK
PATHFINDER
PAWNBROKER
PEARL-DIVER
PEDIATRIST
PEDICURIST
PELTMONGER
PENOLOGIST
PERRUQUIER
PHARMACIST
PHILOLOGER

PIANO TUNER
PICKPOCKET
PLATELAYER
PLAYWRIGHT
POLITICIAN
PORTIONIST
POSTILLION
POSTMASTER
PRESCRIBER
PRIMA DONNA
PRIVATE EYE
PROCURATOR
PROGRAMMER
PRONOUNCER
PROPRIETOR
PROSPECTOR
PROTRACTOR
PROVEDITOR
PUNCTURIST
PYROLOGIST
QUIZ-MASTER
RAILWAYMAN
RAT-CATCHER
RECITALIST
RESEARCHER
RINGMASTER
ROADMENDER
ROPEDANCER
ROUGHRIDER
SAFEBLOWER
SALES FORCE
SALESWOMAN
SCHOOLMARM
SCRUTINEER
SCULPTRESS
SEA-CAPTAIN
SEAMSTRESS
SECOND MATE
SEMINARIST
SERVING-MAN
SEXOLOGIST
SHIP-BROKER
SHIP-HOLDER
SHIPMASTER
SHIPWRIGHT
SHOPFITTER
SHOPKEEPER
SHOPWALKER
SIGNWRITER
SILENTIARY
SILK-MERCER
SILK-WEAVER
SINOLOGIST
SKIRMISHER
SLOP SELLER
SNEAK THIEF
SOAP-BOILER
SPECIALIST
STAFF NURSE
STEERSMATE
STEWARDESS
STIPULATOR
STOCKTAKER

STONE-BORER
STONEMASON
STRATEGIST
STREET-WARD
SUPERCARGO
SUPERVISER
SURCHARGER
SURFACE-MAN
SWAN-KEEPER
SYMPHONIST
TALLY CLERK
TASKMASTER
TAXI-DRIVER
TEA-BLENDER
TEA PLANTER
TECHNICIAN
TECHNOCRAT
THEOGONIST
THEOLOGIAN
THEOLOGIST
THRENODIST
TIMEKEEPER
TRACTARIAN
TRADE UNION
TRAFFIC COP
TRAFFICKER
TRAM-DRIVER
TRANSACTOR
TRANSLATOR
TRAWLERMAN
TREASURESS
TROUBADOUR
TYPESETTER
UNDERTAKER
VETERINARY
VICTUALLER
VIVANDIÈRE
VOCABULIST
WAINWRIGHT
WARRIORESS
WATCHMAKER
WATERGUARD
WHARFINGER
WHITESMITH
WHOLESALER
WINEGROWER
WINE-WAITER
WIREWORKER
WOODCARVER
WOODCUTTER
WOOD-MONGER
WOODWORKER
WOOL-CARDER
WOOL-COMBER
WOOL-DRIVER
WOOL-GROWER
WOOL-SORTER
WOOL-TRADER
WOOL-WINDER
YARDMASTER
ZINC-WORKER
ZOOGRAPHER
ZYMOLOGIST

11

ACCOMPANIST
ACCOUCHEUSE
ACOUSTICIAN
ADJUDICATOR
ALLOPATHIST
ANNUNCIATOR
ANTIQUARIAN
APPLE-GROWER
ARBITRATRIX
ARMY OFFICER
ARQUEBUSIER
ARTILLERIST
AUDIO TYPIST
AUSCULTATOR
BANK CASHIER
BANK MANAGER
BARGEMASTER
BASKETMAKER
BATTI-WALLAH
BATTOLOGIST
BEACHCOMBER
BELL-FOUNDER
BILL-STICKER
BIRD-CATCHER
BIRD-FANCIER
BIRD-WATCHER
BOATBUILDER
BODY SERVANT
BOILERSMITH
BONDSERVANT
BROADCASTER
BULLFIGHTER
CANDLEMAKER
CAR SALESMAN
CAT'S-MEAT-MAN
CHAIR-MENDER
CHALK-CUTTER
CHAMBERMAID
CHIFFONNIER
CHIROLOGIST
CHIROMANCER
CHIROPODIST
CHOIRMASTER
CHRONOLOGER
CINDER-WENCH
CLOCK-SETTER
CLOTH-WORKER
COAL-WHIPPER
COFFIN-MAKER
COLLAR-MAKER
CONDISCIPLE
CONDOTTIERE
CONDUCTRESS
CONFEDERATE
CONGRESSMAN
CONSECRATOR
CONSERVATOR
CONVEYANCER
COPPERSMITH
COSMOGONIST
COSMOLOGIST
CRANE DRIVER

CRIMEWRITER
CUB REPORTER
CYPHER CLERK
DELIVERY MAN
DEMOGRAPHER
DISPENSATOR
DRAUGHTSMAN
DUTY OFFICER
ELECTRICIAN
EMBLEMATIST
EMBROIDERER
ENTERTAINER
ESTATE AGENT
ETHNOLOGIST
ETYMOLOGIST
EXECUTIONER
EXTORTIONER
FACE-PAINTER
FACTORY HAND
FAITH HEALER
FANCY-MONGER
FIELD WORKER
FIGURE-MAKER
FILING CLERK
FINESTILLER
FIRE INSURER
FLAX-DRESSER
FLESH-MONGER
FOURBISSEUR
FRINGE-MAKER
FRUIT PICKER
FUNAMBULIST
GALLEY-SLAVE
GENEALOGIST
GHOSTWRITER
GLASS-BENDER
GLASS-BLOWER
GLASS-CUTTER
GLASS-WORKER
GRAVE-DIGGER
GREENGROCER
HABERDASHER
HAGIOLOGIST
HAIRDRESSER
HAIR STYLIST
HARDWAREMAN
HEDGE-PRIEST
HEDGE-WRITER
HIEROLOGIST
HISTOLOGIST
HORSE DOCTOR
HORSE TRADER
HOSPITALLER
HOTEL-KEEPER
HOUSEMASTER
HOUSEMOTHER
HYMNOLOGIST
ILLUMINATOR
ILLUSIONIST
ILLUSTRATOR
INFANTRYMAN
INSTITUTIST
INTERPRETER

INTERVIEWER
IRON-FOUNDER
IVORY-CARVER
IVORY-TURNER
IVORY-WORKER
KITCHENMAID
LAMPLIGHTER
LAND STEWARD
LAUNDRYMAID
LEADING LADY
LEDGER CLERK
LIFEBOATMAN
LIGHTKEEPER
LINEN DRAPER
LITHOLOGIST
LITHOTOMIST
LORRY DRIVER
MADRIGALIST
MAIDSERVANT
MAMMALOGIST
MASTER BAKER
MECHANICIAN
MEDICINE MAN
MEMORIALIST
MERCHANTMAN
METAL WORKER
MINIATURIST
MONEY-BROKER
MONEY-LENDER
MONOGRAPHER
MULE-SPINNER
MUSIC CRITIC
MUSIC MASTER
MYOGRAPHIST
MYSTERIARCH
MYTHOLOGIST
NECROLOGIST
NECROMANCER
NEEDLEWOMAN
NEUROLOGIST
NEUROTOMIST
NIGHT PORTER
NIGHTWORKER
NOMENCLATOR
NUMISMATIST
OFFICE STAFF
ONION-SELLER
OPERA SINGER
OPHIOLOGIST
ORIENTALIST
ORTHOPEDIST
OSTEOLOGIST
PAMPHLETEER
PANEL-BEATER
PANTOMIMIST
PAPERHANGER
PARLOURMAID
PATHOLOGIST
PATTENMAKER
PEARLFISHER
PETROLOGIST
PETTIFOGGER
PHILATELIST

PHILOLOGIST
PHONOLOGIST
PHYTOLOGIST
POLYPHONIST
PORK BUTCHER
PORTRAITIST
PRECEPTRESS
PRINT-SELLER
PROBATIONER
PROMULGATOR
PROOFREADER
PROPERTY MAN
PROPRIETRIX
QUESTIONARY
RADIOLOGIST
RAG MERCHANT
REPRESENTER
REPUBLISHER
RHETORICIAN
ROADSWEEPER
SAFEBREAKER
SANDWICH MAN
SANSCRITIST
SAXOPHONIST
SCOUTMASTER
SCRAPDEALER
SCRIP-HOLDER
SECRET AGENT
SEDITIONARY
SERVANT GIRL
SERVING-MAID
SHARE-BROKER
SHEEPFARMER
SHEPHERDESS
SHIPBREAKER
SHIPBUILDER
SHIP'S MASTER
SHOPSTEWARD
SILK-THROWER
SILVERSMITH
SLAUGHTERER
SLAVE-DRIVER
SLAVE-HOLDER
SMALLHOLDER
SOCIOLOGIST
STAGE-DRIVER
STEEPLEJACK
STOCKBROKER
STOCKJOBBER
STONECUTTER
STOREKEEPER
SUNDRIESMAN
SYSTEM-MAKER
TAXIDERMIST
TELEGRAPHER
TELEPHONIST
TICKET AGENT
TOASTMASTER
TOBACCONIST
TOOTH-DRAWER
TOPOGRAPHER
TORCH-BEARER
TOWN PLANNER

TOXOPHILITE
TRAIN-BEARER
TRANSCRIBER
TRANSPORTER
TRAVEL AGENT
TYPE-FOUNDER
TYPOGRAPHER
UNDERBEARER
UNDERLETTER
UNDERWRITER
UPHOLSTERER
VERSEMONGER
VINE-DRESSER
WASHERWOMAN
WATCHKEEPER
WAX-CHANDLER
WHEEL-CUTTER
WHEELWRIGHT
WHITEWASHER
WITCH-DOCTOR
WOOL-STAPLER
XYLOPHONIST
ZOOGRAPHIST

12
ACCORDIONIST
ACTOR MANAGER
AMBULANCE MAN
ANAESTHETIST
ANIMALCULIST
ARCHEOLOGIST
ARTILLERYMAN
BALLET DANCER
BALLET MASTER
BANTAMWEIGHT
BELLOWS-MAKER
BIBLIOLOGIST
BIBLIOPEGIST
BIBLIOPOLIST
BOOKING CLERK
BUS CONDUCTOR
CABINET-MAKER
CALLIGRAPHER
CARICATURIST
CARPET-FITTER
CARTOGRAPHER
CATACLYSMIST
CEROGRAPHIST
CHEESEMONGER
CHIEF CASHIER
CHIMNEY-SWEEP
CHIROPRACTOR
CHRONOLOGIST
CHURCHWARDEN
CIRCUIT RIDER
CIVIL SERVANT
CLARINETTIST
CLERK OF WORKS
CLOTH-SHEARER
COACH-BUILDER
COLEOPTERIST
COMMISSIONER
CONCHOLOGIST
CONFECTIONER

CORN CHANDLER
COSMOGRAPHER
COSTERMONGER
CRAFTS-MASTER
CRANIOLOGIST
CRYPTOGAMIST
DANCE HOSTESS
DEEP-SEA DIVER
DEMONOLOGIST
DEMONSTRATOR
DENDROLOGIST
DRAMATURGIST
ECCLESIASTIC
EGYPTOLOGIST
ELECUTIONIST
ENGINE-DRIVER
ENTOMOLOGIST
ENTOMOTOMIST
ENTREPRENEUR
ESCAPOLOGIST
ETHNOGRAPHER
EXPERIMENTER
FAMILY DOCTOR
FARM LABOURER
FILM DIRECTOR
FILM PRODUCER
FIRST OFFICER
FLYING DOCTOR
FOOTPLATEMAN
GEOMETRICIAN
GERIATRICIAN
GLASS-GRINDER
GLOSSOLOGIST
GREASEMONKEY
GUILD BROTHER
GYMNOSOPHIST
GYNECOLOGIST
HAGIOGRAPHER
HALIOGRAPHER
HARNESS-MAKER
HEAD GARDENER
HOMEOPATHIST
HORSE-BREAKER
HORSE-COURSER
HORSE-KNACKER
HOTEL MANAGER
HOUSEBREAKER
HOUSEPAINTER
HOUSE STEWARD
HOUSE SURGEON
HYDROGRAPHER
HYDROPATHIST
HYPOTHECATOR
IMMUNOLOGIST
IMPROPRIATOR
INSTRUCTRESS
INVOICE CLERK
JERRY-BUILDER
JOINT-TRUSTEE
JURISCONSULT
JUVENILE LEAD
KING'S COUNSEL
KNIFE-GRINDER

KNIFE-THROWER
LABOURING MAN
LAND SURVEYOR
LATH-SPLITTER
LEADER-WRITER
LEXICOLOGIST
LITHOGRAPHER
LONGSHOREMAN
LOSS ADJUSTER
LUMBER-DEALER
MAITRE D'HOTEL
MAKE-UP ARTIST
MALACOLOGIST
MANUAL WORKER
MANUFACTURER
MASS PRODUCER
MEAT-SALESMAN
METALLURGIST
MEZZO SOPRANO
MICROSCOPIST
MINERALOGIST
MISCELLANIST
MONEY-CHANGER
MONOGRAPHIST
MORRIS-DANCER
MOSAIC-ARTIST
MOSAIC-WORKER
MYTHOGRAPHER
NEWSPAPERMAN
NUTRITIONIST
OBSTETRICIAN
OFFICE JUNIOR
ONEIROCRITIC
ORCHESTRATOR
ORGAN-BUILDER
ORGAN-GRINDER
ORTHODONTIST
ORTHOGRAPHER
OVARIOTOMIST
PAPER-STAINER
PATTERN-MAKER
PEDIATRICIAN
PHONOGRAPHER
PHOTOGRAPHER
PHRENOLOGIST
PHYSIOLOGIST
PLANT MANAGER
PLOUGHWRIGHT
PLUMBER'S MATE
PLYER-FOR-HIRE
POSTMISTRESS
PRACTITIONER
PRESS OFFICER
PRESTIGIATOR
PRISON WARDER
PRIZE-FIGHTER
PROFESSIONAL
PROPAGANDIST
PROPRIETRESS
PSYCHIATRIST
PSYCHOLOGIST
PUBLICITY MAN
PUPIL-TEACHER

PUPPET-PLAYER
QUARRY MASTER
RACING DRIVER
RADIOGRAPHER
RECEPTIONIST
REMEMBRANCER
RESTAURATEUR
RIDING-MASTER
RIGHT-HAND MAN
RUBBER-GRADER
SALES MANAGER
SCENE-PAINTER
SCENE-SHIFTER
SCHOOLMASTER
SCREENWRITER
SCRIPTWRITER
SCULLERY-MAID
SEED-MERCHANT
SEISMOLOGIST
SHARECROPPER
SHARPSHOOTER
SHIP CHANDLER
SHIP'S HUSBAND
SHOE-REPAIRER
SILVER-BEATER
SLAUGHTERMAN
SNAKE-CHARMER
SOCIAL WORKER
SOIL MECHANIC
SPECIAL AGENT
SPEECHWRITER
SPICE-BLENDER
SPORTSCASTER
SPORTSWRITER
STAGE MANAGER
STATISTICIAN
STENOGRAPHER
STONEBREAKER
STONEDRESSER
STONESQUARER
STREET-TRADER
STREET-WALKER
SUGAR-REFINER
TAX-COLLECTOR
TECHNOLOGIST
TELEGRAPH BOY
TELEGRAPHIST
TEST ENGINEER
THERAPEUTIST
THIEF-CATCHER
TICKET-PORTER
TIMBER TRADER
TOLL-GATHERER
TOURIST AGENT
TOXICOLOGIST
TRADESPEOPLE
TRANSPLANTER
TRICHOLOGIST
UNDERMANAGER
UNDERSERVANT
VETERINARIAN
WAITING-WOMAN
WAREHOUSEMAN

WATER DIVINER
WINE MERCHANT
WOOD-ENGRAVER
WORKS MANAGER
ZINCOGRAPHER

13

ADMINISTRATOR
AGRICULTURIST
ANTIQUE DEALER
ARACHNOLOGIST
ARCHAEOLOGIST
ARITHMETICIAN
ARTICLED CLERK
ASSYRIOLOGIST
BARBER-SURGEON
BIBLIOGRAPHER
CALICO-PRINTER
CAMPANOLOGIST
CARTOGRAPHIST
CHARTOGRAPHER
CHICKEN-FARMER
CHIROGRAPHIST
CHOREOGRAPHER
CHRONOGRAPHER
CIVIL ENGINEER
CLEARSTARCHER
COFFEE-PLANTER
COMETOGRAPHER
CONTORTIONIST
CONTRABANDIST
COTTON-SPINNER
COUNTER-CASTER
COUNTERFEITER
CRANIOSCOPIST
CRYPTOGRAPHER
DANCING MASTER
DEIPNOSOPHIST
DERMATOLOGIST
DIAGNOSTICIAN
DIAMOND-CUTTER
DRAUGHTSWOMAN
DRAWING-MASTER
DRESS DESIGNER
DRILL SERGEANT
ELECTROPLATER
ELECTROTYPIST
EMIGRATIONIST
ENCYCLOPEDIST
ENTOZOOLOGIST
EPIGRAMMATIST
ESTATE MANAGER
FENCING-MASTER
FORTUNE-TELLER
FREIGHT-BROKER
GALVANOLOGIST
GASTRILOQUIST
GLOSSOGRAPHER
GLYPHOGRAPHER
GROUND-BAILIFF
GYNAECOLOGIST
HARBOUR MASTER
HIEROGLYPHIST
HORSE-MILLINER

HOSPITAL NURSE
ICHTHYOLOGIST
INDUSTRIALIST
INTELLIGENCER
JOINT-EXECUTOR
LETTER-CARRIER
LETTER-FOUNDER
LEXICOGRAPHER
LIGHTHOUSE-MAN
MAID-OF-ALL-WORK
MASTER-BUILDER
MASTER MARINER
MATHEMATICIAN
MELODRAMATIST
METAPHYSICIAN
METEOROLOGIST
METOPOSCOPIST
MUSIC MISTRESS
NIGHT-WATCHMAN
OLD-CLOTHES-MAN
ORNITHOLOGIST
ORTHOGRAPHIST
PARK ATTENDANT
PERIODICALIST
PHARMACEUTIST
PHYSIOGNOMIST
PHYSIOGRAPHER
POSTURE-MASTER
POULTRY FARMER
PRIVATEERSMAN
PROCESS-SERVER
PSALMOGRAPHER
PSYCHOANALYST
PTERIDOLOGIST
PUBLIC SPEAKER
QUEEN'S COUNSEL
RACING-TIPSTER
REVOLUTIONARY
REVOLUTIONIST
RUBBER-PLANTER
SAILING MASTER
SCHOOLTEACHER
SCIENCE MASTER
SHOP ASSISTANT
SILK-THROWSTER
SINGING-MASTER
STATION-MASTER
STENOGRAPHIST
STEREOSCOPIST
STETHOSCOPIST
STREET-SWEEPER
SUB-CONTRACTOR

SUPERINTENDER
SUPERNUMERARY
THAUMATURGIST
THIMBLE-RIGGER
TOLL COLLECTOR
TRADE UNIONIST
TRAMCAR-DRIVER
TRAM CONDUCTOR
VENTRILOQUIST
VIOLONCELLIST
WINDOW-CLEANER
WINDOW-DRESSER
WOOLLEN-DRAPER
WRITING-MASTER

14

ADMINISTRATRIX
ANTHROPOLOGIST
AUTOBIOGRAPHER
BACTERIOLOGIST
BALLET MISTRESS
BILLIARD-MARKER
BILLIARD-PLAYER
CHAMBER-COUNSEL
CHIMNEY-SWEEPER
CITIZEN-SOLDIER
CLASSICS MASTER
COLOUR SERGEANT
COMMISSIONAIRE
DANCING PARTNER
DISCOUNT-BROKER
ECCLESIOLOGIST
EDUCATIONALIST
ENCYCLOPAEDIST
EXCHANGE-BROKER
GRAMMATICASTER
HANDICRAFTSMAN
HERESIOGRAPHER
HORTICULTURIST
HOUSE DECORATOR
HOUSE FURNISHER
LANGUAGE MASTER
LEATHER-DRESSER
MANUAL LABOURER
MARKET-GARDENER
MEDICAL OFFICER
MERCHANT-TAILOR
MISCELLANARIAN
MONEY-SCRIVENER
MOTHER-SUPERIOR
MUSIC PUBLISHER
NAVAL PENSIONER

OPTHALMOLOGIST
PAINTER-STAINER
PHARMACOLOGIST
PNEUMATOLOGIST
PSALMOGRAPHIST
RECEPTION CLERK
REPRESENTATIVE
SCHOOLMISTRESS
SHIP'S-CARPENTER
SIDEROGRAPHIST
SPECTACLE-MAKER
SPECTROSCOPIST
SUPERINTENDENT
SYSTEMS ANALYST
TALLOW CHANDLER
WATER-COLOURIST
WEATHER PROPHET

15

ARBORICULTURIST
ASSISTANT MASTER
BOW STREET RUNNER
CROSSING-SWEEPER
CRUSTACEOLOGIST
DANCING MISTRESS
DIAMOND MERCHANT
DOMESTIC SERVANT
FORWARDING AGENT
GENTLEMAN-FARMER
HACKNEY COACHMAN
HEART SPECIALIST
HELMINTHOLOGIST
HIEROGRAMMATIST
HISTORIOGRAPHER
INSTRUMENTALIST
INSURANCE BROKER
MUSICAL DIRECTOR
NUMISMATOLOGIST
PALAEONTOLOGIST
PLATFORM-SPEAKER
PORTRAIT-PAINTER
PROGRAMME SELLER
PROVISION DEALER
RAILWAY ENGINEER
RESURRECTIONIST
SCRIPTURE-READER
SLEEPING PARTNER
STRETCHER-BEARER
TICKET COLLECTOR
TIGHTROPE WALKER

TOOLS

3
AWL
AXE
BIT
DIE
FAN
GAD
GIN
HOD
HOE
JIG
LOY
SAW
ZAX

4
ADZE
BILL
BORE
BROG
BURR
CART
CELT
CRAB
FILE
FORK
FROW
GAGE
HINK
HOOK
JACK
LAST
LOOM
MALL
MAUL
MULE
NAIL
PICK
PIKE
PLOW
RAKE
RASP
RULE
SOCK
SPUD
TRUG
VICE
WHIM

5
ANVIL
AUGER
BEELE
BENCH
BESOM
BETTY
BEVEL
BLADE
BORER
BRACE

BURIN
CHUCK
CHURN
CLAMP
CLAMS
CLASP
CLEAT
CRAMP
CRANE
CROOM
CROZE
CUPEL
DOLLY
DRILL
FLAIL
FLANG
FORGE
GAUGE
GAVEL
GOUGE
HOIST
INCUS
JACKS
JEMMY
JIMMY
KNIFE
LATHE
LEVEL
LEVER
MOWER
PARER
PLANE
PLUMB
PREEN
PRISE
PRONG
PUNCH
QUERN
QUOIN
RATCH
RAZOR
SARSE
SCREW
SPADE
SPIKE
SPILE
SPILL
SWAGE
TEMSE
TOMMY
TONGS
TROMP
TRONE
WEDGE
WINCH

6
BARROW
BENDER
BLOWER

BODKIN
BORCER
BOW-SAW
BRAYER
BROACH
BURTON
CHASER
CHISEL
COLTER
CREVET
CRUSET
DIBBER
DIBBLE
DOFFER
DREDGE
DRIVER
FANNER
FAUCET
FERRET
FOLDER
GIMLET
GRAVER
HACKLE
HAMMER
HARROW
JAGGER
JIGGER
JIG SAW
LADDER
MALLET
MORTAR
MULLER
OLIVER
PALLET
PENCIL
PESTLE
PITSAW
PLANER
PLIERS
PLOUGH
PONTEE
POOLER
RAMMER
RASPER
REAPER
RIDDLE
RIPSAW
RUBBER
SANDER
SAW-SET
SCREEN
SCYTHE
SEGGER
SHEARS
SHOVEL
SICKLE
SIFTER
SKEWER
SLEDGE
SLICER

SQUARE
STIDDY
STITHY
STRIKE
TACKLE
TENTER
TREPAN
TROWEL
TUBBER
TURREL
WIMBLE
WRENCH

7
BOASTER
BRADAWL
CAPSTAN
CATLING
CAUTERY
CHAMFER
CHIP-AXE
CHOPPER
CLEAVER
COULOIR
COULTER
CRAMPON
CRISPER
CROWBAR
CUVETTE
DERRICK
DIAMOND
DOG-BELT
DRUDGER
FISTUCA
FORCEPS
FRETSAW
FRUGGIN
GRADINE
GRAINER
GRAPNEL
GRUB AXE
HACKSAW
HANDSAW
HATCHET
HAY FORK
JOINTER
MANDREL
MATTOCK
NIPPERS
NUT HOOK
PICKAXE
PIERCER
PINCERS
PLUMMET
POLE AXE
POUNDER
PRICKER
SALT-PAN
SCALPEL
SCAUPER

SCRAPER
SCREWER
SCRIBER
SEED LOP
SPADDLE
SPANNER
SPITTLE
SPRAYER
STROCAL
TENONER
THIMBLE
TRESTLE
TRIBLET
T-SQUARE
TWIBILL
TWISTER
WHIP-SAW
WHITTLE
WOOLDER

8
BARK MILL
BAR SHEAR
BEAKIRON
BENCH PEG
BILL HOOK
BISTOURY
BLOOMARY
BLOWLAMP
BLOWPIPE
BOATHOOK
BOWDRILL
BULL NOSE
BUTTERIS
CALIPERS
CANTHOOK
CROW MILL
CRUCIBLE
DIE STOCK
DOWEL BIT
DRILL BOW
EDGE TOOL
FILATORY
FIRE KILN
FLAME GUN
FLAX COMB
GAVELOCK
GEE CRAMP
HANDLOOM
HANDMILL
HAND VICE
HAY KNIFE
HORSE HOE
LAPSTONE
LEAD MILL
MITRE BOX
MOLEGRIP
MUCK RAKE
NUT SCREW
OILSTONE
PAINT PAD
PANEL SAW
PICKLOCK
PINCHERS

PLUMB BOB
POLISHER
POWER SAW
PRONG-HOE
PUNCHEON
REAP HOOK
SAW WREST
SCISSORS
SCUFFLER
SLATE AXE
STILETTO
STRICKLE
TENON SAW
THROSTLE
TOOTH KEY
TWEEZERS
TWIST BIT
WATERCAN
WATER RAM
WEED HOOK
WINDLASS
WINDMILL

9
BELT PUNCH
BENCH HOOK
BOLT AUGER
BOOT CRIMP
CANKER BIT
CANNIPERS
CAN OPENER
CENTRE BIT
COMPASSES
CORKSCREW
COTTON GIN
CRAMP IRON
CURRY COMB
CUTTER BAR
DOG CLUTCH
DRAW KNIFE
DRAW-PLATE
EXCAVATOR
EYELETEER
FILLISTER
FINING POT
FORK CHUCK
GAS PLIERS
HAMMER AXE
HANDBRACE
HANDSCREW
HANDSPIKE
HOLING AXE
HUMMELLER
IMPLEMENT
JACKKNIFE
JACKPLANE
JACKSCREW
LACE FRAME
LAWNMOWER
NAIL PUNCH
NUT WRENCH
PITCH FORK
PLANE IRON
PLANISHER

PLUMBLINE
PLUMBRULE
SCREWJACK
SCRIBE AWL
SHEARLEGS
SHEEP HOOK
STEELYARD
SUGAR MILL
TIN OPENER
TRY SQUARE
TURF SPADE
TURN BENCH
TURNSCREW
WATERMILL

10
BUSH HARROW
CLASPKNIFE
CLAWHAMMER
COLD CHISEL
CRANE'S BILL
CULTIVATOR
DRAY PLOUGH
DRIFT BOLTS
DRILLPRESS
DRILLSTOCK
EMERY WHEEL
FIRING IRON
GRINDSTONE
INSTRUMENT
MASONRY BIT
MASTICATOR
MITRE BLOCK
MOTOR MOWER
MOULD BOARD
PAINTBRUSH
PERFORATOR
PIPE WRENCH
POINTED AWL
SCREW PRESS
SLEEK STONE
SNOWPLOUGH
SPOKESHAVE
STEAM PRESS
STEPLADDER
TENTERHOOK
THUMBSCREW
THUMBSTALL
TILT HAMMER
TRIP HAMMER
TURF CUTTER
TURNBUCKLE
WATERCRANE
WATERGAUGE
WATERLEVEL
WHEEL BRACE

11
BRACE-AND-BIT
BREAST DRILL
CHAFF CUTTER
CHAIN BLOCKS
CHAIN WRENCH
CHEESE PRESS

COUNTERSINK
CRAZING MILL
CRISPING PIN
CROSSCUT SAW
DRILL BARROW
DRILL HARROW
DRILL PLOUGH
FANNING MILL
GRUBBING HOE
HELVEHAMMER
JAGGING IRON
MACHINE TOOL
MONKEY BLOCK
PAINT ROLLER
PLOUGHSHARE
PRUNING HOOK
RABBET PLANE
REAPING-HOOK
SAWING STOOL
SCREWDRIVER
SINGLE-EDGED
SKIM COULTER
SNATCH BLOCK
SPIRIT LEVEL
SQUARING ROD
STEAM HAMMER
STONE HAMMER
STRAW CUTTER
STRIKE BLOCK
STUBBLE RAKE
SWARD CUTTER
SWINGPLOUGH
TAPEMEASURE
TURFING IRON
TWO-FOOT RULE
WARPING HOOK
WARPING POST
WEEDING FORK
WEEDING HOOK
WEEDING RHIM
WHEELBARROW

12
BARKING IRONS
BELT ADJUSTER
BRANDING IRON
BREASTPLOUGH
CAULKING TOOL
COUNTER GAUGE
CRADEL SCYTHE
CRAMPING IRON
CRIMPING IRON
CRISPING IRON
CURLING TONGS
DRILL GRUBBER
DRIVING SHAFT
DRIVING WHEEL
EMERY GRINDER
FLOUR DRESSER
GLASS FURNACE
HYDRAULIC RAM
MANDREL LATHE
MARLINE SPIKE
MONKEY WRENCH

PRUNING KNIFE
PULLEY BLOCKS
RUNNING BLOCK
SCRIBING IRON
SLEDGE HAMMER
SLIDING BEVEL
SOCKET CHISEL
STONE BREAKER
STRAIGHTEDGE
SWINGLE KNIFE
TOUCH NEEDLES
TRENCH PLOUGH
TURFING SPADE
TURNING LATHE
WATER BELLOWS
WEEDING TONGS

13
CHOPPING BLOCK
CHOPPING KNIFE

CYLINDER PRESS
ELECTRIC DRILL
GRAPPLING-IRON
HYDRAULIC JACK
PACKING NEEDLE
SCRIBING BLOCK
SEWING MACHINE
SOLDERING BOLT
SOLDERING IRON
SOWING MACHINE
SPINNING JENNY
SPINNING WHEEL
STOCKING FRAME
SUBSOIL PLOUGH
TWO-HOLE PLIERS
WEEDING CHISEL

14
BLOWING MACHINE
CARDING MACHINE

DRAINING ENGINE
DRAINING PLOUGH
PENUMATIC DRILL
REAPING MACHINE
SMOOTHING PLANE
SWINGLING KNIFE
THRUSTING SCREW
WEEDING FORCEPS

15
CARPENTER'S BENCH
CRIMPING MACHINE
DREDGING MACHINE
DRILLING MACHINE
ENTRENCHING TOOL
PESTLE AND MORTAR
PUMP SCREWDRIVER
WEIGHING MACHINE

MILITARY TERMS

MILITARY TITLES

ROYAL AIR FORCE RANKS

MARSHAL OF THE RAF
AIR CHIEF MARSHAL
AIR MARSHAL
AIR VICE-MARSHAL
AIR COMMODORE
GROUP CAPTAIN
WING COMMANDER
SQUADRON LEADER
FLIGHT LIEUTENANT
FLYING OFFICER
PILOT OFFICER
MASTER PILOT
WARRANT OFFICER
FLIGHT SERGEANT
CHIEF TECHNICIAN
SERGEANT
CORPORAL
JUNIOR TECHNICIAN
SENIOR AIRCRAFTMAN
LEADING AIRCRAFTMAN
AIRCRAFTMAN

ARMY RANKS

FIELD MARSHAL
GENERAL
LIEUTENANT-GENERAL
MAJOR-GENERAL
BRIGADIER
COLONEL
LIEUTENANT-COLONEL
MAJOR
CAPTAIN
LIEUTENANT
SECOND-LIEUTENANT
OFFICER CADET
REGIMENTAL SERGEANT-
    MAJOR
WARRANT OFFICER
SERGEANT-MAJOR
STAFF/COLOUR-SERGEANT
SERGEANT
CORPORAL
LANCE-CORPORAL
PRIVATE

ROYAL NAVY RANKS

ADMIRAL OF THE FLEET
ADMIRAL
VICE-ADMIRAL
REAR-ADMIRAL
COMMODORE
CAPTAIN
COMMANDER
LIEUTENANT-COMMANDER
LIEUTENANT
SUB-LIEUTENANT
MIDSHIPMAN
CADET
WARRANT OFFICER
CHIEF PETTY OFFICER
PETTY OFFICER
LEADING HAND
RATING

BRITISH DECORATIONS AND MEDALS

AIR FORCE CROSS (AFC)
AIR FORCE MEDAL (AFM)
ALBERT MEDAL (AM)
CONSPICUOUS GALLANTRY MEDAL (CGM)
DISTINGUISHED FLYING CROSS (DFC)
DISTINGUISHED FLYING
    MEDAL (DFM)
DISTINGUISHED SERVICE CROSS (DSC)
DISTINGUISHED SERVICE MEDAL (DSM)

GEORGE CROSS (GC)
GEORGE MEDAL (GM)
MEDAL FOR DISTINGUISHED CONDUCT IN THE
    FIELD (DCM)
MILITARY CROSS (MC)
MILITARY MEDAL (MM)
THE DISTINGUISHED SERVICE ORDER (DSO)
VICTORIA CROSS (VC)

US DECORATIONS AND MEDALS

AIR FORCE CROSS
AIRMAN'S MEDAL
BRONZE STAR MEDAL
COAST GUARD MEDAL
DISTINGUISHED SERVICE CROSS
DISTINGUISHED FLYING CROSS
DISTINGUISHED SERVICE MEDAL
LEGION OF MERIT

MEDAL OF HONOR
NAVY CROSS
NAVY/MARINE CORPS MEDAL
PURPLE HEART MEDAL
SILVER STAR MEDAL
SOLDIER'S MEDAL
SUPERIOR SERVICE MEDAL

BATTLES

2
RÉ, ÎLE DE (1627, Anglo-French Wars)

3
ACS (1849, Hungarian Rising)
AIX, ÎLE D' (1758, Seven Years' War)
DEE, BRIG OF (1639, Bishops' War)
GOA (1511, 1570, Portuguese Conquest)
HUÉ (1968, Vietnam War)
ULM (1805, Napoleonic Wars)

4
ACRE (1189–1191, Third Crusade; 1291, Crusader-
Turkish Wars; 1799, French Revolutionary Wars;
1840, Egyptian Revolt)
AGRA (1803, Second British-Maratha War; 1857,
Indian Mutiny)
ALMA (1854, Crimean War)
AONG (1857, Indian Mutiny)
ARAS (1775, First British-Maratha War)
AVUS (198 BC, Second Macedonian War)
BAZA (1489, Spanish-Muslim Wars)
BEDR (623, Islamic Wars)
BEGA (1696, Ottoman Wars)
CUBA (1953, Castro Revolt)
DEEG (1780, First British-Maratha War; 1804, Second
British-Maratha War)
GAZA (332 BC, Alexander's Asiatic Campaigns; 312
BC, Wars of Alexander's Successors; 1917, World
War I)
GELT, THE (1570, Anglo-Scottish Wars)
GUAM (1944, World War II)
JENA (1806, Napoleonic Wars)
KARS (1855, Crimean War)
KIEV (1941, World War II)
KULM (1813, Napoleonic Wars)
LAON (1814, Napoleonic Wars)
LECK, THE (1632, Thirty Years' War)
LENS (1648, Thirty Years' War)
LÓŹ (1914, World War I)
MAIN, THE (9 BC, Germanic War)
MAYA, COLDE (1813, Peninsular War)
METZ (1870, Franco-Prussian War)
NEON (354 BC, Sacred War)
NILE (1798, French Revolutionary Wars)
NIVE (1813, Peninsular War)
NOVI (1799, French Revolutionary Wars)
ONAO (1857, Indian Mutiny)
ORAN (1509, Spanish Invasion of Morocco; 1940,
World War II)
OREL (1943, World War II)
RAAB (1809, Napoleonic Wars)
ROME (387 BC, First Invasion of the Gauls; 408,
Wars of the Western Roman Empire; 472,
Ricimer's Rebellion; 537, 546, Wars of the
Byzantine Empire; 1082, Norman Seizure; 1527,
Wars of Charles V; 1849, Italian Wars of
Independence)
SCIO (1769, Ottoman Wars)

SOHR (1745, War of the Austrian Succession)
ST LÔ (1944, World War II)
TOBA (1868, Japanese Revolution)
TROY (1100 BC)
TRUK (1944, World War II)
VEII (405 BC, Rise of Rome)
ZELA (67 BC, Third Mithridatic War; 47 BC, Wars of
the First Triumvirate)

5
ACCRA (1824, 1825, First British-Ashanti War)
ADUWA (1896, Italian Invasion of Ethiopia)
ALAMO, STORMING OF THE (1836, Texan Rising)
ALLIA, THE (390 BC, The First Invasion of the Gauls)
ALSEN (1864, Schleswig-Holstein War)
ANZIO (1944, World War II)
ARGOS (195 BC, Roman Invasion of Greece)
ARIUS (214 BC, The Wars of the Hellenistic
Monarchies)
ARRAH (1857, Indian Mutiny)
ARRAS (1654, Wars of Louis XIV; 1917, World War I)
A SHAU (1966, Vietnam War)
AURAY (1364, Hundred Years' War)
BAHUR (1752, Seven Years' War)
BANDA (1858, Indian Mutiny)
BANDS, THE (961, Danish Invasion of Scotland)
BASRA (2008, Iraq War)
BEREA (1852, Kaffir Wars)
BETWA, THE (1858, Indian Mutiny)
BOYNE, THE (1690, War of the Grand Alliance)
BREST (1512, War of the Holy League)
BRILL (1572, Netherlands War of Independence)
BURMA (1942, 1943, World War II)
BUXAR (1764, British Conquest of Bengal)
CADIZ (1587, Anglo-Spanish War)
CAIRO (1517, Ottoman Wars)
CARPI (1701, War of the Spanish Succession)
ÇEŞME (1770, Ottoman Wars)
CRÉCY (1346, Hundred Years' War)
CRETE (1941, World War II)
DAK TO (1967, Vietnam War)
DELHI (1297, First Tatar Invasion of India; 1398,
Second Tatar Invasion; 1803, Second British-
Maratha War; 1804, Second British-Maratha War;
1857, Indian Mutiny)
DERNA (2018, Libyan Civil War)
DOUAI (1710, War of the Spanish Succession)
DOURO (1809, Peninsular War)
DOVER (1652, Anglo-Dutch Wars)
DOWNS, THE (1666, Anglo-Dutch Wars)
ELENA (1877, Russo-Turkish War)
EL TEB (1884, British-Sudan Campaigns)
EMESA (272, Wars of the Roman Empire)
ENGEN (1800, French Revolutionary Wars)
EYLAU (1807, Napoleonic Wars)
GENOA (1746, Patriotic Rising; 1795, 1800, French
Revolutionary Wars)
GOITS (1848, Italian Wars of Independence)
GUBAT (1885, British Sudan Campaigns)

HANAU (1813, Napoleonic Wars)
HIPPO (430, Wars of the Western Roman Empire)
IMOLA (1797, French Revoutionary Wars)
ISSUS (333 BC, Alexander's Asiatic Campaigns; 1488, Ottoman Wars)
JASSY (1620, Ottoman Wars)
KAGUL (1770, Ottoman Wars)
KALPI (1858, Indian Mutiny)
KAREE (1900, Second Boer War)
KAZAN (1774, Cossack Rising)
KOLIN (1757, Seven Years' War)
KOTAH (1858, Indian Mutiny)
LAGOS (1693, War of the Grand Alliance)
LA PAZ (1865, Bolivian Civil War)
LARGS (1263, Norse Invasion of Scotland)
LEWES (1264, Barons' Wars)
LEYTE (1944, World War II)
LIÈGE (1914, World War I)
LIGNY (1815, Napoleonic Wars)
LILLE (1708, War of the Spanish Succession)
LISSA (1866, Seven Weeks' War)
LUZON (1945, World War II)
LYONS (197, Civil Wars of the Roman Empire)
MAIDA (1806, Napoleonic Wars)
MALTA (1565, Ottoman Wars; 1798, French Revolutionary Wars; 1942, World War II)
MARNE (1914, 1918, World War I)
MAXEN (1759, Seven Years' War)
MUDKI (1845, First British-Sikh War)
MUNDA (45 BC, Civil War of Caesar and Pompey)
MURSA (351, Civil Wars of the Roman Empire)
MYLEX (36 BC, Wars of the Second Triumvirate)
NAMUR (1914, World War I)
PARIS (1814, Napoleonic Wars; 1870, Franco-Prussian War)
PATAY (1429, Hundred Years' War)
PODOL (1866, Seven Weeks' War)
PRUTH, THE (1770, Ottoman Wars)
RAMLA (1177, Crusader-Turkish Wars)
REDAN, THE GREAT (1855, Crimean War)
REIMS (1814, Napoleonic Wars)
ROUEN (1418, Hundred Years' War)
SEDAN (1870, Franco-Prussian War)
SELBY (1644, English Civil War)
SEOUL (1950, Korean War)
SIRTE (2016, Libyan Civil War)
SLUYS (1340, Hundred Years' War)
SOMME (1916, 1918, World War I)
SPIRA (1703, War of the Spanish Succession)
SPURS (1302, Flemish War; 1513, Anglo-French Wars)
STOKE (1487, Lambert Simnel's Rebellion)
TAMAI (1884, British Sudan Campaigns)
TEXEL (1653, Anglo-Dutch Wars)
TOURS (732, Muslim Invasion of France)
TUNIS (255 BC, First Punic War; 1270, Eighth Crusade)
TURIN (312, Civil Wars of the Roman Empire; 1706, War of the Spanish Succession)
UTICA (49 BC, Civil War of Caesar and Pompey; 694, Muslim Conquest of Africa)
VALMY (1792, French Revolutionary Wars)
VARNA (1444, Anti-Turkish Crusade; 1828, Ottoman Wars)
VARUS, DEFEAT OF (ad 9, Wars of the Roman Empire)
VASAQ (1442, Ottoman Wars)
WANAT (2008, Afghan War)
WAVRE (1815, Napoleonic Wars)
WÖRTH (1870, Franco-Prussian War)
YPRES (1914, 1915, 1917, World War I)
ZENTA (1679, Ottoman Wars)
ZNAIM (1809, Napoleonic Wars)

6

AACHEN (1944, World War II)
ABUKIR (1799, 1801, French Revolutionary Wars)
ABU KRU (1885, British Sudan Campaigns)
ACTIUM (31 BC, Wars of the Second Triumvirate)
ALEPPO (638, Muslim Invasion of Syria; 1400, Tatar Invasion of Syria; 1516, Ottoman Wars)
ALFORD (1645, English Civil War)
ALIWAL (1846, First British-Sikh War)
AMIENS (1870, Franco-Prussian War)
ANGORA (1402, Tatar Invasion of Asia Minor)
ARBELA (331 BC, Alexander's Asiatic Campaigns)
ARCOLA (1796, French Revolutionary Wars)
ARGAON (1803, Second British-Maratha War)
ARKLOW (1798, Irish Rebellion)
ARNHEM (1944, World War II)
ARSOUF (1191, Third Crusade)
ARTOIS (1915, World War I)
ASHTEE (1818, Third British-Maratha War)
ASIAGO (1916, World War I)
ASPERN (1809, Napoleonic Wars)
ASSAYE (1803, Second British-Maratha War)
ATBARA (1898, British Sudan Campaigns)
AZORES (1591, Anglo-Spanish War)
BARDIA (1941, World War II)
BARNET (1471, Wars of the Roses)
BASING (871, Danish Invasion of Britain)
BAYLEN (1808, Peninsular War)
BEAUGÉ (1421, Hundred Years' War)
BENDER (1768, Ottoman Wars)
BERGEN (1759, Seven Years' War)
BEYLAN (1831, Egyptian Revolt)
BILBAO (1937, Spanish Civil War)
BUSACO (1810, Peninsular War)
CALAIS (1346, Hundred Years' War; 1558, Anglo-French Wars)
CAMDEN (1780, American Revolutionary War)
CAMPEN (1759, Seven Years' War)
CHANDA (1818, Third British-Maratha War)
CHIARI (1701, War of the Spanish Succession)
CHIZAI (1372, Hundred Years' War)
DANZIG (1627, Thirty Years' War; 1807, 1813, Napoleonic Wars)
DARGAI (1897, British Northwest Frontier Campaign)
DELPHI (355 BC, Sacred War)
DENAIN (1712, War of the Spanish Succession)
DESSAU (1626, Thirty Years' War)
DIEPPE (1942, World War II)
DJERBA (1560, Ottoman Wars)
DOLLAR (875, Danish Invasions of Scotland)
DUNBAR (1296, 1339, Wars of Scottish

Independence; 1650, Cromwell's Scottish Campaign)
DUNDEE (1899, Second Boer War)
DÜPPEL (1864, Schleswig-Holstein War)
ERBACH (1800, French Revolutionary Wars)
FERKEH (1896, British Sudan Campaigns)
GAZALA (1942, World War II)
GEBORA (1811, Peninsular War)
GERONA (1809, Peninsular War)
GHAZNI (1839, First British-Afghan War)
GISORS (1197, Anglo-French Wars)
GROZKA (1739, Ottoman Wars)
HALLUE (1870, Franco-Prussian War)
HARLAW (1411, Scottish Civil Wars)
HASHIN (1885, British Sudan Campaigns)
HAVANA (1748, War of the Austrian Succession; 1762, Seven Years' War)
HEXHAM (1464, Wars of the Roses)
HÖCHST (1622, Thirty Years' War)
INCHON (1950, Korean War)
INGOGO (1881, First Boer War)
ISMAIL (1790, Ottoman Wars)
ISONZO (1915, World War I)
JERSEY (1550, Anglo-French Wars)
JHANSI (1857, Indian Mutiny)
KHELAT (1839, First British-Afghan War)
KIRKEE (1817, Third British-Maratha War)
KOKEIN (1824, First Burma War)
KOTZIN (1622, 1673, Ottoman Wars)
KRONIA (1738, Ottoman Wars)
KUNDUZ (2015, Afghan War)
LANDAU (1702, War of the Spanish Succession)
LANDEN (1693, War of the Grand Alliance)
LAWARI (1803, Second British-Maratha War)
LE MANS (1871, Franco-Prussian War)
LERIDA (1642, 1647, Thirty Years' War)
LONATO (1796, French Revolutionary Wars)
LUTTER (1626, Thirty Years' War)
LÜTZEN (1632, Thirty Years' War; 1813, Napoleonic Wars)
MADRAS (1746, War of the Austrian Succession; 1758, Seven Years' War)
MADRID (1936, Spanish Civil War)
MAIDAN (1842, First British-Afghan War)
MAJUBA (1881, First Boer War)
MALAGA (1487, Spanish-Muslim Wars; 1704, War of the Spanish Succession)
MALAYA (1941, World War II)
MALDON (991, Danish Invasions of Britain)
MANILA (1898, Spanish-American War)
MANTUA (1797, French Revolutionary Wars)
MARGUS (285, Civil Wars of the Roman Empire)
MEDOLA (1796, French Revolutionary Wars)
MERTON (871, Danish Invasions of Britain)
MEXICO (1520, Conquest of Mexico)
MINDEN (1759, Seven Years' War)
MOHACZ (1526, 1687, Ottoman Wars)
MORAWA (1443, Ottoman Wars)
MOSCOW (1941, World War II)
MUKDEN (1905, Russo-Japanese War; 1948, Chinese Civil War)
MULTAN (1848, Second British-Sikh War)
MUTINA (43 BC, Roman Civil Wars)

MYTTON (1319, Wars of Scottish Independence)
NACHOD (1866, Seven Weeks' War)
NÁJARA (1367, Hundred Years' War)
NASEBY (1645, English Civil War)
NICAEA (1097, First Crusade)
NORWAY (1940, World War II)
OCKLEY (851, Danish Invasions of Britain)
OLMÜTZ (1758, Seven Years' War)
OPORTO (1809, Peninsular War)
ORTHEZ (1814, Peninsular War)
OSTEND (1601, Netherlands War of Independence)
OSWEGO (1756, Seven Years' War)
OTUMBA (1520, Spanish Conquest of Mexico)
PEKING (1214, Tatar Invasion of China)
PLEI ME (1965, Vietnam War)
PLEVNA (1877, Russo-Turkish War)
POLAND (1939, World War II)
PONANI (1780, First British-Mysore War)
PRAGUE (1620, Thirty Years' War; 1757, Seven Years' War)
QUEBEC (1759, 1760, Seven Years' War)
RABAUL (1943, World War II)
RAPHIA (217 BC, Wars of the Hellenistic Monarchies)
RASZYN (1809, Napoleonic Wars)
RHODES (1480, Ottoman Wars)
RIVOLI (1797, French Revolutionary Wars)
ROCROI (1643, Thirty Years' War)
ROLICA (1808, Peninsular War)
RUMANI (1915, World War I)
SACILE (1809, Napoleonic Wars)
SADOWA (1866, Seven Weeks' War)
SAIGON (1968, Vietnam War)
SAINTS, THE (1782, American Revolutionary War)
SANGRO (1943, World War II)
SHILOH (1862, American Civil War)
SICILY (1943, World War II)
SINOPE (1853, Crimean War)
SORATA (1780, Inca Rising)
STE FOY (1760, Seven Years' War)
ST KITS (1667, Anglo-Dutch Wars)
TAURIS (47 BC, Civil War of Caesar and Pompey)
THURII (282 BC, Roman Civil Wars)
TOBRUK (1941, 1942, World War II)
TOFREK (1885, British-Sudan Campaigns)
TORGAU (1760, Seven Years' War)
TOULON (1707, War of the Spanish Succession; 1744, War of the Austrian Succession; 1793, French Revolutionary Wars)
TOWTON (1461, Wars of the Roses)
TSINAN (1948, Chinese Civil War)
TUDELA (1808, Peninsular War)
ULUNDI (1879, Zulu-British War)
USHANT (1794, French Revolutionary Wars)
VENICE (1848, Italian Wars of Independence)
VERDUN (1916, World War I)
VERONA (312, Civil Wars of the Roman Empire)
VIENNA (1529, 1683, Ottoman Wars)
WAGRAM (1809, Napoleonic Wars)
WARSAW (1831, Second Polish Rising; 1914, World War I; 1918, Russo-Polish War; 1939, 1944, World War II)
WERBEN (1631, Thirty Years' War)
WIAZMA (1812, Napoleonic Wars)

ZÜRICH (1799, French Revolutionary Wars)

7

ABRAHAM, PLAINS OF (1759, Seven Years' War)
ABU KLEA (1885, British Sudan Campaigns)
ALBUERA (1811, Peninsular War)
ALGIERS (1775, Spanish-Algerian War; 1816, Bombardment of)
ALIGARH (1803, First British-Maratha War)
ALKMAAR (1573, Netherlands War of Independence; 1799, French Revolutionary Wars)
ALMORAH (1815, British-Gurkha War)
ALNWICK (1093, Anglo-Scottish Wars)
AMOAFUL (1874, Second British-Ashanti War)
ANTIOCH (1097, First Crusade)
ANTWERP (1576, Netherlands War of Independence; 1832, Liberation of Belgium; 1914, World War I)
ARIKERA (1791, Second British-Mysore War)
ASCALON (1099, First Crusade)
ASHDOWN (871, Danish Invasion of Britain)
ATHENRY (1316, Conquest of Ireland)
AUGHRIM (1691, War of the English Succession)
BAGHDAD (1401, Mongul Invasion of Mesopotamia)
BALKANS (1940, 1944, World War II)
BAROSSA (1811, Peninsular War)
BASSANO (1796, French Revolutionary Wars)
BASSEIN (1780, First British-Maratha War)
BATAVIA (1811, Napoleonic Wars)
BAUTZEN (1813, Napoleonic Wars)
BELMONT (1899, Second Boer War)
BENBURB (1646, Great Irish Rebellion)
BÉTHUNE (1707, War of the Spanish Succession)
BIBERAC (1796, French Revolutionary Wars)
BOURBON (1810, Napleonic Wars)
BRESLAU (1757, Seven Years' War)
BRIENNE (1814, Napoleonic Wars)
BULL RUN (1861, 1862, American Civil War)
CADSAND (1357, Hundred Years' War)
CALAFAT (1854, Crimean War)
CALICUT (1790, Second British-Mysore War)
CARIGAT (1791, Second British-Mysore War)
CASSINO (1944, World War II)
CHETATÉ (1854, Crimean War)
COLENSO (1899, Second Boer War)
COLOMBO (1796, French Revolutionary Wars)
CORINTH (394 BC, Corinthian War; 1862, American Civil War)
CORONEL (1914, World War I)
CORUMBA (1877, Paraguayan War)
CORUNNA (1809, Peninsular War)
CRAONNE (1814, Napoleonic Wars)
CRAVANT (1423, Hundred Years' War)
CREFELD (1758, Seven Years' War)
CROTOYE (1347, Hundred Years' War)
CURICTA (49 BC, Civil War of Caesar and Pompey)
DEORHAM (577, Wessex against the Welsh)
DODOWAH (1826, First British-Ashanti War)
DRESDEN (1813, Napleonic Wars)
DUNDALK (1318, Scottish Invasion of Ireland)
DUNKELD (1689, Jacobite Rising)
DUNKIRK (1940, World War II)
DUPPLIN (1332, Baliol's Rising)
ECKMÜHL (1809, Napoleonic Wars)

ELK HORN (1862, American Civil War)
ESSLING (1809, Napoleonic Wars)
EVESHAM (1265, Barons' War)
FALKIRK (1298, Wars of Scottish Independence; 1746, The Forty-five Rebellion)
FERRARA (1815, Napoleon's Hundred Days)
FLEURUS (1622, Thirty Years' War; 1690, War of the Grand Alliance; 1794, French Revolutionary Wars)
FLODDEN (1513, Anglo-Scottish Wars)
FRANLIN (1864, American Civil War)
FULFORD (1066, Norse Invasion of England)
GALICIA (1914, World War I)
GATE PAH (1864, Maori-British War)
GHERAIN (1763, British Conquest of Bengal)
GHOAINE (1842, First British-Afghan War)
GORARIA (1857, Indian Mutiny)
GORLICE (1915, World War I)
GRASPAN (1899, Second Boer War)
GRENADA (1779, American Revolutionary War; 1983, American Invasion)
GUJERAT (1849, Second British-Sikh War)
GWALIOR (1780, First British-Maratha War; 1858, Indian Mutiny)
HAARLEM (1572, Netherlands War of Independence)
HASLACH (1805, Napoleonic Wars)
HOOGHLY, THE (1759, Anglo-Dutch Wars in India)
IWO-JIMA (1945, World War II)
JAMAICA (1655, Anglo-Spanish Wars)
JAVA SEA (1942, World War II)
JITGURH (1815, British Gurkha War)
JUTLAND (1916, World War I)
KALUNGA (1814, British-Gurkha War)
KAMBULA (1879, Zulu War)
KASHGAL (1883, British Sudan Campaigns)
KHARKOV (1942, 1943, World War II)
KHE SANH (1968, Vietnam War)
KILSYTH (1645, English Civil War)
KINEYRI (1848, Second British-Sikh War)
KINLOSS (1009, Danish Invasion of Scotland)
KINSALE (1601, O'Neill's Rebellion)
KRASNOI (1812, Napoleonic Wars)
LA HOGUE (1692, War of the Grand Alliance)
L'ECLUSE (1340, Hundred Years' War)
LEGHORN (1653, Anglo-Dutch Wars)
LEIPZIG (1631, Thirty Years' War; 1813, Napoleonic Wars)
LEUTHEN (1757, Seven Years' War)
LINCOLN, FAIR OF (1217, First Barons' War)
LINDLEY (1900, Second Boer War)
LOCNINH (1967, Vietnam War)
LUCKNOW (1857, Indian Mutiny)
MAIWAND (1880, Second British-Afghan War)
MALAKOV (1855, Crimean War)
MANSÛRA (1250, Seventh Crusade)
MARENGO (1800, French Revolutionary Wars)
MARGATE (1387, Hundred Years' War)
MAROSCH, THE (101, Roman Empire Wars)
MATAPAN, CAPE (1941, World War II)
MEMPHIS (1862, American Civil War)
METHVEN (1306, Wars of Scottish Independence)
MINORCA (1756, Seven Years' War; 1762, American Revolutionary War)
MOGILEV (1812, Napoleonic Wars)

MOSKOWA (1812, Napoleonic Wars)
NAM DONG (1964, Vietnam War)
NANKING (1949, Chinese Civil War)
NEUWIED (1797, French Revolutionary Wars)
NEWBURN (1640, Anglo-Scottish Wars)
NEWBURY (1643, 1644, English Civil War)
NEW ROSS (1798, Irish Rebellion)
NIAGARA (1759, Seven Years' War)
NIVELLE (1813, Peninsular War)
OKINAWA (1945, World War II)
OOSCATA (1768, First British-Mysore War)
OPEQUAN (1864, American Civil War)
ORLÉANS (1428, Hundred Years' War)
PARKANY (1663, Ottoman Wars)
PLASSEY (1757, Seven Years' War)
POLOTSK (1812, Napoleonic Wars)
PRESTON (1648, English Civil War; 1715, The Fifteen Rebellion)
PULTUSK (1806, Napoleonic Wars)
RASTADT (1796, French Revolutionary Wars)
READING (871, Danish Invasions of Britain)
RIO SECO (1808, Peninsular War)
RUMANIA (1916, World War I)
RUSPINA (46 BC, Civil War of Caesar and Pompey)
SABUGAL (1811, Peninsular War)
SAGUNTO (1811, Peninsular War)
SALERNO (1943, World War II)
SAN JUAN (1898, Spanish-American War)
SCUTARI (1474, Ottoman Wars)
SEALION, OPERATION (1940, World War II)
SENEKAL (1900, Second Boer War)
SHARQAT (1918, World War I)
SINUIJU (1951, Korean War)
SKALITZ (1866, Seven Weeks' War)
SOBRAON (1846, First British-Sikh War)
ST DENIS (1567, French Religious Wars; 1837, French-Canadian Rising)
ST LUCIA (1794, French Revolutionary Wars)
SURINAM (1804, Napoleonic Wars)
TALNEER (1818, Third British-Maratha War)
TANJORE (1758, Seven Years' War; 1773, First British-Mysore War)
TARANTO (1940, World War II)
THAPSUS (46 BC, Civil War of Caesar and Pompey)
TREBBIA (1799, French Revolutionary Wars)
TRIPOLI (643, Muslim Conquest of Africa)
TUNISIA (1942, World War II)
UKRAINE (1943, World War II)
VIMEIRO (1808, Peninsular War)
VINAROZ (1938, Spanish Civil War)
VITORIA (1813, Peninsular War)
WARBURG (1760, Seven Years' War)
WARGAOM (1779, First British-Maratha War)
WEPENER (1900, Second Boer War)
WIMPFEN (1622, Thirty Years' War)
WINKOVO (1812, Napoleonic Wars)

8

ABERDEEN (1644, English Civil War)
ABU HAMED (1897, British Sudan Campaigns)
ACAPULCO (1855, Mexican Liberal Rising)
ALICANTE (1706, War of the Spanish Succession)
AMALINDE (1818, Kaffir Wars)

ANTIETAM (1862, American Civil War)
ASIRGHAR (1819, Third British-Maratha War)
ASSUNDUN (1016, Danish Invasions of Britain)
ATLANTIC (1917, World War I)
AULDEARN (1645, English Civil War)
AZIMGHUR (1858, Indian Mutiny)
BAGRADAS (49 BC, Wars of the First Triumvirate)
BASTOGNE (1944, World War II)
BEDA FOMM (1941, World War II)
BELGRADE (1456, 1717, 1789, Ottoman Wars)
BEREZINA (1812, Napoleonic War)
BEYMAROO (1841, First British-Afghan War)
BISMARCK (1941, World War II)
BLENHEIM (1704, War of the Spanish Succession)
BLUEBERG (1806, Napoleonic Wars)
BORODINO (1812, Napoleonic Wars)
BOULOGNE (1544, Anglo-French Wars)
BOUVINES (1214, Anglo-French Wars)
BROOKLYN (1776, American Revolutionary War)
CALCUTTA (1756, Seven Years' War)
CALDIERO (1796, French Revolutionary Wars; 1805, Napoleonic Wars)
CARLISLE (1745, The Forty-five Rebellion)
CARRICAL (1758, Seven Years' War)
CARTHAGE (533, Byzantine Empire Wars)
CASTELLA (1813, Peninsular War)
CAWNPORE (1857, Indian Mutiny)
CHERITON (1644, English Civil War)
CLONTARF (1014, Norse Invasion of Ireland)
COCHEREL (1364, Hundred Years' War)
CORAL SEA (1942, World War II)
CULLODEN (1746, The Forty-five Rebellion)
CZARNOVO (1806, Napoleonic Wars)
DAMASCUS (1918, World War I)
DOMINICA (1782, American Revolutionary War)
DROGHEDA (1641, Great Irish Rebellion; 1649, Cromwell's Campaign in Ireland)
DRUMCLOG (1679, Covenanters' Rising)
EDGEHILL (1642, English Civil War)
ESPINOSA (1808, Peninsular War)
ETHANDUN (878, Danish Invasions of Britain)
FAIR OAKS (1862, American Civil War)
FALLUJAH (2004, Iraq War)
FLANDERS (1940, World War II)
FLORENCE (406, Wars of the Western Roman Empire)
FLUSHING (1809, Napoleonic Wars)
FORMIGNY (1450, Hundred Years' War)
FREIBURG (1644, Thirty Years' War)
FRETEVAL (1194, Anglo-French Wars)
GAULAULI (1858, Indian Mutiny)
GITSCHIN (1866, Seven Weeks' War)
GOODWINS, THE (1666, Anglo-Dutch Wars)
GRAF SPEE (1939, World War II)
GÜNZBURG (1805, Napoleonic Wars)
HASTINGS (1066, Norman Conquest)
HERACLEA (280 BC, Pyrrhus' Invasion of Italy; 313, Roman Civil Wars)
HERRINGS, THE (1429, Hundred Years' War)
HONG KONG (1941, World War II)
INKERMAN (1854, Crimean War)
JEMAPPES (1792, French Revolutionary Wars)
KANDAHAR (1648, Perso-Afghan Wars; 1834, Afghan

Tribal Wars; 1880, Second British-Afghan War)
KATZBACH (1813, Napoleonic Wars)
KHARTOUM (1884, British-Sudan Campaigns)
KIRBEKAN (1885, British Sudan Campaigns)
KORYGAOM (1818, Third British-Maratha War)
KUMANOVO (1912, 1st Balkan War)
LANGPORT (1645, English Civil War)
LANGSIDE (1568, Scottish Civil Wars)
LE CATEAU (1914, World War I)
LEITSKAU (1813, Napoleonic Wars)
LIEGNITZ (1760, Seven Years' War)
LOBOSITZ (1756, Seven Years' War)
LUNCARTY (980, Danish Invasions of Scotland)
LYS RIVER (1918, World War I)
MAFEKING (1899, Second Boer War)
MAHIDPUR (1817, Third British-Maratha War)

MARATHON (490 BC, Persian-Greek Wars)
MEDELLIN (1809, Peninsular War)
MEDENINE (1943, World War II)
MESSINES (1917, World War I)
MONTREAL (1760, Seven Years' War)
MORTLACK (1010, Danish Invasions of Scotland)
MORTMANT (1814, Napoleonic Wars)
MÖSKIRCH (1800, French Revolutionary Wars)
MOUSCRON (1794, French Revolutionary Wars)
MÜHLBERG (1547, German Reformation Wars)
MUSA BAGH (1858, Indian Mutiny)
NAVARINO (1827, Greek War of Independence)
OMDURMAN (1898, British-Sudan Campaigns)
ONESSANT (1778, American Revolutionary War)
OSTROWNO (1812, Napoleonic Wars)
OVERLORD, OPERATION (1944, World War II)
PALO ALTO (1846, American-Mexican War)
PEA RIDGE (1862, American Civil War)
PESHAWAR (1001, Afghan Invasion of India)

PHILIPPI (42 BC, Roman Civil Wars)
POITIERS (507, Gothic Invasion of France; 1356,
    Hundred Years' War)
PORTLAND (1653, Anglo-Dutch Wars)
PYRAMIDS (1798, French Revolutionary Wars)
PYRENEES (1813, Peninsular War)
RICHMOND (1862, American Civil War)
ROSSBACH (1757, Seven Years' War)
ROVEREDO (1796, French Revolutionary Wars)
SAALFELD (1806, Napoleonic Wars)
SAPIENZA (1490, Ottoman Wars)
SARATOGA (1777, American Revolutionary War)
SHOLAPUR (1818, Third British-Maratha War)
SIDASSIR (1799, Third British-Mysore War)
SILISTRA (1854, Crimean War)
SMOLENSK (1708, Great Northern War; 1812,
    Napoleonic Wars; 1941, World War II)
SORAUREN (1813, Peninsular War)
SPION KOP (1900, Second Boer War)
ST ALBANS (1455, 1461, Wars of the Roses)
STANDARD, THE (1138, Anglo-Scottish Wars)
STE CROIX (1807, Napoleonic Wars)
ST GEORGE (1500, Ottoman Wars)
ST MIHIEL (1918, World War I)
STOCKACH (1799, French Revolutionary Wars)
ST PRIVAT (1870, Franco-Prussian War)
STRATTON (1643, English Civil War)
ST THOMAS (1807, Napoleonic Wars)

TALAVERA (1809, Peninsular War)
THETFORD (870, Danish Invasions of England)
TIBERIAS (1187, Crusader-Saracen Wars)
TOULOUSE (1814, Napoleonic Wars)
TORA BORA (2001, Afghan War)
TRINIDAD (1797, French Revolutionary Wars)
TSINGTAO (1914, World War I)
VALLETTA (1798, French Revolutionary Wars)
VALUTINO (1812, Napoleonic Wars)
VERNEUIL (1424, Hundred Years' War)
VILLIERS (1870, Franco-Prussian War)
WATERLOO (1815, Napoleonic Wars)
WIESLOCH (1622, Thirty Years' War)
YORKTOWN (1781, American Revolutionary War;
    1862, American Civil War)
ZORNDORF (1758, Seven Years' War)

9
ABENSBERG (1809, Napoleonic Wars)
AGINCOURT (1415, Hundred Years' War)
AHMADABAD (1780, First British-Maratha War)
AHMED KHEL (1880, Second British-Afghan War)
AIGUILLON (1347, Hundred Years' War)
ALCÁNTARA (1580, Spanish Conquest of Portugal;
    1706, War of the Spanish Succession)
ALRESFORD (1644, English Civil War)
ALTENDORF (1632, Thirty Years' War)
AMSTETTEN (1805, Napoleonic Wars)
ANGOSTURA (1847, American-Mexican War; 1868,
    Paraguayan War)
ASKULTSIK (1828, Ottoman Wars)
AUERSTADT (1806, Napoleonic Wars)
AYLESFORD (456, Jutish Invasion of Britain)
BALACLAVA (1854, Crimean War)
BALLYMORE (1798, Irish Rebellion)
BANGALORE (1791, Second British-Mysore War)
BARCELONA (1705, War of the Spanish Succession;
    1938, Spanish Civil War)
BERGFRIED (1807, Napleonic Wars)
BHURTPORE (1805, Second British-Maratha War;
    1827, Second Siege of)
BLUFF COVE (1982, Falkland Isles)
BOIS-LE-DUC (1794, French Revolutionary Wars)
BORGHETTO (1796, French Revolutionary Wars)
BRENTFORD (1642, English Civil War)
BRIG OF DEE (1639, Bishops' Wars)
BUCHAREST (1771, Ottoman Wars)
BURNS HILL (1847, Kaffir Wars)

BYZANTIUM (318 BC, Wars of Alexander's
    Successors; 323, Civil Wars of the Roman Empire)
CAPE HENRY (1781, American Revolutionary War)
CAPORETTO (1917, World War I)
CASILINUM (554, Byzantine Empire Wars)
CASTILLON (1453, Hundred Years' War)
CHAMPAGNE (1915, World War I)
CHARASIAB (1879, Second British-Afghan War)
CROSSKEYS (1862, American Civil War)
CUDDALORE (1783, American Revolutionary War)
DENNEWITZ (1813, Napoleonic Wars)
DORYLAEUM (1097, First Crusade)
DUNSINANE (1054, Anglo-Scottish Wars)
EBRO RIVER (1938, Spanish Civil War)
EDERSBERG (1809, Napoleonic Wars)

EDGEWORTH (1469, Wars of the Roses)
EL ALAMEIN (1942, World War II)
ELCHINGEN (1805, Napoleonic Wars)
ELLANDUNE (825, Wessex versus Mercia)
EMPINGHAM (1470, Wars of the Roses)
FIVE FORKS (1865, American Civil War)
FRIEDLAND (1807, Napoleonic Wars)
FRONTIERS, BATTLE OF THE (1914, World War I)
GALLIPOLI (1915, World War I)
GIBRALTAR (1704, War of the Spanish Succession;
    1779, American Revolutionary War)
GLADSMUIR (1745, The Forty-five Rebellion)
GLEN FRUIN (1604, Scottish Civil Wars)
GLENLIVET (1594, Huntly's Rebellion)
GRAMPIANS, THE (Roman Invasion of Scotland)
GUINEGATE (1513, Anglo-French Wars)
GUMBINNEN (1914, World War I)
HEILSBERG (1807, Napoleonic Wars)
HOCHKIRCH (1758, Seven Years' War)
HÖCHSTÄDT (1800, French Revolutionary Wars)
JERUSALEM (70 ad, Jewish Wars of Roman Empire;
    637, Muslim Invasion of Syria; 1099, First Crusade;
    1187, Crusader-Turkish Wars; 1917, World War I;
    1948, Israeli-Arab Wars)
JUGDULLUK (1842, First British-Afghan War)
KASSASSIN (1882, Egyptian Revolt)
KIMBERLEY (1899, Second Boer War)
KISSINGEN (1866, Seven Weeks' War)
LADYSMITH (1899, Second Boer War)
LANG'S NECK (1881, First Boer War)
LANSDOWNE (1643, English Civil Wars)
LENINGRAD (1944, World War II)
LEXINGTON (1775, American Revolutionary War;
    1861, American Civil War)
LEYTE GULF (1944, World War II)
LÖWENBERG (1813, Napoleonic Wars)
MAGDEBURG (1631, Thirty Years' War)
MALAVILLY (1799, Third British-Mysore War)
MANGALORE (1783, First British-Mysore War)
MANSFIELD (1864, American Civil War)
MARIA ZELL (1805, Napoleonic Wars)
MARSAGLIA (1693, War of the Grand Alliance)
MILLESIMO (1796, French Revolutionary Wars)
MOHRUNGEN (1807, Napoleonic Wars)
MONTEREAU (1814, Napoleonic Wars)
MONTERREY (1846, Amercian-Mexican War)
MUKWANPUR (1816, British-Gurkha War)
NASHVILLE (1863, American Civil War)
NAULOCHUS (36 BC, Wars of the Second
    Triumvirate)
NAVARRETE (1367, Hundred Years' War)
NEGAPATAM (1746, War of the Austrian Succession;
    1781, Second British Mysore War; 1782, American
    Revolutionary War)
NEW GUINEA (1942, World War II)
NEW MARKET (1864, American Civil War)
NICOPOLIS (1396, Ottoman Wars; 1877, Russo-
    Turkish War)
NUJUFGHUR (1857, Indian Mutiny)
OCEAN POND (1864, American Civil War)
OLTENITZA (1853, Crimean War)
OTTERBURN (1388, Wars of Scottish Independence)
OUDENARDE (1708, War of the Spanish Succession)

PHARSALUS (48 BC, Civil War of Caesar and
    Pompey; 1897, Greco-Turkish Wars)
POLLICORE (1781, First British-Mysore War)
PORTO NOVO (1781, First British-Mysore War)
PRIMOLANÓ (1796, French Revolutionary Wars)
PRINCETON (1777, American Revolutionary War)
RAMILLIES (1706, War of the Spanish Succession)
RAMNUGGUR (1849, Second British-Sikh War)
RATHMINES (1649, Cromwell's Campaign in Ireland)
RHINELAND, THE (1945, World War II)
ROSEBURGH (1460, Anglo-Scottish Wars)
SADULAPUR (1848, Second British-Sikh War)
SALAMANCA (1812, Peninsular War; 1858, Mexican
    Liberal Rising)
SANTANDER (1937, Spanish Civil War)
SARAGOSSA (1700, War of the Spanish Succession;
    1808, Peninsular War)
SEDGEMOOR (1685, Monmouth's Rebellion)
SEVENOAKS (1450, Cade's Rebellion)
SHEERNESS (1667, Anglo-Dutch Wars)
SHERSTONE (1016, Danish Invasion of England)
SHOLINGUR (1781, First British-Mysore War)
SINGAPORE (1942, World War II)
SITABALDI (1817, Third British-Maratha War)
SOUTHWARK (1450, Cade's Rebellion)
STADTLOHN (1623, Thirty Years' War)
STAFFARDA (1690, War of the Grand Alliance)
STORMBERG (1899, Second Boer War)
ST QUENTIN (1557, Franco-Spanish Wars; 1871,
    Franco-Prussian War)
STRALSUND (1628, Thirty Years' War; 1715, Great
    Northern War)
SUDDASAIN (1848, Second British-Sikh War)
TARRAGONA (1811, Peninsular War)
TCHERNAYA (1855, Crimean War)
TOLENTINO (1815, Napoleonic Wars)
TOU MORONG (1966, Vietnam War)
TOURCOING (1794, French Revolutionary Wars)
TRAFALGAR (1805, Napoleonic Wars)
TRAUTENAU (1866, Seven Weeks' War)
TREBIZOND (1461, Ottoman Wars)
TRINKITAT (1884, British-Sudan Campaigns)
VAALKRANZ (1900, Second Boer War)
VAUCHAMPS (1814, Napoleonic Wars)
VICKSBURG (1862, American Civil War)
VIMY RIDGE (1917, World War I)
WAKEFIELD (1460, Wars of the Roses)
WANDIWASH (1760, Seven Years' War; 1780, First
    British-Mysore War)
WORCESTER (1651, English Civil War)
WÜRTZBURG (1796, French Revolutionary Wars)

10

ADRIANOPLE (1205, Fourth Crusade; 1913, First
    Balkan War)
ALEXANDRIA (642, Muslim Invasion of Egypt; 1801,
    British Invasion of Egypt; 1881, Egyptian Revolt)
ANCRUM MOOR (1545, Anglo-Scottish Wars)
ARTOIS-LOOS (1915, World War I)
AUSTERLITZ (1805, Napoleonic Wars)
BALL'S BLUFF (1861, American Civil War)
BEACHY HEAD (1690, War of the Grand Alliance)
BEAUSÉJOUR (1755, Seven Year's War)

BENNINGTON (1777, American Revolutionary War)
BLACKWATER (1598, O'Neill's Rebellion)
BLORE HEATH (1459, Wars of the Roses)
BRANDYWINE (1777, American Revolutionary War)
BRUNANBURH (937, Danish Invasion)
BUENA VISTA (1846, American-Mexican War)
CAMPERDOWN (1797, French Revolutionary Wars)
CEDAR CREEK (1864, American Civil War)
CHARLESTON (1863, American Civil War)
CHEVY CHASE (1388, Wars of Scottish
    Independence)
CHIPPENHAM (878, Danish Invasions of Britain)
COPENHAGEN (1801, French Revolutionary Wars;
    1807, Napoleonic Wars)
DALMANUTHA (1900, Second Boer War)
DOGGER BANK (1781, American Revolutionary War;
    1915, World War I)
DUNGANHILL (1647, Great Irish Rebellion)
DYRRACHIUM (48 BC, Civil War of Caesar and
    Pompey)
ENGLEFIELD (871, Danish Invasion of Britain)
FEROZESHAH (1845, First British-Sikh War)
FETHANLEAG (584, Saxon Conquests)
FUTTEYPORE (1857, Indian Mutiny)
GAINES' MILL (1862, American Civil War)
GERMANTOWN (1777, American Revolutionary War)
GETTYSBURG (1863, American Civil War)
GLEN MALONE (1580, Colonization of Ireland)
GORODECZNO (1812, Napoleonic Wars)
GOTHIC LINE (1944, World War II)
GRANT'S HILL (1758, Seven Years' War)
GRAVELINES (1558, Franco-Spanish Wars)
GRAVELOTTE (1870, Franco-Prussian War)
GUADELOUPE (1794, French Revolutionary Wars)
HABBANIYAH (1941, World War II)
HASTENBECK (1757, Seven Years' War)
HEATHFIELD (633, Mercia against Northumbria)
HELIGOLAND (1807, Napoleonic Wars)
HELIOPOLIS (1800, French Revolutionary Wars)
HELLESPONT (323, War of the Two Empires)
HOLLABRUNN (1805, Napleonic Wars)
INVERLOCHY (1645, English Civil War)
JELLALABAD (1842, First British-Afghan War)
KHOJAH PASS (1842, First British-Afghan War)
KÖNIGGRÄTZ (1866, Seven Weeks' War)
KORNSPRUIT (1900, Second Boer War)
KUNERSDORF (1759, Seven Years' War)
KUT-EL-AMARA (1915, World War I)
LA FAVORITA (1797, French Revolutionary Wars)
LAKE GEORGE (1755, Seven Years' War)
LA ROCHELLE (1372, Hundred Years' War; 1627,
    French Religious Wars)
LA ROTHIÈRE (1814, Napoleonic Wars)
LOUDON HILL (1307, Wars of Scottish
    Independence)
LOUISBOURG (1745, War of the Austrian Succession;
    1758, Seven Years' War)
LÜLEBÜRGAZ (1912, Balkan Wars)
LUNDY'S LANE (1814, War of 1812)
MAASTRICHT (1579, Netherlands War of
    Independence)
MAHARAJPUR (1843, Gwalior Campaign; 1857,
    Indian Mutiny)

MARETH LINE (1943, World War II)
MARIENDAHL (1645, Thirty Years' War)
MARTINIQUE (1794, French Revolutionary Wars;
    1809, Napoleonic Wars)
MASERFIELD (642, Northumbria against Mercia)
MICHELBERG (1805, Napoleonic Wars)
MONTEBELLO (1800, French Revolutionary Wars;
    1859, Italian Wars of Independence)
MONTENOTTE (1796, French Revolutionary Wars)
MONTEVIDEO (1807, Napoleonic Wars; 1843, 1851,
    1863, Uruguayan Civil War)
MONTFAUCON (886, Norman Invasion of France)
MONTMIRAIL (1814, Napoleonic Wars)
MOUNT TABOR (1799, French Revolutionary Wars)
NAROCH LAKE (1916, World War I)
NEERWINDEN (1693, War of the Grand Alliance;
    1793, French Revolutionary Wars)
NEW ORLEANS (1814, War of 1812; 1862, American
    Civil War)
NÖRDLINGEN (1634, 1645, Thirty Year's War)
OSTROLENKA (1853, Crimean War)
PAARDEBERG (1900, Second Boer War)
PANDU NADDI (1857, Indian Mutiny)
PEN SELWOOD (1016, Danish Invasions of Britain)
PEREMBACUM (1780, First British-Mysore War)
PERRYVILLE (1862, American Civil War)
PERSEPOLIS (316 BC, Wars of Alexander's
    Successors)
PETERSBURG (1864, American Civil War)
PIAVE RIVER (1918, World War I)
PONT VALAIN (1370, Hundred Years' War)
PORT ARTHUR (1894, Sino-Japanese War; 1904,
    Russo-Japanese War)
PORT HUDSON (1863, American Civil War)
QALA-I-JANGI (2001, Afghan War)
QUATRE BRAS (1815, Napoleonic Wars)
RAKERSBERG (1416, Ottoman Wars)
RUHR POCKET (1945, World War II)
SANNA'S POST (1900, Second Boer War)
SANTA LUCIA (1842, Rio Grande Rising)
SAVANDROOG (1791, Second British-Mysore War)
SEINE MOUTH (1416, Hundred Years' War)
SEVASTOPOL (1854, Crimean War)
SEVEN PINES (1862, American Civil War)
SHREWSBURY (1403, Percy's Rebellion)
SHROPSHIRE (ad 50, Roman Conquest of Britain)
SIDI REZEGH (1941, World War II)
SOLWAY MOSS (1542, Anglo-Scottish Wars)
STALINGRAD (1942, World War II)
STEENKERKE (1692, War of the Grand Alliance)
STILLWATER (1777, American Revolutionary War)
STONE RIVER (1862, American Civil War)
TALANA HILL (1899, Second Boer War)
TANNENBERG (1914, World War I)
TEL-EL-KEBIR (1882, Egyptian Revolt)
TETTENHALL (910, Danish Invasions of England)
TEWKESBURY (1471, Wars of the Roses)
TIPPERMUIR (1644, English Civil War)
TRAVANCORE (1789, Second British-Mysore War)
WARTEMBERG (1813, Napoleonic Wars)
WATTIGNIES (1793, French Revolutionary Wars)
WILDERNESS, THE (1864, American Civil War)
WINCHESTER (1863, American Civil War)

11

ALAM EL HALFA (1942, World War II)
ALESSANDRIA (1799, French Revolutionary Wars)
AN LAO VALLEY (1966, Vietnam War)
BANNOCKBURN (1314, Wars of Scottish
    Independence)
BELLEAU WOOD (1918, World War I)
BISMARCK SEA (1943, World War II)
BLANQUEFORT (1450, Hundred Years' War)
BRAMHAM MOOR (1408, Northumberland's
    Rebellion)
BREITENFELD (1642, Thirty Years' War)
BRENNEVILLE (1119, Anglo-French Wars)
BUENOS AIRES (1806, 1807, Napoleonic Wars; 1874,
    Mitre's Rebellion)
BUNKER'S HILL (1775, American Revolutionary War)
CAMELODUNUM (43, Roman Invasion of Britain)
CARBIESDALE (1650, English Civil War)
CARENAGE BAY (1778, American Revolutionary War)
CASTIGLIONE (1706, War of the Spanish Succession;
    1796, French Revolutionary Wars)
CHAMPAUBERT (1814, Napoleonic Wars)
CHATTANOOGA (1863, American Civil War)
CHICKAMAUGA (1863, American Civil War)
CHILIANWALA (1849, Second British-Sikh War)
CHRYSOPOLIS (324, War of the Two Empires)
COLDHARBOUR (1864, American Civil War)
DIAMOND HILL (1900, Second Boer War)
DINGAAN'S DAY (1838, Afrikaner-Zulu War)
DRIEFONTEIN (1900, Second Boer War)
DÜRRENSTEIN (1805, Napoleonic Wars)
ELANDS RIVER (1900, Second Boer War)
FARRUKHABAD (1804, Second British-Maratha War)
FERRYBRIDGE (1461, Wars of the Roses)
FISHER'S HILL (1864, American Civil War)
FORT ST DAVID (1758, Seven Years' War)
GIBBEL RUTTS (1798, Irish Rebellion)
GROSS-BEEREN (1813, Napoleonic Wars)
GUADALAJARA (1937, Spanish Civil War)
GUADALCANAL (1942, World War II)
HADRIANOPLE (323, War of the Two Empires; 378,
    Second Gothic Invasion of the East)
HALIDON HILL (1333, Wars of Scottish
    Independence)
HEAVENFIELD (634, Northumbria against the
    British)
HOHENLINDEN (1800, French Revolutionary Wars)
HONDSCHOOTE (1793, French Revolutionary Wars)
ÎLE DE FRANCE (1810, Napoleonic Wars)
ISANDHLWANA (1879, Zulu-British War)
LANGENSALZA (1866, Seven Weeks' War)
LONDONDERRY (1689, War of the Grand Alliance)
LOSTWITHIEL (1644, English Civil War)
MALVERN HILL (1862, American Civil War)
MARSTON MOOR (1644, English Civil War)
MASULIPATAM (1759, Seven Years' War)
MERSA MATRÛH (1942, World War II)
MILL SPRINGS (1862, American Civil War)
MODDER RIVER (1899, Second Boer War)
MONTE LEZINO (1796, French Revolutionary Wars)
MONTMORENCI (1759, Seven Years' War)
MORSHEDABAD (1763, British Conquest of Bengal)
NOISSEVILLE (1870, Franco-Prussian War)

NORTHAMPTON (1460, Wars of the Roses)
PEARL HARBOR (1941, World War II)
PEIWAR KOTAL (1878, Second British-Afghan War)
PHILIPHAUGH (1645, English Civil War)
PIETER'S HILL (1900, Second Boer War)
PONDICHERRY (1748, War of the Austrian
    Succession; 1760, Seven Years' War; 1778, 1783,
    American Revolutionary War)
PRESTONPANS (1745, The Forty-five Rebellion)
QUIBERON BAY (1759, Seven Years' War)
RAJAHMUNDRY (1758, Seven Years' War)
REDDERSBERG (1900, Second Boer War)
RHEINFELDEN (1638, Thirty Years' War)
RIETFONTEIN (1899, Second Boer War)
RORKE'S DRIFT (1879, Zulu-British War)
ROWTON HEATH (1645, English Civil War)
SALDANHA BAY (1796, French Revolutionary Wars)
SAN GIOVANNI (1799, French Revolutionary Wars)
SAUCHIE BURN (1488, Rebellion of the Scottish
    Barons)
SHERIFFMUIR (1715, The Fifteen Rebellion)
SIDI BARRÂNI (1940, World War II)
TAILLEBOURG (1242, Anglo-French Wars)
TARAWA-MAKIN (1943, World War II)
TEL-EL-MAHUTA (1882, Egyptian Revolt)
TELLICHERRY (1780, First British-Mysore War)
TEUTTLINGEN (1643, Thirty Years' War)
TICONDEROGA (1758, Seven Years' War; 1777,
    American Revolutionary War)
TRINCOMALEE (1759, Seven Years' War; 1767, First
    British-Mysore War; 1782, American Revolutionary
    War)
VINEGAR HILL (1798, Irish Rebellion)
WALTERSDORF (1807, Napoleonic Wars)
WEDNESFIELD (911, Danish Invasions of England)
WEISSENBURG (1870, Franco-Prussian War)
WHITE RUSSIA (1943, World War II)

12

ADWALTON MOOR (1643, English Civil War)
ALGEÇIRAS BAY (1801, French Revolutionary Wars)
ARCIS-SUR-AUBE (1814, Napoleonic Wars)
ATHERTON MOOR (1643, English Civil War)
BANDA ISLANDS (1796, French Revolutionary Wars)
BERGEN-OP-ZOOM (1747, War of the Austrian
    Succession; 1799, French Revolutionary Wars)
BLOEMFONTEIN (1900, Second Boer War)
BRADDOCK DOWN (1643, English Civil War)
CHICKAHOMINY (1864, American Civil War)
ELANDSLAAGTE (1899, Second Boer War)
EUTAW SPRINGS (1781, American Revolutionary
    War)
FORT DONELSON (1862, American Civil War)
HAMPTON ROADS (1862, American Civil War)
HARPER'S FERRY (1862, American Civil War)
HEDGELEY MOOR (1464, Wars of the Roses)
HENGESTESDUN (837, Danish Invasions of Britain)
HOMILDON HILL (1402, Anglo-Scottish Wars)
KIRCH-DENKERN (1761, Seven Years' War)
KÖNIGSWARTHA (1813, Napoleonic Wars)
KURSK SALIENT (1943, World War II)
LYNN HAVEN BAY (1781, American Revolutionary
    War)
MAZAR-I SHARIF (2001, Afghan War)

MIDWAY ISLAND (1942, World War II)
MÜNCHENGRÄTZ (1866, Seven Weeks' War)
MURFREESBORO (1862, American Civil War)
NECHTAN'S MERE (685, Northumbrian Invasion of Scotland)
OONDWA NULLAH (1763, British Conquest of Bengal)
PENOBSCOT BAY (1779, American Revolutionary War)
PETERWARDEIN (1716, Ottoman Wars)
PINKIE CLEUGH (1547, Anglo-Scottish Wars)
PORT REPUBLIC (1862, American Civil War)
PRAIRIE GROVE (1862, American Civil War)
RICH MOUNTAIN (1861, American Civil War)
RONCESVALLES (1813, Peninsular War)
ROUNDWAY DOWN (1643, English Civil War)
RULLION GREEN (1666, Covenanters' Rising)
SAN SEBASTIAN (1813, Peninsular War; 1836, First Carlist War)
SECUNDERBAGH (1857, Indian Mutiny)
SERINGAPATAM (1792, Second British-Mysore War; 1799, Third British-Mysore War)
SOUTHWOLD BAY (1672, Anglo-Dutch Wars)
SPOTSYLVANIA (1864, American Civil War)
TET OFFENSIVE, THE (1968, Vietnam War)
WILLIAMSBURG (1862, American Civil War)
WILSON'S CREEK (1861, American Civil War)
WROTHAM HEATH (1554, Wyatt's Insurrection)

13

AIX-LA-CHAPELLE (1795, French Revolutionary Wars)
BADULI-KI-SERAI (1857, Indian Mutiny)
BELLE-ÎLE-EN-MER (1759, 1761, Seven Years' War; 1795, French Revolutionary Wars)
BOROUGHBRIDGE (1322, Rebellion of the Marches)
BOSWORTH FIELD (1485, Wars of the Roses)
CAPE ST VINCENT (1797, French Revolutionary Wars)
CEDAR MOUNTAIN (1862, American Civil War)
CHANDERNAGORE (1757, Seven Years' War)
CIUDAD RODRIGO (1812, Peninsular War)
FALKLAND ISLES (1914, World War I; 1982, Falklands War)
FARQUHAR'S FARM (1899, Second Boer War)
FORT FRONTENAC (1758, Seven Years' War)
FRANKENHAUSEN (1525, Peasants' War)
GLENMARRESTON (683, Angles' Invasion of Britain)
HORNS OF HATTIN (1187, Crusader-Saracen Wars)
INVERKEITHING (1317, Anglo-Scottish Wars)
KASSERINE PASS (1943, World War II)
KILLIECRANKIE (1689, Jacobite Rising)
LITTLE BIG HORN (1876, Sioux Rising)
MAGERSFONTEIN (1899, Second Boer War)
MASURIAN LAKES (1914, 1915, World War I)
MOLINOS DEL REY (1808, Peninsular War)
MOUNT SELEUCUS (353, Civil Wars of the Roman Empire)
NEVILLE'S CROSS (1346, Anglo-Scottish Wars)
NEWTOWN BUTLER (1689, War of the Grand Alliance)
NORTHALLERTON (1138, Anglo-Scottish Wars)
NORTH FORELAND (1666, Anglo-Dutch Wars)
PASSCHENDAELE (1917, World War I)

PELELIU-ANGAUR (1944, World War II)
PHILIPPINE SEA (1944, World War II)
PORTO PRAIA BAY (1781, American Revolutionary War)
ROANOKE ISLAND (1862, American Civil War)
SOUTH MOUNTAIN (1862, American Civil War)
SPANISH ARMADA (1588, Anglo-Spanish War)
SUDLEY SPRINGS (1862, American Civil War)
WHITE OAK SWAMP (1862, American Civil War)
YOUGHIOGHENNY (1754, Seven Years' War)
ZUSMARSHAUSEN (1647, Thirty Years' War)

14

BERWICK-ON-TWEED (1296, Wars of Scottish Independence)
BOTHWELL BRIDGE (1679, Covenanters' Rising)
BRISTOE STATION (1863, American Civil War)
CAPE FINISTERRE (1747, War of the Austrian Succession; 1805, Napoleonic Wars)
CHALGROVE FIELD (1643, English Civil War)
CHÂTEAU-THIERRY (1814, Napoleonic Wars)
CONSTANTINOPLE (668, Muslim Invasion of Europe; 1203–04, Fourth Crusade; 1261, Reconquest by Byzantines; 1422, Ottoman Invasion of Europe; 1453, Turkish Conquest)
CROPREDY BRIDGE (1644, English Civil War)
DRUMMOSSIE MOOR (1746, The Forty-five Rebellion)
FREDERICKSBURG (1862, American Civil War)
FUENTES DE OÑORO (1811, Peninsular War)
KOVEL-STANISLAV (1916, World War I)
LA BELLE FAMILLE (1759, Seven Years' War)
LOOSECOAT FIELD (1470, Wars of the Roses)
MARIANA ISLANDS (1944, World War II)
MORTIMER'S CROSS (1461, Wars of the Roses)
NICHOLSON'S NECK (1899, Second Boer War)
PEACH TREE CREEK (1864, American Civil War)
PUSAN PERIMETER (1950, Korean War)
ROUVRAY-ST-DENIS (1429, Hundred Years' War)
SANTIAGO DE CUBA (1898, Spanish-American War)
SAVAGE'S STATION (1862, American Civil War)
SECESSIONVILLE (1862, American Civil War)
SINAI PENINSULA (1956, Israeli-Arab War)
SOLOMON ISLANDS (1942, World War II)
STAMFORD BRIDGE (1066, Norse Invasion of Britain; 1453, Wars of the Roses)
STIRLING BRIDGE (1297, Wars of Scottish Independence)
VITTORIO VENETO (1918, World War I)

15

ALEUTIAN ISLANDS (1943, World War II)
AMATOLA MOUNTAIN (1846, Kaffir Wars)
APPOMATTOX RIVER (1865, American Civil War)
BATTLE OF BRITAIN (1940, World War II)
BEAVER'S DAM CREEK (1862, American Civil War)
FRANKFURT-ON-ODER (1631, Thirty Years' War)
GROSS-JÄGERSDORF (1757, Seven Years' War)
HELIGOLAND BIGHT (1914, World War I)
KHOORD KABUL PASS (1842, First British-Afghan War)
MALOYAROSLAVETS (1812, Napoleonic Wars)
MISSIONARY RIDGE (1863, American Civil War)
PLAINS OF ABRAHAM (1759, Seven Years' War)

SEVEN DAYS' BATTLE (1862, American Civil War)
SPANISH GALLEONS (1702, War of the Spanish
    Succession)

16
BATAAN-CORREGIDOR (1941, World War II)
BRONKHORST SPRUIT (1880, First Boer War)
CAMBRAI-ST QUENTIN (1918, World War I)
CHANCELLORSVILLE (1863, American Civil War)
FORT WILLIAM HENRY (1757, Seven Years' War)
KINNESAW MOUNTAIN (1864, American Civil War)
MONONGAHELA RIVER (1755, Seven Years' War)
SALUM-HALFAYA PASS (1941, World War II)

17
BURLINGTON HEIGHTS (1813, War of 1812)
DODECANESE ISLANDS (1943, World War II)
GUSTAV-CASSINO LINE (1943, World War II)
INHLOBANE MOUNTAIN (1879, Zulu War)
KWAJALEIN-ENIWETOK (1944, World War II)

LA FÈRE CHAMPENOISE (1814, Napoleonic Wars)
PITTSBURGH LANDING (1862, American Civil War)
POLAND-EAST PRUSSIA (1944, World War II)
VAN TUONG PENINSULA (1965, Vietnam War)

18
GUILFORD COURTHOUSE (1781, American
    Revolutionary War)
MEUSE-ARGONNE FOREST (1918, World War I)

19
CHU PONG-IA DRANG RIVER (1965, Vietnam War)
'GLORIOUS FIRST OF JUNE' (1794, French
    Revolutionary Wars)

20+
RHINE AND THE RUHR POCKET, THE (1945, World
    War II)
SHANNON AND CHESAPEAKE (1813, War of 1812)
THIRTY-EIGHTH PARALLEL (1951, Korean War)

WARS

AFGHAN WAR	2001–PRESENT
AMERICAN CIVIL WAR	1861–65
BALKAN WARS	1912–13
BOER WAR	1880–81, 1899–1902
BOSNIAN CIVIL WAR	1992–95
CRIMEAN WAR	1853–56
ENGLISH CIVIL WAR	1642–49
FALKLANDS WAR	1982
FIRST WORLD WAR	1914–18
FRANCO-PRUSSIAN WAR	1870–71
FRENCH AND INDIAN WAR	1754–63
FRENCH INDOCHINA WAR	1946–54
FRENCH WARS OF RELIGION	1562–98
GALLIC WARS	58–51 BC
GREAT NORTHERN WAR	1700–21
GULF WAR	1991
HUNDRED YEARS WAR	1337–1453
IRAN-IRAQ WAR	1980–88
IRAQ WAR	2003–11
KOREAN WAR	1950–53
LIBYAN CIVIL WAR	2014–PRESENT
MACEDONIAN WARS	214–205 BC, 200–196 BC, 171–168 BC, 149–148 BC
MEXICAN WAR	1846–48
NAPOLEONIC WARS	1805–15
OPIUM WARS	1839–42, 1856–60
PELOPONNESIAN WARS	431–404 BC
PENINSULAR WAR	1808–14
PERSIAN WARS	5th century BC
PUNIC WARS	264–241 BC, 2118–20 BC, 149–146 BC
RUSSIAN CIVIL WAR	1918–21
RUSSO-JAPANESE WAR	1904–05
SAMNITE WARS	343–341 BC, 316–314 BC, 298–290 BC
SECOND GULF WAR	2003–11
SECOND WORLD WAR	1939–45
SEVEN YEARS WAR	1756–63
SINO-JAPANESE WARS	1894–95, 1937–45

SIX DAY WAR	1967
SPANISH-AMERICAN WAR	1898
SPANISH CIVIL WAR	1936–39
THIRTY YEARS WAR	1618–48
VIETNAM WAR	1954–75
WAR OF 1812	1812–14
WAR OF AMERICAN INDEPENDENCE	1775–83
WAR OF THE AUSTRIAN SUCCESSION	1740–48
WAR OF THE SPANISH SUCCESSION	1701–14
WARS OF THE ROSES	1455–85
YOM KIPPUR WAR	1973

ARMOUR

4
JACK
MAIL

5
ARMET
BACYN
BUFFE
CREST
CULET
GIPON
IMBER
JUPEL
JUPON
LAMES
SALET
VISOR

6
ALETES
BASNET
BHANJU
BRACER
BRIDLE
BRUGNE
CALOTE
CAMAIL
CASQUE
CASSIS
CELATE
CHEEKS
CRENEL
CRINET
CUELLO
GORGET
GUSSET
HEAUME

HELMET
MASCLE
MESAIL
MORIAN
MORION
SALADE
SHIELD
TABARD
UMBRIL

7
AILETES
BACINET
BALDRIC
BARBUTE
BASINET
BUCKLER
CHAUCES
CORSLET
CRUPPER
CUIRASS
CUISSES
CULESET
FENDACE
FRONTAL
GAUCHET
GOUCHET
GREAVES
HAUBERK
HOGUINE
LANIERS
MURSAIL
PANACHE
PLACARD
POITRAL
SURCOAT

VISIERE

8
ALLECRET
BARDINGS
BASCINET
BAUDRICK
BRASSARD
BRAYETTE
BUFF COAT
BURGINOT
BURGONET
CABASSET
CHAMPONS
CHANFRON
CHAUCHES
CHAUSSES
COD PIECE
COLLERET
COLLETIN
CORSELET
CRINIERE
GAUNTLET
HALECRET
JAMBEAUX
JAZERANT
PAULDRON
PECTORAL
PLASTRON
SABATONS
SOLARETS
SOLERETS
TESTIERE

9
BAINBERGS
BEINBERGS

CHAIN MAIL
CHAMPFRON
CHAUSSONS
EPAULETTE
HAUSSE-COL
JACK BOOTS
POURPOINT
REREBRACE
SABATYNES

10
AVENTAILLE
BANDED MAIL
BARREL HELM
BRICHETTES
BRIGANDINE
CROISSANTS
ECREVISSES
EMBOITMENT
FLANCHARDS
LAMBREQUIN

11
BREASTPLATE
BREASTSTRAP
BRIGANDYRON
BRIGANTAYLE
CHAPEL DE FER
ESPALLIERES
PLATE ARMOUR

13
ARMING DOUBLET

15
IMBRICATE ARMOUR

WEAPONS

2
NU
V1
V2

3
AXE
BOW
DAG
DAS
GUN
GYN
TNT

4
ADZE
BARB
BILL
BOLO
BOLT
BOMB
CLUB
DIRK
FANG
FOIL
KORA
KRIS
LAWS
MACE
MINE
PIKE
SHOT
TANK
TOCK
TUCK

5
A-BOMB
ANCUS
ANKUS
ANLAS
ARROW
ASWAR
BATON
BIDAG
BILBO
BOLAS
BOSON
BRAND
DRONE
ESTOC
FLAIL
FUSEE
FUSIL
GUPTI
H-BOMB
KERIS
KHORA
KILIG
KILIJ

KNIFE
KUKRI
KYLIE
LANCE
LATCH
MAARS
PILUM
PRODD
RIFLE
SABRE
SHELL
SLING
SPEAR
STAKE
STAVE
SWORD
TACHI
TASER
WADDY

6
AMUKTA
ARMLET
BARKAL
BARONG
BASTON
BODKIN
BULLET
CANNON
CARCAS
CEMTEX
CUDGEL
DAGGER
DAISHO
DRAGON
DUM-DUM
DUSACK
EXOCET
KATANA
KERRIE
KHANDA
KIKUKI
KODOGU
MASSUE
MAZULE
MORTAR
MUSKET
NAPALM
PARANG
PETARD
PISTOL
POP GUN
QILLIJ
QUIVER
RAMROD
RAPIER
ROCKET
SCYTHE
SEMTEX
SUMPIT

TALWAR
VGO GUN

7
ASSEGAI
AWL-PIKE
BALASAN
BALISTA
BAYONET
BELFREY
BILIONG
BOMBARD
BOURDON
BREN GUN
CALIVER
CALTRAP
CARABEN
CARBINE
CARREAU
CHAKRAM
CHALCOS
CHOPPER
CURRIER
CUTLASS
DUDGEON
DUSSACK
FAUCHON
FIRE-POT
GRENADE
HALBARD
HALBART
HALBERD
HAND GUN
HARPOON
KASTANE
KINDJAL
LONG BOW
MISSILE
MUSQUET
PONIARD
PUNT GUN
QUARREL
SHASHQA
SHINKEN
STEN GUN
TORPEDO
TRIDENT

8
AMUSETTE
ARBALEST
ARBALETE
ARQUEBUS
ATOM BOMB
AXE-KNIFE
BASELARD
BASILARD
BLOWPIPE
BUZZBOMB
CALTHORP

CANISTER
CARABINE
CATAPULT
CHACHEKA
CLADIBAS
CLAYMORE
CROSSBOW
DERINGER
DESTRIER
FALCHION
FALCONET
FAUCHARD
FIRELOCK
HACKBUTT
HAIL SHOT
HAQUEBUT
HASSEGAI
HOWITZER
LAND MINE
PETRONEL
POIGNARD
QUERQUER
REPEATER
REVOLVER
SCIMITAR
SHAMSHIR
SHRAPNEL
SPONTOON
SUMPITAN
TOMAHAWK
TOMMY GUN

9
ACK-ACK GUN
ARTILLERY
BADELAIRE
BANDELEER
BANDOLIER
BANNEROLE
BATTLE-AXE
BIG BERTHA
BOOMERANG
CARRONADE
CARTOUCHE
CARTRIDGE
CHAIN SHOT
DETONATOR
DOODLE-BUG
FALCASTRA
FLAGELLUM
FLAMBERGE
FLINTLOCK
GELIGNITE
GRAPESHOT
GUNPOWDER
HARQUEBUS
KNOBSTICK
MATCHLOCK
MAZZUELLE
MILLS BOMB

MUSKETOON
POM-POM GUN
SLUNG SHOT
TRUNCHEON

10
ARTILLATOR
BANDEROLLE
BRANDESTOC
BROAD ARROW
BROADSWORD
CANNON BALL
FIRE-STICKS
FLICK KNIFE
FLYING BOMB
GATLING GUN
KNOBKERRIE
LETTER BOMB
LIMPET MINE
MACHINE GUN
PEA-SHOOTER
POWDERHORN
SIDEWINDER

SMALL SWORD
SWORD STICK

11
ANTI-TANK GUN
ARMOURED CAR
BLUNDERBUSS
HAND GRENADE
KHYBER KNIFE
MISERICORDE
NEUTRON BOMB

12
BATTERING RAM
BREECH LOADER
BRIDLE CUTTER
FIRE CARRIAGE
FLAME-THROWER
HYDROGEN BOMB
LASER AVENGER

13
BRASS KNUCKLES
DUELLING SWORD
GUIDED MISSILE

KNUCKLE DUSTER
THROWING KNIFE

14
DUELLING PISTOL
INCENDIARY BOMB
NUCLEAR WEAPONS
ROCKET LAUNCHER
SAWN-OFF SHOTGUN

15
ANTI-AIRCRAFT GUN

16
BALLISTIC MISSILE

17
ANTI-PERSONNEL MINE

18
HEAT-SEEKING MISSILE

20+
DOUBLE-BARRELLED
   SHOTGUN

TRANSPORT

VEHICLES

2&3
BMX
BUS
CAB
CAR
FLY
GIG
RV
SUV
VAN

4
AUTO
BIKE
CART
DRAG
DRAY
EKKA
HACK
JEEP
LUGE
SHAY
SLED
TAXI
TRAM
TRAP
TUBE
WAIN

5
ARABA
BRAKE
BUGGY
COACH
COUPÉ
CRATE
CYCLE
DANDY
DOOLY
LORRY
METRO
MOPED
MOTOR
PALKI
SEDAN
SULKY
TONGA
TRAIN
TRUCK
WAGON

6
BERLIN
CALASH
CHAISE
DIESEL
FIACRE
GO-CART
HANSOM
HEARSE
HOTROD
HURDLE
JALOPY
JITNEY
LANDAU
LIMBER
LITTER
MAGLEV
MODEL-T
ROCKET
SALOON
SLEDGE
SLEIGH
SNOCAT
SURREY
TANDEM
TANKER
TOURER
TRICAR
WEASEL

7
AUTOBUS
AUTOCAR
BICYCLE
BOB-SLED
BRITZKA
BROWSER
CALÈCHE
CARAVAN
CAROCHE
CHARIOT
COASTER
DOG-CART
DROSHKY
FLIVVER
GROWLER
HACKERY
HARD-TOP
OFF-ROAD
OMNIBUS
OPEN-CAR

PHAETON
PULLMAN
SCOOTER
SHUNTER
SIDE-CAR
TALLY-HO
TAXI-CAB
TILBURY
TRACTOR
TRAILER
TROLLEY
TUMBRIL
TWO-DOOR
UNICORN
VIS-À-VIS
WHISKEY

8
BAROUCHE
BRANCARD
BROUGHAM
CABLE-CAR
CAPE-CART
CARRIAGE
CARRIOLE
CLARENCE
CURRICLE
DEAD-CART
DORMEUSE
FOUR-DOOR
HORSE-BUS
HORSE-CAB
HORSE-VAN
ICE-YACHT
KIBITZKA
MONORAIL
MOTOR-CAR
MOTOR-VAN
OLD CROCK
PONY-CART
PUSH-BIKE
QUADRIGA
RICKSHAW
ROADSTER
RUNABOUT
SOCIABLE
STAFF CAR
STEAM-CAR
TOBOGGAN
TRICYCLE
UNICYCLE

VICTORIA

9
AMBULANCE
BOAT-TRAIN
BOB-SLEIGH
BUBBLECAR
BUCKBOARD
CABRIOLET
CAMPER VAN
CHAR-À -BANC
DILIGENCE
ESTATE-CAR
FUNICULAR
HORSE-CART
HYBRID CAR
LIMOUSINE
MAIL-COACH
MILKFLOAT
MILK TRAIN
MONOCYCLE
MOTOR-BIKE
MOTOR HOME
PALANKEEN
PALANQUIN
RACING CAR
SPORTS CAR
STREET-CAR
STRETCHER
TARANTASS
TIN LIZZIE
TWO-SEATER
WAGONETTE

10
AUTOMOBILE
BAIL GHARRY
BEACHWAGON
BLACK MARIA
FIRE-ENGINE
FOUR-IN-HAND
GOODS TRAIN
JINRICKSHA
LOCAL TRAIN
LOCOMOTIVE
MOTOR-COACH
MOTOR-CYCLE
NIGHT TRAIN
OUTSIDE CAR
PADDYWAGON
PEDAL-CYCLE

PONY-ENGINE
POST-CHAISE
RATTLETRAP
SEDAN-CHAIR
SHANDRYDAN
SINCLAIR C5
SNOWPLOUGH
STAGE-COACH
STAGE-WAGON
STATE COACH
TROLLEY-BUS
TROLLEY-CAR
TWO-WHEELER
VELOCIPEDE

11
BONE-BREAKER
BULLOCK-CART
CONVERTIBLE
DIESEL TRAIN
ELECTRIC CAR
FOUR-WHEELER
GUN-CARRIAGE
JAUNTING-CAR
JINRICKSHAW
LANDAULETTE
MAIL-PHAETON

QUADRICYCLE
SIT-UP-AND-BEG
SOUPED-UP CAR
STEAM-ENGINE
STEAM-ROLLER
THIKA-GHARRY
WHITECHAPEL

12
COACH AND FOUR
DÉSOBLIGEANT
DOUBLE-DECKER
EXPRESS TRAIN
FREIGHT TRAIN
HORSE-AND-CART
LUGGAGE TRAIN
PANTECHNICON
PUFFING BILLY
RAILWAY TRAIN
SINGLE-DECKER
STATION-WAGON
STEAM-OMNIBUS
THROUGH TRAIN

13
CYCLE-RICKSHAW
ELECTRIC TRAIN

GOVERNESS-CART
HORSE-CARRIAGE
PENNYFARTHING
PEOPLE CARRIER
RACING CHARIOT
SHOOTING-BRAKE

14
FOUR-WHEEL DRIVE
PASSENGER TRAIN
RIDING-CARRIAGE
TRACTION ENGINE

15
HACKNEY-CARRIAGE
PRAIRIE-SCHOONER

16
MOTORIZED BICYCLE
UNDERGROUND TRAIN

17
HORSELESS CARRIAGE

18
TRAVELLING CARRIAGE

SHIPS AND BOATS

3
ARK
COG
HOY
TUG

4
ARGO
BARK
BOAT
BRIG
BUSS
DHOW
DORY
GRAB
JUNK
PROA
PUNT
RAFT
SAIC
SNOW
TROW
YAWL

5
BARGE
CANOE
COBLE
DANDY
FERRY

FUNNY
KAYAK
KETCH
LINER
NOBBY
PRAHU
SHELL
SKIFF
SLOOP
SMACK
TRAMP
U-BOAT
UMIAK
XEBEC
YACHT

6
BARQUE
BAWLEY
BIREME
CAIQUE
CARVEL
CUTTER
DINGHY
DOGGER
DUG-OUT
GALLEY
HOOKER
HOPPER
LAUNCH

LORCHA
LUGGER
PACKET
RANDAN
SAMPAN
SEALER
SLAVER
TANKER
TENDER
WHALER

7
BUMBOAT
CARAVEL
CARRACK
CLIPPER
COASTER
COLLIER
CORACLE
CORSAIR
CURRACH
DREDGER
DRIFTER
DROMOND
FELUCCA
FLY-BOAT
FRIGATE
GABBARD
GALLEON
GONDOLA

JANGADA
PINNACE
PIRAGUA
POLACCA
POLACRE
ROWBOAT
SCULLER
STEAMER
TARTANE
TOWBOAT
TRAWLER
TRIREME
WAR SHIP

8
BILANDER
BUDGEROW
COCKBOAT
CORVETTE
CRUMSTER
DAHABIYA
FIRESHIP
FOLDBOAT
GALLIVAT
LIFEBOAT
LONG-BOAT
MAIL-SHIP
NOAH'S ARK
OUTBOARD
SAILBOAT

SCHOONER
SHOWBOAT

9
BUCENTAUR
CARGO-BOAT
CATAMARAN
CRIS-CRAFT
FREIGHTER
HOUSE BOAT
JOLLY-BOAT
LIGHTSHIP
MOTORBOAT
MOTORSHIP
MUD-HOPPER
OUTRIGGER
RIVER-BOAT
ROTOR SHIP
SHIP'S BOAT
SLAVE-SHIP
SPEEDBOAT
STEAMBOAT
STEAMSHIP

STORESHIP
SUBMARINE

10
BANANA-BOAT
BRIGANTINE
PADDLE-BOAT
PICKET BOAT
PIRATE-SHIP
PRISON-SHIP
QUADRIREME
ROWING BOAT
TEA-CLIPPER
TRAIN-FERRY
VIKING-SHIP
WIND-JAMMER

11
BARQUENTINE
CHASSE-MARÉE
COCKLE-SHELL
DOUBLE-CANOE
FISHING-BOAT
HOPPER-BARGE
MAIL-STEAMER

PENTECONTER
PILOT VESSEL
QUINQUEREME
SAILING-SHIP
THREE-MASTER

12
CABIN-CRUISER
ESCORT VESSEL
FISHING SMACK
HOSPITAL SHIP
MERCHANT SHIP
PLEASURE BOAT
SAILING BARGE
STERN-WHEELER

13
HERRING-FISHER
PASSENGER SHIP
TRANSPORT SHIP

14
CHANNEL STEAMER
COASTING VESSEL
FLOATING PALACE
OCEAN GREYHOUND

AIRCRAFT

3
JET

4
KITE

5
PLANE

6
AIR CAR
BOMBER
GLIDER

7
AIRSHIP
BALLOON
BIPLANE
CLIPPER
FIGHTER
JUMP-JET
SHUTTLE

8
AEROSTAT
AIRPLANE
AUTOGIRO
CONCORDE
JUMBO-JET
ROTODYNE
SEA-PLANE
TRIPLANE
TURBO-JET
WARPLANE
ZEPPELIN

9
AEROPLANE
DIRIGIBLE
MAIL-PLANE
MONOPLANE
SAILPLANE
TURBO-PROP

10
FLYING-BOAT
GAS-BALLOON
HELICOPTER
HOVERCRAFT
HYDROPLANE

11
FIRE-BALLOON

12
FREIGHT-PLANE

13
STRATOCRUISER

14
FLYING BEDSTEAD
PASSENGER PLANE

18
MONTGOLFIER BALLOON

INTERNATIONAL AIRPORTS

ARLANDA (Stockholm)
ATATURK (Istanbul)
BARAJAS (Madrid)
BEIJING CAPITAL (Beijing)
CHARLES DE GAULLE (Paris)
CHANGI (Singapore)
CHIANG KAI-SHEK (Taipei)
COINTRIN (Geneva)
DALLAS-FORT WORTH (Dallas)
DOMODEDOVO (Moscow)
DORVAL (Montreal)
DOUGLAS (Charlotte)
DULLES (Washington)
ECHTERDINGEN (Stuttgart)
EL PRAT (Barcelona)
FINDEL (Luxembourg)
FORNEBU (Oslo)
FREDERIC CHOPIN (Warsaw)
GALILEO GALILEI (Pisa)
GATWICK (London)
GEORGE BUSH (Houston)
HARTSFIELD-JACKSON (Atlanta)
HEATHROW (London)
HELSINKI-VANTAA (Helsinki)
HONGQIAO (Shanghai)
HOPKINS (Cleveland)
JOHN F KENNEDY (New York)
(BENITO) JUAREZ (Mexico City)
KIMPO (Seoul)

KING KHALED (Riyadh)
KINGSFORD SMITH (Sydney)
LA GUARDIA (New York)
LEONARDO DA VINCI (FIUMICINO) Rome
LINATE (Milan)
LINDBERGH FIELD (San Diego)
LOGAN (Boston)
LUIS MUÑOZ MARIN (San Juan)
MALPENSA (Milan)
MCCARRAN (Las Vegas)
MIRABEL (Montreal)
NARITA (Tokyo)
NINOY AQUINO (Manila)
O'HARE (Chicago)
OKECIE (Warsaw)
ORLY (Paris)
PEARSON (Toronto)
PORTELA (Lisbon)
RUZYNE (Prague)
ST PAUL (Minneapolis)
SCHIPHOL (Amsterdam)
SHEREMETYEVO (Moscow)
SKY HARBOR (Phoenix)
SOEKARNO HATTA (Jakarta)
STANSTED (London)
SUBANG (Kuala Lumpur)
TEGEL (Berlin)
TULLAMARINE (Melbourne)
WAYNE COUNTY (Detroit)

MOTORING TERMS

2
CC

3
BHP
CAM
FAN
HUB
JET
REV
ROD

4
AXLE
BOOT
BUSH
COIL
GEAR
HORN
LOCK
SUMP
TYRE

5
BRAKE
CHOKE
SERVO
SHAFT
VALVE
WHEEL

6
BIG END
BONNET
CAMBER
CLUTCH
DAMPER
DECOKE
DYNAMO
ENGINE
FILTER
GASKET
HEATER
HUB CAP
IDLING

PISTON
REBORE
STROKE
TAPPET
TORQUE
TUNING

7
BATTERY
BEARING
BRACKET
CHASSIS
DYNAMIC
EXHAUST
FAN BELT
GEARBOX
OIL SEAL

8
ADHESION
BRAKE PAD
BULKHEAD

CALLIPER
CAMSHAFT
CROSS-PLY
CYLINDER
DIPSTICK
FLYWHEEL
FUEL PUMP
IGNITION
KICK-DOWN
KNOCKING
LIVE AXLE
MANIFOLD
MOUNTING
RADIATOR
ROTOR ARM
SELECTOR
SILENCER
SMALL END
STEERING
THROTTLE
TRACK ROD

9
BRAKESHOE
CONDENSER
DISC BRAKE
DRUM BRAKE
GEAR STICK
GENERATOR
HALF-SHAFT
HANDBRAKE
INDUCTION
MISFIRING
OVERDRIVE
OVERSTEER
PROP SHAFT
RADIAL-PLY
SIDE VALVE
SPARK PLUG
TWO-STROKE
UNDERSEAL
WHEELBASE

10
AIR CLEANER
ALTERNATOR
BRAKE FLUID
CRANKSHAFT
DETONATION
DRIVE SHAFT
FOUR-STROKE
GUDGEON PIN
HORSEPOWER

PISTON RING
REV COUNTER
SUSPENSION
TACHOMETER
THERMOSTAT
UNDERSTEER
WINDSCREEN

11
ANTI-ROLL BAR
CARBURETER
CARBURETTOR
COMPRESSION
CROSSMEMBER
DISTRIBUTOR
SERVO SYSTEM
SYNCHROMESH

12
ACCELERATION
CYLINDER HEAD
DIESEL ENGINE
DIFFERENTIAL
SPARKING PLUG
SUPERCHARGER
TRANSMISSION
TURBOCHARGER
VISCOUS DRIVE

13
COOLING SYSTEM

DECARBONIZING
FUEL INJECTION
OVERHEAD VALVE
POWER STEERING
RACK-AND-PINION
SHOCK ABSORBER
SLAVE CYLINDER
SPARK IGNITION

14
FOUR-WHEEL DRIVE
PROPELLER SHAFT
UNIVERSAL JOINT

15
FRONT-WHEEL DRIVE
HYDRAULIC SYSTEM
PETROL INJECTION

17
INDUCTION MANIFOLD
REVOLUTION COUNTER

19
CROWN WHEEL AND PINION

20+
AUTOMATIC TRANSMISSION
INDEPENDENT SUSPENSION
POWER ASSISTED STEERING

INTERNATIONAL CAR REGISTRATIONS

REGISTRATION LETTER	Country
A	Austria
AL	Albania
AUS	Australia
B	Belgium
BDS	Barbados
BG	Bulgaria
BR	Brazil
BRG	Guyana
BRN	Bahrain
BS	Bahamas
BW	Botswana
C	Cuba
CDN	Canada
CH	Switzerland
CI	Côte d'Ivoire
CO	Colombia
CR	Costa Rica
CY	Cyprus
D	Germany
DK	Denmark
DZ	Algeria
E	Spain
EC	Ecuador
F	France
FIN	Finland
FL	Liechtenstein
GB	Great Britain
GCA	Guatemala
GH	Ghana
GR	Greece
H	Hungary
HK	Hong Kong
HKJ	Jordan
I	Italy
IL	Israel
IND	India
IR	Iran
IRL	Ireland
IRQ	Iraq
IS	Iceland
J	Japan
JA	Jamaica
KWT	Kuwait
L	Luxembourg
LAO	Laos
LB	Liberia
LS	Lesotho
M	Malta
MA	Morocco
MAL	Malaysia
MEX	Mexico
MNE	Montenegro

MS	Mauritius	ROK	South Korea
MW	Malawi	RU	Burundi
N	Norway	RWA	Rwanda
NIG	Niger	S	Sweden
NL	Netherlands	SD	Swaziland
NZ	New Zealand	SGP	Singapore
P	Portugal	SLE	Sierra Leone
PA	Panama	SME	Surinam
PAK	Pakistan	SN	Senegal
PE	Peru	SRB	Serbia
PI	Philippines	SYR	Syria
PL	Poland	T	Thailand
PY	Paraguay	TG	Togo
RA	Argentina	TN	Tunisia
RB	Botswana	TR	Turkey
RC	China	TT	Trinidad and Tobago
RCA	Central African Republic	U	Uruguay
RCB	Congo	USA	United States of America
RCH	Chile	UY	Uruguay
RH	Haiti	VN	Vietnam
RI	Indonesia	WAL	Sierra Leone
RIM	Mauritania	WAN	Nigeria
RKS	Kosovo	WS	Western Samoa
RL	Lebanon	YV	Venezuela
RM	Malagasy Republic	Z	Zambia
RMM	Mali	ZA	South Africa
RO	Romania		

NAUTICAL TERMS

3
AFT
BOW
FID
LEE

4
ALEE
BEAM
BITT
BOOM
FORE
HOLD
HULL
KEEL
KNOT
LIST
MATE
POOP
PORT
PROW
STAY
STEM
WAKE
WARP

5
ABAFT

ABEAM
ABOUT
ALOFT
AVAST
BELAY
BELLS
BILGE
BOSUN
CABLE
CAULK
CLEAT
DAVIT
HATCH
HAWSE
STERN
TRICK
TRUCK
WAIST
WEIGH
WINCH

6
BRIDGE
BUNKER
FATHOM
FENDER
FLUKES
FO'C'SLE

GALLEY
HAWSER
JETSAM
LEAGUE
LEEWAY
OFFING
PURSER
SHROUD
YAWING

7
ADMIRAL
BALLAST
BOLLARD
BULWARK
CAPSTAN
CATWALK
COAMING
DRAUGHT
FLOTSAM
GANGWAY
GRAPNEL
GUNWALE
INBOARD
LANYARD
MOORING
QUARTER
RIGGING

SEA MILE
TONNAGE
TOPSIDE
WATCHES

8
BINNACLE
BOWSPRIT
BULKHEAD
COXSWAIN
DOG WATCH
HALYARDS
HATCHWAY
LARBOARD
PITCHING
RATLINES
SCUPPERS
SPLICING
TAFFRAIL
WINDLASS

WINDWARD

9
AMIDSHIPS
COMPANION
CROW'S NEST
FREEBOARD
SHIP'S BELL
STARBOARD
WATER-LINE

10
BATTEN DOWN
DEADLIGHTS
DEADWEIGHT
FIRST WATCH
FORE-AND-AFT
FORECASTLE
NIGHT WATCH

11
MIDDLE WATCH
QUARTER-DECK
WEATHER SIDE

12
DISPLACEMENT
JACOB'S LADDER
MARLINE SPIKE
NAUTICAL MILE
PLIMSOLL LINE

13
QUARTERMASTER

14
SUPERSTRUCTURE

15
COMPANION-LADDER
DAVY JONES' LOCKER

SHIPPING AREAS NAMED IN WEATHER FORECASTS

BAILEY
BISCAY
CROMARTY
DOGGER
DOVER
FAEROES
FAIR ISLE
FASTNET
FISHER
FITZROY
FORTH

FORTIES
GERMAN BIGHT
HEBRIDES
HUMBER
IRISH SEA
LUNDY
MALIN
NORTH UTSIRE
PLYMOUTH
PORTLAND

ROCKALL
SHANNON
SOLE
SOUTH-EAST ICELAND
SOUTH UTSIRE
THAMES
TRAFALGAR
TYNE
VIKING
WIGHT

BRITISH CANALS

4
BUDE

5
CHARD
DERBY
NEATH
CRINAN

6
DUDLEY
EXETER
KETLEY
LYDNEY
OAKHAM
OXFORD
SANKEY
TYRONE

7
CHESTER
EREWASH
REGENTS
SWANSEA
TENNANT

8
BARNSLEY
CARLISLE
COVENTRY
CROMFORD
GRANTHAM
MONKLAND
ROCHDALE
ST HELENS

9
BAYBRIDGE

DROITWICH
ELLESMERE
LANCASTER
LOUTH SHIP
NEWRY SHIP
TAVISTOCK
ULVERSTON

10
BIRMINGHAM
CALEDONIAN
COALISLAND
COOMBE HILL
DONNINGTON
GRAND TRUNK (Trent and
    Mersey)
GRAND UNION
LLANGOLLEN
NOTTINGHAM

PEAK FOREST
SHREWSBURY
TORRINGTON

11
BASINGSTOKE
BRIDGEWATER
STOURBRIDGE

12
CALDON BRANCH (Trent and
Mersey)
CHESTERFIELD
GRAND WESTERN
MACCLESFIELD
THANET BRANCH

13
ABERDEENSHIRE
FORTH AND CLYDE
GRAND JUNCTION
KENNET AND AVON
ROYAL MILITARY
WILTS AND BERKS

14
ASHBY-DE-LA-ZOUCH

GLAMORGANSHIRE
MANCHESTER SHIP
STAFFS AND WORCS
TRENT AND MERSEY

15
ASHTON-UNDER-LYNE
MONTGOMERYSHIRE
RAMSDENS-SIR JOHN
SHROPSHIRE UNION
THAMES AND SEVERN

16
WARWICK AND NAPTON

17
LEEDS AND LIVERPOOL
SOMERSETSHIRE COAL
STRATFORD-UPON-AVON

18
HUDDERSFIELD NARROW
NEWCASTLE-UNDER-LYME
WYRLEY AND ESSINGTON

19
ELLESMERE AND CHESTER

20
LISKEARD AND LOO UNION
PORTSMOUTH AND ARUNDEL
STOURBRIDGE EXTENSION

21
BRIDGEWATER AND TAUNTON
MONMOUTHSHIRE AND BRECON
WORCESTER AND BIRMINGHAM

23+
BRECKNOCK AND ABERGAVENNY
CHELMSFORD AND BLACKWATER
CLIFTON AND KEARSLEY-
FLETCHER
EDINBURGH AND GLASGOW
UNION
GLASGOW, PAISLEY, AND
ADROSSAN
GLOUCESTER AND BERKELEY
SHIP
HEREFORDSHIRE AND
GLOUCESTER
LEICESTER AND NORTHANTS
UNION
SHEFFIELD AND SOUTH
YORKSHIRE

WORLD CANALS

3&4
EST, DE L' (FRANCE)
ERIE (New York State Barge)
(USA)
GOTA (SWEDEN)
KIEL (DENMARK)
MIDI, DU (FRANCE)
SUEZ (EGYPT)

5
EIDER (DENMARK)
GRAND (CHINA)
GRAND (IRELAND)
KINDA (SWEDEN)
LINDO (SWEDEN)
RHINE (GERMANY)
TRENT (CANADA)
UNION (USA)

6
ALBERT (BELGIUM)
ALSACE (FRANCE)
BIRARE (FRANCE)
CENTRE, DU (BELGIUM)
EUROPA (GERMANY)
LEHIGH (USA)
MORRIS (USA)
PANAMA
RIDEAU (CANADA)

SAIMAA (FINLAND)
SANTEE (USA)
VIRIDI (FRANCE)

7
AUGUSTA (USA)
CAPE COD (USA)
CHAMBLY (CANADA)
CHEMUNG (USA)
CORINTH (GREECE)
JULIANA (HOLLAND)
LOUVAIN, DE (BELGIUM)
LUDWIGS (GERMANY)
ORLEANS (FRANCE)
WELLAND (CANADA)

8
MARCHAND (FRANCE)
NOORDZEE (HOLLAND)
TELEMARK (NORWAY)

9
BOURGOGNE (FRANCE)
CHAMPLAIN (USA)
DALSLANDS (SWEDEN)
LANGUEDOC (FRANCE)
MIDDLESEX (USA)
ST QUENTIN (FRANCE)
STECKNITZ (GERMANY)

10
BEREGUARDO (ITALY)
MITTELLAND (GERMANY)
RHONE A SETE (FRANCE)
SCHUYLKILL (USA)
TROLLHATTE (SWEDEN)

11
DISMAL SWAMP (USA)
DORTMUND-EMS (GERMANY)
HOUSTON SHIP (USA)
MARNE AU RHIN, DE LA
(FRANCE)
NORTH BRANCH (USA)
OHIO AND ERIE (USA)
RHINE-DANUBE (GERMANY)
RHONE AU RHIN (FRANCE)
WILLEBROECK (BELGIUM)

12
CROSS-FLORIDA (USA)
FRANCHE-COMTE (FRANCE)
MARNE LATERAL (FRANCE)
MIAMI AND ERIE (USA)
NANTES A BREST (FRANCE)
PENNSYLVANIA (USA)

13
AISNE A LA MARNE (FRANCE)
BEAVER AND ERIE (USA)

MARNE A LA SAONE (FRANCE)
SAMBRE AND OISE (FRANCE)
WABASH AND ERIE (USA)

14
AMSTERDAM-RHINE (HOLLAND)
GHENT-TERNEUZEN (BELGIUM/
  HOLLAND)

15
MARSEILLES-RHONE (FRANCE)

16
BLUE RIDGE PARKWAY (USA)

NORTH HOLLAND SHIP
ST LAWRENCE SEAWAY (USA)
SAULT SAINTE MARIE (USA)
SOUTH HADLEY FALLS (USA)

17
BRUSSELS-CHARLEROI
  (BELGIUM)
CHESAPEAKE AND OHIO (USA)
DELAWARE AND HUDSON (USA)
LATERAL A LA GARONNE
  (FRANCE)
NEW YORK STATE BARGE
  (formerly Erie) (USA)

19+
CHESAPEAKE AND DELAWARE
  (USA)
CHICAGO SHIP AND SANITARY
  (USA)
ILLINOIS AND MICHIGAN
  WATERWAY (USA)
JAMES RIVER AND KANAWHA
  (USA)
PENNSYLVANIA AND ERIE
  (USA)
PENNSYLVANIA AND OHIO
  (USA)

MOTORWAY SERVICE STATIONS

4
LYMM (M6)

5
BIRCH (M62)
BLYTH (A1M)
FLEET (M3)
KEELE (M6)
MAGOR (M4)
TEBAY (M6)

6
CORLEY (M6)
DURHAM (A1M)
EXETER (M5)
GRETNA (A74M)
HESTON (M4)
MEDWAY (M2)
OXFORD (M40)

7
BALDOCK (A1M)
CHESTER (M56)
GORDANO (M5)
KINROSS (M90)
MEMBURY (M4)
READING (M4)
SWANSEY (M4)
TELFORD (M54)
TROWELL (M1)
WARWICK (M40)
WOODALL (M1)

8
ABINGTON (M74)
BOTHWELL (M74)
FRANKLEY (M5)
HAMILTON (M74)
ROWNHAMS (M27)

SANDBACH (M6)
SARN PARK (M4)
STAFFORD (M6)
STIRLING (M9/M80)
TAMWORTH (M42)
THURROCK (M25)
TIBSHELF (M1)
TODHILLS (M42)
WETHERBY (A1M)

9
CHIEVELEY (M4)
DONCASTER (M18)
HAPPENDON (M74)
KNUTSFORD (M6)
LANCASTER (M6)
MAIDSTONE (M20)
RIMINGTON (M61)
SEDGEMOOR (M5)
STRENSHAM (M5)

10
BARTON PARK (A1M)
BOLTON WEST (M61)
BRIDGWATER (M5)
BURTONWOOD (M62)
CULLOMPTON (M5)
FOLKESTONE (M20)
HILTON PARK (M6)
SEVERN VIEW (M48)
SOUTH MIMMS (A1M/
  M25)
SOUTHWAITE (M6)
TODDINGTON (M1)
WASHINGTON (A1M)
WATFORD GAP (M1)
WINCHESTER (M3)

11
CARDIFF GATE (M4)
CARDIFF WEST (M4)
CLACKET LANE (M25)
FERRYBRIDGE (A1M/M62)
HOPWOOD PARK (M42)
MICHAELWOOD (M5)
NORTHAMPTON (M1)
NORTON CANES (M6 Toll)
PONT ABRAHAM (M4)
WOOLLEY EDGE (M1)

12
BEACONSFIELD (M40)
PEASE POTTAGE (M23)
PETERBOROUGH (A1M)
TAUNTON DEANE (M5)

13
DONINGTON PARK (M1)
HARTSHEAD MOOR (M62)
LEIGH DELAMERE (M4)
LONDON GATEWAY (M1)

14
ANNANDALE WATER (A74M)
BURTON-IN-KENDAL (M6)
CHERWELL VALLEY (M40)
KILLINGTON LAKE (M6)
NEWPORT PAGNELL (M1)

15
BIRCHANGER GREEN (M11)
CHARNOCK RICHARD (M6)
HEART OF SCOTLAND (M8)

19
LEICESTER FOREST EAST (M1)
BLACKBURN WITH DARWEN
  (M65)

LOCOMOTIVES

4
DART
ISAR

5
ARROW
BEUTH
CAMEL
COMET
GOTHA
QUEEN
SEEVE

6
DRAGON
METEOR
MINORU
MOABIT
PLANET
ROCKET

7
AMERICA
BATAVIA
CARDEAN
CORSAIR
FIRE FLY
GENERAL
JUPITER
MALLARD
NOVELTY
PHOENIX
TORNADO
WANNSEE

8
ATLANTIC
CYCLOPED
DER ADLER
HERCULES
IRON DUKE
MAJESTIC
PYRACMON
REINGOLD
TOM THUMB
VAUXHALL

9
BLUE GOOSE
IRISH MAIL
NEWCASTLE
NORTH STAR

10
CALEDONIAN
DORCHESTER
EXPERIMENT
LOCOMOTION
SANS PAREIL
WYLAM DILLY

11
HENRY OAKLEY
JEANIE DEANS
ROYAL GEORGE
WILLIAM DEAN

12
GREAT WESTERN

NORTHUMBRIAN
NUNNEY CASTLE
OLD IRONSIDES
PERSEVERENCE
PHILADELPHIA
PINES EXPRESS
PRINCE ALFRED
PUFFING BILLY

13
COALBROOKDALE
GENERAL LOWELL
SAINT NICHOLAS

14
CENTRAL VERMONT
CYRUS K HOLLIDAY
DANTE ALIGHIERI
FLYING SCOTSMAN
ROBERT THE DEVIL

15
BROTHER JONATHAN
PENDENNIS CASTLE

17
DUCHESS OF HAMILTON
PLANET CENTENARIAN
SIR WILLIAM STANIER

18+
BEST FRIEND OF CHARLSTON
EMPIRE STATE EXPRESS
TWENTIETH CENTURY LIMITED
WASHINGTON COUNTY FARMER

CLOTHES, MATERIALS, AND FASHION

CLOTHES

3
ABA
ALB
BAL
BAS
BAT
BIB
BRA
COP
FEZ
HAT
LEI
OBI
TAM

4
ABBA
AGAL
ALBA
APEX
BAJU
BARB
BECK
BELT
BENN
BOTA
BUSK
CACK
CAPE
CLOG
COAT
COPE
COTE
COWL
DAPS
DIDO
DISK
GARB
GETA
GOWN
HAIK
HOOD
HOSE
IZAR
JAMA
KEPI
KILT
MASK
MAXI
MIDI
MINI

MITT
MUFF
MULE
PUMP
ROBE
RUFF
SARI
SASH
SAYA
SHOE
SLIP
SLOP
SOCK
SPAT
SUIT
TABI
TOGA
TOGS
TOPI
TUTU
VAMP
VEIL
VEST
WRAP

5
ABNET
ACTON
AEGIS
AMICE
AMPYX
APRON
ARCAN
ARMET
ARMOR
ASCOT
BARBE
BARRY
BENJY
BERET
BLAKE
BLUEY
BOINA
BOOTS
BURKA
BUSBY
CABAS
CADET
CAPPA
CHALE
CHAPS

CHOGA
CHOLI
CLOAK
CORDY
COTTA
COTTE
CREST
CROWN
CURCH
CYLAS
CYMAR
DERBY
DHOTI
EPHOD
FICHU
FROCK
GANSY
GILET
GIPPO
GLOVE
HABIT
HULLS
IHRAM
JABOT
JAMAH
JEANS
JELAB
JUPON
LAMMY
LODEN
LUNGI
MIDDY
MUFTI
NUBIA
PAGNE
PAGRI
PALLA
PANTS
PARKA
PILCH
PIRNY
PUMPS
SABOT
SAREE
SCARF
SHAKO
SHAWL
SHIFT
SHIRT
SKIRT
SMOCK

SNOOD
STOCK
STOLA
STOLE
TAILS
TEDDY
TIARA
TONGS
TOPEE
TOQUE
TREWS
TUNIC
VISOR
VIZOR
WEEDS

6
ABOLLA
ALMUCE
ANADEM
ANALAV
ANKLET
ANORAK
ARCTIC
ARTOIS
BALKAN
BANYAN
BARRET
BARVEL
BASQUE
BAUTTA
BEANIE
BEAVER
BÈQUIN
BERTHA
BICORN
BIETLE
BIGGIN
BIKINI
BIRRUS
BISHOP
BLAZER
BLIAUD
BLOUSE
BOATER
BODICE
BOLERO
BONNET
BOOTEE
BOWLER
BOXERS

BRACAE	JERKIN	7	CULOTTE
BRACES	JERSEY	AMICTUS	CURCHEF
BRAGAS	JUBBAH	APPAREL	CUTAWAY
BRAIES	JUMPER	ARISARD	DOPATTA
BRETON	KABAYA	ARM BAND	DOUBLET
BRIEFS	KIMONO	BABOOSH	DRAWERS
BROGAN	KIRTLE	BALDRIC	DULBAND
BROGUE	KITTEL	BALTEUS	DUL HOSE
BUSKIN	LAMMIE	BANDEAU	EARMUFF
BYRNIE	LOAFER	BANDORE	ETON CAP
BYRRUS	LUNGEE	BARBUTE	EVERETT
CABAAN	MAGYAR	BAROQUE	FANCHON
CADDIE	MANTEE	BASHLYK	FASHION
CAFTAN	MANTLE	BASINET	FILIBEG
CALASH	MANTUA	BAVETTE	FLATCAP
CALCEI	MITTEN	BAVOLET	GARMENT
CALIGA	MOBCAP	BEDIZEN	GHILLIE
CALPAC	MOGGAN	BELCHER	G STRING
CAMAIL	ONESIE	BERDASH	GUM BOOT
CAMISA	OUTFIT	BERETTA	GUM SHOE
CAMISE	PEG-TOP	BETSIES	GYM SHOE
CAPOTE	PEPLOS	BIRETTA	HANDBAG
CAPUCE	PEPLUM	BOTTINE	HIGH-LOW
CAPUTI	PILEUS	BOX CAPE	HOMBURG
CARACO	PINNER	BOX COAT	HOSIERY
CASQUE	PIRNIE	BRIMMER	JODHPUR
CASTOR	PONCHO	BROIGNE	KLOMPEN
CAUSIA	PUGREE	BURNOUS	LAYETTE
CESTUS	PUTTEE	BUSSKIN	LEOTARD
CHADAR	RAGLAN	CALEÇON	MAILLOT
CHITON	REEFER	CALOTTE	MANTEAU
CHOKER	RUFFLE	CAMOURO	MONTERA
CILICE	SANDAL	CANEZOU	MONTERO
CIMIER	SARONG	CAPE HAT	MUFFLER
CLAQUE	SERAPE	CAPUCHE	OLIVERS
CLOCHE	SHIMMY	CAPULET	OVERALL
COBCAB	SHORTS	CASAQUE	OXFORDS
COCKET	SHROUD	CASSOCK	PANTIES
CORNET	SLACKS	CATSKIN	PARASOL
CORONA	SONTAG	CAUBEEN	PATTERN
CORSET	STEP-IN	CEREVIS	PELISSE
COTHUM	SUN HAT	CHAINSE	PETASOS
COVERT	TABARD	CHALWAR	PIERROT
CRAVAT	TAMISE	CHAPLET	PILLBOX
DIADEM	TIGHTS	CHEMISE	PLUVIAL
DICKEY	TIPPET	CHEVRON	PUGGREE
DIRNDL	TOP HAT	CHIMERE	PYJAMAS
DOLMAN	TOPPER	CHIP HAT	RAIMENT
DOMINO	TRILBY	CHLAMYS	REGALIA
DUSTER	TRUNKS	CHOPINE	ROMPERS
EARCAP	T-SHIRT	CHOU HAT	RUBBERS
FEDORA	TUCKER	CHRISOM	SARAFAN
FILLET	TURBAN	CHUDDAR	SCOGGER
GAITER	TUXEDO	CHUDDER	SHALWAR
GANSEY	TWEEDS	COMMODE	SILK HAT
GARTER	ULSTER	CORONEL	SINGLET
GAUCHO	UNDIES	CORONET	SKI BOOT
GILLIE	UPLIFT	COSSACK	SLIPPER
GUIMPE	VAMPAY	COXCOMB	SLYDERS
HALTER	VESTEE	CREPIDA	SMICKET
HENNIN	WIMPLE	CRISPIN	SNEAKER
HUIPIL	WOOLLY	CUCULLA	SOUTANE
JACKET	ZOUAVE	CUIRASS	SPENCER

SPORRAN
SULTANE
SUN SUIT
SURCOAT
SURTOUT
SWEATER
TANK TOP
TEA GOWN
TOP BOOT
TOP COAT
TRAHEEN
TRICORN
TUNICLE
TWIN SET
UNIFORM
VEILING
WATTEAU
WEDGIES
WING TIE
WOOLLEN
WRAPPER
YASHMAK
Y-FRONTS
ZIMARRA

8
ABBÉ CAPE
ALL-IN-ONE
ANALABOS
ANTELOPE
BABUSHKA
BALADRAN
BALMORAL
BANDANNA
BARBETTE
BASQUINE
BATH ROBE
BEARSKIN
BED SOCKS
BENJAMIN
BIGGONET
BINNOGUE
BLOOMERS
BODY COAT
BOMBARDS
BOOT-HOSE
BOTTEKIN
BREECHES
BURGONET
BURNOOSE
BYCOCKET
CABASSET
CAMISOLE
CANOTIER
CAPE COAT
CAPELINE
CAPRIOLE
CAPUCINE
CAPUTIUM
CARCANET
CARDIGAN
CARDINAL
CAROLINE
CASAQUIN

CATERCAP
CHANDAIL
CHAPERON
CHAQUETA
CHASUBLE
CHAUSSES
CHONGSAM
COLOBIUM
COPATAIN
CORSELET
COUCH HAT
COVERALL
CRUSH HAT
CUCULLUS
DANCE SET
DANDY HAT
DJELLABA
DOM PEDRO
DORMEUSE
DUCK-BILL
DUNCE CAP
DUST COAT
DUTCH CAP
FALDETTA
FLANNELS
FLIMSIES
FOOTWEAR
GAMASHES
GAUNTLET
GUERNSEY
HALF-HOSE
HALF SLIP
HEADGEAR
JACK BOOT
JEGGINGS
JUDO COAT
JUMP SUIT
KERCHIEF
KNICKERS
KNITWEAR
LARRIGAN
LAVA-LAVA
LEGGINGS
LINGERIE
LIRIPIPE
MANTELET
MANTILLA
MOCCASIN
NECKLACE
NIGHTCAP
OPERA HAT
OVERALLS
OVERCOAT
OVERSHOE
PARAMENT
PEASECOD
PEIGNOIR
PHILIBEG
PILEOLUS
PINAFORE
PLASTRON
PLATINUM
PLIMSOLL

PULLOVER
SABOTINE
SKULL-CAP
SLIP-OVER
SNOWSHOE
SOMBRERO
STOCKING
SURPLICE
SWIM SUIT
TAIL COAT
TAILLEUR
TARBOOSH
TOQUETTE
TRAINERS
TRENCHER
TRICORNE
TROUSERS
TWO-PIECE
WOOLLENS
WOOLLIES
ZOOT SUIT

9
AFTERWELT
ALPARGATA
ALPINE HAT
ANKLE BOOT
APON DRESS
ARMILAUSA
BABY SKIRT
BALAYEUSE
BALL DRESS
BALMACAAN
BAMBIN HAT
BANDOLEER
BARCELONA
BEAVERTOP
BED JACKET
BEEGUM HAT
BELL SKIRT
BILLICOCK
BILLYCOCK
BLOUSETTE
BODY LINEN
BOURRELET
BRASSIÈRE
BROADBRIM
BRODEQUIN
BRUNSWICK
BYZANTINE
CABRIOLET
CAPE DRESS
CAPE STOLE
CARTWHEEL
CASENTINO
CASQUETTE
CASSIMERE
CHEMILOON
CHIN-CLOTH
CHIVARRAS
CHOLO COAT
COAT DRESS
COAT SHIRT
COCKED HAT

COOLIE HAT
COPINTANK
CORNERCAP
COVERSLUT
COWBOY HAT
CREEDMORE
CRINOLINE
DOG COLLAR
DOMINICAL
DRESS COAT
DRESS SHOE
DRESS SUIT
DUNGAREES
DUNSTABLE
ESCOFFIAN
FORAGE CAP
FROCK COAT
FULL DRESS
GABARDINE
GABERDINE
GARIBALDI
GLENGARRY
GREATCOAT
HEADDRESS
HEADPIECE
HELMET CAP
HOURI-COAT
HOUSE-COAT
HULA SKIRT
INVERNESS
JOCKEY CAP
JULIET CAP
LOINCLOTH
MILLINERY
NECKCLOTH
NIGHTGOWN
OUTERWEAR
OVERDRESS
OVERSHIRT
OVERSKIRT
PANAMA HAT
PANTALETS
PANTOFFLE
PANTY HOSE
PEA JACKET
PETTICOAT
PILOT COAT
PLUS FOURS
POLONAISE
QUAKER HAT
REDINGOTE
SANBENITO
SHAKSHEER
SHINTIYAN
SHOVEL HAT
SLOPPY JOE
SLOUCH HAT
SNEAKERS
SOU'WESTER
STOMACHER
STRING TIE
SUNBONNET
SURCINGLE

TENT DRESS
THIGH BOOT
TROUSSEAU
TRUNK-HOSE
UNDERCOAT
UNDERGOWN
UNDERVEST
UNDERWEAR
VESTMENTS
VICTORINE
WAISTCOAT
WATCH COAT
WIDE-AWAKE
WITCH'S HAT
WYLIECOAT

10
ANGELUS CAP
APRON TUNIC
BABY BONNET
BASIC DRESS
BATHING CAP
BEER JACKET
BELLBOY CAP
BERRETTINO
BIBI BONNET
BICYCLE BAL
BLOUSE COAT
BOBBY SOCKS
BOSOM SHIRT
BOUDOIR CAP
BRIGANDINE
BRUNCH COAT
BUCKET TOPS
BUMPER BRIM
BUSH JACKET
BUSK JACKET
CALZONERAS
CANVAS SHOE
CAPE COLLAR
CAPPA MAGNA
CARMAGNOLE
CERVELIÈRE
CHARTREUSE
CHATELAINE
CHEMISETTE
CHIGNON CAP
CHOUQUETTE
CLOCK-MUTCH
COOLIE COAT
COQUELUCHE
CORPS PIQUÉ
COSSACK CAP
COTE-HARDIE
COUVRE-CHEF
COVERCHIEF
COVERT COAT
CROSSCLOTH
CUMMERBUND
DANCE DRESS
DESHABILLE
DINNER SUIT
DIPLOIDIAN
DOUILLETTE

DRESS PLAID
DRESS SHIRT
DUFFEL COAT
ECLIPSE TIE
ESPADRILLE
ETON JACKET
EUGÉNIE HAT
FANCY DRESS
FASCINATOR
FLYING SUIT
FORE-AND-AFT
FUSTANELLA
GARMENTURE
GRASS SKIRT
HAREM SKIRT
HUG-ME-TIGHT
JIGGER COAT
LIRIPIPIUM
LOUNGE SUIT
LUMBERJACK
MESS JACKET
NIGHTDRESS
NIGHTSHIRT
OPERA CLOAK
OVERBLOUSE
OVERGAITER
OXFORD BAGS
OXFORD GOWN
PANTALOONS
PICTURE HAT
PITH HELMET
POKE BONNET
PORK PIE HAT
RIDING-HOOD
SERVICE CAP
SHIRTWAIST
SPORTS COAT
SPORT SHIRT
SPORTSWEAR
STICHARION
STRING VEST
SUNDAY BEST
SUSPENDERS
SWEAT SHIRT
THREE-PIECE
TRENCH COAT
UNDERDRESS
UNDERLINEN
UNDERPANTS
UNDERSHIRT
UNDERSKIRT
VELDSCHOEN
WINDSOR TIE
WING COLLAR

11
ALSATIAN BOW
BATHING SUIT
BIB-AND-BRACE
BOILED SHIRT
BOXER SHORTS
BRACONNIÈRE
BREECHCLOTH
BRITISH WARM

CANCAN DRESS
CAVALIER HAT
CHAPEAU BRAS
CHAPEL DE FER
CIRCASSIENE
COMBINATION
CORSET COVER
COWBOY BOOTS
DANCING CLOG
DEERSTALKER
DINNER DRESS
EMPIRE SKIRT
ESPADRILLES
EVENING GOWN
EVENING SLIP
FORMAL DRESS
FORTUNY GOWN
GALLIGASKIN
HOBBLE SKIRT
HOSTESS GOWN
HOUPPELANDE
HUNTING BOOT
MIDDY BLOUSE
NECKERCHIEF
OVERGARMENT
PANTY GIRDLE
RIDING HABIT
RUBBER APRON
RUNNING SHOE
RUSSIAN BOOT
SEWING APRON
SNAP-BRIM HAT
SOUP-AND-FISH
SOUTHWESTER
SPATTERDASH
STOCKING CAP
STRING GLOVE
SWAGGER COAT
TAM-O'SHANTER
TYROLEAN HAT
UNDERGIRDLE
UNDERTHINGS
WALKING SHOE
WEDDING GOWN
WEDDING VEIL
WELLINGTONS
WINDBREAKER
WINDCHEATER

12
AMISH COSTUME
BALKAN BLOUSE
BALLOON SKIRT
BASEBALL BOOT
BATTLE JACKET
BELLY DOUBLET
BLOOMER DRESS
BUSINESS SUIT
CAMICIA ROSSA
CAVALIER BOOT
CHEMISE DRESS
CHEMISE FROCK
CHESTERFIELD
CHUKKER SHIRT

CIGARETTE MIT
CORSET BODICE
COTTAGE CLOAK
CRUSADER HOOD
DINNER JACKET
DIVIDED SKIRT
DORIC CHILTON
DRESS CLOTHES
DRESSING GOWN
EASTER BONNET
ENGLISH DRAPE
EVENING DRESS
EVENING SHOES
EVENING SKIRT
HANDKERCHIEF
HEADKERCHIEF
HELMET BONNET
KNEE BREECHES
LOUNGING ROBE
MANDARIN COAT
MONKEY JACKET
MORNING DRESS
MOTORING VEIL
PEDAL PUSHERS
PENITENTIALS
QUAKER BONNET
ROLL-ON GIRDLE
SCOTCH BONNET
SHIRTWAISTER
SLEEPING COAT
SLEEPING SUIT
SMALLCLOTHES
STOVEPIPE HAT
SUGAR-LOAF HAT
TAILORED SUIT
TEN-GALLON HAT
TROUSERETTES
UNDERCLOTHES
UNDERGARMENT
WIDE-AWAKE HAT
ZOUAVE JACKET

13
ACROBATIC SHOE
AFTER-SKI SOCKS
BACK-STRAP SHOE
BEEFEATER'S HAT
BELLBOY JACKET
BUNGALOW
  APRON
COACHMAN'S COAT
COMBING JACKET
COTTAGE BONNET
DRESSING SAQUE
ELEVATOR SHOES
HAWAIIAN SKIRT
MOTHER HUBBARD
MOURNING DRESS
NORFOLK JACKET
PEEK-A-BOO WAIST
PRINCESS DRESS
SAM BROWNE BELT
SMOKING JACKET
SPORTS CLOTHES

SUSPENDER-BELT
TEDDYBEAR COAT
TRUNK-BREECHES
UNDERCLOTHING

14
AFTERNOON DRESS
BATHING COSTUME
BICYCLE CLIP HAT
CACHE-POUSSIÈRE
CAMOUFLAGE SUIT
CARDIGAN BODICE
CONGRESS GAITOR
CONTINENTAL HAT
DRESSING JACKET
DRESSMAKER SUIT

EGYPTIAN SANDAL
EVENING SWEATER
KNICKERBOCKERS
SHOOTING JACKET

15
CARDIGAN SWEATER
CHAPEAU FRANÇAIS
CHEMISE À LA REINE
CHEVALIER BONNET
ENVELOPE CHEMISE
FAIR ISLE SWEATER
MONTGOMERY BERET

16
BUTCHER BOY BLOUSE

CALMEL'S HAIR SHAWL
CHICKEN SKIN GLOVE
EISENHOWER JACKET
GOING-AWAY COSTUME
SWADDLING CLOTHES

17
CHEMISE À L'ANGLAISE
COAL SCUTTLE BONNET
CONFIRMATION DRESS
FOUNDATION GARMENT
SWALLOW-TAILED COAT

18
BETHLEHEM HEADDRESS
CHARLOTTE CORDAY CAP

MATERIALS

3
ABB
BAN
FUR
NET
REP

4
ACCA
ALMA
BAKU
BRIN
BURE
CALF
CORD
CREA
FELT
FUJI
GROS
HEMP
HIDE
JEAN
LACE
LAMÉ
LAWN
MULL
PELT
ROAN
SILK
SKIN
VAIR
WOOL

5
ABACA
ACELE
ACETA
ARDIL
BAIZE
BASCO

CADIS
CAFFA
CASHA
CLOTH
CRAPE
CRASH
CRISP
CROWN
DENIM
DORIA
FITCH
GAUZE
GENET
GUNNY
HONAN
JUPON
KAPOK
LAINE
LAPIN
LINEN
LINON
LISLE
LUREX
MOIRE
NINON
NYLON
ORLON
PEKIN
PIQUÉ
PLUSH
PRINT
RAYON
SATIN
SCRIM
SERGE
SISAL
SISOL
STRAW
STUFF
SUEDE

SURAH
TAMMY
TISSU
TOILE
TULLE
TWEED
TWILL
UNION
VOILE

6
ALACHA
ALASKA
ALPACA
ANGORA
ARALAC
ARIDEX
ARMURE
BALINE
BARÉGE
BENGAL
BERBER
BIRETZ
BLATTA
BOTANY
BUREAU
BURLAP
BURNET
BURRAH
BYSSUS
CAFFOY
CALICO
CAMACA
CAMLET
CANGAN
CANVAS
CASTOR
CATGUT
CHILLO
CHINTZ

CHROME
CHUNAN
COBURG
CONTRO
COSSAS
CÔTELÉ
CREPON
CROISE
CUBICA
DAMASK
DIAPER
DIMITY
DJERSA
DOMETT
DOWLAS
DUCAPE
ÉPONGE
ERMINE
FABRIC
FAILLE
FISHER
FORFAR
FRIEZE
GALYAC
GALYAK
GRENAI
GURRAH
KERSEY
LAMPAS
LASTEX
LINENE
MADRAS
MELTON
MERINO
MILIUM
MOHAIR
MOUTON
MULMUL
MUSLIN
NAPERY

OXFORD
PAILLE
PONGEE
POPLIN
RIBBON
RUBBER
SAMITE
SATEEN
SAXONY
SENNIT
SHODDY
SISSOL
SKIVER
SOUPLE
TARTAN
TINSEL
TISSUE
TRICOT
TUSSAH
TUSSEH
VELURE
VELVET
VICUNA
WINCEY
WITNEY

7
ACRILON
ACRYLIC
ALAMODE
ART SILK
BAGGING
BATISTE
BATTING
BEMBERG
BRABANT
BUNTING
BUSTIAN
CAMBAYE
CAMBRIC
CANTOON
CAPENET
CARACAL
CARACUL
CATALIN
CHALLIS
CHAMOIS
CHARVET
CHEKMAK
CHEVIOT
CHEYNEY
CHIFFON
COOTHAY
COWHIDE
DAMMASÉ
DELAINE
DOESKIN
DORNICK
DRABBET
DRUGGET
DUCHESS
DURANCE
DUVETYN
EARL GLO

ÉPINGLÉ
ESPARTO
ETAMINE
FAKE FUR
FISHNET
FITCHEW
FLANNEL
FOULARD
FUR FELT
FUSTIAN
GALATEA
GINGHAM
GOBELIN
GROGRAM
GUANACO
GUIPURE
HESSIAN
HOLLAND
JACONET
JAP SILK
KASHMIR
KIDSKIN
LEATHER
LEGHORN
LIBERTY
MINIVER
MOROCCO
NANKEEN
NETTING
OILSKIN
ORGANDY
ORGANZA
OTTOMAN
PAISLEY
PARAGON
PERCALE
PIGSKIN
RACCOON
RAWHIDE
RAW SILK
ROMAINE
SACKING
SAFFIAN
SATINET
SUITING
TAFFETA
TEXTILE
TICKING
TIE SILK
TIFFANY
TUSSORE
VALENCE
VELOURS
VISCOSE
VIYELLA
WEBBING
WOOLLEN
WORSTED

8
AGA BANEE
ALOE LACE
ARMOZEEN
ARMOZINE

ART LINEN
BAGHEERA
BARATHEA
BARRACAN
BAUDEKIN
BEUTANOL
BLANCARD
BOBBINET
BOMBAZET
BOX CLOTH
BUCKSKIN
BUFFSKIN
CALFSKIN
CAPESKIN
CASHMERE
CELANESE
CELENESE
CHAMBRAY
CHARMEEN
CHENILLE
CHIRIMEN
CHIVERET
CORDUROY
COTELINE
CRETONNE
DIAPHANE
DRAP D'ÉTÉ
DUCHESSE
ÉCRU SILK
EOLIENNE
ESTAMENE
EVERFAST
FARADINE
FLORENCE
GOATSKIN
GOSSAMER
HOMESPUN
INDIENNE
KOLINSKY
LAMBSKIN
LUSTRINE
LUSTRING
MARABOUT
MARCELLA
MAROCAIN
MATERIAL
MILANESE
MOGADORE
MOLESKIN
MOQUETTE
MUSLINET
MUSQUASH
NAINSOOK
OILCLOTH
ORGANDIE
PURE SILK
SARCENET
SARSENET
SEALSKIN
SHAGREEN
SHANTUNG
SHIRTING
SHOT SILK

TAPESTRY
TARLATAN
TARLETAN
TOILINET
VALENCIA
WAX CLOTH
WHIPCORD
WILD SILK
ZIBELINE

9
ADA CANVAS
AGRA GAUZE
ASBESTALL
ASTRAKHAN
BARK CLOTH
BARK CREPE
BENGALINE
BOMBAZINE
BOMBYCINE
BOOK CLOTH
BOOK LINEN
BROCATELL
BYRD CLOTH
CALAMANCO
CANNEQUIN
CATALOWNE
CHARMEUSE
CHINA SILK
COTTONADE
COTTON REP
CREPELINE
CRINOLINE
CUT VELVET
DACCA SILK
ÉCRU CLOTH
ÉLASTIQUE
FLANNELET
FUR FABRIC
GABARDINE
GEORGETTE
GRENADINE
GROSGRAIN
HAIRCLOTH
HORSEHAIR
HUCKABACK
LONGCLOTH
MARCELINE
MESSALINE
MOSS CREPE
ORGANZINE
PATCHWORK
PETERSHAM
SACKCLOTH
SAIL CLOTH
SATINETTE
SHARKSKIN
SHEEPSKIN
SNAKESKIN
STOCKINET
SWANSDOWN
TARPAULIN
TOWELLING
TRICOTINE

313

VELVETEEN
WORCESTER

10
ABBOT CLOTH
AIDA CANVAS
ANGOLA YARN
AUSTINIZED
BALBRIGGAN
BARLEYCORN
BAUM MARTEN
BEAVERETTE
BEAVERTEEN
BOOK MUSLIN
BOUCLÉ YARN
BROADCLOTH
BROAD GOODS
CADET CLOTH
CAMBRESINE
CHINO CLOTH
CIRCASSIAN
CONGO CLOTH
CREPE LISSE
DRESS LINEN
GRASS CLOTH
HOP SACKING
HORSECLOTH
IRISH LINEN
MARSEILLES
MOUSSELINE
PEAU DE SOIE
PIECE GOODS
PILOT CLOTH
SEERSUCKER
SUEDE CLOTH
TERRY CLOTH
TOILINETTE
WINCEYETTE

11
ABRADED YARN
AERATED YARN
ALBERT CREPE
ARABIAN LACE
ARMURE-LAINE
BABY FLANNEL
BAG SHEETING
BANDLE LINEN
BASKET CLOTH
BATH COATING
BEDFORD CORD
BOMBER CLOTH
BRUSHED WOOL
CANTON CREPE
CANTON LINEN
CHAMOISETTE
CHEESECLOTH
CHESS CANVAS
CHINA COTTON

CLAY WORSTED
COTTON CREPE
DACCA MUSLIN
DIAPER CLOTH
DOTTED SWISS
DRAP DE BERRY
DREADNOUGHT
DRUID'S CLOTH
DU PONT RAYON
ESKIMO CLOTH
EVERLASTING
FLANNELETTE
HARRIS TWEED
IRISH POPLIN
LEATHERETTE
MARQUISETTE
NAPA LEATHER
NUN'S VEILING
OVERCOATING
PANNE VELVET
POODLE CLOTH
POULT-DE-SOIE
SCOTCH PLAID
SPONGE CLOTH
TOILE DE JOUY
WAFFLE CLOTH

12
ACETATE RAYON
BALLOON CLOTH
BERLIN CANVAS
BOLIVIA CLOTH
BOLTING CLOTH
BRILLIANTINE
BROWN HOLLAND
BRUSHED RAYON
BUTCHER LINEN
CARACUL CLOTH
CAVALRY TWILL
CONVENT CLOTH
COTTON VELVET
CRINKLE CLOTH
CROISÉ VELVET
DENMARK SATIN
DOUBLE DAMASK
DRESS FLANNEL
ELEMENT CLOTH
EMPRESS CLOTH
GLAZED CHINTZ
MUTATION MINK
SHETLAND WOOL
SLIPPER SATIN
SUMMER ERMINE
VISCOSE RAYON
WELSH FLANNEL

13
AIRPLANE CLOTH
AMERICAN CLOTH

ARMURE-SATINÉE
BRITTANY CLOTH
CANTON FLANNEL
CARDINAL CLOTH
CASEMENT CLOTH
CLOISTER CLOTH
COSTUME VELVET
COTTON FLANNEL
COTTON SUITING
COTTON WORSTED
CRUSHED VELVET
DIAGONAL CLOTH
DIAPER FLANNEL
EGYPTIAN CLOTH
END-TO-END CLOTH
LINSEY-WOOLSEY
PATENT LEATHER
RUSSIA LEATHER

14
ALGERIAN STRIPE
AMERICAN COTTON
ARGENTINE CLOTH
BANDOLIER CLOTH
BARONETTE SATIN
BROADTAIL CLOTH
CORKSCREW TWILL
EGYPTIAN COTTON
ELECTORAL CLOTH
FRUIT OF THE LOOM
HONEYCOMB CLOTH
JACQUARD FABRIC
SHEPHERD'S PLAID

15
ABSORBENT COTTON
ADMIRALITY CLOTH
CACHEMIRE DE SOIE
CAMEL'S HAIR CLOTH
EMBROIDERY LINEN
OSTRICH FEATHERS
PARACHUTE FABRIC
SEA-ISLAND COTTON
SHIRTING FLANNEL
TATTERSALL CHECK
TATTERSALL PLAID
TROPICAL SUITING

16
CANDLEWICK FABRIC
CONSTITUTION CORD
MERCERIZED COTTON
TURKISH TOWELLING

17
CROSS-STITCH CANVAS

COSMETICS

4
KOHL

5
ROUGE
TONER

7
BLUSHER
BRONZER
LIP BALM
MASCARA

8
CLEANSER
EYE CREAM
EYELINER
FACE MASK

LIP GLOSS
LIPLINER
LIPSTICK
TWEEZERS

9
COLD CREAM
CONCEALER
EYESHADOW
FACE SCRUB
SPOT CREAM

10
FOUNDATION
NIGHT CREAM

11
LOOSE POWDER

MOISTURIZER

13
EYEBROW PENCIL
EYELASH CURLER
PRESSED POWDER

14
FALSE EYELASHES
LIQUID EYELINER

15+
ANTI-AGEING CREAM
EYE MAKEUP REMOVER
ILLUMINATING CREAM
TINTED MOISTURIZER

HAIRDRESSING

3
BOB
BUN
GEL
WAX
WIG

4
AFRO
COMB
CROP
PERM
SHAG
TINT
TRIM

5
BRAID
BRUSH
PLAIT
QUIFF
RAZOR
SERUM

6
FRINGE
MOHAWK
MOUSSE
MULLET
POMADE
"RACHEL"
TOUPEE

7
BEEHIVE

BLOWDRY
BOWL CUT
BUNCHES
CHIGNON
CREW-CUT
CURLERS
FLAT-TOP
MOHICAN
PAGEBOY
PINCURL
ROLLERS
SHAMPOO
TOPKNOT
UPSWEEP

8
AFRO COMB
CHONMAGE
CLIPPERS
CORN-ROWS
CRIMPERS
CURTAINS
DUCKTAIL
PIGTAILS
PONYTAIL
RINGLETS
SCISSORS
SKINHEAD
SUMO KNOT
UNDERCUT

9
BEATLE CUT
FEATHERED

HAIRBRUSH
HAIRDRYER
HAIRSPRAY
LOWLIGHTS
POMPADOUR

10
DREADLOCKS
FRENCH KNOT
HIGHLIGHTS

11
CONDITIONER
FRENCH PLAIT

12
CURLING TONGS

13
PERMANENT WAVE
SETTING LOTION

14
HAIR EXTENSIONS

15+
HEAT PROTECTION
  SPRAY
LEAVE-IN
  CONDITIONER
PERMANENT COLOUR
SHORT BACK AND
  SIDES
STRAIGHTENING IRONS
TEMPORARY COLOUR

JEWELLERY

3
JET

4
COIL
HORN
JADE
ONYX
OPAL
RUBY

5
AMBER
BADGE
BEADS
BERYL
BEZEL
CAMEO
CHAIN
CLASP
CORAL
DROPS
EBONY
IVORY
PANEL
PASTE
TIARA
TOPAZ

6
AGATES
AMULET
BANGLE
BROOCH
CHOKER
CHROME
COPPER
DIADEM
GARNET
IOLITE
JASPER
LOCKET
MOSAIC
NIELLO
PEARLS
PLIQUE
ROSARY
SCROLL
SPINEL
ZIRCON

7
ABALONE
BANDEAU
CIRCLET
CITRINE
CLUSTER
COLLETS
CORONET
CRYSTAL

EMERALD
GARLAND
KUNZITE
LALIQUE
PENDANT
PERIDOT
PIERCED
PLAQUES
RHODIUM

8
AMETHYST
AMETRINE
AMMONITE
BRACELET
CRUCIFIX
DIAMANTE
EN BRANCH
ENGRAVED
FILIGREE
FIRE OPAL
HAIR COMB
HEMATITE
HORN COMB
INTAGLIO
MAQUETTE
NAIL-HEAD
NECKLACE
OPENWORK
PAILLONS
PASTICHE
REPOUSSE
SAPPHIRE
SARDONYX
SHAGREEN
STAR RUBY

9
ALUMINIUM
BRIOLETTE
CAIRNGORM
CARBUNCLE
CELLULOID
FRENCH JET
LOVE JEWEL
MALACHITE
MARCASITE
MOONSTONE
PEARL DROP
PINNACLED
PORCELAIN
RELIQUARY
SEED PEARL
SIMULATED
STOMACHER
TANZANITE
TERMINALS
TURQUOISE
WING PEARL

10
AQUAMARINE
CANNA BEADS
CHAKRA BEAD
DEMI-PARURE
ENAMELLING
FLEUR-DE-LIS
GOLD THREAD
MEDALLIONS
PENDOLOQUE
QUATREFOIL
ROSE QUARTZ
SHELL CAMEO
SIGNET RING
SILVER GILT
TOURMALINE

11
ALEXANDRITE
CHRYSOBERYL
CHRYSOLITES
CHRYSOPRASE
GOLDEN BERYL
GRANULATION
LAPIS-LAZULI
MICRO MOSAIC
OMBRE ENAMEL
ROCK CRYSTAL
TRANSLUCENT

12
BAROQUE PEARL
BLUE SAPPHIRE
CHALCEDONIES
FACETED STONE
FROSTED GLASS
NEPHRITE DROP
PINK SAPPHIRE
SILVER THREAD
STAR SAPPHIRE

13
CARLO GUILIANO
DOG-TOOTH PEARL
HAIR ORNAMENTS
MOTHER OF PEARL
PECTORAL CROSS
STAR SAPPHIRES
TORTOISESHELL
YELLOW SAPHIRE

14
CABOCHON ZIRCON
MORGANITE BERYL
STERLING SILVER
TREFOIL SETTING

15
CABOCHON EMERALD
CANDY TWIST CHAIN
CHAMPLEVE ENAMEL

CLOISONNE ENAMEL
CORSAGE ORNAMENT
DEMANTOID-GARNET
GREEN TOURMALINE
MANDARINE GARNET
PLASTER MAQUETTE
RHODOLITE GARNET
RUTILATED QUARTZ
TSAVORITE GARNET
WROUGHT WIREWORK

16
CRUCIFORM PENDANT
IRIDESCENT ENAMEL
SOLITAIRE DIAMOND
TABLE CUT DIAMOND

17
ARTICULATED SILVER
CABOCHON TURQUOISE
MARRIAGE JEWELLERY

PLIQUE-A-JOUR ENAMEL
PARAIBA TOURMALINE
TORTOISESHELL COMB

18+
ORANGE BLOSSOM JEWELLERY
PADPARASCHA SAPPHIRE
POLYCHROME CHAMPLEVE
  ENAMELS
RUBELLITE TOURMALINE

FOOD AND DRINK

COOKERY TERMS

4
BARD
BEAT
BLEU (AU)
BOIL
BONE
CHOP
COAT
HANG
HASH
LARD
PIPE
RARE
TOSS

5
BASTE
BERNY
BLANC (À)
BLANC (AU)
BROIL
BROWN
BRULÉ
CARVE
CHILL
CROWN
DAUBE
DRAIN
DRESS
GLAZE
GRILL
KNEAD
MELBA
PLUCK
POACH
POINT (À)
PROVE
PURÉE
REINE (À LA)
ROAST
RUB IN
SAUTÉ
SCALD
STEAM
SWEAT
TRUSS

6
AURORE
BRAISE

CONFIT
CRÉOLE (À LA)
DECANT
DESALT
DIABLE (À LA)
FILLET
FONDUE
GRATIN
GREASE
MAISON
MIGNON
NATURE
REDUCE
SIMMER
ZEPHYR

7
AL DENTE
ARRÊTER
BLANCHE
BLONDIR
CHEMISE (EN)
COLBERT
CROUTON
DEGLAZE
EMINCER
FLAMBER
GRECQUE (À LA)
MARENGO
MÉDICIS
NIÇOISE (À LA)
REFRESH
SUPRÊME
TARTARE (À LA)

8
ALLONGER
ANGLAISE (À L')
APPAREIL
ASSATION
BARBECUE
BELLEVUE (EN)
BRETONNE (À LA)
CATALANE (À LA)
CHAMBORD
CHASSEUR
CHEMISER
CRUDITÉS
DAUPHINE (À LA)
DEVILLED

DUCHESSE (À LA)
EMULSION
ESCALOPE
FLAMANDE (À LA)
INFUSION
JULIENNE
MACERATE
MARINATE
MEUNIÈRE (À LA)
PISTACHE
POT-ROAST
SURPRISE (EN)

9
ACIDULATE
BAKE BLIND
CANELLING
DETAILLER
DIEPPOISE (À LA)
ESPAGNOLE (À L')
FRICASSÉE
KNOCK BACK
LIÉGEOISE (À LA)
LYONNAISE (À LA)
MARINIÈRE (À LA)
MEDALLION
MILANAISE (À LA)

10
ANTILLAISE (À L')
BALLOTTINE
BLANQUETTE
BONNE FEMME
BORDELAISE (À LA)
BOULANGÈRE (À LA)
CHAUD-FROID
DIJONNAISE (À LA)
FLORENTINE (À LA)
PROVENÇALE (À LA)

11
BELLE-HÉLÈNE
BOURGUIGNON
CHARCUTERIE
DAUPHINOISE (À LA)
HOLLANDAISE (À LA)

13
BOURGUIGNONNE (À LA)
CLARIFICATION
DEEP-FAT FRYING

KITCHEN UTENSILS AND TABLEWARE

3
CUP
HOB
JAR
JUG
LID
MUG
PAN
POT
TIN
WOK

4
BOWL
DISH
EWER
FORK
MILL
RACK
SPIT
TRAY

5
BAHUT
BASIN
BOARD
CHOPE
CHURN
FLUTE
GRILL
KNIFE
LADLE
MIXER
MOULD
PELLE
PLATE
PRESS
RUSSE
SIEVE
SPOON
STEEL
STRAW
TONGS
WHISK

6
BASKET
BUCKET
CARAFE
CLOCHE
COOLER
CRIBLE
DIABLE
EGG CUP
FUNNEL
GOBLET
GRADIN
GRATER
KETTLE
MINCER

MORTAR
MUSLIN
PESTLE
PICHET
PITTER
POÊLON
SAUCER
SHAKER
SHEARS
SIPHON
SKEWER
STRING
TAJINE
TOUPIN
TUREEN

7
ALEMBIC
ATTELET
BLENDER
BROILER
CAISSES
CHINOIS
CHIP PAN
CHOPPER
COCOTTE
DRAINER
DREDGER
ÉCUELLE
GRINDER
MARMITE
PITCHER
RAMEKIN
RONDEAU
SALT BOX
SAMOVAR
SKILLET
SKIMMER
SPATULA
SYRINGE
TÂTE-VIN
TOASTER

8
CAQUELON
CAULDRON
COLANDER
CRÊPE PAN
CROCKERY
DAUBIÈRE
EGG TIMER
FLAN RING
HOTPLATE
MAZAGRAN
MOUVETTE
SAUCEPAN
SAUTÉ PAN
SCISSORS
STOCKPOT
STRAINER

TART RING
TASTE-VIN
TRENCHER

9
ALCARRAZA
AUTOCLAVE
BAIN-MARIE
BAKING TIN
CAFETIÈRE
CASSEROLE
COMPOTIER
CORKSCREW
CRUMB TRAY
DÉCOUPOIR
FISH SLICE
FRYING-PAN
KILNER JAR
MANDOLINE
MIJOTEUSE
PASTRY BAG
PIPING BAG
RING MOULD
SALAD BOWL
SAUCEBOAT
SHARPENER
STEAK BATT
TISANIÈRE
TOURTIÈRE

10
APPLE-CORER
CAISSETTES
CASSOLETTE
CHOPSTICKS
CRUET STAND
DIPPING PIN
FISH KETTLE
LIQUIDISER
MUSTARD POT
PERCOLATOR
ROLLING PIN
ROTISSERIE
SALAMANDER
SALT CELLAR
SALTING TUB
SLOW COOKER
STERILIZER
WAFFLE IRON

11
BAKING SHEET
BRAISING PAN
CANDISSOIRE
CHAFING DISH
CHEESECLOTH
COFFEE MAKER
DOUGH TROUGH
DRIPPING PAN
FRUIT STONER

GARGOULETTE
JAMBONNIÈRE
NUTCRACKERS
PASTRY BRUSH
PASTRY WHEEL
SERVING DISH
THERMOMETER
YOGURT-MAKER

12
CARVING KNIFE
DEEP-FAT FRYER

MEASURING JUG
PALETTE KNIFE
PASTRY CUTTER
TURBOT KETTLE

13
BUTCHER'S BLOCK
FOOD PROCESSOR
ICE-CREAM MAKER
KITCHEN SCALES
LARDING NEEDLE
PRESERVING JAR

SACCHAROMETER
VEGETABLE DISH

14
JUICE EXTRACTOR
KNEADING TROUGH
KNIFE SHARPENER
PRESSURE COOKER
TRUSSING NEEDLE

16
MEAT-CARVING TONGS

BAKING

3
BAP
BUN
COB
FAR
PIE

4
BABA
CAKE
CHOU
FLAN
PAVÉ
RUSK
TART

5
BAGEL
BÂTON
BREAD
CRÊPE
FLÛTE
ICING
PLAIT
SABLÉ
SCONE
STICK
TOAST

6
COOKIE
CORNET
ÉCLAIR
LEAVEN
MUFFIN
OUBLIE
ROCHER
TOURTE
WAFFLE

7
BAKLAVA
BANNOCK
BISCUIT
BLOOMER
BRIOCHE
CHAPATI
COTTAGE
CRACKER
CRUMPET
FICELLE
FRITTER
GALETTE
PALMIER
PANCAKE
PRALINE
PRETZEL
STOLLEN
STRUDEL
TARTINE
TARTLET

8
AMANDINE
BAGUETTE
BARM CAKE
BÂTONNET
BISCOTTE
DOUGHNUT
DUCHESSE
DUMPLING
EMPANADA
FROSTING
GRISSINI
SANDWICH
SPLIT TIN
TORTILLA
TURNOVER

9
ALLUMETTE
BARQUETTE
CROISSANT
FEUILLETÉ
FRIANDISE
KUGELHOPF
PETIT FOUR
VOL-AU-VENT

10
CRISPBREAD
FRANGIPANE
PÂTISSERIE
PUFF PASTRY
RELIGIEUSE
SHORTBREAD
SPONGE CAKE

11
CHOUX PASTRY
LINZERTORTE
PETIT-BEURRE
PROFITEROLE

12
LANGUE-DE-CHAT
PUMPERNICKEL
SPONGE FINGER

13
GENOESE SPONGE

14
PAIN AU CHOCOLAT

15
SAVOY SPONGE CAKE

CEREALS

3
RYE

SPELT
WHEAT

FROMENT
SORGHUM

4
BRAN
CORN
OATS
RICE

6
BARLEY
BULGUR
MÉTEIL
MILLET

9
BUCKWHEAT

12
CRACKED WHEAT

5
MAIZE

7
BURGHUL

CHEESES

4
BRIE (France)
CURD (CHEESE)
EDAM (Netherlands)
FETA (Greece)
MESH (Egypt)
SAGA (Denmark)
TOME (France)

5
BANON (France)
BRICK (US)
CABOC (Scotland)
COMTÉ (France)
DANBO (Denmark)
DERBY (England)
FETTA (Greece)
GOUDA (Netherlands)
HERVE (Belgium)
LEIGH (England)
MOLBO (Denmark)
MUROL (France)
NIOLO (Corsica)
ROOMY (Egypt)
TAMIÉ (France)

6
AREESH (Egypt)
ASIAGO (Italy)
BAGNES (Switzerland)
BRESSE (France)
CACHAT (France)
CANTAL (France)
CENDRÉ (France)
CHIMAY (Belgium)
DUNLOP (Scotland)
FOURME (France)
GAPRON (France)
GÉROMÉ (France)
HALUMI (Greece)
HARZER (Germany)
HRAMSA (Scotland)

LEIDEN (Netherlands)
MORVEN (Scotland)
OLIVET (France)
POURLY (France)
ROLLOT (France)
RONCAL (Spain)
SAKURA (Japan)
SALERS (France)
SAMSOË (Denmark)
SBRINZ (Switzerland)
SURATI (India)
TILSIT (Switzerland)
VENACO (Corsica)

7
BONDARD (France)
BONIFAZ (Germany)
BRINZEN (Hungary)
BROCCIO (Corsica)
BROCCIU (Corsica)
BROUSSE (France)
BRUCCIU (Corsica)
BRYNDZA (Hungary)
CABÉCOU (France)
CHEDDAR (England)
CROWDIE (Scotland)
DAUPHIN (France)
DEMI-SEL (France)
DOMYATI (Egypt)
FONTINA (Italy)
GAPERON (France)
GJETÖST (Norway)
GRUYÈRE (France; Switzerland)
JONCHÉE (France)
LANGRES (France)
LEVROUX (France)
LIMBURG (Belgium)
LIVAROT (France)
MAASDAM (Netherlands)
MACQUÉE (France)
MONT-D'OR (France)

MORBIER (France)
MÜNSTER (France)
NANTAIS (France)
PICODON (France)
QUARGEL (Austria)
RICOTTA (Italy)
RODORIC (Belgium)
SAPSAGO (Switzerland)
STILTON (England)
VENDÔME (France)

8
AUVERGNE (France)
AYRSHIRE (Scotland)
BEAUFORT (France)
BEL PAESE (Italy)
BERGKÄSE (Austria)
BOULETTE (France)
CHAOURCE (France)
CHESHIRE (England)
EDELPILZ (Germany)
EMMENTAL (Switzerland)
EPOISSES (France)
LUNEBERG (Austria)
MANCHEGO (Spain)
PARMESAN (Italy)
PECORINO (Italy)
PÉLARDON (France)
REMOUDOU (Belgium)
SCAMORZE (Italy)
TALEGGIO (Italy)
VACHERIN (Switzerland)
VALENÇAY (France)

9
APPENZELL (Switzerland)
BROODKAAS (Netherlands)
CAITHNESS (Scotland)
CAMBOZOLA (Italy; Germany)
CAMEMBERT (France)
CHABICHOU (France)
CHEVRETON (France)

EMMENTHAL (Switzerland)
EXCELSIOR (France)
GAMMELÖST (Norway)
JARLSBERG (Norway)
LA BOUILLE (France)
LEICESTER (England)
LIMBURGER (Belgium)
MAROILLES (France)
MEKKERBEK (Belgium)
MIMOLETTE (France)
PAVÉ D'AUGE (France)
PORT-SALUT (France)
PROVOLONE (Italy)
REBLOCHON (France)
ROQUEFORT (France)

10
CAERPHILLY (Wales)
DANISH BLUE (Denmark)
DOLCELATTE (Italy)
GLOUCESTER (England)
GORGONZOLA (Italy)
KEFALOTYRI (Cyprus)
LANCASHIRE (England)
LEERDAMMER (Netherlands)
MOZZARELLA (Italy)
NEUFCHÂTEL (Switzerland)

PITHIVIERS (France)
RED WINDSOR (England)
SAINGORLON (France)
STRACCHINO (Italy)

11
CARRÉ DE L'EST (France)
COEUR DE BRAY (France)
COULOMMIERS (France)
KATSHKAWALJ (Bulgaria)
PETIT-SUISSE (France)
PONT-L'ÉVÊQUE (France)
SAINTE-MAURE (France)
SAINT-PAULIN (France)
SCHABZIEGER (Switzerland)
TÊTE-DE-MOINE (Switzerland)
WEISSLACKER (Germany)
WENSLEYDALE (England)

12
CACIOCAVALLO (Italy)
RED LEICESTER (England)
SOUMAINTRAIN (France)

13
BACHENSTEINGER (Austria)
SAINT-NECTAIRE (France)

SELLES-SUR-CHER (France)

14
BRILLAT-SAVARIN (France)
FEUILLE DE DREUX (France)
LAGUIOLE-AUBRAC (France)
SAINT-FLORENTIN (France)
SAINT-MARCELLIN (France)
STINKING BISHOP (England)
TRAPPISTENKÄSE (Germany)

15
BOUTON-DE-CULOTTE (France)

16
DOUBLE GLOUCESTER (England)

17
RIGOTTE DE PELUSSIN (France)

18
CHEVROTIN DES ARAVIS (France)
CROTTIN DE CHAVIGNOL
   (France)

19
POULIGNY-SAINT-PIERRE
   (France)

HERBS AND SPICES

3
BAY
RUE

4
BALM
DILL
MINT
SAGE

5
ANISE
BASIL
CHIVE
CLOVE
CUMIN
TANSY
THYME

6
BETONY
BORAGE
BURNET
CICELY
FENNEL
GARLIC
GINGER

LOVAGE
PEPPER
SAVORY
SESAME
SORREL

7
BONESET
CARAWAY
CHERVIL
COMFREY
DITTANY
MUSTARD
OREGANO
PAPRIKA
PARSLEY
PERILLA
PIMENTO
SAFFRON
SALSIFY
TABASCO
VANILLA

8
ALLSPICE
ANGELICA
CAMOMILE

CARDAMOM
CARDAMON
CINNAMON
DROPWORT
FEVERFEW
MARJORAM
ROSEMARY
TARRAGON
TURMERIC

9
CHAMOMILE
CORIANDER
FENUGREEK
SPEARMINT

10+
ASAFOETIDA
BLACK-EYED SUSAN
HERB OF GRACE
HORSERADISH
HOTTENTOT FIG
OYSTER PLANT
PEPPERMINT
POT MARIGOLD
VEGETABLE OYSTER

JOINTS OF MEAT

BEEF

BRISKET
CHUCK
FILLET STEAK
FLANK
FORE RIB
LEG
NECK
RIB
ROLLED RIBS
RUMP
SHIN
SILVERSIDE
SIRLOIN

T-BONE
TOPSIDE
UNDERCUT STEAK

PORK

BELLY
BLADE
HAND
HOCK
LEG
LEG FILLET
LOIN
SHOULDER

SPARE RIB
TENDERLOIN
TROTTER

LAMB

BEST END OF NECK
BREAST
CHUMP
CHUMP CHOPS
LEG
LOIN
SCRAG-END
SHOULDER

TYPES OF PASTA

4
PICI
PIPE
ZITI

5
FIORI
GIGLI
PENNE

6
BIGOLI
DITALI
FETUCE
LAGANE
PILLUS
RISONI
ROTINI
ZITONI

7
BARBINA
CAPELLI
FUSILLI
LASAGNE
LUMACHE
MAFALDE
NOODLES

RAVIOLI
ROTELLE
SPIRALI

8
BUCATINI
DITALINI
DITALONI
FARFALLE
FEDELINI
FETTUCCE
GRAMIGNA
LANTERNE
LINGUINE
MACARONI
RIGATONI
SORPRESE
STELLINE
TAGLIONI
TRENETTE

9
AGNOLOTTI
ANNELLINI
CAPELLINI
MAFALDINE
MANICOTTI

SPAGHETTI
TRIPOLINE
TUFFOLONI

10
CANNELLONI
CONCHIGLIE
CRAVATTINE
FARFALLINE
FETTUCCINE
TAGLIOLINI
TORTELLINI
TORTELLONI
VERMICELLI

11
CAPPELLETTI
ORECCHIETTE
PAPPARDELLE
PERCIATELLI
SPAGHETTINI
SPAGHETTONI
TAGLIATELLE
TORTIGLIONI

12
PAGLIA E FIENO
VERMICELLONI

BEANS AND PEAS

6
LENTIL

7
PEA-BEAN
RED BEAN

8
CHICKPEA
LIMA BEAN
MUNG BEAN

SOYA BEAN
SPLIT PEA
SUGAR PEA

9
BROAD BEAN
FLAGEOLET
GARDEN PEA
HORSE BEAN
MANGETOUT
PETIT POIS

PINTO BEAN

10
ADZUKI BEAN
BEAN SPROUT
BUTTER-BEAN
FRENCH BEAN
KIDNEY BEAN
RUNNER BEAN
STRING BEAN
WAX-POD BEAN

11
HARICOT BEAN

12
SUGAR SNAP PEA

13
BLACK-EYED BEAN
SCARLET RUNNER

VEGETABLES

3
YAM

4
AARD
BEAN
BEET
KALE
LEEK
OKRA
TARO

5
CHARD
CRESS
GOURD
GUMBO
ONION
SAVOY
SWEDE

6
CARROT
CELERY
ENDIVE
FENNEL
LENTIL

MANIOC
MARROW
ORACHE
PEPPER
POTATO
RADISH
SQUASH
TOMATO
TURNIP

7
CABBAGE
CARDOON
CASSAVA
CHAYOTE
CHERVIL
CHICORY
GHERKIN
LETTUCE
MUSTARD
PAK-CHOI
PARSNIP
PUMPKIN
SALSIFY
SEA KALE
SHALLOT
SPINACH

SUCCORY

8
BEETROOT
BROCCOLI
CAPSICUM
CELERIAC
CUCUMBER
EGGPLANT
KOHLRABI
PIMIENTO
RUTABAGA
SCALLION
ZUCCHINI

9
ARTICHOKE
ASPARAGUS
AUBERGINE
CALABRESE
COURGETTE
CURLY KALE
MANGETOUT
SWEET CORN

10
BREADFRUIT

SCORZONERA
WATERCRESS

11
AVOCADO PEAR
CAULIFLOWER
OYSTER PLANT
SPINACH BEET
SWEET POTATO

12
BAMBOO SHOOTS
CORN ON THE COB
MARROW SQUASH

13
CHINESE LEAVES
WATER CHESTNUT

14
BRUSSELS SPROUT
CHINESE CABBAGE
DISHCLOTH GOURD

18
JERUSALEM
  ARTICHOKE

FRUITS AND NUTS

3
FIG

4
BAEL
DATE
KAKI
LIME
NIPA
PEAR
PLUM
SLOE

5
ACORN
APPLE
CAROB
GOURD
GRAPE
GUAVA
LEMON
MANGO
MELON
OLIVE
PEACH
PECAN

6
ALMOND
ANANAS
BABACO
BANANA
CASHEW
CHERRY
CITRON
COB-NUT
CONKER
DAMSON
DURIAN
FEIJOA
GUM NUT
HOGNUT
JUJUBE
LONGAN
LOQUAT
LYCHEE
MEDLAR
MOMBIN
MUSCAT
ORANGE

PAWPAW
PEANUT
PIGNUT
PIPPIN
POMELO
QUINCE
SAL NUT
TOMATO
WALNUT

7
APRICOT
AVOCADO
BULLACE
COCONUT
COLA NUT
COSTARD
CURRANT
FILBERT
GEEBUNG
GENIPAP
KUMQUAT
PALM NUT
PINE NUT
SATSUMA
SOURSOP
TANGELO

8
ARECA NUT
BARBERRY
BAYBERRY
BEECHNUT
BERGAMOT
BETEL-NUT
BILBERRY
BREADNUT
CHESTNUT
COC-DE-MER
COCOANUT
DEWBERRY
EARTH-NUT
HAZELNUT
MANDARIN
MINNEOLA
MULBERRY
PLANTAIN
QUANDONG
RAMBUTAN

SOUR PLUM
SWEETSOP
TAMARIND
TAYBERRY

9
BAKEAPPLE
BEARBERRY
BITTERNUT
BLUEBERRY
BRAZIL NUT
BUTTERNUT
CANDLENUT
CARAMBOLA
CHERIMOYA
CHINCAPIN
COFFEE NUT
CRAB APPLE
CRANBERRY
CROWBERRY
GREENGAGE
GROUNDNUT
GRUGRU NUT
HACKBERRY
IVORY-NUT
JACKFRUIT
KIWI FRUIT
LITCHI NUT
MOCKERNUT
MUSK MELON
MYROBALAN
NECTARINE
PERSIMMON
PINEAPPLE
PISTACHIO
RASPBERRY
SAPODILLA
SOUR GOURD
STAR FRUIT
TAMARILLO
TANGERINE
UGLI FRUIT

10
BLACKBERRY
BREADFRUIT
CHINABERRY
CHOKEBERRY
CLEMENTINE

ELDERBERRY
GOOSEBERRY
GRANADILLA
GRAPEFRUIT
HICKORY NUT
JABOTICABA
LOGANBERRY
MANGOSTEEN
MANZANILLA
MONKEY-NUT
REDCURRANT
SAOUARI NUT
SOUR CHERRY
SOUR ORANGE
STAR-APPLE
STRAWBERRY
TREE TOMATO
WATERMELON
YOUNGBERRY

11
BOYSENBERRY
COQUILLA NUT
HUCKLEBERRY
LINGONBERRY
POMEGRANATE
PRICKLY PEAR
SALMONBERRY
SHARON FRUIT
SPICE-BERRY
WHITE WALNUT

12
BLACKCURRANT
BURRAWANG NUT
MACADAMIA NUT
PASSION FRUIT
SERVICE-BERRY
WHITE CURRANT
WHORTLEBERRY
WINTER CHERRY

13
ALLIGATOR PEAR
DWARF CHESTNUT
HORSE CHESTNUT
QUEENSLAND NUT
SWEET CHESTNUT
WATER CHESTNUT

DESSERTS

4
FOOL
WHIP

5
JELLY

6
CAJETA
JUNKET
KISSEL
MOUSSE
SORBET
SUNDAE
TRIFLE
YOGURT

7
BAKLAVA
COBBLER
COMPOTE
CRUMBLE
CUSTARD
GRANITA
JAM TART
PARFAIT

PAVLOVA
SOUFFLE
SPUMONI
TAPIOCA

8
APPLE PIE
FRUIT CUP
ICE CREAM
PANDOWDY
ROLY POLY
SEMOLINA
TIRAMISU
WATER ICE

9
BAVAROISE
ENTREMETS
FRUIT FLAN
TIPSY CAKE

10
BANOFFI PIE
BLANCMANGE
BROWN BETTY
EGG CUSTARD

FRESH FRUIT
FRUIT SALAD
PEACH MELBA
SHOOFLY PIE
ZABAGLIONE

11
BAKED ALASKA
BANANA SPLIT
EVE'S PUDDING
PLUM PUDDING
RICE PUDDING
SPOTTED DICK
STEWED FRUIT
SUET PUDDING
TREACLE TART

12
APFELSTRUDEL
CREME CARAMEL

13
CREPES SUZETTE
DAIRY ICE CREAM
SPONGE PUDDING
SUMMER PUDDING

14
APPLE CHARLOTTE
CABINET PUDDING
CHARLOTTE RUSSE
FLOATING ISLAND
STEAMED PUDDING

16
CHRISTMAS PUDDING
DEATH BY CHOCOLATE
VIENNOISE PUDDING

17
BLACK FOREST GATEAU
MISSISSIPPI MUD PIE
UPSIDE DOWN
   PUDDING

18
KNICKERBOCKER
   GLORY

21
BREAD AND BUTTER
   PUDDING

CAKES

4
BABA

5
SCONE
TORTE
ECLAIR

6
GATEAU
KUCHEN
MUFFIN
PARKIN

7
BAKLAVA
BANNOCK
BROWNIE
CRULLER
CUPCAKE

HOECAKE
PANCAKE
PAVLOVA
STRUDEL
TEACAKE
YULE LOG

8
DOUGHNUT
FLAPJACK
MERINGUE
PANDOWDY
PLUM CAKE
ROCK CAKE
SEEDCAKE

9
ANGEL CAKE
DROP SCONE

FAIRY CAKE
FRUIT CAKE
GENOA CAKE
LARDY-CAKE
MADELEINE
POUND CAKE
QUEEN CAKE
SHORTCAKE
SWISS ROLL
TIPSY-CAKE

10
ALMOND CAKE
BATTENBURG
CHEESECAKE
DUNDEE CAKE
ECCLES CAKE
FRANGIPANE
KOEKSISTER

LADYFINGER
MARBLE CAKE
SIMNEL CAKE
SPONGE CAKE

11
GINGERBREAD
MADEIRA CAKE
WEDDING CAKE

12
BAKEWELL TART
DANISH PASTRY
MILLEFEUILLE

14
DEVIL'S FOOD CAKE
UPSIDE-DOWN CAKE
VICTORIA SPONGE

SAUCES

3
SOY

4
MINT
NOIR

5
AIOLI
VERTE

6
BATARD
BUTTER
HOISIN

MADERE
MORNAY
ROBERT
TOMATO

7
BLANCHE
COLBERT
MADEIRA
ROUILLE
SOUBISE
SUPREME
TARTARE
VELOUTE

8
ALBUFERA
BARBEQUE
BECHAMEL
CHASSEUR
DUXELLES
NORMANDE
POIVRADE

9
BEARNAISE
LYONNAISE
PICQUANTE
RICHELIEU

10
BORDELAISE
MAYONNAISE
SARLADAISE

11
HOLLANDAISE
VINAIGRETTE

12
SWEET-AND-SOUR

13
BOURGUIGNONNE

EASTERN EUROPEAN DISHES

4
KIEV
UKHA

5
BABKA
BIGOS
BITKI
BLINI
KASHA
LATKE
LOSOS
MIASO
RAKOV
SCHEE
ZRAZY

6
BORSCH
CAVIAR
KULICH
PASKHA

7
BANITSA
BLINTZE
BORSHCH
GOULASH
GRIBNOY
PELMENI
SELEDKA
ZAKUSKY

8
BOTVINYA
DRANNIKY
GROBNAUA
HOLUBTSI
KRABOVIY
KREPLACH
KURINAYA
MYASNOYE
RAZNOSOI
SHASHLYK
SOLYANKA

TURSCHIA

9
BLINCHIKI
CHEBUREKI
POD SHUBOY
STROGANOV
TYUKLEVES

10
BOUZHENINA
OGURTCHIKY
PAPRIKACHE
STOLICHNIY
STROGANOFF

15+
FARSH PO TATARSKY
GOLUBTZY OVOSHNIE
GRIBNY MARINOVANNIE
KOTLETY POZHARSKI
MIASNIE GOLUBTZY
SOLYANKA MIASNAYA

INDIAN DISHES

3
DAL

4
DHAL
NAAN
PURI

5
BHAJI

DORMA
DURMA
KARHI
KOFTA
KORMA
POORI
RAITA
RISTA
TIKKA

6
KARAHI
KORMAH
MADRAS
MASALA
RAITHA
SAMBAL
SAMOSA

7
BIRIANI
BIRYANI
CHAHKEE
CHAPATI
DHANSAK
DO PIAZA
PAPADUM
PARATHA

SHIRMAL

8
POPPADOM
TANDOORI
VINDALOO

9
ALOO BHAJI
GOBHI MHAS
JHAL FARZI
ROGAN JOSH

10
ALOO GOSCHT

BOMBAY ALOO
MALAI SEEKH
METHI GOSHT
MURGH TIKKA
SAMBAL ALOO

11
BARRAH KABAB

12
GOSHT KHUBANI
KADHAI JHINGA
MAKHANI MURGH
MOORGHI KHARI

13
GOSHT GULMARGI
KHEEMA DO-PIAZA
MACHCHI BADAMI
PESHAWARI RAAN
TANDOORI MURGH

14
PESHAWARI GOSHT

15+
MURGH HARA MASALA
MURGH KORMA SHAHI
MURGH-ALOO BHOONA

GREEK DISHES

4
FAVA
FETA
GYRO
PITA

6
DIPLES
OLIVES

7
BAKLAVA
GEMISTA
KAKAVIA

8
DOLMADES
FORMAELA
GIGANDES
GRAVIERA
KEFTEDES
KLEFTIKO

MIZITHRA
MOUSSAKA
OLIVE OIL
SAGANAKI
SOUVLAKI
TIROPITA
TSOUREKI
TZATZIKI
YOUVETSI

9
FASOLAKIA
GIOUVETSI
HILOPITES
HORIATIKI
KOKORETSI
PASTITSIO

10
AVGOLEMONO
DOLMADAKIA
FASSOLATHA

KREATOPITA
LADOLEMONO

11
CRETAN DAKOS
DOLMATHAKIA
FANOUROPITA
HORTA VRASTA
KOURABIEDES
SPANAKOPITA

12
MELOMAKARONA
TARAMASALATA

14
GALAKTOBOUREKO

15
MELITZANOSALATA

17
KOLOKITHOKEFTEDES

CHINESE DISHES

4
MA-LA

5
SATAY

6
DIM SUM
TIAO-MA
TUNG-PO
WONTON
WUN TUN

7
CHA SHAO
FOO YUNG
GAN-CHAO
GAN-SHAO
GUAI-WEI
HANG-YOU
TIANG-ZU
YU-XIANG

8
CHOP SUEY

CHOW MEIN

9
SPARERIBS
STIR FRIED

10
PEKING DUCK
SPRING ROLL

11
MOO SHOO PORK

PANCAKE ROLL

12
EGG FRIED RICE
PRAWN CRACKER
SWEET AND SOUR

13
BIRD'S NEST SOUP
SHARK'S FIN SOUP

15
PEKING ROAST DUCK

YANGCHOW NOODLES

18
CANTONESE ROAST DUCK
CRISPY AROMATIC DUCK
CRISPY FRIED SEAWEED

MEXICAN DISHES

4
MOLE

5
CALDO
ELOTE
PAPAS
SALSA
SOPES
TACOS

6
BIRRIA
CAMOTE
CECINA
COCIDO
FIDEOS
JICAMA
LENGUA
MEMELA
MENUDO
POZOLE
TORTAS
TOTOPO
TRIPAS
VENADO

7
CABRITO
CEVICHE
CHALUPA
CHORIZO
CHURIPO
CODZITO
CORUNDA
CURTIDO
FLAUTAS
GLORIAS
GRINGAS
JOCOQUE
MACHACA
MOLOTES
MORONGA
MULITAS
PANUCHO
POC CHUC
TAMALES

8
ALAMBRES
BARBACOA
BOLILLOS
CALABAZA
CARNITAS
CHARALES
CHILORIO
COACHALA
FRIJOLES
GORDITAS
MILANESA
MIXIOTES
MOLLETES
PAMBAZOS
SALBUTES
TAQUITOS
TLACOYOS
TLAYUDAS
TOSTADAS

9
ATEPOCATE
EMPANADAS
ENCHILADA
ESCAMOLES
GUACAMOLE
HUARACHES
LONGANIZA
NOPALITOS
PICADILLO
ROMERITOS
TORTILLAS
TORTILLAS

10
ARROZ VERDE
CARNE ASADA
CHAPULINES
CHAPULINES
CHILTOMATE
CHORIQUESO
PAPADZULES
PARILLADAS
POLLO ASADO
SOPA AZTECA

11
CHILAQUILES
CUITLACOCHE
ENTOMATADAS
PICO DE GALLO
POLLO PICADO
SOPA DE POLLO
SOPA TARASCA

12
ARROZ CON LIMA
ARROZ ESPAÑOL
BISTEC PICADO
CARNE GUISADA
CHILE RELLENO
CHIMICHANGAS
HUAUNZONTLES
PASTEL AZTECA
QUESO DE CUAJO

13
ARROZ AMARILLO
ARROZ CON POLLO
CAVIAR DE CARPA
QUESO FLAMEADO
RAJAS CON CREMA
SINCRONIZADAS

14
CHILES EN NOGADA
COCHINITA PIBIL
MANCHA MANTELES
POLLO ROSTIZADO
SOPA DE TORTILLA

15+
ARROZ CON CAMARONES
CARNE TAMPIQUEÑA
CHILPACHOLE DE JAIBA
EMPANADA MEXICANA
FRITADAS DE CAMARON
HUEVOS DIVORCIADOS
HUEVOS MOTULEÑOS
HUEVOS RANCHEROS
PEJELAGARTO ASADO
POLLO ENCACAHUATADO
PULPOQUESADILLAS

DRINKS

WINES AND APERTIFS

4
FINO
HOCK
PORT
SACK

5
BYRRH
CRÉPY
FITOU
MÉDOC
MOSEL
RIOJA
TAVEL
TOKAY

6
ALSACE
BANDOL
BAROLO
BARSAC
BEAUNE
CAHORS
CASSIS
CHINON
CLARET
FRANGY
GRAVES
MÁLAGA
SAUMUR
SHERRY
VOLNAY

7
ALIGOTÉ
CAMPARI
CHABLIS
CHIANTI
CLAIRET
CRÉMANT
FALERNO
GAILLAC
MADEIRA
MARGAUX
MARSALA
MARTINI
MOSELLE
ORVIETO
POMMARD
RETSINA
VOUVRAY

8
BORDEAUX
BROUILLY
DUBONNET
GIGONDAS
MERCUREY
MONTAGNY
MONTILLA
MUSCADET
PAUILLAC
RIESLING
ROSÉ WINE
SANCERRE
SANTENAY
VALENÇAY
VERMOUTH

VIN JAUNE

9
BOURGUEIL
CHAMPAGNE
CLAIRETTE
CÔTE-RÔTIE
HERMITAGE
LAMBRUSCO
MEURSAULT
MONTLOUIS
SAUTERNES

10
BARBARESCO
BEAUJOLAIS
BULL'S BLOOD
MANZANILLA
MONTRACHET
RICHEBOURG
RIVESALTES
VINHO VERDE

11
ALOXE-CORTON
AMONTILLADO
MONBAZILLAC
POUILLY-FUMÉ
SAINT JULIEN

12
CÔTES-DU-RHÔNE
ROMANÉE-CONTI
SAINT-EMILION
SAINT ESTEPHE
VALPOLICELLA

VOSNE-ROMANÉE

13
CHÂTEAU D'YQUEM
CHÂTEAU LAFITE
CHÂTEAU LATOUR
ENTRE-DEUX-MERS
POUILLY-FUISSÉ

14
CHÂTEAU MARGAUX
CÔTES-DU-VENTOUX
GEWÜRZTRAMINER

15
CÔTES-DE-PROVENCE
CÔTES-DU-VIVARAIS
CROZES-HERMITAGE
MOREY-SAINT-DENIS

16
CHAMBOLLE-MUSIGNY
GEVREY-CHAMBERTIN
SAVIGNY-LÈS-BEAUNE

17
CÔTES-DU-ROUSSILLON
NUITS-SAINT-GEORGES

18
BLANQUETTE DE
  LIMOUX

19
CHASSAGNE-
  MONTRACHET

COCKTAILS AND MIXED DRINKS

3
FIX
KIR
NOG

4
FIZZ
FLIP
GROG
RAKI
SOUR

5
JULEP
NEGUS
PUNCH
TODDY

6
BEADLE
BISHOP
GIMLET
POSSET

7
MARTINI
SANGRIA
SIDECAR
WALDORF

8
APPLE CAR
DAIQUIRI
GIN AND IT
GIN SLING
HIGHBALL
NIGHTCAP
PINK LADY
WHIZ BANG

9
ALEXANDER
APPLEJACK
BEE'S KNEES
BUCK JONES
BUCKS FIZZ

COMMODORE
MANHATTAN
MINT JULEP
MOONLIGHT
MOONSHINE
MULLED ALE
WHITE LADY

10
ANGEL'S KISS
ARCHBISHOP
BLACK MARIA
BLOODY MARY
HORSE'S NECK
MERRY WIDOW
MULLED WINE
PINA COLADA
RUM COLLINS
TOM COLLINS

11
BEACHCOMBER

BLACK VELVET
FALLEN ANGEL
JOHN COLLINS
WASSAIL BOWL

12
CHURCHWARDEN
ELEPHANT'S EAR
FINE AND DANDY
OLD-FASHIONED
WHITE GIN SOUR

13
CHAMPAGNE BUCK
CORPSE REVIVER
KNICKERBOCKER
MAIDEN'S PRAYER
PLANTER'S PUNCH
PRAIRIE OYSTER

16
BETWEEN THE SHEETS
HARVEY WALLBANGER

BEER AND BEVERAGES

3
ALE

4
MEAD
MILD

5
CIDER
KVASS
LAGER
PERRY
STOUT

6
BITTER
LAMBIC
SHANDY

8

GUINNESS
HYDROMEL

10
BARLEY BEER
BARLEY WINE

SPIRITS

3
GIN
RUM

4
ARAK
MARC
OUZO

5
CHOUM
VODKA

6
BOUKHA
BRANDY
CHICHA
COGNAC
GRAPPA
KIRSCH
MESCAL
METAXA
PASTIS
PERNOD
PULQUE

WHISKY

7
AKVAVIT
AQUAVIT
BACARDI
BOUKHRA
BOURBON
SCHNAPS
TEQUILA
WHISKEY

8

ARMAGNAC
CALVADOS
FALERNUM
SCHNAPPS

9
SLIVOVITZ

10
RYE WHISKEY

11
AGUARDIENTE

LIQUERS

4
SAKÉ
SAKI

5
ANISE
ANRAM

6
CASSIS
KÜMMEL
MÊLISS
QETSCH
SCUBAC
STREGA

7
ALCAMAS
ALLASCH
BAILEYS
CURAÇAO
ESCUBAC
RATAFIA
SAMBUCA

8
ABSINTHE
ADVOCAAT
ANISETTE
DRAMBUIE
PERSICOT
PRUNELLE

9
ARQUEBUSE
COINTREAU
FRAMBOISE
GUIGNOLET
MIRABELLE
TRIPLE SEC

10
BROU DE NOIX
CHARTREUSE
LIMONCELLO
MARASCHINO

11
BENEDICTINE

TRAPPISTINE

12
CHERRY BRANDY
CRÈME DE CACAO
GRAND MARNIER

13
CRÈME DE MENTHE

15
SOUTHERN COMFORT

17
AMARETTO DI
  SARANNO

NON-ALCOHOLIC DRINKS

3
CHA (TEA)
TEA

4
CHAR (TEA)
COLA
MATÉ
SODA

5
LASSI
WATER

6
COFFEE
ORGEAT
TISANE

7
BEEF TEA

CORDIAL
DIABOLO
LIMEADE
SELTZER

8
LEMONADE

9
GRENADINE
MILKSHAKE

ORANGEADE

10
GINGER BEER
TONIC WATER

12
MINERAL WATER

COFFEE DRINKS

AFFOGATO
AMERICANO
BALTIMORE
BLACK EYE
BLACK TIE
BREVE
CA PHE SUA DA
CAFE AU LAIT
CAFE BOMBON
CAFE CREME
CAFE MEDICI
CAFE MELANGE
CAFE MIEL
CAFE MOCHA
CAFE ZORRO
CAPPUCCINO
CARAMEL MACHIATTO
CHAI LATTE
CHOCOLATE DALMATIAN
CINNAMON SPICE MOCHA
CORTADO

DECAF
DIRTY CHAI
EGGNOG LATTE
EISKAFFEE
ESPRESSO ROMANO
FILTER
FRAPPUCCINO
GALAO
GINGERBREAD LATTE
GREEK FRAPPE
GREEN EYE
GUILLERMO
ICED
INDIAN FILTER
INSTANT
IRISH
KOPI SUSU
LATTE
LIQUEUR
MACCHIATO
MAZAGRAN

MOCHA
MOCHASIPPI
POCILLO
PUMPKIN SPICE LATTE
RASPBERRY MOCHA
RED EYE
RED TIE
RED TUX
REGULAR
RISTRETTO
SKINNY LATTE
SOY LATTE
TORPEDO
TRIPLE C'S
TURKISH
VIENNA
WHITE CHOCOLATE MOCHA
YUANYANG
ZEBRA MOCHA

TEAS

GREEN TEAS

AHMAD
BANCHA
CHUNMEE
DRAGON WELL
HOJICHA
GENMAI CHA
GREEN ANJI
GREEN NEEDLE
GREEN PEKOE
GUNPOWDER
GYOKURO
JASMINE
KUKICHA
MATCHA
PIN HEAD
POUCHONG
SENCHA
TEMPLE OF HEAVEN
XUE YA BALLARD

BLACK TEAS

ASSAM
CEYLON
CASTLETON
DARJEELING

DIMBULA
DOOAR
EARL GREY
ENGLISH BREAKFAST
KEEMUM (KEEMUN or KEENUM
KENILWORTH
LAPSANG SOUCHONG
NEPAL
NILGIRI
NUWARA ELIYA
ORANGE PEKOE
RAJA SINHARAJA
ROYAL CHINA BLACK
RUSSIAN CARAVAN
TERAI
TRAVANCORE
TIGERHILL
TURKISH
UVA
YING MING YUNNAN
YUNNAN

WHITE TEAS

GONG MEI
LONG LIFE EYEBROW
PAI MU TAN
PERSIAN MELON

POOBONG
SHOU MEI
SILVER NEEDLE
SNOWBUD
TRIBUTE EYEBROW
WHITE NEEDLE
WHITE PEONY
YIN ZHEN

OOLONG

ALISHAN
CASSIA
DONG DING
GOLDEN CASSIA
GOLD TURTLE
IRON GODDESS
IRON MONK
LISHAN
MAKAIBARI
NARCISSUS
ORIENTAL BEAUTY
PI LO CHUN
POUCHONG
RED ROBE
TI HUAN YIN
WHITE COMB

SPORTS AND RECREATION

SPORTS

4
GOLF
JUDO
PATO
POLO

5
BOWLS
FIVES
KENDO
RALLY
RODEO

6
AIKIDO
BOULES
BOXING
HOCKEY
KARATE
KUNG FU
PELOTA
ROWING
SHINTY
SKIING
TENNIS

7
ANGLING
ARCHERY
BOWLING
CRICKET
CROQUET
CURLING
FENCING
HURLING
JUJITSU
KABADDI
KARTING
NETBALL
RACKETS
SHOT PUT

8
BASEBALL
BIATHLON
CANOEING
COURSING
DRESSAGE

FALCONRY
GYMKHANA
HANDBALL
HURDLING
LACROSSE
LONG JUMP
MARATHON
PETANQUE
PING-PONG
ROUNDERS
SHOOTING
SPEEDWAY
SWIMMING
TUG OF WAR

9
ATHLETICS
BADMINTON
DECATHLON
ICE HOCKEY
MOTO-CROSS
POLE VAULT
SKYDIVING
TAE KWON-DO
WATER POLO
WRESTLING

10
BASKETBALL
DRAG RACING
FLAT RACING
FOXHUNTING
GYMNASTICS
ICE SKATING
REAL TENNIS
RUGBY UNION
TRIPLE JUMP
VOLLEYBALL

11
BEARBAITING
BLOOD SPORTS
BOBSLEDDING
BULLBAITING
DISCUS THROW
HAMMER THROW
HANG-GLIDING

HORSE RACING
HORSE TRAILS
MARTIAL ARTS
MOTOR RACING
PARACHUTING
PENTHATHLON
RUGBY LEAGUE
SEPAK TAKRAW
TABLE TENNIS
TOBOGGANING
WATER SKIING

12
BULLFIGHTING
CABER TOSSING
COCKFIGHTING
ETON WALL GAME
JAVELIN THROW
ORIENTEERING
PIGEON RACING
POINT-TO-POINT
STEEPLECHASE

13
EQUESTRIANISM
HARNESS RACING
SKATEBOARDING
SQUASH RACKETS
WEIGHT LIFTING

14
FOOTBALL LEAGUE
MOUNTAINEERING
STOCK-CAR RACING

15
GREYHOUND RACING

16
AMERICAN FOOTBALL
MOTORCYCLE RACING

18
CLAY-PIGEON SHOOTING
FREESTYLE WRESTLING

19
ASSOCIATION FOOTBALL

GAMES

2 GO	MARBLES MATADOR PACHISI	**10** BACKGAMMON BAT AND TRAP
4 POOL	SNOOKER YAHTZEE	CASABLANCA RUNNING OUT

2
GO

4
POOL

5
BINGO
CAVES
CHESS
CRAPS
DARTS
FIVES
SHOGI
SPOOF

6
CLUEDO
PAC-MAN
QUOITS
TIPCAT

7
DOBBERS
MAHJONG

MARBLES
MATADOR
PACHISI
SNOOKER
YAHTZEE

8
BACCARAT
BIRD CAGE
DADDLUMS
DOMINOES
DRAUGHTS
LIAR DICE
MONOPOLY
ROULETTE
SCRABBLE
SKITTLES
TOTOPOLY

9
AUNT SALLY
BILLIARDS
POKER DICE
SNAKE-EYES
STOOL BALL

10
BACKGAMMON
BAT AND TRAP
CASABLANCA
RUNNING OUT

11
TIDDLYWINKS

12
BAR BILLIARDS
KNUR AND SPELL
SHOVE HA'PENNY

13
SPACE INVADERS

14
TRIVIAL PURSUIT

16
SNAKES AND LADDERS

20
DEVIL AMONG THE TAILORS

CARD GAMES

3
LOO
PAN
RUM

4
BRAG
JASS
KLOB
SNAP
SPIT
VINT

5
BINGO
BOURE
CINCH
COMET
DARDA
OMBRE
PEDRO
PITCH
POKER
POQUE
RUMMY
SAMBA
WHIST
YUKON

6
BOO-RAY
BOSTON
BRIDGE
CASINO
CHEMMY
ÉCARTÉ
EIGHTS
EUCHRE
FAN-TAN
GAIGEL
GO FISH
JULEPE
MAU-MAU
PIQUET
POCHEN
POKINO
QUINZE
RED DOG
SEVENS
SMUDGE
TRUMPS
YABLON

7
AUTHORS
BELOTTE

BEZIQUE
BOLIVIA
CANASTA
COLONEL
COONCAN
OLD MAID
PONTOON
PRIMERA
PRIMERO
SET-BACK
SEVEN-UP
SNOOKER
SOLOMON
SPINADO
TRIUMPH

8
ACE-DEUCE
CANFIELD
CONQUIAN
CRIBBAGE
GIN RUMMY
IMPERIAL
IRISH LOO
KLONDIKE
LAST CARD
LOW PITCH

NAPOLEON
OKLAHOMA
PATIENCE
PINOCHLE
ROCKAWAY
ROLLOVER
SIXTY SIX
SLAPJACK

9
BLACKJACK
DRAW POKER
FORTY FIVE
IN-BETWEEN
OPEN POKER
SOLITAIRE
SOLO WHIST
SPOIL FIVE
STUD POKER
THIRTY ONE
VINGT-ET-UN
WILD JACKS

10
DRAW CASINO
JOKER PITCH
PANGUINGUE
PISHE PASHA
PUT AND TAKE
TABLANETTE
THIRTY FIVE
WELLINGTON

11
BOSTON WHIST
BRIDGE WHIST
CATCH THE TEN
CHEMIN DE FER
CLOSED POKER
CRAZY EIGHTS
DOUBLE RUMMY
FIVE CARD LOO
FIVE HUNDRED
GERMAN WHIST
HUMBUG WHIST
KLABBERJASS
RACING DEMON
ROYAL CASINO
RUSSIAN BANK
SCOTCH WHIST
SLIPPERY SAM
SPADE CASINO

12
AUCTION PITCH
DOMINO FAN-TAN
JACK CHANGE IT
SWEDISH RUMMY

13
AUCTION BRIDGE
CONCENTRATION
HAPPY FAMILIES
OLD MAN'S BUNDLE
SIX SPOT RED DOG
STRAIGHT POKER

14
BACCARET BANQUE
CHINESE BEZIQUE
CONTRACT BRIDGE
FRENCH PINOCHLE
FROGS IN THE POND
RACEHORSE PITCH
RUBICON BEZIQUE
SIX DECK BEZIQUE
SPITE AND MALICE

15
AROUND THE CORNER
AUCTION PINOCHLE
BANKER AND BROKER
HOLLYWOOD EIGHTS

16
CONTINENTAL RUMMY
DOUBLE DUMMY WHIST
EIGHT DECK BEZIQUE
TRENTE ET QUARANTE
TRUMP HUMBUG WHIST

17+
BEAT YOUR NEIGHBOUR
BEGGAR-MY-
  NEIGHBOUR
BEGGAR-YOUR-
  NEIGHBOUR
FIVE HUNDRED BEZIQUE
ROUND THE CORNER
  RUMMY

BRIDGE TERMS

3
BID
FIT

4
ACOL
CALL
DEAL
GAME
LEAD
RUFF
VOID

5
ALERT
DUMMY
ENTRY
GUARD
REBID
TABLE

6
DOUBLE
GERBER

HONOUR
LENGTH
MISFIT
REVOKE
RUBBER
SYSTEM
TENACE
TIMING

7
AUCTION
CONTROL
CUE BIDS
DISCARD
FINESSE
JUMP BID
PARTNER
SIGNALS
STAYMAN
STOPPER

8
CONTRACT

DECLARER
DIRECTOR
LIMIT BID
MCKENNEY
OVERCALL
OVER RUFF
REDOUBLE
RESPONSE
SIDE SUIT

9
BLACKWOOD
DOUBLETON
GRAND SLAM
LAVINTHAL
MAJOR SUIT
MINOR SUIT
OVER TRICK
PART SCORE
SACRIFICE
SINGLETON
SMALL SLAM
SOLID SUIT

10
CONVENTION
FORCING BID
LINE OF PLAY
REVERSE BID
SYSTEM CARD
UNBALANCED
UNDER TRICK
VULNERABLE

11
DOUBLE DUMMY
MATCH POINTS
OPENING LEAD
PARTNERSHIP
THIRD IN HAND

12
BALANCED HAND

BIDDABLE SUIT
BIDDING SPACE
DISTRIBUTION
FOURTH IN HAND
INTERVENTION
JUMP OVERCALL
PLAYING TRICK
SEMI-BALANCED

13
COMMUNICATION
NOT VULNERABLE
PRE-EMPTIVE BID
TAKE OUT DOUBLE
TOUCHING SUITS
TWO-SUITED HAND

14
COMPETITIVE BID

DESTRUCTIVE BID
GRAND SLAM FORCE
REBIDDABLE SUIT

15
CONSTRUCTIVE BID
DUPLICATE BRIDGE
INVITATIONAL BID
PLAYING STRENGTH
THREE-SUITED HAND

16+
CONTESTED AUCTION
MIRROR DISTRIBUTION
NEGATIVE RESPONSE
PHANTOM SACRIFICE
POSITIVE RESPONSE
SINGLE SUITED HAND

POKER HANDS

ROYAL FLUSH
STRAIGHT FLUSH
FOUR OF A KIND

FULL HOUSE
FLUSH
STRAIGHT

THREE OF A KIND
TWO PAIRS
ONE PAIR

DANCES

3
DOG
GIG
JIG
OLE

4
AHIR
BUMP
CANA
HAKA
HORA
JIVE
JOTA
POGO
SHAG
VIRA

5
BARIS
BULBA
CAROL
CEROC
CONGA
CUECA
DANSA
DEBKA

GAVOT
GIGUE
GOPAK
HALOA
HOPAK
KUMMI
L'AG-YA
LIMBO
LOURE
MAMBO
NAZUN
NUMBA
OKINA
POLKA
RUEDA
RUMBA
SALSA
SAMBA
SARBA
SHAKE
SIBEL
SIBYL
STOMP
TANGO
TRATA
TWIST

VELAL
WALTZ

6
ABUANG
AMENER
ATINGA
BATUTA
BOLERO
BOOGIE
CALATA
CANARY
CAN-CAN
CAROLE
CEBELL
CHA CHA
DJOGED
EIXIDA
GANGAR
GIENYS
HUSTLE
JACARA
JARABE
JARANA
KAGURA
KALELA

MINUET
PAVANE
PESSAH
POLSKA
SHIMMY
TIRANA
VALETA
VELETA
YUMARI

7
ABRASAX
ABRAXAS
AHIDOUS
APARIMA
ARNAOUT
BABORÁK
BALL PLA
BAMBUCO
BANJARA
BATUQUE
BHARANG
BOURRÉE
CANARIE
CANARIO
CARIOCA

CINQ PAS
CSARDAS
FORLANA
FOX-TROT
FURIANT
FURLANA
GAVOTTE
GERANOS
GLOCSEN
GOMBEYS
GONDHAL
GOSHIKI
HIMINAU
JABADAO
LAMENTO
LANCERS
LANDLER
LLORONA
MADISON
MAYPOLE
MAZURKA
MEASURE
MILONGA
MUNEIRA
PASILLO
PERICON
PLANXTY
PURPURI
SARDANA
SATACEK
SIKINIK
TANDAVA
TANTARA
TRAIPSE
WAKAMBA

8
ALEGRIAS
Ã MOLESON
AURRESKU
BALZTANZ
BULL-FOOT
CACHUCHA

CAKEWALK
CANACUAS
CANDIOTE
CHARRADA
COURANTE
FANDANGO
GALLIARD
GYMNASKA
HABANERA
HAND JIVE
HORNPIPE
HUAPANGO
MAILEHEN
MOHOBELO
MOONWALK
MUTCHICO
OXDANSEN
PERICOTE
RIGAUDON
RUTUBURI
TSAMIKOS

9
BAGUETTES
BAILECITO
BARN DANCE
BOULANGER
CARDADORA
CLOG DANCE
COTILLION
ECOSSAISE
FARANDOLE
GALLEGADA
HAJDUTÂNC
HORN DANCE
JITTERBUG
KOLOMEJKA
MISTLETOE
MOKOROTLO
PASO DOBLE
PASSEPIED
POLONAISE
QUADRILLE

QUICKSTEP
RENNINGEN
ROCK 'N' ROLL
SARABANDE
SATECKOVA
TAMBORITO
TROYANATS

10
ATNUMOKITA
BANDLTANTZ
BATON DANCE
BERGERETTA
CHANIOTIKO
CHARLESTON
ESPRINGALE
FACKELTANZ
FARANDOULO
FURRY DANCE
GAY GORDONS
HOKEY-COKEY
KYNDELDANS
LAUTERBACH
LOCOMOTION
RUNNING SET
STRATHSPEY
STRIP TEASE
SURUVAKARY
TARANTELLA
TRENCHMORE
TURKEY TROT

11
BABORASCHKA
BLACKBOTTOM
DANSURINGUR
DITHYRAMBOS
FLORAL DANCE
GHARBA DANCE
LAMBETH WALK
LINE DANCING
MORRIS DANCE
PALAIS GLIDE

PAMPERRUQUE
ROCK AND ROLL
SCHOTTISCHE
SQUARE DANCE
TEWRDANNCKH

12
BREAKDANCING
CREUX DE VERVI
DAMHSA NAM BOC
DANSE MACABRE
FUNKY CHICKEN
GREEN GARTERS
REEL O'TULLOCH

13
EIGHTSOME REEL
GHILLIE CALLUM
HIGHLAND FLING

14
BABBITY
  BOWSTER
COUNTRY
  BUMPKIN
MILKMAIDS'
  DANCE
STRIP THE
  WILLOW

15
MILITARY TWO-
  STEP
SELLINGER'S
  ROUND

17
HASTE TO THE
  WEDDING

18
SIR ROGER DE
  COVERLEY

YOGA POSES

3
BOW
CAT
COW

4
BOAT
CROW
EASY
FISH
FROG
GATE
HERO

LION
TREE

5
CAMEL
CHAIR
COBRA
PLANK
STAFF
WHEEL

6
BRIDGE

CHILD'S
CORPSE
LOCUST
MONKEY
PIGEON
PLOUGH
SPHINX

7
COW FACE
DOLPHIN
GARLAND
PERFECT

8
HALF MOON
LOW LUNGE
LOW PLANK
MOUNTAIN
KNEELING
TRIANGLE
WARRIOR I

9
CROCODILE
HAPPY BABY
HANDSTAND

HIGH LUNGE
SIDE PLANK
WARRIOR II

10
BOUND ANGLE
HEAD-TO-KNEE
WARRIOR III

11
GRASSHOPPER

12
ACCOMPLISHED

13
EXTENDED PUPPY
HAND-BALANCING
LEGS-UP-THE-WALL
LOTUS POSITION
PRAYING MANTIS
RECLINING HERO
SHOULDER STAND

14
SALUTATION SEAL
LORD OF THE DANCE

15
BHARADVAJA'S TWIST
CONQUEROR BREATH
UPWARD FACING DOG

16
REVOLVED TRIANGLE

17
DOWNWARD FACING DOG
EXTENDED SIDE ANGLE
SEATED FORWARD BEND

18
INTENSE SIDE STRETCH

19
HALF LORD OF THE FISHES
RECLINING BOUND
  ANGLE

STANDING FORWARD
  BEND

20
WALL-ASSISTED
  HANDSTAND

21
WIDE-LEGGED FORWARD
  BEND

23
STANDING HALF FORWARD
  BEND

24
WALL-ASSISTED
  FOREARMSTAND

26
HIGH LUNGE CRESCENT
  VARIATION
WIDE-ANGLE SEATED FORWARD
  BEND

CRAFTS AND HOBBIES

3
DIY

5
BATIK
BINGO

6
BONSAI
SEWING

7
COLLAGE
COOKERY
CROCHET
KEEP FIT
MACRAMÉ
MOSAICS
ORIGAMI
POTTERY
READING
TATTING
TOPIARY
WEAVING

8
AEROBICS
APPLIQUÉ
BASKETRY
CANEWORK
FRETWORK
KNITTING
LAPIDARY

PAINTING
QUILTING
SPINNING
TAPESTRY
WOODWORK

9
ASTROLOGY
ASTRONOMY
DÉCOUPAGE
GARDENING
GENEALOGY
MARQUETRY
PALMISTRY
PATCHWORK
PHILATELY
RUG MAKING

10
BEE-KEEPING
BEER MAKING
CROSSWORDS
EMBROIDERY
ENAMELLING
KITE FLYING
LACE MAKING
UPHOLSTERY
WINE MAKING

11
ARCHAEOLOGY
BARK RUBBING
BOOK BINDING

CALLIGRAPHY
DRESS MAKING
HANG GLIDING
LEPIDOPTERY
MODEL MAKING
PHOTOGRAPHY
STENCILLING
VINTAGE CARS

12
BEACH COMBING
BIRD WATCHING
BRASS RUBBING
CANDLE-MAKING
FLOWER DRYING
TROPICAL FISH

13
FOSSIL HUNTING
JIGSAW PUZZLES
MODEL RAILWAYS
TRAIN SPOTTING

14
BADGER WATCHING
CAKE DECORATING
COIN COLLECTING
FLOWER PRESSING
GLASS ENGRAVING
PIGEON FANCYING

15
FLOWER ARRANGING

LAMPSHADE MAKING	**16**	**19**
SHELL COLLECTING	AMATEUR DRAMATICS	BUTTERFLY
STAMP COLLECTING	AUTOGRAPH HUNTING	COLLECTING

GAMES POSITIONS

3
END

4
POST
PROP
SLIP
WING

5
GUARD
GULLY
MID-ON
PIVOT

6
ATTACK
BATTER
BOWLER
CENTER
CENTRE
HOOKER
LONG ON
MID-OFF
SAFETY
TACKLE

7
BATSMAN
CATCHER
DEFENCE
FIELDER
FORWARD
LEG SLIP

LONG LEG
LONG OFF
OFFENSE
PITCHER
STRIKER
SWEEPER

8
FULLBACK
HALFBACK
LEFT BACK
LEFT HALF
LEFT WING
MIDFIELD
SPLIT END
TAILBACK
THIRD MAN
TIGHT END
WINGBACK

9
INFIELDER
MID WICKET
NOSE GUARD
NUMBER ONE
NUMBER TWO
RIGHT BACK
RIGHT HALF
RIGHT WING
SCRUM HALF
SHORTSTOP
SQUARE LEG

10

CENTRE BACK
CENTRE HALF
CORNERBACK
COVER POINT
EXTRA COVER
GOAL ATTACK
GOALKEEPER
INSIDE LEFT
LINEBACKER
NUMBER FOUR
OUTFIELDER
SILLY MID-ON
WING ATTACK

11
DEEP FINE LEG
FLANKER BACK
GOAL DEFENCE
GOAL SHOOTER
INSIDE RIGHT
LEFT FIELDER
LEFT FORWARD
NUMBER THREE
OUTSIDE LEFT
QUARTERBACK
RUNNING BACK
SILLY MID-OFF
WING DEFENCE
WING FORWARD

12
FIRST BASEMAN
OUTSIDE RIGHT

LEFT-WING BACK
RIGHT FIELDER
RIGHT FORWARD
SHORT FINE LEG
STAND OFF HALF
THIRD BASEMAN
THREE-QUARTER
WICKETKEEPER
WIDE RECEIVER

13
CENTRE FIELDER
CENTRE FORWARD
POPPING CREASE
RIGHT-WING BACK
SECOND BASEMAN

14
LEFT-CENTRE BACK
LEFT DEFENSEMAN
SHORT SQUARE LEG

15+
FORWARD SHORT
 LEG
LEFT-WING
 FORWARD
RIGHT-CENTRE
 BACK
RIGHT
 DEFENSEMAN
RIGHT-WING
 FORWARD

STADIUMS AND VENUES

ADELAIDE OVAL
 (cricket)
AINTREE (horse
 racing)
ANAHEIM STADIUM,
 CALIFORNIA
 (baseball)
ASCOT (horse racing)
AVIVA STADIUM (rugby
 union)
AZTECA STADIUM,
 MEXICO CITY

(football)
BELFRY, THE (golf)
BELMONT PARK, LONG
 ISLAND (horse
 racing)
BIG FOUR CURLING
 RINK (curling)
BILLY JEAN KING
 NATIONAL TENNIS
 CENTER (tennis)
BRANDS HATCH (motor
 racing)

CAMP NOU,
 BARCELONA
 (football)
CARDIFF ARMS PARK
 (rugby union)
CHELTENHAM (horse
 racing)
CIRCUIT OF SPA-
 FRANCORCHAMPS,
 BELGIUM (motor
 racing)
CROKE PARK, DUBLIN

(Gaelic football,
 hurling)
CRUCIBLE THEATRE,
 SHEFFIELD
 (snooker)
CRYSTAL PALACE
 NATIONAL SPORTS
 CENTRE (athletics)
DAYTONA
 INTERNATIONAL
 SPEEDWAY (motor
 racing, motor cycling)

EDEN GARDENS, KOLKATA (cricket)
EDEN PARK (cricket)
EDGBASTON (cricket)
ELLIS PARK STADIUM (cricket)
EMIRATES ARENA (multi sports)
EMS STADIUM, KOZHIKODE (football)
EPSOM DOWNS (horse racing)
FORUM, THE, CALIFORNIA (multi sports)
GADDAFI STADIUM, LAHORE (cricket)
GELORA BUNG KARNO MAIN STADIUM, JAKARTA (cricket)
HAMPDEN PARK, GLASGOW (football)
HEADINGLEY (cricket)
HUNGARORING (motor racing)
INTERLAGOS (motor racing)
KING BAUDOUIN STADIUM, BRUSSELS (football)
LORDS CRICKET GROUND (cricket)
LUZHNIKI STADIUM, MOSCOW (football)
MADISON SQUARE GARDENS, NEW YORK (multi sports)
MARACANA STADIUM, BRAZIL (football)
MEADOWBANK (athletics)
MELBOURNE CRICKET GROUND (cricket)
MELBOURNE PARK (tennis)
MEMORIAL COLISEUM, LOS ANGELES (most sports)
MERCEDES-BENZ SUPERDOME (most sports)
MGM GRAND GARDEN ARENA, LAS VEGAS (boxing)
MONZA (motor racing)

MOOR PARK, RICKMANSWORTH (golf)
MUNICH OLYMPIC STADIUM (athletics, football)
MURRAYFIELD (rugby union)
NATIONAL SPORTS COMPLEX OLIMPIYSKIY, KIEV (multi sports)
NEWMARKET (horse racing)
ODSAL STADIUM, BRADFORD (rugby league)
OLD TRAFFORD (cricket)
OVAL, THE (cricket)
PRINCIPALITY STADIUM (rugby union, football)
QUEEN'S PARK OVAL (cricket)
ST ANDREWS (golf)
SANTIAGO BERNABEU STADIUM, MADRID (football)
SHANGHAI STADIUM (football)
SILVERSTONE (motor racing)
STADE DE FRANCE (rugby union)
STADE ROLAND GARROS (tennis)
STADE OLIMPICO (football)
STAHOV STADIUM, PRAGUE (gymnastics)
SUZUKA (motor racing)
TRENT BRIDGE (cricket)
TWICKENHAM (rugby union)
WEMBLEY STADIUM (football, rugby)
WIMBLEDON (tennis)
WINDSOR PARK, BELFAST (football)
YAS MARINA (motor racing)

TROPHIES, EVENTS, AND AWARDS

AFRICA CUP OF NATIONS (football)
ALL-IRELAND SENIOR FOOTBALL CHAMPIONSHIPS (Gaelic football)
ALL-IRELAND SENIOR HURLING CHAMPIONSHIP (hurling)
ALPINE WORLD SKI CHAMPIONSHIPS (skiing)
AMERICA'S CUP (sailing)
ASHES (cricket)
BADMINTON HORSE TRIALS (equestrian)
BBC SPORTS PERSONALITY OF THE YEAR (all-round)
BOAT RACE (rowing)
BRITISH CHAMPIONSHIP (most sports)
BRITISH OPEN CHAMPIONSHIP (golf)
BRONZE MEDAL (most sports)
CAMANACHD ASSOCIATION CHALLENGE CUP (shinty)
CHELTENHAM GOLD CUP (horse racing)
CLASSICS (horse racing)
COMMONWEALTH GAMES (athletics)
COPA AMERICA (football)
DAVIS CUP (tennis)
DAYTONA 500 (motor racing)
DECATHLON (athletics)
DERBY (horse racing)
ENGLISH GREYHOUND DERBY (greyhound racing)
EUROPEAN CHAMPION CLUBS CUP (football)
EUROPEAN CHAMPIONS CUP (basketball)
EUROPEAN CHAMPIONSHIP (football)

EUROPEAN CUP WINNERS' CUP (football)
EUROPEAN FOOTBALLER OF THE YEAR (football)
EUROPEAN SUPER CUP (football)
FEDERATION CUP (tennis)
FIFA CLUB WORLD CUP (football)
FIFA WORLD CUP TROPHY (football)
FIS NORDIC WORLD SKI CHAMPIONSHIP (skiing)
FOOTBALL ASSOCIATION CHALLENGE CUP (football)
FOOTBALL ASSOCIATION COMMUNITY SHIELD (football)
FOOTBALL LEAGUE CHAMPIONSHIP (football)
FOOTBALL LEAGUE CUP (football)
FULL CAP (football, rugby)
FWA FOOTBALLER OF THE YEAR (football)
GOLDEN BOOT AWARD (football)
GOLD MEDAL (most sports)
GORDON INTERNATIONAL MEDAL (curling)
GRAND NATIONAL (greyhound racing)
GRAND NATIONAL STEEPLECHASE (horse racing)
GRAND PRIX (motor racing)
HARMSWORTH TROPHY (power boat racing)
HENLEY REGATTA (rowing)
HENRI DELANEY TROPHY (football)
HIGHLAND GAMES (athletics)
IAAF CROSS-COUNTRY CHAMPIONSHIP (athletics)
ICY SMITH CUP (ice hockey)
INDIANAPOLIS 500 (motor racing)

INTERNATIONAL CHAMPIONSHIP (bowls)
ISLE OF MAN TT (motorcycle racing)
JUBILEE TROPHY (tiddlywinks)
KING GEORGE V GOLD CUP (equestrian)
KINNAIRD CUP (fives)
LE MANS 24 HOUR (motor racing)
LOMBARD RALLY (motor rallying)
LONSDALE BELT (boxing)
MACROBERTSON INTERNATIONAL SHIELD
  (croquet)
MAN OF THE MATCH (football)
MARATHON (athletics)
MONTE CARLO RALLY (motor rallying)
MOST VALUABLE PLAYER (American football)
MOTO GP WORLD CHAMPIONSHIP (motorcycle
  racing)
NATIONAL ANGLING CHAMPIONSHIP (angling)
NATIONAL HUNT JOCKEY CHAMPIONSHIP (horse
  racing)
OAKS (horse racing)
OLYMPIC GAMES (most sports)
ONE THOUSAND GUINEAS (horse racing)
OPEN CROQUET CHAMPIONSHIP (croquet)
OXFORD BLUE (most sports)
PALIO DI SIENA (horse racing)
PENTATHLON (athletics)
PFA FOOTBALLER OF THE YEAR (football)
QUEEN ELIZABETH II CUP (equestrian)
RAC TOURIST TROPHY (motor racing)
ROSE BOWL (American football)
ROYAL HUNT CUP (horse racing)
RUGBY LEAGUE CHALLENGE CUP (rugby league)
RUNNERS-UP MEDAL (most sports)
RYDER CUP (golf)

SCOTTISH FOOTBALL ASSOCIATION CUP (football)
SILVER MEDAL (most sports)
SIX NATIONS CHAMPIONSHIP (rugby union)
STANLEY CUP (ice hockey)
ST LEGER (horse racing)
STRATHCONA CUP (curling)
SUPER BOWL (American football)
SUPER CUP (handball)
SWAYTHLING CUP (table tennis)
THOMAS CUP (badminton)
TOUR DE FRANCE (cycling)
TRIPLE CROWN (rugby union)
TWO THOUSAND GUINEAS (horse racing)
UBER CUP (badminton)
UEFA CHAMPIONS LEAGUE (Union of European
  Football Associations) (football)
VINCE LOMBARDI TROPHY (American football)
WALKER CUP (golf)
WIGHTMAN CUP (sailing)
WIMBLEDON (tennis)
WINGFIELD SCULLS (rowing)
WINNERS MEDAL (most sports)
WOODEN SPOON (! most sports)
WORLD INDOOR BOWLS CROWN (bowls)
WORLD JUNIOR CHAMPIONSHIPS (curling)
WORLD LACROSSE CHAMPIONSHIPS (lacrosse)
WORLD MASTERS (darts)
WORLD PROFESSIONAL SNOOKER CHAMPIONSHIP
  (snooker)
WORLD SERIES (baseball)
YELLOW JERSEY (cycling)

OLYMPIC GAMES

4
GOLF
JUDO
LUGE

5
RUGBY

6
BOXING
DIVING
HOCKEY
ROWING
TENNIS

7
ARCHERY
CURLING
FENCING
SAILING

8
BIATHLON

FOOTBALL
HANDBALL
SKELETON
SHOOTING
SWIMMING

9
ATHLETICS
BADMINTON
BOBSLEIGH
ICE HOCKEY
SNOWBOARD
TAEKWONDO
TRIATHLON
WATER POLO

10
BASKETBALL
CYCLING BMX
SHORT TRACK
SKI JUMPING
TRAMPOLINE

VOLLEYBALL

11
CANOE SLALOM
CANOE SPRINT
CYCLING ROAD
TABLE TENNIS

12
ALPINE SKIING
CYCLING TRACK
SPEED SKATING

13
FIGURE SKATING
WEIGHTLIFTING

14
NORDIC COMBINED

15
BEACH VOLLEYBALL
FREESTYLE SKIING

16
ARTISTIC SWIMMING
MARATHON SWIMMING
MODERN PENTATHLON

17
EQUESTRIAN JUMPING
GYMNASTIC ARTISTIC
GYMNASTIC RHYTHMIC

18
CROSS COUNTRY
  SKIING
EQUESTRIAN DRESSAGE
EQUESTRIAN EVENTING
WRESTLING FREESTYLE

19
CYCLING MOUNTAIN
  BIKE
WRESTLING GRECO-
  ROMAN

FIRST CLASS CRICKETING COUNTIES

DERBYSHIRE	HAMPSHIRE	NORTHAMPTONSHIRE	SUSSEX
DURHAM	KENT	NOTTINGHAMSHIRE	WARWICKSHIRE
ESSEX	LANCASHIRE	SOMERSET	WORCESTERSHIRE
GLAMORGAN	LEICESTERSHIRE	SURREY	YORKSHIRE
GLOUCESTERSHIRE	MIDDLESEX		

CRICKETING TERMS AND EXPRESSIONS

3
BAT
BYE
CUT
LBW
RUN
TON

4
BAIL
DUCK
HOOK
OVER
WIDE

5
BOSIE
COVER
GULLY
MID-ON
POINT
SWEEP

6
BEAMER
BOWLED
BOWLER
CAUGHT
CREASE
GOOGLY
HOWZAT!

LEG BYE
LONG ON
MAIDEN
MID-OFF
NO-BALL
RUN OUT
SCORER
SEAMER
UMPIRE
WICKET
YORKER

7
BATSMAN
BOUNCER
CENTURY
COW-SHOT
FIELDER
FINE LEG
FLIPPER
INNINGS
LATE CUT
LEG SLIP
LEG SPIN
LONG HOP
LONG LEG
LONG OFF
OFF SPIN
SHOOTER

STRIKER
STUMPED

8
BOUNDARY
CHINAMAN
HAT-TRICK
HOW'S THAT!
LONGSTOP
SHORT LEG
THE SLIPS
THIRD MAN
TWENTY20

9
BATSWOMAN
HIT WICKET
IN-SWINGER
LEG GLANCE
MID-WICKET
OVERTHROW
SQUARE CUT
SQUARE LEG
STICKY DOG
TEST MATCH
THE COVERS

10
ALL-ROUNDER
FAST BOWLER
GOLDEN DUCK

NON-STRIKER
OUT-SWINGER
SIGHT-SCREEN
SILLY MID-ON
SILLY POINT
TOP-SPINNER
TWELFTH MAN

11
DAISY-CUTTER
SILLY MID-OFF

12
RETURN CREASE
REVERSE SWEEP
STICKY WICKET
STONEWALLING
WICKETKEEPER

13
BATTING CREASE
DEEP SQUARE LEG
NIGHTWATCHMAN
POPPING CREASE

14+
BODY-LINE BOWLING
LEG BEFORE WICKET
LEG-SIDE FIELDER
LEG-THEORY BOWLING
OFFSIDE FIELDER

MAJOR RUGBY UNION CLUBS

3
AYR
GHK
UCD
UCC

4
BATH
CORK
GALA

HULL
NAAS
SALE

5
ESHER
FLYDE
NEATH
WASPS

6
BEDWAS
CURRIE
EALING
EXETER
HAWICK
MALONE

7
BARGOED

BEDFORD
BLAYDON
BRISTOL
CARDIFF
MELROSE
MERTHYR
MOSELEY
NEWPORT
SHANNON
SWANSEA

8
ABERAVON
AMPTHILL
BRIDGEND
COVENTRY
EBBW VALE
LLANELLI
PLYMOUTH
RICHMOND
SARACENS
STIRLING

9
BALLYMENA
BANBRIDGE
CAMBRIDGE
DONCASTER
EDINBURGH
GARRYOWEN
HERIOT'S FP
LANDSDOWE
LEICESTER
NEWCASTLE
OLD WESLEY
ROTHERHAM
WORCESTER

10
BARBARIANS
BLACKHEATH
GLOUCESTER
HARLEQUINS
JERSEY REDS
NOTTINGHAM
PONTYPRIDD
SALE SHARKS
WATSONIANS

11
BOROUGHMUIR
BRISTOL BEARS
HULL IONIANS
LONDON IRISH
LONDON WELSH
NORTHAMPTON
ROSSLYN PARK

12
BEDFORD BLUES
EXETER CHIEFS
OLD BELVEDERE
YOUNG MUNSTER

14
BRIDGEND RAVENS
CORNISH PIRATES
GLASGOW HAWKS
LONDON SCOTTISH
PLYMOUTH ALBION
STIRLING COUNTY

15
CARMARTHEN QUINS
HARTPURY COLLEGE
LEICESTER TIGERS
ROTHERHAM TITANS
TERENURE COLLEGE

16+
BLACKROCK COLLEGE
CORK CONSTITUTION
DONCASTER KNIGHTS
EALING TRAILFINDERS
EDINBURGH ACADEMICALS
NEWCASTLE FALCONS
NORTHAMPTON SAINTS
WORCESTER WARRIORS
YORKSHIRE CARNEGIE

RUGBY LEAGUE CLUBS

4
HULL
YORK

5
LEEDS
LEIGH
WIGAN

6
BATLEY
HULL FC
OLDHAM
WIDNES

7
HALIFAX
HUNSLET
SALFORD
SWINTON

8
BRADFORD
COVENTRY
DEWSBURY
KEIGHLEY
ROCHDALE

ST HELENS

9
DONCASTER
NEWCASTLE
SHEFFIELD
WAKEFIELD

10
CASTLEFORD
WARRINGTON
WHITEHAVEN

11
LEEDS RHINOS

12
DEWSBURY RAMS
HUDDERSFIELD
SWINTON LIONS

13
BARROW RAIDERS
BRADFORD BULLS
COVENTRY BEARS
LONDON BRONCOS
LONDON SKOLARS
WIDNES VIKINGS

WIGAN WARRIORS

14
WORKINGTON TOWN

15+
BARROW-IN-FURNESS
BATLEY BULLDOGS
CASTLEFORD TIGERS
CATALAN DRAGONS
FEATHERSTONE ROVERS
HUDDERSFIELD GIANTS
HULL KINGSTON ROVERS
KEIGHLEY COUGARS
LEIGH CENTURIONS
NEWCASTLE THUNDER
NORTH WALES CRUSADERS
PARIS SAINT GERMAIN
ROCHDALE HORNETS
SALFORD RED DEVILS
SHEFFIELD EAGLES
TORONTO WOLFPACK
TOULOUSE OLYMPIQUE
WAKEFIELD TRINITY
WARRINGTON WOLVES
WEST WALES RAIDERS
YORK CITY KNIGHTS

BRITISH FOOTBALL TEAMS

TEAM	GROUND	NICKNAME
ABERDEEN	PITTODRIE STADIUM	DONS
ACCRINGTON STANLEY	CROWN GROUND	STANLEY
AFC WIMBLEDON	KINGSMEADOW	DONS; WOMBLES
ARSENAL	EMIRATES STADIUM	GUNNERS
ASTON VILLA	VILLA PARK	VILLANS
BARNSLEY	OAKWELL GROUND	TYKES; REDS; COLLIERS
BIRMINGHAM CITY	ST ANDREWS	BLUES
BLACKBURN ROVERS	EWOOD PARK	BLUE & WHITES; ROVERS
BLACKPOOL	BLOOMFIELD ROAD	SEASIDERS, TANGERINES
BOLTON WANDERERS	UNIVERSITY OF BOLTON STADIUM	TROTTERS
BOURNEMOUTH	VITALITY STADIUM	CHERRIES
BRADFORD CITY	VALLEY PARADE	BANTAMS
BRENTFORD	GRIFFIN PARK	BEES
BRIGHTON & HOVE ALBION	FALMER STADIUM	SEAGULLS
BRISTOL CITY	ASHTON GATE	ROBINS
BRISTOL ROVERS	MEMORIAL STADIUM	PIRATES
BURNLEY	TURF MOOR	CLARETS
BURTON ALBION	PIRELLI STADIUM	BREWERS
CARDIFF CITY	CARDIFF CITY STADIUM	BLUEBIRDS
CELTIC	CELTIC PARK	BHOYS
CHARLTON ATHLETIC	THE VALLEY	ADDICKS; ROBINS; VALIANTS
CHELSEA	STAMFORD BRIDGE	BLUES
COVENTRY CITY	RICOH ARENA	SKY BLUES
CRYSTAL PALACE	SELHURST PARK	EAGLES
DERBY COUNTY	PRIDE PARK STADIUM	RAMS
DONCASTER ROVERS	KEEPMOAT STADIUM	ROVERS
DUNDEE FC	DENS PARK	DARK BLUES
EVERTON	GOODISON PARK	TOFFEES
FLETTWOOD TOWN	HIGHBURY STADIUM	FISHERMEN
FULHAM	CRAVEN COTTAGE	COTTAGERS
GILLINGHAM	PRIESTFIELD STADIUM	GILLS
HAMILTON ACADEMICAL	NEW DOUGLAS PARK	ACCIES
HEART OF MIDLOTHIAN	TYNECASTLE STADIUM	HEARTS
HIBERNIAN	EASTER ROAD	HIBEES
HUDDERSFIELD TOWN	KIRKLEES STADIUM	TERRIERS
HULL CITY	KCOM STADIUM	TIGERS
IPSWICH TOWN	PORTMAN ROAD	BLUES; TRACTOR BOYS
KILMARNOCK	RUGBY PARK	KILLIE
LEEDS UNITED	ELLAND ROAD	UNITED
LEICESTER CITY	KING POWER STADIUM	FILBERTS; FOXES
LIVERPOOL	ANFIELD	REDS; POOL
LIVINGSTON	ALMONDVALE STADIUM	LIONS
LUTON TOWN	KENILWORTH ROAD	HATTERS
MANCHESTER CITY	ETIHAD STADIUM	BLUES
MANCHESTER UNITED	OLD TRAFFORD	RED DEVILS
MIDDLESBROUGH	RIVERSIDE STADIUM	BORO
MILLWALL	THE DEN	LIONS
MOTHERWELL	FIR PARK	WELL
NEWCASTLE UNITED	ST JAMES' PARK	MAGPIES
NORWICH CITY	CARROW ROAD	CANARIES
NOTTINGHAM FOREST	CITY GROUND	REDS; FOREST
OXFORD UNITED	KASSAM STADIUM	U'S
PETERBOROUGH UNITED	LONDON ROAD	POSH
PLYMOUTH ARGYLE	HOME PARK	PILGRIMS
PORTSMOUTH	FRATTON PARK	POMPEY
PRESTON NORTH END	DEEPDALE	LILYWHITES; NORTH END
QUEEN'S PARK RANGERS	LOFTUS ROAD	RANGERS; R'S
RANGERS	IBROX STADIUM	GERS
READING	MADEJSKI STADIUM	ROYALS
ROCHDALE	SPOTLAND	DALE

ROTHERHAM UNITED	NEW YORK STADIUM	MILLERS
SCUNTHORPE UNITED	GLANFORD PARK	IRON
SHEFFIELD UNITED	BRAMWELL LANE	BLADES
SHEFFIELD WEDNESDAY	HILLSBOROUGH	OWLS
SHREWSBURY TOWN	NEW MEADOW	SALOP
SOUTHAMPTON	ST MARYS STADIUM	SAINTS
SOUTHEND UNITED	ROOTS HALL	SHRIMPERS
ST JOHNSTONE	McDIARMID PARK	SAINTS
ST MIRREN	ST MIRREN PARK	BUDDIES; PAISLEY SAINTS
STOKE CITY	BET365 STADIUM	POTTERS
STRANRAER	STAIR PARK	BLUES
SUNDERLAND	STADIUM OF LIGHT	BLACK CATS
SWANSEA CITY	LIBERTY STADIUM	SWANS
TOTTENHAM HOTSPUR	TOTTENHAM HOTSPUR STADIUM	SPURS
WALSALL	BESCOT STADIUM	SADDLERS
WATFORD	VICARAGE ROAD	HORNETS
WEST BROMWICH ALBION	HAWTHORNS	THROSTLES; BAGGIES; ALBION
WEST HAM UNITED	LONDON STADIUM	HAMMERS
WIGAN ATHLETIC	DW STADIUM	LATICS
WOLVERHAMPTON	MOLINEUX	WOLVES WANDERERS
WYCOMBE WANDERERS	ADAMS PARK	CHAIRBOYS

EUROPEAN FOOTBALL CLUBS

AUSTRIA

RAPID VIENNA

BELGIUM

FC BRUGES
KAA GENT
KV MECHELEN
ROYAL ANTWERP
STANDARD LIEGE
SV ZULTE WAREGEM

CROATIA

HAJDUK SPLIT

CZECH REPUBLIC

SLAVIA PRAGUE
SPARTA PRAGUE

DENMARK

BRONDBY
FC COPENHAGEN

FRANCE

AUXERRE
BASTIA
BORDEAUX
DIJON EVIAN
LE HAVRE
LILLE
LYONS
MARSEILLES
METZ
MONACO
NANTES

NICE
PARIS SAINT GERMAIN
STRASBOURG

GERMANY

BAYER LEVERKUSEN
BAYERN MUNICH
BORUSSIA
    MÖNCHENGLADBACH
DUISBURG
FC AUGSBURG
FC KAISERSLAUTERN
FC KÖLN
FC NUREMBERG
FC MAINZ
HAMBURGER SV
HERTHA BSC
1899 HOFFENHEIM
KARLSRUHE
MUNICH
SC FREIBURG
SCHALKE 04
WERDER BREMEN
VFB STUTTGART

GREECE

AEK ATHENS
OLYMPIAKOS
PANATHINAIKOS

ITALY

AC MILAN
AS ROMA
BOLOGNA
CAGLIARI

FIORENTINA
INTER MILAN
INTERNAZIONALE
JUVENTUS
LAZIO
NAPOLI
PARMA
SAMPDORIA
VERONA
VICENZA

NETHERLANDS

AJAX
FC TWENTE
FC VOLENDAM
FEYENOORD
PSV EINDHOVEN
RKC WAALWIJK
UTRECHT
VITESSE ARNHEM

PORTUGAL

AMADORA
BELENENSES
BENFICA
BOAVISTA
BRAGA
FARENSE
FC PORTO
GUIMARAES
SETUBAL
SPORTING LISBON

SPAIN

ATHLETIC BILBAO

ATLÉTICO MADRID
BARCELONA
ESPAÑOL
REAL MADRID
REAL SOCIEDAO
REAL ZARAGOZA
SEVILLA
SPORTING GIJÓN
VALENCIA

POLAND

LEGIA WARSAW
POLONIA WARSZAWA
SCASKWROCLAW

ROMANIA

CFR 1907 CLUJ
DINAMO BUCURESTI
RAPID BUCURESTI

RUSSIA

CSKA MOSCOW
DINAMO MOSCOW
SPARTAK MOSCOW

SWEDEN

ZENIT ST PETERSBURG
AIK STOCKHOLM
HELSINGBORGS IF
IF ELFSBORG
IFK GOTHENBURG

UKRAINE

DYNAMO KYIV

AMERICAN FOOTBALL TEAMS

ARIZONA CARDINALS
ATLANTA FALCONS
BALTIMORE RAVENS
BUFFALO BILLS
CAROLINA PANTHERS
CHICAGO BEARS
CINCINNATI BENGALS
CLEVELAND BROWNS
DALLAS COWBOYS
DENVER BRONCOS

DETROIT LIONS
GREEN BAY PACKERS
HOUSTON TEXANS
INDIANAPOLIS COLTS
JACKSONVILLE
  JAGUARS
KANSAS CITY CHIEFS
LOS ANGELES
  CHARGERS
LOS ANGELES RAMS

MIAMI DOLPHINS
MINNESOTA VIKINGS
NEW ENGLAND
  PATRIOTS
NEW ORLEANS SAINTS
NEW YORK GIANTS
NEW YORK JETS
OAKLAND RAIDERS
PHILADELPHIA
  EAGLES

PITTSBURGH
  STEELERS
SAN FRANCISCO 49ERS
SEATTLE SEAHAWKS
TAMPA BAY
  BUCCANEERS
TENNESSEE
  TITANS
WASHINGTON
  REDSKINS

AMERICAN BASEBALL TEAMS

ARIZONA DIAMOND
  BACKS
ATLANTA BRAVES
BALTIMORE ORIOLES
BOSTON RED SOX
CHICAGO CUBS
CHICAGO WHITE SOX
CINCINNATI REDS
CLEVELAND INDIANS

COLORADO ROCKIES
DETROIT TIGERS
HOUSTON ASTROS
KANSAS CITY ROYALS
LOS ANGELES ANGELS
LOS ANGELES
  DODGERS
MIAMI MARLINS
MILWAUKEE

BREWERS
MINNESOTA TWINS
NEW YORK METS
NEW YORK YANKEES
OAKLAND ATHLETICS
PHILADELPHIA
  PHILLIES
PITTSBURGH PIRATES
ST LOUIS CARDINALS

SAN DIEGO PADRES
SAN FRANCISCO
  GIANTS
SEATTLE MARINERS
TAMPA BAY RAYS
TEXAS RANGERS
TORONTO BLUE JAYS
WASHINGTON
  NATIONALS

F1 GRAND PRIX CIRCUITS

Grand Prix	Circuit		
ABU DHABI	Yas Marina	CHINESE	Shangai
ARGENTINA	Termas de Rio Hondo	FRENCH	Circuit Paul Ricard
AUSTRALIAN	Melbourne	GERMAN	Hockenheim
AUSTRIAN	Spielberg	HUNGARIAN	Hungaroring
AZERBAIJAN	Baku	ITALIAN	Monza
BAHRAIN	Sakhir	JAPANESE	Suzuka
BELGIAN	Spa-Francorchamps	MEXICAN	Mexico City
BRAZILIAN	Interlagos, São Paulo	MONACO	Monte Carlo
BRITISH	Silverstone	RUSSIAN	Sochi
CANADIAN	Gilles Villeneuve,	SINGAPORE	Marina Bay Street
	Montreal	SPANISH	Catalunya, Barcelona
		UNITED STATES	Austin

GARDENING

GARDENING TERMS	BULB	CROSS	TILTH
	LIME	CROWN	TRUSS
2	LOAM	FORCE	TUBER
PH	NODE	GENUS	
	PEAT	GRAFT	**6**
3	SNAG	HARDY	ALPINE
BUD	SPIT	MULCH	ANNUAL
POT		PRUNE	CLOCHE
	5	SHRUB	CORDON
4	BLIND	SPORT	DIBBER
BOLE	BLOOM	STAKE	FLORET

HYBRID
MANURE
RUNNER
STRAIN
SUCKER

7
COMPOST
CUTTING
FRIABLE
LATERAL
NEUTRAL
PERGOLA
RHIZOME

8
ACID SOIL
AERATION
BIENNIAL
DEAD-HEAD
PINCH OUT
PRICK OUT
SEEDLING
STANDARD

9
BLANCHING
CHLOROSIS
DECIDUOUS
EVERGREEN
FUNGICIDE
HALF HARDY
HEELING-IN
PERENNIAL
ROOTSTOCK
SIDE SHOOT

10
BASAL SHOOT
CALCAREOUS
FERTILIZER
HERBACEOUS
VARIEGATED

11
GERMINATION
INSECTICIDE
POLLINATION
PROPAGATION

12+
ALKALINE SOIL
BASTARD TRENCHING
BEDDING PLANT
HARDENING OFF

GARDENING FLOWERS

4
FLAX
GEUM
IRIS
SAGE

5
AJUGA
ASTER
ASTER
AVENS
BUGLE
DAISY
HOSTA
INULA
LINUM
LUPIN
PANSY
PEONY
PHLOX
PINKS
POPPY
SEDUM
VIOLA

6
BELLIS
BORAGE
CALTHA
CLEOME
COBAEA
COSMEA
COSMOS
DAHLIA
ECHIUM
IBERIS
MALOPE
NEPETA
PAEONY
RESEDA
SALVIA
SPURGE
STOCKS
VIOLET
YARROW
ZINNIA

7
ALKANET
ALTHAEA
ALYSSUM
ANCHUSA
ANEMONE
ARUNCUS
ASTILBE
BEGONIA
BUGBANE
CAMPION
CATMINT
CELOSIA
CLARKIA
DAY LILY
GAZANIA
GODETIA
HONESTY
IPOMOEA
KINGCUP
LIATRIS
LINARIA
LIRIOPE

LOBELIA
LUNARIA
LYCHNIS
LYTHRUM
MILFOIL
MIMULUS
MONARDA
MULLEIN
NEMESIA
NIGELLA
PAPAVER
PETUNIA
PRIMULA
STACHYS
STATICE
TAGETES
URSINIA
VERBENA

8
ACANTHUS
ACHILLEA
ACONITUM
AGERATUM
ARCTOTIS
BARTONIA
BERGAMOT
BERGENIA
BRUNNERA
CLEMATIS
DIANTHUS
DICENTRA
DROPWORT
ECHINOPS
EREMURUS
ERIGERON
ERYNGIUM
FEVERFEW
FLEABANE
FOXGLOVE
GERANIUM
HELENIUM
HEUCHERA
HIBISCUS
KNAPWEED
KNOTWEED
LARKSPUR
LATHYRUS
LAUATERA
LILY TURF
LIMONIUM
LUNGWORT
MACLEAYA
MYOSOTIS
PHACELIA
PHYSALIS
PRIMROSE
PRUNELLA
SCABIOSA
SCABIOUS
SEA HOLLY
SELF-HEAL
SIDALCEA
SOAPWORT

SOLIDAGO
STOKESIA
SUN PLANT
SWEET PEA
TIARELLA
TICKSEED
TOADFLAX
TROLLIUS
VENIDIUM
VERONICA
VISCARIA

9
ANAPHALIS
AQUILEGIA
ASTRANTIA
BIG BETONY
BUTTERCUP
CALENDULA
CAMPANULA
CANDYTUFT
CARNATION
CENTAUREA
COLUMBINE
COREOPSIS
DICTAMNUS
DIGITALIS
DORONICUM
ECHINACEA
EPIMEDIUM
EUPHORBIA
GOLDEN ROD
HELIOPSIS
HOLLYHOCK
IMPATIENS
KNIPHOFIA
LAMB'S EARS
LIGULARIA
MALCOLMIA
MATTHIOLA
MEADOW RUE
MOLUCELLA
MONKSHOOD
NAVELWORT
NEMOPHILA
NICOTIANA
OENOTHERA
PENSTEMON
POLYGONUM
PORTULACA
PYRETHRUM
RODGERSIA
RUDBECKIA
SAPONARIA
SAXIFRAGE
SNAKEROOT
SPEEDWELL
STONECROP
SUNFLOWER
VERBASCUM

10
ACROLINIUM
AGAPANTHUS

AGROSTEMMA
ALCHEMILLA
AMARANTHUS
BARRENWORT
BELLFLOWER
BISHOP'S HAT
BUSY LIZZIE
CATANANCHE
CHINA ASTER
CIMICIFUGA
CINQUEFOIL
CONEFLOWER
CORN COCKLE
CORNFLOWER
CORTADERIA
CUPID'S DART
DELPHINIUM
FOAM FLOWER
GAILLARDIA
GAYFEATHER
GOAT'S BEARD
GYPSOPHILA
HELIANTHUS
HELIOTROPE
HELLEBORUS
INDIAN PINK
KAFFIR LILY
LENTEN ROSE
LIMNANTHES
LYSIMACHIA
MASTERWORT
MATRICARIA
MECONOPSIS
MIGNONETTE
NASTURTIUM
OMPHALODES
PLATYCODON
PLUME POPPY
POLEMONIUM
POTENTILLA
PULMONARIA
RANUNCULUS
SNAPDRAGON
SNEEZEWORT
SPIDERWORT
THALICTRUM
THUNBERGIA
TROPAEOLUM
WALLFLOWER

11
AFRICAN LILY
ANTIRRHINUM
BABY'S BREATH
BEARD TONGUE
BLAZING STAR
BOUNCING BET
BURNING BUSH
CALCEOLARIA
CENTRANTHUS
CHEIRANTHUS
CONVOLVULUS
CORAL FLOWER
CRANE'S-BILL

FILIPENDULA
FLOSS FLOWER
FORGET-ME-NOT
FOXTAIL LILY
GLOBE FLOWER
HELICHRYSUM
INCARVILLEA
LADY'S MANTLE
LOOSESTRIFE
LOVE-IN-A-MIST
PAMPAS GRASS
PHYSOSTEGIA
POLYGONATUM
POT MARIGOLD
RED HOT POKER
RED VALERIAN
SCHIZANTHUS
SEA LAVENDER
SHASTA DAISY
STOKES' ASTER
STRAW FLOWER
XERANTHEMUM

12
AFRICAN DAISY
ALSTROEMERIA
ANNUAL MALLOW
BABY BLUE EYES
BLUE-EYED MARY
CALLISTEPHUS
ESCHSCHOLZIA
GLOBE THISTLE
HELIOTROPIUM
HEMEROCALLIS
JACOB'S LADDER
LEOPARD'S BANE
MONKEY FLOWER
MORNING GLORY
PERUVIAN LILY
PLANTAIN LILY
SALPIGLOSSIS
SCHIZOSTYLIS
SOLOMON'S SEAL
SPIDER FLOWER
SWEET ALYSSUM
SWEET WILLIAM
TOBACCO PLANT
TRADESCANTIA

13
BALLOON FLOWER
BEAR'S BREECHES
BLANKET FLOWER
BLEEDING HEART
CATHEDRAL BELL
CHRISTMAS ROSE
CHRYSANTHEMUM
DIMORPHOTHECA
MARSH MARIGOLD
OBEDIENT PLANT
PAINTED TONGUE
PRAIRIE MALLOW
SLIPPER FLOWER
VIRGINIA STOCK

14
BELLS OF IRELAND
BLACK-EYED SUSAN
CANTERBURY BELL
CHINESE LANTERN
FLOWER OF AN HOUR
FRENCH MARIGOLD
POOR MAN'S ORCHID
STAR OF THE VELDT
YOUTH AND OLD AGE

15
AFRICAN MARIGOLD
EVENING PRIMROSE
JAPANESE ANEMONE
MICHAELMAS DAISY

16
BACHELOR'S BUTTONS
CALIFORNIAN POPPY
COMMON IMMORTELLE
LIVINGSTONE DAISY
MESEMBRYANTHEMUM
PEARL EVERLASTING
POACHED EGG FLOWER
PURPLE CONEFLOWER

17+
CHINESE BELLFLOWER
CHINESE TRUMPET
 FLOWER
EVERLASTING FLOWER
LOVE-LIES-BLEEDING
MONARCH OF THE
 VELDT
PURPLE LOOSESTRIFE

ROCKERY PLANTS

4
GEUM

5
ASTER
DRABA
DRYAS
MAZUS
PHLOX
SEDUM

6
ACAENA
ARABIS
ERINUS
IBERIS
ONOSMA
OXALIS
SILENE
THRIFT

7
ALYSSUM
ARMERIA
ASTILBE

CAT'S EAR
GENTIAN
LEWISIA
LINNAEA
LYCHNIS
MIMULUS
MORISIA
PIGROOT
PLEIONE
RAMONDA
RAOULIA
SEA PINK
SHORTIA

8
ACHILLEA
ARENARIA
AUBRIETA
DIANTHUS
ERIGERON
ERYSIMUM
FLEABANE
GENTIANA
GERANIUM
GROMWELL
HABERLEA
HEPATICA
ORIGANUM
ROCK ROSE
SANDWORT
SNOWBELL
UVULARIA

9
ANACYCLUS
ANDROSACE
AUBRIETIA
BLOODROOT
CAMPANULA
CANDYTUFT
CERASTIUM
EDELWEISS
HOUSELEEK
HYPERICUM
PENSTEMON
POLYGONUM
ROCK CRESS
SAPONARIA
SAXIFRAGA
SAXIFRAGE
STONECROP
VERBASCUM

10
AETHIONEMA
ALPINE GEUM
ANTENNARIA
BELLFLOWER
CYANANTHUS
LYSIMACHIA
PULSATILLA
SOLDANELLA
THROATWORT
TWIN FLOWER

11
DODECATHEON
DONKEY PLANT
HELICHRYSUM
MOSS CAMPION
ROCKERY PINK
ROCK JASMINE
ROCK MULLEIN
SANGUINARIA
SEMPERVIVUM
VANCOUVERIA
WALDSTEINIA

12
ALPINE YARROW
HELIANTHEMUM
LEONTOPODIUM
LITHOSPERMUM
MONKEY FLOWER
PASQUE FLOWER
ROCK SOAPWORT
SHOOTING STAR
SISYRINCHIUM
ST JOHN'S WORT
WHITLOW GRASS

13+
ALPINE WALLFLOWER
CREEPING JENNY
EVERLASTING FLOWER
INSIDE-OUT FLOWER
MOUNTAIN AVENS
MOUNT ATLAS DAISY
NEW ZEALAND BURR
ROCK CINQUEFOIL
SNOW-IN-SUMMER
SUMMER STARWORT
WHITE ROCK CRESS

BULBS

4
IRIS
IXIA
LILY

5
CANNA
TULIP

6
ALLIUM
CRINUM
CROCUS
LILIUM
NERINE
OXALIS
SCILLA
SORREL
TULIPA

7
ANEMONE
BEGONIA

FREESIA
IPHEION
MUSCARI
QUAMASH

8
BLUEBELL
BRODIAEA
CAMASSIA
CORN LILY
CYCLAMEN
DAFFODIL
ERANTHIS
GALTONIA
HYACINTH
LEUCOJUM
SNOWDROP
SPARAXIS
TIGRIDIA
TRILLIUM
TRITONIA

9
AMARYLLIS
COLCHICUM
CROCOSMIA
GALANTHUS
GLADIOLUS
NARCISSUS
SNOWFLAKE
SWORD LILY
WAKE ROBIN

10
ACIDATHERA
CHIONODOXA
FRITILLARY
HYACINTHUS
INDIAN SHOT
MONTBRETIA
PUSCHKINIA
RANUNCULUS
WINDFLOWER

11
BLAZING STAR
CONVALLARIA
ERYTHRONIUM
FRITILLARIA
STERNBERGIA
TIGER FLOWER

12
AUTUMN CROCUS
CARDIOCRINUM
ORNITHOGALUM

13
GRAPE HYACINTH
STRIPED SQUILL
WINTER ACONITE

14
BELLADONNA LILY
GLORY OF THE SNOW

SUMMER HYACINTH

15
DOG'S-TOOTH VIOLET
FLOWERING GARLIC
HARLEQUIN FLOWER
LILY OF THE VALLEY
STAR OF BETHLEHEM
TURBAN BUTTERCUP

16+
GIANT HIMALAYAN LILY
SPRING STARFLOWER
YELLOW STAR FLOWER

**WATER-GARDEN
PLANTS**

4
GEUM
IRIS
RUSH

5
CALLA
CAREX
CHARA
HOSTA
LEMNA
RHEUM
SEDGE
TRAPA
TYPHA

6
ACORUS
ALISMA
AZOLLA
CALTHA
COTULA
ELODEA
JUNCUS
MENTHA
NUPHAR
PISTIA

7
ARUNCUS
ASTILBE
BOG ARUM
BOG BEAN
BONESET
BULRUSH
BUR-REED
BUTOMUS
CYPERUS
DAY LILY
GUNNERA
LOBELIA
LYCHNIS
LYTHRUM
MIMULUS
ONOCLEA

OSMUNDA
PRIMULA
SCIRPUS
TILLAEA

8
DROPWORT
DUCKWEED
FROG-BIT
GLYCERIA
HORNWORT
HOTTONIA
KNOTWEED
MYOSOTIS
NYMPHAEA
ORONTIUM
POND LILY
PONDWEED
REEDMACE
SAURURUS
TROLLIUS
VERONICA

9
ARROW ARUM
ARROWHEAD
BROOKLIME
CARDAMINE
EICHORNIA
FAIRY MOSS
HAIRGRASS
HYPERICUM
LIGULARIA
PELTANDRA
POLYGONUM
RODGERSIA
ROYAL FERN
STONEWORT
SWEET FLAG
WATER LILY
WATER MINT

10
APONOGETON
ELEOCHARIS
ERIOPHORUM
EUPATORIUM
FONTINALIS
GOAT'S BEARD
GOLDEN CLUB
GOLDEN RAYS
HOUTTUYNIA
KAFFIR LILY
LYSICHITON
LYSIMACHIA
MATTEUCCIA
MENYANTHES
NYMPHOIDES
PONTEDERIA
RANUNCULUS
SAGITTARIA
SPARGANIUM
STRATIOTES
WATER AVENS

WATER GRASS
WILLOW MOSS

11
BLADDERWORT
CALLITRICHE
COTTON GRASS
FILIPENDULA
GLOBE FLOWER
HYDROCHARIS
LOOSESTRIFE
POTAMOGETON
RAGGED ROBIN
UTRICULARIA
WATER FRINGE
WATER VIOLET

12
CUCKOO FLOWER
GOLDFISH WEED
HEMEROCALLIS
LAGAROSIPHON
LIZARD'S TAIL
MONKEY FLOWER
MYRIOPHYLLUM
PELTIPHYLLUM
PICKEREL WEED
PLANTAIN LILY
SCHIZOSTYLIS
SKUNK CABBAGE
WATER LETTUCE
WATER MILFOIL
WATER SOLDIER

ZANTEDESCHIA

13
CERATOPHYLLUM
FLOWERING RUSH
GOLDEN BUTTONS
MARSH MARIGOLD
SENSITIVE FERN
UMBRELLA GRASS
UMBRELLA PLANT
WATER CHESTNUT
WATER HAWTHORN
WATER HYACINTH
WATER PLANTAIN
WATER STARWORT
WHITE ARUM LILY

14
PARROT'S FEATHER
PRICKLY RHUBARB
SWAMP STONECROP
WATER BUTTERCUP

15+
CANADIAN PONDWEED
MARSH ST JOHN'S
  WORT
ORNAMENTAL
  RHUBARB
OSTRICH FEATHER
  FERN
PURPLE LOOSE STRIFE
WATER FORGET-ME-
  NOT

ANGLING TERMS

3
DUN
FLY
NET
PEG
RIB
ROD
TAG
TIP

4
BAIT
BARB
CAST
GAFF
HEMP
HOOK
LEAD
LINE
LURE
PLUG
POLE
REEL
SHOT
TAIL
WORM

5
BLANK
CREEL
FLOAT
FLOSS
JOKER
LEGER
PASTE
QUILL

SPOON
WHISK

6
CASTER
DRY FLY
HACKLE
MAGGOT
MARKER
PALMER
PINKIE
PRIEST
SLIDER
SPIGOT
SQUATT
STRIKE
SWIVEL
WET FLY
ZOOMER

7
ANTENNA
BALE ARM
BRISTLE
DAPPING
DUBBING
KEEP NET
MISSILE
PLUMMET
ROD REST
ROD RING
SPINNER
WAGGLER

8
BACK SHOT
DEAD BAIT
FREELINE

LEGERING
LINE BITE
SPECIMEN
STOP KNOT
SWINGTIP

9
BITE ALARM
BLOODWORM
BLUED HOOK
CLOUD BAIT
DISGORGER
GORGE BAIT
MICRO SHOT
MIDGE HOOK
QUIVERTIP
ROACH POLE
TYING SILK
WAGGY LURE
WIRE TRACE

10
BREAD FLAKE
BREAD PUNCH
CADDIS HOOK
COFFIN LEAD
DOUBLE HOOK
FLYBODY FUR
GROUND BAIT
HAIR-AND-FUR
LANDING NET
SNAP TACKLE
STICK FLOAT
SWIM FEEDER

11
ARLESEY BOMB
BAIT DROPPER

BUBBLE FLOAT
DEVON MINNOW
DOUGH-BOBBIN
FOUL-HOOKED
GALLOWS TOOL
LOADED FLOAT
PATERNOSTER
SPARKLE BODY
WHIP-FINISH
WING-CUTTER

12
BARBLESS HOOK
DETACHED BODY
DRY-FLY HACKLE
PARACHUTE FLY
SLIDING FLOAT

13
BUTT INDICATOR
CENTRE-PIN REEL
FLEXI-TAIL LURE

14
BLOCKEND FEEDER
BREAKING STRAIN
GRUB-SHRIMP HOOK
MULTIPLIER REEL

15+
DANISH DRY FLY HOOK
DETACHED-BODY HOOK
FLAT-BODIED NYMPH
  HOOK
PARACHUTE-FLY HOOK
SWEDISH DRY FLY
  HOOK
YORKSHIRE SEDGE
  HOOK

SEWING TECHNIQUES

6
FACING

7
BASTING
BINDING
CUTWORK
DARNING
MITRING
RUCHING
TUCKING

8
APPLIQUE
COUCHING
LAID WORK
PLEATING
QUILTING
RUFFLING
SHIRRING
SMOCKING

9
DRAWN-WORK
FAGGOTING
GATHERING
PATCHWORK
WHITEWORK

10
CROCHETING
EMBROIDERY
OVERSEWING

SCALLOPING

11
FINE-DRAWING
NEEDLEPOINT
OVERCASTING
OVERLOCKING

12
TOPSTITCHING

SEWING STITCHES

4
TACK

9
CROW'S FOOT
GROS POINT
HEMSTITCH
TOPSTITCH

10
BACKSTITCH

FRENCH KNOT
LOCK STITCH
OVERSTITCH
PETIT POINT
STAY STITCH
STEM STITCH
TENT STITCH
WHIP STITCH

11
BLIND STITCH

CHAIN STITCH
CROSS STITCH
NEEDLEPOINT
SATIN STITCH
TAILOR'S TACK

12
KETTLE STITCH

13
BLANKET STITCH

FEATHER STITCH
RUNNING STITCH

15
LAZY DAISY STITCH

16
BUTTONHOLE STITCH
FLORENTINE STITCH

17
HERRINGBONE STITCH

KNITTING TERMS

4
WARP
YARN

5
CHAIN
GRAFT

6
ARGYLE

7
CROCHET
RASCHEL
RIBBING
WORSTED

8
FAIR ISLE
INCREASE
INTARSIA

9
FISHERMAN
FOUNDATION

10
MOSS STITCH
PURL STITCH
SLIP STITCH

11
CABLE STITCH

PLAIN STITCH
SHELL STITCH

12
GARTER STITCH

13
TRELLIS STITCH

14
DOUBLE KNITTING
STOCKING STITCH

GOLF TERMS

3
ACE
LIE
PAR
PGA
PIN
TEE

4
BITE
BUTT
FORE!
HEEL
HOOK
IRON
LOFT
PUTT
SOLE
SPIN
THIN
TRAP
WOOD

5
APRON
BLADE
BOGEY
CADDY
CLEEK
DORMY
DRIVE
EAGLE
GREEN
MASHY
ROUGH
SHAFT

SLICE
SOLID
SPOOL
SPOON
TEMPO
WEDGE

6
ABSENT
BIRDIE
BISQUE
BUNKER
CADDIE
DORMIE
DRIVER
FLIGHT
FRINGE
GIMLET
HAZARD
JIGGER
MARKER
MASHIE
PUTTER
SCLAFF
SPIKES
SQUARE
STANCE
STROKE
STYMIE
TEE OFF
TEE PEG
ADDRESS

7
AIR SHOT
BRASSIE

DIMPLES
FAIRWAY
GROOVES
HOLE OUT
MIDIRON
NIBLICK
POSTURE
SCRATCH
SCUFFED

8
APPROACH
BACKSPIN
BOUNDARY
CADDY CAR
CHIP SHOT
CLUB FACE
CLUB HEAD
HANDICAP
TAKE AWAY

9
ALBATROSS
ALIGNMENT
BACK SWING
CADDY CART
GREENSOME
HOLE IN ONE
SAND WEDGE
SWEET SPOT
SWING PATH

10
BOTTOM EDGE
GROSS SCORE
OPEN STANCE
STABLEFORD

SWING PLANE
TARGET LINE
TRAJECTORY
VARDON GRIP

11
ANGLE OF TILT
COMPRESSION
STROKE INDEX

12
APPROACH SHOT
BASE BALL GRIP
CAVITY BACKED
CLOSED STANCE
FORWARD SWING
TEEING GROUND
THROUGH SWING

13
DISTANCE PLATE
FOLLOW THROUGH
PITCHING WEDGE
PRIMARY TARGET

14
NINETEENTH HOLE

15
ROYAL AND ANCIENT

17
PITCH MARK REPAIRER
TARGET ORIENTATING

20
STANDARD SCRATCH
  SCORE

PATIENCE GAMES

3
FAN
FLY
USK

4
ACME
CLUB
CONE
DIAL
DUKE
ELBA
EXIT
FORT
FROG

GAPS
GATE
GIZA
GNAT
GOLF
HARP
LILY
MAZE
OPUS
PEEK
TENS
TONI
WOOD
ZEUS

5
ADELA
CLOCK
CRUEL
DEMON
DOVER
GIANT
KINGS
LANES
LINKS
LUCAS
MARIA
NINES
PENTA
SNAKE

SPIKE
STEPS
STEVE
WINGS
YUKON

6
ACES UP
ALASKA
ATHENA
BEETLE
BISLEY
BOX FAN
CADRAN
CARPET

CASSIM
CHEOPS
CICELY
CORONA
DARWIN
DEUCES
DIEPPE
INDIAN
MADAME
MARTHA
MILLIE
MONACO
MRS MOP
MUMBAI
MUNGER
NEEDLE
NESTOR
OCTAVE
RAGLAN
REPAIR
ROBERT
SAXONY
SENATE
SKIPPY
SPIDER
SQUARE
STRATA
TETSOL
TOWERS
TUXEDO
TWENTY
ZODIAC

7
ALI BABA
AMAZONS
ANTARES
ARCHWAY
ARIZONA
BALCONY
BASTION
BIG HARP
BOUDOIR
BOX KITE
BRIGADE
BRISTOL
CARLTON
CASTILE
CITADEL
COLONEL
COLOURS
COMPASS
CORNERS
CZARINA
DIAVOLO
DOROTHY
ECLIPSE
EIGHT ON
ELEVENS
EMPEROR
FIFTEEN
FOURS UP
FREE FAN
GRANADA

KINGDOM
LETTER H
LIMITED
MINERVA
NEW YORK
NUNAVUT
OCTAGON
OSMOSIS
OUTBACK
PAS SEUL
PENGUIN
PIGTAIL
PUSH-PIN
PYRAMID
QUEENIE
RAINBOW
SIBERIA
SIGNORA
SIMPLEX
SPIDIKE
STREETS
TERRACE
THE PLOT
THE WISH
THREE UP
TREFOIL
TWISTER
ZERLINE

8
ALHAMBRA
ARABELLA
ARACNIDA
ASSEMBLY
AUNT MARY
BACKBONE
BATSFORD
BIG APPLE
BIG DOZEN
BIG FORTY
BLOCKADE
BLOCK TEN
BRISBANE
BUSY ACES
CANFIELD
CANISTER
CHEQUERS
CHINAMAN
COLORADO
CONGRESS
CRESCENT
CROMWELL
DEMON FAN
DIPLOMAT
DOUBLETS
DUTCHESS
EIGHT OFF
FAIR LUCY
FIFTEENS
FORECELL
FORTRESS
FORWARDS
FOURSOME
FREECELL

GEOFFREY
GOLD RUSH
HAYSTACK
IDLE ACES
JUNCTION
KINGCELL
KINGSLEY
KING'S WAY
KLONDIKE
LADY JANE
LADY PALK
LEAP YEAR
MOREHEAD
MYSTIQUE
NAPOLEON
PHARAOHS
PRIMROSE
PUTT PUTT
RAW PRAWN
REDHEADS
RESERVES
SALIC LAW
SARATOGA
SCORPION
SHIFTING
SIR TOMMY
SIXTEENS
SOLSTICE
SOMERSET
SQUADRON
ST HELENA
STRATEGY
SURPRISE
TAJ MAHAL
TAKE AWAY
TEN BY ONE
THE SPARK
TRIANGLE
TRILLIUM
TWO CELLS
VERTICAL
VINEYARD
WATERLOO
WINDMILL

9
ACCORDION
ALL IN A ROW
APPLEGATE
BALD EAGLE
BETSY ROSS
BIG BERTHA
BIG SPIDER
BLACK HOLE
CHAMELEON
CHELICERA
CLEOPATRA
CORNELIUS
COURTYARD
DIFFUSION
DOUBLE DOT
EAGLE WING
EASTHAVEN
EIGHTEENS

FAN ALBERT
FIVE PILES
FLORADORA
FOUR BY TEN
FOURTEENS
FOUR WINDS
FORTY-NINE
GARGANTUA
INTERMENT
JOSEPHINE
LADY BETTY
LAFAYETTE
MAMY SUSAN
MARIE ROSE
MATRIMONY
MCCLELLAN
NATIONALE
NUMBER TEN
ORDER TIME
PARALLELS
PELMANISM
PITCHFORK
RIPPLE FAN
ROOSEVELT
SEA TOWERS
SHAMROCKS
SIMON SAYS
SPIDER WEB
STONEWALL
TARANTULA
THIRTEENS
THIRTY SIX
UNLIMITED
WESTCLIFF
WHITEHEAD

10
AGNES SOREL
AGNES THREE
ALEXANDRIA
ANNO DOMINI
BAKER'S GAME
BINARY STAR
BLACK WIDOW
BLIND ALLEY
BREAKWATER
CASTLES END
CHESSBOARD
CIRCLE NINE
CLOVER LEAF
CRISS CROSS
CROSSROADS
DEMONTHIEF
DOUBLE RAIL
EIGHTS DOWN
FAMILY PLOT
FOUR BY FIVE
FOURTEEN UP
GRADATIONS
GREAT WHEEL
HOW THEY RUN
HYPOTENUSE
INQUISITOR
KING ALBERT

LAST CHANCE
LITTLE GATE
LUCKY PILES
MIDSHIPMAN
MISS MUFFET
MONTE CARLO
MOVING LEFT
NUMERATION
ODD AND EVEN
OLD CARLTON
PANTAGRUEL
PARLIAMENT
PATRIARCHS
POINT SABLE
PRECEDENCE
PREFERENCE
PRINCE SERG
QUADRANGLE
RACING ACES
RAINBOW FAN
ROUGE FORTY
ROWS OF FOUR
SCORPION II
SEVEN STEPS
SEVENTEENS
SHADY LANES
SIMPLICITY
SINGLE LEFT
SINGLE RAIL
SPIDERETTE
STOREHOUSE
STRIPTEASE
STRONGHOLD
TARANTELLA
THREE BEARS
THREE CELLS
TOURNAMENT
TRIPLE HARP
TRIPLE LEFT
TRIPLE LINE
TWIN QUEENS
TWO CASTLES
WANING MOON
WAVE MOTION
WAXING MOON
WHEATSHEAF
WHITEHORSE
YUKON KINGS

11
ACE OF HEARTS
ALTERNATION
BAKER'S DOZEN
BASTILLE DAY
BRIDESMAIDS
BUFFALO BILL
CALCULATION
CAPRICIEUSE
CASTLE MOUNT
CIRCLE EIGHT
CONTRADANCE
CORNER SUITE
DOUBLE FIVES
DOUBLET CELL

DOUBLE YUKON
EXILED KINGS
FALLING STAR
FAMOUS FIFTY
FASCINATION
FIFTEEN RUSH
FIRING SQUAD
FORTY DEVILS
FOUR COLOURS
FOUR SEASONS
FOURTEEN OUT
FRED'S SPIDER
FREE PARKING
GERMAN CROSS
GOOD MEASURE
GRANDFATHER
INTERCHANGE
INTERREGNUM
KNOTTY NINES
LADY CADOGAN
LITTLE FORTY
LITTLE GIANT
OSMOTIC CELL
PYRAMID GOLF
RANK AND FILE
RED AND BLACK
RITTENHOUSE
ROUGE ET NOIR
ROYAL FAMILY
ROYAL PARADE
RUSSIAN CELL
SAN JUAN HILL
SEVEN BY FIVE
SEVEN BY FOUR
SEVEN DEVILS
SIMON JESTER
SIMPLE PAIRS
SIMPLE SIMON
SOLID SQUARE
SPECULATION
SPIDERCELLS
SPRINGFIELD
STALACTITES
STRATEGERIE
SUIT ELEVENS
SUSPENSEFUL
TAM O'SHANTER
THIEVES RUSH
THREE DEMONS
TREVI GARDEN
TRIPLE PEAKS
TRIPLE YUKON
YUKON PUZZLE
YUKON SPIDER

12
ACES AND KINGS
ACQUAINTANCE
ALTERNATIONS
AMERICAN TOAD
AULD LANG SYNE
BROWN RECLUSE
CANFIELD RUSH
CURDS AND WHEY

EIGHT BY EIGHT
FLOWER GARDEN
FORTY THIEVES
GRAND DUCHESS
INTELLIGENCE
KINGS AND ACES
LA BELLE LUCIE
LADIES BATTLE
LA NIVERNAISE
LITTLE BILLIE
LITTLE SPIDER
MILLIGAN CELL
MILLIGAN HARP
MISS MILLIGAN
MOUNT OLYMPUS
PATIENT PAIRS
PENELOPE'S WEB
PERSEVERANCE
PYRAMID SEVEN
RIGHT AND LEFT
SCORPION HEAD
SCORPION TAIL
SEVEN BY SEVEN
SIXTY THIEVES
STRATEGY PLUS
SUIT YOURSELF
SWEET SIXTEEN
THIRTEEN DOWN
TOWER OF HANOI
TRIPLE DEMONS
TRUSTY TWELVE
VIRGINIA REEL
WILL O THE WISP
YUKON ONE SUIT

13
AGNES BERNAUER
BATSFORD AGAIN
BLIND PATIENCE
BRITISH SQUARE
CAPTIVE QUEENS
CARRE NAPOLEON
CHINESE SPIDER
DOUBLE OR QUITS
DOUBLE PYRAMID
DOUBLE RUSSIAN
DOUBLE SIGNORA
EIGHTY THIEVES
FIFTEEN PUZZLE
FORTUNE'S FAVOR
FORTY AND EIGHT
GREAT TRIANGLE
HEADS AND TAILS
INDEFATIGABLE
LIGHT AND SHADE
LITTLE THIEVES
LUCKY THIRTEEN
QUEEN VICTORIA
RIGHT TRIANGLE
ROMAN PATIENCE
ROYAL MARRIAGE
SIXTEEN PUZZLE
SPACES AND ACES
SPIDER ONE SUIT

STEPPING STONE
SWISS PATIENCE
THIRTEEN PACKS
THREES COMPANY
THUMB AND POUCH
TRIPLE RUSSIAN

14
CASTLES IN SPAIN
DOUBLE CANFIELD
DOUBLE FREECELL
DOUBLE KINGSLEY
DOUBLE KLONDIKE
DOUBLE SCORPION
DUTCH SOLITAIRE
EMPRESS OF ITALY
FIVE AND DIAMOND
GERMAN PATIENCE
HOUSE IN THE WOOD
HOUSE ON THE HILL
IMPERIAL GUARDS
INDIAN PATIENCE
KINGS AND QUEENS
KLEINE NAPOLEON
LADY OF THE MANOR
LITTLE MILLIGAN
LITTLE NAPOLEON
MIDNIGHT CLOVER
QUEENS AND JACKS
ROYAL COTILLION
SCORPION TOWERS
SCOTCH PATIENCE
SENIOR WRANGLER
SIXES AND SEVENS
SPIDER TWO SUITS
SULTAN OF TURKEY
THIEVES OF EGYPT
THREE BLIND MICE
TRAPDOOR SPIDER
TRIPLE FREECELL
TRIPLE KLONDIKE
TRIPLE SCORPION
TRIPLE TRIANGLE

15
ACEY AND KINGSLEY
BRITISH CANISTER
CHINESE KLONDIKE
DEUCES AND QUEENS
DOUBLE EASTHAVEN
DOUBLE FOURTEENS
DOUBLE SEATOWERS
ETERNAL TRIANGLE
FORTRESS OF MERCY
FOUR LEAF CLOVERS
GLOUCESTERSHIRE
HIDDEN TREASURES
INCOMPATIBILITY
KINGSDOWN EIGHTS
NAPOLEON'S SQUARE
PATIENCE'S REWARD
PERPETUAL MOTION
PHANTOM BLOCKADE
PICTURE PATIENCE

PUSS IN THE CORNER
RESERVED PYRAMID
ROYAL RENDEZVOUS
SELECTIVE CASTLE
SPANISH PATIENCE
THIRTY-NINE STEPS
TRAVELLERS CLOCK
TRIPLE EASTHAVEN
TRIPLE FOURTEENS

16
ALGERIAN PATIENCE
AMERICAN CANISTER
BAVARIAN PATIENCE
BIG SPIDER ONE SUIT
BOXING THE COMPASS
DEMONS AND THIEVES
GENERAL'S PATIENCE
INVERTED FREECELL
PRINCESS PATIENCE

RUSSIAN SOLITAIRE
STREETS AND ALLEYS
SUPERIOR CANFIELD

17
ALEXANDER THE GREAT
BELEAGUERED CASTLE
BIG SPIDER TWO SUITS
BRAZILIAN PATIENCE
CASTLE OF INDOLENCE

CHALLENGE FREECELL
GROUNDS FOR
   DIVORCE
QUADRUPLE CANFIELD
QUADRUPLE KLONDIKE
SINGLE INTERCHANGE
STRAIGHTS AND PAIRS
SUPER FLOWER
   GARDEN
TRIPLE INTERCHANGE

COMPUTER GAMES (*mostly Trademark*)

ADVENTURE
AGE OF EMPIRES
AGE OF WONDERS
ASTEROIDS
BIOSHOCK
BLOBS
BOMBARDER
BROKEN SWORD
CALL OF DUTY
CATCHBALL
CENTIPEDE
CIVILIZATION
DIABLO
DONKEY KONG
DOOM
EXILE
FACTORY
FALLOUT
FIFA SOCCER

FINAL FANTASY
FLIGHT SIMULATOR
FORTNITE
FREECELL
GALAXIA
GEMFIRE
GOD OF WAR
GOLDEN AXE
GRAND THEFT AUTO
GRAN TURISMO
HALF LIFE
HALO
HEBI
LEMMINGS
MADDEN NFL
METAL GEAR SOLID
MINECRAFT
MINE SWEEPER
MISSILE COMMAND

MYST
NEW HORIZONS
ODYSSEY
PAC-MAN
PACPAC
PHANTASY STAR
PIRATES
POKEMON
PONG
PYRAMID
QBI
QUAKE
RED DEAD
   REDEMPTION
RESIDENT EVIL
RINGS OF POWER
SEVEN KINGDOMS
SHINING FORCE
SIMCITY

SONIC THE HEDGEHOG
SPACE INVADERS
SPACEWAR
SPIDER-MAN
STARCRAFT
STREET FIGHTER
SUPER MARIO
   BROTHERS
TETRIS
THE SIMS
THIEF
TOMB RAIDER
TONY HAWK'S PRO
   SKATER
VALIS
WORLD OF WARCRAFT
WORMS
ZELDA

EXTREME SPORTS

BASE-JUMPING
BMXING
BODYBOARDING
BUNGEE JUMPING
DIRTBOARDING
DOWNHILL MOUNTAIN
   BIKING
ENDURANCE RACING
EXTREME IRONING
EXTREME SKIING

FLOWBOARDNING
FREE CLIMBING
HANG GLIDING
IN–LINE SKATING
KITEBOARDING
KITESURFING
MOTO X
MOUNTAINBOARDING
PARAGLIDING
RALLYING

RIVERBOARDING
ROCK CLIMBING
SANDBOARDING
SKATEBOARDING
SKYDIVING
SKYSURFING
SNOWBOARDING
SNOWMOBILES
SNOWSKATE
SUPERCROSS

SURFING
ULTIMATE
   FIGHTING
WAKEBOARDING
WATERSKIING
WHITE–WATER
   RAFTING
WINDSURFING
X–GAMES

MISCELLANEOUS

COLOURS

3
AAL
ABA
DUN
JET
RED
TAN

4
BLEU
BLUE
BOIS
BURE
CUIR
DRAB
EBON
ÉCRU
GOLD
GREY
GRIS
HOPI
IRIS
JADE
LAKE
LARK
NAVY
NOIR
ONYX
OPAL
PIED
PINK
PLUM
PUCE
ROSE
RUBY
SAND
SHOT
VERT

5
AMBER
BEIGE
BLACK
BROWN
CAMEL
CAPRI
CHAIR
COCOA
CORAL
CREAM
CYMAR

DELFT
FLESH
GREEN
GRÈGE
HAZEL
HENNA
IVORY
JASPÉ
JAUNE
JEWEL
KHAKI
LODEN
MAIZE
MAUVE
OCHRE
OLIVE
OMBRÉ
PEACH
PEARL
PÊCHE
PRUNE
ROUGE
SEPIA
SHADE
TAUPE
TOPAZ
UMBER
WHITE

6
ACAJOU
ALESAN
ARGENT
AUBURN
BASANÉ
BISTRE
BLONDE
BRONZE
BURNET
CASTOR
CENDRÉ
CERISE
CHERRY
CHROMA
CITRON
CLARET
COPPER
DORADO
FLAXEN
GARNET
GOLDEN

INDIGO
JASPER
MADDER
MAROON
MATARA
MOTLEY
ORANGE
ORCHID
OYSTER
PASTEL
PEARLY
PIRNED
PURPLE
RACHEL
RAISIN
RESEDA
RUSSET
SALMON
SHRIMP
SILVER
TITIAN
VIOLET
YELLOW
ZIRCON

7
ANAMITE
APRICOT
ARDOISE
AUREATE
BISCUIT
CALDRON
CARAMEL
CARMINE
CHAMOIS
CORBEAU
CRIMSON
EMERALD
FILBERT
FUCHSIA
GRIZZLE
HEATHER
INGÉNUE
JACINTH
JONQUIL
LACQUER
LAVANDE
MAGENTA
MOTTLED
MUSTARD
NACARAT

NATURAL
NEUTRAL
OLD ROSE
PEARLED
PLATINA
SAFFRON
SCARLET
SEA BLUE
SKY BLUE
TEA ROSE
THISTLE
TILE RED
TILLEUL
TUSSORE
VIOLINE

8
ABSINTHE
ALIZARIN
AMARANTH
AURULENT
BABY BLUE
BABY PINK
BORDEAUX
BURGUNDY
CAPUCINE
CHALDERA
CHÂTAINE
CHESTNUT
CIEL BLUE
CINNAMON
CREVETTE
CYCLAMEN
EAU DE NIL
ÉCARLATE
EGGPLANT
EGGSHELL
GRIZZLED
GUN METAL
HAZEL NUT
HYACINTH
LARKSPUR
LAVENDER
MAHOGANY
MOLE GREY
MULBERRY
NAVY BLUE
PEA GREEN
PISTACHE
POPPY RED
PRIMROSE

SAPPHIRE
SEA GREEN
SHAGREEN
SPECTRUM
VIRIDIAN

9
ALICE BLUE
AUBERGINE
AZURE BLUE
BLUE-GREEN
CADET BLUE
CADET GREY
CARNATION
CARNELIAN
CHAMPAGNE
CHOCOLATE
COCHINEAL
DELPH BLUE
DUTCH BLUE
FLESH PINK
GREEN-BLUE
HARLEQUIN
LEAF GREEN
LIME GREEN
MOONSTONE
MOSS GREEN
NILE GREEN
OLIVE DRAB
PARCHMENT
PEARL GREY
RASPBERRY
ROYAL BLUE
TANGERINE
TOMATO RED
TURKEY RED
VERDIGRIS
VERMILION
WALLY BLUE

10
AQUAMARINE
AURICOMOUS
BOIS DE ROSE
CAFÉ AU LAIT
CASTOR GREY
COBALT BLUE
CONGO BROWN
ENSIGN BLUE
LIVER BROWN
MARINA BLUE

356

MARINE BLUE
OXFORD BLUE
PETROL BLUE
POLYCHROME
POWDER BLUE
TERRACOTTA
ZENITH BLUE

11
BOTTLE GREEN
BURNT ALMOND
CARDINAL RED
CLAIR DE LUNE
FOREST GREEN
GOBELIN BLUE
HORIZON BLUE
HUNTER'S PINK
LAPIS LAZULI

LEMON YELLOW
LIPSTICK RED
PARROT GREEN
PEACOCK BLUE
POMEGRANATE
SMOKED PEARL
SOLID COLOUR
ULTRAMARINE
VERSICOLOUR
WALNUT BROWN
YELLOW OCHRE

12
BALL PARK BLUE
CANARY YELLOW
CARROT COLOUR
CASTILIAN RED
CELADON GREEN

HUNTER'S GREEN
HYACINTH BLUE
LOGWOOD BROWN
MIDNIGHT BLUE
OVERSEAS BLUE
SAPPHIRE BLUE
SOLFERINO RED
TYRIAN PURPLE
VERDANT GREEN

13
BISHOP'S PURPLE
BISHOP'S VIOLET
CAMBRIDGE BLUE
MOTHER-OF-PEARL
MULTICOLOURED
PARTI-COLOURED
PEPPER-AND-SALT

PRIMARY COLOUR
TORTOISE SHELL
TURQUOISE BLUE

14
HEATHER MIXTURE
PERIWINKLE BLUE
PISTACHIO GREEN
TURQUOISE GREEN

15
CALEDONIAN BROWN
CHARTREUSE GREEN

16
CHARTREUSE YELLOW

THE SIGNS OF THE ZODIAC

SIGN (Symbol; Element; Dates)

ARIES (Ram; Fire; 21 Mar–19 Apr)
TAURUS (Bull; Earth; 20 Apr–20 May)
GEMINI (Twins; Air; 21 May–21 June)
CANCER (Crab; Water; 22 June–22 July)
LEO (Lion; Fire; 23 July–22 Aug)
VIRGO (Virgin; Earth; 23 Aug–23 Sept)

SIGN (Symbol; Dates)

LIBRA (Scales; Air; 23 Sept–23 Oct)
SCORPIO (Scorpion;Water; 24 Oct–21 Nov)
SAGITTARIUS (Archer; Fire; 22 Nov–21 Dec)
CAPRICORN (Goat; Earth; 22 Dec–19 Jan)
AQUARIUS (Water-carrier; Air; 20 Jan–18 Feb)
PISCES (Fish; Water; 19 Feb–20 Mar)

THE TWELVE SIGNS OF THE CHINESE ZODIAC

RAT (2020)
OX (2021)
TIGER (2022)
RABBIT (2023)
DRAGON (2024)
SNAKE (2025)

HORSE (2026)
SHEEP (2027)
MONKEY (2028)
ROOSTER (2029)
DOG (2030)
PIG (2031)

CALENDARS

GREGORIAN

JANUARY
FEBRUARY
MARCH
APRIL
MAY
JUNE
JULY
AUGUST
SEPTEMBER
OCTOBER
NOVEMBER
DECEMBER

FRENCH REVOLUTIONARY

VENDÉMIAIRE – Vintage (Sept)
BRUMAIRE – Fog (Oct)
FRIMAIRE – Sleet (Nov)
NIVÔSE – Snow (Dec)
PLUVIÔSE – Rain (Jan)
VENTÔSE – Wind (Feb)
GERMINAL – Seed (Mar)
FLORÉAL – Blossom (Apr)
PRAIRIAL – Pasture (May)
MESSIDOR – Harvest (June)
THERMIDOR – Heat (July)
FRUCTIDOR – Fruit (Aug)

HEBREW

SHEVAT (Jan/Feb)
ADAR (Feb/Mar)
NISAN (Mar/Apr)
IYAR (Apr/May)
SIVAN (May/June)
TAMMUZ (June/July)
AV (July/Aug)
ELUL (Aug/Sept)
TISHRI (Sept/Oct)
HESHVAN (Oct/Nov)
KISLEV (Nov/Dec)
TEVET (Dec/Jan)

ISLAMIC

MUHARRAM (Jan)
SAFAR (Feb)
RABIA I (Mar)
RABIA II (Apr)
JUMĀDĀ I (May)
JUMĀDĀ II (June)
RAJAB (July)
SHA'BAN (Aug)
RAMADĀN (Sept)
SHAWWĀL (Oct)
DHŪAL-QA'DAH(Nov)
DHŪAL-HIJJAH(Dec)

CHINESE

XIAO HAN (Jan)
DA HAN (Jan/Feb)
LI CHUN (Feb)
YU SHUI (Feb/Mar)
JING ZHE (Mar)
CHUN FEN (Mar/Apr)
QING MING (Apr)
GU YU (Apr/May)
LI XIA (May)
XIAO MAN (May/June)
MANG ZHONG (June)
XIA ZHI (June/July)
XIAO SHU (July)
DA SHU (July/Aug)
LI QUI (Aug)
CHU SHU (Aug/Sept)
BAI LU (Sept)
QUI FEN (Sept/Oct)
HAN LU (Oct)
SHUANG JIANG (Oct/Nov)
LI DONG (Nov)
XIAO XUE (Nov/Dec)
DA XUE (Dec)
DONG ZHI (Dec/Jan)

BIRTHSTONES

January – GARNET
February – AMETHYST
March – BLOODSTONE/
    AQUAMARINE
April – DIAMOND

May – EMERALD
June – PEARL
July – RUBY
August – SARDONYX/PERIDOT

September – SAPPHIRE
October – OPAL
November – TOPAZ
December – TURQUOISE

WEDDING ANNIVERSARIES

TRADITIONAL	MODERN	TRADITIONAL	MODERN
1st – PAPER	PLASTIC	13th – LACE	TEXTILES
2nd – COTTON	COTTON/CHINA	14th – IVORY	GOLD
3rd – LEATHER	CRYSTAL/GLASS	15th – CRYSTAL	GLASS/WATCHES
4th – FRUIT/FLOWERS	LINEN/SINL	20th – CHINA	PLATINUM
5th – WOOD	SILVERWARE	25th – SILVER	SILVER
6th – IRON	IRON	30th – PEARL	DIAMOND
7th – WOOL/COPPER	WOOL/BRASS	35th – CORAL	JADE
8th – BRONZE/POTTERY	APPLIANCE	40th – RUBY	GARNET
9th – POTTERY/WILLOW	LEATHER	45th – SAPPHIRE	SAPPHIRE
10th – TIN/ALUMINIUM	ALUMINIUM	50th – GOLD	GOLD
11th – STEEL	JEWELLRY	55th – EMERALD	TURQUISE
12th – SILK/LINEN	LINEN/PEARL	60th – DIAMOND	GOLD

PEERAGE

DUKE
MARQUESS/MARQUIS
EARL
VISCOUNT
BARON

DUCHESS
MARCHIONESS
COUNTESS
VISCOUNTESS
BARONESS

HERALDIC TERMS

DIVISIONS OF FIELDS

PER PALE
PER FESS
PER CROSS
PER BEND
PER SALTIRE
PER CHEVRON

DESCRIPTIONS OF FIELDS

PARTY
BARRY
BURELY
BENDY
QUARTERLY
ENTY
FRETTY
GIRONNY
BEZANTY

PARTS OF THE ESCUTCHEON

DEXTER (right)
SINISTER (left)
MIDDLE
CHIEF (top)
FLANK (side)
BASE
NOMBRIL POINT
FESS POINT
HONOUR POINT
TRESSURE (border)

TINCTURES

OR (gold)
ARGENT (silver)
ERMINE
VAIR
POTENT
AZURE (blue)
GULES (red)

SABLE (black)
VERT (green)
PURPURE (purple)

CROSSES

FORMY
PATY
FLORY
MOLINE
BOTONNY
CROSLETTED
FITCHY
SALTIRE

LINES

ENGRAILED
EMBATTLED
INDENTED
INVECTED
WAVY, UNDY

NEBULY
DANCETTY
RAGULY
POTENTÉ
DOVETAILED
URDY

OTHER OBJECTS AND DECORATIONS

LOZENGE
ROUNDEL (circle)
ANNULET (ring)
FOUNTAIN (wavy line on a circle)
BILLET (upright object)
MOLET (star)
RAMPANT (rearing up)
COUCHANT (sleeping or sitting)
PASSANT (standing)
BAR

SEVEN DEADLY SINS

PRIDE
COVETOUSNESS
LUST
ENVY

GLUTTONY
ANGER
SLOTH

SEVEN WONDERS OF THE WORLD

THE PYRAMIDS OF EGYPT
THE COLOSSUS OF RHODES
THE HANGING GARDENS OF BABYLON
THE MAUSOLEUM OF HALICARNASSUS

THE STATUE OF ZEUS AT OLYMPIA
THE TEMPLE OF ARTEMIS AT EPHESUS
THE PHAROS OF ALEXANDRIA

SEVEN VIRTUES

FAITH
FORTITUDE
HOPE
JUSTICE

LOVE (CHARITY)
PRUDENCE
TEMPERANCE

MONEY

1&2	PEAG	SCEAT	TESTON	CUARTILLO
AS	PESO	SCUDI	THALER	DIDRACHMA
D	PICE	SCUDO	TOMAUN	DUPONDIUS
L	PONY	SEMIS	ZECHIN	GOLD BROAD
P	QUID	SOLDO		GOLD NOBLE
S	REAL	STICA	**7**	GOLD PENNY
	RYAL	STYCA	ANGELOT	HALFPENNY
3	TAEL	SYCEE	CAROLUS	PISTAREEN
BIT	UNIK	TICAL	CENTAVA	RIXDOLLAR
BOB		TICCY	DENARII	ROSE-NOBLE
COB	**5**	TOMAN	DRACHMA	SESTERTII
DAM	ANGEL	UNCIA	GUILDER	SOVEREIGN
ECU	ASPER	UNITE	JACOBUS	SPUR ROYAL
FAR	BELGA		MILREIS	YELLOW BOY
KIP	BETSO	**6**	MOIDORE	
LAT	BROAD	AMANIA	NGUSANG	**10**
MIL	CONTO	AUREUS	PISTOLE	EASTERLING
MNA	COPEC	BAWBEE	QUARTER	FIRST BRASS
PIE	CROWN	BEZART	SEXTANS	GOLD STATER
REE	DARIC	CONDOR	STOOTER	QUADRUSSIS
REI	DINAR	COPANG	TESTOON	SESTERTIUM
SHO	DUCAT	COPPER	UNICORN	SILVERLING
SOL	EAGLE	DÉCIME		STOUR-ROYAL
SOU	FRANC	DOBLON	**8**	THREEPENCE
YEN	GROAT	DOLLAR	AMBROSIN	TRIPONDIUS
	LIARD	ESCUDO	DENARIUS	VENEZOLANO
4	LIBRA	FLORIN	DIDRACHM	
ANNA	LITAS	FUORTE	DOUBLOON	**11**
BEKA	LIVRE	GUINEA	DUCATOON	SILVER PENNY
BIGA	LOCHO	GULDEN	FARTHING	SPADE GUINEA
BUCK	LOUIS	KOPECK	FLORENCE	
CASH	MEDIO	MONKEY	JOHANNES	**12**
CENT	MOHAR	NICKEL	KREUTZER	MILL SIXPENCE
DAUM	MOHUR	PAGODE	LOUIS D'OR	SILVER-STATER
DIME	NOBLE	PESETA	MARAVEDI	TETRADRACHMA
DOIT	OBANG	ROUBLE	NAPOLEON	TRIBUTE PENNY
JOEY	PAOLO	SCEATT	PICAYUNE	
KRAN	PENCE	SEQUIN	QUETZALE	**13**
LIRA	PENGO	STATER	SESTERCE	THREEPENNY BIT
MAIL	PENNY	STIVER	SHILLING	
MARK	PLACK	TALARI	SIXPENCE	**14**
MERK	POUND	TALENT		HONG KONG
MITE	QURSH	TANNER	**9**	DOLLAR
OBOL	RUBLE	TESTER	BOLIVIANO	

COLLECTIVE NAMES

ACROBATS – troupe
APES – shrewdness
ASSES – pace
BABOONS – troop
BADGERS – colony
BAKERS – tabernacle
BARBERS – babble
BARMEN – promise
BAYONETS – grove
BEES – erst, swarm

BELLS – change
BISHOPS – bench, psalter
BISON – herd
BREWERS – feast
BUFFALOES – obstinacy
BULLFINCHES – bellowing
BULLOCKS – drove
BUTCHERS – goring
BUTLERS – sneer
CANONS – chapter, dignity

CATERPILLARS – army
CATTLE – herd, drove
CHIMPANZEES – cartload
CHOUGHS – chattering
COBBLERS – cutting
CROCODILES – bask
CROWS – murder
DEANS – decanter, decorum
DOGS – pack
DONS – obscuration

DUCKS – paddling, safe
ELEPHANTS – herd, parade
FERRETS – busyness
FLIES – swarm
GAMBLERS – talent
GEESE – gaggle
GOLDFINCHES – charm
GOVERNESSES – galaxy
GRAMMARIANS – conjunction
HARES – down
HARPISTS – melody
HERONS – serge
HIPPOPOTAMI – bloat
HUNTERS – blast
JELLYFISH – fluther, smack
JUGGLERS – neverthriving
KANGAROOS – troop, herd, mob
KITTENS – litter
LAPWING – desert
LARKS – exaltation
LEOPARDS – leap, lepe

LIONS – pride, sawt, sowse
LOCUSTS – swarm
MAGPIES – tittering
MERCHANTS – faith
MESSENGERS – diligence
MOLES – labour
MULES – span
NIGHTINGALES – watch
ORCHIDS – coterie
OWLS – parliament, stare
PAINTERS – curse, illusion
PARROTS – pandemonium
PEKINGESE – pomp
PENGUINS – parcel
PIGS – litter
PIPERS – skirl
PORPOISES – turmoil
PREACHERS – converting
RABBITS – bury
RACCOONS – gaze
RAVENS – unkindness

RHINOCEROS – crash
ROBBERS – band
SHEEP – flock
SHERIFFS – posse
SHIPS – fleet, armada
SHOEMAKERS – blackening
STARLINGS – murmuration
SWALLOWS – gulp
SWINE – doylt
TAILORS – disguising
TAVERNERS – closing
TROUT – hover
TURKEY – rafter
TURTLES – turn
UNDERTAKERS – unction
WHALES – pod
WIDOWS – ambush
WILDCATS – destruction, dout
WOODPECKERS – descent
WRITERS – worship
ZEBRAS – zeal

TYPEFACES

3
DOW

4
BELL
CITY
GILL
ZAPF

5
ASTER
BEMBO
BLOCK
DORIC
ERBAR
FOLIO
GOUDY
IONIC
KABEL
LOTUS
MITRA
SABON
SWIFT
TIMES

6
AACHEN
ADROIT
AURIGA
BECKET
BODONI
BULMER
CASLON

COCHIN
COOPER
CORONA
FENICE
FUTURA
GLYPHA
GOTHIC
HORLEY
ITALIA
JANSON
LUCIAN
MELIOR
MODERN
OLIVER
ONDINE
OPTIMA
ROMANA

7
ANTIQUE
BASILIA
BAUHAUS
BERNARD
BOOKMAN
BRAMLEY
CANDIDA
CENTURY
CORONET
CUSHING
ELECTRA
FLOREAL
IMPRINT
IRIDIUM

KORINNA
LUBALIN
MADISON
MEMPHIS
NEUZEIT
PLANTIN
RALEIGH
SPARTAN
STEMPEL
TIFFANY
UNIVERS
WEXFORD
WINDSOR

8
BENGUIAT
BERKELEY
BREUGHEL
CLOISTER
CONCORDE
EGYPTIAN
EHRHARDT
FOURNIER
FRANKLIN
FRUTIGER
GALLIARD
GARAMOND
KENNERLY
NOVARESE
OLYMPIAN
PALATINO
PERPETUA

ROCKWELL
SOUVENIR

9
AMERICANA
ATHENAEUM
BARCELONA
BRITANNIC
CALEDONIA
CLARENDON
CLEARFACE
CRITERION
DOMINANTE
EUROSTILE
EXCELSIOR
FAIRFIELD
GROTESQUE
HELVETICA
WORCESTER

10
AVANT GARDE
CHELTENHAM
CHURCHWARD
DEVANAGARI
EGYPTIENNE
LEAMINGTON

11
BASKERVILLE
COPPERPLATE

14
TRUMP MEDIAEVAL

AMERICAN INDIANS

3
FOX
OTO
UTE

4
CREE
CROW
HOPI
HUPA
IOWA
SAUK
TUPI

5
AZTEC
CADDO
CREEK
HAIDA
HURON
KASKA
KIOWA
OMAHA
OSAGE
SIOUX
SLAVE

TETON
WAPPO
YUROK

6
ABNAKI
APACHE
ATSINA
CAYUGA
DAKOTA
DOGRIB
MANDAN
MICMAC
MIXTEC
MOHAWK
NAVAJO
NOOTKA
OJIBWA
ONEIDA
OTTAWA
PAIUTE
PAWNEE
QUAPAW
SALISH
SANTEE
SENECA

TANANA
TOLTEC
YAKIMA

7
ARIKARA
BEOTHUK
CATAWBA
CHINOOK
CHOKTAW
HIDATSA
INGALIK
KUTCHIN
NATCHEZ
SHAWNEE
SHUSWAP
TLINGIT
WICHITA
WYANDOT

8
CHEROKEE
CHEYENNE
COMANCHE
DELAWARE
ILLINOIS

IROQUOIS
KICKAPOO
NEZ PERCÉ
OKANOGAN
ONONDAGA
SHOSHONI
TUTCHONE

9
ALGONQUIN
BLACKFOOT
CHICKASAW
CHIPEWYAN
CHIPPEWAY
MENOMINEE
PENOBSCOT
TAHAGMIUT
TILLAMOOK
TSIMSHIAN
TUSCARORA
WINNEBAGO

10+
KAVIAGMIUT
PASAMAQUODDY
POTAWATOMI

CARTOON CHARACTERS

4
DINO
HUEY

5
BLUTO
DEWEY
GOOFY
HE-MAN
LEWEY
PLUTO
SHE-RA
SNOWY

6
BAM-BAM
BEAVIS
BOO-BOO
DROOPY
POPEYE
SHAGGY
SNOOPY
TINTIN
TOP CAT

7
ATOM ANT

BATFINK
MR JINKS
MR MAGOO
MUTTLEY
NIBBLES
PEBBLES
RAPHAEL

8
BUTT-HEAD
GARFIELD
GODZILLA
HANK HILL
LEONARDO
OLIVE OYL
PORKY PIG
SUPERTED
YOGI BEAR

9
BETTY BOOP
BUGS BUNNY
CHIP 'N' DALE
DAFFY DUCK
DAISY DUCK
DOGTANIAN

ELMER FUDD
PEPE LE PEW
PEGGY HILL
SCOOBY DOO
SPIDERMAN
SYLVESTER

10
ANTHILL MOB
BARNEY BEAR
DEPUTY DAWG
DONALD DUCK
MEG GRIFFIN
PEGLEG PETE
ROAD RUNNER
SCRAPPY DOO
TWEETIE PIE
WILY COYOTE

11
BART SIMPSON
BETTY RUBBLE
FELIX THE CAT
LISA SIMPSON
LOIS GRIFFIN
MICKEY MOUSE

MIGHTY MOUSE
MINNIE MOUSE
PATRICK STAR
PETE HOTHEAD
PINK PANTHER
ROGER RABBIT
SNAGGLEPUSS
TOM AND JERRY
YOSEMITE SAM

12
BARNEY RUBBLE
BRIAN GRIFFIN
CHRIS GRIFFIN
HOMER SIMPSON
MARGE SIMPSON
MICHELANGELO
PETER GRIFFIN
PETER PERFECT

13
DICK DASTARDLY
MAGGIE SIMPSON
STEWIE GRIFFIN

14
CAPTAIN CAVEMAN

CAPTAIN HADDOCK
CAPTAIN PUGWASH
FOGHORN LEGHORN
FRED FLINTSTONE
HONG KONG PHOOEY
MAGILLA GORILLA
SECRET SQUIRREL
SPEEDY GONZALES

TASMANIAN DEVIL

15
HECKLE AND JECKLE
PENELOPE PITSTOP
WILMA FLINTSTONE
WOODY WOODPECKER

16
HUCKLEBERRY HOUND
QUICK DRAW
  MACGRAW

17+
GERALD MCBOING
  BOING

GERTIE THE
  DINOSAUR
SPONGEBOB
  SQUAREPANTS
SQUIDWARD QUINCY
  TENTACLES
TEENAGE MUTANT
  NINJA TURTLES

KNOTS

3
BOW

4
BEND

5
HITCH

6
PRUSIK

7
BOWKNOT
BOWLINE
CAT'S-PAW

8
LOOP-KNOT
LOVE-KNOT

MESH KNOT
REEF KNOT
SLIP-KNOT
WALL-KNOT
WALE-KNOT

9
HALF HITCH
SHEET BEND
THUMB KNOT
TURK'S HEAD
WATER-KNOT

10
CLOVE HITCH
GRANNY KNOT
HAWSER-BEND
SHEEPSHANK
SQUARE KNOT

SHROUD-KNOT

11
CARRICK BEND
DIAMOND KNOT
RUNNING KNOT
SAILOR'S KNOT
TIMBER HITCH
WEAVER'S KNOT
WINDSOR KNOT

12
HANGMAN'S KNOT
HARNESS HITCH
HERCULES KNOT
OVERHAND KNOT
ROLLING HITCH
SURGEON'S KNOT
TRUE-LOVE KNOT

13
ENGLISHMAN'S TIE
MATTHEW WALKER

14
BLACKWALL HITCH
FISHERMAN'S BEND
FISHERMAN'S KNOT
RUNNING BOWLINE

17
BOWLINE ON THE
  BIGHT
FIGURE-OF-EIGHT
  KNOT

26
ROUND TURN AND
  TWO HALF HITCHES

OXFORD COLLEGES

3
NEW

5
JESUS
KEBLE
ORIEL

6
EXETER
MERTON
WADHAM

7
BALLIOL
KELLOGG
LINACRE

LINCOLN
ST ANNE'S
ST CROSS
ST HUGH'S
ST JOHN'S
TRINITY
WOLFSON

8
ALL SOULS
HERTFORD
MAGDALEN
NUFFIELD
PEMBROKE
ST HILDA'S
ST PETER'S

9
ST ANTHONY'S
BRASENOSE
MANSFIELD
THE QUEEN'S
WORCESTER

10
SOMERVILLE
UNIVERSITY

11
REGENT'S PARK
BLACKFRIARS
CAMPION HALL

12
CHRIST CHURCH

ST BENET'S HALL
ST CATHERINE'S
ST EDMUND HALL
WYCLIFFE HALL

13
CORPUS CHRISTI

14
GREEN TEMPLETON

15
ST STEPHEN'S HOUSE

16
HARRIS MANCHESTER
LADY MARGARET HALL

CAMBRIDGE COLLEGES

5
CLARE
JESUS
KING'S

6
DARWIN
GIRTON
SELWYN
QUEENS'

7
CHRIST'S
DOWNING
NEWNHAM
ST JOHN'S
TRINITY

WOLFSON

8
EMMANUEL
HOMERTON
PEMBROKE
ROBINSON

9
CHURCHILL
CLARE HALL
MAGDALENE
ST EDMUND'S

10
HUGHES HALL
PETERHOUSE

RIDLEY HALL

11
FITZWILLIAM
TRINITY HALL

12
SIDNEY SUSSEX
ST CATHARINE'S

13
CORPUS CHRISTI
LUCY CAVENDISH
MURRAY EDWARDS

15
GONVILLE AND CAIUS

IVY LEAGUE COLLEGES

4
YALE

5
BROWN

7
CORNELL
HARVARD

8
COLUMBIA

9
DARTMOUTH
PRINCETON

12
PENNSYLVANIA

LANGUAGE

LANGUAGES OF THE WORLD

2
WU

3
MIN

4
URDU

5
DUTCH
GREEK
HINDI
IRISH
MALAY
ORIYA
TAMIL
WELSH

6
ARABIC
BIHARI
BRETON
DANISH
FRENCH
GAELIC
GERMAN
KOREAN
PAHARI
POLISH
ROMANY
SINDHI
SLOVAK
TELUGU

7
BENGALI
CATALAN

ENGLISH
FRISIAN
ITALIAN
LATVIAN
MARATHI
PUNJABI
RUSSIAN
SLOVENE
SORBIAN
SPANISH
SWEDISH
TURKISH

8
ASSAMESE
GUJARATI
JAPANESE
JAVANESE
KASHMIRI

MANDARIN
ROMANSCH
RUMANIAN
UKRANIAN

9
AFRIKAANS
BULGARIAN
CANTONESE
ICELANDIC
NORWEGIAN
SINHALESE

10
LITHUANIAN
PORTUGUESE
RAJASTHANI
SERBO-CROAT

THE GREEK ALPHABET

ALPHA
BETA
GAMMA
DELTA
EPSILON
ZETA

ETA
THETA
IOTA
KAPPA
LAMBDA
MU

NU
XI
OMICRON
PI
RHO
SIGMA

TAU
UPSILON
PHI
CHI
PSI
OMEGA

THE HEBREW ALPHABET

ALEPH
BETH
GIMEL
DALETH
HE
VAV

ZAYIN
CHETH
TETH
YOD
KAPH
LAMED

MEM
NUN
SAMEKH
AYIN
PE
SADI

KOPH
RESH
SHIN
SIN
TAV

FOREIGN WORDS

AND

Fr.	ET
Ger.	UND
It.	E, ED
Sp.	E
Lat.	ET

BUT

Fr.	MAIS
Ger.	ABER
It.	MA
Sp.	PERO
Lat.	SED

FOR

Fr.	POUR
Ger.	FÜR
It.	PER
Sp.	PARA, POR
Lat.	PER

TO

Fr.	À
Ger.	AUF, NACH
It.	A
Sp.	A
Lat.	AD

WITH

Fr.	AVEC
Ger.	MIT
It.	CON
Sp.	CON
Lat.	CUM

MISTER, MR

Fr.	MONSIEUR, M.
Ger.	HERR, HR., HRN.
It.	SIGNOR, SIG.
Sp.	SEÑOR, SR.
Lat.	DOMINUS.

MADAME, MRS

Fr.	MADAME, MME.
Ger.	FRAU, FR.
It.	SIGNORA, SIG.A., SIG.RA.
Sp.	SEÑORA, SRA.
Lat.	DOMINA

MISS, MS

Fr.	MADEMOISELLE, MLLE
Ger.	FRÄULEIN, FRL.
It.	SIGNORINA, SIG.NA
Sp.	SEÑORITA, SRTA.

FROM

Fr.	DE

Ger.	AUS, VON
It.	DA
Sp.	DE
Lat.	AB

OF

Fr.	DE
Ger.	VON
It.	DI
Sp.	DE
Lat.	DE

GIRL

Fr.	FILLE
Ger.	MÄDCHEN
It.	RAGAZZA
Sp.	CHICA, NIÑA
Lat.	PUELLA

BOY

Fr.	GARÇON
Ger.	JUNGE
It.	RAGAZZO
Sp.	CHICO, NIÑO
Lat.	PUER

BIG

Fr.	GRAND
Ger.	GROSS
It.	GRANDE
Sp.	GRANDE
Lat.	MAGNUS

LITTLE

Fr.	PETIT
Ger.	KLEIN
It.	PICCOLO
Sp.	PEQUEÑO, CHICO, POCO
Lat.	PAUCUS

VERY

Fr.	TRÈS
Ger.	SEHR
It.	MOLTO
Sp.	MUCHO

FASHIONABLE

Fr.	À LA MODE
Ger.	MODISCH
It.	DI MODA
Sp.	DE MODA

GENTLEMAN

Fr.	MONSIEUR
Ger.	HERR
It.	SIGNORE
Sp.	CABALLERO

Lat.	DOMINUS

LADY

Fr.	DAME
Ger.	DAME
It.	SIGNORA
Sp.	SEÑORA
Lat.	DOMINA

MAN

Fr.	HOMME
Ger.	MANN
It.	UOMO
Sp.	HOMBRE
Lat.	HOMO

WOMAN

Fr.	FEMME
Ger.	FRAU
It.	DONNA
Sp.	DOÑA
Lat.	MULIER

WHO

Fr.	QUI
Ger.	WER
It.	CHI
Sp.	QUIEN, QUE
Lat.	QUIS

I

Fr.	JE
Ger.	ICH
It.	IO
Sp.	YO
Lat.	EGO

YOU

Fr.	TU, VOUS
Ger.	DU, SIE, IHR
It.	TU, VOI, LEI
Sp.	TU, VOSOTROS/(AS)
Lat.	TU, VOS

WHAT

Fr.	QUOI, QUEL
Ger.	WAS
It.	CHE COSA
Sp.	QUE
Lat.	QUOD

HE

Fr.	IL
Ger.	ER
It.	EGLI
Sp.	EL
Lat.	IS

SHE

Fr.	ELLE
Ger.	SIE
It.	ELLA
Sp.	ELLA
Lat.	EA

WE

Fr.	NOUS
Ger.	WIR
It.	NOI
Sp.	NOSOTROS/AS
Lat.	NOS

THEY

Fr.	ILS, ELLES
Ger.	SIE
It.	ESSI/E, LORO
Sp.	ELLOS, ELLAS
Lat.	EI, EAE

AT HOME

Fr.	CHEZ NOUS OR À LA MAISON
Ger.	ZU HAUSE
It.	A CASA
Sp.	EN CASA
Lat.	DOMO

HOUSE

Fr.	MAISON
Ger.	HAUS
It.	CASA
Sp.	CASA
Lat.	VILLA, DOMUS

STREET

Fr.	RUE
Ger.	STRASSE
It.	STRADA
Sp.	CALLE
Lat.	VIA

ROAD

Fr.	ROUTE
Ger.	WEG
It.	VIA
Sp.	CAMINO
Lat.	VIA

BY

Fr.	PAR
Ger.	BEI
It.	PER
Sp.	POR
Lat.	PER

BEFORE

Fr.	AVANT
Ger.	VOR
It.	PRIMA
Sp.	(DEL) ANTE
Lat.	ANTE

AFTER

Fr.	APRÈS
Ger.	NACH
It.	DOPO
Sp.	DESPUES
Lat.	POST

UNDER

Fr.	SOUS
Ger.	UNTER
It.	SOTTO
Sp.	(DE)BAJO
Lat.	SUB

OVER

Fr.	SUR
Ger.	OBER
It.	SOPRA, SU
Sp.	SOBRE
Lat.	SUPER

NEAR

Fr.	PRÈS DE
Ger.	NAHE, BEI
It.	VICINO
Sp.	CERCA
Lat.	PROPE

OUT

Fr.	DEHORS
Ger.	AUS
It.	VIA, FUORI
Sp.	FUERA
Lat.	EX

IN

Fr.	DANS
Ger.	IN
It.	IN
Sp.	EN
Lat.	IN

HOW

Fr.	COMMENT
Ger.	WIE
It.	COME
Sp.	COMO
Lat.	QUO MODO

WHY

Fr.	POURQUOI
Ger.	WARUM
It.	PERCHE
Sp.	POR QUÉ
Lat.	CUR

THE

Fr.	LE, LA, LES
Ger.	DER, DIE, DAS
It.	IL, LO, LA, I, GLI, LE
Sp.	EL, LA, LO, LOS, LAS
Lat.	ILLE

A

Fr.	UN, UNE
Ger.	EIN, EINE
It.	UN, UNO, UNA
Sp.	UN, UNA
Lat.	UNUS

RED

Fr.	ROUGE
Ger.	ROT
It.	ROSSO
Sp.	ROJO
Lat.	RUBER

BLUE

Fr.	BLEU
Ger.	BLAU
It.	AZZURRO
Sp.	AZUL
Lat.	CAERULEUS

YELLOW

Fr.	JAUNE
Ger.	GELB
It.	GIALLO
Sp.	AMARILLO
Lat.	FULVUS

GREEN

Fr.	VERT
Ger.	GRÜN
It.	VERDE
Sp.	VERDE
Lat.	VIRIDIS

BLACK

Fr.	NOIR
Ger.	SCHWARZ
It.	NERO
Sp.	NEGRO
Lat.	NIGER

WHITE

Fr.	BLANC OR BLANCHE
Ger.	WEISS
It.	BIANCO
Sp.	BLANCO
Lat.	ALBUS

NUMBERS

	ROMAN NUMERALS	FRENCH	GERMAN	ITALIAN	SPANISH
1	I	UN	EIN	UNO	UNO
2	II	DEUX	ZWEI	DUE	DOS
3	III	TROIS	DREI	TRE	TRES
4	IV	QUATRE	VIER	QUATTRO	CUATRO
5	V	CINQ	FÜNF	CINQUE	CINCO
6	VI	SIX	SECHS	SEI	SEIS
7	VII	SEPT	SIEBEN	SETTE	SIETE
8	VIII	HUIT	ACHT	OTTO	OCHO
9	IX	NEUF	NEUN	NOVE	NUEVE
10	X	DIX	ZEHN	DIECI	DIEZ
20	XX	VINGT	ZWANZIG	VENTI	VEINTE
30	XXX	TRENTE	DREISSIG	TRENTA	TREINTA
40	XL	QUARANTE	VIERZIG	QUARANTA	CUARENTA
50	L	CINQUANTE	FÜNFZIG	CINQUANTA	CINCUENTA
60	LX	SOIXANTE	SECHZIG	SESSANTA	SESENTA
70	LXX	SOIXANTE-DIX	SIEBZIG	SETTANTA	SETENTA
80	LXXX	QUATRE-VINGT	ACHTZIG	OTTANTA	OCHENTA
90	XC	QUATRE-VINGT-DIX	NEUNZIG	NOVANTA	NOVENTA
100	C	CENT	HUNDERT	CENTO	CIEN (CIENTO)
500	D	CINQ CENTS	FÜNFHUNDERT	CINQUECENTO	QUINIENTOS
1000	M	MILLE	TAUSEND	MILLE	MIL

FRENCH PHRASES

5
MÊLÉE – brawl
ON DIT – piece of gossip, rumour

6
DE TROP – unwelcome

7
À LA MODE – fashionable
À PROPOS – to the point
CAP-À -PIE – from head to foot
DE RÈGLE – customary
EN MASSE – all together
EN ROUTE – on the way

8
BÊTE NOIR – person or thing
    particularly disliked
IDÉE FIXE – obsession
MAL DE MER – seasickness
MOT JUSTE – the appropriate
    word

9
DE RIGUEUR – required by
    custom
EN PASSANT – by the way
EN RAPPORT – in harmony
ENTRE NOUS – between you and
    me

10
À BON MARCHÉ – cheap
BILLET DOUX – love letter
DERNIER CRI – latest fashion, the
    last word
NOM DE PLUME – writer's
    assumed name
PENSE À BIEN – think for the
    best

11
AMOUR PROPRE – self- esteem
GARDEZ LA FOI – keep the faith
LÈSE MAJESTÉ – treason
NOM DE GUERRE – assumed
    name
RAISON D'ÊTRE – justification for
    existence
SAVOIR FAIRE – address, tact
TOUR DE FORCE – feat or
    accomplishment of great
    strength

12
FORCE MAJEURE – irresistible
    force or compulsion
HORS DE COMBAT – out of the
    fight, disabled
SANS DIEU RIEN – nothing

without God
VENTRE À TERRE – at great
    speed

14
DOUBLE ENTENDRE – double
    meaning
ENFANT TERRIBLE – child who
    causes embarrassment
NOBLESSE OBLIGE – privilege
    entails responsibility
PREUX CHEVALIER – gallant
    knight
VÉRITÉ SANS PEUR – truth
    without fear

15
AMENDE HONORABLE –
    reparation
CHERCHEZ LA FEMME – look for
    the woman

17
PIÈCE DE RÉSISTANCE – most
    outstanding item; main dish at
    a meal

20+
AUTRE TEMPS, AUTRES MOEURS
    – other times, other manners

LATIN PHRASES

4
FIAT – let it be done or made
IN RE – concerning
STET – let it stand

5
AD HOC – for this special purpose
AD LIB – to speak off the cuff, without notes
AD REM – to the point
CIRCA – about
FECIT – he did it

6
AD USUM – as customary
IN SITU – in its original situation
IN TOTO – entirely
IN VIVO – in life, describing biological occurrences within living bodies
PRO TEM – temporary, for the time being

7
AD FINEM – to the end
A PRIORI – by deduction
CUI BONO? – whom does it benefit?
DE FACTO – in fact
FIAT LUX – let there be light
IN VITRO – in glass, describing biological experiments outside a body
PECCAVI – a confession of guilt (I have sinned)
PER DIEM – by the day
SINE DIE – without a day being appointed
SUB ROSA – confidential
UNA VOCE – with one voice, unanimously

8
ALTER EGO – another self
BONA FIDE – in good faith
EMERITUS – one retired from active official duties
MEA CULPA – an acknowledgement of guilt (I am to blame)
NOTA BENE – observe or note well
PRO FORMA – for the sake of form

9
AD INTERIM – meanwhile
AD LITERAM – to the letter
AD NAUSEAM – to a disgusting, sickening degree
DEI GRATIA – by the grace of God
ET TU, BRUTE – and you, Brutus
EXCELSIOR – still higher
EX OFFICIO – by right of position or office
HIC ET NUNC – here and now
INTER ALIA – among other things
PRO PATRIA – for one's country
STATUS QUO – the existing situation or state of affairs
SUB JUDICE – under consideration
VICE VERSA – the terms being exchanged, the other way round
VOX POPULI – popular opinion

10
ANNO DOMINI – in the year of our Lord
DEO GRATIAS – thanks be to God
EX CATHEDRA – with authority
IN EXTREMIS – in dire straits, at the the point of death
IN MEMORIAM – to the memory of
LOCO CITATO – in the place quoted
POST MORTEM – after death
PRIMA FACIE – at first sight
SINE QUA NON – something indispensable
TERRA FIRMA – solid ground

11
AD INFINITUM – endlessly, to infinity
ANIMO ET FIDE – by courage and faith
DE DIE IN DIEM – from day to day
DE PROFUNDIS – from the depths of misery
EX POST FACTO – after the event
GLORIA PATRI – glory to the Father
LOCUS STANDI – the right to be heard (in a law case)
NON SEQUITUR – an unwarranted conclusion
PAX VOBISCUM – peace be with you
TEMPUS FUGIT – time flies

12
ANTE MERIDIEM – before noon
CAVEAT EMPTOR – let the buyer beware
COMPOS MENTIS – of sane mind
FESTINA LENTE – hasten slowly, be quick without impetuosity
JACTA EST ALEA – the die is cast
PERSEVERANDO – by perseverance
POST MERIDIEM – after noon
SERVABO FIDEM – I will keep faith
VENI, VIDI, VICI – I came, I saw, I conquered
VOLO NON VALEO – I am willing but unable

13
CORPUS DELICTI – body of facts that constitute an offence
DUM SPIRO, SPERO – while I breathe, I hope
IN VINO VERITAS – there is truth in wine, that is, the truth comes out
MODUS OPERANDI – a method of operating
NE FRONTI CREDE – trust not to appearances
VINCIT VERITAS – truth conquers
VIRTUTIS AMORE – by love of virtue

14
CETERIS PARIBUS – other things being equal
EDITIO PRINCEPS – the original edition
IN LOCO PARENTIS – in place of a parent
NIL DESPERANDUM – never despair
PRO BONO PUBLICO – for the public good

15
ANIMO NON ASTUTIA – by courage not by craft
FORTITER ET RECTE – courageously and honourably
FORTUNA SEQUATUR – let fortune follow

INFRA DIGNITATEM – beneath one's dignity
NON COMPOS MENTIS – mentally unsound
OMNIA VINCIT AMOR – love conquers all things
PERSONA NON GRATA – an unacceptable person

16
GLORIA IN EXCELSIS – glory to God in the highest

17
LABOR IPSE VOLUPTAS – labour itself is pleasure
NUNQUAM NON PARATUS – always ready
PROBUM NON PAENITET – honesty repents not
VER NON SEMPER VIRET – spring does not always
flourish

18
NEC TEMERE NEC TIMIDE – neither rashly nor
timidly
PRO REGE, LEGE, ET GREGE – for the king, the law,
and the people
REDUCTIO AD ABSURDUM – reducing to absurdity

19
CANDIDE ET CONSTANTER – fairly and firmly

SOLA NOBILITAS VIRTUS – virtue alone is true
nobility
VIRTUTI NON ARMIS FIDO – I trust to virtue and not
to arms

20+
DE MORTUIS NIL NISI BONUM – speak only good of
the dead
DULCE ET DECORUM EST PRO PATRIA MORI – it is
sweet and seemly to die for one's country
FORTUNA FAVET FORTIBUS – fortune favours the
brave
PATRIA CARA CARIOR LIBERTAS – my country is
dear, but liberty is dearer
QUOD ERAT DEMONSTRANDUM – which was to be
demonstrated
SIC TRANSIT GLORIA MUNDI – thus passes the glory
of the world
TIMEO DANAOS ET DONA FERENTIS – I fear the
Greeks, even when bearing gifts
VIVIT POST FUNERA VIRTUS – virtue survives the
grave

COMMON SAYINGS

PROVERBS

A bad penny always turns up.
A bad workman always blames his tools.
A bird in the hand is worth two in the bush.
Absence makes the heart grow fonder.
A cat has nine lives.
A cat may look at a king.
Accidents will happen in the best regulated families.
A chain is no stronger than its weakest link.
Actions speak louder than words.
A drowning man will clutch at a straw.
A fool and his money are soon parted.
A fool at forty is a fool indeed.
A friend in need is a friend indeed.
All cats are grey in the dark.
All good things must come to an end.
All is fair in love and war.
All roads lead to Rome.
All's grist that comes to the mill.
All's well that ends well.
All that glitters is not gold.
All the world loves a lover.
All work and no play makes Jack a dull boy.
A miss is as good as a mile.
An apple a day keeps the doctor away.
An Englishman's home is his castle.
An Englishman's word is his bond.
A nod is as good as a wink to a blind horse.
Any port in a storm.
Any publicity is good publicity.
A trouble shared is a trouble halved.
Attack is the best form of defence.
A watched pot never boils.
A woman's work is never done.
A young physician fattens the churchyard.

Bad news travels fast.
Beauty is in the eye of the beholder.
Beauty is only skin-deep.
Beggars can't be choosers.
Better be an old man's darling than a young man's slave.
Better be safe than sorry.
Better late than never.
Birds of a feather flock together.
Blood is thicker than water.
Books and friends should be few but good.
Caesar's wife must be above suspicion.
Charity begins at home.
Christmas comes but once a year.
Civility costs nothing.
Cold hands, warm heart.
Constant dripping wears away the stone.
Curiosity killed the cat.
Cut your coat according to your cloth.
Dead men tell no tales.
Death is the great leveller.
Divide and rule.
Do as I say, not as I do.
Do as you would be done by.
Dog does not eat dog.
Don't count your chickens before they are hatched.
Don't cross the bridge till you get to it.
Don't cut off your nose to spite your face.
Don't meet troubles half-way.
Don't put all your eggs in one basket.
Don't spoil the ship for a ha'porth of tar.
Don't teach your grandmother to suck eggs.
Don't throw the baby out with the bathwater.
Don't wash your dirty linen in public.
Early to bed and early to rise, makes a man healthy, wealthy, and wise.
Easier said than done.

East, west, home's best.
Easy come, easy go.
Empty vessels make the greatest sound.
Even a worm will turn.
Every cloud has a silver lining.
Every dog has his day.
Every dog is allowed one bite.
Every man for himself, and the devil take the hindmost.
Everything comes to him who waits.
Experience is the best teacher.
Faith will move mountains.
Familiarity breeds contempt.
Fight fire with fire.
Fine feathers make fine birds.
Fine words butter no parsnips.
Fish and guests smell in three days.
Forewarned is forearmed.
Forgive and forget.
For want of a nail the shoe was lost; for want of a shoe the horse was lost; for want of a horse the rider was lost.
From clogs to clogs in only three generations.
Give a dog a bad name and hang him.
Give him an inch and he'll take a yard.
Great minds think alike.
Great oaks from little acorns grow.
Handsome is as handsome does.
He that fights and runs away, may live to fight another day.
He travels fastest who travels alone.
He who hesitates is lost.
He who lives by the sword dies by the sword.
He who pays the piper calls the tune.
He who sups with the devil should have a long spoon.
History repeats itself.
Honesty is the best policy.
If a job's worth doing, it's worth doing well.

If at first you don't succeed, try, try, try again.

If the mountain will not come to Mahomet, Mahomet must go to the mountain.

If you don't like the heat, get out of the kitchen.

Imitation is the sincerest form of flattery.

In for a penny, in for a pound.

In the country of the blind, the one-eyed man is king.

It is no use crying over spilt milk.

It never rains but it pours.

It's an ill wind that blows nobody any good.

It's too late to shut the stable door after the horse has bolted.

It will all come right in the wash.

It will be all the same in a hundred years.

Jack of all trades, master of none.

Keep something for a rainy day.

Kill not the goose that lays the golden egg.

Least said soonest mended.

Let bygones be bygones.

Let sleeping dogs lie.

Let the cobbler stick to his last.

Life begins at forty.

Life is just a bowl of cherries.

Life is not all beer and skittles.

Look before you leap.

Love is blind.

Love laughs at locksmiths.

Lucky at cards, unlucky in love.

Many a true word is spoken in jest.

Many hands make light work.

March comes in like a lion and goes out like a lamb.

March winds and April showers bring forth May flowers.

Marry in haste, and repent at leisure.

More haste, less speed.

Necessity is the mother of invention.

Needs must when the devil drives.

Ne'er cast a clout till May be out.

Never look a gift horse in the mouth.

No time like the present.

Old habits die hard.

Old sins cast long shadows.

One for sorrow, two for joy; three for a girl, four for a boy; five for silver, six for gold; seven for a secret, not to be told; eight for heaven, nine for hell; and ten for the devil's own sel.

One good turn deserves another.

One man's meat is another man's poison.

One swallow does not make a summer.

Out of sight, out of mind.

Patience is a virtue.

Penny wise, pound foolish.

Prevention is better than cure.

Red sky at night, shepherd's delight; red sky in the morning, shepherd's warning.

Revenge is a dish that tastes better cold.

Revenge is sweet.

See a pin and pick it up, all the day you'll have good luck; see a pin and let it lie, you'll want a pin before you die.

Seeing is believing.

See Naples and die.

Silence is golden.

Spare the rod and spoil the child.

Sticks and stones may break my bones, but words will never hurt me.

Still waters run deep.

St. Swithin's Day, if thou dost rain, for forty days it will remain; St. Swithin's Day, if thou be fair, for forty days 'twill rain no more.

Take a hair of the dog that bit you.

The darkest hour is just before the dawn.

The devil finds work for idle hands to do.

The devil looks after his own.

The early bird catches the worm.

The end justifies the means.

The exception proves the rule.

The hand that rocks the cradle rules the world.

Time is a great healer.

There is honour among thieves.

There is more than one way to skin a cat.

There is no accounting for tastes.

There is safety in numbers.

There's many a good tune played on an old fiddle.

There's many a slip' twixt the cup and the lip.

There's no place like home.

There's no smoke without fire.

The road to hell is paved with good intentions.

Time and tide wait for no man.

Time is a great healer.

Too many cooks spoil the broth.

Truth is stranger than fiction.

Two heads are better than one.

Two wrongs do not make a right.

United we stand, divided we fall.

Waste not, want not.

We must learn to walk before we can run.

What you lose on the swings you gain on the roundabouts.

When poverty comes in at the door, love flies out of the window.

When the cat's away, the mice will play.

When the wine is in, the wit is out.

Where there's a will there's a way.

Why keep a dog and bark yourself?

You can lead a horse to the water, but you can't make him drink.

You cannot run with the hare and hunt with the hounds.

You can't make an omelette without breaking eggs.

You can't teach an old dog new tricks.

You can't tell a book by its cover.

SIMILES

as bald as a coot

as black as pitch

as black as the ace of spades

as blind as a bat

as blind as a mole

as bold as brass

as bright as a button

as busy as a bee

as calm as a millpond

as cheap as dirt

as chirpy as a cricket

as clean as a whistle

as clear as a bell

as clear as crystal

as clear as mud

as cold as charity
as common as muck
as cool as a cucumber
as cross as two sticks
as daft as a brush
as dead as a dodo
as dead as a doornail
as dead as mutton
as deaf as a post
as different as chalk and cheese
as drunk as a lord
as dry as a bone
as dry as dust
as dull as dishwater
as easy as falling off a log
as easy as pie
as fit as a flea
as flat as a pancake
as free as a bird
as free as air
as free as the wind
as fresh as a daisy
as good as gold
as green as grass
as happy as a lark
as happy as a sandboy
as happy as Larry
as happy as the day is long
as hard as nails
as keen as mustard

as large as life
as light as a feather
as like as two peas in a pod
as lively as a cricket
as mad as a hatter
as mad as a March hare
as meek as a lamb
as merry as a cricket
as neat as a new pin
as nutty as a fruitcake
as obstinate as a mule
as old as the hills
as pale as death
as plain as a pikestaff
as plain as the nose on your face
as pleased as Punch
as poor as a church mouse
as poor as Lazarus
as pretty as a picture
as proud as a peacock
as pure as the driven snow
as quick as a flash
as quick as lightning
as quick as thought
as quiet as a mouse
as quiet as the grave
as red as a beetroot
as regular as clockwork
as rich as Croesus
as right as rain

as safe as houses
as sharp as a needle
as sick as a dog
as simple as falling off a log
as slippery as an eel
as snug as a bug in a rug
as sound as a bell
as steady as a rock
as stiff as a board
as stiff as a poker
as stiff as a ramrod
as straight as a die
as straight as an arrow
as stubborn as a mule
as sure as eggs is eggs
as sure as hell
as thick as thieves
as thick as two short planks
as thin as a lath
as thin as a rake
as thin as a stick
as tough as nails
as tough as old boots
as ugly as sin
as warm as toast
as weak as a kitten
as weak as dishwater
as welcome as the flowers in May
as white as a sheet

NURSERY RHYMES

A frog he would a-wooing go,
Heigh ho! says Rowley,
A frog he would a-wooing go,
Whether his mother would let
    him or no.
With a rowley, powley, gammon
    and spinach,
Heigh ho! says Anthony Rowley.

As I was going to St Ives,
I met a man with seven wives.
Each wife had seven sacks
Each sack had seven cats,
Each cat had seven kits,
How many were going to St Ives?

Baa, baa, black sheep,
Have you any wool?
Yes, sir, yes, sir,
Three bags full;
One for the master,
And one for the dame,
And one for the little boy
Who lives down the lane.

Bobby Shafto's gone to sea,
Silver buckles on his knee;
He'll come back and marry me,
Bonny Bobby Shafto!

Come, let's to bed
Says Sleepy-head;
Tarry a while, says Slow;
Put on the pan;
Says Greedy Nan,
Let's sup before we go.

Ding dong, bell,
Pussy's in the well.
Who put her in?
Little Johnny Green.
Who pulled her out?
Little Tommy Stout.

Doctor Foster went to Gloucester
In a shower of rain:
He stepped in a puddle,
Right up to his middle,
And never went there again.

Georgie Porgie, pudding and pie,
Kissed the girls and made them
    cry;
When the boys came out to play,
Georgie Porgie ran away.

Goosey, goosey gander,
Whither shall I wander?
Upstairs and downstairs

And in my lady's chamber.

Hey diddle diddle,
The cat and the fiddle,
The cow jumped over the moon;
The little dog laughed
To see such sport,
And the dish ran away with the
    spoon.

Hickory, dickory, dock,
The mouse ran up the clock.
The clock struck one,
The mouse ran down,
Hickory, dickory, dock.

How many miles to Babylon?
Three score miles and ten.
Can I get there by candle-light?
Yes, and back again.
If your heels are nimble and light,
You may get there by candle-
    light.

Humpty Dumpty sat on a wall,
Humpty Dumpty had a great fall.
All the king's horses and
All the king's men,
Couldn't put Humpty

together again.

Jack and Jill went up the hill
To fetch a pail of water;
Jack fell down and broke his
   crown,
And Jill came tumbling after.

Jack Sprat could eat no fat,
His wife could eat no lean,
And so between them both you
   see,
They licked the platter clean.

Little Bo-peep has lost her sheep,
And can't tell where to find them;
Leave them alone, and they'll
   come home,
Bringing their tails behind them.

Little Boy Blue,
Come blow your horn,
The sheep's in the meadow,
The cow's in the corn.

Little Jack Horner
Sat in the corner,
Eating a Christmas pie;
He put in his thumb,
And pulled out a plum,
And said, What a good boy am I!

Little Miss Muffet
Sat on a tuffet,
Eating her curds and whey;
There came a big spider,
Who sat down beside her
And frightened Miss Muffet
   away.

Little Tommy Tucker,
Sings for his supper:
What shall we give him?
White bread and butter
How shall he cut it
Without a knife?
How will he be married
Without a wife?

Mary, Mary, quite contrary,
How does your garden grow?
With silver bells and cockle shells,
And pretty maids all in a row.

Monday's child is fair of face,
Tuesday's child is full of grace,
Wednesday's child is full of woe,
Thursday's child has far to go,
Friday's child is loving and giving,
Saturday's child works hard for
   his living,
And the child that is born on the
   Sabbath day
Is bonny and blithe, and good
   and gay.

Oh! the grand old Duke of York
He had ten thousand men;

He marched them up to the top
   of the hill,
And he marched them down
   again.
And when they were up they
   were up,
And when they were down they
   were down,
And when they were only half
   way up,
They were neither up nor down.

Old King Cole
Was a merry old soul,
And a merry old soul was he;
He called for his pipe,
And he called for his bowl,
And he called for his fiddlers
   three.

Old Mother Hubbard
Went to the cupboard,
To fetch her poor dog a bone;
But when she got there
The cupboard was bare
And so the poor dog had none.

One, two, Buckle my shoe;
Three, four, Knock at the door.
Five, six, Pick up sticks;
Seven, eight, Close the gate.
Nine, ten, Big fat hen;
Eleven, twelve, Dig and delve.
Thirteen, fourteen, Maids
   a'courting;
Fifteen, sixteen, Maids in the
   kitchen.
Seventeen, eighteen, Maids
   a'waiting;
Nineteen, twenty, My plate's
   empty.

Oranges and lemons,
Say the bells of St Clement's.
You owe me five farthings,
Say the bells of St Martin's.
When will you pay me?
Say the bells of Old Bailey.
When I grow rich,
Say the bells of Shoreditch.
When will that be?
Say the bells of Stepney.
I'm sure I don't know,
Says the great bell at Bow.
Here comes a candle to light you
   to bed,
Here comes a chopper to chop
   off your head.

Peter Piper picked a peck of pick-
led pepper;
A peck of pickled pepper Peter
   Piper picked;
If Peter Piper picked a peck of
   pickled pepper,
Where's the peck of pickled

pepper Peter Piper picked?

Polly put the kettle on,
Polly put the kettle on,
Polly put the kettle on,
We'll all have tea.
Sukey take it off again,
Sukey take it off again,
Sukey take it off again,
They've all gone away.

Pussy cat, pussy cat, where have
you been?
I've been to London to look at
   the queen.
Pussy cat, pussy cat, what did you
there?
I frightened a little mouse under
   her chair.

Ride a cock-horse to Banbury
Cross,
To see a fine lady upon a white
   horse;
Rings on her fingers and bells on
   her toes,
And she shall have music
   wherever she goes.

Ring-a-ring o'roses,
A pocket full of posies,
A-tishoo! A-tishoo!
We all fall down.

Rub-a-dub-dub,
Three men in a tub,
And who do you think they be?
The butcher, the baker,
The candlestick-maker,
And they all sailed out to sea.

See-saw, Margery Daw,
Jacky shall have a new master;
Jacky shall have but a penny a
   day,
Because he can't work any faster.

Simple Simon met a pieman,
Going to the fair;
Says Simple Simon to the pieman,
Let me taste your ware.
Says the pieman to Simple Simon,
Show me first your penny;
Says Simple Simon to the pieman,
Indeed I have not any.

Sing a song of sixpence,
A pocket full of rye;
Four and twenty blackbirds,
Baked in a pie.
When the pie was opened,
The birds began to sing;
Was not that a dainty dish,
To set before the king?

The king was in his countinghouse,

Counting out his money;
The queen was in the parlour,
Eating bread and honey.
The maid was in the garden,
Hanging out the clothes,
When down came a blackbird,
And pecked off her nose.

Solomon Grundy,
Born on a Monday,
Christened on Tuesday,
Married on Wednesday,
Took ill on Thursday,
Worse on Friday,
Died on Saturday,
Buried on Sunday.
This is the end
Of Solomon Grundy.

The lion and the unicorn
Were fighting for the crown;
The lion beat the unicorn
All round about the town.

There was a crooked man, and he
walked a crooked mile,
He found a crooked sixpence
against a crooked stile:
He bought a crooked cat, which
caught a crooked mouse,
And they all lived together in a
little crooked house.

There was an old woman who
lived in a shoe,
She had so many children she
didn't know what to do;
She gave them some broth
without any bread;
She whipped them all soundly
and put them to bed.

The twelfth day of Christmas,
My true love sent to me

Twelve lords a-leaping,
Eleven ladies dancing,
Ten pipers piping,
Nine drummers drumming,
Eight maids a-milking,
Seven swans a-swimming,
Six geese a-laying,
Five gold rings,
Four colly (or calling) birds,
Three French hens,
Two turtle doves, and
A partridge in a pear tree.
Note: There are many variants.
The most common seems to
be:
Twelve drummers drumming
Eleven pipers piping
Ten lords a-leaping
Nine ladies dancing

This little piggy went to market,
This little piggy stayed at home,
This little piggy had roast beef,
This little piggy had none,
And this little piggy cried, Wee-
wee-wee-wee-wee,
I can't find my way home.

Three blind mice, see how they
run!
They all run after the farmer's
wife,
Who cut off their tails with a
carving knife,
Did you ever see such a thing in
your life,
As three blind mice?

Tinker, Tailor,
Soldier, Sailor,
Rich man, Poor man,
Beggarman, Thief.

Tom, Tom, the piper's son,

Stole a pig and away he run;
The pig was eat
And Tom was beat,
And Tom went howling down the
street.

Two little dicky birds,
Sitting on a wall;
One named Peter,
The other named Paul,
Fly away, Peter!
Fly away, Paul!
Come back, Peter!
Come back, Paul!

Wee Willie Winkie runs through
the town
Upstairs and downstairs and in
his nightgown,
Rapping at the window, crying
through the lock,
Are the children all in bed? It's
past eight o'clock.

What are little boys made of?
Frogs and snails
And puppy-dogs' tails,
That's what little boys are made
of.

What are little girls made of?
Sugar and spice
And all that's nice,
That's what little girls are made
of.

Who killed Cock Robin?
I, said the Sparrow,
With my bow and arrow,
I killed Cock Robin.
Who saw him die?
I, said the Fly,
With my little eye,
I saw him die.

COMMON QUOTATIONS

ARNOLD, Matthew (1822–88) British poet

The sea is calm to-night,
The tide is full, the moon lies fair
Upon the Straits.
Dover Beach

A wanderer is man from his birth.
He was born in a ship
On the breast of the river of Time.
The Future

Go, for they call you, Shepherd, from the hill.
The Scholar Gipsy

Tired of knocking at Preferment's door.
The Scholar Gipsy

Before this strange disease of modern life,

With its sick hurry, its divided aims.
The Scholar Gipsy

Truth sits upon the lips of dying men.
Sohrab and Rustum

And see all sights from pole to pole,
And glance, and nod, and bustle by;
And never once possess our soul
Before we die.
A Southern Night

AUDEN, W H (1907–73) British poet

Look, stranger, at this island now
The leaping light for your delight discovers.
Look, Stranger

To the man-in-the-street, who, I'm sorry to say

Is a keen observer of life,
The word Intellectual suggests straight away
A man who's untrue to his wife.
Note on Intellectuals

When it comes, will it come without warning
Just as I'm picking my nose?
Will it knock on my door in the morning,
Or tread in the bus on my toes?
Will it come like a change in the weather?
Will its greeting be courteous or rough?
Will it alter my life altogether?
O tell me the truth about love.
Twelve Songs, XII

AUSTEN, Jane (1775–1817) British novelist

Nobody is healthy in London, nobody can be.
Emma, Ch. 12

Business, you know, may bring money, but friendship hardly ever does.
Emma, Ch. 34

Let other pens dwell on guilt and misery.
Mansfield Park, Ch. 48

A woman, especially if she have the misfortune of knowing anything, should conceal it as well as she can.
Northanger Abbey, Ch. 14

It is a truth universally acknowledged, that a single man in possession of a good fortune must be in want of a wife.
Pride and Prejudice, Ch. 1

Happiness in marriage is entirely a matter of chance.
Pride and Prejudice, Ch. 6

Next to being married, a girl likes to be crossed in love a little now and then.
Pride and Prejudice, Ch. 24

One cannot be always laughing at a man without now and then stumbling on something witty.
Pride and Prejudice, Ch. 40

For what do we live, but to make sport for our neighbours, and laugh at them in our turn?
Pride and Prejudice, Ch. 57

BETJEMAN, John (1906–84) British poet

You ask me what it is I do. Well actually, you know,
I'm partly a liaison man and partly P.R.O.
Essentially I integrate the current export drive
And basically I'm viable from ten o'clock till five.
Executive

I have a vision of the future, chum.
The workers' flats in fields of soya beans
Tower up like silver pencils.
The Planster's Vision

Come, friendly bombs, and fall on Slough
It isn't fit for humans now.
There isn't grass to graze a cow
Swarm over. Death!
Slough

THE BIBLE

And now abideth faith, hope, charity, these three; but the greatest of these is charity.
I Corinthians, 13: 13

O death, where is thy sting? O grave, where is thy victory?
I Corinthians, 15: 55

Vanity of vanities, saith the Preacher, vanity of vanities; all is vanity.
Ecclesiastes, 1: 2

To every thing there is a season, and a time to every purpose under the heaven:
A time to be born, and a time to die; a time to plant, and a time to pluck up that which is planted;
A time to kill, and a time to heal; a time to break down, and a time to build up;
A time to weep, and a time to laugh; a time to mourn, and a time to dance;
...
A time to love, and a time to hate; a time of war, and a time of peace.
Ecclesiastes, 3: 1–8

I returned, and saw under the sun, that the race is not to the swift, nor the battle to the strong, neither yet bread to the wise, nor yet riches to men of understanding, nor yet favour to men of skill; but time and chance happeneth to them all.
Ecclesiastes, 9: 11

Cast thy bread upon the waters: for thou shalt find it after many days.
Ecclesiastes, 11: 1

I am the Lord thy God, which have brought thee out of the land of Egypt, out of the house of bondage.
Thou shalt have no other gods before me.
Thou shalt not make unto thee any graven image, or any likeness of any thing that is in heaven above, or that is in the earth beneath, or that is in the water under the earth:
Thou shalt not bow down thyself to them, nor serve them: for I the Lord thy God am a jealous God, visiting the iniquity of the fathers upon the children unto the third and fourth generation of them that hate me;
And shewing mercy unto thousands of them that love me, and keep my commandments.
Thou shalt not take the name of the Lord thy God in vain; for the Lord will not hold him guiltless that taketh his name in vain.
Remember the sabbath day, to keep it holy.
Six days shalt thou labour, and do all thy work:
But the seventh day is the sabbath of the Lord thy God: in it thou shalt not do any work, thou, nor thy son, nor thy daughter, thy manservant, nor thy maidservant, nor thy cattle, nor thy stranger that is within thy gates:
For in six days the Lord made heaven and earth, the sea, and all that in them is, and rested the seventh day: wherefore the Lord blessed the sabbath day, and hallowed it.

Honour thy father and thy mother: that thy days may be long upon the land which the Lord thy God giveth thee.

Thou shalt not kill.

Thou shalt not commit adultery.

Thou shalt not steal.

Thou shalt not bear false witness against thy neighbour.

Thou shalt not covet thy neighbour's house, thou shalt not covet thy neighbour's wife, nor his manservant, nor his maidservant, nor his ox, nor his ass, nor any thing that is thy neighbour's.
Exodus, 20: 2–17

Eye for eye, tooth for tooth, hand for hand, foot for foot
Exodus, 21: 24

Thou shalt not suffer a witch to live.
Exodus, 22: 18

In the beginning God created the heaven and the earth.

And the earth was without form, and void; and darkness was upon the face of the deep. And the Spirit of God moved upon the face of the waters.

And God said, Let there be light: and there was light.
Genesis, 1: 1–3

And God said, Let us make man in our image, after our likeness: and let them have dominion over the fish of the sea, and over the fowl of the air, and over the cattle, and over all the earth, and over every creeping thing that creepeth upon the earth.
Genesis, 1: 26

And on the seventh day God ended his work which he had made; and he rested on the seventh day from all his work which he had made.
Genesis, 2: 2

But of the tree of the knowledge of good and evil, thou shalt not eat of it: for in the day that thou eatest thereof thou shalt surely die.
Genesis, 2: 17

And the rib, which the Lord God had taken from man, made he a woman, and brought her unto the man.
Genesis, 2: 22

And the Lord said unto Cain, Where is Abel thy brother? And he said, I know not: Am I my brother's keeper?
Genesis, 4: 9

And the Lord said unto him, Therefore whosoever slayeth Cain, vengeance shall be taken on him sevenfold. And the Lord set a mark upon Cain, lest any finding him should kill him.
Genesis, 4: 15

But his wife looked back from behind him, and she became a pillar of salt.
Genesis, 19: 26

And Jacob said to Rebekah his mother, Behold, Esau

my brother is a hairy man, and I am a smooth man.
Genesis, 27: 11

Therefore the Lord himself shall give you a sign; Behold, a virgin shall conceive, and bear a son, and shall call his name Immanuel.
Isaiah, 7: 14

Can the Ethiopian change his skin, or the leopard his spots? Then may ye also do good, that are accustomed to do evil.
Jeremiah, 13: 23

The next day John seeth Jesus coming unto him, and saith, Behold the Lamb of God, which taketh away the sin of the world.
John, 1: 29

So when they continued asking him, he lifted up himself, and said unto them, He that is without sin among you, let him first cast a stone at her.
John, 8: 7

And ye shall know the truth, and the truth shall make you free.
John, 8: 32

In my Father's house are many mansions: if it were not so, I would have told you. I go to prepare a place for you.
John, 14: 2

Greater love hath no man than this, that a man lay down his life for his friends.
John, 15: 13

Now the Lord had prepared a great fish to swallow up Jonah. And Jonah was in the belly of the fish three days and three nights.
Jonah, 1: 17

And it came to pass, as they still went on, and talked, that, behold, there appeared a chariot of fire, and horses of fire, and parted them both asunder; and Elijah went up by a whirlwind into heaven.
II Kings, 2: 11

And it came to pass in those days, that there went out a decree from Caesar Augustus, that all the world should be taxed.
Luke, 2: 1

And she brought forth her firstborn son, and wrapped him in swaddling clothes, and laid him in a manger; because there was no room for them in the inn.
Luke, 2: 7

Then said Jesus, Father, forgive them; for they know not what they do. And they parted his raiment, and cast lots.
Luke, 23: 34

And he asked him, What is thy name? And he answered, saying, My name is Legion: for we are many.
Mark, 5: 9

For what shall it profit a man, if he shall gain the

whole world, and lose his own soul? Or what shall a man give in exchange for his soul?
Mark, 8: 36–37

But he answered and said, It is written, Man shall not live by bread alone, but by every word that proceedeth out of the mouth of God.
Matthew, 4: 4

And he saith unto them, Follow me, and I will make you fishers of men.
Matthew, 4: 19

And if thy right eye offend thee, pluck it out, and cast it from thee: for it is profitable for thee that one of thy members should perish, and not that thy whole body should be cast into hell.
Matthew, 5: 29

Lay not up for yourselves treasures upon earth, where moth and rust doth corrupt, and where thieves break through and steal.
Matthew, 6: 19

Take therefore no thought for the morrow: for the morrow shall take thought for the things of itself. Sufficient unto the day is the evil thereof.
Matthew, 6: 33

Judge not, that ye be not judged.
Matthew, 7: 1

And why beholdest thou the mote that is in thy brother's eye, but considerest not the beam that is in thine own eye?
Matthew, 7: 3

Give not that which is holy unto the dogs, neither cast ye your pearls before swine, lest they trample them under their feet, and turn again and rend you.
Matthew, 7: 6

Because strait is the gate, and narrow is the way, which leadeth unto life, and few there be that find it.
Matthew, 7: 14

And they were offended in him. But Jesus said unto them, A prophet is not without honour, save in his own country, and in his own house.
Matthew, 13: 57

And again I say unto you, It is easier for a camel to go through the eye of a needle, than for a rich man to enter into the kingdom of God.
Matthew, 19: 24

But many that are first shall be last; and the last shall be first.
Matthew, 19: 30

Jesus said unto him, Verily I say unto thee, That this night, before the cock crow, thou shalt deny me thrice.
Matthew, 26: 34

Watch and pray, that ye enter not into temptation: the spirit indeed is willing, but the flesh is weak.
Matthew, 26: 41

Then said Jesus unto him, Put up again thy sword into his place: for all they that take the sword shall perish with the sword.
Matthew, 26: 52

For the lips of a strange woman drop as an honeycomb, and her mouth is smoother than oil:
But her end is bitter as wormwood, sharp as a two-edged sword.
Proverbs, 5: 3–4

Stolen waters are sweet, and bread eaten in secret is pleasant.
Proverbs, 9: 17

He that spareth his rod hateth his son: but he that loveth him chasteneth him betimes.
Proverbs, 13: 24

Pride goeth before destruction, and an haughty spirit before a fall.
Proverbs, 16: 18

For thou shalt heap coals of fire upon his head, and the Lord shall reward thee.
Proverbs, 25: 22

Who can find a virtuous woman? for her price is far above rubies.
Proverbs, 31: 10

And the name of the star is called Wormwood: and the third part of the waters became wormwood; and many men died of the waters, because they were made bitter.
Revelations, 8: 11

Here is wisdom. Let him that hath understanding count the number of the beast: for it is the number of a man; and his number is Six hundred threescore and six.
Revelations, 13: 18

Drink no longer water, but use a little wine for thy stomach's sake and thine often infirmities.
I Timothy, 5: 23

For the love of money is the root of all evil: which while some coveted after, they have erred from the faith, and pierced themselves through with many sorrows.
I Timothy, 6: 10

BLAKE, William (1757–1827) British poet and engraver

To see a World in a grain of sand,
And a Heaven in a wild flower,
Hold Infinity in the palm of your hand,
And Eternity in an hour.
Auguries of Innocence

And did those feet in ancient time
Walk upon England's mountains green?
And was the holy lamb of God
On England's pleasant pastures seen?
Milton, Preface (known as the hymn 'Jerusalem')

I will not cease from mental fight,

Nor shall my sword sleep in my hand,
Till we have built Jerusalem
In England's green and pleasant land.
Milton, Preface (known as the hymn 'Jerusalem')

Love seeketh not itself to please,
Nor for itself hath any care,
But for another gives its ease,
And builds a Heaven in Hell's despair.
Songs of Experience, 'The Clod and the Pebble'

Tiger! Tiger! burning bright
In the forests of the night,
What immortal hand or eye
Could frame thy fearful symmetry?
Songs of Experience, 'The Tiger'

Little Lamb, who made thee?
Dost thou know who made thee?
Songs of Innocence, 'The Lamb'

BRONTË, Charlotte (1816–55) British novelist

Reader, I married him.
Jane Eyre, Ch. 38

BROWNING, Elizabeth Barrett (1806–61) British
poet

'Yes,' I answered you last night;
'No,' this morning, sir, I say.
Colours seen by candle-light
Will not look the same by day.
The Lady's Yes

How do I love thee? Let me count the ways.
Sonnets from the Portuguese, XLIII

I love thee with the breath,
Smiles, tears, of all my life! – and, if God choose,
I shall but love thee better after death.
Sonnets from the Portuguese, XLIII

BROWNING, Robert (1812–89) British poet

Oh, to be in England
Now that April's there,
And whoever wakes in England,
Sees, some morning, unaware,
That the lowest boughs and the brushwood sheaf
Round the elm-tree bole are in tiny leaf,
While the chaffinch sings on the orchard bough
In England—now!
Home Thoughts from Abroad

Rats!
They fought the dogs and killed the cats,
And bit the babies in the cradles.
The Pied Piper of Hamelin

The year's at the spring,
And day's at the morn;
Morning's at seven;
The hill-side's dew-pearled;
The lark's on the wing;
The snail's on the thorn;
God's in His heaven –
All's right with the world.
Pippa Passes, Pt. I

BURNS, Robert (1759–96) Scottish poet

Should auld acquaintance be forgot,
And never brought to min'?
Auld Lang Syne

We'll tak a cup o' kindness yet,
For auld lang syne.
Auld Lang Syne

My love is like a red red rose
That's newly sprung in June:
My love is like the melodie
That's sweetly play'd in tune.
A Red, Red Rose

Wee, sleekit, cow'rin', tim'rous beastie,
O what a panic's in thy breastie!
To a Mouse

The best laid schemes o' mice an' men
Gang aft a-gley,
An' lea'e us nought but grief an' pain
For promis'd joy.
To a Mouse

BYRON, Lord (1788–1824) British poet

While stands the Coliseum, Rome shall stand;
When falls the Coliseum, Rome shall fall;
And when Rome falls – the World.
Childe Harold's Pilgrimage, IV

Man's love is of man's life a thing apart,
'Tis woman's whole existence.
Don Juan, I

'Tis strange – but true; for truth is always strange;
Stranger than fiction: if it could be told,
How much would novels gain by the exchange!
Don Juan, XIV

She walks in beauty, like the night
Of cloudless climes and starry skies;
And all that's best of dark and bright
Meet in her aspect and her eyes.
She Walks in Beauty

Though the night was made for loving,
And the day returns too soon,
Yet we'll go no more a roving
By the light of the moon.
So, we'll go no more a roving

CARROLL, Lewis (Charles Lutwidge Dodgson; 1832–
98) British author

'What is the use of a book,' thought Alice, 'without
pictures or conversation?'
Alice's Adventures in Wonderland, Ch. 1

'Curiouser and curiouser!' cried Alice.
Alice's Adventures in Wonderland, Ch. 2

'You are old, Father William,' the young man said,
'And your hair has become very white;
And yet you incessantly stand on your head –
Do you think at your age, it is right?'
Alice's Adventures in Wonderland, Ch. 5

Twinkle, twinkle, little bat!
How I wonder what you're at!
Up above the world you fly!
Like a teatray in the sky.
Alice's Adventures in Wonderland, Ch. 7

'Off with his head!'
Alice's Adventures in Wonderland, Ch. 8

'Will you walk a little faster?' said a whiting to a snail,
'There's a porpoise close behind us, and he's treading on my tail.'
Alice's Adventures in Wonderland, Ch. 10

'Twas brillig, and the slithy toves
Did gyre and gimble in the wabe;
All mimsy were the borogoves,
And the mome raths outgrabe.
Through the Looking-Glass, Ch. 1

Tweedledum and Tweedledee
Agreed to have a battle;
For Tweedledum said Tweedledee
Had spoiled his nice new rattle.
Through the Looking-Glass, Ch. 4

'The time has come,' the Walrus said,
'To talk of many things:
Of shoes – and ships – and sealing-wax –
Of cabbages – and kings –
And why the sea is boiling hot –
And whether pigs have wings.'
Through the Looking-Glass, Ch. 4

The rule is, jam tomorrow and jam yesterday – but never jam today.
Through the Looking-Glass, Ch. 5

'You look a little shy; let me introduce you to that leg of mutton,' said the Red Queen. 'Alice – Mutton; Mutton – Alice.'
Through the Looking-Glass, Ch. 9

CERVANTES, Miguel de (1547–1616) Spanish novelist

Take care, your worship, those things over there are not giants but windmills.
Don Quixote, Pt. I, Ch. 8

Didn't I tell you, Don Quixote, sir, to turn back, for they were not armies you were going to attack, but flocks of sheep?
Don Quixote, Pt. I, Ch. 18

The best sauce in the world is hunger.
Don Quixote, Pt. II, Ch. 5

Well, now, there's a remedy for everything except death.
Don Quixote, Pt. II, Ch. 10

There are only two families in the world, my old grandmother used to say, The *Haves* and the *Have-Nots*.
Don Quixote, Pt. II, Ch. 20

A private sin is not so prejudicial in the world as a public indecency.

Don Quixote, Pt. II, Ch. 22

CHURCHILL, Sir Winston (1874–1965) British statesman and writer

We shall not flag or fail. We shall fight in France, we shall fight on the seas and oceans, we shall fight with growing confidence and growing strength in the air, we shall defend our island, whatever the cost may be, we shall fight on the beaches, we shall fight on the landing grounds, we shall fight in the fields and in the streets, we shall fight in the hills; we shall never surrender.
Speech, House of Commons, 4 June 1940

This was their finest hour.
Speech, House of Commons, 18 June 1940
  (Referring to the Dunkirk evacuation)

The battle of Britain is about to begin.
Speech, House of Commons, 1 July 1940

Never in the field of human conflict was so much owed by so many to so few.
Speech, House of Commons, 20 Aug 1940 (Referring to the Battle of Britain pilots)

COLERIDGE, Samuel Taylor (1772–1834) British poet

The frost performs its secret ministry,
Unhelped by any wind.
Frost at Midnight

In Xanadu did Kubla Khan
A stately pleasure-dome decree:
Where Alph, the sacred river, ran
Through caverns measureless to man
Down to a sunless sea.
Kubla Khan

And all should cry, Beware! Beware!
His flashing eyes, his floating hair!
Weave a circle round him thrice,
And close your eyes with holy dread,
For he on honey-dew hath fed,
And drunk the milk of Paradise.
Kubla Khan

It is an ancient Mariner,
And he stoppeth one of three.
'By thy long grey beard and glittering eye,
Now wherefore stopp'st thou me?'
The Rime of the Ancient Mariner, I

He holds him with his glittering eye—
The Wedding-Guest stood still,
And listens like a three years' child:
The Mariner hath his will.
The Rime of the Ancient Mariner, I

With my cross-bow
I shot the albatross.
The Rime of the Ancient Mariner, I

As idle as a painted ship
Upon a painted ocean.
The Rime of the Ancient Mariner, II

Water, water, every where,

Nor any drop to drink.
The Rime of the Ancient Mariner, II

Oh sleep! it is a gentle thing,
Beloved from pole to pole!
The Rime of the Ancient Mariner, V

He prayeth best, who loveth best
All things both great and small;
For the dear God who loveth us,
He made and loveth all.
The Rime of the Ancient Mariner, VII

COWARD, Sir Noël (1899–1973) British actor, dramatist, and songwriter

Don't put your daughter on the stage, Mrs
Worthington.
Song title

Mad dogs and Englishmen go out in the mid-day
sun.
Song title

The Stately Homes of England
How beautiful they stand,
To prove the upper classes
Have still the upper hand.
Operette, 'The Stately Homes of England'

Strange how potent cheap music is.
Private Lives

COWPER, William (1731–1800) British poet

John Gilpin was a citizen
Of credit and renown,
A train-band captain eke was he
Of famous London town.
John Gilpin

God moves in a mysterious way
His wonders to perform;
He plants his footsteps in the sea,
And rides upon the storm.
Olney Hymns, 35

I am monarch of all I survey,
My right there is none to dispute;
From the centre all round to the sea
I am lord of the foul and the brute.
Verses supposed to be written by Alexander Selkirk

DICKENS, Charles (1812–70) British novelist

This is a London particular... A fog, miss.
Bleak House, Ch. 3

'God bless us every one!' said Tiny Tim, the last of
all.
A Christmas Carol

Barkis is willin'.
David Copperfield, Ch. 5

Annual income twenty pounds, annual expenditure
nineteen nineteen six, result happiness. Annual income twenty pounds, annual expenditure twenty
pounds ought and six, result misery.
David Copperfield, Ch. 12

I am well aware that I am the 'umblest person
going.
David Copperfield, Ch. 16

Accidents will occur in the best-regulated families.
David Copperfield, Ch. 28

As she frequently remarked when she made any
such mistake, it would be all the same a hundred
years hence.
Martin Chuzzlewit, Ch. 9

All is gas and gaiters.
Nicholas Nickleby, Ch. 49

Oliver Twist has asked for more.
Oliver Twist, Ch. 2

Known by the *sobriquet* of 'The artful Dodger'.
Oliver Twist, Ch. 8

Take example by your father, my boy, and be very
careful o' vidders all your life.
Pickwick Papers, Ch. 13

Poverty and oysters always seem to go together.
Pickwick Papers, Ch. 22

It was the best of times, it was the worst of times, it
was the age of wisdom, it was the age of foolishness, it was the epoch of belief, it was the epoch of
incredulity, it was the season of Light, it was the
season of Darkness, it was the spring of hope, it was
the winter of despair, we had everything before us,
we had nothing before us, we were all going direct
to Heaven, we were all going direct the other way.
A Tale of Two Cities, Bk. I, Ch. 1

It is a far, far, better thing that I do, than I have ever
done; it is a far, far, better rest that I go to, than I
have ever known.
A Tale of Two Cities, Bk. II, Ch. 15

DICKINSON, Emily (1830–86) US poet

Because I could not stop for Death,
He kindly stopped for me;
The carriage held but just ourselves
And Immortality.
The Chariot 'Because I could not stop for Death'

Parting is all we know of heaven,
And all we need of hell.
My Life Closed Twice Before its Close

DONNE, John (1572–1631) English poet

Come live with me, and be my love,
And we will some new pleasures prove
Of golden sands, and crystal brooks,
With silken lines, and silver hooks.
The Bait

No man is an Island, entire of itself; every man is a
piece of the Continent, a part of the main.
Devotions, 17

Any man's death diminishes me, because I am involved in Mankind; And therefore never send to
know for whom the bell tolls; it tolls for thee.
Devotions, 17

Go, and catch a falling star,
Get with child a mandrake root,
Tell me, where all past years are,
Or who cleft the Devil's foot.
Go and Catch a Falling Star

I am two fools, I know,
For loving, and for saying so
In whining Poetry.
The Triple Fool

DOYLE, Sir Arthur Conan (1859–1930) British writer

It is an old maxim of mine that when you have excluded the impossible, whatever remains, however improbable, must be the truth.
The Beryl Coronet

You know my method. It is founded upon the observance of trifles.
The Boscombe Valley Mystery

'Excellent!' I cried. 'Elementary,' said he.
The Crooked Man

It is quite a three-pipe problem.
The Red-Headed League

'Is there any other point to which you would wish to draw my attention?'
'To the curious incident of the dog in the night-time.'
'The dog did nothing in the night-time.' 'That was the curious incident,' remarked Sherlock Holmes.
The Silver Blaze

Mediocrity knows nothing higher than itself, but talent instantly recognizes genius.
The Valley of Fear

DRYDEN, John (1631–1700) British poet and dramatist

But far more numerous was the Herd of such,
Who think too little, and who talk too much.
Absalom and Achitophel, I

None but the Brave deserves the Fair.
Alexander's Feast

Errors, like Straws, upon the surface flow;
He who would search for Pearls must dive below.
All for Love, Prologue

By viewing Nature, Nature's handmaid, art,
Makes mighty things from small beginnings grow.
Annus Mirabilis

ELIOT, T S (1888–1965) US-born British poet and dramatist

Time present and time past
Are both perhaps present in time future,
And time future contained in time past.
Four Quartets, 'Burnt Norton'

We are the hollow men
We are the stuffed men
Leaning together
Headpiece filled with straw. Alas!
The Hollow Men

This is the way the world ends
Not with a bang but a whimper.
The Hollow Men

I have measured out my life with coffee spoons.
The Love Song of J. Alfred Prufrock

Macavity, Macavity, there's no one like Macavity,
There never was a Cat of such deceitfulness and suavity.
He always has an alibi, and one or two to spare:
At whatever time the deed took place – MACAVITY WASN'T THERE!
Old Possum's Book of Practical Cats, Macavity: The Mystery Cat

FITZGERALD, Edward (1809–83) British poet and translator

Here with a Loaf of Bread beneath the Bough,
A Flask of Wine, a Book of Verse – and Thou
Beside me singing in the Wilderness –
And Wilderness is Paradise enow.
The Rubáiyát of Omar Khayyám (1st edn.), XI

Ah, my Belovéd, fill the Cup that clears
TO-DAY of past Regrets and Future Fears: To-morrow!
– Why, To-morrow I may be
Myself with Yesterday's Sev'n thousand Years.
The Rubáiyát of Omar Khayyám (1st edn.), XX

Ah, fill the Cup: – what boots it to repeat
How Time is slipping underneath our Feet:
Unborn TOMORROW, and dead YESTERDAY,
Why fret about them if TODAY be sweet!
The Rubáiyát of Omar Khayyám (1st edn.), XXXVII

The Moving Finger writes; and, having writ,
Moves on: nor all thy Piety nor Wit
Shall lure it back to cancel half a Line,
Nor all thy Tears wash out a Word of it.
The Rubáiyát of Omar Khayyám (1st edn.), LI

FROST, Robert Lee (1875–1963) US poet

My apple trees will never get across
And eat the cones under his pines, I tell him.
He only says, 'Good fences make good neighbours.'
North of Boston, 'Mending Wall'

Two roads diverged in a wood, and I –
I took the one less traveled by,
And that has made all the difference.
The Road Not Taken

The woods are lovely, dark, and deep,
But I have promises to keep,
And miles to go before I sleep,
And miles to go before I sleep.
Stopping by Woods on a Snowy Evening

GILBERT, Sir William Schwenk (1836–1911) British dramatist and comic writer

I'm called Little Buttercup – dear Little Buttercup,
Though I could never tell why.
HMS Pinafore, I

Stick close to your desks and never go to sea,
And you all may be Rulers of the Queen's Navee!
HMS Pinafore, I

I often think it's comical
How Nature always does contrive
That every boy and every gal
That's born into the world alive
Is either a little Liberal
Or else a little Conservative!
Iolanthe, II

As some day it may happen that a victim must be found
I've got a little list – I've got a little list
Of society offenders who might well be underground,
And who never would be missed – who never would be missed!
The Mikado, I

Three little maids from school are we,
Pert as a school-girl well can be,
Filled to the brim with girlish glee.
The Mikado, I

My object all sublime
I shall achieve in time –
To let the punishment fit the crime –
The punishment fit the crime.
The Mikado, II

When constabulary duty's to be done –
A policeman's lot is not a happy one.
The Pirates of Penzance, II

GOLDSMITH, Oliver (1730–74) Irish-born British writer

This is Liberty-Hall, gentlemen.
She Stoops to Conquer, II

Laws grind the poor, and rich men rule the law.
The Traveller

When lovely woman stoops to folly,
And finds too late that men betray,
What charm can soothe her melancholy,
What art can wash her guilt away?
The Vicar of Wakefield, Ch. 9

Conscience is a coward, and those faults it has not strength enough to prevent it seldom has justice enough to accuse.
The Vicar of Wakefield, Ch. 13

GRAY, Thomas (1716–71) British poet

The boast of heraldry, the pomp of pow'r,
And all that beauty, all that wealth e'er gave,
Awaits alike th' inevitable hour,
The paths of glory lead but to the grave.
Elegy Written in a Country Churchyard

Some village-Hampden, that with dauntless breast
The little Tyrant of his fields withstood;
Some mute inglorious Milton here may rest,
Some Cromwell guiltless of his country's blood.
Elegy Written in a Country Churchyard

Far from the madding crowd's ignoble strife,
Their sober wishes never learn'd to stray;
Along the cool sequester'd vale of life
They kept the noiseless tenor of their way.
Elegy Written in a Country Churchyard

Alas, regardless of their doom,
The little victims play!
Ode on a Distant Prospect of Eton College

Yet ah! why should they know their fate?
Since sorrow never comes too late,
And happiness too swiftly flies.
Thought would destroy their paradise.
No more; where ignorance is bliss,
'Tis folly to be wise.
Ode on a Distant Prospect of Eton College

Not all that tempts your wand'ring eyes
And heedless hearts, is lawful prize;
Nor all, that glisters, gold.
Ode on the Death of a Favourite Cat

HOUSMAN, A(lfred) E(dward) (1859–1936) British poet

Loveliest of trees, the cherry now
Is hung with bloom along the bough,
And stands about the woodland ride
Wearing white for Eastertide.
A Shropshire Lad, '1887'

On Wenlock Edge the wood's in trouble;
His forest fleece the Wrekin heaves;
The wind, it plies the saplings double,
And thick on Severn snow the leaves.
A Shropshire Lad, 'The Welsh Marches'

East and west on fields forgotten
Bleach the bones of comrades slain,
Lovely lads and dead and rotten;
None that go return again.
A Shropshire Lad, 'The Welsh Marches'

Malt does more than Milton can
To justify God's ways to man.
A Shropshire Lad, 'The Welsh Marches'

JOHNSON, Samuel (1709–84) British lexicographer and writer

When two Englishmen meet, their first talk is of the weather.
The Idler

Marriage has many pains, but celibacy has no pleasures.
Rasselas, Ch. 26

It is very strange, and very melancholy, that the paucity of human pleasures should persuade us ever to call hunting one of them.
Johnsonian Miscellanies (ed. G. B. Hill), Vol. I

A tavern chair is the throne of human felicity.
Johnsonian Miscellanies (ed. G. B. Hill), Vol. II

Love is the wisdom of the fool and the folly of the wise.
Johnsonian Miscellanies (ed. G. B. Hill), Vol. II

There are few ways in which a man can be more innocently employed than in getting money.
Life of Johnson (J. Boswell), Vol. II

A man will turn over half a library to make one book.
Life of Johnson (J. Boswell), Vol. II

Patriotism is the last refuge of a scoundrel.
Life of Johnson (J. Boswell), Vol. II

There is nothing which has yet been contrived by man, by which so much happiness is produced as by a good tavern or inn.
Life of Johnson (J. Boswell), Vol. II

When a man is tired of London, he is tired of life; for there is in London all that life can afford.
Life of Johnson (J. Boswell), Vol. III

He who praises everybody praises nobody.
Life of Johnson (J. Boswell), Vol. III

No man is a hypocrite in his pleasures.
Life of Johnson (J. Boswell), Vol. IV

KEATS, John (1795–1821) British poet

A thing of beauty is a joy for ever:
Its loveliness increases; it will never
Pass into nothingness; but still will keep
A bower quiet for us, and a sleep
Full of sweet dreams, and health, and quiet breathing.
Endymion, I

St Agnes' Eve – Ah, bitter chill it was!
The owl, for all his feathers, was a-cold;
The hare limp'd trembling through the frozen grass,
And silent was the flock in woolly fold.
The Eve of Saint Agnes, I

And they are gone: aye, ages long ago
These lovers fled away into the storm.
The Eve of Saint Agnes, XLII

Oh what can ail thee, knight at arms
Alone and palely loitering;
The sedge has wither'd from the lake,
And no birds sing.
La Belle Dame Sans Merci

'Beauty is truth, truth beauty,' – that is all
Ye know on earth, and all ye need to know.
Ode on a Grecian Urn

No, no, go not to Lethe, neither twist
Wolf's-bane, tight-rooted, for its poisonous wine.
Ode on Melancholy

My heart aches, and a drowsy numbness pains
My sense.
Ode to a Nightingale

O for a beaker full of the warm South,
Full of the true, the blushful Hippocrene,
With beaded bubbles winking at the brim,
And purple-stained mouth.
Ode to a Nightingale

Thou wast not born for death, immortal Bird!

No hungry generations tread thee down;
The voice I hear this passing night was heard
In ancient days by emperor and clown:
Ode to a Nightingale

Darkling I listen; and, for many a time
I have been half in love with easeful Death,
Call'd him soft names in many a musèd rhyme,
To take into the air my quiet breath;
Now more than ever seems it rich to die,
To cease upon the midnight with no pain,
While thou art pouring forth thy soul abroad
In such an ecstasy!
Ode to a Nightingale

Much have I travell'd in the realms of gold,
And many goodly states and kingdoms seen.
On first looking into Chapman's Homer

Season of mists and mellow fruitfulness,
Close bosom-friend of the maturing sun;
Conspiring with him how to load and bless
With fruit the vines that round the thatch-eaves run.
To Autumn

KIPLING, Rudyard (1865–1936) British writer and poet

For the female of the species is more deadly than the male.
The Female of the Species

If you can talk with crowds and keep your virtue,
Or walk with Kings – nor lose the common touch,
If neither foes nor loving friends can hurt you,
If all men count with you, but none too much;
If you can fill the unforgiving minute
With sixty seconds' worth of distance run,
Yours is the Earth and everything that's in it,
And – which is more – you'll be a Man my son!
If

Ship me somewheres east of Suez, where the best is like the worst,
Where there aren't no Ten Commandments, an' a man can raise a thirst:
The Road to Mandalay

It's Tommy this, an' Tommy that, an' 'Chuck him out, the brute!'
But it's 'Saviour of 'is country' when the guns begin to shoot.
Tommy

They shut the road through the woods
Seventy years ago.
Weather and rain have undone it again,
And now you would never know
There was once a road through the woods.
The Way Through the Woods

LEAR, Edward (1812–88) British artist and writer

Far and few, far and few,
Are the lands where the Jumblies live;
Their heads are green, and their hands are blue,
And they went to sea in a sieve.
The Jumblies

The Owl and the Pussy-Cat went to sea
In a beautiful pea-green boat,
They took some honey, and plenty of money,
Wrapped up in a five-pound note.
The Owl and the Pussy-Cat

They dined on mince, and slices of quince,
Which they ate with a runcible spoon;
And hand in hand, on the edge of the sand,
They danced by the light of the moon.
The Owl and the Pussy-Cat

LONGFELLOW, Henry Wadsworth (1807–82) US poet

The shades of night were falling fast,
As through an Alpine village passed
A youth, who bore, 'mid snow and ice,
A banner with the strange device,
Excelsior!
Excelsior

By the shore of Gitche Gumee,
By the shining Big-Sea-Water,
Stood the wigwam of Nokomis,
Daughter of the Moon, Nokomis,
The Song of Hiawatha, 'Hiawatha's Childhood'

From the waterfall he named her,
Minnehaha, Laughing Water.
The Song of Hiawatha, 'Hiawatha and Mudjekeewis'

He is dead, the sweet musician!
He is the sweetest of all singers!
He has gone from us for ever,
He has moved a little nearer
To the Master of all music,
To the Master of all singing!
O my brother, Chibiabos!
The Song of Hiawatha, 'Hiawatha's Lamentation'

Ships that pass in the night, and speak each other in passing;
Only a signal shown and a distant voice in the darkness;
So on the ocean of life we pass and speak one another,
Only a look and a voice; then darkness again and a silence.
Tales of a Wayside Inn, 'The Theologian's Tale. Elizabeth'

Under a spreading chestnut tree
The village smithy stands;
The smith, a mighty man is he,
With large and sinewy hands;
And the muscles of his brawny arms
Are strong as iron bands.
The Village Blacksmith

MARVELL, Andrew (1621–78) English poet

I have a garden of my own,
But so with roses overgrown,
And lilies, that you would it guess
To be a little wilderness.
The Nymph Complaining for the Death of her Fawn

Had we but world enough, and time,
This coyness, lady, were no crime.
To His Coy Mistress

But at my back I always hear
Time's winged chariot hurrying near;
And yonder all before us lie
Deserts of vast eternity.
To His Coy Mistress

The grave's a fine and private place,
But none, I think, do there embrace.
To His Coy Mistress

MASEFIELD, John (1878–1967) British poet

Quinquireme of Nineveh from distant Ophir
Rowing home to haven in sunny Palestine,
With a cargo of ivory,
And apes and peacocks,
Sandalwood, cedarwood, and sweet white wine.
Cargoes

Dirty British coaster with a salt-caked smoke stack,
Butting through the Channel in the mad March days,
With a cargo of Tyne coal,
Road-rail, pig-lead,
Firewood, iron-ware, and cheap tin trays.
Cargoes

I must down to the seas again, to the lonely sea and the sky,
And all I ask is a tall ship and a star to steer her by,
And the wheel's kick and the wind's song and the white sail's shaking,
And a grey mist on the sea's face and a grey dawn breaking.
Sea Fever

MILTON, John (1608–74) English poet

To sport with Amaryllis in the shade,
Or with the tangles of Neaera's hair.
Lycidas

Fame is the spur that the clear spirit doth raise
(That last infirmity of noble mind)
To scorn delights, and live laborious days.
Lycidas

Of Man's first disobedience, and the fruit
Of that forbidden tree, whose mortal taste
Brought death into the World, and all our woe...
Paradise Lost, Bk. I

What in me is dark
Illumine, what is low raise and support;
That, to the height of this great argument,
I may assert Eternal Providence,
And justify the ways of God to men.
Paradise Lost, Bk. I

To reign is worth ambition, though in Hell:
Better to reign in Hell than serve in Heaven.
Paradise Lost, Bk. I

High on a throne of royal state, which far
Outshone the wealth of Ormuz and of Ind,
Or where the gorgeous East with richest hand

Showers on her kings barbaric pearl and gold,
Satan exalted sat, by merit raised
To that bad eminence.
Paradise Lost, Bk. II

For neither man nor angel can discern
Hypocrisy, the only evil that walks
Invisible, except to God alone.
Paradise Lost, Bk. III

Ask for this great deliverer now, and find him
Eyeless in Gaza at the mill with slaves.
Samson Agonistes

When I consider how my light is spent
Ere half my days in this dark world and wide,
And that one talent which is death to hide
Lodged with me useless.
Sonnet: 'On his Blindness'

NEWBOLT, Sir Henry John (1862–1938) British poet

The sand of the desert is sodden red, –
Red with the wreck of a square that broke; –
The gatling's jammed and the colonel dead,
And the regiment blind with the dust and smoke.
The river of death has brimmed its banks
And England's far and honour a name.
But the voice of a schoolboy rallies the ranks:
'Play up! play up! and play the game!'
Vitaï Lampada

ORWELL, George (Eric Blair; 1903–50) British novelist

Man is the only creature that consumes without producing.
Animal Farm, Ch. 1

Four legs good, two legs bad.
Animal Farm, Ch. 3

All animals are equal but some animals are more equal than others.
Animal Farm, Ch. 10

Who controls the past controls the future. Who controls the present controls the past.
Nineteen Eighty-Four

If you want a picture of the future, imagine a boot stamping on a human face – for ever.
Nineteen Eighty-Four

Big Brother is watching you.
Nineteen Eighty-Four

War is Peace, Freedom is Slavery, Ignorance is Strength.
Nineteen Eighty-Four

Doublethink means the power of holding two contradictory beliefs in one's mind simultaneously, and accepting both of them.
Nineteen Eighty-Four

PARKER, Dorothy (1893–1967) US writer

He lies below, correct in cypress wood,
And entertains the most exclusive worms.
Epitaph for a Very Rich Man

Why is it no one ever sent me yet
One perfect limousine, do you suppose?
Ah no, it's always just my luck to get
One perfect rose.
One Perfect Rose

By the time you say you're his,
Shivering and sighing,
And he vows his passion is
Infinite, undying –
Lady, make a note of this:
One of you is lying.
Unfortunate Coincidence

POPE, Alexander (1688–1744) British poet

The right divine of kings to govern wrong.
The Dunciad, IV

Do good by stealth, and blush to find it fame.
Epilogue to the Satires, Dialogue I

Damn with faint praise, assent with civil leer,
And, without sneering, teach the rest to sneer.
Epistle to Dr. Arbuthnot

Of all the causes which conspire to blind
Man's erring judgment, and misguide the mind,

What the weak head with strongest bias rules, Is
Pride, the never-failing vice of fools.
An Essay on Criticism

A little learning is a dangerous thing;
Drink deep, or taste not the Pierian spring:
There shallow draughts intoxicate the brain,
And drinking largely sobers us again.
An Essay on Criticism

To err is human, to forgive, divine.
An Essay on Criticism

For fools rush in where angels fear to tread.
An Essay on Criticism

Hope springs eternal in the human breast;
Man never is, but always to be blest.
An Essay on Man, I

Know then thyself, presume not God to scan,
The proper study of Mankind is Man.
An Essay on Man, II

Where'er you walk, cool gales shall fan the glade,
Trees, where you sit, shall crowd into a shade:
Where'er you tread, the blushing flow'rs shall rise,
And all things flourish where you turn your eyes.
Pastorals, 'Summer'

SASSOON, Siegfried (1886–1967) British poet and writer

And when the war is done and youth stone dead
I'd toddle safely home and die – in bed.
Base Details

'Good morning; good morning!' the general said
When we met him last week on our way to the line.
Now the soldiers he smiled at are most of 'em dead,
And we're cursing his staff for incompetent swine.
The General

SCOTT, Sir Walter (1771–1832) Scottish writer

O Caledonia! stern and wild,
Meet nurse for a poetic child!
Land of brown heath and shaggy wood,
Land of the mountain and the flood,
Land of my sires! what mortal hand
Can e'er untie the filial band
That knits me to thy rugged strand!
The Lay of the Last Minstrel, VI

To that dark inn, the grave!
The Lord of the Isles, VI

O, young Lochinvar is come out of the west,
Through all the wide Border his steed was the best.
Marmion, V

SHAKESPEARE, William (1564–1616) English dramatist and poet

Our remedies oft in ourselves do lie,
Which we ascribe to heaven.
All's Well that Ends Well, I: 1

Where's my serpent of old Nile?
Antony and Cleopatra, I: 5

My salad days,
When I was green in judgment, cold in blood,

To say as I said then!
Antony and Cleopatra, I: 5

The barge she sat in, like a burnish'd throne,
Burn'd on the water. The poop was beaten gold;
Purple the sails, and so perfumed that
The winds were love-sick with them; the oars were
    silver,
Which to the tune of flutes kept stroke and made
The water which they beat to follow faster,
As amorous of their strokes. For her own person,
It beggar'd all description.
Antony and Cleopatra, II: 2

Age cannot wither her, nor custom stale
Her infinite variety. Other women cloy
The appetites they feed, but she makes hungry
Where most she satisfies.
Antony and Cleopatra, II: 2

She shall be buried by her Antony!
No grave upon the earth shall clip in it
A pair so famous.
Antony and Cleopatra, V: 2

Well said; that was laid on with a trowel.
As You Like It, I: 2

And this our life, exempt from public haunt,
Finds tongues in trees, books in the running brooks,
Sermons in stones and good in everything.
As You Like It, II: 1

All the world's a stage,
And all the men and women merely players;
They have their exits and their entrances;
And one man in his time plays many parts,
His acts being seven ages.
As You Like It, II: 7

Last scene of all,
That ends this strange eventful history,
Is second childishness and mere oblivion;
Sans teeth, sans eyes, sans taste, sans every thing.
As You Like It, II: 7

Men have died from time to time, and worms have
eaten them, but not for love.
As You Like It, IV: 1

Fear no more the heat o' th' sun
Nor the furious winter's rages;
Thou thy worldly task hast done,
Home art gone, and ta'en thy wages.
Golden lads and girls all must,
As chimney-sweepers, come to dust.
Cymbeline, IV: 2

But I have that within which passes show – these
but the trappings and the suits of woe.
Hamlet, I: 2

O! that this too too solid flesh would melt,
Thaw, and resolve itself into a dew.
Or that the Everlasting had not fix'd
His canon 'gainst self-slaughter! O God! O God!
How weary, stale, flat, and unprofitable,
Seem to me all the uses of this world!
Hamlet, I: 2

Frailty, thy name is woman!
Hamlet, I: 2

Foul deeds will rise,
Though all the earth o'erwhelm them, to men's
    eyes.
Hamlet, I: 2

Costly thy habit as thy purse can buy,
But not express'd in fancy; rich, not gaudy;
For the apparel oft proclaims the man.
Hamlet, I: 3

Neither a borrower nor a lender be;
For loan oft loses both itself and friend,
And borrowing dulls the edge of husbandry.
This above all: to thine own self be true,
And it must follow, as the night the day,
Thou canst not then be false to any man.
Hamlet, I: 3

Something is rotten in the state of Denmark.
Hamlet, I: 4

Murder most foul, as in the best it is;
But this most foul, strange, and unnatural.
Hamlet, I: 5

There are more things in heaven and earth, Horatio,
Than are dreamt of in your philosophy.
Hamlet, I: 5

Though this be madness, yet there is method in't.
Hamlet, II: 2

There is nothing either good or bad, but thinking
makes it so.
Hamlet, II: 2

What a piece of work is a man! How noble in reason!
how infinite in faculties! in form and moving, how
express and admirable! in action, how like an angel!
in apprehension, how like a god! the beauty of the
world! the paragon of animals!
Hamlet, II: 2

I am but mad north-north-west; when the wind is
southerly, I know a hawk from a handsaw.
Hamlet, II: 2

The play, I remember, pleas'd not the million; 'twas
caviare to the general.
Hamlet, II: 2

To be, or not to be – that is the question;
Whether 'tis nobler in the mind to suffer
The slings and arrows of outrageous fortune,
Or to take arms against a sea of troubles,
And by opposing end them? To die, to sleep –
No more; and by a sleep to say we end
The heart-ache and the thousand natural shocks
That flesh is heir to, 'tis a consummation
Devoutly to be wish'd. To die, to sleep;
To sleep, perchance to dream. Ay, there's the rub;
For in that sleep of death what dreams may come,
When we have shuffled off this mortal coil,
Must give us pause.
Hamlet, III: 1

The dread of something after death –
The undiscover'd country, from whose bourn
No traveller returns.
Hamlet, III: 1

Thus conscience does make cowards of us all;
Hamlet, III: 1

Madness in great ones must not unwatch'd go.
Hamlet, III: 1

How all occasions do inform against me,
And spur my dull revenge! What is a man,
If his chief good and market of his time
Be but to sleep and feed? a beast, no more.
Hamlet, IV: 4

When sorrows come, they come not single spies,
But in battalions!
Hamlet, IV: 5

There's rosemary, that's for remembrance; pray,
love, remember: and there is pansies, that's for
thoughts.
Hamlet, IV: 5

Alas, poor Yorick! I knew him, Horatio: a fellow of infinite jest, of most excellent fancy.
Hamlet, V: 1

There's a divinity that shapes our ends,
Rough-hew them how we will.
Hamlet, V: 2

Out of this nettle, danger, we pluck this flower,
safety.
Henry IV, Part One, II: 3

The better part of valour is discretion; in the which

better part I have saved my life.
Henry IV, Part One, V: 4

Uneasy lies the head that wears a crown.
Henry IV, Part Two, III: 1

Once more unto the breach, dear friends, once
more;
Or close the wall up with our English dead.
Henry V, III: 1

And gentlemen in England, now a-bed
Shall think themselves accurs'd they were not here,
And hold their manhoods cheap whiles any speaks
That fought with us upon Saint Crispin's day.
Henry V, IV: 3

Men at some time are masters of their fates:
The fault, dear Brutus, is not in our stars,
But in ourselves, that we are underlings.
Julius Caesar, I: 2

Cry 'Havoc!' and let slip the dogs of war.
Julius Caesar, III: 1

Friends, Romans, countrymen, lend me your ears
I come to bury Caesar, not to praise him.
The evil that men do lives after them;
The good is oft interred with their bones.
Julius Caesar, III: 2

If you have tears, prepare to shed them now.
Julius Caesar, III: 2

There is a tide in the affairs of men
Which, taken at the flood, leads on to fortune;
Julius Caesar, IV: 3

How sharper than a serpent's tooth it is
To have a thankless child!
King Lear, I: 4

I am a man
More sinn'd against than sinning.
King Lear, III: 2

The worst is not
So long as we can say 'This is the worst'.
King Lear, IV: 1

As flies to wanton boys are we to th' gods –
They kill us for their sport.
King Lear, IV: 1

When shall we three meet again
In thunder, lightning, or in rain?
Macbeth, I: 1

I have no spur
To prick the sides of my intent, but only
Vaulting ambition, which o'er-leaps itself,
And falls on th' other.
Macbeth, I: 7

Is this a dagger which I see before me,
The handle toward my hand? Come, let me clutch
thee:
I have thee not, and yet I see thee still.
Macbeth, II: 1

Methought I heard a voice cry, 'Sleep no more!'
Macbeth doth murder sleep,' the innocent sleep,
Sleep that knits up the ravell'd sleave of care,
The death of each day's life, sore labour's bath,
Balm of hurt minds, great nature's second course,
Chief nourisher in life's feast.
Macbeth, II: 2

Eye of newt, and toe of frog,
Wool of bat, and tongue of dog,
Adder's fork, and blind-worm's sting,
Lizard's leg, and howlet's wing,
For a charm of powerful trouble,
Like a hell-broth boil and bubble.
Macbeth, IV: 1

Be bloody bold, and resolute, laugh to scorn
The power of man, for none of woman born
Shall harm Macbeth.
Macbeth, IV: 1

Here's the smell of the blood still. All the perfumes
of Arabia will not sweeten this little hand.
Macbeth, V: 1

Tomorrow, and tomorrow, and tomorrow,
Creeps in this petty pace from day to day
To the last syllable of recorded time,
And all our yesterdays have lighted fools
The way to dusty death. Out, out, brief candle!
Life's but a walking shadow, a poor player,
That struts and frets his hour upon the stage,
And then is heard no more; it is a tale
Told by an idiot, full of sound and fury,
Signifying nothing.
Macbeth, V: 5

The devil can cite Scripture for his purpose.
The Merchant of Venice, I: 3

You call me misbeliever, cut-throat dog,
And spit upon my Jewish gaberdine,
And all for use of that which is mine own.
The Merchant of Venice, I: 3

It is a wise father that knows his own child.
The Merchant of Venice, II: 2

Hath not a Jew eyes? Hath not a Jew hands, organs,
dimensions, senses, affections, passions, fed with
the same food, hurt with the same weapons, subject to the same diseases, healed by the same
means, warmed and cooled by the same winter and
summer, as a Christian is? If you prick us, do we not
bleed? If you tickle us, do we not laugh? If you poison us, do we not die? And if you wrong us, shall we
not revenge?
The Merchant of Venice, III: 1

The quality of mercy is not strain'd;
It droppeth as the gentle rain from heaven
Upon the place beneath. It is twice blest;
It blesseth him that gives and him that takes.
The Merchant of Venice, IV: 1

How far that little candle throws his beams!
So shines a good deed in a naughty world.
The Merchant of Venice, V: 1

Why, then the world's mine oyster,
Which I with sword will open.
The Merry Wives of Windsor, II: 2

For aught that I could ever read,
Could ever hear by tale or history,
The course of true love never did run smooth.
A Midsummer Night's Dream, I: 1

Ill met by moonlight, proud Titania.
A Midsummer Night's Dream, II: 1

The lunatic, the lover, and the poet,
Are of imagination all compact.
A Midsummer Night's Dream, V: 1

Doth not the appetite alter? A man loves the meat in
his youth that he cannot endure in his age.
Much Ado About Nothing, II: 3

Comparisons are odorous.
Much Ado About Nothing, III: 5

Reputation, reputation, reputation! O, I have lost
my reputation! I have lost the immortal part of myself, and what remains is bestial.
Othello, II: 3

But he that filches from me my good name
Robs me of that which not enriches him
And makes me poor indeed.
Othello, III: 3

O, beware, my lord, of jealousy;
It is the green-ey'd monster which doth mock
The meat it feeds on.
Othello, III: 3

Then must you speak
Of one that lov'd not wisely, but too well;
Of one not easily jealous, but, being wrought,
Perplexed in the extreme; of one whose hand,
Like the base Indian, threw a pearl away
Richer than all his tribe.
Othello, V: 2

Teach thy necessity to reason thus:
There is no virtue like necessity.
Richard II, I: 3

This royal throne of kings, this sceptred isle,
This earth of majesty, this seat of Mars,
This other Eden, demi-paradise,
This fortress built by Nature for herself
Against infection and the hand of war,
This happy breed of men, this little world,
This precious stone set in the silver sea,
Which serves it in the office of a wall,
Or as a moat defensive to a house,
Against the envy of less happier lands;
This blessed plot, this earth, this realm, this England,
This nurse, this teeming womb of royal kings,
Fear'd by their breed, and famous by their birth.
Richard II, II: 1

Now is the winter of our discontent
Made glorious summer by this sun of York.
Richard III, I: 1

A horse! a horse! my kingdom for a horse.
Richard III, V: 4

From forth the fatal loins of these two foes
A pair of star-cross'd lovers take their life.
Romeo and Juliet, Prologue

O! she doth teach the torches to burn bright
It seems she hangs upon the cheek of night
Like a rich jewel in an Ethiop's ear;
Beauty too rich for use, for earth too dear.
Romeo and Juliet, I: 5

My only love sprung from my only hate!
Too early seen unknown, and known too late!
Romeo and Juliet, I: 5

What's in a name? That which we call a rose
By any other name would smell as sweet.
Romeo and Juliet, II: 2

Good night, good night! Parting is such sweet sorrow
That I shall say good night till it be morrow.
Romeo and Juliet, II: 2

A plague o' both your houses!
They have made worms' meat of me.
Romeo and Juliet, III: 1

How beauteous mankind is! O brave new world
That has such people in't!
The Tempest, V: 1

If music be the food of love, play on,
Give me excess of it, that, surfeiting,
The appetite may sicken and so die.
Twelfth Night, I: 1

Then come kiss me, sweet and twenty;
Youth's a stuff will not endure.
Twelfth Night, II: 3

Dost thou think, because thou art virtuous, there shall be no more cakes and ale?
Twelfth Night, II: 3

Some are born great, some achieve greatness, and some have greatness thrust upon 'em.
Twelfth Night, II: 5

Crabbed age and youth cannot live together:
Youth is full of pleasure, age is full of care;
Youth like summer morn, age like winter weather;
Youth like summer brave, age like winter bare.
The Passionate Pilgrim, XII

Shall I compare thee to a summer's day?
Thou art more lovely and more temperate.
Rough winds do shake the darling buds of May,
And summer's lease hath all too short a date.
Sonnet 18

Let me not to the marriage of true minds
Admit impediments. Love is not love
Which alters when it alteration finds,
Or bends with the remover to remove.
O, no! it is an ever-fixed mark,
That looks on tempests and is never shaken.
Sonnet 116

SHAW, George Bernard (1856–1950) Irish dramatist

When a stupid man is doing something he is ashamed of, he always declares that it is his duty.
Caesar and Cleopatra, III

He knows nothing; and he thinks he knows everything. That points clearly to a political career.
Major Barbara, III

He who can, does. He who cannot, teaches.
Man and Superman, 'Maxims for Revolutionists'

Gin was mother's milk to her.
Pygmalion, III

SHELLEY, Percy Bysshe (1792–1822) British poet

Let there be light! said Liberty,
And like sunrise from the sea,
Athens arose!
Hellas, I

O Wild West Wind, thou breath of Autumn's being,
Thou, from whose unseen presence the leaves dead
Are driven, like ghosts from an enchanter fleeing,
Yellow, and black, and pale, and hectic red,
Pestilence-stricken multitudes.
Ode to the West Wind

I met a traveller from an antique land
Who said: Two vast and trunkless legs of stone
Stand in the desert.
Ozymandias

Hail to thee, blithe Spirit!
Bird thou never wert,
That from Heaven, or near it,
Pourest thy full heart
In profuse strains of unpremeditated art.
To a Skylark

STEVENSON, Robert Louis (1850–94) Scottish writer

Fifteen men on the dead man's chest
Yo-ho-ho, and a bottle of rum!
Drink and the devil had done for the rest –
Yo-ho-ho, and a bottle of rum!
Treasure Island, Ch. 1

Under the wide and starry sky
Dig the grave and let me lie.
Glad did I live and gladly die,
– And I laid me down with a will.
This is the verse you grave for me:
'Here he lies where he longed to be;
Home is the sailor, home from sea,
And the hunter home from the hill.'
Underwoods, Bk. I, 'Requiem'

TENNYSON, Alfred, Baron (1809–92) British poet

'Forward the Light Brigade!'
Was there a man dismay'd?
Not tho' the soldier knew
Some one had blunder'd:
Their's not to make reply,
Their's not to reason why,
Their's but to do and die:
Into the valley of Death

Rode the six hundred.
The Charge of the Light Brigade

An arm
Rose up from out the bosom of the lake,
Clothed in white samite, mystic, wonderful.
Idylls of the King, 'The Passing of Arthur'

And slowly answer'd Arthur from the barge:
'The old order changeth, yielding place to new,
And God fulfils himself in many ways.'
Idylls of the King, 'The Passing of Arthur'

I hold it true, whate'er befall;
I feel it, when I sorrow most;
'Tis better to have loved and lost
Than never to have loved at all.
In Memoriam A.H.H., XXVII

I dreamed there would be Spring no more,
That Nature's ancient power was lost.
In Memoriam A.H.H., LXIX

Kind hearts are more than coronets,
And simple faith than Norman blood.
Lady Clara Vere de Vere, VI

On either side the river lie
Long fields of barley and of rye,
That clothe the wold and meet the sky;
And thro' the field the road runs by
To many-tower'd Camelot.
The Lady of Shalott, Pt. I

'The curse is come upon me,' cried
The Lady of Shalott.
The Lady of Shalott, Pt. III

Dear as remembered kisses after death,
And sweet as those by hopeless fancy feign'd
On lips that are for others: deep as love,
Deep as first love, and wild with all regret;
O Death in Life, the days that are no more.
The Princess, IV

THOMAS, Dylan (1914–53) Welsh poet

Though they go mad they shall be sane,
Though they sink through the sea they shall rise
again.
Though lovers be lost love shall not;
And death shall have no dominion.
And death shall have no dominion

Do not go gentle into that good night,
Old age should burn and rave at close of day;
Rage, rage, against the dying of the light.
Do not go gentle into that good night

Now as I was young and easy under the apple
boughs
About the lilting house and happy as the grass was
green.
Fern Hill

Time held me green and dying
Though I sang in my chains like the sea.
Fern Hill

The hands of the clock have stayed still at half past

eleven for fifty years. It is always opening time in
the Sailors Arms.
Under Milk Wood

It is a winter's tale
That the snow blind twilight ferries over the lakes
And floating fields from the farm in the cup of the
vales.
A Winter's Tale

TWAIN, Mark (Samuel Langhorne Clemens; 1835–
1910) US writer

There are three kinds of lies: lies, damned lies, and
statistics.
Autobiography

The radical invents the views. When he has worn
them out, the conservative adopts them.
Notebooks

Adam was but human – this explains it all. He did
not want the apple for the apple's sake, he wanted
it only because it was forbidden.
Pudd'nhead Wilson's, Ch. 2

WILDE, Oscar Fingal O'Flahertie Wills (1856–1900)
Irish-born British poet and dramatist

I never saw a man who looked
With such a wistful eye
Upon that little tent of blue
Which prisoners call the sky.
The Ballad of Reading Gaol, I:3

Yet each man kills the thing he loves,
By each let this be heard,
Some do it with a bitter look,
Some with a flattering word.
The coward does it with a kiss,
The brave man with a sword!
The Ballad of Reading Gaol, I:7

To love oneself is the beginning of a lifelong romance.
An Ideal Husband, III

Other people are quite dreadful. The only possible
society is oneself.
An Ideal Husband, III

I have invented an invaluable permanent invalid
called Bunbury, in order that I may be able to go
down into the country whenever I choose.
The Importance of Being Earnest, I

All women become like their mothers. That is their
tragedy. No man does. That's his.
The Importance of Being Earnest, I

To lose one parent, Mr Worthing, may be regarded
as a misfortune; to lose both looks like carelessness.
The Importance of Being Earnest, I

I never travel without my diary. One should always
have something sensational to read in the train.
The Importance of Being Earnest, II

No woman should ever be quite accurate about her
age. It looks so calculating.

The Importance of Being Earnest, III

I can resist everything except temptation.
Lady Windermere's Fan, I

It is absurd to divide people into good and bad.
People are either charming or tedious.
Lady Windermere's Fan, I

We are all in the gutter, but some of us are looking
at the stars.
Lady Windermere's Fan, III

A cigarette is the perfect type of a perfect pleasure.
It is exquisite, and it leaves one unsatisfied. What
more can one want?
The Picture of Dorian Gray, Ch. 6

Twenty years of romance makes a woman look like
a ruin; but twenty years of marriage make her something like a public building.
A Woman of No Importance, I

The English country gentleman galloping after a fox
– the unspeakable in full pursuit of the uneatable.
A Woman of No Importance, I

WORDSWORTH, William (1770–1850) British poet

I travelled among unknown men
In lands beyond the sea;
Nor, England! did I know till then
What love I bore to thee.
I Travelled among Unknown Men

I wandered lonely as a cloud
That floats on high o'er vales and hills,
When all at once I saw a crowd,
A host, of golden daffodils.
I Wandered Lonely as a Cloud

For oft, when on my couch I lie
In vacant or in pensive mood,
They flash upon that inward eye
Which is the bliss of solitude.
I Wandered Lonely as a Cloud

I have learned
To look on nature, not as in the hour
Of thoughtless youth; but hearing often-times
The still, sad music of humanity.
Lines composed a few miles above Tintern Abbey

My heart leaps up when I behold
A rainbow in the sky:
So was it when my life began;
So is it now I am a man;
So be it when I shall grow old,
Or let me die!
The Child is Father of the Man;
And I could wish my days to be
Bound each to each by natural piety.
My Heart Leaps Up

Whither is fled the visionary gleam?
Where is it now, the glory and the dream?
Ode. Intimations of Immortality, IV

Fair seed-time had my soul, and I grew up
Fostered alike by beauty and by fear.
The Prelude, I

Bliss was it in that dawn to be alive,
But to be young was very heaven!
The Prelude, XI

YEATS, W(illiam) B(utler) (1865–1939) Irish poet
and dramatist

O chestnut tree, great rooted blossomer,
Are you the leaf, the blossom or the bole?
O body swayed to music; O brightening glance,
How can we know the dancer from the dance?
Among School Children

Wine comes in at the mouth
And love comes in at the eye;
That's all we shall know for truth
Before we grow old and die.
A Drinking Song

For the good are always the merry,
Save by an evil chance,
And the merry love the fiddle,
And the merry love to dance
The Fiddler of Dooney

I will arise and go now, and go to Innisfree,
And a small cabin build there, of clay and wattles
made;
Nine bean rows will I have there, a hive for the
honey bee,
And live alone in the bee-loud glade.
The Lake Isle of Innisfree

Under bare Ben Bulben's head
In Drumcliff churchyard Yeats is laid…
On limestone quarried near the spot
By his command these words are cut:
Cast a cold eye
On life, on death. Horseman, pass by!
Under Ben Bulben, VI

When you are old and gray and full of sleep,
And nodding by the fire, take down this book,
And slowly read, and dream of the soft look
Your eyes had once, and of their shadows deep.
When you are Old

Love fled
And paced upon the mountains overhead
And hid his face amid a crowd of stars.
When you are Old

But I, being poor, have only my dreams;
I have spread my dreams under your feet;
Tread softly because you tread on my dreams.
He Wishes for the Cloths of Heaven

MOTTOES

A DEO ET REGE – By God and the King (Earl of Chesterfield)

AD MAJOREM DEI GLORIAM – to the greater glory of God (The Jesuits)

A MARI USQUE AD MARE – from sea to sea (Canada)

APRES NOUS LE DELUGE – after us the deluge (617 Squadron, 'The Dam Busters', RAF)

ARS LONGA, VITA BREVIS – art is long, life is short (Millais)

AUDI, VIDE, TACE – hear, see, keep silence (United Grand Lodge of Freemasons)

AUSPICIUM MELIORIS AEVI – the sign of a better age (Duke of St Albans, Order of St Michael and St George)

BE PREPARED – Scout Association, 1908

CAVENDO TUTUS – safe by being cautious (Duke of Devonshire)

CHE SERA SERA – what will be will be (Duke of Bedford)

DARE QUAM ACCIPERE – to give rather than to receive (Guy's Hospital)

DE PRAESCIENTIA DEI – from the foreknowledge of God (Barbers' Company, 1461)

DICTUM MEUM PACTUM – my word is my bond (Stock Exchange)

DIEU ET MON DROIT – God and my right (British Sovereigns)

DILIGENT AND SECRET (College of Arms, 1484)

DOMINE DIRIGE NOS – Lord, guide us (City of London)

DOMINUS ILLUMINATIO MEA – the Lord is my light (Oxford University)

DONORUM DEI DISPENSATIO FIDELIS – faithful dispensation of the gifts of God (Harrow School)

ENTALENTÉ À PARLER D'ARMES – equipped to speak of arms (The Heraldry Society, 1957)

ESPÉRANCE EN DIEU – hope in God (Duke of Northumberland)

FIDES ATQUE INTEGRITAS – faith and integrity (Society of Incorporated Accountants and Auditors)

FLOREAT ETONA – may Eton flourish (Eton College)

FOR COUNTRY NOT FOR SELF (226 Squadron, RAF)

GARDEZ BIEN – watch well (Montgomery)

HEAVEN'S LIGHT OUR GUIDE (Order of the Star of India)

HELP (Foundling Hospital, London)

HINC LUCEM ET POCULA SACRA – hence light and sacred cups (Cambridge University)

HONI SOIT QUI MAL Y PENSE – evil be to him who evil thinks (Order of the Garter)

HONNEUR ET PATRIE – honour and country (Order of the Legion of Honour)

ICH DIEN – I serve (Prince of Wales)

IMPERATRICUS AUSPICIIS – imperial in its auspices (Order of the Indian Empire)

IN ACTION FAITHFUL AND IN HONOUR CLEAR (Order of the Companions of Honour, 1917)

IN FIDE SALUS – safety in faith (Star of Rumania)

IN SOMNO SECURITAS – security in sleep (Association of Anaesthetists of Great Britain and Ireland)

JUSTITA VIRTUTUM REGINA – justice is queen of the virtues (Goldsmiths' Company)

LABORARE EST ORARE – to labour is to pray (Benedictine Order)

LABOR VIRIS CONVENIT – labour becomes men (Richard I)

LIFE IN OUR HANDS (Institute of Hospital Engineers)

MIHI ET MEA – to me and mine (Anne Boleyn)

NATION SHALL SPEAK PEACE UNTO NATION (British Broadcasting Corporation)

NEC ASPERA TERRENT – difficulties do not daunt (3rd Foot, 'The Buffs', East Kent Regiment)

NEC CUPIAS NEC METUAS – neither desire nor fear (Earl of Hardwicke)

NEMO ME IMPUNE LACESSIT – no one injures me with impunity (Order of the Thistle)

NOLI ME TANGERE – touch me not (Graeme of Garvock, 103 Squadron, RAF)

NON EST VIVERE SED VALERE VITA – life is not living, but health is life (Royal Society of Medicine)

NON SIBI, SED PATRIAE – not for himself, but for his country (Earl of Romney)

NULLIUS IN VERBA – in no man's words (Royal Society)

PAX IN BELLO – peace in war (Godolphin, Duke of Leeds)

PEACE THROUGH UNDERSTANDING (President Eisenhower)

PER ARDUA AD ASTRA – through endeavour to the stars (RAF motto)

PER CAELUM VIA NOSTRA – our way through heaven (Guild of Air Pilots and Navigators)

PISCATORES HOMINUM – fishers of men (National Society)

POWER IN TRUST (Central Electricity Generating Board)

QUIS SEPARABIT? – who shall separate? (Order of St Patrick)

QUOD PETIS HIC EST – here is what you seek (Institute of British Engineers)

RATIONE ET CONCILIO – by reason and counsel (Magistrates Association)

RERUM COGNOSCERE CAUSAS – to know the causes of things (Institute of Brewing)

SEMPER FIDELIS – always faithful (Devonshire regiment, East Devon Militia)

SEMPER PARATUS – always prepared (207 Squadron, RAF)

SOLA VIRTUS INVICTA – virtue alone is invincible (Duke of Norfolk)

TOUCH NOT THE CAT BOT A GLOVE (Macpherson Clan)

TRIA JUNCTA IN UNO – three joined in one (Order of the Bath)

UNITATE FORTIOR – stronger by union (Building Societies Association; Army and Navy Club)

VER NON SEMPER VIRET – the spring does not always flourish

VERNON SEMPER VIRET – Vernon always flourishes (Lord Lyveden)

WHO DARES WINS (Special Air Service)

WORDS

PALINDROMES

3
AHA
BIB
BOB
DAD
DID
DUD
ERE
EVE
EWE
EYE
GAG
GIG
HAH

HEH
HUH
MAM
MOM
MUM
NUN
OHO
PAP
PEP
PIP
POP
PUP
SIS
SOS

TAT
TIT
TNT
TOT
TUT
WOW

4
BOOB
DEED
KOOK
MA'AM
NOON
PEEP
POOP

SEES
TOOT

5
CIVIC
KAYAK
LEVEL
MADAM
MINIM
RADAR
REFER
ROTOR
SAGAS
SEXES
SHAHS

SOLOS
TENET

6
DENNED
HALLAH
HANNAH
REDDER
TERRET
TUT-TUT

9
MALAYALAM
ROTAVATOR

BACK WORDS

2
AH – HA
AM – MA
AT – TA
EH – HE
HA – AH
HE – EH
HO – OH
IT – TI
MA – AM
MP – PM
NO – ON
OH – HO
ON – NO
PM – MP
TA – AT
TI – IT

3
AND – DNA
BAD – DAB
BAG – GAB
BAN – NAB
BAT – TAB
BIN – NIB
BOG – GOB
BOY – YOB
BUD – DUB

BUN – NUB
BUS – SUB
BUT – TUB
DAB – BAD
DAM – MAD
DEW – WED
DIM – MID
DNA – AND
DOG – GOD
DOH – HOD
DON – NOD
DOT – TOD
DUB – BUD
EEL – LEE
GAB – BAG
GAL – LAG
GAS – SAG
GEL – LEG
GOB – BOG
GOD – DOG
GOT – TOG
GUM – MUG
GUT – TUG
HOD – DOH
JAR – RAJ
LAG – GAL
LAP – PAL
LEE – EEL

LEG – GEL
MAD – DAM
MAR – RAM
MAY – YAM
MID – DIM
MUG – GUM
NAB – BAN
NAP – PAN
NET – TEN
NIB – BIN
NIP – PIN
NIT – TIN
NOD – DON
NOT – TON
NOW – WON
NUB – BUN
PAL – LAP
PAN – NAP
PAR – RAP
PAT – TAP
PAY – YAP
PER – REP
PIN – NIP
PIT – TIP
POT – TOP
PUS – SUP
RAJ – JAR
RAM – MAR

RAP – PAR
RAT – TAR
RAW – WAR
REP – PER
ROT – TOR
SAG – GAS
SUB – BUS
SUP – PUS
TAB – BAT
TAP – PAT
TAR – RAT
TEN – NET
TIN – NIT
TIP – PIT
TOD – DOT
TOG – GOT
TON – NOT
TOP – POT
TOR – ROT
TUB – BUT
TUG – GUT
WAR – RAW
WAY – YAW
WED – DEW
WON – NOW
YAM – MAY
YAP – PAY
YAW – WAY

YOB – BOY

4
ABLE – ELBA
ABUT – TUBA
BARD – DRAB
BATS – STAB
BRAG – GARB
BUNS – SNUB
BUTS – STUB
DEER – REED
DIAL – LAID
DOOM – MOOD
DOOR – ROOD
DRAB – BARD
DRAW – WARD
DRAY – YARD
DUAL – LAUD
EDAM – MADE
EDIT – TIDE
ELBA – ABLE
EMIR – RIME
EMIT – TIME
ERGO – OGRE
ET AL – LATE
EVIL – LIVE
FLOG – GOLF
FLOW – WOLF

GALS – SLAG
GARB – BRAG
GNAT – TANG
GOLF – FLOG
GULP – PLUG
GUMS – SMUG
GUNS – SNUG
HOOP – POOH
KEEL – LEEK
KEEP – PEEK
LAID – DIAL
LAIR – RIAL
LATE – ET AL
LAUD – DUAL
LEEK – KEEL
LEER – REEL
LIAR – RAIL
LIVE – EVIL
LOOP – POOL
LOOT – TOOL
MACS – SCAM
MADE – EDAM
MAPS – SPAM
MAWS – SWAM
MEET – TEEM
MOOD – DOOM
MOOR – ROOM
NAPS – SPAN
NIPS – SPIN
NUTS – STUN
OGRE – ERGO
PALS – SLAP
PANS – SNAP
PART – TRAP
PAWS – SWAP
PEEK – KEEP
PETS – STEP
PINS – SNIP
PLUG – GULP
POOH – HOOP
POOL – LOOP
POTS – STOP
RAIL – LIAR
RAPS – SPAR

RATS – STAR
REED – DEER
REEL – LEER
RIAL – LAIR
RIME – EMIR
ROOD – DOOR
ROOM – MOOR
SCAM – MACS
SLAG – GALS
SLAP – PALS
SMUG – GUMS
SNAP – PANS
SNIP – PINS
SNOT – TONS
SNUB – BUNS
SNUG – GUNS
SPAM – MAPS
SPAN – NAPS
SPAR – RAPS
SPAT – TAPS
SPAY – YAPS
SPIN – NIPS
SPIT – TIPS
SPOT – TOPS
STAB – BATS
STAR – RATS
STEP – PETS
STEW – WETS
STOP – POTS
STUB – BUTS
STUN – NUTS
SWAM – MAWS
SWAP – PAWS
SWAY – YAWS
SWOT – TOWS
TANG – GNAT
TAPS – SPAT
TEEM – MEET
TIDE – EDIT
TIME – EMIT
TIPS – SPIT
TONS – SNOT
TOOL – LOOT
TOPS – SPOT

TORT – TROT
TOWS – SWOT
TRAP – PART
TROT – TORT
TUBA – ABUT
WARD – DRAW
WETS – STEW
WOLF – FLOW
YAPS – SPAY
YARD – DRAY
YAWS – SWAY

5
ANNAM – MANNA
ATLAS – SALTA
CARES – SERAC
DARAF – FARAD
DECAL – LACED
DENIM – MINED
DEVIL – LIVED
FARAD – DARAF
FIRES – SERIF
KEELS – SLEEK
LACED – DECAL
LAGER – REGAL
LEPER – REPEL
LEVER – REVEL
LIVED – DEVIL
LOOPS – SPOOL
MANNA – ANNAM
MINED – DENIM
PACER – RECAP
PARTS – STRAP
POOLS – SLOOP
PORTS – STROP
REBUT – TUBER
RECAP – PACER
REGAL – LAGER
REMIT – TIMER
REPEL – LEPER
REVEL – LEVER
SALTA – ATLAS
SERAC – CARES
SERIF – FIRES

SLEEK – KEELS
SLOOP – POOLS
SMART – TRAMS
SNIPS – SPINS
SPINS – SNIPS
SPOOL – LOOPS
SPOTS – STOPS
STOPS – SPOTS
STRAP – PARTS
STRAW – WARTS
STROP – PORTS
TIMER – REMIT
TRAMS – SMART
TUBER – REBUT
WARTS – STRAW

6
ANIMAL – LAMINA
DELIAN – NAILED
DENIER – REINED
DIAPER – REPAID
DRAWER – REWARD
HARRIS – SIRRAH
LAMINA – ANIMAL
LOOTER – RETOOL
NAILED – DELIAN
PUPILS – SLIP-UP
RECAPS – SPACER
REINED – DENIER
RENNET – TENNER
REPAID – DIAPER
RETOOL – LOOTER
REWARD – DRAWER
SERVES – SEVRES
SEVRES – SERVES
SIRRAH – HARRIS
SLIP-UP – PUPILS
SNOOPS – SPOONS
SPACER – RECAPS
SPOONS – SNOOPS
TENNER – RENNET

8
DESSERTS – STRESSED
STRESSED – DESSERTS

HOMOPHONES

ACCESSARY –
  ACCESSORY
ACCESSORY –
  ACCESSARY
AERIAL – ARIEL
AERIE – AIRY
AIL – ALE
AIR – AIRE, E'ER, ERE,
  EYRE, HEIR
AIRE – AIR, E'ER, ERE,
  EYRE, HEIR
AIRSHIP – HEIRSHIP

AIRY – AERIE
AISLE – I'LL, ISLE
AIT – EIGHT, ATE
ALE – AIL
ALL – AWL, ORLE
ALMS – ARMS
ALTAR – ALTER
ALTER – ALTAR
AMAH – ARMOUR
ANTE – ANTI
ANTI – ANTE
ARC – ARK

AREN'T – AUNT
ARES – ARIES
ARIEL – AERIAL
ARIES – ARES
ARK – ARC
ARMOUR – AMAH
ARMS – ALMS
ASCENT – ASSENT
ASSENT – ASCENT
ATE – AIT, EIGHT
AUK – ORC
AUNT – AREN'T

AURAL – ORAL
AUSTERE – OSTIA
AWAY – AWEIGH
AWE – OAR, O'ER, ORE
AWEIGH – AWAY
AWL – ALL, ORLE
AXEL – AXLE
AXLE – AXEL
AY – AYE, EYE, I
AYAH – IRE
AYE – AY, EYE, I
AYES – EYES

BAA – BAH, BAR
BAAL – BASLE
BAH – BAA, BAR
BAIL – BALE
BALE – BAIL
BALL – BAWL
BALM – BARM
BALMY – BARMY
BAR – BAA, BAH
BARE – BEAR
BARM – BALM
BARMY – BALMY
BARON – BARREN
BARREN – BARON
BASE – BASS
BASLE – BAAL
BASS – BASE
BAUD – BAWD, BOARD
BAWD – BAUD, BOARD
BAWL – BALL
BAY – BEY
BEACH – BEECH
BEAN – BEEN
BEAR – BARE
BEAT – BEET
BEATER – BETA
BEAU – BOH, BOW
BEECH – BEACH
BEEN – BEAN
BEER – BIER
BEET – BEAT
BEL – BELL, BELLE
BELL – BEL, BELLE
BELLE – BEL, BELL
BERRY – BURY
BERTH – BIRTH
BETA – BEATER
BEY – BAY
BHAI – BI, BUY, BY, BYE
BI – BHAI, BUY, BY, BYE
BIER – BEER
BIGHT – BITE, BYTE
BIRTH – BERTH
BITE – BIGHT, BYTE
BLEW – BLUE
BLUE – BLEW
BOAR – BOER, BOOR, BORE
BOARD – BAUD, BAWD
BOARDER – BORDER
BOART – BOUGHT
BOER – BOAR, BOOR, BORE
BOH – BEAU, BOW
BOLE – BOWL
BOLT – BOULT
BOOR – BOAR, BOER, BORE
BOOTIE – BOOTY
BOOTY – BOOTIE
BORDER – BOARDER
BORE – BOAR, BOER, BOOR
BORN – BORNE
BORNE – BORN
BOUGH – BOW
BOUGHT – BOART

BOULT – BOLT
BOW – BEAU, BOH
BOW – BOUGH
BOWL – BOLE
BOY – BUOY
BRAKE – BREAK
BREAD – BRED
BREAK – BRAKE
BRED – BREAD
BREDE – BREED, BREID
BREED – BREDE, BREID
BREID – BREDE, BREED
BRIDAL – BRIDLE
BRIDLE – BRIDAL
BROACH – BROOCH
BROOCH – BROACH
BUNION – BUNYAN
BUNYAN – BUNION
BUOY – BOY
BURGER – BURGHER
BURGHER – BURGER
BURY – BERRY
BUS – BUSS
BUSS – BUS
BUY – BHAI, BI, BY, BYE
BUYER – BYRE
BY – BHAI, BI, BUY, BYE
BYE – BHAI, BI, BUY, BY
BYRE – BUYER
BYTE – BIGHT, BITE
CACHE – CASH
CACHOU – CASHEW
CAIN – CANE, KAIN
CALL – CAUL
CALLAS – CALLOUS, CALLUS
CALLOUS – CALLAS, CALLUS
CALLUS – CALLAS, CALLOUS
CANAPÉ – CANOPY
CANE – CAIN, KAIN
CANOPY – CANAPÉ
CARAT – CARROT, KARAT
CARROT – CARAT, KARAT
CART – CARTE, KART
CARTE – CART, KART
CASH – CACHE
CASHEW – CACHOU
CASHMERE – KASHMIR
CAST – CASTE, KARST
CASTE – CAST, KARST
CAUGHT – COURT
CAUL – CALL
CAW – COR, CORE, CORPS
CEDAR – SEEDER
CEDE – SEED
CEIL – SEEL, SEAL
CELL – SELL, SZELL
CELLAR – SELLER
CENSER – CENSOR, SENSOR
CENSOR – CENSER, SENSOR
CENT – SCENT, SENT
CERE – SEAR, SEER
CEREAL – SERIAL
CESSION – SESSION

CHAW – CHORE
CHEAP – CHEEP
CHECK – CHEQUE, CZECH
CHEEP – CHEAP
CHEQUE – CHECK, CZECH
CHOIR – QUIRE
CHOLER – COLLAR
CHORD – CORD
CHORE – CHAW
CHOTT – SHOT, SHOTT
CHOU – SHOE, SHOO
CHOUGH – CHUFF
CHUFF – CHOUGH
CHUTE – SHOOT, SHUTE
CITE – SIGHT, SITE
CLACK – CLAQUE
CLAQUE – CLACK
CLIMB – CLIME
CLIME – CLIMB
COAL – COLE, KOHL
COARSE – CORSE, COURSE
COLE – COAL, KOHL
COLLAR – CHOLER
COLONEL – KERNEL
COLOUR – CULLER
COME – CUM
COMPLEMENTARY –
   COMPLIMENTARY
COMPLIMENTARY –
   COMPLEMENTARY
COO – COUP
COOP – COUPE
COR – CAW, CORE, CORPS
CORD – CHORD
CORE – CAW, COR, CORPS
CORNFLOUR – CORNFLOWER
CORNFLOWER – CORNFLOUR
CORPS – CAW, COR, CORE
CORSE – COARSE, COURSE
COUNCIL – COUNSEL
COUNSEL – COUNCIL
COUP – COO
COUPE – COOP
COURSE – COARSE, CORSE
COURT – CAUGHT
CREAK – CREEK
CREEK – CREAK
CULLER – COLOUR
CUM – COME
CURB – KERB
CURRANT – CURRENT
CURRENT – CURRANT
CYGNET – SIGNET
CYMBAL – SYMBOL
CZECH – CHECK, CHEQUE
DAM – DAMN
DAMN – DAM
DAW – DOOR, DOR
DAYS – DAZE
DAZE – DAYS
DEAR – DEER
DEER – DEAR
DESCENT – DISSENT

DESERT – DESSERT
DESSERT – DESERT
DEW – DUE
DINAH – DINER
DINE – DYNE
DINER – DINAH
DISSENT – DESCENT
DOE – DOH, DOUGH
DOH – DOE, DOUGH
DONE – DONNE, DUN
DONNE – DONE, DUN
DOOR – DAW, DOR
DOR – DAW, DOOR
DOST – DUST
DOUGH – DOE, DOH
DRAFT – DRAUGHT
DRAUGHT – DRAFT
DROOP – DRUPE
DRUPE – DROOP
DUAL – DUEL
DUCKS – DUX
DUE – DEW
DUEL – DUAL
DUN – DONE, DONNE
DUST – DOST
DUX – DUCKS
DYEING – DYING
DYING – DYEING
DYNE – DINE
EARN – URN
EATEN – ETON
E'ER – AIR, AIRE, ERE, EYRE, HEIR
EERIE – EYRIE
EIDER – IDA
EIGHT – AIT, ATE
EIRE – EYRA
ELATION – ILLATION
ELICIT – ILLICIT
ELUDE – ILLUDE
ELUSORY – ILLUSORY
EMERGE – IMMERGE
EMERSED – IMMERSED
EMERSION – IMMERSION
ERE – AIR, AIRE, E'ER, EYRE, HEIR
ERK – IRK
ERR – UR
ESTER – ESTHER
ESTHER – ESTER
ETON – EATEN
EWE – YEW, YOU
EYE – AY, AYE, I
EYED – I'D, IDE
EYELET – ISLET
EYES – AYES
EYRA – EIRE
EYRE – AIR, AIRE, E'ER, ERE, HEIR
EYRIE – EERIE
FA – FAR
FAIN – FANE, FEIGN
FAINT – FEIGNT
FAIR – FARE
FANE – FAIN, FEIGN
FAR – FA

FARE – FAIR
FARO – PHARAOH
FARTHER – FATHER
FATE – FÊTE
FATHER – FARTHER
FAUGH – FOR, FOUR, FORE
FAUN – FAWN
FAWN – FAUN
FAZE – PHASE
FEAT – FEET
FEET – FEAT
FEIGN – FAIN, FANE
FEIGNT – FAINT
FELLOE – FELLOW
FELLOW – FELLOE
FELT – VELD, VELDT
FETA – FETTER
FÊTE – FATE
FETTER – FETA
FEU – FEW, PHEW
FEW – FEU, PHEW
FIR – FUR
FISHER – FISSURE
FISSURE – FISHER
FIZZ – PHIZ
FLAIR – FLARE
FLARE – FLAIR
FLAW – FLOOR
FLEA – FLEE
FLEE – FLEA
FLEW – FLU, FLUE
FLOE – FLOW
FLOOR – FLAW
FLOUR – FLOWER
FLOW – FLOE
FLOWER – FLOUR
FLU – FLEW, FLUE
FLUE – FLEW, FLU
FOR – FAUGH, FOUR, FORE
FORE – FAUGH, FOR, FOUR
FORT – FOUGHT
FORTE – FORTY
FORTH – FOURTH
FORTY – FORTE
FOUGHT – FORT
FOUL – FOWL
FOUR – FAUGH, FOR, FORE
FOURTH – FORTH
FOWL – FOUL
FRIAR – FRIER
FRIER – FRIAR
FUR – FIR
GAIL – GALE
GAIT – GATE
GALE – GAIL
GALLOP – GALLUP
GALLUP – GALLOP
GAMBLE – GAMBOL
GAMBOL – GAMBLE
GATE – GAIT
GAWKY – GORKY
GENE – JEAN
GIN – JINN

GLADDEN – GLADDON
GLADDON – GLADDEN
GNASH – NASH
GNAT – NAT
GNAW – NOR
GORKY – GAWKY
GRATER – GREATER
GREATER – GRATER
GROAN – GROWN
GROWN – GROAN
HAE – HAY, HEH, HEY
HAIL – HALE
HAIR – HARE
HALE – HAIL
HALL – HAUL
HANDEL – HANDLE
HANDLE – HANDEL
HANGAR – HANGER
HANGER – HANGAR
HARE – HAIR
HART – HEART
HAUD – HOARD, HORDE
HAUL – HALL
HAW – HOARE, WHORE
HAY – HAE, HEH, HEY
HEAR – HERE
HEART – HART
HEH – HAE, HAY, HEY
HEIR – AIR, AIRE, E'ER, ERE, EYRE
HEIRSHIP – AIRSHIP
HERE – HEAR
HEROIN – HEROINE
HEROINE – HEROIN
HEW – HUE
HEY – HAE, HAY, HEH
HIE – HIGH
HIGH – HIE
HIGHER – HIRE
HIM – HYMN
HIRE – HIGHER
HO – HOE
HOAR – HAW, WHORE
HOARD – HAUD, HORDE
HOARSE – HORSE
HOE – HO
HOLE – WHOLE
HOO – WHO
HORDE – HAUD, HOARD
HORSE – HOARSE
HOUR – OUR
HOURS – OURS
HUE – HEW
HYMN – HIM
I – AY, AYE, EYE
I'D – EYED, IDE
IDA – EIDER
IDE – EYED, I'D
IDLE – IDOL
IDOL – IDLE
I'LL – AISLE, ISLE
ILLATION – ELATION
ILLICIT – ELICIT
ILLUDE – ELUDE

397

ILLUSORY – ELUSORY
IMMERGE – EMERGE
IMMERSED – EMERSED
IMMERSION – EMERSION
IN – INN
INCITE – INSIGHT
INDICT – INDITE
INDITE – INDICT
INN – IN
INSIGHT – INCITE
INSOLE – INSOUL
INSOUL – INSOLE
ION – IRON
IRE – AYAH
IRK – ERK
IRON – ION
ISLE – AISLE, I'LL
ISLET – EYELET
JAM – JAMB, JAMBE
JAMB – JAM, JAMBE
JAMBE – JAM, JAMB
JEAN – GENE
JINKS – JINX
JINN – GIN
JINX – JINKS
KAIN – CAIN, CANE
KARAT – CARAT, CARROT
KARST – CAST, CASTE
KART – CART, CARTE
KASHMIR – CASHMERE
KERB – CURB
KERNEL – COLONEL
KEW – KYU, QUEUE
KEY – QUAY
KNAVE – NAVE
KNEAD – NEED
KNEW – NEW, NU
KNIGHT – NIGHT
KNIGHTLY – NIGHTLY
KNIT – NIT
KNOW – NOH, NO
KNOWS – NOES, NOSE
KOHL – COAL, COLE
KYU – KEW, QUEUE
LACKER – LACQUER
LACQUER – LACKER
LAIN – LANE
LANCE – LAUNCE
LANE – LAIN
LAUD – LORD
LAUNCE – LANCE
LAW – LORE
LAY – LEI, LEY
LAYS – LAZE
LAZE – LAYS
LEAD – LED
LEAF – LIEF
LEAH – LEAR, LEER, LEHR
LEAK – LEEK
LEANT – LENT
LEAR – LEAH, LEER, LEHR
LED – LEAD
LEEK – LEAK

LEER – LEAH, LEAR, LEHR
LEHR – LEAH, LEAR, LEER
LEI – LAY, LEY
LEMAN – LEMON
LEMON – LEMAN
LENT – LEANT
LESSEN – LESSON
LESSON – LESSEN
LEY – LAY, LEI
LIAR – LYRE
LIEF – LEAF
LINCS – LINKS, LYNX
LINKS – LINCS, LYNX
LOAD – LODE
LOAN – LONE
LODE – LOAD
LONE – LOAN
LORD – LAUD
LORE – LAW
LUMBAR – LUMBER
LUMBER – LUMBAR
LYNX – LINCS, LINKS
LYRE – LIAR
MA – MAAR, MAR
MAAR – MA, MAR
MADE – MAID
MAID – MADE
MAIL – MALE
MAIN – MAINE, MANE
MAINE – MAIN, MANE
MAIZE – MAZE
MALE – MAIL
MALL – MAUL
MANE – MAIN, MAINE
MANNA – MANNER, MANOR
MANNER – MANNA, MANOR
MANOR – MANNA, MANNER
MAQUIS – MARQUEE
MAR – MA, MAAR
MARC – MARK, MARQUE
MARE – MAYOR
MARK – MARC, MARQUE
MARQUE – MARC, MARK
MARQUEE – MAQUIS
MAUL – MALL
MAW – MOR, MORE, MOOR
MAYOR – MARE
MAZE – MAIZE
MEAN – MESNE, MIEN
MEAT – MEET, METE
MEDAL – MEDDLE
MEDDLE – MEDAL
MEET – MEAT, METE
MESNE – MIEN, MEAN
METAL – METTLE
METE – MEAT, MEET
METTLE – METAL
MEWS – MUSE
MIEN – MESNE, MEAN
MIGHT – MITE
MINER – MINOR
MINOR – MINER
MITE – MIGHT

MOAN – MOWN
MOAT – MOTE
MOCHA – MOCKER
MOCKER – MOCHA
MOOR – MAW, MOR, MORE
MOOSE – MOUSSE
MOR – MAW, MORE, MOOR
MORE – MAW, MOR, MOOR
MORN – MOURN
MORNING – MOURNING
MOTE – MOAT
MOURN – MORN
MOURNING – MORNING
MOUSSE – MOOSE
MOWN – MOAN
MUSCLE – MUSSEL
MUSE – MEWS
MUSSEL – MUSCLE
NAE – NAY, NEAGH, NEIGH, NEY
NASH – GNASH
NAT – GNAT
NAUGHT – NOUGHT
NAVAL – NAVEL
NAVE – KNAVE
NAVEL – NAVAL
NAY – NAE, NEAGH, NEIGH, NEY
NEAGH – NAE, NAY, NEIGH, NEY
NEED – KNEAD
NEIGH – NAE, NAY, NEAGH, NEY
NEUK – NUKE
NEW – KNEW, NU
NEY – NAE, NAY, NEAGH, NEIGH
NIGH – NYE
NIGHT – KNIGHT
NIGHTLY – KNIGHTLY
NIT – KNIT
NO – KNOW, NOH
NOES – KNOWS, NOSE
NOH – KNOW, NO
NONE – NUN
NOR – GNAW
NOSE – KNOWS, NOES
NOUGHT – NAUGHT
NU – KNEW, NEW
NUKE – NEUK
NUN – NONE
NYE – NIGH
OAR – AWE, O'ER, ORE
O'ER – AWE, OAR, ORE
OFFA – OFFER
OFFER – OFFA
OH – OWE
ORAL – AURAL
ORC – AUK
ORE – AWE, OAR, O'ER
ORLE – ALL, AWL
OSTIA – AUSTERE
OUR – HOUR
OURS – HOURS
OUT – OWT
OVA – OVER
OVER – OVA
OWE – OH

OWT – OUT
PA – PAH, PAR, PARR, PAS
PACKED – PACT
PACT – PACKED
PAH – PA, PAR, PARR, PAS
PAIL – PALE
PAIR – PARE, PEAR
PALATE – PALETTE, PALLET
PALE – PAIL
PALETTE – PALATE, PALLET
PALLET – PALATE, PALETTE
PANDA – PANDER
PANDER – PANDA
PAR – PA, PAH, PARR, PAS
PARE – PEAR, PAIR
PARR – PA, PAH, PAR, PAS
PAS – PA, PAH, PAR, PARR
PAW – POOR, PORE, POUR
PAWKY – PORKY
PAWN – PORN
PEA – PEE
PEACE – PIECE
PEAK – PIQUE, PEAKE, PEEK,
  PEKE
PEAL – PEEL
PEAR – PARE, PAIR
PEARL – PURL
PEARLER – PURLER
PEDAL – PEDDLE
PEDDLE – PEDAL
PEE – PEA
PEEK – PEAK, PEAKE, PEKE,
  PIQUE
PEEL – PEAL
PEKE – PEAK, PEAKE, PEEK,
  PIQUE
PER – PURR
PETREL – PETROL
PETROL – PETREL
PHARAOH – FARO
PHASE – FAZE
PHEW – FEU, FEW
PHIZ – FIZZ
PI – PIE, PYE
PIE – PI, PYE
PIECE – PEACE
PILATE – PILOT
PILOT – PILATE
PIQUE – PEAK, PEAKE, PEEK,
  PEKE
PLACE – PLAICE
PLAICE – PLACE
PLAIN – PLANE
PLANE – PLAIN
POLE – POLL
POLL – POLE
POMACE – PUMICE
POMMEL – PUMMEL
POOR – PAW, PORE, POUR
POPULACE – POPULOUS
POPULOUS – POPULACE
PORE – PAW, POOR, POUR
PORKY – PAWKY

PORN – PAWN
POUR – PAW, POOR, PORE
PRAY – PREY
PREY – PRAY
PRINCIPAL – PRINCIPLE
PRINCIPLE – PRINCIPAL
PROFIT – PROPHET
PROPHET – PROFIT
PSALTER – SALTER
PUCKA – PUCKER
PUCKER – PUCKA
PUMICE – POMACE
PUMMEL – POMMEL
PURL – PEARL
PURLER – PEARLER
PURR – PER
PYE – PI, PIE
QUAY – KEY
QUEUE – KEW, KYU
QUIRE – CHOIR
RACK – WRACK
RACKET – RACQUET
RACQUET – RACKET
RAIN – REIGN, REIN
RAINS – REINS
RAISE – RASE
RAP – WRAP
RAPT – WRAPPED
RASE – RAISE
RAW – ROAR
READ – REDE, REED
RECK – WRECK
REDE – READ, REED
REED – READ, REDE
REEK – WREAK
REIGN – RAIN, REIN
REIN – RAIN, REIGN
REINS – RAINS
RENNES – WREN
RETCH – WRETCH
REVERE – REVERS
REVERS – REVERE
RHEUM – ROOM
RHEUMY – ROOMY
RHO – ROW, ROE
RHÔNE – ROAN, RONE
RIGHT – RITE, WRIGHT, WRITE
RING – WRING
RINGER – WRINGER
RITE – RIGHT, WRIGHT, WRITE
ROAM – ROME
ROAN – RHÔNE, RONE
ROAR – RAW
ROE – RHO, ROW
ROLE – ROLL
ROLL – ROLE
ROME – ROAM
RONE – RHÔNE, ROAN
ROOD – RUDE
ROOM – RHEUM
ROOMY – RHEUMY
ROOSE – RUSE
ROOT – ROUTE

RORT – WROUGHT
ROTE – WROTE
ROUGH – RUFF
ROUTE – ROOT
ROW – RHO, ROE
RUDE – ROOD
RUFF – ROUGH
RUNG – WRUNG
RUSE – ROOSE
RYE – WRY
SAIL – SALE
SAIN – SANE, SEINE
SALE – SAIL
SALTER – PSALTER
SANE – SAIN, SEINE
SAUCE – SOURCE
SAUT – SORT, SOUGHT
SAW – SOAR, SORE
SAWN – SORN
SCENE – SEEN
SCENT – CENT, SENT
SCULL – SKULL
SEAL – CEIL, SEEL
SEAM – SEEM
SEAR – CERE, SEER
SEED – CEDE
SEEDER – CEDAR
SEEK – SEIK, SIKH
SEEL – CEIL, SEAL
SEEM – SEAM
SEEN – SCENE
SEER – CERE, SEAR
SEIK – SEEK, SIKH
SEINE – SAIN, SANE
SELL – CELL, SZELL
SELLER – CELLAR
SENSOR – CENSER, CENSOR
SENT – CENT, SCENT
SERF – SURF
SERGE – SURGE
SERIAL – CEREAL
SESSION – CESSION
SEW – SO, SOH, SOW
SEWN – SONE, SOWN
SHAKE – SHEIK
SHEIK – SHAKE
SHIER – SHYER, SHIRE
SHIRE – SHIER, SHYER
SHOE – CHOU, SHOO
SHOO – CHOU, SHOE
SHOOT – SHUTE, CHUTE
SHOT – SHOTT, CHOTT
SHOTT – SHOT, CHOTT
SHUTE – SHOOT, CHUTE
SHYER – SHIER, SHIRE
SIGHT – CITE, SITE
SIGN – SYN
SIGNET – CYGNET
SIKH – SEEK, SEIK
SIOUX – SOU
SITE – CITE, SIGHT
SKULL – SCULL
SKY – SKYE

SKYE – SKY
SLAY – SLEIGH
SLEAVE – SLEEVE
SLEEVE – SLEAVE
SLEIGH – SLAY
SLOE – SLOW
SLOW – SLOE
SO – SEW, SOH, SOW
SOAR – SAW, SORE
SOH – SEW, SO, SOW
SOLE – SOUL
SOME – SUM
SON – SUN, SUNN
SONE – SEWN, SOWN
SONNY – SUNNI, SUNNY
SORE – SAW, SOAR
SORN – SAWN
SORT – SAUT, SOUGHT
SOU – SIOUX
SOUGHT – SAUT, SORT
SOUL – SOLE
SOURCE – SAUCE
SOW – SEW, SO, SOH
SOWN – SEWN, SONE
STAIR – STARE
STAKE – STEAK
STALK – STORK
STARE – STAIR
STEAK – STAKE
STEAL – STEEL
STEEL – STEAL
STOREY – STORY
STORK – STALK
STORY – STOREY
SUITE – SWEET
SUM – SOME
SUN – SON, SUNN
SUNDAE – SUNDAY
SUNDAY – SUNDAE
SUNN – SON, SUN
SUNNI – SONNY, SUNNY
SUNNY – SONNY, SUNNI
SURF – SERF
SURGE – SERGE
SWAT – SWOT
SWEET – SUITE
SWOT – SWAT
SYMBOL – CYMBAL
SYN – SIGN
SZELL – CELL, SELL
TACIT – TASSET
TAI – TAILLE, THAI, TIE
TAIL – TALE
TAILLE – TAI, THAI, TIE
TALE – TAIL
TALK – TORC, TORQUE
TARE – TEAR
TASSET – TACIT
TAUGHT – TAUT, TORT, TORTE
TAUT – TAUGHT, TORT, TORTE
TEA – TEE, TI
TEAM – TEEM
TEAR – TARE

TEE – TEA, TI
TEEM – TEAM
TENNER – TENOR
TENOR – TENNER
TERNE – TURN
THAI – TAI, TAILLE, TIE
THAW – THOR
THEIR – THERE, THEY'RE
THERE – THEIR, THEY'RE
THEY'RE – THEIR, THERE
THOR – THAW
THREW – THROUGH, THRU
THROE – THROW
THRONE – THROWN
THROUGH – THREW, THRU
THROW – THROE
THROWN – THRONE
THRU – THREW, THROUGH
THYME – TIME
TI – TEA, TEE
TIC – TICK
TICK – TIC
TIDE – TIED
TIE – TAI, TAILLE, THAI
TIED – TIDE
TIER – TIRE, TYRE
TIGHTEN – TITAN
TIMBER – TIMBRE
TIMBRE – TIMBER
TIME – THYME
TIRE – TIER, TYRE
TITAN – TIGHTEN
TO – TOO, TWO
TOAD – TOED, TOWED
TOE – TOW
TOED – TOAD, TOWED
TOO – TO, TWO
TOR – TORE
TORC – TALK, TORQUE
TORE – TOR
TORQUE – TALK, TORC
TORT – TAUGHT, TAUT, TORTE
TORTE – TAUGHT, TAUT, TORT
TOW – TOE
TOWED – TOAD, TOED
TROOP – TROUPE
TROUPE – TROOP
TUNA – TUNER
TUNER – TUNA
TURN – TERNE
TWO – TO, TOO
TYRE – TIER, TIRE
UR – ERR
URN – EARN
VAIL – VALE, VEIL
VAIN – VANE, VEIN
VALE – VAIL, VEIL
VANE – VAIN, VEIN
VEIL – VAIL, VALE
VEIN – VAIN, VANE
VELD – FELT, VELDT
VELDT – FELT, VELD
WAE – WAY, WHEY

WAIL – WHALE
WAIN – WANE, WAYNE
WAIST – WASTE
WAIT – WEIGHT
WAIVE – WAVE
WANE – WAIN, WAYNE
WAR – WAUGH, WAW, WORE
WARE – WEAR, WHERE
WARN – WORN
WASTE – WAIST
WATT – WHAT, WOT
WAUGH – WAR, WAW, WORE
WAVE – WAIVE
WAW – WAR, WAUGH, WORE
WAY – WAE, WHEY
WAYNE – WAIN, WANE
WEAK – WEEK
WEAKLY – WEEKLY
WEAR – WARE, WHERE
WEAVE – WE'VE
WE'D – WEED
WEED – WE'D
WEEK – WEAK
WEEKLY – WEAKLY
WEEL – WE'LL, WHEAL, WHEEL
WEIGHT – WAIT
WE'LL – WEEL, WHEAL, WHEEL
WEN – WHEN
WERE – WHIRR
WE'VE – WEAVE
WHALE – WAIL
WHAT – WATT, WOT
WHEAL – WEEL, WE'LL, WHEEL
WHEEL – WEEL, WE'LL, WHEAL
WHEN – WEN
WHERE – WARE, WEAR
WHEY – WAE, WAY
WHICH – WITCH
WHINE – WINE
WHIRR – WERE
WHITE – WIGHT, WITE
WHITHER – WITHER
WHO – HOO
WHOA – WO, WOE
WHOLE – HOLE
WHORE – HAW, HOAR
WIGHT – WHITE, WITE
WINE – WHINE
WITCH – WHICH
WITE – WHITE, WIGHT
WITHER – WHITHER
WO – WHOA, WOE
WOE – WHOA, WO
WORE – WAR, WAUGH, WAW
WORN – WARN
WOT – WATT, WHAT
WRACK – RACK
WRAP – RAP
WRAPPED – RAPT
WREAK – REEK
WRECK – RECK
WREN – RENNES
WRETCH – RETCH

WRIGHT – RIGHT, RITE, WRITE
WRING – RING
WRINGER – RINGER
WRITE – RIGHT, RITE, WRIGHT
WROTE – ROTE
WROUGHT – RORT
WRUNG – RUNG

WRY – RYE
YAW – YORE, YOUR
YAWS – YOURS
YEW – EWE, YOU
YOKE – YOLK
YOLK – YOKE

YORE – YAW, YOUR
YOU – EWE, YEW
YOU'LL – YULE
YOUR – YAW, YORE
YOURS – YAWS
YULE – YOU'LL

TWO-WORD PHRASES

FIRST WORD

ABERDEEN – angus, terrier
ABLE – bodied, rating, seaman
ABSOLUTE – alcohol, humidity, judgment, magnitude, majority, monarchy, music, pitch, temperature, threshold, unit, value, zero
ABSTRACT – expressionism, noun
ACCESS – road, time
ACCOMMODATION – address, bill, ladder, platform
ACHILLES – heel, tendon
ACID – drop, rain, rock, soil, test, value
ACT – as, for, on, out, up
ACTION – committee, group, painting, potential, replay, stations
ACTIVE – centre, list, service, transport, vocabulary, volcano
ADMIRALTY – board, house, islands, mile, range
ADVANCE – booking, copy, guard, man, notice, poll, ratio
AEOLIAN – deposits, harp, islands, mode
AFRICAN – lily, mahogany, time, violet
AGONY – aunt, column
AIR – alert, bag, bed, bladder, brake, bridge, commodore, conditioning, corridor, cover, curtain, cushion, cylinder, dam, embolism, force, gas, gun, hardening, hole, hostess, jacket, letter, mail, marshal, mass, mile, officer, plant, pocket, power, pump, raid, rifle, sac, scoop, scout, shaft, shot, sock, spray, spring, station, terminal, traffic, turbine, valve, vice-marshal
ALL – black, clear, fours, hail, in, one, out, right, square, there, told
ALPHA – centauri, helix, iron, particle, privative, ray, rhythm
ALTAR – boy, cloth, -piece

AMERICAN – aloe, chameleon, cheese, cloth, eagle, football, indian, plan, revolution, samoa, wake
ANCHOR – man, plate, ring
ANCIENT – greek, history, lights, monument
ANGEL – cake, dust, falls, food, shark
ANGLE – bracket, dozer, iron, plate
ANIMAL – husbandry, kingdom, magnetism, rights, spirits, starch
ANT – bear, bird, cow, eater, heap, hill
APPLE – blight, box, brandy, butter, green, isle, jack, maggot, polisher, sauce
ARCTIC – char, circle, fox, hare, ocean, tern, willow
ART – deco, form, nouveau, paper
ARTIFICIAL – insemination, intelligence, respiration
ASH – blond, can, wednesday
ATOMIC – age, clock, cocktail, energy, heat, mass, number, pile, power, structure, theory, volume, weight
AUTOMATIC – camera, pilot, repeat, transmission, typesetting
BABY – boom, buggy, carriage, grand, snatcher, talk, tooth
BACK – boiler, burner, country, door, down, end, light, list, marker, matter, out, passage, pay, rest, room, seat, straight, up, yard
BAD – blood, faith, lands, news
BALL – bearing, boy, cock, game, valve
BANANA – oil, republic, skin, split
BANK – acceptance, account, annuities, bill, card, clerk, discount, holiday, manager, on, rate, statement
BAR – billiards, chart, code,

diagram, fly, girl, graph, line, mitzvah, sinister
BARLEY – sugar, water, wine
BARN – dance, door, owl, swallow
BASE – load, metal, rate
BASKET – case, chair, hilt, maker, weave
BATH – bun, chair, chap, cube, oliver, salts, stone
BATTLE – cruiser, cry, fatigue, royal
BAY – leaf, lynx, rum, street, tree, window
BEACH – ball, boys, buggy, flea, plum
BEAR – down, garden, hug, off, out, up, with
BEAUTY – queen, salon, sleep, spot
BED – jacket, linen
BELL – bronze, buoy, glass, heather, jar, magpie, metal, moth, pull, punch, push, sheep, tent
BELLY – dance, flop, landing, laugh
BERMUDA – grass, rig, shorts, triangle
BEST – boy, end, girl, man, seller
BICYCLE – chain, clip, pump
BIG – apple, band, bang, ben, bertha, brother, business, cheese, chief, deal, dipper, end, screen, shot, stick, time, top, wheel
BINARY – code, digit, fission, form, notation, number, star, weapon
BIRD – call, cherry, dog, pepper, spider, strike, table
BIRTH – certificate, control, rate
BIRTHDAY – honours, suit
BIT – part, rate, slice
BITTER – apple, end, lakes, orange, principle
BLACK – art, bean, bear, beetle, belt, bile, body, book, bottom, box, country, death, diamond,

economy, eye, fly, forest, friar, frost, hills, hole, ice, magic, maria, mark, market, mass, monk, mountains, panther, pepper, prince, pudding, rod, rot, sea, sheep, spot, swan, tie, treacle, velvet, watch, widow

BLANK – cartridge, cheque, endorsement, verse

BLANKET – bath, finish, stitch

BLIND – alley, date, freddie, gut, snake, spot, staggers, stamping

BLISTER – beetle, copper, pack, rust

BLOCK – diagram, in, letter, out, printing, release, sampling, tin, vote

BLOOD – bank, bath, brother, cell, count, donor, feud, fluke, group, heat, money, orange, poisoning, pressure, pudding, red, relation, sport, test, type, vessel

BLUE – baby, bag, billy, blood, cheese, chip, devils, ensign, funk, gum, jay, moon, mountains, murder, nile, pencil, peter, riband, ribbon, vein

BOARDING – house, out, school

BOAT – deck, drill, neck, people, race, train

BOBBY – calf, pin, socks

BODY – blow, building, cavity, corporate, image, language, popping, shop, snatcher, stocking, warmer

BOG – asphodel, cotton, deal, down, in, moss, myrtle, oak, orchid, rush, standard

BON – mot, ton, vivant, voyage

BONE – ash, china, idle, meal, oil, up

BOOBY – hatch, prize, trap

BOOK – club, end, in, into, out, scorpion, token, up

BOTTLE – gourd, green, out, party, tree, up

BOTTOM – drawer, end, house, line, out

BOW – legs, out, tie, window

BOWLING – alley, crease, green

BOX – camera, coat, elder, girder, jellyfish, number, office, pleat, seat, spanner, spring

BRAIN – coral, death, drain, fever, stem, wave

BRAKE – band, drum, fluid, horsepower, light, lining, parachute, shoe, van

BRAND – image, leader, name

BRANDY – bottle, butter, snap

BRASS – band, farthing, hat, neck, rubbing, tacks

BREAK – dance, down, even, in, into, off, out, through, up, with

BRING – about, down, forward, in, off, on, out, over, round, to, up

BRISTOL – board, channel, fashion

BROAD – arrow, bean, church, gauge, jump, seal

BROWN – bear, bomber, fat, owl, paper, rice, shirt, snake, study, sugar

BRUSSELS – carpet, lace, sprout

BUBBLE – bath, car, chamber, float, gum, memory, pack

BUCK – fever, rabbit, up

BUILDING – block, line, paper, society

BULL – mastiff, nose, run, session, snake, terrier, tongue, trout

BURNT – almond, offering, shale, sienna, umber

BUS – boy, lane, shelter, stop

BUTTER – bean, muslin, up

BUZZ – bomb, off, saw, word

CABBAGE – bug, lettuce, moth, palm, palmetto, rose, tree, white

CABIN – boy, class, cruiser, fever

CABLE – car, railway, release, stitch, television

CALL – alarm, box, down, forth, girl, in, loan, money, number, off, out, rate, sign, slip, up

CAMP – david, follower, meeting, oven, site

CANARY – creeper, grass, islands, seed, yellow

CANTERBURY – bell, lamb, pilgrims

CAPE – buffalo, cart, cod, colony, coloured, doctor, dutch, flats, gooseberry, horn, jasmine, peninsula, pigeon, primrose, province, sparrow, town, verde, york

CAPITAL – account, allowance, assets, expenditure, gain, goods, levy, market, punishment, ship, stock, surplus

CARD – file, index, punch, reader, vote

CARDINAL – beetle, flower, number, points, spider, virtues

CARPET – beetle, knight, moth, plot, shark, slipper, snake, tiles

CARRIAGE – bolt, clock, dog, line, trade

CARRIER – bag, pigeon, wave

CARRY – away, back, forward, off, on, out, over, through

CARTRIDGE – belt, clip, paper, pen

CASH – crop, desk, discount, dispenser, flow, in, limit, ratio, register, up

CAST – about, back, down, iron, on, out, steel, up

CAT – burglar, door, hole, litter, rig, scanner

CATCH – basin, crop, on, out, phrase, pit, points, up

CAULIFLOWER – cheese, ear

CENTRE – bit, forward, half, punch, spread, three-quarter

CHAIN – drive, gang, grate, letter, lightning, mail, printer, reaction, rule, saw, shot, stitch, store

CHAMBER – counsel, music, orchestra, organ, pot

CHARGE – account, density, hand, nurse, sheet

CHEESE – cutter, mite, skipper, straw

CHICKEN – breast, feed, louse, out, wire

CHILD – abuse, benefit, care, guidance, labour, minder

CHIMNEY – breast, corner, stack, swallow, sweep, swift

CHINA – aster, bark, clay, ink, rose, sea, tree

CHINESE – block, cabbage, chequers, chippendale, empire, gooseberry, ink, lantern, leaves, puzzle, wall, wax, white, windlass

CHIP – basket, heater, in, log, pan, shot

CHRISTMAS – beetle, box, cactus, card, disease, eve, island, pudding, rose, stocking, tree

CIGARETTE – card, end, holder, lighter, paper

CIRCUIT – binding, board, breaker, judge, rider, training

CITY – blues, company, desk, editor, father, hall, manager, planning, slicker

CIVIL – defence, disobedience, engineer, law, liberty, list, marriage, rights, servant, service, war

CLAW – back, hammer, hatchet, off, setting

CLOCK – golf, off, on, up

CLOSE – call, company, down, harmony, in, out, punctuation, quarters, season, shave, with

CLOSED – book, chain, circuit, corporation, game, primary, scholarship, sentence, set, shop

CLOTHES – moth, peg, pole, prop

CLUB – foot, hand, moss, root, sandwich

COAL – gas, heaver, hole, measures, oil, pot, sack, scuttle, tar, tit

COCONUT – butter, ice, matting, oil, palm, shy

COFFEE – bag, bar, cup, house, mill, morning, nut, shop, table, tree

COLD – call, chisel, cream, cuts, duck, feet, frame, front, shoulder, snap, sore, storage, sweat, turkey, war, warrior, wave, work

COLLECTIVE – agreement, bargaining, farm, fruit, noun, ownership, security, unconscious

COLORADO – beetle, desert, springs

COLOUR – bar, code, contrast, filter, guard, index, line, phase, scheme, sergeant, supplement, temperature

COME – about, across, along, at, away, between, by, forward, in, into, of, off, out, over, round, through, to, up, upon

COMIC – opera, strip

COMMAND – guidance, module, paper, performance, post

COMMERCIAL – art, bank, college, paper, traveller, vehicle

COMMON – cold, denominator, entrance, era, factor, fee, fraction, good, ground, knowledge, law, market, noun, room, sense, stock, time

COMMUNITY – care, centre, chest, service, singing

COMPOUND – eye, flower, fraction, fracture, interest, leaf, number, sentence, time

CON – amore, brio, dolore, espressione, fuoco, man, moto, rod, sordino, spirito, trick

CONTINENTAL – breakfast, climate, divide, drift, quilt, shelf, system

CORAL – fern, reef, sea, snake, tree

CORN – borer, bread, bunting, dolly, exchange, factor, laws, lily, marigold, meal, oil, pone, poppy, rose, row, salad, shock, shuck, silk, whisky

CORONA – australis, borealis, discharge

COTTAGE – cheese, flat, hospital, industry, loaf, piano, pie

COTTON – belt, bush, cake, candy, flannel, grass, on, picker, sedge, stainer, to, waste, wool

COUGH – drop, mixture, up

COUNTRY – club, code, cousin, dance, house, music, seat

COURT – card, circular, dress, martial, roll, shoe

COVER – crop, girl, note, point, version

CRASH – barrier, dive, helmet, out, pad

CREAM – cheese, cracker, puff, sauce, soda, tea

CREDIT – account, card, line, rating, squeeze, standing

CROCODILE – bird, clip, river, tears

CRYSTAL – ball, gazing, microphone, palace, pick-up, set, violet

CUCKOO – bee, clock, shrike, spit

CURTAIN – call, lecture, speech, wall

CUSTARD – apple, pie, powder

CUT – across, along, down, glass, in, off, out, string, up

CUTTY – grass, sark, stool

DANISH – blue, loaf, pastry

DARK – ages, continent, glasses, horse, lantern, reaction, star

DAVY – jones, lamp

DAY – bed, lily, name, nursery, release, return, room, school, shift, trip

DE – facto, fide, luxe, profundis, rigueur, trop

DEAD – beat, centre, duck, end, finish, hand, heart, heat, letter, loss, march, sea, set, weight

DEATH – adder, cap, cell, certificate, duty, grant, knell, mask, penalty, rate, rattle, ray, row, seat, valley, warrant, wish

DECIMAL – classification, currency, fraction, place, point, system

DECK – chair, hand, over, tennis

DENTAL – clinic, floss, hygiene, hygienist, nurse, plaque, surgeon

DESERT – boots, cooler, island, lynx, oak, pea, rat, soil

DIAMOND – anniversary, bird, jubilee, point, snake, wedding, willow

DINNER – jacket, lady, service

DIPLOMATIC – bag, corps, immunity, service

DIRECT – access, action, evidence, labour, method, object, question, speech

DISC – brake, flower, harrow, jockey, plough, wheel

DISPATCH – box, case, rider

DOG – biscuit, box, collar, days, fennel, handler, latin, paddle, rose, star, tag, violet

DONKEY – derby, engine, jacket, vote

DOUBLE – agent, back, bar, bass, bassoon, bill, bond, chin, cream, cross, dutch, entendre, entry, exposure, fault, first, glazing, gloucester, knit, knitting, negation, negative, pneumonia, standard, take, talk, time, up

DOWN – payment, time, under

DRAWING – board, card, pin, room

DRESS – circle, coat, down, parade, rehearsal, shield, shirt, suit, uniform, up

DRESSING – case, gown, room, station, table

DROP – away, cannon, curtain, forge, goal, hammer, kick, leaf, off, scone, shot, tank

DRUM – brake, major, majorette, out, up

DRY – battery, cell, distillation, dock, ice, martini, measure, nurse, out, rot, run, up

DUST – bowl, coat, cover, devil, down, jacket, shot, storm

DUTCH – auction, barn, cap, cheese, courage, doll, door, elm, medicine, oven, treat, uncle

EAR – lobe, piercing, shell, trumpet

EARLY – bird, closing, warning

EARTH – closet, mother, pillar, return, science, up, wax

EASTER – cactus, egg, island, lily

EASY – chair, game, meat, money, street

EGG – cup, roll, slice, spoon, timer, tooth, white

ELECTRIC – blanket, blue, chair, charge, constant, current, eel, eye, field, fire, furnace, guitar, hare, needle, organ, potential, ray, shock, storm

ELEPHANT – bird, grass, seal, shrew

EVENING – class, dress, primrose, star

EX – cathedra, dividend, gratia, libris, officio

EYE – contact, dog, rhyme, shadow, socket, splice

FACE – cloth, out, pack, powder, value

FAIR – copy, game, isle, play, rent, sex

FAIRY – cycle, godmother, lights, penguin, ring, shrimp, swallow, tale

FALL – about, among, away, back, behind, down, for, guy, in, off, on, over, through, to

FALSE – alarm, colours, dawn, imprisonment, pretences, step, teeth

FAMILY – allowance, benefit, bible, circle, doctor, man, name, planning, skeleton, tree

FAN – belt, dance, heater, mail, vaulting

FANCY – dress, goods, man, woman

FAST – food, lane, motion, talk

FATHER – christmas, confessor, time

FIELD – army, artillery, battery, centre, day, emission, event, glasses, hospital, marshal, officer, sports, study, trip, work

FIGURE – on, out, skating

FILM – library, pack, set, star, strip

FILTER – bed, out, paper, press, pump, tip

FINGER – bowl, painting, post, wave

FIRE – alarm, ant, away, brigade, clay, control, department, door, drill, engine, escape, hydrant, insurance, irons, raiser, screen, ship, station, walking, wall, watcher

FIRING – line, order, party, pin, squad

FIRST – aid, base, class, floor, fruits, lady, language, lieutenant, light, mate, name, night, offender, officer, person, post, principle, reading, refusal, school, water

FIVE – hundred, ks, nations, stones, towns

FLAKE – out, white

FLASH – burn, card, eliminator, flood, gun, photography, photolysis, point, set, smelting

FLAT – cap, knot, racing, spin, tuning

FLIGHT – arrow, deck, engineer, feather, formation, lieutenant, line, path, plan, recorder, sergeant, simulator, strip, surgeon

FLYING – boat, bomb, bridge, buttress, circus, colours, doctor, dutchman, fish, fox, frog, jib, lemur, lizard, mare,

officer, picket, saucer, squad, squirrel, start, wing

FOLK – dance, medicine, memory, music, singer, song, tale, weave

FOOD – additive, chain, poisoning, processor

FOOT – brake, fault, rot, rule, soldier

FOREIGN – affairs, aid, bill, correspondent, exchange, legion, minister, mission, office, service

FOUL – play, shot, up

FOURTH – dimension, estate, international, republic, world

FREE – agent, association, church, electron, energy, enterprise, fall, flight, form, gift, hand, house, kick, love, space, speech, state, thought, throw, trade, verse, will, zone

FRENCH – academy, bean, bread, chalk, cricket, cuff, curve, doors, dressing, horn, kiss, knickers, knot, leave, letter, mustard, pleat, polish, seam, stick, toast, windows

FRONT – bench, door, line, man, matter

FRUIT – bat, body, cocktail, cup, fly, knife, machine, salad, sugar, tree

FULL – blood, board, dress, house, moon, nelson, pitch, stop, time, toss

GALLEY – proof, slave

GALLOWS – bird, humour, tree

GAME – bird, chips, fish, fowl, laws, park, point, theory, warden

GARDEN – centre, city, cress, flat, frame, party, snail, suburb, warbler

GAS – burner, chamber, constant, engine, equation, fixture, gangrene, laws, lighter, main, mantle, mask, meter, oil, oven, poker, ring, station, turbine

GENERAL – anaesthetic, assembly, delivery, election, hospital, practitioner, staff, strike, synod, will

GIN – palace, rummy, sling

GINGER – ale, beer, group, snap, up, wine

GIRL – friday, guide, scout

GIVE – away, in, off, onto, out, over, up

GLAD – eye, hand, rags

GLOVE – box, compartment, puppet

GOLD – basis, beetle, brick,

certificate, coast, dust, foil, leaf, medal, mine, note, plate, point, record, reserve, rush, standard, stick

GOLDEN – age, aster, calf, chain, delicious, eagle, fleece, gate, goose, handshake, number, oldie, retriever, rule, section, syrup

GOLF – ball, club, course, links

GOOD – afternoon, day, evening, friday, morning, night, samaritan, sort, turn

GOOSE – barnacle, flesh, step

GRAND – canary, canyon, duchess, duchy, duke, final, guignol, jury, larceny, mal, marnier, master, national, opera, piano, prix, seigneur, siècle, slam, tour

GRANNY – bond, flat, knot, smith

GRASS – box, cloth, court, hockey, moth, roots, snake, tree, widow

GRAVY – boat, train

GREASE – cup, gun, monkey

GREAT – auk, bear, britain, dane, divide, lakes, ouse, plains, seal, tit, trek, war,

GREEN – bean, belt, beret, card, dragon, fingers, light, monkey, mould, paper, pepper, plover, thumb, turtle, woodpecker

GREGORIAN – calendar, chant, telescope, tone

GREY – area, eminence, fox, friar, market, matter, squirrel, warbler, whale, wolf

GROUND – control, cover, engineer, floor, glass, ice, ivy, plan, plate, provisions, rent, rule, swell

GROW – bag, into, on, up

GUIDE – dog, rope

HAIR – dryer, follicle, gel, lacquer, restorer, shirt, slide, spray, trigger

HAPPY – event, hour, medium, release

HARD – cash, cheese, copy, core, court, disk, feeling, hat, hitter, labour, lines, rock, sell, shoulder, standing

HARVEST – home, mite, moon, mouse

HAT – stand, trick

HATCHET – job, man

HEALTH – centre, food, salts, visitor

HEN – harrier, party, run

HIGH – altar, church, comedy, command, commissioner, country, court, day, explosive, fashion, fidelity, german, hat, holidays, jinks, jump, point, priest, school, seas, season, society, spot, street, table, tea, tech, technology, tide, time, treason, water, wire, wycombe

HIGHLAND – cattle, dress, fling, region

HIP – bath, flask, joint, pocket

HIT – list, man, off, on, out, parade

HOLD – back, down, forth, in, off, on, out, over, together, with

HOLY – bible, city, communion, day, father, ghost, grail, island, joe, land, mary, office, orders, place, roller, rood, scripture, see, sepulchre, spirit, war, water, week, writ

HOME – aid, counties, economics, farm, ground, guard, help, loan, office, plate, range, rule, run, secretary, straight, teacher, truth, unit

HORSE – around, bean, brass, chestnut, guards, laugh, mackerel, marine, mushroom, nettle, opera, pistol, sense, trading

HOT – air, dog, line, metal, money, pepper, potato, rod, seat, spot, spring, stuff, up, zone

HOUSE – arrest, guest, lights, martin, moth, organ, party, physician, plant, sparrow, spider

HUMAN – being, capital, interest, nature, resources, rights

HURRICANE – deck, lamp

ICE – age, axe, bag, block, cream, fish, hockey, house, lolly, machine, man, pack, pick, plant, point, sheet, shelf, show, skate, station, water, yacht

ILL – feeling, humour, temper, will

IN – absentia, aeternum, camera, esse, extenso, extremis, memoriam, nomine, perpetuum, personam, re, rem, situ, toto, utero, vacuo, vitro, vivo

INDIA – paper, print, rubber

INDIAN – club, empire, file, hemp, ink, mallow, millet, mutiny, ocean, red, reserve, rope-trick, summer

INNER – city, ear, hebrides, light, man, mongolia, tube

INSIDE – forward, job, lane, track

IRISH – coffee, moss, potato, republic, sea, setter, stew,

terrier, whiskey, wolfhound

IRON – age, chancellor, cross, curtain, filings, guard, hand, horse, lung, maiden, man, out, pyrites, rations

JACK – frost, in, plane, rabbit, robinson, russell, tar, up

KICK – about, in, off, out, pleat, turn, up, upstairs

KIDNEY – bean, machine, stone, vetch

KNIFE – edge, grinder, pleat, switch

LADY – bountiful, chapel, day, fern, mayoress, muck, orchid

LAND – agent, bank, bridge, crab, forces, girl, grant, line, mine, office, rail, reform, tax, up, with

LAST – judgment, name, out, post, quarter, rites, straw, supper, thing

LATIN – america, cross, quarter, square

LAY – aside, away, brother, days, down, figure, in, into, off, on, out, over, reader, to, up

LEADING – aircraftman, article, dog, edge, light, man, note, question, reins

LEAVE – behind, off, out

LEFT – bank, wing

LEMON – balm, cheese, drop, fish, geranium, grass, sole, squash, squeezer, verbena

LETTER – bomb, box, card

LIBERTY – bodice, cap, hall, horse, island, ship

LIE – detector, down, in, to

LIFE – assurance, belt, buoy, cycle, expectancy, form, guards, history, insurance, interest, jacket, peer, preserver, raft, science, span, style

LIGHT – bulb, face, flyweight, heavyweight, horse, into, meter, middleweight, music, opera, out, show, up, welterweight, year

LIVER – fluke, salts, sausage

LIVING – death, fossil, picture, room, wage

LOBSTER – moth, newburg, pot, thermidor

LOCAL – anaesthetic, authority, colour, government, time

LONE – hand, wolf

LONG – arm, beach, face, haul, hop, island, jenny, johns, jump, parliament, shot, suit, tom, vacation, weekend

LOOK – after, back, down, on, over, through, up

LOOSE – change, cover, end

LORD – advocate, chamberlain, chancellor, lieutenant, mayor, muck, protector, provost

LOUNGE – lizard, suit

LOVE – affair, apple, child, feast, game, knot, letter, life, match, nest, potion, seat, set

LOW – church, comedy, countries, frequency, profile, tech, technology, tide

LUNAR – caustic, eclipse, module, month, year

LUNCHEON – club, meat, voucher

MACHINE – bolt, gun, head, shop, tool

MACKEREL – breeze, shark, sky

MAGIC – carpet, eye, lantern, mushroom, number, square

MAGNETIC – circuit, compass, constant, disk, equator, field, flux, induction, ink, lens, moment, needle, north, pick-up, pole, storm, tape

MAIDEN – name, over, voyage

MAIL – drop, order

MAKE – after, away, believe, for, of, off, out, over, with

MALT – extract, liquor, whisky

MANDARIN – chinese, collar, duck

MARCH – brown, hare, past

MARKET – garden, gardening, order, price, rent, research, share, town, value

MARRIAGE – bureau, guidance

MARSH – elder, fern, fever, gas, harrier, hawk, hen, mallow, marigold, orchid, tit

MASTER – builder, cylinder, key, race, sergeant

MATINÉE – coat, idol

MAUNDY – money, thursday

MAY – apple, beetle, blobs, blossom, day, queen, tree

MECHANICAL – advantage, drawing, engineering, instrument

MEDICAL – certificate, examination, examiner, jurisprudence

MEDICINE – ball, chest, lodge, man

MELBA – sauce, toast

MEMORY – bank, mapping, span, trace

MENTAL – age, block, cruelty, disorder, handicap

MERCHANT – bank, navy, prince

MERCY – flight, killing, seat

MESS – about, hall, jacket, kit

MICHAELMAS – daisy, term

MICKEY – finn, mouse

MIDDLE – age, ages, c, class, ear, east, management, name, school, temple

MIDNIGHT – blue, sun

MIDSUMMER – day, madness

MILITARY – academy, honours, law, orchid, pace, police

MILK – bar, chocolate, fever, float, leg, pudding, punch, round, run, shake, stout, tooth

MINT – bush, julep, sauce

MINUTE – gun, hand, mark, steak

MIRROR – canon, carp, finish, image, lens, symmetry, writing

MITRE – block, box, gear, joint, square

MIXED – bag, blessing, doubles, economy, farming, grill, marriage, metaphor

MONEY – market, order, spider, supply

MONKEY – bread, business, climb, flower, jacket, nut, orchid, puzzle, suit, tricks, wrench

MORNING – coat, dress, sickness, star, tea, watch

MOSQUITO – boat, hawk, net

MOSS – agate, layer, pink, rose, stitch

MOTHER – country, goose, hubbard, lode, ship, shipton, superior, tongue, wit

MOTOR – caravan, generator, scooter, vehicle, vessel

MOUNTAIN – ash, cat, chain, devil, goat, laurel, lion, range, sheep, sickness

MUD – bath, dauber, flat, hen, map, pie, puppy, turtle

MUSTARD – gas, oil, plaster

MYSTERY – play, tour

NANSEN – bottle, passport

NARROW – boat, gauge, seas

NATIONAL – accounting, agreement, anthem, assembly, assistance, debt, front, gallery, grid, service, trust

NERVE – cell, centre, fibre, gas, impulse

NEW – broom, forest, guinea, look, maths, moon, penny, testament, town, wave, world, year, york, zealand

NEWS – agency, conference, vendor

NIGHT – blindness, dancer, fighter, nurse, owl, robe, safe, school, shift, watch, watchman

NINETEENTH – hole, man

NOBLE – art, gas, savage

NORFOLK – island, jacket, terrier

NOSE – cone, dive, out, rag, ring

NUCLEAR – bomb, energy, family, fission, fuel, fusion, isomer, physics, power, reaction, reactor, threshold, winter

NURSERY – rhyme, school, slopes, stakes

OFF – chance, colour, key, limits, line, season

OIL – beetle, cake, drum, hardening, paint, painting, palm, rig, rivers, shale, slick, varnish, well

OLD – bailey, bill, bird, boy, contemptibles, country, girl, gold, guard, hand, hat, lady, maid, man, moon, nick, pretender, school, style, testament, world

OLIVE – branch, brown, crown, drab, green, oil

ON – dit, key, line

OPEN – air, book, chain, circuit, court, day, door, house, letter, market, prison, punctuation, sandwich, sesame, university, up, verdict

OPERA – buffa, cloak, glasses, hat, house, seria

OPIUM – den, poppy, wars

ORANGE – blossom, peel, pekoe, stick

ORDINARY – level, rating, ray, seaman, shares

OXFORD – accent, bags, blue, english, frame, group, movement

OYSTER – bed, crab, pink, plant, white

PACK – animal, drill, ice, in, rat, up

PALM – beach, civet, off, oil, sugar, sunday, vaulting, wine

PANAMA – canal, city, hat

PANIC – bolt, button, buying, grass, stations

PAPER – chase, filigree, money, mulberry, nautilus, over, tape, tiger

PAR – avion, excellence, value

PARISH – clerk, council, pump, register

PARTY – line, man, politics, wall

PASSING – bell, note, shot

PASSION – fruit, play, sunday, week

PATCH – board, pocket, quilt, test

PAY – back, bed, dirt, down, for, in, off, out, television, up

PEACE – corps, offering, pipe, river, sign

PEG – climbing, down, leg, out, top

PEN – friend, name, pal

PENNY – arcade, black, whistle

PER – annum, capita, cent, contra, diem, mensem, mill, pro, se

PERSIAN – blinds, carpet, cat, empire, greyhound, gulf, lamb, melon

PETIT – bourgeois, four, jury, larceny, mal, point

PETROL – bomb, pump, station

PETTY – cash, jury, larceny, officer, sessions

PICTURE – card, hat, house, moulding, palace, window, writing

PIECE – goods, out, rate

PILLOW – block, fight, lace, lava, sham, talk

PILOT – balloon, bird, biscuit, cloth, engine, film, fish, house, lamp, light, officer, plant, study, whale

PIN – curl, down, joint, money, rail, tuck, wrench

PINE – cone, end, marten, needle, tar

PINK – elephants, gin, noise, salmon, slip

PIPE – cleaner, down, dream, major, organ, roll, up

PLACE – card, kick, name, setting

PLAIN – chocolate, clothes, flour, sailing, text

PLAY – along, down, off, on, out, up, with

PLYMOUTH – brethren, colony, rock

POCKET – battleship, billiards, borough, gopher, money, mouse

POETIC – justice, licence

PONY – express, trekking

POOR – box, law, mouth, relation, white

POP – art, off, shop

POST – chaise, hoc, horn, house, meridiem, office, road, town

POT – cheese, liquor, marigold, on, plant, roast, shot, still

POTATO – beetle, blight, chip, crisp

POWDER – blue, burn, compact, flask, horn, keg, monkey, puff, room

POWER – cut, dive, drill, factor, line, pack, plant, point, politics, station, steering, structure

PRAIRIE – dog, oyster, provinces, schooner, soil, turnip, wolf

PRAYER – beads, book, meeting, rug, shawl, wheel

PRESS – agency, agent, box, conference, gallery, gang,

release, stud

PRESSURE – cabin, cooker, drag, gauge, gradient, group, head, point, suit

PRICE – commission, control, discrimination, ring, support, tag, war

PRICKLY – ash, heat, pear, poppy

PRIME – cost, meridian, minister, mover, number, rate, time, vertical

PRIVATE – bar, bill, company, detective, enterprise, eye, hotel, income, language, life, member, parts, patient, practice, press, property, school, secretary, sector

PRIVY – chamber, council, purse, seal

PRIZE – court, money, ring

PRO – forma, patria, rata, tempore

PUBLIC – bar, bill, company, convenience, corporation, debt, defender, enemy, enterprise, expenditure, footpath, gallery, holiday, house, law, nuisance, opinion, ownership, prosecutor, relations, school, sector, servant, service, speaking, spending, transport

PUFF – adder, pastry

PULL – about, back, down, in, off, on, out, through, together, up

PURPLE – emperor, gallinule, heart, medic, patch

PUSH – about, along, button, in, off, on, through

PUT – about, across, aside, away, back, by, down, forth, forward, in, off, on, out, over, through, up, upon

QUANTUM – leap, mechanics, number, state, statistics, theory

QUARTER – crack, day, grain, horse, note, plate, round, section, sessions, tone

QUEEN – bee, consort, dowager, mab, mother, olive, post, regent, regnant, substance

QUEER – fish, street

QUESTION – mark, master, time

RAIN – check, gauge, shadow, tree

REAL – ale, estate, life, number, part, presence, property, tennis, wages

RED – admiral, algae, bag, bark, beds, biddy, carpet, cedar, cross, duster, dwarf, ensign, flag, hat, heat, herring, indian,

meat, mullet, pepper, rag, river, rose, salmon, sea, setter, shank, shift, snapper, spider, squirrel, tape

RES – adjudicata, gestae, judicata, publica

RIGHT – about, angle, ascension, away, honourable, off, on, reverend, wing

ROCK – bottom, cake, climbing, garden, plant, salt, steady

ROLLER – bearing, caption, coaster, derby, skate, towel

ROMAN – arch, calendar, candle, catholic, catholicism, collar, empire, holiday, law, mile, nose, numerals

ROOF – garden, rack

ROOM – service, temperature

ROOT – beer, canal, crop, nodule, out, position, up

ROTARY – clothesline, club, engine, plough, press, pump

ROUGH – collie, diamond, out, passage, spin, stuff, up

ROUND – angle, clam, dance, down, hand, off, on, out, robin, table, top, trip, up

ROYAL – academy, assent, blue, burgh, commission, duke, engineers, flush, highness, icing, jelly, marines, navy, purple, road, standard, tennis, warrant, worcester

RUBBER – band, bridge, cement, cheque, goods, plant, stamp, tree

RUN – across, after, along, around, away, down, in, into, off, on, out, over, through, to, up

RUNNING – board, commentary, head, light, mate, repairs, rigging, stitch

RUSSIAN – dressing, empire, revolution, roulette, salad, wolfhound

SAFETY – belt, catch, chain, curtain, factor, film, fuse, glass, lamp, match, net, pin, razor, valve

SALAD – days, dressing

SALLY – army, lunn

SALT – away, bath, cake, dome, flat, lake, lick, marsh, out, pork

SAND – bar, castle, eel, flea, hopper, lance, leek, lizard, martin, painting, shrimp, table, trap, viper, wasp, wedge, yacht

SANDWICH – board, cake, course, islands, man

SAUSAGE – dog, roll

SCARLET – fever, hat, letter,

pimpernel, runner, woman

SCATTER – diagram, pin, rug

SCOTCH – broth, egg, mist, pancake, snap, tape, terrier

SCRAPE – in, through, together

SCRATCH – pad, sheet, test, together, video

SECOND – childhood, class, coming, cousin, fiddle, floor, generation, growth, hand, language, lieutenant, mate, name, nature, reading, sight, string, thought, wind

SECONDARY – colour, emission, picket, processes, qualities, school, stress

SECRET – agent, police, service, society

SEE – about, into, of, off, out, over, through

SENIOR – aircraftman, citizen, management, service

SERVICE – area, charge, industry, module, road, station

SET – about, against, aside, back, down, forth, in, off, on, out, piece, point, square, theory, to, up, upon

SETTLE – down, for, in, with

SHAKE – down, off, up

SHEET – anchor, bend, down, lightning, metal, music

SHOP – around, assistant, floor, steward

SHORE – bird, leave, patrol

SHORT – circuit, cut, fuse, head, list, odds, shrift, story, straw, time, wave

SHOW – bill, business, card, copy, off, stopper, trial, up

SIAMESE – cat, twins

SICK – leave, list, note, pay

SIGN – away, in, language, manual, off, on, out, up

SINGLE – bond, cream, density, entry, file, tax, thread, ticket

SIT – back, down, on, out, over, under, up

SITTING – bull, room, target, tenant

SKI – jump, lift, pants, run, stick, tow

SKIN – diving, effect, flick, food, friction, game, graft, test

SLAVE – ant, coast, cylinder, driver, ship, state, trade

SLIDE – fastener, guitar, over, rest, rule, trombone, valve

SLIP – gauge, rail, ring, road, step, stitch, up

SLOW – burn, handclap, march, motion, time

SMALL – arms, beer, change, fry,

hours, intestine, slam, talk
SMART – aleck, card, money, set
SMOKE – bomb, out, screen, tree
SNEAK – preview, thief
SOB – sister, story, stuff
SOCIAL – climber, science, secretary, security, services, studies, welfare, work
SODA – ash, biscuit, bread, fountain, jerk, lime, nitre, pop, siphon, water
SOFT – drink, fruit, furnishings, goods, landing, line, option, porn, sell, soap, spot, top, touch
SOLAR – eclipse, flare, furnace, heating, month, myth, panel, plexus, power, system, wind, year
SOUND – barrier, bow, check, effect, head, hole, mixer, off, out, wave
SOUR – cherry, cream, gourd, grapes, gum, mash
SPACE – age, blanket, cadet, capsule, character, heater, invaders, opera, platform, probe, shuttle, station
SPAGHETTI – junction, western
SPARK – chamber, coil, erosion, gap, off, plug, transmitter
SPEAK – for, out, to, up
SPECIAL – assessment, branch, case, constable, delivery, effects, jury, licence, pleading, privilege, school, sort
SPEED – limit, trap, up
SPINNING – jenny, mule, top, wheel
SPIRIT – gum, lamp, level, varnish
SPLIT – cane, decision, infinitive, pea, personality, second, shift, tin, up
SPONGE – bag, bath, cake, cloth, down
SPORTS – car, coat, jacket, shirt
SPRING – balance, chicken, fever, lock, mattress, onion, roll, tide
SPUN – silk, sugar, yarn
SQUARE – away, bracket, dance, leg, meal, number, off, root, up
STABLE – door, fly, lad
STAFF – association, college, corporal, nurse, officer, sergeant
STAG – beetle, party
STAGE – direction, door, effect, fright, left, manager, right, whisper
STAMP – act, collecting, duty, mill, out
STAND – by, down, for, in, oil, on, out, over, pat, to, up

STAR – chamber, connection, grass, sapphire, shell, stream, system, thistle, wars
STATUS – quo, symbol
STEEL – band, blue, grey, guitar, wool
STICK – around, at, by, down, insect, out, to, together, with
STICKY – end, wicket
STIRRUP – bone, cup, pump
STOCK – car, certificate, company, exchange, farm, market
STOCKING – cap, filler, frame, mask, stitch
STORAGE – battery, capacity, device, heater
STORM – belt, centre, cloud, collar, cone, door, glass, lantern, petrel, warning, window
STRAIGHT – bat, face, fight, flush, man, off, up
STRAWBERRY – blonde, bush, mark, tomato, tree
STREET – arab, credibility, cry, door, piano, theatre, value
STRIKE – down, fault, note, off, out, pay, through, up
STRING – along, band, bass, bean, course, line, orchestra, quartet, tie, variable
STRIP – cartoon, club, cropping, lighting, mill, mining, out, poker
SUGAR – beet, candy, cane, corn, daddy, diabetes, loaf, maple
SUMMER – holiday, pudding, school, solstice, time
SUN – bath, bear, bittern, blind, block, dance, deck, disc, king, lamp, lounge
SUPREME – being, commander, court, sacrifice
SURFACE – mail, noise, plate, structure, tension
SWAN – dive, maiden, neck, song
SWEAT – gland, off, out, shirt, suit
SWEET – basil, bay, cherry, chestnut, cicely, cider, clover, corn, fern, flag, gale, gum, marjoram, marten, oil, pea, pepper, potato, shop, tooth, william, woodruff
SWISS – chard, cheese, guard, muslin, roll, tournament
TABLE – bay, d'hôte, licence, money, mountain, napkin, salt, talk, tennis, wine
TAIL – coat, covert, end, fan, gate, off, out

TAKE – aback, after, apart, away, back, down, for, in, off, on, out, over, to, up
TALK – about, at, back, down, into, out, round, show
TANK – engine, farming, top, trap, up, wagon
TAX – avoidance, disc, evasion, exile, haven, rate, return, shelter
TEA – bag, biscuit, cloth, cosy, garden, gown, leaf, party, rose, service, towel, trolley
TEAR – away, down, duct, gas, into, off, sheet
TELEPHONE – box, directory, number
TERRA – alba, cotta, firma, incognita, sigillata
TEST – act, ban, case, marketing, match, paper, pilot, tube
THIRD – class, degree, dimension, estate, eyelid, man, party, person, reading, reich, world
THROW – about, in, off, out, over, together, up, weight
TIME – bomb, capsule, clock, immemorial, machine, series, sharing, sheet, signature, switch, trial, zone
TIN – can, god, hat, lizzie, plate, soldier, whistle
TITLE – deed, page, role
TOILET – paper, set, soap, training, water
TONE – cluster, colour, control, down, language, poem, row, up
TOP – boot, brass, dog, drawer, end, gear, hat, management, off, out, up
TORQUE – converter, meter, spanner, wrench
TOUCH – football, judge, off, up
TOWN – clerk, crier, gas, hall, house, meeting, planning
TRACK – down, event, meet, record, rod, shoe
TRADE – acceptance, cycle, discount, gap, journal, name, on, plate, school, secret, union, wind
TRAFFIC – cop, court, island, jam, light, officer, pattern, warden
TREASURY – bench, bill, bond, certificate, note, tag
TRENCH – coat, fever, foot, knife, mortar, mouth, warfare
TRIPLE – alliance, bond, entente, jump, point, time
TURKISH – bath, coffee, delight, empire, tobacco, towel
TURN – against, away, bridge,

down, in, off, on, out, over, to, up

TWELFTH – day, man, night

TWIN – bed, bill, town

UMBRELLA – bird, pine, plant, stand, tree

UNION – card, jack

UNIT – cost, factor, price, trust

UNITED – kingdom, nations, party, provinces

VACUUM – cleaner, flask

VALUE – added, date, judgment

VENETIAN – blind, glass, red

VENTURE – capital, scout

VICAR – apostolic, forane, general

VICE – admiral, chancellor, president, squad, versa

VIDEO – cassette, game, nasty, tape

VIRGIN – birth, islands, mary, wool

VIRGINIA – beach, creeper, deer, reel, stock

VOX – angelica, humana, pop, populi

VULGAR – fraction, latin

WALK – away, into, off, out

WAR – baby, bonnet, bride, chest, correspondent, crime, cry, dance, game, memorial, office, paint, whoop

WASHING – machine, powder, soda

WATCH – cap, chain, committee, fire, night, out

WEATHER – eye, house, map, station, strip, vane, window

WEDDING – breakfast, cake, ring

WEIGH – down, in, up

WELSH – corgi, dresser, harp, mountain, poppy, rabbit, terrier

WET – blanket, cell, dream, fish, fly, look, nurse, pack, rot, steam, suit

WHITE – admiral, area, bear, birch, elephant, ensign, feather, fish, flag, gold, heat, horse, house, knight, lady, lead, lie, light, meat, out, paper, pepper, slave, spirit, stick, tie, whale

WINDOW – box, envelope, sash, seat, tax

WINE – bar, box, cellar, cooler, tasting

WING – chair, collar, commander, covert, loading, nut, shot, tip

WITCH – doctor, hazel

WOLF – cub, spider, whistle

WORD – association, blindness, order, picture, processing,

processor, square

WORK – back, camp, ethic, function, in, off, on, out, over, sheet, station, through, up

WORKING – bee, capital, class, day, dog, drawing, papers, party, substance, week

WRITE – down, in, off, out, up

YELLOW – belly, card, fever, jacket, pages, peril, river, streak

YORKSHIRE – dales, fog, pudding, terrier

YOUNG – blood, fogey, lady, man, pretender, turk

YOUTH – club, custody, hostel

SECOND WORD

ABOUT – bring, cast, come, fall, hang, kick, knock, mess, muck, push, put, right, set, talk, throw

ABSOLUTE – ablative, decree

ACADEMY – french, military, royal

ACCESS – direct, random, sequential

ACCOUNT – bank, budget, capital, charge, control, credit, current, deposit, drawing, expense, joint, savings, short, suspense, trust

ACCOUNTANT – chartered, turf

ACROSS – come, cut, get, put, run

ACT – enabling, homestead, juristic, locutionary, riot, speech, stamp, test

ADMIRAL – fleet, rear, red, vice, white

ADVOCATE – devil's, judge, lord

AGAINST – count, go, set, stack, turn

AGENCY – advertising, employment, mercantile, news, press, travel

AGENT – crown, disclosing, double, estate, forwarding, free, house, land, law, oxidizing, press, reducing, secret, shipping, wetting

AGREEMENT – collective, gentlemen's, national, procedural, standstill, technology

AID – artificial, first, foreign, hearing, home, legal, teaching

ALARM – call, false, fire

ALCOHOL – absolute, allyl, amyl, butyl, ethyl, grain, lauryl, methyl, rubbing, wood

ALE – ginger, real

ALLEY – blind, bowling

ALLIANCE – dual, holy, triple

ALONG – come, cut, get, go,

muddle, play, push, rub, run, sing, string

ANGEL – destroying, hell's, recording

ANGLE – central, complementary, critical, exterior, facial, hour, interior, oblique, plane, right, straight

ANT – amazon, army, bulldog, driver, fire, leafcutter, legionary, pharaoh, slave, velvet, white, wood

APPLE – adam's, balsam, big, bitter, crab, custard, love, may, oak, rose, sugar, thorn

ARCADE – amusement, penny

ARCH – acute, fallen, gothic, horseshoe, keel, lancet, norman, ogee, pointed, roman, skew, triumphal, zygomatic

AREA – catchment, development, goal, grey, mush, no-go, penalty, service

ARMS – canting, order, side, small

ARMY – church, field, sally, salvation, standing, territorial

AROUND – bat, get, go, horse, run, shop, sleep, slop, stick

ART – black, commercial, fine, noble, op, performance, pop

ARTS – graphic, liberal, performing, visual

ASH – bone, fly, mountain, pearl, prickly, soda

ASIDE – brush, lay, put, set

ASSEMBLY – general, legislative, national, unlawful

ATTORNEY – crown, district, prosecuting

AWAY – blow, boil, carry, clear, come, explain, fall, fire, get, give, go, keep, laugh, lay, make, put, right, run, salt, sign, sock, square, take, tear, trail, tuck, turn, walk, while

BABY – blue, jelly, plunket, rhesus, test-tube, war

BACK – answer, bite, bounce, carry, cast, choke, claw, double, fall, fight, get, go, hang, hark, hold, keep, knock, ladder, look, pay, plough, pull, put, ring, set, sit, take, talk

BAG – air, blue, body, carrier, coffee, cool, diplomatic, doggy, duffel, gladstone, grow, ice, jelly, jiffy, lavender, mixed, sag, sleeping, sponge, tea, tote

BALLOON – barrage, hot-air, pilot, trial

BAND – big, brake, brass, citizens', conduction, elastic,

energy, frequency, rubber, steel

BANK – blood, central, clearing, commercial, cooperative, data, dogger, fog, jodrell, land, left, memory, merchant, national, piggy, reserve, savings, soil, sperm

BAR – capstan, coffee, colour, double, heel, horizontal, inner, milk, outer, pinch, private, public, sand, singles, snack, torsion, wine

BARRIER – crash, crush, heat, sonic, sound, thermal, transonic

BASE – air, data, first, lewis, prisoner's, pyrimidine

BASKET – chip, moses, pollen, wastepaper

BASS – black, double, figured, ground, largemouth, rock, sea, smallmouth, stone, string, thorough, walking

BAT – fruit, horseshoe, insectivorous, straight, vampire

BATH – blanket, blood, bubble, hip, mud, salt, sponge, steam, sun, swimming, turkish

BEACON – belisha, landing, radar, radio

BEAN – adsuki, adzuki, black, broad, butter, calabar, castor, cocoa, dwarf, french, green, horse, jack, jumping, kidney, lima, mung, pinto, runner, shell, snap, soya, string, tonka, wax

BEAR – ant, black, brown, cinnamon, great, grizzly, honey, koala, kodiak, little, native, polar, sloth, sun, teddy, water, white, woolly

BEAT – dead, mersey, wing

BEAUTY – bathing, camberwell, spring

BED – air, apple-pie, bunk, feather, oyster, pay, sofa, truckle, trundle, twin, water

BEE – carpenter, cuckoo, hive, leafcutter, mason, mining, queen, spelling, working

BEER – bock, ginger, kaffir, root, small, spruce

BELL – canterbury, diving, lutine, passing, sacring, sanctus, shark, silver

BELT – bible, black, cartridge, chastity, conveyor, copper, cotton, fan, green, life, lonsdale, safety, seat, shelter, stockbroker, storm, suspender, sword

BENCH – front, king's, optical, treasury

BENEFIT – child, disablement, family, fringe, housing, injury, invalidity, maternity, sickness, supplementary, unemployment, widow's

BILL – accommodation, buffalo, demand, double, finance, foreign, old, private, public, reform, treasury, true, twin

BIRD – adjutant, ant, brain-fever, crocodile, diamond, early, elephant, gallows, game, parson, water

BISCUIT – bourbon, captain's, digestive, dog, pilot, sea, ship's, soda, tararua, tea, water

BLACK – all, carbon, gas, ivory, jet, large, penny, platinum

BLOCK – breeze, building, cavity, cylinder, heart, ice, mental, office, psychological, saddle, starting, stumbling, sun, wood

BLOOD – bad, blue, bull's, dragon's, full, whole, young

BOARD – above, admiralty, bulletin, catchment, circuit, cribbage, diving, draft, draining, drawing, emery, full, half, idiot, ironing, notice, patch, running, sandwich, school, skirting, sounding, wobble

BOAT – canal, flying, gravy, jolly, mosquito, narrow, rowing, sailing, sauce, swamp, torpedo

BOMB – atom, borer, buzz, cluster, cobalt, fission, flying, fusion, hydrogen, letter, mills, neutron, nuclear, petrol, smoke, stink, time, volcanic

BOND – bail, chemical, coordinate, covalent, dative, double, electrovalent, english, flemish, granny, herringbone, hydrogen, income, ionic, metallic, pair, peptide, single, treasury, triple

BONE – cannon, cartilage, coffin, crazy, fetter, frontal, funny, haunch, heel, innominate, membrane, occipital, parietal, sphenoid, splint, stirrup, temporal, tympanic, zygomatic

BOOK – black, closed, commonplace, cookery, domesday, doomsday, hymn, open, phrase, prayer, reference, statute, talking

BOTTLE – brandy, feeding, hot-water, klein, nansen, water

BOWL – begging, dust, finger, goldfish, rice

BOX – apple, ballot, black, christmas, coin, deed, dispatch, fuse, fuzz, glove, junction, jury, letter, music, penalty, pillar, poor, press, sentry, shooting, signal, telephone, voice, window, wine, witness

BOY – altar, ball, barrow, best, bevin, blue-eyed, cabin, errand, office, old, principal, rent, tar, teddy, whipping

BRAKE – air, centrifugal, disc, drum, foot, hydraulic, shooting

BRETHREN – bohemian, elder, exclusive, open, plymouth, trinity

BRIDGE – air, auction, bailey, balance, board, cable-stayed, cantilever, clapper, contract, counterpoise, duplicate, flying, four-deal, land, pivot, rainbow, rubber, snow, suspension, swing, transporter, truss, turn, wheatstone

BRIGADE – boys', fire, fur, international

BROTHER – big, blood, lay

BUG – assassin, cabbage, chinch, croton, damsel, debris, flower, ground, harlequin, june, kissing, lace, lightning, maori, mealy, pill, rhododendron, shield, sow, squash, water, wheel

BUGGY – baby, beach, swamp

BUOY – bell, breeches, can, life, nun, spar

BURNER – back, bunsen, gas, lime, welsbach

BUSH – burning, butterfly, calico, cotton, cranberry, creosote, daisy, emu, gooseberry, mint, native, needle, orchard, strawberry, sugar

BUSINESS – big, monkey, show

BY – come, do, get, go, pass, put, stand, stick

CAKE – angel, banbury, barm, cotton, dundee, eccles, fish, genoa, johnny, lardy, layer, madeira, marble, oil, pontefract, pound, rock, salt, sandwich, simnel, sponge, tipsy, upside-down, wedding

CALL – bird, close, cold, curtain, line, photo, roll, toll, trunk

CAMERA – automatic, box, candid, cine, compact, gamma, in, miniature, movie, pinhole, reflex

CAMP – concentration, health, high, holiday, labour, low, motor, transit, work

CANAL – alimentary, anal, caledonian, erie, grand, haversian, mittelland, panama, root, semicircular, spinal, suez, welland

CAP – bathing, cloth, crown, death, dunce, dutch, filler, flat, fool's, funnel, jockey, juliet, legal, liberty, milk, percussion, root, shaggy, stocking, watch, wax

CAPITAL – block, human, risk, small, venture, working

CAPSULE – seed, space, time

CARD – bank, banker's, calling, cheque, christmas, cigarette, court, credit, donor, drawing, flash, green, id, laser, letter, picture, place, playing, postal, punched, show, smart, union, visiting, yellow

CASE – attaché, basket, cot, dispatch, dressing, lower, special, spore, stated, test, upper, wardian, worst, writing

CELL – blood, cadmium, clark, collar, condemned, daniell, death, dry, electrolytic, flame, fuel, germ, gravity, guard, lymph, mast, nerve, padded, parietal, photoelectric, primary, secondary, selenium, solar, somatic, standard, stem, swarm, unit, voltaic, wet

CENTRE – active, attendance, civic, community, cost, daycare, dead, detention, garden, health, music, nerve, remand, shopping, storm

CHAIN – bicycle, branched, closed, daisy, food, golden, grand, gunter's, learner's, markov, mountain, open, safety, side, snigging, straight, surveyor's, watch

CHAIR – bath, boatswain's, deck, easy, electric, rocking, sedan, straight, swivel, windsor, wing

CHAMBER – bubble, cloud, combustion, decompression, echo, float, gas, inspection, ionization, lower, magma, presence, privy, second, spark, star, upper

CHART – bar, breakeven, control, flow, organization, pie, plane

CHASE – paper, wild-goose

CHEST – community, hope, medicine, sea, slop, war, wind

CHILD – foster, latchkey, love, moon

CHINA – bone, cochin, communist, dresden,

nationalist, red, worcester

CHIP – blue, log, potato, silicon

CIRCLE – antarctic, arctic, dip, dress, equinoctial, family, great, hour, hut, meridian, parquet, pitch, polar, turning, vertical, vicious

CLASS – cabin, crystal, evening, first, lower, middle, second, third, universal, upper, working

CLAY – boulder, china, fire, porcelain

CLEF – alto, bass, c, f, g, soprano, tenor, treble, viola

CLERK – articled, bank, desk, filing, parish, shipping, tally, town

CLIP – bicycle, bulldog, cartridge, crocodile, wool

CLOCK – alarm, analogue, atomic, biological, caesium, carriage, cuckoo, digital, grandfather, grandmother, longcase, quartz, settler's, speaking, time, townhall, water

CLOTH – aeroplane, aircraft, altar, bark, covert, face, grass, monk's, nun's, sponge, tea, wire

CLUB – book, chartered, country, glee, golf, indian, jockey, lions, luncheon, monday, provident, pudding, rotary, strip, supper, tramping, youth

COAL – bituminous, brown, cannel, gas, hard, soft, steam, white, wood

COCKTAIL – atomic, fruit, molotov

CODE – area, bar, binary, character, clarendon, colour, country, dialling, genetic, gray, highway, justinian, morse, napoleonic, national, penal, std, time, zip

COLLAR – clerical, dog, eton, head, mandarin, roman, shawl, storm, vandyke, wing

COLOUR – achromatic, chromatic, complementary, cross, local, off, primary, secondary, tone

COLUMN – agony, correspondence, fifth, personal, spinal, steering, vertebral

COMPANY – close, finance, fire, free, holding, joint-stock, limited, parent, private, public, repertory, stock

COMPLEX – electra, inferiority, launch, oedipus, persecution, superiority

CONE – ice-cream, nose, pine, storm, wind

CORD – communication, sash, spermatic, spinal, umbilical

COUNTER – crystal, geiger, proportional, rev, scintillation

COURSE – assault, barge, golf, magnetic, main, refresher, sandwich

COURT – clay, county, crown, district, domestic, grass, hard, high, inferior, justice, juvenile, kangaroo, magistrates', moot, open, police, prize, provost, sheriff, superior, supreme, territorial, tout, traffic, trial, world

COVER – air, dust, extra, first-day, ground, loose

CREAM – barrier, bavarian, clotted, cold, devonshire, double, glacier, ice, pastry, single, sour, vanishing, whipping

CROP – cash, catch, cover, eton, riding, root

CROSS – calvary, celtic, charing, double, fiery, george, greek, iron, jerusalem, latin, lorraine, maltese, northern, papal, patriarchal, red, southern, tau, victoria

CROSSING – level, pedestrian, pelican, zebra

CROW – carrion, hooded, jim

CUP – america's, claret, coffee, davis, egg, fa, fruit, grace, grease, loving, moustache, stirrup, world

CURRENCY – decimal, fractional, managed, reserve

CURRENT – alternating, cromwell, dark, direct, eddy, electric, foucault, humboldt, japan, labrador, peru, thermionic, turbidity

CURTAIN – air, bamboo, drop, iron, safety

CUT – bastard, crew, culebra, gaillard, navy, open, power, short

DASH – em, en, pebble, swung

DAYS – dog, ember, hundred, juridical, lay, rogation, salad

DEATH – black, brain, civil, cot, crib, heat, living, sudden

DECK – 'tween, boat, flight, hurricane, lower, main, poop, promenade, sun, tape

DELIVERY – breech, forward, general, jail, recorded, rural, special

DERBY – crown, donkey,

kentucky, roller, sage
DESK – cash, city, copy, roll-top, writing
DEVIL – dust, mountain, printer's, snow, tasmanian
DIAGRAM – bar, block, indicator, russell, scatter, venn
DIVE – crash, nose, power, swallow, swan
DOCTOR – angelic, barefoot, cape, family, flying, saw, witch
DOG – backing, bird, carriage, coach, eskimo, eye, great, guide, gun, heading, hot, kangaroo, leading, little, native, pariah, pig, police, prairie, raccoon, sausage, sea, shepherd, sled, sniffer, spotted, top, tracker, working
DOOR – back, barn, cat, dutch, fire, folding, front, next, open, overhead, revolving, stable, stage, storm, street, swing, trap
DOWN – back, bear, beat, bog, boil, break, bring, bucket, buckle, call, cast, change, clamp, climb, close, crack, cry, cut, die, do, drag, dress, dust, fall, get, go, hand, hold, hunt, keep, knock, lay, let, lie, live, look, mow, nail, pay, peg, pin, pipe, play, pull, put, ride, round, rub, run, send, set, settle, shake, shoot, shout, simmer, sit, slap, sponge, stand, step, stick, stop, strike, take, talk, tear, tone, track, turn, upside, vote, wash, wear, weigh, wind, write
DRESS – academic, coat, court, evening, fancy, full, highland, morning, pinafore, tent
DRESSING – french, ore, russian, salad, top, well
DRILL – boat, fire, hammer, kerb, pack, power, twist
DRIVE – beetle, chain, disk, fluid, four-wheel, motor, whist
DROP – acid, cough, delayed, dolly, knee, lemon, mail
DUCK – blue, bombay, cold, dead, harlequin, lame, mandarin, muscovy, musk, paradise, ruddy, sea, tufted, wood
DUST – angel, bull, cosmic, gold
DUTY – death, estate, point, stamp
EDGE – deckle, knife, leading, trailing
EGG – curate's, darning, easter, nest, scotch
END – back, best, big, bitter,

book, bottom, business, cigarette, cod, dead, east, fag, gable, land's, loose, rope's, sticky, tag, tail, top, west
ENGINE – aero, beam, bypass, compound, diesel, donkey, external-combustion, fire, gas, heat, internal-combustion, ion, jet, light, overhead-valve, pilot, plasma, radial, reaction, reciprocating, rocket, rotary, side-valve, stationary, stirling, tank, traction, turbojet, v-type, valve-in-head, wankel
ENSIGN – blue, red, white
EVENT – field, happy, media, three-day, track
EVIDENCE – circumstantial, cumulative, direct, hearsay, king's, prima-facie, queen's, state's
EXCHANGE – corn, employment, foreign, ion, labour, part, post, stock
EYE – beady, black, compound, electric, evil, glad, magic, mind's, pheasant's, pineal, pope's, private, red, screw, weather
FACE – bold, en, light, long, old, poker, straight
FACTOR – common, corn, growth, house, load, power, quality, rh, rhesus, safety, unit
FEATHER – cock, contour, flight, shaft, sickle, white
FILE – card, crosscut, indian, single
FINGER – index, lady's, ring
FINISH – blanket, dead, mirror, photo
FIRE – brush, electric, greek, liquid, quick, rapid, red, watch
FLAT – adobe, alkali, cottage, double, garden, granny, mud, salt, studio
FOOD – convenience, fast, health, junk, skin, soul
FORTH – call, go, hold, put, set
FORWARD – bring, carry, centre, come, inside, put
FRACTION – common, complex, compound, continued, decimal, improper, packing, partial, proper, simple, vulgar
FRACTURE – colles', comminuted, compound, greenstick, pott's, simple
FRAME – climbing, cold, garden, half, oxford, portal, sampling, still, stocking
FRIDAY – girl, good, man
FRONT – cold, eyes, national,

occluded, people's, polar, popular, rhodesian, warm, wave
FROST – black, jack, silver, white
FRUIT – accessory, collective, false, forbidden, key, kiwi, multiple, passion, simple, soft, stone, wall
GALLERY – ladies', national, press, public, rogues', shooting, stranger's, tate, whispering, winning
GAP – credibility, deflationary, energy, generation, inflationary, spark, trade, water, wind
GARDEN – bear, botanical, covent, kitchen, knot, market, pebble, rock, roof, tea, winter, zoological
GAS – air, bottled, calor, coal, cs, electrolytic, ideal, inert, laughing, marsh, mustard, natural, nerve, noble, north-sea, perfect, poison, producer, rare, sewage, tear, town, water
GATE – golden, head, iron, kissing, lich, lych, moravian, starting, tail, taranaki, water
GIRL – bachelor, bar, best, call, career, chorus, continuity, cover, dancing, flower, gibson, land, marching, old, sweater
GLASS – bell, burning, cheval, crown, cupping, cut, favrile, field, flint, float, green, ground, hand, lead, liquid, looking, magnifying, milk, murrhine, object, optical, pier, plate, quartz, reducing, ruby, safety, silica, soluble, stained, storm, tiffany, venetian, volcanic, water, wire
GLASSES – dark, field, opera
GOAT – angora, billy, kashmir, mountain, nanny
GOLD – filled, fool's, free, mosaic, old, rolled, white
GREEN – apple, back, bottle, bowling, chrome, crown, gretna, jade, kendal, lime, lincoln, nile, olive, paris, pea, putting, rifle, sea
GROUND – burial, camping, common, home, hunting, middle, proving, recreation, stamping, vantage
GUARD – advance, colour, home, iron, national, old, praetorian, provost, red, security, swiss
GUIDE – brownie, girl, honey, queen's
GUM – acaroid, blue, bubble,

chewing, cow, flooded, ghost, kauri, red, snow, sour, spirit, sugar, sweet, water, white
HALF – better, centre, fly, scrum
HALL – carnegie, city, festival, liberty, mess, music, tammany, town
HAND – charge, club, court, dab, dead, deck, farm, free, glad, helping, hour, iron, lone, minute, old, round, second, shed, sweep, upper, whip
HAT – brass, cocked, cossack, hard, high, old, opera, panama, picture, porkpie, red, sailor, scarlet, shovel, silk, slouch, ten-gallon, tin, top
HEART – bleeding, bullock's, dead, floating, purple, sacred
HEAT – atomic, black, blood, dead, latent, prickly, radiant, red, total, white
HISTORY – ancient, case, life, natural, oral
HITCH – blackwall, clove, harness, magnus, rolling, timber, weaver's
HOLE – air, beam, black, bolt, coal, funk, glory, kettle, lubber's, nineteenth, sound, spider, swallow, water, watering
HOLIDAY – bank, busman's, half, legal, public, roman
HOME – eventide, harvest, mobile, nursing, remand, stately, villa
HORSE – charley, dark, iron, liberty, light, night, pole, post, quarter, river, rocking, saddle, sea, shire, trojan, wheel, white, willing, wooden
HOUR – eleventh, happy, lunch, rush, sidereal, witching, zero
HOUSE – accepting, admiralty, boarding, broiler, bush, charnel, chattel, clearing, coach, coffee, counting, country, custom, discount, disorderly, dower, fashion, forcing, free, full, halfway, ice, issuing, lodging, manor, mansion, meeting, open, opera, picture, post, public, rooming, safe, software, sporting, state, station, storey, terraced, third, town, trinity, upper, wash, wendy, white
HUMOUR – aqueous, gallows, ill, vitreous
HUNT – drag, fox, scavenger, still, treasure
ICE – black, camphor, coconut,

drift, dry, glaze, ground, pack, pancake, shelf, slob, water
IN – all, block, blow, book, break, bring, build, burn, buy, call, cash, cave, check, chip, close, come, dig, do, drag, draw, fall, fill, fit, get, give, go, hand, hang, hold, horn, ink, jack, keep, key, kick, lay, let, lie, listen, live, log, move, muck, pack, pay, phase, pitch, plug, pull, push, put, rake, rein, ring, roll, rope, rub, run, scrape, set, settle, sign, sink, sleep, stand, start, step, suck, swear, take, throw, tie, tuck, tune, turn, weigh, well, whip, work, write, zero, zoom
INTEREST – compound, controlling, human, life, simple, vested
IRON – alpha, angle, beta, cast, channel, corrugated, delta, gamma, gem, grappling, grozing, ingot, lily, malleable, pig, pump, shooting, smoothing, soldering, steam, toggle, wrought
IVY – boston, grape, ground, japanese, poison, weeping
JACK – jumping, man, screw, union, yellow
JACKET – air, bed, bomber, bush, dinner, donkey, dust, eton, flak, hacking, life, mess, monkey, norfolk, pea, reefing, safari, shell, smoking, sports, steam, water, yellow
JELLY – calf's-foot, comb, mineral, petroleum, royal
JOE – gi, holy, sloppy
JUDGMENT – absolute, comparative, last, value
JUMP – broad, high, long, ski, triple, water
KEY – allen, chroma, church, control, dead, function, ignition, master, minor, nut, off, on, prong, shift, skeleton, tuning
KICK – drop, flutter, free, frog, goal, penalty, place, scissors, stab
KNIFE – bowie, carving, case, clasp, flick, fruit, hunting, pallet, sheath, trench
KNOT – black, fisherman's, flat, french, gordian, granny, loop, love, overhand, reef, square, stevedore's, surgeon's, sword, thumb, truelove, wall, windsor
LACE – alençon, bobbin, brussels, chantilly, cluny, mechlin, pillow,

point, sea, torchon
LADY – bag, dinner, first, naked, old, our, painted, white, young
LAMP – aldis, davy, fluorescent, glow, hurricane, incandescent, neon, pilot, safety, spirit, sun, tungsten
LANGUAGE – body, computer, first, formal, machine, natural, programming, second, sign
LANTERN – chinese, dark, friar's, japanese, magic, storm
LEAVE – french, mass, maternity, shore, sick
LETTER – air, begging, black, chain, covering, dead, dominical, form, french, love, open, poison-pen, scarlet
LIBRARY – circulating, film, lending, mobile, subscription
LICENCE – driving, occasional, poetic, special, table
LIFE – future, love, mean, private, real, shelf, still
LIGHT – arc, back, back-up, bengal, brake, courtesy, first, green, inner, klieg, leading, pilot, rear, red, reversing, rush, traffic, white
LIGHTING – indirect, strip, strobe
LIGHTNING – chain, forked, heat, sheet
LIGHTS – ancient, bright, fairy, house, northern, polar, southern
LINE – assembly, bar, bottom, branch, clew, contour, date, fall, firing, flight, front, goal, hard, hindenburg, hot, land, lead, ledger, maginot, main, mason-dixon, number, oder-neisse, off, on, party, picket, plimsoll, plumb, power, production, punch, siegfried, snow, story, timber, water
LINK – cuff, drag, missing
LION – mountain, nemean, sea
LIST – back, check, civil, class, hit, honours, mailing, reserved, short, sick, transfer, waiting
LOCK – combination, fermentation, man, mortise, percussion, scalp, spring, stock, vapour, wheel, yale
LOVE – calf, courtly, cupboard, free, puppy
MACHINE – adding, answering, bathing, fruit, kidney, sewing, slot, time, vending, washing
MAIL – air, chain, electronic, fan, surface
MAIN – ring, spanish, water
MAN – advance, anchor, best,

company, con, confidence, enlisted, family, fancy, front, hatchet, hit, ice, inner, iron, ladies', leading, medicine, muffin, neanderthal, palaeolithic, party, piltdown, rag-and-bone, sandwich, straight, twelfth, yes

MARCH – dead, forced, hunger, long, quick, slow

MARIA – ave, black, henrietta, santa, tia

MARK – bench, black, exclamation, kite, punctuation, question, quotation

MARKET – black, buyers', capital, captive, common, flea, kerb, money, open, sellers', spot, stock

MARRIAGE – civil, common-law, group, mixed

MASK – death, gas, life, loo, oxygen, shadow, stocking

MASTER – careers, grand, harbour, international, old, past, question

MATCH – friction, love, safety, shield, slanging, slow, test

MATE – first, fool's, running, scholar's, second, soul

MATTER – back, end, front, grey, subject, white

MEDICINE – alternative, complementary, dutch, folk, forensic, patent

MILE – admiralty, air, geographical, nautical, roman, sea, statute, swedish

MILL – coffee, pepper, rolling, smock, stamp, strip, water

MITE – bulb, cheese, flour, fowl, gall, harvest, itch, spider, widow's

MONEY – big, blood, call, caution, cob, conscience, danger, easy, folding, gate, head, hot, hush, key, maundy, near, paper, pin, plastic, pocket, prize, ready, seed, ship

MOON – blue, full, harvest, hunter's, mock, new, old

MOTHER – earth, foster, nursing, queen, reverend, solo

MOTION – fast, harmonic, link, perpetual, proper, slow

NAME – brand, christian, day, family, first, given, household, last, maiden, middle, pen, place, proprietary, second, trade

NECK – boat, brass, crew, scoop, swan, v

NEEDLE – cleopatra's, darning,

dip, electric, ice, magnetic, pine, shepherd's

NET – drift, gill, landing, mosquito, pound, safety, shark

NIGHT – first, good, twelfth, walpurgis, watch

NOTE – advice, auxiliary, blue, cover, currency, demand, eighth, gold, grace, leading, passing, postal, promissory, quarter, sick, treasury, whole

NUMBER – accession, algebraic, atomic, back, binary, box, call, cardinal, complex, composite, compound, concrete, e, golden, index, mach, magic, opposite, ordinal, perfect, prime, real, registration, serial, square, telephone, whole, wrong

OFFERING – burnt, peace

OFFICE – box, crown, divine, electronic, employment, foreign, holy, home, land, left-luggage, patent, post, register, war

OIL – camphorated, castor, coconut, cod-liver, corn, crude, diesel, essential, fatty, gas, linseed, macassar, mineral, mustard, nut, olive, palm, peanut, rape, sassafras, shale, sperm, vegetable, whale

OPERA – ballad, comic, grand, horse, light, soap, space

ORANGE – agent, bitter, blood, mock, navel, osage, seville

ORDER – affiliation, apple-pie, attic, banker's, community-service, compensation, enclosed, firing, loose, mail, market, money, pecking, possession, postal, receiving, short, standing, supervision, teutonic, third, word

ORDERS – holy, major, marching, minor, sealed

ORGAN – barrel, electric, electronic, end, great, hammond, hand, house, mouth, pipe, portative, reed, sense, steam

OVER – bind, blow, boil, bowl, bring, carry, chew, do, fall, get, give, gloss, go, hand, hold, keel, lay, look, maiden, make, paper, pass, put, roll, run, see, skate, slide, smooth, spill, stand, take, think, throw, tick, tide, turn, warm, work

OYSTER – bush, pearl, prairie, seed, vegetable

PACK – blister, bubble, cold, face,

film, ice, power, wet

PAD – crash, hard, launching, lily, scratch, shoulder

PAINT – gloss, oil, poster, war

PALACE – buckingham, crystal, gin, picture

PAPER – art, ballot, blotting, bond, bromide, brown, building, carbon, cartridge, cigarette, commercial, crepe, filter, flock, graph, green, india, lavatory, linen, manila, mercantile, music, order, rice, tissue, toilet, tracing, wax, writing

PARK – amusement, car, country, forest, game, hyde, national, safari, science, theme

PARTY – bottle, communist, conservative, firing, garden, hen, house, labour, liberal, national, nationalist, people's, republican, search, stag, tea, third, working

PASSAGE – back, bridge, drake, middle, mona, northeast, northwest, rough, windward

PATH – bridle, flare, flight, glide, primrose, towing

PAY – back, equal, severance, sick, strike, take-home

PEA – black-eyed, desert, pigeon, split, sugar, sweet

PEAR – alligator, anchovy, conference, prickly, williams

PEN – cartridge, catching, data, felt-tip, fountain, quill, sea

PENSION – en, occupational, retirement

PIANO – cottage, grand, player, prepared, square, street, upright

PIE – cottage, custard, humble, mince, mud, pork, shepherd's

PIN – bobby, cotter, drawing, end, firing, gudgeon, panel, rolling, safety, scatter, shear, stick, swivel, taper, wrest, wrist

PIPE – corncob, escape, flue, indian, jet, peace, pitch, rainwater, reed, soil, waste

PITCH – absolute, concert, fever, perfect, wood

PLACE – decimal, high, holy, resting, watering

PLASTER – court, mustard, sticking

PLATE – angle, armour, batten, butt, echo, fashion, futtock, glacis, gold, ground, home, license, nickel, quarter, registration, screw, silver, soup, surface, swash, tin, trade, wall, wobble

PLAY – child's, double, fair, foul, match, miracle, morality, mystery, passion, shadow, stroke

PLEAT – box, french, inverted, kick, knife

POCKET – air, hip, patch, slash, slit

POINT – boiling, breaking, brownie, change, clovis, cover, critical, curie, dead, decimal, dew, diamond, dry, end, equinoctial, fesse, fixed, flash, focal, freezing, gallinas, game, gold, high, ice, limit, match, melting, objective, petit, power, pressure, sample, saturation, set, specie, steam, strong, suspension, transition, trig, triple, turning, vanishing, vantage, west, yield

POLE – barber's, celestial, magnetic, north, south, totem

POLL – advance, deed, gallup, opinion, red, straw

POST – command, finger, first, goal, graded, gradient, hitching, last, listening, newel, observation, registered, staging, tool, trading, winning

POT – chamber, coal, lobster, melting, pepper, watering

POTATO – hot, irish, seed, sweet, white

POWDER – baking, black, bleaching, chilli, curry, custard, face, giant, talcum, tooth, washing

PRESS – drill, filter, fly, folding, gutter, hydraulic, printing, private, racket, stop

PRESSURE – atmospheric, barometric, blood, critical, fluid, osmotic, partial, vapour

PRICE – asking, bid, bride, intervention, list, market, offer, reserve, starting, unit

PROFESSOR – assistant, associate, full, regius, visiting

PUDDING – black, blood, cabinet, christmas, college, eve's, hasty, milk, pease, plum, suet, summer, white, yorkshire

PUMP – air, bicycle, centrifugal, electromagnetic, filter, force, heat, lift, parish, petrol, rotary, stirrup, stomach, suction, vacuum

PUNCH – bell, card, centre, key, milk, planter's, rabbit, suffolk, sunday

PURSE – long, mermaid's,

privy, sea

PUZZLE – chinese, crossword, jigsaw, monkey

QUARTER – empty, first, last, latin

QUESTION – direct, indirect, leading, rhetorical

RABBIT – angora, buck, jack, rock, welsh

RACE – arms, boat, bumping, claiming, drag, egg-and-spoon, master, obstacle, rat, relay, sack, three-legged

RACK – cloud, roof, toast

RATE – bank, base, basic, birth, bit, death, exchange, lapse, mortality, mortgage, piece, poor, prime, tax

RECORDER – flight, incremental, tape, wire

RED – blood, brick, chinese, chrome, congo, indian, turkey, venetian

RELATIONS – community, industrial, labour, public, race

RELIEF – high, low, outdoor, photo

RENT – cost, economic, fair, ground, market, peppercorn

RESERVE – central, gold, indian, nature, scenic

REVOLUTION – american, bloodless, chinese, cultural, february, french, glorious, green, industrial, october, palace, russian

RING – anchor, annual, benzene, engagement, eternity, extension, fairy, gas, growth, guard, keeper, nose, piston, price, prize, retaining, seal, signet, slip, snap, teething, tree, vortex, wedding

ROAD – access, clay, concession, dirt, escape, post, ring, service, slip, trunk

ROD – aaron's, black, blue, con, connecting, control, divining, dowsing, drain, fishing, fly, hot, piston, stair, tie, track, welding

ROLL – barrel, bridge, court, dandy, egg, forward, music, muster, piano, pipe, sausage, snap, spring, swiss, victory, western

ROOM – back, combination, common, composing, consulting, day, dining, drawing, dressing, engine, gun, living, men's, operations, orderly, powder, pump, reception, recreation, rest, robing, rumpus, sitting,

smoking, still, tiring, utility, waiting, withdrawing

ROOT – buttress, club, cube, culver's, mallee, pleurisy, prop, square

ROT – black, brown, dry, foot, soft, wet

ROUND – bring, change, come, milk, rally, scrub, talk

ROW – corn, death, note, skid, tone

ROYAL – annapolis, battle, pair, port, prince, princess, rhyme

RUBBER – cold, crepe, hard, india, pará, smoked, sorbo, synthetic, wild

RULE – chain, foot, global, golden, ground, home, parallelogram, phase, plumb, setting, slide

RUN – bombing, bull, dry, dummy, ground, hen, home, milk, mole, ski, trial

SALAD – corn, fruit, russian, waldorf

SALE – boot, bring-and-buy, car-boot, jumble, rummage, white

SALTS – bath, epsom, health, liver, smelling

SAUCE – apple, béchamel, bread, chilli, cream, hard, hollandaise, melba, mint, mousseline, soy, tartar, white, worcester

SAW – back, band, buzz, chain, circular, compass, coping, crosscut, crown, flooring, fret, gang, panel, scroll, stone, tenon

SCHOOL – approved, board, boarding, choir, comprehensive, correspondence, dame, day, direct-grant, elementary, finishing, first, grammar, high, independent, infant, junior, lower, middle, night, nursery, prep, preparatory, primary, private, public, residential, secondary, special, state, summer, sunday, upper

SCIENCE – behavioural, christian, cognitive, domestic, earth, hard, information, life, natural, physical, policy, political, rural, social, veterinary

SCOUT – air, boy, cub, girl, king's, queen's, sea, talent, venture

SCREEN – big, fire, organ, rood, silver, small, smoke

SCREW – archimedes', cap, coach, grub, ice, interrupted, lag, lead, levelling, lug, machine, micrometer, phillips

SEASON – close, high, off, silly

SEAT – back, box, bucket, country, county, death, ejection, hot, jump, love, mercy, rumble, safe, sliding, window

SECRETARY – company, home, parliamentary, private, social

SERVICE – active, civil, community, dinner, diplomatic, divine, foreign, lip, national, public, room, secret, senior, silver, tea

SET – closed, companion, crystal, data, dead, film, flash, jet, love, nail, open, ordered, permanent, power, saw, smart, solution, toilet, truth

SHAFT – air, butt, drive, escape, propeller

SHEET – balance, charge, crime, dope, flow, fly, ice, scratch, swindle, tear, thunder, time, winding, work

SHIFT – back, blue, day, einstein, function, night, red, sound, split, swing

SHIRT – boiled, brown, dress, hair, sports, stuffed, sweat, tee

SHOE – blocked, brake, court, gym, hot, launching, pile, tennis, track

SHOP – betting, body, bucket, closed, coffee, duty-free, fish-and-chip, junk, machine, open, print, sex, swap, sweet, talking, tuck, union

SHOT – approach, big, booster, direct-mail, drop, foul, jump, long, parthian, passing, pot

SHOW – chat, dumb, floor, ice, light, minstrel, raree, road, talk

SICKNESS – altitude, bush, decompression, falling, milk, morning, motion, mountain, radiation, serum, sleeping, sweating

SIDE – distaff, flip, prompt, spear, sunny

SLEEVE – balloon, batwing, bishop, dolman

SOAP – castile, green, joe, metallic, saddle, soft, sugar, toilet

SODA – caustic, cream, ice-cream, washing

SOLDIER – foot, gallant, old, returned, tin, unknown, wagon, water

SONG – folk, part, patter, prick, swan, theme, torch

SPEECH – curtain, direct, free, indirect, king's, queen's, reported

SPIRIT – holy, proof, surgical, team, white, wood

SPOT – beauty, black, blind, high, hot, leaf, soft, trouble

SQUAD – firing, flying, fraud, snatch, vice

SQUARE – all, bevel, latin, magic, mitre, set, times, word

STAMP – date, postage, rubber, trading

STAND – hall, hat, music, one-night, umbrella

STANDARD – double, gold, lamp, royal, silver

STAR – binary, blazing, dark, dog, double, dwarf, evening, exploding, falling, feather, film, fixed, flare, giant, morning, multiple, neutron, north, pole, pulsating, radio, shooting

START – bump, flying, head

STEAK – minute, t-bone, tartar

STICK – big, cancer, cocktail, control, french, joss, pogo, shooting, ski, swagger, swizzle, walking, white

STITCH – blanket, buttonhole, cable, chain, garter, lock, moss, running, satin, slip, stocking, tent

STOCK – capital, common, dead, joint, laughing, preferred, rolling, virginia

STONE – bath, blarney, cinnamon, coping, foundation, imposing, kidney, mocha, oamaru, paving, philosopher's, precious, rosetta, stepping

STOOL – cucking, cutty, ducking, milking, piano

STRAW – cheese, last, short

STRIKE – bird, general, hunger, official, sit-down, sympathy, token, wildcat

STUDY – brown, case, feasibility, field, motion, nature, pilot, time

STUFF – hot, kids', rough, small, sob

SUGAR – barley, beet, brown, cane, caster, confectioners', fruit, granulated, grape, icing, invert, loaf, maple, milk, palm, spun, wood

SUIT – bathing, birthday, boiler, diving, dress, jump, long, lounge, major, mao, minor, monkey, paternity, pressure, safari, sailor, slack, trouser, wet, zoot

TABLE – bird, coffee, dressing, gate-leg, glacier, high, league, life, multiplication, occasional, operating, pembroke, periodic, pool, refectory, round, sand, tide, water, wool, writing

TALK – baby, double, pep, pillow, sales, small

TAPE – chrome, friction, gaffer, grip, idiot, insulating, magnetic, masking, paper, perforated, punched, red, scotch, ticker, video

TAR – coal, jack, mineral, pine, wood

TENNIS – court, deck, lawn, real, royal, table

TERM – half, hilary, inkhorn, law, lent, michaelmas, trinity

THROUGH – break, carry, come, follow, muddle, pull, push, put, romp, run, scrape, see, walk, work

TICKET – meal, one-way, parking, pawn, platform, return, round-trip, season, single

TIDE – high, low, neap, red, spring

TIE – black, bow, cup, englishman's, string, white, windsor

TIME – big, borrowed, closing, common, compound, core, daylight-saving, double, down, drinking-up, extra, father, four-four, full, high, idle, injury, lighting-up, local, mean, opening, prime, quadruple, question, quick, response, short, six-eight, slow, standard, summer, three-four, triple, two-four, universal

TO – bring, come, fall, go, heave, keep, rise, run, set, speak, stand, stick, take, tumble, turn

TOGETHER – go, hang, hold, live, pull, scrape, scratch, stick, throw

TOM – long, peeping, uncle

TOOTH – baby, egg, milk, sweet, wisdom

TOP – big, double, fighting, humming, peg, round, screw, soft, spinning, tank

TOWN – boom, cape, county, george, ghost, market, new, post, twin

TRADE – carriage, free, rag, slave

TRAIN – boat, dog, gravy, wagon, wave

TRAP – booby, live, poverty, radar, sand, speed, steam, stench, stink, tank

TRIANGLE – bermuda, circular, eternal, pascal's, right, right-angled, spherical

TRICK – con, confidence, dirty, hat, three-card

TRIP – day, ego, field, round

TROT – jog, rising, sitting, turkey

TUBE – capillary, cathode-ray, drift, electron, eustachian, fallopian, geissler, inner, nixie, picture, pitot, pollen, shock, sieve, speaking, static, television, test, vacuum

TURN – about, good, kick, lodging, parallel, stem, three-point

UNDER – down, go, keep, knuckle, sit

WALL – antonine, cavity, cell, chinese, climbing, curtain, fire, hadrian's, hanging, party, retaining, sea, wailing, western

WATCH – black, middle, morning, night

WAVE – brain, electromagnetic, finger, ground, heat, long, longitudinal, medium, new, permanent, radio, seismic, shock, short, sky, sound, standing, stationary, tidal

WAX – chinese, cobbler's, earth, japan, mineral, montan, paraffin, sealing, vegetable

WAY – appian, each, flaminian, fly, fosse, milky, pennine, permanent, under

WHEEL – balance, big, buffing, catherine, crown, disc, driving, emery, escape, ferris, grinding, paddle, potter's, prayer, spinning, steering, stitch, tail, water, wire

WHISKEY – irish, corn, malt

WHISTLE – penny, steam, tin, wolf

WINDOW – bay, bow, compass,

gable, jesse, lancet, launch, picture, radio, rose, sash, storm, weather, wheel

WIRE – barbed, chicken, fencing, high, live, razor

WITH – bear, break, close, deal, go, live, play, settle, sleep, stick

WOMAN – fancy, little, old, painted, scarlet, widow

WORK – field, number, outside, social

YARD – back, main, scotland

YEAR – astronomical, calendar, civil, equinoctial, financial, fiscal, great, holy, leap, light, lunar, new, sabbatical, school, sidereal, solar, tropical

ZONE – economic, enterprise, free, frigid, hot, nuclear-free, skip, smokeless, temperate, time, torrid, twilight

ABBREVIATIONS

AA (Alcoholic Anonymous; Automobile Association)

AAA (Amateur Athletic Association)

AB (able seaman)

ABA (Amateur Boxing Association)

ABP (archbishop)

ABTA (Association of British Travel Agents)

AC (alternating current; account)

ACA (Associate of the Institute of Chartered Accountants)

ACAS (Advisory Conciliation and Arbitration Service)

ACIS (Associate of the Chartered Institute of Secretaries)

AD (anno domini)

ADC (aide-de-camp; amateur dramatic club)

ADJ (adjective)

ADM (Admiral)

ADV (adverb)

AD VAL (ad valorem)

AFA (Amateur Football Association)

AFC (Air Force Cross)

AFM (Air Force Medal)

AGM (annual general meeting)

AI (artificial insemination; artificial intelligence)

AIB (Associate of the Institute of Bankers)

AIDS (Acquired Immune

Deficiency Syndrome)

ALA (Alabama)

AM (ante meridiem)

AMU (atomic mass unit)

ANON (anonymous)

AOB (any other business)

AOC (Air Officer Commanding)

APEX (Association of Professional, Executive, Clerical, and Computer Staff)

APOCR (Apocrypha)

APPROX (approximate)

APT (Advanced Passenger Train)

ARA (Associate of the Royal Academy)

ARAM (Associate of the Royal Academy of Music)

ARCM (Associate of the Royal College of Music)

ARCS (Associate of the Royal College of Science)

ARIBA (Associate of the Royal Institute of British Architects)

ARIZ (Arizona)

ARK (Arkansas)

ASA (Advertising Standards Authority)

ASAP (as soon as possible)

ASH (Action on Smoking and Health)

ASLEF (Associated Society of Locomotive Engineers and Firemen)

AT (atomic)

ATC (air traffic control; Air Training Corps)

ATS (Auxiliary Territorial Service)

ATTN (for the attention of)

ATTRIB (attributive)

AT WT (atomic weight)

AU (Ångstrom unit; astronomical unit)

AUEW (Amalgamated Union of Engineering Workers)

AUG (August)

AV (ad valorem; Authorized Version)

AVDP (avoirdupois)

AVE (avenue)

AWOL (absent without leave)

BA (Bachelor of Arts; British Academy; British Airways; British Association)

BAA (British Airports Authority)

BAFTA (British Academy of Film and Television Arts)

B ARCH (Bachelor of Architecture)

BART (baronet)

BBC (British Broadcasting Corporation)

BC (before Christ)

BCH (Bachelor of Surgery)

BCL (Bachelor of Civil Law)

BCOM (Bachelor of Commerce)

BD (Bachelor of Divinity)

BDA (British Dental Association)

BDS (Bachelor of Dental Surgery)

BE (bill of exchange)
B ED (Bachelor of Education)
B ENG (Bachelor of Engineering)
BHP (brake horsepower)
BIM (British Institute of Management)
B LITT (Bachelor of Letters)
BMA (British Medical Association)
BMC (British Medical Council)
BMJ (British Medical Journal)
BMUS (Bachelor of Music)
BN (billion)
BOC (British Oxygen Company)
BP (bishop)
BPAS (British Pregnancy Advisory Service)
BPHARM (Bachelor of Pharmacy)
BPHIL (Bachelor of Philosophy)
BR (British Rail)
BRCS (British Red Cross Society)
BROS (brothers)
BSC (Bachelor of Science)
BSI (British Standards Institution)
BST (British Standard Time; British Summer Time)
BT (Baronet)
BTA (British Tourist Authority)
BVA (British Veterinary Association)
C (centigrade; circa)
CA (chartered accountant)
CAA (Civil Aviation Authority)
CAD (computer-aided design)
CADCAM (computer-aided design and manufacture)
CAL (California; calorie)
CAM (computer-aided manufacture)
CAMRA (Campaign for Real Ale)
C AND G (City and Guilds)
C AND W (country and western)
CANT (canticles)
CANTAB (of Cambridge – used with academic awards)
CAP (capital)
CAPT (captain)
CARD (Cardinal)
CB (Citizens' Band; Companion of the Bath)
CBE (Commander of the British Empire)
CBI (Confederation of British Industry)
CC (County Council; Cricket Club; cubic centimetre)
CDR (Commander)
CDRE (Commodore)
CE (Church of England; civil engineer)
CEGB (Central Electricity Generating Board)
C ENG (Chartered Engineer)
CENTO (Central Treaty Organization)
CERT (certificate; certified; certify)
CET (Central European Time)
CF (compare)
CFE (College of Further Education)
CFI (cost, freight, and insurance)
CGM (Conspicuous Gallantry Medal)
CH (chapter; church; Companion of Honour)
CHAS (Charles)
CI (curie; Order of the Crown of India)
CIA (Central Intelligence Agency)
CID (Criminal Investigation Department)
CIE (Companion of the Indian Empire)
CIF (cost, insurance, and freight)
CII (Chartered Insurance Institute)
C IN C (Commander in Chief)
CIS (Chartered Institute of Secretaries)
CL (centilitre)
CLLR (councillor)
CM (centimetre)
CMG (Companion of St Michael and St George)
CNAA (Council for National Academic Awards)
CND (Campaign for Nuclear Disarmament)
CO (commanding officer; company; county)
COD (cash on delivery)
C OF E (Church of England)
C OF S (Church of Scotland)
COHSE (Confederation of Health Service Employees)
COL (colonel; Colorado; Colossians)
CONN (Connecticut)
CONT (continued)
COR (Corinthians)
COS (cosine)
CR (credit)
CRO (cathode ray oscilloscope; Criminal Records Office)
CSE (Certificate of Secondary Education)
CSI (Companion of the Star of India)
CSM (Company Sergeant Major)
CU (cubic)
CV (curriculum vitae)
CVO (Commander of the Victorian Order)
CWT (hundredweight)
D (daughter; died; penny)
DA (District Attorney)
DAK (Dakota)
DAN (Daniel)
DBE (Dame Commander of the British Empire)
DC (Detective Constable; direct current; from the beginning)
DCB (Dame Commander of the Bath)
DCL (Doctor of Civil Law)
DCM (Distinguished Conduct Medal)
DCMG (Dame Commander of St Michael and St George)
DCVO (Dame Commander of the Victorian Order)
DD (direct debit; Doctor of Divinity)
DDS (Doctor of Dental Surgery)
DEL (Delaware)
DEPT (department)
DES (Department of Education and Science)
DEUT (Deuteronomy)
DF (Defender of the Faith)
DFC (Distinguished Flying Cross)
DFM (Distinguished Flying Medal)
DG (by the grace of God)
DHSS (Department of Health and Social Security)
DI (Detective Inspector)
DIAL (dialect)
DIP (Diploma)
DIP ED (Diploma in Education)
DIY (do-it-yourself)
D LITT (Doctor of Literature)
DM (Doctor of Medicine)
D MUS (Doctor of Music)
DNB (Dictionary of National Biography)
DO (ditto)
DOA (dead on arrival)
DOB (date of birth)
DOE (Department of the Environment)
DOM (to God, the best and greatest)
DOZ (dozen)
DPHIL (Doctor of Philosophy)
DPP (Director of Public Prosecutions)
DR (debtor; doctor; drive)
DSC (Distinguished Service Cross; Doctor of Science)
DSM (Distinguished Service Medal)
DSO (Distinguished Service Order)
DT (delirium tremens)
DV (God willing)
DVLC (Driver and Vehicle Licensing Centre)
E (East; Easterly; Eastern)
EA (each)

EC (East Central – London postal district)
ECCLES (Ecclesiastes)
ECCLUS (Ecclesiasticus)
ECG (electrocardiogram)
ECS (European Communication Satellite)
EE (Early English)
EEC (European Economic Community)
EEG (electroencephalogram)
EFTA (European Free Trade Association)
EG (for example)
EMA (European Monetary Agreement)
EMF (electromotive force)
ENC (enclosed; enclosure)
ENE (east-northeast)
ENSA (Entertainments National Service Association)
ENT (ear, nose and throat)
EOC (Equal Opportunities Commission)
EOF (end of file)
EP (electroplate; epistle)
EPH (Ephesians)
EPNS (electroplated nickel silver)
EPROM (erasable programmable read only memory)
ER (Edward Rex; Elizabeth Regina)
ESE (east-southeast)
ESN (educationally subnormal)
ESQ (esquire)
ESTH (Esther)
ETA (estimated time of arrival)
ETC (etcetera)
ETD (estimated time of departure)
ET SEQ (and the following one)
EX DIV (without dividend)
EX LIB (from the books)
EXOD (Exodus)
EZEK (Ezekiel)
F (Fahrenheit; franc)
FA (Football Association)
FANY (First Aid Nursing Yeomanry)
FAS (free alongside ship)
FBA (Fellow of the British Academy)
FBI (Federal Bureau of Investigation)
FC (Football Club)
FCA (Fellow of the Institute of Chartered Accountants)
FCII (Fellow of the Chartered Insurance Institute)
FCIS (Fellow of the Chartered Institute of Secretaries)
FCO (Foreign and Commonwealth Office)

FIFA (International Football Federation)
FL (flourished)
FLA (Florida)
FO (Field Officer; Flying Officer; Foreign Office)
FOB (free on board)
FOC (Father of the Chapel; free of charge)
FPA (Family Planning Association)
FRAM (Fellow of the Royal Academy of Music)
FRAS (Fellow of the Royal Astronomical Society)
FRCM (Fellow of the Royal College of Music)
FRCO (Fellow of the Royal College of Organists)
FRCOG (Fellow of the Royal College of Obstetricians and Gynaecologists)
FRCP (Fellow of the Royal College of Physicians)
FRCS (Fellow of the Royal College of Surgeons)
FRCVS (Fellow of the Royal College of Veterinary Surgeons)
FRGS (Fellow of the Royal Geographical Society)
FRIBA (Fellow of the Royal Institute of British Architects)
FRIC (Fellow of the Royal Institute of Chemistry)
FRICS (Fellow of the Royal Institution of Chartered Surveyors)
FRPS (Fellow of the Royal Photographic Society)
FRS (Fellow of the Royal Society)
FRSA (Fellow of the Royal Society of Arts)
FSA (Fellow of the Society of Antiquaries)
FZS (Fellow of the Zoological Society)
G (gram)
GA (Georgia)
GAL (Galatians)
GATT (General Agreement on Tariffs and Trade)
GB (Great Britain)
GBE (Knight/Dame Grand Cross of the British Empire)
GBH (grievous bodily harm)
GC (George Cross)
GCB (Knight/Dame Grand Cross of the Bath)
GCE (General Certificate of Education)
GCHQ (Government Communications Headquarters)
GCIE (Grand Commander of the

Indian Empire)
GCMG (Knight/Dame Grand Cross of St Michael and St George)
GCSE (General Certificate of Secondary Education)
GCVO (Knight/Dame Grand Cross of the Victorian Order)
GDP (gross domestic product)
GDR (German Democratic Republic)
GEO (George)
GER (German)
GHQ (general headquarters)
GIB (Gibraltar)
GLC (Greater London Council)
GM (George Medal; gram)
GMT (Greenwich Mean Time)
GNP (gross national product)
GOM (grand old man)
GP (general practitioner)
GPO (general post office)
H (hour)
HCF (highest common factor)
HEB (Hebrews)
HF (high frequency)
HGV (heavy goods vehicle)
HIH (His/Her Imperial Highness)
HIM (His/Her Imperial Majesty)
HM (headmaster; headmistress; His/Her Majesty)
HMI (His/Her Majesty's Inspector)
HMS (His/Her Majesty's Ship)
HMSO (His/Her Majesty's Stationery Office)
HNC (Higher National Certificate)
HND (Higher National Diploma)
HO (Home Office; house)
HON (honorary; honour; honourable)
HONS (honours)
HON SEC (Honorary Secretary)
HOS (Hosea)
HP (hire purchase; horsepower)
HQ (headquarters)
HR (holiday route; hour)
HRH (His/Her Royal Highness)
HSH (His/Her Serene Highness)
HT (height)
HV (high velocity; high-voltage)
IA (Institute of Actuaries; Iowa)
IAAF (International Amateur Athletic Federation)
IABA (International Amateur Boxing Association)
IATA (International Air Transport Association)
IB (ibidem; Institute of Bankers)
IBA (Independent Broadcasting Authority)
IBID (ibidem)
IC (in charge; integrated circuit)
ICE (Institution of Civil Engineers)
ICHEME (Institute of Chemical

Engineers)
ID (idem; identification)
IE (that is)
IEE (Institution of Electrical Engineers)
IHS (Jesus)
ILL (Illinois)
I MECH E (Institution of Mechanical Engineers)
IMF (International Monetary Fund)
INC (incorporated)
INCL (included; including; inclusive)
IND (Indiana)
INST (instant)
IOM (Isle of Man)
IOW (Isle of Wight)
IPA (International Phonetic Alphabet)
IQ (intelligence quotient)
IR (Inland Revenue)
IRA (Irish Republican Army)
IS (Isaiah)
ISO (Imperial Service Order)
ITA (initial teaching alphabet)
ITAL (italic; italicized)
ITV (Independent Television)
JAM (James)
JC (Jesus Christ; Julius Caesar)
JER (Jeremiah)
JP (Justice of the Peace)
JR (junior)
KAN (Kansas)
KB (King's Bench)
KBE (Knight Commander of the British Empire)
KC (King's Counsel)
KCB (Knight Commander of the Bath)
KCIE (Knight Commander of the Indian Empire)
KCMG (Knight Commander of St Michael and St George)
KCSI (Knight Commander of the Star of India)
KCVO (Knight Commander of the Victorian Order)
KG (kilogram; Knight of the Garter)
KGB (Soviet State Security Committee)
KKK (Ku Klux Klan)
KM (kilometre)
KO (knock-out)
KP (Knight of St Patrick)
KSTJ (Knight of St John)
KT (Knight of the Thistle)
KY (Kentucky)
L (Latin; learner; pound)
LA (Louisiana)
LAT (latitude)
LB (pound)

LBW (leg before wicket)
LCD (liquid crystal display; lowest common denominator)
LCJ (Lord Chief Justice)
LEA (Local Education Authority)
LEV (Leviticus)
LF (low frequency)
LIEUT (Lieutenant)
LITT D (Doctor of Letters; Doctor of Literature)
LJ (Lord Justice)
LJJ (Lords Justices)
LLB (Bachelor of Laws)
LLD (Doctor of Laws)
LLM (Master of Laws)
LOC CIT (in the place cited)
LOQ (he/she speaks)
LPG (liquefied petroleum gas)
LPO (London Philharmonic Orchestra)
LPS (Lord Privy Seal)
LRAM (Licentiate of the Royal Academy of Music)
LS (locus sigilli)
LSD (pounds, shillings, and pence)
LSE (London School of Economics)
LSO (London Symphony Orchestra)
LTD (limited)
LW (long wave)
M (male; married; motorway; thousand)
MA (Master of Arts)
MACC (Maccabees)
MAJ (Major)
MAL (Malachi)
MASH (mobile army surgical hospital)
MASS (Massachusetts)
MATT (Matthew)
MB (Bachelor of Medicine)
MBE (Member of the British Empire)
MC (Master of Ceremonies)
MCC (Marylebone Cricket Club)
MCP (male chauvinist pig)
MD (Doctor of Medicine; Managing Director; Maryland)
ME (Maine)
MEP (Member of the European Parliament)
MET (meteorological; meteorology; metropolitan)
MF (medium frequency)
MG (milligram)
MIC (Micah)
MICH (Michigan)
MINN (Minnesota)
MISS (Mississippi)
ML (millilitre)
M LITT (Master of Letters)

MLR (minimum lending rate)
MM (millimetre)
MO (Medical Officer; Missouri)
MOD (Ministry of Defence)
MOH (Medical Officer of Health)
MONT (Montana)
MP (Member of Parliament; Metropolitan Police; Military Police)
MPG (miles per gallon)
MPH (miles per hour)
MPHIL (Master of Philosophy)
MR (Master of the Rolls)
MRCOG (Member of the Royal College of Obstetricians and Gynaecologists)
MRCP (Member of the Royal College of Physicians)
MRCS (Member of the Royal College of Surgeons)
MRCVS (Member of the Royal College of Veterinary Surgeons)
MS (manuscript; multiple sclerosis)
MSC (Master of Science)
MSM (Meritorious Service Medal)
MSS (manuscripts)
MT (Mount)
MVO (Member of the Victorian Order)
N (North)
NA (North America; not applicable)
NAAFI (Navy, Army, and Air Force Institutes)
NALGO (National and Local Government Officers Association)
NASA (National Aeronautics and Space Administration)
NAT (Nathaniel)
NATO (North Atlantic Treaty Organization)
NATSOPA (National Society of Operative Printers, Graphical and Media Personnel)
NB (note well)
NCB (National Coal Board)
NCO (non-commissioned officer)
NCP (National Car Parks)
NCT (National Childbirth Trust)
NCV (no commercial value)
NDAK (North Dakota)
NE (Northeast)
NEB (Nebraska)
NEC (National Executive Committee)
NEH (Nehemiah)
NEV (Nevada)
NFU (National Farmers' Union)
NGA (National Graphical Association)
NHS (National Health Service)

NI (National Insurance; Northern Ireland)
NNE (north-northeast)
NNW (north-northwest)
NO (not out; number)
NORM (normal)
NOS (numbers)
NP (new paragraph)
NR (near; Northern Region)
NSB (National Savings Bank)
NSPCC (National Society for the Prevention of Cruelty to Children)
NT (National Trust; New Testament)
NUBE (National Union of Bank Employees)
NUGMW (National Union of General and Municipal Workers)
NUJ (National Union of Journalists)
NUM (National Union of Mineworkers)
NUPE (National Union of Public Employees)
NUR (National Union of Railwaymen)
NUS (National Union of Seamen; National Union of Students)
NUT (National Union of Teachers)
NW (Northwest)
NY (New York)
O (Ohio)
OAP (old-age pensioner)
OB (outside broadcast)
OBAD (Obadiah)
OBE (Officer of the British Empire)
OCTU (Officer Cadets Training Unit)
OFM (Order of Friars Minor)
OHMS (On His/Her Majesty's Service)
OKLA (Oklahoma)
OM (Order of Merit)
ONC (Ordinary National Certificate)
OND (Ordinary National Diploma)
ONO (or near offer)
OP (opus)
OP CIT (in the work cited)
OPEC (Organization of Petroleum Exporting Countries)
OPS (operations)
OREG (Oregon)
OS (ordinary seaman; Ordnance Survey)
OSA (Order of St Augustine)
OSB (Order of St Benedict)
OSF (Order of St Francis)
OT (occupational therapy; Old Testament)

OTC (Officers' Training Corps)
OU (Open University)
OUDS (Oxford University Dramatic Society)
OXFAM (Oxford Committee for Famine Relief)
OZ (ounce)
P (page; penny; purl)
PA (Pennsylvania; per annum; personal assistant; public address system)
PAYE (pay as you earn)
PC (per cent; personal computer; police constable)
PD (paid)
PDSA (People's Dispensary for Sick Animals)
PE (physical education)
PEI (Prince Edward Island)
PER PRO (by the agency of)
PG (paying guest; postgraduate)
PHD (Doctor of Philosophy)
PHIL (Philippians)
PL (place; plural)
PLC (public limited company)
PLO (Palestine Liberation Organization)
PM (post meridiem; Prime Minister)
PO (Petty Officer; Pilot Officer; postal order; Post Office)
POW (prisoner of war)
PP (pages; per pro)
PPS (further postscript; Parliamentary Private Secretary)
PR (public relations)
PRAM (programmable random access memory)
PRO (Public Records Office; public relations officer)
PROM (programmable read-only memory)
PROV (Proverbs)
PS (postscript; Private Secretary)
PT (physical training)
PTA (Parent-Teacher Association)
PTO (please turn over)
PVA (polyvinyl acetate)
PVC (polyvinyl chloride)
QB (Queen's Bench)
QC (Queen's Counsel)
QED (which was to be demonstrated)
QM (quartermaster)
QR (quarter; quire)
QT (quart)
QV (which see)
R (king; queen; right; river)
RA (Royal Academy; Royal Artillery)
RAC (Royal Automobile Club)
RADA (Royal Academy of

Dramatic Art)
RAF (Royal Air Force)
RAM (random access memory; Royal Academy of Music)
RAMC (Royal Army Medical Corps)
R AND D (research and development)
RBA (Royal Society of British Artists)
RBS (Royal Society of British Sculptors)
RC (Roman Catholic)
RCA (Royal College of Art)
RCM (Royal College of Music)
RCN (Royal College of Nursing)
RCP (Royal College of Physicians)
RCS (Royal College of Surgeons)
RCVS (Royal College of Veterinary Surgeons)
RD (road)
RE (religious education; Royal Engineers)
REME (Royal Electrical and Mechanical Engineers)
REV (Reverend)
RFC (Royal Flying Corps)
RH (Royal Highness; right hand)
RHA (Royal Horse Artillery)
RI (religous instruction)
RIBA (Royal Institute of British Architects)
RIC (Royal Institute of Chemistry)
RICS (Royal Institution of Chartered Surveyors)
RIP (may he rest in peace)
RK (religious knowledge)
RM (Resident Magistrate; Royal Mail; Royal Marines)
RMA (Royal Military Academy)
RN (Royal Navy)
RNIB (Royal National Institute for the Blind)
RNLI (Royal National Lifeboat Institution)
ROM (read only memory)
ROSPA (Royal Society for the Prevention of Accidents)
RPM (revolutions per minute)
RS (Royal Society)
RSA (Royal Society of Arts)
RSC (Royal Shakespeare Company)
RSM (Regimental Sergeant Major; Royal Society of Medicine)
RSPB (Royal Society for the Protection of Birds)
RSPCA (Royal Society for the Prevention of Cruelty to Animals)
RSVP (please answer)
RT HON (Right Honourable)

RT REV (Right Reverend)
RU (Rugby Union)
RUC (Royal Ulster Constabulary)
S (second; shilling; South)
SA (Salvation Army; sex appeal)
SAE (stamped addressed envelope)
SALT (Strategic Arms Limitation Talks)
SAS (Special Air Service)
SATB (soprano, alto, tenor, bass)
SAYE (save-as-you-earn)
SCD (Doctor of Science)
SE (southeast)
SEC (second; secretary)
SEN (senior; State Enrolled Nurse)
SEQ (the following)
SF (science fiction)
SGT (Sergeant)
SHAPE (Supreme Headquarters Allied Powers Europe)
SI (International System of Units)
SIN (sine)
SLADE (Society of Lithographic Artists, Designers, and Etchers)
SLR (single lens reflex)
SNCF (French National Railways)
SNP (Scottish National Party)
SNR (senior)
SOGAT (Society of Graphical and Allied Trades)
SOP (soprano)
SQ (square)
SRN (State Registered Nurse)
SSE (south-southeast)
SSW (south-southwest)
ST (saint; street)
STD (subscriber trunk dialling)
SW (southwest)
TA (Territorial Army)
TAN (tangent)
TASS (official news agency of the former Soviet Union)
TB (tubercle bacillus)
TCCB (Test and County Cricket Board)
TEFL (teaching English as a foreign language)
TENN (Tennessee)
TEX (Texas)

TGWU (Transport and General Workers' Union)
THESS (Thessalonians)
THOS (Thomas)
TM (trademark; transcendental meditation)
TOPS (Training Opportunities Scheme)
TSB (Trustee Savings Bank)
TT (teetotal; teetotaller)
TU (trade union)
TUC (Trades Union Congress)
TV (television)
UC (upper case)
UCATT (Union of Construction, Allied Trades, and Technicians)
UCCA (Universities Central Council on Admissions)
UCL (University College, London)
UDI (unilateral declaration of independence)
UEFA (Union of European Football Associations)
UHF (ultrahigh frequency)
UHT (ultrahigh temperature)
UK (United Kingdom)
ULT (ultimo)
UN (United Nations)
UNCTAD (United Nations Commission for Trade and Development)
UNESCO (United Nations Educational, Scientific, and Cultural Organization)
UNO (United Nations Organization)
UPOW (Union of Post Office Workers)
US (United States)
USA (United States of America)
USDAW (Union of Shop, Distributive, and Allied Workers)
USSR (Union of Soviet Socialist Republics)
V (verse; versus; volt)
VA (Order of Victoria and Albert; Virginia)
VAT (value-added tax)
VB (verb)
VC (Vice Chancellor; Victoria Cross)
VD (venereal disease)
VDU (visual display unit)
VE (Victory in Europe)
VG (very good)
VHF (very high frequency)
VIP (very important person)
VIZ (namely)
VLF (very low frequency)
VR (Victoria Regina; Volunteer Reserve)
VS (verse)
VSO (Voluntary Service Overseas)
VT (Vermont)
W (west)
WAAC (Women's Army Auxiliary Corps)
WAAF (Women's Auxiliary Air Force)
WC (water closet; West Central)
WI (West Indies; Women's Institute)
WIS (Wisconsin)
WK (week)
WM (William)
WNW (west-northwest)
WO (Warrant Officer)
WP (word processor)
WPC (Woman Police Constable)
WPM (words per minute)
WRAC (Women's Royal Army Corps)
WRAF (Women's Royal Air Force)
WRNS (Women's Royal Naval Service)
WRVS (Women's Royal Voluntary Service)
WSW (west-southwest)
WT (weight)
WW (Word War)
WWF (World Wildlife Fund)
WYO (Wyoming)
XL (extra large)
YHA (Youth Hostels Association)
YMCA (Young Men's Christian Association)
YR (year)
YWCA (Young Women's Christian Association)
ZECH (Zechariah)
ZEPH (Zephania)

EPONYMS

NAME – named after

ACOL – a club in Acol Road, London

ALEXANDER TECHNIQUE – Frederick Matthias (d. 1955) Australian actor who originated it

ANGSTROM – Anders J Ångström (1814–74) Swedish physicist

AXEL – Axel Paulsen (d. 1938) Norwegian skater

BADMINTON – Badminton House, where the game was first played

BAFFIN BAY – William Baffin 17th-century English navigator

BAKELITE – L H Baekeland (1863–1944) Belgian-born US inventor

BAKEWELL TART – Bakewell, Derbyshire

BALACLAVA (HELMET) – Balaklava

BANTING – William Banting (1797–1878) London undertaker

BASKERVILLE TYPE – John Baskerville (1706–75) English printer

BATH OLIVER – William Oliver (1695–1764) a physician at Bath

BEDLINGTON TERRIER – the town Bedlington in Northumberland, where they were first bred

BEEF STROGANOFF – Count Paul Stroganoff 19th-century Russian diplomat

BELISHA BEACON – Leslie Hore-Belisha (1893–1957) British politician

BERTILLON SYSTEM – Alphonse Bertillon (1853–1914) French criminal investigator

BIG BEN – Sir Benjamin Hall, Chief Commissioner of Works in 1856 when it was cast

BIRO – Laszlo Bíró (1900–85) Hungarian inventor

BLACKWOOD – Easeley F Blackwood its US inventor

BO DIDDLEY BEAT – Bo Diddley (1929–2008) US rhythm-and-blues performer and songwriter

BODLEIAN – Sir Thomas Bodley (1545–1613) English scholar who founded it in 1602

BORSTAL – Borstal village, Kent, where the first institution was founded

BOURBON – Bourbon County, Kentucky, where it was first made

BOWLER – John Bowler 19th-century London hatter

BRAMLEY – Matthew Bramley 19th-century English butcher, said to have first grown it

BROUGHAM – Henry Peter, Lord Brougham (1778–1868)

BROWNING GUN – John M Browning (1855–1926) US designer of firearms

CANTON CREPE – Canton, China, where it was originally made

CELSIUS – Anders Celsius (1701–44) Swedish astronomer who invented it

CHESTERFIELD – a 19th-century Earl of Chesterfield

COLT – Samuel Colt (1814–62) US inventor

COS – Kos, the Aegean island of its origin

COX'S ORANGE PIPPIN – R Cox, its English propagator

CRO-MAGNON MAN – the cave Cro-Magnon, Dordogne, France, where the remains were first found

DAIQUIRI – Daiquiri, rum-producing town in Cuba

DEMERARA – Demerara, a region of Guyana

DERBY – 12th Earl of Derby (d. 1834) who founded the horse race at Epsom Downs in 1780

DERRINGER – Henry Deringer, US gunsmith who invented it

DOILY – Doily, a London draper

DOUGLAS FIR – David Douglas (1798–1834) Scottish botanist

DOWNING STREET – Sir George Downing (1623–84) English statesman

DUMDUM – Dum-Dum, town near Calcutta where these bullets were made

EMMENTHAL CHEESE – Emmenthal, a valley in Switzerland

FERRIS WHEEL – G W G Ferris (1859–96) US engineer

FIACRE – the Hotel de St Fiacre, Paris, where these vehicles were first hired out

FOSBURY FLOP – Dick Fosbury US Olympic winner of men's high jump, 1968

GARAND RIFLE – John C Garand (1888–1974) US gun designer

GATLING GUN – R J Gatling (1818–1903) US inventor

GORGONZOLA CHEESE – Gorgonzola, Italian town where it originated

GRANNY SMITH – Maria Ann Smith, known as Granny Smith (d.1870) who first produced them at Eastwood, Sydney

GUILLOTINE – Joseph Ignace Guillotin (1738–1814) French physician

HANSARD – T C Hansard (1752–1828) who compiled the reports until 1889

HANSOM – J A Hansom (1803–82)

HEATH ROBINSON – William Heath Robinson (1872–1944) British cartoonist

HEPPLEWHITE FURNITURE – George Hepplewhite (1727–86) English cabinetmaker

HOBSON'S CHOICE – Thomas Hobson (1544–1631) English liveryman who gave his customers no choice but had them take the nearest horse

HOMBURG – Homburg, Germany, where it was originally made

HONITON LACE – Honiton, Devon, where it was first made

JACK RUSSELL – John Russell (1795–1883) English clergyman who developed the breed

KALASHNIKOV RIFLE – Mikhail Kalashnikov (1919–2013) its designer

KIR – Canon F Kir (1876–1968) mayor of Dijon

LEOTARD – Jules Léotard, French acrobat

LEWIS GUN – I N Lewis (1858–1931) US soldier

LLOYD'S – Edward Lloyd (d. ?1726) at whose coffee house in London the underwriters originally carried on their business

LONSDALE BELT – Hugh Cecil Lowther, 5th Earl of Lonsdale (1857–1944)

LUDDITE – Ned Ludd, an 18th-century Leicestershire workman, who destroyed industrial machinery

MACADAM – John McAdam (1756–1836) Scottish engineer

MACKINTOSH – Charles Macintosh (1760–1843) who invented it

MAGINOT LINE – André Maginot (1877–1932) French minister of war

MASOCHISM – Leopold von Sacher Masoch (1836–95) Austrian novelist

MAUSER – P P von Mauser (1838–1914) German firearms inventor

MILLS BOMB – Sir William Mills (1856–1932) English inventor

MINTON – Thomas Minton (1765–1836) English potter

MOBIUS STRIP – August Möbius (1790–1868) German mathematician

MOOG SYNTHESIZER – Robert Moogorn, US engineer

NEGUS – Col Francis Negus (d. 1732) its English inventor

NISSEN HUT – Lt Col Peter Nissen (1871–1930) British mining engineer

PETRI DISH – J R Petri (1852–1921) German bacteriologist

PILATES – Joseph Pilates (1880–1967) its German inventor

PLIMSOLL LINE – Samuel Plimsoll (1824–98) MP, who advocated its adoption

PULLMAN – George M Pullman (1831–97) the US inventor who first manufactured such coaches

QUEENSBERRY RULES – 9th Marquess of Queensberry, who originated the rules in 1869

ROLLS-ROYCE – its designers: Charles Stewart Rolls (1877–1910) and Sir Frederick Henry Royce (1863–1933)

ROQUEFORT CHEESE – Roquefort village in S France

RUBIK CUBE – Professor Erno Rubik (1944–   ) its Hungarian inventor

RUGBY – the public school at Rugby, where it was first played

SALLY LUNN BUN – an 18th-century English baker who invented it

SALMONELLA – Daniel E Salmon (1850–1914) US veterinary surgeon

SAM BROWNE BELT – Sir Samuel J Browne (1824–1901) British general, who devised such a belt

SANDWICH – John Montagu, 4th Earl of Sandwich (1718–92) who ate sandwiches rather than leave the gambling table for meals

SAXOPHONE – Adolphe Sax (1814–94) Belgian musical-instrument maker, who invented it (1846)

SEALYHAM TERRIER – Sealyham, village in S Wales, where it was bred in the 19th century

SHRAPNEL – H Shrapnel (1761–1842) English army officer, who invented it

SPOONERISM – W A Spooner (1844–1930) English clergyman

STANLEY KNIFE – F T Stanley, US businessman

STAYMAN – Samuel M Stayman (1909–94) US bridge expert

STETSON – John Stetson (1830–1906) US hatmaker

STILTON CHEESE – Stilton, Cambridgeshire, where it was originally sold

TATTERSALL'S – Richard Tattersall (d. 1795) English horseman, who founded the market

TONTINE – Lorenzo Tonti, Neapolitan banker who devised the scheme

TUXEDO – a country club in Tuxedo Park, New York

VENN DIAGRAM – John Venn (1834–1923) English logician

VERNIER – Paul Vernier (1580–1637) French mathematician, who described the scale

VERY LIGHT – Edward W Very (1852–1910) US naval ordnance officer

WALDORF SALAD – the Waldorf–Astoria Hotel, New York City

WELLINGTON BOOTS – the 1st Duke of Wellington

WENDY HOUSE – the house built for Wendy, the girl in J M Barrie's play Peter Pan

WHITWORTH SCREW THREAD – Sir Joseph Whitworth (1803–87) English engineer

WILTON CARPET – Wilton, Wiltshire

WINCHESTER RIFLE – O F Winchester (1810–80) US manufacturer

WORSTED – Worstead, a district in Norfolk

DIALECT WORDS

3
AIT
AN'T
DAP
GAN
GEY
HAP
HEN
KEN
KEP
MIM
NEB
TWP
WUS

4
AGEE
BIDE
BING
BIST
CHAW
CLEM
COOM
COWK
CREE
DARG
DEEK
DUNT
EMPT
FLEY
GIRN
GOWK
GREE
GRIG
HAST
HATH
HEAR
HOLP
INBY
KEYS
LAIK
MECK
MOIL
NARY
NESH
OOSE
PLAT
REDD
REEN
ROUP
SCAG
SILE
SMIT
SOOK
SPAG
STOB
TAMP

TASS
TRIG
TUMP
WAFF
WAME
WEAN
YAWL
YELD

5
ASHET
BEVVY
BIELD
BUROO
CANTY
CHELP
CLECK
COLLY
CUDDY
CUTTY
DIDDY
DOUCE
DUNNY
EMMET
FEEZE
FLITE
GARTH
GUTTY
HADST
HINNY
KECKS
LOSEL
MARDY
MITCH
MODGE
MUTCH
NETTY
NIEVE
NIXER
OXTER
PEART
PLOAT
REEST
REIVE
SHOON
SHOWD
SKELF
SKELP
SKIRL
SNECK
SONSY
SOUGH
SPEEL
SPELK
SPRUE
STANG
THIRL

THOLE
WHEEN

6
ARGUFY
BELIKE
CAGMAG
CLOUGH
CODDER
COLLOP
COOTCH
CROUSE
DREICH
EATAGE
EGGLER
FANKLE
FRATCH
GANSEY
GINNEL
GIRDLE
GOUGER
HAPPEN
HOGGET
HOLDEN
LARRUP
LINHAY
MAUNGY
MESTER
MIDDEN
MISTAL
NOBBUT
PASSEL
PAXWAX
PEERIE
PIZZLE
PLODGE
SCALLY
SCOUSE
SCRAMB
SCROOP
SCRUMP
SHEUCH
SHUGGY
SKELLY
SPENCE
SPUGGY
TACKET
THRAVE
THRAWN
THREAP
WAMBLE
WORRIT

7
BACK END
BOGGART
BRODDLE
CLACHAN

CRACKET
FLEEIN'
FOYBOAT
GRADELY
GROCKLE
GURRIER
HADAWAY
HANDSEL
HIELAND
JIBBONS
JONNOCK
MAMMOCK
PAN LOAF
PEEVERS
SCUNNER
SHINKIN
SHOOGLE
SKELLUM
SKIFFLE
SNICKET
SPAN–NEW
STEAMIE
STOTTER
TAMPING
WHERRET

8
BACKWORD
BARM CAKE
BOBOWLER
CHAMPION
CHOLLERS
DUNNAKIN
FLATLING
FORNENST
GALLUSES
PAMPHREY
POLLIWOG
SOUTHRON

9
BACK GREEN
CAG–HANDED
SOURDOUGH
SPREATHED
WICKTHING
WUTHERING

10
PEELY–WALLY

11
SWEETIEWIFE
WINDLESTRAW

12
CORRIE–FISTED
TATTIE–PEELIN

WORD PAIRS

ALPHA AND OMEGA
APPLES AND PEARS
ASSAULT AND BATTERY
BALL AND CHAIN
BANGERS AND MASH
BAT AND BALL
BIRDS AND BEES
BLACK AND BLUE
BLOOD AND THUNDER
BREAD AND BUTTER
BRICKS AND MORTAR
BRING AND BUY
BROTHERS AND SISTERS
BUBBLE AND SQUEAK
BUCKET AND SPADE
BUTT AND BEN
BUTTONS AND BOWS
CAP AND GOWN
CASH AND CARRY
CATS AND DOGS
CHEESE AND PICKLE
COCKLES AND MUSSELS
COLLAR AND TIE
COPS AND ROBBERS
COW AND GATE
CUT AND THRUST
CUTS AND BRUISES
DUCKING AND DIVING
DUCKS AND DRAKES
DUNGEONS AND DRAGONS
DUST AND ASHES
DUSTPAN AND BRUSH
FAST AND LOOSE

FIFE AND DRUM
FINE AND DANDY
FIRE AND BRIMSTONE
FISH AND CHIPS
FLORA AND FAUNA
FOX AND HOUNDS
FRUIT AND NUT
FRUIT AND VEG
G AND T
GIN AND TONIC
GIVE AND TAKE
GRACE AND FAVOUR
HAIL AND FAREWELL
HAMMER AND TONGS
HAT AND COAT
HEART AND SOUL
HERE AND NOW
HILL AND DALE
HORSE AND CARRIAGE
HOT AND COLD
HUSBAND AND WIFE
KINGS AND QUEENS
KNIFE AND FORK
LADIES AND GENTLEMEN
LEFT AND RIGHT
LOCK AND KEY
LOVE AND KISSES
MUSTARD AND CRESS
NAME AND ADDRESS
NEEDLE AND THREAD
NIGHT AND DAY
NOUGHTS AND CROSSES
ORANGES AND LEMONS

PEN AND INK
PIG AND WHISTLE
PINS AND NEEDLES
RHUBARB AND CUSTARD
ROSE AND CROWN
SALT AND PEPPER
SHAMPOO AND SET
SHOES AND SOCKS
SLAP AND TICKLE
SLUGS AND SNAILS
SNAKES AND LADDERS
SOAP AND WATER
SONG AND DANCE
STEAK AND KIDNEY
STICKS AND STONES
STOP AND GO
STRAWBERRIES AND CREAM
STUFF AND NONSENSE
SUGAR AND SPICE
SWINGS AND ROUNDABOUTS
TABLE AND CHAIRS
THUNDER AND LIGHTNING
TOP AND BOTTOM
TOP AND TAIL
TOWN AND COUNTRY
TRIAL AND ERROR
TRIPE AND ONIONS
TROUBLE AND STRIFE
UP AND UNDER
UPSTAIRS AND DOWNSTAIRS
WAR AND PEACE
WHISKY AND SODA
YOUNG AND OLD

ANAGRAM INDICATORS

ABANDONED
ABERRANT
ABNORMAL
ABOMINATION
ABORTION
ABOUND
ABROAD
ABSTRACT
ABSURD
ACCIDENTAL
ACCOMMODATED
ACCOMMODATION
ACROBATIC
ACTIVELY
ADAPT
ADAPTED
ADDLED
ADJUST
ADJUSTED
ADRIFT

ADULTERATED
AFFECT
AFFECTED
AFFLICT
AFFLICTED
AFLOAT
AFRESH
AFTER A FASHION
AFTER INJURY
AFTERMATH OF
AGITATE
AGITATED
AGITATOR
AGONY
AIEN
AILING
A LA MODE
ALCHEMY
ALIAS
ALL AT SEA

ALL CHANGE
ALL OVER
ALL OVER THE PLACE
ALLOY
ALL ROUND
ALLSORTS
ALL WRONG
ALTERED
ALTERNATIVE
AMALGAM
AMALGAMATE
AMAZING
AMBIGUOUS
AMEND
AMENDED
AMISS
ANALYSIS
ANARCHY
ANEW
ANGRY

ANGUISH
ANIMATED
ANNOYED
ANOMALOUS
ANOMALY
ANOTHER
ANYHOW
ANYWAY
APART
APPALLINGLY
APPEAR
APPOINTED
ARCH
ARISING FROM
AROUND
ARRANGE
ARRANGED
ARRANGEMENT
ARTFUL
ARTIFICIAL
AS A RESULT
ASKEW
ASSAILED
ASSAULTED
ASSEMBLE
ASSEMBLED
ASSEMBLY
ASSORTED
ASTONISHING
ASTRAY
AT FAULT
AT LIBERTY
AT ODDS
ATOMIZED
ATROCIOUS
AT SIXES AND SEVENS
AT VARIANCE
AUTHOR OF
AWFUL
AWFULLY
AWKWARD
AWRY
BAD
BADLY
BARMY
BARNEY
BASH
BASHED
BASTARD
BATS
BATTERED
BEAT
BEATEN–UP
BECOME
BEDEVILLED
BEDLAM
BEDRAGGLED
BEFUDDLE
BEFUDDLED
BELT
BEMUSED
BEND
BENDY

BENT
BERSERK
BEWILDERED
BIBULOUS
BIFF
BIZARRE
BLEND
BLENDED
BLIGHTED
BLITZ
BLOOMER
BLUDGEON
BLUNDER
BLUR
BOTCH
BOTCHED
BOTHER
BOTTLED
BOUNCING
BREAK
BREAKDOWN
BREAKUP
BREW
BROACH
BROADCAST
BROKE
BROKEN
BRUISE
BRUTALIZE
BUCK
BUCKLE
BUCKLED
BUCKLING
BUCKS
BUDGE
BUFFET
BUILD
BUILDING
BUMBLE
BUMP
BUNGLED
BURST
BUST
BUTCHER
BY ACCIDENT
BY ARRANGEMENT
BY MISTAKE
CALAMITOUS
CALAMITOUSLY
CAMOUFLAGED
CAN BE
CANCEL
CAPER
CAPRICIOUS
CAPRICIOUSLY
CARELESSLY
CARNAGE
CASCADE
CASSEROLE
CAST
CAST OFF
CATASTROPHIC
CAUSES

CAVORT
CHANGE
CHANGEABLE
CHANGED
CHAOS
CHAOTIC
CHEW
CHEWED UP
CHICANERY
CHOPPED UP
CHOP SUEY
CHURN
CLUMSILY
CLUMSY
COBBLED
COCKSCREW
COCKTAIL
COIN
COLLAPSE
COLLAPSING
COLLECTION
COMBUSTIBLE
COME TO BE
COME TO GRIEF
COMMOTION
COMPACT
COMPLICATED
COMPONENTS
COMPOSE
COMPOSED
COMPOSER
COMPOSING
COMPOSITION
COMPOUND
COMPRISE
CONCEAL
CONCEALING
CONCOCTION
CONFOUND
CONFOUNDED
CONJURING
CONSTITUENTS
CONSTITUTION
CONSTRUCT
CONSTRUCTION
CONTORTED
CONTRAPTION
CONTRIVANCE
CONTRIVE
CONTRIVED
CONVERSION
CONVERT
CONVERTED
CONVERTIBLE
CONVERTS
CONVULSED
COOK
COOKED
CORRECTED
CORRUPT
CORRUPTED
CORRUPTION
COULD BE

CRACK	DEVELOPMENT	DYNAMITE
CRACKED	DEVIANT	ECCENTRIC
CRACKERS	DEVIATION	EDIT
CRAFTY	DEVILISH	EDITED
CRASH	DEVIOUS	EERIE
CRASHES	DEVISE	EFFECT
CRAZILY	DICKY	EFFECTS
CRAZY	DIFFERENT	EFFERVESCENT
CREATE	DIFFERENTLY	ELBOW
CREATED	DIFFICULT	ELFIN
CRIMINAL	DILAPIDATED	EMANATED
CROOKED	DIRECTED TO	EMBARRASSED
CROSS	DISARRANGE	EMBODY
CRUDE	DISARRANGED	EMEND
CRUMBLE	DISRUPTION	EMENDATION
CRUMBLING	DISSECTED	EMENDED
CRUMPLED	DISSIPATED	EMERGE FROM
CRYPTIC	DISSOLUTE	EMPLOYS
CUNNING	DISSOLVED	ENGENDERING
CURDLED	DISSONANT	ENGENDERS
CURE	DISTILLATION	ENGINEER
CURIOUS	DISTORT	ENSEMBLE
CURIOUSLY	DISTORTED	ENTANGLED
CURLY	DISTORTION	ENTANGLEMENT
CURRY	DISTRACTED	ERRANT
CUT	DISTRACTEDLY	ERRATIC
DAFT	DISTRESSED	ERRING
DAMAGE	DISTRIBUTE	ERRONEOUS
DAMAGED	DISTRIBUTED	ERROR
DANCING	DISTRAUGHT	ERUPTING
DEALT WITH	DISTURB	EVIL
DEBAUCHED	DISTURBANCE	EVOLUTION
DECEIT	DISTURBED	EXCEPTIONAL
DECEPTION	DITHERING	EXCEPTIONALLY
DECIPHERED	DIVERGENCE	EXCITE
DECODED	DIVERGENT	EXCITED
DECOMPOSED	DIVERSIFICATION	EXHIBITS
DEFECTIVE	DIVERSIFIED	EXOTIC
DEFICIENT	DIVERT	EXPLODE
DEFORMED	DIVERTING	EXPLODED
DEFORMITY	DIZZY	EXPLOSION
DELIRIOUS	DO	EXPLOSIVE
DEMENTED	DOCTOR	EXTRACT OF
DEMOLISHED	DOCTORED	EXTRAORDINARILY
DEMOLITION	DODDERY	EXTRAVAGANT
DEPLORABLY	DOTTY	FABRICATED
DEPLOY	DOUBTFUL	FABRICATION
DEPLOYED	DOUBTFULLY	FABULOUS
DERANGED	DOZY	FAILING
DERIVATION	DRAWN	FAILURE
DERIVATIVE OF	DREADFUL	FAKE
DERIVED FROM	DREADFULLY	FALLACIOUS
DESECRATED	DRESS	FALLING
DESIGN	DRESSED	FALSE
DESPOIL	DRESSING	FALSIFIED
DESTROY	DRUB	FALTERING
DESTROYED	DRUNK	FANCIFUL
DETERIORATION	DRUNKEN	FANCY
DEVASTATE	DRUNKENLY	FANTASTIC
DEVASTATED	DUBIOUS	FAR FLUNG
DEVASTATION	DUBIOUSLY	FASHION
DEVELOP	DUD	FASHIONING
DEVELOPER	DUFF	FAULTY

FEBRILE
FERMENT
FERMENTED
FEVERISH
FICTIONAL
FIX
FLEXIBLE
FLIGHTY
FLING
FLIP
FLOUNDER
FLUCTUATING
FLUCTUATION
FLUID
FLURRIED
FLUSTERED
FOGGY
FOMENT
FOOLISH
FOOLISHLY
FOR A CHANGE
FORCED
FOREIGN
FORGE
FORGED
FORM OF
FORMS
FORMULATING
FOUL
FOUND IN
FRACTURED
FRAGMENTS
FRANTIC
FRAUD
FREAK
FREAKISH
FREE
FREELY
FRENZIED
FRENZY
FRET
FRILLY
FRISKY
FROLIC
FUDDLE
FUDDLED
FUDGE
FULMINATE
FUNCTION
FUNNY
FUZZY
GAMBOL
GARBLE
GARBLED
GENERATES
GENERATING
GET-UP
GHASTLY
GIBBERISH
GIDDY
GIVE RISE TO
GIVES
GLEANED FROM

GOING TO
GONE OFF
GO OFF
GO STRAIGHT
GO TO POT
GO TO THE DOGS
GO WRONG
GROTESQUE
GROUND
HACK
HAMMER
HAMMERED
HANKY-PANKY
HAPHAZARD
HAPLESS
HARASSED
HARM
HASH
HASHED
HATCHES
HATCHING
HAVOC
HAYWIRE
HAZE
HELTER-SKELTER
HIDE
HIDING
HIGGLEDY PIGGLEDY
HORRIBLE
HOTCH POTCH
HURT
HYBRID
IDIOTIC
ILL
ILL-COMPOSED
ILL-DISPOSED
ILL-FORMED
ILL-MADE
ILL-TREATED
ILL-USED
IMBECILE
IMPAIRED
IMPERFECT
IMPROPER
IMPROPERLY
INACCURATE
INANE
INCLUDED
INCONSTANT
INDUCE
INFAMOUS
INFIRM
INGREDIENTS OF
INHABITING
INJURED
IN ORDER
INORDINATELY
IN OTHER WORDS
IN REVOLT
IN RUINS
INSANE
IN SHREDS
INTERFERED WITH

INTRICATE
INVALID
INVENTION
INVOLVED
IRREGULAR
IRREGULARITY
IRRITATED
ITINERANT
JAR
JAZZ
JIG
JITTERY
JOG
JOLT
JOSTLED
JUGGLE
JUGGLED
JUMBLE
JUMBLED
KIND OF
KINK
KINKY
KNEAD
KNIT
LABYRINTHINE
LAWLESS
LEAPING
LET LOOSE
LICKED INTO SHAPE
LOOK SILLY
LOOSE
LOOSELY
LOUSY
LUDICROUS
LUNATIC
MAD
MADE FROM
MADE OF
MADE UP
MADLY
MAIM
MAKE
MAKE-UP
MAKING
MALADROIT
MALAISE
MALFORMATION
MALFORMED
MALFUNCTION
MALLEABLE
MALTREAT
MALTREATED
MALTREATMENT
MANAGED
MANAGER
MANGLE
MANGLED
MANIAC
MANIC
MANIFEST
MANIFESTATION
MANIPULATE
MANIPULATED

MANOEUVRE
MARRED
MARSHAL
MASH
MASHED
MASSAGE
MAUL
MAULED
MAYBE
MAY BECOME
MAYHEM
MEANDERING
MEDLEY
MELEE
MEND
MENDED
MERCURIAL
MESS
MESSILY
METAMORPHOSING
METAMORPHOSIS
MIGRANT
MINCE
MINCED
MISALLIANCE
MISCONTRUED
MISDELIVERED
MISGUIDED
MISHANDLED
MISHAP
MISLED
MISREPRESENTATION
MISREPRESENTED
MISSHAPEN
MISTAKE
MISTREATED
MISUSED
MIX
MIXED
MIXTURE
MIX-UP
MOBILE
MODEL
MODELS
MODIFICATION
MODIFIED
MODIFY
MOITHER
MOLEST
MOLESTED
MONKEY WITH
MOULD
MOVED
MOVING
MUCK ABOUT
MUDDLE
MUDDLED
MUTABLE
MUTANT
MUTATION
MUTATIVE
MUTILATE
MUTILATED

MUTILATION
MUTINOUS
MYSTERIOUS
MYSTERIOUSLY
NASTY
NATURALLY
NAUGHTY
NAUSEOUS
NEATLY
NEGLECTED
NEGLIGEE
NEGOTIATED
NEGOTIATION
NERVOUSLY
NEW
NEW FORM OF
NEWLY FORMED
NEWLY MADE
NOBBLED
NOMADIC
NOT EXACTLY
NOT IN ORDER
NOT PROPERLY
NOT RIGHT
NOT STRAIGHT
NOVA
NOVEL
OBLIQUE
OBSCURE
OBSCURED
OBSTREPEROUS
OCCASION
ODD
OF
OFF
OFF-COLOUR
OPEN
OPERATE ON
ORDER
ORDERED
ORDERLY
ORDERS
ORGANIZATION
ORGANIZED
ORIGINALLY
OTHERWISE
OUT
OUTCOME OF
OUTLANDISH
OUT OF
OUTRAGEOUSLY
OVER
OVERTURN
PECULIAR
PERFIDIOUS
PERHAPS
PERPLEXED
PERVERSE
PERVERSELY
PERVERT
PERVERTED
PHONEY
PIE

PLAY
PLAYING TRICKS
PLYING
POLLUTED
POOR
POSING AS
POSITION
POSSIBLY
POTENTIAL
POTENTIALLY
POUND
PREPARATION
PREPARE
PREPARED
PRINT OUT
PROBLEM
PROBLEMATIC
PROBLEMATICAL
PROCESS
PROCESSING
PRODUCES
PRODUCING
PRODUCTION
PROPERLY ORGANIZED
PROPERLY PRESENTED
PSEUDO
PULVERIZED
PUMMELLED
PUT ANOTHER WAY
PUT OUT
PUT RIGHT
PUT STRAIGHT
PUZZLING
QUAKING
QUEASY
QUEER
QUEER LOOKING
QUESTIONABLE
QUIRKY
QUITE DIFFERENT
QUIVERING
RABID
RAGE
RAGGED
RAKISH
RAMBLING
RANDOM
RANSACK
RAVAGED
RAVISH
RAVISHED
REACTIONARY
READJUSTED
REARRANGED
REARRANGEMENT
REASSEMBLED
REASSEMBLY
REBEL
REBELLIOUS
REBUILDING
REBUILT
RECALCITRANT
RECAST

RECIPE
RECKLESS
RECONSTRUCTED
RECTIFICATION
RECTIFIED
REDESIGNED
REDISCOVERED
REELING
REFORMATION
REFORMED
REFRACTORY
REFURBISHED
REGULATED
REGULATION
RELAY
RELAYING
RELEASING
REMADE
REMEDY
REMODELLED
RENDERING
RENDITION
RENOVATED
RENOVATION
REORGANIZATION
REORGANIZED
REPAIR
REPAIRED
REPLACED
REPLACEMENT
REPRESENT
REPRESENTATION
REPRESENTED
REPRESENTING
REPRODUCE
REPRODUCTION
RESHAPED
RESHUFFLE
RESOLUTION
RESOLVE
RESOLVED
RESORT
RESORTING
RESTLESS
RESULT
RESULTING FROM
REVIEW
REVISED
REVOLTING
REVOLUTION
REVOLUTIONARY
REVOLUTIONIZED
REVOLVER
REWRITTEN
RICKETY
RIDICULOUS
RIGGED
RIOT
RIP
RIPPLING
ROCK
ROCKY
ROLLICKING

ROTARY
ROTTEN
ROUGHLY
ROUND
ROVING
ROWDY
RUBBISH
RUDE
RUFFLE
RUFFLED
RUIN
RUINED
RUINOUS
RUM
RUMPLED
RUNNING WILD
RUPTURED
SABORAGE
SACK
SADLY
SALAD
SALVAGED FROM
SATANIC
SAUCY
SAVAGE
SCATTER
SCATTERED
SCHEME
SCRAMBLE
SCRAMBLED
SCRATCH
SCRATCHED
SCRUFFY
SCUFFLE
SCULPTED
SEND OFF/OUT
SENSELESS
SET
SETTING
SETTLEMENT
SHAKE
SHAKEDOWN
SHAKEN
SHAKY
SHAMBLES
SHAPED
SHATTER
SHATTERED
SHELLED
SHIFT
SHIFTING
SHILLY–SHALLY
SHIMMERING
SHIP–SHAPE
SHIVER
SHIVERED
SHOCKED
SHOULD BECOME
SHOWING
SHRED
SHUFFLE
SHUFFLED
SICK

SIFTED
SILLY
SKIDDING
SKIPPING
SKITTISH
SLAP–HAPPY
SLAUGHTER
SLING
SLIP
SLIPPING
SLIPSHOD
SLOPPY
SLOVENLY
SLYLY
SMASH
SMASHED
SMASHING
SOLUTION
SOMEHOW
SOMERSAULT
SORRY STATE
SORT
SORTED OUT
SORT OF
SOUP
SOZZLED
SPASMODIC
SPATTERED
SPELT OUT
SPILL
SPILT
SPIN
SPINNING
SPLASH
SPLICE
SPLICED
SPLINTER
SPLIT
SPOIL
SPOILT
SPORT
SPORTING
SPORTIVE
SPRAY
SPREAD
SPURIOUS
SQUALL
SQUASH
SQUIFFY
SQUIGGLES
STAGGER
STAGGERED
STAMPEDE
START
STATE
STEW
STEWED
STIR
STIRRED
STORM
STORMY
STRAIGHT
STRAIGHTEN

STRANGE
STRAY
STRAYING
STREWN
STRICKEN
STRUGGLE
STRUGGLING
STUPID
STUPIDLY
STYLE
SUBMERGED IN
SUPERFICIAL
SUPERFICIALLY
SURGERY
SURPRISING
SURPRISINGLY
SUSPECT
SWIRL
SWIRLING
TAILOR
TAILORED
TAMPERED WITH
TANGLE
TANGLED
TATTERED
TATTY
TEAR
TEASE
TEMPESTUOUS
TEMPESTUOUSLY
TERRIBLE
TIDIED UP
TIDY
TILT
TIP
TIPSY
TOPSY TURVY
TO RIGHTS
TORMENT
TORN
TORTUOUS
TORTURE
TORTURED
TOSS
TOUCHED
TRAIN
TRAINED
TRANSFERRED
TRANSFORM
TRANSFORMATION
TRANSFORMED
TRANSLATE
TRANSLATED
TRANSLATION
TRANSMUTATION
TRANSMUTE
TRANSMUTED

TRANSPOSE
TRANSPOSED
TRANSPOSITION
TRAVESTY
TREATED
TREMBLING
TRICK
TRICKY
TRIP
TROUBLE
TROUBLED
TROUBLESOME
TUMBLE
TUMBLEDOWN
TUMBLING
TUMULT
TUMULTUOUS
TURBULENT
TURNED
TWIRL
TWIRLING
TWIST
TWISTED
TWISTER
UGLY
UNCERTAIN
UNCOMMON
UNCONVENTIONAL
UNDECIDED
UNDISCIPLINED
UNDOING
UNDONE
UNDULY
UNEASY
UNEVENLY
UNFAMILIAR
UNFIT
UNFORTUNATELY
UNHAPPY
UNNATURAL
UNNATURALLY
UNORTHODOX
UNRAVELLED
UNRELIABLE
UNRESTRAINED
UNRULY
UNSETTLED
UNSETTLING
UNSOUND
UNSTABLE
UNSTEADY
UNSTUCK
UNTIDY
UNUSUAL
UNWIND
UPSET
VACILLATING

VAGABOND
VAGUELY
VANDALIZE
VANDALIZED
VARIABLE
VARIED
VARIETY
VARIOUS
VARIOUSLY
VARY
VERSION OF
VEX
VIA
VIGOROUSLY
VILE
VIOLATE
VIOLENT
VOLATILE
WANDER
WANDERING
WARP
WARPED
WARRING
WAS
WASTED
WAVERING
WEAVE
WEIRD
WELL–FORMED
WELL–ORDERED
WELL–ORGANIZED
WELL–VARIED
WHIP
WHIRL
WHIRLING
WHISK
WICKED
WILD
WILDLY
WIND
WOBBLY
WOOLLY
WORK OUT
WORRIED
WORRY
WOVEN
WRECK
WRECKED
WRENCH
WRESTED FROM
WRETCHED
WRITHING
WRONG
YIELDS
ZANY

SPLIT-WORD INDICATORS

ABOUT
ABSORBED IN
ACCEPTED BY
ACCEPTING
ACCOMMODATED BY
ADMITTED BY
AMID
AROUND
ASSIMILATED BY
BACK
BACKING
BESET BY
CAPTURED BY
CARRIED BY
CIRCUMSCRIBED BY
CLUTCHED BY
CONFINED BY
CONFINED IN
CONTAIN
CONTENT
CONTENTS
CUT BY
CUTTING
DIVIDING
EMBRACED
EMBRACING
ENCIRCLED
ENCIRCLING
ENCLOSED
ENCLOSURE
ENCOMPASSED
ENCOMPASSING
ENGULFED
ENGULFING
ENTERING
ENTRAPPED
ENTRAPPING
ENTRY
ENVELOPED

ENVELOPING
ENVIRONMENT
ENVIRONS
EXTERIOR
FILLED BY
FILLING
FRAMED BY
FRAMED IN
FRAMING
GET ABOUT
GO AROUND
GO IN
GRABBED BY
GRABBING
GRIPPED BY
GRIPPING
HARBOURED
HOLD
HOLDING CAPTIVE
HOLDING PRISONER
HOUSED
HOUSING
IMBIBED
IMPOUND
IMPOUNDED
IMPRISONED
IMPRISONING
INCLUDE
INCLUDED IN
INCORPORATING
INTERIOR
INTERRUPTED
INTERRUPTING
INTERVENING IN
IN TWO WORDS
INVOLVED IN
INVOLVING
KEEPING
LINING

OCCUPIED BY
OCCUPYING
OUTSIDE
PARTED BY
PARTING
POCKETED BY
POCKETING
RECEIVED BY
RECEIVED IN
RECEIVING
RETAINED BY
RETAINING
RINGING
SEPARATED BY
SEPARATING
SET ABOUT
SET IN
SHELTER
SHELTERED BY
SPLIT BY
SPLITTING
STUFFING
SURROUND
SURROUNDED BY
SWALLOWED BY
SWALLOW UP
TAKE IN
TAKEN IN BY
TRAP
TRAPPED BY
TRAPPED IN
TUCKED INTO
UPHEAVAL
WITHIN
WITHOUT
WRAPPED IN
WRAPPING

FIRST NAMES

GIRLS' NAMES

2	MEL	CARY	ILSE	MARA
DI	MIA	CASS	IMMY	MARY
EM	NAN	CATH	INEZ	MAUD
JO	NAT	CERI	IOLA	MAYA
VI	ONA	CISS	IONA	META
	PAM	CLEM	IRIS	MILA
3	PAT	CLEO	IRMA	MIMA
ADA	PEG	CORA	ISLA	MIMI
AMY	PEN	DAFF	IVAH	MINA
ANN	PIA	DALE	JADE	MIRA
AUD	PRU	DANA	JAEL	MOLL
AVA	RAE	DAPH	JANE	MONA
BAB	RIA	DAWN	JEAN	MYRA
BEA	ROS	DOLL	JESS	NADA
BEE	SAL	DORA	JILL	NELL
BEL	SAM	EDEN	JOAN	NEST
CIS	SIB	EDIE	JODI	NEVA
DEB	SUE	EDNA	JODY	NINA
DEE	TIA	EILY	JOSS	NITA
DOT	UNA	EIRA	JUDI	NOLA
EDA	VAL	ELLA	JUDY	NONA
ENA	VIV	ELMA	JUNE	NORA
ETH	WIN	ELSA	KARA	NOVA
EVA	ZOË	EMMA	KATE	OLGA
EVE		ENID	KATH	OONA
FAN	**4**	ERIN	KATY	OPAL
FAY	ABBY	ERYL	KERI	OZZY
FLO	ADAH	ESME	KYLE	PETA
GAY	ADDY	ETTA	LANA	PHIL
GUS	AINE	ETTY	LELA	POLL
IDA	ALDA	EVIE	LENA	PRUE
INA	ALEX	FAYE	LETA	RENA
ISA	ALIX	FERN	LILA	RENE
ITA	ALLY	FIFI	LILI	RHEA
IVY	ALMA	FLOY	LILY	RICA
JAN	ALVA	FRAN	LINA	RIKA
JAY	ALYS	GABI	LISA	RINA
JEN	ANIS	GABY	LISE	RITA
JOY	ANNA	GAIL	LITA	ROMA
KAY	ANNE	GALE	LIZA	RONA
KIM	ANYA	GAYE	LOIS	ROSA
KIT	AVIS	GERT	LOLA	ROSE
LEE	BABS	GILL	LORA	ROXY
LES	BEAT	GINA	LORI	RUBY
LIL	BELL	GLAD	LORN	RUTH
LIZ	BESS	GWEN	LUCE	SARA
LOU	BETA	GWYN	LUCY	SIAN
LYN	BETH	HEBE	LULU	SÍLE
MAE	BINA	HEDY	LYNN	SÍNE
MAY	BRYN	HOPE	LYRA	SKYE
MEG	CARA	ILMA	MAIR	SUZY

TACY	BELLE	ELVIE	JUDOC	MARTA
TARA	BERNY	EMILY	JULIA	MARTI
TESS	BERRY	EMMIE	JULIE	MARTY
THEA	BERTA	EPPIE	KAREN	MATTY
TINA	BERYL	ERICA	KARIN	MAUDE
TONI	BESSY	ERIKA	KATHY	MAURA
TRIS	BETSY	ESMEE	KATIE	MAVIS
TRIX	BETTE	ESSIE	KELDA	MEAVE
TYRA	BETTY	ETHEL	KELLY	MEGAN
VERA	BIDDY	ETHNE	KEREN	MEGGY
VIDA	BONNY	ETTIE	KERRI	MELBA
VINA	BRIDE	EVITA	KERRY	MELVA
VITA	BRITA	FAITH	KEZIA	MERCY
VIVA	BRITT	FANNY	KIRBY	MERLE
WREN	BUNTY	FARON	KITTY	MERRY
WYNN	CANDY	FIONA	KYLIE	MERYL
ZANA	CAREY	FLEUR	LAILA	MILLY
ZARA	CARLA	FLORA	LAURA	MINNA
ZENA	CARLY	FLOSS	LAURI	MINTY
ZITA	CAROL	FREDA	LEIGH	MITZI
ZOLA	CARYL	FREYA	LEILA	MOIRA
ZORA	CARYS	GABBY	LENNY	MOLLY
	CASEY	GAYLE	LEONA	MORAG
5	CATHY	GEMMA	LETTY	MORNA
ABBEY	CELIA	GERDA	LEXIE	MOYNA
ABBIE	CERYS	GERRY	LIANA	MOYRA
ADDIE	CHLOE	GILDA	LIBBY	MYRNA
ADELA	CHRIS	GINNY	LIDDY	MYSIE
ADELE	CILLA	GRACE	LIESL	NADIA
ADLAI	CINDY	GRETA	LILAC	NAHUM
AGGIE	CISSY	GUSTA	LILLA	NANCE
AGNES	CLARA	HAGAR	LINDA	NANCY
AILIE	CLARE	HATTY	LINDY	NANNY
AILIS	CORAL	HAZEL	LIZZY	NAOMI
AILSA	DAISY	HEDDA	LOLLY	NELLY
AIMEE	DARCY	HEIDI	LOREN	NERYS
ALANA	DEBRA	HELEN	LORNA	NESSA
ALEXA	DELIA	HELGA	LORNE	NESTA
ALICE	DELLA	HENNY	LOTTY	NETTA
ALINA	DELMA	HEPSY	LUCIA	NICKY
ALINE	DERYN	HETTY	LUCIE	NIKKI
ALLIE	DIANA	HILDA	LUCKY	NOELE
ALVIE	DIANE	HOLLY	LYDIA	NORAH
AMATA	DILYS	HORRY	LYNDA	NORMA
AMBER	DINAH	HULDA	LYNNE	NUALA
AMICE	DIONE	HYLDA	MABEL	NYREE
ANGEL	DODIE	ILONA	MABLE	ODILE
ANGIE	DOLLY	IRENE	MADDY	OLIFF
ANITA	DONNA	ISMAY	MADGE	OLIVE
ANNIE	DORIA	JACKY	MAEVE	OLLIE
ANNIS	DORIS	JANET	MAGDA	OLWEN
ANONA	DREDA	JANEY	MAIRE	OLWYN
ANWEN	DULCE	JANIE	MAISY	ORIEL
APHRA	EDITH	JANIS	MAMIE	OWENA
APRIL	EFFIE	JAYNE	MANDY	PANSY
ASTRA	ELAIN	JEMMA	MARAH	PATSY
AUDRA	ELENA	JENNA	MARCY	PATTI
AUREA	ELISE	JENNY	MARGE	PATTY
AVERY	ELIZA	JEWEL	MARGO	PAULA
AVICE	ELLEN	JINNY	MARIA	PEACE
AVRIL	ELLIE	JODIE	MARIE	PEARL
BEATA	ELROY	JOSIE	MARLA	PEGGY
BECKY	ELSIE	JOYCE	MARNI	PENNY
BELLA				

PETRA	TILDA	ANNICE	CHERRY	FLOWER
PHEBE	TILLY	ANNIKA	CHERYL	FOSTER
PIPER	TISHA	ANNORA	CICELY	FRANCA
PIPPA	TONIA	ANSTEY	CISSIE	FRANNY
POLLY	TONYA	ANTHEA	CLAIRE	FRIEDA
POPPY	TOPSY	ARIANE	COLINA	GABBIE
QUINN	TOTTY	ARLEEN	CONNIE	GAENOR
RAINA	TRACY	ARLENE	DAGMAR	GARNET
RAINE	TRINA	ARLINE	DANITA	GAYNOR
REINE	TRUDI	ARMINA	DANUTA	GERTIE
RENÉE	TRUDY	ARMINE	DAPHNE	GINGER
RENIE	UNITY	ASHLEY	DAVIDA	GINNIE
RHIAN	VALDA	ASTRID	DAVINA	GISELA
RHODA	VANDA	ATHENE	DEANNA	GLADYS
RHONA	VELDA	AUDREY	DEANNE	GLENDA
RILEY	VELMA	AURIEL	DEBBIE	GLENIS
ROBYN	VENUS	AURIOL	DECIMA	GLENNA
RONNA	VERNA	AURORA	DELWEN	GLENYS
ROSIE	VICKI	AURORE	DELWYN	GLINYS
ROWAN	VICKY	AVERIL	DELYTH	GLORIA
SACHA	VIKKI	BARBIE	DENISE	GLYNIS
SADIE	VILMA	BARBRA	DENNIE	GOLDIE
SALLY	VINNY	BAUBIE	DIANNE	GRACIE
SAMMY	VIOLA	BEATTY	DIONNE	GRANIA
SANDY	VIVIA	BENITA	DORCAS	GRETEL
SARAH	WANDA	BERNIE	DOREEN	GRIZEL
SARAI	WENDA	BERTHA	DORICE	GUSSIE
SARRA	WENDY	BESSIE	DORITA	GWENDA
SELMA	WILLA	BETHAN	DORRIE	HAIDEE
SENGA	WILMA	BETHIA	DOTTIE	HANNAH
SHANA	WYNNE	BEULAH	DULCIE	HARPER
SHANI	XENIA	BIANCA	DYMPNA	HATTIE
SHARI	ZELDA	BILLIE	EARTHA	HAYLEY
SHEBA	ZELMA	BIRDIE	EASTER	HEDWIG
SHENA	ZORAH	BIRGIT	EDWINA	HELENA
SHIRL		BLANCH	EILEEN	HELENE
SHONA	**6**	BLODYN	EILWEN	HENNIE
SIBBY	ADALYN	BLYTHE	EIRIAN	HEPSEY
SIBYL	AGACIA	BOBBIE	EITHNE	HEPSIE
SISSY	AGATHA	BONITA	ELAINE	HERMIA
SONIA	AGNETA	BONNIE	ELINED	HESTER
SONJA	AILEEN	BRENDA	ELINOR	HILARY
SONYA	AILITH	BRIDIE	ELISHA	HONORA
SOPHY	AITHNE	BRIGID	ELISSA	HOWARD
STACY	ALANNA	BRIGIT	ELOISA	HULDAH
SUKEY	ALBINA	BRIONY	ELOISE	IANTHE
SUSAN	ALDITH	BRYONY	ELSPIE	IDONEA
SUSIE	ALEXIA	CANICE	ELUNED	IMOGEN
SYBIL	ALEXIS	CARINA	ELVINA	INGRID
TACEY	ALICIA	CARITA	ELVIRA	ISABEL
TAMAR	ALISON	CARMEL	EMELYN	ISEULT
TAMMY	ALTHEA	CARMEN	EMILIA	ISHBEL
TANIA	ALVINA	CAROLA	ESTHER	ISOBEL
TANSY	AMABEL	CAROLE	EUNICE	ISOLDA
TANYA	AMALIA	CARRIE	EVADNE	ISOLDE
TEGAN	AMALIE	CASSIE	EVELYN	JACKIE
TERRI	AMANDA	CATRIN	EVONNE	JACOBA
TERRY	AMELIA	CECILE	FARRAN	JACQUI
TESSA	AMICIA	CECILY	FARREN	JANICE
TETTY	AMINTA	CELINA	FEDORA	JANINE
THORA	ANDREA	CELINE	FELICE	JANSIS
THYRA	ANDRÉE	CHARIS	FINOLA	JEANIE
TIBBY	ANEIRA	CHERIE	FLAVIA	JEANNE
	ANGELA			

JEHANE	MARISA	ROXANE	VICKIE	BEDELIA
JEMIMA	MARITA	RUBINA	VINNIE	BELINDA
JENNIE	MARLIN	RUTHIE	VIOLET	BERNICE
JESSIE	MARLYN	SABINA	VIVIAN	BETHANY
JOANNA	MARNIE	SALENA	VIVIEN	BETTINA
JOANNE	MARSHA	SALINA	VYVYAN	BETTRYS
JOLEEN	MARTHA	SALOME	WALLIS	BEVERLY
JOLENE	MARTIE	SANDIE	WINNIE	BLANCHE
JUDITH	MARYAM	SANDRA	XANTHE	BLODWEN
JULIET	MATTIE	SARINA	YASMIN	BLOSSOM
KARINA	MAUDIE	SARITA	YVAINE	BRANWEN
KEELEY	MAXINE	SELENA	YVETTE	BRIANNE
KELLIE	MEGGIE	SELINA	YVONNE	BRIDGET
KENDRA	MEGHAN	SERENA	ZANDRA	BRIGHID
KERRIE	MEHALA	SHARON	ZILLAH	BRONWEN
KEZIAH	MELODY	SHAUNA	ZINNIA	BRONWYN
KIRSTY	MERCIA	SHEENA		CAITLIN
LALAGE	MERIEL	SHEILA	**7**	CAMILLA
LAUREL	MIGNON	SHELLY	ABIGAIL	CAMILLE
LAUREN	MILLIE	SHERRI	ADAMINA	CANDACE
LAURIE	MINNIE	SHERRY	ADELINA	CANDICE
LAVENA	MIRIAM	SHERYL	ADELINE	CANDIDA
LAVINA	MONICA	SIBBIE	ADRIANA	CARLEEN
LEANNE	MURIEL	SIDONY	AINSLEY	CARLENE
LEILAH	MYRTLE	SIENNA	AINSLIE	CARMELA
LENNIE	NADINE	SILVIA	AISLING	CAROLYN
LENORE	NELLIE	SIMONA	AISLINN	CECILIA
LEONIE	NERINA	SIMONE	ALBERTA	CECILIE
LESLEY	NESSIE	SINEAD	ALBINIA	CEINWEN
LESLIE	NETTIE	SISLEY	ALBREDA	CELESTE
LETTIE	NICOLA	SISSIE	ALDREDA	CHARITY
LIANNE	NICOLE	SOPHIA	ALEDWEN	CHARLEY
LIESEL	NOELLE	SOPHIE	ALETHEA	CHARLIE
LILIAN	NOREEN	SORCHA	ALFREDA	CHATTIE
LILIAS	ODETTE	STACEY	ALLEGRA	CHRISSY
LILITH	ODILIA	STELLA	ALLISON	CHRISTY
LILLAH	OLIVET	STEVIE	ALOISIA	CLARICE
LILLIE	OLIVIA	SYLVIA	ALOYSIA	CLARRIE
LINNET	OONAGH	SYLVIE	ANNABEL	CLAUDIA
LIZZIE	ORIANA	TAMARA	ANNAPLE	CLODAGH
LLINOS	PAMELA	TAMSIN	ANNETTE	COLETTE
LOLITA	PATTIE	TANITH	ANOUSKA	COLLEEN
LOREEN	PEPITA	TASMIN	ANSELMA	CORALIE
LOTTIE	PETULA	TEGWEN	ANSTICE	CORINNA
LOUISA	PHEMIE	TERESA	ANTOINE	CORINNE
LOUISE	PHOEBE	TESSIE	ANTONIA	CRYSTAL
LUCINA	PORTIA	THECLA	ARIADNE	CYNTHIA
LUELLA	PRISCA	THEKLA	ARIANNA	DAMARIS
MADDIE	PRISSY	THELMA	ARLETTA	DANETTE
MAGGIE	QUEENA	THIRSA	ARLETTE	DARLENE
MAHALA	QUEENY	THIRZA	ASPASIA	DAVINIA
MAIDIE	RACHEL	TIRZAH	AUGUSTA	DEBORAH
MAIRIN	RAMONA	TRACEY	AURELIA	DEIRDRE
MAISIE	REGINA	TRICIA	AUREOLA	DELILAH
MARCIA	RENATA	TRISHA	AUREOLE	DEMELZA
MARCIE	RHONDA	TRIXIE	AVELINE	DESIREE
MARGIE	ROBINA	TRUDIE	BABETTE	DIAMOND
MARGOT	ROISIN	ULRICA	BARBARA	DOLORES
MARIAM	ROSINA	URSULA	BARBARY	DONALDA
MARIAN	ROSITA	VASHTI	BASILIA	DORETTE
MARIEL	ROSLYN	VERENA	BASILIE	DORINDA
MARINA	ROWENA	VERITY	BASILLA	DOROTHY
MARION	ROXANA	VERONA	BEATRIX	DYMPHNA
			BEATTIE	

EILUNED	JOHANNA	MEHALAH	ROSELYN	ARAMINTA
ELDREDA	JONQUIL	MEHALIA	ROSETTA	BEATRICE
ELEANOR	JOSEPHA	MEIRION	ROSSLYN	BERENICE
ELFREDA	JOSETTE	MELANIA	ROXANNA	BEVERLEY
ELFRIDA	JUANITA	MELANIE	ROXANNE	BIRGITTA
ELSPETH	JULIANA	MELINDA	RUPERTA	BRIGITTA
EMELINE	JULITTA	MELIORA	SABRINA	BRIGITTE
EMERALD	JUSTINA	MELISSA	SAFFRON	BRITTANY
ESTELLA	JUSTINE	MELODIE	SANCHIA	BRUNETTA
ESTELLE	KATHRYN	MELVINA	SARANNA	CARLOTTA
EUGENIA	KATRINA	MERILYN	SCARLET	CAROLINA
EUGENIE	KATRINE	MERRION	SEPTIMA	CAROLINE
EULALIA	KETURAH	MICHELE	SHANNON	CATHLEEN
EULALIE	KIRSTEN	MILDRED	SHARRON	CATRIONA
EVELEEN	KRISTEN	MINERVA	SHEILAH	CERIDWEN
EVELINA	KRISTIN	MIRABEL	SHELAGH	CHARISSA
EVELINE	LARAINE	MIRANDA	SHELLEY	CHARLENE
FABIANA	LARISSA	MODESTY	SHIRLEY	CHARMIAN
FELICIA	LAUREEN	MONIQUE	SIBELLA	CHRISSIE
FENELLA	LAURINA	MYFANWY	SIBILLA	CHRISTIE
FEODORA	LAVERNE	NANETTE	SIBYLLA	CLARIBEL
FIDELIA	LAVINIA	NATALIA	SIDONIA	CLARINDA
FLORRIE	LEONORA	NATALIE	SIDONIE	CLARISSA
FLOSSIE	LETITIA	NATASHA	SILVANA	CLAUDINE
FORTUNE	LETTICE	NERISSA	SIOBHAN	CLEMENCE
FRANCES	LILLIAN	NICHOLA	SUSANNA	CLEMENCY
FRANCIE	LILLIAS	NINETTE	SUSANNE	CLOTILDA
FRANKIE	LINDSAY	NOELEEN	SUZANNA	CONCEPTA
FRANNIE	LINDSEY	NOELINE	SUZANNE	CONCETTA
GENEVRA	LINETTE	OCTAVIA	SUZETTE	CORDELIA
GEORGIA	LISBETH	OLYMPIA	SYBELLA	CORNELIA
GEORGIE	LISETTE	OPHELIA	SYBILLA	COURTNEY
GILLIAN	LIZANNE	OTTILIA	TABITHA	CRESSIDA
GINETTE	LIZBETH	OTTILIE	TALITHA	CYTHEREA
GINEVRA	LORAINE	PAMELIA	TATIANA	DANIELLA
GISELLE	LORETTA	PANDORA	THERESA	DANIELLE
GRAINNE	LORETTE	PASCALE	THÉRÈSE	DELPHINE
GRIZZEL	LORINDA	PAULINE	TIFFANY	DIONYSIA
GWLADYS	LOUELLA	PEARLIE	TRISSIE	DOMINICA
GWYNEDD	LOVEDAY	PERDITA	VALERIA	DOROTHEA
GWYNETH	LUCASTA	PERONEL	VALERIE	DOWSABEL
HALCYON	LUCETTA	PETRINA	VANESSA	DRUSILLA
HARRIET	LUCETTE	PHILLIS	VENETIA	ELEANORA
HEATHER	LUCIANA	PHYLLIS	VIVIANA	ELEONORA
HÉLOÏSE	LUCILLA	QUEENIE	YOLANDA	EMANUELA
HEULWEN	LUCILLE	RACHAEL	YOLANDE	EMMELINE
HILLARY	LUCINDA	RAELENE	ZENOBIA	EUPHEMIA
HONORIA	LUCRECE	RAFAELA	ZULEIKA	EUSTACIA
HORATIA	LYNETTE	REBECCA		FAUSTINA
HYPATIA	MABELLA	REBEKAH	**8**	FELICITY
ISADORA	MABELLE	RHONWEN	ADELAIDE	FLORENCE
ISIDORA	MADISON	RICARDA	ADELHEID	FLORETTA
JACINTA	MAHALAH	RICHMAL	ADRIANNE	FLORETTE
JACINTH	MAHALIA	ROBERTA	ADRIENNE	FLORINDA
JANETTA	MALVINA	ROMAINE	ANGELICA	FRANCINE
JANETTE	MANUELA	RONALDA	ANGELINA	FREDRICA
JASMINE	MARILYN	ROSABEL	ANGELINE	FREDRIKA
JEANNIE	MARISSA	ROSALIA	ANGHARAD	GEORGINA
JENIFER	MARLENE	ROSALIE	ANNALISA	GERMAINE
JESSICA	MARTINA	ROSALYN	ANTONINA	GERTRUDE
JILLIAN	MARTINE	ROSANNA	ANTONNIA	GILBERTA
JOCASTA	MATILDA	ROSANNE	APPOLINA	GRETCHEN
JOCELYN	MAUREEN	ROSEANN	APPOLINE	GRISELDA
			ARABELLA	

GULIELMA
GWYNNETH
HADASSAH
HELEWISE
HEPZIBAH
HERMIONE
HORTENSE
HYACINTH
INGEBORG
IOLANTHE
ISABELLA
ISABELLE
JACOBINA
JAMESINA
JEANETTE
JEANNINE
JENNIFER
JESSAMYN
JOSCELIN
JULIANNE
JULIENNE
JULIETTE
KATHLEEN
KIMBERLY
KRISTINA
KRISTINE
LAETITIA
LARRAINE
LAURAINE
LAURETTA
LAURETTE
LAURINDA
LORRAINE
LUCIENNE
LUCRETIA
LUCREZIA
LYNNETTE
MADELINA
MADELINE
MAGDALEN
MAGNOLIA
MARCELLA
MARCELLE
MARGARET
MARIAMNE
MARIANNE
MARIETTA
MARIETTE
MARIGOLD
MARJORIE
MELICENT
MELISENT
MELLONEY
MERCEDES
MEREDITH
MERRILYN
MICHAELA
MICHELLE

MORWENNA
MYRTILLA
PATIENCE
PATRICIA
PAULETTE
PENELOPE
PERPETUA
PHILIPPA
PHILLIDA
PHILLIPA
PHYLLIDA
PRIMROSE
PRUDENCE
PRUNELLA
RAPHAELA
RAYMONDE
RHIANNON
RICHENDA
ROCHELLE
RONNETTE
ROSALEEN
ROSALIND
ROSALINE
ROSAMOND
ROSAMUND
ROSEANNA
ROSEANNE
ROSELINE
ROSEMARY
SAMANTHA
SAPPHIRA
SAPPHIRE
SCARLETT
SHEELAGH
SHUSHANA
STEFANIE
SUSANNAH
TALLULAH
TAMASINE
THEODORA
THERESIA
THOMASIN
TIMOTHEA
TRYPHENA
VERONICA
VICTORIA
VIOLETTA
VIOLETTE
VIRGINIA
VIVIENNE
WALBURGA
WILFREDA
WILFRIDA
WINEFRED
WINIFRED

9
ALBERTINA

ALBERTINE
ALEXANDRA
AMARYLLIS
AMBROSINA
AMBROSINE
ANASTASIA
ANGELIQUE
ANNABELLA
ANNABELLE
ANNELIESE
APOLLONIA
ARTEMISIA
ARTHURINA
ARTHURINE
AUGUSTINA
BATHSHEBA
BENEDICTA
BERNADINA
BERNADINE
BRITANNIA
CARMELITA
CASSANDRA
CATHARINE
CATHERINE
CELESTINA
CELESTINE
CHARLOTTE
CHARMAINE
CHRISTIAN
CHRISTINA
CHRISTINE
CHRISTMAS
CLAUDETTE
CLEMENTIA
CLEOPATRA
COLUMBINA
COLUMBINE
CONSTANCE
CONSTANCY
COURTENAY
DESDEMONA
DOMINIQUE
DONALDINA
ELISABETH
ELIZABETH
EMMANUELA
ERNESTINE
ESMERALDA
ETHELINDA
FIONNUALA
FRANCESCA
FRANCISCA
FREDERICA
FREDERIKA
GABRIELLA
GABRIELLE
GENEVIEVE
GEORGETTE

GEORGIANA
GERALDINE
GHISLAINE
GUENDOLEN
GUINEVERE
GWENDOLEN
GWENDOLYN
GWENLLIAN
HARRIETTE
HENRIETTA
HENRIETTE
HEPHZIBAH
HILDEGARD
HIPPOLYTA
HORTENSIA
HYACINTHA
JACQUELYN
JACQUETTA
JEANNETTE
JESSAMINE
JOSEPHINE
KATHARINE
KATHERINE
KIMBERLEY
LAURENCIA
LAURENTIA
MADELEINE
MAGDALENA
MAGDALENE
MARGARETA
MARGARITA
MEHETABEL
MEHITABEL
MÉLISANDE
MILLICENT
MIRABELLA
MIRABELLE
NICOLETTE
PARTHENIA
PHILLIPPA
PHILOMENA
PLEASANCE
POLLYANNA
PRISCILLA
ROSABELLA
ROSABELLE
ROSALINDA
ROSEMARIE
SERAPHINA
SHUSHANNA
SOPHRONIA
STEPHANIE
THEODOSIA
THEOPHILA
THOMASINA
THOMASINE
VALENTINA
VALENTINE

VÉRONIQUE
VICTORINE
VINCENTIA
WINNIFRED

10
ALEXANDRIA
ALPHONSINE
ANTOINETTE
ARTHURETTA
BERENGARIA
BERNADETTE
BERNARDINA
BERNARDINE
CHRISTABEL
CHRISTIANA
CINDERELLA
CLEMENTINA
CLEMENTINE
CONSTANTIA
DULCIBELLA
ERMINTRUDE
ERMYNTRUDE
ETHELDREDA
EVANGELINA
EVANGELINE
GILBERTINE
GWENDOLINE
HILDEGARDE
JACQUELINE
KINBOROUGH
MARGARETTA
MARGUERITA
MARGUERITE
MARIABELLA
MILBOROUGH
PETRONELLA
PETRONILLA
TEMPERANCE
THEOPHANIA
WILHELMINA
WILLIAMINA

11
ALEXANDRINA
CHRISTIANIA
FIONNGHUALA

12
KERENHAPPUCH
PHILADELPHIA

439

BOYS' NAMES

2	LYN	BRAD	IFOR	OTHO
AL	MAT	BRAM	IGOR	OTIS
CY	MAX	BRET	IOLO	OTTO
ED	MEL	BRYN	IVAN	OWEN
TY	NAT	BURT	IVES	PAUL
	NED	CARL	IVOR	PETE
3	NYE	CARY	JACK	PHIL
ABE	ODO	CERI	JAGO	RAFE
ALF	PAT	CHAD	JAKE	REED
ART	PIP	CHAS	JEFF	RENÉ
ASA	RAB	CHAY	JOCK	RHYS
BAS	RAY	CLEM	JOEL	RICH
BAT	REG	COLE	JOEY	RICK
BAZ	REX	COLM	JOHN	ROLF
BEN	ROB	CONN	JOSÉ	ROLY
BOB	ROD	CURT	JOSH	RORY
BUD	RON	DALE	JUAN	ROSS
CAI	ROY	DANA	JUDD	RUDI
DAI	SAM	DAVE	JUDE	RUDY
DAN	SEB	DAVY	KANE	RUSS
DEE	SID	DEAN	KARL	RYAN
DEL	SIM	DEWI	KEIR	SAUL
DES	STU	DICK	KENT	SEAN
DON	SYD	DION	KIAN	SETH
DUD	TAM	DIRK	KING	SHAW
ELI	TED	DOUG	KIRK	SHEM
ERN	TEL	DREW	KRIS	STAN
GIB	TEX	DUKE	KURT	STEW
GIL	TIM	EARL	KYLE	THEO
GUS	TOM	EBEN	LARS	THOM
GUY	VIC	EDDY	LEON	TOBY
HAL	VIN	EDEN	LIEV	TODD
HAM	WAL	EDOM	LEVI	TONY
HEW	WAT	EMIL	LIAM	TREV
HOB	WIN	ENOS	LORI	TROY
HUW	ZAK	ERIC	LORN	VERE
IAN		ERIK	LUCA	VICK
IKE	**4**	ERLE	LUDO	WADE
IRA	ABEL	ESAU	LUKE	WALT
IVO	ADAM	ESME	LYLE	WARD
JAN	ALAN	EVAN	MARC	WILF
JAY	ALDO	EWAN	MARK	WILL
JED	ALEC	EWEN	MATT	WYNN
JEM	ALED	EZRA	MERV	YVES
JIM	ALEX	FRED	MICK	ZACK
JOB	ALGY	GARY	MIKE	ZANE
JOE	ALUN	GENE	MILO	ZEKE
JON	ALVA	GLEN	MORT	
KAY	AMOS	GLYN	MOSS	**5**
KAI	ANDY	GREG	MUIR	AARON
KEN	ARLO	GWYN	NEAL	ABNER
KIM	ARTY	HAMO	NEIL	ABRAM
KIT	AXEL	HANK	NICK	ADAIR
LEE	BART	HANS	NOAH	ADOLF
LEN	BEAU	HERB	NOEL	AIDAN
LEO	BERT	HUEY	NORM	AIDEN
LES	BILL	HUGH	OLAF	ALAIN
LEW	BING	HUGO	OLAV	ALBAN
LEX	BOAZ	IAGO	OMAR	ALBIN
LOU	BOYD	IAIN	OSSY	ALDEN

ALDIS	CALEB	EMILE	JONAS	OSWIN
ALDUS	CALUM	EMLYN	JUDAH	OWAIN
ALFIE	CAREY	EMRYS	JUDAS	OZZIE
ALGAR	CARLO	ENOCH	JULES	PABLO
ALGER	CAROL	EPPIE	KAROL	PADDY
ALGIE	CASEY	ERNIE	KEITH	PAOLO
ALICK	CECIL	ERROL	KENNY	PARRY
ALLAN	CHRIS	ETHAN	KEVIN	PEDRO
ALLEN	CHUCK	FARON	KIRBY	PERCE
ALVAH	CLARK	FELIX	LABAN	PERCY
ALVAR	CLAUD	FIDEL	LANCE	PERRY
ALVIE	CLIFF	FLOYD	LANTY	PETER
ALVIN	CLINT	FRANK	LARRY	PIERS
ALVIS	CLIVE	GAIUS	LAURI	PIRAN
ALWYN	CLYDE	GARRY	LEIGH	QUINN
AMIAS	COLIN	GARTH	LEROY	RALPH
AMYAS	COLUM	GAVIN	LEWIS	RAMON
ANCEL	CONAN	GEOFF	LLOYD	RANDY
ANDRÉ	CONOR	GERRY	LOGAN	RAOUL
ANGEL	COSMO	GILES	LOREN	RICKI
ANGUS	CRAIG	GLENN	LORIN	RICKY
ANSEL	CUDDY	GRANT	LORNE	RIKKI
ANTON	CYRIL	GREGG	LOUIE	ROALD
ARCHY	CYRUS	GUIDO	LOUIS	ROBIN
ARMIN	DAMON	GYLES	LUCAS	RODDY
ARTIE	DANNY	HAMON	LYULF	RODGE
ASHER	DANTE	HARDY	MADOC	ROGER
ATHOL	DARBY	HARRY	MANNY	ROLLO
AULAY	DARCY	HAYDN	MANUS	ROLLY
AVERY	DARYL	HEATH	MARCO	ROLPH
BARON	DAVID	HEBER	MARIO	ROMAN
BARRY	DENIS	HENRI	MARTY	ROWAN
BASIE	DENNY	HENRY	MASON	ROYAL
BASIL	DENYS	HERVÉ	MATEO	RUFUS
BENET	DERBY	HIRAM	MICAH	RYDER
BENJY	DEREK	HOMER	MICKY	SACHA
BENNY	DERRY	HONOR	MILES	SAMMY
BERNY	DERYK	HORRY	MITCH	SAXON
BERRY	DEWEY	HOWEL	MONTE	SCOTT
BEVIS	DICKY	HUMPH	MONTY	SELBY
BILLY	DIGBY	HYMAN	MORAY	SERGE
BJORN	DONAL	HYMIE	MORTY	SHANE
BLAIR	DONNY	HYWEL	MOSES	SHAUN
BLAKE	DORAN	IDRIS	MOSHE	SHAWN
BLANE	DROGO	INIGO	MUNGO	SILAS
BLASE	DUANE	IRVIN	MYLES	SIMON
BOBBY	DYLAN	IRWIN	MYRON	SOLLY
BONAR	EAMON	ISAAC	NEDDY	SOREN
BORIS	EDDIE	ITHEL	NEILL	STEVE
BOYCE	EDGAR	IZAAK	NEVIL	TAFFY
BRENT	EDWIN	JABEZ	NIALL	TEDDY
BRETT	EDWYN	JACKY	NICKY	TERRI
BRIAN	ELDON	JACOB	NICOL	TERRY
BRICE	ELIAS	JAMES	NIGEL	TIMMY
BROCK	ELIHU	JAMIE	NIKKI	TITUS
BRUCE	ELIOT	JARED	NOLAN	TOLLY
BRUNO	ELLIS	JASON	OGDEN	TOMMY
BRYAN	ELMER	JEMMY	OLAVE	TUDOR
BRYCE	ELTON	JERRY	OLLIE	ULRIC
BYRON	ELVIN	JESSE	ORSON	UPTON
CADEL	ELVIS	JESUS	ORVAL	URBAN
CADEN	ELWYN	JIMMY	OSCAR	URIAH
CAIUS	EMERY	JONAH	OSSIE	VINCE

VITUS	BUSTER	EUGENE	IRVING	MARTYN
WALDO	CADELL	EVELYN	ISAIAH	MARVIN
WALLY	CAESAR	FABIAN	ISRAEL	MARVYN
WAYNE	CALLUM	FARRAN	JACKIE	MELVIN
WILLY	CALVIN	FARREN	JACQUI	MELVYN
WYATT	CARLOS	FERGIE	JARRED	MERLIN
WYNNE	CAROLE	FERGUS	JARROD	MERTON
	CARTER	FINLAY	JARVIS	MERVIN
6	CASPAR	FLURRY	JASPER	MERVYN
ADOLPH	CEDRIC	FRANCO	JAYDEN	MICKEY
ADRIAN	CERDIC	FRASER	JENSON	MILTON
AENEAS	CLAUDE	FRAZER	JEREMY	MORGAN
ALARIC	COLLEY	FREDDY	JEROME	MORRIS
ALBANY	CONNOR	GARETH	JETHRO	MURRAY
ALBERT	CONRAD	GARNET	JOHNNY	NATHAN
ALDOUS	CORMAC	GARRET	JOLYON	NEDDIE
ALDRED	CORNEY	GASPAR	JORDAN	NELSON
ALDWIN	COSIMO	GAWAIN	JOSEPH	NEWTON
ALDWYN	CUDDIE	GEORGE	JOSHUA	NINIAN
ALEXIS	CURTIS	GERALD	JOSIAH	NORMAN
ALFRED	DAFYDD	GERARD	JOSIAS	NORRIS
ALONSO	DAMIAN	GERWYN	JOTHAM	NORTON
ALONZO	DAMIEN	GETHIN	JULIAN	NOWELL
ALURED	DANIEL	GIDEON	JULIUS	OBERON
ANDREW	DANYON	GILROY	JUNIOR	OLIVER
ANGELO	DARREL	GODWIN	JUSTIN	ORRELL
ANSELL	DARREN	GORDON	KELVIN	OSBERT
ANSELM	DARRYL	GRAEME	KENDAL	OSBORN
ANTONY	DECLAN	GRAHAM	KENELM	OSMOND
AQUILA	DENNIS	GREGOR	KENTON	OSMUND
ARCHER	DENZIL	GROVER	KESTER	OSWALD
ARCHIE	DERMOT	GUNTER	KIERAN	PALMER
ARMAND	DERYCK	GUSSIE	LANDON	PARKER
ARNAUD	DEXTER	GUSTAF	LAUNCE	PASCAL
ARNOLD	DICKIE	GUSTAV	LAUREN	PASCOE
ARTHUR	DICKON	GWILYM	LAURIE	PELHAM
ASHLEY	DILLON	GWYLIM	LAWRIE	PHILIP
ASHTON	DONALD	HAMISH	LAYTON	PIERRE
AUBERT	DORIAN	HAMLET	LEMUEL	POLDIE
AUBREY	DOUGAL	HAMLYN	LENNOX	PRINCE
AUGUST	DOUGIE	HAMNET	LESLIE	QUINCY
AUSTEN	DUDLEY	HARLEY	LESTER	RABBIE
AUSTIN	DUGALD	HAROLD	LIONEL	RAFAEL
AYLMER	DUGGIE	HARVEY	LONNIE	RAINER
AYLWIN	DUNCAN	HAYDEN	LOVELL	RAMSAY
BAILEY	DURAND	HAYDON	LOWELL	RAMSEY
BALDIE	DUSTIN	HECTOR	LUCIAN	RANALD
BARNET	DWAYNE	HEDLEY	LUCIEN	RANDAL
BARNEY	DWIGHT	HERBIE	LUCIUS	RAYNER
BARRIE	EAMONN	HERMAN	LUTHER	RAYNOR
BARRON	EASTER	HERVEY	LYNDON	REGGIE
BARTLE	EDMOND	HILARY	LYULPH	REUBEN
BENITO	EDMUND	HOBART	MAGNUS	RICHIE
BENNET	EDWARD	HOLDEN	MALISE	ROBBIE
BERNIE	EGBERT	HONOUR	MALORY	ROBERT
BERTIE	ELDRED	HORACE	MALVIN	RODGER
BETHEL	ELIJAH	HOWARD	MANLEY	RODNEY
BILLIE	ELLERY	HOWELL	MANSEL	ROLAND
BLAINE	ELLIOT	HUBERT	MANUEL	RONALD
BLAISE	EMMETT	HUDSON	MARCEL	RONNIE
BOBBIE	EOGHAN	HUGHIE	MARCUS	RUDOLF
BONAMY	ERNEST	INGRAM	MARIUS	RUPERT
BOTOLF	ESMOND	IRVINE	MARTIN	RUSSEL
BOTULF				

SAMSON	ANEURIN	ERASMUS	LEOLINE	STANLEY
SAMUEL	ANTHONY	EUSTACE	LEONARD	STEPHEN
SEAMUS	ANTONIO	EVERARD	LEOPOLD	STEWART
SEFTON	ARTEMAS	EZEKIEL	LINCOLN	SWITHIN
SELWYN	ARTEMUS	FEARGUS	LINDSAY	TANCRED
SERGEI	ATTICUS	FITZROY	LORENZO	TERENCE
SERGIO	AUBERON	FLORIAN	LUDOVIC	TERTIUS
SEUMAS	AZARIAH	FRANCIS	MALACHI	THORLEY
SEWARD	BALDWIN	FRANKIE	MALACHY	TIMOTHY
SEXTUS	BARCLAY	FREDDIE	MALCOLM	TORQUIL
SHAMUS	BARNABY	FREDRIC	MALLORY	TRAVERS
SHELLY	BARNARD	FULBERT	MANFRED	TRISTAN
SHOLTO	BARRETT	GABRIEL	MANSELL	ULYSSES
SIDNEY	BARTLET	GARRETT	MATTHEW	VAUGHAN
SIMEON	BASTIAN	GARRICK	MAURICE	VINCENT
STEVEN	BEDFORD	GAYLORD	MAXWELL	WALLACE
STEVIE	BENNETT	GEORDIE	MAYNARD	WARWICK
ST JOHN	BENTLEY	GEORGIE	MEIRION	WENDELL
STUART	BERNARD	GERAINT	MERRION	WILBERT
SYDNEY	BERTRAM	GERRARD	MICHAEL	WILFRED
TALBOT	BETHELL	GERSHOM	MILBURN	WILFRID
TAYLOR	BOTOLPH	GERVAIS	MONTAGU	WILLARD
TEDDIE	BRADLEY	GERVASE	MURDOCH	WILLIAM
THOMAS	BRANDAN	GILBERT	MURTAGH	WINDSOR
TOBIAS	BRANDON	GILLEAN	NEVILLE	WINFRED
TRAVIS	BRENDAN	GILLIAN	NICOLAS	WINFRID
TREFOR	CAMERON	GODFREY	NORBERT	WINSTON
TREVOR	CARADOC	GOLDWIN	OBADIAH	WOODROW
TYBALT	CARADOG	GOLDWYN	OLIVIER	WYNDHAM
TYRONE	CARLTON	GRAHAME	ORLANDO	WYNFORD
VAUGHN	CAROLUS	GRAYSON	ORVILLE	ZACHARY
VERNON	CEDRYCH	GREGORY	OSBORNE	
VICTOR	CHARLES	GUNTHER	PADRAIG	**8**
VIRGIL	CHARLEY	GUSTAVE	PATRICK	ADOLPHUS
WALLIS	CHARLIE	GWYNFOR	PHILLIP	ALASDAIR
WALTER	CHAUNCY	HADRIAN	PHINEAS	ALASTAIR
WARNER	CHESTER	HAMMOND	PRESTON	ALGERNON
WARREN	CHRISTY	HARTLEY	QUENTIN	ALISTAIR
WESLEY	CLAYTON	HERBERT	QUINTIN	ALOYSIUS
WILBUR	CLEDWYN	HERMANN	RANDALL	ALPHONSE
WILLIE	CLEMENT	HILLARY	RAPHAEL	ALPHONSO
WILLIS	CLIFTON	HORATIO	RAYMOND	AUGUSTIN
WILMER	CLINTON	HUMBERT	REDVERS	AUGUSTUS
WILMOT	COLUMBA	ICHABOD	REYNARD	AURELIAN
WINNIE	CRISPIN	ISIDORE	REYNOLD	BARDOLPH
WYBERT	CRYSTAL	JACKSON	RICARDO	BARNABAS
WYSTAN	CYPRIAN	JACQUES	RICHARD	BARTLETT
XAVIER	DARRELL	JAPHETH	RODOLPH	BENEDICK
YEHUDI	DECIMUS	JEFFERY	RODRIGO	BENEDICT
	DENHOLM	JEFFREY	ROWLAND	BENJAMIN
7	DERRICK	JILLIAN	ROYSTON	BERENGER
ABRAHAM	DESMOND	JOACHIM	RUDOLPH	BERKELEY
ABSALOM	DIGGORY	JOCELYN	RUSSELL	BERNHARD
ABSOLON	DOMINIC	JOHNNIE	SALAMON	BERTHOLD
ADAMNAN	DONOVAN	KENDALL	SAMPSON	BERTRAND
ADOLPHE	DOUGLAS	KENNETH	SERGIUS	BEVERLEY
AINSLEY	DUNSTAN	KENRICK	SEYMOUR	BONIFACE
AINSLIE	EARNEST	KIMBALL	SHANNON	CAMILLUS
ALBERIC	ELEAZAR	LACHLAN	SHELDON	CAMPBELL
ALDHELM	ELKANAH	LAMBERT	SHELLEY	CARLETON
ALFONSO	ELLIOTT	LAZARUS	SIGMUND	CARTHACH
AMBROSE	EMANUEL	LEANDER	SOLOMON	CHARLTON
ANDREAS	EPHRAIM	LEOFRIC	SPENCER	CHAUNCEY
ANEIRIN				CHRISTIE

CHRYSTAL
CLARENCE
CLAUDIUS
CLIFFORD
CONSTANT
COURTNEY
CRISPIAN
CUTHBERT
DIARMAIT
DIARMUID
DOMINICK
EBENEZER
EMMANUEL
ETHELRED
FARQUHAR
FERNANDO
FLETCHER
FLORENCE
FLUELLEN
FRANKLIN
FREDERIC
FREDRICK
GAMALIEL
GARFIELD
GEOFFREY
GRAYBURN
GRIFFITH
GUSTAVUS
HAMILTON
HANNIBAL
HARRISON
HERCULES
HEREWARD
HEZEKIAH
HUMPHREY

IGNATIUS
IORWERTH
JEDIDIAH
JEPHTHAH
JEREMIAH
JEREMIAS
JERMAINE
JOHANNES
JONATHAN
JOSCELIN
KIMBERLY
KINGSLEY
LANCELOT
LAURENCE
LAWRENCE
LEIGHTON
LLEWELYN
MANASSEH
MANASSES
MARSHALL
MATTHIAS
MELVILLE
MEREDITH
MITCHELL
MOHAMMED
MONTAGUE
MORDECAI
MORTIMER
MUHAMMED
NAPOLEON
NEHEMIAH
NICHOLAS
OCTAVIAN
OCTAVIUS
PERCEVAL

PERCIVAL
PHILEMON
PHINEHAS
RADCLIFF
RANDOLPH
REGINALD
RODERICK
SALVADOR
SEPTIMUS
SHERIDAN
SILVANUS
SINCLAIR
STAFFORD
STANFORD
STIRLING
SYLVANUS
TALIESIN
TERRENCE
THADDEUS
THEOBALD
THEODORE
THORNTON
THURSTAN
THURSTON
TRISTRAM
TURLOUGH
WINTHROP
ZEDEKIAH

9
ALEXANDER
ALPHONSUS
AMBROSIUS
ARCHELAUS
ARCHIBALD

ATHELSTAN
AUGUSTINE
BALTHASAR
BALTHAZAR
BRODERICK
CADWALADR
CHRISTIAN
CHRISTMAS
CORNELIUS
COURTENAY
DIONYSIUS
ENDEAVOUR
ETHELBERT
FERDINAND
FRANCESCO
FRANCISCO
FREDERICK
GERONTIUS
GRANVILLE
GRENVILLE
JEFFERSON
KENTIGERN
KIMBERLEY
LAUNCELOT
LLEWELLYN
MARCELLUS
MARMADUKE
NATHANAEL
NATHANIEL
NICODEMUS
ONUPHRIUS
PEREGRINE
PHILIBERT
RADCLIFFE
SALVATORE

SEBASTIAN
SIEGFRIED
SIGISMUND
SILVESTER
STANISLAS
SYLVESTER
THEODORIC
VALENTINE
ZACCHAEUS
ZACHARIAH
ZACHARIAS
ZECHARIAH
ZEPHANIAH

10
BARRINGTON
CARACTACUS
FORTUNATUS
HIERONYMUS
HILDEBRAND
HIPPOLYTUS
MAXIMILIAN
MONTGOMERY
STANISLAUS
THEOPHILUS
WASHINGTON
WILLOUGHBY

11
BARTHOLOMEW
CADWALLADER
CHRISTOPHER
CONSTANTINE
SACHEVERELL

INDEX

Entries in bold face type (e.g. **COUNTRIES OF THE WORLD** 1) refer to sections, tables, or lists in the text, with their page numbers. Other index entries suggest tables that might be useful (e.g. SHELLS see SEASHELLS, or INSTRUMENT try MUSICAL INSTRUMENTS; TOOLS. We have also included a selection of cue words for cryptic clues (e.g. the word ZERO often indicates the letter O).

F

FAMOUS BUILDINGS AND STRUCTURES 164
FAMOUS SHIPS 208
FASHION see section CLOTHES, MATERIALS, AND FASHION
FASHION DESIGNERS 132
FEAR try PHOBIAS BY FEAR; PHOBIAS BY NAME
FERNS 74
FESTIVAL try RELIGIOUS FESTIVALS
F1 GRAND PRIX CIRCUITS 346
FICTIONAL CHARACTERS 174; see also CARTOON CHARACTERS; CHARACTERS FROM JANE AUSTEN; CHARACTERS FROM LEWIS CARROLL'S 'ALICE' BOOKS; CHARACTERS FROM NURSERY RHYMES; CHARACTERS FROM OPERA; CHARACTERS FROM ROWLING'S 'HARRY POTTER'; CHARACTERS FROM THE TALES OF ROBIN HOOD; CHARACTERS FROM TOLKIEN'S 'LORD OF THE RINGS'; CHARACTERS FROM TROLLOPE; CHARACTERS FROM WALTER SCOTT; DICKENSIAN CHARACTERS; FICTIONAL DETECTIVES; GILBERT AND SULLIVAN; LOVERS OF FACT AND FICTION
FICTIONAL DETECTIVES 198
FIFTY may indicate the letter L (Roman numeral)
FILM STARS try STAGE AND SCREEN PERSONALITIES
FIGURES OF SPEECH 156
FIRST CLASS CRICKETING COUNTIES 342
FIRST NAMES 434–444
FISH 63
FISHING try ANGLING TERMS
FIVE may indicate the letter V (Roman numeral)
FIVE HUNDRED may indicate the letter D (Roman numeral)
FLIGHT try AIRCRAFT; INTERNATIONAL AIRPORTS
FLOWERS 68 try PARTS OF A FLOWER; PLANT PEOPLE; may also indicate a river (something that flows)
FLOWERS see PLANTS AND FLOWERS
FOOD AND DRINK 318–332
FOOTBALL see AMERICAN FOOTBALL TEAMS; BRITISH FOOTBALL TEAMS; EUROPEAN FOOTBALL CLUBS; MAJOR RUGBY UNION CLUBS; RUGBY LEAGUE CLUBS
FOREIGN WORDS 366; see also FRENCH PHRASES; LATIN PHRASES; NUMBERS
FORMER EUROPEAN CURRENCIES 11
FOUR may indicate the letters IV (Roman numeral)
FRENCH PHRASES 368; see also FOREIGN WORDS
FRENCH REGIONS 15
FRUIT, VEGETABLES, AND PULSES 73
FRUITS AND NUTS 325
FUNGI 74
FURNITURE 153
FURNITURE TERMS 154

G

GALLERIES 160
GAMES 334; see also CARD GAMES; COMPUTER GAMES; EXTREME SPORTS; PATIENCE GAMES
GAMES POSITIONS 339

GARB try CLOTHES
GARDEN FLOWERS see GARDENING; see also PLANTS AND FLOWERS
GARDENING 346
GARDENING TERMS see GARDENING
GEAR try CLOTHES
GEMSTONES 241; see also BIRTHSTONES; JEWELLERY
GENDER try ANIMALS AND THEIR GENDER
GEOGRAPHY 1–51
GEOLOGICAL TIME SCALE 236; see also EARLY HOMINIDS; PREHISTORIC ANIMALS
GEOMETRIC FIGURES AND CURVES 227 see also MATHEMATICAL TERMS
GERMAN STATES 16
GILBERT AND SULLIVAN 201
GIRLS' NAMES 434
GIVEN NAME see BOYS' NAMES; GIRLS' NAMES
GLANDS 246
GLASS see TYPES OF GLASS
GODS try AFRICAN MYTHOLOGY; AUSTRALIAN MYTHOLOGY; CELTIC MYTHOLOGY; CENTRAL AND SOUTH AMERICAN MYTHOLOGY; EGYPTIAN MYTHOLOGY; GREEK AND ROMAN MYTHOLOGY; HINDU DEITIES; NORSE MYTHOLOGY; NORTH AMERICAN MYTHOLOGY
GOLF TERMS 352
GOVERNMENT see section HISTORY, POLITICS, GOVERNMENT, AND LAW
GRAND PRIX CIRCUITS 346
GRASSES, SEDGES, AND RUSHES 75
GREEK ALPHABET 365
GREEK DISHES 328
GREEK AND ROMAN MYTHOLOGY 264
GUNNER may indicate the letters RA

H

HAIRDRESSING 315
HAT try CLOTHES
HEADING may indicate the first letter of a word to be used in forming a new word
HEALTH 243–254
HEARD try HOMOPHONES
HEBREW ALPHABET 365
HERALDIC TERMS 359
HERBS AND SPICES 322
HILLS 43
HINDU DEITIES 263
HISTORY, POLITICS, GOVERNMENT, AND LAW 206–215
HOBBIES 338
HOLY may indicate the letters ST
HOMES try ANIMAL HOMES; BRITISH CASTLES; STATELY HOMES
HOMINIDS 237
HOMOPHONES 395; words that sound like other words but have a different spelling, e.g. pear, pair. The following words may indicate a

homophone: sounds like, utter, said, heard, they say.

HOOD see CHARACTERS FROM THE TALES OF ROBIN HOOD

HOP try DANCES

HORSES see BREEDS OF HORSES AND PONIES; POINTS OF A HORSE

HORSES IN HISTORY 208

HUE try COLOURS

HUNDRED may indicate the letter C (Roman numeral)

I

INDIAN DISHES 327

INDIANS see AMERICAN INDIANS

INDIAN STATES AND UNION TERRITORIES 17

INDICATORS see ANAGRAM INDICATORS; SPLIT-WORD INDICATORS

INDUSTRIALISTS 131

INFECTIONS try ANIMAL DISEASES AND INFECTIONS; MEDICAL FIELDS AND SPECIALITIES

IN FRANCE, PARIS, SPAIN etc. may indicate a foreign word e.g. man in Paris = M (monsieur); try FOREIGN WORDS; NUMBERS

INITIALLY may indicate the first letter of a word to be used in forming a new word

INSECTS 66

IN SHORT may indicate an abbreviation

INSTRUMENT try MUSICAL INSTRUMENTS; TOOLS

INTERNATIONAL AIRPORTS 301

INTERNATIONAL CAR REGISTRATIONS 302

INVENTORS 129; try COMPUTER SCIENTISTS; ENTREPRENEURS AND INDUSTRIALISTS; SCIENTISTS

ISLAND GROUPS 35

ISLANDS 34

ITALIAN REGIONS 16

IVY LEAGUE COLLEGES 364

J

JEWELLERY 316; see also BIRTHSTONES; GEMSTONES

JOINTS OF MEAT 323

K

KINGS see RULERS OF ENGLAND; SCOTTISH RULERS; king may also indicate K, R, REX

KITCHEN UTENSILS AND TABLEWARE 319

KNITTING TERMS 351

KNOTS 363

L

LAKES, LOCHS, AND LOUGHS 41

LÄNDER see GERMAN STATES

LANGUAGE 365–370

LANGUAGE try COMPUTER LANGUAGES; FIGURES OF SPEECH; LANGUAGES OF THE WORLD; LITERARY TERMS

LANGUAGES OF THE WORLD 365

LARGE NUMBER may indicate the letters M or D (Roman numerals)

LATIN PHRASES 369

LAW see section HISTORY, POLITICS, GOVERNMENT, AND LAW; try LEGAL TERMS

LEADERS try MILITARY LEADERS; WORLD LEADERS

LEARNER may indicate the letter L

LEFT may indicate L, SINISTER, PORT

LEGAL TERMS 210

LEGEND see ARTHURIAN LEGEND; CHARACTERS FROM THE TALES OF ROBIN HOOD; MYTHOLOGICAL AND IMAGINARY BEINGS; see also AFRICAN MYTHOLOGY; AUSTRALIAN MYTHOLOGY; CELTIC MYTHOLOGY; CENTRAL AND SOUTH AMERICAN MYTHOLOGY; EGYPTIAN MYTHOLOGY; GREEK AND ROMAN MYTHOLOGY; NORSE MYTHOLOGY; NORTH AMERICAN MYTHOLOGY

LIQUEUR see DRINKS

LITERARY TERMS 155

LOCAL AUTHORITIES see ENGLISH COUNTIES, FORMER COUNTIES AND SELECTED LOCAL AUTHORITIES; SCOTTISH REGIONS, COUNTIES, AND SELECTED LOCAL AUTHORITIES; WELSH COUNTIES AND SELECTED LOCAL AUTHORITIES

LOCHS 41

LOCOMOTIVES 307

LOUGHS 41

LOVE may indicate the letter O

LOVERS OF FACT AND FICTION 197

M

MAJOR ARTERIES 243

MAJOR RUGBY UNION CLUBS 342

MAJOR STOCK INDICES 215

MAJOR VEINS 244

MANNED SPACE PROGRAMS 235

MANY may indicate the letters D or M (Roman numerals)

MARSUPIALS 65

MATERIALS 312

MATHEMATICAL TERMS 226; see also GEOMETRIC FIGURES AND CURVES

MEASURES see PAPER MEASURES; WEIGHTS AND MEASURES

MEAT try JOINTS OF MEAT

MEDALS see BRITISH DECORATIONS AND MEDALS; US DECORATIONS AND MEDALS

MEDIC may indicate the letters DR, MD, MO, MB

MEDICAL FIELDS AND SPECIALITIES 243

MEDICINE AND HEALTH 243–254

MEMBERS OF NATO 210

MEMBERS OF THE COMMONWEALTH 209

METEOR SHOWERS 235

MEXICAN DISHES 329

MILITARY LEADERS 80

MILITARY TERMS 283–297

MILITARY TITLES 283

MINERALS 237

MINISTER try CLERGY

MISCELLANEOUS 356–364

MIXED may indicate an anagram

MONEY 360; see also CURRENCIES; FORMER EUROPEAN CURRENCIES

MOTHS 67

MOTORING TERMS 301

MOTORWAY may indicate the letters M, MI (M1)

MOTORWAY SERVICE STATIONS 306

MOTTOES 393

MOUNTAINS AND HILLS 43

MOVED may indicate an anagram

MURDERERS AND ASSASSINS 146

MUSCLES 245

MUSEUMS AND GALLERIES 160

MUSICAL INSTRUMENTS 166

MUSICAL TERMS 165

MUSICIANS AND COMPOSERS 112

MYTH see AFRICAN MYTHOLOGY; AUSTRALIAN MYTHOLOGY; CELTIC MYTHOLOGY; CENTRAL AND SOUTH AMERICAN MYTHOLOGY; EGYPTIAN MYTHOLOGY; GREEK AND ROMAN MYTHOLOGY; NORSE MYTHOLOGY; NORTH AMERICAN MYTHOLOGY

MYTHOLOGICAL AND IMAGINARY BEINGS 269

MYTHOLOGY, RELIGION AND 255–269

N

NAMED NEAREST AND BRIGHTEST STARS 234

NAMES see BOYS' NAMES; GIRLS' NAMES; OLD NAMES OF CAPITAL AND MAJOR CITIES; OLD NAMES OF COUNTRIES; ROMAN NAMES OF CITIES

NATIONAL PARKS 49

NATO, MEMBERS OF 210

NAUTICAL TERMS 303

NEW TESTAMENT see BIBLICAL CHARACTERS; BOOKS OF THE BIBLE

NEW ZEALAND ISLANDS AND TERRITORIES 15

NIGERIAN STATES 17

NIL may indicate the letter O

NOBEL PRIZE WINNERS 134

NOBILITY see PEERAGE

NON-DRINKER may indicate the letters TT

NORSE MYTHOLOGY 265

NORTH may indicate the letter N

NORTH AMERICAN INDIANS see AMERICAN INDIANS

NORTH AMERICAN MYTHOLOGY 266

NOTABLE WINDS 242

NOTE try TONIC SOL-FA; may also indicate one of the letters A, B, C, D, E, F, G

NOTHING may indicate the letter O

NOVEL TITLES 169

NUMBERS 368

NURSERY RHYMES 373; see also CHARACTERS FROM NURSERY RHYMES

NUTS 325

O

OCCUPATIONS 270

OCEANS AND SEAS 39

OLD NAMES OF CAPITAL AND MAJOR CITIES 206

OLD NAMES OF COUNTRIES 206

OLD TESTAMENT see BOOKS OF THE BIBLE; BIBLICAL CHARACTERS

OLYMPIC GAMES 341

ONE may indicate the letter I (Roman numeral)

OPERA see CHARACTERS FROM OPERA; GILBERT AND SULLIVAN

OPERATIONS see SURGICAL OPERATIONS

ORDER try BRITISH DECORATIONS AND MEDALS; RELIGIOUS ORDERS; US DECORATIONS AND MEDALS; may also indicate an anagram

ORES 240

ORGANIC ACIDS 225

OXFORD COLLEGES 363

P

PAKISTANI PROVINCES AND TERRITORIES 17

PALINDROMES 394; words or phrases that read the same backwards as forwards, e.g. able was I ere I saw Elba. The following words may indicate a palindrome: backwards and forwards, both ways

PAPER MEASURES 218; see also BOOK AND PAPER SIZES

PARKS see NATIONAL PARKS

PARTICLES, ELEMENTARY 218

PARTS OF A FLOWER 70

PARTY may indicate the letters DO

PASTA 323

PATIENCE GAMES 352

PATRON SAINTS 257

PEAS 324

PEERAGE 358

PEOPLE 76–148

PHILOSOPHERS 109

PHOBIAS BY FEAR 253

PHOBIAS BY NAME 251

PHRASES see LATIN PHRASES; PROVERBS; SIMILES; TWO-WORD PHRASES

PIGS see BREEDS OF PIGS

PIONEERS 142

PLANETS AND SATELLITES 233

PLANT PEOPLE 71

PLANTS AND FLOWERS 68

PLAYER try GAMES POSITIONS; MUSICIANS AND COMPOSERS; SPORTS; SPORTSMEN AND WOMEN; STAGE AND SCREEN PERSONALITIES

PLAY TITLES 172

PLAYWRIGHTS 97

PLEDGER may indicate the letters TT

POETS 97

POINT may indicate the letters N, S, E, W

CROSSWORD
SOLVER

CONTENTS

INTRODUCTION

This book consists of a set of lists of words specifically designed to help crossword-puzzle solvers. We have included over 100,000 English words organized into words with two letters, words with three letters, four letters, etc., up to fifteen letters. Within each section, the words are arranged alphabetically.

The words chosen include proper nouns, names of people and places, as well as common two- and three-word phrases. We have also given, in many cases, plurals of nouns, comparatives and superlatives of adjectives, and inflections of verbs. In general, '–ize' endings have been used for verbs. It should be noted that '–ise' endings are also possible for these.

While it would be impossible to produce anything like a comprehensive list, we have decided to include some less common variant spellings, for example QUR'AN/KORAN or TSETSE/TZETZE. Likewise, we have also put in some American spellings, for example PEDALING as well as PEDALLING. Note, too, that some words and phrases, although they use identical letters, change their form according to the part of speech and would therefore appear differently in a crossword clue. For example, the verb RUN DOWN would be shown as two words (3,4) whereas the adjective RUN-DOWN would be shown as a single, hyphenated word (3-4). We have included many of these variants.

There are three additional lists in the Appendix: a list of words where Q is not followed by U; a list of words that start with the letter X; and, new for this edition, a list of abbreviations used in texting and messaging,

We hope that the book will prove useful to all who enjoy doing crossword puzzles – and, in particular, to those who enjoy mpleting them.

Anne Stibbs Kerr
Aylesbury, 2019

2

A	**D**	HI	**M**	PE	**U**
AA	DA	H'M	MA	PH	UK
AB	DJ	HO	ME	PI	UM
AC	DO	HQ	MI	PM	UN
AD			MO	PR	UP
AG	**E**	**I**	MP	PS	US
AH	EH	ID	MR	PT	UU
AI	ER	IF	MS	PX	
AM	EU	IM1	MY		**V**
AN	EX	IN		**Q**	VC
AS		IQ	**N**	QC	VD
AT	**F**	IT	NO	QT	VJ
AW	FA				VS
	FE	**J**	**O**	**R**	
B	FM	JP	OF	RE	**W**
BE			OH		WC
BO	**G**	**K**	ON	**S**	WE
BY	GI	KC	OP	SH	
	GO	KO	OR	SO	**X**
C	GP		OW		XU
CB	GS	**L**	OX	**T**	
CD		LA		TA	**Y**
CO	**H**	LO	**P**	TI	YE
CV	HA	LP	PA	TO	YO
	HE	LR	PC	TV	

3

A	B	C			
ABC	BAA	CAB	DAM	EFF	FIX
ABH	BAD	CAD	DAY	EGG	FLU
ABO	BAG	CAM	DDI	EGO	FLY
ACE	BAH	CAN	DDR	EKG	FOB
ACT	BAN	CAP	DDT	ELF	FOE
ADD	BAR	CAR	DEB	ELK	FOG
ADJ	BAT	CAT	DEF	ELM	FOP
ADO	BAY	CAW	DEM	ELT	FOR
ADS	BBC	CDS	DEN	EMO	FOX
ADV	BBM	CIA	DEP	EMU	FRO
AFT	BBQ	CID	DEW	ENC	FRY
AGE	BED	CIS	DID	END	FUG
AGM	BEE	CJD	DIE	EON	FUN
AGO	BEG	CND	DIG	EPS	FUR
AHA	BEN	CNS	DIM	ERA	
AID	BET	COB	DIN	ERE	**G**
AIL	BIB	COD	DIP	ERG	GAB
AIM	BID	COG	DIS	ERR	GAD
AIR	BIG	COL	DIY	ESP	GAG
A LA	BIN	CON	DJS	ESQ	GAL
ALE	BIO-	COO	DNA	EST	GAP
ALL	BIT	COP	DOC	ETC	GAS
AMP	BOA	COS	DOE	EVE	GAY
AND	BOB	COT	DOG	EWE	GCE
ANT	BOD	COW	DOH	EYE	GDP
ANY	BOG	COX	DON		GEC
AOC	BOO	COY	DOR	**F**	GEE
APB	BOP	CPA	DOS	FAB	GEL
APE	BOW	CPS	DOT	FAD	GEM
APP	BOX	CPU	DRY	FAG	GEN
APT	BOY	CRC	D T'S	FAQ	GET
ARB	BPI	CRY	DUB	FAR	GIG
ARC	BPS	CSE	DUD	FAT	GIN
ARK	BRA	CUB	DUE	FAX	GI'S
ARM	BUB	CUD	DUG	FAY	GNP
ART	BUD	CUE	DUN	FBI	GNU
ASH	BUG	CUM	DUO	FED	GOA
ASK	BUM	CUP	DYE	FEE	GOB
ASP	BUN	CUR		FEN	GOD
ASS	BUR	CUT	**E**	FEW	GOO
ATE	BUS	CVS	EAR	FEY	GOP
ATM	BUT	CWM	EAT	FEZ	GOT
AUK	BUY		EBB	FIB	GPS
AWE	BYE	**D**	ECG	FIE	GUM
AWL		DAB	ECT	FIG	GUN
AXE		DAD	EEC	FIN	GUT
AYE			EEK	FIR	GUV
			EEL	FIT	GUY

GYM	HUH	KEG	MAM	NIX	PAT
GYP	HUM	KEN	MAN	NOB	PAW
	HUN	KEY	MAP	NOD	PAY
H	HUT	KID	MAR	NON-	PCS
HAD		KIN	MAS	NOR	PEA
HAE	**I**	KIP	MAT	NOT	PEE
HAG	ICE	KIT	MAW	NOW	PEG
HAH	ICY	KOB	MAY	NRA	PEN
HAM	IDS	KOI	MEH	NSA	PEP
HAN	IFS		MEN	NSU	PER
HAP	ILK	**L**	MET	NTH	PET
HAS	ILL	LAB	MEW	NUB	PEW
HAT	IMP	LAD	MIA	NUN	PHD
HAW	INC	LAG	MID	NUT	PHS
HAY	INF	LAN	MIS		PIE
HE'D	INK	LAP	MIX		PIG
HEH	INN	LAW	MOB	**O**	PIN
HEL	ION	LAX	MOD	OAF	PIP
HEM	IOU	LAY	MOM	OAK	PIS
HEN	IPA	LCD	MOO	OAP	PIT
HEP	IQS	LCM	MOP	OAR	PIX
HER	IRA	LEA	MOS	ODD	PLC
HE'S	IRE	LED	MOT	ODE	PLY
HET	IRK	LEE	MOW	O'ER	PMS
HEW	ISM	LEG	MPS	OFF	POD
HEX	ITS	LEI	MRI	OFT	POP
HEY	ITV	LEO	MRS	OHM	POT
HIB	IUD	LET	MSC	OHO	POW
HIC	IVY	LEV	MUD	OIK	POX
HID		LIB	MUG	OIL	PPS
HIE	**J**	LID	MUM	OLD	PRE-
HIM	JAB	LIE		OMG	PRO
HIN	JAG	LIG	**N**	ONE	PRY
HIP	JAM	LIP	NAB	OOF	PTA
HIS	JAR	LIT	NAD	OPS	PTO
HIT	JAW	LOB	NAG	OPT	PUB
HOB	JAY	LOG	NAN	ORB	PUD
HOD	JET	LOL	NAP	ORE	PUG
HOE	JEW	LOO	NAV	OTT	PUN
HOG	JIB	LOP	NAY	OUR	PUP
HOM	JIG	LOT	NCO	OUT	PUS
HOO	JIT	LOW	NEC	OVA	PUT
HOP	JOB	LOX	NEE	OWE	PVC
HOT	JOG	LPS	NEG	OWL	PYX
HOW	JOT	LSD	NET	OWN	
HOY	JOY	LUG	NEW		**Q**
HQS	JPS	LUV	NFL	**P**	QCS
HRT	JUG		NHS	PAD	QUA
HSI	JUT	**M**	NIB	PAL	
HUB		MAC	NIL	PAN	**R**
HUE	**K**	MAD	NIP	PAP	RAD
HUG		MAG	NIT	PAR	RAF

RAG	RYE	SOP	TMI	**V**	WIN
RAH		SOS	TNT	VAC	WIT
RAI	**S**	SOT	TOD	VAN	WOE
RAJ	SAC	SOU	TOE	VAR	WOK
RAM	SAD	SOW	TOG	VAT	WON
RAN	SAE	SOX	TON	VCR	WOO
RAP	SAG	SOY	TOO	VCS	WOP
RAT	SAP	SPA	TOP	VDU	WOT
RAW	SAT	SPY	TOR	VEG	WOW
RAY	SAW	STD	TOT	VET	WPC
REC	SAY	STY	TOW	VEX	WRY
RED	SDI	SUB	TOY	VGA	
REF	SDP	SUE	TRY	VGC	**Y**
REP	SEA	SUG	TSK	VHF	YAK
REV	SEC	SUM	TUB	VIA	YAM
REX	SEE	SUN	TUC	VIE	YAP
RIA	SEM	SUP	TUG	VIM	YAW
RIB	SET		TUT	VIP	YEA
RID	SEW	**T**	TVS	VIZ	YEN
RIG	SEX	TAB	TWO	VLF	YES
RIM	SHE	TAG		VOW	YET
RIP	SHY	TAN	**U**	VTR	YEW
RNA	SIC	TAP	UFO		YID
ROB	SIN	TAR	UGC	**W**	YIN
ROC	SIP	TAT	UGH	WAD	YOB
ROD	SIR	TAX	UHF	WAG	YOU
ROE	SIS	TEA	UMP	WAN	YTS
ROM	SIT	TEC	UNI-	WAR	
ROT	SIX	TEE	URB	WAS	**Z**
ROW	SKA	TEN	URN	WAX	ZAP
RSE	SKI	THE	USE	WAY	ZED
RSI	SKY	THY	UTC	WEB	ZEN
RUB	SLY	TIA	UTD	WED	ZIG
RUE	SOB	TIC	UVA	WEE	ZIP
RUG	SOD	TIE	UVB	WET	ZOO
RUM	SOH	TIN	UVC	WHO	
RUN	SOL	TIP	UZI	WHY	
RUT	SON	TIT		WIG	

4

A
ABCS
ABED
ABET
ABIA
ABLE
ABLY
ABOS
ABUT
ACAI
ACCT
AC/DC
ACER
ACES
ACHE
ACID
ACME
ACNE
ACRE
ACTS
ADAM
ADEN
ADZE
AEON
AERO-
AFAR
AFRO
AGAL
AGAR
AGED
AGES
AGMS
AGOG
AGRA
AGUE
AHEM
AHOY
AIDE
AIDS
AIMS
AIN'T
AINU
AIRE
AIRS
AIRY
AJAR
AKIN
ALAI

ALAR
ALAS
ALBI
ALIT
ALKY
ALLY
ALMS
ALOE
ALPS
ALSO
ALTO
ALUM
AMBO
AMEN
AMEX
AMID
AMIR
AMIS
AMOK
AMOY
AMPS
ANAL
ANEW
ANKH
ANON
ANSI
ANTE
ANTI-
ANTS
ANUS
APED
APES
APEX
APSE
AQUA
ARAB
ARAN
ARCH
ARCS
ARDS
AREA
AREG
ARIA
ARID
ARKS
ARMS
ARMY
ARSE

ARTS
ARTY
ASBO
ASHY
ASIA
AS IF
ASIR
ASPS
ASTI
AT IT
ATOM
ATOP
AUBE
AUDE
AUKS
AUNT
AURA
AUTO
AVER
AVID
AVON
AVOW
AWAY
AWED
AWLS
AWOL
AWRY
AXED
AXES
AXIS
AXLE
AYAH
AYES

B

BAAS
BABE
BABU
BABY
BACH
BACK
BADE
BAEZ
BAGS
BAIL
BAIT
BAJA
BAKE

BAKU
BALD
BALE
BALI
BALK
BALL
BALM
BAND
BANE
BANG
BANK
BANS
BARB
BARD
BARE
BARI
BARK
BARN
BARS
BASE
BASH
BASK
BASS
BAST
BATH
BATS
BAUD
BAWD
BAWL
BAYS
BEAD
BEAK
BEAM
BEAN
BEAR
BEAT
BEAU
BECK
BEDS
BEEF
BEER
BEES
BEET
BELL
BELT
BEND
BENS
BENT

BERK
BERN
BEST
BETA
BETS
BEVY
BIAS
BIBS
BIDE
BIDS
BIEL
BIER
BIFF
BIFU
BIKE
BILE
BILK
BILL
BIND
BINS
BIRD
BIRL
BIRO
BITE
BITS
BLAB
BLAG
BLAH
BLED
BLEW
BLIP
BLOB
BLOC
BLOG
BLOT
BLOW
BLUE
BLUR
BOAR
BOAS
BOAT
BOBO
BOBS
BODE
BODS
BODY
BOER
BOGS

BOIL
BOLD
BOLE
BOLL
BOLT
BOMA
BOMB
BOND
BONE
BONG
BONN
BONY
BOOB
BOOK
BOOM
BOON
BOOR
BOOS
BOOT
BOPS
BORA
BORE
BORN
BORT
BOSH
BOSS
BOTH
BOUT
BOWL
BOWS
BOYS
BOZO
BRAE
BRAG
BRAN
BRAS
BRAT
BRAY
BREW
BRIM
BRIT
BRNO
BROW
BROZ
BUBO
BUBS
BUCK
BUDS

BUFF	CANE	CLAM	CORD	CYST	DFEE
BUGS	CANS	CLAN	CORE	CZAR	DHAK
BULB	CANT	CLAP	CORK		DHOW
BULK	CAPE	CLAW	CORM	**D**	DIAL
BULL	CAPO	CLAY	CORN	DABS	DICE
BUMF	CAPS	CLEF	COSH	DADO	DICK
BUMP	CARD	CLEW	COST	DADS	DIED
BUMS	CARE	CLIP	COSY	DAFT	DIET
BUNA	CARP	CLOD	COTS	DAGO	DIGS
BUNG	CARS	CLOG	COUP	DAIS	DIKE
BUNK	CART	CLOP	COVE	DALE	DILL
BUNS	CASE	CLOT	COWL	DAME	DIME
BUOY	CASH	CLOY	COWS	DAMN	DINE
BUPA	CASK	CLUB	COXA	DAMP	DINK
BURB	CAST	CLUE	COZY	DAMS	DINS
BURK	CATS	CLUJ	CRAB	DANK	DINT
BURN	CAUL	COAL	CRAG	DARE	DIPS
BURP	CAVE	COAT	CRAM	DARK	DIRE
BURR	CAVY	COAX	CRAP	DARN	DIRK
BURS	CAWS	COBS	CRED	DART	DIRT
BURY	CCTV	COCK	CREW	DASH	DISC
BUSH	CEDE	CODA	CRIB	DATA	DISH
BUSK	CEDI	CODE	CROC	DATE	DISK
BUSS	CELA	CODS	CROP	DAUB	DISS
BUST	CELL	COED	CROW	DAWN	DIVE
BUSY	CENT	COGS	CRUD	DAYS	DMSO
BUTE	CERT	COIF	CRUS	DAZE	DOCK
BUTS	CHAD	COIL	CRUX	D-DAY	DOCS
BUTT	CHAP	COIN	CSES	DEAD	DODO
BUYS	CHAR	COIR	CUBA	DEAF	DOER
BUZZ	CHAT	COKE	CUBE	DEAL	DOES
BYES	CHAV	COLA	CUBS	DEAN	DOFF
BYOB	CHEB	COLD	CUED	DEAR	DOGE
BYRE	CHEF	COLS	CUES	DEBS	DOGS
BYTE	CHER	COLT	CUFF	DEBT	DOHA
	CHEW	COMA	CULL	DECK	DO IT
C	CHIC	COMB	CULM	DEED	DOLE
CABS	CHID	COME	CULT	DEEM	DOLL
CADS	CHIN	COMO	CUNT	DEEP	DOLT
CAEN	CHIP	CONE	CUPS	DEER	DOME
CAFE	CHIT	CONK	CURB	DEFS	DONE
CAGE	CHOP	CONS	CURD	DEFT	DONS
CAKE	CHOU	CONY	CURE	DEFY	DON'T
CALF	CHOW	COOK	CURL	DELE	DOOM
CALI	CHUG	COOL	CURS	DELL	DOOR
CALK	CHUM	COON	CURT	DEMO	DOPE
CALL	CHUR	COOP	CUSP	DENS	DORY
CALM	C-IN-C	COOS	CUSS	DENT	DOSE
CALX	CINE-	COOT	CUTE	DENY	DOSH
CAME	CITE	COPE	CUTS	DERV	DOSS
CAMP	CITY	COPS	CYAN	DESK	DOTE
CAMS	CLAD	COPY	CYME	DEWY	DOTS

DOUR	EARL	EURO	FERN	FOCI	GAGE
DOVE	EARN	EVEN	FESS	FOES	GAGS
DOWN	EARS	EVER	FEST	FOGS	GAIA
DOZE	EASE	EVES	FETE	FOGY	GAIN
DOZY	EAST	EVIL	FEUD	FOHN	GAIT
DRAB	EASY	EWER	FIAT	FOIL	GALA
DRAG	EATS	EWES	FIBS	FOLD	GALE
DRAM	EBBS	EXAM	FIFE	FOLK	GALL
DRAT	ECGS	EXES	FIGS	FOMO	GALS
DRAW	ECHO	EXIT	FIJI	FOND	GAME
DRAY	ECRU	EYED	FILE	FONT	GAMY
DREW	EDAM	EYES	FILL	FOOD	GANG
DRIP	EDDO	EYOT	FILM	FOOL	GAOL
DROP	EDDY	EYRE	FILO	FOOT	GAPE
DRUB	EDEN		FILS	FOPS	GAPS
DRUG	EDGE	**F**	FIND	FORA	GARB
DRUM	EDGY	FACE	FINE	FORD	GARD
DUAL	EDIT	FACT	FINN	FORE	GARY
DUCK	EDTA	FADE	FINS	FORK	GASH
DUCT	EELS	FADO	FIRE	FORM	GASP
DUDE	EFIK	FADS	FIRM	FORT	GATE
DUDS	EGER	FAFF	FIRS	FOUL	GAVE
DUEL	EGGS	FAGS	FISH	FOUR	GAWD
DUES	EGOS	FAIL	FIST	FOWL	GAWK
DUET	EIRE	FAIN	FITS	FOXY	GAWP
DUFF	ELAN	FAIR	FIVE	FRAP	GAYA
DUGS	ELBA	FAKE	FIZZ	FRAU	GAYS
DUKE	ELBE	FALL	FLAB	FRAY	GAZA
DULL	ELIA	FAME	FLAG	FREE	GAZE
DULY	ELKS	FANG	FLAK	FRET	GCES
DUMA	ELMS	FANS	FLAN	FRIT	GCSE
DUMB	ELSE	FAQS	FLAP	FROE	G'DAY
DUMP	EMIR	FARE	FLAT	FROG	GEAR
DUNE	EMIT	FARM	FLAW	FROM	GEEK
DUNG	EMUS	FART	FLAX	FUCK	GELD
DUNK	ENDS	FAST	FLAY	FUEL	GELS
DUNS	ENVY	FATE	FLEA	FUJI	GEMS
DUOS	EONS	FATS	FLED	FULL	GENE
DUPE	EPEE	FAUN	FLEE	FUME	GENK
DUSK	EPIC	FAUX	FLEW	FUMY	GENT
DUST	ERAS	FAWN	FLEX	FUND	GENU
DUTY	ERGO	FAZE	FLIP	FUNK	GERA
DWEM	ERGS	FEAR	FLIT	FURL	GERM
DYAD	ERIE	FEAT	FLOE	FURS	GERS
DYED	ERNE	FEED	FLOG	FURY	GHAT
DYER	ERSE	FEEL	FLOP	FUSE	GHEE
DYES	ESPY	FEES	FLOW	FUSS	GIBE
DYKE	ESTA	FEET	FLUE	FUZZ	GIFT
DYNE	ET AL	FELL	FLUX		GIFU
	ETCH	FELT	FOAL	**G**	GIGS
E	ETON	FEND	FOAM	GAFF	GILD
EACH	EURE	FENS	FOBS	GAGA	GILL

GILT	GREW	HAME	HERM	HONG	**I**
GIMP	GREY	HAMM	HERN	HONK	IAMB
GINS	GRID	HAMS	HERO	HOOD	IBEX
GIRD	GRIM	HAND	HERR	HOOF	IBID
GIRL	GRIN	HANG	HERS	HOOK	IBIS
GIRO	GRIP	HANK	HESS	HOOP	ICBM
GIRT	GRIT	HARD	HEST	HOOT	ICED
GISH	GROG	HARE	HETH	HOPE	ICES
GIST	GROW	HARK	HEWN	HOPI	ICON
GIVE	GRUB	HARL	HICK	HOPS	IDEA
GIZA	GUAM	HARM	HIDE	HORA	IDEM
GLAD	GUFF	HARP	HIED	HORN	IDES
GLEE	GULF	HART	HI-FI	HOSE	IDLE
GLEN	GULL	HARZ	HIGH	HOST	IDLY
GLIB	GULP	HASA	HIKE	HOTS	IDOL
GLOW	GUMS	HASH	HILL	HOUR	IFFY
GLUE	GUNN	HASK	HILT	HOVE	IGBO
GNUS	GUNS	HASP	HIND	HOWE	IKBS
GLUT	GURN	HAST	HINT	HOWF	IKON
GNAT	GURU	HATE	HIPS	HOWL	ILEX
GNAW	GUSH	HATH	HIRE	HOYA	ILLS
GNUS	GUST	HATS	HISS	HUBS	IMAM
GOAD	GUTS	HAUL	HIST	HUED	IMAX
GOAL	GUVS	HAVE	HITS	HUES	IMPI
GOAT	GUYS	HAWK	HIVE	HUFF	IMPS
GOBI	GYBE	HAZE	HOAD	HUGE	INCA
GOBO	GYMS	HAZY	HOAR	HUGO	INCH
GOBS		HEAD	HOAX	HUGS	INDO-
GODS	**H**	HEAL	HOBO	HULA	INDY
GOER	HAAF	HEAP	HOBS	HULK	INFO
GOES	HAAR	HEAR	HOCK	HULL	INKS
GO-GO	HABU	HEAT	HODS	HUME	INKY
GOJI	HACK	HEBE	HOED	HUMP	INNS
GOLD	HADE	HECK	HOER	HUMS	INTI
GOLF	HADJ	HEED	HOES	HUNG	INTO
GONE	HAEM	HEEL	HOGG	HUNK	IONS
GONG	HAFT	HEFT	HOGS	HUNT	IOTA
GOOD	HAGS	HEIR	HOKE	HUON	IOUS
GOOF	HA-HA	HELA	HOKI	HURD	IOWA
GOON	HAIG	HELD	HOLD	HURL	IPOH
GOOP	HAIK	HELL	HOLE	HURT	IRAN
GORE	HAIL	HELM	HOLM	HUSH	IRAQ
GORY	HAIR	HELP	HOLP	HUSK	IRIS
GOSH	HAJJ	HEMP	HOLS	HUSS	IRON
GOUT	HAKE	HEMS	HOLT	HUTS	ISLE
GOWN	HALE	HENS	HOLY	HUTU	ISMS
GRAB	HALF	HENT	HOMA	HWAN	ITCH
GRAF	HALL	HERA	HOME	HWYL	ITEM
GRAM	HALM	HERB	HOMO	HYDE	IUDS
GRAN	HALO	HERD	HOMS	HYMN	
GRAY	HALT	HERE	HOMY	HYPE	**J**
GRAZ	HAMA	HERL	HONE	HYPO	JABS

JACK	KCAL	KURU	LEGS	LOBE	LUVS
JADE	KEEL	KYAT	LEIS	LOBS	LVIV
JAGS	KEEN		LENA	LOCH	LYNX
JAIL	KEEP	**L**	LEND	LOCI	LYON
JAMB	KEGS	LABS	LENS	LOCK	LYRE
JAMS	KELP	LACE	LENT	LOCO	
JAPE	KENS	LACK	LEOS	LODE	**M**
JARS	KENT	LACY	LESS	LODI	MA'AM
JAWS	KEOS	LADE	LEST	LODZ	MACE
JAYS	KEPT	LADS	LETS	LOFT	MACH
JAZZ	KERB	LADY	LEVY	LOGO	MACS
JEEP	KERN	LAGS	LEWD	LOGS	MADE
JEER	KEYS	LAID	LIAR	LOGY	MAFF
JELL	KHAN	LAIN	LIAS	LOIN	MAGI
JENA	KICK	LAIR	LICE	LOLL	MAGS
JERK	KIDS	LAKE	LICK	LONE	MAID
JEST	KIEL	LAKH	LIDO	LONG	MAIL
JETS	KIEV	LAMA	LIDS	LOOK	MAIM
JEWS	KIKE	LAMB	LIED	LOOM	MAIN
JIBE	KILL	LAME	LIEF	LOON	MAKE
JIBS	KILN	LAMP	LIEN	LOOP	MALE
JIGS	KILO	LAND	LIES	LOOS	MALI
JILT	KILT	LANE	LIEU	LOOT	MALL
JINN	KIND	LANK	LIFE	LOPE	MALM
JINX	KINE	LAOS	LIFT	LORD	MALT
JIVE	KING	LAPP	LIKE	LORE	MAMA
JOBS	KINK	LAPS	LILO	LORN	MAMS
JOCK	KIPS	LARD	LILT	LOSE	MANE
JOGS	KIRK	LARK	LILY	LOSS	MANX
JOHN	KISS	LASH	LIMA	LOST	MANY
JOIN	KITE	LASS	LIMB	LOTH	MAPS
JOKE	KITS	LAST	LIME	LOTS	MARE
JOLT	KIVU	LATE	LIMN	LOUD	MARK
JOSH	KIWI	LATH	LIMP	LOUR	MARL
JOVE	KNAP	LAUD	LIMY	LOUT	MARS
JOWL	KNEE	LAUE	LINE	LOVE	MARY
JOYS	KNEW	LAVA	LING	LOWS	MASH
JUDO	KNIT	LAWN	LINK	LUCK	MASK
JUGS	KNOB	LAWS	LINT	LUDO	MASS
JUJU	KNOT	LAYS	LINZ	LUFF	MAST
JULY	KNOW	LAZE	LION	LUGO	MATE
JUMP	KOBE	LAZY	LIPS	LUGS	MATS
JUNE	KOFU	LEAD	LIRA	LULL	MATT
JUNK	KOGI	LEAF	LIRE	LUMP	MAUI
JURA	KOHA	LEAK	LISP	LUND	MAUL
JURY	KOHL	LEAN	LIST	LUNG	MAWS
JUST	KOOK	LEAP	LITE	LUNY	MAYA
JUTE	KOTA	LEAS	LIVE	LURE	MAYS
	KRIS	LEEK	LOAD	LURK	MAZE
K	KUDU	LEER	LOAF	LUSH	MAZY
KALE	KURE	LEES	LOAM	LUST	MEAD
KANO		LEFT	LOAN	LUTE	MEAL

MEAN	MOLE	NAPE	NOSE	OMSK	PAIN
MEAT	MOLL	NAPS	NOSH	ONCE	PAIR
MEEK	MOLT	NARA	NOSY	ONDO	PALE
MEET	MOMS	NARB	NOTE	ONE'S	PALL
MEGA-	MONK	NARC	NOUN	ONLY	PALM
MELK	MONO	NARK	NOUS	ONTO	PALP
MELT	MONS	NARM	NOVA	ONUS	PALS
MEMO	MOOD	NASA	NUBS	ONYX	PANE
MEND	MOON	NATO	NUDE	OOPS	PANG
MENU	MOOR	NAVE	NUKE	OOZE	PANS
MEOW	MOOS	NAVY	NULL	OOZY	PANT
MERE	MOOT	NAYS	NUMB	OPAL	PAPA
MESH	MOPE	NAZI	NUNN	OPEC	PAPS
MESS	MOPS	NCOS	NUNS	OPEN	PARA-
METE	MORE	NEAR	NUPE	OPUS	PARE
METZ	MORN	NEAT	NURD	ORAL	PARK
MEWS	MOSS	NECK	NUTS	ORAN	PARS
MICA	MOST	NEED	NUUK	ORBS	PART
MICE	MOTE	NEEM		OREL	PASS
MICK	MOTH	NE'ER	**O**	ORES	PAST
MIDI	MOTS	NEJD		ORGY	PATE
MIEN	MOVE	NEON	OAFS	ORLY	PATH
MIKE	MOWN	NERD	OAHU	ORNE	PATS
MILD	MOYA	NEST	OAKS	ORSK	PAVE
MILE	MRIA	NETS	OAPS	ORYX	PAWL
MILK	MUCH	NETT	OARS	OSLO	PAWN
MILL	MUCK	NEWS	OATH	OSUN	PAWS
MILT	MUFF	NEWT	OATS	OUCH	PAYE
MIME	MUGS	NEXT	OBAN	OUDH	PCOS
MIND	MULE	NIBS	OBEY	OULU	PEAK
MINE	MULL	NICE	OBOE	OURS	PEAL
MINI	MUMS	NICK	OBVS	OUST	PEAR
MINK	MUON	NIFF	ODDS	OUZO	PEAS
MINT	MURK	NIGH	ODES	OVAL	PEAT
MINX	MUSE	NINE	OGLE	OVEN	PECK
MIPS	MUSH	NIPS	OGRE	OVER	PEED
MIRE	MUSK	NISI	OGUN	OVUM	PEEK
MIRY	MUSS	NITS	OHIO	OWED	PEEL
MISO	MUST	NIUE	OHMS	OWEN	PEEP
MISS	MUTE	NOBS	OH MY	OWLS	PEER
MIST	MUTI	NODE	OH NO	OXEN	PEGS
MITE	MUTT	NODS	OILS	OYEZ	PEGU
MITT	MYNA	NOEL	OILY		PELT
MOAN	MYTH	NOES	OINK	**P**	PENN
MOAT		NO GO	OISE		PENS
MOBS	**N**	NONE	OITA	PACE	PERK
MOCK		NON-U	OKAY	PACK	PERL
MODE	NAFF	NOOK	OKRA	PACT	PERM
MODS	NAGS	NOON	OKTA	PACY	PERT
MOJO	NAHA	NOPE	OMAN	PADS	PERU
MOKE	NAIL	NORD	OMEN	PAGE	PESO
MOLD	NAME	NORM	OMNI-	PAID	PEST
	NANA			PAIL	

PETS	POLY	PULP	RASH	RIOT	RULE
PEWS	POMP	PUMA	RASP	RIPE	RUMP
PHEW	POND	PUMP	RATE	RIPS	RUMS
PHON	PONG	PUNK	RATS	RISE	RUNE
PHOT	PONY	PUNS	RAVE	RISK	RUNG
PHUT	POOF	PUNT	RAYS	RITE	RUNS
PICA	POOH	PUNY	RAZE	RIVE	RUNT
PICK	POOL	PUPA	READ	ROAD	RUSE
PIED	POOP	PUPS	REAL	ROAM	RUSH
PIER	POOR	PURE	REAM	ROAN	RUSK
PIES	POPE	PURI	REAP	ROAR	RUST
PIGS	POPS	PURL	REAR	ROBE	RUTS
PIKE	PORE	PURR	RECK	ROCK	RYES
PILE	PORI	PUSH	REDD	ROCS	
PILL	PORK	PUSS	REDO	RODE	S
PIMP	PORN	PUTT	REDS	RODS	SABA
PINE	PORT	PUTZ	REED	ROEG	SACK
PING	POSE	PYRE	REEF	ROES	SACS
PINK	POSH		REEK	ROLE	SAFE
PINS	POST	Q	REEL	ROLL	SAFI
PINT	POSY	QUAD	REFS	ROME	SAGA
PINY	POTS	QUAY	REGO	ROMO	SAGE
PION	POUF	QUID	REIN	ROMP	SAGO
PIPE	POUR	QUIN	RELY	ROMS	SAGS
PIPS	POUT	QUIP	REND	ROOD	SAID
PISA	POWS	QUIT	RENO	ROOF	SAIL
PISH	PRAM	QUIZ	RENT	ROOK	SAKE
PISS	PRAT	QUOD	REPO	ROOM	SALE
PITH	PRAY		REPS	ROOT	SALK
PITS	PREP	R	REST	ROPE	SALT
PITY	PREY	RACE	REUS	ROPY	SAME
PLAN	PRIG	RACK	REVS	RORT	SAMP
PLAY	PRIM	RACY	RHEA	ROSE	SAN'A
PLEA	PROB	RAFT	RIAL	ROSY	SAND
PLEB	PROD	RAGA	RIBS	ROTA	SANE
PLED	PROF	RAGE	RICE	ROTE	SANG
PLOD	PROG	RAGS	RICH	ROTH	SANK
PLOP	PROM	RAID	RICK	ROTS	SAPS
PLOT	PROP	RAIL	RIDE	ROUE	SARD
PLOW	PROS	RAIN	RIFE	ROUT	SARI
PLOY	PROW	RAKE	RIFF	ROUX	SARK
PLUG	PRUT	RAMP	RIFT	ROVE	SASH
PLUM	PSST	RAMS	RIGA	ROWS	SASS
PLUS	PUBS	RAND	RIGS	RUBS	SATE
PODS	PUCE	RANG	RILE	RUBY	SAVE
POEM	PUCK	RANI	RILL	RUCK	SAWN
POET	PUDS	RANK	RIME	RUDE	SAWS
POKE	PUFF	RANT	RIMS	RUED	SAYS
POKY	PUGS	RAPE	RIMY	RUFF	SCAB
POLE	PUKE	RAPS	RIND	RUGS	SCAG
POLL	PULA	RAPT	RING	RUHR	SCAM
POLO	PULL	RARE	RINK	RUIN	SCAN

SCAR	SHOW	SLOP	SPAM	SUNK	TAUT
SCAT	SHUN	SLOT	SPAN	SUNS	TAXI
SCOT	SHUT	SLOW	SPAR	SUPS	TEAK
SCUD	SIAN	SLUB	SPAS	SURD	TEAL
SCUM	SICK	SLUE	SPAT	SURE	TEAM
SEAL	SIDE	SLUG	SPAY	SURF	TEAR
SEAM	SIFT	SLUM	SPEC	SUSS	TEAS
SEAR	SIGH	SLUR	SPED	SUVA	TEAT
SEAS	SIGN	SLUT	SPEW	SWAB	TEED
SEAT	SIKH	SMOG	SPIC	SWAG	TEEM
SECS	SILK	SMUG	SPIK	SWAM	TELE-
SECT	SILL	SMUT	SPIN	SWAN	TELL
SEED	SILO	SNAG	SPIT	SWAP	TEMA
SEEK	SILT	SNAP	SPIV	SWAT	TEMP
SEEM	SIND	SNIP	SPOD	SWAY	TEND
SEEN	SINE	SNOB	SPOT	SWIG	TENS
SEEP	SING	SNOG	SPRY	SWIM	TENT
SEER	SINH	SNOT	SPUD	SWOP	TERM
SEES	SINK	SNOW	SPUN	SWOT	TERN
SELF	SINO-	SNUB	SPUR	SWUM	TEST
SELL	SINS	SNUG	STAB	SYNC	TEXT
SEME	SION	SOAK	STAG		THAN
SEMI	SIPS	SOAP	STAR	**T**	THAT
SEND	SIRE	SOAR	STAY	TABS	THAW
SENT	SIRS	SOBS	STEM	TACH	THEE
SERA	SITE	SOCA	STEP	TACK	THEM
SERE	SIZE	SOCK	STET	TACO	THEN
SERF	SKEW	SODA	STEW	TACT	THEO-
SETA	SKID	SODS	STIR	TAGS	THEY
SETI	SKIM	SOFA	STOL	TAIL	THIN
SETS	SKIN	SOFT	STOP	TAKE	THIS
SEWN	SKIP	SOIL	STOW	TALC	THOU
SEXY	SKIS	SOLD	STUB	TALE	THRU
SFAX	SKIT	SOLE	STUD	TALK	THUD
SGML	SKUA	SOLO	STUM	TALL	THUG
SHAD	SKYE	SOMA	STUN	TAME	THUN
SHAG	SLAB	SOME	STYE	TAMP	THUS
SHAH	SLAG	SONG	SUBS	TANG	TICK
SHAM	SLAM	SONS	SUCH	TANH	TICS
SHAT	SLAP	SOON	SUCK	TANK	TIDE
SHED	SLAT	SOOT	SUDS	TANS	TIDY
SHEW	SLAV	SOPS	SUED	TAPE	TIED
SHIM	SLAY	SORE	SUER	TAPS	TIER
SHIN	SLED	SORT	SUET	TARE	TIES
SHIP	SLEW	SO SO	SUEZ	TARN	TIFF
SHIT	SLID	SO-SO	SUIT	TARO	TILE
SHOA	SLIM	SOTS	SULK	TARS	TILL
SHOD	SLIP	SOUL	SUMO	TART	TILT
SHOE	SLIT	SOUP	SUMP	TASH	TIME
SHOO	SLOB	SOUR	SUMS	TASK	TINE
SHOP	SLOE	SOWN	SUMY	TA-TA	TING
SHOT	SLOG	SOWS	SUNG	TATS	TINS

TINT	TREK	UP TO	VOID	WELT	WOKS
TINY	TRIM	UPVC	VOLE	WEND	WOLD
TIPS	TRIO	URDU	VOLT	WENT	WOLF
TIRE	TRIP	URFA	VOTE	WEPT	WOMB
TIRO	TROD	URGE	VOWS	WEST	WONT
TITI	TROT	URIC	VTOL	WETA	WOOD
TITS	TRST	URNS		WETS	WOOF
TOAD	TRUE	USED	**W**	WHAM	WOOL
TO BE	TRUG	USER	WADE	WHAP	WOPS
TO DO	TSAR	USES	WADI	WHAT	WORD
TO-DO	TUBA	UTAH	WADS	WHEN	WORE
TODS	TUBE	UVEA	WAFT	WHET	WORK
TOED	TUBS		WAGE	WHEW	WORM
TOES	TUCK	**V**	WAGS	WHEY	WORN
TOFF	TUFT	VACS	WAIF	WHIG	WOVE
TOGA	TUGS	VAIN	WAIL	WHIM	WPCS
TOGO	TULA	VALE	WAIT	WHIP	WRAP
TOGS	TUNA	VAMP	WAKE	WHIR	WREN
TOIL	TUNE	VANE	WALK	WHIT	WRIT
TOLD	TURD	VANS	WALL	WHIZ	WROT
TOLL	TURF	VAPE	WAND	WHOA	WUHU
TOMB	TURN	VARY	WANE	WHOM	WUSS
TOME	TUSH	VASE	WANK	WHOP	
TONE	TUSK	VAST	WANT	WHYS	**X**
TONS	TUTU	VATS	WARD	WICK	XMAS
TOOK	TVEI	VAUD	WARM	WIDE	X-RAY
TOOL	TVER	VDUS	WARN	WIFE	
TOOT	TWAT	VEAL	WARP	WIGS	**Y**
TOPS	TWEE	VEEP	WARS	WIKI	YAKS
TORE	TWIG	VEER	WART	WILD	YAMS
TORN	TWIN	VEIL	WARY	WILL	YANG
TORS	TWIT	VEIN	WASH	WILT	YANK
TORT	TWOS	VELD	WASP	WILY	YAPS
TORY	TYPE	VEND	WATT	WIMP	YARD
TOSA	TYRE	VENT	WAUL	WIND	YARN
TOSH	TYRO	VERB	WAVE	WINE	YAWL
TOSS	TZAR	VERY	WAVY	WING	YAWN
TOTE		VEST	WAXY	WINK	YAWS
TOTO	**U**	VETO	WAYS	WINS	YAZD
TOTS	UCAS	VETS	WEAK	WINY	YEAH
TOUL	UCCA	VIAL	WEAL	WIPE	YEAR
TOUR	UELE	VICE	WEAN	WIRE	YEAS
TOUT	UFOS	VIED	WEAR	WIRY	YELL
TOWN	UGLY	VIES	WEBS	WISE	YELP
TOWS	UH OH	VIEW	WEED	WISH	YENS
TOYS	ULNA	VILE	WEEK	WISP	YETI
TRAD	UNDO	VINE	WEEP	WITH	YEWS
TRAM	UNIT	VINO	WEFT	WITS	YIDS
TRAP	UNIX	VIOL	WEIR	WOAD	YIPS
TRAY	UNTO	VIPS	WELD	WOES	YLEM
TREE	UPON	VISA	WELL	WOKE	YOBS
		VISE	WELS		YOGA

YOGI	YOUR	**Z**	ZERO	ZIPS	ZONE
YOKE	YOWL	ZANY	ZEST	ZITS	ZOOM
YOLK	YOYO	ZEAL	ZIBO	ZIZZ	ZOOS
YOLO	YUAN	ZEBU	ZINC	ZOMG	ZOUK
YORE	YUCK	ZEDS	ZINE	ZOND	ZULU
YORK	YULE	ZEIN	ZION		

5

A	ADEPT	AGUES	ALLOA	ANGST	ARABS
AALII	A DEUX	AHEAD	ALLOT	ANGUS	ARBER
AARAU	AD HOC	AHERN	ALLOW	ANHUI	ARBOR
ABACA	ADIEU	AHWAZ	ALLOY	ANILE	ARDEN
ABACK	ADIOS	AIDED	ALLYL	ANIMA	AREAL
ABAFT	AD LIB	AIDES	ALOFT	ANION	AREAS
ABASE	AD-LIB	AILED	ALOHA	ANISE	ARECA
ABASH	ADMAN	AIMED	ALOIN	ANJOU	ARENA
ABATE	ADMEN	AIOLI	ALONE	ANKLE	ARETE
ABBEY	ADMIT	AIRED	ALONG	ANNAL	ARGIL
ABBOT	ADMIX	AISLE	ALOOF	ANNAM	ARGOL
ABEAM	ADOBE	AISNE	ALOUD	ANNAN	ARGON
ABELE	ADOPT	AITCH	ALPHA	ANNEX	ARGOS
ABHOR	ADORE	AJMER	ALTAI	ANNOY	ARGOT
ABIDE	ADORN	AKURE	ALTAR	ANNUL	ARGUE
ABLED	AD REM	ALACK	ALTER	ANODE	ARIAN
ABODE	ADUKI	ALAMO	*ALTOS	ANOLE	ARIAS
ABOHM	ADULT	ALARM	AMASS	ANOVA	ARICA
A-BOMB	ADUWA	ALARY	AMAZE	ANTED	ARIEL
ABORT	ADZES	ALATE	AMBER	ANTES	ARIEN
ABOUT	AEDES	ALBEE	AMBIT	ANTIC	ARIES
ABOVE	AEGIS	ALBUM	AMBLE	ANTSY	ARISE
ABUJA	AEONS	ALCID	AMBRY	ANVIL	ARLES
ABUSE	AESIR	ALDAN	AMEBA	ANZAC	ARLON
ABYSS	AFFIX	ALDER	AMEND	ANZIO	ARMCO
ACCRA	AFIRE	ALDOL	AMENT	AORTA	ARMED
ACHED	AFOOT	ALECK	AMICE	AOSTA	AROID
ACHES	AFOUL	ALERT	AMIDE	APACE	AROMA
ACIDS	AFROS	ALGAE	AMINE	APART	AROSE
ACKEE	AFTER	ALGAL	AMINO	APEAK	ARRAN
ACORN	AGAIN	ALGID	AMIRS	APERY	ARRAS
ACRES	AGAMA	ALGIN	AMISS	APHID	ARRAY
ACRID	AGAPE	ALGOL	AMITY	APHIS	ARRIS
ACTED	AGATE	ALGOR	AMMAN	APIAN	ARROW
ACTIN	AGAVE	ALIAS	AMNIO	A PIED	ARSES
ACTOR	AGENT	ALIBI	AMONG	APING	ARSIS
ACT UP	AGGER	ALIEN	AMOUR	APISH	ARSON
ACUTE	AGGRO	ALIGN	AMPLE	APORT	ARTEL
ADAGE	AGILE	ALIKE	AMPLY	APPAL	ARTEX
ADAMS	AGING	A LIST	AMUCK	APPEL	ARUBA
ADANA	AGISM	ALIVE	AMUSE	APPLE	ARYAN
ADAPT	AGIST	ALKYD	ANCON	APPLY	ASCII
ADDAX	AGLET	ALKYL	ANDES	APRIL	ASCOT
ADDED	AGLOW	ALLAH	ANGEL	APRON	ASCUS
ADDER	AGNEW	ALLAY	ANGER	APSES	ASDIC
ADDLE	AGONY	ALLEN	ANGLE	APSIS	ASHEN
ADD-ON	AGORA	ALLEY	ANGLO-	APTLY	ASHES
ADD UP	AGREE	ALL IN	ANGRY	AQABA	ASIAN

ASIDE	AXIAL	BANFF	BEAMS	BETAS	BLAZE
ASKED	AXILE	BANGS	BEANO	BETEL	BLEAK
ASKER	AXING	BANJO	BEANS	BEVEL	BLEAR
ASKEW	AXIOM	BANKS	BEARD	BEVVY	BLEAT
ASPEN	AXLES	BANNS	BEARS	BEZEL	BLEED
ASPER	AYAHS	BANTU	BEAST	BHAJI	BLEEP
ASPIC	AZIDE	BARBS	BEATS	BHANG	BLEND
ASSAI	AZINE	BARDS	BEAUS	BIBLE	BLESS
ASSAM	AZOIC	BARED	BEAUT	BICKY	BLEST
ASSAY	AZOLE	BARER	BEAUX	BIDED	BLIDA
ASSEN	AZOTE	BARGE	BEBOP	BIDET	BLIMP
ASSES	AZTEC	BARIC	BECKS	BIERS	BLIND
ASSET	AZURE	BARKS	BEECH	BIFFS	BLING
ASTER		BARMY	BEEFY	BIFID	BLINI
ASTIR	**B**	BARNS	BEERS	BIGHT	BLINK
ASTRO-	BAAED	BARON	BEERY	BIGOT	BLIPS
ASWAN	BABEL	BARRA	BEETS	BIG UP	BLISS
AT ALL	BABES	BARRE	BEFIT	BIHAR	B LIST
ATHOS	BABUL	BARRY	BEFOG	BIJOU	BLITZ
ATLAS	BABUS	BARTH	BEGAN	BIKED	BLOAT
ATOLL	BACCY	BARYE	BEGAT	BIKES	BLOBS
ATOMS	BACKS	BASAL	BEGET	BILGE	BLOCH
ATONE	BACON	BASED	BEGIN	BILLS	BLOCK
ATONY	BADGE	BASEL	BEGOT	BILLY	BLOCS
ATRIA	BADLY	BASER	BEGUM	BINAL	BLOGS
ATRIP	BAGEL	BASES	BEGUN	BINGE	BLOIS
AT SEA	BAGGY	BASHO	BEIGE	BINGO	BLOKE
ATTAR	BAHAI	BASIC	BEING	BIOME	BLOND
ATTIC	BAHIA	BASIL	BEIRA	BIOTA	BLOOD
AUDIO	BAILS	BASIN	BELAY	BIPED	BLOOM
AUDIT	BAIRN	BASIS	BELCH	BIPOD	BLOTS
AUGER	BAIZE	BASRA	BELEM	BIRCH	BLOWN
AUGHT	BAKED	BASSO	BELIE	BIRDS	BLOWS
AUGUR	BAKER	BASTE	BELLE	BIROS	BLOWY
AUNTS	BALAS	BATCH	BELLS	BIRTH	BLUER
AURAL	BALDY	BATED	BELLY	BISON	BLUES
AURAS	BALED	BATHE	BELOW	BITCH	BLUFF
AURIC	BALER	BATHS	BELTS	BITES	BLUNT
AUTOS	BALES	BATIK	BEMBA	BITTY	BLURB
AUXIN	BALKH	BATON	BENCH	BIYSK	BLURT
AVAIL	BALKS	BATTY	BENDS	BIZZY	BLUSH
AVENS	BALLS	BATUM	BENIN	BLACK	BOARD
AVERT	BALLY	BAULK	BENTS	BLADE	BOARS
AVIAN	BALMS	BAWDS	BENUE	BLAIN	BOAST
AVOID	BALMY	BAWDY	BENXI	BLAIR	BOATS
AWAIT	BALSA	BAYED	BERET	BLAME	BOBBY
AWAKE	BALTI	BAYOU	BERKS	BLANC	BOCHE
AWARD	BANAL	BEACH	BERRY	BLAND	BODED
AWARE	BANDA	BEADS	BERTH	BLANK	BODGE
AWASH	BANDS	BEADY	BERYL	BLARE	BOERS
AWFUL	BANDY	BEAKS	BESET	BLASE	BOGEY
AWOKE	BANES	BEAKY	BESOM	BLAST	BOGGY

BOGIE	BOURN	BRISK	BURLY	CAIRN	CATER
BOGOR	BOUSE	BRITS	BURMA	CAIRO	CATTY
BOGUS	BOUTS	BROAD	BURNS	CAJUN	CAULK
BOHEA	BOVID	BROIL	BURNT	CAKED	CAUSE
BOHOL	BOWED	BROKE	BURPS	CAKES	CAVAN
BOILS	BOWEL	BROME	BURRO	CALIX	CAVED
BOISE	BOWER	BRONX	BURRS	CALLA	CAVES
BOLES	BOWIE	BROOD	BURRY	CALLS	CAVIL
BOLLS	BOWLS	BROOK	BURSA	CALOR	CAWED
BOLTS	BOXED	BROOM	BURSE	CALVE	CD-ROM
BOLUS	BOXER	BROTH	BURST	CALYX	CEARA
BOMBE	BOXES	BROWN	BUSBY	CAMEL	CEASE
BOMBS	BOZOS	BROWS	BUSED	CAMEO	CEDAR
BONDI	BRACE	BRUIN	BUSES	CAMPO	CEDED
BONDS	BRACT	BRUIT	BUSHY	CAMPS	CEDER
BONED	BRAES	BRUME	BUSTS	CANAL	CEIBA
BONES	BRAGA	BRUNO	BUSTY	CANDY	CELEB
BONGO	BRAGG	BRUNT	BUTCH	CANEA	CELLA
BONNY	BRAID	BRUSH	BUTTE	CANED	CELLE
BONUS	BRAIL	BRUTE	BUTTS	CANER	CELLO
BONZE	BRAIN	B-SIDE	BUTTY	CANES	CELLS
BOOBS	BRAKE	BUBAL	BUTYL	CANNA	CENSE
BOOBY	BRAND	BUCHU	BUXOM	CANNY	CENTO
BOOED	BRASH	BUCKS	BUYER	CANOE	CENTS
BOOKS	BRASS	BUDDY	BWANA	CANON	CERES
BOOMS	BRATS	BUDGE	BYATT	CANTO	CERIC
BOONS	BRAVE	BUFFS	BYLAW	CANTS	CERTS
BOORS	BRAVO	BUGGY	BYRES	CAPER	CETUS
BOOST	BRAWL	BUGLE	BYTES	CAPES	CEUTA
BOOTH	BRAWN	BUILD	BYTOM	CAPON	CHAFE
BOOTS	BRAXY	BUILT	BYWAY	CAPRI	CHAFF
BOOTY	BRAYS	BULBS		CAPUA	CHAIN
BOOZE	BRAZE	BULGE	**C**	CAPUT	CHAIR
BOOZY	BREAD	BULGY	CABAL	CARAT	CHALK
BORAX	BREAK	BULKS	CABBY	CARDS	CHAMP
BORED	BREAM	BULKY	CABER	CARED	CHANT
BORER	BREDA	BULLA	CABIN	CARES	CHAOS
BORES	BREED	BULLS	CABLE	CARET	CHAPS
BORIC	BRENT	BULLY	CACAO	CARGO	CHARD
BORNE	BREST	BUMPH	CACHE	CARNE	CHARM
BORNO	BREVE	BUMPS	CACTI	CAROB	CHARS
BORNU	BRIAR	BUMPY	CADDY	CAROL	CHART
BORON	BRIBE	BUNCH	CADET	CARPS	CHARY
BOSKY	BRICK	BUNDU	CADGE	CARRY	CHASE
BOSOM	BRIDE	BUNGS	CADIZ	CARTS	CHASM
BOSON	BRIEF	BUNKS	CADRE	CARVE	CHATS
BOSSY	BRIER	BUNNY	CAFES	CASED	CHAVS
BOSUN	BRILL	BUOYS	CAFOD	CASES	CHEAP
BOTCH	BRINE	BURGH	CAGED	CASKS	CHEAT
BOUGH	BRING	BURIN	CAGES	CASTE	CHECK
BOULE	BRINK	BURKE	CAGEY	CASTS	CHEEK
BOUND	BRINY	BURKS	CAINE	CATCH	CHEEP

CHEER	CHUTE	CLOGS	COMBS	COUPS	CRICK
CHEFS	CHYLE	CLONE	COMER	COURT	CRIED
CHEJU	CHYME	CLOSE	COMET	COVEN	CRIER
CHELA	CIDER	CLOTH	COMFY	COVER	CRIES
CHERT	CIGAR	CLOTS	COMIC	COVES	CRIME
CHESS	CIMEX	CLOUD	COMMA	COVET	CRIMP
CHEST	CINCH	CLOUT	COMPO	COVEY	CRISP
CHEWS	CIRCA	CLOVE	CONCH	COVIN	CROAK
CHEWY	CISCO	CLOWN	CONES	COWED	CROAT
CHIBA	CISSY	CLUBS	CONEY	COWER	CROCK
CHICK	CITED	CLUCK	CONGA	COWES	CROFT
CHIDE	CITES	CLUES	CONGE	COWLS	CRONE
CHIEF	CIVET	CLUMP	CONGO	COWRY	CRONY
CHILD	CIVIC	CLUNG	CONIC	COXAL	CROOK
CHILE	CIVIL	CLUNK	CONKS	COXED	CROON
CHILL	CLACK	CLUNY	CONTE	COXES	CROPS
CHIME	CLADE	CLWYD	CONWY	COYLY	CRORE
CHINA	CLAIM	CLYDE	COOED	COYPU	CROSS
CHINE	CLAMP	COACH	COOKS	COZEN	CROUP
CHING	CLAMS	COALS	COOLS	CRABS	CROWD
CHINK	CLANG	COALY	COONS	CRACK	CROWN
CHINS	CLANK	COAST	COOPS	CRAFT	CROWS
CHIOS	CLANS	COATS	CO-OPT	CRAGS	CROZE
CHIPS	CLAPS	COBIA	COOTS	CRAKE	CRUDE
CHIRM	CLARE	COBRA	COPAL	CRAMP	CRUEL
CHIRP	CLARO	COCKS	COPED	CRANE	CRUET
CHIRR	CLARY	COCKY	COPES	CRANK	CRUMB
CHITA	CLASH	COCOA	COPRA	CRAPE	CRUMP
CHITS	CLASP	CODAS	COPSE	CRAPS	CRURA
CHIVY	CLASS	CODED	CORAL	CRASH	CRUSE
CHOCK	CLAVE	CODER	CORDS	CRASS	CRUSH
CHOIR	CLAWS	CODES	CORED	CRATE	CRUST
CHOKE	CLEAN	CODEX	CORER	CRAVE	CRYPT
CHOKO	CLEAR	CODON	CORES	CRAWL	CUBAN
CHOKY	CLEAT	COEDS	CORFU	CRAZE	CUBEB
CHOMP	CLEEK	COGON	CORGI	CRAZY	CUBED
CHOPS	CLEFS	COHSE	CORKS	CREAK	CUBES
CHORD	CLEFT	COIFS	CORMS	CREAM	CUBIC
CHORE	CLERK	COIGN	CORNS	CREDO	CUBIT
CHOSE	CLEWS	COILS	CORNU	CREED	CUDDY
CHOUX	CLICK	COINS	CORNY	CREEK	CUFFS
CHOWS	CLIFF	COKES	CORPS	CREEL	CUING
CHRON-	CLIMB	COLDS	CORSE	CREEP	CULCH
CHUBB	CLIME	COLEY	COSTA	CREME	CULET
CHUCK	CLINE	COLIC	COSTS	CREPE	CULEX
CHUFA	CLING	COLON	COTTA	CREPT	CULLS
CHUFF	CLINK	COLTS	COUCH	CRESS	CULPA
CHUMP	CLINT	COLZA	COUDE	CREST	CULTS
CHUMS	CLIPS	COMAL	COUGH	CRETE	CUMIN
CHUNK	CLOAK	COMAS	COULD	CREWE	CUNTS
CHURL	CLOCK	COMBI	COUNT	CREWS	CUPEL
CHURN	CLODS	COMBO	COUPE	CRIBS	CUPID

CUPPA	DARAF	DELOS	DIODE	DOPED	DRIER
CURBS	DARED	DELTA	DIRER	DOPES	DRIFT
CURCH	DARER	DELVE	DIRGE	DOPEY	DRILL
CURDY	DARES	DEMOB	DIRKS	DORIC	DRILY
CURED	DARKS	DEMON	DIRTY	DOSED	DRINK
CURES	DARKY	DEMOS	DISCO	DOSER	DRIPS
CURET	DARNS	DEMUR	DISCS	DOSES	DRIVE
CURIA	DARTS	DENAR	DISHY	DOTED	DROIT
CURIE	DATED	DENIM	DISKS	DOTER	DROLL
CURIO	DATER	DENSE	DITCH	DOTTY	DROME
CURLS	DATES	DENTS	DITTO	DOUAI	DRONE
CURLY	DATUM	DEPOT	DITTY	DOUBS	DROOL
CURRY	DAUBS	DEPTH	DITZY	DOUBT	DROOP
CURSE	DAUBY	DERBY	DIVAN	DOUGH	DROPS
CURVE	DAUNT	DERMA	DIVED	DOURO	DROSS
CUSEC	DAVIT	DERRY	DIVER	DOUSE	DROVE
CUSHY	DAVOS	DESKS	DIVES	DOVER	DROWN
CUSPS	DAWNS	DETER	DIVOT	DOVES	DRUGS
CUTER	DAZED	DETOX	DIVVY	DOWDY	DRUID
CUTIN	DAZES	DEUCE	DIXIE	DOWEL	DRUMS
CUT IN	DEALS	DEVIL	DIZZY	DOWER	DRUNK
CUTIS	DEALT	DEVON	DJINN	DOWNS	DRUPE
CUT UP	DEANS	DEWAR	DOBBY	DOWNY	DRUSE
CUZCO	DEARS	DHAKA	DOBRO	DOWRY	DRYAD
CYBER	DEARY	DHOLE	DOCKS	DOWSE	DRYER
CYCAD	DEATH	DHOTI	DODGE	DOYEN	DRYLY
CYCLE	DEBAR	DHOWS	DODGY	DOZED	DUALA
CYDER	DEBIT	DIALS	DODOS	DOZEN	DUBAI
CYMAR	DEBTS	DIANA	DOERS	DOZER	DUCAL
CYMRY	DEBUG	DIARY	DO FOR	D PHIL	DUCAT
CYNIC	DEBUT	DIAZO	DOGES	DRABS	DUCHY
CYSTS	DECAF	DICED	DOGGO	DRAFF	DUCKS
CYTON	DECAL	DICER	DOGGY	DRAFT	DUCKY
CZARS	DECAY	DICEY	DOGIE	DRAGS	DUCTS
CZECH	DECKS	DICKS	DOGMA	DRAIL	DUDES
	DECOR	DICKY	DOILY	DRAIN	DUELS
D	DECOY	DICTA	DOING	DRAKE	DUETS
	DECRY	DIETS	DOLBY	DRAMA	DUFFS
DACCA	DEEDS	DIGIT	DOLCE	DRAMS	DUKES
DADDY	DEFER	DIJON	DOLED	DRANK	DULIA
DAGGA	DEGAS	DIKES	DOLLS	DRAPE	DULLY
DAGOS	DE-ICE	DILDO	DOLLY	DRAWL	DULSE
DAILY	DEIFY	DIMER	DOLTS	DRAWN	DUMMY
DAIRY	DEIGN	DIMES	DOMED	DRAWS	DUMPS
DAISY	DEISM	DIMLY	DOMES	DRAYS	DUMPY
DAKAR	DEIST	DINAR	DONEE	DREAD	DUNCE
DALES	DEITY	DINED	DONNA	DREAM	DUNES
DALLY	DEKKO	DINER	DONOR	DREAR	DUNGY
DAMAN	DELAY	DINGO	DOOMS	DREGS	DUNKS
DAMES	DELFT	DINGY	DOONA	DRESS	DUPED
DANCE	DELHI	DINKA	DOORS	DRIBS	DUPER
DANDY	DELLS	DINKY	DOOZY	DRIED	DUPES
DANIO					

DUPLE	EGEST	ENEMY	EVILS	FARAD	FETOR
DURAS	EGGER	ENJOY	EVOKE	FARCE	FETUS
DUREX	EGHAM	ENNIS	EWERS	FARCI	FEUDS
DUROC	EGRET	ENNUI	EXACT	FARCY	FEVER
DURRA	EGYPT	ENROL	EXALT	FARED	FEZES
DURUM	EIDER	ENSUE	EXAMS	FARER	FIATS
DUSKY	EIFEL	ENTER	EXCEL	FARES	FIBRE
DUSTY	EIGER	ENTRY	EXERT	FARLE	FICHU
DUTCH	EIGHT	ENUGU	EXILE	FARMS	FICUS
DUVET	EIKON	ENURE	EXIST	FARTS	FIELD
DWARF	EILAT	ENVOY	EXITS	FASTS	FIEND
DWEEB	EJECT	EOSIN	EXPEL	FATAL	FIERY
DWELL	EKMAN	EPACT	EXTOL	FATED	FIFER
DWELT	ELAND	EPEES	EXTRA	FATES	FIFES
DYERS	ELATE	EPICS	EXUDE	FATTY	FIFTH
DYFED	ELBOW	EPOCH	EXULT	FAUGH	FIFTY
DYING	ELCHE	EPODE	EYING	FAULT	FIGHT
DYKES	ELDER	EPOXY	EYOTS	FAUNA	FILAR
DYLAN	ELECT	EPROM	EYRIE	FAUNS	FILCH
DYULA	ELEGY	EPSOM		FAVUS	FILED
	ELEMI	EQUAL	**F**	FAWNS	FILER
E	ELFIN	EQUIP	FABLE	FAXED	FILES
EAGER	ELGIN	ERASE	FACED	FAZED	FILET
EAGLE	ELIDE	ERBIL	FACER	FEARS	FILLY
EAGRE	ELINT	ERECT	FACES	FEAST	FILMS
EARED	ELITE	ERGOT	FACET	FEATS	FILMY
EARLS	ELOPE	ERNIE	FACIA	FEAZE	FILTH
EARLY	ELUDE	ERODE	FACTS	FECAL	FILUM
EAROM	ELUTE	EROSE	FADDY	FECES	FINAL
EARTH	ELVER	ERRED	FADED	FECIT	FINCH
EASED	ELVES	ERROR	FADER	FEDEX	FINDS
EASEL	EMBAY	ERUCT	FAERY	FED UP	FINED
EASER	EMBED	ERUPT	FAILS	FEEDS	FINER
EASTS	EMBER	ESHER	FAINT	FEIGN	FINES
EATEN	EMBOW	ESKER	FAIRS	FEINT	FINGO
EATER	EMCEE	ESPOO	FAIRY	FELLS	FINIS
EAVES	EMDEN	ESSAY	FAITH	FELON	FINNY
EBBED	EMEND	ESSEN	FAKED	FEMUR	FIORD
E BOAT	EMERY	ESSEX	FAKER	FENCE	FIRED
EBONY	EMIRS	ESTER	FAKES	FENNY	FIRER
ECLAT	EMMEN	ESTOP	FAKIR	FERAL	FIRES
EDEMA	EMMER	ETHER	FALDO	FERIA	FIRMS
EDGED	EMOTE	ETHIC	FALLS	FERMI	FIRRY
EDGER	EMPTY	ETHOS	FALSE	FERNS	FIRST
EDGES	ENACT	ETHYL	FALUN	FERNY	FIRTH
EDICT	ENATE	ETUDE	FAMED	FERRY	FISHY
EDIFY	ENDED	EVADE	FANCY	FESSE	FISTS
EDUCE	ENDER	EVENS	FANGO	FETAL	FITCH
EDUCT	END ON	EVENT	FANGS	FETCH	FITLY
EEJIT	ENDOW	EVERT	FANNY	FETED	FIVER
EERIE	ENDUE	EVERY	FANON	FETES	FIVES
EFFED	ENEMA	EVICT	FANTI	FETID	FIXED

FIXER	FLUID	FOVEA	FUNGI	GANSU	GHOUL
FIXES	FLUKE	FOWEY	FUNKS	GAOLS	GHYLL
FIZZY	FLUKY	FOWLS	FUNKY	GAPED	GIANT
FJELD	FLUME	FOXED	FUNNY	GAPER	GIBER
FJORD	FLUNG	FOXES	FURAN	GAPES	GIBES
FLACK	FLUNK	FOYER	FURRY	GARDA	GIDDY
FLAGS	FLUOR	FRAIL	FURZE	GASES	GIFTS
FLAIL	FLUSH	FRAME	FURZY	GASPS	GIGOT
FLAIR	FLUTE	FRANC	FUSED	GASSY	GIGUE
FLAKE	FLUTY	FRANK	FUSEE	GATED	GIJON
FLAKY	FLYBY	FRAUD	FUSEL	GATES	GILET
FLAME	FLYER	FREAK	FUSES	GAUDY	GILLS
FLAMY	FOALS	FREED	FUSIL	GAUGE	GILTS
FLANK	FOAMY	FREER	FUSSY	GAUNT	GIPSY
FLANS	FOCAL	FREON	FUSTY	GAUSS	GIRLS
FLAPS	FOCUS	FRESH	FUTON	GAUZE	GIRON
FLARE	FOGEY	FRETS	FUZZY	GAUZY	GIRTH
FLASH	FOGGY	FRIAR	FYLDE	GAVEL	GIVEN
FLASK	FOILS	FRIED		GAVLE	GIVER
FLATS	FOISM	FRIER	**G**	GAWKY	GIZMO
FLAWS	FOIST	FRIES	GABBA	GAYER	GLACE
FLAWY	FOLDS	FRILL	GABBY	GAZED	GLADE
FLEAM	FOLIC	FRISE	GABES	GAZER	GLAIR
FLEAS	FOLIO	FRISK	GABLE	GCSES	GLAND
FLECK	FOLKS	FRITT	GABON	GEARS	GLANS
FLEER	FOLLY	FRIZZ	GADID	GECKO	GLARE
FLEET	FONTS	FROCK	GAFFE	GEESE	GLARY
FLESH	FOODS	FROGS	GAFFS	GEEST	GLASS
FLEWS	FOOLS	FROND	GAGED	GELID	GLAZE
FLICK	FOOTS	FRONS	GAGES	GEMMA	GLEAM
FLIER	FOOTY	FRONT	GAILY	GENES	GLEAN
FLIES	FORAY	FROST	GAINS	GENET	GLEBE
FLING	FORCE	FROTH	GAITS	GENIC	GLEEK
FLINT	FORDS	FROWN	GALAH	GENIE	GLEES
FLIPS	FORGE	FROZE	GALAS	GENII	GLEET
FLIRT	FORGO	FRUIT	GALEA	GENOA	GLENN
FLOAT	FOR IT	FRUMP	GALES	GENRE	GLENS
FLOCK	FORKS	FRYER	GALLA	GENTS	GLIDE
FLOES	FORLI	FRY-UP	GALLE	GENUS	GLINT
FLONG	FORME	FUCKS	GALLS	GEODE	GLITZ
FLOOD	FORMS	FUCUS	GAMED	GEOID	GLOAT
FLOOR	FORTE	FUDGE	GAMER	GERMS	GLOBE
FLOPS	FORTH	FUELS	GAMES	GESSO	GLOGG
FLORA	FORTS	FUGAL	GAMEY	GET IT	GLOOM
FLORY	FORTY	FUGGY	GAMIC	GET ON	GLOOP
FLOSS	FORUM	FUGUE	GAMIN	GET TO	GLORY
FLOUR	FOSSA	FULLY	GAMMA	GETUP	GLOSS
FLOUT	FOSSE	FUMED	GAMMY	GET UP	GLOVE
FLOWN	FOULS	FUMER	GAMUT	GHANA	GLUED
FLUED	FOUND	FUMES	GANDA	GHATS	GLUER
FLUES	FOUNT	FUNDS	GANGS	GHENT	GLUEY
FLUFF	FOURS	FUNEN	GANJA	GHOST	GLUME

GLUTS	GRAIN	GUACO	HAGUE	HASN'T	HELOT
GLYPH	GRAMA	GUANO	HA-HAS	HASPS	HELPS
GNARL	GRAMS	GUARD	HAIDA	HASTE	HELVE
GNASH	GRAND	GUAVA	HAIFA	HASTY	HE-MAN
GNATS	GRANS	GUESS	HAIKU	HATCH	HE-MEN
GNOME	GRANT	GUEST	HAILS	HATED	HENAN
GOADS	GRAPE	GUIDE	HAIN'T	HATES	HENCE
GOALS	GRAPH	GUILD	HAIRS	HAUGH	HENGE
GOATS	GRASP	GUILE	HAIRY	HAULM	HENIE
GODLY	GRASS	GUILT	HAITI	HAULS	HENNA
GOERS	GRATE	GUISE	HAJJI	HAUNT	HENRY
GOFER	GRAVE	GULAG	HAKEA	HAUSA	HENZE
GOGGA	GRAVY	GULAR	HAKES	HAVEN	HERAT
GOIAS	GRAYS	GULCH	HAKIM	HAVER	HERBS
GOING	GRAZE	GULES	HALAL	HAVES	HERBY
GOLDS	GREAT	GULFS	HALER	HAVOC	HERDS
GOLEM	GREBE	GULLS	HALIC	HAVRE	HERES
GOLLY	GRECO-	GULLY	HALID	HAWES	HERNE
GOMEL	GREED	GULPS	HALLE	HAWKS	HEROD
GONAD	GREEK	GUMBO	HALLO	HAWSE	HERON
GONDI	GREEN	GUMMA	HALLS	HAYDN	HERTZ
GONER	GREER	GUMMY	HALMA	HAZED	HESSE
GONGS	GREET	GUNGE	HALOS	HAZEL	HET UP
GONNA	GREYS	GUPPY	HALTS	HAZER	HEWED
GOODS	GRIDS	GURUS	HALVE	HAZES	HEWER
GOODY	GRIEF	GUSSY	HAMAL	H-BOMB	HEXAD
GOOEY	GRIFT	GUSTO	HAMMY	HEADS	HEXED
GOOFS	GRIKE	GUSTS	HAMZA	HEADY	HEXER
GOOFY	GRILL	GUSTY	HANAU	HEALY	HEXES
GOOLE	GRIME	GUTSY	HANCE	HEAPS	HEXYL
GOONS	GRIMY	GUTTA	HANDS	HEARD	HICKS
GOOSE	GRIND	GUYED	HANDY	HEART	HIDER
GOOSY	GRINS	GUYOT	HANKS	HEATH	HIDES
GORAL	GRIPE	GWENT	HANKY	HEAVE	HI-FIS
GORED	GRIPS	GWERU	HANOI	HEAVY	HIGHS
GORES	GRIST	GYPSY	HANSA	HEBEI	HIGHT
GORGE	GRITS	GYRAL	HANSE	HEDGE	HIJAZ
GORKI	GROAN		HANTS	HEDGY	HIKED
GORSE	GROAT	**H**	HAPLY	HEELS	HIKER
GOTHA	GROIN		HAPPY	HEFEI	HIKES
GOT UP	GROOM	HABER	HARAM	HEFTY	HILAR
GOUDA	GROPE	HABIT	HARAR	HEGEL	HILLA
GOUGE	GROSS	HACEK	HARDS	HEIRS	HILLS
GOURD	GROUP	HACKS	HARDY	HEIST	HILLY
GOUTY	GROUT	HADAL	HARED	HEJAZ	HILTS
GOWER	GROVE	HADES	HAREM	HEKLA	HILUM
GOWNS	GROWL	HADJI	HARES	HELEN	HILUS
GRABS	GROWN	HADN'T	HARPS	HELIX	HINDI
GRACE	GRUBS	HADST	HARPY	HELLE	HINDS
GRADE	GRUEL	HAFIZ	HARRY	HELLO	HINDU
GRAFT	GRUFF	HAFTS	HARSH	HELLS	HINES
GRAIL	GRUNT	HAGAR	HARTS	HELMS	HINGE
		HAGEN			

HINNY	HOOKY	HUMPS	ILEUM	IRISH	JESUS
HI NRG	HOOPS	HUMPY	ILEUS	IRKED	JETTY
HINTS	HOOTS	HUMUS	ILIAC	IRONS	JEWEL
HIPPO	HOPED	HUNAN	ILIAD	IRONY	JEWRY
HIPPY	HOPEH	HUNCH	ILIUM	ISERE	JIBED
HIRAM	HOPER	HUNKS	IMAGE	ISLAM	JIBES
HIRED	HOPES	HUNTS	IMAGO	ISLAY	JIDDA
HIRER	HORAE	HUPEH	IMAMS	ISLES	JIFFY
HIRST	HORAL	HURDS	IMBED	ISLET	JIHAD
HITCH	HORDE	HURON	IMBUE	ISSUE	JILIN
HIT ON	HOREB	HURRY	IMIDE	ISTLE	JIMMY
HIVED	HORME	HURST	IMINE	ITALO-	JINAN
HIVES	HORNS	HURTS	IMPEL	ITALY	JINGO
HOARD	HORNY	HUSKS	IMPLY	ITCHY	JINJA
HOARY	HORSA	HUSKY	IN ALL	ITEMS	JINKS
HOBBS	HORSE	HUSSY	INANE	IVIED	JINNI
HOBBY	HORST	HUTCH	INAPT	IVIES	JIVED
HOBOS	HORSY	HYADS	INCUR	IVORY	JOCKS
HOCKS	HORUS	HYDRA	INCUS	IZMIR	JOINS
HOCUS	HOSEA	HYDRO	INDEX	IZMIT	JOINT
HOFEI	HOSED	HYENA	INDIA		JOIST
HOFUF	HOSES	HYING	INDIC	**J**	JOKED
HOGAN	HOSTA	HYMEN	INDRE		JOKER
HO-HUM	HOSTS	HYMNS	INDUS	JABOT	JOKES
HOICK	HOTAN	HYPED	INEPT	JACKS	JOLLY
HOIST	HOTEL	HYPER	INERT	JADED	JOLTS
HOKKU	HOTLY	HYPOS	INFER	JADES	JONAH
HOKUM	HOUGH		INFIX	JAFFA	JORUM
HOLDS	HOUND		IN FOR	JAILS	JOULE
HOLES	HOURI	**I**	INGOT	JALAP	JOUST
HOLEY	HOURS	IAMBS	INION	JAMBI	JOVES
HOLLA	HOUSE	I-BEAM	INKED	JAMBS	JOWLS
HOLLO	HOVEL	IBIZA	INK IN	JAMES	JOYED
HOLLY	HOVER	ICIER	INKLE	JAMMU	JUDAS
HOLST	HOWDY	ICILY	IN-LAW	JAMMY	JUDGE
HOMER	HOWLS	ICING	INLAY	JAPAN	JUGAL
HOMES	HOYLE	ICONS	INLET	JAPER	JUGUM
HOMEY	HSIAN	ICTIC	INNER	JAPES	JUICE
HONAN	HUBBY	ICTUS	INPUT	JAUNT	JUICY
HONDO	HUBEI	IDAHO	INSET	JAWED	JUJUS
HONED	HUBLI	IDEAL	INTER	JAZZY	JULEP
HONEY	HUFFY	IDEAS	INTRO	JEANS	JUMBO
HONKS	HUFUF	IDIOM	INUIT	JEEPS	JUMPS
HONKY	HUGER	IDIOT	INURE	JEERS	JUMPY
HONOR	HULKS	IDLED	INURN	JEHOL	JUNCO
HOOCH	HULLO	IDLER	INVAR	JELLO	JUNES
HOODS	HULLS	IDOLS	IODIC	JELLY	JUNKS
HOODY	HULME	IDYLL	IONIC	JEMMY	JUNTA
HOOEY	HUMAN	IGLOO	IOTAS	JENNY	JUNTO
HOO-HA	HUMIC	IKEJA	IRAQI	JEREZ	JURAL
HOOKE	HUMID	IKONS	IRATE	JERKS	JURAT
HOOKS	HUMPH	ILEAC	IRBID	JERKY	JUREL

JUROR	KINGS	KURIL	LATEX	LETUP	LIRAS
JURUA	KININ	KURSK	LATHE	LET UP	LISLE
	KINKS	KUTCH	LATHS	LEVEE	LISTS
K	KINKY	KWARA	LATIN	LEVEL	LITER
KABUL	KIOSK	KWELA	LAUGH	LEVER	LITHE
KALAT	KIRIN	KYOTO	LAVAL	LEVIS	LITRE
KANDY	KIRKS		LAVER	LEWES	LIT UP
KANGA	KIROV	**L**	LAWKS	LEWIS	LIVED
KANSU	KITES	LABEL	LAWNS	LEXIS	LIVEN
KAPOK	KITTY	LACED	LAWNY	LEYTE	LIVER
KAPUT	KITWE	LACER	LAXLY	LHASA	LIVES
KARAT	KIWIS	LACES	LAY-BY	LIANA	LIVID
KAREN	KLONG	LADEN	LAYER	LIARS	LLAMA
KARMA	KNACK	LADER	LAY UP	LIBEL	LLANO
KAROO	KNAVE	LADLE	LAZED	LIBRA	LLOYD
KARST	KNEAD	LAGAN	LAZIO	LIBYA	LOACH
KASAI	KNEED	LAGER	LEACH	LICIT	LOADS
KASHI	KNEEL	LAGOS	LEADS	LICKS	LOAMY
KAUAI	KNEES	LAHTI	LEADY	LIDOS	LOANS
KAURI	KNELL	LAIRD	LEAFY	LIEGE	LOATH
KAYAK	KNELT	LAIRS	LEAKS	LIE IN	LOBAR
KAZAN	KNIFE	LAITY	LEAKY	LIE-IN	LOBBY
KAZOO	KNOBS	LAKER	LEANT	LIENS	LOBED
KBYTE	KNOCK	LAKES	LEAPS	LIEUS	LOBES
KEBAB	KNOLL	LAMAS	LEAPT	LIFER	LOCAL
KEDAH	KNOTS	LAMBS	LEARN	LIFTS	LOCHS
KEDGE	KNOWN	LAMED	LEASE	LIGER	LOCKS
KEELS	KNOWS	LAMER	LEASH	LIGHT	LOCUM
KEENS	KNURL	LAMPS	LEAST	LIKED	LOCUS
KEEPS	KOALA	LANAI	LEAVE	LIKEN	LODEN
KELLS	KOCHI	LANCE	LECCE	LIKES	LODES
KELLY	KOINE	LANDS	LEDGE	LILAC	LODGE
KENNY	KONGO	LANES	LEDGY	LILLE	LOESS
KENYA	KONYA	LANKY	LED ON	LILOS	LOFTS
KERBS	KOOKS	LAOAG	LEECH	LILTS	LOFTY
KERCH	KOOKY	LAOIS	LEEDS	LIMBO	LOGIC
KERRY	KORAN	LA PAZ	LEEKS	LIMBS	LOG IN
KETCH	KOREA	LAPEL	LEERS	LIMED	LOG ON
KEVEL	KORMA	LAPSE	LEERY	LIMEN	LOGOS
KEYED	KRAAL	LAP UP	LEFTY	LIMES	LOINS
KHAKI	KRAFT	LARCH	LEGAL	LIMEY	LOIRE
KHANS	KRAIT	LARGE	LEGER	LIMIT	LOLLY
KHMER	KREMS	LARGO	LEGGY	LINED	LONER
KIANG	KRILL	LARKS	LEGIT	LINEN	LOOKS
KICKS	KRONA	LARNE	LEMMA	LINER	LOOMS
KIKES	KRONE	LAROS	LEMON	LINES	LOONS
KILIM	KROON	LARVA	LEMUR	LINGO	LOONY
KILLS	KUDOS	LASER	LENDL	LININ	LOOPS
KILNS	KUDZU	LASSO	LENIS	LINKS	LOOPY
KILOS	KUFIC	LASTS	LENTO	LINTY	LOOSE
KILTS	KUKRI	LATCH	LEPER	LIONS	LOPED
KINDS	KULAK	LATER	LET ON	LIPID	LOPER

LORAN	LUVVY	MANDE	MEANT	MILAN	MOIST
LORDS	LUXOR	MANED	MEATH	MILCH	MOKES
LOREN	LUZON	MANES	MEATY	MILER	MOKPO
LORIS	LYCEE	MANGE	MECCA	MILES	MOLAL
LORRY	LYING	MANGO	MEDAL	MILKY	MOLAR
LOSER	LYMPH	MANGY	MEDAN	MILLS	MOLDS
LOSSY	LYNCH	MANIA	MEDIA	MIMED	MOLDY
LOTIC	LYRES	MANIC	MEDIC	MIMER	MOLES
LOTTA	LYRIC	MANLY	MEDOC	MIMES	MOLLS
LOTUS	LYSIN	MANNA	MEETS	MIMIC	MOLLY
LOUGH	LYSIS	MANNY	MELEE	MINCE	MOLTO
LOUPE	LYSOL	MANOR	MELON	MINDS	MOLTS
LOUSE	LYTIC	MANSE	MELOS	MINED	MOMMA
LOUSY	LYTTA	MANTA	MEMOS	MINER	MOMMY
LOUTH		MANUS	MENAI	MINES	MONAD
LOUTS	**M**	MAORI	MENDS	MINGY	MONAL
LOVAT	MACAO	MAPLE	MENUS	MINIM	MONCK
LOVED	MACAW	MARAE	MEOWS	MINIS	MONEY
LOVER	MACES	MARCH	MERCA	MINNA	MONKS
LOVES	MACHO	MARES	MERCY	MINOR	MONTH
LOVEY	MACLE	MARKS	MERES	MINSK	MONZA
LOWED	MACON	MARNE	MERGE	MINTS	MOOBS
LOWER	MACRO	MARRY	MERIT	MINUS	MOOCH
LOWLY	MADAM	MARSH	MERRY	MIRED	MOODS
LOYAL	MADLY	MASAI	MERSE	MIRES	MOODY
LUCCA	MAFIA	MASAN	MESIC	MIRID	MOOED
LUCID	MAGIC	MASER	MESNE	MIRTH	MOOLI
LUCKY	MAGMA	MASKS	MESON	MISER	MOONS
LUCRE	MAGUS	MASON	MESSY	MISSY	MOONY
LUFFA	MAIDS	MASSA	METAL	MISTS	MOORS
LUGER	MAINE	MASTS	METED	MISTY	MOOSE
LUMEN	MAINS	MATCH	METER	MITES	MOPED
LUMME	MAINZ	MATED	METHS	MITIS	MOPER
LUMPS	MAIZE	MATER	METOL	MITRE	MOP UP
LUMPY	MAJOR	MATES	ME-TOO	MITTS	MOP-UP
LUNAR	MAKER	MATEY	METRE	MIXED	MORAL
LUNCH	MAKES	MATIN	METRO	MIXER	MORAY
LUNGE	MALAR	MATSU	MEUSE	MIXES	MOREL
LUNGS	MALAY	MATTE	MEWED	MIX-UP	MORES
LUPIN	MALES	MAUVE	MEZZO	MIZAR	MORNS
LUPUS	MALLE	MAXIM	MIAMI	MOANS	MORON
LURCH	MALLS	MAYAN	MIAOW	MOATS	MORPH
LURED	MALMO	MAYBE	MICKS	MOCHA	MOSEY
LURER	MALTA	MAYN'T	MICRO	MOCKS	MOSSI
LURES	MALTY	MAYOR	MIDDY	MODAL	MOSSO
LUREX	MAMAS	MAYST	MIDGE	MODEL	MOSSY
LURGY	MAMBA	MAZES	MID-ON	MODEM	MOSUL
LURID	MAMBO	MBEKI	MIDST	MODES	MOTEL
LUSTS	MAMET	MEADS	MIENS	MOERS	MOTES
LUSTY	MAMEY	MEALS	MIFFY	MOGGY	MOTET
LUTES	MAMMA	MEALY	MIGHT	MOGUL	MOTHS
LUTON	MAMMY	MEANS	MIKES	MOIRE	MOTHY

MOTIF	MUTES	NEEDS	NIVAL	OATEN	OOTID
MOTOR	MUTTS	NEEDY	NIXED	OATHS	OOZED
MOTTO	MUZAK	NEGEV	NOBLE	OBEAH	OPALS
MOULD	MUZZY	NEGRO	NOBLY	OBESE	OP ART
MOULT	MWERU	NEGUS	NODAL	OBOES	OPERA
MOUND	MYALL	NEIGH	NODDY	OCCUR	OPINE
MOUNT	MYNAH	NELLY	NODES	OCEAN	OPIUM
MOURN	MYOMA	NEMAN	NODUS	OCHRE	OPTED
MOUSE	MYOPE	NEMEA	NOHOW	OCREA	OPTIC
MOUSY	MYRRH	NEPAL	NOISE	OCTAD	ORACH
MOUTH	MYTHS	NEPER	NOISY	OCTAL	ORATE
MOVED		NERDS	NOMAD	OCTET	ORBIT
MOVER	**N**	NERVE	NONCE	ODDER	ORDER
MOVES	NAAFI	NERVY	NOOKS	ODDLY	ORGAN
MOVIE	NABOB	NESTS	NO ONE	ODEUM	ORIBI
MOWED	NACRE	NEURO-	NOOSE	ODIUM	ORIEL
MOWER	NADIR	NEUSS	NOPAL	ODOUR	ORION
MOXIE	NAIAD	NEVER	NO-PAR	OFFAL	ORIYA
MOYLE	NAILS	NEVIS	NORMS	OFFER	ORLON
MUCIN	NAIVE	NEWEL	NORSE	OFGAS	ORLOP
MUCKY	NAKED	NEWER	NORTH	OFTEL	ORMER
MUCRO	NALGO	NEWLY	NOSED	OFTEN	ORRIS
MUCUS	NAMED	NEWRY	NOSES	OFWAT	ORURO
MUDDY	NAMES	NEWSY	NOTCH	OGIVE	OSAKA
MUFFS	NAMUR	NEWTS	NOTED	OGLED	OSCAR
MUFTI	NANCY	NEXUS	NOTES	OGLER	OSIER
MUGGY	NANNY	NICAD	NOTUM	OGRES	OSMIC
MULCH	NAPES	NICAM	NOUNS	OILED	OTAGO
MULCT	NAPPA	NICER	NOVAE	OILER	OTHER
MULES	NAPPE	NICHE	NOVAS	OINKS	OTTER
MULEY	NAPPY	NICKS	NOVEL	OKAPI	OUGHT
MULGA	NARES	NIDAL	NO WAY	OKAYS	OUIJA
MULLS	NARKS	NIDUS	NO-WIN	OLDEN	OUJDA
MULTI-	NARKY	NIECE	NOYON	OLDER	OUNCE
MUMMY	NARVA	NIFFY	NUCHA	OLEUM	OUTDO
MUMPS	NASAL	NIFTY	NUDDY	OLIVE	OUTER
MUMSY	NASIK	NIGER	NUDES	OLMEC	OUTGO
MUNCH	NASTY	NIGHT	NUDGE	OMAGH	OUTRE
MUNGO	NATAL	NIHIL	NUKED	OMAHA	OUTRO
MURAL	NATES	NIKKO	NUKUS	OMEGA	OUZEL
MUREX	NATTY	NIMBI	NURSE	OMENS	OVALS
MURKY	NAURU	NIMBY	NUTTY	OMUTA	OVARY
MURRE	NAVAL	NIMES	NYALA	ON AIR	OVATE
MUSED	NAVAR	NINES	NYLON	ON-AIR	OVENS
MUSER	NAVEL	NINNY	NYMPH	ON CUE	OVERS
MUSES	NAVES	NINON		ONEGA	OVERT
MUSHY	NAVVY	NINTH	**O**	ON ICE	OVINE
MUSIC	NAXOS	NIPPY	OAKEN	ONION	OVOID
MUSKY	NAZIS	NISEI	OAKUM	ONSET	OVOLO
MUSTH	NDOLA	NISUS	OARED	ON TAP	OVULE
MUSTY	'NEATH	NITRE	OASES	ON TOW	OWING
MUTED	NECKS	NITTY	OASIS	OOMPH	OWLET

OWNED	PAPPY	PEEPS	PIGGY	PLASM	PONCY
OWNER	PAPUA	PEERS	PIGMY	PLATE	PONDS
OXBOW	PARAS	PEEVE	PIING	PLATY	PONGS
OXEYE	PARCH	PEKOE	PIKER	PLAYS	PONGY
OXFAM	PARED	PELTS	PIKES	PLAZA	POOCH
OXIDE	PARER	PEMBA	PILAF	PLEAD	POOFS
OXIME	PARIS	PENAL	PILED	PLEAS	POOFY
OXLIP	PARKA	PENCE	PILES	PLEAT	POOLE
OZONE	PARKS	PENIS	PILLS	PLEBS	POOLS
	PARKY	PENNA	PILOT	PLICA	POONA
P	PARMA	PENNE	PIMPS	PLIED	POOPS
PACED	PAROL	PENNY	PINCH	PLIER	POPES
PACER	PARRY	PENZA	PINED	PLONK	POPPA
PACES	PARSE	PEONY	PINES	PLOTS	POPPY
PACKS	PARTS	PERAK	PINEY	PLOWS	POPSY
PACTS	PARTY	PERCH	PINGO	PLOYS	POP-UP
PADDY	PASAY	PERES	PINKO	PLUCK	PORCH
PADRE	PASHA	PERIL	PINKS	PLUGS	PORED
PADUA	PASSE	PERKS	PINNA	PLUMB	PORES
PAEAN	PASTA	PERKY	PINNY	PLUME	PORGY
PAEON	PASTE	PERRY	PINSK	PLUMP	PORKY
PAGAN	PASTO	PERSE	PINTA	PLUMS	PORNO
PAGED	PASTS	PER SE	PINTO	PLUMY	PORTS
PAGER	PASTY	PERTH	PINTS	PLUNK	POSED
PAGES	PATCH	PESKY	PINUP	PLUSH	POSER
PAILS	PATEN	PESOS	PIOUS	PLUTO	POSES
PAINS	PATER	PESTO	PIPAL	PLZEN	POSEY
PAINT	PATES	PESTS	PIPED	POACH	POSIT
PAIRS	PATHS	PETAL	PIPER	PO BOX	POSSE
PALEA	PATIO	PETER	PIPES	PODGY	POSTS
PALED	PATNA	PETIT	PIPIT	PODIA	POTTO
PALER	PATSY	PETTY	PIQUE	POEMS	POTTY
PALES	PATTY	PEWEE	PISTE	POESY	POUCH
PALLS	PAUSE	PEWIT	PITCH	POETS	POUFS
PALLY	PAVED	PHASE	PITHY	POGGE	POULT
PALMA	PAVIA	PHIAL	PITON	POILU	POUND
PALMS	PAWED	PHLOX	PITTA	POINT	POUTS
PALMY	PAWKY	PHONE	PIURA	POISE	POWAN
PALSY	PAWNS	PHONO	PIVOT	POKED	POWER
PANDA	PAYEE	PHOTO	PIXEL	POKER	POWYS
PANEL	PEACE	PHUTS	PIXIE	POKES	POXES
PANES	PEACH	PHYLA	PIZZA	POLAR	PRAMS
PANGS	PEAKS	PHYLE	PLACE	POLED	PRANK
PANIC	PEAKY	PIANO	PLAGE	POLES	PRASE
PANNE	PEALS	PIAUI	PLAID	POLIO	PRATE
PANSY	PEARL	PICKS	PLAIN	POLJE	PRATO
PANTS	PEARS	PICKY	PLAIT	POLKA	PRATS
PANTY	PEATS	PICOT	PLANE	POLLS	PRAWN
PAPAL	PEATY	PIECE	PLANK	POLYP	PREEN
PAPAS	PECAN	PIERS	PLANS	POLYS	PREPS
PAPAW	PECKS	PIETA	PLANT	POMMY	PRESA
PAPER	PEDAL	PIETY	PLASH	PONCE	PRESS

PRICE	PUFFS	QUALE	RADOM	RAZOR	RESIN
PRICK	PUFFY	QUALM	RADON	REACH	RESIT
PRICY	PUKED	QUANT	RAFTS	REACT	RESTS
PRIDE	PUKKA	QUARK	RAGAS	READY	RETCH
PRIED	PULER	QUART	RAGED	REALM	RETRO
PRIER	PULLS	QUASH	RAGES	REAMS	RETRO-
PRIGS	PULPS	QUASI-	RAGGA	REARM	RETRY
PRILL	PULPY	QUAYS	RAIDS	REARS	REUSE
PRIME	PULSE	QUEEN	RAILS	REBEL	REVEL
PRIMO	PUMAS	QUEER	RAINS	REBUS	REVET
PRIMP	PUMPS	QUELL	RAINY	REBUT	REVUE
PRINK	PUNCH	QUERN	RAISE	RECAP	REXES
PRINT	PUNKA	QUERY	RAITA	RECON	RHEAS
PRION	PUNKS	QUEST	RAJAH	RECTO	RHEUM
PRIOR	PUNTS	QUEUE	RAKED	RECUR	RHINE
PRISE	PUNTY	QUICK	RAKER	REDAN	RHINO
PRISM	PUPAE	QUIET	RAKES	REDIA	RHONE
PRIVY	PUPAL	QUIFF	RALLY	REDID	RHUMB
PRIZE	PUPAS	QUILL	RAMIE	REEDS	RHYME
PRO-AM	PUPIL	QUILT	RAMPS	REEDY	RIALS
PROBE	PUPPY	QUINE	RAMUS	REEFS	RICIN
PRODS	PUREE	QUINS	RANCE	REEKY	RICKS
PROEM	PURER	QUINT	RANCH	REELS	RIDER
PROFS	PURGE	QUIPS	R AND B	REEVE	RIDES
PROLE	PURRS	QUIRE	R AND D	REFER	RIDGE
PROMO	PURSE	QUIRK	RANDY	REFIT	RIDGY
PROMS	PUSAN	QUIRT	RANEE	REGAL	RIFFS
PRONE	PUSHY	QUITE	RANGE	REICH	RIFLE
PRONG	PUSSY	QUITO	RANGY	REIFY	RIFTS
PROOF	PUT ON	QUITS	RANKS	REIGN	RIGHT
PROPS	PUT-ON	QUOIN	RAPED	REIKI	RIGID
PROSE	PUTTO	QUOIT	RAPES	REIMS	RIGOR
PROST	PUTTS	QUORN	RAPHE	REINS	RILED
PROSY	PUTTY	QUOTA	RAPID	REJIG	RILEY
PROTO-	PYGMY	QUOTE	RARER	REKEY	RILLS
PROUD	PYLON	QUOTH	RASHT	RELAX	RINDS
PROVE	PYOID	QUR'AN	RASPS	RELAY	RINGS
PROWL	PYRAN		RATAL	RELIC	RINKS
PROWS	PYRES	**R**	RATED	REMEX	RINSE
PROXY	PYREX	RABAT	RATEL	REMIT	RIOJA
PRUDE	PYXES	RABBI	RATES	RENAL	RIOTS
PRUNE	PYXIE	RABIC	RATIO	RENEW	RIPEN
PSALM	PYXIS	RABID	RATTY	RENIN	RIPER
PSEUD		RABIN	RAVED	RENTE	RIPON
PSKOV	**Q**	RACED	RAVEL	RENTS	RISEN
PSOAS	QATAR	RACER	RAVEN	REPAY	RISER
PSYCH	QUACK	RACES	RAVER	REPEL	RISES
PUBES	QUADS	RACKS	RAWER	REPLY	RISKS
PUBIC	QUAFF	RADAR	RAWLY	RERAN	RISKY
PUBIS	QUAIL	RADII	RAYON	RERUN	RITES
PUCKS	QUAKE	RADIO	RAZED	RESAT	RITZY
PUDGY	QUAKY	RADIX	RAZER	RESET	RIVAL

RIVEN	ROWAN	SAFER	SAUNA	SCRAM	SERVE
RIVER	ROWDY	SAFES	SAURY	SCRAP	SERVO
RIVET	ROWED	SAGAS	SAUTE	SCREE	SETAL
RIYAL	ROWEL	SAGES	SAVED	SCREW	SET ON
ROACH	ROWER	SAGGY	SAVER	SCRIM	SET TO
ROADS	ROYAL	SAHIB	SAVES	SCRIP	SET-TO
ROANS	RUBLE	SAIDA	SAVIN	SCRUB	SET UP
ROARS	RUCHE	SAIGA	SAVOY	SCRUM	SET-UP
ROAST	RUCKS	SAILS	SAVVY	SCUBA	SEVEN
ROBED	RUDDY	SAINT	SAWED	SCUFF	SEVER
ROBES	RUDER	SAKAI	SAWER	SCULL	SEWED
ROBIN	RUFFE	SAKER	SAXON	SCURF	SEWER
ROBLE	RUFFS	SAKES	SAYER	SCUTE	SEXED
ROBOT	RUGBY	SALAD	SAY SO	SEALS	SEXES
ROCKS	RUING	SALEM	SAY-SO	SEAMS	SHABA
ROCKY	RUINS	SALEP	SCABS	SEAMY	SHACK
RODEO	RULED	SALES	SCADS	SEATS	SHADE
ROGER	RULER	SALIC	SCALD	SEBUM	SHADY
ROGUE	RULES	SALLY	SCALE	SECCO	SHAFT
ROLES	RUMBA	SALOL	SCALL	SECTS	SHAGS
ROLLS	RUMEN	SALON	SCALP	SEDAN	SHAHS
ROMAN	RUMMY	SALOP	SCALY	SEDGE	SHAKE
ROMEO	RUMPS	SALPA	SCAMP	SEDGY	SHAKO
ROMER	RUNES	SALTA	SCAMS	SEDUM	SHAKY
ROMPS	RUNGS	SALTS	SCANS	SEEDS	SHALE
RONDO	RUNIC	SALTY	SCANT	SEEDY	SHALL
ROODS	RUN IN	SALVE	SCAPE	SEERS	SHALT
ROOFS	RUN-IN	SALVO	SCARE	SEGNO	SHALY
ROOKS	RUNNY	SAMAR	SCARF	SEINE	SHAME
ROOMS	RUNTS	SAMBA	SCARP	SEISE	SHAMS
ROOMY	RUNTY	SAMEY	SCARS	SEISM	SHANK
ROOST	RUN-UP	SAMOA	SCART	SEIZE	SHAN'T
ROOTS	RUPEE	SAMOS	SCARY	SELBY	SHAPE
ROPED	RURAL	SANDS	SCAUP	SELES	SHARD
ROPES	RUSHY	SANDY	SCEND	SELVA	SHARE
ROPEY	RUSKS	SANER	SCENE	SEMEN	SHARK
ROSES	RUSSO-	SAPID	SCENT	SEMIS	SHARP
ROSIN	RUSTY	SAPPY	SCHWA	SENNA	SHAVE
ROTAS	RUTTY	SARAN	SCION	SENOR	SHAWL
ROTOR		SARGE	SCOFF	SENSE	SHEAF
ROUEN		SARIN	SCOLD	SENZA	SHEAR
ROUES	S	SARIS	SCONE	SEOUL	SHEDS
ROUGE	SABAH	SARKY	SCOOP	SEPAL	SHEEN
ROUGH	SABER	SAROS	SCOOT	SEPIA	SHEEP
ROUND	SABIN	SASSY	SCOPE	SEPOY	SHEER
ROUPY	SABLE	SATAN	SCORE	SERAC	SHEET
ROUSE	SABOT	SATED	SCORN	SERFS	SHEIK
ROUST	SABRA	SATEM	SCOTS	SERGE	SHELF
ROUTE	SABRE	SATIN	SCOUR	SERIF	SHELL
ROUTS	SACKS	SATYR	SCOUT	SERIN	SHERD
ROVED	SADHU	SAUCE	SCOWL	SEROW	SHEWN
ROVER	SADLY	SAUCY	SCRAG	SERUM	SHIAH

SHIED	SIDES	SKEET	SLINK	SNATH	SONGS
SHIER	SIDLE	SKEIN	SLIPS	SNEAK	SONIC
SHIES	SIEGE	SKELP	SLITS	SNECK	SONNY
SHIFT	SIENA	SKEWS	SLOBS	SNEER	SOOTY
SHILY	SIEVE	SKIDS	SLOES	SNICK	SOPOR
SHINE	SIGHS	SKIED	SLOGS	SNIDE	SOPPY
SHINS	SIGHT	SKIEN	SLOOP	SNIFF	SORES
SHINY	SIGLA	SKIER	SLOPE	SNIPE	SORGO
SHIPS	SIGMA	SKIES	SLOPS	SNIPS	SORRY
SHIRE	SIGNS	SKIFF	SLOSH	SNOBS	SORTS
SHIRK	SIKHS	SKILL	SLOTH	SNOEK	SORUS
SHIRR	SILEX	SKIMP	SLOTS	SNOGS	SOTHO
SHIRT	SILKS	SKINK	SLUED	SNOOD	SOUGH
SHITE	SILKY	SKINS	SLUGS	SNOOK	SOULS
SHITS	SILLS	SKINT	SLUMP	SNOOP	SOUND
SHIVE	SILLY	SKIPS	SLUMS	SNORE	SOUPS
SHLUH	SILOS	SKIRL	SLUNG	SNORT	SOUPY
SHOAL	SILTY	SKIRT	SLUNK	SNOUT	SOUSE
SHOAT	SIMLA	SKITS	SLURP	SNOWS	SOUTH
SHOCK	SIMON	SKIVE	SLURS	SNOWY	SOWED
SHOED	SINAI	SKUAS	SLUSH	SNUBS	SOWER
SHOER	SINCE	SKULK	SLUTS	SNUFF	SOYUZ
SHOES	SINES	SKULL	SLYER	SNUGS	SPACE
SHONA	SINEW	SKUNK	SLYPE	SOAKS	SPADE
SHONE	SINGE	SLABS	SMACK	SOAPS	SPAIN
SHOOK	SINKS	SLACK	SMALL	SOAPY	SPALL
SHOOT	SINUS	SLAGS	SMALT	SOBER	SPAMS
SHOPS	SIOUX	SLAIN	SMARM	SOCHE	SPANK
SHORE	SIRED	SLAKE	SMART	SOCHI	SPARE
SHORN	SIREN	SLANG	SMASH	SOCIO-	SPARK
SHORT	SIRES	SLANT	SMEAR	SOCKS	SPARS
SHOTS	SISAL	SLAPS	SMELL	SOCLE	SPASM
SHOTT	SISSY	SLASH	SMELT	SODAS	SPATE
SHOUT	SITAR	SLATE	SMILE	SOFAR	SPATS
SHOVE	SITED	SLATS	SMIRK	SOFAS	SPAWN
SHOWN	SITES	SLATY	SMITE	SOFIA	SPEAK
SHOWS	SIT-IN	SLAVE	SMITH	SOFTA	SPEAR
SHOWY	SITKA	SLAVS	SMOCK	SOFTY	SPECK
SHRED	SIT ON	SLEDS	SMOKE	SOGGY	SPECS
SHREW	SIT UP	SLEEK	SMOKY	SOILS	SPEED
SHRUB	SIT-UP	SLEEP	SMOLT	SOLAR	SPELL
SHRUG	SITUS	SLEET	SMOTE	SOLED	SPELT
SHUCK	SIVAS	SLEPT	SMUTS	SOLES	SPEND
SHUNT	SIXES	SLEWS	SNACK	SOL-FA	SPENT
SHUSH	SIXMO	SLICE	SNAFU	SOLID	SPERM
SHYED	SIXTE	SLICK	SNAGS	SOLOS	SPICA
SHYER	SIXTH	SLIDE	SNAIL	SOLTI	SPICE
SHYLY	SIXTY	SLIGO	SNAKE	SOLUM	SPICS
SIBIU	SIZAR	SLILY	SNAKY	SOLVE	SPICY
SIBYL	SIZED	SLIME	SNAPS	SOMME	SPIED
SICKO	SIZES	SLIMY	SNARE	SONAR	SPIEL
SIDED	SKATE	SLING	SNARL	SONDE	SPIES

SPIFF	STABS	STIRK	SUDSY	SWILL	TALUS
SPIKE	STACK	STIRS	SUEDE	SWIMS	TAMED
SPIKS	STAFF	STOAT	SUETY	SWINE	TAMER
SPIKY	STAGE	STOCK	SUGAR	SWING	TAMMY
SPILE	STAGS	STOEP	SUING	SWIPE	TAMPA
SPILL	STAGY	STOIC	SUINT	SWIRL	TANGA
SPILT	STAID	STOKE	SUITE	SWISH	TANGO
SPIME	STAIN	STOLE	SUITS	SWISS	TANGY
SPINE	STAIR	STOMA	SULKS	SWOON	TANKS
SPINS	STAKE	STOMP	SULKY	SWOOP	TANSY
SPINY	STALE	STONE	SULLY	SWOPS	TANTA
SPIRE	STALK	STONY	SUMBA	SWORD	TANTO
SPIRY	STALL	STOOD	SUMPS	SWORE	TAPAS
SPITE	STAMP	STOOK	SUNNI	SWORN	TAPED
SPITS	STAND	STOOL	SUNNY	SWOTS	TAPER
SPITZ	STANK	STOOP	SUN-UP	SWUNG	TAPES
SPIVS	STANS	STOPE	SUPER	SYLPH	TAPIR
SPLAT	STARE	STOPS	SUPRA	SYLVA	TAPIS
SPLAY	STARK	STORE	SURAH	SYNOD	TARDY
SPLIT	STARS	STORK	SURAL	SYRIA	TARES
SPOCK	START	STORM	SURAT	SYRUP	TARGA
SPODE	STASH	STORY	SURDS	SYSOP	TARNS
SPOIL	STATE	STOSS	SURER		TAROS
SPOKE	STAVE	STOUP	SURFY	**T**	TAROT
SPOOF	STAYS	STOUR	SURGE	TABBY	TARRY
SPOOK	STEAD	STOUT	SURLY	TABES	TARSI
SPOOL	STEAK	STOVE	SUSHI	TABLE	TARTS
SPOON	STEAL	STRAP	SWABS	TABOO	TARTU
SPOOR	STEAM	STRAW	SWAGE	TABOR	TASKS
SPORE	STEED	STRAY	SWAIN	TACET	TASTE
SPORT	STEEL	STREW	SWALE	TACIT	TASTY
SPOTS	STEEP	STRIA	SWAMI	TACKS	TATAR
SPOUT	STEER	STRIP	SWAMP	TACKY	TATRA
SPRAG	STEIN	STROP	SWANK	TACOS	TATTY
SPRAT	STELE	STRUM	SWANS	TAEGU	TAUNT
SPRAY	STEMS	STRUT	SWAPS	TAFFY	TAUPE
SPREE	STEPS	STUBS	SWARD	TAFIA	TAWER
SPRIG	STERE	STUCK	SWARF	TAIGA	TAWNY
SPRIT	STERN	STUDS	SWARM	TAILS	TAXED
SPRUE	STEWS	STUDY	SWASH	TAINO	TAXER
SPUDS	STEYR	STUFF	SWATH	TAINT	TAXES
SPUME	STICH	STULL	SWATS	TA'IZZ	TAXIS
SPUNK	STICK	STUMP	SWAZI	TAJIK	TAXON
SPURN	STIES	STUNG	SWEAR	TAKEN	TAYRA
SPURS	STIFF	STUNK	SWEAT	TAKER	TAZZA
SPURT	STILE	STUNT	SWEDE	TAKES	T-BONE
SQUAB	STILL	STUPE	SWEEP	TAKIN	TEACH
SQUAD	STILT	STYLE	SWEET	TALCA	TEAKS
SQUAT	STING	SUAVE	SWELL	TALES	TEAMS
SQUAW	STINK	SUCRE	SWEPT	TALKS	TEARS
SQUIB	STINT	SUDAN	SWIFT	TALLY	TEASE
SQUID	STIPE	SUDOR	SWIGS	TALON	TEATS

TECHY	THIEF	TIMID	TOOLS	TREAD	TUBAL
TEENS	THIGH	TINEA	TOOTH	TREAT	TUBAS
TEENY	THINE	TINES	TOOTS	TREEN	TUBBY
TEETH	THING	TINGE	TOPAZ	TREES	TUBER
TELEX	THINK	TINGS	TOPEE	TREKS	TUBES
TELIC	THIOL	TINNY	TOPER	TREND	TUCKS
TELLY	THIRD	TINTS	TOPIC	TRESS	TUDOR
TEMPI	THOLE	TIPSY	TOPOS	TREWS	TUFTS
TEMPO	THONG	TIP UP	TOP UP	TRIAD	TUFTY
TEMPS	THORN	TIRED	TOQUE	TRIAL	TULIP
TEMPT	THOSE	TIREE	TORAH	TRIBE	TULLE
TENCH	THREE	TIRES	TORCH	TRICE	TULSA
TENET	THREW	TIROS	TORIC	TRICK	TUMID
TENON	THROB	TITAN	TORSK	TRIED	TUMMY
TENOR	THROW	TITHE	TORSO	TRIER	TUNAS
TENSE	THRUM	TITLE	TORTS	TRIES	TUNED
TENTH	THUDS	TITRE	TORUN	TRIKE	TUNER
TENTS	THUGS	TITTY	TORUS	TRILL	TUNES
TEPAL	THUJA	TIZZY	TOTAL	TRIMS	TUNIC
TEPEE	THUMB	TOADS	TOTED	TRINE	TUNIS
TEPIC	THUMP	TOADY	TOTEM	TRIOL	TUNNY
TEPID	THUNK	TOAST	TOTER	TRIOS	TUQUE
TERMS	THYME	TODAY	TOTES	TRIPE	TURDS
TERNE	TIARA	TODDY	TOUCH	TRIPS	TURFS
TERNI	TIBET	TO-DOS	TOUGH	TRITE	TURFY
TERNS	TIBIA	TOE-IN	TOURS	TROLL	TURIN
TERRA	TICAL	TOFFS	TOUTS	TRONA	TURKI
TERRY	TICKS	TOGAS	TOWED	TRONK	TURKU
TERSE	TIDAL	TOILE	TOWEL	TROOP	TURNS
TESLA	TIDED	TOILS	TOWER	TROPE	TURPS
TESOL	TIDES	TOKAY	TOWIE	TROTH	TUSKS
TESTA	TIE-IN	TOKEN	TOWNS	TROTS	TUTEE
TESTS	TIE-ON	TOKYO	TOXIC	TROUT	TUTOR
TESTY	TIERS	TOLAN	TOXIN	TROVE	TUTSI
TETRA	TIE UP	TOLLS	TOYED	TRUCE	TUTTI
TEXAS	TIE-UP	TOLYL	TOYER	TRUCK	TUTTY
TEXTS	TIFFS	TOMBS	TRACE	TRUER	TUTUS
THANE	TIGER	TOMES	TRACK	TRUES	TWAIN
THANK	TIGHT	TOMMY	TRACT	TRUGO	TWANG
THAWS	TIGON	TOMSK	TRADE	TRUGS	TWATS
THECA	TIGRE	TONAL	TRAIL	TRULY	TWEAK
THEFT	TIKKA	TONDO	TRAIN	TRUMP	TWEED
THEGN	TILDE	TONED	TRAIT	TRUNK	TWEEN
THEIR	TILED	TONER	TRAMP	TRURO	TWEET
THEME	TILER	TONES	TRAMS	TRUSS	TWERP
THERA	TILES	TONGA	TRANS-	TRUST	TWICE
THERE	TILLS	TONGS	TRAPS	TRUTH	TWIGS
THERM	TILTH	TONIC	TRASH	TRYMA	TWILL
THESE	TILTS	TONNE	TRASS	TRY ON	TWINE
THETA	TIMED	TON UP	TRAVE	TRY-ON	TWINS
THEWS	TIMER	TON-UP	TRAWL	TRYST	TWIRL
THICK	TIMES	TONUS	TRAYS	TSARS	TWIRP

TWIST	UNRIG	VARIA	VINYL	WADER	WEBER
TWITE	UNRIP	VARIX	VIOLA	WADGE	WEDGE
TWITS	UNSAY	VARNA	VIOLS	WADIS	WEDGY
TWIXT	UNSET	VARUS	VIPER	WAFER	WEEDS
TYING	UNSEX	VARVE	VIRAL	WAGED	WEEDY
TYPED	UNTIE	VASES	VIREO	WAGER	WEEKS
TYPES	UNTIL	VAULT	VIRGA	WAGES	WEENY
TYRES	UNZIP	VAUNT	VIRGO	WAGON	WEEPY
TYROL	UP-BOW	V-CHIP	VIRTU	WAHOO	WEIGH
TYROS	UPEND	VEDDA	VIRUS	WAIFS	WEIRD
TYSON	UPOLU	VEDIC	VISAS	WAIST	WEIRS
TZARS	UPPER	VEERY	VISBY	WAIVE	WELCH
TZU-PO	UPSET	VEGAN	VISES	WAJDA	WELDS
	URALS	VEILS	VISEU	WAKED	WELLS
U	URATE	VEINS	VISIT	WAKEN	WELLY
U-BOAT	URBAN	VEINY	VISOR	WAKER	WELSH
UDDER	UREAL	VELAR	VISTA	WAKES	WELTS
UDINE	UREDO	VELUM	VITAL	WALES	WENCH
UGRIC	URGED	VENAL	VITTA	WALKS	WESER
UHURU	URGER	VENDA	VIVID	WALLS	WETLY
UIGUR	URGES	VENIN	VIXEN	WALLY	WHACK
ULCER	URINE	VENOM	V-NECK	WALTZ	WHALE
ULNAR	USAGE	VENTS	VOCAB	WANDS	WHAMS
ULNAS	USERS	VENUE	VOCAL	WANED	WHANG
ULTRA-	USHER	VENUS	VODKA	WANES	WHARF
ULURU	USING	VERBS	VOGUE	WANEY	WHEAL
UMBEL	USUAL	VERGE	VOGUL	WANLY	WHEAT
UMBER	USURP	VERSE	VOICE	WANTS	WHEEL
UMBRA	USURY	VERSO	VOIDS	WARDS	WHELK
UMIAK	UTERI	VERVE	VOILE	WARES	WHELP
UNAPT	UTTER	VESTA	VOLAR	WARPS	WHERE
UNARY	U-TURN	VESTS	VOLES	WARTS	WHICH
UNBAR	UVEAL	VETCH	VOLTA	WARTY	WHIFF
UNCAP	UVULA	VEXED	VOLTS	WASHY	WHIGS
UNCLE	UZBEK	VEXER	VOLVA	WASPS	WHILE
UNCUS		VIALS	VOMER	WASTE	WHIMS
UNCUT	**V**	VIAND	VOMIT	WATCH	WHINE
UNDER	VAASA	VIBES	VOTED	WATER	WHINY
UNDID	VADUZ	VICAR	VOTER	WATTS	WHIPS
UNDUE	VAGAL	VICES	VOTES	WAVED	WHIRL
UNFIT	VAGUE	VICHY	VOUCH	WAVER	WHIRR
UNFIX	VAGUS	VIDAL	VOWED	WAVES	WHIRS
UNIAT	VALES	VIDEO	VOWEL	WAXED	WHISK
UNIFY	VALET	VIEWS	VOWER	WAXEN	WHIST
UNION	VALID	VIGIA	V-SIGN	WAXER	WHITE
UNITE	VALSE	VIGIL	VULVA	WEALD	WHITS
UNITS	VALUE	VILER	VYING	WEALS	WHIZZ
UNITY	VALVE	VILLA		WEARY	WHOLE
UNLAY	VAMPS	VIMEN	**W**	WEAVE	WHOOP
UNMAN	VANDA	VINCA	WACKY	WEBBY	WHORE
UNPEG	VANES	VINES	WADDY		WHORL
UNPIN	VAPID	VINIC	WADED		WHOSE

WICCA	WIPES	WORMS	WURST	YAWNS	YUCCA
WICKS	WIRED	WORMY	WUSIH	Y-AXIS	YUCKY
WIDEN	WIRER	WORRY		YEARN	YUKON
WIDER	WIRES	WORSE	**X**	YEARS	YULAN
WIDES	WISER	WORST	X-AXIS	YEAST	YUMAN
WIDOW	WISPS	WORTH	XENIA	YELLS	
WIDTH	WISPY	WOULD	XENON	YELPS	**Z**
WIELD	WITCH	WOUND	XERIC	YEMEN	ZAIRE
WIGAN	WITHE	WOVEN	XEROX	YERBA	ZAMIA
WIGHT	WITHY	WOWED	XHOSA	YETIS	ZANTE
WILCO	WITTY	WRACK	X-RAYS	YIBIN	ZAPPY
WILDS	WIVES	WRAPS	X-UNIT	YIELD	ZARGA
WILES	WIZEN	WRATH	XYLAN	YIKES	ZARIA
WILLS	WOKEN	WREAK	XYLEM	YODEL	ZARQA
WILLY	WOLDS	WRECK	XYLOL	YOGIC	Z-AXIS
WIMPS	WOLOF	WRENS	XYLYL	YOGIS	ZEBRA
WIMPY	WOMAN	WREST		YOKED	ZEIST
WINCE	WOMBS	WRIED	**Y**	YOKEL	ZENIC
WINCH	WOMEN	WRIER	YACHT	YOKES	ZEROS
WINDS	WONKY	WRING	YAHOO	YOLKS	ZESTY
WINDY	WOODS	WRIST	YAKUT	YOLKY	ZIBET
WINED	WOODY	WRITE	YALTA	YONKS	ZILCH
WINES	WOOED	WRITS	YANAN	YONNE	ZINGY
WINEY	WOOER	WRONG	YANKS	YOUNG	ZIPPY
WINGE	WOOFS	WROTE	YAPOK	YOURS	ZLOTY
WINGS	WOOZY	WROTH	YAPPY	YOUSE	ZOMBA
WINKS	WORDS	WRUNG	YARDS	YOUTH	ZONAL
WINZE	WORDY	WRYER	YARNS	YOWLS	ZONED
WIPED	WORKS	WRYLY	YAWED	YOYOS	ZONES
WIPER	WORLD	WUHAN	YAWLS	YPRES	ZOOID

6

A	ACCENT	ADNOUN	AGE OLD	ALIPED	AMEBIC
AACHEN	ACCEPT	ADORED	AGHAST	ALKALI	AMENDS
AARGAU	ACCESS	ADRIFT	AGNATE	ALKANE	AMHARA
AARHUS	ACCORD	ADROIT	AGOGIC	ALKENE	AMIDIC
ABACUS	ACCOST	ADSORB	AGONIC	ALKYNE	AMIDOL
ABADAN	ACCRUE	ADULTS	AGOUTI	ALLEGE	AMIDST
ABAKAN	ACCUSE	ADVENT	AGREED	ALLELE	AMIENS
ABASED	ACETAL	ADVERB	AIDING	ALLEYS	AMMINE
ABATED	ACETIC	ADVERT	AIKIDO	ALLIED	AMNION
ABATIS	ACETUM	ADVICE	AILING	ALLIER	AMOEBA
ABATOR	ACETYL	ADVISE	AIMING	ALLIES	AMORAL
ABBACY	ACHAEA	ADYGEI	AIRBED	ALLIUM	AMOUNT
ABBESS	ACHENE	ADZHAR	AIRBUS	ALL OUT	AMOURS
ABBEYS	ACHING	AECIUM	AIR-DRY	ALLOYS	AMPERE
ABBOTS	ACIDIC	AEDILE	AIRGUN	ALLUDE	AMPULE
ABDUCT	ACINIC	AEGEAN	AIRIER	ALLURE	AMRITA
ABELIA	ACINUS	AERATE	AIRILY	ALMADA	AMULET
ABIDED	ACNODE	AERIAL	AIRING	AL MARJ	AMUSED
ABIDER	ACORNS	AERIFY	AIRMAN	ALMATY	AMYLUM
ABJECT	ACQUIT	AEROBE	AIRMEN	ALMOND	AMYTAL
ABJURE	ACROSS	AERUGO	AIRWAY	ALMOST	ANABAS
ABKHAZ	ACTING	AETHER	AISLES	ALMUCE	ANADYR
ABLAUT	ACTION	AFFAIR	AKIMBO	ALNICO	ANALOG
ABLAZE	ACTIVE	AFFECT	AKMOLA	ALPACA	ANCHOR
ABOARD	ACTORS	AFFINE	AL-ANON	ALPHAS	ANCONA
ABODES	ACTS UP	AFFIRM	ALARMS	ALPINE	ANDEAN
ABORAL	ACTUAL	AFFLUX	ALASKA	ALSACE	ANDONG
ABOUND	ACUITY	AFFORD	ALBANY	ALSIKE	ANDROS
ABRADE	ACUMEN	AFFRAY	ALBEDO	ALTAIC	ANEMIA
ABROAD	ADAGES	AFGHAN	ALBEIT	ALTAIR	ANEMIC
ABRUPT	ADAGIO	AFIELD	ALBINO	ALTARS	ANERGY
ABSEIL	ADDEND	AFLAME	ALBION	ALTONA	ANGARY
ABSENT	ADDERS	AFL-CIO	ALBITE	ALUDEL	ANGELS
ABSORB	ADDICT	AFLOAT	ALBUMS	ALUMNA	ANGERS
ABSURD	ADDING	AFRAID	ALCOVE	ALUMNI	ANGINA
ABULIA	ADDLED	AFRESH	ALDISS	ALVINE	ANGKOR
ABULIC	ADD-ONS	AFRICA	ALDOSE	ALWAYS	ANGLED
ABUSED	ADDUCE	AFTERS	ALDRIN	AMADOU	ANGLER
ABUSER	ADDUCT	AGADIR	ALECKS	AMATOL	ANGLES
ABUSES	ADEPTS	AGAMIC	ALEGAR	AMAZED	ANGOLA
ABVOLT	ADHERE	AGARIC	ALEPPO	AMAZON	ANGORA
ABWATT	ADIEUS	AGATES	ALERTS	AMBALA	ANHALT
ACACIA	ADIEUX	AGEING	A LEVEL	AMBARY	ANHWEI
ACADIA	ADJOIN	AGEISM	ALGOID	AMBITS	ANIMAL
ACAJOU	ADJURE	AGEIST	AL HASA	AMBLED	ANIMUS
ACARID	ADJUST	AGENCY	ALIBIS	AMBLER	ANKARA
ACARUS	ADMIRE	AGENDA	ALIENS	AMBUSH	ANKING
ACCEDE	ADNATE	AGENTS	ALIGHT	AMEBAS	ANKLES

ANKLET	APLITE	ARMFUL	ASSORT	AUMBRY	BADGES
ANLAGE	APLOMB	ARMIES	ASSUME	AU PAIR	BAFFLE
ANNABA	APNOEA	ARMING	ASSURE	AUREUS	BAGELS
ANNALS	APODAL	ARMLET	ASTANA	AURORA	BAGGED
ANNEAL	APOGEE	ARMOUR	ASSUAN	AUROUS	BAGUIO
ANNECY	APOLLO	ARMPIT	ASTERN	AUSSIE	BAILED
ANNEXE	APPEAL	ARMURE	ASTHMA	AUSTIN	BAILEE
ANNUAL	APPEAR	ARNHEM	ASTRAL	AUSTRO-	BAILER
ANODES	APPEND	ARNICA	ASTRAY	AUTEUR	BAILEY
ANODIC	APPLES	AROMAS	ASTUTE	AUTHOR	BAILOR
ANOINT	APPLET	AROUND	ASWARM	AUTISM	BAIL UP
ANOMIC	APPOSE	AROUSE	ASYLUM	AUTUMN	BAIRNS
ANOMIE	APRILS	ARRACK	ATAXIA	AVATAR	BAITED
ANORAK	APRONS	ARRANT	ATAXIC	AVEIRO	BAKERS
ANOXIA	APULIA	ARRAYS	ATBARA	AVENGE	BAKERY
ANOXIC	AQUILA	ARREST	ATHENS	AVENUE	BAKING
ANQING	ARABIA	ARRIVE	AT HOME	AVERSE	BALATA
ANSATE	ARABIC	ARROBA	AT-HOME	AVIARY	BALBOA
ANSHAN	ARABLE	ARROWS	AT LAST	AVIATE	BALDLY
ANSWER	ARAGON	ARSINE	ATOLLS	AVIDIN	BALEEN
ANTEED	ARARAT	ARTERY	ATOMIC	AVIDLY	BALING
ANTHEM	ARBOUR	ARTFUL	ATONAL	AVOCET	BALKAN
ANTHER	ARCADE	ARTIER	ATONED	AVOWAL	BALKED
ANTICS	ARCANA	ARTIST	ATONER	AVOWED	BALKER
ANTLER	ARCANE	ARTOIS	ATONIC	AVOWER	BALLAD
ANTRIM	ARCHED	ARUNTA	AT REST	AWAKED	BALLET
ANTRUM	ARCHER	ASARUM	ATRIUM	AWAKEN	BALLOT
ANTUNG	ARCHES	ASCEND	ATTACH	AWARDS	BALSAM
ANURAN	ARCHLY	ASCENT	ATTACK	AWEIGH	BALSAS
ANURIA	ARCTIC	ASCOTS	ATTAIN	AWHILE	BALTIC
ANUSES	ARDENT	ASHDOD	ATTEND	AWNING	BAMAKO
ANVILS	ARDOUR	ASHIER	ATTEST	AWOKEN	BAMBOO
ANYANG	ARENAS	ASHLAR	ATTICA	AXENIC	BANABA
ANYHOW	AREOLA	ASHORE	ATTICS	AXILLA	BANANA
ANYONE	ARETES	ASIANS	ATTIRE	AXIOMS	BANDED
ANYWAY	AREZZO	ASIDES	ATTORN	AYE AYE	BANDIT
AORIST	ARGALI	ASKING	ATTRIT	AYMARA	BANDOG
AORTAS	ARGENT	ASLANT	ATTUNE	AZALEA	BANGED
AORTIC	ARGOSY	ASLEEP	ATWOOD	AZORES	BANGER
AOUDAD	ARGOTS	ASMARA	AUBADE	AZOTIC	BANGLE
AOUITA	ARGUED	ASPECT	AUBURN		BANGOR
APACHE	ARGUER	ASPIRE	AUDILE	**B**	BANGUI
APATHY	ARGYLE	ASSAIL	AUDITS	BAAING	BANISH
APEMAN	ARGYLL	ASSAYS	AU FAIT	BABBLE	BANJOS
APERCU	ARIEGE	ASSENT	AU FOND	BABIED	BANJUL
APEXES	ARIGHT	ASSERT	AUGEND	BABIES	BANKED
APHIDS	ARIOSO	ASSESS	AUGERS	BABOON	BANKER
APHTHA	ARISEN	ASSETS	AUGITE	BACKED	BANNED
APIARY	ARISTA	ASSIGN	AUGURY	BACKER	BANNER
APICAL	ARKOSE	ASSISI	AUGUST	BACK UP	BANTAM
APICES	ARMADA	ASSIST	AUKLET	BACKUP	BANTER
APIECE	ARMAGH	ASSIZE	AU LAIT	BADGER	BANYAN

BAOBAB	BASUCO	BEFELL	BESTED	BILLON	BLENDE
BAOTOU	BATHED	BEFOOL	BESTIR	BILLOW	BLENDS
BARBED	BATHER	BEFORE	BESTOW	BILLY-O	BLENNY
BARBEL	BATHOS	BEFOUL	BETAKE	BINARY	BLIGHT
BARBER	BATLEY	BEGGAR	BETHEL	BINATE	BLIMEY
BARBET	BATMAN	BEGGED	BETIDE	BINDER	BLIMPS
BARBIE	BATMEN	BEGONE	BETONY	BINGEN	BLINDS
BARDIC	BATONS	BEGUMS	BETOOK	BINGES	BLINKS
BARELY	BATTED	BEHALF	BETRAY	BINGOS	BLINTZ
BAREST	BATTEN	BEHAVE	BETTED	BINMAN	BLITHE
BARGED	BATTER	BEHEAD	BETTER	BINNED	BLOCKS
BARGEE	BATTLE	BEHELD	BEVELS	BIOGAS	BLOKES
BARGES	BATTUE	BEHEST	BEVIES	BIOGEN	BLONDE
BARING	BAUBLE	BEHIND	BEWAIL	BIONIC	BLOODS
BARIUM	BAUCHI	BEHOLD	BEWARE	BIOPIC	BLOODY
BARKED	BAULKS	BEHOVE	BEXLEY	BIOPSY	BLOOMS
BARKER	BAWLED	BEINGS	BEYOND	BIOTIC	BLOTCH
BARLEY	BAWLER	BEIRUT	BEZIER	BIOTIN	BLOTTO
BARMAN	BAYEUX	BELFRY	BEZOAR	BIPEDS	BLOUSE
BARMEN	BAYING	BELIED	BHOPAL	BIRDIE	BLOWER
BARNET	BAYOUS	BELIEF	BHUTAN	BIRTHS	BLOWSY
BARNEY	BAZAAR	BELIER	BHUTTO	BISCAY	BLOW-UP
BARODA	BEACON	BELIZE	BIAFRA	BISECT	BLOWZY
BARONS	BEADED	BELLES	BIASED	BISHOP	BLUEST
BARONY	BEADLE	BELLOW	BIASES	BISKRA	BLUFFS
BARQUE	BEAGLE	BELONG	BIBLES	BISONS	BLUISH
BARRED	BEAKER	BELSEN	BICEPS	BISQUE	BLUNGE
BARREL	BEAMED	BELTED	BICKER	BISSAU	BLURBS
BARREN	BEARDS	BELTER	BICORN	BISTRE	BLURRY
BARROW	BEARER	BELUGA	BIDDEN	BISTRO	B-MOVIE
BARTER	BEASTS	BEMOAN	BIDETS	BITCHY	BOARDS
BARTON	BEATEN	BEMUSE	BIDING	BITING	BOASTS
BARYON	BEATER	BENDER	BIFFED	BITMAP	BOATED
BARYTE	BEAUNE	BENGAL	BIFFIN	BITOLJ	BOATER
BASALT	BEAUTS	BENGBU	BIGAMY	BITTEN	BOATIE
BASELY	BEAUTY	BENIGN	BIG CAT	BITTER	BOBBED
BASEST	BEAVER	BENONI	BIG END	BLACKS	BOBBER
BASHED	BECAME	BENUMB	BIGGER	BLADES	BOBBIN
BASHES	BECKET	BENZOL	BIGGIE	BLAMED	BOBBLE
BASICS	BECKON	BENZYL	BIGHTS	BLANCH	BOBCAT
BASIFY	BECOME	BERATE	BIGOTS	BLANKS	BOCHUM
BASING	BEDAUB	BEREFT	BIG TOP	BLARED	BODEGA
BASINS	BEDBUG	BERETS	BIGWIG	BLASTS	BODICE
BASION	BEDDED	BERGEN	BIHARI	BLAZED	BODIES
BASKED	BEDDER	BERING	BIKING	BLAZER	BODILY
BASKET	BEDECK	BERLEY	BIKINI	BLAZES	BODING
BASQUE	BEDLAM	BERLIN	BILBAO	BLAZON	BODKIN
BASRAH	BEDPAN	BERTHS	BILGES	BLEACH	BODMIN
BASSES	BEDSIT	BERYLS	BILKED	BLEARY	BOFFIN
BASSET	BEEFED	BESEEM	BILKER	BLEATS	BOGEYS
BASTED	BEETLE	BESIDE	BILLED	BLEEPS	BOGGED
BASTIA	BEFALL	BESOMS	BILLET	BLENCH	BOGGLE

BOGIES	BORROW	BRAIDS	BROMAL	BUMPER	BUSKER
BOGOTA	BORZOI	BRAINS	BROMIC	BUNCHY	BUSKIN
BOILED	BOSKET	BRAINY	BRONCO	BUNDLE	BUSSED
BOILER	BOSNIA	BRAISE	BRONZE	BUNGED	BUSTED
BOLAND	BOSOMS	BRAKED	BRONZY	BUNGEE	BUSTER
BOLDER	BOSOMY	BRAKES	BROOCH	BUNGLE	BUSTLE
BOLDLY	BOSSED	BRANCH	BROODS	BUNION	BUST-UP
BOLERO	BOSSES	BRANDO	BROODY	BUNKED	BUTANE
BOLIDE	BOSTON	BRANDS	BROOKS	BUNKER	BUTENE
BOLSHY	BOSUNS	BRANDT	BROOMS	BUNKUM	BUTLER
BOLSON	BOTANY	BRANDY	BROWNS	BUNK-UP	BUTTED
BOLTED	BOTCHY	BRASHY	BROWSE	BUOYED	BUTTER
BOLTER	BOTFLY	BRASOV	BRUGES	BURBLE	BUTTES
BOLTON	BOTHER	BRASSY	BRUISE	BURBOT	BUTTIE
BOMBAY	BOTTLE	BRAVED	BRUMAL	BURDEN	BUTTON
BOMBED	BOTTOM	BRAVER	BRUMBY	BUREAU	BUXTON
BOMBER	BOUAKE	BRAVES	BRUNCH	BURGAS	BUYERS
BONBON	BOUCLE	BRAVOS	BRUNEI	BURGEE	BUYING
BONDED	BOUGHS	BRAWLS	BRUTAL	BURGER	BUYOUT
BONGOS	BOUGHT	BRAWNY	BRUTES	BURGHS	BUZZED
BONIER	BOUGIE	BRAYED	BRUTON	BURGLE	BUZZER
BONILY	BOULES	BRAYER	BRYONY	BURGOS	BUZZES
BONING	BOULLE	BRAZEN	BUBBLE	BURIAL	BY-BLOW
BONITO	BOUNCE	BRAZER	BUBBLY	BURIED	BYGONE
BON MOT	BOUNCY	BRAZIL	BUCCAL	BURIER	BYLAWS
BONNET	BOUNDS	BREACH	BUCKED	BURLAP	BY-LINE
BONSAI	BOUNTY	BREAKS	BUCKET	BURLER	BYPASS
BONZER	BOURNS	BREAST	BUCKLE	BURLEY	BYPLAY
BOOBED	BOURSE	BRECON	BUDDED	BURNED	BYROAD
BOOGIE	BOVINE	BREECH	BUDDHA	BURNER	BYSSUS
BOOHOO	BOVVER	BREEZE	BUDDLE	BURNET	BYWAYS
BOOING	BOWELS	BREEZY	BUDGED	BURPED	BYWORD
BOOKED	BOWERS	BREGMA	BUDGET	BURPEE	
BOOKIE	BOWERY	BREMEN	BUFFED	BURRED	**C**
BOOMED	BOWFIN	BRETON	BUFFER	BURROS	CABALS
BOOSTS	BOWING	BREVET	BUFFET	BURROW	CABANA
BOOTED	BOWLED	BREWER	BUGGED	BURSAL	CABBIE
BOOTEE	BOWLER	BREXIT	BUGGER	BURSAR	CABERS
BOOTHS	BOWMAN	BRIBER	BUGLER	BURSTS	CABINS
BOOTLE	BOWMEN	BRIDAL	BUGLES	BURTON	CABLED
BOOZED	BOWSAW	BRIDGE	BUILDS	BURYAT	CABLES
BOOZER	BOWSER	BRIDLE	BUKAVU	BUSBAR	CABLET
BOPPED	BOW TIE	BRIERY	BULBAR	BUS BOY	CABMAN
BORAGE	BOWWOW	BRIGHT	BULBIL	BUSBOY	CACHES
BORANE	BOWYER	BRITON	BULBUL	BUSHED	CACHET
BORATE	BOXCAR	BROACH	BULGED	BUSHEL	CACHOU
BORDER	BOXERS	BROADS	BULGES	BUSHES	CACKLE
BOREAL	BOXING	BROCHE	BULKED	BUSIED	CACTUS
BORERS	BOYISH	BROGUE	BULLET	BUSIER	CAD/CAM
BORIDE	BRACED	BROKEN	BUMBLE	BUSILY	CADDIE
BORING	BRACER	BROKER	BUMMED3	BUSING	CADDIS
BORNEO	BRACES	BROLLY	BUMPED	BUSKED	CADENT

CADETS	CAMPER	CARETS	CATNAP	CERVIX	CHERUB
CADGED	CAMPOS	CARGOS	CATNIP	CETANE	CHESTS
CADGER	CAMPUS	CARHOP	CATSUP	CETNIK	CHESTY
CADRES	CANADA	CARIES	CATTLE	CEYLON	CHEWED
CAECUM	CANALS	CARINA	CAUCUS	CHA CHA	CHEWER
CAELUM	CANAPE	CARING	CAUDAD	CHA-CHA	CHICHI
CAEOMA	CANARD	CARLOW	CAUDAL	CHACMA	CHICKS
CAESAR	CANARY	CARMAN	CAUDEX	CHAETA	CHICLE
CAFTAN	CANCAN	CARMEL	CAUDLE	CHAFED	CHICLY
CAGIER	CANCEL	CARNAL	CAUGHT	CHAFER	CHIDED
CAGILY	CANCER	CARNES	CAUSAL	CHAFFY	CHIDER
CAGING	CANDID	CARNET	CAUSED	CHAINS	CHIEFS
CAHIER	CANDLE	CAROBS	CAUSES	CHAIRS	CHIGOE
CAICOS	CANINE	CAROLS	CAVEAT	CHAISE	CHILES
CAIQUE	CANING	CARPAL	CAVE-IN	CHAKRA	CHILLI
CAIRNS	CANKER	CARPED	CAVERN	CHALET	CHILLS
CAJOLE	CANNED	CARPEL	CAVIAR	CHALKS	CHILLY
CAKING	CANNEL	CARPET	CAVING	CHALKY	CHIMED
CALAIS	CANNES	CARPUS	CAVITY	CHAMPS	CHIMES
CALASH	CANNON	CARREL	CAVORT	CHANCE	CHINES
CALCAR	CANNOT	CARROT	CAWING	CHANCY	CHINKS
CALCES	CANOED	CARSON	CAXTON	CHANGE	CHINTZ
CALCIC	CANOES	CARTED	CAYMAN	CHANIA	CHIPPY
CALICO	CANONS	CARTEL	CD-ROMS	CHANTS	CHIRAC
CALIPH	CANOPY	CARTER	CEASED	CHANTY	CHIRPS
CALKED	CANTAL	CARTON	CEDARS	CHAOAN	CHIRPY
CALKIN	CANTED	CARVED	CEDING	CHAPEL	CHISEL
CALLAO	CANTER	CARVER	CELAYA	CHARDS	CHITIN
CALLED	CANTIC	CASABA	CELERY	CHARGE	CHITON
CALLER	CANTLE	CASEFY	CELLAR	CHARMS	CHITTY
CALL-IN	CANTON	CASEIN	CELLOS	CHARTS	CHIVES
CALLOW	CANTOR	CASERN	CELTIC	CHASED	CHOCKA
CALL-UP	CANTOS	CASHED	CEMENT	CHASER	CHOCKS
CALLUS	CANTUS	CASHEW	CENSER	CHASES	CHOICE
CALMED	CANVAS	CASING	CENSOR	CHASMS	CHOIRS
CALMER	CANYON	CASINO	CENSUS	CHASSE	CHOKED
CALMLY	CAPERS	CASKET	CENTAL	CHASTE	CHOKER
CALPAC	CAPIAS	CASLON	CENTER	CHATTY	CHOKES
CALQUE	CAPONS	CASQUE	CENTRE	CHAT UP	CHOLER
CALVED	CAPOTE	CASSIA	CENTUM	CHEATS	CHOLLA
CALVES	CAPPED	CASSIS	CERATE	CHECKS	CHONJU
CALVIN	CAPPER	CASTER	CERCAL	CHECKY	CHOOSE
CAMASS	CAPSID	CASTES	CERCIS	CHEEKS	CHOOSY
CAMBER	CAPTOR	CASTLE	CERCUS	CHEEKY	CHOPPY
CAMDEN	CARAFE	CASTOR	CEREAL	CHEEPS	CHORAL
CAMELS	CARATS	CASTRO	CEREUS	CHEERS	CHORDS
CAMEOS	CARBON	CASUAL	CERISE	CHEERY	CHOREA
CAMERA	CARBOY	CATCHY	CERIUM	CHEESE	CHORES
CAMION	CARDED	CATENA	CERMET	CHEESY	CHORIC
CAMISE	CAREEN	CATGUT	CEROUS	CHEQUE	CHORUS
CAMLET	CAREER	CATION	CERUSE	CHERRY	CHOSEN
CAMPED	CARESS	CATKIN	CERVID	CHERTY	CHOUGH

CHRISM	CLAUSE	CLOWNS	COILER	CONFER	CORKED
CHRIST	CLAWED	CLOYED	COINED	CONGAS	CORKER
CHROMA	CLAWER	CLUBBY	COINER	CONGER	CORMEL
CHROME	CLAYEY	CLUCKS	COIN-OP	CONGES	CORNEA
CHUBBY	CLEATS	CLUCKY	COITAL	CONGOU	CORNEL
CHUCKS	CLEAVE	CLUMPS	COITUS	CONICS	CORNER
CHUKAR	CLEESE	CLUMPY	COLDER	CONIES	CORNET
CHUKKA	CLEFTS	CLUMSY	COLDLY	CONIUM	CORONA
CHUMMY	CLENCH	CLUNGE	COLEUS	CONKED	CORPSE
CHUMPS	CLEOME	CLUNKY	COLEYS	CONKER	CORPUS
CHUNKS	CLERGY	CLUTCH	COLIMA	CONMAN	CORRAL
CHUNKY	CLERIC	COALED	COLLAR	CONMEN	CORSES
CHURCH	CLERKS	COALER	COLLET	CONNED	CORSET
CHURLS	CLEVER	COARSE	COLLIE	CONOID	CORTEX
CHURNS	CLEVIS	COASTS	COLMAR	CONSUL	CORVID
CHUTES	CLICHE	COATED	COLONS	CONTRA-	CORYMB
CICADA	CLICKS	COAXED	COLONY	CONVEX	CORYZA
CICERO	CLIENT	COAXER	COLOUR	CONVEY	COSECH
CIDERS	CLIFFS	COBALT	COLUGO	CONVOY	COSHED
CIGARS	CLIMAX	COBBER	COLUMN	COOING	COSHES
CILICE	CLIMBS	COBBLE	COLURE	COOKED	COSIER
CILIUM	CLIMES	COBNUT	COMATE	COOKER	COSIES
CINDER	CLINAL	COBRAS	COMBAT	COOKIE	COSILY
CINEMA	CLINCH	COBURG	COMBED	COOLED	COSINE
CINEOL	CLINES	COBWEB	COMBER	COOLER	COSMIC
CINQUE	CLINGY	COCCID	COMBOS	COOLIE	COSMOS
CIPHER	CLINIC	COCCUS	COMEDO	COOLLY	COSSET
CIRCLE	CLIP-ON	COCCYX	COMEDY	COOLTH	COSTAL
CIRCUM-	CLIQUE	COCHIN	COMELY	COOPED	CO-STAR
CIRCUS	CLITIC	COCKED	COME ON	COOPER	COSTLY
CIRQUE	CLOACA	COCKLE	COME-ON	COPALM	COTTER
CIRRUS	CLOAKS	COCK-UP	COMERS	COPIED	COTTON
CISKEI	CLOCHE	COCOON	COMETS	COPIER	COUCAL
CITIES	CLOCKS	CODDLE	COMFIT	COPIES	COUGAR
CITIFY	CLODDY	CODGER	COMICS	COPING	COUGHS
CITING	CLOGGY	CODIFY	COMING	COP-OUT	COULEE
CITRAL	CLONAL	CODING	COMITY	COPPED	COULIS
CITRIC	CLONES	COELOM	COMMAS	COPPER	COUNTS
CITRIN	CLONIC	COERCE	COMMIS	COPSES	COUNTY
CITRON	CLONUS	COEVAL	COMMIT	COPTIC	COUPES
CITRUS	CLOSED	COFFEE	COMMON	COPULA	COUPLE
CIVETS	CLOSER	COFFER	COMORO	COQUET	COUPON
CIVICS	CLOSES	COFFIN	COMOSE	CORALS	COURSE
CIVIES	CLOSET	COGENT	COMPEL	CORBAN	COURTS
CLAIMS	CLOTHE	COGGED	COMPER	CORBEL	COUSIN
CLAMMY	CLOTHS	COGNAC	COMPLY	CORDED	COVENS
CLAMPS	CLOUDS	COHEIR	CONCHA	CORDON	COVERS
CLAQUE	CLOUDY	COHERE	CONCHY	CORERS	COVERT
CLARET	CLOUTS	COHORT	CONCUR	CORFAM	COVEYS
CLARKE	CLOVEN	COHOSH	CONDOM	CORGIS	COWAGE
CLASPS	CLOVER	COHUNE	CONDOR	CORING	COWARD
CLASSY	CLOVES	COILED	CONEYS	CORIUM	COWBOY

COWING	CREEPS	CRUSTY	CURTLY	DAGOES	DASHER
COWMAN	CREEPY	CRUTCH	CURTSY	DAHLIA	DASHES
COWMEN	CRENEL	CRUXES	CURVED	DAINTY	DATARY
COWPAT	CREOLE	CRYING	CURVES	DAISES	DATING
COWPEA	CRESOL	CRYPTS	CURVET	DAKOTA	DATIVE
COWPOX	CRESTS	CUBANE	CUSCUS	DALASI	DATURA
COWRIE	CRETAN	CUBBED	CUSPID	DALIAN	DAUBED
COXING	CRETIC	CUBING	CUSSED	DALLAS	DAUBER
COYOTE	CRETIN	CUBISM	CUSSES	DALLES	DAVIES
COYPUS	CREUSE	CUBIST	CUSTOM	DALTON	DAVITS
COZIER	CREWED	CUBITS	CUTELY	DAMAGE	DAWDLE
COZILY	CREWEL	CUBOID	CUTEST	DAMARA	DAWNED
CRABBY	CRICKS	CUCKOO	CUTESY	DAMASK	DAYBOY
CRACKS	CRIERS	CUCUTA	CUTLER	DAMMAR	DAYGLO
CRACOW	CRIKEY	CUDDLE	CUTLET	DAMMED	DAYTON
CRADLE	CRIMEA	CUDDLY	CUTOFF	DAMNED	DAZING
CRAFTS	CRIMES	CUDGEL	CUT OFF	DAMPED	DAZZLE
CRAFTY	CRINGE	CUESTA	CUTOUT	DAMPEN	DEACON
CRAGGY	CRINUM	CUFFED	CUTTER	DAMPER	DEADEN
CRAMBO	CRIPES	CUIABA	CUTUPS	DAMPLY	DEADLY
CRAMPS	CRISES	CULLED	CYANIC	DAMSEL	DEAFEN
CRANED	CRISIS	CULLER	CYBORG	DAMSON	DEALER
CRANES	CRISPS	CULLET	CYCLED	DA NANG	DEARER
CRANIA	CRISPY	CULLIS	CYCLES	DANCED	DEARLY
CRANKS	CRISTA	CULTIC	CYCLIC	DANCER	DEARTH
CRANKY	CRITIC	CUMANA	CYDERS	DANCES	DEATHS
CRANNY	CROAKS	CUMBER	CYGNET	DANDER	DEBARK
CRAPPY	CROCKS	CUNEAL	CYGNUS	DANDLE	DEBASE
CRASIS	CROCUS	CUPIDS	CYMBAL	DANGER	DEBATE
CRATED	CROFTS	CUPOLA	CYMENE	DANGLE	DEBITS
CRATER	CRONES	CUPPAS	CYMOID	DANIEL	DEBRIS
CRATES	CROOKS	CUPPED	CYMOSE	DANISH	DEBTOR
CRATON	CRORES	CUPRIC	CYMRIC	DANKER	DEBUNK
CRAVAT	CROSSE	CUP TIE	CYNICS	DANUBE	DEBUTS
CRAVED	CROTCH	CUPULE	CYPHER	DANZIG	DECADE
CRAVEN	CROTON	CURACY	CYPRUS	DAPHNE	DECALS
CRAWLS	CROUCH	CURARE	CYSTIC	DAPPED	DECAMP
CRAYON	CROUPS	CURATE		DAPPER	DECANE
CRAZED	CROWDS	CURBED	**D**	DAPPLE	DECANT
CRAZES	CROWED	CURDLE	DABBED	DARDIC	DECARE
CREAKS	CROWER	CURFEW	DABBER	DARFUR	DECCAN
CREAKY	CROWNS	CURIAE	DABBLE	DARING	DECEIT
CREAMS	CRUDER	CURING	DACHAU	DARKEN	DECENT
CREAMY	CRUETS	CURIOS	DACITE	DARKER	DECIDE
CREASE	CRUISE	CURIUM	DACOIT	DARKLY	DECILE
CREATE	CRUMBS	CURLED	DACRON	DARNED	DECKED
CRECHE	CRUMBY	CURLER	DACTYL	DARNEL	DECKLE
CREDIT	CRUMMY	CURLEW	DADOES	DARNER	DECOCT
CREDOS	CRUNCH	CURL UP	DAEMON	DARTED	DECODE
CREEDS	CRURAL	CURSED	DAFTER	DARTER	DECOKE
CREEKS	CRUSES	CURSES	DAFTLY	DARWIN	DECORS
CREELS	CRUSTS	CURSOR	DAGGER	DASHED	DECOYS

DECREE	DENEST	DE TROP	DIMMER	DJAMBI	DORIAN
DEDUCE	DENGUE	DETTOL	DIMPLE	DJINNS	DORIES
DEDUCT	DENIAL	DETUNE	DIMPLY	DOABLE	DORMER
DEEMED	DENIED	DEUCED	DIM SUM	DOBBIN	DORMIE
DEEPEN	DENIER	DEVEIN	DIMWIT	DOCENT	DORSAD
DEEPER	DENIMS	DEVICE	DINARS	DOCILE	DORSAL
DEEPLY	DE NIRO	DEVILS	DINERO	DOCKED	DORSET
DEFACE	DENNED	DEVISE	DINERS	DOCKER	DORSUM
DEFAME	DENOTE	DEVOID	DINGHY	DOCKET	DOSAGE
DEFEAT	DENSER	DEVOTE	DINGLE	DOCTOR	DO-SI-DO
DEFECT	DENTAL	DEVOUR	DINING	DODDER	DOSING
DEFEND	DENTED	DEVOUT	DINKUM	DODDLE	DOSSAL
DEFIED	DENTEX	DEWIER	DINNED	DODGED	DOSSED
DEFIER	DENTIL	DEWILY	DINNER	DODGEM	DOSSER
DEFILE	DENTIN	DEWLAP	DIOXAN	DODGER	DOTAGE
DEFINE	DENUDE	DEWORM	DIOXIN	DODGES	DOTARD
DEFORM	DENVER	DEXTER	DIPLEX	DODOES	DOTING
DEFRAY	DEODAR	DHARUK	DIPLOE	DODOMA	DOTTED
DEFTLY	DEPART	DHOTIS	DIPODY	DO DUTY	DOTTER
DEFUSE	DEPEND	DIACID	DIPOLE	DOFFED	DOTTLE
DEGAGE	DEPICT	DIADEM	DIPPED	DOFFER	DOUALA
DEGREE	DEPLOY	DIALED	DIPPER	DOG-EAR	DOUBLE
DEHORN	DEPORT	DIAPER	DIRECT	DOGGED	DOUBLY
DE-ICED	DEPOSE	DIAPIR	DIREST	DOGGER	DOUBTS
DE-ICER	DEPOTS	DIARCH	DIRGES	DOGIES	DOUCHE
DEIFIC	DEPTHS	DIATOM	DIRHAM	DOGLEG	DOUGHY
DEISTS	DEPUTE	DIBBED	DIRNDL	DOGMAS	DOURLY
DEIXIS	DEPUTY	DIBBER	DISARM	DOG TAG	DOUSED
DEJA VU	DERAIL	DIBBLE	DISBAR	DOINGS	DOUSER
DEJECT	DERIDE	DICIER	DISBUD	DOLINE	DOVISH
DE JURE	DERIVE	DICING	DISCOS	DOLING	DOWNED
DELAYS	DERMAL	DICKER	DISCUS	DOLLAR	DOWNER
DELETE	DERMIC	DICTUM	DISEUR	DOLLED	DOWSED
DELIAN	DERMIS	DIDDLE	DISHED	DOLLOP	DOWSER
DELICT	DERRIS	DIEPPE	DISHES	DOLMAN	DOYENS
DELPHI	DESCRY	DIESEL	DISMAL	DOLMAS	DOYLEY
DELTAS	DESERT	DIESIS	DISMAY	DOLMEN	DOZENS
DELUDE	DESIGN	DIETED	DISOWN	DOLOUR	DOZIER
DELUGE	DESIRE	DIETER	DISPEL	DOMAIN	DOZILY
DE LUXE	DESIST	DIFFER	DISTAL	DOMINO	DOZING
DELVED	DESMAN	DIGAMY	DISTIL	DONATE	DRABLY
DELVER	DESMID	DIGEST	DISUSE	DONDER	DRACHM
DEMAND	DESORB	DIGGER	DITHER	DONJON	DRAFFY
DEMEAN	DESPOT	DIGITS	DITTOS	DONKEY	DRAFTS
DEMISE	DESSAU	DIGLOT	DIVANS	DONNED	DRAFTY
DEMIST	DETACH	DIK-DIK	DIVERS	DONORS	DRAGEE
DEMODE	DETAIL	DIKTAT	DIVERT	DOODLE	DRAGGY
DEMONS	DETAIN	DILATE	DIVEST	DOO-DOO	DRAGON
DEMOTE	DETECT	DILDOS	DIVIDE	DOOMED	DRAINS
DEMURE	DETENT	DILUTE	DIVINE	DOPANT	DRAKES
DEMURS	DETEST	DIMITY	DIVING	DOPIER	DRAMAS
DENARY	DETOUR	DIMMED	DIWALI	DOPING	DRAPED

DRAPER	DUCKER	**E**	EFTPOS	ENABLE	ENVIES
DRAPES	DUDEEN	EAGLES	EGESTA	ENAMEL	ENVOYS
DRAWEE	DUDLEY	EAGLET	EGGCUP	ENATIC	ENWIND
DRAWER	DUELED	EALING	EGGNOG	EN BLOC	ENWOMB
DRAWLS	DUELLO	EARFUL	EGOISM	ENCAGE	ENWRAP
DRAWLY	DUENNA	EARING	EGOIST	ENCAMP	ENZYME
DREADS	DUFFEL	EARNED	EGRESS	ENCASE	EOCENE
DREAMS	DUFFER	EARNER	EGRETS	ENCASH	EOGENE
DREAMT	DUGONG	EARTHS	EIGHTH	ENCODE	EOLITH
DREAMY	DUGOUT	EARTHY	EIGHTS	ENCORE	EONISM
DREARY	DUIKER	EARWAX	EIGHTY	ENCYST	EOZOIC
DREDGE	DULCET	EARWIG	EITHER	ENDEAR	EPARCH
DREGGY	DULLED	EASELS	EJECTA	ENDING	EPIRUS
DRENCH	DULLER	EASIER	ELANDS	ENDIVE	EPONYM
DRESSY	DULUTH	EASILY	ELAPID	ENDUED	EPOPEE
DRIERS	DUMBER	EASING	ELAPSE	ENDURE	EPPING
DRIEST	DUMBLY	EASTER	ELATED	ENEMAS	EQUALS
DRIFTS	DUMDUM	EATERS	ELATER	ENERGY	EQUATE
DRIFTY	DUMPED	EATING	ELBOWS	ENFACE	EQUINE
DRILLS	DUMPER	EBBING	ELDERS	ENFOLD	EQUITY
DRINKS	DUNBAR	ECARTE	ELDEST	ENGAGE	ERASED
DRIPPY	DUNCES	ECESIS	ELEGIT	ENGINE	ERASER
DRIVEL	DUNDEE	ECHARD	ELEVEN	ENGRAM	ERBIUM
DRIVEN	DUNITE	ECHOED	ELEVON	ENGULF	ERFURT
DRIVER	DUNKED	ECHOES	ELFISH	ENIGMA	ERLANG
DRIVES	DUNKER	ECHOEY	EL GIZA	ENJOIN	ERMINE
DROGUE	DUNLIN	ECHOIC	ELICIT	ENLACE	ERODED
DROLLY	DUNNED	ECKERT	ELIDED	ENLIST	EROTIC
DRONED	DUNNER	ECLAIR	ELIXIR	ENMESH	ERRAND
DRONES	DUPERY	ECTYPE	ELOPED	ENMITY	ERRANT
DRONGO	DUPING	ECURIE	ELOPER	ENNAGE	ERRATA
DROOPY	DUPLET	ECZEMA	EL PASO	ENNEAD	ERRING
DROPSY	DUPLEX	EDDIED	ELUDED	ENOSIS	ERRORS
DROSSY	DURBAN	EDDIES	ELUDER	ENOUGH	ERSATZ
DROVER	DURBAR	EDGIER	ELYSEE	ENRAGE	ERYNGO
DROVES	DURESS	EDGILY	EMBALM	ENRICH	ESCAPE
DROWSE	DURHAM	EDGING	EMBANK	ENROBE	ESCARP
DROWSY	DURIAN	EDIBLE	EMBARK	ENROOT	ESCHAR
DRUDGE	DURING	EDICTS	EMBERS	ENSIGN	ESCHEW
DRUIDS	DUSTED	EDIRNE	EMBLEM	ENSILE	ESCORT
DRUNKS	DUSTER	EDITED	EMBODY	ENSOUL	ESCROW
DRYADS	DUSTUP	EDITOR	EMBOLY	ENSUED	ESCUDO
DRYERS	DUTIES	EDWARD	EMBOSS	ENSURE	ESKIMO
DRY ICE	DUVETS	EERILY	EMBRYO	ENTAIL	ESPIAL
DRYING	DWARFS	EFFACE	EMERGE	ENTICE	ESPIED
DRY ROT	DYABLE	EFFECT	EMESIS	ENTIRE	ESPIER
DUBBED	DYADIC	EFFETE	EMETIC	ENTITY	ESPRIT
DUBBIN	DYEING	EFFIGY	EMIGRE	ENTOMB	ESSAYS
DUBLIN	DYNAMO	EFFING	EMOTER	ENTRAP	ESTATE
DUCATS	DYNAST	EFFLUX	EMPALE	ENTREE	ESTEEM
DUCKED	DYNODE	EFFORT	EMPIRE	ENVIED	ESTRAY
		EFFUSE	EMPLOY	ENVIER	ETALON

ETCHED	EXPIRE	FALCON	FEASTS	FIANCE	FIRING
ETCHER	EXPIRY	FALLAL	FECULA	FIASCO	FIRKIN
ETHANE	EXPORT	FALLEN	FECUND	FIBBED	FIRMED
ETHENE	EXPOSE	FALLER	FEDORA	FIBBER	FIRMER
ETHICS	EXSERT	FALLOW	FEEBLE	FIBRED	FIRMLY
ETHNIC	EXTANT	FALSER	FEEBLY	FIBRES	FIRSTS
ETHYNE	EXTEND	FALTER	FEEDER	FIBRIL	FIRTHS
ETYMON	EXTENT	FAMILY	FEELER	FIBRIN	FISCAL
EUBOEA	EXTERN	FAMINE	FEIJOA	FIBULA	FISHED
EUCHRE	EXTINE	FAMISH	FEINTS	FICKLE	FISHER
EULOGY	EXTORT	FAMOUS	FEISTY	FIDDLE	FISHES
EUNUCH	EXTRAS	FANDOM	FELINE	FIDDLY	FISTIC
EUREKA	EXUDED	FANGED	FELLED	FIDGET	FITFUL
EURO MP	EYEFUL	FANGIO	FELLER	FIELDS	FITTED
EUROPE	EYEING	FANION	FELLOE	FIENDS	FITTER
EVADED	EYELET	FANJET	FELLOW	FIERCE	FIVERS
EVADER	EYELID	FANNED	FELONS	FIESTA	FIXATE
EVENLY	EYRIES	FANNER	FELONY	FIFTHS	FIXERS
EVENTS		FAN-TAN	FEMALE	FIGHTS	FIXING
EVILER	**F**	FARCES	FEMORA	FIGURE	FIXITY
EVILLY	FABIAN	FARINA	FEMURS	FIJIAN	FIZGIG
EVINCE	FABLED	FARING	FENCED	FILETS	FIZZED
EVOKED	FABLER	FARMED	FENCER	FILIAL	FIZZER
EVOKER	FABLES	FARMER	FENCES	FILING	FIZZLE
EVOLVE	FABRIC	FAR-OFF	FENDED	FILLED	FJORDS
EVZONE	FACADE	FAR-OUT	FENDER	FILLER	FLABBY
EXAMEN	FACETS	FARROW	FENIAN	FILLET	FLACON
EXARCH	FACIAL	FARTED	FENNEC	FILL-IN	FLAGGY
EXCEED	FACIES	FASCIA	FENNEL	FILLIP	FLAGON
EXCEPT	FACILE	FASTED	FENTON	FILMED	FLAILS
EXCESS	FACING	FASTEN	FERBAM	FILMIC	FLAKED
EXCISE	FACTOR	FASTER	FERIAL	FILOSE	FLAKER
EXCITE	FACULA	FAT CAT	FERMAT	FILTER	FLAKES
EXCUSE	FADE-IN	FATHER	FERRET	FILTHY	FLAMBE
EXEDRA	FADING	FATHOM	FERRIC	FIMBLE	FLAMED
EXEMPT	FAECAL	FATTEN	FERULA	FINALE	FLAMER
EXETER	FAECES	FATTER	FERULE	FINALS	FLAMES
EXEUNT	FAENZA	FAUCAL	FERVID	FINDER	FLANGE
EXHALE	FAERIE	FAUCES	FESCUE	FINELY	FLANKS
EXHORT	FAG END	FAUCET	FESTAL	FINERY	FLARED
EXHUME	FAGGED	FAULTS	FESTER	FINEST	FLARES
EXILED	FAGGOT	FAULTY	FETIAL	FINGAL	FLASHY
EXILES	FAILED	FAUNAL	FETING	FINGER	FLASKS
EXILIC	FAILLE	FAUNAS	FETISH	FINIAL	FLATLY
EXITED	FAINTS	FAVOUR	FETTER	FINING	FLATUS
EXODUS	FAIRER	FAWNED	FETTLE	FINISH	FLAUNT
EXONYM	FAIRLY	FAWNER	FEUDAL	FINITE	FLAVIN
EXOTIC	FAITHS	FAXING	FEUDED	FINNED	FLAWED
EXPAND	FAJITA	FAZING	FEZZAN	FINNIC	FLAXEN
EXPECT	FAKERS	FEALTY	FEZZED	FIORDS	FLAYED
EXPEND	FAKING	FEARED	FEZZES	FIORIN	FLAYER
EXPERT	FAKIRS	FEARER	FIACRE	FIPPLE	FLECHE

FLECKS	FOBBED	FORMAN	FRIEND	FULCRA	GAELIC
FLEDGE	FO'C'SLE	FORMAT	FRIERS	FULFIL	GAFFER
FLEECE	FODDER	FORMED	FRIEZE	FULLER	GAFFES
FLEECY	FOETAL	FORMER	FRIGHT	FULL-ON	GAGGED
FLEETS	FOETID	FORMIC	FRIGID	FULMAR	GAGGER
FLENSE	FOETOR	FORMYL	FRIJOL	FUMBLE	GAGGLE
FLESHY	FOETUS	FORNIX	FRILLS	FUMING	GAGING
FLETCH	FOGBOW	FORTES	FRILLY	FUNDED	GAIETY
FLEXED	FOGDOG	FORTIS	FRINGE	FUNDIC	GAIJIN
FLEXES	FOGGED	FORUMS	FRINGY	FUNDUS	GAINED
FLEXOR	FOGGIA	FOSHAN	FRISKS	FUNGAL	GAINER
FLICKS	FOGIES	FOSSIL	FRISKY	FUNGIC	GAINLY
FLIERS	FOIBLE	FOSTER	FRIULI	FUNGUS	GAITER
FLIGHT	FOILED	FOUGHT	FRIVOL	FUNKED	GALATA
FLIMSY	FOLDED	FOULED	FRIZZY	FUNKER	GALATI
FLINCH	FOLDER	FOULER	FROCKS	FUNNEL	GALAXY
FLINTS	FOLIAR	FOULLY	FROGGY	FUN RUN	GALENA
FLINTY	FOLIOS	FOUL-UP	FROLIC	FURFUR	GALERE
FLIRTS	FOLIUM	FOUNTS	FRONDS	FURIES	GALIBI
FLITCH	FOLKIE	FOURTH	FRONTS	FURLED	GALIOT
FLOATS	FOLKSY	FOVEAL	FROSTS	FURLER	GALLED
FLOATY	FOLLOW	FOWLER	FROSTY	FURORE	GALLEY
FLOCKS	FOLSOM	FOWLES	FROTHS	FURRED	GALLIC
FLOCKY	FOMENT	FOXIER	FROTHY	FURROW	GALLON
FLOODS	FONDER	FOXILY	FROWNS	FUSAIN	GALLOP
FLOORS	FONDLE	FOXING	FROWZY	FUSHUN	GALORE
FLOOZY	FONDLY	FOYERS	FROZEN	FUSILE	GALOSH
FLOPPY	FONDUE	FRACAS	FRUGAL	FUSING	GALWAY
FLORAL	FONTAL	FRAMED	FRUITS	FUSION	GALYAK
FLORET	FOODIE	FRAMER	FRUITY	FUSSED	GAMBIA
FLORID	FOOLED	FRAMES	FRUMPS	FUSSER	GAMBIT
FLORIN	FOOTER	FRANCE	FRUMPY	FUSSES	GAMBLE
FLOSSY	FOOTLE	FRANCS	FRUNZE	FUSTIC	GAMBOL
FLOURY	FOOZLE	FRAPPE	FRYERS	FUTILE	GAMELY
FLOWED	FORAGE	FRATER	FRYING	FUTONS	GAMETE
FLOWER	FORAYS	FRAUDS	FRY-UPS	FUTURE	GAMIER
FLUENT	FORBAD	FRAUEN	FU-CHOU	FUZHOU	GAMINE
FLUFFY	FORBID	FRAYED	FUCKED	FUZZED	GAMING
FLUIDS	FORCED	FRAZIL	FUCKER		GAMMAS
FLUKES	FORCER	FREAKS	FUCK-UP	**G**	GAMMED
FLUKEY	FORCES	FREAKY	FUCOID		GAMMON
FLUNKY	FORDED	FREELY	FUDDLE	GABBED	GANDER
FLURRY	FOREGO	FREEST	FUDGED	GABBER	GANGED
FLUTED	FOREST	FREEZE	FUELED	GABBLE	GANGER
FLUTER	FORFAR	FRENCH	FUGARD	GABBRO	GANGES
FLUTES	FORGED	FRENZY	FUGATO	GABION	GANGUE
FLYBYS	FORGER	FRESCO	FUGING	GABLED	GANNET
FLYERS	FORGES	FRESNO	FUGUES	GABLES	GANOID
FLYING	FORGET	FRIARS	FUHRER	GADDED	GANTRY
FLYSCH	FORGOT	FRIARY	FUJIAN	GADDER	GAOLED
FOALED	FORKED	FRIDAY	FUKIEN	GADFLY	GAOLER
FOAMED	FORMAL	FRIDGE	FULANI	GADGET	GAPING
				GADOID	

GAPPED	GEISHA	GINGER	GNAWER	GOVERN	GRINGO
GARAGE	GELADA	GINKGO	GNEISS	GRABEN	GRIPED
GARBED	GELDED	GIRDED	GNOMES	GRACED	GRIPER
GARBLE	GELDOF	GIRDER	GNOMIC	GRACES	GRIPES
GARCON	GELLED	GIRDLE	GNOMON	GRADED	GRISLY
GARDEN	GEMINI	GIRLIE	GNOSIS	GRADER	GRISON
GARGET	GEMMED	GIRTHS	GOADED	GRADES	GRISTS
GARGLE	GENDER	GIUSTO	GOATEE	GRADIN	GRITTY
GARISH	GENERA	GIVE IN	GOBBET	GRADUS	GRIVET
GARLIC	GENEVA	GIVING	GOBBLE	GRAECO-	GROANS
GARNER	GENIAL	GLACIS	GOBIAN	GRAFTS	GROATS
GARNET	GENIES	GLADES	GOBLET	GRAINS	GROCER
GARRET	GENIUS	GLADLY	GOBLIN	GRAINY	GRODNO
GARTER	GENOME	GLAIRY	GODARD	GRAMME	GROGGY
GASBAG	GENRES	GLANCE	GODSON	GRANDS	GROINS
GASCON	GENTLE	GLANDS	GODWIT	GRANGE	GROOMS
GASHED	GENTLY	GLARED	GOFERS	GRANNY	GROOVE
GASHES	GENTRY	GLARES	GOFFER	GRANTS	GROOVY
GASIFY	GEODIC	GLARUS	GOGGLE	GRAPES	GROPED
GASKET	GERBIL	GLASSY	GOITRE	GRAPHS	GROPER
GASKIN	GERMAN	GLAZED	GO-KART	GRASSY	GROPES
GASMAN	GERMEN	GLAZER	GOLDEN	GRATED	GROTTO
GASMEN	GERUND	GLAZES	GOLFER	GRATER	GROTTY
GASPED	GETTER	GLEAMS	GOLLOP	GRATES	GROUCH
GASPER	GETUPS	GLEBES	GOMUTI	GRATIS	GROUND
GASSED	GEYSER	GLEETY	GONADS	GRAVEL	GROUPS
GASSER	GEZIRA	GLIBLY	GONDAR	GRAVEN	GROUSE
GASSES	GHETTO	GLIDED	GONERS	GRAVER	GROUTS
GATEAU	GHIBLI	GLIDER	GONION	GRAVES	GROVEL
GATHER	GHOSTS	GLIDES	GOODLY	GRAVID	GROVES
GAUCHE	GHOULS	GLINTS	GOOFED	GRAYED	GROWER
GAUCHO	GHYLLS	GLIOMA	GOOGLE	GRAYER	GROWLS
GAUGED	GIANTS	GLITCH	GOOGLY	GRAZED	GROWTH
GAUGER	GIAOUR	GLITZY	GOOGOL	GRAZER	GROYNE
GAUGES	GIBBED	GLOATS	GOOIER	GRAZES	GROZNY
GAVAGE	GIBBER	GLOBAL	GOPHER	GREASE	GRUBBY
GAVELS	GIBBET	GLOBES	GORGED	GREASY	GRUDGE
GAVIAL	GIBBON	GLOBIN	GORGER	GREATS	GRUGRU
GAWKED	GIBE AT	GLOOMY	GORGES	GREBES	GRUMPY
GAWKER	GIBEON	GLORIA	GORGON	GREECE	GRUNGE
GAWPED	GIBSON	GLOSSA	GORICA	GREEDY	GRUNGY
GAYEST	GIDDAY	GLOSSY	GORIER	GREENS	GRUNTS
GAZEBO	GIFTED	GLOVED	GORILY	GREYED	GUARDS
GAZING	GIGGLE	GLOVER	GORING	GREYER	GUAVAS
GAZUMP	GIGGLY	GLOVES	GO-SLOW	GRIEVE	GUELPH
GDANSK	GIGOLO	GLOWED	GOSPEL	GRIFFE	GUENON
GDYNIA	GILDED	GLOWER	GOSSIP	GRIGRI	GUESTS
GEARED	GILDER	GLUING	GOTHIC	GRILLE	GUFFAW
GECKOS	GILLED	GLUMLY	GOUGED	GRILLS	GUIANA
GEDACT	GILLIE	GLUTEN	GOUGER	GRILSE	GUIDED
GEE-GEE	GIMLET	GLYCOL	GOUGES	GRIMLY	GUIDER
GEEZER	GIMMAL	GNAWED	GOURDS	GRINDS	GUIDES

GUIDON	HACKLE	HANDEL	HASTEN	HEAVEN	HERDIC
GUILDS	HADEAN	HANDLE	HATBOX	HEAVER	HEREAT
GUILIN	HADITH	HANGAR	HATHOR	HEAVES	HEREBY
GUILTY	HADJES	HANGER	HATING	HEBREW	HEREIN
GUIMPE	HADJIS	HANGRY	HATPIN	HEBRON	HEREOF
GUINEA	HADRON	HANG-UP	HATRED	HECATE	HEREON
GUISES	HAEMAL	HANKER	HATTER	HECKLE	HERERO
GUITAR	HAEMIC	HANKIE	HAULED	HECTIC	HERESY
GULDEN	HAEMIN	HANKOW	HAULER	HECTOR	HERETO
GULLAH	HAERES	HANNAH	HAUNCH	HECUBA	HERIOT
GULLED	HAFTER	HANSEL	HAUNTS	HEDDLE	HERMES
GULLET	HAGBUT	HANSEN	HAVANA	HEDGED	HERMIT
GULLEY	HAGGAI	HANSOM	HAVANT	HEDGER	HERMON
GULPED	HAGGIS	HAPPEN	HAVENS	HEDGES	HERNIA
GULPER	HAGGLE	HAPTEN	HAVEN'T	HEDJAZ	HEROES
GUMBOS	HAIDAN	HAPTIC	HAVING	HEEDED	HEROIC
GUMMED	HAIDUK	HARALD	HAWAII	HEEDER	HEROIN
GUNDOG	HAILED	HARARE	HAWHAW	HEE-HAW	HERONS
GUNG-HO	HAILER	HARASS	HAWICK	HEELED	HERPES
GUNMAN	HAINAN	HARBIN	HAWKED	HEELER	HERREN
GUNMEN	HAIRDO	HARD BY	HAWKER	HEENAN	HERZOG
GUNNED	HAIRIF	HARDEN	HAWSER	HEFTER	HESIOD
GUNNEL	HAJJES	HARDER	HAYBOX	HEGIRA	HESTIA
GUNNER	HAJJIS	HARDIE	HAYMOW	HEIDUC	HETMAN
GUNSHY	HAKIMS	HARDLY	HAZARD	HEIFER	HEWERS
GUNTUR	HALEST	HARD-ON	HAZELS	HEIGHT	HEWING
GUNYAH	HALIDE	HARD UP	HAZIER	HEJIRA	HEXANE
GURGLE	HALITE	HAREEM	HAZILY	HEKATE	HEXING
GURJUN	HALLAH	HAREMS	HAZING	HELENA	HEXONE
GURKHA	HALLEL	HARING	H-BOMBS	HELIOS	HEXOSE
GUSHED	HALLEY	HARKED	HEADED	HELIUM	HEYDAY
GUSHER	HALLOO	HARKEN	HEADER	HELLAS	HIATAL
GUSSET	HALLOS	HARLEM	HEAD-ON	HELLEN	HIATUS
GUSTED	HALLOW	HARLEY	HEALED	HELLER	HICCUP
GUTTED	HALLUX	HARLOT	HEALER	HELLES	HICKEY
GUTTER	HALOES	HARLOW	HEALEY	HELLOS	HICKOK
GUVNOR	HALOID	HARMED	HEALTH	HELMET	HIDDEN
GUYANA	HALTED	HARMER	HEANEY	HELPED	HIDING
GUYING	HALTER	HARNEY	HEAPED	HELPER	HIEING
GUZZLE	HALTON	HAROLD	HEAPER	HELVES	HIEMAL
GYPPED	HALVAH	HARPED	HEARER	HEMMED	HIGGLE
GYPSUM	HALVED	HARPER	HEARSE	HEMMER	HIGHER
GYRATE	HALVES	HARRAR	HEARST	HEMPEN	HIGHLY
GYROSE	HAMATE	HARRIS	HEARTH	HENBIT	HIJACK
	HAMELN	HARROW	HEARTS	HENDRY	HIKERS
H	HAMITE	HARTAL	HEARTY	HENLEY	HIKING
	HAMLET	HARVEY	HEATED	HEPCAT	HILARY
HAAKON	HAMLYN	HASHED	HEATER	HEPTAD	HILLEL
HABANA	HAMMED	HASHES	HEATHS	HERALD	HILLER
HABILE	HAMMER	HASLET	HEATHY	HERBAL	HIMEJI
HABITS	HAMPER	HASSAN	HEAUME	HERDED	HINDER
HACKED	HANDED	HASSLE	HEAVED	HERDER	HINDOO

HINDUS	HOLILY	HORROR	HULLER	HYPHEN	IMPALA
HINGED	HOLISM	HORSEY	HULLOS	HYPING	IMPALE
HINGER	HOLLER	HOSIER	HUMANE		IMPART
HINGES	HOLLOW	HOSING	HUMANS	**I**	IMPEDE
HINTED	HOLMES	HOSTED	HUMBER	IAMBIC	IMPEND
HINTER	HOLMIC	HOSTEL	HUMBLE	IAMBUS	IMPHAL
HIPPED	HOLPEN	HOSTIE	HUMBLY	IBADAN	IMPISH
HIPPER	HOMAGE	HOT AIR	HUMBUG	IBAGUE	IMPORT
HIPPIE	HOMBRE	HOTBED	HUMISM	IBERIA	IMPOSE
HIRING	HOMELY	HOT DOG	HUMMED	IBEXES	IMPOST
HISPID	HOMIER	HOTELS	HUMMEL	IBIBIO	IMPROV
HISSED	HOMILY	HOTIEN	HUMMER	IBISES	IMPUGN
HISSER	HOMING	HOT KEY	HUMMUS	ICE AGE	IMPURE
HISSES	HOMINY	HOTPOT	HUMOUR	ICEBOX	IMPUTE
HI-TECH	HONEST	HOT ROD	HUMPED	ICE CAP	INARCH
HITHER	HONIED	HOTTER	HUMPTY	ICEMAN	INBORN
HITLER	HONING	HOTTIE	HUNGER	ICEMEN	INBRED
HIT MAN	HONKED	HOUDAN	HUNGRY	ICHANG	INCEPT
HIT MEN	HONKER	HOUNDS	HUNKER	I CHING	INCEST
HITTER	HONOUR	HOURIS	HUNTED	ICICLE	INCHED
HIVING	HONSHU	HOURLY	HUNTER	ICIEST	INCHES
HOARDS	HOODED	HOUSED	HUPPAH	ICONIC	INCHON
HOARSE	HOODIE	HOUSEL	HURDLE	ID CARD	INCISE
HOAXED	HOODOO	HOUSES	HURLED	IDEALS	INCITE
HOAXER	HOOFED	HOVELS	HURLER	IDEATE	INCOME
HOAXES	HOOKAH	HOWARD	HURLEY	IDIOCY	INCUBI
HOBART	HOOKED	HOWDAH	HURRAH	IDIOMS	INCUSE
HOBBES	HOOKER	HOWE'ER	HURRAY	IDIOTS	INDEED
HOBBLE	HOOKUP	HOWLED	HURTER	IDLEST	INDENE
HOBNOB	HOOPED	HOWLER	HURTLE	IDLING	INDENT
HOBOES	HOOPER	HOWLET	HUSAIN	IDYLLS	INDIAN
HOCKED	HOOP-LA	HOWRAH	HUSHED	IGLOOS	INDICT
HOCKER	HOOPOE	HOYDEN	HUSH-UP	IGNITE	INDIGO
HOCKEY	HOORAH	HSIANG	HUSKER	IGNORE	INDITE
HODDEN	HOORAY	HUAMBO	HUSSAR	IGUACU	INDIUM
HODDIN	HOOTED	HUBBLE	HUSTLE	IGUANA	INDOLE
HODMAN	HOOTER	HUBBUB	HUSTON	ILESHA	INDOOR
HOEING	HOOVER	HUBCAP	HUXLEY	ILEXES	INDORE
HOGGED	HOOVES	HUBRIS	HUZZAH	ILIGAN	INDRIS
HOGGER	HOPING	HUCKLE	HYADES	ILKLEY	INDUCE
HOGGET	HOPPED	HUDDLE	HYAENA	ILL-USE	INDUCT
HOGNUT	HOPPER	HUDSON	HYALIN	ILOILO	INDULT
HOGTIE	HOPPLE	HUELVA	HYBRID	ILORIN	INFAMY
HOHHOT	HOPPUS	HUESCA	HYBRIS	IMAGES	INFANT
HOICKS	HORACE	HUFFED	HYDRAS	IMBIBE	INFECT
HOIDEN	HORARY	HUGELY	HYDRIA	IMBRUE	INFEST
HOISTS	HORDES	HUGEST	HYDRIC	IMBUED	INFIRM
HOLDEN	HORMIC	HUGGED	HYENAS	IMIDIC	INFLOW
HOLDER	HORMUZ	HUGGER	HYMENS	IMMUNE	INFLUX
HOLDUP	HORNED	HUGHES	HYMNAL	IMMURE	INFORM
HOLD UP	HORNET	HUGHIE	HYMNED	IMPACT	INFUSE
HOLIER	HORRID	HULLED		IMPAIR	INGEST

INGOTS	INULIN	**J**	JEWISH	JUDAEA	KANBAN
INHALE	INURED	JABBED	JHANSI	JUDAIC	KANGAS
INHAUL	INVADE	JABBER	JIBBED	JUDDER	KANPUR
INHERE	INVENT	JABIRU	JIBBER	JUDGED	KANSAS
INHUME	INVERT	JACANA	JIBING	JUDGER	KAOLIN
INJECT	INVEST	JACKAL	JIGAWA	JUDGES	KARATE
INJURE	INVITE	JACKED	JIGGED	JUDOGI	KARATS
INJURY	INVOKE	JACKET	JIGGER	JUDOKA	KARIBA
INK-CAP	INWARD	JACKIE	JIGGLE	JUGATE	KARMIC
INKIER	IODATE	JAFFNA	JIGGLY	JUGGED	KARPOV
INKING	IODIDE	JAGGED	JIGSAW	JUGGLE	KASBAH
INKPAD	IODINE	JAGUAR	JIHADS	JUICED	KASSEL
INLAID	IODISM	JAILED	JILTED	JUICES	KAUNAS
INLAND	IODIZE	JAILER	JILTER	JUJUBE	KAYAKS
IN-LAWS	IODOUS	JAIPUR	JINGLE	JULEPS	KAZAKH
INLAYS	IONIAN	JALAPA	JINGLY	JULIES	KEBABS
INLETS	IONIZE	JALOPY	JINXED	JUMBLE	KEDIRI
INLIER	IONONE	JAMMED	JINXES	JUMP AT	KEEGAN
INMATE	IPECAC	JAMMER	JITTER	JUMPED	KEELED
INMOST	IREFUL	JANGLE	JIVING	JUMPER	KEENED
INNATE	IRENIC	JAPERY	JOBBED	JUNEAU	KEENER
INNING	IRIDIC	JAPURA	JOBBER	JUNGLE	KEENLY
INNUIT	IRISES	JARGON	JOBBIE	JUNGLY	KEEPER
INROAD	IRITIC	JARRAH	JOB LOT	JUNIOR	KEEP ON
INRUSH	IRITIS	JARRED	JOCKEY	JUNKED	KELLER
INSANE	IRKING	JARROW	JOCOSE	JUNKET	KELOID
INSECT	IRONED	JASPER	JOCUND	JUNKIE	KELPIE
INSERT	IRONER	JAUNTS	JOGGED	JUNTAS	KELTIC
INSETS	IRONIC	JAUNTY	JOGGER	JURIED	KELVIN
INSIDE	IRRUPT	JAWARA	JOGGLE	JURIES	KENDAL
INSIST	IRTYSH	JAWING	JOHNNY	JURIST	KENNED
IN SITU	IRVINE	JAZZED	JOHORE	JURORS	KENNEL
INSOLE	ISATIN	JEERED	JOINED	JUSTLY	KENYAN
INSTAR	ISCHIA	JEERER	JOINER	JUTTED	KERALA
INSTEP	ISLAND	JEJUNE	JOINTS	JUTTER	KERMAN
INSTIL	ISLETS	JELLED	JOISTS		KERMES
INSULA	ISOBAR	JENNET	JOKERS	**K**	KERNEL
INSULT	ISOGON	JERBOA	JOKING	KABILA	KERSEY
INSURE	ISOHEL	JERKED	JOLTED	KABYLE	KETENE
INTACT	ISOLEX	JERKER	JORDAN	KADUNA	KETONE
INTAKE	ISOMER	JERKIN	JOSHED	KAFFIR	KETOSE
INTEND	ISOPOD	JERSEY	JOSHES	KAFTAN	KETTLE
INTENT	ISRAEL	JESTED	JOSTLE	KAISER	KEVLAR
INTERN	ISSUED	JESTER	JOTTED	KAIZEN	KEYING
INTIMA	ISSUER	JESUIT	JOTTER	KAKAPO	KEYWAY
INTINE	ISSUES	JET LAG	JOULES	KALISZ	KHALIF
INTONE	ISTRIA	JETSAM	JOUNCE	KALMAR	KHULNA
IN TOTO	ITALIC	JET SET	JOURNO	KALMIA	KHYBER
IN TRIM	ITCHED	JETTED	JOVIAL	KALONG	KIBOSH
INTROS	ITCHES	JETTON	JOYFUL	KALUGA	KICKED
INTUIT	ITHACA	JEWELS	JOYING	KAMALA	KICKER
INUITS	ITSELF	JEWESS	JOYOUS	KANARA	KICK IN

KIDDED	KOPECK	LADLED	LARGER	LAYERS	LEMONY
KIDDER	KOPPIE	LADLER	LARGOS	LAYING	LEMURS
KIDDIE	KOREAN	LADLES	LARIAM	LAYMAN	LENDER
KIDNAP	KORUNA	LADOGA	LARIAT	LAYMEN	LENGTH
KIDNEY	KOSHER	LAGENA	LARINE	LAY-OFF	LENITY
KIELCE	KOSICE	LAGERS	LARISA	LAY OUT	LENSES
KIGALI	KOVROV	LAGGED	LARKED	LAYOUT	LENTEN
KIKUYU	KOWTOW	LAGOON	LARKER	LAZIER	LENTIC
KILLED	KRAALS	LAHORE	LARNAX	LAZILY	LENTIL
KILLER	KRISES	LAICAL	LARVAE	LAZING	LEOBEN
KILTED	KRONER	LAID UP	LARVAL	LEADEN	LEONID
KILTER	KRONOR	LAIRDS	LARYNX	LEADER	LEPERS
KIMONO	KRUGER	LALANG	LASCAR	LEAD-IN	LEPTON
KINASE	KUKRIS	LAMBDA	LASERS	LEAGUE	LESBOS
KINDER	KUMASI	LAMBED	LASHED	LEAKED	LESION
KINDLE	KUMISS	LAMELY	LASHER	LEAKER	LESSEE
KINDLY	KUMMEL	LAMENT	LASHES	LEANED	LESSEN
KINGLY	KUNG FU	LAMEST	LASHIO	LEANER	LESSER
KIOSKS	KUNLUN	LAMINA	LASH-UP	LEAN TO	LESSON
KIPPED	KUOPIO	LAMING	LASKET	LEAN-TO	LESSOR
KIPPER	KURGAN	LAMMAS	LASSES	LEAPED	LETHAL
KIRKBY	KUWAIT	LAMPAS	LASSOS	LEAPER	LETTER
KIRKUK	KWACHA	LANATE	LASTED	LEARNT	LETUPS
KIRMAN	KWANZA	LANCED	LASTER	LEASED	LEVANT
KIRSCH	KYRGYZ	LANCER	LASTLY	LEASER	LEVEES
KIRUNA	KYUSHU	LANCES	LATEEN	LEASES	LEVELS
KISMET		LANCET	LATELY	LEAVED	LEVERS
KISSED	**L**	LANDAU	LATENT	LEAVEN	LEVIED
KISSER	LAAGER	LANDED	LATEST	LEAVER	LEVIER
KISSES	LABELS	LANDES	LATHER	LEAVES	LEVIES
KISUMU	LABIAL	LANGER	LATHES	LECHER	LEVITY
KIT BAG	LABILE	LANGUE	LATINA	LECTIN	LEWDLY
KITSCH	LABIUM	LANGUR	LATINO	LECTOR	LIABLE
KITTED	LABLAB	LANKER	LATINS	LEDGER	LIAISE
KITTEN	LABOUR	LANKLY	LATISH	LEDGES	LIBBER
KLAXON	LABRET	LANNER	LATIUM	LEERED	LIBELS
KNAVES	LABRUM	LANUGO	LATRIA	LEEWAY	LIBERO
KNAWEL	LACHES	LAPDOG	LATTEN	LEGACY	LIBIDO
KNELLS	LACIER	LAPELS	LATTER	LEGATE	LIBRAN
KNIFED	LACILY	LAPPED	LATVIA	LEGATO	LIBYAN
KNIFER	LACING	LAPPER	LAUDED	LEGEND	LICHEN
KNIGHT	LACKED	LAPPET	LAUDER	LEGERS	LICKED
KNIVES	LACKEY	LAPSED	LAUGHS	LEGGED	LICKER
KNOCKS	LACTAM	LAPSER	LAUNCH	LEGION	LIDDED
KNOLLS	LACTIC	LAPSES	LAUREL	LEGIST	LIEGES
KNOTTY	LACUNA	LAPSUS	LAVABO	LEGUAN	LIE-INS
KNOWER	LADDER	LAPTOP	LAVAGE	LEGUME	LIENAL
KOALAS	LADDIE	LAP-TOP	LAVISH	LEIDEN	LIERNE
KODIAK	LA-DI-DA	LARDED	LAWFUL	LEKKER	LIFERS
KOHIMA	LADIES	LARDER	LAWYER	LE MANS	LIFFEY
KOKAND	LADING	LARDON	LAXITY	LEMNOS	LIFTED
KOLYMA	LADINO	LAREDO	LAY-BYS	LEMONS	LIFTER

LIGAND	LISTED	LOGION	LOUSED	LYCHEE	MALADY
LIGATE	LISTEN	LOGJAM	LOUVAR	LYNXES	MALAGA
LIGHTS	LITANY	LOGLOG	LOUVRE	LYRATE	MALANG
LIGNIN	LITCHI	LOG OUT	LOVAGE	LYRICS	MALATE
LIGULA	LITERS	LOIRET	LOVELY	LYRIST	MALAWI
LIGULE	LITHER	LOITER	LOVERS	LYSINE	MALAYA
LIKASI	LITHIA	LOLLED	LOVEYS		MALDON
LIKELY	LITHIC	LOLLER	LOVING	**M**	MALEIC
LIKING	LITMUS	LOLLOP	LOWEST	MACACO	MALICE
LILACS	LITRES	LOMBOK	LOWING	MACAWS	MALIGN
LILIES	LITTER	LOMENT	LOW-KEY	MACEIO	MALLEE
LILLEE	LITTLE	LONDON	LOYANG	MACKAY	MALLET
LIMBER	LIVE-IN	LONELY	LOZERE	MACKLE	MALLOW
LIMBIC	LIVELY	LONERS	L-PLATE	MACRON	MALTED
LIMBOS	LIVERS	LONGAN	LUANDA	MACULA	MALTHA
LIMBUS	LIVERY	LONGED	LUBBER	MADAME	MAMBAS
LIMEYS	LIVING	LONGER	LUBECK	MADAMS	MAMMAL
LIMIER	LIZARD	LOOFAH	LUBLIN	MADCAP	MAMMON
LIMING	LLAMAS	LOOKED	LUCENT	MADDEN	MANAGE
LIMITS	LOADED	LOOKER	LUDLOW	MADDER	MANAMA
LIMNED	LOADER	LOOK-IN	LUFFED	MADE-UP	MANANA
LIMNER	LOAFED	LOOK UP	LUGANO	MADMAN	MANAUS
LIMPED	LOAFER	LOOMED	LUGGED	MADMEN	MANCHE
LIMPER	LOANED	LOONEY	LUGGER	MADRAS	MANCHU
LIMPET	LOANER	LOOPED	LULLED	MADRID	MANEGE
LIMPID	LOATHE	LOOPER	LUMBAR	MADURO	MANFUL
LIMPLY	LOAVES	LOOSED	LUMBER	MAENAD	MANGER
LINAGE	LOBATE	LOOSEN	LUMMOX	MAGGOT	MANGLE
LINDEN	LOBBED	LOOSER	LUMPED	MAGIAN	MANGOS
LINEAL	LOBITO	LOOSES	LUMPEN	MAGNET	MANIAC
LINEAR	LOBOLA	LOOTED	LUNACY	MAGNUM	MANIAS
LINERS	LOBULE	LOOTER	LUNATE	MAGPIE	MANILA
LINEUP	LOCALE	LOPING	LUNGED	MAGUEY	MANISA
LINGER	LOCALS	LOPPED	LUNGER	MAGYAR	MANLEY
LINGUA	LOCATE	LOPPER	LUNGES	MAHOUT	MANNED
LINING	LOCHIA	LOQUAT	LUNULA	MAIDEN	MANNER
LINKED	LOCKED	LORDED	LUPINE	MAIKOP	MANORS
LINKUP	LOCKER	LORDLY	LUPINS	MAILED	MANQUE
LINNET	LOCKET	LORICA	LURING	MAILER	MANTEL
LINTEL	LOCKUP	LOSERS	LURKED	MAI MAI	MANTIC
LINTER	LOCULE	LOSING	LURKER	MAIMED	MANTIS
LIPASE	LOCUMS	LOSSES	LUSAKA	MAIMER	MANTLE
LI PENG	LOCUST	LOTION	LUSHES	MAINLY	MANTUA
LIPIDS	LODGED	LOTTED	LU-SHUN	MAJORS	MANUAL
LIPOID	LODGER	LOUDEN	LUSTED	MAKALU	MANURE
LIPOMA	LODGES	LOUDER	LUSTRE	MAKE DO	MAOISM
LIQUID	LOFTED	LOUDLY	LUTEAL	MAKE IT	MAOIST
LIQUOR	LOFTER	LOUGHS	LUVVIE	MAKERS	MAPLES
LISBON	LOGGED	LOUISE	LUXATE	MAKE UP	MAPPED
LISPED	LOGGER	LOUNGE	LUXURY	MAKE-UP	MAPUTO
LISPER	LOGGIA	LOURED	LYCEES	MAKING	MAQUIS
LISSOM	LOGIER	LOURIE	LYCEUM	MALABO	MARACA

51

MARAUD	MATRON	MELTER	MIAOWS	MINOAN	MODIFY
MARBLE	MATTED	MELTON	MIASMA	MINORS	MODISH
MARBLY	MATTER	MEMBER	MICKEY	MINTED	MODULE
MARCHE	MATURE	MEMOIR	MICMAC	MINTER	MOGULS
MARGAY	MAULED	MEMORY	MICRON	MINUET	MOHAIR
MARGIN	MAULER	MENACE	MICROS	MINUTE	MOHAWK
MARIAN	MAUNDY	MENADO	MIDAIR	MINXES	MOHOLE
MARINA	MAUSER	MENAGE	MIDDAY	MIOSIS	MOIETY
MARINE	MAXIMA	MENDED	MIDDEN	MIOTIC	MOLARS
MARKED	MAXIMS	MENDER	MIDDLE	MIRAGE	MOLDED
MARKER	MAY BUG	MENHIR	MIDGES	MIRING	MOLDER
MARKET	MAY DAY	MENIAL	MIDGET	MIRROR	MOLEST
MARKKA	MAYFLY	MENSES	MIDGUT	MISCUE	MOLISE
MARKUP	MAYHEM	MENTAL	MID-OFF	MISERE	MOLOCH
MARLIN	MAYORS	MENTON	MIDRIB	MISERS	MOLOPO
MARMOT	MAZILY	MENTOR	MIDSTS	MISERY	MOLTED
MAROON	MAZUMA	MEOWED	MIDWAY	MISFIT	MOLTEN
MARQUE	MCEWAN	MERANO	MIERES	MISHAP	MOMENT
MARRED	MEADOW	MERCER	MIFFED	MISHIT	MOMISM
MARRER	MEAGRE	MERELY	MIGHTY	MISLAY	MOMMAS
MARRON	MEALIE	MERGED	MIKADO	MISLED	MONACO
MARROW	MEANER	MERGER	MILADY	MISSAL	MONDAY
MARSHY	MEANLY	MERINO	MILDER	MISSED	MONEYS
MARTEN	MEASLY	MERITS	MILDEW	MISSES	MONGER
MARTIN	MEATUS	MERLIN	MILDLY	MISSIS	MONGOL
MARTYR	MECCAS	MERLON	MILERS	MISSUS	MONIES
MARVEL	MEDALS	MERMAN	MILIEU	MISTED	MONISM
MARY II	MEDDLE	MERSIN	MILIUM	MISTER	MONIST
MASCLE	MEDIAL	MERTON	MILKED	MISUSE	MONKEY
MASCON	MEDIAN	MESCAL	MILKER	MITRAL	MONTHS
MASCOT	MEDICK	MESHED	MILLED	MITRES	MOOING
MASERS	MEDICO	MESHES	MILLER	MITTEN	MOONED
MASERU	MEDICS	MESSED	MILLET	MIXERS	MOORED
MASHED	MEDINA	MESSES	MILORD	MIXING	MOOTED
MASHER	MEDIUM	MESS-UP	MILTER	MIX-UPS	MOOTER
MASHES	MEDLAR	METAGE	MIMICS	MIZZEN	MOPANI
MASHIE	MEDLEY	METALS	MIMING	MOANED	MOPEDS
MASH UP	MEEKER	METEOR	MIMOSA	MOANER	MOPING
MASJID	MEEKLY	METERS	MINCED	MOATED	MOPOKE
MASKED	MEERUT	METHOD	MINCER	MOBBED	MOPPED
MASKER	MEETER	METHYL	MINDED	MOBBER	MOPPET
MASONS	MEGARA	METIER	MINDEL	MOBILE	MORALE
MASQUE	MEGILP	METING	MINDER	MOCKED	MORALS
MASSED	MEGOHM	METOPE	MINERS	MOCKER	MORASS
MASSES	MEKNES	METRES	MINGLE	MOCK UP	MORBID
MASSIF	MEKONG	METRIC	MINIFY	MOCK-UP	MOREEN
MASTER	MELEES	METROS	MINIMA	MOD CON	MORGUE
MASTIC	MELLOW	METTLE	MINIMS	MODELS	MORION
MATADI	MELODY	MEWING	MINING	MODEMS	MORLEY
MATING	MELOID	MEWLER	MINION	MODENA	MORMON
MATINS	MELONS	MEXICO	MINIUM	MODERN	MORNAY
MATRIX	MELTED	MEZZOS	MINNOW	MODEST	MORONI

MORONS	MUESLI	MYOPIA	NATRON	NEWEST	NOGGIN
MOROSE	MUFFED	MYOPIC	NATTER	NEWHAM	NOISES
MORROW	MUFFIN	MYOSIN	NATURE	NEWISH	NOMADS
MORSEL	MUFFLE	MYRIAD	NAUGHT	NEWMAN	NOMISM
MORTAL	MUGABE	MYRICA	NAUSEA	NEWTON	NONAGE
MORTAR	MUGGED	MYRTLE	NAUTCH	NIAMEY	NONCES
MORULA	MUGGER	MYSELF	NAVAHO	NIBBLE	NONEGO
MORYAH	MUKLUK	MYSORE	NAVELS	NIBLET	NOODLE
MOSAIC	MULISH	MYSTIC	NAVIES	NICELY	NOOSES
MOSCOW	MULLAH	MYTHOS	NAZISM	NICEST	NOOTKA
MOSLEM	MULLED	MY WORD	NEARBY	NICETY	NORDIC
MOSQUE	MULLER	MYXOMA	NEARED	NICHES	NORITE
MOSSIE	MULLET		NEARER	NICKED	NORMAL
MOSTLY	MULTAN	**N**	NEARLY	NICKEL	NORMAN
MOTELS	MUMBLE	NAAFIS	NEATEN	NICKER	NORTHS
MOTETS	MUMMER	NABBED	NEATER	NIDIFY	NORWAY
MOTHER	MUNICH	NABLUS	NEATLY	NIECES	NOSHED
MOTIFS	MURALS	NABOBS	NEBULA	NIELLO	NOSH-UP
MOTILE	MURCIA	NACHOS	NECKAR	NIEVRE	NO SIDE
MOTION	MURDER	NACRED	NECKED	NIGGER	NO-SIDE
MOTIVE	MURINE	NADIRS	NECKER	NIGGLE	NOSIER
MOTLEY	MURMUR	NAEVUS	NECTAR	NIGHTS	NOSILY
MOTMOT	MUSCAT	NAGANA	NEEDED	NILGAI	NOSING
MOTORS	MUSCID	NAGANO	NEEDLE	NIMBLE	NOSTOC
MOTOWN	MUSCLE	NAGGED	NEEDN'T	NIMBLY	NOTARY
MOTTLE	MUSCLY	NAGGER	NEGATE	NIMBUS	NOTICE
MOTTOS	MUSEUM	NAGOYA	NEGROS	NINETY	NOTIFY
MOULDS	MUSHES	NAGPUR	NEIGHS	NINGBO	NOTING
MOULDY	MUSING	NAIADS	NEKTON	NINGPO	NOTION
MOULIN	MUSKET	NAILED	NELSON	NINTHS	NOUGAT
MOULTS	MUSKIE	NAILER	NEM CON	NIOBIC	NOUGHT
MOUNDS	MUSLIM	NAKURU	NEPALI	NIP OUT	NOUNAL
MOUNTS	MUSLIN	NAMELY	NEPHEW	NIPPED	NOVARA
MOUSER	MUSSED	NAMING	NEREID	NIPPER	NOVELS
MOUSEY	MUSSEL	NANTES	NEREIS	NIPPLE	NOVENA
MOUSSE	MUSTEE	NAPALM	NERVED	NIPPON	NOVICE
MOUTHS	MUSTER	NAPIER	NERVES	NITRIC	NOWISE
MOUTON	MUSTN'T	NAPKIN	NESTED	NITWIT	NOZZLE
MOVERS	MUTANT	NAPLES	NESTER	NIXING	NUANCE
MOVIES	MUTARE	NAPPED	NESTLE	NO BALL	NUBBLE
MOVING	MUTATE	NAPPER	NETHER	NO-BALL	NUBBLY
MOWERS	MUTELY	NARIAL	NETTED	NOBBLE	NUBILE
MOWING	MUTING	NARKED	NETTLE	NOBLER	NUCHAL
MOWLAM	MUTINY	NARROW	NETTLY	NOBLES	NUCLEI
MUCKED	MUTISM	NARVIK	NEURAL	NOBODY	NUDGED
MUCKER	MUTTER	NASALS	NEURON	NODDED	NUDGER
MUCOID	MUTTON	NASIAL	NEUTER	NODDLE	NUDGES
MUCOUS	MUTUAL	NASION	NEVADA	NOD OFF	NUDISM
MUDCAT	MUTULE	NASSAU	NEVERS	NODOSE	NUDIST
MUDDED	MUZZLE	NATANT	NEW AGE	NODULE	NUDITY
MUDDLE	MYELIN	NATION	NEWARK	NOESIS	NUGGET
MUD PIE	MYNAHS	NATIVE	NEWBIE	NOETIC	NUKING

NUMBAT	ODDS ON	ONLINE	ORIGAN	OUTSET	PALING
NUMBED	ODDS-ON	ONRUSH	ORIGIN	OUTWIT	PALISH
NUMBER	ODENSE	ONSIDE	ORIOLE	OVERDO	PALLAS
NUMBLY	ODESSA	ONWARD	ORISON	OVERLY	PALLED
NUNCIO	ODIOUS	OOCYTE	ORISSA	OVIEDO	PALLET
NURSED	ODOURS	OODLES	ORMOLU	OVISAC	PALLID
NURSES	OEDEMA	OOGAMY	ORNATE	OVOIDS	PALLOR
NUTANT	OEUVRE	OOLITE	ORNERY	OVULAR	PALMAR
NUTLET	OFFALY	OOLOGY	OROIDE	OWELTY	PALMED
NUTMEG	OFFEND	OOLONG	ORPHAN	OWERRI	PALTER
NUTRIA	OFFERS	OOZIER	ORPINE	OWLETS	PALTRY
NUTTED	OFFICE	OOZILY	ORRERY	OWLISH	PAMIRS
NUTTER	OFFING	OOZING	OSCARS	OWNERS	PAMPAS
NUZZLE	OFFSET	OPAQUE	OSCINE	OWNING	PAMPER
NYLONS	OFSTED	OPENED	OSHAWA	OXALIS	PANADA
NYMPHA	OGADEN	OPENER	OSIERS	OXCART	PANAMA
NYMPHS	OGDOAD	OPENLY	OSIJEK	OXFORD	PANDAS
	OGIVAL	OPERAS	OSMIUM	OXIDES	PANDER
O	OGLING	OPERON	OSMOSE	OXTAIL	PANDIT
	OGRESS	OPHITE	OSMOUS	OXYGEN	PANELS
OAFISH	OHMAGE	OPIATE	OSPREY	OYSTER	PANICS
OAKHAM	OIDIUM	OPINED	OSSEIN	OZALID	PANJIM
OAXACA	OILCAN	OPIOID	OSSIFY		PANNED
OBELUS	OILCUP	OPORTO	OSTEAL	**P**	PANTED
OBEYED	OILIER	OPPOSE	OSTEND	PACIFY	PANTRY
OBEYER	OILILY	OPPUGN	OSTIUM	PACING	PANZER
OBJECT	OILING	OPTICS	OSTLER	PACINO	PAOTOW
OBLAST	OILMAN	OPTING	OTHERS	PACKED	PAPACY
OBLATE	OILMEN	OPTION	OTIOSE	PACKER	PAPAIN
OBLIGE	OILRIG	OPUSES	OTITIS	PACKET	PAPAYA
OBLONG	OIL RIG	ORACLE	O'TOOLE	PADANG	PAPERS
OBOIST	OINKED	ORADEA	OTTAVA	PADAUK	PAPERY
OBSESS	OKAYED	ORALLY	OTTAWA	PADDED	PAPHOS
OBTAIN	OLD AGE	ORANGE	OTTERS	PADDLE	PAPIST
OBTECT	OLD BOY	ORATOR	OUNCES	PADRES	PAPPUS
OBTUSE	OLDEST	ORBITS	OUSTED	PAEANS	PAPUAN
OBVERT	OLDHAM	ORCEIN	OUSTER	PAELLA	PAPULE
OCCULT	OLD HAT	ORCHID	OUTAGE	PAEONY	PAPYRI
OCCUPY	OLDISH	ORCHIL	OUTBID	PAGANS	PARADE
OCEANS	OLD LAG	ORCHIS	OUTCRY	PAGING	PARAMO
OCELOT	OLD MAN	ORDAIN	OUTDID	PAGODA	PARANA
O'CLOCK	OLEATE	ORDEAL	OUTFIT	PAHANG	PARANG
OCTANE	O LEVEL	ORDERS	OUTFOX	PAID-UP	PARAPH
OCTANT	OLIVES	ORDURE	OUTGAS	PAINED	PARCEL
OCTAVE	OMASUM	OREBRO	OUTING	PAINTS	PARDON
OCTAVO	OMEGAS	OREGON	OUTLAW	PAIRED	PARENT
OCTETS	ONAGER	ORENSE	OUTLAY	PAJAMA	PARGET
OCTOPI	ONCOST	ORGANS	OUTLET	PALACE	PARIAH
OCTROI	ON EDGE	ORGASM	OUTMAN	PALAIS	PARIAN
OCULAR	ONE-OFF	ORGEAT	OUTPUT	PALATE	PARIES
ODDEST	ONE-WAY	ORGIES	OUTRAN	PALELY	PARING
ODDITY	ONIONS	ORIENT	OUTRUN	PALEST	PARISH
ODD JOB					

PARITY	PAWPAW	PELTER	PETREL	PIFFLE	PIQUET
PARKAS	PAXWAX	PELTRY	PETROL	PIGEON	PIRACY
PARKED	PAYBED	PELVES	PETTED	PIGGED	PIRATE
PARKIN	PAYDAY	PELVIC	PETTER	PIGGIN	PISCES
PARLEY	PAYEES	PELVIS	PEWITS	PIGLET	PISSED
PARODY	PAYING	PENANG	PEWTER	PIGNUS	PISSES
PAROLE	PAYOFF	PENCHI	PHASED	PIGNUT	PISS-UP
PARREL	PAYOLA	PENCIL	PHASES	PIGSTY	PISTIL
PARROT	PAYOUT	PENGPU	PHASIC	PILAFS	PISTOL
PARSEC	PCMCIA	PENMAN	PHENOL	PILEUM	PISTON
PARSED	PEACES	PENNED	PHENOM	PILEUP	PITCHY
PARSEE	PEACHY	PENNEY	PHENYL	PILEUS	PITHOS
PARSER	PEAHEN	PENNON	PHIALS	PILFER	PITIED
PARSON	PEAKED	PEN PAL	PHILAE	PILING	PITIES
PARTED	PEALED	PENTAD	PHIZOG	PILLAR	PITMAN
PARTLY	PEANUT	PENT UP	PHLEGM	PILLOW	PITMEN
PARTON	PEARLS	PENTYL	PHLOEM	PILOSE	PITSAW
PARURE	PEARLY	PENULT	PHOBIA	PILOTS	PITTED
PASHTO	PEBBLE	PENURY	PHOBIC	PILULE	PIVOTS
PASSED	PEBBLY	PEOPLE	PHOBOS	PIMPED	PIXELS
PASSES	PECANS	PEORIA	PHOEBE	PIMPLE	PIXIES
PASSIM	PECKED	PEPLUM	PHONED	PIMPLY	PIZZAS
PASTED	PECKER	PEPPED	PHONES	PINCER	PLACED
PASTEL	PECTEN	PEPPER	PHONEY	PINEAL	PLACER
PASTES	PECTIC	PEPSIN	PHONIC	PINENE	PLACES
PASTOR	PECTIN	PEPTIC	PHONON	PINERY	PLACET
PASTRY	PEDALS	PERFIN	PHOOEY	PINGED	PLACID
PATCHY	PEDANT	PERILS	PHOTIC	PINIER	PLAGAL
PATENT	PEDATE	PERIOD	PHOTON	PINING	PLAGUE
PATERS	PEDDLE	PERISH	PHOTOS	PINION	PLAGUY
PATHAN	PEDLAR	PERKED	PHRASE	PINITE	PLAICE
PATHOS	PEDWAY	PERLIS	PHUKET	PINKED	PLAIDS
PATINA	PEEING	PERMED	PHYLUM	PINKER	PLAINS
PATIOS	PEEKED	PERMIT	PHYSIC	PINKIE	PLAINT
PATMOS	PEELED	PERNIK	PHYSIO	PINKOS	PLAITS
PATOIS	PEELER	PERNOD	PHYTON	PINNED	PLANAR
PATRAS	PEEPBO	PER PRO	PIAFFE	PINNER	PLANED
PATROL	PEEPED	PERRON	PIANOS	PINTAS	PLANER
PATRON	PEEPER	PERSIA	PIAZZA	PINTER	PLANES
PATTED	PEEPUL	PERSON	PICKED	PINTLE	PLANET
PATTEN	PEERED	PERTLY	PICKER	PINUPS	PLANKS
PATTER	PEEVED	PERUKE	PICKET	PINXIT	PLANTS
PAUCAL	PEEWIT	PERUSE	PICKLE	PIPAGE	PLAQUE
PAUNCH	PEGGED	PESADE	PICK-UP	PIPALS	PLASHY
PAUPER	PEG LEG	PESARO	PICNIC	PIPERS	PLASMA
PAUSED	PEKING	PESETA	PIDDLE	PIPING	PLATAN
PAUSER	PELAGE	PESTER	PIDGIN	PIPITS	PLATED
PAUSES	PELITE	PESTLE	PIECED	PIPKIN	PLATEN
PAVANE	PELLET	PETALS	PIECER	PIPPED	PLATER
PAVING	PELMET	PETARD	PIECES	PIPPIN	PLATES
PAWING	PELOTA	PETERS	PIERCE	PIQUED	PLAUEN
PAWNED	PELTED	PETITE	PIERRE	PIQUES	PLAYED

PLAYER	POLEYN	PORKER	PREACH	PROOFS	PUNDIT
PLAZAS	POLICE	POROUS	PRECIS	PROPEL	PUNIER
PLEACH	POLICY	PORTAL	PREFAB	PROPER	PUNISH
PLEASE	POLING	PORTED	PREFER	PROPYL	PUNJAB
PLEATS	POLISH	PORTER	PREFIX	PROSES	PUNKAH
PLEBBY	POLITE	PORTLY	PREPAY	PROTEA	PUNNED
PLEDGE	POLITY	POSERS	PREPPY	PRO TEM	PUNNET
PLEIAD	POLKAS	POSEUR	PRESET	PROTON	PUNTED
PLENTY	POLLAN	POSHER	PRESTO	PROVED	PUNTER
PLENUM	POLLED	POSIES	PRETTY	PROVEN	PUPATE
PLEURA	POLLEN	POSING	PREWAR	PROVIE	PUPILS
PLEVEN	POLLEX	POSSES	PREYED	PROWLS	PUPPED
PLEXOR	POLLUX	POSSET	PREYER	PROZAC	PUPPET
PLEXUS	POLONY	POSSUM	PRICED	PRUDES	PUPPIS
PLIANT	POL POT	POSTAL	PRICES	PRUNED	PURDAH
PLICAL	POLYPS	POSTED	PRICEY	PRUNER	PUREED
PLIERS	POMACE	POSTER	PRICKS	PRUNES	PUREES
PLIGHT	POMADE	POSTIE	PRIDED	PRYING	PURELY
PLINTH	POMMEL	POSTIL	PRIDES	PSALMS	PUREST
PLISSE	POMPOM	POTAGE	PRIEST	PSEUDO-	PURFLE
PLOUGH	POMPON	POTASH	PRIMAL	PSEUDS	PURGED
PLOVER	PONCES	POTATO	PRIMED	PSEUDY	PURGER
PLOWED	PONCEY	POTBOY	PRIMER	PSYCHE	PURGES
PLUCKS	PONCHO	POTEEN	PRIMES	PSYCHO-	PURIFY
PLUCKY	PONDER	POTENT	PRIMLY	PTISAN	PURINE
PLUMED	PONDOK	POTFUL	PRIMUS	PTOSIS	PURISM
PLUMES	PONGED	POTHER	PRINCE	PUBLIC	PURIST
PLUMMY	PONGEE	POTION	PRINTS	PUCKER	PURITY
PLUNGE	PONGID	POTTED	PRIORS	PUDDLE	PURLED
PLURAL	PONIES	POTTER	PRIORY	PUDDLY	PURLER
PLUSES	PONTIC	POUCHY	PRIPET	PUDSEY	PURLIN
PLUTON	PONTIL	POUNCE	PRISED	PUEBLA	PURPLE
PLYING	POODLE	POUNDS	PRISMS	PUEBLO	PURRED
PNEUMA	POOLED	POURED	PRISON	PUFFED	PURSED
POCKED	POOPED	POURER	PRISSY	PUFFER	PURSER
POCKET	POOPER	POUTED	PRIVET	PUFFIN	PURSES
PODDED	POORER	POUTER	PRIZED	PUGGED	PURSUE
PODIUM	POORLY	POWDER	PRIZES	PUKING	PURVEY
PODZOL	POOTLE	POWELL	PRO-AMS	PULLED	PUSHED
POETIC	POP ART	POWERS	PROBED	PULLET	PUSHER
POETRY	POPERY	POWWOW	PROBER	PULLEY	PUSHES
POGROM	POPGUN	POZNAN	PROBES	PULL-IN	PUSH-UP
POINTE	POPISH	PRAGUE	PROFIT	PULL-ON	PUSSES
POINTS	POPLAR	PRAISE	PROJET	PULPED	PUTLOG
POISED	POPLIN	PRANCE	PROLEG	PULPIT	PUT OFF
POISON	POPPAS	PRANKS	PROLES	PULSAR	PUT-OFF
POKERS	POPPED	PRATED	PROLIX	PULSED	PUT OUT
POKIER	POPPER	PRATER	PROLOG	PULSES	PUTRID
POKILY	POPPET	PRAWNS	PROMOS	PUMICE	PUTSCH
POKING	POPPLE	PRAXIS	PROMPT	PUMMEL	PUTTED
POLAND	PORING	PRAYED	PRONGS	PUMPED	PUTTEE
POLDER	PORISM	PRAYER	PRONTO	PUNCHY	PUTTER

PUZZLE	QUIRKY	RAILED	RASHER	RECANT	REFUSE
PYKNIC	QUIVER	RAILER	RASHES	RECAPS	REFUTE
PYLONS	QUOITS	RAILEX	RASHLY	RECAST	REGAIN
PYOSIS	QUORUM	RAINED	RASPED	RECEDE	REGALE
PYRENE	QUOTAS	RAISED	RASPER	RECENT	REGARD
PYRITE	QUOTED	RAISER	RASTER	RECEPT	REGENT
PYRONE	QUOTES	RAISES	RATBAG	RECESS	REGGAE
PYROPE	QWERTY	RAISIN	RATHER	RECIFE	REGIME
PYTHON		RAJAHS	RATIFY	RECIPE	REGINA
PYURIA	**R**	RAJKOT	RATINE	RECITE	REGION
	RABATO	RAJPUT	RATING	RECKED	REGLET
Q	RABAUL	RAKING	RATION	RECKON	REGRET
QATARI	RABBIS	RAKISH	RATIOS	RECODE	REGULO
QINTAR	RABBIT	RAMBLE	RATITE	RECOIL	REHASH
QUACKS	RABBLE	RAMIFY	RATLAM	RECORD	REHEAR
QUAGGA	RABIES	RAMJET	RATOON	RECOUP	REHEAT
QUAGGY	RACEME	RAMMED	RATTAN	RECTAL	REHOME
QUAHOG	RACERS	RAMMER	RAT-TAT	RECTOR	REIGNS
QUAILS	RACHIS	RAMOSE	RATTED	RECTOS	REINED
QUAINT	RACIAL	RAMPUR	RATTER	RECTUM	REJECT
QUAKED	RACIER	RAMROD	RATTLE	RECTUS	REJIGS
QUAKER	RACILY	RAMTIL	RATTLY	REDACT	REJOIN
QUAKES	RACING	RANCHI	RAVAGE	REDBUD	RELAID
QUALMS	RACISM	RANCID	RAVENS	REDCAP	RELATE
QUANGO	RACIST	RANDAN	RAVERS	REDDEN	RELAYS
QUANTA	RACKED	RANDOM	RAVE-UP	REDDER	RELENT
QUARKS	RACKER	RANEES	RAVINE	REDEEM	RELICS
QUARRY	RACKET	RANGED	RAVING	RED EYE	RELICT
QUARTO	RACOON	RANGER	RAVISH	REDFIN	RELIED
QUARTS	RADDLE	RANGES	RAWEST	RED-HOT	RELIEF
QUARTZ	RADIAL	RANKED	RAZING	REDONE	RELINE
QUASAR	RADIAN	RANKER	RAZORS	REDOWA	RELISH
QUAVER	RADIOS	RANKLE	RAZZLE	RED SEA	RELIVE
QUAYLE	RADISH	RANKLY	READER	REDUCE	RELOAD
QUEASY	RADIUM	RANSOM	REALLY	REECHO	REMADE
QUEBEC	RADIUS	RANTED	REALMS	REEFED	REMAIN
QUEENS	RADOME	RANTER	REAMED	REEFER	REMAKE
QUEERS	RADULA	RAPIDS	REAMER	REEKED	REMAND
QUEMOY	RAFFIA	RAPIER	REAPED	REELED	REMARK
QUENCH	RAFFLE	RAPINE	REAPER	REELER	REMEDY
QUESTS	RAFTED	RAPING	REARED	REEVES	REMIND
QUEUED	RAFTER	RAPIST	REARER	REFACE	REMISE
QUEUES	RAGBAG	RAPPED	REASON	REFILL	REMISS
QUICHE	RAGGED	RAPPEL	REBASE	REFINE	REMORA
QUIFFS	RAGING	RAPPER	REBATE	REFITS	REMOTE
QUILLS	RAGLAN	RAPTOR	REBELS	REFLET	REMOVE
QUILTS	RAGMAN	RAREFY	REBIND	REFLEX	RENAME
QUINCE	RAGOUT	RARELY	REBOOT	REFLUX	RENDER
QUINOL	RAGTAG	RAREST	REBORN	REFORM	RENEGE
QUINSY	RAGUSA	RARING	REBUFF	REFUEL	RENNES
QUIRES	RAIDED	RARITY	REBUKE	REFUGE	RENNET
QUIRKS	RAIDER	RASCAL	RECALL	REFUND	RENNIN

RENOWN	RETIRE	RIDDED	ROARED	ROSTER	RUMBLE
RENTAL	RETOLD	RIDDEN	ROARER	ROSTOV	RUMBLY
RENTED	RETOOK	RIDDER	ROASTS	ROSTRA	RUMMER
RENTER	RETOOL	RIDDLE	ROBALO	ROTARY	RUMOUR
RENVOI	RETORT	RIDERS	ROBAND	ROTATE	RUMPLE
REOPEN	RETUNE	RIDGED	ROBBED	ROTGUT	RUMPLY
REPAID	RETURN	RIDGES	ROBBER	ROTORS	RUMPUS
REPAIR	RETUSE	RIDING	ROBBIN	ROTTED	RUNDLE
REPAND	REUSED	RIFFLE	ROBING	ROTTEN	RUNNEL
REPAST	REVAMP	RIFLED	ROBINS	ROTTER	RUNNER
REPEAL	REVEAL	RIFLER	ROBOTS	ROTUND	RUN-OFF
REPEAT	REVERE	RIFLES	ROBSON	ROUBLE	RUN-UPS
REPENT	REVERS	RIGGED	ROBUST	ROUGED	RUNWAY
REPINE	REVERT	RIGGER	ROCHET	ROUNDS	RUPEES
REPLAN	REVEST	RIGHTS	ROCKED	ROUSED	RUPIAH
REPLAY	REVIEW	RIGOUR	ROCKER	ROUSER	RUSHED
REPONE	REVILE	RIG-OUT	ROCKET	ROUTED	RUSHER
REPORT	REVISE	RIJEKA	ROCOCO	ROUTER	RUSHES
REPOSE	REVIVE	RILEYS	RODENT	ROUTES	RUSSET
REPUTE	REVOKE	RILING	RODEOS	ROVERS	RUSSIA
REREAD	REVOLT	RILLET	ROGERS	ROVING	RUSTED
RERUNS	REVUES	RIMINI	ROGUES	ROWANS	RUSTIC
RESALE	REVVED	RIMMED	ROLLED	ROWERS	RUSTLE
RESCUE	REWARD	RIMOSE	ROLLER	ROWING	RUTILE
RESEAT	REWIND	RINGED	ROLL ON	ROYALS	RUTTED
RESEAU	REWIRE	RINGER	ROLL-ON	ROZZER	RWANDA
RESECT	REWORD	RING IN	ROMAIC	RUBATO	RYAZAN
RESEDA	REWORK	RINSED	ROMANO	RUBBED	
RESEED	RHEBOK	RINSER	ROMANS	RUBBER	**S**
RESENT	RHESUS	RINSES	ROMANY	RUBBLE	SABBAT
RESHIP	RHEUMY	RIOTED	ROM-COM	RUBBLY	SABERS
RESIDE	RHEYDT	RIOTER	ROMEOS	RUBIES	SABLES
RESIGN	RHINAL	RIPEST	ROMPED	RUBLES	SABRAS
RESILE	RHODES	RIP-OFF	RONDEL	RUBRIC	SABRES
RESINS	RHODIC	RIPPED	RONDOS	RUCKED	SACHET
RESIST	RHOTIC	RIPPER	ROOFED	RUCKUS	SACKED
RESITS	RHYMED	RIPPLE	ROOKED	RUDDER	SACKER
RESIZE	RHYMES	RIPPLY	ROOKIE	RUDDLE	SACRAL
RESORB	RHYTHM	RIPSAW	ROOMED	RUDELY	SACRED
RESORT	RHYTON	RISERS	ROOMER	RUDEST	SACRUM
RESTED	RIALTO	RISING	ROOSTS	RUEFUL	SADDEN
RESTER	RIBALD	RISKED	ROOTED	RUFFLE	SADDER
RESULT	RIBBED	RISKER	ROOTER	RUFFLY	SADDLE
RESUME	RIBBON	RISQUE	ROOTSY	RUFOUS	SADHUS
RETAIL	RIBERA	RITUAL	ROPIER	RUGGED	SADISM
RETAIN	RIBOSE	RIVALS	ROPILY	RUGOSA	SADIST
RETAKE	RICHER	RIVERS	ROPING	RUGOSE	SAFARI
RETARD	RICHES	RIVETS	ROQUET	RUINED	SAFELY
RETELL	RICHLY	RIYADH	ROSARY	RUINER	SAFEST
RETENE	RICKED	RIYALS	ROSIER	RULERS	SAFETY
RETIAL	RICTAL	ROAMED	ROSILY	RULING	SAGELY
RETINA	RICTUS	ROAMER	ROSINY	RUMBAS	SAGGAR

SAGGED	SANTER	SCANTY	SCREWY	SEEKER	SERENE
SAHARA	SANTOS	SCARAB	SCRIBE	SEEMED	SERIAL
SAHIBS	SAPELE	SCARCE	SCRIMP	SEEMER	SERIES
SAIGON	SAPOTA	SCARED	SCRIPT	SEEMLY	SERIFS
SAILED	SAPPED	SCARER	SCROLL	SEEPED	SERINE
SAILER	SAPPER	SCARES	SCROOP	SEESAW	SERMON
SAILOR	SARGES	SCAREY	SCROTA	SEETHE	SEROSA
SAINTS	SARNIA	SCARFS	SCRUBS	SEFTON	SEROUS
SAIPAN	SARNIE	SCARPS	SCRUFF	SEICHE	SERUMS
SAITHE	SARONG	SCATTY	SCRUMP	SEINES	SERVAL
SALAAM	SARTHE	SCENES	SCRUMS	SEISER	SERVED
SALADS	SASEBO	SCENIC	SCUBAS	SEISIN	SERVER
SALAMI	SASHAY	SCENTS	SCUFFS	SEIZED	SERVES
SALARY	SASHES	SCHEMA	SCULPT	SEIZER	SERVOS
SALIFY	SASSED	SCHEME	SCUMMY	SEJANT	SESAME
SALINE	SASSES	SCHISM	SCUNGY	SELDOM	SESTET
SALIVA	SATEEN	SCHIST	SCURFY	SELECT	SET-OFF
SALLEE	SATING	SCHLEP	SCURRY	SELLER	SETOSE
SALLOW	SATINY	SCHOOL	SCURVY	SELVES	SETTEE
SALMON	SATIRE	SCHORL	SCUTCH	SEMEME	SETTER
SALONS	SATURN	SCHUSS	SCUTUM	SEMITE	SETTLE
SALOON	SATYRS	SCHWAS	SCUZZY	SEMPRE	SET-UPS
SALOOP	SAUCED	SCHWYZ	SCYLLA	SEMTEX	SEVENS
SALTED	SAUCER	SCILLA	SCYTHE	SENARY	SEVERE
SALTER	SAUCES	SCIONS	SEABED	SENATE	SEVRES
SALTUS	SAUGER	SCLAFF	SEA DOG	SENDAI	SEWAGE
SALUKI	SAUNAS	SCLERA	SEALED	SENDER	SEWERS
SALUTE	SAVAGE	SCOFFS	SEALER	SEND UP	SEWING
SALVED	SAVAII	SCOLDS	SEAMAN	SEND-UP	SEXIER
SALVER	SAVANT	SCOLEX	SEAMEN	SENECA	SEXILY
SALVES	SAVERS	SCONCE	SEAMER	SENEGA	SEXING
SALVIA	SAVING	SCONES	SEANCE	SENILE	SEXISM
SALVOR	SAVOIE	SCOOPS	SEARCH	SENIOR	SEXIST
SALVOS	SAVONA	SCORCH	SEARED	SENNAR	SEXPOT
SALYUT	SAVORY	SCORED	SEASON	SENNIT	SEXTET
SAMARA	SAVOUR	SCORER	SEATED	SENORA	SEXTON
SAMBAR	SAVOYS	SCORES	SEATER	SENORS	SEXUAL
SAMBAS	SAWFLY	SCORIA	SEAWAY	SENSED	SHABBY
SAMITE	SAWING	SCORNS	SECANT	SENSES	SHACKS
SAMOAN	SAWYER	SCOTCH	SECEDE	SENSOR	SHADED
SAMOSA	SAXONS	SCOTER	SECOND	SENTRY	SHADES
SAMPAN	SAXONY	SCOTIA	SECRET	SEPALS	SHADOW
SAMPLE	SAYING	SCOUSE	SECTOR	SEPSIS	SHAFTS
SAMSUN	SCABBY	SCOUTS	SECUND	SEPTAL	SHAGGY
SANDAL	SCALAR	SCOWLS	SECURE	SEPTET	SHAKEN
SANDED	SCALDS	SCRAPE	SEDANS	SEPTIC	SHAKER
SANDER	SCALED	SCRAPS	SEDATE	SEPTUM	SHAKES
SANDHI	SCALER	SCRAWL	SEDILE	SEQUEL	SHALOM
SANELY	SCALES	SCREAM	SEDUCE	SEQUIN	SHAMAN
SANEST	SCALPS	SCREED	SEEDED	SERAPH	SHAMED
SANIES	SCAMPI	SCREEN	SEEDER	SERBIA	SHAMMY
SANITY	SCAMPS	SCREWS	SEEING	SEREIN	SHANDY

SHANKS	SHODDY	SIDING	SINNED	SLAGGY	SLOWLY
SHANNY	SHOGUN	SIDLED	SINNER	SLAKED	SLUDGE
SHANSI	SHOOED	SIDLER	SINTER	SLAKER	SLUDGY
SHANTY	SHOO-IN	SIECLE	SIOUAN	SLALOM	SLUICE
SHANXI	SHOOTS	SIEGEN	SIPHON	SLANGY	SLUING
SHAPED	SHORAN	SIEGES	SIPPED	SLANTS	SLUMMY
SHAPES	SHORED	SIENNA	SIPPER	SLAP-UP	SLUMPS
SHARDS	SHORES	SIERRA	SIPPET	SLATED	SLURRY
SHARED	SHORTS	SIESTA	SIRENS	SLATER	SLUSHY
SHARER	SHORTY	SIEVED	SIRING	SLATES	SLYEST
SHARES	SHOULD	SIEVES	SIRIUS	SLAVED	SMACKS
SHARIA	SHOUTS	SIFAKA	SIRRAH	SLAVER	SMALLS
SHARKS	SHOVED	SIFTED	SISERA	SLAVES	SMALTO
SHARPS	SHOVEL	SIFTER	SISKIN	SLAVIC	SMARMY
SHAVED	SHOVER	SIGHED	SISTER	SLAYER	SMEARS
SHAVEN	SHOVES	SIGHER	SITARS	SLEAVE	SMEARY
SHAVER	SHOWED	SIGHTS	SITCOM	SLEAZE	SMEGMA
SHAVES	SHOWER	SIGNAL	SITING	SLEAZY	SMELLS
SHAWLS	SHOW UP	SIGNED	SIT-INS	SLEDGE	SMELLY
SHEARS	SHRANK	SIGNEE	SITTER	SLEEPY	SMELTS
SHEATH	SHREDS	SIGNER	SIT-UPS	SLEETY	SMILAX
SHEAVE	SHREWD	SIGNET	SIXTHS	SLEEVE	SMILED
SHEETS	SHREWS	SIGN ON	SIZING	SLEIGH	SMILER
SHEIKH	SHRIEK	SIGNOR	SIZZLE	SLEUTH	SMILES
SHEILA	SHRIFT	SIKKIM	SKATED	SLEWED	SMILEY
SHEKEL	SHRIKE	SILAGE	SKATER	SLICED	SMIRCH
SHELLS	SHRILL	SILENT	SKATES	SLICER	SMIRKS
SHELVE	SHRIMP	SILICA	SKEINS	SLICES	SMITER
SHENSI	SHRINE	SILKEN	SKELLY	SLICKS	SMITHS
SHERDS	SHRINK	SILTED	SKETCH	SLIDES	SMITHY
SHERIA	SHRIVE	SILVAN	SKEWED	SLIGHT	SMOCKS
SHERPA	SHROUD	SILVER	SKEWER	SLIMLY	SMOGGY
SHERRY	SHRUBS	SIMIAN	SKIBOB	SLINGS	SMOKED
SHEWED	SHRUGS	SIMILE	SKIDOO	SLINKY	SMOKER
SHIELD	SHRUNK	SIMMER	SKIERS	SLIP-ON	SMOKES
SHIEST	SHTOOK	SIMNEL	SKIFFS	SLIPPY	SMOOCH
SHIFTS	SHUCKS	SIMONY	SKIING	SLIP-UP	SMOOTH
SHIFTY	SHUFTI	SIMOOM	SKIKDA	SLIVER	SMUDGE
SHIITE	SHUFTY	SIMPER	SKILLS	SLOGAN	SMUDGY
SHINER	SHUNTS	SIMPLE	SKIMPY	SLOOPS	SMUGLY
SHINNY	SHYEST	SIMPLY	SKINNY	SLOPED	SMUTCH
SHINTO	SHYING	SINDHI	SKIRTS	SLOPER	SMUTTY
SHINTY	SIALIC	SINEWS	SKIVED	SLOPES	SNACKS
SHIRAZ	SIBYLS	SINEWY	SKIVER	SLOPPY	SNAFUS
SHIRES	SICILY	SINFUL	SKIVVY	SLOSHY	SNAGGY
SHIRTS	SICKED	SINGED	SKOPJE	SLOTHS	SNAILS
SHIRTY	SICKEN	SINGER	SKULLS	SLOUCH	SNAKED
SHITTY	SICKER	SINGES	SKUNKS	SLOUGH	SNAKES
SHIVER	SICKIE	SINGLE	SKYCAP	SLOVAK	SNAPPY
SHOALS	SICKLE	SINGLY	SKYLAB	SLOVEN	SNARED
SHOALY	SICKLY	SINING	SKYROS	SLOWED	SNARER
SHOCKS	SIDE-ON	SINKER	SLACKS	SLOWER	SNARES

SNARLS	SODIUM	SOUSED	SPIRAL	SPURTS	STARES
SNARLY	SODOMY	SOUSSE	SPIRES	SPUTUM	STARRY
SNATCH	SOEVER	SOVIET	SPIRIT	SPYING	STARTS
SNAZZY	SOFFIT	SOWERS	SPITAL	SQUABS	STARVE
SNEAKS	SOFTEN	SOWETO	SPITED	SQUADS	STASIS
SNEAKY	SOFTER	SOWING	SPLAKE	SQUALL	STATED
SNEERS	SOFTIE	SPACED	SPLASH	SQUAMA	STATER
SNEEZE	SOFTLY	SPACER	SPLEEN	SQUARE	STATES
SNEEZY	SOIGNE	SPACES	SPLICE	SQUASH	STATIC
SNICKS	SOILED	SPADER	SPLINE	SQUATS	STATOR
SNIDER	SOIREE	SPADES	SPLINT	SQUAWK	STATUE
SNIFFS	SOKOTO	SPADIX	SPLITS	SQUAWS	STATUS
SNIFFY	SOLACE	SPANKS	SPLOSH	SQUEAK	STAVED
SNIPED	SOLDER	SPARED	SPOILS	SQUEAL	STAVES
SNIPER	SOLELY	SPARER	SPOILT	SQUIBS	STAYED
SNIPES	SOLEMN	SPARES	SPOKEN	SQUIDS	STAYER
SNIPPY	SOLENT	SPARID	SPOKES	SQUILL	STAY IN
SNITCH	SOLIDI	SPARKS	SPONGE	SQUINT	STEADS
SNIVEL	SOLIDS	SPARRY	SPONGY	SQUIRE	STEADY
SNOBOL	SOLING	SPARSE	SPOOFS	SQUIRM	STEAKS
SNOOPS	SO LONG	SPASMS	SPOOKS	SQUIRT	STEAMY
SNOOPY	SOLUTE	SPATHE	SPOOKY	SQUISH	STEEDS
SNOOTY	SOLVED	SPAVIN	SPOOLS	STABLE	STEELS
SNOOZE	SOLVER	SPAYED	SPOONS	STABLY	STEELY
SNOOZY	SOMALI	SPEARS	SPOORS	STACKS	STEERS
SNORED	SOMBRE	SPECIE	SPORES	STADIA	STEEVE
SNORER	SOMITE	SPECKS	SPORTS	STAFFS	STEINS
SNORES	SONANT	SPEECH	SPORTY	STAGED	STELAR
SNORTS	SONATA	SPEEDS	SPOT-ON	STAGER	STENCH
SNOTTY	SONNET	SPEEDY	SPOTTY	STAGES	STEPPE
SNOUTS	SONORA	SPEISS	SPOUSE	STAGEY	STEP UP
SNOWED	SONTAG	SPELLS	SPOUTS	STAINS	STEREO
SNUBBY	SOONER	SPERMS	SPRAIN	STAIRS	STERIC
SNUFFY	SOOTHE	SPEWED	SPRANG	STAKED	STERNA
SNUGLY	SOPPED	SPEWER	SPRATS	STAKES	STERNS
SOAKED	SORBET	SPEYER	SPRAWL	STALAG	STEROL
SOAKER	SORBIC	SPHENE	SPRAYS	STALED	STEWED
SOAPED	SORDID	SPHERE	SPREAD	STALER	STICKS
SOARED	SORELY	SPHINX	SPREES	STALKS	STICKY
SOARER	SORREL	SPICED	SPRIER	STALKY	STIFFS
SOARES	SORROW	SPICER	SPRIGS	STALLS	STIFLE
SOBBED	SORTED	SPICES	SPRING	STAMEN	STIGMA
SOBBER	SORTER	SPIDER	SPRINT	STAMPS	STILES
SO BE IT	SORTIE	SPIELS	SPRITE	STANCE	STILLS
SOCAGE	SOTHIC	SPIGOT	SPROUT	STANCH	STILLY
SOCCER	SOUGHS	SPIKED	SPRUCE	STANDS	STILTS
SOCIAL	SOUGHT	SPIKES	SPRUIT	STANZA	STINGS
SOCKED	SOUNDS	SPILLS	SPRUNG	STAPES	STINGY
SOCKET	SOURCE	SPINAL	SPRYLY	STAPLE	STINKS
SOCMAN	SOURED	SPINEL	SPUNKY	STARCH	STINTS
SODDED	SOURER	SPINES	SPURGE	STARED	STIPEL
SODDEN	SOURLY	SPINET	SPURRY	STARER	STIPES

STIRPS	STRIDE	SUBURB	SURFER	SWIVEL	TALENT
STIR UP	STRIFE	SUBWAY	SURFIE	SWIVET	TALION
STITCH	STRIKE	SUCHOU	SURGED	SWOONS	TALKED
STOATS	STRING	SUCKED	SURGER	SWOOPS	TALKER
STOCKS	STRIPE	SUCKER	SURGES	SWOOSH	TALKIE
STOCKY	STRIPS	SUCKLE	SURREY	SWORDS	TALLER
STODGE	STRIPY	SUDDEN	SURTAX	SYDNEY	TALLOW
STODGY	STRIVE	SUFFER	SURVEY	SYLVAN	TALMUD
STOICS	STROBE	SUFFIX	SUSLIK	SYMBOL	TALONS
STOKED	STRODE	SUGARS	SUSSED	SYNCOM	TAMBOV
STOKER	STROKE	SUGARY	SUTTEE	SYNDIC	TAMELY
STOKES	STROLL	SUITED	SUTTON	SYNODS	TAMERS
STOLEN	STROMA	SUITES	SUTURE	SYNTAX	TAMEST
STOLES	STRONG	SUITOR	SUU KYI	SYPHER	TAMING
STOLID	STROPS	SULCUS	SUZHOU	SYPHON	TAMPED
STOLON	STROUD	SULKED	SVELTE	SYRIAN	TAMPER
STONED	STROVE	SULKER	SWABIA	SYRINX	TAMPON
STONER	STRUCK	SULLEN	SWAGER	SYRUPY	TANDEM
STONES	STRUMA	SULTAN	SWAINS	SYSTEM	TANGLE
STOOGE	STRUNG	SULTRY	SWAMIS	SYZRAN	TANGLY
STOOLS	STRUTS	SUMACH	SWAMPS	SYZYGY	TANGOS
STOP-GO	STUBBY	SUMMAT	SWAMPY	SZEGED	TANKER
STOP IN	STUCCO	SUMMED	SWANKS		TANNED
STORAX	STUDIO	SUMMER	SWANKY	T	TANNER
STORED	STUFFY	SUMMIT	SWARDS	TABARD	TANNIC
STORES	STUMER	SUMMON	SWARMS	TABBED	TANNIN
STOREY	STUMPS	SUNBED	SWATCH	TABLED	TANNOY
STORKS	STUMPY	SUNBOW	SWATHE	TABLES	TAOISM
STORMS	STUNTS	SUNDAE	SWATHS	TABLET	TAOIST
STORMY	STUPID	SUNDAY	SWATOW	TABOOS	TAPERS
STOUPS	STUPOR	SUNDER	SWAYED	TABRIZ	TAPING
STOVER	STURDY	SUNDEW	SWAYER	TACKED	TAPIRS
STOVES	STYLAR	SUNDRY	SWEATS	TACKER	TAPPED
STOWED	STYLED	SUN GOD	SWEATY	TACKLE	TAPPER
STRAFE	STYLER	SUNKEN	SWEDEN	TACOMA	TAPPET
STRAIN	STYLES	SUNLIT	SWEDES	TACTIC	TARAWA
STRAIT	STYLET	SUNNED	SWEDOW	TADJIK	TARBES
STRAKE	STYLUS	SUNNIS	SWEENY	TAEJON	TARGET
STRAND	STYMIE	SUNRAY	SWEEPS	TAG END	TARIFF
STRAPS	STYRAX	SUNSET	SWEETS	TAGGED	TARMAC
STRATA	STYRIA	SUNTAN	SWELLS	TAHITI	TAROTS
STRAWS	SUABLE	SUPERB	SWERVE	TAIHOA	TARPAN
STRAWY	SUAKIN	SUPER-G	SWIFTS	TAILED	TARPON
STRAYS	SUBBED	SUPINE	SWILLS	TAILOR	TARRED
STREAK	SUBDUE	SUPPED	SWINES	TAINAN	TARSAL
STREAM	SUBITO	SUPPER	SWINGE	TAIPAN	TARSUS
STREEP	SUBLET	SUPPLE	SWINGS	TAIPEI	TARTAN
STREET	SUBMIT	SUPPLY	SWIPED	TAIWAN	TARTAR
STRESS	SUBORN	SURELY	SWIPES	TAKERS	TARTLY
STREWN	SUBSET	SUREST	SWIRLS	TAKEUP	TASKER
STRICK	SUBTLE	SURETY	SWIRLY	TAKING	TASMAN
STRICT	SUBTLY	SURFED	SWITCH	TALCUM	TASSEL

TASTED	TELPAL	TETUAN	THROAT	TIMBER	TODDLE
TASTER	TELSON	TEUTON	THROBS	TIMBRE	TOE CAP
TASTES	TEMPED	THAMES	THROES	TIMELY	TOEING
TATAMI	TEMPER	THANES	THRONE	TIMERS	TOFFEE
TATARY	TEMPLE	THANKS	THRONG	TIMING	TOGGED
TATTED	TEMPOS	THATCH	THROVE	TINCAL	TOGGLE
TATTER	TEMUCO	THAWED	THROWN	TINDER	TOILED
TATTIE	TENACE	THAWER	THROWS	TINEAL	TOILER
TATTLE	TENANT	THECAL	THRUSH	TINEID	TOILET
TATTOO	TENDED	THEFTS	THRUST	TINGED	TOKENS
TAUGHT	TENDER	THEGNS	THUMBS	TINGLE	TOLEDO
TAUNTS	TENDON	THEINE	THUMPS	TINGLY	TOLLED
TAURUS	TENETS	THEIRS	THWACK	TIN GOD	TOLUCA
TAUTEN	TENNER	THEISM	THWART	TIN HAT	TOLUYL
TAUTER	TENNIS	THEIST	THYMIC	TINIER	TOMATO
TAUTLY	TENONS	THEMES	THYMOL	TINKER	TOMBAC
TAUTOG	TENORS	THEMIS	THYMUS	TINKLE	TOMBOY
TAVERN	TENPIN	THENAR	THYRSE	TINKLY	TOMCAT
TAWDRY	TENREC	THENCE	TIARAS	TINNED	TOM-TOM
TAXEME	TENSED	THEORY	TIBIAE	TIN-POT	TONGAN
TAXIED	TENSER	THERMS	TIBIAS	TINSEL	TONGUE
TAXING	TENSES	THESES	TICINO	TINTED	TONICS
TAXMAN	TENSOR	THESIS	TICKED	TIP-OFF	TONING
TAXMEN	TENTER	THETIC	TICKER	TIPPED	TONKIN
TAYLOR	TENTHS	THICKO	TICKET	TIPPER	TONNES
T-BONES	TENURE	THIEVE	TICKLE	TIPPET	TONSIL
TEABAG	TENUTO	THIGHS	TIC TAC	TIPPLE	TOOLED
TEACUP	TEPEES	THIMBU	TIDBIT	TIPTOE	TOOLER
TEAMED	TEPEFY	THINGS	TIDDLY	TIP-TOP	TOOTED
TEAPOT	TERBIC	THINLY	TIDIER	TIRADE	TOOTER
TEAPOY	TERCEL	THIRDS	TIDILY	TIRANA	TOOTHY
TEARER	TERCET	THIRST	TIDING	TIRING	TOOTLE
TEASED	TEREDO	THIRTY	TIDYED	TISANE	TOP DOG
TEASEL	TERESA	THOLOS	TIE-DYE	TISSUE	TOPEES
TEASER	TERETE	THONGS	TIE-INS	TITANS	TOPEKA
TEASES	TERGAL	THORAX	TIEPIN	TITBIT	TOP HAT
TECHIE	TERGUM	THORIC	TIERCE	TITCHY	TOPHUS
TECHNO	TERMED	THORNS	TIE-UPS	TITFER	TOPICS
TEDDER	TERMLY	THORNY	TIFFIN	TITHER	TOPPED
TEDIUM	TERMOR	THORON	TIFLIS	TITHES	TOPPER
TEEING	TERRET	THOUGH	TIGERS	TITLED	TOPPLE
TEEMED	TERROR	THRALL	TIGHTS	TITLES	TORBAY
TEEPEE	TERUEL	THRASH	TIGRIS	TITTER	TORERO
TEETER	TESTED	THREAD	TILDES	TITTLE	TORIES
TEETHE	TESTER	THREAT	TILERS	TITTUP	TOROID
TEFLON	TESTES	THREES	TILING	TIVOLI	TOROSE
TEGMEN	TESTIS	THRESH	TILLED	TMESIS	TORPID
TEHRAN	TETCHY	THRICE	TILLER	TOASTS	TORPOR
TELEDU	TETHER	THRIFT	TILTED	TOBAGO	TORQUE
TELIAL	TETRAD	THRILL	TILTER	TOBRUK	TORRID
TELIUM	TETRYL	THRIPS	TIMARU	TOCSIN	TORSOS
TELLER	TETTER	THRIVE	TIMBAL	TO DATE	TOSSED

TOSSER	TREADS	TROPPO	TUNE-UP	TWIGGY	UNCLAD
TOSSES	TREATS	TROTHS	TUNGUS	TWILIT	UNCLES
TOSS UP	TREATY	TROTYL	TUNICA	TWINED	UNCLOG
TOSS-UP	TREBLE	TROUGH	TUNICS	TWINER	UNCOIL
TOTALS	TREBLY	TROUPE	TUNING	TWINGE	UNCORK
TOTEMS	TREMOR	TROUTS	TUNNEL	TWIRLS	UNCURL
TOTING	TRENCH	TROVER	TUPELO	TWIRLY	UNDEAD
TOTTED	TRENDS	TROVES	TUPPED	TWIRPS	UNDIES
TOTTER	TRENDY	TROWEL	TURBAN	TWISTS	UNDOER
TOUCAN	TRENTO	TROYES	TURBID	TWISTY	UNDONE
TOUCHE	TREPAN	TRUANT	TURBIT	TWITCH	UNDULY
TOUCHY	TRESSY	TRUCES	TURBOT	TWO-BIT	UNEASE
TOULON	TRIADS	TRUCKS	TUREEN	TWO-PLY	UNEASY
TOUPEE	TRIAGE	TRUDGE	TURFED	TWO-WAY	UNESCO
TOURED	TRIALS	TRUEST	TURGID	TYCOON	UNEVEN
TOURER	TRIBAL	TRUISM	TURGOR	TYMPAN	UNFAIR
TOUSLE	TRIBES	TRUMAN	TURION	TYPHUS	UNFOLD
TOUTED	TRICES	TRUMPS	TURKEY	TYPIFY	UNFREE
TOWAGE	TRICKS	TRUNKS	TURKIC	TYPING	UNFURL
TOWBAR	TRICKY	TRUSTS	TURNED	TYPIST	UNGUAL
TOWELS	TRICOT	TRUSTY	TURNER	TYRANT	UNGUIS
TOWERS	TRIERS	TRUTHS	TURN IN	TYRONE	UNGULA
TOWHEE	TRIFID	TRYING	TURNIP	TYUMEN	UNHAIR
TOWING	TRIFLE	TRY-OUT	TURN ON		UNHAND
TOWNEE	TRIGER	TRYSTS	TURN-ON	U	UNHOLY
TOWNIE	TRIKES	T-SHIRT	TURN UP	UBANGI	UNHOOD
TOXINS	TRILBY	TSINAN	TURN-UP	U-BOATS	UNHOOK
TOXOID	TRILLS	TSONGA	TURRET	UDDERS	UNICEF
TOYAMA	TRIMER	TSOTSI	TURTLE	UDMURT	UNIONS
TOYING	TRIMLY	TSWANA	TURVES	UGANDA	UNIPOD
TRACED	TRINAL	TUAREG	TUSCAN	UGLIER	UNIQUE
TRACER	TRIODE	TUBBED	TUSCHE	UGLIFY	UNISEX
TRACES	TRIOSE	TUBERS	TUSHES	UGRIAN	UNISON
TRACKS	TRIPLE	TUBING	TUSKER	UJJAIN	UNITED
TRACTS	TRIPOD	TUBULE	TUSSAH	ULCERS	UNITER
TRADED	TRIPOS	TUCKED	TUSSIS	ULLAGE	UNJUST
TRADER	TRIPPY	TUCKER	TUSSLE	ULSTER	UNKIND
TRADES	TRITON	TUCK-IN	TUTORS	ULTIMA	UNKNIT
TRAGAL	TRIUNE	TUCSON	TUTSAN	UMBRAL	UNLACE
TRAGIC	TRIVET	TUFFET	TUT-TUT	UMBRIA	UNLAID
TRAGUS	TRIVIA	TUFTED	TUVALU	UMLAUT	UNLASH
TRAILS	TROCAR	TUFTER	TUXEDO	UMPIRE	UNLEAD
TRAINS	TROCHE	TUGGED	TUYERE	UMTATA	UNLESS
TRAITS	TROGON	TUGGER	TWANGS	UNABLE	UNLIKE
TRALEE	TROIKA	TULIPS	TWANGY	UNAWED	UNLIVE
TRAMPS	TROJAN	TUMBLE	TWEAKS	UNBELT	UNLOAD
TRANCE	TROLLS	TUMEFY	TWEEDS	UNBEND	UNLOCK
TRANNY	TROMPE	TUMOUR	TWEEDY	UNBENT	UNMADE
TRASHY	TROOPS	TUMULI	TWEETS	UNBIND	UNMAKE
TRAUMA	TROPES	TUMULT	TWELVE	UNBOLT	UNMASK
TRAVEL	TROPHY	TUNDRA	TWENTY	UNBORN	UNMOOR
TRAWLS	TROPIC	TUNERS	TWERPS	UNCIAL	UNPACK

UNPAID	UPREAR	VACUUM	VENERY	VICARS	VOLANT
UNPICK	UPRISE	VADOSE	VENETO	VICTIM	VOLLEY
UNPLUG	UPROAR	VAGARY	VENIAL	VICTOR	VOLUME
UNREAD	UPROOT	VAGINA	VENICE	VICUNA	VOLUTE
UNREAL	UPSETS	VAINER	VENIRE	VIDEOS	VOLVOX
UNREST	UPSHOT	VAINLY	VENOSE	VIENNA	VOODOO
UNRIPE	UPSIDE	VALAIS	VENOUS	VIENNE	VORTEX
UNROLL	UPTAKE	VALETA	VENTED	VIEWED	VOSGES
UNRULY	UPTICK	VALETS	VENTER	VIEWER	VOSTOK
UNSAFE	UPTILT	VALGUS	VENUES	VIGILS	VOTARY
UNSAID	UPTIME	VALINE	VENULE	VIGOUR	VOTERS
UNSEAL	UPTOWN	VALISE	VERBAL	VIKING	VOTING
UNSEAM	UPTURN	VALIUM	VERBID	VILELY	VOTIVE
UNSEAT	UPWARD	VALLEY	VERDIN	VILEST	VOTYAK
UNSEEN	UPWIND	VALOUR	VERDUN	VILIFY	VOWELS
UNSEXY	URACIL	VALUED	VERGED	VILLAS	VOWING
UNSHIP	URALIC	VALUER	VERGER	VILLUS	VOX POP
UNSNAP	URANIC	VALUES	VERGES	VINERY	VOYAGE
UNSTEP	URANUS	VALVES	VERIFY	VINOUS	VOYEUR
UNSTOP	URANYL	VANDAL	VERILY	VINYLS	V-SIGNS
UNSUNG	URATIC	VANISH	VERISM	VIOLAS	VULGAR
UNSURE	URBANE	VANITY	VERIST	VIOLET	VULVAE
UNTIDY	URCHIN	VAPOUR	VERITY	VIOLIN	VULVAL
UNTIED	UREASE	VARDAR	VERMIN	VIPERS	VULVAS
UNTOLD	UREIDE	VARESE	VERMIS	VIRAGO	VYBORG
UNTRUE	URETER	VARIED	VERNAL	VIRGIN	
UNTUCK	URETIC	VARLET	VERONA	VIRGOS	W
UNUSED	URGENT	VASSAL	VERSED	VIRILE	WADDLE
UNVEIL	URGING	VASTLY	VERSES	VIRTUE	WADERS
UNWARY	URINAL	VAULTS	VERSOS	VISAED	WADGES
UNWELL	UROPOD	VAUNTS	VERSUS	VISAGE	WADING
UNWEPT	URSINE	VECTOR	VERTEX	VISCID	WAFERS
UNWIND	URTEXT	VEERED	VERVET	VISION	WAFFLE
UNWISE	USABLE	VEGANS	VESICA	VISITS	WAFTED
UNWRAP	USAGES	VEILED	VESPER	VISORS	WAFTER
UNYOKE	USANCE	VEILER	VESPID	VISTAS	WAGERS
UPBEAT	USED TO	VEINAL	VESSEL	VISUAL	WAGGED
UPCAST	USEFUL	VEINED	VESTAL	VITALS	WAGGLE
UPDATE	USHERS	VELARS	VESTED	VITRIC	WAGGLY
UPDIKE	USURER	VELATE	VESTRY	VIVACE	WAGING
UPHELD	UTAHAN	VELCRO	VETOED	VIVIFY	WAGONS
UPHILL	UTERUS	VELETA	VETOER	VIXENS	WAILED
UPHOLD	UTMOST	VELLUM	VETOES	VIZIER	WAILER
UPHROE	UTOPIA	VELOCE	VETTED	V-NECKS	WAISTS
UPKEEP	U-TURNS	VELOUR	VEXING	VOCABS	WAITED
UPLAND	UVULAE	VELSEN	VIABLE	VOCALS	WAITER
UPLIFT	UVULAR	VELURE	VIABLY	VOGUES	WAIVED
UPLINK	UVULAS	VELVET	VIAGRA	VOICED	WAIVER
UPLOAD		VENDED	VIANDS	VOICER	WAKING
UPPERS	V	VENDEE	VIBIST	VOICES	WALKED
UPPISH	VACANT	VENDOR	VIBORG	VOIDED	WALKER
UPPITY	VACATE	VENEER	VIBRIO	VOIDER	WALK-IN

WALK-ON	WATERY	WHALER	WIGGLE	WITHIN	XHOSAN
WALK-UP	WATTLE	WHALES	WIGGLY	WIZARD	XIAMEN
WALLAH	WATUSI	WHAMMY	WIGHTS	WOBBLE	XMASES
WALLED	WAVIER	WHARFS	WIGWAG	WOBBLY	X-RAYED
WALLET	WAVILY	WHARVE	WIGWAM	WOEFUL	XUZHOU
WALLOP	WAVING	WHEELS	WILDER	WOKING	XYLENE
WALLOW	WAXIER	WHEEZE	WILDLY	WOLFED	XYLOID
WALNUT	WAXILY	WHEEZY	WILFUL	WOLVER	XYLOSE
WALRUS	WAXING	WHELKS	WILIER	WOLVES	XYSTER
WALTON	WAYLAY	WHELPS	WILLED	WOMBAT	
WAMPUM	WAY-OUT	WHENCE	WILLER	WONDER	**Y**
WANDER	WEAKEN	WHERRY	WILLET	WONSAN	YACHTS
WANGLE	WEAKER	WHEYEY	WILLOW	WONTED	YAGARA
WANING	WEAKLY	WHIFFS	WILSON	WONTON	YAKKED
WANKED	WEALTH	WHIFFY	WILTED	WOODED	YAMMER
WANKER	WEANED	WHILED	WIMBLE	WOODEN	YANGON
WANNED	WEAPON	WHILST	WIMPLE	WOOERS	YANKED
WANNER	WEARER	WHIMSY	WINCED	WOOFER	YANKEE
WANT AD	WEASEL	WHINED	WINCER	WOOGLE	YANTAI
WANTED	WEAVER	WHINER	WINCES	WOOING	YAPPED
WANTER	WEAVES	WHINES	WINCEY	WOOLLY	YAPPER
WANTON	WEBBED	WHINGE	WINDED	WORDED	YARDIE
WAPITI	WEDDED	WHINNY	WINDER	WORKED	YARNED
WARBLE	WEDELN	WHIPPY	WINDOW	WORKER	YARROW
WAR CRY	WEDGED	WHIRLS	WIND UP	WORLDS	YATTER
WARDED	WEDGES	WHISKS	WINGED	WORMED	YAUPON
WARDEN	WEEDED	WHISKY	WINGER	WORMER	YAUTIA
WARDER	WEEDER	WHITBY	WINGES	WORSEN	YAWING
WARIER	WEEING	WHITEN	WINING	WORTHY	YAWNED
WARILY	WEEKLY	WHITER	WINKED	WOUNDS	YAWNER
WARLEY	WEEPER	WHITES	WINKER	WOWING	YEARLY
WARMED	WEEVER	WHIZZY	WINKLE	WRAITH	YEASTY
WARMER	WEEVIL	WHOLLY	WINNER	WRASSE	YELLED
WARMLY	WEE-WEE	WHOOPS	WINNOW	WREATH	YELLER
WARMTH	WEIGHT	WHOOSH	WINTER	WRECKS	YELLOW
WARM-UP	WEIHAI	WHORES	WINTRY	WRENCH	YELPED
WARNED	WEIMAR	WHORLS	WIPING	WRETCH	YELPER
WARNER	WEIRDO	WHYDAH	WIRIER	WRIEST	YEMENI
WARPED	WELDED	WICKED	WIRILY	WRIGHT	YENTAI
WARPER	WELDER	WICKER	WIRING	WRISTS	YEOMAN
WARRED	WELDON	WICKET	WIRRAL	WRISTY	YEOMEN
WARREN	WELKIN	WIDELY	WISDOM	WRITER	YES-MAN
WARSAW	WELKOM	WIDEST	WISELY	WRITHE	YES-MEN
WARTED	WELLED	WIDGET	WISEST	WRONGS	YIELDS
WASHED	WELTER	WIDISH	WISHED	WRYEST	YIPPEE
WASHER	WENDED	WIDNES	WISHER	WRYING	YODELS
WASHES	WESKER	WIDOWS	WISHES	WYVERN	YOGISM
WASHIN	WESTER	WIDTHS	WISMAR		YOGURT
WASTED	WETHER	WIELDY	WITHAL	**X**	YOKELS
WASTER	WETTED	WIFELY	WITHER	XENIAL	YOKING
WASTES	WETTER	WIGEON		XEROMA	YONDER
WATERS	WHACKS	WIGGED			

YORKER	Z	ZAPPER	ZEUGMA	ZIRCON	ZOYSIA
YORUBA	ZABRZE	ZAREBA	ZIGONG	ZITHER	ZURICH
YOUTHS	ZAFFER	ZEALOT	ZIGZAG	ZODIAC	ZWOLLE
YOWLED	ZAGREB	ZEBRAS	ZIMMER	ZOMBIE	ZYDECO
YOWLER	ZAMBIA	ZENIST	ZINCIC	ZONATE	ZYGOMA
YTTRIA	ZANDER	ZENITH	ZINCKY	ZONING	ZYGOSE
YTTRIC	ZANIER	ZEPHYR	ZINNIA	ZONKED	ZYGOTE
YUCCAS	ZANILY	ZEROED	ZIPPED	ZONULE	ZYMASE
YUNNAN	ZAPPED	ZEROES	ZIPPER	ZOOMED	ZOSTER
YUPPIE		ZESTER			ZYRIAN

7

A	ACACIAS	ACTIONS	AERATED	AIRGLOW	AL HUFUF
AALBORG	ACADEME	ACTRESS	AERATOR	AIRGUNS	ALIASES
ABALONE	ACADEMY	ACTUARY	AERIALS	AIRIEST	ALI BABA
ABANDON	ACADIAN	ACTUATE	AEROBIC	AIRINGS	ALIDADE
ABASHED	ACAROID	ACULEUS	AEROGEL	AIRLANE	ALIENEE
ABASING	ACAUDAL	ACUTELY	AEROSOL	AIRLESS	ALIENOR
ABATING	ACAUSAL	ACYCLIC	AETOLIA	AIRLIFT	ALIFORM
ABAXIAL	ACCEDED	ADAGIOS	AFFABLE	AIRLINE	ALIGARH
ABDOMEN	ACCEDER	ADAMANT	AFFABLY	AIRLOCK	ALIGNED
ABELARD	ACCENTS	ADAMAWA	AFFAIRE	AIRMAIL	ALIMENT
ABELIAN	ACCLAIM	ADAPTED	AFFAIRS	AIRMILE	ALIMONY
ABERFAN	ACCORDS	ADAPTER	AFFIANT	AIRPLAY	ALIQUOT
ABETTED	ACCOUNT	ADAPTOR	AFFIXED	AIRPORT	ALIUNDE
ABETTOR	ACCRETE	ADAXIAL	AFFIXES	AIR RAID	ALKALIC
ABEYANT	ACCRUAL	ADDENDA	AFFLICT	AIRSHIP	ALKALIS
ABFARAD	ACCRUED	ADDICTS	AFFRAYS	AIRSICK	ALKANET
ABHENRY	ACCUSED	ADDRESS	AFFRONT	AIRWAYS	ALKMAAR
ABIDING	ACCUSER	ADDUCED	AFGHANS	AITCHES	ALLAYED
ABIDJAN	ACERATE	ADENINE	AFRICAN	AJACCIO	ALLEGED
ABILITY	ACERBIC	ADENOID	AGAINST	ALABAMA	ALLEGRO
ABIOSIS	ACEROSE	ADENOMA	AGAMETE	ALAGOAS	ALLELIC
ABJURED	ACETATE	ADEPTLY	AGEISTS	A LA	ALLERGY
ABJURER	ACETIFY	ADHERED	AGELESS	MODE	ALLHEAL
ABLATOR	ACETONE	ADIPOSE	AGENDAS	ALANINE	ALLONYM
ABLEISM	ACETOUS	ADIVASI	AGENDUM	ALARMED	ALL OVER
ABOLISH	ACHAEAN	ADJOINT	AGGRADE	ALASKAN	ALLOWAY
ABORTED	ACHIEVE	ADJOURN	AGGRESS	ALBANIA	ALLOWED
ABRADED	ACICULA	ADJUDGE	AGILELY	ALBERTA	ALLOYED
ABRADER	ACIDIFY	ADJUNCT	AGILITY	ALBINIC	ALLSEED
ABREACT	ACIDITY	ADJURED	AGITATE	ALBINOS	ALL-STAR
ABREAST	ACNODAL	ADJURER	AGITATO	ALBITIC	ALL-TIME
ABRIDGE	ACOLYTE	ADMIRAL	AGNOMEN	ALBUMEN	ALLUDED
ABRUZZI	ACONITE	ADMIRED	AGONIES	ALBUMIN	ALLURED
ABSCESS	ACOUCHI	ADMIRER	AGONIST	ALCAZAR	ALLURER
ABSCISE	ACQUIRE	ADOPTED	AGONIZE	ALCHEMY	ALLUVIA
ABSCOND	ACREAGE	ADORING	AGRAFFE	ALCOHOL	ALLYING
ABSENCE	ACRILAN	ADORNED	AGRAPHA	ALCOPOP	ALMA-ATA
ABSINTH	ACROBAT	ADRENAL	AGROUND	ALCOVES	ALMANAC
ABSOLVE	ACROGEN	ADULATE	AILERON	AL DENTE	ALMERIA
ABSTAIN	ACRONYM	ADVANCE	AILMENT	ALEMBIC	ALMONDS
ABUSING	ACROTER	ADVENTS	AIMLESS	ALERTED	ALMONER
ABUSIVE	ACRYLIC	ADVERBS	AIRBASE	ALERTLY	ALMS MAN
ABUTTAL	ACRYLYL	ADVERSE	AIRBEDS	A LEVELS	ALOETIC
ABUTTED	ACTABLE	ADVICES	AIR-COOL	ALFALFA	ALOOFLY
ABUTTER	ACTINAL	ADVISED	AIRCREW	ALGARVE	ALPACAS
ABYSMAL	ACTINIA	ADVISER	AIRDRIE	ALGEBRA	ALPHORN
ABYSSAL	ACTINIC	AEGISES	AIRDROP	ALGERIA	ALREADY
ABYSSES	ACTINON	AEONIAN	AIRFLOW	ALGIERS	ALRIGHT

ALSO RAN	AMUSING	ANIMALS	APAGOGE	ARAMAIC	ARRESTS
ALSO-RAN	AMYLASE	ANIMATE	APATITE	ARANEID	ARRIVAL
ALTDORF	AMYLENE	ANIMATO	APELIKE	ARAPAHO	ARRIVED
ALTERED	AMYLOID	ANIMISM	APETALY	ARAROBA	ARRIVER
ALTHAEA	AMYLOSE	ANIMIST	APHAGIA	ARBITER	ARROWED
ALTHING	ANAEMIA	ANIONIC	APHASIA	ARBOURS	ARSENAL
ALTHORN	ANAEMIC	ANISEED	APHESIS	ARBUTUS	ARSENIC
ALUMNAE	ANAGOGE	ANISOLE	APHONIA	ARCADES	ART DECO
ALUMNUS	ANAGRAM	ANKLETS	APHONIC	ARCADIA	ARTICLE
ALUNDUM	ANAHEIM	ANNATES	APHOTIC	ARCANUM	ARTIEST
ALUNITE	ANALOGY	ANNATTO	APHYLLY	ARCHAIC	ARTISAN
ALYSSUM	ANALYSE	ANNELID	APIEZON	ARCHERS	ARTISTE
AMADODA	ANALYST	ANNEXED	APLASIA	ARCHERY	ARTISTS
AMALGAM	ANAMBRA	ANNEXES	APLENTY	ARCHINE	ARTLESS
AMANITA	ANAPEST	ANNOYED	APLITIC	ARCHING	ARTWORK
AMASSED	ANARCHY	ANNUALS	APOCARP	ARCHIVE	ARUGULA
AMASSER	ANATASE	ANNUITY	APOCOPE	ARCHWAY	ARUNDEL
AMATEUR	ANATOMY	ANNULAR	APOGAMY	ARCUATE	ASCARID
AMATORY	ANCHORS	ANNULET	APOGEES	ARDECHE	ASCENTS
AMAZING	ANCHOVY	ANNULUS	APOLOGY	ARDENCY	ASCETIC
AMAZONS	ANCHUSA	ANODIZE	APOLUNE	ARDUOUS	ASCITES
AMBIENT	ANCIENT	ANODYNE	APOMICT	AREAWAY	ASCITIC
AMBLING	ANCONAL	ANOMALY	APOSTIL	ARENITE	ASCRIBE
AMBOYNA	ANDANTE	ANORAKS	APOSTLE	AREOLAR	ASEPSIS
AMENDED	ANDIRON	ANOSMIA	APOTHEM	ARGOLIS	ASEPTIC
AMENDER	ANDORRA	ANOTHER	APPAREL	ARGONNE	ASEXUAL
AMENITY	ANDROID	ANSWERS	APPEALS	ARGOTIC	ASHAMED
AMENTIA	ANEMONE	ANTACID	APPEASE	ARGUING	ASHANTI
AMERICA	ANERGIC	ANTEFIX	APPLAUD	ARIDITY	ASHDOWN
AMHARIC	ANEROID	ANTEING	APPLIED	ARIETTA	ASHFORD
AMIABLE	ANEURIN	ANTENNA	APPLIER	ARISING	ASHIEST
AMIABLY	ANGARSK	ANTHEMS	APPOINT	ARIZONA	ASHTRAY
AMMETER	ANGELIC	ANTHERS	APPRISE	ARMADAS	ASIATIC
AMMONAL	ANGELOU	ANTHILL	APPROVE	ARMBAND	ASININE
AMMONIA	ANGELUS	ANT HILL	APPULSE	ARMENIA	ASKANCE
AMMONIC	ANGERED	ANTHRAX	APRAXIA	ARMFULS	ASOCIAL
AMNESIA	ANGEVIN	ANTIBES	APRAXIC	ARMHOLE	ASPECTS
AMNESTY	ANGINAL	ANTIGEN	APRICOT	ARMIGER	ASPERSE
AMNIOTE	ANGIOMA	ANTIGUA	A PRIORI	ARMLESS	ASPHALT
AMOEBAE	ANGLIAN	ANTIOCH	APROPOS	ARMLOCK	ASPIRED
AMOEBAS	ANGLIFY	ANTIQUE	APSIDAL	ARMOIRE	ASPIRER
AMOEBIC	ANGLING	ANTLERS	APTERAL	ARMOURY	ASPIRIN
AMORIST	ANGOLAN	ANTLION	APTNESS	ARMPITS	ASSAULT
AMOROSO	ANGORAS	ANTONYM	AQUARIA	ARMREST	ASSAYED
AMOROUS	ANGRIER	ANTWERP	AQUATIC	AROUSAL	ASSAYER
AMOUNTS	ANGRILY	ANUROUS	AQUAVIT	AROUSED	ASSEGAI
AMPHORA	ANGUINE	ANXIETY	AQUEOUS	AROUSER	ASSHOLE
AMPLIFY	ANGUISH	ANXIOUS	AQUIFER	ARRAIGN	ASSIZES
AMPOULE	ANGULAR	ANYBODY	ARABIAN	ARRANGE	ASSUAGE
AMPULLA	ANHINGA	ANYMORE	ARABIST	ARRAYAL	ASSUMED
AMPUTEE	ANILINE	ANYWAYS	ARACAJU	ARRAYED	ASSUMER
AMULETS	ANILITY	ANYWISE	ARAL SEA	ARREARS	ASSURED

ASSURER	AUSSIES	BABBLER	BALKING	BARBELL	BATHING
ASSYRIA	AUSTERE	BABOONS	BALLADE	BARBERS	BATH MAT
ASTATIC	AUSTRAL	BABYING	BALLADS	BARBOUR	BATHTUB
ASTOUND	AUSTRIA	BABYISH	BALLARD	BARBUDA	BATHYAL
ASTRIDE	AUTARKY	BABY-SAT	BALLAST	BARBULE	BATISTE
ASTROID	AUTHORS	BABY-SIT	BALLETS	BARCHAN	BATSMAN
ASTYLAR	AUTOCUE	BACCATE	BALLOON	BAR CODE	BATSMEN
ASUNDER	AUTOMAT	BACILLI	BALLOTS	BARENTS	BATTENS
ASYLUMS	AUTOPSY	BACKBAR	BALLS-UP	BARGAIN	BATTERS
ATACTIC	AUTUMNS	BACKERS	BALMIER	BARGEES	BATTERY
ATAVISM	AUXERRE	BACKING	BALMILY	BARGING	BATTIER
ATAVIST	AUXESIS	BACKLOG	BALNEAL	BARILLA	BATTING
ATELIER	AVAILED	BACK OFF	BALONEY	BARKERS	BATTLED
AT HEART	AVARICE	BACKSAW	BALSAMS	BARKING	BATTLES
ATHEISM	AVATARS	BACKUPS	BALTICS	BARMAID	BATWING
ATHEIST	AVENGED	BACOLOD	BALUCHI	BARMIER	BAUBLES
ATHLETE	AVENGER	BACTRIA	BAMBARA	BARNAUL	BAUHAUS
ATHWART	AVENUES	BACULUM	BAMBERG	BARNEYS	BAULKED
ATLANTA	AVERAGE	BADAJOZ	BAMBINO	BARONET	BAUTZEN
ATLASES	AVERRED	BAD DEBT	BAMBOOS	BAROQUE	BAUXITE
ATOMISM	AVERTED	BAD FORM	BANANAS	BAROTSE	BAVARIA
ATOMIST	AVESTAN	BADGERS	BANBURY	BARQUES	BAWDIER
ATOMIZE	AVEYRON	BADNESS	BANDAGE	BARRACK	BAWDILY
ATONING	AVIATOR	BAFFLED	BANDBOX	BARRAGE	BAWLING
ATROPHY	AVIDITY	BAFFLER	BANDEAU	BARRELS	BAYAMON
ATTACHE	AVIGNON	BAFFLES	BANDIED	BARRIER	BAYONET
ATTACKS	AVIONIC	BAGANDA	BANDIER	BARRING	BAYONNE
ATTAINT	AVOCADO	BAGASSE	BANDING	BARROWS	BAYWOOD
ATTEMPT	AVOIDED	BAGGAGE	BANDITS	BARYTES	BAZAARS
ATTIRED	AVOIDER	BAGGIER	BANDUNG	BASCULE	BAZOOKA
ATTRACT	AVOWALS	BAGGILY	BANEFUL	BASENJI	BEACHED
ATTUNED	AVOWING	BAGGING	BANGERS	BASHFUL	BEACHES
AUBERGE	AWAITED	BAGHDAD	BANGING	BASHING	BEACONS
AUCTION	AWAKING	BAG LADY	BANGKOK	BASHKIR	BEADIER
AUDIBLE	AWARDED	BAGPIPE	BANGLES	BASHTAG	BEADILY
AUDIBLY	AWARDEE	BAGWORM	BANKERS	BASILAN	BEADING
AUDITED	AWARDER	BAHAISM	BANKING	BASILAR	BEADLES
AUDITOR	AWESOME	BAHAIST	BANKSIA	BASILIC	BEAGLES
AUGITIC	AWFULLY	BAHAMAS	BANNERS	BASKETS	BEAKERS
AUGMENT	AWKWARD	BAHRAIN	BANNING	BASKING	BEAMING
AUGURAL	AWLWORT	BAILEYS	BANNOCK	BASOTHO	BEARDED
AUGURED	AWNINGS	BAILIFF	BANQUET	BAS-RHIN	BEARERS
AUGUSTA	AXOLOTL	BAILING	BANSHEE	BASSEIN	BEAR HUG
AU PAIRS	AZIMUTH	BAIL OUT	BANTAMS	BASSETS	BEARING
AURALLY	AZURITE	BAILOUT	BANTOID	BASSIST	BEARISH
AUREATE	AZYGOUS	BAINITE	BANYANS	BASSOON	BEASTLY
AUREOLE		BAITING	BAODING	BASTARD	BEATERS
AURICLE	**B**	BALANCE	BAPTISM	BASTING	BEATIFY
AURORAE		BALATON	BAPTIST	BASTION	BEATING
AURORAL	BAALBEK	BALCONY	BAPTIZE	BATCHES	BEATNIK
AURORAS	BABASSU	BALDING	BARBARY	BATFISH	BEAVERS
AUSPICE	BABBITT	BALEFUL	BARBATE	BATHERS	BECAUSE
	BABBLED				

BECKETT	BELOVED	BETIMES	BILLION	BLACKEN	BLOTCHY
BEDBUGS	BELTING	BETOKEN	BILLOWS	BLACKER	BLOTTED
BEDDING	BELT MAN	BETROTH	BILLOWY	BLACKLY	BLOTTER
BEDEVIL	BELTWAY	BETTERS	BILTONG	BLADDER	BLOUSES
BEDEWED	BELYING	BETTING	BIMODAL	BLAMING	BLOW-DRY
BEDFORD	BEMUSED	BETWEEN	BIMORPH	BLANDER	BLOWERS
BEDHEAD	BENARES	BETWIXT	BINDERS	BLANDLY	BLOWFLY
BEDLAMS	BENCHER	BEVELED	BINDERY	BLANKET	BLOWIER
BEDOUIN	BENCHES	BEWITCH	BINDING	BLANKLY	BLOWING
BEDPANS	BENDIGO	BEXHILL	BINNING	BLARING	BLOWOUT
BEDPOST	BENDING	BEYOGLU	BIOCIDE	BLARNEY	BLOW OUT
BEDRAIL	BENEATH	BEZIQUE	BIODATA	BLASTED	BLOW-UPS
BEDROCK	BENEFIT	BHANGRA	BIOFUEL	BLATANT	BLUBBER
BEDROOM	BENELUX	BIASING	BIOHERM	BLATHER	BLUE GUM
BEDSIDE	BENGALI	BIASSED	BIOLOGY	BLAUBOK	BLUEING
BEDSORE	BENNETT	BIAXIAL	BIOMASS	BLAYDON	BLUE JAY
BEDTIME	BENTHOS	BIBCOCK	BIONICS	BLAZERS	BLUE LAW
BEECHES	BENZENE	BIBELOT	BIOPICS	BLAZING	BLUE-SKY
BEEFIER	BENZINE	BICYCLE	BIOPTIC	BLAZONS	BLUETIT
BEEFING	BENZOIC	BIDDING	BIOTECH	BLEAKER	BLUFFED
BEEF TEA	BENZOIN	BIEN HOA	BIOTITE	BLEAKLY	BLUFFER
BEEHIVE	BENZOYL	BIFFING	BIOTOPE	BLEATED	BLUFFLY
BEELINE	BEOGRAD	BIFILAR	BIOTYPE	BLEATER	BLUNDER
BEESWAX	BEQUEST	BIFOCAL	BIPLANE	BLEEDER	BLUNGER
BEETFLY	BERATED	BIG CATS	BIPOLAR	BLEEPED	BLUNTED
BEETLED	BERBERA	BIG DEAL	BIRCHED	BLEEPER	BLUNTLY
BEETLES	BEREAVE	BIG ENDS	BIRCHES	BLEMISH	BLURRED
BEGGARS	BERGAMO	BIGENER	BIRD DOG	BLENDED	BLURTED
BEGGARY	BERMUDA	BIGFOOT	BIRDIES	BLENDER	BLUSHED
BEGGING	BERNESE	BIG GAME	BIRETTA	BLESBOK	BLUSHER
BEGONIA	BERRIES	BIGGEST	BISCUIT	BLESSED	BLUSHES
BEGUILE	BERSEEM	BIGGIES	BISHKEK	BLETHER	BLUSTER
BEHAVED	BERSERK	BIGHEAD	BISHOPS	BLEWITS	B-MOVIES
BEHINDS	BERTHED	BIGHORN	BISMUTH	BLIGHTS	BOARDED
BEIJING	BESEECH	BIG NAME	BISTORT	BLINDED	BOARDER
BEJEWEL	BESIDES	BIGNESS	BISTROS	BLINDLY	BOARISH
BELARUS	BESIEGE	BIGOTED	BITCHED	BLINKED	BOASTED
BELATED	BESMEAR	BIGOTRY	BITCHES	BLINKER	BOASTER
BELAYED	BESPEAK	BIG SHOT	BITCHIN'	BLISTER	BOATERS
BELCHED	BESPOKE	BIG TIME	BITCOIN	BLITZED	BOATING
BELCHES	BESTIAL	BIG TOPS	BIT PART	BLITZES	BOATMAN
BELFAST	BESTING	BIGWIGS	BITTERN	BLOATED	BOATMEN
BELFORT	BEST MAN	BIJAPUR	BITTERS	BLOATER	BOBBERY
BELGAUM	BEST-OFF	BIKANER	BITTIER	BLOCKED	BOBBIES
BELGIAN	BESTREW	BIKINIS	BITUMEN	BLOGGER	BOBBING
BELGIUM	BESTRID	BILBOES	BIVALVE	BLONDER	BOBBINS
BELIEFS	BETAINE	BILIARY	BIVOUAC	BLONDES	BOBBLES
BELIEVE	BETAKEN	BILIOUS	BIZARRE	BLOODED	BOBSLED
BELLBOY	BETHANY	BILKING	BIZERTE	BLOOMED	BOBSTAY
BELLEEK	BETHELS	BILLETS	BLABBED	BLOOMER	BOBTAIL
BELLIES	BETHINK	BILLIES	BLABBER	BLOOPER	BODICES
BELLOWS	BETIDED	BILLING	BLACKED	BLOSSOM	BODKINS

BOFFINS	BOOTING	BOWSHOT	BREEDER	BROOKED	BUGLERS
BOGARDE	BOOTLEG	BOW TIES	BRENDEL	BROTHEL	BUGLOSS
BOGGIER	BOOZERS	BOXCARS	BRENNER	BROTHER	BUILDER
BOGGING	BOOZE UP	BOXROOM	BRENTON	BROWNED	BUILD UP
BOGGLED	BOOZE-UP	BOX SEAT	BRESCIA	BROWNER	BUILT-IN
BOHEMIA	BOOZIER	BOXWOOD	BREVIER	BROWNIE	BUILT-UP
BOHRIUM	BOOZILY	BOYCOTT	BREVITY	BROWSED	BUKHARA
BOILERS	BOOZING	BOYHOOD	BREWAGE	BROWSER	BULBOUS
BOILING	BOPPING	BRABANT	BREWERY	BRUCINE	BULGIER
BOK CHOY	BORACIC	BRABHAM	BREWING	BRUISED	BULGING
BOLDEST	BORAZON	BRACING	BRIBERY	BRUISER	BULIMIA
BOLEROS	BORDERS	BRACKEN	BRICOLE	BRUISES	BULKIER
BOLETUS	BORDURE	BRACKET	BRIDGET	BRUITED	BULKILY
BOLIVAR	BOREDOM	BRADAWL	BRIDOON	BRUMOUS	BULKING
BOLIVIA	BORNEEL	BRAEMAR	BRIGADE	BRUSHED	BULLACE
BOLLARD	BORNITE	BRAGGED	BRIGAND	BRUSHER	BULLATE
BOLOGNA	BOROUGH	BRAGGER	BRIMFUL	BRUSHES	BULLDOG
BOLONEY	BORSCHT	BRAHMAN	BRIMMER	BRUSH-UP	BULLETS
BOLSHIE	BORSTAL	BRAIDED	BRINDLE	BRUSQUE	BULLIED
BOLSTER	BORZOIS	BRAIDER	BRING UP	BRUTISH	BULLIES
BOLTING	BOSCAGE	BRAILLE	BRIOCHE	BRYANSK	BULLION
BOLZANO	BOSNIAN	BRAINED	BRISKER	BUBBLED	BULLISH
BOMBARD	BOSSIER	BRAISED	BRISKET	BUBBLER	BULLOCK
BOMBAST	BOSSILY	BRAKING	BRISKLY	BUBBLES	BULRUSH
BOMBERS	BOSSING	BRAKPAN	BRISTLE	BUBONIC	BULWARK
BOMBING	BOTCHED	BRAMBLE	BRISTLY	BUCKETS	BUMBLED
BONAIRE	BOTCHER	BRAMLEY	BRISTOL	BUCKEYE	BUMBLER
BONANZA	BOTCH-UP	BRANAGH	BRITISH	BUCKING	BUMBOAT
BONBONS	BOTTLED	BRANDED	BRITONS	BUCKLED	BUMMING
BONDAGE	BOTTLES	BRANSON	BRITPOP	BUCKLER	BUMPERS
BONDING	BOTTOMS	BRAN TUB	BRITTLE	BUCKLES	BUMPIER
BONE-DRY	BOTTROP	BRASHER	BROADEN	BUCKRAM	BUMPILY
BONESET	BOTULIN	BRASHLY	BROADER	BUCKSAW	BUMPING
BONFIRE	BOUCHEE	BRASSES	BROADLY	BUCOLIC	BUMPKIN
BONGOES	BOUDOIR	BRASSIE	BROCADE	BUDDIES	BUNCHED
BONIEST	BOULDER	BRAVADO	BROCKET	BUDDING	BUNCHES
BONJOUR	BOUNCED	BRAVAIS	BROGLIE	BUDGETS	BUNDLED
BONKERS	BOUNCER	BRAVELY	BROGUES	BUDGING	BUNDLER
BONNETS	BOUNCES	BRAVERY	BROILED	BUFFALO	BUNDLES
BONNIER	BOUNDED	BRAVEST	BROILER	BUFFERS	BUNGING
BONUSES	BOUNDEN	BRAVING	BROKERS	BUFFETS	BUNGLED
BOOBIES	BOUNDER	BRAVURA	BROMATE	BUFFING	BUNGLER
BOOBING	BOUQUET	BRAWLED	BROMIDE	BUFFOON	BUNGLES
BOOKEND	BOURBON	BRAWLER	BROMINE	BUGABOO	BUNIONS
BOOKING	BOURDON	BRAYING	BROMISM	BUGANDA	BUNKERS
BOOKISH	BOURGES	BRAZIER	BROMLEY	BUGBANE	BUNKING
BOOKLET	BOUYANT	BREADTH	BRONCHI	BUGBEAR	BUNK OFF
BOOMING	BOWHEAD	BREAKER	BRONCOS	BUG-EYED	BUNK-UPS
BOORISH	BOWKNOT	BREAK-IN	BRONZED	BUGGERS	BUNNIES
BOOSTED	BOWLERS	BREATHE	BRONZES	BUGGERY	BUNTING
BOOSTER	BOWLINE	BREATHY	BROODED	BUGGIES	BUOYAGE
BOOTEES	BOWLING	BRECCIA	BROODER	BUGGING	BUOYANT

BUOYING	BUSTING	CADENZA	CALYXES	CAPABLE	CARLINE
BURBLED	BUSTLED	CADGERS	CAMBERS	CAPABLY	CARLING
BURBLER	BUSTLER	CADGING	CAMBIAL	CAP-A-	CARMINE
BURDENS	BUSTLES	CADMIUM	CAMBIST	PIE	CARNAGE
BURDOCK	BUST-UPS	CAESIUM	CAMBIUM	CAPE COD	CARNIFY
BUREAUX	BUSYING	CAESURA	CAMBRAI	CAPELIN	CAROLED
BURETTE	BUTANOL	CAFTANS	CAMBRIC	CAPELLA	CAROLUS
BURGEON	BUTCHER	CAGIEST	CAMELOT	CAPERED	CAROTID
BURGERS	BUTLERS	CAGOULE	CAMERAL	CAPITAL	CAROUSE
BURGESS	BUTLERY	CAHOOTS	CAMERAS	CAPITOL	CARPALE
BURGHAL	BUTTERY	CAIQUES	CAMP BED	CAPORAL	CAR PARK
BURGHER	BUTTIES	CAISSON	CAMPERS	CAPPING	CARPETS
BURGLAR	BUTTING	CAJOLED	CAMPHOR	CAPRICE	CARPING
BURGLED	BUTTOCK	CAJUPUT	CAMPING	CAPSIZE	CAR POOL
BURIALS	BUTTONS	CALABAR	CAMPION	CAPSTAN	CARPORT
BURLIER	BUTYRIC	CALAMUS	CAM RANH	CAPSULE	CARRARA
BURMESE	BUTYRIN	CALCIFY	CAMWOOD	CAPTAIN	CARRICK
BURNERS	BUY INTO	CALCINE	CANAPES	CAPTION	CARRIED
BURNING	BUYOUTS	CALCITE	CANARDS	CAPTIVE	CARRIER
BURNISH	BUZZARD	CALCIUM	CANASTA	CAPTORS	CARRIES
BURNLEY	BUZZERS	CALCULI	CANCANS	CAPTURE	CARRION
BURNOUS	BUZZING	CALDERA	CANCERS	CARABAO	CARROTS
BURNOUT	BYE-BYES	CALDRON	CANDELA	CARABID	CARROTY
BURPING	BYELOVO	CALENDS	CANDIED	CARACAL	CARRY ON
BURRING	BYGONES	CALGARY	CANDIES	CARACAS	CARRY-ON
BURRITO	BY-LINES	CALIBRE	CANDLER	CARACUL	CARSICK
BURROWS	BYRONIC	CALICHE	CANDLES	CARAFES	CARTAGE
BURSARS	BYWORDS	CALICOS	CANDOUR	CARAMBA	CARTELS
BURSARY		CALIPEE	CANELLA	CARAMEL	CARTERS
BURSTER	C	CALIPHS	CANINES	CARAVAN	CARTING
BURTHEN	CABARET	CALKING	CANKERS	CARAVEL	CARTONS
BURTONS	CABBAGE	CALLAIS	CANNERY	CARAWAY	CARTOON
BURUNDI	CABBALA	CALLANT	CANNIER	CARBENE	CARVERS
BURWEED	CABBIES	CALL BOX	CANNILY	CARBIDE	CARVING
BURYING	CABEZON	CALLBOY	CANNING	CARBINE	CASCADE
BUSBIES	CABIMAS	CALLERS	CANNOCK	CARBONS	CASCARA
BUS BOYS	CABINDA	CALLING	CANNONS	CARBOYS	CASEASE
BUSHELS	CABINET	CALL-INS	CANNULA	CARCASS	CASEATE
BUSHIER	CABLING	CALLOUS	CANONRY	CARDIAC	CASEOSE
BUSHING	CABOOSE	CALMEST	CANOPUS	CARDIFF	CASEOUS
BUSHIRE	CAB RANK	CALMING	CANTALA	CARDING	CASERTA
BUSHMAN	CACHETS	CALOMEL	CANTATA	CARDOON	CASHEWS
BUSHPIG	CACKLED	CALORIC	CANTEEN	CAREERS	CASHIER
BUSHTIT	CACKLER	CALORIE	CANTERS	CAREFUL	CASHING
BUSIEST	CACKLES	CALOTTE	CANTHUS	CARFARE	CASINGS
BUSKERS	CADAVER	CALTROP	CANTING	CARGOES	CASINOS
BUSKING	CADDIED	CALUMNY	CANTONS	CARHOPS	CASKETS
BUSSING	CADDIES	CALVARY	CANTORS	CARIBOU	CASPIAN
BUS STOP	CADDISH	CALVING	CANVASS	CARIOCA	CASQUED
BUSTARD	CADELLE	CALYCES	CANYONS	CARIOLE	CASQUES
BUSTERS	CADENCE	CALYCLE	CANZONA	CARIOUS	CASSATA
BUSTIER	CADENCY	CALYPSO	CANZONE	CARJACK	CASSAVA

CASSINO	CAUTION	CESTOID	CHARGES	CHEQUER	CHOCKED
CASSOCK	CAVALLA	CETINJE	CHARIER	CHEQUES	CHOCTAW
CASTERS	CAVALRY	CETOOGY	CHARILY	CHERISH	CHOICER
CASTILE	CAVEATS	CHABLIS	CHARIOT	CHEROOT	CHOICES
CASTING	CAVE-INS	CHABROL	CHARITY	CHERUBS	CHOKERS
CASTLED	CAVEMAN	CHA-CHAS	CHARKHA	CHERVIL	CHOKING
CASTLES	CAVEMEN	CHAFFED	CHARLES	CHESTED	CHOLERA
CAST OFF	CAVERNS	CHAFFER	CHARLIE	CHESTER	CHOLINE
CAST-OFF	CAVES IN	CHAFING	CHARMED	CHEVIOT	CHOLULA
CASTORS	CAVETTO	CHAGRIN	CHARMER	CHEVRON	CHOMPED
CASUIST	CAVILED	CHAINED	CHARNEL	CHEWIER	CHOOSER
CATALAN	CAYENNE	CHAIRED	CHARPOY	CHEWING	CHOPPED
CATALPA	CEASING	CHAISES	CHARQUI	CHIANTI	CHOPPER
CATANIA	CEDILLA	CHALAZA	CHARRED	CHIAPAS	CHORALE
CATARRH	CEILING	CHALCID	CHARTED	CHIASMA	CHORDAL
CATBIRD	CELADON	CHALCIS	CHARTER	CHIBOUK	CHOREAL
CATBOAT	CELEBES	CHALDEA	CHASERS	CHICAGO	CHORION
CATCALL	CELESTA	CHALETS	CHASING	CHICANE	CHORLEY
CATCHER	CELLARS	CHALICE	CHASMAL	CHICANO	CHOROID
CATCHES	CELLIST	CHALKED	CHASSIS	CHICKEN	CHORTLE
CATCH IT	CELLNET	CHALLAH	CHASTEN	CHICORY	CHORZOW
CATCH UP	CELLULE	CHALLIS	CHASTER	CHIDDEN	CHOWDER
CATECHU	CELSIUS	CHALONE	CHATEAU	CHIDING	CHROMIC
CATERED	CEMBALO	CHAMBER	CHATHAM	CHIEFLY	CHROMYL
CATERER	CENACLE	CHAMFER	CHATTED	CHIFFON	CHRONIC
CATFISH	CENSORS	CHAMOIS	CHATTEL	CHIGGER	CHRONON
CATHEAD	CENSUAL	CHAMPAC	CHATTER	CHIGNON	CHUCKED
CATHODE	CENSURE	CHAMPED	CHAYOTE	CHILEAN	CHUCK IN
CATKINS	CENTAUR	CHANCED	CHEAPEN	CHILIAD	CHUCKLE
CATLING	CENTAVO	CHANCEL	CHEAPER	CHILIES	CHUFFED
CATMINT	CENTERS	CHANCES	CHEAPIE	CHILLED	CHUGGED
CATNAPS	CENTIME	CHANCRE	CHEAPLY	CHILLUM	CHUKCHI
CAT'S-	CENTIMO	CHANGDE	CHEATED	CHILUNG	CHUKKER
EAR	CENTNER	CHANGED	CHEATER	CHIMERA	CHUMMED
CAT'S	CENTRAL	CHANGER	CHECHEN	CHIMERE	CHURNED
EYE	CENTRED	CHANGES	CHECKED	CHIMING	CHUTNEY
CAT'S	CENTRES	CHANNEL	CHECK-IN	CHIMNEY	CHUVASH
PAW	CENTRIC	CHANSON	CHECK ON	CHINESE	CHYMOUS
CATSUIT	CENTRUM	CHANTED	CHECKUP	CHINKED	CICADAS
CATTALO	CENTURY	CHANTER	CHEDDAR	CHINOOK	CICHLID
CATTERY	CEPHEUS	CHANTRY	CHEEKED	CHINTZY	CILIARY
CATTIER	CERAMIC	CHAOTIC	CHEEPED	CHINWAG	CILIATE
CATTILY	CERATED	CHAPATI	CHEEPER	CHIPPED	CIMBRIC
CATTISH	CEREALS	CHAPEAU	CHEERED	CHIPPER	CINDERS
CATWALK	CEREBRA	CHAPELS	CHEERIO	CHIRPED	CINDERY
CAUDATE	CERTAIN	CHAPLET	CHEESES	CHIRPER	CINEMAS
CAULINE	CERTIFY	CHAPPAL	CHEETAH	CHIRRUP	CINERIN
CAULKED	CERUMEN	CHAPPED	CHELATE	CHISELS	CIPHERS
CAULKER	CERVINE	CHAPTER	CHEMISE	CHIVIED	CIPOLIN
CAUSING	CESSION	CHARADE	CHEMIST	CHLORAL	CIRCLED
CAUSTIC	CESSPIT	CHARGED	CHENGTU	CHLORIC	CIRCLER
CAUTERY	CESTODE	CHARGER	CHENNAI	CHOC-ICE	CIRCLES

CIRCLET	CLAUSAL	CLOSING	COCOYAM	COLONEL	CONCEIT
CIRCLIP	CLAUSES	CLOSURE	CODDLED	COLONIC	CONCEPT
CIRCUIT	CLAVATE	CLOTHED	CODEINE	COLOSSI	CONCERN
CIRQUES	CLAVIER	CLOTHES	CODFISH	COLOURS	CONCERT
CIRRATE	CLAVIUS	CLOTTED	CODGERS	COLTISH	CONCHAL
CIRSOID	CLAWING	CLOTURE	CODICES	COLUMNS	CONCHES
CISSIES	CLAYPAN	CLOUDED	CODICIL	COMBATS	CONCISE
CISSOID	CLEANED	CLOUTED	CODLING	COMBERS	CONCOCT
CISTERN	CLEANER	CLOWNED	COELIAC	COMBINE	CONCORD
CISTRON	CLEANLY	CLOYING	COEQUAL	COMBING	CONCUSS
CITABLE	CLEANSE	CLUBBED	COERCED	COMB-OUT	CONDEMN
CITADEL	CLEANUP	CLUBMAN	COETZEE	COMBUST	CONDIGN
CITHARA	CLEAN UP	CLUCKED	COEVALS	COMECON	CONDOLE
CITIZEN	CLEARED	CLUMPED	COEXIST	COMEDIC	CONDOMS
CITRATE	CLEARER	CLUNIAC	COFFERS	COMFIER	CONDONE
CITRINE	CLEARLY	CLUPEID	COFFINS	COMFITS	CONDORS
CITRONS	CLEAR UP	CLUSTER	COGENCY	COMFORT	CONDUCE
CIVILLY	CLEAVED	CLUTTER	COGGING	COMFREY	CONDUCT
CIVVIES	CLEAVER	CLYPEAL	COGNACS	COMICAL	CONDUIT
CLACKED	CLEMENT	CLYPEUS	COGNATE	COMINGS	CONDYLE
CLADODE	CLERICS	COACHED	COGNIZE	COMMAND	CONFECT
CLAIMED	CLERKED	COACHES	COHABIT	COMMEND	CONFESS
CLAIMER	CLICHED	COAL GAS	COHERED	COMMENT	CONFIDE
CLAMANT	CLICHES	COALING	COHORTS	COMMODE	CONFINE
CLAMBER	CLICKED	COAL TAR	COILING	COMMONS	CONFIRM
CLAMMED	CLICKER	COAMING	COIMBRA	COMMUNE	CONFORM
CLAMOUR	CLIENTS	COARSEN	COINAGE	COMMUTE	CONFUSE
CLAMPED	CLIMATE	COARSER	COINERS	COMOROS	CONFUTE
CLAMPER	CLIMBED	COASTAL	COINING	COMPACT	CONGEAL
CLANGED	CLIMBER	COASTED	COLBERT	COMPANY	CONGEST
CLANGER	CLINGER	COASTER	COLDEST	COMPARE	CONGIUS
CLANGOR	CLINICS	COATING	COLDISH	COMPASS	CONICAL
CLANKED	CLINKED	COAXIAL	COLDITZ	COMPEER	CONIFER
CLAPPED	CLINKER	COAXING	COLD WAR	COMPERE	CONIINE
CLAPPER	CLINTON	COBBERS	COLICKY	COMPETE	CONJOIN
CLAQUES	CLIPPED	COBBLED	COLITIC	COMPILE	CONJURE
CLARIFY	CLIPPER	COBBLER	COLITIS	COMPING	CONKERS
CLARINO	CLIPPIE	COBWEBS	COLLAGE	COMPLEX	CONKING
CLARION	CLIQUES	COCAINE	COLLARD	COMPLIN	CONNATE
CLARITY	CLIQUEY	COCCOID	COLLARS	COMPONY	CONNECT
CLARKIA	CLOACAL	COCCOUS	COLLATE	COMPORT	CONNERY
CLASHED	CLOAKED	COCHLEA	COLLECT	COMPOSE	CONNING
CLASHER	CLOBBER	COCKADE	COLLEEN	COMPOST	CONNIVE
CLASHES	CLOCHES	COCKIER	COLLEGE	COMPOTE	CONNOTE
CLASPED	CLOCKED	COCKING	COLLIDE	COMPTON	CONQUER
CLASPER	CLOGGED	COCKLES	COLLIER	COMPUTE	CONSENT
CLASSED	CLONMEL	COCKNEY	COLLIES	COMRADE	CONSIGN
CLASSES	CLOPPED	COCKPIT	COLLOID	CONAKRY	CONSIST
CLASSIC	CLOSELY	COCK-UPS	COLLUDE	CONATUS	CONSOLE
CLASSIS	CLOSEST	COCONUT	COLOBUS	CONCAVE	CONSOLS
CLASTIC	CLOSETS	COCOONS	COLOGNE	CONCEAL	CONSORT
CLATTER	CLOSE-UP	COCOTTE	COLOMBO	CONCEDE	CONSULS

CONSULT	CORBEIL	CO-STARS	COWBANE	CRAVING	CRITTER
CONSUME	CORBELS	COSTATE	COWBELL	CRAWLED	CROAKED
CONTACT	CORDAGE	COSTING	COWBIND	CRAWLER	CROAKER
CONTAIN	CORDATE	COSTIVE	COWBIRD	CRAWLEY	CROATIA
CONTEMN	CORDIAL	COSTNER	COWBOYS	CRAYONS	CROCEIN
CONTEND	CORDING	COSTUME	COWDREY	CRAZIER	CROCHET
CONTENT	CORDITE	COTE-	COWERED	CRAZILY	CROCKET
CONTEST	CORDOBA	D'OR	COWFISH	CREAKED	CROFTER
CONTEXT	CORDONS	COTERIE	COWGIRL	CREAMED	CRONIES
CONTORT	CORINTH	COTIDAL	COWHAND	CREAMER	CROOKED
CONTOUR	CORKAGE	COTINGA	COWHERB	CREASED	CROONED
CONTROL	CORKERS	COTONOU	COWHERD	CREASES	CROONER
CONTUSE	CORKING	COTTAGE	COWHIDE	CREATED	CROPPED
CONVENE	CORMOUS	COTTONY	COWLICK	CREATOR	CROPPER
CONVENT	CORNCOB	COUCHED	COWLING	CRECHES	CROQUET
CONVERT	CORNEAL	COUCHER	COWPATS	CREDENT	CROSIER
CONVICT	CORNERS	COUCHES	COWRIES	CREDITS	CROSSED
CONVOKE	CORNETS	COUGARS	COWSHED	CREEDAL	CROSSER
CONVOYS	CORNICE	COUGHED	COWSLIP	CREEPER	CROSSES
COOKERS	CORNIER	COULDN'T	COXCOMB	CREMATE	CROSSLY
COOKERY	CORNISH	COULDST	COYNESS	CREMONA	CROUTON
COOKIES	CORNUAL	COULOIR	COYOTES	CRENATE	CROWBAR
COOKING	CORNUTE	COULOMB	COZENED	CREOLES	CROWDED
COOKOUT	COROLLA	COULTER	COZENER	CREOSOL	CROWING
COOKSON	CORONAE	COUNCIL	COZIEST	CRESSET	CROWNED
COOLANT	CORONAL	COUNSEL	CRABBED	CRESTED	CROYDON
COOLERS	CORONAS	COUNTED	CRACKED	CRETINS	CROZIER
COOLEST	CORONER	COUNTER	CRACKER	CREVICE	CRUCIAL
COOLIES	CORONET	COUNTRY	CRACKLE	CREW CUT	CRUCIFY
COOLING	CORPORA	COUPLED	CRACK UP	CREWING	CRUDELY
COOLISH	CORPSES	COUPLER	CRACKUP	CRIBBED	CRUDEST
COONTIE	CORRADE	COUPLES	CRADLED	CRICKED	CRUDITY
COOPERS	CORRALS	COUPLET	CRADLES	CRICKET	CRUELLY
CO-OPTED	CORRECT	COUPONS	CRAFTED	CRICOID	CRUELTY
COPAIBA	CORREZE	COURAGE	CRAIOVA	CRIMEAN	CRUISED
COPEPOD	CORRIDA	COURIER	CRAMMED	CRIMPED	CRUISER
COPIERS	CORRODE	COURSED	CRAMMER	CRIMPER	CRUISES
COPILOT	CORRUPT	COURSER	CRAMPED	CRIMPLE	CRUMBLE
COPINGS	CORSAGE	COURSES	CRAMPON	CRIMSON	CRUMBLY
COPIOUS	CORSAIR	COURTED	CRANIAL	CRINGED	CRUMPET
COP-OUTS	CORSETS	COURTLY	CRANING	CRINGLE	CRUMPLE
COPPERS	CORSICA	COUSINS	CRANIUM	CRINITE	CRUMPLY
COPPERY	CORTEGE	COUTURE	CRANKED	CRINKLE	CRUNCHY
COPPICE	CORTONA	COUVADE	CRANK UP	CRINKLY	CRUNODE
COPPING	CORVINE	COVERED	CRAPPED	CRINOID	CRUPPER
COPULAR	COSENZA	COVERER	CRAPPIE	CRIOLLO	CRUSADE
COPYCAT	COSHING	COVERTS	CRASHED	CRIPPLE	CRUSHED
COPYING	COSIEST	COVER-UP	CRASHES	CRISPED	CRUSHES
COPYIST	COSINES	COVETED	CRASSLY	CRISPLY	CRUSTAL
COQUINA	COSMINE	COVETER	CRATERS	CRISSAL	CRUZADO
COQUITO	COSMOID	COWARDS	CRATING	CRISSUM	CRYBABY
CORACLE	COSTARD	COWARDY	CRAVATS	CRITICS	CRYOGEN

CRYPTAL	CURIOUS	CYGNETS	DANDIFY	DEALATE	DEEPEST
CRYPTIC	CURLERS	CYMBALS	DANDLED	DEALERS	DEEP FRY
CRYSTAL	CURLEWS	CYNICAL	DANDLER	DEALING	DEFACED
CTENOID	CURLIER	CYPHERS	DANGERS	DEANERY	DEFACER
CUBBING	CURLING	CYPRESS	DANGLED	DEAREST	DE FACTO
CUBICAL	CURRANT	CYPRIOT	DANGLER	DEARIES	DEFAMED
CUBICLE	CURRENT	CYPSELA	DANKEST	DEATHLY	DEFAMER
CUBITAL	CURRIED	CYSTINE	DANSEUR	DEBACLE	DEFAULT
CUCKOLD	CURRIER	CYSTOID	DAPHNIA	DEBASED	DEFEATS
CUCKOOS	CURRIES	CYTHERA	DAPPING	DEBASER	DEFECTS
CUDBEAR	CURRISH	CZARDAS	DAPPLED	DEBATED	DEFENCE
CUDDLED	CURSING	CZARINA	DAPSONE	DEBATER	DEFIANT
CUDGELS	CURSIVE		DARESAY	DEBATES	DEFICIT
CUDLIPP	CURSORS	**D**	DARIOLE	DEBAUCH	DEFILED
CUDWEED	CURSORY	DABBING	DARKEST	DEBITED	DEFILER
CUE BALL	CURTAIL	DABBLED	DARKIES	DEBORAH	DEFILES
CUFFING	CURTAIN	DABBLER	DARKNET	DEBOUCH	DEFINED
CUIRASS	CURTESY	DAB HAND	DARLING	DEBRIEF	DEFINER
CUISINE	CURVING	DACTYLS	DARNING	DEBTORS	DEFLATE
CULCHIE	CUSHIER	DADAISM	DARTING	DECADAL	DEFLECT
CULICID	CUSHION	DADAIST	DASHEEN	DECADES	DEFORCE
CULLING	CUSPATE	DADDIES	DASHIKI	DECAGON	DEFRAUD
CULPRIT	CUSSING	DADROCK	DASHING	DECANAL	DEFROCK
CULTISH	CUSTARD	DAEMONS	DASYURE	DECAPOD	DEFROST
CULTISM	CUSTODY	DAFTEST	DATABLE	DECAYED	DEFUNCT
CULTIST	CUSTOMS	DAGGERS	DATA BUS	DECEASE	DEFUSED
CULTURE	CUTAWAY	DAGLOCK	DATIVAL	DECEIVE	DEFYING
CULVERT	CUTBACK	DAHLIAS	DATIVES	DECENCY	DEGAUSS
CUMBRIA	CUT DOWN	DAHOMAN	DAUBERY	DECIARE	DEGRADE
CUMQUAT	CUTICLE	DAHOMEY	DAUBING	DECIBEL	DEGREES
CUMULET	CUTLASS	DAILIES	DAUNTED	DECIDED	DEHISCE
CUMULUS	CUTLERS	DAIRIES	DAUNTER	DECIDER	DEICIDE
CUNEATE	CUTLERY	DAISIES	DAUPHIN	DECIDUA	DE-ICING
CUNNING	CUTLETS	DAKOTAN	DAWDLED	DECIMAL	DEICTIC
CUP CAKE	CUTOFFS	DALLIED	DAWDLER	DECKING	DEIFIED
CUPOLAS	CUTOUTS	DAMAGED	DAWKINS	DECLAIM	DEIFIER
CUPPING	CUTTACK	DAMAGER	DAWNING	DECLARE	DEIFORM
CUPRITE	CUTTERS	DAMAGES	DAYBOOK	DECLASS	DEIGNED
CUPROUS	CUTTING	DAMMING	DAYBOYS	DECLINE	DEISTIC
CUP TIES	CUTWORK	DAMNIFY	DAY CARE	DECODED	DEITIES
CURABLE	CUTWORM	DAMNING	DAY-CARE	DECORUM	DEJECTA
CURABLY	CWMBRAN	DAMPERS	DAYLONG	DECOYED	DE KLERK
CURACAO	CYANATE	DAMPEST	DAYROOM	DECOYER	DELAINE
CURATES	CYANIDE	DAMPING	DAYTIME	DECREED	DELAYED
CURATOR	CYANINE	DAMPISH	DAZEDLY	DECREER	DELAYER
CURBING	CYANITE	DAMSELS	DAZZLED	DECREES	DELETED
CURCUMA	CYBALER	DAMSONS	DEACONS	DECRIAL	DELIGHT
CURDLED	CYCLING	DANCERS	DEAD END	DECRIED	DELIMIT
CURE-ALL	CYCLIST	DANCING	DEADEYE	DECRIER	DELIVER
CURETTE	CYCLOID	DANDERS	DEADPAN	DECUPLE	DELOUSE
CURFEWS	CYCLONE	DANDIER	DEAD SET	DEDUCED	DELPHIC
CURIOSA	CYCLOPS	DANDIES	DEAF-AID	DEEMING	DELTAIC

DELTOID	DERIDED	DEVISOR	DIEHARD	DIPSHIT	DIVIDED
DELUDED	DERIDER	DEVIZES	DIESELS	DIPTYCH	DIVIDER
DELUDER	DERIVED	DEVOICE	DIETARY	DIREFUL	DIVIDES
DELUGED	DERIVER	DEVOIRS	DIETING	DIRNDLS	DIVINED
DELUGES	DERMOID	DEVOLVE	DIFFUSE	DIRTIED	DIVINER
DELVING	DERRICK	DEVOTED	DIGAMMA	DIRTIER	DIVISOR
DEMANDS	DERVISH	DEVOTEE	DIGESTS	DIRTILY	DIVORCE
DEMERGE	DESCALE	DEWATER	DIGGERS	DISABLE	DIVULGE
DEMERIT	DESCANT	DEWCLAW	DIGGING	DISAVOW	DIZZIER
DEMESNE	DESCEND	DEWDROP	DIGITAL	DISBAND	DIZZILY
DEMIGOD	DESCENT	DEWIEST	DIGNIFY	DISCARD	DNIEPER
DEMIVEG	DESERTS	DEWLAPS	DIGNITY	DISCERN	D-NOTICE
DEMONIC	DESERVE	DEXTRAL	DIGRAPH	DISCOID	DOBRUJA
DEMOTED	DESIGNS	DEXTRAN	DIGRESS	DISCORD	DOCKAGE
DEMOTIC	DESIRED	DEXTRIN	DILATED	DISCUSS	DOCKERS
DEMOUNT	DESIRER	DHAHRAN	DILATOR	DISDAIN	DOCKETS
DEMURER	DESIRES	DIABASE	DILDOES	DISEASE	DOCKING
DENEUVE	DESKTOP	DIABOLO	DILEMMA	DISEUSE	DOCTORS
DENIALS	DESMOID	DIADEMS	DILUENT	DISGUST	DODDERY
DENIERS	DESPAIR	DIAGRAM	DILUTED	DISHFUL	DODDLES
DENIZEN	DESPISE	DIALECT	DILUTEE	DISHIER	DODGEMS
DENMARK	DESPITE	DIALING	DILUTER	DISHING	DODGERS
DENNING	DESPOIL	DIALLED	DIMETER	DISJECT	DODGIER
DENOTED	DESPOND	DIALLER	DIMMERS	DISJOIN	DODGING
DENSELY	DESPOTS	DIALYSE	DIMMEST	DISLIKE	DODOISM
DENSEST	DESSERT	DIAMINE	DIMMING	DISMAST	DOESKIN
DENSITY	DESTINE	DIAMOND	DIMNESS	DISMISS	DOFFING
DENTATE	DESTINY	DIANOIA	DIMORPH	DISOBEY	DOGBANE
DENTINE	DESTOCK	DIAPERS	DIMPLES	DISPLAY	DOGCART
DENTING	DESTROY	DIARCHY	DIMWITS	DISPORT	DOG DAYS
DENTIST	DETAILS	DIARIES	DINERIC	DISPOSE	DOGFISH
DENTOID	DETENTE	DIARIST	DINETTE	DISPUTE	DOGGERY
DENTURE	DETERGE	DIASTER	DINGIER	DISRATE	DOGGIES
DENUDED	DETINUE	DIAZINE	DINGILY	DISROBE	DOGGING
DENUDER	DETOURS	DIAZOLE	DINGLES	DISRUPT	DOGGONE
DENYING	DETRACT	DIBASIC	DINGOES	DISSECT	DOGLEGS
DEONTIC	DETRAIN	DIBBING	DINKIER	DISSENT	DOG ROSE
DEPISER	DETROIT	DIBBLED	DINNERS	DISTAFF	DOG TAGS
DEPLETE	DETRUDE	DIBBLER	DINNING	DISTANT	DOGTROT
DEPLORE	DEUTZIA	DIBBLES	DIOCESE	DISTEND	DOGVANE
DEPLUME	DEVALUE	DICIEST	DIOPTRE	DISTICH	DOGWOOD
DEPOSAL	DEVELOP	DICKENS	DIORAMA	DISTORT	DOILIES
DEPOSED	DEVIANT	DICKIER	DIORITE	DISTURB	DOLEFUL
DEPOSER	DEVIATE	DICKIES	DIOXIDE	DISUSED	DOLLARS
DEPOSIT	DEVICES	DICLINY	DIPHASE	DITCHED	DOLLIES
DEPRAVE	DEVILED	DICTATE	DIPLOID	DITCHER	DOLLING
DEPRESS	DEVILRY	DICTION	DIPLOMA	DITCHES	DOLLISH
DEPRIVE	DEVIOUS	DICTUMS	DIPLONT	DITTANY	DOLLOPS
DEPSIDE	DEVISAL	DIDDLED	DIPNOAN	DITTIES	DOLMENS
DEPUTED	DEVISED	DIDICOY	DIPOLAR	DIURNAL	DOLPHIN
DERANGE	DEVISEE	DIEBACK	DIPPERS	DIVERGE	DOLTISH
DERBIES	DEVISER	DIE-CAST	DIPPING	DIVERSE	DOMAINS

DOMICAL	DOWRIES	DRIP-DRY	DUBNIUM	DWARVES	ECHELON
DOMINEE	DOWSERS	DRIPPED	DUCHESS	DWELLED	ECHIDNA
DONATED	DOWSING	DRIVE IN	DUCHIES	DWELLER	ECHINUS
DONATOR	DOYLEYS	DRIVE-IN	DUCKIES	DWINDLE	ECHOING
DONBASS	DOZENTH	DRIVERS	DUCKING	DYARCHY	ECHOISM
DONEGAL	DOZIEST	DRIVING	DUCTILE	DYELINE	ECLAIRS
DONETSK	DRABBER	DRIZZLE	DUDGEON	DYEWOOD	ECLIPSE
DON JUAN	DRABBLE	DRIZZLY	DUELING	DYNAMIC	ECLOGUE
DONKEYS	DRACHMA	DROLLER	DUELLED	DYNAMOS	ECOCIDE
DONNING	DRACHMS	DRONING	DUELLER	DYNASTY	ECOLOGY
DONNISH	DRAFTED	DRONISH	DUENNAS	DYSURIA	ECONOMY
DOODLED	DRAFTEE	DROOLED	DUFFERS	DYSURIC	ECORCHE
DOODLER	DRAFTER	DROOPED	DUGOUTS	DZONGKA	ECOTONE
DOODLES	DRAGGED	DROPLET	DUKEDOM		ECOTYPE
DOOMING	DRAGGLE	DROP OFF	DULLARD	**E**	ECSTASY
DO-OR-	DRAGNET	DROPOUT	DULLEST	EACH WAY	ECTHYMA
DIE	DRAGONS	DROPPED	DULLING	EAGERLY	ECTOPIA
DOORMAN	DRAGOON	DROPPER	DULOSIS	EAGLETS	ECTOPIC
DOORMAT	DRAINED	DROSHKY	DUMBEST	EARACHE	ECTYPAL
DOORMEN	DRAINER	DROUGHT	DUMMIES	EARBUDS	ECUADOR
DOORWAY	DRAPERS	DROVERS	DUMPERS	EARDRUM	EDACITY
DOPIEST	DRAPERY	DROWNED	DUMPIER	EARFLAP	EDAPHIC
DORMANT	DRAPING	DROWNER	DUMPING	EARHOLE	EDDYING
DORMERS	DRASTIC	DROWSED	DUNDALK	EARLDOM	EDGIEST
DORMICE	DRATTED	DRUBBER	DUNEDIN	EARLIER	EDGINGS
DORNICK	DRAUGHT	DRUDGED	DUNGEON	EARLOBE	EDICTAL
DOSAGES	DRAWBAR	DRUDGER	DUNKING	EARMARK	EDIFICE
DOSSERS	DRAWERS	DRUDGES	DUNKIRK	EARMUFF	EDIFIED
DOSSIER	DRAWING	DRUGGED	DUNNAGE	EARNERS	EDIFIER
DOSSING	DRAWLED	DRUGGET	DUNNEST	EARNEST	EDITING
DOTAGES	DRAWLER	DRUIDIC	DUNNING	EARNING	EDITION
DOTTIER	DRAWS IN	DRUMLIN	DUNNITE	EARPLUG	EDITORS
DOTTING	DRAWS UP	DRUMMED	DUODENA	EARRING	EDUCATE
DOUBLED	DREADED	DRUMMER	DUOTONE	EARSHOT	EEL-LIKE
DOUBLER	DREAMED	DRUNKEN	DUPABLE	EARTHED	EELPOUT
DOUBLES	DREAMER	DRUNKER	DURABLE	EARTHEN	EELWORM
DOUBLET	DREDGED	DRUTHER	DURABLY	EARTHLY	EFFACED
DOUBTED	DREDGER	DRYABLE	DURANGO	EARWIGS	EFFACER
DOUBTER	DRENTHE	DRYADIC	DURMAST	EARWORM	EFFECTS
DOUCHES	DRESDEN	DRY DOCK	DUSKIER	EASEFUL	EFFORTS
DOUGHTY	DRESSED	DRY-EYED	DUSTBIN	EASIEST	EGGCUPS
DOUGLAS	DRESSER	DRY LAND	DUSTERS	EAST END	EGGHEAD
DOURINE	DRESSES	DRYNESS	DUSTIER	EASTERN	EGG ROLL
DOUSING	DRESS UP	DRY-SALT	DUSTING	EASTERS	EGOISTS
DOWABLE	DRIBBLE	DRY-SHOD	DUSTMAN	EASTING	EGOTISM
DOWAGER	DRIBLET	DRYWALL	DUSTMEN	EATABLE	EGOTIST
DOWDIER	DRIED UP	DUALISM	DUSTPAN	EBB TIDE	EGO TRIP
DOWDILY	DRIFTED	DUALIST	DUSTUPS	EBONITE	EIDETIC
DOWN-BOW	DRIFTER	DUALITY	DUTIFUL	EBONIZE	EIDOLON
DOWNERS	DRILLED	DUBBING	DUVETYN	ECBOLIC	EIGHTHS
DOWNIER	DRILLER	DUBIETY	DVANDVA	ECCRINE	EIGHTVO
DOWNING	DRINKER	DUBIOUS	DWARFED	ECDYSIS	EINKORN

EJECTED	EMETICS	ENDUING	ENTICED	EQUALED	ESTORIL
EJECTOR	EMETINE	ENDURED	ENTICER	EQUALLY	ESTREAT
ELAMITE	EMIGRES	END USER	ENTITLE	EQUATED	ESTUARY
ELAPSED	EMINENT	ENDWAYS	ENTOPIC	EQUATOR	ETAGERE
ELASTIC	EMIRATE	ENEMIES	ENTRAIN	EQUERRY	ETAMINE
ELASTIN	EMITTED	ENERGID	ENTRANT	EQUINOX	ETCHERS
ELATION	EMITTER	ENFEOFF	ENTREAT	ERASERS	ETCHING
ELATIVE	EMOTION	ENFIELD	ENTREES	ERASING	ETERNAL
ELBOWED	EMOTIVE	ENFORCE	ENTRIES	ERASION	ETESIAN
ELDERLY	EMPALER	ENGAGED	ENTROPY	ERASURE	ETHANOL
ELEATIC	EMPANEL	ENGAGER	ENTRUST	ERECTED	ETHERIC
ELECTED	EMPATHY	EN GARDE	ENTWINE	ERECTER	ETHICAL
ELECTOR	EMPEROR	ENGINES	E NUMBER	ERECTLY	ETHMOID
ELEGANT	EMPIRES	ENGLAND	ENVELOP	ERECTOR	ETHYLIC
ELEGIAC	EMPIRIC	ENGLISH	ENVENOM	EREMITE	ETRURIA
ELEGIES	EMPLACE	ENGORGE	ENVIOUS	EREPSIN	EUBOEAN
ELEGIST	EMPORIA	ENGRAFT	ENVIRON	ERISTIC	EUCAINE
ELEGIZE	EMPOWER	ENGRAIL	ENVYING	ERITREA	EUGENIC
ELEMENT	EMPRESS	ENGRAIN	ENZYMES	ERMINES	EUGENOL
ELEUSIS	EMPTIED	ENGRAVE	EOBIONT	ERODENT	EUGLENA
ELEVATE	EMPTIER	ENGROSS	EOSINIC	ERODING	EULOGIA
ELEVENS	EMPTIES	ENHANCE	EPARCHY	EROSION	EUNUCHS
ELIDING	EMPTILY	ENIGMAS	EPAULET	EROSIVE	EUPHONY
ELISION	EMPYEMA	ENJOYED	EPEEIST	EROTEMA	EUPHROE
ELITISM	EMULATE	ENJOYER	EPEIRIC	EROTICA	EUPLOID
ELITIST	EMULOUS	ENLARGE	EPERGNE	ERRANCY	EUPNOEA
ELIXIRS	ENABLED	ENLIVEN	EPIBOLY	ERRANDS	EURASIA
ELLIPSE	ENABLER	EN MASSE	EPICARP	ERRATIC	EURATOM
EL MINYA	ENACTED	ENNOBLE	EPICENE	ERRATUM	EURIPUS
EL OBEID	ENACTOR	ENOUNCE	EPICURE	ERRHINE	EUSTASY
ELOPING	ENAMOUR	ENPLANE	EPIDOTE	ERUDITE	EVACUEE
ELUDING	ENCASED	ENQUIRE	EPIGEAL	ERUPTED	EVADING
ELUSION	ENCHAIN	ENQUIRY	EPIGENE	ERZURUM	EVANGEL
ELUSIVE	ENCHANT	ENRAGED	EPIGONE	ESBJERG	EVASION
ELUVIAL	EN CLAIR	ENROBER	EPIGRAM	ESCAPED	EVASIVE
ELUVIUM	ENCLAVE	EN ROUTE	EPIGYNY	ESCAPEE	EVENING
ELYSIAN	ENCLOSE	ENSIGNS	EPIMERE	ESCAPER	EVEREST
ELYSIUM	ENCODED	ENSLAVE	EPISODE	ESCAPES	EVERTOR
ELYTRON	ENCODER	ENSNARE	EPISOME	ESCOLAR	EVESHAM
EMANATE	ENCOMIA	ENSUING	EPISTLE	ESCORTS	EVICTED
EMBARGO	ENCORES	ENSURED	EPITAPH	ESERINE	EVICTOR
EMBASSY	ENCRUST	ENSURER	EPITAXY	ESKIMOS	EVIDENT
EMBLEMS	ENDARCH	ENTASIA	EPITHET	ESPARTO	EVILEST
EMBOLIC	ENDEMIC	ENTASIS	EPITOME	ESPOUSE	EVIL EYE
EMBOLUS	END GAME	ENTEBBE	EPIZOIC	ESPYING	EVILLER
EMBRACE	ENDINGS	ENTENTE	EPIZOON	ESQUIRE	EVINCED
EMBROIL	ENDIVES	ENTERED	EPOCHAL	ESSAYED	EVOKING
EMBRYOS	ENDLESS	ENTERER	EPOCHES	ESSENCE	EVOLUTE
EMENDED	ENDMOST	ENTERIC	EPONYMY	ESSONNE	EVOLVED
EMERALD	ENDORSE	ENTERON	EPSILON	ESTATES	EVOLVER
EMERGED	ENDOWED	ENTHRAL	EQUABLE	ESTHETE	EWE-NECK
EMERSED	ENDOWER	ENTHUSE	EQUABLY	ESTONIA	EXACTED

EXACTLY	EXPOSAL	FAEROES	FARAWAY	FEATURE	FETCHED
EXACTOR	EXPOSED	FAG ENDS	FARCEUR	FEBRILE	FETCHER
EXALTED	EXPOSER	FAGGING	FAR EAST	FEDERAL	FETLOCK
EXALTER	EXPOSES	FAGGOTS	FAR-GONE	FEDORAS	FETTERS
EXAMINE	EXPOUND	FAIENCE	FARMERS	FEEBLER	FETUSES
EXAMPLE	EXPRESS	FAILING	FARMING	FEEDBAG	FEUDING
EXARATE	EXPUNGE	FAILURE	FARNESS	FEEDERS	FEVERED
EXCERPT	EXSCIND	FAINTED	FARRAGO	FEEDING	FEWNESS
EXCIMER	EXTENTS	FAINTER	FARRIER	FEEDLOT	FEYNESS
EXCISED	EXTINCT	FAINTLY	FARTHER	FEELERS	FIANCES
EXCITED	EXTRACT	FAIREST	FARTING	FEELING	FIASCOS
EXCITER	EXTREME	FAIRIES	FARTLEK	FEIGNED	FIBBERS
EXCITON	EXTRUDE	FAIRING	FASCIAL	FEIGNER	FIBBING
EXCITOR	EXUDING	FAIRISH	FASCIAS	FEINTED	FIBROID
EXCLAIM	EXULTED	FAIR SEX	FASCINE	FELAFEL	FIBROIN
EXCLAVE	EXURBIA	FAIRWAY	FASCISM	FELINES	FIBROMA
EXCLUDE	EXUVIAE	FAJITAS	FASCIST	FELLERS	FIBROUS
EXCRETA	EXUVIAL	FALAFEL	FASHION	FELLING	FIBULAE
EXCRETE	EX-WORKS	FALANGE	FASTEST	FELLOWS	FIBULAR
EXCUSAL	EYEBALL	FALASHA	FASTING	FELONRY	FIBULAS
EXCUSED	EYEBATH	FALBALA	FATALLY	FELSITE	FICTILE
EXCUSES	EYEBOLT	FALCATE	FATBACK	FELSPAR	FICTION
EXECUTE	EYEBROW	FALCONS	FAT CATS	FELTING	FIDDLED
EXEGETE	EYELASH	FALKIRK	FATEFUL	FELUCCA	FIDDLER
EXERGUE	EYELESS	FALLACY	FATHEAD	FELWORT	FIDDLES
EXERTED	EYELETS	FALL GUY	FATHERS	FEMALES	FIDEISM
EXHALED	EYELIDS	FALLING	FATHOMS	FEMORAL	FIDEIST
EXHAUST	EYESHOT	FALLOUT	FATIGUE	FENCERS	FIDGETS
EXHIBIT	EYESORE	FALSELY	FATLING	FENCING	FIDGETY
EXHUMED	EYESPOT	FALSEST	FATNESS	FENDERS	FIELDED
EXHUMER	EYEWASH	FALSIES	FATSHAN	FENDING	FIELDER
EXIGENT		FALSIFY	FATTEST	FENLAND	FIERCER
EXILING	**F**	FALSITY	FATTIER	FERGANA	FIERIER
EXISTED	FABIANS	FALSTER	FATTIES	FERMATA	FIESOLE
EXITING	FABRICS	FAMILLE	FATTILY	FERMENT	FIESTAS
EXMOUTH	FACADES	FAMINES	FATTISH	FERMION	FIFTEEN
EXODERM	FACEBAR	FANATIC	FATTISM	FERMIUM	FIFTIES
EXOGAMY	FACE-OFF	FAN BELT	FATUITY	FERNERY	FIGHTER
EXOTICA	FACIALS	FANCIED	FATUOUS	FERRARA	FIG LEAF
EXPANSE	FACINGS	FANCIER	FAUCETS	FERRATE	FIGMENT
EX PARTE	FACTFUL	FANCIES	FAULTED	FERRETS	FIG TREE
EXPENSE	FACTION	FANCILY	FAUVISM	FERRETY	FIGURAL
EXPERTS	FACTORS	FAN CLUB	FAUVIST	FERRIED	FIGURED
EXPIATE	FACTORY	FANFARE	FAUX PAS	FERRIES	FIGURER
EXPIRED	FACTUAL	FANNIES	FAVOURS	FERRITE	FIGURES
EXPIRER	FACULAR	FANNING	FAVRILE	FERROUS	FIGWORT
EXPLAIN	FACULTY	FANTAIL	FAWNING	FERRULE	FILARIA
EXPLANT	FADABLE	FANTAST	FEARFUL	FERTILE	FILBERT
EXPLODE	FADDISH	FANTASY	FEARING	FERVENT	FILCHED
EXPLOIT	FADDISM	FANZINE	FEASTED	FERVOUR	FILCHER
EXPLORE	FADDIST	FARADAY	FEASTER	FESTIVE	FILETED
EXPORTS	FADEOUT	FARADIC	FEATHER	FESTOON	FILIATE

FILIBEG	FISSION	FLEEING	FLUENCY	FOLIOSE	FORGERS
FILINGS	FISSURE	FLEETER	FLUFFED	FOLKISH	FORGERY
FILLETS	FISTULA	FLEMING	FLUIDAL	FOLLIES	FORGING
FILLIES	FITMENT	FLEMISH	FLUIDIC	FONDANT	FORGIVE
FILLING	FITNESS	FLENSER	FLUMMOX	FONDEST	FORGOER
FILL-INS	FITTERS	FLESHED	FLUNKED	FONDLED	FORGONE
FILLIPS	FITTEST	FLESHER	FLUNKEY	FONDLER	FORKFUL
FILMIER	FITTING	FLESHES	FLUORIC	FONDUES	FORKING
FILMILY	FIXABLE	FLESHLY	FLUSHED	FOOCHOW	FORLORN
FILMING	FIXATED	FLEURON	FLUSHER	FOODIES	FORMANT
FILMSET	FIXEDLY	FLEXILE	FLUSHES	FOOLERY	FORMATE
FILTERS	FIXTURE	FLEXING	FLUSTER	FOOLING	FORMATS
FIMBRIA	FIZZIER	FLEXION	FLUTING	FOOLISH	FORMICA
FINABLE	FIZZING	FLEXURE	FLUTIST	FOOTAGE	FORMING
FINAGLE	FLACCID	FLICKED	FLUTTER	FOOTBOY	FORMOSA
FINALES	FLAG DAY	FLICKER	FLUVIAL	FOOTING	FORMULA
FINALLY	FLAGGED	FLIGHTS	FLUXION	FOOTMAN	FORSAKE
FINANCE	FLAGGER	FLIGHTY	FLYABLE	FOOTMEN	FORSOOK
FINBACK	FLAGMAN	FLINGER	FLYAWAY	FOOTPAD	FORSYTH
FINCHES	FLAGONS	FLIPPED	FLYBACK	FOOTSIE	FORTIES
FINDING	FLAILED	FLIPPER	FLYBLOW	FOOT-TON	FORTIFY
FINE ART	FLAKIER	FLIRTED	FLYBOAT	FOOTWAY	FORTUNE
FINE-CUT	FLAKING	FLIRTER	FLYBOOK	FOOZLER	FORWARD
FINESSE	FLAMING	FLITTED	FLY-FISH	FOPPERY	FORWENT
FINFOOT	FLANEUR	FLITTER	FLY HALF	FOPPISH	FOSSILS
FINGERS	FLANGER	FLIVVER	FLYLEAF	FORAGED	FOUETTE
FINICKY	FLANGES	FLOATED	FLYOVER	FORAGER	FOULARD
FININGS	FLANKED	FLOATEL	FLYPAST	FORAGES	FOULEST
FINLAND	FLANKER	FLOATER	FLYTRAP	FORAMEN	FOULING
FINNING	FLANNEL	FLOCCUS	FOALING	FORAYED	FOUL-UPS
FINNISH	FLAPPED	FLOCKED	FOAMIER	FORAYER	FOUNDED
FIREARM	FLAPPER	FLOGGED	FOAMING	FORBADE	FOUNDER
FIREBOX	FLARE-UP	FLOGGER	FOBBING	FORBEAR	FOUNDRY
FIREBUG	FLARING	FLOODED	FO'C'SLES	FORBORE	FOURIER
FIREDOG	FLASHED	FLOODER	FOCUSED	FORCEPS	FOURTHS
FIREFLY	FLASHER	FLOORED	FOCUSER	FORCING	FOUR-WAY
FIREMAN	FLASHES	FLOPPED	FOCUSES	FORDING	FOVEATE
FIREMEN	FLASKET	FLORIDA	FOGGIER	FOREARM	FOVEOLA
FIREPAN	FLAT-BED	FLORINS	FOGGILY	FOREGUT	FOWLING
FIRMEST	FLATLET	FLORIST	FOGGING	FOREIGN	FOXFIRE
FIRMING	FLATTEN	FLORUIT	FOGHORN	FORELEG	FOXHOLE
FIRSTLY	FLATTER	FLOSSED	FOG LAMP	FOREMAN	FOXHUNT
FIRTREE	FLAUNCH	FLOTAGE	FOGYISH	FOREMEN	FOXIEST
FISCALS	FLAVONE	FLOTSAM	FOIBLES	FOREPAW	FOXLIKE
FISCHER	FLAVOUR	FLOUNCE	FOILING	FORERUN	FOXTAIL
FISHERY	FLAWING	FLOURED	FOISTED	FORESAW	FOXTROT
FISH-EYE	FLAYING	FLOUTED	FOLACIN	FORESEE	FRACTAL
FISHGIG	FLEABAG	FLOUTER	FOLDERS	FORESTS	FRACTUS
FISHIER	FLEAPIT	FLOWAGE	FOLDING	FORETOP	FRAENUM
FISHING	FLECKED	FLOWERS	FOLDOUT	FOREVER	FRAGILE
FISHNET	FLEECED	FLOWERY	FOLIAGE	FORFEIT	FRAILER
FISSILE	FLEECES	FLOWING	FOLIATE	FORGAVE	FRAILTY

FRAKTUR	FRISKED	FUNCHAL	GADGETS	GANTLET	GAVOTTE
FRAME UP	FRISKER	FUNDING	GADGETY	GAOLERS	GAWKERS
FRAME-UP	FRISKET	FUNERAL	GADROON	GAOLING	GAWKIER
FRAMING	FRISSON	FUNFAIR	GADWALL	GAPPING	GAWKING
FRANCIS	FRITTER	FUNGOID	GAFFERS	GAP YEAR	GAWPING
FRANKED	FRIZZED	FUNGOUS	GAGAUZI	GARAGED	GAYNESS
FRANKER	FRIZZER	FUNICLE	GAGGING	GARAGES	GAZEBOS
FRANKLY	FRIZZLE	FUNKIER	GAHNITE	GARBAGE	GAZELLE
FRANTIC	FROEBEL	FUNKING	GAINERS	GARBING	GAZETTE
FRAPPES	FROG-BIT	FUNNELS	GAINFUL	GARBLED	GEARBOX
FRAUGHT	FROGMAN	FUNNIER	GAINING	GARBLER	GEARING
FRAYING	FROGMEN	FUNNILY	GAINSAY	GARCONS	GECKOES
FRAZIER	FROLICS	FUN RUNS	GAITERS	GARDENS	GEE-GEES
FRAZZLE	FRONDED	FUNSTER	GALATEA	GARFISH	GEELONG
FREAKED	FRONTAL	FURBISH	GALEATE	GARGETY	GEEZERS
FRECKLE	FRONTED	FURCATE	GALENIC	GARGLED	GEISHAS
FREEBIE	FROSTED	FURCULA	GALICIA	GARGLER	GELATIN
FREEDOM	FROTHED	FURIOSO	GALILEE	GARGLES	GELDING
FREEGAN	FROWARD	FURIOUS	GALIPOT	GARLAND	GELLING
FREEING	FROWNED	FURLING	GALLANT	GARMENT	GEMMATE
FREEMAN	FROWNER	FURLONG	GALLEON	GARNETS	GEMMING
FREEMEN	FROWSTY	FURNACE	GALLERY	GARNISH	GEMMULE
FREESIA	FRUITED	FURNESS	GALLEYS	GARONNE	GEMSBOK
FREEWAY	FRUITER	FURNISH	GALLFLY	GARPIKE	GENAPPE
FREEZER	FRUSTUM	FURRIER	GALLING	GARRETS	GENDERS
FREIGHT	FUCHSIA	FURRING	GALLIUM	GARTERS	GENERAL
FREMONT	FUCHSIN	FURROWS	GALLNUT	GASBAGS	GENERIC
FRENEMY	FUCK ALL	FURROWY	GALLONS	GASCONY	GENESIS
FRESCOS	FUCKERS	FURTHER	GALLOON	GASEOUS	GENETIC
FRESHEN	FUCKING	FURTIVE	GALLOPS	GASHING	GENEVAN
FRESHER	FUCK-UPS	FUSCOUS	GALLOUS	GASKETS	GENIPAP
FRESHET	FUDDLED	FUSIBLE	GALLOWS	GAS MAIN	GENITAL
FRESHLY	FUDDLES	FUSILLI	GALUMPH	GAS MASK	GENITOR
FRESNEL	FUDGING	FUSSIER	GAMBADO	GASOHOL	GENOESE
FRETFUL	FUEGIAN	FUSSILY	GAMBIAN	GASPING	GENTEEL
FRETSAW	FUELING	FUSSING	GAMBIER	GAS PIPE	GENTIAN
FRETTED	FUELLED	FUSSPOT	GAMBITS	GASSIER	GENTILE
FRIABLE	FUELLER	FUSTIAN	GAMBLED	GASSING	GENUINE
FRIBBLE	FUENTES	FUSTIER	GAMBLER	GASTRIC	GEODESY
FRIDAYS	FUGGIER	FUTTOCK	GAMBOGE	GASTRIN	GEOLOGY
FRIDGES	FUKUOKA	FUTURES	GAMBOLS	GATEAUX	GEORDIE
FRIEDAN	FULCRUM	FUZZIER	GAMBREL	GATE-LEG	GEORGIA
FRIENDS	FULGENT	FUZZILY	GAMELAN	GATEWAY	GEORGIC
FRIEZES	FULLEST	FUZZING	GAMETAL	GATHERS	GERBILS
FRIGATE	FULMARS	FYZABAD	GAMIEST	GAUCHOS	GERENUK
FRIGHTS	FULNESS		GANDERS	GAUDERY	GERMANE
FRILLED	FULSOME	**G**	GANDZHA	GAUDIER	GERMANS
FRINGED	FULVOUS		GANGERS	GAUDILY	GERMANY
FRINGES	FUMARIC	GABBING	GANGING	GAUGING	GERUNDS
FRISBEE	FUMBLED	GABBLED	GANGTOK	GAUHATI	GESTALT
FRISEUR	FUMBLER	GABBLER	GANGWAY	GAUTENG	GESTAPO
FRISIAN	FUMBLES	GABFEST	GANNETS	GAUZIER	GESTATE
		GADDING			

GESTURE	GLACIAL	GLUTEUS	GOOGLES	GRANTOR	GRILLES
GETABLE	GLACIER	GLUTTED	GOOIEST	GRANULE	GRIMACE
GETAWAY	GLADDEN	GLUTTON	GOPHERS	GRAPHIC	GRIMIER
GETTING	GLADDER	GLYCINE	GORGING	GRAPNEL	GRIMMER
GEYSERS	GLADDON	GLYPHIC	GORGONS	GRAPPLE	GRIMSBY
GHASTLY	GLAD EYE	GLYPTIC	GORIEST	GRASPED	GRINDER
GHAZALI	GLAMOUR	GNARLED	GORILLA	GRASPER	GRINGOS
GHERKIN	GLANCED	GNASHED	GORIZIA	GRASSED	GRINNED
GHETTOS	GLANCES	GNASHES	GOSHAWK	GRASSES	GRINNER
GHILLIE	GLARING	GNATHIC	GOSLING	GRASS UP	GRIPERS
GHOSTED	GLASGOW	GNAWING	GO-SLOWS	GRATERS	GRIPING
GHOSTLY	GLASSED	GNOCCHI	GOSPELS	GRATIFY	GRIPPED
GIBBETS	GLASSES	GNOMISH	GOSPLAN	GRATING	GRIPPER
GIBBING	GLAZIER	GNOSTIC	GOSPORT	GRAUPEL	GRISTLE
GIBBONS	GLAZING	GOADING	GOSSIPS	GRAVELY	GRISTLY
GIBBOUS	GLEAMED	GO-AHEAD	GOSSIPY	GRAVEST	GRITTED
GIBLETS	GLEANED	GOATEED	GOTLAND	GRAVITY	GRIZZLE
GIDDIER	GLEANER	GOATEES	GOUACHE	GRAVLAX	GRIZZLY
GIDDILY	GLEEFUL	GOBBETS	GOUGING	GRAVURE	GROANED
GIESSEN	GLENCOE	GOBBLED	GOULASH	GRAYEST	GROANER
GIGGLED	GLENOID	GOBBLER	GOURAMI	GRAYING	GROCERS
GIGGLER	GLIADIN	GOBBLES	GOURMET	GRAZIER	GROCERY
GIGGLES	GLIBBER	GOBELIN	GRAB BAG	GRAZING	GROGRAM
GIG LAMP	GLIDERS	GOBIOID	GRABBED	GREASED	GROLIER
GIGOLOS	GLIDING	GOBLETS	GRABBER	GREASER	GROMMET
GILBERT	GLIMMER	GOBLINS	GRABBLE	GREATER	GROOMED
GILDING	GLIMPSE	GODDAMN	GRACILE	GREATLY	GROOMER
GILLIES	GLINTED	GODDESS	GRACING	GREAVES	GROOVED
GIMBALS	GLISTEN	GODHEAD	GRACKLE	GRECIAN	GROOVES
GIMLETS	GLITTER	GODHOOD	GRADATE	GREENED	GROPING
GIMMICK	GLIWICE	GODLESS	GRADING	GREENER	GROSSED
GINGERY	GLOATED	GODLIER	GRADUAL	GREENIE	GROSSER
GINGHAM	GLOATER	GODLIKE	GRAFTED	GREETED	GROSSES
GINGILI	GLOBATE	GODSEND	GRAFTER	GREETER	GROSSLY
GINGIVA	GLOBOID	GOGGLED	GRAINER	GREISEN	GROTTOS
GINSENG	GLOBOSE	GOGGLES	GRAMMAR	GREMIAL	GROUCHY
GIN TRAP	GLOBULE	GOIANIA	GRAMMES	GREMLIN	GROUNDS
GIPSIES	GLORIED	GO-KARTS	GRAMPUS	GRENADA	GROUPED
GIRAFFE	GLORIES	GOLDEYE	GRANADA	GRENADE	GROUPER
GIRASOL	GLORIFY	GOLFERS	GRANARY	GREYEST	GROUPIE
GIRDERS	GLOSSAL	GOLFING	GRANDAD	GREYHEN	GROUSED
GIRDING	GLOSSED	GOLIATH	GRANDEE	GREYING	GROUSER
GIRDLED	GLOSSER	GONADAL	GRANDER	GREYISH	GROUSES
GIRDLER	GLOTTAL	GONDOLA	GRANDLY	GREYLAG	GROUTER
GIRDLES	GLOTTIC	GOODBYE	GRANDMA	GRIBBLE	GROWERS
GIRLISH	GLOTTIS	GOOD DAY	GRANDPA	GRIDDLE	GROWING
GIRONDE	GLOWING	GOODIES	GRANGES	GRIEVED	GROWLED
GIRONNY	GLUCOSE	GOODISH	GRANITE	GRIEVER	GROWLER
GISARME	GLUE EAR	GOOFIER	GRANOLA	GRIFFIN	GROWN-UP
GITTERN	GLUEING	GOOFILY	GRANTED	GRIFFON	GROWTHS
GIVABLE	GLUMMER	GOOFING	GRANTEE	GRILLED	GROYNES
GIZZARD	GLUTEAL	GOOGLED	GRANTER	GRILLER	GRUBBED

GRUBBER	GUNFIRE	HAEMOID	HAMSTER	HARDTOP	HATTERS
GRUDGED	GUNLOCK	HAFNIUM	HAMULAR	HARELIP	HAUBERK
GRUDGER	GUNNELS	HAGFISH	HAMULUS	HARICOT	HAUGHTY
GRUDGES	GUNNERS	HAGGARD	HANAPER	HARIJAN	HAULAGE
GRUFFER	GUNNERY	HAGGISH	HANCOCK	HARKING	HAULIER
GRUFFLY	GUNNING	HAGGLED	HANDBAG	HARLECH	HAULING
GRUMBLE	GUNSHOT	HAGGLER	HANDFUL	HARLOTS	HAUNTED
GRUMOUS	GUNWALE	HAGLIKE	HANDGUN	HARMFUL	HAUNTER
GRUNTED	GURGLED	HAHNIUM	HANDIER	HARMING	HAURAKI
GRUNTER	GURNARD	HAILING	HANDILY	HARMONY	HAUTBOY
GRUYERE	GUSHERS	HAINAUT	HANDING	HARNESS	HAUTEUR
GRYPHON	GUSHING	HAIRCUT	HANDLED	HARPIES	HAVE-A-
G-STRING	GUSSETS	HAIRDOS	HANDLER	HARPING	GO
GUANACO	GUSTIER	HAIRIER	HANDLES	HARPINS	HAWKBIT
GUANASE	GUSTILY	HAIRNET	HANDOUT	HARPIST	HAWKERS
GUANINE	GUSTING	HAIRPIN	HANDSAW	HARPOON	HAWKING
GUARANI	GUTLESS	HAITIAN	HANDSEL	HARRIED	HAWKINS
GUARDED	GUTSIER	HAITINK	HANDSET	HARRIER	HAWKISH
GUARDER	GUTTATE	HAKLUYT	HANDS-ON	HARROWS	HAWORTH
GUAYULE	GUTTERS	HALAKAH	HANDS UP	HARSHER	HAWSERS
GUDGEON	GUTTING	HALAKIC	HANGARS	HARSHLY	HAYCOCK
GUESSED	GUVNORS	HALAVAH	HANGDOG	HARSLET	HAYFORK
GUESSER	GUZZLED	HALBERD	HANGERS	HARTLEY	HAYRACK
GUESSES	GUZZLER	HALCYON	HANGING	HARVARD	HAYSEED
GUESTED	GWALIOR	HALDANE	HANGMAN	HARVEST	HAYWARD
GUFFAWS	GWYNEDD	HALF-CUT	HANGMEN	HARWICH	HAYWIRE
GUIDING	GWYNIAD	HALFWAY	HANGOUT	HARYANA	HAZARDS
GUILDER	GYMNAST	HALF WIT	HANG-UPS	HAS BEEN	HAZIEST
GUINEAN	GYMSLIP	HALF-WIT	HANKIES	HAS-BEEN	HAZLITT
GUINEAS	GYPPING	HALIBUT	HANOVER	HASHING	HEADERS
GUIPURE	GYPSIES	HALIDOM	HANSARD	HASHISH	HEADIER
GUISING	GYRATED	HALIFAX	HANSOMS	HASHTAG	HEADILY
GUITARS	GYRATOR	HALLWAY	HANUMAN	HASIDIC	HEADING
GUIYANG		HALOGEN	HANYANG	HASIDIM	HEADMAN
GUIZHOU	**H**	HALTERE	HA'PENNY	HASSELT	HEADMEN
GUJARAT	HAARLEM	HALTERS	HAPLESS	HASSIUM	HEADPIN
GULCHES	HABDABS	HALTING	HAPLITE	HASSLED	HEADSET
GULDENS	HABITAT	HALVING	HAPLOID	HASSLES	HEADWAY
GULLETS	HABITED	HALYARD	HAP'ORTH	HASSOCK	HEALERS
GULLIES	HABITUE	HAMADAN	HAPPIER	HASTATE	HEALING
GULLING	HABITUS	HAMBURG	HAPPILY	HASTIER	HEALTHS
GULPING	HACHURE	HAMELIN	HAPTENE	HASTILY	HEALTHY
GUMBOIL	HACKBUT	HAMHUNG	HARAPPA	HATBAND	HEAPING
GUMBOOT	HACKERS	HAMITIC	HARBOUR	HATCHED	HEARING
GUMDROP	HACKING	HAMLETS	HARDEST	HATCHEL	HEARKEN
GUMMIER	HACKLER	HAMMERS	HARDIER	HATCHER	HEARSAY
GUMMING	HACKLES	HAMMING	HARDILY	HATCHES	HEARSES
GUMMITE	HACKNEY	HAMMOCK	HARDING	HATCHET	HEARTEN
GUMSHOE	HACKSAW	HAMMOND	HARD NUT	HATEFUL	HEARTHS
GUM TREE	HADAWAY	HAMPDEN	HARD-ONS	HATLESS	HEATERS
GUNBOAT	HADDOCK	HAMPERS	HARD PAD	HATLIKE	HEATHEN
GUNDOGS	HADRIAN	HAMPTON	HARDPAN	HATPINS	HEATHER

HEATING	HEMLOCK	HIDABLE	HOAXERS	HOMONYM	HOTFOOT
HEAVENS	HEMMING	HIDALGO	HOAXING	HONESTY	HOTHEAD
HEAVIER	HENBANE	HIDEOUS	HOBBEMA	HONEYED	HOTLINE
HEAVIES	HENCOOP	HIDINGS	HOBBIES	HONIARA	HOT LINE
HEAVILY	HEN COOP	HIELAND	HOBBISM	HONITON	HOT LINK
HEAVING	HENDRIX	HIGHBOY	HOBBIST	HONKIES	HOTNESS
HEBETIC	HENGELO	HIGHEST	HOBBLED	HONKING	HOTPOTS
HEBRAIC	HENGIST	HIGH HAT	HOBBLER	HONOURS	HOT RODS
HEBREWS	HENNERY	HIGH TEA	HOBLIKE	HOODLUM	HOT SEAT
HECCERS	HENPECK	HIGHWAY	HOBNAIL	HOODOOS	HOT SPOT
HECKLED	HEPARIN	HIJACKS	HOBOISM	HOOGHLY	HOTSPUR
HECKLER	HEPATIC	HILBERT	HOBOKEN	HOOKAHS	HOTTEST
HECTARE	HEPBURN	HILLARY	HOCKING	HOOKERS	HOTTING
HEDGING	HEPTANE	HILLERY	HOCKNEY	HOOKIES	HOUDINI
HEDONIC	HEPTOSE	HILLIER	HODEIDA	HOOKING	HOUMOUS
HEEDFUL	HERALDS	HILLMAN	HODGKIN	HOOKUPS	HOUNDED
HEEDING	HERBAGE	HILLOCK	HOEDOWN	HOORAYS	HOUNDER
HEELING	HERBALS	HIMSELF	HOELIKE	HOOTERS	HOUSING
HEELTAP	HERBERT	HINDGUT	HOFFMAN	HOOTING	HOUSMAN
HEERLEN	HERDING	HINGING	HOGARTH	HOOVERS	HOUSTON
HEFTIER	HEREDES	HINTING	HOGBACK	HOPEFUL	HOUTING
HEFTILY	HERETIC	HIONATE	HOGFISH	HOPHEAD	HOVERED
HEGUMEN	HERISAU	HIPBATH	HOGGING	HOPKINS	HOVERER
HEIFERS	HERITOR	HIPBONE	HOGGISH	HOPLITE	HOWBEIT
HEIFETZ	HERMITS	HIPLESS	HOGLIKE	HOPPERS	HOWDAHS
HEIGH-HO	HERNIAL	HIPLIKE	HOGNOSE	HOPPING	HOWEVER
HEIGHTS	HERNIAS	HIPPEST	HOGWASH	HOPPLER	HOWLAND
HEINOUS	HEROICS	HIPPIES	HOGWEED	HOPSACK	HOWLERS
HEIRDOM	HEROINE	HIPSTER	HOISTED	HORDEIN	HOWLING
HEIRESS	HEROISM	HIRABLE	HOISTER	HORDERN	HOYDENS
HEISTER	HERONRY	HIRCINE	HOKONUI	HORIZON	HOYLAKE
HEITIKI	HERRICK	HIRSUTE	HOKUSAI	HORMONE	HSIA-MEN
HELICAL	HERRING	HIRUDIN	HOLDALL	HORNETS	HSINING
HELICES	HERSELF	HIS NIBS	HOLDERS	HORNIER	HSU-CHOU
HELICON	HERTZOG	HISSING	HOLDING	HORNILY	HUAINAN
HELIPAD	HESIONE	HISTOID	HOLD OUT	HORRIFY	HUAI-NAN
HELLBOX	HESSIAN	HISTONE	HOLDUPS	HORRORS	HUBBIES
HELLCAT	HESSITE	HISTORY	HOLIBUT	HORSENS	HUBCAPS
HELLENE	HETAERA	HITACHI	HOLIDAY	HORSIER	HUDDLED
HELLERY	HETAIRA	HITCHED	HOLIEST	HORSILY	HUDDLER
HELLION	HEXADIC	HITCHER	HOLLAND	HOSANNA	HUDDLES
HELLISH	HEXAGON	HITCHES	HOLLERS	HOSIERS	HUFFIER
HELLUVA	HEXAPLA	HIT LIST	HOLLOWS	HOSIERY	HUFFILY
HELMAND	HEXAPOD	HITTING	HOLMIUM	HOSPICE	HUFFING
HELMETS	HEXOSAN	HITTITE	HOLSTER	HOSTAGE	HUFFISH
HELOISE	HEYDUCK	HOARDED	HOLY SEE	HOSTELS	HUGGING
HELOTRY	HEYSHAM	HOARDER	HOMBURG	HOSTESS	HUHEHOT
HELPFUL	HEYWOOD	HOARIER	HOMERIC	HOSTILE	HULKING
HELPING	HIALEAH	HOARILY	HOME RUN	HOSTING	HULLING
HEMIOLA	HIBACHI	HOARSEN	HOMIEST	HOSTLER	HUMANLY
HEMIPOD	HICCUPS	HOARSER	HOMINID	HOTBEDS	HUMBLED
HEMLINE	HICKORY	HOATZIN	HOMOLOG	HOT DOGS	HUMBLER

HUMBUGS	HYALITE	ILL-BRED	INANELY	INFLATE	INSPIRE
HUMDRUM	HYALOID	ILLEGAL	INANITY	INFLECT	INSTALL
HUMERAL	HYBRIDS	ILLICIT	INAPTLY	INFLICT	INSTANT
HUMERUS	HYDATID	ILLNESS	IN A	INFLOWS	INSTATE
HUMIDLY	HYDRANT	ILL WILL	WORD	INFRACT	INSTEAD
HUMIDOR	HYDRATE	IMAGERY	INBOARD	INFUSED	INSTEPS
HUMMING	HYDRIDE	IMAGINE	INBOUND	INFUSER	INSULAR
HUMMOCK	HYDROID	IMAGISM	INBREED	INGENUE	INSULIN
HUMORAL	HYGIENE	IMAGIST	INCENSE	INGESTA	INSULTS
HUMOURS	HYMNALS	IMAMATE	INCHING	INGOING	INSURED
HUMPING	HYMNING	IMBIBED	INCIPIT	INGRAIN	INSURER
HUNCHED	HYPED UP	IMBIBER	INCISED	INGRATE	INSWING
HUNCHES	HYPHENS	IMBRUTE	INCISOR	INGRESS	INTAKES
HUNDRED	HYPONYM	IMBUING	INCITED	IN-GROUP	INTEGER
HUNGARY		IMITATE	INCITER	INGROWN	INTENSE
HUNGNAM	**I**	IMMENSE	INCLINE	INHABIT	INTERIM
HUNKERS	IAMBICS	IMMERSE	INCLOSE	INHALED	INTERNS
HUNLIKE	IAPETUS	IMMORAL	INCLUDE	INHALER	INTIMAL
HUNNISH	IBERIAN	IMMURED	INCOMES	INHERIT	INTONED
HUNTERS	ICE AGES	IMPACTS	INCROSS	INHIBIT	INTONER
HUNTING	ICEBALL	IMPALAS	INCUBUS	IN-HOUSE	INTROIT
HURDLED	ICEBERG	IMPALED	INCURVE	INHUMAN	INTRUDE
HURDLER	ICE CAPS	IMPALER	INDENTS	INHUMER	INTRUST
HURDLES	ICE-COLD	IMPANEL	IN DEPTH	INITIAL	INURING
HURLING	ICEFALL	IMPASSE	IN-DEPTH	INJURED	INUTILE
HURRAYS	ICELAND	IMPASTE	INDEXED	INJURER	IN VACUO
HURRIED	ICE PACK	IMPASTO	INDEXER	INKATHA	INVADED
HURTFUL	ICE PICK	IMPEACH	INDEXES	INKIEST	INVADER
HURTING	ICE RINK	IMPEDED	INDIANA	INKLING	INVALID
HURTLED	ICHNITE	IMPEDER	INDIANS	INKPADS	INVEIGH
HUSBAND	ICICLED	IMPERIL	INDICAN	INKWELL	INVERSE
HUSHABY	ICICLES	IMPETUS	INDICIA	INLAYER	INVITED
HUSHING	ICINESS	IMPIETY	INDOORS	INMATES	INVITER
HUSKIER	ICTERIC	IMPINGE	INDORSE	INNARDS	IN VITRO
HUSKIES	ICTERUS	IMPIOUS	INDOXYL	INNERVE	INVOICE
HUSKILY	ID CARDS	IMPLANT	INDRAWN	INNINGS	INVOKED
HUSSARS	IDEALLY	IMPLEAD	INDUCED	IN ORDER	INVOKER
HUSSEIN	IDEATUM	IMPLIED	INDUCER	INQUEST	INVOLVE
HUSSIES	IDENTIC	IMPLODE	INDULGE	INQUIET	INWARDS
HUSSISM	IDIOTIC	IMPLORE	INEPTLY	INQUIRE	INWEAVE
HUSSITE	IDOLIZE	IMPORTS	INERTIA	INQUIRY	IODIZER
HUSTLED	IDYLLIC	IMPOSED	INERTLY	INROADS	IONIZED
HUSTLER	IGNEOUS	IMPOSER	INEXACT	INSECTS	IONIZER
HUTCHES	IGNITED	IMPOUND	INFANCY	INSERTS	IPOMOEA
HUTCHIE	IGNITER	IMPRESA	INFANTA	INSHORE	IPSWICH
HUTLIKE	IGNOBLE	IMPRESS	INFANTE	INSIDER	IQUIQUE
HUTMENT	IGNOBLY	IMPREST	INFANTS	INSIDES	IQUITOS
HUYGENS	IGNORED	IMPRINT	INFARCT	INSIGHT	IRANIAN
HWANG HO	IGNORER	IMPROVE	INFERNO	INSIPID	IRATELY
HYAENAS	IGUANAS	IMPULSE	INFIDEL	INSOFAR	IRELAND
HYAENIC	IKEBANA	IMPUTED	INFIELD	INSOLES	IRENICS
HYALINE	ILEITIS	IMPUTER	INFLAME	INSPECT	IRIDIUM

IRKSOME	JACK TAR	JESTERS	JOINTLY	JUNIPER	KEITLOA
IRKUTSK	JACOBIN	JESTING	JOLLIED	JUNKETS	KELVINS
IRON AGE	JACONET	JESUITS	JOLLIER	JUNKIES	KENDREW
IRONIES	JACUZZI	JETFOIL	JOLLIFY	JUNKING	KENNEDY
IRONING	JADEITE	JETPORT	JOLLILY	JUPITER	KENNELS
IRONIST	JAGGERY	JETTIES	JOLLITY	JURISTS	KENNING
IRON ORE	JAGGING	JETTING	JOLTING	JURY BOX	KENOSIS
ISCHIAL	JAGUARS	JEWFISH	JONESES	JURYMAN	KENOTIC
ISCHIUM	JAILERS	JEW'S-	JONQUIL	JUSSIVE	KENTISH
ISFAHAN	JAILING	EAR	JOSHING	JUSTICE	KERATIN
ISLAMIC	JAKARTA	JEZEBEL	JOSTLED	JUSTIFY	KERBING
ISLANDS	JALAPIC	JIANGSU	JOSTLER	JUTLAND	KERNELS
ISOBARS	JALISCO	JIANGXI	JOTTERS	JUTTING	KERNITE
ISOBATH	JAMAICA	JIBBING	JOTTING		KESTREL
ISOCHOR	JAMES II	JIGGERS	JOURNAL	**K**	KESWICK
ISOGAMY	JAMMIER	JIGGING	JOURNEY	KABADDI	KETCHES
ISOGENY	JAMMING	JIGGLED	JOURNOS	KAFFIRS	KETCHUP
ISOHYET	JANE DOE	JIGGLES	JOUSTED	KAFTANS	KETONIC
ISOLATE	JANGLED	JIGSAWS	JOUSTER	KAIFENG	KETOSIS
ISOLINE	JANGLER	JILTING	JOYLESS	KAINITE	KETTLES
ISONOMY	JANITOR	JIM CROW	JOYRIDE	KAISERS	KEYED UP
ISOTONE	JANUARY	JIMJAMS	JUBILEE	KALENDS	KEYHOLE
ISOTOPE	JARGONS	JIMMIES	JUDAEAN	KALININ	KEYNOTE
ISOTOPY	JARRING	JINGLED	JUDAICA	KALMUCK	KEY RING
ISOTRON	JASMINE	JINGLER	JUDAISM	KAMPALA	KHADDAR
ISRAELI	JAUNTED	JINGLES	JUDAIST	KANANGA	KHAKASS
ISSUING	JAVELIN	JINXING	JUDAIZE	KANNADA	KHALIFS
ISTHMUS	JAWBONE	JINZHOU	JUDASES	KANTIAN	KHALKHA
ISTRIAN	JAYWALK	JITTERS	JUDGING	KAOLACK	KHAMSIN
ITALIAN	JAZZIER	JITTERY	JUDOIST	KAPITZA	KHANATE
ITALICS	JAZZILY	JOBBERS	JUGGING	KARACHI	KHARKOV
ITCHIER	JAZZING	JOBBERY	JUGGLED	KARAKUL	KHERSON
ITCHING	JEALOUS	JOBBING	JUGGLER	KARBALA	KHINGAN
ITEMIZE	JEERING	JOBCLUB	JUGULAR	KARELIA	KHOISAN
ITERANT	JEHOVAH	JOBLESS	JUICIER	KAROSHI	KIANGSI
ITERATE	JEJUNAL	JOB LOTS	JUICILY	KARSTIC	KIANGSU
ITHACAN	JEJUNUM	JOCKEYS	JUICING	KASHGAR	KIBBUTZ
IVANOVO	JELLABA	JOCULAR	JUJITSU	KASHMIR	KICKING
IVORIAN	JELLIED	JODHPUR	JUJUBES	KASSALA	KICKOFF
IVORIES	JELLIES	JOGGING	JUKEBOX	KATANGA	KICK OFF
IZHEVSK	JELLIFY	JOGGLED	JUMBLED	KATSINA	KIDDERS
	JELLING	JOGGLER	JUMBLER	KATYDID	KIDDIES
J	JEMMIED	JOGGLES	JUMBLES	KAYAKER	KIDDING
JABBING	JEMMIES	JOG TROT	JUMPERS	KAYSERI	KIDNEYS
JACAMAR	JENNIES	JOHN DOE	JUMPIER	KEATING	KIDSKIN
JACKALS	JERICHO	JOHNSON	JUMPILY	KEELING	KILDARE
JACKASS	JERKIER	JOINDER	JUMPING	KEELSON	KILLERS
JACKDAW	JERKILY	JOINERS	JUMP-OFF	KEENEST	KILLICK
JACKETS	JERKING	JOINERY	JUNDIAI	KEENING	KILLING
JACKING	JERKINS	JOINING	JUNGIAN	KEEPERS	KILLJOY
JACKPOT	JERK OFF	JOINTED	JUNGLES	KEEPING	KILOTON
JACKSON	JERSEYS	JOINTER	JUNIORS	KEEPNET	KILTERS

KIMONOS	KNOW-ALL	LACTATE	LA PALMA	LAXNESS	LEGENDS
KINDEST	KNOW-HOW	LACTEAL	LAPDOGS	LAYERED	LEGGIER
KINDLED	KNOWING	LACTONE	LAPLACE	LAYETTE	LEGGING
KINDLER	KNUCKLE	LACTOSE	LAPLAND	LAY-OFFS	LEGHORN
KINDRED	KNUCKLY	LACUNAE	LA PLATA	LAYOUTS	LEGIBLE
KINETIC	KOBARID	LACUNAR	LAPPING	LAZIEST	LEGIBLY
KINFOLK	KOBLENZ	LACUNAS	LAPSING	L-DRIVER	LEGIONS
KINGCUP	KOFTGAR	LADDERS	LAPWING	LEACHED	LEGLESS
KINGDOM	KOKANEE	LADDIES	LARCENY	LEACHER	LEGNICA
KINGPIN	KOKOBEH	LADDISH	LARCHES	LEADERS	LEG-PULL
KINKIER	KOLDING	LADINGS	LARDERS	LEADING	LEGROOM
KINKILY	KOLKHOZ	LADLING	LARDING	LEAD-INS	LEG ROOM
KINNOCK	KOLOMNA	LAGGARD	LARGELY	LEAD OFF	LEG SIDE
KINSHIP	KONGONI	LAGGING	LARGESS	LEAFAGE	LEGUMES
KINSMAN	KOOKIER	LAGOONS	LARGEST	LEAFIER	LEGUMIN
KINSMEN	KOONING	LAICISM	LARGISH	LEAFLET	LEGWORK
KIPPERS	KOPECKS	LAICIZE	LARIATS	LEAGUED	LE HAVRE
KIPPING	KOPEISK	LALLANS	LARKING	LEAGUES	LEIPZIG
KIRGHIZ	KOUPREY	LAMAISM	LARWOOD	LEAKAGE	LEISTER
KIRUNDI	KOWLOON	LAMAIST	LASAGNA	LEAKIER	LEISURE
KISSERS	KREFELD	LAMBADA	LASAGNE	LEAKING	LEITRIM
KISSING	KREMLIN	LAMBAST	LA SALLE	LEANEST	LEMBERG
KIT BAGS	KRISHNA	LAMBENT	LA SCALA	LEANING	LEMMING
KITCHEN	KRYPTON	LAMBERT	LASCAUX	LEAN-TOS	LEMPIRA
KITSCHY	KUBELIK	LAMBETH	LASHING	LEAPING	LENDERS
KITTENS	KUBRICK	LAMBING	LASH OUT	LEARNED	LENDING
KITTIES	KUCHING	LAMELLA	LASH-UPS	LEARNER	LENGTHS
KITTING	KUMAYRI	LAMENTS	LASSOED	LEASHES	LENGTHY
KLAXONS	KUMQUAT	LAMINAR	LASSOER	LEASING	LENIENT
KLEENEX	KUNDERA	LAMPERN	LAST END	LEATHER	LENTIGO
KNAPPER	KUNMING	LAMPOON	LASTING	LEAVENS	LENTILS
KNAVERY	KUNZITE	LAMPREY	LATAKIA	LEAVING	LEONINE
KNAVISH	KURDISH	LANCERS	LATCHED	LEBANON	LEOPARD
KNEADED	KUTAISI	LANCETS	LATCHES	LECHERS	LEOTARD
KNEADER	KUWAITI	LANCHOW	LATCHET	LECHERY	LEPANTO
KNEECAP	KWANGJU	LANCING	LATENCY	LECTERN	LEPORID
KNEEING	KWAZULU	LANDAUS	LATERAL	LECTION	LEPROSE
KNEELED	KWEILIN	LANDING	LATHERY	LECTURE	LEPROSY
KNEEPAD	KYANIZE	LANDTAG	LATIMER	LEDGERS	LEPROUS
KNEES UP		LANGRES	LATRINE	LEECHES	LERWICK
KNIFING	L	LANGUID	LATTICE	LEERIER	LESBIAN
KNIGHTS		LANGUOR	LATVIAN	LEERING	LESIONS
KNITTED	LABELED	LANIARY	LAUDING	LEE TIDE	LESOTHO
KNITTER	LABIALS	LANKEST	LAUGHED	LEEWARD	LESSEES
KNOBBLY	LABIATE	LANKIER	LAUGHER	LEFTIES	LESSONS
KNOCKED	LABOURS	LANKILY	LAUNDER	LEFTISM	LESSORS
KNOCKER	LABROID	LANOLIN	LAUNDRY	LEFTIST	LETDOWN
KNOCK-ON	LACIEST	LANSING	LAURELS	LEGALLY	LETTERS
KNOCK-UP	LACKEYS	LANTANA	LAWLESS	LEGASPI	LETTING
KNOSSOS	LACKING	LANTERN	LAW LORD	LEGATEE	LETTUCE
KNOTTED	LACONIC	LANYARD	LAWSUIT	LEGATES	LEUCINE
KNOTTER	LACQUER	LAOTIAN	LAWYERS	LEGATOR	LEUCITE
	LACTASE				

LEUCOMA	LIMPEST	LIVABLE	LOLLAND	LOWBROW	LURCHER
LEVATOR	LIMPETS	LIVENED	LOLLARD	LOW BROW	LURCHES
LEVELED	LIMPING	LIVENER	LOLLIES	LOW DOWN	LURGIES
LEVERED	LIMPKIN	LIVIDLY	LOLLING	LOW-DOWN	LURIDLY
LEVERET	LIMPOPO	LIVINGS	LOMBARD	LOWERED	LURKING
LEVYING	LIMULUS	LIVONIA	LONG AGO	LOWLAND	LUSATIA
LEXICAL	LINABLE	LIVORNO	LONGBOW	LOWLIER	LUSTFUL
LEXICON	LINARES	LIZARDS	LONGEST	LOW LIFE	LUSTILY
LIAISED	LINCOLN	LOADING	LONGING	LOWNESS	LUSTING
LIAISON	LINCTUS	LOAFERS	LONGISH	LOW-RISE	LUSTRAL
LIANOID	LINDANE	LOAFING	LONG TON	LOW TIDE	LUSTRES
LIASSIC	LINDENS	LOANING	LOOFAHS	LOYALLY	LUTEOUS
LIBBERS	LINEAGE	LOATHED	LOOKERS	LOYALTY	LUTHIER
LIBELED	LINEATE	LOATHER	LOOKING	LOZENGE	LUVVIES
LIBERAL	LINEMAN	LOATHLY	LOOKOUT	L-PLATES	LYCHEES
LIBEREC	LINEMEN	LOBBIED	LOOK OUT	LUALABA	LYCHNIS
LIBERIA	LINE-OUT	LOBBIES	LOOMING	LUBBOCK	LYCOPOD
LIBERTY	LINEUPS	LOBBING	LOONIER	LUCERNE	LYDDITE
LIBIDOS	LINGCOD	LOBBYER	LOONIES	LUCIDLY	LYING-IN
LIBRARY	LINGOES	LOBELIA	LOOPING	LUCIFER	LYNCEAN
LIBRATE	LINGUAL	LOBSTER	LOOSELY	LUCKIER	LYNCHED
LICENCE	LININGS	LOBULAR	LOOSEST	LUCKILY	LYNCHER
LICENSE	LINKAGE	LOCALES	LOOSING	LUCKNOW	LYRICAL
LICKING	LINKING	LOCALLY	LOOTERS	LUDDITE	
LIE-DOWN	LINKMAN	LOCARNO	LOOTING	LUFFING	**M**
LIESTAL	LINKUPS	LOCATED	LOPPING	LUGANDA	MACABRE
LIFTING	LINNETS	LOCATER	LOQUATS	LUGANSK	MACADAM
LIFTOFF	LINOCUT	LOCHIAL	LORDING	LUGGAGE	MACAQUE
LIFT-OFF	LINSANG	LOCKAGE	LORELEI	LUGGERS	MACEDON
LIGHTED	LINSEED	LOCKERS	LORGNON	LUGGING	MACHETE
LIGHTEN	LINTELS	LOCKETS	LORIENT	LUGHOLE	MACHINE
LIGHTER	LIONESS	LOCKING	LORRIES	LUGSAIL	MACLEAN
LIGHTLY	LIONIZE	LOCKJAW	LOSABLE	LUGWORM	MACRAME
LIGNIFY	LIPETSK	LOCKNUT	LOSINGS	LULLABY	MACULAR
LIGNITE	LIP-READ	LOCKOUT	LOTIONS	LULLING	MADDEST
LIGROIN	LIQUATE	LOCKUPS	LOTTERY	LUMBAGO	MADEIRA
LIGULAR	LIQUEFY	LOCOISM	LOTTING	LUMENAL	MADE OUT
LIGURIA	LIQUEUR	LOCULAR	LOTUSES	LUMPIER	MADISON
LIKABLE	LIQUIDS	LOCUSTS	LOUDEST	LUMPILY	MADNESS
LIKENED	LISBURN	LODGERS	LOUNGED	LUMPING	MADONNA
LIKINGS	LISIEUX	LODGING	LOUNGER	LUMPISH	MADRONA
LILTING	LISPING	LOFTIER	LOUNGES	LUMP SUM	MADURAI
LIMACON	LISTING	LOFTILY	LOURDES	LUMUMBA	MADWORT
LIMBATE	LITCHIS	LOFTING	LOURING	LUNATIC	MAENADS
LIMBURG	LITERAL	LOGBOOK	LOUSIER	LUNCHED	MAESTRI
LIMEADE	LITHELY	LOGGERS	LOUSILY	LUNCHER	MAESTRO
LIMIEST	LITHEST	LOGGIAS	LOUSING	LUNCHES	MAFIOSO
LIMINAL	LITHIUM	LOGGING	LOUTISH	LUNETTE	MAGENTA
LIMITED	LITHOID	LOGICAL	LOUVAIN	LUNGING	MAGGOTS
LIMITER	LITOTES	LOGIEST	LOUVRES	LUOYANG	MAGGOTY
LIMNING	LITTERS	LOGJAMS	LOVABLE	LUPULIN	MAGHREB
LIMOGES	LITURGY	LOGWOOD	LOWBORN	LURCHED	MAGICAL

MAGNATE	MAMMIES	MARACAY	MASBATE	MCENROE	MENTHOL
MAGNETO	MAMMOTH	MARASCA	MASCARA	MEADOWS	MENTION
MAGNETS	MANACLE	MARATHA	MASCOTS	MEALIER	MENTORS
MAGNIFY	MANAGED	MARATHI	MASHHAD	MEANDER	MEOWING
MAGNUMS	MANAGER	MARBLED	MASHING	MEANEST	MERCIES
MAGPIES	MANAGUA	MARBLER	MASKING	MEANING	MERCURY
MAHATMA	MANAKIN	MARBLES	MASONIC	MEASLES	MERGERS
MAHFOUZ	MANATEE	MARBURG	MASONRY	MEASURE	MERGING
MAHICAN	MANDATE	MARCHED	MASQUES	MEATIER	MERITED
MAH JONG	MANDELA	MARCHER	MASSAGE	MEATILY	MERMAID
MAHONIA	MANDREL	MARCHES	MASSAWA	MEDDLED	MERRIER
MAHOUTS	MANGERS	MAREMMA	MASSEUR	MEDDLER	MERRILY
MAIDENS	MANGIER	MARGATE	MASSIFS	MEDIACY	MESARCH
MAILBAG	MANGILY	MARGAUX	MASSING	MEDIANS	MESHING
MAILBOX	MANGLED	MARGINS	MASSIVE	MEDIANT	MESSAGE
MAILING	MANGLER	MARIBOR	MASTERS	MEDIATE	MESSIAH
MAILMAN	MANGLES	MARIMBA	MASTERY	MEDICAL	MESSIER
MAILMEN	MANGOES	MARINAS	MASTIFF	MEDICOS	MESSILY
MAIMING	MANHOLE	MARINER	MASTOID	MEDIUMS	MESSINA
MAINTOP	MANHOOD	MARINES	MASURIA	MEDLARS	MESSING
MAJESTY	MANHOUR	MARITAL	MATADOR	MEDLEYS	MESS-UPS
MAJORCA	MANHUNT	MARKERS	MATCHED	MEDULLA	MESTIZA
MAJORED	MANIACS	MARKETS	MATCHES	MEEKEST	MESTIZO
MAJORLY	MANIKIN	MARKHOR	MATHURA	MEERKAT	METALED
MAKASAR	MANIPUR	MARKING	MATINEE	MEETING	METAMER
MAKE OUT	MAN JACK	MARKUPS	MATLOCK	MEGATON	METEORS
MAKES DO	MANKIND	MARLINE	MATRONS	MEIOSIS	METERED
MAKINGS	MANKINI	MARLINS	MATTERS	MEIOTIC	METHANE
MAKURDI	MANLIKE	MARLITE	MATTING	MEISSEN	METHODS
MALABAR	MAN-MADE	MARMITE	MATTINS	MELANGE	METIERS
MALACCA	MANNERS	MARMOTS	MATTOCK	MELANIC	METONYM
MALAISE	MANNING	MAROONS	MATURED	MELANIN	METOPIC
MALARIA	MANNISH	MARQUEE	MAUDLIN	MELILLA	METRICS
MALATYA	MANNITE	MARQUIS	MAULING	MELILOT	METRIFY
MALAYAN	MANNOSE	MARRIED	MAUNDER	MELISMA	METRIST
MALEATE	MANRESA	MARRIER	MAWKISH	MELODIC	MEXICAN
MALEFIC	MANROPE	MARRING	MAXILLA	MELTAGE	MIAOWED
MALINES	MANSARD	MARROWS	MAXIMAL	MELTING	MIASMAL
MALINKE	MANSELL	MARSALA	MAXIMIN	MEMBERS	MIASMAS
MALLARD	MANSION	MARSHAL	MAXIMUM	MEMENTO	MICELLE
MALLETS	MANTLED	MARSHES	MAXIMUS	MEMOIRS	MICHAEL
MALLEUS	MANTLES	MARTENS	MAXWELL	MEMPHIS	MICKEYS
MALLOWS	MANUALS	MARTIAL	MAY DAYS	MENACED	MICROBE
MALMSEY	MANUKAU	MARTIAN	MAYENNE	MENACER	MICRONS
MALTASE	MANURED	MARTINI	MAYFAIR	MENACES	MIDDENS
MALTESE	MANURER	MARTINS	MAYORAL	MENAGES	MIDDLE C
MALTING	MANX CAT	MARTYRS	MAYOTTE	MENDERS	MIDGETS
MALTOSE	MANXMAN	MARTYRY	MAYPOLE	MENDING	MIDIRON
MALVERN	MAOISTS	MARVELS	MAYWEED	MENDIPS	MIDLAND
MAMILLA	MAPPING	MARXIAN	MAZURKA	MENDOZA	MIDMOST
MAMMALS	MARABOU	MARXISM	MAZZARD	MENFOLK	MIDRIFF
MAMMARY	MARACAS	MARXIST	MBABANE	MENIALS	MIDTERM

MIDWEEK	MINIVER	MITOSIS	MONDAYS	MORTISE	MUD PIES
MIDWEST	MINIVET	MITOTIC	MONEYED	MORULAR	MUEZZIN
MIDWIFE	MINNOWS	MITTENS	MONGOLS	MOSAICS	MUFFING
MIDYEAR	MINORCA	MITZVAH	MONGREL	MOSELEY	MUFFINS
MIGHTN'T	MINSTER	MIXABLE	MONITOR	MOSELLE	MUFFLED
MIGRANT	MINTAGE	MIXED UP	MONKEYS	MOSEYED	MUFFLER
MIGRATE	MINTING	MIXTURE	MONKISH	MOSLEMS	MUGGERS
MIKADOS	MINUETS	MIZORAM	MONOCLE	MOSOTHO	MUGGIER
MILAZZO	MINUSES	MOANERS	MONOMER	MOSQUES	MUGGILY
MILDEST	MINUTED	MOANING	MONSOON	MOSSIER	MUGGING
MILDEWY	MINUTES	MOBBING	MONSTER	MOTHERS	MUGGINS
MILEAGE	MINXISH	MOBILES	MONTAGE	MOTIONS	MUGSHOT
MILIARY	MIOCENE	MOBSTER	MONTANA	MOTIVES	MUGWORT
MILIEUS	MIRACLE	MOCKERS	MONTANE	MOTORED	MUGWUMP
MILIEUX	MIRADOR	MOCKERY	MONTHLY	MOTTLED	MULATTO
MILITIA	MIRAGES	MOCKING	MOOCHED	MOTTOES	MULCHED
MILKERS	MIRRORS	MOCK-UPS	MOOCHER	MOUFLON	MULCTED
MILKIER	MISCALL	MODALLY	MOODIER	MOUILLE	MULLAHS
MILKILY	MISCAST	MOD CONS	MOODILY	MOULDED	MULLEIN
MILKING	MISDEAL	MODELED	MOONEYE	MOULDER	MULLETS
MILKMAN	MISDEED	MODERAS	MOONILY	MOULTED	MULLING
MILKMEN	MISERLY	MODERNS	MOONING	MOULTER	MULLION
MILK RUN	MISFILE	MODESTY	MOONLIT	MOUNTED	MULLITE
MILKSOP	MISFIRE	MODICUM	MOONSET	MOUNTER	MUMBLED
MILLDAM	MISFITS	MODISTE	MOORAGE	MOUNTIE	MUMBLER
MILLERS	MISHAPS	MODULAR	MOORHEN	MOURNED	MUMMERS
MILLINE	MISHEAR	MODULES	MOORING	MOURNER	MUMMERY
MILLING	MISKOLC	MODULUS	MOORISH	MOUSERS	MUMMIES
MILLION	MISLAID	MOFETTE	MOOTING	MOUSIER	MUMMIFY
MILLRUN	MISLEAD	MOGADOR	MOPPETS	MOUSING	MUMMING
MIMESIS	MISNAME	MOGGIES	MOPPING	MOUSSES	MUNCHED
MIMETIC	MISPLAY	MOGILEV	MORAINE	MOUTHED	MUNCHER
MIMICRY	MISREAD	MOHICAN	MORALLY	MOUTHER	MUNDANE
MINABLE	MISRULE	MOIDORE	MORAVIA	MOVABLE	MUNSTER
MINARET	MISSALS	MOISTEN	MORCEAU	MOVABLY	MUNTJAC
MINCERS	MISSIES	MOISTLY	MORDANT	MOVIOLA	MURDERS
MINCING	MISSILE	MOLDIER	MORDENT	MUBARAK	MURDOCH
MINDERS	MISSING	MOLDING	MORDVIN	MUCKIER	MURKIER
MINDFUL	MISSION	MOLDOVA	MOREISH	MUCKILY	MURKILY
MINDING	MISSIVE	MOLLIFY	MORELIA	MUCKING	MURMURS
MINDORO	MISTAKE	MOLLUSC	MORELLO	MUD BATH	MURRAIN
MINERAL	MISTERS	MOLOKAI	MORELOS	MUDDIED	MUSCLED
MINGIER	MISTILY	MOLTING	MORGUES	MUDDIER	MUSCLES
MINGLED	MISTIME	MOMBASA	MORMONS	MUDDILY	MUSEFUL
MINIBAR	MISTING	MOMENTA	MORNING	MUDDING	MUSEUMS
MINIBUS	MISTOOK	MOMENTS	MOROCCO	MUDDLED	MUSHIER
MINICAB	MISTRAL	MOMMIES	MORONIC	MUDDLER	MUSHILY
MINIMAL	MISUSED	MONACAN	MORROWS	MUDDLES	MUSICAL
MINIMAX	MISUSER	MONADIC	MORSELS	MUDFISH	MUSKETS
MINIMUM	MISUSES	MONARCH	MORTALS	MUDFLAP	MUSKIER
MINIMUS	MITCHUM	MONARDA	MORTARS	MUDFLAT	MUSKRAT
MINIONS	MITHRAS	MONCTON	MORTIFY	MUDPACK	MUSLIMS

MUSSELS	NALCHIK	NEGATED	NEW CHUM	NIVEOUS	NOTICES
MUSSING	NAMABLE	NEGATOR	NEW DEAL	NO BALLS	NOTIONS
MUSTANG	NAME DAY	NEGLECT	NEW MOON	NOBBLED	NO TRUMP
MUSTARD	NAMIBIA	NEGRESS	NEWNESS	NOBBLER	NO-TRUMP
MUSTERS	NANJING	NEGRITO	NEWPORT	NOBLEST	NOUGATS
MUSTIER	NANKEEN	NEGROES	NEWTOWN	NOCTUID	NOUGHTS
MUSTILY	NANKING	NEGROID	NEW TOWN	NOCTULE	NOURISH
MUTABLE	NANNIES	NEIGHED	NEW WAVE	NOCTURN	NOUVEAU
MUTABLY	NANNING	NEITHER	NEW YEAR	NODDING	NOVALIS
MUTAGEN	NANTONG	NELLIES	NEW YORK	NODDLES	NOVELLA
MUTANTS	NANTUNG	NELUMBO	NEXUSES	NODICAL	NOVELLE
MUTTONY	NAPHTHA	NEMATIC	NIAGARA	NO DOUBT	NOVELTY
MUZZIER	NAPKINS	NEMESES	NIBBLED	NODULAR	NOVICES
MUZZILY	NAPPIES	NEMESIS	NIBBLER	NODULES	NOVI SAD
MUZZLED	NAPPING	NEOCENE	NIBBLES	NO ENTRY	NOWHERE
MUZZLER	NARKIER	NEOGAEA	NICKELS	NOGGING	NOXIOUS
MUZZLES	NARKING	NEOGENE	NICKING	NOGGINS	NOZZLES
MYALGIA	NARRATE	NEOLITH	NICOBAR	NOISIER	NUANCES
MYALGIC	NARROWS	NEONATE	NICOSIA	NOISILY	NUCLEAR
MYALISM	NARTHEX	NEOTENY	NIFTIER	NOISOME	NUCLEIN
MYANMAR	NARWHAL	NEOTYPE	NIFTILY	NOMADIC	NUCLEON
MYCENAE	NASALLY	NEOZOIC	NIGELLA	NOMBRIL	NUCLEUS
MYCOSIS	NASCENT	NEPHEWS	NIGERIA	NOMINAL	NUCLIDE
MYCOTIC	NASTIER	NEPHRON	NIGGARD	NOMINEE	NUDGING
MYELOID	NASTILY	NEPOTIC	NIGGERS	NONAGON	NUDISTS
MYELOMA	NATIONS	NEPTUNE	NIGGLED	NON-IRON	NUGGETS
MYIASIS	NATIVES	NEREIDS	NIGGLER	NONPLUS	NUGGETY
MYKONOS	NATTIER	NERITIC	NIGHTIE	NON-PROS	NULLIFY
MYNHEER	NATTILY	NERVATE	NIGHTLY	NONSTOP	NULLITY
MYOLOGY	NATURAL	NERVIER	NIIGATA	NON STOP	NULL SET
MYOTOME	NATURES	NERVILY	NILOTIC	NONSUIT	NUMBERS
MYRIADS	NAUGHTY	NERVINE	NIMBLER	NON USER	NUMBING
MYRTLES	NAURUAN	NERVING	NINEPIN	NOODLES	NUMERAL
MYSTERY	NAVARRE	NERVOUS	NINNIES	NOONDAY	NUMMARY
MYSTICS	NAVVIES	NERVURE	NIOBITE	NO-PLACE	NUNATAK
MYSTIFY	NAYARIT	NEST EGG	NIOBIUM	NORFOLK	NUNAVUT
	NEAREST	NESTING	NIOBOUS	NORMANS	NUN BUOY
N	NEARING	NESTLED	NIPPERS	NORWICH	NUNCIOS
NABBING	NEATEST	NESTLER	NIPPIER	NOSEBAG	NUNNERY
NACELLE	NEBULAE	NETBALL	NIPPILY	NOSEGAY	NUPTIAL
NAEVOID	NEBULAR	NETSUKE	NIPPING	NOSHING	NURSERY
NAGGERS	NEBULAS	NETTING	NIPPLES	NOSIEST	NURSING
NAGGING	NECKING	NETTLED	NIRVANA	NOSTRIL	NURTURE
NAHUATL	NECKLET	NETTLES	NITEROI	NOSTRUM	NUTCASE
NAIADES	NECKTIE	NETWORK	NITRATE	NOTABLE	NUTGALL
NAILING	NECROSE	NEUROMA	NITRIDE	NOTABLY	NUTMEGS
NAIPAUL	NECTARY	NEURONE	NITRIFY	NOTCHED	NUTRIAS
NAIROBI	NEEDFUL	NEUTRAL	NITRILE	NOTCHES	NUTTIER
NAIVELY	NEEDIER	NEUTRON	NITRITE	NOTELET	NUTTILY
NAIVETE	NEEDING	NEWBORN	NITROSO	NOTEPAD	NUTTING
NAIVETY	NEEDLED	NEW BORN	NITROUS	NOTHING	NUTWOOD
NAKEDLY	NEEDLES	NEWBURY	NITWITS	NOTICED	NUZZLED

NYMPHAL	OCTUPLE	OMENTUM	OPTIMAL	OSMUNDA	OUTPLAY
NYMPHET	OCULIST	OMICRON	OPTIMUM	OSPREYS	OUTPORT
NYUNGAR	ODDBALL	OMINOUS	OPTIONS	OSSEOUS	OUTPOST
	ODDMENT	OMITTED	OPULENT	OSSETIA	OUTPOUR
O	ODDNESS	OMITTER	OPUNTIA	OSSETIC	OUTPUTS
OAKLAND	ODOROUS	OMNIBUS	OQUASSA	OSSICLE	OUTRAGE
OARFISH	ODYSSEY	ON A	ORACLES	OSSUARY	OUTRANK
OARLOCK	OEDIPAL	WHIM	ORALISM	OSTEOID	OUTRIDE
OARSMAN	OERSTED	ONE EYED	ORANGES	OSTEOMA	OUTRODE
OARSMEN	OESTRUS	ONENESS	ORATION	OSTIOLE	OUTSELL
OATCAKE	OFFBEAT	ONE-OFFS	ORATORS	OSTLERS	OUTSIDE
OATMEAL	OFFENCE	ONEROUS	ORATORY	OSTMARK	OUTSIZE
OBCONIC	OFFERED	ONESELF	ORBITAL	OSTOSIS	OUTSOLD
OBELISK	OFFERER	ONE-STAR	ORBITED	OSTRAVA	OUTSOLE
OBELIZE	OFFHAND	ONE STEP	ORCHARD	OSTRICH	OUTSTAY
OBESITY	OFFICER	ONE-STEP	ORCHIDS	OTOCYST	OUT-TAKE
OBEYING	OFFICES	ONETIME	ORCINOL	OTOLITH	OUTTALK
OBJECTS	OFFINGS	ON-GLIDE	ORDEALS	OTOLOGY	OUT-TRAY
OBLIGED	OFF-LOAD	ONGOING	ORDERED	OTRANTO	OUTVOTE
OBLIGEE	OFF-PEAK	ONITSHA	ORDERER	OTTOMAN	OUTWARD
OBLIGER	OFFSIDE	ON LEAVE	ORDERLY	OUABAIN	OUTWASH
OBLIGOR	OGREISH	ONSHORE	ORDINAL	OUGHTN'T	OUTWEAR
OBLIQUE	OHM'S	ON SIGHT	ORECTIC	OUR LADY	OUTWORK
OBLONGS	LAW	ON STAGE	OREGANO	OUR LORD	OUTWORN
OBLOQUY	OILBIRD	ONTARIO	ORGANIC	OURSELF	OVARIAN
OBOISTS	OILCANS	ONWARDS	ORGANON	OUSTERS	OVARIES
OBOVATE	OILIEST	OOLITIC	ORGANUM	OUSTING	OVATION
OBOVOID	OILRIGS	OOPHYTE	ORGANZA	OUTBACK	OVERACT
OBSCENE	OILSKIN	OOSPERM	ORGASMS	OUTCAST	OVERAGE
OBSCURE	OIL WELL	OOSPORE	ORIENTE	OUTCOME	OVERALL
OBSERVE	OINKING	OOTHECA	ORIFICE	OUTCROP	OVERARM
OBTRUDE	OKAYAMA	OOZIEST	ORIGAMI	OUTDATE	OVERAWE
OBVERSE	OKAYING	OPACITY	ORIGINS	OUTDONE	OVERBID
OBVIATE	OKINAWA	OPALINE	ORINOCO	OUTDOOR	OVERDID
OBVIOUS	OLD BOYS	OPEN-AIR	ORISONS	OUTFACE	OVERDUE
OCARINA	OLD HAND	OPEN DAY	ORIZABA	OUTFALL	OVERFLY
OCCIPUT	OLD LADY	OPENERS	ORKNEYS	OUTFITS	OVERJOY
OCCLUDE	OLD LAGS	OPENING	ORLANDO	OUTFLOW	OVERLAP
OCEANIA	OLD MAID	OPERAND	ORLEANS	OUTGREW	OVERLAY
OCEANIC	OLD NICK	OPERANT	OROGENY	OUTGROW	OVERLIE
OCELLAR	OLDSTER	OPERATE	OROLOGY	OUTHAUL	OVERMAN
OCELLUS	OLDTIME	OPHITIC	OROTUND	OUTINGS	OVERPAY
OCELOTS	OLDUVAI	OPIATES	ORPHANS	OUTLAST	OVERRAN
OCHROID	OLEFINE	OPINING	ORPHREY	OUTLAWS	OVERRUN
OCREATE	O LEVELS	OPINION	ORTOLAN	OUTLAYS	OVERSAW
OCTADIC	OLIVARY	OPOSSUM	ORVIETO	OUTLETS	OVERSEE
OCTAGON	OLIVINE	OPPOSED	OSCULAR	OUTLIER	OVERSET
OCTANES	OLOMOUC	OPPOSER	OSCULUM	OUTLINE	OVERSEW
OCTAVES	OLSZTYN	OPPRESS	OSHOGBO	OUTLIVE	OVERTAX
OCTOBER	OLYMPIA	OPSONIC	OSMIOUS	OUTLOOK	OVERTLY
OCTOPOD	OLYMPIC	OPSONIN	OSMOSIS	OUTMOST	OVERTOP
OCTOPUS	OLYMPUS	OPTICAL	OSMOTIC	OUTPACE	OVERUSE

OVIDUCT	PALATAL	PAPISTS	PARTIED	PAUCITY	PEELING
OVIFORM	PALATES	PAPOOSE	PARTIES	PAULINE	PEEPERS
OVULATE	PALAVER	PAPPIES	PARTING	PAULIST	PEEPING
OWN GOAL	PALE ALE	PAPPOSE	PARTITA	PAUNCHY	PEERAGE
OXALATE	PALERMO	PAPRIKA	PARTITE	PAUPERS	PEERESS
OXAZINE	PALETTE	PAPYRUS	PARTNER	PAUSING	PEERING
OXBLOOD	PALFREY	PARABLE	PARTOOK	PAVANES	PEEVING
OXCARTS	PALINGS	PARADED	PARVENU	PAVINGS	PEEVISH
OXHEART	PALLETS	PARADER	PASCHAL	PAVIOUR	PEEWITS
OXIDANT	PALLIER	PARADES	PASMORE	PAWKIER	PEGGING
OXIDASE	PALLING	PARADOR	PASSADE	PAWKILY	PEG LEGS
OXIDATE	PALLIUM	PARADOX	PASSAGE	PAWNAGE	PELAGIC
OXIDIZE	PALMATE	PARAGON	PASSANT	PAWNING	PELICAN
OXONIAN	PALMIER	PARAIBA	PAS SEUL	PAWPAWS	PELITIC
OXYACID	PALMING	PARAPET	PASS FOR	PAYABLE	PELLETS
OXYSALT	PALMIRA	PARASOL	PASSING	PAYBEDS	PELMETS
OXYTONE	PALMIST	PARATHA	PASSION	PAY DIRT	PELORIA
OYSTERS	PALM OIL	PARBOIL	PASSIVE	PAYLOAD	PELORUS
OZONIZE	PALMYRA	PARCELS	PASSKEY	PAYMENT	PELOTAS
	PALPATE	PARCHED	PASS OFF	PAYOUTS	PELTATE
P	PALSIED	PARDONS	PASS OUT	PAYROLL	PELTING
PABULUM	PAMPEAN	PAREIRA	PASTELS	PAYSLIP	PENALLY
PACHUCA	PANACEA	PARENTS	PASTERN	PEACHES	PENALTY
PACIFIC	PANACHE	PARESIS	PASTE UP	PEACOCK	PENANCE
PACKAGE	PANAMAS	PARETIC	PASTE-UP	PEAFOWL	PENDANT
PACKERS	PAN-ARAB	PARFAIT	PASTIER	PEAHENS	PENDENT
PACKETS	PANCAKE	PARIAHS	PASTIES	PEAKIER	PENDING
PACK ICE	PANCHAX	PARINGS	PASTILY	PEAKING	PENGUIN
PACKING	PANDECT	PARKIER	PASTIME	PEALING	PENISES
PADDIES	PANDITS	PARKING	PASTING	PEANUTS	PEN NAME
PADDING	PANDORE	PARKWAY	PASTORS	PEARLER	PENNANT
PADDLED	PANELED	PARLEYS	PASTURE	PEASANT	PENNATE
PADDLER	PANGAEA	PARLOUR	PATCHED	PEBBLES	PENNIES
PADDLES	PANICKY	PARLOUS	PATCHER	PECCANT	PENNING
PADDOCK	PANICLE	PARODIC	PATCHES	PECCARY	PENNONS
PADLOCK	PANNIER	PAROLED	PATELLA	PECCAVI	PEN PALS
PADRONE	PANNING	PAROLES	PATENCY	PECKERS	PENRITH
PAGEANT	PANOCHA	PARONYM	PATENTS	PECKING	PENROSE
PAGEBOY	PANOPLY	PAROTIC	PATHANS	PECKISH	PENSILE
PAGINAL	PANSIES	PAROTID	PATHWAY	PECTASE	PENSION
PAGODAS	PANTHER	PARQUET	PATIALA	PECTATE	PENSIVE
PAHSIEN	PANTIES	PARRIED	PATIENT	PECTIZE	PENTANE
PAINFUL	PANTILE	PARRIES	PATRIAL	PEDALED	PENTENE
PAINING	PANTING	PARROTS	PATRICK	PEDANTS	PENTODE
PAINTED	PANTOUM	PARSEES	PATRIOT	PEDDLED	PENTOSE
PAINTER	PANZERS	PARSERS	PATROLS	PEDDLER	PEONIES
PAIRING	PAOTING	PARSING	PATRONS	PEDICEL	PEOPLED
PAIR-OAR	PAPAYAS	PARSLEY	PATTENS	PEDICLE	PEOPLES
PAISLEY	PAPEETE	PARSNIP	PATTERN	PEDLARS	PEPPERS
PAJAMAS	PAPERED	PARSONS	PATTERS	PEDOCAL	PEPPERY
PALACES	PAPERER	PARTAKE	PATTIES	PEEBLES	PEP PILL
PALADIN	PAPILLA	PARTIAL	PATTING	PEEKING	PEPPING

PEP TALK	PERVADE	PIANISM	PILEOUS	PIQUING	PLANING
PEPTIDE	PERVERT	PIANIST	PILEUPS	PIRAEUS	PLANISH
PEPTIZE	PESCARA	PIANOLA	PILGRIM	PIRANHA	PLANNED
PEPTONE	PESETAS	PIASTRE	PILLAGE	PIRATED	PLANNER
PERACID	PESKIER	PIAZZAS	PILLARS	PIRATES	PLANTAR
PERCALE	PESSARY	PIBROCH	PILLBOX	PIRATIC	PLANTED
PER CENT	PESTLES	PICADOR	PILLION	PISCARY	PLANTER
PERCEPT	PETARDS	PICARDY	PILLOCK	PISCINA	PLANULA
PERCHED	PETCOCK	PICCOLO	PILLORY	PISCINE	PLAQUES
PERCHER	PETIOLE	PICEOUS	PILLOWS	PISHPEK	PLASMID
PERCHES	PET NAME	PICKAXE	PILOTED	PISSING	PLASMIN
PERCOID	PETRELS	PICKERS	PILSNER	PISS-UPS	PLASMON
PERCUSS	PETRIFY	PICKETS	PILULAR	PISTEUR	PLASTER
PER DIEM	PETROUS	PICKIER	PIMENTO	PISTILS	PLASTIC
PEREIRA	PETSAMO	PICKING	PIMPING	PISTOIA	PLASTID
PERFECT	PETTIER	PICKLED	PIMPLED	PISTOLS	PLATEAU
PERFIDY	PETTILY	PICKLER	PIMPLES	PISTONS	PLATINA
PERFORM	PETTING	PICKLES	PINBALL	PIT A	PLATING
PERFUME	PETTISH	PICK-UPS	PINCERS	PAT	PLATOON
PERFUSE	PETUNIA	PICNICS	PINCHED	PIT-A-	PLATTER
PERGOLA	PFENNIG	PICOTEE	PINCHES	PAT	PLAUDIT
PERHAPS	PHAETON	PICRATE	PINE NUT	PITCHED	PLAY-ACT
PERIDOT	PHALANX	PICRITE	PINETUM	PITCHER	PLAYBOY
PERIGEE	PHALLIC	PICTISH	PINFISH	PITCHES	PLAYERS
PERIGON	PHALLUS	PICTURE	PINFOLD	PITEOUS	PLAYFUL
PERIODS	PHANTOM	PIDDLED	PINGING	PITFALL	PLAYING
PERIQUE	PHARAOH	PIDDOCK	PINGUID	PITHEAD	PLAYLET
PERIWIG	PHARYNX	PIDGINS	PINHEAD	PITHIER	PLAY OFF
PERJURE	PHASING	PIEBALD	PINHOLE	PITHILY	PLAY-OFF
PERJURY	PHASMID	PIECING	PINIEST	PITIFUL	PLAYPEN
PERKIER	PHELLEM	PIE-EYED	PINIONS	PIT PONY	PLEADED
PERKILY	PHILTRE	PIERCED	PINKEST	PIT PROP	PLEADER
PERKING	PHIZOGS	PIERCER	PINKEYE	PITTING	PLEASED
PERLITE	PHLOXES	PIETIES	PINK GIN	PITYING	PLEASER
PERMIAN	PHOBIAS	PIGEONS	PINKIES	PIVOTAL	PLEATED
PERMING	PHOBICS	PIGFISH	PINKING	PIVOTED	PLEATER
PERMITS	PHOCINE	PIGGERY	PINKISH	PIZZAZZ	PLEDGED
PERMUTE	PHOENIX	PIGGIER	PINKOES	PLACARD	PLEDGER
PERPEND	PHONATE	PIGGIES	PINNACE	PLACATE	PLEDGES
PERPLEX	PHONE-IN	PIGGING	PINNATE	PLACEBO	PLEDGET
PERSEID	PHONEME	PIGGISH	PINNIES	PLACING	PLEDGOR
PERSIAN	PHONEYS	PIG IRON	PINNING	PLACKET	PLENARY
PERSIST	PHONICS	PIG LEAD	PINNULE	PLACOID	PLEURAL
PERSONA	PHONIER	PIGLETS	PINTAIL	PLAFOND	PLEURON
PERSONS	PHONING	PIGMENT	PINWORK	PLAGUED	PLIABLE
PERSPEX	PHRASAL	PIGMIES	PINWORM	PLAGUER	PLIANCY
PERTAIN	PHRASED	PIGSKIN	PIONEER	PLAGUES	PLICATE
PERTURB	PHRASES	PIGTAIL	PIOUSLY	PLAINER	PLIGHTS
PERUGIA	PHRATRY	PIGWEED	PIPETTE	PLAINLY	PLINTHS
PERUSAL	PHRENIC	PIKEMAN	PIPPING	PLAINTS	PLODDED
PERUSED	PHYSICS	PIKEMEN	PIPPINS	PLAITED	PLODDER
PERUSER	PHYSIOS	PILEATE	PIQUANT	PLANETS	PLOESTI

PLONKED	POKIEST	POPULAR	POTTERS	PRELUDE	PRINTER
PLOPPED	POLARIS	PORCHES	POTTERY	PREMIER	PRISING
PLOSION	POLEAXE	PORCINE	POTTIER	PREMISE	PRISONS
PLOSIVE	POLECAT	PORIRUA	POTTIES	PREMISS	PRITHEE
PLOTTED	POLEMIC	PORKERS	POTTING	PREMIUM	PRIVACY
PLOTTER	POLICED	PORKIER	POUCHED	PREPACK	PRIVATE
PLOUGHS	POLITIC	PORK PIE	POUCHES	PREPAID	PRIVIER
PLOVDIV	POLLACK	PORTAGE	POULARD	PREPARE	PRIVIES
PLOVERS	POLLARD	PORTALS	POULTRY	PREPONE	PRIVILY
PLOWING	POLLING	PORTEND	POUNCED	PREPOSE	PRIVITY
PLUCKED	POLL TAX	PORTENT	POUNCES	PREPUCE	PRIZING
PLUCKER	POLLUTE	PORTERS	POUNDAL	PRESAGE	PROBANG
PLUGGED	POLTAVA	PORTICO	POUNDED	PRESENT	PROBATE
PLUMAGE	POLYGON	PORTING	POUNDER	PRESIDE	PROBING
PLUMATE	POLYMER	PORTION	POURING	PRESSED	PROBITY
PLUMBED	POLYNYA	PORTRAY	POUTING	PRESSES	PROBLEM
PLUMBER	POLYPOD	POSEURS	POVERTY	PRESSOR	PROCARP
PLUMBIC	POLYPUS	POSHEST	POWDERS	PRESS UP	PROCEED
PLUMING	POMMELS	POSITED	POWDERY	PRESS-UP	PROCESS
PLUMMET	POMMIES	POSITIF	POWERED	PRESTON	PROCTOR
PLUMPED	POMPANO	POSSESS	POWWOWS	PRESTOS	PROCURE
PLUMPER	POMPEII	POSSETS	PRAIRIE	PRESUME	PRODDED
PLUMULE	POMPOMS	POSSUMS	PRAISED	PRETEEN	PRODDER
PLUNDER	POMPOUS	POSTAGE	PRAISER	PRETEND	PRODIGY
PLUNGED	PONCHOS	POSTBAG	PRAISES	PRETEST	PRODUCE
PLUNGER	PONGIER	POSTBOX	PRALINE	PRETEXT	PRODUCT
PLURALS	PONGING	POSTERN	PRANCED	PRETZEL	PROFANE
PLUSHER	PONIARD	POSTERS	PRANCER	PREVAIL	PROFESS
PLUVIAL	PONTIFF	POSTFIX	PRATING	PREVENT	PROFFER
PLYWOOD	PONTINE	POST-GAY	PRATTLE	PREVIEW	PROFILE
POACHED	PONTOON	POSTIES	PRAWNER	PREYING	PROFITS
POACHER	POOCHES	POSTING	PRAYERS	PREZZIE	PRO-FORM
PO BOXES	POODLES	POSTMAN	PRAYING	PRICIER	PROFUSE
POCHARD	POOFIER	POSTMEN	PREBEND	PRICING	PROGENY
POCKETS	POOH-BAH	POSTURE	PRECAST	PRICKED	PROGRAM
PODAGRA	POOLING	POSTWAR	PRECEDE	PRICKER	PROJECT
PODCAST	POOPERS	POTABLE	PRECEPT	PRICKET	PROLATE
PODDING	POOR BOX	POTAGER	PRECESS	PRICKLE	PRO-LIFE
PODESTA	POOREST	POTENCY	PRECISE	PRICKLY	PROLINE
PODGIER	POOR LAW	POTFULS	PRECOOK	PRIDING	PROLONG
PODGILY	POPADUM	POTHEEN	PREDATE	PRIESTS	PROMISE
PODIUMS	POPCORN	POTHERB	PREDICT	PRIMACY	PROMMER
PODOLSK	POPEDOM	POTHOLE	PREEMPT	PRIMARY	PROMOTE
POETESS	POP-EYED	POTHOOK	PREENED	PRIMATE	PROMPTS
POETICS	POPGUNS	POTICHE	PREENER	PRIMERS	PRONATE
PO-FACED	POPLARS	POTIONS	PREFABS	PRIMINE	PRONOUN
POGONIA	POPOVER	POT LUCK	PREFACE	PRIMING	PROOFED
POGROMS	POPPERS	POTLUCK	PREFECT	PRIMMER	PROPANE
POINTED	POPPETS	POTOMAC	PREHEAT	PRIMULA	PROPEND
POINTER	POPPIES	POTSDAM	PRELACY	PRINCES	PROPENE
POISING	POPPING	POTSHOT	PRELATE	PRINKER	PROPHET
POISONS	POP STAR	POTTAGE	PRELIMS	PRINTED	PROPOSE

PROPPED	PUDENDA	PURPURA	QUADRAT	QUILTER	RAFFLER
PRO RATA	PUDGIER	PURPURE	QUADRIC	QUIMPER	RAFFLES
PROSAIC	PUDGILY	PURRING	QUAFFER	QUINARY	RAFTERS
PROSIER	PUERILE	PURSERS	QUAILED	QUINATE	RAFTING
PROSILY	PUFFERY	PURSING	QUAKERS	QUINCES	RAGBAGS
PROSODY	PUFFIER	PURSUED	QUAKILY	QUININE	RAGGING
PROSPER	PUFFILY	PURSUER	QUAKING	QUINONE	RAGOUTS
PROTEAN	PUFFING	PURSUIT	QUALIFY	QUINTAL	RAGTAIL
PROTECT	PUFFINS	PURVIEW	QUALITY	QUINTAN	RAGTIME
PROTEGE	PUGGING	PUSHERS	QUANGOS	QUINTET	RAGWEED
PROTEIN	PULLETS	PUSHIER	QUANTAL	QUINTIC	RAG WEEK
PROTEST	PULLEYS	PUSHILY	QUANTIC	QUIPPED	RAGWORM
PROTIST	PULLING	PUSHING	QUANTUM	QUITTED	RAGWORT
PROTIUM	PULL-INS	PUSHKIN	QUARREL	QUITTER	RAIDERS
PROTONS	PULLMAN	PUSHROD	QUARTAN	QUITTOR	RAIDING
PROTYLE	PULLOUT	PUSH-UPS	QUARTER	QUIVERS	RAILING
PROUDER	PULPIER	PUSSIES	QUARTET	QUIVERY	RAILWAY
PROUDLY	PULPING	PUSTULE	QUARTIC	QUI VIVE	RAIMENT
PROVERB	PULPITS	PUTAMEN	QUARTOS	QUIZZED	RAINBOW
PROVIDE	PULSARS	PUT DOWN	QUASARS	QUIZZER	RAINIER
PROVING	PULSATE	PUT-DOWN	QUASHED	QUIZZES	RAINILY
PROVISO	PULSING	PUT-OFFS	QUASSIA	QUONDAM	RAINING
PROVOKE	PUMPING	PUTREFY	QUAVERS	QUORATE	RAINOUT
PROVOST	PUMPKIN	PUTTERS	QUAVERY	QUORUMS	RAISERS
PROWESS	PUNCHED	PUTTING	QUAYAGE	QUOTHED	RAISING
PROWLED	PUNCHER	PUTTNAM	QUECHUA	QUOTING	RAISINS
PROWLER	PUNCHES	PUT-UPON	QUEENED		RAISINY
PROXIES	PUNCH UP	PUZZLED	QUEENLY	**R**	RAKE-OFF
PROXIMA	PUNCH-UP	PUZZLER	QUEERED	RABBITS	RALEIGH
PRUDENT	PUNDITS	PUZZLES	QUEERER	RABBLER	RALLIED
PRUDERY	PUNGENT	PYAEMIA	QUEERLY	RABBLES	RALLIER
PRUDISH	PUNIEST	PYAEMIC	QUELLED	RACCOON	RALLIES
PRUNING	PUNJABI	PYGMIES	QUELLER	RACEMIC	RALLINE
PRURIGO	PUNKAHS	PYJAMAS	QUERIED	RACHIAL	RAMADAN
PRUSSIA	PUNNETS	PYLORUS	QUERIES	RACIEST	RAMBLED
PSALMIC	PUNNING	PYNCHON	QUERIST	RACISTS	RAMBLER
PSALTER	PUNSTER	PYRALID	QUESTED	RACKETS	RAMBLES
PSYCHED	PUNTERS	PYRAMID	QUESTER	RACKETY	RAMEKIN
PSYCHES	PUNTING	PYRETIC	QUETZAL	RACKING	RAMMING
PSYCHIC	PUPPETS	PYREXIA	QUEUING	RACOONS	RAMMISH
PSYLLID	PUPPIES	PYRITES	QUIBBLE	RACQUET	RAMPAGE
PTERYLA	PUPPING	PYRITIC	QUICHES	RADIALS	RAMPANT
PTYALIN	PURCELL	PYROGEN	QUICKEN	RADIANT	RAMPART
PUBERTY	PURGING	PYROSIS	QUICKER	RADIATE	RAMPION
PUBLISH	PURISTS	PYRRHIC	QUICKIE	RADICAL	RAM RAID
PUCCOON	PURITAN	PYRROLE	QUICKLY	RADICEL	RAMRODS
PUCKERS	PURLIEU	PYTHONS	QUIETEN	RADICES	RAMSONS
PUCKISH	PURLING		QUIETER	RADICLE	RANCHER
PUDDING	PURLOIN	**Q**	QUIETLY	RADIOED	RANCHES
PUDDLED	PURPLES	Q-FACTOR	QUIETUS	RADULAR	RANCOUR
PUDDLER	PURPORT	QINGDAO	QUILMES	RAFFISH	RANDERS
PUDDLES	PURPOSE	QUACKED	QUILTED	RAFFLED	RANDIER

RANDOMS	RAVELLY	RECAPED	REEDING	REISSUE	REPEATS
RANGERS	RAVENER	RECEDED	REEFERS	REJECTS	REPINED
RANGILY	RAVENNA	RECEIPT	REEFING	REJOICE	REPLACE
RANGING	RAVE-UPS	RECEIVE	REEKING	RELAPSE	REPLAYS
RANGOON	RAVINES	RECIPES	RE-ELECT	RELATED	REPLETE
RANKERS	RAVINGS	RECITAL	REELING	RELATER	REPLEVY
RANKING	RAVIOLI	RECITED	REELMAN	RELATOR	REPLICA
RANKLED	RAW DEAL	RECITER	RE-ENTER	RELATUM	REPLIED
RANSACK	RAWHIDE	RECKING	RE-ENTRY	RELAXED	REPLIER
RANSOMS	RAWNESS	RECLAIM	REFACED	RELAXER	REPLIES
RANTERS	RAZZLES	RECLINE	REFEREE	RELAXIN	REPORTS
RANTING	REACHED	RECLUSE	REFILLS	RELAYED	REPOSAL
RAPHIDE	REACHER	RECORDS	REFINED	RELEASE	REPOSED
RAPIDLY	REACHES	RECOUNT	REFINER	RELIANT	REPOSER
RAPIERS	REACTED	RECOVER	REFLATE	RELIEFS	REPOSIT
RAPISTS	REACTOR	RECRUIT	REFLECT	RELIEVE	REPRESS
RAPPING	READERS	RECTIFY	REFORMS	RELINED	REPRINT
RAPPORT	READIED	RECTORS	REFRACT	RELIVED	REPRISE
RAPTURE	READIER	RECTORY	REFRAIN	RELYING	REPROOF
RAREBIT	READIES	RECTRIX	REFRESH	REMAINS	REPROVE
RASBORA	READILY	RECTUMS	REFUGEE	REMAKES	REPTANT
RASCALS	READING	RECURVE	REFUGES	REMANDS	REPTILE
RASHERS	READOUT	RECYCLE	REFUNDS	REMARKS	REPULSE
RASHEST	REAGENT	RED BOOK	REFUSAL	REMARRY	REPUTED
RASPING	REALGAR	RED CARD	REFUSED	REMATCH	REQUEST
RATABLE	REALIGN	REDCOAT	REFUSER	REMNANT	REQUIEM
RATABLY	REALISM	RED DEER	REFUTED	REMODEL	REQUIRE
RATAFIA	REALIST	REDDEST	REFUTER	REMORSE	REQUITE
RAT-A-	REALITY	REDDISH	REGALIA	REMOTER	REREDOS
TAT	REALIZE	REDFISH	REGALLY	REMOULD	RESCIND
RATBAGS	REALTOR	RED FLAG	REGARDS	REMOUNT	RESCUED
RATCHET	REAMERS	REDFORD	REGATTA	REMOVAL	RESCUER
RATE-CAP	REAMING	REDHEAD	REGENCY	REMOVED	RESCUES
RATINGS	REAPERS	RED MEAT	REGENTS	REMOVER	RESERVE
RATIONS	REAPING	REDNECK	REGIMEN	REMOVES	RESHAPE
RATLINE	REARING	REDNESS	REGIMES	RENAMED	RESIDED
RATPACK	REARMED	REDOING	REGINAS	RENDELL	RESIDER
RAT RACE	REASONS	REDONKS	REGIONS	RENDING	RESIDUE
RATTIER	REBADGE	REDOUBT	REGNANT	RENEGED	RESKILL
RATTILY	REBATER	REDOUND	REGOSOL	RENEGER	RESNAIS
RATTING	REBATES	REDPOLL	REGRATE	RENEWAL	RESOLVE
RATTISH	REBIRTH	REDRAFT	REGRESS	RENEWED	RESORTS
RATTLED	REBOUND	REDRESS	REGRETS	RENEWER	RESOUND
RATTLES	REBRAND	REDROOT	REGROUP	RENFREW	RESPECT
RAT TRAP	REBUFFS	REDSKIN	REGULAR	RENTALS	RESPIRE
RAUCOUS	REBUILD	RED SPOT	REGULOS	RENT BOY	RESPITE
RAUNCHY	REBUILT	RED TAPE	REGULUS	RENTERS	RESPOND
RAVAGED	REBUKED	REDUCED	REHOUSE	RENTIER	RESTAGE
RAVAGER	REBUKER	REDUCER	REIFIER	RENTING	RESTATE
RAVAGES	REBUKES	REDWING	REIGATE	REORDER	RESTFUL
RAVELED	REBUSES	REDWOOD	REIGNED	REPAIRS	RESTING
RAVELIN	RECALLS	REEDIER	REINING	REPASTS	RESTIVE

RESTOCK	REVOICE	RIG-OUTS	ROARING	ROOTING	RUBBISH
RESTORE	REVOKED	RIM-FIRE	ROASTED	ROOTLET	RUBDOWN
RESTYLE	REVOKER	RIMLESS	ROASTER	ROPIEST	RUBELLA
RESULTS	REVOLTS	RIMMING	ROBBERS	RORAIMA	RUBEOLA
RESUMED	REVOLVE	RIMROCK	ROBBERY	RORQUAL	RUBICON
RESUMES	REVVING	RINGENT	ROBBING	ROSARIO	RUBIDIC
RETABLE	REWARDS	RINGERS	ROBUSTA	ROSEATE	RUBIOUS
RETAKEN	REWIRED	RINGING	ROCK BUN	ROSEBUD	RUBRICS
RETAKER	REWRITE	RINGLET	ROCKERS	ROSE HIP	RUCHING
RETAKES	REWROTE	RINSING	ROCKERY	ROSELLA	RUCKING
RETCHED	REYNOSA	RIOT ACT	ROCKETS	ROSEOLA	RUCTION
RETHINK	RHAETIC	RIOTERS	ROCKIER	ROSETTA	RUDDERS
RETICLE	RHATANY	RIOTING	ROCKIES	ROSETTE	RUDDIER
RETINAE	RHENIUM	RIOTOUS	ROCKING	ROSIEST	RUDDILY
RETINAL	RHEUMIC	RIPCORD	ROCKOON	ROSINED	RUDERAL
RETINAS	RHIZOID	RIPENED	RODENTS	ROSTERS	RUFFIAN
RETINOL	RHIZOME	RIPENER	RODLIKE	ROSTOCK	RUFFLED
RETINUE	RHODIUM	RIP-OFFS	ROEBUCK	ROSTRAL	RUFFLER
RETIRED	RHOMBIC	RIPOSTE	ROE DEER	ROSTRUM	RUFFLES
RETIRER	RHOMBUS	RIPPING	ROGUERY	ROTATED	RUINING
RETITLE	RHONDDA	RIPPLED	ROGUISH	ROTATOR	RUINOUS
RETORTS	RHUBARB	RIPPLER	ROISTER	ROTIFER	RULABLE
RETOUCH	RHYMING	RIPPLES	ROLL BAR	ROTORUA	RULINGS
RETRACE	RHYTHMS	RIPPLET	ROLLERS	ROTTERS	RUMANIA
RETRACT	RIBBAND	RIPSAWS	ROLLICK	ROTTING	RUMBLED
RETREAD	RIBBING	RIPTIDE	ROLLING	ROTUNDA	RUMBLER
RETREAT	RIBBONS	RISIBLE	ROLLMOP	ROUBAIX	RUMBLES
RETRIAL	RIB CAGE	RISIBLY	ROLL-ONS	ROUBLES	RUMMAGE
RETSINA	RIBWORT	RISINGS	ROLL-TOP	ROUGHEN	RUMMEST
RETURNS	RICHARD	RISKIER	ROLLWAY	ROUGHER	RUMOURS
REUNIFY	RICHEST	RISKILY	ROMAGNA	ROUGHLY	RUMPLED
REUNION	RICHLER	RISKING	ROMANCE	ROUGING	RUNAWAY
REUNITE	RICHTER	RISOTTO	ROMANIA	ROULEAU	RUNCORN
REUSING	RICKETS	RISSOLE	ROMPERS	ROULERS	RUN DOWN
REVALUE	RICKETY	RITUALS	ROMPING	ROUNDED	RUN-DOWN
REVELED	RICKING	RIVALED	RONDEAU	ROUNDEL	RUN INTO
REVELRY	RIDDING	RIVALRY	RONDURE	ROUNDER	RUNNELS
REVENGE	RIDDLED	RIVETED	RONTGEN	ROUNDLY	RUNNERS
REVENUE	RIDDLER	RIVETER	ROOFING	ROUNDUP	RUNNIER
REVERED	RIDDLES	RIVIERA	ROOFTOP	ROUND UP	RUNNING
REVERER	RIDGING	RIVIERE	ROOINEK	ROUSING	RUN-OFFS
REVERIE	RIDOTTO	RIVULET	ROOKERY	ROUTINE	RUN OVER
REVERSE	RIFFLED	ROACHES	ROOKIES	ROUTING	RUNTISH
REVIEWS	RIFFLER	ROADBED	ROOKING	ROWDIER	RUNWAYS
REVILED	RIFLERY	ROAD HOG	ROOMERS	ROWDILY	RUPTURE
REVILER	RIFLING	ROADMAN	ROOMFUL	ROWLOCK	RUSHDIE
REVISAL	RIGGING	ROAD MAP	ROOMIER	ROYALLY	RUSHING
REVISED	RIGHTED	ROADMEN	ROOMILY	ROYALTY	RUSSIAN
REVISER	RIGHTER	ROAD TAX	ROOMING	ROZZERS	RUSTICS
REVIVAL	RIGHTLY	ROADWAY	ROOSTED	RUBBERS	RUSTIER
REVIVED	RIGHT-ON	ROAMERS	ROOSTER	RUBBERY	RUSTILY
REVIVER	RIGIDLY	ROAMING	ROOTAGE	RUBBING	RUSTING

RUSTLED	SALTIER	SAPPORO	SAWMILL	SCOLDED	SCRUMPY
RUSTLER	SALTILY	SAPROBE	SAWN-OFF	SCOLDER	SCRUNCH
RUTLAND	SALTING	SAPSAGO	SAXHORN	SCOLLOP	SCRUPLE
RUTTILY	SALTIRE	SAPWOOD	SAXTUBA	SCONCES	SCUDDED
RUTTING	SALTPAN	SARACEN	SAYINGS	SCOOPED	SCUFFED
RUTTISH	SALTPOT	SARANSK	SCABBLE	SCOOPER	SCUFFLE
RYBINSK	SALUTED	SARATOV	SCABIES	SCOOTED	SCULLED
	SALUTER	SARAWAK	SCALARS	SCOOTER	SCULLER
S	SALUTES	SARCASM	SCALDED	SCOPULA	SCULPIN
SABBATH	SALVAGE	SARCOID	SCALENE	SCORERS	SCUMBLE
SACATON	SALVERS	SARCOMA	SCALIER	SCORIFY	SCUMMER
SACCATE	SALVING	SARCOUS	SCALING	SCORING	SCUPPER
SACCULE	SALVOES	SARDINE	SCALLOP	SCORNED	SCUTATE
SACHETS	SALWEEN	SARDIUS	SCALPED	SCORNER	SCUTTLE
SACKING	SAMISEN	SARKIER	SCALPEL	SCORPER	SCYTHED
SADDEST	SAMNIUM	SARNIES	SCALPER	SCORPIO	SCYTHES
SADDLED	SAMOSAS	SARONGS	SCAMPER	SCOTOMA	SEABIRD
SADDLER	SAMOVAR	SARONIC	SCANDAL	SCOURED	SEACOCK
SADDLES	SAMOYED	SASSABY	SCANDIC	SCOURER	SEA DOGS
SADIRON	SAMPANS	SASSARI	SCANNED	SCOURGE	SEAFOOD
SADISTS	SAMPLED	SASSIER	SCANNER	SCOUSES	SEAGIRT
SADNESS	SAMPLER	SASSING	SCAPOSE	SCOUTED	SEA GULL
SAFARIS	SAMPLES	SATANIC	SCAPULA	SCOUTER	SEAGULL
SAFFIAN	SAMPRAS	SATCHEL	SCARABS	SCOWLED	SEA-LANE
SAFFRON	SAMURAI	SATIATE	SCARCER	SCOWLER	SEALANT
SAFROLE	SANCTUM	SATIETY	SCARIER	SCRAGGY	SEA LEGS
SAGGIER	SANCTUS	SATINET	SCARIFY	SCRAPED	SEALERS
SAGGING	SANDALS	SATIRES	SCARING	SCRAPER	SEALERY
SAGUARO	SANDBAG	SATISFY	SCARLET	SCRAPES	SEALING
SAHARAN	SANDBAR	SATSUMA	SCARPER	SCRAPPY	SEA LION
SAILING	SANDBOX	SATYRIC	SCARRED	SCRATCH	SEAMARK
SAILORS	SANDERS	SATYRID	SCARVES	SCRAWLS	SEAMIER
SAINTED	SAND FLY	SAUCERS	SCATTED	SCRAWLY	SEA MILE
SAINTLY	SANDIER	SAUCIER	SCATTER	SCRAWNY	SEA MIST
SALAAMS	SANDING	SAUCILY	SCENERY	SCREAMS	SEANCES
SALABLE	SANDPIT	SAUCING	SCENTED	SCREECH	SEAPORT
SALAMIS	SANGRIA	SAUNTER	SCEPTIC	SCREEDS	SEARING
SALERNO	SANICLE	SAURIAN	SCEPTRE	SCREENS	SEASICK
SALFORD	SAN JOSE	SAUSAGE	SCHEMED	SCREWED	SEASIDE
SALICIN	SAN JUAN	SAUTEED	SCHEMER	SCREWER	SEASONS
SALIENT	SAN REMO	SAVABLE	SCHEMES	SCREW UP	SEATING
SALLIED	SANTA FE	SAVAGED	SCHERZO	SCRIBAL	SEATTLE
SALLIER	SAO LUIS	SAVAGES	SCHISMS	SCRIBER	SEAWALL
SALLIES	SAPHENA	SAVANNA	SCHLUMP	SCRIBES	SEAWARE
SALLOWS	SAPIENT	SAVANTS	SCHMUCK	SCRIMPY	SEAWAYS
SALMONS	SAPLESS	SAVE-ALL	SCHOLAR	SCRIPTS	SEAWEED
SALOONS	SAPLING	SAVINGS	SCHOOLS	SCROLLS	SECEDED
SALPINX	SAPONIN	SAVIOUR	SCIATIC	SCROOGE	SECEDER
SALSIFY	SAPPERS	SAVOURY	SCIENCE	SCROTUM	SECLUDE
SALTANT	SAPPIER	SAWBILL	SCISSOR	SCRUBBY	SECONDO
SALTBOX	SAPPILY	SAWDUST	SCOFFED	SCRUFFS	SECONDS
SALTERN	SAPPING	SAWFISH	SCOFFER	SCRUFFY	SECRECY

SECRETE	SENORAS	SEVERED	SHAWNEE	SHOOING	SHYLOCK
SECRETS	SENSATE	SEVILLE	SHEARED	SHOOTER	SHYNESS
SECTARY	SENSING	SEXIEST	SHEARER	SHOPPED	SHYSTER
SECTILE	SENSORS	SEXISTS	SHEATHE	SHOPPER	SIALKOT
SECTION	SENSORY	SEXLESS	SHEATHS	SHORING	SIALOID
SECTORS	SENSUAL	SEXPOTS	SHEAVES	SHORTED	SIAMANG
SECULAR	SEPTATE	SEXTANT	SHEBANG	SHORTEN	SIAMESE
SECURED	SEPTETS	SEXTETS	SHE BEAR	SHORTER	SIBERIA
SECURER	SEPTIME	SEXTILE	SHEBEEN	SHORTIE	SIBLING
SEDATED	SEQUELA	SEXTONS	SHEDDER	SHORTLY	SICHUAN
SEDILIA	SEQUELS	SFUMATO	SHEERED	SHOTGUN	SICKBAY
SEDUCED	SEQUENT	SHAANXI	SHEERER	SHOT PUT	SICKBED
SEDUCER	SEQUINS	SHACKED	SHEIKHS	SHOTTEN	SICKEST
SEEDBED	SEQUOIA	SHACKLE	SHEILAS	SHOUTED	SICKING
SEED BED	SERAPHS	SHADIER	SHEKELS	SHOUTER	SICKLES
SEEDIER	SERBIAN	SHADILY	SHELLAC	SHOVELS	SICK PAY
SEEDILY	SERFDOM	SHADING	SHELLED	SHOVING	SIDEARM
SEEDING	SERGIPE	SHADOOF	SHELTER	SHOWERS	SIDECAR
SEEKERS	SERIALS	SHADOWS	SHELVED	SHOWERY	SIDE CAR
SEEKING	SERIATE	SHADOWY	SHELVER	SHOWIER	SIDINGS
SEEMING	SERICIN	SHAFTED	SHELVES	SHOWILY	SIDLING
SEEPAGE	SERIEMA	SHAGGED	SHEPARD	SHOWING	SIEMENS
SEEPING	SERINGA	SHAHDOM	SHEPPEY	SHOWMAN	SIERRAN
SEESAWS	SERIOUS	SHAKERS	SHERBET	SHOWMEN	SIERRAS
SEETHED	SERMONS	SHAKE UP	SHERIFF	SHOWN UP	SIESTAS
SEGMENT	SERPENT	SHAKE-UP	SHERPAS	SHOW OFF	SIEVERT
SEGOVIA	SERPIGO	SHAKHTY	SHEWING	SHOW-OFF	SIEVING
SEISMIC	SERRATE	SHAKIER	SHIELDS	SHRIEKS	SIFTERS
SEIZING	SERRIED	SHAKILY	SHIFTED	SHRIFTS	SIFTING
SEIZURE	SERUMAL	SHAKING	SHIFTER	SHRIKES	SIGHING
SEKONDI	SERVANT	SHALLOP	SHIITES	SHRILLY	SIGHTED
SELENIC	SERVERS	SHALLOT	SHIKOKU	SHRIMPS	SIGHTER
SELFISH	SERVERY	SHALLOW	SHIMMER	SHRINES	SIGHTLY
SELLERS	SERVICE	SHAMANS	SHINDIG	SHRINKS	SIGMATE
SELLING	SERVILE	SHAMBLE	SHINGLE	SHRIVEL	SIGMOID
SELL OFF	SERVING	SHAMING	SHINGLY	SHRIVER	SIGNALS
SELL OUT	SESOTHO	SHAMMED	SHINIER	SHROUDS	SIGNETS
SELL-OUT	SESSILE	SHAMMER	SHINING	SHRUBBY	SIGNIFY
SELTZER	SESSION	SHAMPOO	SHINNED	SHUCKED	SIGNING
SELVAGE	SESTINA	SHANKLY	SHIPPED	SHUCKER	SIGN OFF
SEMATIC	SETBACK	SHANNON	SHIPPER	SHUDDER	SIGNORA
SEMINAL	SET FREE	SHANTOU	SHIPWAY	SHUFFLE	SIGNORE
SEMINAR	SETLINE	SHAPELY	SHIRKED	SHUNNED	SIGNORS
SEMITIC	SETTEES	SHAPING	SHIRKER	SHUNNER	SILENCE
SENATES	SETTERS	SHARERS	SHITBAG	SHUNTED	SILENTS
SENATOR	SETTING	SHARING	SHITTED	SHUNTER	SILESIA
SENDERS	SETTLED	SHARPEN	SHIVERS	SHUSHED	SILICIC
SENDING	SETTLER	SHARPER	SHIVERY	SHUT-EYE	SILICLE
SEND-OFF	SETTLES	SHARPLY	SHOCKED	SHUT-OFF	SILICON
SEND-UPS	SEVENTH	SHATTER	SHOCKER	SHUTOUT	SILIQUA
SENEGAL	SEVENTY	SHAVERS	SHOEING	SHUTTER	SILKIER
SENIORS	SEVERAL	SHAVING	SHOGUNS	SHUTTLE	SILKILY

SILLIER	SKATOLE	SLALOMS	SLIVERS	SMOKIER	SNORING
SILLIES	SKEPTIC	SLAMMED	SLOBBER	SMOKILY	SNORKEL
SILTING	SKETCHY	SLANDER	SLOGANS	SMOKING	SNORTED
SILURID	SKEWERS	SLANGED	SLOGGED	SMOLDER	SNORTER
SILVERS	SKEWING	SLANTED	SLOGGER	SMOTHER	SNOWCAP
SILVERY	SKIABLE	SLAPPED	SLOPING	SMUDGED	SNOWIER
SIMIANS	SKIBOBS	SLAPPER	SLOPPED	SMUDGES	SNOWILY
SIMILAR	SKIDDED	SLASHED	SLOSHED	SMUGGER	SNOWING
SIMILES	SKIDPAN	SLASHER	SLOTTED	SMUGGLE	SNOWMAN
SIMIOUS	SKID ROW	SLASHES	SLOTTER	SMUTCHY	SNOWMEN
SIMPERS	SKIFFLE	SLATING	SLOUCHY	SNACKED	SNUBBED
SIMPLER	SKI JUMP	SLATTED	SLOUGHS	SNAFFLE	SNUBBER
SIMPLEX	SKILFUL	SLAVERS	SLOUGHY	SNAGGED	SNUFFED
SIMULAR	SKI LIFT	SLAVERY	SLOVENE	SNAKILY	SNUFFER
SINALOA	SKILLED	SLAVING	SLOWEST	SNAKING	SNUFFLE
SINCERE	SKILLET	SLAVISH	SLOWING	SNAPPED	SNUFFLY
SINE DIE	SKIMMED	SLAYERS	SLUGGED	SNAPPER	SNUGGLE
SINGING	SKIMMER	SLAYING	SLUICED	SNARING	SOAKAGE
SINGLED	SKIMMIA	SLEDDED	SLUICES	SNARLED	SOAKING
SINGLES	SKIMPED	SLEDDER	SLUMBER	SNARLER	SO-AND-
SINGLET	SKINFUL	SLEDGED	SLUMMED	SNARL UP	SO
SINITIC	SKINNED	SLEDGES	SLUMMER	SNARL-UP	SOAPBOX
SINKERS	SKINNER	SLEEKED	SLUMPED	SNATCHY	SOAPIER
SINKING	SKI POLE	SLEEKER	SLURPED	SNEAKED	SOAPILY
SINLESS	SKIPPED	SLEEKLY	SLURRED	SNEAKER	SOAPING
SINNERS	SKIPPER	SLEEPER	SLYNESS	SNEERED	SOARING
SINNING	SKIPPET	SLEETED	SMACKED	SNEERER	SOBBING
SINUATE	SKIPTON	SLEEVES	SMACKER	SNEEZED	SOBERED
SINUIJU	SKIRRET	SLEIGHS	SMALL AD	SNEEZER	SOBERLY
SINUOUS	SKIRTED	SLEIGHT	SMALLER	SNEEZES	SOCAGER
SINUSES	SKITTER	SLENDER	SMARTED	SNICKED	SOCIALS
SIPHONS	SKITTLE	SLEUTHS	SMARTEN	SNICKER	SOCIETY
SIPPING	SKIVERS	SLEWING	SMARTER	SNIDELY	SOCKETS
SIRLOIN	SKIVING	SLICING	SMARTLY	SNIDEST	SOCKEYE
SIROCCO	SKULKED	SLICKED	SMASHED	SNIFFED	SOCKING
SIRRAHS	SKULKER	SLICKER	SMASHER	SNIFFER	SODDING
SISSIER	SKY BLUE	SLICKLY	SMASHES	SNIFFLE	SOD'S
SISSIES	SKY-BLUE	SLIDING	SMASH-UP	SNIFTER	LAW
SISTERS	SKYCAPS	SLIGHTS	SMATTER	SNIGGER	SOFA BED
SITCOMS	SKYDIVE	SLIMIER	SMEARED	SNIGGLE	SOFTEST
SIT-DOWN	SKY-HIGH	SLIMILY	SMEARER	SNIPERS	SOFTIES
SITTERS	SKYJACK	SLIMMED	SMECTIC	SNIPING	SOGGIER
SITTING	SKYLARK	SLIMMER	SMELLED	SNIPPED	SOGGILY
SITUATE	SKYLINE	SLINGER	SMELTED	SNIPPET	SOILAGE
SIXFOLD	SKYSAIL	SLIP-ONS	SMELTER	SNOGGED	SOILING
SIX-PACK	SKYWALK	SLIPPED	SMIDGIN	SNOOKER	SOIREES
SIXTEEN	SLACKED	SLIPPER	SMILING	SNOOPED	SOJOURN
SIXTIES	SLACKEN	SLIP-UPS	SMIRKED	SNOOPER	SOLACED
SIZABLE	SLACKER	SLIPWAY	SMIRKER	SNOOZED	SOLACER
SIZZLED	SLACKLY	SLITHER	SMITING	SNOOZER	SOLACES
SIZZLER	SLAGGED	SLITTED	SMITTEN	SNOOZES	SOLANUM
SKATING	SLAKING	SLITTER	SMOKERS	SNORERS	SOLARIA

SOLDIER	SOULFUL	SPECTRE	SPLEENS	SPRUCES	STAINER
SOLICIT	SOUNDED	SPEEDED	SPLENIC	SPUMONE	STAINES
SOLIDLY	SOUNDER	SPEEDER	SPLICED	SPUMOUS	STAKING
SOLIDUS	SOUNDLY	SPELLED	SPLICER	SPURNED	STALEST
SOLOIST	SOUPCON	SPELLER	SPLICES	SPURNER	STALING
SOLOMON	SOUPFIN	SPELTER	SPLINTS	SPURRED	STALKED
SOLUBLE	SOURCES	SPENCER	SPLODGE	SPURTED	STALKER
SOLVATE	SOUREST	SPENDER	SPLODGY	SPUTNIK	STALLED
SOLVENT	SOURING	SPEWING	SPLURGE	SPUTTER	STAMBUL
SOLVERS	SOURSOP	SPHENIC	SPOILED	SQUABBY	STAMENS
SOLVING	SOUSING	SPHERAL	SPOILER	SQUACCO	STAMINA
SOMALIA	SOUTANE	SPHERES	SPOKANE	SQUALID	STAMMEL
SOMATIC	SOUTHER	SPICATE	SPONDEE	SQUALLS	STAMMER
SOMEDAY	SOVIETS	SPICERY	SPONGED	SQUALLY	STAMPED
SOMEHOW	SOVKHOZ	SPICIER	SPONGER	SQUALOR	STAMPER
SOMEONE	SOWETAN	SPICILY	SPONGES	SQUARED	STANCES
SOMEWAY	SOZZLED	SPICING	SPONGIN	SQUARER	STANDBY
SOMITAL	SPACING	SPICULE	SPONSON	SQUARES	STAND BY
SONANCE	SPAMMER	SPIDERS	SPONSOR	SQUASHY	STANDER
SONATAS	SPANCEL	SPIDERY	SPOODLE	SQUAWKS	STAND-IN
SONDAGE	SPANDEX	SPIELER	SPOOFER	SQUEAKS	STAND UP
SONGFUL	SPANGLE	SPIGNEL	SPOOKED	SQUEAKY	STAND-UP
SONNETS	SPANGLY	SPIGOTS	SPOONED	SQUEALS	STANLEY
SOOCHOW	SPANIEL	SPIKIER	SPOORER	SQUEEZE	STANNIC
SOOTHED	SPANISH	SPIKILY	SPORRAN	SQUELCH	STANZAS
SOOTHER	SPANKED	SPIKING	SPORTED	SQUIDGY	STAPLED
SOOTIER	SPANKER	SPILLED	SPORTER	SQUIFFY	STAPLER
SOOTILY	SPANNED	SPILLER	SPORULE	SQUILLA	STAPLES
SOPHISM	SPANNER	SPINACH	SPOTLIT	SQUINCH	STARCHY
SOPHIST	SPARING	SPINDLE	SPOTTED	SQUINTS	STARDOM
SOPPIER	SPARKED	SPINDLY	SPOTTER	SQUINTY	STARING
SOPPILY	SPARKLE	SPIN-DRY	SPOTTIFY	SQUIRES	STARKER
SOPPING	SPARRED	SPINETS	SPOUSAL	SQUIRMS	STARKLY
SOPRANO	SPARROW	SPINNER	SPOUSES	SQUIRMY	STARLET
SORBETS	SPARSER	SPINNEY	SPOUTED	SQUIRTS	STARLIT
SORBOSE	SPARTAN	SPIN-OFF	SPOUTER	SQUISHY	STARRED
SORCERY	SPASTIC	SPINOSE	SPRAINS	STABBED	STARTED
SORDINO	SPATHIC	SPINOUS	SPRAINT	STABBER	STARTER
SORGHUM	SPATIAL	SPIN OUT	SPRAWLS	STABILE	STARTLE
SORITES	SPATTER	SPINULE	SPRAWLY	STABLED	START UP
SOROSIS	SPATULA	SPIRAEA	SPRAYED	STABLES	STARVED
SORRIER	SPAWNED	SPIRALS	SPRAYER	STACKED	STARVER
SORRILY	SPAWNER	SPIRANT	SPREADS	STACKER	STASHED
SORROWS	SPAYING	SPIREME	SPRIEST	STADDLE	STASHES
SORTIES	SPEAKER	SPIRITS	SPRIGGY	STADIUM	STATANT
SORTING	SPEARED	SPIROID	SPRINGE	STAFFED	STATELY
SORT-OUT	SPEARER	SPIRULA	SPRINGS	STAFFER	STATICS
SO THERE	SPECIAL	SPITING	SPRINGY	STAGGER	STATING
SOTTISH	SPECIES	SPITTER	SPRINTS	STAGILY	STATION
SOUFFLE	SPECIFY	SPITTLE	SPRITES	STAGING	STATISM
SOUGHED	SPECKLE	SPLASHY	SPROUTS	STAIDLY	STATIST
SOUKOUS	SPECTRA	SPLAYED	SPRUCED	STAINED	STATIVE

STATUED	STICHIC	STORING	STUDDED	SUBTEND	SUNBEDS
STATUES	STICKER	STORMED	STUDENT	SUBTEXT	SUNBELT
STATURE	STICKLE	STOUTER	STUDIED	SUBTLER	SUNBIRD
STATUTE	STICK-ON	STOUTLY	STUDIES	SUBTYPE	SUNBURN
STAUNCH	STICK UP	STOWAGE	STUDIOS	SUBUNIT	SUNDAES
STAVING	STICK-UP	STOWING	STUFFED	SUBURBS	SUNDAYS
STAYERS	STIFFEN	STRAFED	STUFFER	SUBVERT	SUNDIAL
STAYING	STIFFER	STRAFER	STUMBLE	SUBWAYS	SUNDOWN
STEALER	STIFFLY	STRAINS	STUMPED	SUCCEED	SUNFISH
STEALTH	STIFLED	STRAITS	STUMPER	SUCCESS	SUNGLOW
STEAMED	STIFLER	STRANDS	STUNNED	SUCCOUR	SUN GODS
STEAMER	STIGMAS	STRANGE	STUNNER	SUCCUBI	SUNLAMP
STEAM UP	STILLED	STRATAL	STUNTED	SUCCUMB	SUNLESS
STEARIC	STILLER	STRATAS	STUPEFY	SUCCUSS	SUNNIER
STEARIN	STILTED	STRATUM	STUPORS	SUCKERS	SUNNILY
STEELED	STILTON	STRATUS	STUTTER	SUCKING	SUNNING
STEEPED	STIMULI	STRAYED	STYGIAN	SUCKLED	SUNRISE
STEEPEN	STINGER	STRAYER	STYLING	SUCKLER	SUNROOF
STEEPER	STINKER	STREAKS	STYLISH	SUCRASE	SUNSETS
STEEPLE	STINTED	STREAKY	STYLIST	SUCROSE	SUNSPOT
STEEPLY	STINTER	STREAMS	STYLIZE	SUCTION	SUNSTAR
STEERED	STIPEND	STREETS	STYLOID	SUDANIC	SUNTANS
STEERER	STIPPLE	STRETCH	STYLOPS	SUDBURY	SUNTRAP
STELLAR	STIPULE	STRETTA	STYMIED	SUDETES	SUNWISE
STEMMED	STIR-FRY	STRETTO	STYPSIS	SUFFICE	SUPPERS
STEMMER	STIRRED	STREWED	STYPTIC	SUFFOLK	SUPPING
STEMSON	STIRRER	STREWER	STYRENE	SUFFUSE	SUPPLER
STENCIL	STIRRUP	STREWTH	SUAVELY	SUGARED	SUPPORT
STEN GUN	STOCKED	STRIATE	SUAVITY	SUGGEST	SUPPOSE
STENTOR	STOCKER	STRIDES	SUBACID	SUICIDE	SUPREME
STEPDAD	STOICAL	STRIDOR	SUB-AQUA	SUITING	SUPREMO
STEPMUM	STOKERS	STRIKER	SUBARID	SUITORS	SURBASE
STEPPED	STOKING	STRIKES	SUBBASE	SUKHUMI	SURCOAT
STEPPER	STOMACH	STRINGS	SUBBASS	SULCATE	SURFACE
STEPPES	STOMPED	STRINGY	SUBBING	SULKIER	SURFEIT
STEPSON	STOMPER	STRIPED	SUBDUAL	SULKILY	SURFERS
STEPS UP	STONIER	STRIPER	SUBDUCT	SULKING	SURFING
STEREOS	STONILY	STRIPES	SUBDUED	SULLAGE	SURGEON
STERILE	STONING	STRIPEY	SUBEDIT	SULLIED	SURGERY
STERLET	STOOD UP	STRIVEN	SUBERIN	SULPHUR	SURGING
STERNAL	STOOGES	STRIVER	SUBFUSC	SULTANA	SURINAM
STERNER	STOOKER	STROBIC	SUBJECT	SULTANS	SURLIER
STERNLY	STOOPED	STROKED	SUBJOIN	SUMATRA	SURLILY
STERNUM	STOOPER	STROKES	SUBLIME	SUMBAWA	SURMISE
STEROID	STOPGAP	STROLLS	SUBPLOT	SUMMAND	SURNAME
STERTOR	STOPING	STROPHE	SUB ROSA	SUMMARY	SURPASS
STETSON	STOPPED	STROPPY	SUBSETS	SUMMERS	SURPLUS
STEWARD	STOPPER	STRUDEL	SUBSIDE	SUMMERY	SURREAL
STEWART	STORAGE	STUBBED	SUBSIDY	SUMMING	SURREYS
STEWING	STOREYS	STUBBLE	SUBSIST	SUMMITS	SURVEYS
STHENIC	STORIED	STUBBLY	SUBSOIL	SUMMONS	SURVIVE
STIBINE	STORIES	STUCK-UP	SUBSUME	SUNBEAM	SUSPECT

SUSPEND	SWIPPLE	TACKIER	TAMARIN	TASTERS	TEENAGE
SUSSING	SWIRLED	TACKIES	TAMBOUR	TASTIER	TEEPEES
SUSTAIN	SWISHED	TACKILY	TAMPERE	TASTILY	TEGULAR
SUTURAL	SWISHER	TACKING	TAMPICO	TASTING	TEHERAN
SUTURED	SWISHES	TACKLED	TAMPING	TATOUAY	TEKTITE
SUTURES	SWIVELS	TACKLER	TAMPONS	TATTERS	TELAMON
SWABBED	SWIZZLE	TACKLES	TANAGER	TATTIER	TEL AVIV
SWABBER	SWOLLEN	TACNODE	TANBARK	TATTILY	TELEOST
SWABIAN	SWOONED	TACTFUL	TANDEMS	TATTING	TELERAN
SWADDLE	SWOOPED	TACTICS	TANGELO	TATTLED	TELESIS
SWAGGER	SWOPPED	TACTILE	TANGENT	TATTLER	TELEXED
SWAHILI	SWOTTED	TACTUAL	TANGIER	TATTOOS	TELEXES
SWALLOW	SYCOSIS	TADPOLE	TANGLED	TAUNTED	TELFORD
SWAMPED	SYENITE	TADZHIK	TANGLER	TAUNTER	TELLERS
SWANKED	SYLLABI	TAFFETA	TANGLES	TAUNTON	TELLIES
SWANNED	SYLPHIC	TAFFIES	TANGOED	TAUREAN	TELLING
SWANSEA	SYLPHID	TAGGERS	TANGRAM	TAURINE	TELPHER
SWAPPED	SYLVITE	TAGGING	TANKAGE	TAUTEST	TELSTAR
SWAPPER	SYMBOLS	TAG LINE	TANKARD	TAVENER	TEMPERA
SWARMED	SYMPTOM	TAGMEME	TANKERS	TAVERNS	TEMPERS
SWARTHY	SYNAPSE	TAIL END	TANNAGE	TAXABLE	TEMPEST
SWATHED	SYNCARP	TAILING	TANNATE	TAX-FREE	TEMPING
SWATTED	SYNCHRO	TAILORS	TANNERS	TAXICAB	TEMPLES
SWATTER	SYNCOPE	TAINTED	TANNERY	TAXIING	TEMPTED
SWAYING	SYNERGY	TAIYUAN	TANNING	TAXIWAY	TEMPTER
SWEARER	SYNESIS	TAKABLE	TANTRUM	TBILISI	TENABLE
SWEATED	SYNGAMY	TAKEOFF	TAN-TUNG	TBILIZI	TENANCY
SWEATER	SYNODAL	TAKE OFF	TAOISTS	TEABAGS	TENANTS
SWEDISH	SYNODIC	TAKEOUT	TAPERED	TEACAKE	TENCHES
SWEEPER	SYNONYM	TAKE OUT	TAPERER	TEA CAKE	TENDERS
SWEETEN	SYNOVIA	TAKEUPS	TAPETAL	TEACHER	TENDING
SWEETER	SYPHONS	TAKINGS	TAPETUM	TEACH-IN	TENDONS
SWEETIE	SYRINGA	TALCOSE	TAPHOLE	TEA COSY	TENDRIL
SWEETLY	SYRINGE	TALENTS	TAPIOCA	TEACUPS	TENFOLD
SWELLED	SYRPHID	TALIBAN	TAPPETS	TEA GOWN	TENNERS
SWELTER	SYSTEMS	TALIPED	TAPPING	TEALEAF	TENONER
SWERVED	SYSTOLE	TALIPES	TAPROOM	TEAMING	TENPINS
SWERVER	SZILARD	TALIPOT	TAPROOT	TEAPOTS	TENSELY
SWERVES		TALKERS	TARANTO	TEARFUL	TENSEST
SWIFTER	**T**	TALKIES	TARDIER	TEAR GAS	TENSILE
SWIFTLY	TABANID	TALKING	TARDILY	TEARING	TENSING
SWIGGED	TABASCO	TALLAGE	TARGETS	TEAROOM	TENSION
SWIGGER	TABBIES	TALLBOY	TARIFFS	TEASELS	TENSIVE
SWILLED	TABBING	TALLEST	TARMACS	TEASERS	TENTAGE
SWILLER	TABLEAU	TALLIED	TARNISH	TEASHOP	TENUITY
SWIMMER	TABLING	TALLIER	TARRASA	TEASING	TENUOUS
SWINDLE	TABLOID	TALLIES	TARRIED	TEA TREE	TEPIDLY
SWINDON	TABORET	TALLINN	TARRING	TECHILY	TEQUILA
SWINGER	TABORIN	TALLISH	TARSIER	TECHNIC	TERBIUM
SWINGLE	TABULAR	TALLYHO	TARTANS	TECTRIX	TERMING
SWINISH	TACHYON	TAMABLE	TARTARS	TEDIOUS	TERMINI
SWIPING	TACITLY	TAMARAU	TASSELS	TEEMING	TERMITE

TERNARY	THEROUX	THYMINE	TINNILY	TOENAIL	TORMENT
TERNATE	THEURGY	THYROID	TINNING	TOFFEES	TORNADO
TERPENE	THE WASH	THYRSUS	TINTACK	TOGGING	TORONTO
TERRACE	THICKEN	THYSELF	TINTING	TOGGLES	TORPEDO
TERRAIN	THICKER	TIANJIN	TINTYPE	TOHEROA	TORQUAY
TERRANE	THICKET	TIBETAN	TINWARE	TOILETS	TORQUES
TERRENE	THICKIE	TICKERS	TINWORK	TOILING	TORREFY
TERRIER	THICKLY	TICKETS	TIP-OFFS	TOLLING	TORRENT
TERRIFY	THIEVED	TICKING	TIPPERS	TOLUATE	TORREON
TERRINE	THIEVES	TICKLED	TIPPETT	TOLUENE	TORSADE
TERRORS	THIMBLE	TICKLER	TIPPING	TOMBOLA	TORSION
TERSELY	THIN AIR	TICKLES	TIPPLER	TOMBOLO	TORTOLA
TERTIAL	THINNED	TIDBITS	TIPPLES	TOMBOYS	TORTONI
TERTIAN	THINNER	TIDDLER	TIPSIER	TOMCATS	TORTUGA
TESSERA	THIONIC	TIDEWAY	TIPSILY	TOMFOOL	TORTURE
TESTACY	THIONYL	TIDIEST	TIPSTER	TOM-TOMS	TORYISM
TESTATE	THIRSTS	TIDINGS	TIPTOED	TONEPAD	TOSSING
TEST BAN	THIRSTY	TIDYING	TIPTOES	TONETIC	TOSS-UPS
TESTERS	THISTLE	TIE-DIED	TIRADES	TONGUES	TOTALED
TESTIER	THISTLY	TIEPINS	TIREDLY	TONIGHT	TOTALLY
TESTIFY	THITHER	TIFFANY	TISSUES	TONNAGE	TOTE BAG
TESTILY	THORITE	TIGHTEN	TITANIA	TONNEAU	TOTEMIC
TESTING	THORIUM	TIGHTER	TITANIC	TONSILS	TOTTERY
TETANIC	THOUGHT	TIGHTLY	TITBITS	TONSURE	TOTTING
TETANUS	THRALLS	TIGRESS	TITFERS	TONTINE	TOUCANS
TETHERS	THREADS	TIJUANA	TITHING	TOOLING	TOUCHED
TETRODE	THREADY	TILAPIA	TITMICE	TOOTING	TOUCHER
TEXTILE	THREATS	TILBURG	TITOISM	TOOTLED	TOUCHES
TEXTING	THREE	TILLAGE	TITOIST	TOOTLER	TOUGHEN
TEXTUAL	R'S	TILLERS	TITRANT	TOOTLES	TOUGHER
TEXTURE	THRIFTS	TILLING	TITRATE	TOOTSIE	TOUGHLY
THALLIC	THRIFTY	TILTING	TITTERS	TOPARCH	TOUPEES
THALLUS	THRILLS	TIMBALE	TITTIES	TOPAZES	TOURACO
THANKED	THRIVED	TIMBERS	TITULAR	TOPCOAT	TOURING
THAWING	THROATS	TIMBREL	TIZZIES	TOP DOGS	TOURISM
THE ARTS	THROATY	TIMBRES	TLEMCEN	TOP HATS	TOURIST
THEATRE	THRONES	TIME LAG	TOADIED	TOPIARY	TOURNAI
THE BARD	THRONGS	TIME-OUT	TOADIES	TOPICAL	TOURNEY
THEISTS	THROUGH	TIMIDLY	TOADLET	TOPKNOT	TOUSLED
THEOREM	THROWER	TIMPANI	TOASTED	TOPLESS	TOUTING
THERAPY	THROW IN	TINAMOU	TOASTER	TOPMAST	TOWARDS
THEREAT	THROW-IN	TINFOIL	TOASTIE	TOPMOST	TOWBOAT
THEREBY	THRUSTS	TINGING	TOBACCO	TOPONYM	TOWELED
THEREIN	THRUWAY	TINGLED	TOBOLSK	TOPPERS	TOWERED
THEREOF	THUDDED	TINGLER	TOBY JUG	TOPPING	TOWHEAD
THEREON	THULIUM	TIN GODS	TOCCATA	TOPPLED	TOWLINE
THERETO	THUMBED	TIN HATS	TOCSINS	TOPSAIL	TOWPATH
THERMAL	THUMBS	TINIEST	TODDIES	TOPSIDE	TOWROPE
THERMIC	THUMPED	TINKERS	TODDLED	TOPSOIL	TOW ROPE
THERMIT	THUMPER	TINKLED	TODDLER	TOPSPIN	TRABZON
THERMOS	THUNDER	TINKLES	TOE CAPS	TORCHES	TRACERS
THEROID	THWACKS	TINNIER	TOEHOLD	TORFAEN	TRACERY

TRACHEA	TREHALA	TRIPPET	TRUSSER	TURMOIL	TWOFOLD
TRACING	TREKKED	TRIPURA	TRUSSES	TURNERS	TWONESS
TRACKED	TREKKER	TRIREME	TRUSTED	TURNERY	TWOSOME
TRACKER	TREKKIE	TRISECT	TRUSTEE	TURNING	TWO-STAR
TRACTOR	TRELLIS	TRISMIC	TRUSTER	TURNIPS	TWO-STEP
TRADE IN	TREMBLE	TRISMUS	TRYPSIN	TURNKEY	TWO-TIME
TRADE-IN	TREMBLY	TRISOME	TRYPTIC	TURN OFF	TWO-TONE
TRADERS	TREMOLO	TRISOMY	TRYSAIL	TURN-OFF	TYCHISM
TRADING	TREMORS	TRITELY	TRYSTER	TURN-ONS	TYCOONS
TRADUCE	TRENTON	TRITIUM	TSARDOM	TURN OUT	TYLOSIS
TRAFFIC	TREPANG	TRITONE	TSARINA	TURNOUT	TYMPANA
TRAGEDY	TRESSES	TRIUMPH	TSARIST	TURNS UP	TYMPANY
TRAILED	TRESTLE	TRIVETS	T-SHIRTS	TURN-UPS	TYNWALD
TRAILER	TREVISO	TRIVIAL	T-SQUARE	TURPETH	TYPEBAR
TRAINED	TRIABLE	TROCHAL	TSUNAMI	TURRETS	TYPESET
TRAINEE	TRIACID	TROCHEE	TUATARA	TURTLER	TYPHOID
TRAINER	TRIADIC	TRODDEN	TUBBIER	TURTLES	TYPHOON
TRAIPSE	TRIBADE	TROIKAS	TUBBING	TUSCANY	TYPHOUS
TRAITOR	TRIBUNE	TROJANS	TUBIFEX	TUSKERS	TYPICAL
TRAJECT	TRIBUTE	TROLLED	TUBULAR	TUSSIVE	TYPISTS
TRAMCAR	TRICEPS	TROLLEY	TUCKING	TUSSLED	TYRANNY
TRAMMEL	TRICKED	TROLLOP	TUCUMAN	TUSSLES	TYRANTS
TRAMPED	TRICKER	TROMMEL	TUESDAY	TUSSOCK	TYRONIC
TRAMPER	TRICKLE	TROOPED	TUGGING	TUTORED	TZARINA
TRAMPLE	TRICKLY	TROOPER	TUITION	TUTUILA	
TRAMWAY	TRICKSY	TROPHIC	TUMBLED	TUTUOLA	**U**
TRANCES	TRICORN	TROPICS	TUMBLER	TUXEDOS	UDAIPUR
TRANCHE	TRIDENT	TROPISM	TUMBLES	TWADDLE	UGANDAN
TRANSIT	TRIDUUM	TROTTED	TUMBREL	TWANGED	UGLIEST
TRANSOM	TRIED ON	TROTTER	TUMMIES	TWEAKED	UKRAINE
TRAPANI	TRIESTE	TROUBLE	TUMOURS	TWEETED	UKULELE
TRAPEZE	TRIFLED	TROUGHS	TUMULAR	TWEETER	ULANOVA
TRAPPED	TRIFLER	TROUNCE	TUMULTS	TWEETUP	ULAN-UDE
TRAPPER	TRIFLES	TROUPER	TUMULUS	TWELFTH	ULLAGED
TRASHED	TRIGGER	TROUPES	TUNABLE	TWELVES	ULULANT
TRAUMAS	TRILLED	TROUSER	TUNEFUL	TWIDDLE	ULULATE
TRAVAIL	TRILOGY	TROWELS	TUNICLE	TWIDDLY	UMBRAGE
TRAVELS	TRIMBLE	TRUANCY	TUNISIA	TWIGGED	UMBRIAN
TRAVOIS	TRIMMED	TRUANTS	TUNNELS	TWI-HARD	UMBRIEL
TRAWLED	TRIMMER	TRUCKED	TUNNIES	TWIN BED	UMLAUTS
TRAWLER	TRINARY	TRUCKER	TUPPING	TWINGES	UMPIRED
TREACLE	TRINITY	TRUCKLE	TURBANS	TWINING	UMPIRES
TREACLY	TRINKET	TRUDGED	TURBARY	TWINKLE	UMPTEEN
TREADER	TRIOLET	TRUDGEN	TURBINE	TWINNED	UNAIDED
TREADLE	TRIPLED	TRUDGER	TURBOTS	TWIN SET	UNARMED
TREAD ON	TRIPLET	TRUDGES	TURDINE	TWIRLED	UNAWARE
TREASON	TRIPLEX	TRUFFLE	TUREENS	TWIRLER	UNBONED
TREATED	TRIPODS	TRUISMS	TURFING	TWISTED	UNBOSOM
TREATER	TRIPODY	TRUMPED	TURGITE	TWISTER	UNBOUND
TREBLED	TRIPOLI	TRUMPET	TURKEYS	TWITTED	UNBOWED
TREBLES	TRIPPED	TRUNDLE	TURKISH	TWITTER	UNBRACE
TREFOIL	TRIPPER	TRUSSED	TURKMEN	TWIZZLE	UNCAGED

UNCANNY	UNPAGED	UPTAKES	UTTERLY	VARYING	VERSACE
UNCHAIN	UNPOSED	UPTHROW	UVEITIC	VASSALS	VERSANT
UNCINUS	UNQUIET	UPTIGHT	UVEITIS	VASTITY	VERSIFY
UNCIVIL	UNQUOTE	UP TO	UVULARS	VATICAN	VERSION
UNCLASP	UNRAVEL	YOU	UXORIAL	VAUDOIS	VERTIGO
UNCLEAN	UNREADY	UPTURNS		VAULTED	VERVAIN
UNCLEAR	UNREEVE	UPWARDS	**V**	VAULTER	VESICAL
UNCLOAK	UNSCREW	URAEMIA	VACANCY	VAUNTED	VESICLE
UNCLOSE	UNSLING	URAEMIC	VACATED	VAUNTER	VESPERS
UNCOUTH	UNSNARL	URALITE	VACCINE	VECTORS	VESPINE
UNCOVER	UNSOUND	URANIAN	VACUITY	VEDALIA	VESSELS
UNCROSS	UNSTICK	URANIDE	VACUOLE	VEDDOID	VESTIGE
UNCTION	UNSTRAP	URANITE	VACUOUS	VEDETTE	VESTING
UNDERDO	UNSTUCK	URANIUM	VACUUMS	VEERING	VESTRAL
UNDERGO	UNSWEAR	URANOUS	VAGINAL	VEGETAL	VESTURE
UNDOING	UNTHINK	URCHINS	VAGINAS	VEHICLE	VETCHES
UNDRESS	UNTRIED	UREDIAL	VAGRANT	VEILING	VETERAN
UNDYING	UNTRUSS	UREDIUM	VAGUELY	VEINING	VETIVER
UNEARTH	UNTRUTH	URETHRA	VAINEST	VEINLET	VETOING
UNEQUAL	UNTYING	URGENCY	VALANCE	VELAMEN	VETTING
UNFROCK	UNUSUAL	URIDINE	VALENCE	VELIGER	VEXEDLY
UNFUSSY	UNVOICE	URINALS	VALENCY	VELLORE	VIADUCT
UNGODLY	UNWAGED	URINANT	VALERIC	VELOURS	VIBRANT
UNGUENT	UNWOUND	URINARY	VALIANT	VELVETY	VIBRATE
UNGULAR	UP-AND-	URINATE	VALIDLY	VENALLY	VIBRATO
UNHAPPY	UP	URINOUS	VALISES	VENATIC	VICENZA
UNHEARD	UPBRAID	URMSTON	VALLEYS	VENDACE	VICEROY
UNHINGE	UPBUILD	URNLIKE	VALONIA	VENDING	VICINAL
UNHORSE	UPCHUCK	URODELE	VALUERS	VENDORS	VICIOUS
UNICORN	UPDATED	UROLITH	VALUING	VENEERS	VICOMTE
UNIFIED	UPDATER	UROLOGY	VALVATE	VENISON	VICTIMS
UNIFIER	UPDATES	URUAPAN	VALVULE	VENTAGE	VICTORS
UNIFORM	UPDRAFT	URUGUAY	VAMOOSE	VENTING	VICTORY
UNITARY	UPENDED	URUMCHI	VAMPIRE	VENTRAL	VICTRIX
UNITIES	UPFRONT	USELESS	VANADIC	VENTURE	VICTUAL
UNITING	UP FRONT	USHERED	VANDALS	VENULAR	VICUNAS
UNITIVE	UPGRADE	USUALLY	VANILLA	VERANDA	VIDEOED
UNKEMPT	UPHEAVE	USURERS	VANTAGE	VERBENA	VIDICON
UNKNOWN	UPLANDS	USURPED	VANUATU	VERBIFY	VIETNAM
UNLATCH	UPPSALA	USURPER	VANWARD	VERBOSE	VIEWERS
UNLEARN	UPRAISE	UTENSIL	VAPIDLY	VERDANT	VIEWING
UNLEASH	UPRIGHT	UTERINE	VAPOURS	VERDICT	VIKINGS
UNLOOSE	UPRISER	UTILITY	VARIANT	VERDURE	VILLACH
UNLUCKY	UPRIVER	UTILIZE	VARIATE	VERGERS	VILLAGE
UNMAKER	UPSCALE	UT INFRA	VARIETY	VERGING	VILLAIN
UNMANLY	UPSILON	UTOPIAN	VARIOLA	VERGLAS	VILLEIN
UNMEANT	UPSKILL	UTOPIAS	VARIOLE	VERISMO	VILLOUS
UNMORAL	UPSTAGE	UTRECHT	VARIOUS	VERMEIL	VILNIUS
UNMOVED	UPSTART	UTRICLE	VARLETS	VERMONT	VINASSE
UNNAMED	UPSURGE	UT SUPRA	VARMINT	VERNIER	VINEGAR
UNNERVE	UPSWEEP	UTTERED	VARNISH	VERONAL	VINTAGE
UNOWNED	UPSWING	UTTERER	VARSITY	VERRUCA	VINTNER

VIOLATE	VOLAPUK	WAKEFUL	WARM-UPS	WEANING	WENDISH
VIOLENT	VOLCANO	WAKENED	WARNING	WEAPONS	WEST END
VIOLETS	VOLLEYS	WAKENER	WARPAGE	WEARIED	WESTERN
VIOLINS	VOLOGDA	WALCOTT	WARPATH	WEARIER	WESTING
VIOLIST	VOLTAGE	WALKERS	WARPING	WEARILY	WET-LOOK
VIRAGOS	VOLTAIC	WALKIES	WARRANT	WEARING	WETNESS
VIRELAY	VOLUBLE	WALKING	WARRENS	WEASELS	WET SUIT
VIRGATE	VOLUBLY	WALKMAN	WARRING	WEATHER	WETTEST
VIRGINS	VOLUMED	WALK OFF	WARRIOR	WEAVERS	WETTING
VIRGOAN	VOLUMES	WALK-ONS	WARSHIP	WEAVING	WETTISH
VIRGULE	VOLVATE	WALKOUT	WARTHOG	WEBBING	WEXFORD
VIRTUAL	VOMITED	WALK-UPS	WARTIME	WEBFOOT	WHACKED
VIRTUES	VOMITER	WALLABY	WARWICK	WEBSITE	WHACKER
VIRUSES	VOMITUS	WALLAHS	WASHDAY	WEB-TOED	WHALERS
VISAGES	VORLAGE	WALLETS	WASHERS	WEDDING	WHALING
VISAING	VOTABLE	WALLEYE	WASHERY	WEDGING	WHANGEE
VIS-A-	VOUCHED	WALLIES	WASHING	WEDLOCK	WHARVES
VIS	VOUCHER	WALLING	WASHOUT	WEEDIER	WHAT FOR
VISAYAN	VOX POPS	WALLOON	WASHTUB	WEEDILY	WHATNOT
VISCERA	VOYAGED	WALLOPS	WASPILY	WEEDING	WHATSIT
VISCOID	VOYAGER	WALLOWS	WASPISH	WEEKDAY	WHEATEN
VISCOSE	VOYAGES	WALNUTS	WASSAIL	WEEKEND	WHEEDLE
VISCOUS	VOYEURS	WALSALL	WASTAGE	WEENIER	WHEELED
VISIBLE	VULGATE	WALTZED	WASTERS	WEEPING	WHEELER
VISIBLY	VULPINE	WALTZER	WASTING	WEEVILS	WHEELIE
VISIONS	VULTURE	WALTZES	WASTREL	WEEVILY	WHEEZED
VISITED		WANGLED	WATCHED	WEIGELA	WHEEZER
VISITOR	**W**	WANGLER	WATCHER	WEIGHED	WHEEZES
VISTAED		WANGLES	WATCHES	WEIGHER	WHEREAS
VISTULA	WADABLE	WANKERS	WATERED	WEIGHTS	WHEREAT
VITALLY	WADDING	WANKING	WATERER	WEIGHTY	WHEREBY
VITAMIN	WADDLED	WANNABE	WATFORD	WEIRDER	WHEREIN
VITEBSK	WADDLER	WANNESS	WATTAGE	WEIRDIE	WHEREOF
VITIATE	WADDLES	WANNEST	WATTEAU	WEIRDLY	WHEREON
VITORIA	WAFFLED	WANNING	WATTLES	WEIRDOS	WHERETO
VITRAIN	WAFFLES	WANT ADS	WAVELET	WELCHED	WHERRIT
VITRIFY	WAFTAGE	WANTING	WAVEOFF	WELCOME	WHETHER
VITRINE	WAFTING	WAPITIS	WAVERED	WELDERS	WHETTED
VITRIOL	WAGERED	WARBLED	WAVERER	WELDING	WHETTER
VITTATE	WAGERER	WARBLER	WAVIEST	WELFARE	WHICKER
VIVIDLY	WAGGING	WARDENS	WAXBILL	WELL-FED	WHIFFER
VIYELLA	WAGGISH	WARDERS	WAXIEST	WELLIES	WHIFFLE
VIZIERS	WAGGLED	WARDING	WAXLIKE	WELLING	WHILING
V-NECKED	WAGGLES	WARFARE	WAXWING	WELL-OFF	WHIMPER
VOCABLE	WAGONER	WAR GAME	WAXWORK	WELL-SET	WHINERS
VOCALIC	WAGTAIL	WARHEAD	WAYBILL	WELSHED	WHINGED
VOCALLY	WAILFUL	WARIEST	WAYLAID	WELSHER	WHINING
VOCODER	WAILING	WARLIKE	WAYLAIN	WEMBLEY	WHIPPED
VOETSEK	WAISTED	WARLOCK	WAYSIDE	WENCHED	WHIPPER
VOICING	WAITERS	WARLORD	WAYWARD	WENCHER	WHIPPET
VOIDING	WAITING	WARMEST	WEAKEST	WENCHES	WHIPSAW
VOIOTIA	WAIVING	WARMING	WEALTHY	WENDING	

WHIRLED	WILTING	WOLFING	WREAKED	YAKUTSK	ZAMBEZI
WHIRLER	WIMPIES	WOLFISH	WREAKER	YANGTZE	ZAMBIAN
WHIRRED	WIMPISH	WOLFRAM	WREATHE	YANKEES	ZANIEST
WHISKED	WIMPLES	WOMANLY	WREATHS	YANKING	ZAPOTEC
WHISKER	WINCHED	WOMBATS	WRECKED	YAOUNDE	ZAPPIER
WHISKEY	WINCHER	WONDERS	WRECKER	YAPPING	ZAPPING
WHISPER	WINCHES	WONKIER	WRESTED	YARDAGE	ZEALAND
WHISTLE	WINCING	WOODCUT	WRESTER	YARDARM	ZEALOTS
WHITEST	WINDAGE	WOODIER	WRESTLE	YARD ARM	ZEALOUS
WHITHER	WINDBAG	WOODMAN	WREXHAM	YARNING	ZEBRINE
WHITING	WINDIER	WOODSIA	WRIGGLE	YASHMAK	ZEDOARY
WHITLOW	WINDILY	WOOFERS	WRIGGLY	YATHRIB	ZEELAND
WHITSUN	WINDING	WOOFTER	WRINGER	YAWNING	ZENITHS
WHITTLE	WINDOWS	WOOLLEN	WRINKLE	YEAR DOT	ZEOLITE
WHIZZED	WINDROW	WOOMERA	WRINKLY	YEARNED	ZEPHYRS
WHIZZES	WINDSOR	WOOZIER	WRITE-IN	YEARNER	ZERMATT
WHOEVER	WINE BAR	WOOZILY	WRITERS	YELLING	ZEROING
WHOOPED	WINGERS	WORDAGE	WRITE-UP	YELLOWS	ZESTFUL
WHOOPEE	WINGING	WORDIER	WRITHED	YELPING	ZHDANOV
WHOOPER	WINGLET	WORDILY	WRITHER	YENISEI	ZIGZAGS
WHOPPED	WING NUT	WORDING	WRITING	YEREVAN	ZILLION
WHOPPER	WINKERS	WORKBAG	WRITTEN	YESHIVA	ZINCATE
WHORISH	WINKING	WORKBOX	WROCLAW	YEW TREE	ZINCITE
WHORLED	WINKLED	WORKDAY	WRONGED	Y-FRONTS	ZIONISM
WHYALLA	WINKLES	WORKERS	WRONGER	YICHANG	ZIONIST
WICHITA	WINLESS	WORKING	WRONGLY	YIDDISH	ZIP CODE
WICKETS	WINNERS	WORKMAN	WROUGHT	YIELDED	ZIPPERS
WICKING	WINNING	WORKMEN	WRYBILL	YIELDER	ZIPPIER
WICKLOW	WINSOME	WORKOUT	WRYNECK	YINGKOU	ZIPPING
WIDE BOY	WINTERS	WORKSHY	WRYNESS	YINGKOW	ZITHERS
WIDENED	WIRETAP	WORKSOP	WYCH-ELM	YODELED	ZODIACS
WIDENER	WIRIEST	WORKTOP	WYOMING	YOGHURT	ZOISITE
WIDGEON	WISBECH	WORLDLY	WYSIWYG	YONKERS	ZOMBIES
WIDOWED	WISE GUY	WORMIER	WYVERNS	YORKIST	ZONALLY
WIDOWER	WISHFUL	WORMING		YORUBAN	ZONULAR
WIELDED	WISHING	WORN-OUT		YOUNGER	ZOOLOGY
WIELDER	WISPIER	WORRIED	**X**	YOUTUBE	ZOOMING
WIGGING	WISPILY	WORRIER		YOWLING	ZOOTOMY
WIGGLED	WISTFUL	WORRIES	XANTHIC	YTTRIUM	ZORILLA
WIGGLER	WITCHES	WORSHIP	XANTHIN	YUCATAN	ZWICKAU
WIGGLES	WITHERS	WORSTED	XERARCH	YUCKIER	ZYGOSIS
WIGWAMS	WITHOUT	WOTCHER	XEROSIS	YUKONER	ZYGOTIC
WILDCAT	WITLESS	WOULD-BE	XEROTIC	YULE LOG	ZYMOGEN
WILD DOG	WITNESS	WOULDN'T	XEROXED	YUPPIES	ZYMOSIS
WILDEST	WITTIER	WOUNDED	XEROXES	YUPPIFY	ZYMOTIC
WILDING	WITTILY	WOUNDER	XIPHOID		ZYMURGY
WILIEST	WIZARDS	WOUND-UP	X-RAYING		
WILLIES	WIZENED	WRAITHS		**Z**	
WILLING	WOBBLED	WRANGLE	**Y**	ZAGAZIG	
WILLOWS	WOBBLER	WRAPPED		ZAIREAN	
WILLOWY	WOBBLES	WRAPPER	YACHTIE	ZAIRESE	
			YAKKING		

8

A	ABSCISSA	ACCUSTOM	ACTINIDE	AD-	AFFINITY
AARDVARK	ABSEILED	ACCUTRON	ACTINISM	LIBBER	AFFIRMED
AARDWOLF	ABSENCES	ACENTRIC	ACTINIUM	ADMIRALS	AFFIRMER
ABACUSES	ABSENTED	ACERBATE	ACTINOID	ADMIRERS	AFFIXING
ABAMPERE	ABSENTEE	ACERBITY	ACTIVATE	ADMIRING	AFFLATUS
ABATTOIR	ABSENTER	ACERVATE	ACTIVELY	ADMITTED	AFFLUENT
ABBATIAL	ABSENTLY	ACESCENT	ACTIVISM	ADMONISH	AFFORDED
ABBESSES	ABSINTHE	ACHENIAL	ACTIVIST	ADOPTING	AFFOREST
ABDICATE	ABSOLUTE	ACHIEVED	ACTIVITY	ADOPTION	AFFRONTS
ABDOMENS	ABSOLVED	ACHIEVER	ACT OF	ADOPTIVE	AFFUSION
ABDUCENT	ABSOLVER	ACHILLES	GOD	ADORABLE	AFLUTTER
ABDUCTED	ABSORBED	ACHROMAT	ACTUALLY	ADORNING	AFRICANS
ABELMOSK	ABSORBER	ACHROMIC	ACTUATED	ADRIATIC	AGARTALA
ABEOKUTA	ABSTRACT	ACICULAR	ACTUATOR	ADROITLY	AGE
ABERDARE	ABSTRUSE	ACICULUM	ACULEATE	ADULARIA	GROUP
ABERDEEN	ABSURDLY	ACID	ACUTANCE	ADULATOR	AGENCIES
ABERRANT	ABU	DROP	ADAM'S	ADULTERY	AGENESIS
ABETTING	DHABI	ACID-	ALE	ADUMBRAL	AGENETIC
ABETTORS	ABUNDANT	FAST	ADAMSITE	ADVANCED	AGENTIAL
ABEYANCE	ABUTILON	ACIDNESS	ADAPTERS	ADVANCER	AGENTIVE
ABHORRED	ABUTMENT	ACIDOSIS	ADAPTING	ADVANCES	AGERATUM
ABHORRER	ABUTTALS	ACIDOTIC	ADAPTIVE	ADVERTED	AGGRIEVE
ABIDANCE	ABUTTING	ACID	ADDENDUM	ADVISERS	AGIOTAGE
ABINGDON	ACADEMIA	RAIN	ADDICTED	ADVISING	AGITATED
AB	ACADEMIC	ACID	ADDITION	ADVISORY	AGITATOR
INITIO	ACANTHUS	TEST	ADDITIVE	ADVOCAAT	AGITPROP
ABJECTLY	ACAPULCO	ACIERATE	ADDUCENT	ADVOCACY	AGMINATE
ABJURING	ACARPOUS	ACOLYTES	ADDUCING	ADVOCATE	AGNOSTIC
ABKHAZIA	ACCEDING	ACONITIC	ADDUCTOR	ADYNAMIA	AGONIZED
ABLATION	ACCENTED	ACOUSTIC	ADELAIDE	ADYNAMIC	AGRAPHIA
ABLATIVE	ACCENTOR	ACQUAINT	ADENITIS	AEGROTAT	AGRARIAN
ABLUTION	ACCEPTED	ACQUIRED	ADENOIDS	AERATING	AGRESTAL
ABNEGATE	ACCEPTOR	ACQUIRER	ADEQUACY	AERATION	AGRIMONY
ABNORMAL	ACCESSED	ACRE-	ADEQUATE	AERIALLY	AGROLOGY
ABOMASUM	ACCESSES	FOOT	ADHERENT	AEROBICS	AGRONOMY
ABORTING	ACCIDENT	ACRE-	ADHERING	AERODYNE	AGUEWEED
ABORTION	ACCOLADE	INCH	ADHESION	AEROFOIL	AIGRETTE
ABORTIVE	ACCORDED	ACRIDINE	ADHESIVE	AEROGRAM	AIGUILLE
ABOUNDED	ACCORDER	ACRIDITY	ADJACENT	AEROLITE	AILERONS
ABRADANT	ACCOSTED	ACRIMONY	ADJOINED	AEROLOGY	AILMENTS
ABRADING	ACCOUNTS	ACROBATS	ADJUDGED	AERONAUT	AIRBASES
ABRASION	ACCREDIT	ACRODONT	ADJUNCTS	AEROSOLS	AIRBORNE
ABRASIVE	ACCRUING	ACROLEIN	ADJURING	AEROSTAT	AIRBRAKE
ABRIDGED	ACCURACY	ACROLITH	ADJUSTED	AESTHETE	AIRBRICK
ABRIDGER	ACCURATE	ACROMION	ADJUTANT	AFEBRILE	AIRBRUSH
ABROGATE	ACCURSED	ACRONYMS	ADJUVANT	AFFECTED	AIRBURST
ABRUPTLY	ACCUSERS	ACROSTIC	AD-	AFFERENT	AIRBUSES
	ACCUSING	ACRYLICS	LIBBED	AFFIANCE	AIRCRAFT

AIRCREWS	ALGOLOGY	ALMONERS	AMPERAGE	ANECDOTE
AIREDALE	ALGORISM	ALOPECIA	AMPHIPOD	ANECHOIC
AIRFIELD	ALHAMBRA	ALPHABET	AMPHORAE	ANEMONES
AIRFORCE	ALICANTE	ALPHOSIS	AMPHORAS	ANETHOLE
AIR FORCE	ALIENAGE	ALPINISM	AMPOULES	ANEURYSM
AIRFRAME	ALIENATE	ALPINIST	AMPULLAR	ANFINSEN
AIRINESS	ALIENISM	ALSATIAN	AMPUTATE	ANGELENO
AIRLANES	ALIENIST	ALSO-RANS	AMPUTEES	ANGELICA
AIRLIFTS	ALIGHTED	ALTER EGO	AMRAVATI	ANGERING
AIRLINER	ALIGNING	ALTERING	AMRITSAR	ANGINOSE
AIRLINES	ALIQUANT	ALTHOUGH	AMYGDALA	ANGLESEY
AIRLOCKS	ALIZARIN	ALTITUDE	AMYGDALE	ANGLICAN
AIR MILES	ALKAHEST	ALTRUISM	ANABAENA	ANGRIEST
AIRPLANE	ALKALIES	ALTRUIST	ANABASIS	ANGSTROM
AIRPORTS	ALKALIFY	ALUMROOT	ANABATIC	ANGUILLA
AIR RAIDS	ALKALINE	ALVEOLAR	ANABLEPS	ANGULATE
AIRSCREW	ALKALIZE	ALVEOLUS	ANABOLIC	ANHEDRAL
AIRSHIPS	ALKALOID	AMALGAMS	ANACONDA	ANIMATED
AIRSPACE	ALLANITE	AMARANTH	ANAEROBE	ANIMATOR
AIRSPEED	ALLAYING	AMARELLE	ANAGLYPH	ANIMISTS
AIRSTRIP	ALL CLEAR	AMARILLO	ANAGOGIC	ANISETTE
AIRTIGHT	ALLEGING	AMASSING	ANAGRAMS	ANKERITE
AIR-TO-AIR	ALLEGORY	AMATEURS	ANALCITE	ANKYLOSE
AIRWAVES	ALLELISM	AMAZONAS	ANALECTS	ANNALIST
AIRWOMAN	ALLELUIA	AMBEROID	ANALEMMA	ANN ARBOR
AIRWOMEN	ALLEPPEY	AMBIENCE	ANALOGUE	ANNEALED
A LA CARTE	ALLERGEN	AMBITION	ANALYSED	ANNEALER
ALACRITY	ALLERGIC	AMBIVERT	ANALYSER	ANNEXING
ALARMING	ALLEYWAY	AMBROSIA	ANALYSES	ANNOTATE
ALARMISM	ALLIANCE	AMBULANT	ANALYSIS	ANNOUNCE
ALARMIST	ALLOCATE	AMBULATE	ANALYSTS	ANNOYING
ALBACORE	ALLODIAL	AMBUSHED	ANALYTIC	ANNUALLY
ALBANIAN	ALLODIUM	AMBUSHES	ANAPAEST	ANNULATE
ALBINISM	ALLOGAMY	AMENABLE	ANAPHASE	ANNULLED
ALCATRAZ	ALLOPATH	AMENDING	ANAPHORA	ANNULOSE
ALCHEMIC	ALLOTTED	AMERICAN	ANARCHIC	ANODYNES
ALCHEVSK	ALLOTTEE	AMETHYST	ANASARCA	ANOINTED
ALCIDINE	ALLOWING	AMICABLE	ANATHEMA	ANOINTER
ALCOHOLS	ALLOYING	AMICABLY	ANATOLIA	ANOREXIA
ALCOPOPS	ALL RIGHT	AMITOSIS	ANCESTOR	ANSERINE
ALDEHYDE	ALL ROUND	AMITOTIC	ANCESTRY	ANSWERED
ALDERMAN	ALL-ROUND	AMMETERS	ANCHORED	ANTABUSE
ALDERMEN	ALLSPICE	AMMONIAC	ANCIENTS	ANTEATER
ALDERNEY	ALL THERE	AMMONIFY	ANDANTES	ANTECEDE
ALDOXIME	ALLUDING	AMMONITE	ANDERSON	ANTEDATE
ALEATORY	ALLURING	AMMONIUM	ANDESINE	ANTELOPE
ALEHOUSE	ALLUSION	AMNESIAC	ANDESITE	ANTENNAS
ALERTING	ALLUSIVE	AMNIOTIC	ANDIRONS	ANTE-POST
ALFRESCO	ALLUVIAL	AMOEBOID	ANDIZHAN	ANTERIOR
ALGERIAN	ALLUVIUM	AMORETTO	ANDORRAN	ANTEROOM
ALGERINE	ALMANACS	AMORTIZE	ANDROGEN	ANTEVERT
ALGINATE	ALMIGHTY	AMOUNTED	ANDROIDS	ANTHELIX

ANTHESIS	APOSTATE	ARCHIVAL	ARSONIST	ASSIGNAT
ANTHILLS	APOSTLES	ARCHIVES	ARTEFACT	ASSIGNED
ANTIBODY	APPALLED	ARCHNESS	ARTERIAL	ASSIGNEE
ANTIDOTE	APPANAGE	ARCHWAYS	ARTERIES	ASSIGNER
ANTIGENS	APPARENT	ARC LIGHT	ARTESIAN	ASSIGNOR
ANTIHERO	APPEALED	ARCTURUS	ARTFULLY	ASSISTED
ANTI HERO	APPEALER	ARDENNES	ART HOUSE	ASSISTER
ANTI-ICER	APPEARED	ARDENTLY	ARTICLED	ASSONANT
ANTILLES	APPEASED	AREA CODE	ARTICLES	ASSORTED
ANTIMERE	APPELLEE	ARENITIC	ARTIFACT	ASSORTER
ANTIMONY	APPENDED	AREQUIPA	ARTIFICE	ASSUAGED
ANTI-NAZI	APPENDIX	ARETHUSA	ARTINESS	ASSUAGER
ANTINODE	APPESTAT	ARGENTIC	ARTISANS	ASSUMING
ANTINOMY	APPETITE	ARGININE	ARTISTES	ASSURING
ANTIPHON	APPLAUSE	ARGUABLE	ARTISTIC	ASSYRIAN
ANTIQUES	APPLE PIE	ARGUABLY	ARTISTRY	ASTATINE
ANTI-RIOT	APPLIQUE	ARGUMENT	ARYANIZE	ASTERISK
ANTITANK	APPLYING	ARIANISM	ASBESTOS	ASTERISM
ANTONINE	APPOSITE	ARILLATE	ASCENDED	ASTERNAL
ANTONYMS	APPRAISE	ARILLODE	ASCENDER	ASTEROID
ANTRORSE	APPRISED	ARISTATE	ASCETICS	ASTHENIA
ANURESIS	APPROACH	ARKANSAS	ASCIDIAN	ASTHENIC
ANYPLACE	APPROVAL	ARMAGNAC	ASCIDIUM	ASTONISH
ANYTHING	APPROVED	ARMALITE	ASCOCARP	ASTRAGAL
ANYWHERE	APRES-SKI	ARMAMENT	ASCORBIC	ASTURIAS
AORISTIC	APRICOTS	ARMATURE	ASCRIBED	ASTUTELY
APAGOGIC	APTEROUS	ARMBANDS	ASHTRAYS	ASUNCION
APATETIC	APTITUDE	ARMCHAIR	ASNIERES	ATARAXIA
APERIENT	APYRETIC	ARMENIAN	ASPERITY	AT BOTTOM
APERITIF	AQUALUNG	ARMHOLES	ASPERSER	ATHEISTS
APERTURE	AQUANAUT	ARMIDALE	ASPHODEL	ATHENIAN
APHANITE	AQUARIST	ARMORIAL	ASPHYXIA	ATHEROMA
APHELIAN	AQUARIUM	ARMOURED	ASPIRANT	ATHLETES
APHELION	AQUARIUS	ARMOURER	ASPIRATE	ATHLETIC
APHORISM	AQUATICS	ARMS RACE	ASPIRING	ATLANTIC
APHORIST	AQUATINT	AROMATIC	ASPIRINS	ATLANTIS
APHORIZE	AQUEDUCT	AROUSING	ASSAILED	AT LENGTH
APIARIAN	AQUILINE	ARPEGGIO	ASSAILER	ATOM BOMB
APIARIES	ARACHNID	ARRANGED	ASSAMESE	ATOMIZER
APIARIST	ARAPAIMA	ARRANGER	ASSASSIN	ATONABLE
APIOLOGY	ARAWAKAN	ARRAYING	ASSAULTS	ATONALLY
APLASTIC	ARBITERS	ARRESTED	ASSAYING	ATROCITY
APOCRINE	ARBITRAL	ARRESTER	ASSEGAIS	ATROPHIC
APODOSIS	ARBOREAL	ARRIVALS	ASSEMBLE	ATROPINE
APOGAMIC	ARBROATH	ARRIVING	ASSEMBLY	ATTACHED
APOLOGIA	ARCADIAN	ARROGANT	ASSENTED	ATTACHER
APOLOGUE	ARCATURE	ARROGATE	ASSENTOR	ATTACHES
APOMIXIS	ARCHAEAN	ARROWING	ASSERTED	ATTACKED
APOPHYGE	ARCHAISM	ARSENALS	ASSERTER	ATTACKER
APOPLEXY	ARCHAIST	ARSENATE	ASSESSED	ATTAINED
APOSPORY	ARCHAIZE	ARSENIDE	ASSESSOR	ATTEMPTS
APOSTASY	ARCHDUKE	ARSENITE	ASSHOLES	ATTENDED

ATTENDEE	AVENGING	BACKDROP	BALLADRY	BAREFOOT
ATTESTED	AVERAGED	BACKFILL	BALLARAT	BAREILLY
ATTIRING	AVERAGES	BACKFIRE	BALLCOCK	BARENESS
ATTITUDE	AVERMENT	BACKHAND	BALL GAME	BARGAINS
ATTORNEY	AVERRING	BACKINGS	BALLONET	BAR GRAPH
ATTUNING	AVERSION	BACKLASH	BALLOONS	BARITONE
ATYPICAL	AVERSIVE	BACKLESS	BALLOTED	BARLETTA
AUBUSSON	AVERTING	BACKLIST	BALL PARK	BARMAIDS
AUCKLAND	AVIARIES	BACKLOGS	BALLROOM	BARMIEST
AUCTIONS	AVIATION	BACKPACK	BALLS-UPS	BARNACLE
AUDACITY	AVIATORS	BACK SEAT	BALLYHOO	BARNSLEY
AUDIENCE	AVIATRIX	BACKSIDE	BALMIEST	BARNYARD
AUDITING	AVIDNESS	BACKSLID	BALMORAL	BAROGRAM
AUDITION	AVIEMORE	BACKSPIN	BALSAMIC	BARONAGE
AUDITORS	AVIFAUNA	BACKSTAY	BALUSTER	BARONESS
AUDITORY	AVIONICS	BACKSTOP	BANALITY	BARONETS
AUGSBURG	AVOCADOS	BACK TALK	BANDAGED	BARONIAL
AUGURIES	AVOIDING	BACKWARD	BANDAGES	BARONIES
AUGURING	AVOWABLE	BACKWASH	BANDANNA	BAROSTAT
AUGUSTLY	AVULSION	BACKYARD	BANDIEST	BAROUCHE
AUREOLES	AWAITING	BACTERIA	BANDITRY	BARRACKS
AU REVOIR	AWAKENED	BACTERIN	BANDPASS	BARRAGES
AURICLES	AWARDING	BACTRIAN	BANDSMAN	BARRATOR
AURICULA	AWEATHER	BADALONA	BANDSMEN	BARRATRY
AUSPICES	AXILLARY	BAD BLOOD	BANDYING	BARRETTE
AUSTRIAN	AXIOLOGY	BAD DEBTS	BANISHED	BARRIERS
AUTACOID	AXLETREE	BADGERED	BANISTER	BARTERED
AUTARCHY	AYRSHIRE	BADINAGE	BANKABLE	BARTERER
AUTARKIC	AYURVEDA	BADLANDS	BANKBOOK	BARTIZAN
AUTHORED	AZIMUTHS	BADLY-OFF	BANK NOTE	BASEBALL
AUTISTIC	AZOTEMIA	BAD-MOUTH	BANK RATE	BASEHEAD
AUTOBAHN	AZOTEMIC	BAEDEKER	BANKROLL	BASELESS
AUTOCRAT		BAFFLING	BANKRUPT	BASELINE
AUTOCUES	**B**	BAGGAGES	BANNOCKS	BASEMENT
AUTOGAMY		BAGGIEST	BANQUETS	BASENESS
AUTOGIRO	BABBLERS	BAGPIPES	BANSHEES	BASE RATE
AUTOLYSE	BABBLING	BAGUETTE	BANSTEAD	BASICITY
AUTOMATA	BABIRUSA	BAHAMIAN	BANTERED	BASIDIAL
AUTOMATE	BABYHOOD	BAHRAINI	BANTERER	BASIDIUM
AUTOMATS	BABYMOON	BAILABLE	BAPTISMS	BASILARY
AUTONOMY	BABY TALK	BAILIFFS	BAPTISTS	BASILDON
AUTOSOME	BACCARAT	BAILMENT	BAPTIZED	BASILICA
AUTOTOMY	BACCHIUS	BAILSMAN	BARATHEA	BASILISK
AUTOTYPE	BACHELOR	BAKELITE	BARBADOS	BASKETRY
AUTOTYPY	BACILLUS	BAKERIES	BARBARIC	BASOPHIL
AUTUMNAL	BACKACHE	BALANCED	BARBECUE	BASS CLEF
AUTUNITE	BACKBEAT	BALANCER	BARBERRY	BASS DRUM
AUVERGNE	BACKBITE	BALANCES	BARBICAN	BASSINET
AVADAVAT	BACKBONE	BALDNESS	BARBICEL	BASSISTS
AVAILING	BACKCHAT	BALEARIC	BAR CHART	BASSOONS
AVE MARIA	BACKCOMB	BALINESE	BAR CODES	BASSWOOD
AVENGERS	BACKDATE	BALLADES	BAREBACK	BASTARDS

BASTARDY	BECKONER	BELIEVER	BETATRON	BILLHOOK
BASTILLE	BECOMING	BELITTLE	BETIDING	BILLIARD
BASTIONS	BEDAUBED	BELLBIRD	BETRAYAL	BILLIONS
BASTOGNE	BEDAZZLE	BELLBOYS	BETRAYED	BILLOWED
BATANGAS	BEDECKED	BELLOWED	BETRAYER	BILOBATE
BATHETIC	BEDIMMED	BELLOWER	BETTERED	BIMANOUS
BATH MATS	BED LINEN	BELLPULL	BEVATRON	BINAURAL
BATHROBE	BEDOUINS	BELLWORT	BEVELING	BINDINGS
BATHROOM	BEDPLATE	BELLYFUL	BEVELLED	BINDWEED
BATHTUBS	BEDPOSTS	BELMOPAN	BEVERAGE	BIN-LINER
BATHURST	BEDROOMS	BELONGED	BEVERLEY	BINNACLE
BATSWANA	BEDSIDES	BELOVEDS	BEWAILED	BINOMIAL
BATTENED	BEDSORES	BELTWAYS	BEWAILER	BIOASSAY
BATTERED	BEDSTEAD	BEMOANED	BEWARING	BIO-ASSAY
BATTERER	BEDSTRAW	BENADRYL	BEWIGGED	BIOCIDAL
BATTIEST	BEDTIMES	BEN BELLA	BEWILDER	BIOCYCLE
BATTLING	BEDWORTH	BENEFICE	BHATPARA	BIODATAS
BAUHINIA	BEEBREAD	BENEFITS	BIANNUAL	BIOLYSIS
BAULKING	BEECHNUT	BENFLEET	BIARRITZ	BIOLYTIC
BAVARIAN	BEE-EATER	BENGHAZI	BIASSING	BIOMETRY
BAWDIEST	BEEFCAKE	BENGUELA	BIATHLON	BIONOMIC
BAYBERRY	BEEFIEST	BENIGNLY	BIBLICAL	BIOPLASM
BAYONETS	BEEFWOOD	BENTINCK	BIBULOUS	BIOPSIES
BAYREUTH	BEEHIVES	BENTWOOD	BICKERED	BIOSCOPE
BAZOOKAS	BEELINES	BENUMBED	BICKERER	BIOSCOPY
BDELLIUM	BEESWING	BENZOATE	BICOLOUR	BIOTITIC
BEACHING	BEETLING	BEQUEATH	BICONVEX	BIOTYPIC
BEADIEST	BEETROOT	BEQUESTS	BICUSPID	BIPAROUS
BEADINGS	BEFALLEN	BERATING	BICYCLED	BIPHENYL
BEAGLING	BEFITTED	BERCEUSE	BICYCLES	BIPLANES
BEAM-ENDS	BEFOULER	BEREAVED	BICYCLIC	BIRACIAL
BEANPOLE	BEFRIEND	BEREZINA	BIDDABLE	BIRADIAL
BEARABLE	BEGETTER	BERGAMET	BIENNIAL	BIRAMOUS
BEARABLY	BEGGARED	BERIBERI	BIFACIAL	BIRCHING
BEARDING	BEGGARLY	BERKELEY	BIFIDITY	BIRDBATH
BEAR HUGS	BEGINING	BERTHING	BIFOCALS	BIRDCAGE
BEARINGS	BEGINNER	BERYLINE	BIGAMIST	BIRD DOGS
BEARSKIN	BEGOTTEN	BESANCON	BIGAMOUS	BIRDLIKE
BEATABLE	BEGRUDGE	BESIEGED	BIGHEADS	BIRDLIME
BEATIFIC	BEGUILED	BESIEGER	BIG NAMES	BIRDSEED
BEATINGS	BEGUILER	BESMIRCH	BIGNONIA	BIRD'S-EYE
BEATNIKS	BEHAVING	BESOTTED	BIG SHOTS	BIRETTAS
BEAT TIME	BEHEADED	BESOUGHT	BIG STICK	BIRTHDAY
BEAULIEU	BEHOLDEN	BESPOKEN	BIG-TIMER	BIRTHING
BEAUMONT	BEHOLDER	BESTIARY	BIG WHEEL	BISCUITS
BEAUTIES	BELABOUR	BESTOWAL	BIJUGATE	BISECTED
BEAUTIFY	BELAYING	BESTOWED	BILABIAL	BISECTOR
BEAUVAIS	BELCHING	BESTOWER	BILBERRY	BISEXUAL
BEAVERED	BELFRIES	BESTREWN	BILINEAR	BISMARCK
BECALMED	BELGRADE	BESTRIDE	BILLETED	BISTOURY
BECHAMEL	BELIEBER	BESTRODE	BILLFISH	BITCHIER
BECKONED	BELIEVED	BETAKING	BILLFOLD	BITCHILY

BITCHING	BLENCHER	BLUE BOOK	BOLSTERS	BOSPORUS
BITINGLY	BLENDERS	BLUE CHIP	BOLTHOLE	BOSS-EYED
BIT PARTS	BLENDING	BLUE FILM	BOLT HOLE	BOSSIEST
BITSTOCK	BLENHEIM	BLUEFISH	BOLTONIA	BOTANIST
BITTERLY	BLESSING	BLUE FLAG	BOLTROPE	BOTANIZE
BITTERNS	BLIGHTED	BLUEGILL	BOMBARDE	BOTCHERS
BITTIEST	BLIGHTER	BLUE GUMS	BOMBSITE	BOTCHIER
BIVALENT	BLIMPISH	BLUE JAYS	BOMBYCID	BOTCHILY
BIVALVES	BLINDAGE	BLUE LAWS	BONA FIDE	BOTCHING
BIVOUACS	BLINDERS	BLUE MOON	BONANZAS	BOTCH-UPS
BIWEEKLY	BLINDING	BLUENESS	BONEFISH	BOTHERED
BIYEARLY	BLINKERS	BLUFFING	BONEHEAD	BOTRYTIS
BLABBING	BLINKING	BLUNDERS	BONE-IDLE	BOTSWANA
BLACK ART	BLISSFUL	BLUNKETT	BONELESS	BOTTLING
BLACK BOX	BLISTERS	BLUNTING	BONE MEAL	BOTTOMRY
BLACKCAP	BLITHELY	BLURRING	BONFIRES	BOTULISM
BLACKEST	BLITZING	BLURTING	BONHOMIE	BOUDOIRS
BLACK EYE	BLIZZARD	BLUSHERS	BONINESS	BOUFFANT
BLACKFLY	BLOATERS	BLUSHING	BONNIEST	BOUILLON
BLACK ICE	BLOCKADE	BLUSTERY	BONS MOTS	BOULDERS
BLACKING	BLOCKAGE	BOARDERS	BONTEBOK	BOULLION
BLACKISH	BLOCKING	BOARDING	BOOHOOED	BOULOGNE
BLACKLEG	BLOGGERS	BOARFISH	BOOKABLE	BOUNCERS
BLACKOUT	BLOGGING	BOASTERS	BOOKCASE	BOUNCIER
BLACK TIE	BLOKEISH	BOASTFUL	BOOK CLUB	BOUNCILY
BLACK-TIE	BLONDEST	BOASTING	BOOKENDS	BOUNCING
BLACKTOP	BLOODFIN	BOAT HOOK	BOOKINGS	BOUNDARY
BLADDERS	BLOODILY	BOATLOAD	BOOKLETS	BOUNDERS
BLAMABLE	BLOODING	BOA VISTA	BOOKMARK	BOUNDING
BLAMEFUL	BLOOD RED	BOBBINET	BOOKRACK	BOUNTIES
BLANCHED	BLOOMERS	BOBBY PIN	BOOKSHOP	BOUQUETS
BLANDEST	BLOOMERY	BOBOLINK	BOOKWORM	BOUTIQUE
BLANDISH	BLOOMING	BOBRUISK	BOOSTERS	BOUZOUKI
BLANKETS	BLOOPERS	BOBTAILS	BOOSTING	BOW BELLS
BLASTEMA	BLOSSOMS	BOBWHITE	BOOT CAMP	BOWSHOTS
BLASTING	BLOTCHES	BODILESS	BOOTLACE	BOWSPRIT
BLAST-OFF	BLOTTERS	BODLEIAN	BOOTLESS	BOXBERRY
BLASTULA	BLOTTING	BODY BLOW	BOOZE-UPS	BOXBOARD
BLATANCY	BLOWFISH	BODYWORK	BOOZIEST	BOXROOMS
BLAZONED	BLOWHARD	BOEHMITE	BORA BORA	BOYCOTTS
BLAZONRY	BLOWHOLE	BOGEYMAN	BORACITE	BOYISHLY
BLEACHED	BLOWIEST	BOGGIEST	BORDEAUX	BOY SCOUT
BLEACHER	BLOWLAMP	BOGGLING	BORDELLO	BRACELET
BLEAKEST	BLOWOUTS	BOHEMIAN	BORDERED	BRACHIAL
BLEARIER	BLOWPIPE	BOILABLE	BORDERER	BRACHIUM
BLEARILY	BLOW-WAVE	BOLDFACE	BOREHOLE	BRACKETS
BLEATING	BLOWZIER	BOLDNESS	BORINGLY	BRACKISH
BLEEDERS	BLOWZILY	BOLIVIAN	BORNHOLM	BRACTEAL
BLEEDING	BLUDGEON	BOLLARDS	BOROUGHS	BRADAWLS
BLEEPERS	BLUE BABY	BOLLOCKS	BORROWED	BRADBURY
BLEEPING	BLUEBELL	BOLLWORM	BORROWER	BRADFORD
BLENCHED	BLUEBIRD	BOLSHIER	BORSTALS	BRAGGART

BRAGGING	BRIDGEND	BRUISING	BULLHORN	BUTCHERY
BRAHMANI	BRIDGING	BRUITING	BULLNECK	BUTTERED
BRAHMANS	BRIEFING	BRUNCHES	BULLOCKS	BUTTOCKS
BRAIDING	BRIGHTEN	BRUNETTE	BULLRING	BUTTONED
BRAINBOX	BRIGHTON	BRUSHING	BULL'S EYE	BUTTRESS
BRAINIER	BRINDISI	BRUSH OFF	BULL'S-EYE	BUTYRATE
BRAINING	BRIOCHES	BRUSH-OFF	BULLSHIT	BUZZARDS
BRAINPAN	BRISANCE	BRUSH-UPS	BULLYBOY	BUZZWORD
BRAISING	BRISBANE	BRUSSELS	BULLYING	BY-BIDDER
BRAMBLES	BRISKEST	BRUTALLY	BULLY-OFF	BYPASSED
BRANCHED	BRISLING	BRYOLOGY	BULWARKS	BYPASSES
BRANCHES	BRISTLED	BRYOZOAN	BUMBLING	BYRONISM
BRANCHIA	BRISTLES	BUBALINE	BUMPIEST	
BRANDIES	BRITCHES	BUBBLIER	BUMPKINS	**C**
BRANDING	BRITTANY	BUBBLING	BUNCHING	CABARETS
BRANDISH	BROACHED	BUCHSHEE	BUNDLING	CABBAGES
BRAND-NEW	BROACHER	BUCKAROO	BUNGALOW	CABIN BOY
BRASHEST	BROADEST	BUCKBEAN	BUNGHOLE	CABINETS
BRASILIA	BROADWAY	BUCKETED	BUNGLERS	CABLE CAR
BRASSARD	BROCADED	BUCKHORN	BUNGLING	CABLEWAY
BRASS HAT	BROCCOLI	BUCKLERS	BUNTLINE	CABOCHON
BRASSICA	BROCHURE	BUCKLING	BUOYANCY	CABOODLE
BRASSIER	BROILERS	BUCKSHEE	BURAYDAH	CABOOSES
BRASSILY	BROILING	BUCKSHOT	BURBERRY	CABOTAGE
BRATTICE	BROKENLY	BUCKSKIN	BURBLING	CAB RANKS
BRAUNITE	BROLLIES	BUDAPEST	BURDENED	CABRILLA
BRAWLERS	BROMANCE	BUDDHISM	BURGHERS	CABRIOLE
BRAWLING	BROMIDES	BUDDHIST	BURGLARS	CACHALOT
BRAWNIER	BRONCHIA	BUDDLEIA	BURGLARY	CACHEPOT
BRAWNILY	BRONCHOS	BUDGETED	BURGLING	CACHEXIA
BRAZENED	BRONCHUS	BUFFALOS	BURGUNDY	CACHUCHA
BRAZENLY	BRONZING	BUFFERED	BURLIEST	CACKLERS
BRAZIERS	BROOCHES	BUFFETED	BURNOOSE	CACKLING
BRAZILIN	BROODERS	BUFFETER	BURNOUTS	CACTUSES
BREACHED	BROODIER	BUFFOONS	BURRITOS	CADASTER
BREACHES	BROODILY	BUGABOOS	BURROWED	CADAVERS
BREAD BIN	BROODING	BUGBEARS	BURROWER	CADDYING
BREADNUT	BROOKING	BUGGERED	BURSITIS	CADENCES
BREADTHS	BROOKITE	BUILDERS	BURSTING	CADENZAS
BREAKAGE	BROOKLYN	BUILDING	BURTHENS	CADUCEUS
BREAKERS	BROOKNER	BUKOVINI	BUSHBABY	CADUCITY
BREAKING	BROTHELS	BULAWAYO	BUSHBUCK	CADUCOUS
BREAK-INS	BROTHERS	BULGARIA	BUSHIEST	CAERLEON
BREATHER	BROUGHAM	BULGIEST	BUSHVELD	CAESURAS
BREECHES	BROUHAHA	BULKHEAD	BUSINESS	CAFFEINE
BREEDING	BROWBEAT	BULKIEST	BUS STOPS	CAGELING
BREEZILY	BROWNEST	BULL BARS	BUSTIEST	CAGINESS
BRETHREN	BROWNIES	BULLDOGS	BUSTLING	CAGLIARI
BREVETCY	BROWNING	BULLDOZE	BUSYBODY	CAGOULES
BREVIARY	BROWNISH	BULLETIN	BUSYNESS	CAISSONS
BRIBABLE	BROWSING	BULLFROG	BUTANONE	CAJOLERY
BRICKBAT	BRUISERS	BULLHEAD	BUTCHERS	CAJOLING

CAKEWALK	CAMP BEDS	CAPRIOLE	CAROLING	CATALASE
CALABASH	CAMPECHE	CAPSICUM	CAROLLED	CATALYSE
CALABRIA	CAMPFIRE	CAPSIZED	CAROTENE	CATALYST
CALADIUM	CAMPHENE	CAPSTANS	CAROUSAL	CATAMITE
CALAMINE	CAMPINAS	CAPSTONE	CAROUSED	CATAPULT
CALAMINT	CAMPSITE	CAPSULAR	CAROUSEL	CATARACT
CALAMITE	CAMPUSES	CAPSULES	CAR PARKS	CATCALLS
CALAMITY	CAMSHAFT	CAPTAINS	CARPETED	CATCH ALL
CALATHUS	CANADIAN	CAPTIONS	CAR POOLS	CATCH-ALL
CALCIFIC	CANAIGRE	CAPTIOUS	CARPORTS	CATCHFLY
CALCITIC	CANAILLE	CAPTIVES	CARRERAS	CATCHIER
CALCULUS	CANALIZE	CAPTURED	CARRIAGE	CATCHILY
CALCUTTA	CANARIES	CAPTURES	CARRIERS	CATCHING
CALDRONS	CANBERRA	CAPUCHIN	CARRYALL	CATECHIN
CALENDAR	CANCELED	CAPYBARA	CARRYCOT	CATECHOL
CALENDER	CANCROID	CARACARA	CARRYING	CATEGORY
CALF LOVE	CANDIDLY	CARACOLE	CARRY OFF	CATENANE
CALFSKIN	CANFIELD	CARAMELS	CARRYOUT	CATENARY
CALIBRED	CANISTER	CARANGID	CARRY OUT	CATENATE
CALIBRES	CANNABIC	CARAPACE	CARTOONS	CATENOID
CALIPASH	CANNABIN	CARAVANS	CARUNCLE	CATERING
CALIPERS	CANNABIS	CARAWAYS	CARVINGS	CATHEDRA
CALISAYA	CANNIBAL	CARBINES	CARYATID	CATHETER
CALLABLE	CANNIEST	CARBOLIC	CASANOVA	CATHEXIS
CALL GIRL	CANNIKIN	CARBONIC	CASCADED	CATHODES
CALLINGS	CANNONED	CARBONYL	CASCADES	CATHODIC
CALLIOPE	CANNONRY	CARBURET	CASEMATE	CATHOLIC
CALLIPER	CANOEING	CARDAMOM	CASEMENT	CATIONIC
CALLISTO	CANOEIST	CARDENAL	CASEWORK	CAT'S EYES
CALLUSES	CANONESS	CARDIGAN	CASHABLE	CAT'S-FOOT
CALMNESS	CANONIST	CARDINAL	CASHBACK	CAT'S PAWS
CALOR GAS	CANONIZE	CARDIOID	CASH-BOOK	CATSUITS
CALORIES	CANON LAW	CARDITIS	CASH CARD	CATTIEST
CALUTRON	CANOODLE	CAREENED	CASH CROP	CATTLEYA
CALVADOS	CANOPIES	CAREERED	CASH DESK	CATWALKS
CALVARIA	CANTATAS	CAREFREE	CASH FLOW	CAUCASIA
CALYCATE	CANTEENS	CARELESS	CASHIERS	CAUCASUS
CALYCINE	CANTERED	CARESSED	CASHLESS	CAUCUSES
CALYPSOS	CANT HOOK	CARESSER	CASHMERE	CAUDALLY
CALYPTRA	CANTICLE	CARESSES	CASSETTE	CAULDRON
CAMAGUEY	CANTONAL	CAREWORN	CASSOCKS	CAULICLE
CAMBODIA	CANVASES	CARIBOUS	CASTAWAY	CAULKING
CAMBOGIA	CANZONET	CARILLON	CASTINGS	CAUSABLE
CAMBRIAN	CAPACITY	CARINATE	CAST IRON	CAUSALLY
CAMELEER	CAPERING	CARLISLE	CAST-IRON	CAUSERIE
CAMELLIA	CAPESKIN	CARNAUBA	CASTRATE	CAUSEWAY
CAMEROON	CAPE TOWN	CARNIVAL	CASTRATO	CAUTIONS
CAMISOLE	CAPITALS	CAROLINA	CASTRIES	CAUTIOUS
CAMOMILE	CAPITATE	CAROLINE	CASUALLY	CAVALIER
CAMPAGNA	CAPONIZE		CASUALTY	CAVATINA
CAMPAIGN	CAPRICES		CASUISTS	CAVEATOR
CAMPANIA	CAPRIFIG		CATACOMB	CAVEFISH

CAVICORN	CERVELAT	CHARENTE	CHEMNITZ	CHIPMUNK
CAVILING	CERVICAL	CHARGERS	CHEMURGY	CHIPPIES
CAVILLED	CERVICES	CHARGING	CHENILLE	CHIPPING
CAVILLER	CERVIXES	CHARIEST	CHENOPOD	CHIP SHOP
CAVITIES	CESAREAN	CHARIOTS	CHEPSTOW	CHIRPIER
CAVORTED	CESSIONS	CHARISMA	CHEQUERS	CHIRPILY
CEDILLAS	CESSPITS	CHARLADY	CHEROKEE	CHIRPING
CEILINGS	CESSPOOL	CHARLIES	CHEROOTS	CHIRRUPY
CELERIAC	CETACEAN	CHARLOCK	CHERRIES	CHISELED
CELERITY	CEVENNES	CHARLTON	CHERTSEY	CHITCHAT
CELIBACY	CHACONNE	CHARMERS	CHERUBIC	CHIT CHAT
CELIBATE	CHAFFING	CHARMING	CHESHIRE	CHIVALRY
CELLARER	CHAINING	CHARQUID	CHESSMAN	CHIVYING
CELLARET	CHAINMAN	CHARRING	CHESTIER	CHLORATE
CELLISTS	CHAIN SAW	CHARTERS	CHESTILY	CHLORIDE
CELLULAR	CHAIRING	CHARTING	CHESTNUT	CHLORINE
CELULOID	CHAIRMAN	CHARTISM	CHEVRONS	CHLORITE
CEMENTED	CHAIRMEN	CHARTIST	CHEWABLE	CHLOROUS
CEMENTER	CHALAZAL	CHARTRES	CHEWIEST	CHOC-ICES
CEMENTUM	CHALDRON	CHASSEUR	CHEYENNE	CHOCKING
CEMETERY	CHALICES	CHASTELY	CHIASMAL	CHOICELY
CENOTAPH	CHALKIER	CHASTEST	CHIASMIC	CHOICEST
CENOZOIC	CHALKING	CHASTISE	CHIASMUS	CHOIRBOY
CENSORED	CHAMBERS	CHASTITY	CHIASTIC	CHOIRMAN
CENSURED	CHAMBRAY	CHASUBLE	CHICANER	CHOISEUL
CENSURES	CHAMONIX	CHAT SHOW	CHICANOS	CHOLERIC
CENSUSES	CHAMPING	CHATTELS	CHICKENS	CHOMPING
CENTAURS	CHAMPION	CHATTIER	CHICKPEA	CHONGJIN
CENTAURY	CHANCELS	CHATTILY	CHICLAYO	CHOOSIER
CENTAVOS	CHANCERY	CHATTING	CHIGETAI	CHOP CHOP
CENTERED	CHANCIER	CHAUFFER	CHIGGERS	CHOP-CHOP
CENTIARE	CHANCILY	CHEAPEST	CHIGNONS	CHOPPERS
CENTIMES	CHANCING	CHEATING	CHIGWELL	CHOPPIER
CENTRING	CHANDLER	CHECKERS	CHILDISH	CHOPPILY
CENTRIST	CHANGING	CHECKING	CHILDREN	CHOPPING
CENTROID	CHANGSHA	CHECK-INS	CHILIASM	CHOP SUEY
CEPHALAD	CHANGTEH	CHECKOUT	CHILIAST	CHORALES
CEPHALIC	CHANNELS	CHECKUPS	CHILLIER	CHORDATE
CEPHALIN	CHANTIES	CHEDDITE	CHILLIES	CHORDING
CERAMICS	CHANTING	CHEEKIER	CHILLING	CHORIAMB
CERAMIST	CHANUKAH	CHEEKILY	CHILL OUT	CHORTLED
CERASTES	CHAOCHOW	CHEEKING	CHILOPOD	CHORTLES
CERATOID	CHAPATTI	CHEEPING	CHIMAERA	CHORUSED
CERCARIA	CHAPBOOK	CHEERFUL	CHIMBOTE	CHORUSES
CEREBRAL	CHAPERON	CHEERIER	CHIMERAS	CHOW-CHOW
CEREBRIC	CHAPLAIN	CHEERILY	CHIMKENT	CHOW MEIN
CEREBRUM	CHAPLETS	CHEERING	CHIMNEYS	CHRESARD
CEREMENT	CHAPPING	CHEETAHS	CHINAMAN	CHRISMAL
CEREMONY	CHAPTERS	CHEKIANG	CHIN-CHOU	CHRISTEN
CERNUOUS	CHARACIN	CHEMICAL	CHINDWIN	CHROMATE
CEROTYPE	CHARADES	CHEMISES	CHINKING	CHROMITE
CERULEAN	CHARCOAL	CHEMISTS	CHINLESS	CHROMIUM

CHROMOUS	CIVILITY	CLEMATIS	CLUBBING	COCKNEYS
CHUBBIER	CIVILIZE	CLEMENCY	CLUBFEET	COCKPITS
CHUCKING	CIVIL LAW	CLENCHED	CLUBFOOT	COCKSPUR
CHUCKLED	CIVIL WAR	CLENCHES	CLUBHAUL	COCKSURE
CHUCKLER	CLACKING	CLERICAL	CLUCKING	COCKTAIL
CHUCKLES	CLAIMANT	CLERIHEW	CLUELESS	COCONUTS
CHUCK OFF	CLAIMING	CLERKDOM	CLUMPING	COCOONED
CHUGGING	CLAMBAKE	CLERKING	CLUMPISH	CODDLING
CHUKKERS	CLAMMIER	CLEVEITE	CLUMSIER	CODICILS
CHUMMIER	CLAMMILY	CLEVERLY	CLUMSILY	CODIFIED
CHUMMILY	CLAMMING	CLICKING	CLUPEOID	CODIFIER
CHUMMING	CLAMOURS	CLIENTAL	CLUSTERS	CODOMAIN
CHUNKIER	CLAMPING	CLIMATES	CLUSTERY	CODPIECE
CHURCHES	CLANGERS	CLIMATIC	CLUTCHED	CO DRIVER
CHURINGA	CLANGING	CLIMAXED	CLUTCHES	COENURUS
CHURLISH	CLANKING	CLIMAXES	COACHING	COENZYME
CHURNING	CLANNISH	CLIMBERS	COACHMAN	COEQUALS
CHUTZPAH	CLANSMAN	CLIMBING	COACHMEN	COERCING
CHYMOSIN	CLANSMEN	CLINCHED	COACTION	COERCION
CIABATTA	CLAPPERS	CLINCHER	COACTIVE	COERCIVE
CIBORIUM	CLAPPING	CLINCHES	COAGULUM	COEXTEND
CICATRIX	CLAPTRAP	CLINGING	COAHUILA	COGENTLY
CICERONE	CLARINET	CLINICAL	COALESCE	COGITATE
CICHLOID	CLARIONS	CLINKERS	COALFACE	COGNATES
CIMBRIAN	CLASHING	CLINKING	COALFISH	COGNOMEN
CINCHONA	CLASPING	CLIPPERS	COALHOLE	COGWHEEL
CINCTURE	CLASSICS	CLIPPIES	COALMINE	COHERENT
CINEASTE	CLASSIER	CLIPPING	COALPORT	COHERING
CINERAMA	CLASSIFY	CLIQUISH	COARSELY	COHESION
CINERARY	CLASSING	CLITORAL	COARSEST	COHESIVE
CINGULUM	CLASSISM	CLITORIS	COASTERS	COHOBATE
CINNABAR	CLASSIST	CLOAKING	COASTING	COIFFEUR
CINNAMON	CLATTERS	CLOCKING	COATINGS	COIFFURE
CINQUAIN	CLATTERY	CLODDISH	COATROOM	COINAGES
CIPHERED	CLAVICLE	CLOGGING	COAT-TAIL	COINCIDE
CIRCLETS	CLAYLIKE	CLOISTER	COAUTHOR	COINSURE
CIRCLING	CLAYMORE	CLOPPING	COBALTIC	COLANDER
CIRCUITS	CLEAN CUT	CLOSE-SET	COBBLERS	COLD CUTS
CIRCUITY	CLEAN-CUT	CLOSETED	COBBLING	COLD FEET
CIRCULAR	CLEANERS	CLOSE-UPS	COBWEBBY	COLD FISH
CIRCUSES	CLEANEST	CLOSURES	COCA-COLA	COLDNESS
CISLUNAR	CLEANING	CLOTHIER	COCCYGES	COLD SNAP
CISTERNA	CLEANSED	CLOTHING	COCHLEAE	COLD SORE
CISTERNS	CLEANSER	CLOTTING	COCHLEAR	COLD-WELD
CITADELS	CLEAR-CUT	CLOUDIER	COCKADES	COLESLAW
CITATION	CLEAREST	CLOUDILY	COCKAPOO	COLISEUM
CITIFIED	CLEARING	CLOUDING	COCKATOO	COLLAGEN
CITIZENS	CLEAROUT	CLOUDLET	COCKCROW	COLLAGES
CITREOUS	CLEARWAY	CLOUTING	COCK CROW	COLLAPSE
CITRUSES	CLEAVAGE	CLOWNERY	COCKEREL	COLLARED
CITY HALL	CLEAVERS	CLOWNING	COCKEYED	COLLATED
CIVILIAN	CLEAVING	CLOWNISH	COCKIEST	COLLATOR

COLLECTS	COMMONER	CONDUITS	CONTEMPT	COQUETTE
COLLEENS	COMMONLY	CONDYLAR	CONTENTS	COQUILLE
COLLEGES	COMMUNAL	CONFEREE	CONTESTS	CORACLES
COLLIDED	COMMUNED	CONFERVA	CONTEXTS	CORACOID
COLLIDER	COMMUNES	CONFETTI	CONTINUA	CORDIALS
COLLIERS	COMMUTED	CONFIDED	CONTINUE	CORDLESS
COLLIERY	COMMUTER	CONFIDER	CONTINUO	CORDONED
COLLOGUE	COMPACTS	CONFINED	CONTOURS	CORDOVAN
COLLOQUY	COMPADRE	CONFINES	CONTRACT	CORDUROY
COLLUDED	COMPARED	CONFLATE	CONTRAIL	CORDWOOD
COLOMBES	COMPARER	CONFLICT	CONTRARY	CORE TIME
COLOMBIA	COMPARES	CONFOCAL	CONTRAST	CORKWOOD
COLONELS	COMPEERS	CONFOUND	CONTRITE	CORNCOBS
COLONIAL	COMPERED	CONFRERE	CONTRIVE	CORNEOUS
COLONIES	COMPERES	CONFRONT	CONTROLS	CORNERED
COLONIST	COMPETED	CONFUSED	CONTUSED	CORNETTE
COLONIZE	COMPILED	CONFUTED	CONVENED	CORNICES
COLOPHON	COMPILER	CONFUTER	CONVENER	CORNICHE
COLORADO	COMPLAIN	CONGENER	CONVENTS	CORNIEST
COLORANT	COMPLETE	CONGRATS	CONVERGE	CORN PONE
COLOSSAL	COMPLIED	CONGRESS	CONVERSE	CORNWALL
COLOSSUS	COMPLIER	CONIDIAL	CONVERTS	CORONARY
COLOTOMY	COMPLINE	CONIDIUM	CONVEXLY	CORONERS
COLOURED	COMPOSED	CONIFERS	CONVEYED	CORONETS
COLPITIS	COMPOSER	CONJOINT	CONVEYER	CORPORAL
COLUBRID	COMPOTES	CONJUGAL	CONVEYOR	CORRIDOR
COLUMBIA	COMPOUND	CONJUNCT	CONVICTS	CORRODED
COLUMBIC	COMPRESS	CONJURED	CONVINCE	CORRODER
COLUMBUS	COMPRISE	CONJURER	CONVOKED	CORSAGES
COLUMNAR	COMPUTED	CONJUROR	CONVOKER	CORSAIRS
COLUMNED	COMPUTER	CONNACHT	CONVOYED	CORSELET
COMANCHE	COMRADES	CONNIVED	CONVULSE	CORSETED
COMATOSE	CONATION	CONNIVER	COOKABLE	CORSETRY
COMBATED	CONATIVE	CONNOTED	COOKBOOK	CORTEGES
COMBATER	CONCEDED	CONODONT	COOKOUTS	CORTICAL
COMBINED	CONCEITS	CONOIDAL	COOLABAR	CORTICES
COMBINER	CONCEIVE	CONQUEST	COOLANTS	CORTISOL
COMBINES	CONCEPTS	CONSERVE	COOLIBAH	CORUNDUM
COMEBACK	CONCERNS	CONSIDER	COOLNESS	CORVETTE
COMEDIAN	CONCERTO	CONSOLED	COONSKIN	CORYPHEE
COMEDIES	CONCERTS	CONSOLER	COOPTING	COSECANT
COMEDOWN	CONCHOID	CONSOLES	COOPTION	COSINESS
COMELIER	CONCLAVE	CONSOMME	COPILOTS	COSMETIC
COMFIEST	CONCLUDE	CONSORTS	COPLANAR	COSTLIER
COMFORTS	CONCRETE	CONSPIRE	COPPERAS	COSTMARY
COMITIES	CONDENSE	CONSTANT	COPULATE	COST-PLUS
COMMANDO	CONDOLED	CONSTRUE	COPYBOOK	COSTUMES
COMMANDS	CONDOLER	CONSULAR	COPYCATS	COT DEATH
COMMENCE	CONDONED	CONSUMED	COPY-EDIT	COTENANT
COMMENTS	CONDONER	CONSUMER	COPYHOLD	COTERIES
COMMERCE	CONDUCED	CONTACTS	COPYISTS	COTOPAXI
COMMODES	CONDUCER	CONTANGO	COQUETRY	COTSWOLD

COTTAGER	COZINESS	CREATORS	CRONYISM	CRUZEIRO
COTTAGES	CRABBIER	CREATURE	CROOKING	CRY HAVOC
COTYLOID	CRABBING	CREDENCE	CROONERS	CRYOLITE
COUCHANT	CRABWISE	CREDENZA	CROONING	CRYONAUT
COUCHING	CRACKERS	CREDIBLE	CROPPERS	CRYONICS
COUGHING	CRACKING	CREDIBLY	CROPPING	CRYOSTAT
COULISSE	CRACKLED	CREDITED	CROSIERS	CRYOTRON
COUMARIC	CRACKNEL	CREDITOR	CROSSBAR	CRYSTALS
COUMARIN	CRACKPOT	CREEPERS	CROSSBOW	CUBATURE
COUNCILS	CRACKUPS	CREEPIER	CROSSCUT	CUBE ROOT
COUNTERS	CRADLING	CREEPILY	CROSS CUT	CUBICLES
COUNTESS	CRAFTIER	CREEPING	CROSSEST	CUBIFORM
COUNTIES	CRAFTILY	CREMATED	CROSS-EYE	CUBISIST
COUNTING	CRAFTING	CREMATOR	CROSSFIT	CUBISTIC
COUPLETS	CRAGGIER	CREODONT	CROSSING	CUCKOLDS
COUPLING	CRAM-FULL	CREOSOTE	CROSSLET	CUCUMBER
COURANTE	CRAMMERS	CRESCENT	CROSSPLY	CUCURBIT
COURLAND	CRAMMING	CRESTING	CROSTINI	CUDDLIER
COURSING	CRAMPING	CRESYLIC	CROTCHES	CUDDLING
COURTESY	CRAMPONS	CRETONNE	CROTCHET	CUDGELED
COURTIER	CRANE FLY	CREVASSE	CROUCHED	CUFF LINK
COURTING	CRANIATE	CREVICES	CROUPIER	CUL-DE-SAC
COUSCOUS	CRANIUMS	CREW CUTS	CROUPOUS	CULIACAN
COUSTEAU	CRANKIER	CREW NECK	CROUTONS	CULINARY
COVALENT	CRANKING	CRIBBAGE	CROWBARS	CULOTTES
COVENANT	CRANKPIN	CRIBBING	CROWBOOT	CULOUSLY
COVENTRY	CRANNIED	CRICKETS	CROWDING	CULPABLE
COVERAGE	CRANNIES	CRICKING	CROWFOOT	CULPABLY
COVERING	CRAPPIER	CRIMINAL	CROWNING	CULPRITS
COVERLET	CRAPPING	CRIMPING	CROZIERS	CULTIGEN
COVERTLY	CRASHING	CRIMSONS	CRUCIATE	CULTIVAR
COVER-UPS	CRASH PAD	CRINGING	CRUCIBLE	CULTRATE
COVETING	CRAVENLY	CRINKLED	CRUCIFER	CULTURAL
COVETOUS	CRAVINGS	CRINKLES	CRUCIFIX	CULTURED
COWARDLY	CRAWFISH	CRIPPLED	CRUDITES	CULTURES
COWBELLS	CRAWLERS	CRIPPLES	CRUISERS	CULVERIN
COWBERRY	CRAWLING	CRISPATE	CRUISING	CULVERTS
COWERING	CRAYFISH	CRISPIER	CRUMBLED	CUMBERED
COWHANDS	CRAYONED	CRISPING	CRUMBLES	CUMBRIAN
COWHERDS	CRAZIEST	CRISTATE	CRUMHORN	CUMQUATS
COWHIDES	CREAKIER	CRITERIA	CRUMMIER	CUMULOUS
COWLICKS	CREAKILY	CRITICAL	CRUMPETS	CUPBOARD
COWLINGS	CREAKING	CRITIQUE	CRUMPLED	CUP CAKES
CO-WORKER	CREAMERS	CRITTERS	CRUNCHED	CUP FINAL
COWSHEDS	CREAMERY	CROAKILY	CRUSADED	CUPIDITY
COWSLIPS	CREAMIER	CROAKING	CRUSADER	CUPREOUS
COXALGIA	CREAMING	CROATIAN	CRUSADES	CUPULATE
COXALGIC	CREASING	CROCKERY	CRUSHING	CURARIZE
COXCOMBS	CREATINE	CROCOITE	CRUSTIER	CURASSOW
COXSWAIN	CREATING	CROCUSES	CRUSTILY	CURATIVE
COZENAGE	CREATION	CROFTERS	CRUSTOSE	CURATORS
COZENING	CREATIVE	CROMLECH	CRUTCHES	CURCULIO

CURDLING	CYNOSURE	DARK AGES	DEATH ROW	DECRYING
CURE-ALLS	CYPHERED	DARKENED	DEBACLES	DECURVED
CURITIBA	CYPRINID	DARKENER	DEBARKED	DEDICATE
CURLICUE	CYRILLIC	DARKNESS	DEBARRED	DEDUCING
CURLIEST	CYSTEINE	DARKROOM	DEBASING	DEDUCTED
CURRANTS	CYSTITIS	DARK ROOM	DEBATERS	DEED POLL
CURRENCY	CYTASTER	DARLINGS	DEBATING	DEEMSTER
CURRENTS	CYTIDINE	DARTFORD	DEBILITY	DEEPENED
CURRICLE	CYTOLOGY	DATABASE	DEBITING	DEEPENER
CURRIERY	CYTOSINE	DATEABLE	DEBONAIR	DEEP-LAID
CURRYING	CZARINAS	DATELINE	DEBRECEN	DEEPNESS
CURSEDLY		DATE RAPE	DEBUGGED	DEERSKIN
CURTAINS	**D**	DATOLITE	DEBUGGER	DEFACING
CURTNESS		DAUGHTER	DEBUNKED	DEFAMING
CURTSIED	DABBLERS	DAUNTING	DEBUNKER	DEFAULTS
CURTSIES	DABBLING	DAUPHINE	DEBUTANT	DEFEATED
CUSHIEST	DABCHICK	DAUPHINS	DECADENT	DEFEATER
CUSHIONS	DAB HANDS	DAVENTRY	DECAMPED	DEFECATE
CUSHIONY	DACTYLIC	DAWDLERS	DECANOIC	DEFECTED
CUSPIDOR	DAEMONIC	DAWDLING	DECANTED	DEFECTOR
CUSSEDLY	DAFFODIL	DAYBREAK	DECANTER	DEFENCES
CUSTARDS	DAFTNESS	DAYDREAM	DECAYING	DEFENDED
CUSTOMER	DAGESTAN	DAYLIGHT	DECEASED	DEFENDER
CUSTUMAL	DAINTIER	DAYROOMS	DECEIVED	DEFERENT
CUT A DASH	DAINTIES	DAYTIMES	DECEIVER	DEFERRED
CUTAWAYS	DAINTILY	DAY-TO-DAY	DECEMBER	DEFERRER
CUTBACKS	DAIQUIRI	DAZZLING	DECENTLY	DEFIANCE
CUTENESS	DAIRYMAN	DEACONRY	DECENTRE	DEFICITS
CUT GLASS	DAIRYMEN	DEADBEAT	DECIBELS	DEFILERS
CUTICLES	DALESMAN	DEAD BEAT	DECIDING	DEFILING
CUTICULA	DALLYING	DEAD DUCK	DECIDUAL	DEFINING
CUTINIZE	DALMATIA	DEAD ENDS	DECIMALS	DEFINITE
CUT-PRICE	DALMATIC	DEADENED	DECIMATE	DEFLATED
CUTPURSE	DALTONIC	DEADENER	DECIPHER	DEFLATOR
CUTTINGS	DAMAGING	DEADFALL	DECISION	DEFLEXED
CUTWATER	DAMANHUR	DEADHEAD	DECISIVE	DEFLOWER
CUXHAVEN	DAMASCUS	DEAD HEAT	DECKHAND	DEFOREST
CYANITIC	DAMNABLE	DEADLIER	DECK HAND	DEFORMED
CYANOGEN	DAMNABLY	DEADLINE	DECLARED	DEFORMER
CYANOSIS	DAMOCLES	DEADLOCK	DECLARER	DEFRAYAL
CYANOTIC	DAMPENED	DEADNESS	DECLASSE	DEFRAYED
CYBERPET	DAMPENER	DEAD WOOD	DECLINED	DEFRAYER
CYCLADES	DAMPNESS	DEAF-AIDS	DECLINER	DEFTNESS
CYCLAMEN	DANDIEST	DEAFENED	DECLINES	DEFUSING
CYCLISTS	DANDLING	DEAF-MUTE	DECODING	DEGASSER
CYCLONES	DANDRUFF	DEAFNESS	DECOLOUR	DEGRADED
CYCLONIC	DANDYISH	DEALFISH	DECORATE	DEGRADER
CYCLOSIS	DANDYISM	DEALINGS	DECOROUS	DEICIDAL
CYLINDER	DANEWORT	DEANSHIP	DECOYING	DEIFYING
CYMATIUM	DANGLING	DEARESTS	DECREASE	DEIGNING
CYMOGENE	DANKNESS	DEARNESS	DECREPIT	DEJECTED
CYNICISM	DANUBIAN	DEATHBED	DECRETAL	DELAWARE
	DARINGLY			

DELAYING	DENDRITE	DESERVED	DEVOUTLY	DICTATES
DELEGACY	DENDROID	DESERVER	DEWBERRY	DICTATOR
DELEGATE	DENIABLE	DESIGNED	DEWDROPS	DIDACTIC
DELETING	DENIZENS	DESIGNER	DEWINESS	DIDDLING
DELETION	DENOTING	DESINENT	DEWY-EYED	DIDYMIUM
DELICACY	DENOUNCE	DESIRING	DEXTROSE	DIDYMOUS
DELICATE	DENTICLE	DESIROUS	DIABASIC	DIEHARDS
DELIGHTS	DENTINAL	DESISTED	DIABETES	DIELDRIN
DELIRIUM	DENTURES	DESKWORK	DIABETIC	DIERESES
DELIVERY	DENUDATE	DESOLATE	DIABOLIC	DIERESIS
DELOUSED	DENUDING	DESPATCH	DIACIDIC	DIERETIC
DELPHIAN	DEPARTED	DESPISED	DIACONAL	DIES IRAE
DELUDING	DEPENDED	DESPOTIC	DIAGNOSE	DIESTOCK
DELUGING	DEPICTED	DESSERTS	DIAGONAL	DIETETIC
DELUSION	DEPICTER	DESTINED	DIAGRAMS	DIFFERED
DELUSIVE	DEPILATE	DESTRUCT	DIAGRAPH	DIFFRACT
DELUSORY	DEPLETED	DETACHED	DIALECTS	DIFFUSED
DEMAGOGY	DEPLORED	DETACHER	DIALLAGE	DIFFUSER
DEMANDED	DEPLORER	DETAILED	DIALLING	DIGAMIST
DEMANDER	DEPLOYED	DETAINED	DIALOGUE	DIGAMOUS
DEMARCHE	DEPONENT	DETAINEE	DIALYSER	DIGESTED
DEMEANED	DEPORTED	DETAINER	DIALYSIS	DIGESTER
DEMENTED	DEPORTEE	DETECTED	DIALYTIC	DIGESTIF
DEMENTIA	DEPOSING	DETECTER	DIAMANTE	DIGGINGS
DEMERARA	DEPOSITS	DETECTOR	DIAMETER	DIGITATE
DEMERGER	DEPRAVED	DETENTES	DIAMONDS	DIGITIZE
DEMERITS	DEPRAVER	DETERRED	DIANTHUS	DIGITRON
DEMERSAL	DEPRIVED	DETESTED	DIAPASON	DIGRAPHS
DEMESNES	DEPRIVER	DETESTER	DIAPAUSE	DIHEDRAL
DEMIGODS	DEPURATE	DETHRONE	DIAPHONE	DIHEDRON
DEMIJOHN	DEPUTIES	DETONATE	DIAPHONY	DIHYBRID
DEMILUNE	DEPUTING	DETRITAL	DIARCHIC	DILATANT
DEMISTED	DEPUTIZE	DETRITUS	DIARISTS	DILATING
DEMISTER	DERAILED	DEUCEDLY	DIASCOPE	DILATION
DEMIVOLT	DERANGED	DEUTERON	DIASPORA	DILATIVE
DEMOBBED	DERELICT	DEVALUED	DIASPORE	DILATORY
DEMOCRAT	DERIDING	DEVIANCE	DIASTASE	DILEMMAS
DEMOLISH	DERISION	DEVIANTS	DIASTEMA	DILIGENT
DEMONIAC	DERISIVE	DEVIATED	DIASTOLE	DILUTING
DEMONISM	DERISORY	DEVIATOR	DIASTRAL	DILUTION
DEMONIST	DERIVING	DEVILING	DIASTYLE	DILUVIAL
DEMONIZE	DEROGATE	DEVILISH	DIATOMIC	DIMERISM
DEMOTING	DERRICKS	DEVILLED	DIATONIC	DIMERIZE
DEMOTION	DESCALED	DEVISING	DIATRIBE	DIMEROUS
DEMOTIST	DESCANTS	DEVOLVED	DIAZEPAM	DIMETRIC
DEMPSTER	DESCENTS	DEVONIAN	DIBBLING	DIMINISH
DEMURELY	DESCRIBE	DEVOTEES	DICENTRA	DINGDONG
DEMUREST	DESCRIED	DEVOTING	DICHROIC	DINGHIES
DEMURRAL	DESCRIER	DEVOTION	DICKERED	DINGIEST
DEMURRED	DESEEDER	DEVOURED	DICKIEST	DINKIEST
DEMURRER	DESERTED	DEVOURER	DICROTIC	DINOSAUR
DENATURE	DESERTER	DEVOUTER	DICTATED	DIOCESAN

DIOCESES	DISGRACE	DISUNITE	DOGCARTS	DOORWAYS
DIOPSIDE	DISGUISE	DISUNITY	DOG-EARED	DOPAMINE
DIOPTASE	DISHEVEL	DITCHING	DOGFIGHT	DOPINESS
DIOPTRAL	DISHFULS	DITHEISM	DOGGEDLY	DORDOGNE
DIOPTRIC	DISHIEST	DITHEIST	DOGGEREL	DORMANCY
DIORAMIC	DISINTER	DITHERED	DOGGONED	DORMOUSE
DIORITIC	DISJOINT	DITHERER	DOGGY BAG	DORTMUND
DIOXIDES	DISJUNCT	DIURESIS	DOGHOUSE	DOSSIERS
DIPHENYL	DISKETTE	DIURETIC	DOGMATIC	DOTATION
DIPLEGIA	DISLIKED	DIVALENT	DO-GOODER	DOTINGLY
DIPLEXER	DISLIKES	DIVE-BOMB	DOGSBODY	DOTTEREL
DIPLOMAS	DISLODGE	DIVERGED	DOG'S-TAIL	DOTTIEST
DIPLOMAT	DISLOYAL	DIVERTED	DOG TIRED	DOUBLETS
DIPLOPIA	DISMALLY	DIVERTER	DOG-TIRED	DOUBLE UP
DIPLOPIC	DISMAYED	DIVESTED	DOGTOOTH	DOUBLING
DIPLOPOD	DISMOUNT	DIVIDEND	DOGTROTS	DOUBLOON
DIPLOSIS	DISORDER	DIVIDERS	DOGWATCH	DOUBLURE
DIPSTICK	DISOWNED	DIVIDING	DOG WATCH	DOUBTERS
DIPTERAL	DISOWNER	DIVI-DIVI	DOGWOODS	DOUBTFUL
DIPTERAN	DISPATCH	DIVINELY	DOLDRUMS	DOUBTING
DIRECTED	DISPENSE	DIVINERS	DOLERITE	DOUGHNUT
DIRECTLY	DISPERSE	DIVINING	DOLOMITE	DOUNREAY
DIRECTOR	DISPIRIT	DIVINITY	DOLOROSO	DOURNESS
DIRIMENT	DISPLACE	DIVINIZE	DOLOROUS	DOVECOTE
DIRT BIKE	DISPLAYS	DIVISION	DOLPHINS	DOVETAIL
DIRTIEST	DISPOSAL	DIVISIVE	DOMELIKE	DOWAGERS
DIRT ROAD	DISPOSED	DIVISORS	DOMESTIC	DOWDIEST
DIRTYING	DISPOSER	DIVORCED	DOMICILE	DOWNBEAT
DISABLED	DISPROOF	DIVORCEE	DOMINANT	DOWNCAST
DISABUSE	DISPROVE	DIVORCER	DOMINATE	DOWNFALL
DISAGREE	DISPUTED	DIVORCES	DOMINEER	DOWNHAUL
DISALLOW	DISPUTER	DIVULGED	DOMINICA	DOWNHILL
DISANNUL	DISPUTES	DIVULGER	DOMINION	DOWNIEST
DISARMED	DISQUIET	DIZZIEST	DOMINIUM	DOWNLOAD
DISARMER	DISROBED	DJAKARTA	DOMINOES	DOWNPIPE
DISARRAY	DISROBER	DJIBOUTI	DONATING	DOWNPLAY
DISASTER	DISSEISE	DNIESTER	DONATION	DOWNPOUR
DISBURSE	DISSENTS	D-NOTICES	DONATIVE	DOWNSIZE
DISCARDS	DISSEVER	DOCILITY	DON JUANS	DOWNTIME
DISCIPLE	DISSOLVE	DOCKETED	DONLEAVY	DOWNTOWN
DISCLAIM	DISSUADE	DOCKLAND	DOODLING	DOWNTURN
DISCLOSE	DISTAFFS	DOCKSIDE	DOOMSDAY	DOWNWARD
DISCORDS	DISTANCE	DOCKYARD	DOOMSTER	DOWNWASH
DISCOUNT	DISTASTE	DOCTORAL	DOORBELL	DOWNWIND
DISCOVER	DISTINCT	DOCTORED	DOORJAMB	DOXASTIC
DISCREET	DISTRACT	DOCTRINE	DOORKNOB	DOXOLOGY
DISCRETE	DISTRAIN	DOCUMENT	DOORMATS	DOZINESS
DISCUSES	DISTRAIT	DOCUSOAP	DOORNAIL	DRABBEST
DISEASED	DISTRESS	DODDERED	DOORPOST	DRABNESS
DISEASES	DISTRICT	DODDERER	DOORSILL	DRACAENA
DISENDOW	DISTRUST	DODGIEST	DOORSTEP	DRACHMAE
DISGORGE	DISUNION	DOGBERRY	DOORSTOP	DRACHMAS

DRACONIC	DRINKERS	DUELLING	DYNATRON	ECSTATIC
DRAFTEES	DRINKING	DUELLIST	DYSGENIC	ECTODERM
DRAFTIER	DRIPPING	DUE NORTH	DYSLEXIA	ECTOMERE
DRAFTING	DRIVABLE	DUE SOUTH	DYSLEXIC	ECTOSARC
DRAGGIER	DRIVE-INS	DUETTIST	DYSPNOEA	ECUMENIC
DRAGGING	DRIVELED	DUISBURG	DYTISCID	EDACIOUS
DRAGGLED	DRIVEWAY	DUKEDOMS		EDENTATE
DRAGLINE	DRIZZLED	DULCIANA	**E**	EDGEWAYS
DRAGNETS	DROGHEDA	DULCIMER	EARDROPS	EDGINESS
DRAGOMAN	DROLLERY	DULLARDS	EARDRUMS	EDIFICES
DRAGONET	DROLLEST	DULLNESS	EARLDOMS	EDIFYING
DRAGOONS	DROOLING	DUMBBELL	EARLIEST	EDITIONS
DRAGROPE	DROOPILY	DUMB-CANE	EARLOBES	EDMONTON
DRAINAGE	DROOPING	DUMB DOWN	EARMUFFS	EDUCABLE
DRAINING	DROP-DEAD	DUMBNESS	EARNINGS	EDUCATED
DRAMATIC	DROPLETS	DUMB SHOW	EARPHONE	EDUCATOR
DRAPABLE	DROPOUTS	DUMFRIES	EARPIECE	EDUCIBLE
DRATTING	DROPPERS	DUMMY RUN	EARPLUGS	EDUCTION
DRAUGHTS	DROPPING	DUMPIEST	EARRINGS	EDUCTIVE
DRAUGHTY	DROP SHOT	DUMPLING	EARSHOTS	EELGRASS
DRAWABLE	DROPSIED	DUNGAREE	EARTHIER	EERINESS
DRAWBACK	DROPS OFF	DUNGEONS	EARTHILY	EFFACING
DRAWBORE	DROPWORT	DUNGHILL	EARTHING	EFFECTED
DRAWCORD	DROUGHTS	DUODENAL	EARTHNUT	EFFECTER
DRAWDOWN	DROUGHTY	DUODENUM	EASEMENT	EFFECTOR
DRAWINGS	DROWNING	DUOLOGUE	EASINESS	EFFERENT
DRAWLING	DROWSILY	DUPLEXES	EASTERLY	EFFICACY
DRAWTUBE	DROWSING	DURATION	EAST SIDE	EFFIGIAL
DREADFUL	DRUBBING	DURATIVE	EASTWARD	EFFIGIES
DREADING	DRUDGERY	DUSHANBE	EASTWOOD	EFFLUENT
DREAMERS	DRUDGING	DUSKIEST	EASY CARE	EFFUSION
DREAMILY	DRUGGETS	DUSTBINS	EASY MARK	EFFUSIVE
DREAMING	DRUGGING	DUSTBOWL	EBB TIDES	EGESTION
DREARIER	DRUGGIST	DUSTCART	EBBW VALE	EGESTIVE
DREARILY	DRUIDISM	DUSTIEST	ECCLESIA	EGGHEADS
DREDGERS	DRUMBEAT	DUSTPANS	ECDYSIAL	EGGPLANT
DREDGING	DRUMFIRE	DUTCH CAP	ECDYSONE	EGG ROLLS
DRENCHED	DRUMFISH	DUTCHMAN	ECHELONS	EGGSHELL
DRENCHER	DRUMHEAD	DUTIABLE	ECHINATE	EGG TIMER
DRESSAGE	DRUMMERS	DUTY-FREE	ECHINOID	EGOISTIC
DRESSERS	DRUMMING	DWARFING	ECLECTIC	EGOMANIA
DRESSIER	DRUNKARD	DWARFISH	ECLIPSED	EGOTISTS
DRESSILY	DRUNKEST	DWARFISM	ECLIPSER	EGO TRIPS
DRESSING	DRUPELET	DWELLING	ECLIPSES	EGYPTIAN
DRIBBLED	DRY-CLEAN	DWINDLED	ECLIPSIS	EIGHTEEN
DRIBBLER	DRY DOCKS	DYARCHIC	ECLIPTIC	EIGHTIES
DRIBBLES	DRY GOODS	DYESTUFF	ECLOGITE	EISENACH
DRIBLETS	DRY-STONE	DYNAMICS	ECLOSION	EITHER-OR
DRIFTAGE	DUBONNET	DYNAMISM	ECONOMIC	EJECTING
DRIFTERS	DUCKLING	DYNAMIST	ECOTONAL	EJECTION
DRIFTING	DUCKWEED	DYNAMITE	ECOTYPIC	EJECTIVE
DRILLING	DUCTILES	DYNASTIC	ECRASEUR	EKISTICS

ELAPSING	EMBOSSED	ENCLITIC	ENJOYING	ENTOMBED
ELASTANE	EMBOSSER	ENCLOSED	ENKINDLE	ENTOZOIC
ELATERID	EMBRACED	ENCLOSER	ENLARGED	ENTOZOON
ELATERIN	EMBRACER	ENCODING	ENLARGER	ENTR'ACTE
ELBOWING	EMBRACES	ENCOMIUM	ENLISTED	ENTRAILS
EL DORADO	EMBRYOID	ENCROACH	ENLISTER	ENTRANCE
ELDRITCH	EMENDING	ENCUMBER	ENMESHED	ENTRANTS
ELECTING	EMERALDS	ENCYCLIC	ENNEADIC	ENTREATY
ELECTION	EMERGENT	ENDAMAGE	ENNEAGON	ENTRENCH
ELECTIVE	EMERGING	ENDANGER	ENNOBLED	ENTREPOT
ELECTORS	EMERITUS	END-BLOWN	ENNOBLER	ENTRESOL
ELECTRET	EMERSION	ENDBRAIN	ENORMITY	ENTRYISM
ELECTRIC	EMIGRANT	ENDEARED	ENORMOUS	ENTRYWAY
ELECTRON	EMIGRATE	ENDEMIAL	ENQUIRED	ENTWINED
ELECTRUM	EMINENCE	ENDEMISM	ENQUIRER	E NUMBERS
ELEGANCE	EMIRATES	ENDERMIC	ENRAGING	ENURESIS
ELEMENTS	EMISSARY	END GAMES	ENRICHED	ENURETIC
ELENCHUS	EMISSION	ENDOCARP	ENRICHER	ENVELOPE
ELENCTIC	EMISSIVE	ENDODERM	ENROLLED	ENVIABLE
ELEPHANT	EMITTING	ENDOGAMY	ENROLLEE	ENVIABLY
ELEVATED	EMOTIONS	ENDOGENY	ENROLLER	ENVIRONS
ELEVATOR	EMPATHIC	ENDORSED	ENSCHEDE	ENVISAGE
ELEVENTH	EMPERORS	ENDORSEE	ENSCONCE	ENVISION
EL FAIYUM	EMPHASES	ENDORSER	ENSEMBLE	ENWREATH
EL FERROL	EMPHASIS	ENDORSOR	ENSHRINE	ENZOOTIC
ELF LOCKS	EMPHATIC	ENDOSOME	ENSHROUD	EOLITHIC
ELICITED	EMPLOYED	ENDOWING	ENSIFORM	EPAULETS
ELICITOR	EMPLOYEE	ENDPAPER	ENSILAGE	EPHEMERA
ELIDIBLE	EMPLOYER	ENDPLATE	ENSLAVED	EPIBLAST
ELIGIBLE	EMPORIUM	ENDURING	ENSLAVER	EPIBOLIC
ELISIONS	EMPTIEST	END USERS	ENSNARED	EPICALYX
ELITISTS	EMPTYING	ENERGIZE	ENSNARER	EPICOTYL
ELKHOUND	EMPYEMIC	ENERVATE	ENSPHERE	EPICURES
ELLIPSES	EMPYREAL	ENFEEBLE	ENSURING	EPICYCLE
ELLIPSIS	EMPYREAN	ENFILADE	ENSWATHE	EPIDEMIC
ELONGATE	EMULATED	ENFOLDED	ENTAILED	EPIDOTIC
ELOQUENT	EMULATOR	ENFOLDER	ENTAILER	EPIDURAL
ELYTROID	EMULSIFY	ENFORCED	ENTANGLE	EPIFOCAL
EMACIATE	EMULSION	ENFORCER	ENTELLUS	EPIGRAMS
EMANATED	EMULSIVE	ENGADINE	ENTENDRE	EPIGRAPH
EMANATOR	EMULSOID	ENGAGING	ENTENTES	EPILEPSY
EMBALMED	ENABLING	ENGENDER	ENTERING	EPILOGUE
EMBALMER	ENACTING	ENGINEER	ENTHALPY	EPINASTY
EMBARKED	ENACTIVE	ENGINERY	ENTHETIC	EPIPHANY
EMBATTLE	ENACTORY	ENGRAVED	ENTHRONE	EPIPHYTE
EMBEDDED	ENAMELED	ENGRAVER	ENTHUSED	EPISCOPE
EMBEZZLE	ENCAENIA	ENGULFED	ENTICING	EPISODES
EMBITTER	ENCAMPED	ENHANCED	ENTIRELY	EPISODIC
EMBLAZON	ENCASING	ENHANCER	ENTIRETY	EPISTLER
EMBODIED	ENCIPHER	ENIWETOK	ENTITIES	EPISTLES
EMBOLDEN	ENCIRCLE	ENJOINED	ENTITLED	EPISTYLE
EMBOLISM	ENCLAVES	ENJOINER	ENTODERM	EPITAPHS

EPITASIS	ESOTERIC	EUPEPTIC	EXAMINED	EXISTENT
EPITHETS	ESPALIER	EUPHONIC	EXAMINEE	EXISTING
EPITOMIC	ESPECIAL	EUPHORIA	EXAMINER	EXITANCE
EPIZOISM	ESPOUSAL	EUPHORIC	EXAMPLES	EX LIBRIS
EPIZOITE	ESPOUSED	EUPHOTIC	EXARCHAL	EXOCRINE
EPONYMIC	ESPOUSER	EUPHRASY	EXCAVATE	EXOERGIC
EQUALING	ESPRESSO	EUPHUISM	EXCEEDED	EXORABLE
EQUALITY	ESSAYING	EUPHUIST	EXCEEDER	EXORCISE
EQUALIZE	ESSAYIST	EUPNOEIC	EXCELLED	EXORCISM
EQUALLED	ESSENCES	EURASIAN	EXCEPTED	EXORCIST
EQUATING	ESTANCIA	EUROCRAT	EXCERPTS	EXORCIZE
EQUATION	ESTEEMED	EURONOTE	EXCESSES	EXORDIAL
EQUINITY	ESTERASE	EUROPEAN	EXCHANGE	EXORDIUM
EQUIPAGE	ESTERIFY	EUROPIUM	EXCISING	EXOSPORE
EQUIPPED	ESTHETES	EUSTATIC	EXCISION	EXOTERIC
EQUIPPER	ESTIMATE	EUTECTIC	EXCITANT	EXOTOXIC
EQUITANT	ESTONIAN	EUXENITE	EXCITING	EXOTOXIN
EQUITIES	ESTOPPEL	EVACUANT	EXCLUDED	EXPANDED
ERADIATE	ESTOVERS	EVACUATE	EXCLUDER	EXPANDER
ERASABLE	ESTRAGON	EVACUEES	EXCRETAL	EXPECTED
ERASTIAN	ESTRANGE	EVADABLE	EXCRETED	EXPEDITE
ERASURES	ESURIENT	EVALUATE	EXCRETER	EXPELLED
ERECTILE	ET CETERA	EVANESCE	EXCURSUS	EXPELLEE
ERECTING	ETCHINGS	EVANSTON	EXCUSING	EXPELLER
ERECTION	ETERNITY	EVASIONS	EXECRATE	EXPENDED
EREMITIC	ETERNIZE	EVECTION	EXECUTED	EXPENDER
ERETHISM	ETHEREAL	EVENINGS	EXECUTER	EXPENSES
ERGOTISM	ETHERIFY	EVENNESS	EXECUTOR	EXPERTLY
ERIGERON	ETHERIZE	EVENSONG	EXEGESES	EXPIABLE
ERITREAN	ETHERNET	EVENTFUL	EXEGESIS	EXPIATED
ERLANGEN	ETHICIST	EVENTIDE	EXEGETIC	EXPIATOR
ERRANTRY	ETHICIZE	EVENTUAL	EXEMPLAR	EXPIRING
ERUMPENT	ETHIOPIA	EVERMORE	EXEMPLUM	EXPLICIT
ERUPTING	ETHIOPIC	EVERSION	EXEMPTED	EXPLODED
ERUPTION	ETHNARCH	EVERYDAY	EXEQUIES	EXPLODER
ERUPTIVE	ETHOLOGY	EVERYMAN	EXERCISE	EXPLOITS
ERYTHEMA	ETHONONE	EVERYONE	EXERGUAL	EXPLORED
ESCALADE	ETHOXIDE	EVICTING	EXERTING	EXPLORER
ESCALATE	ETHYLATE	EVICTION	EXERTION	EXPONENT
ESCALOPE	ETHYLENE	EVIDENCE	EXERTIVE	EXPORTED
ESCAPADE	ETIOLATE	EVILDOER	EX GRATIA	EXPORTER
ESCAPEES	ETIOLOGY	EVILLEST	EXHALANT	EXPOSING
ESCAPING	ETON CROP	EVILNESS	EXHALING	EXPOSURE
ESCAPISM	ETRUSCAN	EVINCING	EXHAUSTS	EXPUNGED
ESCAPIST	EUCHARIS	EVINCIVE	EXHIBITS	EXPUNGER
ESCHEWAL	EUGENICS	EVOCABLE	EXHORTED	EXTENDED
ESCHEWED	EULACHON	EVOCATOR	EXHORTER	EXTENDER
ESCHEWER	EULOGIES	EVOLVING	EXHUMING	EXTENSOR
ESCORTED	EULOGIST	EVONYMUS	EXIGENCY	EXTERIOR
ESCULENT	EULOGIZE	EXACTING	EXIGIBLE	EXTERNAL
ESKIMOAN	EUONYMUS	EXACTION	EXIGUITY	EXTOLLED
ESKIMOID	EUPEPSIA	EXALTING	EXIGUOUS	EXTOLLER

EXTORTED	FAIR GAME	FARMHAND	FEBRIFIC	FIASCOES
EXTORTER	FAIRINGS	FARMLAND	FEBRUARY	FIBRILAR
EXTRACTS	FAIRLEAD	FARMYARD	FECKLESS	FIBROSIS
EXTRADOS	FAIRNESS	FARNESOL	FECULENT	FIBROTIC
EXTREMES	FAIRWAYS	FAROUCHE	FEDERATE	FICTIONS
EXTRORSE	FAITHFUL	FARRIERS	FEEBLEST	FIDDLING
EXTRUDED	FAIZABAD	FARRIERY	FEEDABLE	FIDELITY
EXULTANT	FALCHION	FARROWED	FEEDBACK	FIDGETED
EXULTING	FALCONER	FARTHEST	FEEDBAGS	FIDUCIAL
EXUVIATE	FALCONET	FARTHING	FEELINGS	FIELD DAY
EYEBALLS	FALCONRY	FASCIATE	FEIGNING	FIELDERS
EYEBROWS	FALDERAL	FASCICLE	FEINTING	FIELDING
EYEGLASS	FALKLAND	FASCISTS	FELDSPAR	FIENDISH
EYELINER	FALL BACK	FASHIONS	FELICITY	FIERCELY
EYEPATCH	FALLFISH	FASTBACK	FELINITY	FIERCEST
EYEPIECE	FALL GUYS	FASTENED	FELLABLE	FIERIEST
EYESHADE	FALLIBLE	FASTENER	FELLATIO	FIFTIETH
EYESIGHT	FALLOUTS	FAST FOOD	FELONIES	FIGHTERS
EYESORES	FALL OVER	FASTNESS	FELSITIC	FIGHTING
EYESTALK	FALMOUTH	FATALISM	FEMININE	FIG LEAFS
EYETEETH	FALSETTO	FATALIST	FEMINISM	FIGMENTS
EYETOOTH	FALTBOAT	FATALITY	FEMINIST	FIGURANT
	FALTERED	FATHEADS	FEMINIZE	FIGURATE
F	FALTERER	FATHERED	FENDERED	FIGURINE
FABULIST	FAMILIAL	FATHERLY	FENESTRA	FIGURING
FABULOUS	FAMILIAR	FATHOMED	FERETORY	FILAGREE
FACEABLE	FAMILIES	FATHOMER	FEROCITY	FILAMENT
FACEBOOK	FAMISHED	FATIGUED	FERREOUS	FILARIAL
FACE CARD	FAMOUSLY	FATIGUES	FERRETED	FILATURE
FACE DOWN	FANAGALO	FATTENED	FERRETER	FILCHING
FACELESS	FANATICS	FATTENER	FERRIAGE	FILECARD
FACE-LIFT	FAN BELTS	FATTIEST	FERRITIN	FILEFISH
FACE PACK	FANCIERS	FAUBOURG	FERRULES	FILENAME
FACETIAE	FANCIEST	FAULTIER	FERRYING	FILETING
FACIALLY	FANCIFUL	FAULTILY	FERRYMAN	FILICIDE
FACILELY	FANCYING	FAULTING	FERRYMEN	FILIFORM
FACILITY	FANCY MAN	FAUSTIAN	FERVENCY	FILIGREE
FACTIONS	FANCY MEN	FAUTEUIL	FERVIDLY	FILIPINO
FACTIOUS	FAN DANCE	FAUXHAWK	FESTERED	FILLETED
FACTOTUM	FANDANGO	FAVONIAN	FESTIVAL	FILLINGS
FADELESS	FANFARES	FAVOURED	FESTOONS	FILMIEST
FADEOUTS	FANLIGHT	FAVOURER	FETATION	FILM STAR
FAEROESE	FANTASIA	FAYALITE	FETCHING	FILTERED
FAHLBAND	FANZINES	FEARLESS	FETIALES	FILTHIER
FAILINGS	FARADISM	FEARSOME	FETICIDE	FILTHILY
FAIL-SAFE	FARADIZE	FEASIBLE	FETISHES	FILTRATE
FAILURES	FARCEUSE	FEASIBLY	FETLOCKS	FIMBRIAL
FAINEANT	FARCICAL	FEASTING	FETTERED	FINAGLER
FAINTEST	FAREWELL	FEATHERS	FETTERER	FINALISM
FAINTING	FAR-FLUNG	FEATHERY	FETTLING	FINALIST
FAINTISH	FARINOSE	FEATURED	FEVERFEW	FINALITY
FAIR COPY	FARMABLE	FEATURES	FEVERISH	FINALIZE

FINANCED	FISHNETS	FLATLETS	FLIRTING	FLYOVERS
FINANCES	FISHSKIN	FLATMATE	FLITTING	FLYPAPER
FINDABLE	FISHTAIL	FLATNESS	FLOATAGE	FLYPASTS
FINDINGS	FISHWIFE	FLAT RACE	FLOATERS	FLYSHEET
FINEABLE	FISSIPED	FLAT SPIN	FLOATING	FLYSPECK
FINE ARTS	FISSURES	FLATTERY	FLOCCOSE	FLYWHEEL
FINE-DRAW	FISTMELE	FLATTEST	FLOCCULE	FLYWHISK
FINE GAEL	FITFULLY	FLATTING	FLOCKING	FOAMIEST
FINENESS	FITMENTS	FLATTISH	FLOGGING	FOAMLIKE
FINESPUN	FITTABLE	FLATWARE	FLOODING	FOB WATCH
FINE SPUN	FITTINGS	FLATWAYS	FLOODLIT	FOCALIZE
FINE-TUNE	FIVEFOLD	FLATWORM	FLOORAGE	FOCUSING
FINGERED	FIVEPINS	FLAUNTED	FLOORING	FOCUSSED
FINGERER	FIVE-STAR	FLAUNTER	FLOOZIES	FOETUSES
FINIALED	FIXATION	FLAUTIST	FLOPPIER	FOGBOUND
FINISHED	FIXATIVE	FLAVOURS	FLOPPILY	FOGGIEST
FINISHER	FIXTURES	FLAWLESS	FLOPPING	FOGHORNS
FINISHES	FIZZIEST	FLAXSEED	FLORALLY	FOG LAMPS
FINITELY	FLABBIER	FLEABAGS	FLORENCE	FOGLIGHT
FINNMARK	FLABBILY	FLEABANE	FLORIDLY	FOIE GRAS
FINOCHIO	FLAG DAYS	FLEABITE	FLORIGEN	FOILABLE
FIREABLE	FLAG FALL	FLEA BITE	FLORISTS	FOILSMAN
FIREARMS	FLAGGING	FLEAPITS	FLOSSING	FOISTING
FIREBACK	FLAGPOLE	FLEAWORT	FLOTILLA	FOLDABLE
FIREBALL	FLAGRANT	FLECKING	FLOUNCED	FOLDAWAY
FIREBOAT	FLAGSHIP	FLECTION	FLOUNCES	FOLDBOAT
FIREBRAT	FLAILING	FLEECING	FLOUNDER	FOLIATED
FIREBUGS	FLAKIEST	FLEETEST	FLOURING	FOLKLORE
FIRE-CURE	FLAMBEAU	FLEETING	FLOURISH	FOLK-ROCK
FIREDAMP	FLAMENCO	FLESHIER	FLOUTING	FOLKTALE
FIREDOGS	FLAMEOUT	FLESHING	FLOWERED	FOLKWAYS
FIRE-PLUG	FLAMINGO	FLESHPOT	FLOWERER	FOLLICLE
FIRESIDE	FLANDERS	FLETCHER	FLUE-CURE	FOLLOWED
FIRETRAP	FLANERIE	FLEXIBLE	FLUENTLY	FOLLOWER
FIREWALL	FLANKING	FLEXIBLY	FLUFFIER	FOLLOW-ON
FIREWEED	FLANNELS	FLEXUOUS	FLUFFING	FOLLOW-UP
FIREWOOD	FLAPJACK	FLEXURAL	FLUIDICS	FOMENTED
FIREWORK	FLAPPING	FLICKERY	FLUIDITY	FOMENTER
FIRMNESS	FLARE-UPS	FLICKING	FLUIDIZE	FONDANTS
FIRMWARE	FLASHERS	FLIMFLAM	FLUMMERY	FONDLING
FIRST AID	FLASHEST	FLIMSIER	FLUNKEYS	FONDNESS
FIRST-DAY	FLASHGUN	FLIMSILY	FLUNKING	FOOLSCAP
FIRTREES	FLASH GUN	FLINCHED	FLUORENE	FOOTBALL
FISCALLY	FLASHIER	FLINCHER	FLUORIDE	FOOTFALL
FISHABLE	FLASHILY	FLINGING	FLUORINE	FOOTGEAR
FISHBOLT	FLASHING	FLINTIER	FLURRIED	FOOTHILL
FISHBOWL	FLATBOAT	FLIP-FLOP	FLURRIES	FOOTHOLD
FISHCAKE	FLATETTE	FLIPPANT	FLUSHING	FOOTLING
FISH FARM	FLAT FEET	FLIPPERS	FLUTISTS	FOOTMARK
FISH-HOOK	FLATFISH	FLIPPEST	FLUTTERS	FOOTNOTE
FISHIEST	FLATFOOT	FLIPPING	FLUTTERY	FOOTPACE
FISHMEAL	FLATHEAD	FLIP SIDE	FLYBLOWN	FOOTPADS

FOOTPATH	FORESKIN	FOUR-BALL	FREESIAS	FROGFISH
FOOTRACE	FORESTAL	FOUR-DEAL	FREE TIME	FROMENTY
FOOTREST	FORESTAY	FOUR-EYED	FREETOWN	FRONDEUR
FOOTROPE	FORESTED	FOUREYES	FREEWARE	FRONTAGE
FOOTSIES	FORESTER	FOURFOLD	FREEWAYS	FRONTIER
FOOTSLOG	FORESTRY	FOUR-LEAF	FREE WILL	FRONTING
FOOTSORE	FORETELL	FOURSOME	FREEZERS	FRONTLET
FOOTSTEP	FORETIME	FOUR-STAR	FREEZE UP	FRONT MAN
FOOTWALL	FORETOLD	FOURTEEN	FREEZE-UP	FRONT MEN
FOOTWEAR	FOREWARN	FOVEOLAR	FREEZING	FROSTIER
FOOTWELL	FOREWENT	FOWLIANG	FREIBURG	FROSTILY
FOOTWORK	FOREWIND	FOWL PEST	FREMITUS	FROSTING
FOOTWORN	FOREWING	FOXGLOVE	FRENETIC	FROTHIER
FORAGING	FOREWORD	FOXHOLES	FRENULUM	FROTHILY
FOR A SONG	FOREYARD	FOXHOUND	FRENZIED	FROTHING
FORAYING	FORFEITS	FOXHUNTS	FREQUENT	FROUFROU
FORBEARS	FORGINGS	FOXINESS	FRESCOES	FROWNING
FORBORNE	FORGIVEN	FOXTROTS	FRESHEST	FROWZIER
FORCE-FED	FORGIVER	FRACTION	FRESHMAN	FRUCTIFY
FORCEFUL	FORGOING	FRACTURE	FRESHMEN	FRUCTOSE
FORCIBLE	FORJUDGE	FRAGMENT	FRETLESS	FRUGALLY
FORCIBLY	FORK-LIFT	FRAGRANT	FRETSAWS	FRUITAGE
FORDABLE	FORMABLE	FRAILEST	FRETTING	FRUIT BAT
FOREARMS	FORMALIN	FRAMABLE	FRETWORK	FRUIT FLY
FOREBEAR	FORMALLY	FRAME-UPS	FREUDIAN	FRUITFUL
FOREBODE	FORMERLY	FRANCIUM	FRIARIES	FRUITIER
FORECAST	FORMLESS	FRANKEST	FRIBBLER	FRUITING
FOREDECK	FORMULAE	FRANKING	FRIBOURG	FRUITION
FOREDOOM	FORMULAS	FRANKISH	FRICTION	FRUMENTY
FOREFEET	FORMWORK	FRANKLIN	FRIENDLY	FRUMPIER
FOREFOOT	FORNICAL	FRASCATI	FRIESIAN	FRUMPISH
FOREGOER	FORSAKEN	FRAULEIN	FRIGATES	FRUSTULE
FOREGONE	FORSAKER	FRAZZLED	FRIGGING	FUCHSIAS
FOREHAND	FORSOOTH	FREAKING	FRIGHTEN	FUCOIDAL
FOREHEAD	FORSWEAR	FREAKISH	FRIGIDLY	FUDDLING
FOREKNOW	FORSWORE	FRECKLED	FRILLIER	FUELLING
FORELAND	FORSWORN	FRECKLES	FRINGING	FUGACITY
FORELEGS	FORTIETH	FREE-BASE	FRIPPERY	FUGGIEST
FORELIMB	FORT KNOX	FREEBIES	FRISBEES	FUGITIVE
FORELOCK	FORTRESS	FREEBOOT	FRISETTE	FUGLEMAN
FOREMAST	FORTUITY	FREEBORN	FRISKIER	FULCRUMS
FOREMOST	FORTUNES	FREEDMAN	FRISKILY	FULLBACK
FORENAME	FORWARDS	FREE-FALL	FRISKING	FULL MOON
FORENOON	FORZANDO	FREEFONE	FRISSONS	FULLNESS
FORENSIC	FOSSETTE	FREEHAND	FRITTATA	FULL-PAGE
FOREPART	FOSTERED	FREEHOLD	FRITTERS	FULL STOP
FOREPEAK	FOSTERER	FREE KICK	FRIULIAN	FULL-TIME
FOREPLAY	FOULNESS	FREELOAD	FRIZZIER	FULL TOSS
FORESAIL	FOUL PLAY	FREE PASS	FRIZZING	FULMINIC
FORESEEN	FOUNDERS	FREE PORT	FRIZZLED	FUMAROLE
FORESEER	FOUNDING	FREEPOST	FRIZZLER	FUMATORY
FORESIDE	FOUNTAIN	FREE REIN	FROCKING	FUMBLING

FUMELESS
FUMIGANT
FUMIGATE
FUMINGLY
FUMITORY
FUNCTION
FUNERALS
FUNERARY
FUNEREAL
FUNFAIRS
FUNGIBLE
FUNGUSES
FUNKIEST
FUNNELED
FUNNIEST
FURBELOW
FURCATED
FURFURAN
FURLABLE
FURLONGS
FURLOUGH
FURNACES
FURRIERS
FURRIERY
FURRIEST
FURROWED
FURROWER
FURTHEST
FURUNCLE
FUSELAGE
FUSIFORM
FUSILIER
FUSSIEST
FUSSPOTS
FUSTIEST
FUTILITY
FUTURISM
FUTURIST
FUTURITY
FUZZIEST

G

GABBLING
GABBROIC
GABONESE
GABORONE
GADABOUT
GADFLIES
GADGETRY
GAFFSAIL
GAINABLE
GAINSAID

GALACTIC
GALANGAL
GALAXIES
GALBANUM
GALENISM
GALENIST
GALICIAN
GALILEAN
GALLANTS
GALLEASS
GALLEONS
GALLERIA
GALLIARD
GALLIPOT
GALLOPED
GALLOPER
GALLOWAY
GALOSHES
GALVANIC
GAMBLERS
GAMBLING
GAMBOLED
GAMECOCK
GAME FOWL
GAMENESS
GAMESTER
GAMINESS
GAMMA RAY
GAMMONER
GANDHIAN
GANG-BANG
GANGLAND
GANGLIAL
GANGLING
GANGLION
GANGRENE
GANGSTER
GANGWAYS
GANISTER
GANTLINE
GANTRIES
GANYMEDE
GAOLBIRD
GAOXIONG
GAPEWORM
GAPINGLY
GARAGING
GARAMOND
GARBLESS
GARBLING
GARBOARD
GARDENED

GARDENER
GARDENIA
GARGANEY
GARGLING
GARGOYLE
GARISHLY
GARLANDS
GARLICKY
GARMENTS
GARNERED
GARRISON
GARROTTE
GASIFIER
GASIFORM
GASLIGHT
GAS MASKS
GASOLIER
GASOLINE
GASSIEST
GASTIGHT
GASTRULA
GASWORKS
GATEFOLD
GATEPOST
GATEWAYS
GATHERED
GATHERER
GAUDIEST
GAULLISM
GAULLIST
GAUNTLET
GAUZIEST
GAVOTTES
GAWKIEST
GAZELLES
GAZETTES
GAZPACHO
GAZUMPED
GAZUMPER
GELATINE
GELATION
GELDINGS
GELIDITY
GEMINATE
GEMOLOGY
GEMSTONE
GENDARME
GENDERED
GENERALS
GENERATE
GENEROUS
GENETICS

GENIALLY
GENITALS
GENITIVE
GENIUSES
GENOCIDE
GENOTYPE
GENTIANS
GENTILES
GENTRIFY
GEODESIC
GEODETIC
GEOGNOSY
GEOMANCY
GEOMETER
GEOMETRY
GEOPHAGY
GEOPHYTE
GEOPONIC
GEORDIES
GEORGIAN
GEOTAXIS
GERANIAL
GERANIOL
GERANIUM
GERMANIC
GERM CELL
GERMINAL
GESTALTS
GESTAPOS
GESTURAL
GESTURED
GESTURER
GESTURES
GET THERE
GHANAIAN
GHERKINS
GHETTOES
GHOSTING
GHOULISH
GIANTESS
GIBBERED
GIBBSITE
GIBINGLY
GIDDIEST
GIFT-WRAP
GIGAFLOP
GIGANTIC
GIGGLING
GILTHEAD
GILTWOOD
GIMCRACK
GIMMICKS

GIMMICKY
GINGERED
GINGERLY
GINGIVAL
GIN RUMMY
GINSBERG
GIN SLING
GIN TRAPS
GIRAFFES
GIRDLING
GIRLHOOD
GISBORNE
GIVEAWAY
GIZZARDS
GLABELLA
GLABROUS
GLACIATE
GLACIERS
GLADBECK
GLADDEST
GLAD HAND
GLADIATE
GLADIOLI
GLADNESS
GLAD RAGS
GLANCING
GLANDERS
GLANDULE
GLASSIER
GLASSINE
GLASSING
GLASSMAN
GLAUCOMA
GLAUCOUS
GLAZIERS
GLAZIERY
GLEAMING
GLEANING
GLENDALE
GLIBBEST
GLIBNESS
GLIMMERS
GLIMPSED
GLIMPSER
GLIMPSES
GLINTING
GLISSADE
GLITCHES
GLITTERS
GLITTERY
GLITZIER
GLOAMING

GLOATING	GODTHAAB	GO TO TOWN	GRAVITON	GROGGIER
GLOBALLY	GOETHITE	GOUACHES	GRAYLING	GROGGILY
GLOBULAR	GO-GETTER	GOURMAND	GREASERS	GROMWELL
GLOBULES	GOGGLING	GOURMETS	GREASIER	GROOMING
GLOBULIN	GOIDELIC	GOUTWEED	GREASILY	GROOVIER
GLOOMFUL	GOINGS ON	GOVERNED	GREASING	GROSBEAK
GLOOMIER	GOINGS-ON	GOVERNOR	GREATEST	GROSCHEN
GLOOMILY	GOITROUS	GRAB BAGS	GREEDIER	GROSSEST
GLORIOUS	GOLD COAT	GRABBING	GREEDILY	GROSSING
GLORYING	GOLD DUST	GRABBLER	GREENERY	GROTTIER
GLOSSARY	GOLDFISH	GRACEFUL	GREENEST	GROTTOES
GLOSSIER	GOLD LEAF	GRACIOUS	GREENFLY	GROUCHED
GLOSSILY	GOLDMINE	GRADABLE	GREENING	GROUCHES
GLOSSING	GOLD RUSH	GRADIENT	GREENISH	GROUNDED
GLOWERED	GOLF BALL	GRADUATE	GREENLET	GROUPIES
GLOW-WORM	GOLF CLUB	GRAECISM	GREENOCK	GROUPING
GLOXINIA	GOLIATHS	GRAFFITI	GREEN TEA	GROUSING
GLUCAGON	GOLLIWOG	GRAFFITO	GREETING	GROVELED
GLUCINUM	GOLLOPER	GRAFTERS	GREMLINS	GROWABLE
GLUCOSIC	GOMBROON	GRAFTING	GRENADES	GROWLERS
GLUMMEST	GONDOLAS	GRAINING	GRENOBLE	GROWLING
GLUMNESS	GONIDIAL	GRAMPIAN	GREY AREA	GROWMORE
GLUTELIN	GONIDIUM	GRANDADS	GREYBACK	GROWN-UPS
GLUTTING	GONOCYTE	GRANDEES	GREYNESS	GRUBBIER
GLUTTONS	GONOPORE	GRANDEST	GRIDDLES	GRUBBILY
GLUTTONY	GOOD BOOK	GRANDEUR	GRIDIRON	GRUBBING
GLYCERIC	GOODBYES	GRAND MAL	GRIDLOCK	GRUDGING
GLYCERIN	GOODLIER	GRANDMAS	GRIEVING	GRUESOME
GLYCEROL	GOODNESS	GRANDPAS	GRIEVOUS	GRUFFEST
GLYCERYL	GOOD TURN	GRANDSON	GRIFFINS	GRUFFISH
GLYCOGEN	GOODWILL	GRANITIC	GRILLAGE	GRUMBLED
GLYCOLIC	GOODWOOD	GRANNIES	GRILLING	GRUMBLER
GLYPTICS	GOOD WORD	GRANTHAM	GRIMACED	GRUMBLES
GNASHERS	GOOFIEST	GRANTING	GRIMACER	GRUMPIER
GNASHING	GOOGLIES	GRANULAR	GRIMACES	GRUMPILY
GNATHION	GOOGLING	GRANULES	GRIMIEST	GRUNTING
GNATHITE	GO PLACES	GRAPHEME	GRIMMEST	GRYPHONS
GNAWABLE	GORDIMER	GRAPHICS	GRIMNESS	G-STRINGS
GNEISSIC	GORGEDLY	GRAPHITE	GRINDERS	GUAIACOL
GNOMONIC	GORGEOUS	GRAPNELS	GRINDERY	GUAIACUM
GOAL LINE	GORGERIN	GRAPPLED	GRINDING	GUARANTY
GOALPOST	GORILLAS	GRAPPLER	GRINNING	GUARDANT
GOATHERD	GORINESS	GRASPING	GRIPPING	GUARDIAN
GOATSKIN	GORLOVKA	GRASSIER	GRISEOUS	GUARDING
GOAT'S-RUE	GORMLESS	GRASSING	GRISETTE	GUERNSEY
GOBBLING	GOSLINGS	GRATEFUL	GRISLIER	GUERRERO
GOBSHITE	GOSPODIN	GRATINGS	GRITTIER	GUESSING
GOD-AWFUL	GOSSAMER	GRATUITY	GRITTILY	GUESTING
GODCHILD	GOSSIPED	GRAVAMEN	GRITTING	GUFFAWED
GODLIEST	GOSSIPER	GRAVELED	GRIZZLED	GUIANESE
GODSENDS	GOSSYPOL	GRAVELLY	GRIZZLER	GUIDABLE
GODSPEED	GOTEBORG	GRAVITAS	GROANING	GUIDANCE

GUILDERS	HABITUDE	HALLOWER	HANNIBAL	HARLOTRY
GUILEFUL	HABITUES	HALLWAYS	HANNOVER	HARMLESS
GUILTIER	HABSBURG	HALMSTAD	HANRATTY	HARMONIC
GUILTILY	HACIENDA	HALO-LIKE	HANUKKAH	HARPINGS
GUJARATI	HACKETTE	HALYARDS	HAPLITIC	HARPISTS
GULFWEED	HACKNEYS	HAMARTIA	HAPLOSIS	HARPOONS
GULLIBLE	HACKSAWS	HAMILTON	HAPPENED	HARRIDAN
GULLIBLY	HACKWORK	HAMMERED	HAPPIEST	HARRIERS
GUMBOILS	HADRONIC	HAMMERER	HAPSBURG	HARRIMAN
GUMBOOTS	HAEMATIC	HAMMOCKS	HAPTERON	HARRISON
GUMBOTIL	HAEMATIN	HAMPERED	HARA-KIRI	HARROWED
GUMDROPS	HAEREMAI	HAMPERER	HARAMBEE	HARROWER
GUMMIEST	HA-ERH-PIN	HAMSTERS	HARANGUE	HARRUMPH
GUMMOSIS	HAFTARAH	HANDBAGS	HARAPPAN	HARRYING
GUMPTION	HAGGADAH	HANDBALL	HARASSED	HARSHEST
GUMSHOES	HAGGADIC	HANDBELL	HARASSER	HARTFORD
GUM TREES	HAGGLING	HANDBILL	HARBOURS	HARTNELL
GUNBOATS	HAILWOOD	HANDBOOK	HARD AT IT	HARUSPEX
GUNFLINT	HAIPHONG	HANDCART	HARDBACK	HARVESTS
GUNMETAL	HAIRBALL	HANDCLAP	HARDBAKE	HAS-BEENS
GUNPAPER	HAIRCUTS	HANDCUFF	HARDBALL	HASIDISM
GUNPOINT	HAIRGRIP	HANDFAST	HARD CASH	HASSLING
GUNSHOTS	HAIRIEST	HANDFEED	HARD COPY	HASSOCKS
GUNSMITH	HAIRLESS	HANDFULS	HARDCORE	HASTEFUL
GUNSTOCK	HAIRLIKE	HANDGRIP	HARD CORE	HASTENED
GUNWALES	HAIRLINE	HANDGUNS	HARD-CORE	HASTENER
GURGLING	HAIRNETS	HANDHOLD	HARD DISK	HASTIEST
GURKHALI	HAIRPINS	HANDICAP	HARDENED	HASTINGS
GUSTIEST	HAIRTAIL	HANDIEST	HARDENER	HATBANDS
GUTSIEST	HAIRWORM	HANDLERS	HARDHACK	HATCHERY
GUTTERED	HAKODATE	HANDLESS	HARDIEST	HATCHETS
GUTTURAL	HALAFIAN	HANDLIKE	HARD LINE	HATCHING
GUYANESE	HALATION	HANDLING	HARDLINK	HATCHWAY
GUYLINER	HALBERDS	HANDLOOM	HARD LUCK	HATEABLE
GUZZLERS	HALCYONE	HANDMADE	HARDNESS	HATFIELD
GUZZLING	HALENESS	HANDOUTS	HARD NUTS	HATHAWAY
GYMKHANA	HALFBACK	HANDOVER	HARD SELL	HATHORIC
GYMNASTS	HALFBEAK	HANDRAIL	HARDSHIP	HATTERAS
GYMSLIPS	HALF COCK	HANDS-OFF	HARD TACK	HAT TRICK
GYNANDRY	HALF-LIFE	HANDSOME	HARDTOPS	HAULIERS
GYNARCHY	HALF-MAST	HANDYMAN	HARD UPON	HAUNCHED
GYPSEOUS	HALF MOON	HANDYMEN	HARDWARE	HAUNCHES
GYRATING	HALF NOTE	HANGBIRD	HARDWOOD	HAUNTING
GYRATION	HALF TERM	HANGCHOW	HAREBELL	HAUSFRAU
GYRATORY	HALF TIME	HANGER-ON	HARELIKE	HAUTBOIS
	HALFTONE	HANGINGS	HARFLEUR	HAUTBOYS
H	HALF-WITS	HANGNAIL	HARGEISA	HAUT-RHIN
	HALF-YEAR	HANGOUTS	HARICOTS	HAVELOCK
HABAKKUK	HALIBUTS	HANGOVER	HARIKARI	HAVE-NOTS
HABANERA	HALLIARD	HANGZHOU	HARINGEY	HAVERING
HABITANT	HALLMARK	HANKERED	HARKENED	HAVILDAR
HABITATS	HALLOWED	HANKERER	HARKENER	HAVOCKER
HABITUAL				

HAWAIIAN	HEATHERY	HELMSMEN	HERODIAS	HIGHVELD
HAWFINCH	HEATLESS	HELOTISM	HERPETIC	HIGHWAYS
HAWKBILL	HEAT PUMP	HELPABLE	HERRINGS	HIJACKED
HAWK-EYED	HEAT RASH	HELPINGS	HERSCHEL	HIJACKER
HAWKLIKE	HEAT WAVE	HELPLESS	HERTFORD	HILARITY
HAWKWEED	HEAVENLY	HELPMANN	HERTZIAN	HILLFORT
HAWTHORN	HEAVIEST	HELPMATE	HESIODIC	HILL FORT
HAYCOCKS	HEAVY-SET	HELPMEET	HESITANT	HILLIARD
HAY FEVER	HEBDOMAD	HELSINKI	HESITATE	HILLIEST
HAYFORKS	HEBETATE	HELVETIA	HESPERIA	HILLOCKS
HAYMAKER	HEBETUDE	HELVETIC	HESPERUS	HILLSIDE
HAYSTACK	HEBRAISM	HELVETII	HESSIANS	HIMATION
HAZARDED	HEBRAIST	HEMIOLIC	HETAERIC	HINAYANA
HAZELHEN	HEBRAIZE	HEMIPODE	HEXAGONS	HINCKLEY
HAZELNUT	HEBRIDES	HEMLINES	HEXAGRAM	HINDERED
HAZINESS	HECATOMB	HEMLOCKS	HEXANOIC	HINDERER
HEADACHE	HECKLERS	HENBANES	HEXAPLAR	HINDMOST
HEADACHY	HECKLING	HENCHMAN	HEXAPODY	HINDUISM
HEADBAND	HECTARES	HENCHMEN	HEZEKIAH	HIPBATHS
HEADFAST	HECTORED	HENEQUEN	HIATUSES	HIP FLASK
HEADGEAR	HEDGEHOG	HENGYANG	HIAWATHA	HIPPARCH
HEADHUNT	HEDGEHOP	HENG-YANG	HIBERNAL	HIPSTERS
HEADIEST	HEDGEROW	HEN HOUSE	HIBERNIA	HIRAGANA
HEADINGS	HEDONICS	HEN PARTY	HIBISCUS	HIRELING
HEADLAND	HEDONISM	HENRYSON	HICCUPED	HIRI MOTU
HEADLESS	HEDONIST	HENSLOWE	HIDDENLY	HIROHITO
HEADLIKE	HEEDLESS	HEPATICA	HIDEAWAY	HISPANIA
HEADLINE	HEELBALL	HEPTAGON	HIDELESS	HISPANIC
HEADLOCK	HEELLESS	HEPTARCH	HIDROSIS	HISTOGEN
HEADLONG	HEELPOST	HEPWORTH	HIDROTIC	HISTORIC
HEADMOST	HEFTIEST	HERACLEA	HIERARCH	HITCHING
HEADRACE	HEGELIAN	HERACLES	HIERATIC	HITHERTO
HEADRAIL	HEGEMONY	HERALDED	HIGHBALL	HIT LISTS
HEADREST	HEIGHTEN	HERALDIC	HIGHBORN	HIVELIKE
HEADROOM	HEIMDALL	HERALDRY	HIGHBOYS	HOACTZIN
HEADSAIL	HEIRLESS	HERBLIKE	HIGHBROW	HOARDING
HEADSETS	HEIRLOOM	HERCULES	HIGHER-UP	HOARIEST
HEADSHIP	HEIRSHIP	HERDSMAN	HIGHJACK	HOARSELY
HEADSMAN	HELIACAL	HERDSMEN	HIGH JUMP	HOARSEST
HEADWARD	HELICOID	HERDWICK	HIGHLAND	HOBBLING
HEADWAYS	HELIPORT	HEREDITY	HIGH LIFE	HOBBYIST
HEADWIND	HELLADIC	HEREFORD	HIGH MASS	HOBNAILS
HEADWORD	HELL-BENT	HEREINTO	HIGHNESS	HOCHHUTH
HEADWORK	HELLCATS	HERESIES	HIGH RISE	HOCKTIDE
HEALABLE	HELLENES	HERETICS	HIGH-RISE	HOGMANAY
HEARABLE	HELLENIC	HEREUNTO	HIGH ROAD	HOGSHEAD
HEAR HEAR	HELLFIRE	HEREUPON	HIGH SEAS	HOISTING
HEARINGS	HELLHOLE	HEREWARD	HIGH SPOT	HOKKAIDO
HEARTIER	HELMETED	HEREWITH	HIGHTAIL	HOLDABLE
HEARTILY	HELMINTH	HERITAGE	HIGH TECH	HOLDALLS
HEATEDLY	HELMLESS	HERMETIC	HIGH TIDE	HOLD DEAR
HEATHENS	HELMSMAN	HERMITIC	HIGH TIME	HOLDFAST

HOLDINGS	HONDURAN	HORSEFLY	HUMBLING	HYSTERIA
HOLDOVER	HONDURAS	HORSEMAN	HUMBOLDT	HYSTERIC
HOLIDAYS	HONEGGER	HORSEMEN	HUMIDIFY	
HOLINESS	HONESTLY	HORSIEST	HUMIDITY	I
HOLISTIC	HONEWORT	HOSANNAS	HUMILITY	IAMBUSES
HOLLANDS	HONEYBEE	HOSEPIPE	HUMMOCKS	ICEBERGS
HOLLERED	HONEYDEW	HOSPICES	HUMMOCKY	ICEBLINK
HOLLIDAY	HONG KONG	HOSPITAL	HUMORIST	ICEBOUND
HOLLOWED	HONIEDLY	HOSPODAR	HUMOROUS	ICEBOXES
HOLLOWER	HONOLULU	HOSTAGES	HUMOURED	ICE CREAM
HOLLOWLY	HONORARY	HOSTELRY	HUMPBACK	ICE LOLLY
HOLOCENE	HONOURED	HOSTLERS	HUMPHREY	ICE PACKS
HOLOGRAM	HONOURER	HOTCHPOT	HUMPLIKE	ICE PICKS
HOLOTYPE	HOODLESS	HOTELIER	HUNCHING	ICE RINKS
HOLOZOIC	HOODLIKE	HOT FLUSH	HUNDREDS	ICE SHEET
HOLSTEIN	HOODLUMS	HOTHEADS	HUNGERED	ICE SKATE
HOLSTERS	HOODWINK	HOTHOUSE	HUNG JURY	ICE WATER
HOLYHEAD	HOOFLESS	HOT LINES	HUNGRIER	ICHTHYIC
HOLYOAKE	HOOFLIKE	HOTPLATE	HUNGRILY	IDEALISM
HOLYTIDE	HOOKLESS	HOT SPOTS	HUNTEDLY	IDEALIST
HOLY WEEK	HOOKLIKE	HOT STUFF	HUNTRESS	IDEALITY
HOLY WRIT	HOOKNOSE	HOT WATER	HUNTSMAN	IDEALIZE
HOMBURGS	HOOKWORM	HOUNDING	HUNTSMEN	IDEATION
HOMEBODY	HOOLIGAN	HOUNSLOW	HURDLERS	IDEATIVE
HOMEBRED	HOOPLIKE	HOUSEBOY	HURDLING	IDEE FIXE
HOME BREW	HOOSEGOW	HOUSEFLY	HURRYING	IDENTIFY
HOME HELP	HOOVERED	HOUSEFUL	HURTLING	IDENTITY
HOMELAND	HOPEFULS	HOUSEMAN	HUSBANDS	IDEOGRAM
HOMELESS	HOPELESS	HOUSEMEN	HUSH-HUSH	IDEOLOGY
HOMELIER	HOPLITIC	HOUSETOP	HUSKIEST	IDIOCIES
HOMELIKE	HORATIAN	HOUSINGS	HUSKLIKE	IDIOLECT
HOMEMADE	HORIZONS	HOVERERS	HUSTINGS	IDLENESS
HOME PAGE	HORMONAL	HOVERING	HUSTLERS	IDOLATER
HOMERIAN	HORMONES	HOWITZER	HUSTLING	IDOLATRY
HOME RULE	HORNBEAM	HRVATSKA	HWANG HAI	IDOLIZED
HOME RUNS	HORNBILL	HSINKING	HYACINTH	IDOLIZER
HOMESICK	HORNBOOK	HUANG HUA	HYDER ALI	IDYLLIST
HOMESPUN	HORNFELS	HUCKSTER	HYDRACID	IGNITING
HOMETOWN	HORNIEST	HUDDLING	HYDRANTH	IGNITION
HOMEWARD	HORNLESS	HUFFIEST	HYDRANTS	IGNITRON
HOMEWORK	HORNLIKE	HUGENESS	HYDRATED	IGNOMINY
HOMICIDE	HORNPIPE	HUGGABLE	HYDRATES	IGNORANT
HOMILIES	HORNTAIL	HUGUENOT	HYDRATOR	IGNORING
HOMILIST	HORNWORT	HULA HOOP	HYDROGEL	IGUANIAN
HOMINESS	HOROLOGE	HULL-LESS	HYDROGEN	ILKESTON
HOMINOID	HOROLOGY	HUMANELY	HYDROMEL	ILLATIVE
HOMODONT	HOROWITZ	HUMANISM	HYGIENIC	ILL-FATED
HOMOGAMY	HORRIBLE	HUMANIST	HYMENEAL	ILLINOIS
HOMOGENY	HORRIBLY	HUMANITY	HYPERNYM	ILLIQUID
HOMOGONY	HORRIDLY	HUMANIZE	HYPNOSIS	ILL-TIMED
HOMOLOGY	HORRIFIC	HUMANOID	HYPNOTIC	ILL-TREAT
HOMONYMS	HORSEBOX	HUMBLEST		ILLUSION

ILLUSORY	IMPOTENT	INDIRECT	INFRINGE	INSISTED
ILMENITE	IMPRINTS	INDOCILE	INFUSING	INSISTER
IMAGINAL	IMPRISON	INDOLENT	INFUSION	INSOLATE
IMAGINED	IMPROPER	INDOLOGY	INFUSIVE	INSOLENT
IMAGINER	IMPROVED	INDORSED	INGATHER	INSOMNIA
IMBECILE	IMPROVER	INDUCING	INGENUES	INSOMUCH
IMBEDDED	IMPUDENT	INDUCTED	INGESTED	INSPIRED
IMBIBING	IMPUGNED	INDUCTOR	INGRATES	INSPIRER
IMITABLE	IMPUGNER	INDULGED	IN-GROUPS	INSPIRIT
IMITATED	IMPULSES	INDULGER	INGROWTH	INSTANCE
IMITATOR	IMPUNITY	INDULINE	INGUINAL	INSTANTS
IMMANENT	IMPURITY	INDUSIAL	INHALANT	INSTINCT
IMMATURE	IMPUTING	INDUSIUM	INHALERS	INSTRUCT
IMMERSED	INACTION	INDUSTRY	INHALING	INSULANT
IMMINENT	INACTIVE	INEDIBLE	INHERENT	INSULATE
IMMOBILE	INASMUCH	INEDIBLY	INHUMANE	INSULTED
IMMODEST	IN CAMERA	INEDITED	INIMICAL	INSULTER
IMMOLATE	INCENSED	INEQUITY	INIQUITY	INSURERS
IMMORTAL	INCEPTOR	INERTIAL	INITIALS	INSURING
IMMOTILE	INCHOATE	INESSIVE	INITIATE	INTAGLIO
IMMUNITY	INCIDENT	INEXPERT	INJECTED	INTARSIA
IMMUNIZE	INCISING	INFAMIES	INJECTOR	INTEGERS
IMMURING	INCISION	INFAMOUS	INJURIES	INTEGRAL
IMPACTED	INCISIVE	INFANTAS	INJURING	INTENDED
IMPAIRED	INCISORS	INFANTRY	INKBERRY	INTENDER
IMPAIRER	INCISURE	INFECTED	INKINESS	INTENTLY
IMPALING	INCITING	INFECTOR	INKSTAND	INTERACT
IMPARITY	INCLINED	INFERIOR	INKWELLS	INTERCOM
IMPARTED	INCLINER	INFERNAL	INLANDER	INTEREST
IMPARTER	INCLINES	INFERNOS	INNATELY	INTERIMS
IMPASSES	INCLOSED	INFERRED	INNER MAN	INTERIOR
IMPEDING	INCLUDED	INFERRER	INNOCENT	INTERLAY
IMPELLED	INCOMING	INFESTED	IN NO TIME	INTERMIT
IMPELLER	INCREASE	INFESTER	INNOVATE	INTERMIX
IMPERIAL	INCUBATE	INFIDELS	INNUENDO	INTERNAL
IMPERIUM	INCUDATE	INFINITE	INOCULUM	INTERNED
IMPETIGO	INCURRED	INFINITY	INOSITOL	INTERNEE
IMPINGED	INDAMINE	INFIXION	INPUTTED	INTERNET
IMPINGER	INDEBTED	INFLAMED	INQUESTS	INTERPOL
IMPISHLY	INDECENT	INFLAMER	INQUIRED	INTERRED
IMPLANTS	INDENTED	INFLATED	INQUIRER	INTERREX
IMPLICIT	INDENTER	INFLATER	INSANELY	INTERSEX
IMPLODED	INDEXERS	INFLEXED	INSANITY	INTERVAL
IMPLORED	INDEXING	IN FLIGHT	INSCRIBE	INTERWAR
IMPLORER	INDICANT	IN-FLIGHT	INSECURE	IN THE BAG
IMPLYING	INDICATE	INFLUENT	INSERTED	IN THE END
IMPOLICY	INDICIAL	INFLUXES	INSERTER	INTIMACY
IMPOLITE	INDICTED	INFORMAL	INSETTED	INTIMATE
IMPORTED	INDICTEE	INFORMED	INSETTER	INTONATE
IMPORTER	INDIGENE	INFORMER	INSIDERS	INTONING
IMPOSING	INDIGENT	INFRA DIG	INSIGHTS	INTRADOS
IMPOSTOR	INDIGOID	INFRARED	INSIGNIA	INTRANET

INTRENCH	ISATINIC	JACOBITE	JIPIJAPA	JUNK MAIL
INTREPID	ISCHEMIC	JACQUARD	JIUJITSU	JUNKYARD
INTRIGUE	ISLAMIST	JACUZZIS	JOCKEYED	JURASSIC
INTRORSE	ISLANDER	JAGGEDLY	JOCOSELY	JURATORY
INTRUDED	ISMAILIA	JAILBAIT	JOCOSITY	JURISTIC
INTRUDER	ISOBARIC	JAILBIRD	JODHPURI	JUSTICES
INTUBATE	ISOCHEIM	JALOPIES	JODHPURS	JUSTNESS
INTUITED	ISOCLINE	JALOUSIE	JOGGLING	JUVENILE
INUNDANT	ISOCRACY	JAMAICAN	JOHN BULL	
INUNDATE	ISOGLOSS	JAMBOREE	JOHNNIES	**K**
INVADERS	ISOGONIC	JAMMIEST	JOINTING	KAI MOANA
INVADING	ISOLABLE	JAMNAGAR	JOINTURE	KAIROUAN
INVALIDS	ISOLATED	JANGLING	JOKINGLY	KAKEMONO
INVASION	ISOLATOR	JANITORS	JOLLIEST	KALAHARI
INVASIVE	ISOLOGUE	JAPANESE	JOLLYING	KAMACITE
INVEIGLE	ISOMERIC	JAPANNED	JOSTLING	KAMAKURA
INVENTED	ISOMETRY	JAPINGLY	JOTTINGS	KAMIKAZE
INVENTOR	ISOMORPH	JAPONICA	JOURNALS	KANARESE
INVERTED	ISOPHONE	JAROSITE	JOURNEYS	KANAZAWA
INVERTER	ISOPLETH	JASMINES	JOUSTING	KANDAHAR
INVESTED	ISOPODAN	JAUNDICE	JOVIALLY	KANGAROO
INVESTOR	ISOPRENE	JAUNTIER	JOYFULLY	KAOLIANG
INVIABLE	ISOSTASY	JAUNTILY	JOYOUSLY	KAOLINIC
INVITING	ISOTHERE	JAUNTING	JOYRIDER	KARELIAN
INVOICED	ISOTHERM	JAVANESE	JOYRIDES	KASHMIRI
INVOICES	ISOTONIC	JAVELINS	JOYSTICK	KATAKANA
INVOKING	ISOTOPES	JAWBONES	JUBILANT	KATMANDU
INVOLUTE	ISOTOPIC	JAYAPURA	JUBILATE	KATOWICE
INVOLVED	ISOTROPY	JAZZIEST	JUBILEES	KATTEGAT
INVOLVER	ISRAELIS	JEALOUSY	JUDAIZER	KAUMATUA
INWARDLY	ISSUABLE	JEHOVIAN	JUDDERED	KAWASAKI
IODATION	ISSUANCE	JEMAPPES	JUDGMENT	KAYAKERS
IODOFORM	ISSYK-KUL	JEMMYING	JUDICIAL	KEDGEREE
IODOPSIN	ISTANBUL	JEOPARDY	JUGGLERS	KEENNESS
IONIZERS	ISTHMIAN	JEREMIAD	JUGGLERY	KEEPSAKE
IONIZING	ISTHMOID	JERKIEST	JUGGLING	KEESHOND
IOTACISM	ITALIANS	JEROBOAM	JUGULARS	KEEWATIN
IRAKLION	ITCHIEST	JESUITIC	JUICIEST	KEIGHLEY
IRISHMAN	ITEMIZED	JET-BLACK	JULIENNE	KELANTAN
IRISHMEN		JETFOILS	JUMBLING	KELOIDAL
IRONBARK	**J**	JETLINER	JUMBO JET	KEMEROVO
IRONCLAD	JABALPUR	JETTISON	JUMPABLE	KENNELED
IRON-GREY	JABBERED	JEWELLED	JUMPED-UP	KENTUCKY
IRON HAND	JABBERER	JEWELLER	JUMPIEST	KERATOID
IRONWARE	JACKBOOT	JEW'S HARP	JUMPSUIT	KERATOSE
IRONWOOD	JACKDAWS	JEZEBELS	JUNAGADH	KERCHIEF
IRONWORK	JACKFISH	JIGGERED	JUNCTION	KERKRADE
IROQUOIS	JACKPOTS	JIGGLING	JUNCTURE	KEROSENE
IRRIGATE	JACKSTAY	JINGLING	JUNGFRAU	KESTEVEN
IRRITANT	JACK TARS	JINGOISM	JUNIPERS	KESTRELS
IRRITATE	JACOBEAN	JINGOIST	JUNKETER	KETAMINE
ISAGOGIC	JACOBIAN	JINJIANG	JUNK FOOD	KETOXIME

KEYBOARD	KIRKWALL	KURTOSIS	LANCELET	LATINIST
KEYHOLES	KISHINEV	KUZNETSK	LANDFALL	LATINITY
KEY MONEY	KISSABLE	KWEICHOW	LANDFORM	LATINIZE
KEYNOTES	KITCHENS	KWEIYANG	LANDINGS	LATITUDE
KEYPUNCH	KLAIPEDA	KYPHOSIS	LANDLADY	LATRINES
KEY RINGS	KLANSMAN	KYPHOTIC	LANDLORD	LATTERLY
KEYSTONE	KLONDIKE		LANDMARK	LATTICES
KHARTOUM	KLYSTRON	**L**	LANDMASS	LAUDABLE
KHMERIAN	KNAPSACK	LABDANUM	LANDMINE	LAUDABLY
KHOIKHOI	KNAPWEED	LABELING	LANDRACE	LAUDANUM
KHUSKHUS	KNEADING	LABELLED	LANDSHUT	LAUGHING
KIAOCHOW	KNEECAPS	LABELLER	LANDSIDE	LAUGHTER
KIBOSHES	KNEE DEEP	LABELLUM	LANDSLIP	LAUNCHED
KICKABLE	KNEE-DEEP	LABILITY	LANDWARD	LAUNCHER
KICKBACK	KNEE-HIGH	LABOURED	LANGLAUF	LAUNCHES
KICKOFFS	KNEE-JERK	LABOURER	LANGUAGE	LAUREATE
KICKSHAW	KNEELING	LABRADOR	LANGUISH	LAUSANNE
KID-GLOVE	KNICKERS	LABURNUM	LANKIEST	LAVATION
KIDNAPED	KNIGHTED	LACANIAN	LANKNESS	LAVATORY
KILKENNY	KNIGHTLY	LACERANT	LANNERET	LAVENDER
KILLDEER	KNITTERS	LACERATE	LANTERNS	LAVISHED
KILLINGS	KNITTING	LACEWING	LANYARDS	LAVISHER
KILLJOYS	KNITWEAR	LACEWORK	LAPBOARD	LAVISHLY
KILOBYTE	KNOCKERS	LACINESS	LAP-CHART	LAWFULLY
KILOGRAM	KNOCKING	LA CORUNA	LAPELLED	LAWGIVER
KILOVOLT	KNOCKOUT	LACRIMAL	LAPIDARY	LAWSUITS
KILOWATT	KNOCK-UPS	LACROSSE	LAPILLUS	LAXATION
KIMONOED	KNOTHOLE	LACTONIC	LAPPETED	LAXATIVE
KINABALU	KNOTTIER	LACUNOSE	LAPSABLE	LAYABOUT
KINDLIER	KNOTTILY	LADDERED	LAPWINGS	LAYERING
KINDLING	KNOTTING	LADYBIRD	LARBOARD	LAYETTES
KINDNESS	KNOTWEED	LADYLIKE	LARGESSE	LAYSHAFT
KINDREDS	KNOWABLE	LADYSHIP	LARKSOME	LAYWOMAN
KINETICS	KNOW-ALLS	LAEVULIN	LARKSPUR	LAYWOMEN
KINGBIRD	KNOWSLEY	LAGGARDS	LARRIGAN	LAZINESS
KINGBOLT	KNUCKLED	LA GUAIRA	LARRIKIN	LAZULITE
KINGDOMS	KNUCKLES	LAH-DI-DAH	LARYNGES	LAZURITE
KINGFISH	KOHINOOR	LAID-BACK	LARYNXES	L-DRIVERS
KINGLIER	KOHLRABI	LAMASERY	LASHINGS	LEACHING
KINGPINS	KOLHAPUR	LAMBASTE	LA SPEZIA	LEADSMAN
KINGSHIP	KOLINSKY	LAMBDOID	LASSOING	LEAD TIME
KING-SIZE	KOMSOMOL	LAMBENCY	LAST POST	LEADWORT
KINGSTON	KOOKIEST	LAMBSKIN	LAST WORD	LEAFIEST
KINGWANA	KOOTENAY	LAME DUCK	LAS VEGAS	LEAF-LARD
KINGWOOD	KORDOFAN	LAMELLAR	LATCHING	LEAFLETS
KINKAJOU	KOSTROMA	LAMENESS	LATCHKEY	LEAGUING
KINKIEST	KOWTOWED	LAMENTED	LATENESS	LEAKAGES
KINSFOLK	KOWTOWER	LAMENTER	LATERALS	LEAKIEST
KINSHASA	KRAKATOA	LAMINATE	LATERITE	LEANINGS
KIRIBATI	KUMAMOTO	LAMPOONS	LATHERED	LEANNESS
KIRIGAMI	KUMQUATS	LAMPPOST	LATINATE	LEAPFROG
KIRKLEES	KUROSAWA	LAMPREYS	LATINISM	LEAP YEAR

LEARNERS	LES CAYES	LIENTERY	LINDWALL	LIVEWARE
LEARNING	LESSENED	LIFE BELT	LINEAGES	LIVE WIRE
LEASABLE	LETDOWNS	LIFEBOAT	LINEALLY	LIVONIAN
LEATHERY	LETHALLY	LIFE BUOY	LINESMAN	LIXIVIUM
LEAVENED	LETHARGY	LIFELESS	LINESMEN	LLANDAFF
LEAVINGS	LETRASET	LIFELIKE	LINGERED	LLANELLI
LECITHIN	LETTERED	LIFELINE	LINGERER	LOADINGS
LECTERNS	LETTERER	LIFELONG	LINGERIE	LOADSTAR
LECTURED	LETTINGS	LIFE PEER	LINGUINE	LOANABLE
LECTURER	LETTUCES	LIFE-SIZE	LINGUIST	LOANWORD
LECTURES	LEUCITIC	LIFESPAN	LINIMENT	LOATHING
LEEBOARD	LEUKEMIA	LIFETIME	LINKABLE	LOBBYING
LEERIEST	LEVANTER	LIFE WORK	LINKAGES	LOBBYISM
LEE SHORE	LEVELING	LIFTABLE	LINKEDIN	LOBBYIST
LEE TIDES	LEVELLED	LIFT-OFFS	LINKWORK	LOBELINE
LEFT-HAND	LEVELLER	LIGAMENT	LINOCUTS	LOBLOLLY
LEFTISTS	LEVERAGE	LIGATION	LINOLEUM	LOBOTOMY
LEFTOVER	LEVERETS	LIGATIVE	LINOTYPE	LOBSTERS
LEFT OVER	LEVERING	LIGATURE	LINSTOCK	LOCALISM
LEFTWARD	LEVIABLE	LIGHT ALE	LIONFISH	LOCALIST
LEFT WING	LEVIGATE	LIGHT BOX	LIONIZED	LOCALITY
LEGACIES	LEVITATE	LIGHTERS	LIONIZER	LOCALIZE
LEGAL AID	LEVKOSIA	LIGHTEST	LIPOGRAM	LOCATING
LEGALESE	LEWDNESS	LIGHTING	LIPOIDAL	LOCATION
LEGALISM	LEWISHAM	LIGNEOUS	LIPSTICK	LOCATIVE
LEGALIST	LEWISITE	LIGNITIC	LIQUESCE	LOCKABLE
LEGALITY	LEXICONS	LIGULATE	LIQUEURS	LOCKOUTS
LEGALIZE	LIAISING	LIGULOID	LISSOMLY	LOCOWEED
LEGATEES	LIAISONS	LIGURIAN	LISTABLE	LOCUTION
LEGATINE	LIAONING	LIKELIER	LISTENED	LODESTAR
LEGATION	LIAOTUNG	LIKENESS	LISTENER	LODGINGS
LEGENDRY	LIAOYANG	LIKENING	LISTEN IN	LODGMENT
LEGGIEST	LIBATION	LIKEWISE	LISTLESS	LODICULE
LEGGINGS	LIBECCIO	LILONGWE	LITANIES	LOESSIAL
LEG-PULLS	LIBELING	LIMA BEAN	LITERACY	LOFTIEST
LEG SIDES	LIBELLED	LIMACINE	LITERALS	LOGBOOKS
LEINSTER	LIBELLEE	LIMASSOL	LITERARY	LOG CABIN
LEISURED	LIBELLER	LIMAVADY	LITERATE	LOGICIAN
LEMMINGS	LIBERALS	LIMBLESS	LITERATI	LOGICISM
LEMONADE	LIBERATE	LIMEKILN	LITHARGE	LOGISTIC
LEMUROID	LIBERIAN	LIMERICK	LITIGANT	LOGOGRAM
LENGTHEN	LIBRETTI	LIMINESS	LITIGATE	LOGOTYPE
LENIENCY	LIBRETTO	LIMITARY	LITTERED	LOGOTYPY
LENINISM	LICENCES	LIMITING	LITTORAL	LOITERED
LENINIST	LICENSED	LIMNETIC	LIVE BAIT	LOITERER
LENITIVE	LICENSEE	LIMONENE	LIVELIER	LOLLARDY
LENTICEL	LICENSER	LIMONITE	LIVELONG	LOLLIPOP
LEOPARDS	LICHENIN	LIMOUSIN	LIVENING	LOLLOPED
LEOTARDS	LICH GATE	LIMPIDLY	LIVERIED	LOMBARDY
LEPIDOTE	LICKINGS	LIMPNESS	LIVERIES	LONDONER
LEPORINE	LICORICE	LINALOOL	LIVERISH	LONDRINA
LESBIANS	LIE-DOWNS	LINCHPIN	LIVETRAP	LONELIER

LONESOME	LOVESICK	LYALLPUR	MAHATMAS	MANDIBLE
LONE WOLF	LOVINGLY	LYCH GATE	MAHOGANY	MANDOLIN
LONGBOAT	LOWBROWS	LYCHGATE	MAIDENLY	MANDORLA
LONGBOWS	LOWERING	LYCH GATE	MAIEUTIC	MANDRAKE
LONGERON	LOWLANDS	LYINGS-IN	MAILABLE	MANDRILL
LONG FACE	LOWLIEST	LYMPHOID	MAILBAGS	MAN-EATER
LONGFORD	LOW-LYING	LYMPHOMA	MAILSHOT	MANEUVER
LONGHAND	LOW TIDES	LYNCHING	MAINLAND	MANFULLY
LONG-HAUL	LOW WATER	LYNCH LAW	MAIN LINE	MANGABEY
LONGHORN	LOYALISM	LYNCHPIN	MAINMAST	MANGANIC
LONGINGS	LOYALIST	LYONNAIS	MAINSAIL	MANGANIN
LONG JUMP	LOZENGES	LYREBIRD	MAINSTAY	MANGIEST
LONG-LIFE	LUCIDITY	LYRICISM	MAINTAIN	MANGLING
LONGSHIP	LUCKIEST	LYRICIST	MAJESTIC	MANGONEL
LONG SHOT	LUCKLESS	LYSOSOME	MAJOLICA	MANGROVE
LONGSPUR	LUCKY DIP	LYSOZYME	MAJORCAN	MANHOLES
LONG SUIT	LUDDITES		MAJORING	MANHOURS
LONG-TERM	LUDHIANA	**M**	MAJORITY	MANHUNTS
LONG TONS	LUGHOLES	MACADMIA	MAKE GOOD	MANIACAL
LONGUEUR	LUGSAILS	MACARONI	MAKING DO	MANICURE
LONG WAVE	LUGWORMS	MACAROON	MALADIES	MANIFEST
LONGWAYS	LUKEWARM	MACERATE	MALAGASY	MANIFOLD
LOOKER-ON	LUMBERED	MACHETES	MALAISES	MANIKINS
LOOKOUTS	LUMBERER	MACHINED	MALARIAL	MANITOBA
LOONIEST	LUMINARY	MACHINES	MALARKEY	MANLIEST
LOONY BIN	LUMINOUS	MACHISMO	MALAYSIA	MANNERED
LOOPHOLE	LUMPFISH	MACKEREL	MAL DE MER	MANNERLY
LOOSEBOX	LUMPIEST	MACRURAL	MALDIVES	MANNHEIM
LOOSE END	LUMP SUMS	MACRURAN	MALENESS	MANNITIC
LOOSENED	LUNATICS	MADDENED	MALIGNED	MANNITOL
LOOSENER	LUNATION	MADHOUSE	MALIGNER	MAN OF WAR
LOP-EARED	LUNCHEON	MADONNAS	MALIGNLY	MAN-OF-WAR
LOP-SIDED	LUNCHING	MADRIGAL	MALINGER	MANORIAL
LOQUITUR	LUNEBURG	MADURESE	MALLARDS	MANPOWER
LORDLIER	LUNGFISH	MAEBASHI	MALPOSED	MANSARDS
LORDOSIS	LUNGWORM	MAENADIC	MALTREAT	MANSHOLT
LORDOTIC	LUNGWORT	MAESTOSO	MALTSTER	MANSIONS
LORDSHIP	LUNULATE	MAESTROS	MALVASIA	MAN-SIZED
LORICATE	LURCHING	MAFIKENG	MAMA'S BOY	MANTILLA
LORIKEET	LURINGLY	MAGAZINE	MAMMOTHS	MANTISES
LORRAINE	LUSATIAN	MAGELLAN	MANACLED	MANTISSA
LOTHARIO	LUSCIOUS	MAGHREBI	MANACLES	MANTLING
LOTHIANS	LUSHNESS	MAGIC EYE	MANAGERS	MAN-TO-MAN
LOUDNESS	LUSTRATE	MAGICIAN	MANAGING	MANUALLY
LOUNGERS	LUSTROUS	MAGNATES	MANASSAS	MANURING
LOUNGING	LUTANIST	MAGNESIA	MANATOID	MANX CATS
LOUSIEST	LUTENIST	MAGNETIC	MANCIPLE	MANYFOLD
LOVEBIRD	LUTEOLIN	MAGNETON	MANDALAY	MAPPABLE
LOVELESS	LUTETIUM	MAGNETOS	MANDAMUS	MAPPINGS
LOVELIER	LUTHERAN	MAGNOLIA	MANDARIN	MAQUETTE
LOVELIES	LUXATION	MAHARAJA	MANDATED	MARABOUS
LOVELORN	LUXURIES	MAHARANI	MANDATES	MARANHAO

MARASMIC	MASSAGES	MEATIEST	MENDABLE	METHYLAL
MARASMUS	MASSEDLY	MECHANIC	MENHADEN	METHYLIC
MARATHON	MASSETER	MECHELEN	MENIALLY	METONYMY
MARAUDER	MASSEURS	MECONIUM	MENINGES	METRICAL
MARBLING	MASSICOT	MEDALLIC	MENISCUS	METRITIS
MARCHERS	MASTERED	MEDDLERS	MEN-OF-WAR	MEUNIERE
MARCHESA	MASTERLY	MEDDLING	MENOLOGY	MEXICALI
MARCHESE	MASTHEAD	MEDELLIN	MEN'S ROOM	MEZEREON
MARCHING	MASTIFFS	MEDIALLY	MENSURAL	MEZEREUM
MARGARIC	MASTITIS	MEDIATED	MENSWEAR	MEZIERES
MARGINAL	MASTODON	MEDIATOR	MENTALLY	MIAOWING
MARIANAO	MASTOIDS	MEDICAID	MENTIONS	MICELLAR
MARIGOLD	MASURIAN	MEDICALS	MEPHITIC	MICHIGAN
MARIMBAS	MATABELE	MEDICARE	MEPHITIS	MICROBAG
MARINADE	MATADORS	MEDICATE	MERCHANT	MICROBES
MARINATE	MATANZAS	MEDICINE	MERCIFUL	MICRODOT
MARINERS	MATCHBOX	MEDIEVAL	MERCURIC	MIDBRAIN
MARIPOSA	MATCHING	MEDIOCRE	MERGENCE	MIDDLE CS
MARITIME	MATERIAL	MEDITATE	MERIDIAN	MIDDLING
MARJORAM	MATERIEL	MEDUSOID	MERINGUE	MIDFIELD
MARKDOWN	MATERNAL	MEEKNESS	MERISTEM	MIDLANDS
MARKEDLY	MATINEES	MEETINGS	MERISTIC	MIDNIGHT
MARKETED	MATRICES	MEGALITH	MERITING	MIDPOINT
MARKETER	MATRIXES	MEGATONS	MERMAIDS	MIDRIFFS
MARKINGS	MATRONAL	MEGAVOLT	MERRIEST	MIDWIVES
MARKSMAN	MATRONLY	MEGAWATT	MERRY MEN	MIGHTIER
MARKSMEN	MATTERED	MELAMINE	MESCALIN	MIGHTILY
MARMOSET	MATTRESS	MELANGES	MESDAMES	MIGRAINE
MAROONED	MATURATE	MELANISM	MESMERIC	MIGRANTS
MAROQUIN	MATURELY	MELANIST	MESOCARP	MIGRATED
MARQUEES	MATURING	MELANITE	MESODERM	MIGRATOR
MARQUESS	MATURITY	MELANOID	MESOGLEA	MILANESE
MARQUISE	MAUBEUGE	MELANOMA	MESOZOIC	MILCH COW
MARRIAGE	MAVERICK	MELANOUS	MESQUITE	MILDEWED
MARRIEDS	MAXILLAR	MELINITE	MESSAGES	MILDNESS
MARRYING	MAXIMIZE	MELLOWED	MESSENIA	MILEAGES
MARSHALS	MAXIMUMS	MELLOWER	MESSIAHS	MILEPOST
MARSH GAS	MAYORESS	MELLOWLY	MESSIEST	MILIARIA
MARTABAN	MAYPOLES	MELODEON	MESSMATE	MILITANT
MARTAGON	MAZATLAN	MELODIES	MESSUAGE	MILITARY
MARTELLO	MAZURKAS	MELODIST	MESTIZOS	MILITATE
MARTIANS	MEA CULPA	MELODIZE	METALING	MILITIAS
MARTINET	MEAGRELY	MELTABLE	METALLED	MILKFISH
MARTINIS	MEALIEST	MELTDOWN	METALLIC	MILKIEST
MARTYRED	MEALWORM	MEMBRANE	METAMALE	MILKMAID
MARVELED	MEANINGS	MEMENTOS	METAMERE	MILK RUNS
MARXISTS	MEANNESS	MEMORIAL	METAPHOR	MILKSOPS
MARYLAND	MEANTIME	MEMORIES	METAZOAN	MILKWEED
MARZIPAN	MEASURED	MEMORIZE	METAZOIC	MILKWORT
MASSACRE	MEASURER	MEMSAHIB	METEORIC	MILKY WAY
MASSAGED	MEASURES	MENACING	METERING	MILLABLE
MASSAGER	MEATBALL	MENARCHE	METHANOL	MILLIAMP

MILLIARD	MISHMASH	MODIFIER	MONOGAMY	MORATORY
MILLIARY	MISJUDGE	MODIOLUS	MONOGENY	MORAVIAN
MILLIBAR	MISLAYER	MODISHLY	MONOGRAM	MORBIDLY
MILLIGAN	MISMATCH	MODULATE	MONOGYNY	MORBIFIC
MILLINER	MISNOMER	MOHAMMED	MONOHULL	MORBIHAN
MILLIONS	MISOGAMY	MOIETIES	MONOLITH	MORDANCY
MILLPOND	MISOGYNY	MOISTURE	MONOLOGY	MOREOVER
MILLRACE	MISOLOGY	MOLALITY	MONOMIAL	MORESQUE
MILTONIC	MISPLACE	MOLASSES	MONOPOLE	MORIBUND
MIMETITE	MISPLEAD	MOLDAVIA	MONOPOLY	MORNINGS
MIMICKED	MISPRINT	MOLDERED	MONORAIL	MOROCCAN
MIMICKER	MISQUOTE	MOLDIEST	MONOSEMY	MORONISM
MINARETS	MISSHAPE	MOLDINGS	MONOSOME	MOROSELY
MINATORY	MISSILES	MOLECULE	MONOTONE	MORPHEME
MINCE PIE	MISSIONS	MOLEHILL	MONOTONY	MORPHEUS
MINDANAO	MISSIVES	MOLESKIN	MONOTYPE	MORPHINE
MINDLESS	MISSOURI	MOLESTED	MONOXIDE	MORPHING
MIND'S EYE	MISSPELL	MOLESTER	MONROVIA	MORRISON
MINERALS	MISSPELT	MOLLUSCS	MONSIEUR	MORTALLY
MINGIEST	MISSPEND	MOLUCCAS	MONSOONS	MORTGAGE
MINGLING	MISSPENT	MOLYBDIC	MONSTERS	MORTIMER
MINICABS	MISSTATE	MOMENTUM	MONTAGES	MORTISER
MINIMIZE	MISTAKEN	MONACHAL	MONTEITH	MORTISES
MINIMOON	MISTAKES	MONADISM	MONTEREY	MORTMAIN
MINIMUMS	MISTIMED	MONAGHAN	MONTREAL	MORTUARY
MINISTER	MISTREAT	MONANDRY	MONTREUX	MOSEYING
MINISTRY	MISTRESS	MONARCHS	MONUMENT	MOSQUITO
MINORCAN	MISTRIAL	MONARCHY	MOOCHING	MOSSIEST
MINORITY	MISTRUST	MONASTIC	MOODIEST	MOTHBALL
MINOTAUR	MISUSAGE	MONAURAL	MOONBEAM	MOTHERED
MINSTERS	MISUSING	MONAZITE	MOONCALF	MOTHERLY
MINSTREL	MITCHELL	MONETARY	MOONFISH	MOTILITY
MINUTELY	MITICIDE	MONETIZE	MOONLESS	MOTIONED
MINUTIAE	MITIGATE	MONEYBOX	MOONRISE	MOTIONER
MINUTING	MITTIMUS	MONGOLIA	MOONSEED	MOTIVATE
MIRACLES	MIXED BAG	MONGOLIC	MOON SHOT	MOTIVITY
MIREPOIX	MIXTURES	MONGOOSE	MOONWORT	MOT JUSTE
MIRRORED	MNEMONIC	MONGRELS	MOORCOCK	MOTORBUS
MIRTHFUL	MOBILITY	MONISTIC	MOORHENS	MOTORCAR
MISANDRY	MOBILIZE	MONITION	MOORINGS	MOTORING
MISAPPLY	MOBOCRAT	MONITORS	MOORLAND	MOTORIST
MISCARRY	MOBSTERS	MONITORY	MOORWORT	MOTORIZE
MISCHIEF	MOCCASIN	MONKEYED	MOOSE JAW	MOTORMAN
MISCIBLE	MOCKABLE	MONKFISH	MOPINGLY	MOTORMEN
MISCOUNT	MODALITY	MON-KHMER	MOQUETTE	MOTORWAY
MISDEEDS	MODELING	MONKHOOD	MORAINAL	MOULDIER
MISERERE	MODELLED	MONMOUTH	MORAINES	MOULDING
MISERIES	MODELLER	MONOACID	MORALISM	MOULMEIN
MISFIRED	MODERATE	MONOCARP	MORALIST	MOULTING
MISFIRES	MODERATO	MONOCLES	MORALITY	MOUNTAIN
MISGUIDE	MODESTLY	MONOCRAT	MORALIZE	MOUNTIES
MISHEARD	MODIFIED	MONOCYTE	MORASSES	MOUNTING

MOURNERS	MUNITION	MYOGRAPH	NATTERED	NEOPRENE
MOURNFUL	MURALIST	MYOLOGIC	NATTIEST	NEOTERIC
MOURNING	MURDERED	MYOSOTIS	NATURALS	NEPALESE
MOUSIEST	MURDERER	MYOTONIA	NATURISM	NEPENTHE
MOUSSAKA	MURICATE	MYOTONIC	NATURIST	NEPHRITE
MOUTHFUL	MURKIEST	MYRIAPOD	NAUPLIUS	NEPOTISM
MOUTHING	MURMANSK	MYSTICAL	NAUSEATE	NEPOTIST
MOVABLES	MURMURED	MYSTIQUE	NAUSEOUS	NERVIEST
MOVEMENT	MURMURER	MYTHICAL	NAUTICAL	NESCIENT
MOVINGLY	MURRAINS	MYTILENE	NAUTILUS	NEST EGGS
MOZZETTA	MURRELET		NAVICERT	NESTLING
MUCHNESS	MURRHINE	**N**	NAVIGATE	NETSPEAK
MUCILAGE	MUSCATEL	NABOBERY	NAVY BLUE	NETTLING
MUCINOUS	MUSCLING	NACELLES	NAZARENE	NETWORKS
MUCKHEAP	MUSCULAR	NACREOUS	NAZARETH	NEURITIC
MUCKIEST	MUSHIEST	NAGALAND	NDJAMENA	NEURITIS
MUCKRAKE	MUSHROOM	NAGASAKI	NEAP TIDE	NEURONIC
MUCKWORM	MUSICALE	NAIL FILE	NEARCTIC	NEUROSES
MUCOSITY	MUSICALS	NAILHEAD	NEAR EAST	NEUROSIS
MUD BATHS	MUSICIAN	NAINSOOK	NEAR MISS	NEUROTIC
MUDDIEST	MUSINGLY	NAISSANT	NEARNESS	NEUTERED
MUDDLING	MUSKETRY	NAMANGAN	NEARSIDE	NEUTRALS
MUDDYING	MUSKIEST	NAME DAYS	NEATNESS	NEUTRINO
MUDFLATS	MUSQUASH	NAMEDROP	NEBRASKA	NEUTRONS
MUDGUARD	MUSTACHE	NAMELESS	NEBULIZE	NEW BLOOD
MUDPACKS	MUSTANGS	NAMESAKE	NEBULOUS	NEW BROOM
MUDSTONE	MUSTELID	NAMETAPE	NECKBAND	NEWCOMER
MUENSTER	MUSTERED	NAMIBIAN	NECKLACE	NEW DEALS
MUEZZINS	MUSTIEST	NANCHANG	NECKLETS	NEW-FOUND
MUFFLERS	MUTATION	NANTERRE	NECKLINE	NEWHAVEN
MUFFLING	MUTENESS	NAPHTHOL	NECKTIES	NEW HAVEN
MUFULIRA	MUTICOUS	NAPHTHYL	NECROSIS	NEWLYWED
MUGGIEST	MUTILATE	NAPIFORM	NECROTIC	NEW MOONS
MUGGINGS	MUTINEER	NARBONNE	NEEDIEST	NEWSCAST
MUG'S GAME	MUTINIED	NARCEINE	NEEDLESS	NEWSPEAK
MUGSHOTS	MUTINIES	NARCISSI	NEEDLING	NEWSREEL
MUGWUMPS	MUTINOUS	NARCOSIS	NEGATING	NEWSROOM
MULATTOS	MUTTERED	NARCOTIC	NEGATION	NEW TOWNS
MULBERRY	MUTTERER	NARKIEST	NEGATIVE	NEW WAVES
MULCHING	MUTUALLY	NARRATED	NEGLIGEE	NEW WORLD
MULCTING	MUZOREWA	NARRATOR	NEGRILLO	NEXT-DOOR
MULETEER	MUZZIEST	NARROWED	NEGRITIC	NHA TRANG
MULHOUSE	MUZZLING	NARROWLY	NEGROISM	NIARCHOS
MULISHLY	MYCELIAL	NASALITY	NEIGHING	NIBBLING
MULLIONS	MYCELIUM	NASALIZE	NEKTONIC	NICENESS
MULTIFID	MYCELOID	NASCENCE	NEMATODE	NICETIES
MULTIPED	MYCETOMA	NASTIEST	NEMBUTAL	NICHROME
MULTIPLE	MYCOLOGY	NATATION	NEOGAEAN	NICKELED
MULTIPLY	MYELINIC	NATIONAL	NEOMYCIN	NICKELIC
MUMBLING	MYELITIS	NATIVISM	NEONATAL	NICKNACK
MUNCHING	MYLONITE	NATIVIST	NEOPHYTE	NICKNAME
MUNIMENT	MYOGENIC	NATIVITY	NEOPLASM	NICOTINE

NIELLIST	NONVOTER	NULL SETS	OBSERVER	OFFSTAGE
NIFTIEST	NONWHITE	NUMBERED	OBSESSED	OFF STAGE
NIGERIAN	NOONTIME	NUMBFISH	OBSIDIAN	OFF-WHITE
NIGGARDS	NORMALLY	NUMBNESS	OBSOLETE	OFT TIMES
NIGGLERS	NORMANDY	NUMERACY	OBSTACLE	OHMMETER
NIGGLING	NORSEMAN	NUMERALS	OBSTRUCT	OILCLOTH
NIGHTCAP	NORSEMEN	NUMERARY	OBTAINED	OILFIELD
NIGHTJAR	NORTHERN	NUMERATE	OBTAINER	OIL-FIRED
NIGHT OWL	NORTHING	NUMEROUS	OBTRUDED	OILINESS
NIHILISM	NOSEBAGS	NUMINOUS	OBTRUDER	OIL PAINT
NIHILIST	NOSEBAND	NUMMULAR	OBTUSELY	OILSKINS
NIHILITY	NOSE BAND	NUMSKULL	OBVIATED	OIL SLICK
NIJMEGEN	NOSECONE	NUNEATON	OBVOLUTE	OILSTONE
NIMBLEST	NOSEDIVE	NUPTIALS	OCARINAS	OIL WELLS
NIMBUSES	NOSEGAYS	NURISTAN	OCCASION	OINTMENT
NINEFOLD	NOSINESS	NURSLING	OCCIDENT	OKAVANGO
NINEPINS	NOSOLOGY	NURTURED	OCCLUSAL	OKLAHOMA
NINETEEN	NOSTRILS	NURTURER	OCCUPANT	OLD FLAME
NINETIES	NOSTRUMS	NUTATION	OCCUPIED	OLD GUARD
NIPPIEST	NOTA BENE	NUT-BROWN	OCCUPIER	OLD HANDS
NIRVANAS	NOTABLES	NUTCASES	OCCURRED	OLD MAIDS
NIRVANIC	NOTARIAL	NUTHATCH	OCEANIAN	OLDSTERS
NITRATES	NOTARIES	NUTHOUSE	OCHREOUS	OLD-TIMER
NITROGEN	NOTARIZE	NUTRIENT	OCOTILLO	OLD WOMAN
NITROSYL	NOTATION	NUTSHELL	OCTAGONS	OLD WOMEN
NIVATION	NOTCHING	NUTTIEST	OCTARCHY	OLD WORLD
NOBBLING	NOTEBOOK	NUZZLING	OCTOBERS	OLEANDER
NOBELIUM	NOTECASE	NYMPHETS	OCTOROON	OLEASTER
NOBILITY	NOTELETS	NYSTATIN	OCULISTS	OLEFINIC
NOBLEMAN	NOTEPADS		ODDBALLS	OLIBANUM
NOBLEMEN	NOTICING	**O**	ODDITIES	OLIGARCH
NOBODIES	NOTIFIED	OAFISHLY	ODDMENTS	OLIGURIA
NOCTURNE	NOTIFIER	OAKVILLE	ODIOUSLY	OLIVE OIL
NODALITY	NOTIONAL	OARLOCKS	ODOMETER	OLYMPIAD
NODOSITY	NOTOGAEA	OATCAKES	ODONTOID	OLYMPIAN
NO-GO AREA	NOTORNIS	OBDURACY	ODYSSEYS	OMDURMAN
NOISIEST	NOVATION	OBDURATE	OENOLOGY	OMELETTE
NOMADISM	NOVELIST	OBEDIENT	OESTRIOL	OMISSION
NOMINATE	NOVELLAS	OBEISANT	OESTRONE	OMITTING
NOMINEES	NOVEMBER	OBELISKS	OESTROUS	OMNIVORE
NOMISTIC	NOVGOROD	OBERLAND	OFF AND ON	OMPHALOS
NOMOLOGY	NOWADAYS	OBITUARY	OFF BREAK	ON AND OFF
NONESUCH	NUBECULA	OBJECTED	OFFENCES	ONCE-OVER
NON-EVENT	NUBILITY	OBJECTOR	OFFENDED	ONCOLOGY
NONJUROR	NUCELLAR	OBLATION	OFFENDER	ONCOMING
NON LICET	NUCELLUS	OBLATORY	OFFERING	ONDAATJE
NONMETAL	NUCLEASE	OBLIGATE	OFF-GLIDE	ONDOGRAM
NON RIGID	NUCLEATE	OBLIGING	OFFICERS	ONE-HORSE
NONSENSE	NUDENESS	OBLIQUES	OFFICIAL	ONE-ON-ONE
NONSTICK	NUDICAUL	OBLIVION	OFFPRINT	ONE-PIECE
NONTOXIC	NUGATORY	OBSCURED	OFFSHOOT	ONE-SIDED
NONUNION	NUISANCE	OBSERVED	OFFSHORE	ONE-TO-ONE

ONE-TRACK	ORATIONS	OUTBREAK	OUT-TAKES	OVERPLAY
ONLOOKER	ORATORIO	OUTBREED	OUTVOTED	OVERRATE
ONRUSHES	ORBITING	OUTBURST	OUTWARDS	OVERRIDE
ON-SCREEN	ORCHARDS	OUTCASTE	OUTWEIGH	OVERRIPE
ONSTREAM	ORCHITIC	OUTCASTS	OUTWORKS	OVERRODE
ONTOGENY	ORCHITIS	OUTCLASS	OVALNESS	OVERRULE
ONTOLOGY	ORDAINED	OUTCOMES	OVARITIS	OVERSEAS
OOGAMOUS	ORDAINER	OUTCRIES	OVATIONS	OVERSEEN
OOGONIAL	ORDERING	OUTCROPS	OVENBIRD	OVERSEER
OOGONIUM	ORDINALS	OUTCROSS	OVENWARE	OVERSELL
OOLOGIST	ORDINAND	OUTDATED	OVERALLS	OVERSHOE
OOPHYTIC	ORDINARY	OUTDOING	OVERARCH	OVERSHOT
OOSPHERE	ORDINATE	OUTDOORS	OVERAWED	OVERSIDE
OOSPORIC	ORDNANCE	OUTFACED	OVERBEAR	OVERSIZE
OOTHECAL	ORENBURG	OUTFALLS	OVERBIDS	OVERSOLD
OOZINESS	ORGANDIE	OUTFIELD	OVERBOOK	OVERSTAY
OPALESCE	ORGANISM	OUTFIGHT	OVERBORE	OVERSTEP
OPAQUELY	ORGANIST	OUTFLANK	OVERCALL	OVERTAKE
OPENCAST	ORGANIZE	OUTFLOWS	OVERCAME	OVERTIME
OPEN-EYED	ORGASMIC	OUTFLUNG	OVERCAST	OVERTIRE
OPEN FIRE	ORIENTAL	OUTFOXED	OVERCOAT	OVERTONE
OPENINGS	ORIFICES	OUTGOING	OVERCOME	OVERTOOK
OPENNESS	ORIGINAL	OUT-GROUP	OVERCOOK	OVERTURE
OPEN-PLAN	ORINASAL	OUTGROWN	OVERCROP	OVERTURN
OPEN SHOP	ORNAMENT	OUT-HEROD	OVERDONE	OVERVIEW
OPENWORK	ORNATELY	OUTHOUSE	OVERDOSE	OVERWIND
OPERABLE	ORNITHIC	OUTLAWED	OVERDRAW	OVERWORK
OPERABLY	OROGENIC	OUTLAWRY	OVERDREW	OVIDUCAL
OPERATED	OROMETER	OUTLINED	OVERFLEW	OVIPOSIT
OPERATIC	ORPHANED	OUTLINES	OVERFLOW	OVULATED
OPERATOR	ORPIMENT	OUTLIVED	OVERGROW	OWLISHLY
OPERETTA	ORRERIES	OUTLOOKS	OVERHAND	OWN GOALS
OPHIDIAN	ORTHODOX	OUTLYING	OVERHANG	OXBRIDGE
OPINICUS	ORTHOEPY	OUTMODED	OVERHAUL	OXIDASIC
OPINIONS	OSCITANT	OUTPOINT	OVERHEAD	OXIDIZED
OPIUMISM	OSCULANT	OUTPOSTS	OVERHEAR	OXIDIZER
OPOSSUMS	OSCULATE	OUTRAGED	OVERHEAT	OXPECKER
OPPILATE	OSNABURG	OUTRAGES	OVERHUNG	OXTONGUE
OPPONENT	OSSIFIED	OUTREACH	OVERKILL	OXYGENIC
OPPOSING	OSSIFIER	OUTRIDER	OVERLAID	OXYMORON
OPPOSITE	OSTEITIC	OUTRIGHT	OVERLAIN	OXYTOCIC
OPPUGNER	OSTEITIS	OUTRIVAL	OVERLAND	OXYTOCIN
OPSONIZE	OSTINATO	OUTSHINE	OVERLAPS	OZONIZER
OPTATIVE	OSTIOLAR	OUTSHONE	OVERLAYS	
OPTICIAN	OSTRACOD	OUTSHOOT	OVERLEAF	**P**
OPTIMISM	OTIOSITY	OUTSIDER	OVERLOAD	PACIFIED
OPTIMIST	OTOSCOPE	OUTSIDES	OVERLONG	PACIFIER
OPTIMIZE	OTTOMANS	OUTSMART	OVERLOOK	PACIFISM
OPTIONAL	OUTBLUFF	OUTSTAND	OVERLORD	PACIFIST
OPULENCE	OUTBOARD	OUTSTARE	OVERMUCH	PACKABLE
ORACULAR	OUTBOUND	OUTSTRIP	OVERPAID	PACKAGED
ORANGERY	OUTBRAVE	OUTSWING	OVERPASS	PACKAGER

PACKAGES	PANACEAS	PARASOLS	PASSABLY	PAWKIEST
PADDLING	PANATELA	PARAVANE	PASSAGES	PAWNSHOP
PADDOCKS	PANCAKES	PAR AVION	PASSBOOK	PAYCHECK
PADLOCKS	PANCREAS	PARAZOAN	PASS BOOK	PAYLOADS
PAEONIES	PANDA CAR	PARCELED	PASSERBY	PAYMENTS
PAGANISM	PANDANUS	PARCENER	PASSIBLE	PAY PHONE
PAGANIST	PANDEMIC	PARCHING	PASSIONS	PAYROLLS
PAGANIZE	PANDERED	PARDONED	PASSKEYS	PAYSLIPS
PAGEANTS	PANDERER	PARDONER	PASSOVER	PEACEFUL
PAGINATE	PANELING	PARENTAL	PASSPORT	PEACOCKS
PAGO PAGO	PANELLED	PARHELIC	PASSWORD	PEAFOWLS
PAGURIAN	PANGOLIN	PARIETAL	PASTERNS	PEA GREEN
PAHOEHOE	PANICKED	PARISHES	PASTE-UPS	PEAKIEST
PAINLESS	PANICLED	PARISIAN	PASTICHE	PEARLIER
PAINTERS	PANMIXIA	PARKIEST	PASTIEST	PEARLITE
PAINTING	PANNIERS	PARKLAND	PASTILLE	PEARMAIN
PAKISTAN	PANNIKIN	PARKWAYS	PASTIMES	PEASANTS
PALADINS	PANOPTIC	PARLANCE	PASTINGS	PEBBLING
PALATALS	PANORAMA	PARLANDO	PASTORAL	PECCABLE
PALATIAL	PANPIPES	PARLEYED	PASTRAMI	PECCANCY
PALATINE	PANSOPHY	PARLEYER	PASTRIES	PECTORAL
PALAVERS	PANTHEON	PARLOURS	PASTURED	PECULATE
PALEFACE	PANTHERS	PARMESAN	PASTURES	PECULIAR
PALENCIA	PANTILES	PARODIED	PATAGIUM	PEDAGOGY
PALENESS	PANTRIES	PARODIES	PATCHIER	PEDALFER
PALETTES	PAPACIES	PARODIST	PATCHILY	PEDALING
PALFREYS	PAPERBOY	PAROLING	PATCHING	PEDALLED
PALINODE	PAPERING	PAROTOID	PATELLAR	PEDANTIC
PALISADE	PAPILLON	PAROXYSM	PATELLAS	PEDANTRY
PALLADIC	PAPISTRY	PARROTED	PATENTED	PEDDLERS
PALLIATE	PAPOOSES	PARRYING	PATENTEE	PEDDLING
PALLIDLY	PARABLES	PARSABLE	PATENTLY	PEDERAST
PALLIEST	PARABOLA	PARSIFAL	PATENTOR	PEDESTAL
PALL MALL	PARADIGM	PARSNIPS	PATERNAL	PEDICURE
PALMETTE	PARADING	PARTAKEN	PATERSON	PEDIFORM
PALMETTO	PARADISE	PARTAKER	PATHETIC	PEDIGREE
PALMIEST	PARADROP	PARTERRE	PATHLESS	PEDIMENT
PALMISTS	PARAFFIN	PARTHIAN	PATHOGEN	PEDIPALP
PALMITIN	PARAGOGE	PARTIBLE	PATHWAYS	PEDOLOGY
PALO ALTO	PARAGONS	PARTICLE	PATIENCE	PEDUNCLE
PALOMINO	PARAGUAY	PARTINGS	PATIENTS	PEEKABOO
PALPABLE	PARAKEET	PARTISAN	PATRIALS	PEELINGS
PALPABLY	PARALLAX	PARTNERS	PATRIOTS	PEEPHOLE
PALPATED	PARALLEL	PART-SONG	PATRONAL	PEEPSHOW
PALTERER	PARALYSE	PART-TIME	PATTERED	PEERAGES
PALTRIER	PARAMENT	PART WORK	PATTERNS	PEERLESS
PALTRILY	PARAMOUR	PARTYING	PATULOUS	PEGBOARD
PAMPERED	PARANOIA	PAR VALUE	PAUNCHES	PEIGNOIR
PAMPERER	PARANOID	PARVENUS	PAVEMENT	PEKINESE
PAMPHLET	PARAPETS	PARZIVAL	PAVILION	PELICANS
PAMPLONA	PARAQUAT	PASADENA	PAVLODAR	PELLAGRA
PANACEAN	PARASITE	PASSABLE	PAVONINE	PELLICLE

PELL-MELL	PERIOTIC	PHANTASM	PICKEREL	PIN MONEY
PELLUCID	PERISARC	PHANTASY	PICKETED	PINNACES
PELVISES	PERISHED	PHANTOMS	PICKETER	PINNACLE
PEMBROKE	PERISHER	PHARAOHS	PICKIEST	PINNIPED
PEMMICAN	PERIWIGS	PHARISEE	PICKINGS	PINOCHLE
PENALIZE	PERJURED	PHARMACY	PICKLING	PINPOINT
PENANCES	PERJURER	PHASE-OUT	PICKLOCK	PINPRICK
PENCHANT	PERKIEST	PHEASANT	PICK ME UP	PINTABLE
PENCILED	PERLITIC	PHENETIC	PICOLINE	PINT-SIZE
PENDANTS	PERMEANT	PHENOLIC	PICTURED	PINWHEEL
PENDULUM	PERMEATE	PHILLIPS	PICTURES	PIONEERS
PENGUINS	PERMUTED	PHILTRES	PIDDLING	PIPE BOMB
PENITENT	PERONEAL	PHIMOSIS	PIEBALDS	PIPECLAY
PENKNIFE	PERORATE	PHISHING	PIE CHART	PIPEFISH
PEN NAMES	PEROXIDE	PHONE BOX	PIECRUST	PIPELINE
PENNANTS	PERSONAL	PHONE-INS	PIEDMONT	PIPE RACK
PENNINES	PERSONAS	PHONEMES	PIERCING	PIPERINE
PENN'ORTH	PERSPIRE	PHONEMIC	PIFFLING	PIPETTES
PENOLOGY	PERSUADE	PHONETIC	PIGGIEST	PIPEWORT
PENSIONS	PERTNESS	PHONIEST	PIGMENTS	PIQUANCY
PENSTOCK	PERUSALS	PHOSGENE	PIGSKINS	PIRACIES
PENTACLE	PERUSING	PHOSPHOR	PIGSTICK	PIRANHAS
PENTAGON	PERUVIAN	PHOTOFIT	PIGSTIES	PIRATING
PENTOMIC	PERVADED	PHOTOMAP	PIGSWILL	PIS ALLER
PENTOSAN	PERVADER	PHOTOPIA	PIGTAILS	PISIFORM
PENUMBRA	PERVERSE	PHOTOPIC	PILASTER	PISOLITE
PENZANCE	PERVERTS	PHOTOSET	PILCHARD	PISS-TAKE
PEOPLING	PERVIOUS	PHRASING	PILEWORT	PITCHERS
PEPPERED	PESHAWAR	PHRATRIC	PILFERED	PITCHING
PEP PILLS	PESKIEST	PHREATIC	PILFERER	PITFALLS
PEP TALKS	PESTERED	PHTHALIC	PILGRIMS	PITHEADS
PEPTIZER	PESTERER	PHTHISIC	PILIFORM	PITHIEST
PER ANNUM	PESTHOLE	PHTHISIS	PILLAGED	PITIABLE
PERCEIVE	PETALINE	PHYLETIC	PILLAGER	PITIABLY
PERCHING	PETALODY	PHYLLITE	PILLIONS	PITILESS
PERFORCE	PETALOID	PHYLLODE	PILLOCKS	PIT PROPS
PERFUMED	PETECHIA	PHYLLOID	PILLOWED	PITTANCE
PERFUMER	PETITION	PHYLLOME	PILOTAGE	PIVOTING
PERFUMES	PETIT MAL	PHYSIBLE	PILOTING	PIXELATE
PERGOLAS	PET NAMES	PHYSICAL	PIMENTOS	PIZZERIA
PERIANTH	PETRARCH	PHYSIQUE	PIMIENTO	PLACABLE
PERIBLEM	PETROLIC	PIACENZA	PINAFORE	PLACARDS
PERICARP	PETROSAL	PIACULAR	PINASTER	PLACATED
PERIDERM	PETTIEST	PIANISTS	PINCE-NEZ	PLACEBOS
PERIDIUM	PETTIFOG	PIANOLAS	PINCHING	PLACE MAT
PERIGEAN	PETULANT	PIASSAVA	PINETREE	PLACENTA
PERIGEES	PETUNIAS	PIASTRES	PINEWOOD	PLACIDLY
PERIGYNY	PETUNTSE	PICADORS	PING-PONG	PLAGUILY
PERILOUS	PEWTERER	PICCANIN	PINHEADS	PLAGUING
PERILUNE	PFENNIGS	PICCOLOS	PINIONED	PLAINEST
PERINEUM	PHAETONS	PICKABLE	PINK GINS	PLAITING
PERIODIC	PHALANGE	PICKAXES	PINKROOT	PLANCHET

PLANFORM	PLEURISY	POKINESS	PONTIFEX	POST HORN
PLANGENT	PLEUSTON	POLANSKI	PONTIFFS	POSTICHE
PLANKING	PLIANTLY	POLARITY	PONTOONS	POSTINGS
PLANKTON	PLIGHTED	POLARIZE	PONYTAIL	POSTLUDE
PLANNERS	PLIGHTER	POLAROID	POOFIEST	POSTMARK
PLANNING	PLIMSOLL	POLEAXED	POOH-POOH	POST-OBIT
PLANOSOL	PLIOCENE	POLECATS	POOLSIDE	POSTPAID
PLANTAIN	PLODDERS	POLEMICS	POOR LAWS	POSTPONE
PLANTERS	PLODDING	POLE STAR	POORLIER	POSTURAL
PLANTING	PLONKING	POLICIES	POORNESS	POSTURED
PLANULAR	PLOPPING	POLICING	POPADUMS	POSTURER
PLASTEEL	PLOSIVES	POLISHED	POPINJAY	POSTURES
PLASTERS	PLOTTING	POLISHER	POPOVERS	POTASSIC
PLASTICS	PLOUGHED	POLISHES	POPPADOM	POTATION
PLASTRAL	PLOUGHER	POLITELY	POPSICLE	POTATOES
PLASTRON	PLUCKIER	POLITICO	POPULACE	POT-AU-FEU
PLATELET	PLUCKILY	POLITICS	POPULATE	POTBELLY
PLATFORM	PLUCKING	POLITIES	POPULISM	POTBOUND
PLATINIC	PLUGGING	POLKA DOT	POPULIST	POTENTLY
PLATINUM	PLUGHOLE	POLLARDS	POPULOUS	POTHOLER
PLATONIC	PLUMBAGO	POLLICAL	PORKIEST	POTHOLES
PLATOONS	PLUMBERS	POLLINIC	PORK PIES	POTLUCKS
PLATTERS	PLUMBERY	POLLSTER	POROSITY	POT PLANT
PLATYPUS	PLUMBING	POLLUTED	PORPHYRY	POTSHERD
PLAUDITS	PLUMBISM	POLLUTER	PORPOISE	POTSHOTS
PLAUSIVE	PLUMBOUS	POLO NECK	PORRIDGE	POTSTONE
PLAYABLE	PLUMMIER	POLONIUM	PORTABLE	POTTERED
PLAYBACK	PLUMPEST	POLTROON	PORTENTS	POTTERER
PLAY BALL	PLUMPING	POLYGALA	PORTHOLE	POTTIEST
PLAYBILL	PLUNGERS	POLYGAMY	PORTICOS	POULTICE
PLAYBOYS	PLUNGING	POLYGENE	PORTIERE	POUNCING
PLAYGOER	PLUSHEST	POLYGLOT	PORTIONS	POUNDAGE
PLAYLIST	PLUTONIC	POLYGONS	PORTLAND	POUNDING
PLAYMATE	PLUVIOUS	POLYGYNY	PORTLIER	POWDERED
PLAY-OFFS	PLYMOUTH	POLYMATH	PORTRAIT	POWDERER
PLAYPENS	POACEOUS	POLYMERS	PORT SAID	POWERFUL
PLAYROOM	POACHERS	POLYPARY	PORT SIDE	POWERING
PLAYSUIT	POACHING	POLYPODY	PORTUGAL	POZIDRIV
PLAYTIME	POCKETED	POLYPOID	POSITING	POZZUOLI
PLEADING	POCKMARK	POLYPOUS	POSITION	PRACTICE
PLEASANT	PODAGRAL	POLYSEMY	POSITIVE	PRACTISE
PLEASING	PODGIEST	POLYURIA	POSITRON	PRAEDIAL
PLEASURE	PODIATRY	POLYURIC	POSOLOGY	PRAESEPE
PLEATING	PODZOLIC	POLYZOAN	POSSIBLE	PRAIRIES
PLEBBIER	POETICAL	POLYZOIC	POSSIBLY	PRAISING
PLEBEIAN	POIGNANT	POMANDER	POSTBAGS	PRALINES
PLECTRUM	POINTERS	POMOLOGY	POSTCARD	PRANCING
PLEDGING	POINTING	PONDERED	POSTCAVA	PRANDIAL
PLEIADES	POISONED	PONDERER	POSTCODE	PRANKISH
PLEIN-AIR	POISONER	PONDWEED	POSTDATE	PRATIQUE
PLEONASM	POITIERS	PONGIEST	POST-FREE	PRATTLED
PLETHORA	POKEWEED	PONIARDS	POSTGRAD	PRATTLER

PREACHED	PRESSMEN	PRIVIEST	PROPHESY	PSALTERS
PREACHER	PRESS-UPS	PRIZE DAY	PROPHETS	PSALTERY
PREAMBLE	PRESSURE	PROBABLE	PROPOLIS	PSEPHITE
PREAXIAL	PRESTIGE	PROBABLY	PROPOSAL	PSORALEA
PREBENDS	PRESUMED	PROBATED	PROPOSED	PSYCHICS
PRECEDED	PRESUMER	PROBATES	PROPOSER	PSYCHING
PRECEPTS	PRETENCE	PROBLEMS	PROPOUND	PTEROPOD
PRECINCT	PRETEXTS	PROCAINE	PROPPING	PTOMAINE
PRECIOUS	PRETORIA	PROCEEDS	PROROGUE	PTYALISM
PRECLUDE	PRETREAT	PROCLAIM	PROSAISM	PUB-CRAWL
PREDATED	PRETTIER	PROCTORS	PROSIEST	PUBLICAN
PREDATOR	PRETTIFY	PROCURED	PROSODIC	PUBLICLY
PREDELLA	PRETTILY	PROCURER	PROSPECT	PUCKERED
PREENING	PRETZELS	PRODDING	PROSTATE	PUDDINGS
PREEXIST	PREVIEWS	PRODIGAL	PROSTYLE	PUDDLING
PRE-EXIST	PREVIOUS	PRODROME	PROTASIS	PUDENDUM
PREFACED	PREZZIES	PRODUCED	PROTEGEE	PUDGIEST
PREFACER	PRIAPISM	PRODUCER	PROTEGES	PUFFBALL
PREFACES	PRICE TAG	PRODUCTS	PROTEINS	PUFFBIRD
PREFECTS	PRICIEST	PROEMIAL	PROTEOSE	PUFFIEST
PREFIXAL	PRICKING	PROFANED	PROTESTS	PUGILISM
PREFIXED	PRICKLED	PROFANER	PROTOCOL	PUGILIST
PREFIXES	PRICKLES	PROFILED	PROTOZOA	PUISSANT
PREGNANT	PRIDEFUL	PROFILES	PROTRACT	PULLMANS
PREJUDGE	PRIE-DIEU	PROFITED	PROTRUDE	PULLOUTS
PRELATES	PRIESTLY	PROFITER	PROUDEST	PULLOVER
PRELATIC	PRIGGERY	PRO FORMA	PROVABLE	PULMONIC
PRELUDER	PRIGGISH	PROFOUND	PROVABLY	PULMOTOR
PRELUDES	PRIGGISM	PROGRAMS	PROVENCE	PULPIEST
PREMIERE	PRIMATES	PROGRESS	PROVENLY	PULPWOOD
PREMIERS	PRIMEVAL	PROHIBIT	PROVERBS	PULSATED
PREMISES	PRIMMEST	PROJECTS	PROVIDED	PULSATOR
PREMIUMS	PRIMNESS	PROLAPSE	PROVIDER	PULSEJET
PREMOLAR	PRIMROSE	PROLIFIC	PROVINCE	PULVINUS
PREMORSE	PRIMULAS	PROLOGUE	PROVISOS	PUMMELED
PRENATAL	PRIMUSES	PROMISED	PROVOKED	PUMPKINS
PREPARED	PRINCELY	PROMISER	PROVOSTS	PUMP ROOM
PREPENSE	PRINCESS	PROMISES	PROWL CAR	PUNCHBAG
PRESAGED	PRINCIPE	PROMISOR	PROWLERS	PUNCHEON
PRESAGER	PRINCIPE	PROMOTED	PROWLING	PUNCHIER
PRESAGES	PRINTERS	PROMOTER	PROXIMAL	PUNCHING
PRESCOTT	PRINTING	PROMPTED	PRUDENCE	PUNCH-UPS
PRESENCE	PRINTOUT	PROMPTER	PRUINOSE	PUNCTATE
PRESENTS	PRIORATE	PROMPTLY	PRUNABLE	PUNCTUAL
PRESERVE	PRIORESS	PRONATOR	PRUNELLA	PUNCTURE
PRESIDED	PRIORIES	PRONOUNS	PRUNELLE	PUNGENCY
PRESIDER	PRIORITY	PROOFING	PRURIENT	PUNINESS
PRESIDIA	PRISMOID	PROPERLY	PRURITIC	PUNISHED
PRESIDIO	PRISONER	PROPERTY	PRURITUS	PUNISHER
PRESS BOX	PRISSIER	PROPHAGE	PRUSSIAN	PUNITIVE
PRESSING	PRISSILY	PROPHASE	PSALMIST	PUNSTERS
PRESSMAN	PRISTINE	PROPHECY	PSALMODY	PUPARIAL

PUPARIUM	PYRAMIDS	QUENCHER	RADIALLY	RAPIDITY
PUPATION	PYRAZOLE	QUERCINE	RADIANCE	RAPTNESS
PUPPETRY	PYRENEAN	QUERYING	RADIATED	RAPTURES
PUPPY FAT	PYRENEES	QUESTING	RADIATOR	RARA AVIS
PUPPYISH	PYRENOID	QUESTION	RADICALS	RAREFIED
PURBLIND	PYREXIAL	QUIBBLED	RADICAND	RAREFIER
PURCHASE	PYRIDINE	QUIBBLER	RADIOING	RARENESS
PUREBRED	PYRIFORM	QUIBBLES	RADISHES	RARITIES
PUREEING	PYROSTAT	QUIBERON	RAFFLING	RASCALLY
PURENESS	PYROXENE	QUICKEST	RAGGEDLY	RASHNESS
PURFLING	PYRROLIC	QUICKIES	RAG TRADE	RASORIAL
PURIFIED	PYRRUVIC	QUICKSET	RAILHEAD	RASPINGS
PURIFIER	PYTHONIC	QUIDDITY	RAILINGS	RAT-ARSED
PURISTIC	PYXIDIUM	QUIDNUNC	RAILLERY	RATCHETS
PURITANS		QUIETEST	RAILROAD	RATIFIED
PURLIEUS	**Q**	QUIETISM	RAILWAYS	RATIFIER
PURPLISH	QUACKERY	QUIETIST	RAINBAND	RATIONAL
PURPOSED	QUACKING	QUIETUDE	RAINBOWS	RATIONED
PURPOSES	QUAD BIKE	QUILL PEN	RAINCOAT	RATSBANE
PURPURIN	QUADRANT	QUILTING	RAINDROP	RATTIEST
PURSLANE	QUADRATE	QUINCUNX	RAINFALL	RATTLING
PURSUANT	QUADROON	QUI NHONG	RAINIEST	RAT TRAPS
PURSUERS	QUAGMIRE	QUINTETS	RAINLESS	RAVAGING
PURSUING	QUAILING	QUINTILE	RAINY DAY	RAVELING
PURSUITS	QUAINTLY	QUIPPING	RAISABLE	RAVELLED
PURULENT	QUALMISH	QUIPSTER	RAKE-OFFS	RAVELLER
PURVEYED	QUANDARY	QUIRKIER	RAKISHLY	RAVENING
PURVEYOR	QUANDONG	QUIRKILY	RALLYING	RAVENOUS
PUSHBIKE	QUANTIFY	QUISLING	RAMAT GAN	RAVISHED
PUSHCART	QUANTITY	QUITTERS	RAMBLERS	RAVISHER
PUSHIEST	QUANTIZE	QUITTING	RAMBLING	RAW-BONED
PUSHOVER	QUARRELS	QUIVERED	RAMBUTAN	RAW DEALS
PUSH-PULL	QUARRIED	QUIVERER	RAMEKINS	RAWHIDES
PUSSYCAT	QUARRIER	QUIXOTIC	RAMENTUM	RAZOR-CUT
PUSTULAR	QUARRIES	QUIZZING	RAMIFIED	REACHING
PUSTULES	QUARTERN	QUOTABLE	RAMOSITY	REACTANT
PUT ABOUT	QUARTERS	QUOTHING	RAMPAGED	REACTING
PUTATIVE	QUARTETS	QUOTIENT	RAMPAGER	REACTION
PUT-DOWNS	QUARTILE		RAMPANCY	REACTIVE
PUTSCHES	QUASHING	**R**	RAMPARTS	REACTORS
PUTTERED	QUATRAIN	RABBITED	RAMSGATE	READABLE
PUT TO SEA	QUAVERED	RABBITER	RAMULOSE	READABLY
PUT-UP JOB	QUAVERER	RABBITRY	RANCAGUA	READIEST
PUZZLERS	QUEASIER	RABIDITY	RANCHERS	READINGS
PUZZLING	QUEASILY	RACCOONS	RANDIEST	READJUST
PYELITIC	QUECHUAN	RACEMISM	RANDOMLY	READOUTS
PYELITIS	QUEENDOM	RACEMOSE	RANKLING	READYING
PYGIDIAL	QUEENING	RACIALLY	RANKNESS	READY-MIX
PYGIDIUM	QUEEREST	RACINESS	RANSOMED	REAFFIRM
PYINKADO	QUEERING	RACK-RENT	RANSOMER	REAGENTS
PYODERMA	QUELLING	RACLETTE	RAPACITY	REALISTS
PYOGENIC	QUENCHED	RACQUETS	RAPESEED	REALIZED

REALIZER	RECREANT	REFERRED	REISSUED	REMITTER
REALNESS	RECREATE	REFERRER	REISSUER	REMNANTS
REAL-TIME	RECRUITS	REFILLED	REISSUES	REMOTELY
REALTORS	RECTALLY	REFINERY	REJECTED	REMOTEST
REAPABLE	RECURRED	REFINING	REJECTER	REMOULDS
REAPPEAR	RECUSANT	REFINISH	REJIGGED	REMOUNTS
REARMING	RECYCLED	REFITTED	REJOICED	REMOVALS
REARMOST	REDACTOR	REFLATED	REJOICER	REMOVERS
REARWARD	RED ALERT	REFLEXES	REJOINED	REMOVING
REASONED	REDBRICK	REFOREST	REKINDLE	RENAMING
REASONER	REDCOATS	REFORMED	RELAPSED	RENDERED
REASSURE	RED CROSS	REFORMER	RELAPSER	RENDERER
REAWAKEN	REDDENED	REFRAINS	RELAPSES	RENDIBLE
REBELLED	REDDITCH	REFUELED	RELATING	RENDZINA
REBOUNDS	REDEEMED	REFUGEES	RELATION	RENEGADE
REBUFFED	REDEEMER	REFUGIUM	RELATIVE	RENEGING
REBUKING	REDEMAND	REFUNDED	RELAUNCH	RENEWALS
REBUTTAL	REDEPLOY	REFUNDER	RELAXANT	RENEWING
REBUTTED	REDESIGN	REFUSALS	RELAXING	RENIFORM
REBUTTER	RED FACED	REFUSING	RELAYING	RENOUNCE
RECALLED	RED-FACED	REFUTING	RELEASED	RENOVATE
RECANTED	RED FLAGS	REGAINED	RELEASER	RENOWNED
RECANTER	RED GIANT	REGAINER	RELEASES	RENTABLE
RECAPPED	REDGRAVE	REGALITY	RELEGATE	RENT BOYS
RECEDING	REDHEADS	REGARDED	RELENTED	RENT-FREE
RECEIPTS	REDIRECT	REGATTAS	RELEVANT	RENTIERS
RECEIVED	RED LIGHT	REGELATE	RELIABLE	RENT-ROLL
RECEIVER	REDNECKS	REGENTAL	RELIABLY	REOFFEND
RECENTLY	REDOLENT	REGICIDE	RELIANCE	REOPENED
RECEPTOR	REDOUBLE	REGIMENS	RELIEVED	REPAIRED
RECESSED	REDOUBTS	REGIMENT	RELIEVER	REPAIRER
RECESSES	REDSHANK	REGIONAL	RELIGION	REPARTEE
RECHARGE	RED SHIFT	REGISTER	RELINING	REPAYING
RECISION	REDSKINS	REGISTRY	RELISHED	REPEALED
RECITALS	REDSTART	REGRATER	RELISHES	REPEALER
RECITERS	REDUCING	REGROWTH	RELIVING	REPEATED
RECITING	REDUVIID	REGULARS	RELOADED	REPEATER
RECKLESS	REDWOODS	REGULATE	RELOCATE	REPELLED
RECKONED	REECHOED	REGULINE	REMAINED	REPELLER
RECKONER	REEDBUCK	REHASHED	REMAKING	REPENTED
RECLINED	REEDIEST	REHASHES	REMANDED	REPENTER
RECLINER	REEDLING	REHEARSE	REMARKED	REPEOPLE
RECLUSES	REEF KNOT	REHEATER	REMARKER	REPETEND
RECOILED	REELABLE	REHOBOAM	REMARQUE	REPHRASE
RECOILER	REELABLY	REHOUSED	REMEDIAL	REPINING
RECOMMIT	RE-EMPLOY	REIGNING	REMEDIED	REPLACED
RECORDED	RE-EXPORT	REIMPORT	REMEDIES	REPLACER
RECORDER	REFACING	REIMPOSE	REMEMBER	REPLAYED
RECOUNTS	REFEREED	REINDEER	REMIGIAL	REPLEVIN
RECOUPED	REFEREES	REINSURE	REMINDED	REPLICAS
RECOURSE	REFERENT	REINVENT	REMINDER	REPLYING
RECOVERY	REFERRAL	REINVEST	REMITTED	REPORTED

REPORTER	RESOLVES	REUNITER	RHAPSODY	RINGETTE
REPOSING	RESONANT	REUSABLE	RHEOBASE	RINGHALS
REPOUSSE	RESONATE	REVALUED	RHEOLOGY	RINGLETS
REPRIEVE	RESORTED	REVAMPED	RHEOSTAT	RING ROAD
REPRINTS	RESORTER	REVAMPER	RHETORIC	RINGSIDE
REPRISAL	RESOURCE	REVEALED	RH FACTOR	RINGWORM
REPRISES	RESPECTS	REVEALER	RHINITIS	RINKHALS
REPROACH	RESPIRED	REVEILLE	RHIZOMES	RINSABLE
REPROOFS	RESPITES	REVELING	RHIZOPOD	RIOT ACTS
REPROVAL	RESPONSE	REVELLED	RHIZOPUS	RIPARIAN
REPROVED	RESTATED	REVELLER	RHODESIA	RIPCORDS
REPROVER	REST CURE	REVENANT	RHODINAL	RIPENESS
REPTILES	REST HOME	REVENGED	RHOMBOID	RIPENING
REPUBLIC	RESTLESS	REVENGER	RHONCHAL	RIPOSTED
REPULSED	RESTORED	REVENUED	RHONCHUS	RIPOSTES
REPULSER	RESTORER	REVEREND	RHUBARBS	RIPPABLE
REPULSES	RESTRAIN	REVERENT	RHYOLITE	RIPPLING
REQUESTS	RESTRICT	REVERIES	RHYTHMIC	RIPTIDES
REQUIEMS	REST ROOM	REVERING	RIBALDRY	RISKIEST
REQUIRED	RESUBMIT	REVERSAL	RIB CAGES	RISOTTOS
REQUIRER	RESULTED	REVERSED	RIBOSOME	RISSOLES
REQUITAL	RESUMING	REVERSER	RICEBIRD	RITENUTO
REQUITED	RETAILED	REVERSES	RICHMOND	RITUALLY
REQUITER	RETAILER	REVERTED	RICHNESS	RIVALING
RESCRIPT	RETAINED	REVERTER	RICKRACK	RIVALLED
RESCUERS	RETAINER	REVIEWAL	RICKSHAW	RIVERBED
RESCUING	RETAKING	REVIEWED	RICOCHET	RIVERINE
RESEARCH	RETARDED	REVIEWER	RIDDANCE	RIVETERS
RESEMBLE	RETARDER	REVILERS	RIDDLING	RIVETING
RESENTED	RETCHING	REVILING	RIDICULE	RIVIERAS
RESERVED	RETICENT	REVISERS	RIESLING	RIVULETS
RESERVER	RETICULE	REVISING	RIFENESS	ROAD HOGS
RESERVES	RETINENE	REVISION	RIFFLING	ROAD RAGE
RESETTER	RETINITE	REVISORY	RIFFRAFF	ROADSHOW
RESETTLE	RETINUED	REVIVALS	RIFLEMAN	ROADSIDE
RESIDENT	RETINUES	REVIVIFY	RIGADOON	ROAD SIGN
RESIDING	RETIRING	REVIVING	RIGATONI	ROADSTER
RESIDUAL	RETORTED	REVOKING	RIGHTFUL	ROAD TEST
RESIDUES	RETORTER	REVOLTED	RIGHTING	ROADWORK
RESIDUUM	RETRACED	REVOLTER	RIGHTISM	ROASTERS
RESIGNAL	RETREADS	REVOLUTE	RIGHTIST	ROASTING
RESIGNED	RETREATS	REVOLVED	RIGHT OFF	ROBINSON
RESIGNER	RETRENCH	REVOLVER	RIGIDITY	ROBOTICS
RESINATE	RETRIALS	REWARDED	RIGORISM	ROBOTISM
RESINOID	RETRIEVE	REWARDER	RIGORIST	ROBUSTLY
RESINOUS	RETROACT	REWINDER	RIGOROUS	ROCAILLE
RESISTED	RETROFIT	REWIRING	RIJSWIJK	ROCHDALE
RESISTER	RETRORSE	REWORDED	RIMOSITY	ROCK BAND
RESISTOR	RETURNED	REWORKED	RINGBOLT	ROCK CAKE
RESOLUTE	RETURNER	REWRITES	RINGBONE	ROCK DASH
RESOLVED	REUNIONS	REYNOLDS	RINGDOVE	ROCKETED
RESOLVER	REUNITED	RHAETIAN	RING-DYKE	ROCKETRY

ROCKFALL	ROSETTES	RUFFIANS	SADDLERS	SAMOVARS
ROCKFISH	ROSEWOOD	RUFFLING	SADDLERY	SAMPHIRE
ROCKFORD	ROSINESS	RUGGEDLY	SADDLING	SAMPLERS
ROCKIEST	ROSINING	RUGOSITY	SADISTIC	SAMPLING
ROCKLING	ROSKILDE	RUINABLE	SAFENESS	SAMURAIS
ROCKROSE	ROSTRUMS	RULEBOOK	SAFE SEAT	SANCTIFY
ROCK SALT	ROTARIAN	RUMANIAN	SAFETIES	SANCTION
ROCKWEED	ROTATING	RUMBLING	SAGACITY	SANCTITY
ROEBUCKS	ROTATION	RUMINANT	SAGGIEST	SANCTUMS
ROENTGEN	ROTATIVE	RUMINATE	SAGITTAL	SANDAKAN
ROGATION	ROTATORY	RUMMAGED	SAILABLE	SANDARAC
ROGATORY	ROTENONE	RUMMAGER	SAILFISH	SANDBAGS
ROLE PLAY	ROTHESAY	RUMMAGES	SAILINGS	SANDBANK
ROLLAWAY	ROTOTILL	RUMOURED	SAILORLY	SANDBARS
ROLL BARS	ROTTENLY	RUMPLING	SAINFOIN	SAND-CAST
ROLL CALL	ROTUNDAS	RUN-ABOUT	SAKHALIN	SAND DUNE
ROLLMOPS	ROUGHAGE	RUNAWAYS	SALAAMED	SAN DIEGO
ROLL OVER	ROUGH-DRY	RUNDOWNS	SALACITY	SANDIEST
ROLLOVER	ROUGHEST	RUNNER UP	SALARIED	SANDPITS
ROLY-POLY	ROUGH-HEW	RUNNER-UP	SALARIES	SANDSHOE
ROMANCED	ROUGHING	RUNNIEST	SALEABLE	SANDSOAP
ROMANCES	ROULETTE	RUPTURED	SALEABLY	SAND TRAP
ROMANIES	ROUND-ARM	RUPTURES	SALEROOM	SANDWELL
ROMAN LAW	ROUNDELS	RURALISM	SALESMAN	SANDWICH
ROMANSCH	ROUNDERS	RURALIST	SALESMEN	SANDWORM
ROMANTIC	ROUNDEST	RURALITY	SALES TAX	SANDWORT
RONDAVEL	ROUNDING	RURALIZE	SALIENCE	SANENESS
RONDELET	ROUNDISH	RUSH HOUR	SALIENTS	SANGAREE
RONTGENS	ROUNDUPS	RUST BELT	SALINGER	SANGUINE
ROOFLESS	ROUTINES	RUSTICAL	SALINITY	SANITARY
ROOF RACK	ROVE-OVER	RUSTIEST	SALIVARY	SANITIZE
ROOFTOPS	ROWDIEST	RUSTLERS	SALIVATE	SANSKRIT
ROOFTREE	ROWDYISM	RUSTLING	SALLYING	SANTA ANA
ROOMIEST	ROW HOUSE	RUTABAGA	SALPICON	SANTAREM
ROOMMATE	ROWLOCKS	RUTHENIC	SALTBUSH	SANTIAGO
ROOM MATE	ROYALISM	RUTHLESS	SALTIEST	SANTONIN
ROOSTERS	ROYALIST	RYDER CUP	SALTILLO	SAO PAULO
ROOSTING	RUBBINGS	RYE-BROME	SALTLICK	SAPIDITY
ROOT BEER	RUBBISHY	RYEGRASS	SALTNESS	SAPIENCE
ROOT CROP	RUBDOWNS		SALTPANS	SAPLINGS
ROOTLESS	RUBELITE	**S**	SALTWORT	SAPONIFY
ROOTLIKE	RUBEOLAR	SAARLAND	SALUTARY	SAPONITE
ROPEWALK	RUBICONS	SABADELL	SALUTING	SAPPHIRE
ROPINESS	RUBICUND	SABBATIC	SALVABLE	SAPPIEST
ROSARIAN	RUBIDIUM	SABOTAGE	SALVABLY	SAPROBIC
ROSARIES	RUBRICAL	SABOTEUR	SALVADOR	SAPROPEL
ROSEBUSH	RUCKSACK	SABULOUS	SALVAGED	SARABAND
ROSEFISH	RUCKUSES	SACKLIKE	SALVAGER	SARACENS
ROSE HIPS	RUDDIEST	SACK RACE	SALZBURG	SARAJEVO
ROSEMARY	RUDENESS	SACREDLY	SAMARIUM	SARDINES
ROSEOLAR	RUDIMENT	SACRISTY	SAMENESS	SARDINIA
ROSE-ROOT	RUEFULLY	SADDENED	SAMIZDAT	SARDONIC

SARDONYX	SCALDING	SCHWERIN	SCRANTON	SEAFRONT
SARGASSO	SCALENUS	SCIAENID	SCRAPERS	SEAGIRTS
SARGODHA	SCALIEST	SCIATICA	SCRAPING	SEAGOING
SARKIEST	SCALLION	SCIENCES	SCRAP MAN	SEA GREEN
SARMATIA	SCALLOPS	SCILICET	SCRAPPED	SEAGULLS
SARRAUTE	SCALPELS	SCIMITAR	SCRATCHY	SEAHORSE
SASHAYED	SCALPERS	SCINCOID	SCRAWLED	SEALABLE
SASH CORD	SCALPING	SCIRRHUS	SCRAWLER	SEA LEVEL
SASSIEST	SCAMMONY	SCISSILE	SCREAMED	SEA LIONS
SASTRUGA	SCAMPISH	SCISSION	SCREAMER	SEALSKIN
SATANISM	SCANDALS	SCISSORS	SCREECHY	SEALYHAM
SATANIST	SCANDIUM	SCIURINE	SCREENED	SEAMIEST
SATCHELS	SCANNERS	SCIUROID	SCREENER	SEA MILES
SATIABLE	SCANNING	SCLAFFER	SCREWIER	SEA MISTS
SATIABLY	SCANSION	SCLERITE	SCREWING	SEAMLESS
SATIATED	SCANTIER	SCLEROID	SCREW TOP	SEAMOUNT
SATIRIST	SCANTILY	SCLEROMA	SCRIBBLE	SEAPLANE
SATIRIZE	SCAPULAR	SCLEROUS	SCRIMPED	SEAPORTS
SATSUMAS	SCAPULAS	SCOFFING	SCRIPTED	SEA POWER
SATURANT	SCARCELY	SCOLDING	SCROFULA	SEAQUAKE
SATURATE	SCARCEST	SCOLLOPS	SCROLLED	SEARCHED
SATURDAY	SCARCITY	SCOOPING	SCROOGES	SEARCHER
SAUCEPAN	SCARGILL	SCOOTERS	SCROTUMS	SEARCHES
SAUCIEST	SCARIEST	SCOOTING	SCROUNGE	SEASCAPE
SAUNTERS	SCARIOUS	SCORCHED	SCRUBBED	SEASHELL
SAUROPOD	SCARRING	SCORCHER	SCRUBBER	SEASHORE
SAUSAGES	SCATHING	SCORCHES	SCRUMPED	SEA SNAKE
SAUTEING	SCATTIER	SCORNFUL	SCRUNCHY	SEASONAL
SAVAGELY	SCATTILY	SCORNING	SCRUPLED	SEASONED
SAVAGERY	SCATTING	SCORPION	SCRUPLES	SEASONER
SAVAGING	SCAVENGE	SCORPIOS	SCRUTINY	SEAT BELT
SAVANNAH	SCENARIO	SCORPIUS	SCUDDING	SEA TROUT
SAVANNAS	SCENTING	SCORSESE	SCUFFING	SEAWALLS
SAVIOURS	SCEPTICS	SCOTCHED	SCUFFLED	SEAWARDS
SAVORIES	SCEPTRES	SCOT-FREE	SCUFFLES	SECEDING
SAVOROUS	SCHEDULE	SCOTLAND	SCULLERS	SECLUDED
SAVOURED	SCHEMATA	SCOTOPIA	SCULLERY	SECONDED
SAVOYARD	SCHEMERS	SCOTOPIC	SCULLING	SECONDER
SAWBONES	SCHEMING	SCOTSMAN	SCULLION	SECONDLY
SAWGRASS	SCHERZOS	SCOTTISH	SCULPSIT	SECRETED
SAWHORSE	SCHIEDAM	SCOURERS	SCULPTOR	SECRETIN
SAWMILLS	SCHILLER	SCOURGED	SCUPPERS	SECRETLY
SAWTOOTH	SCHIZOID	SCOURGER	SCURRIED	SECTIONS
SCABBARD	SCHIZONT	SCOURGES	SCURVILY	SECTORAL
SCABBIER	SCHMALTZ	SCOURING	SCUTTLED	SECURELY
SCABBILY	SCHMUCKS	SCOUTING	SCUTTLES	SECUREST
SCABIOUS	SCHNAPPS	SCOWLING	SCYTHING	SECURING
SCABROUS	SCHOLARS	SCRABBLE	SEABIRDS	SECURITY
SCAFFOLD	SCHOLIUM	SCRAGGED	SEABOARD	SEDATELY
SCALABLE	SCHOOLED	SCRAGGLY	SEABORNE	SEDATING
SCALABLY	SCHOOLIE	SCRAMBLE	SEACOAST	SEDATION
SCALAWAG	SCHOONER	SCRAMMED	SEAFARER	SEDATIVE

SEDIMENT	SENATORS	SET PIECE	SHANDONG	SHINNIED
SEDITION	SENDABLE	SET POINT	SHANGHAI	SHINNING
SEDUCERS	SEND-OFFS	SET RIGHT	SHANTIES	SHIPABLE
SEDUCING	SENILITY	SETSCREW	SHANTUNG	SHIPLOAD
SEDULITY	SENORITA	SETTINGS	SHAPABLE	SHIPMATE
SEDULOUS	SENSIBLE	SETTLERS	SHARABLE	SHIPMENT
SEEDBEDS	SENSIBLY	SETTLE UP	SHARE-OUT	SHIPPERS
SEEDCASE	SENSUOUS	SETTLING	SHARP END	SHIPPING
SEEDCORN	SENTENCE	SEVENTHS	SHARPEST	SHIPWORM
SEEDIEST	SENTIENT	SEVERELY	SHARPISH	SHIPYARD
SEEDLESS	SENTINEL	SEVERING	SHARP-SET	SHIRKERS
SEEDLING	SENTRIES	SEVERITY	SHAVABLE	SHIRKING
SEEDSMAN	SEPALLED	SEWERAGE	SHAVINGS	SHIRRING
SEEDSMEN	SEPALOID	SEXINESS	SHEADING	SHIRTIER
SEESAWED	SEPARATE	SEXOLOGY	SHEARING	SHIRTING
SEETHING	SEPHARDI	SEX ORGAN	SHEATHED	SHITLESS
SEGMENTS	SEPTUPLE	SEXTANTS	SHEBEENS	SHITTIER
SEIGNEUR	SEQUENCE	SEXTUPLE	SHEDABLE	SHITTING
SEISABLE	SEQUINED	SEXUALLY	SHEDDING	SHIVERED
SEISMISM	SEQUOIAS	SHABBIER	SHEEPDIP	SHIVERER
SEIZABLE	SERAGLIO	SHABBILY	SHEEPDOG	SHIZUOKA
SEIZURES	SERAJEVO	SHACKING	SHEEPISH	SHOCKERS
SELANGOR	SERAPHIC	SHACKLED	SHEEREST	SHOCKING
SELECTED	SERAPHIM	SHACKLER	SHEERING	SHODDIER
SELECTOR	SEREMBAN	SHACKLES	SHEETING	SHODDILY
SELENATE	SERENADE	SHADDOCK	SHEIKDOM	SHOEBILL
SELENITE	SERENATA	SHADIEST	SHELDUCK	SHOEHORN
SELENIUM	SERENELY	SHADINGS	SHELLING	SHOELACE
SELFHEAL	SERENITY	SHADOWED	SHELTERS	SHOETREE
SELF-HELP	SERGEANT	SHADOWER	SHELVING	SHOLAPUR
SELFHOOD	SERIALLY	SHAFTING	SHENYANG	SHOOTERS
SELFLESS	SERIATIM	SHAGBARK	SHEPHERD	SHOOTING
SELF-MADE	SERMONIC	SHAGGIER	SHERATON	SHOOT OUT
SELF-PITY	SEROLOGY	SHAGGILY	SHERBETS	SHOOT-OUT
SELF-RULE	SEROSITY	SHAGGING	SHERIFFS	SHOPGIRL
SELFSAME	SEROTINE	SHAGREEN	SHETLAND	SHOPLIFT
SELF-WILL	SERPENTS	SHAKABLE	SHIELDED	SHOPPERS
SELL-OUTS	SERPULID	SHAKEOUT	SHIELDER	SHOPPING
SELVAGES	SERRANID	SHAKE-UPS	SHIELING	SHOPTALK
SEMANTIC	SERRATED	SHAKIEST	SHIFTIER	SHORTAGE
SEMARANG	SERVABLE	SHALLOON	SHIFTILY	SHORT CUT
SEMESTER	SERVANTS	SHALLOTS	SHIFTING	SHORT-DAY
SEMIARID	SERVICED	SHALLOWS	SHIFT KEY	SHORTEST
SEMIDOME	SERVICES	SHAMABLE	SHIITAKE	SHORTIES
SEMINARS	SERVINGS	SHAMBLED	SHILLING	SHORTING
SEMINARY	SERVITOR	SHAMBLES	SHILLONG	SHOTGUNS
SEMIOTIC	SERVQUAL	SHAMEFUL	SHIMMERY	SHOULDER
SEMITICS	SESAMOID	SHAMMIES	SHINBONE	SHOULDN'T
SEMITIST	SESSIONS	SHAMMING	SHINDIGS	SHOUTING
SEMITONE	SET ASIDE	SHAMPOOS	SHINGLER	SHOVELED
SEMOLINA	SETBACKS	SHAMROCK	SHINGLES	SHOVELER
SEMPLICE	SETIFORM	SHANDIES	SHINIEST	SHOWBOAT

SHOWCASE	SICKROOM	SIMPLEST	SKETCHER	SLANTING
SHOWDOWN	SIDEARMS	SIMPLIFY	SKETCHES	SLAP-BANG
SHOWERED	SIDE ARMS	SIMPLISM	SKEWBACK	SLAPDASH
SHOWGIRL	SIDEBAND	SIMULANT	SKEWBALD	SLAPHEAD
SHOWIEST	SIDECARS	SIMULATE	SKEWERED	SLAPPING
SHOWINGS	SIDE DISH	SINAITIC	SKIDDING	SLASHING
SHOW-OFFS	SIDE-FOOT	SINAPISM	SKIDPANS	SLATTERN
SHOWROOM	SIDEKICK	SINCIPUT	SKIJORER	SLAVERED
SHRAPNEL	SIDELINE	SINECURE	SKI JUMPS	SLAVERER
SHREDDED	SIDELONG	SINFONIA	SKI LIFTS	SLAVONIA
SHREDDER	SIDEREAL	SINFULLY	SKILLETS	SLAVONIC
SHREWDER	SIDERITE	SINGABLE	SKIMMERS	SLEAZIER
SHREWDLY	SIDE ROAD	SINGEING	SKIMMING	SLEAZILY
SHREWISH	SIDESHOW	SINGLETS	SKIMPIER	SLEDDING
SHRIEKED	SIDESLIP	SINGLING	SKIMPILY	SLEDGING
SHRIEKER	SIDESMAN	SINGSONG	SKIMPING	SLEEKEST
SHRIEVAL	SIDESTEP	SINGULAR	SKINCARE	SLEEKING
SHRILLER	SIDEWALK	SINISTER	SKIN DEEP	SLEEPERS
SHRIMPER	SIDEWALL	SINKABLE	SKIN-DEEP	SLEEPIER
SHRINKER	SIDEWAYS	SINKHOLE	SKIN-DIVE	SLEEPILY
SHROUDED	SIEGBAHN	SINN FEIN	SKINHEAD	SLEEPING
SHRUGGED	SIFTINGS	SINOLOGY	SKINLESS	SLEETING
SHRUNKEN	SIGHTING	SINUSOID	SKINNIER	SLEEVING
SHUCKING	SIGHTSEE	SIPHONAL	SKINNING	SLEIGHER
SHUDDERS	SIGNALED	SIPHONED	SKIPJACK	SLICKERS
SHUDDERY	SIGNALLY	SIRENIAN	SKI PLANE	SLICKEST
SHUFFLED	SIGNINGS	SIRLOINS	SKI POLES	SLICKING
SHUFFLER	SIGNORAS	SIROCCOS	SKIPPERS	SLIDABLE
SHUFFLES	SIGNPOST	SISSIEST	SKIPPING	SLIGHTED
SHUNNING	SILASTIC	SISSYISH	SKIRMISH	SLIGHTER
SHUNTERS	SILENCED	SISTERLY	SKIRTING	SLIGHTLY
SHUNTING	SILENCER	SISTROID	SKITTISH	SLIM DOWN
SHUSHING	SILENCES	SITARIST	SKITTLES	SLIMIEST
SHUTDOWN	SILENTLY	SIT-DOWNS	SKIVVIED	SLIMMERS
SHUTTERS	SILICATE	SITOLOGY	SKIVVIES	SLIMMEST
SHUTTING	SILICIDE	SITTINGS	SKULKING	SLIMMING
SHUTTLED	SILICIFY	SITUATED	SKULLCAP	SLIMNESS
SHUTTLES	SILICONE	SITZMARK	SKYDIVER	SLINGING
SHYSTERS	SILKIEST	SIX-PACKS	SKYLARKS	SLINKIER
SIANGTAN	SILKWORM	SIXPENCE	SKYLIGHT	SLINKILY
SIBERIAN	SILLABUB	SIXPENNY	SKYLINES	SLINKING
SIBILANT	SILLIEST	SIXTEENS	SKYWARDS	SLIPCASE
SIBILATE	SILOXANE	SIXTIETH	SLACKEST	SLIPKNOT
SIBLINGS	SILURIAN	SIZEABLE	SLACKING	SLIP KNOT
SICILIAN	SILVERED	SIZZLERS	SLAGGING	SLIP OVER
SICKBAYS	SILVERER	SIZZLING	SLAGHEAP	SLIPPAGE
SICKBEDS	SIMBIRSK	SKELETAL	SLAG HEAP	SLIPPERS
SICK CALL	SIMMERED	SKELETON	SLAKABLE	SLIPPERY
SICKENED	SIMONIAC	SKEPTICS	SLAMMING	SLIPPIER
SICKENER	SIMONIST	SKEPTISM	SLANDERS	SLIPPING
SICKLIER	SIMPERED	SKERRICK	SLANGILY	SLIP ROAD
SICKNESS	SIMPERER	SKETCHED	SLANGING	SLIPSHOD

SLIPWAYS	SMELLING	SNEERING	SOAPIEST	SOLONETZ
SLITHERY	SMELTERY	SNEEZING	SOAPLESS	SOLSTICE
SLITTING	SMELTING	SNICKERS	SOAPSUDS	SOLUTION
SLIVERER	SMIRCHED	SNICKING	SOAPWORT	SOLVABLE
SLOBBERY	SMIRCHER	SNIFFING	SOBERING	SOLVENCY
SLOE-EYED	SMIRKING	SNIFFLED	SOBRIETY	SOLVENTS
SLOGGERS	SMITHERY	SNIFFLER	SOB STORY	SOMALIAN
SLOGGING	SMITHIES	SNIFFLES	SO-CALLED	SOMBRELY
SLOPPIER	SMOCKING	SNIFTERS	SOCIABLE	SOMBRERO
SLOPPILY	SMOKABLE	SNIGGERS	SOCIABLY	SOMBROUS
SLOPPING	SMOKIEST	SNIGGERY	SOCIALLY	SOMEBODY
SLOPWORK	SMOLENSK	SNIGGLER	SOCIETAL	SOME HOPE
SLOSHING	SMOOCHED	SNIPPETS	SOCRATIC	SOMERSET
SLOTHFUL	SMOOTHED	SNIPPILY	SODALITE	SOMETIME
SLOTTING	SMOOTHEN	SNIPPING	SODAMIDE	SOMEWHAT
SLOUCHED	SMOOTHER	SNITCHED	SODOMITE	SONANTAL
SLOUCHER	SMOOTHIE	SNITCHES	SODOMIZE	SONATINA
SLOUGHED	SMOOTHLY	SNIVELED	SOFTBALL	SONGBIRD
SLOVAKIA	SMOTHERY	SNIVELLY	SOFT COPY	SONGBOOK
SLOVENIA	SMOULDER	SNOBBERY	SOFTENED	SONGSTER
SLOVENLY	SMUDGILY	SNOBBISH	SOFTENER	SON-IN-LAW
SLOWDOWN	SMUDGING	SNOGGING	SOFTNESS	SONOBUOY
SLOW DOWN	SMUGGEST	SNOOPERS	SOFT SELL	SONORANT
SLOWNESS	SMUGGLED	SNOOPING	SOFT SOAP	SONORITY
SLOWWORM	SMUGGLER	SNOOTIER	SOFT SPOT	SONOROUS
SLUDGIER	SMUGNESS	SNOOTILY	SOFTWARE	SOOTHING
SLUGGARD	SMUTTIER	SNOOZING	SOFTWOOD	SOOTHSAY
SLUGGING	SMUTTILY	SNORKELS	SOGGIEST	SOOTIEST
SLUGGISH	SNACK BAR	SNORTERS	SOISSONS	SOPHISMS
SLUICING	SNACKING	SNORTING	SOJOURNS	SOPHISTS
SLUMMING	SNAFFLED	SNOTTIER	SOLACING	SOPPIEST
SLUMPING	SNAFFLES	SNOTTILY	SOLANDER	SOPRANOS
SLURPING	SNAGGING	SNOWBALL	SOLARIUM	SORBITOL
SLURRING	SNAPBACK	SNOWBIRD	SOLARIZE	SORBONNE
SLUSHIER	SNAPPERS	SNOWDROP	SOLATIUM	SORCERER
SLUTTISH	SNAPPIER	SNOWFALL	SOLDERED	SORDIDLY
SMACKERS	SNAPPILY	SNOWIEST	SOLDERER	SOREDIUM
SMACKING	SNAPPING	SNOWLINE	SOLDIERS	SORENESS
SMALL ADS	SNAPPISH	SNOWSHED	SOLDIERY	SORICINE
SMALLEST	SNAP SHOT	SNOWSHOE	SOLECISM	SOROCABA
SMALL FRY	SNAPSHOT	SNUBBING	SOLECIST	SORORATE
SMALLISH	SNARLING	SNUFFBOX	SOLEMNLY	SORORITY
SMALLPOX	SNARL-UPS	SNUFFERS	SOLENOID	SORPTION
SMALTITE	SNATCHED	SNUFFING	SOLIDAGO	SORRENTO
SMARMIER	SNATCHER	SNUFFLED	SOLIDARY	SORRIEST
SMARTEST	SNATCHES	SNUFFLER	SOLIDIFY	SORROWED
SMARTING	SNAZZIER	SNUFFLES	SOLIDITY	SORROWER
SMASHERS	SNAZZILY	SNUGGERY	SOLIHULL	SORTABLE
SMASHING	SNEAKERS	SNUGGLED	SOLINGEN	SOUCHONG
SMASH-UPS	SNEAKIER	SNUGNESS	SOLITARY	SOUFFLES
SMEARING	SNEAKILY	SO-AND-SOS	SOLITUDE	SOUGHING
SMELLIER	SNEAKING	SOAPBARK	SOLOISTS	SOUL FOOD

SOULLESS	SPEARING	SPITTING	SPOTTILY	SQUEAKED
SOUNDBOX	SPECIALS	SPITTOON	SPOTTING	SQUEAKER
SOUNDING	SPECIFIC	SPLASHED	SPOT-WELD	SQUEALED
SOUND OFF	SPECIMEN	SPLASHER	SPOUTERS	SQUEALER
SOURDINE	SPECIOUS	SPLATTED	SPOUTING	SQUEEGEE
SOURNESS	SPECKLED	SPLATTER	SPRADDLE	SQUEEZED
SOURPUSS	SPECKLES	SPLAYING	SPRAINED	SQUEEZER
SOUTACHE	SPECTATE	SPLENDID	SPRAWLED	SQUEEZES
SOUTHERN	SPECTRAL	SPLENIAL	SPRAWLER	SQUELCHY
SOUTHING	SPECTRES	SPLENIUS	SPRAYERS	SQUIGGLE
SOUTHPAW	SPECTRUM	SPLICERS	SPRAY GUN	SQUIGGLY
SOUVENIR	SPECULAR	SPLICING	SPRAYING	SQUINTED
SOWBREAD	SPECULUM	SPLINTER	SPREADER	SQUINTER
SOYA BEAN	SPEECHES	SPLIT END	SPRIGGER	SQUIRMED
SOY SAUCE	SPEEDIER	SPLIT PEA	SPRINGER	SQUIRMER
SPACE AGE	SPEEDILY	SPLITTER	SPRINKLE	SQUIRREL
SPACE-AGE	SPEEDING	SPLODGES	SPRINTED	SQUIRTED
SPACE BAR	SPEEDWAY	SPLOSHED	SPRINTER	SQUIRTER
SPACE-BAR	SPELAEAN	SPLOSHES	SPRITELY	SQUISHED
SPACEMAN	SPELLING	SPLURGED	SPROCKET	SRI LANKA
SPACEMEN	SPENDERS	SPLURGES	SPROUTED	SRINAGAR
SPACIOUS	SPENDING	SPLUTTER	SPRUCELY	STABBERS
SPAMMING	SPERMARY	SPOILAGE	SPRUCING	STABBING
SPANDREL	SPERMINE	SPOILERS	SPRYNESS	STABLING
SPANGLED	SPERMOUS	SPOILING	SPUNKIER	STACCATO
SPANGLES	SPHAGNUM	SPOLIATE	SPUNKILY	STACKING
SPANIARD	SPHENOID	SPONDAIC	SPURIOUS	STADIUMS
SPANIELS	SPHERICS	SPONDEES	SPURNING	STAFFING
SPANKING	SPHEROID	SPONGERS	SPURRING	STAFFMAN
SPANNERS	SPHERULE	SPONGIER	SPURTING	STAFFORD
SPANNING	SPHINXES	SPONGILY	SPUTTERS	STAGGARD
SPANSPEK	SPHYGMIC	SPONGING	SPYGLASS	STAGGERS
SPARABLE	SPICCATO	SPONSION	SQUABBLE	STAGINGS
SPAR DECK	SPICIEST	SPONSORS	SQUAD CAR	STAGNANT
SPARERIB	SPICULUM	SPOOKIER	SQUADRON	STAGNATE
SPARE RIB	SPIKELET	SPOOKILY	SQUALENE	STAINING
SPARKING	SPIKIEST	SPOOKING	SQUALLED	STAIRWAY
SPARKLED	SPILLAGE	SPOOKISH	SQUALLER	STAKE OUT
SPARKLER	SPILLING	SPOON-FED	SQUAMATE	STALKERS
SPARKLES	SPILLWAY	SPOONFUL	SQUAMOUS	STALKILY
SPARLING	SPINDLES	SPOONING	SQUANDER	STALKING
SPARRING	SPINIFEX	SPORADIC	SQUARELY	STALLING
SPARROWS	SPINNERS	SPORRANS	SQUAREST	STALLION
SPARSELY	SPINNEYS	SPORTFUL	SQUARING	STALWART
SPARSEST	SPINNING	SPORTIER	SQUARISH	STAMFORD
SPASTICS	SPIN-OFFS	SPORTILY	SQUASHED	STAMINAL
SPATTERS	SPINSTER	SPORTING	SQUASHER	STAMMERS
SPATULAR	SPIRACLE	SPORTIVE	SQUASHES	STAMPEDE
SPATULAS	SPIRALED	SPOTLAMP	SQUATTED	STAMPING
SPAWNING	SPIRITED	SPOTLESS	SQUATTER	STANCHED
SPEAKERS	SPITEFUL	SPOTTERS	SQUAWKED	STANCHER
SPEAKING	SPITFIRE	SPOTTIER	SQUAWKER	STANDARD

STANDBYS	STEAMERS	STILLEST	STOPCOCK	STRIKERS
STANDING	STEAMIER	STILLING	STOPGAPS	STRIKING
STAND-INS	STEAMILY	STIMULUS	STOPOVER	STRIMMER
STANDISH	STEAMING	STINGERS	STOPPAGE	STRINGER
STANDOFF	STEAPSIN	STINGIER	STOPPARD	STRIPIER
STAND OUT	STEARATE	STINGILY	STOPPERS	STRIPPED
STANNARY	STEATITE	STINGING	STOPPING	STRIPPER
STANNITE	STEELIER	STINGRAY	STORABLE	STROBILA
STANNOUS	STEELING	STING RAY	STOREYED	STROKING
STANZAIC	STEEPEST	STINKERS	STORMIER	STROLLED
STAPELIA	STEEPING	STINKING	STORMILY	STROLLER
STAPLERS	STEEPLES	STINTING	STORMING	STRONGER
STAPLING	STEERAGE	STIPENDS	STORMONT	STRONGLY
STARCHED	STEERING	STIPPLED	STOUTEST	STROPHES
STARCHER	STEINBOK	STIPPLER	STOWAWAY	STROPHIC
STARCHES	STELLATE	STIPULAR	STRABANE	STRUDELS
STARDUST	STELLIFY	STIRLING	STRADDLE	STRUGGLE
STARFISH	STELLITE	STIRRERS	STRAFING	STRUMMED
STARGAZE	STEMHEAD	STIRRING	STRAGGLE	STRUMMER
STARKERS	STEMMING	STIRRUPS	STRAGGLY	STRUMPET
STARKEST	STENCHES	STITCHED	STRAIGHT	STRUNG-UP
STARLESS	STENCILS	STITCHER	STRAINED	STRUTTED
STARLETS	STEN GUNS	STITCHES	STRAINER	STRUTTER
STARLIKE	STENOSIS	STITCH UP	STRAITEN	STUBBIER
STARLING	STENOTIC	STOCKADE	STRANDED	STUBBILY
STARRIER	STEP DOWN	STOCKCAR	STRANGER	STUBBING
STARRILY	STEPPING	STOCK CAR	STRANGLE	STUBBLED
STARRING	STEPWISE	STOCKIER	STRAPPED	STUBBORN
STARSHIP	STERIGMA	STOCKILY	STRAPPER	STUCCOED
STAR SIGN	STERLING	STOCKING	STRATEGY	STUDBOOK
STARTERS	STERNEST	STOCKIST	STRATIFY	STUDDING
STARTING	STERNSON	STOCKMAN	STRAW MAN	STUDENTS
STARTLED	STERNUMS	STOCKMEN	STRAW MEN	STUD FARM
STARTLER	STERNWAY	STOCKOUT	STRAYING	STUDIOUS
STARVING	STEROIDS	STOCKPOT	STREAKED	STUDWORK
STAR WARS	STETSONS	STOCKTON	STREAKER	STUDYING
STARWORT	STEWARDS	STODGIER	STREAMED	STUFFIER
STASHING	STIBNITE	STODGILY	STREAMER	STUFFILY
STATABLE	STICKERS	STOICISM	STRENGTH	STUFFING
STATELET	STICKFUL	STOLIDLY	STRESSED	STULTIFY
STATICAL	STICKIER	STOMACHS	STRESSES	STUMBLED
STATIONS	STICKILY	STOMACHY	STRETCHY	STUMBLER
STATUARY	STICKING	STOMATAL	STREUSEL	STUMBLES
STATURES	STICKLER	STOMATIC	STREWING	STUMPIER
STATUSES	STICKPIN	STOMPING	STRIATED	STUMPING
STATUTES	STICK-UPS	STONABLE	STRICKEN	STUNNERS
STAYSAIL	STIFFEST	STONE AGE	STRICKLE	STUNNING
STEADIED	STIFLING	STONEFLY	STRICTER	STUNTING
STEADIER	STIGMATA	STONIEST	STRICTLY	STUNT MAN
STEADILY	STILBENE	STONKING	STRIDDEN	STUNT MEN
STEALING	STILBITE	STOOD OUT	STRIDENT	STUPIDER
STEALTHY	STILETTO	STOOPING	STRIGOSE	STUPIDLY

STURDIER	SUCCUBUS	SUNROOFS	SURPLICE	SWIGGING
STURDILY	SUCHLIKE	SUNSHADE	SURPRINT	SWILLING
STURGEON	SUCKLING	SUNSHINE	SURPRISE	SWIMMERS
STUTTERS	SUDANESE	SUNSHINY	SURROUND	SWIMMING
STYLISTS	SUDATORY	SUNSPOTS	SURVEYED	SWIMSUIT
STYLIZED	SUDDENLY	SUNTRAPS	SURVEYOR	SWINDLED
STYLIZER	SUFFERED	SUN VISOR	SURVIVAL	SWINDLER
STYLUSES	SUFFERER	SUNWARDS	SURVIVED	SWINDLES
STYMYING	SUFFICED	SUPADRIV	SURVIVOR	SWINEPOX
STYPTICS	SUFFICER	SUPERBLY	SUSPECTS	SWINGBIN
SUBACUTE	SUFFIXAL	SUPEREGO	SUSPENSE	SWINGERS
SUBADULT	SUFFIXES	SUPERFIX	SUTURING	SWINGING
SUBAGENT	SUFFRAGE	SUPERIOR	SUZERAIN	SWIRLING
SUBCLASS	SUFFUSED	SUPERMAN	SVALBARD	SWISHEST
SUBDUING	SUGARING	SUPERMEN	SVENGALI	SWISHING
SUBERIZE	SUICIDAL	SUPERNAL	SWABBING	SWITCHED
SUBEROSE	SUICIDES	SUPERSEX	SWADDLED	SWITCHER
SUBFLOOR	SUITABLE	SUPERTAX	SWALLOWS	SWITCHES
SUBGENUS	SUITABLY	SUPINATE	SWAMPING	SWIVELED
SUBGROUP	SUITCASE	SUPINELY	SWANKIER	SWOONING
SUBHUMAN	SULAWESI	SUPPLANT	SWANKILY	SWOOPING
SUBJECTS	SULKIEST	SUPPLEST	SWANKING	SWOPPING
SUBLEASE	SULLENER	SUPPLIED	SWANNERY	SWOTTING
SUBMERGE	SULLENLY	SUPPLIER	SWANNING	SYBARITE
SUBMERSE	SULLYING	SUPPLIES	SWANSKIN	SYCAMINE
SUBORDER	SULPHATE	SUPPORTS	SWANSONG	SYCAMORE
SUBORNED	SULPHIDE	SUPPOSED	SWAN SONG	SYCONIUM
SUBORNER	SULPHITE	SUPPOSER	SWAP MEET	SYENITIC
SUBOTICA	SULPHONE	SUPPRESS	SWAPPING	SYLLABIC
SUBOXIDE	SULTANAS	SUPREMOS	SWARMING	SYLLABLE
SUBPLOTS	SULTANIC	SURABAYA	SWASTIKA	SYLLABUB
SUBPOENA	SULTRIER	SURCOATS	SWATCHES	SYLLABUS
SUBPRIME	SULTRILY	SUREFIRE	SWATHING	SYLVATIC
SUBSERVE	SUMATRAN	SURE FIRE	SWATTERS	SYMBIONT
SUBSHRUB	SUMMERED	SURENESS	SWATTING	SYMBOLIC
SUBSIDED	SUMMITAL	SURETIES	SWAYABLE	SYMMETRY
SUBSIDER	SUMMONED	SURFABLE	SWAY-BACK	SYMPATHY
SUBSOLAR	SUM TOTAL	SURFACED	SWEARING	SYMPHILE
SUBSONIC	SUNBAKED	SURFACER	SWEATBOX	SYMPHONY
SUBSTAGE	SUNBATHE	SURFACES	SWEATERS	SYMPOSIA
SUBSUMED	SUNBEAMS	SURFBIRD	SWEATIER	SYMPTOMS
SUBTITLE	SUNBELTS	SURFBOAT	SWEATILY	SYNAPSIS
SUBTLEST	SUNBURNT	SURFLIKE	SWEATING	SYNAPTIC
SUBTLETY	SUNBURST	SURGEONS	SWEEPERS	SYNARCHY
SUBTONIC	SUNDERED	SURGICAL	SWEEPING	SYNCARPY
SUBTOTAL	SUNDIALS	SURICATE	SWEETEST	SYNCLINE
SUBTRACT	SUNDRIES	SURLIEST	SWEETIES	SYNCOPIC
SUBULATE	SUNGLASS	SURMISED	SWEET PEA	SYNDESIS
SUBURBAN	SUNLAMPS	SURMISER	SWEETSOP	SYNDETIC
SUBURBIA	SUNLIGHT	SURMISES	SWELLING	SYNDETON
SUCCINCT	SUNNIEST	SURMOUNT	SWERVING	SYNDICAL
SUCCINIC	SUNRISES	SURNAMES	SWIFTEST	SYNDROME

SYNERGIC	TAJ MAHAL	TAPESTRY	TEACHING	TENDERED
SYNGAMIC	TAKE A BOW	TAPEWORM	TEACH-INS	TENDERER
SYNONYMS	TAKEAWAY	TAPPABLE	TEA CLOTH	TENDERLY
SYNONYMY	TAKE CARE	TAPROOTS	TEAHOUSE	TENDRILS
SYNOPSES	TAKEOFFS	TAPWATER	TEA-MAKER	TENEFIFE
SYNOPSIS	TAKEOUTS	TARAKIHI	TEAM-MATE	TENEMENT
SYNOPTIC	TAKEOVER	TARBOOSH	TEAMSTER	TENERIFE
SYNOVIAL	TAKES OFF	TARDIEST	TEAMWORK	TENESMIC
SYNTONIC	TAKORADI	TARGETED	TEA PARTY	TENESMUS
SYPHILIS	TALAPOIN	TARLATAN	TEARABLE	TEN GURUS
SYPHONED	TALENTED	TARRAGON	TEARAWAY	TENON SAW
SYRACUSE	TALESMAN	TARRYING	TEARDROP	TENORIST
SYRINGED	TALISMAN	TARTARIC	TEAROOMS	TENORITE
SYRINGES	TALKABLE	TARTNESS	TEASE OUT	TENOTOMY
SYSTEMIC	TALK SHOW	TARTRATE	TEASPOON	TENSED UP
SYSTOLIC	TALLBOYS	TASHKENT	TEA TOWEL	TENSIBLE
SYZYGIAL	TALLNESS	TASKWORK	TECHNICS	TENSIONS
SZCZECIN	TALLYING	TASK WORK	TECTONIC	TENTACLE
SZECHWAN	TALLYMAN	TASMANIA	TEDDY BOY	TENURIAL
	TALMUDIC	TASSELED	TEENAGER	TEOCALLI
T	TAMANDUA	TASSELLY	TEE SHIRT	TEOSINTE
TABLEAUS	TAMARACK	TASTABLE	TEESSIDE	TEPHRITE
TABLEAUX	TAMARIND	TASTE BUD	TEETERED	TEPIDITY
TABLEMAT	TAMARISK	TASTEFUL	TEETHING	TERAFLOP
TABLOIDS	TAMBOURS	TASTIEST	TEETOTAL	TERATISM
TABULATE	TAMEABLE	TATARIAN	TEGMINAL	TERATOID
TACITURN	TAMENESS	TATTERED	TELECAST	TERATOMA
TACKIEST	TAMESIDE	TATTIEST	TELECOMS	TERAWATT
TACKLING	TAMPERED	TATTLERS	TELEGONY	TERCEIRA
TACONITE	TAMPERER	TATTLING	TELEGRAM	TEREBENE
TACTICAL	TAMWORTH	TATTOOED	TELEMARK	TERESINA
TACTLESS	TANDOORI	TATTOOER	TELEPLAY	TERMINAL
TADPOLES	TANGENCY	TAUNTING	TELETEXT	TERMINUS
TAFFRAIL	TANGENTS	TAURANGA	TELETYPE	TERMITES
TAGANROG	TANGIBLE	TAUTENED	TELEVISE	TERMITIC
TAGMEMIC	TANGIBLY	TAUTNESS	TELEWORK	TERMLESS
TAHITIAN	TANGIEST	TAUTOMER	TELEXING	TERNOPOL
TAICHUNG	TANGLING	TAUTONYM	TELLABLE	TERPENIC
TAILBACK	TANGOING	TAVERNER	TELLTALE	TERRACES
TAILCOAT	TANGOIST	TAWDRILY	TELLURIC	TERRAINS
TAIL ENDS	TANGSHAN	TAXATION	TELSONIC	TERRAPIN
TAILGATE	TANKARDS	TAX HAVEN	TEMERITY	TERRAZZO
TAILINGS	TANKED UP	TAXINGLY	TEMPERED	TERRIBLE
TAILLESS	TANTALIC	TAXI RANK	TEMPERER	TERRIBLY
TAILORED	TANTALUM	TAXONOMY	TEMPESTS	TERRIERS
TAIL PIPE	TANTALUS	TAXPAYER	TEMPLATE	TERRIFIC
TAILRACE	TANTRUMS	TEABERRY	TEMPORAL	TERTIARY
TAILSKID	TANZANIA	TEA BREAK	TEMPTERS	TERYLENE
TAILSPIN	TAP DANCE	TEA CADDY	TEMPTING	TERZETTO
TAILWIND	TAPE DECK	TEACAKES	TENACITY	TESSERAL
TAIL WIND	TAPENADE	TEACHERS	TENANTRY	TESTABLE
TAINTING	TAPERING	TEA CHEST	TENDENCY	TESTATOR

TEST BANS	THESPIAN	THROTTLE	TIMELESS	TOCCATAS
TEST CARD	THESSALY	THROWING	TIMELIER	TOCOLOGY
TEST CASE	THEURGIC	THROW-INS	TIMEWORK	TODDLERS
TEST-CASE	THE WEALD	THRUMMED	TIMEWORN	TODDLING
TESTICLE	THIAMINE	THRUMMER	TIME ZONE	TOEHOLDS
TESTIEST	THIAZINE	THRUSHES	TIMIDITY	TOENAILS
TEST TUBE	THIAZOLE	THRUSTER	TIMORESE	TOGETHER
TETANIZE	THICKEST	THRUWAYS	TIMOROUS	TOGOLESE
TETCHIER	THICKETS	THUDDING	TINCTURE	TOILETRY
TETCHILY	THICKSET	THUGGERY	TINGLING	TOILETTE
TETHERED	THIEVERY	THUMBING	TINKERED	TOILSOME
TETRACID	THIEVING	THUMBNUT	TINKERER	TOKENISM
TETRAPOD	THIEVISH	THUMPING	TINKLING	TOLERANT
TETRARCH	THIMBLES	THUNDERS	TINNIEST	TOLERATE
TEUTONIC	THIN-FILM	THUNDERY	TINNITUS	TOLIDINE
TEXTBOOK	THINKING	THURIBLE	TINPLATE	TOLL CALL
TEXTILES	THINNESS	THURIFER	TINSELLY	TOLL-FREE
TEXTUARY	THINNEST	THURROCK	TINSMITH	TOLLGATE
TEXTURAL	THINNING	THURSDAY	TINTACKS	TOMAHAWK
TEXTURES	THIONINE	THWACKED	TIPPABLE	TOMATOES
THAILAND	THIOUREA	THWACKER	TIPPLERS	TOMBAUGH
THALAMIC	THIRTEEN	THWARTED	TIPSIEST	TOMBLIKE
THALAMUS	THIRTIES	THWARTER	TIPSTAFF	TOM BROWN
THALLIUM	THISTLES	THYROIDS	TIPSTERS	TOMENTUM
THALLOID	THONBURI	THYRSOID	TIRELESS	TOMMY GUN
THALLOUS	THORACES	TIAN SHAN	TIRESIAS	TOMMYROT
THANKFUL	THORACIC	TIBERIAS	TIRESOME	TOMMY ROT
THANKING	THORAXES	TICKETED	TITANATE	TOMORROW
THANKYOU	THORNIER	TICKLING	TITANISM	TONALITY
THATCHED	THORNILY	TICKLISH	TITANITE	TONE-DEAF
THATCHER	THOROUGH	TICK OVER	TITANIUM	TONELESS
THATCHES	THOUGHTS	TICKTACK	TITANOUS	TONE POEM
THEARCHY	THOUSAND	TICKTOCK	TITCHIER	TONICITY
THEATRES	THRALDOM	TIDDLERS	TITHABLE	TONLE SAP
THEBAINE	THRASHED	TIDEMARK	TITIVATE	TONNAGES
THE BIBLE	THRASHER	TIDEWAYS	TITMOUSE	TONSURES
THE BLUES	THREADED	TIDINESS	TITOGRAD	TOOTHIER
THE BRINY	THREADER	TIE BREAK	TITTERED	TOOTHILY
THEISTIC	THREATEN	TIE-BREAK	TITTERER	TOOTLING
THEMATIC	THREE-D	TIE-DYING	TJIREBON	TOOTSIES
THEOCRAT	THREE-PLY	TIENTSIN	TLAXCALA	TOPARCHY
THEOLOGY	THRENODY	TIGHTEST	TOADFISH	TOP BRASS
THEOREMS	THRESHED	TIGHTWAD	TOADFLAX	TOPCOATS
THEORIES	THRESHER	TIGRAYAN	TOADYING	TOP-DRESS
THEORIST	THRESHES	TILEFISH	TOADYISM	TOP-HEAVY
THEORIZE	THRILLED	TILLABLE	TO AND FRO	TOPKNOTS
THEREMIN	THRILLER	TILLICUM	TO-AND-FRO	TOP-LEVEL
THERMALS	THRIVING	TIMBRELS	TOASTERS	TOP-NOTCH
THERMION	THROBBED	TIMBUKTU	TOASTING	TOPOLOGY
THERMITE	THROMBIN	TIME BOMB	TOBACCOS	TOPONYMY
THEROPOD	THROMBUS	TIMECARD	TOBOGGAN	TOPOTYPE
THESIGER	THRONGED	TIME LAGS	TOBY JUGS	TOPPINGS

TOPPLING	TOWROPES	TRAPEZES	TRIAZINE	TRIREMES
TOP-SHELL	TOXAEMIA	TRAPEZIA	TRIAZOLE	TRISOMIC
TORCHERE	TOXAEMIC	TRAPPERS	TRIBADIC	TRISTICH
TORCHIER	TOXICANT	TRAPPING	TRIBASIC	TRITICUM
TOREADOR	TOXICITY	TRAPPIST	TRIBRACH	TRIUMPHS
TORE DOWN	TRACHEAL	TRAPUNTO	TRIBUNAL	TRIUNITY
TOREUTIC	TRACHEAS	TRASHCAN	TRIBUNES	TROCHAIC
TORMENTS	TRACHEID	TRASHIER	TRIBUTES	TROCHEES
TORNADIC	TRACHOMA	TRASHILY	TRICHINA	TROCHLEA
TORNADOS	TRACHYTE	TRASHING	TRICHITE	TROCHOID
TOROIDAL	TRACINGS	TRAVELED	TRICHOID	TROLLEYS
TORPIDLY	TRACKING	TRAVERSE	TRICHOME	TROLLING
TORQUATE	TRACTATE	TRAVESTY	TRICKERY	TROLLOPS
TORRANCE	TRACTILE	TRAWLERS	TRICKIER	TROMBONE
TORRENTS	TRACTION	TRAWLING	TRICKILY	TROOPERS
TORRIDLY	TRACTIVE	TREADING	TRICKING	TROOPING
TORTELLI	TRACTORS	TREADLER	TRICKLED	TROPHIES
TORTILLA	TRADABLE	TREADLES	TRICTRAC	TROPICAL
TORTIOUS	TRADE GAP	TREASURE	TRICYCLE	TROTLINE
TORTOISE	TRADE OFF	TREASURY	TRIDENTS	TROTTERS
TORTUOUS	TRADE-OFF	TREATIES	TRIFLING	TROTTING
TORTURED	TRAD JAZZ	TREATING	TRIFOCAL	TROUBLED
TORTURER	TRADUCED	TREATISE	TRIGGERS	TROUBLER
TORTURES	TRADUCER	TREATIZE	TRIGLYPH	TROUBLES
TOTALING	TRAFFORD	TREBLING	TRIGONAL	TROUNCED
TOTALITY	TRAGOPAN	TREE FERN	TRIGRAPH	TROUPERS
TOTALIZE	TRAILERS	TREELESS	TRILBIES	TROUPIAL
TOTALLED	TRAILING	TREELINE	TRILEMMA	TROUSERS
TOTE BAGS	TRAINEES	TREENAIL	TRILLING	TRUCKERS
TOTEMISM	TRAINERS	TREFOILS	TRILLION	TRUCKING
TOTEMIST	TRAINING	TREKKING	TRILLIUM	TRUCKLED
TOTTERED	TRAIN SET	TREMBLED	TRIMARAN	TRUDGING
TOTTERER	TRAIPSED	TREMBLER	TRIMETER	TRUE-BLUE
TOUCHIER	TRAITORS	TREMBLES	TRIMMERS	TRUEBORN
TOUCHILY	TRAMLINE	TREMOLOS	TRIMMEST	TRUE-LIFE
TOUCHING	TRAMMELS	TRENCHER	TRIMMING	TRUELOVE
TOUGHEST	TRAMPING	TRENCHES	TRIMNESS	TRUE LOVE
TOULOUSE	TRAMPLED	TRENDIER	TRIMORPH	TRUENESS
TOURAINE	TRAMPLER	TRENDIES	TRINIDAD	TRUFFLES
TOURISTS	TRANNIES	TRENDIFY	TRINKETS	TRUISTIC
TOURISTY	TRANQUIL	TRENDILY	TRIOXIDE	TRUJILLO
TOURNEYS	TRANSACT	TRENDING	TRIPLANE	TRUMPERY
TOUSLING	TRANSECT	TREPHINE	TRIPLETS	TRUMPETS
TOWELING	TRANSEPT	TRESPASS	TRIPLING	TRUMPING
TOWELLED	TRANSFER	TRESSURE	TRIPLOID	TRUNCATE
TOWERING	TRANSFIX	TRESTLES	TRIPODAL	TRUNDLED
TOWN HALL	TRANSITS	TRIADISM	TRIPOSES	TRUNNION
TOWNSHIP	TRANSKEI	TRIAL RUN	TRIPPERS	TRUSSING
TOWNSMAN	TRANSMIT	TRIANGLE	TRIPPING	TRUSTEES
TOWNSMEN	TRANSOMS	TRIARCHY	TRIPTANE	TRUSTFUL
TOWPATHS	TRANSUDE	TRIASSIC	TRIPTYCH	TRUSTIER
TOWPLANE	TRAPDOOR	TRIAXIAL	TRIPWIRE	TRUSTIES

TRUSTILY	TURN-OFFS	TWOPENNY	UNBIDDEN	UNFETTER
TRUSTING	TURNOUTS	TWO-PHASE	UNBODIED	UNFILIAL
TRUTHFUL	TURNOVER	TWO-PIECE	UNBOLTED	UNFOLDED
TSARINAS	TURNPIKE	TWO-SIDED	UNBRIDLE	UNFOLDER
TSESSEBI	TURNSOLE	TWOSOMES	UNBROKEN	UNFORCED
TSINGHAI	TURRETED	TWO-STEPS	UNBUCKLE	UNFORMED
TSINGTAO	TUSKLIKE	TWO-TIMED	UNBURDEN	UNFREEZE
T-SQUARES	TUSSLING	TWO-TIMER	UNBUTTON	UNFURLED
TSUSHIMA	TUSSOCKS	TYMPANIC	UNCAPPED	UNGAINLY
TUBBIEST	TUSSOCKY	TYMPANUM	UNCHASTE	UNGUENTS
TUBELESS	TUTELAGE	TYNESIDE	UNCHURCH	UNGULATE
TUBERCLE	TUTELARY	TYPECAST	UNCIFORM	UNHANDED
TUBEROSE	TUTORAGE	TYPE CAST	UNCINATE	UNHEALED
TUBEROUS	TUTORIAL	TYPEFACE	UNCLENCH	UNHINGED
TUBIFORM	TUTORING	TYPE FACE	UNCLE SAM	UNHORSED
TUBULATE	TV DINNER	TYPE-HIGH	UNCLE TOM	UNIATISM
TUBULOUS	TWADDLER	TYPHONIC	UNCLOTHE	UNIAXIAL
TUCKERED	TWANGING	TYPHOONS	UNCOINED	UNICORNS
TUCOTUCO	TWEAKING	TYPIFIED	UNCOMMON	UNICYCLE
TUESDAYS	TWEETERS	TYPIFIER	UNCORKED	UNIFORMS
TUG OF WAR	TWEETING	TYPOLOGY	UNCOUPLE	UNIFYING
TUG-OF-WAR	TWEEZERS	TYRAMINE	UNCTUOUS	UNIONISM
TUMBLERS	TWELFTHS	TYROLESE	UNDAMPED	UNIONIST
TUMBLING	TWELVEMO	TYROSINE	UNDERACT	UNIONIZE
TUMBRELS	TWENTIES	TZARINAS	UNDERAGE	UNIPOLAR
TUMIDITY	TWIDDLED	TZATZIKI	UNDERARM	UNIQUELY
TUMOROUS	TWIDDLER		UNDERBID	UNITEDLY
TUMULOSE	TWIDDLES	**U**	UNDERBUY	UNIVALVE
TUNELESS	TWIGGING	UBIQUITY	UNDERCUT	UNIVERSE
TUNGSTEN	TWILIGHT	UBI SUPRA	UNDERDOG	UNIVOCAL
TUNGSTIC	TWIN BEDS	UGLIFIER	UNDERFUR	UNKENNEL
TUNGUSIC	TWINKLED	UGLINESS	UNDERLAY	UNKINDER
TUNICATE	TWINKLER	UIGURIAN	UNDERLET	UNKINDLY
TUNISIAN	TWINNING	UKULELES	UNDERLIE	UNKNOWNS
TUNNELED	TWIN SETS	ULCERATE	UNDERLIP	UNLAWFUL
TUNNELER	TWIRLERS	ULCEROUS	UNDERPAY	UNLIKELY
TUPPENCE	TWIRLING	ULTERIOR	UNDERPIN	UNLIMBER
TUPPENNY	TWISTERS	ULTIMATA	UNDERSEA	UNLISTED
TURBANED	TWISTIER	ULTIMATE	UNDERSET	UNLOADED
TURBINES	TWISTING	ULTRAISM	UNDERTOW	UNLOADER
TURBOCAR	TWITCHED	ULTRAIST	UNDERUSE	UNLOCKED
TURBOFAN	TWITCHER	UMBONATE	UNDULANT	UNLOOSED
TURBOJET	TWITCHES	UMBRAGES	UNDULATE	UNLOOSEN
TURGIDLY	TWITTERS	UMBRELLA	UNEARNED	UNLOVELY
TURKOMAN	TWITTERY	UMPIRING	UNEASIER	UNMANNED
TURMERIC	TWITTING	UNABATED	UNEASILY	UNMARKED
TURNABLE	TWOCCING	UNAWARES	UNENDING	UNMASKED
TURNCOAT	TWO-EDGED	UNBACKED	UNERRING	UNMASKER
TURNCOCK	TWOFACED	UNBARRED	UNEVENLY	UNMUZZLE
TURN DOWN	TWO FACED	UNBEATEN	UNFAIRER	UNNERVED
TURNINGS	TWOPENCE	UNBELIEF	UNFAIRLY	UNOPENED
TURNKEYS	TWO PENCE	UNBIASED	UNFASTEN	UNPACKED

UNPACKER	UNZIPPED	URUSHIOL	VANADIUM	VENOSITY
UNPEOPLE	UP-ANCHOR	USEFULLY	VANADOUS	VENTOLIN
UNPICKED	UP-AND-UPS	USHERING	VANGUARD	VENTOUSE
UNPLACED	UPCOMING	USUFRUCT	VANILLIC	VENTURED
UNPOLLED	UPDATING	USURIOUS	VANILLIN	VENTURER
UNPRICED	UPENDING	USURPERS	VANISHED	VENTURES
UNPROFOR	UPGRADED	USURPING	VANISHER	VENUSIAN
UNPROVEN	UPGRADER	UTENSILS	VANQUISH	VERACITY
UNREASON	UPGROWTH	UTERUSES	VAPIDITY	VERACRUZ
UNRIDDLE	UPHEAVAL	UTILIZED	VAPORIZE	VERANDAS
UNRIFLED	UPHOLDER	UTILIZER	VAPOROUS	VERBALLY
UNROLLED	UPLIFTED	UTTERING	VAPOURER	VERBATIM
UNSADDLE	UPLIFTER	UVULITIS	VARACTOR	VERBIAGE
UNSEATED	UP-MARKET	UXORIOUS	VARANASI	VERBOTEN
UNSEEDED	UPPERCUT		VARIABLE	VERCELLI
UNSEEING	UPRAISER	**V**	VARIABLY	VERDANCY
UNSEEMLY	UPRISING	VACANTLY	VARIANCE	VERDICTS
UNSETTLE	UPROOTED	VACATING	VARIANTS	VERIFIED
UNSHAPEN	UPROOTER	VACATION	VARICOSE	VERIFIER
UNSHAVEN	UPSETTER	VACCINAL	VARIETAL	VERISTIC
UNSOCIAL	UPSTAGED	VACCINES	VARIFORM	VERITIES
UNSPOKEN	UPSTAIRS	VACCINIA	VARIOLAR	VERJUICE
UNSTABLE	UPSTARTS	VACUOLAR	VARIORUM	VERLIGTE
UNSTEADY	UPSTREAM	VACUUMED	VARISTOR	VERMOUTH
UNSTRING	UPSTROKE	VADODARA	VARITYPE	VERONESE
UNSUBTLE	UPSURGES	VAGABOND	VARMINTS	VERONICA
UNSUITED	UPSWINGS	VAGARIES	VASCULAR	VERRUCAE
UNSWATHE	UPTHRUST	VAGINATE	VASCULUM	VERRUCAS
UNTANGLE	UP TO DATE	VAGOTOMY	VASELINE	VERSICLE
UNTAPPED	UP-TO-DATE	VAGRANCY	VASTERAS	VERSIONS
UNTAUGHT	UPTURNED	VAGRANTS	VASTNESS	VERTEBRA
UNTHREAD	URALITIC	VAINNESS	VAUCLUSE	VERTEXES
UNTIDILY	URANITIC	VALANCED	VAULTERS	VERTICAL
UNTIMELY	URANYLIC	VALANCES	VAULTING	VERTICES
UNTIRING	URBANELY	VALDIVIA	VAUNTING	VERTICIL
UNTITLED	URBANITY	VAL-D'OISE	VEGETATE	VESICANT
UNTOWARD	URBANIZE	VALENCIA	VEHEMENT	VESICATE
UNTRENDY	URETERAL	VALERIAN	VEHICLES	VESICLES
UNTRUTHS	URETHANE	VALIANCE	VEILEDLY	VESPERAL
UNUSABLE	URETHRAL	VALIDATE	VELARIZE	VESPIARY
UNVALUED	URETHRAS	VALIDITY	VELOCITY	VESTIGES
UNVEILED	URGENTLY	VALLETTA	VENALITY	VESTMENT
UNVERSED	URGINGLY	VALORIZE	VENATION	VESTRIES
UNVOICED	URINATED	VALOROUS	VENDETTA	VESTURAL
UNWALLED	URNFIELD	VALUABLE	VENDIBLE	VESUVIAN
UNWASHED	UROCHORD	VALUATOR	VENEERED	VESUVIUS
UNWEIGHT	UROLOGIC	VALVULAR	VENEERER	VETERANS
UNWIELDY	UROPODAL	VAMBRACE	VENERATE	VEXATION
UNWINDER	UROSCOPY	VAMOOSED	VENEREAL	VEXILLUM
UNWISHED	UROSTYLE	VAMPIRES	VENETIAN	VEXINGLY
UNWONTED	URSULINE	VAMPIRIC	VENGEFUL	VIADUCTS
UNWORTHY	URTICATE	VANADATE	VENOMOUS	VIA MEDIA

VIATICAL	VIRAGOES	VOLATILE	WALKMANS	WASHDAYS
VIATICUM	VIRGINAL	VOLCANIC	WALKOUTS	WASHED-UP
VIBRANCY	VIRGINIA	VOLCANOS	WALKOVER	WASHOUTS
VIBRATED	VIRIDIAN	VOLITION	WALLAROO	WASHROOM
VIBRATOR	VIRIDITY	VOLITIVE	WALLASEY	WASTABLE
VIBRATOS	VIRILISM	VOLLEYED	WALLEYED	WASTEFUL
VIBRIOID	VIRILITY	VOLLEYER	WALL-LIKE	WASTRELS
VIBRISSA	VIROLOGY	VOLPLANE	WALLOPED	WATCHDOG
VIBRONIC	VIRTUOSI	VOLTAGES	WALLOPER	WATCHFUL
VIBURNUM	VIRTUOSO	VOLTAISM	WALLOWED	WATCHING
VICARAGE	VIRTUOUS	VOLUTION	WALLOWER	WATCHMAN
VICARIAL	VIRULENT	VOLVULUS	WALLSEND	WATCHMEN
VICELIKE	VISCACHA	VOMERINE	WALRUSES	WATERAGE
VICENARY	VISCERAL	VOMITING	WALTZING	WATER BAG
VICEROYS	VISCOUNT	VOMITIVE	WANDERED	WATERBED
VICINITY	VISIONAL	VOMITORY	WANDERER	WATER ICE
VICTORIA	VISITANT	VONNEGUT	WANDEROO	WATERING
VICTUALS	VISITING	VOORSKOT	WANGANUI	WATERLOO
VIDEOFIT	VISITORS	VORACITY	WANGLING	WATERMAN
VIDEOING	VISUALLY	VORONEZH	WANTONLY	WATER RAT
VIENNESE	VITALISM	VORTEXES	WARANGAL	WATER SKI
VIETCONG	VITALIST	VORTICAL	WARBLERS	WATER-SKI
VIETMINH	VITALITY	VORTICES	WARBLING	WATERWAY
VIEWLESS	VITALIZE	VOTARESS	WAR CRIES	WATT-HOUR
VIGILANT	VITAMINS	VOTARIES	WAR CRIME	WAVE BAND
VIGNETTE	VITELLIN	VOTARIST	WAR DANCE	WAVEFORM
VIGOROSO	VITIABLE	VOUCHERS	WARDENRY	WAVELIKE
VIGOROUS	VITIATED	VOUCHING	WARDRESS	WAVERERS
VILENESS	VITIATOR	VOUSSOIR	WARDROBE	WAVERING
VILIFIED	VITI LEVU	VOWELIZE	WARDROOM	WAVINESS
VILIFIER	VITILIGO	VOYAGERS	WARDSHIP	WAXBERRY
VILLAGER	VITREOUS	VOYAGING	WARFARIN	WAXINESS
VILLAGES	VITULINE	VULGARLY	WAR GAMES	WAXPLANT
VILLAINS	VIVACITY	VULTURES	WARHEADS	WAXWORKS
VILLAINY	VIVARIUM	VULVITIS	WARHORSE	WAYBILLS
VILLATIC	VIVA VOCE	VUVUZELA	WARINESS	WAYFARER
VILLEINS	VIVIFIER		WARLOCKS	WAYLAYER
VINCULUM	VIVISECT	**W**	WARLORDS	WEAKENED
VINDALOO	VIXENISH		WARMNESS	WEAKENER
VINEGARY	VLADIMIR	WADDLING	WARNINGS	WEAKFISH
VINEYARD	VOCALESE	WAFFLING	WAR PAINT	WEAKLING
VINNITSA	VOCALISE	WAGERING	WARPATHS	WEAKNESS
VINOSITY	VOCALISM	WAGGLING	WARPLANE	WEANLING
VINTAGER	VOCALIST	WAGON-LIT	WARRANTS	WEAPONED
VINTAGES	VOCALITY	WAGTAILS	WARRANTY	WEAPONRY
VINTNERS	VOCALIZE	WAINSCOT	WARRIGAL	WEARABLE
VIOLABLE	VOCATION	WAITRESS	WARRIORS	WEARIEST
VIOLATED	VOCATIVE	WAKASHAN	WARSHIPS	WEARYING
VIOLATOR	VOICE BOX	WAKAYAMA	WARTBURG	WEASELED
VIOLENCE	VOICEFUL	WAKELESS	WARTHOGS	WEASELLY
VIPERINE	VOIDABLE	WAKENING	WASHABLE	WEDDINGS
VIPEROUS	VOIDANCE	WALKABLE	WASHBOWL	WEDGWOOD
		WALKAWAY		

WEEDIEST	WHEEZILY	WHOMEVER	WING NUTS	WOODCHAT
WEEKDAYS	WHEEZING	WHOOPEES	WINGOVER	WOODCOCK
WEEKENDS	WHENEVER	WHOOPING	WINGSPAN	WOODCUTS
WEEKLIES	WHEREVER	WHOOSHES	WINKLING	WOODENLY
WEENIEST	WHETTING	WHOPPERS	WINNABLE	WOODIEST
WEIGHING	WHEYFACE	WHOPPING	WINNINGS	WOODLAND
WEIGHTED	WHICKERS	WHOREDOM	WINNIPEG	WOODLARK
WEIGHTER	WHIFFIER	WICKEDLY	WINNOWED	WOODLICE
WEIRDEST	WHIGGERY	WIDE BOYS	WINNOWER	WOODNOTE
WELCHING	WHIGGISH	WIDE-EYED	WINTERED	WOODPILE
WELCOMED	WHIMBREL	WIDENESS	WINTERER	WOOD PULP
WELCOMER	WHIMPERS	WIDENING	WINTRIER	WOODRUFF
WELCOMES	WHIMSIES	WIDE OPEN	WINTRILY	WOODRUSH
WELDABLE	WHINCHAT	WIDE-OPEN	WIPED OUT	WOODSHED
WELL-BRED	WHINGING	WIDGEONS	WIREDRAW	WOODSMAN
WELL DONE	WHINNIED	WIDOWERS	WIRELESS	WOODSMEN
WELL-DONE	WHINNIES	WIELDERS	WIRETAPS	WOODWIND
WELLHEAD	WHIPCORD	WIELDING	WIRE WOOL	WOODWORK
WELL HEAD	WHIP HAND	WIGGINGS	WIREWORK	WOODWORM
WELL-HUNG	WHIPLASH	WIGGLING	WIREWORM	WOOLLENS
WELL-KNIT	WHIPLIKE	WILD BOAR	WIRE-WOVE	WOOLLIER
WELL-NIGH	WHIPPETS	WILD CARD	WIRINESS	WOOLLIES
WELL READ	WHIPPING	WILDCATS	WISEACRE	WOOLLILY
WELL-READ	WHIPWORM	WILD-EYED	WISE GUYS	WOOLPACK
WELL-TO-DO	WHIRLING	WILDFIRE	WISENESS	WOOLSACK
WELL-WORN	WHIRRING	WILDFOWL	WISHBONE	WOOZIEST
WELSHERS	WHISKERS	WILDLIFE	WISPIEST	WORDBOOK
WELSHING	WHISKERY	WILDNESS	WISTERIA	WORD-DEAF
WENCHING	WHISKIES	WILD OATS	WITCHERY	WORDIEST
WEREWOLF	WHISKING	WILD WEST	WITCHING	WORDLESS
WESLEYAN	WHISPERS	WILFULLY	WITHDRAW	WORDPLAY
WEST BANK	WHISTLED	WILINESS	WITHDREW	WORKABLE
WESTERLY	WHISTLER	WILLABLE	WITHERED	WORKADAY
WESTERNS	WHISTLES	WILLIWAW	WITHERER	WORKBAGS
WESTWARD	WHITE ANT	WINCHING	WITHHELD	WORKBOOK
WESTWOOD	WHITECAP	WINDABLE	WITHHOLD	WORKDAYS
WET DREAM	WHITE-EYE	WINDBAGS	WITTIEST	WORKED UP
WET NURSE	WHITEFLY	WINDBURN	WIZARDRY	WORKINGS
WET SUITS	WHITE-HOT	WINDFALL	WOBBLIER	WORKLOAD
WETTABLE	WHITE LIE	WINDGALL	WOBBLING	WORKOUTS
WETTINGS	WHITENED	WINDHOEK	WOEFULLY	WORKROOM
WEYMOUTH	WHITENER	WINDIEST	WOLFFISH	WORKSHOP
WHACKING	WHITEOUT	WINDLASS	WOLFLIKE	WORKTOPS
WHARFAGE	WHITE-TIE	WINDMILL	WOMANISH	WORLD CUP
WHATEVER	WHITINGS	WINDPIPE	WOMANIST	WORM CAST
WHATNOTS	WHITLOWS	WINDSAIL	WOMANIZE	WORM GEAR
WHATSITS	WHITTLED	WINDSOCK	WOMBLIKE	WORMHOLE
WHEATEAR	WHITTLER	WINDWARD	WONDERED	WORMIEST
WHEEDLED	WHIZ-BANG	WINE BARS	WONDERER	WORMLIKE
WHEEDLER	WHIZZING	WINESKIN	WONDROUS	WORMSEED
WHEELIES	WHIZZ KID	WINGLESS	WONKIEST	WORMWOOD
WHEELING	WHODUNIT	WINGLIKE	WOODBINE	WORRIERS

WORRYING	WRIGGLED	X-RAY TUBE	YOUNGEST	ZIONISTS
WORSENED	WRIGGLER	XYLIDINE	YOUNGISH	ZIP CODES
WORSE-OFF	WRIGGLES	XYLOCARP	YOURSELF	ZIPPIEST
WORSHIPS	WRINGERS	XYLOTOMY	YOUTHFUL	ZIRCONIA
WORSTING	WRINGING		YTTERBIA	ZIRCONIC
WORST-OFF	WRINKLED	**Y**	YUCKIEST	ZLATOUST
WORTHIER	WRINKLES	YACHTING	YUGOSLAV	ZODIACAL
WORTHIES	WRISTLET	YAHOOISM	YULE LOGS	ZOMBIISM
WORTHILY	WRITE-INS	YAKITORI	YULETIDE	ZONATION
WORTHING	WRITE OFF	YAMMERED	YVELINES	ZONETIME
WOUNDING	WRITE-OFF	YAMMERER		ZOOCHORE
WRANGLED	WRITE-UPS	YARDARMS	**Z**	ZOOGLOEA
WRANGLER	WRITHING	YARN-DYED	ZAANSTAD	ZOOLATER
WRANGLES	WRITINGS	YASHMAKS	ZAIBATSU	ZOOLATRY
WRAPOVER	WRONGFUL	YEANLING	ZANINESS	ZOOMETRY
WRAPPERS	WRONGING	YEARBOOK	ZANZIBAR	ZOOM LENS
WRAPPING	WURZBURG	YEARLING	ZAPPIEST	ZOONOSIS
WRATHFUL		YEARLONG	ZARAGOZA	ZOOPHILE
WREAKING	**X**	YEARNING	ZARATITE	ZOOPHYTE
WREATHED	XANTHATE	YEASTILY	ZEALOTRY	ZOOSPERM
WRECKAGE	XANTHEIN	YELLOWED	ZECCHINO	ZOOSPORE
WRECKERS	XANTHENE	YEOMANLY	ZENITHAL	ZOOTOMIC
WRECKING	XANTHINE	YEOMANRY	ZEOLITIC	ZOOTOXIC
WRENCHED	XANTHOMA	YIELDING	ZEPPELIN	ZOOTOXIN
WRENCHES	XANTHOUS	YODELING	ZERO HOUR	ZUCCHINI
WRESTING	XENOGAMY	YODELLED	ZHEJIANG	ZUGZWANG
WRESTLED	XENOLITH	YODELLER	ZHITOMIR	ZULULAND
WRESTLER	XEROSERE	YOKELISH	ZIBELINE	ZWIEBACK
WRETCHED	XEROXING	YOKOHAMA	ZILLIONS	ZYGOTENE
WRETCHES	XIANGTAN	YOKOSUKA	ZIMBABWE	ZYMOLOGY

9

A	ABSTAINER	ACHIEVING	ADDRESSER	ADVENTURE
AARON'S ROD	ABSTINENT	ACICULATE	ADDRESSES	ADVERBIAL
ABACTINAL	ABSTRACTS	ACID HOUSE	ADDUCTION	ADVERSARY
ABANDONED	ABSURDISM	ACIDIFIED	ADEMPTION	ADVERSELY
ABASEMENT	ABSURDITY	ACIDIFIER	ADENOIDAL	ADVERSITY
ABASHEDLY	ABUNDANCE	ACIDOPHIL	ADENOSINE	ADVERTING
ABATEMENT	ABU SIMBEL	ACID TESTS	ADHERENCE	ADVERTISE
ABATTOIRS	ABUSIVELY	ACIDULATE	ADHERENTS	ADVISABLE
ABCOULOMB	ABUTMENTS	ACIDULOUS	ADHESIONS	ADVISEDLY
ABDICABLE	ABYSSINIA	ACINIFORM	ADHESIVES	ADVOCATED
ABDICATED	ACADEMICS	ACOUSTICS	ADIABATIC	ADVOCATES
ABDICATOR	ACANTHINE	ACQUIESCE	AD INTERIM	AEOLIPILE
ABDOMINAL	ACANTHOID	ACQUIRING	ADIPOCERE	AEPYORNIS
ABDUCTING	ACANTHOUS	ACQUITTAL	ADJACENCY	AEROBATIC
ABDUCTION	ACARIASIS	ACQUITTED	ADJECTIVE	AERODROME
ABERRANCE	ACAROLOGY	ACQUITTER	ADJOINING	AEROLOGIC
ABHORRENT	ACCEDENCE	ACROBATIC	ADJOURNED	AEROMETER
ABHORRING	ACCENTING	ACRODROME	ADJUDGING	AEROMETRY
ABIDINGLY	ACCENTUAL	ACROGENIC	ADJUSTING	AEROPAUSE
ABILITIES	ACCEPTANT	ACRONYMIC	ADJUTANCY	AEROPHONE
A BIT THICK	ACCEPTING	ACROPETAL	ADJUTANTS	AEROPLANE
ABJECTION	ACCESSING	ACROPOLIS	AD-LIBBING	AEROSPACE
ABLUTIONS	ACCESSION	ACROSPIRE	ADMEASURE	AESTHESIA
ABNEGATOR	ACCESSORY	ACROSTICS	ADMINICLE	AESTHETES
ABOLISHED	ACCIDENCE	ACTINOPOD	ADMIRABLE	AESTHETIC
ABOLISHER	ACCIDENTS	ACTIVATED	ADMIRABLY	AESTIVATE
ABOLITION	ACCIPITER	ACTIVATOR	ADMIRALTY	AETHEREAL
ABOMINATE	ACCLAIMED	ACTIVISTS	ADMISSION	AETIOLOGY
ABORIGINE	ACCLIVITY	ACTRESSES	ADMISSIVE	AFFECTING
ABORTIONS	ACCOLADES	ACTS OF GOD	ADMITTING	AFFECTION
ABOUNDING	ACCOMPANY	ACTUALITY	ADMIXTURE	AFFECTIVE
ABOUT TURN	ACCORDANT	ACTUALIZE	AD NAUSEAM	AFFIANCED
ABOUT-TURN	ACCORDING	ACTUARIAL	ADNOMINAL	AFFIDAVIT
ABRASIONS	ACCORDION	ACTUARIES	ADOPTIONS	AFFILIATE
ABRASIVES	ACCOSTING	ACTUATING	ADORATION	AFFIRMING
ABRIDGING	ACCOUNTED	ACTUATION	ADORNMENT	AFFIXTURE
ABROGATED	ACCRETION	ACUMINATE	ADRENALIN	AFFLICTED
ABROGATOR	ACCRETIVE	ACUMINOUS	ADSORBATE	AFFLUENCE
ABSCESSES	ACCRUMENT	ACUTENESS	ADSORBENT	AFFORDING
ABSCONDED	ACCUMBENT	ACYCLOVIR	ADULATION	AFFRICATE
ABSCONDER	ACELLULAR	ADAMANTLY	ADULATORY	AFFRONTED
ABSEILING	ACESCENCE	ADAPTABLE	ADULTERER	AFLATOXIN
ABSENTEES	ACETAMIDE	ADDICTION	ADUMBRATE	AFORESAID
ABSENTING	ACETIFIER	ADDICTIVE	AD VALOREM	A FORTIORI
ABSOLVING	ACETYLATE	ADDITIONS	ADVANCING	AFRIKAANS
ABSORBENT	ACETYLENE	ADDITIVES	ADVANTAGE	AFRIKANER
ABSORBING	ACETYLIDE	ADDRESSED	ADVECTION	AFRO-ASIAN
ABSTAINED	ACHEULIAN	ADDRESSEE	ADVENTIVE	AFTERBODY

AFTERCARE	ALCHEMIST	ALLOPHONE	AMBITIOUS	ANACLINAL
AFTERDAMP	ALCHEMIZE	ALLOPLASM	AMBLESIDE	ANACLISIS
AFTERDECK	ALCOHOLIC	ALLOTMENT	AMBLYOPIA	ANACLITIC
AFTERGLOW	ALDEBARAN	ALLOTROPE	AMBLYOPIC	ANACONDAS
AFTERHEAT	ALDEBURGH	ALLOTROPY	AMBROSIAL	ANACRUSIS
AFTERLIFE	ALDERSHOT	ALLOTTING	AMBROTYPE	ANAEROBIC
AFTERMATH	ALEHOUSES	ALLOWABLE	AMBULANCE	ANALECTIC
AFTERNOON	ALEMANNIC	ALLOWABLY	AMBUSHING	ANALEPTIC
AFTERWORD	ALEPH-NULL	ALLOWANCE	AMENDABLE	ANALGESIA
AGE GROUPS	ALERTNESS	ALLOWEDLY	AMENDMENT	ANALGESIC
AGGRAVATE	ALFILARIA	ALLUSIONS	AMENITIES	ANALOGIES
AGGREGATE	ALGARROBA	ALLUVIUMS	AMERASIAN	ANALOGIST
AGGRESSOR	ALGEBRAIC	ALMA MATER	AMERICANA	ANALOGIZE
AGGRIEVED	ALGECIRAS	ALMANDINE	AMERICANS	ANALOGOUS
AGITATING	ALGOMETER	ALMSHOUSE	AMERICIUM	ANALOGUES
AGITATION	ALGOMETRY	ALMS-HOUSE	AMERINDIC	ANALYSAND
AGITATORS	ALGONQUIN	ALONGSIDE	AMETHYSTS	ANALYSING
AGNOLOTTI	ALGORITHM	ALOOFNESS	AMETROPIA	ANALYTICS
AGNOMINAL	ALICE BAND	ALPENGLOW	AMIANTHUS	ANAMNESIS
AGNOSTICS	ALICYCLIC	ALPHABETS	AMIDSHIPS	ANANDROUS
AGONISTIC	ALIENABLE	ALSATIANS	AMINO ACID	ANANTHOUS
AGONIZING	ALIENATED	ALTERABLE	AMMOCOETE	ANAPAESTS
AGREEABLE	ALIENATOR	ALTERCATE	AMMONIATE	ANAPESTIC
AGREEABLY	ALIGHTING	ALTER EGOS	AMMONICAL	ANAPHORAL
AGREEMENT	ALIGNMENT	ALTERNATE	AMMONITIC	ANAPLASIA
AGRIGENTO	ALIPHATIC	ALTIMETER	AMNESIACS	ANAPLASTY
AGRONOMIC	ALKALOSIS	ALTIMETRY	AMNESTIES	ANAPTYXIS
AGTERSKOT	ALLA BREVE	ALTIPLANO	AMOEBAEAN	ANARCHISM
AHMEDABAD	ALLAHABAD	ALTISSIMO	AMORALITY	ANARCHIST
AILANTHUS	ALLANTOIC	ALTITUDES	AMOROUSLY	ANARTHRIA
AIMLESSLY	ALLANTOID	ALTRICIAL	AMORPHISM	ANATHEMAS
AIRBRAKES	ALLANTOIS	ALTRUISTS	AMORPHOUS	ANATOLIAN
AIRFIELDS	ALL-AROUND	ALUMINATE	AMORTIZED	ANATOMIES
AIRFORCES	ALL AT ONCE	ALUMINIUM	AMOUNTING	ANATOMIST
AIR GUITAR	ALLEGEDLY	ALUMINIZE	AMPERSAND	ANATOMIZE
AIR-INTAKE	ALLELUIAS	ALUMINOUS	AMPHIBIAN	ANCESTORS
AIRLETTER	ALL ENDS UP	ALVEOLARS	AMPHIBOLE	ANCESTRAL
AIRLIFTED	ALLENTOWN	ALVEOLATE	AMPHIGORY	ANCHORAGE
AIRLINERS	ALLERGIES	AMAGASAKI	AMPHIOXUS	ANCHORESS
AIRPLANES	ALLERGIST	AMARYLLIS	AMPLIFIED	ANCHORING
AIRPOCKET	ALLETHRIN	AMAUROSIS	AMPLIFIER	ANCHORITE
AIRSTREAM	ALLEVIATE	AMAUROTIC	AMPLITUDE	ANCHOVIES
AIRSTRIPS	ALLEYWAYS	AMAZEMENT	AMPUTATED	ANCILLARY
AIRWORTHY	ALLIANCES	AMAZINGLY	AMSTERDAM	ANCIPITAL
AITCHBONE	ALLIGATOR	AMAZONIAN	AMUSEMENT	ANDALUSIA
ALABAMIAN	ALLOCATED	AMAZONITE	AMUSINGLY	ANDANTINO
ALABASTER	ALLOGRAFT	AMBERGRIS	AMYGDALIN	ANDRADITE
ALARM BELL	ALLOGRAPH	AMBERJACK	AMYLOPSIN	ANDROLOGY
ALARMISTS	ALLOMETRY	AMBIENCES	ANABANTID	ANDROMEDA
ALBATROSS	ALLOMORPH	AMBIGUITY	ANABIOSIS	ANECDOTAL
ALBERTITE	ALLOPATHY	AMBIGUOUS	ANABOLISM	ANECDOTES
ALBESCENT	ALLOPHANE	AMBITIONS	ANABOLITE	ANECDOTIC

ANEMOLOGY	ANORTHITE	APELDOORN	APPOINTED	ARCOGRAPH
ANEUPLOID	ANOSMATIC	APENNINES	APPOINTEE	ARCTOGAEA
ANGEL CAKE	ANOXAEMIA	APERIODIC	APPOINTER	ARCTURIAN
ANGELFISH	ANOXAEMIC	APERITIFS	APPOINTOR	ARCUATION
ANGELICAL	ANSWERING	APERTURES	APPORTION	ARDUOUSLY
ANGIOGRAM	ANTALKALI	APETALOUS	APPRAISAL	AREA CODES
ANGIOLOGY	ANTARCTIC	APHERESIS	APPRAISED	ARGENTINA
ANGLE IRON	ANTEATERS	APHIDIOUS	APPRAISER	ARGENTINE
ANGLESITE	ANTECHOIR	APHORISMS	APPREHEND	ARGENTITE
ANGLEWORM	ANTEDATED	APHYLLOUS	APPRESSED	ARGENTOUS
ANGLICANS	ANTEFIXAL	APICULATE	APPRISING	ARGILLITE
ANGLICISM	ANTELOPES	APISHNESS	APPROBATE	ARGUMENTS
ANGLICIZE	ANTENATAL	APIVOROUS	APPROVING	ARMADILLO
ANGOSTURA	ANTENNULE	APLANATIC	APPULSIVE	ARMAMENTS
ANGUISHED	ANTEROOMS	APOCOPATE	APRIL FOOL	ARMATURES
ANHYDRIDE	ANTHELION	APOCRYPHA	APRIORITY	ARMCHAIRS
ANHYDRITE	ANTHEMION	APODICTIC	APTITUDES	ARMISTICE
ANHYDROUS	ANTHODIUM	APOENZYME	AQUALUNGS	ARMOURERS
ANIMALISM	ANTHOLOGY	APOGAMOUS	AQUAPLANE	ARMOURIES
ANIMALIST	ANTHOTAXY	APOLOGIAS	AQUARELLE	ARMS RACES
ANIMALITY	ANTHOZOAN	APOLOGIES	AQUARIUMS	AROMATIZE
ANIMALIZE	ANTHURIUM	APOLOGIST	AQUATINTS	ARPEGGIOS
ANIMATEUR	ANTICHLOR	APOLOGIZE	AQUEDUCTS	ARRAIGNED
ANIMATING	ANTICLINE	APOPHASIS	AQUILEGIA	ARRAIGNER
ANIMATION	ANTIDOTES	APOPHYSIS	AQUITAINE	ARRANGING
ANIMATISM	ANTIGENIC	APOPTOSIS	ARABESQUE	ARRESTING
ANIMISTIC	ANTIKNOCK	APOSTATES	ARABINOSE	ARRIVISTE
ANIMOSITY	ANTIMERIC	APOSTOLIC	ARACHNOID	ARROGANCE
ANISOGAMY	ANTIMONIC	APPALLING	ARAGONESE	ARROGATED
ANKLEBONE	ANTIMONYL	APPALOOSA	ARAGONITE	ARROGATOR
ANKYLOSIS	ANTINODAL	APPARATUS	ARAUCANIA	ARROWHEAD
ANNALISTS	ANTINOMIC	APPARITOR	ARAUCARIA	ARROWROOT
ANNAPOLIS	ANTIPATHY	APPEALING	ARBITRAGE	ARROWWOOD
ANNAPURNA	ANTIPHONY	APPEARING	ARBITRARY	ARROWWORM
ANNEALING	ANTIPODAL	APPEASING	ARBITRATE	ARSENICAL
ANNELIDAN	ANTIPODES	APPELLANT	ARBITRESS	ARSENIOUS
ANNOTATED	ANTIQUARY	APPELLATE	ARBOREOUS	ARSONISTS
ANNOTATOR	ANTIQUATE	APPENDAGE	ARBORETUM	ARTEFACTS
ANNOUNCED	ANTIQUITY	APPENDANT	ARBOVIRUS	ARTEMISIA
ANNOUNCER	ANTISERUM	APPENDING	ARCHAISMS	ARTERIOLE
ANNOYANCE	ANTITOXIC	APPENZELL	ARCHAIZER	ARTERITIS
ANNUITANT	ANTITOXIN	APPERTAIN	ARCHANGEL	ARTHRITIC
ANNUITIES	ANTIVENIN	APPETENCE	ARCHDUCAL	ARTHRITIS
ANNULLING	ANTIVIRAL	APPETITES	ARCHDUCHY	ARTHROPOD
ANNULMENT	ANTIWORLD	APPETIZER	ARCHDUKES	ARTICHOKE
ANOESTRUS	ANTONIONI	APPLAUDED	ARCHENEMY	ARTICLING
ANOINTING	ANXIETIES	APPLAUDER	ARCHETYPE	ARTICULAR
ANOMALIES	ANXIOUSLY	APPLE CART	ARCHFIEND	ARTIFACTS
ANOMALOUS	ANY AMOUNT	APPLEJACK	ARCHICARP	ARTIFICER
ANONYMITY	APARTHEID	APPLE PIES	ARCHITECT	ARTIFICES
ANONYMOUS	APARTMENT	APPLIANCE	ARCHIVIST	ARTILLERY
ANOPHELES	APATHETIC	APPLICANT	ARCHIVOLT	ARTLESSLY

ARYTENOID	ASSURGENT	ATTENUATE	AUTOMATIC	BACKCROSS
ASCENDANT	ASTERISKS	ATTESTANT	AUTOMATON	BACKDATED
ASCENDING	ASTEROIDS	ATTESTING	AUTONOMIC	BACK DOORS
ASCENSION	ASTHMATIC	AT THE TIME	AUTOPHYTE	BACKDROPS
ASCERTAIN	ASTOUNDED	ATTITUDES	AUTOPSIES	BACKFIRED
ASCOSPORE	ASTRADDLE	ATTORNEYS	AUTOSOMAL	BACKHANDS
ASCRIBING	ASTRAKHAN	ATTRACTED	AUTOTIMER	BACKPACKS
ASEPALOUS	ASTROCYTE	ATTRACTOR	AUTOTOMIC	BACKPEDAL
ASEXUALLY	ASTRODOME	ATTRIBUTE	AUTOTOXIC	BACK PEDAL
ASHAMEDLY	ASTROLABE	ATTRITION	AUTOTOXIN	BACK SEATS
ASHKENAZI	ASTROLOGY	ATTRITIVE	AUTOTYPIC	BACK SHIFT
ASHKHABAD	ASTRONAUT	AUBERGINE	AUXILIARY	BACKSIDES
ASININITY	ASTRONOMY	AUBRIETIA	AVAILABLE	BACKSIGHT
ASPARAGUS	ASYLLABIC	AU COURANT	AVAILABLY	BACKSLIDE
ASPERSION	ASYMMETRY	AUCTIONED	AVALANCHE	BACKSPACE
ASPERSIVE	ASYMPTOTE	AUCTORIAL	AVERAGING	BACKSTAGE
ASPHALTED	ASYNDETIC	AUDACIOUS	AVERSIONS	BACKSWEPT
ASPHALTIC	ASYNDETON	AUDIENCES	AVERTIBLE	BACKTRACK
ASPHALTUM	AT A GLANCE	AUDIO BOOK	AVIFAUNAL	BACKWARDS
ASPHYXIAL	ATARACTIC	AUDIOLOGY	AVIRULENT	BACKWATER
ASPIRANTS	ATAVISTIC	AUDIPHONE	AVOCATION	BACKWOODS
ASPIRATED	ATHEISTIC	AUDITIONS	AVOIDABLE	BACKYARDS
ASPIRATES	ATHENAEUM	AUGMENTED	AVOIDANCE	BACTERIAL
ASPIRATOR	ATHLETICS	AUGMENTOR	AVUNCULAR	BACTERIUM
ASSAILANT	ATLANTEAN	AU NATUREL	AWAKENING	BACTEROID
ASSAILING	ATMOLYSIS	AUNT SALLY	AWARDABLE	BADGERING
ASSASSINS	ATMOMETER	AURICULAR	AWARENESS	BADMINTON
ASSAULTED	ATMOMETRY	AUSCHWITZ	AWESTRUCK	BAGATELLE
ASSAULTER	ATOM BOMBS	AUSTENITE	AWFULNESS	BAGGINESS
ASSAYABLE	ATOMICITY	AUSTERELY	AWKWARDLY	BAG LADIES
ASSEMBLED	ATOMISTIC	AUSTERITY	AXIOMATIC	BAHUVRIHI
ASSEMBLER	ATOMIZERS	AUSTRALIA	AYAHUASCA	BAILIWICK
ASSENTING	ATONALISM	AUTARCHIC	AYATOLLAH	BAIN-MARIE
ASSERTING	ATONALITY	AUTARKIES	AYUTTHAYA	BAKHTARAN
ASSERTION	ATONEMENT	AUTHENTIC	AZEDARACH	BALACLAVA
ASSERTIVE	AT ONE TIME	AUTHORESS	AZEOTROPE	BALAKLAVA
ASSESSING	ATONICITY	AUTHORIAL	AZIMUTHAL	BALALAIKA
ASSESSORS	AT PRESENT	AUTHORITY		BALANCING
ASSIDUITY	ATROCIOUS	AUTHORIZE	**B**	BALCONIES
ASSIDUOUS	ATROPHIED	AUTOCLAVE	BAAGANDJI	BALEFULLY
ASSIGNING	ATTACHING	AUTOCRACY	BABY TEETH	BALKANIZE
ASSISTANT	ATTACKERS	AUTOCRATS	BABY TOOTH	BALLASTED
ASSISTING	ATTACKING	AUTOCROSS	BACCHANAL	BALLCOCKS
ASSOCIATE	ATTAINDER	AUTOECISM	BACCIFORM	BALLERINA
ASSONANCE	ATTAINING	AUTOFOCUS	BACHELORS	BALL GAMES
ASSORTING	ATTEMPTED	AUTOGRAFT	BACILLARY	BALLISTIC
ASSUAGING	ATTEMPTER	AUTOGRAPH	BACKACHES	BALLOONED
ASSUASIVE	ATTENDANT	AUTOICOUS	BACKBENCH	BALLOTING
ASSUMABLE	ATTENDING	AUTOLYSIN	BACKBITER	BALLOTINI
ASSURABLE	ATTENTION	AUTOLYSIS	BACKBOARD	BALLPOINT
ASSURANCE	ATTENTIVE	AUTOLYTIC	BACKBONES	BALLROOMS
ASSUREDLY	ATTENUANT	AUTOMATED	BACKCLOTH	BALLYMENA

BALMINESS	BARITONES	BEACHHEAD	BEHAVIOUR	BETHOUGHT
BALTHAZAR	BAR KOCHBA	BEACHSIDE	BEHEADING	BETOKENED
BALTIMORE	BARNACLES	BEACHWEAR	BEHOLDERS	BETRAYALS
BAMBOOZLE	BARN DANCE	BEADINESS	BEHOLDING	BETRAYERS
BANBRIDGE	BARNSTORM	BEAN FEAST	BELATEDLY	BETRAYING
BANDAGING	BARNYARDS	BEARBERRY	BELEAGUER	BETROTHAL
BANDANNAS	BAROGRAPH	BEARDLESS	BELEMNITE	BETROTHED
BANDEROLE	BAROMETER	BEARISHLY	BELGRAVIA	BETTERING
BANDICOOT	BARONETCY	BEARNAISE	BELIEVERS	BETTER-OFF
BANDOLEER	BAROSCOPE	BEAR'S-FOOT	BELIEVING	BEVELLING
BANDOLIER	BARRACKED	BEARSKINS	BELITTLED	BEVERAGES
BANDSTAND	BARRACUDA	BEASTLIER	BELITTLER	BEWAILING
BANDWAGON	BARRETTES	BEATIFIED	BELLATRIX	BEWITCHED
BANDWIDTH	BARRICADE	BEATITUDE	BELLICOSE	BHAGALPUR
BANEBERRY	BARRISTER	BEAUMARIS	BELLOWING	BHARATIYA
BANEFULLY	BARROW BOY	BEAU MONDE	BELLYACHE	BHAVNAGAR
BANGALORE	BARTENDER	BEAUTEOUS	BELLY FLOP	BHUTANESE
BANISHING	BARTERING	BEAUTIFUL	BELONGING	BIALYSTOK
BANISTERS	BASEBALLS	BEAUX-ARTS	BELVEDERE	BIBLIOTIC
BANJA LUKA	BASEBOARD	BEAVERING	BEMOANING	BICIPITAL
BANKBOOKS	BASELINES	BEBEERINE	BENCHMARK	BICKERING
BANK DRAFT	BASEMENTS	BEBINGTON	BENCH MARK	BICONCAVE
BANK NOTES	BASE METAL	BECCAFICO	BENEFICES	BICYCLING
BANKROLLS	BASE RATES	BECKONING	BENEFITED	BICYCLIST
BANKRUPTS	BASHFULLY	BECQUEREL	BENEVENTO	BIDENTATE
BANNISTER	BASICALLY	BEDAUBING	BENGALESE	BIELEFELD
BANQUETED	BASIFIXED	BEDECKING	BENGALINE	BIFARIOUS
BANQUETTE	BASILICAN	BEDEVILED	BENIGHTED	BIFOLIATE
BANTERING	BASILICAS	BEDFELLOW	BENIGNANT	BIFURCATE
BANTUSTAN	BASILISKS	BEDRAGGLE	BENIGNITY	BIGAMISTS
BAPTISMAL	BASIPETAL	BEDRIDDEN	BENIN CITY	BIGARREAU
BAPTIZING	BAS RELIEF	BED-SITTER	BENTONITE	BIG DIPPER
BARBADIAN	BAS-RELIEF	BEDSPREAD	BENZIDINE	BIGENERIC
BARBARIAN	BASS CLEFS	BEDSTEADS	BERBERINE	BIG-TIMERS
BARBARISM	BASSINETS	BEEFEATER	BEREAVING	BIGUANIDE
BARBARITY	BASTINADO	BEEFINESS	BEREZNIKI	BIG WHEELS
BARBARIZE	BATH CHAIR	BEEFSTEAK	BERIOSOVA	BIJECTION
BARBAROUS	BATHOLITH	BEEKEEPER	BERKELIUM	BIJECTIVE
BARBECUED	BATHROBES	BEELZEBUB	BERKSHIRE	BILABIALS
BARBECUES	BATHROOMS	BEERINESS	BERYLLIUM	BILABIATE
BARBICANS	BATHWATER	BEERSHEBA	BESEECHED	BILATERAL
BARBITONE	BATTALION	BEESTINGS	BESETTING	BILHARZIA
BARCAROLE	BATTENING	BEETLE OFF	BESIEGING	BILINGUAL
BARCELONA	BATTERIES	BEETROOTS	BESMEARED	BILIRUBIN
BAR CHARTS	BATTERING	BEFALLING	BESPATTER	BILLBOARD
BARE BONES	BATTINESS	BEFITTING	BESTIALLY	BILLETING
BAREFACED	BATTLEAXE	BEGETTING	BESTIRRED	BILLFOLDS
BARE FACED	BATTLE CRY	BEGGARING	BESTOWING	BILLHOOKS
BARGAINED	BAWDINESS	BEGINNERS	BESTREWED	BILLIARDS
BARGAINER	BAYONETED	BEGINNING	BETE NOIRE	BILLIONTH
BARGE POLE	BAY WINDOW	BEGRUDGED	BETE-NOIRE	BILLOWING
BAR GRAPHS	BEACH BALL	BEGUILING	BETHLEHEM	BILLY GOAT

BILOCULAR	BLACKHEAD	BLOCKAGES	BOARHOUND	BOOKSTALL
BIMONTHLY	BLACK HOLE	BLOCKHEAD	BOAT HOOKS	BOOKSTAND
BIN-LINERS	BLACK ISLE	BLOCK VOTE	BOATHOUSE	BOOK TOKEN
BINOCULAR	BLACKJACK	BLONDNESS	BOATSWAIN	BOOKWORMS
BINOMIALS	BLACK LEAD	BLOOD BANK	BOAT TRAIN	BOOMERANG
BINTURONG	BLACKLEGS	BLOODBATH	BOBBEJAAN	BOOMSLANG
BINUCLEAR	BLACKLIST	BLOOD FEUD	BOBBY PINS	BOONDOCKS
BIOGRAPHY	BLACKMAIL	BLOOD HEAT	BOBSLEIGH	BOORISHLY
BIOHAZARD	BLACK MASS	BLOODLESS	BOBTAILED	BOOTBLACK
BIOLOGIST	BLACKNESS	BLOOD LUST	BOCCACCIO	BOOTHROYD
BIOMETRIC	BLACKOUTS	BLOODROOT	BODACIOUS	BOOTLACES
BIONOMICS	BLACKPOLL	BLOODSHED	BODY BLOWS	BOOTMAKER
BIONOMIST	BLACKPOOL	BLOODSHOT	BODYCHECK	BOOTSTRAP
BIOSPHERE	BLACK SPOT	BLOOD TYPE	BODYGUARD	BOOZINESS
BIOSTATIC	BLACKTAIL	BLOODWORM	BOGGINESS	BORDELLOS
BIOSTROME	BLAMELESS	BLOSSOMED	BOHEMIANS	BORDERING
BIPARTITE	BLANCHING	BLOTCHIER	BOILINGLY	BOREHOLES
BIPINNATE	BLANDNESS	BLOTCHILY	BOLDFACED	BORN-AGAIN
BIRDHOUSE	BLANKETED	BLOW-DRIED	BOLECTION	BORROWERS
BIRD HOUSE	BLANKNESS	BLOW-DRIES	BOLEGNESE	BORROWING
BIRD'S-FOOT	BLASPHEME	BLOWFLIES	BOLIVIANO	BOSSA NOVA
BIRTHDAYS	BLASPHEMY	BLOWHARDS	BOLLINGER	BOSSINESS
BIRTHMARK	BLASTEMIC	BLOWHOLES	BOLLYWOOD	BOTANICAL
BIRTHRATE	BLASTULAR	BLOWLAMPS	BOLOMETER	BOTANISTS
BIRTHROOT	BLATANTLY	BLOWPIPES	BOLSHEVIK	BOTANIZED
BIRTHWORT	BLATHERED	BLOWTORCH	BOLSHIEST	BOTCHIEST
BISECTING	BLAZONING	BLOWZIEST	BOLSTERED	BOTHERING
BISECTION	BLEACHERS	BLUBBERED	BOLSTERER	BOTTLE-FED
BISECTRIX	BLEACHING	BLUDGEONS	BOLTHOLES	BOTULINUS
BISERRATE	BLEAKNESS	BLUEBEARD	BOMBARDED	BOUILLONS
BISEXUALS	BLEARIEST	BLUEBELLS	BOMBARDON	BOULEVARD
BISHOPRIC	BLEMISHED	BLUEBERRY	BOMBASTIC	BOUNCIEST
BISMUTHAL	BLEMISHER	BLUEBIRDS	BOMBAZINE	BOUNDLESS
BISMUTHIC	BLEMISHES	BLUE-BLACK	BOMBPROOF	BOUNTEOUS
BISULCATE	BLENCHING	BLUE BLOOD	BOMBSHELL	BOUNTIFUL
BITCHIEST	BLENNIOID	BLUE BOOKS	BOMBSIGHT	BOURGEOIS
BITTERNUT	BLESSEDLY	BLUE CHIPS	BOMBSITES	BOUTIQUES
BITTINESS	BLESSINGS	BLUE FILMS	BONA FIDES	BOWERBIRD
BIVALENCY	BLETHERED	BLUEGRASS	BONEBLACK	BOW LEGGED
BIZARRELY	BLIGHTERS	BLUE JEANS	BONE CHINA	BOW-LEGGED
BLABBERED	BLIGHTING	BLUE PETER	BONEHEADS	BOWSPRITS
BLACKBALL	BLIND DATE	BLUEPRINT	BONINGTON	BOWSTRING
BLACK BELT	BLINDFISH	BLUESTONE	BON VIVANT	BOW WINDOW
BLACKBIRD	BLINDFOLD	BLUFFNESS	BOOBY TRAP	BOX AND COX
BLACKBUCK	BLINDNESS	BLUNDERED	BOOHOOING	BOXING DAY
BLACKBURN	BLIND SPOT	BLUNDERER	BOOKCASES	BOX NUMBER
BLACKCOCK	BLINKERED	BLUNTNESS	BOOK CLUBS	BOX OFFICE
BLACKDAMP	BLISTERED	BLURREDLY	BOOKMAKER	BOYCOTTED
BLACKENED	BLIZZARDS	BLUSTERED	BOOKMARKS	BOYFRIEND
BLACK EYES	BLOCKADED	BLUSTERER	BOOKPLATE	BOYLE'S LAW
BLACKFACE	BLOCKADER	BOARDROOM	BOOKSHELF	BOY SCOUTS
BLACKFISH	BLOCKADES	BOARDWALK	BOOKSHOPS	BRACELETS

BRACHIATE	BRIC-A-BRAC	BRUNSWICK	BULL'S-EYES	BYPASSING
BRACINGLY	BRICKWORK	BRUSH-OFFS	BULLY BEEF	BY-PRODUCT
BRACKETED	BRICKYARD	BRUSHWOOD	BULLYBOYS	BYSTANDER
BRACKNELL	BRICOLAGE	BRUSHWORK	BULLY-OFFS	BY THE BOOK
BRACTEATE	BRIEFCASE	BRUSQUELY	BULRUSHES	BYZANTINE
BRACTEOLE	BRIGADIER	BRUTALITY	BUMBLEBEE	BYZANTIUM
BRAGGARTS	BRIGHOUSE	BRUTALIZE	BUMIPUTRA	
BRAINIEST	BRILLIANT	BRUTISHLY	BUMPINESS	**C**
BRAINLESS	BRIMSTONE	BRYLCREEM	BUMPTIOUS	CABALLERO
BRAINSICK	BRININESS	BRYOPHYTE	BUNDABERG	CABIN BOYS
BRAINWASH	BRIOLETTE	BRYTHONIC	BUNDESRAT	CABINETRY
BRAINWAVE	BRIQUETTE	BUBBLE GUM	BUNDESTAG	CABLE CARS
BRAIN WAVE	BRISKNESS	BUBBLIEST	BUNGALOWS	CABLEGRAM
BRAINWAVE	BRISTLING	BUCCANEER	BUNGHOLES	CABLE-LAID
BRAKE SHOE	BRITANNIA	BUCHAREST	BUNKHOUSE	CABOODLES
BRAKESMAN	BRITANNIC	BUCKBOARD	BUOYANTLY	CABRIOLET
BRAMBLING	BRITICISM	BUCKETING	BUPRESTID	CACHECTIC
BRANCHIAL	BRITISHER	BUCKHOUND	BURDENING	CACODEMON
BRANCHING	BRITTONIC	BUCKTEETH	BURGEONED	CACOETHES
BRANDLING	BROACHING	BUCKTHORN	BURGESSES	CACOETHIC
BRAND NAME	BROADBAND	BUCKTOOTH	BURLESQUE	CACOPHONY
BRANTFORD	BROAD BEAN	BUCKWHEAT	BURLINESS	CACUMINAL
BRASHNESS	BROADBILL	BUCKYBALL	BURMA ROAD	CAECILIAN
BRASS BAND	BROADCAST	BUCKYTUBE	BURNINGLY	CAESAREAN
BRASS NECK	BROADENED	BUDDH GAYA	BURNISHED	CAFETERIA
BRASSERIE	BROAD JUMP	BUDDHISTS	BURNISHER	CAIRNGORM
BRASS HATS	BROADLEAF	BUDGETARY	BURNOUSES	CAITHNESS
BRASSIERE	BROADLOOM	BUDGETING	BURROUGHS	CALABOOSE
BRASSIEST	BROADNESS	BUFFALOES	BURROWING	CALAMANCO
BRAVENESS	BROADSIDE	BUFFERING	BURSARIAL	CALCANEAL
BRAWNIEST	BROADTAIL	BUFFETING	BURSARIES	CALCANEUS
BRAZENING	BROCADING	BUGGER ALL	BURSIFORM	CALCICOLE
BRAZILEIN	BROCHETTE	BUGGERING	BURTHENED	CALCIFIED
BRAZILIAN	BROCHURES	BUGLE CALL	BUSHELLER	CALCIFUGE
BREACHING	BROKERAGE	BUGLEWEED	BUSHINESS	CALCIMINE
BREAD BINS	BROMELIAD	BUHRSTONE	BUSHWHACK	CALCULATE
BREADLINE	BROMEOSIN	BUILDINGS	BUTADIENE	CALCULOUS
BREADROOT	BROMINATE	BUJUMBURA	BUTCHERED	CALENDARS
BREAKABLE	BROMOFORM	BULGARIAN	BUTENANDT	CALENDERS
BREAKAGES	BRONCHIAL	BULGINESS	BUTESHIRE	CALENDULA
BREAKAWAY	BRONZE AGE	BULGINGLY	BUTHELEZI	CALENTURE
BREAKBEAT	BROODIEST	BULKHEADS	BUTTERBUR	CALIBRATE
BREAKDOWN	BROOKABLE	BULKINESS	BUTTERCUP	CALIPHATE
BREAKEVEN	BROOKLIME	BULLDOZED	BUTTERFAT	CALL A HALT
BREAKFAST	BROOKWEED	BULLDOZER	BUTTERFLY	CALL BOXES
BREAKNECK	BROOMCORN	BULLETINS	BUTTERINE	CALL GIRLS
BREATHILY	BROOMRAPE	BULLFIGHT	BUTTERING	CALLOSITY
BREATHING	BROSCOPIC	BULLFINCH	BUTTERNUT	CALLOUSLY
BREECHING	BROTHERLY	BULLFROGS	BUTTONING	CALMATIVE
BRENTWOOD	BROUGHAMS	BULLHORNS	BUXOMNESS	CALORIFIC
BREXITEER	BROWN RICE	BULLISHLY	BUZZWORDS	CALUMNIES
BRIARROOT	BRUNETTES	BULLRINGS	BYDGOSZCZ	CALVARIES

CALVINISM	CANTONESE	CAREFULLY	CASH DESKS	CATECHIST
CALVINIST	CANVASSED	CARESSING	CASHIERED	CATECHIZE
CALVITIES	CANVASSER	CARETAKER	CASSAREEP	CATERWAUL
CAMBISTRY	CANVASSES	CARIBBEAN	CASSATION	CATHARSES
CAMBRIDGE	CAPACIOUS	CARIBBEES	CASSEROLE	CATHARSIS
CAMELHAIR	CAPACITOR	CARILLONS	CASSETTES	CATHARTIC
CAMELLIAS	CAPARISON	CARINTHIA	CASSIMERE	CATHEDRAL
CAMEMBERT	CAPE VERDE	CARIOSITY	CASSINGLE	CATHEPSIN
CAMERAMAN	CAPILLARY	CARMELITE	CASSOCKED	CATHETERS
CAMERAMEN	CAP IN HAND	CARNALIST	CASSOULET	CATHOLICS
CAMERA SHY	CAPITULAR	CARNALITY	CASSOWARY	CATOPTRIC
CAMISOLES	CAPITULUM	CARNATION	CAST ABOUT	CATTERIES
CAMPAIGNS	CAPRICCIO	CARNELIAN	CASTANETS	CATTINESS
CAMPANILE	CAPRICORN	CARNIVALS	CASTAWAYS	CATTLEMAN
CAMPANULA	CAPSAICIN	CARNIVORE	CASTIGATE	CAUCASOID
CAMPFIRES	CAPSICUMS	CARNOTITE	CASTILIAN	CAUDATION
CAMPHORIC	CAPSIZING	CAROLLING	CASTOR OIL	CAUGHT OUT
CAMPSITES	CAPSULATE	CAROTIDAL	CASTRATED	CAULDRONS
CAMSHAFTS	CAPTAINCY	CAROUSALS	CASTRATOR	CAUSALGIA
CANAANITE	CAPTAINED	CAROUSELS	CASUARINA	CAUSALITY
CANAL BOAT	CAPTIVATE	CAROUSING	CASUISTIC	CAUSATION
CANALIZED	CAPTIVITY	CARPACCIO	CASUISTRY	CAUSATIVE
CANAVERAL	CAPTURING	CARPENTER	CATABASIS	CAUSEWAYS
CANCELING	CARAPACES	CARPENTRY	CATABATIC	CAUTERANT
CANCELLED	CARBAMATE	CARPETBAG	CATABOLIC	CAUTERIZE
CANCELLER	CARBANION	CARPETING	CATACLYSM	CAUTIONED
CANCEROUS	CARBAZOLE	CARPOLOGY	CATACOMBS	CAVALCADE
CANDIDACY	CARBINEER	CARRAGEEN	CATALEPSY	CAVALIERS
CANDIDATE	CARBOLIZE	CARREFOUR	CATALOGUE	CAVENDISH
CANDLEMAS	CARBONADO	CARRIAGES	CATALONIA	CAVERNOUS
CANDLENUT	CARBONATE	CARRYALLS	CATALYSER	CAVILLERS
CANDYTUFT	CARBONIZE	CARRYCOTS	CATALYSIS	CAVILLING
CANESCENT	CARBONOUS	CARRY-OVER	CATALYSTS	CAVORTING
CANICULAR	CARBON TAX	CARTAGENA	CATALYTIC	CEASEFIRE
CANISTERS	CARBUNCLE	CARTESIAN	CATAMARAN	CEASE-FIRE
CANKEROUS	CARBURIZE	CARTHORSE	CATAMENIA	CEASELESS
CANNELURE	CARCASSES	CARTILAGE	CATAMOUNT	CELANDINE
CANNERIES	CARCINOMA	CARTOGRAM	CAT-AND-DOG	CELEBRANT
CANNIBALS	CARDBOARD	CARTOUCHE	CATAPHYLL	CELEBRATE
CANNINESS	CARDIGANS	CARTRIDGE	CATAPLASM	CELEBRITY
CANNONADE	CARDINALS	CART TRACK	CATAPLEXY	CELESTIAL
CANNONING	CARD INDEX	CARTULARY	CATAPULTS	CELESTITE
CANNULATE	CARDPHONE	CARTWHEEL	CATARACTS	CELIBATES
CANOEISTS	CARD PUNCH	CARYATIDS	CATARRHAL	CELLARAGE
CANONICAL	CARDPUNCH	CARYOPSIS	CATATONIA	CELLARMAN
CANONIZED	CARDSHARP	CASANOVAS	CATATONIC	CELLOIDIN
CANOODLED	CARD SHARP	CASCADING	CATCALLED	CELLULASE
CAN OPENER	CARD TABLE	CASEATION	CATCH CROP	CELLULOID
CANTABILE	CAREENING	CASEBOUND	CATCHIEST	CELLULOSE
CANTALOUP	CAREERING	CASE STUDY	CATCHMENT	CELTICIST
CANTERING	CAREERISM	CASH CARDS	CATCHWORD	CEMENTING
CANTICLES	CAREERIST	CASH CROPS	CATECHISM	CEMENTITE

CENOTAPHS	CHANCROID	CHELASHIP	CHISELLER	CHURCHMAN
CENSORIAL	CHANCROUS	CHELATION	CHISIMAIO	CHURRASCO
CENSORING	CHANDELLE	CHELICERA	CHITINOID	CICATRICE
CENSURING	CHANDLERS	CHELIFORM	CHITINOUS	CICATRIZE
CENTAURUS	CHANDLERY	CHELONIAN	CHIVALRIC	CICERONES
CENTENARY	CHANGCHOW	CHEMICALS	CHLORACNE	CIGARETTE
CENTERING	CHANGCHUN	CHEMISORB	CHLORDANE	CIGARILLO
CENTESIMO	CHANNELED	CHEMISTRY	CHLORELLA	CILIATION
CENTIGRAM	CHANTEUSE	CHEMOSTAT	CHLORIDES	CILIOLATE
CENTIPEDE	CHANTILLY	CHEMPADUK	CHLORIDIC	CIMMERIAN
CENTRALLY	CHAPERONS	CHEMURGIC	CHLORITIC	CINCTURES
CENTRIOLE	CHAPLAINS	CHENGCHOW	CHLOROSIS	CINEMATIC
CENTRISTS	CHAPLETED	CHEONGSAM	CHLOROTIC	CINEPHILE
CENTURIAL	CHARABANC	CHEQUERED	CHOCK-FULL	CINERARIA
CENTURIES	CHARACTER	CHERBOURG	CHOCOLATE	CINEREOUS
CENTURION	CHARBROIL	CHERISHED	CHOCOLATY	CINGULATE
CERACEOUS	CHARCOALS	CHERISHER	CHOIRBOYS	CIPHERING
CERATODUS	CHARINESS	CHERNOZEM	CHOKEABLE	CIRALPINE
CERCARIAL	CHARITIES	CHERRY PIE	CHOLEROID	CIRCADIAN
CEREBROID	CHARIVARI	CHESTIEST	CHOMSKIAN	CIRCASSIA
CEREBRUMS	CHARLATAN	CHESTNUTS	CHONDRIFY	CIRCINATE
CERECLOTH	CHARLOTTE	CHEVALIER	CHONDRITE	CIRCUITAL
CERTAINLY	CHARMEUSE	CHEVRETTE	CHONDROMA	CIRCUITRY
CERTAINTY	CHARTABLE	CHICALOTE	CHONDRULE	CIRCULARS
CERTIFIED	CHARTERED	CHICANERY	CHONGQING	CIRCULATE
CERTITUDE	CHARWOMAN	CHICKADEE	CHOOSIEST	CIRRHOSED
CERUSSITE	CHARWOMEN	CHICKPEAS	CHOPHOUSE	CIRRHOSIS
CESAREANS	CHASTENED	CHICKWEED	CHOPLOGIC	CIRRHOTIC
CESSATION	CHASTENER	CHIEFTAIN	CHOPPIEST	CIRRIPEDE
CETACEANS	CHASTISED	CHIHUAHUA	CHOPSTICK	CITATIONS
CHABAZITE	CHASUBLES	CHILBLAIN	CHORIONIC	CITIZENRY
CHA-CHA-CHA	CHATELAIN	CHILDHOOD	CHORISTER	CITY HALLS
CHAETOPOD	CHATOYANT	CHILDLESS	CHOROLOGY	CITY-STATE
CHAFFINCH	CHAT SHOWS	CHILDLIKE	CHORTLING	CIVICALLY
CHAGRINED	CHATTERED	CHILIADAL	CHORUSING	CIVILIANS
CHAIN GANG	CHATTERER	CHILLIEST	CHOWKIDAR	CIVILIZED
CHAIN MAIL	CHATTIEST	CHINATOWN	CHRISTIAN	CIVILIZER
CHAIN SAWS	CHAUFFEUR	CHINAWARE	CHRISTMAS	CIVIL LIST
CHAIRLIFT	CHEAPENED	CHINGLISH	CHROMATIC	CIVIL WARS
CHAIR LIFT	CHEAP-JACK	CHINKIANG	CHROMATID	CLADOGRAM
CHALCOGEN	CHEAPNESS	CHINSTRAP	CHROMATIN	CLAIMABLE
CHALKIEST	CHECHENIA	CHINTZIER	CHROMOGEN	CLAIMANTS
CHALLENGE	CHECKABLE	CHIPBOARD	CHRONAXIE	CLAMBAKES
CHAMELEON	CHECKERED	CHIPMUNKS	CHRONICLE	CLAMBERED
CHAMFERER	CHECKLIST	CHIPOLATA	CHRYSALID	CLAMMIEST
CHAMOMILE	CHECKMATE	CHIPPINGS	CHRYSALIS	CLAMOROUS
CHAMPAGNE	CHECKOUTS	CHIROPODY	CHTHONIAN	CLAMOURED
CHAMPAIGN	CHECKROOM	CHIROPTER	CHUBBIEST	CLAMPDOWN
CHAMPERTY	CHEEKBONE	CHIRPIEST	CHUCKLING	CLAMP DOWN
CHAMPIONS	CHEEKIEST	CHIRRUPER	CHUMMIEST	CLAPBOARD
CHAMPLEVE	CHEERIEST	CHISELING	CHUNGKING	CLARENDON
CHANCIEST	CHEERLESS	CHISELLED	CHUNKIEST	CLARIFIED

CLARIFIER	CLOCKWORK	COCCYGEAL	COLD FRAME	COLOSTRUM
CLARINETS	CLOG DANCE	COCHINEAL	COLD FRONT	COLOUR BAR
CLASSICAL	CLOISONNE	COCHLEATE	COLD SNAPS	COLOUREDS
CLASSIEST	CLOISTERS	COCK-A-HOOP	COLD SORES	COLOURFUL
CLASSLESS	CLOISTRAL	COCKATIEL	COLD STEEL	COLOURING
CLASSMATE	CLONICITY	COCKATOOS	COLD SWEAT	COLOURIST
CLASSROOM	CLOSE CALL	COCKED HAT	COLECTOMY	COLOURWAY
CLATHRATE	CLOSEDOWN	COCKERELS	COLERAINE	COLTISHLY
CLATTERED	CLOSE KNIT	COCKFIGHT	COLICROOT	COLTSFOOT
CLAVICLES	CLOSE-KNIT	COCKHORSE	COLICWEED	COLUBRINE
CLAVICORN	CLOSENESS	COCKINESS	COLLAGIST	COLUMBIAN
CLAYMORES	CLOSETING	COCKLEBUR	COLLAPSAR	COLUMBINE
CLAYSTONE	CLOTHIERS	COCKNEYFY	COLLAPSED	COLUMBITE
CLAYTONIA	CLOUDBANK	COCKROACH	COLLAPSES	COLUMBIUM
CLEANABLE	CLOUDIEST	COCKSCOMB	COLLARING	COLUMELLA
CLEANNESS	CLOUDLESS	COCKSFOOT	COLLATING	COLUMNIST
CLEANSERS	CLOUD NINE	COCKTAILS	COLLATION	COLWYN BAY
CLEANSING	CLOYINGLY	COCOONING	COLLATIVE	COMATULID
CLEARANCE	CLUBBABLE	CODIFYING	COLLEAGUE	COMBATANT
CLEAR-EYED	CLUBHOUSE	CODPIECES	COLLECTED	COMBATING
CLEARINGS	CLUMSIEST	COELOSTAT	COLLECTOR	COMBATIVE
CLEARNESS	CLUSTERED	COENOBITE	COLLEGIAL	COMBATTED
CLEARWAYS	CLUTCH BAG	COENOCYTE	COLLEGIAN	COMBINING
CLEARWING	CLUTCHING	COENOSARC	COLLEGIUM	COMBUSTOR
CLEAVAGES	CLUTTERED	COEQUALLY	COLLIDING	COME ABOUT
CLEMENTLY	CLYDEBANK	COERCIBLE	COLLIGATE	COMEBACKS
CLENCHING	CNIDARIAN	COEVALITY	COLLIMATE	COMEDIANS
CLERGYMAN	COACHWORK	COEXISTED	COLLINEAR	COMEDOWNS
CLERGYMEN	COADJUTOR	COFFEE BAR	COLLINSIA	COMELIEST
CLERIHEWS	COADUNATE	COFFEEPOT	COLLISION	COME OFF IT
CLERKSHIP	COAGULANT	COFFERDAM	COLLOCATE	COMFORTED
CLEVELAND	COAGULASE	COGITATED	COLLODION	COMFORTER
CLIENTELE	COAGULATE	COGITATOR	COLLOIDAL	COMICALLY
CLIMACTIC	COALESCED	COGNATION	COLLOTYPE	COMMANDED
CLIMAXING	COALFACES	COGNITION	COLLUDING	COMMANDER
CLIMB DOWN	COALFIELD	COGNITIVE	COLLUSION	COMMANDOS
CLIMB-DOWN	COALHOLES	COGNIZANT	COLLUSIVE	COMMENCED
CLINCHERS	COALHOUSE	COGNOMENS	COLLUVIAL	COMMENDAM
CLINCHING	COALITION	COGWHEELS	COLLUVIUM	COMMENDED
CLINGFILM	COALMINER	COHABITED	COLLYRIUM	COMMENSAL
CLINGFISH	COALMINES	COHERENCE	COLOCYNTH	COMMENTED
CLINICIAN	COARCTATE	COIFFEURS	COLOMBIAN	COMMENTER
CLINOSTAT	COARSENED	COIFFURED	COLONELCY	COMMINGLE
CLINQUANT	COASTLINE	COIFFURES	COLONIALS	COMMINUTE
CLINTONIA	COAT TAILS	COINCIDED	COLONISTS	COMMISSAR
CLIPBOARD	COAXINGLY	COINTREAU	COLONIZED	COMMITTAL
CLIP JOINT	COBALTITE	COKULORIS	COLONIZER	COMMITTED
CLIPPINGS	COBALTOUS	COLANDERS	COLONNADE	COMMITTEE
CLITELLUM	COCA-COLAS	COLCHICUM	COLORIFIC	COMMITTER
CLOAKROOM	COCAINISM	COLCOTHAR	COLOR LINE	COMMODITY
CLOBBERED	COCAINIZE	COLD CREAM	COLOSTOMY	COMMODORE
CLOCKWISE	COCCOLITH	COLD-DRAWN	COLOSTRAL	COMMONAGE

COMMONERS	CONCEIVED	CONFRERES	CONSTABLE	CONVERSED
COMMON LAW	CONCENTRE	CONFUCIAN	CONSTANCE	CONVERSER
COMMON-LAW	CONCEPTUS	CONFUSING	CONSTANCY	CONVERTED
COMMOTION	CONCERNED	CONFUSION	CONSTANTA	CONVERTER
COMMUNING	CONCERTED	CONFUTING	CONSTANTS	CONVEXITY
COMMUNION	CONCERTOS	CONGEALED	CONSTRAIN	CONVEYERS
COMMUNISM	CONCIERGE	CONGENIAL	CONSTRICT	CONVEYING
COMMUNIST	CONCILIAR	CONGER EEL	CONSTRUCT	CONVICTED
COMMUNITY	CONCISELY	CONGERIES	CONSTRUED	CONVINCED
COMMUNIZE	CONCISION	CONGESTED	CONSTRUER	CONVINCER
COMMUTATE	CONCLAVES	CONGOLESE	CONSULATE	CONVIVIAL
COMMUTERS	CONCLUDED	CONGRUENT	CONSULTED	CONVOKING
COMMUTING	CONCOCTED	CONGRUITY	CONSULTEE	CONVOLUTE
COMPACTED	CONCOCTER	CONGRUOUS	CONSULTER	CONVOYING
COMPACTER	CONCORDAT	CONHOIDAL	CONSUMERS	CONVULSED
COMPACTLY	CONCOURSE	CONICALLY	CONSUMING	COOKHOUSE
COMPANDER	CONCRETED	CONJOINED	CONTACTED	COOKSTOWN
COMPANIES	CONCUBINE	CONJOINER	CONTACTOR	COOPERAGE
COMPANION	CONCURRED	CONJUGANT	CONTAGION	COOPERATE
COMPARING	CONCUSSED	CONJUGATE	CONTAGIUM	COORDINAL
COMPASSES	CONDEMNED	CONJURERS	CONTAINED	COPARTNER
COMPELLED	CONDEMNER	CONJURING	CONTAINER	COPESTONE
COMPELLER	CONDENSED	CONNECTED	CONTEMNER	COPIOUSLY
COMPENDIA	CONDENSER	CONNECTOR	CONTENDED	COPOLYMER
COMPERING	CONDIGNLY	CONNEMARA	CONTENDER	COPROLITE
COMPETENT	CONDIMENT	CONNIVENT	CONTENTED	COPULATED
COMPETING	CONDITION	CONNIVING	CONTESTED	COPYBOOKS
COMPILERS	CONDOLING	CONNOTING	CONTESTER	COPYRIGHT
COMPILING	CONDONING	CONNUBIAL	CONTINENT	COQUETTES
COMPLAINT	CONDUCING	CONQUERED	CONTINUAL	CORALLINE
COMPLETED	CONDUCIVE	CONQUEROR	CONTINUED	CORALLOID
COMPLETER	CONDUCTED	CONQUESTS	CONTINUER	CORALROOT
COMPLEXES	CONDUCTOR	CONSCIOUS	CONTINUOS	CORBICULA
COMPLIANT	CONDYLOID	CONSCRIPT	CONTINUUM	COR BLIMEY
COMPLYING	CONDYLOMA	CONSENSUS	CONTORTED	CORDIALLY
COMPONENT	CONFERRED	CONSENTED	CONTOURED	CORDIFORM
COMPORTED	CONFERRER	CONSENTER	CONTRACTS	CORDONING
COMPOSERS	CONFERVAL	CONSERVED	CONTRAILS	COREOPSIS
COMPOSING	CONFESSED	CONSERVER	CONTRALTO	CORIANDER
COMPOSITE	CONFESSOR	CONSERVES	CONTRASTS	CORKBOARD
COMPOSTED	CONFIDANT	CONSIGNED	CONTRASTY	CORKSCREW
COMPOSURE	CONFIDENT	CONSIGNEE	CONTRIVED	CORMORANT
COMPOUNDS	CONFIDING	CONSIGNOR	CONTUMACY	CORN BREAD
COMPRISAL	CONFINING	CONSISTED	CONTUMELY	CORNBREAD
COMPRISED	CONFIRMED	CONSOCIES	CONTUSING	CORNCRAKE
COMPUTERS	CONFITURE	CONSOLING	CONTUSION	CORNELIAN
COMPUTING	CONFLATED	CONSOLUTE	CONTUSIVE	CORNERING
COMRADELY	CONFLICTS	CONSONANT	CONUNDRUM	CORNETIST
CONCAVITY	CONFLUENT	CONSORTED	CONVECTOR	CORNFIELD
CONCEALED	CONFORMAL	CONSORTER	CONVENERS	CORNFLOUR
CONCEDING	CONFORMED	CONSORTIA	CONVENING	CORNSTALK
CONCEITED	CONFORMER	CONSPIRED	CONVERGED	COROLLARY

CORPORALE	COTYLEDON	CRANKCASE	CRIPPLING	CRUMBLING
CORPORALS	COUCHETTE	CRANKIEST	CRISPIEST	CRUMMIEST
CORPORATE	COUNSELED	CRAPPIEST	CRISPNESS	CRUMPLING
CORPOREAL	COUNTABLE	CRAPULOUS	CRITERION	CRUNCHIER
CORPOSANT	COUNTDOWN	CRASH-DIVE	CRITICISM	CRUNCHILY
CORPULENT	COUNTERED	CRASH-LAND	CRITICIZE	CRUNCHING
CORPUSCLE	COUNTLESS	CRASH TEAM	CRITIQUES	CRUSADERS
CORRALLED	COUNT NOUN	CRASSNESS	CROCHETED	CRUSADING
CORRASION	COUNTRIES	CRATEROUS	CROCHETER	CRUSTIEST
CORRASIVE	COUP D'ETAT	CRAYONING	CROCODILE	CRYBABIES
CORRECTED	COUPLINGS	CRAYONIST	CROISSANT	CRYOMETER
CORRECTLY	COURGETTE	CRAZINESS	CROMLECHS	CRYOMETRY
CORRECTOR	COURT CARD	CREAKIEST	CROOKEDLY	CRYONAUTS
CORRELATE	COURTELLE	CREAMCUPS	CROP-EARED	CRYOPHYTE
CORRIDORS	COURTEOUS	CREAMIEST	CROQUETTE	CRYOSCOPE
CORRODANT	COURTESAN	CREATIONS	CROSSBARS	CRYOSCOPY
CORRODING	COURTIERS	CREATURAL	CROSSBEAM	CRYPTOGAM
CORROSION	COURTLIER	CREATURES	CROSSBILL	CTENIDIUM
CORROSIVE	COURTROOM	CREDENDUM	CROSSBOWS	CUBBYHOLE
CORRUGATE	COURTSHIP	CREDITING	CROSSBRED	CUBBY HOLE
CORRUPTED	COURT SHOE	CREDITORS	CROSS-EYED	CUBE ROOTS
CORRUPTER	COURTYARD	CREDULITY	CROSSFIRE	CUBISISTS
CORRUPTLY	COUTURIER	CREDULOUS	CROSSHEAD	CUB SCOUTS
CORSELETS	COVALENCY	CREEPIEST	CROSSINGS	CUCKOLDED
CORTICATE	COVENANTS	CREMATING	CROSS-LINK	CUCULLATE
CORTISONE	COVERALLS	CREMATION	CROSSNESS	CUCUMBERS
CORUSCATE	COVERINGS	CREMATORY	CROSSOVER	CUDDLIEST
CORVETTES	COVERLESS	CRENATION	CROSS TALK	CUDGELING
CORYDALIS	COVERLETS	CRENULATE	CROSSTREE	CUDGELLED
CORYMBOSE	COVER NOTE	CREOLIZED	CROSSWALK	CUDGELLER
COSEISMAL	COVERTURE	CREOPHAGY	CROSSWIND	CUFF LINKS
COSMETICS	COWABUNGA	CREOSOTED	CROSSWISE	CUIRASSES
COSMIC RAY	COWARDICE	CREOSOTIC	CROSSWORD	CUL-DE-SACS
COSMOGONY	CO-WORKERS	CREPITANT	CROSSWORT	CULLENDER
COSMOLOGY	COXCOMBRY	CREPITATE	CROTCHETS	CULMINANT
COSMONAUT	COYOTILLO	CRESCENDO	CROTCHETY	CULMINATE
COSMOTRON	CRAB APPLE	CRESCENTS	CROUCHING	CULTIVATE
COSSETTED	CRABBEDLY	CRETINISM	CROUPIERS	CULTURIST
COSTA RICA	CRABBIEST	CRETINOID	CROWBERRY	CUMBERING
CO-STARRED	CRABSTICK	CRETINOUS	CROWN LAND	CUMBRANCE
COSTLIEST	CRACKDOWN	CREVASSES	CROWNWORK	CUNEIFORM
COSTOTOMY	CRACKLING	CREWELIST	CROW'S FEET	CUNNINGLY
COST PRICE	CRACKPOTS	CREW NECKS	CROW'S FOOT	CUPBEARER
COSTUMIER	CRACKSMAN	CRIBELLUM	CROW'S NEST	CUPBOARDS
COTANGENT	CRACKSMEN	CRICKETER	CRUCIALLY	CUP FINALS
COT DEATHS	CRAFTIEST	CRIME WAVE	CRUCIBLES	CUPOLATED
COTE D'AZUR	CRAFTSMAN	CRIMINALS	CRUCIFIED	CURATIVES
COTENANCY	CRAFTSMEN	CRIMPLENE	CRUCIFIER	CURDINESS
COTILLION	CRAFTWORK	CRIMSONED	CRUCIFORM	CURETTAGE
COTTAGERS	CRAGGIEST	CRINKLIER	CRUDITIES	CURIOSITY
COTTONADE	CRAIGAVON	CRINKLING	CRUELTIES	CURIOUSLY
COTTON GIN	CRANBERRY	CRINOLINE	CRUMBLIER	CURLICUES

CURLINESS	CYRENAICA	DAVENPORT	DECALCIFY	DECUSSATE
CURLPAPER	CYSTEINIC	DAYDREAMS	DECALOGUE	DEDICATED
CURRENTLY	CYSTOCARP	DAYDREAMY	DECAMPING	DEDICATEE
CURRICULA	CYSTOCELE	DAYFLOWER	DECANTERS	DEDICATOR
CURRYCOMB	CYSTOLITH	DAYLIGHTS	DECANTING	DEDUCIBLE
CURSIVELY	CYSTOTOMY	DAY SCHOOL	DECAPODAL	DEDUCTING
CURSORIAL	CYTOLYSIN	DEACONESS	DECASTYLE	DEDUCTION
CURSORILY	CYTOLYSIS	DEADBEATS	DECATHLON	DEDUCTIVE
CURTAILED	CYTOPLASM	DEAD DUCKS	DECEITFUL	DEED POLLS
CURTAINED	CYTOPLAST	DEADENING	DECEIVERS	DEEDS POLL
CURTILAGE		DEAD HEART	DECEIVING	DEEPENING
CURTSYING	**D**	DEAD HEATS	DECEMBERS	DEEP FRIED
CURVATURE	DACHSHUND	DEADLIEST	DECENCIES	DEEP SOUTH
CUSHINESS	DACTYLICS	DEADLIGHT	DECENNIAL	DEERGRASS
CUSHIONED	DADAISTIC	DEADLINES	DECEPTION	DEERHOUND
CUSPIDATE	DAFFODILS	DEADLOCKS	DECEPTIVE	DEFALCATE
CUSPIDORS	DAILY HELP	DEADLY SIN	DECIDABLE	DEFAULTED
CUSTODIAL	DAINTIEST	DEAD MARCH	DECIDEDLY	DEFAULTER
CUSTODIAN	DAIQUIRIS	DEAFBLIND	DECIDUOUS	DEFEATING
CUSTOMARY	DAIRY FARM	DEAFENING	DECILLION	DEFEATISM
CUSTOMERS	DAIRYMAID	DEAF-MUTES	DECIMALLY	DEFEATIST
CUSTOMIZE	DALAI LAMA	DEALATION	DECIMATED	DEFECATED
CUT A CAPER	DALLIANCE	DEAMINATE	DECIMATOR	DEFECATOR
CUT AND RUN	DALMATIAN	DEANERIES	DECIMETRE	DEFECTING
CUTANEOUS	DALTONISM	DEATHBEDS	DECISIONS	DEFECTION
CUTICULAR	DAMASCENE	DEATHBLOW	DECK CARGO	DEFECTIVE
CUTLASSES	DAMNATION	DEATH DUTY	DECKCHAIR	DEFECTORS
CUTPURSES	DAMNATORY	DEATHLESS	DECKHANDS	DEFENDANT
CUTTHROAT	DAMNEDEST	DEATHLIKE	DECKHOUSE	DEFENDERS
CUT-THROAT	DAMPENING	DEATH MASK	DECLAIMED	DEFENDING
CUTTINGLY	DAMP SQUIB	DEATH RATE	DECLAIMER	DEFENSIVE
CYANAMIDE	DAMSELFLY	DEATH TOLL	DECLARANT	DEFERENCE
CYANOTYPE	DANDELION	DEATH TRAP	DECLARING	DEFERMENT
CYBERCAFE	DANDIFIED	DEATH WISH	DECLINATE	DEFERRING
CYBERNATE	DANGEROUS	DEAUVILLE	DECLINING	DEFIANTLY
CYBERPUNK	DAREDEVIL	DEBARKING	DECLIVITY	DEFICIENT
CYBERPUNT	DARKENING	DEBARMENT	DECOCTION	DEFINABLE
CYCLAMATE	DARK HORSE	DEBARRING	DECOLLATE	DEFINIENS
CYCLOIDAL	DARKROOMS	DEBATABLE	DECOLLETE	DEFLATING
CYCLONITE	DARMSTADT	DEBAUCHED	DECOMPOSE	DEFLATION
CYCLOPSES	DARTBOARD	DEBAUCHEE	DECONTROL	DEFLECTED
CYCLORAMA	DARTMOUTH	DEBAUCHER	DECORATED	DEFLECTOR
CYCLOTRON	DASHBOARD	DEBAUCHES	DECORATOR	DEFOLIANT
CYLINDERS	DASHINGLY	DEBENTURE	DECOUPAGE	DEFOLIATE
CYMBALIST	DASTARDLY	DEBOUCHED	DECREASED	DEFORMING
CYMOGRAPH	DATABASES	DEBRIEFED	DECREASES	DEFORMITY
CYMOPHANE	DATA BUSES	DEBUGGING	DECREEING	DEFRAUDED
CYNICALLY	DATEDNESS	DEBUNKERS	DECREMENT	DEFRAUDER
CYNOSURES	DATELINES	DEBUNKING	DECRETIVE	DEFRAYING
CYPHERING	DATE STAMP	DEBUTANTE	DECRETORY	DEFROCKED
CYPRESSES	DAUGHTERS	DECADENCE	DECUMBENT	DEFROSTED
CYPRINOID	DAUNTLESS	DECAGONAL	DECURRENT	DEFROSTER

DEGRADING	DENTALIUM	DESCENDED	DETESTING	DIALOGISM
DEGREE-DAY	DENTATION	DESCENDER	DETHRONED	DIALOGIST
DEHISCENT	DENTIFORM	DESCRIBED	DETHRONER	DIALOGIZE
DEHYDRATE	DENTISTRY	DESCRIBER	DETONATED	DIALOGUER
DEJECTION	DENTITION	DESCRYING	DETONATOR	DIALOGUES
DELEGABLE	DENTURIST	DESECRATE	DETRACTED	DIAMAGNET
DELEGATED	DEODORANT	DESERTERS	DETRACTOR	DIAMETERS
DELEGATES	DEODORIZE	DESERTING	DETRAINED	DIAMETRAL
DELETIONS	DEOXIDIZE	DESERTION	DETRIMENT	DIAMETRIC
DELICIOUS	DEPARDIEU	DESERVING	DETRITION	DIANDROUS
DELIGHTED	DEPARTING	DESICCANT	DETRUSION	DIANOETIC
DELIGHTER	DEPARTURE	DESICCATE	DEUTERIDE	DIAPHONIC
DELIMITED	DEPASTURE	DESIGNATE	DEUTERIUM	DIAPHRAGM
DELINEATE	DEPENDANT	DESIGNERS	DEVALUATE	DIAPHYSIS
DELIRIANT	DEPENDENT	DESIGNING	DEVALUING	DIARRHOEA
DELIRIOUS	DEPENDING	DESINENCE	DEVASTATE	DIASTASIC
DELIRIUMS	DEPICTING	DESIRABLE	DEVELOPED	DIASTASIS
DELIVERED	DEPICTION	DESIRABLY	DEVELOPER	DIASTATIC
DELIVERER	DEPICTIVE	DESISTING	DEVIATING	DIASTOLIC
DELOUSING	DEPICTURE	DESMIDIAN	DEVIATION	DIATHERMY
DELUSIONS	DEPILATOR	DES MOINES	DEVIATORY	DIATHESIS
DEMAGOGIC	DEPLETING	DESOLATED	DEVILFISH	DIATHETIC
DEMAGOGUE	DEPLETION	DESOLATER	DEVILLING	DIATOMITE
DEMANDANT	DEPLETIVE	DESPAIRED	DEVILMENT	DIATRIBES
DEMANDING	DEPLORING	DESPERADO	DEVIOUSLY	DIATROPIC
DEMANTOID	DEPLOYING	DESPERATE	DEVISABLE	DIAZONIUM
DEMARCATE	DEPORTEES	DESPISING	DEVITRIFY	DIAZOTIZE
DEMEANING	DEPORTING	DESPOILED	DEVOLVING	DIBROMIDE
DEMEANOUR	DEPOSABLE	DESPOILER	DEVOTEDLY	DICHASIAL
DEMIJOHNS	DEPOSITED	DESPOTISM	DEVOTIONS	DICHASIUM
DEMIMONDE	DEPOSITOR	DESPUMATE	DEVOURING	DICHOGAMY
DEMISABLE	DEPRAVING	DESTINIES	DEVOUTEST	DICHOTOMY
DEMISTING	DEPRAVITY	DESTITUTE	DEXEDRINE	DICHROISM
DEMITASSE	DEPRECATE	DESTROYED	DEXTERITY	DICHROITE
DEMOBBING	DEPRESSED	DESTROYER	DEXTEROUS	DICHROMIC
DEMOCRACY	DEPRESSOR	DESUETUDE	DEXTRORSE	DICKERING
DEMOCRATS	DEPRIVING	DESULTORY	DIABETICS	DICKYBIRD
DEMOTIONS	DEPURATOR	DETACHING	DIABLERIE	DICLINISM
DEMULCENT	DEPUTIZED	DETAILING	DIABOLISM	DICLINOUS
DEMULSIFY	DERAILING	DETAINEES	DIABOLIST	DICROTISM
DEMURRAGE	DERELICTS	DETAINING	DIABOLIZE	DICTATING
DEMURRING	DE RIGUEUR	DETECTING	DIACONATE	DICTATION
DEMYSTIFY	DERISIBLE	DETECTION	DIACRITIC	DICTATORS
DENDRITIC	DERIVABLE	DETECTIVE	DIACTINIC	DIDACTICS
DENIGRATE	DERMATOID	DETECTORS	DIAERESES	DIETETICS
DENITRATE	DERMATOME	DETENTION	DIAERESIS	DIETICIAN
DENITRIFY	DEROGATED	DETERGENT	DIAGNOSED	DIETITIAN
DENOTABLE	DERRING-DO	DETERMENT	DIAGNOSES	DIFFERENT
DENOUNCED	DERRINGER	DETERMINE	DIAGNOSIS	DIFFERING
DENOUNCER	DERVISHES	DETERRENT	DIAGONALS	DIFFICULT
DENSENESS	DESCALING	DETERRING	DIALECTAL	DIFFIDENT
DENSITIES	DESCANTER	DETERSIVE	DIALECTIC	DIFFUSELY

DIFFUSING	DIRECTRIX	DISEMBARK	DISPLAYED	DIURETICS
DIFFUSION	DIRECT TAX	DISEMBODY	DISPLAYER	DIURNALLY
DIFFUSIVE	DIREFULLY	DISENABLE	DISPLEASE	DIVALENCY
DIGASTRIC	DIRIGIBLE	DISENGAGE	DISPORTED	DIVERGENT
DIGENESIS	DIRT BIKES	DISENTAIL	DISPOSING	DIVERGING
DIGENETIC	DIRT CHEAP	DISESTEEM	DISPRAISE	DIVERSELY
DIGESTANT	DIRTINESS	DISFAVOUR	DISPROVAL	DIVERSIFY
DIGESTING	DIRT ROADS	DISFIGURE	DISPROVED	DIVERSION
DIGESTION	DIRT TRACK	DISFOREST	DISPUTANT	DIVERSITY
DIGESTIVE	DIRTY WORK	DISGORGED	DISPUTING	DIVERTING
DIGITALIN	DISABLING	DISGORGER	DISREGARD	DIVERTIVE
DIGITALIS	DISABLIST	DISGRACED	DISRELISH	DIVESTING
DIGITIZED	DISABUSAL	DISGRACER	DISREPAIR	DIVIDABLE
DIGITIZER	DISABUSED	DISGUISED	DISREPUTE	DIVIDENDS
DIGITOXIN	DISACCORD	DISGUISER	DISROBING	DIVINABLE
DIGLOTTIC	DISAFFECT	DISGUISES	DISRUPTED	DIVISIBLE
DIGNIFIED	DISAFFIRM	DISGUSTED	DISRUPTER	DIVISIONS
DIGNITARY	DISAGREED	DISHCLOTH	DISSECTED	DIVORCEES
DIGNITIES	DISAPPEAR	DISHONEST	DISSECTOR	DIVORCING
DIGRAPHIC	DISARMING	DISHONOUR	DISSEISIN	DIVORCIVE
DIGRESSED	DISASTERS	DISH TOWEL	DISSEISOR	DIVULGING
DIGRESSER	DISAVOWAL	DISHWATER	DISSEMBLE	DIVULSION
DILATABLE	DISAVOWED	DISINFECT	DISSENTED	DIVULSIVE
DILATANCY	DISAVOWER	DISINFEST	DISSENTER	DIXIELAND
DILIGENCE	DISBANDED	DISK DRIVE	DISSIDENT	DIZZINESS
DILUTIONS	DISBARRED	DISKETTES	DISSIPATE	DJAJAPURA
DIMENSION	DISBELIEF	DISLIKING	DISSOLUTE	DOBSONFLY
DIMIDIATE	DISBRANCH	DISLOCATE	DISSOLVED	DOCK BRIEF
DIMISSORY	DISBURDEN	DISLODGED	DISSOLVER	DOCKETING
DIM-WITTED	DISBURSED	DISMANTLE	DISSONANT	DOCKYARDS
DINGDONGS	DISBURSER	DISMASTED	DISSUADED	DOCTORATE
DINGINESS	DISCALCED	DISMAYING	DISSUADER	DOCTORING
DINING CAR	DISCARDED	DISMEMBER	DISTANCED	DOCTRINAL
DINOCERAS	DISCARDER	DISMISSAL	DISTANCES	DOCTRINES
DINOSAURS	DISCERNED	DISMISSED	DISTANTLY	DOCUMENTS
DINOTHERE	DISCERNER	DISOBEYED	DISTEMPER	DODDERERS
DIOECIOUS	DISCHARGE	DISOBEYER	DISTENDED	DODDERING
DIOESTRUS	DISCIPLES	DISOBLIGE	DISTENDER	DODECAGON
DIPHTHONG	DISCLIMAX	DISORDERS	DISTICHAL	DODGE CITY
DIPLOIDIC	DISCLOSED	DISOWNING	DISTILLED	DOG COLLAR
DIPLOMACY	DISCLOSER	DISPARAGE	DISTILLER	DOG-EAT-DOG
DIPLOMATE	DISCOIDAL	DISPARATE	DISTINGUE	DOGFIGHTS
DIPLOMATS	DISCOLOUR	DISPARITY	DISTORTED	DOGFISHES
DIPLOTENE	DISCOMFIT	DISPELLED	DISTORTER	DOGGY BAGS
DIPSTICKS	DISCOMMON	DISPELLER	DISTRAINT	DOGHOUSES
DIPSWITCH	DISCOUNTS	DISPENSED	DISTRICTS	DOGLEGGED
DIPTEROUS	DISCOURSE	DISPENSER	DISTURBED	DOGMATICS
DIRECTING	DISCOVERT	DISPERSAL	DISTURBER	DOGMATISM
DIRECTION	DISCOVERY	DISPERSED	DISUNITED	DOGMATIST
DIRECTIVE	DISCREDIT	DISPERSER	DITHERING	DOGMATIZE
DIRECTORS	DISCUSSED	DISPLACED	DITHYRAMB	DO-GOODERS
DIRECTORY	DISDAINED	DISPLACER	DITTANDER	DOG PADDLE

DOLEFULLY	DOWNFALLS	DRIVE HOME	DUOLOGUES	EARLY BIRD
DOLERITIC	DOWNGRADE	DRIVELING	DUPLEXITY	EARMARKED
DOLGELLAU	DOWNPOURS	DRIVELLED	DUPLICATE	EARNESTLY
DOLLY BIRD	DOWNRANGE	DRIVELLER	DUPLICITY	EARPHONES
DOLOMITES	DOWNRIGHT	DRIVE-TIME	DURALUMIN	EARPIECES
DOLOMITIC	DOWNSPOUT	DRIVEWAYS	DURICRUST	EARTHIEST
DOLTISHLY	DOWNSTAGE	DRIZZLING	DUSKINESS	EARTHLIER
DOMESTICS	DOWNSWING	DROLLNESS	DUSTBOWLS	EARTHLING
DOMICILED	DOWNTHROW	DROMEDARY	DUSTCARTS	EARTHRISE
DOMICILES	DOWNTURNS	DROPLIGHT	DUSTSHEET	EARTHSTAR
DOMINANCE	DOWNWARDS	DROPPINGS	DUST STORM	EARTHWARD
DOMINATED	DRACONIAN	DROPSICAL	DUTCH BARN	EARTHWORK
DOMINATOR	DRAFTIEST	DROPSONDE	DUTCH CAPS	EARTHWORM
DOMINICAL	DRAFTSMAN	DRUBBINGS	DUTCH OVEN	EASTBOUND
DOMINICAN	DRAFTSMEN	DRUGGISTS	DUTIFULLY	EAST ENDER
DOMINIONS	DRAGGIEST	DRUGSTORE	DUTY-FREES	EASTER EGG
DONATIONS	DRAGHOUND	DRUMBEATS	DWARF STAR	EASTERNER
DONCASTER	DRAGOMANS	DRUM MAJOR	DWELLINGS	EASTLEIGH
DONNISHLY	DRAGONESS	DRUM ROLLS	DWINDLING	EASTWARDS
DONORSHIP	DRAGONFLY	DRUMSTICK	DYER'S-WEED	EASY CHAIR
DOODLEBUG	DRAGONISH	DRUNKARDS	DYNAMETER	EASYGOING
DOOHICKEY	DRAGOONED	DRUNKENLY	DYNAMITED	EASY GOING
DOOJIGGER	DRAINABLE	DUALISTIC	DYNAMITER	EASY TERMS
DOOMSAYER	DRAINPIPE	DUBIOUSLY	DYNAMITIC	EAVESDROP
DOORBELLS	DRAMAMINE	DUBITABLE	DYNAMOTOR	EBULLIENT
DOORFRAME	DRAMATICS	DUBROVNIK	DYNASTIES	ECCENTRIC
DOORKNOBS	DRAMATIST	DUCHESSES	DYSENTERY	ECHOLALIA
DOORNAILS	DRAMATIZE	DUCKBOARD	DYSGENICS	ECHOLALIC
DOORPLATE	DRAPERIED	DUCKLINGS	DYSLECTIC	ECLAMPSIA
DOORSTEPS	DRAPERIES	DUCTILITY	DYSPEPSIA	ECLAMPTIC
DORDRECHT	DRAUGHTER	DUDE RANCH	DYSPEPTIC	ECLIPSING
DORMITORY	DRAVIDIAN	DUELLISTS	DYSPHAGIA	ECOLOGIST
DORMOBILE	DRAWBACKS	DUFFEL BAG	DYSPHAGIC	ECONOMICS
DORONICUM	DRAWKNIFE	DULCIMERS	DYSPHASIA	ECONOMIES
DORYPHORE	DRAWPLATE	DUMBARTON	DYSPHASIC	ECONOMIST
DOSIMETER	DREAMBOAT	DUMBBELLS	DYSPHONIA	ECONOMIZE
DOSIMETRY	DREAMLAND	DUMBFOUND	DYSPHONIC	ECOSPHERE
DOSSHOUSE	DREAMLESS	DUMB SHOWS	DYSPHORIA	ECOSYSTEM
DOTTINESS	DREAMLIKE	DUMMY RUNS	DYSPHORIC	ECSTASIES
DOUBLE BED	DREAMTIME	DUMPINESS	DYSPLASIA	ECSTATICS
DOUBLED UP	DREARIEST	DUMPLINGS	DYSPNOEAL	ECTOBLAST
DOUBLETON	DRENCHING	DUNCE'S CAP	DYSTHYMIA	ECTOMERIC
DOUBLOONS	DRESS CODE	DUNE BUGGY	DYSTHYMIC	ECTOMORPH
DOUBTABLE	DRESS DOWN	DUNGANNON	DYSTROPHY	ECTOPHYTE
DOUBTLESS	DRESSIEST	DUNGAREES	DZUNGARIA	ECTOPLASM
DOUGHNUTS	DRESSINGS	DUNGENESS		ECTOPROCT
DOUGHTIER	DRIBBLING	DUNKERQUE	E	ECUMENISM
DOVECOTES	DRIFTWOOD	DUNSINANE	EACH OTHER	EDDYSTONE
DOVETAILS	DRILLABLE	DUNSTABLE	EAGERNESS	EDELWEISS
DOWDINESS	DRINKABLE	DUODECIMO	EAGLE-EYED	EDEMATOUS
DOWITCHER	DRIP-DRIED	DUODENARY	EAGLEWOOD	EDIBILITY
DOWNCOMER	DRIPSTONE	DUODENUMS	EARLINESS	EDIFICIAL

EDINBURGH	ELECTRODE	EMBRACERY	ENCHANTER	ENGRAVERS
EDITORIAL	ELECTRONS	EMBRACING	ENCHILADA	ENGRAVING
EDUCATING	ELECTUARY	EMBRASURE	ENCHORIAL	ENGROSSED
EDUCATION	ELEGANTLY	EMBROCATE	ENCIRCLED	ENGROSSER
EDUCATIVE	ELEMENTAL	EMBROIDER	ENCLOSING	ENGULFING
EDUCATORS	ELEOPTENE	EMBROILED	ENCLOSURE	ENHANCING
EDUCATORY	ELEPHANTS	EMBROILER	ENCOMIAST	ENHANCIVE
EDWARDIAN	ELEVATING	EMBRYONIC	ENCOMIUMS	ENIGMATIC
EFFECTING	ELEVATION	EMENDABLE	ENCOMPASS	ENJOINING
EFFECTIVE	ELEVATORS	EMENDATOR	ENCOUNTER	ENJOYABLE
EFFECTUAL	ELEVENSES	EMERGENCE	ENCOURAGE	ENJOYABLY
EFFERENCE	ELEVENTHS	EMERGENCY	ENCRINITE	ENJOYMENT
EFFICIENT	ELICITING	EMIGRANTS	ENCRUSTED	ENKINDLER
EFFLUENCE	ELIMINANT	EMIGRATED	ENDAMOEBA	ENLARGING
EFFLUENTS	ELIMINATE	EMINENCES	ENDEARING	ENLIGHTEN
EFFLUVIAL	ELIZABETH	EMINENTLY	ENDEAVOUR	ENLISTING
EFFLUVIUM	ELLESMERE	EMISSIONS	ENDLESSLY	ENLIVENED
EFFORTFUL	ELLIPSOID	EMMENTHAL	ENDOBLAST	ENLIVENER
EFFULGENT	EL MANSURA	EMOLLIENT	ENDOCRINE	ENMESHING
EFFUSIONS	ELOCUTION	EMOLUMENT	ENDOERGIC	ENNOBLING
EGG BEATER	ELONGATED	EMOTIONAL	ENDOLYMPH	EN PASSANT
EGGPLANTS	ELOPEMENT	EMOTIVELY	ENDOMORPH	ENQUIRIES
EGGSHELLS	ELOQUENCE	EMOTIVISM	ENDOPHYTE	ENQUIRING
EGG TIMERS	ELSEWHERE	EMPANELED	ENDOPLASM	ENRAGEDLY
EGLANTINE	ELUCIDATE	EMPATHIZE	ENDORSING	EN RAPPORT
EGOMANIAC	ELUSIVELY	EMPENNAGE	ENDOSCOPE	ENRAPTURE
EGOTISTIC	ELUTRIATE	EMPHASIZE	ENDOSCOPY	ENRICHING
EGREGIOUS	EMACIATED	EMPHYSEMA	ENDOSPERM	ENROLLING
EGYPTIANS	EMANATING	EMPIRICAL	ENDOSPORE	ENROLMENT
EIDERDOWN	EMANATION	EMPLOYEES	ENDOSTEAL	ENSCONCED
EIGHTFOLD	EMANATIVE	EMPLOYERS	ENDOSTEUM	ENSEMBLES
EIGHTIETH	EMANATORY	EMPLOYING	ENDOTOXIC	ENSHRINED
EINDHOVEN	EMBALMERS	EMPORIUMS	ENDOTOXIN	ENSLAVING
EIRENICON	EMBALMING	EMPOWERED	ENDOWMENT	ENSNARING
EISEGESIS	EMBARGOED	EMPRESSES	ENDURABLE	ENSTATITE
EJACULATE	EMBARGOES	EMPTIABLE	ENDURANCE	ENSUINGLY
EKISTICAL	EMBARKING	EMPTINESS	ENERGETIC	ENTAILING
ELABORATE	EMBARRASS	EMPYREUMA	ENERGIZED	ENTAMOEBA
EL ALAMEIN	EMBASSIES	EMULATING	ENERGIZER	ENTANGLED
ELAN VITAL	EMBATTLED	EMULATION	ENERGUMEN	ENTANGLER
ELASTANCE	EMBAYMENT	EMULATIVE	ENERVATED	ENTELECHY
ELASTOMER	EMBEDDING	EMULSIONS	ENERVATOR	ENTENDRES
ELATERITE	EMBEDMENT	EMUNCTORY	EN FAMILLE	ENTERABLE
ELATERIUM	EMBELLISH	ENACTMENT	ENFEEBLED	ENTERALLY
ELBOWROOM	EMBEZZLED	ENAMELING	ENFEEBLER	ENTERITIS
ELBOW ROOM	EMBEZZLER	ENAMELLED	ENFILADED	ENTERTAIN
ELDERSHIP	EMBODYING	ENAMELLER	ENFILADES	ENTHRONED
ELECTIONS	EMBOLISMS	ENAMOURED	ENFOLDING	ENTHUSING
ELECTORAL	EMBOSOMED	ENCAMPING	ENFORCING	ENTHYMEME
ELECTRESS	EMBOSSING	ENCAUSTIC	ENGINEERS	ENTITLING
ELECTRICS	EMBOWMENT	ENCHAINED	ENGLACIAL	ENTOBLAST
ELECTRIFY	EMBRACEOR	ENCHANTED	ENGRAMMIC	ENTOMBING

ENTOPHYTE	EPIPHYTIC	ESCALADER	EUCHARIST	EXCALIBUR
ENTOURAGE	EPIROGENY	ESCALATED	EUCLIDEAN	EXCAUDATE
ENTRAINED	EPISCOPAL	ESCALATOR	EUDEMONIA	EXCAVATED
ENTRANCED	EPISTASIS	ESCALOPES	EUDEMONIC	EXCAVATOR
ENTRANCES	EPISTATIC	ESCAPABLE	EUKARYOTE	EXCEEDING
ENTRAPPED	EPISTAXIS	ESCAPADES	EULOGISTS	EXCELLENT
ENTRAPPER	EPISTEMIC	ESCAPISTS	EULOGIZED	EXCELLING
ENTREATED	EPITAPHIC	ESCHEWING	EUPHEMISM	EXCELSIOR
ENTRECHAT	EPITAXIAL	ESCORTING	EUPHEMIST	EXCEPTING
ENTRECOTE	EPITHETIC	ESKISEHIR	EUPHEMIZE	EXCEPTION
ENTREMETS	EPITOMIST	ESOPHAGUS	EUPHONIUM	EXCEPTIVE
ENTRE NOUS	EPITOMIZE	ESPERANTO	EUPHONIZE	EXCERPTER
ENTRUSTED	EPIZOOTIC	ESPIONAGE	EUPHORBIA	EXCESSIVE
ENTRYWAYS	EPONYMOUS	ESPLANADE	EUPHRATES	EXCHANGED
ENTWINING	EQUAL-AREA	ESPOUSALS	EUPLASTIC	EXCHANGER
ENUCLEATE	EQUALIZED	ESPOUSING	EURHYTHMY	EXCHANGES
ENUMERATE	EQUALIZER	ESPRESSOS	EUROCRATS	EXCHEQUER
ENUNCIATE	EQUALLING	ESSAOUIRA	EUROPHILE	EXCIPIENT
ENVELOPED	EQUATABLE	ESSAYISTS	EUROPOORT	EXCISABLE
ENVELOPES	EQUATIONS	ESSENTIAL	EUTHENICS	EXCISEMAN
ENVIOUSLY	EQUERRIES	ESSLINGEN	EUTHENIST	EXCISIONS
ENVISAGED	EQUINOXES	ESTABLISH	EUTHERIAN	EXCITABLE
ENVYINGLY	EQUIPMENT	ESTAMINET	EUTROPHIC	EXCITEDLY
ENZYMATIC	EQUIPOISE	ESTATE CAR	EVACUATED	EXCLAIMED
EPARCHIAL	EQUIPPING	ESTEEMING	EVACUATOR	EXCLAIMER
EPHEDRINE	EQUISETUM	ESTHETICS	EVADINGLY	EXCLUDING
EPHEMERAL	EQUITABLE	ESTIMABLE	EVAGINATE	EXCLUSION
EPHEMERID	EQUITABLY	ESTIMATED	EVALUATED	EXCLUSIVE
EPHEMERIS	EQUIVOCAL	ESTIMATES	EVALUATOR	EXCORIATE
EPHEMERON	EQUIVOQUE	ESTIMATOR	EVAPORATE	EXCREMENT
EPICENISM	ERADICANT	ESTOPPAGE	EVAPORITE	EXCRETING
EPICENTRE	ERADICATE	ESTRANGED	EVASIVELY	EXCRETION
EPICRISIS	ERECTABLE	ESTRANGER	EVENTUATE	EXCRETIVE
EPICRITIC	ERECTIONS	ESTUARIAL	EVERGREEN	EXCRETORY
EPICUREAN	ERECTNESS	ESTUARIES	EVERSIBLE	EXCULPATE
EPICURISM	EREMITISM	ESTUARINE	EVERYBODY	EXCURRENT
EPICYCLIC	ERGOGRAPH	ESURIENCE	EVICTIONS	EXCURSION
EPIDEMICS	ERGOMETER	ETCETERAS	EVIDENTLY	EXCURSIVE
EPIDERMAL	ERGONOMIC	ETERNALLY	EVILDOERS	EXCUSABLE
EPIDERMIS	ERISTICAL	ETHERIZER	EVILDOING	EXCUSABLY
EPIDURALS	EROGENOUS	ETHICALLY	EVINCIBLE	EXECRABLE
EPIGENOUS	EROSIONAL	ETHIOPIAN	EVOCATION	EXECRABLY
EPIGRAPHY	EROTICISM	ETHMOIDAL	EVOCATIVE	EXECRATED
EPIGYNOUS	EROTICIZE	ETHNARCHY	EVOLUTION	EXECUTANT
EPILEPTIC	ERRONEOUS	ETHNOGENY	EVOLVABLE	EXECUTING
EPILOGIST	ERSTWHILE	ETHNOLOGY	EXACTABLE	EXECUTION
EPILOGUES	ERUDITELY	ETHOLOGIC	EXACTNESS	EXECUTIVE
EPIMYSIUM	ERUDITION	ETHYLENIC	EXALTEDLY	EXECUTORS
EPINASTIC	ERUPTIBLE	ETIOLATED	EXAMINERS	EXECUTORY
EPIPHANIC	ERUPTIONS	ETIQUETTE	EXAMINING	EXECUTRIX
EPIPHRAGM	ERYTHRISM	ETRAMETER	EXANIMATE	EXEGETICS
EPIPHYSIS	ERYTHRITE	ETYMOLOGY	EXANTHEMA	EXEMPLARY

EXEMPLIFY	EXPLICATE	EXTREMIST	FAINEANCE	FASCICULE
EXEMPTING	EXPLODING	EXTREMITY	FAINTNESS	FASCIITIS
EXEMPTION	EXPLOITED	EXTRICATE	FAIRBANKS	FASCINATE
EXEQUATUR	EXPLOITER	EXTRINSIC	FAIRYLAND	FASCISTIC
EXERCISED	EXPLORERS	EXTROVERT	FAIRY-LIKE	FASHIONED
EXERCISER	EXPLORING	EXTRUDING	FAIRY RING	FASHIONER
EXERCISES	EXPLOSION	EXTRUSION	FAIRY-TALE	FASTENERS
EXERTIONS	EXPLOSIVE	EXTRUSIVE	FAITHFULS	FASTENING
EXFOLIATE	EXPONENTS	EXUBERANT	FAITHLESS	FATALISTS
EXHALABLE	EXPONIBLE	EXUBERATE	FALANGISM	FATEFULLY
EXHAUSTED	EXPORTERS	EXUDATION	FALANGIST	FATHEADED
EXHAUSTER	EXPORTING	EXUDATIVE	FALCONERS	FATHERING
EXHIBITED	EXPOSABLE	EYEBALLED	FALCONINE	FATHOMING
EXHIBITOR	EXPOSITOR	EYEBRIGHT	FALDSTOOL	FATIGABLE
EXHORTING	EXPOSURES	EYELASHES	FALLACIES	FATIGUING
EXISTENCE	EXPOUNDED	EYELETEER	FALLALERY	FATTENING
EXODONTIA	EXPOUNDER	EYE OPENER	FALL APART	FATTINESS
EXOENZYME	EXPRESSED	EYE-OPENER	FALLOPIAN	FATUITOUS
EX OFFICIO	EXPRESSER	EYEPIECES	FALSEHOOD	FATUOUSLY
EXOGAMOUS	EXPRESSES	EYE SHADOW	FALSENESS	FAULTIEST
EXOGENOUS	EXPRESSLY	EYES RIGHT	FALSIFIED	FAULTLESS
EXONERATE	EXPULSION	EYESTRAIN	FALSIFIER	FAVEOLATE
EXORCISER	EXPULSIVE	EYE STRAIN	FALSITIES	FAVOURING
EXORCISMS	EXPUNGING		FALTERING	FAVOURITE
EXORCISTS	EXPURGATE	**F**	FAMAGUSTA	FAWNINGLY
EXORCIZED	EXQUISITE	FABACEOUS	FAMILIARS	FEARFULLY
EXOSMOSIS	EXSECTION	FABIANISM	FAMILY MAN	FEATHERED
EXOSMOTIC	EXSERTILE	FABRICATE	FAMILY MEN	FEATURING
EXOSPHERE	EXSERTION	FABRIKOID	FANATICAL	FEBRICITY
EXOSTOSIS	EXSICCATE	FACE CARDS	FANCINESS	FEBRIFUGE
EXOTICISM	EXSTROPHY	FACECLOTH	FANCY-FREE	FEBRILITY
EXPANDING	EXTEMPORE	FACE-LIFTS	FANCYWORK	FECULENCE
EXPANSILE	EXTENDING	FACE PACKS	FANDANGLE	FECUNDATE
EXPANSION	EXTENSION	FACEPLATE	FANDANGOS	FECUNDITY
EXPANSIVE	EXTENSITY	FACE-SAVER	FANLIGHTS	FEDERATED
EXPATIATE	EXTENSIVE	FACETIOUS	FAN-TAILED	FEEDSTOCK
EXPECTANT	EXTENUATE	FACE VALUE	FANTASIES	FEEDSTUFF
EXPECTING	EXTERIORS	FACSIMILE	FANTASIZE	FEE EARNER
EXPEDIENT	EXTERNALS	FACTIONAL	FANTASTIC	FEELINGLY
EXPEDITED	EXTIRPATE	FACTITIVE	FARADIZER	FEE-PAYING
EXPEDITER	EXTOLLING	FACTORAGE	FARANDOLE	FELICIFIC
EXPELLANT	EXTOLMENT	FACTORIAL	FAREWELLS	FELONIOUS
EXPELLING	EXTORTING	FACTORIES	FARMHANDS	FEMINISTS
EXPENDING	EXTORTION	FACTORING	FARMHOUSE	FENESTRAL
EXPENSIVE	EXTORTIVE	FACTORIZE	FARMSTEAD	FENUGREEK
EXPERTISE	EXTRABOLD	FACTUALLY	FARMVILLE	FERMANAGH
EXPIATING	EXTRACTED	FACULTIES	FARMYARDS	FERMENTED
EXPIATION	EXTRACTOR	FADDINESS	FARRAGOES	FERMENTER
EXPIATORY	EXTRADITE	FADDISHLY	FARROWING	FEROCIOUS
EXPLAINED	EXTRAVERT	FADEDNESS	FAR-SEEING	FERRETING
EXPLAINER	EXTREMELY	FAGACEOUS	FARTHINGS	FERROCENE
EXPLETIVE	EXTREMISM	FAGGOTING	FASCICLED	FERROTYPE

FERTILITY	FILOSELLE	FISHCAKES	FLAUTISTS	FLUCTUATE
FERTILIZE	FILTERING	FISHERIES	FLAVOROUS	FLUFFIEST
FERVENTLY	FILTER TIP	FISHERMAN	FLAVOURED	FLUIDIZER
FESTERING	FILTHIEST	FISHERMEN	FLAVOURER	FLUKINESS
FESTIVALS	FIMBRIATE	FISH FARMS	FLEABITES	FLUMMOXED
FESTIVITY	FINALISTS	FISHGUARD	FLEDGLING	FLUORESCE
FESTOONED	FINALIZED	FISHINESS	FLEETNESS	FLUOROSIS
FETICIDAL	FINANCIAL	FISH KNIFE	FLEETWOOD	FLUORSPAR
FETISHISM	FINANCIER	FISHPLATE	FLENSBURG	FLURRYING
FETISHIST	FINANCING	FISH SLICE	FLESHIEST	FLUSTERED
FETISHIZE	FINE-GRAIN	FISH STICK	FLESHINGS	FLUTTERED
FETTERING	FINE PRINT	FISSILITY	FLESHPOTS	FLUTTERER
FETTUCINE	FINE-TOOTH	FISTULOUS	FLEURETTE	FLUXIONAL
FEUDALISM	FINE-TUNED	FIXATIONS	FLEXIONAL	FLUXMETER
FEUDALIST	FINGERING	FIXATIVES	FLEXITIME	FLY-FISHER
FEUDALITY	FINGERTIP	FIXED-HEAD	FLICKERED	FLY HALVES
FEUDALIZE	FINICKETY	FIXED STAR	FLIGHTIER	FLYING FOX
FEUDATORY	FINISHING	FIZZINESS	FLIGHTILY	FLYLEAVES
FEVERWORT	FINISTERE	FLABBIEST	FLIMSIEST	FLYSHEETS
FIBONACCI	FIRE ALARM	FLABELLUM	FLINCHING	FLYWEIGHT
FIBREFILL	FIREBALLS	FLACCIDLY	FLINTIEST	FLYWHEELS
FIBRIFORM	FIREBOXES	FLAGELLAR	FLINTLOCK	FLYWHISKS
FIBRINOUS	FIREBRAND	FLAGELLUM	FLIP-FLOPS	FOAMINESS
FICTIONAL	FIREBREAK	FLAGEOLET	FLIPPANCY	FOCUSABLE
FIDEISTIC	FIREBRICK	FLAGPOLES	FLOATABLE	FOCUSSING
FIDGETING	FIRECREST	FLAGRANCE	FLOAT-FEED	FOETATION
FIDUCIARY	FIRE DRILL	FLAGRANCY	FLOCCULUS	FOETICIDE
FIELD ARMY	FIRE-EATER	FLAGSHIPS	FLOGGINGS	FOGGINESS
FIELD DAYS	FIREFIGHT	FLAGSTAFF	FLOODABLE	FOLIATION
FIELDFARE	FIREFLIES	FLAGSTONE	FLOODGATE	FOLIOLATE
FIELD GOAL	FIREGUARD	FLAG-WAVER	FLOOD TIDE	FOLK DANCE
FIELDSMAN	FIRE IRONS	FLAKINESS	FLOOR SHOW	FOLKLORIC
FIELDSMEN	FIRELIGHT	FLAMELIKE	FLOPHOUSE	FOLK MUSIC
FIELD-TEST	FIREPLACE	FLAMINGOS	FLOPPIEST	FOLKTALES
FIELD TRIP	FIRE-PLUGS	FLAMMABLE	FLOPTICAL	FOLLICLES
FIELDWORK	FIREPOWER	FLANNELED	FLORIATED	FOLLOWERS
FIFTEENTH	FIREPROOF	FLAPJACKS	FLORIDITY	FOLLOWING
FIFTIETHS	FIRESIDES	FLARE PATH	FLORISTIC	FOLLOW-UPS
FIG LEAVES	FIRESTONE	FLASHBACK	FLOS FERRI	FOMENTING
FIGURE OUT	FIRESTORM	FLASHBULB	FLOTATION	FOOD CHAIN
FIGURINES	FIRETHORN	FLASHCUBE	FLOTILLAS	FOOD STAMP
FILAMENTS	FIRETRAPS	FLASHGUNS	FLOUNCING	FOODSTUFF
FILIATION	FIREWATER	FLASHIEST	FLOUNDERS	FOOLERIES
FILICIDAL	FIREWORKS	FLASHOVER	FLOURMILL	FOOLHARDY
FILLETING	FIRMAMENT	FLATMATES	FLOWCHART	FOOLISHLY
FILLISTER	FIRSTBORN	FLAT SPINS	FLOWERAGE	FOOLPROOF
FILMINESS	FIRST FOOT	FLATTENED	FLOWERBED	FOOTBALLS
FILM SPEED	FIRSTHAND	FLATTENER	FLOWERING	FOOTBOARD
FILM STARS	FIRST LADY	FLATTERED	FLOWERPOT	FOOTFALLS
FILM STOCK	FIRSTLING	FLATTERER	FLOWINGLY	FOOT FAULT
FILMSTRIP	FIRST NAME	FLATULENT	FLOWMETER	FOOTHILLS
FILOPLUME	FIRST-RATE	FLAUNTING	FLUCTUANT	FOOTHOLDS

FOOTLOOSE	FOREWORDS	FOVEOLATE	FRENCHMEN	FRUSTRATE
FOOTNOTES	FORFEITED	FOXGLOVES	FREQUENCE	FRYING PAN
FOOTPATHS	FORFEITER	FOXHOUNDS	FREQUENCY	FUGACIOUS
FOOTPLATE	FORFICATE	FOXHUNTER	FRESHENED	FUGITIVES
FOOT-POUND	FORGATHER	FRACTIONS	FRESHENER	FUKUSHIMA
FOOTPRINT	FORGEABLE	FRACTIOUS	FRESHNESS	FULFILLED
FOOTRACES	FORGERIES	FRACTURAL	FRETBOARD	FULFILLER
FOOTSTALK	FORGETFUL	FRACTURED	FRETFULLY	FULGURITE
FOOTSTALL	FORGETTER	FRACTURES	FRETWORKS	FULGUROUS
FOOTSTEPS	FORGIVING	FRAGILITY	FRIARBIRD	FULLBACKS
FOOTSTOOL	FORGOTTEN	FRAGMENTS	FRICASSEE	FULL-BLOWN
FORAMINAL	ORLORNLY	FRAGONARD	FRICATIVE	FULL BOARD
FORBEARER	FORMALISM	FRAGRANCE	FRIESIANS	FULL DRESS
FORBIDDEN	FORMALIST	FRAILTIES	FRIESLAND	FULLERENE
FORBIDDER	FORMALITY	FRAMBOISE	FRIGHTFUL	FULL-FACED
FORCEABLE	FORMALIZE	FRAMEWORK	FRIGIDITY	FULL-GROWN
FORCE FEED	FORMATION	FRANCHISE	FRILLIEST	FULL HOUSE
FORCE-FEED	FORMATIVE	FRANCOLIN	FRISKIEST	FULL MARKS
FORCEMEAT	FORMATTED	FRANGIBLE	FRITTERED	FULL MONTY
FORCINGLY	FORMICARY	FRANGLAIS	FRITTERER	FULL MOONS
FOREARMED	FORMULAIC	FRANKABLE	FRIVOLITY	FULL-SCALE
FOREBEARS	FORMULARY	FRANKFORT	FRIVOLLER	FULL STOPS
FOREBODED	FORMULATE	FRANKNESS	FRIVOLOUS	FULMINANT
FOREBODER	FORMULISM	FRATERNAL	FRIZZIEST	FULMINATE
FOREBRAIN	FORMULIST	FRAUDSTER	FRIZZLING	FULSOMELY
FORECASTS	FORNICATE	FREE AGENT	FROCK COAT	FUMAROLIC
FORECLOSE	FORSAKING	FREE-BASED	FROGMARCH	FUMIGATED
FORECOURT	FORSYTHIA	FREEBOARD	FROGMOUTH	FUMIGATOR
FOREFRONT	FORTALEZA	FREEHOLDS	FROGSPAWN	FUNCTIONS
FOREGOING	FORTALICE	FREE HOUSE	FROLICKED	FUNDAMENT
FOREHANDS	FORTHWITH	FREE KICKS	FROLICKER	FUNGICIDE
FOREHEADS	FORTIETHS	FREELANCE	FRONTAGES	FUNGIFORM
FOREIGNER	FORTIFIED	FREE-LIVER	FRONTALLY	FUNGISTAT
FOREJUDGE	FORTIFIER	FREEMASON	FRONT DOOR	FUNICULAR
FORELOCKS	FORTITUDE	FREEPHONE	FRONTIERS	FUNICULUS
FORENAMED	FORTNIGHT	FREE PORTS	FRONT LINE	FUNNELING
FORENAMES	FORTUNATE	FREE-RANGE	FRONT-PAGE	FUNNELLED
FORENSICS	FORT WORTH	FREESHEET	FRONT ROOM	FUNNINESS
FOREREACH	FORTY-FIVE	FREE STATE	FROSTBITE	FUNNY BONE
FORESHANK	FORWARDED	FREESTONE	FROSTIEST	FUNNY FARM
FORESHEET	FORWARDER	FREESTYLE	FROSTWORK	FURBISHED
FORESHOCK	FORWARDLY	FREE TRADE	FROTHIEST	FURBISHER
FORESHORE	FOSSILIZE	FREE VERSE	FROWSTIER	FURCATION
FORESIGHT	FOSSORIAL	FREEWHEEL	FROWZIEST	FURIOUSLY
FORESKINS	FOSTERAGE	FREE WORLD	FRUCTUOUS	FURLOUGHS
FORESTALL	FOSTERING	FREEZABLE	FRUGALITY	FURNISHED
FORESTERS	FOUNDERED	FREEZE-DRY	FRUIT BATS	FURNISHER
FORETASTE	FOUNDLING	FREIGHTED	FRUITCAKE	FURNITURE
FORETOKEN	FOUNDRIES	FREIGHTER	FRUITERER	FURRINESS
FORETOOTH	FOUNTAINS	FREMANTLE	FRUITIEST	FURROWING
FOREWOMAN	FOURSOMES	FRENCHIFY	FRUITLESS	FURTHERED
FOREWOMEN	FOUR-WHEEL	FRENCHMAN	FRUMPIEST	FURTHERER

FURTIVELY	GAOLBIRDS	GAZUMPING	GERMANIUM	GLANDULAR
FUSELAGES	GARBOLOGY	GEARBOXES	GERMANIZE	GLARINGLY
FUSILLADE	GARDENERS	GEAR LEVER	GERMANOUS	GLASSIEST
FUSIONISM	GARDENIAS	GEARSHIFT	GERM CELLS	GLASSWARE
FUSIONIST	GARDENING	GEAR STICK	GERMICIDE	GLASSWORK
FUSSINESS	GARGOYLED	GEARWHEEL	GERMINANT	GLASSWORT
FUSTINESS	GARGOYLES	GEHLENITE	GERMINATE	GLEANABLE
FUTURISTS	GARIBALDI	GELIGNITE	GERMISTON	GLEANINGS
FUZZINESS	GARLANDED	GELLIGAER	GERUNDIAL	GLEEFULLY
	GARNERING	GELSEMIUM	GERUNDIVE	GLENGARRY
G	GARNISHED	GEMMATION	GESTATION	GLIDINGLY
GABARDINE	GARNISHER	GEMUTLICH	GESTATORY	GLIMMERED
GABERDINE	GARNISHES	GENDARMES	GESTURING	GLIMPSING
GABIONADE	GARNITURE	GENEALOGY	GETTING ON	GLISSADER
GADABOUTS	GARRISONS	GENE CLONE	GEYSERITE	GLISSANDO
GADOLINIC	GARROTTED	GENERABLE	GHASTLIER	GLISTENED
GADROONED	GARROTTER	GENERALLY	GHETTOIZE	GLITTERED
GAINFULLY	GARROTTES	GENERATED	GHOSTLIER	GLITZIEST
GAINSAYER	GARRULITY	GENERATOR	GHOST TOWN	GLOBALISM
GALACTOSE	GARRULOUS	GENIALITY	GIANT STAR	GLOBALIST
GALANTINE	GAS FITTER	GENITALIC	GIBBERING	GLOBALIZE
GALAPAGOS	GAS HEATER	GENITALLY	GIBBERISH	GLOBE FISH
GALEIFORM	GASHOLDER	GENITIVAL	GIBRALTAR	GLOBOSITY
GALENICAL	GASLIGHTS	GENITIVES	GIDDINESS	GLOMERATE
GALINGALE	GAS MANTLE	GENOCIDAL	GIFT HORSE	GLOMERULE
GALLANTLY	GASOLINIC	GENOTYPIC	GIGAHERTZ	GLOOMIEST
GALLANTRY	GASOMETER	GENTEELLY	GIGANTISM	GLORIFIED
GALLERIED	GASOMETRY	GENTILITY	GILSONITE	GLORIFIER
GALLERIES	GASPINGLY	GENTLEMAN	GILT-EDGED	GLORY HOLE
GALLICISM	GASSINESS	GENTLEMEN	GIMMICKRY	GLOSSIEST
GALLICIZE	GASTRITIC	GENTLE SEX	GINGER ALE	GLOSSITIC
GALLINULE	GASTRITIS	GENUFLECT	GINGERING	GLOSSITIS
GALLIPOLI	GASTROPOD	GENUINELY	GINGER NUT	GLOTTIDES
GALLIVANT	GASTRULAR	GEODESIST	GIN SLINGS	GLOTTISES
GALLIWASP	GATECRASH	GEOGRAPHY	GIPSYWORT	GLOWERING
GALLONAGE	GATEHOUSE	GEOLOGIST	GIRANDOLE	GLOWINGLY
GALLOPING	GATEPOSTS	GEOLOGIZE	GIRL GUIDE	GLOW-WORMS
GALLSTONE	GATESHEAD	GEOMANCER	GIRLISHLY	GLUCOSIDE
GALUMPHED	GATHERING	GEOMANTIC	GIRONDISM	GLUTAMINE
GALVANISM	GAUCHERIE	GEOMETRIC	GIRONDIST	GLUTENOUS
GALVANIZE	GAUDINESS	GEOMETRID	GIVEAWAYS	GLUTINOUS
GALWEGIAN	GAUGEABLE	GEOPHYTIC	GIVEN NAME	GLYCERIDE
GAMBOGIAN	GAUGEABLY	GEOPONICS	GLABELLAR	GLYCERINE
GAMBOLING	GAULEITER	GEORGETTE	GLADDENED	GLYCOSIDE
GAMECOCKS	GAUNTLETS	GEOSTATIC	GLADDENER	GOAL LINES
GAMMADION	GAUNTNESS	GEOTACTIC	GLADIATOR	GOALMOUTH
GAMMA RAYS	GAUZINESS	GEOTROPIC	GLADIOLUS	GOALPOSTS
GANDHIISM	GAWKINESS	GERANIUMS	GLAIREOUS	GOATHERDS
GANG-BANGS	GAZA STRIP	GERIATRIC	GLAMORGAN	GOATSKINS
GANGLIONS	GAZEHOUND	GERMANDER	GLAMORIZE	GO-BETWEEN
GANGPLANK	GAZETTEER	GERMANISM	GLAMOROUS	GODESBERG
GANGSTERS	GAZIANTEP	GERMANITE	GLANDERED	GODFATHER

GODLESSLY	GOVERNESS	GREASIEST	GROOMSMAN	GUILDSMAN
GODLINESS	GOVERNING	GREAT-AUNT	GROOVIEST	GUILELESS
GODMOTHER	GOVERNORS	GREAT BEAR	GROPINGLY	GUILLEMOT
GODPARENT	GRACELESS	GREAT BELT	GROSGRAIN	GUILLOCHE
GO-GETTERS	GRADATION	GREATCOAT	GROSSNESS	GUILTIEST
GOGGLE BOX	GRADIENTS	GREAT DANE	GROTESQUE	GUILTLESS
GOING-OVER	GRADUALLY	GREATNESS	GROTTIEST	GUINEA PIG
GOLDCREST	GRADUATED	GREEDIEST	GROUCHIER	GUITARIST
GOLDEN AGE	GRADUATES	GREENAWAY	GROUCHILY	GULPINGLY
GOLDENEYE	GRADUATOR	GREENBACK	GROUCHING	GUMMATOUS
GOLDENROD	GRAMPUSES	GREEN BEAN	GROUNDAGE	GUMMINESS
GOLDFIELD	GRANARIES	GREEN BELT	GROUNDING	GUMSHIELD
GOLDFINCH	GRANDADDY	GREEN EYED	GROUNDNUT	GUN COTTON
GOLD MEDAL	GRANDIOSE	GREENGAGE	GROUNDSEL	GUNPOWDER
GOLD-MINER	GRANDIOSO	GREENHEAD	GROUPINGS	GUNRUNNER
GOLDMINES	GRAND JURY	GREENHORN	GROUPWARE	GUNSMITHS
GOLD PLATE	GRANDNESS	GREENLAND	GROVELING	GUSHINGLY
GOLDSMITH	GRAND PRIX	GREENLING	GROVELLED	GUSTATORY
GOLF BALLS	GRAND SLAM	GREENNESS	GROVELLER	GUSTINESS
GOLF CLUBS	GRANDSONS	GREENROOM	GRUBBIEST	GUTTERING
GOLF LINKS	GRANITITE	GREEN ROOM	GRUBSTAKE	GYMKHANAS
GOLLIWOGS	GRANIVORE	GREENSAND	GRUELLING	GYMNASIUM
GOMPHOSIS	GRANOLITH	GREENWICH	GRUFFNESS	GYMNASTIC
GONDOLIER	GRANTABLE	GREENWOOD	GRUMBLERS	GYNAECOID
GONIATITE	GRANULATE	GREETINGS	GRUMBLING	GYNARCHIC
GONOPHORE	GRANULITE	GREGARINE	GRUMPIEST	GYNOECIUM
GONORRHEA	GRANULOMA	GREGORIAN	GUANABARA	GYNOPHORE
GOODLIEST	GRAPESHOT	GRENADIER	GUANGDONG	GYRATIONS
GOOD LOOKS	GRAPEVINE	GRENADINE	GUANIDINE	GYRFALCON
GOODNIGHT	GRAPHITIC	GREY AREAS	GUANOSINE	GYROSCOPE
GOOD-SIZED	GRAPPELLI	GREYBEARD	GUARANTEE	
GOOD TIMES	GRAPPLING	GREYHOUND	GUARANTOR	**H**
GOOD WORDS	GRASPABLE	GREY-STATE	GUARDABLE	HABERGEON
GOOFINESS	GRASSIEST	GREYWACKE	GUARDEDLY	HABITABLE
GOOSANDER	GRASSLAND	GREY WATER	GUARDIANS	HABITABLY
GOOSEFOOT	GRASSQUIT	GRIDIRONS	GUARDRAIL	HABITUATE
GOOSENECK	GRATICULE	GRIEVANCE	GUARDROOM	HACIENDAS
GOOSESTEP	GRATIFIED	GRILLROOM	GUARDSMAN	HACKAMORE
GOOSINESS	GRATIFIER	GRIMACING	GUARDSMEN	HACKBERRY
GORAKHPUR	GRATINGLY	GRIMALKIN	GUARD'S VAN	HACKNEYED
GORGEABLE	GRATITUDE	GRIMINESS	GUATEMALA	HADROSAUR
GORGONIAN	GRAVELING	GRINDELIA	GUAYAQUIL	HAECCEITY
GORILLIAN	GRAVELISH	GRIPINGLY	GUERRILLA	HAEMATEIN
GORILLOID	GRAVELLED	GRISAILLE	GUESSABLE	HAEMATITE
GOSPELLER	GRAVENESS	GRISLIEST	GUESSWORK	HAEMATOID
GOSSIPING	GRAVESEND	GRISTLIER	GUESTROOM	HAEMATOMA
GOTHICISM	GRAVESIDE	GRISTMILL	GUFFAWING	HAEMOCOEL
GO THROUGH	GRAVEYARD	GRITTIEST	GUIDELINE	HAEMOCYTE
GO TO EARTH	GRAVIDITY	GRIZZLING	GUIDEPOST	HAEMOSTAT
GOTTINGEN	GRAVITATE	GROCERIES	GUIDINGLY	HAGBUTEER
GOURMANDS	GRAVY BOAT	GROGGIEST	GUILDFORD	HAGGADIST
GOUTINESS	GREASE GUN	GRONINGEN	GUILDHALL	HAGGARDLY

HAGGISHLY	HAMADRYAD	HARBOURED	HASTENING	HEALTHIER
HAGIARCHY	HAMADRYAS	HARBOURER	HASTINESS	HEALTHILY
HAGIOLOGY	HAMAMATSU	HARDBACKS	HATCHABLE	HEARKENED
HAG-RIDDEN	HAMBURGER	HARDBOARD	HATCHBACK	HEARKENER
HAIDAR ALI	HAMERSLEY	HARDBOUND	HATCHLING	HEARTACHE
HAILSTONE	HAM-FISTED	HARD CIDER	HATCHMENT	HEARTBEAT
HAILSTORM	HAMMERING	HARD CORES	HATCHWAYS	HEARTBURN
HAIRBRUSH	HAMMERTOE	HARD COURT	HATEFULLY	HEARTENED
HAIRCLOTH	HAMMURABI	HARDCOVER	HAT TRICKS	HEARTFELT
HAIRGRIPS	HAMPERING	HARD DISKS	HAUGHTIER	HEARTHRUG
HAIRINESS	HAMPSHIRE	HARD DRINK	HAUGHTILY	HEARTIEST
HAIRLINES	HAMPSTEAD	HARDENING	HAVE A BASH	HEARTLAND
HAIRPIECE	HAMSTRING	HARDHEADS	HAVENLESS	HEARTLESS
HAIR SHIRT	HAMSTRUNG	HARDHOUSE	HAVERSACK	HEARTSICK
HAIR SLIDE	HANDBASIN	HARDIHOOD	HAVERSIAN	HEARTSOME
HAIRSTYLE	HANDBILLS	HARDINESS	HAVERSINE	HEARTWOOD
HALEAKALA	HANDBOOKS	HARD-LINER	HAWKSBILL	HEARTWORM
HALESOWEN	HANDBRAKE	HARD LINES	HAWSEHOLE	HEATHERED
HALFBACKS	HANDCARTS	HARD-NOSED	HAWSEPIPE	HEATHFOWL
HALF-BAKED	HANDCLAPS	HARDSHIPS	HAWTHORNE	HEATHLAND
HALF BOARD	HANDCLASP	HARD TIMES	HAWTHORNS	HEATHLIKE
HALF-BREED	HANDCRAFT	HARDWOODS	HAYMAKING	HEAT PUMPS
HALF-CASTE	HANDCUFFS	HAREBELLS	HAYSTACKS	HEAT WAVES
HALF CROWN	HANDICAPS	HARKENING	HAZARDING	HEAVINESS
HALF DOZEN	HANDINESS	HARLEQUIN	HAZARDOUS	HEAVISIDE
HALF-DOZEN	HANDIWORK	HARMATTAN	HEADACHES	HEAVY-DUTY
HALF-HITCH	HANDLEBAR	HARMFULLY	HEADBANDS	HEBRAIZER
HALF LIGHT	HANDLOOMS	HARMONICA	HEADBOARD	HEBRIDEAN
HALF-LIGHT	HANDOVERS	HARMONICS	HEADDRESS	HECTOGRAM
HALF-LIVES	HANDRAILS	HARMONIES	HEADFIRST	HECTORING
HALF MOONS	HANDS DOWN	HARMONIST	HEAD FIRST	HEDGE FUND
HALF NOTES	HANDSHAKE	HARMONIUM	HEADINESS	HEDGEHOGS
HALFPENCE	HANDSPIKE	HARMONIZE	HEADLANDS	HEDGEROWS
HALFPENNY	HANDSTAND	HARMOTOME	HEADLIGHT	HEDONISTS
HALF-PLATE	HANGERS ON	HARNESSED	HEADLINED	HEEDFULLY
HALFTONES	HANGERS-ON	HARNESSER	HEADLINER	HEELPIECE
HALF-TRUTH	HANGNAILS	HARNESSES	HEADLINES	HEFTINESS
HALITOSIS	HANGOVERS	HARPOONED	HEADPIECE	HEGEMONIC
HALLELUJA	HANKERING	HARPOONER	HEADREACH	HEGUMENOS
HALLIARDS	HANSEATIC	HARQUEBUS	HEADRESTS	HEILBRONN
HALL-JONES	HAPHAZARD	HARRIDANS	HEADSCARF	HEIMDALLR
HALLMARKS	HAPHTARAH	HARROGATE	HEADSHIPS	HEINOUSLY
HALLOWEEN	HAPLESSLY	HARROVIAN	HEADSTALL	HEIRESSES
HALLOWE'EN	HAPLOLOGY	HARROWING	HEADSTAND	HEIRLOOMS
HALLOWING	HAPPENING	HARSHNESS	HEAD START	HELGOLAND
HALLOWMAS	HAPPINESS	HARTBEEST	HEADSTOCK	HELICALLY
HALLSTATT	HAPPY HOUR	HARTSHORN	HEADSTONE	HELICLINE
HALMAHERA	HARANGUED	HARUSPICY	HEADWARDS	HELIOSTAT
HALOBIONT	HARANGUER	HARVESTED	HEADWINDS	HELIOTYPE
HALOPHYTE	HARANGUES	HARVESTER	HEADWORDS	HELIOZOAN
HALOTHANE	HARASSING	HASDRUBAL	HEALINGLY	HELIPORTS
HALTINGLY	HARBINGER	HASHEMITE	HEALTHFUL	HELLDIVER

HELLEBORE	HETAERISM	HIGH TABLE	HOBBESIAN	HOME TRUTH
HELLENIAN	HETAERIST	HIGH TIDES	HOBGOBLIN	HOMEWARDS
HELLENISM	HETAIRISM	HIGH-TONED	HOBNAILED	HOMEYNESS
HELLENIST	HETERODOX	HIGH WATER	HOBNOBBED	HOMICIDAL
HELLENIZE	HETERONYM	HIJACKERS	HO CHI MINH	HOMICIDES
HELLHOUND	HETEROSIS	HIJACKING	HODOMETER	HOMILETIC
HELLISHLY	HEURISTIC	HILARIOUS	HODOMETRY	HOMOGRAFT
HELPFULLY	HEXACHORD	HILLBILLY	HODOSCOPE	HOMOGRAPH
HELPMATES	HEXAGONAL	HILLOCKED	HOGGISHLY	HOMOLYSIS
HELVELLYN	HEXAGRAMS	HILLSIDES	HOGSHEADS	HOMOLYTIC
HELVETIAN	HEXAMETER	HILVERSUM	HOHENLOHE	HOMONYMIC
HELVETIUS	HEXAPODIC	HIMALAYAS	HOIDENISH	HOMOPHILE
HEMIALGIA	HEXASTICH	HIMYARITE	HOI POLLOI	HOMOPHONE
HEMICYCLE	HEXASTYLE	HINDBRAIN	HOLARCTIC	HOMOPHONY
HEMINGWAY	HEXATEUCH	HINDERING	HOLDOVERS	HOMOPHYLY
HEMISTICH	HEYERDAHL	HINDOOISM	HOLD WATER	HOMOPLASY
HEMITROPE	HEY PRESTO	HINDRANCE	HOLE IN ONE	HOMOPOLAR
HEMSTITCH	HIBERNATE	HINDSIGHT	HOLIDAYED	HOMOSPORY
HENDIADYS	HIBERNIAN	HINDU KUSH	HOLINSHED	HOMOTAXIC
HEN HOUSES	HICCUPING	HINDUSTAN	HOLLANDER	HOMOTAXIS
HENPECKED	HICKORIES	HINGELESS	HOLLANDIA	HONEYBEES
HEOMANIAC	HIDDENITE	HINGELIKE	HOLLERING	HONEYCOMB
HEPATITIS	HIDEAWAYS	HIP FLASKS	HOLLOWEST	HONEYEDLY
HEPTAGONS	HIDEBOUND	HIP POCKET	HOLLOWING	HONEY-LIKE
HEPTARCHY	HIDEOUSLY	HIPPOCRAS	HOLLYHOCK	HONEYMOON
HERACLEAN	HIERARCHY	HIPPOLYTA	HOLLYWOOD	HONEYTRAP
HERALDING	HIERODULE	HIPPOLYTE	HOLOCAINE	HONKY-TONK
HERALDIST	HIEROGRAM	HIRELINGS	HOLOCAUST	HONORARIA
HERBALIST	HIEROLOGY	HIROSHIGE	HOLOCRINE	HONORIFIC
HERBARIAL	HIFALUTIN	HIROSHIMA	HOLOGRAMS	HONOR ROLL
HERBARIUM	HIGHBALLS	HIRUNDINE	HOLOGRAPH	HONOURING
HERBICIDE	HIGHBROWS	HISPIDITY	HOLOPHYTE	HOODOOISM
HERBIVORE	HIGH CHAIR	HISTAMINE	HOLOTYPIC	HOOFBOUND
HERCULEAN	HIGH-CLASS	HISTIDINE	HOLSTEINS	HOOK NOSED
HERCYNIAN	HIGH COURT	HISTOGENY	HOLSTERED	HOOK-NOSED
HEREAFTER	HIGHER-UPS	HISTOGRAM	HOLY GHOST	HOOKWORMS
HERETICAL	HIGH-FLIER	HISTOLOGY	HOLY GRAIL	HOOLIGANS
HEREUNDER	HIGH-FLOWN	HISTORIAN	HOLYSTONE	HOOTNANNY
HERITABLE	HIGH-FLYER	HISTORIES	HOLY WATER	HOOVERING
HERITABLY	HIGH-GRADE	HIT AND RUN	HOME ALONE	HOPE CHEST
HERITRESS	HIGH HOPES	HIT-AND-RUN	HOME FRONT	HOPEFULLY
HERMITAGE	HIGH HORSE	HITCHCOCK	HOMEGROWN	HOP GARDEN
HERMITIAN	HIGH JINKS	HITCHHIKE	HOME GUARD	HOPLOLOGY
HERNIATED	HIGH JUMPS	HITLERISM	HOME HELPS	HOPSCOTCH
HERODOTUS	HIGHLANDS	HIT-OR-MISS	HOMELANDS	HOREHOUND
HESELTINE	HIGH-LEVEL	HIT PARADE	HOMELIEST	HORNBILLS
HESITANCY	HIGHLIGHT	HIT WICKET	HOMEMAKER	HORNINESS
HESITATED	HIGH POINT	HOARDINGS	HOME MOVIE	HORNPIPES
HESITATER	HIGH-RISES	HOARFROST	HOMEOPATH	HORNSTONE
HESPERIAN	HIGH ROADS	HOARHOUND	HOMEOWNER	HOROLOGIC
HESSONITE	HIGH-SPEED	HOARINESS	HOMESTEAD	HOROSCOPE
HESYCHAST	HIGH SPOTS	HOATCHING	HOMETOWNS	HOROSCOPY

HORRIFIED	HOYDENISH	HYDANTOIN	IDIOLECTS	IMMOLATOR
HORSEBACK	HSUAN T'UNG	HYDATHODE	IDIOMATIC	IMMORALLY
HORSE FAIR	HUBRISTIC	HYDERABAD	IDIOPATHY	IMMORTALS
HORSEHAIR	HUCKABACK	HYDRANGEA	IDIOPHONE	IMMOVABLE
HORSEHIDE	HUCKSTERS	HYDRASTIS	IDOLATERS	IMMOVABLY
HORSELESS	HUE AND CRY	HYDRATION	IDOLIZING	IMMUNIZED
HORSELIKE	HUFFINESS	HYDRAULIC	IGNESCENT	IMMUNIZER
HORSEMINT	HUGH CAPET	HYDRAZINE	IGNITABLE	IMMUTABLE
HORSEPLAY	HU-HO-	HYDRAZOIC	IGNORAMUS	IMMUTABLY
HORSESHIT	HAO-T'E	HYDRIODIC	IGNORANCE	IMPACTING
HORSESHOE	HUMANISTS	HYDROCELE	IGNORATIO	IMPACTION
HORSETAIL	HUMANIZED	HYDROFOIL	IGUANODON	IMPAIRING
HORSEWEED	HUMANIZER	HYDROLOGY	ILEOSTOMY	IMPARTIAL
HORSEWHIP	HUMANKIND	HYDROLYSE	ILL AT EASE	IMPARTING
HORSINESS	HUMAN-LIKE	HYDROLYTE	ILLAWARRA	IMPASSION
HORTATIVE	HUMANNESS	HYGIENIST	ILLEGALLY	IMPASSIVE
HORTATORY	HUMANOIDS	HYPERBOLA	ILLEGIBLE	IMPATIENS
HOSPITALS	HUMAN RACE	HYPERBOLE	ILLEGIBLY	IMPATIENT
HOSPITIUM	HUMBLEBEE	HYPERCUBE	ILL-GOTTEN	IMPEACHED
HOSTELLER	HUMBUGGER	HYPERTEXT	ILLIBERAL	IMPEACHER
HOSTESSES	HUMDINGER	HYPHENATE	ILLICITLY	IMPEDANCE
HOSTILELY	HUMECTANT	HYPNOTISM	ILLNESSES	IMPELLENT
HOSTILITY	HUMERUSES	HYPNOTIST	ILLOGICAL	IMPELLING
HOTELIERS	HUMIDNESS	HYPNOTIZE	ILL-OMENED	IMPENDING
HOTFOOTED	HUMILIATE	HYPOCRISY	ILLUSIONS	IMPERFECT
HOTHEADED	HUMONGOUS	HYPOCRITE	IMAGINARY	IMPERILED
HOTHOUSES	HUMORISTS	HYSTERICS	IMAGINING	IMPERIOUS
HOTPLATES	HUMOURFUL		IMAGISTIC	IMPETRATE
HOT POTATO	HUMOURING	**I**	IMBALANCE	IMPETUOUS
HOTTENTOT	HUMPBACKS	IBUPROFEN	IMBECILES	IMPETUSES
HOT WATERS	HUMPINESS	ICE CREAMS	IMBEDDING	IMPIETIES
HOURGLASS	HUNCHBACK	ICE HOCKEY	IMBRICATE	IMPINGING
HOUSEBOAT	HUNDREDTH	ICELANDER	IMBROGLIO	IMPIOUSLY
HOUSEBOYS	HUNGARIAN	ICELANDIC	IMIDAZOLE	IMPLANTED
HOUSECARL	HUNGERING	ICE SHEETS	IMITATING	IMPLANTER
HOUSECOAT	HUNGRIEST	ICE SKATED	IMITATION	IMPLEADER
HOUSEHOLD	HUNKY DORY	ICE-SKATED	IMITATIVE	IMPLEMENT
HOUSELEEK	HUNKY-DORY	ICE-SKATER	IMITATORS	IMPLICATE
HOUSELESS	HUNNISHLY	ICE SKATES	IMMANENCE	IMPLODING
HOUSELINE	HURRICANE	ICHNEUMON	IMMANENCY	IMPLORING
HOUSEMAID	HURRIEDLY	ICHNOLOGY	IMMEDIACY	IMPLOSION
HOUSEROOM	HURTFULLY	ICHTHYOID	IMMEDIATE	IMPLOSIVE
HOUSETOPS	HUSBANDED	ICONOLOGY	IMMENSELY	IMPOLITIC
HOUSEWIFE	HUSBANDER	IDEALISTS	IMMENSITY	IMPORTANT
HOUSEWORK	HUSBANDRY	IDEALIZED	IMMERSING	IMPORTERS
HOUSTONIA	HUSH MONEY	IDEALIZER	IMMERSION	IMPORTING
HOVERPORT	HUSKINESS	IDENTICAL	IMMIGRANT	IMPORTUNE
HOW ARE YOU	HYACINTHS	IDENTIKIT	IMMIGRATE	IMPOSABLE
HOWITZERS	HYBRIDISM	IDEOGRAMS	IMMINENCE	IMPOSTORS
HOWLINGLY	HYBRIDITY	IDEOLOGUE	IMMINGHAM	IMPOSTURE
HOWSOEVER	HYBRIDIZE	IDEOMOTOR	IMMODESTY	IMPOTENCE
HOWTOWDIE	HYBRISTIC	IDIOBLAST	IMMOLATED	IMPOUNDED

IMPOUNDER	INCOME TAX	INDULGENT	INGESTING	INQUIRING
IMPRECATE	INCOMMODE	INDULGING	INGESTION	INQUORATE
IMPRECISE	INCORRECT	INEBRIANT	INGESTIVE	INSCRIBED
IMPRESSED	INCORRUPT	INEBRIATE	INGLENOOK	INSCRIBER
IMPRESSER	INCREASED	INEBRIETY	INGRAINED	INSECTEAN
IMPRESSES	INCREASER	INEFFABLE	INGROWING	INSELBERG
IMPRINTED	INCREASES	INEFFABLY	INHABITED	INSENSATE
IMPRINTER	INCREMENT	INELASTIC	INHALANTS	INSERTING
IMPROBITY	INCRETION	INELEGANT	INHALATOR	INSERTION
IMPROMPTU	INCUBATED	INEPTNESS	INHAMBANE	IN-SERVICE
IMPROVING	INCUBATOR	INERTNESS	INHARMONY	INSETTING
IMPROVISE	INCUBUSES	INFANTILE	IN HARNESS	INSIDE JOB
IMPRUDENT	INCULCATE	INFARCTED	INHERENCE	INSIDE OUT
IMPUDENCE	INCULPATE	INFATUATE	INHERITED	INSIDIOUS
IMPUGNING	INCUMBENT	INFECTING	INHERITOR	INSINCERE
IMPULSION	INCURABLE	INFECTION	INHIBITED	INSINUATE
IMPULSIVE	INCURABLY	INFECTIVE	INHIBITER	INSIPIDLY
IMPUTABLE	INCURIOUS	INFERABLE	INHIBITOR	INSISTENT
IN A BAD	INCURRENT	INFERENCE	INITIALED	INSISTING
WAY	INCURRING	INFERIORS	INITIALER	IN SO FAR
INABILITY	INCURSION	INFERRING	INITIALLY	AS
INAMORATA	INCURSIVE	INFERTILE	INITIATED	INSOLENCE
INANIMATE	INCURVATE	INFESTING	INITIATES	INSOLUBLE
INANITIES	INDECENCY	INFIELDER	INITIATOR	INSOLVENT
INANITION	INDECORUM	INFIGHTER	INJECTING	INSOMNIAC
INAPTNESS	INDELIBLE	INFIRMARY	INJECTION	INSPECTED
INAUDIBLE	INDELIBLY	INFIRMITY	INJECTIVE	INSPECTOR
INAUDIBLY	INDEMNIFY	INFLAMING	INJURABLE	INSPIRING
INAUGURAL	INDEMNITY	INFLATING	INJURIOUS	INSTAGRAM
IN BETWEEN	INDENTING	INFLATION	INJUSTICE	INSTALLED
INCAPABLE	INDENTION	INFLECTED	INKSTANDS	INSTALLER
INCAPABLY	INDENTURE	INFLECTOR	INMIGRANT	INSTANCED
INCARNATE	INDEXICAL	INFLICTED	INNER CITY	INSTANCES
INCAUTION	INDIAN INK	INFLICTER	INNERMOST	INSTANTER
INCENSING	INDICATED	INFLUENCE	INNER TUBE	INSTANTLY
INCENTIVE	INDICATOR	INFLUENZA	INNERVATE	INSTIGATE
INCEPTION	INDICTING	INFORMANT	INNKEEPER	INSTILLED
INCEPTIVE	INDIGENCE	INFORMERS	INN KEEPER	INSTILLER
INCESSANT	INDIGNANT	INFORMING	INNOCENCE	INSTINCTS
INCIDENCE	INDIGNITY	INFRACTOR	INNOCUOUS	INSTITUTE
INCIDENTS	INDIGOTIC	INFRADIAN	INNOVATED	INSULATED
INCIPIENT	INDISPOSE	INFRINGED	INNOVATOR	INSULATOR
INCISIONS	INDOCHINA	INFRINGER	INNSBRUCK	INSULTING
INCISURAL	INDOLENCE	INFURIATE	INNUENDOS	INSURABLE
INCLEMENT	INDONESIA	INFUSCATE	INOCULATE	INSURANCE
INCLINING	INDORSING	INFUSIBLE	INORGANIC	INSURGENT
INCLOSING	INDRAUGHT	INFUSIONS	INOTROPIC	INSWINGER
INCLOSURE	INDUCIBLE	INFUSORIA	IN PATIENT	INTAGLIOS
INCLUDING	INDUCTILE	IN GENERAL	IN-PATIENT	INTEGRAND
INCLUSION	INDUCTING	INGENIOUS	INPUTTING	INTEGRANT
INCLUSIVE	INDUCTION	INGENUITY	INQUILINE	INTEGRATE
INCOGNITO	INDUCTIVE	INGENUOUS	INQUIRIES	INTEGRITY

INTELLECT	IN THE DARK	INVERTING	ISOCHORIC	JACKSMELT
INTENDANT	IN THE LINE	INVESTING	ISOCLINAL	JACKSNIPE
INTENDEDS	IN THE SOUP	INVIDIOUS	ISOCRATIC	JACOBITES
INTENDING	IN THE SWIM	INVIOLACY	ISOGAMETE	JAILBIRDS
INTENSELY	INTIMATED	INVIOLATE	ISOGAMOUS	JAILBREAK
INTENSIFY	INTIMATES	INVISIBLE	ISOGENOUS	JAILHOUSE
INTENSION	INTORSION	INVISIBLY	ISOLATING	JALANDHAR
INTENSITY	IN TRANSIT	INVOCABLE	ISOLATION	JAMBOREES
INTENSIVE	INTRICACY	INVOICING	ISOLATIVE	JAM-PACKED
INTENTION	INTRICATE	INVOLUCEL	ISOLOGOUS	JANISSARY
INTER ALIA	INTRIGUED	INVOLUCRE	ISOMERISM	JANSENISM
INTERBRED	INTRIGUER	INVOLVING	ISOMERIZE	JANSENIST
INTERCEDE	INTRIGUES	IODOMETRY	ISOMEROUS	JANUARIES
INTERCEPT	INTRINSIC	IONOPAUSE	ISOMETRIC	JAPANNING
INTERCITY	INTRODUCE	IPSO FACTO	ISONIAZID	JAPONICAS
INTERCOMS	INTROITAL	IRASCIBLE	ISOOCTANE	JARGONIZE
INTERCROP	INTROJECT	IRASCIBLY	ISOPROPYL	JAUNDICED
INTERDICT	INTROVERT	IRIAN JAYA	ISOSCELES	JAUNTIEST
INTERESTS	INTRUDERS	IRIDOTOMY	ISOSMOTIC	JAYWALKED
INTERFACE	INTRUDING	IRISH BULL	ISOSTATIC	JAYWALKER
INTERFERE	INTRUSION	IRISH STEW	ISOSTERIC	JEALOUSLY
INTERFILE	INTRUSIVE	IRONBOUND	ISOTACTIC	JEERINGLY
INTERFUSE	INTRUSTED	IRON CROSS	ISOTHERAL	JELLY BEAN
INTERIORS	INTUITING	IRON HORSE	ISOTHERMS	JELLYFISH
INTERJECT	INTUITION	IRONSIDES	ISOTROPIC	JELLY ROLL
INTERLACE	INTUITIVE	IRONSTONE	ISRAELITE	JEREMIADS
INTERLARD	INTUMESCE	IRONWORKS	ISTHMUSES	JERKINESS
INTERLEAF	INUNCTION	IROQUOIAN	ITALICIZE	JERKINGLY
INTERLINE	INUNDATED	IRRADIANT	ITCHINESS	JEROBOAMS
INTERLINK	INUNDATOR	IRRADIATE	ITCHY FEET	JERUSALEM
INTERLOCK	INUTILITY	IRRAWADDY	ITCHY PALM	JESTINGLY
INTERLOPE	INVADABLE	IRREGULAR	ITEMIZING	JESUITISM
INTERLUDE	INVALIDED	IRRIGABLE	ITERATION	JET ENGINE
INTERMENT	INVALIDLY	IRRIGATED	ITERATIVE	JET-SETTER
INTERNEES	INVARIANT	IRRIGATOR	ITINERANT	JET STREAM
INTERNING	INVASIONS	IRRITABLE	ITINERARY	JEWELFISH
INTERNIST	INVECTIVE	IRRITABLY	ITINERATE	JEWELLERS
INTERNODE	INVEIGHED	IRRITANTS	ITSY BITSY	JEWELLERY
INTERPLAY	INVEIGHER	IRRITATED	ITSY-BITSY	JEWELLING
INTERPOSE	INVEIGLED	IRRITATOR	IVY LEAGUE	JEW'S HARPS
INTERPRET	INVEIGLER	IRRUPTION		JIB-HEADED
INTERRING	INVENTING	IRRUPTIVE	**J**	JITTERBUG
INTERRUPT	INVENTION	ISAGOGICS		JOBCENTRE
INTERSECT	INVENTIVE	ISALLOBAR	JABBERERS	JOB CENTRE
INTERVALS	INVENTORS	ISCHAEMIA	JABBERING	JOBSWORTH
INTERVENE	INVENTORY	ISINGLASS	JABORANDI	JOCKEYING
INTERVIEW	INVERARAY	ISLAMABAD	JACARANDA	JOCKSTRAP
INTERWOVE	INVERNESS	ISLANDERS	JACKASSES	JOCULARLY
INTESTACY	INVERSELY	ISLE OF MAN	JACKBOOTS	JOCUNDITY
INTESTATE	INVERSION	ISLINGTON	JACK FROST	JOE PUBLIC
INTESTINE	INVERSIVE	ISOBARISM	JACKFRUIT	JOINTRESS
IN THE CLUB	INVERTASE	ISOBATHIC	JACK KNIFE	JOINTWORM
			JACKSHAFT	

JOLLINESS	KAMA SUTRA	KILLARNEY	KOTA BHARU	LAMINARIA
JONKOPING	KAMCHATKA	KILLBOARD	KOWTOWING	LAMINATED
JORDANIAN	KAMILAROI	KILLIFISH	KOZHIKODE	LAMINATES
JOSS STICK	KAMPUCHEA	KILLINGLY	KRASNODAR	LAMINATOR
JOURNEYED	KANAMYCIN	KILOBYTES	KRAUTROCK	LAMINITIS
JOURNEYER	KANGAROOS	KILOCYCLE	KRIVOY ROG	LAMP-BLACK
JOVIALITY	KAOHSIUNG	KILOGRAMS	KRONSTADT	LAMPOONED
JOYLESSLY	KAOLINITE	KILOHERTZ	KUIBYSHEV	LAMPOONER
JOYRIDERS	KARABINER	KILOLITRE	KURDISTAN	LAMPPOSTS
JOYRIDING	KARAGANDA	KILOMETRE	KURRAJONG	LAMPSHADE
JOYSTICKS	KARAKORAM	KILOWATTS	KWANGTUNG	LANCASTER
JUBILANCE	KARAKORUM	KIMBERLEY	KYMOGRAPH	LANCEWOOD
JUDDERING	KARLSRUHE	KINDLIEST		LANCINATE
JUDGEABLE	KARNATAKA	KINEMATIC	**L**	LAND AGENT
JUDGEMENT	KARYOGAMY	KINGLIEST	LABELLING	LANDAULET
JUDGESHIP	KARYOSOME	KINGMAKER	LABELLOID	LANDFALLS
JUDGINGLY	KARYOTYPE	KING'S EVIL	LABIALISM	LANDLORDS
JUDGMENTS	KATABATIC	KING'S HEAD	LABIALITY	LANDMARKS
JUDICABLE	KATANGESE	KING'S LYNN	LABIALIZE	LANDMINES
JUDICATOR	KATHIAWAR	KINGSTOWN	LABORIOUS	LAND OF NOD
JUDICIARY	KAWAGUCHI	KINKINESS	LABOUR DAY	LANDOWNER
JUDICIOUS	KEEP ORDER	KINSWOMAN	LABOURERS	LAND ROVER
JUICINESS	KEEPSAKES	KIRGHIZIA	LABOURING	LANDSCAPE
JUKEBOXES	KEEP STATE	KIRKCALDY	LABOURISM	LANDSLIDE
JULLUNDUR	KELTICISM	KIROVABAD	LABOURIST	LANDSLIPS
JUMBO JETS	KELTICIST	KISANGANI	LABOURITE	LANDWARDS
JUMPINESS	KENNELING	KISSINGER	LABRADORS	LANGOUSTE
JUMP START	KENNELLED	KITCHENER	LABURNUMS	LANGUAGES
JUMP-START	KENTLEDGE	KITTENISH	LABYRINTH	LANGUEDOC
JUMPSUITS	KEPT WOMAN	KITTIWAKE	LACCOLITH	LANGUIDLY
JUNCTIONS	KEPT WOMEN	KLEENEXES	LACERABLE	LANKINESS
JUNCTURES	KERATITIS	KNACKERED	LACERATED	LANOLATED
JUNGLE GYM	KERATOSIS	KNAPSACKS	LACERTIAN	LANTHANUM
JUNKETING	KERBSTONE	KNAVERIES	LACHRYMAL	LAODICEAN
JUNOESQUE	KERCHIEFS	KNAVISHLY	LACINIATE	LAPLANDER
JURIDICAL	KERFUFFLE	KNIFE EDGE	LACQUERED	LARCENIES
JURY BOXES	KETONURIA	KNIFE-EDGE	LACQUERER	LARCENIST
JUSTICIAR	KETTERING	KNIGHTING	LACTATION	LARCENOUS
JUSTIFIED	KEYBOARDS	KNIPHOFIA	LADDERING	LARGENESS
JUSTIFIER	KEYHOLDER	KNITTABLE	LADIES' MAN	LARGHETTO
JUTLANDER	KEYSTONES	KNOBBLIER	LADIES' MEN	LARKSPURS
JUVENILES	KEYSTROKE	KNOCKDOWN	LADYBIRDS	LARVICIDE
JUVENILIA	KIBBUTZES	KNOCKOUTS	LADYSHIPS	LARYNGEAL
JUXTAPOSE	KIBBUTZIM	KNOTGRASS	LAEVULOSE	LASHINGLY
	KICKBACKS	KNOTTIEST	LAGOMORPH	LAS PALMAS
K	KICK-START	KNOWINGLY	LALLATION	LASSITUDE
KADAITCHA	KID GLOVES	KNOWLEDGE	LAMAISTIC	LAST-DITCH
KADIYEVKA	KIDNAPING	KNOXVILLE	LAMBASTED	LASTINGLY
KAGOSHIMA	KIDNAPPED	KNUCKLING	LAMBSKINS	LAST RITES
KAISERDOM	KIDNAPPER	KONIOLOGY	LAME DUCKS	LAST STRAW
KALAMAZOO	KIDSTAKES	KOOKINESS	LAMENTING	LAST THING
KALANCHOE	KIESERITE	KOSCIUSKO	LAMINABLE	LATCHKEYS

LATECOMER	LEE SHORES	LIBERATED	LIMITABLE	LITURGICS
LATERALLY	LEFTOVERS	LIBERATOR	LIMITLESS	LITURGIES
LATERITIC	LEFTWARDS	LIBERTIES	LIMNOLOGY	LITURGISM
LATHERING	LEGALIZED	LIBERTINE	LIMOUSINE	LITURGIST
LATIMERIA	LEGATIONS	LIBIDINAL	LIMPIDITY	LIVELIEST
LATINIZER	LEGENDARY	LIBRARIAN	LIMPINGLY	LIVERPOOL
LATITUDES	LEGGINESS	LIBRARIES	LINCHPINS	LIVERWORT
LATTER-DAY	LEGGINGED	LIBRATION	LINEAMENT	LIVERYMAN
LAUDATION	LEGIONARY	LIBRATORY	LINEARITY	LIVERYMEN
LAUDATORY	LEGISLATE	LIBRETTOS	LINEATION	LIVESTOCK
LAUGHABLE	LEG-WARMER	LIBRIFORM	LINEOLATE	LIVE WIRES
LAUGHABLY	LEICESTER	LICENSEES	LINGERERS	LIVIDNESS
LAUNCHING	LEISURELY	LICENSING	LINGERING	LJUBLJANA
LAUNCH PAD	LEITMOTIF	LICHENOID	LINGUISTS	LLANDUDNO
LAUNDERED	LEITMOTIV	LICHENOUS	LINGULATE	LOADSTARS
LAUNDERER	LEMNISCUS	LIDOCAINE	LINKOPING	LOADSTONE
LAUNDRESS	LEMON CURD	LIEGE LORD	LINOLEATE	LOAMINESS
LAUNDRIES	LEMON SOLE	LIENTERIC	LINOTYPER	LOAN SHARK
LAUREATES	LEND-LEASE	LIFE BELTS	LIONIZING	LOANWORDS
LAVISHING	LENGTHIER	LIFEBLOOD	LIPOLYSIS	LOATHSOME
LAWGIVING	LENGTHILY	LIFEBOATS	LIPOLYTIC	LOBECTOMY
LAWLESSLY	LENIENTLY	LIFE BUOYS	LIP READER	LOCAL CALL
LAWNMOWER	LENINABAD	LIFE CYCLE	LIP-READER	LOCALIZED
LAWN PARTY	LENINAKAN	LIFEGUARD	LIPSTICKS	LOCALIZER
LAW SCHOOL	LENINGRAD	LIFELINES	LIQUATION	LOCAL TIME
LAXATIVES	LENIN PEAK	LIFE PEERS	LIQUEFIED	LOCATABLE
LAYABOUTS	LEPONTINE	LIFE-SAVER	LIQUEFIER	LOCATIONS
LAY FIGURE	LEPTOSOME	LIFESPANS	LIQUIDATE	LOCKERBIE
LAYPERSON	LEPTOTENE	LIFE STORY	LIQUIDITY	LOCKSMITH
LAY READER	LESSENING	LIFESTYLE	LIQUIDIZE	LOCOMOTOR
LAY SISTER	LETHALITY	LIFETIMES	LIQUORICE	LOCUTIONS
LAZARETTO	LETHARGIC	LIGAMENTS	LISPINGLY	LODESTARS
LAZYBONES	LETTERBOX	LIGATURES	LISTENERS	LODESTONE
LEADERENE	LETTERING	LIGHT BULB	LISTENING	LODGEABLE
LEAD TIMES	LEUCOCYTE	LIGHTENED	LISTERISM	LOFTINESS
LEAFINESS	LEUCOTOMY	LIGHT-FAST	LIST PRICE	LOGAOEDIC
LEAFLETED	LEUKAEMIA	LIGHTNESS	LITERALLY	LOGARITHM
LEAF MOULD	LEVANTINE	LIGHTNING	LITERATIM	LOG CABINS
LEAFSTALK	LEVELLERS	LIGHT RAIL	LITHENESS	LOGICALLY
LEAKINESS	LEVELLING	LIGHTSHIP	LITHIASIS	LOGICIANS
LEAP YEARS	LEVIATHAN	LIGHTS OUT	LITHOLOGY	LOGISTICS
LEARNABLE	LEVIGATOR	LIGHTS-OUT	LITHOPONE	LOGOGRIPH
LEARNEDLY	LEVITATED	LIGHT YEAR	LITHOTOMY	LOGOMACHY
LEASEBACK	LEVITATOR	LIGNIFORM	LITHUANIA	LOINCLOTH
LEASEHOLD	LEXICALLY	LIKELIEST	LITIGABLE	LOITERERS
LEASTWAYS	LEXINGTON	LILY-WHITE	LITIGANTS	LOITERING
LEAVENING	LIABILITY	LIMA BEANS	LITIGATED	LOLLINGLY
LECHEROUS	LIBATIONS	LIME GREEN	LITIGATOR	LOLLIPOPS
LECTORATE	LIBELLANT	LIMELIGHT	LITIGIOUS	LOLLOPING
LECTURERS	LIBELLING	LIMERICKS	LITTERBIN	LOMBARDIC
LECTURING	LIBELLOUS	LIMESTONE	LITTERING	LONELIEST
LEERINGLY	LIBERALLY	LIMEWATER	LITTORALS	LONE WOLFS

LONG BEACH	LOWERABLE	LYREBIRDS	MAGNIFIER	MALTSTERS
LONGBOATS	LOWER CASE	LYRICALLY	MAGNITUDE	MALVOISIE
LONGCLOTH	LOWERMOST	LYRICISMS	MAGNOLIAS	MAMA'S BOYS
LONG EATON	LOWESTOFT	LYRICISTS	MAHAJANGA	MAMILLARY
LONGEVITY	LOWLANDER	LYSIMETER	MAHARAJAH	MAMILLATE
LONGEVOUS	LOWLINESS	LYSOSOMAL	MAHARAJAS	MAMMALIAN
LONG FACES	LOW-MINDED		MAHARANIS	MAMMALOGY
LONGICORN	LOW-NECKED	**M**	MAIDSTONE	MAMMOGRAM
LONGINGLY	LOW SEASON	MACARONIC	MAIDUGURI	MAMMONISM
LONGITUDE	LOYALISTS	MACAROONS	MAILBOXES	MAMMONIST
LONG JOHNS	LOYALTIES	MACEDOINE	MAILCOACH	MANACLING
LONG-LIVED	LUBRICANT	MACEDONIA	MAIL ORDER	MAN-AT-ARMS
LONG-RANGE	LUBRICATE	MACERATED	MAILSHOTS	MANCHURIA
LONGSHIPS	LUBRICITY	MACERATER	MAINFRAME	MANCUNIAN
LONGSHORE	LUBRICOUS	MACHINATE	MAINLINED	MANDARINS
LONG SHOTS	LUCIFERIN	MACHINERY	MAIN LINES	MANDATARY
LONG SINCE	LUCKINESS	MACHINING	MAINMASTS	MANDATING
LONGUEUIL	LUCKY DIPS	MACHINIST	MAINSAILS	MANDATORY
LONGUEURS	LUCRATIVE	MACHMETER	MAINSHEET	MANDIBLES
LOOK AFTER	LUCUBRATE	MACKENZIE	MAINSTAYS	MANDOLINS
LOOK-ALIKE	LUDICROUS	MACKERELS	MAJESTICS	MANDRAKES
LOOK ALIVE	LUFTWAFFE	MACROCOSM	MAJESTIES	MANDRILLS
LOOKING UP	LULLABIES	MACROCYST	MAJOR-DOMO	MAN-EATERS
LOOM-STATE	LULLINGLY	MACROCYTE	MAJORETTE	MAN-EATING
LOONINESS	LUMBERING	MACRUROID	MAJOR SUIT	MANEUVERS
LOONY BINS	LUMBERMAN	MACRUROUS	MAJUSCULE	MAN FRIDAY
LOOPHOLES	LUMBERMEN	MADDENING	MAKE A MOVE	MANGALORE
LOOSE ENDS	LUMBRICAL	MADELEINE	MAKE MERRY	MANGANATE
LOOSE-LEAF	LUMINAIRE	MAD HATTER	MAKE PEACE	MANGANESE
LOOSENESS	LUMINANCE	MADHOUSES	MAKE READY	MANGANITE
LOOSENING	LUMINESCE	MADREPORE	MAKESHIFT	MANGANOUS
LOQUACITY	LUMPINESS	MADRIGALS	MAKEYEVKA	MANGETOUT
LORDLIEST	LUNATICAL	MAELSTROM	MALACHITE	MANGINESS
LORDSHIPS	LUNISOLAR	MAGAZINES	MALADROIT	MANGROVES
LORGNETTE	LUNITIDAL	MAGDEBURG	MALAGUENA	MANHANDLE
LORRY PARK	LURIDNESS	MAGICALLY	MALANDERS	MANHATTAN
LOS ALAMOS	LURKINGLY	MAGIC EYES	MALATHION	MANHUNTER
LOST CAUSE	LUSTFULLY	MAGICIANS	MALAYALAM	MANICURED
LOTTERIES	LUSTINESS	MAGIC WAND	MALAYSIAN	MANICURES
LOUDMOUTH	LUTANISTS	MAGISTERY	MALDIVIAN	MANIFESTO
LOUISBURG	LUTHERISM	MAGISTRAL	MALFORMED	MANIFESTS
LOUISIANA	LUXEMBURG	MAGMATISM	MALGRE LUI	MANIFOLDS
LOUNGE BAR	LUXURIANT	MAGNESIAN	MALIC ACID	MANIZALES
LOUSEWORT	LUXURIATE	MAGNESITE	MALICIOUS	MANLINESS
LOUSINESS	LUXURIOUS	MAGNESIUM	MALIGNANT	MANNEQUIN
LOVEBIRDS	LYCHGATES	MAGNETICS	MALIGNING	MANNERISM
LOVECHILD	LYME REGIS	MAGNETISM	MALIGNITY	MANNERIST
LOVE FEAST	LYMINGTON	MAGNETITE	MALLEABLE	MANNISHLY
LOVELIEST	LYMPHATIC	MAGNETIZE	MALLEMUCK	MANOEUVRE
LOVE MATCH	LYONNAISE	MAGNETRON	MALLEOLAR	MANOMETER
LOVING CUP	LYOPHILIC	MAGNIFICO	MALLEOLUS	MANOMETRY
LOW COMEDY	LYOPHOBIC	MAGNIFIED	MALTINESS	MANSFIELD

MANTILLAS	MASCULINE	MEANDERER	MELUNGEON	MESMERIZE
MANUBRIAL	MASOCHISM	MEANDROUS	MEMBRANES	MESOMORPH
MANUBRIUM	MASOCHIST	MEANS TEST	MEMORABLE	MESOPAUSE
MANY-SIDED	MASSACRED	MEANTIMES	MEMORABLY	MESOPHYLL
MAPLE LEAF	MASSACRER	MEANWHILE	MEMORANDA	MESOPHYTE
MARACAIBO	MASSACRES	MEASURING	MEMORIALS	MESSALINE
MARATHONS	MASSAGING	MEATBALLS	MEMORIZED	MESSENGER
MARAUDERS	MASSIVELY	MEATINESS	MEMORIZER	MESSIANIC
MARAUDING	MASS MEDIA	MECHANICS	MEMSAHIBS	MESSIEURS
MARCASITE	MASTERDOM	MECHANISM	MENADIONE	MESSINESS
MARCH HARE	MASTERFUL	MECHANIST	MENAGERIE	MESTRANOL
MARCH-PAST	MASTERING	MECHANIZE	MEN-AT-ARMS	METABOLIC
MARCO POLO	MASTER KEY	MEDALLION	MENDACITY	METALLINE
MARDI GRAS	MASTHEADS	MEDALLIST	MENDELIAN	METALLING
MARE'S NEST	MASTICATE	MEDIAEVAL	MENDELISM	METALLIST
MARGARINE	MASTICATE	MEDIATING	MENDICANT	METALLIZE
MARGARITA	MATAMOROS	MEDIATION	MENISCOID	METALLOID
MARGARITE	MATCHLESS	MEDIATIVE	MENOPAUSE	METALWORK
MARGINATE	MATCHMARK	MEDIATIZE	MEN'S ROOMS	METAMERAL
MARIEHAMN	MATCH PLAY	MEDIATORS	MENSTRUAL	METAMERIC
MARIENBAD	MATCHWOOD	MEDICABLE	MENSTRUUM	METAPHASE
MARIGOLDS	MATELASSE	MEDICABLY	MENTAL AGE	METAPHORS
MARIJUANA	MATERIALS	MEDICALLY	MENTALISM	METAPLASM
MARINADES	MATERNITY	MEDICATED	MENTALITY	METAXYLEM
MARINATED	MATEYNESS	MEDICINAL	MENTIONED	METEORITE
MARITALLY	MATRIARCH	MEDICINES	MENTIONER	METEOROID
MARKDOWNS	MATRICIDE	MEDITATED	MENTORIAL	METHADONE
MARKETEER	MATRIMONY	MEDITATOR	MEPACRINE	METHODISM
MARKETERS	MATRONAGE	MEDULLARY	MERBROMIN	METHODIST
MARKETING	MATSUMOTO	MEGACYCLE	MERCAPTAN	METHODIZE
MARK TWAIN	MATSUYAMA	MEGADEATH	MERCENARY	METHOXIDE
MARMALADE	MATTERING	MEGAHERTZ	MERCERIZE	METHYLATE
MARMOREAL	MATUTINAL	MEGALITHS	MERCHANTS	METHYLENE
MARMOSETS	MAULSTICK	MEGAPHONE	MERCILESS	METRALGIA
MAROONING	MAUNDERED	MEGASPORE	MERCURATE	METRICIZE
MARQUETRY	MAUNDERER	MEGASTORE	MERCURIAL	METRIC TON
MARQUISES	MAURITIAN	MEGHALAYA	MERCUROUS	METRIFIER
MARRAKECH	MAURITIUS	MELANESIA	MERGANSER	METROLOGY
MARRIAGES	MAUSOLEAN	MELANOSIS	MERIDIANS	METRONOME
MARROWFAT	MAUSOLEUM	MELATONIN	MERINGUES	MEZZANINE
MARSEILLE	MAVERICKS	MELBOURNE	MERITEDLY	MEZZOTINT
MARSHALCY	MAWKISHLY	MELIORATE	MERITLESS	MICACEOUS
MARSHALED	MAXILLARY	MELIORISM	MEROCRINE	MICHOACAN
MARSUPIAL	MAXIMALLY	MELITOPOL	MEROZOITE	MICROBIAL
MARSUPIUM	MAXIMIZED	MELLOWEST	MERRIMENT	MICROBLOG
MARTINETS	MAXIMIZER	MELLOWING	MERRINESS	MICROCHIP
MARTINMAS	MAYFLOWER	MELODIOUS	MERSEBURG	MICROCOPY
MARTYRDOM	MAYORALTY	MELODIZER	MESCALINE	MICROCOSM
MARTYRING	MAYORSHIP	MELODRAMA	MESENTERY	MICROCYTE
MARVELING	MBUJIMAYI	MELTDOWNS	MESICALLY	MICRODONT
MARVELLED	MCCARTNEY	MELTINGLY	MESMERISM	MICROFILM
MARZIPANS	MEANDERED	MELTWATER	MESMERIST	MICROMESH

MICROPYLE	MILOMETER	MISMANAGE	MOLECULES	MONOPHONY
MICROSOME	MILWAUKEE	MISNOMERS	MOLEHILLS	MONOPLANE
MICROTOME	MIMICKING	MISONEISM	MOLESKINS	MONOPSONY
MICROTOMY	MINARETED	MISONEIST	MOLESTERS	MONORAILS
MICROTONE	MINCEMEAT	MISPLACED	MOLESTING	MONOSOMIC
MICROWAVE	MINCE PIES	MISPRINTS	MOLLIFIED	MONOSTICH
MIDDLE AGE	MINCINGLY	MISQUOTED	MOLLIFIER	MONOSTOME
MIDDLEMAN	MINEFIELD	MISREPORT	MOLLUSCAN	MONOTONIC
MIDDLEMEN	MINELAYER	MISSHAPEN	MOLYBDATE	MONOTREME
MIDDLESEX	MINIATURE	MISSILERY	MOLYBDOUS	MONOTYPER
MIDDLETON	MINIBUSES	MISSIONER	MOMENTARY	MONOTYPIC
MIDHEAVEN	MINIDRESS	MISSTATED	MOMENTOUS	MONOXIDES
MIDNIGHTS	MINIMALLY	MISTAKING	MOMENTUMS	MONSIGNOR
MIDPOINTS	MINIMIZED	MISTIMING	MONACHISM	MONSTROUS
MIDSTREAM	MINIMIZER	MISTINESS	MONADNOCK	MONTAUBAN
MIDSUMMER	MINISCULE	MISTLETOE	MONARCHAL	MONT BLANC
MID-WICKET	MINISKIRT	MISTRIALS	MONASTERY	MONTERREY
MIDWIFERY	MINISTERS	MITICIDAL	MONATOMIC	MONTHLIES
MIDWINTER	MINITRACK	MITIGABLE	MONEYBAGS	MONTICULE
MIFFINESS	MINNESOTA	MITIGATED	MONEYLESS	MONTREUIL
MIGHTIEST	MINOR SUIT	MITIGATOR	MONEYWORT	MONUMENTS
MIGRAINES	MINSTRELS	MITREWORT	MONGERING	MONZONITE
MIGRATING	MINT JULEP	MNEMONICS	MONGOLIAN	MOODINESS
MIGRATION	MINUSCULE	MOANINGLY	MONGOLISM	MOONBEAMS
MIGRATORY	MINUTE GUN	MOBILIZED	MONGOLOID	MOON-FACED
MILCH COWS	MINUTE MAN	MOBOCRACY	MONGOOSES	MOONINESS
MILESTONE	MIRRORING	MOCCASINS	MONITORED	MOONLIGHT
MILITANCY	MIRTHLESS	MOCKERIES	MONITRESS	MOONRAKER
MILITANTS	MISADVISE	MOCKINGLY	MONKEYING	MOONSCAPE
MILITARIA	MISBEHAVE	MODELLING	MONKEY NUT	MOONSHINE
MILITATED	MISBELIEF	MODERATED	MONKSHOOD	MOON SHOTS
MILK FLOAT	MISCALLED	MODERATES	MONOBASIC	MOONSTONE
MILKINESS	MISCHANCE	MODERATOR	MONOCHORD	MOOT POINT
MILKMAIDS	MISCHIEFS	MODERATOS	MONOCLINE	MORACEOUS
MILK SHAKE	MISCOUNTS	MODERNISM	MONOCOQUE	MORADABAD
MILK TOOTH	MISCREANT	MODERNIST	MONOCRACY	MORALISTS
MILLBOARD	MISCREATE	MODERNITY	MONOCULAR	MORALIZED
MILLENARY	MISDEALER	MODERNIZE	MONOCYTIC	MORALIZER
MILLENNIA	MISDIRECT	MODIFIERS	MONODRAMA	MORATORIA
MILLEPEDE	MISERABLE	MODIFYING	MONOGENIC	MORBIDITY
MILLEPORE	MISERABLY	MODILLION	MONOGRAMS	MORDACITY
MILLERITE	MISFIRING	MODULATED	MONOGRAPH	MORDANTLY
MILLIBARS	MISGIVING	MODULATOR	MONOLATER	MORECAMBE
MILLIGRAM	MISGOVERN	MOGADISHU	MONOLATRY	MORGANITE
MILLINERS	MISGUIDED	MOISTENED	MONOLAYER	MORMONISM
MILLINERY	MISGUIDER	MOISTENER	MONOLITHS	MORPHEMES
MILLIONTH	MISHANDLE	MOISTNESS	MONOLOGIC	MORPHEMIC
MILLIPEDE	MISINFORM	MOLDAVIAN	MONOLOGUE	MORPHOSIS
MILLIVOLT	MISJUDGED	MOLDAVITE	MONOMANIA	MORSE CODE
MILLPONDS	MISJUDGER	MOLDERING	MONOMERIC	MORTALITY
MILLSTONE	MISLAYING	MOLDINESS	MONOMETER	MORTAL SIN
MILLWHEEL	MISLEADER	MOLECULAR	MONOPHAGY	MORTGAGED

MORTGAGEE	MUGGINESS	MUTILATED	NASHVILLE	NEOPHYTES
MORTGAGES	MUGGINSES	MUTILATOR	NASTINESS	NEOPHYTIC
MORTGAGOR	MULATTOES	MUTINEERS	NATIONALS	NEOPLASTY
MORTICIAN	MULETEERS	MUTINYING	NATROLITE	NEOTENOUS
MORTIFIED	MULLINGAR	MUTTERERS	NATTERING	NEPHELINE
MORTIFIER	MULLIONED	MUTTERING	NATTINESS	NEPHOGRAM
MOSAICIST	MULTICIDE	MUTUALITY	NATURALLY	NEPHOLOGY
MOSCHATEL	MULTIFOIL	MUTUALIZE	NATURISTS	NEPHRITIC
MOSQUITOS	MULTIFOLD	MUZZINESS	NAUGHTIER	NEPHRITIS
MOSS-GROWN	MULTIFORM	MYCENAEAN	NAUGHTILY	NEPHROSIS
MOSSINESS	MULTIHULL	MYDRIASIS	NAUSEATED	NEPHROTIC
MOTHBALLS	MULTIPARA	MYDRIATIC	NAUTILOID	NEPTUNIAN
MOTH EATEN	MULTIPLES	MYOGLOBIN	NAVICULAR	NEPTUNIUM
MOTH-EATEN	MULTIPLET	MYOGRAPHY	NAVIGABLE	NERVE CELL
MOTHERING	MULTIPLEX	MYOLOGIST	NAVIGABLY	NERVELESS
MOTHPROOF	MULTITUDE	MYROBALAN	NAVIGATED	NERVINESS
MOTIONING	MUMMIFIED	MYSTAGOGY	NAVIGATOR	NERVOUSLY
MOTIVATED	MUNDANELY	MYSTERIES	NEAP TIDES	NESCIENCE
MOTOCROSS	MUNICIPAL	MYSTICISM	NEAR THING	NESTLINGS
MOTORBIKE	MUNIMENTS	MYSTIFIED	NEBULIZER	NESTORIAN
MOTORBOAT	MUNITIONS	MYSTIFIER	NECESSARY	NETANYAHU
MOTORCADE	MURDERERS	MYSTIQUES	NECESSITY	NETWORKED
MOTORCARS	MURDERESS	MYTHICIZE	NECKBANDS	NEUCHATEL
MOTORHOME	MURDERING	MYTHOLOGY	NECKCLOTH	NEURALGIA
MOTORISTS	MURDEROUS	MYXOEDEMA	NECKLACES	NEURALGIC
MOTORIZED	MURKINESS	MYXOVIRUS	NECKLINES	NEUROGLIA
MOTORWAYS	MURMURING		NECKPIECE	NEUROLOGY
MOULDABLE	MUSACEOUS	**N**	NECROLOGY	NEUROPATH
MOULDERED	MUSCADINE	NAHUATLAN	NECROTOMY	NEUROTICS
MOULDIEST	MUSCARINE	NAILBRUSH	NECTARIAL	NEUROTOMY
MOULDINGS	MUSCATELS	NAIL FILES	NECTARINE	NEUTERING
MOUNTABLE	MUSCLEMAN	NAIVENESS	NEEDFULLY	NEUTRALLY
MOUNTAINS	MUSCLEMEN	NAIVETIES	NEEDINESS	NEUTRETTO
MOUSETAIL	MUSCOVADO	NAKEDNESS	NEFARIOUS	NEVER MIND
MOUSETRAP	MUSCOVITE	NAMECHECK	NEGATIONS	NEVERMORE
MOUSINESS	MUSEOLOGY	NAMEPLATE	NEGATIVED	NEW BROOMS
MOUSTACHE	MUSHINESS	NAME PLATE	NEGATIVES	NEWCASTLE
MOUTHFULS	MUSHROOMS	NAMESAKES	NEGLECTED	NEWCOMERS
MOUTHPART	MUSICALLY	NANNY GOAT	NEGLECTER	NEW FOREST
MOUTHWASH	MUSIC HALL	NANOMETER	NEGLIGEES	NEW GUINEA
MOVEABLES	MUSICIANS	NANTUCKET	NEGLIGENT	NEW JERSEY
MOVEMENTS	MUSKETEER	NAPHTHENE	NEGOTIANT	NEWLYWEDS
MOVIE STAR	MUSKINESS	NAPPINESS	NEGOTIATE	NEWLY WEDS
MOVIETONE	MUSKMELON	NARCISSUS	NEGRITUDE	NEWMARKET
MOVING VAN	MUSLIMISM	NARCOTICS	NEIGHBOUR	NEW MEXICO
MUCIC ACID	MUSTACHES	NARCOTISM	NEMERTEAN	NEW ROMNEY
MUCKHEAPS	MUSTACHIO	NARCOTIZE	NEODYMIUM	NEWSAGENT
MUCKINESS	MUSTELINE	NARRATING	NEOLITHIC	NEWSGROUP
MUCKRAKER	MUSTERING	NARRATION	NEOLOGISM	NEWSHOUND
MUCRONATE	MUSTINESS	NARRATIVE	NEOLOGIST	NEWSINESS
MUDDINESS	MUTAGENIC	NARRATORS	NEOLOGIZE	NEWSPAPER
MUDGUARDS	MUTATIONS	NARROWING	NEON LIGHT	NEWSPRINT

NEWSREELS	NOCTILUCA	NOTOCHORD	NYMPHALID	OBVIATING
NEWSROOMS	NOCTURNAL	NOTOGAEAN	NYSTAGMIC	OBVIATION
NEWSSHEET	NOCTURNES	NOTORIETY	NYSTAGMUS	OBVIOUSLY
NEWSSTAND	NO-GO AREAS	NOTORIOUS		OCCASIONS
NEWTONIAN	NOISELESS	NOT PROVEN	**O**	OCCIPITAL
NEW YORKER	NOISINESS	NOTRE DAME	OAST HOUSE	OCCLUDENT
NICARAGUA	NOMINALLY	NOURISHED	OBBLIGATO	OCCLUSION
NICCOLITE	NOMINATED	NOURISHER	OBCORDATE	OCCLUSIVE
NICHOLSON	NOMINATOR	NOVELETTE	OBEDIENCE	OCCULTISM
NICKELING	NOMOCRACY	NOVELISTS	OBEISANCE	OCCULTIST
NICKELLED	NOMOGRAPH	NOVELTIES	OBELISCAL	OCCUPANCY
NICKELOUS	NONAGONAL	NOVEMBERS	OBFUSCATE	OCCUPANTS
NICKNACKS	NONEDIBLE	NOVITIATE	OBJECTIFY	OCCUPIERS
NICKNAMED	NONENTITY	NOVOCAINE	OBJECTING	OCCUPYING
NICKNAMES	NON-EVENTS	NOXIOUSLY	OBJECTION	OCCURRENT
NICOTIANA	NON-FINITE	NUCLEATOR	OBJECTIVE	OCCURRING
NICOTINIC	NONILLION	NUCLEOLAR	OBJECTORS	OCELLATED
NICTITATE	NONLINEAR	NUCLEOLUS	OBJET D'ART	OCHLOCRAT
NIFTINESS	NONPAREIL	NUCLEONIC	OBJURGATE	OCTAGONAL
NIGGARDLY	NONPAROUS	NUEVO LEON	OBLATIONS	OCTAMETER
NIGHTCAPS	NONRACIAL	NUISANCES	OBLIGABLE	OCTENNIAL
NIGHTCLUB	NONSMOKER	NUKU'ALOFA	OBLIGATED	OCTILLION
NIGHTFALL	NONVERBAL	NULLIFIED	OBLIGATOR	OCTOPUSES
NIGHTGOWN	NONWHITES	NULLIFIER	OBLIQUITY	ODALISQUE
NIGHTHAWK	NORMALITY	NULLIPARA	OBLIVIOUS	ODD-JOB MAN
NIGHTLIFE	NORMALIZE	NULLIPORE	OBNOXIOUS	ODD MAN OUT
NIGHTLONG	NORMATIVE	NULLITIES	OBREPTION	ODD MEN OUT
NIGHTMARE	NORTH DOWN	NUMBERING	OBSCENELY	ODOMETERS
NIGHT OWLS	NORTHEAST	NUMBER ONE	OBSCENITY	ODOURLESS
NIGHT SOIL	NORTHERLY	NUMBER TEN	OBSCURANT	OESTROGEN
NIGHTTIME	NORTH POLE	NUMBSKULL	OBSCURELY	OFF CHANCE
NIGHTWEAR	NORTHWARD	NUMERABLE	OBSCURING	OFF COLOUR
NIGROSINE	NORTHWEST	NUMERABLY	OBSCURITY	OFFENBACH
NIHILISTS	NORTHWICH	NUMERATOR	OBSEQUENT	OFFENDERS
NIKOLAYEV	NORWEGIAN	NUMERICAL	OBSEQUIES	OFFENDING
NINETEENS	NOSEBLEED	NUMMULITE	OBSERVANT	OFFENSIVE
NINETIETH	NOSECONES	NUMSKULLS	OBSERVERS	OFFERINGS
NIPPINESS	NOSEDIVED	NUNNERIES	OBSERVING	OFFERTORY
NIPPONESE	NOSEDIVES	NUREMBERG	OBSESSING	OFFHANDED
NISI PRIUS	NOSE PIECE	NURSELING	OBSESSION	OFFICE BOY
NISSEN HUT	NOSTALGIA	NURSEMAID	OBSESSIVE	OFFICIALS
NITPICKER	NOSTALGIC	NURSERIES	OBSOLESCE	OFFICIANT
NITRAMINE	NOSTOLOGY	NURSLINGS	OBSTACLES	OFFICIARY
NITRATION	NOTARIZED	NURTURING	OBSTETRIC	OFFICIATE
NITRIDING	NOT AT HOME	NUTHOUSES	OBSTINACY	OFFICIOUS
NIVERNAIS	NOTATIONS	NUTRIENTS	OBSTINATE	OFF-LOADED
NO ACCOUNT	NOTEBOOKS	NUTRIMENT	OBSTRUENT	OFF-ROADER
NO-ACCOUNT	NOTEPAPER	NUTRITION	OBTAINING	OFF SEASON
NOBILIARY	NOTHING ON	NUTRITIVE	OBTRUDING	OFFSHOOTS
NOBLENESS	NOTIFYING	NUTSHELLS	OBTRUSION	OFFSPRING
	NO-TILLAGE	NUTTINESS	OBTRUSIVE	
		NYASALAND	OBVERSION	

OFF-STREET	ONOMASTIC	ORDER ARMS	OUTBRAVED	OVERCOATS
OFF THE PEG	ONRUSHING	ORDERLIES	OUTBREAKS	OVERCROWD
OGBOMOSHO	ONSLAUGHT	ORDINANCE	OUTBURSTS	OVERDOING
OILFIELDS	ON THE BEAM	ORGANELLE	OUTCASTES	OVERDOSED
OIL PAINTS	ON THE HOOF	ORGANISMS	OUTERMOST	OVERDOSES
OIL SLICKS	ON THE MEND	ORGANISTS	OUTFACING	OVERDRAFT
OIL TANKER	ON THE NAIL	ORGANIZED	OUTFITTED	OVERDRAWN
OINTMENTS	ON THE SPOT	ORGANIZER	OUTFITTER	OVERDRESS
OKLAHOMAN	ON THE TROT	ORGANZINE	OUTFOUGHT	OVERDRIVE
OLDENBURG	ONTOGENIC	ORGIASTIC	OUTFOXING	OVERFLOWN
OLD FLAMES	OOGENESIS	ORIENTALS	OUTGOINGS	OVERFLOWS
OLD MASTER	OOGENETIC	ORIENTATE	OUTGROWTH	OVERGLAZE
OLD SCHOOL	OOLOGICAL	ORIGINALS	OUTHOUSES	OVERGROWN
OLD STAGER	OPEN-ENDED	ORIGINATE	OUTLASTED	OVERHANGS
OLD-TIMERS	OPEN-FACED	ORNAMENTS	OUTLAWING	OVERHAULS
OLEACEOUS	OPEN HOUSE	ORNITHINE	OUTLAYING	OVERHEADS
OLEANDERS	OPENING UP	OROGRAPHY	OUTLINING	OVERHEARD
OLECRANAL	OPEN ORDER	OROLOGIST	OUTLIVING	OVERISSUE
OLECRANON	OPEN SHOPS	ORPHANAGE	OUTNUMBER	OVERJOYED
OLEOGRAPH	OPERATING	ORPHANING	OUT-OF-DATE	OVERLADEN
OLEORESIN	OPERATION	ORRIS ROOT	OUT OF STEP	OVERLOADS
OLFACTION	OPERATIVE	ORTANIQUE	OUTPLAYED	OVERLORDS
OLFACTORY	OPERATORS	ORTHODOXY	OUTRAGING	OVERLYING
OLIGARCHY	OPERCULAR	ORTHOEPIC	OUTRANKED	OVERNIGHT
OLIGOCENE	OPERCULUM	ORTHOPTER	OUTRIDDEN	OVERPAINT
OLIGOPOLY	OPERETTAS	ORTHOPTIC	OUTRIDERS	OVERPOWER
OLIVE DRAB	OPHIOLOGY	OSCILLATE	OUTRIDING	OVERPRICE
OLIVENITE	OPPONENCY	OSCITANCY	OUTRIGGER	OVERPRINT
OLYMPIADS	OPPONENTS	OSMOMETER	OUTRUNNER	OVERPROOF
OLYMPIANS	OPPORTUNE	OSMOMETRY	OUTSIDERS	OVERRATED
OMBUDSMAN	OPPOSABLE	OSNABRUCK	OUTSKIRTS	OVERREACH
OMBUDSMEN	OPPOSABLY	OSSICULAR	OUTSOURCE	OVERREACT
OMELETTES	OPPOSITES	OSSIFRAGE	OUTSPOKEN	OVERRIDER
OMINOUSLY	OPPRESSED	OSSIFYING	OUTSPREAD	OVERRULED
OMISSIBLE	OPPRESSOR	OSTENSIVE	OUTSTARED	OVERSCORE
OMISSIONS	OPTICALLY	OSTEOLOGY	OUTSTAYED	OVERSEERS
OMNIBUSES	OPTICIANS	OSTEOPATH	OUTTALKED	OVERSEXED
OMNIRANGE	OPTIMISTS	OSTEOTOME	OUTVOTING	OVERSHOES
OMOPHAGIA	OPTIMIZED	OSTEOTOMY	OUTWARDLY	OVERSHOOT
OMOPHAGIC	OPTOMETER	OSTRACISM	OUT WITH IT	OVERSIGHT
ON ACCOUNT	OPTOMETRY	OSTRACIZE	OUTWITTED	OVERSIZED
ON A STRING	OPULENTLY	OSTRICHES	OUTWORKER	OVERSKIRT
ONCE A WEEK	ORANGEADE	OTHERNESS	OVATIONAL	OVERSLEEP
ONCE-OVERS	ORANGEISM	OTHERWISE	OVEN-READY	OVERSLEPT
ONCOGENIC	ORANGEMAN	OTOCYSTIC	OVERACTED	OVERSPEND
ONDOGRAPH	ORANGE TIP	OTOLITHIC	OVERAWING	OVERSPILL
ONDOMETER	ORANG-UTAN	OTOLOGIST	OVERBLOWN	OVERSTATE
ONEROUSLY	ORATORIES	OTOSCOPIC	OVERBOARD	OVERSTOCK
ONION DOME	ORATORIOS	OUBLIETTE	OVERBORNE	OVERTAKEN
ONIONSKIN	ORBICULAR	OUR FATHER	OVERBUILD	OVERTAXED
ONLOOKERS	ORCHESTRA	OURSELVES	OVERCHECK	OVERTHREW
ONLOOKING	ORDAINING	OUT-AND-OUT	OVERCLOUD	OVERTHROW

OVERTONES	PALEMBANG	PAPILLOMA	PARODISTS	PATCHIEST
OVERTRADE	PALESTINE	PAPILLOTE	PARODYING	PATCHOULI
OVERTRICK	PALISADES	PAPYRUSES	PAROICOUS	PATCHWORK
OVERTRUMP	PALLADIAN	PARABLAST	PAROLABLE	PATELLATE
OVERTURES	PALLADIUM	PARABOLAS	PARONYMIC	PATENTEES
OVERVIEWS	PALLADOUS	PARABOLIC	PAROTITIS	PATENTING
OVERWEIGH	PALLIASSE	PARACHUTE	PAROXYSMS	PATERNITY
OVERWHELM	PALLIATED	PARADIGMS	PARQUETRY	PATHOLOGY
OVERWRITE	PALLIATOR	PARADISAL	PARRICIDE	PATIENTLY
OVIFEROUS	PALMATION	PARADISES	PARROTING	PATRIARCH
OVIPAROUS	PALM BEACH	PARADOXES	PARSIMONY	PATRICIAN
OVOTESTIS	PALMETTOS	PARAGOGIC	PARSONAGE	PATRICIDE
OVULATING	PALMISTRY	PARAGRAPH	PARTAKING	PATRIMONY
OVULATION	PALMITATE	PARAKEETS	PARTERRES	PATRIOTIC
OWNERSHIP	PALOMINOS	PARALLELS	PARTHENON	PATRISTIC
OXIDATION	PALPATING	PARALYSED	PARTIALLY	PATROL CAR
OXIDATIVE	PALPATION	PARALYSER	PARTICLES	PATROLLED
OXIDIZING	PALPEBRAL	PARALYSES	PARTI PRIS	PATROLLER
OXYGENATE	PALPITATE	PARALYSIS	PARTISANS	PATROLMAN
OXYGENIZE	PALTRIEST	PARALYTIC	PARTITION	PATROLMEN
OYSTER BED	PAMPERING	PARAMATTA	PARTITIVE	PATRONAGE
OZOCERITE	PAMPHLETS	PARAMEDIC	PARTNERED	PATRONESS
	PANATELAS	PARAMETER	PARTRIDGE	PATRONIZE
P	PANDA CARS	PARAMORPH	PART-SONGS	PATTERING
PACEMAKER	PANDEMICS	PARAMOUNT	PART WORKS	PATTERNED
PACHYDERM	PANDERING	PARAMOURS	PARTY LINE	PAULOWNIA
PACHYTENE	PANDURATE	PARANOIAC	PARTY WALL	PAUPERISM
PACIFIERS	PANEGYRIC	PARAPLASM	PAS DE DEUX	PAUPERIZE
PACIFISTS	PANELLING	PARASITES	PASO DOBLE	PAUSINGLY
PACIFYING	PANELLIST	PARASITIC	PASSBOOKS	PAVEMENTS
PACKAGERS	PANHANDLE	PARATAXIS	PASSED OUT	PAVILIONS
PACKAGING	PANICKING	PARATHION	PASSENGER	PAWKINESS
PACKED-OUT	PANMUNJOM	PARBOILED	PASSERINE	PAWNSHOPS
PACKHORSE	PANNIKINS	PARBUCKLE	PASSERSBY	PAYCHECKS
PADERBORN	PANOPLIED	PARCELING	PASSIONAL	PAYMASTER
PADLOCKED	PANORAMAS	PARCELLED	PASSIVELY	PAY PACKET
PAEDERAST	PANORAMIC	PARCENARY	PASSIVISM	PAY PHONES
PAEDOLOGY	PANSOPHIC	PARCHMENT	PASSIVIST	PEACEABLE
PAGANIZER	PANTHEISM	PARDONERS	PASSIVITY	PEACEABLY
PAGEANTRY	PANTHEIST	PARDONING	PASSOVERS	PEACE PIPE
PAILLASSE	PANTHEONS	PARDUBICE	PASSPORTS	PEACETIME
PAILLETTE	PANTOMIME	PAREGORIC	PASSWORDS	PEARLIEST
PAINFULLY	PANTY HOSE	PARENTAGE	PASTICHES	PEARLITIC
PAINTBALL	PAPARAZZI	PARENTING	PASTILLES	PEARLIZED
PAINTERLY	PAPARAZZO	PARGETING	PASTINESS	PEARMAINS
PAINTINGS	PAPERBACK	PARHELION	PASTORALE	PEASANTRY
PAINTWORK	PAPERBOYS	PARI PASSU	PASTORALS	PEA SOUPER
PAKISTANI	PAPER CLIP	PARISIANS	PASTORATE	PECCARIES
PALANQUIN	PAPER TAPE	PARLEYING	PASTURAGE	PECTINATE
PALATABLE	PAPERWORK	PARLOR CAR	PASTURING	PECULATED
PALATABLY	PAPETERIE	PARNASSUS	PATAGONIA	PECULATOR
PALEFACES	PAPILLARY	PAROCHIAL	PATCHABLE	PECUNIARY

PEDAGOGIC	PENTAGONS	PERISPERM	PETERSHAM	PHONEMICS
PEDAGOGUE	PENTAGRAM	PERISTOME	PETIOLATE	PHONETICS
PEDALLING	PENTARCHY	PERISTYLE	PETIOLULE	PHONEY WAR
PEDATIFID	PENTECOST	PERITONEA	PETIT FOUR	PHONINESS
PEDERASTS	PENTHOUSE	PERITRACK	PETITIONS	PHONOGRAM
PEDERASTY	PENTOTHAL	PERJURERS	PETRI DISH	PHONOLITE
PEDESTALS	PENTOXIDE	PERJURIES	PETRIFIED	PHONOLOGY
PEDICULAR	PENUMBRAL	PERJURING	PETRIFIER	PHONOTYPE
PEDICURES	PENUMBRAS	PERKINESS	PETROLEUM	PHONOTYPY
PEDIGREED	PENURIOUS	PERMALLOY	PETROLOGY	PHOSPHATE
PEDIGREES	PEPPERING	PERMANENT	PETTICOAT	PHOSPHENE
PEDIMENTS	PEPPER POT	PERMEABLE	PETTINESS	PHOSPHIDE
PEDUNCLED	PEPSINATE	PERMEANCE	PETTISHLY	PHOSPHINE
PEEPHOLES	PEPTIDASE	PERMEATED	PETTY CASH	PHOSPHITE
PEERESSES	PEPTONIZE	PERMEATOR	PETULANCE	PHOTOCELL
PEEVISHLY	PERBORATE	PER MENSEM	PFORZHEIM	PHOTOCOPY
PEGGED OUT	PERCALINE	PERMITTED	PHAGOCYTE	PHOTOGRAM
PEGMATITE	PER CAPITA	PERMITTER	PHALANGER	PHOTONICS
PEKINESES	PERCEIVED	PERMUTING	PHALANGES	PHOTOSTAT
PEKINGESE	PERCEIVER	PERPETUAL	PHALANXES	PHOTOTUBE
PEKING MAN	PERCHANCE	PERPIGNAN	PHALAROPE	PHOTOTYPE
PELLITORY	PERCHERON	PERPLEXED	PHALLUSES	PHRENITIC
PELMANISM	PERCOLATE	PERSECUTE	PHANTASMS	PHRENITIS
PELTATION	PERCUSSOR	PERSEVERE	PHARISAIC	PHTHALEIN
PEMPHIGUS	PERDITION	PERSIMMON	PHARISEES	PHYCOLOGY
PENALIZED	PEREGRINE	PERSISTED	PHARYNXES	PHYLLITIC
PENALTIES	PERENNATE	PERSISTER	PHASE-OUTS	PHYLLOMIC
PENCHANTS	PERENNIAL	PERSONAGE	PHEASANTS	PHYLOGENY
PENCILING	PERFECTED	PERSONALS	PHELLOGEN	PHYSICALS
PENCILLED	PERFECTER	PERSONATE	PHENACITE	PHYSICIAN
PENCILLER	PERFECTLY	PERSONIFY	PHENAZINE	PHYSICIST
PENDRAGON	PERFIDIES	PERSONNEL	PHENETOLE	PHYSIQUES
PENDULOUS	PERFORATE	PERSPIRED	PHENOCOPY	PHYTOTRON
PENDULUMS	PERFORMED	PERSUADED	PHENOLATE	PIANISTIC
PENEPLAIN	PERFORMER	PERSUADER	PHENOLOGY	PICKETING
PENETRANT	PERFUMERY	PERTAINED	PHENOMENA	PICKINESS
PENETRATE	PERFUMING	PERTINENT	PHENOTYPE	PICK-ME-UPS
PEN FRIEND	PERFUSION	PERTURBED	PHENOXIDE	PICK PURSE
PENINSULA	PERFUSIVE	PERTUSSIS	PHEROMONE	PICNICKED
PENITENCE	PERICLASE	PERVADING	PHILANDER	PICNICKER
PENITENTS	PERICLINE	PERVASIVE	PHILATELY	PICOLINIC
PENKNIVES	PERICYCLE	PERVERTED	PHILIPPIC	PICTORIAL
PENNILESS	PERILYMPH	PERVERTER	PHILOLOGY	PICTURING
PENNINITE	PERIMETER	PESSARIES	PHLEBITIC	PIECE-DYED
PENN'ORTHS	PERIMETRY	PESSIMISM	PHLEBITIS	PIECEMEAL
PENNY-WISE	PERIMORPH	PESSIMIST	PHLYCTENA	PIECEWORK
PENNYWORT	PERINATAL	PESTERING	PHNOM PENH	PIE CHARTS
PEN PUSHER	PERIODATE	PESTICIDE	PHOENICIA	PIECRUSTS
PENSILITY	PERIPHERY	PESTILENT	PHOENIXES	PIERCABLE
PENSIONED	PERISCOPE	PETAL-LIKE	PHONATION	PIERIDINE
PENSIONER	PERISHERS	PETALODIC	PHONATORY	PIGGERIES
PENSIVELY	PERISHING	PETECHIAL	PHONE BOOK	PIGGISHLY

PIGGYBACK	PITHINESS	PLAYFULLY	PNEUMONIA	POLO SHIRT
PIGGYBANK	PITOT TUBE	PLAYGOERS	PNEUMONIC	POLTROONS
PIGHEADED	PIT PONIES	PLAYGROUP	POCKETFUL	POLYAMIDE
PIG-HEADED	PITTANCES	PLAYHOUSE	POCKETING	POLYANDRY
PIGTAILED	PITUITARY	PLAYMAKER	POCKMARKS	POLYBASIC
PIKEPERCH	PITYINGLY	PLAYMATES	PODGINESS	POLYCARPY
PIKESTAFF	PIZZICATO	PLAYROOMS	POETASTER	POLYESTER
PILASTERS	PLACARDED	PLAYTHING	POETESSES	POLYGLOTS
PILCHARDS	PLACATING	PLEADABLE	POETICIZE	POLYGONAL
PILFERAGE	PLACATION	PLEADINGS	POGO STICK	POLYGONUM
PILFERERS	PLACATORY	PLEASABLE	POIGNANCY	POLYGRAPH
PILFERING	PLACEBOES	PLEASANCE	POINCIANA	POLYMATHS
PILLAGERS	PLACE CARD	PLEASEDLY	POINT DUTY	POLYMERIC
PILLAGING	PLACE MATS	PLEASURES	POINTEDLY	POLYMORPH
PILLAR BOX	PLACEMENT	PLEBBIEST	POINTLESS	POLYMYXIN
PILLBOXES	PLACENTAE	PLEBEIANS	POINTSMAN	POLYNESIA
PILLORIED	PLACENTAL	PLECTRUMS	POISONERS	POLYPHASE
PILLORIES	PLACENTAS	PLENARILY	POISON GAS	POLYPHONE
PILLOWING	PLACIDITY	PLENITUDE	POISONING	POLYPHONY
PIMPERNEL	PLACODERM	PLENTEOUS	POISON IVY	POLYPLOID
PINACEOUS	PLAIN-LAID	PLENTIFUL	POISONOUS	POLYPTYCH
PINAFORES	PLAINNESS	PLEONASMS	POKEBERRY	POLYSOMIC
PINCHBECK	PLAINSMAN	PLEURITIC	POKER FACE	POLYTHENE
PINCHCOCK	PLAINSONG	PLEXIFORM	POKERWORK	POLYTONAL
PINEAPPLE	PLAINTIFF	PLICATION	POLAR BEAR	POLYTYPIC
PINETREES	PLAINTIVE	PLIGHTING	POLARIZED	POLYVINYL
PINEWOODS	PLANARIAN	PLIMSOLLS	POLARIZER	POMACEOUS
PINIONING	PLANATION	PLOUGHBOY	POLAROIDS	POMANDERS
PINNACLES	PLANETARY	PLOUGHING	POLEAXING	POMERANIA
PINNATION	PLANETOID	PLOUGHMAN	POLEMICAL	POMPADOUR
PINPOINTS	PLANE TREE	PLOUGHMEN	POLE VAULT	POMPOSITY
PINPRICKS	PLANGENCY	PLUCKIEST	POLICE DOG	POMPOUSLY
PINSTRIPE	PLANISHER	PLUGBOARD	POLICEMAN	PONDERING
PINTABLES	PLANTABLE	PLUGHOLES	POLICEMEN	PONDEROUS
PINTADERA	PLANTAINS	PLUMBABLE	POLISHING	PONDOLAND
PINWHEELS	PLASMAGEL	PLUMBEOUS	POLITBURO	PONTIANAK
PIONEERED	PLASMASOL	PLUMBICON	POLITESSE	PONTYPOOL
PIOUSNESS	PLASTERED	PLUMB LINE	POLITICAL	PONYTAILS
PIPE DREAM	PLASTERER	PLUMMETED	POLITICOS	POORHOUSE
PIPELINES	PLATELETS	PLUMMIEST	POLKA DOTS	POORLIEST
PIPE RACKS	PLATE RACK	PLUMPNESS	POLLARDED	POORLY OFF
PIPERONAL	PLATFORMS	PLUNDERED	POLLINATE	POOR WHITE
PIPESTONE	PLATINIZE	PLUNDERER	POLLINIUM	POPE'S NOSE
PIPSQUEAK	PLATINOID	PLURALISM	POLLSTERS	POPINJAYS
PIQUANTLY	PLATINOUS	PLURALIST	POLL TAXES	POPLITEAL
PIRATICAL	PLATITUDE	PLURALITY	POLLUCITE	POPPYCOCK
PIROUETTE	PLAUSIBLE	PLURALIZE	POLLUTANT	POPPYHEAD
PISS-TAKES	PLAUSIBLY	PLUS FOURS	POLLUTING	POPSICLES
PISTACHIO	PLAY-ACTED	PLUSHNESS	POLLUTION	POPULARLY
PITCH-DARK	PLAYBACKS	PLUTOCRAT	POLLYANNA	POPULATED
PITCHFORK	PLAY DOUGH	PLUTONIUM	POLONAISE	POPULISTS
PITEOUSLY	PLAYED-OUT	PNEUMATIC	POLO NECKS	PORBEAGLE

PORCELAIN	POTBOILER	PRECISION	PRESCRIPT	PRIME RATE
PORCUPINE	POT-BOILER	PRECLUDED	PRESENCES	PRIME TIME
PORIFERAN	POTENTATE	PRECOCIAL	PRESENTED	PRIMIPARA
PORKINESS	POTENTIAL	PRECOCITY	PRESENTEE	PRIMITIVE
POROMERIC	POTHOLERS	PRECONIZE	PRESENTER	PRIMROSES
PORPHYRIN	POTHOLING	PRECOOKED	PRESENTLY	PRINCEDOM
PORPOISES	POTHUNTER	PRECURSOR	PRESERVED	PRINCETON
PORRINGER	POT PLANTS	PREDATING	PRESERVER	PRINCIPAL
PORTACRIB	POTPOURRI	PREDATION	PRESERVES	PRINCIPLE
PORTADOWN	POT POURRI	PREDATORS	PRESETTER	PRINTABLE
PORTATIVE	POTSHERDS	PREDATORY	PRESHRUNK	PRINTINGS
PORT BLAIR	POTTERIES	PREDICANT	PRESIDENT	PRINTOUTS
PORTENDED	POTTERING	PREDICATE	PRESIDING	PRISMATIC
PORTERAGE	POTTINESS	PREDICTED	PRESIDIUM	PRISONERS
PORTFOLIO	POULTERER	PREDICTOR	PRESS-GANG	PRISSIEST
PORTHOLES	POULTICES	PREDIGEST	PRESS GANG	PRITCHETT
PORTICOES	POULTRIES	PRE-EMPTED	PRESSINGS	PRIVATEER
PORTIONED	POUNDINGS	PRE-EMPTOR	PRESSMARK	PRIVATELY
PORTLIEST	POURBOIRE	PREFACING	PRESSROOM	PRIVATION
PORT LOUIS	POUTINGLY	PREFATORY	PRESS-STUD	PRIVATIVE
PORTO NOVO	POVERTIES	PREFERRED	PRESSURED	PRIVATIZE
PORTRAITS	POWDERING	PREFIGURE	PRESSURES	PRIVILEGE
PORTRAYAL	POWDER KEG	PREFIXING	PRESSWORK	PRIZE DAYS
PORTRAYED	POWER BASE	PREFLIGHT	PRESTIGES	PROACTIVE
PORTRAYER	POWERBOAT	PREGNABLE	PRESTRESS	PROBABLES
PORT SUDAN	POWER DIVE	PREGNANCY	PRESTWICH	PROBATING
PORTULACA	POWERLESS	PREHEATED	PRESTWICK	PROBATION
POSITIONS	PRACTICAL	PREJUDGED	PRESUMING	PROBATIVE
POSITIVES	PRACTICES	PREJUDGER	PRETENCES	PROBEABLE
POSITRONS	PRACTISED	PREJUDICE	PRETENDED	PROBINGLY
POSSESSED	PRAESIDIA	PRELATISM	PRETENDER	PROBOSCIS
POSSESSOR	PRAGMATIC	PRELATIST	PRETERITE	PROCEDURE
POSSIBLES	PRANKSTER	PRELATURE	PRETTIEST	PROCEEDED
POSTAXIAL	PRATINGLY	PRELUDIAL	PREVAILED	PROCEEDER
POSTCARDS	PRATTLERS	PRELUSION	PREVAILER	PROCESSED
POSTCODES	PRATTLING	PRELUSIVE	PREVALENT	PROCESSES
POSTDATED	PRAYERFUL	PREMATURE	PREVENTED	PROCESSOR
POSTERIOR	PRAYER RUG	PREMIERED	PREVENTER	PROCLITIC
POSTERITY	PREACHERS	PREMIERES	PREVIEWED	PROCONSUL
POSTHASTE	PREACHIFY	PREOCCUPY	PREVISION	PROCREANT
POST HORNS	PREACHING	PREORDAIN	PRICELESS	PROCREATE
POSTICOUS	PREAMBLES	PREPACKED	PRICE TAGS	PROCTORED
POSTILION	PREBENDAL	PREPARING	PRICINESS	PROCURERS
POSTMARKS	PRECANCEL	PREPAYING	PRICKLIER	PROCURING
POSTNATAL	PRECEDENT	PREPOTENT	PRICKLING	PRODIGALS
POSTPONED	PRECEDING	PREPUTIAL	PRIESTESS	PRODIGIES
POSTPONER	PRECENTOR	PRERECORD	PRIMAEVAL	PRODROMAL
POSTULANT	PRECEPTOR	PRESAGING	PRIMARIES	PRODUCERS
POSTULATE	PRECINCTS	PRESBYTER	PRIMARILY	PRODUCING
POSTURING	PRECIPICE	PRESCHOOL	PRIMATIAL	PROFANELY
POTASSIUM	PRECISELY	PRESCIENT	PRIME COST	PROFANING
POTATIONS	PRECISIAN	PRESCRIBE	PRIMENESS	PROFANITY

PROFESSED	PROPOSING	PRUSSIATE	PUNCHBALL	PYONGYANG
PROFESSOR	PROPRIETY	PRYTANEUM	PUNCH BOWL	PYORRHOEA
PROFFERED	PROPTOSIS	PSALMISTS	PUNCHIEST	PYRAMIDAL
PROFFERER	PROPYLITE	PSALMODIC	PUNCH LINE	PYRETHRIN
PROFILING	PROROGUED	PSEUDONYM	PUNCTILIO	PYRETHRUM
PROFITEER	PROSCRIBE	PSORIASIS	PUNCTUATE	PYRIDOXAL
PROFITING	PROSECTOR	PSORIATIC	PUNCTURED	PYROGENIC
PROFLUENT	PROSECUTE	PSYCHICAL	PUNCTURER	PYROLITIC
PROFUSELY	PROSELYTE	PSYCHOSES	PUNCTURES	PYROLYSIS
PROFUSION	PROSIMIAN	PSYCHOSIS	PUNGENTLY	PYROMANCY
PROGESTIN	PROSINESS	PSYCHOTIC	PUNISHING	PYROMANIA
PROGNOSES	PROSODIST	PTARMIGAN	PUPILLAGE	PYROMETER
PROGNOSIS	PROSPECTS	PTERYGOID	PUPILLARY	PYROMETRY
PROGRAMED	PROSPERED	PTOLEMAIC	PUPPETEER	PYROXENIC
PROGRAMER	PROSTATES	PUB-CRAWLS	PUPPYHOOD	PYROXYLIN
PROGRAMME	PROSTATIC	PUBESCENT	PUPPY LOVE	
PROJECTED	PROSTRATE	PUBLICANS	PURCHASED	**Q**
PROJECTOR	PROTAMINE	PUBLIC BAR	PURCHASER	QUADRANTS
PROLACTIN	PROTANDRY	PUBLICIST	PURCHASES	QUADRATIC
PROLAMINE	PROTECTED	PUBLICITY	PUREBREDS	QUADRIFID
PROLAPSED	PROTECTOR	PUBLICIZE	PURGATION	QUADRILLE
PROLAPSES	PROTESTER	PUBLISHED	PURGATIVE	QUADRUPED
PROLEPSIS	PROTHESIS	PUBLISHER	PURGATORY	QUADRUPLE
PROLEPTIC	PROTHETIC	PUCKERING	PURIFIERS	QUADRUPLY
PROLIXITY	PROTHORAX	PUCKISHLY	PURIFYING	QUAGMIRES
PROLOGUES	PROTOCOLS	PUDGINESS	PURLOINED	QUAKERISM
PROLONGED	PROTOGYNY	PUERILISM	PURLOINER	QUAKINESS
PROLONGER	PROTONEMA	PUERILITY	PURPORTED	QUALIFIED
PROLUSION	PROTOSTAR	PUERPERAL	PURPOSELY	QUALIFIER
PROLUSORY	PROTOTYPE	PUFF ADDER	PURPOSING	QUALITIES
PROMENADE	PROTOXIDE	PUFFINESS	PURPOSIVE	QUARRELED
PROMINENT	PROTOZOAN	PUGILISTS	PURSUANCE	QUARRYING
PROMISING	PROTRUDED	PUGNACITY	PURULENCE	QUARTERED
PROMOTERS	PROUDNESS	PUISSANCE	PURVEYING	QUARTERLY
PROMOTING	PROUSTITE	PULLOVERS	PURVEYORS	QUARTZITE
PROMOTION	PROVENCAL	PULL ROUND	PUSHBIKES	QUATRAINS
PROMOTIVE	PROVENDER	PULLULATE	PUSHCARTS	QUAVERING
PROMPTING	PROVIDENT	PULMONARY	PUSHCHAIR	QUEASIEST
PRONATION	PROVIDERS	PULMONATE	PUSH CHAIR	QUEBECKER
PRONENESS	PROVIDING	PULPINESS	PUSHINESS	QUEBECOIS
PRONGHORN	PROVINCES	PULSATILE	PUSHINGLY	QUEBRACHO
PRONOUNCE	PROVISION	PULSATING	PUSSYFOOT	QUEEN-SIZE
PROOFREAD	PROVISORY	PULSATION	PUSTULANT	QUEERNESS
PROPAGATE	PROVOKING	PULSATIVE	PUSTULATE	QUENCHING
PROPAGULE	PROVOLONE	PULSATORY	PUTREFIED	QUERCETIN
PRO PATRIA	PROWESSES	PULVERIZE	PUTREFIER	QUERETARO
PROPELLED	PROWL CARS	PULVILLUS	PUTRIDITY	QUERULOUS
PROPELLER	PROXIMATE	PULVINATE	PUTTERING	QUESTIONS
PROPHETIC	PROXIMITY	PUMICEOUS	PUTTYROOT	QUEUE-JUMP
PROPONENT	PRUDENTLY	PUMMELING	PUT-UP JOBS	QUIBBLERS
PROPOSALS	PRUDISHLY	PUMMELLED	PUY DE DOME	QUIBBLING
PROPOSERS	PRURIENCE	PUMP ROOMS	PYCNIDIUM	QUICKENED

QUICKLIME	RAILHEADS	REACTANCE	RECLUSION	RED INDIAN
QUICKNESS	RAILROADS	REACTIONS	RECLUSIVE	RED LIGHTS
QUICKSAND	RAIN CHECK	READDRESS	RECOGNIZE	REDOLENCE
QUICKSTEP	RAINCOATS	READINESS	RECOILING	REDOUBLED
QUIESCENT	RAINDROPS	READY-MADE	RECOLLECT	REDOUNDED
QUIETENED	RAINFALLS	REALIGNED	RECOMMEND	RED-PENCIL
QUIETISTS	RAIN GAUGE	REALISTIC	RECOMPOSE	RED PEPPER
QUIETNESS	RAININESS	REALITIES	RECONCILE	REDRESSED
QUIETUSES	RAINMAKER	REALIZING	RECONDITE	REDRESSER
QUILLWORT	RAINPROOF	REANIMATE	RECONVERT	REDUCIBLE
QUINIDINE	RAINSTORM	REAPPOINT	RECORDERS	REDUCTASE
QUINOLINE	RAINWATER	REARGUARD	RECORDING	REDUCTION
QUINONOID	RAJASTHAN	REAR LIGHT	RECOUNTAL	REDUNDANT
QUINTUPLE	RAMIFYING	REARRANGE	RECOUNTED	RE-ECHOING
QUIRKIEST	RAMPAGING	REARWARDS	RECOUPING	REEDINESS
QUISLINGS	RAMPANTLY	REASONING	RECOVERED	RE-EDUCATE
QUITCLAIM	RANCIDITY	REASSURED	RE-COVERED	REEF KNOTS
QUITTANCE	RANCOROUS	REASSURER	RECOVERER	REEKINGLY
QUIVERFUL	RANDINESS	REBATABLE	RECREANTS	RE-ELECTED
QUIVERING	RANDOMIZE	REBELLING	RECREATED	RE-ENFORCE
QUIXOTISM	RANGINESS	REBELLION	RE-CREATOR	RE-ENTRANT
QUIZZICAL	RANSACKED	REBINDING	RECREMENT	RE-ENTRIES
QUODLIBET	RANSACKER	REBOUNDED	RECRUITED	RE-EXAMINE
QUOTATION	RANSOMERS	REBOUNDER	RECRUITER	REFECTION
QUOTIDIAN	RANSOMING	REBUFFING	RECTANGLE	REFECTORY
QUOTIENTS	RANTINGLY	REBUKABLE	RECTIFIED	REFERABLE
	RAPACIOUS	REBUTTALS	RECTIFIER	REFERENCE
R	RAPID-FIRE	REBUTTING	RECTITUDE	REFERENDA
RABBINATE	RAPIDNESS	RECALLING	RECTOCELE	REFERRALS
RABBITING	RAPTORIAL	RECANTING	RECTORATE	REFERRING
RABBITTED	RAPTUROUS	RECAPPING	RECTORIAL	REFILLING
RACEHORSE	RARE EARTH	RECAPTION	RECTORIES	REFINABLE
RACETRACK	RASCALITY	RECAPTURE	RECUMBENT	REFINANCE
RACIALISM	RASPBERRY	RECASTING	RECURRENT	REFITTING
RACIALIST	RASPINGLY	RECEIVERS	RECURRING	REFLATING
RACKETEER	RASTERIZE	RECEIVING	RECUSANCY	REFLATION
RACONTEUR	RATEPAYER	RECENSION	RECUSANTS	REFLECTED
RADIAL-PLY	RATIFYING	RECEPTION	RECYCLING	REFLECTOR
RADIANCES	RATIONALE	RECEPTIVE	REDACTION	REFLEXIVE
RADIANTLY	RATIONING	RECESSING	RED ALERTS	REFORMERS
RADIATING	RATTINESS	RECESSION	REDBREAST	REFORMING
RADIATION	RATTLEBOX	RECESSIVE	REDBRICKS	REFORMISM
RADIATIVE	RAUCOUSLY	RECHARGED	REDBRIDGE	REFORMIST
RADIATORS	RAUNCHIER	RECHARGER	RED CARPET	REFRACTED
RADICALLY	RAUNCHILY	RECHAUFFE	REDDENING	REFRACTOR
RADIOGRAM	RAUWOLFIA	RECHERCHE	REDEEMERS	REFRAINED
RADIOLOGY	RAVELLING	RECIPIENT	REDEEMING	REFRAINER
RADIO STAR	RAVISHING	RECITABLE	REDELIVER	REFRESHED
RAFFINOSE	RAZORBACK	RECKONING	REDEVELOP	REFRESHER
RAFFISHLY	RAZORBILL	RECLAIMED	RED GIANTS	REFUELING
RAFFLESIA	RAZOR EDGE	RECLINATE	RED-HANDED	REFUELLED
RAIL GAUGE	REACHABLE	RECLINING	RED-HEADED	REFULGENT

REFUNDING	RELAXABLE	REPAIRMAN	REPUGNANT	RESOURCES
REFURBISH	RELAXEDLY	REPARABLE	REPULSING	RESPECTED
REFUSABLE	RELEASING	REPARABLY	REPULSION	RESPECTER
REFUSE BIN	RELEGATED	REPARTEES	REPULSIVE	RESPIRING
REFUSE TIP	RELENTING	REPAYABLE	REPUTABLE	RESPONDED
REFUTABLE	RELEVANCE	REPAYMENT	REPUTABLY	RESPONDER
REGAINING	RELEVANCY	REPEALING	REPUTEDLY	RESPONSER
REGARDANT	RELIEF MAP	REPEATERS	REQUESTED	RESPONSES
REGARDFUL	RELIEVING	REPEATING	REQUESTER	RESTATING
REGARDING	RELIGIONS	REPECHAGE	REQUIRING	REST CURES
REGENCIES	RELIGIOSE	REPELLENT	REQUISITE	RESTFULLY
REGICIDAL	RELIGIOUS	REPELLING	REQUITING	REST HOMES
REGICIDES	RELIQUARY	REPENTANT	REREDOSES	RESTIFORM
REGIMENTS	RELISHING	REPENTING	RERUNNING	RESTIVELY
REGISTERS	RELIVABLE	REPERTORY	RESALABLE	RESTOCKED
REGISTRAR	RELOADING	REPHRASED	RESCINDED	RESTORERS
REGRESSED	RELOCATED	REPLACING	RESCINDER	RESTORING
REGRESSOR	RELUCTANT	REPLAYING	RESCUABLE	RESTRAINT
REGRETFUL	REMAINDER	REPLEADER	RESECTION	REST ROOMS
REGRETTED	REMAINING	REPLENISH	RESEMBLED	RESULTANT
REGRETTER	REMANDING	REPLETION	RESEMBLER	RESULTING
REGROUPED	REMANENCE	REPLETIVE	RESENTFUL	RESUMABLE
REGULABLE	REMARKING	REPLICATE	RESENTING	RESURFACE
REGULARLY	REMARRIED	REPLY-PAID	RESERPINE	RESURGENT
REGULATED	REMEDYING	REPORTAGE	RESERVING	RESURRECT
REGULATOR	REMINDERS	REPORTERS	RESERVIST	RETAILERS
REHASHING	REMINDFUL	REPORTING	RESERVOIR	RETAILING
REHEARSAL	REMINDING	REPOSEDLY	RESETTING	RETAINERS
REHEARSED	REMINISCE	REPOSEFUL	RESETTLED	RETAINING
REHEARSER	REMISSION	REPOSSESS	RESHUFFLE	RETALIATE
REHOUSING	REMISSIVE	REPREHEND	RESIDENCE	RETARDANT
REIMBURSE	REMITTING	REPRESENT	RESIDENCY	RETARDATE
REINFORCE	REMODELED	REPRESSED	RESIDENTS	RETARDING
REINSTALL	REMONTANT	REPRESSER	RESIDUARY	RETELLING
REINSTATE	REMONTOIR	REPRESSOR	RESIGNING	RETENTION
REINSURED	REMOULDED	REPRIEVED	RESILIENT	RETENTIVE
REINSURER	REMOUNTED	REPRIEVER	RESINATED	RETHOUGHT
REISSUING	REMOVABLE	REPRIEVES	RESISTANT	RETICENCE
REITERANT	REMOVABLY	REPRIMAND	RESISTERS	RETICULES
REITERATE	REMSCHEID	REPRINTED	RESISTING	RETICULUM
REJECTING	RENASCENT	REPRINTER	RESISTORS	RETINITIS
REJECTION	RENDERING	REPRISALS	RESITTING	RETORSION
REJECTIVE	RENDITION	REPROBACY	RESNATRON	RETORTING
REJIGGING	RENEGADES	REPROBATE	RESOLUBLE	RETORTION
REJOICING	RENEWABLE	REPROCESS	RESOLVENT	RETOUCHED
REJOINDER	RENEWEDLY	REPRODUCE	RESOLVING	RETOUCHER
REJOINING	RENOUNCED	REPROVING	RESONANCE	RETRACING
REKINDLED	RENOUNCER	REPTILIAN	RESONATED	RETRACTED
RELAPSING	RENOVATED	REPTILOID	RESONATOR	RETRACTOR
RELATABLE	RENOVATOR	REPUBLICS	RESORBENT	RETREADED
RELATIONS	REOPENING	REPUBLISH	RESORTING	RETREATAL
RELATIVES	REPAIRING	REPUDIATE	RESOUNDED	RETREATED

RETRIEVAL	RHEOSTATS	RITUALIZE	ROPE TRICK	RUFESCENT
RETRIEVED	RHEOTAXIS	RIVALLING	ROQUEFORT	RUFFIANLY
RETRIEVER	RHEUMATIC	RIVALRIES	ROSACEOUS	RUINATION
RETROCEDE	RH FACTORS	RIVALROUS	ROSCOMMON	RUINOUSLY
RETROFIRE	RHIGOLENE	RIVERBEDS	ROSEWATER	RULEBOOKS
RETROFLEX	RHINELAND	RIVERBOAT	ROSINWEED	RUMBLINGS
RETROPACK	RHINOLOGY	RIVERHEAD	ROSTELLUM	RUMINANTS
RETROUSSE	RHIZOBIUM	RIVERSIDE	ROTAMETER	RUMINATED
RETURNING	RHIZOIDAL	ROADBLOCK	ROTARIANS	RUMINATOR
REUNITING	RHIZOTOMY	ROADHOUSE	ROTATABLE	RUMMAGING
REUTILIZE	RHODAMINE	ROADSHOWS	ROTATIONS	RUMP STEAK
REVALUING	RHODESIAN	ROADSTEAD	ROTAVATOR	RUN-ABOUTS
REVAMPING	RHODOLITE	ROADSTERS	ROTHERHAM	RUN ACROSS
REVEALING	RHODONITE	ROAD TAXES	ROTIFERAL	RUN-AROUND
REVELATOR	RHODOPSIN	ROAD TESTS	ROTOVATOR	RUNCINATE
REVELLING	RHOMBOIDS	ROADWORKS	ROTTERDAM	RUNNERS-UP
REVELMENT	RHOMBUSES	ROAD WORKS	ROTUNDITY	RUNNER-UPS
REVELROUS	RHOTACISM	ROAST BEEF	ROUGHCAST	RUNNYMEDE
REVENGING	RHOTACIST	ROASTINGS	ROUGH DEAL	RUNTINESS
REVERABLE	RHYMESTER	ROBBERIES	ROUGHENED	RUN TO SEED
REVERENCE	RHYOLITIC	ROBOT-LIKE	ROUGH-HEWN	RUPTURING
REVERENDS	RHYTHMICS	ROCHESTER	ROUGHNECK	RUSH HOURS
REVERSALS	RIBOSOMAL	ROCKBOUND	ROUGHNESS	RUSHINESS
REVERSING	RICE PADDY	ROCK CAKES	ROUGHSHOD	RUSHINGLY
REVERSION	RICE PAPER	ROCKERIES	ROUNDELAY	RUSHLIGHT
REVERTING	RICKSHAWS	ROCKETEER	ROUNDHEAD	RUSH LIGHT
REVERTIVE	RICOCHETS	ROCKETING	ROUNDNESS	RUSSETISH
REVETMENT	RIDDANCES	ROCKFALLS	ROUNDSMAN	RUSTICATE
REVIEWERS	RIDERLESS	ROCKINESS	ROUNDSMEN	RUSTICITY
REVIEWING	RIDGELING	ROCK 'N'	ROUND TRIP	RUSTINESS
REVISABLE	RIDGEPOLE	ROLL	ROUND-TRIP	RUSTPROOF
REVISIONS	RIDICULED	ROCK PLANT	ROUNDWORM	RUTABAGAS
REVIVABLE	RIDICULER	ROCKSHAFT	ROUTINELY	RUTACEOUS
REVIVABLY	RIFLEBIRD	ROENTGENS	ROUTINISM	RUTHENIAN
REVOCABLE	RIGHTEOUS	ROGUERIES	ROUTINIST	RUTHENIUM
REVOCABLY	RIGHT-HAND	ROGUISHLY	ROVING EYE	RUTILATED
REVOKABLE	RIGHTISTS	ROISTERER	ROWAN TREE	RUTTINESS
REVOKABLY	RIGHTNESS	ROLE MODEL	ROWDINESS	RUWENZORI
REVOLTING	RIGHTSIZE	ROLE PLAYS	ROW HOUSES	
REVOLVERS	RIGHTWARD	ROLL CALLS	ROYAL BLUE	**S**
REVOLVING	RIGHT WING	ROLLINGLY	ROYALISTS	SABADILLA
REVULSION	RIGMAROLE	ROMANCING	ROYALTIES	SABOTAGED
REVULSIVE	RING A BELL	ROMAN NOSE	RUBBERIZE	SABOTEURS
REWARDING	RING ROADS	ROMANTICS	RUBBISHED	SACCHARIN
REWIRABLE	RIO BRANCO	ROMPINGLY	RUBESCENT	SACCULATE
REWORDING	RIO GRANDE	ROOF RACKS	RUBRICATE	SACKCLOTH
REWORKING	RIOTOUSLY	ROOKERIES	RUBRICIAN	SACK RACES
REWRITING	RIPOSTING	ROOMINESS	RUCKSACKS	SACRAMENT
REYKJAVIK	RISE ABOVE	ROOMMATES	RUDACEOUS	SACRARIUM
RHAPSODIC	RISKINESS	ROOT CROPS	RUDBECKIA	SACRED COW
RHEOMETER	RITUALISM	ROOTINESS	RUDDINESS	SACRIFICE
RHEOMETRY	RITUALIST	ROOTSTOCK	RUDIMENTS	SACRILEGE

SACRISTAN	SALTWORKS	SASKATOON	SCARFSKIN	SCOLECITE
SADDENING	SALVAGING	SASSAFRAS	SCARIFIED	SCOLIOSIS
SADDLEBAG	SALVATION	SASSENACH	SCARIFIER	SCOLIOTIC
SADDLEBOW	SAMARITAN	SATANISTS	SCARINGLY	SCOLLOPED
SAFEGUARD	SAMARKAND	SATELLITE	SCARPERED	SCOMBROID
SAFE HOUSE	SANATORIA	SATIATING	SCATOLOGY	SCOPOLINE
SAFELIGHT	SANCTIONS	SATIATION	SCATTERED	SCOPULATE
SAFETY NET	SANCTUARY	SATINWOOD	SCATTERER	SCORBUTIC
SAFETY PIN	SANDALLED	SATIRICAL	SCATTIEST	SCORCHERS
SAFFLOWER	SANDBANKS	SATIRIZED	SCAVENGED	SCORCHING
SAFRANINE	SANDBLAST	SATIRIZER	SCAVENGER	SCORECARD
SAGACIOUS	SAND-BLIND	SATISFIED	SCENARIOS	SCORIFIER
SAGEBRUSH	SANDBOXES	SATISFIER	SCENARIST	SCORPIOID
SAGE DERBY	SAND DUNES	SATURABLE	SCENTLESS	SCORPIONS
SAGE GREEN	SAND FLIES	SATURATED	SCEPTICAL	SCOTCH EGG
SAGITTATE	SANDHURST	SATURATER	SCHEDULAR	SCOTCHING
SAILBOARD	SANDINESS	SATURDAYS	SCHEDULED	SCOUNDREL
SAILCLOTH	SANDPAPER	SATURNIAN	SCHEDULES	SCOURGING
SAILOR HAT	SANDPIPER	SATURNIID	SCHEELITE	SCOURINGS
SAILPLANE	SANDSHOES	SATURNINE	SCHEMATIC	SCRABBLED
SAINTE FOY	SANDSTONE	SATURNISM	SCHILLING	SCRABBLER
SAINT GALL	SANDSTORM	SAUCEPANS	SCHISTOSE	SCRAGGIER
SAINTHOOD	SAND TRAPS	SAUCINESS	SCHIZOPOD	SCRAGGILY
SAINT JOHN	SANFORIZE	SAUNTERED	SCHLEPPED	SCRAGGING
SAINTLILY	SANGFROID	SAUNTERER	SCHLIEREN	SCRAMBLED
SAINT-OUEN	SANITARIA	SAUTERNES	SCHLIERIC	SCRAMBLER
SAINT PAUL	SANITIZED	SAVOURING	SCHMALTZY	SCRAMBLES
SAINT'S DAY	SAN MARINO	SAXIFRAGE	SCHNAUZER	SCRAMMING
SALAAMING	SANS SERIF	SAXOPHONE	SCHNITZEL	SCRAPABLE
SALACIOUS	SANTA CRUZ	SCABBARDS	SCHNORKEL	SCRAPBOOK
SALAD DAYS	SANTANDER	SCABBIEST	SCHOLARLY	SCRAP HEAP
SALAMANCA	SANTONICA	SCABIETIC	SCHOLIAST	SCRAPINGS
SALARYMAN	SAPHENOUS	SCAFFOLDS	SCHOOLBOY	SCRAP IRON
SALERATUS	SAPIENTLY	SCAGLIOLA	SCHOOLING	SCRAPPIER
SALEROOMS	SAPODILLA	SCALAWAGS	SCHOONERS	SCRAPPILY
SALESGIRL	SAPPHIRES	SCALDFISH	SCIENTIAL	SCRAPPING
SALESROOM	SAPPINESS	SCALINESS	SCIENTISM	SCRATCHED
SALES SLIP	SAPRAEMIA	SCALLIONS	SCIENTIST	SCRATCHER
SALES TALK	SAPRAEMIC	SCALLOPED	SCIMITARS	SCRATCHES
SALIMETER	SAPROLITE	SCALLOPER	SCINTILLA	SCRAWLING
SALIMETRY	SAPROZOIC	SCALLYWAG	SCIOMANCY	SCRAWNIER
SALISBURY	SAPSUCKER	SCAMPERED	SCIRRHOID	SCRAWNILY
SALIVATED	SARABANDE	SCAMPERER	SCIRRHOUS	SCREAMING
SALMONOID	SARABANDS	SCANTIEST	SCLERITIC	SCREECHED
SALOON BAR	SARACENIC	SCANTLING	SCLERITIS	SCREECHER
SALPIFORM	SARCASTIC	SCANTNESS	SCLEROSAL	SCREECHES
SALTATION	SARCOCARP	SCAPA FLOW	SCLEROSED	SCREENING
SALTINESS	SARDINIAN	SCAPEGOAT	SCLEROSES	SCREWBALL
SALTLICKS	SARGASSUM	SCAPHOPOD	SCLEROSIS	SCREWIEST
SALTPETRE	SARTORIAL	SCAPOLITE	SCLEROTIC	SCREW TOPS
SALT SPOON	SARTORIUS	SCARABOID	SCOLDABLE	SCREWWORM
SALTWATER	SASHAYING	SCARECROW	SCOLDINGS	SCRIBBLED

SCRIBBLER	SEAWORTHY	SEMESTERS	SERENADED	SHACKLING
SCRIBBLES	SEBACEOUS	SEMESTRAL	SERENADER	SHADINESS
SCRIMMAGE	SECATEURS	SEMI-BANTU	SERENADES	SHADOW-BOX
SCRIMPILY	SECESSION	SEMIBREVE	SERGEANCY	SHADOWIER
SCRIMPING	SECLUDING	SEMICOLON	SERGEANTS	SHADOWING
SCRIMSHAW	SECLUSION	SEMIFINAL	SERIALISM	SHAGGIEST
SCRIPTURE	SECLUSIVE	SEMIFLUID	SERIALIZE	SHAKE A LEG
SCROLLING	SECONDARY	SEMILUNAR	SERICEOUS	SHAKEDOWN
SCROUNGED	SECONDERS	SEMIOTICS	SERIGRAPH	SHAKEOUTS
SCROUNGER	SECONDING	SEMIRIGID	SERIOUSLY	SHAKINESS
SCRUBBERS	SECRETARY	SEMISOLID	SERMONIZE	SHALLOWED
SCRUBBIER	SECRETING	SEMISWEET	SEROLOGIC	SHALLOWER
SCRUBBING	SECRETION	SEMITONES	SEROTINAL	SHALLOWLY
SCRUBLAND	SECRETIVE	SEMITONIC	SEROTONIN	SHAMANISM
SCRUFFIER	SECRETORY	SEMIVOCAL	SERRATION	SHAMANIST
SCRUMHALF	SECTARIAN	SEMIVOWEL	SERRIFORM	SHAMATEUR
SCRUM HALF	SECTILITY	SENESCENT	SERRULATE	SHAMBLING
SCRUMMAGE	SECTIONAL	SENESCHAL	SERVERIES	SHAMBOLIC
SCRUMPING	SECTIONED	SENIORITY	SERVICING	SHAMELESS
SCRUNCHED	SECTORIAL	SENORITAS	SERVIETTE	SHAMPOOED
SCRUNCHIE	SECUNDINE	SENSATION	SERVILELY	SHAMPOOER
SCRUPLING	SECURABLE	SENSELESS	SERVILITY	SHANGRI-LA
SCUFFLING	SEDATIVES	SENSILLUM	SERVITORS	SHAN STATE
SCULLIONS	SEDENTARY	SENSITIVE	SERVITUDE	SHAPELESS
SCULPTORS	SEDIMENTS	SENSITIZE	SESSILITY	SHAPELIER
SCULPTURE	SEDITIOUS	SENSORIUM	SESSIONAL	SHARECROP
SCUPPERED	SEDUCIBLE	SENTENCED	SETACEOUS	SHARE SHOP
SCURRYING	SEDUCTION	SENTENCES	SET FIRE TO	SHAREWARE
SCUTATION	SEDUCTIVE	SENTIENCE	SET PIECES	SHARKSKIN
SCUTCHEON	SEEDINESS	SENTIMENT	SET SPEECH	SHARPENED
SCUTELLAR	SEEDLINGS	SENTINELS	SETSQUARE	SHARPENER
SCUTELLUM	SEEMINGLY	SENTRY BOX	SET SQUARE	SHARP-EYED
SCUTIFORM	SEESAWING	SEPARABLE	SET THEORY	SHARPNESS
SCUTTLING	SEGMENTAL	SEPARABLY	SETTLED IN	SHATTERED
SEABOARDS	SEGMENTED	SEPARATED	SETTLINGS	SHATTERER
SEA BREEZE	SEGREGATE	SEPARATES	SET-TOP BOX	SHEARLING
SEA CHANGE	SEIGNEURS	SEPARATOR	SEVENFOLD	SHEATFISH
SEAFARING	SELACHIAN	SEPHARDIC	SEVENTEEN	SHEATHING
SEAFRONTS	SELECTING	SEPIOLITE	SEVENTIES	SHEEPDIPS
SEAHORSES	SELECTION	SEPTARIAN	SEVERABLE	SHEEPDOGS
SEAL-POINT	SELECTIVE	SEPTARIUM	SEVERALLY	SHEEPFOLD
SEALYHAMS	SELECTORS	SEPTEMBER	SEVERALTY	SHEEPSKIN
SEAMINESS	SELENIOUS	SEPTENARY	SEVERANCE	SHEEPWALK
SEAPLANES	SELF-ABUSE	SEPTICITY	SEX APPEAL	SHEERLEGS
SEA POWERS	SELF-DOUBT	SEPTUPLET	SEXENNIAL	SHEERNESS
SEARCHING	SELF-DRIVE	SEPULCHRE	SEX OBJECT	SHEFFIELD
SEASCAPES	SELFISHLY	SEPULTURE	SEX ORGANS	SHEIKHDOM
SEA SHANTY	SELLOTAPE	SEQUACITY	SEXTUPLET	SHELDUCKS
SEASHELLS	SELL SHORT	SEQUENCER	SEXUALITY	SHELF LIFE
SEASONING	SEMANTICS	SEQUENCES	SFORZANDO	SHELLFIRE
SEAT BELTS	SEMAPHORE	SEQUESTER	SGRAFFITO	SHELLFISH
SEA URCHIN	SEMBLANCE	SERAGLIOS	SHABBIEST	SHELTERED

SHELTERER	SHOT TOWER	SIDERITIC	SINCERELY	SKINFLINT
SHEPHERDS	SHOULDERS	SIDEROSIS	SINCERITY	SKIN GRAFT
SHERBORNE	SHOVELING	SIDEROTIC	SINECURES	SKINHEADS
SHIELDING	SHOVELLED	SIDESHOWS	SINGAPORE	SKINNIEST
SHIFTIEST	SHOWCASES	SIDESLIPS	SINGINGLY	SKIN-TIGHT
SHIFT KEYS	SHOWDOWNS	SIDESTEPS	SINGLETON	SKI PLANES
SHIFTLESS	SHOWERING	SIDESWIPE	SINGSONGS	SKIPPERED
SHILLINGS	SHOWGIRLS	SIDETRACK	SINGULARS	SKITTERED
SHIMMERED	SHOWINESS	SIDEWARDS	SINGULTUS	SKIVVYING
SHINBONES	SHOWPIECE	SIGHTABLE	SINHALESE	SKULLCAPS
SHININESS	SHOW PIECE	SIGHTINGS	SINISTRAL	SKYDIVERS
SHINNYING	SHOWPLACE	SIGHTLESS	SINOLOGUE	SKYDIVING
SHIPBOARD	SHOWROOMS	SIGHT-READ	SINUOSITY	SKYJACKED
SHIPMATES	SHOW TRIAL	SIGHTSEER	SINUOUSLY	SKYJACKER
SHIPMENTS	SHREDDERS	SIGMATION	SINUSITIS	SKYLARKED
SHIPOWNER	SHREDDING	SIGNAL BOX	SIPHONAGE	SKYLARKER
SHIPSHAPE	SHREWDEST	SIGNALING	SIPHONING	SKYLIGHTS
SHIPWRECK	SHRIEKING	SIGNALIZE	SISYPHEAN	SKYROCKET
SHIPYARDS	SHRILLEST	SIGNALLED	SIT AT HOME	SKYWRITER
SHIRTIEST	SHRINKAGE	SIGNALLER	SITATUNGA	SLACKENED
SHIRTTAIL	SHRINKING	SIGNALMAN	SITUATING	SLACKNESS
SHITTIEST	SHRIVELED	SIGNALMEN	SITUATION	SLAGHEAPS
SHIVERING	SHROUDING	SIGNATORY	SITZKREIG	SLANDERED
SHOCKABLE	SHRUBBERY	SIGNATURE	SIX-FOOTER	SLANDERER
SHODDIEST	SHRUGGING	SIGNBOARD	SIXPENCES	SLANTWISE
SHOEHORNS	SHUBUNKIN	SIGNIFIED	SIXTEENMO	SLAPHAPPY
SHOELACES	SHUDDERED	SIGNIFIER	SIXTEENTH	SLAPSTICK
SHOEMAKER	SHUFBOARD	SIGNORINA	SIXTH FORM	SLATINESS
SHOESHINE	SHUFFLERS	SIGNPOSTS	SIXTIETHS	SLATTERNS
SHOETREES	SHUFFLING	SIKKIMESE	SIZARSHIP	SLAUGHTER
SHOOT-'EM-	SHUNNABLE	SILENCERS	SKAGERRAK	SLAVERING
UP	SHUTDOWNS	SILENCING	SKEDADDLE	SLAVISHLY
SHOOTINGS	SHUTTERED	SILICATES	SKELETONS	SLAVONIAN
SHOOT-OUTS	SHUTTLING	SILICEOUS	SKEPTICAL	SLEAZIEST
SHOP FLOOR	SIBILANCE	SILICOSIS	SKETCHERS	SLEEKNESS
SHORELESS	SIBILANTS	SILIQUOSE	SKETCHIER	SLEEPIEST
SHORELINE	SIBYLLINE	SILKALINE	SKETCHILY	SLEEPLESS
SHORTAGES	SICCATIVE	SILKINESS	SKETCHING	SLEEPWALK
SHORTCAKE	SICKENING	SILKWORMS	SKETCHPAD	SLICEABLE
SHORT CUTS	SICK LEAVE	SILLABUBS	SKEWBALDS	SLICKNESS
SHORTENED	SICKLIEST	SILLINESS	SKEWERING	SLIDE RULE
SHORTENER	SICKROOMS	SILTATION	SKEW-WHIFF	SLIGHTEST
SHORTFALL	SIC PASSIM	SILVERING	SKIASCOPE	SLIGHTING
SHORTHAND	SIDEBOARD	SIMAROUBA	SKIASCOPY	SLIMINESS
SHORT-HAUL	SIDEBURNS	SIMILARLY	SKIDPROOF	SLINGSHOT
SHORTHORN	SIDE-DRESS	SIMMERING	SKIJORING	SLINKIEST
SHORT LIST	SIDE ISSUE	SIMPATICO	SKILFULLY	SLIPCASES
SHORTNESS	SIDEKICKS	SIMPERING	SKIMMINGS	SLIPKNOTS
SHORT SLIP	SIDELIGHT	SIMPLETON	SKIMPIEST	SLIPNOOSE
SHORT-TERM	SIDELINED	SIMULACRA	SKIN-DIVED	SLIPPAGES
SHORT TIME	SIDELINES	SIMULATED	SKIN DIVER	SLIPPIEST
SHORT WAVE	SIDE ORDER	SIMULATOR	SKIN FLICK	SLIP ROADS

SLIPSHEET	SNAIL MAIL	SOAPSTONE	SOLOTHURN	SOUP SPOON
SLITHERED	SNAKEBITE	SOAPSUDSY	SOLSTICES	SOUR CREAM
SLIVOVITZ	SNAKEROOT	SOARINGLY	SOLUTIONS	SOUTH BEND
SLOBBERED	SNAKESKIN	SOBBINGLY	SOLUTREAN	SOUTHDOWN
SLOBBERER	SNAKINESS	SOBERNESS	SOLVATION	SOUTHEAST
SLOPINGLY	SNAPPABLE	SOBRIQUET	SOMBREROS	SOUTHERLY
SLOPPIEST	SNAPPIEST	SOB SISTER	SOMEPLACE	SOUTHPAWS
SLOUCH HAT	SNAPSHOTS	SOCIALISM	SOMETHING	SOUTH POLE
SLOUCHILY	SNARE DRUM	SOCIALIST	SOMETIMES	SOUTHPORT
SLOUCHING	SNARINGLY	SOCIALITE	SOMEWHERE	SOUTHWARD
SLOUGHING	SNATCHILY	SOCIALITY	SOMMELIER	SOUTHWARK
SLOVAKIAN	SNATCHING	SOCIALIZE	SOMNOLENT	SOUTHWEST
SLOVENIAN	SNAZZIEST	SOCIETIES	SONGBIRDS	SOUVENIRS
SLOWCOACH	SNEAKIEST	SOCIOLOGY	SONGBOOKS	SOU'WESTER
SLOWDOWNS	SNICKERED	SOCIOPATH	SONG CYCLE	SOVEREIGN
SLOW MATCH	SNIDENESS	SODA WATER	SONGOLOLO	SOVIETISM
SLOWWORMS	SNIFFLERS	SODOMITES	SONGSTERS	SOVIETIST
SLUDGIEST	SNIFFLING	SOFTENING	SONIC BOOM	SOVIETIZE
SLUGGARDS	SNIGGERED	SOFT FRUIT	SONNETEER	SOYA BEANS
SLUMBERED	SNIPEFISH	SOFT GOODS	SON-OF-A-	SPACEBAND
SLUMBERER	SNITCHING	SOFT METAL	GUN	SPACED OUT
SLUSH FUND	SNIVELING	SOFT-PEDAL	SONS-IN-LAW	SPACELESS
SLUSHIEST	SNIVELLED	SOFT SPOTS	SOOTINESS	SPACEPORT
SMALL ARMS	SNIVELLER	SOFT TOUCH	SOPHISTER	SPACESHIP
SMALL BEER	SNOOKERED	SOFTWOODS	SOPHISTIC	SPACESUIT
SMALLNESS	SNOOTIEST	SOGGINESS	SOPHISTRY	SPACE-TIME
SMALL TALK	SNOTTIEST	SOI-DISANT	SOPHOMORE	SPACEWALK
SMALL-TIME	SNOWBALLS	SOJOURNED	SOPORIFIC	SPADEFISH
SMARMIEST	SNOWBERRY	SOJOURNER	SOPPINESS	SPADEWORK
SMART ALEC	SNOW-BLIND	SOLAR CELL	SOPRANINO	SPAGHETTI
SMART CARD	SNOWBLINK	SOLARIUMS	SORCERERS	SPANGLING
SMARTENED	SNOWBOUND	SOLAR YEAR	SORCERESS	SPANIARDS
SMARTNESS	SNOWDONIA	SOLDERING	SORCEROUS	SPANKINGS
SMASHABLE	SNOWDRIFT	SOLDIERED	SORE POINT	SPARENESS
SMATTERER	SNOWDROPS	SOLDIERLY	SORITICAL	SPARE PART
SMEAR TEST	SNOWFALLS	SOLDIER ON	SORRINESS	SPARERIBS
SMELLIEST	SNOWFIELD	SOLECISMS	SORROWFUL	SPARE TYRE
SMILINGLY	SNOWFLAKE	SOLEMNIFY	SORROWING	SPARINGLY
SMIRCHING	SNOW GOOSE	SOLEMNITY	SORTILEGE	SPARKLERS
SMOKELESS	SNOWINESS	SOLEMNIZE	SORTITION	SPARKLING
SMOKINESS	SNOWSHOER	SOLENODON	SOSNOWIEC	SPARK PLUG
SMOLDERED	SNOWSHOES	SOLFATARA	SOSTENUTO	SPARTEINE
SMOOCHING	SNOWSTORM	SOLFEGGIO	SOTTO VOCE	SPASMODIC
SMOOTHEST	SNOW-WHITE	SOLFERINO	SOUBRETTE	SPATIALLY
SMOOTHIES	SNUB-NOSED	SOLICITED	SOULFULLY	SPATTERED
SMOOTHING	SNUFFLING	SOLICITOR	SOUL MUSIC	SPATULATE
SMOTHERED	SNUGGLING	SOLIDNESS	SOUNDABLE	SPEAKABLE
SMUGGLERS	SOAKINGLY	SOLILOQUY	SOUNDINGS	SPEAKEASY
SMUGGLING	SOAPBERRY	SOLIPSISM	SOUNDLESS	SPEARHEAD
SMUTTIEST	SOAPBOXES	SOLIPSIST	SOUNDNESS	SPEARMINT
SNACK BARS	SOAPINESS	SOLITAIRE	SOUNDPOST	SPEARWORT
SNAFFLING	SOAP OPERA	SOLONCHAK	SOUND POST	SPECIALLY

SPECIALTY	SPINULOSE	SPORULATE	SQUEEGEES	STAMP MILL
SPECIFICS	SPIRALING	SPOT CHECK	SQUEEZERS	STANCHING
SPECIFIED	SPIRALLED	SPOTLIGHT	SQUEEZING	STANCHION
SPECIFIER	SPIRILLAR	SPOTTABLE	SQUELCHED	STANDARDS
SPECIMENS	SPIRILLUM	SPOTTIEST	SQUELCHER	STAND FIRM
SPECTACLE	SPIRITING	SPRAINING	SQUIDGIER	STAND OVER
SPECTATED	SPIRITOSO	SPRAWLING	SQUIFFIER	STANDPIPE
SPECTATOR	SPIRITOUS	SPRAY GUNS	SQUIGGLER	STAPEDIAL
SPECULATE	SPIRITUAL	SPREADING	SQUIGGLES	STAR-APPLE
SPEECH DAY	SPIROGYRA	SPRIGHTLY	SQUINTING	STARBOARD
SPEECHIFY	SPITFIRES	SPRINGBOK	SQUIRMING	STARBURST
SPEEDBOAT	SPIT IT OUT	SPRINGIER	SQUIRRELS	STARCHIER
SPEEDIEST	SPITTOONS	SPRINGILY	SQUIRTERS	STARCHILY
SPEEDSTER	SPLASHIER	SPRINGING	SQUIRTING	STARCHING
SPEED TRAP	SPLASHILY	SPRINKLED	SQUISHIER	STARE DOWN
SPEEDWAYS	SPLASHING	SPRINKLER	SQUISHING	STARGAZER
SPEEDWELL	SPLATTING	SPRINKLES	SQUITTERS	STARKNESS
SPELLABLE	SPLAYFOOT	SPRINTERS	STABILITY	STARLIGHT
SPELLBIND	SPLEENFUL	SPRINTING	STABILIZE	STARLINGS
SPELLINGS	SPLEENISH	SPRITSAIL	STABLE BOY	STARRIEST
SPELUNKER	SPLENDOUR	SPROCKETS	STAGE DOOR	STAR SIGNS
SPENDABLE	SPLENETIC	SPROUTING	STAGEHAND	STARTLING
SPERMATIC	SPLENITIS	SPUNKIEST	STAGE HAND	STATE DUMA
SPERMATID	SPLINTERS	SPUTTERED	STAGE NAME	STATEHOOD
SPHAGNOUS	SPLINTERY	SPUTTERER	STAGGERED	STATELESS
SPHAGNUMS	SPLIT ENDS	SQUABBLED	STAGGERER	STATEMENT
SPHENODON	SPLIT PEAS	SQUABBLER	STAGHOUND	STATEROOM
SPHERICAL	SPLIT RING	SQUABBLES	STAGINESS	STATESIDE
SPHEROIDS	SPLITTING	SQUAD CARS	STAGNANCY	STATESMAN
SPHERULAR	SPLOSHING	SQUADRONS	STAGNATED	STATESMEN
SPHINCTER	SPLURGING	SQUALIDLY	STAG PARTY	STATIONED
SPHYGMOID	SPLUTTERS	SQUALLIER	STAIDNESS	STATIONER
SPICINESS	SPODUMENE	SQUALLING	STAINABLE	STATISTIC
SPICULATE	SPOKEN FOR	SQUAMOSAL	STAINLESS	STATOCYST
SPIDERMAN	SPOKESMAN	SQUARE LEG	STAIRCASE	STATOLITH
SPIDERWEB	SPONGE BAG	SQUARE ONE	STAIRHEAD	STATUETTE
SPIELBERG	SPONGIEST	SQUARROSE	STAIRWELL	STATUS QUO
SPIKENARD	SPONSORED	SQUASHIER	STALEMATE	STATUTORY
SPIKE-RUSH	SPOOKIEST	SQUASHILY	STALENESS	STAUNCHED
SPIKINESS	SPOONBILL	SQUASHING	STALINISM	STAUNCHER
SPILLIKIN	SPOON-FEED	SQUATNESS	STALINIST	STAUNCHLY
SPILLWAYS	SPOONFULS	SQUATTERS	STALL-FEED	STAVANGER
SPINDLIER	SPOONSFUL	SQUATTEST	STALLIONS	STAVROPOL
SPIN-DRIED	SPOROCARP	SQUATTING	STALWARTS	ST BERNARD
SPINDRIFT	SPOROCYST	SQUAWKERS	STAMINATE	STEADFAST
SPIN-DRYER	SPOROCYTE	SQUAWKING	STAMINODE	STEADIEST
SPINELESS	SPOROGONY	SQUEAKERS	STAMINODY	STEADYING
SPININESS	SPOROZOAN	SQUEAKIER	STAMMERED	STEAMBOAT
SPINNAKER	SPORTIEST	SQUEAKING	STAMMERER	STEAMED-UP
SPINNERET	SPORTS CAR	SQUEALERS	STAMPEDED	STEAMIEST
SPINOSITY	SPORTSMAN	SQUEALING	STAMPEDER	STEAM IRON
SPINSTERS	SPORTSMEN	SQUEAMISH	STAMPEDES	STEAMROLL

STEAMSHIP	STINKWOOD	STOREROOM	STRINGENT	STYLOBATE
STEATITIC	STIPIFORM	STORMIEST	STRINGIER	STYLOLITE
STEEL BAND	STIPITATE	STORNOWAY	STRINGILY	STYLOPIZE
STEELHEAD	STIPPLING	STORYBOOK	STRINGING	STYPTICAL
STEELIEST	STIPULATE	STORY LINE	STRIP CLUB	STYROFOAM
STEEL WOOL	STIR-FRIED	STORYLINE	STRIPIEST	SUABILITY
STEELWORK	STIRRABLE	STOUTNESS	STRIPLING	SUAVENESS
STEELYARD	STITCHING	STOVEPIPE	STRIPPERS	SUBALPINE
STEEPENED	STOCKADED	STOWAWAYS	STRIPPING	SUBALTERN
STEEPNESS	STOCKADES	STRADDLED	STROBILUS	SUBARCTIC
STEERABLE	STOCKCARS	STRADDLER	STROLLERS	SUBATOMIC
STEERSMAN	STOCK CUBE	STRAGGLED	STROLLING	SUBCLIMAX
STEERSMEN	STOCKFISH	STRAGGLER	STROMATIC	SUBCORTEX
STELLULAR	STOCKHOLM	STRAIGHTS	STRONGARM	SUBDEACON
STENCILED	STOCKIEST	STRAINERS	STRONGBOX	SUBDIVIDE
STENOTYPE	STOCKINET	STRAINING	STRONGEST	SUBDUABLE
STENOTYPY	STOCKINGS	STRALSUND	STRONGYLE	SUBDUEDLY
STEPCHILD	STOCKISTS	STRANGELY	STRONTIAN	SUBEDITED
STERADIAN	STOCKPILE	STRANGERS	STRONTIUM	SUBEDITOR
STERILANT	STOCKPORT	STRANGEST	STROPPIER	SUBFAMILY
STERILITY	STOCKPOTS	STRANGLED	STRUCTURE	SUBJACENT
STERILIZE	STOCKROOM	STRANGLER	STRUGGLED	SUBJECTED
STERNMOST	STOCK TAKE	STRANGLES	STRUGGLER	SUBJOINED
STERNNESS	STOCKYARD	STRANGURY	STRUGGLES	SUB JUDICE
STERNPOST	STODGIEST	STRANRAER	STRUMATIC	SUBJUGATE
STEVEDORE	STOICALLY	STRAPLESS	STRUMMING	SUBLEASED
STEVENAGE	STOKEHOLD	STRAPPING	STRUMPETS	SUBLEASES
STICK AT IT	STOKEHOLE	STRATAGEM	STRUNG-OUT	SUBLESSEE
STICKIEST	STOLIDITY	STRATEGIC	STRUTTING	SUBLESSOR
STICKLERS	STOMACHED	STRAW POLL	STRYCHNIC	SUBLIMATE
STICKPINS	STOMACHIC	STREAKERS	STUBBIEST	SUBLIMELY
STICKSEED	STONECHAT	STREAKIER	STUDBOOKS	SUBLIMITY
STICKWEED	STONE-COLD	STREAKILY	STUDHORSE	SUBLUNARY
STICKY BUN	STONECROP	STREAKING	STUFFIEST	SUBMARINE
STICKY END	STONE-DEAD	STREAMERS	STUMBLING	SUBMENTAL
STIFFENED	STONE-DEAF	STREAMING	STUMPIEST	SUBMERGED
STIFFENER	STONEFISH	STREETCAR	STUPEFIED	SUBMITTAL
STIFFNESS	STONELESS	STREISAND	STUPEFIER	SUBMITTED
STIGMATIC	STONE-LILY	STRENGTHS	STUPIDEST	SUBMITTER
STILETTOS	STONEWALL	STRENUOUS	STUPIDITY	SUBMUCOSA
STILLBORN	STONEWARE	STRESSFUL	STUPOROUS	SUBNORMAL
STILL LIFE	STONEWORK	STRESSING	STURDIEST	SUBORNING
STILLNESS	STONEWORT	STRETCHED	STURGEONS	SUBPHYLAR
STILL ROOM	STONINESS	STRETCHER	STUTTERED	SUBPHYLUM
STILTEDLY	STOPCOCKS	STRETCHES	STUTTERER	SUBPOENAS
STIMULANT	STOPLIGHT	STRETFORD	STUTTGART	SUBREGION
STIMULATE	STOPOVERS	STRIATION	STYLEBOOK	SUBROGATE
STINGIEST	STOPPABLE	STRICTEST	STYLELESS	SUBSCRIBE
STINGRAYS	STOPPAGES	STRICTURE	STYLIFORM	SUBSCRIPT
STINK-BOMB	STOPPERED	STRIDENCE	STYLISHLY	SUBSIDIES
STINKHORN	STOP PRESS	STRIDENCY	STYLISTIC	SUBSIDING
STINKWEED	STOPWATCH	STRIKE PAY	STYLIZING	SUBSIDIZE

SUBSISTED	SULLIABLE	SUPPORTER	SWALLOWER	SYBARITIC
SUBSISTER	SULPHATES	SUPPOSING	SWAMPLAND	SYCAMORES
SUBSOCIAL	SULPHIDES	SUPPURATE	SWANKIEST	SYCOPHANT
SUBSOILER	SULPHITIC	SUPREMACY	SWAN'S DOWN	SYKTYVKAR
SUBSTANCE	SULPHURET	SUPREMELY	SWAN'S-DOWN	SYLLABARY
SUBSTRATA	SULPHURYL	SUPREMITY	SWANSONGS	SYLLABIFY
SUBSTRATE	SULTANATE	SURAKARTA	SWAP MEETS	SYLLABISM
SUBSUMING	SULTRIEST	SURCHARGE	SWARTHIER	SYLLABLES
SUBSYSTEM	SUMMARIES	SURCINGLE	SWARTHILY	SYLLABUBS
SUBTENANT	SUMMARILY	SURCULOSE	SWASTIKAS	SYLLEPSIS
SUBTENDED	SUMMARIZE	SURE THING	SWATHABLE	SYLLEPTIC
SUBTILIZE	SUMMATION	SURFACING	SWAYINGLY	SYLLOGISM
SUBTITLED	SUMMERING	SURFBOARD	SWAZILAND	SYLLOGIZE
SUBTITLES	SUMMING-UP	SURFEITED	SWEARWORD	SYLPHLIKE
SUBTOTALS	SUMMONING	SURFEITER	SWEATBAND	SYLVANITE
SUBVERTED	SUMMONSED	SURFPERCH	SWEATIEST	SYMBIOSIS
SUBVERTER	SUMMONSES	SURGEONCY	SWEATSHOP	SYMBIOTIC
SUBWOOFER	SUMPTUARY	SURGERIES	SWEEPBACK	SYMBOLISM
SUCCEEDED	SUMPTUOUS	SURLINESS	SWEEPINGS	SYMBOLIST
SUCCEEDER	SUNBATHED	SURMISING	SWEET CORN	SYMBOLIZE
SUCCENTOR	SUNBATHER	SURPASSED	SWEETENER	SYMBOLOGY
SUCCESSES	SUNBURNED	SURPLICES	SWEETMEAT	SYMPATHIN
SUCCESSOR	SUNDERING	SURPLUSES	SWEETNESS	SYMPATRIC
SUCCINATE	SUNDOWNER	SURPRISED	SWEET PEAS	SYMPHONIC
SUCCOURED	SUNDSVALL	SURPRISER	SWEET TALK	SYMPHYSIS
SUCCOURER	SUNFLOWER	SURPRISES	SWELLFISH	SYMPODIAL
SUCCULENT	SUN LOUNGE	SURRENDER	SWELLINGS	SYMPODIUM
SUCCUMBED	SUNNINESS	SURROGACY	SWELTERED	SYMPOSIAC
SUCCUMBER	SUNSHADES	SURROGATE	SWEPT-BACK	SYMPOSIUM
SUCKLINGS	SUNSTROKE	SURROUNDS	SWEPTWING	SYNAGOGUE
SUCTIONAL	SUNTANNED	SURTITLES	SWERVABLE	SYNALEPHA
SUCTORIAL	SUN VISORS	SURVEYING	SWIFTNESS	SYNCHRONY
SUDORIFIC	SUPERABLE	SURVEYORS	SWIMMABLE	SYNCLINAL
SUFFERERS	SUPERCOOL	SURVIVALS	SWIMMERET	SYNCOPATE
SUFFERING	SUPEREGOS	SURVIVING	SWINDLERS	SYNCRETIC
SUFFICING	SUPERFINE	SURVIVORS	SWINDLING	SYNCYTIUM
SUFFIXION	SUPERHEAT	SUSPECTED	SWINEHERD	SYNDACTYL
SUFFOCATE	SUPERHERO	SUSPECTER	SWINGEING	SYNDICATE
SUFFRAGAN	SUPERIORS	SUSPENDED	SWING-WING	SYNDROMES
SUFFRAGES	SUPERNOVA	SUSPENDER	SWINISHLY	SYNDROMIC
SUFFUSING	SUPERPOSE	SUSPENSOR	SWISS ROLL	SYNECTICS
SUFFUSION	SUPERSEDE	SUSPICION	SWITCHING	SYNERESIS
SUFFUSIVE	SUPERSIZE	SUSTAINED	SWITCH OFF	SYNERGISM
SUGAR BEET	SUPERSTAR	SUSTAINER	SWIVELING	SYNERGIST
SUGAR CANE	SUPERVENE	SUSURRANT	SWIVELLED	SYNIZESIS
SUGARCANE	SUPERVISE	SUSURRATE	SWORDBILL	SYNKARYON
SUGGESTED	SUPINATOR	SUZERAINS	SWORDFISH	SYNOEKETE
SUGGESTER	SUPPERADD	SWADDLING	SWORDPLAY	SYNONYMIC
SUITCASES	SUPPLIANT	SWAGGERED	SWORDSMAN	SYNOVITIC
SULCATION	SUPPLIERS	SWAGGERER	SWORDSMEN	SYNOVITIS
SULKINESS	SUPPLYING	SWAHILIAN	SWORDTAIL	SYNTACTIC
SULLENEST	SUPPORTED	SWALLOWED	SYBARITES	SYNTHESES

SYNTHESIS	TAKING OFF	TAUTONYMY	TELLTALES	TERRORFUL
SYNTHETIC	TALIGRADE	TAXACEOUS	TELLURATE	TERRORISM
SYPHERING	TALISMANS	TAX HAVENS	TELLURIAN	TERRORIST
SYPHILOID	TALKATIVE	TAXIDERMY	TELLURIDE	TERRORIZE
SYPHILOMA	TALKING-TO	TAXIMETER	TELLURION	TERSENESS
SYPHONING	TALK SHOWS	TAXI RANKS	TELLURITE	TERVALENT
SYRINGEAL	TALL ORDER	TAXONOMIC	TELLURIUM	TESSERACT
SYRINGING	TALL STORY	TAXPAYERS	TELLURIZE	TESSITURA
SYSTALTIC	TALMUDISM	TEA BREAKS	TELLUROUS	TESTAMENT
	TALMUDIST	TEACHABLE	TELOPHASE	TESTATORS
T	TAMARINDS	TEA CHESTS	TELPHERIC	TESTATRIX
TABESCENT	TAMIL NADU	TEA CLOTHS	TEMAZEPAM	TEST CARDS
TABLATURE	TAMOXIFEN	TEA COSIES	TEMPERATE	TEST CASES
TABLELAND	TAMPERING	TEAGARDEN	TEMPERING	TESTICLES
TABLEMATS	TANDOORIS	TEAHOUSES	TEMPLATES	TESTIFIED
TABLEWARE	TANGERINE	TEAKETTLE	TEMPORARY	TESTIFIRE
TABLE WINE	TANNERIES	TEALEAVES	TEMPORIZE	TESTIMONY
TABULABLE	TANTALATE	TEAMSTERS	TEMPTABLE	TESTINESS
TABULATED	TANTALITE	TEARAWAYS	TEMPTRESS	TESTINGLY
TABULATOR	TANTALIZE	TEARDROPS	TENACIOUS	TEST MATCH
TACAMAHAC	TANTALOUS	TEARFULLY	TENACULUM	TEST PILOT
TACHYLYTE	TANZANIAN	TEARINGLY	TENANCIES	TEST TUBES
TACITNESS	TAP DANCER	TEASINGLY	TENDEREST	TETCHIEST
TACKINESS	TAP DANCES	TEASPOONS	TENDERING	TETE-A-TETE
TACTFULLY	TAPE DECKS	TEA TASTER	TENDERIZE	TETHERING
TACTICIAN	TAPEWORMS	TEA TOWELS	TENDINOUS	TETRAGRAM
TACTILITY	TAPHONOMY	TECHINESS	TENEBRISM	TETRALOGY
TAENIASIS	TARANTISM	TECHNICAL	TENEBRIST	TETRAPODY
TAGMEMICS	TARANTULA	TECHNIQUE	TENEBROUS	TETRARCHY
TAILBACKS	TARAXACUM	TECTONICS	TENEMENTS	TETROXIDE
TAILBOARD	TARDINESS	TEDDY BEAR	TENNESSEE	TEXTBOOKS
TAILCOATS	TARGETING	TEDDY BOYS	TENOR CLEF	THALASSIC
TAILGATED	TARMACKED	TEDIOUSLY	TENSENESS	THANJAVUR
TAILGATES	TARNISHED	TEENAGERS	TENSILITY	THANKLESS
TAILLIGHT	TARNISHER	TEE SHIRTS	TENSIONAL	THANKYOUS
TAIL-LIGHT	TARPAULIN	TEETERING	TENSORIAL	THATCHERS
TAILORING	TARRAGONA	TELECASTS	TENTACLES	THATCHING
TAILPIECE	TARTARIZE	TELEGENIC	TENTATION	THEACEOUS
TAIL PIPES	TARTAROUS	TELEGONIC	TENTATIVE	THEARCHIC
TAILPLANE	TASIMETER	TELEGRAMS	TENUOUSLY	THEATRICS
TAILSPINS	TASIMETRY	TELEGRAPH	TEPHRITIC	THE BROADS
TAILSTOCK	TASK FORCE	TELEMETER	TEREBINTH	THECODONT
TAILWHEEL	TASMANIAN	TELEMETRY	TERMAGANT	THE CREEPS
TAILWINDS	TASMAN SEA	TELEOLOGY	TERMINALS	THEME PARK
TAIWANESE	TASTE BUDS	TELEPATHY	TERMINATE	THEME SONG
TAKAMATSU	TASTELESS	TELEPHONE	TERPINEOL	THEOCRACY
TAKEAWAYS	TASTINESS	TELEPHONY	TERRAFORM	THEOCRASY
TAKE LEAVE	TATTINESS	TELESCOPE	TERRAPINS	THEOMANIA
TAKE NOTES	TATTOOING	TELESCOPY	TERRARIUM	THEORISTS
TAKEOVERS	TATTOOIST	TELESTICH	TERRIFIED	THEORIZED
TAKE STEPS	TAUTENING	TELEVISED	TERRIFIER	THEORIZER
TAKE STOCK	TAUTOLOGY	TELLINGLY	TERRITORY	THEOSOPHY

THERAPIES	THROTTLED	TINDERBOX	TOOTHIEST	TOUGH LUCK
THERAPIST	THROTTLER	TINGALING	TOOTHLESS	TOUGHNESS
THERAPSID	THROTTLES	TINKERING	TOOTHPICK	TOURCOING
THEREFORE	THROWAWAY	TINNINESS	TOOTHSOME	TOURISTIC
THEREINTO	THROWBACK	TIN OPENER	TOOTHWORT	TOUT A FAIT
THEREUPON	THROWSTER	TINTERWEB	TOOWOOMBA	TOWELLING
THEREWITH	THRUMMING	TIP AND RUN	TOP DOLLAR	TOWN CLERK
THERMOSES	THRUSTERS	TIPPERARY	TOP DRAWER	TOWN CRIER
THESAURUS	THRUSTING	TIPSINESS	TOP FLIGHT	TOWN HALLS
THESPIANS	THUMBNAIL	TIREDNESS	TOP-FLIGHT	TOWN HOUSE
THE STATES	THUMBTACK	TITCHIEST	TOPIARIAN	TOWNSCAPE
THEURGIST	THUNDERED	TIT FOR TAT	TOPIARIST	TOWNSHIPS
THICKENED	THUNDERER	TITILLATE	TOPICALLY	TOXAPHENE
THICKENER	THURINGIA	TITIVATED	TOPMINNOW	TOXICALLY
THICKHEAD	THURSDAYS	TITIVATOR	TOPOLOGIC	TOXICOSIS
THICKLEAF	THWACKING	TITLE DEED	TOPONYMIC	TOXOPHILY
THICKNESS	THWARTING	TITLE PAGE	TOP SECRET	TRABEATED
THIGHBONE	THYLACINE	TITLE ROLE	TOP-SECRET	TRABECULA
THINKABLE	THYMIDINE	TITRATION	TORCHWOOD	TRACEABLE
THINK TANK	THYRATRON	TITTERING	TOREADORS	TRACHYTIC
THINNINGS	THYRISTOR	T-JUNCTION	TOREUTICS	TRACKABLE
THIO-ETHER	THYROXINE	TOADSTONE	TORMENTED	TRACKLESS
THIOPHENE	TICKETING	TOADSTOOL	TORMENTIL	TRACK SUIT
THIRD-RATE	TIC TAC MAN	TOAMASINA	TORMENTOR	TRACTABLE
THIRSTIER	TIDAL WAVE	TOAST RACK	TORNADOES	TRADE GAPS
THIRSTILY	TIDEMARKS	TOBOGGANS	TORPEDOED	TRADEMARK
THIRTIETH	TIDEWATER	TOCANTINS	TORPEDOES	TRADE NAME
THITHERTO	TIED HOUSE	TOGLIATTI	TORPIDITY	TRADE-OFFS
THONINESS	TIE-DYEING	TOLERABLE	TORRIDITY	TRADESMAN
THORNBACK	TIGER LILY	TOLERABLY	TORSIONAL	TRADESMEN
THORNBILL	TIGHTENED	TOLERANCE	TORTILLAS	TRADE WIND
THORNIEST	TIGHTENER	TOLERATED	TORTOISES	TRADITION
THOUSANDS	TIGHTEN UP	TOLERATOR	TORTRICID	TRADUCERS
THRALLDOM	TIGHTKNIT	TOLLBOOTH	TORTURERS	TRADUCING
THRASHING	TIGHTNESS	TOLLGATES	TORTURING	TRAFALGAR
THREADFIN	TIGHTROPE	TOLLHOUSE	TOTALIZER	TRAGEDIAN
THREADING	TIGHT SPOT	TOLL HOUSE	TOTALLING	TRAGEDIES
THREEFOLD	TIGRESSES	TOMAHAWKS	TOTAQUINE	TRAINABLE
THREESOME	TIME BOMBS	TOMBOYISH	TOTEM POLE	TRAININGS
THREE-STAR	TIME LAPSE	TOMBSTONE	TO THE FORE	TRAIN SETS
THREONINE	TIME-LAPSE	TOMMY GUNS	TOTTERING	TRAIPSING
THRESHERS	TIMELIEST	TOMORROWS	TOTTING UP	TRAMLINES
THRESHING	TIME LIMIT	TONBRIDGE	TOUCHABLE	TRAMMELER
THRESHOLD	TIMEPIECE	TONE POEMS	TOUCHDOWN	TRAMPLING
THRIFTIER	TIMESAVER	TONKA BEAN	TOUCH DOWN	TRANSCEND
THRIFTILY	TIME SHEET	TONOMETER	TOUCHIEST	TRANSEPTS
THRILLERS	TIMETABLE	TONOMETRY	TOUCHLINE	
THRILLING	TIME ZONES	TONSILLAR	TOUCHMARK	
THROATIER	TIMISOARA	TONSORIAL	TOUCH-TYPE	
THROATILY	TIMOCRACY	TOOL-MAKER	TOUCHWOOD	
THROBBING	TIMPANIST	TOOTHACHE	TOUGHENED	
THRONGING	TINCTURES	TOOTHCOMB	TOUGHENER	

TRANSEUNT	TREMULOUS	TRILLIONS	TRUNDLING	TURNSTONE
TRANSFERS	TRENCHANT	TRILOBATE	TRUNK CALL	TURNTABLE
TRANSFORM	TRENCHERS	TRILOBITE	TRUNKFISH	TURPITUDE
TRANSFUER	TRENDIEST	TRILOGIES	TRUNK ROAD	TURQUOISE
TRANSFUSE	TRENGGANU	TRIMARANS	TRUSTABLE	TUSCARORA
TRANSIENT	TREPANNED	TRIMEROUS	TRUST FUND	TUTIORISM
TRANSLATE	TREPHINED	TRIMESTER	TRUSTIEST	TUTIORIST
TRANSMUTE	TREPHINES	TRIMETRIC	TRYING OUT	TUTORIALS
TRANSONIC	TREPONEMA	TRIMMINGS	TRY SQUARE	TUT-TUTTED
TRANSPIRE	TRIALLIST	TRINITIES	TSETSE FLY	TV DINNERS
TRANSPORT	TRIAL RUNS	TRINOMIAL	TSITSIHAR	TWAYBLADE
TRANSPOSE	TRIANGLES	TRIOELEIN	TUBBINESS	TWENTIETH
TRANSSHIP	TRIATHLON	TRIPLEXES	TUBULATOR	TWICE-LAID
TRANSVAAL	TRIATOMIC	TRIPTYCHS	TUCKER BAG	TWICE-TOLD
TRAPDOORS	TRIAZOLIC	TRIPWIRES	TUCKER-BAG	TWIDDLING
TRAPEZIAL	TRIBADISM	TRISECTED	TUCKERING	TWINKLING
TRAPEZIUM	TRIBALISM	TRISECTOR	TUG-OF-LOVE	TWISTABLE
TRAPEZIUS	TRIBALIST	TRISERIAL	TUGS-OF-WAR	TWISTEDLY
TRAPEZOID	TRIBESMAN	TRITENESS	TUILERIES	TWISTIEST
TRAPPINGS	TRIBESMEN	TRITURATE	TUITIONAL	TWITCHING
TRAPPISTS	TRIBOLOGY	TRIUMPHAL	TULIP TREE	TWITTERED
TRASHCANS	TRIBUNALS	TRIUMPHED	TULIPWOOD	TWITTERER
TRASHIEST	TRIBUNARY	TRIUMPHER	TULLAMORE	TWO-BY-FOUR
TRATTORIA	TRIBUNATE	TRIVALENT	TUMBLE-DRY	TWO-HANDED
TRAUMATIC	TRIBUTARY	TRIVIALLY	TUMESCENT	TWOPENCES
TRAVAILED	TRICEPSES	TRIWEEKLY	TUMULUSES	TWO-SEATER
TRAVELING	TRICHITIC	TROCHLEAR	TUNEFULLY	TWO-STROKE
TRAVELLED	TRICHOMIC	TROMBONES	TUNGSTITE	TWO-TIMERS
TRAVELLER	TRICHOSIS	TRONDHEIM	TUNGUSIAN	TWO-TIMING
TRAVERSAL	TRICHROIC	TROOPSHIP	TUNING PEG	TYMPANIST
TRAVERSED	TRICKIEST	TROOSTITE	TUNNELERS	TYMPANUMS
TRAVERSER	TRICKLING	TROPISTIC	TUNNELING	TYNEMOUTH
TRAVERSES	TRICKSTER	TROPOLOGY	TUNNELLED	TYNESIDER
TREACHERY	TRICLINIC	TROSSACHS	TUNNELLER	TYPEFACES
TREADMILL	TRICOLOUR	TROUBLING	TUPPENCES	TYPEWRITE
TREASURED	TRICOTINE	TROUBLOUS	TURBIDITY	TYPHLITIC
TREASURER	TRICROTIC	TROUNCING	TURBINATE	TYPHLITIS
TREASURES	TRICUSPID	TROUSSEAU	TURBOJETS	TYPHOIDAL
TREATABLE	TRICYCLES	TROWELLER	TURBOPROP	TYPHOIDIN
TREATISES	TRICYCLIC	TRPORIFIC	TURBULENT	TYPICALLY
TREATMENT	TRIDACTYL	TRUCK FARM	TURFINESS	TYPIFYING
TREE FERNS	TRIENNIAL	TRUCKLING	TURGIDITY	TYRANNIES
TREENWARE	TRIENNIUM	TRUCKLOAD	TURKESTAN	TYRANNIZE
TREE SHREW	TRIFOLIUM	TRUCK STOP	TURNABOUT	TYRANNOUS
TREHALOSE	TRIFORIAL	TRUCULENT	TURN ABOUT	TZETZE FLY
TREILLAGE	TRIFORIUM	TRUELOVES	TURNCOATS	
TRELLISES	TRIGGERED	TRUE NORTH	TURNCOCKS	**U**
TREMATODE	TRIGONOUS	TRUMP CARD	TURNOVERS	UITLANDER
TREMBLING	TRIHEDRAL	TRUMPETED	TURNPIKES	UKRAINIAN
TREMOLITE	TRIHEDRON	TRUMPETER	TURNROUND	ULAN BATOR
TREMOROUS	TRIHYDRIC	TRUNCATED	TURN ROUND	ULCERATED
TREMULANT	TRILINEAR	TRUNCHEON	TURNSTILE	ULMACEOUS

ULOTRICHY	UNDECIDED	UNEARTHLY	UNLEASHED	UNSTOPPED
ULTIMATUM	UNDERBODY	UNEASIEST	UNLIMITED	UNSTRIPED
ULTRADIAN	UNDERBRED	UNEATABLE	UNLOADERS	UNSTUDIED
ULTRA HIGH	UNDERCLAY	UNELECTED	UNLOADING	UNTANGLED
ULULATION	UNDERCOAT	UNEQUALLY	UNLOCKING	UNTENABLE
ULYANOVSK	UNDERCOOK	UNETHICAL	UNLOOSING	UNTENURED
UMBELLATE	UNDERDOGS	UNFAILING	UNLUCKILY	UNTOUCHED
UMBELLULE	UNDERDONE	UNFAIREST	UNMARRIED	UNTREATED
UMBILICAL	UNDERFEED	UNFANCIED	UNMASKING	UNTUTORED
UMBILICUS	UNDERFELT	UNFEELING	UNMATCHED	UNTYPICAL
UMBRELLAS	UNDERFOOT	UNFEIGNED	UNMEANING	UNUSUALLY
UMPTEENTH	UNDERFUND	UNFITNESS	UNMINDFUL	UNVEILING
UNABASHED	UNDERGIRD	UNFLEDGED	UNMUSICAL	UNWATCHED
UNADOPTED	UNDERGOER	UNFOLDING	UNNATURAL	UNWEARIED
UNADVISED	UNDERGONE	UNFOUNDED	UNNERVING	UNWEIGHED
UNALLOYED	UNDERHAND	UNFROCKED	UNNOTICED	UNWELCOME
UNANIMITY	UNDERHUNG	UNFURLING	UNOPPOSED	UNWILLING
UNANIMOUS	UNDERLAIN	UNGUARDED	UNPACKING	UNWINDING
UNAPTNESS	UNDERLAYS	UNGUINOUS	UNPICKING	UNWITTING
UNASHAMED	UNDERLIER	UNHANDING	UNPLUGGED	UNWORLDLY
UNASSUMED	UNDERLINE	UNHAPPILY	UNPLUMBED	UNWRITTEN
UNAUDITED	UNDERLING	UNHARNESS	UNPOLITIC	UNZIPPING
UNBALANCE	UNDERMINE	UNHEALTHY	UNPOPULAR	UP AND DOWN
UNBARRING	UNDERMOST	UNHEARD OF	UNPOWERED	UP-AND-DOWN
UNBEKNOWN	UNDERPAID	UNHEARD-OF	UNRAVELED	UPBRAIDED
UNBENDING	UNDERPASS	UNHINGING	UNREALISM	UPBRAIDER
UNBINDING	UNDERPLAY	UNHORSING	UNREALITY	UPBUILDER
UNBLESSED	UNDERPLOT	UNHURRIED	UNREFINED	UP-COUNTRY
UNBOSOMED	UNDERPROP	UNICOLOUR	UNRELATED	UPGRADING
UNBOUNDED	UNDERRATE	UNIFIABLE	UNRESERVE	UPHEAVALS
UNBRIDLED	UNDERSEAL	UNIFORMED	UNRIDDLER	UPHOLDERS
UNBUCKLED	UNDERSELL	UNIFORMLY	UNROLLING	UPHOLDING
UNCANNIER	UNDERSHOT	UNIJUGATE	UNROUNDED	UPHOLSTER
UNCANNILY	UNDERSIDE	UNINSURED	UNRUFFLED	UPLIFTING
UNCEASING	UNDERSOIL	UNION FLAG	UNSADDLED	UPLIGHTER
UNCERTAIN	UNDERSOLD	UNIONISTS	UNSAVOURY	UPPER CASE
UNCHARGED	UNDERTAKE	UNIONIZED	UNSCATHED	UPPERCUTS
UNCHARTED	UNDERTINT	UNION JACK	UNSCREWED	UPPER HAND
UNCHECKED	UNDERTOAD	UNION SHOP	UNSEATING	UPPERMOST
UNCLIMBED	UNDERTONE	UNIPAROUS	UNSECURED	UPRIGHTLY
UNCONCERN	UNDERTOOK	UNIPLANAR	UNSELFISH	UPRISINGS
UNCORKING	UNDERWEAR	UNIRAMOUS	UNSERIOUS	UPROOTING
UNCOUNTED	UNDERWENT	UNISEXUAL	UNSETTLED	UPSETTING
UNCOUPLED	UNDERWING	UNISONOUS	UNSHACKLE	UPSTAGING
UNCOUTHLY	UNDESIRED	UNITARIAN	UNSHEATHE	UP THE ANTE
UNCOVERED	UNDIVIDED	UNIT TRUST	UNSIGHTED	UP THE DUFF
UNCREATED	UNDOUBTED	UNIVALENT	UNSIGHTLY	UP THE POLE
UNCROWDED	UNDRESSED	UNIVERSAL	UNSKILFUL	URANINITE
UNCROWNED	UNDULANCE	UNIVERSES	UNSKILLED	URBAN MYTH
UNDAUNTED	UNDULATED	UNKINDEST	UNSPARING	URCEOLATE
UNDECAGON	UNDULATOR	UNKNOWING	UNSPOTTED	URINATING
UNDECEIVE	UNEARTHED	UNLEARNED	UNSPRAYED	URINATION

URINATIVE	VAMPIRISM	VENERATOR	VIAREGGIO	VIRGINITY
UROCHROME	VANASPATI	VENEZUELA	VIBRANTLY	VIRGULATE
UROGENOUS	VANCOUVER	VENGEANCE	VIBRATILE	VIRTUALLY
UROLITHIC	VANDALISM	VENIALITY	VIBRATING	VIRTUOSIC
UROLOGIST	VANDALIZE	VENTILATE	VIBRATION	VIRTUOSOS
UROPYGIAL	VANGUARDS	VENTRICLE	VIBRATIVE	VIRULENCE
UROPYGIUM	VANISHING	VENTURERS	VIBRATORS	VIRULENCY
UROSCOPIC	VAPIDNESS	VENTURING	VIBRISSAL	VISCIDITY
URSA MAJOR	VAPORETTO	VENUSBERG	VICARAGES	VISCOSITY
URTICARIA	VAPORIFIC	VERACIOUS	VICARIATE	VISCOUNTS
URUGUAYAN	VAPORIZED	VERANDAED	VICARIOUS	VISIONARY
USABILITY	VAPORIZER	VERATRINE	VICARSHIP	VISITABLE
USELESSLY	VAPOURISH	VERBALISM	VICEGERAL	VISUAL AID
USHERETTE	VARANGIAN	VERBALIST	VICENNIAL	VISUALIZE
USUALNESS	VARIABLES	VERBALIZE	VICEREGAL	VITACEOUS
UTILITIES	VARIANCES	VERBASCUM	VICEREINE	VITALIZER
UTILIZING	VARIATION	VERBOSELY	VICE VERSA	VITAMINIC
UTRICULAR	VARICELLA	VERBOSITY	VICIOUSLY	VITELLINE
UTTERABLE	VARICOSIS	VERDIGRIS	VICKSBURG	VITIATING
UTTERANCE	VARIEGATE	VERDUROUS	VICTIMIZE	VITIATION
UTTERLESS	VARIETIES	VERIDICAL	VICTORIAN	VITRIFIED
UVAROVITE	VARIFOCAL	VERIFYING	VICTORIES	VITRIFORM
UXORICIDE	VARIOLATE	VERITABLE	VICTUALED	VITRIOLIC
	VARIOLITE	VERITABLY	VIDELICET	VIVACIOUS
V	VARIOLOID	VERMICIDE	VIDEODISC	VIVARIUMS
VACANCIES	VARIOLOUS	VERMIFORM	VIDEO GAME	VIVA VOCES
VACATABLE	VARIOUSLY	VERMIFUGE	VIDEO TAPE	VIVERRINE
VACATIONS	VARISCITE	VERMILION	VIDEOTAPE	VIVIDNESS
VACCINATE	VARITYPER	VERMINOUS	VIENTIANE	VOCALISTS
VACCINIAL	VARNISHED	VERMONTER	VIEWPOINT	VOCALIZER
VACILLANT	VARNISHER	VERNALIZE	VIGESIMAL	VOCATIONS
VACILLATE	VARNISHES	VERNATION	VIGILANCE	VOCATIVES
VACUOLATE	VARSITIES	VERRUCOSE	VIGILANTE	VOICELESS
VACUOUSLY	VARYINGLY	VERSATILE	VIGNETTES	VOICE MAIL
VACUUMING	VASECTOMY	VERSIFIER	VILIFYING	VOICE-OVER
VAGABONDS	VASOMOTOR	VERSIONAL	VILLAGERS	VOJVODINA
VAGINITIS	VASSALAGE	VERS LIBRE	VILLIFORM	VOL-AU-VENT
VAGOTONIA	VASSALIZE	VERTEBRAE	VILLOSITY	VOLCANISM
VAGUENESS	VECTORIAL	VERTEBRAL	VIMINEOUS	VOLCANIZE
VAINGLORY	VEERINGLY	VERY LIGHT	VINACEOUS	VOLCANOES
VALENCIES	VEGETABLE	VESICULAR	VINCENNES	VOLGOGRAD
VALENTINE	VEGETATED	VESTIBULE	VINDICATE	VOLLEYING
VALIANTLY	VEHEMENCE	VESTIGIAL	VINEYARDS	VOLTE-FACE
VALIDATED	VEHICULAR	VESTMENTS	VIOLATING	VOLTMETER
VALIDNESS	VEINSTONE	VESTRYMAN	VIOLATION	VOLUMETER
VALLATION	VELODROME	VETCHLING	VIOLATIVE	VOLUMETRY
VALLECULA	VELVETEEN	VEXATIONS	VIOLATORS	VOLUNTARY
VALUABLES	VENDETTAS	VEXATIOUS	VIOLENTLY	VOLUNTEER
VALUATION	VENDITION	VEXEDNESS	VIOLINIST	VOODOOISM
VALUELESS	VENEERING	VEXILLARY	VIRESCENT	VOODOOIST
VALVELESS	VENERABLE	VEXILLATE	VIRGINALS	VORACIOUS
VAMOOSING	VENERATED	VIABILITY	VIRGINIAN	VORTICISM

VORTICIST	WAREHOUSE	WAVELLITE	WESTWARDS	WHITENESS
VOUCHSAFE	WARHORSES	WAVEMETER	WET DREAMS	WHITENING
VOYEURISM	WARM FRONT	WAXWORKER	WET-NURSED	WHITE ROSE
VULCANIAN	WARMONGER	WAYFARERS	WET NURSES	WHITEWALL
VULCANITE	WARRANTED	WAYFARING	WHACKINGS	WHITEWASH
VULCANIZE	WARRANTEE	WAYLAYING	WHALEBOAT	WHITEWOOD
VULGARIAN	WARRANTER	WEAKENING	WHALEBONE	WHITTLERS
VULGARISM	WARRANTOR	WEAKER SEX	WHANGAREI	WHITTLING
VULGARITY	WASHBASIN	WEAK-KNEED	WHEAT GERM	WHIZZ-BANG
VULGARIZE	WASHBOARD	WEAKLINGS	WHEATWORM	WHIZZ KIDS
VULNERARY	WASHCLOTH	WEALTHIER	WHEEDLING	WHODUNITS
VULTURINE	WASHED-OUT	WEALTHILY	WHEELBASE	WHODUNNIT
VULTUROUS	WASHINESS	WEAPONEER	WHEELWORK	WHOLEFOOD
VULVIFORM	WASHING-UP	WEARINESS	WHEREFORE	WHOLEMEAL
	WASHROOMS	WEARINGLY	WHEREUPON	WHOLENESS
W	WASHSTAND	WEARISOME	WHEREWITH	WHOLE NOTE
WACKINESS	WASPINESS	WEARPROOF	WHERRYMAN	WHOLESALE
WAD MEDANI	WASPISHLY	WEASELING	WHETSTONE	WHOLESOME
WAFER-THIN	WASSAILER	WEATHERED	WHICHEVER	WHOSOEVER
WAGE SLAVE	WASTELAND	WEATHERER	WHICKERED	WIDE-ANGLE
WAGGISHLY	WATCHDOGS	WEB-FOOTED	WHIFFIEST	WIDE-AWAKE
WAGONETTE	WATCHWORD	WEB OFFSET	WHIMPERED	WIDOWHOOD
WAGONLOAD	WATER BIRD	WEDNESDAY	WHIMPERER	WIDTHWISE
WAILINGLY	WATERBUCK	WEEDINESS	WHIMSICAL	WIELDABLE
WAINSCOTS	WATER BUTT	WEEKENDED	WHININGLY	WIESBADEN
WAISTBAND	WATER-COOL	WEEKENDER	WHINNYING	WIGWAGGER
WAISTCOAT	WATERFALL	WEEKNIGHT	WHINSTONE	WILD BOARS
WAISTLINE	WATERFORD	WEEPINESS	WHIPPER-IN	WILDFIRES
WAIT FOR IT	WATERFOWL	WEEPINGLY	WHIPPINGS	WILLEMITE
WAKEFIELD	WATERHOLE	WEIGHABLE	WHIP ROUND	WILLINGLY
WAKEFULLY	WATER ICES	WEIGH DOWN	WHIP-ROUND	WILLPOWER
WAKE-ROBIN	WATER JUMP	WEIGHTILY	WHIPSTALL	WILTSHIRE
WALBRZYCH	WATERLESS	WEIGHTING	WHIPSTOCK	WINCINGLY
WALCHEREN	WATER LILY	WEIRDNESS	WHIRLIGIG	WINDBLOWN
WALKABOUT	WATERLINE	WELCOMING	WHIRLPOOL	WIND-BORNE
WALKAWAYS	WATER MAIN	WELL-ACTED	WHIRLWIND	WINDBOUND
WALK ON AIR	WATERMARK	WELL-AWARE	WHISKERED	WINDBREAK
WALKOVERS	WATERMILL	WELLBEING	WHISPERED	WINDBURNT
WALLABIES	WATER PIPE	WELL-FOUND	WHISPERER	WINDFALLS
WALLBOARD	WATER POLO	WELL-KNOWN	WHISTLING	WIND GAUGE
WALLCHART	WATER RATE	WELL-LINED	WHITE ANTS	WINDINESS
WALLOPING	WATER RATS	WELL-MEANT	WHITEBAIT	WINDINGLY
WALLOWING	WATERSHED	WELL OILED	WHITECAPS	WINDMILLS
WALLPAPER	WATER-SICK	WELL-OILED	WHITEDAMP	WINDOW BOX
WALVIS BAY	WATERSIDE	WELL-TIMED	WHITEFISH	WINDPIPES
WANDERERS	WATER VOLE	WELL-TRIED	WHITE FLAG	WINDROWER
WANDERING	WATERWAYS	WERNERITE	WHITEHALL	WINDSOCKS
WAR CLOUDS	WATERWEED	WESLEYANS	WHITE HEAT	WINDSTORM
WAR CRIMES	WATERWORN	WESTBOUND	WHITE HOPE	WINDSWEPT
WAR DANCES	WATTMETER	WESTERING	WHITE LEAD	WINEGLASS
WARDROBES	WAVE BANDS	WESTERNER	WHITE LIES	WINEMAKER
WARDROOMS	WAVEGUIDE	WESTMEATH	WHITE MEAT	WINEPRESS

WINGSPANS	WOMAN-LIKE	WORLDWIDE	XENOPHOBE	ZEBRA-LIKE
WINNEBAGO	WOMENFOLK	WORM CASTS	XERICALLY	ZEBRAWOOD
WINNOWING	WOMEN'S LIB	WORM-EATEN	XERODERMA	ZEEBRUGGE
WINSOMELY	WONDERFUL	WORM GEARS	XEROPHILY	ZEELANDER
WINTERING	WONDERING	WORMHOLES	XEROPHYTE	ZEITGEIST
WINTRIEST	WOODBLOCK	WORRIEDLY	XYLOGRAPH	ZEPPELINS
WIRADHURI	WOODBORER	WORRISOME	XYLOPHONE	ZESTFULLY
WIRE-GAUGE	WOODCHUCK	WORRYWART		ZEUGMATIC
WIREWORKS	WOODCOCKS	WORSENING	Y	ZHANGZHOU
WIREWORMS	WOODCRAFT	WORSHIPED	YACHTINGS	ZHENGZHOU
WISCONSIN	WOODINESS	WORTHIEST	YACHTSMAN	ZIGZAGGED
WISECRACK	WOODLOUSE	WORTHLESS	YACHTSMEN	ZIGZAGGER
WISHBONES	WOODPRINT	WOUNDABLE	YAMMERING	ZINKENITE
WISPINESS	WOODSCREW	WOUNDWORT	YANKEEISM	ZIONISTIC
WISTFULLY	WOOD SCREW	WRANGLERS	YARDSTICK	ZIRCALLOY
WITCH-HUNT	WOODSHEDS	WRANGLING	YAROSLAVL	ZIRCONIUM
WITCHLIKE	WOODSMOKE	WRAPPINGS	YAWNINGLY	ZITHERIST
WITH A WILL	WOODSTOCK	WREATHING	YEA AND NAY	ZOOGLOEAL
WITHDRAWN	WOOLLIEST	WRECKFISH	YEARBOOKS	ZOOGRAPHY
WITHERING	WOOZINESS	WRENCHING	YEARLINGS	ZOOLOGIST
WITHERITE	WORCESTER	WRESTLERS	YEARNINGS	ZOOMETRIC
WITHSTAND	WORDBREAK	WRESTLING	YELLOWFIN	ZOOPHILIA
WITHSTOOD	WORDINESS	WRIGGLING	YELLOWING	ZOOPHILIC
WITLESSLY	WORKBENCH	WRINKLING	YELLOWISH	ZOOPHOBIA
WITNESSED	WORKBOOKS	WRISTBAND	YESTERDAY	ZOOPHYTIC
WITNESSER	WORKFORCE	WRISTLETS	YIELDABLE	ZOOPLASTY
WITNESSES	WORKHORSE	WRISTLOCK	YODELLING	ZOOSPORIC
WITTICISM	WORKHOUSE	WRITE-OFFS	YOHIMBINE	ZOOSTEROL
WITTINESS	WORKLOADS	WRONGDOER	YORKSHIRE	ZOOTOMIST
WOBBLIEST	WORK OF ART	WRONGNESS	YOUNGSTER	ZUCCHINIS
WOEBEGONE	WORKPIECE	WROUGHT-UP	YTTERBITE	ZUGSPITZE
WOKINGHAM	WORKPLACE	WULFENITE	YTTERBIUM	ZUIDER ZEE
WOLFHOUND	WORKROOMS	WUPPERTAL		ZYGOMATIC
WOLFSBANE	WORKSHEET	WYANDOTTE	Z	ZYGOPHYTE
WOLFSBURG	WORKSHOPS	WYCH-HAZEL	ZACATECAS	ZYGOSPORE
WOLVERINE	WORK-STUDY		ZAMBEZIAN	ZYMOGENIC
WOMANHOOD	WORKTABLE	X	ZAMBOANGA	ZYMOLOGIC
WOMANIZED	WORLD BANK	XENOCRYST	ZANZIBARI	ZYMOLYSIS
WOMANIZER	WORLDLIER	XENOGRAFT	ZAPOTECAN	ZYMOLYTIC
WOMANKIND	WORLDLING	XENOPHILE	ZEALOUSLY	ZYMOMETER

10

A	ABSORBENCY	ACETOMETER	ADIRONDACK	AECIOSPORE
ABANDONING	ABSORBENTS	ACETYLENIC	ADJECTIVAL	AERENCHYMA
ABBREVIATE	ABSORPTION	ACHIEVABLE	ADJECTIVES	AEROBATICS
ABDICATING	ABSORPTIVE	ACHONDRITE	ADJOURNING	AEROBIOSIS
ABDICATION	ABSTAINERS	ACHROMATIC	ADJUDICATE	AEROBIOTIC
ABDICATIVE	ABSTAINING	ACHROMATIN	ADJUNCTIVE	AERODROMES
ABERRATION	ABSTEMIOUS	ACIDIFYING	ADJURATION	AERO-ENGINE
ABHORRENCE	ABSTENTION	ACIDIMETER	ADJURATORY	AEROGRAMME
ABIOGENIST	ABSTERGENT	ACIDOMETER	ADJUSTABLE	AEROGRAPHY
ABIRRITANT	ABSTINENCE	ACIERATION	ADJUSTMENT	AEROLOGIST
ABIRRITATE	ABSTRACTED	ACOTYLEDON	ADMINISTER	AEROMETRIC
ABJURATION	ABUNDANTLY	ACQUAINTED	ADMIRATION	AERONAUTIC
ABLE-BODIED	ABYSSINIAN	ACQUIESCED	ADMIRINGLY	AEROPHAGIA
ABLE SEAMAN	ACCELERANT	ACQUIRABLE	ADMISSIBLE	AEROPHOBIA
ABLE SEAMEN	ACCELERATE	ACQUITTALS	ADMISSIONS	AEROPHOBIC
ABNEGATION	ACCENTUATE	ACQUITTING	ADMITTANCE	AEROPLANES
ABNEY LEVEL	ACCEPTABLE	ACROBATICS	ADMITTEDLY	AEROSPHERE
ABNORMALLY	ACCEPTABLY	ACROMEGALY	ADMIXTURES	AEROSTATIC
ABOLISHING	ACCEPTANCE	ACRONYCHAL	ADMONISHED	AEROTOWING
ABOMINABLE	ACCEPTEDLY	ACROPHOBIA	ADMONISHER	AESTHETICS
ABOMINABLY	ACCESSIBLE	ACROPHOBIC	ADMONITION	AESTIVATOR
ABOMINATED	ACCESSIONS	ACTABILITY	ADMONITORY	AFFABILITY
ABOMINATOR	ACCESS ROAD	ACTINIFORM	ADOLESCENT	AFFECTEDLY
ABORIGINAL	ACCESS TIME	ACTINOLITE	ADORNMENTS	AFFECTIONS
ABORIGINES	ACCIDENTAL	ACTINOMERE	ADRENALINE	AFFECTLESS
ABORTICIDE	ACCIPITRAL	ACTINOZOAN	ADRENERGIC	AFFETTUOSO
ABORTIONAL	ACCLAIMING	ACTIONABLE	ADROITNESS	AFFIDAVITS
ABORTIVELY	ACCOMPLICE	ACTIVATING	ADSORBABLE	AFFILIATED
ABOUT-TURNS	ACCOMPLISH	ACTIVATION	ADSORPTION	AFFILIATES
ABOVEBOARD	ACCORDABLE	ACTIVENESS	ADULTERANT	AFFINITIES
ABOVE BOARD	ACCORDANCE	ACTIVITIES	ADULTERATE	AFFINITIVE
ABRASIVELY	ACCORDIONS	ACTOMYOSIN	ADULTERERS	AFFLICTING
ABREACTION	ACCOSTABLE	ACT THE	ADULTERESS	AFFLICTION
ABRIDGABLE	ACCOUNTANT	GOAT	ADULTERINE	AFFLICTIVE
ABRIDGMENT	ACCOUNTING	ADACTYLOUS	ADULTEROUS	AFFORDABLE
ABROGATING	ACCREDITED	ADAMANTINE	ADUMBRATED	AFFORESTED
ABROGATION	ACCRESCENT	ADAM'S	ADVANTAGES	AFFRICATES
ABRUPTNESS	ACCRETIONS	APPLE	ADVENTITIA	AFFRONTING
ABSCISSION	ACCUMBENCY	ADAPTATION	ADVENTURER	AFICIONADO
ABSCONDING	ACCUMULATE	ADDICTIONS	ADVENTURES	AFRIKANDER
ABSOLUTELY	ACCURATELY	ADDIS ABABA	ADVERBIALS	AFRIKANERS
ABSOLUTION	ACCUSATION	ADDITIONAL	ADVERTENCE	AFTERBIRTH
ABSOLUTISM	ACCUSATIVE	ADDRESSEES	ADVERTISED	AFTERBRAIN
ABSOLUTORY	ACCUSINGLY	ADDRESSING	ADVERTISER	AFTERGLOWS
ABSOLVABLE	ACCUSTOMED	ADDUCEABLE	ADVOCATING	AFTERIMAGE
ABSORBABLE	ACEPHALOUS	ADENECTOMY	ADVOCATION	AFTERLIVES
ABSORBANCE	ACETABULUM	ADENOVIRUS	ADVOCATORY	AFTERMATHS
ABSORBEDLY	ACETIC ACID	ADEQUATELY	ADZUKI BEAN	AFTERNOONS

AFTERPAINS	ALGORISMIC	ALTERNATOR	AMYGDALOID	ANGLOPHILE
AFTERPIECE	ALGORITHMS	ALTIMETERS	AMYLACEOUS	ANGLOPHOBE
AFTERSHAFT	ALIENATING	ALTOGETHER	AMYLOLYSIS	ANGLOPHONE
AFTERSHAVE	ALIENATION	ALTRINCHAM	ANABOLITIC	ANGLO-SAXON
AFTERSHOCK	ALIGNMENTS	ALTRUISTIC	ANACHORISM	ANGULARITY
AFTERTASTE	ALIMENTARY	AMALGAMATE	ANACOUSTIC	ANGULATION
AFTERWARDS	ALKALINITY	AMANUENSES	ANACRUSTIC	ANGWANTIBO
AGAMICALLY	ALKYLATION	AMANUENSIS	ANADROMOUS	ANIMADVERT
AGAPANTHUS	ALLARGANDO	AMATEURISH	ANAGLYPHIC	ANIMALCULE
AGGLUTININ	ALLEGATION	AMATEURISM	ANALGESICS	ANIMAL FARM
AGGRANDIZE	ALLEGIANCE	AMBASSADOR	ANALOGICAL	ANIMATEDLY
AGGRAVATED	ALLEGORIES	AMBIVALENT	ANALYSABLE	ANISOTROPY
AGGREGATED	ALLEGORIST	AMBOCEPTOR	ANAMNESTIC	ANKYLOSAUR
AGGREGATES	ALLEGORIZE	AMBULACRAL	ANAMORPHIC	ANNALISTIC
AGGRESSION	ALLEGRETTO	AMBULACRUM	ANAPAESTIC	ANNEXATION
AGGRESSIVE	ALLERGENIC	AMBULANCES	ANAPLASTIC	ANNIHILATE
AGGRESSORS	ALLEVIATED	AMBULATION	ANAPTYCTIC	ANNO DOMINI
AGITATIONS	ALLEVIATOR	AMBULATORY	ANARCHISTS	ANNOTATING
AGREEMENTS	ALLIACEOUS	AMELIORANT	ANARTHROUS	ANNOTATION
AGRONOMICS	ALLIGATORS	AMELIORATE	ANASARCOUS	ANNOTATIVE
AGRONOMIST	ALLITERATE	AMENDMENTS	ANASTIGMAT	ANNOUNCERS
AGRYPNOTIC	ALLOCATING	AMERINDIAN	ANASTOMOSE	ANNOUNCING
AHMEDNAGAR	ALLOCATION	AMIABILITY	ANATOMICAL	ANNOYANCES
AIDE-DE-	ALLOCUTION	AMIANTHINE	ANATOMISTS	ANNULATION
CAMP	ALLOGAMOUS	AMINO ACIDS	ANATOMIZER	ANNULLABLE
AIR-HOSTESS	ALLOMERISM	AMMONIACAL	ANATROPOUS	ANNULMENTS
AIR-LETTERS	ALLOMEROUS	AMMUNITION	ANCESTRESS	ANNUNCIATE
AIR-LIFTING	ALLOMETRIC	AMOEBIASIS	ANCESTRIES	ANOINTMENT
AIR MARSHAL	ALLOPATHIC	AMOEBOCYTE	ANCHORAGES	ANORTHITIC
AIRPOCKETS	ALLOPATRIC	AMORTIZING	ANCHORITES	ANSWERABLE
AIR WAYBILL	ALLOPHONIC	AMPELOPSIS	ANDALUSITE	ANSWERABLY
AKTYUBINSK	ALLOTMENTS	AMPERE-HOUR	ANDERLECHT	ANTAGONISM
ALACRITOUS	ALLOTROPIC	AMPERE-TURN	ANDROECIAL	ANTAGONIST
ALARM CLOCK	ALLOWANCES	AMPERSANDS	ANDROECIUM	ANTAGONIZE
ALARMINGLY	ALL-PURPOSE	AMPHEATRIC	ANDROGENIC	ANTARCTICA
ALBESCENCE	ALL-ROUNDER	AMPHIASTER	ANECDOTAGE	ANTEBELLUM
ALBUMENIZE	ALL THE	AMPHIBIANS	ANECDOTIST	ANTECEDENT
ALBUMINATE	TIME	AMPHIBIOUS	ANEMICALLY	ANTEDATING
ALBUMINOID	ALLUREMENT	AMPHIBOLIC	ANEMOCHORE	ANTE-MORTEM
ALBUMINOUS	ALLUSIVELY	AMPHIBRACH	ANEMOGRAPH	ANTEPENULT
ALCHEMISTS	ALMA MATERS	AMPHICTYON	ANEMOMETER	ANTHOPHORE
ALCHERINGA	ALMIGHTIER	AMPHIGORIC	ANEMOMETRY	ANTHRACENE
ALCOHOLICS	ALMIGHTILY	AMPHIMACER	ANEMOPHILY	ANTHRACITE
ALCOHOLISM	ALMS-HOUSES	AMPHIMIXIS	ANEMOSCOPE	ANTHRACOID
ALCOHOLIZE	ALONGSHORE	AMPHOTERIC	ANESTHESIA	ANTHROPOID
ALDERMANIC	ALPENSTOCK	AMPLIFIERS	ANESTHETIC	ANTIBARYON
ALEXANDRIA	ALPESTRINE	AMPLIFYING	ANEURYSMAL	ANTIBIOSIS
ALGEBRAIST	ALTARPIECE	AMPUTATING	ANGELOLOGY	ANTIBIOTIC
ALGOLAGNIA	ALTAZIMUTH	AMPUTATION	ANGIOSPERM	ANTIBODIES
ALGOLAGNIC	ALTERATION	AMUSEMENTS	ANGLEPOISE	ANTICHRIST
ALGONQUIAN	ALTERATIVE	AMYGDALATE	ANGLICISMS	ANTICIPANT
ALGOPHOBIA	ALTERNATED	AMYGDALINE	ANGLICIZED	ANTICIPATE

ANTICLIMAX	APOTHECIAL	ARCHBISHOP	ASCOMYCETE	ASTOMATOUS
ANTICLINAL	APOTHECIUM	ARCHDEACON	ASCRIBABLE	ASTONISHED
ANTIDROMIC	APOTHEOSES	ARCHERFISH	ASCRIPTION	ASTOUNDING
ANTIFREEZE	APOTHEOSIS	ARCHESPORE	ASEXUALITY	ASTRAGALUS
ANTIFUNGAL	APOTROPAIC	ARCHETYPAL	ASPARAGINE	ASTRINGENT
ANTIHEROES	APPALACHIA	ARCHETYPES	ASPERITIES	ASTROLOGER
ANTILEPTON	APPARELLED	ARCHIMEDES	ASPERSIONS	ASTROMETRY
ANTILOGISM	APPARENTLY	ARCHITECTS	AS PER	ASTRONAUTS
ANTIMATTER	APPARITION	ARCHITRAVE	USUAL	ASTRONOMER
ANTIMERISM	APPEALABLE	ARCHIVISTS	ASPHALTING	ASTUTENESS
ANTIMONIAL	APPEARANCE	ARCHOPLASM	ASPHALTITE	ASYMMETRIC
ANTIMONOUS	APPEASABLE	ARCTOGAEAN	ASPHYXIANT	ASYMPTOTIC
ANTIPHONAL	APPENDAGES	ARC WELDING	ASPHYXIATE	AT ALL
ANTIPODEAN	APPENDICES	ARENACEOUS	ASPIDISTRA	TIMES
ANTIPROTON	APPENDICLE	AREOGRAPHY	ASPIRATING	AT A
ANTIPYRINE	APPENDIXES	AREOLATION	ASPIRATION	STRETCH
ANTIQUATED	APPERCEIVE	ARGENTEUIL	ASPIRATORY	ATHERMANCY
ANTI-SEMITE	APPETIZERS	ARGILLITIC	ASSAILABLE	ATMOSPHERE
ANTISEPSIS	APPETIZING	ARGUMENTUM	ASSAILANTS	ATOMICALLY
ANTISEPTIC	APPLAUDING	ARISTOCRAT	ASSAILMENT	ATOMIC BOMB
ANTISOCIAL	APPLE CARTS	ARITHMETIC	ASSAULTING	ATOMIC PILE
ANTISTATIC	APPLIANCES	ARMADILLOS	ASSEMBLAGE	ATROCITIES
ANTITHESIS	APPLICABLE	ARMAGEDDON	ASSEMBLIES	ATROPHYING
ANTITRADES	APPLICANTS	ARMIPOTENT	ASSEMBLING	ATTACHABLE
ANTITRAGUS	APPLICATOR	ARMISTICES	ASSERTIBLE	ATTACHMENT
ANXIOLYTIC	APPOINTEES	ARNHEM LAND	ASSERTIONS	ATTAINABLE
APARTMENTS	APPOINTING	ARRAIGNING	ASSESSABLE	ATTAINMENT
APGAR SCORE	APPOSITION	ARRHYTHMIA	ASSESSMENT	ATTEMPTING
APHORISTIC	APPOSITIVE	ARROGANTLY	ASSET VALUE	ATTENDANCE
APHRODISIA	APPRAISALS	ARROGATING	ASSEVERATE	ATTENDANTS
APICULTURE	APPRAISING	ARROGATION	ASSIBILATE	ATTENTIONS
APIOLOGIST	APPRAISIVE	ARROGATIVE	ASSIGNABLE	ATTENUATED
APLACENTAL	APPRECIATE	ARROWHEADS	ASSIGNMENT	ATTENUATOR
APOCALYPSE	APPRENTICE	ARTFULNESS	ASSIMILATE	ATTESTABLE
APOCARPOUS	APPROACHED	ARTHRALGIA	ASSISTANCE	AT THE
APOCHROMAT	APPROACHES	ARTHRALGIC	ASSISTANTS	READY
APOCRYPHAL	APPROXIMAL	ARTHRITICS	ASSOCIABLE	ATTORNMENT
APOLITICAL	APRIL FOOLS	ARTHROMERE	ASSOCIATED	ATTRACTING
APOLOGETIC	APTERYGIAL	ARTICHOKES	ASSOCIATES	ATTRACTION
APOLOGISTS	AQUAMARINE	ARTICULATE	ASSONANTAL	ATTRACTIVE
APOLOGIZED	AQUAPHOBIA	ARTIFICERS	ASSORTMENT	ATTRIBUTED
APOLOGIZER	AQUAPLANED	ARTIFICIAL	ASSUMPTION	ATTRIBUTER
APOPHTHEGM	AQUAPLANES	ART NOUVEAU	ASSUMPTIVE	ATTRIBUTES
APOPHYSATE	ARABESQUES	ARTY-CRAFTY	ASSURANCES	ATYPICALLY
APOPHYSIAL	ARACHNIDAN	ASAFOETIDA	ASTATICISM	AUBERGINES
APOPLECTIC	ARAKAN YOMA	ASARABACCA	ASTERIATED	AUCTIONEER
APOSEMATIC	ARAUCANIAN	ASBESTOSIS	ASTERISKED	AUCTIONING
APOSTASIES	ARBITRABLE	ASCARIASIS	ASTEROIDAL	AUDIBILITY
APOSTATIZE	ARBITRATED	ASCENDANCY	ASTHENOPIA	AUDIOGENIC
APOSTOLATE	ARBITRATOR	ASCENDANTS	ASTHENOPIC	AUDIOMETER
APOSTROPHE	ARCHAISTIC	ASCETICISM	ASTHMATICS	AUDIOMETRY
APOTHECARY	ARCHANGELS	ASCOGONIUM	ASTIGMATIC	AUDITIONED

AUDITORIUM	AXIOLOGIST	BALLOONING	BARRENWORT	BEDEVILING
AUGMENTING	AYATOLLAHS	BALLOONIST	BARRICADED	BEDEVILLED
AUREOMYCIN	AZEOTROPIC	BALLPOINTS	BARRICADER	BEDFELLOWS
AURICULATE	AZERBAIJAN	BALLYMONEY	BARRICADES	BED OF
AURIFEROUS	AZOBENZENE	BALNEOLOGY	BARRISTERS	NAILS
AUSCULTATE		BALUSTRADE	BARROW BOYS	BED OF
AUSFORMING	**B**	BAMBOOZLED	BARTENDERS	ROSES
AUSPICIOUS	BABY-MINDER	BAMBOOZLER	BARYCENTRE	BEDRAGGLED
AUSTENITIC	BABY SITTER	BANALITIES	BARYSPHERE	BED-SITTERS
AUSTERLITZ	BABY-SITTER	BANANA SKIN	BASALTWARE	BEDSPREADS
AUSTRALIAN	BACCHANALS	BANDERILLA	BASE METALS	BEEFEATERS
AUSTRALOID	BACITRACIN	BANDLEADER	BASILICATA	BEEF TOMATO
AUSTRALORP	BACKBITERS	BANDMASTER	BASKETBALL	BEER GARDEN
AUTARCHIES	BACKBITING	BANDOLEERS	BASKET-STAR	BEFOREHAND
AUTECOLOGY	BACKCLOTHS	BANDSTANDS	BASKETWORK	BEFOULMENT
AUTHORIZED	BACKCOMBED	BANDWAGONS	BAS-RELIEFS	BEFRIENDED
AUTHORIZER	BACKDATING	BANFFSHIRE	BASSE-TERRE	BEGGARWEED
AUTHORSHIP	BACKFIRING	BANGLADESH	BASSETERRE	BEGINNINGS
AUTOCHTHON	BACKGAMMON	BANISHMENT	BASS GUITAR	BEGRUDGING
AUTOCRATIC	BACKGROUND	BANK DRAFTS	BASSOONIST	BEHIND BARS
AUTOECIOUS	BACKHANDED	BANKROLLED	BASTARDIZE	BEHINDHAND
AUTOGAMOUS	BACKHANDER	BANKRUPTCY	BASUTOLAND	BEHIND TIME
AUTOGENOUS	BACKLASHES	BANKRUPTED	BATH CHAIRS	BELABOURED
AUTOGRAPHS	BACK MATTER	BANNERETTE	BATHOMETER	BELIEVABLE
AUTOGRAPHY	BACK NUMBER	BANQUETING	BATHOMETRY	BELIEVABLY
AUTOMATICS	BACKPACKER	BAPTISTERY	BATHYMETRY	BELITTLING
AUTOMATING	BACKSLIDER	BARBARIANS	BATHYSCAPH	BELIZE CITY
AUTOMATION	BACKSPACES	BARBARISMS	BATON ROUGE	BELLADONNA
AUTOMATISM	BACKSTAIRS	BARBARIZED	BATTALIONS	BELLARMINE
AUTOMATIST	BACKSTITCH	BARBECUING	BATTLEAXES	BELLETRIST
AUTOMATONS	BACK STREET	BARBED WIRE	BATTLEDORE	BELLINZONA
AUTOMATOUS	BACKSTROKE	BARBELLATE	BATTLEMENT	BELL-RINGER
AUTOMOBILE	BACKWARDLY	BAREHEADED	BATTLESHIP	BELL THE
AUTOMOTIVE	BACKWATERS	BARELEGGED	BAYONETING	CAT
AUTONOMIST	BACULIFORM	BARGAINING	BAY WINDOWS	BELLWETHER
AUTONOMOUS	BADEN-BADEN	BARGE POLES	BEACH BALLS	BELL WETHER
AUTOPHYTIC	BAD HAIR	BARIUM MEAL	BEACH BUGGY	BELLYACHED
AUTOPLASTY	DAY	BARLEYCORN	BEACHCHAIR	BELLYACHES
AUTOSTRADA	BAD-MOUTHED	BARLEY WINE	BEACHFRONT	BELLY DANCE
AUTOTOMIZE	BAFFLEMENT	BAR MITZVAH	BEACHHEADS	BELLY FLOPS
AUTUMNALLY	BAGGAGE CAR	BARN DANCES	BEANSPROUT	BELLY LAUGH
AUXOCHROME	BAHAWALPUR	BARNSTAPLE	BEAR GARDEN	BELONGINGS
AVALANCHES	BAINBRIDGE	BAROMETERS	BEASTLIEST	BELORUSSIA
AVANT GARDE	BALACLAVAS	BAROMETRIC	BEATIFYING	BENCH MARKS
AVANT-GARDE	BALALAIKAS	BARONESSES	BEATITUDES	BENCH PRESS
AVARICIOUS	BALDERDASH	BARONETAGE	BEAUJOLAIS	BENEDICITE
AVELLANEDA	BALDHEADED	BARRACKING	BEAUTICIAN	BENEFACTOR
AVENTURINE	BALIKPAPAN	BARRACUDAS	BEAUTIFIED	BENEFICENT
AVICULTURE	BALLASTING	BARRAMUNDA	BEAUTY SPOT	BENEFICIAL
AVOCATIONS	BALLERINAS	BARRAMUNDI	BECOMINGLY	BENEFITING
AVUNCULATE	BALLFLOWER	BARRATROUS	BECQUERELS	BENEVOLENT
AWAKENINGS	BALLISTICS	BARRENNESS	BEDCLOTHES	BENIGNANCY

BENNINGTON	BILL OF	BITTERNESS	BLIND DRUNK	BLUNDERING
BENZOCAINE	FARE	BITTERWEED	BLINDFOLDS	BLUSHINGLY
BENZODRINE	BILL OF	BITTERWOOD	BLIND SPOTS	BLUSTERERS
BENZOFURAN	SALE	BITUMINIZE	BLISSFULLY	BLUSTERING
BEQUEATHED	BILLY GOATS	BITUMINOUS	BLISTERING	BOARDROOMS
BEQUEATHER	BIMESTRIAL	BIVALVULAR	BLITHENESS	BOARDWALKS
BERIBBONED	BIMETALLIC	BIVOUACKED	BLITHERING	BOASTFULLY
BERLIN WALL	BINOCULARS	BLABBERING	BLITHESOME	BOASTINGLY
BERTOLUCCI	BINUCLEATE	BLACKAMOOR	BLOCKADING	BOATHOUSES
BESEECHING	BIOCELLATE	BLACK BELTS	BLOCKCHAIN	BOATSWAINS
BESMEARING	BIODYNAMIC	BLACKBERRY	BLOCKHEADS	BOAT TRAINS
BESMIRCHED	BIOECOLOGY	BLACKBIRDS	BLOCKHOUSE	BOBBY SOCKS
BESPEAKING	BIOGENESIS	BLACKBOARD	BLOCK VOTES	BOBSLEIGHS
BESSARABIA	BIOGENETIC	BLACK BOXES	BLONDENESS	BODY DOUBLE
BESTIALITY	BIOGRAPHER	BLACK DEATH	BLOOD BANKS	BODYGUARDS
BESTIALIZE	BIOGRAPHIC	BLACKENING	BLOODBATHS	BODY SEARCH
BESTIARIES	BIOLOGICAL	BLACKGUARD	BLOOD COUNT	BOILER SUIT
BESTIRRING	BIOLOGISTS	BLACKHEADS	BLOOD DONOR	BOISTEROUS
BESTREWING	BIOMEDICAL	BLACKHEART	BLOOD FEUDS	BOLLOCKS-UP
BESTRIDDEN	BIOPHYSICS	BLACK HOLES	BLOOD GROUP	BOLL WEEVIL
BESTRIDING	BIOPLASMIC	BLACKJACKS	BLOODHOUND	BOLOMETRIC
BEST-SELLER	BIOPOIESIS	BLACKLISTS	BLOODINESS	BOLSHEVIKS
BETELGEUSE	BIORHYTHMS	BLACK MAGIC	BLOOD LUSTS	BOLSHEVISM
BETHINKING	BIOSTATICS	BLACK MARIA	BLOOD MONEY	BOLSTERING
BETOKENING	BIPARIETAL	BLACK POWER	BLOOD SPORT	BOMBARDIER
BETROTHALS	BIPARTISAN	BLACK SHEEP	BLOODSTAIN	BOMBARDING
BETROTHING	BIPETALOUS	BLACKSHIRT	BLOODSTOCK	BOMBAY DUCK
BETTERMENT	BIQUADRATE	BLACKSMITH	BLOODSTONE	BOMBSHELLS
BETWS-Y-	BIRD OF	BLACKSNAKE	BLOOD TYPES	BONDHOLDER
COED	PREY	BLACK SPOTS	BLOODY MARY	BONEHEADED
BEWILDERED	BIRKENHEAD	BLACKTHORN	BLOOMSBURY	BONE MARROW
BEWITCHING	BIRMINGHAM	BLACK WATCH	BLOSSOMING	BONESHAKER
BIANNULATE	BIRTHMARKS	BLACK WIDOW	BLOTCHIEST	BONKBUSTER
BIBLIOPOLE	BIRTHPLACE	BLADDERNUT	BLOW-BY-	BON VIVANTS
BIBLIOTICS	BIRTH-RATES	BLANCMANGE	BLOW	BOOBY PRIZE
BIBLIOTIST	BIRTHRIGHT	BLANKETING	BLOW-DRYING	BOOBY TRAPS
BICHLORIDE	BIRTHSTONE	BLANK VERSE	BLOWZINESS	BOOKBINDER
BICYCLISTS	BIRTWISTLE	BLASPHEMED	BLUBBERING	BOOKKEEPER
BIENNIALLY	BISEXUALLY	BLASPHEMER	BLUDGEONED	BOOKMAKERS
BIFURCATED	BISHOPBIRD	BLASTOCOEL	BLUDGEONER	BOOKMOBILE
BIGAMOUSLY	BISHOPRICS	BLASTOCYST	BLUE BABIES	BOOKPLATES
BIG BROTHER	BISMUTHOUS	BLASTODERM	BLUEBEARDS	BOOKSELLER
BIG DIPPERS	BISSEXTILE	BLASTOMERE	BLUEBOTTLE	BOOKSTALLS
BIJOUTERIE	BISULPHATE	BLASTOPORE	BLUE CHEESE	BOOK TOKENS
BILBERRIES	BISULPHIDE	BLATHERING	BLUE-COLLAR	BOOMERANGS
BILINGUALS	BISULPHITE	BLEACHABLE	BLUE DEVILS	BOOTBLACKS
BILIVERDIN	BISYMMETRY	BLEARINESS	BLUE MURDER	BOOTLEGGED
BILL AND	BITARTRATE	BLEATINGLY	BLUE-PENCIL	BOOTLEGGER
COO	BITCHINESS	BLEMISHING	BLUEPRINTS	BOOTLOADER
BILLBOARDS	BIT OF	BLETHERING	BLUETHROAT	BOOTSTRAPS
BILLET-DOUX	FLUFF	BLIND ALLEY	BLUE TONGUE	BORDERLAND
BILLIONTHS	BITTERLING	BLIND DATES	BLUNDERERS	BORDERLINE

BORGERHOUT	BRAWNINESS	BROOMSTICK	BUSTAURANT	CALCULATOR
BORROWINGS	BRAZENNESS	BROWBEATEN	BUSYBODIES	CALCULUSES
BOTANIZING	BREADBOARD	BROWNED-OFF	BUTCHERING	CALDERDALE
BOTCHINESS	BREADCRUMB	BROWNFIELD	BUTTER BEAN	CALEDONIAN
BOTHERSOME	BREADFRUIT	BROWNSTONE	BUTTERCUPS	CALIBRATED
BOTRYOIDAL	BREADLINES	BRUTALIZED	BUTTERFISH	CALIBRATOR
BOTTLE BANK	BREAKAWAYS	BRYOLOGIST	BUTTERMILK	CALIFORNIA
BOTTLE-FEED	BREAKDOWNS	BRYOPHYTIC	BUTTERWORT	CALIPHATES
BOTTLENECK	BREAKFASTS	BUBBLE WRAP	BUTTON-DOWN	CALL CENTRE
BOTTLE SHOP	BREAKFRONT	BUBONOCELE	BUTTONHOLE	CALL IT A
BOTTOMLESS	BREAKWATER	BUCCANEERS	BUTTONHOOK	DAY
BOTTOM LINE	BREASTBONE	BUCCINATOR	BUTTONWOOD	CALLOWNESS
BOTTOMMOST	BREASTWORK	BUCHENWALD	BUTTRESSED	CALORICITY
BOULEVARDS	BREATHABLE	BUCKBOARDS	BUTTRESSES	CALUMNIATE
BOUNCINESS	BRECCIATED	BUCKET SEAT	BY-ELECTION	CALUMNIOUS
BOUNDARIES	BREEZINESS	BUCKET SHOP	BY-PRODUCTS	CALVINISTS
BOWDLERISM	BRICKLAYER	BUCKINGHAM	BYSTANDERS	CALYPTRATE
BOWDLERIZE	BRIDEGROOM	BUDGERIGAR		CAMEMBERTS
BOW WINDOWS	BRIDESMAID	BUFFER ZONE	**C**	CAMERAWORK
BOX NUMBERS	BRIDEZILLA	BUFFLEHEAD	CABANATUAN	CAMERLENGO
BOX OFFICES	BRIDGEABLE	BUFFOONERY	CABIN CLASS	CAMOUFLAGE
BOYCOTTING	BRIDGEHEAD	BULLDOZERS	CACCIATORE	CAMPAIGNED
BOYFRIENDS	BRIDGEPORT	BULLDOZING	CACHINNATE	CAMPAIGNER
BOYISHNESS	BRIDGETOWN	BULLFIGHTS	CACK-HANDED	CAMPANILES
BRACHIOPOD	BRIDGEWORK	BULLHEADED	CACOGENICS	CAMPESTRAL
BRACHYLOGY	BRIDGWATER	BULLNECKED	CACOGRAPHY	CAMPGROUND
BRACHYURAN	BRIGANTINE	BULLROARER	CACOMISTLE	CAMPHORATE
BRACKETING	BRIGHTENER	BULLY COURT	CACOPHONIC	CAMPOBELLO
BRADYKININ	BRIGHTNESS	BUMBLEBEES	CACTACEOUS	CANAL BOATS
BRAGGINGLY	BRIGHTWORK	BUNCHINESS	CADAVERINE	CANALIZING
BRAHMANISM	BRILLIANCE	BUNKHOUSES	CADAVEROUS	CANCELLATE
BRAINCHILD	BRILLIANCY	BUNYA-BUNYA	CADET CORPS	CANCELLING
BRAIN DRAIN	BRIQUETTES	BUON GIORNO	CAERPHILLY	CANDELABRA
BRAININESS	BRITISHERS	BURBERRIES	CAESAREANS	CANDIDATES
BRAINSTORM	BROAD BEANS	BURDENSOME	CAESPITOSE	CANDLEFISH
BRAINWAVES	BROADCASTS	BUREAUCRAT	CAFETERIAS	CANDLEPINS
BRAKE SHOES	BROADCLOTH	BURGENLAND	CALABASHES	CANDLEWICK
BRANCHIATE	BROADENING	BURGEONING	CALABOOSES	CANDLEWOOD
BRANDISHED	BROAD GAUGE	BURGLARIES	CALAMANDER	CANDYFLOSS
BRANDISHER	BROADSHEET	BURGUNDIAN	CALAMITIES	CANKERWORM
BRAND NAMES	BROADSIDES	BURLESQUED	CALAMITOUS	CANNABINOL
BRANDY SNAP	BROADSWORD	BURLESQUER	CALAMONDIN	CANNELLONI
BRASHINESS	BROCATELLE	BURLESQUES	CALAVERITE	CANNONADES
BRASS BANDS	BROKEN DOWN	BURLINGTON	CALCAREOUS	CANNONBALL
BRASSBOUND	BROKEN-DOWN	BURNISHING	CALCEIFORM	CANONICATE
BRASSED OFF	BROKENNESS	BURTHENING	CALCIFEROL	CANONICITY
BRASSERIES	BROMSGROVE	BUSHBABIES	CALCIFUGAL	CANONIZING
BRASSIERES	BRONCHIOLE	BUSHHAMMER	CALCIFYING	CANOODLING
BRASSINESS	BRONCHITIC	BUSHMASTER	CALCITONIN	CAN OPENERS
BRASS TACKS	BRONCHITIS	BUSHRANGER	CALCSINTER	CANTABRIAN
BRATISLAVA	BRONX CHEER	BUSINESSES	CALCULABLE	CANTALOUPE
BRAVISSIMO	BROODINESS	BUS STATION	CALCULATED	CANTALOUPS

CANTATRICE	CARNASSIAL	CATAMARANS	CENSURABLE	CHALKINESS
CANTERBURY	CARNATIONS	CATAMENIAL	CENTENNIAL	CHALLENGED
CANTILEVER	CARNELIANS	CATAPLASIA	CENTESIMAL	CHALLENGER
CANTILLATE	CARNIVORES	CATAPULTED	CENTIGRADE	CHALLENGES
CANTONMENT	CAROLINIAN	CATARRHINE	CENTIGRAMS	CHALYBEATE
CANVASBACK	CAROTENOID	CATASTASIS	CENTILITRE	CHAMBER POT
CANVASSERS	CARPATHIAN	CAT BURGLAR	CENTILLION	CHAMELEONS
CANVASSING	CARPELLARY	CATCALLING	CENTIMETRE	CHAMOMILES
CAOUTCHOUC	CARPELLATE	CATCH A	CENTIPEDES	CHAMPIGNON
CAPABILITY	CARPENTERS	CRAB	CENTIPOISE	CHAMPIONED
CAPACITATE	CARPOPHORE	CATCH CROPS	CENTRALISM	CHANCELLOR
CAPACITIES	CARPOSPORE	CATCHINESS	CENTRALITY	CHANCERIES
CAPACITIVE	CARRIER BAG	CATCHPENNY	CENTRALIZE	CHANCINESS
CAPACITORS	CARRYING-ON	CATCHWORDS	CENTRE-FIRE	CHANDELIER
CAPARISONS	CARRY-OVERS	CATECHESIS	CENTRE-FOLD	CHANDIGARH
CAPE COLONY	CARSON CITY	CATECHISMS	CENTRE HALF	CHANGEABLE
CAP-HAITIEN	CARTHORSES	CATECHISTS	CENTRE PASS	CHANGEABLY
CAPITALISM	CARTHUSIAN	CATECHIZED	CENTRICITY	CHANGELESS
CAPITALIST	CARTILAGES	CATEGORIES	CENTRIFUGE	CHANGELING
CAPITALIZE	CARTOMANCY	CATEGORIZE	CENTROMERE	CHANGEOVER
CAPITATION	CARTOONIST	CATENARIAN	CENTROSOME	CHANGE OVER
CAPITATIVE	CARTRIDGES	CATENATION	CENTURIONS	CHANNEL-HOP
CAPITULATE	CART TRACKS	CATENULATE	CEPHALONIA	CHANNELLED
CAPPUCCINO	CARTWHEELS	CATHEDRALS	CEPHALOPOD	CHANNELLER
CAPREOLATE	CARUNCULAR	CATHOLICON	CEREBELLAR	CHAPERONED
CAPRICIOUS	CARYATIDAL	CATOPTRICS	CEREBELLUM	CHAPFALLEN
CAPRICORNS	CASABLANCA	CAT'S	CEREBRALLY	CHAPLAINCY
CAPTAINING	CASCARILLA	CRADLE	CEREDIGION	CHARABANCS
CAPTIOUSLY	CASE-HARDEN	CATTLE GRID	CEREMONIAL	CHARACTERS
CAPTIVATED	CASEINOGEN	CAULESCENT	CEREMONIES	CHARDONNAY
CAPTIVATOR	CASEWORKER	CAUTERIZED	CEROGRAPHY	CHARGEABLE
CARAMELIZE	CASHIERING	CAUTIONARY	CERTIFYING	CHARGE CARD
CARAVAGGIO	CASSEROLES	CAUTIONING	CERTIORARI	CHARGE HAND
CARBOLATED	CASSIOPEIA	CAUTIOUSLY	CERUMINOUS	CHARIOTEER
CARBONATED	CASTIGATED	CAVALCADES	CERVICITIS	CHARITABLE
CARBON COPY	CASTIGATOR	CAVALRYMAN	CESSATIONS	CHARITABLY
CARBONIZED	CASTING OFF	CAVALRYMEN	CESSIONARY	CHARLADIES
CARBUNCLES	CASTRATING	CAVITATION	CETOLOGIST	CHARLATANS
CARCINOGEN	CASTRATION	CAVITY WALL	CHAGRINING	CHARLESTON
CARDIALGIA	CASUALNESS	CEASE-FIRES	CHAIN GANGS	CHARMINGLY
CARDIALGIC	CASUALTIES	CEILOMETER	CHAINPLATE	CHARTERING
CARDIOGRAM	CASUS BELLI	CELEBRATED	CHAIN-REACT	CHARTREUSE
CARDIOLOGY	CATABOLISM	CELEBRATOR	CHAIN SMOKE	CHASTENING
CARD READER	CATABOLITE	CELLOBIOSE	CHAIN-SMOKE	CHASTISING
CARDSHARPS	CATACLINAL	CELLOPHANE	CHAIN STORE	CHATELAINE
CAREERISTS	CATACLYSMS	CELLULITIS	CHAIR LIFTS	CHATOYANCY
CARELESSLY	CATAFALQUE	CELLULOSIC	CHAIRWOMAN	CHATTERBOX
CARETAKERS	CATALECTIC	CEMETERIES	CHAIRWOMEN	CHATTERERS
CARICATURE	CATALEPTIC	CENOTAPHIC	CHALCEDONY	CHATTERING
CARJACKING	CATALOGUED	CENSORABLE	CHALCIDICE	CHAUDFROID
CARMARTHEN	CATALOGUER	CENSORIOUS	CHALCOCITE	CHAUFFEURS
CARNALLITE	CATALOGUES	CENSORSHIP	CHALKBOARD	CHAUVINISM

CHAUVINIST	CHILD'S	CHRYSOTILE	CLARIFYING	CLOVE HITCH
CHEAPENING	PLAY	CHUBBINESS	CLASP KNIFE	CLOVERLEAF
CHEAPSKATE	CHILIASTIC	CHUCKER-OUT	CLASSIC CAR	CLOWNISHLY
CHEBOKSARY	CHILLINESS	CHUCKWALLA	CLASSICISM	CLOYEDNESS
CHECKLISTS	CHIMERICAL	CHUKKA BOOT	CLASSICIST	CLUBFOOTED
CHECKMATED	CHIMNEYPOT	CHUMMINESS	CLASSIFIED	CLUBHOUSES
CHECKMATES	CHIMPANZEE	CHUNKINESS	CLASSIFIER	CLUMSINESS
CHECKPOINT	CHINABERRY	CHURCHGOER	CLASSMATES	CLUSTERING
CHECKROOMS	CHINATOWNS	CHURCHYARD	CLASSROOMS	CLUTCH BAGS
CHEEKBONES	CHINCHILLA	CHURLISHLY	CLATTERING	CLUTTERING
CHEEKINESS	CHINQUAPIN	CHYLACEOUS	CLAVICHORD	CLYDESDALE
CHEEKPIECE	CHINSTRAPS	CICATRICES	CLAVICULAR	CNIDOBLAST
CHEERFULLY	CHINTZIEST	CICATRICLE	CLAY PIGEON	COACERVATE
CHEERINESS	CHIPOLATAS	CICATRIZER	CLEANSABLE	COACTIVITY
CHEESECAKE	CHIROMANCY	CIGARETTES	CLEAN SHEET	COADJUTANT
CHEESED OFF	CHIRPINESS	CINCHONINE	CLEAN SWEEP	COADJUTORS
CHEESINESS	CHISELLERS	CINCHONISM	CLEARANCES	COAGULABLE
CHEKHOVIAN	CHISELLING	CINCHONIZE	CLEFT STICK	COAGULATED
CHELICERAL	CHITARRONE	CINCINNATI	CLEMENTINE	COALBUNKER
CHELMSFORD	CHITTAGONG	CINDERELLA	CLERESTORY	COALESCENT
CHELTENHAM	CHIVALROUS	CINERARIUM	CLERICALLY	COALESCING
CHEMICALLY	CHLAMYDATE	CINNAMONIC	CLEVER DICK	COALFIELDS
CHEMISETTE	CHLORAMINE	CINQUEFOIL	CLEVERNESS	COALHOUSES
CHEMOTAXIS	CHLORINATE	CIRCUITOUS	CLIENTELES	COALITIONS
CHEQUEBOOK	CHLOROFORM	CIRCULATED	CLINGINESS	COAPTATION
CHEQUE CARD	CHOANOCYTE	CIRCULATOR	CLINGSTONE	COARSENESS
CHERISHING	CHOCKSTONE	CIRCUMCISE	CLINICALLY	COARSENING
CHERNOVTSY	CHOCOHOLIC	CIRCUMFLEX	CLINKSTONE	COASTGUARD
CHERRYWOOD	CHOCOLATES	CIRCUMFUSE	CLINOMETER	COASTLINES
CHERUBICAL	CHOICENESS	CIRCUMVENT	CLINOMETRY	COAT HANGER
CHESAPEAKE	CHOKEBERRY	CISMONTANE	CLIPBOARDS	COAT OF
CHESSBOARD	CHONDRITIC	CISTACEOUS	CLIP JOINTS	ARMS
CHESTINESS	CHOPHOUSES	CISTERCIAN	CLOAKROOMS	COCHABAMBA
CHEVALIERS	CHOPPINESS	CITRIC ACID	CLOBBERING	COCHINEALS
CHEVROTAIN	CHOPSTICKS	CITRONELLA	CLOCKMAKER	COCKABULLY
CHEWING GUM	CHORIAMBIC	CITRULLINE	CLOCK TOWER	COCKALORUM
CHEW THE	CHORISTERS	CITY FATHER	CLODDISHLY	COCKCHAFER
CUD	CHRISTENED	CITY-STATES	CLODHOPPER	COCKED HATS
CHEW THE	CHRISTENER	CIVILITIES	CLOGGINESS	COCKFIGHTS
FAT	CHRISTIANS	CIVILIZING	CLOISTERED	COCKHORSES
CHEW THE	CHROMATICS	CLACTONIAN	CLOSE CALLS	COCKNEYISM
RAG	CHROMATIST	CLADISTICS	CLOSED BOOK	COCKSCOMBS
CHICHESTER	CHROMOMERE	CLADOCERAN	CLOSEDOWNS	COCONUT SHY
CHICKEN POX	CHROMONEMA	CLAMBERING	CLOSED SHOP	CODSWALLOP
CHIEFTAINS	CHROMOSOME	CLAMMINESS	CLOSE SHAVE	COELACANTH
CHIFFCHAFF	CHRONICITY	CLAMOURING	CLOSE THING	COENOCYTIC
CHIFFONIER	CHRONICLED	CLAMPDOWNS	CLOTHBOUND	COEQUALITY
CHIHUAHUAS	CHRONICLER	CLANGOROUS	CLOTHES PEG	COERCIVELY
CHILBLAINS	CHRONICLES	CLANNISHLY	CLOUDBANKS	COERCIVITY
CHILDBIRTH	CHRONOGRAM	CLANSWOMAN	CLOUDBERRY	COEXISTENT
CHILDISHLY	CHRONOLOGY	CLAPPED-OUT	CLOUDBURST	COEXISTING
	CHRYSOLITE	CLARABELLA	CLOUDINESS	COFFEE BARS

COFFEEPOTS	COLORATURA	COMMONABLE	COMPRESSED	CONDENSING
COFFEE SHOP	COLOR LINES	COMMONALTY	COMPRESSES	CONDESCEND
COFFERDAMS	COLOSSALLY	COMMONNESS	COMPRESSOR	CONDIMENTS
COGITATING	COLOSSUSES	COMMON NOUN	COMPRISING	CONDITIONS
COGITATION	COLOURABLE	COMMON ROOM	COMPROMISE	CONDOLENCE
COGITATIVE	COLOUR BARS	COMMONWEAL	COMPULSION	CONDUCIBLE
COGNIZABLE	COLOURFAST	COMMOTIONS	COMPULSIVE	CONDUCTING
COGNIZANCE	COLOUR FAST	COMMUNIONS	COMPULSORY	CONDUCTION
COHABITANT	COLOURINGS	COMMUNIQUE	COMPUTABLE	CONDUCTIVE
COHABITING	COLOURLESS	COMMUNISTS	CONCEALING	CONDUCTORS
COHERENTLY	COLUMBINES	COMMUTABLE	CONCEDEDLY	CONEFLOWER
COHESIVELY	COLUMELLAR	COMMUTATOR	CONCEIVING	CONFECTION
COIMBATORE	COLUMNISTS	COMPACTING	CONCENTRIC	CONFERENCE
COINCIDENT	COMANCHEAN	COMPANIONS	CONCEPCION	CONFERMENT
COINCIDING	COMBATABLE	COMPARABLE	CONCEPTION	CONFERRING
COLATITUDE	COMBATANTS	COMPARABLY	CONCEPTIVE	CONFERVOID
COLCHESTER	COMBATTING	COMPARATOR	CONCEPTUAL	CONFESSING
COLCHICINE	COMBINABLE	COMPARISON	CONCERNING	CONFESSION
COLD CHISEL	COMBUSTION	COMPASSION	CONCERTINA	CONFESSORS
COLD FISHES	COMEDIENNE	COMPATIBLE	CONCERTINO	CONFIDANTS
COLD FRAMES	COME-HITHER	COMPATIBLY	CONCESSION	CONFIDENCE
COLD FRONTS	COMELINESS	COMPATRIOT	CONCESSIVE	CONFIRMING
COLDSTREAM	COMESTIBLE	COMPELLING	CONCHIOLIN	CONFISCATE
COLD TURKEY	COME TO	COMPENDIUM	CONCHOLOGY	CONFLATING
COLEMANITE	HAND	COMPENSATE	CONCIERGES	CONFLATION
COLEOPTILE	COME TO	COMPETENCE	CONCILIATE	CONFLICTED
COLEORHIZA	MIND	COMPETENCY	CONCINNITY	CONFLUENCE
COLLAGENIC	COMFORTERS	COMPETITOR	CONCINNOUS	CONFORMERS
COLLAPSING	COMFORTING	COMPLACENT	CONCLAVIST	CONFORMING
COLLARBONE	COMIC OPERA	COMPLAINED	CONCLUDING	CONFORMIST
COLLAR STUD	COMIC STRIP	COMPLAINER	CONCLUSION	CONFORMITY
COLLATERAL	COMMANDANT	COMPLAINTS	CONCLUSIVE	CONFOUNDED
COLLATIONS	COMMANDEER	COMPLEMENT	CONCOCTING	CONFOUNDER
COLLEAGUES	COMMANDERS	COMPLETELY	CONCOCTION	CONFRONTED
COLLECTING	COMMANDING	COMPLETING	CONCOCTIVE	CONFRONTER
COLLECTION	COMMEASURE	COMPLETION	CONCORDANT	CONFUSABLE
COLLECTIVE	COMMENCING	COMPLETIST	CONCORDATS	CONFUSEDLY
COLLECTORS	COMMENDING	COMPLETIVE	CONCOURSES	CONGEALING
COLLEGIATE	COMMENTARY	COMPLEXION	CONCRETELY	CONGENERIC
COLLIERIES	COMMENTATE	COMPLEXITY	CONCRETING	CONGENITAL
COLLIMATOR	COMMENTING	COMPLIANCE	CONCRETION	CONGER EELS
COLLISIONS	COMMERCIAL	COMPLICATE	CONCRETIVE	CONGESTION
COLLOCATED	COMMISSARS	COMPLICITY	CONCRETIZE	CONGESTIVE
COLLOQUIAL	COMMISSARY	COMPLIMENT	CONCUBINES	CONGLOBATE
COLLOQUIES	COMMISSION	COMPONENTS	CONCURRENT	CONGREGATE
COLLOQUIUM	COMMISSURE	COMPORTING	CONCURRING	CONGRESSES
COLLOTYPIC	COMMITMENT	COMPOSITES	CONCUSSING	CONGRUENCE
COLONIZERS	COMMITTALS	COMPOSITOR	CONCUSSION	CONIFEROUS
COLONIZING	COMMITTEES	COMPOSTING	CONCUSSIVE	CONJECTURE
COLONNADED	COMMITTING	COMPOUNDED	CONDEMNING	CONJOINING
COLONNADES	COMMODIOUS	COMPOUNDER	CONDENSATE	CONJOINTLY
COLORATION	COMMODORES	COMPREHEND	CONDENSERS	CONJUGABLE

CONJUGATED	CONTAINERS	CONVERGENT	CORMOPHYTE	COTTONSEED
CONJUGATOR	CONTAINING	CONVERGING	CORMORANTS	COTTONTAIL
CONNECTING	CONTENDERS	CONVERSANT	CORNACEOUS	COTTONWOOD
CONNECTION	CONTENDING	CONVERSELY	CORNCOCKLE	COTTON WOOL
CONNECTIVE	CONTENTING	CONVERSING	CORNCRAKES	COUCHETTES
CONNIVANCE	CONTENTION	CONVERSION	CORNED BEEF	COUCH GRASS
CONQUERING	CONTESTANT	CONVERTERS	CORNELIANS	COULOMETER
CONQUERORS	CONTESTING	CONVERTING	CORNFLAKES	COUNCILLOR
CONSCIENCE	CONTEXTUAL	CONVEYABLE	CORNFLOWER	COUNCILMAN
CONSCRIPTS	CONTEXTURE	CONVEYANCE	CORNSTARCH	COUNCILMEN
CONSECRATE	CONTIGUITY	CONVICTING	CORNUCOPIA	COUNCIL TAX
CONSENSUAL	CONTIGUOUS	CONVICTION	CORNWALLIS	COUNSELLED
CONSENTING	CONTINENCE	CONVICTIVE	CORONATION	COUNSELLOR
CONSEQUENT	CONTINENTS	CONVINCING	CORPORATOR	COUNTDOWNS
CONSERVING	CONTINGENT	CONVOCATOR	CORPOREITY	COUNTERACT
CONSIDERED	CONTINUANT	CONVOLUTED	CORPULENCE	COUNTERING
CONSIDERER	CONTINUING	CONVULSING	CORPUSCLES	COUNTERSPY
CONSIGNEES	CONTINUITY	CONVULSION	CORRALLING	COUNTESSES
CONSIGNING	CONTINUOUS	CONVULSIVE	CORRECTING	COUNT NOUNS
CONSIGNORS	CONTINUUMS	COOCH BEHAR	CORRECTION	COUNTRYMAN
CONSISTENT	CONTORTING	COOKHOUSES	CORRECTIVE	COUNTRYMEN
CONSISTING	CONTORTION	COOL-HEADED	CORRELATED	COUNTY TOWN
CONSISTORY	CONTOURING	COOPERATED	CORRELATES	COUPS
CONSOCIATE	CONTRABAND	COOPERATOR	CORRESPOND	D'ETAT
CONSOLABLE	CONTRABASS	COOPTATION	CORRIENTES	COURAGEOUS
CONSONANCE	CONTRACTED	COOPTATIVE	CORRIGENDA	COURGETTES
CONSONANTS	CONTRACTOR	COORDINATE	CORRIGIBLE	COURSEBOOK
CONSORTIAL	CONTRADICT	COPARCENER	CORROBOREE	COURT CARDS
CONSORTING	CONTRAFLOW	COPENHAGEN	CORRODIBLE	COURTESANS
CONSORTIUM	CONTRALTOS	COPPER BELT	CORRUGATED	COURTESIES
CONSPECTUS	CONTRARIES	COPPERHEAD	CORRUPTING	COURTHOUSE
CONSPIRACY	CONTRARILY	COPROLALIA	CORRUPTION	COURTLIEST
CONSPIRING	CONTRASTED	COPROLITIC	CORRUPTIVE	COURTSHIPS
CONSTABLES	CONTRAVENE	COPROPHAGY	CORSETIERE	COURTYARDS
CONSTANTAN	CONTRIBUTE	COPULATING	CORUSCATED	COUTURIERS
CONSTANTIA	CONTRITELY	COPULATION	COS LETTUCE	COVARIANCE
CONSTANTLY	CONTRITION	COPULATIVE	COSMICALLY	COVENANTAL
CONSTIPATE	CONTRIVING	COPY EDITOR	COSMIC RAYS	COVENANTED
CONSTITUTE	CONTROLLED	COPYHOLDER	COSMODROME	COVENANTEE
CONSTRAINT	CONTROLLER	COPYRIGHTS	COSMOGONAL	COVENANTER
CONSTRUCTS	CONTROVERT	COPYWRITER	COSMOGONIC	COVENANTOR
CONSTRUING	CONTUSIONS	COQUELICOT	COSMONAUTS	COVER NOTES
CONSUETUDE	CONUNDRUMS	COQUETRIES	COSSETTING	COVER POINT
CONSULATES	CONVALESCE	COQUETTISH	COSTA RICAN	COVETOUSLY
CONSULSHIP	CONVECTION	COR ANGLAIS	CO-STARRING	COWCATCHER
CONSULTANT	CONVECTIVE	CORDIALITY	COSTLINESS	CRAB APPLES
CONSULTING	CONVECTORS	CORDIERITE	COST PRICES	CRACKBERRY
CONSUMMATE	CONVENABLE	CORDILLERA	COSTUMIERS	CRACKBRAIN
CONTACTING	CONVENANCE	CORDON BLEU	COTANGENTS	CRACKDOWNS
CONTACTUAL	CONVENIENT	CORIACEOUS	COTILLIONS	CRADLE SONG
CONTAGIONS	CONVENTION	CORINTHIAN	COTTAGE PIE	CRAFTINESS
CONTAGIOUS	CONVENTUAL	CORKSCREWS	COTTON GINS	CRANE FLIES

CRANESBILL
CRANIOLOGY
CRANIOTOMY
CRANKSHAFT
CRAPULENCE
CRAQUELURE
CRASH-DIVED
CRASH-DIVES
CRAVENNESS
CRAYFISHES
CREAKINESS
CREAMERIES
CREAMINESS
CREATININE
CREATIONAL
CREATIVELY
CREATIVITY
CREDITABLE
CREDITABLY
CREDIT CARD
CREDIT NOTE
CREEPINESS
CREMATIONS
CREMATORIA
CRENELLATE
CREOSOTING
CREPE PAPER
CRESCENDOS
CRESCENTIC
CRETACEOUS
CREWELWORK
CRIBRIFORM
CRICKETERS
CRIMINALLY
CRIMSONING
CRINKLIEST
CRINOLINES
CRISPATION
CRISPINESS
CRISSCROSS
CRITERIONS
CRITICALLY
CRITICISMS
CRITICIZED
CRITICIZER
CROAKINESS
CROCHETING
CROCODILES
CROISSANTS
CROQUETTES
CROSSBONES
CROSSBREED

CROSSCHECK
CROSSHATCH
CROSS-INDEX
CROSSPATCH
CROSSPIECE
CROSS-REFER
CROSSROADS
CROSS-SLIDE
CROSSTREES
CROSSWALKS
CROSSWINDS
CROSSWORDS
CROWDED OUT
CROWN COURT
CROWN DERBY
CROWNPIECE
CROW'S
  NESTS
CRUCIFIXES
CRUCIFYING
CRUMBLIEST
CRUNCHIEST
CRUSTACEAN
CRUSTINESS
CRYOGENICS
CRYOPHILIC
CRYOSCOPIC
CRYPTOLOGY
CRYPTOZOIC
CRYSTAL SET
CTENOPHORE
CUBBYHOLES
CUCKOLDING
CUCKOOPINT
CUCKOO SPIT
CUCULIFORM
CUDDLESOME
CUDGELLING
CUERNAVACA
CULLENDERS
CULTIVABLE
CULTIVATED
CULTIVATOR
CULTURALLY
CUMBERSOME
CUMMERBUND
CUMULATION
CUMULATIVE
CUMULIFORM
CUPBEARERS
CURABILITY

CURATE'S
  EGG
CURATORIAL
CURMUDGEON
CURRENCIES
CURRICULAR
CURRICULUM
CURTAILING
CURTAINING
CURVACEOUS
CURVATURES
CUSHIONING
CUSSEDNESS
CUSTARD PIE
CUSTODIANS
CUSTOMIZED
CUSTOM MADE
CUSTOM-MADE
CUTTHROATS
CUTTLEBONE
CUTTLEFISH
CUT UP
  ROUGH
CYANOGENIC
CYBERNETIC
CYBERSPACE
CYCLAMATES
CYCLICALLY
CYCLOMETER
CYCLOMETRY
CYCLORAMIC
CYCLOSTOME
CYCLOSTYLE
CYLINDROID
CYMBALISTS
CYMIFEROUS
CYSTECTOMY
CYSTOSCOPE
CYSTOSCOPY
CYTOCHROME
CYTOLOGIST

D
DACHSHUNDS
DAIL EIRANN
DAILY BREAD
DAIMYO BOND
DAINTINESS
DAIRY FARMS
DAIRYMAIDS
DAISY WHEEL
DALAI LAMAS

DALMATIANS
DAMAGEABLE
DAMP COURSE
DAMP SQUIBS
DAMSELFISH
DANDELIONS
DAPPLE-GREY
DAREDEVILS
DARJEELING
DARK HORSES
DARLINGTON
DARTBOARDS
DASHBOARDS
DAUGAVPILS
DAUGHTERLY
DAYDREAMED
DAYDREAMER
DAY-NEUTRAL
DAY NURSERY
DAY SCHOOLS
DAY-TRIPPER
DEACONSHIP
DEACTIVATE
DEAD CENTRE
DEAD LETTER
DEADLINESS
DEADLY SINS
DEAD-NETTLE
DEAD RINGER
DEALERSHIP
DEATHBLOWS
DEATH MASKS
DEATH RATES
DEATH'S-
  HEAD
DEATH SQUAD
DEATH TOLLS
DEATH TRAPS
DEATHWATCH
DEBASEMENT
DEBAUCHEES
DEBAUCHERY
DEBAUCHING
DEBENTURES
DEBILITATE
DEBOUCHING
DEBRIEFING
DEBUTANTES
DECADENTLY
DECAHEDRAL
DECAHEDRON
DECAMPMENT

DECAPITATE
DECATHLONS
DECEIVABLE
DECELERATE
DECEPTIONS
DECIMALIZE
DECIMATING
DECIMATION
DECIPHERED
DECIPHERER
DECISIONAL
DECISIVELY
DECKCHAIRS
DECLAIMING
DECLARABLE
DECLASSIFY
DECLENSION
DECLINABLE
DECOCTIONS
DECOLLATOR
DECOLONIZE
DECOLORANT
DECOLORIZE
DECOMPOSED
DECOMPOSER
DECOMPOUND
DECOMPRESS
DECORATING
DECORATION
DECORATIVE
DECORATORS
DECOROUSLY
DECOUPLING
DECREASING
DECREEABLE
DECREE NISI
DECRESCENT
DECUMBENCE
DEDICATING
DEDICATION
DEDICATORY
DEDUCTIBLE
DEDUCTIONS
DEEP FREEZE
DEEP FRYING
DEEP-ROOTED
DEEP-SEATED
DE-ESCALATE
DEFACEABLE
DEFACEMENT
DEFALCATOR
DEFAMATION

DEFAMATORY	DELECTABLE	DENOTATION	DERAILLEUR	DESTROYING
DEFAULTERS	DELECTABLY	DENOTATIVE	DERAILMENT	DESTRUCTOR
DEFAULTING	DELEGATING	DENOTEMENT	DERBYSHIRE	DETACHABLE
DEFEASANCE	DELEGATION	DENOUEMENT	DEREGULATE	DETACHMENT
DEFEASIBLE	DELIBERATE	DENOUNCING	DERISIVELY	DETAINABLE
DEFEATISTS	DELICACIES	DENSIMETER	DERISORILY	DETAINMENT
DEFECATING	DELICATELY	DENSIMETRY	DERIVATION	DETECTABLE
DEFECATION	DELIGHTFUL	DENTIFRICE	DERIVATIVE	DETECTIVES
DEFECTIONS	DELIGHTING	DENUDATION	DERMATITIS	DETERGENCY
DEFENDABLE	DELIMITING	DENUNCIATE	DERMATOGEN	DETERGENTS
DEFENDANTS	DELINEATED	DENVER BOOT	DERMATOMIC	DETERMINED
DEFENSIBLE	DELINEATOR	DEODORANTS	DERMATOSIS	DETERMINER
DEFENSIBLY	DELINQUENT	DEODORIZED	DEROGATING	DETERRENCE
DEFENSIVES	DELIQUESCE	DEODORIZER	DEROGATION	DETERRENTS
DEFERMENTS	DELIVERIES	DEONTOLOGY	DEROGATIVE	DETESTABLE
DEFERRABLE	DELIVERING	DEOXIDIZER	DEROGATORY	DETESTABLY
DEFICIENCY	DELOCALIZE	DEPARTMENT	DESALINATE	DETHRONING
DEFILEMENT	DELPHINIUM	DEPARTURES	DESALINIZE	DETONATING
DEFINITELY	DELTIOLOGY	DEPENDABLE	DESCENDANT	DETONATION
DEFINITION	DELUSIONAL	DEPENDABLY	DESCENDENT	DETONATIVE
DEFINITIVE	DELUSIVELY	DEPENDANTS	DESCENDING	DETONATORS
DEFINITUDE	DEMAGOGUES	DEPENDENCE	DESCRIBING	DETOXICANT
DEFLAGRATE	DEMANDABLE	DEPENDENCY	DESECRATED	DETOXICATE
DEFLECTING	DEMARCATED	DEPICTIONS	DESECRATOR	DETRACTING
DEFLECTION	DEMARCATOR	DEPILATION	DESERTIONS	DETRACTION
DEFLECTIVE	DEMEANOURS	DEPILATORY	DESERVEDLY	DETRACTIVE
DEFLOWERED	DEMENTEDLY	DEPLETABLE	DESHABILLE	DETRACTORS
DEFLOWERER	DEMICANTON	DEPLORABLE	DESICCANTS	DETRAINING
DEFOLIANTS	DEMIVIERGE	DEPLORABLY	DESICCATED	DETRIMENTS
DEFOLIATED	DEMOBILIZE	DEPLOYMENT	DESICCATOR	DETRUNCATE
DEFOLIATOR	DEMOCRATIC	DEPOLARIZE	DESIDERATA	DEUTOPLASM
DEFORESTED	DEMODULATE	DEPOPULATE	DESIDERATE	DEUX-SEVRES
DEFORESTER	DEMOGRAPHY	DEPORTABLE	DESIGNABLE	DEVASTATED
DEFORMABLE	DEMOISELLE	DEPORTMENT	DESIGNATED	DEVASTATOR
DEFRAUDING	DEMOLISHED	DEPOSITARY	DESIGNATOR	DEVELOPERS
DEFRAYABLE	DEMOLISHER	DEPOSITING	DESIGNEDLY	DEVELOPING
DEFROCKING	DEMOLITION	DEPOSITION	DESISTANCE	DEVIATIONS
DEFROSTERS	DEMONETIZE	DEPOSITORS	DESOLATELY	DEVILISHLY
DEFROSTING	DEMONIACAL	DEPOSITORY	DESOLATING	DEVITALIZE
DEFUNCTIVE	DEMONOLOGY	DEPRECATED	DESOLATION	DEVOCALIZE
DEGENERACY	DEMORALIZE	DEPRECATOR	DESPAIRING	DEVOLUTION
DEGENERATE	DEMOTIVATE	DEPRECIATE	DESPATCHED	DEVOTEMENT
DEGRADABLE	DEMURENESS	DEPRESSANT	DESPATCHER	DEVOTIONAL
DEGRESSION	DEMURRABLE	DEPRESSING	DESPATCHES	DEVOUTNESS
DEHISCENCE	DENATURANT	DEPRESSION	DESPERADOS	DEXTRALITY
DEHUMANIZE	DENDRIFORM	DEPRESSIVE	DESPICABLE	DIABOLICAL
DEHUMIDIFY	DENDROGRAM	DEPRIVABLE	DESPICABLY	DIACAUSTIC
DEHYDRATED	DENDROLOGY	DEPURATION	DESPOILING	DIACHRONIC
DEHYDRATOR	DENEGATION	DEPURATIVE	DESPONDENT	DIACRITICS
DEJECTEDLY	DENIGRATED	DEPUTATION	DESQUAMATE	DIACTINISM
DELAMINATE	DENIGRATOR	DEPUTIZING	DESSIATINE	DIADROMOUS
DELAWAREAN	DENOMINATE	DERACINATE	DESTROYERS	DIAGENESIS

DIAGNOSING	DILAPIDATE	DISCARDING	DISFIGURER	DISPLEASED
DIAGNOSTIC	DILATATION	DISC BRAKES	DISGORGING	DISPORTING
DIAGONALLY	DILEMMATIC	DISCERNING	DISGRACING	DISPOSABLE
DIAKINESIS	DILETTANTE	DISCHARGED	DISGRUNTLE	DISPOSSESS
DIALECTICS	DILETTANTI	DISCHARGER	DISGUISING	DISPRAISER
DIALYSABLE	DILIGENTLY	DISCHARGES	DISGUSTING	DISPROVING
DIAPASONAL	DILLYDALLY	DISC HARROW	DISHABILLE	DISPUTABLE
DIAPEDESIS	DIMENSIONS	DISCIPLINE	DISHARMONY	DISPUTABLY
DIAPEDETIC	DIMINISHED	DISC JOCKEY	DISHCLOTHS	DISQUALIFY
DIAPHANOUS	DIMINUENDO	DISCLAIMED	DISHEARTEN	DISQUIETED
DIAPHRAGMS	DIMINUTION	DISCLAIMER	DISHONESTY	DISRESPECT
DIAPHYSIAL	DIMINUTIVE	DISCLOSING	DISH TOWELS	DISRUPTING
DIARRHOEAL	DIMORPHISM	DISCLOSURE	DISHWASHER	DISRUPTION
DIASTALSIS	DIMORPHOUS	DISCOMFORT	DISINCLINE	DISRUPTIVE
DIASTALTIC	DINERS CLUB	DISCOMMODE	DISINHERIT	DISSATISFY
DIATHERMIC	DINING CARS	DISCOMPOSE	DISJOINTED	DISSECTING
DIATROPISM	DINING ROOM	DISCONCERT	DISK DRIVES	DISSECTION
DIBASICITY	DINNER BELL	DISCONNECT	DISLIKABLE	DISSEMBLED
DICHLORIDE	DIPETALOUS	DISCONTENT	DISLOCATED	DISSEMBLER
DICHROMATE	DIPHOSGENE	DISCOPHILE	DISLODGING	DISSENSION
DICKENSIAN	DIPHTHERIA	DISCORDANT	DISLOYALLY	DISSENTERS
DICKEY BIRD	DIPHTHONGS	DISCOUNTED	DISLOYALTY	DISSENTING
DICKYBIRDS	DIPHYLETIC	DISCOUNTER	DISMALNESS	DISSERVICE
DICTAPHONE	DIPHYLLOUS	DISCOURAGE	DISMANTLED	DISSIDENCE
DICTATIONS	DIPHYODONT	DISCOURSED	DISMANTLER	DISSIDENTS
DICTATRESS	DIPLODOCUS	DISCOURSER	DISMASTING	DISSIMILAR
DICTIONARY	DIPLOMATIC	DISCOURSES	DISMISSALS	DISSIPATED
DICTOGRAPH	DIPSOMANIA	DISCOVERED	DISMISSING	DISSIPATER
DICYNODONT	DIRECTIONS	DISCOVERER	DISMISSIVE	DISSOCIATE
DIDYNAMOUS	DIRECTIVES	DISCREETLY	DISMOUNTED	DISSOLUBLE
DIE-CASTING	DIRECTNESS	DISCREPANT	DISOBEYING	DISSOLVING
DIE-HARDISM	DIRECTOIRE	DISCRETELY	DISOBLIGED	DISSONANCE
DIELECTRIC	DIRECTRESS	DISCRETION	DISORDERED	DISSUADING
DIETICIANS	DIRIGIBLES	DISCURSIVE	DISORDERLY	DISSUASION
DIFFERENCE	DIRT FARMER	DISCUSSANT	DISOWNMENT	DISSUASIVE
DIFFICULTY	DIRT TRACKS	DISCUSSING	DISPARAGED	DISTANCING
DIFFIDENCE	DIRTY TRICK	DISCUSSION	DISPARAGER	DISTENDING
DIFFRACTED	DISABILITY	DISDAINFUL	DISPASSION	DISTENSION
DIFFUSIBLE	DISABUSING	DISDAINING	DISPATCHED	DISTICHOUS
DIGESTIBLE	DISALLOWED	DISEMBOGUE	DISPATCHES	DISTILLATE
DIGESTIONS	DISAPPOINT	DISEMBOWEL	DISPELLING	DISTILLERS
DIGESTIVES	DISAPPROVE	DISEMBROIL	DISPENSARY	DISTILLERY
DIGITALISM	DISARRANGE	DISEMPOWER	DISPENSERS	DISTILLING
DIGITALIZE	DISASTROUS	DISENCHANT	DISPENSING	DISTINCTLY
DIGITATION	DISAVOWALS	DISENDOWER	DISPERMOUS	DISTORTING
DIGITIFORM	DISAVOWING	DISENGAGED	DISPERSING	DISTORTION
DIGITIZERS	DISBANDING	DISENTHRAL	DISPERSION	DISTORTIVE
DIGITIZING	DISBARMENT	DISENTITLE	DISPERSIVE	DISTRACTED
DIGNIFYING	DISBARRING	DISENTWINE	DISPERSOID	DISTRACTER
DIGRESSING	DISBELIEVE	DISEPALOUS	DISPIRITED	DISTRAINED
DIGRESSION	DISBENEFIT	DISFEATURE	DISPLACING	DISTRAINEE
DIGRESSIVE	DISBURSING	DISFIGURED	DISPLAYING	DISTRAINOR

DISTRAUGHT
DISTRESSED
DISTRIBUTE
DISTRUSTED
DISTRUSTER
DISTURBING
DISULFIRAM
DISULPHATE
DISULPHIDE
DISUNITING
DISUTILITY
DISYLLABIC
DITHEISTIC
DITHIONITE
DIVARICATE
DIVE-BOMBED
DIVE-BOMBER
DIVERGENCE
DIVERGENCY
DIVERSIONS
DIVERTEDLY
DIVERTIBLE
DIVESTIBLE
DIVESTMENT
DIVINATION
DIVINATORY
DIVING BELL
DIVINITIES
DIVISIONAL
DIVISIVELY
DIVULGENCE
DIYARBAKIR
DOCENTSHIP
DOC MARTENS
DOCTORATES
DOCTRINISM
DOCUMENTED
DODECANESE
DOG BISCUIT
DOGCATCHER
DOG COLLARS
DOGGEDNESS
DOGMATISTS
DOGMATIZER
DOGSBODIES
DOLCELATTE
DOLLARFISH
DOLL'S
 HOUSE
DOLLY BIRDS
DOLOROUSLY
DOMINATING

DOMINATION
DOMINATIVE
DOMINATRIX
DOMINEERED
DOMINICANS
DONER KEBAB
DONKEYWORK
DONNYBROOK
DOORKEEPER
DOORPLATES
DORCHESTER
DORSIGRADE
DOSIMETRIC
DOSSHOUSES
DO THE
 TRICK
DOTTED LINE
DOUBLE BASS
DOUBLE BEDS
DOUBLE BIND
DOUBLE CHIN
DOUBLE DATE
DOUBLE-HUNG
DOUBLE-PARK
DOUBLE-REED
DOUBLE-STOP
DOUBLE TAKE
DOUBLE-TALK
DOUBLE TIME
DOUBLETREE
DOUBTFULLY
DOUGHTIEST
DOVETAILED
DOWN-AND-
 OUT
DOWN AT
 HEEL
DOWNGRADED
DOWNLOADED
DOWN-MARKET
DOWNPLAYED
DOWNSIZING
DOWNSPOUTS
DOWNSTAIRS
DOWNSTREAM
DRAGONHEAD
DRAGONROOT
DRAGOONAGE
DRAGOONING
DRAINPIPES
DRAMATISTS
DRAMATIZED

DRAMATIZER
DRAMATURGE
DRAMATURGY
DRAWBRIDGE
DRAWING PIN
DRAWSTRING
DREADFULLY
DREADLOCKS
DREAMBOATS
DREAMINESS
DREAMINGLY
DREAMLANDS
DREAM WORLD
DREARINESS
DRESSINESS
DRESSMAKER
DRILLSTOCK
DRIP-DRYING
DRIVELLERS
DRIVELLING
DROLLERIES
DROOPINESS
DROSOPHILA
DROSSINESS
DROWSINESS
DRUGSTORES
DRUM MAJORS
DRUMSTICKS
DRUPACEOUS
DRY BATTERY
DRY-CLEANED
DRY CLEANER
DUBITATION
DUCKBOARDS
DUFFEL BAGS
DUFFEL COAT
DUMBSTRUCK
DUMBWAITER
DUNCE'S
 CAPS
DUNDERHEAD
DUODECIMAL
DUODENITIS
DUPABILITY
DUPLICABLE
DUPLICATED
DUPLICATES
DUPLICATOR
DURABILITY
DURATIONAL
DUSSELDORF
DUST JACKET

DUSTSHEETS
DUST STORMS
DUTCH BARNS
DUTCH OVENS
DUTCH TREAT
DUTCH UNCLE
DYNAMISTIC
DYNAMITING
DYSENTERIC
DYSPLASTIC
DYSPROSIUM
DYSTROPHIC
DZERZHINSK

E
EAGLESTONE
EARLY BIRDS
EARMARKING
EARTHBOUND
EARTHINESS
EARTHLIEST
EARTHLIGHT
EARTHLINGS
EARTHQUAKE
EARTHSHINE
EARTHWARDS
EARTHWORKS
EARTHWORMS
EAR TRUMPET
EAST ANGLIA
EAST BERLIN
EAST ENDERS
EASTER EGGS
EASTERNERS
EASTERTIDE
EAST GERMAN
EAST INDIAN
EAST INDIES
EASTWARDLY
EASY CHAIRS
EASY DOES
 IT
EASY STREET
EASY VIRTUE
EBRACTEATE
EBULLIENCE
EBULLITION
EBURNATION
ECCENTRICS
ECCHYMOSIS
ECHINODERM
ECHOPRAXIA

ECOCENTRIC
ECOLOGICAL
ECOLOGISTS
ECONOMICAL
ECONOMISTS
ECONOMIZED
ECONOMIZER
ECOSPECIES
ECOSYSTEMS
ECOTOURISM
ECTODERMAL
ECTOENZYME
ECTOGENOUS
ECTOMORPHY
ECUADORIAN
ECUMENICAL
ECZEMATOUS
EDENTULOUS
EDIFYINGLY
EDITORIALS
EDITORSHIP
EDULCORATE
EDWARDIANS
EFFACEABLE
EFFACEMENT
EFFECTIBLE
EFFECTUATE
EFFEMINACY
EFFEMINATE
EFFERVESCE
EFFETENESS
EFFICIENCY
EFFLORESCE
EFFORTLESS
EFFRONTERY
EFFULGENCE
EFFUSIVELY
EGOCENTRIC
EGYPTOLOGY
EIDERDOWNS
EIGHTEENMO
EIGHTEENTH
EIGHTH NOTE
EIGHTIETHS
EISENSTADT
EISTEDDFOD
EJACULATED
EJACULATOR
ELABORATED
ELABORATOR
ELAEOPTENE
ELASTICITY

ELASTICIZE	EMBRASURED	ENCODEMENT	ENGLISHMEN	ENUMERATOR
ELATEDNESS	EMBRASURES	ENCOUNTERS	ENGRAVINGS	ENUNCIABLE
ELDERBERRY	EMBRECTOMY	ENCOURAGED	ENGROSSING	ENUNCIATED
ELEATICISM	EMBROIDERY	ENCOURAGER	ENGULFMENT	ENUNCIATOR
ELECAMPANE	EMBROILING	ENCROACHED	ENHARMONIC	ENVELOPING
ELECTIVITY	EMBRYOGENY	ENCROACHER	ENJAMBMENT	ENVISAGING
ELECTORATE	EMBRYOLOGY	ENCRUSTANT	ENJOINMENT	ENZYMOLOGY
ELECTRICAL	EMENDATION	ENCUMBERED	ENJOYMENTS	EOSINOPHIL
ELECTRODES	EMENDATORY	ENCYCLICAL	ENLACEMENT	EPEIROGENY
ELECTROJET	EMETICALLY	ENCYSTMENT	ENLISTMENT	EPENTHESIS
ELECTRONIC	EMIGRATING	ENDANGERED	ENLIVENING	EPENTHETIC
ELEMENTARY	EMIGRATION	ENDEARMENT	ENORMITIES	EPEXEGESIS
ELEVATIONS	EMIGRATIVE	ENDEAVOURS	ENORMOUSLY	EPEXEGETIC
ELEVEN-PLUS	EMISSARIES	ENDOCARPAL	ENPHYTOTIC	EPIBLASTIC
ELICITABLE	EMISSIVITY	ENDOCRINAL	ENRAGEMENT	EPICANTHUS
ELIMINABLE	EMMENTALER	ENDOCRINIC	ENRAPTURED	EPICARDIAC
ELIMINATED	EMMETROPIA	ENDODERMAL	ENRICHMENT	EPICARDIUM
ELIMINATOR	EMMETROPIC	ENDODERMIC	ENROLMENTS	EPICENTRAL
ELLIPTICAL	EMOLLIENCE	ENDODERMIS	ENSANGUINE	EPICENTRES
ELONGATING	EMOLLIENTS	ENDODONTIA	ENSCONCING	EPICUREANS
ELONGATION	EMOLUMENTS	ENDODONTIC	ENSHRINING	EPICYCLOID
ELONGATIVE	EMPALEMENT	ENDOENZYME	ENSHROUDED	EPIDEICTIC
ELOPEMENTS	EMPANELING	ENDOGAMOUS	ENSIGNSHIP	EPIDEMICAL
ELOQUENTLY	EMPANELLED	ENDOGENOUS	ENTAILMENT	EPIDIDYMAL
EL SALVADOR	EMPHASIZED	ENDOMORPHY	ENTANGLING	EPIDIDYMIS
ELUCIDATED	EMPIRICISM	ENDOPHYTIC	ENTEROTOMY	EPIGASTRIC
ELUCIDATOR	EMPIRICIST	ENDORSABLE	ENTERPRISE	EPIGENESIS
ELUTRIATOR	EMPLOYABLE	ENDOSCOPIC	ENTHRALLED	EPIGENETIC
ELUVIATION	EMPLOYMENT	ENDOSMOSIS	ENTHRALLER	EPIGLOTTAL
EMACIATION	EMPOWERING	ENDOSMOTIC	ENTHRONING	EPIGLOTTIS
EMANATIONS	EMULSIFIED	ENDOSTOSIS	ENTHUSIASM	EPIGRAPHER
EMANCIPATE	EMULSIFIER	ENDOWMENTS	ENTHUSIAST	EPIGRAPHIC
EMARGINATE	EMULSIONED	END PRODUCT	ENTICEMENT	EPILEPTICS
EMASCULATE	ENACTMENTS	ENDURINGLY	ENTICINGLY	EPILEPTOID
EMBALMMENT	ENAMELLING	ENERGETICS	ENTIRENESS	EPIMORPHIC
EMBANKMENT	ENAMELLIST	ENERGIZING	ENTODERMAL	EPINEURIAL
EMBARGOING	ENAMELWARE	ENERVATING	ENTOMBMENT	EPINEURIUM
EMBARKMENT	ENAMELWORK	ENERVATION	ENTOMOLOGY	EPIPHONEMA
EMBEZZLERS	ENCAMPMENT	ENERVATIVE	ENTOPHYTIC	EPIPHYSEAL
EMBEZZLING	ENCASEMENT	ENFACEMENT	ENTOURAGES	EPIROGENIC
EMBITTERED	ENCASHABLE	ENFEEBLING	ENTRAINING	EPISCOPACY
EMBITTERER	ENCASHMENT	ENFILADING	ENTRANCING	EPISCOPATE
EMBLAZONED	ENCEPHALIC	ENFLEURAGE	ENTRAPMENT	EPISIOTOMY
EMBLAZONRY	ENCEPHALON	ENFOLDMENT	ENTRAPPING	EPISPASTIC
EMBLEMATIC	ENCHAINING	ENFORCEDLY	ENTREATIES	EPISTERNUM
EMBLEMENTS	ENCHANTERS	ENGAGEMENT	ENTREATING	EPISTOLARY
EMBODIMENT	ENCHANTING	ENGAGINGLY	ENTRENCHED	EPITAPHIST
EMBOLDENED	ENCHILADAS	ENGENDERED	ENTRENCHER	EPITHELIAL
EMBOLISMIC	ENCIPHERER	ENGENDERER	ENTRUSTING	EPITHELIUM
EMBONPOINT	ENCIRCLING	ENGINEERED	ENTRY-LEVEL	EPITOMIZED
EMBOSSMENT	ENCLOSABLE	ENGINE ROOM	ENUCLEATOR	EPITOMIZER
EMBOUCHURE	ENCLOSURES	ENGLISHMAN	ENUMERATED	EPOXY RESIN

EPSOM SALTS	ESTHETICAL	EVACUATING	EXCLUDABLE	EXPATIATOR
EQUABILITY	ESTIMATING	EVACUATION	EXCLUSIVES	EXPATRIATE
EQUALIZERS	ESTIMATION	EVACUATIVE	EXCOGITATE	EXPECTABLE
EQUALIZING	ESTIMATIVE	EVALUATING	EXCORIATED	EXPECTANCY
EQUANIMITY	ESTIMATORS	EVALUATION	EXCRESCENT	EXPEDIENCE
EQUANIMOUS	ESTIPULATE	EVALUATIVE	EXCRETIONS	EXPEDIENCY
EQUATIONAL	ESTRANGING	EVANESCENT	EXCRUCIATE	EXPEDIENTS
EQUATORIAL	ETERNALITY	EVANGELISM	EXCULPABLE	EXPEDITING
EQUESTRIAN	ETERNALIZE	EVANGELIST	EXCULPATED	EXPEDITION
EQUIPOTENT	ETERNITIES	EVANGELIZE	EXCURSIONS	EXPELLABLE
EQUITATION	ETHANEDIOL	EVANSVILLE	EXCUSATORY	EXPENDABLE
EQUIVALENT	ETHEREALLY	EVAPORABLE	EXECRATING	EXPERIENCE
EQUIVOCATE	ETHNICALLY	EVAPORATED	EXECRATION	EXPERIMENT
ERADIATION	ETHNOGENIC	EVAPORATOR	EXECRATIVE	EXPERTNESS
ERADICABLE	ETHNOLOGIC	EVECTIONAL	EXECUTABLE	EXPIRATION
ERADICATED	ETHOLOGIST	EVEN-HANDED	EXECUTANTS	EXPIRATORY
ERADICATOR	ETHYLATION	EVENING ALL	EXECUTIONS	EXPLAINING
ERECTILITY	ETIOLATION	EVENING OUT	EXECUTIVES	EXPLETIVES
ERETHISMIC	EUBACTERIA	EVENTFULLY	EXEMPTIBLE	EXPLICABLE
ERGONOMICS	EUCALYPTOL	EVENTUALLY	EXEMPTIONS	EXPLICABLY
ERGOSTEROL	EUCALYPTUS	EVERGLADES	EXENTERATE	EXPLICATED
ERICACEOUS	EUCHLORINE	EVERGREENS	EXERCISING	EXPLICATOR
ERINACEOUS	EUDEMONICS	EVERY OTHER	EXHALATION	EXPLICITLY
EROGENEITY	EUDEMONISM	EVERYTHING	EXHAUSTING	EXPLOITERS
EROTEMATIC	EUDIOMETER	EVERYWHERE	EXHAUSTION	EXPLOITING
EROTICALLY	EUDIOMETRY	EVIDENTIAL	EXHAUSTIVE	EXPLOSIONS
EROTOGENIC	EUGENICIST	EVIL-MINDED	EXHIBITING	EXPLOSIVES
EROTOMANIA	EUHEMERISM	EVISCERATE	EXHIBITION	EXPORTABLE
ERRATICISM	EUHEMERIST	EVOCATIONS	EXHIBITIVE	EXPOSITION
ERUBESCENT	EUHEMERIZE	EVOLVEMENT	EXHIBITORS	EXPOSITORY
ERUCTATION	EULOGISTIC	EXACERBATE	EXHIBITORY	EXPOUNDING
ERUCTATIVE	EULOGIZING	EXACTINGLY	EXHILARANT	EXPRESSAGE
ERUPTIONAL	EUPATORIUM	EXACTITUDE	EXHILARATE	EXPRESSING
ERUPTIVITY	EUPHAUSIID	EXAGGERATE	EXHUMATION	EXPRESSION
ERYSIPELAS	EUPHEMISMS	EXALTATION	EXIGENCIES	EXPRESSIVE
ERYTHRITOL	EUPHEMIZER	EXAMINABLE	EXIGUOUSLY	EXPRESSWAY
ESCADRILLE	EUPHONIOUS	EXASPERATE	EXISTENCES	EXPULSIONS
ESCALATING	EUPHONIUMS	EX CATHEDRA	EXOBIOLOGY	EXPUNCTION
ESCALATION	EUPHORIANT	EXCAVATING	EXOCENTRIC	EXPURGATED
ESCALATORS	EUPHUISTIC	EXCAVATION	EXODONTIST	EXPURGATOR
ESCAPEMENT	EURE-ET-	EXCAVATORS	EXONERATED	EXSANGUINE
ESCAPOLOGY	LOIR	EXCEEDABLE	EXONERATOR	EXSICCATOR
ESCARPMENT	EURHYTHMIC	EXCELLENCE	EXORBITANT	EXTENDIBLE
ESCHAROTIC	EUROCHEQUE	EXCELLENCY	EXORCIZING	EXTENSIBLE
ESCRITOIRE	EUROCLYDON	EXCEPTABLE	EXOSPOROUS	EXTENSIONS
ESCUTCHEON	EURODOLLAR	EXCEPTIONS	EXOTHERMIC	EXTENUATED
ESKILSTUNA	EUROMARKET	EXCHANGING	EXOTICALLY	EXTENUATOR
ESPADRILLE	EURYPTERID	EXCITATION	EXOTICNESS	EXTERNALLY
ESPECIALLY	EURYTHMICS	EXCITATIVE	EXPANDABLE	EXTINCTION
ESPLANADES	EURYTROPIC	EXCITEMENT	EXPANSIBLE	EXTINCTIVE
ESSENTIALS	EUSTACHIAN	EXCITINGLY	EXPANSIONS	EXTINGUISH
ESTATE CARS	EUTHANASIA	EXCLAIMING	EXPATIATED	EXTIRPATED

EXTIRPATOR	FACTUALIST	FATHERHOOD	FETCHINGLY	FIREBREAKS
EXTORTIONS	FAHRENHEIT	FATHERLAND	FETIPAROUS	FIREBRICKS
EXTRACTING	FAINTINGLY	FATHERLESS	FETISHISTS	FIRE DRILLS
EXTRACTION	FAIR COPIES	FATHER-LIKE	FETTUCCINE	FIRE-EATERS
EXTRACTIVE	FAIR DINKUM	FATHOMABLE	FEUILLETON	FIRE-EATING
EXTRACTORS	FAIRGROUND	FATHOMETER	FEVERISHLY	FIRE ENGINE
EXTRADITED	FAIR-MINDED	FATHOMLESS	FFESTINIOG	FIRE ESCAPE
EXTRAMURAL	FAIR-SPOKEN	FAT-SOLUBLE	FIANNA FAIL	FIREGUARDS
EXTRANEOUS	FAIRYLANDS	FATTENABLE	FIBREBOARD	FIREPLACES
EXTRAVERTS	FAIRY LIGHT	FAULTINESS	FIBREGLASS	FIRE-RAISER
EXTRICABLE	FAIRY TALES	FAVOURABLE	FIBRINOGEN	FIRESTORMS
EXTRICATED	FAISALABAD	FAVOURABLY	FIBROBLAST	FIRING LINE
EXTROVERTS	FAITHFULLY	FAVOURITES	FIBROSITIS	FIRST CLASS
EXTRUSIONS	FALLACIOUS	FEARLESSLY	FICKLENESS	FIRST-CLASS
EXUBERANCE	FALLOW DEER	FEARNOUGHT	FICTIONIST	FIRST FLOOR
EXULTANTLY	FALLOWNESS	FEATHER BED	FICTITIOUS	FIRST NAMES
EXULTATION	FALSE ALARM	FEATHER BOA	FIDDLEHEAD	FIRST NIGHT
EXULTINGLY	FALSEHOODS	FEATHERING	FIDDLEWOOD	FISH FINGER
EXUVIATION	FALSE SCENT	FEBRIFUGAL	FIELD EVENT	FISH KNIVES
EYEBALLING	FALSE START	FEBRUARIES	FIELDMOUSE	FISHMONGER
EYE-CATCHER	FALSE TEETH	FECKLESSLY	FIELDSTONE	FISH SLICES
EYEDROPPER	FALSIFYING	FECUNDATOR	FIELD-TESTS	FISH STICKS
EYEGLASSES	FAMILIARLY	FEDERALISM	FIELD TRIPS	FISSIPEDAL
EYE-OPENERS	FAMILY NAME	FEDERALIST	FIENDISHLY	FISTICUFFS
EYE SHADOWS	FAMILY TREE	FEDERALIZE	FIERCENESS	FIT OF
EYEWITNESS	FAMISHMENT	FEDERATING	FIFTEENTHS	ANGER
	FAMOUSNESS	FEDERATION	FIFTY FIFTY	FIT OF
F	FANATICISM	FEDERATIVE	FIFTY-FIFTY	PIQUE
FABRICATED	FANATICIZE	FEEBLENESS	FIGURATION	FIT THE
FABRICATOR	FANCIFULLY	FEET OF	FIGURATIVE	BILL
FABULOUSLY	FANCY DRESS	CLAY	FIGUREHEAD	FITZGERALD
FACECLOTHS	FANCY WOMAN	FEIGNINGLY	FILARIASIS	FIVE-FINGER
FACE-HARDEN	FANCY WOMEN	FELICITATE	FILE SERVER	FIXED-POINT
FACE POWDER	FANTASIZED	FELICITIES	FILIALNESS	FIXED STARS
FACE-SAVERS	FANTOCCINI	FELICITOUS	FILIBUSTER	FLABBINESS
FACE-SAVING	FARCICALLY	FELIXSTOWE	FILMSETTER	FLABELLATE
FACE TO	FAR EASTERN	FELLMONGER	FILMSTRIPS	FLACCIDITY
FACE	FARFETCHED	FELLOWSHIP	FILTERABLE	FLAGELLANT
FACE-TO-	FARMHOUSES	FELT-TIP	FILTER TIPS	FLAGELLATE
FACE	FARMSTEADS	PEN	FILTHINESS	FLAGITIOUS
FACE VALUES	FARSIGHTED	FEMALENESS	FILTRATION	FLAGRANTLY
FACILENESS	FASCIATION	FEMININITY	FINALIZING	FLAGSTAFFS
FACILITATE	FASCICULAR	FENESTELLA	FINANCIERS	FLAGSTONES
FACILITIES	FASCICULUS	FER-DE-	FINE-TUNING	FLAG-WAVING
FACSIMILES	FASCINATED	LANCE	FINGER BOWL	FLAMBOYANT
FACTITIOUS	FASHIONING	FERMENTING	FINGERLING	FLAMEPROOF
FACT OF	FASTENINGS	FEROCITIES	FINGERNAIL	FLAMINGOES
LIFE	FASTIDIOUS	FERRITE-ROD	FINGERTIPS	FLANNELING
FACTORABLE	FASTIGIATE	FERTILIZED	FINISTERRE	FLANNELLED
FACTORIZED	FASTNESSES	FERTILIZER	FINNO-UGRIC	FLARE PATHS
FACTORSHIP	FATALISTIC	FESTOONERY	FIRE ALARMS	FLASHBACKS
FACTUALISM	FATALITIES	FESTOONING	FIREBRANDS	FLASHBOARD

FLASHBULBS	FLOPHOUSES	FONDLINGLY	FORMALIZED	FRACTURING
FLASHCUBES	FLOPPINESS	FONTANELLE	FORMALIZER	FRAGMENTAL
FLASHINESS	FLOPPY DISK	FOOD STAMPS	FORMATIONS	FRAGMENTED
FLASHLIGHT	FLORENTINE	FOODSTUFFS	FORMATTING	FRAGRANCES
FLASH POINT	FLORIBUNDA	FOOTBALLER	FORMIC ACID	FRAGRANTLY
FLATFISHES	FLORISTICS	FOOTBRIDGE	FORMIDABLE	FRAMEWORKS
FLAT-FOOTED	FLOTATIONS	FOOT-CANDLE	FORMIDABLY	FRANCHISED
FLAT RACING	FLOUNDERED	FOOT FAULTS	FORMLESSLY	FRANCHISES
FLATTENING	FLOURISHED	FOOTLIGHTS	FORMULATED	FRANCISCAN
FLATTERERS	FLOURISHER	FOOTPLATES	FORMULATOR	FRANCONIAN
FLATTERING	FLOURISHES	FOOTPRINTS	FOR MY	FRANGIPANI
FLATULENCE	FLOURMILLS	FOOTSTOOLS	MONEY	FRATERNITY
FLAVESCENT	FLOUTINGLY	FORBEARING	FORNICATED	FRATERNIZE
FLAVOURFUL	FLOWCHARTS	FORBIDDING	FORNICATOR	FRATRICIDE
FLAVOURING	FLOWERBEDS	FORCEDNESS	FORSTERITE	FRAUDULENT
FLAWLESSLY	FLOWER GIRL	FORCEFULLY	FORSWEARER	FRAUENFELD
FLEA-BITTEN	FLOWERLESS	FORE AND	FORTE-PIANO	FRAXINELLA
FLEA MARKET	FLOWER-LIKE	AFT	FORTHRIGHT	FRAY BENTOS
FLECTIONAL	FLOWERPOTS	FOREARMING	FORTIFIERS	FREAKINESS
FLEDGLINGS	FLUCTUATED	FOREBODING	FORTIFYING	FREAKISHLY
FLEECINESS	FLUFFINESS	FORECASTED	FORTISSIMO	FREDERICIA
FLEETINGLY	FLUGELHORN	FORECASTER	FORTNIGHTS	FREE AGENTS
FLESHINESS	FLUID OUNCE	FORECASTLE	FORTRESSES	FREE-BASING
FLESH WOUND	FLUMMOXING	FORECLOSED	FORT SUMTER	FREEBOARDS
FLETCHINGS	FLUORIDATE	FORECOURSE	FORTUITISM	FREEBOOTER
FLEUR-DE-	FLUORINATE	FORECOURTS	FORTUITIST	FREE CHURCH
LIS	FLUSTERING	FOREDOOMED	FORTUITOUS	FREEDWOMAN
FLEUR-DE-	FLUTTERING	FOREFATHER	FORTY-NINER	FREE FOR
LYS	FLY-BY-	FOREFINGER	FORTY WINKS	ALL
FLICKERING	NIGHT	FOREGATHER	FORWARDING	FREE-FOR-
FLICK KNIFE	FLYCATCHER	FOREGOINGS	FOSSILIZED	ALL
FLIGHT DECK	FLY-FISHING	FOREGROUND	FOSTERLING	FREE-HANDED
FLIGHTIEST	FLYING BOAT	FOREIGN AID	FOUDROYANT	FREEHOLDER
FLIGHTLESS	FLYING FISH	FOREIGNERS	FOUNDATION	FREE HOUSES
FLIGHT PATH	FLYSPECKED	FOREIGNISM	FOUNDERING	FREELANCED
FLIMSINESS	FLYSWATTER	FOREMOTHER	FOUNDLINGS	FREELANCER
FLINTINESS	FLYWEIGHTS	FOREORDAIN	FOURCHETTE	FREELANCES
FLINTLOCKS	FOAMFLOWER	FORERUNNER	FOUR-COLOUR	FREE-LIVING
FLINTSHIRE	FOAM RUBBER	FORESEEING	FOUR-HANDED	FREELOADED
FLIPPANTLY	FOB WATCHES	FORESHADOW	FOURIERISM	FREELOADER
FLIRTATION	FOCAL POINT	FOREST-LIKE	FOURIERIST	FREEMARTIN
FLIRTINGLY	FOCUS GROUP	FORETELLER	FOUR-IN-	FREEMASONS
FLOATATION	FOLIACEOUS	FOREWARNED	HAND	FREE PARDON
FLOCCULANT	FOLK DANCER	FOREWARNER	FOUR-POSTER	FREE PASSES
FLOCCULATE	FOLK DANCES	FORFEITERS	FOURRAGERE	FREE-SPOKEN
FLOCCULENT	FOLKESTONE	FORFEITING	FOURSQUARE	FREE-TRADER
FLOODGATES	FOLKLORIST	FORFEITURE	FOUR-STROKE	FREIGHTAGE
FLOODLIGHT	FOLKSINESS	FORGETTING	FOURTEENTH	FREIGHTERS
FLOOD TIDES	FOLLICULAR	FORGIVABLE	FOXHUNTERS	FREIGHTING
FLOORBOARD	FOLLICULIN	FORGIVABLY	FOXHUNTING	FRENCH BEAN
FLOOR CLOTH	FOLLOWABLE	FORKEDNESS	FOX TERRIER	FRENCH HORN
FLOOR SHOWS	FOLLOWINGS	FORMALISTS	FRACTIONAL	FRENCH KISS

FRENCH LOAF	FULFILLING	GALVANIZER	GENERALIZE	GIFTEDNESS
FRENZIEDLY	FULFILMENT	GAMEKEEPER	GENERATING	GIFT HORSES
FREQUENTED	FULIGINOUS	GAMETOCYTE	GENERATION	GILLINGHAM
FREQUENTER	FULL-BODIED	GAME WARDEN	GENERATIVE	GINGER ALES
FREQUENTLY	FULL HOUSES	GANG-BANGED	GENERATORS	GINGER BEER
FRESHENING	FULL-LENGTH	GANG-BANGER	GENERATRIX	GINGER NUTS
FRESHWATER	FULL-RIGGED	GANGLIONIC	GENEROSITY	GINGIVITIS
FRIABILITY	FULL-SAILED	GANGPLANKS	GENEROUSLY	GIPPY TUMMY
FRICANDEAU	FULLY-GROWN	GANGRENOUS	GENETICIST	GIRL FRIDAY
FRICASSEES	FULMINATED	GANGSTA RAP	GENICULATE	GIRLFRIEND
FRICATIVES	FULMINATOR	GANTT CHART	GENIUS LOCI	GIRL GUIDES
FRICTIONAL	FUMATORIUM	GARAGE SALE	GENTLEFOLK	GIVEN NAMES
FRIENDLESS	FUMBLINGLY	GARBAGE CAN	GENTLENESS	GIVE RISE
FRIENDLIER	FUMIGATING	GARDEN CITY	GENTRIFYED	TO
FRIENDLIES	FUMIGATION	GARGANTUAN	GEOCENTRIC	GLACIALIST
FRIENDLILY	FUNCTIONAL	GARISHNESS	GEOCHEMIST	GLACIATION
FRIENDSHIP	FUNCTIONED	GARLANDING	GEODYNAMIC	GLACIOLOGY
FRIGHTENED	FUNDHOLDER	GARNIERITE	GEOGNOSTIC	GLADDENING
FRIGHTENER	FUNEREALLY	GARNISHING	GEOGRAPHER	GLADIATORS
FRILLINESS	FUNGICIDAL	GARRISONED	GEOLOGICAL	GLAGOLITIC
FRISKINESS	FUNGICIDES	GARROTTING	GEOLOGISTS	GLAIRINESS
FRITILLARY	FUNICULARS	GAS FITTERS	GEOMETRIZE	GLAMORIZED
FRITTERING	FUNICULATE	GASHOLDERS	GEOMORPHIC	GLAMORIZER
FRIZZINESS	FUNNELLING	GASIFIABLE	GEOPHAGIST	GLANCINGLY
FROCK COATS	FUNNY BONES	GASOMETERS	GEOPHAGOUS	GLANDEROUS
FROGHOPPER	FUNNY FARMS	GASOMETRIC	GEOPHYSICS	GLASS FIBRE
FROLICKING	FURBISHING	GAS STATION	GEORGETOWN	GLASSHOUSE
FROLICSOME	FURNISHING	GASTRALGIA	GEORGE TOWN	GLASSINESS
FRONTALITY	FURTHERING	GASTRALGIC	GEOSCIENCE	GLASS-MAKER
FRONTBENCH	FURUNCULAR	GASTROLITH	GEOSTATICS	GLASSWORKS
FRONT DOORS	FUSIBILITY	GASTRONOME	GEOTHERMAL	GLASWEGIAN
FRONT ROOMS	FUSILLADES	GASTRONOMY	GEOTROPISM	GLAUCONITE
FRONTWARDS	FUSTANELLA	GASTROTOMY	GERATOLOGY	GLAZING-BAR
FROSTBOUND	FUTURISTIC	GAS TURBINE	GERIATRICS	GLEAMINGLY
FROSTINESS	FUTUROLOGY	GATEHOUSES	GERMANIZER	GLENROTHES
FROTHINESS	FUZZY LOGIC	GATEKEEPER	GERMICIDAL	GLIMMERING
FROWNINGLY		GATHERABLE	GERMICIDES	GLIOMATOUS
FROWZINESS	**G**	GATHERINGS	GERMINABLE	GLISTENING
FROZENNESS		GAUCHENESS	GERMINATED	GLITTERATI
FRUCTIFIED	GABARDINES	GAULTHERIA	GERMINATOR	GLITTERING
FRUCTIFIER	GADOLINITE	GAUSSMETER	GERUNDIVAL	GLOATINGLY
FRUITCAKES	GADOLINIUM	GAZETTEERS	GESTATIONS	GLOBALISTS
FRUITERERS	GAFF-RIGGED	GEAR LEVERS	GESUNDHEIT	GLOCHIDIUM
FRUIT FLIES	GAILLARDIA	GELATINIZE	GET HITCHED	GLOMERULAR
FRUITFULLY	GAINLINESS	GELATINOID	GET-UP-AND-	GLOMERULUS
FRUITINESS	GAINSAYING	GELATINOUS	GO	GLOOMINESS
FRUIT SALAD	GALASHIELS	GELDERLAND	GHASTLIEST	GLORIFYING
FRUSTRATED	GALLICIZER	GEMINATION	GHOSTLIEST	GLORIOUSLY
FRUSTRATER	GALLOGLASS	GEMMACEOUS	GHOST TOWNS	GLORY HOLES
FRUTESCENT	GALLSTONES	GEMOLOGIST	GHOSTWRITE	GLOSSARIAL
FRYING PANS	GALLUP POLL	GENERALIST	GIANT PANDA	GLOSSARIES
FUDDY-DUDDY	GALUMPHING	GENERALITY	GIARDIASIS	GLOSSARIST
	GALVANIZED			

GLOSSINESS	GOOD NATURE	GRAPHITIZE	GRENADIERS	GUARD'S
GLOTTIDEAN	GOODS TRAIN	GRAPHOLOGY	GRENADINES	VANS
GLOUCESTER	GOODY-GOODY	GRAPH PAPER	GRESSORIAL	GUERRILLAS
GLUCOSIDAL	GOOGOLPLEX	GRAPTOLITE	GREYHOUNDS	GUESSINGLY
GLUMACEOUS	GOOSEBERRY	GRASSFINCH	GREY MARKET	GUESTHOUSE
GLUTTINGLY	GOOSEFLESH	GRASSINESS	GREY MATTER	GUESTROOMS
GLUTTONOUS	GOOSESTEPS	GRASS ROOTS	GRIEVANCES	GUIDELINES
GLYCOGENIC	GORGEOUSLY	GRASS WIDOW	GRIEVINGLY	GUILDHALLS
GLYCOLYSIS	GORGONZOLA	GRATEFULLY	GRIEVOUSLY	GUILEFULLY
GLYCOSIDIC	GORMANDIZE	GRATIFYING	GRIM REAPER	GUILLEMOTS
GLYCOSURIA	GORMLESSLY	GRATUITIES	GRINDSTONE	GUILLOTINE
GLYCOSURIC	GORNO-ALTAI	GRATUITOUS	GRIPPINGLY	GUILTINESS
GNASHINGLY	GOTHICALLY	GRAUBUNDEN	GRISLINESS	GUINEA FOWL
GOALKEEPER	GO TOGETHER	GRAVELLING	GRISTLIEST	GUINEA PIGS
GOALMOUTHS	GO TO	GRAVESTONE	GRITTINESS	GUITARFISH
GOALSCORER	GROUND	GRAVETTIAN	GROANINGLY	GUITARISTS
GOATSBEARD	GO TO	GRAVEYARDS	GROGGINESS	GUJRANWALA
GO-BETWEENS	PIECES	GRAVIMETER	GROTESQUES	GULF STREAM
GODFATHERS	GOVERNABLE	GRAVIMETRY	GROTTINESS	GUNRUNNERS
GOD-FEARING	GOVERNANCE	GRAVITATED	GROUCHIEST	GUNRUNNING
GODMOTHERS	GOVERNMENT	GRAVITATER	GROUND BAIT	GURGLINGLY
GODPARENTS	GRACEFULLY	GRAVY BOATS	GROUND CREW	GYMNASIAST
GOGGLE-EYED	GRACIOUSLY	GRAVY TRAIN	GROUNDLESS	GYMNASIUMS
GOINGS-OVER	GRADATIONS	GREASE GUNS	GROUNDLING	GYMNASTICS
GOLD-BEATER	GRADUALISM	GREASEWOOD	GROUNDMASS	GYMNOSPERM
GOLD DIGGER	GRADUALIST	GREASINESS	GROUNDNUTS	GYNANDROUS
GOLDEN AGES	GRADUATING	GREATCOATS	GROUND PLAN	GYNOPHORIC
GOLDEN HOUR	GRADUATION	GREAT DANES	GROUND RENT	GYPSOPHILA
GOLDEN MEAN	GRAININESS	GREAT-NIECE	GROUND RULE	GYROSCOPES
GOLDEN RULE	GRAMICIDIN	GREAT STOUR	GROUNDSMAN	GYROSCOPIC
GOLDENSEAL	GRAMINEOUS	GREAT-UNCLE	GROUNDSMEN	GYROSTATIC
GOLDFIELDS	GRAMMARIAN	GREEDINESS	GROUNDWORK	
GOLDILOCKS	GRAMOPHONE	GREEDY-GUTS	GROUPTHINK	**H**
GOLD MEDALS	GRANADILLA	GREEK CROSS	GROVELLERS	HABILIMENT
GOLD-MINING	GRANDCHILD	GREENBACKS	GROVELLING	HABILITATE
GOLD-PLATED	GRAND OPERA	GREEN BEANS	GRUBBINESS	HABITATION
GOLD RUSHES	GRANDPAPPY	GREEN BELTS	GRUBSTAKES	HABITUALLY
GOLDSMITHS	GRAND PIANO	GREENBRIER	GRUDGINGLY	HABITUATED
GOLDTHREAD	GRAND SLAMS	GREENFINCH	GRUESOMELY	HACKBUTEER
GOLF COURSE	GRANDS PRIX	GREENFLIES	GRUMPINESS	HACKNEYISM
GONDOLIERS	GRANDSTAND	GREENGAGES	GRUNTINGLY	HADHRAMAUT
GONGOOZLER	GRANGERISM	GREENHEART	GUADELOUPE	HAECKELIAN
GONIOMETER	GRANGERIZE	GREENHORNS	GUANAJUATO	HAEMAGOGUE
GONIOMETRY	GRANNY KNOT	GREENHOUSE	GUANTANAMO	HAEMATINIC
GONOCOCCAL	GRANOPHYRE	GREEN LIGHT	GUARANTEED	HAEMATITIC
GONOCOCCUS	GRANT-IN-	GREEN PAPER	GUARANTEES	HAEMATOSIS
GONOPHORIC	AID	GREEN POUND	GUARANTIES	HAEMATURIA
GONORRHOEA	GRANULATED	GREENSBORO	GUARANTORS	HAEMATURIC
GOOD FRIDAY	GRANULATOR	GREENSHANK	GUARDHOUSE	HAEMOLYMPH
GOOD HUMOUR	GRANULITIC	GREENSTONE	GUARDRAILS	HAEMOLYSIN
GOODLINESS	GRAPEFRUIT	GREEN THUMB	GUARDROOMS	HAEMOLYSIS
GOOD LOOKER	GRAPEVINES	GREGARIOUS		HAEMOLYTIC

HAEMOPHILE	HANDMAIDEN	HATCHELLER	HEATHBERRY	HEMIPTERAN
HAGIOCRACY	HAND-ME-	HATCHERIES	HEATHENDOM	HEMIPTERON
HAGIOLATER	DOWN	HATCHET JOB	HEATHENISH	HEMISPHERE
HAGIOLATRY	HANDPICKED	HATCHET MAN	HEATHENISM	HEMITROPIC
HAGIOLOGIC	HANDSHAKES	HATCHET MEN	HEATHENIZE	HEMOGLOBIN
HAGIOSCOPE	HANDSOMELY	HATSHEPSUT	HEAT RASHES	HEMOPHILIA
HAILSTONES	HANDSPRING	HATTERSLEY	HEAT SHIELD	HEMORRHAGE
HAILSTORMS	HANDSTANDS	HAUBERGEON	HEATSTROKE	HEMORRHOID
HAIRPIECES	HANDSTROKE	HAUGHTIEST	HEAT STROKE	HENCEFORTH
HAIR SHIRTS	HANKERINGS	HAUNTINGLY	HEAVEN-SENT	HENDECAGON
HAIR SLIDES	HANKY-PANKY	HAUSTELLUM	HEAVENWARD	HENOTHEISM
HAIRSPRING	HANOVERIAN	HAUSTORIAL	HEAVY-LADEN	HENOTHEIST
HAIRSTREAK	HAPLOLOGIC	HAUSTORIUM	HEAVY METAL	HEN PARTIES
HAIRSTYLES	HAPPENINGS	HAUTE-LOIRE	HEAVY WATER	HEPARINOID
HALBERDIER	HAPPY EVENT	HAUTE-MARNE	HEBDOMADAL	HEPHAESTUS
HALF A	HAPPY HOURS	HAVE A	HEBETATION	HEPHAISTOS
CROWN	HARANGUING	HEART	HEBETATIVE	HEPTAGONAL
HALF-BOTTLE	HARASSMENT	HAVE A	HEBRAISTIC	HEPTAMETER
HALF-BREEDS	HARBINGERS	POINT	HECTICALLY	HEPTARCHIC
HALF-CASTES	HARBOURAGE	HAVERSACKS	HECTOGRAPH	HEPTASTICH
HALF CROWNS	HARBOURING	HAZARDABLE	HEDONISTIC	HEPTATEUCH
HALF-LENGTH	HARD-BITTEN	HAZARD-FREE	HEEDLESSLY	HEPTATHLON
HALF-ROTTEN	HARD-BOILED	HEADBOARDS	HEIDELBERG	HERACLIDAN
HALF-SISTER	HARD CIDERS	HEADCHEESE	HEIGHTENED	HERACLITUS
HALF-TRUTHS	HARDHEADED	HEADHUNTED	HEIGHTENER	HERBACEOUS
HALF VOLLEY	HARD LABOUR	HEADHUNTER	HEISENBERG	HERBALISTS
HALF-WITTED	HARD-LINERS	HEADLIGHTS	HELIANTHUS	HERBICIDAL
HALLELUJAH	HARD LIQUOR	HEADLINING	HELICOPTER	HERBIVORES
HALLMARKED	HARD PALATE	HEADMASTER	HELIGOLAND	HEREABOUTS
HALOGENATE	HARELIPPED	HEAD OF	HELIOGRAPH	HEREDITARY
HALOGENOID	HARGREAVES	HAIR	HELIOLATER	HEREDITIST
HALOGENOUS	HARLEQUINS	HEADPHONES	HELIOLATRY	HERESIARCH
HALOPHYTIC	HARMLESSLY	HEADPIECES	HELIOMETER	HERETOFORE
HALTER-LIKE	HARMONICAS	HEADSPRING	HELIOMETRY	HERMITAGES
HALTERNECK	HARMONIOUS	HEADSQUARE	HELIOPOLIS	HERMOSILLO
HAMBURGERS	HARMONIUMS	HEADSTONES	HELIOTAXIS	HEROICALLY
HAMMERFEST	HARMONIZED	HEADSTREAM	HELIOTROPE	HEROPHILUS
HAMMERHEAD	HARMONIZER	HEADSTRONG	HELIOTYPIC	HESITANTLY
HAMMERLESS	HARMSWORTH	HEADWATERS	HELLACIOUS	HESITATING
HAMMER-LIKE	HARNESSING	HEADWORKER	HELLBENDER	HESITATION
HAMSHACKLE	HARPOONING	HEALTH FOOD	HELLENIZER	HESITATIVE
HAMSTRINGS	HARRISBURG	HEALTHIEST	HELLESPONT	HESPERIDES
HANDBALLER	HARROWMENT	HEARING AID	HELLRAISER	HESPERIDIN
HANDBARROW	HARTEBEEST	HEARKENING	HELMET-LIKE	HETERODONT
HANDBRAKES	HARTLEPOOL	HEARTBEATS	HELMINTHIC	HETERODOXY
HANDCUFFED	HARUSPICAL	HEARTBREAK	HELPLESSLY	HETERODYNE
HANDICRAFT	HARVESTERS	HEARTENING	HEMELYTRAL	HETEROGAMY
HAND IN	HARVESTING	HEARTHRUGS	HEMELYTRON	HETEROGONY
HAND	HARVESTMAN	HEARTINESS	HEMICYCLIC	HETEROLOGY
HANDLEABLE	HASH BROWNS	HEARTSEASE	HEMIHEDRAL	HETERONOMY
HANDLEBARS	HASTEFULLY	HEARTTHROB	HEMIPLEGIA	HETEROTOPY
HANDLELESS	HATCHBACKS	HEATEDNESS	HEMIPLEGIC	HEULANDITE

HEURISTICS	HILDESHEIM	HOLINESSES	HOMUNCULUS	HOT FLUSHES
HEXADECANE	HILLINGDON	HOLLOWNESS	HONESTNESS	HOTFOOTING
HEXAEMERIC	HIMYARITIC	HOLLYHOCKS	HONEYBUNCH	HOUSEBOATS
HEXAEMERON	HINAYANIST	HOLOCAUSTS	HONEYCOMBS	HOUSEBOUND
HEXAHEDRAL	HINDENBURG	HOLOENZYME	HONEYDEWED	HOUSECOATS
HEXAHEDRON	HINDERMOST	HOLOFERNES	HONEY-EATER	HOUSECRAFT
HEXAMERISM	HINDRANCES	HOLOGRAPHY	HONEYMOONS	HOUSEFLIES
HEXAMEROUS	HINDUSTANI	HOLOHEDRAL	HONORARIUM	HOUSE GUEST
HEXAMETERS	HINTERLAND	HOLOPHYTIC	HONORIFICS	HOUSEHOLDS
HEXAMETRIC	HIPHUGGERS	HOLUS-BOLUS	HONOURABLE	HOUSEMAIDS
HEXANGULAR	HIPPARCHUS	HOLY ISLAND	HONOURABLY	HOUSE OF
HEXAVALENT	HIP POCKETS	HOLY SPIRIT	HONOURLESS	GOD
HIBERNACLE	HIPPOCRENE	HOMEBODIES	HOODLUMISM	HOUSE PARTY
HIBERNATED	HIPPODROME	HOME-BREWED	HOODWINKED	HOUSEPLANT
HIBERNATOR	HIPPOGRIFF	HOMECOMING	HOODWINKER	HOUSE-PROUD
HIBISCUSES	HIPPOLYTAN	HOME GUARDS	HOOKEDNESS	HOUSE-TRAIN
HIDDENNESS	HIPPOLYTUS	HOMELINESS	HOOTENANNY	HOUSEWIVES
HIERARCHAL	HIPPOMENES	HOMEMAKERS	HOPE CHESTS	HOVERCRAFT
HIEROCRACY	HISPANIOLA	HOMEMAKING	HOPELESSLY	HOVERINGLY
HIERODULIC	HISTAMINIC	HOME MOVIES	HOPPING MAD	HOVERTRAIN
HIEROGLYPH	HISTIOCYTE	HOME OFFICE	HORIZONTAL	HOW DO YOU
HIEROLOGIC	HISTOGRAMS	HOMEOPATHS	HORNBLENDE	DO
HIERONYMIC	HISTOLYSIS	HOMEOPATHY	HORNEDNESS	HUA KUO-
HIERONYMUS	HISTOLYTIC	HOMEOTYPIC	HORN-RIMMED	FENG
HIEROPHANT	HISTORIANS	HOMESTEADS	HOROLOGIST	HUCKLEBONE
HIGHBINDER	HISTORICAL	HOME TRUTHS	HOROLOGIUM	HUDDLESTON
HIGH CHAIRS	HISTRIONIC	HOMEWORKER	HOROSCOPES	HUGUENOTIC
HIGH CHURCH	HIT-AND-	HOMILETICS	HOROSCOPIC	HULLABALOO
HIGH COURTS	MISS	HOMOCERCAL	HORRENDOUS	HUMANENESS
HIGH-FLIERS	HITCHHIKED	HOMOCYCLIC	HORRIDNESS	HUMANISTIC
HIGH-FLYING	HITCHHIKER	HOMOEOPATH	HORRIFYING	HUMANITIES
HIGH-HANDED	HITHERMOST	HOMOEROTIC	HORROR FILM	HUMANIZING
HIGH HORSES	HIT PARADES	HOMOGAMOUS	HORSEBOXES	HUMBERSIDE
HIGHJACKER	HIT THE	HOMOGENATE	HORSEFLESH	HUMBLENESS
HIGH JUMPER	ROAD	HOMOGENIZE	HORSEFLIES	HUMBLINGLY
HIGHLANDER	HIT THE	HOMOGENOUS	HORSELAUGH	HUMBUGGERY
HIGHLIGHTS	SACK	HOMOGONOUS	HORSELEECH	HUMDINGERS
HIGH MASSES	HOARSENESS	HOMOGRAPHS	HORSE OPERA	HUMIDIFIED
HIGH-MINDED	HOBBYHORSE	HOMOLOGATE	HORSEPOWER	HUMIDIFIER
HIGHNESSES	HOBGOBLINS	HOMOLOGIZE	HORSE SENSE	HUMIDISTAT
HIGH-OCTANE	HOBNOBBING	HOMOLOGOUS	HORSESHOES	HUMILIATED
HIGH POINTS	HOCHHEIMER	HOMOLOSINE	HORSEWOMAN	HUMILIATOR
HIGH PRIEST	HOCUS-POCUS	HOMONYMITY	HORSEWOMEN	HUMORESQUE
HIGH RELIEF	HODGEPODGE	HOMOOUSIAN	HOSPITABLE	HUMORISTIC
HIGH SCHOOL	HOGARTHIAN	HOMOPHONES	HOSPITABLY	HUMOROUSLY
HIGH SEASON	HOITY-TOITY	HOMOPHONIC	HOSPITALET	HUMOURLESS
HIGH STREET	HOKEY COKEY	HOMOPLASTY	HOSTELLERS	HUMOURSOME
HIGH-STRUNG	HOKEY-POKEY	HOMORGANIC	HOSTELLING	HUMPBACKED
HIGHWAYMAN	HOLDERSHIP	HOMOSEXUAL	HOSTELRIES	HUNCHBACKS
HIGHWAYMEN	HOLES IN	HOMOZYGOTE	HOT-BLOODED	HUNDREDTHS
HIJACKINGS	ONE	HOMOZYGOUS	HOTCHPOTCH	HUNGRINESS
HILDEBRAND	HOLIDAYING	HOMUNCULAR	HOT DESKING	HUNTINGDON

HUNTRESSES	ICONOCLASM	IMMATERIAL	IMPOLITELY	INAUGURATE
HUNTSVILLE	ICONOCLAST	IMMATURELY	IMPORTANCE	INBREEDING
HURDY-GURDY	ICONOLATER	IMMATURITY	IMPORTUNED	INCANDESCE
HURLY-BURLY	ICONOLATRY	IMMEMORIAL	IMPORTUNER	INCAPACITY
HURRICANES	ICONOMATIC	IMMERSIBLE	IMPOSINGLY	INCAPARINA
HURRYINGLY	ICONOSCOPE	IMMIGRANTS	IMPOSITION	INCARNATED
HUSBANDING	IDEALISTIC	IMMIGRATED	IMPOSSIBLE	INCAUTIOUS
HUSBANDMAN	IDEALIZING	IMMIGRATOR	IMPOSSIBLY	INCENDIARY
HUSBANDMEN	IDEATIONAL	IMMINENTLY	IMPOSTROUS	INCENTIVES
HYACINTHUS	IDEMPOTENT	IMMISCIBLE	IMPOSTURES	INCEPTIONS
HYALOPLASM	IDENTIFIED	IMMOBILITY	IMPOTENTLY	INCESSANCY
HYALURONIC	IDENTIFIER	IMMOBILIZE	IMPOUNDAGE	INCESTUOUS
HYBRIDIZER	IDENTIKITS	IMMODERACY	IMPOUNDING	INCHOATION
HYDRANGEAS	IDENTITIES	IMMODERATE	IMPOVERISH	INCHOATIVE
HYDRASTINE	IDEOGRAPHY	IMMODESTLY	IMPREGNATE	INCIDENTAL
HYDRAULICS	IDEOLOGIES	IMMOLATING	IMPRESARIO	INCINERATE
HYDROCORAL	IDEOLOGIST	IMMOLATION	IMPRESSING	INCIPIENCE
HYDROFOILS	IDEOLOGUES	IMMORALIST	IMPRESSION	INCIPIENCY
HYDROGRAPH	IDIOLECTAL	IMMORALITY	IMPRESSIVE	INCISIVELY
HYDROLOGIC	IDIOPATHIC	IMMORTELLE	IMPRIMATUR	INCITATION
HYDROLYSER	IDIOPHONIC	IMMOTILITY	IMPRINTING	INCITEMENT
HYDROLYSIS	IDOLATRIZE	IMMUNIZING	IMPRISONED	INCITINGLY
HYDROLYTIC	IDOLATROUS	IMMUNOLOGY	IMPRISONER	INCIVILITY
HYDROMANCY	IGNES FATUI	IMPAIRMENT	IMPROBABLE	INCLEMENCY
HYDROPONIC	IGNOBILITY	IMPALEMENT	IMPROBABLY	INCLINABLE
HYGIENISTS	IGNOMINIES	IMPALPABLE	IMPROPERLY	INCLOSURES
HYPERBOLAS	IJSSELMEER	IMPANATION	IMPROVABLE	INCLUDABLE
HYPERBOLES	ILL-ADVISED	IMPANELLED	IMPROVISED	INCLUSIONS
HYPERBOLIC	ILLEGALITY	IMPARTIBLE	IMPROVISER	INCOHERENT
HYPERMEDIA	ILLEGALIZE	IMPASSABLE	IMPRUDENCE	INCOMMODED
HYPERSPACE	ILLITERACY	IMPATIENCE	IMPUDENTLY	INCOMPLETE
HYPHENATED	ILLITERATE	IMPEACHING	IMPUISSANT	INCONSTANT
HYPNOTISTS	ILL-NATURED	IMPECCABLE	IMPULSIONS	INCRASSATE
HYPNOTIZED	ILLOCUTION	IMPECCABLY	IMPUNITIES	INCREASING
HYPOCRITES	ILL-STARRED	IMPEDANCES	IMPURITIES	INCREDIBLE
HYPODERMIC	ILL-TREATED	IMPEDIMENT	IMPUTATION	INCREDIBLY
HYPOTENUSE	ILLUMINANT	IMPEDINGLY	IMPUTATIVE	INCREMENTS
HYPOTHESES	ILLUMINATE	IMPENDENCE	IN ABSENTIA	INCRESCENT
HYPOTHESIS	ILLUMINATI	IMPENITENT	INACCURACY	INCUBATING
HYSTERICAL	ILLUMINISM	IMPERATIVE	INACCURATE	INCUBATION
	ILLUMINIST	IMPERIALLY	INACTIVATE	INCUBATIVE
I	ILLUSORILY	IMPERILLED	INACTIVELY	INCUBATORS
IAMBICALLY	ILLUSTRATE	IMPERSONAL	INACTIVITY	INCULCATED
IATROGENIC	IMAGINABLE	IMPERVIOUS	IN ADDITION	INCULCATOR
ICEBREAKER	IMBALANCES	IMPETRATOR	INADEQUACY	INCULPABLE
ICE BREAKER	IMBECILITY	IMPISHNESS	INADEQUATE	INCULPATED
ICE LOLLIES	IMBIBITION	IMPLACABLE	INAMORATAS	INCUMBENCY
ICE-SKATERS	IMBRICATED	IMPLANTING	IN ANY	INCUMBENTS
ICE-SKATING	IMBROGLIOS	IMPLEMENTS	EVENT	INCUNABULA
ICHINOMIYA	IMITATIONS	IMPLICATED	INAPPOSITE	INCURRABLE
ICHTHYOSIS	IMMACULACY	IMPLICITLY	INAPTITUDE	INCURRENCE
ICHTHYOTIC	IMMACULATE	IMPLOSIONS	INARTISTIC	INCURSIONS

INDECENTLY	INEXPERTLY	INGRESSIVE	INOPERABLE	INSTITUTES
INDECISION	INEXPIABLE	INGUSHETIA	INORDINACY	INSTITUTOR
INDECISIVE	INEXPLICIT	INHABITANT	INORDINATE	INSTRUCTED
INDECOROUS	IN EXTREMIS	INHABITING	INOSCULATE	INSTRUCTOR
INDEFINITE	INFALLIBLE	INHALATION	IN-PATIENTS	INSTRUMENT
INDELICACY	INFALLIBLY	INHARMONIC	INQUIETUDE	INSUFFLATE
INDELICATE	INFARCTION	INHERENTLY	INQUISITOR	INSULARISM
INDENTURED	INFATUATED	INHERITING	INSALIVATE	INSULARITY
INDENTURES	INFECTIONS	INHIBITING	INS AND	INSULATING
INDEXATION	INFECTIOUS	INHIBITION	OUTS	INSULATION
INDIAN CORN	INFELICITY	INHIBITIVE	INSANITARY	INSULATORS
INDICATING	INFERENCES	IN HOT	INSATIABLE	INSURANCES
INDICATION	INFERNALLY	WATER	INSATIABLY	INSURGENCE
INDICATIVE	INFIBULATE	INHUMANELY	INSCRIBING	INSURGENCY
INDICATORS	INFIDELITY	INHUMANITY	INSECURELY	INSURGENTS
INDICATORY	INFIELDERS	INHUMATION	INSECURITY	INTANGIBLE
INDICTABLE	INFIGHTING	INIMITABLE	INSEMINATE	INTANGIBLY
INDICTMENT	INFILTRATE	INIMITABLY	INSENSIBLE	INTEGRABLE
INDIGENOUS	INFINITELY	INIQUITIES	INSENSIBLY	INTEGRATED
INDIRECTLY	INFINITIVE	INIQUITOUS	INSENTIENT	INTEGRATOR
INDISCREET	INFINITUDE	INITIALING	INSERTABLE	INTEGUMENT
INDISCRETE	INFLATABLE	INITIALIZE	INSERTIONS	INTELLECTS
INDISPOSED	INFLATEDLY	INITIALLED	INSIDE JOBS	INTENDANCE
INDISTINCT	INFLECTING	INITIATING	INSIDE LANE	INTENDANCY
INDIVIDUAL	INFLECTION	INITIATION	INSIGHTFUL	INTENDMENT
INDOCILITY	INFLECTIVE	INITIATIVE	INSINUATED	INTENTIONS
INDOLENTLY	INFLEXIBLE	INITIATORY	INSINUATOR	INTENTNESS
INDOLOGIST	INFLEXIBLY	INJECTABLE	INSIPIDITY	INTERACTED
INDONESIAN	INFLICTING	INJECTIONS	INSISTENCE	INTER ALIOS
INDOPHENOL	INFLICTION	INJUNCTION	INSOBRIETY	INTERBRAIN
INDUCEMENT	INFLICTIVE	INJUNCTIVE	INSOLATION	INTERBREED
INDUCTANCE	INFLUENCED	INJURY TIME	INSOLENTLY	INTERCEDED
INDUCTIONS	INFLUENCER	INJUSTICES	INSOLVABLE	INTERCEDER
INDULGENCE	INFLUENCES	IN MEMORIAM	INSOLVENCY	INTERDICTS
INDUSTRIAL	INFLUENZAL	INNER CHILD	INSOLVENTS	INTERESTED
INDUSTRIES	INFORMALLY	INNER TUBES	INSOMNIACS	INTERFACED
INEBRIATED	INFORMANTS	INNKEEPERS	INSOMNIOUS	INTERFACES
INEBRIATES	INFORMEDLY	INNOCENTLY	INSOUCIANT	INTERFERED
INEDUCABLE	INFRACLASS	INNOMINATE	INSPECTING	INTERFERER
INEDUCABLY	INFRACTION	INNOVATING	INSPECTION	INTERFERON
INEFFICACY	INFRASONIC	INNOVATION	INSPECTIVE	INTERFLUVE
INELEGANCE	INFREQUENT	INNOVATIVE	INSPECTORS	INTERGRADE
INELIGIBLE	INFRINGING	INNOVATORS	INSPIRABLE	INTERGROUP
INELOQUENT	INFURIATED	INNUENDOES	INSPIRITER	INTERLACED
INEPTITUDE	INFUSORIAL	INNUMERACY	INSTALLING	INTERLAKEN
INEQUALITY	INGESTIBLE	INNUMERATE	INSTALMENT	INTERLEAVE
INEQUITIES	INGLENOOKS	INOCULATED	INSTANCING	INTERLINER
INEVITABLE	INGLORIOUS	INOCULATOR	INSTIGATED	INTERLOPER
INEVITABLY	INGOLSTADT	IN ONE	INSTIGATOR	INTERLUDES
INEXISTENT	INGRATIATE	PIECE	INSTILLING	INTERLUNAR
INEXORABLE	INGREDIENT	IN ONE'S	INSTILMENT	INTERMARRY
INEXORABLY	INGRESSION	CUPS	INSTITUTED	INTERMENTS

INTERMEZZI	INTUITABLE	IRRADIATED	JAM SESSION	JUNCACEOUS
INTERMEZZO	INTUITIONS	IRRADIATOR	JAMSHEDPUR	JUNCTIONAL
INTERMODAL	INUNDATING	IRRATIONAL	JANITORIAL	JUNKETINGS
INTERNALLY	INUNDATION	IRREGULARS	JARDINIERE	JURY-RIGGED
INTERNMENT	INUREDNESS	IRRELATIVE	JAUNTINESS	JUST AS
INTERNODAL	INVAGINATE	IRRELEVANT	JAWBREAKER	WELL
INTERNSHIP	INVALIDATE	IRRELIGION	JAYWALKERS	JUSTICIARY
INTERPHASE	INVALID CAR	IRRESOLUTE	JAYWALKING	JUSTIFYING
INTERPHONE	INVALIDING	IRREVERENT	JEALOUSIES	JUST IN
INTERPLEAD	INVALIDISM	IRRIGATING	JELLY BEANS	CASE
INTERPOSAL	INVALIDITY	IRRIGATION	JELLY ROLLS	JUST-IN-
INTERPOSED	INVALUABLE	IRRIGATIVE	JEOPARDIZE	TIME
INTERPOSER	INVARIABLE	IRRITATING	JERRY-BUILD	JUVENILITY
INTERREGNA	INVARIABLY	IRRITATION	JERRY-BUILT	JUXTAPOSED
INTERSPACE	INVARIANCE	IRRITATIVE	JERSEY CITY	
INTERSTATE	INVEIGHING	IRRUPTIONS	JESUITICAL	**K**
INTERSTICE	INVEIGLING	ISENTROPIC	JET ENGINES	KABARAGOYA
INTERTIDAL	INVENTIBLE	ISKENDERUN	JET-SETTERS	KALGOORLIE
INTERTWINE	INVENTIONS	ISOANTIGEN	JETTISONED	KANSAS CITY
INTERVENED	INVERACITY	ISOCHEIMAL	JIANG ZEMIN	KANTIANISM
INTERVENER	INVERCLYDE	ISOCHRONAL	JIGGERMAST	KAPFENBERG
INTERVIEWS	INVERSIONS	ISOCHROOUS	JINGDEZHEN	KARA-KALPAK
INTERWEAVE	INVERTIBLE	ISOCYANIDE	JINGOISTIC	KARAMANLIS
INTERWOVEN	INVESTABLE	ISODYNAMIC	JITTERBUGS	KARLSKRONA
INTESTINAL	INVESTMENT	ISOGAMETIC	JOB CENTRES	KARYOGAMIC
INTESTINES	INVETERACY	ISOGLOSSAL	JOBSHARING	KARYOLYMPH
IN THE	INVETERATE	ISOGLOTTIC	JOCKSTRAPS	KARYOLYSIS
EVENT	INVIGILATE	ISOLEUCINE	JOCULARITY	KARYOLYTIC
IN THE	INVIGORATE	ISOMETRICS	JOGJAKARTA	KARYOPLASM
MONEY	INVINCIBLE	ISOMORPHIC	JOLLY ROGER	KARYOTYPIC
INTIMACIES	INVINCIBLY	ISOPIESTIC	JOSS STICKS	KASHMIRIAN
INTIMATELY	INVIOLABLE	ISOSEISMAL	JOURNALESE	KAZAKHSTAN
INTIMATING	INVITATION	ISOTHERMAL	JOURNALISM	KEEP TABS
INTIMATION	INVITATORY	ISOTROPOUS	JOURNALIST	ON
INTIMIDATE	INVITINGLY	ISRAELITES	JOURNALIZE	KENILWORTH
INTINCTION	INVOCATION	ITALIANATE	JOURNEYING	KENNELLING
INTOLERANT	INVOCATORY	ITALICIZED	JOURNEYMAN	KENTUCKIAN
INTONATION	INVOLUCRAL	ITCHY PALMS	JOURNEYMEN	KERATINIZE
INTOXICANT	INVOLUTION	ITINERANCY	JOYFULNESS	KERATOTOMY
INTOXICATE	IODIZATION	IVORY TOWER	JOYOUSNESS	KERCHIEFED
IN TRAINING	IODOMETRIC		JUBILANTLY	KERFUFFLES
INTRAMURAL	IONIZATION	**J**	JUBILATION	KERMANSHAH
INTRENCHED	IONOSPHERE		JUDGMENTAL	KERSEYMERE
INTREPIDLY	IRENICALLY	JACKANAPES	JUDICATIVE	KETTLEDRUM
INTRIGUING	IRIDACEOUS	JACKHAMMER	JUDICATORY	KEYBOARDED
INTRODUCED	IRIDECTOMY	JACK-KNIFED	JUDICATURE	KEYBOARDER
INTRODUCER	IRIDESCENT	JACK KNIVES	JUDICIALLY	KEYPUNCHED
INTROSPECT	IRISH STEWS	JACKRABBIT	JUGGERNAUT	KEYPUNCHER
INTROVERTS	IRISHWOMAN	JACK THE	JUIZ DE	KEYPUNCHES
INTRUSIONS	IRONICALLY	LAD	FORA	KHABAROVSK
INTRUSTING	IRONMONGER	JACOBITISM	JUMBLE SALE	KIDNAPPERS
INTUBATION	IRRADIANCE	JAGUARONDI	JUMBLINGLY	KIDNAPPING

KIDNEY BEAN	**L**	LANDSCAPED	LEBENSRAUM	LEUCOPLAST
KIESELGUHR	LABIONASAL	LANDSCAPES	LECTIONARY	LEVERKUSEN
KILMARNOCK	LABIOVELAR	LANDSLIDES	LECTORSHIP	LEVIATHANS
KILOLITRES	LABORATORY	LANGLAUFER	LEEUWARDEN	LEVIGATION
KILOMETRES	LABOR UNION	LANGUISHED	LEFT-HANDED	LEVITATING
KILOMETRIC	LABOUR CAMP	LANGUISHER	LEFT-HANDER	LEVITATION
KIMBERLITE	LABOUR DAYS	LANGUOROUS	LEFT-WINGER	LEXICALITY
KINCARDINE	LABOUREDLY	LANIFEROUS	LEGAL EAGLE	LEXICOLOGY
KINDLINESS	LABYRINTHS	LANTHANIDE	LEGALISTIC	LIBATIONAL
KINDNESSES	LACERATING	LAPAROTOMY	LEGALIZING	LIBERALISM
KINEMATICS	LACERATION	LAP DANCING	LEGATESHIP	LIBERALIST
KINGFISHER	LACERATIVE	LAPIDARIAN	LEGATORIAL	LIBERALITY
KINGLINESS	LACHRYMOSE	LAPIDARIES	LEGIBILITY	LIBERALIZE
KINGMAKERS	LACKLUSTRE	LARGE-SCALE	LEGISLATED	LIBERATING
KING-OF-	LACQUERING	LA ROCHELLE	LEGISLATOR	LIBERATION
ARMS	LACRIMATOR	LARVICIDAL	LEGITIMACY	LIBERATORS
KING'S	LACTESCENT	LARYNGITIC	LEGITIMATE	LIBERTINES
BENCH	LACTIC ACID	LARYNGITIS	LEGITIMISM	LIBIDINOUS
KIRITIMATI	LACTOGENIC	LASCIVIOUS	LEGITIMIST	LIBRARIANS
KIROVOGRAD	LACTOMETER	LAST MINUTE	LEGITIMIZE	LIBRETTIST
KISS OF	LACTOSCOPE	LATECOMERS	LEGUMINOUS	LIBREVILLE
LIFE	LACUNOSITY	LATENT HEAT	LEG-WARMERS	LICENSABLE
KITAKYUSHU	LACUSTRINE	LATTERMOST	LEISHMANIA	LICENTIATE
KITH AND	LADY-KILLER	LAUGHINGLY	LEITMOTIVS	LICENTIOUS
KIN	LADY'S-	LAUNCESTON	LEMNISCATE	LIE IN
KITTIWAKES	SMOCK	LAUNCH PADS	LEMON GRASS	STATE
KLAGENFURT	LAMARCKIAN	LAUNDERING	LEMON SOLES	LIEUTENANT
KLANGFARBE	LAMARCKISM	LAUNDROMAT	LENGTHENED	LIFE CYCLES
KNEECAPPED	LAMASERIES	LAUNDRYMAN	LENGTHENER	LIFEGUARDS
KNEE-LENGTH	LAMBASTING	LAURACEOUS	LENGTHIEST	LIFE JACKET
KNICK-KNACK	LAMBDACISM	LAUREATION	LENGTHWAYS	LIFELESSLY
KNIFE-EDGES	LAMBREQUIN	LAURENTIAN	LENTAMENTE	LIFE-SAVING
KNIGHTHEAD	LAMB'S	LAVATIONAL	LENTICULAR	LIFESTYLES
KNIGHTHOOD	TAILS	LAVATORIAL	LENTISSIMO	LIGHT BULBS
KNOBBLIEST	LAMELLATED	LAVATORIES	LEOPARDESS	LIGHTENING
KNOBKERRIE	LAMENTABLE	LAVISHNESS	LEPIDOLITE	LIGHTERAGE
KNOCKABOUT	LAMENTABLY	LAW-ABIDING	LEPRECHAUN	LIGHTHOUSE
KNOCK-KNEED	LAMINATING	LAW-BREAKER	LEPTOSOMIC	LIGHTNINGS
KOEKSISTER	LAMINATION	LAWFULNESS	LESBIANISM	LIGHTSHIPS
KOMMUNARSK	LAMPOONERY	LAWNMOWERS	LESSEESHIP	LIGHT YEARS
KOMSOMOLSK	LAMPOONING	LAWN TENNIS	LETCHWORTH	LIGNOCAINE
KOOKABURRA	LAMPSHADES	LAWRENCIUM	LETHBRIDGE	LIKELIHOOD
KRAGUJEVAC	LANCASHIRE	LAY BROTHER	LET'S FACE	LIKE-MINDED
KRAMATORSK	LANCEOLATE	LAY FIGURES	IT	LIKENESSES
KREMENCHUG	LAND AGENTS	LAYPERSONS	LETTER BOMB	LILIACEOUS
KRIEGSPIEL	LAND FORCES	LAY READERS	LETTERHEAD	LIMICOLINE
KRISHNAISM	LANDING NET	LAY SISTERS	LEUCOCYTES	LIMICOLOUS
KRUGERRAND	LANDLADIES	LEADERSHIP	LEUCOCYTIC	LIMITARIAN
KU KLUX	LANDLOCKED	LEAF-HOPPER	LEUCODERMA	LIMITATION
KLAN	LANDLUBBER	LEAFLETING	LEUCOMAINE	LIMOUSINES
	LANDMASSES	LEASEBACKS	LEUCOPENIA	LINEAMENTS
	LAND ROVERS	LEAVENINGS	LEUCOPENIC	LINECASTER

LINGUIFORM	LOCALISTIC	LOWBROWISM	MACHINE GUN	MALEFACTOR
LINGUISTIC	LOCALITIES	LOWER CLASS	MACHINISTS	MALEFICENT
LINLITHGOW	LOCALIZING	LOWER HOUSE	MACH NUMBER	MALEVOLENT
LINSEED OIL	LOCKER ROOM	LOWERINGLY	MACKINTOSH	MALFEASANT
LIPOMATOUS	LOCK KEEPER	LOWLANDERS	MACROCOSMS	MALIGNANCY
LIPOPHILIC	LOCKSMITHS	LOW-PITCHED	MACROCYTIC	MALINGERED
LIP-READING	LOCKSTITCH	LOW PROFILE	MACROGRAPH	MALINGERER
LIP SERVICE	LOCOMOTION	LOW-TENSION	MACROPHAGE	MALODOROUS
LIQUEFYING	LOCOMOTIVE	LOXODROMIC	MACROSPORE	MALPIGHIAN
LIQUESCENT	LOCULATION	LUBRICANTS	MACULATION	MALTED MILK
LIQUIDATED	LODESTONES	LUBRICATED	MADAGASCAN	MALTHUSIAN
LIQUIDATOR	LOGANBERRY	LUBRICATOR	MADAGASCAR	MALTREATED
LIQUIDIZED	LOGARITHMS	LUBRICIOUS	MADCHESTER	MALTREATER
LIQUIDIZER	LOGGERHEAD	LUBUMBASHI	MADREPORAL	MALVACEOUS
LIQUORICES	LOGICALITY	LUCUBRATOR	MAELSTROMS	MANAGEABLE
LISSOMNESS	LOGISTICAL	LUGGAGE VAN	MAGIC WANDS	MANAGEABLY
LISTENABLE	LOGOGRAPHY	LUGUBRIOUS	MAGISTRACY	MANAGEMENT
LISTLESSLY	LOGOPAEDIC	LULUABOURG	MAGISTRATE	MANAGERESS
LIST PRICES	LOGORRHOEA	LUMBERJACK	MAGNA CARTA	MANAGERIAL
LITERALISM	LOGROLLING	LUMBER-ROOM	MAGNETITIC	MANCHESTER
LITERALIST	LOINCLOTHS	LUMBERYARD	MAGNETIZED	MANCHINEEL
LITERARILY	LOIR-ET-	LUMBRICOID	MAGNETIZER	MANCHURIAN
LITERATELY	CHER	LUMINARIES	MAGNIFIERS	MANCUNIANS
LITERATION	LONELINESS	LUMINOSITY	MAGNIFYING	MANEUVERED
LITERATURE	LONGBENTON	LUMINOUSLY	MAGNITUDES	MAN FRIDAYS
LITHOGRAPH	LONGHAIRED	LUMISTEROL	MAGNUM OPUS	MANFULNESS
LITHOLOGIC	LONG-HEADED	LUNAR MONTH	MAIDENHAIR	MANGOSTEEN
LITHOMARGE	LONG ISLAND	LURCHINGLY	MAIDENHEAD	MANHANDLED
LITHOPHYTE	LONGITUDES	LUSCIOUSLY	MAIDENHOOD	MANIACALLY
LITHOTOMIC	LONG-JUMPER	LUSTRATION	MAIDEN NAME	MANICURING
LITHOTRITY	LONGWINDED	LUSTRATIVE	MAIN CHANCE	MANICURIST
LITHUANIAN	LOOK-ALIKES	LUSTREWARE	MAIN CLAUSE	MANIFESTED
LITIGATING	LOPHOPHORE	LUSTROUSLY	MAINFRAMES	MANIFESTLY
LITIGATION	LOQUACIOUS	LUTINE BELL	MAINLINING	MANIFESTOS
LITTERBINS	LORDLINESS	LUXEMBOURG	MAINSPRING	MANIFOLDER
LITTERLOUT	LORGNETTES	LUXURIANCE	MAINSTREAM	MANIPULATE
LITTLE BELT	LORRY PARKS	LUXURIATED	MAINTAINED	MANNEQUINS
LITTLE ROCK	LOS ANGELES	LYCOPODIUM	MAINTAINER	MANNERISMS
LITURGICAL	LOSS LEADER	LYMPHOCYTE	MAISONETTE	MANOEUVRED
LIVABILITY	LOST CAUSES	LYOPHILIZE	MAJOR-DOMOS	MANOEUVRER
LIVELIHOOD	LOTUS-EATER		MAJORETTES	MANOEUVRES
LIVELINESS	LOUDHAILER	**M**	MAJORITIES	MAN OF
LIVING ROOM	LOUDMOUTHS		MAJOR SUITS	STRAW
LIVINGSTON	LOUISVILLE	MAASTRICHT	MAJUSCULAR	MANOMETERS
LIVING WAGE	LOUNGE BARS	MAASTRICHT	MAKE A	MANOMETRIC
LIVING WILL	LOUNGE SUIT	MACADAMIZE	POINT	MANOR HOUSE
LLANGOLLEN	LOVABILITY	MACEBEARER	MAKESHIFTS	MANSERVANT
LOADSTONES	LOVE AFFAIR	MACEDONIAN	MAKEWEIGHT	MANTELTREE
LOBOTOMIES	LOVELINESS	MACERATING	MALACOLOGY	MANTICALLY
LOBSTERPOT	LOVEMAKING	MACERATION	MALADDRESS	MANUSCRIPT
LOBULATION	LOVING CUPS	MACERATIVE	MALAPROPOS	MANZANILLA
LOCAL DERBY	LOW-ALCOHOL	MACHINABLE	MALCONTENT	MARASCHINO

MARCESCENT	MASTICABLE	MEDICATIVE	MERCAPTIDE	METHYLDOPA
MARCH-PASTS	MASTICATED	MEDIOCRITY	MERCIFULLY	METICULOUS
MARCONI RIG	MASTICATOR	MEDITATING	MERIDIONAL	METOESTRUS
MARE'S	MASTURBATE	MEDITATION	MERRYMAKER	METRICALLY
NESTS	MATCHBOARD	MEDITATIVE	MERSEY BEAT	METRICIZED
MARGARITAS	MATCHBOXES	MEDIUM WAVE	MERSEYSIDE	METRIC TONS
MARGINALIA	MATCHMAKER	MEDULLATED	MESENCHYME	METRONOMES
MARGINALLY	MATCH POINT	MEERSCHAUM	MESENTERIC	METRONOMIC
MARGUERITE	MATCHSTICK	MEFLOQUINE	MESENTERON	METRONYMIC
MARINATING	MATERIALLY	MEGAGAMETE	MESITYLENE	METROPOLIS
MARINATION	MATERNALLY	MEGALITHIC	MESMERISTS	METTLESOME
MARIONETTE	MATO GROSSO	MEGAPHONES	MESMERIZED	MEXICO CITY
MARKEDNESS	MATOZINHOS	MEGAPHONIC	MESMERIZER	MEZZANINES
MARKETABLE	MATRIARCHS	MEGASPORIC	MESOCRATIC	MEZZOTINTS
MARKETABLY	MATRIARCHY	MEITNERIUM	MESODERMAL	MIAMI BEACH
MARKETEERS	MATRICIDAL	MELANCHOLY	MESOLITHIC	MICHAELMAS
MARKET TOWN	MATRICIDES	MELANESIAN	MESOMORPHY	MICROCHIPS
MARKSWOMAN	MATRILOCAL	MELANISTIC	MESOPHYTIC	MICROCLINE
MARLACIOUS	MATTERHORN	MELANOCYTE	MESOSPHERE	MICROCOSMS
MARQUISATE	MATTRESSES	MELANOSITY	MESOTHORAX	MICROCYTIC
MARROWBONE	MATURATION	MELBURNIAN	MESSENGERS	MICROFICHE
MARSHALING	MATURATIVE	MELIACEOUS	METABOLISM	MICROFILMS
MARSHALLED	MAUDLINISM	MELIORABLE	METABOLITE	MICROGRAPH
MARSHALLER	MAUNDERING	MELIORATOR	METABOLIZE	MICROMETER
MARSHINESS	MAURITANIA	MELISMATIC	METACARPAL	MICROMETRY
MARSUPIALS	MAUSOLEUMS	MELLOPHONE	METACARPUS	MICRONESIA
MARTELLATO	MAXILLIPED	MELLOWNESS	METACENTRE	MICROPHONE
MARTENSITE	MAXIMALIST	MELODRAMAS	METAFEMALE	MICROPHYTE
MARTIAL ART	MAXIMIZING	MELTING POT	METAGALAXY	MICROPRINT
MARTIALISM	MAXISINGLE	MEMBERSHIP	METALLURGY	MICROPYLAR
MARTIALIST	MAYONNAISE	MEMBRANOUS	METAMERISM	MICROSCOPE
MARTIAL LAW	MAYORESSES	MEMORANDUM	METAPHORIC	MICROSCOPY
MARTINGALE	MEADOWLARK	MEMORIZING	METAPHRASE	MICROSEISM
MARTINICAN	MEAGRENESS	MENACINGLY	METAPHRAST	MICROSOMAL
MARTINIQUE	MEANDERING	MENAGERIES	METAPHYSIC	MICROSPORE
MARVELLING	MEANINGFUL	MENARCHEAL	METAPLASIA	MICROTOMIC
MARVELLOUS	MEANS TESTS	MENDACIOUS	METASTABLE	MICROTONAL
MARVELMENT	MEASLINESS	MENDICANCY	METASTASIS	MICROWAVES
MARXIANISM	MEASURABLE	MENDICANTS	METASTATIC	MIDAS TOUCH
MASCARPONE	MEASURABLY	MENINGITIC	METATARSUS	MIDDELBURG
MASOCHISTS	MEASUREDLY	MENINGITIS	METATHEORY	MIDDLE-AGED
MASQUERADE	MECHANICAL	MEN OF	METATHESIS	MIDDLE AGES
MASSACRING	MECHANISMS	STRAW	METATHETIC	MIDDLEBROW
MASSASAUGA	MECHANIZED	MENOPAUSAL	METATHORAX	MIDDLE EAST
MASSETERIC	MECHANIZER	MENOPAUSIC	METEORITES	MIDDLE NAME
MASTECTOMY	MECONOPSIS	MENSTRUATE	METEORITIC	MIDDLE WEST
MASTER CARD	MEDALLIONS	MENSTRUOUS	METHIONINE	MIDLOTHIAN
MASTERHOOD	MEDALLISTS	MENSURABLE	METHODICAL	MIDSECTION
MASTER KEYS	MEDDLESOME	MENTAL AGES	METHODISTS	MIDSHIPMAN
MASTERMIND	MEDDLINGLY	MENTAL NOTE	METHODIZER	MIDSHIPMEN
MASTERSHIP	MEDICAMENT	MENTIONING	METHUSELAH	MIDWESTERN
MASTERWORK	MEDICATION	MERCANTILE	METHYLATOR	MIGHTINESS

MIGNONETTE	MINUTE HAND	MITIGATIVE	MONOCLINAL	MORALISTIC
MIGRAINOID	MINUTENESS	MITTERRAND	MONOCLINIC	MORALITIES
MIGRATIONS	MIRACIDIAL	MIXABILITY	MONOCRATIC	MORALIZERS
MILEOMETER	MIRACIDIUM	MIXED GRILL	MONOCYCLIC	MORALIZING
MILESTONES	MIRACULOUS	MIXOLYDIAN	MONOCYTOID	MORATORIUM
MILITANTLY	MIRTHFULLY	MIZZENMAST	MONOECIOUS	MORAYSHIRE
MILITARILY	MISAPPLIED	MOBILE HOME	MONOGAMIST	MORBIDNESS
MILITARISM	MISBEHAVED	MOBILIZING	MONOGAMOUS	MORDACIOUS
MILITARIST	MISBEHAVER	MOBOCRATIC	MONOGENOUS	MORDVINIAN
MILITARIZE	MISCALLING	MOCK-HEROIC	MONOGRAPHS	MORGANATIC
MILITATING	MISCARRIED	MODERATELY	MONOGYNIST	MOROSENESS
MILITATION	MISCASTING	MODERATING	MONOGYNOUS	MORPHEUSES
MILITIAMAN	MISCELLANY	MODERATION	MONOHYBRID	MORPHINISM
MILK FLOATS	MISCHANCES	MODERATORS	MONOLITHIC	MORPHOLOGY
MILK SHAKES	MISCH METAL	MODERNISMS	MONOLOGIST	MORTAL SINS
MILK TOOTHS	MISCONDUCT	MODERNISTS	MONOLOGUES	MORTGAGEES
MILLENNIAL	MISCOUNTED	MODERNIZED	MONOMANIAC	MORTGAGING
MILLENNIUM	MISCREANTS	MODERNIZER	MONOMEROUS	MORTGAGORS
MILLEPEDES	MISERICORD	MODERNNESS	MONOPHOBIA	MORTICIANS
MILLESIMAL	MISFORTUNE	MODIFIABLE	MONOPHOBIC	MORTIFYING
MILLIGRAMS	MISGIVINGS	MODISHNESS	MONOPHONIC	MORTUARIES
MILLILITRE	MISHANDLED	MODULATING	MONOPLANES	MOSQUITOES
MILLIMETRE	MISHEARING	MODULATION	MONOPLEGIA	MOSTAGANEM
MILLIONTHS	MISJOINDER	MODULATIVE	MONOPLEGIC	MOTHERHOOD
MILLIPEDES	MISJUDGING	MOGADISCIO	MONOPODIAL	MOTHERLESS
MILLSTONES	MISLEADING	MOHAMMEDAN	MONOPODIUM	MOTHER'S
MILLSTREAM	MISMANAGED	MOISTENING	MONOPOLIES	BOY
MILLWHEELS	MISMANAGER	MOISTURIZE	MONOPOLISM	MOTHER'S
MILLWORKER	MISMATCHED	MOLLIFYING	MONOPOLIST	DAY
MILLWRIGHT	MISMATCHES	MOLLUSCOID	MONOPOLIZE	MOTHER-TO-
MILOMETERS	MISOGAMIST	MOLYBDENUM	MONOPTEROS	BE
MIMEOGRAPH	MISOGYNIST	MONADISTIC	MONOTHEISM	MOTHERWELL
MINATORILY	MISOGYNOUS	MONADOLOGY	MONOTHEIST	MOTHERWORT
MINDLESSLY	MISOLOGIST	MONANDROUS	MONOTONOUS	MOTIONLESS
MIND READER	MISPLACING	MONANTHOUS	MONOVALENT	MOTIVATING
MINEFIELDS	MISPRINTED	MONARCHIES	MONSIGNORS	MOTIVATION
MINERALIZE	MISPRISION	MONARCHISM	MONSTRANCE	MOTIVATIVE
MINERALOGY	MISQUOTING	MONARCHIST	MONTE CARLO	MOTIVELESS
MINERAL OIL	MISREADING	MONEGASQUE	MONTEGO BAY	MOTONEURON
MINESTRONE	MISSIONARY	MONETARISM	MONTENEGRO	MOTORBIKES
MINIATURES	MISSOURIAN	MONETARIST	MONTEVIDEO	MOTORBOATS
MINIMALIST	MISSPELLED	MONEYBOXES	MONTGOMERY	MOTORCADES
MINIMIZING	MISSTATING	MONEYMAKER	MONTMARTRE	MOTORCYCLE
MINISTERED	MISSUPPOSE	MONEY ORDER	MONTPELIER	MOTORIZING
MINISTRANT	MISTAKABLE	MONGRELISM	MONTSERRAT	MOTOR LODGE
MINISTRIES	MISTAKABLY	MONGRELIZE	MONUMENTAL	MOTS JUSTES
MINNESOTAN	MISTAKENLY	MONILIFORM	MONZONITIC	MOULDBOARD
MINORITIES	MISTRESSES	MONITORIAL	MOONFLOWER	MOULDERING
MINOR SUITS	MISTRUSTED	MONITORING	MOONSCAPES	MOULDINESS
MINSTRELSY	MISTRUSTER	MONKEY NUTS	MOONSTONES	MOUNTEBANK
MINT JULEPS	MITIGATING	MONOCARPIC	MOONSTRUCK	MOURNFULLY
MINUSCULAR	MITIGATION	MONOCHROME	MOOT POINTS	MOUSETRAPS

MOUSSELINE	MYCETOZOAN	NATURALIZE	NETIQUETTE	NIHILISTIC
MOUSTACHES	MYCOLOGIST	NATUROPATH	NETTLE RASH	NIMBLENESS
MOUTH ORGAN	MYCOPLASMA	NAUGHTIEST	NETTLESOME	NINCOMPOOP
MOUTHPIECE	MYCORRHIZA	NAUSEATING	NETWORKING	NINETEENTH
MOVABILITY	MYCOSTATIN	NAUSEATION	NEURECTOMY	NINETIETHS
MOVIE STARS	MYOCARDIAL	NAUSEOUSLY	NEUROBLAST	NINETY-NINE
MOVING VANS	MYOCARDIUM	NAUTICALLY	NEUROCOELE	NINGSIA HUI
MOZAMBIQUE	MYOGRAPHIC	NAVIGATING	NEUROGENIC	NIPPLEWORT
MOZZARELLA	MYOPICALLY	NAVIGATION	NEUROLEMMA	NISSEN HUTS
MPUMALANGA	MYRIAPODAN	NAVIGATORS	NEUROPATHY	NITPICKERS
MUCKRAKERS	MYRTACEOUS	NEAPOLITAN	NEUROTOXIN	NITPICKING
MUCKRAKING	MYSTAGOGIC	NEAR MISSES	NEUTRALISM	NITRIC ACID
MUDDLINGLY	MYSTAGOGUE	NEAR THINGS	NEUTRALIST	NITROMETER
MUDSKIPPER	MYSTERIOUS	NEBULOSITY	NEUTRALITY	NO-ACCOUNTS
MUDSLINGER	MYSTICALLY	NEBULOUSLY	NEUTRALIZE	NOBEL PRIZE
MUHAMMADAN	MYSTIFYING	NECROLATRY	NEUTROPHIL	NOBILITIES
MUJAHEDDIN	MYTHICIZER	NECROMANCY	NEVER-NEVER	NO-MAN'S-
MULBERRIES	MYTHOMANIA	NECROPHOBE	NEW BEDFORD	LAND
MULIEBRITY	MYTHOPOEIA	NECROPOLIS	NEW BRITAIN	NOM DE
MULISHNESS	MYTHOPOEIC	NEEDLEFISH	NEW ENGLAND	PLUME
MULTIBIRTH	MYXOEDEMIC	NEEDLESSLY	NEWFANGLED	NOMINALISM
MULTIMEDIA	MYXOMATOUS	NEEDLEWORK	NEW IRELAND	NOMINALIST
MULTIPLANE	MYXOMYCETE	NE'ER-DO-	NEW ORLEANS	NOMINATING
MULTIPLIED		WELL	NEWS AGENCY	NOMINATION
MULTIPLIER	**N**	NEGATIVELY	NEWSAGENTS	NOMINATIVE
MULTISTAGE	NAIL-BITING	NEGATIVING	NEWSCASTER	NOMOGRAPHY
MULTITUDES	NAIRNSHIRE	NEGATIVISM	NEWSHOUNDS	NOMOLOGIST
MUMBLINGLY	NAMBY-PAMBY	NEGATIVIST	NEWSLETTER	NOMOTHETIC
MUMBO JUMBO	NAMEPLATES	NEGLECTFUL	NEWSPAPERS	NONALIGNED
MUMMIFYING	NANNY GOATS	NEGLECTING	NEWSREADER	NONCHALANT
MUNIFICENT	NANOSECOND	NEGLIGENCE	NEWSSHEETS	NONDRINKER
MURPHY'S	NAPKIN RING	NEGLIGIBLE	NEWSSTANDS	NONESUCHES
LAW	NAPOLEONIC	NEGLIGIBLY	NEWSVENDOR	NONETHICAL
MUSCOVITES	NARCISSISM	NEGOTIABLE	NEWSWORTHY	NONFACTUAL
MUSCULARLY	NARCISSIST	NEGOTIATED	NEWTON'S	NONFERROUS
MUSHROOMED	NARCOLEPSY	NEGOTIATOR	LAW	NONFICTION
MUSICAL BOX	NARRATABLE	NEIGHBOURS	NEW ZEALAND	NONJOINDER
MUSIC HALLS	NARRATIONS	NEMATOCYST	NICARAGUAN	NONMEDICAL
MUSICOLOGY	NARRATIVES	NEOLOGICAL	NICKELLING	NO-NONSENSE
MUSKETEERS	NARROW BOAT	NEOLOGISMS	NICKNAMING	NONPAREILS
MUSKETRIES	NARROWNESS	NEON LIGHTS	NICOTINISM	NONPAYMENT
MUSTACHIOS	NASTURTIUM	NEOPLASTIC	NIDICOLOUS	NONPLUSSED
MUSTARD GAS	NATATIONAL	NEPENTHEAN	NIDIFUGOUS	NONSMOKERS
MUTABILITY	NATIONALLY	NEPHOGRAPH	NIGHTCLUBS	NONSMOKING
MUTATIONAL	NATIONHOOD	NEPHOSCOPE	NIGHTDRESS	NONSTARTER
MUTILATING	NATIONWIDE	NEPHRALGIA	NIGHTLIGHT	NONSTATIVE
MUTILATION	NATIVISTIC	NEPHRALGIC	NIGHTMARES	NON-STRIKER
MUTILATIVE	NATIVITIES	NEPHRIDIAL	NIGHTSHADE	NONTYPICAL
MUTINOUSLY	NATTERJACK	NEPHRIDIUM	NIGHT SHIFT	NONVIOLENT
MUTUAL FUND	NATURAL GAS	NEPHROTOMY	NIGHTSHIRT	NORMALIZED
MYASTHENIA	NATURALISM	NEPOTISTIC	NIGHTSTICK	NORRKOPING
MYASTHENIC	NATURALIST	NETHERMOST	NIGRESCENT	NORTHBOUND

NORTHERNER
NORTH POLES
NORTHWARDS
NOSEBLEEDS
NOSEDIVING
NOSOGRAPHY
NOSOLOGIST
NOSTOLOGIC
NOSY PARKER
NOTABILITY
NOTARIZING
NOTATIONAL
NOTEWORTHY
NOTICEABLE
NOTICEABLY
NOTIFIABLE
NOTTINGHAM
NOUAKCHOTT
NOURISHING
NOVACULITE
NOVA SCOTIA
NOVELETTES
NOVELISTIC
NOVITIATES
NUCLEATION
NUCLEONICS
NUCLEOSIDE
NUCLEOTIDE
NUDIBRANCH
NULLIFYING
NUMBERLESS
NUMBSKULLS
NUMERATION
NUMERATIVE
NUMERATORS
NUMEROLOGY
NUMEROUSLY
NUMISMATIC
NUMMULITIC
NUNCIATURE
NURSELINGS
NURSEMAIDS
NURSERYMAN
NURSERYMEN
NURTURABLE
NUTATIONAL
NUTCRACKER
NUTRITIOUS
NYCTALOPIA
NYCTINASTY
NYMPHOLEPT

O
OAFISHNESS
OAST HOUSES
OBDURATELY
OBEDIENTLY
OBEISANCES
OBELISKOID
OBERHAUSEN
OBFUSCATED
OBITUARIES
OBITUARIST
OBJECTIONS
OBJECTIVES
OBJETS
D'ART
OBJURGATOR
OBLIGATING
OBLIGATION
OBLIGATIVE
OBLIGATORY
OBLIGINGLY
OBLITERATE
OBSEQUIOUS
OBSERVABLE
OBSERVABLY
OBSERVANCE
OBSESSIONS
OBSESSIVES
OBSTETRICS
OBSTRUCTED
OBSTRUCTER
OBTAINABLE
OBTAINMENT
OBTUSENESS
OBVOLUTION
OBVOLUTIVE
OCCASIONAL
OCCASIONED
OCCIDENTAL
OCCUPATION
OCCURRENCE
OCEANARIUM
OCEANGOING
OCEANOLOGY
OCELLATION
OCHLOCRACY
OCTAHEDRAL
OCTAHEDRON
OCTAMEROUS
OCTANGULAR
OCTAVALENT
OCTODECIMO

OCULOMOTOR
ODALISQUES
ODD-PINNATE
ODIOUSNESS
ODONTALGIA
ODONTALGIC
ODONTOLOGY
OEDEMATOUS
OENOLOGIST
OESOPHAGUS
OESTRADIOL
OFFENSIVES
OFFICE BOYS
OFFICIALLY
OFFICIATED
OFFICIATOR
OFF-LICENCE
OFF-LOADING
OFF-PUTTING
OFFSETTING
OFF THE
CUFF
OFF THE
HOOK
OFF-THE-
WALL
OIL-BEARING
OIL TANKERS
OLDE WORLDE
OLD MAIDISH
OLD MASTERS
OLD SCHOOLS
OLD SCRATCH
OLEAGINOUS
OLEOGRAPHY
OLIGARCHIC
OLIGOCLASE
OLIGOPSONY
OLIGURETIC
OLIVACEOUS
OLIVE GREEN
OMMATIDIAL
OMMATIDIUM
OMNIPOTENT
OMNISCIENT
OMNIVOROUS
ONCOLOGIST
ONE ANOTHER
ONE-MAN
BAND
ONE-SIDEDLY
ONOMASTICS

ONSLAUGHTS
ON THE
ALERT
ON THE
CARDS
ON THE
ROCKS
ON THE
ROPES
ON THE
SPREE
ON THE
WAGON
OOPHORITIC
OOPHORITIS
OOPS-A-
DAISY
OPALESCENT
OPAQUENESS
OPEN-HANDED
OPEN LETTER
OPEN MARKET
OPEN-MINDED
OPEN SEASON
OPEN SECRET
OPEN SESAME
OPERA BUFFA
OPERA HOUSE
OPERATIONS
OPERATIVES
OPERETTIST
OPHICLEIDE
OPHTHALMIA
OPHTHALMIC
OPPILATION
OPPOSINGLY
OPPOSITION
OPPRESSING
OPPRESSION
OPPRESSIVE
OPPRESSORS
OPPROBRIUM
OPTICAL ART
OPTIMISTIC
OPTIMIZING
OPTIONALLY
OPTOMETRIC
ORANGEWOOD
ORANGUTANG
ORATORICAL
ORCHESTRAL
ORCHESTRAS

ORDER PAPER
ORDINANCES
ORDINARILY
ORDINATION
ORDONNANCE
ORDOVICIAN
ORGANICISM
ORGANICIST
ORGANISMAL
ORGANIZERS
ORGANIZING
ORGANOLOGY
ORIENTATED
ORIGINALLY
ORIGINATED
ORIGINATOR
ORIMULSION
ORNAMENTAL
ORNAMENTED
ORNATENESS
ORNITHOPOD
ORNITHOSIS
OROGRAPHER
OROGRAPHIC
OROLOGICAL
ORPHANAGES
ORTHOCLASE
ORTHOGENIC
ORTHOGONAL
OSCILLATED
OSCILLATOR
OSCULATION
OSCULATORY
OSMIRIDIUM
OSMOMETRIC
OSSIFEROUS
OSTENSIBLE
OSTENSIBLY
OSTEOBLAST
OSTEOCLAST
OSTEOPATHS
OSTEOPATHY
OSTEOPHYTE
OSTRACIZED
OSTRACIZER
OSTRACODAN
OTOLOGICAL
OUANANICHE
OUBLIETTES
OUIJA BOARD
OUTBALANCE
OUTBIDDING

OUTBRAVING
OUTCLASSED
OUTFIELDER
OUTFITTERS
OUTFITTING
OUTFLANKED
OUTGENERAL
OUTGROWING
OUTGROWTHS
OUT-HERODED
OUTLANDISH
OUTLASTING
OUT OF
  COURT
OUT OF
  DOORS
OUT OF
  ORDER
OUT OF
  PLACE
OUT OF
  SIGHT
OUT OF
  SORTS
OUTPATIENT
OUTPERFORM
OUTPLAYING
OUTPOINTED
OUTPOURING
OUTRAGEOUS
OUTRANKING
OUTRIGGERS
OUTRIVALED
OUTRUNNING
OUTSELLING
OUTSHINING
OUTSMARTED
OUTSTARING
OUTSTATION
OUTSTAYING
OUTSTRETCH
OUTSWINGER
OUTTALKING
OUTWEIGHED
OUTWITTING
OUTWORKERS
OVARIOTOMY
OVERACTING
OVERACTIVE
OVERARCHED
OVERBOOKED
OVERBURDEN

OVERCHARGE
OVERCOMING
OVERDOSAGE
OVERDOSING
OVERDRAFTS
OVEREXPOSE
OVERFLIGHT
OVERFLOWED
OVERFLYING
OVERHAULED
OVERIJSSEL
OVERLAPPED
OVERLOADED
OVERLOOKED
OVERMANNED
OVERMASTER
OVERMATTER
OVERPASSES
OVERPLAYED
OVERRATING
OVERRIDDEN
OVERRIDING
OVERRULING
OVERSEEING
OVERSHADOW
OVERSIGHTS
OVERSPILLS
OVERSPREAD
OVERSTATED
OVERSTAYED
OVERSTRUNG
OVERTAXING
OVER THE
  TOP
OVERTHROWN
OVERTHROWS
OVERTHRUST
OVERTOPPED
OVERTURNED
OVERWEIGHT
OVERWORKED
OVIPOSITOR
OVULATIONS
OXIDIMETRY
OXYCEPHALY
OXYGENATED
OXYGENIZER
OXYGEN MASK
OXYGEN TENT
OYSTER BEDS
OZONOLYSIS

P
PACE BOWLER
PACEMAKERS
PACHYDERMS
PACIFIC RIM
PACK ANIMAL
PACKSADDLE
PACKTHREAD
PADDLEFISH
PADLOCKING
PAEDERASTS
PAEDERASTY
PAEDIATRIC
PAGANISTIC
PAGINATION
PAILLASSES
PAINKILLER
PAINLESSLY
PAINTBRUSH
PAKISTANIS
PALAEOCENE
PALAEOGENE
PALAEOLITH
PALAEOZOIC
PALANQUINS
PALATALIZE
PALATIALLY
PALATINATE
PALEACEOUS
PALIMPSEST
PALINDROME
PALLBEARER
PALLIASSES
PALLIATING
PALLIATION
PALLIATIVE
PALLIDNESS
PALMACEOUS
PALMETTOES
PALM SUNDAY
PALPATIONS
PALPEBRATE
PALPITATED
PALSY-WALSY
PALTRINESS
PALYNOLOGY
PANAMA CITY
PANAMANIAN
PAN-ARABISM
PANCAKE DAY
PANCREASES
PANCREATIC

PANCREATIN
PANEGYRICS
PANEGYRIST
PANEGYRIZE
PANELLISTS
PANGENESIS
PANGENETIC
PANHANDLED
PANHANDLER
PANHANDLES
PANICULATE
PANJANDRUM
PANTALOONS
PANTHEISTS
PANTOGRAPH
PANTOMIMES
PANTOMIMIC
PAPANDREOU
PAPAVERINE
PAPERBACKS
PAPERBOARD
PAPER CHASE
PAPER CLIPS
PAPERINESS
PAPER KNIFE
PAPER MONEY
PAPER TIGER
PAPISTICAL
PARABIOSIS
PARABIOTIC
PARABOLIST
PARABOLIZE
PARABOLOID
PARACHUTED
PARACHUTES
PARADIDDLE
PARAGRAPHS
PARAGUAYAN
PARALLELED
PARALOGISM
PARALOGIST
PARALYSING
PARALYTICS
PARAMARIBO
PARAMECIUM
PARAMEDICS
PARAMETERS
PARAMETRIC
PARAMNESIA
PARANOIACS
PARANORMAL
PARAPHRASE

PARAPHYSIS
PARAPLEGIA
PARAPLEGIC
PARAPODIUM
PARAPRAXIS
PARASELENE
PARASITISM
PARASITIZE
PARASITOID
PARASTICHY
PARATACTIC
PARATROOPS
PARBOILING
PARCELLING
PARCEL POST
PARCHMENTS
PARDONABLE
PARDONABLY
PARENCHYMA
PARENTERAL
PARENTHOOD
PARI-MUTUEL
PARISH-PUMP
PARKING LOT
PARK KEEPER
PARLIAMENT
PARLOR CARS
PARONYMOUS
PAROXYSMAL
PARRICIDAL
PARRICIDES
PARROTFISH
PARSONAGES
PARTIALITY
PARTICIPLE
PARTICULAR
PARTITIONS
PARTITIVES
PARTNERING
PARTRIDGES
PARTURIENT
PARTY LINES
PARTY PIECE
PARTY WALLS
PARVOVIRUS
PASQUINADE
PASSAGEWAY
PASSENGERS
PASSIONATE
PASTEBOARD
PASTELLIST
PASTEURISM

PASTEURIZE	PEDESTRIAN	PEPPER POTS	PERITONEAL	PERVERTING
PAST MASTER	PEDIATRICS	PEPPERWORT	PERITONEUM	PESCADORES
PASTY-FACED	PEDICULATE	PEPSINOGEN	PERITRICHA	PESSIMISTS
PATCHINESS	PEDICULOUS	PEPTIZABLE	PERIWINKLE	PESTICIDAL
PATCHWORKS	PEDICURIST	PEPTONIZER	PERMAFROST	PESTICIDES
PATENTABLE	PEDIMENTAL	PERACIDITY	PERMANENCE	PESTILENCE
PATERNALLY	PEDOLOGIST	PERCEIVING	PERMANENCY	PETERSBURG
PATHFINDER	PEEPING TOM	PERCENTAGE	PERMANENTS	PETIT FOURS
PATHOGENIC	PEGMATITIC	PERCENTILE	PERMEATING	PETITIONED
PATISSERIE	PEJORATION	PERCEPTION	PERMEATION	PETITIONER
PATRIARCHS	PEJORATIVE	PERCEPTIVE	PERMEATIVE	PETIT POINT
PATRIARCHY	PELLAGROUS	PERCEPTUAL	PERMETHRIN	PETITS POIS
PATRICIANS	PELLICULAR	PERCIPIENT	PERMISSION	PETRIFYING
PATRICIATE	PELLUCIDLY	PERCOLATED	PERMISSIVE	PETROGLYPH
PATRICIDAL	PENALIZING	PERCOLATOR	PERMITTING	PETROLATUM
PATRICIDES	PENCILLING	PERCUSSION	PERNAMBUCO	PETROPOLIS
PATRILOCAL	PENDENTIVE	PERCUSSIVE	PERNICIOUS	PETTICOATS
PATRIOTISM	PENDERECKI	PEREMPTORY	PERNICKETY	PETULANTLY
PATROL CARS	PENETRABLE	PERENNIALS	PERORATION	PHAGOCYTES
PATROLLING	PENETRALIA	PERFECTING	PEROXIDASE	PHAGOCYTIC
PATRONIZED	PENETRANCE	PERFECTION	PERPETRATE	PHAGOMANIA
PATRONIZER	PENETRATED	PERFECTIVE	PERPETUATE	PHALANGEAL
PATRONYMIC	PENETRATOR	PERFIDIOUS	PERPETUITY	PHALANGIST
PATTERNING	PEN FRIENDS	PERFOLIATE	PERPLEXING	PHALLICISM
PAWNBROKER	PENICILLIN	PERFORABLE	PERPLEXITY	PHALLICIST
PAYMASTERS	PENINSULAR	PERFORATED	PERQUISITE	PHANEROGAM
PAY PACKETS	PENINSULAS	PERFORATOR	PERSECUTED	PHANTASIES
PAY-PER-	PENITENTLY	PERFORMERS	PERSECUTOR	PHANTASMAL
VIEW	PENMANSHIP	PERFORMING	PERSEVERED	PHARISAISM
PAY STATION	PENNINE WAY	PERICLINAL	PERSIAN CAT	PHARMACIES
PEACE CORPS	PENNY BLACK	PERICYCLIC	PERSIENNES	PHARMACIST
PEACEFULLY	PENNYCRESS	PERIDERMAL	PERSIFLAGE	PHARYNGEAL
PEACEMAKER	PENNYROYAL	PERIDOTITE	PERSIMMONS	PHELLODERM
PEACE PIPES	PENNYWORTH	PERIGYNOUS	PERSISTENT	PHENACAINE
PEACHINESS	PENOLOGIST	PERIHELION	PERSISTING	PHENACETIN
PEACH MELBA	PEN PUSHERS	PERILOUSLY	PERSONABLE	PHENFORMIN
PEARL DIVER	PENSIONARY	PERIMETERS	PERSONALLY	PHENOCRYST
PEARLINESS	PENSIONERS	PERIMETRIC	PERSONAGES	PHENOMENAL
PEAR-SHAPED	PENSIONING	PERIMYSIUM	PERSONALLY	PHENOMENON
PEASHOOTER	PENTAGONAL	PERIODICAL	PERSONALTY	PHENOTYPIC
PEA SHOOTER	PENTAGRAMS	PERIOSTEUM	PERSONATOR	PHILATELIC
PEA SOUPERS	PENTAMETER	PERIPETEIA	PERSPIRING	PHILIPPICS
PEBBLEDASH	PENTAQUINE	PERIPHERAL	PERSUADING	PHILIPPINE
PECCADILLO	PENTASTICH	PERIPHYTON	PERSUASION	PHILISTINE
PECTIZABLE	PENTATEUCH	PERIPTERAL	PERSUASIVE	PHILOSOPHY
PECULATING	PENTATHLON	PERISARCAL	PERTAINING	PHLEBOTOMY
PECULATION	PENTHOUSES	PERISCOPES	PERTHSHIRE	PHLEGMATIC
PECULIARLY	PENTIMENTO	PERISCOPIC	PERTINENCE	PHLOGISTIC
PEDAGOGISM	PENTSTEMON	PERISHABLE	PERTURBING	PHLOGISTON
PEDAGOGUES	PEPPERCORN	PERISTOMAL	PERVERSELY	PHLOGOPITE
PEDANTRIES	PEPPER MILL	PERISTYLAR	PERVERSION	PHOCOMELIA
PEDERASTIC	PEPPERMINT	PERISTYLES	PERVERSITY	PHOENICIAN

PHONE BOOKS	PICCALILLI	PISTILLATE	PLAYGROUPS	POLITICIAN
PHONE BOXES	PICCANINNY	PISTON RING	PLAYHOUSES	POLITICIZE
PHONEYNESS	PICHICIEGO	PITCH-BLACK	PLAYSCHOOL	POLLARDING
PHONEY WARS	PICKPOCKET	PITCHFORKS	PLAYTHINGS	POLLINATED
PHONICALLY	PICNICKERS	PITCHINESS	PLAYWRIGHT	POLLINATOR
PHONOGRAPH	PICNICKING	PITCHSTONE	PLEASANTER	POLLINOSIS
PHONOLITIC	PICRIC ACID	PITH HELMET	PLEASANTLY	POLLUTANTS
PHONOMETER	PICROTOXIC	PITILESSLY	PLEASANTRY	POLONAISES
PHONOSCOPE	PICROTOXIN	PITOT TUBES	PLEASINGLY	POLYANTHUS
PHONOTYPIC	PICTOGRAPH	PITTSBURGH	PLEBISCITE	POLYATOMIC
PHOSGENITE	PIED-A-	PITYRIASIS	PLEIOTROPY	POLYBASITE
PHOSPHATES	TERRE	PLACARDING	PLEONASTIC	POLYCARPIC
PHOSPHATIC	PIERCINGLY	PLACE CARDS	PLESIOSAUR	POLYCHAETE
PHOSPHORIC	PIGEONHOLE	PLACEMENTS	PLEURODONT	POLYCHROME
PHOSPHORUS	PIGEON-TOED	PLAGIARISM	PLEUROTOMY	POLYCHROMY
PHOTOFLOOD	PIGGYBACKS	PLAGIARIST	PLEXIGLASS	POLYCLINIC
PHOTOGENIC	PIGGYBANKS	PLAGIARIZE	PLIABILITY	POLYCOTTON
PHOTOGRAPH	PIGMENTARY	PLAINCHANT	PLODDINGLY	POLYCYCLIC
PHOTOLYSIS	PIGSTICKER	PLAIN FLOUR	PLOUGHBOYS	POLYDACTYL
PHOTOLYTIC	PIKESTAFFS	PLAINTIFFS	PLOUGHLAND	POLYDIPSIA
PHOTOMETER	PILE DRIVER	PLANCHETTE	PLUCKINESS	POLYDIPSIC
PHOTOMETRY	PILGRIMAGE	PLANETARIA	PLUMB LINES	POLYGAMIST
PHOTOMURAL	PILIFEROUS	PLANE TREES	PLUMMETING	POLYGAMOUS
PHOTONASTY	PILLORYING	PLANGENTLY	PLUNDERERS	POLYGRAPHS
PHOTONOVEL	PILLOWCASE	PLANIMETER	PLUNDERING	POLYGYNIST
PHOTOPHILY	PILLOW TALK	PLANIMETRY	PLUNDEROUS	POLYGYNOUS
PHOTOPHORE	PILOT LIGHT	PLANK-SHEER	PLUPERFECT	POLYHEDRAL
PHOTOSTATS	PIMPERNELS	PLANKTONIC	PLURALISTS	POLYHEDRON
PHOTOTAXIS	PIMPLINESS	PLANOMETER	PLURALIZER	POLYMATHIC
PHOTOTONIC	PINA COLADA	PLANOMETRY	PLUTOCRACY	POLYMERASE
PHOTOTONUS	PINCERLIKE	PLANTATION	PLUTOCRATS	POLYMERISM
PHOTOTYPIC	PINCHPENNY	PLASMAGENE	PNEUMATICS	POLYMERIZE
PHRASEBOOK	PINCUSHION	PLASMODIUM	POCKETABLE	POLYMEROUS
PHRENOLOGY	PINEAPPLES	PLASMOLYSE	POCKETBOOK	POLYNESIAN
PHTHISICAL	PINE MARTEN	PLASMOSOME	POCKETFULS	POLYNOMIAL
PHYLACTERY	PINFEATHER	PLASTERERS	POCKMARKED	POLYPHAGIA
PHYLLODIAL	PINGUIDITY	PLASTERING	PODIATRIST	POLYPHONIC
PHYLLOXERA	PINNATIFID	PLASTIC ART	POETASTERS	POLYPLOIDY
PHYLOGENIC	PINNATIPED	PLASTICINE	POETICALLY	POLYPODOUS
PHYSIATRIC	PINPOINTED	PLASTICITY	POGO STICKS	POLYRHYTHM
PHYSICALLY	PINSTRIPED	PLASTICIZE	POIGNANTLY	POLYSEMOUS
PHYSICIANS	PINSTRIPES	PLAT DU	POINSETTIA	POLYTHEISM
PHYSICISTS	PIONEERING	JOUR	POINT-BLANK	POLYTHEIST
PHYSIOCRAT	PIPED MUSIC	PLATE GLASS	POKER-FACED	POLYVALENT
PHYSIOLOGY	PIPE DREAMS	PLATELAYER	POLAR BEARS	POMERANIAN
PHYTOGENIC	PIPERAZINE	PLATE RACKS	POLARITIES	POMIFEROUS
PHYTOPHAGY	PIPERIDINE	PLATITUDES	POLARIZING	POMOLOGIST
PHYTOTOXIN	PIPSISSEWA	PLATTELAND	POLEMICIST	PONDERABLE
PIANISSIMO	PIPSQUEAKS	PLATYPUSES	POLES APART	POND-SKATER
PIANOFORTE	PIROUETTED	PLAY-ACTING	POLE VAULTS	PONTEFRACT
PICARESQUE	PIROUETTES	PLAYFELLOW	POLITBUROS	PONTEVEDRA
PICCADILLY	PISTACHIOS	PLAYGROUND	POLITENESS	PONTIFICAL

PONTYPRIDD	POSTMASTER	PREBENDARY	PREHOMINID	PRETENSION
POOH-POOHED	POSTMORTEM	PRECARIOUS	PREJUDGING	PRETTIFIED
POOL MALEBO	POST OFFICE	PRECAUTION	PREJUDICED	PRETTINESS
POORHOUSES	POSTPARTUM	PRECEDENCE	PREJUDICES	PREVAILING
POPE'S	POSTPONING	PRECEDENTS	PRELEXICAL	PREVALENCE
NOSES	POSTSCRIPT	PRECENTORS	PREMARITAL	PREVENIENT
POPISHNESS	POSTULANCY	PRECEPTIVE	PREMAXILLA	PREVENTING
POPULARITY	POSTULANTS	PRECESSION	PREMEDICAL	PREVENTION
POPULARIZE	POSTULATED	PRECIOSITY	PRENATALLY	PREVENTIVE
POPULATING	POSTULATES	PRECIOUSLY	PRENOMINAL	PREVIEWING
POPULATION	POSTULATOR	PRECIPICED	PREPACKAGE	PREVIOUSLY
PORCUPINES	POTABILITY	PRECIPICES	PREPACKING	PREVISIONS
PORIFEROUS	POTATO CHIP	PRECIPITIN	PREPAREDLY	PREVOCALIC
PORK BARREL	POTBELLIED	PRECISIONS	PREPAYABLE	PRICKLIEST
PORNOCRACY	POTBELLIES	PRECLUDING	PREPAYMENT	PRIEST-HOLE
POROUSNESS	POTBOILERS	PRECLUSION	PREPOSSESS	PRIESTHOOD
PORPHYROID	POTENTATES	PRECLUSIVE	PREPOTENCY	PRIESTLIER
PORTAMENTO	POTENTIATE	PRECOCIOUS	PREP SCHOOL	PRIGGISHLY
PORTCULLIS	POTENTILLA	PRECONCERT	PRESAGEFUL	PRIMA DONNA
PORTENDING	POTENTNESS	PRECOOKING	PRESBYOPIA	PRIMA FACIE
PORTENTOUS	POTHUNTERS	PRECURSORS	PRESBYOPIC	PRIMAQUINE
PORTFOLIOS	POTPOURRIS	PRECURSORY	PRESBYTERY	PRIME MOVER
PORT-GENTIL	POULTERERS	PREDACIOUS	PRESCHOOLS	PRIME RATES
PORTIONING	POULTRYMAN	PREDECEASE	PRESCIENCE	PRIMITIVES
PORTLAOISE	POURPARLER	PREDESTINE	PRESCRIBED	PRIMORDIAL
PORTLINESS	POWDER KEGS	PREDICABLE	PRESCRIBER	PRIMORDIUM
PORTOBELLO	POWDER PUFF	PREDICATED	PRESCRIPTS	PRINCEDOMS
PORT OF	POWDER ROOM	PREDICATES	PRESENT DAY	PRINCELING
CALL	POWER BASES	PREDICTING	PRESENT-DAY	PRINCESSES
PORTRAYALS	POWERBOATS	PREDICTION	PRESENTERS	PRINCIPALS
PORTRAYING	POWER DIVES	PREDICTIVE	PRESENTING	PRINCIPIUM
PORTSMOUTH	POWERFULLY	PREDISPOSE	PRESERVERS	PRINCIPLED
PORT TALBOT	POWERHOUSE	PRE-EMINENT	PRESERVING	PRINCIPLES
PORTUGUESE	POWER PLANT	PRE-EMPTING	PRESETTING	PRINTMAKER
POSITIONAL	POWER POINT	PRE-EMPTION	PRESIDENCY	PRIORITIES
POSITIONED	POZZUOLANA	PRE-EMPTIVE	PRESIDENTS	PRIORITIZE
POSITIVELY	PRACTICALS	PRE-EMPTORY	PRESIDIUMS	PRISMATOID
POSITIVISM	PRACTISING	PREEXISTED	PRESIGNIFY	PRISMOIDAL
POSITIVIST	PRAESIDIUM	PREFECTURE	PRESS AGENT	PRISON CAMP
POSSESSING	PRAGMATICS	PREFERABLE	PRESS BARON	PRISON GATE
POSSESSION	PRAGMATISM	PREFERABLY	PRESS BOXES	PRISSINESS
POSSESSIVE	PRAGMATIST	PREFERENCE	PRESSGANGS	PRIVATEERS
POSSESSORS	PRAIRIE DOG	PREFERMENT	PRESSINGLY	PRIVATIONS
POSSESSORY	PRANCINGLY	PREFERRING	PRESS-STUDS	PRIVATIZED
POST-BELLUM	PRANKSTERS	PREFIGURED	PRESSURING	PRIVILEGED
POST-CYCLIC	PRASELENIC	PREFRONTAL	PRESSURIZE	PRIVILEGES
POSTDATING	PRATINCOLE	PREGLACIAL	PRESUMABLE	PRIVY PURSE
POSTERIORS	PRAYER RUGS	PREGNANTLY	PRESUMABLY	PRIZEFIGHT
POSTHUMOUS	PREACHMENT	PREHEATING	PRESUMEDLY	PROCAMBIAL
POSTILIONS	PREADAMITE	PREHENSILE	PRESUPPOSE	PROCAMBIUM
POSTLIMINY	PREAMBULAR	PREHENSION	PRETENDERS	PROCEDURAL
POSTMARKED	PREARRANGE	PREHISTORY	PRETENDING	PROCEDURES

PROCEEDING	PROLONGING	PROSCENIUM	PROVINCIAL	PUNISHABLE
PROCESSING	PROMENADED	PROSCRIBED	PROVISIONS	PUNISHMENT
PROCESSION	PROMENADER	PROSECUTED	PROVITAMIN	PUNITIVELY
PROCESSORS	PROMENADES	PROSECUTOR	PRUDENTIAL	PUPIPAROUS
PROCLAIMED	PROMETHIUM	PROSELYTES	PRURIENTLY	PUPPETEERS
PROCLIVITY	PROMINENCE	PROSELYTIC	PSALMODIST	PURCHASERS
PROCONSULS	PROMISSORY	PROSPECTED	PSALTERIES	PURCHASING
PROCREATED	PROMONTORY	PROSPECTOR	PSALTERIUM	PURGATIVES
PROCREATOR	PROMOTABLE	PROSPECTUS	PSEPHOLOGY	PURITANISM
PROCRYPTIC	PROMOTIONS	PROSPERING	PSESPHITIC	PURLOINING
PROCTOLOGY	PROMPTBOOK	PROSPERITY	PSEUDOCARP	PURPLENESS
PROCTORIAL	PROMPTNESS	PROSPEROUS	PSEUDONYMS	PURPORTING
PROCUMBENT	PROMULGATE	PROSTHESIS	PSILOCYBIN	PURPOSEFUL
PROCURATOR	PRONEPHRIC	PROSTHETIC	PSITTACINE	PURSUANCES
PRODIGALLY	PRONEPHROS	PROSTITUTE	PSITTACISM	PURSUIVANT
PRODIGIOUS	PRONOMINAL	PROSTOMIUM	PSYCHIATRY	PURVEYANCE
PRODUCIBLE	PRONOUNCED	PROSTRATED	PSYCHOLOGY	PUSH-BUTTON
PRODUCTION	PRONOUNCER	PROTANOPIA	PSYCHOPATH	PUSHCHAIRS
PRODUCTIVE	PRONUCLEAR	PROTANOPIC	PSYCHOTICS	PUT A STOP
PROFESSING	PRONUCLEUS	PROTECTING	PTOLEMAIST	TO
PROFESSION	PRO-OESTRUS	PROTECTION	PUB-CRAWLED	PUTREFYING
PROFESSORS	PROPAGABLE	PROTECTIVE	PUBERULENT	PUTRESCENT
PROFFERING	PROPAGANDA	PROTECTORS	PUBESCENCE	PUTRESCINE
PROFICIENT	PROPAGATED	PROTECTORY	PUBLIC BARS	PUZZLEMENT
PROFITABLE	PROPAGATOR	PROTEINASE	PUBLICISTS	PUZZLINGLY
PROFITABLY	PROPELLANT	PRO TEMPORE	PUBLICIZED	PYCNOMETER
PROFITEERS	PROPELLENT	PROTESTANT	PUBLISHERS	PYOGENESIS
PROFITLESS	PROPELLERS	PROTESTERS	PUBLISHING	PYORRHOEAL
PROFLIGACY	PROPELLING	PROTHALLIC	PUERPERIUM	PYRACANTHA
PROFLIGATE	PROPENSITY	PROTHALLUS	PUERTO RICO	PYRETHROID
PROFOUNDLY	PROPERNESS	PROTOCTIST	PUGILISTIC	PYRIDOXINE
PROFUNDITY	PROPER NOUN	PROTOHUMAN	PUGNACIOUS	PYRIMIDINE
PROGENITOR	PROPERTIED	PROTONEMAL	PUISSANCES	PYROGALLIC
PROGLOTTIS	PROPERTIES	PROTOPATHY	PULLULATED	PYROGALLOL
PROGNOSTIC	PROPHECIES	PROTOPLASM	PULSATIONS	PYROGRAPHY
PROGRAMERS	PROPHESIER	PROTOPLAST	PULSIMETER	PYROLUSITE
PROGRAMING	PROPHESIED	PROTOSTELE	PULVERABLE	PYROMANCER
PROGRAMMED	PROPHESIES	PROTOTYPAL	PULVERIZED	PYROMANIAC
PROGRAMMER	PROPIONATE	PROTOTYPES	PULVERIZER	PYROMANTIC
PROGRAMMES	PROPITIATE	PROTOXYLEM	PUMMELLING	PYROMETRIC
PROGRESSED	PROPITIOUS	PROTOZOANS	PUNCH BALLS	PYROPHORIC
PROGRESSES	PROPONENTS	PROTRACTED	PUNCHBOARD	PYROSTATIC
PROHIBITED	PROPORTION	PROTRACTOR	PUNCH BOWLS	PYROXENITE
PROHIBITER	PROPOSABLE	PROTRUDENT	PUNCH-DRUNK	PYRRHOTITE
PROJECTILE	PROPOSITUS	PROTRUDING	PUNCHINESS	PYTHAGORAS
PROJECTING	PROPOUNDED	PROTRUSILE	PUNCH LINES	
PROJECTION	PROPOUNDER	PROTRUSION	PUNCTATION	**Q**
PROJECTIVE	PROPRIETOR	PROTRUSIVE	PUNCTILIOS	QARAGHANDY
PROJECTORS	PROPULSION	PROVENANCE	PUNCTUALLY	QUADRANGLE
PROKARYOTE	PROPULSIVE	PROVENCALE	PUNCTUATED	QUADRANTAL
PROLAPSING	PROPYLAEUM	PROVERBIAL	PUNCTUATOR	QUADRATICS
PROLOCUTOR	PROROGUING	PROVIDENCE	PUNCTURING	QUADRATURE

QUADRICEPS	RACEHORSES	RATIONALES	RECHRISTEN	RED INDIANS
QUADRILLES	RACETRACKS	RATIONALLY	RECIDIVISM	REDIRECTED
QUADRISECT	RACHMANISM	RAT-RUNNING	RECIDIVIST	REDISCOUNT
QUADRIVIAL	RACIALISTS	RATTLETRAP	RECIPIENCE	REDOUBLING
QUADRUPEDS	RACKETEERS	RAUNCHIEST	RECIPIENTS	REDOUNDING
QUADRUPLED	RACK-RENTER	RAVAGEMENT	RECIPROCAL	RED PEPPERS
QUADRUPLET	RACONTEURS	RAVENOUSLY	RECITATION	REDRESSING
QUADRUPLEX	RADARSCOPE	RAVISHMENT	RECITATIVE	REDUCTIONS
QUAINTNESS	RADIATIONS	RAWALPINDI	RECKLESSLY	REDUNDANCY
QUALIFIERS	RADICALISM	RAWINSONDE	RECKONINGS	RE-EDUCATED
QUALIFYING	RADIO ALARM	RAZZMATAZZ	RECLAIMANT	RE-ELECTING
QUANDARIES	RADIOGENIC	REACTIONAL	RECLAIMING	RE-ELECTION
QUANTIFIED	RADIOGRAMS	REACTIVATE	RECLINABLE	RE-ENFORCER
QUANTIFIER	RADIOGRAPH	REACTIVELY	RECOGNIZED	RE-ENTRANCE
QUANTITIES	RADIOLYSIS	REACTIVITY	RECOGNIZEE	RE-EXAMINER
QUARANTINE	RADIOMETER	READERSHIP	RECOGNIZER	RE-EXPORTER
QUARRELING	RADIOMETRY	READJUSTED	RECOGNIZOR	REFEREEING
QUARRELLED	RADIOPAQUE	READJUSTER	RECOILLESS	REFERENCER
QUARRELLER	RADIOPHONY	READY MONEY	RECOMMENCE	REFERENCES
QUARTERAGE	RADIOSCOPE	REAFFIRMED	RECOMPENSE	REFERENDUM
QUARTER DAY	RADIOSCOPY	REAFFOREST	RECONCILED	REFILLABLE
QUARTERING	RADIOSONDE	REAL ESTATE	RECONCILER	REFINEMENT
QUARTERSAW	RADIOTOXIC	REALIGNING	RECONSIDER	REFINERIES
QUATERNARY	RAFSANJANI	REALIZABLE	RECORDABLE	REFINISHER
QUATERNION	RAGAMUFFIN	REALIZABLY	RECORDINGS	REFLECTING
QUATREFOIL	RAGGEDNESS	REALLOCATE	RECOUNTING	REFLECTION
QUEASINESS	RAILROADED	REANIMATED	RECOUPABLE	REFLECTIVE
QUEENSLAND	RAIN CHECKS	REAPPEARED	RECOUPMENT	REFLECTORS
QUENCHABLE	RAIN FOREST	REAPPRAISE	RECOVERIES	REFLEXIVES
QUESTINGLY	RAIN GAUGES	REARGUARDS	RE-COVERING	REFORESTED
QUESTIONED	RAINMAKING	REARMAMENT	RECREATING	REFRACTING
QUESTIONER	RAINSTORMS	REARRANGED	RECREATION	REFRACTION
QUEZON CITY	RAISE A	REARRANGER	RECRUDESCE	REFRACTIVE
QUICKENING	DUST	REASONABLE	RECRUITING	REFRACTORY
QUICKSANDS	RAJYA SABHA	REASONABLY	RECTANGLES	REFRAINING
QUICKSTEPS	RAKISHNESS	REASSEMBLE	RECTIFIERS	REFRESHFUL
QUID PRO	RAMPAGEOUS	REASSURING	RECTIFYING	REFRESHING
QUO	RAMSHACKLE	REBELLIONS	RECUMBENCE	REFRINGENT
QUIESCENCE	RANCH HOUSE	REBELLIOUS	RECUPERATE	REFUELLING
QUIETENING	RANCIDNESS	REBIRTHING	RECURRENCE	REFUGEEISM
QUINTUPLET	RANDOMNESS	REBOUNDING	RED ADMIRAL	REFULGENCE
QUIRKINESS	RANSACKING	REBUILDING	RED-BLOODED	REFUNDABLE
QUITTANCES	RANSOMEWARE	REBUKINGLY	REDBREASTS	REFUTATION
QUIZMASTER	RANUNCULUS	REBUTTABLE	REDCURRANT	REGAINABLE
QUONSET HUT	RAPPORTEUR	RECALLABLE	REDECORATE	REGALEMENT
QUOTATIONS	RARE EARTHS	RECAPTURED	REDEDICATE	REGARDABLE
	RAREFIABLE	RECEIVABLE	REDEEMABLE	REGARDLESS
R	RATABILITY	RECENTNESS	REDEEMABLY	REGELATION
RABBINICAL	RAT-A-TAT-	RECEPTACLE	REDELIVERY	REGENERACY
RABBITFISH	TAT	RECEPTIONS	REDEMPTION	REGENERATE
RABBITTING	RATE-CAPPED	RECESSIONS	REDEPLOYED	REGENSBURG
RACECOURSE	RATIFIABLE	RECHARGING	RED HERRING	REGENTSHIP

REGIMENTAL	RELUCTANCE	REPERTOIRE	RESHIPMENT	RETHINKING
REGIMENTED	REMAINDERS	REPETITION	RESHUFFLED	RETICENTLY
REGIONALLY	REMANDMENT	REPETITIVE	RESHUFFLES	RETICULATE
REGISTERED	REMARKABLE	REPHRASING	RESIDENCES	RETIREMENT
REGISTERER	REMARKABLY	REPLICATED	RESIGNEDLY	RETOUCHING
REGISTRANT	REMARRYING	REPORTABLE	RESILEMENT	RETRACTILE
REGISTRARS	REMEDIABLE	REPORTEDLY	RESILIENCE	RETRACTING
REGISTRIES	REMEDIABLY	REPOSITION	RESILIENCY	RETRACTION
REGRESSING	REMEDIALLY	REPOSITORY	RESISTANCE	RETRACTIVE
REGRESSION	REMEDILESS	REPRESSING	RESISTIBLY	RETREADING
REGRESSIVE	REMEMBERED	REPRESSION	RESISTLESS	RETREATING
REGRETTING	REMEMBERER	REPRESSIVE	RESOLUTELY	RETRENCHED
REGROUPING	REMINISCED	REPRIEVING	RESOLUTION	RETRIEVERS
REGULARITY	REMISSIBLE	REPRIMANDS	RESOLVABLE	RETRIEVING
REGULARIZE	REMISSIONS	REPRINTING	RESONANCES	RETROCHOIR
REGULATING	REMISSNESS	REPROACHED	RESONANTLY	RETROGRADE
REGULATION	REMITTABLE	REPROACHER	RESONATING	RETROGRESS
REGULATIVE	REMITTANCE	REPROACHES	RESONATION	RETROSPECT
REGULATORS	REMITTENCE	REPROBATER	RESONATORS	RETROVERSE
REGULATORY	REMODELING	REPROBATES	RESORCINOL	RETROVIRUS
REHEARSALS	REMODELLED	REPRODUCED	RESORPTION	RETURNABLE
REHEARSING	REMODELLER	REPRODUCER	RESORPTIVE	REUNIONISM
REIMBURSED	REMONETIZE	REPROVABLE	RESOUNDING	REUNIONIST
REIMBURSER	REMORSEFUL	REPTILIANS	RESPECTERS	REUNITABLE
REINFORCED	REMOTENESS	REPUBLICAN	RESPECTFUL	REUTLINGEN
REINSTATED	REMOULDING	REPUDIABLE	RESPECTING	REVANCHISM
REINSTATOR	REMOUNTING	REPUDIATED	RESPECTIVE	REVANCHIST
REINSURING	REMOVAL VAN	REPUDIATOR	RESPIRABLE	REVEALABLE
REISSUABLE	REMUNERATE	REPUGNANCE	RESPIRATOR	REVEALEDLY
REITERATED	RENDERABLE	REPULSIONS	RESPONDENT	REVEALMENT
REJECTABLE	RENDERINGS	REPURCHASE	RESPONDING	REVEGETATE
REJECTIONS	RENDEZVOUS	REPUTATION	RESPONSIVE	REVELATION
REJOINDERS	RENDITIONS	REQUESTING	RESPONSORY	REVENGEFUL
REJUVENATE	RENEWABLES	REQUIESCAT	RES PUBLICA	REVERENCED
REKINDLING	RENOUNCING	REQUIRABLE	RESTAURANT	REVERENCER
RELATIONAL	RENOVATING	REQUISITES	RESTHARROW	REVERENCES
RELATIVELY	RENOVATION	REQUITABLE	RESTLESSLY	REVERENTLY
RELATIVISM	RENOVATIVE	RESCHEDULE	RESTOCKING	REVERSIBLE
RELATIVIST	RENOWNEDLY	RESCINDING	RESTORABLE	REVERTIBLE
RELATIVITY	RENT STRIKE	RESCISSION	RESTRAINED	REVETMENTS
RELAXATION	REORGANIZE	RESCISSORY	RESTRAINER	REVIEWABLE
RELEGATING	REPAIRABLE	RESEARCHED	RESTRAINTS	REVILEMENT
RELEGATION	REPARATION	RESEARCHER	RESTRICTED	REVILINGLY
RELENTLESS	REPARATIVE	RESEARCHES	RESUMPTION	REVISIONAL
RELEVANTLY	REPATRIATE	RESEMBLANT	RESUMPTIVE	REVITALIZE
RELIEF MAPS	REPAYMENTS	RESEMBLING	RESUPINATE	REVIVALISM
RELIEF ROAD	REPEALABLE	RESENTMENT	RESURFACED	REVIVALIST
RELIEVABLE	REPEATABLE	RESERVABLE	RESURGENCE	REVIVIFIED
RELINQUISH	REPEATEDLY	RESERVEDLY	RETAINABLE	REVIVINGLY
RELISHABLE	REPELLENCE	RESERVISTS	RETAINMENT	REVOCATION
RELOCATING	REPELLENTS	RESERVOIRS	RETALIATED	REVOCATIVE
RELOCATION	REPENTANCE	RESETTLING	RETALIATOR	REVOKINGLY

REVOLUTION	RING-TAILED	ROUNDHOUSE	RUTHERFORD	SAINT-LOUIS
REVOLVABLE	RIPPLINGLY	ROUND ROBIN	RUTHLESSLY	SAINT LUCIA
REVOLVABLY	RIP-ROARING	ROUND-TABLE		SAINT'S
REWARDABLE	RISIBILITY	ROUND TRIPS	S	DAYS
REWARD CARD	RISING DAMP	ROUSEDNESS	SABBATICAL	SALABILITY
RHAPSODIES	RITARDANDO	ROUSSILLON	SABOTAGING	SALAD CREAM
RHAPSODIST	RITORNELLO	ROUSTABOUT	SABULOSITY	SALAMANDER
RHAPSODIZE	RIVER BASIN	ROUTE MARCH	SACCHARASE	SALBUTAMOL
RHEOLOGIST	ROADBLOCKS	ROWING BOAT	SACCHARATE	SALESCLERK
RHEOMETRIC	ROADHOUSES	ROYAL FLUSH	SACCHARIDE	SALESGIRLS
RHEOSTATIC	ROAD ROLLER	ROYALISTIC	SACCHARIFY	SALES PITCH
RHEOTACTIC	ROADRUNNER	RUB' AL	SACCHARINE	SALES SLIPS
RHEOTROPIC	ROAD-TESTED	KHALI	SACCHAROID	SALES TAXES
RHETORICAL	ROADWORTHY	RUBBER BAND	SACCHAROSE	SALESWOMAN
RHEUMATICS	ROBUSTNESS	RUBBERNECK	SACERDOTAL	SALESWOMEN
RHEUMATISM	ROCK BOTTOM	RUBBER TREE	SACRAMENTO	SALICORNIA
RHEUMATOID	ROCK GARDEN	RUBBISH BIN	SACRAMENTS	SALICYLATE
RHINESTONE	ROCK PLANTS	RUBBISHING	SACRED COWS	SALIFEROUS
RHINOCEROS	ROCK SALMON	RUBBLEWORK	SACREDNESS	SALIFIABLE
RHINOSCOPY	ROISTERERS	RUBESCENCE	SACRIFICED	SALIMETRIC
RHIZOGENIC	ROISTEROUS	RUBIACEOUS	SACRIFICER	SALIVATING
RHIZOMORPH	ROLE MODELS	RUBIGINOUS	SACRIFICES	SALIVATION
RHIZOPODAN	ROLE-PLAYED	RUBRICATOR	SACRILEGES	SALLOWNESS
RHOMBOIDAL	ROLLED GOLD	RUDDERHEAD	SACRISTANS	SALMANAZAR
RHUMBATRON	ROLLICKING	RUDDERLESS	SACRISTIES	SALMONELLA
RHYMESTERS	ROLLING PIN	RUDDERPOST	SACROILIAC	SALMON LEAP
RHYTHMICAL	ROLY-POLIES	RUEFULNESS	SACROSANCT	SALOON BARS
RIBBONFISH	ROMAN BLIND	RUFESCENCE	SADDLEBACK	SALOPETTES
RIBOFLAVIN	ROMANESQUE	RUFFIANISM	SADDLEBAGS	SALPINGIAN
RICKETTSIA	ROMAN NOSES	RUGBY UNION	SADDLEBILL	SALTARELLO
RICOCHETED	ROOD SCREEN	RUGGEDIZED	SADDLERIES	SALTCELLAR
RIDGEPOLES	ROOF GARDEN	RUGGEDNESS	SADDLE-SORE	SALTIGRADE
RIDICULING	ROPE LADDER	RUMBLINGLY	SADDLETREE	SALT SHAKER
RIDICULOUS	ROSANILINE	RUMINATING	SAFARI PARK	SALUBRIOUS
RIEMANNIAN	ROSEMALING	RUMINATION	SAFEGUARDS	SALUTARILY
RIFLE RANGE	ROSE WINDOW	RUMINATIVE	SAFE HOUSES	SALUTATION
RIFT VALLEY	ROSTELLATE	RUMPUS ROOM	SAFETY BELT	SALUTATORY
RIGHTABOUT	ROTARY CLUB	RUNNER BEAN	SAFETY LAMP	SALVERFORM
RIGHT ANGLE	ROTATIONAL	RUN-OF-	SAFETY NETS	SALZGITTER
RIGHTFULLY	ROTISSERIE	PAPER	SAFETY PINS	SAMARITANS
RIGHT OF	ROTOVATORS	RUN THROUGH	SAHARANPUR	SAMARSKITE
WAY	ROTTENNESS	RUN-THROUGH	SAILBOARDS	SAMOTHRACE
RIGHTWARDS	ROTTWEILER	RUPESTRIAN	SAILOR SUIT	SAN ANTONIO
RIGMAROLES	ROUGHENING	RUPTURABLE	SAILPLANES	SANATORIUM
RIGORISTIC	ROUGHHOUSE	RURITANIAN	SAINT-CLOUD	SANCTIFIED
RIGOROUSLY	ROUGH HOUSE	RUSHLIGHTS	SAINT CROIX	SANCTIFIER
RINDERPEST	ROUGHNECKS	RUSSOPHILE	SAINT-DENIS	SANCTIMONY
RING BINDER	ROUGH PAPER	RUSSOPHOBE	SAINT	SANCTIONED
RING FINGER	ROUGHRIDER	RUSTICATED	JOHN'S	SANCTIONER
RINGLEADER	ROUGH STUFF	RUSTICATOR	SAINT KILDA	SANCTITUDE
RINGMASTER	ROUNDABOUT	RUSTLINGLY	SAINT KITTS	SANDALWOOD
RING-NECKED	ROUNDHEADS	RUTHENIOUS	SAINT LOUIS	SANDBAGGED

SANDBAGGER	SAXOPHONIC	SCIENTISTS	SCRUBBIEST	SECULARITY
SANDCASTLE	SCABBINESS	SCILLONIAN	SCRUFFIEST	SECULARIZE
SAND CASTLE	SCAFFOLDER	SCIOMANCER	SCRUMMAGED	SECUNDINES
SANDERLING	SCALEBOARD	SCIOMANTIC	SCRUMMAGER	SECUREMENT
SANDGROUSE	SCALLOPING	SCLEROTIUM	SCRUMMAGES	SECURENESS
SAND MARTIN	SCALLYWAGS	SCLEROTOMY	SCRUNCHING	SECURITIES
SANDPIPERS	SCALOPPINE	SCOFFINGLY	SCRUPULOUS	SEDAN CHAIR
SANDSTORMS	SCALPELLIC	SCOLDINGLY	SCRUTINEER	SEDATENESS
SANDWICHED	SCAMPERING	SCOLLOPING	SCRUTINIES	SEDUCINGLY
SANDWICHES	SCANDALIZE	SCOREBOARD	SCRUTINIZE	SEDUCTRESS
SANFORIZED	SCANDALOUS	SCORECARDS	SCULLERIES	SEDULOUSLY
SANFORIZED	SCANSORIAL	SCORNFULLY	SCULPTRESS	SEEMLINESS
SANGUINARY	SCANTINESS	SCORNINGLY	SCULPTURAL	SEERSUCKER
SANGUINELY	SCAPEGOATS	SCORPAENID	SCULPTURED	SEETHINGLY
SANITARIAN	SCAPEGRACE	SCORPIONIC	SCULPTURES	SEE-THROUGH
SANITARILY	SCARABAEID	SCOTCH EGGS	SCUNTHORPE	SEGMENTARY
SANITARIUM	SCARABAEUS	SCOTCH MIST	SCUPPERING	SEGMENTING
SANITATION	SCARCEMENT	SCOTCH SNAP	SCURRILITY	SEGREGABLE
SANITIZING	SCARCENESS	SCOTCH TAPE	SCURRILOUS	SEGREGATED
SANSKRITIC	SCARCITIES	SCOTTICISM	SCURVINESS	SEGREGATOR
SANTA CLARA	SCARECROWS	SCOUNDRELS	SCUTELLATE	SEISMICITY
SANTA CLAUS	SCAREDY CAT	SCOWLINGLY	SCYPHIFORM	SEISMOLOGY
SANTA MARIA	SCARIFYING	SCRABBLING	SCYPHOZOAN	SELECTIONS
SANTA MARTA	SCARLATINA	SCRAGGIEST	SEA ANEMONE	SELECTNESS
SAPIENTIAL	SCARPERING	SCRAMBLING	SEABORGIUM	SELENOLOGY
SAPONIFIER	SCATHINGLY	SCRAPBOOKS	SEA BREEZES	SELF-ACTING
SAPPANWOOD	SCATTER-GUN	SCRAP HEAPS	SEA CAPTAIN	SELF-ACTION
SAPPHIRINE	SCATTERING	SCRAP METAL	SEA CHANGES	SELF-DENIAL
SAPROGENIC	SCATTINESS	SCRAP PAPER	SEALED-BEAM	SELF-ESTEEM
SAPROLITIC	SCAVENGERS	SCRAPPIEST	SEALING WAX	SELF-FEEDER
SAPROPELIC	SCAVENGING	SCRATCHIER	SEAMANLIKE	SELFLESSLY
SAPROPHYTE	SCENICALLY	SCRATCHILY	SEAMANSHIP	SELF-REGARD
SAPROTROPH	SCEPTICISM	SCRATCHING	SEAMSTRESS	SELF-SEEKER
SARCOPHAGI	SCHAERBEEK	SCRATCH PAD	SEARCHABLE	SELF-STYLED
SARMENTOSE	SCHEDULING	SCRATCHPAD	SEA SERPENT	SELF-WILLED
SARRACENIA	SCHEMATISM	SCRAWNIEST	SEASONABLE	SELL-BY
SASH WINDOW	SCHEMATIZE	SCREECHING	SEASONABLY	DATE
SATELLITES	SCHEMINGLY	SCREENABLE	SEASONEDLY	SELLOTAPED
SATINWOODS	SCHERZANDO	SCREENINGS	SEASONINGS	SEMAPHORES
SATIRIZING	SCHIPPERKE	SCREENPLAY	SEA URCHINS	SEMAPHORIC
SATISFYING	SCHISMATIC	SCREEN TEST	SEBIFEROUS	SEMATOLOGY
SATURATING	SCHIZOCARP	SCREWBALLS	SEBORRHOEA	SEMIANNUAL
SATURATION	SCHIZOGONY	SCRIBBLERS	SECOND BEST	SEMIBREVES
SATURNALIA	SCHLEPPING	SCRIBBLING	SECOND-HAND	SEMICIRCLE
SATYRIASIS	SCHNITZELS	SCRIMMAGED	SECONDMENT	SEMICOLONS
SAUERKRAUT	SCHOLASTIC	SCRIMMAGER	SECOND-RATE	SEMIFINALS
SAUNTERING	SCHOOLGIRL	SCRIMMAGES	SECOND WIND	SEMINALITY
SAUSAGE DOG	SCHOOLMARM	SCRIPTURAL	SECRETAIRE	SEMINARIAL
SAVAGENESS	SCHOOLMATE	SCROFULOUS	SECRETIONS	SEMINARIAN
SAVAGERIES	SCHOOLWORK	SCROLLWORK	SECTIONING	SEMINARIES
SAXICOLOUS	SCHUMACHER	SCROUNGERS	SECULARISM	SEMIQUAVER
SAXOPHONES	SCIENTIFIC	SCROUNGING	SECULARIST	SEMIVOWELS

SEMIWEEKLY	SETSQUARES	SHELTERING	SHOW TRIALS	SILK SCREEN
SENATORIAL	SETTING OUT	SHENANIGAN	SHREVEPORT	SILLY BILLY
SENEGALESE	SETTLEABLE	SHEPHERDED	SHREWDNESS	SILVERFISH
SENEGAMBIA	SETTLEMENT	SHERARDIZE	SHREWISHLY	SILVERWARE
SENESCENCE	SEVASTOPOL	SHERBROOKE	SHREWSBURY	SILVERWEED
SENSATIONS	SEVENTIETH	SHIBBOLETH	SHRIEVALTY	SIMFEROPOL
SENSE ORGAN	SEVERANCES	SHIFTINESS	SHRILLNESS	SIMILARITY
SENSIBILIA	SEVERENESS	SHIFTINGLY	SHRINKABLE	SIMILITUDE
SENSITIZED	SEVERITIES	SHIFT STICK	SHRINK-WRAP	SIMONIACAL
SENSITIZER	SEXAGENARY	SHILLELAGH	SHRIVELING	SIMPLE LIFE
SENSUALISM	SEXAGESIMA	SHIMMERING	SHRIVELLED	SIMPLENESS
SENSUALIST	SEXIVALENT	SHIPBOARDS	SHROPSHIRE	SIMPLETONS
SENSUALITY	SEX OBJECTS	SHIPMASTER	SHROUD-LAID	SIMPLICITY
SENSUOUSLY	SEXOLOGIST	SHIP-RIGGED	SHROVETIDE	SIMPLIFIED
SENTENCING	SEXPARTITE	SHIPWRECKS	SHUDDERING	SIMPLIFIER
SENTENTIAL	SEXTILLION	SHIPWRIGHT	SHUNT-WOUND	SIMPLISTIC
SENTIMENTS	SEXTUPLETS	SHIRE HORSE	SHUTTERING	SIMULACRUM
SEPARATELY	SEYCHELLES	SHIRTFRONT	SIALAGOGIC	SIMULATING
SEPARATING	SHABBINESS	SHIRTTAILS	SIALAGOGUE	SIMULATION
SEPARATION	SHADOWIEST	SHISH KEBAB	SIAMESE CAT	SIMULATIVE
SEPARATISM	SHAGGED OUT	SHOALINESS	SIBILATION	SIMULATORS
SEPARATIST	SHAGGINESS	SHOCKINGLY	SICKLEBILL	SINCIPITAL
SEPARATIVE	SHAKEDOWNS	SHOCKPROOF	SICKLINESS	SINECURISM
SEPARATORS	SHALLOWEST	SHODDINESS	SICKNESSES	SINECURIST
SEPARATRIX	SHALLOWING	SHOEMAKING	SICK PARADE	SINE QUA
SEPTENNIAL	SHAMANISMS	SHOESHINES	SIDEBOARDS	NON
SEPTICALLY	SHAMANISTS	SHOESTRING	SIDE DISHES	SINEWINESS
SEPTICIDAL	SHAMATEURS	SHOGUN BOND	SIDE EFFECT	SINFULNESS
SEPTIC TANK	SHAMEFACED	SHOOT A	SIDE ISSUES	SINGHALESE
SEPTILLION	SHAMEFULLY	LINE	SIDELIGHTS	SINGLE FILE
SEPULCHRAL	SHAMPOOING	SHOPAHOLIC	SIDELINING	SINGLENESS
SEPULCHRES	SHANGHAIED	SHOPKEEPER	SIDE ORDERS	SINGLETONS
SEQUACIOUS	SHANTYTOWN	SHOPLIFTED	SIDEROLITE	SINGULARLY
SEQUENCING	SHAPELIEST	SHOPLIFTER	SIDEROSTAT	SINHAILIEN
SEQUENTIAL	SHARE PRICE	SHOPSOILED	SIDESADDLE	SINISTROUS
SEQUESTRAL	SHARPENERS	SHOPWALKER	SIDE STREET	SINN FEINER
SEQUESTRUM	SHARPENING	SHOPWORKER	SIDESTROKE	SINOLOGIST
SERBO-CROAT	SHATTERING	SHORE LEAVE	SIDESWIPED	SINUSOIDAL
SERENADING	SHEARWATER	SHOREWARDS	SIDESWIPER	SISTERHOOD
SERENENESS	SHEATHBILL	SHORTBREAD	SIDESWIPES	SITOSTEROL
SERIALIZED	SHEATHINGS	SHORTENING	SIDETRACKS	SITUATIONS
SERIGRAPHY	SHEEPISHLY	SHORTFALLS	SIDEWINDER	SIX-FOOTERS
SERIOCOMIC	SHEEP'S	SHORT LISTS	SIGHTSEERS	SIX-SHOOTER
SERMONICAL	EYES	SHORT-LIVED	SIGNALIZED	SIXTEENTHS
SERMONIZED	SHEEPSHANK	SHORT-RANGE	SIGNALLING	SIXTH FORMS
SERMONIZER	SHEEPSHEAD	SHORT STORY	SIGNATURES	SIXTH SENSE
SEROLOGIST	SHEEPSKINS	SHOULDERED	SIGNIFYING	SKATEBOARD
SERPENTINE	SHEET MUSIC	SHOVELHEAD	SIGNORINAS	SKEDADDLED
SERVICEMAN	SHEIKHDOMS	SHOVELLING	SIGNPOSTED	SKEPTICISM
SERVICEMEN	SHELF LIVES	SHOVELNOSE	SILENTNESS	SKETCHABLE
SERVIETTES	SHELLPROOF	SHOW JUMPER	SILHOUETTE	SKETCHBOOK
SERVOMOTOR	SHELLSHOCK	SHOWPIECES	SILICULOSE	SKETCHIEST

SKETCHPADS	SLUICEGATE	SNOOTINESS	SOLICITORS	SPACEWOMAN
SKIMPINESS	SLUMBERERS	SNORKELLED	SOLICITOUS	SPACIOUSLY
SKIN DIVERS	SLUMBERING	SNORTINGLY	SOLICITUDE	SPADICEOUS
SKIN DIVING	SLUMBEROUS	SNOTTINESS	SOLIDARITY	SPALLATION
SKIN FLICKS	SLUSH FUNDS	SNOWBALLED	SOLIDIFIED	SPARE PARTS
SKINFLINTS	SLUSHINESS	SNOW-CAPPED	SOLIDIFIER	SPARE TYRES
SKIN GRAFTS	SMALL HOURS	SNOWDRIFTS	SOLID-STATE	SPARK PLUGS
SKINNINESS	SMALL PRINT	SNOWFIELDS	SOLITAIRES	SPARSENESS
SKIPPERING	SMALL-SCALE	SNOWFLAKES	SOLITARIES	SPARTANISM
SKIRMISHED	SMALL-TIMER	SNOWMAKING	SOLITARILY	SPATCHCOCK
SKIRMISHER	SMARAGDITE	SNOWMOBILE	SOLSTITIAL	SPATIALITY
SKIRMISHES	SMART ALECK	SNOWPLOUGH	SOLUBILITY	SPATTERING
SKITTERING	SMARTENING	SNOWSTORMS	SOLUBILIZE	SPEARHEADS
SKITTISHLY	SMARTINGLY	SNUBBINGLY	SOLVOLYSIS	SPECIALISM
SKYJACKERS	SMATTERING	SNUFFINESS	SOMALILAND	SPECIALIST
SKYJACKING	SMEARINESS	SNUFFINGLY	SOMATOLOGY	SPECIALITY
SKYLARKING	SMEAR TESTS	SOAP BUBBLE	SOMATOTYPE	SPECIALIZE
SKYROCKETS	SMELLINESS	SOAP OPERAS	SOMBRENESS	SPECIATION
SKYSCRAPER	SMIRKINGLY	SOBERINGLY	SOMERSAULT	SPECIESISM
SKYWRITING	SMOKEHOUSE	SOBRIQUETS	SOMNOLENCE	SPECIFYING
SLACKENING	SMOKESTACK	SOB STORIES	SONGSTRESS	SPECIOSITY
SLANDERERS	SMOLDERING	SOCIALISTS	SONGWRITER	SPECIOUSLY
SLANDERING	SMOOTHABLE	SOCIALITES	SONIC BOOMS	SPECTACLES
SLANDEROUS	SMOOTHBORE	SOCIALIZED	SONIFEROUS	SPECTATING
SLANGINESS	SMOOTHNESS	SOCIALIZER	SONOROUSLY	SPECTATORS
SLANTINGLY	SMOTHERING	SOCIALNESS	SONS-OF-	SPECULATED
SLASHINGLY	SMOULDERED	SOCIAL WORK	GUNS	SPECULATOR
SLATTERNLY	SMUDGINESS	SOCIOMETRY	SOOTHINGLY	SPEECH DAYS
SLAVE TRADE	SMUTTINESS	SOCIOPATHY	SOOTHSAYER	SPEECHLESS
SLAVOPHILE	SNAIL'S	SODDENNESS	SOPHOMORES	SPEEDBOATS
SLEAZINESS	PACE	SOFT-BOILED	SORDIDNESS	SPEEDINESS
SLEEPINESS	SNAKEMOUTH	SOFT-FINNED	SORORICIDE	SPEED LIMIT
SLEEPYHEAD	SNAPDRAGON	SOFT FRUITS	SORORITIES	SPEED TRAPS
SLEEVELESS	SNAPPINESS	SOFT-HEADED	SOUBRIQUET	SPELEOLOGY
SLENDERIZE	SNAPPINGLY	SOFT OPTION	SOULLESSLY	SPELLBOUND
SLIDE RULES	SNAPPISHLY	SOFT PALATE	SOUNDPROOF	SPELUNKING
SLIGHTNESS	SNARE DRUMS	SOFT-SOAPED	SOUNDTRACK	SPEND LIMIT
SLINGSHOTS	SNARLINGLY	SOFT-SPOKEN	SOUP SPOONS	SPERMACETI
SLINKINESS	SNAZZINESS	SOJOURNERS	SOUR GRAPES	SPERMATIUM
SLINKINGLY	SNEAKINESS	SOJOURNING	SOURPUSSES	SPERMICIDE
SLIPPINESS	SNEAKINGLY	SOLAR CELLS	SOUSAPHONE	SPERM WHALE
SLIPPINGLY	SNEAK THIEF	SOLAR PANEL	SOUTHBOUND	SPERRYLITE
SLIPSTREAM	SNEERINGLY	SOLAR YEARS	SOUTH DOWNS	SPHALERITE
SLITHERING	SNEEZEWORT	SOLDERABLE	SOUTHERNER	SPHENOIDAL
SLOBBERING	SNICKERING	SOLDIERING	SOUTH KOREA	SPHERICITY
SLOPPINESS	SNIFFINGLY	SOLECISTIC	SOUTHWARDS	SPHEROIDAL
SLOPWORKER	SNIGGERING	SOLEMNIZED	SOU'WESTERS	SPHERULITE
SLOTHFULLY	SNIPPINESS	SOLEMNIZER	SOVEREIGNS	SPHINCTERS
SLOUCH HATS	SNIVELLERS	SOLEMNNESS	SPACECRAFT	SPICEBERRY
SLOW MOTION	SNIVELLING	SOLENOIDAL	SPACE PROBE	SPIDERWEBS
SLOW-WITTED	SNOBBISHLY	SOLFATARIC	SPACESHIPS	SPIDERWORT
SLUGGISHLY	SNOOKERING	SOLICITING	SPACESUITS	SPINAL CORD

SPINDLIEST	SPOTTINESS	STAGEHANDS	STAY-AT-	STIGMATISM
SPIN-DRYING	SPREADABLE	STAGE NAMES	HOME	STIGMATIST
SPINESCENT	SPRINGBOKS	STAGGERING	STAYCATION	STIGMATIZE
SPINNAKERS	SPRINGHAAS	STAGNANTLY	ST BERNARDS	STILLBIRTH
SPIRACULAR	SPRINGHEAD	STAGNATING	STEADINESS	STILL LIFES
SPIRALLING	SPRINGIEST	STAGNATION	STEAKHOUSE	STIMULABLE
SPIRITEDLY	SPRING ROLL	STAG NIGHTS	STEALTHIER	STIMULANTS
SPIRITLESS	SPRINGTAIL	STAIRCASES	STEALTHILY	STIMULATED
SPIRITUALS	SPRING TIDE	STAIRWELLS	STEAMBOATS	STIMULATOR
SPIRITUOUS	SPRINGTIME	STALACTITE	STEAM-CHEST	STINGINESS
SPIROGRAPH	SPRINGWOOD	STALAGMITE	STEAMINESS	STINGINGLY
SPIROMETER	SPRINKLERS	STALEMATED	STEAM IRONS	STINK-BOMBS
SPIROMETRY	SPRINKLING	STALEMATES	STEAMSHIPS	STINKINGLY
SPITEFULLY	SPRUCENESS	STALKINESS	STEAMTIGHT	STINKSTONE
SPLANCHNIC	SPUMESCENT	STALWARTLY	STEEL BANDS	STIPELLATE
SPLASHBACK	SPUNKINESS	STAMMERERS	STEELINESS	STIPULABLE
SPLASHDOWN	SPURIOUSLY	STAMMERING	STEELWORKS	STIPULATED
SPLASHIEST	SPUTTERING	STAMPEDING	STEEPENING	STIPULATOR
SPLATTERED	SPYGLASSES	STANCHABLE	STELLIFORM	STIR-FRYING
SPLEENWORT	SQUABBLING	STANCHIONS	STEM-WINDER	STIRRINGLY
SPLENDIDLY	SQUALIDITY	STANDPIPES	STENCILING	STIRRUP CUP
SPLINTERED	SQUALLIEST	STANDPOINT	STENCILLED	STITCHWORT
SPLIT HAIRS	SQUAMATION	STANDSTILL	STENCILLER	STOCHASTIC
SPLIT LEVEL	SQUAMULOSE	STARCHIEST	STENOGRAPH	STOCKADING
SPLIT-LEVEL	SQUANDERED	STARFISHES	STENOTYPIC	STOCK CUBES
SPLIT RINGS	SQUANDERER	STARFLOWER	STENTORIAN	STOCKINESS
SPLUTTERED	SQUARE DEAL	STARGAZERS	STEPFAMILY	STOCKPILED
SPLUTTERER	SQUARE KNOT	STARGAZING	STEPFATHER	STOCKPILER
SPOILSPORT	SQUARE MEAL	STARRINESS	STEPLADDER	STOCKPILES
SPOKESHAVE	SQUARENESS	STARRY-EYED	STEPMOTHER	STOCKROOMS
SPOLIATION	SQUARE ROOT	STARVATION	STEPPARENT	STOCK-STILL
SPONGE BAGS	SQUASHIEST	STARVELING	STEPSISTER	STOCKYARDS
SPONGE CAKE	SQUEAKIEST	STATECRAFT	STEREOBATE	STODGINESS
SPONGINESS	SQUEEZABLE	STATEMENTS	STEREOGRAM	STOKEHOLDS
SPONSORIAL	SQUEEZEBOX	STATEROOMS	STEREOPSIS	STOMACHING
SPONSORING	SQUELCHIER	STATIONARY	STEREOTOMY	STOMATITIC
SPOOKINESS	SQUELCHING	STATIONERS	STEREOTYPE	STOMATITIS
SPOONERISM	SQUETEAGUE	STATIONERY	STEREOTYPY	STOMATOPOD
SPORANGIAL	SQUIDGIEST	STATIONING	STERICALLY	STOMODAEAL
SPORANGIUM	SQUIFFIEST	STATISTICS	STERILIZED	STOMODAEUM
SPOROPHORE	SQUISHIEST	STATOBLAST	STERILIZER	STONE-BLIND
SPOROPHYLL	STABILATOR	STATOSCOPE	STERNWARDS	STONE FRUIT
SPOROPHYTE	STABILIZED	STATUESQUE	STERTOROUS	STONEHENGE
SPOROZOITE	STABILIZER	STATUETTES	STEVEDORES	STONEMASON
SPORTINESS	STABLE BOYS	STATUS ZERO	STEWARDESS	STONY BROKE
SPORTINGLY	STABLEFORD	STATUTABLE	STICKINESS	STOOPINGLY
SPORTIVELY	STABLENESS	STATUTE LAW	STICK SHIFT	STOPPERING
SPORTS CARS	STAFF NURSE	STAUNCHEST	STICKTIGHT	STOREHOUSE
SPORTSWEAR	STAG BEETLE	STAUNCHING	STICKY ENDS	STOREROOMS
SPOT CHECKS	STAGECOACH	STAUROLITE	STIFFENERS	STORKSBILL
SPOTLESSLY	STAGECRAFT	STAVESACRE	STIFFENING	STORMBOUND
SPOTLIGHTS	STAGE DOORS	STAVESACRE	STIFLINGLY	STORM CLOUD

STORMINESS	STRIP CLUBS	SUBJECTING	SUBTENDING	SUMMARIZED
STORMPROOF	STRIPLINGS	SUBJECTION	SUBTERFUGE	SUMMARIZER
STORY LINES	STRIPTEASE	SUBJECTIVE	SUBTILIZER	SUMMATIONS
STRABISMAL	STROKE PLAY	SUBJOINING	SUBTITULAR	SUMMERTIME
STRABISMUS	STRONGHOLD	SUBJUGABLE	SUBTLENESS	SUMMERWOOD
STRADDLING	STRONGNESS	SUBJUGATED	SUBTLETIES	SUMMINGS-UP
STRAGGLERS	STRONG ROOM	SUBJUGATOR	SUBTRACTED	SUMMONABLE
STRAGGLIER	STROPPIEST	SUBKINGDOM	SUBTRACTER	SUMMONSING
STRAGGLING	STRUCTURAL	SUBLEASING	SUBTRAHEND	SUNBATHERS
STRAIGHTEN	STRUCTURED	SUBLETTING	SUBTROPICS	SUNBATHING
STRAIGHTER	STRUCTURES	SUBLIMABLE	SUBTYPICAL	SUNDAY BEST
STRAITENED	STRUGGLING	SUBLIMATED	SUBVENTION	SUNDERLAND
STRAITNESS	STRUTHIOUS	SUBLIMATES	SUBVERSION	SUNDOWNERS
STRAMONIUM	STRYCHNINE	SUBLIMINAL	SUBVERSIVE	SUNFLOWERS
STRANGLERS	STUBBINESS	SUBLINGUAL	SUBVERTING	SUNGLASSES
STRANGLING	STUBBORNER	SUBMARINER	SUCCEEDING	SUNLOUNGER
STRASBOURG	STUBBORNLY	SUBMARINES	SUCCESSFUL	SUN LOUNGES
STRATAGEMS	STUDIOUSLY	SUBMEDIANT	SUCCESSION	SUPERBNESS
STRATEGICS	STUFFINESS	SUBMERGING	SUCCESSIVE	SUPERCARGO
STRATEGIES	STULTIFIED	SUBMERSION	SUCCESSORS	SUPERCLASS
STRATEGIST	STULTIFIER	SUBMISSION	SUCCINCTLY	SUPERDUPER
STRATIFIED	STUMPINESS	SUBMISSIVE	SUCCOURING	SUPER DUPER
STRATIFORM	STUNNINGLY	SUBMITTING	SUCCULENCE	SUPERFLUID
STRATOCRAT	STUPEFYING	SUBMONTANE	SUCCULENTS	SUPERGIANT
STRAWBERRY	STUPENDOUS	SUBOCEANIC	SUCCUMBING	SUPERGRASS
STRAWBOARD	STUPIDNESS	SUBOPTIMAL	SUCCUSSION	SUPERHUMAN
STRAW POLLS	STURDINESS	SUBORBITAL	SUCCUSSIVE	SUPERLUNAR
STREAKIEST	STUTTERERS	SUBORDINAL	SUCKERFISH	SUPERMODEL
STREAMLINE	STUTTERING	SUBPOENAED	SUCKING PIG	SUPERNOVAS
STREET ARAB	STYLISTICS	SUBPROGRAM	SUDDENNESS	SUPERORDER
STREETCARS	STYLOGRAPH	SUBREPTION	SUFFERABLE	SUPEROXIDE
STREETWISE	STYLOLITIC	SUBROUTINE	SUFFERANCE	SUPERPOWER
STRELITZIA	STYPTICITY	SUB-SAHARAN	SUFFERINGS	SUPERSEDED
STRENGTHEN	SUBACETATE	SUBSCRIBED	SUFFICIENT	SUPERSEDER
STRESS MARK	SUBACIDITY	SUBSCRIBER	SUFFOCATED	SUPERSONIC
STRETCHERS	SUBALTERNS	SUBSECTION	SUFFRAGISM	SUPERSTARS
STRETCHIER	SUBAQUATIC	SUBSEQUENT	SUFFRAGIST	SUPERTONIC
STRETCHING	SUBAQUEOUS	SUBSIDENCE	SUGAR DADDY	SUPERVENED
STRIATIONS	SUBCALIBRE	SUBSIDIARY	SUGARINESS	SUPERVISED
STRICTNESS	SUBCLAVIAN	SUBSIDIZED	SUGGESTING	SUPERVISOR
STRICTURES	SUBCOMPACT	SUBSIDIZER	SUGGESTION	SUPINENESS
STRIDENTLY	SUBCULTURE	SUBSISTENT	SUGGESTIVE	SUPPLANTED
STRIDULATE	SUBDIVIDED	SUBSISTING	SUICIDALLY	SUPPLANTER
STRIDULOUS	SUBDIVIDER	SUBSPECIES	SULLENNESS	SUPPLEJACK
STRIGIFORM	SUBDUCTION	SUBSTANCES	SULPHA DRUG	SUPPLEMENT
STRIKINGLY	SUBEDITING	SUBSTATION	SULPHATION	SUPPLENESS
STRING BEAN	SUBEDITORS	SUBSTITUTE	SULPHONATE	SUPPLETION
STRINGENCY	SUBGENERIC	SUBSTRATUM	SULPHURATE	SUPPLETIVE
STRINGENDO	SUBGLACIAL	SUBSUMABLE	SULPHURIZE	SUPPLETORY
STRINGHALT	SUBHEADING	SUBTANGENT	SULPHUROUS	SUPPLIABLE
STRINGIEST	SUBJACENCY	SUBTENANCY	SULTANATES	SUPPLIANCE
STRIPAGRAM	SUBJECTIFY	SUBTENANTS	SULTRINESS	SUPPLIANTS

SUPPLICANT	SVERDLOVSK	SYMPATHIES	TACHYMETRY	TATTOOISTS
SUPPLICATE	SWAGGERERS	SYMPATHIZE	TACITURNLY	TAUNTINGLY
SUPPORTERS	SWAGGERING	SYMPHONIES	TACTICALLY	TAUROMACHY
SUPPORTING	SWALLOWING	SYMPHONIST	TACTICIANS	TAUTOMERIC
SUPPORTIVE	SWANKINESS	SYMPHYSIAL	TACTLESSLY	TAUTONYMIC
SUPPOSABLE	SWAN-UPPING	SYMPHYSTIC	TAENIACIDE	TAWDRINESS
SUPPOSEDLY	SWARTHIEST	SYMPOSIUMS	TAENIAFUGE	TAXABILITY
SUPPRESSED	SWASHINGLY	SYNAGOGUES	TAGLIATELE	TAXATIONAL
SUPPRESSOR	SWEARINGLY	SYNCARPOUS	TAILBOARDS	TAXIDERMAL
SUPPURATED	SWEARWORDS	SYNCHRONIC	TAILGATING	TAXIMETERS
SUPRARENAL	SWEATBANDS	SYNCLASTIC	TAILLIGHTS	TAXONOMIST
SURCHARGED	SWEAT GLAND	SYNCOPATED	TAILORBIRD	TAX SHELTER
SURCHARGER	SWEATINESS	SYNCOPATOR	TAILOR-MADE	TEA CADDIES
SURCHARGES	SWEATSHIRT	SYNCRETISM	TAILPIECES	TEAGARDENS
SUREFOOTED	SWEATSHOPS	SYNCRETIST	TAJIKISTAN	TEAM SPIRIT
SURFACTANT	SWEEPINGLY	SYNCRETIZE	TAKE IN	TEA PARTIES
SURFBOARDS	SWEEPSTAKE	SYNDICATED	HAND	TEARJERKER
SURFCASTER	SWEETBREAD	SYNDICATES	TAKINGNESS	TEA SERVICE
SURFEITING	SWEETBRIER	SYNDICSHIP	TALCAHUANO	TEA TROLLEY
SURGICALLY	SWEETENERS	SYNECDOCHE	TALEBEARER	TECHNETIUM
SURINAMESE	SWEETENING	SYNECOLOGY	TALISMANIC	TECHNICIAN
SURJECTION	SWEETHEART	SYNERGETIC	TALKING-TOS	TECHNIQUES
SURJECTIVE	SWEETMEATS	SYNOECIOUS	TAMABILITY	TECHNOCRAT
SURMISABLE	SWEET TOOTH	SYNONYMITY	TAMAULIPAS	TECHNOLOGY
SURMISEDLY	SWELTERING	SYNONYMIZE	TAMBOURINE	TECTRICIAL
SURMOUNTED	SWERVINGLY	SYNONYMOUS	TANANARIVE	TEDDY BEARS
SURMOUNTER	SWIMMINGLY	SYNTACTICS	TANGANYIKA	TEENY WEENY
SURPASSING	SWINEHERDS	SYNTHESIST	TANGENTIAL	TELECASTER
SURPLUSAGE	SWINGINGLY	SYNTHESIZE	TANGERINES	TELEGNOSIS
SURPRISING	SWING SHIFT	SYNTHETISM	TANGLEMENT	TELEGRAPHS
SURREALISM	SWIRLINGLY	SYNTHETIST	TANTALIZED	TELEGRAPHY
SURREALIST	SWISHINGLY	SYPHILITIC	TANTALIZER	TELEMETRIC
SURRENDERS	SWISS CHARD	SYSTEMATIC	TANTALUSES	TELEPATHIC
SURROGATES	SWITCHABLE	SYSTEMIZER	TANTAMOUNT	TELEPHONED
SURROUNDED	SWITCHBACK		TAP DANCERS	TELEPHONER
SURVEYABLE	SWITCH CARD	**T**	TAP DANCING	TELEPHONES
SURVIVABLE	SWITCHED-ON	TABERNACLE	TAPERINGLY	TELESCOPED
SUSCEPTIVE	SWITCHGEAR	TABESCENCE	TAPESTRIED	TELESCOPES
SUSPECTING	SWIVELLING	TABLECLOTH	TAPESTRIES	TELESCOPIC
SUSPENDERS	SWOONINGLY	TABLE	TARANTELLA	TELESCRIPT
SUSPENDING	SWORDCRAFT	D'HOTE	TARANTULAS	TELEVISING
SUSPENSION	SWORD DANCE	TABLELANDS	TARDIGRADE	TELEVISION
SUSPENSIVE	SWORDSTICK	TABLE LINEN	TARMACKING	TELEVISUAL
SUSPENSOID	SYCOPHANTS	TABLESPOON	TARNISHING	TELEWRITER
SUSPENSORY	SYLLABUSES	TABULARIZE	TARPAULINS	TELIOSPORE
SUSPICIONS	SYLLOGISMS	TABULATING	TASIMETRIC	TELLING-OFF
SUSPICIOUS	SYLLOGIZER	TABULATION	TASK FORCES	TELOPHASIC
SUSTAINING	SYLPHIDINE	TACHOGRAPH	TASKMASTER	TELPHERAGE
SUSTENANCE	SYLVESTRAL	TACHOMETER	TASTEFULLY	TEMPERABLE
SUSTENTION	SYMBIONTIC	TACHOMETRY	TATTERSALL	TEMPERANCE
SUTHERLAND	SYMBOLIZED	TACHYLYTIC	TATTLETALE	TEMPORIZED
SUZERAINTY	SYMMETRIZE	TACHYMETER	TATTLINGLY	TEMPORIZER

TEMPTATION	TETRAPLOID	THORNINESS	TILLANDSIA	TOMOGRAPHY
TEMPTINGLY	TETRAPODIC	THOROUGHLY	TIMBERHEAD	TONALITIES
TENABILITY	TETRARCHIC	THOUGHTFUL	TIMBERLINE	TONELESSLY
TENDENCIES	TETRASPORE	THOUGHT-OUT	TIMBERWORK	TONGUE-TIED
TENDERABLE	TETRASTICH	THOUSANDTH	TIMBERYARD	TONIC SOL-
TENDERFEET	TETRATOMIC	THRASH PUNK	TIMEKEEPER	FA
TENDERFOOT	TEWKESBURY	THREADBARE	TIMELESSLY	TONIC WATER
TENDERIZED	TEXTUALISM	THREADWORM	TIME LIMITS	TONOMETRIC
TENDERIZER	TEXTUALIST	THREATENED	TIMELINESS	TOOL-MAKING
TENDERLOIN	TEXTURALLY	THREATENER	TIMEPIECES	TOOTHACHES
TENDERNESS	THANKFULLY	THREEPENCE	TIMESAVING	TOOTHBRUSH
TENDRILLAR	THEATRICAL	THREE-PHASE	TIME-SAVING	TOOTHCOMBS
TENEMENTAL	THEME PARKS	THREE-PIECE	TIMESERVER	TOOTHINESS
TENGRI KHAN	THEME SONGS	THREESOMES	TIME SHEETS	TOOTHPASTE
TENNESSEAN	THEMSELVES	THRENODIES	TIME SIGNAL	TOOTHPICKS
TENOTOMIST	THENARDITE	THRESHOLDS	TIME SWITCH	TOPAZOLITE
TENSIMETER	THEOCRATIC	THRIFTIEST	TIMETABLED	TOPGALLANT
TENTACULAR	THEODOLITE	THRIFTLESS	TIMETABLES	TOP-HEAVILY
TENTERHOOK	THEOLOGIAN	THROATIEST	TIMEWORKER	TOPICALITY
TERATOLOGY	THEOLOGIES	THROATLASH	TIMOROUSLY	TOPOGRAPHY
TERENGGANU	THEOLOGIZE	THROMBOGEN	TIMPANISTS	TOPOLOGIST
TERMAGANCY	THEOPHOBIA	THROMBOSES	TINCTORIAL	TOPPING OUT
TERMAGANTS	THEORETICS	THROMBOSIS	TINGALINGS	TOPSY-TURVY
TERMINABLE	THEORIZING	THROMBOTIC	TINGLINGLY	TORBERNITE
TERMINALLY	THEOSOPHIC	THROTTLING	TIN OPENERS	TORCHLIGHT
TERMINATED	THERAPISTS	THROUGHOUT	TIRELESSLY	TORMENTING
TERMINATOR	THEREAFTER	THROUGHPUT	TIRESOMELY	TORMENTORS
TERMINUSES	THEREUNDER	THROUGHWAY	TITANESQUE	TORPEDOING
TERRACOTTA	THERMALIZE	THROWBACKS	TITILLATED	TORRENTIAL
TERRA FIRMA	THERMIONIC	THUMBNAILS	TITIVATING	TORTELLINI
TERRAMYCIN	THERMISTOR	THUMBSCREW	TITIVATION	TORT-FEASOR
TERREPLEIN	THERMOGRAM	THUMBSTALL	TITLE DEEDS	TORTUOSITY
TERRE-VERTE	THERMOPILE	THUMBTACKS	TITLE PAGES	TORTUOUSLY
TERRIFYING	THERMOSTAT	THUMPINGLY	TITLE ROLES	TORTUREDLY
TERRORISTS	THEROPODAN	THUNDER BAY	TITRATABLE	TOTEMISTIC
TERRORIZED	THESSALIAN	THUNDERERS	TITUBATION	TOTEM POLES
TERRORIZER	THETICALLY	THUNDERFLY	T-JUNCTIONS	TOTIPOTENT
TERRYCLOTH	THICKENERS	THUNDERING	TOADSTOOLS	TOUCH-AND-
TESSELLATE	THICKENING	THUNDEROUS	TOBOGGANED	GO
TESTACEOUS	THIEVINGLY	THURINGIAN	TOBOGGANER	TOUCHDOWNS
TESTAMENTS	THIEVISHLY	THWARTEDLY	TOCOPHEROL	TOUCHINESS
TESTICULAR	THIMBLEFUL	TICKERTAPE	TOILETRIES	TOUCHINGLY
TESTIFYING	THIMEROSAL	TICKING OFF	TOILET ROLL	TOUCHLINES
TEST PILOTS	THINK TANKS	TICKLISHLY	TOLERANTLY	TOUCHPAPER
TESTUDINAL	THIOURACIL	TIDAL WAVES	TOLERATING	TOUCHSTONE
TETCHINESS	THIRD PARTY	TIEBREAKER	TOLERATION	TOUCH-TYPED
TETE-A-	THIRD WORLD	TIED HOUSES	TOLERATIVE	TOUGHENING
TETES	THIRSTIEST	TIEMANNITE	TOLLBOOTHS	TOURMALINE
TETRABASIC	THIRTEENTH	TIGHTENING	TOLLUIDINE	TOURNAMENT
TETRABRACH	THIRTIETHS	TIGHTROPES	TOLUIC ACID	TOURNIQUET
TETRACHORD	THIXOTROPY	TIGLIC ACID	TOMBSTONES	TOWER BLOCK
TETRAGONAL	THORIANITE	TILIACEOUS	TOMFOOLERY	TOWN CLERKS

TOWN CRIERS	TRANSIENCY	TRIANGULAR	TRISKELION	TRYINGNESS
TOWN HOUSES	TRANSISTOR	TRIBRACHIC	TRISTICHIC	TRYPTOPHAN
TOWNSCAPES	TRANSITION	TRICHIASIS	TRITANOPIA	TUBERCULAR
TOWNSVILLE	TRANSITIVE	TRICHINIZE	TRITANOPIC	TUBERCULIN
TOWNSWOMAN	TRANSITORY	TRICHINOUS	TRITURABLE	TUBEROSITY
TOXALBUMIN	TRANSKEIAN	TRICHOCYST	TRITURATOR	TUB-THUMPER
TOXICOLOGY	TRANSLATED	TRICHOGYNE	TRIUMPHANT	TUBULARITY
TRABEATION	TRANSLATOR	TRICHOLOGY	TRIUMPHING	TUBULATION
TRABECULAR	TRANSLUNAR	TRICHOTOMY	TRIVALENCY	TUFFACEOUS
TRACHEIDAL	TRANSMUTED	TRICHROISM	TRIVANDRUM	TUGS-OF-
TRACHEITIS	TRANSMUTER	TRICHROMAT	TRIVIALITY	LOVE
TRACHYTOID	TRANSPIRED	TRICKINESS	TRIVIALIZE	TULARAEMIA
TRACK EVENT	TRANSPLANT	TRICKINGLY	TROCHANTER	TULARAEMIC
TRACKLAYER	TRANSPOLAR	TRICKSTERS	TROGLODYTE	TUMBLEDOWN
TRACKSUITS	TRANSPORTS	TRICOLOURS	TROLLEYBUS	TUMBLEWEED
TRACTILITY	TRANSPOSED	TRICOSTATE	TROLLEY BUS	TUMESCENCE
TRACTIONAL	TRANSPOSER	TRICROTISM	TROMBONIST	TUMULOSITY
TRADEMARKS	TRANSPUTER	TRIDENTATE	TROOPSHIPS	TUMULTUOUS
TRADE NAMES	TRANSUDATE	TRIDENTINE	TROPAEOLIN	TUNELESSLY
TRADE PRICE	TRANSVALUE	TRIFLINGLY	TROPAEOLUM	TUNING FORK
TRADE ROUTE	TRANSVERSE	TRIFOLIATE	TROPICALLY	TUNING PEGS
TRADE UNION	TRAPEZIUMS	TRIFURCATE	TROPICBIRD	TUNNELLING
TRADE WINDS	TRAPEZOIDS	TRIGEMINAL	TROPOLOGIC	TUPPERWARE
TRADITIONS	TRASHINESS	TRIGGERING	TROPOPAUSE	TURBOPROPS
TRADUCIBLE	TRAUMATISM	TRIGLYPHIC	TROPOPHYTE	TURBULENCE
TRAFFIC JAM	TRAUMATIZE	TRIGRAPHIC	TROTSKYISM	TURGESCENT
TRAFFICKED	TRAVAILING	TRIHYDRATE	TROTSKYIST	TURNABOUTS
TRAFFICKER	TRAVELLERS	TRILATERAL	TROTSKYITE	TURNAROUND
TRAGACANTH	TRAVELLING	TRILINGUAL	TROUBADOUR	TURNBUCKLE
TRAGEDIANS	TRAVELOGUE	TRILITERAL	TROUBLEDLY	TURNROUNDS
TRAGICALLY	TRAVELSICK	TRILLIONTH	TROUSSEAUS	TURNSTILES
TRAGICOMIC	TRAVERSING	TRILOBITES	TROUSSEAUX	TURNTABLES
TRAILINGLY	TRAVERTINE	TRILOCULAR	TROWBRIDGE	TURPENTINE
TRAITOROUS	TRAVESTIES	TRIMESTERS	TROY WEIGHT	TURQUOISES
TRAJECTILE	TREADMILLS	TRIMESTRAL	TRUCK FARMS	TURTLEBACK
TRAJECTION	TREAD WATER	TRIMONTHLY	TRUCKLOADS	TURTLEDOVE
TRAJECTORY	TREASURERS	TRIMORPHIC	TRUCK STOPS	TURTLENECK
TRAMONTANE	TREASURIES	TRINOCULAR	TRUCULENCE	TUT-TUTTING
TRAMPOLINE	TREASURING	TRIOECIOUS	TRUMP CARDS	TWELVE-TONE
TRANCELIKE	TREATMENTS	TRIPARTITE	TRUMPETERS	TWENTIETHS
TRANQUILLY	TREBLE CLEF	TRIPHAMMER	TRUMPETING	TWIN-BEDDED
TRANSACTED	TREEHOPPER	TRIPHTHONG	TRUNCATING	TWINFLOWER
TRANSACTOR	TREMENDOUS	TRIPHYLITE	TRUNCATION	TWINKLINGS
TRANSCRIBE	TRENCHANCY	TRIPINNATE	TRUNCHEONS	TWISTINGLY
TRANSCRIPT	TRENCH COAT	TRIPLE JUMP	TRUNK CALLS	TWITTERATI
TRANSDUCER	TRENDINESS	TRIPLETAIL	TRUNK ROADS	TWITTERING
TRANSEPTAL	TREPANNING	TRIPLICATE	TRUNK ROUTE	TYMPANITES
TRANSFEREE	TREPHINING	TRIPLICITY	TRUSTFULLY	TYMPANITIC
TRANSFEROR	TREPPANNER	TRIPPINGLY	TRUST FUNDS	TYMPANITIS
TRANSFIXED	TRESPASSED	TRIPTEROUS	TRUSTINESS	TYPECASTER
TRANSGRESS	TRESPASSER	TRIRADIATE	TRUTHFULLY	TYPESCRIPT
TRANSIENCE	TRESPASSES	TRISECTING	TRUTH-VALUE	TYPESETTER

TYPEWRITER	UNBURDENED	UNDERSTOCK	UNHALLOWED	UNPLEASANT
TYPHLOLOGY	UNCANNIEST	UNDERSTOOD	UNHAMPERED	UNPREPARED
TYPHOGENIC	UNCARED-FOR	UNDERSTUDY	UNHANDSOME	UNPROMPTED
TYPING POOL	UNCARPETED	UNDERTAKEN	UNHERALDED	UNPROVIDED
TYPOGRAPHY	UNCIVILITY	UNDERTAKER	UNHOLINESS	UNPROVOKED
TYPOLOGIST	UNCOMMONLY	UNDERTONES	UNHOPED-FOR	UNPUNCTUAL
TYRANNICAL	UNCONFINED	UNDERTRICK	UNHYGIENIC	UNPUNISHED
TYRANNIZED	UNCOUPLING	UNDERTRUMP	UNICAMERAL	UNRAVELING
TYRANNIZER	UNCOVERING	UNDERVALUE	UNICOSTATE	UNRAVELLED
TYROCIDINE	UNCREDITED	UNDERWATER	UNICYCLIST	UNRAVELLER
TYROSINASE	UNCRITICAL	UNDERWIRED	UNIFOLIATE	UNREACTIVE
	UNCTUOSITY	UNDERWORLD	UNIFORMITY	UNREADABLE
U	UNCTUOUSLY	UNDERWRITE	UNILATERAL	UNREADABLY
UBIQUITOUS	UNDECEIVED	UNDERWROTE	UNILOCULAR	UNRELIABLE
ULCERATING	UNDECEIVER	UNDETERRED	UNIMPOSING	UNRELIEVED
ULCERATION	UNDEFEATED	UNDIRECTED	UNIMPROVED	UNREQUITED
ULCERATIVE	UNDEFENDED	UNDISPUTED	UNINFORMED	UNRESERVED
ULTIMATELY	UNDENIABLE	UNDRESSING	UNINSPIRED	UNRESOLVED
ULTIMATUMS	UNDENIABLY	UNDULATING	UNINTENDED	UNRIVALLED
ULTRAFICHE	UNDERACTED	UNDULATION	UNIONISTIC	UNRULINESS
ULTRAISTIC	UNDERBELLY	UNDULATORY	UNIONIZING	UNSADDLING
ULTRASHORT	UNDERBRUSH	UNEARTHING	UNIQUENESS	UNSANITARY
ULTRASONIC	UNDERCOATS	UNEASINESS	UNISEPTATE	UNSCHOOLED
ULTRASOUND	UNDERCOVER	UNECONOMIC	UNITARIANS	UNSCRAMBLE
ULTRAVIRUS	UNDERCROFT	UNEDIFYING	UNITEDNESS	UNSCREENED
UMBILICATE	UNDERDRAIN	UNEDUCATED	UNIT TRUSTS	UNSCREWING
UMBILIFORM	UNDERFLOOR	UNEMPLOYED	UNIVALENCY	UNSCRIPTED
UMBRAGEOUS	UNDERGLAZE	UNENVIABLE	UNIVERSITY	UNSEALABLE
UMPIRESHIP	UNDERGOING	UNEQUALLED	UNJUSTNESS	UNSEASONED
UMPTEENTHS	UNDERGROWN	UNERRINGLY	UNKINDNESS	UNSEEINGLY
UNABRIDGED	UNDERLINED	UNEVENNESS	UNKNOWABLE	UNSETTLING
UNACCENTED	UNDERLINGS	UNEVENTFUL	UNLAWFULLY	UNSHAKABLE
UNADJUSTED	UNDERLYING	UNEXAMPLED	UNLEARNING	UNSOCIABLE
UNAFFECTED	UNDERMINED	UNEXPECTED	UNLEASHING	UNSPEAKING
UN-AMERICAN	UNDERMINER	UNEXPLODED	UNLEAVENED	UNSPECIFIC
UNASSISTED	UNDERNAMED	UNFAIRNESS	UNLETTERED	UNSTEADILY
UNASSUMING	UNDERNEATH	UNFAITHFUL	UNLICENSED	UNSTINTING
UNATTACHED	UNDERPANTS	UNFAMILIAR	UNLOCKABLE	UNSTOPPING
UNATTENDED	UNDERPRICE	UNFATHERED	UNLOOSENED	UNSTRAINED
UNAVAILING	UNDERPROOF	UNFEMININE	UNMANNERED	UNSTRESSED
UNBALANCED	UNDERQUOTE	UNFETTERED	UNMANNERLY	UNSTRIATED
UNBEARABLE	UNDERRATED	UNFINISHED	UNMEASURED	UNSUITABLE
UNBEARABLY	UNDERSCORE	UNFLAGGING	UNMEDIATED	UNSURFACED
UNBEATABLE	UNDERSEXED	UNFORESEEN	UNMERCIFUL	UNSWERVING
UNBECOMING	UNDERSHIRT	UNFORGIVEN	UNMORALITY	UNTANGLING
UNBELIEVER	UNDERSHOOT	UNFRIENDLY	UNNUMBERED	UNTHANKFUL
UNBENDABLE	UNDERSIZED	UNFROCKING	UNOCCUPIED	UNTHINKING
UNBLINKING	UNDERSKIRT	UNFRUITFUL	UNOFFICIAL	UNTIDINESS
UNBLUSHING	UNDERSLUNG	UNGENEROUS	UNORIGINAL	UNTIRINGLY
UNBOSOMING	UNDERSPEND	UNGRATEFUL	UNORTHODOX	
UNBUCKLING	UNDERSTAND	UNGRUDGING	UNPATENTED	
UNBUNDLING	UNDERSTATE	UNGUENTARY	UNPLAYABLE	

UNTOWARDLY	USURPATIVE	VARITYPIST	VIBRAPHONE	VISCOMETRY
UNTRUSTING	USURPINGLY	VARNISHING	VIBRATIONS	VISCOUNTCY
UNTRUTHFUL	UTILIZABLE	VASTNESSES	VICEGERENT	VISIBILITY
UNWIELDILY	UTO-AZTECAN	VAUDEVILLE	VICEREINES	VISITATION
UNWINDABLE	UTOPIANISM	VAUNTINGLY	VICINITIES	VISITORIAL
UNWORKABLE	UTTERANCES	VEGETABLES	VICOMTESSE	VISUAL AIDS
UNWORTHILY	UXORICIDAL	VEGETARIAN	VICTIMIZED	VISUALIZED
UNYIELDING	UZBEKISTAN	VEGETATING	VICTIMIZER	VISUALIZER
UP-AND-		VEGETATION	VICTIMLESS	VITALISTIC
UNDER	**V**	VEGETATIVE	VICTORIANA	VITAL SIGNS
UPBRAIDING	VACANTNESS	VEHEMENTLY	VICTORIANS	VITRESCENT
UPBRINGING	VACATIONED	VELOCIPEDE	VICTORIOUS	VITRIFYING
UPHOLSTERY	VACATIONER	VELOCITIES	VICTUALING	VITRIOLIZE
UP IN THE	VACCINATED	VELUTINOUS	VICTUALLED	VITUPERATE
AIR	VACILLATED	VENATIONAL	VICTUALLER	VIVIPARITY
UPLIFTMENT	VACILLATOR	VENDETTIST	VIDEODISCS	VIVIPAROUS
UPON MY	VACUUM PUMP	VENERATING	VIDEO NASTY	VIVISECTOR
WORD	VAGAZZLING	VENERATION	VIDEOPHILE	VOCABULARY
UPPER CLASS	VAGINISMUS	VENEZUELAN	VIDEOPHONE	VOCAL CORDS
UPPER CRUST	VAGOTROPIC	VENGEANCES	VIDEOTAPED	VOCATIONAL
UPPER EGYPT	VAL-DE-	VENGEFULLY	VIETNAMESE	VOCIFERANT
UPPER HOUSE	MARNE	VENOMOUSLY	VIEWFINDER	VOCIFERATE
UPPER VOLTA	VALENTINES	VENOUSNESS	VIEWPOINTS	VOCIFEROUS
UPPISHNESS	VALIDATING	VENTILABLE	VIGILANTES	VOETSTOETS
UPROARIOUS	VALIDATION	VENTILATED	VIGILANTLY	VOICE BOXES
UPSETTABLE	VALIDATORY	VENTILATOR	VIGNETTING	VOICE-OVERS
UPSIDE DOWN	VALLADOLID	VENTRICLES	VIGNETTIST	VOICEPRINT
UPSTANDING	VALLECULAR	VENTRICOSE	VIGOROUSLY	VOLAPUKIST
UP THE	VALPARAISO	VERBALIZED	VIJAYAWADA	VOLATILITY
SPOUT	VALUATIONS	VERBALIZER	VILLAINOUS	VOLATILIZE
UP THE	VALVULITIS	VERBAL NOUN	VILLANELLA	VOL-AU-
STAKE	VAMPIRE BAT	VERIFIABLE	VILLANELLE	VENTS
UP THE	VANADINITE	VERKRAMPTE	VILLANOVAN	VOLITIONAL
STICK	VANDALIZED	VERMICELLI	VINA DEL	VOLLEYBALL
UPWARDNESS	VAN DER	VERMICIDAL	MAR	VOLT-AMPERE
URAL-ALTAIC	POST	VERMICULAR	VINDICABLE	VOLTE-FACES
URBANENESS	VANISHMENT	VERNACULAR	VINDICATED	VOLUBILITY
UREDOSORUS	VANQUISHED	VERNISSAGE	VINDICATOR	VOLUMETRIC
UREDOSPORE	VANQUISHER	VERSAILLES	VINDICTIVE	VOLUMINOUS
URETHRITIC	VAPORIZING	VERTEBRATE	VINIFEROUS	VOLUNTEERS
URETHRITIS	VAPOURABLE	VERTICALLY	VINYLIDENE	VOLUPTUARY
URINALYSIS	VARIATIONS	VERY LIGHTS	VIOLACEOUS	VOLUPTUOUS
UROCHORDAL	VARICELLAR	VESICATION	VIOLATIONS	VORARLBERG
UROGENITAL	VARICOCELE	VESICULATE	VIOLINISTS	VORTICELLA
UROSCOPIST	VARICOSITY	VESPERTINE	VIRAGINOUS	VOTIVENESS
URTICARIAL	VARICOTOMY	VESTIBULAR	VIRESCENCE	VOUCHSAFED
URTICATION	VARIEDNESS	VESTIBULES	VIROLOGIST	VULCANIZED
USEFULNESS	VARIEGATED	VESTMENTAL	VIRTUALITY	VULCANIZER
USHERETTES	VARIFOCALS	VESTMENTED	VIRTUOSITY	VULGARIZED
USQUEBAUGH	ANGLO-SAXON	VETERINARY	VIRTUOUSLY	VULGARIZER
USTULATION	VARIOLITIC	VIBRACULAR	VIRULENTLY	VULGARNESS
USURPATION	VARIOMETER	VIBRACULUM	VISCOMETER	VULNERABLE

VULNERABLY	WATERCRAFT	WELL I	WHITE HOUSE	WINE COOLER
VULPECULAR	WATERCRESS	NEVER	WHITE MAGIC	WINEMAKING
	WATERFALLS	WELLINGTON	WHITE METAL	WINTERFEED
W	WATERFOWLS	WELL-JUDGED	WHITE PAPER	WINTERTHUR
WADDLINGLY	WATERFRONT	WELL-SPOKEN	WHITE SAUCE	WINTERTIME
WADING POOL	WATERHOLES	WELLSPRING	WHITESMITH	WINTRINESS
WAGE SLAVES	WATERINESS	WELL-TURNED	WHITE TRASH	WIRE-HAIRED
WAGGA WAGGA	WATER JUMPS	WELL-WISHER	WHITEWATER	WIRELESSES
WAGGLINGLY	WATER LEVEL	WELL-WORDED	WHITLEY BAY	WIREWORKER
WAGONS-LITS	WATER MAINS	WENTLETRAP	WHITTLINGS	WISECRACKS
WAINWRIGHT	WATERMARKS	WEREWOLVES	WHOLEFOODS	WISHY-WASHY
WAISTBANDS	WATERMELON	WEST BENGAL	WHOLE NOTES	WITCHCRAFT
WAISTCOATS	WATER METER	WESTERLIES	WHOLESALER	WITCH-HAZEL
WAISTLINES	WATERMILLS	WESTERNERS	WHOREHOUSE	WITCH-HUNTS
WAITPERSON	WATER PIPES	WESTERNISM	WICKEDNESS	WITHDRAWAL
WAKEY WAKEY	WATERPOWER	WESTERNIZE	WICKERWORK	WITHDRAWER
WALKABOUTS	WATERPROOF	WEST INDIAN	WICKET GATE	WITHHOLDER
WALK OF	WATER RATES	WEST INDIES	WIDE-SCREEN	WITNESS BOX
LIFE	WATERSCAPE	WESTPHALIA	WIDESPREAD	WITNESSING
WALLCHARTS	WATERSHEDS	WEST RIDING	WIDOW'S	WITTENBERG
WALLFLOWER	WATER SKIER	WET BLANKET	MITE	WITTICISMS
WALLPAPERS	WATERSPOUT	WET-NURSING	WIFELINESS	WOBBLINESS
WALL STREET	WATER TABLE	WHARFINGER	WILDCATTED	WOEFULNESS
WALL-TO-	WATERTIGHT	WHATSOEVER	WILDEBEEST	WOLFHOUNDS
WALL	WATER VOLES	WHEELBASES	WILDERNESS	WOLFRAMITE
WANDERINGS	WATERWHEEL	WHEELCHAIR	WILDFOWLER	WOLLONGONG
WANDERLUST	WATERWINGS	WHEELHOUSE	WILFULNESS	WOMANIZERS
WANDSWORTH	WATERWORKS	WHEELIE BIN	WILLEMSTAD	WOMANIZING
WANTONNESS	WATTLEBIRD	WHEEZINESS	WILLOWHERB	WOMENSWEAR
WAREHOUSES	WAVELENGTH	WHEEZINGLY	WILLY-NILLY	WONDERLAND
WARMING PAN	WAVERINGLY	WHENSOEVER	WILMINGTON	WONDERMENT
WARMONGERS	WAXED PAPER	WHEREFORES	WINCEYETTE	WONDERWORK
WARRANTIES	WEAKLINESS	WHETSTONES	WINCHESTER	WOODBLOCKS
WARRANTING	WEAK-MINDED	WHICKERING	WINDBREAKS	WOODCARVER
WARRINGTON	WEAKNESSES	WHIMPERING	WIND-BROKEN	WOODCUTTER
WASHBASINS	WEAK-WILLED	WHIPLASHES	WINDEDNESS	WOODENNESS
WASHCLOTHS	WEALTHIEST	WHIP-ROUNDS	WINDFLOWER	WOODLANDER
WASHING DAY	WEARYINGLY	WHIPSTITCH	WINDGALLED	WOODPECKER
WASHINGTON	WEATHERING	WHIRLABOUT	WIND GAUGES	WOODWORKER
WASHSTANDS	WEATHERMAN	WHIRLIGIGS	WINDJAMMER	WOOKEY HOLE
WASTEFULLY	WEATHERMEN	WHIRLINGLY	WINDLASSES	WOOLGROWER
WASTELANDS	WEAVERBIRD	WHIRLPOOLS	WINDOWPANE	WOOLLINESS
WASTE PAPER	WEDNESDAYS	WHIRLWINDS	WINDOW-SHOP	WORDLESSLY
WATCHFULLY	WEEDKILLER	WHIRLYBIRD	WINDOWSILL	WORKAHOLIC
WATCHMAKER	WEEKENDERS	WHISPERERS	WINDSCREEN	WORKBASKET
WATCH NIGHT	WEEKENDING	WHISPERING	WINDSHIELD	WORK-HARDEN
WATCHSTRAP	WEEKNIGHTS	WHIST DRIVE	WIND SLEEVE	WORKHORSES
WATCHTOWER	WEIGHTLESS	WHITEBOARD	WINDSTORMS	WORKING DAY
WATCHWORDS	WELL-ARGUED	WHITE DWARF	WINDSUCKER	WORKINGMAN
WATER BIRDS	WELL-CHOSEN	WHITE FLAGS	WIND-SURFER	WORKPEOPLE
WATERBORNE	WELL-EARNED	WHITE HOPES	WIND TUNNEL	WORKPLACES
WATER BUTTS	WELL-HEELED	WHITE HORSE	WINEBIBBER	WORKPLACES

WORK-TO-
  RULE
WORLD-CLASS
WORLDLIEST
WORLD POWER
WORLD-WEARY
WORRYINGLY
WORRYWARTS
WORSHIPFUL
WORSHIPING
WORSHIPPED
WORSHIPPER
WORTHINESS
WORTHWHILE
WOUNDINGLY
WRAITHLIKE
WRATHFULLY
WRETCHEDLY
WRISTBANDS

WRISTWATCH
WRITHINGLY
WRONGDOERS
WRONGDOING
WRONGFULLY
WUNDERKIND

X

XANTHATION
XENOGAMOUS
XENOLITHIC
XENOPHOBIA
XENOPHOBIC
XEROGRAPHY
XEROPHYTIC
XIPHOSURAN
XOCHIMILCO
X-RADIATION

X-RAY
  BINARY
XYLOGRAPHY
XYLOPHONES
XYLOPHONIC
XYLOTOMIST
XYLOTOMOUS

Y

YARBOROUGH
YARDSTICKS
YEASTINESS
YELLOWBARK
YELLOWBIRD
YELLOWCAKE
YELLOWLEGS
YELLOWTAIL
YELLOWWEED
YELLOWWOOD

YESTERDAYS
YESTERYEAR
YIELDINGLY
YLANG-YLANG
YOGYAKARTA
YOSHKAR-OLA
YOUNGBERRY
YOUNGSTERS
YOUNGSTOWN
YOURSELVES
YOUTHFULLY
YUGOSLAVIA

Z

ZAPOROZHYE
ZENER DIODE
ZIGZAGGING
ZINCOGRAPH

ZOOGRAPHER
ZOOGRAPHIC
ZOOLATROUS
ZOOLOGICAL
ZOOLOGISTS
ZOOM LENSES
ZOOMORPHIC
ZOOPHAGOUS
ZOOPHILISM
ZOOPHILOUS
ZOOPHOBOUS
ZOOPLASTIC
ZWITTERION
ZYGODACTYL
ZYGOMYCETE
ZYGOSPORIC
ZYMOLOGIST

11

A	ACCESSORIAL	ACQUIESCING	ADVENTUROUS	AGGRAVATION
ABANDONEDLY	ACCESSORIES	ACQUIREMENT	ADVERBIALLY	AGGREGATING
ABANDONMENT	ACCESSORILY	ACQUISITION	ADVERSARIAL	AGGREGATION
ABBEVILLIAN	ACCIPITRINE	ACQUISITIVE	ADVERSARIES	AGGRIEVEDLY
ABBREVIATED	ACCLAMATION	ACQUITTANCE	ADVERSATIVE	AGNOSTICISM
ABBREVIATOR	ACCLAMATORY	ACRIFLAVINE	ADVERSITIES	AGONIZINGLY
ABDICATIONS	ACCLIMATIZE	ACRIMONIOUS	ADVERTENTLY	AGONY
ABERRATIONS	ACCLIVITIES	ACROCARPOUS	ADVERTISERS	COLUMN
ABERYSTWYTH	ACCLIVITOUS	ACROMEGALIC	ADVERTISING	AGORAPHOBIA
ABIETIC	ACCOMMODATE	ACTINICALLY	ADVERTORIAL	AGORAPHOBIC
ACID	ACCOMPANIED	ACTINOMETER	AEOLIAN	AGRARIANISM
ABIOGENESIS	ACCOMPANIER	ACTINOMETRY	HARP	AGRICULTURE
ABIOGENETIC	ACCOMPANIST	ACTINOMYCIN	AERODYNAMIC	AGROBIOLOGY
ABLUTIONARY	ACCOMPLICES	ACTUALITIES	AEROGRAMMES	AGROLOGICAL
ABNORMALITY	ACCORDANCES	ACUMINATION	AERONAUTICS	AGROSTOLOGY
ABOLISHMENT	ACCORDINGLY	ACUPRESSURE	AEROSTATICS	AIDE-
ABOMINATING	ACCOUNTABLE	ACUPUNCTURE	AEROSTATION	MEMOIRE
ABOMINATION	ACCOUNTANCY	ADAM'S	AESTIVATION	AIDES-DE-
ABORIGINALS	ACCOUNTANTS	APPLES	AETIOLOGIST	CAMP
ABORTIONIST	ACCULTURATE	ADAPTATIONS	AFFECTATION	AILUROPHILE
ABRACADABRA	ACCUMULABLE	ADIAPHORISM	AFFECTINGLY	AILUROPHOBE
ABRANCHIATE	ACCUMULATED	ADIAPHORIST	AFFECTIONAL	AIMLESSNESS
ABRIDGMENTS	ACCUMULATOR	ADIAPHOROUS	AFFECTIVITY	AIRCRAFTMAN
ABROGATIONS	ACCUSATIONS	AD INFINI-	AFFILIATING	AIRCRAFTMEN
ABSENTEEISM	ACCUSATIVAL	TUM	AFFILIATION	AIRLESSNESS
ABSORBINGLY	ACCUSATIVES	ADIPOCEROUS	AFFIRMATION	AIRSICKNESS
ABSORPTANCE	ACCUSTOMING	ADJOURNMENT	AFFIRMATIVE	AIR TERMI-
ABSTENTIONS	ACETANILIDE	ADJUDICATED	AFFLICTIONS	NAL
ABSTENTIOUS	ACETYLATION	ADJUDICATOR	AFFORESTING	AIX-LES-
ABSTRACTING	ACHIEVEMENT	ADJUSTMENTS	AFFRANCHISE	BAINS
ABSTRACTION	ACHONDRITIC	ADMIRATIONS	AFFRICATIVE	ALARM
ABSTRACTIVE	ACHROMATISM	ADMONISHING	AFGHANISTAN	CLOCKS
ABSTRICTION	ACHROMATIZE	ADMONITIONS	AFICIONADOS	ALBATROSSES
ABSURDITIES	ACHROMATOUS	ADOLESCENCE	AFRO-ASI-	ALBUMINURIA
ABUSIVENESS	ACID-FORM-	ADOLESCENTS	ATIC	ALBUQUERQUE
ACADEMICALS	ING	ADOPTIONISM	AFTERBIRTHS	ALCOHOL-
ACADEMICIAN	ACIDIFIABLE	ADOPTIONIST	AFTERBURNER	FREE
ACADEMICISM	ACIDIMETRIC	ADULTERATED	AFTEREFFECT	ALDERMASTON
ACARPELLOUS	ACIDOPHILIC	ADULTERATOR	AFTERSHAVES	ALDERPERSON
ACATALECTIC	ACIDOPHILUS	ADUMBRATING	AFTERTASTES	ALDOSTERONE
ACAULESCENT	ACIDULATION	ADUMBRATION	AGAMOSPERMY	ALESSANDRIA
ACCELERANDO	ACINACIFORM	ADUMBRATIVE	AGELESSNESS	ALGEBRAICAL
ACCELERATED	ACKNOWLEDGE	ADVANCEMENT	AGGLOMERATE	ALGINIC
ACCELERATOR	ACLINIC	ADVANCINGLY	AGGLUTINANT	ACID
ACCENTUATED	LINE	ADVENTURERS	AGGLUTINATE	ALGOLAGNIST
ACCEPTANCES	ACOUSTICIAN	ADVENTURESS	AGGRADATION	ALGORITHMIC
ACCEPTATION	ACQUAINTING	ADVENTURISM	AGGRANDIZER	ALKALIMETER
ACCESSIONAL	ACQUIESCENT	ADVENTURIST	AGGRAVATING	ALKALIMETRY

ALKALIZABLE	AMMONIATION	ANGLICIZING	ANTICYCLONE
ALL-AMERICAN	AMONTILLADO	ANGLO-INDIAN	ANTIFEBRILE
ALLANTOIDAL	AMOROUSNESS	ANGLOPHILES	ANTIFCULING
ALLEGATIONS	AMOR PATRIAE	ANGLOPHILIA	ANTIMISSILE
ALLEGIANCES	AMORPHOUSLY	ANGLOPHOBES	ANTIMYCOTIC
ALLEGORICAL	AMORTIZABLE	ANGLOPHOBIA	ANTINEUTRON
ALLEVIATING	AMOUR-PROPRE	ANGLO-SAXONS	ANTINUCLEAR
ALLEVIATION	AMPHETAMINE	ANIMALCULAR	ANTINUCLEON
ALLEVIATIVE	AMPHIBIOTIC	ANIMOSITIES	ANTIOXIDANT
ALLOCATIONS	AMPHIBOLITE	ANISEIKONIA	ANTIPATHIES
ALLOGRAPHIC	AMPHIBOLOGY	ANISEIKONIC	ANTIPHONARY
ALLOMORPHIC	AMPHICHROIC	ANISODACTYL	ANTIPHRASIS
ALLOPLASMIC	AMPHICTYONY	ANISOGAMOUS	ANTIPYRESIS
ALLOPURINOL	AMPHISBAENA	ANISOMEROUS	ANTIPYRETIC
ALL-POWERFUL	AMPHISTYLAR	ANISOMETRIC	ANTIQUARIAN
ALL-ROUNDERS	AMPHITRICHA	ANISOTROPIC	ANTIQUITIES
ALLUREMENTS	AMPLEXICAUL	ANNABERGITE	ANTIRRHINUM
ALMIGHTIEST	AMPLIFIABLE	ANNEXATIONS	ANTI-SEMITES
ALPHABETIZE	AMPUTATIONS	ANNIHILABLE	ANTI-SEMITIC
ALTARPIECES	AMYL NITRITE	ANNIHILATED	ANTISEPTICS
ALTERATIONS	AMYLOPECTIN	ANNIHILATOR	ANTITUSSIVE
ALTERCATION	ANACHRONISM	ANNIVERSARY	ANTOFAGASTA
ALTERNATELY	ANACOLUTHIA	ANNOTATIONS	ANTONOMASIA
ALTERNATING	ANACOLUTHIC	ANNUNCIATOR	ANXIOUSNESS
ALTERNATION	ANACOLUTHON	ANOINTMENTS	APATOSAURUS
ALTERNATIVE	ANADIPLOSIS	ANOMALISTIC	APHETICALLY
ALTERNATORS	ANAEMICALLY	ANOMALOUSLY	APHRODISIAC
ALTITUDINAL	ANAESTHESIA	ANONYMOUSLY	APICULTURAL
ALTOCUMULUS	ANAESTHETIC	ANORTHOSITE	APOCALYPSES
ALTOGETHERS	ANALEMMATIC	ANTAGONISMS	APOCALYPTIC
ALTOSTRATUS	ANALYSATION	ANTAGONISTS	APOCOPATION
ALUMINOSITY	ANAMORPHISM	ANTAGONIZED	APOCYNTHION
ALVEOLATION	ANAPHYLAXIS	ANTALKALINE	APOLOGETICS
AMABOKOBOKO	ANARCHISTIC	ANTECEDENCE	APOLOGIZING
AMALGAMATED	ANASTOMOSIS	ANTECEDENTS	APOMORPHINE
AMARANTHINE	ANASTOMOTIC	ANTECHAMBER	APONEUROSIS
AMBASSADORS	ANCIENTNESS	ANTEPENDIUM	APONEUROTIC
AMBIGUGUITY	ANCILLARIES	ANTEVERSION	APOPHYLLITE
AMBIGUOUSLY	ANDROGENOUS	ANTHERIDIAL	APOSIOPESIS
AMBITIOUSLY	ANDROGYNOUS	ANTHERIDIUM	APOSIOPETIC
AMBIVALENCE	ANDROSPHINX	ANTHEROZOID	A POSTERIORI
AMBLYGONITE	ANEMOGRAPHY	ANTHOCYANIN	APOSTROPHES
AMELIORATED	ANEMOMETERS	ANTHOLOGIES	APOTHEOSIZE
AMELIORATOR	ANEMOMETRIC	ANTHOLOGIST	APPALLINGLY
AMENABILITY	ANESTHETICS	ANTHOLOGIZE	APPARATCHIK
AMENORRHOEA	ANESTHETIST	ANTHRACITIC	APPARATUSES
AMERICANISM	ANESTHETIZE	ANTHRACNOSE	APPARELLING
AMERICANIZE	ANFRACTUOUS	ANTIBIOTICS	APPARITIONS
AMETHYSTINE	ANGELICALLY	ANTICATHODE	APPEALINGLY
AMICABILITY	ANGIOMATOUS	ANTICIPATED	APPEARANCES
AMINOPHENOL	ANGIOPLASTY	ANTICIPATOR	APPEASEMENT
AMINOPYRINE	ANGLICANISM	ANTICLASTIC	APPELLATION

APPELLATIVE	ARENICOLOUS	ASSUMPTIONS	AUDITORIUMS
APPERTAINED	ARGENTINEAN	ASSUREDNESS	AUGMENTABLE
APPLICATION	ARGYLLSHIRE	ASSYRIOLOGY	AURIGNACIAN
APPLICATIVE	ARISTOCRACY	ASTATICALLY	AUSCULTATOR
APPLICATORY	ARISTOCRATS	ASTERISKING	AUSTERENESS
APPOINTMENT	ARMED FORCES	ASTIGMATISM	AUSTERITIES
APPORTIONED	ARMIPOTENCE	ASTONISHING	AUSTRALASIA
APPORTIONER	ARMOURED CAR	ASTRAPHOBIA	AUSTRALIANA
APPRECIABLE	ARMOUR PLATE	ASTRAPHOBIC	AUSTRALIANS
APPRECIABLY	AROMATICITY	ASTRINGENCY	AUSTRONESIA
APPRECIATED	ARONOMASTIC	ASTRINGENTS	AUTHORITIES
APPREHENDED	ARRAIGNMENT	ASTROBOTANY	AUTHORIZING
APPRENTICED	ARRANGEMENT	ASTROLOGERS	AUTOCHANGER
APPRENTICES	ARRESTINGLY	ASTROMETRIC	AUTOCRACIES
APPROACHING	ARTERIALIZE	ASTRONAUTIC	AUTOGENESIS
APPROBATION	ARTHROMERIC	ASTRONOMERS	AUTOGENETIC
APPROBATIVE	ARTHROSPORE	ASTROSPHERE	AUTOGRAPHED
APPROPRIATE	ARTICULATED	ATELECTASIS	AUTOGRAPHIC
APPROVINGLY	ARTICULATOR	ATHEISTICAL	AUTOKINETIC
APPROXIMATE	ARTILLERIES	ATHERMANOUS	AUTOMOBILES
APPURTENANT	ARTIODACTYL	ATHLETICISM	AUTOPLASTIC
AQUACULTURE	ARTLESSNESS	ATLANTICISM	AUTOTROPHIC
AQUAEROBICS	ARYTENOIDAL	ATMOSPHERES	AUXANOMETER
AQUAMARINES	ASCENSIONAL	ATMOSPHERIC	AUXILIARIES
AQUAPLANING	ASCERTAINED	ATOMIC PILES	AVOIRDUPOIS
AQUARELLIST	ASCETICALLY	ATOMIZATION	AVUNCULARLY
AQUATICALLY	ASKING PRICE	ATRABILIOUS	AWESOMENESS
AQUICULTURE	ASPERGILLUS	ATROCIOUSLY	AWKWARDNESS
ARABICA BEAN	ASPHYXIATED	ATTACHE CASE	AXIOLOGICAL
ARALIACEOUS	ASPHYXIATOR	ATTACHMENTS	AXONOMETRIC
ARAN ISLANDS	ASPIDISTRAS	ATTAINMENTS	AZERBAIJANI
ARBITRAGEUR	ASPIRATIONS	ATTEMPTABLE	AZOTOBACTER
ARBITRAMENT	ASSASSINATE	ATTENDANCES	
ARBITRARILY	ASSEMBLAGES	ATTENTIVELY	**B**
ARBITRATING	ASSEMBLYMAN	ATTENUATING	BABY-MINDERS
ARBITRATION	ASSEMBLYMEN	ATTENUATION	BABY ON BOARD
ARBITRATORS	ASSENTATION	ATTESTATION	BABY'S-BREATH
ARBORESCENT	ASSERTIVELY	ATTITUDINAL	BABY-SITTERS
ARCHAEOLOGY	ASSESSMENTS	ATTRACTABLE	BABY-SITTING
ARCHAEOZOIC	ASSESSORIAL	ATTRACTIONS	BACCHANALIA
ARCHAICALLY	ASSEVERATED	ATTRIBUTING	BACCIFEROUS
ARCHANGELIC	ASSIDUOUSLY	ATTRIBUTION	BACCIVOROUS
ARCHBISHOPS	ASSIGNATION	ATTRIBUTIVE	BACILLIFORM
ARCHDEACONS	ASSIGNMENTS	ATTRITIONAL	BACKBENCHER
ARCHDIOCESE	ASSIMILABLE	AUCTIONEERS	BACKBENCHES
ARCHDUCHESS	ASSIMILATED	AUDACIOUSLY	BACKCOMBING
ARCHEGONIUM	ASSOCIATING	AUDIOLOGIST	BACK COUNTRY
ARCHENEMIES	ASSOCIATION	AUDIOMETRIC	BACKGROUNDS
ARCHENTERIC	ASSOCIATIVE	AUDIOTYPING	BACKHANDERS
ARCHENTERON	ASSORTATIVE	AUDIOTYPIST	BACK NUMBERS
ARCHIPELAGO	ASSORTMENTS	AUDIO-VISUAL	BACKPACKERS
ARDUOUSNESS	ASSUAGEMENT	AUDITIONING	BACKPACKING

BACK PASSAGE	BARONETCIES	BELARUSSIAN	BILLETS-DOUX
BACKPEDALED	BAROTSELAND	BELATEDNESS	BILLIONAIRE
BACKROOM BOY	BARQUENTINE	BELEAGUERED	BILLOWINESS
BACKSLAPPER	BARREL ORGAN	BELL-BOTTOMS	BILLS OF FARE
BACKSLIDERS	BARRICADING	BELLICOSITY	BILLS OF SALE
BACKSLIDING	BASHFULNESS	BELLIGERENT	BIMETALLISM
BACK STREETS	BASINGSTOKE	BELL-RINGING	BIMOLECULAR
BACKSTROKES	BASKERVILLE	BELLYACHING	BIOCATALYST
BACK TO FRONT	BASS GUITARS	BELLY BUTTON	BIOCENOLOGY
BACKTRACKED	BASSOONISTS	BELLY DANCER	BIODYNAMICS
BACTERAEMIA	BASTARDIZED	BELLY DANCES	BIOENGINEER
BACTERICIDE	BASTINADOED	BELLY LAUGHS	BIOFEEDBACK
BADDERLOCKS	BASTINADOES	BENEDICTINE	BIOGRAPHERS
BAD-MOUTHING	BASTNAESITE	BENEDICTION	BIOGRAPHIES
BAGGAGE CARS	BATHING SUIT	BENEDICTORY	BIOPHYSICAL
BAGGAGE ROOM	BATHOLITHIC	BENEFACTION	BIPARTITION
BAHIA BLANCA	BATHOMETRIC	BENEFACTORS	BIQUADRATIC
BAKER'S DOZEN	BATHYMETRIC	BENEFICENCE	BIQUARTERLY
BALANCEABLE	BATHYSPHERE	BENEFICIARY	BIRD-BRAINED
BALEFULNESS	BATSMANSHIP	BENEVOLENCE	BIRDS OF PREY
BALL BEARING	BATTLE CRIES	BENIGHTEDLY	BIRD-WATCHER
BALLBREAKER	BATTLEFIELD	BEQUEATHING	BIROBIDZHAN
BALLETOMANE	BATTLEMENTS	BEREAVEMENT	BIRTHPLACES
BALLOONISTS	BATTLE ROYAL	BERGSCHRUND	BIRTHRIGHTS
BALLOT PAPER	BATTLESHIPS	BESMIRCHING	BIRTHWEIGHT
BALUCHISTAN	BATTY RIDERS	BESPATTERED	BISEXUALISM
BALUSTRADES	BEACHCHAIRS	BEST-SELLERS	BISEXUALITY
BAMBOOZLING	BEACHCOMBER	BEST-SELLING	BISYMMETRIC
BANANA SKINS	BEAN COUNTER	BETA-BLOCKER	BIT OF FLUFFS
BANDMASTERS	BEANSPROUTS	BETES-NOIRES	BITTERSWEET
BANGLADESHI	BEARISHNESS	BETULACEOUS	BITTER SWEET
BANK ACCOUNT	BEAR'S-BREECH	BEWILDERING	BIVOUACKING
BANKER'S CARD	BEASTLINESS	BHUBANESWAR	BLACKAMOORS
BANK HOLIDAY	BEAUHARNAIS	BIAS BINDING	BLACKBALLED
BANKROLLING	BEAUTEOUSLY	BIBLIOLATRY	BLACKBOARDS
BANKRUPTING	BEAUTICIANS	BIBLIOMANCY	BLACK COMEDY
BANNOCKBURN	BEAUTIFULLY	BIBLIOMANIA	BLACK FOREST
BANTERINGLY	BEAUTIFYING	BIBLIOPHILE	BLACKGUARDS
BARBARITIES	BEAUTY QUEEN	BIBLIOPHISM	BLACK HUMOUR
BARBARIZING	BEAUTY SLEEP	BIBLIOTHECA	BLACKLEGGED
BARBAROUSLY	BEAUTY SPOTS	BICARBONATE	BLACKLISTED
BARBASTELLE	BEAVERBOARD	BICENTENARY	BLACKMAILED
BARBITURATE	BECKENBAUER	BICEPHALOUS	BLACKMAILER
BARCOO RIVER	BED AND BOARD	BICONCAVITY	BLACK MARIAS
BAREFACEDLY	BEDEVILLING	BIEDERMEIER	BLACK MARKET
BARIUM MEALS	BEDEVILMENT	BIFOLIOLATE	BLACK MASSES
BARLEY SUGAR	BEFITTINGLY	BIFURCATING	BLACK MUSLIM
BARLEY WATER	BEFRIENDING	BIFURCATION	BLACK PEPPER
BAR MITZVAHS	BEGUILEMENT	BIG BUSINESS	BLACKSHIRTS
BARNSTORMED	BEGUILINGLY	BIKER JACKET	BLACKSMITHS
BARNSTORMER	BEHAVIOURAL	BILATERALLY	BLACK WIDOWS
BAROGRAPHIC	BELABOURING	BILIOUSNESS	BLADDERWORT

BLAMELESSLY
BLAMEWORTHY
BLANCMANGES
BLANK CHEQUE
BLASPHEMERS
BLASPHEMIES
BLASPHEMING
BLASPHEMOUS
BLASTOGENIC
BLASTOMERIC
BLASTOPORIC
BLENCHINGLY
BLEPHARITIC
BLEPHATITIS
BLESSEDNESS
BLIND ALLEYS
BLINDFOLDED
BLINDSTOREY
BLOCKBUSTER
BLOCKHOUSES
BLOOD COUNTS
BLOOD GROUPS
BLOODHOUNDS
BLOODLESSLY
BLOOD PLASMA
BLOOD SPORTS
BLOODSTAINS
BLOODSTREAM
BLOODSUCKER
BLOOD VESSEL
BLOOMINGTON
BLOTCHINESS
BLUDGEONING
BLUEBERRIES
BLUE-BLOODED
BLUEBOTTLES
BLUE CHEESES
BLUE-EYED BOY
BLUE MURDERS
BLUNDERBUSS
BLURREDNESS
BOBSLEIGHED
BODHISATTVA
BODY-CENTRED
BODY POLITIC
BOGNOR REGIS
BOILERMAKER
BOILERPLATE
BOILER SUITS
BOLLOCKS-UPS
BOLL WEEVILS
BOMBARDIERS

BOMBARDMENT
BONDHOLDERS
BONE MARROWS
BONESHAKERS
BOOBY PRIZES
BOOKBINDERS
BOOKBINDERY
BOOKBINDING
BOOKISHNESS
BOOKKEEPERS
BOOKKEEPING
BOOKMOBILES
BOOKSELLERS
BOOMERANGED
BOORISHNESS
BOOTLEGGERS
BOOTLEGGING
BORDERLANDS
BORDERLINES
BOTANICALLY
BOTHERATION
BOTTLE BANKS
BOTTLEBRUSH
BOTTLE GREEN
BOTTLENECKS
BOUNDLESSLY
BOUNTEOUSLY
BOURGEOISIE
BOURNEMOUTH
BOWDLERIZED
BOYOMA FALLS
BOYSENBERRY
BRACE AND BIT
BRACHIATION
BRACTEOLATE
BRADYCARDIA
BRADYCARDIC
BRAGGADOCIO
BRAHMAPUTRA
BRAIN DRAINS
BRAINLESSLY
BRAINSTORMS
BRAINS TRUST
BRAINTEASER
BRAINWASHED
BRAINWASHER
BRANCHIOPOD
BRANDENBURG
BRANDISHING
BRATTISHING
BRAZZAVILLE
BREADBASKET

BREADBOARDS
BREADCRUMBS
BREADFRUITS
BREADTHWAYS
BREADWINNER
BREAKFASTED
BREAK THE ICE
BREASTPLATE
BREATHALYSE
BREATHINESS
BRECONSHIRE
BREECHBLOCK
BREMERHAVEN
BRIDGEBOARD
BRISTLETAIL
BRITTLENESS
BRITTLE-STAR
BROADCASTER
BROAD CHURCH
BROAD GAUGES
BROADMINDED
BROADSHEETS
BROADSWORDS
BROMINATION
BRONCHIOLAR
BRONTOSAURI
BRONX CHEERS
BRONZE MEDAL
BROOMSTICKS
BROTHERHOOD
BROWBEATING
BROWNSTONES
BRUCELLOSIS
BRUSQUENESS
BRUTALITIES
BRUTALIZING
BRUTISHNESS
BRYOLOGICAL
BUCARAMANGA
BUCKET SEATS
BUCKET SHOPS
BUCKLER-FERN
BUCOLICALLY
BUDGERIGARS
BUENOS AIRES
BUFFER STATE
BUFFER STOCK
BUFFER ZONES
BULBIFEROUS
BULLDOG CLIP
BULLETPROOF
BULLFIGHTER

BULLFINCHES
BULLISHNESS
BULLSHITTED
BULL TERRIER
BUMPTIOUSLY
BUNDELKHAND
BUPIVACAINE
BUREAUCRACY
BUREAUCRATS
BURGOMASTER
BURKINA-FASO
BURLESQUING
BURNISHABLE
BUSHWHACKER
BUSINESS END
BUSINESSMAN
BUSINESSMEN
BUS STATIONS
BUSTAURANTS
BUTCHERBIRD
BUTTER BEANS
BUTTERFLIES
BUTTONHOLED
BUTTONHOLES
BUTTONMOULD
BUTTRESSING
BUTYRACEOUS
BY-ELECTIONS
BYELORUSSIA

C

CABINETWORK
CABORA BASSA
CACHE MEMORY
CACOGRAPHIC
CACOPHONOUS
CALCEOLARIA
CALCICOLOUS
CALCIFEROUS
CALCIFUGOUS
CALCINATION
CALCULATING
CALCULATION
CALCULATORS
CALEFACIENT
CALEFACTION
CALEFACTORY
CALIBRATING
CALIBRATION
CALIFORNIAN
CALIFORNIUM
CALLIGRAPHY

CALLIPYGIAN	CARBONIZING	CATAFALQUES	CENTROSOMIC
CALLOUSNESS	CARBON PAPER	CATALOGUING	CEPHALALGIA
CALORIMETER	CAR-BOOT SALE	CATAPLASTIC	CERARGYRITE
CALORIMETRY	CARBORUNDUM	CATAPULTING	CEREBRATION
CALUMNIATED	CARBOXYLASE	CATASTROPHE	CEREBROSIDE
CALVINISTIC	CARBOXYLATE	CAT BURGLARS	CEREMONIALS
CALYPTROGEN	CARBUNCULAR	CATCHPHRASE	CEREMONIOUS
CAMARADERIE	CARBURETTOR	CATCHWEIGHT	CEROGRAPHIC
CAMERA-READY	CARBYLAMINE	CATECHISMAL	CEROPLASTIC
CAMOUFLAGED	CARCASSONNE	CATECHISTIC	CERTAINTIES
CAMOUFLAGES	CARCINOGENS	CATECHIZING	CERTIFIABLE
CAMPAIGNERS	CARDINALATE	CATEGORICAL	CERTIFICATE
CAMPAIGNING	CARD INDEXES	CATEGORIZED	CETOLOGICAL
CAMPANOLOGY	CARDIOGRAPH	CATERPILLAR	CHAETOGNATH
CAMPANULATE	CARDPUNCHES	CATERWAULED	CHAFFINCHES
CAMPGROUNDS	CARDUACEOUS	CATHETERIZE	CHAFING DISH
CAMPO GRANDE	CAREFULNESS	CATHOLICISM	CHAIN LETTER
CANALICULAR	CARESSINGLY	CATHOLICITY	CHAIN-SMOKED
CANALICULUS	CARICATURED	CATHOLICIZE	CHAIN-SMOKER
CANDELABRUM	CARICATURES	CATTLE GRIDS	CHAIN STITCH
CANDIDACIES	CARMINATIVE	CAULIFLOWER	CHAIN STORES
CANDLEBERRY	CARNIVOROUS	CAUSABILITY	CHAIRPERSON
CANDLELIGHT	CAROLINGIAN	CAUSATIVELY	CHALCANLITE
CANDLEPOWER	CARPOGONIAL	CAUSTICALLY	CHALCEDONIC
CANDLESTICK	CARPOGONIUM	CAUSTICNESS	CHALKBOARDS
CANDLEWICKS	CARPOLOGIST	CAUTERIZING	CHALLENGERS
CANINE TEETH	CARRAGEENAN	CAVACO SILVA	CHALLENGING
CANINE TOOTH	CARRIAGEWAY	CAVALIERISM	CHAMBERLAIN
CANNIBALISM	CARRIER BAGS	CAVERNOUSLY	CHAMBERMAID
CANNIBALIZE	CARSICKNESS	CAVITY WALLS	CHAMBER POTS
CANNONBALLS	CARTOGRAPHY	CAVO-RELIEVO	CHAMELEONIC
CANTHARIDES	CARTOONISTS	CEASELESSLY	CHAMPERTOUS
CANTILEVERS	CARTWHEELED	CELEBRATING	CHAMPIONING
CAPACIOUSLY	CARUNCULATE	CELEBRATION	CHANCELLERY
CAPACITANCE	CARVEL-BUILT	CELEBRATIVE	CHANCELLORS
CAPILLARIES	CARVING FORK	CELEBRITIES	CHANCROIDAL
CAPILLARITY	CASE HISTORY	CEMENTATION	CHANDELIERS
CAPITALISTS	CASE STUDIES	CEMENT MIXER	CHANGELINGS
CAPITALIZED	CASEWORKERS	CENOSPECIES	CHANGEOVERS
CAPITAL LEVY	CASSITERITE	CENTENARIAN	CHANNELLING
CAPITATIONS	CASTELLATED	CENTENARIES	CHANTERELLE
CAPITULATED	CASTER SUGAR	CENTENNIALS	CHANTICLEER
CAPITULATOR	CASTIGATING	CENTIMETRES	CHAOTICALLY
CAPRICCIOSO	CASTIGATION	CENTRALIZED	CHAPERONAGE
CAPRICORNUS	CASTING VOTE	CENTREBOARD	CHAPERONING
CAPSULATION	CASTLEREAGH	CENTRE-FOLDS	CHARCUTERIE
CAPTIVATING	CASTOR SUGAR	CENTREPIECE	CHARGE CARDS
CAPTIVATION	CATACAUSTIC	CENTRIFUGAL	CHARGE HANDS
CARABINIERE	CATACHRESIS	CENTRIFUGES	CHARGE NURSE
CARAVANNING	CATACLASTIC	CENTRIPETAL	CHARGE SHEET
CARBAMIDINE	CATACLYSMIC	CENTROBARIC	CHAR-GRILLED
CARBONATION	CATADROMOUS	CENTROMERIC	CHARIOTEERS

CHARISMATIC	CHLOROPRENE	CIRCULATION	CLOTHESLINE
CHASTISABLE	CHLOROQUINE	CIRCULATIVE	CLOTHES PEGS
CHATELAINES	CHOANOCYTAL	CIRCULATORY	CLOUDBURSTS
CHATTANOOGA	CHOCK-A-BLOCK	CIRCUMCISED	CLOUD-CAPPED
CHAUFFEURED	CHOIRMASTER	CIRCUMLUNAR	CLOYINGNESS
CHAULMOOGRA	CHOIR SCHOOL	CIRCUMPOLAR	CLUSTER BOMB
CHAUVINISTS	CHOKECHERRY	CIRCUMSPECT	COADUNATION
CHEAPSKATES	CHOLESTEROL	CIRENCESTER	COADUNATIVE
CHECKMATING	CHOLINERGIC	CITIZENSHIP	COAGULATING
CHECKPOINTS	CHORDOPHONE	CITRONELLAL	COAGULATION
CHEERLEADER	CHOREODRAMA	CITY FATHERS	COAGULATIVE
CHEERLESSLY	CHOREOGRAPH	CIVIL RIGHTS	COALBUNKERS
CHEESECAKES	CHOROGRAPHY	CIVVY STREET	COALESCENCE
CHEESECLOTH	CHRISMATORY	CLAIRVOYANT	COALITIONAL
CHEF D'OEUVRE	CHRISTENDOM	CLAMATORIAL	COALSCUTTLE
CHELICERATE	CHRISTENING	CLANDESTINE	COARCTATION
CHELIFEROUS	CHRISTINGLE	CLARINETIST	COASTGUARDS
CHELYABINSK	CHRISTMASES	CLASP KNIVES	COAT HANGERS
CHEMOSMOSIS	CHRISTOLOGY	CLASS ACTION	COATS OF ARMS
CHEMOSMOTIC	CHROMATINIC	CLASSICISTS	COBBLESTONE
CHEMOSPHERE	CHROMINANCE	CLASSIFYING	COCCIDIOSIS
CHEMOTACTIC	CHROMOGENIC	CLAVICHORDS	COCCIFEROUS
CHEMOTROPIC	CHROMONEMAL	CLAY PIGEONS	COCK-A-LEEKIE
CHEQUE CARDS	CHROMOPHORE	CLEAN-LIMBED	COCKCHAFERS
CHEREMKHOVO	CHROMOPLASM	CLEANLINESS	COCKLESHELL
CHERISHABLE	CHROMOPLAST	CLEAN-SHAVEN	COCKLE SHELL
CHESHIRE CAT	CHROMOSOMAL	CLEAN SWEEPS	COCKROACHES
CHESSBOARDS	CHROMOSOMES	CLEAR-HEADED	CODICILLARY
CHEVAL GLASS	CHRONICALLY	CLEAR THE AIR	COD-LIVER OIL
CHIAROSCURO	CHRONICLERS	CLEETHORPES	COEDUCATION
CHIASTOLITE	CHRONICLING	CLEFT PALATE	COEFFICIENT
CHICANERIES	CHRONOGRAPH	CLEFT STICKS	COELENTERIC
CHICHIHAERH	CHRONOMETER	CLEISTOGAMY	COELENTERON
CHICKENFEED	CHRONOMETRY	CLERGYWOMAN	COERCIONARY
CHICKEN FEED	CHRONOSCOPE	CLEVER DICKS	COERCIONIST
CHIFFONIERS	CHRYSALISES	CLIENT STATE	COESSENTIAL
CHILDMINDER	CHRYSAROBIN	CLIFFHANGER	COEXISTENCE
CHIMNEYPOTS	CHRYSOBERYL	CLIMACTERIC	COEXTENSION
CHIMPANZEES	CHRYSOLITIC	CLIMATOLOGY	COEXTENSIVE
CHINCHILLAS	CHRYSOPRASE	CLINANDRIUM	COFFEE BREAK
CHINESE LEAF	CHURCHGOERS	CLINOMETRIC	COFFEE HOUSE
CHINOISERIE	CHURCHGOING	CLOCK TOWERS	COFFEE SHOPS
CHIPPENDALE	CHURCHWOMAN	CLODHOPPERS	COFFEE TABLE
CHIROGRAPHY	CHURCHYARDS	CLOISTERING	COGITATIONS
CHIROPODIST	CICATRICIAL	CLOSED SHOPS	COGNITIVELY
CHIROPTERAN	CICATRIZANT	CLOSEFISTED	COGNITIVIST
CHITCHATTED	CINDERELLAS	CLOSE-HAULED	COGNIZANCES
CHLAMYDEOUS	CINEMASCOPE	CLOSE SEASON	COGNOSCENTI
CHLORINATED	CIRCULARITY	CLOSE SHAVES	COINCIDENCE
CHLORINATOR	CIRCULARIZE	CLOSING TIME	COINSURANCE
CHLOROPHYLL	CIRCULAR SAW	CLOSTRIDIAL	COLD-BLOODED
CHLOROPLAST	CIRCULATING	CLOSTRIDIUM	COLD CHISELS

COLD COMFORT	COMMINATORY	COMPLIANTLY	CONDOLATORY
COLD-HEARTED	COMMINUTION	COMPLICATED	CONDOLENCES
COLD STORAGE	COMMISERATE	COMPLIMENTS	CONDOMINIUM
COLEOPTERAN	COMMISSIONS	COMPORTMENT	CONDONATION
COLLABORATE	COMMISSURAL	COMPOSITION	CONDUCTANCE
COLLAPSIBLE	COMMITMENTS	COMPOSITORS	CONDUCTIBLE
COLLARBONES	COMMODITIES	COMPOUNDING	CONDUCTRESS
COLLAR STUDS	COMMON NOUNS	COMPRESSING	CONFABULATE
COLLECTABLE	COMMONPLACE	COMPRESSION	CONFECTIONS
COLLECTANEA	COMMON ROOMS	COMPRESSIVE	CONFEDERACY
COLLECTEDLY	COMMON SENSE	COMPRESSORS	CONFEDERATE
COLLECTIONS	COMMOTIONAL	COMPRISABLE	CONFERENCES
COLLECTIVES	COMMUNALISM	COMPROMISED	CONFERMENTS
COLLEMBOLAN	COMMUNALIST	COMPROMISER	CONFESSEDLY
COLLENCHYMA	COMMUNALITY	COMPROMISES	CONFESSIONS
COLLIGATION	COMMUNALIZE	COMPTOMETER	CONFIDENCES
COLLIGATIVE	COMMUNICANT	COMPTROLLER	CONFIDENTLY
COLLIMATION	COMMUNICATE	COMPULSIONS	CONFIDINGLY
COLLOCATING	COMMUNIONAL	COMPUNCTION	CONFINEMENT
COLLOCATION	COMMUNIQUES	COMPUTATION	CONFISCABLE
COLOGARITHM	COMMUNISTIC	COMPUTERATE	CONFISCATED
COLONIALISM	COMMUNITIES	COMPUTERIZE	CONFISCATOR
COLONIALIST	COMMUTATION	COMRADESHIP	CONFLATIONS
COLONIZABLE	COMMUTATIVE	CONCATENATE	CONFLICTING
COLONOSCOPY	COMMUTATORS	CONCAVITIES	CONFLICTION
COLORATURAS	COMPACT DISC	CONCEALMENT	CONFLICTIVE
COLORIMETER	COMPACTEDLY	CONCEITEDLY	CONFLUENCES
COLOUR-BLIND	COMPACTNESS	CONCEIVABLE	CONFORMABLE
COLOURISTIC	COMPANY TOWN	CONCEIVABLY	CONFORMABLY
COLTISHNESS	COMPARATIVE	CONCENTRATE	CONFORMANCE
COLUMBARIUM	COMPARISONS	CONCEPTACLE	CONFORMISTS
COMBATIVELY	COMPARTMENT	CONCEPTIONS	CONFOUNDING
COMBINATION	COMPASSABLE	CONCERNEDLY	CONFRONTING
COMBINATIVE	COMPATRIOTS	CONCERTANTE	CONFUSINGLY
COMBUSTIBLE	COMPELLABLE	CONCERTEDLY	CONFUTATION
COMESTIBLES	COMPENDIOUS	CONCERTGOER	CONFUTATIVE
COME-UPPANCE	COMPENDIUMS	CONCERTINAS	CONGEALMENT
COMFORTABLE	COMPENSATED	CONCESSIBLE	CONGELATION
COMFORTABLY	COMPENSATOR	CONCESSIONS	CONGENIALLY
COMFORTLESS	COMPETENTLY	CONCILIATED	CONGESTIBLE
COMIC OPERAS	COMPETITION	CONCILIATOR	CONGREGATED
COMIC STRIPS	COMPETITIVE	CONCLUSIONS	CONGREGATOR
COMMANDANTS	COMPETITORS	CONCOCTIONS	CONGRESSMAN
COMMANDMENT	COMPILATION	CONCOMITANT	CONGRESSMEN
COMME IL FAUT	COMPLACENCE	CONCORDANCE	CONGRUENTLY
COMMEMORATE	COMPLACENCY	CONCUBINAGE	CONGRUITIES
COMMENDABLE	COMPLAINANT	CONCURRENCE	CONJECTURAL
COMMENDABLY	COMPLAINERS	CONDEMNABLE	CONJECTURED
COMMENTATED	COMPLAINING	CONDENSABLE	CONJECTURER
COMMENTATOR	COMPLAISANT	CONDITIONAL	CONJECTURES
COMMERCIALS	COMPLEMENTS	CONDITIONED	CONJOINEDLY
COMMINATION	COMPLEXIONS	CONDITIONER	CONJUGALITY

CONJUGATING	CONSTRICTOR	CONTROLLING	COROLLARIES
CONJUGATION	CONSTRUCTED	CONTROVERSY	CORONAGRAPH
CONJUGATIVE	CONSTRUCTOR	CONTUMELIES	CORONATIONS
CONJUNCTION	CONSULSHIPS	CONTUSIONED	CORONERSHIP
CONJUNCTIVA	CONSULTANCY	CONURBATION	CORPORALITY
CONJUNCTIVE	CONSULTANTS	CONVALESCED	CORPORATELY
CONJUNCTURE	CONSUMERISM	CONVENIENCE	CORPORATION
CONJURATION	CONSUMMATED	CONVENTICLE	CORPORATIVE
CONNECTIBLE	CONSUMMATOR	CONVENTIONS	CORPOREALLY
CONNECTICUT	CONSUMPTION	CONVERGENCE	CORPUSCULAR
CONNECTIONS	CONSUMPTIVE	CONVERGENCY	CORRECTABLE
CONNOISSEUR	CONTACT LENS	CONVERSABLE	CORRECTIONS
CONNOTATION	CONTACTLESS	CONVERSANCE	CORRECTIVES
CONNOTATIVE	CONTAINMENT	CONVERSIONS	CORRECTNESS
CONSCIENCES	CONTAMINANT	CONVERTIBLE	CORRELATING
CONSCIOUSLY	CONTAMINATE	CONVEXITIES	CORRELATION
CONSCRIPTED	CONTEMNIBLE	CONVEYANCER	CORRELATIVE
CONSECRATED	CONTEMPLATE	CONVEYANCES	CORRIGENDUM
CONSECRATOR	CONTENTEDLY	CONVICTABLE	CORROBORATE
CONSECUTION	CONTENTIONS	CONVICTIONS	CORROSIVELY
CONSECUTIVE	CONTENTIOUS	CONVINCIBLE	CORRUGATION
CONSENSUSES	CONTENTMENT	CONVIVIALLY	CORRUPTIBLE
CONSENTIENT	CONTESTANTS	CONVOCATION	CORRUPTIONS
CONSEQUENCE	CONTEXTURAL	CONVOCATIVE	CORRUPTNESS
CONSERVABLE	CONTINENTAL	CONVOLUTION	CORS ANGLAIS
CONSERVANCY	CONTINGENCE	CONVOLVULUS	CORTICATION
CONSERVATOR	CONTINGENCY	CONVULSIONS	CORUSCATING
CONSIDERATE	CONTINGENTS	COOKERY BOOK	CORUSCATION
CONSIDERING	CONTINUALLY	COOK ISLANDS	COSIGNATORY
CONSIGNABLE	CONTINUANCE	COOPERATING	COS LETTUCES
CONSIGNMENT	CONTINUATOR	COOPERATION	COSMETICIAN
CONSISTENCY	CONTORTIONS	COOPERATIVE	COSMOGONIES
CONSOLATION	CONTRACTILE	COOPERATORS	COSMOGONIST
CONSOLATORY	CONTRACTING	COOPER CREEK	COSMOLOGIST
CONSOLIDATE	CONTRACTION	COORDINATED	COSMOPOLITE
CONSONANCES	CONTRACTIVE	COORDINATES	COTERMINOUS
CONSONANTAL	CONTRACTORS	COORDINATOR	COTES-DU-NORD
CONSORTIUMS	CONTRACTUAL	COPARCENARY	COTONEASTER
CONSPECIFIC	CONTRACTURE	COPING STONE	COTTAGE LOAF
CONSPICUOUS	CONTRAFLOWS	COPLANARITY	COTTON CANDY
CONSPIRATOR	CONTRAPTION	COPPERPLATE	COTTONTAILS
CONSTANTINE	CONTRARIETY	COPPERSMITH	COTYLEDONAL
CONSTELLATE	CONTRASTING	COPROCESSOR	COUNCIL AREA
CONSTERNATE	CONTRASTIVE	COPROPHILIA	COUNCILLORS
CONSTIPATED	CONTRAVENED	COPYWRITERS	COUNSELLING
CONSTITUENT	CONTRAVENER	CORACIIFORM	COUNSELLORS
CONSTITUTED	CONTRAYERVA	CORDILLERAS	COUNTENANCE
CONSTITUTER	CONTRETEMPS	CORMOPHYTIC	COUNTERFEIT
CONSTRAINED	CONTRIBUTED	CORNERSTONE	COUNTERFOIL
CONSTRAINER	CONTRIBUTOR	CORNFLOWERS	COUNTERMAND
CONSTRAINTS	CONTRIVANCE	CORNICULATE	COUNTERMINE
CONSTRICTED	CONTROLLERS	CORNUCOPIAS	COUNTERMOVE

COUNTERPANE
COUNTERPART
COUNTERPLOT
COUNTERSANK
COUNTERSIGN
COUNTERSINK
COUNTERSUNK
COUNTERTYPE
COUNTERVAIL
COUNTERWORD
COUNTERWORK
COUNTRIFIED
COUNTRY CLUB
COUNTRY SEAT
COUNTRYSIDE
COUNTY COURT
COUNTY TOWNS
COUP DE GRACE
COURTEOUSLY
COURTHOUSES
COURTLINESS
COVENANTING
COVER CHARGE
COWCATCHERS
CRABBEDNESS
CRACKERJACK
CRANBERRIES
CRANIOMETER
CRANIOMETRY
CRANKSHAFTS
CRASH COURSE
CRASH-DIVING
CRASH HELMET
CRASH-LANDED
CRAZY PAVING
CREAM CHEESE
CREDENTIALS
CREDIBILITY
CREDIT CARDS
CREDIT NOTES
CREDULOUSLY
CREMATORIUM
CRENELLATED
CRENULATION
CREOPHAGOUS
CREPITATION
CREPUSCULAR
CRESTFALLEN
CRIMINALITY
CRIMINOLOGY
CRINKLEROOT
CRINKLINESS

CRITICIZING
CROCIDOLITE
CROCODILIAN
CROOKEDNESS
CROP-DUSTING
CROSSBREEDS
CROSS-GARNET
CROSS-LEGGED
CROSSPIECES
CROSS-STITCH
CROWDEDNESS
CROWN COLONY
CROWN COURTS
CROWNED HEAD
CROWN JEWELS
CROWN PRINCE
CRUCIFEROUS
CRUCIFIXION
CRUNCHINESS
CRUSTACEANS
CRUSTACEOUS
CRYOBIOLOGY
CRYOHYDRATE
CRYOSURGERY
CRYOTHERAPY
CRYPTICALLY
CRYPTOGAMIC
CRYPTOGENIC
CRYPTOGRAPH
CRYPTOZOITE
CRYSTAL BALL
CRYSTALLINE
CRYSTALLITE
CRYSTALLIZE
CRYSTALLOID
CRYSTAL SETS
CTENOPHORAN
CUCKOO CLOCK
CULMIFEROUS
CULMINATION
CULPABILITY
CULTIVATING
CULTIVATION
CULTIVATORS
CUMMERBUNDS
CUNNILINGUS
CUPELLATION
CUPRIFEROUS
CUPRONICKEL
CURATORSHIP
CURIOSITIES
CURIOUSNESS

CURMUDGEONS
CURRICULUMS
CURRY POWDER
CURTAILMENT
CURTAIN CALL
CURVILINEAR
CUSPIDATION
CUSTARD PIES
CUSTOMARILY
CUSTOM-BUILT
CUSTOMIZING
CUT-AND-DRIED
CUTTING EDGE
CYANIDATION
CYANOHYDRIN
CYBERNATION
CYBERNETICS
CYBERPHOBIA
CYCADACEOUS
CYCLOALKANE
CYCLOHEXANE
CYCLOPLEGIA
CYCLOSPORIN
CYCLOSTYLED
CYCLOTHYMIA
CYCLOTHYMIC
CYLINDRICAL
CYPERACEOUS
CYPRINODONT
CYPRIPEDIUM
CYSTICERCUS
CYSTOCARPIC
CYSTOSCOPIC
CYTOGENESIS
CYTOKINESIS
CYTOLOGICAL
CYTOLOGISTS
CYTOPLASMIC
CZESTOCHOWA

D

DACTYLOLOGY
DAGGERBOARD
DAIL EIREANN
DAIRY CATTLE
DAIRY FARMER
DAISY WHEELS
DAMAN AND DIU
DAMNABILITY
DAMP COURSES
DANGER MONEY
DANGEROUSLY

DAPPLE-GREYS
DARDANELLES
DAREDEVILRY
DAR ES SALAAM
DATABLENESS
DAUNTLESSLY
DAWSON CREEK
DAYDREAMERS
DAYDREAMING
DEACCESSION
DEACTIVATOR
DEAD LETTERS
DEAD MARCHES
DEAD RINGERS
DEAD SOLDIER
DEAF-AND-DUMB
DEALERSHIPS
DEAMINATION
DEATH DUTIES
DEATHLESSLY
DEATHLINESS
DEATH RATTLE
DEATH'S-HEADS
DEATH SQUADS
DEATTRIBUTE
DEBARKATION
DEBASEDNESS
DEBASEMENTS
DEBILITATED
DEBOUCHMENT
DEBRIDEMENT
DECALCIFIER
DECALESCENT
DECANEDIOIC
DECAPITATED
DECAPITATOR
DECARBONIZE
DECEITFULLY
DECELERATED
DECELERATOR
DECEPTIVELY
DECEREBRATE
DECILLIONTH
DECIMALIZED
DECIPHERING
DECKLE-EDGED
DECLAMATION
DECLAMATORY
DECLARATION
DECLARATIVE
DECLARATORY
DECLENSIONS

DECLINATION	DELIBERATED	DEODORIZING	DESPATCHING
DECLINATORY	DELIBERATOR	DEOXYGENATE	DESPERADOES
DECLIVITIES	DELICIOUSLY	DEOXYRIBOSE	DESPERATELY
DECLIVITOUS	DELINEATING	DEPARTMENTS	DESPERATION
DECOLLATION	DELINEATION	DEPLORINGLY	DESPOILMENT
DECOLLETAGE	DELINEATIVE	DEPLUMATION	DESPONDENCY
DECOLONIZED	DELINQUENCY	DEPOLARIZER	DESPUMATION
DECOMPOSING	DELINQUENTS	DEPOPULATED	DESSERT WINE
DECORATIONS	DELIRIOUSLY	DEPORTATION	DESTABILIZE
DECORTICATE	DELITESCENT	DEPOSITIONS	DESTINATION
DECREPITATE	DELIVERABLE	DEPRAVATION	DESTITUTION
DECREPITUDE	DELIVERANCE	DEPRAVITIES	DESTROYABLE
DECRESCENCE	DELIVERYMAN	DEPRECATING	DESTRUCTION
DECRETALIST	DELIVERYMEN	DEPRECATION	DESTRUCTIVE
DECUSSATION	DELPHINIUMS	DEPRECATIVE	DESULTORILY
DEDICATEDLY	DEMAGNETIZE	DEPRECATORY	DETACHMENTS
DEDICATIONS	DEMAGOGUERY	DEPRECIABLE	DETERIORATE
DEDUCTIVELY	DEMARCATING	DEPRECIATED	DETERMINANT
DEEP FREEZES	DEMARCATION	DEPRECIATOR	DETERMINATE
DEERSTALKER	DEMOCRACIES	DEPREDATION	DETERMINERS
DE-ESCALATED	DEMOCRATIZE	DEPRESSIBLE	DETERMINING
DEFALCATION	DEMODULATOR	DEPRESSIONS	DETERMINISM
DEFECTIVELY	DEMOGRAPHER	DEPRIVATION	DETERMINIST
DEFENCELESS	DEMOGRAPHIC	DEPUTATIONS	DETESTATION
DEFENSIVELY	DEMOLISHING	DERAILMENTS	DETONATIONS
DEFERENTIAL	DEMOLITIONS	DERANGEMENT	DETRAINMENT
DEFICIENTLY	DEMONETIZED	DERECOGNIZE	DETRIBALIZE
DEFINIENDUM	DEMONICALLY	DEREGULATED	DETRIMENTAL
DEFINITIONS	DEMONOLATER	DERELICTION	DEUTERANOPE
DEFLECTIONS	DEMONOLATRY	DERIVATIONS	DEUTEROGAMY
DEFLORATION	DEMONSTRATE	DERIVATIVES	DEUTSCHMARK
DEFLOWERING	DEMORALIZER	DERMATOLOGY	DEVALUATION
DEFOLIATING	DEMOTIVATED	DESALINATED	DEVASTATING
DEFOLIATION	DEMOUNTABLE	DESCENDABLE	DEVASTATION
DEFORCEMENT	DEMULSIFIER	DESCENDANTS	DEVASTATIVE
DEFORESTING	DEMUTUALIZE	DESCENDIBLE	DEVELOPABLE
DEFORMATION	DEMYSTIFIED	DESCRIBABLE	DEVELOPMENT
DEFORMITIES	DENIGRATING	DESCRIPTION	DEVIOUSNESS
DEFRAUDMENT	DENIGRATION	DESCRIPTIVE	DEVITALIZED
DEGENERATED	DENITRATION	DESECRATING	DEVOLVEMENT
DEGENERATES	DENOMINABLE	DESECRATION	DEVOTEDNESS
DEGLUTINATE	DENOMINATED	DESEGREGATE	DEVOURINGLY
DEGLUTITION	DENOMINATOR	DESENSITIZE	DEXTEROUSLY
DEGRADATION	DENOTATIONS	DESERVINGLY	DIACRITICAL
DEHUMANIZED	DENOUEMENTS	DESEXUALIZE	DIADELPHOUS
DEHYDRATING	DENSIMETRIC	DESICCATING	DIAGNOSABLE
DEHYDRATION	DENTAL FLOSS	DESICCATION	DIAGNOSTICS
DEICTICALLY	DENTAL PLATE	DESICCATIVE	DIALECTICAL
DEIFICATION	DENTICULATE	DESIDERATUM	DIALOGISTIC
DELECTATION	DENTILABIAL	DESIGNATING	DIALYSATION
DELEGATIONS	DENUMERABLE	DESIGNATION	DIAMAGNETIC
DELETERIOUS	DENUNCIATOR	DESIGNATIVE	DIAMONDBACK

DIAPHORESIS	DINNER TABLE	DISCIPLINES	DISJUNCTION
DIAPHORETIC	DINOSAURIAN	DISC JOCKEYS	DISJUNCTIVE
DIAPOPHYSIS	DIOPTOMETER	DISCLAIMERS	DISJUNCTURE
DIARTHROSIS	DIOPTOMETRY	DISCLAIMING	DISLOCATING
DIASTROPHIC	DIPHOSPHATE	DISCLOSURES	DISLOCATION
DIATESSARON	DIPHTHEROID	DISCOGRAPHY	DISLODGMENT
DIATOMICITY	DIPHTHONGAL	DISCOLOURED	DISMANTLING
DIATONICISM	DIPHYCERCAL	DISCOMFITED	DISMASTMENT
DICEPHALISM	DIPLOCOCCAL	DISCOMFITER	DISMEMBERED
DICEPHALOUS	DIPLOCOCCUS	DISCOMFORTS	DISMEMBERER
DICHOGAMOUS	DIPLOMATIST	DISCOMMODED	DISMISSIBLE
DICHOTOMIES	DIPROTODONT	DISCOMPOSED	DISMOUNTING
DICHOTOMIST	DIPSOMANIAC	DISCONTINUE	DISOBEDIENT
DICHOTOMIZE	DIPSWITCHES	DISCORDANCE	DISOBLIGING
DICHOTOMOUS	DIRECT DEBIT	DISCOTHEQUE	DISORDERING
DICHROMATIC	DIRECTIONAL	DISCOUNTING	DISORGANIZE
DICHROSCOPE	DIRECTORATE	DISCOURAGED	DISPARAGING
DICOTYLEDON	DIRECTORIAL	DISCOURAGER	DISPARATELY
DICTAPHONES	DIRECTORIES	DISCOURSING	DISPARITIES
DICTATIONAL	DIRECT TAXES	DISCOURTESY	DISPATCH BOX
DICTATORIAL	DIRT FARMERS	DISCOVERERS	DISPATCHING
DIDACTICISM	DIRTY OLD MAN	DISCOVERIES	DISPENSABLE
DIE-CASTINGS	DIRTY OLD MEN	DISCOVERING	DISPIRITING
DIFFERENCES	DIRTY TRICKS	DISCREDITED	DISPLEASING
DIFFERENTIA	DISABLEMENT	DISCREPANCY	DISPLEASURE
DIFFERENTLY	DISACCREDIT	DISCUSSIBLE	DISPOSITION
DIFFIDENTLY	DISACCUSTOM	DISCUSSIONS	DISPROVABLE
DIFFRACTING	DISAFFECTED	DISEMBARKED	DISPUTATION
DIFFRACTION	DISAFFOREST	DISEMBODIED	DISQUIETING
DIFFRACTIVE	DISAGREEING	DISENCUMBER	DISQUIETUDE
DIFFUSENESS	DISALLOWING	DISENGAGING	DISREGARDED
DIFFUSIVITY	DISAPPEARED	DISENTANGLE	DISREGARDER
DIGESTIONAL	DISAPPROVAL	DISENTHRALL	DISRELISHED
DIGITIGRADE	DISAPPROVED	DISFIGURING	DISROBEMENT
DIGNITARIES	DISAPPROVER	DISFORESTED	DISRUPTIONS
DIGRESSIONS	DISARMAMENT	DISGRACEFUL	DISSECTIBLE
DIHYBRIDISM	DISARRANGED	DISGRUNTLED	DISSECTIONS
DILAPIDATED	DISASSEMBLE	DISGUISABLE	DISSEMBLERS
DILAPIDATOR	DISASSEMBLY	DISGUSTEDLY	DISSEMBLING
DILATOMETER	DISAVOWEDLY	DISHEVELLED	DISSEMINATE
DILATOMETRY	DISBANDMENT	DISHONESTLY	DISSEMINULE
DILETTANTES	DISBELIEVED	DISHONOURED	DISSENSIONS
DIMENSIONAL	DISBELIEVER	DISHONOURER	DISSENTIENT
DIMERCAPROL	DISBURSABLE	DISHWASHERS	DISSENTIOUS
DIMIDIATION	DISCERNIBLE	DISILLUSION	DISSEPIMENT
DIMINISHING	DISCERNIBLY	DISILLUSIVE	DISSIMILATE
DIMINUENDOS	DISCERNMENT	DISINCLINED	DISSIMULATE
DIMINUTIONS	DISCHARGING	DISINFECTED	DISSIPATING
DIMINUTIVES	DISC HARROWS	DISINFECTOR	DISSIPATION
DINING ROOMS	DISCIPLINAL	DISINTEREST	DISSIPATIVE
DINING TABLE	DISCIPLINED	DISINTERRED	DISSOCIABLE
DINNER BELLS	DISCIPLINER	DISJOINABLE	DISSOCIATED

DISSOLUTELY
DISSOLUTION
DISSOLUTIVE
DISSOLVABLE
DISSONANCES
DISSUADABLE
DISSYLLABIC
DISSYLLABLE
DISSYMMETRY
DISTASTEFUL
DISTEMPERED
DISTENSIBLE
DISTILLABLE
DISTINCTION
DISTINCTIVE
DISTINGUISH
DISTORTIONS
DISTRACTING
DISTRACTION
DISTRACTIVE
DISTRAINING
DISTRESSFUL
DISTRESSING
DISTRIBUTED
DISTRIBUTOR
DISTRUSTFUL
DISTRUSTING
DISTURBANCE
DISULPHURIC
DITHYRAMBIC
DITTOGRAPHY
DIVARICATOR
DIVE-BOMBERS
DIVE-BOMBING
DIVERGENCES
DIVERGENTLY
DIVERSIFIED
DIVERSIFIER
DIVERSIFORM
DIVERSIONAL
DIVERTINGLY
DIVESTITURE
DIVINATIONS
DIVINE RIGHT
DIVING BELLS
DIVINGBOARD
DIVISIONISM
DIVISIONIST
DIVORCEABLE
DIVORCEMENT
DOCTRINAIRE
DOCUMENTARY

DOCUMENTING
DODDERINGLY
DODECAGONAL
DODECAPHONY
DOGBERRYISM
DOG BISCUITS
DOGCATCHERS
DOLABRIFORM
DOLEFULNESS
DOLL'S HOUSES
DOLORIMETRY
DOMESTICATE
DOMESTICITY
DOMICILIARY
DOMICILIATE
DOMINEERING
DOORKEEPERS
DOORKNOCKER
DOORSTOPPER
DORMITORIES
DOTTED LINES
DOUBLE AGENT
DOUBLE BINDS
DOUBLE-BLIND
DOUBLE BLUFF
DOUBLE-CHECK
DOUBLE CHINS
DOUBLE CREAM
DOUBLE-CROSS
DOUBLE DATED
DOUBLE DATES
DOUBLE-DUTCH
DOUBLE-EDGED
DOUBLE-FACED
DOUBLE FAULT
DOUBLE-GLAZE
DOUBLE-QUICK
DOUBLE-SPACE
DOUBLESPEAK
DOUBLE TAKES
DOUBLETHINK
DOUROUCOULI
DOVETAILING
DOWN-AND-OUTS
DOWNGRADING
DOWNHEARTED
DOWNLOADING
DOWNPATRICK
DOWN PAYMENT
DOWNPLAYING
DOWN-TO-EARTH
DOWNTRODDEN

DOXOLOGICAL
DRAGONFLIES
DRAMATIZING
DRAMATURGIC
DRASTICALLY
DRAUGHTSMAN
DRAUGHTSMEN
DRAWBRIDGES
DRAWING PINS
DRAWING ROOM
DRAWSTRINGS
DREADNOUGHT
DREAMLESSLY
DREAM TICKET
DREAM WORLDS
DRESS CIRCLE
DRESSMAKERS
DRESSMAKING
DRILLMASTER
DROMEDARIES
DRUNKENNESS
DRY CLEANERS
DRY-CLEANING
DSCONTINUER
DUAL-PURPOSE
DUBIOUSNESS
DUDE RANCHES
DUFFEL COATS
DUMBFOUNDED
DUMBFOUNDER
DUMBWAITERS
DUNDERHEADS
DUNE BUGGIES
DUNFERMLINE
DUPLEX HOUSE
DUPLICATING
DUPLICATION
DUPLICATIVE
DUPLICATORS
DUST JACKETS
DUTCH TREATS
DUTCH UNCLES
DUTIABILITY
DUTIFULNESS
DYNAMICALLY
DYNAMOMETER
DYNAMOMETRY
DYSFUNCTION
DYSFUNCTION

E
EAGER BEAVER

EARNESTNESS
EARTHENWARE
EARTH-GRAZER
EARTHLINESS
EARTHQUAKES
EAR TRUMPETS
EASEFULNESS
EAST ANGLIAN
EASTERN CAPE
EASTERNMOST
EAST GERMANY
EAST LOTHIAN
EATING APPLE
EBULLIENTLY
ECCLESIARCH
ECCRINOLOGY
ECHCHYMOSED
ECHOPRACTIC
ECLECTICISM
ECOFRIENDLY
ECONOMETRIC
ECONOMIZING
ECOSPECIFIC
ECTOBLASTIC
ECTOGENESIS
ECTOMORPHIC
ECTOPLASMIC
ECTOSARCOUS
EDAPHICALLY
EDIFICATION
EDIFICATORY
EDITORIALLY
EDUCABILITY
EDUCATIONAL
EFFECTIVELY
EFFECTUALLY
EFFECTUATED
EFFERVESCED
EFFICACIOUS
EFFICIENTLY
EGALITARIAN
EGOCENTRISM
EGOMANIACAL
EGOTISTICAL
EGREGIOUSLY
EIDETICALLY
EIFFEL TOWER
EIGHTEENTHS
EINSTEINIAN
EINSTEINIUM
EISTEDDFODS
EJACULATING

EJACULATION	EMBARKATION	ENCROACHING	ENLISTMENTS
EJACULATIVE	EMBARRASSED	ENCUMBERING	ENLIVENMENT
EJACULATORY	EMBELLISHED	ENCUMBRANCE	ENNEAHEDRAL
EJECTOR SEAT	EMBELLISHER	ENCYCLICALS	ENNEAHEDRON
ELABORATELY	EMBITTERING	ENDANGERING	ENNISKILLEN
ELABORATING	EMBLAZONING	ENDEARINGLY	ENNOBLEMENT
ELABORATION	EMBLEMATIZE	ENDEARMENTS	ENNOBLINGLY
ELABORATIVE	EMBOLDENING	ENDEAVOURED	ENRAPTURING
ELASTICALLY	EMBOLECTOMY	ENDEAVOURER	ENSHROUDING
ELASTIC BAND	EMBRACEABLE	ENDEMICALLY	ENSLAVEMENT
ELASTOMERIC	EMBRACEMENT	ENDLESSNESS	ENSNAREMENT
ELASTOPLAST	EMBROCATION	ENDOBLASTIC	ENTABLATURE
ELBOW GREASE	EMBROIDERED	ENDOCARDIAL	ENTABLEMENT
ELDERFLOWER	EMBROIDERER	ENDOCARDIUM	ENTEROSTOMY
ELECTIONEER	EMBROILMENT	ENDOCENTRIC	ENTEROVIRUS
ELECTORATES	EMBRYECTOMY	ENDOCRANIUM	ENTERPRISER
ELECTORSHIP	EMBRYOGENIC	ENDOCRINOUS	ENTERPRISES
ELECTRIC EYE	EMENDATIONS	ENDODONTICS	ENTERTAINED
ELECTRICIAN	EMERGENCIES	ENDODONTIST	ENTERTAINER
ELECTRICITY	EMIGRATIONS	ENDOMETRIAL	ENTHRALLING
ELECTRIFIED	EMMENAGOGIC	ENDOMETRIUM	ENTHRALMENT
ELECTRIFIER	EMMENAGOGUE	ENDOMORPHIC	ENTHUSIASMS
ELECTROCUTE	EMOTIONALLY	ENDONEURIUM	ENTHUSIASTS
ELECTROFORM	EMOTIONLESS	ENDOPLASMIC	ENTICEMENTS
ELECTROLYSE	EMOTIVENESS	ENDORSEMENT	ENTITLEMENT
ELECTROLYTE	EMPANELLING	ENDOSCOPIST	ENTOBLASTIC
ELECTRONICS	EMPANELMENT	ENDOSPERMIC	ENTOMBMENTS
ELECTROTYPE	EMPERORSHIP	ENDOSPOROUS	ENTOMOPHILY
ELEGIACALLY	EMPHASIZING	ENDOTHECIAL	ENTRAINMENT
ELEPHANTINE	EMPIRICALLY	ENDOTHECIUM	ENTREATMENT
ELEPHANTOID	EMPLACEMENT	ENDOTHELIAL	ENTRENCHING
ELICITATION	EMPLOYMENTS	ENDOTHELIUM	ENTRUSTMENT
ELIGIBILITY	EMPOWERMENT	ENDOTHERMIC	ENTWINEMENT
ELIMINATING	EMPTY-HANDED	END PRODUCTS	ENUCLEATION
ELIMINATION	EMPTY-HEADED	ENFORCEABLE	ENUMERATING
ELIMINATIVE	EMULOUSNESS	ENFORCEMENT	ENUMERATION
ELIZABETHAN	EMULSIFYING	ENFRANCHISE	ENUMERATIVE
ELLIPSOIDAL	EMULSIONING	ENGAGEMENTS	ENUNCIATING
ELLIPTICITY	ENARTHROSIS	ENGENDERING	ENUNCIATION
ELONGATIONS	ENCAMPMENTS	ENGINEERING	ENUNCIATIVE
ELUCIDATING	ENCAPSULATE	ENGLISH HORN	ENVELOPMENT
ELUCIDATION	ENCEPHALOMA	ENGORGEMENT	ENVIOUSNESS
ELUCIDATIVE	ENCEPHALOUS	ENGRAILMENT	ENVIRONMENT
ELUCIDATORY	ENCHAINMENT	ENGROSSEDLY	ENZYMOLYSIS
ELUSIVENESS	ENCHANTMENT	ENGROSSMENT	ENZYMOLYTIC
ELUTRIATION	ENCHANTRESS	ENHANCEMENT	EPHEMERALLY
EMANATIONAL	ENCHONDROMA	ENLARGEABLE	EPIDERMISES
EMANCIPATED	ENCOMIASTIC	ENLARGEMENT	EPIDIASCOPE
EMANCIPATOR	ENCOMPASSED	ENLIGHTENED	EPIGASTRIUM
EMASCULATED	ENCOUNTERED	ENLIGHTENER	EPIGENESIST
EMASCULATOR	ENCOUNTERER	ENLISTED MAN	EPIGRAPHIST
EMBANKMENTS	ENCOURAGING	ENLISTED MEN	EPIPHYTOTIC

EPITHALAMIC	ETHNOGENIST	EXCESSIVELY	EXPEDITIONS
EPITHELIOMA	ETHNOGRAPHY	EXCITEDNESS	EXPEDITIOUS
EPITOMIZING	ETHNOLOGIST	EXCITEMENTS	EXPENDITURE
EPOCH-MAKING	ETIOLOGICAL	EXCLAMATION	EXPENSIVELY
EQUIANGULAR	ETYMOLOGIES	EXCLAMATORY	EXPERIENCED
EQUIDISTANT	ETYMOLOGIST	EXCLUSIVELY	EXPERIENCES
EQUILATERAL	EUCHARISTIC	EXCOGITATOR	EXPERIMENTS
EQUILIBRANT	EUCHROMATIC	EXCORIATING	EXPLAINABLE
EQUILIBRATE	EUCHROMATIN	EXCORIATION	EXPLANATION
EQUILIBRIST	EUDIOMETRIC	EXCREMENTAL	EXPLANATORY
EQUILIBRIUM	EUGENICALLY	EXCRESCENCE	EXPLICATING
EQUINOCTIAL	EUPHEMISTIC	EXCRESCENCY	EXPLICATION
EQUIPOLLENT	EURHYTHMICS	EXCULPATING	EXPLICATIVE
EQUIVALENCE	EUROCENTRIC	EXCULPATION	EXPLOITABLE
EQUIVALENCY	EUROCHEQUES	EXCULPATORY	EXPLORATION
EQUIVALENTS	EURODOLLARS	EX-DIRECTORY	EXPLORATORY
EQUIVOCALLY	EUROPEANISM	EXECRATIONS	EXPLOSIVELY
EQUIVOCATED	EUROPEANIZE	EXECUTIONER	EXPONENTIAL
ERADICATING	EURO-SCEPTIC	EXECUTORIAL	EXPORTATION
ERADICATION	EURYTHERMAL	EXEMPLARILY	EXPOSEDNESS
ERADICATIVE	EVACUATIONS	EXEMPLIFIED	EXPOSITIONS
ERADICATORS	EVAGINATION	EXEMPLIFIER	EX POST FACTO
ERASTIANISM	EVALUATIONS	EXERCISABLE	EXPOSTULATE
ERGATOCRACY	EVANESCENCE	EXFOLIATION	EXPRESSIBLE
EROSIVENESS	EVANGELICAL	EXFOLIATIVE	EXPRESSIONS
EROTOMANIAC	EVANGELISTS	EXHAUSTIBLE	EXPRESSWAYS
ERRATICALLY	EVANGELIZED	EXHIBITIONS	EXPROPRIATE
ERRONEOUSLY	EVANGELIZER	EXHILARATED	EXPURGATING
ERUBESCENCE	EVAPORATING	EXHILARATOR	EXPURGATION
ERUCTATIONS	EVAPORATION	EXHORTATION	EXPURGATORY
ERYSIPELOID	EVAPORATIVE	EXHORTATIVE	EXQUISITELY
ERYTHEMATIC	EVASIVENESS	EXHUMATIONS	EXSICCATION
ERYTHRISMAL	EVENING STAR	EXISTENTIAL	EXSICCATIVE
ERYTHROCYTE	EVENTUALITY	EXONERATING	EXSTIPULATE
ESCAPEMENTS	EVENTUATION	EXONERATION	EXTEMPORIZE
ESCAPE WHEEL	EVERLASTING	EXONERATIVE	EXTENSIONAL
ESCARPMENTS	EVISCERATED	EXORABILITY	EXTENSIVELY
ESCHATOLOGY	EVISCERATOR	EXORBITANCE	EXTENUATING
ESCUTCHEONS	EXACERBATED	EXOSKELETAL	EXTENUATION
ESEMPLASTIC	EXAGGERATED	EXOSKELETON	EXTENUATORY
ESOPHAGUSES	EXAGGERATOR	EXOTERICISM	EXTERIORIZE
ESOTERICISM	EXALTEDNESS	EXPANSIVELY	EXTERMINATE
ESSENTIALLY	EXAMINATION	EXPATIATING	EXTERNALISM
ESTABLISHED	EXANIMATION	EXPATIATION	EXTERNALIST
ESTABLISHER	EXASPERATED	EXPATRIATED	EXTERNALITY
ESTATE AGENT	EXASPERATER	EXPATRIATES	EXTERNALIZE
ESTREMADURA	EXCAVATIONS	EXPECTANTLY	EXTIRPATING
ETHANEDIOIC	EXCEEDINGLY	EXPECTATION	EXTIRPATION
ETHEREALITY	EXCELLENTLY	EXPECTATIVE	EXTIRPATIVE
ETHEREALIZE	EXCEPTIONAL	EXPECTORANT	EXTOLLINGLY
ETHICALNESS	EXCERPTIBLE	EXPECTORATE	EXTRACTABLE
ETHNOBOTANY	EXCERPTTION	EXPEDIENTLY	EXTRACTIONS

EXTRADITING
EXTRADITION
EXTRAPOLATE
EXTRAVAGANT
EXTRAVAGATE
EXTRAVASATE
EXTREMENESS
EXTREMITIES
EXTRICATING
EXTRICATION
EXTROVERTED
EXUBERANTLY
EYE-CATCHING

F
FABRICATING
FABRICATION
FABRICATIVE
FACE-CENTRED
FACETIOUSLY
FACILITATED
FACILITATOR
FACT-FINDING
FACTORIZING
FACTORY FARM
FACTS OF LIFE
FACTUALNESS
FACULTATIVE
FAIRGROUNDS
FAIR-WEATHER
FAIRY LIGHTS
FAITH HEALER
FAITHLESSLY
FALCONIFORM
FALLIBILITY
FALLING STAR
FALSE ALARMS
FALSE BOTTOM
FALSE STARTS
FALSIFIABLE
FALSTAFFIAN
FALTERINGLY
FAMILIARITY
FAMILIARIZE
FAMILY NAMES
FAMILY TREES
FANATICALLY
FANTASIZING
FARCICALITY
FARINACEOUS
FARNBOROUGH
FARRAGINOUS

FAR-REACHING
FARTHERMOST
FARTHINGALE
FASCINATING
FASCINATION
FASCINATIVE
FASHIONABLE
FAST-BREEDER
FAST-FORWARD
FATEFULNESS
FATHER-IN-LAW
FATHERLANDS
FATUOUSNESS
FAULT-FINDER
FAULTLESSLY
FAVOURINGLY
FAVOURITISM
FAWNINGNESS
FEARFULNESS
FEASIBILITY
FEATHER BEDS
FEATHER BOAS
FEATHEREDGE
FEATURE FILM
FEATURELESS
FECUNDATION
FECUNDATORY
FEDERALISTS
FEDERATIONS
FELDSPATHIC
FELICITATED
FELICITATOR
FELLOWSHIPS
FELT-TIP PENS
FEMME FATALE
FENESTRATED
FERMENTABLE
FEROCIOUSLY
FERRICYANIC
FERRIFEROUS
FERRIS WHEEL
FERROCYANIC
FERRUGINOUS
FERTILIZERS
FERTILIZING
FERULACEOUS
FERVENTNESS
FESTINATION
FESTSCHRIFT
FETISHISTIC
FEUDALISTIC
FIBRE OPTICS

FIBROMATOUS
FIBROUSNESS
FICTIONALLY
FIDGETINGLY
FIELD-EFFECT
FIELD EVENTS
FIELD HOCKEY
FIELD-HOLLER
FIELD-TESTED
FIELDWORKER
FIFTH COLUMN
FIFTH-DEGREE
FIGURED BASS
FIGUREHEADS
FILAMENTARY
FILIBUSTERS
FILL THE BILL
FILMOGRAPHY
FILMSETTING
FILTHY LUCRE
FILTRATABLE
FIMBRIATION
FINANCIALLY
FIN DE SIECLE
FINE-GRAINED
FINES HERBES
FINGERBOARD
FINGER BOWLS
FINGERNAILS
FINGERPLATE
FINGERPRINT
FINGERSTALL
FIRE BRIGADE
FIRECRACKER
FIRE ENGINES
FIRE ESCAPES
FIRE FIGHTER
FIRE HYDRANT
FIRELIGHTER
FIREPROOFED
FIRE-RAISERS
FIRE-RAISING
FIRE STATION
FIRING SQUAD
FIRMAMENTAL
FIRST COUSIN
FIRST-DEGREE
FIRST-FOOTER
FIRST NATION
FIRST NIGHTS
FIRST PERSON
FIRST STRIKE

FIRST-STRING
FISHEYE LENS
FISH-EYE LENS
FISH FARMING
FISH FINGERS
FISHMONGERS
FISSIONABLE
FISSIPAROUS
FLABBERGAST
FLAGELLANTS
FLAGELLATED
FLAMBOYANCE
FLANNELETTE
FLANNELLING
FLASHLIGHTS
FLASH POINTS
FLAT-CHESTED
FLATTERABLE
FLAUNTINGLY
FLAVOURINGS
FLAVOURLESS
FLAVOURSOME
FLEA MARKETS
FLEET STREET
FLESHLINESS
FLESH WOUNDS
FLETCHERISM
FLEURS-DE-LIS
FLEXIBILITY
FLEXITARIAN
FLICK KNIVES
FLIGHT DECKS
FLIGHTINESS
FLIGHT PATHS
FLINCHINGLY
FLIRTATIONS
FLIRTATIOUS
FLOATATIONS
FLOCCULENCE
FLOODLIGHTS
FLOORBOARDS
FLOOR CLOTHS
FLOORWALKER
FLOPPY DISKS
FLORESCENCE
FLORILEGIUM
FLOUNDERING
FLOURISHING
FLOWCHARTED
FLOWER GIRLS
FLOWERINESS
FLUCTUATING

FLUCTUATION
FLUID OUNCES
FLUORESCEIN
FLUORESCENT
FLUORIDATED
FLUOROMETER
FLUOROMETRY
FLUOROSCOPE
FLUOROSCOPY
FLYCATCHERS
FLYING BOATS
FLYING FOXES
FLYING SQUAD
FLYING START
FLYSWATTERS
FOCAL LENGTH
FOLK DANCERS
FOLLICULATE
FOMENTATION
FOOLISHNESS
FOOL'S ERRAND
FOOTBALLERS
FOOTBRIDGES
FOOT FAULTED
FOOT-LAMBERT
FOOT-POUNDAL
FOOTSLOGGED
FOPPISHNESS
FORAMINIFER
FORASMUCH AS
FORBEARANCE
FORBIDDANCE
FOREBODINGS
FORECASTERS
FORECASTING
FORECLOSING
FORECLOSURE
FOREFATHERS
FOREFINGERS
FOREGROUNDS
FOREMANSHIP
FOREQUARTER
FORERUNNERS
FORESEEABLE
FORESHORTEN
FORESIGHTED
FORESTALLED
FORESTALLER
FORESTATION
FORETELLING
FORETHOUGHT
FORE-TOPMAST

FORE-TOPSAIL
FOR EVERMORE
FOREWARNING
FORFEITABLE
FORGATHERED
FORGETFULLY
FORGET-ME-NOT
FORGETTABLE
FORGIVENESS
FORGIVINGLY
FORJUDGMENT
FORLORN HOPE
FORLORNNESS
FORMALISTIC
FORMALITIES
FORMALIZING
FORMATIONAL
FORMATIVELY
FORMICATION
FORMULAICLY
FORMULARIZE
FORMULATING
FORMULATION
FORMULISTIC
FORNICATING
FORNICATION
FORSWEARING
FORTHCOMING
FORTIFIABLE
FORTNIGHTLY
FORTUNATELY
FORT WILLIAM
FORWARDNESS
FOSSILIZING
FOSTERINGLY
FOUL-MOUTHED
FOUNDATIONS
FOUNTAIN PEN
FOURDRINIER
FOUR-POSTERS
FOURTEENTHS
FOX TERRIERS
FRACTIONARY
FRACTIONATE
FRACTIONIZE
FRACTIOUSLY
FRACTURABLE
FRAGMENTARY
FRAGMENTING
FRAME OF MIND
FRANCHISING
FRANCISCANS

FRANCOPHILE
FRANCOPHOBE
FRANCOPHONE
FRANKFURTER
FRANKLINITE
FRANTICALLY
FRATERNALLY
FRATERNIZED
FRATERNIZER
FRATRICIDAL
FRATRICIDES
FRAUDULENCE
FREDERICTON
FREDRIKSTAD
FREEBOOTERS
FREE-FLOATER
FREE-FOR-ALLS
FREE-HEARTED
FREEHOLDERS
FREELANCING
FREELOADERS
FREELOADING
FREEMASONIC
FREEMASONRY
FREE PARDONS
FREE-SWIMMER
FREETHINKER
FREEWHEELED
FREEZE-DRIED
FRENCH BEANS
FRENCH BREAD
FRENCH DOORS
FRENCH FRIES
FRENCH HORNS
FRENCH LEAVE
FRENCH TOAST
FRENCHWOMAN
FREQUENCIES
FREQUENTING
FRETFULNESS
FREUDIANISM
FRIENDLIEST
FRIENDSHIPS
FRIGHTENING
FRIGHTFULLY
FRINGILLINE
FRIVOLITIES
FRIVOLOUSLY
FROGMARCHED
FRONDESCENT
FRONTOLYSIS
FRONT-RUNNER

FROSTBITTEN
FRUCTIFYING
FRUGIVOROUS
FRUITLESSLY
FRUIT SALADS
FRUSTRATING
FRUSTRATION
FRUTESCENCE
FULGURATING
FULGURATION
FULL-BLOODED
FULL-FLEDGED
FULL-MOUTHED
FULMINATING
FULMINATION
FULMINATORY
FULSOMENESS
FUNAMBULIST
FUN AND GAMES
FUNCTIONARY
FUNCTIONING
FUNDAMENTAL
FUNDHOLDING
FUNGIBILITY
FUNGISTATIC
FURALDEHYDE
FURIOUSNESS
FURNISHINGS
FURTHERANCE
FURTHERMORE
FURTHERMOST
FURTIVENESS

G

GAFF-TOPSAIL
GAINFULNESS
GALLANTNESS
GALLANTRIES
GALL BLADDER
GALLINACEAN
GALLIVANTED
GALLUP POLLS
GALVANIZING
GAMEKEEPERS
GAMEKEEPING
GAMETANGIAL
GAMETANGIUM
GAMETOGENIC
GAMETOPHORE
GAMETOPHYTE
GAMOGENESIS
GAMOGENETIC

GANG-BANGING
GARAGE SALES
GARBAGE CANS
GARDEN PARTY
GARNISHMENT
GARRISONING
GARRULOUSLY
GASEOUSNESS
GAS STATIONS
GASTRECTOMY
GASTRONOMES
GASTRONOMIC
GASTROPODAN
GASTROSCOPE
GASTROSCOPY
GASTROSTOMY
GASTROTRICH
GAS TURBINES
GATECRASHED
GATECRASHER
GATEKEEPERS
GEANTICLINE
GEGENSCHEIN
GELATINIZER
GEMMIPAROUS
GEMMULATION
GEMOLOGICAL
GENDARMERIE
GENEALOGIES
GENEALOGIST
GENE LIBRARY
GENERALIZED
GENERALIZER
GENERALNESS
GENERALSHIP
GENERATIONS
GENERATION X
GENERICALLY
GENETICALLY
GENETIC CODE
GENETICISTS
GENTEELNESS
GENTIANELLA
GENTLEMANLY
GENTLEWOMAN
GENTLEWOMEN
GENTRIFYING
GENUFLECTED
GENUFLECTOR
GENUINENESS
GEOCHEMICAL
GEODYNAMICS

GEOGRAPHERS
GEOGRAPHIES
GEOMAGNETIC
GEOPHYSICAL
GEOPOLITICS
GEOSTRATEGY
GEOSTROPHIC
GEOSYNCLINE
GEOTECTONIC
GERATOLOGIC
GERMANENESS
GERMINATING
GERMINATION
GERM WARFARE
GERONTOLOGY
GERRYMANDER
GESTATIONAL
GESTICULATE
GET CRACKING
GET-TOGETHER
GHASTLINESS
GHOSTBUSTER
GHOSTLINESS
GHOSTWRITER
GIANT KILLER
GIANT PANDAS
GIBBERELLIN
GIBBOUSNESS
GIFT-WRAPPED
GIGANTESQUE
GILA MONSTER
GILLYFLOWER
GINGER BEERS
GINGERBREAD
GINGER GROUP
GIRL FRIDAYS
GIRLFRIENDS
GIRLISHNESS
GIVE-AND-TAKE
GLADIOLUSES
GLAMORIZING
GLAMOROUSLY
GLARINGNESS
GLASSBLOWER
GLASSCUTTER
GLASSHOUSES
GLASS-MAKING
GLASS-WORKER
GLASTONBURY
GLAUCONITIC
GLEEFULNESS
GLOBEFLOWER

GLOBIGERINA
GLOCHIDIATE
GLOMERATION
GLOMERULATE
GLORIFIABLE
GLOSSECTOMY
GLOSSOLALIA
GLOTTAL STOP
GLOVE PUPPET
GLOWERINGLY
GLUE-SNIFFER
GLUTATHIONE
GLYPHOGRAPH
GNATCATCHER
GOALKEEPERS
GOALKEEPING
GO BALLISTIC
GODCHILDREN
GODDAUGHTER
GODFORSAKEN
GODLESSNESS
GOLD-BEATING
GOLD DIGGERS
GOLD-DIGGING
GOLDEN EAGLE
GOLDEN SYRUP
GOLDFINCHES
GOLF COURSES
GONIOMETRIC
GONOCOCCOID
GONORRHOEAL
GOOD EVENING
GOOD LOOKERS
GOOD-LOOKING
GOOD MORNING
GOOD-NATURED
GOOD OFFICES
GORDIAN KNOT
GORMANDIZED
GORMANDIZER
GOSSIPINGLY
GO TO THE DOGS
GOURMANDISE
GOURMANDISM
GOVERNESSES
GOVERNMENTS
GRACELESSLY
GRADABILITY
GRADATIONAL
GRADE SCHOOL
GRADUALNESS
GRADUATIONS

GRAECO-ROMAN
GRAMMARIANS
GRAMMATICAL
GRAMOPHONES
GRANDADDIES
GRAND BAHAMA
GRAND CANARY
GRANDE-TERRE
GRANDFATHER
GRANDIOSITY
GRAND JURIES
GRAND MASTER
GRANDMOTHER
GRAND OPERAS
GRANDPARENT
GRAND PIANOS
GRAND RAPIDS
GRANDSTANDS
GRANGEMOUTH
GRANGERIZER
GRANITEWARE
GRANIVOROUS
GRANNY KNOTS
GRANOLITHIC
GRANOPHYRIC
GRANULARITY
GRANULATION
GRANULATIVE
GRANULOCYTE
GRAPEFRUITS
GRAPHICALLY
GRAPHOLOGIC
GRAPHOMOTOR
GRASSHOPPER
GRASS WIDOWS
GRAVESTONES
GRAVIMETRIC
GRAVITATING
GRAVITATION
GRAVITATIVE
GREASEPAINT
GREASY SPOON
GREAT CIRCLE
GREAT-NEPHEW
GREENBOTTLE
GREENGROCER
GREENHOUSES
GREENLANDER
GREENOCKITE
GREEN PAPERS
GREEN PEPPER
GRETNA GREEN

GRIDDLECAKE
GRIMACINGLY
GRINDELWALD
GRINDSTONES
GRISTLINESS
GRIZZLY BEAR
GROTESQUELY
GROTESQUERY
GROUCHINESS
GROUND CREWS
GROUND FLOOR
GROUND GLASS
GROUNDLINGS
GROUND PLANS
GROUND RENTS
GROUND RULES
GROUNDSHEET
GROUNDSPEED
GROUND STAFF
GROUNDSWELL
GROUPUSCULE
GRUELLINGLY
GRUMBLINGLY
GUADALAJARA
GUADALCANAL
GUARDEDNESS
GUARDHOUSES
GUELDER-ROSE
GUESSTIMATE
GUESTHOUSES
GUEST WORKER
GUILELESSLY
GUILLOTINED
GUILLOTINER
GUILLOTINES
GUILTLESSLY
GULLIBILITY
GUN CARRIAGE
GUNSMITHING
GURGITATION
GUTLESSNESS
GUTTA-PERCHA
GUTTER PRESS
GUTTERSNIPE
GUTTURALIZE
GYNAECOLOGY
GYPSIFEROUS
GYROCOMPASS
GYROSCOPICS
GYROSTATICS

H
HABERDASHER
HABILITATOR
HABITATIONS
HABITUATING
HABITUATION
HABITUDINAL
HADROSAURUS
HAEMACHROME
HAEMATOCELE
HAEMATOCRIT
HAEMATOLOGY
HAEMATOZOON
HAEMOCHROME
HAEMOCYANIN
HAEMOGLOBIN
HAEMOPHILIA
HAEMOPHILIC
HAEMOPTYSIS
HAEMORRHAGE
HAEMOSTASIA
HAEMOSTASIS
HAEMOSTATIC
HAGGADISTIC
HAGGARDNESS
HAGGISHNESS
HAGIOGRAPHA
HAGIOGRAPHY
HAGIOLOGIST
HAGIOSCOPIC
HAIRBREADTH
HAIRBRUSHES
HAIRDRESSER
HAIRPIN BEND
HAIR-RAISING
HAIRSPRINGS
HAIRSTYLIST
HAIR TRIGGER
HAIRWEAVING
HALBERSTADT
HALCYON DAYS
HALF-BROTHER
HALF-CENTURY
HALF-HEARTED
HALF-HOLIDAY
HALFPENNIES
HALF-SISTERS
HALF VOLLEYS
HALLMARKING
HALLUCINATE
HALOPHYTISM
HALTEMPRICE

HALTERNECKS
HALTINGNESS
HAMILTONIAN
HAMMERSMITH
HAMMERSTEIN
HAMMOCK-LIKE
HANDBREADTH
HANDCUFFING
HANDFASTING
HANDICAPPED
HANDICAPPER
HANDICRAFTS
HAND IN GLOVE
HAND LUGGAGE
HANDMAIDENS
HAND-ME-DOWNS
HANDWRITING
HANDWRITTEN
HANG GLIDING
HAPHAZARDLY
HAPLESSNESS
HAPLOGRAPHY
HAPPY EVENTS
HAPPY MEDIUM
HARASSINGLY
HARBOURLESS
HARD-AND-FAST
HARDECANUTE
HARD-HEARTED
HARD-HITTING
HARDICANUTE
HARD PALATES
HARD-PRESSED
HARDWEARING
HARDY ANNUAL
HAREBRAINED
HARMFULNESS
HARMONISTIC
HARMONIZING
HARNESSLESS
HARNESS-LIKE
HARPOON-LIKE
HARPSICHORD
HARRIS TWEED
HARROWINGLY
HARTEBEESTS
HARUM SCARUM
HARUM-SCARUM
HARVEST HOME
HARVESTLESS
HARVEST MOON
HATCHET JOBS

HATCHET-LIKE
HATEFULNESS
HAUGHTINESS
HAUSTELLATE
HAUTES-ALPES
HAUTE-SAVOIE
HAUTE-VIENNE
HAWKISHNESS
HAZARDOUSLY
HEADDRESSES
HEADHUNTERS
HEADHUNTING
HEADMASTERS
HEALTH FOODS
HEALTHFULLY
HEALTHINESS
HEARING AIDS
HEART ATTACK
HEARTBROKEN
HEARTHSTONE
HEARTLESSLY
HEARTSOMELY
HEARTTHROBS
HEATHENNESS
HEAT SHIELDS
HEAVENWARDS
HEAVY-HANDED
HEAVYWEIGHT
HEBDOMADARY
HEBEPHRENIA
HEBEPHRENIC
HEBRAICALLY
HECKELPHONE
HECTOGRAPHY
HEDGEHOPPER
HEEDFULNESS
HEGELIANISM
HEIGHTENING
HEINOUSNESS
HELICHRYSUM
HELICOGRAPH
HELICOPTERS
HELIOCHROME
HELIOGRAPHS
HELIOGRAPHY
HELIOLITHIC
HELIOMETRIC
HELIOSTATIC
HELIOTACTIC
HELIOTROPES
HELIOTROPIC
HELIOTROPIN

HELLEBORINE	HETEROLYTIC	HIPPOCRATIC	HOMOPTEROUS
HELLENISTIC	HETEROPHONY	HIPPOPOTAMI	HOMO SAPIENS
HELLISHNESS	HETEROPHYTE	HIPPO REGIUS	HOMOSEXUALS
HELMINTHOID	HETEROPOLAR	HIRSUTENESS	HOMOSPOROUS
HELPFULNESS	HETEROSPORY	HISPANICISM	HOMOTHALLIC
HELPING HAND	HETEROSTYLY	HISPANICIST	HOMOTHERMAL
HELSINGBORG	HETEROTAXIS	HISPANICIZE	HOMOZYGOSIS
HEMERALOPIA	HETEROTOPIA	HISTAMINASE	HOMOZYGOTIC
HEMERALOPIC	HETEROTOPIC	HISTIOCYTIC	HONEYCOMBED
HEMIANOPSIA	HETEROTYPIC	HISTOLOGIST	HONEYMOONED
HEMIELYTRAL	HEXADECIMAL	HISTORIATED	HONEYMOONER
HEMIELYTRON	HEXAGONALLY	HISTORICISM	HONEYSUCKER
HEMIHYDRATE	HEXAHYDRATE	HISTORICIST	HONEYSUCKLE
HEMIMORPHIC	HEXASTICHIC	HISTORICITY	HONORARIUMS
HEMIPTEROUS	HEXASTICHON	HISTRIONICS	HONOURS LIST
HEMISPHERES	HEXATEUCHAL	HITCHHIKERS	HOODWINKING
HEMISPHERIC	HIBERNATING	HITCHHIKING	HOOLIGANISM
HEMITERPENE	HIBERNATION	HOBBLEDEHOY	HOPEFULNESS
HEMITROPISM	HIBERNICISM	HOBBYHORSES	HOPLOLOGIST
HEMOPHILIAC	HIDE-AND-SEEK	HOGGISHNESS	HORIZONLESS
HEMORRHAGES	HIDEOUSNESS	HOLKAR STATE	HORIZONTALS
HEMORRHOIDS	HIERARCHIES	HOLLANDAISE	HORNBLENDIC
HEMSTITCHER	HIERARCHISM	HOLOBLASTIC	HORNET'S NEST
HEPPLEWHITE	HIEROCRATIC	HOLOCAUSTAL	HORNSWOGGLE
HEPTAHEDRAL	HIEROGLYPHS	HOLOGRAPHIC	HORROR FILMS
HEPTAHEDRON	HIEROLOGIST	HOLOHEDRISM	HORS D'OEUVRE
HEPTAMEROUS	HIGH COMMAND	HOLOMORPHIC	HORSE DOCTOR
HEPTANGULAR	HIGHFALUTIN	HOLOTHURIAN	HORSELAUGHS
HEPTAVALENT	HIGH JUMPERS	HOMECOMINGS	HORSE OPERAS
HERBIVOROUS	HIGHLANDERS	HOMEOPATHIC	HORSERADISH
HERCEGOVINA	HIGHLIGHTED	HOMEOSTASIS	HORTATORILY
HERCULANEUM	HIGHLIGHTER	HOMEOSTATIC	HOSPITALITY
HEREDITABLE	HIGH-PITCHED	HOMERICALLY	HOSPITALIZE
HEREDITABLY	HIGH-POWERED	HOMESTEADER	HOSPITALLER
HEREINAFTER	HIGH PRIESTS	HOME STRETCH	HOSTILITIES
HERETICALLY	HIGH PROFILE	HOMICIDALLY	HOT-CROSS BUN
HERMENEUTIC	HIGH-RANKING	HOMOCENTRIC	HOTHEADEDLY
HERMOUPOLIS	HIGH SCHOOLS	HOMOEOPATHS	HOT POTATOES
HERO WORSHIP	HIGH SHERIFF	HOMOEOPATHY	HOT-TEMPERED
HERPESVIRUS	HIGH-TENSION	HOMOEROTISM	HOURGLASSES
HERPETOLOGY	HIGH TREASON	HOMOGENEITY	HOUSE ARREST
HERRINGBONE	HIGHWAY CODE	HOMOGENEOUS	HOUSEBROKEN
HERZEGOVINA	HIGH WYCOMBE	HOMOGENIZED	HOUSEFATHER
HESITATIONS	HILARIOUSLY	HOMOGENIZER	HOUSEHOLDER
HESPERIDIAN	HILLBILLIES	HOMOGRAPHIC	HOUSEKEEPER
HESPERIDIUM	HINDERINGLY	HOMOIOUSIAN	HOUSE LIGHTS
HESYCHASTIC	HINDQUARTER	HOMOLOGICAL	HOUSEMASTER
HETAERISTIC	HINSHELWOOD	HOMOLOGIZER	HOUSEMOTHER
HETEROCLITE	HIPPEASTRUM	HOMOMORPHIC	HOUSEPARENT
HETEROECISM	HIPPOCAMPAL	HOMOPHONOUS	HOUSEPLANTS
HETEROGRAFT	HIPPOCAMPUS	HOMOPHYLLIC	HOUSEWIFELY
HETEROLYSIS	HIPPOCRATES	HOMOPLASTIC	HOUSEWIFERY

HOUSEWORKER	**I**	IMMIGRATION	IMPORTATION
HOVERCRAFTS	ICEBREAKERS	IMMOBILIZED	IMPORTUNATE
HOW DO YOU DOS	ICHNOGRAPHY	IMMOBILIZER	IMPORTUNING
HSIN-HAI-LIEN	ICHTHYOLOGY	IMMORTALITY	IMPORTUNITY
HUCKLEBERRY	ICONOCLASTS	IMMORTALIZE	IMPOSITIONS
HUCKSTERISM	ICONOGRAPHY	IMMUNOASSAY	IMPRACTICAL
HUDIBRASTIC	ICONOLOGIST	IMMUNOGENIC	IMPRECATION
HUGUENOTISM	ICOSAHEDRAL	IMMUNOLOGIC	IMPRECATORY
HULLABALOOS	ICOSAHEDRON	IMPANELLING	IMPRECISION
HUMAN RIGHTS	IDENTICALLY	IMPARTATION	IMPREGNABLE
HUMDRUMNESS	IDENTIFYING	IMPARTIALLY	IMPREGNABLY
HUMIDIFIERS	IDEOLOGICAL	IMPASSIONED	IMPREGNATED
HUMIDIFYING	IDIOBLASTIC	IMPASSIVELY	IMPREGNATOR
HUMILIATING	IDIOGRAPHIC	IMPASSIVITY	IMPRESARIOS
HUMILIATION	IDIOMORPHIC	IMPASTATION	IMPRESSIBLE
HUMILIATIVE	IDIOTICALLY	IMPATIENTLY	IMPRESSIONS
HUMILIATORY	IDOLATRIZER	IMPEACHABLE	IMPRESSMENT
HUMMINGBIRD	IDOLIZATION	IMPEACHMENT	IMPRIMATURS
HUNCHBACKED	IDYLLICALLY	IMPECUNIOUS	IMPRISONING
HUNGER MARCH	IGNIS FATUUS	IMPEDIMENTA	IMPROPRIATE
HUNNISHNESS	IGNOMINIOUS	IMPEDIMENTS	IMPROPRIETY
HURRIEDNESS	IGNORAMUSES	IMPENITENCE	IMPROVEMENT
HURTFULNESS	ILE-DE-FRANCE	IMPERATIVES	IMPROVIDENT
HUSBANDLESS	ILL-ASSORTED	IMPERFECTLY	IMPROVINGLY
HYACINTHINE	ILL-FAVOURED	IMPERFORATE	IMPROVISING
HYDNOCARPIC	ILLIBERALLY	IMPERIALISM	IMPRUDENTLY
HYDRARGYRIC	ILLIMITABLE	IMPERIALIST	IMPUGNATION
HYDRARGYRUM	ILL-MANNERED	IMPERILLING	IMPUISSANCE
HYDROCARBON	ILLOGICALLY	IMPERIOUSLY	IMPULSIVELY
HYDROCYANIC	ILL-TEMPERED	IMPERMANENT	IMPUTATIONS
HYDROGENATE	ILL-TREATING	IMPERMEABLE	INADVERTENT
HYDROGENIZE	ILLUMINANCE	IMPERSONATE	INADVISABLE
HYDROGENOUS	ILLUMINATED	IMPERTINENT	INALIENABLE
HYDROGRAPHY	ILLUMINATOR	IMPETRATION	INALTERABLE
HYDROLOGIST	ILLUSIONARY	IMPETRATIVE	INATTENTION
HYDROLYSATE	ILLUSIONISM	IMPETUOSITY	INATTENTIVE
HYDROMANCER	ILLUSIONIST	IMPETUOUSLY	INAUGURATED
HYDROMANTIC	ILLUSTRATED	IMPINGEMENT	INAUGURATOR
HYDROMEDUSA	ILLUSTRATOR	IMPIOUSNESS	INAUTHENTIC
HYDROMETEOR	ILLUSTRIOUS	IMPLAUSIBLE	INCALESCENT
HYDROPHOBIA	ILLUVIATION	IMPLAUSIBLY	INCANTATION
HYDROPONICS	I'M A DUTCHMAN	IMPLEADABLE	INCAPSULATE
HYPERACTIVE	IMAGINARILY	IMPLEMENTAL	INCARCERATE
HYPERMARKET	IMAGINATION	IMPLEMENTED	INCARDINATE
HYPHENATING	IMAGINATIVE	IMPLEMENTER	INCARNATING
HYPHENATION	IMBRICATION	IMPLICATING	INCARNATION
HYPNOTIZING	IMITABILITY	IMPLICATION	INCERTITUDE
HYPODERMICS	IMITATIONAL	IMPLICATIVE	INCESSANTLY
HYPOSTATIZE	IMITATIVELY	IMPLORATION	INCIDENTALS
HYPOTHERMIA	IMMEDIATELY	IMPLORATORY	INCINERATED
	IMMEDICABLE	IMPLORINGLY	INCINERATOR
	IMMIGRATING	IMPORTANTLY	INCIPIENTLY

INCLINATION	INDIGNATION	INFANTRYMAN	INITIATRESS
INCLUSIVELY	INDIGNITIES	INFANTRYMEN	INJUDICIOUS
INCOERCIBLE	INDIRECTION	INFATUATION	INJUNCTIONS
INCOGNIZANT	INDIVIDUALS	INFERENTIAL	INJURIOUSLY
INCOHERENCE	INDIVIDUATE	INFERIORITY	IN-LINE SKATE
INCOME TAXES	INDIVISIBLE	INFERNALITY	INNER CITIES
INCOMMODING	INDIVISIBLY	INFERTILITY	INNERVATION
INCOMPETENT	INDOCHINESE	INFESTATION	INNOCUOUSLY
INCOMPLIANT	INDO-HITTITE	INFILTRATED	INNOVATIONS
IN CONDITION	INDO-IRANIAN	INFILTRATOR	INNS OF COURT
INCONGRUITY	INDOMITABLE	INFINITIVAL	INNUMERABLE
INCONGRUOUS	INDOMITABLY	INFINITIVES	INNUTRITION
INCONSONANT	INDO-PACIFIC	INFIRMARIES	INOBSERVANT
INCONSTANCY	INDORSEMENT	INFIRMITIES	INOCULATING
INCONTINENT	INDUBITABLE	INFLAMINGLY	INOCULATION
INCORPORATE	INDUBITABLY	INFLAMMABLE	INOCULATIVE
INCORPOREAL	INDUCEMENTS	INFLECTIONS	INOFFENSIVE
INCORRECTLY	INDUCTILITY	INFLICTIONS	INOFFICIOUS
INCREASABLE	INDUCTIONAL	INFLUENCING	INOPERATIVE
INCREASEDLY	INDUCTIVELY	INFLUENTIAL	INOPPORTUNE
INCREDULITY	INDULGENCES	INFOMERCIAL	IN PERPETUUM
INCREDULOUS	INDULGENTLY	INFORMALITY	INQUILINISM
INCREMENTAL	INDULGINGLY	INFORMATION	INQUILINOUS
INCRIMINATE	INDUPLICATE	INFORMATIVE	INQUIRINGLY
INCULCATING	INDUSTRIOUS	INFORMINGLY	INQUISITION
INCULCATION	INEBRIATING	INFRACOSTAL	INQUISITIVE
INCULPATING	INEBRIATION	INFRACTIONS	INQUISITORS
INCULPATION	INEDIBILITY	INFRANGIBLE	IN-RESIDENCE
INCUNABULAR	INEFFECTIVE	INFREQUENCY	INSALUBRITY
INCURIOSITY	INEFFECTUAL	INFURIATING	INSCRIBABLE
INCURVATION	INEFFICIENT	INFURIATION	INSCRIPTION
INCURVATURE	INELEGANTLY	INFUSIONISM	INSCRIPTIVE
INDECIDUOUS	INELOQUENCE	INFUSIONIST	INSCRUTABLE
INDEFINABLE	INELUCTABLE	INGENIOUSLY	INSCRUTABLY
INDEFINABLY	INELUCTABLY	INGENUOUSLY	INSECTARIUM
INDEHISCENT	INEQUITABLE	INGRAINEDLY	INSECTICIDE
INDEMNIFIED	INEQUITABLY	INGRATIATED	INSECTIVORE
INDEMNIFIER	INERTIA REEL	INGRATITUDE	INSEMINATED
INDEMNITIES	INESCAPABLE	INGREDIENTS	INSEMINATOR
INDENTATION	INESCAPABLY	INGURGITATE	INSENSITIVE
INDENTURING	INESSENTIAL	INHABITABLE	INSENTIENCE
INDEPENDENT	INESTIMABLE	INHABITANCY	INSEPARABLE
INDEX FINGER	INESTIMABLY	INHABITANTS	INSEPARABLY
INDIA RUBBER	INEXACTNESS	INHALATIONS	INSERTIONAL
INDICATABLE	INEXCUSABLE	INHERITABLE	INSESSORIAL
INDICATIONS	INEXCUSABLY	INHERITANCE	INSIDE TRACK
INDICATIVES	INEXISTENCE	INHIBITABLE	INSIDIOUSLY
INDICTMENTS	INEXPEDIENT	INHIBITEDLY	INSINCERELY
INDIFFERENT	INEXPENSIVE	INHIBITIONS	INSINCERITY
INDIGESTION	INFANTICIDE	INITIALLING	INSINUATING
INDIGESTIVE	INFANTILISM	INITIATIONS	INSINUATION
INDIGNANTLY	INFANTILITY	INITIATIVES	INSINUATIVE

INSISTENTLY	INTERCOSTAL	INTERWEAVER	INVOLUCRATE
INSOUCIANCE	INTERCOURSE	INTIMATIONS	INVOLUNTARY
INSPECTABLE	INTERDENTAL	INTIMIDATED	INVOLVEMENT
INSPECTIONS	INTERDICTOR	INTIMIDATOR	IONOSPHERIC
INSPECTORAL	INTERESTING	INTOLERABLE	IPECACUANHA
INSPIRATION	INTERFACING	INTOLERABLY	IRIDESCENCE
INSPIRATIVE	INTERFERING	INTOLERANCE	IRISH COFFEE
INSPIRATORY	INTERFUSION	INTONATIONS	IRON CURTAIN
INSPIRINGLY	INTERJECTED	INTOXICABLE	IRONMONGERS
INSTABILITY	INTERJECTOR	INTOXICANTS	IRONMONGERY
INSTALMENTS	INTERLACING	INTOXICATED	IRON RATIONS
INSTATEMENT	INTERLARDED	INTOXICATOR	IRRADIATING
INSTIGATING	INTERLINEAR	INTRA-ATOMIC	IRRADIATION
INSTIGATION	INTERLINGUA	INTRACOSTAL	IRRADIATIVE
INSTIGATIVE	INTERLINING	INTRACTABLE	IRRECUSABLE
INSTIGATORS	INTERLINKED	INTRACTABLY	IRREDENTISM
INSTINCTIVE	INTERLOCKED	INTRADERMAL	IRREDENTIST
INSTITUTING	INTERLOCKER	INTRAVENOUS	IRREDUCIBLE
INSTITUTION	INTERLOPERS	INTRENCHING	IRREDUCIBLY
INSTITUTIVE	INTERMEZZOS	INTREPIDITY	IRREFUTABLE
INSTRUCTING	INTERMINGLE	INTRICACIES	IRREFUTABLY
INSTRUCTION	INTERMITTOR	INTRICATELY	IRREGULARLY
INSTRUCTIVE	INTERNALITY	INTRODUCING	IRRELEVANCE
INSTRUCTORS	INTERNALIZE	INTROVERTED	IRRELIGIOUS
INSTRUMENTS	INTERNECINE	INTRUDINGLY	IRREMOVABLE
INSUFFLATOR	INTERNEURON	INTRUSIONAL	IRREPARABLE
INSUPERABLE	INTERNMENTS	INTUITIONAL	IRREPARABLY
INSUPERABLY	INTERNSHIPS	INTUITIVELY	IRRESOLUBLE
INTAGLIATED	INTERNUNCIO	INTUITIVISM	IRRETENTIVE
INTEGRATING	INTERPOLATE	INTUITIVIST	IRREVERENCE
INTEGRATION	INTERPOSING	INTUMESCENT	IRREVOCABLE
INTEGRATIVE	INTERPRETED	INUNDATIONS	IRREVOCABLY
INTEGUMENTS	INTERPRETER	INVAGINABLE	IRRITATIONS
INTELLIGENT	INTERRACIAL	INVALIDATED	ISAAC NEWTON
INTEMPERATE	INTERRADIAL	INVALIDATOR	ISOCHRONIZE
INTENSIFIED	INTERREGNAL	INVENTIONAL	ISODIAPHERE
INTENSIFIER	INTERREGNUM	INVENTIVELY	ISOELECTRIC
INTENSIONAL	INTERRELATE	INVENTORIAL	ISOGEOTHERM
INTENSIVELY	INTERROBANG	INVENTORIES	ISOLABILITY
INTENTIONAL	INTERROGATE	INVERTEBRAL	ISOLECITHAL
INTERACTING	INTERRUPTED	INVESTIGATE	ISOMAGNETIC
INTERACTION	INTERRUPTER	INVESTITIVE	ISOMETRICAL
INTERACTIVE	INTERSECTED	INVESTITURE	ISOMETROPIA
INTERATOMIC	INTERSEXUAL	INVESTMENTS	ISOMORPHISM
INTERBEDDED	INTERSPERSE	INVIABILITY	ISORHYTHMIC
INTERCALARY	INTERSTICES	INVIDIOUSLY	ISOTONICITY
INTERCALATE	INTERTRIBAL	INVIGILATED	ITACOLUMITE
INTERCEDING	INTERTWINED	INVIGILATOR	ITALICIZING
INTERCEPTED	INTERVENING	INVIGORATED	ITEMIZATION
INTERCEPTOR	INTERVIEWED	INVIGORATOR	ITHYPHALLIC
INTERCESSOR	INTERVIEWEE	INVITATIONS	ITINERARIES
INTERCHANGE	INTERVIEWER	INVOCATIONS	

ITINERATION
IVORY TOWERS

J
JACKHAMMERS
JACK-KNIFING
JACKRABBITS
JACTITATION
JAM SESSIONS
JANISSARIES
JAWBREAKERS
JAYAWARDENE
JEHOSHAPHAT
JELLYFISHES
JEOPARDIZED
JETTISONING
JOHORE BAHRU
JOIE DE VIVRE
JOURNALISTS
JOURNALIZER
JOYLESSNESS
JUDAIZATION
JUDGMENT DAY
JUDICATURES
JUDICIOUSLY
JUGGERNAUTS
JUGULAR VEIN
JUMBLE SALES
JUSTICESHIP
JUSTICIABLE
JUSTIFIABLE
JUSTIFIABLY
JUVENESCENT
JUXTAPOSING

K
KALASHNIKOV
KALININGRAD
KANCHIPURAM
KARLOVY VARY
KERB CRAWLER
KETTLEDRUMS
KEYBOARDERS
KEYBOARDING
KEYPUNCHERS
KIDNEY BEANS
KILIMANJARO
KILLER WHALE
KIND-HEARTED
KINDREDNESS
KINETICALLY
KINETOPLAST

KINGFISHERS
KISS OF DEATH
KITCHENETTE
KITCHENWARE
KITTENISHLY
KLEPTOMANIA
KNEECAPPING
KNICK-KNACKS
KNIGHTHOODS
KNUCKLEBONE
KOOKABURRAS
KRASNOYARSK
KRISTIANSEN
KRUGERRANDS
KRUGERSDORP
KUALA LUMPUR
KUMARATUNGE
KWANGCHOWAN
KWASHIORKOR
KYANIZATION
KYMOGRAPHIC

L
LABIODENTAL
LABORIOUSLY
LABOR UNIONS
LABOURINGLY
LABOUR PARTY
LABRADOODLE
LABRADORITE
LACCOLITHIC
LACERATIONS
LACERTILIAN
LACINIATION
LACONICALLY
LACQUERWARE
LACRIMATION
LACRIMATORY
LACTALBUMIN
LACTATIONAL
LACTESCENCE
LACTIFEROUS
LADY-KILLERS
LAEVOGYRATE
LAGOMORPHIC
LAICIZATION
LAKE DWELLER
LAKE SUCCESS
LAMELLATION
LAMELLICORN
LAMELLIFORM
LAMELLOSITY

LAMENTATION
LAMENTINGLY
LAMINAR FLOW
LAMMERGEIER
LAMPROPHYRE
LANARKSHIRE
LANCASTRIAN
LANCINATION
LANDHOLDING
LANDING GEAR
LANDING NETS
LANDLUBBERS
LANDSCAPING
LANDSCAPIST
LANGUISHING
LAPAROSCOPY
LAPIS LAZULI
LARGE-MINDED
LARKISHNESS
LARYNGOLOGY
LARYNGOTOMY
LATITUDINAL
LAUDABILITY
LAUGHING GAS
LAUNDERETTE
LAURUSTINUS
LAW-BREAKERS
LAWBREAKING
LAWLESSNESS
LAWN PARTIES
LAY BROTHERS
LEADING LADY
LEAF-CLIMBER
LEAPFROGGED
LEARNEDNESS
LEASEHOLDER
LEATHERBACK
LEATHERETTE
LEATHERHEAD
LEATHERWOOD
LEAVENWORTH
LEAVE TAKING
LECHEROUSLY
LECITHINASE
LECTURESHIP
LEFT-HANDERS
LEFT-WINGERS
LEGAL TENDER
LEGATIONARY
LEGERDEMAIN
LEGIONARIES
LEGIONNAIRE

LEGISLATING
LEGISLATION
LEGISLATIVE
LEGISLATORS
LEGISLATURE
LEGITIMIZED
LEMON SQUASH
LENGTHENING
LENGTHINESS
LENTIGINOUS
LEPIDOSIREN
LEPRECHAUNS
LEPROSARIUM
LEPTORRHINE
LESE-MAJESTY
LET OFF STEAM
LETTER BOMBS
LETTERBOXES
LETTERHEADS
LETTERPRESS
LEUCOCRATIC
LEUCODERMAL
LEUCORRHOEA
LEUCOTOMIES
LEVEL-HEADED
LIABILITIES
LIANYUNGANG
LIBELLOUSLY
LIBERAL ARTS
LIBERALIZED
LIBERALIZER
LIBERALNESS
LIBERATRESS
LIBERTARIAN
LIBERTICIDE
LIBERTINISM
LIBRATIONAL
LIBRETTISTS
LICENTIATES
LICKSPITTLE
LIE DETECTOR
LIEUTENANCY
LIEUTENANTS
LIFE JACKETS
LIFE OF RILEY
LIFE STORIES
LIGAMENTOUS
LIGHT-FOOTED
LIGHT-HEADED
LIGHTHOUSES
LIGHTWEIGHT
LIKABLENESS

LILLIPUTIAN
LILY-LIVERED
LIMITATIONS
LIMITLESSLY
LIMNOLOGIST
LIMP-WRISTED
LINDISFARNE
LINEAMENTAL
LINE DANCING
LINE DRAWING
LINEN BASKET
LINE OF SIGHT
LINE PRINTER
LINERTRAINS
LINGERINGLY
LINGUISTICS
LION-HEARTED
LIONIZATION
LIPOPROTEIN
LIPOSUCTION
LIQUEFIABLE
LIQUESCENCE
LIQUIDAMBAR
LIQUIDATING
LIQUIDATION
LIQUIDATORS
LIQUIDIZERS
LIQUIDIZING
LISTERIOSIS
LITERALNESS
LITERATURES
LITHOGRAPHS
LITHOGRAPHY
LITHOLOGIST
LITHOMETEOR
LITHOPHYTIC
LITHOSPHERE
LITHOTOMIST
LITTERATEUR
LITTERLOUTS
LITTLE WOMAN
LITURGISTIC
LIVABLENESS
LIVELIHOODS
LIVING ROOMS
LLOYD WEBBER
LO AND BEHOLD
LOATHSOMELY
LOBSTERPOTS
LOCAL COLOUR
LOCALIZABLE
LOCAL OPTION

LOCKER ROOMS
LOCK KEEPERS
LOCOMOTIVES
LOCUM TENENS
LOGARITHMIC
LOGGERHEADS
LOGISTICIAN
LOGOGRAPHER
LOGOGRIPHIC
LOGOMACHIST
LOGOPAEDICS
LOITERINGLY
LOLLIPOP MAN
LOLLIPOP MEN
LONDONDERRY
LONG JUMPERS
LONGSIGHTED
LONGWEARING
LOOSE CANNON
LOOSE CHANGE
LOOSESTRIFE
LOPHOBRANCH
LORD PROVOST
LORD'S PRAYER
LOSS LEADERS
LOTUS-EATERS
LOUDHAILERS
LOUDMOUTHED
LOUDSPEAKER
LOUNGE SUITS
LOUTISHNESS
LOVE AFFAIRS
LOW COMEDIES
LOWER SAXONY
LOW-PRESSURE
LOW PROFILES
LOW-SPIRITED
LOXODROMICS
LOYALTY CARD
LUBRICATING
LUBRICATION
LUBRICATIVE
LUBRICATORS
LUCRATIVELY
LUCUBRATION
LUDICROUSLY
LUDWIGSBURG
LUGGAGE RACK
LUGGAGE VANS
LUMBERINGLY
LUMBERJACKS
LUMBER-ROOMS

LUMBERYARDS
LUMBRICALIS
LUMINESCENT
LUNAR MONTHS
LUSTFULNESS
LUTHERANISM
LUXULIANITE
LUXURIANTLY
LUXURIATING
LUXURIATION
LUXURIOUSLY
LYMPHANGIAL
LYMPHOBLAST
LYMPHOCYTIC
LYTHRACEOUS

M
MACADAMIZER
MACHICOLATE
MACHINATION
MACHINE CODE
MACHINEGUNS
MACHINE TOOL
MACROBIOTIC
MACROCOSMIC
MACROGAMETE
MACROPHAGIC
MACROSCOPIC
MADDENINGLY
MADEIRA CAKE
MADRIGALIAN
MADRIGALIST
MAGDALENIAN
MAGGOTINESS
MAGHERAFELT
MAGIC BULLET
MAGISTERIAL
MAGISTRALLY
MAGISTRATES
MAGLEMOSIAN
MAGNANIMITY
MAGNANIMOUS
MAGNETIZING
MAGNIFIABLE
MAGNIFICENT
MAHARASHTRA
MAIDENHEADS
MAIDEN NAMES
MAIDSERVANT
MAILING LIST
MAIN CLAUSES
MAINSPRINGS

MAINTAINING
MAINTENANCE
MAIN-TOPMAST
MAINTOPSAIL
MAISONETTES
MAKE-BELIEVE
MAKES A POINT
MAKHACHKALA
MALADJUSTED
MALADROITLY
MALAPROPIAN
MALAPROPISM
MALCONTENTS
MALEDICTION
MALEDICTIVE
MALEFACTION
MALEFACTORS
MALEFICENCE
MALEVOLENCE
MALFEASANCE
MALFUNCTION
MALICIOUSLY
MALIGNANTLY
MALINGERERS
MALINGERING
MALOCCLUDED
MALONIC ACID
MALPOSITION
MALPRACTICE
MALTED MILKS
MALTREATING
MAMMALOGIST
MAMMIFEROUS
MAMMOGRAPHY
MAMMONISTIC
MANAGEMENTS
MANDATORILY
MANDOLINIST
MANEUVERING
MANHANDLING
MANICHAEISM
MANICURISTS
MANIFESTING
MANIFESTOES
MANIPULATED
MANIPULATOR
MANNERISTIC
MANNISHNESS
MANOEUVRING
MANOR HOUSES
MANSERVANTS
MANTELPIECE

MANTELSHELF	MASTOIDITIS	MELIORATION	MESOPOTAMIA
MANTOUX TEST	MASTROIANNI	MELIORATIVE	MESOSPHERIC
MANUFACTORY	MASTURBATED	MELLIFEROUS	MESOTHELIAL
MANUFACTURE	MATCHLESSLY	MELLIFLUOUS	MESOTHELIUM
MANUSCRIPTS	MATCHMAKERS	MELODICALLY	MESOTHORIUM
MARASCHINOS	MATCHMAKING	MELODIOUSLY	METABOLISMS
MARCESCENCE	MATCH POINTS	MELTABILITY	METACENTRIC
MARCHIONESS	MATCHSTICKS	MELTING POTS	METAGENESIS
MAR DEL PLATA	MATERIALISM	MEMBERSHIPS	METAGENETIC
MARE CLAUSUM	MATERIALIST	MEMORABILIA	METALLOCENE
MARE LIBERUM	MATERIALITY	MEMORANDUMS	METALLOIDAL
MARGINALITY	MATERIALIZE	MEMORIALIST	METALLURGIC
MARGINATION	MATERNALISM	MEMORIALIZE	METALWORKER
MARICULTURE	MATHEMATICS	MEMORIZABLE	METAMORPHIC
MARINE CORPS	MATINEE IDOL	MENAQUINONE	METANEPHROS
MARIONETTES	MATRIARCHAL	MENDELEVIUM	METAPHYSICS
MARKETPLACE	MATRICULANT	MENDEL'S LAWS	METAPLASMIC
MARKET PRICE	MATRICULATE	MENORRHAGIA	METASTASIZE
MARKET TOWNS	MATRILINEAL	MENORRHAGIC	METATHERIAN
MARKOV CHAIN	MATRIMONIAL	MENSTRUATED	METATHESIZE
MARLBOROUGH	MAUDLINNESS	MENSURATION	METEMPIRICS
MARQUESSATE	MAUNDY MONEY	MENSURATIVE	METEOROLOGY
MARQUISETTE	MAURITANIAN	MENTALISTIC	METHODOLOGY
MARRAM GRASS	MAWKISHNESS	MENTALITIES	METHYLAMINE
MARROWBONES	MAYONNAISES	MENTAL NOTES	METHYLATION
MARSHALLING	MEADOWSWEET	MENTHACEOUS	METONYMICAL
MARSHMALLOW	MEANDERINGS	MENTHOLATED	METRICATION
MARTENSITIC	MEANINGLESS	MENTIONABLE	METRICIZING
MARTIAL ARTS	MEASURELESS	MEPROBAMATE	METROLOGIST
MARTINETISH	MEASUREMENT	MERCENARIES	METROSEXUAL
MARTINETISM	MECHANICIAN	MERCENARILY	MICHIGANDER
MARTYROLOGY	MECHANISTIC	MERCHANDISE	MICHIGANITE
MASCULINIST	MECHANIZING	MERCHANTMAN	MICKEY MOUSE
MASCULINITY	MECKLENBURG	MERCHANTMEN	MICROCOCCUS
MASKING TAPE	MEDIASTINAL	MERCILESSLY	MICROCOSMIC
MASOCHISTIC	MEDIASTINUM	MERCURATION	MICROFICHES
MASONICALLY	MEDICAMENTS	MERCURIALLY	MICROFILMED
MASQUERADED	MEDICATIONS	MERITOCRACY	MICROGAMETE
MASQUERADER	MEDICINALLY	MERITORIOUS	MICROGRAPHY
MASQUERADES	MEDICINE MAN	MEROBLASTIC	MICROGROOVE
MASSACHUSET	MEDICINE MEN	MERRYMAKERS	MICROMETERS
MASSIVENESS	MEDIEVALISM	MERRYMAKING	MICROMETRIC
MASS-PRODUCE	MEDIEVALIST	MESALLIANCE	MICROPHONES
MASTER CARDS	MEDITATIONS	MESENCHYMAL	MICROPHONIC
MASTERCLASS	MEERSCHAUMS	MESMERIZING	MICROPHYTIC
MASTERFULLY	MEGACEPHALY	MESOBENTHOS	MICROREADER
MASTERMINDS	MEGALOBLAST	MESOCEPHALY	MICROSCOPES
MASTERPIECE	MEGALOMANIA	MESOGASTRIC	MICROSCOPIC
MASTERWORKS	MEGALOPOLIS	MESOMORPHIC	MICROSECOND
MASTICATING	MEIOTICALLY	MESONEPHRIC	MICROSPORIC
MASTICATION	MELANCHOLIA	MESONEPHROS	MICROTOMIST
MASTICATORY	MELANCHOLIC	MESOPHYLLIC	MIDDLEBROWS

MIDDLE CLASS	MISCONSTRUE	MONASTICISM	MORRIS DANCE
MIDDLE NAMES	MISCOUNTING	MONETARISTS	MORTALITIES
MIDDLE-SIZED	MISCREATION	MONEYLENDER	MORTARBOARD
MIDNIGHT SUN	MISDESCRIBE	MONEYMAKERS	MORTISE LOCK
MIGRATIONAL	MISDIRECTED	MONEYMAKING	MOSQUITO NET
MILITARISTS	MISE-EN-SCENE	MONEY ORDERS	MOTHERBOARD
MILITARIZED	MISERLINESS	MONEY SUPPLY	MOTHER-IN-LAW
MILLEFLEURS	MISFEASANCE	MONITORSHIP	MOTHER'S BOYS
MILLENARIAN	MISFORTUNES	MONOCHASIAL	MOTHER'S RUIN
MILLENIALS	MISGOVERNOR	MONOCHASIUM	MOTHERS-TO-BE
MILLILITRES	MISGUIDANCE	MONOCHROMAT	MOTHPROOFED
MILLIMETRES	MISGUIDEDLY	MONOCHROMIC	MOTORCYCLES
MILLIMICRON	MISHANDLING	MONOCLINISM	MOTOR LODGES
MILLIONAIRE	MISINFORMED	MONOCLINOUS	MOUNTAINEER
MILLISECOND	MISJUDGMENT	MONOCULTURE	MOUNTAINOUS
MIMEOGRAPHS	MISMANAGING	MONOGENESIS	MOUNTAINTOP
MIMETICALLY	MISMATCHING	MONOGENETIC	MOUNTBATTEN
MIMOSACEOUS	MISOGYNISTS	MONOGRAMMED	MOUNTEBANKS
MINAS GERAIS	MISONEISTIC	MONOGRAPHER	MOUTHORGANS
MIND-BENDING	MISPRINTING	MONOGRAPHIC	MOUTHPIECES
MIND-BLOWING	MISREMEMBER	MONOHYDRATE	MOUTHWASHES
MINDFULNESS	MISREPORTED	MONOHYDROXY	MOXIBUSTION
MIND READERS	MISSING LINK	MONOLATROUS	MUCOPROTEIN
MIND READING	MISSISSAUGA	MONOLINGUAL	MUCRONATION
MINERALIZER	MISSISSIPPI	MONOMANIACS	MUDDLEDNESS
MINERAL OILS	MISSPELLING	MONOMORPHIC	MUDSLINGING
MINESWEEPER	MISSPENDING	MONONUCLEAR	MUHAMMADANS
MINIATURIST	MISTRUSTFUL	MONOPHAGOUS	MULTANGULAR
MINIATURIZE	MISTRUSTING	MONOPHTHONG	MULTINOMIAL
MINIMUM WAGE	MITHRIDATIC	MONOPOLISTS	MULTIPARITY
MINISTERIAL	MITOTICALLY	MONOPOLIZED	MULTIPAROUS
MINISTERING	MIXED GRILLS	MONOPOLIZER	MULTIPLEXER
MINISTERIUM	MOBILE HOMES	MONOSTICHIC	MULTIPLYING
MINISTRANTS	MOBILE PHONE	MONOSTROPHE	MULTIRACIAL
MINNEAPOLIS	MOBILIZABLE	MONOSTYLOUS	MULTISCREEN
MINOR PLANET	MOCKINGBIRD	MONOTERPENE	MULTISTOREY
MINUTE STEAK	MODERNISTIC	MONOTHEISTS	MULTIVALENT
MIRACLE PLAY	MODERNIZING	MONOVALENCE	MUM'S THE WORD
MIRROR IMAGE	MODULATIONS	MONSEIGNEUR	MUNDANENESS
MIRTHLESSLY	MOHAMMEDANS	MONSTRANCES	MUNICIPALLY
MISALLIANCE	MOISTURIZED	MONSTROSITY	MUNIFICENCE
MISANTHROPE	MOISTURIZER	MONSTROUSLY	MURDERESSES
MISANTHROPY	MOLESTATION	MONS VENERIS	MURDEROUSLY
MISAPPLYING	MOLLIFIABLE	MONTENEGRAN	MURMURINGLY
MISBEGOTTEN	MOLLYCODDLE	MONTPELLIER	MUSCLE-BOUND
MISBEHAVING	MOLYBDENITE	MOONLIGHTER	MUSCOVY DUCK
MISCARRIAGE	MOLYBDENOUS	MORAVIANISM	MUSCULARITY
MISCARRYING	MOMENTARILY	MORIBUNDITY	MUSCULATURE
MISCELLANEA	MONARCHICAL	MORNING COAT	MUSEUM PIECE
MISCHIEVOUS	MONARCHISTS	MORNING STAR	MUSHROOMING
MISCIBILITY	MONASTERIAL	MORONICALLY	MUSICALNESS
MISCONCEIVE	MONASTERIES	MORPHOLOGIC	MUSIC CENTRE

MUSKELLUNGE	NATUROPATHS	NEVER-NEVERS	NONCREATIVE
MUSTACHIOED	NATUROPATHY	NEVER SAY DIE	NONDESCRIPT
MUTAGENESIS	NAUGHTINESS	NEW PLYMOUTH	NONENTITIES
MUTILATIONS	NEANDERTHAL	NEWPORT NEWS	NONETHELESS
MUTTERINGLY	NEAR EASTERN	NEW POTATOES	NONEXISTENT
MUTTONCHOPS	NEARSIGHTED	NEWSCASTERS	NONFEASANCE
MUTUAL FUNDS	NECESSARIES	NEWSLETTERS	NONHARMONIC
MYCOLOGICAL	NECESSARILY	NEWSREADERS	NONILLIONTH
MYCOPROTEIN	NECESSITATE	NEWSVENDORS	NONINVASIVE
MYCORRHIZAL	NECESSITIES	NEW YEAR'S DAY	NONIRRITANT
MYELOMATOID	NECESSITOUS	NEW YEAR'S EVE	NONMETALLIC
MYOCARDITIS	NECKERCHIEF	NICENE CREED	NONOPERABLE
MYRIAPODOUS	NECROBIOSIS	NICKELODEON	NONPARTISAN
MYRMECOLOGY	NECROBIOTIC	NICTITATION	NONPLUSSING
MYSTERY PLAY	NECROLOGIST	NIETZSCHEAN	NONRESIDENT
MYSTERY TOUR	NECROMANCER	NIGHTINGALE	NONSENSICAL
MYSTIFIEDLY	NECROMANTIC	NIGHTLIGHTS	NON SEQUITUR
MYTHOLOGIES	NECROPHILIA	NIGHTMARISH	NONSTANDARD
MYTHOLOGIST	NECROPHILIC	NIGHT-PORTER	NONSTARTERS
MYTHOLOGIZE	NECROPHOBIA	NIGHT SCHOOL	NONVERBALLY
MYTHOMANIAC	NECROPHOBIC	NIGHTSHADES	NONVIOLENCE
MYTHOPOEISM	NEEDFULNESS	NIGHT SHIFTS	NORMALIZING
MYTHOPOEIST	NEEDLEPOINT	NIGHTSHIRTS	NORTHAMPTON
MYXOMATOSIS	NEEDLEWOMAN	NIGHTSTICKS	NORTH DAKOTA
	NEEDLEWOMEN	NIGRESCENCE	NORTHEASTER
N	NE'ER-DO-WELLS	NINCOMPOOPS	NORTHERNERS
NAILBRUSHES	NEFARIOUSLY	NINETEENTHS	NORTH ISLAND
NAIL VARNISH	NEGLIGENTLY	NINETY-NINES	NORTHUMBRIA
NAKHICHEVAN	NEGOTIATING	NISHINOMIYA	NORTHWESTER
NAMEDROPPED	NEGOTIATION	NITRIFIABLE	NOSOGRAPHER
NAMEDROPPER	NEGOTIATORS	NITROGENIZE	NOSOGRAPHIC
NAPHTHALENE	NEIGHBOURLY	NITROGENOUS	NOSOLOGICAL
NAPKIN RINGS	NEOCOLONIAL	NITROMETRIC	NOSY PARKERS
NARAYANGANJ	NEOLOGISTIC	NITROSAMINE	NOTABLENESS
NARCISSISTS	NEPHELINITE	NITTY-GRITTY	NOTHINGNESS
NARCISSUSES	NEPHOLOGIST	NIZHNI TAGIL	NOTHING TO IT
NARCOLEPTIC	NEPHRECTOMY	NOBEL PRIZES	NOTICE BOARD
NARRATOLOGY	NE PLUS ULTRA	NOCICEPTIVE	NOTOCHORDAL
NARROW BOATS	NERVE CENTRE	NOCTILUCENT	NOTORIOUSLY
NARROW GAUGE	NERVELESSLY	NOCTURNALLY	NOTOTHERIUM
NASOFRONTAL	NERVOUSNESS	NOISELESSLY	NOURISHMENT
NASOGASTRIC	NETHERLANDS	NOISOMENESS	NOVOSIBIRSK
NASOPHARYNX	NEUROFIBRIL	NOMADICALLY	NOXIOUSNESS
NASTURTIUMS	NEUROLOGIST	NO-MAN'S-LANDS	NUCLEAR-FREE
NATIONALISM	NEUROMATOUS	NOMENCLATOR	NUCLEIC ACID
NATIONALIST	NEUROPATHIC	NOMINATIONS	NUCLEOPLASM
NATIONALITY	NEUROPTERAN	NOMINATIVES	NUEVO LAREDO
NATIONALIZE	NEUROTICISM	NOMOGRAPHER	NULL AND VOID
NATION STATE	NEUROTOMIST	NOMOGRAPHIC	NULLIFIDIAN
NATURALISTS	NEUTRALIZED	NOMOLOGICAL	NULLIPAROUS
NATURALIZED	NEUTRALIZER	NOMS DE PLUME	NUMBERPLATE
NATURALNESS	NEUTRON BOMB	NONCHALANCE	NUMERATIONS

NUMERICALLY	OCHLOCRATIC	OPERABILITY	OSTEOPATHIC
NUMISMATICS	OCHLOPHOBIA	OPERATIONAL	OSTEOPHYTIC
NUMISMATIST	OCTAHEDRITE	OPHIOLOGIST	OSTEOPLASTY
NUNCUPATIVE	OCTILLIONTH	OPHTHALMIAC	OSTRACIZING
NURSING HOME	ODDS AND ENDS	OPINIONATED	OSTRACODERM
NUTCRACKERS	ODONTOBLAST	OPINION POLL	OSTRACODOUS
NUTRITIONAL	ODONTOGRAPH	OPPORTUNELY	OUAGADOUGOU
NYCTINASTIC	ODONTOPHORE	OPPORTUNISM	OUIJA BOARDS
NYCTITROPIC	ODORIFEROUS	OPPORTUNIST	OUTBALANCED
NYCTOPHOBIA	ODOROUSNESS	OPPORTUNITY	OUTBUILDING
NYCTOPHOBIC	OENOLOGICAL	OPPOSITIONS	OUTCLASSING
NYMPHOLEPSY	OESOPHAGEAL	OPPROBRIOUS	OUTDISTANCE
NYMPHOMANIA	OESTROGENIC	OPTICAL DISC	OUTERCOURSE
	OFFENSIVELY	OPTOMETRIST	OUTFIELDERS
O	OFFERTORIES	ORANGUTANGS	OUTFIGHTING
OARSMANSHIP	OFFHANDEDLY	ORCHESTRATE	OUTFLANKING
OBFUSCATING	OFFICE BLOCK	ORDER-DRIVEN	OUT-HERODING
OBFUSCATION	OFFICIALDOM	ORDERLINESS	OUTNUMBERED
OBITER DICTA	OFFICIALESE	ORDER PAPERS	OUT OF BOUNDS
OBJECTIVELY	OFFICIATING	ORDINATIONS	OUT OF POCKET
OBJECTIVISM	OFFICIATION	ORGANICALLY	OUT-OF-THE-WAY
OBJECTIVIST	OFFICIOUSLY	ORIEL WINDOW	OUTPATIENTS
OBJECTIVITY	OFF-LICENCES	ORIENTALISM	OUTPOINTING
OBJET TROUVE	OIL PAINTING	ORIENTALIST	OUTPOURINGS
OBJURGATION	OIL-SEED RAPE	ORIENTALIZE	OUTRIVALLED
OBJURGATORY	OLD-WOMANISH	ORIENTATING	OUTSMARTING
OBLIGATIONS	OLEOGRAPHIC	ORIENTATION	OUT SOURCING
OBLIQUITOUS	OLIGARCHIES	ORIGINALITY	OUTSPOKENLY
OBLITERATED	OLIGOCHAETE	ORIGINAL SIN	OUTSTANDING
OBLITERATOR	OLIGOTROPHY	ORIGINATING	OUTSTRIPPED
OBLIVIOUSLY	OLIVE BRANCH	ORIGINATION	OUTWEIGHING
OBNOXIOUSLY	OMINOUSNESS	ORIGINATORS	OVERACHIEVE
OBSCENITIES	OMMATOPHORE	ORNAMENTING	OVERANXIOUS
OBSCURATION	OMNIFARIOUS	ORNITHOLOGY	OVERARCHING
OBSCURITIES	OMNIPOTENCE	ORNITHOPTER	OVERBALANCE
OBSERVANCES	OMNIPRESENT	ORTHOCENTRE	OVERBEARING
OBSERVATION	OMNISCIENCE	ORTHODONTIC	OVERBIDDING
OBSERVATORY	ONAGRACEOUS	ORTHOGRAPHY	OVERBOOKING
OBSESSIONAL	ONCOLOGICAL	ORTHOPAEDIC	OVERCHARGED
OBSOLESCENT	ONE-MAN BANDS	ORTHOPTERAN	OVERCHARGES
OBSTINATELY	ONEROUSNESS	ORTHOSCOPIC	OVERCLOUDED
OBSTIPATION	ONTOLOGICAL	ORTHOSTICHY	OVERCROPPED
OBSTRUCTING	OPALESCENCE	ORTHOTROPIC	OVERCROWDED
OBSTRUCTION	OPEN-AND-SHUT	OSCILLATING	OVERDEVELOP
OBSTRUCTIVE	OPENHEARTED	OSCILLATION	OVERDRAUGHT
OBTRUSIVELY	OPENING TIME	OSCILLATORS	OVERDRAWING
OBVIOUSNESS	OPEN LETTERS	OSCILLATORY	OVERDRESSED
OCCASIONING	OPEN-MOUTHED	OSCILLOGRAM	OVEREXPOSED
OCCIDENTALS	OPEN SEASONS	OSMOTICALLY	OVERFLOWING
OCCULTATION	OPEN SECRETS	OSTENTATION	OVERGARMENT
OCCUPATIONS	OPEN SESAMES	OSTEOCLASIS	OVERHAULING
OCCURRENCES	OPEN VERDICT	OSTEOLOGIST	OVERHEARING

OVERINDULGE	PAINFULNESS	PARAGRAPHIA	PARTY PIECES
OVERLAPPING	PAINKILLERS	PARAGRAPHIC	PARTY POOPER
OVERLOADING	PAINSTAKING	PARALDEHYDE	PAS-DE-CALAIS
OVERLOOKING	PALAEARCTIC	PARALEIPSIS	PASQUINADER
OVERMANNING	PALATINATES	PARALLACTIC	PASSIBILITY
OVERPLAYING	PALEOGRAPHY	PARALLELING	PASSIONLESS
OVERPOWERED	PALEOLITHIC	PARALLELISM	PASSION PLAY
OVERPRODUCE	PALESTINIAN	PARALLELIST	PASSIONTIDE
OVERPROTECT	PALIMPSESTS	PARALLELLED	PASSIVENESS
OVERREACHED	PALINDROMES	PARALYMPICS	PASTEBOARDS
OVERREACTED	PALINDROMIC	PARAMEDICAL	PASTEURIZED
OVERRUNNING	PALLBEARERS	PARAMORPHIC	PASTEURIZER
OVERSELLING	PALLIATIVES	PARAMOUNTCY	PAST MASTERS
OVERSTAFFED	PALM SPRINGS	PARAPHRASED	PAST PERFECT
OVERSTATING	PALPABILITY	PARAPHRASES	PASTURELAND
OVERSTAYING	PALPITATING	PARAPLASTIC	PATCH POCKET
OVERSTEPPED	PALPITATION	PARAPLEGICS	PATELLIFORM
OVERSTOCKED	PAMPAS GRASS	PARASAILING	PATERNALISM
OVERSTUFFED	PAMPHLETEER	PARATHYROID	PATERNALIST
OVERTOPPING	PAN-AMERICAN	PARATROOPER	PATERNOSTER
OVERTURNING	PANCAKE ROLL	PARATYPHOID	PATHFINDERS
OVERWEENING	PANCHEN LAMA	PARENTHESES	PATHFINDING
OVERWHELMED	PANDEMONIAC	PARENTHESIS	PATHOLOGIST
OVERWORKING	PANDEMONIUM	PARENTHETIC	PATISSERIES
OVERWROUGHT	PANDORA'S BOX	PARESTHESIA	PATRIARCHAL
OVIPOSITION	PANEGYRICAL	PARESTHETIC	PATRILINEAL
OWNER-DRIVER	PANHANDLERS	PARI-MUTUELS	PATRIMONIAL
OXFORDSHIRE	PANHANDLING	PARIPINNATE	PATROL WAGON
OXIDATIONAL	PANHELLENIC	PARISH CLERK	PATRONIZING
OXIDIMETRIC	PANIC ATTACK	PARISHIONER	PATRON SAINT
OXIDIZATION	PANJANDRUMS	PARKING LOTS	PATRONYMICS
OXYCEPHALIC	PANTELLERIA	PARK KEEPERS	PAUNCHINESS
OXYGENATING	PANTHEISTIC	PARLIAMENTS	PAVING STONE
OXYGENATION	PANTOGRAPHS	PARLOUR GAME	PAWNBROKERS
OXYGEN MASKS	PANTOGRAPHY	PAROCHIALLY	PAWNBROKING
OXYGEN TANKS	PANTOMIMIST	PARONOMASIA	PAY ENVELOPE
OXYGEN TENTS	PAPER CHASES	PARSON'S NOSE	PAY STATIONS
OXYHYDROGEN	PAPER-CUTTER	PART COMPANY	PEACH MELBAS
OXYSULPHIDE	PAPERHANGER	PARTIALNESS	PEACOCK BLUE
OZONIFEROUS	PAPER KNIVES	PARTICIPANT	PEARL DIVERS
OZONIZATION	PAPER TIGERS	PARTICIPATE	PEARLY GATES
OZONOSPHERE	PAPERWEIGHT	PARTICIPIAL	PEASHOOTERS
	PAPIER-MACHE	PARTICIPLES	PECCABILITY
P	PAPYRACEOUS	PARTICULARS	PECCADILLOS
PACE BOWLERS	PARABLASTIC	PARTICULATE	PECTINATION
PACIFICALLY	PARACETAMOL	PARTING SHOT	PECTIZATION
PACKAGE DEAL	PARACHUTING	PARTITIONED	PECULATIONS
PACKAGE TOUR	PARACHUTIST	PARTITIONER	PECULIARITY
PACK ANIMALS	PARADOXICAL	PARTITIVELY	PECUNIARILY
PACKING CASE	PARAGENESIS	PARTNERSHIP	PEDESTRIANS
PAEDIATRICS	PARAGENETIC	PARTURIENCY	PEDICULOSIS
PAEDOLOGIST	PARAGLIDING	PARTURITION	PEDICURISTS

PEDOLOGICAL	PERFECTIBLE	PERSECUTING	PHILATELIST
PEDUNCULATE	PERFORATING	PERSECUTION	PHILHELLENE
PEEPING TOMS	PERFORATION	PERSECUTIVE	PHILIPPINES
PEEVISHNESS	PERFORATIVE	PERSECUTORS	PHILISTINES
PELARGONIUM	PERFORMABLE	PERSEVERANT	PHILOLOGIST
PELLUCIDITY	PERFORMANCE	PERSEVERING	PHILOSOPHER
PELOPONNESE	PERFUNCTORY	PERSIAN CATS	PHLEBOTOMIC
PENALTY AREA	PERICARDIUM	PERSISTENCE	PHONETICIAN
PENDULOUSLY	PERICARPIAL	PERSNICKETY	PHONOGRAMIC
PENETRALIAN	PERICLASTIC	PERSONALISM	PHONOGRAPHS
PENETRATING	PERICRANIAL	PERSONALIST	PHONOGRAPHY
PENETRATION	PERICRANIUM	PERSONALITY	PHONOLOGIST
PENETRATIVE	PERIDOTITIC	PERSONALIZE	PHONOMETRIC
PENICILLATE	PERIGORDIAN	PERSONATION	PHONOTYPIST
PENICILLIUM	PERIHELIONS	PERSONATIVE	PHOSPHATASE
PENITENTIAL	PERIMORPHIC	PERSONIFIED	PHOSPHATIZE
PENNYWEIGHT	PERINEURIUM	PERSPECTIVE	PHOSPHORATE
PENNYWORTHS	PERIODICALS	PERSPICUITY	PHOSPHORISM
PENOLOGICAL	PERIODICITY	PERSPICUOUS	PHOSPHORITE
PENSIONABLE	PERIODONTAL	PERSUADABLE	PHOSPHOROUS
PENSIVENESS	PERIODONTIC	PERSUASIONS	PHOTOACTIVE
PENTADACTYL	PERIOD PIECE	PERTINACITY	PHOTOCOPIED
PENTAHEDRON	PERIOSTITIC	PERTINENTLY	PHOTOCOPIER
PENTAMEROUS	PERIOSTITIS	PERTURBABLE	PHOTOCOPIES
PENTAMETERS	PERIPATETIC	PERTURBABLY	PHOTO FINISH
PENTANGULAR	PERIPETEIAN	PERVASIVELY	PHOTOGRAPHS
PENTATHLONS	PERIPHERALS	PERVERSIONS	PHOTOGRAPHY
PENTAVALENT	PERIPHERIES	PERVERTEDLY	PHOTOMETRIC
PENTECOSTAL	PERIPHRASES	PERVERTIBLE	PHOTONASTIC
PENTLANDITE	PERIPHRASIS	PESSIMISTIC	PHOTO-OFFSET
PENULTIMATE	PERISHABLES	PESTERINGLY	PHOTOPERIOD
PENURIOUSLY	PERISHINGLY	PESTIFEROUS	PHOTOPHOBIA
PEOPLE MOVER	PERISPERMAL	PESTILENCES	PHOTOPHOBIC
PEPPERCORNS	PERISTALSIS	PETITIONARY	PHOTOSETTER
PEPPER MILLS	PERISTALTIC	PETITIONERS	PHOTOSPHERE
PEPPERMINTS	PERITHECIUM	PETITIONING	PHOTOSTATIC
PEPTIC ULCER	PERITONEUMS	PETRODOLLAR	PHOTOTACTIC
PEPTIZATION	PERITONITIC	PETROGRAPHY	PHOTOTROPIC
PERAMBULATE	PERITONITIS	PETROLOGIST	PHRASAL VERB
PERCEIVABLE	PERIWINKLES	PETTIFOGGER	PHRASEBOOKS
PERCENTAGES	PERLOCUTION	PETTISHNESS	PHRASEOGRAM
PERCEPTIBLE	PERMANENTLY	PHAGOMANIAC	PHRASEOLOGY
PERCEPTIBLY	PERMISSIBLE	PHAGOPHOBIA	PHTHIRIASIS
PERCHLORATE	PERMISSIBLY	PHAGOPHOBIC	PHYCOLOGIST
PERCHLORIDE	PERMUTATION	PHALANSTERY	PHYCOMYCETE
PERCIPIENCE	PERORATIONS	PHANEROZOIC	PHYLLOCLADE
PERCOLATING	PERPETRATED	PHARMACISTS	PHYLLOTAXIS
PERCOLATION	PERPETRATOR	PHARYNGITIS	PHYLOTACTIC
PERCOLATIVE	PERPETUALLY	PHELLOGENIC	PHYSIATRICS
PERCOLATORS	PERPETUATED	PHENETIDINE	PHYSICALISM
PEREGRINATE	PERPLEXEDLY	PHENOLOGIST	PHYSICALIST
PERENNIALLY	PERQUISITES	PHILANDERER	PHYSIOGNOMY

PHYTOGRAPHY	PLAGIOCLASE	PLUG-AND-PLAY	POLYHYDROXY
PICKPOCKETS	PLAINSPOKEN	PLUM PUDDING	POLYNUCLEAR
PICKWICKIAN	PLAINTIVELY	PLUNDERABLE	POLYPEPTIDE
PICTORIALLY	PLANETARIUM	PLURALISTIC	POLYPHONOUS
PICTURE BOOK	PLANETOIDAL	PLURALITIES	POLYPLOIDAL
PICTURE CARD	PLANIMETRIC	PLUTOCRATIC	POLYSTYRENE
PICTURESQUE	PLANISPHERE	PLUVIOMETER	POLYTECHNIC
PIECE OF CAKE	PLANO-CONVEX	PLUVIOMETRY	POLYTHEISTS
PIECE OF WORK	PLANOGAMETE	PNEUMECTOMY	POLYTROPHIC
PIEDMONTITE	PLANOGRAPHY	PNEUMOGRAPH	POLYVALENCY
PIEDS-A-TERRE	PLANOMETRIC	POCKETBOOKS	POLYZOARIUM
PIEZOMETRIC	PLANTAGENET	POCKETKNIFE	POMEGRANATE
PIGEONHOLED	PLANTATIONS	POCKET KNIFE	POMICULTURE
PIGEONHOLES	PLANTIGRADE	POCKET MONEY	POMOLOGICAL
PIGGISHNESS	PLASMAGENIC	POCOCURANTE	POMPOUSNESS
PIGHEADEDLY	PLASMODESMA	POCTOSCOPIC	PONDEROUSLY
PIGSTICKING	PLASMOLYSIS	PODIATRISTS	PONDICHERRY
PILE DRIVERS	PLASMOLYTIC	PODOPHYLLIN	PONTIFICALS
PILGRIMAGES	PLASTER CAST	POINSETTIAS	PONTIFICATE
PILLAR BOXES	PLASTICALLY	POINTEDNESS	POOH-POOHING
PILLOWCASES	PLASTIC ARTS	POINTE-NOIRE	POPULARIZED
PILLOW FIGHT	PLASTICIZER	POINTILLISM	POPULARIZER
PILOCARPINE	PLASTOMETER	POINTILLIST	POPULATIONS
PILOT LIGHTS	PLASTOMETRY	POINTLESSLY	PORK BARRELS
PINA COLADAS	PLATELAYERS	POINT OF VIEW	PORNOGRAPHY
PINCUSHIONS	PLATINOTYPE	POISONOUSLY	PORPHYRITIC
PINEAL GLAND	PLATS DU JOUR	POLARIMETER	PORTABILITY
PINE MARTENS	PLATYRRHINE	POLARIMETRY	PORTERHOUSE
PINNATISECT	PLAYER PIANO	POLARISCOPE	PORTMANTEAU
PINOCYTOSIS	PLAYFELLOWS	POLARIZABLE	PORT MORESBY
PINPOINTING	PLAYFULNESS	POLEMICALLY	PORTO ALEGRE
PIPE CLEANER	PLAYGROUNDS	POLE VAULTED	PORT OF ENTRY
PIPE OF PEACE	PLAYING CARD	POLE VAULTER	PORT OF SPAIN
PIPERACEOUS	PLAY ON WORDS	POLICE STATE	PORTRAITIST
PIPISTRELLE	PLAYSCHOOLS	POLICEWOMAN	PORTRAITURE
PIRATICALLY	PLAYWRIGHTS	POLICEWOMEN	PORTRAYABLE
PIROUETTING	PLAYWRITING	POLITICALLY	PORTS OF CALL
PISCATORIAL	PLEASANTEST	POLITICIANS	POSITIONING
PISCIVOROUS	PLEASURABLE	POLITICIZED	POSITIVISTS
PISTON RINGS	PLEASURABLY	POLITICKING	POSITRONIUM
PITCHBLENDE	PLEASUREFUL	POLLEN COUNT	POSSESSIONS
PITCHFORKED	PLEBEIANISM	POLLINATING	POSSESSIVES
PITCHOMETER	PLEBISCITES	POLLINATION	POSSIBILITY
PITEOUSNESS	PLECTOGNATH	POLLOTARIAN	POSTAL ORDER
PITH HELMETS	PLEISTOCENE	POLTERGEIST	POSTERITIES
PITIFULNESS	PLENTEOUSLY	POLYANDROUS	POSTER PAINT
PITUITARIES	PLENTIFULLY	POLYCHASIUM	POSTGLACIAL
PLACABILITY	PLEOCHROISM	POLYGAMISTS	POSTMARKING
PLAGIARISMS	PLEOMORPHIC	POLYGENESIS	POSTMASTERS
PLAGIARISTS	PLICATENESS	POLYGENETIC	POSTMORTEMS
PLAGIARIZED	PLOUGHSHARE	POLYGLOTISM	POSTNUPTIAL
PLAGIARIZER	PLOUGHSTAFF	POLYGRAPHIC	POST OFFICES

POSTPONABLE	PREDIGESTED	PRESSURIZER	PROCHRONISM
POSTSCRIPTS	PREDISPOSAL	PRESTIGIOUS	PROCLAIMING
POSTULATING	PREDISPOSED	PRESTISSIMO	PROCONSULAR
POSTULATION	PREDOMINANT	PRESTONPANS	PROCREATING
POTATO CHIPS	PREDOMINATE	PRESTRESSED	PROCREATION
POTATO CRISP	PRE-EMINENCE	PRESUMINGLY	PROCRUSTEAN
POTENTIALLY	PRE-EXISTENT	PRESUMPTION	PROCTOSCOPE
POTTING SHED	PRE-EXISTING	PRESUMPTIVE	PROCTOSCOPY
POVERTY TRAP	PREFATORILY	PRESUPPOSED	PROCURATION
POWDER PUFFS	PREFECTURAL	PRETENDEDLY	PROCUREMENT
POWDER ROOMS	PREFECTURES	PRETENSIONS	PRODIGALITY
POWER BROKER	PREFERENCES	PRETENTIOUS	PRODUCTIONS
POWERHOUSES	PREFIGURING	PRETERITION	PROFANATION
POWERLESSLY	PREGNANCIES	PRETERITIVE	PROFANATORY
POWER PLANTS	PREHISTORIC	PRETTIFYING	PROFANENESS
POWER POINTS	PRE-IGNITION	PRETTY PENNY	PROFANITIES
PRACTICABLE	PREJUDGMENT	PREVALENTLY	PROFESSEDLY
PRACTICABLY	PREJUDICIAL	PREVARICATE	PROFESSIONS
PRACTICALLY	PREJUDICING	PREVENTABLE	PROFICIENCY
PRAEDIALITY	PRELIMINARY	PREVENTABLY	PROFITEERED
PRAESIDIUMS	PRELITERACY	PREVENTIVES	PROFITEROLE
PRAGMATISTS	PRELITERATE	PRICKLINESS	PROFLIGATES
PRAIRIE DOGS	PREMATURELY	PRICKLY HEAT	PROFUSENESS
PRATTLINGLY	PREMEDITATE	PRICKLY PEAR	PROGENITIVE
PRAYER WHEEL	PREMIERSHIP	PRIESTCRAFT	PROGENITORS
PREARRANGED	PREMIUM BOND	PRIESTLIEST	PROGNATHISM
PREARRANGER	PREMONITION	PRIMA DONNAS	PROGNATHOUS
PRECAMBRIAN	PREMONITORY	PRIMATOLOGY	PROGRAMMERS
PRECAUTIONS	PREMUNITION	PRIME MOVERS	PROGRAMMING
PRECAUTIOUS	PREOCCUPIED	PRIME NUMBER	PROGRESSING
PRECESSIONS	PREORDAINED	PRIMIPARITY	PROGRESSION
PRECIPITANT	PREPARATION	PRIMIPAROUS	PROGRESSIVE
PRECIPITATE	PREPARATIVE	PRIMITIVELY	PROHIBITING
PRECIPITOUS	PREPARATORY	PRIMITIVISM	PROHIBITION
PRECISENESS	PREPOSITION	PRIMITIVIST	PROHIBITIVE
PRECLINICAL	PREPOSITIVE	PRINCIPALLY	PROHIBITORY
PRECLUDABLE	PREP SCHOOLS	PRINTING INK	PROJECTILES
PRECONCEIVE	PRERECORDED	PRIORITIZED	PROJECTIONS
PRECONTRACT	PREROGATIVE	PRISON CAMPS	PROKOPYEVSK
PRECRITICAL	PRESBYTERAL	PRIVATIZING	PROLATENESS
PREDATORILY	PRESCRIBING	PRIZEFIGHTS	PROLEGOMENA
PREDECEASED	PRESENTABLE	PROBABILISM	PROLETARIAN
PREDECESSOR	PRESENTABLY	PROBABILIST	PROLETARIAT
PREDESTINED	PRESENT ARMS	PROBABILITY	PROLIFERATE
PREDICAMENT	PRESENTIENT	PROBATIONAL	PROLIFEROUS
PREDICATING	PRESENTMENT	PROBATIONER	PROLONGMENT
PREDICATION	PRESERVABLE	PROBLEMATIC	PROMENADING
PREDICATIVE	PRESS AGENCY	PROBOSCIDES	PROMINENCES
PREDICATORY	PRESS AGENTS	PROBOSCISES	PROMINENTLY
PREDICTABLE	PRESS BARONS	PROCEEDINGS	PROMISCUITY
PREDICTABLY	PRESSGANGED	PROCEPHALIC	PROMISCUOUS
PREDICTIONS	PRESSURIZED	PROCESSIONS	PROMISINGLY

PROMOTIONAL	PROTANDROUS	PTERIDOLOGY	PYROMANIACS
PROMPTITUDE	PROTECTIONS	PTERODACTYL	PYROTECHNIC
PROMULGATED	PROTECTORAL	PTOCHOCRACY	PYRRHULOXIA
PROMULGATOR	PROTECTRESS	PUB-CRAWLING	PYRROLIDINE
PROMYCELIUM	PROTEOLYSIS	PUBLICATION	PYTHAGOREAN
PRONOUNCING	PROTEOLYTIC	PUBLIC HOUSE	PYTHONESQUE
PROOFREADER	PROTEROZOIC	PUBLICIZING	
PROOF SPIRIT	PROTESTANTS	PUBLIC WORKS	**Q**
PROPAGATING	PROTHROMBIN	PUBLISHABLE	QUADRANGLES
PROPAGATION	PROTOGYNOUS	PUCKISHNESS	QUADRENNIAL
PROPAGATIVE	PROTOLITHIC	PUERTO RICAN	QUADRENNIUM
PROPAGATORS	PROTOPATHIC	PULAU PINANG	QUADRILLION
PROPELLANTS	PROTOSTELIC	PULCHRITUDE	QUADRUPEDAL
PROPER NOUNS	PROTRACTILE	PULL STRINGS	QUADRUPLETS
PROPHESYING	PROTRACTING	PULLULATING	QUADRUPLING
PROPHYLAXES	PROTRACTION	PULLULATION	QUALIFIABLE
PROPHYLAXIS	PROTRACTIVE	PULSATILITY	QUALITATIVE
PROPINQUITY	PROTRACTORS	PULVERIZING	QUANGOCRACY
PROPITIABLE	PROTRUDABLE	PULVERULENT	QUANTIFIERS
PROPITIATED	PROTRUSIONS	PUMPKINSEED	QUANTIFYING
PROPITIATOR	PROTUBERANT	PUNCHED CARD	QUANTUM LEAP
PROPORTIONS	PROVABILITY	PUNCTILIOUS	QUARANTINED
PROPOSITION	PROVIDENCES	PUNCTUALITY	QUARRELLING
PROPOUNDING	PROVIDENTLY	PUNCTUATING	QUARRELSOME
PROPRANOLOL	PROVINCIALS	PUNCTUATION	QUARTER DAYS
PROPRIETARY	PROVISIONAL	PUNCTURABLE	QUARTERDECK
PROPRIETIES	PROVISIONED	PUNISHINGLY	QUARTER-HOUR
PROPRIETORS	PROVISIONER	PUNISHMENTS	QUARTERLIES
PROROGATION	PROVISORILY	PUNTA ARENAS	QUARTER NOTE
PROSAICALLY	PROVOCATION	PURCHASABLE	QUAVERINGLY
PROSAICNESS	PROVOCATIVE	PURCHASE TAX	QUEENLINESS
PROS AND CONS	PROVOKINGLY	PUREBLOODED	QUEEN MOTHER
PROSCENIUMS	PROXIMATELY	PURGATORIAL	QUEEN'S BENCH
PROSCRIBING	PROXIMATION	PURIFICATOR	QUERULOUSLY
PROSECUTING	PRUDENTNESS	PURITANICAL	QUESTIONARY
PROSECUTION	PRUDISHNESS	PURPLE HEART	QUESTIONERS
PROSECUTORS	PRUSSIC ACID	PURPOSELESS	QUESTIONING
PROSELYTISM	PSEUDOMORPH	PUSHINGNESS	QUESTION TAG
PROSELYTIZE	PSILOMELANE	PUSSYFOOTED	QUEUE-JUMPED
PROSENCHYMA	PSITTACOSIS	PUSSY WILLOW	QUEUE-JUMPER
PROSPECTING	PSYCHEDELIA	PUSTULATION	QUIBBLINGLY
PROSPECTIVE	PSYCHEDELIC	PUTREFIABLE	QUICK-CHANGE
PROSPECTORS	PSYCHIATRIC	PUTRESCENCE	QUICK-FREEZE
PROSTATITIS	PSYCHICALLY	PYCNOMETRIC	QUICKSILVER
PROSTHETICS	PSYCHOBILLY	PYELOGRAPHY	QUICK-WITTED
PROSTITUTED	PSYCHODRAMA	PYLORECTOMY	QUID PRO QUOS
PROSTITUTES	PSYCHOGENIC	PYRANOMETER	QUIESCENTLY
PROSTITUTOR	PSYCHOGRAPH	PYRARGYRITE	QUINCUNCIAL
PROSTRATING	PSYCHOMETRY	PYROCLASTIC	QUINDECAGON
PROSTRATION	PSYCHOMOTOR	PYROGALLATE	QUINTANA ROO
PROTAGONISM	PSYCHOPATHS	PYROGRAPHER	QUINTILLION
PROTAGONIST	PSYCHOPATHY	PYROGRAPHIC	QUINTUPLETS

QUIVERINGLY	RATIONALIZE	RECOLLECTED	REFORMATION
QUIZMASTERS	RATTLESNAKE	RECOMBINANT	REFORMATIVE
QUIZZICALLY	RATTLETRAPS	RECOMMENDED	REFORMATORY
QUONSET HUTS	RAUCOUSNESS	RECOMMENDER	REFRACTABLE
QUOTABILITY	RAUNCHINESS	RECOMPENSED	REFRAINMENT
QUOTE-DRIVEN	RAVEN-HAIRED	RECOMPENSER	REFRANGIBLE
	RAVISHINGLY	RECONCILING	REFRESHMENT
R	REACH-ME-DOWN	RECONDITION	REFRIGERANT
RABBIT HUTCH	REACTIONARY	RECONNOITRE	REFRIGERATE
RABBIT PUNCH	REACTIONISM	RECONSTRUCT	REFRINGENCY
RABELAISIAN	REACTIVATED	RECOVERABLE	REFURBISHED
RACECOURSES	READABILITY	RECREATIONS	REFUTATIONS
RACE MEETING	READDRESSED	RECREMENTAL	REGENERABLE
RACQUETBALL	READERSHIPS	RECRIMINATE	REGENERATED
RADIATIONAL	READJUSTING	RECRUITABLE	REGIMENTALS
RADICALNESS	READ-THROUGH	RECRUITMENT	REGIMENTING
RADIOACTIVE	READY-TO-WEAR	RECTANGULAR	REGIONALISM
RADIO ALARMS	READY-WITTED	RECTIFIABLE	REGIONALIST
RADIO BEACON	REAFFIRMING	RECTILINEAR	REGISTERING
RADIOCARBON	REALIGNMENT	RECUPERATED	REGISTRABLE
RADIOGRAPHY	REALIZATION	RECUPERATOR	REGRETFULLY
RADIOLARIAN	REALPOLITIK	RECURRENCES	REGRETTABLE
RADIOLOGIST	REANIMATING	RECURRENTLY	REGRETTABLY
RADIOLUCENT	REANIMATION	RECURRINGLY	REGULARIZED
RADIOMETRIC	REAPPEARING	REDACTIONAL	REGULATIONS
RADIOPACITY	REAPPORTION	RED ADMIRALS	REGURGITANT
RADIOPHONIC	REAPPRAISAL	RED CRESCENT	REGURGITATE
RADIOSCOPIC	REAPPRAISED	REDCURRANTS	REIFICATION
RADIOTHERMY	REAR ADMIRAL	REDECORATED	REIMBURSING
RAFFISHNESS	REARRANGING	REDEPLOYING	REINCARNATE
RAGAMUFFINS	REASSURANCE	REDEVELOPED	REINFORCING
RAILROADING	REASSUREDLY	REDEVELOPER	REINSTATING
RAIN FORESTS	REBARBATIVE	RED HERRINGS	REINSURANCE
RAISON D'ETRE	RECALESCENT	REDIFFUSION	REINTRODUCE
RALLENTANDO	RECANTATION	REDIRECTING	REITERATING
RAMAN EFFECT	RECAPTURING	REDIRECTION	REITERATION
RAMBOUILLET	RECEIVABLES	REDOUBTABLE	REITERATIVE
RANCH HOUSES	RECEPTACLES	REDOUBTABLY	REJUVENATED
RANCOROUSLY	RECEPTIVELY	REDRESSABLE	REJUVENATOR
RANGE FINDER	RECEPTIVITY	REDUCTIONAL	RELATEDNESS
RANK AND FILE	RECESSIONAL	REDUNDANTLY	RELAXATIONS
RAPACIOUSLY	RECIDIVISTS	REDUPLICATE	RELIABILITY
RAPSCALLION	RECIPROCATE	RE-EDUCATING	RELIEF ROADS
RAPTUROUSLY	RECIPROCITY	RE-EDUCATION	RELIGIONISM
RAREFACTION	RECITATIONS	RE-ELECTIONS	RELIGIOSITY
RASPBERRIES	RECITATIVES	REFECTORIES	RELIGIOUSLY
RASTAFARIAN	RECLAIMABLE	REFERENDUMS	RELIQUARIES
RATE-CAPPING	RECLAMATION	REFERENTIAL	RELISHINGLY
RATIOCINATE	RECLINATION	REFINEMENTS	RELUCTANTLY
RATIONALISM	RECOGNITION	REFLECTANCE	RELUCTIVITY
RATIONALIST	RECOGNIZING	REFLECTIONS	REMAINDERED
RATIONALITY	RECOILINGLY	REFORESTING	REMEMBERING

REMEMBRANCE	REPROCESSED	RESTITUTION	REVERSIONER
REMINISCENT	REPRODUCERS	RESTITUTIVE	REVISIONISM
REMINISCING	REPRODUCING	RESTIVENESS	REVISIONIST
REMITTANCES	REPROGRAPHY	RESTORATION	REVITALIZED
REMODELLING	REPROVINGLY	RESTORATIVE	REVIVALISTS
REMONSTRANT	REPUBLICANS	RESTRAINING	REVIVIFYING
REMONSTRATE	REPUBLISHER	RESTRICTING	REVOCATIONS
REMORSELESS	REPUDIATING	RESTRICTION	REVOLTINGLY
REMOVAL VANS	REPUDIATION	RESTRICTIVE	REVOLUTIONS
REMUNERABLE	REPUDIATIVE	RESTRUCTURE	REVOLVINGLY
REMUNERATED	REPUDIATORY	RESURFACING	RHABDOMANCY
REMUNERATOR	REPULSIVELY	RESURRECTED	RHABDOMYOMA
RENAISSANCE	REPUTATIONS	RESUSCITATE	RHAMNACEOUS
RENEGOTIATE	REQUEST STOP	RETALIATING	RHAPSODIZED
RENOVATIONS	REQUIREMENT	RETALIATION	RHEOLOGICAL
RENTABILITY	REQUISITION	RETALIATIVE	RHEOTROPISM
RENT STRIKES	REQUITEMENT	RETALIATORY	RHETORICIAN
REORGANIZED	RERADIATION	RETARDATION	RHEUMATICKY
REORGANIZER	RESCHEDULED	RETARDATIVE	RHINESTONES
REPARATIONS	RESCINDABLE	RETARDINGLY	RHINOLOGIST
REPARTITION	RESCINDMENT	RETENTIVELY	RHINOPLASTY
REPATRIATED	RESCISSIBLE	RETENTIVITY	RHINOSCOPIC
REPELLINGLY	RESEARCHERS	RETICULATED	RHIZOMATOUS
REPENTANTLY	RESEARCHING	RETINACULAR	RHIZOPODOUS
REPERTOIRES	RESECTIONAL	RETINACULUM	RHIZOSPHERE
REPERTORIAL	RESEMBLANCE	RETINOSCOPY	RHODE ISLAND
REPERTORIES	RESENTFULLY	RETIREMENTS	RHOTACISTIC
REPETITIONS	RESERVATION	RETOUCHABLE	RHYTHMICITY
REPETITIOUS	RESHUFFLING	RETRACEABLE	RICE PADDIES
REPLACEABLE	RESIDENTIAL	RETRACEMENT	RICKETINESS
REPLACEMENT	RESIGNATION	RETRACTABLE	RICKETTSIAL
REPLENISHED	RESILIENTLY	RETRACTIONS	RICOCHETING
REPLENISHER	RESISTANCES	RETRENCHING	RICOCHETTED
REPLETENESS	RESISTENCIA	RETRIBUTION	RIFLE RANGES
REPLEVIABLE	RESISTINGLY	RETRIBUTIVE	RIFT VALLEYS
REPLICATING	RESISTIVITY	RETRIEVABLE	RIGHT-ANGLED
REPLICATION	RESOLUTIONS	RETRIEVABLY	RIGHT ANGLES
REPLICATIVE	RESOURCEFUL	RETROACTION	RIGHTEOUSLY
REPOSSESSED	RESPECTABLE	RETROACTIVE	RIGHT-HANDED
REPOSSESSOR	RESPECTABLY	RETROLENTAL	RIGHT-HANDER
REPREHENDED	RESPIRATION	RETRO-ROCKET	RIGHT-MINDED
REPREHENDER	RESPIRATORS	RETROVERTED	RIGHTS ISSUE
REPRESENTED	RESPIRATORY	REUPHOLSTER	RIGHTS OF WAY
REPRESSIBLE	RESPLENDENT	REUSABILITY	RIGHT-WINGER
REPRESSIONS	RESPONDENCE	REVALUATION	RIGOR MORTIS
REPRIEVABLE	RESPONDENTS	REVEALINGLY	RING BINDERS
REPRIMANDED	RESPONSIBLE	REVELATIONS	RING FINGERS
REPRIMANDER	RESPONSIBLY	REVENGINGLY	RINGLEADERS
REPROACHFUL	RESPONSIONS	REVERBERANT	RINGMASTERS
REPROACHING	RESTATEMENT	REVERBERATE	RINSABILITY
REPROBATION	RESTAURANTS	REVERENCING	RIOTOUSNESS
REPROBATIVE	RESTFULNESS	REVERENTIAL	RITUALISTIC

RIVER BASINS
ROADHOLDING
ROAD MANAGER
ROAD PRICING
ROAD ROLLERS
ROAD TESTING
ROCK-AND-ROLL
ROCK GARDENS
ROCKHAMPTON
RODENTICIDE
RODOMONTADE
ROENTGEN RAY
ROGUISHNESS
ROLE PLAYING
ROLLERBLADE
ROLLER BLIND
ROLLER SKATE
ROLLER TOWEL
ROLLICKINGS
ROLLICKSOME
ROLLING MILL
ROLLING PINS
ROLLTOP DESK
ROMAN CANDLE
ROMANTICISM
ROMANTICIST
ROMANTICIZE
ROOD SCREENS
ROOF GARDENS
ROOM SERVICE
ROPE LADDERS
ROSE WINDOWS
ROTARIANISM
ROTISSERIES
ROTOGRAVURE
ROTTENSTONE
ROTUNDITIES
ROUGHCASTER
ROUGH-SPOKEN
ROUNDABOUTS
ROUNDEDNESS
ROUND ROBINS
ROUSTABOUTS
ROWING BOATS
ROYAL TENNIS
RUBBER BANDS
RUBBER DUCKS
RUBBER PLANT
RUBBER STAMP
RUBBER TREES
RUBBISH BINS
RUBEFACIENT

RUBEFACTION
RUBICUNDITY
RUBRICATION
RUDESHEIMER
RUDIMENTARY
RUGBY LEAGUE
RULE OF THUMB
RUMBUSTIOUS
RUMINATIONS
RUMMAGE SALE
RUMPUS ROOMS
RUNNER BEANS
RUNNING JUMP
RUNNING MATE
RUN-THROUGHS
RUNTISHNESS
RUSSOPHOBIA
RUSSOPHOBIC
RUSTICATING
RUSTICATION
RUSTPROOFED
RUTTISHNESS

S

SAARBRUCKEN
SABBATARIAN
SABBATICALS
SACCULATION
SACRAMENTAL
SACRIFICIAL
SACRIFICING
SACRILEGIST
SACROILIACS
SADDENINGLY
SADDLECLOTH
SAFARI PARKS
SAFEBREAKER
SAFE-CONDUCT
SAFE-DEPOSIT
SAFEGUARDED
SAFEKEEPING
SAFETY BELTS
SAFETY CATCH
SAFETY-FIRST
SAFETY GLASS
SAFETY LAMPS
SAFETY MATCH
SAFETY RAZOR
SAFETY VALVE
SAGACIOUSLY
SAGITTARIAN
SAGITTARIUS

SAILING BOAT
SAILOR SUITS
SAINT ALBANS
SAINT-BRIEUC
SAINT GALLEN
SAINT HELENA
SAINT HELENS
SAINT HELIER
SAINTLINESS
SAINT MARTIN
SAINT MORITZ
SAINT THOMAS
SALACIOUSLY
SALAMANDERS
SALEABILITY
SALESCLERKS
SALESPEOPLE
SALESPERSON
SALICACEOUS
SALIENTNESS
SALINOMETER
SALINOMETRY
SALMONBERRY
SALMON TROUT
SALPINGITIC
SALPINGITIS
SALTATORIAL
SALTCELLARS
SALT SHAKERS
SALUTATIONS
SALVABILITY
SALVADORIAN
SALVAGEABLE
SALVATIONAL
SAL VOLATILE
SAMURAI BOND
SAN ANTONIAN
SANATORIUMS
SANCTIFYING
SANCTIONING
SANCTUARIES
SANDBAGGING
SANDBLASTED
SANDBLASTER
SAND-CASTING
SANDCASTLES
SANDPAPERED
SANDWICHING
SAN FERNANDO
SANGUINARIA
SANGUINEOUS
SANITARIUMS

SAN MARINESE
SAN SALVADOR
SANSEVIERIA
SANSKRITIST
SAPONACEOUS
SAPOTACEOUS
SAPROPHYTIC
SARCOMATOID
SARCOPHAGUS
SARDONICISM
SARGASSO SEA
SARTORIALLY
SASH WINDOWS
SATANICALLY
SATELLITIUM
SATIABILITY
SATIRICALLY
SATISFIABLE
SATURNALIAS
SAUDI ARABIA
SAURISCHIAN
SAUROPODOUS
SAUSAGE DOGS
SAUSAGE MEAT
SAUSAGE ROLL
SAVABLENESS
SAVING GRACE
SAVINGS BANK
SAVOIR-FAIRE
SAVOURINGLY
SAXOPHONIST
SCAFFOLDING
SCALARIFORM
SCAMMONIATE
SCANDALIZED
SCANDALIZER
SCANDINAVIA
SCARABAEOID
SCARBOROUGH
SCAREDY CATS
SCAREMONGER
SCARLATINAL
SCATOLOGIST
SCATTERABLE
SCENOGRAPHY
SCEPTICALLY
SCHEMATIZED
SCHISMATICS
SCHISTOSITY
SCHISTOSOME
SCHIZOPHYTE
SCHLESINGER

SCHOLARSHIP	SEARCHINGLY	SELF-PITYING	SEQUESTRATE
SCHOLIASTIC	SEARCHLIGHT	SELF-RELIANT	SERENDIPITY
SCHOOLCHILD	SEARCH PARTY	SELF-RESPECT	SERIALIZING
SCHOOLHOUSE	SEASICKNESS	SELF-SEALING	SERICULTURE
SCHOOLMARMS	SEBORRHOEAL	SELF-SEEKERS	SERIES-WOUND
SCHOOLMATES	SECESSIONAL	SELF-SEEKING	SERIOUSNESS
SCHWEINFURT	SECONDARILY	SELF-SERVICE	SERMONIZING
SCIENCE PARK	SECOND-CLASS	SELF-STARTER	SERPIGINOUS
SCIENTISTIC	SECOND-GUESS	SELF-WINDING	SERRULATION
SCIENTOLOGY	SECOND HANDS	SELL-BY DATES	SERTULARIAN
SCINTILLATE	SECONDMENTS	SELLOTAPING	SERVICEABLE
SCIRRHOSITY	SECOND-RATER	SELL-THROUGH	SERVICEABLY
SCLERODERMA	SECOND SIGHT	SEMANTICIST	SERVICE FLAT
SCLEROMETER	SECRET AGENT	SEMASIOLOGY	SERVICE ROAD
SCLEROTIOID	SECRETARIAL	SEMIAQUATIC	SERVOMOTORS
SCOPOLAMINE	SECRETARIAT	SEMIARIDITY	SESQUIOXIDE
SCOREBOARDS	SECRETARIES	SEMICIRCLES	SETTLEMENTS
SCORIACEOUS	SECRETIVELY	SEMIDIURNAL	SEVENTEENTH
SCORPAENOID	SECULARIZED	SEMIFLUIDIC	SEVENTIETHS
SCOTCH BROTH	SECULARIZER	SEMIMONTHLY	SEXAGESIMAL
SCOTCH MISTS	SEDAN CHAIRS	SEMIOTICIAN	SEXLESSNESS
SCOTCH TAPED	SEDENTARILY	SEMIPALMATE	SEXOLOGISTS
SCOTOMATOUS	SEDIMENTARY	SEMIQUAVERS	SEXTODECIMO
SCOURGINGLY	SEDIMENTOUS	SEMISKILLED	SHADOW-BOXED
SCOUTMASTER	SEDITIONARY	SEMITONALLY	SHADOWGRAPH
SCRAGGINESS	SEDITIOUSLY	SEMITRAILER	SHADOWINESS
SCRAPPINESS	SEDUCTIVELY	SEMITROPICS	SHALLOWNESS
SCRATCHCARD	SEGREGATING	SEMIVOCALIC	SHAMANISTIC
SCRATCHIEST	SEGREGATION	SEMPERVIVUM	SHAMELESSLY
SCRATCHINGS	SEGREGATIVE	SEMPITERNAL	SHANGHAIING
SCRATCHPADS	SEIGNIORAGE	SENSATIONAL	SHANKS'S PONY
SCRAWNINESS	SEISMICALLY	SENSELESSLY	SHANTYTOWNS
SCREAMINGLY	SEISMOGRAPH	SENSE ORGANS	SHAPELESSLY
SCREENPLAYS	SEISMOLOGIC	SENSIBILITY	SHAPELINESS
SCREENSAVER	SEISMOSCOPE	SENSITIVELY	SHAREHOLDER
SCREEN TESTS	SELAGINELLA	SENSITIVITY	SHARPBENDER
SCREWDRIVER	SELECTIVELY	SENSITIZING	SHARP-WITTED
SCRIMMAGING	SELECTIVITY	SENSUALISTS	SHAVING FOAM
SCRIMPINESS	SELENOGRAPH	SENSUALNESS	SHEATH KNIFE
SCRIPTORIUM	SELF-ASSURED	SENTENTIOUS	SHEET ANCHOR
SCRUBBINESS	SELF-CENTRED	SENTIMENTAL	SHELLACKING
SCRUMHALVES	SELF-COMMAND	SENTRY BOXES	SHENANIGANS
SCRUMMAGING	SELF-CONCEPT	SEPARATIONS	SHEPHERDESS
SCRUMPTIOUS	SELF-CONTROL	SEPARATISTS	SHEPHERDING
SCRUTINEERS	SELF-DEFENCE	SEPTAVALENT	SHIBBOLETHS
SCRUTINIZED	SELF-DENYING	SEPTICAEMIA	SHIFTLESSLY
SCRUTINIZER	SELF-EVIDENT	SEPTICAEMIC	SHIFT STICKS
SCUBA DIVING	SELF-IMPOSED	SEPTIC TANKS	SHIMONOSEKI
SCULPTURING	SELF-INDUCED	SEPTIFRAGAL	SHIP BISCUIT
SCYPHISTOMA	SELFISHNESS	SEPTIVALENT	SHIPBUILDER
SEA ANEMONES	SELF-LOADING	SEQUESTERED	SHIPWRECKED
SEA CAPTAINS	SELF-LOCKING	SEQUESTRANT	SHIPWRIGHTS

SHIRE HORSES	SIGHT-READER	SIX-SHOOTERS	SMART ALECKY
SHIRTFRONTS	SIGHTSCREEN	SIXTH-FORMER	SMARTY-PANTS
SHIRTSLEEVE	SIGHTSEEING	SIZABLENESS	SMATTERINGS
SHISH KEBABS	SIGNAL BOXES	SKATEBOARDS	SMILINGNESS
SHIVERINGLY	SIGNALIZING	SKEDADDLING	SMITHEREENS
SHOCKHEADED	SIGNATORIES	SKELETONIZE	SMITHSONITE
SHOCK TROOPS	SIGNIFIABLE	SKELETON KEY	SMOKESCREEN
SHOESTRINGS	SIGNIFICANT	SKEPTICALLY	SMOKESTACKS
SHOPKEEPERS	SIGNPOSTING	SKETCHINESS	SMOOTH-FACED
SHOPLIFTERS	SILHOUETTED	SKILFULNESS	SMORGASBORD
SHOPLIFTING	SILHOUETTES	SKIMMED MILK	SMOULDERING
SHOP STEWARD	SILICON CHIP	SKIRMISHERS	SNAPDRAGONS
SHOPWALKERS	SILLIMANITE	SKIRMISHING	SNIPERSCOPE
SHORT CHANGE	SILLY SEASON	SKULDUGGERY	SNORKELLING
SHORT-CHANGE	SILVER BIRCH	SKYJACKINGS	SNOWBALLING
SHORTCOMING	SILVERINESS	SKYROCKETED	SNOWMOBILES
SHORT CORNER	SILVER MEDAL	SKYSCRAPERS	SNOWPLOUGHS
SHORTHANDED	SILVER PAPER	SLAUGHTERED	SOAP BUBBLES
SHORT-HANDED	SILVER PLATE	SLAUGHTERER	SOCIABILITY
SHORT-LISTED	SILVERPOINT	SLAVE DRIVER	SOCIALISTIC
SHORT SHRIFT	SILVERSMITH	SLAVE LABOUR	SOCIALIZING
SHORT-SPOKEN	SIMMERINGLY	SLAVISHNESS	SOCIOLOGIST
SHORT-WINDED	SIMPERINGLY	SLEEPING BAG	SOCIOMETRIC
SHOULDERING	SIMPLIFYING	SLEEPING CAR	SOCIOPATHIC
SHOWERPROOF	SIMPLON PASS	SLEEPLESSLY	SOFTHEARTED
SHOW JUMPERS	SIMULACRUMS	SLEEPWALKED	SOFT LANDING
SHOW JUMPING	SIMULATIONS	SLEEPWALKER	SOFT OPTIONS
SHOWMANSHIP	SINE QUA NONS	SLEEPYHEADS	SOFT PALATES
SHOW OF HANDS	SINFONIETTA	SLENDERIZED	SOFT-SOAPING
SHOWSTOPPER	SINGAPOREAN	SLENDERNESS	SOFT TOUCHES
SHRINKINGLY	SINGLE-BLIND	SLEUTHHOUND	SOLANACEOUS
SHRIVELLING	SINGLE-CROSS	SLICED BREAD	SOLARIMETER
SHRUBBERIES	SINGLE-PHASE	SLICE OF LIFE	SOLAR PANELS
SHRUBBINESS	SINGLE-SPACE	SLICKENSIDE	SOLAR PLEXUS
SHUFFLE PLAY	SINGLE-TRACK	SLIDE-ACTION	SOLAR SYSTEM
SHUTTLECOCK	SINGULARITY	SLIDING DOOR	SOLEMNITIES
SIAMESE CATS	SINGULARIZE	SLIGHTINGLY	SOLEMNIZING
SIAMESE TWIN	SINISTRORSE	SLIPPED DISC	SOLIDIFYING
SICKENINGLY	SINKING FUND	SLIPSTREAMS	SOLILOQUIES
SIDE EFFECTS	SINLESSNESS	SLOOP-RIGGED	SOLILOQUIST
SIDESADDLES	SINN FEINISM	SLOPINGNESS	SOLILOQUIZE
SIDESLIPPED	SINOLOGICAL	SLOT MACHINE	SOLIPSISTIC
SIDESTEPPED	SINOLOGISTS	SLOUCHINESS	SOLMIZATION
SIDESTEPPER	SINO-TIBETAN	SLOUCHINGLY	SOLUBLENESS
SIDE STREETS	SINUOSITIES	SLOWCOACHES	SOLVABILITY
SIDESWIPING	SINUOUSNESS	SLUMGULLION	SOMATICALLY
SIDETRACKED	SISTERHOODS	SMALL CHANGE	SOMATOLOGIC
SIDE-WHEELER	SISTER-IN-LAW	SMALLHOLDER	SOMATOPLASM
SIENKIEWICZ	SITTING BULL	SMALL-MINDED	SOMERSAULTS
SIERRA LEONE	SITTING DUCK	SMALL SCREEN	SOMNOLENTLY
SIERRA MADRE	SITTING ROOM	SMALL-TIMERS	SONGFULNESS
SIGHTLINESS	SITUATIONAL	SMART ALECKS	SON-OF-A-BITCH

SOOTHSAYERS	SPERMOPHILE	SPREADSHEET	STATELY HOME
SOPHISTRIES	SPERM WHALES	SPRINGBOARD	STATESWOMAN
SORORICIDAL	SPESSARTITE	SPRING-CLEAN	STATISTICAL
SORROWFULLY	SPHEROMETER	SPRINGFIELD	STATOLITHIC
SOTTISHNESS	SPHERULITIC	SPRINGINESS	STATUTE BOOK
SOUBRIQUETS	SPHINCTERAL	SPRING ONION	STATUTORILY
SOUGHT-AFTER	SPHINGOSINE	SPRING ROLLS	STAUNCHABLE
SOUL BROTHER	SPHRAGISTIC	SPRING TIDES	STAUNCHNESS
SOULFULNESS	SPINA BIFIDA	SPRINKLINGS	STAUROLITIC
SOUNDLESSLY	SPINAL CORDS	SPUMESCENCE	STAUROSCOPE
SOUNDTRACKS	SPINELESSLY	SQUANDERERS	STAY-AT-HOMES
SOUP KITCHEN	SPINESCENCE	SQUANDERING	STEADFASTLY
SOUSAPHONES	SPINIFEROUS	SQUARE DANCE	STEALTHIEST
SOUTH AFRICA	SPINSTERISH	SQUARE KNOTS	STEAM-BOILER
SOUTHAMPTON	SPINY-FINNED	SQUARE MEALS	STEAM-ENGINE
SOUTH DAKOTA	SPIRACULATE	SQUARE ROOTS	STEAMROLLER
SOUTHEASTER	SPIRIFEROUS	SQUASHINESS	STEAM SHOVEL
SOUTHERNERS	SPIRIT LEVEL	SQUEAMISHLY	STEAROPTENE
SOUTH ISLAND	SPIRITUALLY	SQUELCHIEST	STEATOLYSIS
SOUTHWESTER	SPIRKETTING	SQUIGGLIEST	STEATOPYGIA
SOVEREIGNTY	SPIROCHAETE	SQUIREARCHY	STEATOPYGIC
SOVIETISTIC	SPIROMETRIC	SQUIRMINGLY	STEELWORKER
SPACE HEATER	SPITSTICKER	STABILIZERS	STEEPLEJACK
SPACE PROBES	SPLASHBOARD	STABILIZING	STEERAGEWAY
SPARINGNESS	SPLASHDOWNS	STADIOMETER	STELLARATOR
SPARROWHAWK	SPLASH GUARD	STAFF NURSES	STENCILLING
SPASTICALLY	SPLASHINESS	STAGE FRIGHT	STENOGRAPHY
SPATHACEOUS	SPLATTERING	STAGE-MANAGE	STENOHALINE
SPEAKEASIES	SPLAYFOOTED	STAGESTRUCK	STENOPHAGUS
SPEAKERSHIP	SPLENDOROUS	STAGGERBUSH	STENOTROPIC
SPEARHEADED	SPLENECTOMY	STAGING POST	STENOTYPIST
SPECIALISMS	SPLENETICAL	STAG PARTIES	STEPBROTHER
SPECIALISTS	SPLINTERING	STAKEHOLDER	STEPHANOTIS
SPECIALIZED	SPLIT SECOND	STALACTITES	STEPLADDERS
SPECIALNESS	SPLUTTERING	STALACTITIC	STEPPARENTS
SPECIFIABLE	SPOILSPORTS	STALAGMITES	STEPSISTERS
SPECIFICITY	SPOKESWOMAN	STALAGMITIC	STEREOGRAPH
SPECTACULAR	SPONDYLITIS	STALEMATING	STEREOMETRY
SPECTRALITY	SPONGE CAKES	STALLHOLDER	STEREOSCOPE
SPECULATING	SPONSORSHIP	STANDARDIZE	STEREOSCOPY
SPECULATION	SPONTANEITY	STANDOFFISH	STEREOTAXIS
SPECULATIVE	SPONTANEOUS	STANDPOINTS	STEREOTYPED
SPECULATORS	SPOONERISMS	STANLEY POOL	STEREOTYPER
SPEECHIFIED	SPOROGENOUS	STARA ZAGORA	STEREOTYPES
SPEECHIFIER	SPOROGONIAL	STAR CHAMBER	STEREOTYPIC
SPEED LIMITS	SPOROGONIUM	STARCHINESS	STERILIZERS
SPEEDOMETER	SPOROPHYTIC	STAR-CROSSED	STERILIZING
SPELLBINDER	SPORTSWOMAN	STAR-STUDDED	STERLITAMAK
SPENDTHRIFT	SPORULATION	STARTER HOME	STERNUTATOR
SPERMATHECA	SPOT CHECKED	STARTLINGLY	STETHOSCOPE
SPERMATOZOA	SPOTTED DICK	STARVELINGS	STETHOSCOPY
SPERMICIDES	SPREAD-EAGLE	STATELINESS	STEWARDSHIP

STICHICALLY	STRAININGLY	STYLOGRAPHY	SUBSIDIZERS
STICHOMETRY	STRAITLACED	STYLOPODIUM	SUBSIDIZING
STICKHANDLE	STRANGENESS	STYLOSTIXIS	SUBSISTENCE
STICK INSECT	STRANGULATE	SUBASSEMBLY	SUBSPECIFIC
STICKLEBACK	STRAPHANGER	SUBAUDITION	SUBSTANDARD
STICK SHIFTS	STRATEGISTS	SUBAXILLARY	SUBSTANTIAL
STIFF-NECKED	STRATHCLYDE	SUBBASEMENT	SUBSTANTIVE
STIGMATICAL	STRATIFYING	SUBCHLORIDE	SUBSTATIONS
STIGMATIZED	STRATOCRACY	SUBCOMPACTS	SUBSTITUENT
STIGMATIZER	STRATOPAUSE	SUBCONTRACT	SUBSTITUTED
STILLBIRTHS	STRAWFLOWER	SUBCONTRARY	SUBSTITUTES
STILTEDNESS	STRAWWEIGHT	SUBCORTICAL	SUBSTRATIVE
STIMULATING	STREAKINESS	SUBCULTURAL	SUBSUMPTION
STIMULATION	STREAMLINED	SUBCULTURES	SUBSUMPTIVE
STIMULATIVE	STREETLIGHT	SUBDELIRIUM	SUBTERFUGES
STIPENDIARY	STREET VALUE	SUBDIACONAL	SUBTRACTING
STIPULATING	STRENUOSITY	SUBDIVIDING	SUBTRACTION
STIPULATION	STRENUOUSLY	SUBDIVISION	SUBTRACTIVE
STIPULATORY	STRESS MARKS	SUBDOMINANT	SUBTROPICAL
STIRRUP CUPS	STRETCHABLE	SUBDUEDNESS	SUBURBANITE
STIRRUP PUMP	STRETCHIEST	SUBHEADINGS	SUBVENTIONS
STOCKBROKER	STRETCHMARK	SUBIRRIGATE	SUBVERSIVES
STOCKHOLDER	STRIDULATED	SUBJECTABLE	SUCCEDANEUM
STOCKJOBBER	STRIDULATOR	SUBJUGATING	SUCCEEDABLE
STOCK MARKET	STRIKEBOUND	SUBJUGATION	SUCCESSIONS
STOCKPILING	STRING BEANS	SUBJUNCTION	SUCCESSORAL
STOCKTAKING	STRINGBOARD	SUBJUNCTIVE	SUCCOURABLE
STOICALNESS	STRINGENTLY	SUBLIMATING	SUCH AND SUCH
STOMACHACHE	STRINGINESS	SUBLIMATION	SUCKING PIGS
STOMACHICAL	STRINGPIECE	SUBLITTORAL	SUCTION PUMP
STOMACH PUMP	STRIP MINING	SUBLUXATION	SUDETENLAND
STOMATOLOGY	STRIP-SEARCH	SUBMARGINAL	SUFFERINGLY
STONECUTTER	STRIPTEASES	SUBMARINERS	SUFFICIENCY
STONE FRUITS	STROBE LIGHT	SUBMERSIBLE	SUFFOCATING
STONE-GROUND	STROBOSCOPE	SUBMISSIONS	SUFFOCATION
STONEMASONS	STRONGBOXES	SUBMITTABLE	SUFFOCATIVE
STONE'S THROW	STRONGHOLDS	SUBMULTIPLE	SUFFRAGETTE
STONEWALLED	STRONG POINT	SUBORDINARY	SUFFUMIGATE
STONEWALLER	STRONG ROOMS	SUBORDINATE	SUGGESTIBLE
STONEWORKER	STRUCTURING	SUBORNATION	SUGGESTIONS
STOOLPIGEON	STRUCTURIST	SUBORNATIVE	SUITABILITY
STOPWATCHES	STRUTTINGLY	SUBPOENAING	SULPHA DRUGS
STOREHOUSES	STUBBORNEST	SUBREGIONAL	SULPHUREOUS
STOREKEEPER	STUDENTSHIP	SUBROGATION	SUMMARINESS
STORE KEEPER	STUDIEDNESS	SUBROUTINES	SUMMARIZING
STORM CLOUDS	STUDIO COUCH	SUBSCAPULAR	SUMMATIONAL
STORYTELLER	STULTIFYING	SUBSCRIBERS	SUMMERHOUSE
STOURBRIDGE	STUMBLINGLY	SUBSCRIBING	SUMMERINESS
STRAGGLIEST	STUNTEDNESS	SUBSECTIONS	SUMPTUOUSLY
STRAIGHTEST	STUPIDITIES	SUBSEQUENCE	SUNDRENCHED
STRAIGHT-OUT	STYLISHNESS	SUBSERVIENT	SUNLESSNESS
STRAIGHTWAY	STYLIZATION	SUBSIDENCES	SUNNY-SIDE UP

SUPERABOUND	SURFCASTING	SYLLABOGRAM	TACHYCARDIA
SUPERCHARGE	SURGEONFISH	SYLLOGISTIC	TACHYMETRIC
SUPERFAMILY	SURMOUNTING	SYMBOLISTIC	TACITURNITY
SUPERFETATE	SURPASSABLE	SYMBOLIZING	TACTFULNESS
SUPERFICIAL	SURPRISEDLY	SYMBOLOGIST	TAGLIATELLE
SUPERFLUITY	SURREALISTS	SYMMETRICAL	TAKE AGAINST
SUPERFLUOUS	SURREBUTTAL	SYMPATHETIC	TAKE-HOME PAY
SUPERIMPOSE	SURREBUTTER	SYMPATHIZED	TALEBEARERS
SUPERINDUCE	SURRENDERED	SYMPATHIZER	TALENT SCOUT
SUPERINTEND	SURRENDERER	SYMPETALOUS	TALKABILITY
SUPERIORITY	SURROGATION	SYMPHONIOUS	TALKING BOOK
SUPERJACENT	SURROUNDING	SYMPTOMATIC	TALLAHASSEE
SUPERLATIVE	SURVEILLANT	SYNAGOGICAL	TALL STORIES
SUPERLUNARY	SURVIVAL KIT	SYNCHROMESH	TAMABLENESS
SUPERMARKET	SUSCEPTANCE	SYNCHRONISM	TAMBOURINES
SUPERNATANT	SUSCEPTIBLE	SYNCHRONIZE	TANGIBILITY
SUPERNORMAL	SUSPENDIBLE	SYNCHRONOUS	TANTALIZING
SUPERSCRIBE	SUSPENSEFUL	SYNCHROTRON	TAPE MACHINE
SUPERSCRIPT	SUSPENSIONS	SYNCOPATING	TAPE MEASURE
SUPERSEDEAS	SUSPICIONAL	SYNCOPATION	TARANTELLAS
SUPERSEDING	SUSTAINABLE	SYNDESMOSIS	TARNISHABLE
SUPERSEDURE	SUSTAINEDLY	SYNDESMOTIC	TARRADIDDLE
SUPERSONICS	SUSTAINMENT	SYNDICALISM	TARTAR SAUCE
SUPERSTRUCT	SUSURRATION	SYNDICALIST	TASKMASTERS
SUPERTANKER	SWALLOWABLE	SYNDICATING	TASTELESSLY
SUPERVENING	SWALLOW DIVE	SYNDICATION	TAUTOLOGIES
SUPERVISING	SWALLOWTAIL	SYNECDOCHIC	TAUTOLOGIZE
SUPERVISION	SWALLOWWORT	SYNECOLOGIC	TAUTOMERISM
SUPERVISORS	SWARTHINESS	SYNKARYONIC	TAXIDERMIST
SUPERVISORY	SWEAT GLANDS	SYNTHESIZED	TAX SHELTERS
SUPPLANTING	SWEATSHIRTS	SYNTHESIZER	TEARFULNESS
SUPPLEMENTS	SWEEPSTAKES	SYNTHETICAL	TEARJERKERS
SUPPLICANTS	SWEETBREADS	SYPHILITICS	TEA SERVICES
SUPPLICATED	SWEETHEARTS	SYPHILOLOGY	TEA TROLLEYS
SUPPORTABLE	SWEET PEPPER	SYSSARCOSIS	TECHNICALLY
SUPPOSITION	SWEET POTATO	SYSSARCOTIC	TECHNICIANS
SUPPOSITIVE	SWEET-TALKED	SYSTEMATICS	TECHNICOLOR
SUPPOSITORY	SWINDLINGLY	SYSTEMATISM	TECHNOCRACY
SUPPRESSANT	SWINISHNESS	SYSTEMATIST	TECHNOCRATS
SUPPRESSING	SWISS CHARDS	SYSTEMATIZE	TECHNOPHILE
SUPPRESSION	SWISS CHEESE	SZOMBATHELY	TECHNOPHOBE
SUPPRESSIVE	SWISS CLOCKS		TEDIOUSNESS
SUPPRESSORS	SWITCHBACKS	T	TEENYBOPPER
SUPPURATING	SWITCHBLADE	TABERNACLES	TEETOTALISM
SUPPURATION	SWITCHBOARD	TABLECLOTHS	TEETOTALLER
SUPPURATIVE	SWITZERLAND	TABLESPOONS	TEGUCIGALPA
SUPREMACIST	SWOLLEN HEAD	TABLE TENNIS	TELEBANKING
SUPREMATISM	SWOLLENNESS	TABULATIONS	TELECOMMUTE
SUPREMATIST	SWORD DANCER	TACHEOMETER	TELECOTTAGE
SUPREMENESS	SWORD DANCES	TACHOGRAPHS	TELEGNOSTIC
SURBASEMENT	SWORDFISHES	TACHOMETERS	TELEGRAPHED
SURCHARGING	SYCOPHANTIC	TACHOMETRIC	TELEGRAPHER

TELEGRAPHIC	TERRORIZING	THERMOSCOPE	TIMEKEEPERS
TELEKINESIS	TERTIUM QUID	THERMOSTATS	TIMESERVERS
TELEKINETIC	TESSELLATED	THERMOTAXIC	TIMESERVING
TELEOLOGISM	TESTABILITY	THERMOTAXIS	TIME-SHARING
TELEOLOGIST	TESTAMENTAL	THESAURUSES	TIME SIGNALS
TELEPATHIST	TESTICULATE	THICKHEADED	TIMETABLING
TELEPHONING	TESTIMONIAL	THICKNESSES	TINDERBOXES
TELEPHONIST	TESTIMONIES	THICK-WITTED	TIN PAN ALLEY
TELEPRINTER	TEST MATCHES	THIGMOTAXIS	TIN-PAN ALLEY
TELESCOPING	TETANICALLY	THIMBLEFULS	TIRUNELVELI
TELESELLING	TETRADYMITE	THIMBLEWEED	TITANICALLY
TELEVISIONS	TETRAHEDRAL	THINGAMAJIG	TITILLATING
TELEWORKING	TETRAHEDRON	THIN-SKINNED	TITILLATION
TELLING-OFFS	TETRAMERISM	THIOCYANATE	TITILLATIVE
TELUKBETUNG	TETRAMEROUS	THIOPENTONE	TITLEHOLDER
TEMERARIOUS	TETRAPLEGIA	THIRD DEGREE	TITTERINGLY
TEMPERAMENT	TETRARCHATE	THIRD-DEGREE	TOAST MASTER
TEMPERATURE	TETRASPORIC	THIRD PERSON	TOBACCONIST
TEMPESTUOUS	TETRAVALENT	THIRSTINESS	TOBOGGANING
TEMPORALITY	THALIDOMIDE	THIRTEENTHS	TOFFEE APPLE
TEMPORARILY	THALLOPHYTE	THISTLEDOWN	TOFFEE-NOSED
TEMPORIZING	THANKLESSLY	THIXOTROPIC	TOILET PAPER
TEMPTATIONS	THAUMATROPE	THORACOTOMY	TOILET ROLLS
TEMPTRESSES	THEATREGOER	THOROUGHPIN	TOILET WATER
TENACIOUSLY	THEATRICALS	THOUGHTLESS	TOLBUTAMIDE
TENDENTIOUS	THEIRSELVES	THOUSANDTHS	TOMBOYISHLY
TENDERFOOTS	THENCEFORTH	THRASH METAL	TONSILLITIS
TENDERIZING	THEOBROMINE	THREADINESS	TOOTH POWDER
TENEBROSITY	THEOCENTRIC	THREATENING	TOPDRESSING
TENNIS COURT	THEODOLITES	THREEPENCES	TOPOGRAPHER
TENNIS ELBOW	THEODOLITIC	THRIFTINESS	TOPOGRAPHIC
TENORRHAPHY	THEODORAKIS	THRILLINGLY	TORCHBEARER
TENSIBILITY	THEOLOGIANS	THROATINESS	TORMENTEDLY
TENSIOMETER	THEOLOGICAL	THROBBINGLY	TORONTONIAN
TENTATIVELY	THEOLOGIZER	THROMBOCYTE	TORSIBILITY
TENTERHOOKS	THEOPHOBIAC	THROUGHPUTS	TORTICOLLAR
TENUOUSNESS	THEOREMATIC	THROUGHWAYS	TORTICOLLIS
TEPEFACTION	THEORETICAL	THUMBSCREWS	TORTURESOME
TERATOGENIC	THEOSOPHISM	THUNDERBIRD	TORTURINGLY
TERATOLOGIC	THEOSOPHIST	THUNDERBOLT	TORTUROUSLY
TEREBIC ACID	THERAPEUTIC	THUNDERCLAP	TOTALIZATOR
TERMINATING	THEREABOUTS	THYROIDITIS	TOTEMICALLY
TERMINATION	THEREMINIST	THYROTROPIN	TOTIPALMATE
TERMINATIVE	THERETOFORE	THYRSANURAN	TOTIPOTENCY
TERMINATORY	THERIOMORPH	TICKINGS OFF	TOUCHPAPERS
TERMINOLOGY	THERMIONICS	TICK-TACK-TOE	TOUCHSTONES
TERRESTRIAL	THERMOCLINE	TIDDLYWINKS	TOUCH-TYPING
TERRICOLOUS	THERMOGRAPH	TIEBREAKERS	TOUCH-TYPIST
TERRIGENOUS	THERMOLYSIS	TIED COTTAGE	TOUCHY-FEELY
TERRITORIAL	THERMOLYTIC	TIGHTFISTED	TOUR DE FORCE
TERRITORIES	THERMOMETER	TIGHT-LIPPED	TOURMALINIC
TERRORISTIC	THERMOMETRY	TIME CAPSULE	TOURNAMENTS

TOURNIQUETS	TRANSFUSIVE	TRESPASSING	TRUEHEARTED
TOUT LE MONDE	TRANSHUMANT	TRESTLETREE	TRUK ISLANDS
TOWER BLOCKS	TRANSISTORS	TRESTLEWORK	TRUMPETWEED
TOWN PLANNER	TRANSITABLE	TRIABLENESS	TRUNK ROUTES
TOWNSPEOPLE	TRANSITIONS	TRIANGULATE	TRUSTEESHIP
TOXICOGENIC	TRANSITIVES	TRIBULATION	TRUSTWORTHY
TOXOPHILITE	TRANS-JORDAN	TRIBUTARIES	TRYPANOSOME
TOXOPLASMIC	TRANSLATING	TRIBUTARILY	TRYPSINOGEN
TRACHEOTOMY	TRANSLATION	TRICERATOPS	TSELINOGRAD
TRACK EVENTS	TRANSLATORS	TRICHINOSIS	TSETSE FLIES
TRACKLAYERS	TRANSLOCATE	TRICHLORIDE	TUBERCULATE
TRACK RECORD	TRANSLUCENT	TRICHOMONAD	TUBERCULOUS
TRACKSUITED	TRANSMITTAL	TRICHOTOMIC	TUB-THUMPERS
TRADE PRICES	TRANSMITTED	TRICKLE-DOWN	TUB-THUMPING
TRADE ROUTES	TRANSMITTER	TRICKLINGLY	TUDORBETHAN
TRADES UNION	TRANSMUTING	TRICKSINESS	TUMBLE-DRIED
TRADESWOMAN	TRANSPADANE	TRICUSPIDAL	TUMBLE DRIER
TRADE UNIONS	TRANSPARENT	TRIGGERFISH	TUMBLE DRYER
TRADING POST	TRANSPIERCE	TRILLIONTHS	TUMBLE-DRYER
TRADITIONAL	TRANSPIRING	TRIMETROGON	TUMEFACIENT
TRADUCEMENT	TRANSPLANTS	TRIMORPHISM	TUMEFACTION
TRADUCINGLY	TRANSPONDER	TRINCOMALEE	TUNEFULNESS
TRAFFICATOR	TRANSPORTED	TRINIDADIAN	TUNING FORKS
TRAFFIC JAMS	TRANSPORTER	TRIPALMITIN	TURBINATION
TRAFFICKERS	TRANSPOSING	TRIPLICATES	TURBOCHARGE
TRAFFICKING	TRANSPUTERS	TRIQUETROUS	TURBULENTLY
TRAGEDIENNE	TRANSSEXUAL	TRISTICHOUS	TURGESCENCE
TRAGICOMEDY	TRANSURANIC	TRISULPHIDE	TURKISH BATH
TRAILBLAZER	TRANSVAALER	TRITURATION	TURNAROUNDS
TRAINBEARER	TRANSVALUER	TRIUMVIRATE	TURRICULATE
TRAMPOLINER	TRANSVERSAL	TRIVIALIZED	TURTLEDOVES
TRAMPOLINES	TRAPSHOOTER	TROCHOPHORE	TURTLENECKS
TRANQUILITY	TRAUMATIZED	TROCORNERED	TUTTI FRUTTI
TRANSACTING	TRAVEL AGENT	TROGLODYTES	TWELVEMONTH
TRANSACTION	TRAVELOGUES	TROGLODYTIC	TWITCHINGLY
TRANSALPINE	TRAVERSABLE	TROJAN HORSE	TYNE AND WEAR
TRANSCEIVER	TREACHERIES	TROMBONISTS	TYPECASTING
TRANSCENDED	TREACHEROUS	TROMPE L'OEIL	TYPESCRIPTS
TRANSCRIBED	TREACLINESS	TROPHICALLY	TYPESETTERS
TRANSCRIBER	TREASONABLE	TROPHOBLAST	TYPE SETTING
TRANSCRIPTS	TREASONABLY	TROPHOZOITE	TYPEWRITERS
TRANSECTION	TREASURABLE	TROPICALITY	TYPEWRITING
TRANSFERASE	TREBLE CLEFS	TROPICALIZE	TYPEWRITTEN
TRANSFERRED	TRELLISWORK	TROPISMATIC	TYPICALNESS
TRANSFERRIN	TREMBLINGLY	TROPOPHYTIC	TYPING POOLS
TRANSFIGURE	TREMULOUSLY	TROPOSPHERE	TYPOGRAPHER
TRANSFINITE	TRENCHANTLY	TROTSKYISTS	TYPOGRAPHIC
TRANSFIXING	TRENCH COATS	TROUBADOURS	TYPOLOGICAL
TRANSFIXION	TRENCHERMAN	TROUBLESOME	TYRANNICIDE
TRANSFORMED	TRENCHERMEN	TROUBLE SPOT	TYRANNIZING
TRANSFORMER	TRENDSETTER	TROUBLINGLY	TYROTHRICIN
TRANSFUSION	TREPIDATION	TRUCULENTLY	TZETZE FLIES

U

ULOTRICHOUS
ULTRAFILTER
ULTRAMARINE
ULTRAMODERN
ULTRASONICS
ULTRAVIOLET
ULVERIZABLE
UMBELLULATE
UNACCOUNTED
UNADVISEDLY
UNALTERABLE
UNAMBIGUOUS
UNAMBITIOUS
UNANIMOUSLY
UNANNOUNCED
UNAVAILABLE
UNAVOIDABLE
UNAWARENESS
UNBALANCING
UNBALLASTED
UNBELIEVERS
UNBLEMISHED
UNBREAKABLE
UNBURDENING
UNCALLED-FOR
UNCATCHABLE
UNCERTAINLY
UNCERTAINTY
UNCHARTERED
UNCHASTENED
UNCHRISTIAN
UNCIVILIZED
UNCLEANNESS
UNCOMMITTED
UNCONCERNED
UNCONCLUDED
UNCONFIDENT
UNCONNECTED
UNCONSCIOUS
UNCONSULTED
UNCONTESTED
UNCONTRIVED
UNCONVERTED
UNCONVINCED
UNCORRECTED
UNCOUNTABLE
UNCOUTHNESS
UNCRUSHABLE
UNDECEIVING
UNDECIDABLE
UNDECIDEDLY

UNDEMANDING
UNDERACTING
UNDERBIDDER
UNDERCHARGE
UNDEREXPOSE
UNDERGROUND
UNDERGROWTH
UNDERLETTER
UNDERLINING
UNDERMANNED
UNDERMINING
UNDERPASSES
UNDERPAYING
UNDERPINNED
UNDERPLAYED
UNDERRATING
UNDERSCORED
UNDERSELLER
UNDERSHIRTS
UNDERSIGNED
UNDERSTAIRS
UNDERSTATED
UNDERTAKERS
UNDERTAKING
UNDERTHRUST
UNDERVALUED
UNDERVALUER
UNDERWEIGHT
UNDERWRITER
UNDESIGNING
UNDESIRABLE
UNDESIRABLY
UNDEVELOPED
UNDISCLOSED
UNDISCUSSED
UNDISTORTED
UNDOUBTEDLY
UNDREAMED-OF
UNDRINKABLE
UNDULATIONS
UNEQUALNESS
UNEQUIVOCAL
UNESSENTIAL
UNEXPLAINED
UNEXPRESSED
UNFAILINGLY
UNFALTERING
UNFLAPPABLE
UNFLAPPABLY
UNFLINCHING
UNFORTUNATE
UNFULFILLED

UNGODLINESS
UNGUICULATE
UNGULIGRADE
UNHAPPINESS
UNHEALTHILY
UNICELLULAR
UNIFICATION
UNIFORMNESS
UNINHABITED
UNINHIBITED
UNINITIATED
UNINSPIRING
UNINSULATED
UNIPERSONAL
UNIPOLARITY
UNIVERSALLY
UNJUSTIFIED
UNKEMPTNESS
UNKNOWINGLY
UNKNOWNNESS
UNLOOKED-FOR
UNLOOSENING
UNLUCKINESS
UNMANLINESS
UNMITIGATED
UNNATURALLY
UNNECESSARY
UNOBTRUSIVE
UNORGANIZED
UNPALATABLE
UNPATRIOTIC
UNPERTURBED
UNPOLITICAL
UNPRACTICAL
UNPRACTISED
UNPRINTABLE
UNPROCESSED
UNPROFESSED
UNPROMISING
UNPUBLISHED
UNQUALIFIED
UNRAVELLING
UNRAVELMENT
UNREALISTIC
UNREASONING
UNREFLECTED
UNREHEARSED
UNRELENTING
UNREMITTING
UNRIGHTEOUS
UNSATISFIED
UNSATURATED

UNSAVOURILY
UNSCHEDULED
UNSCRAMBLED
UNSCRAMBLER
UNSCRATCHED
UNSHAKEABLE
UNSOCIALIST
UNSPARINGLY
UNSPEAKABLE
UNSPEAKABLY
UNSPECIFIED
UNSPONSORED
UNSTOPPABLE
UNSURPASSED
UNSURPRISED
UNSUSPECTED
UNTERWALDEN
UNTHEORIZED
UNTHINKABLE
UNTOUCHABLE
UNTRAVELLED
UNUTTERABLE
UNUTTERABLY
UNVARNISHED
UNWARRANTED
UNWATCHABLE
UNWHOLESOME
UNWILLINGLY
UNWITNESSED
UNWITTINGLY
UP-AND-COMING
UPHOLSTERED
UPHOLSTERER
UPRIGHTNESS
UPS AND DOWNS
UPSTRETCHED
URANOGRAPHY
URINIFEROUS
UROCHORDATE
URTICACEOUS
USELESSNESS
UTILITARIAN
UTILITY ROOM
UTILIZATION
UTRICULITIS

V

VACATIONERS
VACATIONING
VACCINATING
VACCINATION
VACILLATING

VACILLATION	VERBALIZING	VISCOUSNESS	WARM-HEARTED
VACUOLATION	VERBAL NOUNS	VISIBLENESS	WARMING PANS
VACUOUSNESS	VEREENIGING	VISIONARIES	WAR OF NERVES
VACUUM FLASK	VERISIMILAR	VISITATIONS	WARRANTABLE
VACUUM PUMPS	VERMICULATE	VISUALIZING	WASHABILITY
VAGABONDAGE	VERMICULITE	VITICULTURE	WASH DRAWING
VAGABONDISM	VERMINATION	VITRESCENCE	WASHERWOMAN
VAGINECTOMY	VERMIVOROUS	VITRIFIABLE	WASHERWOMEN
VAGRANTNESS	VERNACULARS	VITUPERATOR	WASHING DAYS
VALEDICTION	VERRUCOSITY	VIVACIOUSLY	WASPISHNESS
VALEDICTORY	VERSATILITY	VIVISECTION	WATCHKEEPER
VALIDATIONS	VERSICOLOUR	VLAARDINGEN	WATCHMAKERS
VALLE D'AOSTA	VERTEBRATES	VLADIKAVKAZ	WATCHMAKING
VALUATIONAL	VERTICALITY	VLADIVOSTOK	WATCHSTRAPS
VAMPIRE BATS	VERTIGINOUS	VOCIFERANCE	WATCHTOWERS
VANDALISTIC	VESTIGIALLY	VOCIFERATED	WATER CANNON
VANDALIZING	VETERANS DAY	VOCIFERATOR	WATER CLOSET
VANISHINGLY	VEXATIOUSLY	VOLCANICITY	WATERCOLOUR
VANQUISHING	VEXILLOLOGY	VOLCANOLOGY	WATERCOURSE
VAPORESCENT	VIBRACULOID	VOLTAMMETER	WATERED-DOWN
VAPORIMETER	VIBRAPHONES	VOLUNTARIES	WATERFRONTS
VAPORIZABLE	VIBRATILITY	VOLUNTARILY	WATERING CAN
VAPOUR TRAIL	VIBRATINGLY	VOLUNTARISM	WATER LEVELS
VARGAS LLOSA	VIBRATIONAL	VOLUNTARIST	WATER LILIES
VARIABILITY	VICARIOUSLY	VOLUNTEERED	WATERLOGGED
VARIATIONAL	VICEGERENCY	VOODOOISTIC	WATER MEADOW
VARICELLATE	VICEROYALTY	VOORTREKKER	WATERMELONS
VARICELLOID	VICEROYSHIP	VORACIOUSLY	WATERPROOFS
VARIEGATION	VICHYSSOISE	VORTIGINOUS	WATER SKIERS
VARIOLATION	VICIOUSNESS	VOUCHSAFING	WATER SKIING
VARIOUSNESS	VICISSITUDE	VOYEURISTIC	WATERSPOUTS
VASCULARITY	VICTIMIZING	VULCANIZING	WATER SUPPLY
VASCULARIZE	VICTUALLING	VULGARITIES	WATER TABLES
VASECTOMIES	VIDEOPHONIC	VULGARIZING	WATER VAPOUR
VASODILATOR	VIDEOTAPING	VULGAR LATIN	WATERWHEELS
VASOPRESSIN	VIEWFINDERS		WATHAWURUNG
VATICAN CITY	VINAIGRETTE	**W**	WAVELENGTHS
VEGETARIANS	VINDICATING	WADING POOLS	WAYWARDNESS
VELOCIPEDES	VINDICATION	WAGGISHNESS	WEALTHINESS
VENDIBILITY	VINDICATORY	WAINSCOTING	WEARABILITY
VENEREOLOGY	VINEDRESSER	WAINSCOTTED	WEAR AND TEAR
VENESECTION	VINEGARROON	WAITING GAME	WEATHERCOCK
VENTILATING	VINEYARDIST	WAITING LIST	WEATHER SHIP
VENTILATION	VINICULTURE	WAITING ROOM	WEATHER VANE
VENTILATIVE	VINIFICATOR	WAITRESSING	WEATHER-WISE
VENTILATORS	VIOLABILITY	WAKEFULNESS	WEDDING RING
VENTILATORY	VIOLONCELLO	WALKS OF LIFE	WEIGHBRIDGE
VENTRICULAR	VIRGIN BIRTH	WALLFLOWERS	WEIGHTINESS
VENTRICULUS	VIRIDESCENT	WALLPAPERED	WELCOMENESS
VENTURESOME	VIROLOGICAL	WANDERINGLY	WELDABILITY
VERACIOUSLY	VISCOMETRIC	WANNE-EICKEL	WELL-ADAPTED
VERATRIDINE	VISCOUNTESS	WARM-BLOODED	WELL-ADVISED

WELL AND GOOD
WELLBEHAVED
WELL-DEFINED
WELL-ENDOWED
WELL-FOUNDED
WELL-GROOMED
WELLINGTONS
WELL-MEANING
WELL-ROUNDED
WELLSPRINGS
WELL-WISHERS
WELL-WISHING
WELWITSCHIA
WENSLEYDALE
WESLEYANISM
WEST COUNTRY
WESTERNIZED
WESTERNMOST
WEST GERMANY
WEST LOTHIAN
WESTMINSTER
WESTPHALIAN
WET BLANKETS
WETTABILITY
WHEEDLINGLY
WHEELBARROW
WHEELCHAIRS
WHEELHOUSES
WHEELWRIGHT
WHEREABOUTS
WHERESOEVER
WHEREWITHAL
WHIFFLETREE
WHIMSICALLY
WHIPPING BOY
WHIRLYBIRDS
WHIST DRIVES
WHITEBOARDS
WHITE-COLLAR
WHITE DWARFS
WHITE HORSES
WHITE KNIGHT
WHITE METALS
WHITE PAPERS
WHITE PEPPER
WHITE RUSSIA
WHITE-SLAVER

WHITE SPIRIT
WHITETHROAT
WHITEWASHED
WHITEWASHER
WHITEWASHES
WHITSUNTIDE
WHOLE NUMBER
WHOLESALERS
WHOREHOUSES
WICKET GATES
WILDEBEESTS
WILDFOWLING
WILDPOSTING
WILLINGNESS
WINDCHEATER
WINDFALL TAX
WINDJAMMERS
WINDOW BOXES
WINDOWPANES
WINDOW SHADE
WINDOWSILLS
WINDSCREENS
WINDSHIELDS
WIND-SUCKING
WIND-SURFERS
WIND-SURFING
WIND TUNNELS
WIND TURBINE
WINEBIBBING
WINNINGNESS
WINNING POST
WINNIPEGGER
WINSOMENESS
WINTERGREEN
WIRE NETTING
WIRE-TAPPING
WISDOM TEETH
WISDOM TOOTH
WISECRACKED
WISECRACKER
WISHFULNESS
WISTFULNESS
WITCHDOCTOR
WITCH-HUNTER
WITHDRAWALS
WITHDRAWING
WITHHOLDING

WITHOUT FAIL
WITHSTANDER
WITLESSNESS
WITNESSABLE
WIZARD PRANG
WOBBLE BOARD
WOLFISHNESS
WOLF WHISTLE
WOMANLINESS
WONDERFULLY
WONDERINGLY
WONDERLANDS
WOOD ALCOHOL
WOODCARVING
WOODCUTTERS
WOODCUTTING
WOODEN SPOON
WOODPECKERS
WOODTURNING
WOODWORKING
WOOLGROWING
WORD-PERFECT
WORKABILITY
WORKAHOLICS
WORKAHOLISM
WORKBASKETS
WORKBENCHES
WORKING DAYS
WORKING WEEK
WORKMANLIKE
WORKMANSHIP
WORKSTATION
WORLD-BEATER
WORLDLINESS
WORLDLY-WISE
WORLD POWERS
WORLD SERIES
WORSHIPABLE
WORSHIPPERS
WORSHIPPING
WORTHLESSLY
WRIGGLINGLY
WRITING DESK
WRONGDOINGS
WRONGHEADED
WROUGHT IRON

X

XANTHOPHYLL
X CHROMOSOME
XENOGENESIS
XENOGENETIC
XENOGLOSSIA
XENOMORPHIC
XEROGRAPHER
XEROGRAPHIC
XEROMORPHIC
XEROPHILOUS
XEROPHYTISM
XYLOCARPOUS
XYLOGRAPHER
XYLOGRAPHIC
XYLOPHAGOUS
XYLOPHONIST

Y

YACHTSWOMAN
Y CHROMOSOME
YELLOW FEVER
YELLOWKNIFE
YELLOW PAGES
YELLOWSTONE
YEVTUSHENKO
YOUTH HOSTEL
YTTRIFEROUS
YUGOSLAVIAN
YUWAALARAAY

Z

ZANTHOXYLUM
ZEALOUSNESS
ZESTFULNESS
ZHANGJIAKOU
ZINCIFEROUS
ZINCOGRAPHY
ZOOCHEMICAL
ZOOMORPHISM
ZOOPLANKTON
ZOOTECHNICS
ZYGOMORPHIC
ZYGOTICALLY
ZYMOGENESIS
ZYMOTICALLY

12

A	ACCUSATORIAL	AFFILIATIONS	ALPHANUMERIC
ABBREVIATING	ACETALDEHYDE	AFFINITY CARD	ALSTROEMERIA
ABBREVIATION	ACHIEVEMENTS	AFFIRMATIONS	ALTERABILITY
ABELIAN GROUP	ACHILLES' HEEL	AFFIRMATIVES	ALTERCATIONS
ABOLITIONARY	ACHILL ISLAND	AFORETHOUGHT	ALTERNATIONS
ABOLITIONISM	ACHLAMYDEOUS	AFRIKANERDOM	ALTERNATIVES
ABOLITIONIST	ACHLORHYDRIA	AFRO-AMERICAN	ALTHORP HOUSE
ABOMINATIONS	ACKNOWLEDGED	AFTERBURNING	ALTIMETRICAL
ABORTIONISTS	ACKNOWLEDGER	AFTEREFFECTS	AMALGAMATING
ABORTION PILL	ACOUSTICALLY	AFTER THE FACT	AMALGAMATION
ABRACADABRAS	ACQUAINTANCE	AFTERTHOUGHT	AMATEURISHLY
ABSENT MINDED	ACQUIESCENCE	AGAMOGENESIS	AMBASSADRESS
ABSENT-MINDED	ACQUISITIONS	AGAMOGENETIC	AMBIDEXTROUS
ABSOLUTENESS	ACROSTICALLY	AGARICACEOUS	AMBITENDENCY
ABSOLUTE ZERO	ACTINOMETRIC	AGE OF CONSENT	AMBIVALENTLY
ABSORPTIVITY	ACTINOMYCETE	AGGLOMERATED	AMELIORATING
ABSTEMIOUSLY	ADAPTABILITY	AGGLUTINABLE	AMELIORATION
ABSTRACTEDLY	ADDER'S TONGUE	AGGLUTINOGEN	AMELIORATIVE
ABSTRACTIONS	ADDITIONALLY	AGGRAVATIONS	AMERICANISMS
ABSTRACT NOUN	ADHESIVENESS	AGGREGATIONS	AMERICANIZED
ABSTRUSENESS	ADJECTIVALLY	AGGRESSIVELY	AMERICANIZER
ACADEMICALLY	ADJOURNMENTS	AGONY COLUMNS	AMITOTICALLY
ACADEMICIANS	ADJUDICATING	AGORAPHOBICS	AMORTIZATION
ACANTHACEOUS	ADJUDICATION	AGRICULTURAL	AMORTIZEMENT
ACCELERATING	ADJUDICATORS	AGROFORESTRY	AMPHETAMINES
ACCELERATION	ADMINISTERED	AILUROPHILIA	AMPHIBRACHIC
ACCELERATIVE	ADMINISTRATE	AILUROPHOBIA	AMPHICOELOUS
ACCELERATORS	ADSCITITIOUS	AIR COMMODORE	AMPHICTYONIC
ACCENTUATING	ADULTERATING	AIR-CONDITION	AMPHIDIPLOID
ACCENTUATION	ADULTERATION	AIRHOSTESSES	AMPHISBAENIC
ACCESS COURSE	ADUMBRATIONS	AIR TERMINALS	AMPHITHEATRE
ACCIACCATURA	ADVANTAGEOUS	ALCOHOLICITY	AMPHITHECIUM
ACCIDENTALLY	ADVENTITIOUS	ALHAMBRESQUE	AMPHITROPOUS
ACCLAMATIONS	ADVISABILITY	ALICE SPRINGS	AMPULLACEOUS
ACCLIMATIZED	AERIFICATION	ALIENABILITY	AMYGDALOIDAL
ACCLIMATIZER	AERODONETICS	ALIMENTATION	ANACHRONISMS
ACCOMMODATED	AERODYNAMICS	ALIMENTATIVE	ANAESTHETICS
ACCOMPANISTS	AEROEMBOLISM	ALKALIMETRIC	ANAESTHETIST
ACCOMPANYING	AEROMECHANIC	ALL-IMPORTANT	ANAESTHETIZE
ACCOMPLISHED	AERONAUTICAL	ALL-INCLUSIVE	ANAGOGICALLY
ACCOMPLISHER	AERONEUROSIS	ALLITERATION	ANAGRAMMATIC
ACCORDIONIST	AESTHETICIAN	ALLITERATIVE	ANALPHABETIC
ACCOUPLEMENT	AESTHETICISM	ALLOMORPHISM	ANALYTICALLY
ACCOUTREMENT	AETHEREALITY	ALLUSIVENESS	ANAMORPHOSIS
ACCUMULATING	AETIOLOGICAL	ALMIGHTINESS	ANAPHRODISIA
ACCUMULATION	AFFECTATIONS	ALPHABETICAL	ANAPHYLACTIC
ACCUMULATIVE	AFFECTEDNESS	ALPHABETIZER	ANARCHICALLY
ACCUMULATORS	AFFECTIONATE	ALPHA-BLOCKER	ANASTIGMATIC

ANATHEMATIZE	ANTIQUARIANS	ARBORESCENCE	ASTROBIOLOGY
ANATOMICALLY	ANTIRACHITIC	ARBORIZATION	ASTROCOMPASS
ANCHORPERSON	ANTI-SEMITISM	ARCHDEACONRY	ASTROGEOLOGY
ANCIEN REGIME	ANTITHETICAL	ARCHDIOCESAN	ASTROLOGICAL
ANDROSTERONE	ANTONOMASTIC	ARCHDIOCESES	ASTRONAUTICS
ANEMOGRAPHIC	ANURADHAPURA	ARCHEOLOGIES	ASTRONOMICAL
ANEMOPHILOUS	AORISTICALLY	ARCHESPORIAL	ASTROPHYSICS
ANESTHETISTS	APAGOGICALLY	ARCHETYPICAL	ASYMPTOMATIC
ANESTHETIZED	APERIODICITY	ARCHIPELAGIC	ASYNCHRONISM
ANGLO-INDIANS	APHRODISIACS	ARCHIPELAGOS	ASYNCHRONOUS
ANGLOPHILIAC	APICULTURIST	ARCHITECTURE	ATHEROMATOUS
ANGUILLIFORM	APLANOSPHERE	ARCHOPLASMIC	ATHLETE'S FOOT
ANGULARITIES	APOCHROMATIC	ARCTIC CIRCLE	ATHLETICALLY
ANIMADVERTED	APOCYNACEOUS	ARGILLACEOUS	ATHWARTSHIPS
ANIMAL RIGHTS	APOGEOTROPIC	ARISTOCRATIC	ATLANTIC CITY
ANIMATRONICS	APOSTROPHIZE	ARMOURED CARS	ATMOSPHERICS
ANNEXATIONAL	APOTHECARIES	ARMOUR-PLATED	ATOMIC ENERGY
ANNIHILATING	APPALACHIANS	AROMATHERAPY	ATTACHE CASES
ANNIHILATION	APPARATCHIKS	AROMATICALLY	ATTENBOROUGH
ANNIHILATIVE	APPARENTNESS	ARRAIGNMENTS	ATTESTATIONS
ANNOUNCEMENT	APPASSIONATO	ARRANGEMENTS	ATTESTED MILK
ANNUNCIATION	APPEASEMENTS	ARSENOPYRITE	ATTITUDINIZE
ANNUNCIATIVE	APPELLATIONS	ARTESIAN WELL	ATTRACTIVELY
ANTAGONISTIC	APPENDECTOMY	ARTHROPODOUS	ATTRIBUTABLE
ANTAGONIZING	APPENDICITIS	ARTHROSPORIC	AUDIOLOGICAL
ANTANANARIVO	APPENDICULAR	ARTICULATELY	AUDIOMETRIST
ANTECHAMBERS	APPERCEPTION	ARTICULATING	AUGMENTATION
ANTEDILUVIAN	APPERCEPTIVE	ARTICULATION	AUGMENTATIVE
ANTEMERIDIAN	APPERTAINING	ARTICULATORY	AULD LANG SYNE
ANTE MERIDIEM	APPETIZINGLY	ARTIFICIALLY	AUSCULTATION
ANTHOLOGICAL	APPLAUDINGLY	ARTILLERYMAN	AUSPICIOUSLY
ANTHOLOGISTS	APPLICATIONS	ARTISTICALLY	AUSTRALASIAN
ANTHROPOIDAL	APPOGGIATURA	ASCENSION DAY	AUSTRONESIAN
ANTHROPOLOGY	APPOINTMENTS	ASCERTAINING	AUTHENTICATE
ANTI-AIR-CRAFT	APPORTIONING	ASCOMYCETOUS	AUTHENTICITY
ANTICATALYST	APPRAISINGLY	ASH WEDNESDAY	AUTISTICALLY
ANTICIPATING	APPRECIATING	ASKING PRICES	AUTOANTIBODY
ANTICIPATION	APPRECIATION	ASPHYXIATING	AUTOEXPOSURE
ANTICIPATIVE	APPRECIATIVE	ASPHYXIATION	AUTOGRAPHING
ANTICIPATORY	APPREHENDING	ASSASSINATED	AUTOHYPNOSIS
ANTICLERICAL	APPREHENSION	ASSEMBLY LINE	AUTOHYPNOTIC
ANTICLIMAXES	APPREHENSIVE	ASSEVERATING	AUTOMOBILIST
ANTICYCLONES	APPRENTICING	ASSEVERATION	AUTONOMOUSLY
ANTICYCLONIC	APPROACHABLE	ASSIBILATION	AUTOROTATION
ANTIHALATION	APPROPRIABLE	ASSIGNATIONS	AUTOXIDATION
ANTIMACASSAR	APPROPRIATED	ASSIMILATING	AVAILABILITY
ANTIMAGNETIC	APPROXIMATED	ASSIMILATION	AVANT GARDISM
ANTINEUTRINO	APPURTENANCE	ASSIMILATIVE	AVARICIOUSLY
ANTIPARALLEL	A PRETTY PENNY	ASSOCIATIONS	AVICULTURIST
ANTIPARTICLE	APRON STRINGS	ASTONISHMENT	AVITAMINOSIS
ANTIPATHETIC	AQUICULTURAL	ASTOUNDINGLY	AVOGADRO'S LAW
ANTIPERIODIC	ARBITRAGEURS	ASTRINGENTLY	

AWE-INSPIRING
AZATHIOPRINE

B
BABY CARRIAGE
BACCHANALIAN
BACKBENCHERS
BACKBREAKING
BACKHANDEDLY
BACK OF BEYOND
BACK PASSAGES
BACKPEDALING
BACKPEDALLED
BACKROOM BOYS
BACKSLAPPERS
BACKSLAPPING
BACKTRACKING
BACKWARDNESS
BACKWOODSMAN
BACKWOODSMEN
BACTERICIDAL
BACTERIOLOGY
BAGGAGE ROOMS
BAKING POWDER
BALANCED DIET
BALANCE SHEET
BALCONY SCENE
BALL BEARINGS
BALLOTTEMENT
BALNEOLOGIST
BALTIC STATES
BANDARANAIKE
BANDERILLERO
BANDJARMASIN
BANK ACCOUNTS
BANKER'S CARDS
BANKER'S ORDER
BANK HOLIDAYS
BANKRUPTCIES
BANTAMWEIGHT
BARBARIANISM
BARBARICALLY
BARBITURATES
BARLEY SUGARS
BARNSTORMERS
BARNSTORMING
BARORECEPTOR
BARQUISIMETO
BARRANQUILLA
BARREL ORGANS
BASIDIOSPORE
BASTARDIZING

BASTINADOING
BATAN ISLANDS
BATCH PROCESS
BATHING SUITS
BATHYSPHERES
BATTERING RAM
BATTLEFIELDS
BATTLE ROYALS
BEACH BUGGIES
BEACHCOMBERS
BEACONSFIELD
BEAT A RETREAT
BEATIFICALLY
BEAUTY QUEENS
BECHUANALAND
BEDAZZLEMENT
BEDFORDSHIRE
BEGGARLINESS
BEGRUDGINGLY
BEHAVIOURISM
BEHAVIOURIST
BELEAGUERING
BELGIAN CONGO
BELITTLEMENT
BELITTLINGLY
BELLETRISTIC
BELLIGERENCE
BELLIGERENCY
BELLIGERENTS
BELLY BUTTONS
BELLY DANCERS
BELLY-LANDING
BELOW THE BELT
BENEDICTINES
BENEDICTIONS
BENEFACTIONS
BENEFACTRESS
BENEFICENTLY
BENEFICIALLY
BENEVOLENTLY
BENZALDEHYDE
BENZOPHENONE
BENZOQUINONE
BEREAVEMENTS
BERWICKSHIRE
BESPECTACLED
BEVERLY HILLS
BEWILDERMENT
BEWITCHINGLY
BIAURICULATE
BIBLIOGRAPHY
BIBLIOMANIAC

BIBLIOPHILES
BICOLLATERAL
BIELSKO-BIALA
BIFLAGELLATE
BIFURCATIONS
BILHARZIASIS
BILINGUALISM
BILL OF HEALTH
BILL OF LADING
BILL OF RIGHTS
BIOCATALYTIC
BIOCHEMISTRY
BIODIVERSITY
BIOECOLOGIST
BIOFLAVONOID
BIOGEOGRAPHY
BIOGRAPHICAL
BIOLOGICALLY
BIOMECHANICS
BIONOMICALLY
BIOPHYSICIST
BIOSYNTHESIS
BIOSYNTHETIC
BIPROPELLANT
BIRD'S-EYE
 VIEW
BIRD-WATCHERS
BIREFRINGENT
BIRTH CONTROL
BISMUTHINITE
BLABBERMOUTH
BLACK AND
 BLUE
BLACKBALLING
BLACKBERRIES
BLACK COUNTRY
BLACKCURRANT
BLACK ECONOMY
BLACK ENGLISH
BLACKGUARDLY
BLACK-HEARTED
BLACKLEGGING
BLACKLISTING
BLACKMAILERS
BLACKMAILING
BLACK MUSLIMS
BLACK PUDDING
BLADDERWRACK
BLAENAU GWENT
BLAMEFULNESS
BLANK CHEQUES
BLARNEY STONE

BLAST FURNACE
BLASTODERMIC
BLASTOSPHERE
BLINDFOLDING
BLISSFULNESS
BLISTERINGLY
BLOCKBUSTERS
BLOCK LETTERS
BLOEMFONTEIN
BLOOD BROTHER
BLOODLETTING
BLOODSTAINED
BLOODSTREAMS
BLOODSUCKERS
BLOODTHIRSTY
BLOOD VESSELS
BLOODY-MINDED
BLUE-EYED BOYS
BLUESTOCKING
BLUNDERINGLY
BLUSTERINGLY
BOARDING CARD
BOASTFULNESS
BOBSLEIGHING
BODY LANGUAGE
BODY SNATCHER
BODY STOCKING
BOILING POINT
BOISTEROUSLY
BOLSTERINGLY
BOMBACACEOUS
BOMBARDMENTS
BOOBY-TRAPPED
BOOK-LEARNING
BOOMERANGING
BOROSILICATE
BOTTOM DRAWER
BOUGAINVILLE
BOUNCY CASTLE
BOWDLERIZING
BOWLING ALLEY
BOWLING GREEN
BRACHYLOGOUS
BRACKISHNESS
BRAINS TRUSTS
BRAIN SURGEON
BRAINTEASERS
BRAINWASHING
BREADWINNERS
BREAKFASTING
BREASTSTROKE
BREATHALYSER

BREATHALYZER	CALLIGRAPHER	CARPOLOGICAL	CHALCOGRAPHY
BREATHTAKING	CALLIGRAPHIC	CARPOPHAGOUS	CHALCOPYRITE
BREECHLOADER	CALLISTHENIC	CARRIAGEWAYS	CHAMBERLAINS
BREWER'S YEAST	CALL OF NATURE	CARTE BLANCHE	CHAMBERMAIDS
BRIGHTSIZING	CALORIMETRIC	CARTOGRAPHER	CHAMBER MUSIC
BRILLIANTINE	CALUMNIATING	CARTOGRAPHIC	CHAMPIONSHIP
BRINKMANSHIP	CALUMNIATION	CARTWHEELING	CHANGCHIAKOW
BRISTLE-GRASS	CAMELOPARDUS	CARVING FORKS	CHANGELESSLY
BROADCASTERS	CAMI-KNICKERS	CARVING KNIFE	CHANGE OF LIFE
BROADCASTING	CAMOUFLAGING	CASH AND CARRY	CHANGING ROOM
BRONCHOSCOPE	CAMP FOLLOWER	CASH REGISTER	CHAPLAINCIES
BRONCHOSCOPY	CANALIZATION	CASTELLATION	CHAPTERHOUSE
BRONCOBUSTER	CANCELLATION	CASTING VOTES	CHARACTERFUL
BRONTOSAURUS	CANDELABRUMS	CATACHRESTIC	CHARACTERIZE
BRONZE MEDALS	CANDLESTICKS	CATADIOPTRIC	CHARGE NURSES
BROTHERHOODS	CANDY-STRIPED	CATASTROPHES	CHARGE SHEETS
BROTHER-IN-LAW	CANNIBALIZED	CATASTROPHIC	CHARLATANISM
BROWNIE POINT	CANNON FODDER	CATCHPHRASES	CHARNEL HOUSE
BUENAVENTURA	CANONIZATION	CATECHETICAL	CHASTISEMENT
BUFFER STATES	CANTABRIGIAN	CATEGORIZING	CHASTITY BELT
BUFFER STOCKS	CANTANKEROUS	CATERPILLARS	CHATTERBOXES
BULLDOG CLIPS	CAPABILITIES	CATERWAULING	CHAUFFEURING
BULLET-HEADED	CAPACITATION	CAT'S WHISKERS	CHAUVINISTIC
BULLFIGHTERS	CAPARISONNED	CAULIFLOWERS	CHECKERBERRY
BULLFIGHTING	CAPE PROVINCE	CAUSE CELEBRE	CHECKERBLOOM
BULLHEADEDLY	CAPERCAILLIE	CAUTIOUSNESS	CHEERFULNESS
BULLSHITTING	CAPILLACEOUS	CAVEAT EMPTOR	CHEERLEADERS
BULL TERRIERS	CAPITAL GAINS	CELEBRATIONS	CHEESEBURGER
BUNSEN BURNER	CAPITALIZING	CEMENT MIXERS	CHEESEPARING
BUREAUCRATIC	CAPITULATING	CENSORIOUSLY	CHEESE-PARING
BURGLAR ALARM	CAPITULATION	CENTENARIANS	CHEFS D'OEUVRE
BURSERACEOUS	CAPRICIOUSLY	CENTRALIZING	CHEMOSPHERIC
BUSINESSLIKE	CAPTIOUSNESS	CENTRAL KAROO	CHEMOTHERAPY
BUSINESS SUIT	CARAVANSERAI	CENTREPIECES	CHEMOTROPISM
BUTTERSCOTCH	CARBOHYDRATE	CENTROCLINAL	CHEQUERBOARD
BUTTONHOLING	CARBONACEOUS	CENTROSPHERE	CHERUBICALLY
BUYER'S MARKET	CARBON COPIES	CENTUPLICATE	CHESHIRE CATS
BYELORUSSIAN	CARBON DATING	CEPHALOMETER	CHESTERFIELD
	CARBON PAPERS	CEPHALOMETRY	CHIAROSCUROS
C	CARBURETTORS	CEPHALOPODAN	CHIEF JUSTICE
CABBAGE WHITE	CARCINOGENIC	CEPHALOPODIC	CHIEF OF STAFF
CABIN CRUISER	CARD-CARRYING	CEREMONIALLY	CHILDBEARING
CABINET-MAKER	CARDIOGRAPHY	CEROGRAPHIST	CHILD BENEFIT
CABLE RAILWAY	CARDIOLOGIST	CERRO DE PASCO	CHILDISHNESS
CACHINNATION	CARDIOMEGALY	CERTIFICATED	CHILDMINDERS
CAENOGENESIS	CARELESSNESS	CERTIFICATES	CHILDMINDING
CAENOGENETIC	CARIBBEAN SEA	CHAIN LETTERS	CHILD PRODIGY
CALAMITOUSLY	CARICATURING	CHAIN-SMOKERS	CHILPANCINGO
CALCULATIONS	CARICATURIST	CHAIN-SMOKING	CHIMNEYPIECE
CALENDAR YEAR	CARILLONNEUR	CHAIRMANSHIP	CHIMNEYSTACK
CALIBRATIONS	CARPETBAGGER	CHAIRPERSONS	CHIMNEYSWEEP
CALISTHENICS	CARPET KNIGHT	CHAISE LONGUE	CHIROGRAPHER

CHIROGRAPHIC	CIRCULAR SAWS	CLOTHESHORSE	COLOURLESSLY
CHIROPODISTS	CIRCUMCISING	CLOTHESLINES	COLOUR SCHEME
CHIROPRACTIC	CIRCUMCISION	CLOTHES-PRESS	COLUMNIATION
CHIROPRACTOR	CIRCUMFLUOUS	CLOTTED CREAM	COMBINATIONS
CHITCHATTING	CIRCUMFUSION	CLOVE HITCHES	COMBUSTIBLES
CHITTERLINGS	CIRCUMNUTATE	CLOVERLEAVES	COME A CROPPER
CHIVALROUSLY	CIRCUMSCRIBE	CLOWNISHNESS	COME-UPPANCES
CHLORAMBUCIL	CIRCUMSTANCE	CLUB SANDWICH	COMFORTINGLY
CHLORENCHYMA	CIRCUMVENTED	CLUSTER BOMBS	COMMANDEERED
CHLORINATING	CIRCUMVENTER	COACERVATION	COMMANDMENTS
CHLORINATION	CIRROCUMULUS	COACHBUILDER	COMMEMORATED
CHLOROFORMED	CIRROSTRATUS	COACH STATION	COMMEMORATOR
CHLOROHYDRIN	CITIZENS' BAND	COALITIONIST	COMMENCEMENT
CHLOROPICRIN	CITRICULTURE	COALSCUTTLES	COMMENDATION
CHOCOLATE BOX	CIVIL DEFENCE	COBBLESTONES	COMMENDATORY
CHOIRMASTERS	CIVILIZATION	COCKFIGHTING	COMMENSALISM
CHOIR SCHOOLS	CIVIL LIBERTY	COCKLESHELLS	COMMENSURATE
CHOLERICALLY	CIVIL SERVANT	COCONUT SHIES	COMMENTARIAL
CHONDRIOSOME	CIVIL SERVICE	COCOS ISLANDS	COMMENTARIES
CHOREOGRAPHS	CLAIRVOYANCE	CODEPENDENCY	COMMENTATING
CHOREOGRAPHY	CLAIRVOYANTS	CODIFICATION	COMMENTATORS
CHOROGRAPHER	CLANGOROUSLY	COEFFICIENTS	COMMERCIALLY
CHOROGRAPHIC	CLANNISHNESS	COELENTERATE	COMMISERATED
CHRISTCHURCH	CLAPPERBOARD	COENESTHESIA	COMMISERATOR
CHRISTENINGS	CLARINETTIST	COENESTHESIS	COMMISSARIAL
CHRISTIAN ERA	CLASS ACTIONS	COENESTHETIC	COMMISSARIAT
CHRISTIANITY	CLASSICALITY	COERCIVENESS	COMMISSARIES
CHRISTIANIZE	CLASSICISTIC	COFFEE BREAKS	COMMISSIONAL
CHRISTMAS BOX	CLASSIFIABLE	COFFEE HOUSES	COMMISSIONED
CHRISTMAS EVE	CLASSIFIED AD	COFFEE KLATCH	COMMISSIONER
CHRIST'S-THORN	CLAUDICATION	COFFEE TABLES	COMMITTEEMAN
CHROMATICISM	CLEAR-SIGHTED	COHABITATION	COMMITTEEMEN
CHROMATICITY	CLEFT PALATES	COHESIVENESS	COMMODIOUSLY
CHROMATOGRAM	CLERESTORIED	COINCIDENCES	COMMON MARKET
CHROME YELLOW	CLERESTORIES	COINCIDENTAL	COMMONPLACES
CHROMOPHORIC	CLERK OF WORKS	COLD SHOULDER	COMMONWEALTH
CHROMOSPHERE	CLIENT STATES	COLEOPTEROUS	COMMUNICABLE
CHRONOGRAPHS	CLIFFHANGERS	COLLABORATED	COMMUNICABLY
CHRONOLOGIES	CLIFFHANGING	COLLABORATOR	COMMUNICANTS
CHRONOLOGIST	CLIMACTERICS	COLLECTIVELY	COMMUNICATED
CHRONOMETERS	CLIMATICALLY	COLLECTIVISM	COMMUNICATOR
CHRONOMETRIC	CLIMATOLOGIC	COLLECTIVIST	COMMUNIONIST
CHRONOSCOPIC	CLIMBING IRON	COLLECTIVITY	COMMUTATIONS
CHURCHWARDEN	CLINKER-BUILT	COLLECTIVIZE	COMPACT DISCS
CHURLISHNESS	CLIQUISHNESS	COLLECTORATE	COMPANIONATE
CHURRASCARIA	CLODDISHNESS	COLLOCATIONS	COMPANIONWAY
CHYMOTRYPSIN	CLOSE-CROPPED	COLLOIDALITY	COMPARTMENTS
CINCHONIDINE	CLOSED SEASON	COLLOQUIALLY	COMPASS POINT
CINEMATHEQUE	CLOSE-GRAINED	COLLYWOBBLES	COMPATRIOTIC
CIRCUITOUSLY	CLOSE SEASONS	COLONIALISTS	COMPELLINGLY
CIRCULARIZED	CLOSING PRICE	COLONIZATION	COMPENSATING
CIRCULARIZER	CLOSING TIMES	COLORIMETRIC	COMPENSATION

COMPENSATIVE
COMPENSATORY
COMPETITIONS
COMPILATIONS
COMPLACENTLY
COMPLAINANTS
COMPLAISANCE
COMPLEMENTED
COMPLETENESS
COMPLEXITIES
COMPLICATING
COMPLICATION
COMPLIMENTED
COMPONENTIAL
COMPOSITIONS
COMPOS MENTIS
COMPREHENDED
COMPRESSIBLE
COMPROMISING
COMPTROLLERS
COMPULSIVELY
COMPULSORILY
COMPUNCTIOUS
COMPUTATIONS
COMPUTERIZED
CONCATENATED
CONCELEBRATE
CONCENTRATED
CONCENTRATES
CONCENTRATOR
CONCEPTIONAL
CONCEPTUALLY
CONCERTGOERS
CONCERT GRAND
CONCERTINAED
CONCERT PITCH
CONCHIFEROUS
CONCHOLOGIST
CONCILIATING
CONCILIATION
CONCILIATORS
CONCILIATORY
CONCLUSIVELY
CONCOMITANCE
CONCOMITANTS
CONCORDANCES
CONCRESCENCE
CONCUPISCENT
CONCURRENCES
CONCURRENTLY
CONDEMNATION
CONDEMNATORY

CONDENSATION
CONDESCENDED
CONDITIONERS
CONDITIONING
CONDOMINIUMS
CONDUCTIVITY
CONDUPLICATE
CONFABULATED
CONFABULATOR
CONFECTIONER
CONFEDERATED
CONFEDERATES
CONFERENTIAL
CONFESSIONAL
CONFIDENTIAL
CONFINEMENTS
CONFIRMATION
CONFIRMATORY
CONFISCATING
CONFISCATION
CONFISCATORY
CONFORMATION
CONFOUNDEDLY
CONFRATERNAL
CONFUCIANISM
CONFUCIANIST
CONFUTATIONS
CONGENIALITY
CONGENITALLY
CONGLOBATION
CONGLOMERATE
CONGLUTINANT
CONGLUTINATE
CONGRATULATE
CONGREGATING
CONGREGATION
CONGREGATIVE
CONIDIOPHORE
CONJECTURING
CONJUGATIONS
CONJUNCTIONS
CONJUNCTIVAL
CONJUNCTIVES
CONJUNCTURAL
CONJUNCTURES
CONNECTIONAL
CONNING TOWER
CONNOISSEURS
CONNOTATIONS
CONNUBIALITY
CONQUISTADOR
CONSCIONABLE

CONSCRIPTING
CONSCRIPTION
CONSECRATING
CONSECRATION
CONSECRATORY
CONSENTIENCE
CONSEQUENCES
CONSEQUENTLY
CONSERVATION
CONSERVATISM
CONSERVATIVE
CONSERVATORY
CONSIDERABLE
CONSIDERABLY
CONSIGNATION
CONSIGNMENTS
CONSISTENTLY
CONSISTORIAL
CONSOCIATION
CONSOLATIONS
CONSOLIDATED
CONSOLIDATOR
CONSPECTUSES
CONSPIRACIES
CONSPIRATORS
CONSTABULARY
CONSTIPATION
CONSTITUENCY
CONSTITUENTS
CONSTITUTING
CONSTITUTION
CONSTITUTIVE
CONSTRAINING
CONSTRICTING
CONSTRICTION
CONSTRICTIVE
CONSTRICTORS
CONSTRUCTING
CONSTRUCTION
CONSTRUCTIVE
CONSTRUCTORS
CONSULTATION
CONSULTATIVE
CONSUMMATELY
CONSUMMATING
CONSUMMATION
CONSUMMATIVE
CONSUMPTIONS
CONSUMPTIVES
CONTAGIOUSLY
CONTAINERIZE
CONTAMINANTS

CONTAMINATED
CONTAMINATOR
CONTEMPLATED
CONTEMPLATOR
CONTEMPORARY
CONTEMPORIZE
CONTEMPTIBLE
CONTEMPTIBLY
CONTEMPTUOUS
CONTENTIONAL
CONTERMINOUS
CONTESTATION
CONTEXTUALLY
CONTIGUOUSLY
CONTINENTALS
CONTINGENTLY
CONTINUALITY
CONTINUATION
CONTINUATIVE
CONTINUINGLY
CONTINUOUSLY
CONTORTIONAL
CONTRABASSES
CONTRACTIBLE
CONTRACTIONS
CONTRADICTED
CONTRADICTER
CONTRAPTIONS
CONTRAPUNTAL
CONTRARINESS
CONTRARIWISE
CONTRAVENING
CONTRIBUTING
CONTRIBUTION
CONTRIBUTIVE
CONTRIBUTORS
CONTRIBUTORY
CONTRIVANCES
CONTROLLABLE
CONTROVERTER
CONTUMACIOUS
CONTUMELIOUS
CONURBATIONS
CONVALESCENT
CONVALESCING
CONVECTIONAL
CONVENIENCES
CONVENIENTLY
CONVENTICLES
CONVENTIONAL
CONVERGENCES
CONVERSATION

CONVERSIONAL
CONVERTIBLES
CONVEYANCING
CONVEYER BELT
CONVINCINGLY
CONVIVIALITY
CONVOCATIONS
CONVOLUTEDLY
CONVOLUTIONS
CONVULSIVELY
COOKERY BOOKS
COOKING APPLE
COOPERATIVES
COORDINATELY
COORDINATING
COORDINATION
COPOLYMERIZE
COPROPHAGOUS
COPROPHILOUS
COPTIC CHURCH
COQUETTISHLY
CORDUROY ROAD
CORESPONDENT
CORNERSTONES
CORN EXCHANGE
CORNISH PASTY
COROLLACEOUS
CORPORALSHIP
CORPORATIONS
CORPOREALITY
CORRECTITUDE
CORRECTIVELY
CORRELATIONS
CORRELATIVES
CORRESPONDED
CORROBORATED
CORROBORATOR
CORRUGATIONS
COSMETICALLY
COSMETICIANS
COSMOLOGICAL
COSMOPOLITAN
COSTERMONGER
COST OF LIVING
COST THE EARTH
COTYLEDONARY
COTYLEDONOUS
COUNTENANCED
COUNTENANCES
COUNTERACTED
COUNTERBLAST
COUNTERCHECK

COUNTERCLAIM
COUNTERFOILS
COUNTERPANES
COUNTERPARTS
COUNTERPARTY
COUNTERPOINT
COUNTERPOISE
COUNTERPROOF
COUNTERPUNCH
COUNTERSHAFT
COUNTERSIGNS
COUNTERTENOR
COUNTRY CLUBS
COUNTRY DANCE
COUNTRY SEATS
COUNTY COURTS
COUPS DE GRACE
COURAGEOUSLY
COURT MARTIAL
COURT-MARTIAL
COVENT GARDEN
COVER CHARGES
COVERED WAGON
COVETOUSNESS
COWARDLINESS
CRACKBRAINED
CRANIOLOGIST
CRANIOMETRIC
CRASH BARRIER
CRASH HELMETS
CRASH LANDING
CREEPY-CRAWLY
CREMATIONISM
CREMATIONIST
CREMATORIUMS
CRENELLATION
CRISSCROSSED
CRISSCROSSES
CROP-SPRAYING
CROSSBENCHER
CROSS BENCHER
CROSSBENCHES
CROSSCHECKED
CROSS-COUNTRY
CROSSCURRENT
CROSS-DRESSER
CROSS-EXAMINE
CROSS-GRAINED
CROSSPATCHES
CROSS-SECTION
CROWNED HEADS
CROWN PRINCES

CRUSH BARRIER
CRYOPLANKTON
CRYPTANALYST
CRYPTOGRAPHY
CRYPTOLOGIST
CRYSTAL BALLS
CRYSTAL CLEAR
CRYSTAL GAZER
CRYSTALLITIC
CRYSTALLIZED
CUCKOO CLOCKS
CUMULATIVELY
CUMULONIMBUS
CUPBOARD LOVE
CURARIZATION
CURATORSHIPS
CURMUDGEONLY
CURTAILMENTS
CURTAIN CALLS
CURVACEOUSLY
CUT AND THRUST
CUTTLEFISHES
CYCLOPENTANE
CYCLOSTOMATE
CYCLOSTYLING
CYSTICERCOID
CYTOCHEMICAL
CYTOGENETICS
CYTOSKELETON
CYTOTAXONOMY
CZECHOSLOVAK

D

DACTYLICALLY
DAEMONICALLY
DAIRY FARMERS
DANGER SIGNAL
DANISH PASTRY
DARBY AND JOAN
DAY NURSERIES
DEACTIVATION
DEAF-MUTENESS
DEATH FUTURES
DEATH RATTLES
DEATH WARRANT
DEBARKATIONS
DEBAUCHERIES
DEBILITATING
DEBILITATION
DEBILITATIVE
DEBT OF HONOUR
DECALCOMANIA

DECALESCENCE
DECAPITATING
DECAPITATION
DECARBONIZER
DECASYLLABIC
DECASYLLABLE
DECELERATING
DECELERATION
DECENTRALIST
DECENTRALIZE
DECIMALIZING
DECIPHERABLE
DECIPHERMENT
DECISION TREE
DECISIVENESS
DECLAMATIONS
DECLARATIONS
DECLASSIFIED
DECLENSIONAL
DECLINATIONS
DECLINOMETER
DECOLLETAGES
DECOLONIZING
DECOLORATION
DECOMMISSION
DECOMPOSABLE
DECOMPRESSED
DECONGESTANT
DECONTROLLED
DECORATIVELY
DECORTICATOR
DEDUCIBILITY
DEERSTALKERS
DE-ESCALATING
DE-ESCALATION
DEFAMATORILY
DEFICIENCIES
DEFINITENESS
DEFINITIONAL
DEFINITIVELY
DEFLAGRATION
DEFLATIONARY
DEFLATIONIST
DEFLOCCULATE
DEFORMATIONS
DEFORMEDNESS
DEFRAUDATION
DEGENERATING
DEGENERATION
DEGENERATIVE
DEGRADATIONS
DEHUMANIZING

DEHUMIDIFIER	DEONTOLOGIST	DETHRONEMENT	DILATATIONAL
DEJECTEDNESS	DEPARTMENTAL	DETOXICATION	DILATOMETRIC
DELAMINATION	DEPENDENCIES	DETRUNCATION	DILATORINESS
DELIBERATELY	DEPILATORIES	DETUMESCENCE	DILETTANTISH
DELIBERATING	DEPOLITICIZE	DEUTERANOPIA	DILETTANTISM
DELIBERATION	DEPOPULATING	DEUTERANOPIC	DILLYDALLIED
DELIBERATIVE	DEPOPULATION	DEUTOPLASMIC	DIMINISHABLE
DELICATESSEN	DEPORTATIONS	DEUTSCHE MARK	DIMINISHMENT
DELIGHTFULLY	DEPOSITORIES	DEUTSCHMARKS	DINING TABLES
DELIMITATION	DEPRAVEDNESS	DEVALUATIONS	DINNER JACKET
DELIMITATIVE	DEPRECIATING	DEVELOPMENTS	DIOPTRICALLY
DELIQUESCENT	DEPRECIATION	DEVIATIONISM	DIPHTHERITIC
DELITESCENCE	DEPRECIATORY	DEVIATIONIST	DIPHTHONGIZE
DELTIOLOGIST	DEPREDATIONS	DEVILISHNESS	DIPLOBLASTIC
DEMAGNETIZED	DEPRESSINGLY	DEVIL-MAY-CARE	DIPLOCARDIAC
DEMAGNETIZER	DEPRIVATIONS	DEVITALIZING	DIPLOMATISTS
DEMENTEDNESS	DERACINATION	DEXTROGYRATE	DIPROPELLANT
DEMILITARIZE	DERANGEMENTS	DIABOLICALLY	DIPSOMANIACS
DEMIMONDAINE	DEREGULATING	DIAGEOTROPIC	DIRECT DEBITS
DEMOCRATIZED	DEREGULATION	DIAGRAMMATIC	DIRECT OBJECT
DEMODULATION	DERELICTIONS	DIALECTICIAN	DIRECTORATES
DEMOGRAPHERS	DERESTRICTED	DIALECTOLOGY	DIRECTORSHIP
DEMOGRAPHICS	DERISIVENESS	DIALLING CODE	DIRECT SPEECH
DEMOLISHMENT	DERIVATIONAL	DIALLING TONE	DIRIGIBILITY
DEMONETIZING	DERIVATIVELY	DIALYTICALLY	DISABILITIES
DEMONIACALLY	DERMATOPHYTE	DIAMAGNETISM	DISABLEMENTS
DEMONOLOGIST	DEROGATORILY	DIAPOPHYSIAL	DISACCHARIDE
DEMONOPOLIZE	DESALINATING	DIARTHRODIAL	DISADVANTAGE
DEMONSTRABLE	DESALINATION	DIASTROPHISM	DISAFFECTION
DEMONSTRABLY	DESCRIPTIONS	DIATHERMANCY	DISAFFILIATE
DEMONSTRATED	DESEGREGATED	DIATOMACEOUS	DISAGGREGATE
DEMONSTRATOR	DESENSITIZED	DIATONICALLY	DISAGREEABLE
DEMOTIVATING	DESENSITIZER	DIAZOMETHANE	DISAGREEABLY
DEMOTIVATION	DESERVEDNESS	DIBRANCHIATE	DISAGREEMENT
DEMYSTIFYING	DESIDERATION	DICARBOXYLIC	DISALLOWABLE
DENATURALIZE	DESIDERATIVE	DICHROMATISM	DISALLOWANCE
DENATURATION	DESIGNATIONS	DICHROSCOPIC	DISAMBIGUATE
DENBIGHSHIRE	DESIRABILITY	DICTATORSHIP	DISANNULMENT
DENDROLOGIST	DESPAIRINGLY	DICTIONARIES	DISAPPEARING
DENG XIAOPING	DESPOLIATION	DIDACTICALLY	DISAPPOINTED
DENICOTINIZE	DESPONDENTLY	DIENCEPHALIC	DISAPPOINTER
DENOMINATING	DESPOTICALLY	DIENCEPHALON	DISAPPROVING
DENOMINATION	DESQUAMATION	DIESEL ENGINE	DISARRANGING
DENOMINATIVE	DESSERTSPOON	DIETETICALLY	DISASSEMBLER
DENOMINATORS	DESSERT WINES	DIFFERENTIAL	DISASSOCIATE
DENOUNCEMENT	DESTABILIZED	DIFFICULTIES	DISASTROUSLY
DENSITOMETER	DESTINATIONS	DIGITAL CLOCK	DISBELIEVERS
DENSITOMETRY	DESTRUCTIBLE	DIGITAL WATCH	DISBELIEVING
DENTAL PLATES	DESULPHURIZE	DIGITIZATION	DISBURSEMENT
DENTILINGUAL	DETERIORATED	DIGRESSIONAL	DISCIPLESHIP
DENUNCIATION	DETERMINABLE	DILAPIDATION	DISCIPLINARY
DENUNCIATORY	DETERMINANTS	DILATABILITY	DISCIPLINING

DISCLAMATION	DISINTERMENT	DISTILLERIES	DOUBLE DAGGER
DISCOGRAPHER	DISINTERRING	DISTINCTIONS	DOUBLE-DATING
DISCOLOURING	DISJOINTEDLY	DISTINCTNESS	DOUBLE-DEALER
DISCOMFITING	DISLOCATIONS	DISTORTIONAL	DOUBLE-DECKER
DISCOMFITURE	DISLODGEMENT	DISTRACTEDLY	DOUBLE-DOTTED
DISCOMMODING	DISLOYALTIES	DISTRACTIBLE	DOUBLE FAULTS
DISCOMMODITY	DISMEMBERING	DISTRACTIONS	DOUBLE-GLAZED
DISCOMPOSING	DISMOUNTABLE	DISTRAINABLE	DOUBLE-HEADER
DISCOMPOSURE	DISOBEDIENCE	DISTRAINMENT	DOUBLE-PARKED
DISCONCERTED	DISOPERATION	DISTRIBUTARY	DOUBLE-TALKED
DISCONNECTED	DISORGANIZED	DISTRIBUTING	DOUBLE-TONGUE
DISCONNECTER	DISORGANIZER	DISTRIBUTION	DOUGHNUTTING
DISCONSOLATE	DISORIENTATE	DISTRIBUTIVE	DOWN PAYMENTS
DISCONTENTED	DISPENSARIES	DISTRIBUTORS	DOWNSHIFTING
DISCONTINUED	DISPENSATION	DISTURBANCES	DOWN SHIFTING
DISCORDANTLY	DISPENSATORY	DITTOGRAPHIC	DRACONIANISM
DISCOTHEQUES	DISPIRITEDLY	DIURETICALLY	DRACONICALLY
DISCOUNTABLE	DISPLACEABLE	DIVARICATION	DRAG ONE'S
DISCOURAGING	DISPLACEMENT	DIVERSIFYING	FEET
DISCOURTEOUS	DISPOSITIONS	DIVERSIONARY	DRAMATICALLY
DISCOVERABLE	DISPOSSESSED	DIVERTICULAR	DRAMATIZABLE
DISCOVERTURE	DISPOSSESSOR	DIVERTICULUM	DRAUGHTBOARD
DISCREDITING	DISPUTATIONS	DIVERTIMENTO	DRAWING BOARD
DISCREETNESS	DISPUTATIOUS	DIVINGBOARDS	DRAWING ROOMS
DISCRETENESS	DISQUALIFIED	DIVINIZATION	DREADFULNESS
DISCRIMINANT	DISQUALIFIER	DIVISIBILITY	DREADNOUGHTS
DISCRIMINATE	DISQUIETEDLY	DIVISIVENESS	DRESS CIRCLES
DISCURSIVELY	DISQUISITION	DOCTRINALITY	DRESSING DOWN
DISCUSSIONAL	DISREGARDFUL	DOCTRINARIAN	DRESSING GOWN
DISDAINFULLY	DISREGARDING	DODECAHEDRAL	DRESSING ROOM
DISEMBARKING	DISRELISHING	DODECAHEDRON	DRY BATTERIES
DISEMBARRASS	DISREPUTABLE	DODECAPHONIC	DUCKING STOOL
DISEMBOWELED	DISREPUTABLY	DOGMATICALLY	DUMBFOUNDING
DISENCHANTED	DISRUPTIVELY	DO-IT-YOURSELF	DUMORTIERITE
DISENCHANTER	DISSATISFIED	DOMESDAY BOOK	DUTCH AUCTION
DISENDOWMENT	DISSEMBLANCE	DOMESTICABLE	DUTCH COURAGE
DISENTANGLED	DISSEMINATED	DOMESTICALLY	DUTY-FREE SHOP
DISESTABLISH	DISSEMINATOR	DOMESTICATED	DWARFISHNESS
DISFORESTING	DISSENTIENCE	DOMESTICATOR	DYNAMOMETRIC
DISFRANCHISE	DISSERTATION	DOMINO EFFECT	DYSTELEOLOGY
DISGORGEMENT	DISSEVERANCE	DONKEY JACKET	
DISGUSTINGLY	DISSIMILARLY	DONKEY'S YEARS	**E**
DISHEVELMENT	DISSIMULATED	DOORKNOCKERS	EAGER BEAVERS
DISHONOURING	DISSIMULATOR	DOORSTEPPING	EARSPLITTING
DISINCENTIVE	DISSOCIATING	DOORSTOPPERS	EARTHSHAKING
DISINFECTANT	DISSOCIATION	DORSIVENTRAL	EAST AYRSHIRE
DISINFECTING	DISSOCIATIVE	DORSOVENTRAL	EAST BERLINER
DISINFECTION	DISSOLUTIONS	DOUBLE-ACTING	EASTER CACTUS
DISINFLATION	DISSYMMETRIC	DOUBLE AGENTS	EASTER ISLAND
DISINGENUOUS	DISTEMPERING	DOUBLE BASSES	EASTER-LEDGES
DISINHERITED	DISTILLATION	DOUBLE-BEDDED	EAST FLANDERS
DISINTEGRATE	DISTILLATORY	DOUBLE BLUFFS	EAST GERMANIC

EAST KILBRIDE	ELECTRICIANS	EMPHATICALLY	ENTEROKINASE
EASY ON THE	ELECTRIFYING	EMPLACEMENTS	ENTERPRISING
EYE	ELECTROCUTED	EMULSIFIABLE	ENTERTAINERS
EAT HUMBLE PIE	ELECTROGRAPH	ENANTIOMORPH	ENTERTAINING
EATING APPLES	ELECTROLYSER	ENARTHRODIAL	ENTHRONEMENT
EAT ONE'S	ELECTROLYSIS	ENCEPHALITIC	ENTHUSIASTIC
WORDS	ELECTROLYTES	ENCEPHALITIS	ENTHYMEMATIC
EAU DE COLOGNE	ELECTROLYTIC	ENCHANTMENTS	ENTICINGNESS
EAVESDROPPED	ELECTROMETER	ENCIPHERMENT	ENTOMOLOGIST
EAVESDROPPER	ELECTROMETRY	ENCIRCLEMENT	ENTOMOLOGIZE
EBULLIOSCOPY	ELECTRONVOLT	ENCLITICALLY	ENTRANCEMENT
ECCENTRICITY	ELECTROPHONE	ENCOMPASSING	ENTRANCINGLY
ECCLESIASTIC	ELECTROPLATE	ENCOUNTERING	ENTREATINGLY
ECCLESIOLOGY	ELECTROSCOPE	ENCROACHMENT	ENTRENCHMENT
ECHINOCOCCUS	ELECTROSHOCK	ENCRUSTATION	ENTREPRENEUR
ECHINODERMAL	ELECTROTONIC	ENCUMBRANCER	ENUMERATIONS
ECHOLOCATION	ELECTROTONUS	ENCUMBRANCES	ENVIABLENESS
ECLECTICALLY	ELECTROTYPER	ENCYCLOPEDIA	ENVIRONMENTS
ECLIPTICALLY	ELEEMOSYNARY	ENCYCLOPEDIC	ENVISAGEMENT
ECOLOGICALLY	ELEPHANT'S-EAR	ENDAMAGEMENT	ENZOOTICALLY
ECONOMETRICS	ELEVENTH HOUR	ENDANGERMENT	ENZYMOLOGIST
ECONOMICALLY	ELIZABETHANS	ENDEAVOURING	EOSINOPHILIC
ECOTERRORIST	ELLIPTICALLY	ENDOCARDITIC	EPENCEPHALIC
ECOTYPICALLY	ELOCUTIONARY	ENDOCARDITIS	EPENCEPHALON
ECSTATICALLY	ELOCUTIONIST	ENDOMORPHISM	EPHEMERALITY
ECTOPARASITE	ELOQUENTNESS	ENDOPARASITE	EPICUREANISM
ECUMENICALLY	ELYSEE PALACE	ENDORSEMENTS	EPICYCLOIDAL
EDACIOUSNESS	EMANCIPATING	ENDOSKELETAL	EPIDEMIOLOGY
EDITORIALIST	EMANCIPATION	ENDOSKELETON	EPIGLOTTIDES
EDITORIALIZE	EMANCIPATIVE	ENDOTHELIOID	EPIGLOTTISES
EDULCORATION	EMANCIPATORY	ENDOTHELIOMA	EPIGRAMMATIC
EFFECTUALITY	EMARGINATION	ENDOTHERMISM	EPIMORPHOSIS
EFFECTUATING	EMASCULATING	ENDURABILITY	EPISCOPALIAN
EFFECTUATION	EMASCULATION	ENERGETICIST	EPISCOPALISM
EFFEMINATELY	EMASCULATIVE	ENFEEBLEMENT	EPISODICALLY
EFFERVESCENT	EMBARKATIONS	ENFRANCHISED	EPISTEMOLOGY
EFFERVESCING	EMBARRASSING	ENFRANCHISER	EPITHALAMIUM
EFFLORESCENT	EMBELLISHING	ENGAGINGNESS	EQUALITARIAN
EFFORTLESSLY	EMBEZZLEMENT	ENGENDERMENT	EQUALIZATION
EFFUSIOMETER	EMBITTERMENT	ENGINE DRIVER	EQUATABILITY
EFFUSIVENESS	EMBLAZONMENT	ENGLISH HORNS	EQUESTRIENNE
EGOISTICALLY	EMBRANCHMENT	ENGLISHWOMAN	EQUIDISTANCE
EGYPTOLOGIST	EMBROCATIONS	ENGRAFTATION	EQUILIBRATOR
EISTEDDFODIC	EMBROIDERIES	ENGROSSINGLY	EQUIPOLLENCE
EJACULATIONS	EMBROIDERING	ENHANCEMENTS	EQUIVALENTLY
EJECTOR SEATS	EMBRYOLOGIST	ENLARGEMENTS	EQUIVOCALITY
ELABORATIONS	EMIGRATIONAL	ENLIGHTENING	EQUIVOCATING
ELASMOBRANCH	EMOTIONALISM	ENLIVENINGLY	EQUIVOCATION
ELASTICATION	EMOTIONALIST	ENORMOUSNESS	EQUIVOCATORY
ELASTIC BANDS	EMOTIONALITY	ENSHRINEMENT	ERGASTOPLASM
ELECTRICALLY	EMOTIONALIZE	ENSILABILITY	ERYTHROBLAST
ELECTRIC EYES	EMPATHICALLY	ENTANGLEMENT	ERYTHROCYTIC

ERYTHROMYCIN
ESCAPE CLAUSE
ESCAPOLOGIST
ESCUTCHEONED
ESOTERICALLY
ESSENTIALISM
ESSENTIALIST
ESSENTIALITY
ESTABLISHING
ESTATE AGENCY
ESTATE AGENTS
ESTHETICALLY
ESTRANGEMENT
ETERNITY RING
ETERNIZATION
ETHERIZATION
ETHNOCENTRIC
ETHNOGRAPHER
ETHNOGRAPHIC
ETHNOLOGICAL
ETHNOLOGISTS
ETHOXYETHANE
ETHYL ALCOHOL
ETYMOLOGICAL
ETYMOLOGISTS
EUCALYPTUSES
EUHEMERISTIC
EUPHONICALLY
EUPHORICALLY
EUSTATICALLY
EVANGELISTIC
EVANGELIZING
EVAPORIMETER
EVENING DRESS
EVEN-TEMPERED
EVENTFULNESS
EVERY MAN JACK
EVISCERATING
EVISCERATION
EVOLUTIONARY
EVOLUTIONISM
EVOLUTIONIST
EXACERBATING
EXACERBATION
EXACTINGNESS
EXAGGERATING
EXAGGERATION
EXAGGERATIVE
EXAMINATIONS
EXASPERATING
EXASPERATION
EXCELLENCIES

EXCHANGEABLE
EXCHANGE RATE
EXCITABILITY
EXCLAMATIONS
EXCLUSIONARY
EXCOGITATION
EXCOGITATIVE
EXCORIATIONS
EXCRESCENCES
EXCRUCIATING
EXCRUCIATION
EXCURSIONIST
EXECUTIONERS
EXECUTORSHIP
EXEGETICALLY
EXEMPLIFYING
EXENTERATION
EXHAUSTIVELY
EXHIBITIONER
EXHILARATING
EXHILARATION
EXHILARATIVE
EXHORTATIONS
EXIGUOUSNESS
EXOBIOLOGIST
EXOPEPTIDASE
EXOPHTHALMIC
EXOPHTHALMOS
EXORBITANTLY
EXOTERICALLY
EXPANSIONARY
EXPANSIONISM
EXPANSIONIST
EXPATRIATING
EXPATRIATION
EXPECTATIONS
EXPECTORATED
EXPECTORATOR
EXPEDIENTIAL
EXPERIENCING
EXPERIENTIAL
EXPERIMENTAL
EXPERIMENTED
EXPERIMENTER
EXPERT SYSTEM
EXPLANATIONS
EXPLANTATION
EXPLICITNESS
EXPLOITATION
EXPLOITATIVE
EXPLORATIONS
EXPOSITIONAL

EXPOSITORILY
EXPOSTULATED
EXPOSTULATOR
EXPRESSIONAL
EXPRESSIVELY
EXPRESSIVITY
EXPROPRIABLE
EXPROPRIATED
EXPROPRIATOR
EXPURGATIONS
EXSANGUINITY
EX-SERVICEMAN
EX-SERVICEMEN
EXTEMPORIZED
EXTEMPORIZER
EXTENDEDNESS
EXTENSOMETER
EXTERMINABLE
EXTERMINATED
EXTERMINATOR
EXTERNALIZED
EXTEROCEPTOR
EXTINGUISHED
EXTINGUISHER
EXTORTIONARY
EXTORTIONATE
EXTORTIONIST
EXTRADITABLE
EXTRADITIONS
EXTRAMARITAL
EXTRAMUNDANE
EXTRANEOUSLY
EXTRANUCLEAR
EXTRAPOLATED
EXTRAPOLATOR
EXTRASENSORY
EXTRAUTERINE
EXTRAVAGANCE
EXTRAVAGANZA
EXTROVERSION
EXTROVERSIVE
EYEWITNESSES

F
FABRICATIONS
FABULOUSNESS
FACELESSNESS
FACILITATING
FACILITATION
FACILITATIVE
FACTIONALISM
FACTIONALIST

FACTIOUSNESS
FACTORY FARMS
FACTUALISTIC
FAINT-HEARTED
FAIT ACCOMPLI
FAITHFULNESS
FAITH HEALERS
FAITH HEALING
FALLACIOUSLY
FALLING STARS
FALSE BOTTOMS
FAMILIARIZED
FAMILIARIZER
FAMILIARNESS
FAMILY CIRCLE
FAMILY DOCTOR
FANCIFULNESS
FARADIZATION
FARSIGHTEDLY
FASCINATEDLY
FASTIDIOUSLY
FATHER FIGURE
FATHERLINESS
FATHERS-IN-LAW
FATIGABILITY
FAULT-FINDING
FAUTE DE MIEUX
FEARLESSNESS
FEARSOMENESS
FEATHERBRAIN
FEATURE FILMS
FEBRIFACIENT
FECKLESSNESS
FEDERALISTIC
FEEBLEMINDED
FEEL THE PINCH
FELDSPATHOSE
FELICITATING
FELICITATION
FELICITOUSLY
FEMINIZATION
FENESTRATION
FENNELFLOWER
FERLINGHETTI
FERMENTATION
FERMENTATIVE
FERRICYANIDE
FERRIS WHEELS
FERROCYANIDE
FERROSILICON
FERTILIZABLE
FEVERISHNESS

FIBRILLATION	FLAMMABILITY	FORGET-ME-NOTS	FRONT-RUNNERS
FIBRILLIFORM	FLATTERINGLY	FORMALDEHYDE	FRUCTIFEROUS
FIBRINOGENIC	FLAVOPROTEIN	FORMLESSNESS	FRUITFULNESS
FIBRINOLYSIN	FLEET ADMIRAL	FORMULARIZER	FRUIT MACHINE
FIBRINOLYSIS	FLICKERINGLY	FORMULATIONS	FRUMPISHNESS
FIBRINOLYTIC	FLITTERMOUSE	FORT-DE-FRANCE	FRUSTRATIONS
FIBROBLASTIC	FLOATABILITY	FORTUITOUSLY	FUDDY-DUDDIES
FICTIONALIZE	FLOCCULATION	FOSSILIZABLE	FULLER'S EARTH
FICTITIOUSLY	FLOORWALKERS	FOUNDATIONAL	FULLY-FLEDGED
FIDDLE-FADDLE	FLORICULTURE	FOUNTAINHEAD	FULMINATIONS
FIDDLESTICKS	FLOWCHARTING	FOUNTAIN PENS	FUNCTIONALLY
FIELD GLASSES	FLUCTUATIONS	FOURIERISTIC	FUNDAMENTALS
FIELD MARSHAL	FLUIDEXTRACT	FOURTH-DEGREE	FURFURACEOUS
FIELD-TESTING	FLUIDIZATION	FOURTH ESTATE	FURUNCULOSIS
FIELDWORKERS	FLUORESCENCE	FOURTH OF JULY	FUTILITARIAN
FIENDISHNESS	FLUORIDATING	FRACTIONALLY	FUTUROLOGIST
FIFTH COLUMNS	FLUORIDATION	FRACTIONATOR	
FIGURATIVELY	FLUORINATION	FRAMES OF MIND	**G**
FIGURE-GROUND	FLUOROCARBON	FRANCHE-COMTE	GALACTAGOGUE
FIGURE SKATER	FLUOROMETRIC	FRANCO GERMAN	GALACTOMETER
FILIBUSTERED	FLUOROSCOPIC	FRANGIBILITY	GALACTOMETRY
FILIBUSTERER	FLUTTERINGLY	FRANKFURTERS	GALL BLADDERS
FILM PREMIERE	FLUVIOMARINE	FRANKINCENSE	GALLINACEOUS
FILTER-TIPPED	FLYING DOCTOR	FRATERNALISM	GALLIVANTING
FINALIZATION	FLYING PICKET	FRATERNITIES	GALVANICALLY
FINGERBOARDS	FLYING SAUCER	FRATERNIZING	GALVANOMETER
FINGERPLATES	FLYING SQUADS	FRAUDULENTLY	GALVANOMETRY
FINGERPRINTS	FOCALIZATION	FREAKISHNESS	GALVANOSCOPE
FINGERSTALLS	FOLKLORISTIC	FREE CHURCHES	GALVANOSCOPY
FIRE BRIGADES	FOOL'S-PARSLEY	FREE-FLOATING	GAMESMANSHIP
FIRECRACKERS	FOOT-AND-MOUTH	FREESTANDING	GAMETOPHORIC
FIRE FIGHTERS	FOOT FAULTING	FREE-SWIMMING	GAMETOPHYTIC
FIRE FIGHTING	FOOTSLOGGING	FREETHINKERS	GAMOPETALOUS
FIRE HYDRANTS	FORBEARINGLY	FREETHINKING	GAMOPHYLLOUS
FIRELIGHTERS	FORBIDDINGLY	FREEWHEELING	GAMOSEPALOUS
FIREPROOFING	FORCE-FEEDING	FREEZE-DRYING	GARBAGE TRUCK
FIRE STATIONS	FORCEFULNESS	FREIGHTLINER	GARDEN CITIES
FIRING SQUADS	FORCIBLENESS	FRENCH KISSES	GASIFICATION
FIRST COUSINS	FORE-AND-AFTER	FRENCH LOAVES	GASTIGHTNESS
FIRST-FOOTING	FORECLOSABLE	FRENCH POLISH	GASTRONOMIST
FIRST-NIGHTER	FORECLOSURES	FRENETICALLY	GASTROPODOUS
FIRST OFFENCE	FOREGONENESS	FREQUENTABLE	GASTROSCOPIC
FIRST REFUSAL	FOREKNOWABLE	FREUDIAN SLIP	GASTRULATION
FISH AND CHIPS	FORENSICALLY	FRIENDLINESS	GATECRASHERS
FISH HATCHERY	FOREORDAINED	FRIGHTENABLE	GATECRASHING
FISSIPALMATE	FORESHADOWED	FROGMARCHING	GAVANIZATION
FISSIROSTRAL	FORESHADOWER	FRONDESCENCE	GEANTICLINAL
FLAGELLATING	FORESTALLING	FRONTBENCHER	GENDER-BENDER
FLAGELLATION	FORESTALMENT	FRONTBENCHES	GENEALOGICAL
FLAGELLIFORM	FORESTAYSAIL	FRONTIERSMAN	GENEALOGISTS
FLAMBOYANTLY	FORETRIANGLE	FRONTIERSMEN	GENERALITIES
FLAME-THROWER	FORGATHERING	FRONTISPIECE	GENERALIZING

GENERAL STAFF
GENEROSITIES
GENEROUSNESS
GENICULATION
GENOTYPICITY
GENUFLECTING
GENUFLECTION
GEOCHEMISTRY
GEOGRAPHICAL
GEOLOGICALLY
GEOMAGNETISM
GEOMECHANICS
GEOPHYSICIST
GEOPOLITICAL
GEOSYNCLINAL
GERANIACEOUS
GERIATRICIAN
GERMANOPHILE
GERMANOPHOBE
GERONTOCRACY
GESTICULATED
GESTICULATOR
GET ONE'S
 CARDS
GET-TOGETHERS
GHOULISHNESS
GIANT KILLERS
GIBRALTARIAN
GIFT-WRAPPING
GIGANTICALLY
GIGANTICNESS
GINGERLINESS
GLABROUSNESS
GLACIOLOGIST
GLADIATORIAL
GLASSBLOWERS
GLASS-BLOWING
GLASS CEILING
GLASSCUTTERS
GLAUCOMATOUS
GLIMMERINGLY
GLISTENINGLY
GLITTERINGLY
GLOBETROTTER
GLOCKENSPIEL
GLORIOUSNESS
GLOSSOGRAPHY
GLOTTAL STOPS
GLOVE PUPPETS
GLUCOGENESIS
GLUCOGENETIC
GLUE-SNIFFERS

GLUE-SNIFFING
GLUTTONOUSLY
GLYCOGENESIS
GLYCOGENETIC
GLYCOPROTEIN
GLYPHOGRAPHY
GLYPTOGRAPHY
GNOMONICALLY
GNOTOBIOTICS
GOBBLEDEGOOK
GOBBLEDYGOOK
GOLDEN EAGLES
GOLDEN FLEECE
GOLDFISH BOWL
GOLD STANDARD
GONADOTROPIN
GOOD-HUMOURED
GOODY-GOODIES
GOOSEBERRIES
GOOSE PIMPLES
GOOSESTEPPED
GO OVER THE
 TOP
GORGEOUSNESS
GORMANDIZING
GOSSIPMONGER
GOVERNMENTAL
GOVERNORSHIP
GRACEFULNESS
GRACIOUSNESS
GRADE SCHOOLS
GRADUALISTIC
GRALLATORIAL
GRAMMATOLOGY
GRAM-NEGATIVE
GRAM-POSITIVE
GRANDFATHERS
GRAND MASTERS
GRANDMOTHERS
GRANDPARENTS
GRANODIORITE
GRANULOCYTIC
GRAPHOLOGIST
GRASSHOPPERS
GRATEFULNESS
GRATIFYINGLY
GRATUITOUSLY
GREASY SPOONS
GREAT BRITAIN
GREAT CIRCLES
GREAT RED SPOT
GREEN FINGERS

GREENGROCERS
GREENGROCERY
GREEN PEPPERS
GREGARIOUSLY
GRIEVOUSNESS
GRIZZLY BEARS
GROSSULARITE
GROUND FLOORS
GROUNDLESSLY
GROUNDSHEETS
GROUND STAFFS
GROUND STROKE
GROUNDSWELLS
GROUP CAPTAIN
GROUP THERAPY
GROVELLINGLY
GROWING PAINS
GRUESOMENESS
GUADALQUIVIR
GUARANTEEING
GUARDIANSHIP
GUERRILLAISM
GUESSTIMATES
GUEST WORKERS
GUILLOTINING
GUINEA-BISSAU
GUN CARRIAGES
GUTTERSNIPES
GUTTURALNESS
GYNAECOCRACY
GYROMAGNETIC

H

HABEAS CORPUS
HABERDASHERS
HABERDASHERY
HABILITATION
HABITABILITY
HABITATIONAL
HABITUALNESS
HACKING COUGH
HAEMATEMESIS
HAEMATOBLAST
HAEMATOCRYAL
HAEMATOGENIC
HAEMATOLOGIC
HAEMATOLYSIS
HAEMATOXYLIC
HAEMATOXYLIN
HAEMATOXYLON
HAEMOPHILIAC
HAEMOPOIESIS

HAEMOPOIETIC
HAEMORRHAGIC
HAEMORRHOIDS
HAGIOGRAPHER
HAGIOGRAPHIC
HAGIOLATROUS
HAIRDRESSERS
HAIRDRESSING
HAIRPIN BENDS
HAIR-RESTORER
HAIR'S BREADTH
HAIRSPLITTER
HAIR TRIGGERS
HALF-BROTHERS
HALF-HOLIDAYS
HALF MEASURES
HALF-TIMBERED
HALFWAY HOUSE
HALF-WITTEDLY
HALLOWEDNESS
HALLSTATTIAN
HALLUCINATED
HALLUCINATOR
HALLUCINOGEN
HALLUCINOSIS
HALOGENATION
HAMBLETONIAN
HAMMARSKJOLD
HAMMERHEADED
HAMPEREDNESS
HAMSTRINGING
HANDICAPPING
HANDKERCHIEF
HAND OVER FIST
HANDSOMENESS
HAPPENSTANCE
HAPPY-GO-LUCKY
HAPPY MEDIUMS
HAPTOTROPISM
HARD CURRENCY
HARD FEELINGS
HARD SHOULDER
HARE COURSING
HARLEQUINADE
HARLEY STREET
HARMLESSNESS
HARMONICALLY
HARMONIOUSLY
HARMONIZABLE
HARPSICHORDS
HARQUEBUSIER
HARTHACANUTE

HARVEST HOMES	HEMIHYDRATED	HEXAGRAMMOID	HOMOTHALLISM
HARVEST MOONS	HEMIMORPHISM	HEXAHYDRATED	HOMOZYGOUSLY
HATCHET-FACED	HEMIMORPHITE	HIBERNACULUM	HONEYMOONERS
HAUTE COUTURE	HEMIPARASITE	HIBERNIANISM	HONEYMOONING
HAUTE CUISINE	HEMISPHEROID	HIDDEN AGENDA	HONEYSUCKLED
HAUTE-GARONNE	HEMOPHILIACS	HIERARCHICAL	HONEYSUCKLES
HAUTS-DE-SEINE	HENDECAGONAL	HIERATICALLY	HOPELESSNESS
HAZARD LIGHTS	HENOTHEISTIC	HIEROGLYPHIC	HORIZONTALLY
HEADQUARTERS	HERALDICALLY	HIEROPHANTIC	HORNET'S NESTS
HEADSHRINKER	HERBACEOUSLY	HIGH FIDELITY	HORN OF PLENTY
HEADSTRONGLY	HERD INSTINCT	HIGH-HANDEDLY	HORRENDOUSLY
HEART ATTACKS	HERE AND THERE	HIGHLIGHTING	HORRIBLENESS
HEARTBREAKER	HEREDITAMENT	HIGHLY-STRUNG	HORRIFICALLY
HEART DISEASE	HEREDITARILY	HIGH-MINDEDLY	HORRIFYINGLY
HEARTENINGLY	HEREINBEFORE	HIGH-PRESSURE	HORS DE COMBAT
HEART FAILURE	HERITABILITY	HIGH PROFILES	HORS D'OEUVRES
HEARTRENDING	HERMANNSTADT	HIGH SHERIFFS	HORSEMANSHIP
HEARTSTRINGS	HERMENEUTICS	HIGH-SOUNDING	HORSE TRADING
HEART TO HEART	HERMENEUTIST	HIGH-SPIRITED	HORSE-TRADING
HEART-TO-HEART	HERMETICALLY	HINAYANISTIC	HORSEWHIPPED
HEARTWARMING	HERMITICALLY	HINDQUARTERS	HORSEWHIPPER
HEATHENISHLY	HERMOTENSILE	HIPPOCRENIAN	HORTICULTURE
HEAVENLINESS	HEROD ANTIPAS	HIPPOPOTAMUS	HORTUS SICCUS
HEAVYHEARTED	HEROICALNESS	HIRE PURCHASE	HOSPITALIZED
HEAVY PETTING	HERPES ZOSTER	HISTOGENESIS	HOT-CROSS BUNS
HEAVYWEIGHTS	HERPETOLOGIC	HISTOGENETIC	HOT-GOSPELLER
HEBDOMADALLY	HERRINGBONES	HISTOLOGICAL	HOUSE ARRESTS
HEBETUDINOUS	HERSTMONCEUX	HISTORICALLY	HOUSEBREAKER
HEBRAIZATION	HESITATINGLY	HIT A BAD	HOUSEFATHERS
HECTOCOTYLUS	HETEROCERCAL	PATCH	HOUSEHOLDERS
HECTOGRAPHIC	HETEROCYCLIC	HOBBLEDEHOYS	HOUSE HUSBAND
HEDGEHOPPING	HETERODACTYL	HOBSON-JOBSON	HOUSEKEEPERS
HEDGE SPARROW	HETEROECIOUS	HOHENZOLLERN	HOUSEKEEPING
HEEDLESSNESS	HETEROGAMETE	HOLIDAYMAKER	HOUSEMASTERS
HEILONGJIANG	HETEROGAMOUS	HOLISTICALLY	HOUSEMOTHERS
HEILUNGKIANG	HETEROGENOUS	HOLOPHRASTIC	HOUSE OF CARDS
HEIR APPARENT	HETEROGONOUS	HOLOPLANKTON	HOUSE OF LORDS
HELICOIDALLY	HETEROGRAPHY	HOLY OF HOLIES	HOUSEPARENTS
HELIOCENTRIC	HETEROGYNOUS	HOME COUNTIES	HOUSE PARTIES
HELIOCHROMIC	HETEROLOGOUS	HOME FROM HOME	HOUSE SPARROW
HELIOGABALUS	HETEROMEROUS	HOMELESSNESS	HOUSE-TO-HOUSE
HELIOGRAPHER	HETERONOMOUS	HOMEOMORPHIC	HOUSE-TRAINED
HELIOGRAPHIC	HETERONYMOUS	HOMEOPATHIST	HOUSEWARMING
HELIOGRAVURE	HETEROOUSIAN	HOMESICKNESS	HOUSEY HOUSEY
HELIOLATROUS	HETEROPHYLLY	HOMING PIGEON	HOUSEY-HOUSEY
HELIOTHERAPY	HETEROPLASTY	HOMOCHROMOUS	HUBBLE-BUBBLE
HELIOTROPISM	HETEROSEXISM	HOMOGENIZING	HUDDERSFIELD
HELLENICALLY	HETEROSEXUAL	HOMOGONOUSLY	HUGGER-MUGGER
HELLGRAMMITE	HETEROTACTIC	HOMOLOGATION	HUMANITARIAN
HELPING HANDS	HETEROZYGOTE	HOMOMORPHISM	HUMANIZATION
HELPLESSNESS	HETEROZYGOUS	HOMOPOLARITY	HUMILIATIONS
HEMICHORDATE	HEXACOSANOIC	HOMOTAXIALLY	HUMMINGBIRDS

HUMOROUSNESS	IDIOSYNCRASY	IMPERMANENCE	INCARNATIONS
HUMPTY DUMPTY	IDOLATROUSLY	IMPERSONALLY	INCAUTIOUSLY
HUNGER STRIKE	IGNITABILITY	IMPERSONATED	INCENDIARISM
HURDY-GURDIES	ILLEGAL ENTRY	IMPERSONATOR	INCESTUOUSLY
HURSTMONCEUX	ILLEGALITIES	IMPERTINENCE	INCIDENTALLY
HUSEIN IBN-ALI	ILLEGIBILITY	IMPETIGINOUS	INCINERATING
HYALOPLASMIC	ILLEGITIMACY	IMPLANTATION	INCINERATION
HYBRIDIZABLE	ILLEGITIMATE	IMPLEMENTING	INCINERATORS
HYDNOCARPATE	ILLIBERALITY	IMPLICATIONS	INCISIVENESS
HYDRASTININE	ILLITERATELY	IMPLICITNESS	INCIVILITIES
HYDROCARBONS	ILLOGICALITY	IMPOLITENESS	INCLINATIONS
HYDROCEPHALY	ILL-TREATMENT	IMPONDERABLE	INCLINOMETER
HYDROCHLORIC	ILLUMINATING	IMPORTATIONS	INCOGNIZANCE
HYDRODYNAMIC	ILLUMINATION	IMPOVERISHED	INCOHERENTLY
HYDROFLUORIC	ILLUMINATIVE	IMPOVERISHER	INCOMMODIOUS
HYDROGENATOR	ILLUSIONISTS	IMPRECATIONS	INCOMMUTABLE
HYDROGEN BOMB	ILLUSORINESS	IMPREGNATING	INCOMPARABLE
HYDROGEOLOGY	ILLUSTRATING	IMPREGNATION	INCOMPARABLY
HYDROGRAPHER	ILLUSTRATION	IMPRESSIONAL	INCOMPATIBLE
HYDROGRAPHIC	ILLUSTRATIVE	IMPRESSIVELY	INCOMPATIBLY
HYDROKINETIC	ILLUSTRATORS	IMPRISONMENT	INCOMPETENCE
HYDROLYSABLE	IMAGINATIONS	IMPROPRIATOR	INCOMPETENTS
HYDROMEDUSAN	IMBECILITIES	IMPROVEMENTS	INCOMPLETELY
HYDROTHERAPY	IMMACULATELY	IMPROVIDENCE	INCOMPLIANCE
HYGIENICALLY	IMMEASURABLE	IMPUTABILITY	INCOMPUTABLE
HYPERCORRECT	IMMEASURABLY	INACCESSIBLE	INCONCLUSIVE
HYPERMARKETS	IMMEMORIABLE	INACCESSIBLY	INCONFORMITY
HYPNOTHERAPY	IMMERSIONISM	INACCURACIES	INCONSEQUENT
HYPNOTICALLY	IMMERSIONIST	INACCURATELY	INCONSISTENT
HYPOCHONDRIA	IMMETHODICAL	INACTIVATION	INCONSOLABLE
HYPOCRITICAL	IMMOBILIZING	INADEQUACIES	INCONSOLABLY
HYPOTHETICAL	IMMODERATELY	INADEQUATELY	INCONSONANCE
HYSTERECTOMY	IMMODERATION	INADMISSIBLE	INCONSUMABLE
HYSTERICALLY	IMMORALITIES	INADMISSIBLY	INCONTINENCE
	IMMORTALIZED	INADVERTENCE	INCONVENIENT
I	IMMORTALIZER	INAPPLICABLE	INCOORDINATE
ICE-CREAM SODA	IMMOVABILITY	INAPPLICABLY	INCORPORABLE
ICHNEUMON FLY	IMMUNE SYSTEM	INARTICULATE	INCORPORATED
ICHNOGRAPHIC	IMMUNIZATION	IN ATTENDANCE	INCORPORATOR
ICHNOLOGICAL	IMMUNOLOGIST	INAUDIBILITY	INCORPOREITY
ICHTHYOLOGIC	IMMUTABILITY	INAUGURATING	INCORRIGIBLE
ICHTHYOPHAGY	IMPARTIALITY	INAUGURATION	INCORRIGIBLY
ICONOCLASTIC	IMPEDIMENTAL	INAUSPICIOUS	INCRASSATION
ICONOGRAPHER	IMPENETRABLE	INCALCULABLE	INCREASINGLY
ICONOGRAPHIC	IMPENITENTLY	INCALCULABLY	INCRETIONARY
ICONOLATROUS	IMPERATIVELY	INCALESCENCE	INCRIMINATED
ICONOLOGICAL	IMPERCEPTION	INCANDESCENT	INCRIMINATOR
IDEALIZATION	IMPERCEPTIVE	INCANTATIONS	INCRUSTATION
IDENTIFIABLE	IMPERFECTION	INCAPABILITY	INCUBATIONAL
IDENTITY CARD	IMPERFECTIVE	INCAPACITATE	INCUMBENCIES
IDEOLOOGICAL	IMPERIALISTS	INCARCERATED	INCURABILITY
IDIOMORPHISM	IMPERISHABLE	INCARCERATOR	INDEBTEDNESS

INDECISIVELY	INEXPEDIENCE	INORDINATELY	INTERDICTION
INDECLINABLE	INEXPERIENCE	INOSCULATION	INTERDICTIVE
INDECOROUSLY	INEXPERTNESS	INQUISITIONS	INTERESTEDLY
INDEFEASIBLE	INEXPLICABLE	INSALIVATION	INTERFERENCE
INDEFENSIBLE	INEXPLICABLY	INSALUBRIOUS	INTERFERTILE
INDEFENSIBLY	INEXPRESSIVE	INSCRIPTIONS	INTERFLUVIAL
INDEFINITELY	INEXTENSIBLE	INSECTICIDAL	INTERGLACIAL
INDEHISCENCE	INEXTIRPABLE	INSECTICIDES	INTERJECTING
INDELIBILITY	INEXTRICABLE	INSECTIVORES	INTERJECTION
INDELICATELY	INEXTRICABLY	INSEMINATING	INTERJECTORY
INDEMNIFYING	INFANTICIDAL	INSEMINATION	INTERLACEDLY
INDENTATIONS	INFANTICIDES	IN SHORT ORDER	INTERLAMINAR
INDEPENDENCE	INFANT SCHOOL	INSINUATIONS	INTERLARDING
INDEPENDENCY	INFATUATEDLY	INSOLUBILITY	INTERLINKING
INDEPENDENTS	INFATUATIONS	INSPECTINGLY	INTERLOCKING
INDEX FINGERS	INFECTIOUSLY	INSPECTIONAL	INTERLOCUTOR
INDEX FUTURES	INFELICITOUS	INSPECTORATE	INTERMARRIED
INDIANAPOLIS	INFESTATIONS	INSPIRATIONS	INTERMEDIACY
INDIAN SUMMER	INFIBULATION	INSPIRITMENT	INTERMEDIARY
INDICATIVELY	INFIDELITIES	INSTALLATION	INTERMEDIATE
INDIFFERENCE	INFILTRATING	INSTILLATION	INTERMINABLE
INDIGENOUSLY	INFILTRATION	INSTITUTIONS	INTERMINABLY
INDIGESTIBLE	INFILTRATIVE	INSTRUCTIBLE	INTERMINGLED
INDIGESTIBLY	INFILTRATORS	INSTRUCTIONS	INTERMISSION
INDIRECTNESS	INFLAMMATION	INSTRUMENTAL	INTERMISSIVE
INDISCIPLINE	INFLAMMATORY	INSUFFERABLE	INTERMITTENT
INDISCREETLY	INFLATIONARY	INSUFFERABLY	INTERMIXABLE
INDISCRETION	INFLATIONISM	INSUFFICIENT	INTERMIXTURE
INDISPUTABLE	INFLATIONIST	INSUFFLATION	INTERNALIZED
INDISPUTABLY	INFLECTIONAL	INSURABILITY	INTERNUNCIAL
INDISSOLUBLE	INFLORESCENT	INSURGENCIES	INTEROCEPTOR
INDISSOLUBLY	INFOTAINMENT	INSURRECTION	INTERPELLANT
INDISTINCTLY	INFREQUENTLY	INTELLECTION	INTERPELLATE
INDIVIDUALLY	INFRINGEMENT	INTELLECTIVE	INTERPLEADER
INDIVIDUATOR	INFUNDIBULAR	INTELLECTUAL	INTERPOLATED
INDOCTRINATE	INFUNDIBULUM	INTELLIGENCE	INTERPOLATER
INDO-EUROPEAN	INFUSIBILITY	INTELLIGIBLE	INTERPOSABLE
INDOLEACETIC	INGLORIOUSLY	INTELLIGIBLY	INTERPRETERS
INDOMETHACIN	INGRATIATING	INTEMPERANCE	INTERPRETING
INDRE-ET-LOIRE	INGRATIATION	INTENSIFIERS	INTERPRETIVE
INDUSTRIALLY	INHABITATION	INTENSIFYING	INTERREGNUMS
INEFFABILITY	INHARMONIOUS	INTERACTIONS	INTERROGATED
INEFFACEABLE	INHERITANCES	INTERCEPTING	INTERROGATOR
INEFFICIENCY	INHOSPITABLE	INTERCEPTION	INTERRUPTING
INELASTICITY	INHOSPITABLY	INTERCEPTIVE	INTERRUPTION
INEQUALITIES	INHUMANITIES	INTERCEPTORS	INTERRUPTIVE
INERADICABLE	INIMICALNESS	INTERCESSION	INTERSECTING
INERADICABLY	INIQUITOUSLY	INTERCESSORY	INTERSECTION
INERTIA REELS	INNOVATIONAL	INTERCHANGED	INTERSPATIAL
INESCUTCHEON	INNUTRITIOUS	INTERCHANGES	INTERSPERSED
INESSENTIALS	INOBSERVANCE	INTERCONNECT	INTERSTADIAL
INEXACTITUDE	INOCULATIONS	INTERCURRENT	INTERSTELLAR

INTERSTITIAL	INVIGORATION	JACOB'S LADDER	KRISTIANSTAD
INTERTEXTURE	INVIGORATIVE	JE NE SAIS	KYRGYZ STEPPE
INTERTWINING	INVISIBILITY	QUOI	
INTERVENTION	INVITATIONAL	JEOPARDIZING	**L**
INTERVIEWEES	INVOCATIONAL	JET-PROPELLED	LABORATORIES
INTERVIEWERS	INVOLUCELATE	JIGSAW PUZZLE	LABOUR MARKET
INTERVIEWING	INVOLUTIONAL	JOHANNESBURG	LABOUR OF LOVE
INTERVOCALIC	INVULNERABLE	JOURNALISTIC	LABOURSAVING
INTERWEAVING	INVULNERABLY	JUDICATORIAL	LABYRINTHINE
IN THE LONG	INVULTUATION	JUGULAR VEINS	LACERABILITY
RUN	IRASCIBILITY	JUNIOR SCHOOL	LACHRYMOSITY
INTIMIDATING	IRISH COFFEES	JURISCONSULT	LACTOPROTEIN
INTIMIDATION	IRONING BOARD	JURISDICTION	LADY'S FINGERS
INTOLERANTLY	IRRADIATIONS	JURISDICTIVE	LADY'S-SLIPPER
INTONATIONAL	IRRATIONALLY	JURISPRUDENT	LAISSEZ-FAIRE
INTOXICATING	IRREDEEMABLE	JUSTIFYINGLY	LAKE DISTRICT
INTOXICATION	IRREDEEMABLY	JUVENESCENCE	LAMENTATIONS
INTOXICATIVE	IRREFRAGABLE		LANDED GENTRY
INTRACARDIAC	IRREGULARITY	**K**	LANDING CRAFT
INTRACRANIAL	IRRELEVANCES	KALEIDOSCOPE	LANDING FIELD
INTRANSIGENT	IRRELEVANTLY	KARYOKINESIS	LANDING STAGE
INTRANSITIVE	IRRELIEVABLE	KARYOKINETIC	LANDING STRIP
INTRANUCLEAR	IRREMEDIABLE	KARYOPLASMIC	LANDLUBBERLY
INTRAPRENEUR	IRREMEDIABLY	KEEP ONE'S	LANGUISHMENT
INTRAUTERINE	IRREMISSIBLE	HEAD	LANGUOROUSLY
INTRIGUINGLY	IRRESISTIBLE	KEEP THE PEACE	LANTERN-JAWED
INTRODUCIBLE	IRRESISTIBLY	KERATOGENOUS	LANTERNSLIDE
INTRODUCTION	IRRESOLUTELY	KERATOPLASTY	LAPIS LAZULIS
INTRODUCTORY	IRRESOLUTION	KERB CRAWLERS	LARYNGOSCOPE
INTROJECTION	IRRESOLVABLE	KERB CRAWLING	LARYNGOSCOPY
INTROJECTIVE	IRRESPECTIVE	KEYNESIANISM	LASCIVIOUSLY
INTROVERSION	IRRESPIRABLE	KEY SIGNATURE	LASER PRINTER
INTROVERSIVE	IRRESPONSIVE	KILLER WHALES	LAST JUDGMENT
INTUITIONISM	IRREVERENTLY	KILOWATT-HOUR	LATEENRIGGED
INTUITIONIST	IRREVERSIBLE	KINAESTHESIA	LATICIFEROUS
INTUMESCENCE	IRREVERSIBLY	KINAESTHETIC	LATINIZATION
INTUSSUSCEPT	IRRIGATIONAL	KINDERGARCHY	LAUNDERETTES
INVAGINATION	IRRITABILITY	KINDERGARTEN	LAUNDRYWOMAN
INVALIDATING	ISOCHROMATIC	KING'S COUNSEL	LAUREATESHIP
INVALIDATION	ISODIAMETRIC	KING'S ENGLISH	LEADING LIGHT
INVERCARGILL	ISOLATIONISM	KINROSS-SHIRE	LEAPFROGGING
INVERTEBRACY	ISOLATIONIST	KITCHENETTES	LEASEHOLDERS
INVERTEBRATE	ISOTOPICALLY	KLEPTOMANIAC	LEATHERINESS
INVERTED SNOB	ITALIANESQUE	KLIPSPRINGER	LEAVE TAKINGS
INVESTIGABLE		KNACKER'S YARD	LECTURESHIPS
INVESTIGATED	**J**	KNEE BREECHES	LEGALIZATION
INVESTIGATOR	JACK-IN-THE-	KNIGHT ERRANT	LEGIONNAIRES
INVESTITURES	BOX	KNIGHT-ERRANT	LEGISLATRESS
INVIGILATING	JACK-O'-	KNOX-JOHNSTON	LEGISLATURES
INVIGILATION	LANTERN	KOMI REPUBLIC	LEGITIMATELY
INVIGILATORS	JACK ROBINSON	KOTA KINABALU	LEGITIMATION
INVIGORATING	JACKSONVILLE	KREMLINOLOGY	LEGITIMATIZE

LEGITIMISTIC	LITTLE FINGER	LYMPHANGITIC	MALFUNCTIONS
LEGITIMIZING	LITTLE PEOPLE	LYMPHANGITIS	MALIGNANCIES
LENTICELLATE	LITURGICALLY	LYMPHOMATOID	MALIMPRINTED
LEOPARD'S-BANE	LIVERPUDLIAN	LYSERGIC ACID	MALLEABILITY
LEPIDOPTERAN	LIVER SAUSAGE		MALNOURISHED
LEPIDOPTERON	LIVERY STABLE	**M**	MALNUTRITION
LETTER OPENER	LIVING FOSSIL	MACCLESFIELD	MALOCCLUSION
LEUCOCYTOSIS	LOCAL DERBIES	MACHINATIONS	MALPRACTICES
LEUCOCYTOTIC	LOCALIZATION	MACHINE CODES	MALTESE CROSS
LEUCOPOIESIS	LOCAL OPTIONS	MACHINE TOOLS	MALTREATMENT
LEUCOPOIETIC	LOCI CLASSICI	MACKINTOSHES	MAMMALOGICAL
LEUCORRHOEAL	LOCKSMITHERY	MACROCLIMATE	MAN-ABOUT-TOWN
LEVALLOISIAN	LOCKSTITCHES	MACROCYTOSIS	MANAGERESSES
LEXICOGRAPHY	LODGING HOUSE	MACROGRAPHIC	MANAGERIALLY
LEXICOLOGIST	LOGANBERRIES	MACRONUCLEUS	MANDARIN DUCK
LIBERALISTIC	LOGANIACEOUS	MACROPHYSICS	MANEUVERABLE
LIBERALITIES	LOGISTICALLY	MACROPTEROUS	MANGEL-WURZEL
LIBERALIZING	LOLLAPALOOZA	MADEMOISELLE	MANIFESTABLE
LIBERAL PARTY	LOMENTACEOUS	MAGIC LANTERN	MANIPULATING
LIBERTARIANS	LONELY HEARTS	MAGISTRACIES	MANIPULATION
LIBERTICIDAL	LONESOMENESS	MAGISTRATURE	MANIPULATIVE
LIBIDINOUSLY	LONG-DISTANCE	MAGNETICALLY	MANIPULATORY
LICENSE PLATE	LONG DIVISION	MAGNETIC HEAD	MANNERLINESS
LICENTIATION	LONG DRAWN OUT	MAGNETIC POLE	MANOEUVRABLE
LICENTIOUSLY	LONG-DRAWN-OUT	MAGNETIC TAPE	MAN OF LETTERS
LICHTENSTEIN	LONGITUDINAL	MAGNETIZABLE	MANSION HOUSE
LIE DETECTORS	LONGSHOREMAN	MAGNETOGRAPH	MANSLAUGHTER
LIFELESSNESS	LONGSHOREMEN	MAGNETOMETER	MANSPLAINING
LIGHT BRIGADE	LONG-STANDING	MAGNETOMETRY	MANTELPIECES
LIGHT-HEARTED	LONG VACATION	MAGNIFICENCE	MANUFACTURAL
LIGHTWEIGHTS	LONGWINDEDLY	MAGNILOQUENT	MANUFACTURED
LIMNOLOGICAL	LOOKING GLASS	MAGNITOGORSK	MANUFACTURER
LINCOLNSHIRE	LOOSE-JOINTED	MAGNUM OPUSES	MARCASITICAL
LINE DRAWINGS	LOOSE-TONGUED	MAIDENLINESS	MARIE GALANTE
LINE-ENGRAVER	LOPHOPHORATE	MAIDEN SPEECH	MARITIME ALPS
LINEN BASKETS	LOQUACIOUSLY	MAIDEN VOYAGE	MARKET FORCES
LINE PRINTERS	LOSS ADJUSTER	MAID OF HONOUR	MARKET GARDEN
LINE PRINTING	LOST PROPERTY	MAIDSERVANTS	MARKETPLACES
LINES OF SIGHT	LOT-ET-GARONNE	MAILING LISTS	MARKET PRICES
LINGUA FRANCA	LOUDSPEAKERS	MAINE-ET-LOIRE	MARKSMANSHIP
LIQUEFACIENT	LOUGHBOROUGH	MAINTAINABLE	MARLINESPIKE
LIQUEFACTION	LOVECHILDREN	MAITRE D'HOTEL	MARRIAGEABLE
LIQUEFACTIVE	LOWER AUSTRIA	MAJESTICALLY	MARSEILLAISE
LIRIODENDRON	LOWER CLASSES	MAJOR GENERAL	MARSHALL PLAN
LISTLESSNESS	LOW-WATER MARK	MAKE ENDS MEET	MARSHMALLOWS
LITERALISTIC	LUDWIGSHAFEN	MALACOLOGIST	MARSUPIALIAN
LITERARINESS	LUGGAGE RACKS	MALAPROPISMS	MARVELLOUSLY
LITERATENESS	LUGUBRIOUSLY	MALEDICTIONS	MASQUERADERS
LITHOGRAPHED	LUMBERJACKET	MALEFACTRESS	MASQUERADING
LITHOGRAPHER	LUMINESCENCE	MALEVOLENTLY	MASSOTHERAPY
LITHOGRAPHIC	LUNCHEONETTE	MALFEASANCES	MASS-PRODUCED
LITTERATEURS	LUSCIOUSNESS	MALFORMATION	MASS-PRODUCER

MASTECTOMIES	MENSTRUATING	METROLOGICAL	MINIMUM WAGES
MASTER-AT-ARMS	MENSTRUATION	METROPOLISES	MINISTRATION
MASTERLINESS	MEPHITICALLY	METROPOLITAN	MINISTRATIVE
MASTERMINDED	MERCANTILISM	METRORRHAGIA	MINOR PLANETS
MASTER OF ARTS	MERCANTILIST	MEZZO-RELIEVO	MINUTE STEAKS
MASTERPIECES	MERCHANDISED	MEZZO-SOPRANO	MIRACLE PLAYS
MASTERSTROKE	MERCHANDISER	MICROANALYST	MIRROR IMAGES
MASTIGOPHORE	MERCHANTABLE	MICROBALANCE	MIRTHFULNESS
MASTURBATING	MERCHANT BANK	MICROBIOLOGY	MISADVENTURE
MASTURBATION	MERCHANT NAVY	MICROCEPHALY	MISALIGNMENT
MATABELELAND	MERCIFULNESS	MICROCIRCUIT	MISALLIANCES
MATERIALISTS	MERCURIALIZE	MICROCLIMATE	MISANTHROPES
MATERIALIZED	MERCY KILLING	MICROFILMING	MISANTHROPIC
MATERIALIZER	MERETRICIOUS	MICROGRAPHER	MISAPPREHEND
MATHEMATICAL	MERISTEMATIC	MICROGRAPHIC	MISBEHAVIOUR
MATINEE IDOLS	MEROPLANKTON	MICROGRAVITY	MISCALCULATE
MATRIARCHIES	MERRY-GO-ROUND	MICROHABITAT	MISCARRIAGES
MATRICLINOUS	MESENTERITIS	MICRONUCLEUS	MISCEGENETIC
MATRICULATED	MESENTERONIC	MICROPHYSICS	MISCELLANIES
MATRICULATOR	MESMERICALLY	MICROSCOPIST	MISCELLANIST
MATRONLINESS	MESOCEPHALIC	MICROSECONDS	MISCONCEIVED
MATTER-OF-FACT	MESOGASTRIUM	MICROSEISMIC	MISCONCEIVER
MATURATIONAL	MESOGNATHISM	MICROSTOMOUS	MISCONDUCTED
MAXIMIZATION	MESOGNATHOUS	MIDDLE COURSE	MISCONSTRUED
MEALY-MOUTHED	MESOMORPHISM	MIDDLE FINGER	MISDEMEANANT
MEAN BUSINESS	MESOMORPHOUS	MIDDLE GROUND	MISDEMEANOUR
MEANDERINGLY	MESOPOTAMIAN	MIDDLE SCHOOL	MISDIRECTING
MEANINGFULLY	MESOTHORACIC	MIDDLEWEIGHT	MISDIRECTION
MEASUREMENTS	MESSAGE STICK	MID GLAMORGAN	MISE-EN-SCENES
MECAMYLAMINE	METAGALACTIC	MIDSUMMER DAY	MISINFORMANT
MECHANICALLY	METAGNATHISM	MIDWESTERNER	MISINFORMING
MEDALLIONIST	METAGNATHOUS	MIFEPRISTONE	MISINTERPRET
MEDICAMENTAL	METALANGUAGE	MIGHT AND MAIN	MISJUDGEMENT
MEDICINE BALL	METALLICALLY	MILFORD HAVEN	MISJUDGMENTS
MEDIOCRITIES	METALLURGIST	MILITARISTIC	MISLEADINGLY
MEDITATINGLY	METALWORKERS	MILITARIZING	MISPLACEMENT
MEDITATIVELY	METALWORKING	MILLEFEUILLE	MISPRONOUNCE
MEETINGHOUSE	METAMORPHISM	MILLENARIANS	MISQUOTATION
MEGACEPHALIC	METAMORPHOSE	MILLIONAIRES	MISREPORTING
MEGALOCARDIA	METAPHORICAL	MILTON KEYNES	MISREPRESENT
MEGALOMANIAC	METAPHRASTIC	MIMEOGRAPHED	MISSING LINKS
MELANCHOLIAC	METAPHYSICAL	MIND-BOGGLING	MISSIONARIES
MELANCHOLILY	METASOMATISM	MINDLESSNESS	MISSPELLINGS
MELODRAMATIC	METATHORACIC	MINE DETECTOR	MISSTATEMENT
MELTING POINT	METEMPIRICAL	MINERALOGIST	MISTREATMENT
MEMORABILITY	METEORICALLY	MINERAL WATER	MITHRIDATISM
MEMORIALIZER	METEOROGRAPH	MINESWEEPERS	MIXED-ABILITY
MEMORIZATION	METHACRYLATE	MINESWEEPING	MIXED DOUBLES
MEN-ABOUT-TOWN	METHODICALLY	MINIATURISTS	MIXED ECONOMY
MENAGE A TROIS	METHOTREXATE	MINICOMPUTER	MIXED FARMING
MENDACIOUSLY	METICULOUSLY	MINIFICATION	MNEMONICALLY
MEN OF LETTERS	METONIC CYCLE	MINIMIZATION	MOBILIZATION

MOCKINGBIRDS	MORALIZATION	MULTIPLICAND	NAVIGABILITY
MODERATENESS	MORALIZINGLY	MULTIPLICATE	NAVIGATIONAL
MODIFICATION	MORBIFICALLY	MULTIPLICITY	NEBULIZATION
MODIFICATORY	MORNING COATS	MULTIPURPOSE	NEBULOUSNESS
MODULABILITY	MORNING DRESS	MULTITASKING	NECESSITATED
MODUS VIVENDI	MORNING GLORY	MULTIVALENCY	NECKERCHIEFS
MOHAVE DESERT	MORPHALLAXIS	MULTIVARIATE	NECROLOGICAL
MOISTURIZING	MORPHOLOGIES	MUNICIPALITY	NECROMANCERS
MOLLIFYINGLY	MORPHOLOGIST	MUNICIPALIZE	NECROPHILIAC
MOLLYCODDLED	MORRIS DANCER	MUNIFICENTLY	NECROPHILISM
MONADELPHOUS	MORRIS DANCES	MUSEUM PIECES	NECROPOLISES
MONARCHISTIC	MORTARBOARDS	MUSICAL BOXES	NEEDLESSNESS
MONASTICALLY	MORTGAGEABLE	MUSIC CENTRES	NEGATIVENESS
MONETIZATION	MORTIFYINGLY	MUSICIANSHIP	NEGATIVE POLE
MONEYCHANGER	MORTISE LOCKS	MUSICOLOGIST	NEGATIVE SIGN
MONEY-GRUBBER	MOSQUITO NETS	MYRMECOPHILE	NEGATIVISTIC
MONEYLENDERS	MOTHERFUCKER	MYSTERIOUSLY	NEGLECTFULLY
MONEYLENDING	MOTHERLINESS	MYSTERY PLAYS	NEGOTIATIONS
MONEY SPINNER	MOTHER NATURE	MYSTERY TOURS	NEIGHBOURING
MONEY-SPINNER	MOTHERS-IN-LAW	MYSTIFYINGLY	NEMATOCYSTIC
MONISTICALLY	MOTHER TONGUE	MYTHOLOGICAL	NEOANTHROPIC
MONKEY-PUZZLE	MOTHPROOFING	MYTHOLOGISTS	NEOCLASSICAL
MONKEY WRENCH	MOTIONLESSLY	MYTHOLOGIZER	NEOLOGICALLY
MONOCHLORIDE	MOTIVATIONAL	MYXOMYCETOUS	NEOTERICALLY
MONOCHROMIST	MOTORCYCLIST		NEPHELOMETER
MONODRAMATIC	MOTORIZATION	**N**	NEPHOLOGICAL
MONOFILAMENT	MOTOR SCOOTER	NAIL SCISSORS	NERVE CENTRES
MONOGAMISTIC	MOULDABILITY	NAMBY-PAMBIES	NERVE-RACKING
MONOGAMOUSLY	MOUNTAINEERS	NAMEDROPPERS	NETHERLANDER
MONOMANIACAL	MOUNTAIN LION	NAMEDROPPING	NETTLE RASHES
MONOMETALLIC	MOUNTAINSIDE	NANOPLANKTON	NEURASTHENIA
MONOMETRICAL	MOUNTAINTOPS	NANSEN BOTTLE	NEURASTHENIC
MONOMORPHISM	MOURNFULNESS	NARCISSISTIC	NEUROANATOMY
MONOPETALOUS	MOUTHBROODER	NARCOTICALLY	NEUROBIOLOGY
MONOPHTHONGS	MOUTH-TO-MOUTH	NARRAGANSETT	NEUROLOGICAL
MONOPHYLETIC	MOVABLE FEAST	NARROW GAUGES	NEUROLOGISTS
MONOPHYLLOUS	MUCILAGINOUS	NARROW-MINDED	NEUROPTEROUS
MONOPOLISTIC	MUCOPURULENT	NARROW SQUEAK	NEUROSCIENCE
MONOPOLIZING	MUDDLE-HEADED	NASALIZATION	NEUROSURGEON
MONOSEPALOUS	MULLIGATAWNY	NATIONAL DEBT	NEUROSURGERY
MONOSPERMOUS	MULTICHANNEL	NATIONAL HUNT	NEUROTICALLY
MONOSTROPHIC	MULTIFACETED	NATIONALISTS	NEUROTOMICAL
MONOSYLLABIC	MULTIFARIOUS	NATIONALIZED	NEUTRALIZING
MONOSYLLABLE	MULTIFOLIATE	NATIONAL PARK	NEUTRON BOMBS
MONOTHEISTIC	MULTIFORMITY	NATION STATES	NEVERTHELESS
MONOTONOUSLY	MULTIGRAVIDA	NATIVITY PLAY	NEW BRUNSWICK
MONOTRICHOUS	MULTILAMINAR	NATURALISTIC	NEW CALEDONIA
MONTPARNASSE	MULTILATERAL	NATURALIZING	NEWFOUNDLAND
MONUMENTALLY	MULTILINGUAL	NATUROPATHIC	NEW HAMPSHIRE
MOONLIGHTERS	MULTINUCLEAR	NAUSEATINGLY	NEWS AGENCIES
MOONLIGHTING	MULTIPARTITE	NAUSEOUSNESS	NEWSPAPERMAN
MORALITY PLAY	MULTIPLIABLE	NAUTICAL MILE	NEW TESTAMENT

NEWTOWNABBEY
NEW ZEALANDER
NIAGARA FALLS
NICOTINAMIDE
NIDIFICATION
NIETZSCHEISM
NIGHTDRESSES
NIGHTINGALES
NIMBOSTRATUS
NITROBENZENE
NITROMETHANE
NOCTAMBULISM
NOCTAMBULIST
NOCTILUCENCE
NOCTURNALITY
NOLENS VOLENS
NOMENCLATURE
NOMINALISTIC
NONADDICTIVE
NONAGENARIAN
NONALCOHOLIC
NONALIGNMENT
NONCHALANTLY
NONCOMBATANT
NONCOMMITTAL
NONCONDUCTOR
NONCORRODING
NONE SO PRETTY
NONESSENTIAL
NONEXISTENCE
NONEXPLOSIVE
NONFICTIONAL
NONFLAMMABLE
NONIDENTICAL
NONIDIOMATIC
NONMALIGNANT
NONOPERATIVE
NONPOISONOUS
NONPOLITICAL
NONRESIDENCE
NON RESIDENCE
NONRESIDENTS
NONRESISTANT
NONSCHEDULED
NONSECTARIAN
NON SEQUITURS
NONSTRATEGIC
NONTECHNICAL
NONVIOLENTLY
NORTH AMERICA
NORTH BRABANT
NORTHEASTERN

NORTHEASTERS
NORTHERNMOST
NORTH HOLLAND
NORTHUMBRIAN
NORTHWESTERN
NOTEWORTHILY
NOTICE BOARDS
NOTIFICATION
NOURISHINGLY
NOUVEAU RICHE
NOVOKUZNETSK
NUBIAN DESERT
NUCLEOPHILIC
NUMBERPLATES
NUMEROUSNESS
NUMINOUSNESS
NUMISMATISTS
NURSERY RHYME
NURSING HOMES
NUSA TENGGARA
NUTRITIONIST
NUTRITIOUSLY
NUTS AND BOLTS
NYCTITROPISM
NYMPHOLEPTIC
NYMPHOMANIAC

O

OBERAMMERGAU
OBITER DICTUM
OBJECT LESSON
OBLANCEOLATE
OBLATE SPHERE
OBLIGATIONAL
OBLIGATORILY
OBLITERATING
OBLITERATION
OBLITERATIVE
OBSCURANTISM
OBSCURANTIST
OBSEQUIOUSLY
OBSERVATIONS
OBSOLESCENCE
OBSOLETENESS
OBSTETRICIAN
OBSTREPEROUS
OBSTRUCTIONS
OCCASIONALLY
OCCUPATIONAL
OCEANOGRAPHY
OCTOGENARIAN
OCTOSYLLABIC

OCTOSYLLABLE
ODONTOGRAPHY
ODONTOLOGIST
ODONTOPHORAL
OESOPHAGUSES
OFFICE BLOCKS
OFFICEHOLDER
OFF ONE'S
  HANDS
OFF-THE-RECORD
OIL PAINTINGS
OKLAHOMA CITY
OLD-FASHIONED
OLD MAN'S
  BEARD
OLD PRETENDER
OLD SCHOOL TIE
OLD TESTAMENT
OLD WIVES'
  TALE
OLEORESINOUS
OLIGOTROPHIC
OLYMPIC GAMES
OMNIPRESENCE
ONEIROCRITIC
ONE-SIDEDNESS
ONE-TRACK MIND
ONE-UPMANSHIP
ONOMASIOLOGY
ONOMATOPOEIA
ONOMATOPOEIC
ON THE RAMPAGE
ONYCHOPHORAN
OOPHORECTOMY
OPEN-HANDEDLY
OPENING TIMES
OPEN-MINDEDLY
OPEN QUESTION
OPEN SANDWICH
OPEN VERDICTS
OPERA GLASSES
OPERATICALLY
OPHIOLOGICAL
OPHTHALMITIS
OPINION POLLS
OPPORTUNISTS
OPPOSABILITY
OPPOSITENESS
OPPOSITIONAL
OPPRESSINGLY
OPPRESSIVELY
OPSONIZATION

OPTIMIZATION
ORANGE ROUGHY
ORATORICALLY
ORBICULARITY
ORCHESTRA PIT
ORCHESTRATED
ORCHIDACEOUS
ORDINARINESS
ORGAN GRINDER
ORGANICISTIC
ORGANIZATION
ORGANOGRAPHY
ORGANOLEPTIC
ORGANOLOGIST
ORIEL WINDOWS
ORIENTALISTS
ORIENTATIONS
ORIENTEERING
ORNAMENTALLY
OROGENICALLY
OROLOGICALLY
ORTHOCEPHALY
ORTHODONTICS
ORTHOGENESIS
ORTHOGENETIC
ORTHOGRAPHER
ORTHOGRAPHIC
ORTHOMORPHIC
ORTHOPAEDICS
ORTHOPAEDIST
ORTHOPTEROUS
ORTHORHOMBIC
ORTHOTROPISM
ORTHOTROPOUS
OSCILLATIONS
OSCILLOGRAPH
OSCILLOSCOPE
OSSIFICATION
OSTENTATIOUS
OSTEOBLASTIC
OSTEOCLASTIC
OSTEOLOGICAL
OSTEOMALACIA
OSTEOPLASTIC
OSTRACIZABLE
OTHERWORLDLY
OUTBALANCING
OUTBUILDINGS
OUTDISTANCED
OUTGENERALED
OUTLANDISHLY
OUTMANOEUVRE

OUTNUMBERING	PALATABILITY	PARISH CLERKS	PEDIATRICIAN
OUTRAGEOUSLY	PALATIALNESS	PARISHIONERS	PEEBLESSHIRE
OUTRIVALLING	PALAZZO PANTS	PARISYLLABIC	PEJORATIVELY
OUTSTRETCHED	PALEOGRAPHER	PARKING LIGHT	PENALIZATION
OUTSTRIPPING	PALEONTOLOGY	PARKING METER	PENALTY AREAS
OVERBALANCED	PALETTE KNIFE	PARLOUR GAMES	PENDENTE LITE
OVERBURDENED	PALINGENESIS	PAROCHIALISM	PENITENTIARY
OVERCAPACITY	PALINGENETIC	PARSIMONIOUS	PENNSYLVANIA
OVERCAUTIOUS	PALPITATIONS	PARSON'S NOSES	PENNULTIMATE
OVERCHARGING	PALYNOLOGIST	PART EXCHANGE	PENNY PINCHER
OVERCLOUDING	PAMPHLETEERS	PARTHIAN SHOT	PENNY WHISTLE
OVERCRITICAL	PANCAKE ROLLS	PARTIALITIES	PENTARCHICAL
OVERCROPPING	PANCHROMATIC	PARTICIPANTS	PEPTIC ULCERS
OVERCROWDING	PANDANACEOUS	PARTICIPATED	PERADVENTURE
OVERDRESSING	PANDEMONIUMS	PARTICIPATOR	PERAMBULATED
OVEREMPHATIC	PANHELLENISM	PARTICULARLY	PERAMBULATOR
OVERESTIMATE	PANHELLENIST	PARTING SHOTS	PERCEPTIONAL
OVEREXPOSING	PANOPTICALLY	PARTISANSHIP	PERCEPTIVELY
OVERGENEROUS	PANTECHNICON	PARTITIONING	PERCEPTIVITY
OVERINDULGED	PANTISOCRACY	PARTNERSHIPS	PERCOLATIONS
OVERMASTERED	PANTOGRAPHER	PART OF SPEECH	PERCUTANEOUS
OVERPOPULATE	PANTOGRAPHIC	PARTY POOPERS	PEREGRINATOR
OVERPOWERING	PAPERHANGERS	PASQUEFLOWER	PEREMPTORILY
OVERREACHING	PAPERHANGING	PASSE PARTOUT	PERFECT PITCH
OVERREACTING	PAPERWEIGHTS	PASSE-PARTOUT	PERFIDIOUSLY
OVERREACTION	PAPULIFEROUS	PASSIONATELY	PERFOLIATION
OVERSHADOWED	PARABOLOIDAL	PASSION PLAYS	PERFORATIONS
OVERSHOOTING	PARACHRONISM	PASTEURIZING	PERFORMANCES
OVERSIMPLIFY	PARACHUTISTS	PAST PERFECTS	PERFORMATIVE
OVERSLEEPING	PARADE GROUND	PATCH POCKETS	PERICARDITIC
OVERSTEPPING	PARADIGMATIC	PATERNALISTS	PERICARDITIS
OVERSTOCKING	PARADISE LOST	PATERNOSTERS	PERICYNTHION
OVERTHROWING	PARADISIACAL	PATHETICALLY	PERILOUSNESS
OVERWHELMING	PARAESTHESIA	PATHOGENESIS	PERIMORPHISM
OWNER-DRIVERS	PARAESTHETIC	PATHOGENETIC	PERINEPHRIUM
OXYACETYLENE	PARAHYDROGEN	PATHOLOGICAL	PERINEURITIC
OXYGENIZABLE	PARALANGUAGE	PATHOLOGISTS	PERINEURITIS
	PARALLEL BARS	PATRIARCHATE	PERIODICALLY
P	PARALLELISMS	PATRIARCHIES	PERIODONTICS
PACIFICATION	PARALLELLING	PATRICLINOUS	PERIOD PIECES
PACKAGE DEALS	PARALOGISTIC	PATROL WAGONS	PERIONYCHIUM
PACKAGE TOURS	PARALYSATION	PATRON SAINTS	PERIPHERALLY
PACKING CASES	PARAMAGNETIC	PAVING STONES	PERIPHRASTIC
PADDLING POOL	PARAMILITARY	PAY ENVELOPES	PERITRICHOUS
PAEDOGENESIS	PARAMORPHISM	PEACEFULNESS	PERMACULTURE
PAEDOGENETIC	PARAPHRASING	PEAK DISTRICT	PERMANENT WAY
PAEDOLOGICAL	PARAPHRASTIC	PEANUT BUTTER	PERMANGANATE
PAGANIZATION	PARASITICIDE	PEARL HARBOUR	PERMEABILITY
PAINTBRUSHES	PARASITOLOGY	PEASE PUDDING	PERMISSIVELY
PALAEOBOTANY	PARATHYROIDS	PECCADILLOES	PERMITTIVITY
PALAEOGRAPHY	PARATROOPERS	PECKING ORDER	PERMUTATIONS
PALAEOLITHIC	PARENTHESIZE	PEDANTICALLY	PERNICIOUSLY

PERPETRATING	PHILANDERERS	PHOTOTHERAPY	PLATONICALLY
PERPETRATION	PHILANDERING	PHOTOTHERMIC	PLAUSIBILITY
PERPETRATORS	PHILANTHROPY	PHOTOTROPISM	PLAYER PIANOS
PERPETUATING	PHILATELISTS	PHRASAL VERBS	PLAYING CARDS
PERPETUATION	PHILHARMONIC	PHRASEOGRAPH	PLAYING FIELD
PERPETUITIES	PHILISTINISM	PHRENOLOGIST	PLAYS ON WORDS
PERPLEXITIES	PHILODENDRON	PHYCOLOGICAL	PLEASANTNESS
PERSECUTIONS	PHILOLOGICAL	PHYLETICALLY	PLEASANTRIES
PERSEVERANCE	PHILOLOGISTS	PHYSICALNESS	PLEASINGNESS
PERSISTENTLY	PHILOSOPHERS	PHYSIOCRATIC	PLEIOTROPISM
PERSONA GRATA	PHILOSOPHIES	PHYSIOGNOMIC	PLEOMORPHISM
PERSONALIZED	PHILOSOPHIZE	PHYSIOGRAPHY	PLIMSOLL LINE
PERSONIFYING	PHLEBOTOMIST	PHYSIOLOGIES	PLODDINGNESS
PERSPECTIVES	PHONEMICALLY	PHYSIOLOGIST	PLOUGHSHARES
PERSPICACITY	PHONE-TAPPING	PHYSOSTOMOUS	PLUMBIFEROUS
PERSPIRATION	PHONETICALLY	PHYTOGENESIS	PLUM PUDDINGS
PERSPIRATORY	PHONETICIANS	PHYTOGENETIC	PLUTOCRACIES
PERSPIRINGLY	PHONOGRAPHER	PHYTOHORMONE	PLUVIOMETRIC
PERSUASIVELY	PHONOLOGICAL	PHYTOPHAGOUS	PNEUMOCOCCUS
PERTINACIOUS	PHONOLOGISTS	PICCANINNIES	PNEUMOTHORAX
PERTURBATION	PHONOTACTICS	PICKERELWEED	POET LAUREATE
PERTURBINGLY	PHOSPHATURIA	PICTURE BOOKS	POINTILLISTS
PERVERSENESS	PHOSPHATURIC	PICTURE CARDS	POINT OF ORDER
PERVERSITIES	PHOSPHOLIPID	PIECE OF EIGHT	POINTS OF VIEW
PERVIOUSNESS	PHOSPHORESCE	PIECES OF WORK	POINT-TO-POINT
PESTILENTIAL	PHOSPHORITIC	PIGEONHOLING	POLARIMETRIC
PETALIFEROUS	PHOTOACTINIC	PIGMENTATION	POLARIZATION
PETERBOROUGH	PHOTOCATHODE	PILOT OFFICER	POLAROGRAPHY
PETIT LARCENY	PHOTOCHEMIST	PINEAL GLANDS	POLE POSITION
PETRIFACTION	PHOTOCHROMIC	PINK ELEPHANT	POLE VAULTERS
PETRODOLLARS	PHOTOCOMPOSE	PIPE CLEANERS	POLE VAULTING
PETROGRAPHER	PHOTOCOPIERS	PIPES OF PEACE	POLICE STATES
PETROGRAPHIC	PHOTOCOPYING	PISCICULTURE	POLICYHOLDER
PETROLOGICAL	PHOTOCURRENT	PITCHFORKING	POLITICIZING
PETROLOGISTS	PHOTODYNAMIC	PITIABLENESS	POLLEN COUNTS
PETROZAVODSK	PHOTOENGRAVE	PITILESSNESS	POLLING BOOTH
PETTIFOGGING	PHOTOGEOLOGY	PITTER-PATTER	POLTERGEISTS
PETTY LARCENY	PHOTOGRAPHED	PLACENTATION	POLYANTHUSES
PETTY OFFICER	PHOTOGRAPHER	PLACE SETTING	POLYCENTRISM
PHAGOCYTOSIS	PHOTOGRAPHIC	PLAGIARISTIC	POLYCHAETOUS
PHANEROGAMIC	PHOTOGRAVURE	PLAGIARIZING	POLYCYTHEMIA
PHANEROPHYTE	PHOTOKINESIS	PLAGIOCLIMAX	POLYEMBRYONY
PHARMACOLOGY	PHOTOKINETIC	PLAIN-CLOTHES	POLYETHYLENE
PHARYNGOLOGY	PHOTOMETRIST	PLAIN SAILING	POLYISOPRENE
PHARYNGOTOMY	PHOTOMONTAGE	PLANETARIUMS	POLYMORPHISM
PHELLODERMAL	PHOTONEUTRON	PLANETESIMAL	POLYMORPHOUS
PHENANTHRENE	PHOTONUCLEAR	PLANISPHERIC	POLYPETALOUS
PHENOLOGICAL	PHOTOPHILOUS	PLANO-CONCAVE	POLYPHYLETIC
PHENOMENALLY	PHOTOPOLYMER	PLANOGRAPHIC	POLYPHYODONT
PHI BETA KAPPA	PHOTOREALISM	PLASTERBOARD	POLYRHYTHMIC
PHILADELPHIA	PHOTOSPHERIC	PLASTER CASTS	POLYSEPALOUS
PHILADELPHUS	PHOTOSTATTED	PLASTOMETRIC	POLYSULPHIDE

POLYSYLLABIC
POLYSYLLABLE
POLYSYNDETON
POLYTECHNICS
POLYTHEISTIC
POLYTONALIST
POLYTONALITY
POLYURETHANE
POMEGRANATES
PONS ASINORUM
PONTA DELGADA
PONTIFICATED
PONTIFICATES
PONY-TREKKING
POOR RELATION
POOR-SPIRITED
POPOCATEPETL
POPULAR FRONT
POPULARIZING
POPULOUSNESS
PORNOGRAPHER
PORNOGRAPHIC
PORPHYROPSIN
PORT ADELAIDE
PORT-AU-PRINCE
PORTCULLISES
PORTE-COCHERE
PORTENTOUSLY
PORTERHOUSES
PORT HARCOURT
PORTMANTEAUS
PORTMANTEAUX
PORTS OF ENTRY
POSITIVENESS
POSITIVE POLE
POSITIVISTIC
POSSESSIVELY
POSTAGE STAMP
POSTAL ORDERS
POSTDILUVIAL
POSTDILUVIAN
POSTDOCTORAL
POSTER COLOUR
POSTER PAINTS
POSTGRADUATE
POSTHUMOUSLY
POSTMERIDIAN
POST MERIDIEM
POSTPONEMENT
POSTPOSITION
POSTPOSITIVE
POSTPRANDIAL

POTATO BEETLE
POTATO CRISPS
POTENTIALITY
POTTER'S WHEEL
POTTING SHEDS
POTTY-TRAINED
POVERTY TRAPS
POWER BROKERS
POWERFULNESS
POWER-SHARING
POWER STATION
PRACTICALITY
PRACTITIONER
PRAGMATISTIC
PRAISEWORTHY
PRASEODYMIUM
PRAYER WHEELS
PREAMPLIFIER
PREARRANGING
PREBENDARIES
PRECARIOUSLY
PRECEDENTIAL
PRECENTORIAL
PRECEPTORATE
PRECEPTORIAL
PRECESSIONAL
PRECIOUSNESS
PRECIPITANCE
PRECIPITATED
PRECIPITATES
PRECIPITATOR
PRECISIANISM
PRECISIONISM
PRECISIONIST
PRECLASSICAL
PRECOCIOUSLY
PRECOGNITION
PRECOGNITIVE
PRECONCEIVED
PRECONDITION
PRECONSCIOUS
PREDECEASING
PREDECESSORS
PREDESTINATE
PREDESTINING
PREDETERMINE
PREDICAMENTS
PREDICTIVELY
PREDIGESTING
PREDIGESTION
PREDILECTION
PREDISPOSING

PREDOMINANCE
PREDOMINATED
PREDOMINATOR
PRE-ECLAMPSIA
PRE-EMINENTLY
PRE-EMPTIVELY
PRE-EXISTENCE
PREFABRICATE
PREFECTORIAL
PREFERENTIAL
PREFORMATION
PREGNABILITY
PREJUDGEMENT
PREJUDGMENTS
PREMARITALLY
PREMAXILLARY
PREMEDITATED
PREMEDITATOR
PREMENSTRUAL
PREMIERSHIPS
PREMIUM BONDS
PREMONITIONS
PREOCCUPYING
PREORDAINING
PREPARATIONS
PREPAREDNESS
PREPONDERANT
PREPONDERATE
PREPOSITIONS
PREPOSSESSED
PREPOSTEROUS
PRERECORDING
PREREQUISITE
PREROGATIVES
PRESBYTERATE
PRESBYTERIAL
PRESBYTERIAN
PRESBYTERIES
PRESCRIPTION
PRESCRIPTIVE
PRESENTATION
PRESENTATIVE
PRESENTIMENT
PRESERVATION
PRESERVATIVE
PRESIDENCIES
PRESIDENTIAL
PRESS CUTTING
PRESS GALLERY
PRESSGANGING
PRESSINGNESS
PRESS RELEASE

PRESSURIZING
PRESUMPTIONS
PRESUMPTUOUS
PRESUPPOSING
PRETTY-PRETTY
PREVAILINGLY
PREVARICATED
PREVARICATOR
PREVENTIVELY
PREVIOUSNESS
PRICKLY PEARS
PRIDE OF PLACE
PRIESTLINESS
PRIEST-RIDDEN
PRIGGISHNESS
PRIME NUMBERS
PRIMOGENITOR
PRIMORDIALLY
PRIMULACEOUS
PRIMUM MOBILE
PRINCELINESS
PRINCE REGENT
PRINCE RUPERT
PRINCIPAL BOY
PRINCIPALITY
PRINTABILITY
PRIORITIZING
PRISMATOIDAL
PRIVATE PARTS
PRIVY COUNCIL
PRIZEFIGHTER
PROBATIONARY
PROBATIONERS
PROBLEMATIZE
PROBOSCIDEAN
PROCATHEDRAL
PROCESSIONAL
PROCLAMATION
PROCLIVITIES
PROCONSULATE
PROCTOLOGIST
PRODIGIOUSLY
PRODUCTIONAL
PRODUCTIVELY
PRODUCTIVITY
PROFANATIONS
PROFESSIONAL
PROFESSORIAL
PROFICIENTLY
PROFITEERING
PROFITLESSLY
PROFIT MARGIN

PROFOUNDNESS
PROFUNDITIES
PROGESTERONE
PROGRAMMABLE
PROGRAMMATIC
PROGRESSIONS
PROGRESSIVES
PROHIBITIONS
PROJECTIONAL
PROLEGOMENAL
PROLEGOMENON
PROLETARIANS
PROLIFERATED
PROLIFICALLY
PROLIFICNESS
PROLONGATION
PROMISED LAND
PROMONTORIES
PROMULGATING
PROMULGATION
PROMULGATORS
PRONOMINALLY
PRONOUNCEDLY
PROOFREADERS
PROOFREADING
PROPAEDEUTIC
PROPAGANDISM
PROPAGANDIST
PROPAGANDIZE
PROPENSITIES
PROPHESIABLE
PROPHYLACTIC
PROPITIATING
PROPITIATION
PROPITIATIVE
PROPITIATORY
PROPITIOUSLY
PROPORTIONAL
PROPORTIONED
PROPOSITIONS
PROROGATIONS
PROSCRIPTION
PROSCRIPTIVE
PROSECUTABLE
PROSECUTIONS
PROSELYTIZED
PROSELYTIZER
PROSOPOPOEIA
PROSPECTUSES
PROSPEROUSLY
PROSTITUTING
PROSTITUTION

PROSTRATIONS
PROTACTINIUM
PROTAGONISTS
PROTECTIVELY
PROTECTORATE
PROTESTATION
PROTESTINGLY
PROTHALAMION
PROTHONOTARY
PROTOHISTORY
PROTOMORPHIC
PROTOPLASMIC
PROTOPLASTIC
PROTOSEMITIC
PROTOTHERIAN
PROTOTROPHIC
PROTOZOOLOGY
PROTRACTEDLY
PROTUBERANCE
PROVERBIALLY
PROVIDENTIAL
PROVINCETOWN
PROVINCIALLY
PROVISIONING
PROVOCATIONS
PRUDENTIALLY
PRUSSIAN BLUE
PSEPHOLOGIST
PSEUDONYMITY
PSEUDONYMOUS
PSEUDOPODIUM
PSYCHIATRIST
PSYCHOACTIVE
PSYCHOBABBLE
PSYCHOGNOSIS
PSYCHOGRAPHY
PSYCHOLOGIES
PSYCHOLOGISM
PSYCHOLOGIST
PSYCHOLOGIZE
PSYCHOMETRIC
PSYCHOPATHIC
PSYCHOSEXUAL
PSYCHOSOCIAL
PSYCHROMETER
PTERIDOPHYTE
PTERIDOSPERM
PTERODACTYLS
PUBLICATIONS
PUBLIC HOUSES
PUBLIC SCHOOL
PUBLIC SECTOR

PUBLIC SPIRIT
PUGNACIOUSLY
PULL A FAST
  ONE
PULVERULENCE
PUMPERNICKEL
PUNCHED CARDS
PUNITIVENESS
PURIFICATION
PURIFICATORY
PURISTICALLY
PURPLE HEARTS
PURPOSE-BUILT
PURPOSEFULLY
PURSE STRINGS
PUSSYFOOTING
PUSSY WILLOWS
PUT INTO WORDS
PUT ONE'S OAR
  IN
PUTREFACTION
PUTREFACTIVE
PYELOGRAPHIC
PYRIDOXAMINE
PYROCATECHOL
PYROCHEMICAL
PYROELECTRIC
PYROGNOSTICS
PYROLIGNEOUS
PYROMANIACAL
PYROMORPHITE
PYROPHYLLITE
PYROSULPHATE
PYROTECHNICS

Q

QUADRAGESIMA
QUADRANGULAR
QUADRAPHONIC
QUADRILLIONS
QUADRINOMIAL
QUADRIPLEGIA
QUADRIPLEGIC
QUADRIVALENT
QUADRUMANOUS
QUALIFYINGLY
QUANTIFIABLE
QUANTITATIVE
QUANTIZATION
QUANTUM LEAPS
QUAQUAVERSAL
QUARANTINING

QUARTER-BOUND
QUARTERFINAL
QUARTERLIGHT
QUARTER NOTES
QUARTER PLATE
QUARTERSTAFF
QUEEN CONSORT
QUEEN MOTHERS
QUELQUE CHOSE
QUESTIONABLE
QUESTIONABLY
QUESTION MARK
QUESTION TAGS
QUESTION TIME
QUEUE-JUMPERS
QUEUE-JUMPING
QUINDECAPLET
QUINQUENNIAL
QUINQUENNIUM
QUINTESSENCE
QUIXOTICALLY
QUIZZICALITY

R

RABBIT WARREN
RABBLE-ROUSER
RACE MEETINGS
RACEMIZATION
RADICALISTIC
RADIO BEACONS
RADIOBIOLOGY
RADIOCHEMIST
RADIOELEMENT
RADIOGRAPHER
RADIOGRAPHIC
RADIOISOTOPE
RADIOLOGICAL
RADIOLOGISTS
RADIONUCLIDE
RADIOTHERAPY
RAISE THE ROOF
RAISON D'ETRES
RALLENTANDOS
RAMBUNCTIOUS
RAMENTACEOUS
RAMIFICATION
RANGE FINDERS
RANKINE SCALE
RAPHAELESQUE
RAPSCALLIONS
RASTAFARIANS
RATIFICATION

RATIOCINATOR
RATIONALISTS
RATIONALIZED
RATIONALIZER
RATTLESNAKES
RAVENOUSNESS
RAYLEIGH DISC
RAZZLE-DAZZLE
REACH-ME-DOWNS
REACTIVATING
REACTIVATION
REACTIVENESS
READDRESSING
READJUSTABLE
READJUSTMENT
REAFFIRMANCE
REAFFORESTED
REALIGNMENTS
REALIZATIONS
REALLOCATION
REAL PROPERTY
REAPPEARANCE
REAPPRAISALS
REAPPRAISING
REAR ADMIRALS
REASSURANCES
REASSURINGLY
REAUMUR SCALE
REBELLIOUSLY
RECALCITRANT
RECALESCENCE
RECANTATIONS
RECAPITALIZE
RECAPITULATE
RECEIVERSHIP
RECEPTIONIST
RECESSIONALS
RECIDIVISTIC
RECIPROCALLY
RECIPROCATED
RECIPROCATOR
RECKLESSNESS
RECOGNITIONS
RECOGNIZABLE
RECOGNIZABLY
RECOGNIZANCE
RECOLLECTING
RECOLLECTION
RECOLLECTIVE
RECOMMENDING
RECOMMISSION
RECOMMITMENT

RECOMPENSING
RECONCILABLE
RECONCILABLY
RECONNOITRED
RECONNOITRER
RECONSECRATE
RECONSIDERED
RECONSTITUTE
RECONVERSION
RECORD PLAYER
RECREATIONAL
RECRIMINATED
RECRIMINATOR
RECUPERATING
RECUPERATION
RECUPERATIVE
RED BLOOD CELL
REDECORATING
REDEMANDABLE
REDEMPTIONAL
REDEPLOYMENT
REDEVELOPING
REDINTEGRATE
REDISTRIBUTE
RED-LETTER DAY
REDUCIBILITY
REDUNDANCIES
REDUPLICATED
REEFER JACKET
RE-EMPLOYMENT
RE-EXAMINABLE
REFLATIONARY
REFLECTINGLY
REFLECTIONAL
REFLECTIVITY
REFORMATIONS
REFRACTIONAL
REFRACTORILY
REFRESHINGLY
REFRESHMENTS
REFRIGERANTS
REFRIGERATED
REFRIGERATOR
REFURBISHING
REFUTABILITY
REGENERATING
REGENERATION
REGENERATIVE
REGISTRATION
REGULARIZING
REGURGITATED
REHABILITATE

REIMBURSABLE
REIMPOSITION
REIMPRESSION
REINCARNATED
REINVESTMENT
REITERATIONS
REJECTIONIST
REJUVENATING
REJUVENATION
RELATIONSHIP
RELATIVISTIC
RELENTLESSLY
RELINQUISHED
RELINQUISHER
REMAINDERING
REMAINDERMAN
REMEMBRANCER
REMEMBRANCES
REMINISCENCE
REMONSTRANCE
REMONSTRATED
REMONSTRATOR
REMORSEFULLY
REMOVABILITY
REMUNERATING
REMUNERATION
REMUNERATIVE
RENAISSANCES
RENEGOTIABLE
RENEWABILITY
RENFREWSHIRE
RENOUNCEMENT
RENUNCIATION
RENUNCIATIVE
REORGANIZING
REPARABILITY
REPATRIATING
REPATRIATION
REPERCUSSION
REPERCUSSIVE
REPLACEMENTS
REPLENISHING
REPLICATIONS
REPOSITORIES
REPOSSESSING
REPOSSESSION
REPREHENDING
REPREHENSION
REPREHENSIVE
REPREHENSORY
REPRESENTING
REPRESSIVELY

REPRIMANDING
REPROACHABLE
REPROACHABLY
REPROCESSING
REPRODUCIBLE
REPRODUCTION
REPRODUCTIVE
REPROGRAPHIC
REPUTABILITY
REQUEST STOPS
REQUIREMENTS
REQUISITIONS
RESCHEDULING
RESEARCHABLE
RESEMBLANCES
RESERVATIONS
RESERVEDNESS
RESETTLEMENT
RESIDENTIARY
RESIDENTSHIP
RESIGNATIONS
RESIGNEDNESS
RESINIFEROUS
RESINOUSNESS
RESOLUBILITY
RESOLUTENESS
RESOLUTIONER
RESOLVEDNESS
RESOUNDINGLY
RESOURCELESS
RESPECTFULLY
RESPECTIVELY
RESPLENDENCE
RESPONSIVELY
RESPONSORIAL
RESTATEMENTS
RESTAURATEUR
RESTLESSNESS
RESTORATIONS
RESTORATIVES
RESTRAINABLE
RESTRAINEDLY
RESTRICTEDLY
RESTRICTIONS
RESTRUCTURED
RESUPINATION
RESURRECTING
RESURRECTION
RESUSCITABLE
RESUSCITATED
RESUSCITATOR
RETICULATION

RETINOSCOPIC
RETRACTILITY
RETRENCHABLE
RETRENCHMENT
RETROCESSION
RETROCESSIVE
RETROFLEXION
RETROGRESSED
RETRO-ROCKETS
RETROVERSION
REUNIONISTIC
REVALUATIONS
REVEGETATION
REVELATIONAL
REVERBERATED
REVERBERATOR
REVERENDSHIP
REVERENTNESS
REVERSIONARY
REVISABILITY
REVISIONISTS
REVITALIZING
REVIVABILITY
REVIVALISTIC
REVOCABILITY
REVOKABILITY
REVULSIONARY
RHAPSODISTIC
RHAPSODIZING
RHESUS FACTOR
RHETORICALLY
RHETORICIANS
RHINOCEROSES
RHINOCEROTIC
RHINOLOGICAL
RHINOPLASTIC
RHIZOCARPOUS
RHODODENDRON
RHOMBOHEDRAL
RHOMBOHEDRON
RHYMING SLANG
RHYTHMICALLY
RHYTHM METHOD
RIBONUCLEASE
RICHTER SCALE
RICOCHETTING
RIDICULOUSLY
RIGHTFULNESS
RIGHT-HANDERS
RIGHT-HAND MAN
RIGHT-HAND MEN

RIGHTS ISSUES
RIGHT-WINGERS
RIGOROUSNESS
RING-STREAKED
RIO DE JANEIRO
ROAD MANAGERS
ROBBEN ISLAND
ROCKING CHAIR
ROCKING HORSE
ROCKUMENTARY
ROLLER BLINDS
ROLLER SKATED
ROLLER-SKATER
ROLLER SKATES
ROLLER TOWELS
ROLLICKINGLY
ROLLING MILLS
ROLLING STOCK
ROLLING STONE
ROLL OF HONOUR
ROLLTOP DESKS
ROMAN CANDLES
ROMAN NUMERAL
ROMANTICALLY
ROMANTICISTS
ROMANTICIZED
ROOMING HOUSE
ROOTLESSNESS
ROSE-COLOURED
ROSTROPOVICH
ROTARY TILLER
ROUGH DIAMOND
ROUND BRACKET
ROUND THE BEND
ROUTE MARCHES
ROYAL FLUSHES
ROYAL SOCIETY
RUBBER BRIDGE
RUBBER DINGHY
RUBBERNECKED
RUBBER PLANTS
RUBBER STAMPS
RULES OF THUMB
RUMINATINGLY
RUMINATIVELY
RUMMAGE SALES
RUMOURMONGER
RUNNING JUMPS
RUNNING MATES
RUN OF THE
  MILL

RUN-OF-THE-
  MILL
RURALIZATION
RUSTPROOFING
RUTHLESSNESS

S
SABBATARIANS
SACCHARINITY
SACRILEGIOUS
SADISTICALLY
SAFE AS HOUSES
SAFEBREAKERS
SAFEGUARDING
SAFETY ISLAND
SAFETY RAZORS
SAFETY VALVES
SAILING BOATS
SAINT ANDREWS
SAINT AUSTELL
SAINT-ETIENNE
SAINT LAURENT
SAINT LEONARD
SAINT-NAZAIRE
SAINT-QUENTIN
SAINT VINCENT
SALAMANDRINE
SALESMANSHIP
SALES PITCHES
SALIFICATION
SALINOMETRIC
SALMON LADDER
SALMON TROUTS
SALPIGLOSSIS
SALT LAKE CITY
SALUTARINESS
SALUTATORILY
SALVATIONISM
SALVATIONIST
SAMARITANISM
SAMOA ISLANDS
SANCTIFIABLE
SANCTIONABLE
SANDBLASTING
SAND BLASTING
SANDPAPERING
SAN FRANCISCO
SANGUINARILY
SANGUINENESS
SANGUINOLENT
SANITARINESS
SAN PEDRO SULA

SAN SEBASTIAN
SANTALACEOUS
SANTO DOMINGO
SAONE-ET-LOIRE
SAPINDACEOUS
SAPONIFIABLE
SAPROPHAGOUS
SARCOMATOSIS
SARDONICALLY
SARSAPARILLA
SASKATCHEWAN
SATIRIZATION
SATISFACTION
SATISFACTORY
SATISFYINGLY
SATURABILITY
SAUDI ARABIAN
SAUSAGE ROLLS
SAVING GRACES
SAVINGS BANKS
SAXONY-ANHALT
SAXOPHONISTS
SCALABLENESS
SCANDALIZING
SCANDALOUSLY
SCANDINAVIAN
SCAREMONGERS
SCARIFICATOR
SCARLET FEVER
SCARLET WOMAN
SCARLET WOMEN
SCATOLOGICAL
SCATTERBRAIN
SCENESHIFTER
SCENOGRAPHER
SCENOGRAPHIC
SCHAFFHAUSEN
SCHEMATIZING
SCHIZOMYCETE
SCHIZOPHYTIC
SCHIZOTHYMIA
SCHIZOTHYMIC
SCHOLARSHIPS
SCHOLASTICAL
SCHOOLFELLOW
SCHOOLHOUSES
SCHOOL-LEAVER
SCHOOLMASTER
SCHORLACEOUS
SCIENCE PARKS
SCINTILLATED
SCINTILLATOR

SCLERENCHYMA
SCLEROMETRIC
SCOLOPENDRID
SCORNFULNESS
SCOTCH TAPING
SCOTCH WHISKY
SCOTLAND YARD
SCOUTMASTERS
SCRATCHINESS
SCRATCH PAPER
SCREWDRIVERS
SCRIMSHANDER
SCRIPTWRITER
SCROBICULATE
SCRUPULOUSLY
SCRUTINIZING
SCURRILOUSLY
SCUTELLATION
SEAMSTRESSES
SEARCH ENGINE
SEARCHLIGHTS
SEASONALNESS
SEASON TICKET
SEATON VALLEY
SECESSIONISM
SECESSIONIST
SECLUDEDNESS
SECOND COMING
SECOND COUSIN
SECOND-DEGREE
SECOND NATURE
SECOND PERSON
SECOND-STRING
SECRET AGENTS
SECRETARIATS
SECRETIONARY
SECRET POLICE
SECTARIANISM
SECTIONALISM
SECTIONALIST
SECTIONALIZE
SECULARISTIC
SECULARIZING
SECURITY RISK
SEDULOUSNESS
SEGMENTATION
SEINE-ET-MARNE
SEISMOGRAPHS
SEISMOGRAPHY
SEISMOLOGIST
SEISMOSCOPIC
SELENOGRAPHY

SELENOLOGIST
SELF-ABSORBED
SELF-ANALYSIS
SELF-ASSEMBLY
SELF-CATERING
SELF-COLOURED
SELF-DESTRUCT
SELF-EDUCATED
SELF-EFFACING
SELF-EMPLOYED
SELF-INTEREST
SELFLESSNESS
SELF PORTRAIT
SELF-PORTRAIT
SELF-RELIANCE
SELF-REPROACH
SELF-STARTERS
SELKIRKSHIRE
SELLING PLATE
SELLING POINT
SEMANTICALLY
SEMICIRCULAR
SEMIDETACHED
SEMIDIAMETER
SEMIFINALIST
SEMIFLUIDITY
SEMINIFEROUS
SEMIOTICIANS
SEMIPALMATED
SEMIPRECIOUS
SEMITROPICAL
SEMIVITREOUS
SEMPITERNITY
SENARMONTITE
SENSIBLENESS
SENSITOMETER
SENSITOMETRY
SENSORIMOTOR
SENSUOUSNESS
SEPARABILITY
SEPARATENESS
SEPARATISTIC
SEPTILATERAL
SEPTILLIONTH
SEPTUAGESIMA
SEPTUPLICATE
SEQUENTIALLY
SEQUESTRABLE
SEQUESTRATED
SEQUESTRATOR
SERIAL NUMBER
SERICULTURAL

SERINGAPATAM
SERONEGATIVE
SEROPOSITIVE
SERVICEBERRY
SERVICE FLATS
SERVICE ROADS
SESQUIALTERA
SET BY THE
  EARS
SEVENTEENTHS
SEVENTY-EIGHT
SEVERANCE PAY
SEXAGENARIAN
SEXCENTENARY
SEXTILLIONTH
SEXTUPLICATE
SHADOW-BOXING
SHAHJAHANPUR
SHAMATEURISM
SHAMEFACEDLY
SHAMEFULNESS
SHARECROPPER
SHAREHOLDERS
SHARPSHOOTER
SHARP-SIGHTED
SHARP-TONGUED
SHATTERINGLY
SHATTERPROOF
SHAVING CREAM
SHEATH KNIVES
SHEEPISHNESS
SHEEPSHEARER
SHEET ANCHORS
SHELLACKINGS
SHELLSHOCKED
SHEPHERD'S PIE
SHETLAND PONY
SHIFTINGNESS
SHIJIAZHUANG
SHILLY-SHALLY
SHIMMERINGLY
SHIPBUILDERS
SHIPBUILDING
SHIPWRECKING
SHIRTSLEEVES
SHIRTWAISTER
SHOCKABILITY
SHOCKINGNESS
SHOCKING PINK
SHOOTING STAR
SHOP STEWARDS
SHORT-CHANGED

SHORT-CHANGER
SHORT CIRCUIT
SHORTCOMINGS
SHORT-LISTING
SHORTSIGHTED
SHORT STORIES
SHORT-WAISTED
SHOT IN THE
  ARM
SHOW BUSINESS
SHOWSTOPPERS
SHOWSTOPPING
SHREWISHNESS
SHUDDERINGLY
SHUFFLEBOARD
SHUTTLECOCKS
SIAMESE TWINS
SICK HEADACHE
SIDEROSTATIC
SIDESLIPPING
SIDESTEPPING
SIDETRACKING
SIDE-WHEELERS
SIDE WHISKERS
SIDI-BEL-ABBES
SIERRA NEVADA
SIGHT-READERS
SIGHT-READING
SIGNIFICANCE
SIGN LANGUAGE
SILHOUETTING
SILICIFEROUS
SILICON CHIPS
SILIQUACEOUS
SILVERFISHES
SILVER LINING
SILVER MEDALS
SILVERSMITHS
SILVICULTURE
SIMILARITIES
SIMPLE-MINDED
SIMULTANEITY
SIMULTANEOUS
SINANTHROPUS
SINGLE-ACTING
SINGLE-ACTION
SINGLE-DECKER
SINGLE-HANDED
SINGLE-MINDED
SINGULARNESS
SINISTERNESS
SINISTRORSAL

SINKING FUNDS	SNEAK THIEVES	SPACE CAPSULE	SPLENOMEGALY
SIPHONOPHORE	SNICKERINGLY	SPACE HEATERS	SPLIT SECONDS
SIPHONOSTELE	SNIGGERINGLY	SPACE SHUTTLE	SPOKESPEOPLE
SISTERLINESS	SNOBBISHNESS	SPACE STATION	SPOKESPERSON
SISTERS-IN-LAW	SNOOPERSCOPE	SPACIOUSNESS	SPONGIOBLAST
SITTING DUCKS	SOCIALIZABLE	SPEAKING TUBE	SPOON-FEEDING
SITTING ROOMS	SOCIAL WORKER	SPEARHEADING	SPORADICALLY
SITUATIONISM	SOCIOLOGICAL	SPECIALISTIC	SPOROGENESIS
SKELETON KEYS	SOCIOLOGISTS	SPECIALITIES	SPORTFULNESS
SKELMERSDALE	SOCIOMETRIST	SPECIALIZING	SPORTIVENESS
SKIPPING-ROPE	SODA FOUNTAIN	SPECIFICALLY	SPORTSPERSON
SKITTISHNESS	SOFT LANDINGS	SPECIOUSNESS	SPOT-CHECKING
SKYROCKETING	SOFT-PEDALING	SPECTACULARS	SPOTLESSNESS
SLANDEROUSLY	SOFT-PEDALLED	SPECTROGRAPH	SPOTLIGHTING
SLAUGHTERING	SOLARIZATION	SPECTROMETER	SPOTTED DICKS
SLAUGHTEROUS	SOLAR SYSTEMS	SPECTROMETRY	SPREAD-EAGLED
SLAVE DRIVERS	SOLICITATION	SPECTROSCOPE	SPREADSHEETS
SLAVONICALLY	SOLICITOUSLY	SPECTROSCOPY	SPRINGBOARDS
SLEDGEHAMMER	SOLIDIFIABLE	SPECULATIONS	SPRING ONIONS
SLEEPING BAGS	SOLIFLUCTION	SPEECHIFYING	SPURIOUSNESS
SLEEPING CARS	SOLILOQUIZED	SPEECHLESSLY	SQUAMOUSNESS
SLEEPING PILL	SOLITARINESS	SPEEDOMETERS	SQUARE DANCES
SLEEPWALKERS	SOLITUDINOUS	SPEEDWRITING	SQUARE-RIGGED
SLEEPWALKING	SOLVENT ABUSE	SPELEOLOGIST	SQUARE-RIGGER
SLENDERIZING	SOMATOLOGIST	SPELLBINDERS	SQUEAKY-CLEAN
SLIDING DOORS	SOMATOPLEURE	SPELLBINDING	SQUEEZEBOXES
SLIDING SCALE	SOMERSAULTED	SPELLCHECKER	SQUELCHINGLY
SLIPPERINESS	SOMNAMBULANT	SPENDTHRIFTS	SQUIRRELFISH
SLIPPINGNESS	SOMNAMBULATE	SPERMATHECAL	STADDLESTONE
SLIPSTREAMED	SOMNAMBULISM	SPERMATOCYTE	STAFF OFFICER
SLOANE RANGER	SOMNAMBULIST	SPERMATOZOAL	STAGECOACHES
SLOTHFULNESS	SON ET LUMIERE	SPERMATOZOID	STAGE-MANAGED
SLOT MACHINES	SONG AND DANCE	SPERMATOZOON	STAGE MANAGER
SLOVENLINESS	SONOROUSNESS	SPERMOGONIUM	STAGE WHISPER
SLUGGARDNESS	SOOTHINGNESS	SPHRAGISTICS	STAGGERINGLY
SLUGGISHNESS	SOPHISTICATE	SPHYGMOGRAPH	STAGING POSTS
SLUMBERINGLY	SOPORIFEROUS	SPICK AND SPAN	STAINABILITY
SLUTTISHNESS	SOUL BROTHERS	SPICK-AND-SPAN	STAINED GLASS
SMALL FORTUNE	SOULLESSNESS	SPIEGELEISEN	STAKEHOLDERS
SMALLHOLDERS	SOUND BARRIER	SPINSTERHOOD	STALACTIFORM
SMALLHOLDING	SOUND EFFECTS	SPIRITEDNESS	STALLHOLDERS
SMASH-AND-GRAB	SOUNDPROOFED	SPIRIT LEVELS	STALWARTNESS
SMILACACEOUS	SOUP KITCHENS	SPIRITUALISM	STAMMERINGLY
SMOKESCREENS	SOUSAPHONIST	SPIRITUALIST	STANDARDIZED
SMOOTH-SPOKEN	SOUTH AMERICA	SPIRITUALITY	STANDARDIZER
SMORGASBORDS	SOUTHEASTERN	SPIRITUALIZE	STANDARD LAMP
SNAGGLETOOTH	SOUTHERNMOST	SPIRITUOSITY	STANDARD TIME
SNAKE CHARMER	SOUTHERNWOOD	SPIROGRAPHIC	STANDING ROOM
SNAP FASTENER	SOUTH HOLLAND	SPITEFULNESS	STANDOFF HALF
SNAPPISHNESS	SOUTH OSSETIA	SPLASH GUARDS	STAND-OFF HALF
SNEAKINGNESS	SOUTH SHIELDS	SPLATTERPUNK	STANLEY KNIFE
SNEAK PREVIEW	SOUTHWESTERN	SPLENDIDNESS	STANNIFEROUS

STAR CHAMBERS	STIGMATIZING	STREETWALKER	SUBERIZATION
STAR-SPANGLED	STILBOESTROL	STRENGTHENED	SUBINFEUDATE
STARTING GATE	STILETTO HEEL	STRENGTHENER	SUBJECTIVELY
STATELY HOMES	STINKINGNESS	STREPTOCOCCI	SUBJECTIVISM
STATEN ISLAND	STIPULATIONS	STREPTOMYCIN	SUBJECTIVIST
STATIONARILY	STIRRUP PUMPS	STRETCHINESS	SUBJECTIVITY
STATION BREAK	STOCKBREEDER	STRETCHMARKS	SUBJUNCTIVES
STATION HOUSE	STOCKBROKERS	STRIDULATING	SUBMAXILLARY
STATION WAGON	STOCKHOLDERS	STRIDULATION	SUBMERSIBLES
STATISTICIAN	STOCK-IN-TRADE	STRIDULATORY	SUBMISSIVELY
STAYING POWER	STOCKJOBBERS	STRIKINGNESS	SUBMITTINGLY
STEAK TARTARE	STOCKJOBBERY	STRIP CARTOON	SUBNORMALITY
STEAL THE SHOW	STOCK MARKETS	STRIP MININGS	SUBORDINATED
STEALTHINESS	STOICHIOLOGY	STROBE LIGHTS	SUBORDINATES
STEAMROLLERS	STOKE-ON-TRENT	STROBILATION	SUBPRINCIPAL
STEAM SHOVELS	STOMACHACHES	STROBOSCOPES	SUBSCRIPTION
STEATOPYGOUS	STOMACH PUMPS	STROBOSCOPIC	SUBSCRIPTIVE
STEATORRHOEA	STONECUTTING	STROMATOLITE	SUBSEQUENTLY
STEEPLECHASE	STONEMASONRY	STRONG-MINDED	SUBSERVIENCE
STEEPLEJACKS	STONEWALLERS	STRONG POINTS	SUBSIDIARIES
STELLIFEROUS	STONEWALLING	STRONG-WILLED	SUBSIDIARILY
STENOGRAPHER	STONY-HEARTED	STRONTIANITE	SUBSIDIARITY
STENOGRAPHIC	STOOLPIGEONS	STROPHANTHIN	SUBSIDIZABLE
STENOTHERMAL	STOREKEEPERS	STROPHANTHUS	SUBSISTINGLY
STEPBROTHERS	STOREKEEPING	STRUCTURALLY	SUBSTANTIATE
STEPCHILDREN	STORM TROOPER	STRUGGLINGLY	SUBSTANTIVAL
STEPDAUGHTER	STORMY PETREL	STRYCHNINISM	SUBSTANTIVES
STEREOCHROME	STORYTELLERS	STUBBORNNESS	SUBSTITUTING
STEREOCHROMY	STORYTELLING	STUDDINGSAIL	SUBSTITUTION
STEREOGRAPHY	STOUTHEARTED	STUDIOUSNESS	SUBSTITUTIVE
STEREOISOMER	STOVEPIPE HAT	STUFFED SHIRT	SUBSTRUCTURE
STEREOMETRIC	STRADIVARIUS	STUPEFACIENT	SUBTEMPERATE
STEREOPHONIC	STRAGGLINGLY	STUPEFACTION	SUBTERRANEAN
STEREOPTICON	STRAIGHTAWAY	STUPEFYINGLY	SUBTRACTIONS
STEREOSCOPIC	STRAIGHTEDGE	STUPENDOUSLY	SUBURBANITES
STEREOTACTIC	STRAIGHTENED	STUTTERINGLY	SUBVERSIVELY
STEREOTROPIC	STRAIGHTENER	STYLOGRAPHIC	SUCCEDANEOUS
STEREOTYPING	STRAIGHTNESS	STYRACACEOUS	SUCCEEDINGLY
STEREOVISION	STRAINEDNESS	SUBALTERNATE	SUCCESSFULLY
STERILIZABLE	STRAITJACKET	SUBANTARCTIC	SUCCESSIONAL
STERNUTATION	STRANGLEHOLD	SUBAURICULAR	SUCCESSIVELY
STERNUTATIVE	STRANGULATED	SUBCELESTIAL	SUCCINCTNESS
STERNUTATORY	STRAPHANGERS	SUBCLIMACTIC	SUCTION PUMPS
STERNWHEELER	STRAPHANGING	SUBCOMMITTEE	SUDORIFEROUS
STERTOROUSLY	STRATICULATE	SUBCONSCIOUS	SUFFRAGETTES
STETHOSCOPES	STRATIGRAPHY	SUBCONTINENT	SUFFRUTICOSE
STETHOSCOPIC	STRATOCRATIC	SUBCUTANEOUS	SUGAR DADDIES
STICHOMETRIC	STRATOSPHERE	SUBDEACONATE	SUGGESTINGLY
STICK INSECTS	STRAWBERRIES	SUBDIACONATE	SUGGESTIVELY
STICKLEBACKS	STREAMLINING	SUBDIVISIONS	SUITABLENESS
STICKY WICKET	STREETS AHEAD		SULPHONAMIDE
STIGMASTEROL	STREET VALUES		SULPHURATION

SUMMARIZABLE	SURROUNDINGS	**T**	TEMPERATURES
SUMMERHOUSES	SURVEILLANCE	TABERNACULAR	TENANT FARMER
SUMMER SCHOOL	SURVEYORSHIP	TABLE MANNERS	TEN-GALLON HAT
SUNDAY SCHOOL	SURVIVAL KITS	TABLE-TURNING	TERATOLOGIST
SUPERABILITY	SUSCEPTIVITY	TACHEOMETRIC	TERCENTENARY
SUPERANNUATE	SUSPICIOUSLY	TACHYCARDIAC	TEREBINTHINE
SUPERCHARGED	SUSTAININGLY	TACTLESSNESS	TERGIVERSATE
SUPERCHARGER	SWAGGERINGLY	TADZHIKISTAN	TERMINATIONS
SUPERCILIARY	SWALLOW DIVES	TALCUM POWDER	TERRIBLENESS
SUPERCILIOUS	SWASHBUCKLER	TALENT SCOUTS	TERRIFICALLY
SUPEREMINENT	SWEEPINGNESS	TALKING POINT	TERRIFYINGLY
SUPERFICIARY	SWEET-AND-SOUR	TAMBOURINIST	TERRITORIALS
SUPERGLACIAL	SWEET PEPPERS	TANGENTIALLY	TESSELLATION
SUPERGRASSES	SWEET POTATOS	TAPE MEASURES	TESTAMENTARY
SUPERIMPOSED	SWEET-TALKING	TAPE RECORDER	TESTIMONIALS
SUPERLATIVES	SWELTERINGLY	TAPE STREAMER	TESTOSTERONE
SUPERMARKETS	SWIMMING BATH	TARAMASALATA	TEST-TUBE BABY
SUPERNATURAL	SWIMMING POOL	TARDENOISIAN	TETANIZATION
SUPERPOSABLE	SWING THE LEAD	TARTARIC ACID	TETRACHORDAL
SUPERSEDABLE	SWITCHBLADES	TASTEFULNESS	TETRACYCLINE
SUPERSESSION	SWITCHBOARDS	TAUROMACHIAN	TETRAHEDRITE
SUPERSTITION	SWIZZLE STICK	TAUTOLOGICAL	TETRAPTEROUS
SUPERSTRATUM	SWORD DANCERS	TAX COLLECTOR	TETRASTICHIC
SUPERTANKERS	SYLLABICALLY	TAXIDERMISTS	TETRAVALENCY
SUPERVENIENT	SYMBOLICALLY	TECHNICALITY	TEUTONICALLY
SUPPLEMENTAL	SYMBOLOGICAL	TECHNOBABBLE	THALAMICALLY
SUPPLEMENTED	SYMMETALLISM	TECHNOGRAPHY	THALASSAEMIA
SUPPLEMENTER	SYMPATHIZERS	TECHNOLOGIES	THALLOPHYTIC
SUPPLETORILY	SYMPATHIZING	TECHNOLOGIST	THANKFULNESS
SUPPLICATING	SYNAESTHESIA	TECTONICALLY	THANKSGIVING
SUPPLICATION	SYNAESTHETIC	TEENYBOPPERS	THAUMATOLOGY
SUPPLICATORY	SYNAPTICALLY	TEETER-TOTTER	THEANTHROPIC
SUPPOSITIONS	SYNARTHROSIS	TEETOTALLERS	THEATREGOERS
SUPPOSITIOUS	SYNCHROFLASH	TELAESTHESIA	THEATRICALLY
SUPPRESSIBLE	SYNCHRONIZED	TELAESTHETIC	THE HERMITAGE
SUPRAGLOTTAL	SYNCHRONIZER	TELAUTOGRAPH	THEISTICALLY
SUPRALIMINAL	SYNCHROSCOPE	TELEGRAPHERS	THEMATICALLY
SUPRAORBITAL	SYNCLINORIUM	TELEGRAPHESE	THEOCENTRISM
SUPRAPROTEST	SYNDACTYLISM	TELEGRAPHING	THEOPHYLLINE
SUPREMACISTS	SYNDETICALLY	TELEMEDICINE	THEORETICIAN
SUPREME BEING	SYNDICALISTS	TELEOLOGICAL	THEORIZATION
SUPREME COURT	SYNDIOTACTIC	TELEOLOGISTS	THERAPEUTICS
SUREFOOTEDLY	SYNODIC MONTH	TELEPHONE BOX	THE REAL THING
SURFACE-TO-AIR	SYNONYMOUSLY	TELEPHONISTS	THEREINAFTER
SURMOUNTABLE	SYNOPTICALLY	TELEPRINTERS	THERMOCOUPLE
SURPASSINGLY	SYNTHESIZERS	TELEPROMPTER	THERMOGENOUS
SURPRISINGLY	SYNTHESIZING	TELESHOPPING	THERMOGRAPHY
SURREALISTIC	SYNTONICALLY	TELEUTOSPORE	THERMOLABILE
SURREJOINDER	SYSTEMATIZED	TELEVISIONAL	THERMOMETERS
SURRENDERING	SYSTEMATIZER	TELGENICALLY	THERMOMETRIC
SURROUNDEDLY	SYSTEMICALLY	TELLUROMETER	THERMOSCOPIC
		TEMPERAMENTS	THERMOS FLASK

THERMOSIPHON	TONELESSNESS	TRANSDUCTION	TRENDSETTERS
THERMOSPHERE	TONSILLOTOMY	TRANSFERABLE	TRENDSETTING
THERMOSTABLE	TOOTHBRUSHES	TRANSFERENCE	TREPHINATION
THERMOSTATIC	TOPDRESSINGS	TRANSFERRING	TRIBESPEOPLE
THERMOTROPIC	TOP-HEAVINESS	TRANSFIGURED	TRIBULATIONS
THEURGICALLY	TOPOGRAPHERS	TRANSFORMERS	TRICHINIASIS
THICK-SKINNED	TORMENTINGLY	TRANSFORMING	TRICHOCYSTIC
THIEVISHNESS	TORREFACTION	TRANSFORMISM	TRICHOGYNIAL
THIGMOTACTIC	TORTUOUSNESS	TRANSFORMIST	TRICHOLOGIST
THIGMOTROPIC	TOTALITARIAN	TRANSFUSIBLE	TRICHOPTERAN
THINGAMAJIGS	TOTALIZATORS	TRANSFUSIONS	TRICHROMATIC
THIOSINAMINE	TOURIST CLASS	TRANSGRESSED	TRICK OR TREAT
THIOSULPHATE	TOUT ENSEMBLE	TRANSGRESSOR	TRIFURCATION
THIRD PARTIES	TOWER HAMLETS	TRANSHUMANCE	TRIGGER HAPPY
THOROUGHBRED	TOWER OF BABEL	TRANSITIONAL	TRIGGER-HAPPY
THOROUGHFARE	TOWN PLANNERS	TRANSITORILY	TRIGLYCERIDE
THOROUGHNESS	TOWN PLANNING	TRANSLATABLE	TRIGONOMETRY
THOUGHTFULLY	TOXICOLOGIST	TRANSLATIONS	TRILINGUALLY
THREE QUARTER	TOXOPHILITIC	TRANSLUCENCE	TRIMOLECULAR
THREE-QUARTER	TRACEABILITY	TRANSLUCENCY	TRIPARTITION
THREE-WHEELER	TRACE ELEMENT	TRANSMIGRANT	TRIPHTHONGAL
THROMBOCYTIC	TRACHEOPHYTE	TRANSMIGRATE	TRIPLE-TONGUE
THUNDERBOLTS	TRACHEOSTOMY	TRANSMISSION	TRIPLICATION
THUNDERCLAPS	TRACHOMATOUS	TRANSMISSIVE	TRIPOLITANIA
THUNDERCLOUD	TRACING PAPER	TRANSMITTERS	TRIUMPHANTLY
THUNDERFLASH	TRACK RECORDS	TRANSMITTING	TRIUMVIRATES
THUNDERINGLY	TRACTABILITY	TRANSMOGRIFY	TRIVIALITIES
THUNDEROUSLY	TRACUCIANIST	TRANSMUNDANE	TRIVIALIZING
THUNDERSTONE	TRADESCANTIA	TRANSMUTABLE	TROCHAICALLY
THUNDERSTORM	TRADESPEOPLE	TRANSOCEANIC	TROCHOIDALLY
THUNDER STORM	TRADING POSTS	TRANSPARENCY	TROJAN HORSES
TICKLISHNESS	TRADING STAMP	TRANSPIRABLE	TROLLEYBUSES
TIED COTTAGES	TRADITIONIST	TRANSPLANTED	TROMBIDIASIS
TIME CAPSULES	TRADUCIANISM	TRANSPLANTER	TROOP CARRIER
TIME EXPOSURE	TRAFFICATORS	TRANSPONDERS	TROPHALLAXIS
TIME HONOURED	TRAFFIC LIGHT	TRANSPORTERS	TROPOPHILOUS
TIME-HONOURED	TRAGEDIENNES	TRANSPORTING	TROUBLEMAKER
TIMELESSNESS	TRAILBLAZING	TRANSPORTIVE	TROUBLE SPOTS
TIME SWITCHES	TRAILER HOUSE	TRANSPOSABLE	TROUSER PRESS
TIMOROUSNESS	TRAINBEARERS	TRANSUDATORY	TRUSTABILITY
TIRELESSNESS	TRAIN SPOTTER	TRANSVAALIAN	TRUSTEESHIPS
TIRESOMENESS	TRAINSPOTTER	TRANSVERSELY	TRUSTFULNESS
TITANIFEROUS	TRAITOROUSLY	TRANSVESTISM	TRUTHFULNESS
TITLEHOLDERS	TRAJECTORIES	TRANSVESTITE	TRYPANOSOMAL
TITTLE-TATTLE	TRAMPISHNESS	TRANSYLVANIA	TRYPARSAMIDE
TOASTING FORK	TRANQUILLITY	TRAPSHOOTING	TUBERCULOSIS
TOASTMASTERS	TRANQUILLIZE	TRAUMATIZING	TUMBLE-DRYERS
TOBACCONISTS	TRANSACTIONS	TRAVEL AGENCY	TUMBLE-DRYING
TOFFEE APPLES	TRANSCENDENT	TRAVEL AGENTS	TUMULTUOUSLY
TOGETHERNESS	TRANSCENDING	TREBLE CHANCE	TUNELESSNESS
TOMFOOLERIES	TRANSCRIBING	TREELESSNESS	TUNNEL VISION
TONE LANGUAGE	TRANSCURRENT	TREMENDOUSLY	TURBELLARIAN

TURBIDIMETER	UNCOMMONNESS	UNFATHOMABLY	UNREFLECTIVE
TURBOCHARGED	UNCONFORMITY	UNFAVOURABLE	UNREGENERACY
TURBOCHARGER	UNCONSENTING	UNFAVOURABLY	UNREGENERATE
TURKISH BATHS	UNCONSIDERED	UNFLAGGINGLY	UNRESERVEDLY
TURKMENISTAN	UNCONVINCING	UNFLATTERING	UNRESPONSIVE
TURNING POINT	UNCOVENANTED	UNFORGIVABLE	UNRESTRAINED
TUVA REPUBLIC	UNCRITICALLY	UNFORTUNATES	UNRESTRICTED
TU-WHIT TU-	UNCTUOUSNESS	UNFREQUENTED	UNSANCTIONED
WHOO	UNDECEIVABLE	UNGAINLINESS	UNSATURATION
TWILIGHT ZONE	UNDEMOCRATIC	UNGOVERNABLE	UNSCIENTIFIC
TWISTABILITY	UNDERACHIEVE	UNGRATEFULLY	UNSCRAMBLING
TWO-FACEDNESS	UNDERBELLIES	UNHESITATING	UNSCRUPULOUS
TWO-WAY MIRROR	UNDERCHARGED	UNHYPHENATED	UNSEARCHABLE
TYPIFICATION	UNDERCLOTHES	UNIDENTIFIED	UNSEASONABLE
TYPOGRAPHERS	UNDERCURRENT	UNIFOLIOLATE	UNSEASONABLY
TYRANNICALLY	UNDERCUTTING	UNILATERALLY	UNSEEMLINESS
TYRANNICIDAL	UNDERDEVELOP	UNIMAGINABLE	UNSEGREGATED
	UNDERDRAWING	UNIMPRESSIVE	UNSETTLEMENT
U	UNDERDRESSED	UNINFLUENCED	UNSTEADINESS
UBIQUITOUSLY	UNDEREXPOSED	UNINTERESTED	UNSTRATIFIED
UGLIFICATION	UNDERGARMENT	UNIONIZATION	UNSTRUCTURED
UGLY CUSTOMER	UNDERGROUNDS	UNISEXUALITY	UNSUCCESSFUL
UGLY DUCKLING	UNDERNOURISH	UNITARIANISM	UNSUPPORTIVE
ULTRAMONTANE	UNDERPAYMENT	UNIVERSALISM	UNSUSPECTING
ULTRAMUNDANE	UNDERPINNING	UNIVERSALIST	UNTENABILITY
UMBILICATION	UNDERPLAYING	UNIVERSALITY	UNTHINKINGLY
UNACCEPTABLE	UNDERSCORING	UNIVERSALIZE	UNTIMELINESS
UNACCUSTOMED	UNDERSELLING	UNIVERSITIES	UNTOUCHABLES
UNACQUAINTED	UNDERSHERIFF	UNKINDLINESS	UNTOWARDNESS
UNAFFECTEDLY	UNDERSTAFFED	UNLAWFULNESS	UNTRAMMELLED
UNAFFORDABLE	UNDERSTATING	UNLIKELIHOOD	UNWIELDINESS
UNAGGRESSIVE	UNDERSTUDIED	UNLIKELINESS	UNWORTHINESS
UNANSWERABLE	UNDERSTUDIES	UNMANAGEABLE	UNWRITTEN LAW
UNAPOLOGETIC	UNDERSURFACE	UNMEASURABLE	UPHOLSTERERS
UNAPPEALABLE	UNDERTAKINGS	UNMISTAKABLE	UPHOLSTERING
UNASSAILABLE	UNDERTRAINED	UNMISTAKABLY	UPPER AUSTRIA
UNASSOCIATED	UNDERUTILIZE	UNMODERNIZED	UPRIGHT PIANO
UNASSUMINGLY	UNDERVALUING	UNOFFICIALLY	UPROARIOUSLY
UNATTAINABLE	UNDERWRITERS	UNPARALLELED	UP-TO-DATENESS
UNATTRACTIVE	UNDERWRITING	UNPERFORATED	URANOGRAPHER
UNATTRIBUTED	UNDERWRITTEN	UNPLEASANTLY	URANOGRAPHIC
UNBELIEVABLE	UNDESIRABLES	UNPOPULARITY	URBANIZATION
UNBELIEVABLY	UNDETERMINED	UNPREJUDICED	URETHROSCOPE
UNBIASEDNESS	UNDISCHARGED	UNPRINCIPLED	URETHROSCOPY
UNCELEBRATED	UNECONOMICAL	UNPRODUCTIVE	URINOGENITAL
UNCHALLENGED	UNEMPLOYABLE	UNPROFITABLE	USER FRIENDLY
UNCHARITABLE	UNEMPLOYMENT	UNPUBLICIZED	USER-FRIENDLY
UNCHARITABLY	UNEVENTFULLY	UNQUESTIONED	USUFRUCTUARY
UNCHASTENESS	UNEXPRESSIVE	UNREASONABLE	USURIOUSNESS
UNCINARIASIS	UNEXPURGATED	UNREASONABLY	UTILITY ROOMS
UNCLASSIFIED	UNFAITHFULLY	UNRECKONABLE	UTTAR PRADESH
UNCOMMERCIAL	UNFATHOMABLE	UNRECOGNIZED	UXORIOUSNESS

V
VACCINATIONS
VACILLATIONS
VACUUM FLASKS
VACUUM-PACKED
VAINGLORIOUS
VALEDICTIONS
VALENCIENNES
VALORIZATION
VALUABLENESS
VANQUISHABLE
VANQUISHMENT
VANTAGEPOINT
VANTAGE POINT
VAPORESCENCE
VAPORIZATION
VAPOROUSNESS
VAPOUR TRAILS
VARICOLOURED
VASODILATION
VAUDEVILLIAN
VAUDEVILLIST
VEGETATIONAL
VELARIZATION
VELOCIRAPTOR
VENERABILITY
VENERATIONAL
VENGEFULNESS
VENIPUNCTURE
VENTRICOSITY
VERBENACEOUS
VERIDICALITY
VERIFICATION
VERIFICATIVE
VERTEBRATION
VERTICILLATE
VESICULATION
VESTAL VIRGIN
VIBRAPHONIST
VICE-CHAIRMAN
VICISSITUDES
VICTORIANISM
VICTORIA PLUM
VICTORIOUSLY
VIDEO NASTIES
VIGOROUSNESS
VILIFICATION
VILLAGE GREEN
VILLAHERMOSA
VILLEURBANNE
VINDICTIVELY
VINICULTURAL

VIN ORDINAIRE
VIOLONCELLOS
VIRGIN'S-BOWER
VIRIDESCENCE
VIRTUOUSNESS
VISCEROMOTOR
VISCOUNTCIES
VISITATIONAL
VISITATORIAL
VISITING CARD
VISITORS' BOOK
VITALIZATION
VITICULTURAL
VITICULTURER
VITREOUSNESS
VITUPERATION
VITUPERATIVE
VIVIFICATION
VIVISECTIONS
VIXENISHNESS
VOCABULARIES
VOCALIZATION
VOCIFERATING
VOCIFERATION
VOCIFEROUSLY
VOIDABLENESS
VOLCANICALLY
VOLTA REDONDA
VOLUMINOSITY
VOLUMINOUSLY
VOLUNTARYISM
VOLUNTARYIST
VOLUNTEERING
VOLUNTEERISM
VOLUPTUARIES
VOLUPTUOUSLY
VOMITURITION
VOTE OF THANKS
VOWELIZATION
VULCANIZABLE

W
WAGES COUNCIL
WAITING LISTS
WAITING ROOMS
WALKIE-TALKIE
WALKING STICK
WALLCOVERING
WALL PAINTING
WALLPAPERING
WANKEL ENGINE
WAREHOUSEMAN

WARMONGERING
WARS OF NERVES
WARWICKSHIRE
WASH DRAWINGS
WASTEFULNESS
WASTE PRODUCT
WATCHFULNESS
WATER BISCUIT
WATER BUFFALO
WATER CANNONS
WATER CLOSETS
WATERCOLOURS
WATERCOURSES
WATERING CANS
WATERING HOLE
WATERMANSHIP
WATER MEADOWS
WATERPROOFED
WATTENSCHEID
WAYS AND MEANS
WEATHERBOARD
WEATHER-BOUND
WEATHERCOCKS
WEATHERGLASS
WEATHERPROOF
WEATHER SHIPS
WEATHER VANES
WEDDING RINGS
WEIGHBRIDGES
WEIGHTLESSLY
WEIGHT LIFTER
WELFARE STATE
WELL-ADJUSTED
WELL-ASSORTED
WELL-ATTENDED
WELL BALANCED
WELL-BALANCED
WELL-DESERVED
WELL DISPOSED
WELL-DISPOSED
WELL-EDUCATED
WELL-EQUIPPED
WELL-FAVOURED
WELL-GROUNDED
WELL-INFORMED
WELL-MANNERED
WELL-PROVIDED
WELL-RECEIVED
WELL-SITUATED
WELL-TEMPERED
WELSH RAREBIT
WELTERWEIGHT

WENSLEYDALES
WEST BROMWICH
WESTERLINESS
WESTERN ISLES
WESTERNIZING
WESTERN SAMOA
WEST FLANDERS
WEST MIDLANDS
WEST VIRGINIA
WETTING AGENT
WHEELBARROWS
WHEELWRIGHTS
WHENCESOEVER
WHEREWITHALS
WHIGGISHNESS
WHIMPERINGLY
WHIMSICALITY
WHIPPING BOYS
WHIPPOORWILL
WHITE KNIGHTS
WHITE-LIVERED
WHITE SLAVERY
WHITEWASHING
WHITE WEDDING
WHOLEHEARTED
WHOLE NUMBERS
WHORTLEBERRY
WICKET KEEPER
WIDE RECEIVER
WIFE SWAPPING
WIGTOWNSHIRE
WILDERNESSES
WILLIAMSBURG
WILL-O'-THE-
  WISP
WINDCHEATERS
WINDING SHEET
WINDOW SHADES
WIND TURBINES
WINEGLASSFUL
WINGLESSNESS
WINSTON-SALEM
WINTERBOURNE
WINTER SPORTS
WISCONSINITE
WISECRACKING
WITCHDOCTORS
WITCH-HUNTING
WITCHING HOUR
WITHDRAWABLE
WITHEREDNESS
WITH OPEN ARMS

WITH PLEASURE
WITHSTANDING
WITNESS BOXES
WOLF WHISTLES
WOLLASTONITE
WOMANISHNESS
WONDER-WORKER
WONDROUSNESS
WOODENHEADED
WOOLGATHERER
WOOLLY-HEADED
WORDLESSNESS
WORD OF HONOUR
WORKER-PRIEST
WORKING CLASS

WORKING ORDER
WORKING PARTY
WORKING WEEKS
WORKINGWOMAN
WORKSHIFTING
WORKSTATIONS
WORLD-BEATERS
WORLD-BEATING
WORLDSHAKING
WORLD WIDE WEB
WORM'S EYE
  VIEW
WRATHFULNESS
WRETCHEDNESS
WRISTWATCHES

WRITER'S CRAMP
WRITING DESKS
WRITING PAPER
WRONGFULNESS

X

X CHROMOSOMES
XERODERMATIC
XIPHISTERNUM

Y

Y CHROMOSOMES
YELLOWHAMMER
YIELDINGNESS

YINDJIBARNDI
YOUTHFULNESS
YOUTH HOSTELS

Z

ZINCOGRAPHER
ZINCOGRAPHIC
ZOOCHEMISTRY
ZOOGEOGRAPHY
ZOOSPERMATIC
ZOOTOMICALLY
ZWITTERIONIC
ZYGAPOPHYSIS
ZYGOMORPHISM

13

A
ABBREVIATIONS
ABERDEENSHIRE
ABNORMALITIES
ABOLITIONISTS
ABORTIFACIENT
ABSORBABILITY
ACCELEROMETER
ACCENTUATIONS
ACCEPTABILITY
ACCESSIBILITY
ACCESSORINESS
ACCIDENT-PRONE
ACCLIMATIZING
ACCOMMODATING
ACCOMMODATION
ACCOMMODATIVE
ACCOMPANIMENT
ACCOMPLISHING
ACCOUTREMENTS
ACCREDITATION
ACCULTURATION
ACCUMULATIONS
ACETIFICATION
ACETYLCHOLINE
ACHILLES'
  HEELS
ACIDIFICATION
ACKNOWLEDGING
ACOTYLEDONOUS
ACQUAINTANCES
ACQUIESCENTLY
ACQUIRED TASTE
ACQUISITIVELY
ACRIMONIOUSLY
ACROBATICALLY
ACRYLONITRILE
ACTINOMORPHIC
ACTINOMYCOSIS
ACTINOMYCOTIC
ACTINOTHERAPY
ACTINOURANIUM
ACTUALIZATION
ADDITIONALITY
ADDRESSOGRAPH
ADENOIDECTOMY
ADIAPHORISTIC
ADMEASUREMENT

ADMINISTERING
ADMINISTRATOR
ADMISSIBILITY
ADMONISHINGLY
ADNYAMATHANHA
ADSORBABILITY
ADVANCED LEVEL
ADVENTURESSES
ADVENTUROUSLY
ADVERTISEMENT
AEROMECHANICS
AESTHETICALLY
AFFENPINSCHER
AFFIRMATIVELY
AFFORESTATION
AFTERTHOUGHTS
AGGIORNAMENTO
AGGLOMERATING
AGGLOMERATION
AGGLOMERATIVE
AGGLUTINATION
AGGLUTINATIVE
AGGRAVATINGLY
AGREEABLENESS
AGRICULTURIST
AGROBIOLOGIST
AIR COMMODORES
AIRCRAFTWOMAN
AIRWORTHINESS
AIX-EN-
  PROVENCE
ALBURY-WODONGA
ALCOHOLICALLY
ALCOHOLOMETER
ALDUS MANUTIUS
ALGEBRAICALLY
ALLEGORICALLY
ALLOCHTHONOUS
ALPHA AND
  OMEGA
ALTAI REPUBLIC
ALTERNATIVELY
ALUMINIFEROUS
ALUMINOTHERMY
AMALGAMATIONS
AMBASSADORIAL
AMBIDEXTERITY
AMBIGUGUITIES

AMBIGUOUSNESS
AMBITIOUSNESS
AMERICANIZING
AMERICAN SAMOA
AMNIOCENTESIS
AMORPHOUSNESS
AMPHIBLASTULA
AMPHIPROSTYLE
AMPHITHEATRES
AMPHITRICHOUS
AMPLIFICATION
AMUSEMENT PARK
ANACHRONISTIC
ANAEROBICALLY
ANAESTHETISTS
ANAESTHETIZED
ANAGRAMMATISM
ANAGRAMMATIST
ANAGRAMMATIZE
ANAL RETENTIVE
ANAPHORICALLY
ANAPHRODISIAC
ANATHEMATIZED
ANATOMIZATION
ANCHORPERSONS
ANDHRA PRADESH
ANEMOMETRICAL
ANESTHETIZING
ANFRACTUOSITY
ANGIOSPERMOUS
ANGLICIZATION
ANGLO-AMERICAN
ANGLO-CATHOLIC
ANIMADVERSION
ANIMADVERTING
ANIMALIZATION
ANISOMETROPIA
ANNEXATIONISM
ANNEXATIONIST
ANNIVERSARIES
ANNOUNCEMENTS
ANSWERABILITY
ANTAGONIZABLE
ANTHRAQUINONE
ANTHROPOMETRY
ANTHROPOPATHY
ANTHROPOPHAGI
ANTHROPOSOPHY

ANTI-APARTHEID
ANTIBACTERIAL
ANTICLIMACTIC
ANTICLINORIUM
ANTICLOCKWISE
ANTI-COMMUNIST
ANTIGENICALLY
ANTIHISTAMINE
ANTILOGARITHM
ANTIMACASSARS
ANTIMONARCHIC
ANTINOMICALLY
ANTIPERSONNEL
ANTIPRAGMATIC
ANTIPSYCHOTIC
ANTISPASMODIC
ANTISUBMARINE
APATHETICALLY
APERIODICALLY
APHELIOTROPIC
APLANATICALLY
APOCHROMATISM
APODICTICALLY
APOGEOTROPISM
APOSTROPHIZED
APPLE PIE
  ORDER
APPLICABILITY
APPORTIONABLE
APPORTIONMENT
APPRECIATIONS
APPREHENSIBLE
APPREHENSIONS
APPROPRIATELY
APPROPRIATING
APPROPRIATION
APPROXIMATELY
APPROXIMATING
APPROXIMATION
APPURTENANCES
AQUICULTURIST
ARABIAN DESERT
ARABIC NUMERAL
ARACHNOPHOBIA
ARBITRARINESS
ARBORICULTURE
ARCHAEOLOGIST
ARCHBISHOPRIC

ARCHIDIACONAL
ARCHIMANDRITE
ARCHIPELAGOES
ARCHITECTONIC
ARCHITECTURAL
ARGENTIFEROUS
ARGILLIFEROUS
ARGUMENTATION
ARGUMENTATIVE
ARGYLL AND
 BUTE
ARISTOCRACIES
ARITHMETICIAN
AROMATIZATION
ARRIERE-PENSEE
ARTERIOVENOUS
ARTESIAN WELLS
ARTICULATIONS
ARTIFICIALITY
ARTS AND
 CRAFTS
ARUNDINACEOUS
ASCERTAINABLE
ASCERTAINMENT
ASCHAFFENBURG
ASPERGILLOSIS
ASSASSINATING
ASSASSINATION
ASSAULT COURSE
ASSEMBLY LINES
ASSERTIVENESS
ASSET-STRIPPER
ASSEVERATIONS
ASSIDUOUSNESS
ASSIGNABILITY
ASSYRIOLOGIST
ASTHENOSPHERE
ASTHMATICALLY
ASTIGMATISTIC
ASTONISHINGLY
ASTRODYNAMICS
ASTROPHYSICAL
ASYNDETICALLY
ATACAMA DESERT
ATAVISTICALLY
ATHEISTICALLY
ATOMISTICALLY
ATROCIOUSNESS
ATTAINABILITY
ATTENTIVENESS
AT THE SAME
 TIME

ATTITUDINIZER
ATTRIBUTIVELY
AUBERVILLIERS
AUDACIOUSNESS
AUGMENTATIONS
AUNG SAN SUU
 KYI
AUSTRALASIANS
AUSTRO-ASIATIC
AUTECOLOGICAL
AUTHENTICALLY
AUTHENTICATED
AUTHENTICATOR
AUTHORITARIAN
AUTHORITATIVE
AUTHORIZATION
AUTOBIOGRAPHY
AUTOCATALYSIS
AUTOCHTHONISM
AUTOCHTHONOUS
AUTOMATICALLY
AUTOMATIC DOOR
AUTONOMICALLY
AUTOSTABILITY
AUXILIARY VERB
AXIOMATICALLY

B

BABY CARRIAGES
BACCALAUREATE
BACK FORMATION
BACKPEDALLING
BACKWARDATION
BACTERIOLYSIS
BACTERIOLYTIC
BACTERIOPHAGE
BALANCED DIETS
BALANCE SHEETS
BALKANIZATION
BALLISTICALLY
BALL LIGHTNING
BALNEOLOGICAL
BALSAMIFEROUS
BAMBOOZLEMENT
BANDSPREADING
BANKER'S
 ORDERS
BANTAMWEIGHTS
BARBAROUSNESS
BARBOUR JACKET
BAREFACEDNESS
BASIDIOMYCETE

BASOTHO-QWAQWA
BATTERING RAMS
BATTLE CRUISER
BATTLE-SCARRED
BEAST OF
 BURDEN
BEATIFICATION
BEAUFORT SCALE
BEAUTY PARLOUR
BEHAVIOURALLY
BEHAVIOURISTS
BELISHA BEACON
BELLES-LETTRES
BELLY-LANDINGS
BELO HORIZONTE
BENEFICIARIES
BENEFIT IN
 KIND
BERCHTESGADEN
BEWILDERINGLY
BIBLIOGRAPHER
BIBLIOGRAPHIC
BICENTENARIES
BIDIRECTIONAL
BIG BANG THE-
 ORY
BIGHEADEDNESS
BIGNONIACEOUS
BILLS OF
 HEALTH
BILLS OF
 LADING
BILLS OF
 RIGHTS
BIODEGRADABLE
BIOECOLOGICAL
BIOENERGETICS
BIOMETRICALLY
BIOSTATICALLY
BIOTECHNOLOGY
BIRD OF
 PASSAGE
BIRD'S-EYE
 VIEWS
BIREFRINGENCE
BLABBERMOUTHS
BLACK AND
 WHITE
BLACKBERRYING
BLACK COMEDIES
BLACKCURRANTS
BLACKGUARDISM

BLACK MOUNTAIN
BLACK PUDDINGS
BLAMELESSNESS
BLANDISHMENTS
BLANTYRE-LIMBE
BLASPHEMOUSLY
BLAST FURNACES
BLASTOGENESIS
BLIND MAN'S
 BUFF
BLOOD BROTHERS
BLOODCURDLING
BLOODLESSNESS
BLOOD PRESSURE
BLOOD RELATION
BLOTTING PAPER
BLUE MOUNTAINS
BLUE-PENCILLED
BLUESTOCKINGS
BLUNDERBUSSES
BOARDING CARDS
BOARDINGHOUSE
BOBO-DIOULASSO
BODY SNATCHERS
BODY STOCKINGS
BOILING POINTS
BOMBASTICALLY
BOOBY TRAPPING
BOON COMPANION
BORAGINACEOUS
BORDERS REGION
BOTTLE-FEEDING
BOTTOM DRAWERS
BOUGAINVILLEA
BOUILLABAISSE
BOUNDLESSNESS
BOUNTEOUSNESS
BOUNTIFULNESS
BOUSTROPHEDON
BOWLING ALLEYS
BOWLING GREENS
BRACHYCEPHALY
BRACHYPTEROUS
BRAINLESSNESS
BRAINSTORMING
BRASS FARTHING
BRASSICACEOUS
BRASS KNUCKLES
BROADMINDEDLY
BROKEN-HEARTED
BROMELIACEOUS
BRONCHIAL TUBE

BRONCHOSCOPIC
BROTHERLINESS
BROTHERS-IN-
LAW
BROWNIE GUIDES
BROWNIE POINTS
BRUTALIZATION
BUBONIC PLAGUE
BUDGET DEFICIT
BUILDING BLOCK
BULLETIN BOARD
BUMPTIOUSNESS
BUNGEE JUMPING
BUNSEN BURNERS
BURDEN OF
PROOF
BUREAUCRACIES
BUREAUCRATISM
BURGLAR ALARMS
BURNT OFFERING
BURY ST
EDMUNDS
BUSH CARPENTER
BUSH TELEGRAPH
BUSINESS CLASS
BUSINESS SUITS
BUSINESSWOMAN
BUTCHER'S-
BROOM
BUTTER-FINGERS
BUTYRALDEHYDE

C
CABIN CRUISERS
CABINET-MAKERS
CABLE RAILWAYS
CAICOS ISLANDS
CALCARIFEROUS
CALCIFICATION
CALCULABILITY
CALENDAR MONTH
CALENDAR YEARS
CALLIGRAPHIST
CALLISTHENICS
CALORIFICALLY
CAMBRIDGE BLUE
CAMPANOLOGIST
CAMP FOLLOWERS
CAMPYLOBACTER
CANARY ISLANDS
CANCELLATIONS
CANNIBALISTIC

CANNIBALIZING
CANONIZATIONS
CAPACIOUSNESS
CAPARISONNING
CAPITAL LEVIES
CAPITULATIONS
CAPRIFICATION
CARAVANSERAIS
CARBOHYDRATES
CARBON DIOXIDE
CARBONIFEROUS
CARBONIZATION
CARBON-NEUTRAL
CARBURIZATION
CARCINOMATOID
CARDIGANSHIRE
CARDINAL POINT
CARDIOGRAPHER
CARDIOGRAPHIC
CARDIOLOGICAL
CARICATURISTS
CARNIFICATION
CARPETBAGGERS
CARPET SWEEPER
CARRICKFERGUS
CARRIER PIGEON
CARTILAGINOUS
CARTOGRAPHERS
CARVING KNIVES
CASE HISTORIES
CASH DISPENSER
CASH REGISTERS
CASSEGRAINIAN
CASUISTICALLY
CATASTROPHISM
CATASTROPHIST
CATCHMENT AREA
CATECHIZATION
CATECHOLAMINE
CATEGORICALLY
CATER-CORNERED
CATHARTICALLY
CAT-O'-NINE-
TAILS
CAUTERIZATION
CAYENNE PEPPER
CAYMAN ISLANDS
CELLULAR RADIO
CENTRAL REGION
CENTRE FORWARD
CEPHALIZATION
CEPHALOMETRIC

CEPHALOTHORAX
CEREBRAL PALSY
CEREBROSPINAL
CEREMONIALISM
CEREMONIALIST
CEREMONIOUSLY
CERTIFICATION
CERTIFICATORY
CERTIFIED MAIL
CERTIFIED MILK
CHAFING DISHES
CHAIN REACTION
CHAIN STITCHES
CHAIRMANSHIPS
CHAISE LONGUES
CHALCOGRAPHER
CHALCOGRAPHIC
CHALLENGEABLE
CHAMPIONSHIPS
CHANCELLERIES
CHANDERNAGORE
CHANDRASEKHAR
CHANGEABILITY
CHANGE OF
HEART
CHANGE RINGING
CHANGING ROOMS
CHANNEL TUNNEL
CHANTRY CHAPEL
CHARACTERIZED
CHARACTERLESS
CHARGEABILITY
CHARGE ACCOUNT
CHARLOTTETOWN
CHARNEL HOUSES
CHARTER MEMBER
CHASTISEMENTS
CHASTITY BELTS
CHATEAUBRIAND
CHEERLESSNESS
CHEMISORPTION
CHEMORECEPTOR
CHESTERFIELDS
CHEVAL GLASSES
CHIAROSCURISM
CHIAROSCURIST
CHIEF JUSTICES
CHIEFS OF
STAFF
CHIEFTAINSHIP
CHILDLESSNESS
CHIMNEYBREAST

CHIMNEY CORNER
CHIMNEYPIECES
CHIMNEYSTACKS
CHIMNEYSWEEPS
CHIROPRACTORS
CHLAMYDOSPORE
CHLOROBENZENE
CHLOROFORMING
CHLOROMYCETIN
CHLOROPLASTIC
CHONDRIOSOMAL
CHONDROMATOUS
CHOREOGRAPHED
CHOREOGRAPHER
CHOREOGRAPHIC
CHRISTIANIZER
CHRISTIAN NAME
CHRISTMAS CAKE
CHRISTMAS CARD
CHRISTMASTIDE
CHRISTMAS TIME
CHRISTMAS TREE
CHRISTOLOGIST
CHROMATICALLY
CHROMATICNESS
CHROMATOLYSIS
CHROMATOPHORE
CHROMOPLASMIC
CHROMOPROTEIN
CHROMOSPHERIC
CHRONOBIOLOGY
CHRONOGRAPHER
CHRONOGRAPHIC
CHRONOLOGICAL
CHRYSANTHEMUM
CHURCHWARDENS
CICATRIZATION
CINEMATICALLY
CINEMATOGRAPH
CIRCULARIZING
CIRCUMAMBIENT
CIRCUMCISIONS
CIRCUMFERENCE
CIRCUMFLEXION
CIRCUMSCRIBED
CIRCUMSPECTLY
CIRCUMSTANCES
CIRCUMVALLATE
CIRCUMVENTING
CIRCUMVENTION
CIUDAD GUAYANA
CIVIL ENGINEER

CIVILIZATIONS
CIVIL SERVANTS
CLAIRAUDIENCE
CLANDESTINELY
CLAPPERBOARDS
CLARIFICATION
CLARINETTISTS
CLASSIFIED ADS
CLASSLESSNESS
CLASS STRUGGLE
CLAUSTROPHOBE
CLAVICHORDIST
CLEARANCE SALE
CLEAR-HEADEDLY
CLEARINGHOUSE
CLEISTOGAMOUS
CLERKS OF
  WORKS
CLIMACTERICAL
CLIMATOLOGIST
CLIMBING FRAME
CLIMBING IRONS
CLOSED-CIRCUIT
CLOSED SEASONS
CLOSING PRICES
CLOTHES HANGER
CLOTHESHORSES
CLUSTER-BOMBED
COACHBUILDERS
COACH STATIONS
COBELLIGERENT
COCAINIZATION
COCKER SPANIEL
COCKTAIL STICK
CODECLINATION
CODIFICATIONS
COEDUCATIONAL
COLD-BLOODEDLY
COLD-HEARTEDLY
COLLABORATING
COLLABORATION
COLLABORATIVE
COLLABORATORS
COLLATERALIZE
COLLETIVISTIC
COLLOQUIALISM
COLOUR SCHEMES
COMBAT FATIGUE
COMBINING FORM
COMMANDEERING
COMMANDERSHIP
COMMAND MODULE

COMMEMORATING
COMMEMORATION
COMMEMORATIVE
COMMENCEMENTS
COMMENDATIONS
COMMENSURABLE
COMMERCIALISM
COMMERCIALIST
COMMERCIALITY
COMMERCIALIZE
COMMISERATING
COMMISERATION
COMMISERATIVE
COMMISSARIATS
COMMISSIONERS
COMMISSIONING
COMMUNALISTIC
COMMUNAUTAIRE
COMMUNICATING
COMMUNICATION
COMMUNICATIVE
COMMUNICATORY
COMMUNITARIAN
COMMUNITY HOME
COMMUNIZATION
COMPANIONABLE
COMPANIONABLY
COMPANIONSHIP
COMPANIONWAYS
COMPARABILITY
COMPARATIVELY
COMPARTMENTAL
COMPASSIONATE
COMPASS POINTS
COMPATIBILITY
COMPATRIOTISM
COMPENDIOUSLY
COMPETITIVELY
COMPLAININGLY
COMPLAISANTLY
COMPLEMENTARY
COMPLEMENTING
COMPLICATEDLY
COMPLICATIONS
COMPLIMENTARY
COMPLIMENTING
COMPOSITIONAL
COMPREHENDING
COMPREHENSION
COMPREHENSIVE
COMPRESSIONAL
COMPUTABILITY

COMPUTATIONAL
COMPUTERIZING
CONCATENATING
CONCATENATION
CONCAVO-CONVEX
CONCENTRATING
CONCENTRATION
CONCENTRATIVE
CONCENTRICITY
CONCEPTUALISM
CONCEPTUALIST
CONCEPTUALIZE
CONCERT GRANDS
CONCERTINAING
CONCESSIONARY
CONCHOLOGICAL
CONCHOLOGISTS
CONCOMITANTLY
CONCRETE MIXER
CONCRETIONARY
CONCUPISCENCE
CONDEMNATIONS
CONDEMNED CELL
CONDENSED MILK
CONDESCENDING
CONDESCENSION
CONDITIONALLY
CONDUCIVENESS
CONDUCTOR RAIL
CONDYLOMATOUS
CONFABULATING
CONFABULATION
CONFABULATORY
CONFECTIONARY
CONFECTIONERS
CONFECTIONERY
CONFEDERACIES
CONFEDERATING
CONFEDERATION
CONFESSIONALS
CONFESSIONARY
CONFIGURATION
CONFIRMATIONS
CONFISCATIONS
CONFLAGRATION
CONFLAGRATIVE
CONFORMATIONS
CONFRATERNITY
CONFRONTATION
CONGLOMERATES
CONGLOMERATIC
CONGRATULATED

CONGRATULATOR
CONGREGATIONS
CONGRESSIONAL
CONGRESSWOMAN
CONJUGATIONAL
CONJUNCTIONAL
CONNECTING ROD
CONNING TOWERS
CONNOTATATIVE
CONQUISTADORS
CONSANGUINITY
CONSCIENTIOUS
CONSCIOUSNESS
CONSECUTIVELY
CONSEQUENTIAL
CONSERVANCIES
CONSERVATIVES
CONSERVATOIRE
CONSIDERATELY
CONSIDERATION
CONSISTENCIES
CONSOLIDATING
CONSOLIDATION
CONSPICUOUSLY
CONSPIRATRESS
CONSTELLATION
CONSTELLATORY
CONSTERNATION
CONSTITUTIONS
CONSTRAINEDLY
CONSTRICTIONS
CONSTRUCTIBLE
CONSTRUCTIONS
CONSULTANCIES
CONSULTATIONS
CONSUMMATIONS
CONTACT LENSES
CONTAINERIZED
CONTAMINATING
CONTAMINATION
CONTAMINATORS
CONTEMPLATING
CONTEMPLATION
CONTEMPLATIVE
CONTENTIOUSLY
CONTEXTUALISM
CONTEXTUALIZE
CONTINGENCIES
CONTINUATIONS
CONTORTIONIST
CONTRABANDIST
CONTRABASSIST

CONTRABASSOON
CONTRACEPTION
CONTRACEPTIVE
CONTRACTILITY
CONTRACTIONAL
CONTRACTUALLY
CONTRADICTING
CONTRADICTION
CONTRADICTIVE
CONTRADICTORY
CONTRAPUNTIST
CONTRAVENTION
CONTRIBUTIONS
CONTROVERSIAL
CONTROVERSIES
CONVALESCENCE
CONVALESCENTS
CONVERSATIONS
CONVERSAZIONE
CONVERTIPLANE
CONVEXO-CONVEX
CONVEYER BELTS
CONVOCATIONAL
CONVOLVULUSES
COOKING APPLES
COOPERATIVELY
CORDUROY ROADS
CORELIGIONIST
CO-RESPONDENCY
CO-RESPONDENTS
CORN EXCHANGES
CORPS DE
  BALLET
CORPUS CHRISTI
CORRESPONDENT
CORRESPONDING
CORRIGIBILITY
CORROBORATING
CORROBORATION
CORROBORATIVE
CORROBORATORS
CORRODIBILITY
CORROSIVENESS
CORRUPTIONIST
COSIGNATORIES
COSMOPOLITANS
COSMOPOLITISM
COST-EFFECTIVE
COSTERMONGERS
COTERMINOUSLY
COTTAGE CHEESE
COTTAGE LOAVES

COTTON-PICKING
COUNTENANCING
COUNTERACTING
COUNTERACTION
COUNTERACTIVE
COUNTERATTACK
COUNTERBLASTS
COUNTERCHARGE
COUNTERCLAIMS
COUNTERFEITED
COUNTERFEITER
COUNTERMANDED
COUNTERPOINTS
COUNTERPOISED
COUNTERPOISES
COUNTERSIGNED
COUNTERTENORS
COUNTERWEIGHT
COUNTINGHOUSE
COUNTRY COUSIN
COUNTRY DANCES
COUNTY BOROUGH
COUNTY COUNCIL
COURT CIRCULAR
COURTEOUSNESS
COURT MARTIALS
COURTS-MARTIAL
COVERED WAGONS
CRAFTSMANSHIP
CRANIOLOGICAL
CRASH BARRIERS
CRASH LANDINGS
CRASSULACEOUS
CREAM OF
  TARTAR
CREDIT ACCOUNT
CREDIT SQUEEZE
CREME DE
  MENTHE
CRIMINOLOGIST
CRISSCROSSING
CROSSBENCHERS
CROSSBREEDING
CROSSCHECKING
CROSSCURRENTS
CROSS-DRESSERS
CROSS-DRESSING
CROSS-EXAMINED
CROSS-EXAMINER
CROSS-HATCHING
CROSS-PURPOSES
CROSS-QUESTION

CROSS-REFERRED
CROSS-SECTIONS
CROSS-STITCHES
CROWDSOURCING
CROWN COLONIES
CROWN IMPERIAL
CROWN PRINCESS
CRUISE MISSILE
CRUISERWEIGHT
CRUSH BARRIERS
CRYOBIOLOGIST
CRYPTANALYSIS
CRYPTANALYTIC
CRYPTOCLASTIC
CRYPTOGRAPHER
CRYPTOGRAPHIC
CRYPTOZOOLOGY
CRYSTAL GAZERS
CRYSTAL GAZING
CRYSTALLINITY
CRYSTALLIZING
CUMULOSTRATUS
CURTAIN RAISER
CUSTODIANSHIP
CUT ONE'S
  LOSSES
CYANOBACTERIA
CYBERNETICIST
CYLINDRICALLY
CYTOCHEMISTRY
CYTOTAXONOMIC
CZECH REPUBLIC

D
DADAISTICALLY
DADDY LONGLEGS
DAGUERREOTYPE
DAGUERREOTYPY
DAMAGEABILITY
DAMNIFICATION
DANDIFICATION
DARK CONTINENT
DASTARDLINESS
DAUGHTER-IN-
  LAW
DEAD-CAT
  BOUNCE
DEAD RECKONING
DEATH WARRANTS
DEBTS OF
  HONOUR
DECAPITATIONS

DECEITFULNESS
DECENTRALIZED
DECEPTIVENESS
DECEREBRATION
DECK PASSENGER
DECLAMATORILY
DECLARATORILY
DECLASSIFYING
DECOMPOSITION
DECOMPRESSING
DECOMPRESSION
DECOMPRESSIVE
DECONGESTANTS
DECONTAMINANT
DECONTAMINATE
DECONTROLLING
DECORTICATION
DECREPITATION
DEDUCTIBILITY
DEFECTIVENESS
DEFENSIBILITY
DEFENSIVENESS
DEFERENTIALLY
DEFIBRILLATOR
DEFORESTATION
DEGLUTINATION
DEHYDROGENASE
DEHYDROGENATE
DEHYDROGENIZE
DELETERIOUSLY
DELIBERATIONS
DELICATESSENS
DELICIOUSNESS
DELINQUENCIES
DELIQUESCENCE
DELIRIOUSNESS
DEMAGNETIZING
DEMAGOGICALLY
DEMERARA SUGAR
DEMERITORIOUS
DEMILITARIZED
DEMOCRATIZING
DEMOLITIONIST
DEMONOLOGICAL
DEMONSTRATING
DEMONSTRATION
DEMONSTRATIVE
DEMONSTRATORS
DENATIONALIZE
DENDRITICALLY
DENDROLOGICAL
DENOMINATIONS

DENSITOMETRIC
DENTAL SURGEON
DENTICULATION
DENUNCIATIONS
DEODORIZATION
DEONTOLOGICAL
DEOXIDIZATION
DEOXYGENATION
DEPENDABILITY
DEPERSONALIZE
DEPRECATINGLY
DEPRECATORILY
DEPRESSOMOTOR
DERMATOLOGIST
DERMATOPHYTIC
DERMATOPLASTY
DESCRIPTIVELY
DESCRIPTIVISM
DESEGREGATING
DESEGREGATION
DESENSITIZING
DESPICABILITY
DESSERTSPOONS
DESTABILIZING
DESTRUCTIVELY
DESULTORINESS
DETACHABILITY
DETERIORATING
DETERIORATION
DETERIORATIVE
DETERMINATION
DETERMINATIVE
DETERMINISTIC
DETESTABILITY
DETRIMENTALLY
DEUTEROGAMIST
DEVASTATINGLY
DEVELOPMENTAL
DEVIATIONISTS
DEVOLUTIONARY
DEVOTIONALITY
DEXTEROUSNESS
DEXTROGLUCOSE
DIAGEOTROPISM
DIAGNOSTICIAN
DIALECTICIANS
DIALLING CODES
DIALLING TONES
DIALYSABILITY
DIAMETRICALLY
DIAPHRAGMATIC
DIATHERMANOUS

DIATONIC SCALE
DIAZOTIZATION
DICHLAMIDEOUS
DICTATORIALLY
DICTATORSHIPS
DIEFFENBACHIA
DIESEL ENGINES
DIFFERENTIALS
DIFFERENTIATE
DIFFUSIBILITY
DIGESTIBILITY
DIGITAL CAMERA
DILAPIDATIONS
DILLYDALLYING
DIMENSIONLESS
DIM-WITTEDNESS
DINNER JACKETS
DINNER SERVICE
DIPHENYLAMINE
DIPSOMANIACAL
DIRECT CURRENT
DIRECT OBJECTS
DIRECTORSHIPS
DISADVANTAGED
DISADVANTAGES
DISAFFECTEDLY
DISAFFILIATED
DISAFFIRMANCE
DISAFFORESTED
DISAGREEMENTS
DISAPPEARANCE
DISAPPOINTING
DISARTICULATE
DISASSOCIATED
DISBURDENMENT
DISBURSEMENTS
DISCHARGEABLE
DISCIPLINABLE
DISCOLORATION
DISCOMMODIOUS
DISCOMPOSEDLY
DISCONCERTING
DISCONCERTION
DISCONFORMITY
DISCONNECTING
DISCONNECTION
DISCONNECTIVE
DISCONTENTING
DISCONTINUING
DISCONTINUITY
DISCONTINUOUS
DISCOUNT STORE

DISCOURTESIES
DISCREDITABLE
DISCREDITABLY
DISCREPANCIES
DISCRETIONARY
DISCRIMINATED
DISCRIMINATOR
DISEMBODIMENT
DISEMBOWELING
DISEMBOWELLED
DISENABLEMENT
DISENGAGEMENT
DISENTAILMENT
DISENTANGLING
DISFIGUREMENT
DISFRANCHISED
DISGRACEFULLY
DISHARMONIOUS
DISHONOURABLE
DISHONOURABLY
DISILLUSIONED
DISINCENTIVES
DISINFECTANTS
DISINHERITING
DISINTEGRABLE
DISINTEGRATED
DISINTEGRATOR
DISINTERESTED
DISINTERMENTS
DISINVESTMENT
DISMANTLEMENT
DISMEMBERMENT
DISOBEDIENTLY
DISOBLIGINGLY
DISORIENTATED
DISPARAGEMENT
DISPARAGINGLY
DISPASSIONATE
DISPATCH BOXES
DISPENSATIONS
DISPLACEMENTS
DISPOSABILITY
DISPOSITIONAL
DISPOSSESSING
DISPOSSESSION
DISPOSSESSORY
DISPROPORTION
DISPUTABILITY
DISQUALIFYING
DISQUISITIONS
DISRESPECTFUL
DISSATISFYING

DISSEMINATING
DISSEMINATION
DISSEMINATIVE
DISSEPIMENTAL
DISSERTATIONS
DISSIMILARITY
DISSIMILATION
DISSIMILATIVE
DISSIMILATORY
DISSIMILITUDE
DISSIMULATING
DISSIMULATION
DISSIMULATIVE
DISSOLUBILITY
DISSOLUTENESS
DISTASTEFULLY
DISTILLATIONS
DISTINCTIVELY
DISTINGUISHED
DISTINGUISHER
DISTRESSINGLY
DISTRIBUTABLE
DISTRIBUTIONS
DISTRUSTFULLY
DITRANSITIVES
DIVERSIFIABLE
DIVISIONALIZE
DIVISION LOBBY
DOCTRINAIRISM
DOCUMENTARIES
DOCUMENTARILY
DOCUMENTARIST
DOCUMENTATION
DODECAPHONISM
DODECAPHONIST
DOGMATIZATION
DOG'S BREAK-
FAST
DOLLARIZATION
DOME OF THE
ROCK
DOMESTICATING
DOMESTICATION
DOMESTICATIVE
DOMESTICITIES
DONKEY JACKETS
DOSIMETRICIAN
DOTHEBOYS HALL
DOUBLE-CHECKED
DOUBLE-CROSSED
DOUBLE-CROSSER
DOUBLE-CROSSES

DOUBLE-DEALERS
DOUBLE-DEALING
DOUBLE-DECKERS
DOUBLE FEATURE
DOUBLE FIGURES
DOUBLE-GLAZING
DOUBLE-JOINTED
DOUBLE OR
 QUITS
DOUBLE-PARKING
DOUBLE-TALKING
DOWNHEARTEDLY
DOWNING STREET
DOWN'S
 SYNDROME
DRAINING BOARD
DRAMATIC IRONY
DRAMATIZATION
DRAWING BOARDS
DRESSING GOWNS
DRESSING ROOMS
DRESSING TABLE
DRINKING WATER
DRUM MAJORETTE
DRYOPITHECINE
DUALISTICALLY
DUCKING STOOLS
DUCTLESS GLAND
DUMFRIESSHIRE
DUPLICABILITY
DUQUE DE
 CAXIAS
DUTCH AUCTIONS
DWELLING HOUSE
DYED-IN-THE-
 WOOL
DYSFUNCTIONAL
DYSMENORRHOEA

E
EAST-NORTHEAST
EAST-SOUTHEAST
EAVESDROPPERS
EAVESDROPPING
ECCENTRICALLY
ECCLESIASTICS
ECCLESIOLATER
ECCLESIOLATRY
ECONOMIZATION
ECTOPARASITIC
ECUMENICALISM
EDITORIALIZER

EDUCATED GUESS
EFFECTIVENESS
EFFERVESCENCE
EFFERVESCIBLE
EFFICACIOUSLY
EFFLORESCENCE
EGOCENTRICITY
EGOTISTICALLY
EGREGIOUSNESS
EGYPTOLOGICAL
EIGHTEEN HOLES
ELABORATENESS
ELECTIONEERER
ELECTRIC CHAIR
ELECTRIC FENCE
ELECTRIC SHOCK
ELECTRIFIABLE
ELECTROCUTING
ELECTROCUTION
ELECTROGRAPHY
ELECTROMAGNET
ELECTROMERISM
ELECTROMETRIC
ELECTROMOTIVE
ELECTROPHILIC
ELECTROPHONIC
ELECTROPHORUS
ELECTROPLATER
ELECTROSCOPIC
ELECTROSTATIC
ELECTROVALENT
ELEPHANTIASIC
ELEPHANTIASIS
ELEPHANT'S-
 FOOT
ELLESMERE PORT
EMBARRASSMENT
EMBELLISHMENT
EMBRYOLOGICAL
EMBRYONICALLY
EMILIA-ROMAGNA
EMINENCE GRISE
EMOTIONLESSLY
EMPHYSEMATOUS
EMPIRE-BUILDER
EMPIRICALNESS
EMPLOYABILITY
EMULSION PAINT
ENCAPSULATION
ENCAUSTICALLY
ENCEPHALOGRAM
ENCHANTRESSES

ENCOMPASSMENT
ENCOURAGEMENT
ENCOURAGINGLY
ENCROACHINGLY
ENCROACHMENTS
ENCULTURATION
ENCULTURATIVE
ENCUMBERINGLY
ENCYCLOPEDIAS
ENCYCLOPEDISM
ENCYCLOPEDIST
ENDOCRINOLOGY
ENDODONTOLOGY
ENDOLYMPHATIC
ENDOMETRIOSIS
ENDOPARASITIC
ENDOPEPTIDASE
ENERGETICALLY
ENFRANCHISING
ENGINE DRIVERS
ENIGMATICALLY
ENLIGHTENMENT
ENROLLED NURSE
ENTANGLEMENTS
ENTERTAINMENT
ENTHRALLINGLY
ENTHRONEMENTS
ENTOMOLOGICAL
ENTOMOLOGISTS
ENTOMOPHAGOUS
ENTOMOPHILOUS
ENTOMOSTRACAN
ENTREPRENEURS
ENUNCIABILITY
ENVIRONMENTAL
ENZYMOLOGICAL
EPIGRAMMATISM
EPIGRAMMATIST
EPIGRAMMATIZE
EPILEPTICALLY
EPIPHENOMENAL
EPIPHENOMENON
EPIPHYTICALLY
EPISCOPALIANS
EPITOMIZATION
EPIZOOTICALLY
EQUESTRIANISM
EQUILIBRATION
EQUILIBRISTIC
EQUIMOLECULAR
EQUIPONDERANT
EQUIPONDERATE

EQUIPOTENTIAL
EQUITABLENESS
EQUIVOCATIONS
ERGONOMICALLY
ERRONEOUSNESS
ERYSIPELATOUS
ESCAPOLOGISTS
ESCHATOLOGIST
ESPIRITO SANTO
ESPRIT DE
 CORPS
ESTABLISHMENT
ESTIMABLENESS
ESTRANGEMENTS
ETHNOCENTRISM
ETHNOGRAPHERS
ETHOLOGICALLY
ETIOLOGICALLY
EUROCOMMUNISM
EUSPORANGIATE
EVAPORABILITY
EVENTUALITIES
EVERLASTINGLY
EVERY WHICH
 WAY
EVOCATIVENESS
EXAGGERATEDLY
EXAGGERATIONS
EXAMINATIONAL
EXANTHEMATOUS
EXASPERATEDLY
EXCEPTIONABLE
EXCEPTIONALLY
EXCESSIVENESS
EXCHANGE RATES
EXCLAMATIONAL
EXCLAMATORILY
EXCLUDABILITY
EXCLUSIVENESS
EXCOMMUNICATE
EXCURSIVENESS
EXCUSABLENESS
EXECRABLENESS
EXEMPLARINESS
EXEMPLIFIABLE
EXEMPLI GRATIA
EXHIBITIONISM
EXHIBITIONIST
EXPANSIBILITY
EXPANSIONISTS
EXPANSIVENESS
EXPECTORATING

EXPECTORATION
EXPEDITIONARY
EXPEDITIOUSLY
EXPENDABILITY
EXPENSIVENESS
EXPERIMENTING
EXPERT SYSTEMS
EXPLANATORIES
EXPLANATORILY
EXPLOSIVENESS
EXPONENTIALLY
EXPORTABILITY
EXPOSTULATING
EXPOSTULATION
EXPOSTULATORY
EXPRESSIONISM
EXPRESSIONIST
EXPROPRIATING
EXPROPRIATION
EXPROPRIATORS
EXQUISITENESS
EXTEMPORARILY
EXTEMPORIZING
EXTENDIBILITY
EXTENSIBILITY
EXTENSIVENESS
EXTENUATINGLY
EXTERMINATING
EXTERMINATION
EXTERMINATIVE
EXTERMINATORS
EXTERNALIZING
EXTEROCEPTIVE
EXTERRITORIAL
EXTINGUISHANT
EXTINGUISHERS
EXTINGUISHING
EXTORTIONABLE
EXTORTIONISTS
EXTRACELLULAR
EXTRAGALACTIC
EXTRAJUDICIAL
EXTRAORDINARY
EXTRAPOLATING
EXTRAPOLATION
EXTRAPOLATIVE
EXTRAPOSITION
EXTRAVAGANCES
EXTRAVAGANTLY
EXTRAVAGANZAS
EXTRAVAGATION
EXTRAVASATION

EXTRAVASCULAR
EXTRINSICALLY
EYEBROW PENCIL
EYE-CATCHINGLY

F

FACETIOUSNESS
FACTORABILITY
FACTORIZATION
FAITHLESSNESS
FALLOPIAN TUBE
FALSIFICATION
FAMILIARITIES
FAMILIARIZING
FAMILY DOCTORS
FAMILY SUPPORT
FANTASTICALLY
FASCICULATION
FASCINATINGLY
FASCISTICALLY
FATHEADEDNESS
FATHER FIGURES
FAULTLESSNESS
FEATHERBEDDED
FEATHERSTITCH
FEATHER-VEINED
FEATHERWEIGHT
FEATURE-LENGTH
FEEDING BOTTLE
FELICITATIONS
FELLOW FEELING
FELONIOUSNESS
FEMMES FATALES
FEROCIOUSNESS
FERRIMAGNETIC
FERROCHROMIUM
FERROCONCRETE
FERROELECTRIC
FERROMAGNETIC
FERTILIZATION
FEUDALIZATION
FEUILLETONISM
FEUILLETONIST
FIBROVASCULAR
FICTIONALIZED
FIELD MARSHALS
FIELD OF
  VISION
FIGHTER-BOMBER
FIGURED BASSES
FIGURE OF
  EIGHT

FIGURE SKATERS
FIGURE-SKATING
FILIBUSTERING
FILING CABINET
FILM PREMIERES
FILTERABILITY
FINANCIAL YEAR
FINE-TOOTH
  COMB
FINGERPRINTED
FIRST MINISTER
FIRST OFFENDER
FISH-EYE
  LENSES
FISSION-FUSION
FLABBERGASTED
FLAGELLANTISM
FLAME-THROWERS
FLAVOPURPURIN
FLEET ADMIRALS
FLESH AND
  BLOOD
FLIGHT CAPITAL
FLIRTATIOUSLY
FLOATING-POINT
FLOATING VOTER
FLOODLIGHTING
FLORIANOPOLIS
FLORICULTURAL
FLORISTICALLY
FLOURISHINGLY
FLYING COLOURS
FLYING DOCTORS
FLYING OFFICER
FLYING PICKETS
FLYING SAUCERS
FOLLOW-THROUGH
FONTAINEBLEAU
FOOD POISONING
FOOD PROCESSOR
FOOLHARDINESS
FOOL'S
  PARADISE
FOOTBALL POOLS
FORAMINIFERAL
FORBIDDEN CITY
FOREIGN OFFICE
FOREJUDGEMENT
FOREKNOWINGLY
FOREKNOWLEDGE
FORENSICALITY
FOREORDAINING

FORESHADOWING
FORESHORTENED
FOREWARNINGLY
FORGETFULNESS
FORGIVINGNESS
FORKLIFT TRUCK
FORMALIZATION
FORMATIVENESS
FORMIDABILITY
FORTIFICATION
FORTITUDINOUS
FORTUNE HUNTER
FORTUNE-TELLER
FOSSILIFEROUS
FOSSILIZATION
FOUNDATIONARY
FRACTIONATION
FRACTIOUSNESS
FRACTOCUMULUS
FRACTOSTRATUS
FRAGMENTATION
FRANCHISEMENT
FREDERIKSBERG
FREEZING POINT
FREIGHTLINERS
FRENCH WINDOWS
FREQUENTATION
FREQUENTATIVE
FREUDIAN SLIPS
FRIDGE-FREEZER
FRIGHTENINGLY
FRIGHTFULNESS
FRINGE BENEFIT
FRIVOLOUSNESS
FRONTBENCHERS
FRONTISPIECES
FRONTOGENESIS
FRUITLESSNESS
FRUIT MACHINES
FRUMENTACEOUS
FULL-FASHIONED
FUNCTIONALISM
FUNCTIONALIST
FUNCTIONARIES
FUNDAMENTALLY
FUNNY BUSINESS
FUTURE PERFECT

G

GALLICIZATION
GALLOWS HUMOUR
GALVANOMETRIC

GALVANOSCOPIC
GALVANOTROPIC
GAMBREL-ROOFED
GAMETOGENESIS
GAMMA GLOBULIN
GARBAGE TRUCKS
GARDEN PARTIES
GARRULOUSNESS
GASTROSCOPIST
GEIGER COUNTER
GELANDESPRUNG
GELSENKIRCHEN
GENDER-BENDERS
GENERALISSIMO
GENERAL STRIKE
GENERATION GAP
GENTIANACEOUS
GENUFLECTIONS
GEOCHRONOLOGY
GEODYNAMICIST
GEO-ENGINEERED
GEOMETRICALLY
GEOMORPHOLOGY
GEOPOLITICIAN
GEOSTATIONARY
GEOTACTICALLY
GEOTROPICALLY
GERIATRICIANS
GERMANIZATION
GERMAN MEASLES
GERMANOPHILIA
GERMANOPHOBIA
GERONTOCRATIC
GERONTOLOGIST
GERRYMANDERED
GESTICULATING
GESTICULATION
GESTICULATIVE
GHETTO BLASTER
GLACIOLOGICAL
GLAMORIZATION
GLAMOROUSNESS
GLOBETROTTERS
GLOBETROTTING
GLOBULIFEROUS
GLOCKENSPIELS
GLORIFICATION
GLOSSOGRAPHER
GLUTINOUSNESS
GLYPHOGRAPHER
GLYPHOGRAPHIC
GLYPTOGRAPHER

GLYPTOGRAPHIC
GO-AS-YOU-
  PLEASE
GOING STRAIGHT
GOLDEN HAMSTER
GOLDEN JUBILEE
GOLDEN WEDDING
GOLDFISH BOWLS
GOOD AFTERNOON
GOOD-NATUREDLY
GOOD SAMARITAN
GOOSESTEPPING
GOVERNABILITY
GRACELESSNESS
GRADE CROSSING
GRAMINIVOROUS
GRAMMAR SCHOOL
GRAMMATICALLY
GRAM-MOLECULAR
GRANDCHILDREN
GRANDDAUGHTER
GRANDILOQUENT
GRANULOMATOUS
GRAPHEMICALLY
GRAPHICALNESS
GRAPHIC DESIGN
GRAPHOLOGISTS
GRAPPLING IRON
GRATIFICATION
GRAVEYARD SLOT
GRAVITATIONAL
GREAT YARMOUTH
GREEN-FINGERED
GROTESQUENESS
GROUND STROKES
GROUP CAPTAINS
GROUP PRACTICE
GUARDIAN ANGEL
GUATEMALA CITY
GUBERNATORIAL
GUIDED MISSILE
GUILELESSNESS
GUILTLESSNESS
GUNPOWDER PLOT
GYMNOSPERMISM
GYMNOSPERMOUS
GYNAECOCRATIC
GYNAECOLOGIST
GYNANDROMORPH

H
HACKING COUGHS

HAEMATOGENOUS
HAEMATOLOGIST
HAEMODIALYSIS
HAEMOPHILIOID
HAEMORRHOIDAL
HAGIOGRAPHIES
HAILE SELASSIE
HAIR-RESTORERS
HAIR-SPLITTING
HALE AND
  HEARTY
HALF-HEARTEDLY
HALFWAY HOUSES
HALICARNASSUS
HALLUCINATING
HALLUCINATION
HALLUCINATORY
HAMILCAR BARCA
HANDBRAKE TURN
HANDKERCHIEFS
HANG SENG
  INDEX
HAPHAZARDNESS
HARD-HEARTEDLY
HARD-LUCK
  STORY
HARD OF
  HEARING
HARD SHOULDERS
HARMONIZATION
HARUN AL-
  RASHID
HAVE NO TIME
  FOR
HAZARDOUSNESS
HEADSHRINKERS
HEALTHFULNESS
HEALTH VISITOR
HEARTBREAKING
HEARTBROKENLY
HEART DISEASES
HEARTLESSNESS
HEARTSICKNESS
HEARTSOMENESS
HEART-TO-
  HEARTS
HEATH ROBINSON
HEAVY HYDROGEN
HEAVY INDUSTRY
HEDGE SPARROWS
HEEBIE-JEEBIES
HEIRS APPARENT

HELLENIZATION
HELMINTHIASIS
HELMINTHOLOGY
HELTER SKELTER
HELTER-SKELTER
HEMICELLULOSE
HENDECAHEDRON
HEPTADECANOIC
HEPTAMETRICAL
HERBIVOROUSLY
HEREDITAMENTS
HEREFORDSHIRE
HERMAPHRODITE
HERNIORRHAPHY
HEROIC COUPLET
HERPES SIMPLEX
HERPETOLOGIST
HERTFORDSHIRE
HETEROGENEITY
HETEROGENEOUS
HETEROGENESIS
HETEROGENETIC
HETEROGRAPHIC
HETEROMORPHIC
HETEROPLASTIC
HETEROPTEROUS
HETEROSEXUALS
HETEROSPOROUS
HETEROSTYLOUS
HETEROTHALLIC
HETEROTROPHIC
HETEROZYGOSIS
HEURISTICALLY
HIERACOSPHINX
HIEROGLYPHICS
HIEROGLYPHIST
HIGH-AND-
  MIGHTY
HIGH CHURCHMAN
HIGHER-RATE
  TAX
HIGH EXPLOSIVE
HIGHLAND FLING
HIGH-PRESSURED
HIGH-WATER
  MARK
HILARIOUSNESS
HILDEBRANDIAN
HILDEBRANDINE
HISTOCHEMICAL
HOBSON'S
  CHOICE

HO CHI MINH
  CITY
HOIDENISHNESS
HOLE-AND-
  CORNER
HOLIDAYMAKERS
HOLIDAYMAKING
HOLY COMMUNION
HOME ECONOMICS
HOMEOMORPHISM
HOMILETICALLY
HOMOCHROMATIC
HOMOEROTICISM
HOMOGENEOUSLY
HOMOIOTHERMIC
HOMOLOGICALLY
HOMOLOGRAPHIC
HOMOOUSIANISM
HOMOSEXUALITY
HONEYDEW MELON
HONORIFICALLY
HORNS OF
  PLENTY
HORRIFICATION
HORRIPILATION
HORSE CHESTNUT
HORSEWHIPPING
HORTICULTURAL
HOSPITALIZING
HOT-GOSPELLERS
HOT-GOSPELLING
HOT-HEADEDNESS
HOUSEBREAKERS
HOUSEBREAKING
HOUSEHOLD NAME
HOUSEHUSBANDS
HOUSEMISTRESS
HOUSES OF
  CARDS
HOUSE SPARROWS
HOUSEWARMINGS
HOYDENISHNESS
HUCKLEBERRIES
HUMANITARIANS
HUMILIATINGLY
HUNDREDWEIGHT
HUNGER MARCHER
HUNGER MARCHES
HUNGER STRIKER
HUNGER STRIKES
HUNTING GROUND
HURRICANE LAMP

HYALURONIDASE
HYBRIDIZATION
HYDRAULICALLY
HYDROCEPHALIC
HYDROCEPHALUS
HYDROCHLORIDE
HYDRODYNAMICS
HYDROELECTRIC
HYDROGENATION
HYDROGEN BOMBS
HYDROKINETICS
HYDROLYSATION
HYPERCRITICAL
HYPOCHONDRIAC

I

IATROGENICITY
ICE-CREAM
  SODAS
ICHTHYOLOGIST
ICONOMATICISM
IDEALIZATIONS
IDENTICAL TWIN
IDENTITY CARDS
IDEOLOGICALLY
IDIOMATICALLY
IDIOSYNCRATIC
IGNOMINIOUSLY
ILL-CONSIDERED
ILLE-ET-
  VILAINE
ILLOCUTIONARY
ILLUMINATIONS
ILLUSIONISTIC
ILLUSTRATIONS
ILLUSTRIOUSLY
IMAGINATIVELY
IMAGISTICALLY
IMITATIVENESS
IMMATERIALISM
IMMATERIALIST
IMMATERIALITY
IMMATERIALIZE
IMMIGRATIONAL
IMMISCIBILITY
IMMORTALIZING
IMMUNIZATIONS
IMMUNOGENETIC
IMMUNOTHERAPY
IMPALPABILITY
IMPARIPINNATE
IMPARTIBILITY

IMPASSABILITY
IMPASSIONEDLY
IMPASSIVENESS
IMPECCABILITY
IMPECUNIOUSLY
IMPERCEPTIBLE
IMPERCEPTIBLY
IMPERFECTIONS
IMPERFORATION
IMPERIALISTIC
IMPERIOUSNESS
IMPERMISSIBLE
IMPERSONALITY
IMPERSONALIZE
IMPERSONATING
IMPERSONATION
IMPERSONATORS
IMPERTINENTLY
IMPERTURBABLE
IMPERTURBABLY
IMPETUOUSNESS
IMPLACABILITY
IMPONDERABLES
IMPORTUNATELY
IMPOSSIBILITY
IMPOVERISHING
IMPRACTICABLE
IMPRACTICABLY
IMPRACTICALLY
IMPRESSIONISM
IMPRESSIONIST
IMPROBABILITY
IMPROPRIATION
IMPROPRIETIES
IMPROVABILITY
IMPROVIDENTLY
IMPROVISATION
IMPULSIVENESS
INADVERTENTLY
INAPPROPRIATE
INATTENTIVELY
INAUGURATIONS
INCANDESCENCE
INCANTATIONAL
INCAPACITATED
INCAPSULATION
INCARCERATING
INCARCERATION
INCARDINATION
INCLINATIONAL
INCOMBUSTIBLE
INCOME SUPPORT

INCOMMUNICADO
INCOMPETENTLY
INCONCEIVABLE
INCONCEIVABLY
INCONDENSABLE
INCONGRUITIES
INCONGRUOUSLY
INCONSEQUENCE
INCONSIDERATE
INCONSISTENCY
INCONSPICUOUS
INCONSTANCIES
INCONTESTABLE
INCONTESTABLY
INCONVENIENCE
INCONVERTIBLE
INCONVINCIBLE
INCORPORATING
INCORPORATION
INCORPORATIVE
INCORPOREALLY
INCORRECTNESS
INCORRUPTIBLE
INCORRUPTIBLY
INCREDIBILITY
INCREDULOUSLY
INCREMENTALLY
INCRIMINATING
INCRIMINATION
INCRIMINATORY
INCRUSTATIONS
INCULPABILITY
INDEFATIGABLE
INDEFATIGABLY
INDENTURESHIP
INDEPENDENTLY
INDESCRIBABLE
INDESCRIBABLY
INDETERMINACY
INDETERMINATE
INDETERMINISM
INDETERMINIST
INDIAN SUMMERS
INDIFFERENTLY
INDISCERNIBLE
INDISCRETIONS
INDISPENSABLE
INDISPENSABLY
INDISPOSITION
INDISTINCTIVE
INDIVIDUALISM
INDIVIDUALIST

INDIVIDUALITY	INOFFENSIVELY	INTERCLAVICLE	INTRANSIGENCE
INDIVIDUALIZE	INOPERABILITY	INTERCOLUMNAR	INTRAPERSONAL
INDIVIDUATION	INOPPORTUNELY	INTERCURRENCE	INTRATELLURIC
INDOCTRINATED	INORGANICALLY	INTEREST GROUP	INTRAVASATION
INDOCTRINATOR	INQUISITIONAL	INTERESTINGLY	INTRAVENOUSLY
INDOLEBUTYRIC	INQUISITIVELY	INTERFACIALLY	INTRINSICALLY
INDUPLICATION	INQUISITORIAL	INTERFERINGLY	INTRODUCTIONS
INDUSTRIALISM	INSATIABILITY	INTERGALACTIC	INTROGRESSION
INDUSTRIALIST	INSCRIPTIONAL	INTERGRADIENT	INTROSPECTION
INDUSTRIALIZE	INSECTIVOROUS	INTERJECTIONS	INTROSPECTIVE
INDUSTRIOUSLY	INSENSIBILITY	INTERLACEMENT	INTUITIVENESS
INEDUCABILITY	INSENSITIVELY	INTERLAMINATE	INVARIABILITY
INEFFECTIVELY	INSENSITIVITY	INTERLOCUTION	INVENTIVENESS
INEFFECTUALLY	INSIDIOUSNESS	INTERLOCUTORS	INVENTORIABLE
INEFFICACIOUS	INSIGNIFICANT	INTERLOCUTORY	INVERTEBRATES
INEFFICIENTLY	INSOLVABILITY	INTERLUNATION	INVERTED COMMA
INELIGIBILITY	INSPECTORATES	INTERMARRIAGE	INVERTED SNOBS
INEVITABILITY	INSPECTORSHIP	INTERMARRYING	INVERTIBILITY
INEXHAUSTIBLE	INSPIRATIONAL	INTERMEDIATOR	INVESTIGATING
INEXHAUSTIBLY	INSPIRITINGLY	INTERMINGLING	INVESTIGATION
INEXORABILITY	INSTABILITIES	INTERMISSIONS	INVESTIGATIVE
INEXPENSIVELY	INSTALLATIONS	INTERMITTENCE	INVESTIGATORS
INEXPERIENCED	INSTANTANEOUS	INTERNALIZING	INVIDIOUSNESS
INEXPRESSIBLE	INSTIGATINGLY	INTERNATIONAL	INVINCIBILITY
INEXPRESSIBLY	INSTINCTIVELY	INTEROCEPTIVE	INVIOLABILITY
INFALLIBILITY	INSTITUTIONAL	INTEROPERABLE	INVOLUNTARILY
INFANT PRODIGY	INSTRUCTIONAL	INTEROSCULATE	IONIAN ISLANDS
INFECTIVENESS	INSTRUCTIVELY	INTERPELLATOR	IRONING BOARDS
INFERENTIALLY	INSUBORDINATE	INTERPERSONAL	IRRATIONALITY
INFILTRATIONS	INSUBSTANTIAL	INTERPOLATING	IRRECLAIMABLE
INFINITESIMAL	INSUFFICIENCY	INTERPOLATION	IRRECOVERABLE
INFLAMMATIONS	INSUPPORTABLE	INTERPOLATIVE	IRRECOVERABLY
INFLECTEDNESS	INSURRECTIONS	INTERPOSINGLY	IRREFRANGIBLE
INFLEXIBILITY	INSUSCEPTIBLE	INTERPOSITION	IRRELIGIONIST
INFLORESCENCE	INTANGIBILITY	INTERPRETABLE	IRREPLACEABLE
INFLUENCEABLE	INTEGRABILITY	INTERRACIALLY	IRREPLEVIABLE
INFLUENTIALLY	INTEGUMENTARY	INTERRELATION	IRREPRESSIBLE
INFORMATIONAL	INTELLECTUALS	INTERROGATING	IRREPRESSIBLY
INFORMATIVELY	INTELLIGENTLY	INTERROGATION	IRRESPONSIBLE
INFRINGEMENTS	INTEMPERATELY	INTERROGATIVE	IRRESPONSIBLY
INFURIATINGLY	INTENTIONALLY	INTERROGATORS	IRRETRIEVABLE
INGENUOUSNESS	INTERACTIONAL	INTERROGATORY	IRRETRIEVABLY
INGRAINEDNESS	INTERACTIVELY	INTERRUPTIBLE	ISOAGGLUTININ
INGURGITATION	INTERACTIVITY	INTERRUPTIONS	ISODIMORPHISM
INHOSPITALITY	INTERBREEDING	INTERSECTIONS	ISODIMORPHOUS
INIMITABILITY	INTERCALARILY	INTERSPERSING	ISOELECTRONIC
INJUDICIOUSLY	INTERCALATION	INTERSPERSION	ISOGEOTHERMAL
INLAND REVENUE	INTERCALATIVE	INTERSTRATIFY	ISOLATIONISTS
INNER MONGOLIA	INTERCELLULAR	INTERTROPICAL	ISOMERIZATION
INNOCUOUSNESS	INTERCEPTIONS	INTERVENTIONS	ISOSPONDYLOUS
INNOVATIONIST	INTERCESSIONS	INTRACELLULAR	ITALICIZATION
INOCULABILITY	INTERCHANGING	INTRAMUSCULAR	

J
JACK-O'-
  LANTERNS
JARGONIZATION
JEFFERSON CITY
JELLIFICATION
JET PROPULSION
JIGGERY-POKERY
JIGSAW PUZZLES
JOB'S
  COMFORTER
JOLLIFICATION
JUDICIOUSNESS
JUGLANDACEOUS
JUNIOR SCHOOLS
JURISPRUDENCE
JUSTICIARSHIP
JUSTIFICATION
JUSTIFICATORY
JUXTAPOSITION

K
KALEIDOSCOPES
KALEIDOSCOPIC
KANGAROO COURT
KANGCHENJUNGA
KARL-MARX-
  STADT
KERATOPLASTIC
KETTLEDRUMMER
KEY SIGNATURES
KIDDERMINSTER
KIDNEY MACHINE
KINDERGARTENS
KIND-HEARTEDLY
KINEMATICALLY
KINETIC ENERGY
KINETONUCLEUS
KING'S
  COUNSELS
KING'S
  EVIDENCE
KIRKCUDBRIGHT
KITCHEN GARDEN
KITTY-CORNERED
KLEPTOMANIACS
KNAVE OF
  HEARTS
KNIGHTS-ERRANT
KNOWLEDGEABLE
KNOWLEDGEABLY

KNUCKLE-DUSTER
KWANGSI-CHUANG

L
LABIALIZATION
LABORIOUSNESS
LABOURS OF
  LOVE
LACKADAISICAL
LACTOBACILLUS
LADY BOUNTIFUL
LADY-IN-
  WAITING
LAEVOROTATION
LAEVOROTATORY
LAMELLIBRANCH
LANCE CORPORAL
LANDING FIELDS
LANDING STAGES
LANDING STRIPS
LANDOWNERSHIP
LANTERNSLIDES
LAPAROSCOPIES
LARYNGOLOGIST
LARYNGOSCOPIC
LASER PRINTERS
LATCHKEY CHILD
LATEROVERSION
LATIN AMERICAN
LAUGHINGSTOCK
LAUNDRY BASKET
LEADING LADIES
LEADING LIGHTS
LEAMINGTON SPA
LEATHERJACKET
LECHEROUSNESS
LEGISLATORIAL
LEISHMANIASIS
LEISURELINESS
LEPIDOPTERIST
LEPIDOPTEROUS
LEPTOCEPHALUS
LEPTOPHYLLOUS
LETHARGICALLY
LETTER OPENERS
LETTER-PERFECT
LETTERPRESSES
LEVEL CROSSING
LEXICOGRAPHER
LEXICOGRAPHIC
LEXICOLOGICAL
LIBRARIANSHIP

LICENSE PLATES
LICENSING LAWS
LIEBFRAUMILCH
LIECHTENSTEIN
LIFE PRESERVER
LIFESTREAMING
LIGHT AIRCRAFT
LIGHT-FINGERED
LIGHT-HEADEDLY
LIGNIFICATION
LIMITLESSNESS
LINE-ENGRAVING
LINGUA FRANCAS
LIPARI ISLANDS
LITHOGRAPHING
LITIGIOUSNESS
LITTLE FINGERS
LIVERY COMPANY
LIVERY STABLES
LIVING FOSSILS
LOATHSOMENESS
LODGING HOUSES
LOGOGRAMMATIC
LONDON BRIGADE
LONG HOT
  SUMMER
LONGSUFFERING
LONG VACATIONS
LONS-LE-SAU-
  NIER
LOSS ADJUSTERS
LOTHIAN REGION
LOWER EAST
  SIDE
LOW-PASS
  FILTER
LOW-WATER
  MARKS
LUBRICATIONAL
LUDICROUSNESS
LUNATIC FRINGE
LUNCHEONETTES
LYMPHADENITIS
LYMPHATICALLY
LYMPHOBLASTIC
LYMPHOCYTOSIS
LYMPHOCYTOTIC
LYMPHOPOIESIS
LYMPHOPOIETIC

M
MACARONICALLY

MACHIAVELLIAN
MACHICOLATION
MACHINABILITY
MACHINEGUNNED
MACRENCEPHALY
MACROCLIMATIC
MACROECONOMIC
MACROMOLECULE
MACRONUTRIENT
MADE-TO-
  MEASURE
MADHYA PRADESH
MADRIGALESQUE
MAGIC LANTERNS
MAGISTERIALLY
MAGNANIMOUSLY
MAGNETIC FIELD
MAGNETIC HEADS
MAGNETIC NORTH
MAGNETIC POLES
MAGNETIC TAPES
MAGNETIZATION
MAGNETOMETRIC
MAGNETOMOTIVE
MAGNETOSPHERE
MAGNIFICATION
MAGNIFICENTLY
MAGNILOQUENCE
MAGNITUDINOUS
MAGNOLIACEOUS
MAIDS OF
  HONOUR
MAJOR GENERALS
MALACOLOGICAL
MALACOSTRACAN
MALADJUSTMENT
MALADMINISTER
MALADROITNESS
MALFORMATIONS
MALFUNCTIONED
MALICIOUSNESS
MALIMPRINTING
MALTHUSIANISM
MANAGEABILITY
MANDARIN DUCKS
MANGEL-WURZELS
MANIFESTATION
MANIPULATABLE
MANIPULATIONS
MANTELSHELVES
MANUFACTURERS
MANUFACTURING

MANY-SIDEDNESS
MARAGING STEEL
MARCHIONESSES
MARKETABILITY
MARKET GARDENS
MARRIAGE LINES
MARRONS GLACES
MARTYRIZATION
MARTYROLOGIST
MASSACHUSETTS
MASSIF CENTRAL
MASS-PRODUCING
MASTERFULNESS
MASTERMINDING
MASTERS-AT-
  ARMS
MASTERS OF
  ARTS
MASTERSTROKES
MASTIGOPHORAN
MASTOIDECTOMY
MATCHLESSNESS
MATERFAMILIAS
MATERIALISTIC
MATERIALIZING
MATERNALISTIC
MATHEMATICIAN
MATRICULATING
MATRICULATION
MATRILOCALITY
MATURE STUDENT
MAXILLIPEDARY
MEALS ON
  WHEELS
MEANINGLESSLY
MEASURABILITY
MECHANIZATION
MEDIATIZATION
MEDIATORIALLY
MEDIEVALISTIC
MEDITERRANEAN
MEETINGHOUSES
MEGACEPHALOUS
MEGALOBLASTIC
MEGALOMANIACS
MEGALOPOLITAN
MELODIOUSNESS
MELODRAMATIST
MELTING POINTS
MELTON MOWBRAY
MENINGOCOCCUS
MENSTRUATIONS

MENSURATIONAL
MENTAL ILLNESS
MERCENARINESS
MERCERIZATION
MERCHANDISING
MERCHANT BANKS
MERCILESSNESS
MERCURIALNESS
MERCUROCHROME
MERCY KILLINGS
MERITOCRACIES
MERITORIOUSLY
MERRY-GO-
  ROUNDS
MERTHYR TYDFIL
MESENCEPHALIC
MESENCEPHALON
MESMERIZATION
MESSIANICALLY
METABOLICALLY
METABOLIZABLE
METACHROMATIC
METALANGUAGES
METALLIFEROUS
METALLIZATION
METALLOGRAPHY
METALLURGICAL
METALLURGISTS
METAMERICALLY
METAMORPHOSED
METAMORPHOSES
METAMORPHOSIS
METAPHOSPHATE
METAPHYSICIAN
METASTABILITY
METEMPIRICIST
METENCEPHALIC
METENCEPHALON
METEOROLOGIST
METHODIZATION
METHODOLOGIES
METHODOLOGIST
METHYL ALCOHOL
METRONIDAZOLE
METROPOLITANS
MEZZO-SOPRANOS
MICROANALYSIS
MICROANALYTIC
MICROCEPHALIC
MICROCHEMICAL
MICROCLIMATIC
MICROCOMPUTER

MICRODETECTOR
MICRONUTRIENT
MICROORGANISM
MICROPARASITE
MICROPHYSICAL
MICROTONALITY
MIDDLEBROWISM
MIDDLE EASTERN
MIDDLE ENGLAND
MIDDLE FINGERS
MIDDLE PASSAGE
MIDDLESBROUGH
MIDDLE SCHOOLS
MIDDLEWEIGHTS
MIDDLE WESTERN
MID-LIFE
  CRISES
MID-LIFE
  CRISIS
MIDWAY ISLANDS
MILK CHOCOLATE
MILLENNIALIST
MILLENNIUM BUG
MILLIONAIRESS
MIMEOGRAPHING
MINE DETECTORS
MINERALOGICAL
MINERALOGISTS
MINERAL WATERS
MINICOMPUTERS
MINISTERIALLY
MIRABILE DICTU
MIRROR WRITING
MIRTHLESSNESS
MISADVENTURES
MISCALCULATED
MISCEGENATION
MISCELLANEOUS
MISCHIEVOUSLY
MISCONCEIVING
MISCONCEPTION
MISCONDUCTING
MISCONSTRUING
MISDEMEANOURS
MISERABLENESS
MISGOVERNMENT
MISJUDGEMENTS
MISMANAGEMENT
MISPROPORTION
MISQUOTATIONS
MISSISSIPPIAN
MISSTATEMENTS

MISTRUSTFULLY
MISTRUSTINGLY
MISUNDERSTAND
MISUNDERSTOOD
MITOCHONDRIAL
MITOCHONDRION
MIXED BLESSING
MIXED METAPHOR
MOBILE LIBRARY
MOBILIZATIONS
MODERNIZATION
MODIFIABILITY
MODIFICATIONS
MODUS OPERANDI
MOHAMMEDANISM
MOLLIFICATION
MOLLYCODDLING
MOMENT OF
  TRUTH
MONEYCHANGERS
MONEY-GRUBBERS
MONEY-GRUBBING
MONEY-SPINNERS
MONKEY-PUZZLES
MONMOUTHSHIRE
MONOCHROMATIC
MONOCOTYLEDON
MONOGRAMMATIC
MONOMETALLISM
MONOMETALLIST
MONOMOLECULAR
MONONUCLEOSIS
MONOPHTHONGAL
MONOPSONISTIC
MONOSYLLABISM
MONOSYLLABLES
MONOTREMATOUS
MONSTROSITIES
MONS VENERISES
MONUMENTALITY
MOONLIGHT FLIT
MORALITY PLAYS
MORAL MAJORITY
MORNING PRAYER
MORPHEMICALLY
MORPHOGENESIS
MORPHOGENETIC
MORPHOLOGICAL
MORPHOPHONEME
MORRIS DANCERS
MORTIFICATION
MOTHER COUNTRY

MOTHER-OF-
  PEARL
MOTHER TONGUES
MOTION PICTURE
MOTORCYCLISTS
MOTOR SCOOTERS
MOUNTAIN LIONS
MOUNTAINSIDES
MOUNTEBANKERY
MOUTH WATERING
MOUTH-WATERING
MOVABLE FEASTS
MOVING PICTURE
MUHAMMADANISM
MULTICELLULAR
MULTICOLOURED
MULTINATIONAL
MULTIPLE STORE
MULTITUDINOUS
MULTIVIBRATOR
MUMMIFICATION
MURDEROUSNESS
MUSICAL CHAIRS
MUSICOLOGICAL
MYCOBACTERIUM
MYRMECOLOGIST
MYSTIFICATION
MYTHICIZATION

N
NARCOANALYSIS
NARCOTIZATION
NARROW SQUEAKS
NATIONAL DEBTS
NATIONALISTIC
NATIONALITIES
NATIONALIZING
NATIONAL PARKS
NATIONAL TRUST
NATIVITY PLAYS
NATURAL NUMBER
NAUTICAL MILES
NEARSIGHTEDLY
NECESSARY EVIL
NECESSITARIAN
NECESSITATING
NECESSITATION
NECESSITATIVE
NECESSITOUSLY
NECKERCHIEVES
NECROPHILIACS
NEFARIOUSNESS

NEGATIVE POLES
NEGLIGIBILITY
NEGOTIABILITY
NEGRI SEMBILAN
NEIGHBOURHOOD
NEMATHELMINTH
NEOCLASSICISM
NEOCLASSICIST
NEOPLASTICISM
NERVELESSNESS
NERVOUS SYSTEM
NEUROFIBRILAR
NEUROMUSCULAR
NEUROSURGICAL
NEUROVASCULAR
NEW PROVIDENCE
NEW SOUTH
  WALES
NEW TECHNOLOGY
NICKELIFEROUS
NIGGARDLINESS
NIGHTCLUBBING
NIGHTMARISHLY
NIGHT WATCHMAN
NITRIFICATION
NITROBACTERIA
NITROGLYCERIN
NITROPARAFFIN
NO-CLAIMS
  BONUS
NO HOLDS
  BARRED
NOISELESSNESS
NOLI-ME-
  TANGERE
NOLLE PROSEQUI
NOMENCLATURES
NOMOGRAPHICAL
NOMOLOGICALLY
NONAGENARIANS
NONAGGRESSION
NONAPPEARANCE
NONATTENDANCE
NONCOMBATANTS
NONCOMPLIANCE
NONCONCURRENT
NONCONDUCTORS
NONCONFORMISM
NONCONFORMIST
NONCONFORMITY
NONCONTAGIOUS
NONCOOPERATOR

NONFUNCTIONAL
NONINDUSTRIAL
NONINFECTIOUS
NONPRODUCTIVE
NONRETURNABLE
NONSENSICALLY
NO OIL
  PAINTING
NORADRENALINE
NORFOLK ISLAND
NORFOLK JACKET
NORMALIZATION
NORTHALLERTON
NORTH AYRSHIRE
NORTH CAROLINA
NORTHEASTERLY
NORTHEASTWARD
NORTH OSSETIAN
NORTH SOMERSET
NORTH TYNESIDE
NORTHWESTERLY
NORTHWESTWARD
NOSOLOGICALLY
NOSTALGICALLY
NOTICEABILITY
NOTIFICATIONS
NOTORIOUSNESS
NUCLEAR ENERGY
NUCLEAR FAMILY
NUCLEAR WINTER
NUCLEONICALLY
NUCLEOPLASMIC
NUCLEOPROTEIN
NUISANCE VALUE
NULLIFICATION
NUMEROLOGICAL
NUMISMATOLOGY
NURSERY RHYMES
NURSERY SCHOOL
NYMPHAEACEOUS
NYMPHOMANIACS

O
OBJECTIONABLE
OBJECTIONABLY
OBJECTIVENESS
OBJECTIVISTIC
OBJECT LESSONS
OBLATE SPHERES
OBLIVIOUSNESS
OBNOXIOUSNESS
OBSERVATIONAL

OBSERVATORIES
OBSESSIVENESS
OBSTETRICALLY
OBSTETRICIANS
OBSTRUCTIONAL
OBSTRUCTIVELY
OBTAINABILITY
OBTRUSIVENESS
OCCASIONALISM
OCCIDENTALISM
OCCIDENTALIST
OCCIDENTALIZE
OCCLUSIVENESS
OCEANOGRAPHER
OCEANOGRAPHIC
OCTOGENARIANS
ODONTOBLASTIC
ODONTOGLOSSUM
ODONTOGRAPHIC
ODONTOLOGICAL
OFFENSIVENESS
OFFHANDEDNESS
OFFICEHOLDERS
OFFICIOUSNESS
OLD AGE
  PENSION
OLD-BOY
  NETWORK
OLD SCHOOL
  TIES
OLD WIVES'
  TALES
OLIGOPOLISTIC
OLIVE BRANCHES
OMMATOPHOROUS
ONE-NIGHT
  STAND
ONE-TRACK
  MINDS
ON THE
  PREMISES
ONTOGENICALLY
ONTOLOGICALLY
OPENHEARTEDLY
OPEN THE DOOR
  TO
OPERATIONALLY
OPERATIVENESS
OPHTHALMOLOGY
OPISTHOBRANCH
OPPORTUNENESS
OPPORTUNISTIC

OPPORTUNITIES
OPPOSITIONIST
OPPROBRIOUSLY
ORANGE BLOSSOM
ORCHESTRA PITS
ORCHESTRATING
ORCHESTRATION
ORDINARY LEVEL
ORDZHONIKIDZE
ORGAN GRINDERS
ORGANIZATIONS
ORGANOGENESIS
ORGANOGENETIC
ORGANOGRAPHIC
ORGANOLOGICAL
ORGANOTHERAPY
ORIENTALISTIC
ORIENTATIONAL
ORNAMENTATION
ORNITHISCHIAN
ORNITHOLOGIST
ORTHOCEPHALIC
ORTHOEPICALLY
ORTHOGNATHISM
ORTHOGNATHOUS
ORTHOHYDROGEN
ORTHOSTICHOUS
OSCILLOGRAPHY
OSTENSIBILITY
OSTEOMALACIAL
OSTEOMYELITIS
OTHER-DIRECTED
OUTBOARD MOTOR
OUTDISTANCING
OUTGENERALING
OUTGENERALLED
OUTMANOEUVRED
OUTSPOKENNESS
OUTSTANDINGLY
OVERABUNDANCE
OVERAMBITIOUS
OVERBALANCING
OVERBEARINGLY
OVERBURDENING
OVERCONFIDENT
OVERCRITICIZE
OVERCULTIVATE
OVERDEVELOPED
OVERELABORATE
OVEREMPHASIZE
OVERESTIMATED
OVERESTIMATES

OVERINDULGING
OVERMASTERING
OVERPOPULATED
OVERREACTIONS
OVERSHADOWING
OVERSTATEMENT
OVERSUBSCRIBE
OVERWEENINGLY
OVOVIVIPAROUS
OWNER-OCCUPIED
OWNER-OCCUPIER
OYSTERCATCHER

P

PADDLE STEAMER
PADDLING POOLS
PAEDIATRICIAN
PAINSTAKINGLY
PAINTBALL GAME
PALAEOECOLOGY
PALAEOGRAPHIC
PALAEONTOLOGY
PALAEOZOOLOGY
PALEOGRAPHERS
PALETTE KNIVES
PALYNOLOGICAL
PANCHROMATISM
PANDORA'S
 BOXES
PANIC DISORDER
PANIC STATIONS
PANIC-STRICKEN
PANORAMICALLY
PANSOPHICALLY
PANTECHNICONS
PAPAVERACEOUS
PAPILLOMATOUS
PARABOLICALLY
PARADE GROUNDS
PARADOXICALLY
PARAGOGICALLY
PARALLELOGRAM
PARALYTICALLY
PARAMAGNETISM
PARANOIACALLY
PARAPHERNALIA
PARASITICALLY
PARASITICIDAL
PARASYNTHESIS
PARASYNTHETON
PARENT COMPANY
PARENTHETICAL

PAR EXCELLENCE
PARKING LIGHTS
PARKING METERS
PARKING TICKET
PARKINSON'S
 LAW
PARLIAMENTARY
PARROT-FASHION
PART EXCHANGES
PARTHENOCARPY
PARTICIPATING
PARTICIPATION
PARTICIPIALLY
PARTI-COLOURED
PARTICULARISM
PARTICULARIST
PARTICULARITY
PARTICULARIZE
PARTS OF
 SPEECH
PASSEMENTERIE
PASSIONFLOWER
PASSIONLESSLY
PASSIVIZATION
PATENT LEATHER
PATERFAMILIAS
PATERNALISTIC
PATHOGNOMONIC
PATRIOTICALLY
PATRISTICALLY
PATRONIZINGLY
PAY-AND-
 DISPLAY
PEACEABLENESS
PEACE DIVIDEND
PEACE OFFERING
PECKING ORDERS
PECTORAL CROSS
PECULIARITIES
PEDAGOGICALLY
PEDESTRIANIZE
PEDIATRICIANS
PEDUNCULATION
PELOPONNESIAN
PELTIER EFFECT
PEMBROKESHIRE
PENALTY CORNER
PENEPLANATION
PENETRABILITY
PENETRATINGLY
PENETRATIVELY
PENICILLATION

PENITENTIALLY
PENNILESSNESS
PENNSYLVANIAN
PENNY-DREADFUL
PENNY-FARTHING
PENNY-PINCHERS
PENNY-PINCHING
PENNY WHISTLES
PENTANOIC ACID
PEOPLE CARRIER
PEPPER-AND-
 SALT
PEPTONIZATION
PERAMBULATING
PERAMBULATION
PERAMBULATORS
PERAMBULATORY
PERCUSSION CAP
PERCUSSIONIST
PEREGRINATION
PERFECTIONISM
PERFECTIONIST
PERFUNCTORILY
PERICARPOIDAL
PERICHONDRIUM
PERIODIC TABLE
PERIOPERATIVE
PERISHABILITY
PERISSODACTYL
PERMANENT WAVE
PERMANENT WAYS
PERMUTATIONAL
PERPENDICULAR
PERSEVERATION
PERSONALISTIC
PERSONALITIES
PERSONALIZING
PERSONIFIABLE
PERSPECTIVISM
PERSPICACIOUS
PERVASIVENESS
PERVERTEDNESS
PETROCHEMICAL
PETROL STATION
PETROPAVLOVSK
PETTY OFFICERS
PHALLOCENTRIC
PHARMACEUTICS
PHARMACOGNOSY
PHARMACOPOEIA
PHARYNGOSCOPE
PHARYNGOSCOPY

PHELLOGENETIC
PHENCYCLIDINE
PHENOMENALISM
PHENOMENALIST
PHENOMENOLOGY
PHENOTHIAZINE
PHENYLALANINE
PHI BETA
  KAPPAS
PHILANTHROPIC
PHILHELLENISM
PHILOSOPHICAL
PHILOSOPHIZED
PHILOSOPHIZER
PHI-PHENOMENON
PHOSPHORYLASE
PHOTOCHEMICAL
PHOTOCOMPOSER
PHOTODYNAMICS
PHOTOELECTRIC
PHOTOELECTRON
PHOTOEMISSION
PHOTOEMISSIVE
PHOTOENGRAVER
PHOTO FINISHES
PHOTOGRAPHERS
PHOTOGRAPHING
PHOTOPERIODIC
PHOTORECEPTOR
PHOTOSTATTING
PHRASEOGRAPHY
PHRASEOLOGIST
PHRENOLOGICAL
PHYCOMYCETOUS
PHYLLOQUINONE
PHYSICALISTIC
PHYSICAL JERKS
PHYSIOGNOMIES
PHYSIOGNOMIST
PHYSIOGRAPHER
PHYSIOGRAPHIC
PHYSIOLOGICAL
PHYSIOLOGISTS
PHYSIOTHERAPY
PHYSOCLISTOUS
PHYSOSTIGMINE
PHYTOPLANKTON
PICTURESQUELY
PICTURE WINDOW
PIECES OF
  EIGHT
PIEZOELECTRIC

PIGEON-CHESTED
PIGHEADEDNESS
PILOT OFFICERS
PINK ELEPHANTS
PINKING SHEARS
PISCICULTURAL
PITCHED BATTLE
PLACE SETTINGS
PLAGIOTROPISM
PLAINTIVENESS
PLASTIC BULLET
PLATINIFEROUS
PLATINIRIDIUM
PLATINIZATION
PLATINUM-BLOND
PLATITUDINIZE
PLATITUDINOUS
PLATYHELMINTH
PLAYING FIELDS
PLENTEOUSNESS
PLENTIFULNESS
PLIMSOLL LINES
PLOUGHMANSHIP
PLURALIZATION
PNEUMATICALLY
PNEUMATOLYSIS
PNEUMATOMETER
PNEUMATOMETRY
PNEUMATOPHORE
PNEUMOGASTRIC
PNEUMONECTOMY
POETIC JUSTICE
POETIC LICENCE
POETS LAUREATE
POINTLESSNESS
POINTS OF
  ORDER
POINT-TO-
  POINTS
POISONOUSNESS
POLE POSITIONS
POLICE OFFICER
POLICE STATION
POLIOMYELITIS
POLLING BOOTHS
POLLINIFEROUS
POLYADELPHOUS
POLYCHROMATIC
POLYCOTYLEDON
POLYDACTYLOUS
POLYEMBRYONIC
POLYGALACEOUS

POLYGONACEOUS
POLYPHOSPHATE
POLYPROPYLENE
POLYPROTODONT
POLYSYLLABLES
POLYSYLLOGISM
POLYSYNTHESIS
PONDERABILITY
PONDEROUSNESS
PONTIFICATING
POOR RELATIONS
PORCELLANEOUS
PORNOGRAPHERS
PORT ELIZABETH
POSITIVE POLES
POSSIBILITIES
POSTAGE STAMPS
POSTCLASSICAL
POSTER COLOURS
POSTE RESTANTE
POSTGRADUATES
POSTMAN'S
  KNOCK
POST OFFICE
  BOX
POSTOPERATIVE
POSTPONEMENTS
POTATO BEETLES
POTENTIOMETER
POTTER'S
  WHEELS
POTTY-TRAINING
POWERLESSNESS
POWER POLITICS
POWER STATIONS
POWER STEERING
PRACTICAL JOKE
PRACTITIONERS
PRAGMATICALLY
PRAYER MEETING
PRAYING MANTIS
PREADAPTATION
PREADOLESCENT
PRECAUTIONARY
PRECEPTORSHIP
PRECIOUS METAL
PRECIOUS STONE
PRECIPITATELY
PRECIPITATING
PRECIPITATION
PRECIPITATIVE
PRECIPITOUSLY

PRECONCEPTION
PRECONDITIONS
PRECONIZATION
PREDATORINESS
PREDETERMINED
PREDETERMINER
PREDICABILITY
PREDICATIVELY
PREDILECTIONS
PREDOMINANTLY
PREDOMINATING
PREDOMINATION
PREFABRICATED
PREFABRICATOR
PREFERABILITY
PREFIGURATION
PREFIGURATIVE
PREFIGUREMENT
PREJUDGEMENTS
PRELIMINARIES
PRELIMINARILY
PREMATURENESS
PREMEDICATION
PREMEDITATION
PREMEDITATIVE
PREOCCUPATION
PREORDINATION
PREPARATORILY
PREPONDERANCE
PREPONDERATED
PREPOSITIONAL
PREPOSSESSING
PREPOSSESSION
PRE-RAPHAELITE
PREREQUISITES
PRESBYTERIANS
PRESCRIPTIBLE
PRESCRIPTIONS
PRESENTATIONS
PRESENTIMENTS
PRESERVATIVES
PRESS AGENCIES
PRESS CUTTINGS
PRESS RELEASES
PRESSURE GROUP
PRESSURE POINT
PRESUMPTIVELY
PRETENTIOUSLY

PRETERNATURAL	PROMENADE DECK	PSYCHIATRISTS	QUANTUM THEORY
PREVARICATING	PROMINENTNESS	PSYCHOANALYSE	QUARTERFINALS
PREVARICATION	PROMISCUOUSLY	PSYCHOANALYST	QUARTERMASTER
PREVARICATORS	PROMISED LANDS	PSYCHOANALYZE	QUARTERSTAFFS
PRICELESSNESS	PROMISINGNESS	PSYCHOBIOLOGY	QUARTERSTAVES
PRIMARY COLOUR	PROMOTIVENESS	PSYCHODYNAMIC	QUARTZIFEROUS
PRIMARY SCHOOL	PRONOMINALIZE	PSYCHOGENESIS	QUEEN'S
PRIMARY STRESS	PRONOUNCEABLE	PSYCHOGENETIC	CONSORT
PRIME MERIDIAN	PRONOUNCEMENT	PSYCHOGNOSTIC	QUEEN'S
PRIME MINISTER	PRONUNCIATION	PSYCHOGRAPHIC	COUNSEL
PRIMITIVENESS	PROPAGABILITY	PSYCHOHISTORY	QUEEN'S
PRIMITIVISTIC	PROPAGANDISTS	PSYCHOKINESIS	ENGLISH
PRIMOGENITURE	PROPAGANDIZED	PSYCHOKINETIC	QUERULOUSNESS
PRINCE CONSORT	PROPAGATIONAL	PSYCHOLOGICAL	QUESTIONINGLY
PRINCIPAL BOYS	PROPAROXYTONE	PSYCHOLOGISTS	QUESTION MARKS
PRINTED MATTER	PROPHETICALLY	PSYCHOMETRICS	QUESTIONNAIRE
PRINTING PRESS	PROPHYLACTICS	PSYCHOPHYSICS	QUICK-TEMPERED
PRISONER OF	PROPITIATIOUS	PSYCHOSOMATIC	QUINDECENNIAL
WAR	PROPORTIONATE	PSYCHOSURGERY	QUINQUAGESIMA
PRISON VISITOR	PROPORTIONING	PSYCHOTHERAPY	QUINQUEVALENT
PRIVATE MEMBER	PROPOSITIONAL	PSYCHOTICALLY	QUINTILLIONTH
PRIVATE SCHOOL	PROPOSITIONED	PSYCHROPHILIC	QUINTUPLICATE
PRIVATE SECTOR	PROPRIETARILY	PTERIDOLOGIST	QUODLIBETICAL
PRIVATIZATION	PROPRIETORIAL	PTERIDOPHYTIC	QUOTATION MARK
PRIZEFIGHTERS	PROPRIOCEPTOR	PUBLIC COMPANY	
PRIZEFIGHTING	PROSCRIPTIONS	PUBLIC SCHOOLS	**R**
PROBABILISTIC	PROSELYTIZERS	PULVERIZATION	RABBIT HUTCHES
PROBABILITIES	PROSELYTIZING	PUNCTILIOUSLY	RABBIT PUNCHES
PROCESS-SERVER	PROSOPOPOEIAL	PUNISHABILITY	RABBIT WARRENS
PROCLAMATIONS	PROSTAGLANDIN	PURITANICALLY	RABBLE-ROUSING
PROCONSULATES	PROSTATECTOMY	PURPLE PASSAGE	RACK-AND-
PROCRASTINATE	PROTECTIONISM	PURPOSELESSLY	PINION
PROCTOLOGICAL	PROTECTIONIST	PURPOSIVENESS	RADIOACTIVATE
PRODUCIBILITY	PROTECTORATES	PUSILLANIMITY	RADIOACTIVITY
PROFESSIONALS	PROTEINACEOUS	PUSILLANIMOUS	RADIOCHEMICAL
PROFESSORIATE	PROTESTANTISM	PUT OUT OF	RADIOGRAPHERS
PROFESSORSHIP	PROTESTATIONS	SIGHT	RADIOISOTOPIC
PROFITABILITY	PROTHETICALLY	PYRHELIOMETER	RADIOTELEGRAM
PROFIT MARGINS	PROTOCHORDATE	PYROPHOSPHATE	RADIOTELETYPE
PROFIT SHARING	PROTOHISTORIC		RAG-AND-BONE
PROGNOSTICATE	PROTOLANGUAGE	**Q**	MAN
PROGRESSIONAL	PROTUBERANCES	QUADRICIPITAL	RAINBOW NATION
PROGRESSIVELY	PROTUBERANTLY	QUADRILATERAL	RAMIFICATIONS
PROGRESSIVISM	PROVINCIALISM	QUADRILLIONTH	RANCOROUSNESS
PROGRESSIVIST	PROVINCIALITY	QUADRIPARTITE	RANDOMIZATION
PROHIBITIVELY	PROVING GROUND	QUADRISECTION	RAPPROCHEMENT
PROJECTIONIST	PROVISIONALLY	QUADRIVALENCY	RAPTUROUSNESS
PROLEPTICALLY	PROVOCATIVELY	QUADRUPLICATE	RAREFACTIONAL
PROLIFERATING	PROXIMATENESS	QUADRUPLICITY	RATEABLE VALUE
PROLIFERATION	PSEPHOLOGICAL	QUALIFICATION	RATIOCINATION
PROLIFERATIVE	PSEPHOLOGISTS	QUALIFICATORY	RATIONALISTIC
PROLONGATIONS	PSEUDOMORPHIC	QUALITATIVELY	RATIONALIZING

RATUSHINSKAYA
REACTIONARIES
READJUSTMENTS
READ-WRITE
  HEAD
REAFFIRMATION
REAFFORESTING
REALISTICALLY
REAPPOINTMENT
REARRANGEMENT
RECALCITRANCE
RECAPITULATED
RECEPTIONISTS
RECEPTION ROOM
RECESSIVENESS
RECIPROCALITY
RECIPROCATING
RECIPROCATION
RECIPROCATIVE
RECOGNITIONAL
RECOLLECTIONS
RECOMBINATION
RECOMMENDABLE
RECOMPENSABLE
RECOMPOSITION
RECONCILEMENT
RECONCILINGLY
RECONDITENESS
RECONDITIONED
RECONDITIONER
RECONNOITRING
RECONSIDERING
RECONSTITUENT
RECONSTITUTED
RECONSTRUCTED
RECONSTRUCTOR
RECORD-CHANGER
RECORD LIBRARY
RECORD PLAYERS
RECRIMINATING
RECRIMINATION
RECRIMINATIVE
RECRIMINATORY
RECRUDESCENCE
RECRYSTALLIZE
RECTIFICATION
RED BLOOD
  CELLS
REDEEMABILITY
REDEVELOPMENT
REDISTRIBUTED

RED-LETTER
  DAYS
REDUPLICATING
REDUPLICATION
REDUPLICATIVE
REEFER JACKETS
RE-ENFORCEMENT
RE-EXAMINATION
RE-EXPORTATION
REFERENCE BOOK
REFLEXIVENESS
REFORESTATION
REFORMATIONAL
REFORMATORIES
REFRACTOMETER
REFRACTOMETRY
REFRIGERATING
REFRIGERATION
REFRIGERATIVE
REFRIGERATORS
REFURBISHMENT
REGARDFULNESS
REGIMENTATION
REGISTRARSHIP
REGISTRATIONS
REGRETFULNESS
REGURGITATING
REGURGITATION
REHABILITATED
REIGN OF
  TERROR
REIMBURSEMENT
REIMPORTATION
REINCARNATING
REINCARNATION
REINFORCEMENT
REINSTATEMENT
REJUVENESCENT
RELATIONSHIPS
RELIGIOUSNESS
RELINQUISHING
REMINISCENCES
REMISSIBILITY
REMONSTRANCES
REMONSTRATING
REMONSTRATION
REMONSTRATIVE
REMORSELESSLY
REMOTE CONTROL
RENATIONALIZE
RENEGOTIATION
RENSSELAERITE

RENUNCIATIONS
REPEATABILITY
REPELLINGNESS
REPERCUSSIONS
REPLENISHMENT
REPOSEFULNESS
REPREHENDABLE
REPREHENSIBLE
REPREHENSIBLY
REPRESENTABLE
REPROACHFULLY
REPROACHINGLY
REPRODUCTIONS
REPROGRAPHICS
REPUBLICANISM
REPUBLICANIZE
REPUBLICATION
REPUBLISHABLE
REPULSIVENESS
REQUISITIONED
REQUISITIONER
RESENTFULNESS
RESISTIBILITY
RESISTIVENESS
RESOLVABILITY
RESOURCEFULLY
RESPIRABILITY
RESPIRATIONAL
RESPLENDENTLY
RESTAURANT CAR
RESTAURATEURS
RESTRAININGLY
RESTRICTIVELY
RESTRUCTURING
RESURRECTIONS
RESUSCITATING
RESUSCITATION
RESUSCITATIVE
RETAINABILITY
RETENTIVENESS
RETICULATIONS
RETINOSCOPIST
RETROACTIVELY
RETROACTIVITY
RETROGRESSING
RETROGRESSION
RETROGRESSIVE
RETROSPECTION
RETROSPECTIVE
RETURNABILITY
REUNIFICATION
REUTILIZATION

REVEALABILITY
REVELATIONIST
REVERBERATING
REVERBERATION
REVERBERATIVE
REVERBERATORY
REVERENTIALLY
REVERSIBILITY
REVOLUTIONARY
REVOLUTIONIST
REVOLUTIONIZE
RHABDOMANTIST
RHAPSODICALLY
RHIZOCEPHALAN
RHIZOMORPHOUS
RHODOCHROSITE
RHODODENDRONS
RIBEIRAO PRETO
RIGHTEOUSNESS
RIGHT TRIANGLE
ROAD ALLOWANCE
ROCK-AND-
  ROLLER
ROCKING CHAIRS
ROCKING HORSES
ROGUES'
  GALLERY
ROLLER COASTER
ROLLER-SKATERS
ROLLER SKATING
ROLLING STONES
ROLL OF
  HONOURS
ROLL-ON ROLL-
  OFF
ROMAN CATHOLIC
ROMAN NUMERALS
ROMANTICIZING
ROOMING HOUSES
RORSCHACH TEST
ROTARY TILLERS
ROTTEN BOROUGH
ROUGH AND
  READY
ROUGH-AND-
  READY
ROUGH DIAMONDS
ROUND BRACKETS
ROUND-THE-
  CLOCK
ROYAL HIGHNESS
RUBBERNECKING

RUBBER-STAMPED
RUMOURMONGERS
RUTHERFORDIUM
RYUKYU ISLANDS

S
SABRE-RATTLING
SACCHARIMETER
SACCHAROMETER
SACRIFICEABLE
SACRIFICIALLY
SACRIFICINGLY
SACROSANCTITY
SADOMASOCHISM
SADOMASOCHIST
SAFETY CATCHES
SAFETY CURTAIN
SAFETY ISLANDS
SAFETY MATCHES
SAGACIOUSNESS
SAINT LAWRENCE
SAKHA REPUBLIC
SALACIOUSNESS
SALAD DRESSING
SALPINGECTOMY
SALVATION ARMY
SALVATIONISTS
SAM BROWNE
  BELT
SAN BERNARDINO
SANCTIMONIOUS
SAND-BLINDNESS
SANDWICH BOARD
SAN FRANCISCAN
SANGUINOLENCY
SANITARY TOWEL
SAN LUIS
  POTOSI
SANTA CATARINA
SAPROGENICITY
SARCASTICALLY
SARCOPHAGUSES
SATANICALNESS
SATIRICALNESS
SATISFACTIONS
SATURNINENESS
SCANDALMONGER
SCARIFICATION
SCATTERBRAINS
SCENESHIFTERS
SCEPTICALNESS
SCHEMATICALLY

SCHIZOCARPOUS
SCHIZOGENESIS
SCHIZOGENETIC
SCHIZOMYCETIC
SCHIZOPHRENIA
SCHIZOPHRENIC
SCHOLARLINESS
SCHOLASTICATE
SCHOLASTICISM
SCHOOLFELLOWS
SCHOOL-LEAVERS
SCHOOLMARMISH
SCHOOLMASTERS
SCHOOLTEACHER
SCIENTOLOGIST
SCILLY ISLANDS
SCINTILLATING
SCINTILLATION
SCLEROPROTEIN
SCOLOPENDRINE
SCORCHED EARTH
SCORIFICATION
SCRIPTWRITERS
SCRIPTWRITING
SCULPTURESQUE
SEANAD EIREANN
SEA OF
  TROUBLES
SEARCH PARTIES
SEARCH WARRANT
SEASON TICKETS
SEAWORTHINESS
SECESSIONISTS
SECLUSIVENESS
SECONDARINESS
SECOND COUSINS
SECOND-GUESSED
SECOND THOUGHT
SECRETARYSHIP
SECRETIVENESS
SECRET SERVICE
SECURITY RISKS
SEDENTARINESS
SEDIMENTARILY
SEDIMENTATION
SEDIMENTOLOGY
SEDITIOUSNESS
SEDUCTIVENESS
SEGREGATIONAL
SEINE-MARITIME
SEISMOGRAPHER
SEISMOGRAPHIC

SEISMOLOGISTS
SELECTIVENESS
SELENOGRAPHER
SELENOGRAPHIC
SELF-ABASEMENT
SELF-ADDRESSED
SELF-ANNEALING
SELF-APPOINTED
SELF-ASSERTION
SELF-ASSERTIVE
SELF-ASSURANCE
SELF-CONFESSED
SELF-CONFIDENT
SELF-CONSCIOUS
SELF-CONTAINED
SELF-DECEPTION
SELF-DECEPTIVE
SELF-DEFEATING
SELF-EVIDENTLY
SELF-IMPORTANT
SELF-INDUCTION
SELF-INDUCTIVE
SELF-INDULGENT
SELF-INFLICTED
SELF-KNOWLEDGE
SELF-PITYINGLY
SELF-POSSESSED
SELF-PROPELLED
SELF-RESTRAINT
SELF-RIGHTEOUS
SELF-SACRIFICE
SELF-SATISFIED
SELLER'S
  MARKET
SELLING-PLATER
SELLING POINTS
SEMASIOLOGIST
SEMIAUTOMATIC
SEMICONDUCTOR
SEMICONSCIOUS
SEMIDETACHEDS
SEMIFINALISTS
SEMIPALATINSK
SEMIPARASITIC
SEMIPERMEABLE
SEMIPORCELAIN
SEMPER FIDELIS
SEMPER PARATUS
SENIOR CITIZEN
SENSATIONALLY
SENSELESSNESS
SENSITIVENESS

SENSITIZATION
SENTENTIOUSLY
SENTIMENTALLY
SEQUENTIALITY
SEQUESTRATING
SEQUESTRATION
SERBO-CROATIAN
SERGEANT MAJOR
SERIALIZATION
SERIAL NUMBERS
SERICULTURIST
SERJEANT AT
  LAW
SERVICE CHARGE
SEVENTH HEAVEN
SEVEN-YEAR
  ITCH
SEWING MACHINE
SEXAGENARIANS
SEXPLOITATION
SHAKESPEAREAN
SHAMELESSNESS
SHAPELESSNESS
SHARP PRACTICE
SHARPSHOOTERS
SHEEPSHEARING
SHEPHERDESSES
SHIFTLESSNESS
SHIP'S
  CHANDLER
SHIRTWAISTERS
SHOCK ABSORBER
SHOOTING MATCH
SHOOTING STARS
SHOOTING STICK
SHOP ASSISTANT
SHORT-CHANGING
SHORT CIRCUITS
SHORT-TEMPERED
SHOULDER BLADE
SHOULDER STRAP
SHROVE TUESDAY
SICK HEADACHES
SIDESPLITTING
SIERRA LEONEAN
SIGHTLESSNESS
SIGMOIDOSCOPE
SIGMOIDOSCOPY
SIGNATURE TUNE
SIGNIFICANTLY
SIGNIFICATION
SIGNIFICATIVE

SILENT PARTNER
SILVER BIRCHES
SILVER JUBILEE
SILVER-TONGUED
SILVER WEDDING
SILVICULTURAL
SIMPLE MACHINE
SINGLE-DECKERS
SINGULARITIES
SIPHONOSTELIC
SIT ON THE
  FENCE
SITTING PRETTY
SITTING TARGET
SIXTEENTH NOTE
SKEET SHOOTING
SKIRTING BOARD
SLAP AND
  TICKLE
SLEDGEHAMMERS
SLEEPING PILLS
SLEEP LEARNING
SLEEPLESSNESS
SLEIGHT OF
  HAND
SLIDING SCALES
SLIPSTREAMING
SMALL FORTUNES
SMALLHOLDINGS
SMELLING SALTS
SMOOTH-TONGUED
SNAKE CHARMERS
SNAP FASTENERS
SNEAK PREVIEWS
SNOW BLINDNESS
SOCIAL CHAPTER
SOCIAL CLIMBER
SOCIALIZATION
SOCIAL SCIENCE
SOCIAL SERVICE
SOCIAL WORKERS
SOCIOECONOMIC
SOCIOLINGUIST
SODA FOUNTAINS
SOFT-PEDALLING
SOLAR CONSTANT
SOLDERING IRON
SOLDIERLINESS
SOLEMNIZATION
SOLICITATIONS
SOLICITORSHIP
SOLILOQUIZING

SOLVAY PROCESS
SOMATOPLASTIC
SOMATOPLEURAL
SOMERSAULTING
SOMNAMBULANCE
SOMNAMBULATOR
SOMNAMBULISTS
SONS-OF-
  BITCHES
SOPHISTICALLY
SOPHISTICATED
SOPHISTICATES
SOPHISTICATOR
SOPORIFICALLY
SORROWFULNESS
SOUL-SEARCHING
SOUNDING BOARD
SOUNDLESSNESS
SOUNDPROOFING
SOUTH CAROLINA
SOUTHEAST ASIA
SOUTHEASTERLY
SOUTHEASTWARD
SOUTHEND-ON-
  SEA
SOUTHERLINESS
SOUTHERN OCEAN
SOUTH TYNESIDE
SOUTHWESTERLY
SOUTHWESTWARD
SOVIETIZATION
SPACE INVADERS
SPACE SHUTTLES
SPACE STATIONS
SPASMODICALLY
SPEAKING TUBES
SPECIAL BRANCH
SPECIAL SCHOOL
SPECIFICATION
SPECIFICATIVE
SPECTACULARLY
SPECTROGRAPHY
SPECTROMETRIC
SPECTROSCOPES
SPECTROSCOPIC
SPECULATIVELY
SPEECH THERAPY
SPELEOLOGICAL
SPELEOLOGISTS
SPENDING MONEY
SPERMATICALLY
SPERMATOPHORE

SPERMATOPHYTE
SPHERICALNESS
SPHEROIDICITY
SPHINGOMYELIN
SPHYGMOGRAPHY
SPINE-CHILLING
SPINELESSNESS
SPINNING JENNY
SPINNING WHEEL
SPIRITUALISTS
SPIRITUALIZER
SPIT AND
  POLISH
SPITTING IMAGE
SPLAYFOOTEDLY
SPLENDIFEROUS
SPLINTER GROUP
SPONTANEOUSLY
SPORTSMANLIKE
SPORTSMANSHIP
SPREAD BETTING
SPREAD-EAGLING
SPRIGHTLINESS
SPRING CHICKEN
SPRING-CLEANED
SQUANDERINGLY
SQUARE-BASHING
SQUARE BRACKET
SQUEAMISHNESS
SQUIREARCHIES
STABILIZATION
STAFF OFFICERS
STAFFORDSHIRE
STAFF SERGEANT
STAGE MANAGERS
STAGE-MANAGING
STAGE WHISPERS
STALKING-HORSE
STAMINIFEROUS
STANDARDIZING
STANDARD LAMPS
STANDING ORDER
STANDOFFISHLY
STAPHYLOCOCCI
STARCH-REDUCED
STARTING BLOCK
STARTING GATES
STARTING PRICE
STATELESSNESS
STATE-OF-THE-
  ART
STATESMANLIKE

STATESMANSHIP
STATION BREAKS
STATION HOUSES
STATIONMASTER
STATION WAGONS
STATISTICALLY
STATISTICIANS
STEADFASTNESS
STEAMROLLERED
STEEPLECHASER
STEEPLECHASES
STEERING WHEEL
STENOGRAPHERS
STENOPETALOUS
STENOPHYLLOUS
STEPPING-STONE
STERCORACEOUS
STEREOGRAPHIC
STEREOSCOPIST
STEREOTROPISM
STEREOTYPICAL
STERILIZATION
STICKING POINT
STICK IN THE
  MUD
STICK-IN-THE-
  MUD
STIFF UPPER
  LIP
STILETTO HEELS
STIMULATINGLY
STIPENDIARIES
STIRLINGSHIRE
STOCKBREEDERS
STOCKBREEDING
STOCK EXCHANGE
STOICHIOMETRY
STOLONIFEROUS
STOMATOPLASTY
STOP AT
  NOTHING
STORM TROOPERS
STORMY PETRELS
STOVEPIPE HATS
STRAIGHTEDGES
STRAIGHTENING
STRAIGHT-FACED
STRAIGHT FIGHT
STRAIGHT RAZOR
STRAITJACKETS
STRANGLEHOLDS
STRANGULATING

STRANGULATION	SUBSTRUCTURES	SUSTENTACULAR	TASTELESSNESS
STRATEGICALLY	SUBTILIZATION	SWASHBUCKLING	TATAR REPUBLIC
STRATIGRAPHER	SUBVENTIONARY	SWEET NOTHINGS	TAX-DEDUCTIBLE
STRATIGRAPHIC	SUFFICIENCIES	SWIMMING BATHS	TAXONOMICALLY
STRATOCUMULUS	SUFFOCATINGLY	SWIMMING POOLS	TAYSIDE REGION
STRATOSPHERIC	SUFFRAGANSHIP	SWIZZLE STICKS	TEAR A STRIP
STRAW-COLOURED	SUFFRAGETTISM	SWOLLEN HEADED	OFF
STREETWALKERS	SUFFUMIGATION	SWORDSMANSHIP	TECHNOLOGICAL
STRENGTHENING	SULPHADIAZINE	SYBARITICALLY	TECHNOLOGISTS
STRENUOUSNESS	SULPHURIC ACID	SYLLABOGRAPHY	TEETER-TOTTERS
STREPTOCARPUS	SUMMARIZATION	SYLLEPTICALLY	TELAUTOGRAPHY
STREPTOCOCCAL	SUMMER SCHOOLS	SYLLOGISTICAL	TELECOMMUTING
STREPTOCOCCUS	SUMPTUOUSNESS	SYLLOGIZATION	TELEGRAPH POLE
STREPTOKINASE	SUNDAY SCHOOLS	SYMBOLIZATION	TELEMARKETING
STRIKEBREAKER	SUPERABUNDANT	SYMMETRICALLY	TELENCEPHALIC
STRIP CARTOONS	SUPERADDITION	SYMPATHECTOMY	TELENCEPHALON
STRIP LIGHTING	SUPERANNUATED	SYMPATHOLYTIC	TELEPHOTO LENS
STROBILACEOUS	SUPERCALENDER	SYMPATRICALLY	TELEPROMPTERS
STROMATOLITIC	SUPERCHARGERS	SYMPHONICALLY	TELEUTOSPORIC
STRUCTURALISM	SUPERCHARGING	SYMPHYSICALLY	TELEVISIONARY
STRUCTURALIST	SUPERCOLUMNAR	SYNARTHRODIAL	TEMPERABILITY
STUDENTS'	SUPERCRITICAL	SYNCHRONISTIC	TEMPERAMENTAL
UNION	SUPEREMINENCE	SYNCHRONIZING	TEMPERATENESS
STUDIO COUCHES	SUPERFETATION	SYNDICALISTIC	TEMPESTUOUSLY
STUFFED SHIRTS	SUPERFICIALLY	SYNTACTICALLY	TEMPORARINESS
STYLISTICALLY	SUPERFLUIDITY	SYNTHETICALLY	TEMPORIZATION
SUBCOMMITTEES	SUPERFLUOUSLY	SYPHILOLOGIST	TEMPORIZINGLY
SUBCONTINENTS	SUPERHUMANITY	SYRINGOMYELIA	TENACIOUSNESS
SUBCONTRACTED	SUPERIMPOSING	SYRINGOMYELIC	TENANT FARMERS
SUBCONTRACTOR	SUPERINTENDED	SYSTEMATIZING	TENDENTIOUSLY
SUBDIVISIONAL	SUPERLATIVELY	SYSTEMATOLOGY	TENDERHEARTED
SUBEQUATORIAL	SUPERNATATION	SYSTEMIZATION	TENDERIZATION
SUBIRRIGATION	SUPERNUMERARY	SYZYGETICALLY	TEN-GALLON
SUBJECT MATTER	SUPERORDINATE		HATS
SUBLIEUTENANT	SUPERPHYSICAL	**T**	TENPIN BOWLING
SUBMACHINE GUN	SUPERPOSITION	TACHISTOSCOPE	TENTATIVENESS
SUBORDINATING	SUPERSENSIBLE	TACHYPHYLAXIS	TERGIVERSATOR
SUBORDINATION	SUPERSTITIONS	TAKE A BACK	TERMINABILITY
SUBORDINATIVE	SUPERSTITIOUS	SEAT	TERMINATIONAL
SUBPOPULATION	SUPERVENIENCE	TAKE THE	TERMINOLOGIES
SUBREPTITIOUS	SUPPLANTATION	PLEDGE	TERMINOLOGIST
SUBSCRIPTIONS	SUPPLEMENTARY	TALKATIVENESS	TERPSICHOREAN
SUBSERVIENTLY	SUPPLEMENTING	TALKING POINTS	TERRACED HOUSE
SUBSIDIZATION	SUPPLICATIONS	TANGENTIALITY	TERRESTRIALLY
SUBSTANTIALLY	SUPPLY TEACHER	TANTALIZATION	TERRORIZATION
SUBSTANTIATED	SUPPOSITIONAL	TANTALIZINGLY	TESTIFICATION
SUBSTANTIATOR	SUPPOSITORIES	TAPE RECORDERS	TETARTOHEDRAL
SUBSTANTIVELY	SUPRANATIONAL	TAR AND	TETRABASICITY
SUBSTANTIVIZE	SURFACE-ACTIVE	FEATHER	TETRACHLORIDE
SUBSTITUTABLE	SURREPTITIOUS	TARN-ET-	TETRADYNAMOUS
SUBSTITUTIONS	SURROGATESHIP	GARONNE	TETRASTICHOUS
SUBSTRUCTURAL	SURVIVABILITY	TARTARIZATION	TETRASYLLABIC

TETRASYLLABLE
THALASSOCRACY
THANKLESSNESS
THANKSGIVINGS
THEANTHROPISM
THEANTHROPIST
THEATRICALITY
THE CUT OF A
CARD
THE GONDOLIERS
THE LION'S
SHARE
THE MAGIC
FLUTE
THENCEFORWARD
THEOLOGICALLY
THEORETICALLY
THERIOMORPHIC
THERMOCHEMIST
THERMODYNAMIC
THERMOGENESIS
THERMOGRAPHER
THERMOGRAPHIC
THERMONUCLEAR
THERMOPLASTIC
THERMOSETTING
THERMOS FLASKS
THERMOSTATICS
THERMOTHERAPY
THERMOTROPISM
THETFORD MINES
THIGMOTROPISM
THORACOPLASTY
THOROUGHBREDS
THOROUGHFARES
THOROUGHGOING
THOROUGHPACED
THOUGHTLESSLY
THOUGHT POLICE
THREATENINGLY
THREE-CORNERED
THREE-DAY
EVENT
THREE LINE
WHIP
THREMMATOLOGY

THUNDERCLOUDS
THUNDERSHOWER
THUNDERSTORMS
THUNDERSTRUCK
THYROIDECTOMY
TIME AFTER
TIME
TIME-AND-
MOTION
TIME-CONSUMING
TIME EXPOSURES
TIME SIGNATURE
TINTINNABULAR
TINTINNABULUM
TITILLATINGLY
TITTLE-TATTLED
TITTLE-TATTLER
TOAD-IN-THE-
HOLE
TOASTING FORKS
TOILET-TRAINED
TOLERABLENESS
TOLERATIONISM
TOLERATIONIST
TONE LANGUAGES
TONGUE TWISTER
TONSILLECTOMY
TOOTHSOMENESS
TOPOGRAPHICAL
TOPOLOGICALLY
TORRE DEL
GRECO
TORTOISESHELL
TOTIPALMATION
TOXICOLOGICAL
TOXICOLOGISTS
TOXOPLASMOSIS
TRACE ELEMENTS
TRACHEOTOMIST
TRADE UNIONISM
TRADE UNIONIST
TRADING ESTATE
TRADING STAMPS
TRADITIONALLY
TRAFFIC CIRCLE
TRAFFIC ISLAND
TRAFFIC LIGHTS
TRAFFIC WARDEN
TRAGICOMEDIES
TRAILER HOUSES
TRANQUILLIZED

TRANQUILLIZER
TRANSACTINIDE
TRANSACTIONAL
TRANSATLANTIC
TRANSCAUCASIA
TRANSCENDENCE
TRANSCENDENCY
TRANSCRIBABLE
TRANSCRIPTION
TRANSFIGURING
TRANSFORMABLE
TRANSGRESSING
TRANSGRESSION
TRANSGRESSIVE
TRANSGRESSORS
TRANSISTORIZE
TRANSLATIONAL
TRANSLATORIAL
TRANSLITERATE
TRANSLOCATION
TRANSMIGRATOR
TRANSMISSIBLE
TRANSMISSIONS
TRANSMITTANCE
TRANSMITTANCY
TRANSMUTATION
TRANSPARENTLY
TRANSPIRATION
TRANSPIRATORY
TRANSPLANTING
TRANSPORTABLE
TRANSPORT CAFE
TRANSPORTEDLY
TRANSPOSITION
TRANSSHIPMENT
TRANSVESTITES
TRANSYLVANIAN
TRAPEZOHEDRAL
TRAPEZOHEDRON
TRAUMATICALLY
TREACHEROUSLY
TREASURERSHIP
TREASURE-TROVE
TREASURY NOTES
TREMULOUSNESS
TREPONEMATOUS
TRIANGULARITY
TRIANGULATION
TRIATOMICALLY
TRIBOELECTRIC
TRICENTENNIAL
TRICHOLOGISTS

TRICHOMONADAL
TRICHROMATISM
TRIGONOMETRIC
TRILATERATION
TRILINGUALISM
TRIMETHADIONE
TRIPLOBLASTIC
TRIPOLITANIAN
TRISACCHARIDE
TROOP CARRIERS
TROPHALLACTIC
TROPHOBLASTIC
TROUBLEMAKERS
TRUCIAL STATES
TRUSTWORTHILY
TRUTH-FUNCTION
TUBERCULATION
TUBUAI ISLANDS
TUBULIFLOROUS
TURBOCHARGERS
TURBOCHARGING
TURBO-ELECTRIC
TURING MACHINE
TURNING CIRCLE
TURNING POINTS
TWO-WAY
MIRRORS
TYPOGRAPHICAL
TYRANNIZINGLY
TYRANNOSAURUS
TYRANNOUSNESS

U
UGLY DUCKLINGS
ULTRANATIONAL
UMBELLIFEROUS
UMBILICAL CORD
UNACCOMPANIED
UNACCOUNTABLE
UNACCOUNTABLY
UNADULTERATED
UNADVENTUROUS
UNADVISEDNESS
UNASHAMEDNESS
UNBELIEVINGLY
UNBENDINGNESS
UNBLESSEDNESS
UNCEASINGNESS
UNCEREMONIOUS
UNCERTAINNESS

UNCHALLENGING
UNCHARISMATIC
UNCIRCUMCISED
UNCLEANLINESS
UNCOMFORTABLE
UNCOMFORTABLY
UNCOMPENSATED
UNCOMPETITIVE
UNCOMPLAINING
UNCOMPLICATED
UNCONCERNEDLY
UNCONDITIONAL
UNCONDITIONED
UNCONFORMABLE
UNCONSCIOUSLY
UNCONSTRAINED
UNCONSUMMATED
UNCONTENTIOUS
UNCOORDINATED
UNCROWNED KING
UNDECIDEDNESS
UNDERACHIEVED
UNDERACHIEVER
UNDERBREEDING
UNDERCARRIAGE
UNDERCHARGING
UNDERCURRENTS
UNDERDRAINAGE
UNDEREDUCATED
UNDEREMPLOYED
UNDERESTIMATE
UNDEREXPOSING
UNDEREXPOSURE
UNDERGARMENTS
UNDERGRADUATE
UNDERHANDEDLY
UNDER MILK
  WOOD
UNDERMININGLY
UNDERPAINTING
UNDERPINNINGS
UNDERSTANDING
UNDERSTRENGTH
UNDERSTUDYING
UNDISCIPLINED
UNDISTRIBUTED
UNEARTHLINESS
UNEMBARRASSED
UNENFORCEABLE
UNENLIGHTENED
UNEQUIVOCALLY
UNEXCEPTIONAL

UNEXPERIENCED
UNFALTERINGLY
UNFAMILIARITY
UNFASHIONABLE
UNFEELINGNESS
UNFLINCHINGLY
UNFORESEEABLE
UNFORGETTABLE
UNFORGETTABLY
UNFORTUNATELY
UNFOUNDEDNESS
UNGUARDEDNESS
UNHEALTHINESS
UNICAMERALISM
UNICAMERALIST
UNILATERALISM
UNILLUSTRATED
UNIMPEACHABLE
UNIMPEACHABLY
UNINHABITABLE
UNINHIBITEDLY
UNINTELLIGENT
UNINTENTIONAL
UNINTERRUPTED
UNITED KINGDOM
UNITED NATIONS
UNIVERSALNESS
UNIVERSAL TIME
UNMENTIONABLE
UNMUSICALNESS
UNNATURALNESS
UNNECESSARILY
UNOBTRUSIVELY
UNPATRONIZING
UNPRECEDENTED
UNPREDICTABLE
UNPRESSURIZED
UNPRETENTIOUS
UNQUALIFIABLE
UNQUESTIONING
UNREADABILITY
UNRELENTINGLY
UNRELIABILITY
UNREMITTINGLY
UNREPRESENTED
UNRUFFLEDNESS
UNSAVOURINESS
UNSELFISHNESS
UNSERVICEABLE
UNSIGHTLINESS
UNSOCIABILITY
UNSUBSTANTIAL

UNSUITABILITY
UNSUSTAINABLE
UNTHREATENING
UNTRADITIONAL
UNTRANSFORMED
UNWARRANTABLE
UNWILLINGNESS
UNWRITTEN LAWS
UPRIGHT PIANOS
UP TO THE
  MINUTE
UP-TO-THE-
  MINUTE
URETHROSCOPIC
UTI POSSIDETIS
UTTERABLENESS

V

VACILLATINGLY
VACUUM CLEANER
VALUE-ADDED
  TAX
VALUE JUDGMENT
VALUELESSNESS
VANTAGE POINTS
VAPOURABILITY
VAPOURISHNESS
VARICOSE VEINS
VARIOLIZATION
VASOINHIBITOR
VAULTING HORSE
VEGETARIANISM
VENEREOLOGIST
VENETIAN BLIND
VENTRILOQUIAL
VENTRILOQUISM
VENTRILOQUIST
VENTRILOQUIZE
VERACIOUSNESS
VERBALIZATION
VERBIFICATION
VERITABLENESS
VERMICULATION
VERMINOUSNESS
VERNACULARISM
VERNALIZATION
VERSIFICATION
VESTAL VIRGINS
VESTMANAEYJAR
VEXATIOUSNESS
VEXED QUESTION
VEXILLOLOGIST

VICARIOUSNESS
VICE PRESIDENT
VICIOUS CIRCLE
VICTIMIZATION
VICTORIA CROSS
VICTORIA PLUMS
VILIFICATIONS
VINDICABILITY
VINICULTURIST
VIOLONCELLIST
VIRGINIA BEACH
VIRGIN ISLANDS
VISCOUNTESSES
VISIONARINESS
VISITING CARDS
VISITORS'
  BOOKS
VISUALIZATION
VITRIFICATION
VITRIOLICALLY
VIVACIOUSNESS
VIVISECTIONAL
VOCIFERATIONS
VOICELESSNESS
VOLATILIZABLE
VOLCANIZATION
VOLCANOLOGIST
VOLUNTARINESS
VOLUNTARISTIC
VOTE OF
  CENSURE
VOTES OF
  THANKS
VOUCHSAFEMENT
VRAISEMBLANCE
VULCANIZATION
VULGARIZATION
VULNERABILITY

W

WALKIE-TALKIES
WALKING PAPERS
WALKING STICKS
WALL PAINTINGS
WALTHAM FOREST
WARM-HEARTEDLY
WASHINGTONIAN
WASTE PRODUCTS
WATCH THE
  CLOCK
WATER BISCUITS
WATER BUFFALOS

WATERING HOLES
WATERING PLACE
WATERPROOFING
WATER SOFTENER
WATER SUPPLIES
WATTLE AND
  DAUB
WEARISOMENESS
WEATHER-BEATEN
WEATHERBOARDS
WEIGHT LIFTERS
WEIGHT LIFTING
WELFARE STATES
WELL-APPOINTED
WELL-CONNECTED
WELL-DEVELOPED
WELL-PRESERVED
WELL-QUALIFIED
WELL-SUPPORTED
WELL-THOUGHT-
  OF
WELTERWEIGHTS

WEST BERKSHIRE
WESTERN SAHARA
WEST GLAMORGAN
WEST-NORTHWEST
WEST-SOUTHWEST
WEST YORKSHIRE
WETTING AGENTS
WHEELER-DEALER
WHIMSICALNESS
WHIPPOORWILLS
WHITE ELEPHANT
WHITE WEDDINGS
WHOLESOMENESS
WHOOPING COUGH
WICKET KEEPERS
WIDE-AWAKENESS
WILDCAT STRIKE
WILHELMSHAVEN
WILL-O'-THE-
  WISPS
WILLOW PATTERN

WINDING SHEETS
WINDOW-DRESSER
WINDOW-SHOPPED
WINDOW-SHOPPER
WING COMMANDER
WITHDRAWNNESS
WITHERINGNESS
WITWATERSRAND
WOLVERHAMPTON
WOMEN'S
  STUDIES
WONDERFULNESS
WONDER-WORKING
WOODCRAFTSMAN
WOOLGATHERING
WORD BLINDNESS
WORD PROCESSOR
WORK-HARDENING
WORSHIPPINGLY
WORTHLESSNESS
WRONGHEADEDLY

X
XANTHOCHROISM
XEROPHTHALMIA
XEROPHTHALMIC
XINJIANG UYGUR

Y
YACHTSMANSHIP
YEOMAN SERVICE
YOUNG MARRIEDS

Z
ZEBRA CROSSING
ZEUGMATICALLY
ZIGZAGGEDNESS
ZINJANTHROPUS
ZOOGEOGRAPHER
ZOOGEOGRAPHIC
ZOOSPORANGIAL
ZOOSPORANGIUM
ZYGAPOPHYSEAL
ZYGODACTYLISM
ZYGODACTYLOUS

14

A
ABOVE-MEN-
  TIONED
ABSENT-MIND-
  EDLY
ABSORBEFACIENT
ABSTEMIOUSNESS
ABSTRACTEDNESS
ABSTRACTIONISM
ACCLIMATIZABLE
ACCOMMODATIONS
ACCOMPANIMENTS
ACCOMPLISHABLE
ACCOMPLISHMENT
ACCOUNTABILITY
ACCUMULATIVELY
ACHONDROPLASIA
ACHROMATICALLY
ACKNOWLEDGMENT
ACQUIRED
  TASTES
ACROSS THE
  BOARD
ACROSS-THE-
  BOARD
ACTION STA-
  TIONS
ADENOCARCINOMA
ADMINISTRATION
ADMINISTRATIVE
ADMINISTRATORS
ADMINISTRATRIX
ADULT EDUCA-
  TION
ADVANCED LEV-
  ELS
ADVANTAGEOUSLY
AEROBALLISTICS
AEROMECHANICAL
AFFECTIONATELY
AFOREMENTIONED
AGGLOMERATIONS
AGGRANDIZEMENT
AGGRESSIVENESS
AGRICULTURISTS
AGROBIOLOGICAL
AGUASCALIENTES

AIR-CONDI-
  TIONED
AIR VICE-MAR-
  SHAL
ALCOHOLIZATION
ALLEGORIZATION
ALL-IN WRES-
  TLING
ALLITERATIVELY
ALLOPATHICALLY
ALLOPATRICALLY
ALLOTROPICALLY
ALL OVER THE
  SHOP
ALPES MARI-
  TIMES
ALPHABETICALLY
ALSACE-LOR-
  RAINE
ALTRUISTICALLY
AMARANTHACEOUS
AMATEURISHNESS
AMBASSADORSHIP
AMBASSADRESSES
AMBIDEXTROUSLY
AMERICAN IN-
  DIAN
AMMONIFICATION
AMPHIARTHROSIS
AMPHIBOLOGICAL
AMPHIPROSTYLAR
AMUSEMENT
  PARKS
ANACARDIACEOUS
ANAESTHETIZING
ANAMNESTICALLY
ANAMORPHOSCOPE
ANATHEMATIZING
ANCIENT MARI-
  NER
ANDORRA LA
  VELLA
ANGINA PECTO-
  RIS
ANGLO-AMERI-
  CANS
ANGLO-CATHO-
  LICS

ANIMADVERSIONS
ANISODACTYLOUS
ANTAGONIZATION
ANTHROPOLOGIST
ANTHROPOMETRIC
ANTHROPOPATHIC
ANTHROPOSOPHIC
ANTICHLORISTIC
ANTICIPATORILY
ANTIDEPRESSANT
ANTIHISTAMINES
ANTILOGARITHMS
ANTIMONARCHIST
ANTIPERSPIRANT
ANTIPHLOGISTIC
ANTIPRAGMATISM
ANTIQUATEDNESS
ANTIREPUBLICAN
ANTISEPTICALLY
ANTITHETICALLY
APARTMENT
  HOUSE
APOLOGETICALLY
APOPLECTICALLY
APOSTROPHIZING
APPENDECTOMIES
APPENDICECTOMY
APPLES AND
  PEARS
APPORTIONMENTS
APPRECIATIVELY
APPREHENSIVELY
APPRENTICESHIP
APPROPRIATIONS
APPROVED
  SCHOOL
APPROXIMATIONS
ARABIC NUMER-
  ALS
ARCHAEOLOGICAL
ARCHAEOLOGISTS
ARCHBISHOPRICS
ARCHETYPICALLY
ARCHIDIACONATE
ARCHIEPISCOPAL
ARCHIMANDRITES
ARCHITECTONICS
ARITHMETICALLY

ARITHMETICIANS
ARRONDISSEMENT
ARTICULATENESS
ARTIODACTYLOUS
AS CLEAR AS A
  BELL
AS DRUNK AS A
  LORD
AS SAFE AS
  HOUSES
ASSASSINATIONS
ASSAULT
  COURSES
ASSET-STRIP-
  PING
ASSOCIATIONISM
AS THE CASE
  MAY BE
ASTIGMATICALLY
ASTROLOGICALLY
ASTRONAVIGATOR
ASTRONOMICALLY
ASTROPHYSICIST
ASYMMETRICALLY
ASYMPTOTICALLY
AT DAGGERS
  DRAWN
ATTRACTIVENESS
AUF WIEDERSE-
  HEN
AUSPICIOUSNESS
AUTHENTICATING
AUTHENTICATION
AUTHENTICITIES
AUTHORITARIANS
AUTHORIZATIONS
AUTOBIOGRAPHER
AUTOBIOGRAPHIC
AUTOCRATICALLY
AUTOIONIZATION
AUTOMATIC
  PILOT
AUTOPHYTICALLY
AUTORADIOGRAPH
AUTOSUGGESTION
AUTOSUGGESTIVE
AUXILIARY
  VERBS

AWE-INSPIR-
INGLY

B
BACCALAUREATES
BACHELOR OF
ARTS
BACK FORMA-
TIONS
BACKHANDEDNESS
BACK-SEAT
DRIVER
BACTERIOLOGIST
BACTERIOPHAGIC
BACTERIOSTASIS
BACTERIOSTATIC
BALANCE OF
POWER
BALANCE OF
TRADE
BALSAMINACEOUS
BANANA REPUB-
LIC
BANNER HEAD-
LINE
BAROMETRICALLY
BASIDIOSPOROUS
BASTARDIZATION
BATCH PRO-
CESSED
BATHING MA-
CHINE
BATTLE CRUIS-
ERS
BE-ALL AND
END-ALL
BEASTS OF BUR-
DEN
BEATIFICATIONS
BEAUTIFICATION
BEAUTY PAR-
LOURS
BEHIND THE
TIMES
BELISHA BEA-
CONS
BERBERIDACEOUS
BERKSHIRE
DOWNS
BESIDE THE
POINT

BEST BEFORE
DATE
BIBLIOGRAPHERS
BIBLIOGRAPHIES
BIG GAME HUNT-
ING
BIOCLIMATOLOGY
BIODEGRADABLES
BIOENGINEERING
BIOGENETICALLY
BIOGRAPHICALLY
BIOLUMINESCENT
BIPARTISANSHIP
BIRD OF PARA-
DISE
BIRDS OF PAS-
SAGE
BITUMINIZATION
BLACK MARKET-
EER
BLANK CAR-
TRIDGE
BLOCK AND
TACKLE
BLOOD POISON-
ING
BLOOD PRES-
SURES
BLOOD RELA-
TIONS
BLOOD SACRI-
FICE
BLOODTHIRSTILY
BLUE-PENCIL-
LING
BOARDINGHOUSES
BOARDING
SCHOOL
BOIS DE BOU-
LOGNE
BOISTEROUSNESS
BOLOMETRICALLY
BOON COMPAN-
IONS
BOUCHES-DU-
RHONE
BOUGAINVILLEAS
BOUILLABAISSES
BOULEVERSEMENT
BOWDLERIZATION
BRACHYCEPHALIC
BRACHYDACTYLIA

BRACHYDACTYLIC
BREAD-AND-BUT-
TER
BREAKFAST
TABLE
BREATHLESSNESS
BREMSSTRAHLUNG
BRIGHT AND
EARLY
BRONCHIAL
TUBES
BRONCHIECTASIS
BRONCHOSCOPIST
BRUSSELS
SPROUT
BUILDING
BLOCKS
BULLETIN
BOARDS
BULLHEADEDNESS
BUREAU DE
CHANGE
BURNT OFFER-
INGS
BUSMAN'S HOLI-
DAY

C
CADAVEROUSNESS
CALAMINE LO-
TION
CALENDAR
MONTHS
CALLIGRAPHISTS
CAMPANOLOGISTS
CAMPANULACEOUS
CANTANKEROUSLY
CAPITALIZATION
CAPITAL LET-
TERS
CAPPARIDACEOUS
CAPRICIOUSNESS
CARBON MONOX-
IDE
CARCINOMATOSIS
CARDINAL
POINTS
CARDIOVASCULAR
CARPET SWEEP-
ERS
CARRIER PI-
GEONS

CARRYING
CHARGE
CARTOGRAPHICAL
CARTRIDGE
PAPER
CASEMENT WIN-
DOW
CASH AND CAR-
RIES
CASH DISPENS-
ERS
CATCHMENT
AREAS
CATECHETICALLY
CATEGORIZATION
CATHEDRAL
CLOSE
CATHERINE
WHEEL
CATHODE RAY
TUBE
CAUGHT UN-
AWARES
CAUSES CEL-
EBRES
CENSORIOUSNESS
CENTRAL HEAT-
ING
CENTRALIZATION
CENTRE FOR-
WARDS
CENTRIFUGATION
CERCOPITHECOID
CHAIN REAC-
TIONS
CHAISES
LONGUES
CHANGEABLENESS
CHANTRY CHAP-
ELS
CHARACTER
ACTOR
CHARACTERISTIC
CHARACTERIZING
CHARGE AC-
COUNTS
CHARITABLENESS
CHARLATANISTIC
CHARTER MEM-
BERS
CHECHENO-IN-
GUSH

CHEMOSYNTHESIS
CHEMOSYNTHETIC
CHEMOTHERAPIST
CHEST OF DRAWERS
CHICKENHEARTED
CHIEF CONSTABLE
CHIEF EXECUTIVE
CHIEF INSPECTOR
CHIEFTAINSHIPS
CHILD PRODIGIES
CHIMNEYBREASTS
CHIMNEY CORNERS
CHINCHERINCHEE
CHINESE LANTERN
CHINLESS WONDER
CHLOROPHYLLOID
CHLOROPHYLLOUS
CHLOROTHIAZIDE
CHLORPROMAZINE
CHLORPROPAMIDE
CHOLINESTERASE
CHOREOGRAPHERS
CHOREOGRAPHING
CHRISTIAN NAMES
CHRISTMAS BOXES
CHRISTMAS CAKES
CHRISTMAS CARDS
CHRISTMAS TREES
CHRISTOLOGICAL
CHROMATOGRAPHY
CHROMATOPHORIC
CHRYSANTHEMUMS
CIGARETTE PAPER
CINCHONIZATION
CINEMATOGRAPHY
CIRCUIT BREAKER
CIRCULAR LETTER
CIRCUMAMBIENCE
CIRCUMAMBULATE
CIRCUMFERENCES
CIRCUMLOCUTION
CIRCUMLOCUTORY
CIRCUMNAVIGATE
CIRCUMNUTATION
CIRCUMSCISSILE
CIRCUMSCRIBING
CIRCUMSPECTION
CIRCUMSTANTIAL
CIRCUMVOLUTION
CIRCUMVOLUTORY
CIVIL ENGINEERS
CLARIFICATIONS

CLASS-CONSCIOUS
CLASSIFICATION
CLASSIFICATORY
CLAUSTROPHOBIA
CLAUSTROPHOBIC
CLEARANCE SALES
CLEARINGHOUSES
CLEAR-SIGHTEDLY
CLIMBING FRAMES
CLOAK-AND-DAGGER
CLOTHES HANGERS
CLUB SANDWICHES
CLUSTER BOMBING
COCK-A-DOODLE-DOO
COCKER SPANIELS
COCKTAIL LOUNGE
COCKTAIL STICKS
COESSENTIALITY
COFFEE KLATCHES
COINCIDENTALLY
COLD SHOULDERED
COLLAPSIBILITY
COLLECTIVE FARM
COLLECTIVE NOUN
COLLECTOR'S ITEM
COLLOQUIALISMS
COLORADO BEETLE
COLOURFASTNESS
COLOURLESSNESS
COMBINING FORMS
COMBUSTIBILITY
COMFORTABLY OFF
COMFORT STATION
COMMAND MODULES
COMMENSURATION
COMMERCIALIZED
COMMISERATIONS
COMMISSIONAIRE
COMMITTEE STAGE
COMMON FRACTION
COMMON-OR-GARDEN
COMMUNICATIONS
COMMUNITY CHEST
COMMUNITY HOMES
COMPLEMENTIZER
COMPREHENSIBLE
COMPREHENSIBLY
COMPREHENSIONS
COMPREHENSIVES
COMPULSIVENESS
CONCATENATIONS
CONCAVO-CONCAVE

CONCELEBRATION
CONCENTRATIONS
CONCEPTUALIZED
CONCESSIONAIRE
CONCRETE JUNGLE
CONCRETE MIXERS
CONCRETE POETRY
CONCRETIZATION
CONDEMNED CELLS
CONDENSABILITY
CONDITIONALITY
CONDUCTOR RAILS
CONDUPLICATION
CONFABULATIONS
CONFEDERATIONS
CONFIDENTIALLY
CONFIGURATIONS
CONFLAGRATIONS
CONFORMABILITY
CONFRONTATIONS
CONGLOMERATION
CONGLUTINATIVE
CONGRATULATING
CONGRATULATION
CONGRATULATORY
CONGREGATIONAL
CONJUNCTIVITIS
CONNECTING RODS
CONQUISTADORES
CONSANGUINEOUS
CONSCRIPTIONAL
CONSERVATIONAL
CONSERVATIVELY
CONSERVATOIRES
CONSERVATORIES
CONSIDERATIONS
CONSOLIDATIONS
CONSPIRATORIAL
CONSTABULARIES
CONSTANTINOPLE
CONSTELLATIONS
CONSTITUENCIES
CONSTITUTIONAL
CONSTRUCTIONAL
CONSTRUCTIVELY
CONSTRUCTIVISM
CONSTRUCTIVIST
CONSUETUDINARY
CONTAGIOUSNESS
CONTAINERIZING
CONTEMPORARIES
CONTEMPORARILY

CONTEMPTUOUSLY
CONTINENTALISM
CONTINENTALIST
CONTINENTALITY
CONTORTIONISTS
CONTRACEPTIVES
CONTRACT BRIDGE
CONTRADICTIONS
CONTRAINDICANT
CONTRAINDICATE
CONTRAPOSITION
CONTRAPUNTALLY
CONTRAVENTIONS
CONTRIBUTORIAL
CONTROVERTIBLE
CONTUMACIOUSLY
CONTUMELIOUSLY
CONVENTIONALLY
CONVERSATIONAL
CONVERTIBILITY
CONVEXO-CONCAVE
COPPER-BOTTOMED
CORELIGIONISTS
CORNISH PASTIES
CORPORATION TAX
CORRESPONDENCE
CORRESPONDENTS
CORRUPTIBILITY
CORTICOSTEROID
CORTICOSTERONE
CORTICOTROPHIN
COUNTERACTIONS
COUNTERATTACKS
COUNTERBALANCE
COUNTERFEITERS
COUNTERFEITING
COUNTERMANDING
COUNTERMEASURE
COUNTERMENSURE
COUNTERPOISING
COUNTERSHADING
COUNTERSIGNING
COUNTERSINKING
COUNTERVAILING
COUNTINGHOUSES
COUNTRY COUSINS
COUNTY COUNCILS
COURAGEOUSNESS
COURT-MARTIALED
COURT OF INQUIRY
COVERING LETTER
CRADLE SNATCHER

CRAMP ONE'S STYLE
CREDIBILITY GAP
CREDITABLENESS
CREDIT ACCOUNTS
CREDIT SQUEEZES
CREEPY-CRAWLIES
CRIMINAL RECORD
CRIMINOLOGICAL
CRIMINOLOGISTS
CROCODILE TEARS
CROSS-COUNTRIES
CROSS-EXAMINERS
CROSS-EXAMINING
CROSS-FERTILIZE
CROSS-POLLINATE
CROSS REFERENCE
CROSS-REFERENCE
CROSS-REFERRING
CROSS-SECTIONAL
CROWN AND ANCHOR
CRUISE MISSILES
CRYPTAESTHESIA
CRYPTOCURRENCY
CRYPTOGRAPHERS
CUCURBITACEOUS
CURRENT ACCOUNT
CURRICULA VITAE
CURRUGATED IRON
CURTAIN RAISERS
CURVILINEARITY
CYANOCOBALAMIN
CYBERNETICALLY
CYTOTAXONOMIST
CZECHOSLOVAKIA

D

DAGUERREOTYPER
DAGUERREOTYPES
DANISH PASTRIES
DATA PROCESSING
DAUGHTERLINESS
DAUGHTERS-IN-LAW
DAY OF RECKONING
DEAD MAN'S HANDLE
DEAD TO THE WORLD
DECEIVABLENESS
DECENTRALIZING
DECIMALIZATION
DECLASSIFIABLE
DECLENSIONALLY
DECLINE AND FALL
DECOLONIZATION

DECOLORIZATION
DECONTAMINATED
DECONTAMINATOR
DEFENESTRATION
DEFLOCCULATION
DEGENERATENESS
DEHUMANIZATION
DELECTABLENESS
DELIBERATENESS
DELIGHTFULNESS
DELOCALIZATION
DEMILITARIZING
DEMISEMIQUAVER
DEMOBILIZATION
DEMOCRATICALLY
DEMONETIZATION
DEMONSTRATIONS
DEMORALIZATION
DENATIONALIZED
DENOMINATIONAL
DENTAL SURGEONS
DEPLORABLENESS
DEPOLARIZATION
DEPOSIT ACCOUNT
DERMATOLOGICAL
DERMATOLOGISTS
DERMATOPLASTIC
DEROGATORINESS
DESTRUCTIONIST
DETERMINEDNESS
DEVIL'S ADVOCATE
DEVITALIZATION
DEXTROROTATION
DEXTROROTATORY
DIABOLICALNESS
DIAGNOSTICALLY
DIALECTOLOGIST
DIAMOND JUBILEE
DIAMOND WEDDING
DIAPHANOUSNESS
DIAPHOTOTROPIC
DICHROMATICISM
DICOTYLEDONOUS
DIELECTRICALLY
DIESEL-ELECTRIC
DIEU ET MON DROIT
DIFFERENTIABLE
DIFFERENTIATED
DIFFERENTIATOR
DIFFRACTOMETER
DIGITALIZATION
DIG ONE'S HEELS IN

DIMENHYDRINATE
DIMENSIONALITY
DINITROBENZENE
DINNER SERVICES
DINOFLAGELLATE
DIPLOMATICALLY
DIPLOSTEMONOUS
DIRECTIONALITY
DIRECT TAXATION
DISAFFILIATING
DISAFFILIATION
DISAFFORESTING
DISAPPEARANCES
DISAPPOINTEDLY
DISAPPOINTMENT
DISAPPROBATION
DISAPPROVINGLY
DISARRANGEMENT
DISARTICULATOR
DISASSOCIATING
DISASSOCIATION
DISBELIEVINGLY
DISCIPLINARIAN
DISCOLORATIONS
DISCOMPOSINGLY
DISCONNECTEDLY
DISCONNECTIONS
DISCONSOLATELY
DISCONSOLATION
DISCONTENTEDLY
DISCONTENTMENT
DISCONTINUANCE
DISCOUNTENANCE
DISCOUNT STORES
DISCOURAGEMENT
DISCOURAGINGLY
DISCOURTEOUSLY
DISCRIMINATING
DISCRIMINATION
DISCRIMINATORY
DISCURSIVENESS
DISEMBARKATION
DISEMBOGUEMENT
DISEMBOWELLING
DISEMBOWELMENT
DISENCHANTMENT
DISENFRANCHISE
DISENTHRALMENT
DISEQUILIBRIUM
DISESTABLISHED
DISFEATUREMENT
DISFIGUREMENTS

DISFORESTATION
DISFRANCHISING
DISGRUNTLEMENT
DISHEARTENMENT
DISILLUSIONING
DISINCLINATION
DISINFESTATION
DISINGENUOUSLY
DISINHERITANCE
DISINTEGRATING
DISINTEGRATION
DISINTEGRATIVE
DISJOINTEDNESS
DISORDERLINESS
DISORIENTATING
DISORIENTATION
DISPARAGEMENTS
DISPENSABILITY
DISPENSATIONAL
DISPUTATIOUSLY
DISQUALIFIABLE
DISQUIETEDNESS
DISRESPECTABLE
DISSERTATIONAL
DISSERVICEABLE
DISSIMULATIONS
DISSOCIABILITY
DISSOLVABILITY
DISSUASIVENESS
DISTENSIBILITY
DISTINGUISHING
DISTRIBUTIONAL
DISTRIBUTIVELY
DIURETICALNESS
DIVERTICULITIS
DIVERTICULOSIS
DIVERTISSEMENT
DNEPROPETROVSK
DOG IN THE MANGER
DO-IT-YOURSELFER
DOMESTIC ANIMAL
DOUBLE BREASTED
DOUBLE-BREASTED
DOUBLE-CHECKING
DOUBLE-CROSSERS
DOUBLE-CROSSING
DOUBLE ENTENDRE
DOUBLE FEATURES
DOUBTING THOMAS
DOWN IN THE DUMPS
DRAINING BOARDS
DRAMATIZATIONS

DRESSING TABLES
DRESS REHEARSAL
DRIVING LICENCE
DROP IN THE OCEAN
DRUM MAJORETTES
DUCKS AND DRAKES
DUCTLESS GLANDS
DWELLING HOUSES
DYER'S-GREENWEED
DYNAMOELECTRIC
DYSMENORRHOEAL

E

ECCENTRICITIES
ECCLESIASTICAL
ECCLESIOLOGIST
ECONOMETRICIAN
EDITIO PRINCEPS
EDUCATIONALIST
EFFERVESCENTLY
EFFERVESCINGLY
EFFORTLESSNESS
EGALITARIANISM
EGOCENTRICALLY
ELDER STATESMAN
ELDER STATESMEN
ELECTIONEERING
ELECTRA COMPLEX
ELECTROCHEMIST
ELECTROCUTIONS
ELECTRODEPOSIT
ELECTRODYNAMIC
ELECTROGRAPHIC
ELECTROKINETIC
ELECTRONICALLY
ELECTRONIC MAIL
ELECTROSTATICS
ELECTROSURGERY
ELECTROTHERMAL
ELECTROVALENCY
ELEMENTARINESS
ELLIPTICALNESS
EMBARRASSINGLY
EMBARRASSMENTS
EMBELLISHMENTS
EMBLEMATICALLY
EMOTIONALISTIC
EMPHATICALNESS
EMULSIFICATION
EMULSION PAINTS
ENANTIOMORPHIC
ENCAPSULATIONS

ENCEPHALOGRAPH
ENCOURAGEMENTS
ENDOCRINE GLAND
ENDOCRINOLOGIC
ENDOPHYTICALLY
ENDOSMOTICALLY
ENFANT TERRIBLE
ENFORCEABILITY
ENGAGEMENT RING
ENHARMONICALLY
ENLIGHTENINGLY
ENROLLED NURSES
ENTEROGASTRONE
ENTERPRISINGLY
ENTERTAININGLY
ENTERTAINMENTS
ENTOMOSTRACOUS
EPEXEGETICALLY
EPICONTINENTAL
EPIDEMIOLOGIST
EPIGENETICALLY
EPIGRAPHICALLY
EPISTEMOLOGIST
EQUIPONDERANCE
EQUIVOCATINGLY
ERYTHROBLASTIC
ERYTHROPOIESIS
ERYTHROPOIETIC
ESCAPE VELOCITY
ESCHATOLOGICAL
ESTABLISHMENTS
ESTATE AGENCIES
ESTERIFICATION
ETERNALIZATION
ETHERIFICATION
ETHNOCENTRISMS
ETHNOLOGICALLY
ETYMOLOGICALLY
EULOGISTICALLY
EUPHONICALNESS
EUPHORBIACEOUS
EUPHUISTICALLY
EUSTACHIAN TUBE
EUTROPHICATION
EVANGELICALISM
EVANGELIZATION
EVAPORATED MILK
EVEN-HANDEDNESS
EVENING DRESSES
EVIL-MINDEDNESS
EVOLUTIONISTIC
EXACERBATINGLY

EXAGGERATINGLY
EXASPERATINGLY
EXCEPTIONALITY
EXCLAUSTRATION
EXCOMMUNICABLE
EXCOMMUNICATED
EXCOMMUNICATOR
EXCRUCIATINGLY
EXHAUSTIBILITY
EXHAUSTIVENESS
EXHIBITIONISTS
EXHILARATINGLY
EXISTENTIALISM
EXISTENTIALIST
EXOTHERMICALLY
EXPANSIONISTIC
EXPENSE ACCOUNT
EXPERIMENTALLY
EXPOSTULATIONS
EXPRESSIONISTS
EXPRESSIONLESS
EXPRESSIVENESS
EXPROPRIATIONS
EXTEMPORANEOUS
EXTENDED FAMILY
EXTENSIONALITY
EXTINGUISHABLE
EXTINGUISHMENT
EXTORTIONATELY
EXTRACANONICAL
EXTRACTABILITY
EXTRANEOUSNESS
EXTRAVEHICULAR
EYEBROW PENCILS

F

FACTITIOUSNESS
FACTORY FARMING
FAINT-HEARTEDLY
FAIR-MINDEDNESS
FAIRY GODMOTHER
FAITS ACCOMPLIS
FALLACIOUSNESS
FALLOPIAN TUBES
FALSE PRETENCES
FALSIFICATIONS
FAMILY PLANNING
FARSIGHTEDNESS
FASTIDIOUSNESS
FATALISTICALLY
FATHERS AND SONS
FAVOURABLENESS

FEATHERBEDDING
FEATHERBRAINED
FEATHERWEIGHTS
FEDERALIZATION
FEEDING BOTTLES
FEEL THE DRAUGHT
FELICITOUSNESS
FEMININE ENDING
FEMME DE CHAMBRE
FERMENTABILITY
FERRIMAGNETISM
FERROMAGNESIAN
FERROMAGNETISM
FERROMANGANESE
FICTIONALIZING
FICTITIOUSNESS
FIDEICOMMISSUM
FIELDS OF VISION
FIELD TELEGRAPH
FIFTH COLUMNIST
FIGHTING CHANCE
FIGURATIVENESS
FIGURE OF SPEECH
FIGURES OF EIGHT
FILING CABINETS
FILLING STATION
FINANCIAL YEARS
FINE-TOOTH COMBS
FINGER PAINTING
FINGERPRINTING
FINSTERAARHORN
FIRST OFFENDERS
FISSIONABILITY
FLABBERGASTING
FLIGHT-RECORDER
FLIGHT SERGEANT
FLOATING VOTERS
FLOG A DEAD HORSE
FLORICULTURIST
FLOWER-OF-AN-HOUR
FLYING BUTTRESS
FLYING DUTCHMAN
FLYING OFFICERS
FOLLOW MY LEADER
FOLLOW-MY-LEADER
FOLLOW-THROUGHS
FOOD PROCESSORS
FORBIDDEN FRUIT
FORBIDDINGNESS
FOREIGN AFFAIRS
FOREORDAINMENT
FORESHORTENING

FORETHOUGHTFUL
FORE-TOPGALLANT
FORKLIFT TRUCKS
FORTHRIGHTNESS
FORTIFICATIONS
FORTUITOUSNESS
FORTUNE HUNTERS
FORTUNE-TELLERS
FORWARD-LOOKING
FOUNDING FATHER
FOUR-LETTER WORD
FRATERNIZATION
FREE ENTERPRISE
FREEZING POINTS
FRENCH DRESSING
FRENCH POLISHED
FRIDGE-FREEZERS
FRIENDLESSNESS
FRINGE BENEFITS
FROZEN SHOULDER
FRUCTIFICATION
FULLY-FASHIONED
FUNCTIONALISTS
FUNDAMENTALISM
FUNDAMENTALIST
FUNDAMENTALITY
FUNERAL PARLOUR
FURFURALDEHYDE
FUTURISTICALLY

G

GALACTOPOIESIS
GALACTOPOIETIC
GALVANOTROPISM
GASTROVASCULAR
GAVE UP THE GHOST
GEIGER COUNTERS
GELATINIZATION
GENEALOGICALLY
GENERALISSIMOS
GENERALIZATION
GENERAL STRIKES
GENTRIFICATION
GEOCENTRICALLY
GEO-ENGINEERING
GEOGRAPHICALLY
GERMAN SHEPHERD
GERONTOLOGICAL
GERRYMANDERING
GESTICULATIONS
GET ONE'S OWN BACK
GHETTO BLASTERS

GLANDULAR FEVER
GLOBE ARTICHOKE
GLOBETROTTINGS
GLORIFICATIONS
GLORY-OF-THE-SNOW
GLOSSY MAGAZINE
GLUCOCORTICORD
GOLDEN JUBILEES
GOLDEN WEDDINGS
GOLD-OF-PLEASURE
GOOD-FOR-NOTHING
GOOD-HUMOUREDLY
GOOD SAMARITANS
GRACE-AND-FAVOUR
GRADE CROSSINGS
GRAMMAR SCHOOLS
GRAMMATICALITY
GRAMMATOLOGIST
GRANDDAUGHTERS
GRANDILOQUENCE
GRANGERIZATION
GRAPHITIZATION
GRAPPLING HOOKS
GRAPPLING IRONS
GRASP THE NETTLE
GRATIFICATIONS
GRATUITOUSNESS
GREGARIOUSNESS
GREGORIAN CHANT
GROUNDLESSNESS
GROUP PRACTICES
GUARDIAN ANGELS
GUIDED MISSILES
GUY FAWKES NIGHT
GYNAECOLOGICAL
GYNAECOLOGISTS
GYROSTABILIZER

H

HABERDASHERIES
HAEMACYTOMETER
HAEMAGGLUTININ
HAEMATOBLASTIC
HAEMATOGENESIS
HAEMATOPOIESIS
HAEMATOPOIETIC
HAEMATOTHERMAL
HAEMOCYTOMETER
HALFPENNYWORTH
HALFWITTEDNESS
HALICARNASSIAN
HALLUCINATIONS

HALLUCINOGENIC
HANDICRAFTSMAN
HANDSOME SALARY
HANGING GARDENS
HAPAX LEGOMENON
HARD CURRENCIES
HARD-HEADEDNESS
HARMONIOUSNESS
HARPSICHORDIST
HEAD LIKE A SIEVE
HEADMASTERSHIP
HEADSTRONGNESS
HEARTRENDINGLY
HEARTWARMINGLY
HEATHENISHNESS
HEBRAISTICALLY
HEGIRA CALENDAR
HELL FOR LEATHER
HELTER-SKELTERS
HEMEL HEMPSTEAD
HEMISPHEROIDAL
HENRIETTA MARIA
HEREDITABILITY
HEREDITARINESS
HERMAPHRODITES
HERMAPHRODITIC
HERMAPHRODITUS
HEROIC COUPLETS
HERO WORSHIPPED
HERPES LABIALIS
HETEROCHROMOUS
HETEROGONOUSLY
HETEROLECITHAL
HETEROMORPHISM
HETERONOMOUSLY
HETERONYMOUSLY
HETEROPHYLLOUS
HETEROPOLARITY
HETEROSEXUALLY
HIERARCHICALLY
HIGH COMMISSION
HIGH COURT JUDGE
HIGH EXPLOSIVES
HIGH-HANDEDNESS
HIGHLAND FLINGS
HIGH-MINDEDNESS
HIGH-PRESSURING
HIGH-PRINCIPLED
HIGH SPEED TRAIN
HIGH TECHNOLOGY
HIGH WATER MARKS

HIPPOPOTAMUSES
HISTOCHEMISTRY
HISTOLOGICALLY
HISTOLYTICALLY
HISTOPATHOLOGY
HISTOPLASMOSIS
HISTORICALNESS
HISTORIOGRAPHY
HISTRIONICALLY
HOEK VAN HOLLAND
HOLDING COMPANY
HOLD NO BRIEF FOR
HOLIER-THAN-THOU
HOMOCHROMATISM
HOMOGENIZATION
HOMOIOUSIANISM
HOMOPHONICALLY
HONEYDEW MELONS
HONOURABLENESS
HORATIUS COCLES
HORIZONTALNESS
HORRENDOUSNESS
HORROR-STRICKEN
HORSE CHESTNUTS
HORSE LATITUDES
HORTICULTURIST
HOSPITABLENESS
HOT-WATER BOTTLE
HOUSEHOLD NAMES
HOUSEMAID'S KNEE
HOUSE OF COMMONS
HOUSING PROJECT
HUMIDIFICATION
HUMOURLESSNESS
HUNGER MARCHERS
HUNGER STRIKERS
HUNTING GROUNDS
HURRICANE LAMPS
HYDROCELLULOSE
HYDROCORTISONE
HYDROGENOLYSIS
HYDROLOGICALLY
HYDROMAGNETICS
HYDROMECHANICS
HYPERBOLICALLY
HYPERSENSITIVE
HYPOCHONDRIACS
HYPOCRITICALLY
HYPODERMICALLY
HYPOTHETICALLY
HYSTERECTOMIES

I
ICEBERG LETTUCE
ICHNEUMON FLIES
ICHTHYOPHAGOUS
IDEALISTICALLY
IDENTICAL TWINS
IDENTIFICATION
IDEOLOOGICALLY
IDIOSYNCRASIES
ILLEGALIZATION
ILLEGITIMATELY
ILLIMITABILITY
ILLUSTRATIONAL
ILLUSTRATIVELY
IMMETHODICALLY
IMMOBILIZATION
IMMUNOGENETICS
IMMUNOGLOBULIN
IMMUNOREACTION
IMPARISYLLABIC
IMPEACHABILITY
IMPERCEPTIVITY
IMPERMEABILITY
IMPERSONATIONS
IMPERTURBATION
IMPLAUSIBILITY
IMPLEMENTATION
IMPOLITENESSES
IMPRACTICALITY
IMPREGNABILITY
IMPRESSIONABLE
IMPRESSIONABLY
IMPRESSIONALLY
IMPRESSIONISTS
IMPRESSIVENESS
IMPROVISATIONS
INADVISABILITY
INALIENABILITY
INALTERABILITY
INAPPRECIATIVE
INAPPREHENSIVE
INAPPROACHABLE
INARTICULATELY
INARTISTICALLY
INAUSPICIOUSLY
INCANDESCENTLY
INCAPACITATING
INCAPACITATION
INCAUTIOUSNESS
INCESTUOUSNESS
INCOMMENSURATE
INCOMMODIOUSLY

INCOMMUNICABLE
INCOMPLETENESS
INCOMPRESSIBLE
INCONCLUSIVELY
INCONSIDERABLE
INCONSISTENTLY
INCONVENIENCED
INCONVENIENCES
INCONVENIENTLY
INCOORDINATION
INDECIPHERABLE
INDECIPHERABLY
INDECOROUSNESS
INDEFINITENESS
INDESTRUCTIBLE
INDESTRUCTIBLY
INDETERMINABLE
INDETERMINABLY
INDIAN ELEPHANT
INDIFFERENTISM
INDIFFERENTIST
INDIGENOUSNESS
INDIRECT OBJECT
INDIRECT SPEECH
INDISCRIMINATE
INDISPOSITIONS
INDISTINCTNESS
INDIVIDUALISTS
INDIVIDUALIZED
INDIVIDUALIZER
INDIVISIBILITY
INDOCTRINATING
INDOCTRINATION
INDOMITABILITY
INDUBITABILITY
INDUSTRIALISTS
INDUSTRIALIZED
INEFFECTUALITY
INELUCTABILITY
INERTIA SELLING
INESSENTIALITY
INESTIMABILITY
INEXCUSABILITY
INFECTIOUSNESS
INFLAMMABILITY
INFLAMMATORILY
INFRALAPSARIAN
INFRANGIBILITY
INFRASTRUCTURE
INGRATIATINGLY
INHABITABILITY
INHARMONIOUSLY

INHERITABILITY
INITIALIZATION
IN LOCO PARENTIS
INNUMERABILITY
INQUISITIONIST
INSANITARINESS
INSCRUTABILITY
INSEPARABILITY
INSIDER DEALING
INSIGNIFICANCE
INSTITUTIONARY
INSTRUCTORSHIP
INSUFFICIENTLY
INSUPERABILITY
INSUPPRESSIBLE
INSURMOUNTABLE
INSURRECTIONAL
INTEGRATIONIST
INTELLECTUALLY
INTELLIGENTSIA
INTENTIONALITY
INTERCESSIONAL
INTERCOMMUNION
INTERDEPENDENT
INTEREST GROUPS
INTERFERENTIAL
INTERFEROMETER
INTERFEROMETRY
INTERFERTILITY
INTERGRADATION
INTERJECTIONAL
INTERLOCUTRESS
INTERMEDIARIES
INTERMIGRATION
INTERMITTENTLY
INTERMITTINGLY
INTERMOLECULAR
INTERNAL MARKET
INTERNATIONALE
INTERNATIONALS
INTERPELLATION
INTERPENETRANT
INTERPENETRATE
INTERPLANETARY
INTERPOLATIONS
INTERPOSITIONS
INTERPRETATION
INTERPRETATIVE
INTERRELATIONS
INTERROGATIONS
INTERROGATIVES
INTERSECTIONAL

INTERSEXUALITY
INTERSPERSEDLY
INTERTWININGLY
INTERVENTIONAL
INTOLERABILITY
INTO THE BARGAIN
INTOXICATINGLY
INTRACTABILITY
INTRACUTANEOUS
INTRAMOLECULAR
INTRANSIGENTLY
INTRANSITIVELY
INTRODUCTORILY
INVERTED COMMAS
INVESTIGATIONS
INVIGORATINGLY
IODOMETRICALLY
IRRECONCILABLE
IRRECONCILABLY
IRREDUCIBILITY
IRREFUTABILITY
IRREGULARITIES
IRREMOVABILITY
IRREPARABILITY
IRREPROACHABLE
IRREPROACHABLY
IRRESOLUBILITY
IRREVOCABILITY
ISOPIESTICALLY

J

JACK-IN-THE-BOXES
JOB'S COMFORTERS
JOLLIFICATIONS
JOURNALIZATION
JURISDICTIONAL
JUSTICIABILITY
JUSTIFIABILITY

K

KAISERSLAUTERN
KAMENSK-URALSKI
KANGAROO COURTS
KEEP ONE'S CHIN UP
KEEP ONE'S HAND IN
KERATINIZATION
KEYHOLE SURGERY
KIDNEY MACHINES
KINDERGARTENER
KITCHEN GARDENS
KNICKERBOCKERS
KNIGHT-ERRANTRY

KNOCK ON THE HEAD
KNUCKLE-DUSTERS
KOSOVO-METOHIJA

L

LABOUR EXCHANGE
LAMELLIROSTRAL
LANCE CORPORALS
LAND ON ONE'S FEET
LARGE INTESTINE
LARGER THAN LIFE
LARYNGOLOGICAL
LARYNGOSCOPIST
LASCIVIOUSNESS
LATITUDINARIAN
LAUGHING STOCKS
LAUNDRY BASKETS
LAW OF THE JUNGLE
LEADING ARTICLE
LEADING STRINGS
LEAVE OF ABSENCE
LEFT-HANDEDNESS
LEFT IN THE LURCH
LEGALISTICALLY
LEGERDEMAINIST
LEGION OF HONOUR
LEGITIMIZATION
LENDING LIBRARY
LET'S CALL IT A DAY
LETTER OF CREDIT
LEVEL CROSSINGS
LEXICOGRAPHERS
LIBERALIZATION
LIBERAL STUDIES
LIBERTARIANISM
LIBIDINOUSNESS
LICENTIATESHIP
LICENTIOUSNESS
LIFE EXPECTANCY
LIFE PRESERVERS
LIGHT AIRCRAFTS
LIGNOCELLULOSE
LIKE-MINDEDNESS
LINE ONE'S POCKET
LINGUISTICALLY
LISTEN TO REASON
LITHOLOGICALLY
LITTLE BY LITTLE
LITTLE GREEN MEN
LOCAL AUTHORITY
LOCUS CLASSICUS
LONGITUDINALLY

LONG-SUFFERANCE
LONGWINDEDNESS
LOOKING GLASSES
LOVING KINDNESS
LOXODROMICALLY
LUGUBRIOUSNESS

M
MACADAMIZATION
MACHINEGUNNING
MACROECONOMICS
MACROEVOLUTION
MACROMOLECULAR
MAGNETIC FIELDS
MAGNIFICATIONS
MAHALLA EL KUBRA
MAKE ALLOWANCES
MAKE THE RUNNING
MAKE UP ONE'S MIND
MALACOPHYLLOUS
MALACOSTRACOUS
MALE CHAUVINIST
MALFUNCTIONING
MALPIGHIACEOUS
MALTESE CROSSES
MANIFESTATIONS
MAN IN THE STREET
MANIPULABILITY
MANNERLESSNESS
MANOMETRICALLY
MANUFACTURABLE
MARCHING ORDERS
MARKET GARDENER
MARKET RESEARCH
MARTYROLOGICAL
MASON-DIXON LINE
MASSAGE PARLOUR
MASSOTHERAPIST
MASS PRODUCTION
MATERNITY LEAVE
MATHEMATICALLY
MATHEMATICIANS
MATTER OF COURSE
MATTER-OF-FACTLY
MATURE STUDENTS
MAUNDY THURSDAY
MEANINGFULNESS
MECHANOTHERAPY
MEDDLESOMENESS
MEDITATIVENESS
MEGALOCEPHALIC
MEGALOMANIACAL

MEGAPHONICALLY
MEGASPOROPHYLL
MELANCHOLINESS
MENDACIOUSNESS
MENTAL HOSPITAL
MEPHISTOPHELES
MERCAPTOPURINE
MERCHANT NAVIES
MERETRICIOUSLY
MESDEMOISELLES
METACHROMATISM
METALLOGRAPHER
METALLOGRAPHIC
METAMORPHOSING
METAPHORICALLY
METAPHYSICALLY
METAPSYCHOLOGY
METASTATICALLY
METEMPSYCHOSIS
METEOROGRAPHIC
METEOROLOGICAL
METEOROLOGISTS
METHAEMOGLOBIN
METHODICALNESS
METHODOLOGICAL
METICULOUSNESS
MICROBAROGRAPH
MICROBIOLOGIST
MICROCEPHALOUS
MICROCHEMISTRY
MICROCIRCUITRY
MICROCOMPUTERS
MICROECONOMICS
MICROMETEORITE
MICROORGANISMS
MICROPARASITIC
MICROPROCESSOR
MICROPYROMETER
MICROSTOMATOUS
MICROSTRUCTURE
MIDDLE-DISTANCE
MIGHT-HAVE-BEENS
MILITARIZATION
MILITARY POLICE
MILLENARIANISM
MINERALIZATION
MISAPPLICATION
MISAPPREHENDED
MISAPPROPRIATE
MISCALCULATING
MISCALCULATION
MISCONCEPTIONS

MISINFORMATION
MISINTERPRETED
MISINTERPRETER
MISREPRESENTED
MISREPRESENTER
MIXED ECONOMIES
MIXED METAPHORS
MOCK-HEROICALLY
MOCK TURTLE SOUP
MODERNIZATIONS
MOMENTS OF TRUTH
MONGRELIZATION
MONKEY BUSINESS
MONKEY WRENCHES
MONOCARPELLARY
MONOCHROMATISM
MONOLITHICALLY
MONOPOLIZATION
MONOPROPELLANT
MONOSACCHARIDE
MOONLIGHT FLITS
MORALISTICALLY
MORGANATICALLY
MORNING GLORIES
MORPHOPHONEMIC
MOTHER SUPERIOR
MOTIONLESSNESS
MOTION PICTURES
MOTIVELESSNESS
MOUNTAINEERING
MOVING PAVEMENT
MOVING PICTURES
MUCOMEMBRANOUS
MUCOUS MEMBRANE
MULTIFACTORIAL
MULTIFARIOUSLY
MULTILATERALLY
MULTINATIONALS
MULTIPLE STORES
MULTIPLICATION
MULTIPLICATIVE
MUNICIPALITIES
MUSTARD PLASTER
MYELENCEPHALIC
MYELENCEPHALON
MYOCARDIOGRAPH
MYOGRAPHICALLY
MYRMECOLOGICAL
MYRMECOPHAGOUS
MYRMECOPHILOUS
MYSTAGOGICALLY
MYSTERIOUSNESS

N

NANSEN PASSPORT
NARCOSYNTHESIS
NARRATIVE VERSE
NASOPHARYNGEAL
NASTY BIT OF WORK
NATIONAL ANTHEM
NATIVE AMERICAN
NATURAL HISTORY
NATURALIZATION
NATURAL SCIENCE
NEANDERTHAL MAN
NEBUCHADNEZZAR
NEGLECTFULNESS
NEIGHBOURHOODS
NEOCOLONIALISM
NEOCOLONIALIST
NERVOUS SYSTEMS
NEUROPATHOLOGY
NEUTRALIZATION
NEWFOUNDLANDER
NEWS CONFERENCE
NEWSWORTHINESS
NIGHT BLINDNESS
NIL DESPERANDUM
NINE DAYS' WONDER
NITROCELLULOSE
NITROGLYCERINE
NOBLESSE OBLIGE
NOLO CONTENDERE
NONATTRIBUTIVE
NONCOMMITTALLY
NONCONFORMISTS
NONCOOPERATION
NONCOOPERATIVE
NONDISJUNCTION
NONEQUIVALENCE
NONINFLAMMABLE
NONPROGRESSIVE
NON PROSEQUITUR
NONRESIDENTIAL
NONRESTRICTIVE
NONSTIMULATING
NORFOLK JACKETS
NORTHERN LIGHTS
NORTH-NORTHEAST
NORTH-NORTHWEST
NORTHUMBERLAND
NOTEWORTHINESS
NOUVEAUX RICHES
NO-WIN SITUATION
NUCLEAR REACTOR

NUCLEAR WINTERS
NURSERY SCHOOLS
NUTRITIOUSNESS
NYCTAGINACEOUS
NYMPHOMANIACAL

O

OBSEQUIOUSNESS
OBSERVABLENESS
OBSTREPEROUSLY
OBSTRUCTIONISM
OBSTRUCTIONIST
OCCUPATIONALLY
OCEAN GRAYHOUND
OCEANOGRAPHERS
OEDIPUS COMPLEX
OLD MAN OF THE SEA
OLD PEOPLE'S HOME
OLD TIME DANCING
OLIGARCHICALLY
OLIGOPSONISTIC
ONE-ARMED BANDIT
ONEIROCRITICAL
ONE-NIGHT STANDS
ON ONE'S BEAM ENDS
ON THE OTHER HAND
ON THE THRESHOLD
OPEN-HANDEDNESS
OPEN-MINDEDNESS
OPEN SANDWICHES
OPEN UNIVERSITY
OPERATING TABLE
OPERATIONALISM
OPHTHALMOSCOPE
OPHTHALMOSCOPY
OPPOSITE NUMBER
OPPRESSIVENESS
OPTIMISTICALLY
ORCHESTRATIONS
ORDINARY LEVELS
ORDINARY SEAMAN
ORDNANCE SURVEY
ORGANIZATIONAL
ORGANIZED CRIME
ORGANOGRAPHIST
ORGANOMETALLIC
ORNITHOLOGICAL
ORNITHOLOGISTS
OROBANCHACEOUS
OROGRAPHICALLY
ORTHOCHROMATIC
ORTHODOX CHURCH

ORTHOGENICALLY
ORTHOGRAPHICAL
ORTHOPHOSPHATE
OSCILLOGRAPHIC
OSMOMETRICALLY
OSTENTATIOUSLY
OSTEOARTHRITIC
OSTEOARTHRITIS
OSTEOLOGICALLY
OTOLARYNGOLOGY
OUTBOARD MOTORS
OUTGENERALLING
OUTLANDISHNESS
OUTMANOEUVRING
OUTRAGEOUSNESS
OVERCAPITALIZE
OVERCOMPENSATE
OVERDEVELOPING
OVERENTHUSIASM
OVERESTIMATING
OVERESTIMATION
OVERINDULGENCE
OVERPOPULATION
OVERPOWERINGLY
OVERPRODUCTION
OVERPROTECTION
OVERSIMPLIFIED
OVERSTATEMENTS
OVERSUBSCRIBED
OVER-THE-COUNTER
OVERWHELMINGLY
OWNER-OCCUPIERS
OXYHAEMOGLOBIN
OYSTERCATCHERS

P

PACHYDERMATOUS
PACKAGE HOLIDAY
PADDLE STEAMERS
PAEDIATRICIANS
PAEDOMORPHOSIS
PAGANISTICALLY
PALAEANTHROPIC
PALAEETHNOLOGY
PALAEOBOTANIST
PALATALIZATION
PALEONTOLOGIST
PAN-AMERICANISM
PANCAKE LANDING
PANGENETICALLY
PANHELLENISTIC
PAPILLOMATOSIS

PARABOLIZATION	PERSONAL COLUMN	PICTURE WINDOWS
PARALLELEPIPED	PERSONAL ESTATE	PIEZOCHEMISTRY
PARALLELOGRAMS	PERSONAL STEREO	PILGRIM FATHERS
PARAPHERNALIAS	PERSON-TO-PERSON	PINCER MOVEMENT
PARAPSYCHOLOGY	PERSUADABILITY	PINNATIPARTITE
PARASITOLOGIST	PERSUASIVENESS	PINS AND NEEDLES
PARATACTICALLY	PERTINACIOUSLY	PISCICULTURIST
PARENCHYMATOUS	PETIT BOURGEOIS	PITCH-BLACKNESS
PARSIMONIOUSLY	PETIT LARCENIST	PITCHED BATTLES
PARTHENOCARPIC	PETROCHEMICALS	PLAIN CHOCOLATE
PARTICULARIZED	PETROCHEMISTRY	PLANCK CONSTANT
PARTICULARIZER	PETROLEUM JELLY	PLASTER OF PARIS
PARTURIFACIENT	PETROL STATIONS	PLASTIC BULLETS
PASSENGER TRAIN	PETTY BOURGEOIS	PLASTICIZATION
PASSING THE BUCK	PETTY LARCENIES	PLASTIC SURGEON
PASSIONATENESS	PHANTASMAGORIA	PLASTIC SURGERY
PASSIONFLOWERS	PHANTASMAGORIC	PLATINOCYANIDE
PASSIVE SMOKING	PHARMACEUTICAL	PLATINUM BLONDE
PASTEURIZATION	PHARMACOLOGIST	PLATITUDINIZER
PAST PARTICIPLE	PHARMACOPOEIAL	PLEA BARGAINING
PATE DE FOIE GRAS	PHARMACOPOEIAS	PLEONASTICALLY
PATENT MEDICINE	PHARMACOPOEIST	PLETHYSMOGRAPH
PATHOLOGICALLY	PHARYNGOLOGIST	PLUMBER'S FRIEND
PAVEMENT ARTIST	PHARYNGOSCOPIC	PNEUMATIC DRILL
PEACE OFFERINGS	PHENOBARBITONE	PNEUMOBACILLUS
PENITENTIARIES	PHENOTYPICALLY	PNEUMOCONIOSIS
PENNY DREADFULS	PHILANTHROPIST	PNEUMODYNAMICS
PENNY-FARTHINGS	PHILATELICALLY	POIKILOTHERMAL
PENNY-HALFPENNY	PHILOLOGICALLY	POLEMONIACEOUS
PEPPERCORN RENT	PHILOSOPHIZING	POLICE OFFICERS
PERAMBULATIONS	PHLEGMATICALLY	POLICE STATIONS
PERCEIVABILITY	PHONOLOGICALLY	POLITICIZATION
PERCEPTIBILITY	PHOSPHOPROTEIN	POLLING STATION
PERCUSSION CAPS	PHOSPHORESCENT	POLYCARPELLARY
PERCUSSIONISTS	PHOSPHOROSCOPE	POLYCHROMATISM
PEREGRINATIONS	PHOTOCHEMISTRY	POLYMERIZATION
PEREMPTORINESS	PHOTOCONDUCTOR	POLYNUCLEOTIDE
PERFECT BINDING	PHOTOENGRAVING	POLYPHONICALLY
PERFECTIBILITY	PHOTOGENICALLY	POLYSACCHARIDE
PERFECTIONISTS	PHOTOGRAMMETRY	POLYSYNTHESISM
PERFIDIOUSNESS	PHOTOPERIODISM	PONTOON BRIDGES
PERIMETRICALLY	PHOTOSENSITIVE	POOR-SPIRITEDLY
PERISCOPICALLY	PHOTOSENSITIZE	POPULARIZATION
PERLOCUTIONARY	PHOTOSYNTHESIS	PORPHYROGENITE
PERMANENT WAVES	PHOTOSYNTHETIC	PORTENTOUSNESS
PERMISSIBILITY	PHOTOTYPICALLY	PORTULACACEOUS
PERMISSIVENESS	PHRASEOGRAPHIC	POSSESSIVENESS
PERNICIOUSNESS	PHRASEOLOGICAL	POSTMILLENNIAL
PERNICKETINESS	PHTHALOCYANINE	POSTPOSITIONAL
PEROXIDE BLONDE	PHYTOGEOGRAPHY	POTENTIALITIES
PERPENDICULARS	PHYTOPATHOLOGY	PRACTICABILITY
PERSONABLENESS	PHYTOSOCIOLOGY	PRACTICALITIES

PRACTICAL JOKER
PRACTICAL JOKES
PRAISEWORTHILY
PRAYER MEETINGS
PREADOLESCENCE
PREARRANGEMENT
PRECARIOUSNESS
PRECIOUS METALS
PRECIOUS STONES
PRECIPITATIONS
PRECOCIOUSNESS
PRECONCEPTIONS
PREDACIOUSNESS
PREDESTINARIAN
PREDESTINATION
PREDETERMINATE
PREDETERMINERS
PREDETERMINING
PREDICTABILITY
PREDISPOSITION
PREFABRICATING
PREFABRICATION
PREFERENTIALLY
PREFIGURATIONS
PREMEDITATEDLY
PREOCCUPATIONS
PREORDINATIONS
PREPONDERANTLY
PREPONDERATING
PREPONDERATION
PREPOSSESSIONS
PREPOSTEROUSLY
PRE-RAPHAELITES
PRESCRIPTIVELY
PRESCRIPTIVISM
PRESCRIPTIVIST
PRESENCE OF MIND
PRESENTATIONAL
PRESENT PERFECT
PRESERVABILITY
PRESIDENT-ELECT
PRESS GALLERIES
PRESSURE COOKER
PRESSURE GROUPS
PRESSURE POINTS
PRESSURIZATION
PRESUMPTUOUSLY
PRESUPPOSITION
PREVARICATIONS
PREVENTIVENESS
PRIMA BALLERINA
PRIMARY COLOURS

PRIMARY SCHOOLS
PRIME MINISTERS
PRINCE CHARMING
PRINCES CONSORT
PRINCIPALITIES
PRINCIPAL PARTS
PRINTED CIRCUIT
PRISONERS OF WAR
PRISON VISITORS
PRIVATE MEMBERS
PRIVATE SCHOOLS
PRIVATE SOLDIER
PRO BONO PUBLICO
PROCRASTINATED
PROCRASTINATOR
PROCRYPTICALLY
PRODIGIOUSNESS
PRODUCTION LINE
PRODUCTIVENESS
PROFESSIONALLY
PROFESSORIALLY
PROFESSORSHIPS
PROGESTATIONAL
PROGNOSTICATED
PROGNOSTICATOR
PROGRAMME MUSIC
PROHIBITIONARY
PROHIBITIONISM
PROHIBITIONIST
PROJECTIONISTS
PROLETARIANISM
PROLIFERATIONS
PROMENADE DECKS
PRONOUNCEMENTS
PRONUNCIATIONS
PROPAEDEUTICAL
PROPAGANDIZING
PROPER FRACTION
PROPITIOUSNESS
PROPORTIONALLY
PROPORTIONMENT
PROPOSITIONING
PROPRIETORALLY
PROPRIOCEPTIVE
PROSENCEPHALON
PROSPEROUSNESS
PROSTHETICALLY
PROSTHODONTICS
PROSTHODONTIST
PROTECTIONISTS
PROTECTIVENESS
PROTHONOTARIAL

PROTOZOOLOGIST
PROTRACTEDNESS
PROTRUSIVENESS
PROVENTRICULAR
PROVENTRICULUS
PROVIDENTIALLY
PROVINCIALISMS
PROVING GROUNDS
PSEUDOMORPHISM
PSYCHOANALYSED
PSYCHOANALYSIS
PSYCHOANALYSTS
PSYCHOANALYTIC
PSYCHOANALYZER
PSYCHOCHEMICAL
PSYCHODRAMATIC
PSYCHODYNAMICS
PSYCHOLINGUIST
PSYCHOLOGISTIC
PSYCHONEUROSIS
PSYCHONEUROTIC
PSYCHOPHYSICAL
PSYCHOSOMATICS
PSYCHOSURGICAL
PSYCHOTECHNICS
PTERIDOLOGICAL
PUBLIC NUISANCE
PUBLIC-SPIRITED
PUGILISTICALLY
PUGNACIOUSNESS
PURCHASABILITY
PURPLE PASSAGES
PURPOSEFULNESS
PURSE STRINGSES
PUT THE SCREWS ON
PYELONEPHRITIS
PYRAMID SELLING
PYRHELIOMETRIC
PYROMETALLURGY
PYROMETRICALLY
PYROPHOTOMETER
PYROPHOTOMETRY
PYROTECHNICSES
PYRRHIC VICTORY

Q
QUADRAGENARIAN
QUADRILATERALS
QUALIFICATIONS
QUANTIFICATION
QUANTITATIVELY
QUARTERMASTERS

QUEEN'S COUNSELS
QUEEN'S EVIDENCE
QUESTION MASTER
QUESTIONNAIRES
QUICK ON THE DRAW
QUINQUEFOLIATE
QUINQUEPARTITE
QUINQUEVALENCY
QUINTESSENTIAL
QUOTATION MARKS

R
RADIOBIOLOGIST
RADIOCHEMISTRY
RADIO FREQUENCY
RADIOSENSITIVE
RADIOTELEGRAPH
RADIOTELEMETRY
RADIOTELEPHONE
RADIOTELEPHONY
RADIO TELESCOPE
RADIOTHERAPIST
RAILWAY STATION
RAMBUNCTIOUSLY
RAMPAGEOUSNESS
RANUNCULACEOUS
RAPPROCHEMENTS
RASTAFARIANISM
RATEABLE VALUES
RATE OF EXCHANGE
READY FOR ACTION
REAFFIRMATIONS
REAL-TIME SYSTEM
REARRANGEMENTS
REAR VIEW MIRROR
REASONABLENESS
REBELLIOUSNESS
RECAPITULATING
RECAPITULATION
RECAPITULATIVE
RECEPTION ROOMS
RECKLINGHAUSEN
RECOMMENCEMENT
RECOMMENDATION
RECOMMENDATORY
RECONCILIATION
RECONCILIATORY
RECONDITIONING
RECONNAISSANCE
RECONSTITUTING
RECONSTITUTION
RECONSTRUCTING

RECONSTRUCTION
RECONSTRUCTIVE
RECORD-BREAKING
RECOVERABILITY
RECREATION ROOM
RECRIMINATIONS
RECRUDESCENCES
RECTANGULARITY
RECTIFICATIONS
REDEVELOPMENTS
REDINTEGRATION
REDINTEGRATIVE
REDISTRIBUTING
REDISTRIBUTION
REFERENCE BOOKS
REFLECTIVENESS
REFRACTIVENESS
REFRACTOMETRIC
REFRACTORINESS
REFRANGIBILITY
REGARDLESSNESS
REGISTERED POST
REGISTER OFFICE
REGISTRATIONAL
REGISTRY OFFICE
REGRESSIVENESS
REGULARIZATION
REHABILITATING
REHABILITATION
REHABILITATIVE
REIGNS OF TERROR
REIMBURSEMENTS
REINCARNATIONS
REINFORCEMENTS
REINSTALLATION
REINSTATEMENTS
REINTRODUCTION
REJUVENESCENCE
RELATIVE CLAUSE
RELENTLESSNESS
RELINQUISHMENT
REMARKABLENESS
REMEMBRANCE DAY
REMONETIZATION
REMORSEFULNESS
REMUNERABILITY
REMUNERATIVELY
REORGANIZATION
REPETITIVENESS
REPLACEABILITY
REPORTED SPEECH

REPRESENTATION
REPRESENTATIVE
REPRESSIVENESS
REPRIMANDINGLY
REQUISITIONARY
REQUISITIONING
RESPECTABILITY
RESPECTFULNESS
RESPONSIBILITY
RESPONSIVENESS
RESTAURANT CARS
RESTRICTEDNESS
RESTRICTIONIST
RESURRECTIONAL
RETRACTABILITY
RETRIEVABILITY
RETROGRADATION
RETROGRADATORY
RETRO-OPERATIVE
RETROSPECTIVES
REVERBERATIONS
REVEREND MOTHER
REVISED VERSION
REVITALIZATION
REVIVIFICATION
REVOLUTIONIZED
REVOLUTIONIZER
RHEUMATIC FEVER
RHINENCEPHALIC
RHINENCEPHALON
RHIZOCEPHALOUS
RHYTHM AND BLUES
RICINOLEIC ACID
RIDICULOUSNESS
RIGHT TRIANGLES
RIO GRANDE DO SUL
ROADWORTHINESS
ROARING FORTIES
ROCKET-LAUNCHER
ROCKY MOUNTAINS
ROENTGENOPAQUE
ROLLER COASTERS
ROMAINE LETTUCE
ROMAN CATHOLICS
RORSCHACH TESTS
ROTTEN BOROUGHS
ROUGH-AND-TUMBLE
RUBBER DINGHIES
RUBBER-STAMPING
RUBBING ALCOHOL
RUDIMENTARILLY
RUNNING REPAIRS

RUN THE GAUNTLET
RUSH ONE'S FENCES

S
SACRAMENTALISM
SACRAMENTALIST
SACRAMENTALITY
SACRAMENTARIAN
SACRILEGIOUSLY
SADOMASOCHISTS
SAFE-DEPOSIT BOX
SAFETY CURTAINS
SALAD DRESSINGS
SALUBRIOUSNESS
SANCTIFICATION
SANDWICH BOARDS
SANDWICH COURSE
SANGUINARINESS
SANITARY TOWELS
SANTIAGO DE CUBA
SAPONIFICATION
SATELLITE STATE
SATISFACTIONAL
SATISFACTORILY
SAVE ONE'S BREATH
SAVINGS ACCOUNT
SAWN-OFF SHOTGUN
SAXIFRAGACEOUS
SCANDALIZATION
SCANDALMONGERS
SCANDALOUSNESS
SCATTERBRAINED
SCHEMATIZATION
SCHISMATICALLY
SCHIZOMYCETOUS
SCHIZOPHRENICS
SCHIZOPHYCEOUS
SCHOOLCHILDREN
SCHOOLMISTRESS
SCHOOLTEACHERS
SCIENCE FICTION
SCIENTIFICALLY
SCINTILLOMETER
SCOTCH WHISKIES
SCREEN PRINTING
SCRUBBING BRUSH
SCRUPULOUSNESS
SCRUTINIZINGLY
SCURRILOUSNESS
SEARCH WARRANTS
SEASONABLENESS
SECOND-GUESSING

SECOND THOUGHTS
SECULARIZATION
SEGREGATIONIST
SELF-ABNEGATION
SELF-ABSORPTION
SELF-ANALYTICAL
SELF-CONFIDENCE
SELF-CONTROLLED
SELF-DESTRUCTED
SELF-DISCIPLINE
SELF-EFFACEMENT
SELF-EMPLOYMENT
SELF-GOVERNMENT
SELF-IMPORTANCE
SELF-INDUCTANCE
SELF-INDULGENCE
SELF-INFLICTION
SELF-INTERESTED
SELF-JUSTIFYING
SELF-POSSESSION
SELF-PROTECTION
SELF-RESPECTFUL
SELF-RESPECTING
SELF-SUFFICIENT
SELF-SUPPORTING
SEMAPHORICALLY
SEMASIOLOGICAL
SEMICENTENNIAL
SEMICONDUCTION
SEMICONDUCTORS
SEMIELLIPTICAL
SEMIPARASITISM
SENIOR CITIZENS
SENSATIONALISM
SENSATIONALIST
SENTIMENTALISM
SENTIMENTALIST
SENTIMENTALITY
SENTIMENTALIZE
SEPARATE TABLES
SEPARATIVENESS
SEPTUAGENARIAN
SEQUESTRATIONS
SERGEANT-AT-ARMS
SERGEANT MAJORS
SERIALIZATIONS
SERIOCOMICALLY
SERJEANT-AT-ARMS
SERVICEABILITY
SERVICE CHARGES
SERVICE STATION
SERVOMECHANISM

SESQUIPEDALIAN
SEWING MACHINES
SHAGGY-DOG STORY
SHAMEFACEDNESS
SHEET LIGHTNING
SHEPHERD'S-PURSE
SHERARDIZATION
SHETLAND PONIES
SHIHCHIACHUANG
SHILLY-SHALLIED
SHILLYSHALLIER
SHIP'S CHANDLERS
SHOCK ABSORBERS
SHOCK TREATMENT
SHOOTING STICKS
SHOP ASSISTANTS
SHOPPING CENTRE
SHORT-CIRCUITED
SHORTSIGHTEDLY
SHOTGUN WEDDING
SHOULDER BLADES
SHOULDER STRAPS
SIDEWALK ARTIST
SIGMOIDOSCOPIC
SIGNATURE TUNES
SIGNIFICATIONS
SILENT PARTNERS
SILICIFICATION
SILVER JUBILEES
SILVER WEDDINGS
SILVICULTURIST
SIMAROUBACEOUS
SIMPLE FRACTURE
SIMPLE INTEREST
SIMPLE MACHINES
SIMPLIFICATION
SIMPLIFICATIVE
SIMPLISTICALLY
SIMULTANEOUSLY
SINGLE-BREASTED
SINGLE-MINDEDLY
SINKIANG-UIGHUR
SINKING FEELING
SIPHONOPHOROUS
SITTING TARGETS
SIXTEENTH NOTES
SKATE ON THIN ICE
SKIRTING BOARDS
SLANDEROUSNESS
SLAP ON THE WRIST
SLATTERNLINESS
SLAUGHTERHOUSE

SLIPSHODDINESS
SLOTTED SPATULA
SLUGGARDLINESS
SLUMBEROUSNESS
SMALL INTESTINE
SOCIAL CLIMBERS
SOCIAL SCIENCES
SOCIAL SECURITY
SOCIAL SERVICES
SOCIOLOGICALLY
SOCIOPOLITICAL
SODIUM CHLORIDE
SOLDERING IRONS
SOLICITOUSNESS
SOLIDIFICATION
SOMNAMBULATION
SOMNAMBULISTIC
SOPHISTICATION
SOUL-DESTROYING
SOUNDING BOARDS
SOUTHEASTWARDS
SOUTHERN LIGHTS
SOUTH-SOUTHEAST
SOUTH-SOUTHWEST
SOUTHWESTWARDS
SPATIOTEMPORAL
SPEAKERS' CORNER
SPECIALIZATION
SPECIAL LICENCE
SPECIAL SCHOOLS
SPECIFICATIONS
SPECTROGRAPHIC
SPECTROSCOPIST
SPEECHLESSNESS
SPERMATOGONIAL
SPERMATOGONIUM
SPERMATOPHORAL
SPERMATOPHYTIC
SPERMATORRHOEA
SPERMIOGENESIS
SPERMIOGENETIC
SPHEROIDICALLY
SPHYGMOGRAPHIC
SPINNING WHEELS
SPINTHARISCOPE
SPIRITLESSNESS
SPIRITUALISTIC
SPIROCHAETOSIS
SPIRONOLACTONE
SPITTING IMAGES
SPLINTER GROUPS
SPONGIOBLASTIC

SPORADICALNESS
SPRECHSTIMMUNG
SPRING CHICKENS
SPRING-CLEANING
SQUADRON LEADER
SQUARE BRACKETS
STAFF SERGEANTS
STAGE DIRECTION
STAMPING GROUND
STANDARD-BEARER
STANDING ORDERS
STANDOFF HALVES
ST ANDREW'S CROSS
STAPHYLOCOCCAL
STAPHYLOCOCCUS
STAPHYLOPLASTY
STARTING BLOCKS
STARTING PISTOL
STARTING PRICES
START SOMETHING
STATE'S EVIDENCE
STATIONARINESS
STATIONMASTERS
STATUESQUENESS
STEAMROLLERING
STEAMTIGHTNESS
STEERING WHEELS
STEPPING-STONES
STERCORICOLOUS
STERCULIACEOUS
STEREOMETRICAL
STEREOSPECIFIC
STERTOROUSNESS
STICKING POINTS
STIGMATIZATION
STINGING NETTLE
STIPPLING BRUSH
STIR ONE'S STUMPS
STOCHASTICALLY
STOCKBROKERAGE
STOCK EXCHANGES
STOCKING-FILLER
STOICHIOMETRIC
STOLEN PROPERTY
STOPS AT NOTHING
STORE DETECTIVE
STORM IN A TEACUP
STRAIGHT FIGHTS
STRAIGHT JACKET
STRATICULATION
STRATIFICATION
STRAWBERRY MARK

STREET-CREDIBLE
STREPTOTHRICIN
STRETCHABILITY
STRETCHER PARTY
STRIDULOUSNESS
STRIKEBREAKERS
STRIKEBREAKING
STRONG LANGUAGE
STRONG-MINDEDLY
STUDENTS' UNIONS
STULTIFICATION
STUMBLING BLOCK
STUPENDOUSNESS
SUBALTERNATION
SUBCONSCIOUSLY
SUBCONTINENTAL
SUBCONTRACTING
SUBCONTRACTORS
SUBCUTANEOUSLY
SUBINFEUDATION
SUBINFEUDATORY
SUBJECTABILITY
SUBJECTIVISTIC
SUBJECT-RAISING
SUBLIEUTENANCY
SUBLIEUTENANTS
SUBMACHINE GUNS
SUBMERSIBILITY
SUBMICROSCOPIC
SUBMISSIVENESS
SUBSIDIARINESS
SUBSTANTIALISM
SUBSTANTIALIST
SUBSTANTIALITY
SUBSTANTIATING
SUBSTANTIATION
SUBSTANTIATIVE
SUBTERRESTRIAL
SUBVERSIVENESS
SUCCESSFULNESS
SUCCESSIVENESS
SUGGESTIBILITY
SUGGESTIVENESS
SULPHANILAMIDE
SULPHATHIAZOLE
SULPHISOXAZOLE
SULPHONMETHANE
SULPHURIZATION
SULPHUROUSNESS
SUPERABUNDANCE

SUPERANNUATION
SUPERCILIOUSLY
SUPERCONDUCTOR
SUPERELEVATION
SUPERFICIALITY
SUPERINCUMBENT
SUPERINDUCTION
SUPERINTENDENT
SUPERINTENDING
SUPERNATURALLY
SUPERNORMALITY
SUPERPHOSPHATE
SUPERSATURATED
SUPERSCRIPTION
SUPERSONICALLY
SUPERSTRUCTURE
SUPPLY TEACHERS
SUPPORTABILITY
SUPPORTING PART
SUPRAMOLECULAR
SUPRASEGMENTAL
SUREFOOTEDNESS
SURGICAL SPIRIT
SURPASSINGNESS
SURPRISINGNESS
SUSCEPTIBILITY
SUSPENDIBILITY
SUSPENSIVENESS
SUSPICIOUSNESS
SWIMMING TRUNKS
SWORD-SWALLOWER
SYMBIONTICALLY
SYMBOLICALNESS
SYMMETRIZATION
SYMPATHIZINGLY
SYMPTOMATOLOGY
SYNCHRONICALLY
SYNCRETIZATION
SYNERGETICALLY
SYNONYMOUSNESS
SYNTHESIZATION
SYNTHETIZATION
SYPHILITICALLY
SYSTEMATICALLY
SYSTEMS ANALYST

T

TACHISTOSCOPIC
TAKE IN GOOD PART
TALK OF THE DEVIL
TARTAN TROUSERS
TAUTOLOGICALLY

TECHNICALITIES
TELANGIECTASIS
TELANGIECTATIC
TELAUTOGRAPHIC
TELEGRAPH POLES
TELEMETRICALLY
TELEOLOGICALLY
TELEPATHICALLY
TELEPHONE BOXES
TELESCOPICALLY
TELETYPESETTER
TERCENTENARIES
TERGIVERSATION
TERGIVERSATORY
TERMINOLOGICAL
TERRACED HOUSES
TERRITORIALISM
TERRITORIALIST
TERRITORIALITY
TERRITORIALIZE
TERROR-STRICKEN
TEST-TUBE BABIES
TETRAETHYL LEAD
THAUMATROPICAL
THE AMBASSADORS
THE FOUR SEASONS
THE LIFE OF RILEY
THEOCENTRICITY
THEOCRATICALLY
THEOLOGIZATION
THEOSOPHICALLY
THERIANTHROPIC
THERMAESTHESIA
THERMOCHEMICAL
THERMODYNAMICS
THERMOELECTRIC
THERMOELECTRON
THERMOJUNCTION
THERMOMAGNETIC
THERMOPLASTICS
THIOCYANIC ACID
THOUGHTFULNESS
THREE-DAY EVENTS
THREE-HALFPENCE
THREE-LINE WHIPS
THREE-POINT TURN
THRIFTLESSNESS
THROMBOPLASTIC
THROMBOPLASTIN
THYMELAEACEOUS
THYROTOXICOSIS
TICKLED TO DEATH

TIERRA DEL FUEGO
TIME IMMEMORIAL
TIME SIGNATURES
TITTLE-TATTLING
TOAD OF TOAD HALL
TOILET TRAINING
TO-ING AND FRO-ING
TONGUE TWISTERS
TORTOISESHELLS
TRACTION ENGINE
TRADE UNIONISTS
TRADING ESTATES
TRADITIONALISM
TRADITIONALIST
TRADUCIANISTIC
TRAFFIC CALMING
TRAFFIC CIRCLES
TRAFFIC ISLANDS
TRAFFIC WARDENS
TRAGICOMICALLY
TRAITOROUSNESS
TRANQUILLIZERS
TRANQUILLIZING
TRANSCAUCASIAN
TRANSCENDENTAL
TRANSCENDENTLY
TRANSCENDINGLY
TRANSCRIPTIONS
TRANSFERENTIAL
TRANSFORMATION
TRANSFORMATIVE
TRANSGRESSIBLE
TRANSGRESSIONS
TRANSISTORIZED
TRANSITIONALLY
TRANSITIVENESS
TRANSITORINESS
TRANS-JORDANIAN
TRANSLITERATED
TRANSLITERATOR
TRANSMIGRATION
TRANSMIGRATIVE
TRANSMIGRATORY
TRANSMISSIVITY
TRANSMOGRIFIED
TRANSMUTATIONS
TRANSPARENCIES
TRANSPLANTABLE
TRANSPORTATION
TRANSPORT CAFES
TRANSPOSITIONS
TRANSVALUATION

TRANSVERSENESS
TRAUMATIZATION
TRAVEL AGENCIES
TRAVELLER'S TALE
TRAVELSICKNESS
TREAD THE BOARDS
TREASURE ISLAND
TREASURE TROVES
TREMENDOUSNESS
TRICHINIZATION
TRICHOMONIASIS
TRICHOTOMOUSLY
TRICK OR TREATED
TRIDIMENSIONAL
TRINITROCRESOL
TRINITROPHENOL
TRISOCTAHEDRAL
TRISOCTAHEDRON
TRISTAN DA CUNHA
TRIVIALIZATION
TROPIC OF CANCER
TROUBLESHOOTER
TROUSER PRESSES
TUMULTUOUSNESS
TUNBRIDGE WELLS
TURBOGENERATOR
TURF ACCOUNTANT
TURKISH DELIGHT
TURN A DEAF EAR TO
TURNING CIRCLES
TWO-DIMENSIONAL
TYRANNICALNESS

U
UBIQUITOUSNESS
ULTIMOGENITURE
ULTRAMODERNISM
ULTRAMODERNIST
ULTRAMONTANISM
ULTRAMONTANIST
ULTRASONICALLY
ULTRASTRUCTURE
UMBILICAL CORDS
UNACCOMMODATED
UNACCOMPLISHED
UNACCOUNTED-FOR
UNAPPRECIATIVE
UNAPPROACHABLE
UNAPPROPRIATED
UNAVOIDABILITY
UNBEARABLENESS
UNBECOMINGNESS

UNCOMPROMISING
UNCONSCIONABLE
UNCONSCIONABLY
UNCONTAMINATED
UNCONTROLLABLE
UNCONVENTIONAL
UNCONVINCINGLY
UNCORROBORATED
UNDERACHIEVERS
UNDERACHIEVING
UNDERCARRIAGES
UNDERESTIMATED
UNDERESTIMATES
UNDERGRADUATES
UNDERMENTIONED
UNDERNOURISHED
UNDERSECRETARY
UNDERSTANDABLE
UNDERSTANDABLY
UNDERSTANDINGS
UNDERSTATEMENT
UNDERVALUATION
UNDESIRABILITY
UNECONOMICALLY
UNENTHUSIASTIC
UNEVENTFULNESS
UNEXPECTEDNESS
UNFAITHFULNESS
UNFLAPPABILITY
UNFRIENDLINESS
UNFRUITFULNESS
UNGRATEFULNESS
UNHANDSOMENESS
UNHOLY ALLIANCE
UNICELLULARITY
UNIDENTIFIABLE
UNIDIRECTIONAL
UNIFORMITARIAN
UNINCORPORATED
UNINTELLIGENCE
UNINTELLIGIBLE
UNIPERSONALITY
UNIVERSALISTIC
UNIVERSAL JOINT
UNKNOWABLENESS
UNMENTIONABLES
UNPLEASANTNESS
UNPRACTICALITY
UNPREMEDITATED

UNPREPAREDNESS
UNPROFESSIONAL
UNQUESTIONABLE
UNQUESTIONABLY
UNRECOGNIZABLE
UNRESERVEDNESS
UNRESTRAINEDLY
UNSATISFACTORY
UNSCRUPULOUSLY
UNTHANKFULNESS
UNTHINKABILITY
UNTOUCHABILITY
UPSIDE-DOWNNESS
UPSTANDINGNESS
UPWARDLY-MOBILE
UST-KAMENOGORSK
UTILITARIANISM

V
VACUUM CLEANERS
VALERIANACEOUS
VALETUDINARIAN
VALUE JUDGMENTS
VASOINHIBITORY
VAULTING HORSES
VEGETABLE KNIFE
VEGETATIVENESS
VENDING MACHINE
VENETIAN BLINDS
VENTRILOQUISTS
VENTURE CAPITAL
VERISIMILITUDE
VERTICILLASTER
VERTICILLATION
VESPERTILIONID
VESTED INTEREST
VEXED QUESTIONS
VICE-CHANCELLOR
VICE-PRESIDENCY
VICIOUS CIRCLES
VICTORIOUSNESS
VIEW ON THE STOUR
VILLAINOUSNESS
VINDICTIVENESS
VISHAKHAPATNAM
VITRIFIABILITY
VITRIOLIZATION
VITUPERATIVELY
VIVISECTIONIST
VOCIFEROUSNESS
VOLATILIZATION
VOLCANOLOGICAL

VOLUMETRICALLY
VOLUMINOUSNESS
VOLUPTUOUSNESS
VOROSHILOVGRAD
VOTES OF CENSURE
VULGAR FRACTION
VULGARIZATIONS
VULVOVAGINITIS

W
WARRANTABILITY
WARRANT OFFICER
WASHING MACHINE
WATERCOLOURIST
WATERING PLACES
WATERPROOFNESS
WATER-REPELLENT
WATER-RESISTANT
WATER SOFTENERS
WATERTIGHTNESS
WEAK-MINDEDNESS
WEATHERABILITY
WEATHERPROOFED

WEATHER STATION
WEIGHTLESSNESS
WE LIVE AND LEARN
WELL-ACCUSTOMED
WELL-ACQUAINTED
WELL-DOCUMENTED
WESTERNIZATION
WET ONE'S WHISTLE
WHEELER-DEALERS
WHEELER-DEALING
WHIMSICALITIES
WHIPPERSNAPPER
WHITE BLOOD CELL
WHITE ELEPHANTS
WHOLE-HEARTEDLY
WHORTLEBERRIES
WILDCAT STRIKES
WILD GOOSE CHASE
WILD-GOOSE CHASE
WILLIAM AND MARY
WIND INSTRUMENT
WINDOW DRESSING
WINDOW-SHOPPERS

WINDOW-SHOPPING
WIND-POLLINATED
WING COMMANDERS
WOMEN'S MOVEMENT
WORCESTER SAUCE
WORD PROCESSING
WORD PROCESSORS
WORKING PARTIES
WORLD-WEARINESS
WORMWOOD SCRUBS
WORSHIPFULNESS
WORTHWHILENESS

X
XANTHOPHYLLOUS
XEROPHYTICALLY

Y
YOUTH HOSTELLER

Z
ZEBRA CROSSINGS
ZINGIBERACEOUS

15

A
A BUNDLE OF NERVES
ACANTHOCEPHALAN
ACCLIMATIZATION
ACCOMMODATINGLY
ACCOMPLISHMENTS
ACHONDROPLASTIC
ACHROMATIZATION
ACIDIMETRICALLY
ACKNOWLEDGEABLE
ACKNOWLEDGMENTS
ACOUSTIC COUPLER
ACQUISITIVENESS
ADMINISTRATIONS
A DROP IN THE OCEAN
AERODYNAMICALLY
AFFRANCHISEMENT
AGAINST THE GRAIN
AGGLUTINABILITY
AGRANULOCYTOSIS
AIR CHIEF MARSHAL
AIR-CONDITIONING
AIRCRAFT CARRIER
AIR VICE-MARSHALS
ALGORITHMICALLY
ALIMENTARY CANAL
ALIVE AND KICKING
ALPHABETIZATION
ALUMINOSILICATE
AMARYLLIDACEOUS
AMBASSADORSHIPS
AMERICAN INDIANS
AMERICANIZATION
A MONTH OF SUNDAYS
AMUSEMENT ARCADE
ANABOLIC STEROID
ANARCHISTICALLY
ANCYLOSTOMIASIS
ANIMAL HUSBANDRY
ANIMATED CARTOON
ANOMALISTICALLY
ANTARCTIC CIRCLE
ANTEPENULTIMATE
ANTHROPOCENTRIC
ANTHROPOGENESIS
ANTHROPOGENETIC
ANTHROPOLOGICAL
ANTHROPOLOGISTS

ANTHROPOMETRIST
ANTHROPOMORPHIC
ANTICHOLINERGIC
ANTICLERICALISM
ANTI-IMPERIALISM
ANTI-IMPERIALIST
ANTILOGARITHMIC
ANTINATIONALIST
ANTIPERISTALSIS
ANTIPERSPIRANTS
APARTMENT HOUSES
APOCALYPTICALLY
APPRENTICESHIPS
APPROACHABILITY
APPROPRIATENESS
APPROVED SCHOOLS
ARCHIEPISCOPATE
ARCHITECTURALLY
ARGUMENTATIVELY
ARTERIALIZATION
ASCLEPIADACEOUS
ASSIMILATIONIST
ASSOCIATE DEGREE
ASTRONAUTICALLY
ASTRONAVIGATION
ASTROPHYSICISTS
ATHEROSCLEROSIS
ATHEROSCLEROTIC
ATMOSPHERICALLY
AT THE DROP OF A HAT
ATTORNEY GENERAL
AUDIOMETRICALLY
AUTHORITATIVELY
AUTOBIOGRAPHIES
AUTOCORRELATION
AUTOGRAPHICALLY
AUTOMATIC PILOTS
AUTORADIOGRAPHY
AUTOTRANSFORMER
AVERSION THERAPY

B
BACHELOR'S DEGREE
BACK-SEAT DRIVERS
BACTERIOLOGICAL
BACTERIOLOGISTS
BACTERIOPHAGOUS
BALLROOM DANCING

BANANA REPUBLICS
BANNER HEADLINES
BANQUETING HOUSE
BASIDIOMYCETOUS
BATCH PROCESSING
BATHING MACHINES
BATHOMETRICALLY
BATHYMETRICALLY
BEATEN AT THE POST
BED AND BREAKFAST
BENEFIT OF CLERGY
BIBLIOGRAPHICAL
BIBLIOPHILISTIC
BINOCULAR VISION
BIOASTRONAUTICS
BIOGEOGRAPHICAL
BIOLUMINESCENCE
BIOTECHNOLOGIST
BIRDS OF A FEATHER
BIRDS OF PARADISE
BISYMMETRICALLY
BLACK MARKETEERS
BLACKWATER FEVER
BLAMEWORTHINESS
BLANK CARTRIDGES
BLOCK AND TACKLES
BLOOD-AND-THUNDER
BOARDING SCHOOLS
BONDED WAREHOUSE
BOW STREET RUNNER
BRAKE HORSE POWER
BREAKING THE NEWS
BRING AND BUY SALE
BROADMINDEDNESS
BROKEN-HEARTEDLY
BRUSSELS SPROUTS
BUBBLE AND SQUEAK
BUILDING SOCIETY
BUREAU DE CHANGES
BUSMAN'S HOLIDAYS
BUTTERFLY STROKE

C
CABLE TELEVISION
CANNIBALIZATION
CAPRIFOLIACEOUS
CARDIOPULMONARY
CARPOMETACARPUS

CARRYING CHARGES
CASEMENT WINDOWS
CATEGORIZATIONS
CATHERINE WHEELS
CATHETERIZATION
CATHODE RAY TUBES
CATHOLICIZATION
CENTRE OF GRAVITY
CEPHALOCHORDATE
CEPHALOTHORACIC
CEREBROVASCULAR
CEREMONIOUSNESS
CHAPTER AND VERSE
CHARACTERISTICS
CHARENT-MARITIME
CHARGE D'AFFAIRES
CHECKING ACCOUNT
CHEMICAL WARFARE
CHEMOTACTICALLY
CHEMOTROPICALLY
CHENOPODIACEOUS
CHESTS OF DRAWERS
CHIEF CONSTABLES
CHIEF INSPECTORS
CHINESE CHEQUERS
CHINESE LANTERNS
CHINLESS WONDERS
CHLORAMPHENICOL
CHOLECALCIFEROL
CHOLECYSTECTOMY
CHONDRIFICATION
CHROMATOGRAPHER
CHROMATOGRAPHIC
CHROMATOPHOROUS
CHRONOGRAMMATIC
CHRONOLOGICALLY
CHUCK-WILL'S-WIDOW
CHURCH OF ENGLAND
CIGARETTE HOLDER
CIGARETTE PAPERS
CINEMATOGRAPHER
CINEMATOGRAPHIC
CIRCUIT BREAKERS
CIRCULARIZATION
CIRCUMAMBULATOR
CIRCUMFERENTIAL
CIRCUMLOCUTIONS
CIRCUMNAVIGABLE
CIRCUMNAVIGATED
CIRCUMNAVIGATOR
CIRCUMSCRIPTION
CIRCUMSTANTIATE

CIRCUMVALLATION
CLANDESTINENESS
CLASSIFICATIONS
CLAUSTROPHOBICS
CLEAR-HEADEDNESS
CLERMONT-FERRAND
CLOUD-CUCKOO-LAND
COCK-A-DOODLE-DOOS
COCKNEYFICATION
COCKTAIL LOUNGES
COCKTAIL SAUSAGE
COFFEE-TABLE BOOK
COLD-BLOODEDNESS
COLD-HEARTEDNESS
COLD-SHOULDERING
COLLECTIVE FARMS
COLLECTIVE NOUNS
COLLECTOR'S ITEMS
COLLISION COURSE
COLORADO BEETLES
COLOUR BLINDNESS
COMBINATION LOCK
COMEDY OF MANNERS
COME INTO ONE'S OWN
COMFORT STATIONS
COMITY OF NATIONS
COMMERCIALISTIC
COMMERCIALIZING
COMMISSIONAIRES
COMMITTEE STAGES
COMMODIFICATION
COMMON FRACTIONS
COMMUNALIZATION
COMMUNICABILITY
COMMUNITY CENTRE
COMMUNITY CHESTS
COMPASSIONATELY
COMPETITIVENESS
COMPLICATEDNESS
COMPREHENSIVELY
COMPRESSIBILITY
COMPUTERIZATION
CONCEPTUALISTIC
CONCEPTUALIZING
CONCESSIONAIRES
CONCRETE JUNGLES
CONFECTIONERIES
CONFIDENCE TRICK
CONFIDENTIALITY
CONFIGURATIONAL
CONFRATERNITIES
CONGLOMERATIONS

CONGRATULATIONS
CONSCIENCE MONEY
CONSCIENTIOUSLY
CONSCRIPTIONIST
CONSENTING ADULT
CONSERVATIONISM
CONSERVATIONIST
CONSIDERATENESS
CONSPICUOUSNESS
CONSTITUTIONALS
CONSUMER DURABLE
CONTEMPORANEITY
CONTEMPORANEOUS
CONTEMPTIBILITY
CONTENTIOUSNESS
CONTORTIONISTIC
CONTRACTIBILITY
CONTRAINDICATED
CONTROVERSIALLY
CONVENIENCE FOOD
CONVENTIONALISM
CONVENTIONALIST
CONVENTIONALITY
CONVENTIONALIZE
CONVOLVULACEOUS
CORRELATIVENESS
CORRESPONDINGLY
COSMOPOLITANISM
COST-EFFECTIVELY
COTTAGE HOSPITAL
COTTAGE INDUSTRY
COUNTERATTACKED
COUNTERATTACKER
COUNTERBALANCED
COUNTERBALANCES
COUNTERCLAIMANT
COUNTERIRRITANT
COUNTER IRRITANT
COUNTERMEASURES
COUNTERPROPOSAL
COURT-MARTIALING
COURT-MARTIALLED
COURTS OF INQUIRY
COVERING LETTERS
CREASE RESISTANT
CREATIVE WRITING
CREDIBILITY GAPS
CRICKET PAVILION
CRIMINAL CLASSES
CROSS-FERTILIZED
CROSSOPTERYGION
CROSS-QUESTIONED

CROSS-QUESTIONER
CROSS-REFERENCES
CROSSWORD EDITORS
CROWN PRINCESSES
CRYSTALLIZATION
CRYSTALLOGRAPHY
CUCKOO IN THE NEST
CURRENT ACCOUNTS
CURRICULUM VITAE
CUT AND COME AGAIN
CYTOMEGALOVIRUS

D
DAYLIGHT ROBBERY
DAYS OF RECKONING
DECALCIFICATION
DECARBONIZATION
DECARBOXYLATION
DECIPHERABILITY
DECOMPOSABILITY
DECONTAMINATING
DECONTAMINATION
DECONTAMINATIVE
DECONTEXTUALIZE
DEFINITE ARTICLE
DEHYDROGENATION
DELIRIUM TREMENS
DELIVER THE GOODS
DEMAGNETIZATION
DEMOCRATIZATION
DEMONSTRABILITY
DEMONSTRATIONAL
DEMONSTRATIVELY
DEMULSIFICATION
DEMYSTIFICATION
DENATIONALIZING
DENITRIFICATION
DEPARTMENTALISM
DEPARTMENTALIZE
DEPARTMENT STORE
DEPARTURE LOUNGE
DEPENDENT CLAUSE
DEPOSIT ACCOUNTS
DERMATOGLYPHICS
DERMATOPHYTOSIS
DESCRIPTIVENESS
DESENSITIZATION
DESEXUALIZATION
DESTABILIZATION
DESTRUCTIBILITY
DESTRUCTIVENESS
DETRIBALIZATION

DEVELOPMENT AREA
DEVIL'S ADVOCATES
DEVITRIFICATION
DIALECTOLOGICAL
DIAMAGNETICALLY
DIAMOND JUBILEES
DIAMOND WEDDINGS
DIAPHOTOTROPISM
DICHOTOMIZATION
DIESEL-HYDRAULIC
DIFFERENTIATING
DIFFERENTIATION
DIGITAL COMPUTER
DIRECTION FINDER
DISADVANTAGEOUS
DISAPPOINTINGLY
DISAPPOINTMENTS
DISARTICULATION
DISCIPLINARIANS
DISCONCERTINGLY
DISCONTINUATION
DISCONTINUITIES
DISCONTINUOUSLY
DISCOUNTENANCED
DISCOURAGEMENTS
DISCRETIONARILY
DISENCUMBERMENT
DISENTANGLEMENT
DISESTABLISHING
DISHEARTENINGLY
DISHEARTENMENTS
DISILLUSIONMENT
DISINCLINATIONS
DISINFLATIONARY
DISINTERESTEDLY
DISORDERLY HOUSE
DISORGANIZATION
DISPASSIONATELY
DISREPUTABILITY
DISRESPECTFULLY
DISSATISFACTION
DISSATISFACTORY
DISSERTATIONIST
DISSIMILARITIES
DISTASTEFULNESS
DISTINCTIVENESS
DISTINGUISHABLE
DISTRACTIBILITY
DISTRUSTFULNESS
DITHYRAMBICALLY
DIVERSIFICATION
DIVISION LOBBIES

DO-IT-YOURSELFERS
DOLICHOCEPHALIC
DOMESTIC ANIMALS
DOMESTIC SCIENCE
DOMESTIC SERVANT
DOMESTIC SERVICE
DORSIVENTRALITY
DOUBLE-BARRELLED
DOUBLE ENTENDRES
DOUBLE STANDARDS
DOUBLE WHITE LINE
DRAUGHTSMANSHIP
DRESSING STATION
DRESS REHEARSALS
DRIVE-BY SHOOTING
DRIVING LICENCES
DRUIDICAL CIRCLE
DUAL CARRIAGEWAY
DUAL CITIZENSHIP
DUTCH ELM DISEASE

E
EARTHSHATTERING
EAT ONE'S HEART OUT
ECCLESIASTICISM
ECCLESIOLOGICAL
EDUCATED GUESSES
EDUCATIONALISTS
ELECTRIC BLANKET
ELECTRIFICATION
ELECTROACOUSTIC
ELECTROANALYSIS
ELECTROANALYTIC
ELECTROCHEMICAL
ELECTRODIALYSIS
ELECTRODYNAMICS
ELECTROKINETICS
ELECTROLYSATION
ELECTROMAGNETIC
ELECTRONEGATIVE
ELECTROPHORESIS
ELECTROPHORETIC
ELECTROPOSITIVE
ELECTROSURGICAL
ELEVATED RAILWAY
EMANCIPATIONIST
EMINENCES GRISES
ENANTIOMORPHISM
ENCEPHALOGRAPHY
ENCHONDROMATOUS
ENCOMIASTICALLY
ENDOCRINE GLANDS

ENDOCRINOLOGIST
ENDOTHERMICALLY
ENDOWMENT POLICY
ENFRANCHISEMENT
ENGAGEMENT RINGS
ENTENTE CORDIALE
ENTREPRENEURIAL
ENVIRONMENTALLY
EPIDEMIOLOGICAL
EPISCOPALIANISM
EPISTEMOLOGICAL
EPITHELIOMATOUS
EQUALITARIANISM
ETERNAL TRIANGLE
ETHEREALIZATION
ETHNIC CLEANSING
ETHNOCENTRICITY
EUCHARISTICALLY
EUDIOMETRICALLY
EUPHEMISTICALLY
EUROPEANIZATION
EUSTACHIAN TUBES
EVERLASTINGNESS
EXCEPTIONALNESS
EXCHANGEABILITY
EXCLAMATION MARK
EXCOMMUNICATING
EXCOMMUNICATION
EXCOMMUNICATIVE
EXEMPLIFICATION
EXEMPLIFICATIVE
EXHIBITIONISTIC
EXPEDITIOUSNESS
EXPENSE ACCOUNTS
EXPERIMENTALISM
EXPERIMENTALIST
EXPERIMENTATION
EXPOSTULATINGLY
EXPRESSIONISTIC
EXTEMPORARINESS
EXTEMPORIZATION
EXTERIORIZATION
EXTERNALIZATION
EXTRACURRICULAR
EXTRALINGUISTIC
EXTRAORDINARILY

F

FAIRY GODMOTHERS
FAMILIARIZATION
FAMILY ALLOWANCE
FASHIONABLENESS

FATHER CHRISTMAS
FEATURELESSNESS
FELLOW TRAVELLER
FEUILLETONISTIC
FIDEICOMMISSARY
FIFTH COLUMNISTS
FIGURES OF SPEECH
FILLING STATIONS
FINISHING SCHOOL
FIRST LIEUTENANT
FLIBBERTIGIBBET
FLIGHT SERGEANTS
FLIRTATIOUSNESS
FOLDING ONE'S ARMS
FOOT-POUND-SECOND
FOREIGN EXCHANGE
FORESIGHTEDNESS
FORKED LIGHTNING
FORMULARIZATION
FOUNDATION STONE
FOUNDING FATHERS
FOUR-DIMENSIONAL
FOUR-LETTER WORDS
FOURTH DIMENSION
FRACTIONIZATION
FRAGMENTARINESS
FRANKFURT AM MAIN
FREE ASSOCIATION
FRENCH POLISHING
FRIENDLY SOCIETY
FROM STEM TO STERN
FULL-BLOODEDNESS
FUNDAMENTALISTS
FUNERAL DIRECTOR
FUNERAL PARLOURS
FUTILITARIANISM

G

GAME SET AND MATCH
GASTROENTERITIC
GASTROENTERITIS
GASTRONOMICALLY
GENERAL DELIVERY
GENERAL ELECTION
GENERALIZATIONS
GENERAL PRACTICE
GENTLEMAN-AT-ARMS
GENTLEMAN FARMER
GENTLEMANLINESS
GENTLEMEN-AT-ARMS
GERMAN SHEPHERDS
GET ONE'S SKATES ON

GIVE ONESELF AWAY
GIVE THE GAME AWAY
GLOBE ARTICHOKES
GLOSSY MAGAZINES
GLOUCESTERSHIRE
GLUCONEOGENESIS
GNOTOBIOTICALLY
GOLDEN HANDSHAKE
GOLDEN RETRIEVER
GOOD-FOR-NOTHINGS
GOOD-NATUREDNESS
GO OFF THE DEEP END
GORNO-BADAKHSHAN
GOVERNOR-GENERAL
GRAPHIC DESIGNER
GREGORIAN CHANTS
GUTTURALIZATION
GYNANDROMORPHIC

H

HACKNEY CARRIAGE
HAEMAGGLUTINATE
HAEMOFLAGELLATE
HAEMOGLOBINURIA
HALF-HEARTEDNESS
HALL OF RESIDENCE
HALLUCINATIONAL
HAMAMELIDACEOUS
HAMMER AND SICKLE
HARD-HEARTEDNESS
HARD LUCK STORIES
HARMONISTICALLY
HARVEST FESTIVAL
HAVE A BONE TO PICK
HEARTBREAK HOUSE
HEARTBREAKINGLY
HEARTBROKENNESS
HEAVY-HANDEDNESS
HEIR PRESUMPTIVE
HELIOCENTRICITY
HELIOMETRICALLY
HELIOTROPICALLY
HELLENISTICALLY
HELMINTHOLOGIST
HENDECASYLLABIC
HENDECASYLLABLE
HERBIVOROUSNESS
HEREDITARIANISM
HERMAPHRODITISM
HERMENEUTICALLY
HERO-WORSHIPPING
HETEROCHROMATIC

HETEROCHROMATIN
HETEROGENEOUSLY
HETEROSEXUALITY
HEXACHLOROPHENE
HEXYLRESORCINOL
HIGH COMMISSIONS
HIGHER EDUCATION
HIMACHAL PRADESH
HIPPOCRATIC OATH
HISPANICIZATION
HISTORIC PRESENT
HISTORIOGRAPHER
HISTORIOGRAPHIC
HOLOBLASTICALLY
HOLOGRAPHICALLY
HOLY ROMAN EMPIRE
HOMEOPATHICALLY
HOMOCENTRICALLY
HOMOGENEOUSNESS
HOMOPLASTICALLY
HOPE AGAINST HOPE
HORTICULTURALLY
HOSPITALIZATION
HOT-WATER BOTTLES
HOUSEHOLDERSHIP
HOUSEHOLD TROOPS
HOUSEWIFELINESS
HOUSING PROJECTS
HUMANITARIANISM
HUMANITARIANIST
HUNTINGDONSHIRE
HYDROBROMIC ACID
HYDROGENIZATION
HYDROMECHANICAL
HYDROMETALLURGY
HYPERCRITICALLY

I
ICEBERG LETTUCES
IDIOMORPHICALLY
IMMEASURABILITY
IMMERSION HEATER
IMMORTALIZATION
IMMUNOCHEMISTRY
IMMUNOGENICALLY
IMMUNOLOGICALLY
IMPECUNIOUSNESS
IMPENETRABILITY
IMPERISHABILITY
IMPONDERABILITY
IMPRESCRIPTIBLE
IMPRESSIONISTIC

IMPROBABILITIES
IMPROVISATIONAL
INACCESSIBILITY
INADMISSIBILITY
INAPPLICABILITY
INAPPROPRIATELY
INATTENTIVENESS
IN BLACK AND WHITE
INCALCULABILITY
INCIDENTAL MUSIC
INCOMMENSURABLE
INCOMMUNICATIVE
INCOMMUTABILITY
INCOMPARABILITY
INCOMPATIBILITY
INCOMPREHENSION
INCOMPREHENSIVE
INCOMPUTABILITY
INCONSEQUENTIAL
INCONSIDERATELY
INCONSIDERATION
INCONSISTENCIES
INCONSOLABILITY
INCONSPICUOUSLY
INCONVENIENCING
INCORRIGIBILITY
INCREDULOUSNESS
INDECENT ASSAULT
INDEFEASIBILITY
INDEFENSIBILITY
INDEMNIFICATION
INDETERMINISTIC
INDIAN ROPE-TRICK
INDIGESTIBILITY
INDIRECT OBJECTS
INDISCRETIONARY
INDISPUTABILITY
INDISSOLUBILITY
INDIVIDUALISTIC
INDIVIDUALIZING
INDUSTRIALIZING
INDUSTRIOUSNESS
INEFFACEABILITY
INEFFECTIVENESS
INEXPENSIVENESS
INEXPLICABILITY
INEXTENSIBILITY
INEXTRICABILITY
INFANT PRODIGIES
INFINITESIMALLY
INFRASTRUCTURES

INFUNDIBULIFORM
INJUDICIOUSNESS
INOFFENSIVENESS
INOPPORTUNENESS
INQUISITIVENESS
INQUISITORIALLY
INSENSIBILITIES
INSIGNIFICANTLY
INSTALLMENT PLAN
INSTANTANEOUSLY
INSTRUMENTALISM
INSTRUMENTALIST
INSTRUMENTALITY
INSTRUMENTATION
INSUBORDINATELY
INSUBORDINATION
INSURANCE POLICY
INSURRECTIONARY
INSURRECTIONISM
INSURRECTIONIST
INTELLECTUALISE
INTELLECTUALISM
INTELLECTUALIST
INTELLECTUALITY
INTELLECTUALIZE
INTELLIGIBILITY
INTENSIFICATION
INTERCHANGEABLE
INTERCHANGEABLY
INTERCLAVICULAR
INTERCOLLEGIATE
INTERCONNECTION
INTERDEPENDENCE
INTERFEROMETRIC
INTERLAMINATION
INTERLOCUTORILY
INTERNALIZATION
INTERNAL REVENUE
INTERNATIONALES
INTERNATIONALLY
INTEROSCULATION
INTERPENETRABLE
INTERPRETATIONS
INTERROGATINGLY
INTERROGATIONAL
INTERROGATIVELY
INTERROGATORIES
INTERROGATORILY
INTERSCHOLASTIC
INTERVENTIONISM
INTERVENTIONIST
IN THE LAST RESORT

INTRANSIGENTIST
INTROSPECTIONAL
INTROSPECTIVELY
INTUSSUSCEPTION
INTUSSUSCEPTIVE
INVESTIGATIONAL
INVOLUNTARINESS
INVOLUNTATARILY
INVULNERABILITY
IRREDEEMABILITY
IRREFRAGABILITY
IRREMISSIBILITY
IRRESISTIBILITY
IRRESOLVABILITY
IRREVERSIBILITY

J
JACK-OF-ALL-TRADES
JAPANESE LANTERN
JEHOVAH'S WITNESS
JUMPING-OFF PLACE
JURISPRUDENTIAL
JUXTAPOSITIONAL

K
KABARDINO-BALKAR
KEEPS ONE'S HAND IN
KIND-HEARTEDNESS

L
LABOUR EXCHANGES
LABOUR INTENSIVE
LABOUR-INTENSIVE
LABYRINTHICALLY
LACKADAISICALLY
LADIES-IN-WAITING
LAISSEZ-FAIREISM
LARGE INTESTINES
LATERAL THINKING
LAUGHING JACKASS
LEADING ARTICLES
LEADING QUESTION
LET ONE'S HAIR DOWN
LETTERS OF CREDIT
LEVEL-HEADEDNESS
LIGHT-HEADEDNESS
LIGHT MACHINE GUN
LIGHTNING STRIKE
LIKE THE CLAPPERS
LILY OF THE VALLEY
LIVERY COMPANIES

LOCAL GOVERNMENT
LOGARITHMICALLY
LOIRE-ATLANTIQUE
LOPHOBRANCHIATE
LOURENCO MARQUES

M
MACHINE-READABLE
MACROCOSMICALLY
MACROSCOPICALLY
MACROSPORANGIUM
MAD AS A MARCH HARE
MAGNANIMOUSNESS
MAGNETOCHEMICAL
MAGNETO ELECTRIC
MAGNIFYING GLASS
MALACOPTERYGIAN
MALASSIMILATION
MALE CHAUVINISTS
MALPRACTITIONER
MANIC-DEPRESSIVE
MANIFESTATIONAL
MANNERISTICALLY
MANOEUVRABILITY
MARKET GARDENERS
MARKET GARDENING
MARRIAGEABILITY
MARSHALLING YARD
MARXISM-LENINISM
MARXIST-LENINIST
MASSAGE PARLOURS
MASTER CRAFTSMAN
MASTER OF SCIENCE
MATERIALIZATION
MEANINGLESSNESS
MECHANISTICALLY
MEGALOCEPHALOUS
MELANCHOLICALLY
MELLIFLUOUSNESS
MEMORIALIZATION
MENDING ONE'S WAYS
MENISPERMACEOUS
MENSTRUAL PERIOD
MENTAL DEFECTIVE
MENTAL HOSPITALS
MENTALISTICALLY
MEPHISTOPHELEAN
MEROBLASTICALLY
METACINNABARITE
METAGENETICALLY
METALINGUISTICS
METALLURGICALLY

METAMATHEMATICS
METHODISTICALLY
METROPOLITANISM
MICROBIOLOGICAL
MICROBIOLOGISTS
MICROELECTRONIC
MICROPHOTOGRAPH
MICROPROCESSORS
MICROSCOPICALLY
MICROSPORANGIUM
MICROSPOROPHYLL
MIDDLE OF NOWHERE
MIDDLE-OF-THE-ROAD
MINIATURIZATION
MISAPPLICATIONS
MISAPPREHENDING
MISAPPREHENSION
MISAPPREHENSIVE
MISAPPROPRIATED
MISCALCULATIONS
MISCELLANEOUSLY
MISCHIEVOUSNESS
MISCONSTRUCTION
MISINTERPRETING
MISREPRESENTING
MISTRUSTFULNESS
MOBILE LIBRARIES
MODERNISTICALLY
MOLOTOV COCKTAIL
MONCHEN-GLADBACH
MONEY FOR OLD ROPE
MONOGRAPHICALLY
MONOUNSATURATED
MONTE CARLO RALLY
MONTMORILLONITE
MOOG SYNTHESIZER
MOONLIGHT SONATA
MORNING SICKNESS
MORPHOLOGICALLY
MORPHOPHONEMICS
MOTHER COUNTRIES
MOTHER SUPERIORS
MOVING STAIRCASE
MULTITUDINOUSLY
MUSCULOSKELETAL
MUSTARD AND CRESS
MUSTARD PLASTERS
MUTATIS MUTANDIS
MYTHOLOGIZATION

N
NAGORNO-KARABAKH

NATIONAL ANTHEMS
NATIONAL GALLERY
NATIONALIZATION
NATIONAL SERVICE
NATURAL SCIENCES
NEARSIGHTEDNESS
NEEDLE AND THREAD
NEGATIVE-RAISING
NEIGHBOURLINESS
NEOARSPHENAMINE
NEOLOGISTICALLY
NEUROHYPOPHYSIS
NEUROPATHICALLY
NEUROPHYSIOLOGY
NEUROPSYCHIATRY
NEUROPSYCHOLOGY
NEUROSURGICALLY
NEWS CONFERENCES
NIGHTMARISHNESS
NINE DAYS' WONDERS
NITROCHLOROFORM
NITROGENIZATION
NOMOGRAPHICALLY
NON COMPOS MENTIS
NONCONTRIBUTING
NONCONTRIBUTORY
NON INTERVENTION
NONINTOXICATING
NONPRODUCTIVITY
NON-PROFIT-MAKING
NONSENSICALNESS
NONSTANDARDIZED
NORTH COUNTRYMAN
NOTWITHSTANDING
NOUVELLE CUISINE
NO-WIN SITUATIONS
NUCLEAR FAMILIES
NUCLEAR REACTORS
NUCLEOSYNTHESIS
NUMBER-CRUNCHING

O

OBJECTIFICATION
OBSERVATION POST
OBSTRUCTIONISTS
OBSTRUCTIVENESS
OESTROGENICALLY
OLD AGE PENSIONER
OLD PEOPLE'S HOMES
OLIGOSACCHARIDE
OMNIDIRECTIONAL
ONCE IN A BLUE MOON

ONE-ARMED BANDITS
ONE'S HEART BLEEDS
ON THE BACK BURNER
OPEN-AND-SHUT CASE
OPENHEARTEDNESS
OPERATING SYSTEM
OPHTHALMOLOGIST
OPHTHALMOSCOPIC
OPINIONATEDNESS
OPISTHOGNATHISM
OPISTHOGNATHOUS
OPPOSITE NUMBERS
OPTICAL ILLUSION
OPTOELECTRONICS
ORIENTALIZATION
ORNITHORHYNCHUS
ORTHOCHROMATISM
ORTHOPSYCHIATRY
OSTEOPATHICALLY
OUT OF THE PICTURE
OVERCAPITALIZED
OVERCOMPENSATED
OVERDEVELOPMENT
OVERSIMPLIFYING
OXYTETRACYCLINE

P

PAINSTAKINGNESS
PALAEOBOTANICAL
PALAEOGRAPHICAL
PALAEONTOGRAPHY
PALAEONTOLOGIST
PALAEOZOOLOGIST
PALEONTOLOGISTS
PANCAKE LANDINGS
PANTHEISTICALLY
PARAGENETICALLY
PARAGRAPHICALLY
PARALLACTICALLY
PARASITOLOGICAL
PARASYMPATHETIC
PARENT COMPANIES
PARENTHETICALLY
PARLIAMENTARIAN
PARTHENOGENESIS
PARTHENOGENETIC
PARTICULARISTIC
PARTICULARITIES
PARTICULARIZING
PASSIFLORACEOUS
PASSIONLESSNESS

PAST PARTICIPLES
PATENT MEDICINES
PATHETIC FALLACY
PAVEMENT ARTISTS
PAYING IN ADVANCE
PELICAN CROSSING
PENTATONIC SCALE
PENTOTHAL SODIUM
PEPPERCORN RENTS
PEREGRINE FALCON
PERFUNCTORINESS
PERIODONTICALLY
PERIPATETICALLY
PERISTALTICALLY
PEROXIDE BLONDES
PERPENDICULARLY
PERPETUAL MOTION
PERSONAL COLUMNS
PERSONALITY CULT
PERSONALIZATION
PERSONAL PRONOUN
PERSONAL STEREOS
PERSONA NON GRATA
PERSONIFICATION
PERSPICACIOUSLY
PERSPICUOUSNESS
PESSIMISTICALLY
PHANTASMAGORIAS
PHARMACODYNAMIC
PHARMACOGNOSIST
PHARMACOGNOSTIC
PHARMACOLOGICAL
PHARMACOLOGISTS
PHARYNGOLOGICAL
PHENOLPHTHALEIN
PHENYLKETONURIA
PHILANTHROPISTS
PHILOSOPHICALLY
PHLEBOSCLEROSIS
PHOSPHATIZATION
PHOSPHOCREATINE
PHOSPHORESCENCE
PHOTOCONDUCTION
PHOTODEGRADABLE
PHOTOELASTICITY
PHOTOGRAMMETRIC
PHOTOJOURNALISM
PHOTOJOURNALIST
PHOTOLITHOGRAPH
PHOTOMECHANICAL
PHOTOMETRICALLY
PHOTOMICROGRAPH

PHOTOMULTIPLIER
PHOTOSENSITIZED
PHOTOTELEGRAPHY
PHOTOTOPOGRAPHY
PHOTOTRANSISTOR
PHOTOTYPESETTER
PHOTOTYPOGRAPHY
PHOTOZINCOGRAPH
PHYSICOCHEMICAL
PHYSIOTHERAPIST
PHYTOGEOGRAPHER
PHYTOPLANKTONIC
PICTURE-POSTCARD
PICTURESQUENESS
PIEZOMETRICALLY
PINCER MOVEMENTS
PITHECANTHROPUS
PLASMOLYTICALLY
PLASTIC SURGEONS
PLATINUM BLONDES
PLATYHELMINTHIC
PLEASURABLENESS
PLENIPOTENTIARY
PLEUROPNEUMONIA
PLIGHT ONE'S TROTH
PLOUGHMAN'S LUNCH
PLUMBAGINACEOUS
PLUMBER'S FRIENDS
PLUTOCRATICALLY
PNEUMATIC DRILLS
POIKILOTHERMISM
POISON-PEN LETTER
POLICE CONSTABLE
POLITICAL ASYLUM
POLLING STATIONS
POLYGENETICALLY
POLYGRAPHICALLY
POLYUNSATURATED
PORTMANTEAU WORD
POST OFFICE BOXES
POVERTY-STRICKEN
POWER OF ATTORNEY
PRAYING MANTISES
PREACHIFICATION
PRECANCELLATION
PRECIPITOUSNESS
PREDISPOSITIONS
PREFERENTIALITY
PREHISTORICALLY
PREPOSITIONALLY
PRESBYTERIANISM

PRESCRIPTIVISTS
PRESENCE CHAMBER
PRESENTABLENESS
PRESENTATIONISM
PRESENTATIONIST
PRESS CONFERENCE
PRESSURE COOKERS
PRESTIDIGITATOR
PRESTIGIOUSNESS
PRESUMPTIVENESS
PRESUPPOSITIONS
PRETENTIOUSNESS
PRETERNATURALLY
PRIMA BALLERINAS
PRIMARY STRESSES
PRINCE CHARMINGS
PRINTED CIRCUITS
PRINTING PRESSES
PRIVATE PROPERTY
PRIVATE SOLDIERS
PRIVY COUNCILLOR
PROBLEMATICALLY
PROCRASTINATING
PROCRASTINATION
PRODUCTION LINES
PROFESSIONALISM
PROFESSIONALIST
PROGENITIVENESS
PROGNOSTICATING
PROGNOSTICATION
PROGNOSTICATIVE
PROGNOSTICATORS
PROGRESSIVENESS
PROHIBITIONISTS
PROHIBITIVENESS
PROLETARIANNESS
PROMISCUOUSNESS
PROPER FRACTIONS
PROPORTIONALITY
PROPORTIONATELY
PROPYLENE GLYCOL
PROSELYTIZATION
PROSENCHYMATOUS
PROTOZOOLOGICAL
PROVOCATIVENESS
PSEPHOLOGICALLY
PSEUDOMUTUALITY
PSYCHEDELICALLY
PSYCHIATRICALLY
PSYCHOACOUSTICS
PSYCHOANALYSING

PSYCHOBIOLOGIST
PSYCHOGENICALLY
PSYCHOLOGICALLY
PSYCHOMETRICIAN
PSYCHOPATHOLOGY
PSYCHOSEXUALITY
PSYCHOTECHNICAL
PSYCHOTHERAPIST
PSYCHOTOMIMETIC
PTOLEMAIC SYSTEM
PUBLIC COMPANIES
PUBLIC NUISANCES
PUBLIC OWNERSHIP
PUBLIC RELATIONS
PULCHRITUDINOUS
PUNCTILIOUSNESS
PUNCTUATION MARK
PURITANICALNESS
PURPOSELESSNESS
PUSILLANIMOUSLY
PUT ONE'S FOOT DOWN
PUT OUT MORE FLAGS
PYROELECTRICITY

Q
QUADRUPLICATION
QUARRELSOMENESS
QUARTER SESSIONS
QUATERCENTENARY
QUEEN'S EVIDENCES
QUESTION MASTERS
QUICK-WITTEDNESS
QUINQUAGENARIAN
QUINTUPLICATION
QUODLIBETICALLY

R
RADIOACTIVATION
RADIOBIOLOGICAL
RADIOLOCATIONAL
RADIOMICROMETER
RADIOPHONICALLY
RADIOSCOPICALLY
RADIOTELEGRAPHY
RADIOTELEPHONIC
RADIO TELESCOPES
RADIOTHERAPISTS
RAILWAY STATIONS
RATE OF EXCHANGES
RATIONALIZATION
REAFFORESTATION
REAL-ESTATE AGENT

REARGUARD ACTION
RECAPITULATIONS
RECOGNIZABILITY
RECOMMENDATIONS
RECONCILABILITY
RECONNAISSANCES
RECONSIDERATION
RECONSTRUCTIBLE
RECONSTRUCTIONS
RECORD LIBRARIES
RECREATION ROOMS
REDOUBTABLENESS
REFRESHER COURSE
REGISTERED NURSE
REGISTER OFFICES
REGISTRY OFFICES
REGIUS PROFESSOR
REINDUSTRIALIZE
RELATIVE CLAUSES
RELATIVE PRONOUN
REMORSELESSNESS
REPETITIOUSNESS
REPRESENTATIONS
REPRESENTATIVES
REPROACHFULNESS
REPRODUCIBILITY
RESOURCEFULNESS
RESPECTABLENESS
RESPONSIBLENESS
RESTRICTIVENESS
RESURRECTIONARY
RESURRECTIONISM
RESURRECTIONIST
RESURRECTION MEN
RETROGRESSIVELY
RETROSPECTIVELY
REVEREND MOTHERS
REVOLUTIONARIES
REVOLUTIONARILY
REVOLUTIONIZING
RHOMBENCEPHALON
RIBONUCLEIC ACID
RIGHT-HANDEDNESS
RIGHT-MINDEDNESS
RITUALISTICALLY
ROBIN GOODFELLOW
ROGUES' GALLERIES
ROMANTICIZATION
ROUGH-AND-TUMBLES
ROUND-SHOULDERED

ROYAL HIGHNESSES
RUMBUSTIOUSNESS
RUSSIAN ROULETTE

S

SADOMASOCHISTIC
SALES RESISTANCE
SANCTIMONIOUSLY
SANDWICH COURSES
SAPROPHYTICALLY
SARRACENIACEOUS
SATURATION POINT
SAVINGS ACCOUNTS
SAWN-OFF SHOTGUNS
SCARBOROUGH FAIR
SCHISTOSOMIASIS
SCHOOL OF THOUGHT
SCINTILLATINGLY
SCLERODERMATOUS
SCRUMPTIOUSNESS
SEA ISLAND COTTON
SECONDARY MODERN
SECONDARY SCHOOL
SECONDARY STRESS
SECOND CHILDHOOD
SECOND-IN-COMMAND
SECURITY COUNCIL
SEINE-SAINT-DENIS
SELECT COMMITTEE
SELF-CENTREDNESS
SELF-CONFIDENTLY
SELF-CONSCIOUSLY
SELF-DESTRUCTING
SELF-DESTRUCTION
SELF-DISCIPLINED
SELF-EXAMINATION
SELF-EXPLANATORY
SELF-IMPORTANTLY
SELF-IMPROVEMENT
SELF-INDULGENTLY
SELF-LIQUIDATING
SELF-POLLINATION
SELF-POSSESSEDLY
SELF-REPROACHFUL
SELF-RIGHTEOUSLY
SELF-SACRIFICING
SELF-SUFFICIENCY
SENSATIONALISTS
SENSE OF OCCASION
SENTENTIOUSNESS
SENTIMENTALISTS
SENTIMENTALIZED

SEPTUAGENARIANS
SERGEANTS-AT-ARMS
SERVICE STATIONS
SERVOMECHANICAL
SERVOMECHANISMS
SESQUICARBONATE
SHARP-WITTEDNESS
SHILLY-SHALLYING
SHOOTING GALLERY
SHOOTING MATCHES
SHOPPING CENTRES
SHORT-CIRCUITING
SHORT-HANDEDNESS
SHORTHAND TYPIST
SHOTGUN WEDDINGS
SHOWING ONE'S HAND
SHRINKING VIOLET
SHRINK RESISTANT
SICKNESS BENEFIT
SIDEWALK ARTISTS
SIESMOLOGICALLY
SIMPLE FRACTURES
SIMPLICIDENTATE
SIMPLIFICATIONS
SINGULARIZATION
SINISTRODEXTRAL
SITUATION COMEDY
SITUATION ETHICS
SLAUGHTERHOUSES
SLEEPING PARTNER
SLOTTED SPATULAS
SLOUGH OF DESPOND
SLOW ON THE UPTAKE
SMALL INTESTINES
SMALL-MINDEDNESS
SMELLS OF THE LAMP
SOCIAL DEMOCRATS
SOCIALISTICALLY
SOCIOLINGUISTIC
SOFT FURNISHINGS
SOFTHEARTEDNESS
SOLEMNIFICATION
SOUNDED THE ALARM
SOW DRAGON'S TEETH
SPANISH-AMERICAN
SPANISH OMELETTE
SPECIALIZATIONS
SPECIAL LICENCES
SPECIAL PLEADING
SPECIFIC GRAVITY

SPECULATIVENESS
SPEECHIFICATION
SPEECH THERAPIST
SPERMATOGENESIS
SPERMATOGENETIC
SPINNING JENNIES
SPLIT INFINITIVE
SPONTANEOUSNESS
SPUR-OF-THE-MOMENT
SQUADRON LEADERS
SQUARE THE CIRCLE
STAGE DIRECTIONS
STAMPING GROUNDS
STANDARD-BEARERS
STANDARDIZATION
STANDOFFISHNESS
STAND ONE'S GROUND
STAPHYLOPLASTIC
STAPHYLORRHAPHY
STAR-OF-BETHLEHEM
STARS AND STRIPES
STARVATION WAGES
STATE DEPARTMENT
STEREOCHEMISTRY
STEREOISOMERISM
STEREOISOMETRIC
STICKING PLASTER
STINGING NETTLES
STOCKBROKER BELT
STOCKING-FILLERS
STOICHIOLOGICAL
STORE DETECTIVES
STRAIGHTFORWARD
STRAIGHTJACKETS
STRATIFICATIONS
STRAWBERRY MARKS
STRETCHER-BEARER
STUMBLING BLOCKS
SUBORDINATENESS
SUBSISTENCE CROP
SUBSPECIFICALLY
SUBSTANTIVENESS
SUGGESTIBLENESS
SULPHUREOUSNESS
SUNRISE INDUSTRY
SUPERADDITIONAL
SUPERCONDUCTION
SUPERCONDUCTIVE
SUPERCONDUCTORS
SUPERFLUOUSNESS
SUPERIMPOSITION
SUPERINCUMBENCE

SUPERINDUCEMENT
SUPERINTENDENCE
SUPERINTENDENCY
SUPERINTENDENTS
SUPERLATIVENESS
SUPERNATURALISM
SUPERNATURALIST
SUPERNUMERARIES
SUPERSTITIOUSLY
SUPERSTRUCTURAL
SUPERSTRUCTURES
SUPPLEMENTARILY
SUPPLEMENTATION
SUPPLY AND DEMAND
SUPPORTING PARTS
SURREPTITIOUSLY
SUSCEPTIBLENESS
SWIMMING COSTUME
SWIM WITH THE TIDE
SWORD OF DAMOCLES
SYCOPHANTICALLY
SYLLABIFICATION
SYMBOL-FORMATION
SYMBOLISTICALLY
SYMMETRICALNESS
SYMPATHETICALLY
SYMPATHOMIMETIC
SYMPTOMATICALLY
SYNCHRONIZATION
SYNCHRONOUSNESS
SYNECDOCHICALLY
SYNECOLOGICALLY
SYNOPTIC GOSPELS
SYSTEMATIZATION
SYSTEMS ANALYSTS

T

TACHOMETRICALLY
TACHYMETRICALLY
TAKEN FOR GRANTED
TAKE TO ONE'S HEELS
TARSOMETATARSAL
TARSOMETATARSUS
TECHNOLOGICALLY
TECHNOSTRUCTURE
TELEGRAPHICALLY
TELEPHONE NUMBER
TELEPHOTOGRAPHY
TELEPHOTO LENSES
TELESTEREOSCOPE
TELETYPESETTING
TEMPERAMENTALLY

TEMPESTUOUSNESS
TEN COMMANDMENTS
TENDENTIOUSNESS
TENDERHEARTEDLY
TERMINOLOOGICAL
TERRITORIAL ARMY
TETRABRANCHIATE
THALASSOTHERAPY
THAT'S MORE LIKE IT
THE BACK OF BEYOND
THE COAST IS CLEAR
THEOREMATICALLY
THE POWERS THAT BE
THERAPEUTICALLY
THERIANTHROPISM
THERMIONIC VALVE
THERMOBAROGRAPH
THERMOCHEMISTRY
THERMOSTABILITY
THICKHEADEDNESS
THICK-WITTEDNESS
THOUGHTLESSNESS
THREE-LEGGED RACE
THREE-POINT TURNS
THROMBOEMBOLISM
THYROCALCITONIN
TIGHTFISTEDNESS
TIGHTROPE WALKER
TIMES IMMEMORIAL
TOOK SOME BEATING
TOPOGRAPHICALLY
TOTALITARIANISM
TO THE MANNER BORN
TOWER OF STRENGTH
TRACTION ENGINES
TRADITIONALISTS
TRAINING COLLEGE
TRANSCRIPTIONAL
TRANSFERABILITY
TRANSFIGURATION
TRANSFIGUREMENT
TRANSFORMATIONS
TRANSGRESSINGLY
TRANSILLUMINATE
TRANSISTORIZING
TRANSLATABILITY
TRANSLITERATING
TRANSLITERATION
TRANSMOGRIFYING
TRANSMUTATIONAL
TRANSPARENTNESS
TRANSPLANTATION

TRANSPOSABILITY
TRANSPOSITIONAL
TRANSUBSTANTIAL
TREACHEROUSNESS
TREASONABLENESS
TRIBROMOETHANOL
TRICHLOROETHANE
TRICK OR TREATING
TRINITROBENZENE
TRINITROTOLUENE
TROPICALIZATION
TROUBLESHOOTERS
TROUBLESOMENESS
TRUSTWORTHINESS
TRYPANOSOMIASIS
TURF ACCOUNTANTS
TYPOGRAPHICALLY
TYRANNOSAURUSES

U
ULTRACENTRIFUGE
ULTRAFILTRATION
ULTRAMICROMETER
ULTRAMICROSCOPE
ULTRAMICROSCOPY
ULTRASTRUCTURAL
UNBELIEVABILITY
UNCEREMONIOUSLY
UNCHALLENGEABLE
UNCOMMUNICATIVE
UNCOMPLIMENTARY
UNCONCERNEDNESS
UNCONDITIONALLY
UNCONNECTEDNESS
UNCONSCIOUSNESS
UNDEMONSTRATIVE
UNDERCAPITALIZE
UNDEREMPLOYMENT
UNDERESTIMATING
UNDERESTIMATION
UNDERHANDEDNESS
UNDERPRIVILEGED
UNDERPRODUCTION

UNDERSTATEMENTS
UNDER-THE-COUNTER
UNDISTINGUISHED
UNEMPLOYABILITY
UNEQUIVOCALNESS
UNEXCEPTIONABLE
UNEXCEPTIONABLY
UNFLINCHINGNESS
UNFORTUNATENESS
UNHOLY ALLIANCES
UNINTERRUPTEDLY
UNIVERSAL JOINTS
UNKNOWN QUANTITY
UNOBTRUSIVENESS
UNPARLIAMENTARY
UNPRECEDENTEDLY
UNPREMEDITATION
UNPRETENTIOUSLY
UNPROFITABILITY
UNPRONOUNCEABLE
UNSOPHISTICATED
UNWHOLESOMENESS

V
VALETUDINARIANS
VALUE-ADDED TAXES
VASCULARIZATION
VASOCONSTRICTOR
VEGETABLE KNIVES
VEGETABLE MARROW
VENDING MACHINES
VENEREAL DISEASE
VENTRILOQUISTIC
VENTURESOMENESS
VERTIGINOUSNESS
VESPERTILIONINE
VESTED INTERESTS
VICE-CHANCELLORS
VICISSITUDINARY
VICTORIA CROSSES
VIDEOCONFERENCE
VIRGINIA CREEPER
VITAL STATISTICS

VIVISECTIONISTS
VOYEURISTICALLY
VULGAR FRACTIONS

W
WALRUS MOUSTACHE
WARM-BLOODEDNESS
WARM-HEARTEDNESS
WAR OF JENKIN'S EAR
WARRANT OFFICERS
WASHING MACHINES
WEATHER BOARDING
WEATHER FORECAST
WEATHERPROOFING
WEATHER STATIONS
WELL-CONSTRUCTED
WELL-ESTABLISHED
WELL-INTENTIONED
WHIPPERSNAPPERS
WHISTLE-STOP TOUR
WHITE BLOOD CELLS
WHITED SEPULCHRE
WHITE MAN'S BURDEN
WILD-GOOSE CHASES
WIND INSTRUMENTS
WIND-POLLINATION
WINDSCREEN WIPER
WISHFUL THINKING
WRONGHEADEDNESS

X
XENOMORPHICALLY
XEROGRAPHICALLY

Y
YOURS FAITHFULLY
YOUTH HOSTELLERS
YOUTH HOSTELLING

Z
ZYGOPHYLLACEOUS

APPENDICES

MESSAGING ABBREVIATIONS

AAP	ALWAYS A PLEASURE	B-DAY	BIRTHDAY
ABT	ABOUT	BF	BEST FRIEND
ABT2	ABOUT TO	BF	BOYFRIEND
ACK	ACKNOWLEDGE	BFF	BEST FRIENDS FOREVER
ADD	ADDRESS	BFN	BYE FOR NOW
ADDY	ADDRESS	BHL8	BE HOME LATE
ADMIN	ADMINISTRATOR	BIO	BIO BREAK
ADN	ANY DAY NOW	BISLY	BUT I STILL LOVE YOU
ADR	ADDRESS	BK	BACK
AFAIC	AS FAR AS I'M CONCERNED	BOL	BEST OF LUCK
		BOYF	BOYFRIEND
AFAIK	AS FAR AS I KNOW	BRB	BE RIGHT BACK
AFK	AWAY FROM KEYBOARD	BRD	BORED
AIGHT	ALRIGHT	BTAIM	BE THAT AS IT MAY
AITR	ADULT IN THE ROOM	BTW	BY THE WAY
ALOL	ACTUALLY LAUGHING OUT LOUD	BW	BEST WISHES
		BYKT	BUT YOU KNEW THAT
AMG	AH, MY GOD!	C U	SEE YOU
AML	ALL MY LOVE	CBF	CAN'T BE FUCKED
ASAP	AS SOON AS POSSIBLE	CD9	PARENTS ARE AROUND
ASL	AGE, SEX, LOCATION?	CIAO	GOODBYE
ASLMH	AGE, SEX, LOCATION, MUSIC, HOBBIES?	CID	CONSIDER IT DONE
		CMON	COME ON
ATM	AT THE MOMENT	CODE 9	PARENTS ARE AROUND
ATST	AT THE SAME TIME	CONGRATS	CONGRATULATIONS
AWESO	AWESOME	COO	COOL
AWOL	ABSENT WITHOUT LEAVE	COS	BECAUSE
AYK	AS YOU KNOW	CR8	CREATE
AYSOS	ARE YOU STUPID OR SOMETHING	CSL	CAN'T STOP LAUGHING
		CU	SEE YOU
AYTMTB	AND YOU'RE TELLING ME THIS BECAUSE?	CYA	SEE YOU
		CYL	SEE YOU LATER
B2W	BACK TO WORK	CYT	SEE YOU TOMORROW
B4	BEFORE	DB	DEAR (OR DARLING) BROTHER
B4N	BYE FOR NOW		
B8	BAIT	DD	DEAR (OR DARLING) DAUGHTER
B9	BOSS IS WATCHING		
BBIAB	BE BACK IN A BIT	DGA	DON'T GO ANYWHERE
BBIAF	BE BACK IN A FEW		
BBIAM	BE BACK IN A MINUTE	DH	DEAR (OR DARLING) HUSBAND
BBL	BE BACK LATER		
BBT	BE BACK TOMORROW	DIKU	DO I KNOW YOU?
BC	BECAUSE	DLTM	DON'T LIE TO ME
BCOS	BECAUSE	DNR	DINNER
BDAY	BIRTHDAY	DNT	DON'T

DS	DEAR (*OR* DARLING) SON	HMU	HIT ME UP
DURS	DAMN YOU'RE SEXY	HRU	HOW ARE YOU?
		IAC	IN ANY CASE
DUSL	DO YOU SCREAM LOUD?	IANAL	I AM NOT A LAWYER
DV8	DEVIATE	IC	I SEE
DW	DEAR OR DARLING WIFE	IDC	I DON'T CARE
E1	EVERYONE	IDK	I DON'T KNOW
EMA	E-MAIL ADDRESS	IDUNNO	I DON'T KNOW
EMSG	E-MAIL MESSAGE	IIRC	IF I REMEMBER CORRECTLY
ENUF	ENOUGH	ILBL8	I'LL BE LATE
EVA	EVER	ILU	I LOVE YOU
EVO	EVOLUTION	IM	INSTANT MESSAGE
EZ	EASY	IMHO	IN MY HUMBLE OPINION
EZY	EASY	IMNSHO	IN MY NOT SO HUMBLE OPINION
F2F	FACE TO FACE	IMO	IN MY OPINION
FF	FRIENDS FOREVER	IMS	I AM SORRY
FFS	FOR FUCK'S SAKE	IOH	I'M OUTTA HERE
FO	FUCK OFF	IRC	INSTANT RELAY CHAT
FTW	FOR THE WIN	IRL	IN REAL LIFE
FWD	FORWARD	JFDI	JUST FUCKING DO IT
FWIW	FOR WHAT IT'S WORTH	JJ	JUST JOKING
FYEO	FOR YOUR EYES ONLY	JK	JUST KIDDING
FYI	FOR YOUR INFORMATION	JKBNR	JUST KIDDING, BUT NOT REALLY
FYM	FOR YOUR MISINFORMATION	JMHO	JUST MY HUMBLE OPINION
G2G	GOT TO GO	JTLYK	JUST TO LET YOU KNOW
GB	GOODBYE	K	OKAY
GBH	GREAT BIG HUG	KEWL	COOL
GF	GIRLFRIEND	KISS	KEEP IT SIMPLE STUPID
GG	GOOD GAME	KIT	KEEP IN TOUCH
GJ	GOOD JOB	KPC	KEEPING PARENTS CLUELESS
GL	GOOD LUCK		
GNIGHT	GOOD NIGHT	L8	LATE
GNITE	GOOD NIGHT	L8R	LATER
GR8	GREAT	L8RG8R	LATER, GATOR
GRATZ	CONGRATULATIONS	LEMENO	LET ME KNOW
GRL	GIRL	LKITR	LITTLE KID IN THE ROOM
GTG	GOT TO GO	LMAO	LAUGHING MY ASS OFF
GTG	WE'RE GOOD TO GO		
GUD	GOOD	LMFAO	LAUGHING MY FUCKING ASS OFF
H8	HATE		
HAGS	HAVE A GREAT SUMMER		
HAK	HUGS AND KISSES	LMIRL	LET'S MEET IN REAL LIFE
HBDAY	HAPPY BIRTHDAY		
HF	HAVE FUN		

LOL	LAUGHING OUT LOUD	O4U	ONLY FOR YOU
LOLZ	LAUGHING OUT LOUD	OATUS	ON A TOTALLY UNRELATED SUBJECT
LTNS	LONG TIME NO SEE		
M4C	MEET FOR COFFEE	OIC	OH, I SEE
M8	MATE	OLL	ONLINE LOVE
MEGO	MY EYES GLAZE OVER	OMDB	OVER MY DEAD BODY
		OMG	OH MY GOD
MEH	I FEEL MEDIOCRE ABOUT THAT	OMG	OH MY GOSH
		OMW	ON MY WAY
MF	MALE OR FEMALE?	ONL	ONLINE
MIRL	MEET IN REAL LIFE	ONNA	OH NO, NOT AGAIN
MKAY	MMM, OKAY	OOTO	OUT OF THE OFFICE
MOOS	MEMBER OF THE OPPOSITE SEX	OP	ON PHONE
		ORLY	OH REALLY?
MORF	MALE OR FEMALE	OT	OFF TOPIC
MOS	MOTHER OVER SHOULDER	OTL	OUT TO LUNCH
MSG	MESSAGE	OTOH	ON THE OTHER HAND
MTFBWY	MAY THE FORCE BE WITH YOU	OTT	OVER THE TOP
		OTW	OFF TO WORK
MYOB	MIND YOUR OWN BUSINESS	OVA	OVER
		P911	PARENT ALERT
NOOB	NEWBIE	PAL	PARENT(S) IS/ARE LISTENING
N1	NICE ONE		
N2M	NOTHING TOO MUCH	PAW	PARENT(S) IS/ARE WATCHING
NANA	NOT NOW, NO NEED		
NBD	NO BIG DEAL	PBB	PARENT(S) BEHIND BACK
NE	ANY	PEEPS	PEOPLE
NE1	ANYONE	PIC	PICTURE
NEWB	NEWCOMER (OR ROOKIE OR AMATEUR)	PIR	PARENT(S) IN ROOM
		PL8	PLATE
NM	NEVER MIND	PLOS	PARENT(S) LOOKING OVER SHOULDER
NMP	NOT MY PROBLEM		
NO1	NO ONE	PLS	PLEASE
NOOB	NEWCOMER (OR ROOKIE OR AMATEUR)	PLZ	PLEASE
		PM	PERSONAL MESSAGE
NOOBIE	NEWCOMER (OR ROOKIE OR AMATEUR)	PMFJI	PARDON ME FOR JUMPING IN
NOYB	NONE OF YOUR BUSINESS	PMJI	PARDON MY JUMPING IN
NP	NO PROBLEM	POMS	PARENT(S) OVER MY SHOULDER
NSFW	NOT SAFE FOR WORK		
NTIM	NOT THAT IT MATTERS	POOF	GOODBYE
NUB	NEWCOMER OR ROOKIE OR AMATEUR	POS	PARENT(S) OVER SHOULDER
NUFF	ENOUGH SAID	POS	PIECE OF SHIT
NVM	NEVER MIND	PPL	PEOPLE
NVR	NEVER	PROPS	PROPER RESPECT AND RECOGNITION
O GAWD	OH GOD		
O RLY	OH, REALLY?		

PRT	PARTY
PRW	PARENT(S) IS/ARE WATCHING
PU	THAT STINKS!
PZ	PEACE
PZA	PIZZA
QFT	QUOTED FOR TRUTH
QL	QUIT LAUGHING
QSO	CONVERSATION
QT	CUTIE
QTPI	CUTIE PIE
RBTL	READING BETWEEN THE LINES
RL	REAL LIFE
RLY	REALLY
ROFL	ROLLING ON FLOOR, LAUGHING
ROFLMAO	ROLLING ON FLOOR, LAUGHING MY ASS OFF
RSN	REAL SOON NOW
RTFM	READ THE FUCKING MANUAL
RU	ARE YOU?
RU/18	ARE YOU OVER 18?
RUMOF	ARE YOU MALE OR FEMALE?
RUOK	ARE YOU OKAY?
RUT	ARE YOU THERE?
RX	REGARDS
RYO	ROLL YOUR OWN
S2R	SEND TO RECEIVE
S2S	SORRY TO SAY
SFSG	SO FAR SO GOOD
SH^	SHUT UP
SIG2R	SORRY, I GOT TO RUN
SK8	SKATE
SK8NG	SKATING
SK8R	SKATER
SK8RBOI	SKATER BOY
SMEM	SEND ME AN EMAIL
SMIM	SEND ME AN INSTANT MESSAGE
SOHF	SENSE OF HUMOUR FAILURE
SORG	STRAIGHT OR GAY
SPK	SPEAK
SPST	SAME PLACE SAME TIME
SQ	SQUARE
SRSLY	SERIOUSLY
SRY	SORRY
STR8	STRAIGHT
SUP	WHAT'S UP?
SUX	SUCKS (OR IT SUCKS)
SYS	SEE YOU SOON
T:)T	THINK HAPPY THOUGHTS
T+	THINK POSITIVE
T4BU	THANKS FOR BEING YOU
TAFN	THAT'S ALL FOR NOW
TAH	TAKE A HIKE
TAW	TEACHERS ARE WATCHING
TBC	TO BE CONTINUED
TBD	TO BE DETERMINED
TBH	TO BE HONEST
TFH	THREAD FROM HELL
TGIF	THANK GOD IT'S FRIDAY
THNQ	THANK YOU
THNX	THANKS
THX	THANKS
TLK2UL8R	TALK TO YOU LATER
TM	TRUST ME
TMI	TOO MUCH INFORMATION
TOM	TOMORROW
TTFN	TA TA FOR NOW
TTG	TIME TO GO
TTLY	TOTALLY
TTT	TO THE TOP
TTYL	TALK TO YOU LATER
TU	THANK YOU
TVM	THANK YOU VERY MUCH
TY	THANK YOU
TYVM	THANK YOU VERY MUCH
UL	YOU WILL
UN4TUN8	UNFORTUNATE
UNCRTN	UNCERTAIN
UOK	ARE YOU OK?
UR	YOU'RE (OR YOUR)
UR2YS4ME	YOU ARE TOO WISE FOR ME
URA*	YOU ARE A STAR
URH	YOU ARE HOT
^URS	UP YOURS
USU	USUALLY

UT2L	YOU TAKE TOO LONG	WRK	WORK
VM	VOICE MAIL	WRT	WITH RESPECT TO
VRY	VERY	WRU@	WHERE ARE YOU AT?
W/	WITH	WTB	WANT TO BUY
W/E	WHATEVER	WTF	WHAT THE FUCK?
W/END	WEEKEND	WTG	WAY TO GO
W@	WHAT?	WTT	WANT TO TRADE
W3	WWW (WEB ADDRESS)	WUF	WHERE YOU FROM?
W8	WAIT	WUP	WHAT'S UP?
WAN2TLK	WANT TO TALK	WUT	WHAT
WB	WELCOME BACK	WUTEVA	WHATEVER
WBU	WHAT ABOUT YOU?	WYCM	WILL YOU CALL ME?
WC	WELCOME	WYP	WHAT'S YOUR PROBLEM?
WC	WHO CARES?	WYRN	WHAT'S YOUR REAL NAME?
WDYMBT	WHAT DO YOU MEAN BY THAT?	WYWH	WISH YOU WERE HERE
WE	WHATEVER	X	KISS
WF	WAY FUN	XLNT	EXCELLENT
WFM	WORKS FOR ME	XOXO	HUGS AND KISSES
WH5	WHO, WHAT, WHEN, WHERE, WHY	XTC	ECSTASY
		YMMV	YOUR MILEAGE MAY VARY
WK	WEEK	Z	SAID
WKD	WEEKEND	ZUP	WHAT'S UP?
WKD	WICKED	ZZZ	SLEEPING, BORED

WORDS THAT CONTAIN Q NOT FOLLOWED BY U

ANQING – CITY IN CHINA

AQABA – PORT IN JORDAN, ON THE GULF OF AQABA

AQMOLA – FORMER NAME OF ASTANA, CAPITAL OF KAZAKHSTAN

BASOTHO-QWAQWA – FORMER BANTU HOMELAND IN SOUTH AFRICA

CHONGQING – CITY IN CHINA

DIMASHQ – ARABIC NAME FOR DAMASCUS, CAPITAL OF SYRIA

FAQIR – MUSLIM OR HINDU HOLY MAN

INQILAB – URDU WORD FOR REVOLUTION

IQBAL – SIR MOHAMMED IQBAL, INDIAN MUSLIM POET, PHILOSOPHER, AND POLITICAL LEADER

IRAQ – COUNTRY IN THE MIDDLE EAST

IRAQI – 1 INHABITANT OF IRAQ 2 RELATING TO IRAQ

JIANG QING – CHINESE COMMUNIST POLITICIAN, WIDOW OF MAO TSE-TUNG

LAILAT-UL-QADR – ANNUAL NIGHT OF PRAYER AND STUDY FOR MUSLIMS

MASQAT – ARABIC NAME FOR MUSCAT, CAPITAL OF OMAN

MBAQANGA – STYLE OF BLACK POPULAR MUSIC IN SOUTH AFRICA

QABIS – ARABIC NAME FOR GABÉS, PORT IN TUNISIA

QABIS BIN SAID – SULTAN OF OMAN

QADDAFI – MOAMAR AL-QADDAFI (MUAMMAR GADDAFI), FORMER LEADER OF LIBYA

QADDISH – JEWISH PRAYER, ESPECIALLY FOR THE DEAD

QADI – MUSLIM JUDGE

QAIRWAN – HOLY CITY IN TUNISIA

QANTAS – AUSTRALIAN NATIONAL AIRLINE (QUEENSLAND AND NORTHERN TERRITORY AERIAL SERVICES)

QAT – TYPE OF BUSH FOUND IN ETHIOPIA

QATAR – COUNTRY IN ARABIA

QATTARA DEPRESSION – DEPRESSION IN THE SAHARA

QAWWALI – MUSLIM RELIGIOUS SONG

QESHM – IRANIAN ISLAND

QIAN LONG – CHINESE EMPEROR

QIBLA – THE DIRECTION OF MECCA

QINGDAO – PORT IN CHINA

QINGHAI – PROVINCE OF CHINA

QINTAR – ALBANIAN COIN

QIQIHAR – CITY IN CHINA

QISHM – IRANIAN ISLAND

QOM – HOLY CITY IN IRAN

QOPH – HEBREW LETTER Q

QORMA – INDIAN DISH OF MEAT AND VEGETABLES

QU QIU BAI – CHINESE COMMUNIST LEADER AND WRITER

QWAQWA – FORMER BANTU HOMELAND IN SOUTH AFRICA

QWERTY – STANDARD LAYOUT OF ENGLISH TYPEWRITER/COMPUTER KEYBOARD

SERCQ – FRENCH NAME FOR SARK IN THE CHANNEL ISLANDS

SI-MA QIAN – ANCIENT CHINESE HISTORIAN

ZAQAZIQ – CITY IN EGYPT

ZARQA – CITY IN JORDAN

WORDS THAT START WITH X

XANTHATE – SALT OR ESTER OF XANTHIC ACID

XANTHEIN – YELLOW PIGMENT FOUND IN FLOWERS

XANTHENE – CRYSTALLINE COMPOUND USED IN DYES

XANTHIC – RELATING TO XANTHIC ACID

XANTHIN – ORANGE-YELLOW PIGMENT FOUND IN PLANTS

XANTHINE – CRYSTALLINE COMPOUND FOUND IN URINE

XANTHIPPE – THE WIFE OF SOCRATES; ANY NAGGING OR QUARRELSOME WOMAN

XANTHISM – ABNORMAL YELLOWNESS OF SKIN, FUR, ETC.

XANTHOCHROID – RELATING TO RACES HAVING LIGHT HAIR AND PALE SKIN

XANTHOCHROISM – EXCESSIVE YELLOWNESS IN GOLDFISH, ETC.

XANTHOMA – YELLOW-BROWN PATCH OR NODULE ON THE SKIN

XANTHOPHYLL – YELLOW PIGMENT FOUND IN PLANTS

XANTHOUS – RELATING TO RACES HAVING LIGHT HAIR AND PALE SKIN

XANTHUS – THE CHIEF CITY OF ANCIENT LYCIA IN ASIA MINOR

XAVIER – ST FRANCIS XAVIER, SPANISH JESUIT MISSIONARY

XEBEC – SMALL THREE-MASTED SHIP

XENIA – **1** GIFT OR OFFERING **2** INFLUENCE OF POLLEN UPON THE DEVELOPED FRUIT

XENOCRATES – GREEK PHILOSOPHER

XENOCRYST – CRYSTAL OF DIFFERENT ORIGIN FOUND IN IGNEOUS ROCK

XENOGAMY – CROSS-FERTILIZATION

XENOGENEIC – DERIVED FROM AN INDIVIDUAL OF A DIFFERENT SPECIES

XENOGENESIS – PRODUCTION OF OFFSPRING UNLIKE EITHER PARENT

XENOGLOSSIA – ABILITY TO SPEAK A LANGUAGE ONE HAS NEVER LEARNED

XENOGRAFT – GRAFT OF TISSUE FROM AN INDIVIDUAL OF A DIFFERENT SPECIES

XENOLITH – ROCK FRAGMENT OF DIFFERENT ORIGIN FOUND IN IGNEOUS ROCK

XENOMORPHIC – (OF A MINERAL) HAVING A DIFFERENT FORM FROM THE SURROUNDING ROCK

XENON – GASEOUS CHEMICAL ELEMENT

XENOPHANES – GREEK PHILOSOPHER AND POET

XENOPHILE – PERSON WHO LIKES FOREIGN PEOPLE OR THINGS

XENOPHOBE – PERSON WHO DISLIKES FOREIGN PEOPLE OR THINGS

XENOPHOBIA – FEAR OR HATRED OF FOREIGN PEOPLE AND THINGS

XENOPHON – GREEK GENERAL AND HISTORIAN

XERANTHEMUM – SEVERAL MEDITERRANEAN PLANTS, ESPECIALLY THE IMMORTELLE

XERARCH – (OF PLANT SUCCESSIONS) ORIGINATING IN A DRY HABITAT

XERES – FORMER NAME OF JEREZ IN SPAIN

XERIC – (OF PLANTS) GROWING IN DRY CONDITIONS

XERODERMA – ABONORMAL DRYNESS OF THE SKIN

XEROGRAPHY – PHOTOCOPYING PROCESS

XEROMORPHIC – (OF PLANTS) HAVING PROTECTION AGAINST EXCESSIVE WATER LOSS

XEROPHILOUS – ADAPTED TO A DRY HABITAT

XEROPHTHALMIA – DRYNESS IN THE EYE

XEROPHYTE – PLANT THAT IS ADAPTED TO DRY CONDITIONS

XEROSERE – PLANT SUCCESSION ORIGINATING IN A DRY HABITAT

XEROSIS – ABNORMAL DRYNESS OF SKIN OR OTHER TISSUES

XEROSTOMIA – ABNORMAL DRYNESS OF THE MOUTH

XEROX – TRADENAME FOR A PHOTOCOPYING PROCESS

XHOSA – BANTU PEOPLE AND LANGUAGE OF SOUTH AFRICA

XI – GREEK LETTER X

XIA GUI – CHINESE LANDSCAPE PAINTER

XI AN – CITY IN CHINA

XIANG – RIVER IN CHINA

XIMENES – XIMENES DE CISNEROS, SPANISH CARDINAL AND STATESMAN

XINGÚ – RIVER IN BRAZIL

XINING – CITY IN CHINA

XINJIANG UYGUR – ADMINISTRATIVE DIVISION OF CHINA

XIPHISTERNUM – THE LOWEST PART OF THE BREAST BONE

XIPHOID – (OF BODILY PARTS) SWORD-SHAPED

XIPHOSURAN – HORSESHOE CRAB

XIZANG – CHINESE NAME FOR TIBET

XMAS – CHRISTMAS

XOANON – CARVED IMAGE OF A GOD

XOCHIMILCO – TOWN AND LAKE IN MEXICO

X-RAY – ELECTROMAGNETIC RADIATION OF VERY SHORT WAVELENGTH, USED IN MEDICAL DIAGNOSIS ETC.

XUTHUS – SON OF HELLEN IN GREEK MYTHOLOGY

XUZHOU – CITY IN CHINA

XYLAN – YELLOW CARBOHYDRATE FOUND IN WOOD AND STRAW

XYLEM – PLANT TISSUE THAT CONDUCTS WATER AND NUTRIENTS

XYLENE – LIQUID HYDROCARBON USED AS A SOLVENT

XYLIDINE – XYLENE DERIVATIVE USED IN DYES

XYLOCARP – FRUIT WITH A HARD WOODY SHELL

XYLOGENOUS – (OF INSECTS ETC.) LIVING IN OR ON WOOD

XYLOGRAPH – ENGRAVED WOODEN BLOCK OR PRINT MADE FROM ONE

XYLOGRAPHY – ART OF PRINTING FROM WOODEN BLOCKS

XYLOID – RELATING TO OR LIKE WOOD

XYLOPHAGOUS – (OF INSECTS ETC.) FEEDING ON WOOD

XYLOPHONE – TUNED WOODEN PERCUSSION INSTRUMENT

XYLORIMBA – LARGE XYLOPHONE

XYLOSE – SUGAR FOUND IN WOOD AND STRAW, USED IN FOOD FOR DIABETICS

XYLOTOMOUS – (OF INSECTS ETC.) BORING INTO WOOD

XYLOTOMY – PREPARATION OF WOOD SECTIONS FOR MICROSCOPE EXAMINATION

XYLYL – DERIVED FROM XYLENE

XYST – **1** (IN ANCIENT GREECE) COVERED PORTICO USED FOR ATHLETICS **2** (IN ANCIENT ROME) TREELINED GARDEN WALK

XYSTER – SURGICAL FILE FOR SCRAPING BONE